DHRUV P. SINGH

(303) 440-8639
OR 492-4036

BUSINESS LAW TEXT AND CASES

THE LEGAL ENVIRONMENT

FOURTH EDITION

Joseph L. Frascona
University of Colorado—Professor Emeritus

Edward J. Conry
University of Colorado at Denver

Gerald R. Ferrera
Bentley College

Terry L. Lantry
Colorado State University

Bill M. Shaw
The University of Texas at Austin

George J. Siedel
The University of Michigan

George W. Spiro
University of Massachusetts, Amherst

Arthur D. Wolfe
Michigan State University

Allyn and Bacon
Boston London Toronto Sydney Tokyo Singapore

Series Editor: *Henry Reece*
Developmental Editor: *Judith S. Fifer*
Series Editorial Assistant: *Katherine Grubbs*
Senior Editorial-Production Administrator: *Elaine M. Ober*
Composition Buyer: *Linda Cox*
Manufacturing Buyer: *Megan Cochran*
Cover Administrator: *Linda K. Dickinson*
Cover Designer: *Bruce Kennett*
Editorial-Production Service: *York Production Services*

Library of Congress Cataloging-in-Publication Data

Business law: the legal environment, text and cases / Joseph L. Frascona . . . [et al.]. — 4th ed.
p. cm.
Rev. ed. of : Business law / Joseph L. Frascona. 3rd ed. c1987.
Includes index.
ISBN 0-205-12586-2
1. Commercial Law—United States. I. Frascona, Joseph L. II. Frascona, Joseph L. Business Law.
KF889.F68 1991
346.73 07—dc20 90-1148
[347.3067] CIP

MAG 92 NBAR .0120 BW. -.0020
25661 FRASCONA LAW 4/E ISBN 0-205-12566-2

Printed in the United States of America
10 9 8 7 6 5 4 3 2 1 95 94 93 92 91 90

THE AUTHORS

Joseph L. Frascona, J.D.

Professor Emeritus of Business Law at the University of Colorado, formerly a member of its faculty teaching Legal Issues for Executives in its Executive M.B.A. Program, and the past Director of the Graduate School of Banking at Colorado. He is a member of the New York, Colorado, and Federal Bars; a past president of the American Business Law Association; a member of the Rocky Mountain Business Law Association; and is on the Commercial Arbitration Panel of the American Arbitration Association. Professor Frascona was formerly an Associate Attorney in the Office of the Attorney General of the United States and General Counsel to the Office of the Foreign Liquidation Commission, U.S. Department of State, in England. He is the author of numerous books and articles on business law and international law; many articles are in the current edition of *Encyclopedia Americana.* At present he is legal consultant to business and industry, and is Of Counsel to the law firm of Frascona, Joiner, & Smittkamp. He has a B.S. from City College, City University of New York, and a J.D. from Harvard University.

Edward J. Conry, M.B.A., J.D.

Associate Professor of Business Law and Ethics, University of Colorado at Denver. He has both worked in and served as consultant to business. He has written extensively on business ethics, consumerism, and real estate topics. Professor Conry is a past president of the Rocky Mountain Business Law Association; Founding Chair of the Ethics Section of the American Business Law Association; has served as staff editor for the *American Business Law Journal;* and is the author of numerous books and articles. During 1981–1982 he was the Research Fellow in Business Ethics at Yale University. He is co-author of the Allyn and Bacon text, *The Legal Environment of Business.* He has a B.A. from California State University at Fullerton, an M.B.A. from the University of California, Berkeley, and a J.D. from the University of California, Davis.

Gerald R. Ferrera, J.D.

Professor of Business Law and Chairman of the Law Department, Bentley College. He is a past president of the North Atlantic Regional Business Law Association and is on the board of editors of the *Business Law Review.* He is a co-author of the Allyn and Bacon text, *The Legal Environment of Business,* and the author of numerous articles on business law and the legal environment. He has consulted to professional and business associations and is a member of the Massachusetts and Federal Bars. Professor Ferrera earned his B.S. from Boston College, an M.S. in Taxation from Bentley College, and a J.D. from the New England School of Law.

Terry L. Lantry, J.D.

Professor of Accounting and Business Law at Colorado State University. He is a member of the Colorado and Indiana State Societies of Certified Public Accountants and of the Colorado, Indiana, and Federal Bars. He is a past president of the American Business Law Association. Professor Lantry is the author or co-author of numerous articles, monographs, and textbooks. He has a B.A. and J.D. from Valparaiso University and an M.B.A. from Indiana University.

Bill Shaw, J.D., L.L.M.

Professor of Business Law at The University of Texas at Austin. He is particularly interested in environmental law and corporate social responsibility and has written extensively on these topics. Professor Shaw is a member of the editorial board of the *Journal of Business Ethics,* a former editor of the *American Business Law Journal,* and is currently serving as President of the American Business Law Association. He is a member of the Texas and Louisiana Bars. He earned a B.S. and M.B.A. at Louisiana Tech University, a J.D. at Tulane University, and an L.L.M. at the University of Texas at Austin.

George J. Siedel, J.D., D.C.L.S.

Professor of Business Law at The University of Michigan. He is Chief Editor of the *Michigan Real Property Review* and has served as a staff and special editor of the *American Business Law Journal.* The author of numerous books and articles, Professor Siedel has received the Award of Excellence for the best paper presented at the Midwest Business Law Association Annual Meeting, and the University of Michigan Faculty Recognition Award for teaching and research. He has served as Visiting Professor of Business Law at Stanford University and has been elected a Visiting Fellow at Wolfson College, Cambridge University, England. Professor Siedel has a B.A. from The College of Wooster, a J.D. from The University of Michigan, and a Diploma in Comparative Legal Studies from Cambridge University, England.

George W. Spiro, J.D.

Associate Academic Dean and Executive Director of the School of Management, and Professor of Business Law and Management at the University of Massachusetts at Amherst. He specializes in labor relations and labor studies and has written primarily on the interfaces of law, management theory, jurisprudence, and labor studies. Professor Spiro has a B.S. in Personnel and Industrial relations and an M.S. in Labor Studies from the University of Massachusetts at Amherst, and a J.D. from Syracuse University.

Arthur D. Wolfe, J.D.

Professor of Business, Law, and Public Policy at Michigan State University. He has served as Editor-in-Chief of the *American Business Law Journal,* and, together with Professor Bill Shaw, received the 1981 Holmes-Cardozo Award given by the American Business Law Association for scholarly presentation at its annual meeting. He is a member of the Indiana, Ohio, and U.S. Virgin Islands Bars. He is co-author of five books on business law and the legal environment, and has published articles on law, business policy, and ethics. He has been a Visiting Scholar with the Business and Public Policy Group at the University of California, Berkeley (1985–1986), and at the J.L. Kellogg School of Management at Northwestern University (1989–1990). He earned a B.A. in history and a J.D. from Ohio State University, and an M.A. in Economics from the University of Illinois.

CONTENTS

PREFACE

This fourth edition is not just another book on business law. It continues its three-fold thrust. *First,* this book pushes back the frontiers of the law of business, reflecting not only what the law is but also where it is developing and expanding. *Second,* this book takes the position that law is a limitation on freedom to act, particularly in freedom of contract, as reflected by current common law, case law, statute, and judicial decision. *Third,* this is a *teaching book,* written specifically *for,* and not at, students.

Users of this fourth edition will find: the text has been extensively revised, reworded, and much of the material reorganized and subdivided; everything has been updated and made more readable for better student comprehension; former terms and many new ones together with definitions have been checked and reworded for accuracy and better clarity; and a substantial amount of new material has been added. Much of this is the result of the constructive comments and suggestions made by reviewers, faculty, and students throughout the country, for which we are grateful. Many terms are defined in the margins of the text, and some are included in more than one Part for completeness of understanding of each individual Part.

A few of the many major items may be of interest. There are approximately 350 short cases, and 57 long cases at the ends of the chapters, many being new. Each of the case opinions has been edited to show the "essential" facts and the judge's reasoning. Several new forms, charts, and diagrams have been added for a total of 114. New extensive material has been added on women's rights, the status and liability of auditors, and in the law of corporations, bankruptcy, sales, and business law in the international marketplace. There is a completely new chapter on constitutional law. Also, there is distinctively authoritative ethics material, unlike the typical listing of quasi-ethical issues so common today, based on the findings in the field of moral psychology and on the work of Professor Conry as the Research Fellow in Business Ethics at Yale University 1981–1982. *The unique feature of this material is that it is designed to help students form their own beliefs, now and in later life, about what is right and wrong conduct in business.* The ethics material in the first Part gives students the analytic tools needed to engage in mature ethical analysis. Subsequent Parts ask students to apply these tools to a variety of ethical issues. The final Part provides an in depth exploration of the citizen's duty to obey the law. We recommend that instructors who wish to integrate ethics into their courses cover, at a minimum, the first and final end-of-part discussions.

Appendices include: An Explanation of the Civil Trial Process; the United States Constitution, and Amendments; the Uniform Partnership Act (1914); Uniform Limited Partnership Act (1916); (Revised) Uniform Limited Partnership Act, as Amended (1985); and the Uniform Commercial Code (1978 Text).

A note on sexism. The text has been thoroughly reviewed by editors skilled in the use of gender-inclusive language to eliminate gender from the text wherever practicable. There is no generic singular for "they" or "them." One solution to this problem is to use "he or she," "his or her." However, such wording can become awkward, especially when repeated frequently. To avoid cumbersome structures, sentences have been worded, as much as possible, to avoid gender references. In cases where it is not feasible to solve the problem in this way, the singular pronoun "he" or the adjective "his" has been used. This usage is also true in legal definitions, case opinions, and statutes where the language cannot be changed. We have done our best in this regard.

The eight professors who are the contributing authors have written the following portions of this book: Conry, Part 9, and the Part discussions on Ethics and Business Law; Ferrera, Parts 3 and 8, except for chapter 19; Frascona, chapters 3 and 19, and Parts 11 and 12; Lantry, Part 2; Shaw, Part 6 and chapter 37; Siedel, Parts 4 and 10; Spiro, Parts 1 and 7, except for chapter 37; and Wolfe, Part 5 and Appendix A.

The innovative design of the text, Instructor's Manual, and Student Study Guide/Workbook as an integrated unit has been accomplished by the use of a matrix analysis which allows the instructor to integrate case materials from the text and application questions from the Student Study Guide/Workbook into the lecture formats provided in the Instructor's Manual.

A comprehensive student study guide programmed learning format is available. It provides for self-paced instruction and contains practice examinations. Included in the student study guide are exercises with answers covering terminology, concepts, and applications of law. A Student Study Guide/Workbook for *Business Law, Text and Cases, The Legal Environment* is available either at your bookstore or by special order through your bookstore.

The total educational package, including a special Instructor's Annotated Edition, makes *Business Law, Text and Cases, The Legal Environment* a true teaching text, the only one available on the market.

Acknowledgments

As in all research and writing, there are always those persons—silent and unsung—whose efforts, patience, and sacrifices are quietly intertwined into the final product. The authors are deeply grateful for help afforded them by their families in this process. Also, the authors wish to acknowledge with thanks the excellent assistance of Associate Professor Barbara Bintliff, Librarian of the School of Law, University of Colorado, and the library staffs of both the various Schools of Law and the various Colleges and Schools of Business helpful to the authors. Professor Ferrera wishes to acknowledge the invaluable assistance of his research associate, Adjunct Professor Margo E.K. Reder of Bentley College.

Helpful reviewers and faculty have contributed to the excellence of the four editions of this book with their constructive comments and perceptive suggestions. Some of them are the following. Thank you all very much: John J. Balek, Morton College; Caryn Beck-Dudley, Utah State University; Robert W. Bing, William Paterson College of New Jersey; Earl W. Coblyn, University of the District of Columbia; Wallace Conard, Columbus Technical Institute; James C. Fetterman, St. Louis University; Edward J. Gac, University of Colorado at Boulder; Sally Genson, Milwaukee Area Technical College, North Campus; Christopher L. Hamilton, Golden West College; Nancy Hauserman, University of Iowa; Lewis D. Howell, Tennessee State University; J. Roland Kelley, Tarrant County Junior College, Northeast Campus; Mike R. LaFrance, Kirkwood Community College; William F. Lynch, Niagra University; Peter J. Musante III, Milwaukee Area Technical College; Gregory Naples, William Rainy Harper College; Michael Noonan, Frostburg State College; Gena Ousley, Chaffey College; William Parks, Orange Coast College-Costa Mesa; Paul Peckosh, Loras College; George N. Plavac, Cuyahoga Community College; Hank Ramp, Merced College; Roger Reinsch, Emporia State University; F. Durwood Ruegger, University of Southern Mississippi; Gabe Sanders, Jersey City State College; Gary R. Schwartz, Harrisburg Area Community College; J. Gregory Service, Broward Community College; Arthur F. Stelley, Hankamer School of Business, Baylor University; Zachary Taylor Jr., La Grange College; William S. Vanderpool, Appalachian State University; Lamont Walton, Michigan State University; Edd Welsh, Phoenix College.

We also wish to thank those professors who took time from their busy schedules to respond to our publisher's telephone survey: Harold Anderson, Arizona Western College; Emmett Arnold, Augusta College; Adolpho Benavizes, La Grange College; Sharon Benson, Shoreline Community College; Joe Demaio, Catawba Valley Technical College; Vernon Dorweiler, Michigan Tech University; Roger Fish, Cumberland University; Annadawn Hopkins, Shoreline Community College; Richard Hungate, Whitworth College; John Lowry, Oklahoma State University Technical Institute; Thomas McKenna, Lawrence Institute of Technology; Berry Miller, Golden Gate University; Chuck Nolan, College of Santa Fe; Michael Noonan, Frostburg State University; David Poindexter, Michigan Tech University; William Sheehy, Lawrence Institute of Technology; Jamie Sullivan, College of Santa Fe; Zachary Taylor, La Grange College; Timothy Welsh, Catonsville Community College; and David Zessin, Hope College.

Very special thanks are due to William Parks, Orange Coast College; Edward Gac, University of Colorado at Boulder; and Mary Wilder, University of Denver, Westminster Law Library for their invaluable assistance in preparation of the Instructor's Annotated Edition.

In addition, we wish to thank Judith Fifer, our developmental editor at Allyn and Bacon, for her immense patience and immeasurable assistance during the revision process.

The authors also wish to acknowledge with appreciation the permissions to reprint the following material: the 1978 text of the Uniform Commercial Code and some Official Comments to various sections therein copyrighted 1978 by and reprinted herein with the permission of both The American Law Institute and the National Conference of Commissioners on Uniform State Laws; various sections from the RESTATEMENTS (SECOND) OF AGENCY, copyrighted 1958, CONFLICT OF LAWS, copyrighted 1969, CONTRACTS, copyrighted 1982, TORTS, copyrighted 1965, and TRUSTS, copyrighted 1959, by and reprinted herein with the permission of The American Law Institute; the texts of the Uniform Partnership Act, copyrighted 1914, the Uniform Limited Partnership Act, copyrighted 1916, and the (Revised) Uniform Limited Partnership Act, copyrighted 1976 and as Amended in 1985, by and reprinted herein with the permission of the National Conference of Commissioners on Uniform State Laws; various sections from the 1983 Revised Model Business Corporation Act, copyrighted 1983 by and reprinted with the permission of the American Bar Foundation.

To the Student

Congratulations *to you* as a student for wishing to learn about the law of business! You and other students have motivated us authors to write this book for you to enjoy, find interesting and stimulating, and serve you well both in and outside the classroom.

This book is not designed to make you a lawyer but, rather, to help you recognize and understand the legal significance of the business transactions occurring around you and in which you will participate, and to know when to call a lawyer. It is so written as to cause you to *want* to read it and to hold your attention and interest as you proceed through the book, building on what you have read as you go along.

This text has not been "leveled down," but has been authoritatively written to "lift up" the subject in a very innovative, current, and useful manner. The book is continually addressed to you, involving you in the text discussion. It will challenge you, as well as the instructor, by its smooth and deceptively easy style. Everything has been done to be helpful to you, as a student. Easily understandable language is used throughout the text, which is thoroughly up to date.

Each of the book's twelve Parts begins with a very brief overview statement of the chapters in that Part and a summary paragraph covering the whole Part. Each chapter begins with a list of the learning objectives for that chapter. Then comes an introduction leading you into the subject of that chapter. The text reads easily and logically as the subject is developed progressively. Many legal forms, charts, and diagrams are used at points in the book where they will be helpful. As you read through the text, guides and definitions of important legal terms appear in the margins highlighting topics discussed in the text.

Important legal terms are clearly defined and printed in bold type *as soon as they appear* in the text so that you can quickly understand their meaning and how they are used. They are included in the Glossary at the end of the book. Many factual examples appear in the text as you read along, illustrating how the legal principles apply.

A great many condensed court cases occur throughout the text showing how the courts use these principles in live situations. There is an introductory sentence leading into each case indicating the point of that case and tying the case into the text. First the "Facts" are presented, then the "Decision," which presents the court's reasoning in reaching a decision. These cases (with their citations) are carefully selected so as to be interesting to you and are *not* a lot of legal verbiage. Most of them are recent cases.

At the end of each chapter is a Summary Statement, briefly pointing up some of the high points that you should have learned from the chapter. This is helpful in your review of what you have read. Following the summary is a carefully selected *long* interesting case that will give you the "feel" of a court's thinking as the court analyzes the facts and moves toward its decision. The case illustrates the application of an important legal principle that you have learned as you read through the chapter. Like the first famous long case in the book, all these long cases should be very interesting to you. Many of these are *the* outstanding cases on the subject, guiding the courts and followed by the courts as new cases are later considered.

In this text we have presented four different kinds of material. *First,* there is textual material which presents a statement of the general rules of law applicable to most of the important areas of business activity. These rules are both legislative and judicial in origin.

However, presenting the written rules is only a starting point. A *second* type of information illustrates how some of the important rules are applied by those in charge of rule application, either the state or federal governments or private individuals. This rule application is illustrated by presenting both short and long excerpts from mostly appellate case opinions. These case opinions demonstrate how the abstract statements presented by the written rules of law are applied to reality. The cases literally breathe life into the rules and are absolutely necessary to an understanding of how the laws "work." Therefore, you are encouraged to read them carefully.

Third, we have presented at the end of the chapters review questions and case problems and also a long important case. Some of these review case problems are actual cases; others, created by us, should not be viewed as portraying an actual occurrence.

Fourth, at the end of each Part is a discussion of business ethics as it is applicable in the context of business law. The portion at the end of Part 1 introduces you to the ethics material as it applies in each of the following Parts.

At the back of the book are six appendices to provide you ready access to source material. Appendix A is "An Explanation of the Civil Trial Process." This explains in detail how a civil case proceeds and how the judgment is appealed. Appendix B is "the United States Constitution, As Amended," Appendix C is the "Uniform Partnership Act (1914)," Appendix D is the "Uniform Limited Partnership Act (1916)," Appendix E is the "(Revised) Uniform Limited Partnership Act, as Amended (1976)," Appendix F is the "Uniform Commercial Code (1978 Text)." Throughout the book many footnote references are made to the Code, which is here in its complete up-to-date form.

This is followed by an extensive "Glossary of Legal Terms and Definitions." Next is a "Table of Cases" listing the cases (with page references) that have occurred throughout the book, followed by an Index to the book.

BUSINESS LAW
TEXT AND CASES

THE LEGAL ENVIRONMENT

PART 1

THE FOUNDATIONS OF LEGAL SYSTEMS

PREVIEW

Part 1 of this text introduces you to the subject matter of law, the nature and functions of law in our nation, and the impact on our lives of the Constitution of the United States. You will learn as you progress through this text how law is used to improve our society.

We begin our discussion with an attempt to provide a workable definition of law. Next we move to an outline of the workings of the United States legal system. We then consider the Constitution of the United States as interpreted and applied by the federal and state courts, especially the Supreme Court of the United States. Finally we turn to two subjects that are of increasing importance to managers—criminal law and the law of torts.

We conclude with a consideration of business ethics as it relates to the text material in this part.

CHAPTER

1

THE NATURE OF LEGAL SYSTEMS AND LAW

After you have read this chapter, you should be able to:

1. Define "legal system."
2. Identify the various concepts of law proposed by Aristotle, Saint Thomas Aquinas, and Friedrich Karl von Savigny.
3. Explain natural law.
4. Explain the historical school of jurisprudence.
5. Explain why contemporary social scientists study our legal system.
6. Define "norm."
7. Distinguish between formal and informal norms.
8. Explain the meaning of the word "sanctions" and how it applies.
9. Define "law."
10. Explain social engineering.

BUSINESS DECISIONS and the LAW

Every citizen of the United States knows just how important it is to adhere to the law. Regardless of size, every business is faced with a myriad of laws. Business people must be attentive to laws regulating the employment relationship, regulating the payment of creditors, regulating the environment, and regulating how we prepare contracts for the sale of goods.

All the laws regulating our lives, including our business lives, are premised on a belief that we all share in our constitutional form of government. This constitutional government came into being because of the hard work and bravery of some courageous people who in 1776 declared themselves independent of Great Britain. For the colonists, it was an open statement to the world that they wanted to be viewed as an independent political entity, free of British rule. The colonists declared their independence with these words.

> When in the course of human events, it becomes necessary for one people to dissolve the political bonds which have connected them with another, and to assume among the powers of the earth, the separate and equal station to which the laws of nature and of nature's god entitle them, a decent respect to the opinions of mankind requires that they should declare the causes which impel them to separation.
>
> We hold these truths to be self evident, that all men are created equal; that they are endowed by their creator with certain inalienable rights; that among these are

> life, liberty and the pursuit of happiness. That to secure these rights, governments are instituted among men, deriving their just powers from the consent of the governed.

The writing of these words signaled the beginning of a war between the colonies and Great Britain. We have been enjoying the benefits of the colonists' effort ever since. They were demanding to live a life of *happiness, liberty,* and *equality.* They were also demanding that they be able to determine their own future through a system of government that derived its powers from the people governed. As a result, we have government officials who are in office only as long as the electorate keeps them there. We have a system of rules that insists on equality in the workplace and in our day to day lives. The liberty and happiness that we enjoy can be traced to the words and deeds of the colonists.

The all-important Declaration of Independence was written by Thomas Jefferson. Jefferson worked in conjunction with Benjamin Franklin and John Adams. We owe Jefferson a good deal of thanks. He was not only the author of the Declaration of Independence but also the U.S. Minister to France, Vice-President, and subsequently President. During his presidency, he was responsible for the Louisiana Purchase.

Jefferson's final achievement was the founding of the University of Virginia. He not only planned the institution but also designed the facility, hired the faculty, and helped in its overall administration. Thomas Jefferson was also a lawyer by training. As we embark upon the collegiate study of business law, we can be certain that Thomas Jefferson would approve.

Introduction

You are about to embark on a study of the subject of law. You may be surprised to discover that the search for an accurate, all-encompassing definition of law has gone on for thousands of years and will not end as long as people continue to think about the subject. Today researchers are studying legal systems throughout the world to make them work better for all of us. While you may not have an exact definition of law in mind as you pick up this textbook, you certainly are affected by law each and every day.

Every nation in the world has a legal system, and law touches each of us as we go about the business of participating in society. If we are to be effective citizens and participate fully in society, it becomes important for each of us to have a *knowledge* about and a concern for law.

The Importance of Law

legal system
A set of laws adopted by a society or group of people

Legal systems have always been an important part of every society. In thousands of instances each day, the **legal system** helps us resolve conflicts, punish individuals who violate societal norms, and solve some of our most pressing problems. Indeed, as our society becomes more complex, we tend to rely more heavily on law to guide our conduct.

Just as individuals look to the law as a guide in their personal affairs, so do business people look to the law in their business activities. In the United States today there are more than two million corporations doing business. Many of these corporations are so large that what they do has an impact on the entire world. Examples of firms with a worldwide reach are Ford Motor Company and American Telephone and Telegraph Company. As large as these firms are, they look to the law to help structure their operations. Even though there may be significant differences in the laws of the countries in which these firms do business, the firms' managers expect certain rules imposed by society to be followed in doing business. Without some shared expectations about how people will behave—as spelled out by a society's legal system—how could a businessperson expect to run an organization, even for a day?

For example, assume that General Electric agrees to deliver 3,000 citizens band radios to Ajax, Inc., in Newark, New Jersey, and another 3,000 radios to LeFleur, Inc., in Paris, France. The sales manager at GE needs to be able to rely on the laws of contracts and sales in both nations so he can properly manufacture and deliver the radios and make a profit. He needs to know that if Ajax or LeFleur decides not to make payments when they are due, the court in Newark or Paris will make them perform as agreed or make some other fair adjustment. The following case illustrates how important the law is in resolving even the most controversial and difficult problem, when emotions are running high on both sides. The issue is whether one can burn a flag and still claim the protection of the first amendment to the Constitution. It also provides us with an opportunity to learn some legal terms that will be used repeatedly in the text.

FACTS

Johnson took part in a political demonstration to protect the policies of the Reagan administration. The demonstration ended near the Dallas City Hall. Johnson unfurled the American flag, doused it with kerosene and set it on fire. While the flag burned, the demonstrators chanted slogans. No person was physically injured or threatened with injury although many people were offended by the flag burning. Johnson was convicted with violating a Texas statute (flag desecration). The question to the Supreme Court is whether the State can punish Johnson for flag burning. Is this consistent with first amendment free speech?

DECISION

Johnson's conviction cannot stand. He was convicted for engaging in expressive conduct. The State's interest in preventing breaches of the peace does not support his conviction because Johnson's conduct did not threaten to disturb the peace. The government may not prohibit expression merely because it disagrees with its message. Further, the government may not prohibit the expression merely because of the mode one chooses to express an idea.

Texas v. Johnson, 109 S.Ct. 2533 (1989).

appellant
A party who appeals a case decision against him or her

respondent (appelle)
A party against whom an appeal is taken

plaintiff
The party who initiates a civil suit by filing a complaint in the proper court

defendant
The party against whom a civil suit (or criminal action) is brought

In this text you will be reading a number of summarized cases like *Texas v. Johnson*. Cases are legal decisions that have been made by judges. In Figure 1.1, there is an illustration of the parts of a case; this particular case, *Texas v. Johnson,* was decided by the U.S. Supreme Court and written by Justice Brennan. Since *Texas v. Johnson* is a criminal case, the state of Texas (rather than an individual) is the **appellant,** or party that is appealing the case from the lower court; Johnson is the **respondent** or **appellee,** or party against whom the appeal is taken. At the lower court level, a civil case is brought by a **plaintiff,** who initiates a lawsuit; the **defendant** is the party against whom a civil suit or criminal action is brought. Each case has a *citation,* a series of numbers and letters that are used to find that case in a law library. (See Figure 1.1.)

Law is an important element of society, both in our private lives and in the world of work. As vital as law is to our lives, however, many students are not given an opportunity

FIGURE 1.1 The Parts of a Case

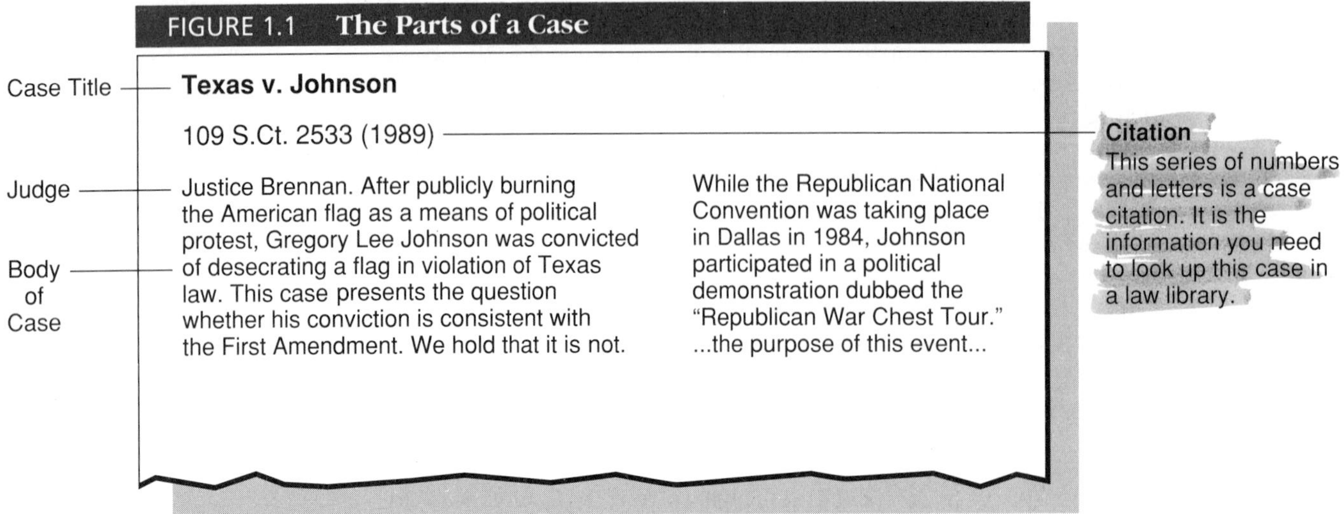

to study it in any formal way before they attend college. In fact, many people are not exposed to law even during their years as undergraduates. To many, law remains a mystery understood only by a select number of craftsmen known as lawyers or judges.

Case Title
Texas v. Johnson
109 S.Ct. 2533 (1989)
Citation
This series of numbers and letters is a case citation. It is the information you need to look up this case in a law library.
Judge
Body of Case
Justice Brennan. After publicly burning the American flag as a means of political protest, Gregory Lee Johnson was convicted of desecrating a flag in violation of Texas law. This case presents the question whether his conviction is consistent with the First Amendment. We hold that it is not.
While the Republican National Convention was taking place in Dallas in 1984, Johnson participated in a political demonstration dubbed the "Republican War Chest Tour." ...the purpose of this event...

We hope to take some of the mystery out of law through the pages of this text. We plan to do this by giving you a look at law as a major institution in our society. You will learn how law affects our society and how we can make social changes by using law. Our focus will be on those portions of law that are of most immediate value to someone in business. We start by familiarizing you with some basic notions about law and legal systems. These concepts provide a foundation upon which you can build.

What Is Law?

Anthropologists, philosophers, historians, sociologists, and political scientists are only a few of the kinds of scholar who have tried to give an accurate definition of the term "law."[1] A practicing lawyer would probably give yet another definition. Your own idea of law might include legal craftsmen, such as judges, police, bailiffs, and lawyers; the places where these craftsmen work, such as courts and jails; and the endless stream of books they refer to, such as *Black's Law Dictionary,* the criminal codes, and the *Uniform Commercial Code.* Indeed, each of these is a part of the legal system in the United States. But this is not the whole picture. The historical background of law plays a large part in our understanding.

natural law
An ideal or cosmic law

Aristotle built upon the Greek notion that the world was ordered by cosmic law or, to use his term, **natural law.** He simply meant that there is a law higher than that which is made by mortals—a kind of ideal law. Aristotle tried to connect moral principles and legal principles.

As part of their philosophies of law, Aristotle and Saint Thomas Aquinas shared a belief in a transcendent law given to society. Both men saw a relationship between moral

[1]For a more complete picture of the various perspectives on law, see the original works by any of these philosophers or one of the many fine texts on jurisprudence, such as J. Feinberg and H. Gross, *Law in Philosophical Perspective* (Encino, Calif.: Dickenson Publishing, 1977); or C. Morris, *The Great Legal Philosophers* (Philadelphia: University of Pennsylvania, 1959).

justice and law. Others also have worked with the concept of natural law. To pursue this perspective on the law somewhat further, you might examine the works of Emmanuel Kant or John Locke. But if this perspective is unsatisfactory, your thoughts may be closer to those of Friedrich Karl von Savigny.

Savigny was instrumental in developing the **historical school of jurisprudence.** This school of thought suggests that law evolves as a result of a particular nation's entire history; that lawyers or judges simply interpret the historical direction of the nation. Even legislators, Savigny would suggest, merely put into words that which is embedded in the larger web of a given nation's history. The name that Savigny gave this expression of the spirit of the people is *Volksgeist.* Critics of the historical school of jurisprudence in general and of Savigny in particular ask whether law simply reflects the common consciousness of the nation, as he suggests, or helps to mold the future.

historical school of jurisprudence
A school of thought suggesting that law evolves from a nation's history

The most important feature of Savigny's work for our purposes is that it marked a move away from traditional generalizations about law toward a more careful pattern of study of society. Indeed, contemporary social scientists are indebted to Savigny for his work. Students interested in learning more about the historical school of jurisprudence might look into the writings of Sir Henry Maine, another legal philosopher of similar persuasion. He believed that one could analyze various historical stages of legal development.

Why Is Law Investigated?

There are a number of different ways of viewing law, each of which has a particular strength or weakness. Yet contemporary legal scholars are always searching for new and workable models of law that might be useful in organizing and analyzing the information that they are continually uncovering. Why are social scientists dissatisfied with the traditional models?

Today's rapidly changing world presents us with issues that were rare or unheard of only a few years ago. This is particularly true in the world of work. In our society, people are calling upon business to have a heightened sense of social responsibility, and law is ever more frequently the vehicle used to move business people in the desired direction. Products liability[2] cases reflect this trend.

We have all been disappointed by products at some time in our lives. Some of us have found unusual substances in soft drink bottles or have been hurt by machines that contained defective parts. For many years consumers had little recourse against companies that put defective or harmful products on the market. For example, in the case of *MacPherson v. Buick Motor Co.,*[3] a person was injured when a wheel on an automobile collapsed because of a defect and thus caused an accident. In order to recover damages caused by such an incident, the court said, the driver had to prove that the company failed to use reasonable care (the same care an ordinary prudent person would use in these circumstances) in assembling the car or, to use the legal terms, that the company was **negligent** in manufacturing the car. The driver also had to defend against the company's assertion that he was **contributorily negligent**—that he failed to exercise reasonable care as a driver and so could not blame the motor company for his misfortune.[4]

negligence
In conduct, failure to use the degree of care demanded by the circumstances; in tort law, negligent conduct proximately causing injury to another person's interest

contributory negligence
Plaintiff's conduct that falls below the standard to which he or she should conform for his or her own protection and that is a legally contributing cause with the defendant's negligence causing the plaintiff's harm

[2]Products liability is discussed on pp. 90–91 and 562–571.

[3]111 N.E. 1050 (N.Y. 1916). For a short abstract of this case, see p. 91.

[4]For a full discussion of the tort of negligence, see pp. 83–89.

Needless to say, it was difficult to establish that the company did not use reasonable care in assembling the car. The problem of defending against the company's assertion of contributory negligence merely complicated the situation. In recent years, the buying public has demanded that this burden be lifted in instances where a particular product is unreasonably dangerous to the consumer, so people have turned to law to resolve this difficulty. The legal system has responded to this social pressure by increasing business responsibility. In more than 60 percent of our states, those who sell products that will reach the consumer virtually unchanged are responsible for injury if the product is defective, even if due care was used in manufacturing the item.

You can expect to see changes in this and almost every other area of law discussed in this text. Clearly, law is not a set of unchanging rules; rather, it changes to reflect movements in our society and, at times, even leads the way for change. The following case illustrates a change in the common law awarding damages for emotional trauma and upset from witnessing an automobile accident.

FACTS

David Legg negligently drove his automobile on Blue Grass Road. At the same time, a young girl named Erin lawfully crossed the same road. Erin was killed as a result of David's driving. The death was witnessed by Erin's sister and mother. They both sued for damages for emotional trauma. David argues that since he did not actually hit either the mother or the sister that there is no common law basis for emotional trauma.

DECISION

Mother and sister prevail. They may collect damages for the emotional trauma resulting from witnessing an accident in which close relatives are injured. The possibility that witnesses might feign trauma to collect damages does not justify the court acting differently. The court recognizes that it is creating a new concept of duty by including a right to recover for emotionally caused injury. Earlier one could only recover for injury if there was a physical impact.

Dillon v. Legg, 441 P.2d 912 (Cal. 1968).

Because the range of disputes that are considered amenable to solution through legal systems continues to grow, and because the complexity of the issues within the range increases all the time, we need to study our legal machinery constantly to make sure that it is functioning at its best. Social scientists who study the legal system perform that task. They seek new models of law because the older models do not enable them to study how law and legal systems really function.

How Is Law Perceived?

As we discussed above, there are a number of different ways of understanding what is meant by the term "law." In this section we present a view shared by a significant number of contemporary writers about the subject. We begin by learning certain fundamental concepts.

► Norm

norm
A group's standard of behavior

A **norm** is a standard shared by members of a group about how they should behave. We all adhere to standards of behavior that we learned as members of a family, a town, and our society as a whole. Many of us have learned these standards so well that we do not even consciously think about them unless we deviate from the norm.

Recently a music group called Motley Crue created quite a stir when they violated a norm by wearing exaggerated makeup and having unusual hairstyles. Many people consider such actions outrageous and look upon them with scorn. Other simple examples of norms are that people should have three meals a day, that dogs in fire stations should be dalmatians, and that nurses should wear white uniforms while working in hospitals.

The kind of norms just mentioned are largely "informal." That means that although they define how a person should behave, they are really casual in that enforcement is not usually strict and punishment for deviation is minor. The norm dictating that forks be placed on the left side of a plate is another informal norm. Although you might raise some eyebrows or be chastised for failing to follow the correct procedure, you probably would receive, at worst, nothing more than a serious reprimand.

Norms may be very "formal," and deviation may be punished severely. Any number of standards for performance fit into this category. As a society we do not approve of one person taking another's life, nor do we approve of embezzlement, forgery, and arson. In each case society has defined the norm in legal words, in something we call the "criminal code." Violations of the code bring punishments ranging from fines to loss of one's own life.

Norms and Freedom of Choice

The term **sanction** may be used to describe the techniques for maintaining social control over the members of a group. As was suggested above, a violation of a society's criminal code can bring a sanction ranging from a fine to loss of one's own life. In the following case the court upheld a state's habitual criminal statute.

sanction
A group's technique for controlling its members

FACTS

Jimmy F. Freeman was convicted of third degree burglary with punishment fixed at not less than 3 years nor more than 6 years confinement in a state penitentiary. He was also found to be a habitual criminal, which increased the punishment for burglary to life imprisonment. Tennessee has a habitual criminal statute. Freeman appeals, arguing that the Tennessee statute violates the Eighth Amendment to the U.S. Constitution.

DECISION

This statute does not violate the U.S. Constitution. The Tennessee legislature has selected crimes it obviously deems to be the most serious [and] likely to be repeated. [The U.S. Supreme Court] recognizes that a state may impose harsher or milder penalties for a given crime than its sister states according to its own notions of severity.

State of Tennessee v. Freeman, 669 S.W. 2d 688 (Tenn. Ct. App., 1983).

In the above case failure to adhere to the norm brought punishment to the individual. Sanctions are often used by our legal systems. We punish our wrongdoers.

Psychologists tell us that there are also rewards. When a person does something particularly good, he or she is rewarded. Children know that if they do certain chores they will be rewarded by their mother or father. A sales employee knows that achieving a certain level of sales in a month will mean receiving a bonus, which is a reward. An employee who works hard all year long may expect a reward in the form of a raise in pay or a promotion.

Basically, people are free to choose how they behave. Whether you wear a sport jacket and tie to school or a sweatshirt and blue jeans is a matter of your own choice. Not all people choose to follow the norms prescribed by their peer group or by society. A course in psychology would probably help you begin to understand the reasons for that kind of decision. Here it is important to note that all of us have a range of choices from which we may choose our behavior. If we choose within the norms, we are rewarded; a choice outside the norms results in a sanction.

Conflict Between Norms

Difficult choices arise when the norms of one group of people come into conflict with society's formal norms. In certain groups—particularly among young people—individuals are pressured to conform to norms that advocate drinking or the use of drugs. The larger society has norms that severely punish such behavior; hence, there is a potential for conflict. In the following case the norm of a school was upheld by the court as superior to the norm as perceived by a student.

FACTS

A high school student delivered a speech nominating a fellow student for elective office. The speech was attended by approximately 600 students, many of whom were 14 years old. During the entire speech, the student referred to his candidate in terms of an elaborate, graphic, and explicit sexual metaphor. The student was given copies of teacher reports of his conduct and was given a chance to explain his conduct. He admitted that he deliberately used sexual innuendo and was suspended for 3 days. Review of the disciplinary action by the school district grievance procedure affirmed the discipline. The student contends that his suspension was in violation of due process.

DECISION

The high school student was given adequate due process. In the case of an academic dismissal, due process does not rise to the level of a penal sanction calling for the full panoply of procedural due process protections applicable to a criminal prosecution.

Bethel School District #403 v. Fraser, 478 U.S. 675 (1986).

The strains can be great in business as well. A company may be able to maximize profits by polluting the atmosphere instead of purchasing expensive pollution control equipment, and many firms have a norm dictating that managers should try to maximize the company's profits. Even so, in the United States today, many norms have developed that apply powerful sanctions to firms that destroy the environment. Managers may find themselves in a terrible bind, torn between competing norms.

Law as a Form of Norm

Some social scientists argue persuasively that law can exist in any number of situations. For example, in a family, parents "make laws" that children must obey; in a company, the personnel director makes rules that employees must obey. In fact, whenever a group gets together, law may appear. These laws, which are not supported by the official sanctions of the government, are called "private laws" and are generated in "private legal systems."

This text, however, takes the position that law is one type of norm or, more specifically, that *norms established by the official leaders of society may be characterized as* ***law.*** We will limit our discussion to the study of the U.S. legal system—those norms established by any part of our government—and we will not discuss private legal systems, except to note that they are actively studied by people interested in the sociology of law.

law
Norms established by the official leaders of society; also those interests recognized and secured by society

Legal Systems

Once you understand the concept of law, you can imagine a number of different *ways* of putting together the laws of a particular society. Lawmakers can put together laws to create a very democratic or a very autocratic society. For example, in the United States the system of government allows individual citizens to participate extensively in creating laws. On the other hand, in Iran the legal system was dominated for years by the whims of its leader Ayatollah Khomeini. In fact, there are an enormous number of different ways to construct a legal system.

Karl Llewellyn (1893–1962) developed what he called the **law-government continuum** to illustrate the point that legal systems can be constructed in an infinite number of ways. He suggested that, in a legal system at the government end of the continuum, decisions would be made according to the arbitrary whim of a leader. Laws would exist or disappear depending on the leader's mood. Llewellyn called this extreme situation the *government pole,* while the other end of the continuum was the *law pole,* as diagrammed in Figure 1.2. At the law pole, the rules of law would be so complete that there would be no need for human judgment. Whim would play no role in such a system.

law-government continuum
A method of showing the numerous ways of constructing legal systems

Both ends of the continuum are extreme systems, and it is difficult to imagine any modern legal system at either extreme. It is possible, however, to place nations closer to one pole than the other.[5] For example, countries controlled by a dictator are closer to the government pole than to the law pole. The United States and Great Britain are closer to the law pole.

Our text will focus on the legal system of the United States. However, students should remember that the laws of other nations may vary significantly from ours. For students interested in legal history, some legal systems predate the U.S. legal system—for example, the Code of Hammurabi (2000 B.C.) and the Mosaic Code (1200 B.C.). The laws of other nations are very important for future business managers. Many firms in the

FIGURE 1.2 The Law-Government Continuum

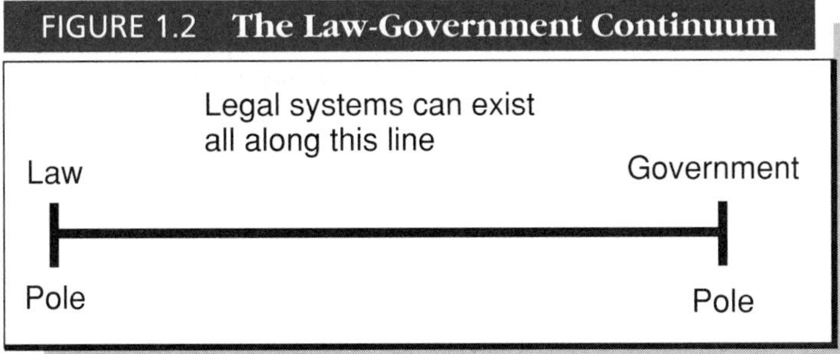

[5]For a more complete explanation, see H. Richard Hartzler, *Justice, Legal Systems and Social Structure* (Port Washington, N.Y.: Kennikat Press, 1977), p. 62.

United States actively do business all over the world. The laws governing business transactions vary from nation to nation. Managers should be very careful not to assume that rules of law and interpretation of them are the same worldwide. In the following early case the English court reflected upon the laws of other nations in deciding the law of liability for negligence in England in connection with impure food.

FACTS

A woman became ill while drinking some carbonated beverages. She traced the illness to the fact that she had swallowed a bit of decomposed snail which was found in the bottle of soda. She did not see the impurity at first because of the dark color of the bottle. Will she be allowed to recover from the manufacturer, defendant, who contended that, since they did not directly enter into a contract with her, the plaintiff should not recover.

DECISION

Yes, there is a sufficient degree of connection between the consumer and the manufacturer.

After looking at the laws of several nations and the laws of Great Britain, the court announced that "a manufacturer of products . . . who sells those products in the form intended for the consumption of the ultimate consumer, and with the knowledge that the absence of reasonable care in the preparation will result in an injury to the consumer's life or property, owes a duty to the consumer to take that reasonable care."

Donoghue v. Stevenson (1932) L.R., A.C. 562.

Social Engineering

social engineering Using the law to bring about societal change

One of the beauties of our legal system is that it is flexible. New laws are continually being created and old laws set aside or amended. This enables us to work within the system in building our nation. Working within the legal system to bring about desired change is quite common. This process of development and control through law was called **social engineering** by the late Roscoe Pound (1870–1964), a legal scholar. In speaking of legal systems, Pound said:[6]

> Today, in my judgment, the most important problem which confronts the jurist is the theory of interests. A legal system attains the ends of the legal order (1) by recognizing certain interests, individual, public and social; (2) by defining the limits within which these interests shall be recognized legally and given effect through legal precepts; and (3) by endeavoring to secure the interests so recognized within defined limits. I should define an interest, for the present purpose, as a demand or desire which human beings either individually or in groups . . . seek to satisfy, of which, therefore, the ordering of human relations must take account.

Thus, under this concept, law can be defined as those interests recognized and secured by society, such recognition and security being established by a legal system.

Social engineering is clearly evident today in the area of minority rights. The United States has citizens from many different ethnic backgrounds; most of us can think of several different examples of ethnic minority groups, such as Hispanics, Native Americans

---

[6]Roscoe Pound, *My Legal Philosophy,* edited by Julius Rosenthal Foundation (Boston: Boston Book Company, 1941), p. 247.

or African Americans. Difficulties often arise because minority groups are, by definition, a small part of the population and because their habits and characteristics derived from their backgrounds are often different from those of the majority. One problem that minority groups face is discrimination in employment. That minority groups are "different" from the majority does not mean that they are "bad" or "useless," but some people take this view; the effect of this error can be devastating on an individual. Many victims of discrimination have no way of supporting their families, even if they have valuable skills. Minority groups facing this kind of problem have increasingly turned to law craftsmen for help. In the following case the court declared and applied the law prohibiting discrimination on the basis of color.

FACTS

The married plaintiffs, Andrew and Ophelia Faraca, wanted to be employed by the Georgia Retardation Center. Andrew had several favorable interviews and was told that he was the best-qualified applicant. All that remained was to route his application to Personnel; there was no doubt that his application would be accepted. Andrew was Caucasian. Ophelia was black. This latter fact caused a Dr. Clements, defendant, another official at the Center, to reject Andrew because of his concern of possible adverse reaction by the public and from legislators of the state to a racially mixed couple. Plaintiffs request an injunction against defendant from engaging in discriminatory employment practices, and seek a court award of money against the defendant. Does this racial discrimination require monetary relief?

DECISION

Monetary relief is warranted here. The civil rights laws cover refusal to enter into a contract, and the director was properly held liable for compensatory damages for refusal to employ plaintiff on the grounds that it would not be proper to have a racially mixed couple in the cottage administrator position.

Faraca v. Clements, 506 F.2d 956 (5th. Cir. 1975).

The earliest form of such help came from the Constitution of the United States, which has been the major vehicle for reducing discrimination. While we will be discussing the Constitution in more detail in Chapter 3, you should know that the Fourteenth Amendment, which provides all people with equal protection of the laws, has been a powerful force for ensuring the civil rights of all of our citizens. The Constitution is not the only source of aid. Federal legislation, such as the Civil Rights Act of 1964, prohibits discrimination based on race, color, sex, or national origin. Federal agencies have also been called upon to help. The Equal Employment Opportunity Commission provides help to employees who feel that they have been discriminated against on the job because they are members of a minority group.

In recent years, women have been looking to the law to help them obtain rights equal to those of men. The equal rights movement, as it is popularly called, has tried to obtain passage of a constitutional amendment guaranteeing that equality of rights shall not be abridged because of sex.

Summary Statement

1. It is important for every citizen to have a knowledge of, and a concern for, law.
2. Our society relies upon law as society becomes more complex.
3. An all-encompassing definition of law has not yet been agreed upon.
4. Different theories of jurisprudence exist.

5. Law changes, and determining why law changes is a fertile field of research.
6. Norms are behavior standards shared by members of a group. Sanctions are techniques for maintaining social control over group members.
7. Law is a kind of norm and is defined as norms established by the official leaders of society; law is also those interests recognized and secured by society.
8. In our system of government, the individual participates extensively in creating laws.
9. The U.S. legal system is close to the "law pole continuum."
10. Our legal system is involved in social engineering.
11. Our legal system deserves our support.

The point made in this chapter is that there is a difference among morals, norms, and law. The famous English case that follows here illustrates the idea that what one might consider morally right does not necessarily protect one in a criminal action.

REGINA v. DUDLEY AND STEPHENS
[1884] L.R., Q.B. 61

Lord Coleridge, C.J. The . . . verdict . . . [for the crime of murder] as it is finally settled before us is as follows:

On July 5, 1884, . . . Thomas Dudley and Edward [sic] Stephens, with one Brooks, . . . English seamen, and the deceased also an English boy, between seventeen and eighteen years of age, . . . were cast away in a storm on the high seas 1,600 miles from the Cape of Good Hope, and were compelled to put into an open boat belonging to the said yacht. That in this boat they had no supply of water and no supply of food, except two 1 lb. tins of turnips . . . [and a small turtle which they caught]. That on the twelfth day the remains of the turtle were entirely consumed, and for the next *eight days* they had nothing to eat. That they had no fresh water. . . . That the boat was drifting on the ocean, and was probably more than 1,000 miles away from land. That on the eighteenth day, when they had been seven days without food and five without water, the prisoners spoke to Brooks as to what should be done if no succour came, and suggested that some one be sacrificed to save the rest, but Brooks dissented, and the boy to whom they were understood to refer, was not consulted. That on the 24th of July, the day before the act now in question, the prisoner Dudley proposed to Stephens and Brooks that lots should be cast who should be put to death to save the rest, but Brooks refused to consent, and it was not put to the boy. . . . Dudley proposed that if there was no vessel in sight by the morrow morning the boy should be killed. That next day, the 25th of July, no vessel appearing, . . . the prisoner Stephens agreed to the act, but Brooks dissented from it. That the boy was then lying at the bottom of the boat quite helpless and extremely weakened by famine and by drinking sea water, and unable to make any resistance, nor did he ever assent to his being killed. . . . That Dudley, with the assent of Stephens, went to the boy, and telling him that his time was come, put a knife into his throat and killed him then and there; that the three men fed upon the body . . . of the boy . . . ; that on the fourth day after the act had been committed the boat was picked up by a passing vessel, and the prisoners rescued. . . . That they were carried to the port of Falmouth, and committed for trial at Exeter. That if the men had not fed upon the body of the boy they would probably not have survived to be so picked up and rescued, but would within the four days have died of famine. . . . That at the time of the act in question there was no sail in sight, nor any reasonable prospect of relief. That under these circumstances there appeared to the prisoners every probability that unless they then fed or very soon fed upon the boy or one of themselves they would die of starvation. That there was no appreciable chance of saving life except by killing some one for the others to eat. . . . [If] upon the whole matter the Court shall be of opinion that the killing of Richard Parker be felony and murder, then the jurors say that Dudley and Stephens were each guilty of felony and murder as alleged in the indictment.

... [This case differs from killing done] in the service of ... [the] Sovereign and in the defense of ... [the] country. Now it is admitted that the deliberate killing of this unoffending and unresisting boy was clearly murder, unless the killing can be justified by some well-recognized excuse admitted by the law. It is further admitted that there was in this case no such excuse, unless the killing was justified by what has been called "necessity." But the temptation to the act which existed here was not what the law has ever called necessity. Nor is this to be regretted. Though law and morality are not the same, the many things may be immoral which are not necessarily illegal, yet the absolute divorce of law from morality would be of fatal consequence; and such divorce would follow if the temptation to murder in this case were to be held by law an absolute defense of it. It is not so....

It must not be supposed that in refusing to admit temptation to be an excuse for crime it is forgotten how terrible the temptation was; how awful the suffering; how hard in such trials to keep the judgment straight and the conduct pure. We are often compelled to set up standards we cannot reach ourselves. ... A man has no right to ... allow compassion for the criminal to change or weaken in any manner the legal definition of the crime. It is therefore our duty to declare that the prisoners' act in this case was willful murder, that the facts as stated in the verdict are no legal justification of the homicide; and to say that in our unanimous opinion the prisoners are upon this special verdict guilty of murder.

Questions and Case Problems

1. Alan Bakke applied to the Medical School at the University of California at Davis under the regular admissions program for one of 100 seats. He was rejected. Under a special admissions procedure, certain minority group members with lesser academic credentials were admitted. Does this represent reverse discrimination? Does this illustrate social engineering? [*Regents of the University of California v. Alan Bakke,* 438 U.S. 265 (1978).]
2. Justice Byron White of the U.S. Supreme Court made the following statement: "The imposition and execution of the death penalty are obviously cruel in the dictionary sense. But the penalty has not been considered cruel and unusual in the constitutional sense because it was thought justified by the social ends it was deemed to serve." Is capital punishment a reasonable way to punish people? [*Furman v. Georgia,* 408 U.S. 238 (1972).]
3. Esop, a native of Baghdad, is aboard a ship docked in Great Britain. While in port he was indicted for committing an unnatural act which from his background he did not know was wrongful or illegal. Should he be punished? [*Rex v. Esop,* 7 Car. & P. 456 (1836).]
4. A passenger runs to catch a train that is leaving a railroad station. In an attempt to help the potential passenger, a trainman pulled the man aboard and dislodged a package from his arms. The package, which contained fireworks, exploded and overturned some distant scales that fell upon plaintiff and injured her. The courts have for years argued the question of to what extent one person should be liable to another where the injury is not clearly foreseeable. What practical norm might you create that would allow you to answer the question posed? Would you hold the Long Island Railroad responsible for the injury to the woman hurt by the scales? [*Palsgraf v. Long Island R. Co.,* 162 N.E. 99 (N.Y. 1928).]
5. "In each of the cases before us, minors of the Negro race, through their legal representatives, seek the aid of the courts in obtaining admission to the public

schools of their community on a nonsegregated basis. In each instance, they had been denied admission to the schools attended by white children under laws requiring or permitting segregation according to race. This segregation was alleged to deprive the plaintiffs of equal protection." Does segregation of children on the basis of race, even though physical and other factors may be equal, represent discriminatory and illegal treatment? [*Brown v. Board of Education,* 347 U.S. 483 (1954).]

6. A group of picketers decided that the best place to communicate their ideas was in a local shopping mall. The owners of the mall moved to stop the picketers from trespassing in the mall. The Supreme Court ruled that "the mall was the equivalent of a main street business district and the state should not exclude members of the public wishing to [picket]." What norm is illustrated in this case? [*Amalgamated Food Employees Local 590 v. Logan Valley Plaza,* 391 U.S. 308 (1968).]

7. Musicians are being interviewed on a radio station. During the interview, the musicians used the words "fooling around with his wife." Some of the listeners think that the words mean that the plaintiff was engaged in an affair with the defendant. The plaintiff thinks that the use of these words should be punished. If you were designing a legal system, would this kind of action be punishable? Would this be a violation of a norm? Explain. [*Matherson v. Marchello,* 473 N.Y.S. 2d 998 (N.Y. 1984).]

8. A television commercial attempting to illustrate the moisturizing capacity of a shaving cream is demonstrated to be capable of making it possible to shave sandpaper. In fact, sandpaper is not used. Rather, Plexiglas with sand sprinkled on it is used. What rule would you establish as head of the Federal Trade Commission (FTC)? What norm is illustrated? [*Colgate-Palmolive Co. v. FTC,* 310 F.2d 89 (1962).]

9. In a letter Thomas Jefferson said: "I know of no safe depository of the ultimate powers of the society but the people themselves." [A. C. Lipscomb, ed., *The Writings of Thomas Jefferson* (Washington, D.C.: T. Jefferson Memorial Association, 1903) XV 276–79.] Why might Thomas Jefferson have made this statement?

10. *Regina v. Dudley and Stephens,* excerpted at the beginning of this section, illustrates a case in which a judge is trying to apply the law without allowing his personal reaction to the facts to enter into his judgment. Is this always appropriate?

CHAPTER 2

ORGANIZATION OF THE U.S. LEGAL SYSTEM

After you have read this chapter, you should be able to:

1. Identify and explain several techniques for resolving disputes.
2. Explain the advantages and disadvantages of arbitration, mediation, and conciliation.
3. Explain the roles of different kinds of law craftsmen: lawyers, judges, paralegals.
4. Identify the different kinds of state and federal courts.
5. Explain the process of beginning a lawsuit.
6. Distinguish between statutory law, common law, administrative law, case law, and constitutional law.

BUSINESS DECISIONS and the LAW

Do you know that the first justice on the Supreme Court to have a degree from a law school was Oliver Wendell Holmes, Jr.? Before then justices served apprenticeships before practicing law as did all other lawyers.

Few people have had as profound an effect on the law as has Oliver Wendell Holmes, Jr. He lived a long and productive life. In fact, he became a member of the Supreme Court at age sixty and was still serving at age ninety. During his career as a justice in our highest court, he had the opportunity to work on such critical business issues as minimum wage laws, labor contract issues such as the "yellow dog" contract, and issues involving freedom of speech. His decisions were so thoughtful and thought-provoking that he has almost become the image of what law practitioners think of when they imagine a judge. His wisdom and clarity of thought help us understand the importance of the court system in resolving disputes.

For example, in the early part of this century, the question of working hours was hotly debated. Men, women, and even children worked under adverse conditions for lengthy periods of time. The State of New York had passed a statute establishing maximum hours for bakers. In 1905, the Supreme Court rejected the statute, the majority arguing that any such statute would be an impermissible infringement on one's freedom of contract.* Holmes understood

**Lochner v. New York*, 198 U.S. 45 (1905).

the need for social legislation and argued in his dissenting opinion that the Constitution permits the states to regulate hours of work through use of police power since people's health and safety were at stake.

Justice Holmes was a model legal practitioner and scholar. He understood that the law needed to be practical and to deal in reality. He had compassion and an understanding of law in our daily lives. He worked in the state courts of Massachusetts and in the highest federal court in the land.

Introduction

In Chapter 1 we discussed basic notions about law and the nature of legal systems. In this chapter we will discuss the U.S. legal system, its operation, and alternatives to the use of the legal system in order to resolve civil disputes.

In a society as large as our own, people are bound to have conflicting ideas about how things ought to be done. Indeed, even in a relatively small group such as a family or business organization, it is likely that from time to time individuals will disagree. Fortunately, most of the time these disagreements can be settled promptly and with no formal proceeding necessary. But what happens when the problem is complex or difficult to resolve? For example, what happens when a truck owned by Kross Kuntrie Freight, Inc., collides with another truck owned by One Way, Inc., and both drivers deny that they are the cause of the accident?

Suppose that in the situation just mentioned one of the drivers decides that the best way to resolve the dispute is to start a fight with the other driver and the fight results in serious injury to that other driver. Furthermore, what happens if some of the cargo is damaged as a result of the accident? Who should be held responsible—the trucking firm, the individual drivers, the seller, or the purchaser? As we will see, these perplexing issues can be resolved in a number of ways.

Response of the Law

In the next few pages we will first examine the nonjudicial procedures that people use to resolve grievances among themselves. Then we will look at the legal forums available for resolving disputes. This material is preparation for treatment in later chapters of the substantive rules applied to particular cases. We will focus primarily on a branch of the U.S. legal system known as civil procedure, although we will first look at alternatives to using law, such as compromise, arbitration, or mediation.

No time will be spent in this chapter on the U.S. criminal law. But students should bear in mind that the procedures used for resolving criminal cases are markedly different from those described here, as illustrated by the following case, which discusses the burden of proof of the prosecution in a criminal case.

FACTS

On January 3, 1982, agents of the U.S. Customs Service conducted a surveillance of a house in Key Largo, Florida. Customs officials observed several people running empty-handed from the area around the house down to the boat, returning from the boat carrying large bundles. Bales of marijuana were found in and around an enclosed garage. Several people were arrested including defendant. Defendant was found on the second floor of a house hiding in a closet. After arrest and conviction defendant argues that there was insufficient evidence to support his conviction.

DECISION

It is not necessary that the evidence exclude every reasonable hypothesis of innocence or be wholly inconsistent with every conclusion except that of guilt, provided that a jury could find that the evidence establishes guilt beyond a reasonable doubt. A jury is free to choose among reasonable constructions of the evidence.

U.S. v. Pintado, 715 F.2d 1501 (11th Cir. 1983).

Most of the events mentioned in the introduction to this chapter would be handled in the civil courts of the United States. *Civil* courts deal with disputes between parties which are not concerned with offenses against society and are not punishable by society. *Criminal* courts deal with individuals who have wronged *society* by committing a crime defined by one of the various criminal codes. In our truck driver incident the fight might result in criminal charges of assault and/or battery being filed. All the other disputes would involve interpreting contracts between the parties or ascribing the fault to one of the drivers for causing the accident or deciding who bears the burden for damaged cargo. They would all lie within the purview of a *civil* court of law and would be resolved by the parties either nonjudicially or by the use of the legal procedures discussed later. (See pp. 28–32 and Appendix A.)

Alternative Mechanisms—Nonjudicial, or Use of the Legal System

Suppose you purchase a stereo system from a reputable store in your community and the system simply does not live up to your expectations. What do you do? It is highly unlikely that your first response would be to sue the department store. Rather, you would probably begin by taking the set back to the store and asking for a refund or a replacement. You have a grievance and you are looking for the simplest, most direct route toward a solution. Most reliable stores would be willing to replace the set or refund your money if the cause of the difficulty could not be traced to something you had done. That is the simple case. But let's make the problem more difficult. Suppose you discover a large scratch on the speaker cabinet. You know you did not cause the scratch. But what if the retail dealer thinks that the scratch looks like something you might have done through your carelessness in unpacking the speaker and, thus, the dealer is unwilling to take it back or refund your money? What can you do without resorting to the courts?

Nonjudicial Mechanisms

▶ Compromise

The chances are you would still not run off to your lawyer in preparation for a lawsuit. Even if you did, a responsible attorney would not instantly file a suit. Rather, a more logical solution would be to seek a **compromise.** A compromise is an agreement resolving a dispute reached through concessions offered by the aggrieved parties. In the case of the stereo, you might start with requesting a refund, or you might indicate that you would be willing to accept the unit at a reduced cost with the defect. Likewise, the retailer might agree to offer you a discount if you kept the damaged speaker. Each of you has moved slightly from your original position to some acceptable middle ground. The dispute is over and each party is satisfied with the result.

compromise
An agreement resolving a dispute outside of court reached through concessions offered by the aggrieved parties

Why should a businessperson ever compromise? There are a number of good reasons for settling a dispute through compromise. The first reason has to do with the cost of litigation. Hiring a lawyer to resolve a simple business disagreement is an expensive proposition. A lawyer's fee could easily exceed the value of the item in question. For example, a five-dollar discount in the cost of the speaker is far simpler to grant and far less costly than consulting a lawyer on the issue.

A second reason for compromise is the speed of resolution. Litigation takes time. Civil courts in certain parts of the country have extremely heavy workloads, and it is possible that they would be unable to hear a case for months; in some cases years might go by before the issue is heard. A compromise satisfactory to both parties is rapid—indeed, even instantaneous.

► Arbitration

arbitration
A method for deciding disputes outside of court by persons called arbitrators, appointed by the disputing parties

Another alternative to litigation is **arbitration.** Arbitration is the process of resolving a dispute by using a third party chosen for his or her neutrality to decide the disputed issue or issues. Arbitration usually implies that the parties agree to be bound by the decision of the intermediary. For example, in the case of the scratched stereo, if you and the retailer could not agree on a precise compromise position, you both might have chosen to arbitrate the dispute. That is, you both could have called upon a neutral third party to decide what should be done. In the following case the court declared that the new Missouri Uniform Arbitration Act should be followed.

FACTS

On June 1973 Tri-City Construction Company entered into a construction contract with the city of Kansas City, Kansas, for sewer improvements. In August 1973 Tri-City signed a subcontract with Alliett and Williams for a portion of the work. A dispute arose alleging money due under the subcontract in various courts. A proceeding was brought to compel the judge to proceed to a final determination on a petition to confirm the arbitrator's award. The arbitrator had decided the case under the new Missouri Uniform Arbitration Act. Should the Missouri Courts enforce private arbitration decisions which are otherwise in accord with the law?

DECISION

Yes. Adoption of the Uniform Arbitration Act in this state is a legislative recognition of the growing use of arbitration as a means of resolving disputes quickly with relatively low cost to the parties.

State ex rel. Tri-City Construction Company v. Marsh, 668 S.W.2d 148 (Mo. App. 1984).

Anyone can be an arbitrator of a dispute. All that is required is that the parties to the dispute have trust in the chosen neutral and that the neutral have the intelligence necessary to understand the dimensions of the particular problem presented. The case of the scratched stereo is relatively simple, but not all issues amenable to arbitration are so simple to resolve. For example, labor relations disputes often involve multimillion-dollar business operations and complex employee contracts. When such affairs demand the attention of an arbitrator, the individual chosen must have special skills. There are a number of ways of locating individuals with the desired experience. One possibility is to contact a local university and find a professor with the skills required. Another, somewhat more direct, route is to contact a specialized arbitration organization, such as the American Arbitration Association. They in turn will help you select an appropriate individual for your particular needs.

The practice of arbitration is not so clearly defined as formal legal procedure. An arbitrator may hold an informal hearing with the disputing parties or may be very formal and require that the parties prepare evidence, bring forward witnesses, and the like. Furthermore, an arbitrator may serve one company on a permanent basis, agreeing to handle all complaints presented over a year, or may serve a given firm only once. Arbitration has many of the same advantages that compromise has. *First,* arbitration is a rapid way of dealing with disputes. Once an arbitrator is located, it is merely a matter of scheduling an appropriate hearing time and waiting for a decision to be made. Thus the problem of the overburdened court is eliminated.

Second, although arbitration is more costly than compromise, it still is not as costly as settling a dispute in court. This is because it is not necessary to have a lawyer present to argue a case in front of an arbitrator, there does not need to be as much preparation, and no papers need to be filed.

Third, arbitration can generate goodwill. If compromise does not lead to a solution, arbitration may be an easy way to settle the dispute without generating a great deal of hostility. For example, a retail department store may want to maintain good customer relations with the residents of the town in which it is located. If the store or the grievant feels that a compromise solution to their problem cannot be found without sacrificing future relations, they might still agree to arbitrate. The arbitrator need not worry about hostility being directed toward him or her, since the relationship is short-term.

Fourth, the parties may call upon experts in particular areas to decide disputes. Judges often are unfamiliar with highly complex, technical areas, and the parties may feel more comfortable having their dispute argued before an expert.

► Mediation

Sometimes the disputing parties would like the help of a third individual but would not like to feel bound to follow the solution proposed by arbitration. In that case an alternative mechanism for dispute resolution is **mediation.** Mediation generally follows a twelve-stage pattern outlined in Table 2.1. Mediation is the process of intervention of a third party between two disputing parties for the purpose of moving them closer to a compromise position. Neither side is bound by what the mediator suggests.

mediation
The process of using a third party to bring disputants closer to resolution of their differences

TABLE 2.1 **The Twelve Stages of Mediation**

Stage	Action
1	Initial contacts with the disputing parties
2	Selecting a strategy to guide mediation
3	Collecting and analyzing background information
4	Designing a detailed plan for mediation
5	Building trust and cooperation
6	Beginning the mediation session
7	Defining issues and setting an agenda
8	Uncovering hidden interests of the disputing parties
9	Generating options for settlement
10	Assessing options for settlement
11	Final bargaining
12	Achieving formal settlement

Source: L. Riskin and J. Westbrook, *Dispute Resolution and Lawyers* (St. Paul: West Publishing, 1987), reprinted with permission of The West Publishing Company.

The most familiar contemporary illustration of mediation is one drawn from international relations. Former presidential advisor Henry Kissinger used the term "shuttle diplomacy" to describe his efforts to mediate the differences of opinion in a Middle East controversy. President Carter did the same in the Egyptian-Israeli dispute in 1979, as did President Reagan's representative Philip Habib in the Israel/Palestine Liberation Organization evacuation of the PLO from Beirut, Lebanon, in 1982. Some examples of mediation may be as close as the college you are attending. Many schools have people known as "ombudsmen" on campus. These are people who were chosen for their rapport with students, faculty, and administrators and for their ability to act as an intermediary (or mediator) in disputes that may arise among these three groups. Another example of a mediator might come from the area of labor law. Many firms turn to state-run mediation services when contract negotiations break down.

As is the case in arbitration, the profession of mediator is ill-defined. Mediators might be highly skilled persons with a great deal of expertise in a particular subject area, or they might simply be persons respected for their neutrality. Mediation might be a full-time position with the state or federal government, or it might be a part-time position for a university professor or someone in the clergy.

Using the Legal System: The Craftsmen

▶ Lawyers

If compromise, arbitration, or mediation should fail to result in a solution, the next step might be to turn to the law. For most people this means turning to a lawyer. In the next few pages we will review the roles that various individuals play in the legal system.

lawyer
A person who is licensed to practice law by advising and representing clients in legal matters

A **lawyer** is an individual trained as an advocate to represent clients in the legal process. The training involved normally amounts to four years of college followed by three years of law school. Students come to law from all college majors—from business to fine arts. Law schools look for inquisitive, thoughtful students in their admissions process. Even after this rather lengthy period of study, almost all states require that potential lawyers pass a bar examination that tests their understanding of basic legal concepts and special understanding of particular states' laws. Although most people imagine that lawyers spend the majority of their time in court, this is not true. In the following case the court indicated that discussion giving legal advice is practicing law, which occurs outside the courtroom, but that the activities of the defendants, nonlawyers, were not of that character and did not constitute practicing law.

FACTS

The defendants maintained an office in Portland and advertised in the Portland papers. One sample ad read as follows: "Divorce. Join the thousands of people who have been successful in securing their own non-contested divorce. Oregon Divorce Council."

The plaintiff, Oregon State Bar, brought suit to enjoin the defendants from practicing law through advertising and sale of do-it-yourself divorce kits. None of the defendants is a lawyer. May they be stopped?

DECISION

Some of their activities may continue. The defendants did not actually practice law by publishing and advertising and selling such kits. But any *discussion* they might have with the parties is a violation of the law.

Oregon State Bar v. Gilchrist, 538 P.2d 913 (Or. 1975).

Lawyers enter into a relationship with a client based upon the client's trust that the lawyer will help to resolve the client's concerns in an expeditious manner. This trust is called a **fiduciary** relationship. In the following case the court points out that an attorney must be very careful how he or she handles a client's money. The court also points out that the conduct of the attorney with respect to his client's funds violated trust in him as a lawyer.

fiduciary
A person with a duty to act primarily for the benefit of another

FACTS

The lawyer admits that he (1) failed to obtain written directions for disbursement of $18,000 of his client's funds, (2) delivered the $18,000 to another without obtaining a receipt, and (3) received $2,000 in reimbursement for expenses for which he maintained no substantiating records. He maintains that he acted in good faith in accordance with his client's oral directions and neither injured his client nor violated any rules or statutes governing professional conduct. Did the attorney breach the trust?

DECISION

The attorney's failure to maintain adequate records warrants discipline (and) the attorney is publicly reprimanded. The rules of professional conduct specify "Unless the client otherwise directs in writing, [the attorney] shall promptly deposit his client's funds. It is largely irrelevant that an attorney may have violated the rule in good faith and without damage to his client."

Fitzsimmons v. State Bar of California, 667 P.2d 700 (Cal. 1983).

Many problems simply do not require that a lawyer spend time in court. For example, the procedures involved in many real estate transactions require the talents of an attorney but often do not require his or her appearance before a judge. Similarly, many problems require a great deal of out-of-court time in relation to the time spent in court. For example, many states have uncontested or no-fault divorce statutes. An attorney may spend days working out the dimensions of the separation agreement with the couple and only a few minutes in the actual courtroom appearance.

Furthermore, some lawyers take jobs requiring that they use their legal training to perform other kinds of tasks. Some people, for example, use their training in large corporations as managers. Others are employed in government agencies working on administrative law problems. Still others teach law and do extensive research into perplexing contemporary problems. All of the foregoing should not lead you to the conclusion that lawyers rarely use the courts. Rather, you should realize that there are many opportunities for people to use their law-trained minds both inside and outside the courtroom. Lawyers are officers of the court in that they carry out official duties and, in a trial, have a duty to assist the court in the administration of justice.

► Judges

There are two systems of courts in the United States: state and federal. This leads us to the fact that there are two systems of **judges,** state and federal. If some of you have had contact with a judge, it is likely that it was a judge working in the state system. Many communities have municipal court judges who handle routine minor cases such as illegal parking and other traffic violations. The municipal judge may also decide simple disorderly conduct or shoplifting cases.

judge
The government officer who presides over a court

Another kind of state judge that many people are familiar with is the "justice of the peace." J.P.s usually have the power to hear minor violations of the law and often have the power to perform civil marriage ceremonies. J.P. courts have come under increasing criticism in the last few years because the judges are often not trained in law or legal processes and are often merely political appointees.

At the higher levels of court, state judges are often elected for a long term in office. The reason for the long term is to free the judge from being concerned that unpopular (but fair) decisions will potentially cost him or her a job. At these upper levels, judges are usually well trained in law, often having practiced or taught law for several years, and have undergone careful scrutiny by the state bar association.

The length of time in office for federal judges is defined by the U.S. Constitution, which states that all federal judges serve in office so long as they maintain good behavior. Thus federal judges may hold their offices for an unlimited period of time. This makes it important that the individuals be carefully chosen for the position. All federal judges are nominated by the President of the United States and are confirmed by the Senate before they sit on the bench.

One additional kind of judge is an "administrative law judge." Many federal administrative agencies have the power to create rules and regulations that have the force of law. For example, the Federal Communications Commission creates rules to govern citizens band radios. Some of these agencies have established tribunals that determine whether accused persons have violated their rules. Those who decide are specialists called administrative law judges. The following case illustrates the power of an administrative law judge.

FACTS

Ms. Holding, an employee, was injured in a one-vehicle accident involving a truck owned by the alleged employer. A third party was driving the truck when its brakes failed and it struck a pole. The employee sustained many injuries. Conflicting testimony was given about the accident before an administrative law judge. A question was presented concerning the judge's discretion to discount the claimant's testimony because the claimant lacked credibility.

DECISION

The administrative law judge is the sole judge of witness credibility. Although the administrative law judge may not reject a claimant's testimony simply because it is motivated by self-interest, the administrative law judge may reject it if it is self-contradictory, inconsistent with other evidence, or directly impeached.

Holding v. Industrial Commission of Arizona, 679 P.2d 571 (Ariz. App. 1984).

Other Law Craftsmen

It would take almost an entire volume to describe in detail all of the different jobs people do in order to make the legal system function. Many of these make interesting and rewarding careers. Inside the courthouse, people hold such law-related positions as clerk, bailiff, court reporter, and some larger courts have law librarians and judicial administration officers as well. Outside the courtroom, law crafts abound. These include positions such as police officer, corrections officials, and legislative research aides.

Paralegals

paralegal
An individual trained to assist lawyers in their practice

An emerging occupation for people interested in law but not interested in attending years of law school is that of the **paralegal.** This position is also referred to as a legal assistant or lawyer's assistant. Persons in paralegal positions assist lawyers in a number of different ways. They may complete preliminary interviews with clients, thus saving the lawyer a great deal of time. After proper training, paralegals may do legal research, file and prepare papers with the proper court authorities, and generally perform other tasks under the supervision of an attorney. Since the job title "paralegal" is relatively new, the exact tasks that any individual can expect to do will vary with the inclinations of the paralegal's employer. Paralegal work is often a research-oriented position with a great deal of client contact. At many colleges, the program offering training in this field and resulting in certification is called a paralegal or legal assistant program.

Using the Legal System: The Courts

It was mentioned above that the United States has a dual system of **courts.** What this means is that each state has a court structure and the federal government also has a court structure. The courts may be diagrammed as shown in Figures 2.1 and 2.2.

court
A judicial tribunal

► State Courts

State Inferior Courts **State inferior courts** are the lowest order of state courts and they are sharply limited in **jurisdiction.** Jurisdiction is the power of a court to hear and to decide a case involving a person or subject matter properly brought before the court. Every state decides what configuration of courts it needs to deal with the case load that it faces. Therefore it would be difficult to list every kind of inferior court. However, typically, states have *probate courts* designed to work on the estates of the deceased. They also have *small claims courts,* which can hear cases involving relatively small amounts of money, the amount varying from state to state. *Traffic courts, criminal courts, police courts, mayor's courts, magistrate's courts, municipal* or *city courts, justice of the peace courts,* and *county courts* are other relatively common inferior courts. Note that the word "inferior" refers to the fact that these courts are the lowest in the state system, not that they are of lesser quality. These inferior courts are *trial* courts, but they may not hear cases outside their jurisdiction. For example, a traffic court may not hear a case involving the probate (proof) of a will, nor may a small claims court hear controversies that exceed a certain dollar limit.

state inferior court
The lowest order of state trial court

jurisdiction
The power of a court to hear and decide a case involving a person or subject matter properly brought before the court

FIGURE 2.1 State Court System

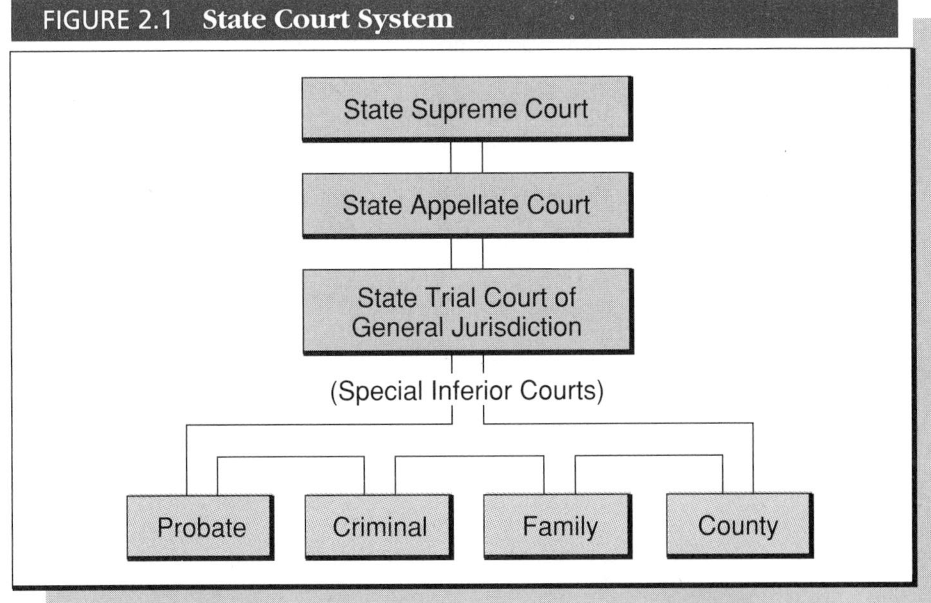

FIGURE 2.2 **Federal Court System**

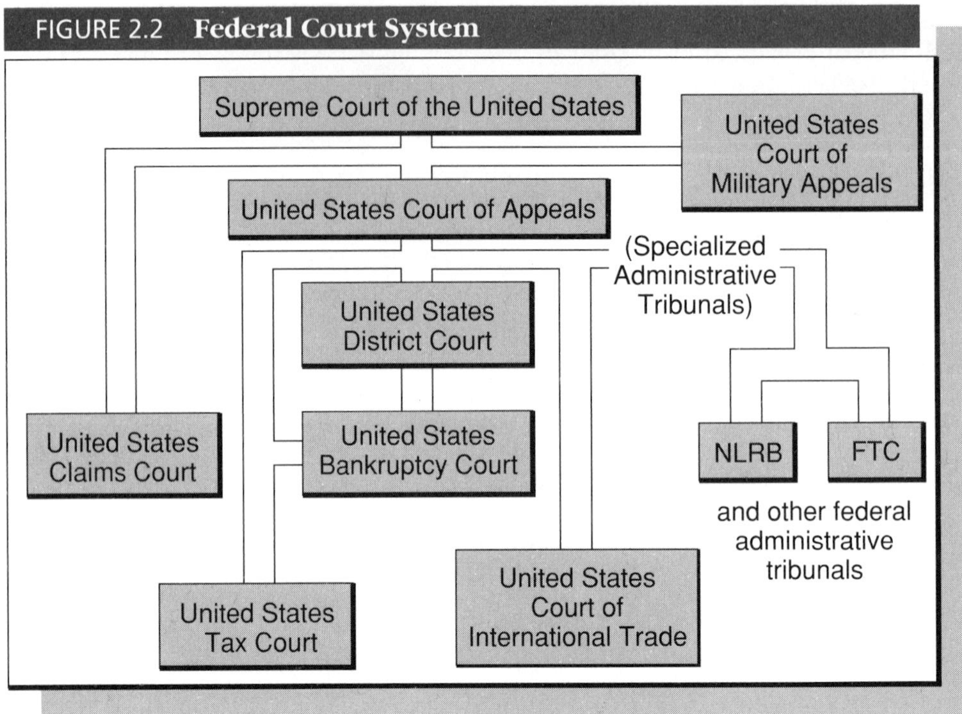

state court of general jurisdiction
The highest order of state trial court

State Courts of General Jurisdiction **State courts of general jurisdiction** have many different names, such as *circuit court, superior court, district court,* or *court of common pleas.* In all states these represent the highest *trial* level court. Since all cases begin in a trial level court, they begin at an inferior court that can hear the case or, if appropriate, a court of general jurisdiction. Also, if a lawyer gets an unsatisfactory result in the inferior court and wishes to further argue a point of law, he or she may appeal to the court of general jurisdiction. These courts are called general jurisdiction courts because they may hear any type of case. However, if there is an inferior court that can hear the case, they will allow it to hear the case first. Technically, its only limitation is territorial. For example, a Texas court of general jurisdiction would not hear a case involving an incident that took place in New York and that involved disputants also from New York.

question of fact
A dispute over what happened

question of law
A dispute over the legal effect of what happened

State (Intermediate) Appellate Courts **Questions of fact** (for example, did the person sign the paper?) are settled in trial courts and many cannot be appealed. But lawyers and judges often disagree on the meaning of particular points of law, and these **questions of law** (for example, should the witness have been required to answer a question?) may be appealed to the next higher level court—(intermediate) appellate courts. They are intermediate, or in between, the trial court and the court above the intermediate court—for example, the supreme court. Since (intermediate) appellate courts are not involved in disputes over factual issues, a jury is not required. Lawyers argue points of law in front of a panel of judges (usually three). Just as with inferior courts, the need for intermediate appellate courts varies from state to state depending on case load requirements.

State Supreme Court If a question of law is particularly troublesome, lawyers may appeal to the highest level court—the supreme court of the state. Students should note that the highest state court does not always have the name "supreme court"; sometimes it has a different name. The supreme court, again, is not involved in disputes over questions of fact and so does not require a jury. Rather, a panel of between five and nine judges, depending upon the state, listens to the lawyers argue their points of law. If there is no federal issue involved in a case (such as a federal constitutional question), the determination of law by the state supreme court would terminate a case. There then could be no appeal to the federal court system. However, in certain limited instances (for example, the validity of a federal statute is questioned in the state court proceedings), the U.S. Supreme Court may certify for review a decision by the state supreme court.

► Federal Courts

The U.S. Constitution authorizes the creation of the federal court system. Article III, section I of the Constitution says: "The Judicial Power of the United States shall be vested in one Supreme Court and in such inferior courts as the Congress may from time to time ordain and establish." This has resulted in the formation of the U.S. Supreme Court, which derives its power from the U.S. Constitution, and, over the years, the formation by Congress of all the lower federal courts.

Federal District Courts The **federal district court** is the *trial* level court of the federal system. At this point you may wonder how one decides whether to use the state or federal trial level court. The answer is found in the procedural law. In order for a federal district court to hear a case, the case must fall into one of the following categories: (1) One category is that it may be a federal question (that is, it must be a question arising out of a federal law, treaty, or the federal Constitution). (2) Another category is to have a question that deals with a federal law that has no dollar requirements, such as civil rights issues or copyrights. (3) A final category requires that the disputants be from different states or from a state and a foreign nation *and* the amount in controversy must be *over* $50,000. If there are more than two disputants, no plaintiff (the person bringing the case to court) and no defendant (the person against whom the case is brought) can be from the same state. These requirements are known as subject matter requirements, because they literally define which subjects the federal courts will hear and which will be heard by state courts. In addition to subject matter jurisdiction, courts must also have jurisdiction over the person (**in personam**) or property (**in rem**) in dispute, and there are additional rules of civil procedure that define these requirements.

federal district court
The trial level court of the federal legal system

in personam
Against the person

in rem
Against the thing

U.S. Court of Appeals There are thirteen courts of appeals in the federal system, often called the federal "circuit courts of appeals." Just as with intermediate appellate courts in the state system, the court of appeals does not have "original" jurisdiction over cases. That is, it is not the first court to hear a particular federal case. Rather, the district court or some other federal inferior court holds the trial and the appellate court hears appeals on questions of law. Each of the cases brought before it is heard by a panel of three judges.

U.S. Supreme Court Of course, the highest court within the federal system is the Supreme Court of the United States. In rare cases it has original jurisdiction—for example, in cases involving ambassadors and in controversies between two or more states or between a state and citizens of another state. But the vast majority of its time is spent on appeals made to it from other courts. The Supreme Court is established by the U.S. Constitution and is composed of nine justices, one being the chief justice, each of whom has lifetime tenure in the job. These justices hear certain appeals to it and also decide which limited number of cases they will certify for review by it during the upcoming year. The term used to denote a review by the Supreme Court, and indeed by any appellate court, is "certiorari."

The Supreme Court considers not only cases from the federal district courts and courts of appeals, but also those cases where a state's highest court has rendered a final judgment in a case in which the validity of a state statute has been drawn into question on the ground of its being repugnant to the U.S. Constitution. In a recent case the U.S. Supreme Court considered the validity of a Minnesota statute that allowed state taxpayers, in computing their state income tax, to deduct expenses incurred in providing "tuition, textbooks, and transportation" for their children attending an elementary or secondary school. Petitioners were Minnesota taxpayers who claimed that the statute violated the Establishment Clauses of the First and Fourteenth Amendments of the U.S. Constitution prohibiting Congress from making any law "respecting an establishment of religion." They claimed that parents had taken the tax deduction for expenses incurred in sending their children to parochial schools, and that the statute thereby violated the Establishment Clause by providing financial assistance to sectarian institutions. The Supreme Court held that the Minnesota statute was valid and constitutional. The tax deduction has as its secular purpose ensuring that the state's citizenry is well educated. The deduction does not have the primary effect of advancing the sectarian aims of nonpublic schools. It is only one of many deductions available under Minnesota laws for educational expenses incurred by all parents, whether their children attend public schools or private sectarian or nonsectarian schools.[1]

Other Federal Courts and Administrative Tribunals There are several additional federal courts, each with limited subject matter jurisdiction. The U.S. *tax court* is a specialized federal court dealing with questions that arise concerning federal taxation. Before using the tax court, individuals must first exhaust their administrative remedies through the Internal Revenue Service. The U.S. *claims court* hears cases that deal with claims made by individuals against the U.S. government. As mentioned previously, many administrative agencies are also administrative tribunals that are also part of this federal system. Examples are the National Labor Relations Board and the Federal Trade Commission. Appeals from these special courts (except claims court) and administrative tribunals are heard first by the U.S. court of appeals and later, if further litigation is needed, by the U.S. Supreme Court. The U.S. Court of Military Appeals is worth noting here as a separate federal court. It is important to note that the U.S. Supreme Court can review decisions of the U.S. court of military appeals.

Using the Legal System: The Lawsuit

Once the proper court is chosen by your attorney, he or she must begin the case by notification of the grievance to the court and the person or group you wish to proceed against. Instituting a lawsuit is a complex branch of a discipline known as civil (or criminal) procedure. In the next few pages we will sketch an outline of the proceedings

[1]*Mueller and Noyes v. Allen, Jr.*, et al., 463 U.S. 388 (1983).

in a civil lawsuit. Later in this book there is a detailed outline of the civil trial process. (See pp. A 1243–1249).

Parties to the Suit

In addition to the various law craftsmen described earlier in this chapter, the two primary parties are the **plaintiff** and **defendant.** The plaintiff is the person who has a grievance and begins a civil lawsuit. The defendant is the party against whom the lawsuit (or criminal action) is brought and who must be notified of the case.

plaintiff
The party who initiates a civil suit by filing a complaint in the proper court

defendant
The party against whom a civil suit (or criminal action) is brought

Complaint and Response

The plaintiff must notify both the court and the defendant that he or she wishes to begin a lawsuit. In order to do this the plaintiff prepares papers known as **pleadings.** The initial paper prepared is called the **complaint** (see Figure 2.3), which sets forth in detail the cause of action that the plaintiff has against the defendant. It states the position of the plaintiff in clear and concise language. The plaintiff's attorney or paralegal assistant then takes the papers to the appropriate court. The plaintiff's attorney usually also prepares a **summons** (see Figure 2.4) which, usually along with a copy of the complaint, is served (delivered) upon the defendant.

pleadings
The formal documents filed with a court that usually include the complaint, answer, and motions regarding them

complaint
The first pleading in a civil action

summons
A writ or process served on the defendant in a civil action notifying him or her of the action and summoning him or her to appear and plead

The summons sets forth the place for the trial as determined by the court, and the complaint tells the defendant why he or she is being sued. Service of the summons upon the defendant is necessary for the court to have jurisdiction over the defendant and to try the case. Obviously care must be taken to ensure that the defendant is actually notified, so ideally a court officer or other proper person must personally serve the summons upon the defendant or, in a proper case, mail it to the defendant via registered mail.

Upon receiving the summons and complaint, the defendant then has several alternatives. The simplest thing to do, although probably the least wise, would be to disregard the summons. This would result in a *default* judgment being filed against the defendant. A default means that the defendant has automatically lost the case.

A wiser course of action would be for the defendant to choose a lawyer and turn over the summons and complaint to the lawyer. Lawyers can be located through friends or through the state or local bar associations. If the defendant cannot afford a lawyer, there are a number of organizations that may provide assistance. In criminal cases the court would appoint a lawyer to ensure that the defendant receives competent legal assistance in protecting his or her rights. In civil cases certain organizations might wish to assist—for example, legal aid societies, legal service corporations, the American Civil Liberties Union, and special interest groups such as public interest research groups.

The defendant's lawyer would then choose from a number of options. Often the lawyer will file an *answer* to the complaint by agreeing with, or denying, each of the points raised in the plaintiff's pleading. The defendant may add some additional points or may even choose to **counterclaim,** which means a cause of action asserted by the defendant against the plaintiff. The entire process is designed to focus attention on those points about which there is disagreement.

counterclaim
A claim asserted by the defendant against the plaintiff's claim in a civil action

Of course, lawyers should make every effort to resolve cases before they come to trial. It may be clear from the pleadings that a ground for compromise exists, and lawyers often negotiate with each other compromise solutions that are in the best interests of all the parties to the dispute. Compromise solutions to civil disputes are encouraged by the courts, and it is possible to compromise at any time prior to the trial.

FIGURE 2.3 **Example of a Complaint/Pleading**

IN THE DISTRICT COURT IN AND FOR THE

COUNTY OF BOULDER AND

STATE OF COLORADO

Civil Action No.___________

```
QUICK COMMERCIAL LOANS,        )
INC. A Colorado Corporation,)
                               )
               Plaintiff,      )          COMPLAINT ON
                               )
v.                             )          PROMISSORY NOTE
                               )
GERALD K. JONES,               )
                               )
               Defendant.      )
```

COMES NOW the Plaintiff, by and through its counsel, FISH, FISH, and LAKE, and complains and alleges as follows:

1. That the amount involved herein is in excess of $1,000.00.

2. That venue is proper in this Court because Defendant resided at 621 Pine Street, Boulder, Colorado (Boulder County) as of the commencement of this action.

3. That the Defendant, on or about March 30, 1989 executed and delivered to Plaintiff a Promissory Note, a copy of which is attached hereto and hereby made a part of this Complaint.

4. That the Defendant on or about March 30, 1989 received $5,000.00 as a loan under the terms of the Promissory Note above referenced.

5. That the Defendant has refused to make payments when due and there remains yet due and payable the sum of $3,652.19.

WHEREFORE, Plaintiff demands Judgment against the Defendant in the amount of $3,652.19 together with interest and legal fees as provided in said note, for the costs of suit and collection of the Judgment, interest on the entire amount due at the legal rate from date of Judgment and such other relief as the Court may deem just and proper.

FISH, FISH and LAKE
Attorneys at Law

____
By: Frank R. Fish, Jr. #2232
1909 Pearl Street, Suite 1300
Boulder, Colorado 80302
Telephone: (303) 499-1058

Plaintiff's Address

828 Arapahoe Street
Boulder, Colorado 80302

FIGURE 2.4 Example of a Summons

Court Filing Stamp

IN THE...DISTRICT.......COURT
IN AND FOR
...................COUNTY OF...BOULDER................
AND STATE OF COLORADO

Civil Action No. .... Div. ....

QUICK COMMERCIAL LOANS, INC.
A Colorado Corporation

Plaintiff..........,

vs.

GERALD K. JONES

Defendant...........

SUMMONS

THE PEOPLE OF THE STATE OF COLORADO
TO THE ABOVE NAMED DEFENDANT.........., GREETINGS:

You are hereby summoned and required to file with the clerk an answer to the complaint within 20 days after service of this summons upon you. If you fail so to do, judgment by default will be taken against you for the relief demanded in the complaint.

If service upon you is made outside the State of Colorado, or by publication, or if a copy of the complaint be not served upon you with this summons, you are required to file your answer to the complaint within 30 days after service of this summons upon you.

Warning: If this summons does not contain the docket number of the civil action, then the complaint may not now be on file with the clerk of the court. The complaint must be filed within ten days after the summons is served, or the court will be without jurisdiction to proceed further and the action will be deemed dismissed without prejudice and without further notice. Information from the court concerning this civil action may not be available until ten days after the summons is served.

This is an action* in debt, as set forth more fully in the Complaint.

Dated.......January 20......................, 19.....90.....

FISH, FISH and LAKE
Attorneys at Law

....
Clerk of said Court

By..
Deputy Clerk

....
Attorney for Plaintiff
Frank R. Fish, Jr. #2232
1909 Pearl Street, Suite 1300
Boulder, Colorado 80302
Address of Attorney 499-1058

(Seal of Court)

*This summons is issued pursuant to Rule 4, C.R.C.P., as amended. If the summons is published or served without a copy of the complaint, after the word "action" state the relief demanded. If body execution is sought the summons must state, "This is an action founded upon tort."

Appearing in Court

evidence
A fact from which an inference can be drawn of another fact

jury
Trial jury, a group of people selected to decide the facts in a trial

challenge
In a jury trial, objection by a party to an action to persons chosen for service on a jury to try a case who have not been selected properly, or who are not qualified or impartial

peremptory challenge
A challenge to an individual juror for which no cause need be stated. Only a limited number of peremptory challenges are allowed in each case

cross-examination
A party's initial examination of a witness other than the party's own in a trial

verdict
A jury's finding of fact

judgment
The final decision of a case by a court

If the lawyers cannot settle out of court and if the pleadings have been finalized, it is time to prepare for trial. Each of the lawyers marshals as much **evidence** as possible in anticipation of the courtroom appearance. If there are both questions of law (for example, was the writing a contract?) *and* questions of fact (was the defendant negligent?) to be decided, then there is a need to have a **jury.** Either party may demand a jury; but if both parties decide not to have a jury, the judge alone will decide the questions of fact. If no dispute exists as to the facts of a case (that is, what happened), then there is no need for a jury and the case can be tried in front of a judge. Choosing a jury must be done with the utmost care to avoid bias.

In a recent important criminal case shattering precedent, *Batson v. Kentucky,* 106 S.Ct. 1712 (1986), the U.S. Supreme Court, in reversing and remanding for further proceedings the conviction by an all white jury of a black defendant, held that purposeful racial discrimination in the selection of a jury denies a defendant the "protection that a trial by jury is intended to secure," namely a jury of one's peers. The prosecutor had exercised its **peremptory challenges** to exclude four blacks from the jury. Prior to this case, a black defendant who alleged discriminatory exclusion of black jurors had the burden of showing that the prosecution invariably used peremptory challenges to exclude blacks *in case after case*—"a crippling burden of proof." In this case the court held that, if the defendant can show a pattern of discriminatory challenges *in that defendant's trial alone,* then the prosecutor has the burden of demonstrating a nonracial motive for making such challenges.

Once the jury is chosen the trial may begin. Each side presents its evidence to the judge and jury. Lawyers must be careful that they present their views without violating the rules of evidence for the admission of materials to the court. Lawyers not only present their best evidence, but they try to find flaws in their opponents' evidence. For example, oral evidence that is presented by a witness for the plaintiff may be rebutted through skillful **cross-examination** by the defendant's lawyer—the process of questioning an opposing witness following his or her original testimony.

When both sides have concluded their presentation, including their summations, the judge makes a statement to the jury explaining what law they must consider in coming to a verdict. These explanations to the jury are called the jury instructions.

The jury then retires to a private room in the courthouse or elsewhere to deliberate the **verdict.** When this is done, they return to the court and announce their decision. The judge then renders **judgment.**

The losing side then has a set period of time within which it must decide whether or not to appeal to a higher court. Again, the appeal must be based upon a disagreement about a point of *law,* either substantive or some procedural violation. Generally, there can be no appeal of questions of *fact.* For example, if we go back to the case of the scratched stereo, a question of *fact* would be: Who scratched the speaker cabinet? A question of *law* might be centered around the interpretation of some aspect of contract law, such as determination of the meaning of unconscionable contracts, or whether the conduct of the parties created a contract.

On appeal, the case is heard by a panel of judges. Normally a party has the right to one appeal. Prior to the hearing date, each lawyer submits a written report outlining his or her position on the disputed point of law. This document is called a *brief.* On the day of the hearing, each lawyer argues the points of law before the panel of judges, and the panel at some later time files a written decision. This decision may in certain instances be appealed to the next highest court in the particular system. Sooner or later final resolutions of the dispute occur either because the parties are satisfied or because there are no additional grounds or opportunities for appeal.

The Law Relevant to the Situation

▶ Statutory Law

The form of law that most people think of when asked to answer the question "What is a law?" is **statutory law.** Federal statutory laws are bills passed by the U.S. House of Representatives and Senate, signed by the president, and not declared unconstitutional by the court system. Each of the states also has statutory laws, passed through their equivalents of the House and Senate and signed by the governor and allowed to stand by the courts. Furthermore, cities, towns, and other municipalities have the authority to pass *ordinances,* which are forms of statutory law. One simple example of a statute is the law that requires some businesses to close on Sundays. But statutory law is not the only source of law.

statutory law
Bills passed by a legislature and signed into law by the president or governor

▶ Common Law

In the previous chapter we discussed how norms of a society can become translated into law. When settlers came to America, there obviously were no American laws for them to follow; but they did have norms for behavior based on the laws of their native lands. Many of these norms, mostly from England, have been incorporated by reference into the laws of the United States, both federal and state. This happens when courts of law refer to these norms and use them in deciding cases. Norms may not be in statutory form but are reflected in the principles of law made by courts in their decisions. Judges often refer to these principles as **common law,** the common concept of justice *not in statutory form.* And the principles are just as binding as statutory law. The early colonies in America had the common law of England, much of which continues as a part of the law in the states today, except for Louisiana, where the civil code or Roman law influence continues.

common law
Principles of nonstatutory law reflecting the customs and usages of society and found in judicial decisions

Society has left to the courts the power to make law in certain areas without statutory help. Examples of such legal areas of law are torts, contracts, and agency. Society can change the common law by legislation. For example, the common law age of majority was twenty-one years; today in almost all states by legislation the age of majority generally has been changed to eighteen years.

Along with common law, the United States has also drawn upon the British system of equity. Equity involves the court's ability to do what is just in situations where specific rules of law are not applicable. Common law rules in Great Britain resolved situations with certainty but the results were sometimes harsh. A chancellor (or judge) sitting in equity could sometimes fashion a more appropriate remedy than a law court and take care of problem cases when the existing law was inadequate. Equitable remedies are available to U.S. judges in their decision making.

A second great system of law is the Roman or Civil Law. Roman Law is legislative, in the form of a written code, and the judge has the function of applying the pertinent code provision of rule or principle to the particular facts in the case before him or her. In contrast, the common law is nonlegislative, consisting of those principles of nonstatutory law reflecting the customs and usages of society and found in judicial decisions.

▶ Administrative Law

Chapter 35, on **administrative law,** is devoted to discussion of the administrative rules and regulations that implement constitutional and statutory law. For the time being it is important to realize that both state and federal administrative agencies have the power to make such rules, all of which have the strength of law. There are a number of reasons

administrative law
Rules and regulations created by an administrative agency, thereby becoming law

for granting administrative bodies the power to make rules that have the force of law. One of the most important reasons is that administrative agencies have expertise that goes far beyond the expertise of the legislative bodies who would otherwise have to create the rules. There are literally hundreds of administrative agencies, including the Federal Trade Commission (FTC) and the National Labor Relations Board (NLRB).

► Case Law

stare decisis
A principle of law stating that earlier cases that are similar should, if possible, be followed to decide current issues before the court

Every time a case is heard, a judge is asked to interpret the law in light of a new set of facts and apply case precedent if it is still applicable—a doctrine called **stare decisis.** When a judge is called upon to interpret the meaning of a word in a statute or administrative rule, or even interpret what a previous judge has said, the judge is in a position to "make law." All the decisions judges write are filed in court reports by court reporters, and their interpretations become binding on lower courts in the same jurisdiction as the lower courts consider future cases on the same point of law. In effect, the legislatures and administrative agencies leave to the judges the task of making more meaningful and clear these pronouncements, which need such attention when they create law. Judges, in doing their job, make the law known as **case law.**

case law
The law that comes from decided cases

► Our Constitutional Form of Government

Each of the states that comprise the United States has its own state constitution. These constitutions describe the structure of state government. In a similar fashion, the federal government is structured in accordance with the model described in the U.S. Constitution.

The federal Constitution describes the structure of the three major components of our government. The components are the legislative, executive, and judicial branches. In addition, the Constitution contains a series of amendments. The first ten amendments are known as the Bill of Rights. The balance of the amendments describe the various changes we have made to our governance structure over time.

Legislative Branch The legislative branch of our federal government, the Congress, has the power to make laws. There are two branches of the Congress. They are the House of Representatives and the Senate. As most students are aware, a major step in the creation of law is to introduce a bill to either the House or the Senate. In some cases, the Constitution specifies which branch should act on a bill first. For example, Article 1, Section 7 of the federal Constitution states: "All bills for raising revenue shall originate in the House of Representatives."

Congress has many important powers that are enumerated in the Constitution. In Article 1, Section 8 of the Constitution, some of these powers are listed. Many of these powers have a profound effect on business. For example, Congress has the power to establish taxes to pay the debts of the United States and to promote the general welfare and provide for our defense needs. Congress has the power to establish post offices. Congress has the power to grant patents and copyrights, and has the right to establish uniform laws on the subject of bankruptcies.

Executive Branch Article 2 of the Constitution defines the executive branch of the government. Of course, the executive power is vested in the office of the President of the United States. The Constitution defines how a president is elected. For example, while most of you are aware of the fact that a president is elected for a four-year term, you may not recall that only a natural born citizen of the United States is eligible to serve as president. Furthermore, that a person must be at least thirty-five years old in order to hold the office of president.

The president today is also commander in chief of the Army, Navy, and Air Force. The president has the power to make treaties, provided the president gets the concurrence of two-thirds of the Senate. Furthermore, the president has, with the concurrence of the Senate, the right to appoint ambassadors.

Judicial Branch The nature of the judiciary has been discussed in great detail earlier in this chapter. Perhaps at this point it would be well to add that all cases involving ambassadors, or other public ministers and consuls as well as those cases in which a state is a party come under the original jurisdiction of the Supreme Court.

Summary Statement

1. There are alternatives to the legal system for resolving disputes. Not all problems need to be brought to a lawyer. Compromise, arbitration, and mediation are natural alternatives. If the dispute cannot be settled in any other way, the legal system presents the forum for grievance resolution.
2. Lawyers and judges are not the only persons who serve and are employed in the U.S. legal system. Other legal craftsmen include police officers and paralegals.
3. The basic design of all state legal systems is the same, and in both the federal and state systems we have courts of general and special jurisdictions and courts of trial and review.
4. The legal process is a series of interrelated actions that are normally taken in an attempt to resolve controversies over the applicability of law in a given situation.
5. Law that can be applied to a dispute varies. The law of any one state consists of the U.S. Constitution, the public acts of Congress, its own state constitution, the public acts of its own legislature, case decisions of the Supreme Court of the United States on a constitutional question, case decisions of its own courts, federal and state administrative law, and the private law of individuals within its boundaries.
6. The structure of the federal Constitution consists of three components—legislative, executive, and judicial branches. The first ten amendments to the Constitution are known as the Bill of Rights.

The following is a case illustrating the worldwide scope of trade and the need for arbitration in the United States. It also shows how the law is concerned with justice.

SOLER CHRYSLER-PLYMOUTH, INC. v. MITSUBISHI MOTORS CORPORATION
473 U.S. 614, 87 L.Ed.2d 444 (1985)

The principal question presented by these cases is the arbitrability of a valid arbitration clause in an agreement embodying an international commercial transaction.

I

Mitsubishi Motors Corporation (Mitsubishi) is a Japanese corporation which manufactures automobiles and has its principal place of business in Tokyo, Japan. Mitsubishi is the product of a joint venture between, on the one hand, Chrysler International, S.A. (CISA), a Swiss corporation registered in Geneva and wholly owned by Chrysler Corporation, and, on the other, Mitsubishi Heavy Industries, Inc., a Japanese corporation. The aim of the joint venture was the distribution through Chrysler dealers outside the continental United States of vehicles manufactured by Mitsubishi and bearing Chrysler and Mitsubishi trademarks. Soler Chrysler-Plymouth, Inc. (Soler), is a Puerto Rico corporation.

On October 31, 1979, Soler entered into a Distributor Agreement with CISA which provided for the sale by Soler of Mitsubishi-manufactured vehicles within a designated area, including metropolitan San Juan. [App. 18.] On the same date, CISA, Soler, and Mitsubishi entered into a Sales Procedure Agreement (Sales Agreement) which, referring to the Distributor Agreement provided for the direct sale of Mitsubishi products to Soler and governed the terms and conditions of such sales. Paragraph VI of the Sales Agreement, labeled "Arbitration of Certain Matters," provides: "All disputes, controversies or differences which may arise between [Mitsubishi] and [Soler] out of or in relation to Articles I-B through V of this Agreement or for the breach thereof, shall be finally settled by arbitration in Japan in accordance with the rules and regulations of the Japan Commercial Arbitration Association."

Initially, Soler did a brisk business in Mitsubishi-manufactured vehicles. As a result of its strong performance, its minimum sales volume, specified by Mitsubishi and CISA, and agreed to by Soler, for the 1981 model year was substantially increased. In early 1981, however, the new-car market slackened. Soler ran into serious difficulties in meeting the expected sales volume, and by the spring of 1981 it felt itself compelled to request that Mitsubishi delay or cancel shipment of several orders. About the same time, Soler attempted to arrange for transshipment of a quantity of its vehicles for sale in the continental United States and Latin America. Mitsubishi and CISA, however, refused permission for any such diversion, citing a variety of reasons, and no vehicles were transshipped. Attempts to work out these difficulties failed. Mitsubishi eventually withheld shipment of 966 vehicles, apparently representing orders placed for May, June, and July 1981 production, responsibility for which Soler disclaimed in February 1982. [App. 131.]

The following month, Mitsubishi brought an action against Soler in the United States District of Puerto Rico under the Federal Arbitration Act and the Convention.

Soler denied the allegations and counterclaimed against both Mitsubishi and CISA.

The District Court ordered Mitsubishi and Soler to arbitrate. Soler claimed that it did not have to submit statutory anti-trust claims to arbitration.

The United States Court of Appeals for the First Circuit affirmed in part and reversed in part.

We granted certiorari primarily to consider whether an American court should enforce an agreement to resolve antitrust claims by arbitration when that agreement arises from an international transaction. [469 U.S. 916, 105 S.Ct. 291, 83 L.Ed.2d 227 (1984).]

As international trade has expanded in recent decades, so too has the use of international arbitration to resolve disputes arising in the course of that trade. The controversies that international arbitral institutions are called upon to resolve have increased in diversity as well as in complexity. Yet the potential of these tribunals for efficient disposition of legal disagreements arising from commercial relations has not yet been tested. If they are to take a central place in the international legal order, national courts will need to "shake off the old judicial hostility to arbitration" [*Kulukundis Shipping Co. v. Amtorg Trading Corp.*, 126 F.2d 978, 985 (2d Cir. 1942)], and also their customary and understandable unwillingness to cede jurisdiction of a claim arising under domestic law to a foreign or transnational tribunal. To this extent, at least, it will be necessary for national courts to subordinate domestic notions of arbitrability to the international policy favoring commercial arbitration.

Accordingly, we "require this representative of the American business community to honor its bargain" [*Alberto-Culver Co. v. Scherk*, 484 F.2d 611, 620 (7th Cir. 1973) (Stevens, J., dissenting)], by holding this agreement to arbitrate "enforce[able] . . . in accord with the explicitly provisions of the Arbitration Act." [*Sherk*, 417 U.S. at 520, 94 S.Ct. at 2457.]

The judgment of the Court of Appeals is affirmed in part and reversed in part, and the cases are remanded for further proceedings consistent with this opinion.

It is so ordered.

Questions and Case Problems

1. What is the difference between arbitration and mediation?
2. What is the difference between statutory law and common law?
3. Just before leaving office, John Adams, President of the United States, appointed forty-two Federalists. The Senate confirmed these appointments, but the new president told his Secretary of State, James Madison, not to deliver seventeen of these commissions. William Marbury was to have received one of the commissions. Marbury appealed to the Supreme Court of the United States for his appointment under legislation passed by Congress which was contrary to the U.S. Constitution. Must legislation that is contrary to a constitution give way to the constitution under our system of law? [*Marbury v. Madison,* 1 Cranch 137 (1803).]
4. Dr. Sabates, on behalf of his professional association, contracted with International Medical Centers, Inc. (IMC) to provide ophthalmologic services for IMC patients. A condition of Sabates' employment was that he was to meet the qualifications and standards for staff membership at International Hospital. Although IMC assured Sabates that his application for permanent staff privileges at the hospital would be promptly processed, his temporary privileges were allowed to expire resulting in IMC terminating its contract with Sabates. Sabates objected to this breach of contract. What mechanisms might be used by the parties to resolve their dispute? [*Sabates, M.D. v. International Medical Centers,* 450 So.2d 514 (Fla. 1984).]
5. Standard Oil Company of New Jersey and thirty-three other corporations, John D. Rockefeller, William Rockefeller, and five other individuals decided to seek a reversal of a decree in a lower court that attempted to dissolve a holding company that was believed to be a violation of a certain federal antitrust law because its actions were in restraint of trade. The statute did not define "in restraint of trade." The court developed a rule of reason that gave meaning to the words "restraint of trade." This rule of reason is an example of what type of law? [*Standard Oil Company of New Jersey v. United States,* 221 U.S. 1 (1910).]
6. Robbins had transported construction and road building materials for at least thirty years, but had never before sought an ICC (Interstate Commerce Commission) authorization. Lacking this authorization in the past, Robbins often had to pay "civil forfeitures" for unlawful operations.

   In March 1982, Robbins applied for an ICC certificate authorizing him to operate as a motor common carrier. According to the Department of Commerce, ICC had to consider the nature and extent of past violations, whether Robbins had made sincere efforts to correct his past mistakes, and so forth. In considering the matter, is the court dealing with a question of fact or law? Explain. [*Department of Transportation Federal Highway Administration v. Interstate Commerce Commission,* 733 F.2d 105 (D.C. Cir. 1984).]
7. Tompkins, a citizen of Pennsylvania, was injured on a dark night by a passing train of the Erie Railroad. He claimed the accident occurred through the train company's negligence. The action was brought in the U.S. district court. The case resulted in a battle over the appropriate law to apply since there was a diversity of citizenship. It was held in the case that the federal court had to apply state law to determine whether Tompkins's complaint contained a cause of action, and it could not create by case decision a federal right for Tompkins. This means there is one type of law that the federal system does not have. What is this law? [*Erie Railroad v. Tompkins,* 304 U.S. 64 (1938).]

8. Alleging negligence, appellant filed in the county court at law an original petition seeking $4,750 in damages for personal injuries. In her pleading she filed a supplemental petition, a deceptive trade practice claim, and prayed for treble damages. Appellee's argument is based upon the premises that plaintiff's petition should be contained in one instrument in writing and that a party may not adopt by reference in an amended pleading a statement from a prior pleading. The appellee did not specially *plead* in writing the appellant's impropriety, and now seeks to assert the impropriety in an oral motion to dismiss appellant's petition. Based on this information, should the appellant's pleading fail? [*Hawkins v. Anderson,* 672 S.W.2d 293 (Tex. 1984).]
9. In order to make the law in certain legal areas uniform among the various states, each state appoints lawyer "Commissioners" to a national body called the National Conference of Commissioners on Uniform State Laws, which drafts proposed uniform laws for consideration by each state. One of the uniform laws presented to the states for adoption is the Uniform Commercial Code. When a state legislature adopts the Code making it the law of the state, is this law an example of common law, statutory law, administrative law, or some other form of law? Explain the difference between the form of law you chose and these other forms of law.
10. More and more business transactions are international in nature, and many of them call for the use of international arbitration. What is arbitration and will U.S. courts recognize such international arbitration clauses? [*Soler Chrysler-Plymouth, Inc. v. Mitsubishi Motors Corporation,* 473 U.S. 614 (1985).]

CHAPTER 3

CONSTITUTIONAL LAW

After you have read this chapter, you should be able to:

1. Briefly review the background of the formation of the United States of America and the creation of its Constitution.
2. Understand the purpose and structure of the Constitution.
3. Distinguish the overall division of the respective constitutional powers of the federal government and the states, and the constitutional limitations on those powers.
4. Realize the importance of the U.S. Supreme Court, through its judicial opinions and case decisions, in the interpretation, application, and preservation of the principles expressed in the Constitution.
5. Have a keen and well-informed appreciation of the impact of the Constitution and Supreme Court decisions on societal and business life in the United States.
6. Have a specific knowledge of the extensive congressional power over interstate commerce.
7. Understand the various enumerated and implied constitutional rights associated with the following subjects:
   a. Religion
   b. Freedom of speech and the press
   c. Private association with others
   d. Privacy
   e. Unreasonable searches and seizures
   f. Due process of law
   g. Eminent domain
   h. Equal protection of the laws
   i. Nonimpairment of the obligation of contracts.

BUSINESS DECISIONS and the LAW

You, as a future business person who may be operating at any level, particularly the management level, should become keenly aware of the present and potential impact upon your business of the U.S. Constitution and of congressional statutes and administrative regulations that implement it. For example, let us look at the Commerce Clause in Article I, Section 8, Clause 3 of the Constitution. While it states that Congress has the sole power "to regulate Commerce with foreign Nations and among the States," this federal power is so extensive that, under U.S. Supreme Court decisions, it applies to *any* activity of *any* kind in *any* state that *affects* interstate commerce. Since your business activity will usually in some way affect interstate commerce, your awareness of federal statutory and administrative regulatory law pertinent to your business is a must.

The power of Congress extends to *intrastate* economic activities that affect interstate commerce. Labor conditions as well as civil rights in commerce come within the Clause. The interstate movement of people is commerce, so as your firm's employees travel outside a state your firm is engaged in interstate commerce and is subject to that federal power. The power extends to the regulation of local incidents in a facility such as a motel or hotel that might have a substantial and harmful effect on interstate commerce, as is illustrated in the

Heart of Atlanta Motel v. United States case in this chapter.[1] The Supreme Court has held that the rental of real property is an activity affecting interstate commerce, the local rental of an apartment unit being merely an element of a much broader commercial market in rental properties, as illustrated in *Robert Russell v. United States*, 417 U.S. 858 (1985). If you contemplate doing business abroad by exporting or importing, the "foreign Nations" part of the Clause comes into play. Chapter 57, "Business Law in the International Marketplace," describes how congressional statutes, federal administrative regulations, and Supreme Court decisions govern and condition your business activity.

Introduction

Imagine the excitement of the early American colonists in 1776 when, having suffered great hardships and injustices, and imbued with a desire to become free of England, their colonial representatives dared to declare as "Representatives of the United States of America, in General Congress assembled, . . . that these colonies are Free and Independent States . . . And for the support of the declaration, with a firm reliance on the protection of Divine Providence, we mutually pledge to each other our lives, our fortunes, and our sacred honor."

Then imagine the further excitement of the representatives of the thirteen new sovereign states, who had experienced great difficulty with the weak Articles of Confederation, when they met in Philadelphia in May 1787, for the purpose of supplementing and strengthening the Articles. In September 1787 they produced a world-shaking final draft of a document that had a startling preamble:

> We the people of the United States, in order to form a more perfect union, establish justice, insure domestic tranquillity, provide for the common defense, promote the general welfare, and secure the blessings of liberty to ourselves and our posterity, do ordain and establish this Constitution for the United States of America.

However, ratification of the constitutional draft with its democratic scheme of government was a difficult matter, resolved in large part by the information provided by a series of letters written by Alexander Hamilton, James Madison, and John Jay; these letters are collectively called The Federalist Papers and were fundamental to the establishment of the Constitution.

Although most of the earliest state constitutions emphasized the securing of individual liberties in their "bills of rights," such securities were not included in the draft constitution. Accordingly, some of the states made the inclusion of these rights a condition to ratification; in 1791 these rights were included in the first ten amendments, called the Bill of Rights. Most of this chapter will be concerned with these rights and with the Fourteenth Amendment, as interpreted and applied by the U.S. Supreme Court.

With compromises hammered out of the red-hot steel of intense conflict, the Constitution of the United States was produced. The document was ratified by nine states by midsummer in 1788, with the last state ratifying in 1790; the new government took

---

[1]See page 46.

office in April 1789. The Constitution, including the Preamble and all amendments, is found in Appendix B on pp. 1247–1253.

First, we will briefly discuss the purpose and structure of the federal government under the Constitution; then, the powers enumerated and implied in the Constitution; and finally, certain selected constitutional rights of the people.

The Purpose and Structure of the Federal Government Under the Constitution

► Purpose

The experience of the colonies under English rule and the period under the Articles of Confederation taught the framers of the Constitution that what was needed was a federal constitution that provided for a central form of government with the powers necessary to operate, but subject to limitations on those powers.

All federal power is derived from the Constitution. State power is derived from each state's constitution, except as otherwise provided in the federal constitution, and from common law. In the event of conflict between federal and state law, the federal law is supreme. Article VI, Clause 2 provides in part:

> This Constitution, and the Laws of the United States which shall be made in Pursuance thereof; and all Treaties made, or which shall be made, under the Authority of the United States, shall be the supreme law of the land; and all the Judges in every State shall be bound thereby, any Thing in the Constitution or Laws of any State to the Contrary notwithstanding.

Under the Tenth Amendment, "The powers not delegated to the United States by the Constitution, nor prohibited by it to the States, are reserved to the States respectively, or to the people." In addition, the Twenty-first Amendment, Section 2, illustrates a power specifically reserved to the states: "The transportation or importation into any State, Territory, or Possession of the United States for delivery therein of Intoxicating Liquors, in violation of the laws thereof, is hereby prohibited." Thus we see that the Constitution consists of delegated powers, and that the states retain nondelegated powers. But no federal law and no state constitution or law is valid if it violates the federal Constitution.

► Structure

Article III, Section 1 of the Constitution provides for three branches of government: the legislative branch (the Congress); the executive branch (the President); and the judicial branch (the Supreme Court and "such inferior federal courts as the Congress may from time to time ordain and establish"). In this way, each branch has its own area of specific powers, and each is prevented from interfering with another branch.

The Legislative Branch Article I, Section 1 provides: "All legislative Powers herein granted shall be vested in a Congress of the United States. . . ." Section 8 expressly enumerates specific powers of Congress, and Section 9 expressly prohibits congressional action in certain areas. Some of the Section 8 powers will be discussed later.

The Constitution does not make any express provision for administrative agencies to assist the Congress. However, just as delegation is necessary when additional time and expertise are required, so the Congress has created many federal administrative agencies to assist it in carrying out its constitutional duties. These agencies are in large number and have great regulatory power dealing for the most part with the public. Congress may reasonably delegate some of its responsibilities, but it may not delegate its *legislative powers* to make statutory law.

The Executive Branch Article II, Section 1 provides: "The executive Power shall be vested in a President of the United States of America." Sections 2 and 3 specify the powers of the president. There has always been concern over alleged attempts by Congress to encroach upon the powers of the president, and vice versa. A recent instance is the Ethics in Government Act of 1978, which provides for the appointment of an "independent counsel" to prosecute certain high-ranking government officials for violation of federal criminal laws. In *Morrison, Independent Counsel, v. Olsen, Schmults, and Dinkins,* 108 S.Ct. 2597 (1988), the Supreme Court held the Act constitutional; the Court held that it did not violate the principle of separation of powers by unduly interfering with the executive branch's role to make appointments, and did not violate the judicial role as described in Article III.

Although the Constitution does not expressly state that the president has the power and responsibility to *conduct* the foreign affairs of the United States, traditionally the president has exercised this power. He or she is the "executive power" under Article II; Section 1, Clause 1, and Section 2 enumerate a limited number of foreign affairs powers that are granted to the president. Today it is understood that Congress has implied power to *influence* foreign affairs (Article I, Section 8, Clauses 1, 3, 10, 11, 12, 13, 18, and Article II, Section 2, Clause 2).

The Judicial Branch Article III, Section 1 provides: "The judicial Power of the United States, shall be vested in one supreme Court, and in such inferior Courts as the Congress may from time to time ordain and establish." Section 2 specifies the powers and jurisdiction of the federal courts, and both Sections 2 and 3 provide for specific federal crimes. The functions of the federal courts are to integrate the Constitution and federal laws, to declare what is the law of the land, determine the constitutional validity of federal laws and of state laws when challenged, and to try civil and criminal cases as provided in Sections 2 and 3. The Supreme Court has the power of "judicial review," which means that it has the final power and authority to determine whether federal or state law violates the Constitution. The Court, as well as the Congress, has the power to *influence* foreign affairs.

► The Pre-emption of Federal Authority

We have already discussed the federal supremacy clause under Article VI and the reservation of state powers under the Tenth Amendment. However, there are many subject areas where both the federal government and a state may *concurrently* participate by statute and regulation. For example, both the federal government and the state have concurrent powers to tax, the Congress establishing federal taxes and the state providing for state taxes. If there is *no* conflict between the concurrent powers, then Congress has not **pre-empted** the subject area, and each power can be constitutionally, and therefore validly, exercised. If there *is* conflict, Congress has pre-empted the *particular* subject matter area and the congressional power prevails over the state power that now is unconstitutionally and illegally exercised. Many federal statutes contain express or implied exemptions for states.

pre-emption
To retain exclusively, supersede; the doctrine adopted by the U.S. Supreme Court that certain matters are of such a national character that federal laws pre-empt or take precedence over state laws

Often it is difficult to determine whether Congress, by statute or regulation, intended to pre-empt all or merely part of the subject matter area. In the following case, the question is whether the power of the federal government to regulate the safety of nuclear energy pre-empts the power of the state to authorize an award of **punitive damages** to an employee who was injured in a nuclear energy plant. Notice that the Supreme Court distinguishes between regulatory authority over the *safety aspects* of nuclear development, which Congress has pre-empted, and the *power to award punitive damages* for injury sustained in the operation of such development, which Congress has not pre-empted.

punitive damages
The money judicially awarded to an injured party in excess of compensatory damages to punish for malicious, wanton, or intentional wrongful conduct

FACTS

Karen Silkwood was a laboratory analyst for Kerr-McGee at its Cimarron plant near Crescent, Oklahoma. The plant fabricated plutonium fuel pins for use as reactor fuel in nuclear power plants. Accordingly, the plant was subject to licensing and regulation by the Nuclear Regulatory Commission (NRC) pursuant to the Atomic Energy Act. During a three-day period in November 1974, Silkwood was contaminated by plutonium from the Cimarron plant. On November 13 Silkwood was killed in an unrelated automobile accident.

Bill Silkwood, Karen's father, brought a federal lawsuit as administrator of her estate. The action was based on common-law tort principles under Oklahoma law and was designed to recover for the contamination injuries to Karen's person and property.

The jury returned a verdict in favor of Mr. Silkwood, finding punitive damages of $10 million. The trial court entered judgment against Kerr-McGee for that amount.

Kerr-McGee appealed. The Court of Appeals for the Tenth Circuit reversed holding that, because of the federal statutes regulating the Kerr-McGee plant, "punitive damages may not be awarded in this case." The Court of Appeals determined that *such awards were pre-empted by federal law.*

Mr. Silkwood appealed, seeking review of the Court of Appeals' ruling with respect to the punitive damages award.

DECISION

The judgment of the Court of Appeals with respect to punitive damages was reversed by the Supreme Court, which held that a punitive damage award was not pre-empted by federal law. In the words of the Court,

> . . . state law can be pre-empted in either of two general ways. If Congress evidences an intent to occupy a given field, any state law falling within that field is pre-empted. If Congress has not entirely displaced state regulation over the matter in question, state law is still pre-empted to the extent it actually conflicts with federal law, that is, when it is impossible to comply with both state and federal law, . . . or where the state law stands as an obstacle to the accomplishment of the full purposes and objectives of Congress. . . . We consider each of these in turn . . .
>
> . . . Congress . . . intended that the Federal Government should regulate the radiological *safety* aspects involved in the construction and operation of a nuclear plant. [Thus, we concluded that] the Federal Government has occupied the *entire field of nuclear safety concerns,* except the limited powers expressly ceded to the States.
>
> Congress [failed] to provide any federal remedy for persons injured by such conduct. . . . It is difficult to believe that Congress would, without comment, remove all means of judicial recourse for those injured by illegal conduct. . . . Congress assumed that persons injured by nuclear accidents were free to utilize existing state tort law remedies. . . . Punitive damages have long been a part of traditional state tort law.
>
> . . . But insofar as damages for radiation injuries are concerned, pre-emption should not be judged on the basis that the Federal Government has so completely occupied the field of safety that state remedies are foreclosed, but on whether there is an irreconcilable conflict between the federal and state standards or whether the imposition of a State standard in a damages action would frustrate the objectives of the federal law. We perceive no such conflict or frustration in the circumstances of this case. . . . Nor does exposure to punitive damages frustrate any purpose of the federal remedial scheme.
>
> We conclude that the award of punitive damages in this case is not pre-empted by federal law.

Silkwood, Administrator of the Estate of Silkwood v. Kerr-McGee Corp. et al., 464 U.S. 238 (1984).

Amendment of the Federal Constitution

Article V provides the method by which the Constitution can be amended. There are now twenty-six amendments; the Eighteenth Amendment, which prohibited the manufacture, sale, or transportation of "intoxicating liquors," was repealed by the Twenty-first Amendment. The first ten amendments, the Bill of Rights, are limitations on *federal* powers. The Supreme Court has established by judicial decision that the greater part of the Bill of Rights is applied *to the states* through the Fourteenth Amendment. This means that the Fourteenth Amendment limits the power of the States as well as the federal government, to deny not only the rights therein stated but also the added rights in the Bill of Rights.

The broad principles of the Constitution permit judicial interpretation and application so as to include additional rights. The following case illustrates the implied constitutional right of access to criminal trials.

FACTS

Section 16A of Chapter 278 of the Massachusetts General Laws, as construed by the Massachusetts Supreme Judicial Court, *requires* trial judges, at trials for specified sexual offenses involving a victim under the age of 18, to *exclude* the press and general public from the courtroom during the testimony of that victim. . . . The Globe Newspaper Co. (Globe) unsuccessfully attempted to gain access to a rape trial conducted in a Massachusetts superior court. The criminal defendant in that trial had been charged with the rape of three girls who were minors at the time of trial. . . . The trial court, relying on Section 16A, ordered the exclusion of the press and general public from the courtroom during the trial. . . .

The Globe appealed to the Supreme Judicial Court. . . . The provision was designed, the court determined, "to encourage young victims of sexual offenses to come forward; once they have come forward, the statute is designed to preserve their ability to testify by protecting them from undue psychological harm at trial." Relying on these twin purposes, the court concluded that Section 16A *required* the closure of sex-offense trials only during the testimony of minor victims; during other portions of such trials, closure was "a matter within the judge's sound discretion." . . . The Globe appealed to the Supreme Court of the United States.

DECISION

[W]e reverse, and hold that the *mandatory* closure rule contained in Section 16A violates the First Amendment. The question presented is whether the statute thus construed violates the First Amendment as applied to the States through the Fourteenth Amendment. . . . [This] Court's recent decision in *Richmond Newspapers* firmly established for the first time that the press and general public have a constitutional right of access to criminal trials. . . . [T]his right of access is embodied in the First Amendment, and applied to the States through the Fourteenth Amendment. . . . Of course, this right of access to criminal trials is not explicitly mentioned in terms in the First Amendment. . . . "Congress shall make no law . . . abridging the freedom of . . . the press . . . " But we have long eschewed any "narrow, literal conception" of the Amendment's terms . . . .

[T]he Framers were concerned with broad principles, and wrote against a background of shared values and practices. The First Amendment is thus broad enough to encompass those rights that, while not unambiguously enumerated in the very terms of the Amendment, are nonetheless necessary to the enjoyment of other First Amendment rights. Underlying the First Amendment right of access to criminal trials is the common understanding that "a major purpose of that Amendment was to protect the free discussion of governmental affairs." . . . By offering such protection, the First Amendment serves to ensure that the individual citizen can effectively participate in and contribute to our republican system of self-government.

Two features of the criminal justice system together serve to explain why a right of access to *criminal trials* in particular is properly afforded protection by the First Amendment. First, the criminal trial historically has been open to the press and general public....

Second, the right of access to criminal trials plays a particularly significant role in the functioning of the judicial process and the government as a whole....

Although the right of access to criminal trials is of constitutional stature, it is not absolute.... But the circumstances under which the press and public can be barred from a criminal trial are limited; the State's justification in denying access must be a weighty one. Where, as in the present case, the State attempts to deny the right of access in order to inhibit the disclosure of sensitive information, it must be shown that the denial is necessitated by a compelling governmental interest, and is narrowly tailored to serve that interest.

Reversed. The State of Massachusetts did not prove it had such a compelling interest, and the Supreme Court reversed the lower court's decision.

Globe Newspaper Co. v. Superior Court for the County of Norfolk, 457 U.S. 596 (1982).

Federal Powers Under the Constitution

Constitutional Limitation on Federal Powers

Since the Constitution consists of powers delegated to the federal government by the people, the Constitution as amended is the sole source of federal powers and limitations on such powers. The Tenth Amendment specifically provides that "The powers not delegated to the United States by the Constitution, nor prohibited by it to the States, are reserved to the States respectively, or to the people." The Constitution also sets forth limitations on, and denials of, federal powers that cannot interfere with constitutional rights.

Also, throughout the Constitution there are specific denials of power to Congress as the legislative arm of the government. For example, the rights stated in the Fifteenth and Nineteenth Amendments "shall not be denied or abridged by the United States or by any State...." The language of the Twenty-first Amendment, Section 2, provides "The transportation or importation into any State... for delivery therein of Intoxicating Liquors, in violation of the laws thereof, is hereby prohibited." The Supreme Court of the United States has interpreted it to recognize state desire to promote temperance in alcohol consumption and state power to shield itself from importation of intoxicating liquors into the state. Accordingly, a state statute or regulation for this purpose, while affecting interstate commerce and within the Commerce Clause of Article I, Section 8, Clause 3, is not in violation of congressional power to regulate interstate commerce. However, if the state statute or regulation restricting the importation of intoxicating liquor is *not* for such a purpose but, rather, is to *discriminate* in favor of local industry from industry outside the state, it is an illegal unconstitutional restraint on interstate commerce in violation of the Commerce Clause.

Let us briefly consider three of the federal *financial* powers—namely to tax, to borrow, and to spend—and then the great Commerce Clause.

The Power to Tax According to Article I, Section 8, Clause 1, Congress has the power to "lay and collect Taxes, Duties, Imposts and Excises... but all Duties, Imposts and Excises shall be uniform throughout the United States" But capitation (poll) and other direct taxes must be apportioned among the States according to census population (Section 9, Clause 4). As stated in the Sixteenth Amendment, another congressional taxing power is "on incomes, from whatever source derived, without apportionment among the several States, and without regard to any census or enumeration." Pursuant to its power, Congress has imposed many indirect taxes, such as those on gasoline, cigarettes, property on death (estate tax), and making gifts. However, Congress cannot impose a "tax or duty on articles exported from another State" (Article I, Section 9, Clause 5). The federal power to tax does not preclude the states from levying taxes as they wish, subject to federal constitutional limitations. Federal and state taxes must be for a *public* purpose.

The Power to Borrow According to Article I, Section 8, Clause 2, "The Congress shall have the power to borrow Money on the credit of the United States." There is no constitutional limitation on the purpose for such borrowing. The power and extent to which states may borrow is also not subject to any constitutional limitation and is authorized and limited only by state constitution and statute.

The Power to Spend Although the Constitution does not expressly provide for a federal power to spend federal funds, it is nevertheless recognized that the power to spend is impliedly coupled with the limited power to tax and "to pay the Debts and to provide for the common Defense and general Welfare of the United States" (Article I, Section 8, Clause 1). Also, the power to spend when coupled with the power under Clause 5 to "coin Money, regulate the Value thereof" has been the basis for congressional power to establish the federal banking system, the Federal Reserve system, and various federal lending programs.

The Supreme Court has held that "While the United States is not concerned with, and has no power to regulate, local political activities as such of state officials, it does have power to fix the terms upon which its money allotments to states shall be disbursed." [*Oklahoma v. United States Civil Service Commission,* 330 U.S. 127, 143 (1947); *South Dakota v. Dole,* 107 S.Ct. 2793 (1987).]

The Commerce Clause

The Congress shall have power "[t]o regulate Commerce with foreign nations, and among the several States, and with the Indian tribes" (Article I, Section 8, Clause 3). Note that the power is to regulate *interstate* commerce. The simplicity and brevity of the Clause is misleading as to its extremely broad power. The Supreme Court stated in *Garcia v. San Antonio Metropolitan Transit Authority, et al.,* 105 S.Ct. 1005 (1985): "It long has been settled that Congress' authority under the Commerce Clause extends to *intrastate* economic activities that *affect* interstate commerce" [Emphasis added]. Almost every activity *affects* interstate commerce and therefore comes within the purview of the Commerce Clause. Congress has used the Commerce Clause to enact much regulatory legislation concerned with commercial activity and civil rights, which it could not otherwise do. Even labor conditions in commerce come within the Clause. The federal Fair Labor Standards Act of 1938 (as amended), known as the Wage-Hour Law and with the purpose of establishing fair labor standards in employment in and affecting interstate and foreign commerce, was upheld as a valid congressional exercise of the commerce power.

In the much-cited case of *Heart of Atlanta Motel v. United States,* 379 U.S. 241 (1964), the Commerce Clause was used to regulate civil rights and to make racial discrimination illegal. The Supreme Court held that Title II of the Civil Rights Act of 1964 is a valid exercise of congressional power under the Commerce Clause, and that it applies to a place of accommodation serving interstate travelers (a large motel that refused to rent accommodations to blacks). The Court stated that, even if the motel was of a purely "local" character, the power of Congress over interstate commerce can extend to the regulation of local matters that might have a "substantial and harmful effect" upon that commerce. It held that the interstate movement of persons is "commerce" that concerns more than one state.

The Commerce Clause limits the manner in which states may legitimately compete for interstate trade, for in the process of competition no state may discriminatorily tax the products manufactured or the business operations performed in any other state. The collision between state laws and the Commerce Clause occurs frequently—for example, when a state, pursuant to its police powers, seeks to protect and encourage new and growing businesses in the state by discriminating against out-of-state commercial activities. Such discrimination immediately creates a confrontation with the Commerce Clause as well as with the constitutional prohibition against states laying any imposts or duties on imports or exports.

The state's *legislative intent* is of great importance in this connection. The Supreme Court stated in the case below, *Kassell v. Consolidated Freightways Corporation of Delaware,* "[i]n considering a Commerce Clause challenge to a state regulation, the judicial task is to balance the burden imposed on [interstate] commerce against the local benefits sought to be achieved by the State's lawmakers."

FACTS

By statute, Iowa prohibited the use of 55-foot single-trailer trucks and 60-foot double-trailer trucks, unlike all other states in the Midwest and West. Consolidated Freightways Corporation of Delaware (Consolidated), a trucking company that carries commodities through Iowa on interstate highways, filed suit alleging that Iowa's statutory scheme unconstitutionally burdened interstate commerce. Because Consolidated could not use its 65-foot doubles to move goods through Iowa, it had to use shorter truck units, detach the trailers of a 65-foot double and shuttle each through Iowa separately, or divert 65-foot doubles around Iowa.

Iowa defended the law as a reasonable safety measure. The United States District Court found that the evidence established that 65-foot doubles were as safe as the shorter truck units, and held that the state law impermissibly burdened interstate commerce. The Court of Appeals affirmed and Iowa appealed.

DECISION

The U.S. Supreme Court held that the Iowa truck-length limitations *did* unconstitutionally burden interstate commerce. The Court found that Iowa did not substantiate its claimed safety interest, and that its regulations "impair significantly the federal interest in efficient and safe interstate transportation." The regulation was found to have a disproportionate effect on out-of-state residents and businesses, and the Court concluded that the statute had been designed, not to ban dangerous trucks, but "rather to discourage interstate truck traffic . . . This purpose, being *protectionist* in nature, is impermissible under the Commerce Clause. Iowa may not shunt off its fair share of the burden of maintaining interstate truck routes, nor may it create increased hazards on the highways of neighboring States in order to decrease the hazards on Iowa highways." Because Iowa had imposed this burden without any significant countervailing safety interest, its statute was found to violate the Commerce Clause. Affirmed.

Kassell v. Consol. Freightways Corp. of Del., 450 U.S. 662 (1981).

Certain Selected Constitutional Rights of the People

► The Ninth Amendment

As we saw in the *Globe Newspaper Co.* case on page 44 concerning a person's right of access to a criminal trial, the broad principles of the Constitution permit the Supreme Court to recognize and enunciate rights not specifically stated in the Constitution. This makes for a "living Constitution" that enables the Supreme Court *not* to create new law by judicial legislation but, rather, to apply the general principles of the Constitution to circumstances that necessitate the recognition of nonenumerated rights. This is reflected in the Ninth Amendment, which provides: "The enumeration in the Constitution, of certain rights, shall not be construed to deny or disparage others retained by the people."

The First Amendment

Religion "Congress shall make no law respecting an establishment of religion, or prohibiting the free exercise thereof. . . . " Note that this is a constitutional limitation on *congressional* power.

In the following case, the Supreme Court stated: "One fixed principle in this field is our consistent *rejection* of the argument that 'any program which in some manner aids an institution with a religious affiliation' violates the Establishment Clause."

FACTS

Minnesota, like every other state, provides its citizens with free elementary and secondary schooling. Minnesota . . . permits state taxpayers to claim a deduction from gross income for certain expenses incurred in educating their children. The deduction is limited to actual expenses incurred for the "tuition, textbooks and transportation" of dependents attending elementary or secondary schools. [Minn. Stat. sec. 290.09, subd.22 (1982).]

Petitioners—certain Minnesota taxpayers—sued in the United States District Court for the District of Minnesota claiming that sec. 290.09, subd. 22, violated the Establishment Clause by providing financial assistance to sectarian institutions. They named as defendants, respondents here, the Commissioner of the Department of Revenue of Minnesota and several parents who took advantage of the tax deduction for expenses incurred in sending their children to parochial schools. The District Court held that the statute "does not have a primary effect of either advancing or inhibiting religion." On appeal, the Court of Appeals affirmed, concluding that the Minnesota statute substantially benefited a "broad class of Minnesota citizens." The U.S. Supreme Court granted certiorari.

DECISION

Affirmed.

The Supreme Court applied a "three-part test" to the Minnesota statute, to determine whether it impermissibly advanced or inhibited religion:

> First, the statute must have a secular legislative purpose; second, its principal or primary effect must be one that neither advances nor inhibits religion . . . ; finally, the statute must not foster 'an excessive government entanglement with religion.'

The Court decided that the statute met the first part of the test, since the state's effort to help parents meet the rising costs of education serves the purpose of ensuring that the citizens of the state are well educated. In the second part of the test, the Court found that the educational tax deduction is only one among many deductions—such as those for medical expenses or charitable contributions—available in Minnesota. The Court approved the Minnesota legislature's judgment that a tax deduction for education would encourage desirable expenditures for educational purposes. Further, the deduction is available to *all* parents, including those whose children attend public schools and those whose children attend either sectarian or nonsectarian private schools. Another important factor was that the aid is available to the individual parents themselves, and does not go directly to the schools. For the third part of the test, the Court found "no difficulty" in concluding that the Minnesota statute did not "excessively entangle" the state in religion. The judgment of the Court of Appeals was affirmed.

Mueller et al. v. Allen, 463 U.S. 388 (1983).

Note that the Court stressed that there is a difference between state financial assistance transmitted *directly* to parochial schools, which is a violation of the Establishment Clause and therefore unconstitutional, and that transmitted *directly* to *parents,* who cause the funds to go *indirectly* to parochial schools attended by their children.

The Establishment Clause also prohibits Congress, and the states by the inclusion of the First Amendment in the Fourteenth Amendment, from making any law prohibiting the *free exercise* of religion. In the following case, the question before the Court was whether the state had violated the free exercise portion of the clause.

FACTS

After two and one-half years, Hobbie informed her employer that she was joining the Seventh-day Adventist Church and that, for religious reasons, she would no longer be able to work at the employer's jewelry store on her Sabbath. When she refused to work scheduled shifts on Friday evenings and Saturdays, she was discharged. She then filed a claim for unemployment compensation, which was denied by a claims examiner for "misconduct connected with [her] work" under the applicable Florida statute, and the Unemployment Appeals Commission (Appeals Commission) affirmed. The Florida Fifth District Court of Appeals affirmed the Appeals Commission's order. The U.S. Supreme Court granted certiorari.

DECISION

The judgment of the Florida Fifth District Court of Appeals is *reversed.* Florida's refusal to award unemployment compensation benefits to Hobbie violated the Free Exercise Clause of the First Amendment. The Court said that, "[w]hen a State denies receipt of a benefit because of conduct mandated by religious belief, thereby putting substantial pressure on an adherent to modify his behavior and to violate his beliefs, that denial must be subjected to *strict scrutiny* and can be justified only by proof of a *compelling state interest*" [Emphasis added]. The Court found no such "compelling state interest," and no merit to the state's argument that awarding benefits to Hobbie would violate the Establishment Clause of the First Amendment, since the accommodation of religious practices in this instance would not "entangle the State in an unlawful fostering of religion."

Hobbie v. Unemployment Appeals Comm'n of Fla., et al., 480 U.S. 136 (1987).

Freedom of Speech and of the Press We are concerned here with free speech and free press as guaranteed by the First Amendment as a limitation on congressional power. "Congress shall make no law abridging the freedom of speech, or the press." As previously discussed, First Amendment rights have been applied to the states through the Due Process Clause of the Fourteenth Amendment with its limitation on *state* power.

There has been much conflicting discussion over the meanings of the two words "speech" and "press". Generally, we may say that both words are concerned with freedom of *expression.* Speech is not only an oral or written expression; it may also be a person's conduct made with the intent to communicate a message which will be understood by those who viewed it. First Amendment protection is enjoyed not only by the sender, but also by the prospective recipient of the message.

It is clear that freedom of the press connotes the freedom of the media, such as printed publications (newspapers and magazines), radio, television, and motion pictures, to express ideas, information, and opinion. "Press" also includes, with certain limitations, the right to collect information for media expression.

"Commercial speech" is speech that concerns economic matters, such as advertisements and commercial transactions relating to products and services. It is included in, and has the protection of, the First Amendment. Society, with its consumers, has a public interest in the free flow of commercial information, even if the message provokes controversy, as in the following *Sable* case involving use of the telephone media to advertise obscene material. False advertising is not protected by the right of commercial speech, and can be prohibited by state statute and municipal ordinance. However, where professional organizations have tried to prevent the advertising of the prices of goods like prescription drugs, or services like lawyers' fees, the Supreme Court has held that both the sender *and* the recipient (the consumer) have a right to such commercial information, which qualifies as protected speech.

defamation
A person's unprivileged, wrongful publication to a second person of a false and defamatory statement concerning a third person, harmful to the third person's reputation

However, there are limitations on freedom of speech, such as expressions that involve **defamation;** those that inflict injury; or those that tend to incite an immediate breach of the peace. A person does not have the right to falsely shout "fire" in a crowded theatre, nor to cause unnecessary, outrageously loud noises in the middle of the night in a residential neighborhood.

Federal or state governmental regulation of speech must promote a substantial governmental interest in the free flow of information, and the regulation must not extend beyond what is reasonably necessary to achieve that interest. The basic question is, Does the governmental regulation (federal or state) substantially further a legitimate government interest, and are less onerous alternatives available?

The following case, which was shocking to some, illustrates the freedom to commercialize indecent telephone messages.

FACTS

In 1983 Sable Communications of California (Sable) began offering sexually oriented prerecorded telephone messages (popularly known as "dial-a-porn") through the Pacific Bell telephone networks. Those who called the adult message number were charged a special fee, which was divided between Pacific and Sable. Special telephone lines designed to handle large volumes of calls simultaneously were used. In 1988 the federal Communications Act was amended by section 223(b), which imposed a blanket prohibition on "indecent" as well as "obscene" interstate commercial telephone messages. Sable sued the Federal Communications Commission in the United States District Court, challenging the indecency and obscenity provisions of section 223(b) as *unconstitutional* under the First Amendment on free speech, and asked for an injunction against enforcement of the section's ban on such messages. The District Court refused to grant an injunction banning obscene telephone messages for commercial purposes, and held that it was constitutional for Congress to prohibit obscene messages. But the Court struck down the "indecent speech" provision as being overbroad and unconstitutional; the Court said, "while the Government unquestionably has a legitimate interest in protecting children from exposure to indecent dial-a-porn messages, section 223(b) is not narrowly drawn to achieve any such purpose. Its flat-out ban of indecent speech is contrary to the First Amendment." Sable appealed the Court's ruling which upheld the section 223(b) prohibition of *obscene* telephone commercial messages.

DECISION

The U.S. Supreme Court affirmed the District Court's judgment, holding that Congress has the power to prohibit transmission of obscene commercial telephonic communications.

"Sexual expression that is indecent but not obscene is protected by the First Amendment. The Government has a *legitimate interest* in shielding minors from the influence of literature that is not obscene by adult standards; . . . but to withstand constitutional scrutiny, it must do so by narrowly drawn regulations designed to serve those interests without unnecessarily interfering with First Amendment freedoms. Section 223(b)'s prohibition on obscenity is legislation not reasonably restricted to the evil with which it is said to deal. The Government may not reduce the adult population to only what is fit for children. There is nothing to indicate that there is no constitutionally acceptable less restrictive means, short of a total ban, to achieve the Government's interest in protecting minors.

"Sable has the burden of complying with the prohibition on obscene messages established by local standards of different communities."

Sable Communications of California v. Federal Communications Commission, et al., 109 S.Ct. 2829, 106 L.Ed.2d 93 (1989).

Right to Private Association with Others The First Amendment does not expressly state a "right of association." However, the Supreme Court has held that "the right to engage in activities protected by the First Amendment *implies* a corresponding right to associate with others in pursuit of a wide variety of political, social, economic, educational, religious, and cultural ends. Impediments to the exercise of one's right to choose one's associates can violate this right of association protected by the First Amendment."

In the case of *Board of Directors of Rotary International, et al. v. Rotary Club of Duarte, et al.,* 107 S.Ct. 1940 (1987), the Duarte Club had admitted women to membership in violation of International's charter restricting membership to men. The U.S. Supreme Court said admitting women to Duarte would not unduly interfere with the objective of International nor with the present members' freedom of private association. The Court held that the California Unruh Civil Rights Act was constitutionally applied to Rotary International prohibiting it from revoking the local Duarte Club's charter.

▶ The Fourth Amendment

Article IV of the Fourth Amendment provides:

> The right of the people to be secure in their persons, houses, papers, and effects, against unreasonable searches and seizures, shall not be violated, and no warrants shall issue, but upon probable cause, supported by oath or affirmation, and particularly describing the place to be searched, and the persons or things to be seized.

Right of Privacy A person has an *interest* in having his or her private life protected from unlawful government intrusion. In general, this is called the right of privacy. Although the Constitution does not expressly state a right of privacy, the broad principles of the Constitution nevertheless permit the Supreme Court to recognize and enunciate rights not specifically stated in the Constitution. This was the basis for the Court's recognition of the implied constitutional right of access to criminal trials in the *Globe Newspaper Co.* case discussed on p. 44. We see here the implied Constitutional right of privacy as a reflection of the rights granted in the First, Fourth, and Fourteenth Amendments. A person must have *manifested an expectation of privacy* with respect to his or her person or property to acquire the protection of the Fourth Amendment.

This right is the subject of much current discussion and litigation, particularly in the areas of abortion and living wills. (See discussion of wills on p. 1150.) In the following case concerning AIDS, a state court considered the invasion of this right of privacy. In *Rasmussen v. South Florida Blood Services, Inc.,* 500 So.2d 533 (Fla. 1987), Rasmussen, while hospitalized for injuries suffered from an automobile accident, received extensive blood transfusions from South Florida Blood Services. He later was diagnosed as having AIDS and eventually died of that disease. In an attempt to prove that the source of his AIDS was the medical treatment he received because of injuries sustained in the accident, Rasmussen demanded from South Florida Blood Services "any and all records, documents, and other material indicating the names and addresses of the 51 blood donors to South Florida Blood Services" with *no restrictions on their use.* The Supreme Court of Florida refused to permit the disclosure of such names, preserving the confidentiality of the donors' identities, stating: "We conclude, therefore, that the disclosure sought here implicates *constitutionally protected privacy interests*" [Emphasis added].

The Right Against Unreasonable Searches and Seizures The Fourth Amendment's prohibition is also against *unreasonable* searches and seizures by the government of persons or property without a warrant. When such unlawful conduct occurs, there may be a violation of both the constitutional right of privacy as well as the constitutional right against unlawful search and seizure.

Rights Under the Fifth and Fourteenth Amendments

The Right of Due Process of Law The right of due process of law is stated in two places in the Constitution. The Fifth Amendment, as a part of the Bill of Rights, is a limitation on *federal* power and provides, among other rights, that no person shall be "deprived of life, liberty, or property, without due process of law." The Fourteenth Amendment is a limitation on *state* power and provides: "Nor shall any State deprive any person of life, liberty or property without due process of law."

The phrase due process of law means that both governmental law and the process of its administration must be reasonable and fair, consistent with traditional notions of fair play and substantial justice, basically impartial and free from arbitrary governmental action. A person *must* have a "property interest" in the matter that he or she claims is constitutionally protected. Property is a tangible thing (for example, land or chattel) or an intangible interest or right in a thing (such as the title to something, interest in a job or pension benefits, a sales license, or governmental conferred entitlement). Accordingly, a property interest is a recognized and protected *property right.* Much due process litigation involves what is called "procedural due process," which means that governmental action must be *procedurally* fair in resolving a question of whether or not there has been an infringement of a constitutional right, such as a person receiving notice and an opportunity to be heard.

States have the power to establish price-control regulation without violating the Due Process Clause if it is for a legitimate rational public purpose and is not arbitrary or discriminatory. Protection of consumer welfare is a legitimate and rational goal of price or rate regulation. For example, a city rent control ordinance intended to prevent unreasonable rent increases caused by the city's housing shortage is a legitimate exercise of the city's *police power.*

The Fifth and Fourteenth Amendments also protect "liberty," which means a person's freedom of action and choice with respect to his or her personal life. Governmental infringement of liberty is subject to the right of due process of law. We see this often in criminal cases where the process in a trial is challenged by the defendant as unfair and is claimed to be a violation of the defendant's constitutionally protected right of due process of law.

The Power of Eminent Domain The Fifth Amendment provides: "Nor shall private property be taken for public use, without just compensation." This clause recognizes the inherent power of government to "take" private property for public use—which is called "eminent domain." But notice that there are two limitations on this power to take: the taking must be *for public use,* also known as "public purpose," and *just compensation must be paid.* The exercise of this power by a state is pursuant to its police power. Taking private property for a private purpose is void and unconstitutional as a violation of both the taking clause and the due process clause. Just compensation is measured by the market value of the property at the time of the taking.

The power of eminent domain is currently used for community planning—for example, in urban renewal, redevelopment, and highway construction. Usually, condemnation proceedings are initiated to obtain title to the land and to determine the fair value of the property taken. The reasonable exercise of land-use regulatory power is proper as long as it serves a public purpose.

In a taking-of-property case, the court must balance the nature and importance of the government's interest against the nature and extent of the economic loss of the property owner.

In *The City of Oakland v. The Oakland Raiders, et al.,* 220 Cal.Rptr. 153 (Cal. 1985), the City of Oakland sued to acquire the National Football League franchise owned by the Oakland Raiders, thereby prohibiting the Raiders from transferring its franchise from Oakland to another location. The California Court of Appeals held that the right of eminent domain can extend to personal property, including a franchise. However, the Court said that California's right of eminent domain in this case was not so substantial as to supersede the congressional power to regulate interstate commerce under the Commerce Clause of Article I, Section 8. The Court said, "Professional football is such a nationwide business and so completely involved in interstate commerce that acquisition of a franchise by an individual state through eminent domain would impermissibly burden interstate commerce." The decision was let stand by the U.S. Supreme Court.

The Right of Equal Protection of the Laws The Fourteenth Amendment states: "Nor shall any State . . . deny any person within its jurisdiction the equal protection of the laws." Both the states as well as the federal government are prohibited from denying such equal protection. Equal protection means government must treat similarly situated persons in a similar manner, unless there is a reasonable and rational ground for classifying and treating them differently in furtherance of a *legitimate governmental interest or purpose.* As soon as government action treats similarly situated people differently, the Fourteenth Amendment becomes applicable in order to determine whether the action is constitutionally valid.

The level or standard of judicial scrutiny in equal protection cases depends upon the nature of the *statutory classification* allegedly discriminated against:
(1) classifications based on race or national origin, or affecting fundamental rights, are *strictly construed;* (2) classifications based on sex or illegitimacy are given an *intermediate scrutiny;* (3) any other statutory classification will be given *minimal scrutiny. Majidi v. Palmer,* 530 N.E.2d 66, 68 (Ill.App. 2d Dist. 1988).

► The Right Not to Have the Obligation of Contracts Impaired

Article I, Section 10 provides: "No State shall . . . pass any . . . Law impairing the Obligation of Contracts." Persons, states, and the federal government have the inherent power to make contracts that create obligations of performance and rights to such performance. The very existence of the clause recognizes the freedom of contract. The clause is a limitation on state power to retroactively impair a contractual obligation. However, states have inherent power to pass laws for the protection of the public safety, health, and morals, and for eminent domain.

A famous nineteenth-century case involving this clause is *Dartmouth College v. Woodstock,* 4 Wheaton 518 (1819). In that case the U.S. Supreme Court held that the charter of Dartmouth College was a contract between the state and the *private* college, protected against attempted revocation and impairment by the state legislature. Today, states that grant private charters, such as corporate charters, expressly reserve in the charter contract the state's right to repeal, modify, and otherwise limit the charter.

Summary Statement

1. All federal power is derived only from the U.S. Constitution, delegated by the states to the federal government.
2. All state power is derived from each state's constitution, except as otherwise provided in the federal Constitution, and common law.
3. In the event of conflict between federal and state law, the federal law is supreme.
4. The powers not delegated to the United States by the Constitution, nor prohibited by it to the states, are reserved to the states respectively, or to the people.
5. No federal law, nor any state constitution or law, is valid if it violates the U.S. Constitution.
6. The first ten amendments to the U.S. Constitution are called the Bill of Rights; they are limitations on *federal* power. By decision of the U.S. Supreme Court, most of these amendments are now included within the purview of the Fourteenth Amendment, limiting *state* power in these areas.
7. The U.S. Supreme Court has the power of "judicial review", which means that it has the *final* power and authority to determine whether federal or state law violates the Constitution.
8. Congress has, among its financial powers, the power to tax, to borrow on the credit of the United States, and to spend federal funds.
9. The broad principles of the Constitution permit the Supreme Court to recognize and enunciate rights not specifically stated in the Constitution, making for a "living" Constitution so as to apply these principles in the circumstances that necessitate the recognition of nonenumerated rights.
10. *Interstate commerce:* Congress has the power to regulate foreign and interstate commerce and, by U.S. Supreme Court decision, this power extends to *intrastate* economic activities that *affect* interstate commerce. However, Congress will not exercise its power over such intrastate activities unless they have a substantial and harmful effect on interstate commerce.
11. *Religion:* Congress is expressly prohibited, and by inclusion of most of the Bill of Rights within the purview of the Fourteenth Amendment the states are also prohibited, from making any law respecting an establishment of religion, or prohibiting its free exercise.
12. *Freedom of speech and the press:* Under the First Amendment, Congress is expressly prohibited from making any law abridging the freedom of speech, or of the press, nor can any state make such a law because of the Fourteenth Amendment. "Speech" includes "commercial speech" concerning economic matters. There are limitations on freedom of speech, including state tort law regarding defamation and criminal laws prohibiting obscene speech.
13. *Private association with others:* The right to private association with others is an *implied* constitutional right.
14. *Privacy:* A right of privacy is, in general, a person's interest in his or her private life protected from unlawful government intrusion; it is another *implied* constitutional right.
15. *Unreasonable searches and seizures of persons or property:* When such unlawful conduct occurs, there is often a violation of both the right of privacy and the right against unreasonable search and seizure.
16. *Due process of law:* The phrase "due process of law" means that both governmental "law" and the "process" of its administration must be reasonable and fair, consistent with traditional notions of fair play and substantial justice, basically impartial and free from arbitrary *governmental* action. The process must be procedurally fair.

17. *Eminent domain:* The Constitution has expressly recognized the inherent power of government to "take" *private* property for "public" use, for which "just compensation" (market value) must be paid.
18. *Equal protection of the laws:* This right stated in the Fourteenth Amendment is a limitation on state power that disallows classification upon the basis of race or national origin, or affecting fundamental rights.
19. *The obligation of contracts is not to be impaired:* Federal and state governments cannot impair private contracts or contractual obligations, except for a state's police power.

The following case caused shock and indignation, when the U.S. Supreme Court decided that the act of burning the U.S. flag was protected as "free expression" under the First Amendment.

TEXAS, PETITIONER v. GREGORY LEE JOHNSON
109 S.Ct. 2533 (1989)

Justice Brennan. After publicly burning the American flag as a means of political protest, Gregory Lee Johnson was convicted of desecrating a flag in violation of Texas law. This case presents the question whether his conviction is consistent with the First Amendment. We hold that it is not.

I

While the Republican National Convention was taking place in Dallas in 1984, Johnson participated in a political demonstration dubbed the "Republican War Chest Tour."... [T]he purpose of this event was to protest the policies of the Reagan administration and of certain Dallas-based corporations.... He did accept an American flag handed to him by a fellow protestor who had taken it from a flag pole outside one of the targeted buildings.

The demonstration ended in front of Dallas City Hall, where Johnson unfurled the American flag, doused it with kerosene, and set it on fire. While the flag burned, the protestors chanted, "America, the red, white, and blue, we spit on you."... No one was physically injured or threatened with injury, though several witnesses testified that they had been seriously offended by the flag-burning.

Johnson ... was charged with the desecration of a venerated object in violation of Tex. Penal Code Ann. Sec. 42.09 (a)(3) (1989). After a trial, he was convicted, sentenced to one year in prison, and fined $2,000. The Court of Appeals for the Fifth District of Texas at Dallas affirmed Johnson's conviction, ... but the Texas Court of Criminal Appeals reversed, ... holding that the States could not, consistent with the First Amendment, punish Johnson for burning the flag in these circumstances.

The Court of Criminal Appeals began by recognizing that Johnson's conduct was symbolic speech protected by the First Amendment: ... The act for which appellant was convicted was clearly "speech" contemplated by the First Amendment. To justify Johnson's conviction for engaging in symbolic speech, the State asserted two interests: preserving the flag as a symbol of national unity and preventing breaches of the peace. The Court of Criminal Appeals held that neither interest supported his conviction.... The Texas court concluded that furthering this interest by curtailing speech was impermissible.... Noting that the State had not shown that the flag was in "grave and immediate danger" of being stripped of its symbolic value, the Texas court also decided that the flag's special status was not endangered by Johnson's conduct.

As to the State's goal of preventing breaches of the peace, the court concluded that the flag-desecration statute was not drawn narrowly enough to encompass only those flag-burnings that were likely to result in a serious disturbance of the peace. And in fact, the court emphasized, the flag burning in this particular case did not threaten such a reaction. . . . One cannot equate "serious offense" with incitement to breach the peace.

Johnson was convicted of flag desecration for burning the flag rather than for uttering insulting words. . . . We must first determine whether Johnson's burning of the flag constituted expressive conduct, permitting him to invoke the First Amendment in challenging his conviction. If his conduct was expressive, we next decide whether the State's regulation is related to the suppression of free expression. . . . If it is, then we must ask whether this interest justifies Johnson's conviction under a more demanding standard. . . .

The First Amendment literally forbids the abridgement only of "speech," but we have long recognized that its protection does not end at the spoken or written word. [W]e have acknowledged that conduct may be "sufficiently imbued with elements of communication to fall within the scope of the First and Fourteenth Amendments."

In deciding whether particular conduct possesses sufficient communicative elements to bring the First Amendment into play, we have asked whether "[a]n intent to convey a particularized message was present, and [whether] the likelihood was great that the message would be understood by those who viewed it." Hence, we have recognized the expressive nature of students' wearing of black armbands to protest American military involvement in Vietnam, . . . of a sit-in by blacks in a "whites only" area to protest segregation, . . . of the wearing of American military uniforms in a dramatic presentation criticizing American involvement in Vietnam, . . . and of picketing about a wide variety of causes. . . .

Especially pertinent to this case are our decisions recognizing the communicative nature of conduct relating to flags. Attaching a peace sign to the flag, . . . saluting the flag, . . . displaying a red flag, . . . we have held, all may find shelter under the First Amendment. . . . (treating flag "contemptuously" by wearing pants with small flag sewn into their seat is expressive conduct). . . .

We have not automatically concluded, however, that any action taken with respect to our flag is expressive. Instead, in characterizing such action for First Amendment purposes, we have considered the context in which it occurred. . . . Johnson's conduct was expressive conduct. Johnson burned an American flag as part—indeed, as the culmination—of a political demonstration that coincided with the convening of the Republican Party and its renomination of Ronald Reagan for President. The expressive, overtly political nature of this conduct was both intentional and overwhelmingly apparent. . . . In these circumstances, Johnson's burning of the flag was conduct "sufficiently imbued with elements of communication," to implicate the First Amendment.

. . . [W]e must decide whether Texas has asserted an interest in support of Johnson's conviction that is unrelated to the suppression of expression. . . . The State offers two separate interests to justify this conviction: preventing breaches of the peace, and preserving the flag as a symbol of nationhood and national unity. We hold that the first interest is not implicated on this record and that the second is related to the suppression of expression.

Whether Johnson's treatment of the flag violated Texas law thus depended on the likely communicative impact of his expressive conduct. . . . this restriction on Johnson's expression is content-based. . . . Johnson's political expression was restricted because of the content of the message he conveyed. We must therefore subject the State's asserted interest in preserving the special symbolic character of the flag to "the most exacting scrutiny." . . .

If there is a bedrock principle underlying the First Amendment, it is that the Government may not prohibit the expression of an idea simply because society finds the idea itself offensive or disagreeable.

We have not recognized an exception to this principle even where our flag has been involved. . . . "[T]he constitutionally guaranteed 'freedom to be intellectually . . . diverse or even contrary,' and the 'right to differ as to things that touch the heart of the existing order,' encompass the freedom to express publicly one's opinions about our flag, including those opinions which are defiant or contemptuous." . . . Nor may the Government, we have held, compel conduct that would evince respect for the flag. . . .

In short, nothing in our precedents suggests that a State may foster its own view of the flag by prohibiting expressive conduct relating to it. . . .

The way to preserve the flag's special role is not to punish those who feel differently about these matters. It is to persuade them that they are wrong.

Johnson was convicted for engaging in expressive conduct. The State's interest in preventing breaches of the peace does not support his conviction because Johnson's conduct did not threaten to disturb the peace. Nor does the State's interest in preserving the flag as a symbol of nationhood and national unity justify his criminal conviction for engaging in political expression. The judgment of the Texas Court of Criminal Appeals is therefore affirmed.

Questions and Case Problems

1. A Hawaii statute imposes a tax on the annual gross income of airlines operating within the State, and declares that such tax is a means of taxing an airline's personal property. Section 7(a) of the federal Airport Development Acceleration Act of 1973 (ADAA) prohibits a State from levying a tax, "directly or indirectly, on persons traveling in air commerce or on the carriage of persons traveling in air commerce or on the sale of air transportation or on the gross receipts derived therefrom," but provides that property taxes are not included in this prohibition. Aloha Airlines and Hawaiian Airlines each brought an action for refund of taxes assessed under the Hawaii statute, claiming that the statute was pre-empted by Section 7(a), and that the Hawaiian statute is not a property tax but a tax on gross receipts. Was the Hawaiian statute pre-empted by Section 7(a) and was the Hawaiian statute a property tax or a gross receipts tax? Explain fully. [*Aloha Airlines, Inc. v. Director of Taxation of Hawaii,* 464 U.S. 7 (1983).]
2. The state of Hawaii imposes a 20 percent excise tax on sales of liquor at wholesale. In order to encourage the development of the Hawaiian liquor industry, two items are exempted from the tax: *okolehao,* a brandy distilled from the root of an indigenous shrub of Hawaii, and a fruit wine manufactured in Hawaii. There is competition between these domestic exempt beverages with nonexempt liquor products from outside Hawaii. Bacchus Imports, Ltd., and Eagle Distributors, Inc., are liquor wholesalers who sell to licensed retailers at their wholesale price plus the 20 percent excise tax. They challenge the tax as being unconstitutional in violation of the Commerce Clause and the Twenty-first Amendment. Do you think the tax is unconstitutional as violative of the Commerce Clause and the Twenty-first Amendment? Explain your answer. [*Bacchus Imports, Ltd., et al. v. Dias, Director of Taxation of Hawaii, et al.,* 468 U.S. 263 (1984).]
3. It is the stated policy of the University of Missouri to encourage the activities of student organizations. The university officially recognizes over 100 student groups and provides university facilities for meetings of registered student organizations, supported in part by student fees. Cornerstone is an organization of evangelical Christian students from various denominational backgrounds. From 1973 to 1977 it was a registered religious student group with university permission to conduct its meetings in university facilities. In 1977 the university informed the group that it could no longer meet in university buildings, its decision based on a regulation adopted in 1972 that prohibits the use of university buildings or grounds "for purposes of religious worship or religious teaching." Eleven university students who were members of Cornerstone sued the university in a U.S. District Court, challenging the regulation as unconstitutional on the grounds that the university's discrimination against religious activity and expression violated their rights to *free exercise of religion, equal protection, and freedom of speech* under the First and Fourteenth Amendments to the Constitution. Is the university regulation unconstitutional? Explain fully. [*Widmar, et al. v. Vincent, et al.,* 454 U.S. 263 (1981).]

4. A Texas statute exempts from its sales tax "periodicals that are published or distributed by a religious faith and that consist wholly of writings promulgating the teaching of the faith and books that consist wholly of writings sacred to a religious faith." Texas Monthly, Inc., publishes a general interest magazine. It is not a religious faith magazine and does not contain only articles promulgating (publishing) the teaching of a religious faith. It was required to collect and remit to the state the applicable sales tax on the prices of qualifying subscription sales. Texas Monthly paid sales taxes pursuant to the statute under protest and sued the State of Texas in a state court to recover those payments. Texas Monthly claims that the tax statute is in violation of the Establishment of Religion Clause of the First Amendment and, therefore, unconstitutional. Is the Texas tax statute unconstitutional? Explain fully. [*Texas Monthly v. Bob Bullock, Comptroller of Public Accounts of the State of Texas, et al.,* 109 S.Ct. 890 (1989).]
5. In Virginia, a pharmacist is licensed by the State Board of Pharmacy, a state regulatory agency, with the power to revoke or suspend a pharmacist for unprofessional conduct. A section of a Virginia statute provides that it is unprofessional conduct for a pharmacist to advertise the prices of prescription drugs. Plaintiffs are prescription drug users, including two nonprofit organizations with many members who use prescription drugs. They claim that they will greatly benefit if the prohibition were lifted and pharmacists freely allowed to advertise. They sued the State Board in a U.S. District Court, challenging the constitutionality of the Virginia statute section as violative of the First and Fourteenth Amendments concerning commercial speech. Is the Virginia statutory section unconstitutional? Explain fully. [*Virginia State Board of Pharmacy, et al. v. Virginia Citizens Consumer Council, Inc., et al.,* 425 U.S. 748 (1976).]
6. Hunter Marine Corp., a manufacturer of sailboats, advertised its new boat, the "Hunter 45," in *Yachting,* a nationally distributed magazine sold in New York State. The advertisement stated that a "Cruise Pac" came with the boat consisting of, among other things, a cockpit table and a mast winch. Kenneth McDonald saw the advertisement, visited the Hunter plant, and then purchased a Hunter 45 boat from North Shore Yacht Sales, Inc., an independent dealer in Hunter products. The sales contract had a typed list of certain equipment included in the sale and the words "plus any and all equipment or hardware nationally advertised in *Yachting.*" The cockpit table and mast winch were not delivered with the boat to McDonald. The prototype of Hunter 45 was not completed at the time of the advertisement. McDonald sued to obtain an injunction against Hunter prohibiting it from "advertising any Hunter products within the State of New York." New York General Business Law permits a private party to bring an action to enjoin false advertising, meaning "advertising which is misleading in a material respect" which injured that party. Was the *Yachting* advertisement commercial speech, was the advertisement false, and was the New York law a reasonable regulation of commercial expression permissible under the U.S. Constitution? Explain fully. [*McDonald v. North Shore Yacht Sales, Inc.,* 513 N.Y.S.2d 590 (1987).]
7. Heights Medical Center, Inc., (Center) sued Peralta to recover $5,600 allegedly due under Peralta's guaranty of a hospital debt incurred by one of his employees. Peralta has no meritorious defense to Center's claim. A summons was issued but was not properly served on Peralta and, under Texas law, was of no legal effect. Peralta did not appear or answer, and a default judgment was entered against Peralta for the amount claimed. The judgment was recorded in the county property records, a writ of attachment was issued, and Peralta's real property was sold at auction to satisfy the

judgment. Sometime later, Peralta initiated legal proceedings to set aside the default judgment and obtain adequate relief, claiming that he had been deprived of a constitutional right by reason of the improper service of summons, default judgment, and loss of his property. Has Peralta been deprived of any constitutional right? Explain fully. [*Peralta v. Heights Medical Center,* 108 S.Ct. 896 (1988).]

8. The City of San Jose enacted a rent control ordinance during a city housing shortage with the stated purpose of "alleviating some of the more immediate needs created by San Jose's housing situation. These needs include but are not limited to the prevention of excessive and unreasonable rent increases, the alleviation of undue hardship upon individual tenants, and the assurance to landlords of a fair and reasonable return on the value of their property." The ordinance also provides that a landlord may increase the annual rent charged to tenants. If the rent exceeds a specified formula, a hearing is required before a mediation hearing officer to determine whether the landlord's proposed increase is reasonable. In making his or her determination, the hearing officer is to consider, among various stated factors, the "hardship to a tenant." The number of hardship tenants varies among the rentals of the various landlords. The landlords instituted a civil action against the City of San Jose seeking a court declaration that the ordinance, particularly the "tenant hardship" provision, is invalid under the federal Constitution on the following grounds: (a) Provision for a hearing officer is a violation of the Due Process Clauses of the Fifth and Fourteenth Amendments; (b) The ordinance's classification scheme of landlords who have varying numbers (or none) of hardship tenants is a violation of the Equal Protection Clause of the Fourteenth Amendment.

Is the ordinance unconstitutional on any of the above grounds? Discuss each ground separately, and explain fully. [*Pennell and Tri-County Apartment House Owners Ass'n v. City of San Jose and City Council of San Jose,* 108 S.Ct. 849 (1988).]

9. The West Virginia Constitution in relevant part establishes a general principle of uniform taxation so that all property, both real and personal, shall be taxed in proportion to its value. The Webster County tax assessor, from 1975 to 1986, valued petitioners' real property on the basis of its recent purchase price. Other properties not recently transferred were assessed based on their previous assessments with minor modifications. This system resulted in gross disparities in the assessed value of generally comparable property. Each year, the County Commission affirmed the assessments. Petitioners sued the County Commission, claiming that the county's assessment system systematically and intentionally discriminated against the petitioners in violation of the Equal Protection Clause of the Fourteenth Amendment. Does the county's assessment system violate the Equal Protection Clause? Explain fully. [*Allegheny Pittsburgh Coal Co. and East Kentucky Energy Corp., et al. v. County Commission of West County, West Virginia,* 488 U.S. 336 (1989).]

10. In *Texas v. Johnson,* excerpted at the beginning of this section, explain fully why the U.S. Supreme Court held that the Texas statute could not be constitutionally applied to convict Johnson.

CHAPTER 4

CRIMINAL LAW

After you have read this chapter, you should be able to:

1. Distinguish between criminal law and tort law.
2. Identify the different categories of crime: felony, misdemeanor, violation, treason.
3. Explain the difference between legality and morality.
4. Describe the requisites for crime.
5. Explain several defenses to criminal acts.
6. Explain several different business crimes: arson, forgery, bad checks, embezzlement, burglary.

1, 2, 4, 5

BUSINESS DECISIONS and the LAW

Ford Motor Company has a long record of selling quality, mass-produced automobiles. Its history can be traced back to 1913 when a man named Henry Ford established a bold new system of manufacturing automobiles. His new idea was to incorporate the assembly-line process into the business of building cars. Ford had heard of the technique of scientific management and was quite impressed with the notion that a workplace could be designed to bring work to the workers rather than workers to the work. Today we all know this new idea by its name—the assembly line.

Ford was also largely responsible for refining the gasoline-driven motor. He worked on his idea and received a good deal of encouragement from a man named Thomas Edison. Edison thought that creating and refining a car that would carry its own fuel with it was an excellent idea. One must wonder how these early pioneers would have reacted to a recent criminal case against Ford Motor Company.

Three young women were driving a Ford Pinto when the Pinto was hit in the rear by a van; the Pinto exploded, killing the young women. The state alleged that the company and its officials knew that the gasoline tanks on the Pinto had a tendency to explode when struck from behind. Not only did the state allege that the company knew of this tendency, but it set out to prove that Ford Motor Company should be held criminally responsible. It was an attempt to break new ground. In effect the state was arguing that society as a whole was offended by Ford Motor Company's action. Their alleged action was producing and selling a defective product.

Federal and state prosecutors are increasingly turning to criminal law as a way to regulate corporate behavior. We hear of companies paying bribes to do business in other lands, companies that falsify records to the Internal Revenue Service or to the Securities and Exchange Commission, and we are collectively offended. Criminal law provides a very powerful tool for changing behavior. But should criminal law be used to deal with defective products?

In the case involving the Pinto, the state wished to show that Ford had knowledge about the safety hazard but did not act appropriately to correct the situation. The jury deliberated for more than twenty-four hours after spending more than ten weeks in trial. Their decision was unanimous: Ford Motor Company was not guilty. In spite of this verdict, Ford finally yielded to public and government pressure and in the summer of 1978 voluntarily recalled almost two million Pintos to improve the gas tank safety.

To counter future risk, Ford continues to aggressively research and develop each of its new cars. In order for companies to flourish, they must make a strong effort to satisfy the public about their commitment to safety. On the other hand, corporate executives must learn about criminal law and understand that corporations can be brought to trial for designing dangerous products.

Sources: "Ford Acquitted in Pinto Trial of Charges of Reckless Homicide in Deaths of Three Girls," *Wall Street Journal*, March 14, 1980, p. 5; "Jury Clears Ford in Three Pinto Deaths," *New York Times*, March 14, 1980, p. 1.

Introduction

In the preceding chapters of this part, we discussed legal systems and utilization of those systems and alternatives used to resolve *civil* disputes. In this chapter we will discuss the nature of criminal law as a wrong to the *public* interest and, in the next chapter, discuss the law of torts concerned with wrongs to *private interests*.

Unfortunately, the number of crimes committed in the United States provides convincing evidence of the necessity for spending some time discussing criminal law. The FBI reported that in 1940 there were approximately 100 crimes committed per 100,000 population; 118 crimes per 100,000 in 1950; 145 in 1960, and 180 in 1965. Subsequent figures available from the FBI indicate that in 1975 over 11 million serious crimes were committed (approximately 5,000 per 100,000 population). The number of crimes continues to be a problem. By 1987 approximately one violent crime was being committed every 21 *seconds* somewhere in the United States and one property crime (for example, theft of another's goods) was being committed every three *seconds*.[1]

Alarming as these figures are, they tell only part of the story. Increasingly, business organizations have had to face the reality that the number of "white-collar" crimes is also increasing. These are offenses such as embezzlement or larceny.

[1]See FBI statistics, *Uniform Crime Reports*, 1975, 1980, and 1987 (Washington, D.C.: Government Printing Office), as well as *New York Times*, June 10, 1971, p. 22, col. 3, and June 9, 1972, p. 1, col. 2.

The substantive law of crime is concerned with defining what duties we owe to society and what rights we have as members of society. Thus, a study of criminal law is important to us so that we may know our legal rights and duties.

Moreover, because crime has a significant impact upon us as individuals and has an impact upon business, it is important for us to have an exposure to this area of law.

Concern of the Law

Society is concerned not only with disputes among persons for wrongs committed by them on each other for which they seek relief against each other, but also with wrongs to society and its members for which punishment should be imposed.

Most of this book discusses civil law and civil procedure. In this chapter we will examine briefly "the other half of the law" known as criminal law. A **crime** is an act, committed or omitted, in violation of a public law governing it.[2] For example, a robbery or a traffic violation is a crime. The major difference between a crime and a **tort** is that a crime is an offense against the state (a public wrong) in which the state prosecutes the individual; whereas a tort is a civil (private) wrong to a person other than breach of contract and the injured party must be the one to bring the civil lawsuit. An example of a tort is negligence. One who negligently drives a car is civilly liable to the pedestrian injured by such negligence.

crime
An act, committed or omitted, in violation of a public law governing it

tort
A civil (private) noncontractual wrong for which a court will give a remedy

In a criminal offense the society as a whole takes action against a person who has violated a formalized norm. Most of society dislikes murder, burglary, arson, and other such criminal offenses, and collectively we have delegated the responsibility of dealing with accused criminals to various governmental prosecutors. If an individual is found to be guilty of an offense, he or she is punished by the government. We are saying that society as a whole has found the act reprehensible. Some acts are reprehensible to both society as a whole *and* to private individuals who are hurt. Therefore, certain acts are considered both torts and crimes. For example, *A* shoots and wounds *B*. *A* can be prosecuted for *criminal* assault and battery, and *B* can sue *A* civilly for damages for the torts of *civil* assault and battery.

Categories of Crime

► Felony

A **felony** is the most serious category of crime. It is a crime for which, usually, the punishment can be more than one year in prison. Some states have an alternative definition for felony: any crime punishable by death or imprisonment in the state prison. Examples of felonies include murder, robbery, and rape. In some states a convicted felon loses certain citizenship rights, such as the right to vote and to hold public office.

felony
A serious crime for which, usually, the punishment can be more than one year in prison

► Misdemeanor

Another kind of criminal act is a **misdemeanor.** It is a crime for which the punishment is imprisonment for less than one year and the possibility of a fine, usually in a city or county jail. Once again, an alternative definition adopted by some jurisdictions is that a

misdemeanor
A crime for which the punishment is less than one year in prison and the possibility of a fine

[2] *Shick v. United States,* 195 U.S. 65 (1904).

misdemeanor is any crime not punishable by death or imprisonment in a state prison. Examples of misdemeanors include shoplifting and petty larceny.

Violation or Infraction

Some jurisdictions have an additional classification for offenses of lesser importance, such as parking or traffic citations. These are called *violations* or *infractions* and are generally distinguished by the minimal nature of the punishment, such as a fine. Usually they are classified as misdemeanors.

Treason

treason
A felony specifically defined by the U.S. Constitution

Treason is a felony that is specifically defined in the U.S. Constitution as "levying war against them [the states], or in adhering to their enemies, giving them aid and comfort."[3]

Requisites for Crime

Morality Versus Criminality

Just as in the law of torts, certain acts may seem reprehensible to you, but they may be only morally wrong and not criminal in nature. You will not be treated as a criminal if you do not yield your seat in a crowded bus to an elderly individual, or if you fail to remember an engagement (even if it's a promise to witness your best friend's wedding). Similarly, commission of certain infractions generally is insufficient to label someone a moral bankrupt. For example, few would argue that overtime parking at a meter is an indication of immorality.

Act and Intent

Every crime requires either an act or an omission (failure to act) when action is required by law. This very simple statement is an extremely important base of criminal law. If people could be punished without having committed an act required by law, we would be liable to punishment just for our thoughts. In addition, all people are charged with the responsibility of knowing the law. The following case illustrates that ignorance of the law is no excuse.

FACTS

Students were involved in a long-standing dispute. They agreed to meet in a parking lot. When the victim arrived at the designated spot, he encountered his adversary and several other individuals. The victim was forced into a van, then taken to a selected spot and severely beaten. The defendants claimed that they thought that they might be charged with assault, but did not know that they could be charged with kidnapping. Is ignorance of the law an excuse?

DECISION

No. One is obliged to discover whether a contemplated activity is criminal. And if he acts without such knowledge, he runs the risk of violation and consequent criminal prosecution.

State of Iowa v. Clark, 346 N.W. 2d 510 (Ia. 1984).

mens rea
The mental element required for a crime

This mental element of intent stated by the court in the decision is sometimes given the name **mens rea.** However, students should not confuse *mens rea* with *motive.* You

[3]U.S. CONST., art. III, sec. 3.

do not have to prove a motive to prove a crime. Different kinds of intent are required for different crimes. Some crimes require *specific intent,* which means they require the proof that the accused intended to commit the particular wrongful act proscribed by law. For example, a general definition of forgery is the false making or materially altering, with intent to defraud, of any writing which, if genuine, might apparently be of legal efficacy. To be guilty of forgery you must have the intent to defraud. If you are merely reproducing an item with the honest belief that you have permission, you will not be held criminally responsible.

Some crimes require only *general intent* but not *specific intent.* This means that you do not have to have the particular intent to commit a certain crime but only an intent to be doing what you did. An example of a crime usually involving simply general intent is robbery. Robbery often is defined as "taking property from the person or presence of another by use of force or threatening the imminent use of force." Note that no specific intent is spelled out in such statutory language.

Sometimes the mere agreement to commit an offensive act is regarded as violative of the law. For example, if two individuals communicate to each other the desire to commit embezzlement, they have committed a crime. That crime is known as *conspiracy.* Notice that the act of communicating this desire is enough to warrant a criminal charge. Some states also require an overt act.

Ability to Commit Crime—Defenses

▶ Insanity

The classic defense to crime is that the actor was insane at the time the actor committed the offense. There are a number of definitions of legal insanity. Traditionally two tests were employed to prove insanity. The first is the *McNaghten test.* Under this older rule, the persons accused would have to prove that either they did not know the nature of the act, or if they did know the nature of the act they did not know that it was wrong. A second traditional test is the *irresistible impulse test.* This requires that defendants prove that they were suffering from a mental disease that caused them to act in the criminal way (irresistible impulse) even though they knew right from wrong.

More recently, two additional tests have been added. According to the *Durham test,* insanity is demonstrated by proof that the actor was suffering from a mental condition and that the act was a result of that condition. The *American Law Institute Model Code test* suggests that a person is not responsible if, as a result of his mental disease, he lacked substantial capacity "to appreciate the criminality of his conduct or to conform his conduct to the requirements of the law." The ALI Model Code test was used in the judge's instructions to the jury in the 1982 criminal trial of John W. Hinckley, Jr., for the alleged attempted assassination of President Reagan in 1981. Additionally the term "mental disease" does "not include an abnormality manifested only by repeated criminal or otherwise anti-social conduct."[4]

▶ Minors

At common law there existed a sliding scale for determining the responsibility of children (minors) for the commission of a crime. Under seven years old, a child is

---

[4]American Law Institute Model Penal Code Proposed Official Draft, May 4, 1962, sec. 4.01.

conclusively presumed not to have the ability to commit a crime. Between seven and fourteen, the child is presumed incompetent to commit a crime, but the state may rebut the presumption. Finally, between fourteen and adulthood, the child is presumed to have the ability, but he or she may rebut that presumption. The trend in many states is to treat some minors as adults if they are charged with serious crimes. (See Figure 4.1.)

► Duress

duress

Wrongful inducement to do that which a reasonable person would have been unable to resist

If a defendant commits a wrongful act because he or she was induced to do so by the use of, or threat to use, unlawful force against the defendant or another, which a reasonable person would have been unable to resist, the defendant can assert the defense of **duress.** For example, if someone orders you to rob a bank while holding a gun at you and threatening your life if you do not cooperate, you can later use the defense of duress to charges of robbery leveled at you by the state.

FACTS

On March 3, 1981, a robbery occurred at Arth Drugstore. The night delivery man was preparing to unload his van when he was approached by a masked man. He then heard two clicks that sounded like the activation of the working parts of a gun. The delivery man triggered a silent alarm and the police came and arrested the alleged robber. The robber testified that he was forced to commit the robbery by Smith who, he said, was a dangerous person. He provided evidence that Smith was a dangerous person who was capable of forcing someone to commit a crime. But Smith was not at the scene of the crime. Is this a defense?

DECISION

Yes. Duress is one of several defenses to criminal offense. The whole issue is one of criminal culpability. That is, the law defines situations in which a person will not be deemed responsible for his or her acts because there is a justifiable reason for committing them or because the person was incapable of forming an intent. However, in this case, insufficient evidence was presented to demonstrate duress by Smith. Judgment of trial court against robber, affirmed.

Sanders v. State, 466 N.E.2d 424 (Ind. 1984)

► Corporate Responsibility

For years, society was unsure whether to hold corporations liable for criminal acts. The answer today is generally yes, as in the Ford Pinto case. Although corporations obviously

FIGURE 4.1 **Scale of Responsibility of Minors for Committing a Crime**

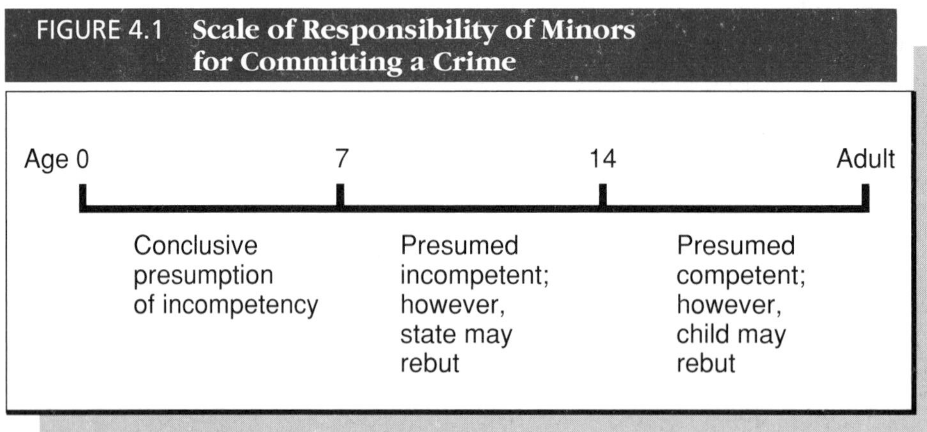

cannot be imprisoned, they can be fined for offenses. An officer of the corporation will be held criminally liable only if he or she actually committed the wrongful act or directed that the act be done.

► Other Defenses

Intoxication or drug use is often used as a defense to criminal culpability. However, voluntary drunkenness will not help you avoid liability. For example, if Carol, a student, voluntarily indulges her drug habit and then commits a crime, most courts would still find her guilty of the crime she committed. *Consent*—that is, voluntary agreement to do what would otherwise be the commission of a crime—may sometimes be a defense. For example, bodily harm that might otherwise be criminal in nature is consented to by the participants in a boxing match.

Select Crimes Relevant to Business

For a more complete treatment of any of the following business crimes,[5] see *Corpus Juris Secundum* or *American Jurisprudence,* two of the many excellent legal encyclopedias that are available.

► Arson

Arson may be defined as the willful and malicious burning of the dwelling house of another. This is a common law definition, which today has been extended to include one's own house and the buildings of another, depending on the particular state statute. Recall that common law consisted of those norms of behavior that became embodied in the case law over time. Each state has its own statutory definition of arson. For example, West Virginia Code 61-31-1 states: "Any person who willfully and maliciously sets fire to or burns or causes to be burned or aids, counsels or procures the burning of any dwelling house whether occupied, unoccupied or vacant, or any kitchen, shop, barn, stable or other outhouse that is parcel thereof, or belonging to or adjoining thereto, whether the property of himself or another shall be guilty of arson in the first degree."

arson
The willful and malicious burning of the dwelling house of another (at common law); today, by statute, arson includes one's own house and the buildings of another

► Crimes Involving Computer Use

All business students are aware of the growing importance of computers in the world of management. Because computers contain many different kinds of information, it is possible for an adventurous individual to commit a host of different crimes. If a person steals a particular program that the computer can use, he or she has stolen property of value, that is, committed "theft." If this program is a trade secret and the individual uses the program for personal advantage, he or she may have committed the crime of "misappropriation of a trade secret." Of course, stealing competitors' lists from a computer file might also qualify as a misappropriation of a trade secret.

Embezzlement is another crime that increasingly involves the use of a computer. Employees with access to computers in banks, for example, may learn how to transfer money from one account to another. If the employee abuses this understanding and trust

---

[5]The definitions that follow are useful *for teaching purposes only*. Students with legal problems are reminded that the best source of advice for their particular problems is an attorney.

and takes the money owed by the bank to its customers, the employee may have committed embezzlement.

FACTS

Evans and Smith were employed as salespeople in the investment division of Central Fidelity Bank. They submitted their resignations in August 1981 and began to work with a competing bank at the end of the month. When they left Central, they took with them a computer printout belonging to the bank. The printout, known as a customer security list, reflects the securities held in safekeeping and the owners' names. According to a bank officer, such a list would be useful as a sales tool to produce profits for many years to come. Is the taking of computer time and services in the form of printouts larceny?

DECISION

Yes. Computer lists can be considered property. The evidence respecting the nature and use of the customer security list supplied proof that the list had value. Further, in 1978 the General Assembly of Virginia passed a law that stated, in part: "Computer time or services or data processing services or information or data stored in connection therewith is hereby defined to be property which may be the subject of larceny."

Evans v. Commonwealth of Va., 308 S.E.2d 126 (Va. 1983)

► Misappropriation of Trade Secrets

Recently a number of cases have come to the courts that involve an employee or some other individual copying a company secret and using that secret for personal advantage and without permission. This is a particularly troublesome problem when the secret "involves a formula, pattern, device, or bit of information critical to the success of the business involved."[6] These kinds of secrets are called "trade secrets," and the crime of copying and using these trade secrets without permission is called "misappropriation of trade secrets." In the following case the court held that there was no trade secret and, therefore, the alleged crime of misappropriation of trade secrets had not occurred.

FACTS

Robinson, defendant, on the pretext of becoming a dealer for Energy Management, Inc., gained access to a partial list of Energy's customers. He then formed a competing company and used this list to his advantage. Energy never took precautions to maintain the secrecy of the list. The defendant was tried for committing the crime of misappropriation of a trade secret. Is this a misappropriation of a trade secret?

DECISION

No. In deciding whether a secret is a trade secret, one must examine (1) the extent to which the information is known outside the business; (2) the extent to which it is known by employees and others involved in the business; and (3) the extent of measures taken by the employer to guard the secrecy of the information. Here, no attempt was made to guard the secrecy of the list, so there is no trade secret here. Therefore the defendant is not guilty of the alleged crime.

Commonwealth v. Robinson, 388 N.E.2d 705 (Mass. 1979)

---

[6] RESTATEMENT (SECOND) OF TORTS, sec. 757 (1965).

► Forgery

The false making or altering, with intent to defraud, of any writing which, if genuine, might be of legal efficacy is known as common law **forgery.** In a business setting, forgery might include altering public records, issuing false certificates, or falsifying a doctor's prescription. Altering of checks is also considered forgery and is a particularly common form of forgery.

forgery
The unauthorized act of imitating or altering a writing with the intent to defraud and impose liability

► Issuing Bad Checks

As stated in the consolidated laws of New York, a person is guilty of issuing a bad **check** when (a) as a **drawer** or representative drawer, he or she writes a check knowing that there are not sufficient funds to cover it; (b) he or she intends or believes at the time of making the check that payment will be refused by the **drawee** upon presentation; and (c) payment is refused by the drawee upon presentation.

check
A negotiable "draft drawn on a bank payable on demand" UCC 3-104(2)(b)

drawer
The person who initially draws or creates and signs a draft

drawee
The person on whom a draft is drawn and ordered to pay

► Embezzlement and Larceny

Embezzlement and larceny are two closely related crimes. **Embezzlement** involves depriving someone of his or her property through breach of a trust relationship.[7] Note that the property is generally obtained lawfully but later converted to the embezzler's own use. **Larceny** is a common law crime that involves the taking and carrying away of the personal property of another by someone who does not have the right to do so. Notice that there is no relationship of trust between the parties to larceny. In the following case an employee had a position of authority and violated his employer's trust.

embezzlement
Depriving someone of his or her property through breach of a trust relationship

larceny
The taking and carrying away of the personal property of another without the right to do so

FACTS

Boueri was a Vice President of Caesar's Palace in charge of hosting affluent guests. As part of his job, he would arrange complimentary air fare and other services for such people. At the grand jury hearing, evidence was presented that Boueri had authorized tickets for several people who neither received tickets nor money, and Boueri kept the refund money received from the travel agency for unused tickets. Boueri sought dismissal of the grand jury indictment for embezzlement, claiming the tickets were not the property of Caesar's Palace, thereby making embezzlement impossible.

DECISION

The court decided embezzlement was possible. Although Caesar's Palace did not furnish Boueri with a cash box from which to embezzle funds, Caesar's Palace did entrust Boueri with power and authority through which he could possess his employer's funds. Therefore, embezzlement was possible.

State of Nevada v. Boueri, 672 P.2d 33 (Nev. 1983)

It is interesting to note that the Supreme Court of the United States has held that where a state legislature specifically authorizes cumulative punishment under two statutes, regardless of whether those two statutes proscribe the same conduct, under the Blockburger case [*Blockburger v. United States,* 284 U.S. 299 (1932)] cumulative punishments may be imposed in a single trial under such statutes [*Missouri v. Hunter,* 459 U.S. 359 (1983)].

[7] 26 AM. JUR. 2D *Embezzlement,* secs. 1–7 (1966).

Burglary Versus Robbery

robbery
The taking of money or goods of value from the person of another or in his or her presence, against that person's will, by force or fear

burglary
The breaking and entering in the night of the structure (e.g., building) of another with the intent to commit a felony therein

Two crimes that are often confused by laypersons but that are actually quite different are burglary and robbery. Both are common law crimes. **Robbery** is the taking of money or goods of value from the person of another or in his or her presence, against that person's will, by force or fear. In effect, it is an aggravated larceny. **Burglary,** however, is the breaking and entering in the night of the home of another with the intent to commit *any* felony therein. Many states have amended the burglary statute or have alternative laws to deal with burglary-type offenses during the daylight hours. Most states now say burglary can involve any structure, not just a home.

Commercial Bribing

bribery
The offering, giving, receiving, or soliciting of anything of value to influence action as an official or in discharge of legal or public duty

All states have laws regulating **bribery.** Some have special statutes that regulate bribery in a business setting. For example, New York sec. 180.00 states: ". . . guilty of commercial bribing when he confers, or offers or agrees to confer, any benefit upon any employee, agent or fiduciary without the consent of the latter's employer or principal, with intent to influence his conduct in relation to his employer's or principal's affairs." The federal Foreign Corrupt Practices Act of 1977[8] condemns foreign corrupt payments as a form of bribery.

Preparatory Crimes

attempt
In criminal law, a preparatory crime

Sometimes merely preparing to commit a crime results in a criminal offense being committed. *Solicitation* involves inciting someone else to commit a felony. It is a common law crime. Contemporary laws would include inciting to commit misdemeanors as solicitation. **Attempt** is a preparatory crime. Here an actor has the specific intent to commit a crime; makes some act toward accomplishing the crime which goes beyond mere preparation; and has the apparent ability to complete the crime but is stopped by something beyond the actor's control.

Violation of the Antitrust Laws

Violation of the antitrust laws can be a crime. Antitrust laws are discussed in Chapter 34.

Summary Statement

1. Crime has a significant impact on society, and an individual will want to know his or her legal rights and duties as defined by criminal law.
2. There is a difference in rights and duties as defined by the substantive areas of crime, tort, and contract law.
3. Crimes have been categorized according to the seriousness of the end result of the crime—a felony being the most serious, followed by misdemeanor and violation.
4. In criminal law, act plus intent (mens rea) determine whether or not a crime was committed; motive is not a requisite element.

---

[8]For a discussion of this act, see pp. 947–948.

5. Society has certain rights shown in its statutory criminal law, but these rights are limited by defenses to crimes. Some defenses are insanity, minority, consent, duress.
6. Certain crimes have special significance for business. These include arson, larceny, forgery, embezzlement, burglary, computer crimes, and misappropriation of trade secrets. Statutory definitions of the various crimes differ from state to state.

The following case illustrates corporate and corporate executives' responsibility for criminal wrongdoing.

UNITED STATES v. PARK
421 U.S. 658 (1975)

Burger, C. J. Acme Markets Inc. is a national retail food chain with approximately 36,000 employees, 874 retail outlets, and four specialty warehouses. Its headquarters is located in Philadelphia, Pennsylvania. In a five count information filed in the U.S. District Court . . . the government charged Acme and respondent, its president, with violations of the Food, Drug, and Cosmetic Act. Each count of the information alleged that the defendants had received food that had been shipped in interstate commerce and that, while the food was being held for sale in Acme's Baltimore warehouse following shipment in interstate commerce, they caused it to be held in the building accessible to rodents and to be exposed to contamination by rodents. These acts were alleged to have resulted in the food being adulterated (in violation of the law). . . . Acme pleaded guilty to each of the counts of the information. Respondent pleaded not guilty.

Respondent was the only defense witness. He testified that, although all of Acme's employees were in a sense under his general direction, the company had an organizational structure for responsibilities for certain functions according to which different phases of its operation were assigned to individuals who, in turn, have staff and departments under them. He identified those individuals responsible for sanitation, and related that upon receipt of the January 1972 FDA letter he had conferred with the Vice President for Legal Affairs, who informed him that the Baltimore division vice president was investigating the situation immediately and would be taking corrective action and would be preparing a summary of the corrective action through reply to the letter. Respondent stated that he did not believe there was anything he could have done more constructively than what he found was being done.

The jury found respondent guilty on all counts of the information . . . the Court of Appeals reversed the conviction and remanded for a new trial.

We granted certiorari because of an apparent conflict among the Courts of Appeals with respect to the standard of liability of corporate officers under the federal Food, Drug, and Cosmetic Act. We reverse.

We cannot agree with the Court of Appeals that it was incumbent upon the District Court to instruct the jury that the government had the burden of establishing "wrongful action" in the sense in which the Court of Appeals used that phrase. The concept of a "responsible relationship" to or a "responsible share in a violation of" the Act indeed imports some measure of blameworthiness; but it is equally clear that the government establishes a prima facie case when it introduces evidence sufficient to warrant a finding by the trier of the facts that the defendant had, by reason of his position in the corporation, responsibility and authority either to prevent in the first instance, or promptly correct, the violation complained of, and that he failed to do so. The failure thus to fulfill the duty imposed by the interaction of the corporate agent's authority and the statute furnishes a sufficient causal link. The considerations which prompted the imposition of this duty, and the scope of the duty, provide the measure of culpability.

Therefore, we reverse.

Questions and Case Problems

1. William Doucette can clearly remember that he stabbed and killed Ronald Landry after they arrived at their motel room together. However, he does not seem to be consistent in his explanation of why he killed the victim. Doucette had been drinking rather heavily and states that he was incoherent at the time of the stabbing. Do you think he can successfully use the defense of intoxication? Explain your answer. [*Commonwealth v. Doucette,* 462 N.E.2d 1084 (Mass. 1983).]
2. Burns, whose house was insured against fire, decided that it would cost him less to rebuild his house rather than to repair the old one. A cheap way of getting rid of the old house would be to burn it to the ground, which was exactly what Burns did. Under which circumstances would this be an act of arson and when would it not be? Explain your answer. [*Burns v. The State,* 305 S.E.2d 398 (Ga. 1983).]
3. One afternoon, at 4 P.M., Patricia DeWall and her cousin looked over some used cars on Russ DeVine's car lot. On DeWall's request, DeVine gave her permission to take a car for a test drive to a motel nearby. However, DeWall and her cousin also stopped at some other local businesses and failed to be back before DeVine's closing hours. They decided to take a spin and took a 300-mile drive. When they arrived back in the early morning hours, they left the car in DeVine's lot with the keys locked in it. Was this a crime? Explain. [*State of South Dakota v. DeWall,* 343 N.W.2d 790 (S.D. 1984).]
4. Howard Babits was working as a clerk in a store when he accepted a credit card from a person who he knew was not the person named on the card. Was this an offense? Explain. [*People of the State of New York v. Babits,* 469 N.Y.S.2d 537 (N.Y. 1983).]
5. Luther Butler was observed breaking the vent window of a parked automobile on a public street, entering the car, and kneeling on the front passenger's seat facing the dashboard when he was interrupted and fled. He was later caught possessing a pair of pliers. The only damage to the car was the broken vent window. Did Butler commit the crime of larceny? Why or why not? [*People of the State of New York v. Butler,* 465 N.Y.S.2d 477 (N.Y. 1983).]
6. Dianne and Earline occasionally let Montrae and Ricky stay in their apartment overnight. Ricky even kept some clothes and personal effects in the apartment, and T.S.J. often visited when Ricky was there. One morning after Dianne and Earline had left the apartment the night before, someone had broken through the lock in the back door and taken a sweater, two cameras, etc. It was proved that Ricky, Montrae, and T.S.J. were responsible for the break-in. The two roommates testified that neither T.S.J., Ricky nor Montrae had permission to enter the apartment that night, although T.S.J. was not aware of this. In addition, T.S.J. did not know that the property taken did not belong to Ricky or Montrae and he did not see how the back door was opened by Ricky. Given these facts, did T.S.J. commit a crime? Explain your answer. [*T.S.J. v. State of Florida,* 439 So.2d 966 (Fla. 1983).]
7. Defendant was the president of the union that represented the Wellston firefighters, and he strongly supported a proposed tax increase for the districts they were serving. On March 26, City of Pagedale and others filed suit against the Wellston Fire Protection District seeking to eliminate this tax proposition due to an illegal election.

   William Speiser, Mayor of Pagedale, was the principal witness against defendant. On March 31 and April 1 defendant offered him money and other benefits in return for which the City of Pagedale would withdraw from the lawsuit. Assuming no money or benefits were passed, has a crime been committed? Explain. [*State of Missouri v. Walker,* 657 S.W.2d 704 (Mo. 1983).]

8. Defendants were charged with purchasing and "aiding" in the concealment of certain intellectual property contained in and on two video cassettes of a movie entitled "Star Wars." Note that no charge was made that the video cassettes themselves were stolen property. Is the taping of a movie in this manner a criminal taking of property? [*Commonwealth v. Yourawski,* 425 N.E.2d 298 (Mass. 1981).]
9. Gillies murdered a person and then used the victim's bank card to obtain money from the victim's automatic teller machine. Is it a computer crime to use someone else's bank credit car to obtain funds? [*State v. Gillies,* 662 P.2 1007 (Ariz. 1983).]
10. Consider the case of *United States v. Park,* excerpted at the beginning of this section. Do you think that a corporation and its corporate president should be held criminally liable for acts of the corporation's employees?

C H A P T E R

5

THE LAW OF TORTS

3, 4, 5, 7,

After you have read this chapter, you should be able to:

1. Identify and explain the concept of tort.
2. Distinguish between a tort and a crime.
3. Distinguish between an intentional tort and a negligent tort.
4. Explain the torts of assault and battery.
5. Define at least an additional kind of intentional tort.
6. Explain defenses to intentional torts.
7. Define negligent torts.
8. Explain proximate cause as a legal concept.
9. Explain the concept of immunity from tort liability.

BUSINESS DECISIONS and the LAW

On March 24, 1989, the supertanker *Exxon Valdez* struck a reef. The resulting hole in the side of the ship permitted more than eleven million gallons of crude oil to spill into Prince William Sound in Alaska. The natural beauty of this area is an important national resource. The cost of cleaning such an area is enormous. No one is seriously questioning that the area should be cleaned up and no one doubts that the source of the oil spill was the hole in Exxon Corporation's tanker. But there is a good deal of disagreement about why the accident occurred, exactly who should be blamed, and how much of a clean-up is required.

Some groups are arguing that Exxon should pay the full cost of cleaning the environment. According to a newspaper account, certain environmental groups believe the Exxon and six of its partners in the Alaska Pipeline Services Company misrepresented their ability to prevent or control a spill. The National Wildlife Federation and the Natural Resources Defense Fund estimate that a complete clean-up—which would of necessity include restoring the damaged wildlife and thoroughly cleaning the shoreline—would cost at least a billion dollars.

Other people are placing the alleged blame more squarely on the shoulders of Joseph Hazelwood, the captain of the ship. Hazelwood had criminal charges pending against him. It was alleged that he was drinking prior to the incident and that the drinking was a cause of the accident. However, a jury found him not guilty of the alcohol charge but guilty of negligent discharge of oil.

Still others would place at least part of the blame on the Coast Guard. For example, why didn't the Coast Guard track the *Valdez* when it veered out of the normal shipping channel?

We all have an inherent standard of conduct by which we judge behavior. How would you evaluate responsibility in this situation? Would you ascribe blame to the corporation, the individual employee, or the government through the Coast Guard?

One of the jobs of the law in torts is to determine just this sort of responsibility for alleged wrong behavior. We know that the damage has been done and that someone must assume or at least share responsibility for it. But it is up to the law of torts to decide who it will be.

Corporations and individuals do not often face problems of the magnitude of those involving the *Exxon Valdez.* All of us have heard of people who claim to have found foreign objects in their food or who have bought a defective product. If damage results, it is the law that assesses the cause of the wrong and the remedy. Products liability cases are also the province of tort law.

Finally, on occasion, people act intentionally to commit a wrong. Paralleling criminal assault and battery there is a tort action for redressing those kinds of personal wrongs.

Sources: Linda Deutsch, "Jury Finds Skipper Not Guilty on Alcohol Charge," Boston *Globe,* March 23, 1990, p. 1; Richard Behar, "Joe's Bad Trip," *Time,* July 24, 1989, pp. 42–47; "Environmental Groups Sue Exxon," *Hampshire Gazette,* August 18, 1989.

Introduction

In Chapter 4 we discussed criminal law, which is concerned with wrongs to the *public* interest. In Chapters 1 and 2 we discussed legal systems and utilization of those systems and alternatives in order to resolve *civil* disputes. In this chapter we will discuss the law of torts, which is one of the areas concerned with civil disputes and wrongs to the interests of *persons* (individuals or legal entities such as corporations). Another area concerned with civil disputes is the law of contracts, discussed in Part 2.

tort
A civil (private) noncontractual wrong for which a court will give a remedy

The word **tort** is not a part of the vocabulary of most people. Yet, torts are committed every day in almost every community in the United States. In fact, the chances of you or a member of your family having committed a tort or being otherwise involved in a tort action at one time or another are reasonably high. The reason is that the number of different kinds of torts is very large. The next few paragraphs will give you some examples of the kind of problem included within the subject matter of torts.

The most common kind of tort action in the United States is the typical automobile accident. It happens in every large city every single day. Driver *X* drives his car in a careless manner and dents the fender of driver *Y*'s car. Add passengers to either car or more automobiles or trucks to the accident and you have made the tort more complex—but it is still a tort action.

If the drivers of the cars involved in the accident get out of their cars and exchange more than driver's licenses and ultimately end up in a fight, this too can result in a tort action. If driver *X* is hurt badly and is rushed to a hospital, where the doctor in charge carelessly administers the wrong drug or performs the wrong operation, this can result in a tort.

If driver *X,* recuperating in the hospital, is served food with an unwanted foreign object (such as a cigarette butt in his milk) or becomes sick from being carelessly served spoiled food, there is a chance for a tort action. If, in reconstructing the accident, the police discover that the incident was caused by a poorly constructed steering column rather than the driver's carelessness, once again there is a possible tort action.

Torts exist in the business world in the form of trademark infringement, copyright abuse, products liability, and more. Almost any time a person acts below a generally accepted standard of behavior, he or she is risking becoming involved in a tort action.

Response of the Law

All of us are involved in incidents at one time or another for which we are at fault. These incidents may be as simple as accidentally tripping someone in a hallway or as severe as an automobile accident involving damages that might exceed a million dollars. In the vast majority of these cases nobody is accused of being a criminal although someone may have angered others or even cost them large sums of money. However, both a tort *and* a crime may arise from the same act or facts.

Assuming that a **wrong** has been committed, and there is neither a crime involved nor a contractual arrangement existing, our legal system has developed a body of rules for redressing these wrongs. William L. Prosser (1898–1971) was the foremost scholar of his time concerning the law of torts. He said that a precise definition of tort was difficult if not impossible to provide but suggested that, "broadly speaking, a tort is a civil wrong, other than breach of contract, for which the court will provide a remedy in the form of an action for **damages**." It is an area that is at once exciting and rapidly changing. We will look at the three major subdivisions of tort law—intentional torts, negligent torts, and strict liability torts—and see how it is evolving. (See Figure 5.1.)

wrong
The illegal invasion of another person's interest

damages
The money judicially awarded to an injured party for another's wrongful conduct

Intentional Torts

While we are free to do as we please in the United States, if we *intentionally* hurt others in the process, we can be held responsible. Certain acts are so repulsive that all members of our society agree to punish the wrongdoer through the vehicle of criminal law. But, for example, assume *X* punches you in the nose and society demands that *X* spend some time in jail for violating the criminal law. The problem of paying your doctor's bills remains even if society is satisfied that *X* is behind bars. You, as the individual damaged, still are personally unsatisfied even though society as a whole has achieved relief. For this reason there are several *intentional* torts that parallel criminal acts. However, the causes of action are different, and students should not confuse criminal actions with their parallel intentional tort actions. If an intentional tort has been committed, an individual may collect an amount of money beyond that which merely "repairs the wrongdoing." The injured party may collect **punitive damages.** Punitive damages are designed to punish the wrongdoer *civilly.*

punitive (exemplary) damages
The money judicially awarded to an injured party in excess of compensatory damages to punish for malicious, wanton, or intentional wrongful conduct

► Battery and Assault

One of the incidents cited in the first part of this chapter was a fist fight between two individuals. This is an example of a battery. A **battery** is committed when an individual acts *intentionally* to cause a harmful or offensive bodily contact with another and a

battery
An act by a person intentionally causing harmful or offensive bodily contact with another

FIGURE 5.1 **The Concept of Wrongs**

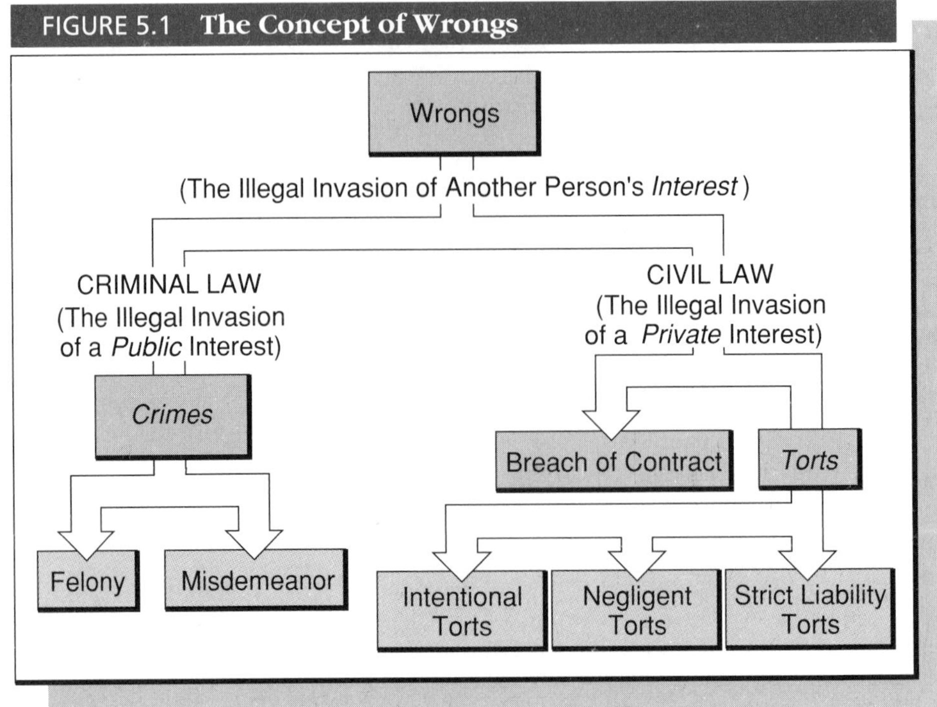

harmful or offensive bodily *contact* directly or indirectly results.[1] The following case illustrates that an intentional offensive bodily contact with another sustains a claim of battery.

FACTS

The plaintiff worked for a firm named Alford Photo Industries. During the course of her employment, plaintiff was approached by the president of the firm and asked what she was doing. She showed him. Then he put his hand under her coat and touched her without her consent. She was so upset by the touching that she immediately asked for and received permission to leave the plant. The president admitted that he touched and hugged female employees but claimed that his conduct was just a friendly act of an employer. The plaintiff sued for the tort of battery.

DECISION

Plaintiff was entitled to damages for battery. The president of the firm had engaged in outrageous conduct and intentionally inflicted distress on the plaintiff by touching her without consent.

Pease v. Alford Photo Indus., 667 F.Supp. 1188 (W.D. Tenn. 1987).

assault
An unprivileged act by a person intentionally causing another to apprehend an immediate harmful or offensive bodily contact to the other

Note that the court is not concerned with the fact that no physical injury resulted. It is concerned with *intentional* harm and the factual issue of *bodily contact,* which is what differentiates battery from assault. An **assault** is an unprivileged act by a person intentionally causing another to *apprehend* that an immediate harmful or offensive

[1] See, generally, Restatement (Second) of Torts sec. 13 (1965).

bodily contact will occur to the other. In order for an assault to exist, it is not necessary that the actor have the ability to carry out the intended threat, as long as the actor has the *apparent* ability to do so. It is necessary only that the receiver of the threat believes that the actor has the ability to carry out the threat. Battery and assault are separate torts that may occur separately or at the same time. It should be noted that civil battery and assault can also be separate crimes of criminal assault and battery, because the wrong is also to a member of society and, therefore, a wrong to the public interest.

► False Imprisonment

False imprisonment, often called *false arrest,* is another intentional tort that may be of concern to business people. False imprisonment may be defined as the unprivileged act of intentionally restraining the movement of another who is aware of such restraint. As with other intentional torts, the actor must have the requisite intent to confine another. Further, the confined party must know he or she is restrained. For example, if you were working with a friend taking inventory of goods in a warehouse and accidently locked your friend in the warehouse, this would not be false imprisonment. You simply do not have the requisite intent. If your friend had continued to work while you left on an errand and had been unaware of having been locked up, this also would not be false imprisonment. In the following case locking a person in a room was not false imprisonment.

false imprisonment (false arrest)
An unprivileged act intentionally restraining the movement of another who is aware of such restraint

FACTS

Plaintiff employee was asked to come down to the donut shop. She was not told why. Upon arrival she was asked by her employer to accompany him into the baking room, which was located at the rear of the store. A Mr. Ralph Bell was also present in the room. Her employer asked the plaintiff to sit down. She indicated that they closed the door and locked it by putting a "little latch on." She stated that the two men told her that they had proof that spotters going from store to store had purchased two dozen donuts from her, but that her register had not shown the sale. Based on these facts, is there a case for false imprisonment?

DECISION

No. In the tort of false imprisonment, it is not enough for the plaintiff to have felt "compelled" to remain in the baking room in order to protect her reputation. The evidence must establish a restraint against the plaintiff's will, as where she yields to force, to the threat of force or to the assertion of authority. In the present case, our search of the record reveals no evidence that plaintiff yielded to constraint of a physical threat, express or applied, or to physical force of any kind.

Lopez v. Winchell's Donut House, 466 N.E.2d 1309 (Ill. 1984).

► Invasion of Privacy

There are a number of additional intentional torts. However, brief mention should be made of one other intentional tort that may occur in a business setting. A tort that has increased in importance in recent years is the *intentional invasion of one's privacy.* Here, the cause of action often arises in a business situation when a company unauthorizedly uses an individual's name or likeness for profit.[2] One example might be using your picture in an advertisement without your permission. Another type of invasion occurs when objectionable, highly private information about an individual is made public without the individual's permission. Still another type of invasion occurs

---

[2]*Carlisle v. Fawcett Publications, Inc.,* 201 Cal.App.2d 733 (1962).

when there is unwarranted intrusion into someone's private life, as is illustrated by the following case.

FACTS

Ralph Nader, plaintiff, is a well-known advocate for automobile safety and consumer protection. Nader sued General Motors Corporation, defendant, claiming that the defendant through its agents was invading his privacy by, among other things, (1) wiretapping his telephone and eavesdropping on private conversations, as well as (2) conducting ongoing and harassing investigations. The defendant's actions arose because of Nader's decision to publish a book entitled *Unsafe At Any Speed.* Did these activities by the defendant constitute the tort of invasion of privacy?

DECISION

Yes. Judgment for the plaintiff, Nader. In order for there to be a cause of action for invasion of the plaintiff's privacy, the plaintiff must show that the actions of General Motors Corporation were intrusive and for the purpose of gathering information not normally available on inquiry. This occurred here.

Nader v. General Motors Corp., 255 N.E.2d 765 (N.Y. 1970).

In an effort to control invasions of privacy, the federal government has passed a number of new laws. The Fair Credit Reporting Act gives people the right to examine files compiled about them pertaining to their credit record. Incorrect files must be changed. Later the Privacy Act was passed, which placed severe restrictions on the use of private records by federal agencies.

► Some Other Intentional Torts

A few other intentional torts should be mentioned here briefly.

1. *Malicious prosecution* is concerned with a person's initiation or procurement of criminal proceedings against an innocent person, done without probable cause and with malice, the proceedings terminating in favor of the accused person.
2. *Mental and emotional disturbance* is a relatively new and developing tort consisting of outrageous conduct interfering with another person's mental and emotional tranquility.
3. *Deceit* occurs when a person knowingly misrepresents a material fact, intending to mislead another person by inducing him to rely on the misrepresentation and to act in a particular business transaction, causing financial damage to him or her.
4. *Trespass to chattels* is concerned with a person's wrongful interference with another person's possession of **chattels** (for example, an automobile or furniture) causing damage to the other person's interest in the chattels.
5. *Conversion* is a more serious type of wrongful interference with another person's possession of chattels by wrongfully exercising control and dominion over them.
6. *Trespass to land* is concerned with a person's wrongful interference with another person's possession of land.
7. *Public nuisance* and *private nuisance* are concerned with a person's unreasonable, substantial interference with either the *public's* use and enjoyment of *public* land (e.g., blocking a public highway), or with a *private* person's use and enjoyment of his or her *private* land (e.g., excessive and continuous loud noise or offensive odors from a neighbor).

chattel
A tangible, movable thing

8. Miscellaneous torts concerned with unfair trade practices, such as *fraudulent marketing* of goods or services (for example, Sam markets and sells goods or services to Paul, misrepresenting that they are made or provided by Ralph when, instead, they are from Zelda); and wrongful *imitation of physical appearance* of goods.

► Defenses to Intentional Torts

Occasionally there exists a legally justifiable reason for committing what would otherwise be an intentional tort. Some of these reasons provide enough protection for the actor so that he or she is shielded from what would otherwise be wrongful with resulting liability. These reasons create a *privilege* so to act.

Privilege A **privilege** is that which exempts a person from liability for his or her conduct which, but for the exemption, would subject the person to liability for such conduct. A privilege may be in the form of consent to such conduct by the person affected or by operation of law.

privilege
That which exempts a person from liability for his or her conduct which, but for the exemption, would subject the person to liability for such conduct

1. *Consent.* A person's **consent** to the illegal invasion of his or her interest by another person privileges such invasion. The person consenting must have had full capacity to consent and have acted freely, without fraud or mistake, in assenting to the invasion. For example, in all body contact sports the participants consent to body contact by each other, thus precluding the commission of the tort of battery. This is the subject of the following case.

consent
A person's approval of something, made with full capacity, freely, and without fraud or mistake; in torts, such approval permitting what would otherwise be an intentional tort

FACTS

Plaintiff entered into a boxing match with the defendant while attending a carnival in the hope of winning some prize money. The match resulted in injury to the plaintiff by the defendant. Plaintiff sued for battery.

DECISION

Judgment for defendant. There is no battery. An assent which satisfied the stated rules constitutes consent and prevents an invasion from being tortious and, therefore, is not actionable.

Hudson v. Craft, 204 P.2d 1 (Cal. 1949).

It should be clear that consent is not present if assent was induced through fraudulent means. For example, if a person **assents** to eat a tablet that he or she believes to be an aspirin and that was intentionally misrepresented to be such when in fact it was actually LSD, the victim has not consented to the negative consequences and has a valid cause of action for tort. Finally, consent may be expressly stated or may be implied from the situation.

assent
A person's manifestation of approval of something

2. *By operation of law.* There are various privileges given by operation of law and without the consent of the person whose interest is threatened with invasion or has been invaded.
   a. Self-defense. If there is an assault, the person assaulted has the privilege of self-defense, which includes the right to self-help by that person by the use of such physical force as is reasonably required under the circumstances to

protect that person from the threatened battery. If the threat is danger of substantial bodily harm or danger to life itself, the person assaulted may use force amounting to substantial bodily harm or death to the assaulting party.[3] The following case illustrates reasonable conduct in self-defense when there is reasonable belief of danger of substantial bodily harm.

FACTS

Plaintiffs, Lynn Richard Bray, his mother, Nina Landry, and his stepfather, Robert Landry, appealed from a judgment dismissing their claim for damages against T. H. Isbell, owner of the Sunset Motor Inn, and John Daniel Wells, the Inn's general maintenance man. Plaintiffs seek damages for injuries Bray suffered when Wells shot him after Bray broke into a vending machine on the premises of the Sunset Inn. The trial court concluded that Bray was 100 percent at fault.

Bray broke into a vending machine and stole the coin box. Mrs. Gastineau, the Inn's manager, saw Bray and immediately alerted her son, Wells, who was asleep on the couch in the apartment. Wells went to the back door of the apartment and saw Bray breaking into the machine with a tire tool which prompted Wells to obtain his mother's pistol. When he shouted at the intruders, Bray and his companion ran toward their parked car carrying the money box, a tire tool, and a lug wrench. Wells shouted to them to drop their weapons, and go inside the Inn so he could call the police. Instead, Bray ran past their car. When they were approximately 75 yards away, Wells fired three warning shots, one of which struck Bray in the lower back. Plaintiff contends that Wells' use of force against Bray was unreasonable under the circumstances. Was the force unreasonable?

DECISION

No. The judgment of the trial court is affirmed. The law is well settled that a plaintiff cannot recover damages for a battery if he is at fault in provoking the difficulty in which he is injured. This court believes the use of force in this matter was reasonable. If the defendant shot to run these people off so they wouldn't come back, and steal, and/or harm his mother, or, if he shot, as the court believes he did, thinking he was threatened by the object in perpetrator's hand, the defendant used what the court believes was reasonable force. We believe that the record supports the trial judge's determination that Wells used reasonable force under the circumstances.

Bray et al. v. Isbell, 458 So. 2d 594 (La. App. 1984).

The privilege of self-defense extends to one person protecting a second person from a third person.

b. Possessory interests in property. A person whose possessory interest in property is superior to that of a person threatening to interfere with such property interest has the privilege to use such physical force as is reasonably required under the circumstances as protection against such interference, but the force may not amount to substantial bodily harm or death. An example is a person threatening to commit a trespass to land or chattels of another who has a superior right to possession of such land or chattels. However, if the threatening person also threatens assault, then the privilege of self-defense becomes available to the person assaulted.

A person with a superior right to possess land or chattels which are in another person's possession has a privilege of recapturing such property. Whether the first person may use physical force to recapture depends upon

[3]See, generally, Restatement (Second) of Torts secs. 63–76 (1965).

whether or not the person in possession initially obtained possession rightfully or wrongfully. If the person in possession was initially rightfully in possession, then physical force cannot be used to recapture. For example, if you defaulted in making an installment payment on your automobile and your creditor, with the right to repossess the automobile on your default, seeks to repossess it, the creditor cannot use physical force on you to do so if you refuse to consent to the creditor's repossession. You were initially rightfully in possession. However, if the person in possession initially obtained possession wrongfully, and the person with a superior right to possession seeking to recapture the property acts promptly to repossess after wrongful dispossession has occurred, then reasonable force may be used, but not amounting to substantial bodily harm or death. For example, if you see a thief running off with your tires, you can chase the thief and use reasonable physical force on the thief to recapture your tires.

Another illustration of this privilege to recapture chattels is in the area of merchandising. Some states allow shopkeepers the privilege of detaining an individual suspected of shoplifting.

Negligent Torts

In this section we turn to the largest subdivision of the law of torts, in terms of the number of cases litigated each year. It is the branch of the law that uses *fault* rather than *intent* for imposing liability. However, not all incidents for which a person is at fault result in legal liability. There are a number of issues to consider before legal liability may be established.

The person found responsible for committing a negligent tort will not have to pay punitive damages as does the wrongdoer in the case of an intentional tort. Instead, the responsible party will probably have to pay only an amount of money that will rectify the negligent act. It is often said that the object of damages is to make the injured party "whole again."

► Negligent Torts and Morality

As small children, we are directed by our parents in our activities. When we make a mistake, we are punished and taught the correct behavior. As we grow older, we discover that the community in which we live has standards of behavior to which we must adhere. However, no one ever can or does tell us the precise behavior deemed acceptable for every conceivable situation. Nonetheless, a certain standard of conduct prevails in all situations, and if we fail to live up to the prevalent standard of conduct, we will be held responsible either morally or legally.

On occasion, certain behavior will fail to meet the community's standard of care but will not be a legal wrong. For example, assume that Franklin Moneypockets is a multimillionaire. Years ago Franklin had his life saved by Ben Pennyless, an extremely poor individual. If Franklin knows of Ben's financial plight, many of us would expect that Franklin would come to Ben's aid. However, there is no legal responsibility to do so. This is because there is *no legal duty* that extends from Franklin to Ben no matter how strong the moral obligation seems to be. The following elements are involved in suing for the tort of negligence: a duty of care and its breach; causation, called *proximate cause;* and damage, or loss or harm.

► Legal Duty

This leads us to the first step of establishing tort liability through *negligence.* There can be an established case of negligence only where there is a *legal duty that extends between the parties.* The question of whether such a legal duty exists is strictly a question of law and not a question of fact subject to jury interpretation.

► Standard of Care

negligence (conduct)
Failure to use the degree of care demanded by the circumstances

negligence (tort)
Negligent conduct proximately causing injury to another person's interest

On the assumption that a legal duty exists, the second step would be to establish that the person committing the *tort* of negligence *acted below the prevailing standard of care.* The term we use to describe such *conduct* is **negligence.** Negligence (careless conduct) is the failure to use the degree of care demanded by the circumstances[4] at the time of the act or failure to act. Another definition for negligence is the failure to use the care which an ordinary, prudent person would use under the same or similar circumstances to avoid causing injury to another or to protect another from injury.[5] Negligence (careless conduct) should be distinguished from the **tort of negligence,** which occurs when (1) a person's negligent conduct (2) proximately causes (3) injury to another person's interest. Until negligence proximately causes such injury, the tort does not exist. In the following case failure to exercise reasonable care was not shown; therefore, there being no negligence, no tort of negligence had occurred.

FACTS

Pritchard testified during his deposition that he descended the steps in a shopping mall, engaged in a telephone conversation at a telephone approximately 1½ to 2 feet from the bottom step, and slipped on a melted or partially melted ice cream cone within several inches of the bottom step immediately upon completing his telephone call. The melted ice cream extended out from the base of the bottom step to approximately 6 to 8 inches beyond the base and extended nearly the entire length of the step. The appellant testified that he did not see the ice cream prior to his telephone call. The complaint alleges negligent maintenance and inspection of the area in which appellant fell, and negligent use of floor materials. Were the defendant-appellees shopping mall proprietors negligent?

DECISION

No. Pritchard produced no admissible evidence whatsoever showing that mall maintenance persons knew or should have known of the substance. While the affidavit and deposition testimony in this case demonstrate the absence of knowledge of the substance on the part of the appellees, appellant has failed to produce any admissible evidence to demonstrate that the substance was on the floor for a length of time sufficient for knowledge of it to be imputed to the appellees. Thus the trial court correctly ruled that appellees had pierced the allegations of Pritchard's complaint, and that Pritchard had failed to produce the responsive evidence creating an issue of fact as to mall personnel's liability for negligent maintenance.

Pritchard v. Wilson, 316 S.E.2d 604 (Ga. App. 1984).

A question that must naturally arise is, How do you determine if a person is acting as an ordinary, prudent person would act under the same or similar circumstances? The answer to that question lies within the province of the jury. In each case that comes before it, the jury listens to the fact pattern as shown by the evidence and as explained

---

[4]*Fort Smith Gas Co. v. Cloud,* 75 F.2d 413 (1935).

[5]*Hewlett v. Schadel,* 68 F.2d 502 (1934).

by the lawyers and decides whether the parties were acting above or below the standard. If the actor was below the standard, he or she is negligent.

Not only is the standard of care a difficult thing to measure for the reason noted above, but the standard varies for other reasons as well. For example, if an individual has certain special skills which he or she is using (usually those licensed), such as a physician or beautician, then that individual must adopt as a personal standard of conduct the standard of care of the reasonable person within that profession or specialty. The question faced by the jury would be, What would the reasonable and prudent doctor have done under the same or similar circumstances? This is called the *reasonable person test.*

Obviously, the standard is not a precise line, and that is one of the major issues of debate in a negligence trial. Lawyers may present expert witnesses to testify on the issue of negligence in the particular situation. For example, the lawyer may get a physician to testify before the jury about the standard of conduct among doctors. Lawyers may also be able to put together a fact pattern in which the facts speak for themselves, which is called **res ipsa loquitur.** This involves inferring negligence from the fact pattern. For example, a tack in a can of beans bought at a store implies negligence by the manufacturer. In the case that follows, res ipsa loquitur is used to establish responsibility for property damage.

res ipsa loquitur
The thing speaks for itself

FACTS

Three insurance companies acting on behalf of Davies Supply and Manufacturing Company brought this action against the U.S. Government. Davies' property was damaged because of a fire at Tinker Air Force Base. The equipment was provided to the government under a contract with Davies. The cause of the fire was traced to a specific tank being used for electroplating. The liquid in the tank was heated by a quartz immersion heater which thermostatically controlled the heat of the liquid. The evidence established that the fire started when the liquid in the tank escaped. This permitted the heater to reach a temperature perhaps as high as 1,000° and to ignite a fire. At trial, three possible explanations of how the liquid escaped were proposed. The doctrine of res ipsa loquitur was used to establish responsibility. The Government argues that it was not enough for the insurance company to show that the fire was caused by the heater, but that they had to show which of the three possibilities was the cause of the event.

DECISION

The doctrine of res ipsa loquitur applies in this case. It permits the inference of negligence on the part of the government sufficient to establish a case for Davies. To invoke the doctrine Davies must show (1) the event is of a kind which ordinarily does not occur in the absence of someone's negligence; (2) accident was caused by something within the exclusive control of the defendant; and (3) the accident was not due to any voluntary act or contribution by Davies. The insurance company wins.

Federal Ins. v. the United States, 538 F.2d 300 (1976).

Yet another way of building a case of negligence is by illustrating that trade rules were not adhered to, or in select cases that a statute was violated. Once again, it is for the jury to decide if a person was acting as he or she should. It may well be that the jury will decide that, even if a person followed trade standards or adhered to a statute, the person's conduct was still negligent.

Condition and Use of Land Chapter 47, Real Property and Its Ownership, discusses the duty and standard of care and liability for the condition and use of land.

► Proximate Cause of Injury by Negligence

proximate cause
The cause of an injury without which the injury would not have occurred

After negligence is proved, the third step is to prove that the negligent conduct in question was the **proximate cause** of the injury. Proximate cause refers to the *legal cause* of the injury. The definition of proximate cause most often quoted is "that cause which in natural and continuous sequence, unbroken by an intervening cause, produces the injury, and without which the result would not have occurred." The courts often discuss the issue of the *foreseeability* of the incident when determining proximate cause. However, the terms "proximate cause" and "foreseeability" are not interchangeable. Foreseeability of injury from negligence is an element in proximate cause. The following well-reasoned case makes this distinction.

FACTS

Plaintiff, a longshoreman, employee of the defendant vessel owner, was injured while working aboard ship. The defendant failed to provide adequate flooring to support the weight of a loaded handtruck used by the plaintiff. The flooring collapsed and the plaintiff and the loaded handtruck fell into the hole. The plaintiff, in trying to get the truck and load out of the hole, strained the muscles in his rib cage. He sued for this injury, claiming that the *inadequate flooring* was the proximate cause of his injury. Defendant claimed that he could not reasonably *foresee* that plaintiff would go into the hole and, therefore, he should not be liable because the inadequate flooring was not the proximate cause of plaintiff's injury; his going into the hole was the nonforeseeable proximate cause.

In a suit for negligence against the defendant, the court found that the flooring was insufficient and the proximate cause of plaintiff's injury. Defendant appealed.

DECISION

In this case for the tort of negligence, there was no error in finding that the insufficient flooring was the *proximate cause* of plaintiff injury. Foreseeability was an element of proximate cause. The court held that the failure to furnish adequate flooring prompted the plaintiff, when he fell, to act as he did. Plaintiff's attempt to lift the truck out of the hole was a normal response of a worker under the circumstances and, therefore, foreseeable. It was part of the flooring collapse, which was the proximate cause of plaintiff's injury. Plaintiff wins.

Dewey v. A. R. Klaveness & Co., 379 P.2d 560 (Or. 1963).

► Defenses to the Tort of Negligence

In an accident it is often the case that each party blames the other for the occurrence. Sometimes only one party is at fault, but at other times each party's fault may contribute to the incident. At still other times one party or the other may assume a risk as part of the activity in which they are participating. These points lead us to a discussion of the defenses to the charge of negligence.

contributory negligence
Plaintiff's conduct that falls below the standard to which he or she should conform for his or her own protection and that is a legally contributing cause with the defendant's negligence causing the plaintiff's harm

Contributory Negligence Suppose you were involved in a minor car accident and that you were at fault. Suppose, further, that you knew that the driver of the other car was not driving very carefully either. Would you willingly agree to pay for all the damage done? Probably not! **Contributory negligence** may be the doctrine you use to protect yourself. It is "conduct on the part of the plaintiff which falls below the standard to which he should conform for his own protection, and which is a legally contributing cause cooperating with the negligence of the defendant in bringing about the plaintiff's harm."[6]

---

[6] RESTATEMENT (SECOND) OF TORTS sec. 464 (1965).

In the following case the plaintiff's contributory negligence prevented him from obtaining a judgment against the defendant who was negligent.

FACTS

Defendant put a pole across the road while making repairs to his home. Plaintiff was riding a horse at top speed and it tripped over the pole. Plaintiff sued defendant for negligence.

DECISION

Judgment for defendant. Contributory negligence was present. One is not to cast oneself upon an obstruction which had been made by the fault of another, and avail oneself of it, if one does not use common and ordinary caution to be in the right.

Butterfield v. Forester, K.B. 11 E 60 (1809).

Last Clear Chance and Comparative Negligence As we have seen, in the simplest of negligence cases there is merely one argument:

1. *X* accuses and proves *Y* negligent.

In the case of contributory negligence, the problem becomes slightly more difficult:

1. *X* accuses and proves *Y* negligent, but
2. *Y* claims *X* was negligent also (that is, contributory negligence).

In yet another possible ripple, we can add a third stage, which would look like this:

1. *X* accuses and proves *Y* negligent.
2. *Y* claims *X* was negligent also (contributory negligence).
3. *X* says "I may have been contributorily negligent, but you (*Y*) had the *last clear chance* to avoid the incident."

Indeed, *last clear chance* is a well established line of defense to a charge of contributory negligence. Along with each of these charges comes the difficulty of proof. Each claim of negligence, contributory negligence, or last clear chance must be substantiated using the patterns of proof we have been discussing throughout this chapter. This is why even seemingly simple automobile accidents can result in large, elaborate, and costly trials. It is almost an endless cycle with each of the participants claiming the other is at fault.

Some jurisdictions have established a system of **comparative negligence.** Under this system the jury is not required to determine ultimate responsibility, as it must in a system using negligence, contributory negligence, and last clear chance. Rather, comparative negligence merely asks the jury to apportion the percentage of fault among the parties to the case. Thus driver *X* may be 30 percent at fault and must pay 30 percent of the cost, while driver *Y* is 70 percent at fault and pays 70 percent of the cost. In contrast, in many jurisdictions *any* amount of contributory negligence will preclude recovery by the contributorily negligent party.

comparative negligence
A statute or doctrine in which negligence is measured in terms of percentage

Assumption of Risk One final defense that is frequently used by attorneys is **assumption of risk.** This involves a situation in which a person *knowing* of the risk of harm agrees to voluntarily assume the risk of harm. The effect of this defense is that the

assumption of risk
Voluntarily assuming a known risk of harm

defendant may claim that the plaintiff agreed to subject himself or herself to potential danger, and therefore plaintiff, if injured, may not be successful in collecting damages. In the following case the injured plaintiff did not assume any risk because he was not aware of the specific danger.

FACTS

Plaintiff, Vierra, was injured when a piece of steel dislodged from a broken tool being used by the defendant and flew several feet striking him in the eye. Plaintiff knew only of the danger from flying particles of concrete within a range of seven feet. However, he was standing more than nine feet from the tool. In the trial court judgment was rendered for the defendant. Plaintiff appealed, claiming error in that the court should not have instructed the jury on the doctrine of assumption of risk.

DECISION

The lower court was not correct in its instructions; reversed, for Vierra. "The basic question in this case is whether the trial court was justified, under the facts, in instructing on the doctrine of assumption of risk. We have concluded that it was in error . . . and therefore reversible to have instructed on this doctrine. The application of the doctrine of assumption of the risk requires that the evidence show that the victim appreciated the *specific* danger involved. He does not assume any risk he does not know or appreciate." Here, the plaintiff appreciated the *specific* danger from flying concrete but not from flying steel.

Vierra v. Fifth Avenue Rental Service, 383 P.2d 777 (Cal. 1963).

immunity
Exemption from liability

Immunities On occasion, certain categories of persons are granted an **immunity** from tort liability. There must be a very special underlying policy reason for granting such an immunity, and these immunities are greatly limited in number and scope. Historically, both *charitable organizations* and *governmental organizations* were granted such a shield. The policy reason for this was that both these groups were working so much for the public good that they should not be subject to tort liability. Further, governmental liability was based on the common law principle that the "King can do no wrong." Over the years these two immunities have come under severe attack. Charitable organizations are often big businesses and can insure against loss. Thus the underlying reason for protection is less strong today. Governmental immunity has always been stronger than charitable immunity, but even it, as the following case illustrates, has come under attack.

FACTS

The plaintiff, Peggy Copeland, brings this action against the Housing Authority of Spartanburg, defendant. She alleges that she is entitled to recover damages because of the negligence of the defendant in failing to repair a gas furnace which emitted flames causing her furniture to be burned. The trial court overruled the doctrine of sovereign immunity and that the defendant could be held liable. Defendant appealed. Is sovereign immunity still applicable in South Carolina?

DECISION

Reversed, judgment for the defendant, the Housing Authority. The court held that the doctrine of sovereign immunity is still applicable in South Carolina. If the law is to be changed, such change should come from the legislature. The court reaffirmed in this case the doctrine of sovereign immunity.

Copeland v. Housing Authority of Spartanburg, 316 S.E.2d 408 (S.C. 1984).

Indeed, under the Federal Tort Claims Act the federal government can be held liable for *negligent* torts. Even under this act, the government cannot be sued for intentional or strict liability torts. Further, most high-ranking government officials are immune provided they do not act with malice.

There is also an *intra-family immunity*. In order to promote family harmony, there was a common law immunity between parent and child. However, today this immunity is limited to negligent torts. Thus, children can sue their parents for intentional torts.

Finally, there was a *husband/wife* immunity based on the old common law policy that considers husband and wife as one in law. Recently some states have rejected husband/wife immunities entirely in response to a number of pressures. Some insurance companies are concerned with the continued weakening of this immunity. They are worried that some husbands and wives will join in collusive suits designed to fraudulently collect money.

Liability Without Regard to Negligence or Fault: Strict Liability

In the first part of this chapter we spoke of torts that were intentional in nature. Next we turned to torts that were caused through someone's negligence. In this section we turn to those instances in which courts are not concerned with negligence at all. Rather, they believe that the particular action was of such a nature that the defendant should accept responsibility without reference to their standard of conduct.

► Hazardous Activities

The courts state that if you are engaged in activity involving danger of serious harm to another person or property—a danger that cannot be eliminated even using due care and which is not a matter of common usage—you may be held **strictly liable** without reference to your standard of care. This is illustrated in the following famous English case.

strict liability
Absolute liability irrespective of the absence of negligence or fault

FACTS

Defendants owned a mill and, in order to supply it with water, constructed a reservoir on some nearby land. Plaintiff owned a nearby coal mine which was inundated by water that escaped from the reservoir. There is proof that the defendant used a great deal of care in building the reservoir. Plaintiff sued for damage caused to his land.

DECISION

Judgment for plaintiff. "We think . . . that the person who for his own purpose brings on his lands . . . anything likely to do mischief if it escapes must keep it at his peril, and if he does not do so, is answerable for all the damage which is a natural consequence of its escape."

Rylands v. Fletcher, [1868] L.R., 3 H.L. 330.

► Animals

Another area in which there is strict liability without reference to negligence is in the keeping of wild animals. Thus people who want to keep exotic pets such as snakes or tigers are in most cases responsible for their pets' activity even if they use due care in keeping them restrained. This rule does not apply to animals kept in a zoo, used for the entertainment or education of the public.[7]

► Workers' Compensation

State workers' compensation laws impose upon an employer strict liability to most employees for personal injury in the course of and arising out of employment, except for self-inflicted injury and intoxication. This subject is discussed in Chapter 19, Employment.

► Products Liability

Products liability is one of the most rapidly growing fields of tort liability in the United States today. (See p. 562–571.) Until recently, people injured while using a product had to demonstrate that the producer was negligent in manufacturing the product. The plaintiff had the difficult task of proving that the manufacturer had fallen below the standard of care required. As you can imagine, this was a difficult task. For example, if you were hurt because of a defect in your car, you would have to collect evidence that the person who put together your particular automobile was negligent at the particular time that person was working on your car.

Even if you could accomplish that task, you still had to avoid the defenses to a charge of negligence, such as contributory negligence. You had to prove that you did not contribute to the carelessness of the situation resulting in the accident. These problems are being resolved today through the application of the doctrine of *strict liability* in tort to those who put products on the market. That is, in certain areas, the courts will impose liability on the manufacturer without reference to negligence.

privity
A mutuality of relationship between persons or between persons and a particular transaction

At first, the scope of products liability was sharply limited to a select number and kinds of products. The first cases demanded that there had to be direct contact between the manufacturer and purchaser, called **privity.** This meant that, if you purchased a defective product from a middleman or retailer, you could not sue the manufacturer. You lacked privity with the manufacturer. Gradually, the privity doctrine gave way in select cases, such as those involving drugs or poisoned foods.

Soon even this requirement gave way, and you now can sue a manufacturer in some instances without having privity of contract with the manufacturer. Today manufacturers of a chattel that they know or reasonably should believe to be inherently dangerous for the use supplied are strictly liable for harm caused by the chattel unless they give adequate warning of the danger. An example is an explanatory label on a container of poison. Also, manufacturers are held liable for manufacturing a chattel which, they should realize, if negligently manufactured, would create an unreasonable risk of substantial bodily harm when used for the purpose for which it was manufactured. In this case, what is important is the risk of harm from the imperfect manufacture of the chattel rather than the inherently dangerous character of the chattel. For example, a glass coffee urn is not inherently dangerous, but its negligent manufacture could cause it to be an unreasonable risk of substantial bodily harm to a consumer. This trend in the case law has caused concern to many manufacturers since they are increasingly subject to lawsuits brought by injured consumers. In the following famous case the court made new law by extending the duty to manufacture carefully to the remote consumer, thereby hurdling the privity of contract rule.

---

[7]See 4 Am. Jur.2d *Animals* § 80 (1962).

FACTS

The defendant, Buick Motor Company, purchased automobile wheels from a wheel manufacturer. A wheel was defective and the defendant could, by reasonable care, have discovered the defect. However, the defendant did not exercise such care and overlooked the defect. The defendant attached the wheel to one of its automobiles, which was sold to a retailer who, in turn, resold the car to the plaintiff consumer, who was unaware of the defective wheel. The wheel collapsed because of the defect, causing the car to collapse, and the plaintiff was injured. Plaintiff sued the defendant for such injury.

DECISION

Judgment for plaintiff. The defendant manufacturer owed a duty of care to the remote plaintiff consumer. "We hold that when the nature of a thing is such that it is reasonably certain to place life and limb in peril when negligently made, it is then a thing of danger. [If]...its nature gives warning of the consequences to be expected [then]...the manufacturer is under a duty to make it carefully." The court extended the manufacturer's duty under the facts to the remote consumer, plaintiff, even though there was no privity of contract between the plaintiff and the defendant.

MacPherson v. Buick Motor Company, 111 N.E. 1050 (N.Y. 1916).

Protection of Inventions, Authorship, Identification of Products, Certain Contractual Business Relationships, and Reputation Through Tort Law

At the beginning of this chapter it was suggested that tort law provided a wide range of protection to persons. Before we close this chapter, brief mention should be made of the use of tort law to protect personal and business creations, certain contractual business relationships, and reputation.

▶ Inventions, Authorship, and Identification of Products

A **patent** protects an invention for a nonrenewable period of seventeen years. The tort for using a person's invention without permission is *patent infringement.* Under the new federal copyright law effective 1978, a **copyright** protects original works in a tangible medium of expression, such as literary, musical and dramatic works, television or radio shows.[8] Copyright laws sharply limit a person's ability to reproduce others' work since in doing so there may be infringement on the copyright holder's proprietary interests. Finally, a **trademark** or trade name is an identifying designation by which a marketer differentiates his or her goods from those of another. It may take the form of a name or symbol. Trademarks are governed by the Lanham Act, also known as the Trademark Act of 1946, and are for renewable periods of twenty years. *Copyright infringement* and *trademark infringement* are torts.

patent
A governmental grant of protection of an invention

copyright
A governmental grant of protection of original works in a tangible medium of expression

trademark
An identifying designation differentiating one's goods from those of another

The original reason for these protections can be traced at least to the U.S. Constitution, which states in Article I, section 8, clause 8, that Congress shall have the power "to promote the progress of science and useful arts, by securing for limited times

[8]Beginning with 1978, with certain limitations and variations, the period of protection is the author's life plus fifty years after his or her death; or, if there are two or more authors, then for the life of the last surviving author plus fifty years after his or her death. There is special provision for works prior to 1978.

to authors and inventors the exclusive right to their respective writings and discoveries." In the following case the common law copyright of unpublished works prior to the 1976 Copyright Act was not preempted (taken away) by the Act.

FACTS

The motion picture "Animal House," a satire on college fraternity life, was filmed in late 1977. The picture was a commercial success, grossing, according to the plaintiff's complaint, over $60 million in film rentals. The success of Animal House led defendants MCA Incorporated and ABC to produce a television series as a sequel to the film. The pilot episode of the television series, which was entitled "Delta House," was broadcast on January 28, 1979.

Plaintiff, Meta-Film Associates, is the assignee of the rights in an *unpublished* screenplay entitled "Frat Rats." Plaintiff, asserting that Animal House and the Delta House television series were copied from Frat Rats, instituted this action in 1979. A first amended complaint, filed in February of 1980, contains a count which states that the defendants committed a common law copyright infringement. Is this a copyright infringement?

DECISION

Yes. Defendants argue that plaintiff's common law copyright claim is preempted [taken away] by the Copyright Act of 1976. This argument is premised on defendant's contention that a cause of action for copyright infringement does not arise until the allegedly infringing work is exhibited to the public. Animal House was not released until the summer of 1978. Defendants contend that since this date was subsequent to the effective date of the Act, the Act preempts any common law copyright claims that plaintiff might otherwise have possessed. While this argument is superficially appealing, the court cannot accept defendant's view on the law on the point.

Prior to the advent of the Copyright Act of 1976, a dichotomy existed in the American copyright law between published and unpublished works. Unpublished works were protected by the state law of common law copyright. This protection began at the moment of creation and terminated upon publication when common law copyright was lost. Thereafter protection was available, if at all, only through federal or statutory copyright. The Act which became effective on January of 1978 eliminated this dichotomy. Under the Act, almost all works become exclusively the subject of statutory copyright, irrespective of whether they are published or unpublished. Common law copyright for works prior to the Act is not preempted.

Meta-Film Assoc., Inc. v. MCA, Inc. et al., 586 F.Supp. 1346 (1984).

► Certain Contractual Business Relationships

People have a right to deal and contract with whom they please, and also to refuse to do so if they please, unless their conduct is wrongful because it breaches a duty to another person or is contrary to law. It is wrongful intentionally to induce other persons to breach their contracts with third persons or to induce other persons to refuse to deal or to continue a business relationship with third persons, thereby causing damage to such third persons. These are the torts of *inducing breach of contract* and *inducing refusal to deal*.

► Reputation

Persons have an interest in their reputations, and they have a right to freedom from false disparagement of their reputations. It is wrongful intentionally, without privilege, to publish matter that is false and disparages another person's reputation, thereby causing damage to that person's reputation. Published matter is disparaging if it tends to belittle or diminish the esteem in which the defamed person is held by third persons or by the community. **Slander** is an oral disparagement, while **libel** generally is a written disparagement or any form other than oral. The tort is called *defamation*. In the following case the plaintiff claims libel *per se*.

slander

A defamatory publication by spoken words, gestures, or other nonpermanent form

libel

A defamatory publication in written or other permanent form

FACTS

The plaintiff, James Cantrell, filed this action to recover actual and punitive damages from ABC television. The complaint alleges that the plaintiff suffered injury to his reputation because of a nationally broadcast show entitled "Newsmagazine 20/20." The segment was entitled "Arson and Profit" and it concerned an investigation of an alleged arson for profit conspiracy involving a group of real estate owners. During the show Cantrell was interviewed. It was alleged that ABC and their employees made several statements about Cantrell including: "We filmed their conversation from this van. . . . During the course of the conversation, Cantrell actually instructed Lance on how to get the most insurance money from an arson fire." Cantrell alleges that the statements made were false, malicious, and defamatory. Motion to dismiss the case by the defendant.

DECISION

Libel per se is generally defined as words so obviously and naturally hurtful to the aggrieved person that the proof of their injurious character is unnecessary. Four categories of words which are libel per se are: (1) those imputing the commission of a criminal offense, (2) those imputing infection with a communicable disease, (3) those imputing inability to perform or want of integrity in discharge of duties of office or employment, and (4) those prejudicing a particular party in his profession or trade. The clear message conveyed is that the plaintiff had engaged in criminal conduct. The motion to dismiss is denied.

Cantrell v. American Broadcasting Co., 529 F. Supp. 746 (1981).

Summary Statement

1. Tort law has a significant impact on our society, and an individual will want to know his or her legal rights and duties as defined by tort law.
2. There is a difference between rights and duties as defined by the legal areas of tort, crime, and contract.
3. There are three major subdivisions of tort liability: intentional torts, negligent torts, and strict liability.
4. Intentional torts include assault and battery, false imprisonment, and invasion of privacy.
5. There are defenses to the commission of intentional torts, among which are consent, self-defense, and privilege.
6. Negligent torts involve careless behavior and require that a complainant prove three things: a legal duty of care, a breach of a standard of care, and proximate cause of damage or harm.
7. There are defenses to liability for negligent torts, among which are contributory negligence, last clear chance, comparative negligence, assumption of risk, and immunities.
8. Society has imposed strict liability in certain instances upon suppliers of chattels irrespective of any lack of privity with the injured user.

9. Governmental protection is extended to certain intellectual property (such as copyrights) and to the rights of persons in their contractual relationships and in their reputations.

The following case deals with strict liability for asbestos-related injury. The corporation attempted to use a defense called "state of the art."

BESHADA ET AL. v. JOHNS-MANVILLE PRODUCTS CORPORATION
447 A.2d 207 (N.J. 1982)

Pashman, J. The sole question here is whether defendants in a products liability case based on strict liability for failure to warn may raise a "state of the art" defense. Defendants assert that the danger of which they failed to warn was undiscovered at the time the product was marketed and that it was undiscoverable given the state of scientific knowledge at that time.

These six consolidated cases are personal injury and wrongful death actions brought against manufacturers and distributors of asbestos products. Plaintiffs are workers, or the survivors of deceased workers, who claim to have been exposed to asbestos for varying periods of time. They allege that as a result of that exposure, they contracted asbestosis and other asbestos related illnesses.

These cases involve asbestos exposure dating back to perhaps as far as the 1930s. The suits are first arising now because of the long latent period between exposure and the discernible symptoms of asbestos. Plaintiffs have raised a variety of legal theories to support their claims for damages. The important claim, for purposes of this appeal, is strict liability for failure to warn. Prior to the 1960s, defendants' products allegedly contain no warning of their hazardous nature. Defendants responded by asserting the state of the art defense. They allege that no one knew or could have known that asbestos was dangerous when it was marketed.

We conclude that plaintiffs' position is consistent with our holding in *Freund* and prior cases and will achieve the various policies underlying strict liability. The burden of illness from dangerous products such as asbestos should be placed upon those who profit from its production and, more generally, upon society at large, which reaps the benefits of the various products our economy manufactures. That burden should not be imposed exclusively on the innocent victim. Although victims must in any case suffer the pain involved, they should be spared the burdensome financial consequences of unfit products. At the same time, we believe this position will serve the salutary goals of increasing product safety research and simplifying tort trials.

Defendants have argued that it is unreasonable to impose a duty on them to warn of the unknowable. Failure to warn of a risk which one could not have known existed is not unreasonable conduct. But this argument is based on negligence principles. We are not saying what defendants should have done. That is negligence .... We impose strict liability because it is unfair for the distributors of a defective product not to compensate its victims. As between those innocent victims and the distributors, it is the distributors—and the public who consumes their product—who should bear the unforeseen costs of the product.

The judgment of the trial court is reversed; the plaintiffs' motion to strike the state of the art defense is granted.

Questions and Case Problems

1. Plaintiff was a welfare applicant. Defendant, Easton Publishing Co., published an article concerning the private lives of the plaintiff and her family based on information supplied by the Department of Public Welfare. From this article, 17

people identified the plaintiff and her family. Assuming that the facts in the article were collected without the plaintiff's knowledge, is this an invasion of privacy? [*Harris by Harris v. Easton Publishing Co.*, 483 A.2d 1377 (Pa. 1984).]

2. Comprecare was a Colorado Corporation and health maintenance organization where plaintiff, Paula Rederscheid, had an insurance policy that should cover her corrective oral surgery. When defendant, Comprecare, failed to pay for this surgery, plaintiff experienced distress and anxiety. Does plaintiff have any recourse? Explain. [*Rederscheid v. Comprecare, Inc.*, 667 P.2d 766 (Colo. 1983).]
3. Isaacs, M.D., was working at Huntington Memorial Hospital. One day when leaving work, he was shot at and injured in the hospital's parking lot. This had never happened to Isaacs before, neither had the hospital ever been involved in such an incident. However, since Isaacs was injured, what result if he sues the hospital for negligence? Explain. [*Isaacs, M.D. v. Huntington Memorial Hospital,* 204 Cal. Rptr. 765 (Cal. 1984).]
4. Twelve-year-old Kenneth A. Demeri was running his unregistered, uninsured motor cycle in Lynn Park. He did not have a license and his father did not allow him to ride the bike alone. When crossing the public road on his way home, Kenneth did not see the automobile before it was too late. As a result of the collision, Kenneth suffered severe and permanent injuries. Who is in this case liable for negligence—if anyone? Explain. [*Demeri v. Morris,* 477 A.2d 426 (N.J. 1983).]
5. Mr. Tate, a farmer, was delivering eggs to defendant the day after a heavy snowfall. After the delivery, he fell on the defendant's private, unshoveled driveway and fractured his wrist. The defendant said it was their practice to let snow and ice melt away naturally, which was the reason for the state of the driveway. Even though Mr. Tate frequently used this driveway, what result in a suit against defendant for negligence? Explain. [*Tate v. Rice et al.*, 315 S.E.2d 385 (Va. 1984).]
6. Linda Lee was a part-time medical assistant working in Dr. Morales' office. One day, she was called into his office in the presence of a co-worker and the doctor's son. A small amount of money was missing and Dr. Morales asked if she took the money. Lee replied "no." The doctor got mad and was accusing and threatening Lee. He said, "If you leave, I'll call the police, and the police will be here in a minute." Lee was scared and remained in his office. May Lee sue Dr. Morales for false imprisonment? Explain. [*Morales v. Lee,* 668 S.W.2d 867 (Tex. 1984).]
7. Plaintiff Douglas A. Campbell was a passenger in a car owned by defendant Carla M. Hundley and driven by defendant Tammye S. Van Roekel, 17 years old. Even though they all knew that Van Roekel was intoxicated, they let her drive, and the predictable happened—they struck a utility pole causing injuries to Campbell's nose. Since Van Roekel's intoxication was the proximate cause of the accident, may Campbell recover damages? Explain. [*Campbell v. Van Roekel,* 347 N.W.2d 406 (Iowa. 1984).]
8. A young lady orders baked beans in Boston. "I started to eat [them] and there were two or three dark pieces which I thought were hard beans; that is, baked more than the others, and I put it in my mouth [and bit down and hurt myself]." If there was no evidence of negligence on the part of the dining hall which baked the food, may she recover damages? [*Friend v. Childs Dining Hall, Co.,* 120 N.E. 407 (Mass. 1918).]
9. A credit reporting agency's report on a corporation misidentified one of the corporation's affiliates. This incorrectly reported the number of employees, amount of sales, and value of inventory. Is this libel per se? [*Sunward v. Dun & Bradstreet, Inc.,* 568 F. Supp. 602 (1983).]

10. In the case of *Beshada, et al. v. Johns-Manville Products Corp.*, excerpted at the beginning of this section, the court indicated that products liability could be imposed by law without reference to negligence. It could even be argued that tort law is being used as a tool for social change. The case also would seem to suggest that the law should place the burden of payment on those who are best able to prevent the loss. Does this standard satisfy you? Assume that you are a member of top management of a major manufacturing firm. Would your answer be the same?

PART 1 THE FOUNDATIONS OF LEGAL SYSTEMS

ETHICS AND BUSINESS LAW

Introduction

Now that you have completed studying the material on the foundations of legal systems, we want to introduce the subject of *ethics,* particularly the *business ethics* that underpins business law.

► Organization

At the end of each part of this book there is a short discussion of business ethics as it relates to the business law discussed in that particular part. The discussion in this part is the longest and is the foundation for all the others. Subsequent end-of-part materials are organized in a different way. They first present an overview of a variety of ethical issues, next an in-depth discussion of a particular issue, and last business ethics dilemmas to be resolved by students.

► Ethics and Morality Defined

Philosophy is the study of the basic issues of life; it is characterized by the clarity and logical consistency of the assumptions and reasoning used. One branch of philosophy is *ethics.* It examines the *rightness or wrongness of conduct.* Business ethics is, of course, concerned with examining the rightness or wrongness of *business* conduct. While some thinkers attach different meanings to the words ethics and morals, we will use them interchangeably in this and the other end-of-part sections.

► The Goals of These Materials

All the end-of-part materials are designed to help students study business law in ways that increase their ability to make ethical decisions. Specifically, the materials try to equip students to do the following:

1. Spot ethical issues in business,
2. Analyze ethical problems rigorously,
3. Define personal (i.e., one's own) standards of ethical behavior in business,
4. Act in conformity with these self-chosen personal ethical standards.

The following section describes in detail the way the critical study of business law and the study of these materials can move students closer to personal ethical competence.

Ethical Competence and the Critical Study of Business Law

▶ Ability to Spot Ethical Issues

One of the objectives of this book is to equip you to spot the *legal* problems that typically arise in the conduct of business. By studying legal topics, you learn to spot the business situations that raise legal problems. Since laws have been created to handle situations where ethical issues are significant, the study of business law is also the study of situations where ethics is important. Since law and ethics overlap extensively, and both are vitally concerned with *what is right and wrong,* the study of business law topics will increase your ability to spot ethical issues in business.

In addition, each of the other end-of-part discussions provides an overview of the principal ethical issues related to the law discussed in that part. By comparing the ethics overview with the legal topics, you should quickly begin to see the strong relationship between situations raising legal issues and situations raising ethical issues.

▶ Ability to Analyze Ethical Problems Rigorously

The skills that you use in analyzing the law, particularly appellate cases and the end of chapter problems, are the same skills that are required for ethical analysis. In particular, the ability to *reason* about facts, and about rules of conduct, are skills common to both legal analysis and ethical analysis. Thus, when you increase your ability to engage in legal reasoning, you also increase your ability to analyze ethical problems rigorously.

The material presented later in this first end-of-part discussion is designed to help you engage in the type of ethical reasoning used by philosophers. In many ways it is similar to legal reasoning.

▶ Develop Individual Ethical Standards

A major problem in business is that many people do not have personal beliefs about what is ethical or unethical conduct in business. Since business law is a very sophisticated statement of society's ethical standards for business, studying it can help individuals form personal beliefs about what is ethical in business.

We call the evaluation of business law to develop personal ethical beliefs "critical study." This requires that students try to understand the ethical goals that particular laws seek to advance. Critical study also asks students to assess the law's ethical strengths and weaknesses, its alternatives, and its consequences. This approach contrasts with studying the law with the single objective of learning the rules. Critical study can give you the ethical experience and insight needed to develop mature personal beliefs about what is right and wrong in business.

In addition, other end-of-part materials present in-depth discussions of a few pivotal ethical issues. These issues were very carefully selected. Most were picked because they greatly influence large numbers of business ethics decisions. Other in-depth discussions help students see more clearly the ethical content of the law. Further, each end-of-part contains problems related to the in-depth issue. These in-depth discussions and the related problems encourage students to begin articulating their own beliefs.

▶ Action Consistent with Ethical Beliefs

Even when persons know what they believe is right or wrong conduct in business, their actions are often not consistent with their ethical beliefs. Philosophers sometimes call the ability to act on our ethical beliefs "will," or "integrity," or "moral character." Moral psychologists have studied this problem and found that people who casually state as their beliefs the "views of their peer group" or "what they think most people believe" are easily pressured into violating such beliefs. Beliefs, like these, which are not carefully thought out are called *conventional wisdom*. In contrast, those who cautiously adopt a belief after critically examining its strengths and weaknesses, its alternatives and its consequences, are much more likely to act in ways consistent with their ethical beliefs.

Research in moral psychology indicates that age and education also are major factors contributing to the "moral maturity" required to act consistently with one's ethical beliefs. Education that stresses differing styles of reasoning generally produces the most maturity. However, courses in business usually focus on a single style of reasoning. Thus, courses in economics, finance, marketing, and management typically share the common objective of identifying that conduct which is economically most profitable. In contrast, business law is a course rich with differing styles of reasoning. Thus, this course may be the best in the business curriculum for promoting moral maturity and thus the ability to act in ways consistent with one's ethical beliefs.

The end-of-part materials foster moral maturity by explicitly articulating different, and frequently conflicting, styles of moral reasoning. Students are then asked to apply these differing styles to the problems at the end of each part. Repetition of this activity is intended to encourage the development of moral maturity.

Another goal of this material is to encourage you to adopt this critical way of thinking as a *habit* to be used for the rest of your business life. The research in moral psychology suggests that most people stop growing after they leave school. If you develop the habit of critically thinking about the law, about your own business behavior, and about the behavior of other persons and organizations, this on-going critical thinking will help you to grow for the rest of your life. It will make you more and more powerful in making and implementing business ethics decisions.

Perhaps you can see that society very much needs individuals who can manage business in ways that are ethical. As a manager, you will undoubtedly confront situations where, acting alone, you must decide whether an action is morally right or wrong. But unless you deliberately try to develop mature ethical beliefs in advance, you are likely to find it difficult to decide and difficult to act on your decisions. We are convinced that the critical study of business law, the careful study of the end-of-part materials, and the development of this mental habit are the best ways for you to develop the ethical competence essential for professional management.

► Business Law and Markets in Critical Study

The context of *managerial* decision making is what distinguishes business ethics from other types of ethics. Managers try to decide what is right and wrong in an environment shaped in large part by the free market and by business law. They must therefore have a firm grasp of the ethical attributes both of the market and of the law as they attempt to control business behavior. Both of these social systems seek to compel, or at least encourage, ethical conduct in business.

Often, it is difficult to discern the ethical goals behind *particular* market transactions or business laws. In large part this is because students do not clearly understand the *general* ethical goals of the market and of business law. Since critical study of business law focuses on understanding the ethical goals behind laws, it is essential to understand the ethical grounding of markets and the law. The following two sections describe the ethical attributes of the market and of the law.

The Ethical Character of the Free Market

▶ How the Market Works

In the view of Adam Smith, a Scottish moralist, the theory of the free market assumes that consumers select from the range of goods and services offered in the marketplace those which each desires most. All of these choices tell producers (business) by the dollars that consumers spend what consumers want.

Producers who are not sensitive to the needs and desires of consumers are likely to lose business to more sensitive competitors and perhaps even be driven out of business. On the other hand, those businesses that are highly skilled at serving consumer needs are likely to grow and generate significant profits. This rivalry—competition for the consumer's dollars—is the driving force of the market.

When there are lots of producers, the rivalry is more intense; it often causes price reductions, or product innovations, in attempts to win or keep customers. Rivalry may be substantially reduced if there are *few producers.*

Often, the marketplace controls business behavior by making unethical conduct unprofitable. If, for example, a tire manufacturer sells dangerous tires, its reputation among consumers will decline and sales will probably fall. Similarly, if Sears sells power lawnmowers that last only a single season, consumers will become upset and future sales of Sears lawnmowers, and perhaps other items, will decline. The free-market process then is a very potent force in directing business conduct in ethically desirable directions. The following are some of the ethical attributes of profits earned in the free market:

1. Profits are the product of a system that, because of its efficiency, advances the ethical goal of increasing the *material well-being of society.* It does this by offering rewards (wealth) to those who efficiently satisfy society's material needs. This profit incentive fosters innovation and tends to place society's resources in the hands of talented individuals motivated to become rich or motivated to some society.
2. Profits are the product of a system that has the effect of maximizing personal liberty. Because the free market places economic decision making in the hands of many consumers and many producers, few have very great economic power over individuals. This contrasts with centrally planned economies where a few persons make most of the economic decisions.
3. These profits are justified by merit. That is, because rewards are in proportion to social contribution, the profits are morally justified by the extent to which the individual or firm has contributed to society.

▶ Imperfections in the Free Market System

While the market mechanism is quite powerful, it is widely acknowledged to be seriously imperfect. When the economic system is imperfect, some or all of its ethical attributes may not be achieved. Thus, an imperfect market may not advance society's material well-being or it may reduce personal liberty, or it may cause the profits earned not to be proportional to one's social contribution. Some of these market imperfections with their adverse ethical effect are described below:

1. Either *too few sellers or too few buyers* can lead to **market power.** Market power is the ability to be insensitive to customers or suppliers—without a reduction in profits. For example, if there were only a single seller of heating fuel in the country, it might become insensitive to consumer desires and yet not lose business.

Consumers would not have other heating fuel businesses to turn to for better service. Thus, a solitary seller (one not subject to rivalry) has the effect of reducing the personal liberty of consumers and its profits are not justified by merit.

2. **Barriers to entry into business** can cause either few sellers or few buyers. A barrier to entry is an artificial condition that prohibits or discourages new entrants into a field of business. Often the law creates barriers to entry. For example, in Utah you must pay a fee and pass a test before you can install lawn sprinkling systems in residential yards. This law discourages entrants into this business and thus reduces rivalry. Perhaps it allows the fewer persons in the business to increase the price for their services. Thus, the profits earned in this line of business may not fairly reflect the social contribution of this business.
3. If either of the participants in the marketplace transaction operates with **imperfect knowledge** about the market or the transaction, this can create an imperfection. For example, if you bought a new car from your local Ford dealer when another dealer ten miles away would have sold you the same car for $2,000 less, but you didn't know it, an imperfection would exist. You would suffer a $2,000 injury, the local dealer would have an inappropriately high profit, and the other dealer would have inappropriately low revenues. This imperfection keeps the economic system from placing resources in the hands of those who use them most efficiently. Thus the material well-being of society is less.
4. Market imperfections called **externalities** may exist when *costs or benefits go to the wrong party*. The most widely used example is pollution. If a factory dumps its waste into a local river, it *benefits* by saving money over what it would cost if the factory paid to have the waste trucked to a nonpolluting waste disposal site. The *cost* of this pollution is borne, not by the manufacturer, but by the other users of the river.
5. **Agency costs** arise when there is a separation of ownership and management. Thus, in large corporations ownership is held by vast numbers of shareholders while the senior managers often own no stock. In these settings it is often tempting for the managers to act for their own benefit instead of the benefit of the owners of the corporation. When they engage in this conduct, they produce the market imperfection of agency costs. Thus if the president of a corporation hires his son instead of a better qualified applicant, he helps his family at the expense of the corporation's owners. Actions that have been characterized as creating agency costs include nepotism, pay raises for friends, subcontracting with relatives, poison pills, and golden parachutes. The most pervasive agency cost is promoting friends into high-paid but unnecessary jobs.

While there are some other widely recognized imperfections, these examples of market power, barriers to entry, imperfect knowledge externalities, and agency costs illustrate the point that the marketplace is sometimes flawed. When flaws are serious, then it is likely that one or several of the ethical objectives in the marketplace may not be advanced in particular transactions.

The Ethical Character of the Law

Jurisprudence is the study of the *philosophy of law* as opposed to the study of only the rules of law. An understanding of jurisprudence is essential to the critical study of business law because it illuminates the ethical ideas that underpin our business law. Jurisprudence is characterized by fairly well-defined schools of thought. Although these schools agree on many points, they conflict on others. The following are three schools of jurisprudential thought.

► Natural Law Jurisprudence

As we discussed in Chapter 1, natural law jurisprudence was articulated by Aristotle and Saint Thomas Aquinas. The core idea of this school of thought is that *there are truths about right law that humanity can come to know, usually by the use of the reasoning mind.* The following are some examples of natural law conclusions:

1. Do good and avoid evil. (Aquinas)
2. Keep your promises. (Grotius)
3. Apply the law equally to all persons. (The Constitution of the United States)
4. Do not lie. (The Bible)
5. Repay those whom you have carelessly injured. (Grotius)

Natural law is not necessarily written law; it exists independent of laws made by people and is in fact superior to them. For example, there were in Nazi Germany many laws designed to persecute the Jews. Some persons who obeyed these written laws were, after the Allied victory in World War II, convicted at the Nuremburg trials of violating natural law even though they obeyed the written laws of their country. *Natural law seeks justice as its most fundamental goal.*

► Historical School Jurisprudence

As we also discussed in Chapter 1, the core idea of historical jurisprudence is that law is an expression of the historical "spirit of the people." That is, the unique history of each nation produces something similar to a consensus of the population, or *Volksgeist,* on *what the law ought to be.* Legislators and judges then simply give their voice to this *Volksgeist* by creating law. The philosophical justification of historical law is that it *reflects the will of those governed.* Thus this law is sometimes viewed as being justified by *consent.*

► Positive Law Jurisprudence

The core idea of positive law jurisprudence is simply that, in order to be legitimate, a law need only be the end product of the authorized process of the government in power. *Order is the primary goal* underlying positive law jurisprudence.

► The Law and the Market-Mechanism

Business law is concerned with these traditional jurisprudential objectives and also with facilitating the operation of the marketplace. Thus as the legal system regulates business, its chief purposes are (1) to achieve the traditional jurisprudential objectives of *justice, order,* and *advancing the popular will,* and also (2) to achieve the market-related objectives of *efficiency, liberty,* and *merit.*

The Law as a Cure for Market Imperfections One common response to market imperfections is to enact laws to cure them. Indeed, your study of business law will focus on many laws designed to minimize the impact of market imperfections. For example, labor law in large part attempts to redress the market power that a single employer has when there are very many persons willing to do the work. Antitrust laws sometimes deal with problems related to barriers to entry. Law responds to the problem of imperfect consumer information. These are described in Chapter 27 on consumer rights; in many instances these laws require *full disclosure* as a cure for imperfect information. Thus, the Truth-in-Lending Act requires disclosure of the actual interest rate on certain consumer loans. Externalities are, of course, a major focus of Chapter 37 on environmental law. Products liability law can also be viewed as addressing the issue of human injury as an externality. The law of business organizations addresses the problem of agency costs. Clearly the law is a powerful resource for minimizing the imperfections in the market process.

Imperfections in the Legal System The legal system has its imperfections, and, because of this, business law sometimes fails to compel ethical conduct. The following are some of the principal reasons for such failure:

1. Often it is quite profitable to violate the law. The potential for illegal profits can create great pressures that many are unable to resist, so they violate the law.
2. Frequently, the penalties for violating laws regulating business are weak deterrents. Some studies have shown that, generally, fines are too small to motivate businesses to comply. And some observers note that, for large businesses, the decision makers (corporate executives) are seldom the ones subject to punishment. More commonly, any fine merely reduces the money available for shareholders.
3. Enforcement of laws regulating business is often haphazard. In some areas, such as civil law, enforcement by injured private parties may be too time-consuming or expensive. Administrative laws may not be adequately enforced because the governmental agency's budget is too small. Also, when a new political party takes office, enforcement policies for administrative laws may change.
4. Laws regulating business conduct are often much more complex than other laws and this makes it difficult for some, particularly small, businesses to know what the law is.
5. The process of creating new laws or modifying existing laws can be influenced through political campaign contributions and lobbying so that the law may not accurately reflect the will of those governed.
6. Laws regulating business often appear to lack the *apparent* legitimacy of many other areas of the law. Laws regulating crimes, torts, adoption, and inheritance seem to most persons clearly worthy of their support. Such laws have such a strong natural law component that the desired conduct might occur even in the absence of written laws. In contrast, many business laws appear to unsophisticated persons as lacking visible legitimacy. For example, people often see nothing wrong when competing merchants agree to charge the same price. Business law condemns this, and often other, conduct that is not, in the minds of the legally uneducated, obviously wrong.

Because of the growing awareness of the flaws in the legal system, many persons now argue that something more than just obeying the law is expected from business; many assert that business managers must better evaluate the ethical character of their decisions.

Traditional Ethical Thinking

You will be able to better engage in the critical study of business law if you develop the ability to think and reason the way some philosophers do. This thinking has two fundamental attributes. First, it is directed toward a goal, often called "the good." Second, it uses a consistent "style of reasoning."

▶ The Good

The *good* is the principal object toward which moral life is directed. It is the principal ethical standard for evaluating ethical reasoning and business conduct. While philosophers disagree about what the good ought to be, their varying conclusions and thinking can be quite useful to persons trying to sort out their own ethical values. If you can learn to perceive which good is implicit in a particular law or economic activity, your powers of ethical analysis will greatly increase. More significantly, if you can begin seeing the *conflicts* among goods, and the ways in which legal and economic systems weigh and choose between the conflicting goods, you will become skilled in the critical analysis of business law and business decisions.

We have described the principal goods of the marketplace—material well being, liberty, and merit. In addition we have identified some traditional goods implicit in the legal system—justice, order, and consent. There are many other goods, such as respect for human dignity, love, pleasure, power, and status.

One attribute of *any* good is its perspective. Perspective answers the question, whose good—that of the decision maker or that of others? If you were to conclude that pleasure were the good, then you would need to decide whose pleasure you would want to maximize. One perspective is the *self.* This perspective would cause you to maximize a good for your own benefit. The second perspective is *others.* The other may be a *group,* perhaps a majority of the membership of a particular group, or a minority, or it may be God, or anyone (or thing) other than the decision maker. Thus the good of pleasure would have an "other" perspective if you sought to maximize the pleasure of the other employees in your firm.

▶ The Roots of Ethical Reasoning

While there are a variety of ethical theories and categories, two are most fundamental. The first judges the rightness or wrongness of conduct by weighing the *consequences* of the conduct. The second rejects the importance of consequences and focuses on *duty.* This second style holds that there is an ethical character to acts themselves that determines whether one has a duty to do them.

You would evaluate lying differently using these categories for ethical analysis. The *consequentialist* views lying as morally neutral. If the consequences of a particular lie are good, then the act of lying is good. In contrast, an analysis based on *duty* is likely to conclude that lying is inherently evil and cannot be justified by good consequences. This conflict between consequences and duty is captured by the question, "Can the ends ever justify the means?" Duty says no, while consequences sometimes say yes.

▶ Illustration

It will help you to better understand the styles of ethical reasoning if we are able to use them to assess a particular business law and apply them to a concrete business decision. The process of critical study of business law will also become clearer as you see the way a law is evaluated for its ethical content. The following fact pattern illustrates a business ethics problem which we can use in discussing the principal ethical concepts.

Assume you are the manager of production for the swing shift of a small firm. You supervise ten production line workers but you have been told one worker must be laid off. Nine of your workers are college women and men who are earning extra spending money while attending school. Three drive brand new cars: two Corvettes and one BMW. Several are saving money for trips to Europe and Asia. All the college students achieve between 105 and 115 percent of their individual production goals. The other worker is a thirty-eight-year-old divorced mother of four children. All of her salary is used to purchase such basic necessities as food, housing, and clothing for her family. She achieves only 85 percent of her production goal because she is not as physically coordinated as the younger workers. If the mother is fired, you forecast that she will be able to collect welfare support equal to about one half her salary, and it will take her up to two years to find another job. If any of the college students are fired, you forecast that they will be able to find similar employment immediately. Whom should you fire? We will refer to this dilemma as "the mother of four" problem.

The business law we assess is described in the case on strict liability for products at the end of Chapter 5, *Beshada v. Johns-Manville Products Corp.* Recall that the case held Johns-Manville liable to those injured by asbestos even though it was not proven that Johns-Manville was at fault. This will be referred to as the "*strict liability law.*" We will examine this law using the differing styles of ethical analysis in the same way you might critically examine other business laws. After evaluating the law we will evaluate the problem of the divorced mother of four. One of our objectives is to help you see how the critical examination of the law can increase your ability to deal with business ethics problems that may not directly involve the law.

In discussing the application of different ethical concepts to the business problem and the law, we will try to communicate only a basic flavor rather than present an exhaustive analysis. Sometimes this may mean making assumptions with which you do not agree. But once you see the rough outlines of the analysis associated with a particular ethical concept, you should be able to forecast the outcome of an analysis based on differing assumptions.

► Styles of Ethical Reasoning

Egoism One type of *consequential* thinking with a large business following is called *egoism.* Its perspective is self-centered. Egoists generally judge conduct against *the good of their self-interested pleasure.* Often they engage in cost/benefit analysis to identify which alternative generates the most pleasure for them. Egoists claim that people are selfish, and that philosophy, economics, and law must take this into account. It is a *consequential* type of thinking that judges the rightness or wrongness of conduct by weighing the consequences of the conduct. If the consequences of particular conduct will further the egoist's pleasure, then the conduct is ethically right and fair. It is a philosophy where "the end justifies the means."

The most obvious type of egoism is *hedonistic egoism.* In this expression of egoism, individuals seek physical pleasures associated with their senses of sight, sound, touch, taste, and smell. Enjoying good food is an example of hedonistic egoism. A less obvious form of egoism is sometimes called *psychological egoism.* What the individual seeks here is not necessarily physical pleasure but psychological comfort. Thus someone may buy a new BMW, not for the physical pleasures it generates but for the psychological satisfaction flowing from the envy of others. A student may earn a bachelor's degree because he or she wants to be free from worry about unemployment. Individuals with a conscience may avoid evil, not because of its wrongness but because they don't want to feel guilty.

The ethical nature of the *strict liability law* with respect to manufacturers of products is dependent on the position occupied by the hedonistic egoist. If this egoist is a Johns-Manville Company shareholder, the law can be judged *unethical* because the Company's liability reduces the hedonistic egoist's income and the physical pleasures money can buy. If the hedonistic egoist is a person injured by asbestos, the law is *ethical* because it allows one to recover money for the injury. If the hedonistic egoist is not involved in the litigation, the law is probably good because it promotes order by specifying who pays when chance causes injury. Order benefits everyone, including hedonistic egoists.

For the hedonistic egoist, *the problem of the mother of four* is easily resolved by *ignoring the plight of the mother and her family and applying the standard of self-interested pleasure.* Since firing the mother will increase the department's productivity, this is the path most likely to result in a pay raise for the egoist head of the department. This pay raise can then be used to purchase material things and services that increase the hedonistic pleasure of the decision maker egoist.

It is difficult to predict how a person acting out of psychological egoism would respond to the dilemma of the mother of four. Someone seeking peace of mind might fire the college student to avoid guilt about dismissing the mother of four. On the other hand, persons seeking respect from their bosses might identify the mother of four to be let go so their superiors will think of them as tough-minded.

Utilitarianism Utilitarian theory is another form of *consequential ethics.* It has been important in philosophy since the nineteenth century, when one of its greatest proponents, John Stuart Mill, lived and wrote. Utilitarianism says an action is morally right if it produces the greatest amount of good for the greatest number of people affected by the act. Conversely, an action is wrong if it affects the majority adversely. Note that this focus is more on *whose* good rather than on *which* good. Utilitarian theory, like egoism, uses cost/benefit analysis. However, utilitarian analysis is based on a calculation of how an action will affect *others* in the long run. A variety of "goods" can be the object of utilitarianism. For example, Jeremy Bentham argued that the greatest pleasure for the greatest number is the best standard. Personal liberty is another good that might be sought by some utilitarians.

Capitalism is to a very large extent utilitarian. In Adam Smith's view of capitalism, self-interested behavior (egoism) causes producers in the marketplace to allocate scarce resources in ways that produce a utilitarian good—the greatest material benefit for the greatest number of consumers. Thus capitalism is a distinctive system that, at least in Smith's theory, links the "self"-interest and "other"-interested views.

In assessing the *strict liability law,* the utilitarian would again look at what produces the greatest good for the greatest number. On the benefit side, the law helps the party injured. On the cost side, the law increases costs for many consumers. If there were no such law, the loss would be borne by the injured party—just one person. With this law, many must bear the burden of higher prices for asbestos. Therefore it is quite arguable that the greatest good for the greatest number occurs when there is no law of strict liability.

A utilitarian who analyzes the problem of the mother of four children might try to separately assess costs and benefits, reasoning as follows. There is a *cost* to society in firing the mother. But there is little cost in firing one of the college students because the student will easily find another job. Therefore on the cost side, the greatest good for the greatest number probably occurs when a college student is dismissed. In reasoning about the *benefits* side, a utilitarian might conclude that the more productive workers will make the department and the company more profitable. The efficiency associated with keeping the most productive persons active in the workplace is likely to support economic growth, and perhaps lower prices. Thus the benefit side of the analysis suggests dismissing the mother may be the best strategy. In balancing the costs against the benefits, many utilitarians would be likely to conclude that dismissing the mother generates the best consequences for more people.

Egoism and utilitarianism are two major *consequential* systems often motivating business behavior. There are also major systems of *duty based ethics* with great influence in business. Two are discussed next.

Kant's Philosophy Kant believed that consequences are difficult to forecast and that they often lead to ethically wrong conduct. **Kantian ethics** are based on the conclusion that persons are autonomous moral entities who, by practical reasoning, give to themselves moral law. From this base, Kant sought to discover the existence of an ultimate moral law that all persons should strive to obey.

Basically, Kant's philosophy states a test that may be used to determine whether an action, or principle of action, is moral. It can be paraphrased as follows: The conduct or principle must be *universalizable*. This means that for it to be moral, everyone must be able to follow a principle or mode of conduct without generating an inconsistent, self-defeating, or irrational situation. Thus if everyone is commanded to do an act, the performance by some must not preclude or interfere with the performance of the act by others. In Kant's words, "Act only according to that maxim by which you can at the same time will [i.e., intend] that it should become a universal law."

In his book, *Fundamental Principles of the Metaphysics of Morals,* Kant illustrates this idea by applying it to lying. He writes:

> The shortest but most infallible way to find the answer to the question as to whether a deceitful promise is consistent with duty is to ask myself: Would I be content that my maxim (of extricating myself from difficulty by a false promise) should hold as a universal law for myself as well as for others? And could I say to myself that everyone may make a false promise when he is in a difficulty from which he otherwise cannot escape? I immediately see that I could will (i.e., intend) the lie but not a universal law to lie. For with such a universal law there would be no promises at all inasmuch as it would be . . . [useless] to make a . . . [promise]. Thus my maxim would destroy itself as soon as it was made a universal law.

The idea of testing one's conduct by universalizing it is the central idea of this philosophical good and can be looked at in three ways:

1. One ought never to act unless one is willing to have one's act, or the axiom on which it is based, become universal law.
2. One is obligated to treat every individual as an *end* and never exclusively as a *means.*
3. One must act as though one were a person who both makes the law and is bound by the law—one who is *both subject and sovereign.* That is, one must act in ways consistent with the way one desires others to act.

Formulations 1 and 3 are straightforward restatements of the universalizing idea, the idea that we must be consistent in demanding of ourselves what we demand of others, that we not treat ourselves as exceptions to the rules we desire others to follow. The second expression may not appear on the surface to be closely connected. Yet if we ask how we would like to be treated, we are likely to state the second expression. And to be consistent we must therefore accord to other persons this treatment. This duty to treat other persons as ends, not means, also rests on the observation that humans, as moral beings, must be treated with moral dignity. This would mean that I could not disregard your moral judgments or deprive you of the opportunity to exercise them.

A Kantian analysis of the *strict liability law* would ask several questions but the one yielding the most clear-cut answer is the means/ends question. It is clear that allowing some to benefit without compensating the party injured is a way by which the injured party is used exclusively as a means (to lower prices) and not as an end. A Kantian would support the strict liability law.

A Kantian might analyze the problem of the mother of four children along the following lines. Is dismissing any of the workers treating them as means and not as ends? Would it be appropriate to make as a universal law that the lowest producing employee ought to be the one dismissed when layoffs are required? Since this law is likely to make the organization more efficient, it may therefore reduce the risks that additional layoffs will be required. Making a universal law of the opposite—laying off the most productive worker—probably is self-defeating, since that would make the firm more inefficient, thereby increasing the need for further layoffs, and eventually probably destroying and eliminating the firm. Since this is self-defeating, it fails Kant's test of universality. Accordingly, a Kantian may conclude that laying off the mother of four is ethical, consistent with duty.

Religious Ethics For many business persons their religious views are the primary source of standards for judging rightness or wrongness. For this reason it is useful to consider the attributes of religious ethics. Judeo-Christian ethics is certainly the dominant ethic of this country, and many of its conclusions about business ethics overlap those of the other major religions of the world such as Islam, Hinduism, and Buddhism. You can see the ethics content, rather than the religious content, of Judeo-Christian ethics more clearly if you focus on those aspects that describe people's relationships with one another as opposed to those that describe their relationship with God. For example, the first three of the Christian Ten Commandments deal with people's relationship with God while the last seven deal with relations among persons.

The character of this ethic is largely based on *duty*. It consistently imposes duties on believers that must be followed simply because of the source and inherent correctness of the duty. The command, "Thou shalt not steal" is an example. On the other hand, many religious denominations interpret religious duties in a utilitarian way, as almost exclusively means, as steps on a path leading to eternal salvation.

The perspective of this ethic is primarily, but not exclusively, "other" oriented. Exhortations to "Honor thy father and mother"; "Do unto others as you would have them do unto you"; and the central command from Jesus to "Love one another as I have loved you" all display the "other" orientation. Again, however, in some denominations the focus on salvation evokes a self-oriented perspective.

Some of the Judeo-Christian precepts have *direct* application to business. For example, the commandment against lying has pervasive implications for nearly all business activities and particular importance for such functions as advertising.

Other Judeo-Christian concepts influence business behavior *indirectly*. For example, special concern for the weakest members of society is a part of this ethic. Many business decisions by persons who embrace this ethic reflect this special concern for the poor.

To a large degree the Judeo-Christian ethic rejects materialism, particularly material excesses such as conspicuous consumption. This ethic encourages participation in the market economy when the motivating impulse is other-oriented service rather than egoistic greed. Even when profits are earned honestly and thus reflect the amount of service rendered, this ethic speaks to the *use* of this earned profit.

When evaluating the strict liability law, it is likely that someone applying the Judeo-Christian ethic would conclude that the injured person ought to be compensated. Selling products can generally be viewed as Judeo-Christian service to humanity. This definition of service however would probably not be met if a product, such as asbestos, seriously injured others. Thus the activity of selling products that cause serious injury violates the Judeo-Christian ethic. If you sold a product that, unknown to you, caused injury to another, the "other" orientation, implicit in the command to love others, would probably require that, at the least, you compensate them for their injury. In another line of analysis, the injured party might be viewed as one of society's disadvantaged members who are entitled to special treatment and therefore the injured party ought to be compensated. These two lines of analysis lead to the same conclusion—the strict liability law is ethical.

In applying the Judeo-Christian ethic to the problem of the mother of four children, we minimize injury—and therefore maximize love—by dismissing one of the college students who will find other work quite soon. Also, the disadvantaged status of the mother argues for special treatment. So again two lines of analysis lead to the same Judeo-Christian conclusion.

The ethical theories we have described cannot give you "the" answer to every moral dilemma that you or other people in business face; mature persons must ultimately decide for themselves. However, ethical theory can prove quite helpful in defining the exact *nature* of the moral problems. And it offers insight into the *manner* in which philosophers who have given great thought to moral systems might *solve* a problem. Together with an understanding of the ethics of the law and of markets, this ethical theory equips students to engage in the critical study of business law.

Solving Ethics Problems

Like the other end-of-part discussions in this book, this one presents four problems for you to consider and discuss. The problems present the kinds of ethical issues frequently confronted by today's managers. Unless you are unusually mature or have substantial work experience, you may not be able to reach firm conclusions about what you ought to do in considering these problems.

The following suggestions may help as you first try to analyze business ethics issues. After you've analyzed a variety of ethics problems using these procedures, you may find it more comfortable to use a different approach. But as you start out, try to follow this procedure.

1. After reading the problem, determine whether the *marketplace* plays an important role in the problem. If it does, decide what goals the market tries to advance and whether you think market imperfections are present.
2. Determine whether *a law* plays an important role in the problem. If it does, try to decide what jurisprudential goal, or "good," the law seeks to advance and whether, based on your standards, the legal system is working appropriately.
3. Ask if there are *philosophic goods* other than those associated with the *market* or the *law* that are important in the problem. Once you have identified the relevant

philosophic goods present in the problem, decide whether there are conflicts among the goods. That is, does the achievement of one good, such as egoistic pleasure, eliminate the possibility of achieving another good, such as order?

4. If you conclude that *goods* are *in conflict,* you must decide which good is more important. You will find your judgment improved if you assess the alternative goods using the four styles of ethical reasoning (egoism, utilitarianism, Kant's philosophy, religious ethics) discussed previously. After you have used the four styles of reasoning, decide what you personally believe is ethical (fair or right) conduct in response to the problem.

► An Illustration of Ethics Problem Analysis

The following paragraphs depict one person's attempt to follow this process in evaluating the divorced mother of four problem.

The Market's Role: The marketplace plays a critical role in this problem. The market here tries to advance the material well-being of society by creating incentives to keep employed only the most talented members of the workforce, so the divorced mother should be fired.

The Law's Role: This problem does not involve the law directly.

An Egoistic Analysis: Self-interest for the manager requires that the divorced mother be fired. This alternative increases the output per dollar spent. Thus, the manager looks more effective and is therefore more likely to win pay raises and promotions.

A Utilitarian Analysis: The greatest good for the greatest number occurs when the divorced mother is let go. This is because the total wealth of society is increased when the most talented are employed. This wealth benefits those who work and it also pays for the welfare system.

A Kantian Analysis: There is a duty to the organization to act in its best interest. Also, since firing the most productive worker is self-defeating if made universal, there is a duty to fire the divorced mother. Both these lines of analysis suggest the same conclusion, *fire the divorced mother.*

Religious Analysis: Since the divorced mother is poor, she is entitled to special status and, therefore, if no one else is significantly injured, she *should not be fired.*

Personal Belief: As the manager of production, I believe that the way this society generates the greatest total material well-being is by hiring only the most productive people. Hiring the least productive people is self-defeating for firms and society because this reduces the size of society's pie of wealth. In general, we ought to hire and keep the most productive people.

However, I think this case represents an exception to the general rule. The way we cut the pie may be more important than the reduction in the size of the pie. I weigh two factors in coming to this conclusion. First, our Judeo-Christian heritage asks us to be particularly sensitive to the weakest members of society. I think the mother qualifies for this treatment. Second, the four children will be affected by this decision. The trauma they would endure if their mother were fired cannot be eliminated by society's welfare system. Therefore, I think we ought to *keep the divorced mother.*

Additionally, as the manager, I must realize that the authority to fire anyone is coupled with the understanding that I will act in the best interest of the company. Since in keeping the mother I will not be doing that, I am obligated to obtain consent from the organization. I would meet with my boss and try to persuade my boss that the company ought to keep the divorced mother.

Ethical Problems for Discussion

The following problems give you the opportunity to engage in ethical reasoning using the four styles of reasoning—egoism, utilitarianism, Kant's philosophy, and religious ethics.

1. Suppose you are the owner of a company and need to hire a production line worker. Also suppose the two best applicants include an old high school friend, but the other applicant is clearly better qualified for the job. You and your friend are the same sex, while the other applicant is a member of the opposite sex. Assume that you would rather have the good company of your friend than any increased profits created by selecting the best qualified applicant. You also know that hiring your friend would violate the federal law that prohibits discrimination on the basis of sex. Should you violate this law in these circumstances? Why or why not?
2. Suppose you own one of three gasoline stations in a small rural town located more than fifty miles away from the nearest competition. Further, assume that the other two station owners have agreed to raise prices fifteen cents per gallon. They approach you and ask you to join them. You know that this conduct is illegal. After a very careful analysis you conclude that if you participate your income will double. You and your family definitely need the money. Assume that there is absolutely no risk that you would be caught. If you believe that such conduct is unfair or wrong, would you be willing to give up the additional income? If you do believe the conduct unfair and wrong, do you think the greater wrong is violating the law or causing someone an economic injury?
3. Assume that you are the personnel manager of a firm. Your new employees are instructed not to discuss their salaries with other employees. ("Pay secrecy" is, in fact, a reality of organizational life.) Assume you have interviewed a great candidate for the unique position of sales representative. The market salary for this position is $20,000. However, this applicant, when asked about her salary expectations, said, "I'd feel good if I could land a job at $17,500." You know you could pay her this amount without violating any equal employment opportunity or equal pay laws because there is only one position like this in the organization. Also, you have been instructed to hire people at the lowest possible salary. What will you do and why?
4. Assume that you are the northeastern regional sales manager for a company. Suppose your boss, the national sales manager, quit recently. His boss, the president, has announced that he will pick one of the six regional sales managers for promotion. You judge that it will be a close race, but only between you and the southwestern regional manager, Kirk. You are aware that the president has very strict sexual standards. You know that Kirk has been living with three girlfriends at different periods over the last year. Will you weave this information into your conversation with the president if you think it will help you win the promotion?

PART 2

CONTRACTS

PREVIEW

While a contract can be simply stated as "a promise which the law recognizes as creating a legal obligation of performance," *the finding of a contract* requires that a proper contractual purpose be manifested by genuineness of assent, by parties with capacity to contract, who have exchanged consideration. A contract will be *enforced* if its contractual purpose is not in conflict with public policy and, in certain instances, only if the contract is in writing or there is a proper written note or memorandum of the oral contract. Legal obligations to perform a contract end by performance or by other methods of discharge. A contract is property which, in certain instances, can be transferred to third parties. The property interest in the contract is protected by law.

Business ethics as it relates to the text material discussed in these chapters is considered at the end of this part. Also, the international dimensions of contracts to buy and sell goods are discussed at the end of the part.

CHAPTER 6

CONCEPT OF CONTRACTUAL AGREEMENT

After you have read this chapter, you should be able to:

1. Discuss the concept of "freedom of contract" and its current applications.
2. Understand the distinction between the terms "promise" and "agreement."
3. Explain why every contract requires the existence of an agreement based on a proper promise or promises.
4. Become familiar with those words and phrases that are currently used in the law of contracts.
5. Be able to identify what concepts of contract law are summarized in legal terms or phrases.

BUSINESS DECISIONS and the LAW

The main theme of Chapter 6 is the legal limitations that exist on the freedom to contract. An example is the Proposition 103 insurance-reform initiative in California.

California insurance commissioner Roxani Gillespie ordered that auto insurers in the state limit annual premium increases to the inflation rate, as part of issuing a series of generally proconsumer regulations implementing the Proposition 103 insurance-reform initiative.

The cap on rates is bound to be challenged in court by insurers on the grounds that it would unconstitutionally deprive them of a chance to make a fair profit. State auto insurance rates have been frozen for some time because of a separate insurance-department order.

The cap on rates is also an ironic twist in the battle to implement Proposition 103, which voters approved in November 1988, but which has been bogged down in court and regulatory proceedings ever since. The initiative's main impetus was to reduce rates. But the insurance commissioner said that implementing the exact language of the initiative would cause many rates to rise sharply, which thus prompted her to impose the cap. "I am convinced that following the letter of the statute will cause rates for many Californians to escalate significantly," she said. "I also believe this result is contrary to what the promoters of Proposition 103 promised and contrary to its intent."

The industry condemned the idea of a cap. Insurers have argued that they are suffering heavy losses from their auto lines and that sharp increases in rates are needed to cover rising liability costs.

"That would be grossly unconstitutional," said David Snyder, an attorney for the American Insurance Association, a property and casualty insurance trade group in Washington, D.C. "It violates a California Supreme court decision that says rates have to be fair. It violates the language of Proposition 103 that says rates have to be adequate. And it violates economic sense, because losses in California are skyrocketing."

The regulation, which generally mirrors guidelines established in Proposition 103, also upset long-established procedures for how insurers set rates in California and around the country. Insurers have historically based rates mainly on where an insured person lives. In contrast, the new rules require that insurers must primarily consider an insured person's driving record, miles driven annually, and driving experience. The commissioner said she would allow insurers to consider other factors that may relate to where a person lives, such as population density or litigation rates, but that each such factor should be given less weight than any of the first three when computing a rate.

The industry has contended that eliminating the so-called territorial rating would result in suburban and rural motorists paying higher rates and urban drivers paying less. The commissioner previously indicated she shared such concerns.

The state's roughly 400 auto insurers have sixty days to file new rate applications comporting with the new regulations, a timetable that some industry spokesmen said would be a hardship, especially on small companies. The commissioner will thereafter have an additional ninety days to see that they go into effect.

Consumer groups and Proposition 103 proponents were guardedly optimistic. "It is historic. This is the first effort to eliminate territorial rating in the nation and have rates based on factors within an individual's control," said Harvey Rosenfield, a Santa Monica, California, consumer activist who was the main architect of the initiative. He said that the commissioner's concerns that Proposition 103 would, literally applied, cause rate increases were "completely unjustified" and that no hard data existed to back up such claims.

Mr. Rosenfield and others were concerned, however, that insurers might take advantage of the multitude of rating factors that the commissioner has permitted them to consider—twenty-five in all—and produce unduly higher rates for urban dwellers.

The new rules also ban the use of such traditional insurance-rating factors as age, sex, and marital status. Regulators had expressed concerns that their use constituted illegal discrimination. The rules also implement a section of Proposition 103 that gives drivers with no more than one moving violation in three years a 20 percent discount off standard rates. About 90 percent of the drivers in the state qualify for that special rate, however, which suggests that the discount may be achieved mostly by raising rates for bad drivers.

Source: Richard Schmitt, "California Auto Insurers Told to Limit Premium Increases to Rate of Inflation," *Wall Street Journal*, December 6, 1989, p. A2; reprinted by permission of *Wall Street Journal*,

Elements needed for a contract:

	CHAPTER
1. **MUTUAL ASSENT WITH A PROMISE OR PROMISES**	**6, 7, 8**
2. Consideration	9
3. Capacity to contract	10
4. Legality	11

Introduction

The U.S. Constitution guarantees to each of us the *freedom to contract.*[1] Such a guaranty ensures that you and I may become personally involved in the legal environment in which we all reside. We do this every day by creating *rights and duties* for ourselves and others. This direct participation by us in our legal environment takes place when we buy groceries at the store, rent an apartment, buy a car, enroll in a course at a university, or do many other activities.

Generally, a right is that which one is legally entitled to have, or to do, or to receive from others within limits prescribed by law. Generally, a duty is a legal obligation owing from one person to another.

Without freedom to contract, which is called "freedom of contract," business in the United States as we know it would cease to exist and our ability to maintain our standard of living would be reduced. It is important, therefore, that every person understand, use wisely, and preserve such a basic freedom so necessary to our way of life.

The important point you should note in this chapter and throughout Part 2 is that *the concept of freedom to contract has legal limitations.* It is not an absolute freedom.

The Agreement—A Prerequisite to a Contract

The law specifies what promises can form the basis of a contract. Some promises create only an "agreement," while some create a "contract" in which the promises create legal obligations to perform them. Thus there is a difference between the words "agreement" and "contract." To have a contract, there must be (1) **mutual assent** with a promise or promises, (2) **consideration,** (3) **capacity** to contract, and (4) **legality.** Obviously, if a person does not have the capacity to make a promise creating a legal obligation, there is no contract. Also, if a promise is to do that which society condemns as illegal, such a promise does not create a contract because there is no legal obligation to perform the promise. These four elements will be discussed in separate chapters.

mutual assent
The meeting of the minds of both or all the parties to a contract

consideration
The legal price bargained for a promise and inducing a party to enter into a contract

capacity
The legal ability to make a contract

legality
Something that does not violate a statute or public policy as declared by the courts

[1]U.S. CONST., art. I, sec. 10: "No State shall . . . pass any . . . law impairing the obligation of contracts. . . ."

► How You Might View It

agreement
A manifestation of mutual assent between parties by offer and acceptance

"We agreed." "We shook hands." "You said you would do it!" "But Mom, Dad said I could have the car tonight." To the casual observer these statements imply the existence of an **agreement.** Each statement suggests that some accord or understanding might exist. In a nonlegal sense we might have an agreement or understanding.

► What the Dictionary Says

The dictionary defines an "agreement" as an "arrangement" and notes certain equivalent words—namely, "bargain," "compact," and "contract."[2]

► What the Law Says

Uniform Commercial Code
A body of statutory law governing commercial transactions concerning personal property (movable things)

Two bodies of law are applicable here: the **Uniform Commercial Code** (statutory law) and the common law (the nonstatutory law common to the people and to society). The Code defines an agreement as a "bargain in fact" between parties. It also defines a contract in Article 1 Section 201(11) resulting from the agreement of the parties. Whether an agreement has *legal consequences* is determined by the Code, when applicable, or by the *common law of contracts.*[3] Whether an agreement will result in a *contract,* which imposes *legal obligations on the parties,* is also determined by the Code and the common law of contracts.[4] (See Figure 6.1.)

goods
Tangible, movable things

The Uniform Commercial Code An application of the Uniform Commercial Code definition of an agreement is found in UCC 2–106. In that Article, an agreement must be for the present or future sale of **goods** to result in a contract. This Code Article limits the subject matter of a sales contract to goods and excludes land and services. Another

FIGURE 6.1 Law Governing Contracts

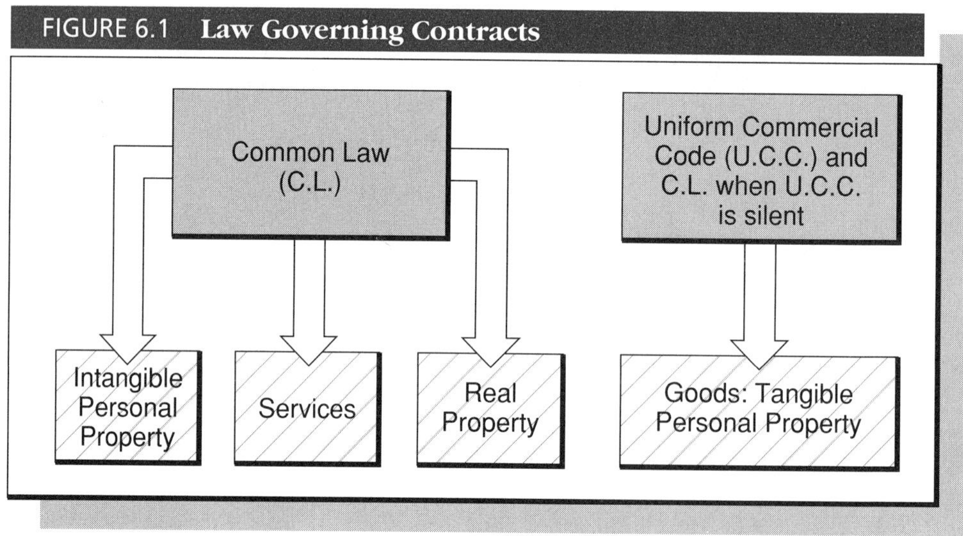

[2]*The Random House Dictionary,* 2nd ed. (New York: Random House, 1987), p. 40.

[3]UCC 1–201(3). This means Article 1, Part 2, Section 1(3).

[4]UCC 1–201(11).

application is found in UCC 2–204. There the Code requires that an agreement exist before a contract can be formed. Both definitions and applications under the Code lead to the conclusion that the words "agreement" and "contract" have different meanings under the Code—that agreement is a part of, and necessary to, a contract.

The Common Law Under the **common law,** certain arrangements or understandings with regard to social obligations or illegal activities might be recognized as agreements but not as contracts. This is done because the purpose of the understanding is considered by society to be of minor legal importance, or it conflicts with what law seeks to prevent others from doing because society has determined such conduct to be undesirable. Thus under the common law, a contract and an agreement have different meanings—again, agreement being a part of, and necessary to, a contract.

common law
Principles of nonstatutory law reflecting the customs and usages of society and found in judicial decisions

contract
A promise that the law recognizes as creating a legal obligation of performance

Definition of Contract

A **contract** is *a promise that the law recognizes as creating a legal obligation of performance.* A promise creates such a legal obligation and thereby becomes a contract when the four elements previously stated have occurred. A minimum of two persons, called *parties* (one on each side of the contract), is required in order to have a contract. There can be any number of parties to a contract. Usually these parties are individuals, partnerships, corporations or governments. The definition of contract requires a promise. Thus we have the rule that a contract can be formed only if we have at least one promise and at least two parties. In the following case the court found that, since the defendant had not made a promise, he had not made a contract.

FACTS

This is an action for damages. Stanley Smith and Sons, a construction company, contracted with Limestone College to construct a gymnasium on campus. The building was completed on or before October 1, 1976, at a cost to the College of $655,178. On October 1, 1976 the campus experienced extraordinary heavy rainfall which caused damage to the gymnasium. Stanley Smith and Sons construction company repaired the damage at a cost of $37,255.24 and seeks recovery under an express contract.

DECISION

The court held for Limestone College. The court said a contract is an obligation which arises from actual agreement of the parties manifested by words, oral or written, or by conduct. If the agreement is manifested by words, the contract is said to be express. If it is manifested by conduct, it is said to be implied. In either case, the parties must manifest a mutual intent to be bound. Without the actual agreement of the parties, there is no contract. The Board (Limestone College) never expressly promised to pay for the repairs and therefore there is no express contract upon which Stanley Smith and Sons construction company can achieve recovery.

Stanley Smith and Sons v. Limestone College, 322 S.E.2d 474 (S.C. 1984).

Certain promises will not be enforced by law as legal obligations. Social obligations, promises that violate a strongly felt public policy, and usually promises to do illegal acts or promises that will produce **unconscionable** results are not enforced by law as contracts. Except for these types of promise, all other promises normally can form the basis for a contract. In the following case the court held that the contract was unconscionable and against public policy.

unconscionable
Offensive to the conscience; immoderate, too one-sided

FIGURE 6.2 **Basic Contract Rule**

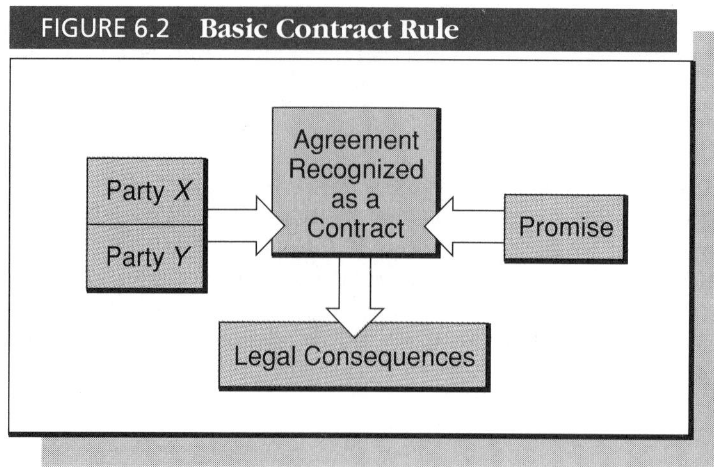

FACTS

Clifton and Cora Jones, welfare recipients, agreed to buy a home freezer for $900 from Star Credit Corporation through a salesman representing Your Shop At Home Service, Inc. After adding time credit charges, credit life insurance, credit property insurance and sales tax, the purchase price came to a total of $1,234.80. So far Clifton and Cora Jones have paid $619.88 toward the purchase. Star Credit claims that with added credit charges paid for an extension of time Clifton and Cora still owe a balance of $819.81. The freezer unit, when purchased, had a maximum retail value of approximately $300. Clifton and Cora Jones sued to have the sales contract reformed on the ground that the contract was unconscionable as a matter of law. The question is whether this transaction and the resulting contract could be considered unconscionable within the meaning of Section 2–302 of the Uniform Commercial Code.

DECISION

The Court held that selling a freezer for $900 ($1,439.69 including credit charges and $18 sales tax) that had an actual retail value of $300 was unconscionable as a matter of law under the Uniform Commercial Code.

Section 2–302 of the Uniform Commercial Code enacts the moral sense of the community into the law of commercial transactions. It authorizes the court to find that a contract or a clause of a contract was "unconscionable at the time it was made," and upon so finding the court may refuse to enforce the contract, remove the objectionable clause, or limit the application of the clause to avoid an unconscionable result. The prevention of oppression and unfair surprise is the principle embodied in this section. It is apparent that Star Credit has been adequately and amply compensated, already having been paid more than $600 for a $300 freezer unit. In accordance with the statute, the application of the payment provision should be limited to amounts already paid by Clifton and Cora and the contract should be rewritten to change the payments called for to equal the amount of payment actually so paid by Clifton and Cora.

Jones v. Star Credit Corp., 59 Misc. 2d 189 (N.Y. 1969).

Types of Contract

▶ Formal and Informal Contracts

A written promise that the law will enforce because it is in a certain required form is called a **formal contract.** Examples of formal contracts would be a contract under seal, a **recognizance,** and various types of negotiable commercial paper such as a **check** and a negotiable **promissory note.**

formal contract
A contract that must be in a certain form

recognizance
An obligation acknowledged by a person in a court to do something, such as to appear in court at a later time; for example, a personal bond

check
A negotiable "draft drawn on a bank payable on demand" UCC 3–104(2)(b)

promissory note
A written promise to pay money

Required Form for a Negotiable Instrument Figure 6.3 illustrates a check. A negotiable instrument must (a) be in writing and signed by the drawer or maker. It must (b) contain an unconditional order or promise (c) to pay a sum certain in money. It must (d) be payable on demand or at a definite time. It must (e) be payable to order or bearer. Chapters 29 to 33 are devoted to the concept of a negotiable instrument as a *formal* contract later in this book.

An informal or **simple contract** contains a promise that the law does not require to be in any particular form—e.g., a promise to employ a person. It may or may not be in writing; if in writing, it may be long or short. Figure 6.4 is an example of a simple contract, with identification of (a) mutual assent, (b) the consideration, (c) the parties, and (d) legality. In this section of the text, our discussion of contracts will be limited to the informal or simple contract.

simple contract
A contract that need not be in any particular form

Elements of a Simple Contract

As was previously mentioned, the elements necessary for a promise to become a simple contract are: (a) mutual assent, (b) consideration, (c) capacity to contract, and (d) legality. Accordingly, we will first examine the promise that leads to mutual assent and an agreement.

► The Promise

Perspective As we discussed on pages 119–121, a contract requires an agreement predicated upon a promise that is legally enforceable. Every agreement, therefore, is not necessarily a contract. Only certain promises will be enforced as contracts.

The Character of a Promise The expression of a **promise** necessary to the formation of a contract looks to the future and is one person's assurance to another or others that something in the future shall happen or not happen. "I'll build the bridge" or "the can will not leak" are examples. The word "promise" need not occur.

promise
An assurance or undertaking that something shall or shall not happen

The Number of Promises While we must have at least one promise to create a contract, the contract can contain any number of promises. If the promise seeks the performance of an act (for example, digging a ditch), or a forbearance (refraining from doing something), the contract, if it comes into being, will be called a **unilateral contract** because there is only *one* promise. For example, John promises to pay Ray

unilateral contract
A contract in which the consideration for a promise is an act or a forbearance

FIGURE 6.3 A Check

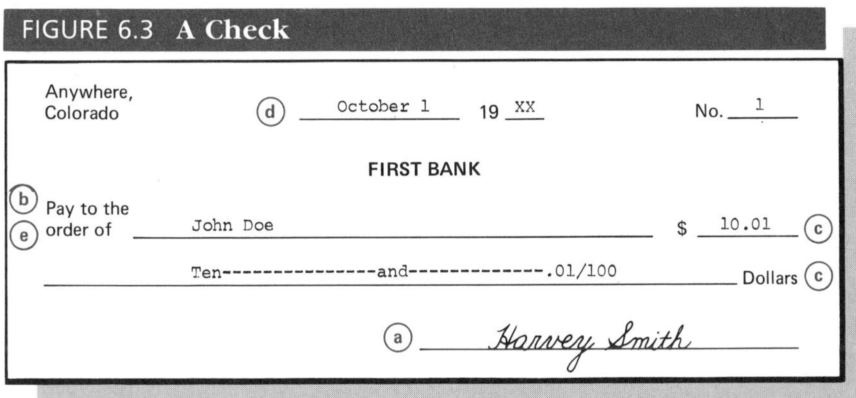

Anywhere, Colorado
(d) October 1 19 XX
No. 1
FIRST BANK
(b) (e) Pay to the order of John Doe
$ 10.01 (c)
Ten---------------and-------------.01/100 Dollars (c)
(a) Harvey Smith

FIGURE 6.4 A Simple Contract

Agreement(a) between Barnes(c) and Smith(c) whereby this day Smith has sold(a) and Barnes has bought(a) the entire crop of Niagara grapes(b), same to be clean and free of mildew and fungi diseases, now growing(d)... Terms $1,000.00 cash(b), payment as follows: Net 30.

Date______ Signature ________________ buyer

Signature ________________ seller

Elements needed for a contract:
(a) mutual assent with a promise or promises
(b) consideration
(c) the parties (relates to capacity to contract)
(d) legality

bilateral contract
A contract in which the consideration is mutual promises

promisor
The person who makes a promise

promisee
The person to whom a promise is made

obligor
The person who owes a legal obligation

obligee
The person to whom a legal obligation is owed

express contract
An actual agreement of parties, the terms of which are stated in distinct and explicit language, either oral or in writing

implied contract
An explicit agreement found from acts or conduct making it reasonable to conclude that a contract exists

$3,000 if Ray will paint John's house by the end of August, or Carl promises to pay Darlene $10,000 if Darlene will not sue Edward. If the promise seeks a return promise that is given and the contract comes into existence, the contract will be called a **bilateral contract** because there is *more than one* promise. For example, Art promises to pay Bill $200 for certain services to be rendered by Bill and Bill promises to render such services.

Communication of the Promise The promise necessary to the formation of a contract must be *communicated* to another party before it can act as an effective basis for forming a contract. The person who initiates the process for formation of a contract by making the original promise is called the **promisor.** The person to whom a promise has been made is called the **promisee.**

The person who has the duty to carry out the promise is called the **obligor.** The person who has the right to the benefit of the promise is called the **obligee.** (In a contract, Ray promises to pay Bob $100. Ray is the promisor and obligor. Bob is the promisee and obligee.)

An agreement that expressly manifests by oral or written words the terms of a promise in a unilateral contract situation, and the return promise in a bilateral contract situation, is called an **express contract,** provided that the other requirements of a contract are present. The promise in a written express contract can be pieced together if one document refers to another—for example, if one letter refers to another letter. Figure 6.4 illustrates an example of an express contract.

An agreement that can be *inferred* only from the conduct of persons and that has the other requirements of a contract is called a *contract implied in fact.* For example, Joe enters Dee's drugstore, picks up a magazine for sale, waves it in the air to get Dee's attention, and Dee nods her head. Upon leaving the store, Joe will have communicated to Dee a promise to pay for the magazine and Dee will have accepted the promise—all by action.

FIGURE 6.5 **Promises, Parties, and Contracts**

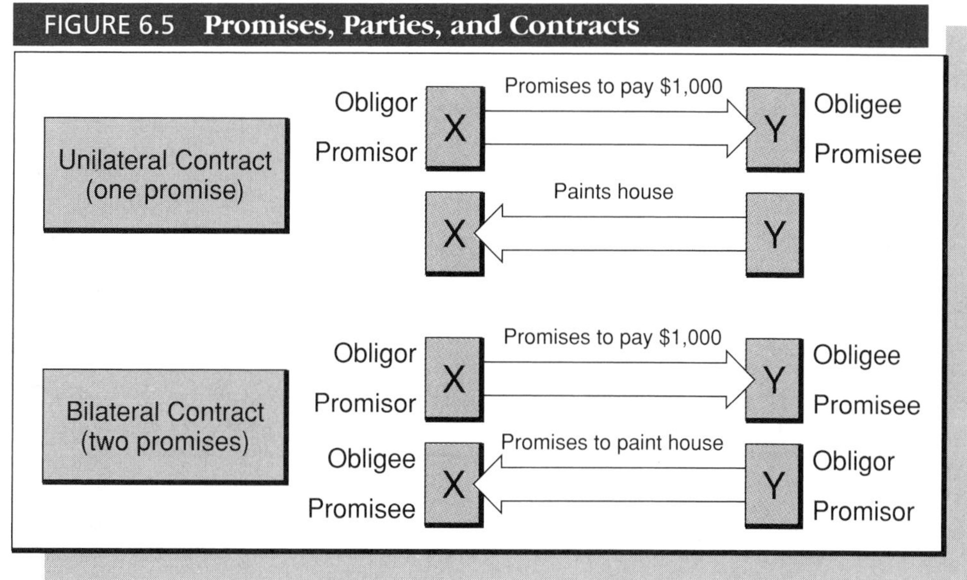

Apart from the way of proving the fact that an agreement has been made, there is no difference at all in legal effect between express contracts and contracts implied in fact. There is still a true contract whether the undertaking or agreement is actually manifested by words or conduct.

The Implied Promise When no promise was intended, yet one is *implied* in law to prevent **unjust enrichment,** and an agreement is found by law, we have a contract implied in law, or **quasi contract.** The implied contract is not expressed in words but is inferred or implied from the circumstances. This is illustrated by the following case.

unjust enrichment
A legal doctrine that prevents persons from profiting or enriching themselves inequitably at the expense of others

quasi contract
A legal fiction invented by the common law to provide for a contract remedy where, in fact, there is no contract but where justice requires recovery as though there had been a promise

FACTS

John A. Artukovich & Sons, Inc., leased a crane to Ashton Company for use in Tucson, Arizona. Ashton hired Reliance Truck to transport the crane. Reliance Truck sought permission from Ashton to use the crane prior to the time the crane was to be delivered in Tucson, Arizona. Ashton told Reliance Truck to obtain permission from Artukovich, the leasor. Without having received permission, Reliance Truck used the crane and then delivered it to Ashton. Reliance Truck did not attempt to pay a rental fee for this use. Artukovich sued Reliance Truck under the theory of unjust enrichment.

DECISION

The court held for John A. Artukovich & Sons, Inc. The court stated the "contracts implied-in-law" or "quasi-contracts," also called "constructive contracts," are inferred by law as a matter of reason and justice from acts and conduct of the parties and circumstances surrounding the transactions and are imposed for the purpose of bringing about justice without reference to the intentions of the parties. The court noted that unjust enrichment did not depend upon the existence of a valid contract nor was it necessary for one to suffer a loss that corresponded with another's gain. Therefore the court held that Reliance Truck was liable to Artukovich under a theory of unjust enrichment because Reliance Truck had received a benefit by unauthorizedly using the crane to perform a contract.

John A. Artukovich & Sons, Inc. v. Reliance Truck, 614 P.2d 327 (Ariz. 1980).

Figure 6.6 summarizes how a supplied promise results in a particular contract.

joint liability
Occurs when parties together obligate themselves to perform the same promise

several liability
Occurs when the same performance is separately promised by each party

Joint and Several Promises We can have any number of parties in a contract. Also we can have any number of promises in a contract. When we relate parties to promises, we have three basic relationships present.

When more than one party appears on either side of a contract, depending upon their intentions, their promises will be considered **joint, several,** or *joint and several.*

If there is only *one promise* and more than one party *together* obligate themselves to perform the *same* promise, the parties' obligation is *joint;* their obligation is to perform together, *jointly.* They are *collectively liable* and can be sued only together. Art and Bill contract with Carla. ("We promise to purchase from Carla.") Art and Bill are jointly liable to Carla.

If the same performance is separately promised by each party, the obligation is *several,* performable by each of the several parties. They are *individually liable* and can be sued individually. Art and Bill contract with Carla. ("Each of us promises to buy from Carla.") Art and Bill are *severally* liable to Carla.

If the promise is in terms of "I promise" rather than "we promise," and it is undertaken by more than one party, the obligation assumed is *joint and several,* so that the parties are liable and can be sued together or individually. The following case illustrates how the total language of a document will be reviewed by a court to determine whether an obligation is joint or several.

FACTS

The pertinent provisions of a guaranty agreement were as follows:

> . . . When any such drafts, loans, or paper, or any renewal thereof, shall become and remain due and unpaid, the *undersigned* will on demand, pay the amount due thereon. It is understood that if this Guaranty Agreement is executed by more than one person, liability of each of the undersigned by reason of notice herein provided or otherwise shall not affect the continuing obligation of any other.

It is argued that this language creates a joint liability among guarantors, and when one is released, all are released.

DECISION

Whether the liability of several promisors, whose interests are separate, is joint or several depends on the intention of the parties. Where an instrument provides that "we or either of us" promise to pay, the liability of the parties will then be deemed to be joint and several. The court held that when the provisions in the guaranty agreement are considered in total there is no indication that only joint liability was intended.

FIGURE 6.6 **Supplied Promise and Resultant Contract**

Promise Supplied by Words	Promise Supplied by Conduct	Promise Supplied by Law
Express Contract	Implied in Fact Contract	Implied in Law Contract

The language used in the agreement refers to the undersigned and a whole paragraph is devoted to stating that if the agreement is executed by more than one person the liability of each will be joint and several. After considering this language, the court held that the obligation here is joint and several and that the release of one guarantor would not operate as a release of remaining guarantors.

Guynn v. Corpus Christi Bank & Trust, 620 S.W.2d 188 (Tex. 1981).

The Objective Test

In express and implied-in-fact contracts, the law looks to the **objective evidence** that parties normally manifest in a bargain situation in order to determine whether a contract has been formed and then whether it is express or implied in fact. This objective evidence is governed by an objective standard. The standard is what would a reasonable person conclude from the words and/or conduct of another.

objective evidence
The words and conduct of the party, not the secret thoughts of the party

If I **subjectively** (personally) do not want a contract but my actions or words, oral or written, would lead a reasonable person to understand or presume that I do intend a contract, that presumption will control. A promise communicated in a bargain setting raises a strong presumption that a contractual intent is present. The following case so holds. In this situation the president thought he would not be held liable on the note, but a reasonable person looking at the form of the signature could reasonably conclude he intended to be personally liable.

subjectively
Existing only in one's mind

FACTS

The sole issue presented by Thomas E. Green is as follows:

> Whether the trial court erred in holding that the Guaranty signed by Thomas E. Green was an individual Guaranty and therefore making him personally liable for the debts of Safety Signal of Tennessee, Inc. up to the aggregate sum of $2,500.00 for which amount the court entered judgment against the defendant.

At the end of the continuing guaranty document the following appeared:

> *s/s Thomas E. Green*
> *President, Safety Signal of Tenn.*

The form contains two lines for signatures of guarantors. On the first line, the signature of Thomas E. Green was signed in script. On the second line, the words "President, Safety Signal of Tenn., In(c)" are printed by hand with an ink pen. Appellant relies upon his testimony that his intention was to sign for the corporation and not as an individual. No other evidence was offered as to the mutual intent of the parties.

DECISION

The court held for Cone Oil Company, Inc. The court noted that it is possible for an officer of a corporation to avoid personal liability by signing his name and adding his title and the name of the corporation. However, such a signature does not produce the presumptive effect of a signature in which the name of the corporation appears first followed by the word "by" or "per." In the former case, additional evidence such as text of the instrument or evidence of the joint intent of the parties would be required to establish that only the corporation was to be bound. In the latter case, the intention of the parties is self-evident from the form of the signature. Since no additional evidence of intent was offered, the court held that a secret unexpressed intent of one party to the contract cannot bind the other party who has no notice of the secret intent.

Cone Oil Co., Inc. v. Green, 669 S.W.2d 662 (Tenn. 1983).

► Risk

When one makes a promise, one assumes all the risks associated with its performance. One cannot after the fact be excused from performing the promise because it has become more difficult to perform than one originally contemplated, or it seems to be less profitable for one to perform it. In the following case insurance agents and managers assume the risk that a loss ratio would prevent them from receiving a bonus.

FACTS

In consolidated actions, insurance agents and agency managers brought suit against an insurance company, contending they were entitled to certain bonus renewal commissions pursuant to their employment agreements. In their employment agreements, the following clause appears:

> 10. Company shall pay to Agent a bonus of 2 percent of all his premiums, (excluding Crop, Hail and Tobacco Fidater) in his territory, if a production quota assigned by the Company is reached and if the Company loss ratio (annual statement to Insurance Department) for the year in question does not exceed 63 percent.

Losses reported exceeded 63 percent so the insurance company did not pay the bonus. The agents contend that if recovery of losses paid by the insurance company from parties responsible for losses were included in the calculation of the loss ratio it would be below 63 percent and they would be entitled to a bonus.

DECISION

The court held for the insurance company. The court said that in the present case the loss ratio precondition was bargained for and understood. By entering into their respective agreements the agents *accepted the risk* that the loss ratio might exceed 63 percent for a given year and that their bonus renewal commissions would not be paid.

Fraver v. North Carolina Farm Bureau Mutual Ins. Co., 318 S.E.2d 340 (N.C. 1984).

factual impossibility
The facts prevent performance of the promise

Where the promise cannot be fulfilled because of **factual impossibility** of carrying it out, one is excused from the consequence of the promise. For example, John, an artist, agrees to paint Al's portrait. Before the portrait is finished, John is injured in an automobile accident and is now blind. John is no longer bound to his contract to paint the portrait. *Subsequent illegality* of the contractual obligation contained in the promise (a later event making performance illegal) and *destruction of the subject matter* of the promise (the building to be painted burns) will in proper cases *excuse* the promisor from the risk consequence involved in making the promise.

► Classification of Agreements and Contracts

void agreement
An agreement that the law will not enforce as a legal obligation

Void Agreement A **void agreement** is one that the law will not enforce as a legal obligation, nor does the law recognize its performance as a duty. It is not a contract because the promise or promises do not create a legal obligation of performance. An example is an agreement to commit a crime or to perpetrate a fraud. In the following case the court held that the agreement to support a live-in mate was void because its enforcement would be in violation of a public policy found in a state statute.

FACTS

Mrs. Hewitt appealed the order of a trial court dismissing her complaint which asked that the court grant her a just, fair share of the property, earnings, and profits of Mr. Hewitt, order a proper division for support and maintenance of herself and their minor children, or in the alternative, divide the joint property of the parties and impress a trust on other properties acquired through the joint efforts of Mrs. Hewitt and her husband. The complaint alleges that Mrs. Hewitt became pregnant by Mr. Hewitt out of wedlock, that Mr. Hewitt told Mrs. Hewitt they would live together as husband and wife and that no formal marriage ceremony was necessary, that Mr. Hewitt stated that he would share his life, future earnings and property with her, that they announced their marriage to their respective parents and thereafter lived together as husband and wife in the community for seventeen years during which Mrs. Hewitt helped him complete his professional education and helped in his professional practice, bore him children and performed other motherly and wifely duties. The appellate court reversed the trial court and held for Mrs. Hewitt. The case is now before the Supreme Court to hear the appeal of Mr. Hewitt.

DECISION

The court held for Mr. Hewitt, noting that the situation alleged here was not the kind of arm's length bargain envisioned by traditional contract principles, but an intimate arrangement of a fundamentally different kind. The issue, realistically is whether it is appropriate for this court to grant a legal status to a private arrangement substituting for the institution of marriage sanctioned by the State. The question whether change is needed in the law governing the rights of parties in this delicate area of marriage-like relationships involves evaluation of sociological data and alternatives the court believes best suited to the superior investigative and fact-finding facilities of the legislative branch in the exercise of its traditional authority to declare public policy in the domestic relations field. That belief is reinforced by the fact that judicial recognition of mutual property rights between unmarried cohabitants would, in this court's opinion, clearly violate the policy of the recently enacted Illinois Marriage and Dissolution of Marriage Act. The court, therefore, holds that Mrs. Hewitt's agreement with Mr. Hewitt is void and unenforceable.

Hewitt, et al. v. Hewitt, 394 N.E.2d 1204 (Ill. 1979).

Voidable Contract A voidable agreement can result in a **voidable contract.** However, it gives one or more of the parties to a contract the alternative of avoiding it or of enforcing it. (Ray fraudulently induced Bob to enter into a contract. It is voidable by Bob.) In the following case the court held that there were sufficient facts on the basis of which the contract could be found to be voidable.

voidable contract
A contract that can be avoided by one or more of the parties

FACTS

Arthur Murray, Inc. is a national franchisor of dancing schools. J. P. Davenport is a franchisee in Florida. Davenport made various contacts with Mrs. Vokes, a widow without family, and sold to her 2302 hours of dance lessons for a total cash outlay of $31,090.45 over a period of less than sixteen months. Mrs. Vokes alleges the sales contracts were entered into by her because of means and methods by Davenport and his associates which, though legally permissible, went beyond the unsavory perimeter of "sales puffing" and went well into the forbidden area of undue influence, the suggestion of falsehood, the suppression of truth, and the free exercise of rational judgment, if what Mrs. Vokes alleged was true. From the time of her first contact with the dancing school, she was influenced unwittingly by a constant and continuous barrage of flattery, false praise, excessive compliments, to such extent that, in her estimation, it would be not only inequitable, but unconscionable, for a court to allow such contracts to stand. Mrs. Vokes asked the court to declare the contracts null and void. Her complaint was dismissed for failure to state a cause of action, and Mrs. Vokes appealed.

DECISION

The lower court was reversed and judgment was entered for Mrs. Vokes. The court said that although it is true that generally a misrepresentation, to be actionable, must be one of fact rather than opinion, there are significant qualifications to this rule and they are applicable in this case. It does not apply where there is a fiduciary relationship between the parties or where there has been some artifice or trick employed by the representor, or where the parties do not in general deal at arm's length, or where the representee does not have equal opportunity to become apprised of the truth or falsity of the fact represented. It is reasonable to suppose that Arthur Murray and Davenport had "superior knowledge" as to whether Mrs. Vokes had the potential to become a good dancer and whether she was noticeably improving as the lessons progressed. One could infer from the undenied statements of the complaint that the flowery compliments heaped upon her by Davenport proceeded as much or more from the urge to "ring the cash register" as from any honest or realistic appraisal of her dancing ability or a factual representation of her progress. In the court's view, Mrs. Vokes is entitled to her day in court and the order dismissing Mrs. Vokes' complaint with prejudice should be and is dismissed.

Vokes v. Arthur Murray, Inc., and J. P. Davenport, 212 So.2d 906 (Fla. 1968).

unenforceable contract
A contract that the courts will not enforce

Unenforceable Agreement An unenforceable agreement is an agreement that cannot be successfully sued upon or proved. It cannot be enforced in the courts. If it is a contract, it is called an **unenforceable contract.**

executed contract
A contract that has been performed by all the parties to it

Executed Contract An **executed contract** is a contract that has been completely performed by all the parties to it.

executory contract
A contract that has not been performed by all the parties to it

Executory Contract In an **executory contract** something has not been accomplished. The contract can be completely executory, i.e., all of the parties to it have not performed their respective duties. A contract can also be partially executory—i.e., one party has performed but the other party has not performed. For example, John painted a house as he agreed to do for Mike. Mike has not yet paid John for his work. The obligation of John has been executed. The obligation of Mike remains executory.

unconscionable contract
A contract in which one of the parties is in too unequal or one-sided a bargaining position

Unconscionable Contract An **unconscionable contract** for the *sale of goods* under the Uniform Commercial Code is a contract which the court may refuse to enforce or which the court may modify because one of the parties is in too unequal a bargaining position at the time the contract was made. The crucial test is whether the bargain is so one-sided in its benefit to one party as to strike the conscience of the court.[5] For an example of such a contract see *Jones v. Star Credit Corp.*, 59 Misc.2d 189 (N.Y. 1969).

While freedom of contract is basic to our way of life, we see a number of developments in our law, perhaps best represented by the Uniform Commercial Code, which temper the results of an application of freedom of contract contained in the words

FIGURE 6.7 **Legal Consequence Table**

Valid Contract	Void Agreement	Voidable Contract	Unenforceable Agreement
Legal Consequence	No Legal Consequence	Avoidable Legal Consequence	No Legal Consequence

[5]UCC 2–302.

"buyer beware." Certainly the concept of the unconscionable contract is designed to soften the harshness of the marketplace.

A total concept of freedom, it could be argued, would allow each state to develop its own law of contracts. The purpose of the statutory Uniform Commercial Code is, because of the needs of commerce and the economy, to bring uniformity in all states to the law of commercial transactions concerning personal property, such as in sales of goods, which is a part of contract law.

Other statutes that have as their purpose the protection of the consumer make inroads on the concept of freedom of contract. Some of them are the Consumer Product Safety Act and the Truth-in-Packaging Act, discussed in Chapter 28; the Federal Trade Commission Act, discussed in Chapter 34; the Securities Acts, discussed in Chapter 45, and other Acts discussed in the chapters of Part 7, Government Regulation of Business.

The labor relations acts—i.e., the Wagner Act, the Taft-Hartley Act, and the Landrum-Griffin Act, discussed in Chapter 36, Labor Law—have their impact on the freedom of labor and management to contract.

The conclusions to be drawn from observation of the evolutionary process of contract law are that the concept of *freedom* of contract has been questioned and found wanting, that the concept of **caveat emptor** (let the buyer beware) continues to erode and is being replaced by the concept of **caveat venditor** (let the seller beware).

caveat emptor
Let the buyer beware

caveat venditor
Let the seller beware

Summary Statement

1. The concept of freedom to contract is not unlimited. The understandings we reach with others in our daily lives are not always contracts. The law does not give legal importance to social obligations.
2. In law, the word "contract" has a very special meaning separate from what we find in the dictionary.
3. In application, the definition of a contract as a promise that creates a legal obligation of performance becomes quite complex.
4. The promise creates a legal obligation and becomes a contract when four things are present: (1) mutual assent, (2) consideration, (3) capacity to contract, and (4) legality.
5. While we require at least one promise and two parties as a minimum for a contract, any number of parties, relationships, and promises can become part of a contract.
6. The importance of the need to communicate the promise by language and/or action before a contract is formed has been illustrated. The objective analysis of the actions of the parties was developed as a critical concept to determine if there is a manifested meeting of the minds.
7. The importance of terminology as a way of expressing conceptual ideas about contracts has also been illustrated.
8. This chapter has evaluated the concept and evolution of contract law and indicated the path of its future development.

The following case has been chosen for you to read because it represents current thinking on what *freedom of contract* should really mean. The implications of the case are far-reaching, and no doubt you will have a strong feeling for or against the court's decision. The case highlights the importance of contract law both to an individual and to business organizations.

JOHNSON v. MOBIL OIL CORPORATION
415 F.Supp. 264 (1976)

Johnson brought this action against Mobil Oil Corporation to recover for losses suffered when the service station he operated was destroyed by fire. Johnson alleges that the fire was caused by events following Mobil's delivery of gasoline containing water, and seeks to recover for the loss of inventory and other **consequential damages.** Mobil moves for a partial summary judgment dismissing Johnson's claim for consequential damages. Mobil seeks to limit any recovery to the difference of the value of the gasoline as gasoline and its value as watered gasoline.

consequential (special) damages
The money judicially awarded to an injured party for loss that the breaching party reasonably could foresee would be a result of his or her breach

Mobil relies on a clause contained in a contract between itself and Johnson which reads as follows: *"In no event shall seller be liable for prospective profits or special, indirect, or consequential damages."*

Johnson opposes the motion on the ground that the clause excluding consequential damages is unconscionable.

The court noted that the law in Michigan was such that unreasonable terms in a contract for goods and services used by a significant segment of the public and obtainable from limited sources would not be enforced as a matter of public policy. In the eyes of the court this *might* represent a departure from the majority view in a direction away from the freedom to contract but was the law in Michigan.

substantive unconscionability
Contract terms that cause one of the parties to be in too unequal or one-sided a bargaining position

procedural unconscionability
Circumstances, other than the contract terms, that cause the enforcement of the contract to be unreasonably excessive

prima facie
At first sight

Since gasoline is used by a significant body of consumers and is available from limited sources, the court felt the question of unconscionability was properly before it.

The court noted that unconscionability can be shown in two ways: by proving either **substantive unconscionability** or **procedural unconscionability.**

The court noted that under the Uniform Commercial Code the clause of the contract in question would not be **prima facie** unconscionable in a commercial setting. Thus a finding of substantive unconscionability might not be present.

On the other hand, the court found procedural unconscionability present. The court noted that Johnson could not read, except perhaps for certain items in the sports section of the newspaper, and therefore could not understand the significance of the clause in question. Moreover, the court found that neither was the clause brought to Johnson's attention nor was its legal significance explained to him.

The court found the clause to be unconscionable and not binding on Johnson. In the court's words:

> However, before a contracting party with the immense bargaining power of the Mobil Oil Corporation may limit its liability vis-à-vis an uncounseled layman, as it seeks to do in this case, to "difference money damages," it has an affirmative duty to obtain the voluntary, knowing assent of the other party. This could easily have been done in this case by explaining to plaintiff in layman's terms the meaning and possible consequences of the disputed clause. Such a requirement does not detract from the freedom to contract, unless that phrase denotes the freedom to impose the onerous terms of one's carefully drawn printed document on an unsuspecting contractual partner. Rather, freedom of contract is enhanced by a requirement that both parties be aware of the burdens they are assuming. The notion of free will has little meaning as applied to one who is ignorant of the consequences of his acts.

Motion of Mobil Oil Corporation denied.

Questions and Case Problems

1. Welborn was retired but worked for Snider 's neighbor, Walter Boyd, doing odd jobs around Boyd's house and yard. On the day Welborn was hurt, Snider and his son Ollie were building a shed in their backyard. Welborn walked over to visit with them while they were taking a break from their work, at about 2:30 in the afternoon. When the Sniders returned to their work, Welborn accompanied them. The Sniders had one more post to raise for their shed. The three men picked it up, with Welborn at the front, Snider in the middle, and Ollie at the rear. Ollie slipped and dropped the pole, causing Snider to lose control and drop it also. The pole fell on Welborn, fracturing several of his ribs and rendering him unconscious. He was taken to the hospital, treated, and released about two weeks later. Welborn sued Snider, alleging that Snider entered into an implied in fact contract with Welborn whereby for the consideration of Welborn's assistance in raising the post, Snider impliedly promised to support the rear of the post, said contract being breached. Welborn seeks damages. What result? [*Welborn v. Snider,* 431 So.2d 1198 (Ala. 1983).]

2. Kennedy, a general contractor, obtained a quotation from Moore-Handley, a distributor for Westinghouse products, to provide various electrical equipment called for by specifications. Kennedy negotiated with Moore-Handley as to price, achieved a price reduction in quoted price and then issued a purchase order to Moore-Handley. This purchase order called for Moore-Handley to provide equipment "per the attached bill of materials," and the attached bill of materials was a complete copy of the Moore-Handley written quotation. On the back of the first page of the quotation sent with the purchase order were certain provisions, printed in red, limiting Moore-Handley's liability for consequential and delay damages. Kennedy's contention is that the court should not have found the limiting conditions on the back of the front page of the quotation to be part of the overall contract. Is Kennedy correct? [*Kennedy Electric Co. v. Moore-Handley, Inc.,* 437 So.2d 76 (Ala. 1983).]

3. A lease contained the following paragraph:

> At the expiration of this Second Supplemental Lease Extension Agreement on May 1, 1983, the second party [lessee] shall have the privilege of an option for the further extension of this lease for an additional period of 10 years from and after May 1, 1983. Both parties agree that the rental terms and conditions for this lease shall be renegotiated as of May 1, 1983 for the 10 year term beginning on that date. The rental terms and conditions shall be negotiated upon a basis which is satisfactory and acceptable to both parties. Both parties agree to negotiate such terms consistent with conditions existing on May 1, 1983, to provide rental terms and conditions substantially the same as those now existing, with appropriate adjustments, however, satisfactory to both parties and covering the ten year term beginning May 1, 1983.

The parties could not agree as to rent in the renewed lease. The lessee seeks to have the contract enforced. The lessor alleges the clause is not sufficient to create a contract. Who should prevail? [*R. A. S., Inc., v. Crowley,* 351 N.W.2d 414 (Neb. 1984).]

4. Knack, a cook, is suing under an Arizona workers' compensation statute for injuries sustained on a job. The State Industrial Commission contends that Knack was hired to perform a series of unilateral contracts to act as cook in various states for an employer who provided services to railroad track-laying crews. Both parties agree that the terms of the agreement were communicated in Arizona. The State Industrial Commission contends that the contract was not formed until the acts were performed in other states. The State Industrial Commission maintains that Knack is not entitled to the protection of the workers' compensation statutes of Arizona since the contract was not formed in Arizona. On the other hand, Knack contends that a bilateral contract, in which he promised to act as a cook and his employer promised to pay for his services as a cook, was formed in Arizona, one of the conditions of the contract being that the performance of his services as a cook was to take place in various other states. What result? [*Knack v. Industrial Commission of Arizona,* 503 P.2d 373 (Ariz. 1972).]

5. The parties were close personal friends while residents in St. Joseph, Missouri. In 1972 the Etchisons moved to a mobile home located on 23 acres owned by their uncle. Two years later, the Etchisons discussed with the Leesons the possibility of the Leesons moving on the same acreage so that their personal association could continue and the Leesons could aid the Etchisons in taking care of the partially disabled uncle. The Etchisons agreed to deed three acres to the Leesons if they came, conditioned upon the Etchisons inheriting the 23 acres. The Leesons sold their home and purchased a mobile home that they put on the three acres after making substantial improvements, such as putting in a foundation and driveway. The uncle died. The Etchisons inherited the 23 acres. The Leesons were evicted. Are the Leesons entitled to three acres of land? [*Leeson v. Etchison,* 650 S.W.2d 681 (Mo. 1983).]

6. Perry Lucas was initially hired by his brother to do minor work on a project. After Perry worked for a short time he claimed he entered into a contract with his brother to perform certain remodeling tasks. The following oral conversation became part of the court record:

A. I was asked if I could build the kitchen, lay tiles on the floor, lay tiles around the bar, do some minor repairs, lay tiles in the bathroom, fix the ceilings in the dining room, bathrooms, and kitchen, and work for half the bid (made by one Larcomb) and I said yes. I was asked if it would include the work that I had already done, and I said yes.
Q. Then, under your new contract, did you proceed to do work?
A. Yes, sir.
Q. What did you do?
A. Exactly what we talked about.
Q. You did all those things?
A. Yes, sir.

The judge instructed the jury that there was no express building contract. Was the judge correct? [*Lucas v. Constantini,* 469 N.E.2d 927 (Ohio 1983).]

7. Clayton sold his radio station. Suit is being brought against the Communications Capital Corporation, buyer, upon a promissory note given by a now-bankrupt corporation formed by the Communications Capital. The contract of sale stipulated that the balance of the purchase price was to be paid by a note of either the buyer or a corporation formed by the buyer. Communications Capital contends that the contract was executed and that it was discharged when the note was issued to Clayton upon formation of the corporation. What result? [*Clayton v. Communications Capital Corp.,* 440 P.2d 330 (Ariz. 1968).]

8. Strickland set out to bribe a judge named Woods to throw a case. The judge contacted the state's attorney and told him of the bribe offer. The judge was advised to play along with Strickland. The judge agreed. A $2,500 bribe was delivered to the judge by Strickland. Strickland was subsequently indicted for bribery, pleaded guilty, and was sentenced to imprisonment for a term of four years. Three months after the criminal trial, Strickland seeks return of the $2,500. Is he entitled to the return of his money? [*State of Maryland v. Strickland,* 400 A. 2d 451 (Md. 1979).]

9. The marriage of Mary Q. Griffin (the mother) and Clarence A. Griffin (the father) was dissolved on September 14, 1979. The decree of dissolution between the father and mother contained the following provision with regard to education: "Both parents shall fully and equally participate in the education of their child. Schools shall be selected jointly." The father alleges that the mother planned to enroll their child in the Vidya School in Boulder over the father's objection. The father further alleged that the Vidya School was sponsored by the Boulder Tibetan Buddhist Community and that enrollment of his son in such a community would hamper his development by placing him outside the broad stream of the American cultural community. A Colorado statute allocates the authority to make child-rearing decisions following an award of custody as follows: "Except as otherwise agreed by the parties in writing at the time of the custody decree, the custodian may determine the child's upbringing, including his education. . . ." Custody was awarded to the mother. The father contends that the parties have agreed to joint authority over their son's education, thereby limiting the mother's power under the statute to control education decisions. Who prevails? [*Griffin v. Griffin*, 699 P.2d 407 (Colo. 1985).]

10. In *Johnson v. Mobil Oil Corporation*, excerpted at the beginning of this section, the court held that a contracting party having immense bargaining power has an affirmative duty to explain in layperson's terms the meaning and possible consequences of a contractual obligation to be assumed by another contracting party who is an uncounseled layperson. Evaluate this holding by the court.

CHAPTER 7

FORMATION OF A CONTRACT

After you have read this chapter, you should be able to:

1. Discuss the law of offer and acceptance, recognizing that it acts as a limitation on the freedom to contract.
2. Recognize that the law of offer and acceptance is evolving and moving to facilitate broad social objectives.
3. Appreciate how the promise necessary to the formation of a contract is absorbed into an offer.
4. Understand the complexity of the creation of an offer that places a power in another.
5. Note how the law of offer and acceptance can create rights and duties not previously recognized by law.
6. Note the critical importance of the agency authorized to communicate the acceptance.
7. Realize the critical impact that the Uniform Commercial Code has had upon the law of offer and acceptance.

BUSINESS DECISIONS and the LAW

When companies advertise for workers in today's market, they may find they have no choice but to hire from a new labor pool. The supply of America's once-plentiful workers is tightening. U.S.-born white male workers, once the bulwark of American business, are becoming scarce. Women, blacks, Hispanics, and immigrants have become the mainstay of the labor supply. As the twenty-first century approaches, their sheer numbers will reshape much of American corporate life.

Work-force shortages of the 1990s may accomplish what the activism of the 1960s could not: getting corporations deeply involved in broad social issues. As they are forced more and more to look for workers among groups they once could afford to ignore, companies are starting to find themselves caught up in such issues as education, child care, illiteracy, care for the elderly, broken homes, and teenage pregnancies.

Many executives think the problem is not that companies will do too much but too little. Smaller companies may not be able to afford programs to remedy shortages of workers or skills. Larger concerns may resist the cost of taking on added burdens in the face of foreign competition. Some simply choose to ignore the social conditions now keeping women, minorities, and immigrants from participating fully in the work force.

At the heart of the issue is demographic change. The baby boom that swelled the labor force for the past two decades is being abruptly replaced by a baby bust.

Work-force growth will slump to 1 percent a year in the 1990s. Nearly two-thirds of the new entrants will be women; an additional 20 percent will be nonwhite or immigrant men. White, native-born males will make up only 15 percent of the new entries to the labor force from now through the next century.

Companies that once rejected applicants without necessary skills now may go out of their way to find out what employees can do. "We don't want to screen anyone out," says Sharon Canter, a spokesperson for Manpower, Inc. "There's always something they can do. We are looking to uncover skills and abilities that workers don't even know they have."

The same situation has occurred at Gannett Company. "We are looking a lot harder in places that we haven't focused our attention on; the disabled, retired, older workers," says Madelyn Jennings, senior vice president for personnel. "It has nothing to do with altruism or concern about society. It has to do with survival."

The fear is that, increasingly, the workers available to do a given job will not be able to handle it. The Hudson Institute predicts that 41 percent of jobs created through the end of the century will be "high-skill" ones, versus just 24 percent of existing jobs. Yet many new workers lack even basic skills. The Department of Education recently asked a group of twenty-one- to twenty-four-year-olds to decipher a bus schedule; only a quarter of whites who were asked could do so, and only 7 percent of Hispanics and 3 percent of blacks.

More and more companies are thus deciding they have to get involved in education. "If we can't expand the pool of qualified people, we won't get the people we need," says Eastman Kodak president Kay Whitmore.

Kodak executives are helping restructure the Rochester, New York, school system. General Electric is working on programs to get more minority teachers into colleges and universities. Sears Roebuck and fourteen other companies have funded a model school that works with center-city students. According to Paula Banks, president of the Sears Roebuck Foundation, the hope is that "it will be a learning laboratory, improvements will find their way into the school system, and that will affect the work force that we see."

Institutions are also beginning to grapple seriously for the first time with issues of parents and work. B. Joseph White, associate dean of University of Michigan's business school, explains that the issue is not training the workers but keeping them. "The challenge is getting women who choose to have children through their childbearing years without driving them out of the corporation." And that evidently means getting companies more involved in family life. "In the past, you left your children and family at the front door. That's not going to be possible anymore," contends Honeywell's Barbara Jerich.

With child care in such short supply, companies are coming to believe they will have to fill the gap. Campbell Soup, which has an on-site day-care center that wins high marks, hears each week from five or six major companies wanting to know how the program works.

Source: Amanda Bennett, "As Pool of Skilled Help Tightens, Firms Move to Broaden Their Role, the Second Century," *Wall Street Journal*, May 8, 1989, pp. A1–4; reprinted by permission of *Wall Street Journal*,

Elements needed for a contract:

	CHAPTER
1. MUTUAL ASSENT WITH A PROMISE OR PROMISES	6, 7, 8
2. Consideration	9
3. Capacity to contract	10
4. Legality	11

Introduction

The preceding chapter discussed the importance of a promise and the necessity of having an agreement between parties in order to have a contract. We saw that an agreement is a manifestation of **mutual assent** between parties by their offer and acceptance. This chapter will discuss the offer that contains the promise, the acceptance, what they are, how they work, and how they create an agreement and a resulting contract with its rights and duties.

mutual assent
The meeting of the minds of both or all the parties to a contract

The offer and acceptance is critical to the formation of a simple express, or implied-in-fact, contract. One reason is that the offer normally contains the promise required for the formation of a contract. Another reason is that by offer and acceptance there is an apparent meeting of the minds of the parties resulting in an agreement. Before we can have a contract, except for the implied-in-law (quasi) contract, we need an offer.

The importance of offer and acceptance to the formation of a contract is apparent from the role the concept is designed to play in the law of contracts. (Al offers to sell a house to Bo for $100,000, and Bo accepts. Al is promising to sell and Bo is promising to buy the house.) Figure 7.1 illustrates how a promise is merged into an offer.

Necessary to the finding of an offer is the satisfaction of two tests: a *certainty of terms test* and an *intention test*. The law, having given us the freedom to contract and the ability to create *rights and duties*, is concerned that we truly *want* to assume certain duties that would not otherwise be imposed upon us by law, and that we truly want to gain rights that we would not otherwise be entitled to by law. To satisfy its concerns, the law limits our freedom to contract until the two tests necessary for the existence of an offer are satisfied—the certainty of terms and intention tests. These two tests will be examined later.

The important point in this chapter is the concern of the law for determining from the parties' conduct whether or not the minds of the parties have apparently met in order to have a contract. The need to determine this factor objectively has resulted in the law of offer and acceptance.

The Offer

The terms of an offer must be communicated to an offeree before we place in the offeree the power to accept and to create a contract—to bring a contract into existence.

FIGURE 7.1 **Promise Merged into an Offer**

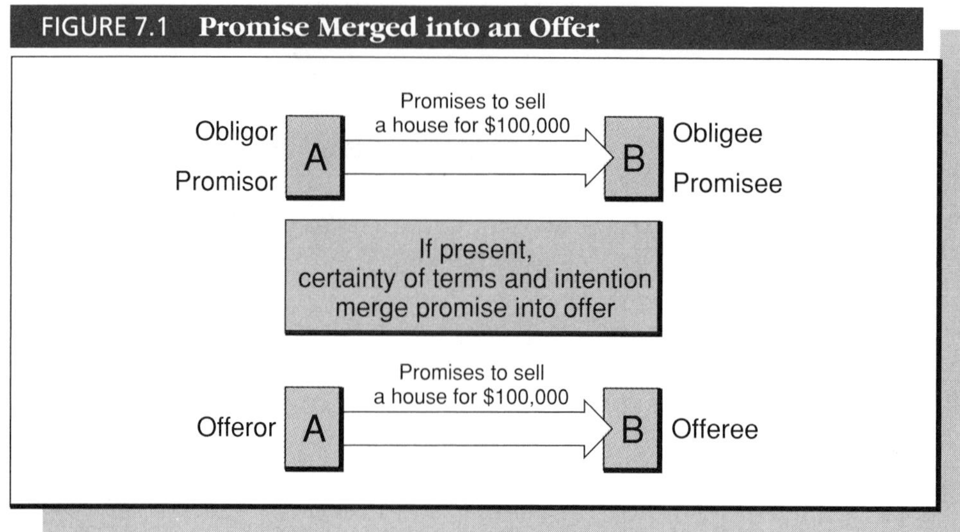

Once the terms of an offer are communicated to an offeree, the power to bring a contract into existence does not last forever. It ends with the passage of time, or it can end prematurely through acts of the parties to the proposed contract.

The Uniform Commercial Code has brought major changes to the common law of offer and of acceptance where the subject matter of the offer is goods. These changes will be discussed later in this chapter.

An important point to watch for in this chapter is how the law of offer and acceptance is *evolving* to accomplish social objectives.

► Offer Contains a Promise

offer
A promise proposed in exchange for another's act, forbearance, or return promise

offeror
The promisor making an offer

offeree
The promisee to whom an offer is made

An **offer** is a promise proposed with the expectation that it will provoke an exchange of another's act, forbearance, or return promise. The offer gives the offeree the legal power to accept the offer and to bring a contract into existence. Except for the *inverted unilateral contract* in which there is an act in search of a promise, the offer will contain the promise necessary to the formation of a contract. The promisor—the person who makes the promise contained in the offer—becomes an **offeror.** The promisee—the person to whom the promise is made—becomes the **offeree** when the promisee receives the offer. It should be recognized that in the law of contracts the promise is merged into the concept of offer. The following case deals with an inverted unilateral contract. It involves an idea for a film for which a promise to pay was enforced as a contract.

FACTS

Blaustein is suing Richard and Elizabeth Burton for breach of contract, unjust enrichment, breach of confidential relationship, services rendered, and benefits conferred on the grounds that the Burtons had used Blaustein's idea for filming *The Taming of the Shrew* without compensating Blaustein. Blaustein had come to the Burtons and had explained to them his ideas about making the film.

DECISION

The court held the Burtons liable for breach of contract on the basis that they had breached an inverted unilateral contract. The court noted that a contract for the conveyance of, and payment for, an idea may be either express or implied where an idea has been conveyed with the expectation that compensation will be paid by the recipient if the idea is used. The recipient may thereafter gratuitously promise to pay a reasonable compensation for the idea and create a valid obligation. This is what happened in this case when an inverted unilateral contract was created. The conveyance of the idea was the act in search of a promise to compensate.

Blaustein v. Burton, 88 Cal.Rptr. 319 (Cal. 1970).

► Certainty of Terms Test

certainty of terms test
The promise must have certainty of terms in what it promises and what it asks for

Before a proper promise[1] can result in an offer, it must have **certainty of terms**. A promise can undertake only two things: an act or a forbearance (refraining from doing something). The promise can ask from the offeree only three things in exchange: an act, a forbearance, or the offeree's return promise. The promise must tell the offeree what the offeree is to do (an act) or refrain from doing (a forbearance), and what the offeror will do or will not do. (I'll pay you $100 for digging the ditch. The offeror's promise is to do an act—to pay $100; the offeree is to do an act—to dig the ditch.) If the offer does not objectively manifest the promise, it will fail for uncertainty of terms and no contract can be formed.

One can understand why advertisements are not intended to be offers. Advertisements normally state what the promisee is required to do, but they do not normally state what the promisor/offeror will do because no limit is placed upon what the promisor will be required to do. Is the promisor willing to sell one item, 200 items, or an infinite quantity? This question is not answered in the typical advertisement; therefore it is not an offer. Normally an advertisement is construed as soliciting or inviting offers. (Al reads an advertisement in the local newspaper for frying chickens at 59 cents per pound. When Al takes a chicken to the checkout counter, Al is making an offer to the store through its clerk to buy the chicken for 59 cents per pound.) However, advertisements can be offers when it is obvious from the way they are phrased that this is the intent of the advertiser and when the advertisement leaves nothing open to negotiation. (Al advertises in a large Chicago newspaper that Al will pay a specified reward to anyone who gives Al certain information within one year. Bo sees a copy of the advertisement one month later and immediately sends the requested information to Bo. The advertisement is an offer by Al. There is a contract between Al and Al will have to pay the reward to Bo.) Under a rule promulgated by the Federal Trade Commission, goods advertised as *specials* must be available for purchase at the advertised price unless a specific quantity is indicated in the advertisement. A raincheck must be provided for later purchase if the item is unavailable for a reason beyond the control of the store. The following case illustrates how the consumer is entitled to a *statutory remedy* when the requirements of the rule are not observed by the seller.

FACTS

J. C. Penney Company ran an advertisement in a newspaper which stated that it had a number of small appliances including a waffle baker for sale at $9.99. The sale was advertised as a closeout with limited quantities available. The specific number of items for sale did not appear in the advertisement. Weaver sought to purchase a waffle baker and was

[1]See p. 121. In Chapter 6 we noted that social obligations, illegal objectives, and objectives violative of public policy contained in promises would not be enforced as contracts.

told that they had all been sold. Mr. Weaver asked for a raincheck giving him the right to purchase a waffle baker for $9.99 in the future, but since Penney was not going to stock the item in the future they refused his request. Mr. Weaver sued Penney claiming a violation of a substantive rule of the Ohio Department of Commerce pursuant to the Ohio Consumer Sales Practice Act. The lower court held for J. C. Penney Company and the case is before the court on appeal.

DECISION

The court decided for Weaver, stating that a failure to state a specific quantity of waffle bakers available for sale and a refusal to issue a raincheck or place an order for the waffle baker at $9.99 constituted a deceptive sales practice under rule 3-01.03(A)(2)(d) which provides: it is a deceptive act or practice to (d) fail to give rainchecks to consumers after the original quantity of goods is exhausted or to refuse to take orders for the advertised goods or services at the advertised price to be delivered within a reasonable period of time, unless the supplier has clearly and adequately disclosed the specific quantity of advertised goods or services available. The court noted that for a deceptive act or practice the statute provided that the consumer could rescind the transaction or recover actual damages or $100.

Weaver v. J. C. Penney Company, 372 N.E.2d 633 (Ohio 1977).

auction
A public sale of property by public outcry to the highest bidder

Similar points can be raised regarding catalogs or requests for bids to be made by contractors on jobs. These are not offers but invitations to make offers. Generally, a bid is an offer; but special rules apply to **auctions** of property. In an auction "with reserve," the auctioneer reserves the right to accept or reject any bid and a bid is an offer. In an auction "without reserve," the auctioneer does not reserve such right and a bid is an acceptance of the auctioneer's offer to sell. In both auctions a bid may be withdrawn until the auctioneer announces completion of the sale.[2]

cost-plus contract
A contract in which the price is the cost of production or performance (whatever it turns out to be) plus an agreed-upon profit

Under the common law, if the promise contained in the offer includes a formula that will in the future provide the terms of the certainty of terms test, the offer will not fail for uncertainty of terms. An example of a contract that contains a formula that provides certainty of terms is a **cost-plus contract.**

► Intention Test

intention test
The promise must cause the offeree reasonably to believe that the promise was intended to be an offer

One must intend to make an offer before an offer legally exists. Whatever form the certainty of terms statement takes, it must be done with the intent to make an offer. The certainty of terms statement taken alone is not enough to be construed as an offer.

The **intention test** is concerned with a person's expression and its interpretation by a reasonable person to whom it was made that the expression was intended to be an offer. The person making the expression may not have intended it to be an offer; but if the expression is interpreted as an offer by the reasonable person to whom it was made, then it is an offer. The intention test will not result in an offer without certainty of terms being satisfied. *Both* the certainty of terms test and the intention test must be satisfied before an offer will exist. In the following case the court found an expression to be reasonably understood as manifesting an intent to make an offer.

[2]See RESTATEMENT (SECOND) OF CONTRACTS sec. 28 (1982) and UCC 2-328.

FACTS

George Braun, who was an employee of Northeast Station and Services, Inc., was a victim of a robbery on the business premises where he was employed. In response to the robbery, Northeast Station and Services posted the following at the place of the robbery:

> "NOTICE $5,000 REWARD" and in print less than one-eighth size of those words "A reward of up to $5,000 will be paid for information leading to the arrest and conviction of anyone robbing this station or attendant on duty."

George Braun gave information which led to the arrest and conviction of the robber. Northeast Station and Services contends that the language in the *small print* does not evidence an intent to make an offer.

DECISION

The court held for George Braun. The court said that parties purporting to act seriously in making an offer will be taken to have intended that the offer will have meaning and the court will attempt to ascertain the meaning intended and give it effect. The clear purpose and intention of the notices posted by Northeast Station and Services was to convey an offer of a $5,000 reward, thus to compensate responsive effort beyond the ordinary value of services sought to be performed. The language in the small print should only be read to limit the amount of the reward to a maximum of $5,000 in the event there are multiple claimants to the reward.

Braun v. Northeast Station and Services, Inc., 461 N.Y.S.2d 623 (N.Y. 1983).

► Bringing the Contract into Existence

If certainty of terms and intention tests of an offer are satisfied, and if the offer has been communicated to the offeree, the offeror has given the offeree the ability to bring a contract into existence by the offeree's acceptance of the offer. In the *unilateral contractual situation*, the contract comes into existence by the offeree's acceptance in performing, or refraining from doing, the requested act. In the *bilateral contractual situation*, the contract comes into existence by the offeree's acceptance in giving the requested return promise, to the offeror. (Angela asks Bill to paint Angela's fence. Bill paints Angela's fence. Angela asks Bill to promise to pay the selling price Angela is asking for Angela's used car and Bill so promises. In each case, Bill, by doing what was requested in the offer, created a contract.)

► Communicating the Offer: Express and Implied Terms

In order for the offeree to bring a contract into existence, the offeree must have notice of the offer. This requires that the offer be communicated to the offeree in some fashion. The offeror may communicate the offer to the offeree directly or through some third party or other agency. If the offeree does what the offeror requests without notice of the offer, no contract results because, since the offeree did not rely on any offer, there is no acceptance.

The terms of an offer can be distributed to the general public at large by announcements, such as for rewards, or to particular members of the public by use of tickets or stubs, such as terms on the back of airline tickets or claim tickets. In the following case the court held that a **bailee,** in a **bailment** contract,[3] could not limit its liability by a ticket unless its terms are called to the attention of the **bailor.**

bailee
The person to whom goods are bailed

bailment
A delivery of goods by a bailor to a bailee which are to be returned to the bailor or as the bailor directs, in accordance with the bailment agreement

bailor
The person who bails goods

[3]The subject of bailments is considered in Chapter 21.

FACTS

The Brooks alleged that they sustained damage to their couch and chair pillow covers left with Angelo's Cleaners for cleaning. The trial court found that the items were damaged because of improper drycleaning by Angelo's Cleaners. Angelo's Cleaners contends relief from liability by the inclusion of a disclaimer of responsibility to warrant work contained on the reverse side of the cleaning ticket.

DECISION

The court held for the Brooks and noted that no notice was given to the Brooks that there was a risk attendant to drycleaning the covers and that Angelo's Cleaners intended to disclaim responsibility for their own negligence. Under such circumstances, the disclaimer is ineffective.

Brooks, et al. v. Angelo's Cleaners, 477 N.Y.S.2d 922 (N.Y. 1984).

► Duration of the Offer

In the absence of a time period stated in the offer, an offer expires after the passage of a *reasonable time*. The reasonable time period can be short or long, depending upon whether the subject matter of the offer is perishable or fluctuating greatly in value over short periods of time. Also, the offer expires and ceases to exist if the offeror or offeree becomes mentally ill (insane) or dies. If performance of the contemplated contract to be formed in the future becomes illegal—normally because of enactment of a criminal statute—the offer which looks to the formation of the future contract expires because of the subsequent illegality. Destruction of the specific subject matter of an offer before acceptance occurs by performance causes the offer to expire, and since there is no offer to accept there cannot be a contract. (See Figure 7.2.) In the following case an offer ends by the expiration of a stated period of time.

FACTS

Sullivan became interested in purchasing a tract of land owned by Economic Research Properties. Sullivan, through his agent Hone, mailed a written offer to Economic Research Properties for acceptance through February 4, 1980. Economic Research Properties made several changes to the offer including extending the time for acceptance through February 14, 1980 so as to allow sufficient time for the counteroffer to reach Sullivan via the mails and for him to execute it. On February 19, 1980, Economic Research Properties called Sullivan and advised him that negotiations were terminated. This oral conversation was confirmed by telegram on February 25, 1980. The trial court specifically found that no contract for sale existed because "Sullivan failed to accept timely, within the time specified, the counteroffer for

FIGURE 7.2 **Stated Time Periods Measuring Duration of Offer**

Dated Offer	Undated Offer	Delayed Undated Offer
May 1. Stated time period 10 days. Offer ends on May 11.	Received June 6. Stated time period 20 days. Offer ends on June 26.	Received June 9, should have been received June 6. Stated time period 20 days. With notice of delay, offer ends on June 26. Without notice of delay, offer ends June 29.

a contract submitted by Economic Research Properties." The case is before this court on appeal.

DECISION

The court held for Economic Research Properties. The court recognized the general principle that the acceptance of an offer, to result in a contract, must be absolute and unconditional, identical with the terms of the offer and in the mode, at the place and within the time expressly or impliedly required by the offer. The court stated that there can be no question that when an offer is made for a time limited in the offer itself, no acceptance afterwards will make it binding. Any offer without consideration may be withdrawn at any time before acceptance; and an offer which in its terms limits the time of acceptance is withdrawn by the expiration of the time.

Sullivan v. Economic Research Properties, 455 So.2d 630 (Fla. 1984).

The offer can end also by revocation, rejection and counteroffer. These means of ending an offer are equally applicable to the potential bilateral or unilateral contract.

Revocation of an offer occurs when the offeror recalls the offer. Revocation takes place when notice is received by the offeree that the offer no longer exists. Actual notice of the ending of the offer need not be received by the offeree from the offeror to cause the offer to end. For example, if the offeree finds out that the subject matter of the offer has been disposed of by the offeror, the offer is revoked. Revocation also occurs when the offeror delivers a notice of revocation to the offeree's place of business, personal residence, or **agent** with authority or apparent authority to receive notices for the offeree. The notice of revocation is effective whether or not it is read by the offeree. However, a public offer, as in reward situations, is revoked when a revocation is distributed using the same means that were used to communicate the offer.

revocation
The offeror's recalling of the offeree's power to accept as contained in the offer

agent
A person authorized to act on behalf of another and subject to the other's control

Rejection of an offer occurs by the offeree's act refusing the offer. Rejection takes effect when a rejection or counteroffer to an original offer is received by an offeror. The same requirements for notice discussed for revocation are applicable for rejection and counteroffer. A **rejection** is some expression by the offeree that indicates that the offeree is not interested in the offer. A **counteroffer** is an offer made by the offeree that changes the terms of the original offer and, therefore, under the common law is a rejection of the original offer. A type of counteroffer is the "conditional acceptance"—there is a purported acceptance of the offer but the acceptance is conditioned upon the assent of the offeror to additional or different terms.

rejection
The offeree's expression refusing the offer

counteroffer
An offer that rejects a previous offer

Two kinds of irrevocable offer that are of great importance in business are the *option* and the *firm offer*.

Option, Under the Common Law Under the common law, an *option contract* is a contract to keep an offer stated therein open for a definite time. The offer is irrevocable and is called an **option.** The option offer looks to the formation of a future contract. The effect of an option contract is to prevent the offeror from withdrawing the option offer for a stated period of time or until a specified date, unless the offeror wishes to take the risk of being sued for breach of the option contract. The offeree must pay (give consideration) for the option in order to have an option contract. (I'll sell you this land for $30,000, and I'll keep my offer open for ninety days if you will pay me $1,000—which the offeree then pays. There is a contract to keep the offer to sell open for ninety days.)

option
The irrevocable offer in an option contract

In the situation where the offer requests solely an act (and not a return promise) in order to create a unilateral contract, the offeror can revoke the offer only before the offeree starts to perform. Once the offeree has started to perform the requested act, an

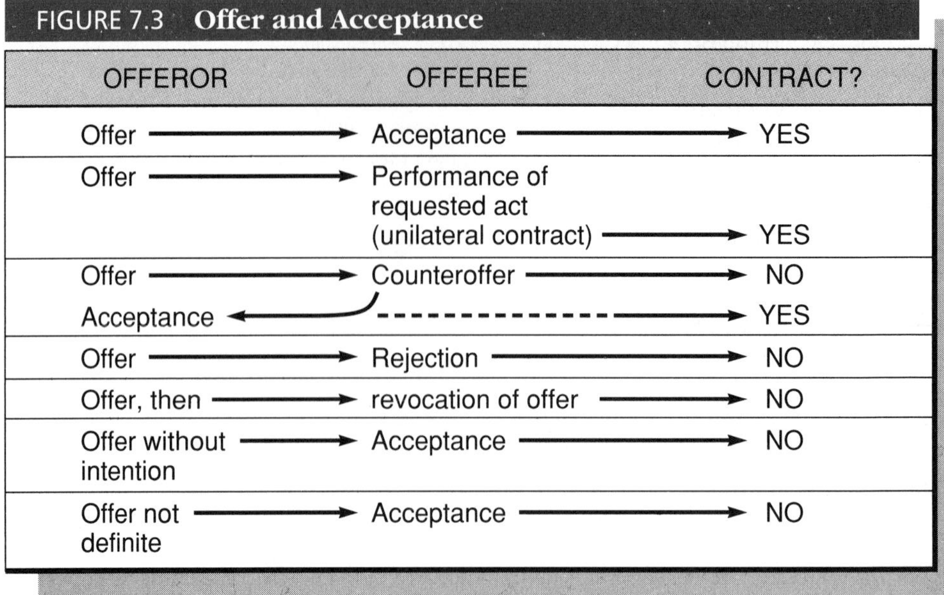

FIGURE 7.3 **Offer and Acceptance**

OFFEROR	OFFEREE	CONTRACT?
Offer →	Acceptance →	YES
Offer →	Performance of requested act (unilateral contract) →	YES
Offer →	Counteroffer →	NO
Acceptance ←	- - - - - - - - →	YES
Offer →	Rejection →	NO
Offer, then →	revocation of offer →	NO
Offer without intention →	Acceptance →	NO
Offer not definite →	Acceptance →	NO

reasonable amount of time in which the offeree may complete performance of the act necessary to bring the unilateral contract into existence. The offeror cannot revoke the offer prior to the expiration of that time, because to do so would be unfair to the offeree who has started to perform the requested act. (Cathy offers to pay Beck $150 for painting a tall pipe. When Beck has started to paint the pipe, Cathy cannot revoke the offer. Beck's beginning to paint created an option contract.) In the following case the employer could not revoke its offer for a unilateral contract pension plan once the employee had begun to comply with the offer.

FACTS

Miller, a retired employee, brought suit against his employer, Dictaphone Corporation, for breach of contract with regard to an employee pension plan. Originally Miller had agreed to enter into the pension plan and allow deductions from his pay. He had worked for some seven months before he received notice from his employer of the potential change in benefits. The employer informed the employee that he would not be covered by the pension plan. Miller contended that Dictaphone could not revoke its unilateral contract offer to include him in the pension plan. Dictaphone contended it could revoke its offer.

DECISION

The court held for Miller and said that the signing of the plan and the employee's engaging in work for the employer constituted substantial performance, after which the employer's unilateral contract offer, embodied in the original announcement for enrollment in the pension plan, could not be revoked. The court held that an offer for a unilateral contract may not be revoked after substantial performance has taken place.

Miller v. Dictaphone Corp., 334 F.Supp. 840 (1971).

[4]See Restatement (Second) of Contracts sec. 45 (1982).

Firm Offer, Under the Code The Uniform Commercial Code governs commercial transactions concerning personal property, for example a sale of goods. To the extent that the Code conflicts with the common law, the Code governs. The common law supplements the Code and applies if the Code does not provide to the contrary. For example, the Code does not define an offer and, therefore, the common law of contracts applies.

We have just discussed the common law of option for which consideration is required. The Uniform Commercial Code[5] has its version of the common law option when the transaction involves the sale of goods. The Code provides that a written offer signed by a **merchant** to buy or sell goods which gives assurance that it will be held open is not revocable for a stated time or, if no time is stated, for a reasonable time. The maximum amount of time that the offer will not be revocable is three months. Such an offer is called a **firm offer.** (I'll sell you this machine for $900, and I'll keep my offer open for sixty days—which is in writing and signed by the merchant offeror.)

The offeree need not pay (give consideration) for the firm offer to make it binding upon the offeror, as is necessary to the creation of the option contract under the common law. But if consideration is given, there will be an option as well as a firm offer. However, the offeror will not be bound to the firm offer if it is contained in a form supplied by the offeree and the offeror has not **signed** the clause containing the firm offer provision.[6]

merchant

A person who deals in goods or, by occupation, holds himself or herself out as having knowledge or skill in a transaction concerning goods, or who uses someone who holds himself or herself out as having such knowledge or skill in a transaction concerning goods

firm offer

A merchant's signed irrevocable offer to buy or sell goods, giving assurance that it will be kept open; consideration is not required, and its maximum time is three months

signed

"Includes any symbol executed or adopted by a party with present intention to authenticate a writing" UCC 1-201(39)

► Under the Uniform Commercial Code

As under the common law of contracts, the Uniform Commercial Code Article on Sales of goods places a heavy reliance upon the intention test—that is, the intent of the parties to make an offer.[7] This can be seen in the Code's reliance upon conduct of the parties in determining whether an offer was made[8] and the Code's lack of concern with regard to the moment when the offer effectively formed the basis for springing a contract into existence.[9]

The Code deemphasizes the certainty of terms test and is willing to rely heavily upon flexible terms like "reasonable" and "seasonable" in the determination of what the offeror has stated will be done or not done and what the offeree must do or not do.[10] The Code also relies heavily upon "course of dealing" and "usage of trade" in interpreting terminology used in an offer.[11]

The approach used in the Uniform Commercial Code provides significant differences from the common law of offer. The changes are limited to offers which have goods as their subject matter.

---

[5]UCC 2-205.

[6]Offers irrevocable by statute: bids for state, municipality or other governmental body; preincorporation stock subscription agreements. See Revised Model Business Corporation Act sec. 6.20(a) (1984).

[7]UCC 2-204(3).

[8]UCC 2-204(1), 1–201(3).

[9]UCC 2-204(2).

[10]UCC 1-204.

[11]UCC 1-205.

Code Offer Under the Uniform Commercial Code an offer will not fail for uncertainty of terms if price is not stated[12] if the parties intend a contract for sale with price to be established in the future. Nor will a contract of purchase fail though no quantity is specified if the contract provides for a portion of the seller's "output" or for the buyer's "needs" or "requirements."

In each case the Code establishes and relies upon formulae external to the offer to establish the terms of price and quantity. In the case of price, the market itself establishes the terms. The controlling price will always be a reasonable price for like goods as the goods would have sold for at the time and place of delivery. In the case of quantity, past ability to produce (an output contract) or consume (a requirements contract) the items in question provides the formula which will determine quantity.[13]

In the following case a requirements contract was deemed *not* to fail because of indefiniteness.

FACTS

The legal controversy centers on the following agreement:

March 9, 1977
Mr. John B. Stacks
Route 1
Damacus, Arkansas

Dear Mr. Stacks:
With further reference to our conversations in regard to our supplying you with motor gasoline at your gasoline outlet which is now under construction in Bee Branch, I have listed below the points which we discussed Sunday, February 20, 1977:

1. We agree to furnish you fuel in an amount up to 50,000 gallons per month. We will withhold this amount from our various allotments. The amounts will be subject to allocation adjustments by the Federal Energy Administration.
2. We will be your exclusive supplier upon the following terms: (a) Costs will be laid-in costs per gallon plus $.01 per gallon; (b) gallons will be temperature corrected; and (c) billing terms will be net 4 days from invoice.
3. If the Federal Energy Administration allocation falls below 96%, terms in "a" will be negotiated and revised upward.

The above is, in substance, the terms upon which we agreed in our meeting. Please sign below after our signatures and return the original to me.

F & S Petroleum Company, Inc.

/s/ Dee Francy, President
/s/ John B. Stacks

Stacks contends the foregoing agreement is indefinite and fails to obligate Stacks for gasoline subsequently supplied to Stacks' outlet.

F & S Petroleum sued Stacks for gasoline supplied at the sales price stipulated in the agreement. Judgment was rendered for Stacks and F & S Petroleum appeals.

DECISION

The court held for F & S Petroleum. Under the Uniform Commercial Code, a requirements contract is simply an agreement by the buyer to buy the buyer's good faith requirements exclusively from the seller. The buyer, who will determine quantity, is required to operate the buyer's plant or conduct business in good faith according to commercial standards of fair dealing in the trade so that the buyer's requirements will approximate a reasonably foreseeable figure and not be indefinite. The fact that the agreement left open the number of gallons to be purchased monthly does not support invalidation of the agreement.

Stacks v. F & S Petroleum Co., 641 S.W.2d 726 (Ark. 1982).

The end result of this approach is to use reliable formulae to ensure commercial honesty and restrict sharp business practices and yet facilitate the transaction of business.

---

[12]UCC 2-305.

[13]UCC 2-306.

The Acceptance

▶ The Concept

An **acceptance** is the offeree's assent to the offer by performing the act or forbearance, or by giving a return promise, in reliance on and in compliance with the offer. By accepting an offer, the offeree has brought a contract into existence.

acceptance
The offeree's expressed assent to the offer in reliance on and in compliance with the offer

In the bilateral contractual situation, the contract comes into existence the moment the return promise requested is effectively communicated to the offeror.

In the unilateral contractual situation, the contract comes into existence the moment the requested act or forbearance has been performed. If the offer requires notice of performance by the offeree, then such notice must be given. However, on performance of the act or forbearance, there is an acceptance and the contract immediately comes into existence irrespective of whether or not notice has been given. While the offer may not expressly require notice, it may impliedly require notice if the offeree reasonably can believe that the offeror will not learn of his or her performance within a reasonable time in the ordinary course of affairs. Failure to give such notice causes the offeror to be **discharged** from his or her contract. It should be noted that, once performance is begun by the offeree, the offer is irrevocable by the offeror and can be accepted only by full performance. In the following case full performance of the act did not occur; so, without an acceptance, there was no unilateral contract.

discharge
Termination of a contractual duty to perform a promise

FACTS

This breach of contract action is based on a series of communications by U.S. Steel Corporation to the workers at its Mahoning Valley plants. The workers allege these communications constitute a promise by the company to keep the mills operating if and so long as the workers made the mills profitable. Due to continuing losses, U.S. Steel closed the mills and the workers seek damages.

DECISION

The court held for U.S. Steel and stated that the alleged contract must either be unilateral or bilateral—that is, parties must either exchange a promise for a promise or a promise for an act. In this action, plaintiffs' allegation can be simplified as follows: the company promised to keep the plants operational as long as they remained profitable, and the workers in fact made the plants profitable. Therefore, the contract must be of the unilateral type. At the time the alleged promise was made by the company, the workers did not immediately execute the contract in full—profitability would have to be achieved over a long period of hard work. This means that the contract would not come into existence until the workers had *fully performed* their side of the contract making the plant profitable. A unilateral contract does not come into existence until one party to it has done all that is necessary on that party's part. In this case, that did not happen.

United Steel Workers of America, Local No. 1330 et al. v. U.S. Steel Corp., 492 F.Supp. 1 (1980).

To be effective, the acceptance must be unqualified or unconditional (no new terms added) under the common law and made by the offeree. An attempt to accept an offer by someone other than the offeree will not cause a contract to come into existence. Only the intended offeree can accept the offer.

The offeree usually has the choice of accepting or rejecting the offer. Inaction on the part of the offeree normally results in the offer expiring because of the passage of time. Unless otherwise indicated by language or circumstances, an offer by mail is not **seasonably** accepted if an acceptance is mailed anytime after midnight on the day on which the offer is received.

seasonably
"An action is taken seasonably when it is taken at or within the time agreed or if no time is agreed at or within a reasonable time" UCC 1-204(3)

course of dealing
"A sequence of previous conduct between the parties to a particular transaction which is fairly to be regarded as establishing a common basis of understanding for interpreting their expressions and other conduct" UCC 1-205(1)

Unless otherwise agreed, silence is not normally a manifestation of assent and is not an acceptance. If, however, past **course of dealing** has made silence an acceptance, active rejection of the offer by the offeree will be necessary to prevent the silence from being an acceptance and resulting in the formation of a contract. Silence plus the offeree's use of the subject matter of the offer normally results in an implied acceptance of the offer under the common law. However, by statute, unsolicited items received through the mail can be used without creating a contract. Silence or inaction of a manufacturing or merchandise distributing company soliciting offers by salespersons for acceptance at the home office will be treated as an acceptance if rejection of the offer is not given to the offeror within a reasonable period of time. In the following case the defendant's silence in not objecting to the renewal of an insurance policy did not constitute an acceptance of such policy contract.

FACTS

This is an appeal from a judgment awarding to the J. C. Durick Insurance Company premiums allegedly due on an insurance contract sold by Andrus. Andrus's apartment building was insured against fire loss under a policy sold by J. C. Durick Insurance which had expired and contained two provisions for automatic renewal. Some two months before the expiration date, J. C. Durick Insurance wrote Andrus recommending increasing coverage for the building. Andrus telephoned J. C. Durick Insurance and told it that if he could not obtain insurance for just $24,000, which was the outstanding balance on his mortgage, he would be forced to obtain insurance elsewhere. J. C. Durick Insurance sent Adrus a new policy with a face amount of $48,000. This policy contained the provision that Andrus could "cancel the new policy by returning the policy itself or the last policy receipt. Absent that, the policy would be automatically accepted through the inaction of Andrus." Andrus did not respond and was sued for nonpayment of premiums which had fallen due under the purported insurance contract.

J. C. Durick Insurance contends that Andrus's silence was an acceptance of its offer to reinsure creating a new contract, and that Andrus was liable for premiums under it. Andrus contends that his silence was not an acceptance.

DECISION

The court held for Andrus and stated that an offeror cannot force the offeree to speak or be bound by his silence. Silence gives consent oniy where there is a duty to speak. There is no such duty here. The past dealings of the parties establish no course of conduct, and the record is silent as to custom within the industry, or the defendant's familiarity therewith. Under these circumstances there was no acceptance, hence no contract and no premiums.

J. C. Durick Ins. v. Andrus, 424 A.2d 249 (Vt. 1980).

There are exceptional instances where the offeree cannot refuse to accept the offer. These instances arise primarily because of statutory law, the typical example of which would be antidiscrimination laws that prevent an individual who has solicited offers from the public to refuse to accept the tendered offer because of color, religion, sex, race, or nationality. This is a further inroad on the freedom to contract but an inroad approved of by legislative bodies for some more important, usually public, purpose.

► Communication of the Acceptance

medium
An agency, instrument, means, or channel

Expressly Authorized Medium If the offeree uses the expressly authorized **medium** for accepting the offer, the acceptance becomes effective when sent. The contract is formed the moment the message is delivered to the indicated medium. For example, the acceptance would be effective the moment the letter was mailed, the telegram handed to the telegraph clerk, or the acceptance spoken into the phone. The acceptance is effective though it might never be received by the offeror. However, if the offeror specifies or makes the use of a particular medium for communicating the acceptance a condition of acceptance, then the use of any other medium will result in a counteroffer. (Al's letter to Bo states "reply only by telephone." Bo replies by letter. There is no acceptance.)

The offeror can require actual receipt of the acceptance as necessary to the formation of a contract. In this circumstance a contract can result only if the acceptance is actually received while the offer continues in existence.

Both the common law and the Uniform Commercial Code are in agreement on the above points.[14] In the following case the company's offer required receipt of acceptance to be effective as an acceptance, and, since the offeree died before his acceptance was effective, there was no acceptance. The offer had expired by the offeree's death.

FACTS

On February 24, 1984, Koch enrolled in a group insurance policy that provided for $100,000 accidental death benefits. In 1985, American Heritage sent Koch a premium notice that included an application to increase his accidental death benefits to $150,000. Koch signed the application on March 26, 1985 and on March 29, 1985 Mrs. Koch mailed the application and a check for the additional premiums to American Heritage's agent, Kirk-Van Orsdel, Inc. (Orsdel). Orsdel received the application and additional premiums on April 3, 1985, and negotiated the check the following day. On April 16, 1985, Koch died in an automobile accident. American Heritage paid $100,000, representing the proceeds of the original policy. Mrs. Koch contends she is entitled to $150,000 based upon the application she mailed. She contends a contract was formed under the "mailbox rule" which provides that when a party makes an offer through the mail, the contract is created when a written acceptance by the offeree, properly addressed and stamped, is deposited with the post office. The application provided that the increased coverage would "become effective upon the first day of the month following the *receipt* of my premium payment."

DECISION

The court held for American Heritage. The court said the "mailbox rule" does not apply if the offer, as here, contains a stipulation that the acceptance must be received before the contract is complete. The plain language of this offer requires that acceptance be actually received before calculating when coverage began. Since Koch's application and additional premiums were not received by Orsdel until April 3, 1985, the increased coverage would not have become effective until May 1, 1985, after Koch's death.

American Heritage Life Ins. Co. v. Koch, 721 S.W.2d 611 (Tex. 1986).

Impliedly Authorized Medium If the offeror does not require actual receipt of the acceptance and does not indicate the communication medium, the medium used by the offeror to send the offer becomes impliedly authorized as a medium for acceptance. Also, impliedly authorized is any medium customarily used for transactions of that nature at the place where the offer was received.

Deposit Rule The use of the expressly or impliedly authorized means by the offeree to communicate the acceptance will cause the acceptance to become effective and brings

deposit rule
An acceptance is effective when sent, though never received, if an authorized medium is timely used by the offeree

[14]UCC 2-206(1).

the contract into existence the moment the acceptance is delivered to the medium of communication. Again, the acceptance is effective though it might never be received by the offeror.

Unauthorized Medium Any medium not expressly nor impliedly authorized is unauthorized. If the offer requires the use exclusively of a specific medium for acceptance, the offeree's use of an unauthorized medium is not an acceptance but, instead, is a rejection and a counteroffer. If the offer does not require such an exclusive medium but suggests or invites a medium, then the offeree's use of an unauthorized medium is an acceptance *when sent*, not when received by the offeror. Such receipt, however, must be within the time expectations that the offeror had for receipt from the impliedly authorized agency. (Al uses the mail asking for an acceptance by mail. It takes three days for the letter to get to Bud without delay. Al's expectation, at the outside, for the receipt of the acceptance by mail is probably six days. If Bud uses a telegram and the telegraphed acceptance arrives within six days after the offer was sent by Al, under the common law the telegram is treated as an acceptance. However, if the telegram arrives ten days after the offer was sent by Al, under the common law the telegram will be treated as a counteroffer.)

Timeliness In order for the acceptance to be timely in the expressly and impliedly authorized medium situations, it should be capable of being received within the stated time required by the offeror, and in the absence of a stated time, then within a reasonable time. If the acceptance is not timely, then the offer expires, and the offeree's late-attempted acceptance is a new offer.

The only difference in the unauthorized situation is that the acceptance must be received within the stated time required by the offer or, in the absence of a stated time, within a reasonable time.

► Under the Uniform Commercial Code

Under the Code,[15] unless the offeror clearly requires otherwise, if the offeree uses a medium reasonable in the circumstances to communicate an acceptance, such use will spring a contract into existence immediately when the acceptance is sent even though it is never received by the offeror.

A medium reasonable in the circumstances is one which the offeree calculates will enable the timely receipt of the acceptance by the offeror—for example, mail, telegram, telephone, depending on the circumstances.

A Code change in the common law is that an offer to buy goods to be shipped may be accepted either by shipment, creating a unilateral contract, or by a prompt promise to ship, creating a bilateral contract. Under the common law, such a promise to ship would have been construed as a counteroffer.

In addition, the seller's shipment of nonconforming goods will be an acceptance and result in a contract unless the seller clearly indicates that such shipment is a counteroffer being made for the accommodation of the buyer. Under the common law such a shipment would always have resulted in a counteroffer.

---

[15] UCC 2-206.

Confirmation and Additional Terms in Acceptance Under the Code,[16] the offeree's written confirmation of an offer is an acceptance. This is not so under the common law, because a confirmation merely acknowledges receipt of the offer and does not assent to the offer.

Also under the Code, a definite and reasonable expression of acceptance can act as an acceptance though it states terms additional to or different from those offered, unless the offeree clearly indicates that the offeree is making a counteroffer. In such a case, there is a contract to the extent that the terms of the offer are accepted, and the additional terms stated by the offeree are a counteroffer by the offeree. Under the common law the result is always a counteroffer in the described situation. (Sue offers to sell Bud 1,000 raincoats at $20 each. Bud replies that he will take 500 at $20 and 500 at $18 each. Under the common law of contracts, there is no acceptance and no contract. Under the Code, there is an acceptance and a contract for 500 at $20 each and a counteroffer for 500 at $18 each.)

The Code provides formulas to determine what the terms of the contract will be. Between the parties, the changes must be consented to by the offeror before they become part of the contract.

Between merchants, the additional terms automatically become part of the contract unless (a) the offer expressly limits acceptance to the terms of the offer, (b) the changes materially alter the offer, or (c) notification of objection to changes in the terms of the offer has already been given or is given within a reasonable time after notice of them is received. In the above example, Bud's counteroffer of $18 materially alters the offer.

If parties by their conduct recognize the existence of a contract, then there is a contract. The terms of the contract will be established by the writings of the parties where agreement exists and also by supplementary terms incorporated under any other provision of the Code, as has been illustrated in this chapter for open quantity and price terms. In the following case the court recognized that a contract existed by the conduct of the parties.

FACTS

Alliance Wall Corporation, seller, and Ampat Midwest Corporation, buyer, entered into an agreement for the sale of over two hundred aluminum panels. A purchase order was received by the seller which stated upon release of production ship "you (Alliance) truck" FOB Okmulgee, Oklahoma. The seller acknowledged the purchase order.

On September 1 the buyer sent the release of production and wrote "Shipment should occur as soon as possible and certainly within seven (7) weeks of the date of this release." The seller responded in writing stating that the "tentative shipping date was November 6, 1981." On October 5, 1981, the buyer was informed by the seller that the tentative shipping date was now to be November 20, 1981. On October 22, 1981, the seller received a letter from the buyer dated October 14, 1981 stating that the revised shipping date was not acceptable. This letter demanded better service and threatened to charge to the seller any expenses experienced by the buyer due to its inability to meet its contractual commitments because of lack of materials. To this letter the seller replied, stating "Any threat to charge us with expenses will not be accepted and if you do not withdraw your threat we will not fill your order and you can purchase your material requirements elsewhere. We very frankly are exerting all possible pressure on our supplier to speed up their delivery of aluminum and

[16] UCC 2-207.

our plant personnel has been alerted to the urgency of your order. However, we cannot and will not work under threats." The goods were shipped November 20, 1981 and were received on November 23, 1981. The goods were used and a partial payment on purchase price was made. Ampat Midwest, buyer, now contends that no contract exists between it and Alliance Wall, seller, for the purchase of the aluminum panels.

DECISION

The court held for the seller, Alliance Wall. The court said that the parties did not agree to a material term, the shipment date. This failure to agree prevented the formation of a contract at that time. The court noted that in the usual case, the seller's written confirmation "operates as an acceptance even though it states terms additional or different from those offered." In such cases the material terms of the contract are the buyer's terms. This rule, however, does not apply where the parties disagree as to "dickered for" terms like shipping date in this case. In such a case, a contract formation does not occur until both sides have at least partially performed. Here, the goods were shipped and received, and the price partially paid. *This was conduct by both parties sufficient to establish a contract.*

Therefore the terms of the contract consist of the terms upon which the parties agreed together with the "gap-filler" provisions of the Uniform Commercial Code. The relevant "gap-filler," for purposes of this case, is the time for shipment. In absence of an agreed-upon time for delivery, the Code prescribes that it shall be a "reasonable time." As of the time of the formation of the contract, a reasonable time under the circumstances was within a reasonable time after the seller was able to obtain its raw materials. This was November 20, 1981, the actual date of shipment.

Alliance Wall Corp. v. Ampat Midwest Corp., 477 N.E.2d 1206 (Ohio 1984).

Summary Statement

1. The offer contains the required promise necessary for the formation of a contract.
2. To be effective, an offer must be communicated to the offeree, be intended to be an offer, and in addition must contain certainty of terms (intentions test and certainty of terms test).
3. Offers do not last forever. Some expire after the passage of a stated period of time; some end after the passage of a reasonable time; and others end by the death or mental incompetence (insanity) of the offeror or offeree.
4. Offers can also end by revocation, rejection and counteroffer, and subsequent illegality.
5. The concepts of option and of firm offer limit the ability of the offeror to revoke the offer without being responsible to the offeree for damages for breach of contract on the offeree's acceptance.
6. The Uniform Commercial Code has vastly changed the impact of the common law on offers that have goods as their subject matter. The purpose of these changes is to facilitate commercial transactions and promote commercial honesty.
7. The act of acceptance springs a contract into existence.
8. The acceptance must be unqualified and made with the intent to accept.
9. An authorized means for communicating an acceptance must be used in order for the deposit rule to be applicable.
10. The use of an unauthorized means for communicating the acceptance can result in a counteroffer.
11. The Uniform Commercial Code significantly changes the common law of acceptance when the subject matter of the contract is goods.

12. In addition to the Uniform Commercial Code, other statutes have an impact on the law of offer and acceptance in order to accomplish other goals.
13. The law of offer and acceptance conceptually sets a limit on the freedom of contract by the requirements needed to be fulfilled before a contract can come into existence.
14. This area of contract law is still evolving.

The point made in Chapter 6 that it may be unlawful *not* to contract is illustrated by the following case. Because of a right guaranteed to one party by statute, another party loses the right not to contract. The point being made by this case is that the freedom to contract does not necessarily include the freedom not to contract.

McDONALD v. VERBLE
622 F.2d 1227 (1980)

The McDonalds, husband and wife, are black citizens of the United States. The Verbles are white citizens of the United States, who were owners of property located in McArthur Park, Sandusky, Ohio (hereinafter McArthur Park property).

On or about July 3, 1975, in response to an advertisement the McDonalds called the Verbles and inquired about the property. The McDonalds were informed that the purchase price was $26,500.

On the evening of July 3, 1975 the McDonalds met the Verbles at the McArthur Park property and observed the exterior of the residence and the inside of two apartments. Later that evening the McDonalds called the Verble residence and informed Mrs. Verble that they had called about buying the McArthur Park property. The McDonalds did not receive a return phone call from the Verbles.

On Sunday, July 6, 1975 the McDonalds called the Verble residence to inquire as to the status of the property and were informed by Mr. Verble that two men were going to purchase the property. The McDonalds informed Verble that they were interested in purchasing the property. The McDonalds did not hear from the Verbles again.

The McDonalds observed that the newspaper advertisement for the sale of the property continued to appear on July 8 and 9, 1975. Thereafter the McDonalds contacted Owens, a longtime white friend of the McDonalds, to seek his help in purchasing the McArthur Park property and to ascertain whether or not the Verbles were discriminating against them on the basis of color or race. The McDonalds asked Owens to call the Verbles, make an appointment to see the property, and submit an offer to purchase the property.

On July 15, 1975 the Verbles listed the property for sale with a broker for $29,500. During the conversation between Verble and the broker on July 15, 1975, Mr. Verble told the broker that he preferred not to sell the property to blacks.

At a later date, Owens, the friend of the McDonalds, was shown the McArthur Park property by the broker. After Owens had contact with the broker, the McDonalds visited the broker's office and inquired about property for sale in the McArthur Park area and, after much evasion, the broker indicated that the McArthur Park property was for sale, but that he was interested in purchasing the property for himself. The McDonalds then told the broker that they wanted to purchase the property. The broker informed the McDonalds that the purchase price of the McArthur Park property was $29,500. In a written offer to purchase dated July 24, 1975, the McDonalds offered to purchase the McArthur Park property for $26,500, effective until July 28, 1975.

Owens testified that the broker called him and told him that the owners had a buyer, but that the owners did not want to sell to that party and that the owners might take an offer of $27,500. Owens conferred with the McDonalds who told him not to offer more than $27,500. Owens executed an offer to purchase the property for $27,500 on July 28, 1975, and the broker informed him the same day that the offer had been accepted by the Verbles. On that same day the Verbles rejected the McDonalds' offer to purchase the property for $26,500. The broker thereafter called the McDonalds and told them that their offer had been rejected. The broker admitted that after Owens placed his offer for $27,500, he did not contact the McDonalds to inform them of the offer or encourage them to "up" their own bid.

After the McDonalds were informed that their offer had been rejected, they contacted the NAACP (National Association for the Advancement of Colored People) who indicated their lawyer would look into the matter. The NAACP lawyer contacted the Verbles concerning the McDonalds' claims of discrimination on August 1, 1975. In a letter dated August 4, 1975, the broker informed the NAACP that if the present purchaser of the property was unable to complete the transaction, the Verbles were willing to sell the property to the McDonalds for $27,500.

On August 11, 1975 Owens informed the broker that he was withdrawing his offer to purchase the property. The broker informed the McDonalds that the other offer had fallen through so on August 12, 1975 the McDonalds submitted an offer to purchase the McArthur Park property for $26,500. The Verbles rejected the McDonalds' offer, as well as a subsequent offer for $27,500 submitted by the McDonalds on August 15, 1975. The Verbles said they would take nothing less than $29,500. Mr. Verble admitted at the trial that the only offers he ever got for the property were those of Owens and the McDonalds.

The McDonalds allege in their action that the Verbles had refused to sell them the McArthur Park property for racially discriminatory reasons. The Court entered a restraining order preventing the Verbles from selling the property to anyone other than the McDonalds. The Verbles subsequently withdrew their rejection of the McDonalds' offer and accepted their $27,500 offer. The McDonalds took possession of the property after executing a purchase agreement with the Verbles. The McDonalds testified that they were upset, embarrassed, and humiliated by the actions of the Verbles, which they perceived to be based on race.

Since 1866, when Congress sought to spell out the civil rights of the newly freed slaves, federal law has recognized the right to purchase and own a house as a fundamental part of American citizenship. Since 1968 the federal law has provided that it is unlawful to refuse to sell or rent after a bona fide offer is made, or to refuse to negotiate for the sale or rental of, or otherwise make unavailable or deny, a dwelling to any person because of race, color, religion, sex, or national origin.

Black citizens, who saw a promise of freedom in the Thirteenth Amendment to the United States Constitution, must be assured by Congress that their dollars will purchase the same thing as a white citizen's dollars. The court held that the Verbles had effectively implemented their initial indication "they preferred not to sell the property to blacks" when they rejected the McDonalds' offer of $27,500 on August 15, 1975, although the Verbles had previously wanted to sell to a white buyer at the same price.

The Verbles' prior discriminatory conduct was not altered by the subsequent sale of the property by the Verbles to the McDonalds nor did the sale wipe out the need for consideration of damages. The case is sent back to the District Court for determination of damages, costs, and attorney fees in favor of the McDonalds.

Questions and Case Problems

emancipated minor
A minor whose parents have given up their rights to take care of the minor and to have custody of and to claim the minor's earnings

1. A widow and her 18-year-old son lived together until 1976. The son began associating and staying overnight with people his mother did not like and of whom she did not approve. Arguments over his associations and conduct resulted in mother and son agreeing that he should move out and support himself. Shortly after moving the son was shot and was taken to a hospital where expenses were incurred. At the time of admission to the hospital his mother signed a consent to an operation, anesthetics, and other medical services form. The document contained no language of a promise, express or implied, to pay for services. At that time, in Nebraska a person 18 years of age was a minor. The hospital seeks to recover from the mother the cost of medical services rendered to the son. Should the hospital recover from the mother? [*Accent Service Company, v. Ebsen,* 306 N.W.2d 575 (Neb. 1981).]

2. Lefkowitz is suing the Great Minneapolis Surplus Store, Inc. for refusal to sell to him a fur piece which it had offered for sale in a newspaper advertisement that read as follows: "Saturday 9 a.m. sharp, three brand new fur coats worth $139.50, first come, first served. $1 each." The store's contention is that a newspaper advertisement offering items of merchandise for sale at a named price is not an offer and may be withdrawn without notice. Lefkowitz was first in line but was refused when he offered $1 for the fur coat advertised. Is the contention of the store correct, or does Lefkowitz have a contract to buy the fur coat for $1? [*Lefkowitz v. Great Minneapolis Surplus Store*, Inc., 86 N.W.2d 689 (Minn. 1957).]

3. On January 23, 1986, Wilkens filed a lawsuit against Butler seeking damages for personal injuries sustained in an automobile accident that occurred on February 10, 1984. In February 1986 Butler made an offer to settle the case for $4,500. This offer was never withdrawn formally. In February 1987 Wilkens notified Butler that she would accept his offer. Was this a timely acceptance? [*Wilkens v. Butler*, 369 S.E.2d 267 (Ga. 1988).]

4. Homeowners sued a construction company for the negligent design and construction of their residence. On July 21, 1982 they mailed to the construction company an offer to accept $10,000 in settlement of their claim. On August 16, 1982 the construction company made a counteroffer of $7,000 on the condition it be accepted that day. The counteroffer was rejected by the homeowners. On August 21, 1982 the homeowners wrote to the construction company, informing them that they were revoking their offer of July 21, 1982. The construction company received the letter the following day but nevertheless on August 25, 1982 sent the homeowners a letter accepting their offer of July 21, 1982. Did the construction company create a valid contract by its letter of acceptance or had the offer been revoked? [*T. M. Cobb Co. v. Superior Court of Marin County*, 682 P.2d 338 (Cal. 1984).]

5. Ivey's Plumbing and Electric Co., Inc., brought this action against a material supplier for refusal to supply materials at a price originally quoted on an "Estimate Sheet." The material supplier knew that Ivey's would rely on the "Estimate Sheet" in bidding for a job with a general contractor. Is the quotation by the material supplier irrevocable for a reasonable time or simply an offer to sell subject to revocation by the seller at any time prior to the buyer's acceptance? [*Ivey's Plumbing & Electric Co., Inc. v. Petrochem Maintenance*, 463 F.Supp. 543 (Miss. 1978).]

6. Louisiana-Pacific Corp. operates a woodpulp mill and produces a by-product known as rayon rejects. The sole business of Pulprint, Inc., was purchasing rayon rejects from Louisiana-Pacific for resale. Deliveries of rayon rejects were scheduled throughout the year, but no annual price was set. Prices were negotiated each quarter depending upon current market conditions. Louisiana-Pacific refused to continue to make deliveries of rayon rejects to Pulprint. Is a failure by the parties to set a firm price fatal to the finding of a contract? [*Pulprint, Inc. v. Louisiana-Pacific Corp.*, 477 N.Y.S.2d 540 (N.Y. 1984).]

7. Roberts, insurance agent, sent Buske a policy that was a renewal of one which Buske's father previously held. Buske had not ordered or requested issuance of this policy, but he accepted it and paid the premium. At a later date, just prior to the expiration date of the renewed policy, a second unsolicited renewal was sent by

Roberts to Buske and attached to it was a printed notice stating that, if Buske did not wish to accept it, he must return it or be liable for the premium. Buske made no response. Roberts inquired about the premium by telephone with Buske. Buske informed him that he had purchased another policy elsewhere. Roberts sues on the second renewal. What result? [*Roberts v. Buske*, 298 N.E.2d 795 (Ill. 1973).]

8. Pacific Photocopy brought an action to recover damages for Canon's breach of an alleged contract to appoint Pacific Photocopy as an authorized dealer for Canon's photocopy products. The issue is whether a contract exists between the parties notwithstanding that the writing that was to be the contract was signed by Pacific Photocopy *but not by Canon* and contained a provision requiring approval by Canon's executive office. What result? [*Pacific Photocopy v. Canon U.S.A., Inc.*, 646 P.2d 647 (Or. 1982), petition for review denied, 652 P.2d 810 (Or. 1982).]

9. CIC sought to enforce a reorganization plan tendered by CAC, wherein money loaned by CAC would be converted into other long-term debts and stock. A proposal for the reorganization was delivered to CIC on September 27. By the terms of the proposal, the entire plan of reorganization was to be completed by November 1. Contained in this proposal were the following words: "Will you kindly examine this proposal and let us know your reaction to it at the earliest possible time. We wish to point out that it is not an inflexible proposal, but we also point out that a recapitalization along these lines is imperative." CIC prepared a written acceptance of the offer, dated it October 8, but deliberately withheld mailing the letter until October 19; it was not received by the offeror CAC until October 21. The offeror contends that the offer expired before it was accepted due to the passage of a reasonable amount of time. What result? You decide. [*Central Invest. Corp. of Denver v. Container Advertising Co.*, 471 P.2d 647 (Colo. 1970).]

10. In *McDonald v. Verble*, excerpted at the beginning of this section, the court held that one could lose one's right not to contract in order to further a legislative purpose contained in a statute. It is quite appropriate to use business law as a tool for social change. Evaluate the above statement of the court's holding.

CHAPTER

8

RELIEF FROM CONTRACTUAL OBLIGATIONS

After you have read this chapter, you should be able to:

1. Discuss the law associated with the law of relief from contractual obligation and recognize that it acts as a legal safeguard on the freedom to contract.
2. Recognize that the law of genuineness of assent is a strongly felt force in society.
3. Understand the philosophical importance of the fact that the promise forming the basis of a contract must be fairly and voluntarily given.
4. Realize how the concept of unconscionability has given new importance to the exercise of free will in the contractual setting.
5. Recognize that this area of law is still evolving.

BUSINESS DECISIONS and the LAW

In the past, banks exercised a great deal of control over the decision to lend funds to businesses and over the resolution of any problems that arose in connection with those loans. However, more recently, borrowers began to initiate lawsuits against the banks, alleging fraud or a lack of good faith in making the loans. Some banks faced large damage awards made by juries. These actions are known as lender liability suits.

In one such suit, the owner of a small family apple orchard sued Bank of America for allegedly encouraging him to incur new debt. A jury held for the small businessman, awarding him $20 million in damages for lost business and property and $6 million in punitive damages.

Other similar suits have been reversed on appeal, however. In 1989, the California Court of Appeals overturned a $50 million lender-liability judgment against the Bank of America. In that case, the jury had found the bank guilty of fraud, violation of fiduciary duty, and intentionally causing emotional distress to a tomato farmer and his family. The jury had awarded the family $20 million in compensatory damages and $30 million in punitive damages. On appeal, a three-judge panel found there was insufficient evidence to support the family's case. Some observers believe that lender liability suits have gotten out of hand, and that appeals courts are trying to restore the balance.

Lender liability suits can be based on a variety of legal theories, including breach of fiduciary duty, fraud, or breach of the duty of good faith in lending. The issue of good faith and honesty in fact is discussed throughout this chapter.

Sources: Sam Zuckerman, "Bank of America Is Winner in Appeal of a Second Lender-Liability Lawsuit," *American Banker* CLIV:221, November 13, 1989; "An Apple Grower Takes a Bite Out of B of A," *Business Week*, November 1, 1985, p. 115; Janine S. Hiller, "Good Faith Lending," *American Business Law Journal* 26/4, Winter 1989, p. 783.

Elements needed for a contract:

	CHAPTER
1. MUTUAL ASSENT WITH A PROMISE OR PROMISES	6, 7, 8
2. Consideration	9
3. Capacity to contract	10
4. Legality	11

Introduction

genuineness of assent
Reality of consent to an offer or acceptance

In the formative stage of a simple express or implied-in-fact contract, the concern of the law is to determine whether or not the parties to the contract truly intended to create rights and duties not otherwise imposed by law. The preceding chapter developed an objective test to determine the existence of a contract. The law also approaches the parties through a subjective test to ascertain whether they are acting with free will or **genuineness of assent** in their manifestations of mutual assent—that is, offer and acceptance.

It is not the intent of the law to protect the fool from folly. The intent of the law is to protect the freedom of voluntary action of the individual. As it provides relief from contractual obligations, the law looks at the parties as individuals and applies a subjective test that considers the traits and characteristics of the individual.

The importance of this chapter to the concept of freedom to contract is with regard to what the law means by a promise voluntarily made as being basic to the formation of a contract. A proper promise voluntarily and fairly made is necessary to the formation of an enforceable contract.

Concern of the Law

manifestation of mutual assent
Offer and acceptance

After it has been determined that the requirements of offer and acceptance have been satisfied, the concern of the law is to see whether or not the **manifestations of mutual assent** to a contract were freely given. In the requirements necessary to satisfy offer and acceptance, parties who choose to contract must pass an objective test (certainty of terms and intention tests). (Ann, evidencing a serious contractual intent, offers to sell her car to Bea for $2,000. Bea accepts the offer with the intent to buy the car.)

Genuineness of assent presents parties to a contract with a second test that must be passed before a contract at its formative stage becomes enforceable. Was the offer and/or acceptance an act of free will? The answer to the question necessarily is very subjective (personal). Each individual has a different strength of will.

Both the objective and subjective tests must be satisfied in order to successfully form an enforceable contract.

Result

If genuineness of assent is not present (the manifestation of mutual assent was not an act of free will), then the party to the contract not exercising free will has the right to **rescind**—to cancel or annul—what objectively appears to be a contract.

rescind
To cancel, annul

The act of avoidance must be timely or it is lost. Conduct that is inconsistent with avoidance will reaffirm the contract. This is illustrated by the following case.

FACTS

Tidwell and Critz are medical doctors who allegedly entered into an oral agreement to form a medical association to practice radiotherapy in Atlanta, Georgia. Shortly after the purported agreement Tidwell began to work with Critz. Later Critz presented Tidwell with a second agreement prepared by Critz's attorney which created an employer-employee relationship between Tidwell and Critz and provided that Tidwell would be compensated for his association with Critz in the amount of $1,000 per month, "plus such bonus amounts" as Critz approved. The agreement further provided that either party could terminate his association by giving 30 days notice. Tidwell objected to this agreement contending it did not reflect their previous "partnership" understanding. Tidwell contends he signed it three months after review by his lawyer because Critz threatened to end his association with Tidwell and have his privilege to practice at Georgia Baptist Hospital taken away. Tidwell continued to work for Critz for some nine months until Critz terminated his association with Tidwell because of Tidwell's poor work performance and his inability to cooperate with other hospital employees. Tidwell seeks to avoid the written agreement on the grounds of duress and seeks an accounting for profits under the purported partnership association. Critz contended that he did not use duress.

DECISION

The court held for Critz. Tidwell waived any claimed duress, which would have allowed him to avoid the contract, surrounding the signing of the agreement with Critz to be his employee when Tidwell ratified the contract by accepting compensation under the agreement without apparent complaint until termination of employment. Contracts made under duress are not ordinarily void, but merely voidable, and may be ratified. Once ratified such contracts cannot be avoided.

Tidwell v. Critz, 282 S.E.2d 104 (Ga. 1981).

In the case of fraud[1] (intentional misrepresentation), one can rescind or waive one's power to avoid the contract and, instead, seek damages for the tort of deceit.[2] (Sam sold

[1]For a discussion of fraud, see p. 164.

[2]For the tort of deceit, see p. 80.

a twelve-year-old tractor to Bill intentionally misrepresenting it to be ten years old. Bill kept the tractor and sued Sam for deceit for the difference in value between a ten-year-old tractor and a twelve-year-old tractor.) Under the Code,[3] a party can rescind *and* seek damages. A mistake in drafting a contract will be corrected by **reformation.**[4]

reformation

An action to correct a writing so as to reflect correctly the intentions of the parties that mistakenly were not properly expressed in the writing

mistake

Believing a fact to exist when it does not exist, or believing a fact not to exist when it does exist

Mistake

In certain situations one can avoid the consequences of the offer or acceptance by proving a **mistake.** A mistake of *law* does not allow one to avoid a contract; we are all presumed to know the law. A mistake of *fact* may justify avoidance of a contract. If only one party is mistaken without the other party knowing of the mistake, avoidance of the contract is not allowed. (Al contracts to sell certain goods to Betty, forgetting that he had already sold them to Bud. Al cannot avoid for his mistake of fact.) If the other party knows a mistake is being made by a party to a contract, avoidance by the mistaken party is usually allowed. This is the situation of *unilateral mistake*—one party making the mistake. The law seeks to prevent one from knowingly taking advantage of the mistake of another. The following case illustrates how an insurance company was not allowed to escape liability on a malpractice policy because of a mistake of the insured.

FACTS

Associates, Inc., established an architecture and engineering business and contracted for malpractice insurance with Continental Casualty Company. The policy required continuous coverage in order that claims made in a policy year for prior years' negligent acts be covered. While the policy was in effect, Associates contracted for work on a construction project. Due to a lack of business, Associates was unable to maintain its insurance and cancelled the policy. Three years later it renewed its policy with the Continental Casualty but was not informed that it could have purchased a "prior acts" endorsement. Continental Casualty also had never informed them of the effect of the continuous coverage requirement. After renewal of their insurance policy, Associates was sued for negligence on the previous construction project. The insurance company refuses to defend Associates, citing absence of continuous coverage or prior acts endorsement as justification for its inaction. Associates seeks an order requiring the insurance company to defend them.

DECISION

The court held for Associates, Inc. Where there is a mistake by one party and inequitable conduct by the other, an insurance contract can be reformed. Associates was mistaken in its assumption that it was covered by malpractice for past acts at the time it was insured and at the time it renewed its insurance policy. Continental Casualty, having handled Associates' insurance needs for ten years, owed a duty to inform it as to what coverage it actually had and how it could obtain complete coverage. Continental Casualty's silence justifies this court in reforming the current insurance contract so that Associates is insured for the suit by the construction company.

Stein, Hinkle, Dawe, and Assoc. v. Continental Casualty Co., 313 N.W.2d 299 (Mich. 1981).

---

[3]UCC 2-720, 2-721.

[4]For a discussion of reformation, see p. 273.

Figure 8.1 should be helpful as a summary chart of invalidations.

In the mutual or bilateral mistake situation, both parties to the contract are mistaken and either party can avoid the contract. It is most commonly said that the minds of the parties never met. Most often this occurs in a situation of ambiguity. In an ambiguous fact situation, the fact is capable of two meanings. Each of the contracting parties associates with a different fact meaning. Objectively their minds seem to have met but subjectively no meeting of the minds has taken place. Additionally, if both parties assume a fact to be in existence when it is not in existence, or not to be in existence when it is in existence, mutual mistake occurs.

The area of mistake reflects the concern of the law that the parties contract knowing the reality of the situation. Without this assurance, the law cannot ascertain if the parties to the contract would have entered into it voluntarily. On the other hand, as between two innocent parties, the one causing his or her own distortion of reality and the other party contracting in reality, the court will hold for the latter and against the former. Thus if a

FIGURE 8.1 **Invalidating Table**

Category of Invalidation	Result		Reason for Determination of Invalidation
	Void	Voidable	
Unilateral mistake with notice		X	Unfairness to party mistaken
Bilateral mistake		X	No meeting of the minds
Misrepresentation of a material fact *Innocent* *Negligent*		X	No assurance that the misled party would have manifested assent if reality were known
Fraud in the *inducement*		X	Same as above
Fraud in the *procurement* (factum, execution, or essence)	X		No free manifestation of assent
Concealment		X	No assurance that party would have manifested assent if reality were known
Duress – *knowing character of transaction*		X	No free manifestation of assent, but knowledge of reality
Duress – *not knowing character of transaction*	X		No free manifestation of assent
Undue Influence		X	Unfair persuasion
Unconscionable		X	Unfair result: one-sided

person negligently signs a contract misinterpreting its impact or terms, or mistakenly assumes that he or she is contracting with a named party but is actually contracting with someone else, the person, nevertheless, will be bound to the contract.

Misrepresentation

misrepresentation
An assertion of what is not true

When one unintentionally misrepresents a material fact and this induces another to enter into a contract, the misled party can avoid the contract if the party reasonably relied upon the **misrepresentation.** This is so because the law cannot assure itself that, if the true state of affairs had been known, the misled party would have freely entered into the contract. In the following case the plaintiff sought to avoid the contract alleging that the defendant knew, or should have known, that its representation was false. The court held that the complaint sufficiently stated a cause of action justifying avoidance.

FACTS

Whipp purchased an automobile business from Iverson, believing the business included the Oldsmobile agency and franchise. Whipp alleged that Iverson knew, or should have known, that the franchise was not saleable as part of the business. General Motors refused to transfer the franchise to Whipp who then returned the business to Iverson and demanded rescission of the purchase contract. Iverson contends the complaint failed to allege that Iverson intentionally made false representations that Whipp would receive the franchise and therefore there was no basis for Whipp's suit.

DECISION

The court held for Whipp, noting that, in an action for deceit, the basis for responsibility is the intent to deceive, proved by the fact that the speaker believes the statement to be false or the representation is made without any belief in its truth. Recovery in damages is also allowed for fraud not amounting to deceit where there was a representation of fact or the speaker is supposed to possess complete knowledge of the facts. In negligence actions, Iverson need only fail to exercise ordinary care in making a representation or in ascertaining facts, but, like other cases of negligence, it requires a duty of care or an assumption of a duty. Recovery is allowed even though representations are innocently made, because it would be unjust to allow one making false representations to retain the fruits of a bargain induced by them. A misrepresentation may be innocent, negligent, or known to be false. If innocently made, the contract is still voidable. Since Iverson here was alleged to know or should have known that the franchise was not saleable as part of the business, the order overruling the demurrer was sustained.

Whipp v. Iverson, 168 N.W.2d 201 (Wis. 1969).

Fraud

fraud
In contracts, a misrepresentation of fact, known to be false, intentionally made to induce another person to make or refrain from making a contract, and reasonably relied on by the other person

An *intentional* misrepresentation of a fact bringing about a contractual mistake is called **fraud.** (See Figure 8.2 for elements of fraud.) If the intentional misrepresentation of fact is to induce the formation of a contract, it is called "fraud in the inducement." Fraud in the inducement causes the resulting contract to be voidable at the election of the party defrauded who innocently reasonably relied on the fraud. Alternatively, the party defrauded may sue to recover damages under the common law. The statement of an opinion by a person who does not profess to be an expert normally is not a statement of a material fact and cannot be reasonably relied on. (Al says, "This is the best car on the market." The statement exaggerates the value of one's wares and is an opinion.)

FIGURE 8.2 **Elements of Fraud**

1. A representation.
2. Falsity of representation.
3. Materiality of that representation.
4. Speaker's knowledge of falsity of representation or ignorance of truth.
5. The speaker's intent that it should be relied on.
6. The hearer is ignorant of the falsity of the representation.
7. The hearer relies on the representation.
8. The hearer has a right to rely on the representation.
9. Consequent and proximate injury was caused by reliance on the representation.

However, if the intentional misrepresentation of fact is of the nature of what is to be done and the defrauded party innocently relied on the fraud without negligence on his or her part, it is called *fraud in the procurement* (or fraud in the *factum, execution,* or in the *essence*) and no contract is made. This happens because the defrauded party did not manifest assent to the misrepresented transaction but was assenting to another transaction. (Art misrepresents to Bud that the form to be signed by Bud is a receipt, when in fact it is a promissory note. If Bud reasonably believes the paper is a receipt, and Bud is not negligent in Bud's exercise of reasonable care to ascertain what the paper is, there is fraud in the procurement and no contract or note of any legal effect comes into being.) In this illustration the transaction is void, rather than voidable as when one is fraudulently induced to make a contract. If the defrauded party is negligent (e.g., the misrepresentation could have been discovered on a reasonable examination by the defrauded party), it is fraud in the inducement causing the contract to be voidable by the defrauded party.

Concealment

Both in misrepresentation and in fraud there is action that distorts reality. In concealment normally there is passive inaction, a failure to disclose. Concealment may also occur by actively hiding the facts—for example, the owner of a house covers a wall damaged by termites so that a prospective buyer of the house will not see the damage. In the following case of passive inaction, a failure to disclose was deemed to be fraud in the inducement.

FACTS

A seller of a water conditioning business appealed the judgment of the lower court in favor of the buyers granting rescission (avoidance) of a contract for sale of the business. The buyers alleged fraud by seller's failure to disclose a security arrangement and an agreement with a manufacturer of the water conditioner's subsidiary. Said agreement provided that leases of water conditioners through the business could not be sold or assigned or given as security other than to the subsidiary. Upon taking control of the business, the buyers converted 34 leases to sales. Learning of this, the subsidiary took over the business. The buyers immediately sought rescission of the purchase contract for the business. Judgment was rendered for the buyer and the seller appealed.

DECISION

The court held for the buyers. An inadvertent failure to disclose the security interest and agreement which posed restraints on the free conduct of the business amounts to fraud. The sellers owed an express duty to inform the buyers of these provisions which made the conduct of the business impossible without the consent of the manufacturer's subsidiary.

Cady v. Pitts, 625 P.2d 1089 (Idaho 1981).

A growing body of law is accumulating that requires parties to disclose facts whenever justice, equity, and fair dealing demand it so that the law can be assured that the parties are exercising free will in the contractual setting.[5] This is especially true under the Uniform Commercial Code, as illustrated by the following case.

FACTS

A buyer purchased a refrigerator from a merchant. An invoice was signed by the buyer at the bottom. Beneath the customer's signature is the clearly marked printed wording "see reverse side for guaranty." The "reverse side" contains a 90-day warranty for parts installed by the dealer and then states in bold letters that: "EXCEPT AS EXPRESSLY PROVIDED ABOVE, THERE IS NO WARRANTY OR GUARANTY OF MERCHANTABILITY, OR FITNESS FOR A PARTICULAR PURPOSE, OR OF ANY OTHER KIND, EXPRESS OR IMPLIED, WITH RESPECT TO THE SERVICES PERFORMED OR PARTS FURNISHED BY US. . . ." This information on the reverse side is in extremely light print and is difficult to read, especially inasmuch as it is against the backdrop of the darker print and writing on the front side of this "invoice." The refrigerator failed and ceased to function within two and one-half years after purchase. The buyer sues for breach of an implied warranty of merchantability. The seller contends the language on the back of the invoice effectively disclaims the implied warranty of merchantability.

DECISION

The court held for the buyer, noting that the language on the back of the invoice is obscured to the extent that it is in print so light, that against the background of the written and printed portion of the front of this "invoice" it is almost illegible—certainly very difficult to read. The disclaimer not being conspicuous is not effective to exclude an implied warranty of merchantability.

LUPA v. Jock's, 500 N.Y.S.2d 962 (N.Y. 1986).

duress
Wrongful inducement to do that which a reasonable person would have been unable to resist

Duress

Duress is wrongful pressure by threat that induces one to enter into a contract, without freedom of choice, because of fear that the threatened, wrongful act will be carried out. Its effect is to make a contract voidable by the injured party if he or she knew the character of the transaction. If the injured party did not know the character of the transaction, there is no contract. (John is wrongfully induced to sign a paper evidencing a contract. If John knew the contents of the paper, the contract is voidable by him. If he did not know, there is no contract.) The most crude form of duress that prevents the

[5]See Chapter 27, Consumer Law A, for a discussion of the Magnuson-Moss Warranty-Federal Trade Commission Improvements Act.

exercise of free will is when one is threatened with criminal or tortious conduct if a contract is not formed. More subtle forms of duress are recognized where free will is controlled by threat to bring criminal action, or by abuse of civil legal process (excessive and improper use of the right to sue in an attempt to exhaust someone into submission), or by threat to withhold goods. The key to understanding duress is to recognize that the law is identifying conduct of one party that is wrongful and calculated to control the will of another in the contractual setting. The threat of a justifiable civil suit does not constitute duress nor prevent the other party's free exercise of will. In the following case a threat of criminal sanction did not constitute duress nor prevent the other party's exercise of freedom.

FACTS

Willig failed to observe an agreement made between himself and the 150 Crown Street Tenants' Association to place money in the hands of someone to make repairs to a building necessitated by his prior gross mismanagement. Thereafter, the Housing and Development Administration (HDA) commenced an action against Willig for correction of 300 building violations. An order by the court to make repairs was ignored by Willig, so HDA brought contempt proceedings. Willig agreed to turn over the deteriorating buildings to a court-appointed trustee and to pay a $20,000 fine to be used for repair of the building. A stay of a 30-day jail sentence was entered when Willig made this agreement. Approximately six months later, the agreement not having been carried out, the HDA moved for judgment on the agreement and vacation of the stay of the 30-day jail sentence. During this latter proceeding, Willig was asked to sign a new agreement which the judge said if not signed would result in Willig serving 30 days in jail. Willig signed the new agreement but failed to comply with it and brings this suit against HDA and several of the trustees of the Tenants Association to have it set aside on the basis that he entered into the new agreement under duress.

DECISION

The court held for the Housing and Development Administration. The law is well settled that threats of arrest or imprisonment may constitute such duress as will render a contract entered into voidable at the election of the person threatened. It is immaterial whether such person was guilty or innocent of the act for which arrest or imprisonment was threatened in order for there to be duress. On the other hand, it does not constitute duress to do what one has the legal right to do. All that the judge did was to inform Willig that, if he did not enter into the agreement, the judge would grant the motion to vacate a prior stay of the 30-day jail sentence. This is not a situation of duress which will avoid a contract.

Willig v. Rapaport, et al. 438 N.Y.S.2d 872 (N.Y. 1981).

Undue Influence

The law recognizes **undue influence**—that because of closeness of relationship (e.g., fiduciary, close friend, confidant), age, physical or mental condition, the will of a person can be manipulated. If, because of the unique relationship, contemplated undue contractual advantage is taken of the manipulated party by unfair persuasion, the contract can be avoided. Mere persuasion is proper and does not cause the contract to be voidable. In the following case the court held that there was a **fiduciary** relationship between the parties that was violated by the undue influence of the party with the fiduciary duty to act for the benefit of the others.

undue influence
Unfair persuasion by one who, because of his or her relationship with another, dominates the other

fiduciary
A person with a duty to act primarily for the benefit of another

FACTS

This is an action by the conservator of the estate of the decedent, Conrad Schaneman, Sr., to set aside and cancel a deed of real estate executed by Conrad Schaneman, Sr. in favor of his eldest son. Schaneman, Sr. was born in Russia and could neither read nor write the English language. He was the father of eight sons and five daughters, all living heirs. Over the years the family had been close-knit, especially the father and the sons. In 1974, the eldest son advised his brothers and sisters that he would henceforth manage his father's business matters and that they no longer need be concerned in that regard. Thereafter, the eldest son was the primary person who advised his father on business matters and handled his father's business matters. On March 18, 1975 Schaneman, Sr. was for all intents and purposes an invalid. Schaneman, Sr.'s children testified that during 1975 their father seemed mentally confused. In 1977, one of the children discovered that the eldest son's name was on Schaneman, Sr.'s bank account as a joint tenant with right of survivorship. It was also discovered that the eldest son was listed as a joint tenant with right of survivorship on a certificate of deposit purchased with Schaneman, Sr.'s money. Schaneman, Sr. had also executed a power of attorney in favor of the eldest son. Before his death, Schaneman, Sr. testified that he never agreed to sell the farm to the eldest son but decided to give the eldest son the farm since he had asked for it several times out of the presence of his other children and that he could not refuse anything to his eldest son since the eldest son was his best boy. Schaneman, Sr. also testified that his eldest son had told him not to tell the other children about the gift, but to keep it quiet. Schaneman, Sr. said the eldest son dictated everything and told him what to do. The lower court held in favor of the conservator, finding that the execution of the deed was a result of fraud and undue influence, and set aside the deed. The eldest son appealed.

DECISION

In affirming the judgment for the conservator, the court held that evidence indicating that, due to age and physical infirmities, Schaneman, Sr. was, for all intents and purposes, an invalid at the time of the conveyance of the farm, that Schaneman, Sr.'s mental acuity was impaired at times and that he sometimes suffered from disorientation and lapse of memory, that Schaneman, Sr. was subject to the influence of the eldest son who was acting in a confidential relationship, that opportunity to exercise undue influence existed, that there was a disposition on the part of the son to exercise undue influence, and that the conveyance of the farm appeared to be the effect of such influence, was sufficient to establish a prima facie case of undue influence and to cast upon the eldest son the burden of going forward with the evidence which he did not do.

Schaneman v. Schaneman, 291 N.W.2d 412 (Neb. 1980).

The Uniform Commercial Code

unconscionable
Offensive to the conscience; immoderate, too one-sided

Under the Uniform Commercial Code,[6] the court is allowed to test the subjective question of the exercise of free will in the commercial setting. The question the court answers is whether or not the contract is **unconscionable.** The test is whether, in light of the general commercial background and the commercial needs of the particular trade or case, the clauses are so one-sided as to be unconscionable under the circumstances existing at the time of the making of the contract. If the conclusion is yes, the contract can be avoided. In the area of genuineness of assent, the law's concern is to give relief from contractual obligations not fairly and voluntarily assumed.

---

[6]UCC 2-302.

Summary Statement

1. Not only must the requirements of manifestation of mutual assent be satisfied before there is an *enforceable* contract, but genuineness of assent must also exist.
2. In the absence of genuineness of assent, a contract can be avoided through rescission, and in some instances damages will be given.
3. The traditional areas wherein problems of exercise of free will may result are mistake, misrepresentation, fraud, concealment, duress, and undue influence.
4. The Uniform Commercial Code in its development of the concept of unconscionability has given renewed importance to problems involving the exercise of free will in a contractual setting.

The most modern form of relief from contractual obligation can be found in the application of avoidance of contractual responsibility found in the Uniform Commercial Code.[7] The following case is included in depth to illustrate how the concept of unconscionability is applied in a commercial setting.

WILLE v. SOUTHWESTERN BELL TELEPHONE COMPANY
549 P.2d 903 (Kan. 1976)

The question before the court is whether an advertiser can recover damages for breach of contract from a telephone company for an omission in the yellow pages of its telephone directory when the contract entered into by the parties limits the company's liability for errors and omissions to an amount equal to the cost of advertisement. The trial court granted summary judgment for the telephone company, and the advertiser has appealed.

The facts of the case are that Wille has operated a heating and air conditioning business in Wichita for some thirteen years and has had some listing in the yellow pages of the phone directory for his business over this period of time.

In the year involved in this case Wille was in the process of expanding his business and sought additional telephone listings. Additional listing were given by the telephone company but one of the telephone numbers was inadvertently omitted from the directory. Upon learning of the omission Wille began advertising the omitted number on television, incurring expenditures of some $5,000.

The written contract contained a *conspicuous* clause which limited the telephone company's damages in case of breach of contract:

> The applicant agrees that the Telephone Company shall not be liable for errors in/or omissions of the directory advertising beyond the amount paid for the directory advertising omitted, or in which errors occur, for the issue life of the directory involved.

Wille contends the **exculpatory clause** is contrary to public policy and should not be enforced. He asserts unconscionability of contract in two respects: the party's unequal bargaining position, and the form of the contract and the circumstances of its execution.

exculpatory clause
A clause that relieves a party from liability

The court noted that the traditional view is that competent adults may make contracts on their own terms, provided they are neither illegal nor contrary to public policy. Absent fraud, mistake, or duress, a party who has fairly and voluntarily entered into such a contract is bound thereby, notwithstanding that it is unwise or dis-

[7] UCC 2-302.

advantageous to him. However, such a rule is tempered by the principle of unconscionability.

The UCC neither defines the concept of unconscionability nor provides the elements or perimeters of the doctrine. To define the doctrine is to limit its application, and to limit its application is to defeat its purpose.

Aids to a determination of whether a contract is unconscionable include:

1. Use of printed form or boilerplate contracts drawn skillfully by the party in the strongest economic position, which establish industrywide standards offered on a take-it-or-leave-it basis to the party in the weaker economic position.
2. A significant cost-price disparity or excessive price.
3. A denial of basic rights and remedies to a buyer of consumer goods.
4. Inclusion of penalty clauses.
5. Circumstances surrounding execution of the agreement including its commercial setting, purpose, and effect.
6. Hiding of disadvantageous clauses in a mass of fine print trivia or in places which are inconspicuous.
7. Phrasing clauses in language that is incomprehensible to a layman or that divert his attention from the problems raised by them or the rights given up through them.
8. Overall imbalance in the obligations and rights imposed by the bargain.
9. Exploitation of the underprivileged, unsophisticated, uneducated, and illiterate.
10. Inequality of bargaining or economic power.

The doctrine of unconscionability is used to police the excesses of certain parties who abuse their right to contract freely. It is directed against one-sided, oppressive, unfairly surprising contracts and not against the consequences per se of uneven bargaining power or even a simple old-fashioned bad bargain.

In this case the contract was not unconscionable because the form of the agreement directed the reader's attention to the clause limiting damages. The clause was clearly legible and was phrased in common words and was not one-sided. Moreover, the advertiser was an experienced businessman, and the omission arose from a clerical error which in its commercial setting was reasonably contemplated as falling within the purview of and purpose of the clause.

Judgment for the telephone company was affirmed. (Note: While the Uniform Commercial Code does not actually apply since a sale of goods is not involved in this case, the court borrowed the concept of unconscionability from it to decide the case.)

Questions and Case Problems

1. The Aluminum Company of America (ALCOA) entered into a contract with Essex Group, Inc., whereby Essex agreed to supply alumina (aluminum ore) to ALCOA who agreed to convert it into molten aluminum requiring intensive use of oil fuel. This molten aluminum would then be repossessed by Essex for further processing. ALCOA sought reformation or modification of the contract in the face of a potential $60 million dollar loss brought about by an unforeseeable rise in labor production costs due to an unexpected rise in OPEC's pricing system. ALCOA contends that unforeseeable rise in costs constituted a mutual mistake of fact justifying reformation or modification in the face of both parties contemplating a risk variance of only three cents per pound. Is ALCOA correct? [*Aluminum Co. of America v. Essex Group, Inc.*, 499 F.Supp. 53 (1980).]
2. Two ships, both named *Peerless,* were leaving Bombay, India, one in October and the other in December. An offer was made to sell 125 bales of a commodity to be shipped from Bombay, India, to arrive on the ship *Peerless.* The buyer accepted the offer and had in mind the ship that sailed in October. The seller, on the other hand, believed that the agreement referred to the ship *Peerless* that was sailing in December. Each party, seller and buyer, believed in good faith that a different ship

was intended in the contract. What result? [*Raffles v. Wichelhaus,* (English) 2 Hurlstone and Coltman 906 (1864).]

3. First National Bank in Havre brought an action to collect the amount due on a promissory note signed by Nelson and to foreclose a mortgage securing repayment of the promissory note. In his answer, Nelson pleaded fraud as a defense. The answer made certain representations regarding the terms and nature of the note. Was fraud properly pleaded by Nelson or should Nelson sue his attorney? [*First National Bank in Havre v. Nelson,* 741 P.2d 420 (Mont. 1987).]
4. Burger Chef Systems, Inc., and its former parent company, General Foods Corporation, appeal a jury verdict awarding $175,859.23 in compensatory damages to Rita O'Neal, a former Burger Chef franchisee. The award of damages was based on a theory of wrongful nondisclosure. The alleged wrongful nondisclosure was the failure to disclose that General Foods had decided to sell Burger Chef Systems. Was General Foods under a duty to disclose to potential franchisees of Burger Chef Systems that it intended to sell the franchise operation? [*O'Neal v. Burger Chef Systems,* 860 F.2d 1341 (1988).]
5. Inmates who were convicted of offenses arising out of a jail break appealed the conviction on the grounds that certain agreements had not been enforced. The first alleged agreement was with the Commissioner of Corrections, made while the Commissioner was a hostage. It was that the inmates would not be punished for crimes arising out of the jail break attempt. The second alleged agreement was an order issued by a federal judge, in the presence of the inmates and their hostage, that no action be taken against the inmates for their participation in the jail break. Can the agreements be avoided? [*United States v. Gorham,* 523 F.2d 1088 (1975).]
6. In 1971 Sambo's Restaurants, Inc. petitioned the City of Ann Arbor, Michigan, for site plan approval for construction of a Sambo's Restaurant. When the City Council balked at accepting the proposal and it appeared that approval of the project would not be forthcoming, Sambo's agreed not to use the name in connection with the restaurant. Approval by the City Council followed quickly. After six years of small profits operating under the name of "Jolly Tiger," the restaurant applied to the City for sign permits to display the name "Sambo's." Those permits were granted and the signs erected. The permits were subsequently revoked by the City as in contravention of the earlier "agreement." Sambo's refuses to take down the signs. Can Sambo's avoid the earlier "agreement" because of duress? [*Sambo's Restaurants v. City of Ann Arbor,* 663 F.2d 686 (1981).]
7. After a 99-year-old aunt executed a deed conveying certain property to her nephew and his wife, the aunt commenced an action seeking a determination that the deed was null and void and a judgment directing reconveyance of the property. The aunt initiated the conveyance and selected the price and was not dependent upon the nephew or his wife in personal or business affairs, although the aunt had respect for the nephew's judgment and trust in his character. The property was worth more than the $5,000 she asked for from the nephew. Does this case present a fiduciary relationship that would allow the contract to be avoided because of the differences in value exchanged? [*Bruno v. Bruno, et al.,* 422 N.E.2d 1369 (Mass. 1981).]
8. Religious counselor appealed a judgment of the lower court rescinding a partnership agreement between the counselor and the devotee with regard to the financial purchase of apartments. Evidence was introduced to show that the devotee had fallen in love with the counselor and that several times a week she received treatment from the counselor that involved intense spiritual and emotional pressure. The devotee advanced $13,000 for the purchase of the building and the counselor

only $2,987.50. Originally the devotee did not want to enter into the partnership but the counselor changed her mind by noting that she was ungrateful for all he had done for her and that her refusal violated the tenets of her faith. Can the partnership be rescinded? [*Ferguson v. Jeanes,* 619 P.2d 369 (Wash. 1981).]

adhesion contract

A standard form contract in which the weaker party has no realistic choice or opportunity to bargain

9. Patient's father brought action against hospital and radiological association for a declaratory judgment that he did not owe the association for the expense of interpretation of X rays of his son's wrist. The son was injured in a motorcycle accident and taken to a hospital for treatment of his injuries. Upon admittance to the hospital, the father signed a form containing the following language: "I hereby authorize and direct the above-named surgeon and/or his associates to provide such additional services for me as he or they may deem reasonable and necessary, including, but not limited to, the administration and maintenance of the anesthesia, and the performance of services involving pathology and radiology, and I hereby consent thereto. I understand that the above mentioned . . . are independent contractors and as such are the agents, servants or employees of myself." The father alleges that the consent form is an **adhesion contract** and thus is void. He states that the form is a standardized form which was presented to him by a party with greater bargaining power. He contends there was no bargaining between the parties as to its contents; rather, if he wanted medical treatment for his son, then he had to sign the form presented. This lack of negotiation, he contends, makes the contract unenforceable. What result? [*Rumple v. Bloomington Hospital,* 422 N.E.2d 1309 (Ind. 1981).]

10. In *Johnson v. Mobil Oil Corporation,* 415 F.Supp. 264 (1976) (see p. 132), the court held that a contracting party having immense bargaining power has an affirmative duty to explain in layman's terms the meaning and possible consequences of a contractual obligation to be assumed by another contracting party who is an uncounseled layman. Because this was not done, a clause limiting liability was declared null and void. In *Wille v. Southwestern Bell Telephone Company,* excerpted at the beginning of this section, a clause limiting liability was deemed valid and binding. Reconcile the two cases. Why in one instance deny the freedom to contract and in the next instance enforce it? Are the cases inconsistent?

CHAPTER 9

CONSIDERATION/ VALUE GIVEN FOR A PROMISE

After you have read this chapter, you should be able to:

1. Discuss the law of consideration, recognizing that it acts as a limitation on the freedom to contract.
2. Recognize that the law is moving in the direction of not requiring consideration in more and more instances so as to achieve a better sense of fairness to the parties involved and a better understanding of their intentions about assuming legal obligations.
3. Appreciate the differences among the requirements of consideration, manifestation of mutual assent, and genuineness of assent.
4. Note the exceptions to the requirement of consideration in both the common law and the Uniform Commercial Code.
5. Apply the objective tests used to determine whether consideration exists.

BUSINESS DECISIONS and the LAW

The bargain theory of consideration is the giving up of a right one has by law to do or *not* to do something (forbearance), or the assumption of a legal duty to do or not to do something not otherwise imposed by law.

Recently International Business Machines Corporation (IBM) found itself in a position where it has to bargain with its employees to cut costs. IBM appears to be trying to reduce its workforce by 10,000 to 15,000, almost entirely in the United States, where growth has been stagnant for several years. Despite a series of early retirement programs that induced some 22,000 people to leave the company, IBM still employs 223,000 in the United States and 387,000 worldwide.

Rumors have circulated about further cutbacks at the company, that apparently found that expenses are far too high. To reduce costs, IBM had to find a better way of aiming the early retirement incentives at weak performers. Under earlier programs, which were offered to everyone in certain sectors of the company, many of IBM's best people left. IBM also found certain programs in disarray because the bulk of those employees involved had left.

It was hoped that the company could find better ways to keep expenses below those of earlier programs. In the past the company gave some employees nearly three years' pay as incentive to leave the company, an extremely generous inducement.

Some have said the program could be as generous as "7, 7, and 1," meaning that in calculating retirement benefits, seven years would be added to the employee's age and length of service, and the employee would get a bonus of one year's pay. One anonymous company employee said that the gallows humor now rampant at the company has turned that into "7, 7, 1, 1, and 2," meaning seven years added to age, seven to service, a one-year bonus, and "you have one minute to think about it, and you have to take two people with you".

Source: Paul Carroll, "IBM Expected to Unveil Plan to Cut Costs," *Wall Street Journal*, December 5, 1989, pp. A3, A16; reprinted by permission of *Wall Street Journal*,

Elements needed for a contract:

	CHAPTER
1. Mutual assent with a promise or promises	6, 7, 8
2. CONSIDERATION	**9**
3. Capacity to contract	10
4. Legality	11

Introduction

consideration
The legal price bargained for a promise and inducing a party to enter into a contract

In the preceding chapters of this part, we discussed the promise and one of the four elements required for a contract, namely mutual assent of the parties. We now consider the second element—consideration. **Consideration** as *value* and as the *price for a promise* is a basic requirement for a contract. The concept of consideration is: What did the promisor request and receive for his or her promise to which the promisor was not already legally entitled? (Al promises Betty $10 for mowing Al's lawn. Mowing the lawn is the consideration/value for Al's promise, which, stated legally, says "In consideration of your mowing my lawn, I'll pay you $10.")

However, the law, by case decision and by statute, is reflecting a trend in public policy of making more and more exceptions to this requirement in order to achieve a better sense of fairness to the parties in particular transactions and a better understanding of their intentions about assuming legal obligations.

The fact that the requirement of consideration must be satisfied to have a *simple contract* can be better understood by learning how the concept of consideration developed and how it relates to the *freedom to contract.*

contract under seal
A contract that has a symbol attached to it attesting that it is a binding obligation

A type of formal contract, a **contract under seal,** did not require consideration to prove its validity or enforceability. It was presumed that a person who pressed a signet ring into wax on a contractual document became committed to the obligation evidenced by the document, truly intending to be so bound.

FIGURE 9.1 **Consideration**

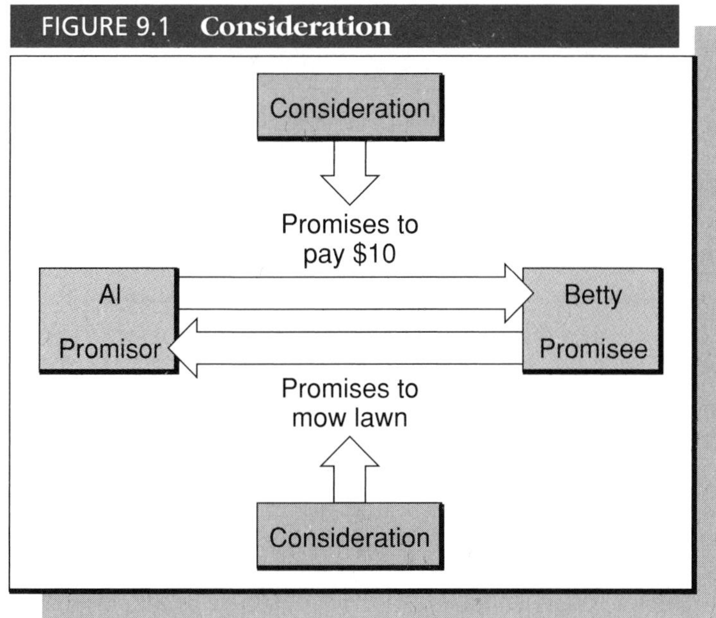

A signet ring bearing some symbol normally was restricted in use to nobles. Merchants wishing to engage in trade and commerce found it necessary to prove to the court that they truly wanted and intended to be bound to a contractual obligation. In most cases merchants were not nobles and therefore could not resort to the use of a seal to satisfy the concerns of the law. Thus the concept of consideration developed to substitute for the necessity of a seal to show that a common person intended to be bound to a contractual obligation.

Historically, then, it is easily seen why the requirement of consideration is important to the freedom to contract. It is a *further limitation on our ability to create a contract.* By requiring that consideration be present, as well as manifestation of mutual assent and genuineness of assent, the law can be more satisfied that the parties to a contract *want to be bound to the obligation.* Otherwise, consideration as value would not be requested and given for promise. Today numerous exceptions to the requirement of consideration are being discovered through case development and the Uniform Commercial Code.

Consideration—A Third Test to Determine Intent to Contract

In previous chapters we discussed the concern of the law to determine whether the parties to a contract truly wanted and intended to be bound to an obligation. There are three tests to make this determination, all of which are necessary elements in order to have a contract: (1) manifestation of mutual assent by offer and acceptance, (2) genuineness of assent, and (3) consideration. We have already discussed the first two, and now we will consider the third, consideration.

Unlike the concept of genuineness of assent, wherein a subjective test was applied to determine whether the parties' manifestation of mutual assent was an act of free will, consideration requires the satisfaction of two objective requisites. One is that **detriment**

detriment
The doing, or forbearing from doing, something by a party who had no previous legal obligation so to do or refrain from doing

FIGURE 9.2 Test for Court to Determine Whether Parties Truly Intended to Be Bound to an Obligation

1. Manifestation of mutual assent by offer and acceptance [Chapter 7]
2. Genuineness of assent [Chapter 8]
3. Consideration [Chapter 9]

be given for the return obligation by both parties to the contract under the assumption that detriment to one party is normally of benefit to another party. The other requisite is that the detriment be bargained for. (Jan contracted with Bill to dig a ditch for Bill. Jan's digging is a detriment to Jan given by Jan in return for Bill's promissory obligation to pay Jan. Jan's digging is a benefit to Bill and Bill's payment is a benefit to Jan. Jan and Bill bargained for the digging and payment.)

The detriment by one party is the price, value, or consideration for the promise of the other party justifying enforcement of the promise. The detriment also indicates the intent to contract, as does the promise requesting the detriment.

The Bargain Theory

Under the common law, the basic theory of consideration was the bargain theory with one major exception, *promissory estoppel*. Only the bargain theory demands the satisfaction of the requirements of detriment bargained for, to be explained next. When applicable, the exception requires something different to show that consideration is present. The concern of the promissory estoppel is different from that which is traditional to the concept of consideration. The concern is that equity and justice be done in the contractual setting rather than the concern about whether the parties intended to commit themselves to a contractual obligation.

► Detriment Bargained For

Detriment is the giving up of a legal right one has by law to do or not do something (forbearance), or the assumption of a legal duty to do or not do something not otherwise imposed by law. In the following case the plaintiff gave up a legal right that she honestly believed she had, even though its exercise would not have produced a result in her favor. Her forbearance constituted a detriment to her and consideration for the defendant's promise, making it a contract.

FACTS

A mother brought suit against a claimed putative father to recover for breach of an oral agreement under which he was to pay birth expenses and to support a child upon condition that the mother would refrain from instituting bastardy proceedings. The putative father did not carry out his part of the oral agreement and, in a subsequent bastardy proceeding, upon medical proof in the form of blood tests, it was shown that he could not have fathered the child.

The mother contends that her forbearance was a detriment to her and consideration for the putative father's promise to pay. The putative father contends that, since he was not the father, there was no detriment to the mother and, therefore, no contract.

DECISION

The court found for the mother and enforced the agreement. Forbearance to sue for a lawful claim or demand is sufficient consideration where the promise to pay is for a forbearance. The party forbearing must have an honest intention to prosecute litigation which is not frivolous, vexatious, or unlawful and which he or she believes to be well founded. The court found in this case that the mother believed the putative father to actually be the father of the child, and therefore her forbearance to sue was valid, good, and sufficient consideration.

Fiege v. Boehm, 123 A.2d 316 (Md. 1956).

► Forms of Detriment

The certainty of terms test (see p. 141) illustrates some forms that detriment can take. Consideration is unique in that it requires that the offer and acceptance contain bargained-for legal rights and duties. Detriment need not have economic value. In the following case the court held that detriment can consist of an implied promise to forbear from repossessing a car.

FACTS

The evidence showed that a grandson of Cheney entered into a retail installment sales contract with Zimmerman Ford, Inc., to purchase an automobile and that he forged his grandmother's signature as a co-signer on the contract to purchase the car. Thereafter, Zimmerman Ford obtained a replacement contract with the real signature of Cheney. Cheney, the grandmother, testified that she knew her signature was forged on the first contract and that she knew her grandson would not be able to keep the car unless she signed the replacement contract. Cheney now contends she received no consideration to support her promise to pay the pre-existing debt of her grandson.

DECISION

The court held for Zimmerman Ford, Inc. The court found sufficient evidence of mutual consideration consisting of Zimmerman Ford's implied promise to forbear from repossessing the car in exchange for Cheney's promise to pay if the grandson did not. An agreement to forbear need not be in express terms or for an exact period of time; the terms may be gathered from the surrounding circumstances from which forbearance for a reasonable time may be implied.

Zimmerman Ford, Inc. v. Cheney, 271 N.E.2d 682 (Ill. 1971).

Bargained For Whether or not detriment has been bargained for is decided by whether it was mutually requested. This determination will be made objectively by looking at the facts of the contractual setting and deciding as a reasonable person whether the request has been made. This is illustrated by the following case.

FACTS

This is an admiralty action concerning the sinking of a harbor tug, the result of the negligence of a pilot hired by Steam Tanker, Amoco, said negligence being imputed to the Steam Tanker, Amoco. Immediately after the harbor tug sank and Steam Tanker, Amoco's vessel had docked, the pilot presented the captain of Steam Tanker, Amoco's vessel with a pilotage agreement, the pertinent part of which read: "It is agreed between Pilot and the Vessel, her owners . . . etc. that the Pilot . . . will not be held personally liable for any damage whatsoever . . . caused by Vessel . . . [due] to Pilot's negligence. . . ." The captain signed the agreement without reading it as was his custom. At the time the agreement was entered into, the pilot's association to which the pilot belonged offered a 15 percent discount on pilot fees to any vessel using an association pilot and a 15 percent discount on billing was given to Steam Tanker, Amoco. Steam Tanker, Amoco contends that it is not an agreement since it never received consideration for the right it purportedly gave up not to sue the pilot for damage experienced due to his negligence.

DECISION

The court held for Steam Tanker, Amoco. *The court said that consideration must be bargained for by the promisor and given by the promisee in exchange for the promise.* In this case the pilotage discount was not bargained for by Steam Tanker, Amoco as consideration for its agreement to relieve the pilot from liability for negligence and the discount was not given in exchange for the exculpatory agreement. Such discounts were given to any vessel using an association pilot, regardless of a vessel's acceptance of the exculpatory clause. Furthermore, the signing of the pilotage agreement after the services had been rendered was intended to be a receipt for services rendered and not a contract. The court stated that it was not likely that *after* the grounding took place the captain would have agreed without consideration to an exculpatory clause which would have left the ship *solely* responsible for heavy damage.

Gulf Towing Co., Inc. v. Steam Tanker, Amoco, N.Y., 648 F.2d 242 (1981).

Adequacy and Mutuality of Obligations

If only one party to a proposed contract has been requested to give detriment, no binding contractual obligation will be formed, under the general principle that if one party is not bound to a contract (did not give consideration), the other is not bound.

Adequacy of consideration does not deal with a problem of economic value directly. However, where the detriment exchanged is economically worthless or greatly disproportionate in value, it will not be adequate consideration if it can be shown it was not intended to be consideration. Adequacy questions for the most part limit themselves to questions of whether consideration was intended or whether a contract was intended at all. (For example, perhaps a gift was intended and the purpose of the gift was not meant to be consideration for any promise.) This is illustrated by the following case where the consideration exchanged is of disproportionate value yet the court finds a contract to exist.

FACTS

Ruby Trump Ruffner died leaving the residue of her estate to St. Andrews Episcopal Church. Twenty-one months before her death, she executed a contract transferring stock representing a controlling interest in High Lawn Memorial Park Company to an escrow agent retaining the income from the stock for her life and upon her death to transfer the stock to one Ballard should he survive. The stated consideration for the transfer was that Ballard "covenants and agrees to immediately assume the full management of High Lawn Memorial Park corporation as may be necessary in and about its proper operation and with a full effort towards its profitable operation." Newell, trustee of the church, brings this action to have the alleged contract set aside on the ground that it lacks consideration, and that the friendship between Ruby and Ballard was the basis for undue influence by Ballard on Ruby in causing Ruby to make the transaction. The lower court rendered judgment for Newell, and High Lawn Memorial Park appeals.

DECISION

The court held for High Lawn Memorial Park Co. The doctrine of failure of consideration in the law of contracts is certainly a nebulous one. Cases can be found where the slightest consideration is adequate to support a contract while others can be found in which substantial consideration has been held insufficient. In this case, it was held that, though Ballard was a friend of Ruby and already employed by High Lawn Memorial Park he could have withdrawn from management at any time but contracted with Ruby not to do so. Such is the nature of consideration. Though Ruby may have given disproportionately more than she got, she did receive consideration of some value for the contract. There is insufficient evidence of undue influence here.

Newell v. High Lawn Memorial Park Co., 264 S.E.2d 454 (W. Va. 1980).

► Applications

Past Consideration Under the bargain theory, "past consideration" is no consideration. Thus, detriment given to support a prior contract cannot be used or brought forward to support a new contract. (Al promises to pay Bud an additional $1,000 if Bud will perform the contract previously made by them. Bud's obligation to perform the previous contract is not a detriment for Al's new promise. Al's promise is not a contract.) Nor can one already under a legal duty offer the performance of that duty as consideration for a contract. The right already exists for the other contracting party. Therefore, a promise not to commit a tort or crime, or a promise by a public official to perform a public duty, cannot act as consideration for a contract. In the following case giving incriminating evidence to stop a crime was not deemed to be performance of a pre-existing duty.

FACTS

In 1982, executives of Gulf Oil Corporation received a letter announcing that one of its plant facilities would be sabotaged by explosive charges unless $15,000,000 was paid, whereupon the bombs would be deactivated. The executives were told not to inform the authorities and were sent a sample bomb. The letter closed with "Gentlemen, THE CLOCK IS RUNNING." The FBI investigated the extortion attempt and arrested McBride and others. Shortly after McBride's arrest, he stated he would give the government everything it needed in exchange for his girlfriend's release and nonprosecution. An assistant United States Attorney drafted an agreement which gave McBride's girlfriend statutory immunity. This agreement was accepted by McBride and he gave all requested information to the authorities. Subsequent to these events, McBride's girlfriend was indicted and now McBride's girlfriend moves to dismiss her indictment on the grounds that it is in violation of the Government's agreement not to prosecute her. The Government argued that the agreement fails as a contract because of lack of consideration.

DECISION

The court held for McBride on the consideration issue. The court said that the argument that McBride, in promising to locate and describe explosives, was not furnishing consideration but merely fulfilling a preexisting duty to refrain from criminal activity could not be upheld. McBride, the court said, had no duty to provide the Government incriminating evidence. In doing so, he relinquished his rights under the Fifth Amendment to the United States Constitution and thereby suffered a detriment. He was induced to suffer that detriment by the Government's promise not to prosecute his girlfriend. The court held that McBride's promise clearly fits the well-established definition of consideration: a promise to act or forbear that is bargained for and exchanged for a return promise.

United States v. McBride, 571 F.Supp. 596 (S.D. Tex. 1983).

liquidated debt
A debt whose amount has been agreed to by the parties or is ascertainable by a standard

unliquidated debt
A debt whose amount has not been ascertained

Liquidated and Unliquidated Debt In a **liquidated debt,** the amount of the debt has been agreed to by the parties or is ascertainable by a standard. For example, a five-cent deposit on a beverage bottle is the amount agreed to by the buyer and the retailer as the liquidated debt for not returning the bottle. In an **unliquidated debt,** the amount of the debt is unascertained. (Pursuant to the contract, Al performed services for Bea. The contract did not state what amount Bea was to pay Al.) In a disputed debt or claim, the person against whom the debt is asserted honestly and reasonably believes it not to be valid, but the claimant disagrees. (Al performs a service for Bea and claims $150 as its value, but Bea honestly and reasonably believes and contends that she never requested the service.)

An attempt to discharge a liquidated debt by doing something less than what is required by the contract (even though accepted) is ineffective, unless a gift is made by the creditor of the remaining legal duty not performed. The doing of something more than what was initially bargained for will discharge the debt. Thus when a creditor promises to discharge the debtor if the debtor will pay a lesser amount at an earlier date, this is something more than the debtor was obligated to do, and, therefore, if the debtor does this, the debtor is discharged from the debt.

composition
(Outside of bankruptcy) an agreement among some or all of the creditors with their insolvent or financially embarrassed debtor, each to take something less than what is owed to him or her and, on the debtor's performance, the debtor is discharged fully as to those creditors who are parties to the agreement

A **composition** (agreement) outside of bankruptcy will discharge liquidated debts. The agreement by some or all of the creditors with their insolvent or financially embarrassed debtor (a person whose assets are less than his or her liabilities or who ceases to pay or cannot pay debts as they come due), each to take something less than what is owed to him, is sufficient new legal detriment bargained for to bind the creditors to the new agreement which, when performed, will discharge the previous liquidated debts. The mutual promises of the creditors provide the consideration for each other. This reflects public policy.

accord and satisfaction
A new contract (accord) that discharges a party from a previous contractual obligation; the old contract is discharged (satisfied)

An acceptance of something less than what is demanded satisfies and discharges an unliquidated debt because each of the parties to the contract has suffered detriment by foregoing the opportunity to have a court determination of what is owed. This type of discharge is a form of compromise that is technically called an **accord and satisfaction.** The parties are in "accord" with their new contract, which the parties intend of itself to

FIGURE 9.3 **Consideration for Debt**

DEBT	Consideration present?
LIQUIDATED (amount certain)	
Discharge by doing less →	No
if remainder a gift →	Yes
Discharge by doing more →	Yes
Discharge by agreement outside of bankruptcy →	Yes
UNLIQUIDATED (amount uncertain)	
Discharge by doing less →	Yes; accord and satisfaction
DISPUTED	
Payment by debtor →	Yes

"satisfy" the obligation of the old contract and thus discharge the old contract. (For a discussion of accord and of accord and satisfaction, see p. 245.)

Payment by the debtor of a disputed debt is consideration for the creditor's promise of discharge on such payment. The debtor is experiencing a forbearance in that the debtor is giving up the defense of not being liable for the agreed upon larger amount, which the debtor honestly and reasonably believes is not owing. (Carl and Dora disagree on what Dora owes Carl. Carl claims it is $100 and Dora honestly and reasonably believes it is $50. Carl promises to discharge Dora from Dora's debt if Dora will pay Carl $75, which Dora does. Carl's promise is supported by Dora's forbearance to refuse to pay more than $50 and Dora's payment of $75 as consideration and is a contract binding on Carl.) It is irrelevant whether Carl's claim or Dora's defense was correct. Payment by the debtor of a disputed claim results in an accord and satisfaction and a discharge of the debtor's obligation to the creditor.

Promissory Estoppel

The concept of **promissory estoppel** is an exception to the bargain theory of consideration. It requires that certain elements exist: (1) an existing promise (2) made with the expectation that it will be relied upon (3) and justifiably relied upon substantially (4) to the injury of the promisee should the promise not be enforced. In the typical situation, no detriment or benefit is given by one of the parties to the contract. Under the bargain theory of consideration there would be no contract because of lack of mutuality of obligation. However, in limited circumstances, a contract will be found on the ground of promissory estoppel because of the need to promote strongly felt public policy, justice, and equity. In the following case a promise was enforced to avoid injustice.

promissory estoppel
An equitable principle of preventing injustice by enforcing a gratuitous promise as a contract, without consideration and agreement, the promisor reasonably expecting that his or her promise would be justifiably relied upon substantially by the promisee

FACTS

A county in the state of Florida advertised for bids for a road resurfacing. The bid instructions provided that all bidders were to submit bids for both of two alternatives, *A* and *B*. One bidder bid only on alternative *A* because the county inadvertently failed to include in the bidder's information the instruction to bid for both alternatives. The county awarded the project to this bidder who submitted the low bid only on alternative *A*. Baxter's Asphalt and Concrete, Inc., the lowest bidder on alternatives *A* and *B*, sought an injunction against the awarding of the bid. While the injunction action was pending, the county allowed the project to be completed by the low bidder on only alternative *A*. The injunction, issued too late, ordered the bid process to be readvertised. Baxter's Asphalt and Concrete now sues under promissory estoppel for damages.

DECISION

The court held for Baxter's Asphalt and Concrete, Inc. The court found that where the government solicited bids promising the contract to the lowest bidder, the lowest bidder could reasonably rely on the government's promise. Whereas here the lowest bidder for alternatives *A* and *B* did rely to its detriment, it was entitled to reliance damages to include the costs of preparing its bid and the legal costs associated with defending its interest, but not alleged loss of profits, said loss being speculative.

Baxter's Asphalt and Concrete, Inc., v. Liberty County, 421 So.2d 505 (Fla. 1982).

The evidence of the need to do **equity** and fair dealing is causing the courts to apply the concept to the promises made in a business transaction in limited circumstances. The following case illustrates the application of promissory estoppel in enforcing a business promise.

equity
Principles of justice and fairness that developed when the relief at common law was inadequate

FACTS

The Vogels, a married couple, bought a used home in Mississippi from another married couple. Mr. Vogel desired a warranty against defects, and as part of the negotiated transaction, the sellers paid for and delivered to the buyers a document entitled Home Buyers Protection Plan issued by American Warranty Home Service Corporation. American Warranty published a brochure that stated that the policyholder would be protected against major repair bills resulting from hidden defects. Mr. Vogel read the brochure and relied upon it in his decision to purchase the home. The actual insurance policy contained limited warranties for repairs. Nine months after taking possession of the home, major repairs became necessary due to hidden defects. The insurance company refused to pay for the repairs under the limited warranty. To determine whether the terms of the brochure could constitute covenants between the Vogels and American Warranty, the court turned to the Restatement's definition of promissory estoppel.

DECISION

The court held for the Vogels. The court concluded that a Mississippi state court would hold an insurer estopped [barred] to deny that an insurance contract contained a clause that the insurer represented (in its brochure) to be among its terms after the insured relied on that representation.

Vogel v. American Warranty Home Service Corp., 695 F.2d 877 (1983).

In limited situations, promises between closely related parties have been enforced under the concept of promissory estoppel because of the need of justice.

► Pledge of a Gift

A pledge to a charitable or benevolent institution (for example, to a church or to United Way) is not enforceable under the bargain theory of consideration because the one making the promise to give a gift has not bargained for anything (detriment) in return. For example, Al promises to contribute $100 toward the cost of a new organ for a church. A promise has been made. It is calculated to be relied upon. It may be justifiably relied upon. If relied on, the institution will suffer loss if it is not carried out, and there is a strongly felt public policy to assist such organizations by enforcing the promise as an obligation by promissory estoppel.

Moral Obligation

A person may be motivated to do, or to refrain from doing, something and thereby experience an "obligation" to cause this to happen or not to happen. The obligation may be a "legal obligation" or a "moral obligation." When a promise is made to perform, it becomes important to determine whether there is a legal or a moral obligation to perform under the law of contracts. We have seen that, under the bargain theory of contracts, a promise requesting and receiving a detriment or benefit creates a legal obligation to perform the promise and the promise is then called a contract. A previous moral obligation does not involve a detriment or benefit and, not being consideration, it is not sufficient to cause a promise to perform the moral obligation to become a contract. (Ann's promise to Ben to pay $100 to Ben for Ben's previous love and affection; Don's promise to Ed to pay Ed for Fran's previous injury to Ed; Al's promise to Bud to pay Jay's previous debt to Bud.) All of these promises do not create legal obligations to perform and, therefore, are not binding as contracts.

Statutes

In situations where contractual obligations have been discharged by the passage of a **statute of limitations** or a proceeding in bankruptcy, a promise to pay a debt due under the discharged contract will reinstate the debt even though this runs counter to the rule that "past consideration" is no consideration. The new promise is enforceable in accordance with its terms. (Art owes Ben three debts of $600 each. All of the debts are barred by the statute of limitations. Art writes Ben, "I promise to pay you one of those $600 debts that I owe; the other two I shall not pay." Art's promise of $600 is binding.)

statute of limitations
A statute limiting the time in which a claim may be asserted in court; expiration bars enforcement of the claim

In most cases the new promise must be in writing. There is some justification for this holding when one recognizes that good and adequate consideration was given in the previous contract, and that the court is merely requiring a promisor to abide by the new promise and to carry out what the promisor was obligated to carry out previously before having been discharged by operation of law. However, the new promise may be implied from the debtor's conduct, such as the debtor's part payment of the debt. (For example, Ann owes Betty a debt of $1,000, barred by the statute of limitations. Ann orally promises to pay the debt in monthly installments of $10, and subsequently pays $5 on account of the first installment. The part payment, though excepted from a statute requiring a writing, binds Ann only to pay in monthly installments.) The same is true by the debtor's issuance of new collateral security for the debt, or acknowledgement of the debt. (Al owes Bev $400 and sends Bev a post-dated check for $200, stating that it is sent as part payment of the debt. The delivery of the check operates as a new promise to pay the debt and payment of the check by the drawee bank on the subsequent date shown on the check operates as a second new promise by Al. The bank's authority to pay was revocable, and Al could have stopped payment.)

If the debtor has several debts with the same creditor, the effect of the debtor's unqualified part payment depends upon whether or not the debtor has specified the particular debt to which the payment is to be applied. If the debtor has so specified, the creditor must apply the payment to that debt, and if the statute has run on that debt the part payment reinstates the barred debt and the statute starts running anew. If the debtor has not so specified, then the creditor may apply the payment to any of the debts; but the creditor's application of the payment to a debt on which the statute has run does not reinstate the barred debt nor halt the statute.

The new federal Bankruptcy Reform Act of 1978, Section 524(c)(d), as amended in 1984, makes new special provision for a debtor who wishes to reinstate, wholly or partially, the debtor's obligation discharged in bankruptcy. The subject is discussed in Chapter 52, Bankruptcy under the Bankruptcy Reform Act of 1978,[1] to which reference should be made at this time. Bankruptcy is solely a federal matter; there are no state bankruptcy laws.

The Uniform Commercial Code

Under the Uniform Commercial Code, consideration is no longer required in the following instances: to support a "firm offer"[2] (UCC 2-205); to support an agreement that modified a contract for the sale of goods (UCC 2-209(1)); to discharge a claim arising out

[1] See "reaffirmation," p. 1093.

[2] See p. 147.

of an alleged breach of contract if the aggrieved party has signed and delivered a written waiver or renunciation (UCC 1-107). In other sections of the Code, consideration has been dispensed with for other purposes.[3]

Figure 9.4 shows the basics of consideration that have been discussed in this chapter. The "bargain theory" includes the elements of a detriment that is bargained for. Promissory estoppel has four elements, as shown in the figure. Note that there are several situations both under the common law and under the Uniform Commercial Code where consideration is not required.

Summary Statement

1. Consideration is a necessary element to the existence of a contract, though there are numerous exceptions.
2. Under the bargain theory of consideration, two objective tests must be satisfied before consideration will be found. These are (a) detriment and (b) bargained for.
3. Detriment bargained for requires that the giving of a detriment be a condition for bringing the contract into existence.
4. Detriment can be recited as a formula: doing or refraining from doing something that one was under no previous legal obligation to do or not do.
5. Mutuality of obligation requires that if one is not bound to a contract, the other party to the contract is not bound.
6. Adequacy of consideration deals with a question of intention.
7. Past consideration is no consideration, with exceptions.
8. An unliquidated debt can be discharged by compromise.
9. Promissory estoppel is applied in situations where the doing of equity is required.
10. Moral obligation is not consideration for a subsequent promise to perform the previous moral obligation.

FIGURE 9.4 **The Basics of Consideration**

Theory	Exception	Contracts without Consideration	
Bargain	Promissory Estoppel	Moral Obligation	U.C.C.
1. Detriment	1. Promise	1. Waiver of Statute of Limitations	1. Firm Offer
2. Bargained for	2. Induce Reliance	2. Waiver of Bankruptcy Discharge	2. Modification of Sales Contract
	3. Justified Reliance	3. Extreme Moral Obligation	3. Discharge by Written Waiver or Renunciation
	4. Injury		4. Other

[3]See Commercial Paper, UCC 3-605; Letters of Credit, UCC 5-105.

11. The Uniform Commercial Code in many instances has dispensed with requiring that consideration be present in order to have a contract.

The following case is included in depth to illustrate why consideration exists in contract law.

BAEHR v. PENN-O-TEX OIL CORP.
104 N.W.2d 661 (Minn. 1960)

Baehr sued Penn-O-Tex Oil Corporation for rent because of an alleged breach of contract. Baehr leased gasoline filling stations to Kemp, who was heavily in debt to Penn-O-Tex. Baehr received a letter from Kemp stating that his (Kemp's) assets were all tied up by Penn-O-Tex and this was why he had not paid the rent due on the leased stations.

A short time after receiving Kemp's letter, Baehr called the agent of Penn-O-Tex and asked about payment of the filling station rents. Penn-O-Tex told Baehr "that Mr. Kemp's affairs were in a very mixed up form but that he would get them straightened out and mail *Baehr* ... checks for the rent".

Hearing nothing further, Baehr wrote a letter to Penn-O-Tex asking what he had to do to get his rent checks and added "or will I have to give it to an attorney to sue?"

Penn-O-Tex wrote Baehr indicating that they were trying to help Kemp "but in no way were they operating the business." The letter denied knowledge of or responsibility for any rent due Baehr.

After receiving the letter, Baehr called Penn-O-Tex demanding payment of the rent.

Penn-O-Tex's agent said that Penn-O-Tex would pay the rent. He would take it up with the home office.

The rent was never paid by Penn-O-Tex, and the communications described took place over an eighteen-month period of time.

The court reasoned that if it accepted Baehr's version of the statements made by Penn-O-Tex's agent as recorded, there was an unequivocal assurance given that the rents would be paid—a promise.

But the court noted "the fact that a promise is given does not necessarily mean a contract was made." Not every promise is legally enforceable. It is not practical nor reasonable to expect full performance of every assurance given whether it be thoughtless, casual, and gratuitous, or deliberately and seriously made.

The test, the court stated, that has been developed by the common law for determining the enforceability of promises is the doctrine of consideration. Consideration requires that a contractual promise be the product of a bargain. It means a negotiation resulting in the voluntary assumption of an obligation by one party upon condition of an act or forbearance by the other (legal value) [detriment]. Consideration thus ensures that the promise enforced as a contract is not accidental, casual, or gratuitous but has been uttered intentionally as the result of some deliberation, manifested by reciprocal bargaining or negotiation. In this view, the requirement of consideration is no mere technicality, historic anachronism, or arbitrary formality. It is an attempt to be as reasonable as we can in deciding which promises constitute contracts.

Consideration, as essential evidence of the parties' intent to create a legal obligation, must be something adopted and regarded by the parties as such. In substance, a contractual promise must be of logical form: "If ... [consideration] is given ... then I promise. ..."

In this case, though a promise was made by Penn-O-Tex, a contract was not created. While Baehr suffered detriment by forbearing to sue Kemp, such detriment was not bargained for by Penn-O-Tex. Hence Baehr did not give consideration for Penn-O-Tex's promise. The voluntary relinquishment of a legal right is not consideration. Nor did the court find factually that there was evidence that either party took Penn-O-Tex's assurances seriously or acted upon them in any way. Judgment for Penn-O-Tex Oil Corporation.

Questions and Case Problems

1. Hiers-Wright Associates entered into a contract with Manufacturers Hanovers Mortgage, Inc., to repair water damage in two buildings. The contract required Hiers-Wright to repair pipes, replace sheetrock and fix other items affected by the freeze, all for $24,000. When Hiers-Wright began to repair the buildings, it discovered that winter weather had wreaked massive water damage that was greater than had been anticipated. It informed Manufacturers Hanover that it was experiencing large cost overruns and Manufacturers Hanover agreed to reimburse Hiers-Wright for these costs. When the work was completed, Hiers-Wright was paid $24,000 by Manufacturers Hanover. Can Hiers-Wright successfully sue Manufacturers Hanover for the cost overruns? [*Hiers-Wright Assoc. v. Manufacturers Hanover Mortgage, Inc.*, 356 S.E.2d 903 (Ga. 1987).]
2. An agreement was made between prisoners and a director of a department of correction who was a hostage of a prisoner and who gave the prisoners absolute immunity from prosecution if they would cease engaging in further violence in a prison uprising. The prisoners subsequently were tried and convicted for the criminal acts, and they then sued the U.S. Government for breach of contract. Judgment for prisoners and the Government appealed. What result? [*United States v. Bridgeman,* 523 F.2d 1099 (1975).]
3. Jessee instituted suit against Smith seeking $2,673.26 for labor performed pursuant to an oral contract. The trial court sustained Smith's motion to strike Jessee's evidence of the oral contract on the basis that the labor price Jessee claimed was "exorbitant" and, hence, contrary to public policy. Did the trial court err in substituting its judgment for what should be consideration when it feels the underlying bargain is foolish or exorbitant? [*Jessee v. Smith,* 278 S.E.2d 793 (Va. 1981).]
4. Upon receipt of a certified check from a bank, subcontractors on a construction project signed the following receipt:

   > "RECEIVED of The Omaha National Bank the sum of______ Dollars______ in payment of the above order. In consideration of said payment the undersigned hereby acknowledges that the mortgage in favor of The Omaha National Bank in the above property constitutes a prior **lien,** superior to any lien which the undersigned may now have or hereafter may acquire. . . ."

   lien
   A legal right in another's property as security for the performance of an obligation

   The bank had the right to pay the general contractor first and for the general contractor to pay the subcontractors. Subcontractors contend there was no consideration for the agreement to subordinate their liens. Are they correct? [*Omaha National Bank v. Goddard Realty, Inc.*, 316 N.W.2d 306 (Neb. 1982).]
5. An 83-year-old married woman contended that she was enticed and induced to leave her apartment and move in with a 79-year-old widower in a house on land which at the time he owned. At a later date, the widower deeded to the woman a fee simple (the greatest bundle of ownership rights in, and powers over, realty) interest in the house and land, reserving a life estate (ownership of property for the length of life) to himself. Shortly thereafter relationships became strained and an agreement was entered into. The agreement stated, "It is mutually agreed by and between the parties hereto that during the remainder of their lifetimes, they shall live together in harmony in the above-described residential premises. Neither shall have the right to dispossess the other from these premises." Shortly after the signing of this

agreement, the widower changed the locks on the doors of the house and refused to allow the woman to reenter. The woman claims that she has a right to reside in the house and brings this suit to enforce the contract. What result? [*Maszewski v. Piskadlo,* 318 So.2d 226 (Fla. 1975).]

6. The following provision appeared in an agreement:

> The Contractor shall transport in contractor's truck such tonnage of beets as may be loaded by the Company from piles at receiving stations of the Company, and unload said beets at such factory or factories as may be designated by the Company. The term of this contract shall be from October 1, 1980 until February 15, 1981.

De Los Santos had been transporting beets under the agreement for approximately two months when in early December 1980 the Great Western Sugar Co. informed De Los Santos that his services were no longer needed. De Los Santos sues for lost profits that would have been earned had he been allowed to continue to haul beets. Does De Los Santos have a contract that he can enforce against Great Western Sugar Co.? [*De Los Santos v. Great Western Sugar Co.,* 348 N.W.2d 842 (Neb. 1984).]

7. The following letter, written on company stationery and addressed to Harry Cohen, was sent and received:

> Dear Mr. Cohen:
>
> This will confirm our understanding that you will continue to purchase from us all the scrap that generates from the operation of our plant at fair market price, as long as you live on the same basis as we have dealt between us in the past.
>
> We are very pleased with your service and hope you can continue to deal with us for many years to come.
> Sincerely yours,
>
> WOOD BROS. STEEL STAMPING CO.
>
> /s/ Arthur Lasser, President
>
> AL:amh
>
> CC: Ralph Cohen

Later in the year Wood Brothers began to reduce the amount of scrap metal it sold to Cohen. Still later in the year all scrap metal sales ceased. Cohen filed a complaint for breach of contract. In their answer to the complaint, Wood Brothers contend there is no contract because of lack of mutuality of obligation. Is there or is there not mutuality of obligation? [*Cohen v. Wood Bros. Steel Stamping Co.,* 529 N.E.2d 1068 (Ill. 1988).]

8. Dyke Industries, Inc., supplied Mike Waldrop with materials for a house he was building for his sister, Brenda Wilson. For several years, Waldrop and Dyke Industries had conducted business on an open account. During construction of her house, Wilson made payments on her brother's account; these were delivered to

Dyke Industries by her brother. On February 8, 1984, Wilson mailed a check to Dyke Industries in the amount of $2,699.51 and added a notation stating "Customer No. 1525—Wilson Job—Paid in Full." Before cashing the check, Dyke Industries informed Wilson that $1,218.34 would still be owing on her account. Brenda did not dispute this amount other than to say she had previously written a check to Waldrop for this amount. Waldrop denies he ever received this check. Dyke Industries cashed the $2,699.51 check and sued Wilson for $1,218.34. Was the cashing of the check an accord and satisfaction of an unliquidated debt? [*Dyke Industries, Inc. v. Waldrop*, 697 S.W.2d 936 (Ark. 1985).]

9. In an action to foreclose a mortgage, Virgie E. Tinsley's Enterprises, Inc., appeals from an order of the Supreme Court, Suffolk County, dated August 18, 1983, which denied its motion to dismiss the complaint against it on the ground that the action was barred by the statute of limitations. The mortgage in question was executed on April 1, 1974 and provided for the payment of any unpaid balance of the $10,000 principal on or before April 1, 1976. On April 15, 1978, some two years after the note remained unpaid, Tinsley's signed a written memorandum promising to pay the mortgage debt. Action was brought by Aleci in April 1982. In New York the applicable statute of limitations on mortgage debt is six years. On appeal, should the court bar the action by the running of the statute of limitations? [*Aleci v. Virgie E. Tinsley's Enterprises,* 476 N.Y.S.2d 595 (N.Y. 1984).]

10. In *Baehr v. Penn-O-Tex Oil Corp.*, excerpted at the beginning of this section, the court said "the requirement of consideration is no mere technicality, historic anachronism, or arbitrary formality. It is an attempt to be as reasonable as we can in deciding which promises constitute contracts." Evaluate this statement.

C H A P T E R

10

CAPACITY/ABILITY TO CREATE A CONTRACT

After you have read this chapter, you should be able to:

1. Discuss the concept of capacity to make a contract and explain what purpose it serves in the law of contracts.
2. Recognize that there are individuals (a) who have no capacity to contract, (b) who have a limited capacity to contract, and (c) who can avoid the consequences of contract.
3. Be aware of the similarities and differences in the way classes of individuals avoid and ratify contracts.
4. Understand that necessaries occupy a unique position with regard to avoidance of contracts.
5. Perceive the current movement of the law to expand contractual capacity.

Business Decisions and the Law

Alan Otten is a highly respected reporter for the *Wall Street Journal.* Although he has covered stories on every conceivable issue and event since the Truman Administration, one of his most moving, written in 1985, began:

"Every few days now, I go to visit my ninety-year-old mother in a nearby nursing home, more to salve my own conscience probably than to do her any meaningful service. For her, in fact, there is little I can do. She lies on her side in bed, legs drawn rigidly into a fetal position, blinks at me uncomprehendingly as I prattle on about family doings, and rarely utters a sound except a shriek of pain when the attendants turn her from side to side in their constant battle to heal her terrible bedsores. She must be hand-fed, and her incontinency requires a urethral catheter."

Mr. Otten further remarks that this is the scenario for more and more elderly patients. The aged end their days in nursing homes and hospitals with little hope that there will ever be a full recovery in ever-increasing numbers.

Today more than ever, the issue of the capacity of the aged to contract gains importance. How law will deal with this issue of contractual capacity is addressed in the case of *Paskvan v. Mesich.*

Source: Roy Hoopes, "Turning Out the Light," *Modern Maturity,* June–July 1988, p. 29; reprinted with permission from *Modern Maturity.* Copyright 1988, American Association of Retired Persons.

Elements needed for a contract:

	CHAPTER
1. Mutual assent with a promise or promises	6, 7, 8
2. Consideration	9
3. CAPACITY TO CONTRACT	**10**
4. Legality	11

contractual capacity
The legal ability to make a contract

Introduction

In the preceding chapters of this part we discussed two of the four elements required for a contract: mutual assent and consideration. We now consider the third element—a party's capacity to contract. The existence of the necessary **contractual capacity** of the parties is an element necessary to the formation of a contract. It is important to note that the capacity to create a contract provides yet another barrier to our freedom to create, through a contract, rights and duties not otherwise imposed by law.

The law associated with the capacity to create a contract recognizes that there are certain situations in which one should not be allowed to contract. Moreover, there is a recognition that certain persons should be given a chance to escape the consequences of a contract because they need protection. These are the important value judgments that have resulted in the law that determines one's capacity to create a contract.

A study of the law relating to the capacity to create a contract is a study of who has no capacity to contract, who has limited capacity to contract, and who can avoid the consequences of a contract.

adjudged
The result of a formal legal process

void
Of no legal effect

trust
A legal device whereby legal title to property is held by one person (a trustee) for the benefit of a beneficiary

surety
A person who promises the creditor to pay the principal's debt or to perform his or her obligation on the principal's nonperformance

voidable contract
A contract that can be avoided by one or more of the parties

Protection—Limited or No Capacity

When one is **adjudged** mentally incompetent (insane), any attempt to contract is **void.** The party has no capacity to contract. A **trust** will normally give a trustee a limited power to contract to further the purpose of the trust. A corporation, which contracts through agents, can enter into contracts that only further the purpose contained in the corporate charter. Convicted felons in some states have a limited capacity to contract. In some states a married woman cannot act as a **surety** for her husband's debts. Enemy and unlawful aliens cannot contract or sue on contracts. Minors, often called infants, who are so young that they cannot understand the significance of a contract have no capacity to contract.

These various situations, which run the full spectrum from no ability to contract to partial inability to contract, exist for various purposes—mainly protection and punishment. (See Figure 10.1.)

Protection—Right to Avoid

A **voidable contract** is one that is subject to being avoided by a party or the parties and, on avoidance, is discharged. (Art fraudulently induces Betty to contract with Art. Betty has

FIGURE 10.1 Incapacity Table

Category of Person	Incapacity		Reason for Determination of Incapacity	Agreement Result
	Total	Limited		
Adjudged mentally incompetent (insane)	Yes		Inability to protect oneself	Void
Mentally incompetent (insane)		Yes	Inability to protect oneself	Voidable
Trustee		Yes	To ensure that the purpose of a trust is carried out	Void
Corporation		Yes	To ensure that the purpose of a corporation is carried out	Void
Convicted felons		Yes	Punishment	Void
Married women in special situations		Yes	Protection from undue influence	Void
Minors of a tender age	Yes		Inability to protect oneself	Void
Minors not of a tender age		Yes	Inability to protect oneself	Voidable
Intoxicated	Yes	Yes	The degree of intoxication determines whether incapacity is total or limited	Void or Voidable
Enemy or unlawful aliens	Yes		Punishment	Void
Felon in jail		Yes in some states	Public policy	Void

a power of avoidance, so the contract is voidable by Betty.) It *is* a good contract until it is avoided.

Those persons who are minors under the law (below the age of eighteen in most states, below twenty-one in a few states)[1] can avoid (rescind) their contracts. Avoidance of the contractual obligation is possible by those who are induced to enter into a contract because of insane delusions or by those who are so under the influence of drugs or alcoholic beverages that they do not know they are entering into a contract. Only the party with the power of avoidance can avoid the contract, e.g., the minor, not the adult; the insane person after becoming sane, but not the other contracting party.

The purpose for giving the right to avoid a contract is the value judgment of the law that these classes of people need protection from what might turn out to be an improvident act. This principle of law is in a state of evolution. In the following case a

[1]The law disregards fractions of a day. Thus, a person born at 1:00 P.M. on November 11, 1970 becomes eighteen at the beginning of the day of November 10, 1988.

contract was set aside (avoided) because of a party's limited mental capacity and business competence.

FACTS

This is an action to set aside certain business transacted by one deemed to be limited in mental capacity and business competence. The court found that Mesich ingratiated himself into the confidence of Paskvan and fraudulently took advantage of Paskvan's mental and physical infirmities and incompetency to induce the business which has been transacted. Both Paskvan and Mesich immigrated to the United States from Austria, had known each other for many years, had common tastes and interests, and both spoke the Croatian language. Paskvan was unable to read or write English, and because of his injuries it was extremely difficult for him to understand matters read or related to him; he relied upon Mesich for explanations. The eyesight of Paskvan was also impaired due to an unsuccessful operation on cataracts. He was also quite hard of hearing.

DECISION

The court held for Paskvan. The court set aside the contract. The court stated that, where it is established that the mind of a party to a transaction has become infirm or his comprehension weakened by age, accident, or illness, the usual presumption of normality and capacity to contract is dissipated. The weakness of mind may not amount to absolute incapacity to transact any business at all, and the mental infirmity need not have been established judicially in order to require the person who has received benefits from dealings with one so afflicted to prove that they were not affected thereby. If one does not have sufficient understanding to protect one's own interests and mental strength to compete in the marketplace, he lacks capacity to transact ordinary business, and dealings with him may be viewed with caution.

Paskvan v. Mesich, 227 F.2d 646 (1955).

disaffirm
To nullify one's previous consent

Avoidance is the **disaffirming** of a contract. This is done by a party to the contract manifesting that he or she no longer intends to be bound by a contract previously made by him or her. The following case illustrates one way to manifest an intent to avoid a contract.

FACTS

Christine M. Hagen was on February 4, 1984 and at all relevant times (16) sixteen years of age. On this date, Christine and Brian were husband and wife and they entered into (1) a "Sales and Service" contract and (2) a "Retail Installment Contract and Security Agreement" with Bramley's Water Conditioning. Well before Christine's eighteenth birthday she was sued for breach of the contracts by Bramley's. She contested the contracts by her answer to Bramley's complaint. Bramley contended (1) that the contracts were not disaffirmed and (2) that Christine's marriage prevented her from disaffirming as a minor.

DECISION

The court held that the contracts were disaffirmed and noted that a minor can disaffirm a contract by contesting the enforcement of the contract in court. The court also noted that contracts of a minor are voidable at the minor's election and marriage does not change this longstanding rule of law. The purpose of the rule of law is to protect minors whose "mind and judgment are immature and need to be sheltered from their own imprudence and folly." A married sixteen-year-old is no more mature than an unmarried one.

Bramley's Water Conditioning v. Hagen, 501 N.E.2d 38 (Ohio 1985).

Avoidance (Disaffirmance) by Minors

When disaffirming a contract, a minor must return the consideration received by the minor if the minor still has it. Disaffirmance by a minor for contracts concerning personal property (a movable thing, along with interests and rights in the thing) can occur anytime during minority and within a *reasonable time* after reaching **majority.** For real property (land and immovable things attached to land, along with interests and rights in the land, also a freehold interest in land) contracts, most states require minors to wait until reaching majority and then give to them as new adults a reasonable time thereafter in which to disaffirm. Statutes usually specify what is a reasonable time. Unless a statute provides otherwise, an individual is a minor until the beginning day of the individual's eighteenth birthday. In the following case, a minor was able to disaffirm a contract seven years after it was made for her by her parents.

majority
The legal age at which a minor becomes an adult

FACTS

An internationally known model and actress, Brooke Shields, brought action against Gross, a photographer, revoking her parents' consent granting Gross unrestricted right to use, reuse and/or publish or republish photographs taken by him of her when she was 10 years old in a series of photographs of her unclothed in a bathtub. In a lower court action, the court held that Shields could not disaffirm the contract made on her behalf by her mother. Gross informed Shields that he intended to publish the pictures in Playboy magazine. Shields appealed.

DECISION

The court held for Shields and reversed the decision of the lower court. The court noted that, absent a specific provision in a statute denying a minor a right to disaffirm, the general rule is that a minor has a right to disaffirm a contract even when the contract has been entered into on behalf of the minor by a parent or guardian. In this case, the statutes cited by Gross which require consent of a parent or guardian in the making of a contract by a minor with an adult did not specifically take away a minor's right to disaffirm the contract and, therefore, did not prevent Shields from disaffirming the contract.

Shields v. Gross, 451 N.Y.S.2d 419 (N.Y. 1982).

The minor is entitled to get back all that was given by the minor as consideration for the contract, unless what was given was tangible personal property that was sold to another for value without notice that the property once belonged to a minor. This result

FIGURE 10.2 **Minor's Contract**

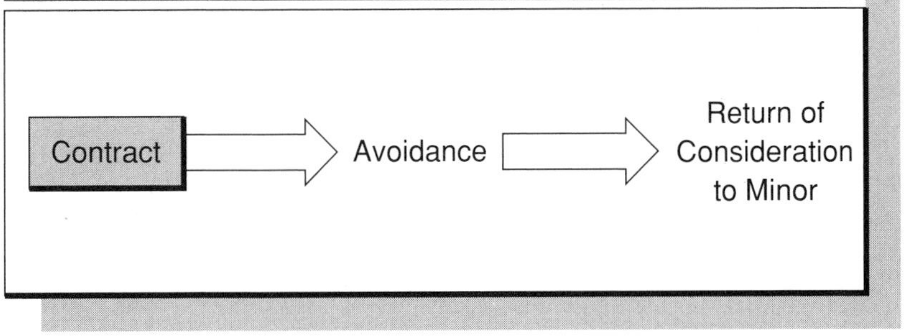

Contract → Avoidance → Return of Consideration to Minor

is based upon section 2-403 of the Uniform Commercial Code. (Isaac, a minor, sold his skis to Art, an adult, in exchange for Art's typewriter. Art then sold the skis to Pat, who was unaware of Isaac's infancy. Isaac disaffirmed the transaction. Pat keeps the skis.)

Avoidance by Others

Mentally incompetent (insane) persons, alcoholics, or drug addicts, if they qualify for the right to avoid a contract, must exercise the right within a reasonable time and must give back to the other party the consideration received or its equivalent value if they still have it, except as otherwise provided by case law or statute.

If the other party knew and took advantage of the disabled party, the disabled party, like the minor, can avoid the contract and must return only that portion of the consideration the disabled party received and still has, and the disabled party, in turn, has the right to receive back what the disabled party gave as consideration. This is illustrated by the following case involving a mentally incompetent person.

FACTS

A committee for an incompetent party to a land sale contract brought an action attempting to set aside a conveyance of property to a purchaser. In an earlier proceeding the circuit court had confirmed the sale of the children's interest in the land as being fair and held that the incompetency of the mother in making the contract of sale was adequately protected in the court's review of the sales price of the land with regard to the children.

DECISION

The court held for the committee for the incompetent party. The court erred in not hearing evidence on the issue of whether the purchaser knew of the incompetency in order to determine whether the incompetent party would be entitled to have the contract set aside without reimbursing the purchaser. When the consideration is fair, the contract has been executed and the other party acts in good faith without knowledge of the incompetency, the contract will be set aside only if the incompetent party can be reimbursed. However, where the competent party has knowledge of the incompetency and overreaches the incompetent party, the contract will be set aside and the competent party will not be entitled to reimbursement.

Upton v. Hall, 300 S.E.2d 777 (Va. 1983).

Necessaries

necessaries
Those things needed for survival and to maintain social position in life

Minors are responsible for their contracts for **necessaries.** What is a "necessary" is a question of fact. All authorities agree that those things *actually needed* for survival (food, clothing, shelter, medical care, and burial expenses for spouses) are necessaries. The following case illustrates this point.

FACTS

Cidis, a duly licensed optometrist, was requested by Carol Ann White, 19 years of age and a minor under New York law at that time, to furnish her with contact lenses. She advised Cidis that she urgently desired them as soon as possible. She agreed to pay $225 for the lenses and gave the doctor her personal check for $100. After examining Ms. White's eyes, Cidis immediately ordered the lenses from his laboratory and incurred an indebtedness of $110. The examination was held on Thursday evening, the lenses were ordered on Friday and received by the doctor on Saturday. On Monday morning, Carol called and disaffirmed her contract on advice of her father and stopped payment on her check. The contact lenses could be used by no one but Carol. Ms. White contends the contact lenses are not a necessary.

DECISION

The court held for Cidis, noting that the term "necessaries" as used in the law relating to the liability of minors is a relative term, somewhat flexible, except when applied to such things as are obviously requisite for the maintenance of existence, and also depends on the social position and situation in life of the minor. The contact lenses are a necessary for Carol White.

Cidis v. White, 336 N.Y.S.2d 362 (N.Y. 1972).

Generally, for the minor those things needed to maintain a social status equal to the station in life of one's peers are deemed to be necessaries. The flexibility of the concept as it has been applied to minors has resulted in contracts that indirectly provide survival needs (for example, employment agency services, tools) and tuition fees for an undergraduate college education being considered necessaries. Something is not a necessary for a minor if the parents are willing and able to provide, or have already provided, what would otherwise be necessaries. A contract by a minor for these items is considered not to be for a necessary. However, if a minor is not emancipated and his or her parents have not provided the minor with necessaries, the parents may become liable under agency law for necessaries purchased by the minor. In the following case the court held that vinyl siding on a house was not a necessary.

FACTS

Dalton seeks a personal money judgment against Janet Bundy for $3,380 for siding placed on a house owned by her and acquired from her parents. Dalton placed the vinyl siding on the house in question under a written contract with Janet's parents, not knowing that twelve-year-old Janet was the owner of the house. Janet's parents have declared bankruptcy and Dalton says he is entitled to recover against Janet under the doctrine of "necessaries."

DECISION

The court held for Bundy, noting that the doctrine of "necessaries" gets around the defense of minority when a person has provided necessaries to a minor in reliance upon the minor's credit and not upon the credit of another. Dalton relied upon the credit of the parents, not the minor child. Furthermore, there is no showing that these house improvements were "necessaries." While housing is in general a necessary, that is not to say that adding additional siding to a house falls into that category.

Dalton v. Bundy, as Guardian, 666 S.W.2d 443 (Mo. 1984).

While those who have the right to avoid a contract can avoid a contract for necessaries, they must keep the necessaries; and they remain liable to the other party to pay a reasonable value for the items or services provided. Reasonable value will normally be something less than the usual contract price.

Ratification

Ratification is the opposite of avoidance. In the law of contracts, it is a party's manifestation of intent to continue to be bound by a contract that the party could have avoided. The ratifying party waives his or her power of avoidance.

ratification
In contracts, a person's waiver of his or her power of avoidance

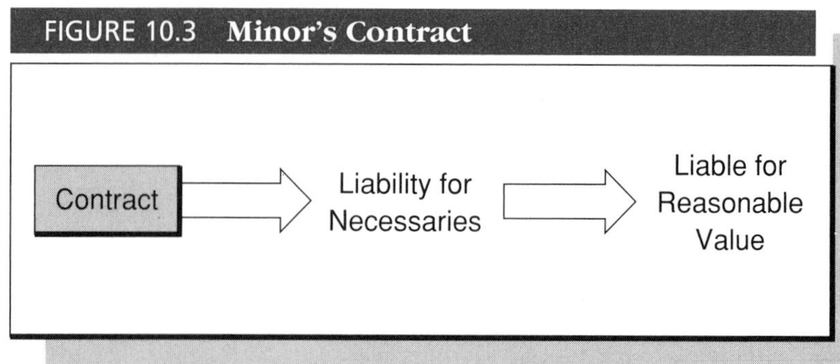

FIGURE 10.3 Minor's Contract

Ratification by a minor can occur immediately upon the minor reaching the age of majority. For mentally ill persons or those under the disability of alcohol or drugs, ratification can take place only after the disability is removed, or through the action of a **guardian** or other legal representative. Ratification may be made by conduct, as is illustrated by the following case in which a minor's conduct after majority ratified his contract made during minority.

guardian

A person legally entrusted with the custody and/or the property of another

FACTS

On November 17, 1973, Jones, who was then seventeen years old, signed a contract with Dressel. The contract allowed Jones to use Dressel's recreational skydiving facilities, which included use of an airplane to ferry skydivers to the parachute jumping site. A promise not to sue and a clause exempting Dressel from liability were included in the contract. On December 28, 1973, Jones attained the age of eighteen. Ten months later, on October 19, 1974, he suffered serious personal injuries in an airplane crash shortly after the takeoff of an airplane provided by Dressel for skydiving purposes. On November 21, 1975, nearly two years after attaining his majority, Jones sued Dressel in negligence for injuries experienced in the crash. Based upon the exculpatory agreement, judgment was granted for Dressel. Jones contends he disaffirmed the contract with Dressel by filing suit a reasonable time after he attained his majority; Jones appealed the decision of the lower court.

DECISION

The court held for Dressel, noting that a minor may disaffirm a contract made during his minority within a reasonable time after attaining his majority or he may, after becoming of legal age, by acts recognizing the contract, ratify it. Affirmance is not merely a matter of intent. It may be determined by the actions of minors who accept the benefits of a contract after reaching the age of majority, or who are silent or acquiesce in the contract for a considerable length of time. What constitutes ratification or disaffirmance is a question of law. Jones ratified the contract, as a matter of law, by accepting the benefits of the contract when he used Dressel's facilities on October 19, 1974. Since the contract was ratified, the factual issue of whether the suit for personal injuries was filed within a reasonable time after attaining his majority and constituted disaffirmance of the contract, is not relevant. Jones, therefore, cannot sue for negligence because the exculpatory clause is enforceable.

Jones v. Dressel, 623 P.2d 370 (Colo. 1981).

Minor's Misrepresentation of Age

It has been said that the right of a minor to disaffirm a contract, while shielding the minor, could be used by the minor as a sword against an adult. Thus if the minor

FIGURE 10.4 **Minor's Contract**

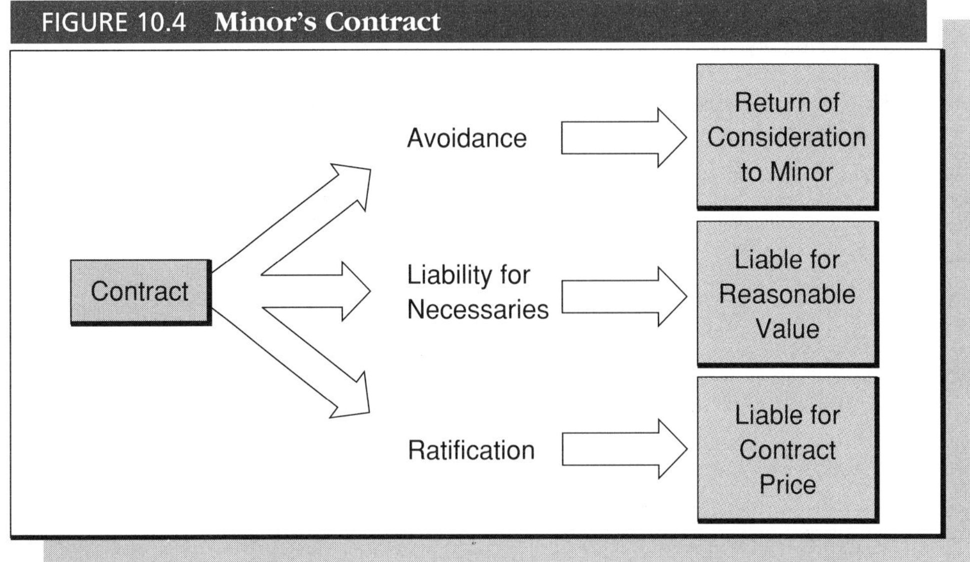

misrepresented his or her age and induced the adult to enter into a contract thinking the minor was an adult, the minor would have the possibility of avoidance but the adult would be bound to the contract.

In earlier common law, the court did not allow adults to sue minors (who generally are responsible for their own crimes and torts) for the damage caused by misrepresentation. The principle was that one could not do indirectly what one could not do directly. Allowing the suit in tort would have the indirect effect of holding minors to the contract which they were capable of avoiding.

Today in misrepresentation cases a compromise—known as **restitution**—seems to be developed by case law which retains the right of the minor to avoid the contract but requires the minor to return the total consideration given by the adult for the contract. However, restitution is not allowed in some states. Also, in some cases the minor's misrepresentation causes the contract to be voidable by the adult party to the contract. This is illustrated by the following case.

restitution
A legal remedy restoring one to his or her original position prior to the particular transaction

FACTS

Manasquan Savings and Loan Association sued to recover on a loan of $22,000 made to Mayer and her husband on a real estate mortgage to build a home. Mayer, who was nineteen and a minor at the time of taking out the loan, recited in an affidavit of title in three places that she was of the age of majority in seeking a loan. After the loan was made, she and her husband built the home, separated, abandoned the property, and defaulted on the mortgage payments. In a subsequent foreclosure suit on the mortgage, Mayer counterclaimed, asserting her infancy and disaffirmance of the mortgage agreement, and she demanded a return from Manasquan of personal funds used by her in making the mortgage payments and improving the premises.

DECISION

The court held for Manasquan Savings and Loan Association because Mayer misrepresented her age. Infancy is no defense to an action to recover money advanced to an infant on the basis of misrepresentation of majority reasonably relied upon by a lender. While Mayer here tenders her entire interest in the real estate to Manasquan for the return of her advances, the difficulty is that Manasquan cannot be made whole. It is entitled to be made whole, and Manasquan is entitled to complete foreclosure free of any claim of Mayer except that she may have an interest in surplus funds.

Manasquan Sav. and Loan Ass'n v. Mayer, 236 A.2d 407 (N.J. 1967).

Special Cases

In some cases a minor cannot disaffirm a contract completely or can only partially disaffirm it. A minor's contracts that, by statute, cannot be disaffirmed include purchases of corporate investments, insurance policy purchases, contract of marriage, and enlistment in the armed forces. In a few states a married minor cannot disaffirm his or her contracts. A minor's contracts that can be only partially disaffirmed would be partnership contracts. While the contract creating the partnership can be avoided, the capital committed by the minor to the partnership must remain available to the creditors of the partnership.

► Emancipation of a Minor

emancipated minor

A minor whose parents have given up their rights to take care of the minor and to have custody of and to claim the minor's earnings

Emancipation means freedom from something. An **emancipated minor** is a minor whose parents have given up their rights to take care of the minor and to have custody of and claim to the minor's earnings. The minor has now become self-supporting. The minor may declare emancipation either expressly, or impliedly as by marriage or voluntary enlistment in military service. An emancipated minor has capacity to contract and, in the absence of statute to the contrary, still has the power of avoidance.

Summary Statement

1. Certain classes of persons have no capacity to contract, others have limited capacity to contract, and still others can escape the consequence of a contract.
2. The right to avoid a contract is in a process of evolving in two directions: (1) contract law is becoming more specific about who can avoid a contract; and (2) it is limiting the right to avoid a contract.
3. Avoidance requires the avoiding party's express or implied manifestation of intent no longer to be bound by the contract that must be made within a reasonable time.
4. A minor may disaffirm during minority or within a reasonable time after attaining majority, except that for real property contracts disaffirmance can occur only within a reasonable time after attaining majority.
5. Generally, the minor must return what the minor has received or its equivalent value if the minor still has it in order to disaffirm and to get restitution (except for UCC 2-403). This is also true for a disadvantaged party with limited capacity to contract.
6. In cases of a minor's misrepresentation of age, or of contracts by those not known to be incapacitated, all consideration must be returned by such persons in order to avoid their contracts. For contracts where the subject matter is necessaries, such persons must keep what they have received and pay for their reasonable value.
7. An emancipated minor still has the power to disaffirm a contract.

8. Ratification is the waiver of a power to avoid a contract. A minor can ratify only after attaining majority; others within a reasonable time after their disability has been removed.

The following case is included in depth to illustrate the value judgment that the law needs to protect people in the legal area of capacity. The case also illustrates the current trend in this area of law making limitations on who and what will be protected and how protection will be afforded. At the time of this case, a minor was a person below twenty-one years of age.

GASTONIA PERSONNEL CORPORATION v. ROGERS
172 S.E.2d 19 (N.C. 1970)

Rogers was graduated from high school when he was seventeen. By the time he was nineteen years old he was emancipated and married. He needed only "one quarter, or twenty-two hours" for completion of the course requirements at Gaston Tech for an A.S. degree in civil engineering. His wife was employed as a computer programmer at First Federal Savings and Loan. He and she were living in a rented apartment. They were expecting a baby in September. Rogers had to quit school and go to work.

For assistance in obtaining suitable employment, Rogers went to the office of the Gastonia Personnel Corporation, an employment agency. Rogers signed a contract which contained the following: "If I ACCEPT employment offered me by an employer as a result of a lead ... from you within twelve (12) months of such lead ... I will be obligated to pay you as per the terms of (this) contract."

After making several phone calls, the employment agency was successful in obtaining an interview for Rogers for a draftsman job. Rogers was interviewed and hired.

Gastonia Personnel has sued for its service charge, and the defense of Rogers was infancy (below twenty-one years of age at that time).

The court held the infant liable for the service charge. The court noted that the early common law recognized that "an infant may bind himself to pay for his necessary meat, drinks, apparell, necessary physicke, and such other necessaries, and likewise for his good teaching or instruction whereby he may profit himself afterwards." The court continued by recognizing the ancient rule of the common law that an infant's contract, unless for "necessaries" or unless authorized by statute, is voidable by the infant, at his election.

Such other necessaries, the court noted, traditionally meant those articles suitable to the infant's degree and estate. The court also stated that today such other necessaries has become a very flexible concept.

The dominant purpose of the law in permitting infants to disaffirm their contracts is to protect children and those of tender years from their own improvidence, or want of discretion, and from the wiles of designing men.

Society, the court said, has a moral obligation to protect the interest of infants from overreaching adults. But this protection must not become a straightjacket, stifling the economic and social advancement of infants who have the need and maturity to contract. Nor should infants be allowed to turn that protective legal shield into a weapon to wield against fair-dealing adults. It is in the interest of society to have its members contribute actively to the general economic and social welfare, if this can be accomplished consistently with the protection of those persons unable to protect themselves in the marketplace.

The court concluded that the common law rule by judges centuries ago was in need of modification. One of the great virtues of the common law is its dynamic nature that makes it adaptable to the requirements of society at the time of its application in court.

While the court noted that prior decisions were to the effect that the "necessaries" of an infant, his wife, and child include only such necessities of life as food, clothing, shelter, medical attention, etc., its view is that the concept of "necessaries" should be enlarged to include such articles of property and such services as are reasonably necessary to enable an infant to earn money required to provide the necessities of life for himself and those legally dependent upon him.

Questions and Case Problems

1. McCoy was discharged from the U.S. Army in 1960 because of his mental condition and has been, and still is, receiving psychiatric treatment and medication ever since at a V. A. hospital. It was generally known in the community where McCoy resided that he was mentally incapable of handling his affairs. Fidelity Financial Services, Inc., entered into negotiations for an automobile loan to McCoy in the presence of a car dealer who wanted to sell McCoy a car. The car was sold to McCoy, who borrowed the purchase money from Fidelity. McCoy gave Fidelity a promissory note and a chattel mortgage (a nonpossessory security interest) on the car as security for the loan. The transaction took about 45 minutes and Fidelity stated that McCoy acted and appeared normal. The note was not paid and Fidelity sued McCoy on the note and to enforce the chattel mortgage. McCoy asserted his insanity at the time the note and mortgage were executed by him. Fidelity never called the car dealer to testify. In the lower court, the note was annulled and the chattel mortgage cancelled because of McCoy's insanity. Fidelity appealed. What result? [*Fidelity Fin. Services v. McCoy,* 392 So.2d 118 (La. 1980).]
2. William Nicholas died leaving three children. He left his entire estate to the Bank of America in trust until his youngest child reached the age of 40 years. The will directed the trustee to operate ranch and employ one Nicholi as ranch manager subject to the trustee's discretion to act in the best interests of the beneficiaries. The trustee now seeks an order to sell all livestock raised on the ranch to maximize sales proceeds. Nicholi objects to the sale of breeding cattle as not being in the best interest of the trust for a variety of valid reasons. Does the trustee under the circumstances have the right to contract for the sale of all the cattle? [In re *Estate of Nicholas,* 223 Cal.Rptr. 410 (Cal. 1986).]
3. From 1920 to July 1965, Iota Chapter of Kappa Alpha Theta, Inc., a nonprofit corporation, owned real property in Ithaca, New York. In 1965, because of the national sorority's discriminatory membership policies that excluded those of certain religious and ethnic groups, the chapter's active membership voted to end its affiliation with the national, surrender its charter, and sell its principal asset, the real property. In 1966, the board of directors entered into a trust agreement with defendant, Cornell University, whereby $115,000, the proceeds of the sale, was transferred to Cornell University to hold as trustee in a scholarship fund provided that if IOTA was reactivated, the balance of the funds in trust would be returned to the sorority. In January 1967, IOTA changed its name to IOTA Alumnae, Inc. In January 1980, IOTA was reincorporated for purposes of re-establishing Kappa Alpha Theta at Cornell. IOTA Alumnae argued that the 1966 trust agreement was beyond the power of IOTA to contract and hence invalid. The bylaws in 1965 read "the board of directors shall have entire charge and control of the corporation and its affairs, funds and property." Was the action of the board invalid? [*IOTA Alumnae, Inc. v. Cornell University,* 453 N.Y.S.2d 879 (1982).]
4. In March 1978, Milda Sandstrom was convicted of murder in the first degree. She wished to appeal her conviction. She was not indigent and wished to employ counsel of her own choosing. This she did. Payment of attorney's fees was made by a trustee

of her estate, appointed after the contract was made. Now the trustee seeks return of the fees contending that Milda was civilly dead because of her conviction and could therefore not create a valid contract of employment with the attorney. What result? [*Matter of Trusteeship of Sandstrom,* 696 P.2d 958 (Kan. 1985).]

5. Husband, owner of a corporation, obtained a $30,000 loan from a bank to the corporation to finance his business. When the note came due, he sought an extension. The bank determined that neither the corporation nor its owner personally qualified for an extension. Wife of the husband had considerable assets of her own. The bank agreed to an extension on the loan to the corporation if both the husband and wife as sureties guaranteed its payment, which they did. The state in which the transaction took place has a Married Women's Act, which protects married women from the improvidence or predatory conduct of their husbands and from the husbands' creditors. Was the guaranty of the corporation debt beyond the wife's capacity to contract? [*National Bank of Rochester v. Meadowbrook Heights, Inc.,* 265 N.W.2d 43 (Mich. 1978).]

6. Alonso was refused employment as fruit picker when he could not prove to the owner of a farm that he was an alien lawfully in the United States to work as a farm laborer during the harvest season. Is this a violation of a freedom to contract? [*Alonso v. State of California,* 123 Cal.Rptr. 536, cert. denied 425 U.S. 903 (1976).]

7. On August 21, 1981 William Todd Wallace, then 16 years old, purchased a 1977 Datsun automobile from Whitley's Discount Auto Sales for $3,080. Wallace paid $1,200 in cash from Social Security benefits and financed the remaining $1,880 with a car loan from Richmond County Bank. According to the credit application, Wallace's age was 18 which was untrue. Whitley's indorsed the credit application. After Wallace and the Datsun had been involved in two car accidents while Wallace was still under 18, Wallace returned the Datsun to Whitley's and demanded payment of all monies paid. Can Wallace disaffirm the contract and, if so, what money must be returned to Wallace? [*Gillis v. Whitley's Discount Auto Sales, Inc.,* 319 S.E.2d 661 (N.C. 1984).]

8. In July a minor contracted to buy a 1968 Oldsmobile for $1,250 from Lemke. The minor paid $1,000 to Lemke and the remainder was to be paid at $25 per week. In September, after the minor had paid a total of $1,100, a connecting rod on the car's engine snapped. The minor had the car repaired but never paid the bill. In October the minor disaffirmed the contract on the grounds that he was a minor. The repair garage repossessed the engine. The car, without engine, sitting in front of the house of the father of the minor, was repeatedly vandalized and became unsalvageable. The minor sued to recover his payments on the car and Lemke counterclaimed for the amount still owed on the purchase price. Who wins? [*Halbman, Jr., v. Lemke,* 298 N.W.2d 562 (Wis. 1980).]

9. This action against a mentally incompetent widow, through her guardian, was based upon a contract that she entered into with Melbourne and Sons for the conduct of her deceased husband's funeral services. At the time of the contract, the estate of the husband was insolvent, and the funeral director could not observe any mental impairment on the part of the widow. Are funeral services a necessary? What is the measure of recovery if they are found to be necessaries? [*Charles Melbourne and Sons, Inc. v. Jesset,* 163 N.E.2d 773 (Ohio 1960).]

10. In the case of *Gastonia Personnel Corp. v. Rogers,* excerpted at the beginning of this section, the court implied that traditional cases of incapacity should be viewed on individual merits. What implications does this have for the law governing one's ability to make a contract?

C H A P T E R

11

PUBLIC POLICY AND CONTRACTUAL PURPOSE

After you have read this chapter, you should be able to:

1. Ascertain that the subject matter reflects a value judgment that the courts should scrutinize contractual purposes for the good of society.
2. Recognize that there are both traditional and nontraditional contractual purposes that do not further the interests of society.
3. Note how the concept of public policy and contractual purpose limits the freedom of individuals to contract.
4. Discuss the most recent development of importance in the area of contractual purpose and public policy, namely, "unconscionability."
5. Recognize that the law of public policy and contractual purpose is evolving to facilitate a broad social objective—greatest good.

BUSINESS DECISIONS and the LAW

In the past, gambling was viewed as morally reprehensible, and all states had laws making it illegal. Today, with states increasingly squeezed for new sources of revenue, gambling has come to be viewed as an important income-producing activity.

Until 1964, lotteries were illegal everywhere in the United States. In 1968, New Hampshire initiated a state-sponsored lottery; today, thirty-three states, plus the District of Columbia, Puerto Rico, and the Virgin Islands, have lotteries, and per capita ticket sales have grown 13 percent a year after inflation. In 1988, lotteries generated sales of $15.6 billion, of which the states retained about $6 billion. Columnist George F. Will estimated that lottery earnings have grown an average of 17.5 percent annually, a rate of growth comparable to that of the computer industry.* The downside of gambling is now being pointed out by economists, psychologists, and other experts. One management consultant estimates that Americans spend more on gambling than they do on health insurance, dentists, shoes, foreign travel, or household appliances.**

For some, gambling is a compulsion that experts consider as addictive and socially destructive as narcotics. Compulsive gambling takes a heavy toll on society, in both monetary and human terms. Individual stories range from the executive who embezzles from the company in order to gamble, to the person who writes scores of worthless checks to buy lottery tickets. It is estimated that there are as many as twelve million addicted gamblers in the United States.

Apart from the issue of compulsive gambling, experts argue that the burden of raising state revenues through lotteries falls more heavily on low-income and less well-educated consumers. Many bettors do not realize that lotteries pay out only 50 percent of the money taken in, as compared to 90 percent for slot machines and 80 percent at horse racetracks. Still other experts are concerned that, by its very nature, gambling runs counter to the work ethic that has produced America's prosperity, and that there is an inherent danger in the majority of Americans coming to believe that sheer luck will benefit them more than hard work.

Still, there is no sign of let-up in the trend toward ever-increasing legalization of gambling. Some states are currently testing the waters of legalized sports betting. Oregon has a lottery game in which players can bet on the outcome of National Football League games, and New Hampshire and California are considering other types of sports betting. A similar measure in Kentucky was vetoed by the governor after intense lobbying by racetrack owners and officials.

New technology has helped to stimulate "gambling fever"—from video gambling devices that allow patrons to play "mega-bingo" games telecast by satellite, to video slot machines and "simulcast" horse races that allow patrons to bet on a number of races at once.

In this chapter, you will learn what kinds of agreements are enforceable as contracts, and what kinds of agreements, such as gambling agreements, have traditionally been held to be unenforceable as against public policy.

*George F. Will, "In the Grip of Gambling," *Newsweek,* May 8, 1989, p. 78.
**Dan Cordtz, "Betting the Country," 159:4 *Financial World,* (February 20, 1990): 23–26.
Sources: Pauline Yoshihashi, "More States Like Odds on Sports Betting Despite Fierce Opposition to Legalization," *Wall Street Journal,* February 1, 1990, p. B1; "America's Gambling Fever," *Business Week,* April 24, 1989, pp. 112–20; "Lotteries Lure Some Die-Hard Fans," *Wall Street Journal,* June 23, 1989, p. B1; Gwenda Blair, "Betting Against the Odds," *The New York Times Magazine,* September 25, 1988, pp. 57–81.

Introduction

In the preceding chapters of this part we discussed three of the four elements required for a contract: mutual assent, consideration, and capacity to contract. We will now consider the fourth element, legality.

Elements needed for a contract:

	CHAPTER
1. Mutual assent with a promise or promises	6, 7, 8
2. Consideration	9
3. Capacity to contract	10
4. LEGALITY	**11**

The importance of **public policy** and contractual purpose is evident in that this area of contract law requires that the interests of society or the community be balanced against the interests of individuals in the contractual setting. The end result of this balancing or weighing process directed toward the greatest good is that an agreement between individuals may be held to be unenforceable as a contract because it works against the good of the community. (See Figure 11.1)

public policy
The concept of law under which the freedom to act is limited for the good of the community

The study of public policy and contractual purpose reveals a further restriction upon an individual's freedom to contract. The rights of a "third party"—society—must be considered.

What Is Illegal?

It can be said that if a contractual purpose looks to the doing of something that is **illegal,** then that agreement violates public policy and will not be **enforced** as a contract by the courts. It is a void agreement; there is no contract because there is no legal duty to perform a promise.

illegal
Contrary to law

enforce
To compel performance

What is illegal in the contractual setting is a contractual purpose that is directed toward the commission of a tort or a crime.

Crime and Tort

The definition of a **crime** can be found in criminal codes. Generally it is a wrong against society. A **tort** is normally defined by the common law—by case decision. Generally it is a civil (private), noncontractual wrong against person or property. In the following case the court refused to enforce the agreement because it was an agreement to insure against the results of criminal acts.

crime
An act, committed or omitted, in violation of a public law governing it

tort
A civil (private) noncontractual wrong for which a court will give a remedy

FACTS

In 1977, McBrearty became a member of the United States Taxpayers Union (USTU). In the "Declaration of Client Membership Agreement," USTU promised that, in the event a client member should be incarcerated for a time, USTU would meet all necessary, personal and family obligations of the member plus all costs incurred in the defense of the member. In

FIGURE 11.1 **Contracts – Public Policy Violations**

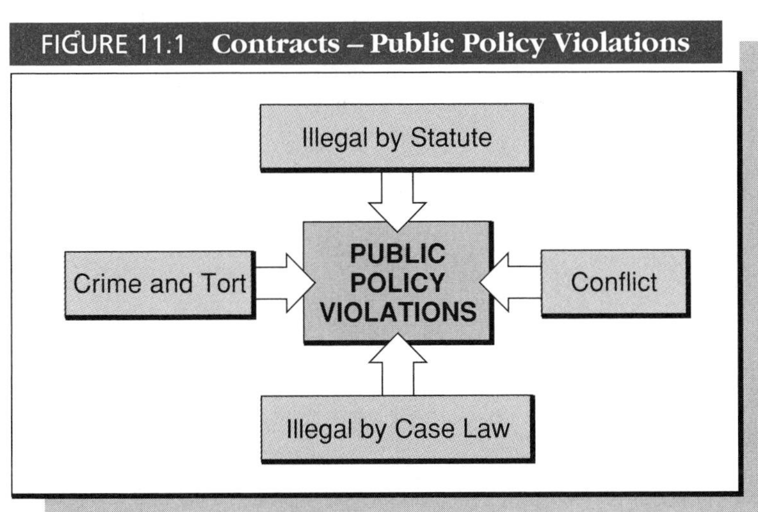

1979, following McBrearty's conviction for violation of the federal tax laws, McBrearty was incarcerated for a period of four months. USTU failed to fulfill its promises and McBrearty sued for breach of contract.

DECISION

The court held for USTU. The court noted that generally an agreement which contravenes some recognized public policy is void. USTU's promise amounted to an agreement to insure against the results of criminal acts. Such a bargain contravenes public policy and is unenforceable.

McBrearty v. United States Taxpayers Union, 668 F.2d 450 (8th Cir. 1982).

Illegality by Statute

statute
Law created by a legislative body and approved by the executive

Something declared by **statute** not to be a proper contractual purpose is deemed to be in violation of public policy and unenforceable.

► Revenue Versus Regulatory Licenses

If licensing is required by statute to protect the public, such as licensing of medical doctors or lawyers to practice a profession or real estate brokers or beauticians to engage in a business, the absence of such a license will cause their agreements with clients to not become a contract. However, if the sole purpose of the license is to raise revenue for the state, the agreement is enforceable as a contract. Examples are sales licenses to sell merchandise.

In the following case a landlord was prevented from enforcing a lease because the landlord did not have an occupancy permit.

FACTS

A landlord sued two prospective tenants to recover rent and damages under a one-year lease. The tenants never took possession of the premises, which were not registered as a residence and did not have an occupancy permit as required by the housing code. The tenants tried to find a subtenant. A subsequent inspection of the premises by a code enforcement officer revealed that the house did not comply with the housing code. The tenants decided, therefore, that they could not legally find a subtenant and concluded that the lease was void.

DECISION

The court held for the two prospective tenants, concluding that the municipal requirements that the house be registered and have an occupancy permit were measures to promote public welfare. Because the landlord violated these measures, he would not receive the benefit of his bargain to collect rent from the tenants.

Noble v. Alis, 474 N.E.2d 109 (Ind. 1985).

► Sunday Agreements

nullity
Of no legal effect

In certain states, by statute, any attempt to form a contract on Sunday is a **nullity.** Negotiations of contracts on Sunday are allowed. Exceptions exist in these statutes for contracts directed toward humanitarian purposes—for example, the sale of a life-saving drug or acts of charity or necessity. Normally, however, these statutes prohibit the formation on Sunday of those ordinary contracts that allow one to earn a living. This is an illustration of a state reasonably exercising its police power in order to promote the public comfort, health, safety, morals, and welfare of society.

► Usury Law

usury
Charging a rate of interest on a loan higher than that permitted by statute

Most states have declared by statute a maximum rate of interest that it is unlawful to exceed in a contract to lend money. Various penalties exist for violation of this statutory provision, ranging from loss of interest to loss of interest and principal. In some states, corporations can borrow money at any rate of interest. If no rate of interest has been stated in a contract, then the **legal rate of interest** will apply. The declared legal rate of interest by statute may be less than the maximum rate.

legal rate of interest
The maximum rate of interest fixed by statute where no rate of interest is fixed by the contract

Discounting loans, service charges, points, requiring insurance, and other charges must all be taken into account to determine whether the maximum rate has been exceeded. In the following case the court held that usury had occurred.

FACTS

Strawn Furniture Company, Inc. compounded interest [charged interest on the unpaid interest] by using the following formula: the amount of the indebtedness was multiplied by 10% to obtain the yearly amount of interest; that amount was then divided by 360 and then multiplied by 30 to obtain the amount of unpaid interest for the month which was added to the principal. Each succeeding month the interest was compounded using the same formula. The evidence is uncontradicted that the compounding of interest in this case resulted in an annual percentage rate of 10.76%. The usurious rate of interest in Arkansas is an annual rate of interest above 10%.

DECISION

Affirmed, judgment for the debtor, Austin. It is well settled that compounding interest will render a contract usurious if it effectively raises the annual rate of interest above 10%.

Strawn Furniture Company v. L. K. Austin, 655 S.W.2d 397 (Ark. 1983).

Revolving charge account[1] plans are in the nature of credit sales on a revolving basis. In most states, and under the 1974 Uniform Consumer Credit Code,[2] such plans are not considered to involve the lending of money but, rather, the revolving extension of credit over time in a sales transaction for a price. There is a difference between a sale for cash and for credit in the revolving charge account. This concept is called the "time-price differential" theory. Any amount may be charged; it is immaterial whether the enhanced price be ascertained by the simple addition of a lump sum to the cash price, or by a percentage thereon. The transaction is not usurious.

Exceptions Lending by certain financial institutions such as small loan companies in some states can be at a rate of interest that would exceed the normal maximum rate.

---

[1]" 'Revolving charge account' means an arrangement between a seller and a buyer pursuant to which (1) the seller may permit the buyer to purchase goods or services on credit either from the seller or pursuant to a seller credit card, (2) the unpaid balances of amounts financed arising from purchases and the credit service and other appropriate charges are debited to an account, (3) a credit service charge if made is not precomputed but is computed on the outstanding unpaid balances of the buyer's account from time to time, and (4) the buyer has the privilege of paying the balances in installments." [Uniform Consumer Credit Code, sec. 2.108 (1974).]

[2]Ibid. sec. 2.201(1).

Discrimination

It is interesting that there are statutes that require a contracting party to contract with another party on a nondiscriminatory basis. The primary impact areas are employment, housing, and the service industry—for example businesses providing food, drink, lodging. What is violative of public policy in these areas is not in doing something but in having not done something. One is required not to discriminate on the basis of color, race, national origin, religion, sex, or age. This subject is discussed in Chapter 19 on Employment. The difficulty in proving discrimination in employment is illustrated by the two steps necessary to prove unlawful discrimination: first, the employment standards or requirements must cause a result that is discriminatory; second, the employer must produce evidence of business justification of such standards or requirements. However, the employer is not required to prove the business justification of such standards or requirements. If these standards or requirements are justified, the employee has the opportunity to show that there are means without similar discriminatory effect that are available that would serve the employer's legitimate interest just as well.

In the following case the court held that the plaintiff was entitled to back pay, interest, and attorney's fees because of the failure of the defendant to enter into a contract of employment with her.

FACTS

A former employee, Thurber, brought this action against Reilly's, her former employer, alleging discrimination against her on the basis of gender in violation of the federal Civil Rights Act of 1964 and the antidiscrimination statutes of Massachusetts. Thurber was originally employed as a waitress with the understanding that she had bartending experience and would be interested in applying for any bartending positions which became available. Several times she asked to be promoted to a bartender's position which became available periodically. Despite Reilly's knowledge of her desire to be employed as a bartender, her previous work experience in that capacity, and her job seniority, Reilly's refused to promote her to the position of bartender trainee and consistently hired males for these positions. Thurber seeks damages for failure to employ her as a bartender trainee.

DECISION

The court held for Thurber for back pay. The facts of this case show that Reilly's intentionally discriminated against Thurber on the basis of gender (sex). Under the Civil Rights Act of 1964, failure to promote (employ) on the basis of sex discrimination entitles the one discriminated against to attorney's fees, interest on damages award, and back pay, here based on the higher compensation of a bartender trainee.

Thurber v. Jack Reilly's, Inc., 521 F.Supp. 238 (D. Mass. 1981).

It may be statutorily unlawful not to contract, as is illustrated by the previously discussed case of *Faraca v. Clements* (see p. 13) involving discrimination in which the court held the defendant liable for damages for refusal to employ because of the plaintiff's color.

"Contracts" of Chance

"contract" of chance
An agreement creating a risk of loss

What is called a **"contract" of chance** is really an agreement creating a risk of loss rather than the legal shifting of an existing risk of loss from a possible future event (for example, insurance against loss of property by fire). In the contract of chance, the parties do not have any legal interest in the subject matter at the time the agreement is made.

Gambling or wagering agreements meet the criteria of a contract of chance. State lotteries, which are becoming more common for revenue raising purposes, by statute result in legal contracts. Insurance contracts are nothing more than contracts that share existing risks. Buying stock, hedging contracts, and transactions in futures are speculative but valid business contracts. In the great majority of states, contracts of chance are against public policy and are void agreements. In the following case trades in commodity futures were not wagering agreements and were lawful.

FACTS

An attorney, Lindwall, invested in commodities futures. ACLI is a futures commission merchant. On September 10, 1980, Lindwall executed a Risk Disclosure statement, a Customer's Agreement, an Authorization to Transfer Funds, and a Non-Hedge Commodity Accountant Information letter. ACLI opened the account to invest in strategic metals. When Lindwall discovered he could not presently invest in strategic metals, he chose to trade commodities futures contracts. The trading began in October 1980 and ended in July 1981. On July 22, 1981, the last trading day in contracts for July delivery, Lindwall held open oats contracts for July delivery. Lindwall had either to buy the commodity with $60,000 cash or enter off-the-board transactions at prices above market prices. Lindwall liquidated his position resulting in losses of $4,171.50 for which ACLI sues as a debt owed to ACLI. Lindwall contends there was no intent to deliver the oats, thus the agreement was illegal and unenforceable. Judgment was rendered for ACLI and Lindwall appealed.

DECISION

The court affirmed judgment for ACLI. The court held that trading commodities futures does not constitute gambling. The customer's agreement stated: "Orders are to be received and executed with the understanding that actual delivery is contemplated." If Lindwall subjectively rejected the prospect of delivery, contrary to the written contract, his own uncommunicated intentions cannot render the actions of ACLI unlawful. An agreement is illegal only if parties intend at the time of the agreement that no delivery of the commodity shall be made.

ACLI Int'l Commodity Servs., Inc. v. Lindwall, 347 N.W.2d 522 (Minn. 1984).

The Uniform Commercial Code

The broad and general concept of **unconscionability,** as it appears in UCC 2–302 (enacted by statute in states), has allowed for a *flexible* determination of what contractual purpose is a violation of public policy.

unconscionable
Offensive to the conscience; immoderate, too one-sided

Likewise, in Section 208 of the Restatement (Second) of Contracts (modeled after UCC 2–302), the general concept of unconscionablity is stated. In both the Restatement and UCC 2–302, provision is made for rendering the agreement void or unenforceable as a contract or for enforcing the remainder of the contract without its unconscionable clauses or terms.

In the following case an **exculpatory clause** in a contract was held to be unconscionable and against public policy and, therefore, void.

exculpatory clause
A clause that relieves one from liability

FACTS

On February 18, 1985, Helen Stanek wrote a $197 personal check payable to Western Glass Company drawn on her account with the National Bank of Detroit. The next day, February 19, 1985, Helen went to the bank and issued a stop payment order on the check. According to bank records, the stop payment order was entered into National Bank of Detroit's computer system five minutes later. Sometime the same day (February 19, 1985), Western Glass negotiated the check at the bank's main office. The teller's stamp on the check indicates that it was the ninth transaction of the day for that particular teller. Helen seeks recovery of the $197 from the bank. The bank filed a motion for summary disposition and in support of the motion cited the following language which appeared on the stop payment order:

> It is understood that this stop payment order is not effective if said check shall have been accepted, certified or cashed at any one of the Bank's offices or otherwise paid by the Bank as provided under the Uniform Commercial Code without actual notice of this stop payment order or before the Bank has a reasonable time to act under this order. It is agreed that "reasonable time" as used herein shall mean one (1) full banking day.

DECISION

The court held for Stanek. The court said "No agreement can disclaim a bank's responsibility for its own failure to exercise ordinary care or can limit the measure of damages for such lack of care or failure." Such a provision in a bank contract is a void exculpatory clause.

Stanek v. National Bank of Detroit, 430 N.W.2d 819 (Mich. 1988).

► Other Statutes

Under federal legislation, antitrust acts prohibit contracts that reduce competition, such as contracts in unreasonable restraint of trade. (See Chapter 34, Antitrust Law.) A variety of consumer protection legislation, such as labeling requirements promulgated by the Federal Trade Commission, make sales of mislabeled products unlawful.

Illegality by Case Law—Reflection of Community Standards

What is violative of public policy has also developed by case law (common law). What contracts violate community standards of morals and ethics is flexible. The court will look to the values of the community, and that community may be the nation or it may be the block you live on. There are some well established concepts of what is a violation of public policy in this area.

► Restraint of Trade

A national value judgment is presumed to exist that suggests that competition is good and that any contract that has the elimination of competition as its purpose is bad. Thus any contract whose sole purpose is the elimination of competition violates public policy.

If the agreement not to compete exists to protect some other worthwhile purpose, such as the goodwill in the sale of a business, then it is deemed to be not in violation of public policy if it is reasonable for the benefit of the person to be protected.

Thus if a business and its goodwill are being sold, whether or not the restraint provision in the contract for sale is in reasonable restraint of trade is tested by what is reasonable in time, geographical area, and subject matter for the benefit and protection of the buyer. (Sam sells his drugstore to Bill who would not want Sam to open (1) another competing drugstore (2) across the street (3) within the next six months. A restraint provision to this effect in the contract for sale would be reasonable in (1) subject matter, (2) geographical area, and (3) time.)

If the restraint provision is in an employment contract, it must be reasonable only to the extent of the protection needed by the person to be benefited. It must not be unduly harsh and burdensome on the employee. In the following case the court held there was no substantial right that could qualify for a restraint of trade.

FACTS

An employer brought an action to enjoin a former employee from competing with it. The parties had entered into a contract which sought to prevent the employee from competing for a five-year period following termination of employment. In the course of employment, the employee was taught how to install vinyl tops and became proficient in that craft. Subsequently, the employee voluntarily terminated employment and became employed by a competing vinyl top shop. The trial court granted the injunction and the employee appeals.

DECISION

The court reversed the trial court's judgment and held for the employee. The court said it would not enforce a negative covenant unless (1) the employer had a protected interest, (2) the restriction was reasonably related to that interest, (3) the restriction was reasonable in time and place, and (4) the restriction imposed no undue hardship. In this case the court concluded that the employer had no protected interest. In order to have such an interest, the employer must possess a substantial right in its business sufficiently unique to warrant the type of protection contemplated by a noncompetition agreement. Here the employee learned no more than the normal skills of the vinyl top installation trade. A simple labor skill, without more, was simply not enough to give an employer a substantial protectable right unique in his business.

DeVoe v. Cheatham, et al., 413 So.2d 1141 (Ala. 1982).

► Corruption

Agreements that cause a **fiduciary** to ignore duties owed to others and agreements that have a tendency to corrupt a public official are against public policy. This judgment seeks to prevent self-dealing on the part of fiduciaries and partiality in treatment by public officials.

fiduciary
A person with a duty to act primarily for the benefit of another

► Promise Detrimental to Marital Relationship

A promise by a person contemplating marriage or by a married person, other than as part of an enforceable separation agreement, is unenforceable on grounds of public policy if it would change some essential incident of the marital relationship in a way detrimental to the public interest in the marriage relationship. For example, the following agreement is deemed detrimental to the public interest because Art may have to be supported by the state should the agreement be enforced. Art and Betty, who are about to marry, make an antenuptial agreement in which Art promises to leave their home at any time on notice by Betty and to make no further claims against Betty, and Betty promises thereupon to pay Art $100,000. Also, a promise that tends unreasonably to encourage divorce or separation is unenforceable on grounds of public policy. For example, John, who is married to Ann, promises to pay Ann $50,000 in return for Ann's promise to obtain a divorce. Such promises of John and Ann will be deemed to encourage divorce and will be unenforceable on grounds of public policy.

Conflict

substantive law
That part of the law that creates, defines, and regulates rights

Areas of **substantive law** usually complement each other. If areas of substantive law were in conflict with each other, the logic of the law would be impaired. It follows, therefore, that contract law should complement the law of crime and tort.

► Contract Against Liability for Illegality

It would be against public policy to allow contracting parties, by the contract, to relieve themselves from liability for the consequences of criminal action. However, it is lawful to limit one's liability for negligent acts by contract, but not for acts of gross negligence, as illustrated by the following case in which a waiver of liability for negligence was upheld but was deemed inadequate as a shield against an action for gross negligence.

FACTS

On September 9, 1978, Gillespie and a friend went to Westboro Speedway to race the friend's midget racing car. In order to gain access to the track area, Gillespie signed a form purporting to release certain parties, which include Papale, from any injuries he sustained while at the track. While driving around the track the car spun out on a curve, flipped over, and came to rest upside down upon one of the vertical posts. As a result of that accident, Gillespie was rendered a permanent quadriplegic. Gillespie sues for damages and Papale offers the release in defense.

DECISION

The court held for Gillespie. The court granted summary judgment for Papale on the issue of ordinary negligence. Under pertinent state law, the release executed by Gillespie was sufficient to prevent any suit for ordinary negligence. However, this court ruled that such a release was inadequate to shield against an action for gross negligence. Accordingly, the court permitted Gillespie to amend his complaint to allege gross negligence.

Gillespie v. Papale, 541 F.Supp. 1042 (D. Mass. 1982).

Exculpatory clauses, such as the one illustrated in the Gillespie case, generally are not enforced in contracts when a party to the contract has imposed the clause because of a superior bargaining position or where a public service or a specific legal duty is the subject matter of the contract.

► Legality of Purpose

The law always presumes that parties to a contract intend a lawful result. If the purpose of the contract can be interpreted either as lawful or unlawful, the lawful result will be preferred. If the contractual purpose is unlawful (e.g., violative of public policy), the general rule is that the court will leave the parties where it finds them. The court will not lend its aid to enforce the agreement.

divisible contract
A contract that provides that performance of less than all the obligations on one side will become due by performance of less than all the obligations on the other side

Divisible Contract A contract can consist of more than one promise or more than one act. If the contractual promises and/or acts can be divided into lawful contractual purposes and unlawful contractual purposes without destroying the substance of the agreement, the lawful contractual purposes will be enforced.

Exceptions

There are certain exceptions to the general principle that the court will not aid the parties to an illegal agreement and will leave them where the court finds them. A party to an illegal agreement may enforce it if the person is one of the class of individuals for whose protection the agreement was made illegal. For example, a bank can enforce an agreement for an investment made illegal by banking regulation in order to protect a depositor's assets. Additionally, a party who withdraws from an illegal agreement before its purpose is carried out is entitled to return of the consideration given by him or her for the agreement. A party who was misled or pressured into an illegal agreement may rescind it. Normally, parties equal in legal fault or guilt will not be aided, and, while ignorance of law is generally no excuse, a party who is ignorant of facts making a bargain illegal will be given relief as justice (equity) requires relief to be given. For instance, an innocent party agreeing to take part in what would be a bigamous marriage will be able to sue the party with guilty knowledge for breach of contract based upon mutual promises to marry. In the following case the court reformed a note to reflect a lawful rate of interest because justice and equity required it.

FACTS

Borrowers brought an action requesting that a judge declare void a loan which they had obtained from lenders. The lenders extended the loan at a rate of interest which turned out to be usurious. Before the loan was advanced, the lenders were advised in writing by a Massachusetts attorney that the mortgage note and the mortgage to secure it were not in violation of Massachusetts' usury statutes. The judge declined to void the loan and entered a judgment reforming the mortgage note by reducing the stated interest rate to the maximum permissible limit. The borrowers argue that the loan was void and that the judge was powerless to reform the mortgage note.

DECISION

The court found for the lenders. Reformation is available to parties where there has been mutual mistake which is material to an instrument and where no rights of third parties are affected. It is of no critical importance whether the mutual mistake is one of fact or law; it is sufficient that it is material and that it is of a type which can be remedied in equity. In this case, the parties freely entered into the transaction at arm's length in the mistaken belief that the interest rate provided in the note was proper and legal and, under these circumstances, the judge is allowed to exercise discretion in granting relief.

Beach Assoc. v. Fauser et al., 401 N.E.2d 858 (Mass. 1980).

Summary Statement

1. The rights of society, as they are impacted by a contract, are given due consideration by the law.
2. There are three aspects of identified contractual purposes that work against the greatest good of society: (1) torts and crimes; (2) contractual purposes declared so by statutes; and (3) contractual purposes deemed unconscionable at common law by case decision.
3. Traditional areas identified as having contractual purposes that violate public policy are licensing, Sunday agreements, usury, contracts of chance, unreasonable restraint of trade, corruption, and conflict.

4. Nontraditional areas having contractual purposes violative of public policy that are growing in importance are governmental regulation, discrimination, and unconscionability.
5. Exceptions exist to defined areas of public policy violations such as in lending institutions and usury, speculative business contracts, and exculpatory clauses.
6. Exceptions exist to the normal result that the court leaves the parties in "illegal" agreement where it finds them. This occurs when the one who seeks to enforce it was the one to be protected or when one withdraws or when one was "forced" into the agreement.
7. The end of what is necessary to protect society is not yet in sight.

The following case is included in depth as an illustration of how the interests of society, here represented by a child's welfare, can restrict the ability of individuals to contract.

IN THE MATTER OF BABY M
357 A.2d 1227 (N.J. 1988)

In this matter the court is asked to determine the validity of a contract that purports to provide a new way of bringing children into a family. For a fee of $10,000, a woman agrees to be artificially inseminated with the semen of another woman's husband; she is to conceive a child, carry it to term, and after birth surrender it to the natural father and his wife. The intent of the contract is that the child's natural mother will thereafter be forever separated from her child. The wife of the natural father is to adopt the child, and she and the natural father are to be regarded as its parents for all purposes. The contract providing for this is called a "surrogacy contract," and the natural mother is called the "surrogate mother."

The court invalidated the surrogacy contract because it conflicted with the law and public policy of the State of New Jersey. Recognition was given to the depth of yearning of infertile couples to have their own children, but the payment of money to a "surrogate" mother was found to be illegal, perhaps criminal, and potentially degrading to women. Although in this case custody was granted to the natural father, the evidence having clearly proved such custody to be in the best interests of the infant, both the termination of the surrogate mother's parental rights and the adoption of the child by the wife/stepparent was voided. The "surrogate" was restored as the mother of the child. The issue of the natural mother's visitation rights was remanded to the trial court, since the issue was not reached below and the record before this court is not sufficient for it to decide the issue *de novo.*

The court found no offense to present state laws where a woman voluntarily and without payment agrees to act as a "surrogate" mother, provided that she is not subject to a binding agreement to surrender her child. This holding by the court does not preclude the legislature from altering the current statutory scheme, within constitutional limits, so as to permit surrogacy contracts. Under current law, however, the surrogacy agreement before the court is illegal and invalid.

It is illegal and invalid first because it conflicts with statutory provisions which:

1. Prohibit the use of money in connection with adoptions;
2. Require proof of parental unfitness or abandonment before termination of parental rights; and
3. Make surrender of custody and consent to adoption revocable in private placement adoptions.

It is illegal and invalid also because the contract's basic premise, that the natural parents can decide in advance of birth which one is to have custody of the child, bears no relationship to the settled law that the child's best interest shall determine custody.

Questions and Case Problems

1. A woman sued the estate of deceased for unpaid salary and other compensation for personal services rendered the deceased for two years prior to his death. The woman had left her husband to live with the deceased, a married man. Deceased's gross estate was valued at over several hundred thousand dollars and the woman seeks $29,200. The woman rendered housekeeping, farming, and nursing services to the deceased. The woman also engaged in an adulterous relationship with the deceased. Can she recover for her services? [In re *Estate of Steffes,* 290 N.W.2d 697 (Wis. 1980).]
2. Baron & Co., Inc., entered into an agreement with a corporation whose assets were placed in a trust administered by the Bank of New Jersey as a liquidating trustee. The agreement provided that Baron would attempt to secure a ready, willing, and able buyer for real property owned by the corporation for a finder's fee. Baron found a qualified buyer and claims its finder's fee. The Bank of New Jersey claims that Baron is not entitled to a finder's fee because Baron was not licensed as a broker in New Jersey where the real property is located. Baron claims that it is still entitled to a finder's fee because it used a broker licensed in New Jersey as an independent consultant. Is Baron entitled to a finder's fee? [*Baron and Co. Inc. v. Bank of New Jersey,* 504 F.Supp. 1199 (1981).]
3. Jim Edgar, Secretary of State, appeals from a judgment of a circuit court that held the following state statute unconstitutional:

   > No person . . . may keep open, operate or assist in keeping open or operating any established place of business for the purpose of buying, selling, bartering or exchanging, or offering for sale, barter or exchange, any motor vehicle, whether new or used, on the First day of the week, commonly called Sunday. . . .

   Fireside Chrysler-Plymouth Mazda contends the statute denies them equal protection of the law in violation of the Fourteenth Amendment of the U.S. Constitution. They argue there is no reasonable basis to single out auto dealers for a Sunday closing law. Edgar argues that the law does not create an unreasonable classification and the law is a reasonable restriction in a compendium of rules that specifically governs a class licensee to engage in the sale of automobiles. Who should prevail? [*Fireside Chrysler-Plymouth Mazda, Inc. v. Edgar, Secretary of State,* 464 N.E.2d 275 (Ill. 1984).]
4. A bank made a loan commitment to Abramowitz to loan Abramowitz $400,000 for one year, at 9 percent interest with a 1 percent point or "service fee." The $4,000 service fee was shown on a closing statement as a "discount." The $4,000 service fee was deducted in full from the loan proceeds. During the year Abramowitz was charged and paid $36,347.78 in interest. Abramowitz therefore paid more than $40,000 or 10 percent of his $400,000 loan. By statute, the maximum rate of interest that could be charged was 10 percent. Was the loan usurious? [*Abramowitz v. Barnett Bank of West Orlando,* 394 So.2d 1033 (Fla. 1981).]
5. A bank filed a suit against Larkins for failure to make required payments as provided in a retail installment contract. Larkins counterclaimed alleging a usurious rate of interest in the contract. The subject matter of the contract was a mobile home. The contract provided for a cash price of $15,000 or a deferred payment price of $24,225.12. Larkins bought the mobile home for the deferred payment price and the seller sold the contract to Larkins. Is the contract usurious? [*First National Bank of Ottawa v. Larkins,* 444 N.E.2d 818 (Ill. 1983).]

6. An insurance company brought an action for an injunction against its former employee, Rezatto, alleging that the employee breached the employment contract by engaging in the insurance business in the same area as the employer within ten years after termination of employment. Rezatto had agreed at the outset of employment not to compete for the ten-year-period. Should the injunction be issued? [*1st American Systems, Inc. v. Rezatto,* 311 N.W.2d 51 (S.D. 1981).]
7. Sacks was employed by Dallas Gold and Silver Exchange, Inc. (DGSE) as an assistant controller-credit manager in October 1982. In 1983 he was promoted to controller. His duties as controller included the preparation of a quarterly statements for DGSE's landlord to determine proper rental payments. The rent was based upon a percentage of DGSE's sales. Upon assuming his role as controller, Sacks found that the previously submitted statements were falsified to show lesser rental amounts owed. Sacks suggested one way out of the problem was to "cook" the books (keep two sets of records). His boss told him to take care of the matter and he filed a false report. Sacks received part of a bonus and part payment on overtime due him. With auditors on the horizon, Sacks quit his job and now sues DGSE for compensation due him. Should Sacks recover? [*Sacks v. Dallas Gold and Silver Exch., Inc.,* 720 S.W.2d 177 (Tex. 1986).]
8. Burne, as beneficiary under an insurance policy, sued for double indemnity accidental death benefits because of the death of the insured [the person whose risk has been assumed by another]. The insured had been struck by an automobile and was kept alive in a vegetative state for four and a half years before he died. The policy provided that the accidental death benefits would be paid only if death occurred within ninety days of the accident, and that such benefits would not be paid if death occurred during a time when premiums were being waived due to the insured's disability. Will the beneficiary be allowed to recover the insurance? [*Burne v. Franklin Life Ins. Co.,* 301 A.2d 799 (Pa. 1973).].
9. In 1979, the Arizona Department of Transportation gave notice that it would sell a parcel of property at public auction. The notice stated that the successful bidder would be required to pay $500 as an initial deposit and also to pay 20 percent of the purchase price as a down payment before the close of the transaction. The notice further stated that the buyer would have 30 days from notice of approval of sale to close the transaction. Renaissance Homes, Ltd., was the successful bidder at public auction and subsequently received 120 days extension to close the transaction from the bank who was acting as agent for the transaction in return for a $15,000 earnest money deposit. This deposit was returned by the bank to Renaissance Homes, because of a dispute by Renaissance Homes with the Department. When Renaissance Homes did not close the transaction, the bank paid the $15,000 to the Arizona Department of Transportation as earnest money forfeited for breach of contract, and by this suit the bank seeks to recover the $15,000 from Renaissance Homes. The bank's agreement with Renaissance Homes for the 120-day extension was in violation of Arizona's competitive bidding statutes. The trial court found in favor of Renaissance Homes. The bank appeals. Should the bank be allowed to recover the $15,000? [*Chicago Title Insurance Co. v. Renaissance Homes, Ltd.,* 679 P.2d 517 (Ariz. 1983).]
10. In the Baby M case, excerpted at the beginning of this section, the court held that the consideration of the child's best interest should prevail over the freedom of choice of the natural parents to determine its custody. Discuss the merits and demerits of the legal system acting as the final judge on what is for the greatest good in the contractual setting.

CHAPTER

12

CONTRACTUAL FORM

REQUIREMENT OF A WRITING FOR ENFORCEABILITY, STATUTE OF FRAUDS

After you have read this chapter, you should be able to:

1. Recognize that the law tries to assure itself that it is not being misled when it enforces a contract.
2. Understand that the law has developed many exceptions to the rule that certain contracts must be in writing or that there must be a written memorandum of an oral contract in order for the contract to be enforced.
3. Note how the concept of contractual form limits the freedom of individuals to contract.
4. Appreciate the interrelationships among the statute of frauds, the parol evidence rule, and rules of interpretation.
5. Discuss how the evolution of the law associated with the concept of the statute of frauds may be leading to a substantial limitation in its application.

BUSINESS DECISIONS and the LAW

As reflected in a series of law cases, purchasers of new houses have experienced the following problems: wet basements, furnaces installed without ducts, foundations crumbling, ceilings falling, sewage backing up under the house, leaky showers, splits in cement driveways, splits in brick fireplaces, and splits in kitchen walls. There are also untold other real-life "horror stories" of homeowners who find themselves in terrible situations with building contractors.

Today, home repair and remodeling demands have led to the growth of new and inexperienced contracting companies—and to flaring tempers and many consumer complaints. In 1988 the U.S. Better Business Bureau received enough complaints about home improvement to have that topic become the fourth largest category of gripes.

To aid property owners in specifying their expectations in writing, the American Homeowners Foundation has formulated a prototype contract for homeowners. The document provides for listing a detailed work description, materials to be used, starting and completion dates, and a payment schedule. It also aids homeowners in selecting the right contractor for their needs.

Most problems arise over matters that are never discussed in advance. Complaints relate to what is assumed, but never agreed upon orally or in writing by either party. The document is an effort to force both parties to address all aspects of the contractual relationship. Although oral contracts can be enforceable, the above situations point out the wisdom of having a contract in writing.

Introduction

In the preceding chapters of this part we discussed the four elements required for a contract: mutual assent, consideration, capacity to contract, and legality. In order to prevent fraud by persons who assert that certain contracts were made when, in fact, they were not made, certain contracts must be proved by a proper writing before the courts will recognize and enforce them. Accordingly, we will now consider the contractual form and proof necessary for the enforcement of certain contracts.

Jim claims that he had a contract with Mary, who denies this. Was there a contract, and if so what were its terms? Would this kind of problem be solved if the law required that, for the purpose of proving a contract and its terms, *all* contracts must be in writing or that there be a written memorandum of an oral contract? Obviously it would be very inconvenient, and all transactions would be much slowed down if such a writing were required for *all* contracts. Also, the opportunity to escape from being bound by a contract that had been made is present by showing that there is no writing. Or should only selected kinds of contract be required to be proved by a writing?

The Statute of Frauds

The original Statute of Frauds was passed in 1677 by the English Parliament adopting "An Act for Prevention of Frauds and Perjuries." This statute was repealed in England in 1954, except as to land sale and guaranty contracts. In the United States, individual states modeled statutes of frauds after the Act passed by Parliament. Today, any statutory provision in the law requiring that a contract be proved only by a proper writing is called a **statute of frauds.** Its purpose is to prevent fraud by perjured testimony (false testimony given under oath in a judicial proceeding) in proving the existence of a contract. The statute applies only to certain selected kinds of alleged contracts which, over many years, have been the subject of much fraud in proving their existence.

statute of frauds
A statute requiring that certain kinds of contract be proved only by a proper writing

enforceable contract
A contract that can be proved and enforced by the courts

Compliance with the statute's requirement of proof by a writing is necessary for a contract to be enforced. Failure to comply with the statute does not affect a contract's validity, only its **enforceability.** The courts will not enforce the contract if it cannot be proved by a proper writing.

Often when a contract does exist but cannot be proved because a required writing does not exist, fraud has been perpetrated upon a contracting party and fraud has not been prevented. Therefore, to be safe, one is well advised to have all contracts in writing, to the extent possible, and not be caught in the pitfall of the statute of frauds requirements.

While there are contracts for which there must be a writing to be proved, numerous exceptions exist that allow many of these kinds of contract to be proved orally. Even if the writing does not exist to support these contracts, the party who cannot enforce the contract is not always without a remedy.

If the subject matter of a contract does not fall within the statute of frauds, the contract can be proved orally. Such oral proof of a contract must be sufficiently definite that a court can ascertain that the elements necessary for the formation of a contract are present.

There is a distinction between a contract to sell land, and a collateral (additional) contract that refers to the sales contract. The first contract is within the statute of frauds and must be proved by a writing to be enforceable. The second contract is not within the statute of frauds and need not be proved by a writing to be enforceable. In the following case note how the court sought to achieve justice by treating the case as one of tort for **fraud** rather than as a contract case.

fraud

In contracts, a misrepresentation of fact, known to be false, intentionally made to induce another person to make or refrain from making a contract, and reasonably relied on by the other person

FACTS

Kett, purchasers of real property, brought this action against the sellers on an oral promise allegedly made by the sellers, collateral to the sales contract, to make certain specific repairs to the real property sold. Kett alleged they were induced to buy the home when the sellers orally agreed to repair a leaky shower, splits in the cement driveway, split bricks in the fireplace, and split kitchen walls. The sellers raised the statute of frauds as a defense, contending that the alleged collateral oral promise was under that part of the statute of frauds concerning the sale of real property and, therefore, was unenforceable because the alleged oral promise could not be proved by a proper writing. The sellers referred to a deposit receipt, signed by the sellers, which stated "This [sales] agreement contains the entire agreement and all representations not herein set forth are deemed waived." In the lower court, the sellers' motion for summary judgment was granted, and the purchasers appealed.

DECISION

Reversed, for the purchasers, and sent back to the lower court for trial. The court reasoned that the written sales contract was the final expression of the parties and the alleged oral collateral promise was not a part of it. However, this is not an action to enforce a contract for the sale of real property and, therefore, the statute of frauds does not apply. Nor is this an action for damages for breach of the sales contract. The property has been sold and paid for. This is an action in tort for fraud by the alleged sellers' collateral oral promise made to induce Kett to buy, and made without any intention to perform—a promissory fraud.

Kett v. Graeser, 50 Cal.Rptr. 727 (1966).

► Contracts Within the Statute

Traditionally, and under the law of contracts, the following kinds of contract cannot be proved unless there is a proper writing: (1) contracts that cannot be performed within one year; (2) contracts concerning the sale of real property; (3) a promise given in consideration of marriage but not between the parties to be married; (4) a promise to answer for the duty (debt, default, or miscarriages) of another; (5) a promise by an **executor** or **administrator** to answer personally for the debt of a **decedent's** estate; and now, under the Uniform Commercial Code, (6) a contract for the sale of goods for $500 or more.[1]

executor (executrix)

A court-appointed man (woman) designated in a decedent's will as the decedent's personal representative

administrator (administratrix)

A court-appointed man (woman) who acts as the intestate's personal representative

decedent

One who is dead

► One Year Plus

For a bilateral contract that will require more than one year to perform from the date of its formation, there must be a writing for the contract to be enforceable. When computing time, the day upon which the contract is formed is not counted. Thus a contract made on the first day of the month to start on the third day of the month and to run for one year would require a writing to render it enforceable. The contract runs

[1]UCC 2–201. Other Code sections requiring a writing are UCC 8–319, sale of securities; 9–203 (1)(a), security agreement; and 1–206, sale of other personal property.

FIGURE 12.1 Statute of Frauds (Contracts That Cannot Be Proved Without a Proper Writing)

1. Contracts that cannot be performed within one year.
2. Contracts concerning the sale of real property.
3. A promise given in consideration of marriage but not between the parties to be married.
4. A promise to answer for the duty (debt, default, or miscarriage) of another.
5. A promise by an executor or administrator to answer personally for the debt of a decedent's estate.
6. A contract for the sale of goods for $500 or more (Uniform Commercial Code).

for one year and one day. The extra day is the second day of the month. (See Figure 12.2.) A writing will not be required when it is possible that the consideration promised can be given within one year. A promise to work for one's lifetime is capable of performance in one year because one might die within a year.

In the following case the oral contract was provable because the defendant was unable to show that the promise could not be performed within one year.

FACTS

The Augusta Bank and Trust orally contracted with Broomfield to level four thousand acres of Broomfield's land. Broomfield never paid the Augusta for the performed work and the Augusta brought an action for breach of contract. Broomfield contended that because the bank had estimated that it would take a year to level two thousand acres, the project to level four thousand acres could not be completed within one year. Broomfield therefore argued that the statute of frauds applied, making the oral contract unenforceable.

DECISION

The court found for the Augusta Bank and Trust. The court rejected Broomfield's argument, noting that it was not established that performance could not possibly have been completed within one year; thus the contract did not fall within the statute of frauds.

Augusta Bank and Trust v. Broomfield, 643 P.2d 100 (Kan. 1982).

If the contract is unilateral and the act has been performed, though the promise for the act will take more than one year to perform, no writing will be required to prove its existence. For example, if Jan gave money to Bill as requested in return for the promise of Bill to repay the loan with interest in eighteen months, no writing would be necessary to enforce the promise.

▶ Real Property

easement
An irrevocable right to the limited use of another's land

A writing is needed to prove a contract that concerns itself with the sale of land or of an interest in land. A lease of land, **easement,** and real property mortgage are illustrations

FIGURE 12.2 **One Year Plus Contract**

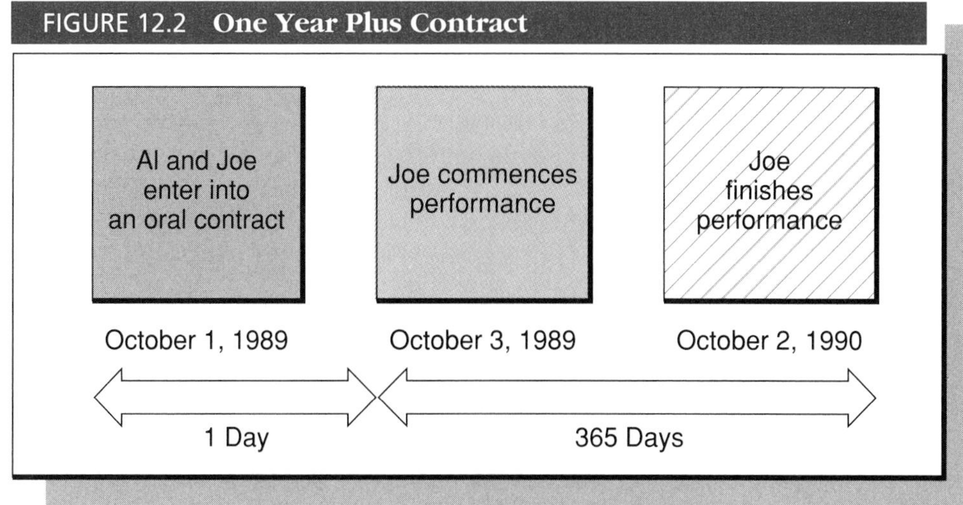

of interests in land. However, by statute, leases for not more than one year are often not included within the statute and are enforceable without a writing.

Contractual purposes that touch, or are collateral to, an interest in land need not be in writing to be enforced. Thus a commission agreement with a broker who is to produce a purchaser of real property (absent a statutory requirement for a writing), or a contract to paint or repair a house on land, touch an interest in land but are not concerned with the sale of an interest in land and, therefore, need not be in writing to be enforceable.[2]

However, if there is an oral contract for the sale of land and the seller conveys the title to the land to the buyer, who is to pay the purchase price to the seller later, the contract is no longer within the statute of frauds. The reason is that the purpose, for protecting the seller against a fraudulent charge that he or she made a contract, is no longer applicable since the seller has conveyed the title to the buyer. Therefore the seller can enforce the oral contract against the buyer for the purchase price without proof by any writing.

Also, while there is a difference of view, in many states if the seller delivers possession to the buyer and the buyer either makes payment or, with the seller's consent, makes substantial improvements on the land, the contract is no longer within the statute of frauds.

► Marriage

The exchange of promises to marry are enforceable and can be proved without a writing. However, a writing is required to prove a promise containing additional consideration other than to marry. For example, Adam orally promises Brenda, a divorcee, to pay for the education of Brenda's son if Brenda will marry Adam, which Brenda then does. Adam's oral promise will be unenforceable.

[2]For more detail on what is an interest in land, see pp. 986–987.

► Debt, Default, and Miscarriage

default
A failure to perform a legal duty

A promise to answer for (be responsible for) the duty (debt, **default,** or miscarriage) of another is unenforceable unless proved by a writing. A father orally promises a retailer that if the retailer will extend credit to his son and his son does not pay, then the father will pay the retailer. Or a sister promises the university that if her brother does not build the building pursuant to his contract with the university, the sister will be liable for her brother's default in not performing his contract. In both of these examples, the promises of the father and the sister must be proved by a writing for them to be enforceable.

However, for a promise to come within this part of the statute of frauds, *all* of the following three things must occur:

1. The promise must be made to the obligee, the person to whom the obligation is owing. Thus the retailer and the university are the obligees—the retailer is the creditor and the university is the entity for whom the building was to be built. If the father had made the promise to his son, or the sister had made the promise to her brother, their promises would *not* be made to the obligees and would *not* be within the statute and, therefore, would be enforceable without a writing. (See Figure 12.3.)

FIGURE 12.3 **Promises Within and Without the Statute of Frauds (promise must be made *to the obligee*)**

Within the Statute of Frauds Writing Required	Without the Statute of Frauds No Writing Required
Father orally promises retailer. Son If the retailer sells to the son on credit, the father will pay the son's debt owed to the retailer if the son does not pay the retailer.	Father orally promises son. Retailer If the son buys from the retailer on credit and fails to pay the retailer, the father will pay his son's debt owed to the retailer. (The father's promise is not made to the obligee, retailer.)
Sister orally promises university. Brother *If her brother defaults*, the sister will perform her brother's obligation to the university.	Sister orally promises brother. University *If her brother defaults*, the sister will perform her brother's obligation to the university. (The sister's promise is not made to the obligee, the university.)

2. The promise must not assume another's obligation of performance but, rather, must be to perform if another did not perform. Thus the father and the sister promised to perform if the son and the brother did not perform. If instead the father had promised to be liable with his son as a co-debtor, or the sister promised to build the building with her brother, the promises of the father and the sister would *not* be to answer for the debt or default of another (the son and the brother), and their promises would not be within the statute. They would have assumed the obligations, and their promises would be enforceable without a writing. (See Figure 12.4.)
3. The promise must be made primarily for the benefit of another, namely the obligor, and not for the promisor. Thus if the father's promise was made primarily so that his son could buy goods on credit from the retailer and supply them to the father, or if the sister's promise was made primarily so that the sister could lease and occupy the building from the university, the promises of the father and the sister would not be primarily for the benefit of the son and the brother, and their promises would not be within the statute. They would be enforceable without a writing. This is illustrated by the following case.

FACTS

From February 19, 1974 through June 13, 1974, Barboza delivered gravel to Liberty Contractors Company, Inc.'s construction site. Liberty's subcontractor had run up a bill with Barboza for $13,332.60. At this point, Barboza stopped delivering gravel. A responsible officer of Liberty told Barboza orally to continue delivering gravel to the construction site

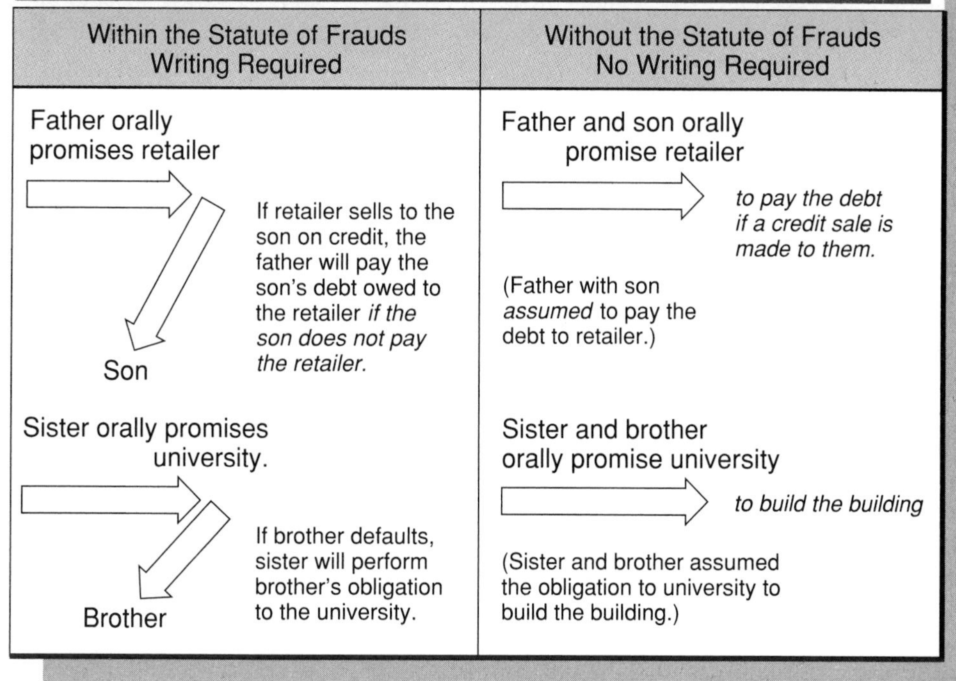
FIGURE 12.4 Promises Within and Without the Statute of Frauds (promise must *not be to assume* another's obligation of performance)
Within the Statute of Frauds
Writing Required
Without the Statute of Frauds
No Writing Required
Father orally promises retailer
If retailer sells to the son on credit, the father will pay the son's debt owed to the retailer *if the son does not pay the retailer.*
Son
Father and son orally promise retailer
to pay the debt if a credit sale is made to them.
(Father with son *assumed* to pay the debt to retailer.)
Sister orally promises university.
If brother defaults, sister will perform brother's obligation to the university.
Brother
Sister and brother orally promise university
to build the building
(Sister and brother assumed the obligation to university to build the building.)

and they would pay the $13,332.60 owed by the subcontractor. Evidence during the trial showed (1) Liberty needed Barboza's gravel badly; (2) Barboza's gravel was the right grade for the job; and (3) the job was behind schedule when the promise was made. Liberty seeks a directed verdict.

DECISION

The court found for Barboza. The court said that to the extent Liberty's promise was an undertaking to pay the debt of another it was, unless committed to writing, unenforceable under the statute of frauds. If, however, Liberty's undertaking fell into a class of cases in which the essence of the transaction is to obtain some benefit for the promisor from the promisee, the statute of frauds would not apply. A contract that all or part of a duty of a third person to the promisee shall be satisfied is not within the statute of frauds as a promise to answer for the duty of another if the consideration for the promise is in fact, or apparently desired by the promisee, mainly for the promisor's own economic advantage, rather than in order to benefit the third person. The directed verdict is denied and the question of fact should go to the jury.

Barboza et al., v. Liberty Contractors Co., 469 N.E.2d 1303 (Mass. 1984).

The term *miscarriage* means misdoing, a miscarriage of justice. An example is a bonding or insurance company promising to an employer that, if an employee cashier embezzles the employer's money, the company will pay the employer its loss. There must be a writing to prove the company's promise.

▶ Decedent's Estate

A special application of answering for the duty (debt, default, or miscarriage) of another is recognized—namely, for the obligations of a deceased person. The process of winding up the affairs of a decedent are normally handled by an executor or an administrator, who pays the decedent's debts out of the money in the decedent's estate. If this personal representative promises to become personally responsible for a debt of the decedent's estate, there must be a writing proving the promise.

Sale of Goods

▶ The Uniform Commercial Code

Under UCC 2–201, a writing is necessary to prove a contract for the sale of goods for $500 or more. However, such a writing is not required if (1) part payment for or part delivery of the goods has been accepted; (2) the goods are to be specially manufactured for the buyer, are not suitable for sale to others in the ordinary course of the seller's business, and the seller has either substantially begun their manufacture or made commitments to procure them; or (3) the oral contract has been admitted in court proceedings.[3] Under (1) and (3) above, the contract is enforceable without a writing only to the extent of goods for such part payment or goods delivered, and to the extent of such court admission. In the following case the question was whether part payment by the buyer of goods had been made causing the oral contract for sale to be enforceable.

---

[3]For a more detailed discussion of these exceptions, see p. 455.

FACTS

Sedmak, an automobile enthusiast, orally contracted with Charlie's Chevrolet, an automobile retailer, for a specified optioned Corvette to be manufactured by Chevrolet in limited quantities to commemorate the selection of Corvette as the Indianapolis 500 Pace Car. Sedmak made a $500 deposit with Charlie's for purchase of the car. Charlie's refused to deliver the car to Sedmak and offered Sedmak a chance to bid on it. Sedmak filed this suit for delivery of the car.

DECISION

The court found for Sedmak, the automobile enthusiast. The court held that where, as here, there is no dispute as to quantity, part payment for a single indivisible commercial unit validates an oral contract. The purpose of the statute of frauds is to prevent the enforcement of alleged promises that were never made; it is not and never has been to justify contractors in repudiating promises that were in fact made. Enforcement of the oral contract here carries out the purpose of the statute of frauds.

Sedmak III v. Charlie's Chevrolet, Inc., 622 S.W.2d 694 (Mo. 1981).

By statute (the Uniform Commercial Code), all that the writing needs are (1) an overall expression of an intent to contract; (2) the statement of some quantity of goods; and (3) the signature of the party (or his agent) against whom the contract is to be enforced. Any symbol may be used or adopted by a party as a signature if done with the intention of authenticating the writing. However, as between merchants, if a merchant does not object seasonably (within ten days) to a sufficient writing from the other merchant after receipt, he will be deemed to have authenticated it as his own, causing the contract to be proved and enforceable against him. In the following case all three of these items were present, and the court held that the plaintiff's letter was sufficient to comply with the Code's requirement of a proper writing.

FACTS

A buyer, Fortune Furniture Manufacturing Co., and a seller, Mid-South Plastic Fabric Company, agreed orally, respectively, to purchase and to supply plastic products. The president of Fortune told the sales representative of Mid-South to send him a letter containing the terms of the oral contract. The following letter was sent:

Mr. Sidney Widcock, President
Fortune Furn. Mfg. Co., Inc.
Okolona, Mississippi 38860

Dear Sid:
This is to confirm the agreement entered into this date between Phil on behalf of Mid-South Plastic Co., Inc. and you on behalf of Fortune Furn. Mfg. Co., Inc. We agree to maintain expanded and 21-ounce plastic in the warehouse of Mid-South Furniture Suppliers, Inc. in sufficient amounts to supply all the plastics for your plant's use, and if for any reason we do not have the necessary plastic you will be at liberty to purchase the plastic from any other source and we will pay the difference in price between the other source and our current price. We also agree to pay Fortune a 2 percent rebate on the gross sales price of our plastic as an advertisement aid to your company, which rebate to be paid at your request. We assure that all fabrics you need will be in our warehouse at all times and we appreciate your agreeing to buy all of your plastics from us.

Very truly yours,
/s/W. E. Walker, President

In a suit by the seller for the balance of the purchase price, the buyer entered a **counterclaim** based on Walker's letter. The seller's contention to the buyer's counterclaim is that the letter does not satisfy the statute of frauds. Judgment was entered in favor of the seller regarding the counterclaim in that the letter did not satisfy the statute of frauds. The buyer appealed.

counterclaim
A claim asserted by the defendant against the plaintiff's claim in a civil action

DECISION

Judgment reversed, for the buyer, Fortune, on its counterclaim. The court noted there are only three requirements to make a memorandum sufficient to take the case outside of the statute of frauds provision of the Uniform Commercial Code. Those requirements are (1) the memorandum must evidence a contract for sale of goods; (2) it must be signed by the party against whom enforcement is sought; and (3) it must specify a quantity. The court held that the letter in question satisfied all three requirements.

Fortune Furniture Mfg. Co., v. Mid-South Plastic Fabric Co., 310 So.2d 725 (Miss. 1975).

The Required Writing

The best writing to prove a contract is the written contract. However, if the contract is oral, what kind of a writing or written memorandum of the oral contract will be sufficient to prove the oral contract? The difference between a written contract and a written memorandum of an oral contract is that the written contract is a formally drawn document intentionally drafted to meet the requirements of the statute of frauds whereas a written memorandum as originally recorded was not intended by its form to meet the requirements of the statute of frauds.

▶ The Common Law of Contracts

A writing that will satisfy the requirements of the statute of frauds can be in any form. (It does not need to be labeled a "contract.") It can be pieced together if one document refers to another (e.g., one letter refers to another letter). To be complete, however, the memorandum of an oral contract must (1) identify the parties to the contract and their relationship (for example, seller and buyer); (2) identify the subject matter of the contract; (3) indicate that a contract was made; and (4) state all the terms and conditions of each promise and to whom made (for example, price and credit terms). The writing must be signed by the party charged with having made the contract—namely, the party against whom the enforcement of the contract is sought. For example, if *Al* orally contracts with *Bo* and *Al* wishes to enforce the contract against *Bo, Al* must prove that a memorandum was signed by *Bo* or by *Bo's* lawfully authorized agent. *Bo* is the party charged by *Al* with having made the contract. In the following case an advertisement failed as a writing because it lacked an essential term.

FACTS

McBride, a former employee of a municipality, brought this action against the municipality to recover damages for breach of an oral contract of employment. The employee had been employed for a little over five months when the employment was terminated despite the employee's insistence that the employment period was to be for eighteen months. The employee had learned of the position through a newspaper advertisement placed by the municipality. The advertisement did not mention the salary to be paid the person hired. No formal written employment contract was entered into by the parties. The municipality asserted that the employment contract, to be performed in eighteen months, and not being in writing, was within the statute of frauds and thus unenforceable.

DECISION

The court held for the City of McCook. Since the alleged contract by its terms was not to be performed within one year from the making thereof, it was subject to the statute of frauds and would be unenforceable unless some sufficient memorandum existed to prove it. A classified advertisement published in the McCook Daily Gazette not containing the essential term of salary is not a sufficient memorandum.

McBride v. City of McCook, 321 N.W.2d 905 (Neb. 1982).

► Effect of the Parol Evidence Rule

Common Law Under the common law, when there is a written contract, it cannot be contradicted (added to or varied) by any prior or contemporaneous oral (**parol**) agreement or by a prior written agreement. This is called the **parol evidence rule.** All the terms and conditions should have been included in (integrated into) the writing.

parol
Oral

parol evidence rule
A rule of law providing that, when there is a written contract, it cannot be contradicted (added to or varied) by any prior or contemporaneous oral agreement, or by a prior written agreement

The parol evidence rule should not be confused with the statute of frauds, just discussed. Each has a different purpose. The statute of frauds is concerned with requiring written proof that a contract exists. The parol evidence rule is concerned with preventing contradiction of a written contract that has been already proven to exist.

However, there are exceptions when certain oral evidence can be introduced in a legal action seeking to enforce a written contract. Under the common law, oral evidence could be introduced to prove the nonexistence of a contract. This is done most often by proving the absence of one of the elements necessary to the formation of a contract—namely, genuineness of assent (see Chapter 8). Oral evidence can also be introduced (1) to show that the written contract violates public policy (see Chapter 11); (2) to show that a condition that was to occur before the contract was to be enforced failed to happen; (3) to show that the contract is voidable; (4) to show that the contract was discharged by a subsequent oral or written agreement; and (5) to show the meaning of ambiguous language in a contract or to fill in obvious gaps in an *incomplete* written contract.

In the following case the court permitted oral proof of fraud even though a written contract existed that stated (an integration clause) it contained the entire agreement.

FACTS

Betz Laboratories, Inc., purchased a building and subsequently brought suit against Hines, the seller, to recover some $80,000. Betz Laboratories made known to Hines a particular need for the floor of the building to be able to bear a loading capacity of at least 750 pounds per square foot. Hines orally stated that the floor would meet Betz's needs. A written con-

FIGURE 12.5 **Exceptions to Parol Evidence Rule**

When one attempts to show:

1. Absence of genuineness of assent;
2. A condition that was to occur before the contract was to be enforced failed to happen;
3. The written contract violates public policy;
4. The contract is voidable;
5. The contract was discharged by a subsequent oral or written agreement; and/or
6. The meaning of ambiguous language in a contract or to fill in obvious gaps in an incomplete written contract.

tract was signed by Betz Laboratories and Hines. It contained the following language: "This agreement contains the whole agreement between the Seller and Buyer and there are no other terms, obligations, covenants, representations, statements or conditions, oral or otherwise, of any kind whatsoever." Subsequently Betz found the floor unfit for its purposes and alleged fraud in the inducement in the making of the contract in its suit to recover the cost of repairs. Hines objects to oral evidence being introduced with regard to its statement to Betz Laboratories in the face of the written contract.

DECISION

Evidence of fraud in the inducement is outside the parol evidence rule and, therefore, admissible. The court found for Betz Laboratories, holding that it is always competent to aver and prove that an engagement in writing was induced by fraudulent oral representations of material facts that affect the consideration. The purpose in such case is not to alter or vary the terms of the writing by parol evidence but to strike the writing down, just as though it had never been in existence, or to strike down such part of it as is dependent on the fraud, if the balance of the contract can be sustained as enforceable. To give effect to an integration clause permits language to shield a party from the consequences of fraud, contrary to public policy.

Betz Laboratories, Inc. v. Hines, 647 F.2d 402 (3rd Cir. 1981).

course of dealing

"A sequence of previous conduct between the parties to a particular transaction which is fairly to be regarded as establishing a common basis of understanding for interpreting their expressions and other conduct" UCC 1–205(1)

usage of trade

"Any practice or method of dealing having such regularity of observance in a place, vocation, or trade as to justify an expectation that it will be observed with respect to the transaction in question" UCC 1–205(2)

The Uniform Commercial Code UCC 2–202 broadens the traditional parol evidence rule by permitting the introduction of **course of dealing** and **usage of trade** orally to explain terms in a written contract where the subject matter is goods. A course of dealing is a sequence of previous conduct between parties to an agreement that is fairly to be regarded as establishing a common basis of understanding for interpreting their expressions. Usage of trade is a usage having such regularity of observance in a place, vocation, or trade as to justify an expectation that it will be observed with respect to a particular agreement. Additional terms can be introduced orally despite the writing when the court is not convinced that the writing was intended to be the complete and exclusive agreement of the parties to the contract.

Interpretation

In interpreting a written contract, usually ordinary words are given their ordinary meaning and technical words their technical meaning. Each part (that is, each paragraph in the contract) will be interpreted so that it is compatible with the primary purpose of the contract. Special terms will prevail over general terms, and written terms will prevail over printed terms in a form contract. In the following case typewritten provisions of a contract prevail over printed portions that were inconsistent.

FACTS

A dispute over the payment for additional electrical usage came about as the result of certain provisions in a lease. Paragraph 10A(4) of the printed form lease provided:

> 10. Utilities and Services. A. Lessor agrees to furnish or cause to be furnished to the Demised Premises, in common with other lessees where appropriate, the following services.... (4) Electricity for normal office usage, it being agreed that all additional electricity costs stemming from such causes as, but not limited to, Lessee's operation of special equipment from Lessee's extraordinary usage of heating and air conditioning shall be paid by Lessee....

Two typewritten paragraphs appear at the end of the lease which read as follows:

> 37. Lessor agrees rent shall be inclusive of hot water, electricity and air conditioning charges.
> 38. In event electrical charges are determined to be less than Lessor has projected, an appropriate credit will be applied to the Lease.

The lessee contends that the lease rental includes all electricity and air conditioning charges. The landlord claims that such charges are not included in the rental.

DECISION

Judgment for the lessee. The court said these typewritten paragraphs reflect a clear intent that the stated rental should include all electricity and air conditioning charges. The typewritten provisions of a contract ordinarily prevail over printed portions which are inconsistent. Such is the case here.

The Natural Kitchen, Inc. v. American Transworld Corp., 449 So.2d 855 (Fla. 1984).

All writings making up the contract are interpreted together as a whole agreement. As was stated and explained in Chapter 11, Public Policy and Contractual Purpose, a legal rather than an illegal result will be presumed. Conduct with regard to terminology and circumstances surrounding the creation of the contract will be considered in interpreting words. Usage of trade, or custom, is used to explain ambiguous terms, and such terminology is construed when needed against the interest of the party who wrote the contract.

Result If No Writing, in General

A defendant who raises the defense of the lack of a writing where required by the statute of frauds renders the contract unenforceable because it cannot be proved by a writing. It should be remembered that an oral contract not within the statute of frauds is enforceable if proved without any writing.

Quasi Contract

In many instances where performance has been rendered under an oral agreement that is not provable, recovery can be obtained for unjust enrichment under the theory of a contract implied in law, namely a quasi contract. (See p. 125).

Partial Performance

Partial performance, as we have seen in the sale of goods under the Code (see p. 224), can be proved. Under the common law of contracts, when, with the permission of the owner (seller), one (buyer) has taken possession of land under an oral contract and either pays part or all of the purchase price or vastly improves the property, the court, if convinced of the existence of an oral contract, will enforce it without a writing.

Full Performance

Full performance of all duties by both parties to the contract prevents the introduction of the plea of the statute of frauds. The defense of the statute of frauds applies only to **executory contracts**; it does not apply to executed contracts because there is no longer any contract to enforce.

executory contract
A contract that has not been performed by all the parties to it

▶ Equity

To promote justice and fairness should the situation demand it, a court can employ equity and thereby waive the requirement of compliance with the statute of frauds. An example is promissory estoppel, discussed in Chapter 9 (p. 181).

Summary Statement

1. As a practical matter, all contracts should be in writing.
2. Most oral contracts can be proved orally.
3. If the writing is the contract, previous oral or written evidence or contemporaneous oral evidence should not be heard that would contradict its terms.
4. There are six types of contract (the first five being under the law of contracts), which must be proved by a writing: (a) contracts that cannot be performed within one year; (b) sale of real property; (c) marriage consideration; (d) debt, default, or miscarriage of another; (e) executor's or administrator's promise; and (f), under the Uniform Commercial Code the sale of goods for $500 or more.
5. Under the common law, oral evidence can be introduced irrespective of the content of a writing in five general instances: (a) violation of public policy; (b) failure of conditions; (c) voidable contracts; (d) discharge by subsequent oral or written agreement; and (e) ambiguity and incompleteness.
6. The parol evidence rule under the Code is more liberal than the common law in allowing oral testimony to explain terms in a written contract where the subject matter is goods.
7. Under the common law, there are four requirements for a writing that will satisfy the requirements of the statute of frauds if the contract is oral. The writing must: (a) identify the parties and their relationship, (b) describe the subject matter, (c) indicate that a contract was made, and (d) state all the terms and conditions of each promise and to whom made. The writing becomes effective when it is signed by the party to be charged with its performance.
8. There are three exceptions under the Code to the necessity for a writing to prove an oral contract for the sale or purchase of goods for $500 or more: (a) part performance; (b) specially manufactured goods; and (c) admitting the contract in court proceedings.
9. Under the Code, if the contract for the sale of goods is oral, for a writing to be sufficient there are only three requirements: (a) quantity of goods; (b) a writing showing intent to contract; and (c) signature. Between merchants, the writing of one may become that of the other. The signature on a writing must be that of the party sought to be charged with the contract.
10. There are a limited number of rules of interpretation of a writing.
11. There are numerous exceptions that allow enforcement of contracts normally not provable because of the lack of a writing.
12. Equity—through the concept of part performance, quasi contract, and promissory estoppel—has provided remedies when parties can prove contracts at law in the absence of a writing.

The following case illustrates how the court applied promissory estoppel.

KIELY v. ST. GERMAIN
670 P.2d 764 (Colo. 1983)

In October 1978, St. Germain and the Boshouwers began discussing the possibility of St. Germain joining the color film processing business then operated by Boshouwers and his wife. At that time St. Germain had been employed by the Public Service Company of Colorado for approximately 12 years.

On December 8, 1978, St. Germain and Boshouwers visited the office of St. Germain's lawyer. In response to questions by the attorney, both parties stated that they had reached an agreement on all major terms of a new business venture. Those terms included payment of a monthly salary to St. Germain of $1,500 and an agreement by Boshouwers to sell stock to St. Germain in the corporation that ran the film processing business and which was to guarantee the salary to be paid to St. Germain.

St. Germain's attorney then drafted a document containing these provisions and both parties assured him that a "firm deal" was in existence. *Neither party executed the document* [Emphasis added]; however, at the conclusion of the meeting Boshouwers made the following statements: "Well, now we have a deal and you can tell your employer . . . that you are leaving." St. Germain terminated his employment with the Public Service Company later that same day.

St. Germain then obtained a second mortgage on his house to finance the purchase of the stock, took a prearranged vacation with his family and, on January 17, 1979, tendered a document containing the terms of the December 8, 1978 oral agreement to Boshouwers for signature. At this point, Boshouwers denied that the parties had an oral agreement.

St. Germain sued and sought damages on claims of breach of an oral contract or, alternatively, promissory estoppel. Boshouwers raised an affirmative defense asserting that the Colorado Statute of Frauds which provides that "a contract for the sale of securities is not enforceable" unless proved by a proper writing.

The trial court concluded that St. Germain was entitled to lost wages and legal service costs based on promissory estoppel, but barred his claim for lost profits relating to the purchase of the corporate stock. The appeals court found for St. Germain on all issues and the Supreme Court of Colorado reviewed the case to consider the assertion that the doctrine of promissory estoppel may be invoked to enforce an alleged oral agreement in the face of a statute of frauds defense.

The court noted that the doctrine of promissory estoppel is part of the common law of Colorado and that it has been given most recent expression in Section (90)(1) of the *Restatement (Second) of Contracts,* as follows:

> A promise which the promisor should reasonably expect to induce action or forbearance on the part of the promisee or a third person and which does induce such action or forbearance is binding if injustice can be avoided only by enforcement of the promise. *The remedy granted for breach may be limited as justice requires.* [Emphasis added]

The court pointed out that the doctrine of promissory estoppel encourages fair dealing and discourages conduct which unreasonably causes foreseeable economic loss because of action or inaction induced by a specific promise. The doctrine represents in part a modest extension of the basic contract principle that one who makes promises must be required to keep them. The doctrine is grounded upon principles of fair dealing. Fraudulent conduct by the promisor is not an element of promissory estoppel. When injustice to a promisee who reasonably and justifiably relies on a promise can be prevented only by recognizing a right of recovery from the promisor, neither the lack of a written contract nor the absence of fraudulent conduct can defeat the claim for recompense.

The policies furthered by the statute of frauds were to represent a forceful effort to prevent the perpetration of fraud by the device of perjury. However laudable this goal, courts, when faced with inequity by its strict application, have found ways to circumvent it. The doctrine of promissory estoppel is but one principle developed by the courts to prevent parties from employing the statute of frauds to defeat just claims. [The Colorado Statute, reflecting the Uniform Commercial Code, provides] "... the principles of law and equity, including ... the law relative to ... estoppel shall supplement its provisions."

Section 139 of the *Restatement (Second) of Contracts*, the court noted, states as follows:

> (1) A promise which the promisor should reasonably expect to induce action or forbearance on the part of the promisee or a third person and which does induce the action or forbearance is *enforceable* not withstanding the Statute of Frauds if injustice can be avoided only by enforcement of the promise. The remedy granted for breach is to be limited as justice requires. [Emphasis added]
> (2) In determining whether injustice can be avoided only by enforcement of the promise, the following circumstances are significant: (a) the availability and adequacy of other remedies, particularly cancellation and restitution; (b) the definite and substantial character of the action or forbearance in relation to the remedy sought; (c) the extent to which the action or forbearance corroborates evidence of the making and terms of the promise, or the making and terms are otherwise established by clear and convincing evidence; (d) the reasonableness of the action or forbearance; (e) the extent to which the action or forbearance was foreseeable by the promisor.

By this rationale the court held that it affirmed the trial court's award of lost wages and legal service costs and remanded the case to the trial court for a determination of an award of lost profits under Section 139 of the *Restatement (Second) of Contracts* in the circumstances of this case.

Questions and Case Problems

1. After submitting a low bid of $239,975, West Ark Construction Co. was awarded a contract to build an apartment project for Sellers and Win. Upon completion of the project, West Ark was paid $239,975 plus $8,275.30 for change orders. West Ark now sues Sellers and Win for fraud claiming that if West Ark rebated Sellers and Win the $25,000 Sellers and Win had paid for the construction site, Sellers and Win promised orally to pay West Ark $260,000 for the project despite the $239,975 term written in the contract. Sellers and Win assert that the trial court erroneously admitted into evidence conversations between the parties concerning and leading up to the oral construction contract and indicating fraudulent misrepresentations. Did the court err? [*Sellers v. West-Ark Constr. Co.*, 676 S.W.2d 726 (Ark. 1984).]
2. Manning brought this action against Metal Stamping Corp. under a written contract for commissions related to a successful bid by Metal Stamping for the manufacture of Illinois license plates. Metal Stamping offered to prove orally that part of the agreement with Manning was that Manning was to bribe, and did bribe, the late secretary of state to obtain the contract. Manning objects to the introduction of the oral evidence as a violation of the parol evidence rule. What result? [*Manning v. Metal Stamping Corp.*, 396 F.Supp. 1376, aff'd 530 F.2d 980 (N.D. Ill. 1975).]
3. Virgil Dixon attended an auction sale at the advertised time and location and was the highest and last bidder on a tract of land having bid $8,700. Immediately following the sale, Dixon gave the auctioneer a check for $1,305 as a 15 percent down payment on the property and signed a memorandum of sale prepared by the auctioneer. The written memorandum of sale contained the terms of sale, a description of the property and the names of the seller and buyer. Dixon subsequently sued for specific performance of the contract and the seller replies that there was no written contract

of sale entered into by the buyer and seller in compliance with the statute of frauds. The statute of frauds provides that "When lands, tenements or hereditaments are sold or leased at public auction and the auctioneer, his clerk or agent make a memorandum of the property and the price thereof at which it is sold or leased, the terms of sale, the name of the purchaser or lessee, and the name of the person on whose account the sale or lease is made; such memorandum is [a] note of the contract." Who is right—Dixon or the seller? [*Dixon v. Hill,* 456 So.2d 313 (Ala. 1984).]

4. Leucadia, Inc., through its agent, orally placed orders for fuel for three buildings located in New York City. As of December 26, 1977, unpaid fuel bills amounted to $18,105.38. As of December 27, 1977, Leucadia delivered a letter to Plymouth Rock Fuel Corp. indicating that Leucadia would no longer pay for contracts previously entered into by its agent. Upon suit by Plymouth Rock Fuel, Leucadia asserted the statute of frauds as a defense. Is Plymouth Rock Fuel entitled to be paid? [*Plymouth Rock Fuel Corp. v. Leucadia, Inc.,* 474 N.Y.S.2d 79 (N.Y. 1984).]
5. Landowners brought action against lessees of adjoining land seeking to enjoin lessees from discharging irrigation waste water upon their land. Adjoining landowners intervened, seeking to quiet title to alleged oral easement over land for purpose of discharging water and to enjoin landowners from interfering with its discharge. Can the "oral" easement be upheld? [*Darsaklis et al. v. Schildt et al.,* 358 N.W.2d 186 (Neb. 1984).]
6. A husband brought a suit for divorce. The wife in her answer prayed that, if he should be granted the divorce, she be awarded custody of their minor child, her husband to be required to perform specifically an alleged oral contract made prior to their marriage to adopt her daughter of a previous marriage, and that she be awarded temporary and permanent alimony in support of their minor child. The wife's daughter filed a petition to intervene to require the husband to specifically perform the alleged oral agreement to adopt her as his child. Can the oral agreement be proved? [*Maddox v. Maddox,* 161 S.E.2d 870 (Ga. 1968).]
7. Thomas was awarded a finder's fee of $25,000 to be paid to Thomas for procuring a buyer for the sale of controlling stock of a company. The stock was held by executors in trust for themselves as beneficiaries of the trust for various decedents. Hill, representing the executors, was the one who made the oral promise to Thomas to pay him $25,000 if he could find a desirable buyer. The executors asserted the defense of the statute of frauds when Thomas sued them for the commission. Hill and others are appealing the award to Thomas. Is there a promise to answer for the debt of a decedent? [*Hill v. Thomas,* 462 S.W.2d 922 (Ky. 1970).]
8. Evalyn and Charles Tice were married in Las Vegas, Nevada, on December 31, 1979. Previously Evalyn had received an alimony award from her first husband in the amount of $72,000. The divorce decree provided that the alimony would terminate upon her death or remarriage. At the time of her marriage to Charles, there was $44,500 remaining to be paid. On July 18, 1980, Evalyn filed a divorce petition against Charles, alleging that Charles had orally agreed to indemnify her for the alimony that she would lose as a result of their marriage and that this promise was made as an inducement for the marriage. The question presented is whether a person who induces another to marry by the oral promise to reimburse any lost alimony is liable to pay alimony awarded under a previous divorce decree. [*Tice v. Tice,* 672 P.2d 1168 (Okl. 1983).]
9. St. Germain had contacted the Boshouwers to see if they were interested in his becoming a part owner in their business. After a period of negotiations, the parties

met to draw up a final agreement. At the meeting's end, the Boshouwers stated they had a final agreement wherein St. Germain was to receive a certain salary for six months and was to buy 49 percent of the corporation's outstanding stock. The parties were to sign the agreement when St. Germain started work. St. Germain took out a second mortgage on his house to raise the money for the stock purchase and terminated his employment. The Boshouwers then told St. Germain they were no longer interested in the agreement but they would hire St. Germain at a smaller salary. In this state, sale of securities is covered by a statute of frauds. Can St. Germain enforce the contract? [*St. Germain v. Boshouwers,* 646 P.2d 952 (Colo. 1982).]

10. It has been said that the statute of frauds has perpetrated as much fraud (inequity) as it has prevented. *Kiely v. St. Germain,* excerpted at the beginning of this section, is a case that illustrates how the court attempted to prevent fraud (inequity). Evaluate the pros and cons of the court's action.

CHAPTER

13

CONTRACTUAL DUTIES OF PERFORMANCE, NONPERFORMANCE, AND DISCHARGE

After you have read this chapter, you should be able to:

1. Discuss the law of contractual duties, recognizing that it is directed at ending a contract.
2. Recognize that the law of contractual duties is evolving and is constantly balancing the rights of society and the rights of the immediate parties to the contract.
3. Understand the complexity of determining when one should be allowed to be discharged of a contractual obligation when in breach of contract.
4. Note the role of conditions in contract law.
5. List the methods of discharge.
6. Appreciate the thrust of the Uniform Commercial Code in this area of law.

BUSINESS DECISIONS and the LAW

Bankruptcy laws have been a tempting escape for people who regret the signature they have put on a contract. Bankruptcy is supposed to wipe the slate clean, not only of credit card balances and business debts but also of contractual obligations.

That effect of the bankruptcy laws has been recently called into question in a ruling by a Los Angeles bankruptcy judge. In 1986 a Los Angeles rock band called Concrete Blonde signed a contract with I.R.S. Records to produce seven albums. Although its first record was a modest success, Concrete Blonde's second has yet to be released. The reason? It seems the young band had run up some production expenses, which advances from I.R.S. Records could not cover. By the end of last summer the band claimed to owe some $77,000 to I.R.S. Records for advances and was more than $21,000 in the red to its lawyer, manager, and accountant.

The band's success, meanwhile, has attracted interest from competing labels willing to offer far more lucrative terms than those it had with I.R.S. Records. In September of 1987 the members of the band filed for personal bankruptcy in Los Angeles under Chapter 7 of the Bankruptcy Code. Under the rules of Chapter 7, the estate's trustee can either assume or reject all debtors' contracts. If he or she does not act, a contract is automatically rejected sixty days after the bankruptcy filing. Since a trustee cannot play lead guitar or sing harmony, assumption is out.

Thus the contract, in theory, should be canceled. At least that is what the band's bankruptcy lawyers thought.

The bankruptcy judge ruled that since earnings from postpetition services are outside the pie that is cut up for creditors, the contract generating those earnings could not be considered the property of the estate; thus the trustee was not empowered to reject the record contract. Since the contract is separate from the bankrupt estate, any royalties from the band's records also remain outside the estate's grasp. In so ruling, the judge put the royalties outside the grasp of the creditors also.

The decision is being appealed. It will be interesting to follow the case to see if bankruptcy can be used merely to break a contract.

Source: Deidre Fanning, "How Clean the Slate?" *Forbes,* March 21, 1988, p. 71; excerpted by permission of *Forbes* magazine © Forbes Inc., 1988.

Introduction

In the preceding chapters of this part we discussed the creation and enforceability of contracts and found that a contract created duties of performance. We will now consider what these duties are, when performance of such duties occurs, and how these duties are ended or discharged.

The duties assumed when a contract is created do not last forever. The law, as it has provided for the creation of a contract, also provides for its ending. As it was important for an individual to know how to create a right, it is equally important to know how to discharge (end) an obligation assumed under a contract.

Society has a concern that contractual duties be performed. To bring assurance to the community that contractual obligations will be carried out, the law cannot lightly discharge an individual from duties assumed by contract.

There is, however, a line of reasonableness between an individual's need to be discharged from a specific contractual obligation and society's interest in seeing that all contractual obligations be enforced. This line constantly shifts as law reflects the collective judgment of the community.

The important point in this chapter is the concern of the law for providing means and ways whereby contractual obligations are terminated.

The Concept of Performance

The expectations of parties when they contract is that they will receive what was promised in a contract. A substitute performance provided by a remedy or something less than complete **performance** was not thought of by the parties when the contract was made. We are, however, human beings and as such not always reliable. The law has taken this into account when it determines what will be required when complete performance of a contractual obligation is not forthcoming.

performance
The fulfillment of a contractual obligation

discharge
Termination of a contractual duty to perform a promise

executed contract
A contract that has been performed by all the parties to it

► Performance

Performance means complete performance. If one party to a contract has completely performed his other obligation under the contract, that party is **discharged.** The original expectation has been met and the law requires no further obligation. As far as the party is concerned, his or her part of the contract is **executed** (performed). If all parties to the contract have completely performed, the contract is executed and all the parties are discharged.

If the parties have not performed, the contract is **executory;** if only one party has not performed, as to that party's obligation the contract is executory. Only when the contract is executory and there is wrongful nonperformance of a promise is there a **breach of contract** by the nonperforming party. In the following case the contract of the debtor on a promissory note was executory and he would be liable only as he failed to pay each installment.

executory contract
A contract that has not been performed by all the parties to it

breach of contract
Wrongful nonperformance of a contractual promise

FACTS

Debtor signed four promissory notes. There were no installments due on three of the four notes and the fourth note was at most in default as to only one or two installments. None of the notes contained a clause specifically stating that each note was dependent upon the others and that the default in the payment of an installment under one note permitted acceleration for all other notes. Creditor sought judgment for all notes.

DECISION

The court found for the debtor, noting that the majority rule is that a unilateral contract for the payment of money is not subject to the rule of anticipatory breach particularly when the suit is upon a promissory note. The rationale for such a rule is to avoid what would, in effect, be a rewriting of the terms of the note to permit recovery prior to the date on which it is due. At most, the debtor is responsible only for the installments not paid on one note. As to the other notes, the debtor has not breached his contractual obligations.

Parliament Industries, Inc. v. William H. Vaughan and Co., 430 A. 2d 981 (Pa. 1981).

▶ Tender of Performance

A contracting party's **tender** of performance has the effect of performance. A tender is an unconditional offer by one contracting party to perform, with present ability to do so. (Al, pursuant to the contract, tenders the goods to Bert, who is to pay Al.) A party's improper refusal to accept a valid tender of performance causes the tendering party to be discharged of his or her contract to perform (Bert's refusal to receive the goods in the above example); except that when the refused tender is of payment of money, then the debt continues but interest on the debt stops running.

tender
In contracts, an unconditional offer by one contracting party to perform, with present ability to do so; as a verb, to proffer, make available

It should be mentioned that, if the debtor has several debts with the same creditor and tenders a payment that the creditor accepts, the creditor must apply the payment to the particular debt specified by the debtor or, if the debtor does not so specify, then the creditor can apply it to any of the debts due or past due.[1]

▶ Substantial Performance

Performance means complete performance. Sometimes the expectations of the parties are not met in that they receive only substantial or partial performance. The test of whether there is substantial performance or partial performance is often called the "main purpose" rule—has the main purpose of the contract been performed or not defeated? If the answer is yes, then there is substantial performance; if it is no, then there is partial performance. The answer is determined by the facts in each case.

[1]To see how this applies with respect to the statute of limitations, see p. 183.

FIGURE 13.1 **Performance**

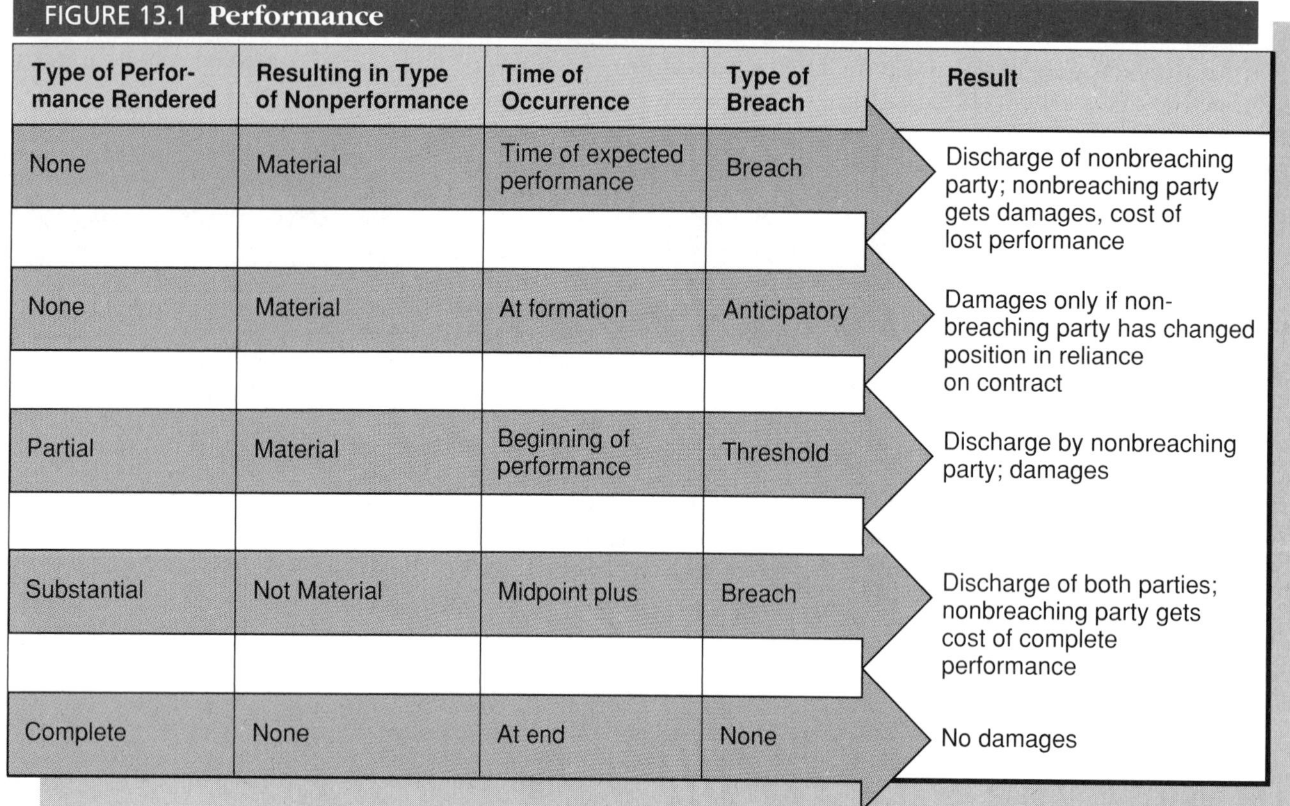

Type of Performance Rendered	Resulting in Type of Nonperformance	Time of Occurrence	Type of Breach	Result
None	Material	Time of expected performance	Breach	Discharge of nonbreaching party; nonbreaching party gets damages, cost of lost performance
None	Material	At formation	Anticipatory	Damages only if non-breaching party has changed position in reliance on contract
Partial	Material	Beginning of performance	Threshold	Discharge by nonbreaching party; damages
Substantial	Not Material	Midpoint plus	Breach	Discharge of both parties; nonbreaching party gets cost of complete performance
Complete	None	At end	None	No damages

substantial performance
Incomplete performance that is sufficient to accomplish, and does not defeat, the main purpose of a contract

forfeiture
To lose a legal right as a penalty

Substantial performance is a performance slightly less than complete performance. The main purpose of the contract has been performed or not defeated. The nonperformance is not material and there is a nonmaterial breach of contract. When substantial performance has been rendered but it cannot be returned to the performing party and the breach of contract is not intentional, the law will allow both parties to be discharged by giving to the party in breach what he or she was originally entitled to less what it will cost the nonbreaching party to get complete performance elsewhere. For example, Bert substantially performs his contract to construct a building for Clara. Bert painted the front door brown instead of yellow. There is substantial performance and a nonmaterial breach by Bert. Clara must pay to Bert the contract price less what it will cost to repaint the door yellow. This prevents a **forfeiture** and is considered a just result in law. Bert will not lose his right to recover most of the agreed upon contract price for Clara's slight inconvenience. The expectations of the parties have been approximately met.

► Partial Performance

partial performance
Incomplete performance that is insufficient to accomplish, or that defeats, the main purpose of a contract

Partial performance is only slight performance. The nonperformance is material and there is a material breach of contract. The expectations of the nonbreaching party have not even approximately been met. The main purpose of the contract has not been performed or has been defeated.

A material breach normally happens at the threshold or beginning stages for time of performance under the contract. Since the expectation of future performance is dim and will not be forthcoming, the nonbreaching party can be discharged from the obligation and seek **damages.** (See pp. 270–72.) In the following case of partial performance the plaintiff was not allowed to recover for building just the shell of an office addition.

damages
The money judicially awarded to an injured party for another's wrongful conduct

FACTS

In a complaint against Glasheen for breach of payment of a construction contract of a warehouse, Waters included a claim for work partially performed on an office addition pursuant to a separate oral agreement. Waters abandoned work before installing a floor and roof.

DECISION

Judgment for Glasheen. The court held that party who has partially performed a contract and who has materially defaulted in completing it is not entitled to recover for part performance unless a legal excuse can be established for not completing the work.

Waters v. Glasheen, 478 N.Y.S. 2d 437 (N.Y. 1984).

▶ Nonperformance

If no performance is given as of the date of expected performance under the contract, the nonbreaching party is discharged. The nonbreaching party also can **cover** his or her lost performance, and also can seek damages. (See Figure 13.1.)

cover
To seek a substitute performance of a contract

Threat of Nonperformance A threatened nonperformance of a bilateral contract is an anticipatory repudiation resulting in an **anticipatory breach.** However, the party not in breach is not discharged unless the nonbreaching party materially changes his or her position in reliance on the anticipatory repudiation. The nonbreaching party may immediately bring a suit for damages for such breach. (On September 1, Art hires Bud as a secretary to begin work on September 10. On September 5, Art tells Bud he will not need Bud. Bud immediately gets a job with Clara. Art cannot withdraw his anticipatory repudiation, which he could have done before Bud obtained employment elsewhere. Art is liable to Bud for his anticipatory breach.) There cannot be an anticipatory breach of a proposed unilateral contract because, until performance of the act or forbearance occurs, there is no acceptance and no contract. For example, a promissory note is a unilateral contract by the maker to pay the money at the maturity date, and, therefore, the maker cannot anticipatorily repudiate and breach his or her contract prior to the maturity date.

anticipatory breach
A party's material breach of contract made by the party's repudiation before performance is due

▶ Failure Midway

If a failure to perform happens midway through the contract but before substantial performance occurs, the party not in breach is not automatically discharged. For example, *A* contracts with *B* for twenty tons of coal to be delivered by *B* to *A* over twenty months at one ton per month. *A* is not automatically discharged if *B* misses the eleventh delivery. *A* must wait until, perhaps, the time for delivery of the twelfth installment and its nondelivery before the breach will be material. After the passage of a reasonable time such that a reasonable person would assume that the remainder of performance was not forthcoming, the nonbreaching party's discharge will then take place.

Personal Satisfaction

If one has agreed to perform an obligation to the personal satisfaction, judgment, or taste of the other contracting party, he or she will not have performed the obligation nor be discharged from the contract until the other party has acknowledged that the personal standard has been met.

If, however, the obligation involves a matter of mechanical fitness or suitability for a particular purpose, a reasonable person test will be applied to determine whether satisfactory performance had been rendered resulting in discharge of the performing party. The following case is one of personal satisfaction as determined by interpreting the word "opinion."

FACTS

In May 1976, Martin Marietta Aluminum and Action Engineering entered into a written agreement for the construction of a lime storage facility. Paragraph 7 of the contract provided that if in MMA's opinion Action fails to carry on the work diligently and on schedule . . . MMA shall have the right . . . to terminate the contract forthwith. Under the original progress schedule, work was to be completed by November 1, 1976. Delays required a revised completion date of December 25, 1976. On December 1, 1976, without advance notice, MMA terminated the contract based on its opinion that the job could not be completed by the revised deadline. Action sued MMA for wrongful termination. The lower court judged MMA's termination under an objective standard of reasonableness. The court found that Action could have had the job 89 percent complete by December 25, 1976 and since this performance would have been substantial, MMA's termination was unreasonable. MMA appeals.

DECISION

Reversed, judgment for MMA. The court noted that Section 228 of the Restatement (Second) of Contracts provides

> When it is a condition of an obligor's duty that he be satisfied with respect to the obligee's performance or with respect to something else, and it is practicable to determine whether a reasonable person in the position of the obligor would be satisfied, an interpretation is preferred under which the condition occurs if such a reasonable person in the position of the obligor would be satisfied.

The court noted that Section 228 states only a preference for interpreting an ambiguous contractual provision and that Comment (a) to the section indicates that if it is clear that the contract intends to leave a decision to one party subject only to the requirement of good faith, then the court should not imply an additional requirement of reasonableness. Here, the court said, the contract did not use the usual terminology of "satisfaction" clauses, but used the term opinion. The term "opinion" implies a personal subjective determination made in good faith. The case, therefore, is remanded back to the trial court to determine if MMA terminated the contract in good faith.

Action Engineering v. Martin Marietta Aluminum, 670 F.2d 456 (3rd Cir. 1983).

Time of the Essence

The time for performance of a contract is normally a reasonable time under the circumstances if no time is stated in the contract. If time is of the essence because it is expressly made so by the contract or because a nontimely performance will be valueless, any performance other than on time results in a material breach and a *discharge* of the nonbreaching party. In the following case the court held that time is of the essence in exercising a simple option.

FACTS

On December 19, 1964, the Fraziers, lessees, entered into a primary lease for eight years with the lessor. The lease contained the following provision:

> Five years after the start of lease, Lessee has the option to request Lessor to expand the building. . . . If the option to expand is exercised, it is understood that this lease inclusive of all options, shall be beginning anew.

On February 20, 1980, the Fraziers wrote the lessor as follows: "As per the lease . . . I choose to expand the building. . . ." On March 5, 1980, the lessor wrote the Fraziers:

> This is to advise you that your letter of February 20, 1980 is not acceptable. . . . Unless a new lease containing terms acceptable to us has been negotiated . . . we will expect you to surrender quiet and peaceable possession to us on August 31, 1980.

The Fraziers seek a declaration that they are entitled to an extension of their lease.

DECISION

Judgment for the lessor. The chancellor noted that the request for extension was made February 20, 1980, some fifteen years and five months after the start of the lease, whereas the option stated "Five years after the start of lease. . . ." The chancellor concluded it was manifestly unreasonable for the Fraziers to exercise the option some ten plus years beyond its terms. In a simple option, given without additional consideration, the optionee (the one who has the option) is free to exercise or ignore it whereas until the option expires the optionor (the one who gave the option) is bound. For this reason time is of the essence in exercising a simple option.

Frazier v. Northeast Mississippi Shopping Center, Inc., 458 So.2d 1051 (Miss. 1984).

Impossibility of Performance

▶ Concept

Impossibility of performance discharges one's obligation assumed by contract. Impossibility means "it cannot factually be done" as opposed to "it is more difficult or less profitable for me to do it." This is often called "prospective failure of consideration."

impossibility
Performance cannot factually be done

▶ When Impossible

There are four situations where the law deems that factually something cannot be done:

1. The personal services of the obligor are so necessary to the performance of the contract that the death or incapacitation of the obligor can make a personal service obligation impossible of performance. (Mary, a famous painter, agrees to paint Joe's portrait. Mary dies. Mary's estate is not liable to Joe for Mary's failure to paint Joe's portrait);
2. **Commercial frustration** is experienced and the contract is deemed "commercially impracticable" (see *Transatlantic Financing Corp. v. United States* on p. 250);
3. The subject matter essential to the performance of the contract is destroyed. (Al and Bud enter into a contract for the sale by Al to Bud of a famous oil painting by an old master. The painting is destroyed by fire before delivery to Bud. Al is excused from performing the obligation under the contract because it is impossible for Al to perform); and
4. The performance of the obligation is deemed, after the formation of the contract but before the date of performance, to violate public policy.

commercial frustration
An excuse offered by a party to a contract justifying nonperformance of an obligation, usually because performance has been made impossible in fact

The following case illustrates impossibility of performance because the performance became illegal before it was to be done, which resulted in a discharge of the contract.

FACTS

McDonnell Douglas Corporation had a contract with Iran to deliver military aircraft parts. After the Islamic revolution, the U.S. Department of the Treasury promulgated the following regulation:

> No property subject to the jurisdiction of the United States or which is in its possession or control of persons subject to the jurisdiction of the United States in which . . . Iran has any interest of any nature whatsoever, may be transferred, paid, exported, withdrawn or otherwise dealt in except as authorized.

McDonnell Douglas asked the court for a declaratory judgment that it is not liable to Iran for breach of contract, since the contract had become impossible to perform due to the new regulation.

DECISION

The court held that, due to the new regulation, McDonnell Douglas could no longer legally export the military aircraft parts to Iran. Therefore McDonnell Douglas was excused from performance of the contract because of supervening "legal impossibility."

McDonnell Douglas Corp. v. Islamic Republic of Iran, 591 F.Supp. 293 (E.D. Mo. 1984).

The Concept of Conditions

condition
An uncertain event on the occurrence of which a contractual obligation is made contingent or dependent

dependent promise
A promise the performance of which is dependent upon the occurrence of a condition

independent promise
A promise the performance of which is not dependent upon the occurrence of a condition

The duty to perform a promise arises when the contract is created. The time for performance is normally at a later time. If a **condition** must happen before one is required to perform, the promise forming the basis of the contract is deemed dependent for its performance upon the occurrence of the condition. For example, Art's promise to pay Bill for digging a ditch is an offer for a unilateral contract and is performable when the condition (the act) occurs—namely, when Bill has dug the ditch. Art's promise is a **dependent promise,** dependent for its performance on condition of Bill's digging the ditch. A promise that forms the basis of a contract and renders the promisor unconditionally responsible to carry out the obligation contained in the promise is an **independent promise.** In the above example, if Art's promise asked for and received Bill's promise to dig the ditch, Bill's promise is not dependent upon any condition. Bill's promise is an independent promise. A dependent promise can be discharged by the happening or nonhappening of a condition. An independent promise is discharged by its performance.

In the unilateral contract situation, if Bill never dug the ditch, Art's dependent promise has never been accepted and is no longer binding on Art; in the bilateral contract situation, when Bill dug the ditch, Bill's independent promise to perform is discharged, and Art's dependent promise is to pay Bill. In the following case the husband was discharged from performing his dependent promise because the condition did not occur.

FACTS

The Olands owned property that the Hills were interested in buying as a homesite. The parties met twice and signed a document by which Mr. Oland agreed to sell the property to the Hills for $15,000 with a $4,000 downpayment. The Hills were told before they entered into the contract that Mrs. Oland's approval was necessary. Mrs. Oland did not give approval and said to the Hills, "If it was the Lord's will that the Hills moved up there, it would be so."

DECISION

Judgment for the Olands. The court said the event on which Mr. Oland's performance was conditioned, the giving of his wife's consent, did not occur. Failure of this condition to happen meant no contract came into existence that could be specifically enforced.

Hill v. Oland, 655 P.2d 1088 (Or. 1982).

► Kinds of Conditions

Conditions are either express, implied in fact, or implied in law, and they can be classified as precedent, concurrent, or subsequent. Conditions are normally introduced by words like "if," "when," "after," "as soon as," "provided that," "on condition that."

An *express* condition becomes part of a contract by words, written or oral. It is expressly stated. ("I'll repair your watch *if* you deliver it to me." Delivery is an express condition.) *Implied in fact* conditions are part of the contract though not expressed. They are inferred by the promissee because they are necessary for performance of the promisor's promise. (If Alice wants her watch fixed by Buck as Buck promised to do, Alice has to deliver her watch to Buck. Delivery is the condition implied in fact. If Alice cannot deliver her watch to Buck, Buck has no duty to perform his promise to repair.) *Implied in law* conditions exist to ensure fairness between parties. (Alice and Buck enter into a contract for the sale of goods to Buck; nothing is said about the time for payment of price. Payment upon delivery is implied in law. Delivery is the condition implied in law.) Implied in law conditions need only be substantially performed.

A **condition precedent** requires something to occur or not to occur before the performance of a promissory duty is required (e.g., "dig the ditch and then I'll pay you"). **Concurrent conditions** are mutual conditions that are required to happen theoretically simultaneously (e.g., unpaid seller is to deliver the goods at the same time that payment is made). On the other hand, a duty to perform will be excused upon the occurrence or nonoccurrence of a **condition subsequent.** For example, a contract for transportation of goods provides that, after delivery, any claim for damage to the goods must be made within thirty days. The carrier's promissory duty to pay for any such damage will be excused if the condition subsequent, namely thirty days, expires before any claim is made. (See Figure 13.2 for kinds of conditions.)

condition precedent
A condition that must occur or not occur before a dependent promise becomes performable

concurrent condition
A condition that must occur at the same time as another condition

condition subsequent
A condition, on the occurrence or nonoccurrence of which, after a promise becomes performable, excuses the duty of performance

The Concept of Discharge

As we have seen, discharge takes place by performance or by the occurrence or nonoccurrence of a condition. Discharge can also take place by acts of the parties or by operation of law.

► Discharge by Acts of the Parties

Novation Novation, which will be discussed fully in Chapter 14, is an act by the parties to a contract who mutually discharge their obligations under their contract so that a new contract with a new party can replace it. It is (1) a new contract with (2) a new party (3) immediately discharging the old contract. It is also an accord and satisfaction. The following case illustrates how a court can find a novation based upon the actions of the creditor.

novation
A new contract in which one of the parties was not a party to the old contract and which immediately discharges the old contract

FIGURE 13.2 **Kinds of Conditions**

	When	How
Condition Precedent	Before performance can occur	Buck says, "Deliver the watch; then I'll fix it." (Delivery is the *condition precedent.*)
Concurrent Conditions	Simultaneously	When Buck delivers the fixed watch, Alice pays him. (Delivery and payment are *concurrent.*)
Condition subsequent	Occurs after the performance of the contract	Buck's receipt says, any claim for mistakes or faulty repairs must be made within 30 days.
	Form	**How**
Express Condition	Written or oral	Buck says, "I'll repair your watch if you deliver it to me." (Delivery is the *express condition*.)
Implied in Fact Condition	Not expressed	Alice wants Buck to repair the watch; Alice must deliver the watch in order for Buck to be obligated to repair it. (Delivery is the *implied in fact* condition.)
Implied in Law Condition	Not expressed; ensures fairness	Alice wants Buck to repair her watch; neither says anything about the time of payment. Payment upon Buck's delivery of the watch to Alice is a condition *implied in law.*

FACTS

Bracero purchased property from the Federal Deposit Insurance Corporation (FDIC) and acquired a loan from Girod to develop the property. Bracero gave Girod Bracero's promissory note secured by a mortgage on the real property purchase for repayment of the loan. Bracero sold the property to Development, Inc. for the price of the outstanding debt secured by the mortgage in favor of Girod. Pursuant to the terms of the sale, instead of paying Bracero directly, Development, Inc. retained the purchase price and agreed to use the money to cancel Bracero's debt with Girod and agreed to develop the property. Subsequently Girod advanced significant sums to Development, Inc. to complete the project. Development, Inc. defaulted on paying off Bracero's debt. Bracero's contention is that when it sold the project to Development, Inc., its liability on the mortgage note was discharged by Development, Inc.'s assumption of Bracero's debt under the consenting eye of Girod. In effect, Bracero contends that when it was unwilling to finish the project it provided Girod with a more palatable and viable alternative to foreclosure. In exchange for the freedom to walk away from the project and its construction loan liabilities, Bracero offered a new debtor, a fresh face, willing to finish the project and take over the then-existing debt owed by Bracero to Girod. Bracero contends that Girod consented to this arrangement. Girod contends they never entered into a novation to discharge Bracero's debt.

DECISION

Judgment was rendered in favor of Bracero. The court held that novation by substitution of debtor requires certain and positive proof that the creditor had the deliberate purpose of accepting the new debtor and thereby extinguishing any cause of action against the original debtor upon the debt. The court held that Girod did in fact tacitly but clearly consent to the novation by opening its arms wide to finance Development, Inc. while waving a fair goodbye to Bracero. In so holding, the court noted that novation today is much broader than its Roman law genesis, which was conceived simply as a way of extinguishing obligations between individuals, and more in line with its German legal foundations, which allowed substitution of debtors so as not to impractically affect the flow of commerce as was the effect of Roman law.

Federal Deposit Ins. Corp. v. Prann, 694 F.Supp. 1027 (D.P.R. 1988).

Accord, and Accord and Satisfaction When a subsequent new contract is made between the same parties, it is called an **accord.** The old contract still exists and will be discharged only by performance of the new contract. For example, Mel defaults on his promissory note held by the bank and he gives the bank his renewal note, the bank keeping both notes. Mel is still obligated on the original note, as well as on the new note which is an accord with the bank. However, if at the time of its formation the new contract satisfies the old contract and thereby causes its discharge, the new contract is called an **accord and satisfaction.** In the above example, if the bank returned the old note to Mel the old note is discharged and the renewal note is an accord and satisfaction.

accord
A new contract providing that, on its performance, a previous contract as well as the new contract are discharged

accord and satisfaction
A new contract (accord) that discharges a party from a previous contractual obligation; the old contract is discharged (satisfied)

Account Stated One person may have a right against another person for payment under their contract. Such a right is called an **account.** When they have settled their account and the matured items have been expressly or impliedly agreed to, the account is called an **account stated** discharging each of the matured items in the account. (At various times during one month, Alan ordered and received goods from Bess, seller. When Bess has totaled the monthly amount owing by Alan, the total is the account. When Alan assents to the total either expressly or by Alan's silence, the balance becomes an account stated causing Alan's contract debts to Bess for *each* of the contracted items to be discharged, the account stated replacing them.)

account
A right to payment under a contract

account stated
An account that has been settled and the matured items and balance expressly or impliedly agreed to by the parties

Mutual Rescission, Waiver, and Release Some other acts of the parties may cause a discharge. If the parties mutually agree to discharge each other from obligations assumed by a contract, mutual **rescission** occurs.

rescission
Cancellation

An oral agreement for mutual rescission is enforceable and will discharge an enforceable, executory written contract even if the written contract is within the statute of frauds and even if the written contract provides that it can be mutually rescinded or modified only in writing. (Jones and Smith enter into a written employment contract for two years, which is within the statute of frauds and is enforceable being in writing. Four months later they orally agree to rescind the contract. The oral agreement of rescission is enforceable discharging the written contract.)

However, if an oral agreement for mutual rescission of a written contract involves a retransfer of the subject matter that brings the oral rescission agreement within the statute of frauds, the oral rescission agreement would be unenforceable and the written contract will not be discharged. (Solomon and Brown contract in writing for the sale of a desk to Brown for $600, the contract being within the statute of frauds under the Uniform Commercial Code but enforceable because the contract is in writing. Delivery of the desk and payment are made. Ten days later they orally agree that, if Brown is not satisfied with the desk, the contract for sale is rescinded. No redelivery or repayment is made. If Brown becomes dissatisfied, since the oral agreement for rescission involves the retransfer of the $600 desk it is within the statute of frauds and, being oral, it is unenforceable.)

If one party knowingly accepts a defective performance, this is a waiver of the nonperformance and is a discharge of the other party's duty to perform. One party can also extinguish a claim to performance by releasing the other party.

Intentional Material Alteration of a Written Contract A written contract that is intentionally and materially altered by a party to a contract without the consent of other contracting party discharges the other party.

Destruction of a Sealed Contract The intentional physical destruction of a contract under seal by the person entitled to its performance discharges the person obligated to perform under the contract.

Substituted Contract A substituted contract is a contract that is itself accepted by the obligee in satisfaction of the obligor's existing duty. The substituted contract discharges the original duty, and breach of the substituted contract does not give rise to a right to enforce the original duty.

Discharge by Operation of Law

statute of limitations
A statute limiting the time in which a claim may be asserted in court; expiration bars enforcement of the claim

Statute of Limitations By statute in each state, the law gives a specific limited time period for the bringing of a suit for breach of contract. The time varies from three to ten years, depending upon whether the contract was oral or written. These time periods are contained in what is called a **statute of limitations.** The time period starts from the moment of breach of the contract, but it is suspended for periods when the breaching party is not within the jurisdiction of the court. If the statute of limitations runs, this acts as a barrier to suit for the nonperformance of a contract that is now unenforceable and thus, in effect, discharges the party who is in breach of contract.

judgment
The final decision of a case by a court

Bankruptcy Discharge A discharge in bankruptcy acts as a barrier to the enforcement of a contract. It terminates the bankrupt debtor's duty to perform and, therefore, is a discharge of such duty. (For a discussion of bankruptcy, see Chapter 52.)

arbitration
A method for deciding disputes outside of court by persons called arbitrators, appointed by the disputing parties

Judgment Contracts are also discharged by mergers into **judgments** of claims for performance of a contractual duty. (*A* sues *B* for nonperformance and obtains a judgment. The contract is discharged and is merged into the judgment.)

Arbitration Award Contracts are also discharged by an **arbitration** award by an arbitrator on the existence and violation of a contractual duty which merges the duty into the award and discharges the duty. (For a discussion of arbitration, see pp. 20–21.)

Figure 13.3 illustrates a summary chart on discharge of contracts.

The Uniform Commercial Code

Performance under the Code

The Code does not require performance to one's personal satisfaction but, rather, requires a good faith performance[2] in all applicable cases, thus requiring that the reasonable expectations of a contracting party be met. Nonperformance is excused if

[2]UCC 1–203.

FIGURE 13.3 **Discharge of Contracts**

By Act of the Parties	Reason
Complete Performance	Nothing remains to be done
Substantial Performance	Avoidance of forfeiture
Material Breach of Contract	Nonperformance of contract's main purpose at nonbreaching party's election
Novation	Substitution of a new party
Accord and Satisfaction	New contract discharging old contract
Account Stated	Matured items in the account are discharged
Mutual Rescission	Mutual agreement of cancellation
Waiver	Acceptance of defective performance
Release	Giving up right
Intentional Material Alteration of a Written Contract	Fraud
Destruction of a Sealed Contract	Fraud
Substitute Contract	Mutual agreement

By Operation of Law	Reason
Death	Impossibility
Commercial Frustration	Impossibility
Destruction of Subject Matter	Impossibility
Subsequent Illegality of the Contract	Violation of public policy
Failure of Condition	No duty to perform
Statute of Limitations	Unenforceable contract
Bankruptcy	Public policy
Judgment	Merger of contractual duty
Arbitration Award	Merger of contractual duty

performance as agreed has been made impractical by either the occurrence of a contingency the nonoccurrence of which was a basic assumption on which the contract was made, or by compliance in good faith with any applicable foreign or domestic governmental regulation or order.[3] If a contingency affects only part of the capacity of the seller to perform, an allocation of production and deliveries among customers must be made and notification of delay or any limited allocation of goods must be given to customers. This is illustrated by the following case.

[3]UCC 2–615(a).

FACTS

Terry, a gasoline dealer, sued Atlantic Richfield Co. for breach of contract. Atlantic Richfield, in a time of gasoline shortage, was required to allocate gasoline supplies among its dealers, including Terry. Atlantic Richfield found it impossible to fully meet its contractual commitments to its dealers due to the energy crisis. Atlantic Richfield allocated its supplies among its customers on a quota-percentage basis based upon the previous year's gallon usage.

DECISION

Judgment for Atlantic Richfield. The court noted that under the Uniform Commercial Code as it is enacted in California, partial performance will discharge one from his obligation to multiple customers when suppliers inadvertently become short, making full performance impossible. What is required is that the party allocating scarce supplies act in good faith and proceed in a fair and reasonable manner. The court concluded that the quota system met the criteria for discharging the contractual obligation of Atlantic Richfield.

Terry v. Atlantic Richfield Co., 140 Cal.Rptr. 510 (1977).

► Discharge Under the Code

In the case of a material breach, meaning a failure to provide perfect tender by any deviation from the promised performance,[4] the Code provides that the nonbreaching party may cancel a contract reserving, however, remedies for nonperformance.[5] The following case discusses the requirement of perfect tender.

FACTS

Following a mobile home show, Ramirez agreed to buy from Autosport a new camper. Autosport required two weeks to prepare the new van. The contract provided for delivery on or about August 3, 1978. On that date, Ramirez arrived to pick up the van but found it was not quite ready. On August 14, Ramirez arrived to accept delivery of the van but found Autosport touching up scratch marks with paint and that cushions in the van were wet because the windows had been left open. Ramirez agreed to accept the van if he could withhold $2,000 of the purchase price. Autosport said "no" but agreed to replace the cushions. On October 5, the van still was not ready and Ramirez rejected it. On November 20, Ramirez sought rescission of the contract and Autosport counterclaimed for breach of contract.

DECISION

Judgment for Ramirez. The court said that underlying the Uniform Commercial Code is the recognition of the revolutionary change in business practices in this century. The purchase of goods is no longer a simple transaction in which a buyer purchases individually made goods from a seller in a face-to-face transaction. Our economy depends on a complex system for the manufacture, distribution, and sale of goods, a system in which manufacturers and consumers rarely meet. Faceless manufacturers mass produce goods for unknown consumers who purchase these goods from merchants exercising little or no control over the quality of production. In an age of assembly lines, we are accustomed to cars with scratches, television sets without knobs and other products with all kinds of defects. Buyers no longer expect a "perfect tender." If a

---

[4]UCC 2–703(f), 711(i).

[5]UCC 2–106(3).

merchant sells defective goods, the reasonable expectation of the parties is that the buyer will return the goods and the seller will repair or replace them. Recognizing the commercial reality, the Code permits a seller to cure imperfect tenders. Should the seller fail to cure the defects, whether substantial or not, the balance shifts again in favor of the buyer, who has the right to cancel or seek damages. Such is the case here and Ramirez may cancel the contract.

Ramirez v. Autosport, 440 A.2d 1345 (N.J. 1981).

In the case of a party's repudiation by anticipatory breach, the Code nevertheless seeks to encourage performance by the repudiating party. Therefore the Code permits the repudiating party to retract the repudiation before the performance is due if, meanwhile, the party not in breach has not cancelled the contract or materially changed his or her position in reliance on the repudiation.[6] However, the party not in breach, upon such repudiation, can ask for additional assurances—for example, a bond.[7] If such assurances are not forthcoming, the nonbreaching party can discharge himself or herself by **cancellation.**

cancellation
The nullification of a contractual obligation

Termination of a contract occurs without a breach but, rather, by one party exercising a power (for example, exercising a power of avoidance caused by a contract fraudulently induced). Termination acts as a discharge of all parties to a contract, reserving, however, to the party not in breach any remedies for a prior breach or defective performance.[8]

The Code provides for a four-year statute of limitations for a sales contract which, in effect, can discharge the contract by its running.[9] Moreover, unlike the common law of contracts, a written waiver or renunciation of an obligation owed under a sales contract acts as a discharge even though it is not supported by consideration.[10] But if a written contract provides that it cannot be modified or rescinded except by a signed writing, an oral agreement to mutually rescind will not act as a discharge of the contract.[11]

Summary Statement

1. Normally parties to a contract expect complete performance, but the law recognizes other types of performance—namely, substantial and partial. Partial performance when coupled with a damage award will discharge contracts.
2. In special cases, such as anticipatory breach, personal satisfaction, and time of the essence, a party can be discharged from performing his or her side of the contractual commitment.
3. Four situations exist in law that are deemed factual situations of impossibility that will discharge one's duty assumed by contract.

[6]UCC 2–611.

[7]UCC 2–609.

[8]UCC 2–106(4).

[9]UCC 2–725.

[10]UCC 1–107.

[11]UCC 2–209(2).

4. There are conditions precedent, concurrent, subsequent, and also express, implied in fact, and implied in law. The failure of a condition may cause a contract obligation to cease to exist or never to come into existence.
5. Discharge of obligations assumed by contract can happen by acts of the parties through novation, an accord and satisfaction, mutual rescission, waiver, release, intentional material alteration of a written contract, and destruction of a sealed contract.
6. By operation of law, a contract can be discharged by (in effect) the running of the statute of limitations, discharge in bankruptcy, judgment, and arbitration award.
7. The primary interest of the Code is to encourage a good-faith performance of contractual obligations.

The following case illustrates how the interest of society in seeing that contracts are performed is balanced against impossibility of performance.

TRANSATLANTIC FINANCING CORP. v. UNITED STATES
363 F.2d 312 (D.C. Cir. 1966)

This case involves an appeal from a judgment entered in favor of the United States. Transatlantic sued the United States for additional cost of carriage pursuant to a contract for the shipment of wheat on the vessel *S.S. Christos* from Texas to Iran.

The carriage cost of $43,972 above and beyond the contract price of $305,842.92 resulted from an extension of a 10,000 mile voyage by about 3,000 miles around the Cape of [Good Hope] Africa after the closing of the Suez Canal by the Egyptian government through obstruction by sunken vessels. This action by the Egyptian government took place on November 2, 1956, shortly after the invasion of Egypt by Israel on October 29, 1956 and the invasion of the canal zone by Britain and France on October 31, 1956. The canal had been nationalized by Egypt on July 26, 1956.

It was on October 2, 1956 that the contract was made by Transatlantic and the United States in an atmosphere of international tension. On October 27, 1956 the *S.S. Christos* sailed from Galveston, Texas, for Bandar Shapur, Iran, on a course which would have taken her through Gibraltar and the Suez Canal.

On November 7, 1956 a representative of Transatlantic contacted the United States government, requesting instructions concerning the disposition of the cargo and an agreement for payment of additional compensation for a voyage around the Cape of Good Hope. The United States informed Transatlantic that they were expected to perform their obligation assumed by contract without additional compensation. The *Christos* changed course following this discussion and delivered the wheat in December at Bandar Shapur, Iran. Transatlantic seeks additional compensation denied to them by the United States District Court.

This court affirmed the judgment of the district court denying relief to Transatlantic.

The court recognized Transatlantic's argument that implicit in the contract was the contemplation that the *Christos* would use the "usual and customary" route to deliver the wheat (a constructive condition); such route would normally include passage through the Suez Canal; and when that route was closed, the contract was impossible to perform as originally contemplated; and because of the need for altered performance, additional compensation was owed.

The court rejected Transatlantic's argument, holding that "a thing is impossible in legal contemplation when it is not practicable, and a thing is impracticable when it can only be done at an excessive and unreasonable cost." The court noted that this approach ultimately represents the ever-shifting line drawn by courts hopefully responsive to commercial practices and mores, at which the community's interest in having contracts enforced according to their terms is outweighed only by the commercial senselessness of requiring performance.

In order to apply the ever-shifting line to excuse one from performance of obligations assumed by contract by applying the doctrine of impossibility the court noted the need to satisfy three reasonably definable steps. First, a contingency, something unexpected, must have occurred. Second, the risk of the unexpected occurrence must not have been allocated either by agreement or custom. Finally, occurrence of the contingency must have rendered performance commercially impracticable.

The court held the timing of the closing of the canal met the first requirement of an unexpected event. The contingency of foreclosure of the route was to a certain extent, in the eyes of the court, somewhat foreseen by Transatlantic (international tension) and, since the continued passage of the canal was not made an express condition of the contract, it could be argued to have been assumed by them. Thus, requirement two could be interpreted adversely against Transatlantic.

The court, however, decided the case based upon the third element, of commercial impracticability. The court pointed out that (any) increased cost and difficulty of performance never constitutes impracticability. Justification for relief in this case would require more of a variation between expected cost and the actual cost of performing by the available alternative route.

Questions and Case Problems

1. A contract of sale of a broadcasting corporation provided that a certain purchase price was to be paid by the buyer by executing a personal note or by executing a note by a corporation formed by the buyer. The corporation was formed and it issued the note. The corporation was unable to pay the note, and the seller sued the buyer for payment. What result? [*Clayton v. Communications Capital Corp.,* 440 P.2d 330 (Ariz. 1968).]

2. On October 5, 1976, the parties signed a written contract for the Vincenzis to construct a three-family house on land owned by the Cerros. The contract price was $91,000, to be paid in five installments as various stages of the work were finished. The house was to be completed within 150 days from the date of the execution of the contract, which would make the projected completion date March 4, 1977. Except for $2,000 withheld for incomplete items, the first four scheduled payments were made. The Cerros refused to make the final installment payment because the house was not substantially completed until November 9, 1977 and $2,060.40 was needed to repair stress cracks in foundation walls as well as $1,527 and $533.40 for five minor items. The Cerros contend that the doctrine of substantial performance is inapplicable because the Vincenzis were guilty of willful or intentional breach of contract by failing to complete all the work required. Are the Cerros correct? [*Vincenzi et al. v. Cerro et al.,* 442 A.2d 1352 (Conn. 1982).]

3. This is a Uniform Commercial Code case involving repossession of collateral (a car) by a bank that subsequently disposed of the collateral by private sale and seeks to recover a deficiency in an amount owed on a note by Bledsoe. Bledsoe had borrowed from the bank to purchase a car and signed a note. On November 15, 1979 the first payment on the note was due. Bledsoe was in the process of getting a divorce from his wife and closed his checking account with the bank so his wife could not withdraw funds. The account was closed on October 17, 1979. The bank repossessed the car on October 23, 1979. Bledsoe contends he does not owe the bank a deficiency because the bank wrongfully repossessed the car. Is Bledsoe correct? [*Bank of Cabot v. Bledsoe,* 653 S.W.2d 144 (Ark. 1983).]

4. Parker signed a contract for $25,000 worth of dancing lessons from the defendant. A clause in the contract read "NONCANCELLABLE NEGOTIABLE CONTRACT" and "I UNDERSTAND THAT NO REFUNDS WILL BE MADE." Parker had some lessons, and then he was involved in an automobile accident and suffered injuries that prevent him from dancing. Parker sued for a refund of his money less the cost of completed lessons. Can Arthur Murray, Inc. enforce the contract? [*Parker v. Arthur Murray, Inc.*, 295 N.E.2d 487 (Ill. 1973).]
5. The Lemays leased a specific piece of property from a landlord and then subleased it to a subtenant. The Lemays failed to give the landlord timely notice of intent to renew and the landlord began negotiations directly with the subtenant. The Lemays brought suit seeking a declaratory judgment that they should be able to renew their lease, and seeking to enjoin the landlord from terminating the lease and dealing with the subtenant. Should the Lemays prevail? [*Lemay et al. v. Rouse et al.*, 444 A.2d 553 (N.H. 1982).]

confession of judgment
A party's consent to jurisdiction and judgment of a court without a trial in a civil case

6. Air Power, Inc., had obtained a **judgment by confession** against Omega Equipment Corp. in the amount of $26,544.37. To collect its judgment, Air Power caused various items of Omega Equipment's property to be attached. Before any of the property was attached, Omega Equipment had delivered to Air Power's attorney a cashier's check, marked "paid in full in settlement of all claims." Air Power informed Omega Equipment that the cashier's check had been negotiated (transferred), but that Air Power considered it only partial payment. If the balance was not forthcoming, the attached property would be sold. Omega Equipment seeks an injunction to prevent the sale of the attached property. Should the injunction be given? [*Air Power, Inc. v. Omega Equipment Corp.*, 459 A.2d 1120 (Md. 1983).]
7. Willie Samuels was hired by Motor Convoy as a yard employee. Samuels requested a transfer to a driving position and Motor Convoy denied his request. Samuels subsequently filed an EEOC charge of discrimination against Motor Convoy. Samuels contended white employees with less seniority were receiving preferred work assignments over black employees like himself. Samuels executed an EEOC conciliation agreement with Motor Convoy. Under the terms of the agreement, Motor Convoy agreed to assign all jobs in a fair and equitable manner and Samuels waived his right to sue the company. Samuels read the agreement and consulted with an EEOC representative before signing it. Subsequently Samuels sued Motor Convoy. Is Samuels barred from suing Motor Convoy for discrimination in his employment contract, namely, for back wages for the time period he was not employed as a driver, because of his promise not to sue? [*Freeman v. Motor Convoy, Inc.*, 700 F.2d 1339 (1983).]
8. Husband and wife opened a joint checking account, which became overdrawn. Husband gave two notes totaling $181,000 to the bank to cover some loans and the overdraft. When activity in the account ceased, there remained an overdraft of $75,983.06. The wife had written checks on the account totaling $82,252.31. Deposits made to the account while it was active were applied to the overdrafts of husband by the bank. The wife contends she should not owe $16,811.43 since her overdrafts should have been reduced proportionately by the deposits. Must the bank apply part of the deposits to the wife's overdrafts? [*United States Trust Co. of New York v. McSweeney Ill*, 457 N.Y.S.2d 276 (N.Y. 1982).]
9. After being employed by an insurance company for over 10 years, employees were required to sign new employment contracts with more restrictive noncompetition clauses or to be discharged. The employees refused to sign, and their employment was terminated. A master found the employees had performed their obligations under their original contract of employment "fully, faithfully, and competently," and

that the insurance company had discharged them in violation of their employment contract. After discharge, the master found that the employees had violated the original contract noncompetition clause. The master concluded this barred the employees from recovery for breach of contract. Is the master correct? [*Ward v. American Mutual Liab. Ins. Co.*, 433 N.E.2d 1342 (Mass. 1983).]

10. In *Transatlantic Financing Corp. v. United States*, excerpted at the beginning of this section, the court held that the concept of impossibility ultimately represents an ever-shifting line drawn by courts responsive to commercial practices and mores, which shows that the community's interest in having contracts enforced according to their terms is outweighed only by commercial senselessness of requiring performance. Discuss the significance of this statement.

CHAPTER 14

CONTRACTUAL RIGHTS, THIRD PARTIES, AND REMEDIES FOR BREACH OF CONTRACT

After you have read this chapter, you should be able to:

1. Discuss the law associated with contractual rights, recognizing that the concern of the law in this area is to enhance and protect contract rights gained by exercising the freedom of contract.
2. Appreciate that exercising one's freedom of contract and assuming duties is not viewed lightly by the law.
3. Understand how third parties become associated with a contract.
4. Realize that a remedy is normally a substitute for the right acquired by contract.
5. Note that the Uniform Commercial Code does not differ substantially from the common law in this area of contractual rights.

BUSINESS DECISIONS and the LAW

W. Richard Barnhart, a retired executive of U.S. Steel, wrote a letter to PaineWebber, Inc., accusing them of exposing his ninety-eight-year-old mother to too much risk and cost by putting her into a bond fund. PaineWebber offered him a deal: The firm would pay $1,000 if he would keep mum about the settlement. Barnhart wanted more, and filed for arbitration with the National Association of Securities Dealers. PaineWebber has refused to discuss the incident and has since upped the ante to $1,250.

The retired steel executive had $42,000 to invest for his mother, who lives in a nursing home. Early last year, he says, he responded for his mother, then ninety-seven, to a PaineWebber mailing that promoted high-rate certificates of deposit. But instead of CDs, he says, PaineWebber broker Ronald Walchack recommended funneling $37,000 of the money into Massachusetts Financial Services' Lifetime Government Income Trust.

Barnhart says the broker called the bond fund as "safe as the government securities it owned." Barnhart accuses the broker of neglecting to mention that the value of fund shares could gyrate along with bond prices, and that there could be steep fees to redeem charges.

Walchack, reached at his Pittsburgh office by newspaper reporters, said he did not "have any of the details here" and declined to elaborate. In a letter to Barnhart, PaineWebber has denied that the broker mishandled the account.

The only reason PaineWebber made him an offer, Barnhart maintains, is because he "screamed and pushed" and wrote a clear, forceful complaint. Now he says he will accept nothing less than the $1,500 it would take to pay the fund's exit fees—even though he says PaineWebber has told him the firm's policy is never to settle for 100 percent of a client's claim.

According to Barnhart, all he wants to do is "get out of this and reinvest my mom's money."

This case is far from unique. Brokerage firms have routinely paid off small investors to settle disputes involving investments, although most investors are not aware of such settlements. Such payments usually cost the firms less than the risk of bad publicity, legal fees, and brokers' time. New rules from the Securities and Exchange Commission will open the arbitration process to public scrutiny. Although the new process has yet to be worked out in detail, it is expected that the proceedings will publicize names, hearing results, and damages.

Brokerage firm clients will find it tougher to sue their brokers due to a recent Supreme Court decision that held that arbitration agreements are binding in disputes over securities purchases. Suing their brokers can be costly and time-consuming for investors also.

It is still often worth the effort, particularly if the investor has a strong case. Firms who believe the investor is serious and will file an arbitration case usually settle, especially if the dispute involves less than $20,000 (the approximate cost of taking a case through arbitration).

Arbitration is one of many ways to achieve an effective remedy.

Source: Michael Siconolfi, "Squeaky Investor Gets the Grease, Some Brokerage Firms Admit," *Wall Street Journal*, May 24, 1989, p. C1; reprinted by permission of *Wall Street Journal*, © Dow Jones & Company, Inc. (1989). All Rights Reserved Worldwide.

Introduction

In the last chapter we discussed the contracting parties' contractual duties of performance. We will now consider their contractual rights, how contractual rights and duties may be transferred to or otherwise acquired by third persons, and the legal effect and remedies for breach of contract.

property
A thing; also an interest or right in a thing

interest
A person's desire that has been legally recognized as dominant over a similar desire of another person

right
A legal claim by the owner of an interest that others shall not interfere with the owner's interest

The creation of a simple contract creates property, rights, and duties. **Property** usually refers to a thing, which may be either tangible (e.g., that house, that bag, that typewriter is my property) or intangible (e.g., that account receivable, that copyright, that patent, that idea is my property). It belongs to me; I have an interest in it, a right to it, and other persons have a duty not to interfere with my property. Legally, then, property is a thing, and also an interest or a right in a thing, recognized by law.

My desire to enjoy a thing exclusively has been recognized as proper by society. An **interest** is a person's desire that has been legally recognized as dominant over a similar desire of another person. For example, an owner's title to a house is a legal interest in that house recognized by law.

I have the right to claim that others will not interfere with my legal interest. So a **right** is a legal claim by the owner of an interest that others shall not interfere with that interest. For example, the owner of a house has the right to claim that others are not to interfere with the owner's enjoyment of the house.

Other persons have a legal obligation to respect my legal interest and not to interfere with it. So a **duty** is a legal obligation not to interfere with another person's legal interest. For example, other persons have a duty not to interfere with my enjoyment of my house.

duty
A legal obligation not to interfere with another person's interest

Thus the creation of a simple contract gives to each of the immediate parties to the contract: (1) an *interest* in the other party's performance of what he or she contracted to do; (2) a *right* to have the other party not violate that interest by his or her failure to perform; and (3) a *duty* to perform the contract and not fail to perform.

These interests, rights, and duties can be transferred to third persons who are not immediate parties to the original contract. Often interests in things are transferred for the purpose of security. For example, I borrow $100 from you and deliver my ring to you as security, and you now have a security interest in the ring that includes the right to sell it if I don't pay you. A contract right can be transferred or assigned and a contract duty can be transferred or delegated to a third person. Also, the contract may provide for a benefit to a third person who, as a third-party beneficiary of the contract, thereby obtains a right to enforce the contract to which he or she is not a party. For example, a husband contracts with an insurance company and obtains a policy of life insurance in which his wife is named as the beneficiary on his death.

The important point in this chapter is the concern of the law with enhancing and protecting the rights that parties gained by exercising the freedom of contract.

The Concept of Parties

As was discussed in Chapter 6 (p. 126), there can be any number of parties to a contract. The obligations of the immediate parties to the contract may be *joint, several,* or *joint and several.*

Unless the contracting parties agree otherwise, if two or more parties *together* are obligated to perform the *same* duty to the *same* person, the obligation is *joint* (collective). They can sue and be sued only together. If each of the several parties *separately* promises to perform the *same* obligation, the obligation is *several* (independent). Each of them can sue and be sued separately. The obligation to perform a duty can be both *joint and several.* (See Figure 14.1.)

Only the parties to a contract have **privity of contract**—the right to enforce a contract—with two exceptions to be discussed, namely, *assignments* and *third-party creditor or donee beneficiary contracts.*

privity of contract
A legal relationship between two or more parties created by their contract

Rights

Rights under a contract are normally capable of transfer by the process of **assignment**. The party to a contract who assigns the right under a contract is called an **assignor,** and the person who receives the right is called an **assignee.** For example, Bill owes Sam $10, and Sam assigns to Ed his right against Bill for the $10. Sam is the assignor and Ed is the assignee.

assignment
The transfer of a contract right

assignor
The transferor of a contract right

assignee
The person to whom a contract right is transferred

An assignment can take any form as long as the original party to the contract indicates a present intent to transfer a contract right to another. In the following case the court found that the purported assignment failed because the debtor attempting to assign retained control over the subject matter of the assignment.

FIGURE 14.1 **Joint and Several Obligation**

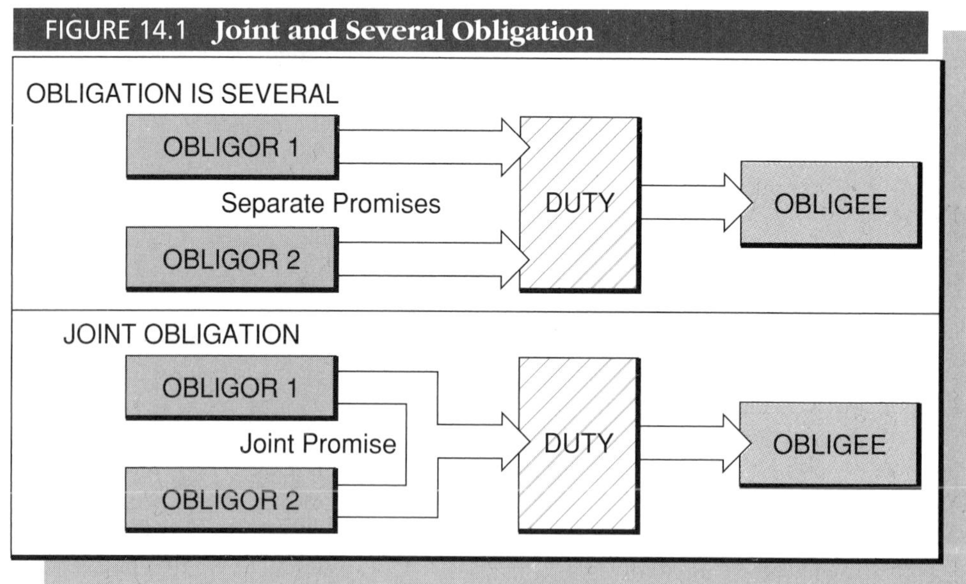

FACTS

On March 22, 1974, a debtor made to a bank a demand promissory note. On April 8, 1974, in order to secure the payment of the note, the debtor granted the bank a security interest in, among other things, "accounts receivable . . . now owned or hereafter acquired." A financing statement evidencing the bank's security interest was filed with the Minnesota Secretary of State on April 29, 1974. The debtor established with the bank a "collateral account" into which all payments on accounts receivable made to the debtor would be deposited. Without the debtor's consent, the bank could not use the funds in the collateral account for any purpose other than to satisfy the debtor's liability to the bank in the event of default on the loan. Notice was given by the debtor, to a debtor of the debtor, to make future payments on contracts to the bank. Accordingly, the debtor of the debtor made the bank the payee on its checks and the bank deposited the proceeds of the checks to the "collateral account." The United States filed a tax lien on the collateral account for taxes owed by the debtor. The bank claims it has priority over the United States to the funds in the collateral account.

DECISION

Judgment for the United States Internal Revenue Service. The court said that although under Minnesota law "no particular form or words are required" for an assignment, an intent to transfer must be manifested and the assignor must not retain control over the fund or any power of revocation. In the present case, the letter from the debtor to its debtor would have been sufficient to establish an assignment of the accounts receivable had there been manifested the necessary intent to transfer the accounts receivable and relinquishment of all control over them and their proceeds. Since the debtor retained some control over the collateral account, all things necessary to perfect the assignment were not accomplished.

Guaranty State Bank of St. Paul v. Lindquist, 304 N.W.2d 278 (Minn. 1981).

When an effective assignment has been accomplished, the assignee has the assignor's right to enforce the contract against the party who had contracted with the assignor. In the above example of Sam's assignment to Ed, Ed has Sam's right to enforce the contract against Bill. (See Figure 14.2.)

FIGURE 14.2 Assignments of Rights and Delegation of Duties

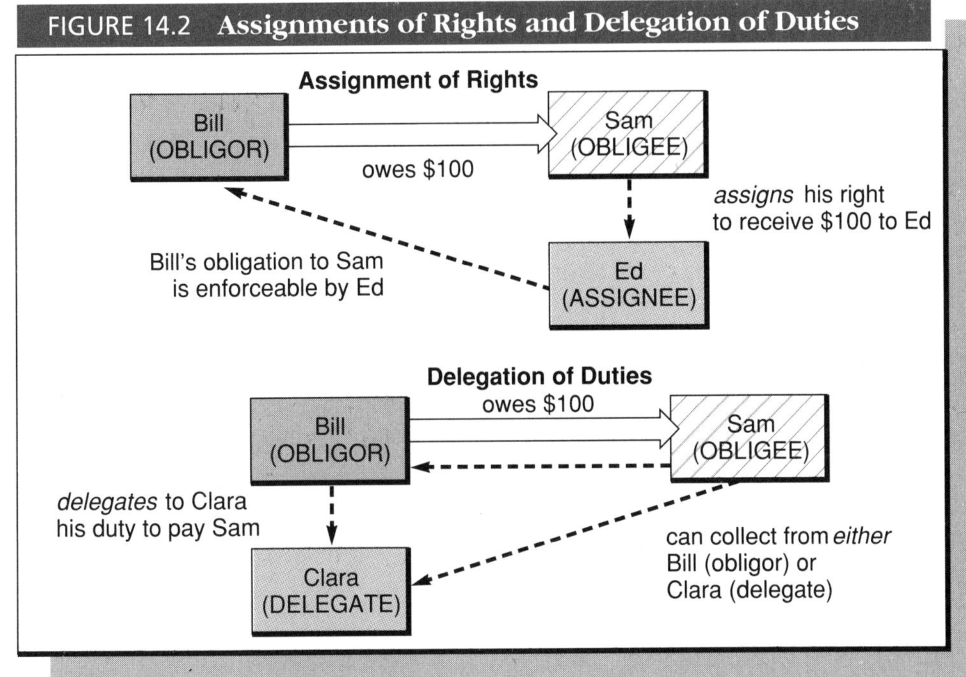

Duties

While contract rights are assignable, contract duties are only **delegable.** A contractual mechanical or ministerial duty requiring no special factor or person with special abilities necessary to performance is normally freely delegable. Examples of persons with special abilities are lawyers, doctors, certified public accountants, and famous artists. When a party to a contract delegates a contractual duty to another, that party, as the original **obligor,** remains responsible for seeing that the duty is performed. The **obligee,** the one holding the right to performance, can hold responsible either the obligor or the obligor's consenting delegate for nonperformance of the owed duty. In this way a third party (the delegate) not originally a party to "the contract" can become responsible for its performance. In the above example of Sam and Bill, if Bill delegates to Clara his duty to pay Sam $10 and Clara agrees to pay Sam, Bill is still liable to Sam (and now Clara is also liable to Sam).[1]

delegation
The transfer of one's duty to another, the transferor still being responsible for the duty

obligor
The person who owes a legal obligation

obligee
The person to whom a legal obligation is owed

Special Rules for Assignment and Delegation

▶ Notice to Obligor of Assignment

Notice of an assignment of a right not for the purpose of security is normally given by an assignee to the obligor who owes a duty under the contract in order to cut off defenses of the obligor that may occur subsequently. Notice is also given to prevent the discharge of the obligor by the obligor's innocent performance of the obligor's contractual duty for

[1]Clara is now liable to Sam who becomes a "third-party creditor beneficiary," a topic discussed on pp. 264–65.

the benefit of the obligee. For example, Dora owes money to Cathy, who assigns her right to the money to Ed. Dora is unaware of the assignment and Dora pays Cathy. Dora is discharged from the debt, and Ed has no right against Dora, but only against Cathy. If Ed had notified Dora of the assignment, then Dora must pay only Ed. The following case illustrates this point.

FACTS

On October 31, 1973, a lessor leased seven trucks to a lessee and secured the lease by taking delivery of six savings certificates issued by State Federal Savings and Loan Association to the lessee. The lessee subsequently encountered financial straits and notified State Federal Savings and Loan Association that it had lost the certificates and desired to effect an early withdrawal of the funds. Without notice of the lessee's pledge of the certificates to the lessor, State Federal Savings and Loan Association disbursed the funds to the lessee. The lessor contends as true owner of the certificates by pledge (assignment) State Federal Savings and Loan Association should have to pay the value of the certificates to the lessor.

DECISION

Judgment for State Federal Savings and Loan Association. The court held that the general rule applicable to this case is that an assignee must notify a debtor prior to the debtor's payment to the assignor in order to bind the debtor to the obligation asserted by the assignee; otherwise, the debtor is discharged of the debt by its innocent payment to the assignor.

Equilease Corp. v. State Fed. Sav. and Loan Ass'n, 647 F.2d 1069 (10th Cir. 1981).

Obligor's Defense Against the Assignee

Since the assignee takes rights under the contract through the assignor, any defenses arising from the contract itself are not cut off by the assignee giving notice to the obligor of the assignment to the assignee of the contract right. The assignee gets only what the assignor has. For example, Al fraudulently induces Betty to contract with him. Thus the contract is voidable by Betty against Al. Later, Al assigns to Chris his right against Betty for $100 owing by Betty to Al under the contract. Betty can avoid the contract and assert fraud as a defense to Chris's claim against Betty.

If a defense separate from the contract arises between the obligor and the obligee-assignor after notice is given by the assignee to the obligor, such defense is cut off. This is not the result if the "separate defense" came into being before notice of the assignment was given to the obligor.

Discharge

If the obligor performs the duty owing to the assignor before the obligor receives notice from the assignee of the assignment of the right, the assignee has no claim against the obligor. The obligor having performed his or her contractual obligation innocent of the assignment is **discharged** of the obligation. The assignee's claim is directed at the assignor for breach of the assignor's warranty not to defeat or impair the value of the assignment. When a person claims to be the assignee, the obligor has the right to request such person to furnish the obligor reasonable proof of assignment to him or her.

discharge
In contracts, termination of a contractual duty to perform a promise

Since most assignments are made for the purpose of security for a debt, when this occurs the Uniform Commercial Code then governs and provides in Article 9 on Secured Transactions that, if the assignee of an account receivable wishes the obligor to pay directly to the assignee, the assignee must not only give the obligor notice of the assignment but the assignee must also demand payment from the obligor. If this is done, then the obligor must pay only the assignee. Notice of assignment alone is not enough to prevent the obligor from paying the assignor and thereby being discharged. In the following case notice was given and demand made by the assignee and the debtor's subsequent payment to the assignor did not discharge the debtor's obligation to pay the assignee.

FACTS

Employee of a claims service settled an uninsured motorist's claim for an Insurance Company with the insured. A memo was delivered to the insured addressed "to whom it may concern, a $4,300 settlement draft will be issued by insurance company in the first week in May 1982." Insured obtained a loan from a bank and assigned to the bank the settlement payment as security for the loan payment. The bank called the employee of the claim service and asked the employee to inform the insurance company of the assignment. The employee of the claim service sent a letter to the insurance company informing them of the assignment. On May 3, the bank called the insurance company and relayed the request that the insurance company should send the insured's check to the bank. On May 12, the mother of the insured called the insurance company and asked that they stop payment on the insured's check sent to the bank. The insurance company stopped payment on the check, and issued a second check to the insured which was cashed by the insured. No funds have been paid by the insured to the bank to pay off the loan. The bank sues the insurance company to recover the proceeds of the first check.

DECISION

Judgment for the bank. The court reasoned that an obligor is liable to an assignee for the debt assigned if the obligor pays that debt to the obligee-assignor after either actual or constructive notice of the assignment and the assignee's demand of payment by the obligor. Both by letter and by telephone call, the insurance company obligor had constructive notice of the assignment and of the assignee-bank's demand of payment. Therefore the company's payment to the insured does not relieve it from liability to the assignee-bank for the proceeds of the settlement claim.

Security State Bank of Aitkin v. Morlock, 355 N.W.2d 441 (Minn. 1984).

► Warranty

The **warranty** an assignor makes to an assignee is that the contract is valid and that the right exists that the assignor can assign. The assignor also warrants there will be no interference with the assignee's perfection of the right. By the assignor later accepting performance from the obligor of the duty owed under a contract, the assignor has interfered with the assignee's right. An assignor does not warrant that the obligor is solvent (pays his or her debts), nor that the obligor will perform the obligation due under the contract.

warranty
An express or implied assurance that certain facts exist

► Priority Among Successive Assignees When the Assignment Is Not Made for the Purpose of Security

If an assignor wrongfully assigns a right for value to several successive assignees who are innocent of a prior assignment, there exist several claimants. As among the claimants, only one is entitled to performance of the duty owed by the obligor. Under the American rule in the majority of the states and the Restatement (Second) of Contracts, Section 174, generally the first assignee in time has the best claim. Under the English rule, the first assignee to give notice to the obligor of the assignment to him or her has the best claim to the right. However, irrespective of the rights of several assignees among themselves, performance by the innocent obligor to any assignee discharges the obligor of the obligation.

► Nonassignability

Certain rights acquired under a contract are nonassignable. Assignment may be prohibited by law. For example, in some states the assignment of future wages and personal injury claims is prohibited. Also, if the contract expressly or impliedly precludes assignment, it is personal in character, and the contract rights are not assignable by the obligee without the consent of the obligor. The contract is personal to the obligor.

A contract is impliedly personal in character and nonassignable when either (1) it involves the personal taste, skill, judgment, character, credit, or fancy of the obligor or (2) assignment would materially change the duties of the obligor or impose additional material risks or burdens upon the obligor or change the obligor's duty.

For example, the contracts of lawyers and public accountants with their clients are personal in character and nonassignable by the clients as obligees of such professional services because of the skill and judgment of the lawyer and the accountant obligors. The clients cannot assign their rights to such legal and accounting services without the consent of the lawyer and the accountant.

Basically, assignment by the obligee here is not allowed because it violates the obligor's freedom of contract. However, a right as to what is due under an executed nonassignable contract is enforceable by the assignee. For example, the fire insurance contract on Dot's house prohibited assignment of the contract. A fire occurred and Dot assigned to Ed Dot's right to the insurance proceeds due Dot under the policy. Ed can enforce Dot's right to the proceeds. The contract had not been assigned; only the right to the proceeds had been assigned.

► Nondelegability

Certain duties imposed by the contract cannot be delegated. Delegation may be prohibited by law. Also, if the contract expressly or impliedly precludes delegation, it is personal in character, and the contract duties are not delegable by the obligor without the consent of the obligee. The contract is personal to the obligee.

A contract is impliedly personal in character and nondelegable when either (1) it involves the personal taste, skill, judgment, character, credit, or fancy of the obligor or (2) delegation would materially alter the performance due to the obligee.

In the lawyer and accountant example given above, their contracts are impliedly personal and nondelegable for the same reason. The lawyer and the accountant are obligors with contractual duties to render professional services, and they cannot delegate their duties without the consent of their clients, obligees.

Basically, delegation here is not allowed because it violates the obligee's freedom to contract. In the following case the court held that, since the contract was not for personal service, contract duties were delegable.

FACTS

Bedortha is the owner of a tree farm. One Mooney had been performing management services on the farm for Bedortha. Mooney requested that Bedortha enter into a contract for management services and harvesting trees with a corporation for which Mooney worked and in which Mooney owned stock. The contract was entered into and subsequently assigned by Bedortha to Emerald Christmas Tree Company, a successor corporation. Bedortha wishes to avoid the contract with the successor corporation on the basis that the duties were nondelegable because of Bedortha's personal reliance on the services of Mooney.

DECISION

Judgment for Emerald Christmas Tree Company. The court noted that the contract Bedortha made was not with Mooney personally but with the corporation for which Mooney worked. In fact, Bedortha was shown to have talked with one Santiago about the contract and knew that Santiago was also maintaining and harvesting trees for the corporation and would later take charge of the operation. Such evidence is sufficient to support a finding that the contract was not for personal services and, therefore, was delegable.

Emerald Christmas Tree Co. v. Bedortha, 674 P.2d 76 (Or. 1984).

► Some Code Provisions

Assignment We have already seen that the Uniform Commercial Code requires that, when an assignment is made for the purpose of security, the assignee is to give notice to the obligor of the assignment and to demand performance directly to the assignee to assure that the obligor must perform only to the assignee. If the obligor, not knowing of any assignee prior to the demanding assignee, performs to the latter, the obligor is discharged.[2]

While the Code permits a buyer in a contract to agree that the buyer will not assert against an assignee who takes an assignment for value and in good faith any claim or defense that the buyer may have against the seller, such provisions have been invalidated in consumer credit transactions.[3] In the following case the court held that the contract granted the buyer the right to assert against the seller as well as the seller's assignee-holder of the retail installment contract all the buyer's claims and defenses arising out of the sale.

FACTS

Hinojosa purchased a new pickup truck from Castellow Chevrolet Oldsmobile, Inc., a dealership, and signed a retail installment contract providing that the purchase price would be paid in 36 monthly payments and that other terms and conditions would apply. The contract was assigned by the dealership to General Motors Acceptance Corporation (G.M.A.C.). The vehicle was purchased for personal use and not for resale. It is undisputed that this transaction was a retail installment transaction subject to provisions of the Texas Credit Code (a statute). Hinojosa contends that the retail installment contract violates the Texas Credit Code. Above Hinojosa's signature appeared the following in bold print:

NOTICE

ANY HOLDER OF THIS CONSUMER CREDIT CONTRACT IS SUBJECT TO ALL CLAIMS AND DEFENSES WHICH THE DEBTOR COULD ASSERT AGAINST THE SELLER OF GOODS OR SERVICES OBTAINED PURSUANT HERETO OR WITH THE PROCEEDS HEREOF

On the back of the contract in paragraph 7(c) the following was provided:

> 7. It is mutually understood and agreed that (c) except where the seller is also the manufacturer of said property, buyer will not assert against any subsequent holder as assignee of this contract any claim or defense which the buyer may have against the manufacturer or a seller other than the

[2]See p. 260; see also p. 261 for priorities among successive assignees.

[3]UCC 9–201; see also pp. 676–677 for Federal Trade Commission Rule.

> seller of said property obtained pursuant hereto.
>
> The Texas Credit Code reads:
>
> No retail installment contract . . . shall (6) Provide that the buyer agrees not to assert against the seller or holder of . . . any claim or defense arising out of the sale. . . .
>
> DECISION
>
> Judgment for Hinojosa. The court found that a reasonable construction of the contract requires that the buyer have the right to assert against the seller, as well as any holder (assignee) of the retail sales contract, all claims and defenses arising out of the sale. The provision on the back of the contract, being in violation of the Texas Credit Code, does not limit the buyer in this right.
>
> *Hinojosa v. Castellow Chevrolet Oldsmobile, Inc. and G.M.A.C.*, 678 S.W.2d 707 (Tex. 1984).

Also under the Code,[4] a right as to what is due under an executed contract is assignable, and its assignment cannot be prohibited by the contract. (Jan contracts with Burt to supply goods to Burt, who is to pay Jan $1,000. The contract provides that neither the contract nor Jan's right to the $1,000 is assignable. Jan supplies the goods to Burt. The contract is nonassignable; nevertheless, Jan's right [account receivable] to the $1,000 is assignable by Jan to Carl, Jan's creditor.)

Delegation The common law of delegation is changed by the Uniform Commercial Code,[5] which provides that, in the absence of anything to the contrary, an assignment in general terms is also a delegation of the assignor's duties, and the assignee's acceptance is a promise to perform them. When both contractual right and duty are simultaneously assigned and delegated to a third party by one of the parties to the contract, the other original party to the contract affected thereby may demand additional assurances, such as a bond or deposit, from the third party that the contractual duty assumed by the third party will be performed.

Other Third Parties

▶ Third-Party Donee and Creditor Beneficiaries—Intended Beneficiaries

beneficiary
A person who is to receive a benefit

donee
The recipient of a gift

donor
The person who makes a gift

creditor
One to whom money is owed

There are three types of **beneficiaries** to a contract: donee, creditor, and incidental. The first two are intended beneficiaries; that is, the contract provides that they are to receive certain contract rights. This is not true of the incidental beneficiary.

A **donee** beneficiary of a contract is a third person who has been given the right under the contract as a gift by a contracting party. For example, the life insurance policy of a husband designates his wife as the beneficiary with the right to receive the policy proceeds on the husband's death. See Figure 14.3 for a clear picture of a third party donee beneficiary contract.

A **creditor** beneficiary is a third person (Carl) who is given the right under the contract (between Sam and Bill) to obtain performance by one of the contracting parties

[4]UCC 2–210 and 9–318(4).

[5]Ibid.

FIGURE 14.3 **Third-Party Donee Beneficiary Contract**

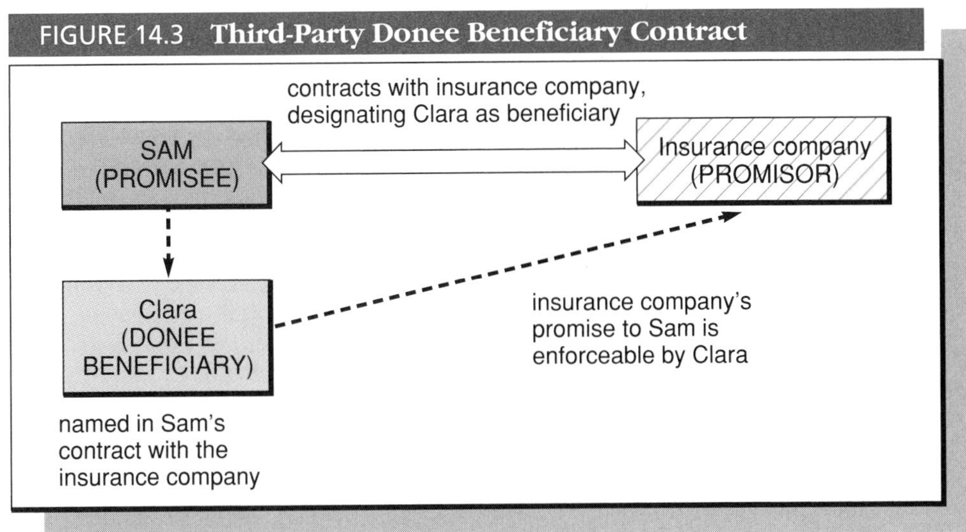

(Bill) of an obligation owing to the other contracting party (Sam) in discharge of the latter's (Sam's) duty to the third person (Carl). For example, Sam contracts with Bill to sell his house to Bill, who agrees to pay Sam's mortgage (real property security) debt to Carl, the mortgagee (secured creditor). Carl is a third-party creditor beneficiary of the contract between Bill and Sam and Bill is now liable to Carl for Sam's *duty* to pay Carl on the mortgage debt. Sam is still liable to Carl on Sam's mortgage contract with Carl, but when Bill fully pays Carl on the debt, Sam is then discharged of Sam's debt to Carl. (See Figure 14.4.)

A third-party *incidental* beneficiary has no enforceable claim to any right under contract to which the beneficiary is not a party but anticipates a benefit if the contract is performed. Beneficiaries can enforce the contracts naming them as beneficiaries and to which they are not parties only when the contract right is created for their benefit as creditors or donees. In the following case the court held that the plaintiff was an

FIGURE 14.4 **Third-Party Creditor Beneficiary Contract**

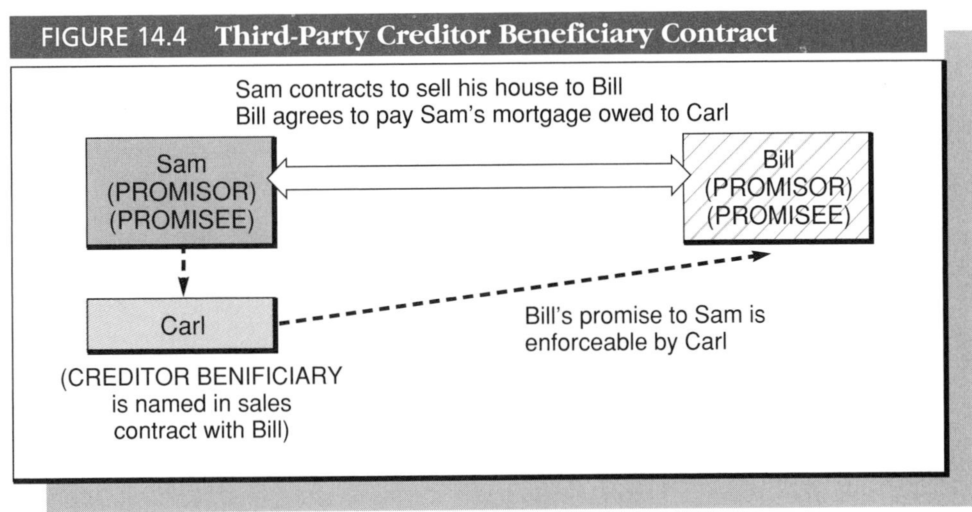

incidental beneficiary because the contract was devoid of any contemplation of a third party.

FACTS

American Financial Corporation leased a UNIVAC computer system and supporting equipment to Sci-Tek and TDC. One of the requirements of the lease was that Sci-Tek and TDC were required to enter into a maintenance contract for the leased equipment. Sci-Tek contracted with the Computer Sciences Corporation to maintain and repair the leased computers. Thereafter, Sci-Tek and TDC ran into financial difficulties and eventually became insolvent. American Financial seeks recovery from Computer Sciences, contending it breached its maintenance contract with Sci-Tek/TDC thereby causing damage to the computer system. Nowhere in the contract was the name of American Financial Corporation mentioned.

DECISION

Judgment for Computer Sciences Corporation. The court noted that there are two theories to prove a third-party beneficiary. One theory requires that the third-party beneficiary must be *wholly* disclosed within the "four corners" of the contract. Another theory suggests that the third-party beneficiary status can be ascertained wholly from extrinsic evidence. The court stated that extrinsic facts and circumstances surrounding the execution of the contract can be examined for purposes of ascertaining third-party beneficiary status only when the language of the contract shows that it was entered into for the benefit of a third party, even though it may not specifically identify the party. Such is not the case here. Nothing in the maintenance agreement contemplates or even hints at the existence of a third party who might have some right to or benefits from Computer Sciences Corporation's performance. The rationale for the court's theory is premised on the following:

> To allow the unilateral intent of one party, without safeguards, to determine the existence of a third-party beneficiary would thwart the power that contracting parties should have to control their legal relations, particularly in a commercial setting.

American Fin. Corp. v. Computer Sciences Corp., 558 F.Supp. 1182 (D.Del. 1983).

► Novation

novation
A new contract in which one of the parties was not a party to the old contract and which immediately discharges the old contract

In a **novation,** (1) a *new* contract is made in which (2) one of the parties was not a party to the old contract, and (3) the new contract immediately discharges the old contract. A new party is substituted for one of the parties under the former contract. The new party may be a new debtor or a new creditor, usually a new debtor. For example, the bank creditor holds the debtor's land as security for the debt; the bank discharges the debtor's contract; and the bank takes in its place the new contract of the buyer of the land, who contracts with the bank to pay the bank on the new debt, the bank holding the same land as security for the buyer's debt. (See Figure 14.5.)

The consideration given by one of the original parties to the contract (the bank in the example) for the substitution of a new third party (Clara in the example) who assumes the duty to perform the obligations of the original contract is the discharge of the other original contracting party (Art in the example). In the following case the court held that there was a new contract of novation that bound the new party to the terms of the old contract.

FACTS

Taylor & Martin, Inc., seeks to recover the purchase price of a refrigerated semi-trailer unit sold to Hiland Dairy, Inc., at an auction conducted by Taylor & Martin. Hiland Dairy registered to bid at Taylor & Martin's auction but was outbid on a five-unit lot of Hobbs re-

FIGURE 14.5 **Novation**

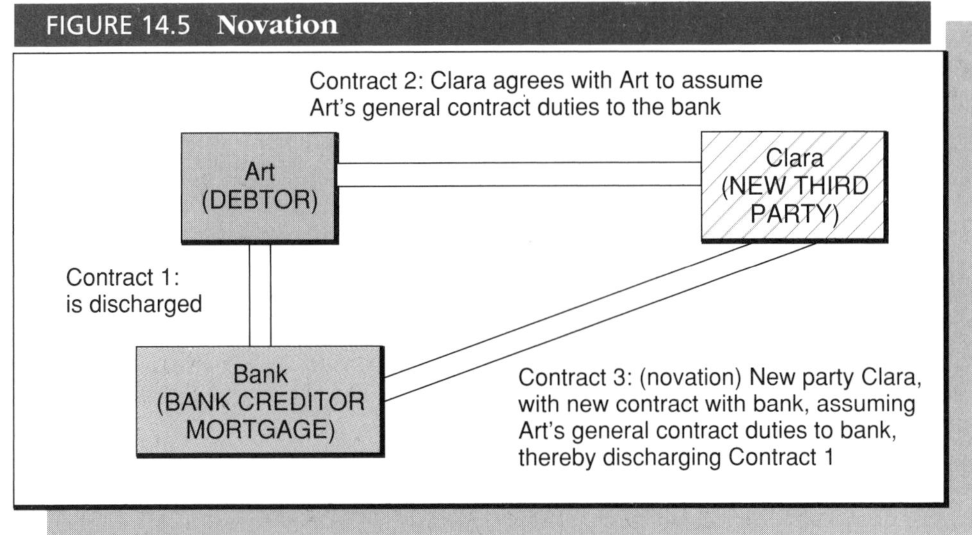
Contract 2: Clara agrees with Art to assume
Art's general contract duties to the bank
Art
(DEBTOR)
Clara
(NEW THIRD
PARTY)
Contract 1:
is discharged
Bank
(BANK CREDITOR
MORTGAGE)
Contract 3: (novation) New party Clara,
with new contract with bank, assuming
Art's general contract duties to bank,
thereby discharging Contract 1

frigerated semi-trailers. After the lot was "struck off," Hiland Dairy approached the successful bidder and arranged to purchase four of the units. Both the successful bidder and Hiland Dairy went to one of Taylor & Martin's employees and had her mark through the successful bidder's bidding number on the auction's memorandum and substitute Hiland Dairy's bidding number. One of the terms of the auction sales contract was that a buyer of a sales item assumes "full responsibility" for the item at the time it is sold. In the process of transporting the trucks, Hiland Dairy discovered that one of the trucks had been stolen off the auction lot after the auction sale. Hiland Dairy, Inc. refuses to pay for this truck.

DECISION

Judgment for Taylor & Martin, Inc. The court said that in order to constitute a contract of novation subjecting the new party to the terms of the old contract, there must be (1) a previous contractual obligation (2) extinguished by a new contract, effected by substitution of parties or of undertaking (3) with the consent of all the parties, the debtor, the creditor, and the third party. Assent to the terms of a novation need not be shown by express words, but may be inferred from the facts and circumstances attending the transaction and the conduct of the parties thereafter. Further, a person substituted as a party to a contract who agrees to perform the original obligation becomes bound by all the terms of the contract to the same extent as the original party. Here we have a sale when the auctioneer announced it by the fall of the hammer. The mark through the auction memo indicates the substitution of a new party for the obligation of the old contract. All parties consent to the novation. Under the terms of the contract, Hiland Dairy bore the risk of loss upon sale and must pay for the stolen unit.

Taylor & Martin, Inc. v. Hiland Dairy, Inc., 676 S.W.2d 859 (Mo. 1984).

Creation of Third-Party Intended Relationships

▶ At the Time the Contract Is Formed

The rights of a third-party beneficiary in the contract in which the beneficiary is named are created at the time the contract is formed. A donee beneficiary's rights arise the moment the contracting party who owns the right acknowledges that the right is being held for the beneficiary. If the contracting party reserves the right to change beneficiaries, the beneficiary's right is subject to divestment (termination) should the contracting party change the beneficiary. For example, Hal takes out a life insurance policy naming Wendy, his wife, as a donee beneficiary, Hal reserving the right to change the beneficiary. Hal can inform the insurance company to change the beneficiary. If the contracting party does not reserve this right in a life insurance policy, the interest of the beneficiary is vested (fixed and irrevocable), and change cannot be made without the beneficiary's consent.

The interests of creditor beneficiaries normally vest in the contract after they have knowledge of it and move in reliance upon the right given. The beneficiary must be a creditor of the party (promisee) to whom the assuming party's (promisor) contract obligation is owed. For example, Donna takes out a policy of car collision insurance with Ink Insurance Company, naming Dollars Bank as beneficiary, from whom Donna had borrowed the money to buy the car. Dollars Bank is the third-party creditor beneficiary of the policy, Ink Insurance is the assuming party promisor, and Donna is the debtor promisee. In summary, the assuming party's promise is made to the debtor promisee to perform the debtor's duty to the creditor third party.

In the following case the court held that a creditor of a corporation could be a third-party creditor beneficiary of individual shareholders' binding promises to a corporation to pay its debts.

FACTS

Snyder alleges in substance as follows: Before February 3, 1967, she was an employee of General Aviation and had loaned it $4,602.50 and that the corporation also owed her $800 for back salary plus interest on both debts. Freeman and Croom were, at the time these debts were owed, officers, directors and sole shareholders of the corporation. On February 3, 1967, Freeman and Croom contracted in writing on behalf of General Aviation with Colucci that the latter would pay General Aviation the sum of $10,000 for a 50 percent interest in the corporation. Part of the agreement reads as follows:

> Out of monies coming to the corporation . . ., the corporation shall pay accrued salary to Mrs. Snyder, [Plaintiff] of approximately $800, . . . and to Mrs. Snyder [Plaintiff] notes payable in the amount of $4,602.50 plus interest; . . .

Snyder further alleges that, after the execution of the agreement and pursuant thereto, Colucci paid $10,000 to Freeman and Croom for General Aviation, but Freeman and Croom failed to pay Snyder the funds owed her. Snyder seeks payment from Freeman and Croom.

DECISION

Judgment for Snyder. The court said that unless otherwise agreed between promisor and promisee, the beneficiary (Snyder) of a promise (made by Colucci) is an intended beneficiary if recognition of a right to performance in the beneficiary is appropriate to effectuate the intention of the parties (Colucci and General Aviation) and the performance of the promise will satisfy an obligation of the promisee (General Aviation) to pay money to the beneficiary (Snyder). This type of promise is referred to as a creditor beneficiary promise. In such a case, the promisee (General Aviation) is surety for the promisor (Colucci), the promise is an asset of the promisee, and a direct action by the beneficiary (Snyder) against the promisor is appropriate to carry out the intention of promisor and promisee. The agreement here is tantamount to a promise by the signatories, to cause the corporation to receive the capital and to pay Snyder.

Snyder v. Freeman, 266 S.E.2d 593 (N.C. 1980).

Since beneficiaries take their rights through a contracting party, they are subject to all the terms of the contract. If the contract provides that only the original parties to the contract may enforce it, then, although the right is created in the beneficiary as of the time of the formation of the contract, since right cannot be directly enforced by the beneficiary.

FIGURE 14.6 **Rights of Third Parties: Beneficiary, Assignee, Novation**

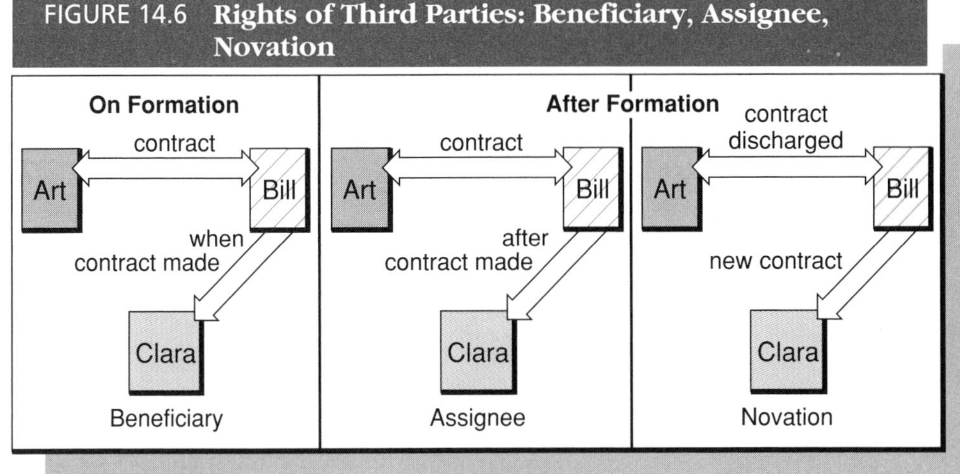

► After the Contract Is Formed

Rights taken under a contract by novation or assignment occur after a contract is formed. (See Figure 14.6.) A contract may prohibit assignment by the creditor obligee of the obligee's right to payment of money from the debtor, or the contract may prohibit assignment of one party's right to performance other than to pay money by the other party. With respect to the prohibition of assignment of the right to payment of money, some courts hold that such a prohibition is contrary to public policy and of no legal effect because it limits the assignor's freedom to contract with third persons. Other courts hold that the prohibition is valid.

With respect to the prohibition of assignment of the right to performance other than to pay money, such a provision is valid and will cause the contract to be "personal in character" and nonassignable without the consent of the other party obligor.

A contractual promise to assign future contract rights in an existing contract gives only an expectation to an assignee that can be enforced in the future.

Remedies

► The Concept of Remedy

We are still considering rights, but these are new rights contained in remedies for breach of contract. When a right is acquired by contract, the legal system will seek to protect it. If the one who owes the duty wrongfully does not perform, a **breach of contract** exists for which the law provides relief by giving a **remedy**. The various remedies available are money damages, specific performance by order or **injunction,** restitution, and reformation. These will be considered in turn.

breach of contract
Wrongful nonperformance of a contractual promise

remedy
The means by which a right is enforced or protected

injunction
A court order requiring a person to do or not to do something

Since the party enforcing the remedy may in all probability not get the original right due him or her under the contract, it should be recognized that the right that the remedy affords is a second type of right with its corresponding duty. For example, Sam contracts to dig a ditch for Bud. Bud has a right to have the ditch dug by Sam. On Sam's wrongful refusal to dig the ditch, Bud now has a remedy for Sam's breach of contract and, thus, a new right against Sam for one of the three remedies.

Damages

A breach of contract is a wrongful nonperformance of a contractual duty. The word **damage** means loss or harm. **Damages** means the money judicially awarded (by the court) to an **injured** party for another's wrongful conduct. If a breach of contract has occurred but the injured party cannot show that he or she actually suffered damage, a symbolic award of **nominal damages** can be obtained. Usually the money award is $1. (Al unauthorizedly walks over Betty's land without damaging the land. Betty's possessory interest in the land has been wrongfully invaded, and Betty can obtain nominal damages against Al.)

Damages are determined as of the time of the breach, except that for an **anticipatory repudiation** and breach, damages are determined as of the time performance was to have occurred. For example, Ed employs Lee on Wednesday, and Lee is to report for work on the following Monday. On Thursday Ed tells Lee not to report for work. Ed has committed an anticipatory repudiation and breach of the contract. If Lee sues Ed on Friday, damages will be fixed as of Monday when Lee was to have begun work.

When loss due to breach of contract is something other than nominal, one is entitled to recover **compensatory damages,** compensating for damage actually sustained. One measure of compensatory damages is the difference between fair market value (the cost of a substitute performance) and the contract price. Another measure of compensatory damages (for a defective performance rather than no performance) is the difference between the value of a performance as promised or warranted and the actual value received. Compensatory damages could also be lost profits on lost sales or the cost necessary to make a defective performance whole.

Consequential (special) damages for loss foreseeable from a breach of contract are recoverable. For example, if Ann knows Bill's plant will be shut down if a promised machine is not delivered by a promised date by Ann. Ann can be held liable for Bill's loss of profit from lost production as a consequence of Ann's nonperformance and breach of contract. Consequential damages, when applicable, are given in addition to compensatory damages.

Incidental damages are another form of consequential damages and are usually incurred in a reasonable effort by the injured party, whether successful or not, to avoid loss. For example, an injured contracting party pays brokerage fees in arranging or attempting to arrange a substitute transaction for the one that the other contracting party failed to perform.

The following case shows that no matter what we call damages it is the purpose of the court to redress the wrong suffered by the party who has not breached the contract.

damage
Loss or harm

damages
The money judicially awarded to an injured party for another's wrongful conduct

injury
The wrongful invasion of another person's interest

nominal damages
The money judicially awarded to an injured party when no damage has occurred from another's wrongful conduct

anticipatory repudiation
A party's manifestation of an intent not to perform a contractual obligation, made before his or her performance is due

compensatory damages
The money judicially awarded to an injured party to compensate for damage caused by another's wrongful conduct

consequential (special) damages
The money judicially awarded to an injured party for loss that the breaching party reasonably could foresee would be a result of his or her breach

incidental damages
The money judicially awarded to a nonbreaching party for expenses reasonably incurred by the nonbreaching party on the other party's breach

quantum meruit
An action for services rendered based on an implied promise to pay plaintiff as much as plaintiff reasonably deserved for the plaintiff's services

FACTS

Hastoupis, a skilled baker, immigrated to this country from Greece and met an uncle, the decedent. Hastoupis moved in with the decedent and rendered personal services to him for many years. The decedent orally promised to leave Hastoupis one-half of his estate in his will. When the decedent was in poor health, he persuaded Hastoupis to give up his plans for acquiring his own bakery by again stating that he would leave Hastoupis one-half of his estate. The decedent died but did not mention Hastoupis in his will. The trial judge held that justice and equity required that judgment be rendered for Hastoupis on a theory of **quantum meruit**. The dollar value of the judgment amounted to $375,000. Gargas, the representative of the decedent's estate, appealed.

DECISION

Affirmed, judgment for Hastoupis. The court reasoned that the measure of damages for the reasonable value of Hastoupis's services is premised on principles of restitution, that is, the party liable in restitution for monetary damages must pay an amount equal to the benefits conferred upon him. The promisee possesses a protected restitution interest because the promisor (the decedent), who is treated for purposes of the analysis as the contract breaker, has been unjustly enriched. The ascertainment of the fair market value of services so unusual in nature and so uncommon in ordinary experience is doubtless a matter of some difficulty, but the problem lies primarily in the domain of fact and its solution to a large extent is left to the good sense, practical wisdom and sound judgment of the trier of fact, mindful of the evidence and guided by the correct principles of law.

Hastoupis v. Gargas, Executor, 398 N.E.2d 745 (Mass. 1980).

Punitive (exemplary) damages are given in certain tort actions, but not for contract loss. Punitive damages seek to punish a wrongdoer and they need bear no relationship to actual damages (compensatory and/or consequential). Victims of intentional torts can receive punitive damages awards. Under the common law, if one is defrauded into making a contract, one can either (1) avoid the contract; or (2) affirm the contract, sue for the tort of **deceit,** and obtain punitive damages. In the following case punitive damages were not awarded, both because the action was for breach of contract, and because the defendant had not intentionally committed a tort.

punitive (exemplary) damages
The money judicially awarded to an injured party in excess of compensatory damages to punish for malicious, wanton, or intentional wrongful conduct

deceit
Briefly, a tort consisting of contractual fraud causing loss (for a full definition see the Glossary)

FACTS

McIntosh and Magna Systems, Inc., entered into an agreement providing that, in return for McIntosh's assistance in the development, acquisition, marketing, production and distribution of Magna's educational materials, Magna would reserve an annual fee of $35,000 for three years on McIntosh's behalf and provide the option of purchasing 25 percent of Magna's authorized stock in lieu of payment of fees. McIntosh alleged that McIntosh had performed all obligations but Magna refused to perform. Among the counts of McIntosh's complaint was one seeking punitive damages.

DECISION

Judgment for Magna Systems, Inc. as not liable for punitive damages. The court noted that as a general rule, courts would not award punitive damages for actions grounded solely in contract, only when the breach itself constituted an independent and willful tort accompanied by fraud, malice, wantonness or oppression, would recovery of punitive damages be permitted for a breach of contract. Here, the court was unable to identify any independent cause of action sounding in tort arising simply from Magna's breach of contract.

McIntosh v. Magna Systems, Inc., 539 F.Supp. 1185 (N.D. Ill. 1982).

Triple damages, a form of punitive damages, are assessed against violators of the federal Sherman Antitrust Act.[6]

Liquidated damages is the judicial award of the money agreed upon by the contracting parties as compensation for a breach of contract before the breach is experienced. For example, a contract for the sale of real estate may provide that, if the buyer does not pay the purchase price at the time of the closing of the deal, the buyer's money deposit shall be the liquidated damages. If the liquidated damages provision

liquidated damages
The money judicially awarded in the amount as agreed to by the parties in their contract at the time it was made as reasonable compensation for damage that may be caused by the wrongful conduct of one of the parties in the future

[6]For a discussion of the Sherman Antitrust Act, see pp. 727–730.

bears some reasonable relationship to the actual damage, it will be awarded for breach of the contract. If the liquidated damages provision is excessive, it will be denied. Such excessive damages agreements are considered penalties that are not enforced by law.

Mitigation If the nonbreaching party to the contract can lessen the damage caused by a breaching party, the nonbreaching party will be required by law so to act as to minimize the damage. For example, if an employer wrongfully discharged an employee under a contract with three months remaining, the employee has a duty to seek employment elsewhere for the three-month period and thereby reduce the employee's loss of wages under the first contract. In the following case the defendant could not prove that the plaintiff had failed to minimize the damage.

FACTS

In 1974, Stewart, by virtue of having taught in the school district since 1959, was a permanent tenured teacher. In June 1974, it was found that the defendant Board of Education had wrongfully terminated Stewart's teaching contract. Stewart was awarded damages of back pay plus 6 percent interest. Stewart made no effort to secure a teaching position in the community during the five years she had been unemployed. The Board of Education of Ritenour Consolidated School District introduced evidence that teaching jobs in Stewart's subject matter were available in the community, but it was shown that applicants outnumbered the jobs available and that none of the jobs filled were hired in Stewart's age bracket. The Board of Education contends that Stewart's damage award should be reduced because of Stewart's failure to mitigate damages.

DECISION

Judgment for Stewart. The court said the employer had the burden to prove the employee's failure to mitigate damages. This burden is met when the employer proves that (a) one or more discoverable opportunities for comparable employment were available in a location as, or more convenient than, the place of former employment, (b) the improperly discharged employee unreasonably made no attempt to apply for any such job, and (c) it was reasonably likely that the former employee would obtain one of those comparable jobs. What the evidence showed was that there was not a reasonable likelihood that Stewart could have received a job. Stewart's age and higher starting salary requirements made the finding of a teaching job slim at best. The Board of Education has failed to meet its burden of proof.

Stewart v. Board of Educ. of Ritenour Consol. School Dist., 630 S.W.2d 130 (Mo. 1982).

Specific Performance

specific performance
The exact performance of a contract by a party as ordered by a court

If damages will adequately compensate one for a breach of contract, an order from a court with equity power to **specifically perform** the contract will not be given. If the subject matter of the contract is land or a unique item of personal property, an order to specifically perform the contract will be given by a court with equity powers. Normally, before one is entitled to an equitable remedy, one must show that (1) his or her remedy at law for damages is inadequate; (2) such equitable relief will not work an extreme hardship on the party in breach; (3) there is an enforceable contract; and (4) the court can grant such an effective remedy.

In contracts for personal services, a mandatory injunction ordering specific performance by a party will not be issued. Such an injunction would be in violation of the U.S. Constitution prohibition of "involuntary servitude" and also would be difficult to enforce. Also, a prohibitory injunction ordering that an act not be done will not be issued unless there is a threat of irreparable harm to the wronged party. Failure to comply with an injunction invites punishment for contempt of court.

► Restitution

Restitution is a remedy that is an alternative to damages for material breach of contract. One cannot have both restitution and damages, nor restitution and specific performance. It is available against a party in default, for a party who may not enforce the contract because of the statute of frauds, and to a party upon his or her avoidance of a voidable contract. In restitution, the parties to the breached contract return what they have received, or the value of what was given if what was given cannot be returned. The objective is to restore the contracting parties to the positions they occupied before the contract was formed.

restitution
A legal remedy restoring a party to his or her original position prior to the particular transaction

► Reformation

The remedy of **reformation** is not concerned with breach of contract, but it should be mentioned here. A written contract that, because of the parties' mutual mistake, does not state the parties' real agreement, generally will be reformed to reflect their real agreement by an action in a court with equity powers. For the purpose of reformation (changing the writing to reflect the real agreement) resort can be made to parol evidence as an exception to the parol evidence rule.[7] The result is that the contract can be reformed and enforced based upon the real agreement of the parties.

reformation
An action to correct a writing so as to reflect correctly the intentions of the parties that mistakenly were not properly expressed in the writing

► Election of Remedies

A party suing for breach of contract will be required to select a remedy. If one seeks damages, one is not entitled to restitution. If one seeks restitution, one is not entitled to specific performance. One can join an action for specific performance with a request for damages. In the following case the court held that when one seeks restitution one is entitled to restorative restitutive damages.

FACTS

Gregg fraudulently induced Head & Seemann, Inc., to sell to Gregg a home which Gregg occupied for five months before being ejected by a court order. Head & Seemann sought damages for the five months lost use of the property. At issue was whether a defrauded party who obtains rescission and restitution of real estate may also recover the rental value and out-of-pocket expenses for the period of lost possession. The trial court held that the election of remedies doctrine barred an additional action for rental value and out-of-pocket expenses. Head & Seemann appealed.

DECISION

Rescission and an action for restorative damages are not inconsistent remedies. Reversed, judgment for Head & Seemann, Inc., seller. The election of remedies doctrine is an equitable principle barring one from maintaining inconsistent theories or forms of relief. The classic application of the election of remedies doctrine is that a defrauded party has the election of

[7]For a discussion of the parol evidence rule, see p. 227.

either rescission or affirming the contract and seeking damages. Thus, it appears superficially that, if a claimant chooses to seek rescission, the claimant may not sue for incidental expenses. Rescission is always coupled with restitution. Restitution to a rescinding fraud victim includes everything the victim has reasonably paid out or given up in the transaction—here the rental value of the premises.

Head & Seemann, Inc. v. Gregg, 311 N.W.2d 667 (Wis. 1981).

Under the Uniform Commercial Code

Generally Special damages under the Uniform Commercial Code are called consequential damages and can be recovered.[8] Under the Code, an action by the seller for the price of goods sold can be maintained when the goods are damaged or destroyed and risk of loss has passed to the buyer.[9]

Specifically The remedies of an unpaid seller under the Code are (1) actions directed toward the goods for security for payment of price; (2) mitigation of damage by reselling the goods; (3) suit for price and incidental damages; (4) damages; and (5) cancellation of the contract.

Under the Code, the remedies of a buyer are (1) damages; (2) specific performance; (3) obtaining a security interest in goods and sale of the goods; and (4) cancellation of the contract.[10]

Summary Statement

1. The creation of a simple contract creates property, rights, and duties.
2. An obligation assumed by contract may be joint, several, or joint and several. Each of the contracting parties has rights and duties.
3. Rights are normally freely assignable unless the contract is personal in character. Duties are normally freely delegable if mechanical or ministerial in nature, but they are not delegable if the contract is personal in character.
4. A contract is personal in character if it expressly or impliedly precludes assignment or delegation.
5. The assignee gets only what the assignor has.
6. There are three types of third-party beneficiaries: donee, creditor, and incidental.
7. Rights of a third-party beneficiary arise at the moment the contract is created.
8. Rights taken by contract through the process of novation or assignment occur after the contract is formed.
9. When an assignment of a contract right is not made for the purpose of security, if the assignee notifies the obligor of the assignment, the obligor must pay only to the assignee. If no such notice is given and the obligor innocently pays the obligee assignor, the obligor is discharged.

---

[8]UCC 2–714 and 2–715.

[9]UCC 2–509 and 2–510.

[10]For detailed information on Code remedies in sales of goods, see pp. 514–532.

10. When the assignment is made for the purpose of security, under the Code the assignee must notify the obligor of the assignment and demand payment so that the obligor must pay only the assignee. If no such demand is made, the obligor may pay the obligee assignor and be discharged.
11. Under the Uniform Commercial Code, rights for what is due under an executed contract remain assignable; and the right to payment cannot be made nonassignable.
12. The remedies available for breach of a sales contract are numerous and varied under the Uniform Commercial Code. Under the common law of contracts, remedies for breach of contract are damages, specific performance, and restitution.
13. There are five types of damages: nominal, compensatory, consequential, punitive, and liquidated. Restitution is a remedy that is an alternative to damages and to specific performance.
14. One must mitigate damage.
15. The remedy of specific performance is given in limited circumstances.
16. The law associated with contractual rights seeks to enhance and protect rights created by one's exercise of the freedom to contract.

This chapter has made the point that the creation of a contract creates rights that can be transferred to or acquired by third parties and that the law will protect. The following case illustrates how personal service contracts not normally considered assignable can, in certain instances, be assigned and how the law protects rights.

MUNCHAK CORPORATION v. CUNNINGHAM
457 F.2d 721 (4th Cir. 1972)

This is a suit by owners and operators of a professional basketball club to enjoin one of its players from performing services as a player for any other basketball club.

Cunningham, a basketball player of special, exceptional and unique knowledge, skills and ability, was under contract to play basketball for the Philadelphia 76ers. Cunningham's contract was about to run out with the 76ers, although they had a right under the contract to prevent him from playing basketball with any club for one year if he did not renew his contract with them.

A team called the Cougars entered into contract negotiations by intermediaries with Cunningham whereby they agreed to compensate Cunningham if he sat out a year under the "penalty" clause in the Philadelphia contract and, if he agreed for a stipulated compensation, to play for them for an extended period of time after the one-year suspension was over.

Cunningham entered into a contract with the Cougars, then owned by Southern Sports Corporation, on the terms previously indicated, but required in his contract with Southern Sports that it be prohibited from assigning its contractual right to his services to another "club" without his consent. This contract contained no prohibition against its assignment to another owner of the same club.

Subsequent to the contract, Southern Sports assigned its franchise to the plaintiffs, Munchak Corporation. Cunningham was not asked to consent, nor has he consented to this assignment. The club "Cougars" still remains the same, only the ownership has changed.

Cunningham wishes now to remain with the 76ers. His contention is that his contract with the Cougars was not assignable and that, by reason of a purported assignment, he is excused from performance of the previous contract with the Cougars.

The court recognized that, generally, the right to performance of a personal service contract requiring special skills and based upon the personal relationship between parties cannot normally be assigned without the consent of the parties rendering those services. However, the court held that such contracts may be assigned when the character of the performance and the obligation will not be changed. Change of ownership of a franchise does not change the character of the performance or obligation assumed by contract. The right is assignable and will be enforced by granting the injunction.

Questions and Case Problems

1. Charles and Linda Austin executed a promissory note in favor of Town & Country Bank of Springfield on January 27, 1981. On February 26, 1981, Charles Austin signed a document entitled "Assignment" wherein he purportedly assigned to the Town & Country Bank of Springfield any proceeds which may result from settlement of an automobile accident between Charles Austin and Hazel Snyder, who was insured by Country Mutual Life Insurance Co. Could Charles Austin assign this right to the Town & Country Bank of Springfield? [*Town & Country Bank of Springfield v. Country Mut. Life Ins. Co.,* 459 N.E.2d 639 (Ill. 1984).]
2. Potential buyers had contracted to buy a house with a specific condition precedent that the contract was subject to the buyer receiving a conventional real estate mortgage loan. The bank involved subsequently withdrew its loan commitment and the potential buyer of the house rescinded the contract. The seller sued the bank for money damages. Is the seller a third party beneficiary of the bank's original loan commitment to the potential buyer? [*Khabbaz v. Swartz,* 319 N.W.2d 279 (Iowa 1982).]
3. Following an accident and in exchange for valuable consideration, the husband of a woman killed in the automobile accident involving another car executed releases in favor of the driver of the other car and his insurance company. The releases also contained language releasing all other possible parties in the action for damages arising from the accident. The language was: "any and all other persons, associations and corporations, whether herein named or referred to or not. . . ." The husband was represented by counsel and freely executed the releases in consideration for the sum paid. The husband then brought suit against the manufacturer of the wife's automobile for the fatal injuries. The automobile manufacturer moved for summary judgment asserting that the releases acted to prevent the husband from bringing suit against it. What type of beneficiary is the manufacturer, if any? [*White v. Gen. Motors Corp.,* 541 F.Supp. 190 (1982).]
4. Boulevard National Bank of Miami lent money to Air Metal Industries, Inc. To secure the loans, Air Metal purported to assign to the Bank certain accounts receivable it had with a contractor. At a later date Air Metal assigned as security to a surety company all its accounts receivable to reimburse the surety company in the event Air Metal defaulted on certain contracts and the surety company had to pay damages on its performance bond. In July 1963 the surety company notified the contractor of the assignment of his account, the surety having had to pay on its performance bond. In August 1963 the Bank notified the contractor of the assignment and its claim thereunder. The contractor paid remaining funds owed to Air Metal Industries, Inc. to the surety company and the Bank sues the contractor on the basis that it had the preferred and prior right to payment. What result, if we are in a jurisdiction using the English Rule? Will the Bank win? [*Boulevard Nat'l Bank of Miami v. Air Metal Indus., Inc.,* 176 S.2d 94 (Fla. 1965).]
5. In 1979 Dauterive entered into a contract to act as an exclusive franchisor of Wellcraft Marine, Inc., products through July 15, 1980. In July 1979 the "gas crunch"

hit the country and Louisiana boat dealers were particularly hard hit. In March 1980 Wellcraft established a new dealership that infringed on Dauterive's territory. When Dauterive learned of this action by Wellcraft, he sold his business and sued Wellcraft for damages for breach of the franchise agreement. One of the elements of damages sought was loss of profit. Dauterive contends he should recover the same amount of profit as he made in 1979, which was $15,850. Should Dauterive recover for loss of profits and if so, how much profit? [*Wellcraft Marine, Inc. v. Dauterive,* 482 So.2d 1002 (La. 1986).]

6. Agee engaged a law firm to examine title to unimproved property that Agee had contracted to purchase, and to effect a conveyance if title proved marketable. The law firm's attorneys engaged in real estate transactions and were aware of the inflationary trends in interest rates and construction costs. The lawyers failed to discover that there was no recorded access to the property and this delayed obtaining a bank loan commitment until an easement of necessity was awarded in a judicial action. In a subsequent suit by Agee, the law firm was required to pay as damages the increase in construction and financing costs arising from the delay in obtaining bank financing. The law firm appeals. Who wins? [*Myerberg, Sawyer & Rue, P.A., et al. v. Agee,* 446 A.2d 69 (Md. 1982).]

7. The U.S. Government entered into a contract with Bubble Up Delaware, Inc., whereby the Government would provide Bubble Up with $1,000,000, and in turn Bubble Up agreed to employ 300 hard-core unemployed persons for a period of nine months. The contract contained a damages clause that obligated Bubble Up to refund $2,500 to the Government for every employment opportunity short of 300. Is the clause a valid liquidated damages clause or an invalid penalty clause? [*In re Bubble Up Delaware, Inc.,* 684 F.2d 1259 (1982).]

8. On March 6, 1982, Southern Offshore Yachts executed a yacht purchase agreement whereby Fast agreed to buy and Southern agreed to sell a customized Tayana 37 cruising yacht, to be manufactured in Taiwan in accordance with blueprints and a customizing narration statement approved by Fast. The purchase price was $99,572. On or about October 22, 1982, Fast inspected a boat offered for delivery and found it to deviate substantially from the blueprints and specifications approved by Fast. The yacht was rejected as nonconforming. In October 1983 Fast inspected a second yacht offered for delivery and found various defects that he asked to be repaired. Upon failure to repair the boat, Fast brought an action for specific performance (delivery of the boat). Southern Offshore Yachts seeks discharge from its contract because of Fast's failure to pay the final 10 percent due under the contract under a theory of anticipatory repudiation. Should Fast get the boat? [*Fast v. Southern Offshore Yachts,* 587 F.Supp. 1354 (1984).]

9. Under date of February 12, 1962, Blethen, an assignee of Howard Manor, executed instructions addressed to Prudential Escrows of Palm Springs:

> You are . . . authorized and instructed to advise American Express, Diners Club and Carte Blanc that all sums due Howard Manor, Palm Springs, California, are to be paid direct to this **escrow,** commencing April 1, 1962 to apply on final payment of a Note owed to me.

escrow
The conditional delivery of property to a person who is to deal with it on the occurrence of specified conditions

On April 5, 1962, Continental Bank entered into a written agreement with "Howard Manor," which set forth the terms under which "Howard Manor" would sell to the bank "such assets belonging to Assignor as may be acceptable to the bank." Notice of assignment of accounts receivable by Howard Manor, assignor, to Continental Bank, assignee, was filed with the County Recorder of Riverside County on April 9,

1962. $14,506.06 of Diners Club accounts were assigned to the bank. Diners Club was not aware of the assignment by Howard Manor to the bank. Diners Club paid Prudential Escrows on its accounts who then disbursed the money to Blethen. Who had priority as to the accounts—Blethen or Continental Bank? [*Continental Bank v. Blethen,* 86 Cal.Rptr. 485 (Cal. 1970).]

10. In *Munchak Corporation v. Cunningham,* excerpted at the beginning of this section, the court enforced the assigned right to personal services by preventing the basketball player from playing basketball for any club but the Cougars. Evaluate the action by the court.

PART 2: CONTRACTS

ETHICS AND BUSINESS LAW

Introduction

This end-of-part discussion, like the others in this book, is designed to encourage you to begin forming personal beliefs about what is right or wrong conduct in business. The discussion here builds on the material in the first end-of-part discussion; you may find it helpful to review that.

This material has several goals. The overview section is designed to help you see the range of ethical issues associated with this area of the law. The in-depth discussion is intended to provide you with a background for forming your own beliefs about a single very important ethical issue in business. The problems at the end of this part are designed to build your skill in ethical analysis while exploring further the in-depth issue.

Overview of Ethical Issues in Contract Law

Promises are the heart of contract law. But is it ethical to break a promise just because it does not constitute a contract? This situation arises in a variety of ways. For example, a promise may become unenforceable because of the statute of frauds, or the statute of limitations. But do you think this changes its *moral* character? Similarly, a promise not supported by consideration may not be legally enforceable but may still constitute an *ethical* obligation. Businesspersons are frequently called on to decide whether or not they are justified in breaking a promise that is not enforceable in court.

An almost opposite ethical issue arises when legally enforceable promises are unfair. In contract law, a promise is enforceable if consideration is present, but it need not be adequate or fair. Stated another way, courts will enforce contracts even if the items exchanged are unequal in economic value. This doctrine compels persons to look out for their own self-interests. Both the legal doctrine and its consequences (making people more careful in looking out for their own self-interests) keep people out of court. But some are injured when they contract on terms that are very unfavorable. Is it ethical to enforce your contract rights if this causes financial injury to others?

Another ethical issue is associated with contractual capacity. Is it ethical for a minor to disaffirm a fair contract for the purchase of non-necessaries? This law is designed to protect those who have limited capacity, yet disaffirmance can do very serious injury to an innocent party on the other side of the contract. This presents knowledgeable persons who lack capacity with a dilemma: should they assert their legal rights when it benefits them yet injures others?

The law of remedies can be viewed as a system for defining liability for breaking your promise. In business, situations frequently arise where it is more profitable to breach and pay damages than to fulfill a contractual duty. For example, assume you contracted to deliver 10 railroad boxcars of frozen chickens at $1.75 per chicken. Then a nearby soup company encountered an emergency that caused it to offer you $2.00 per chicken. If the market value was still at $1.75, you could, assuming there were no consequential damages, breach without being liable for damages and still earn an extra 25 cents per chicken. But would this be ethical? Do additional profits justify breaking your promise? It is clear that contract law raises a range of ethical issues for businesspersons. You may find it helpful to use the evaluation process described in the first end-of-part to evaluate some of these difficult ethics problems.

In-Depth Discussion of a Basic Issue: Truth Telling

Your study of the law of contracts has also been the study of the way the courts view truth telling in the context of contract law. Fraud, concealment, and other types of misrepresentation are legal ideas that confront the ethical issue of truth telling.

► When Does Deception Constitute Lying?

Exactly when is it that we have failed to tell the truth? Obviously, when we state as true something that is untrue, we have lied. Suppose you say to me, "Please sign this lease document right now because I'm in a hurry to get home; the rental amount in the lease is $295 per month." If the rental amount stated in the lease is actually $395 and you know it and intend to deceive, then clearly you have lied (and probably committed fraud). However, once we depart from this type of clear-cut situation, truth telling and/or lying become more difficult for most of us to define.

Material Omissions Would it be lying for you to ask the prospective tenant to sign the lease after stating the true monthly rent but without disclosing that the lease agreement gave you, the landlord, the right to keep the cleaning deposit even if the apartment were left spotless at the end of the lease? In other words, is it a lie if you leave out of your description important information about the transaction?

Would it matter to you that the party injured by your material omission is someone with whom you have a relationship of trust, such as an elderly relative? Notice that the law imposes greater obligations on fiduciaries—those who occupy positions of trust. Can you ethically justify treating strangers differently from those you know better?

Concealment Do you think your obligation to tell the whole story is increased because someone has asked a question about a particular issue such as the cleaning deposit? Can you justify not telling the tenant about the cleaning deposit clause in the lease on the grounds that the tenant failed to ask?

Fraudulent Misrepresentation Suppose I ask you, "How much will the utilities for the apartment cost?" If you do not know, would it be a lie for you to say, "They are about average for an apartment this size"?

Puffing There are truth-telling issues associated with the use of broad, flowery language such as, "It is a *wonderful* place for you to live!" "Wonderful" is a very vague term. Courts call such terms puffing. Generally, people are not liable for false puffing. If you knew the noise, distractions, price, and distance from campus made your apartment a bad place for this tenant to live, would the vagueness of the term "wonderful" make it ethical for you to use it?

Affirmative Nondisclosure If someone clearly misunderstands reality, and you are doing business with them, are you obligated to correct their perception? Suppose I said to you, "I like the apartment because it is only twenty-five minutes from campus." If you knew that during most times of the day the actual travel time in congested traffic was sixty-five minutes, would you be lying if you remained silent?

► Asserted Justifications for Lying

A Right to the Truth Many people believe that they are not obligated to give information to everyone. Thus if the owner of a competing apartment building asked you for information about the rental rates in your building, do you think you have a duty to disclose that information? Most people would say, no. Some of these people conclude that since there is not a right to the information, we can also deceive the competitor, perhaps by giving him wrong information about our rental rates. Do you think this is ethical?

Protecting Others Sometimes people lie to others to protect their feelings. Suppose I say, "I am sure I will meet lots of members of the opposite sex in this apartment complex whom I can date, don't you think so?" If you think I will not because I am an unappealing person, should you tell me so? Would it be ethically wrong to lie to me by agreeing with my statement? Do you think it makes any difference if your reason, or motive, for lying to me were to rent the apartment rather than to protect my feelings?

Profits In business, the most frequent justification for lying is profits. When there is money to be made by legal lying, many will do it. Will you?

Ethical Reasoning About Truth Telling

► Markets

The market assumes that the parties to business transactions have complete information about both the market and the particular transaction. If one party lacks this information, it is called a *market imperfection*. When a market imperfection is present, the market may not achieve all of its moral goals. It is clear that markets are based upon the assumption of truth telling.

► The Law

The legal system generally seeks the same objectives as the market when it regulates business conduct. Legislative and judicial penalties for fraud, concealment, and other types of misrepresentation promote truth telling in business transactions. But the legal and market systems are imperfect. They do not always compel the conduct that they were intended to foster. Thus it is often profitable to lie.

► Consequential Ethical Reasoning

For many persons, whether or not one may lie is based on the results of the lying. If these people are purely self-interested, they are egoists who may lie only if there is a benefit to them. Additional rental income would be such a benefit. Of course more sophisticated egoists would refuse to lie because they fear a reputation for lying will cause them injury resulting in loss of benefits.

Others who look at consequences judge the impact of lying on *all* the people affected not just themselves. These people are *utilitarians*. Thus a utilitarian might decline to lie if it would injure the tenant and his family of five. That might be because only one landlord is benefited while five tenants are injured.

Kantian Philosophy and Religious Ethics

Some people embrace certain things as "good" in and of themselves, without regard for the consequences. Truth telling is one of these. The Kantian is always under a duty to tell the truth without regard for the consequences.

Similarly, those who hold religious beliefs judge truth telling to be fundamentally good. Religious writings from the Bible, to the Koran, to the Gita all condemn lying.

Solving Ethics Problems

Like the other end-of-part discussions in this book, this one presents problems for you to consider. These problems have three goals. The first is to give you the opportunity to further explore the in-depth issue. The second goal is to give you experience in ethical reasoning about the law and about related management problems. The third goal is to let you see how thinking critically about the law can increase your ability to make ethical decisions. To facilitate this, the problems begin by asking you to analyze the law for its ethical content and then shift to looking at related problems in managerial ethics.

For a discussion of the ethical roles of markets and the law and examples of the four styles of ethical reasoning—egoism, utilitarianism, Kantian philosophy, and religious ethics—read the business ethics material at the end of Part 1.

Problems

1. In *Dalton v. Bundy,* discussed in Chapter 10 (p. 195), the Bundy parents placed the title of their home in the name of their 12-year-old daughter, Janet Bundy. Later they contracted for the purchase of vinyl siding for $3,380 for the house. After the siding was installed, they declared bankruptcy. The seller of the vinyl siding sued Janet for the value of the siding. Janet defended by asserting her minority and prevailed. Assess the conduct of Janet's parents using the four styles of ethical reasoning. Do you think the conduct of the Bundy parents was a form of lying? If you conclude they engaged in deception, how do you reconcile that ethical conclusion with the outcome of this case? Is the law here attempting to balance another ethical good against the ethical good of truth telling? Can you articulate what the other "good" is?
2. In May of 1978, the St. George, Staten Island, Branch of Citibank conducted a "Fire Sale Promotion" offering free checking to new customers opening a Citibank checking and savings account along with a checking plus line of credit. The only advertisements of this promotional campaign were signs in windows and on counters of the Staten Island branch. In August of 1979, the bank decided to terminate the free checking privileges of selected depositors. Did the bank's signs misrepresent the nature of its offer by failing to disclose its reserved right to terminate free checking at its own discretion? Is the bank's conduct ethical?
3. In *McBride v. City of McCook,* discussed in Chapter 12 (pp. 226–27), the city advertised in the local newspaper a job opening that would purportedly last for a period of 18 months. McBride took the job but was terminated after just five months. When McBride sued for the loss of income for the other 13 months, the city asserted the statute of frauds, stating that since the contract required more than one year to complete and there was no writing, the purported 18-month contract was unenforceable. Who won the lawsuit? Assume that there was an oral agreement for a job

for 18 months, then assess the conduct of the city using the four styles of ethical reasoning. Do *you* think the city acted ethically? If you conclude that the city acted unethically, how do you reconcile this with the outcome of the case? Do you think the law is sometimes compelled to have arbitrary rules even if they lead to unfair results in a minority of situations?

4. Joe is the owner of a small manufacturing firm. A retailer is interested in purchasing 100 air compressors from Joe for immediate delivery. The retailer is pressed for time and asks Joe about prior safety testing, price, terms of credit, the tank's capacity, and the delivery schedule. Joe responds truthfully to nearly all the inquiries, but he intentionally omits discussing safety testing because there has not been any. The retailer is in such a hurry that he does not notice the omission. Assess Joe's conduct using the four styles of ethical reasoning.

INTERNATIONAL DIMENSIONS

The contract to buy and sell goods is the starting point of international trade.

Offer and Acceptance

An international sales contract comes into being when one party, the exporter, makes an offer to the other party, the importer, and the importer accepts it. The offer and the acceptance have to match for the agreement to be formalized.

The principle of offer and acceptance is simple, but in practice, it is often more complex. For example, Ed, an exporter, sends out his quotation on a standard form incorporating his general conditions. Irene, an importer, accepts the offer but sends her reply on a form referring to her own standard purchasing conditions. The two sets of conditions—those of Ed and those of Irene—will likely differ on various points.

Under most legal systems, it will be considered that no enforceable agreement has come into being in such a situation. The conditional "acceptance" in this example (Irene's reply on her own form) is a counteroffer that the other party may accept or refuse. If Ed reacts by sending the goods without mentioning the conditions, he has probably implicitly agreed to Irene's terms.

Form of the Contract

In general, export agreements do not have to follow any particular form, although the precise requirements vary from one country to another. In many countries a legally binding contract arises from an agreement between the exporter and the importer that can be manifested in many different ways: a formal document, a series of telexes, an exchange of messages between computers, a telephone conversation or simply an oral agreement during contact at a trade fair. In other countries—for example, in Eastern Europe—contracts must usually be written documents.

Consideration

Most commercial contracts impose obligations on both parties in the trading transaction. One party supplies a product (the exporter); the other pays (the importer). English law gives considerable importance to this simple merchant principle and refuses to recognize contracts unless they are clearly two-sided in this way. This is called the "doctrine of consideration." Over the years, however, so many exceptions to the doctrine have been allowed that the exceptions almost outweigh the principle.

The doctrine is also applied in varying degrees by countries such as the United States and Australia that inherited the principles of English law (often referred to as the "common law" tradition).

Other countries such as France and Italy have modelled their legal systems on Roman law principles (referred to as the "civil law" countries) and do not apply this concept. However, they have another doctrine that affects contracts: the theory of "cause." The general idea behind this concept is that contracts should enjoy the blessing of judicial recognition only if they have some serious purpose and are not contrary to the public good.

Many developing countries that inherited aspects of their legal systems from one of the former colonial powers are also affected by one or the other of these doctrines.

Trade Terms and the Contract

Export sales revolve around the movement of goods from one country to another. How to divide the costs and risks of that movement of goods between the exporter and the importer is one of the most important questions to be resolved by the contract of sale.

Standard codifications called trade terms help to resolve this problem. The parties choose the most appropriate term from the list and refer to it in their contract. The best known of these codifications is a set of provisions called "Incoterms," drawn up by the International Chamber of Commerce (ICC). The Swedish freight forwarders association offers a variant referred to as "Combiterms," which adds detailed cost breakdowns to the basic ICC provisions.

The main trade bodies in the United States have recommended use of the Incoterms since they were most recently revised in 1980. However, many U.S. exporters still apply the Revised American Foreign Trade Definitions of 1941. These adopt many of the same titles as Incoterms (such as FOB—"free on board") but interpret them differently.

The socialist countries of Eastern Europe apply the general conditions of contract of the Council for Mutual Economic Assistance (CMEA) for trade among each other. They use Incoterms for business transactions with non-CMEA trading partners.

Performance Payment Under a Contract

Trade terms describe how goods are to be delivered, but they leave many important questions unanswered. For example, they do not say when ownership switches from the exporter to the importer, or when and how payment is to be made.

If the exporter and the importer do not deal with points such as payment expressly in their sales agreement, these questions will be regulated by the law applicable to the contract.

Reference should be made to Part 12, "Business Law in the International Marketplace," where the legal aspects of engaging in transnational business and the United Nations Convention on Contracts for the International Sale of Goods are analyzed and discussed.

PART 3

AGENCY AND EMPLOYMENT

18 TERMINATION OF AGENCY

Terminating the agency relationship by acts of the parties, by operation of law, and when equity and fairness require. How the law prevents premature termination of the agency relationship.

19 EMPLOYMENT

Various state and federal laws affecting employers and employees, employer use of detection tests, and unfair discrimination against women in the workforce because of their sex. Labor law is covered in Chapter 36.

PREVIEW

An agency relationship is created by agreement for the purpose of transacting business affairs by one party with a person acting on behalf of another. The primary objective of the agency is to give authority and power to an agent to create a contract between the principal and a third person. In the process, various rights, duties, and liabilities are created on the part of the principal, agent, and third person.

As with other legal relationships, the law provides for termination of the agency relationship through freedom of individual action and by operation of law.

Any discussion of employment involves not only the agency relationship between employer and employee, covered in Chapters 15–18, but also an examination of the regard that society has for employees as reflected in federal and state legislation affecting their employment, protection from injury, compensation for injury, and financial security. Chapter 19 is concerned with such legislation.

Business ethics as it relates to the material in these chapters is considered at the end of the part, as are international dimensions of these topics.

CHAPTER

15

NATURE AND CREATION OF AGENCY

After you have read this chapter, you should be able to:

1. Define the agency relationship and identify the source of agency law.
2. Describe the relationship of agency law to business transactions.
3. Understand how an agent's conduct may affect the liabilities of the agent, the principal, and the third person.
4. Explain why it is important to determine whether an agent is a servant.
5. Distinguish an agent from
   a) An independent contractor
   b) A real estate broker
   c) A bailee
   d) A trustee
6. Distinguish a general power of attorney from a limited power of attorney.
7. Describe the relationship of agency law to business associations.
8. Explain who may be a principal and who may be an agent.
9. Distinguish a general from a special agent.
10. Explain how an agency is created.
11. Define ratification and describe its five elements.
12. Explain who must prove the agency relationship.

BUSINESS DECISIONS and the LAW

Consider this scenario: Mary and Sam both work for Leslie, the sole proprietor of a consulting firm. Leslie, while driving to work, is struck by a car, which leaves her mentally and physically incapacitated. Who may immediately assume responsibility for the business? Leslie's husband? Mary and Sam, because they were Leslie's agents and employees? Leslie's attorney? Answer: It depends upon whom Leslie chose in a durable power of attorney.

This instrument is defined as a statutory written power of attorney conferred on the agent by the principal, which is not affected by the principal's subsequent disability or incapacity. (This is in contrast to the common law power of attorney, which terminates upon the principal's disability or incapacity.)

This simple inexpensive document is essential in a complete estate plan and is especially useful in the business setting. In the case of a business, the durable power of attorney makes the transition after such disability orderly since it is clear who is to succeed the principal. The agent in a durable power of attorney is able to go beyond mere bill paying if the parties so designate. The principal may grant powers as broad as he or she desires. In our hypothetical case, Leslie could name one or all of these parties as agents in a durable power of attorney—or she might decide to look outside this group altogether.

This chapter will explain the various types of powers of attorney and their application to business transactions.

Introduction

agent
A person authorized to act on behalf of another and subject to the other's control

agency
A legal relationship between two persons who agree that one is to act on behalf of the other, subject to the other's control

All around us are **agents,** persons acting on behalf of others. During your business career and private life you will have various dealings with agents. As an employee, you may be involved as an agent in the selling of goods or services to the general public. As a consumer, you will go to the marketplace for your "daily bread" and there deal with persons representing others. In these transactions the work process is delivered to society through the "hands of agents."

Because the laws of **agency** enter into all forms of business activity, this chapter will explain the nature of the agency relationship within the corporation, partnership, and sole proprietorship.

The rights and duties of the parties involved in agency create a series of potential lawsuits. This chapter will examine and illustrate this liability exposure.

In order for you to recognize an agency problem, it is necessary to distinguish other types of somewhat similar business relationships. This chapter will explain the reasons for the difference based upon agency law.

An important point to watch for in the chapter is how the law applies the value judgment that someone who uses another person to create rights and duties should be liable for the consequences of that other person's acts.

Nature of the Agency Relationship

► Agency Concept

Business associations rely on their employees and other representatives to contract and to act on the association's behalf in the delivering of goods and services. The relationships formed by this process have legal consequences governed by agency law.

► Source of Agency Law

principal
A person who has authorized an agent to act on his or her behalf and subject to his or her control

The source of agency law is the common law created through each state's judicial system where the agency agreement was made.[1] Rights and duties conflict in this three-party relationship (the business or individual is referred to as the **principal** in agency law; the representative acting under the authority and on behalf of the principal is called the *agent;* and the person with whom the agent contracts is called the *third party*). The courts, in resolving these disputes, establish a body of law relevant to almost every business transaction. To a much lesser extent, statutes assist in the creation of agency law. Statutory laws have adopted agency principles to provide a legislative remedy to aggrieved parties.

Throughout Part 3, reference will be made to the Restatement of Agency, which is an authoritative general compilation of the common law of agency throughout the country and constantly referred to in judicial decisions and opinions.

Business Organizations and Agency Law

Agreements that are commonly made in dealings with business associations frequently involve agency issues. For example, a salesperson (agent) who contracts with the

---

[1] Restatement (Second) of Conflict of Laws sec. 291 (1969).

customer (third party), on behalf of a company (principal), is acting pursuant to an agency relationship, and a consequent series of rights and duties arises for all parties to the transaction.

The laws governing the *operation* of the corporation, partnership, and the sole proprietorship illustrate the application of agency laws.

Corporations

The **corporation** is an artificial person or legal entity created by law.[2] State statutory law has authorized it to deliver goods and services through the "hands of agents" acting on its behalf. Ordinarily, the officers of a corporation and certain other designated employees are those agents through whom the corporation acts.[3] The board of directors is not an agent of the corporation because it is not under the direct control of the stockholders, and the board makes its own managerial decisions.[4]

corporation
A legal entity created by statute authorizing an association of persons to carry on an enterprise

Partnerships

Partnerships are governed by the Uniform Partnership Act[5] and the owners' partnership agreement. The UPA sec. 9(1) provides: "Every partner is an agent of the partnership for the purpose of its business . . ." and thus establishes the statutory foundation for the application of agency law to partnership transactions.[6]

partnership
An association of two or more persons to carry on as co-owners of a business for profit

Sole Proprietorships

A sole proprietor has the legal right to and exclusive ownership of his or her business. The agency relationship occurs when the proprietor owner hires employees or other representatives to contract with customers on the proprietor's behalf. For example, a real estate broker who owns houses (principal) hires a salesperson (agent) to sell the houses. The contract that the agent (salesperson) makes with the buyer (third person) to sell the buyer a house will bind the proprietor principal (broker).

Most business transactions involve one person acting for another person and, therefore, agency law applies. All parties concerned in the agency relationship should understand the legal consequences of their actions. This chapter will help you to identify the agency issues.

---

[2]BLACK'S LAW DICTIONARY 307 (5th ed. 1979); in this book, see Part 8B, Business Organizations: Corporations; in *Trustees of Dartmouth College v. Woodward,* 4 Wheat (U.S.) 518,636, 4 L.Ed. 629,659 (1819), Chief Justice Marshall stated, "A corporation is an artificial being, intangible, and existing only in contemplation of law."

[3]Revised Model Business Corporation Act, sec. 3.02, General Powers: "Each corporation shall have power to conduct its business, carry on its operations, . . . to elect directors and appoint officers, employees, and agents of the corporation [and] define their duties . . .;" and *Phoenix Sav. and Loan, Inc. v. Aetna Casualty & Surety Co.,* 266 F.Supp. 465 (1966).

[4]RESTATEMENT (SECOND) OF AGENCY sec. 14C. (1958): "Neither the board of directors nor an individual director . . . is an agent of the corporation."

[5]The Act has been adopted in all states except Louisiana.

[6]See Part 8A, Business Organizations: General Partnerships and Special Ventures.

Definition of Agency

fiduciary
A person with a duty to act primarily for the benefit of another

Agency is a **fiduciary** relationship based upon an express or implied agreement whereby one party (the agent) is authorized to act on behalf and under the control of another (the principal) when the agent consents so to act.[7] Basically, agency is a legal relationship between two persons who agree that one (agent) is to act on behalf of the other (principal), subject to the other's control. Throughout Part 3, we will often use the following abbreviations: *P* (principal), *A* (agent), *T* (third party). This relationship may be diagrammed as in Figure 15.1.

Liability under the Agency Relationship

Although agency may appear to be a simple legal relationship, the following examples illustrate possible grounds for liability through agency.

authority
An agent's power to act for the principal in accordance with the principal's manifestation of consent to the agent

actual authority
Express and implied authority

apparent authority
The power of a person (*A*) to act as though *A* were an agent, created by another's (*P*'s) manifestation to a third person (*T*) that *A* is *P*'s agent

► *T* v. *P*

The intended result of creating an agency is to make the principal liable and to protect the agent from personal liability to third parties. When an agent acts within the scope of the agent's **actual** or **apparent authority** and makes a contract with a third party on behalf of a disclosed principal, the agent is not liable on the contract to either the third party or the principal. Only the principal is liable to the third party.

Whether a principal is a disclosed principal, partially disclosed principal, or an undisclosed principal depends upon the knowledge of the third party (*T*). If *T* knows or reasonably should know:

1. that *A* is an agent for a principal and *T* knows who the principal is, the latter is a disclosed principal;
2. that *A* is an agent for a principal but *T* does not know who the principal is, the latter is a partially disclosed principal;

FIGURE 15.1 **Relationships among Principal, Agent, and Third Party**

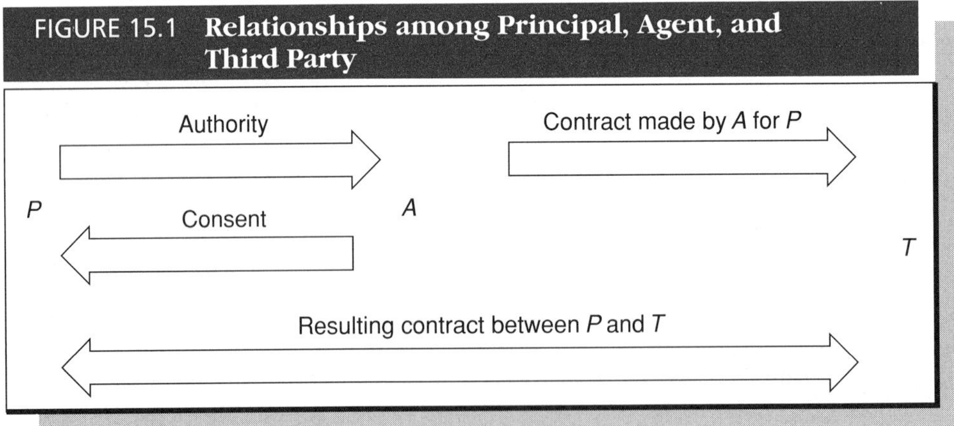

[7] Restatement (Second) of Agency sec. 1 (1958); and *Tonka Corp. v. Commissioner of Taxation,* 169 N.W.2d 589, 593 (Minn. 1969).

3. if *T* does not know or reasonably should not know that *A* is an agent for a principal, the latter is an undisclosed principal. (See p. 328 for the libility of an undisclosed principal.)

The law of agency applicable to disclosed principals is, generally, equally applicable to partially disclosed principals, except that both the agent and the partially disclosed principal generally are parties to the contract with a third person.

► *P* v. *T*

If an authorized agent makes a contract on behalf of a disclosed principal, the resulting contract is between *P* and *T*; and *P* may sue *T* for its breach. For example, the business association (*P*) may sue on its contract with a customer (*T*) authorizedly made by its salesperson (*A*). (*A* is a salesperson for *P*'s shoe store and sells a pair of shoes to *T*, who is now liable to *P* for the price.)

► *T* v. *A*

The agent must carefully comply with agency law or the agent may incur personal liability for making an authorized contract. For example, if the agent does not disclose the principal or the agency status but purports to act on the agent's own behalf, the agent is a party to the contract with *T*.

The agent may also be personally liable for committing a tort against the third party. For example, a principal instructs an agent to slander a competitor, which the agent does.

► *A* v. *T*

The agent may sue the third party in contract or in tort in certain circumstances. The third party is liable to the agent in contract if the agent did not disclose to the third party that the agent was acting for a principal. The third party intended to contract with the agent and, therefore, the third party is liable to the agent on the contract.

The third party is liable to the agent in tort if the third party wrongfully injures the agent or the agent's property.

► *A* v. *P*

The agent normally has an employment contract with the principal and can sue the principal for its breach. For example, *P* may wrongfully discharge or not pay *A* a due commission. It should be carefully noted that, under Section 441 of the Restatement (Second) of Agency: "Unless the relationship of the parties, the triviality of the services, or other circumstances indicate that the parties have agreed otherwise, it is inferred that (*P*) promises to pay for services which he requests or permits another to perform for him as an agent."

► *P* v. *A*

When the principal authorizes the agent to act on the principal's behalf, various legal duties come into existence obligating the agent to perform in a certain manner. Violation of these implied fiduciary duties will allow the principal to sue the agent. The next chapter will discuss these duties.

► Employer and Employee or Master and Servant Relationship

To the extent that a person has the right of control, or exercises control, over another person, he or she is liable for the other person's conduct. The principal's control may or may not be over the agent's *physical* conduct. If control is not over physical conduct, then the principal is not liable for the agent's physical conduct. (*P* retains *A,* a real estate broker, to produce a willing and able buyer of *P*'s house and land. *A* drives his own car negligently and hits *X,* a pedestrian. *P* is not liable to *X;* only *A* is liable to *X. P* did not have the right to control the physical conduct of *A,* a special agent, in driving *A*'s automobile.)

However, if a principal has the right to control, or exercises control, over the physical conduct of the principal's agent, the principal is liable to third persons for physical harm caused to them by the agent's wrongful physical conduct. Such an agent is called a "servant," or often "employee," and the principal is called a "master," or often "employer." (*P*'s truck driver negligently drives into *T* while delivering *P*'s goods. Since *P* has the right to control *A*'s physical conduct, *A* is a servant and *P* is liable to *T* for *T*'s physical injury caused by *A*'s negligence.) Most agents are servants.

The terms of master and servant are used in the employment relationship only to determine the liability of an employer principal for the physical harm caused to third persons by the servant employee's torts. This legal relationship exists when the master (principal) controls the physical conduct of the servant (agent). The master is held responsible for the negligence of the servant causing the physical injury to the third party[8] while the servant was acting within the scope of his or her employment.[9]

Agency Distinguished from Other Business Relationships

► Independent Contractor

independent contractor

A person who contracts independently for him- or herself to render a result, and who is not acting on behalf of another nor subject to another's control

For agency to exist, the principal must have the right to exercise control, or actually exercise control, over the agent. An **independent contractor** hired to accomplish a physical result is not an agent primarily because the independent contractor is not under the supervision and control of the hiring party. Independent contractors act independently on their own and make their own contracts. Notice the court's reasoning in the following case in making the legal distinction between employees and independent contractors.

FACTS

Hall hired Davey, who was the partner of Amear, to work around his house. Hall would tell Davey what needed to be done, and then Davey or Amear would accomplish the work. Davey and Amear controlled their own hours and methods of doing the work. Hall asked Davey to install fiberglass over spaces formed by exposed beams connecting the carport and the house. It was Amear's idea to climb out on the beams to install it. Once he was on the beams, he fell and severly injured himself. Amear claimed that he was an employee and that Hall had failed to provide and maintain safe working conditions. Hall claimed that Amear was an independent contractor. The trial court entered judgment in favor of Hall, and Amear appealed.

DECISION

Judgment of the trial court affirmed. The test in determining whether a person employed is a servant or an independent contractor is whether the employer, under the contract, whether oral or written, has the right to direct the time, the manner, the methods, and the means of the execution of the work. The evi-

---

[8]*Smalich v. Westfall,* 269 A.2d 476 (Pa. 1970).

[9]See pp. 330–33 for a full discussion of the master-servant relationship.

dence demanded a finding that Amear was an independent contractor.

An individual contractor is expected to determine for himself whether his place of employment is safe or unsafe, and ordinarily may not recover against the owner for injuries sustained in the performance of the contract. Unless the owner and an injured employee have a relationship of master/servant, the employer is generally not responsible for injuries occasioned by the methods by which work is done by the employee. It is also the general rule that the employer is under no duty to take affirmative steps to guard or protect the individual contractor's employees against the consequences of the contractor's negligence or to provide for their safety.

Amear v. Hall, 296 S.E.2d 611 (Georgia 1982).

An independent contractor may become an agent if he or she is subject to the control of the principal in the performance of service. The degree of control the principal exercises over the hired party is decisive, and the courts will disregard the professional status of the hired party and examine the facts of the situation on the issue of control.

Some independent contractors retain their status when retained to act. Examples are doctors, certified public accountants, and engineers. If control should be exercised over their conduct, then they become agents. Examples are hiring a doctor to be an employee in the employer's plant, hiring the CPA as the treasurer or comptroller of a firm, and hiring the engineer as a member of the employer's staff.

Some independent contractors lose this status as such while they are retained to do a job; they become agents. Examples are lawyers, real estate **brokers, auctioneers,** and **factors.** They become "special agents" or "professional agents."

broker
A person authorized to represent another and to negotiate for him or her with others

auctioneer
A person licensed by law to sell property of another at a public sale

factor
A person in business for him- or herself with authority to buy goods, or to sell goods in his or her possession, in his or her own name for another

Real Estate Broker A real estate broker is licensed by the state to represent sellers in the sale of their real property (land). The broker is compensated for this service on a commission basis. A real estate broker has very limited authority—generally to state the asking price and identify the owner's property—and in such capacity the broker is an agent. The broker may be given authority to represent the seller and to contract on the seller's behalf rather than just to negotiate for the seller.[10]

► Bailee

Bailed property is goods delivered by a bailor to another (the bailee) to be returned to the bailor or as the bailor directs.[11] As business associations continue to rent equipment, the incidents of bailed property become very common. A bailee is not an agent, but he or she can become an agent if the bailee has possession with authority to buy, sell, or otherwise deal with the bailed goods on behalf of the bailor.

bailment
Delivery of goods by a bailor to a bailee, which are to be returned to the bailor or as the bailor directs, in accordance with the bailment agreement

► Trustee

A **trustee**[12] is a party to whom the legal title of property has been transferred for the purpose of managing the property for a beneficiary. Although the trustee acts on behalf of the beneficiary, generally the trustee is not an agent because of the following factors:

trustee
A person who holds title to property in trust for the benefit of someone

[10] *Knudson v. Weeks,* 394 F.Supp. 963 (Okla. 1975).

[11] See Part 4, Personal Property and Bailments; see also *English v. Dhane,* 286 S.W.2d 666 (Tex. 1956).

[12] See Part 11, Wills and Decedents' Estates, and Trusts, Chapter 55.

1. The trustee has title to the property held in trust, while an agent normally does not have title to any property.
2. The trustee does not have authority to make the beneficiary a party to a contract with anyone, while an agent has the authority to make the disclosed principal a party to the contract.
3. The trustee acts in its own name as trustee, while the agent usually acts in the name of the principal.
4. The trust is not revocable by the trustee, while an agency usually is revocable by the agent or the principal.[13]

However, in a grantor/trust the grantor (the transferor of the property) has the right to control the management of the property during the grantor's life. In this instance and to that extent, the trustee to whom the property has been transferred is an agent of the grantor. For a trustee to be an agent, the trustee must, under the terms of the trust, be subject to the control of another. The grantor is a **settlor** here, transferring property to a trustee and creating an express **trust.**

settlor
The person who has created an express trust

trust
A legal device whereby legal title to property is held by one person (a trustee) for the benefit of a beneficiary

The following case illustrates that the settlor, unlike a principal, has no control over the trustee nor the property in the trust unless the trust instrument so provides.

FACTS

On September 29, 1965, the settlor gave the lessee-optionee, defendant, a 50-year lease and an option to purchase, during the sixth year of the lease, on 31 acres of land. On March 1, 1971, the settlor granted the lessee-optionee a 5-year extension of its option to September 29, 1976. On December 6, 1973, the settlor conveyed the property to the trustee, plaintiff, in trust for various members of his family, signing a trust agreement and conveying the property to the trustee by a warranty deed, which was promptly recorded. The lessee-optionee had actual notice of the creation of the trust by at least April, 1975, when it began making its monthly lease payments directly to the trustee. On March 1, 1976, the settlor signed an instrument purporting to grant the lessee-optionee another five-year extension of its option to September 29, 1981. The trustee was unaware of this action and did not participate in it. On July 3, 1979, the trustee brought this action against the lessee-optionee to determine the validity of the attempted extension of the last option. Can a settlor who has created a trust by conveying property that is subject to an option to sell thereafter extend the period of the option without the participation or consent of the trustee?

DECISION

No. Judgment for the plaintiff, trustee. A trust is a form of ownership in which the legal title to property is vested in a trustee, who has equitable duties to hold and manage it for the benefit of the beneficiaries. The trustee under a valid trust deed has exclusive control of the trust property, subject only to the limitations imposed by law or the trust instrument. Once the settlor has created the trust, he is no longer the owner of the trust property and has only such ability to deal with it as is expressly reserved to him in the trust instrument. If we gave legal effect to the settlor's extension of this option in contravention of the existence and terms of the trust, we would prejudice the interests of the beneficiaries, blur some fundamental principles of trust law, and cast doubt upon whether it is the trustee or the settlor who is empowered to manage and dispose of the trust property in a valid revocable trust.

Continental Bank & Trust Company v. Country Club Mobile Estates, 632 P.2d 869 (Utah 1981).

[13]*Cassedy v. Connecticut Gen. Life Ins. Co.*, 56 Misc. 2d 970 (N.Y. 1968); and RESTATEMENT (SECOND) OF TRUSTS sec. 8 (1957).

Power of Attorney

A written authorization to act as an agent is called a **power of attorney.** There are two types based upon the extent of the authority given to the agent: the limited power of attorney and the full, or general, power of attorney.

power of attorney
Written authority by a principal to an agent

► Limited Power of Attorney

When the power to act or contract is restricted to a certain period of time and to specific transactions, it is a *limited power of attorney*. (See Figure 15.2.) For example, *P* authorizes *A* to withdraw a specified amount of money from *P*'s personal checking account while *P* is in the hospital. The restrictions here are to a certain amount and during hospitalization.

► General Power of Attorney

An authorization to do any and all things necessary to carry on with the principal's legal affairs is a *general power of attorney*. (See Figure 15.3.) In the following case notice how the court strictly interprets the terms of the power of attorney.

FACTS

A general power of attorney executed by Bankerd authorized King to "convey, grant, bargain and/or sell" the subject property "on such terms as to him may seem best." The single issue presented in this case is whether a power of attorney authorizing the agent to "convey, grant, bargain and/or sell" the principal's property authorizes the agent to make a gratuitous transfer of that property.

DECISION

Broadly defined, a power of attorney is a written document by which one party, as principal, appoints another as agent (attorney in fact) and confers upon the latter the authority to perform certain specified acts or kinds of acts on behalf of the principal. This instrument, which delineates the extent of the agent's authority, is a contract of agency that creates a principal-agent relationship. An agent holding a broad power of attorney lacks the power to make a gift of the principal's property, unless that power (1) is expressly conferred, (2) arises as a necessary implication from the conferred powers, or (3) is clearly intended by the parties, as evidenced by the surrounding facts and circumstances.

Because an agent must act for the benefit of his principal, we decline to interpret this broad, all-encompassing language as authority for the agent to make a gift of the principal's property.

King v. Bankerd, 492 A.2d 608 (1985).

► Durable Power of Attorney

The common law provides for the termination of a power of attorney upon the principal's incapacity. (See pp. 345–47.) This rule presents two potential problems: (1) the agent may be held personally liable on a contract made with a third party on behalf of an incompetent principal under the agent's implied warranty to the third party that the agent's principal has contractual capacity; and (2) the principal's intent to provide for the management of his or her assets in the event of an emergency physical or mental disability will not be accomplished.

To resolve this dilemma, the majority of states authorize by statute a **durable power of attorney** defined in the Uniform Probate Code as a writing that "contains the words 'this Power of Attorney shall not be affected by the subsequent disability or incapacity of

durable power of attorney
A statutory written power of attorney that will not terminate upon the principal's incapacity

FIGURE 15.2 Limited Power of Attorney

Form **2848** (Rev. October 1982) Department of the Treasury Internal Revenue Service

Power of Attorney and Declaration of Representative
▶ See separate instructions

OMB No. 1545-0150
Expires 9-30-85

Part I Power of Attorney

Taxpayer(s) name, identifying number, and address including ZIP code (Please type or print)

For IRS Use Only	
File So.	
Level	
Receipt	
Powers	
Blind T.	
Action	
Ret. Ind.	

hereby appoints (name(s), CAF number(s), address(es), including ZIP code(s), and telephone number(s) of individual(s))*

as attorney(s)-in-fact to represent the taxpayer(s) before any office of the Internal Revenue Service for the following tax matter(s) (specify the type(s) of tax and year(s) or period(s) (date of death if estate tax)):

Type of tax (Individual, corporate, etc.)	Federal tax form number (1040, 1120, etc.)	Year(s) or period(s) (Date of death if estate tax)

The attorney(s)-in-fact (or either of them) are authorized, subject to revocation, to receive confidential information and to perform any and all acts that the principal(s) can perform with respect to the above specified tax matters (excluding the power to receive refund checks, and the power to sign the return (see regulations section 1.6012–1(a)(5), Returns made by agents), unless specifically granted below).

Send copies of notices and other written communications addressed to the taxpayer(s) in proceedings involving the above tax matters to:

1 ☐ the appointee first named above, or
2 ☐ (names of not more than two of the above named appointees) ....

Initial here ▶ .... if you are granting the power to receive, but not to endorse or cash, refund checks for the above tax matters to:

3 ☐ the appointee first named above, or
4 ☐ (name of one of the above designated appointees) ▶

This power of attorney revokes all earlier powers of attorney and tax information authorizations on file with the Internal Revenue Service for the same tax matters and years or periods covered by this power of attorney, except the following:

(Specify to whom granted, date, and address including ZIP code, or refer to attached copies of earlier powers and authorizations.)

Signature of or for taxpayer(s)
(If signed by a corporate officer, partner, or fiduciary on behalf of the taxpayer, I certify that I have the authority to execute this power of attorney on behalf of the taxpayer.)

(Signature) (Title, if applicable) (Date)

(Signature) (Title, if applicable) (Date)

*An organization, firm, or partnership may not be designated as a taxpayer's representative.

For Privacy Act and Paperwork Reduction Act Notice, see page 1 of separate instructions. Form **2848** (Rev. 10-82)

FIGURE 15.3 **General Power of Attorney**

GENERAL POWER OF ATTORNEY

1. *Appointment of Attorney-In-Fact.* KNOW ALL MEN BY THESE PRESENTS, that I, ... , residing at . . . . make, constitute, and appoint . . . . , residing at . . . . to be my lawful attorney-in-fact for me and to do any and all acts which I could do if personally present.

2. *No Limitation on Attorney-In-Fact's Powers.* I intend to give my attorney-in-fact the fullest powers possible and do not intend, by the enumeration of his powers to limit or reduce them in any fashion.

3. *Enumeration of Attorney-In-Fact's Powers.* Among the powers granted to my attorney-in-fact are:

(a) *Receive Goods and Money.* To demand and sue for and recover and receive all debts, rents, interest, money, goods, and chattels due to me or that may become due to me or which belong to me or to which I may be entitled to possession. In connection with these powers my attorney-in-fact is authorized to execute and deliver receipts, releases, and discharges. My attorney-in-fact is also empowered to make, endorse, accept, or deliver in my name or his name commercial paper, agreements, and other instruments that he deems necessary to carry out the powers granted to him by these presents.

(b) *Conduct Business.* To carry on the business of . . . . presently conducted by me under the trade name ". . . . ." at . . . . In connection with the conduct of my business, my attorney-in-fact may recover all debts due or that become due to the business, pay all debts that the business may owe or which may become due to others, enter into agreements and other written instruments, employ people to further the conduct of the business, pay all taxes due from the business, and do all other acts that my attorney-in-fact deems necessary to carry on the business.

(c) *Appear in Actions and Suits.* To appear, answer, and defend all actions and suits that may be brought against me in my name, and in my stead, to compromise, settle or adjust them or any other claims against me in any manner that my attorney-in-fact deems proper.

(d) *Sell, Transfer, or Purchase Securities.* To purchase, sell, or transfer stocks and bonds of any kind in my name or that of my attorney-in-fact and to execute and deliver any instruments required in connection with the purchase, sale, or transfer.

(e) *Manage Real Estate.* To take possession of any real estate that belongs to me or to which I may be entitled to possession and to receive any rents or profits that may be due from the real estate. In connection with these powers, my attorney-in-fact is empowered to enter into new leases for any term, renew or extend existing leases for any term, and to sell, convey, or mortgage any real estate affected by these presents. My attorney-in-fact is also empowered to commence and prosecute for me and in my name any suits or actions for the recovery of the possession of any real estate belonging to me or to which I may be entitled and for the rents and profits due from such real estate or from any other real estate which is the subject of these presents.

(f) *Appoint Other Attorneys-In-Fact.* To constitute. appoint. and authorize in my attorney-in-fact's place and stead with full power of revocation other attorneys-in-fact for me to exercise any or all of the powers granted to my attorney-in-fact by these presents.

4. *Closing Paragraph.* IN WITNESS WHEREOF, I have hereunto set my hand and seal the . . . . day of . . . . , 19 . . . .

. . . .
Principal

the principal' . . . or similar words showing the intent of the principal that the authority conferred shall . . . continue beyond the principal's incapacity." Both principal and agent must be of legal age and competent at the time the power of attorney was signed.

The durable power of attorney remains in duration until either the principal revokes it, it expires by its terms, or the principal or agent dies. Consider the business use of a durable power of attorney by an elderly person, or its importance to an individual going to a hospital for serious surgery or to a healthy person, to include a durable power of attorney as part of a complete estate plan in the event of an unforeseen emergency. In each instance both the principal and the agent know the powers granted will not terminate upon incapacity. The scope of the powers conferred on the agent should conform to the desires of the principal; they may be as limited or as broad as the situation demands.

Capacity to Be Principal, Agent

▶ Principal

Generally, if a person has the legal capacity to act, the person can act through an agent. (See Chapter 10, Capacity/Ability to Create a Contract.) If the principal has limited capacity, the appointment of an agent is void or voidable in accordance with contract law. For example, *P,* a minor, authorizes *A,* an adult, to purchase in *P*'s name a television set from a merchant. Both the appointment of the agent and the purchase contract made under it are voidable by the minor. The contract may be ratified by the minor after the minor reaches majority.

▶ Agent

Any person may act as an agent, even if he or she lacks contractual capacity. The contract is between the principal and the third party; the agent is not a party to the contract. Thus, although a minor/agent can avoid the contract with the principal who appointed the minor as an agent, the minor has the power to bind the principal with a third party. The minor's power of avoidance is personal to the minor and is not available to the principal. By statutory law, an agent may be a partnership or a corporation.

Classification of Agents

Agents are classified in accordance with the extent of their authority. There are two classes of agents, *general* and *special,* both of whom receive a delegation of authority from the principal to perform on its behalf. If an agent exceeds the scope of the agent's authority, the agent is personally liable and the principal is not bound.

▶ General Agent

general agent
An agent authorized to conduct a series of transactions involving a continuity of service

A **general agent** has been defined as "an agent authorized to conduct a series of transactions involving a continuity of service."[14] An example of a general agent is the manager of a retail hardware store employed to perform all the acts connected with managing the store. Limiting the agent's authority to the hardware store does not make the agency special. The continuity of service would involve such acts as personnel responsibility, buying merchandise, and dealing with customer relations on a daily basis. Other examples of general agents are sales personnel, truck drivers, secretaries, and clerks on salary.

---

[14] RESTATEMENT (SECOND) OF AGENCY sec. 3 (1958); and *Kelly v. U.S. Steel Corp. and Thew Shovel Co.,* 170 F.Supp. 649 (1959).

A **universal agent** is a sort of unlimited general agent, and is an agent authorized the principal to transact all business of every kind. This is usually given in an emergency situation and can be created only by clear and unambiguous language. It is rarely used but, if used, it should be limited to a stated period of time. For example, "to do anything that must be done during my stay in the hospital."

universal agent
An agent authorized by the principal to transact all business of every kind.

► Special Agent

"A **special agent** is an agent authorized to conduct a single transaction or a series of transactions not involving continuity of service."[15] A power of attorney given by a stockholder to a broker to sell a stock certificate is an example of a special agency. The single transaction of selling stock will terminate the broker's authority. There is no continuity of service involved in the sale transaction.

special agent
An agent authorized to conduct a single transaction or series of transactions not involving continuity of service

Creating the Agency

► Appointment—Consent of the Principal and Agent

The agency relationship is based on an implied or express agreement between the principal and the agent, as found in the facts of each case. For example, *P* expressly appoints *A* to act for and on behalf of *P,* and *A* consents. An agency relationship may be created in an informal manner without compensation being paid to the agent. Although the agency relationship usually is contractual, it may be a gratuitous undertaking by the agent.[16] If the agency is created by a contract between the principal and the agent, the law of contracts applies to its enforcement.[17]

► Form

Unless state statutory law requires a writing, the appointment of an agent may be oral or by conduct. For example, if *P* authorizes *A* to sell *P*'s land, by statute the appointment must be in writing.

► Ratification

Ratification by one person of an unauthorized act by another person does not create agency because there is no initial agreement between the two persons that one is to act for the other. In agency one is to act for another in the future, however short or long a period of time. A court has defined this doctrine as follows: "Ratification is the affirmation by a person of a prior act which did not bind him but which was done on his account and is given effect as if originally authorized by him."[18]

ratification
In agency, a person's manifested consent to be bound by another's previously unauthorized act made in the person's name and not binding on him or her

---

[15] Restatement (Second) of Agency sec. 3 (1958).

[16] *Groh v. Shelton,* 428 S.W.2d 911 (Mo. 1968).

[17] *Automotive Finance Co. v. Kesk, Inc.,* 200 So.2d 136 (La. 1967).

[18] Restatement (Second) of Agency sec. 82 (1958).

Ratification becomes important when an agent exceeds his or her authority when dealing in the principal's name with a third party, or when a person, not an agent, acts on behalf of another in the latter's name. In both cases, unless the principal ratifies his or her actions with the third party, the principal is not liable but the agent is personally liable on the contract. The doctrine of ratification may be useful when a principal, with knowledge of the unauthorized transaction, accepts the benefit or affirms the "agent's" conduct and thereby becomes bound with the same effect as though the agent had authority so to act. (An unauthorized real estate agent, in *P*'s name, signs a purchase and sale agreement with *T* to sell *P*'s house above its appraised market value; if *P* wants the benefit of this contract, *P*'s subsequent written ratification will bind *P* and *T*.)

The court in the following case refused to apply the doctrine of ratification because the principal did not have full knowledge of the unauthorized transaction.

FACTS

In 1971, Mrs. Thropp opened a margin trading account with Bache Halsey Stuart Shields, Inc., a securities brokerage firm, placing in its care securities worth approximately $40,000. . . . Mrs. Thropp is not a sophisticated investor. She expected Gregory, a broker in Bache's office, to manage her account and make investment decisions on her behalf.

Mrs. Thropp opened the Bache account in her name alone, although her husband was present at her initial meeting with Gregory. . . . Subsequently, Jack Thropp forged his wife's signature on a completely blank power of attorney form, which he then either mailed or delivered to Gregory.

Between September 21, 1971, and April 21, 1972, Jack Thropp ordered Gregory to sell his wife's stock for cash, in a series of transactions which eventually depleted the margin account. During this seven-month period, Mr. Thropp ordered Bache to issue seven checks in his wife's name. . . . He then forged his wife's indorsement, cashed the checks, and spent the money.

Mrs. Thropp inadvertently discovered her husband's forgeries in December, 1972, when she found a letter from Bache addressed to Mr. Thropp. When Mrs. Thropp quickly confronted her husband, he "confessed" that he had stolen nearly $40,000 from her account and had used the money to pay his gambling debts. He also told her that he held a power of attorney over her account and assured her that Gregory had not been involved in depleting her account.

In 1975 Mrs. Thropp first learned of Gregory's involvement, and in December, 1975 she filed this suit against Bache for negligence in handling her security account. Bache claimed as a defense that Mrs. Thropp ratified the actions of Mr. Thropp and Bache.

DECISION

To establish ratification, one must show action by the principal, taken with full knowledge of the facts, which manifests his intention to adopt the unauthorized transaction. . . . Mrs. Thropp did not learn of Gregory's involvement until 1975. Thus it cannot be said that she ratified Bache's actions. Nor can it be said that she ratified her husband's forgeries. The fact that she remained his wife is not the sort of "action" ratification requires. Judgment for Mrs. Thropp.

Thropp v. Bache Halsey Stuart Shields, Inc., 650 F.2d 817 (1981).

Elements of Ratification For ratification, the principal must intend to affirm the transaction and the following conditions must be satisfied:

1. The principal must have had *legal capacity* both when the unauthorized transaction was made by the agent and when ratification occurred.

2. The principal must ratify the *entire* contract; *P* cannot accept the benefits and reject the obligations. For example, *A*, without authorization, sold *P*'s merchandise on credit, payable in installments. *P* cannot ratify the sale and exclude the installment sale provision. *P* has to ratify the contract in its entirety or not at all.
3. The transaction to be ratified must be legal. For example, a loan unauthorizedly obtained by *A* on *P*'s behalf that violates a usury statute cannot be ratified.
4. The agent must disclose to the third person the identity of the principal on whose behalf the agent purports to act. It is not necessary that the person who is acting as an agent have any authority at this time. Ratification will not apply in the case of an undisclosed principal. For example, if *A* never informed *T* that he was selling a boat on *P*'s behalf, *P* cannot ratify the contract made by *A* with *T*. The reason is that *T* never intended to contract with *P*, and it would be unfair to permit *P* to impose himself upon *T* by ratification. *T* intended to contract with *A*.
5. The ratification must occur before the third person withdraws. For example, if *T* sues *A* for breach of contract because *A* never had the authority, *P* cannot then decide to ratify the contract.

The following case illustrates that for the doctrine of ratification to apply, the person making the contract must represent himself or herself as the principal's agent.

FACTS

Ralph Bruffey, President of Bruffey, became interested in obtaining an office computer to handle office billing and accounting work in early 1977. He had telephone and personal conversations with Edwin C. Van Allen, then Burroughs' zone sales manager. The computer was delivered to Bruffey on June 30, 1977, and installed July 6, 1977. Bruffey paid in full for the equipment and support services by July 11, 1977. However, Bruffey was unsatisfied with the continued performance of the computer. On September 28, 1978, Bruffey rescinded the agreement with Burroughs and the computer has remained, unused, in Bruffey's office.

The programming was actually done by Edwin Van Allen, then the Burroughs zone manager. Van Allen concealed from Burroughs that he was preparing Bruffey's programs from Burroughs, with Bruffey's complicity, but his involvement was later revealed. Van Allen was told by Burroughs to finish up as soon as he could. Bruffey, contending that this direction by Burroughs to Van Allen constituted a ratification by Burroughs and that Burroughs is barred from asserting defective programs as a defense, sued defendant for breach of contract, seeking rescission and damages. Did Burroughs ratify the software contract?

DECISION

The doctrine of ratification provides that a contract made by an agent without authority may, by words, conduct or silence, subsequently be approved by the principal, retroactively conferring authority on the agent. The doctrine applies only if the transaction is originally entered into on behalf of a principal, who subsequently ratifies it, and the person making it represents himself as the principal's agent.

In this case *there was never any contract between Bruffey and Van Allen, supposedly on behalf of Burroughs, in which Van Allen* [ever] *represented himself to be acting for Burroughs.* [Emphasis added] . . . If plaintiff bases its ratification theory on some later oral agreement with Van Allen, the undisputed facts are that *Van Allen never purported to act, and Bruffey never believed he was acting, on behalf of Burroughs.* [Emphasis added] Bruffey knew that what Van Allen was doing was not authorized by Burroughs; indeed, he helped Van Allen conceal it from Burroughs for a time. . . . The ratification doctrine, as well as similar theories of apparent agency or agency by estoppel, are not applicable.

Bruffey Contracting Co., Inc. v. Burroughs Corp. 522 F.Supp. 769 (Md. 1981).

► Agency by Operation of Law

The courts will infer an agency if it appears from the facts that there was an implied intention to create one.

Marital Relationship The marital relationship does not, in itself, create authority for one spouse to act for the other. However, if a wife customarily orders household supplies, authority or apparent authority to purchase things needed in the household can be inferred.[19] A husband is under a legal duty to financially provide the necessities of life for his family. A wife or child to whom a husband or parent has failed to provide the necessities has the power to contract for the purpose of necessities.[20]

Proving the Agency Relationship

When an agency question is relevant to a case, the burden of proving that the agency relationship existed is on the party who claims it existed.[21] As illustrated in the combinations of agency liability, this may be the principal, agent, or third party. The agency relationship is not presumed and must be proved by the evidence. For example, if *T* sues *P*, claiming that *A* acted as *P*'s agent, *T* has the burden of proving the agency between *P* and *A*.

Summary Statement

1. The source of agency law is the common law.
2. Corporations, partnerships, and sole proprietorships all act through agents.
3. Agency is a fiduciary relationship based on an express or implied agreement whereby one party, the agent, is authorized to act on behalf and under the control of the principal.
4. If a principal has the right to control, or exercises control, over the physical conduct of the agent, the principal is liable to third persons for physical harm caused to them by the agent's wrongful physical conduct. Such an agent is called a *servant* or *employee,* and the principal is called a *master.*
5. The terms master and servant are used in the employment relationship only to determine the liability of an employer principal for the physical harm caused to third persons by the servant employee's torts.
6. An independent contractor is hired to accomplish a physical result and is not under the direct supervision and control of the hiring party.
7. A real estate broker is an independent contractor but, when retained by a client, the broker becomes a special agent and generally has authority only to state the asking price and identify the owner's property.
8. A power of attorney is a written authorization to act as an agent. A limited power is restrictive, a general power is not.
9. Any person with legal capacity to act can act through an agent.
10. Any person can act as an agent even if the person lacks contractual capacity.

---

[19] Restatement (Second) of Agency sec. 22, comment b (1958); and *Melton v. Mire,* 268 So.2d 123 (La. 1972).

[20] Restatement of Restitution sec. 113 (1937).

[21] *Reed v. Bunger,* 122 N.W.2d 290 (Iowa 1963).

11. A *general agent* is authorized to conduct a series of transactions involving a continuity of service.
12. A *special agent* is authorized to conduct a single transaction or a series of transactions not involving continuity of service.
13. The agency relationship is based on an implied or express agreement between the principal and the agent.
14. The relationship of master and servant is a type of agency. One can be a servant even though the service is gratuitously performed.
15. Ratification is a person's affirmation of an unauthorized act having the effect of binding the ratifying party as though the act had been authorized previously.
16. The agency relationship is not presumed, and the burden of proving it is on the party who claims it exists.

In the following case notice how the right to control another's physical conduct is the decisive factor in determining whether a person is a servant or an agent.

MASSEY v. TUBE ART DISPLAY, INC.
551 P.2d 1387 (Wash. 1976)

Tube Art Display, Inc. (Tube Art) appeals from a judgment entered on a jury verdict awarding $134,000 in damages to John Massey, doing business as Olympic Research & Design Associates (Massey).

A recently opened branch office of McPherson's Realty Company desired to move a sign from its previous location to a site adjacent to its new quarters. An agreement was reached with Tube Art, the owner of the sign, to transport and re-install it on the corner of the building's parking lot... Later, a Tube Art employee laid out the exact size and location for the excavation by marking a 4 by 4 foot square on the asphalt surface with yellow paint. The dimensions of the hole, including its depth of 6 feet, were indicated with spray paint inside the square. After the layout was painted on the asphalt, Tube Art engaged a backhoe operator, Richard F. Redford, to dig the hole.

In response to Tube Art's desire that the job be completed on the 16th of February, 1972, Redford began digging in the early evening hours at the location designated by Tube Art. At approximately 9:30 p.m. the bucket of Redford's backhoe struck a small natural gas pipeline. After examining the pipe and finding no indication of a break or leak, he concluded that the line was not in use and left the site. Shortly before 2 a.m. on the following morning, an explosion and fire occurred in the building serviced by that gas pipeline. As a result, two people in the building were killed and most of its contents were destroyed. Was Tube Art liable for the deaths? The court held it was not. In determining whether one acting for another is a servant or independent contractor, several factors must be taken into consideration. These are listed in Restatement (Second) of Agency Section 220(2) (1958), as follows:

a. The extent of control which, by the agreement, the master may exercise over the details of the work;
b. Whether or not the one employed is engaged in a distinct occupation or business;
c. The kind of occupation, with reference to whether, in the locality, the work is usually done under the direction of the employer or by a specialist without supervision;
d. The skill required in the particular occupation;
e. Whether the employer or the workman supplies the instrumentalities, tools, and the place of work for the person doing the work;

f. The length of time for which the person is employed;
g. The method of payment, whether by the time or by the job;
h. Whether or not the work is a part of the regular business of the employer;
i. Whether or not the parties believe they are creating the relation of master and servant; and
j. Whether the principal is or is not in business.

All of these factors are of varying importance in determining the type of relationship involved and, with the exception of the element of control, not all the elements need be present. It is the right to control another's physical conduct that is the essential and oftentimes decisive factor in establishing vicarious liability whether the person controlled is a servant or a nonservant agent. Redford was left no discretion with regard to the placement of the excavations that he dug. Rather, it was his skill in digging holes pursuant to the exact dimensions prescribed that caused him to be preferred over other backhoe operators. We therefore find no disputed evidence of the essential factor—the right to control, nor is there any dispute that control was exercised over the most significant decision—the size and location of the hole....

Tube Art exercised control over where the hole was to be dug, the day it was to be dug, and how deep the hole was to be. Moreover, it was not unreasonable to expect Tube Art to know that gas pipes might very well be lurking in the vicinity of the proposed excavation. In such a case it was incumbent upon Tube Art to ascertain where other service pipes might be. Failing this, Tube Art can not now disclaim liability. Rather, where the danger to others is great, a duty is imposed upon an employer to make such provision against negligence as may be commensurate with the obvious danger. It is a duty which cannot be delegated to another so as to avoid liability for its neglect.

Questions and Case Problems

1. This action was initiated by the Jay County Rural Electric Membership Corp., (hereinafter REMC), against the Aetna Casualty & Surety Co., and Harold Floyd, REMC's general manager, seeking recovery on a comprehensive dishonesty bond, alleging fraudulent and dishonest acts committed by the REMC's general manager, Harold Floyd. Floyd was indebted to REMC for funds expended by Floyd for his personal use. Floyd points out that the corporate minutes show three resolutions authorizing certain types of expenditure and that the board of directors had read and approved a list of checks written during the previous month. Did the board of directors ratify the general manager, Harold Floyd's, conduct? [*Harold Floyd, Aetna Casualty & Surety Co. v. Jay County Rural Electric Membership Corp.,* 405 N.E.2d 630 (Ind. 1980).]
2. Mr. Dunbar was a brother-in-law and business associate of Mr. Judy and assisted with his financial affairs. Mr. Judy was physically frail and suffered from senility, occasional forgetfulness, restlessness, and nervousness. However, he was not mentally incompetent. On November 24, 1969 Mr. Judy executed a general power of attorney in favor of Mr. Dunbar to facilitate the handling of his financial and business affairs. On February 17, 1970 Mr. Dunbar delivered to Kanawha Valley Bank certain signature cards, bearing his signature and that of Mr. Judy, for the purpose of creating joint checking and savings accounts with survivorship. In May of 1970, at the direction of Mr. Dunbar, $30,000 was placed in the joint savings account, which money came from matured U.S. treasury bills owned by Mr. Judy. When Mr. Judy died in August of 1970 there was $32,571.82 in the joint savings account and $4,646.26 in the joint checking account. The purpose of this action by the bank was to determine the

ownership of funds in the two joint bank accounts, which were in the names of Mr. Judy and Mr. Dunbar, and which had rights of survivorship. Was there a presumption of constructive fraud, which existed as a result of the power of attorney and fiduciary relationship between Mr. Judy and Mr. Dunbar that precluded the defendant from becoming the surviving owner of the funds in the two bank accounts? [*Kanawha Valley Bank v. Friend,* 253 S.E.2d 528 (W.Va. 1979).]

3. Janice McComey resided in an apartment building located at 314 North Curson Street in Los Angeles. That building was owned by Robert Christopher Co., a partnership comprised of Robert Carangi and Josephine Carangi. Mr. Carangi hired Victor Vinney to paint and repair the building. On the afternoon of November 5, 1975, McComey left the building to go shopping. As Nikki Cordet, McComey's daughter, placed her foot on the second step, she stepped on a tool, her body rolled and she fell. After she fell, she and her mother noticed that the light fixtures in that portion of the common area had been disconnected. They also noticed two tools on the floor between the front door and steps. Cordet filed a complaint for damages to recover for the injuries she sustained in the fall. Robert Christopher Co. answered the complaint denying any liability as the negligence, if any, was that of an independent contractor. Was the employer/defendant liable for the negligence of Vinney, the independent contractor? [*Cordet v. Robert Christopher Co.,* 210 Cal.Rptr. 517 (Cal. 1985).]

4. Plaintiff, Bicknell, Inc., sued John J. Havlin, defendant, an insurance agent, alleging negligence in failing to place proper insurance coverage on two buildings leased to Bicknell. Havlin described himself as experienced in the insurance business. Havlin made recommendations for particular types of coverage and, when asked what would be sufficient coverage for the buildings, he stated "let's slap 50,000 on each building."

A fire broke out on June 3, 1974, in one of Bicknell's two new rented warehouses. The fire loss amounted to $103,275.91. The insurance carrier paid Bicknell $50,000, the amount of the endorsement of April 4, 1974. Did Havlin, as Bicknell's insurance agent, violate a duty of care in not providing Bicknell with sufficient insurance coverage? [*Bicknell, Inc. v. Havlin,* 402 N.E.2d 116 (Mass. 1980).]

5. Plaintiff Roland Bradley was a sergeant in the U.S. Air Forçe assigned to Shaw Air Force Base. Bradley contends that, as a result of seeing a real estate broker's signs on a lot near Shaw Air Force Base, he contacted the broker and one of its agents, John Pate, came to their residence located on Shaw Air Force Base and after observing that they were black refused to show them the dwelling. The broker's president approved of Pate's action. Bradley seeks damages against the defendant and also an injunction permanently restraining and denying defendant from refusing to show, negotiate, and sell real estate to plaintiffs and others in similar situations. The broker corporation asserts that Pate was an independent contractor and not an agent of John M. Brabham Agency, Inc. Decide. [*Bradley v. John M. Brabham Agency, Inc.,* 463 F.Supp. 27 (S.C. 1978).]

6. A & M had contracted with Melancon in February, 1970, to furnish subterranean termite control for Melancon's house for a period of two years. In December 1970 Melancon sold the house to Ruiz. In connection with the sale Melancon turned over his contract with A & M to Ruiz and instructed him to pay the renewal fee when it became due in February 1972. Ruiz contacted A & M and informed them that he found termites in the house. Although the contract and warranty were issued to Melancon, Ruiz testified that A & M's representative, with apparent authority to do so, told him the contract could be kept in effect by paying the renewal fee. A & M not only did not deny this statement but also accepted the renewal fee from Ruiz and contacted him to arrange the annual inspection and treatment pursuant to the contract. Did A & M ratify its agent's agreement? [*Melancon and Ruiz v. A & M Pest Control Serv. Co., Inc.*, 325 So.2d 391 (La. 1976).]

7. Fielding Home for Funerals (FHF) brought suit to collect the proceeds of a life insurance policy from the insurance company. Although it is undisputed that the policy had lapsed prior to the death of the named insured due to nonpayment of premiums, FHF contends that the insurance company is estopped to assert the lapse of the policy since it had represented to FHF that the policy was in force and, as a consequence of reliance on such representation, the FHF acted to its detriment. The appellant accepted assignment of the proceeds of the policy from the policy beneficiary as payment for the funeral and burial expenses of the insured. A former employee testified that she had been secretary and insurance clerk of appellant. A former employee of FHF called the insurance company on the telephone to ascertain whether the policy in question was in fôrce and was informed by the person answering that it was. She could not identify that person by name. Can it be presumed that a person is authorized to speak for a business as its agent when the caller cannot identify the person by name? [*Fielding Home for Funerals, as assignee for the life insurance policy of Green, v. Public Savings Life Ins. Co.*, 245 S.E. 2d 238 (S.C. 1978).]

8. To entertain its patrons when they were not absorbed in watching the races, Bay State's raceway furnished music. For this purpose, it retained Famous Music Box, Inc., which, as an independent contractor, supplied the music. Bay State's president had instructed his subordinates in Bay State to instruct Famous Music Box not to play any copyrighted music. Despite this admonition, on August 24, 1972 and January 6, 1973 such music was played at a time when monitors in the field spotted and recorded such transgressions. Was Bay State responsible for the infringing performances by an independent contractor? [*Famous Music Corp., et al. v. Bay State Harness Horse Racing and Breeding Association, Inc.*, 554 F.2d 1213 (1st Cir. 1977).]

9. During the fall of 1975, Sierra Pacific Industries, plaintiff, purchased, for a lump sum, various timberlands and six other pieces of real property, including the subject of this dispute, a ten acre parcel in Willow Creek on which five duplexes and two single family units are located. After the acquisition, Sierra Pacific requested the assistance of Joseph H. Carter, a real estate broker, in selling the nontimberland properties, including the Willow Creek parcel. Acting in reliance on Carter's representation as to the value of the Willow Creek parcel, Sierra Pacific commissioned him to sell it for an asking price of $85,000 of which Sierra Pacific would receive $80,000 and Carter $5,000. Pursuant to the agreement, Carter showed the Willow Creek property to several prospective buyers but was for a time unable to secure a sale at the asking price of $85,000. Finally, in June of 1976, Carter sold the property for that amount to his daughter and son-in-law and retained a $5,000 commission without informing Sierra Pacific of his relationship with the buyers. Sierra Pacific instituted a fraud action against Carter for the $5,000 commission paid to Carter based on the foregoing facts. Decide. [*Sierra Pacific Indus. v. Carter*, 163 Cal.Rptr. 764 (Cal. 1980).]

10. The case of *Massey v. Tube Art Display, Inc.*, excerpted at the beginning of this section, held that there was no disputed evidence over the right to control the physical conduct of the backhoe operator. Discuss the court's analysis in reaching the conclusion that Tube Art could not disclaim liability.

C H A P T E R

16

DUTIES OF PRINCIPAL AND AGENT TO EACH OTHER

After you have read this chapter, you should be able to:

1. Define the following kinds of authority:
   a) Express authority
   b) Implied authority
      (1) Incidental authority
      (2) Customary authority
   c) Apparent authority
2. Know whose duty it is to determine the extent of the agent's authority.
3. Explain the effect of limitations on the agent's authority.
4. Explain the instances when an agent may delegate authority to another.
5. List and explain the five duties an agent owes to a principal.
6. List and explain the four duties a principal owes to an agent.
7. Explain the effect of proper exercise of the agent's authority.
8. Explain the meaning of a fiduciary.

BUSINESS DECISIONS and the LAW

In the arena of investing, the customer is the principal, and the brokerage firm is the agent, as E.F. Hutton & Company, Inc., recently found out.

In a class action the customers sued, claiming that E.F. Hutton engaged in a practice of paying its customers from geographically remote banks. This activity delayed the receipt by customers of their funds, which benefitted E.F. Hutton by providing the firm with additional days for accumulation of interest in its bank accounts. The customers alleged that this violated the fiduciary duties owed to them, including the duty of loyalty, the duty to promptly and fully inform, the duty of an agent not to place itself in a position that conflicts with that of the principal, and the duty not to prefer its interests above those of the principal.

Although the terms of the agency were not defined by the parties, E.F. Hutton concedes that such principal-agent relationship exists with its customers. This, of course, means that E.F. Hutton owes its customers an elevated duty of care.

It remains to be seen how the court will interpret the scope of the fiduciary duty, and whether E.F. Hutton's actions breached this duty.

This chapter will explain the various legal duties resulting from the principal-agent relationship.

Source: *Goodrich v. E.F. Hutton Group, Inc.*, 542 A.2d 1200 (Del. 1988).

Introduction

In the preceding chapter of this part we discussed the nature of agency, its creation, and how it is distinguished from other business relationships, particularly the independent contractor. In this chapter, we will discuss the various kinds of authority, apparent authority, and the duties of principal and agent to each other.

It is almost certain that at some time in your life you will find yourself involved in a business agency relationship either as a principal or as an agent.

The agency relationship creates rights and duties for both parties not previously existing, both by the act of creating the agency and in its day-to-day operation.

The concept of authority and power implicit in the agency relationship can lead to the creation of rights, duties, and great potentiality for loss. Accordingly, it is very important to consider carefully your obligations before entering into an agency relationship. For your own well-being and future conduct, you, as a student, need to understand the perspective in this chapter.

Agent's Authority

▶ Scope of Agent's Authority

An agent may properly contract with a third party only if authorized by the principal in words or other conduct. Agents have no power to create their own authority nor to extend its scope. The essence of **authority** is a person's (principal's) consent to another (agent) to act on the principal's behalf.

authority
An agent's power to act for the principal in accordance with the principal's manifestation of consent to the agent

The following types of authority will help you to identify authority and decide whether the agent is acting with the principal's consent.[1]

Express Authority If the principal specifies orally or in writing what the agent is to do, the agent has **express authority** to act. For example, if *P* tells his stockbroker *A* to sell *P*'s stock at a certain price, *A* has been given express authority to sell the stock at a specified price.

express authority
An agent's authority specifically expressed in the principal's manifestation to the agent

Implied Authority The agent's duty is to carry out his or her express authority as reasonably understood by the agent. The agent must interpret the principal's words of consent in order to understand what they mean. The principal's words imply to the agent, and the agent infers from those words what the agent reasonably understands he or she is to do. Thus we have **implied** (or inferred) **authority.** Implied authority can be described as incidental or customary.

implied authority
An agent's authority that the agent reasonably can understand he or she has from the principal's manifestation to the agent, but not expressed therein

1. *Incidental authority.* An agent is authorized from the circumstances to perform those acts that are reasonably necessary to carry out the express authority. Suppose an agent is authorized to use a company car on a business trip to effect a sale with a third party. The salesperson/agent has implied **incidental authority** to charge the gasoline used to the principal.
2. *Customary authority.* The traditional trade or professional practice in which the agent acts creates an implied authorization to conform with the general custom. This is referred to as **customary authority.**

incidental authority
Implied authority to do what is incidental in carrying out the express authority

customary authority
Implied authority to do those acts that conform to the general custom or usage

[1]See RESTATEMENT (SECOND) OF AGENCY sec. 7, comment c (1958), where express and implied authority are discussed.

By agreement between the principal and the agent, the agent may not have incidental and customary authority. Some common examples of implied authority may be helpful.

1. In authority "to sell" personal property, if the agent has received possession of the property, then the agent's implied authority is to contract in the principal's name and sell and transfer the title to the property. If the agent has not received possession, the agent's implied authority is solely to produce a willing and able buyer. In authority "to sell" real property, if the agent's authority is in writing (for example, if the agent has power of attorney) and there is nothing to the contrary, the implied authority is to contract in the principal's name and sell and transfer the title to the property. If the authority is oral, the implied authority is solely to produce a willing and able buyer.
2. Authority to receive payment implies authority to receive only cash for the entire amount or to take a check as conditional payment—on condition that it is paid. Authority to receive payment does not authorize the agent to accept credit.
3. Authority to sign checks and other negotiable instruments in the name of a principal is not implied easily, in the absence of special circumstances (e.g., in an emergency).

Apparent Authority[2] Agency and authority are created by the principal's expression of consent to the agent. If *P* represents to *T*, a third person, that *A* is *P*'s agent, there is neither agency nor authority because *P* never expressed consent to *A* that *A* was to be *P*'s agent. But as far as *T* is concerned, *A* apparently is *P*'s agent because of *P*'s representation to *T*. Therefore, *A* is an apparent agent with **apparent authority** to act for *P* in accordance with *P*'s representation to *T*. The extent of *A*'s apparent authority will depend upon *T*'s reasonable understanding of *P*'s representation to *T*. If *A* acts within the scope of *A*'s apparent authority, *P* will be bound to *T* by *A*'s conduct with the same effect as though *A* had authority so to act. Under apparent authority, sometimes called "ostensible authority," the principal's expression of consent is to the third person rather than to the agent. Apparent authority has replaced estoppel when *P*'s manifestation to *T* is that *A* is *P*'s agent.

apparent authority
The power of a person (*A*) to act as though *A* were an agent, created by another's (*P*'s) manifestation to a third person (*T*) that *A* is *P*'s agent

A person may be an agent with authority and, at the same time, have apparent authority. For example, *P* employs *A* as a salesperson in *P*'s store, and *P* informs *T* that *A* is *P*'s salesperson. *A*'s authority and apparent authority are to act as a salesperson is reasonably expected to act.

An intent to authorize an act may be found from the principal's conduct. For example, a store clerk who reasonably appears to a vendor/third party to have authority to purchase supplies from the vendor has apparent authority to do so, and the owner of the store will be liable to the vendor on a sale.

The following case illustrates how the agent's apparent authority can take the form of conduct that reasonably causes the third party to believe that the principal consents to the agent acting on its behalf.

FACTS

Oak Hill Raquet Club contracted with Emmark Collaborative, Inc., for the design, construction, and construction management of the Oak Hill project. Emmark then entered into a subcontract with Emmenegger Construction Company, Inc. Emmenegger was to do the concrete work on the project. Emmark was the construction manager for the Oak Hill project. Fred Alsbach was the job superintendent for the project and directed activities on the job site. There is

[2] See Restatement (Second) of Agency sec. 8 (1958), where apparent authority is discussed.

some dispute as to who is Alsbach's employer. Ames, a concrete worker, was not certain for whom he was working. He dealt exclusively with Alsbach and did not meet or talk to Emmenegger. Ames has not been paid for his concrete work and claims that his contract was with Emmenegger, which is denied by Emmenegger. Did Alsbach have authority to bind Emmenegger to the contract with Ames? Judgment was rendered for Ames and Emmenegger appealed.

DECISION

Yes. Affirmed, judgment for Ames. "Apparent authority to do an act is created as to a third party by written or spoken words or any other conduct of the principal which reasonably interpreted, causes the third party to believe that the principal consents to have the act done on his behalf by the person purporting to act for him." Ames dealt exclusively with Alsbach, and they discussed matters pertaining to work, and particularly billing and payment, in Emmenegger's trailer. The bill for the January work was made out to "Emmenegger Constr. Co.," and was submitted by Ames to Alsbach in the trailer. This bill was approved for payment by Leo Kuntz, Emmenegger's corporate vice president, and was later submitted for payment by Alsbach on an Emmenegger purchase order. If doubt existed as to Alsbach's authority to bind defendant, it was removed by Kuntz' action in approving the January bill for payment. This indicated consent by the principal (Emmenegger) to actions of its agent (Alsbach).

Emmenegger Constr. Co., Inc. v. Frank King, et al. 431 N.E.2d 738 (Ill. 1982).

► Legal Effect of a Contract Properly Executed by an Agent

If an agent acts within the express or implied authority in the name of the principal, there is a contract between the third party and the principal. Accordingly, a salesperson is not personally liable for a breach of warranty for goods made to a customer/third party because the sales contract is made with the principal through the agent; the agent is not a party to the contract.

► Third Party's Duty to Determine the Extent of the Agent's Authority

The third party is under a legal obligation not only to identify the existence of the agent's authority but also to determine its extent. If the agent exceeds this authority, the principal will not be bound. Suppose a life insurance agent changes the terms of a life insurance contract without the consent of the company. It is the customer/third party's responsibility to determine whether the agent had the power to change the insurance contract. A third party who fails to do so acts at its peril.

The third party cannot rely upon statements made by the agent unless the principal has invited the third party to do so. For example, a customer is invited by the store owner to rely upon the salesperson's statement of the price of goods.

The following case illustrates how a third party can bind a principal for authorized acts, even though the third party does not inquire into the extent of the agent's authority.

FACTS

Loper Lumber Company, a corporate owner of timber, brings this action to recover payment for timber cut and removed from its land pursuant to an agreement made by Windham, through his agent. Windham refused to pay on the grounds that Loper Lumber made no inquiry as to the extent of the agent's authority, and they were thereby released from responsibility for the agent's authorized act. If the agent does not exceed his authority, does a third party have an obligation to determine the extent of the authority?

DECISION

No. Judgment for Loper. While a third party dealing with an agent is held to be subject to the burden of ascertaining the extent of the powers of the agent, it seems that where the agent is, in fact, acting within the scope of the authority granted to him, the principal ought to be bound for the acts of the agent, whether the third party made any inquiry as to the extent of the agent's authority or not. The decision as to the principal's liability ought to rest on the actual extent of the authority granted to the agent and not on the fact that the third party dealing with the agent made inquiry to ascertain the agent's authority.

Loper Lumber Co. v. Windham, 282 So.2d 256 (Ala. 1973).

► Limitation on the Agent's Authority

As between the principal and the agent, any expressed limitations on the scope of the agent's authority are valid. However, a third party without knowledge of the private and secret limitations is not bound by them. The third party has the duty of determining the extent of an agent's authority, but since the third party cannot determine the secret limitations on such authority made by the principal, the limitations are not effective as to the third party. If the agent has express, implied, or apparent authority to act, the agent can make a contract with the third party that will bind the principal.

For instance, if it is customary in the used car trade to warrant a used car for thirty and the principal instructs the salesperson/agent to warrant the car for only fourteen days, unless disclosed to the customer/third party the latter can assume that the agent has authority to give a thirty-day warranty. The agent has such apparent authority.

In the following case the court found no apparent authority on the part of an attorney/agent to settle his client's case.

FACTS

Plaintiff was injured when the vehicle in which she was a passenger was struck by a vehicle driven by defendant. Plaintiff retained John D. Logsdon, an attorney, to represent her in a personal injury action. At a pretrial conference, defendant admitted liability, leaving the nature and extent of plaintiff's injuries as the only triable issues. Settlement negotiations ensued. The court and Mr. Logsdon approved a settlement and the court dismissed plaintiff's action. Unknown to all parties or the court, Logsdon had apparently forged plaintiff's indorsement to the settlement draft made payable to plaintiff and to Logsdon as her attorney, and he received the proceeds. Plaintiff brought this action to set aside the judgment. The trial court denied the plaintiff's motion to set aside the judgment and dismissed her action. Plaintiff appealed. Did the attorney, Logsdon, have apparent authority to settle the action?

DECISION

No. Reversed, motion to set aside the judgment allowed.... It is clear that the relation of attorney and client is one of agency and the general rules of law that apply to agency apply to that relation.... The liability of the principal for the acts and contracts of his agent is not limited to such acts and contracts of the agent as are expressly authorized.... All such acts and contracts of an agent as are within the apparent scope of authority conferred upon him, although no actual authority to do such acts or to make such contracts has been conferred, are also binding upon the principal.

Apparent authority, or ostensible authority as it is also called, is that which, though not actually granted, the principal knowingly permits the agent to exercise or which he holds him out as possessing. An apparent agent is one who, with or without authority, reasonably appears to third persons to be authorized to act as the agent of another.

In the present case there is no evidence of apparent authority on the part of Logsdon to settle plaintiff's case other than his retention as her attorney. There being no evidence, other than Logsdon's employment as plaintiff's attorney, of Logsdon's apparent authority to settle plaintiff's action, we hold that the trial court abused its discretion in denying plaintiff's motion to set aside the judgment of dismissal.

Miotk v. Rudy, 605 P.2d 587 (Kan. 1980).

► Delegation of Authority by Agent

When a principal selects an agent to contract with others on his or her behalf, the principal does so on the personal qualifications of the agent.[3] The agent generally will exercise discretion, special skill, or judgment in the performance of the agent's contract with the principal and the agent's fiduciary duties on behalf of the principal. Hence, it usually is held that an agent does not have implied (or apparent) authority to delegate the agent's authority to another (subagent) without the consent of the principal.

If the agent's discretion, special skill, or judgment are not required for the agent's performance, unless the principal has indicated to the contrary, the agent has implied (and apparent) authority to **delegate** his or her performance to a **subagent.** On delegation, the subagent is an agent both of the agent appointing him or her and also of the agent's principal. The subagent has two principals who are both liable for the subagent's conduct, the appointing agent being ultimately liable. For example, *P* insurance company appoints *A* as its general manager in a particular geographical area, *A* agreeing to be responsible for personnel hired by *A*. *A* employs insurance salespersons working out of *A*'s office. The salespersons sell insurance in *P*'s name to third persons, binding *P* to them. The salespersons are subagents with *A* and *P* as their principals. Both *A* and *P* are liable for the salespersons' conduct but, as between *A* and *P*, *A* is ultimately liable.

delegation
The transfer of one's duty to another, the transferor still being responsible for the duty

subagent
The person appointed by an agent and as to whom the appointing agent is a principal

An agent's delegation of his or her authority to a subagent is different from an agent's appointment of another agent. The appointed agent and the appointing agent have only one principal—namely, the person who created the original agency. For example, *P* owns a retail store and employs *A* as general manager. *A* appoints *S* as a salesperson in the store. *P* is the principal, and both *A* and *S* are the principal's agents. *S* is not an agent of *A*, who is not liable for *S*'s conduct. Only *P* is liable for the conduct of *A* and *S*.

Agents may delegate their authority in the following four instances:

1. Ministerial or Mechanical Duties In certain cases the act to be performed by the agent does not require anything more than a ministerial (nondiscretionary) or mechanical duty. For example, a general agent parking attendant may delegate the duty to collect parking tickets because it requires no special skill, discretion, or judgment. The following case illustrates how the showing of land is a ministerial act and can be delegated to a subagent.

---

[3]See RESTATEMENT (SECOND) OF AGENCY secs. 17, 18, and 19 (1958), where delegable acts and powers are discussed.

FACTS

Heritage Land Sales entered an agreement with Freeport Ridge Estates, defendant, to act as Freeport's broker for the sale of real estate in the Bahamas. Heritage was to get a commission on each lot sold. Reckner was retained by Heritage to fly prospective buyers from the United States to Grand Bahama Island to view lots that were for sale. Reckner sued Freeport for services rendered. Was Reckner a subagent of Freeport?

DECISION

Yes. Judgment for Reckner. Heritage, as the agent of Freeport, had the implied authority to delegate its authority to a subagent, Reckner, regarding the ministerial act of showing land and flying prospective purchasers to Grand Bahama Island. In his capacity as a subagent, Reckner can look directly to the principal for his compensation.

Freeport Ridge Estates, Ltd. v. Reckner, 266 So.2d 129 (Fla. 1972).

The principal may prohibit the delegation of even a ministerial act, providing it is clearly indicated to the agent. It is usually good practice to do so because the principal is responsible to compensate the subagent.

2. Business Custom It is implied that the agent has authority to delegate if the trade or profession in which the agency is to be performed has an established custom to employ subagents. In the following case, a limited partner brought suit against his attorneys for negligent representation. The attorneys claim they delegated their duty to subagents. There is no professional custom for attorneys to employ subagents.

FACTS

Quintel Corporation (Quintel) sued Citibank for violations of federal securities laws in connection with Quintel's investment in Flag Associates (Flag), a real estate limited partnership. The complaint alleges that the general partners of Flag and Citibank made certain misrepresentations to Quintel upon which it relied in investing in Flag. Quintel alleges that certain of the defendants failed to disclose their ownership of approximately 80 acres of undeveloped land adjacent to the property being acquired by Flag, and that Quintel's funds were used to purchase the undeveloped land. . . .

An agreement was reached between Citibank, and Alperstein and Conboy, Quintel's lawyers, which resulted in the allocation of the legal work that had to be completed on behalf of the limited partnership and Quintel. Pursuant to that agreement, Alperstein and Goldstick relied upon Conboy and Citibank to protect the limited partner's (Quintel's) interest in the Flag transaction.

Did Alperstein and Goldstick have authority to delegate their fiduciary duty to the subagents Conboy and Citibank without the principal's (Quintel's) consent?

DECISION

No. Judgment for Quintel. A lawyer cannot delegate his fiduciary duties to another in an effort to avoid responsibility for the manner in which they are undertaken. It is a rule of the first importance governing the conduct of a lawyer that his relationship to his client should be personal; that his responsibility should be direct. Without specific authority from his principal, an agent has no power to delegate his trust. The relationship of principal and agent does not exist between the principal and a subagent. The complaint does not allege that Quintel, as Alperstein's client, was a party to the agreement or consented to it.

Quintel Corp. v. Citibank N.A., 589 F.Supp. 1235 (1984).

For example, if it is customary in the real estate agency business to have subagents show the house and accept counteroffers, the agent would be authorized to do so.

3. Unforeseen Emergency If the circumstances surrounding the agent's acts create a sudden emergency, and it is impracticable for the agent to communicate with the principal, the agent may appoint a subagent to protect the principal's interest and do what the agent reasonably can believe the principal would want done if the principal were aware of the circumstances. To illustrate, if the principal delivers perishable food to a carrier/agent with instructions to transport and sell it to a third party, if the carrier/agent cannot communicate with the principal that the third party refuses to purchase it, and if the food will be worthless unless refrigerated in a warehouse, the carrier/agent has authority to store it and charge the principal's account, the warehouse-worker being a subagent of the principal to care for the food.

4. Contemplated Conduct of Principal's Business So Requires Although not expressed in the agency contract, if it is reasonably inferred from the principal's business that the parties contemplated the appointment of subagents, then the agent may delegate his or her authority. For example, a general insurance agent ordinarily has the power to appoint subagents to sell insurance for the company. Also, an agent corporation has implied authority to act through its officers and other employees, and an agent partnership through its partners.

Duties and Liabilities of Principal and Agent

▶ Agent to Principal

fiduciary
A person with a duty to act primarily for the benefit of another

The basis of liability resulting from an agency relationship is contractual. The agreement, express or implied, between the agent and the principal creates a series of rights and duties.[4] An understanding of this contract is necessary for both parties to perform properly. The following duties are imposed upon the agent in compliance with the contract and the **fiduciary** relationship. They may be expressed in the contract, but frequently are implied. The principal may sue the agent in contract or tort, depending on the nature of the duty violated. In general, the agent has five duties to the principal.

1. Loyalty The agreement between the principal and agent creates a fiduciary relationship. An agent acts solely for the benefit of the principal, and the agent thereby incurs a duty of loyalty that is imposed on all fiduciaries.

For example, if *A* has been authorized to negotiate the sale price and sell a house for *P*, and *A* sold the house to a friend, *T*, below the fair market value, *A* has committed a breach of duty to *P*.

An agent cannot enter into a contract with a third party that would create a *conflict of interest* with the principal. The purpose of the agent's contracts with others is to benefit the principal. Even though this may not be expressed in the agency contract, it is implied by the fiduciary relationship.

For instance, if *A* is *P*'s agent and *A* convinces *P* to sell his product to *T*, a corporation in which *A* owns a substantial amount of stock, of which *P* is unaware, *A* has violated *A*'s

---

[4]See Restatement (Second) of Agency secs. 376–409 (1958) for a discussion of the duties an agent owes to a principal.

duty of loyalty to *P*. *A* is liable even if *A* acts in good faith and believes the transaction is appropriate. However, if *P* knew of *A*'s interest in the corporation, there is no breach.

Notice how the court in the following case *presumes fraud* when an agent has an interest in a transaction in conflict with the principal's interest.

FACTS

Argovitz was employed as an agent of Billy Sims, a professional football player. Argovitz told Sims that he had applied for a United States Football League franchise with the Houston Gamblers. Sims was unaware, however, of Argovitz's extensive ownership interest in the new Houston Gamblers organization. Meanwhile, during the spring of 1983, Argovitz continued contract negotiations on behalf of Sims with the Detroit Lions of the National Football League. Argovitz and the Lions were very close to an agreement, although Argovitz represented to Sims that the negotiations were not proceeding well. Argovitz then sought an offer for Sims' services from the Gamblers. The Gamblers offered Sims $3.5 million over a five-year period. Argovitz told Sims that he thought the Lions would match the Gamblers' offer; however, he did not seek a final offer from the Lions and then present the terms of both packages to Sims. Sims, convinced that the Lions were not negotiating in good faith, signed with the Gamblers. Five months later, Sims signed a second contract with the Lions. The Lions and Sims brought an action against Argovitz, seeking to invalidate Sims' contract with the Gamblers on the ground that Argovitz breached his fiduciary duty when negotiating the contract with the Gamblers.

DECISION

The relationship between a principal and agent is fiduciary in nature, and as such imposes a duty of loyalty, good faith, and fair and honest dealing on the agent. A fiduciary relationship arises not only from a formal principal-agent relationship but also from informal relationships of trust and confidence. In light of the express agency agreement, and the relationship between Sims and Argovitz, Argovitz clearly owed Sims the fiduciary duties of an agent at all times. An agent's duty of loyalty requires that he not have a personal stake that conflicts with the principal's interest in a transaction in which he represents his principal. A fiduciary violates the prohibition against self-dealing not only by dealing with himself on his principal's behalf, but also by dealing on his principal's behalf with a third party in which he has an interest. Where an agent has an interest adverse to that of his principal in a transaction in which he purports to act on behalf of his principal, the transaction is voidable by the principal unless the agent disclosed all material facts within the agent's knowledge that might affect the principal's judgment. Once it has been shown that an agent had an interest in a transaction involving his principal, antagonistic to the principal's interest, fraud on the part of the agent is presumed. Argovitz had an ownership interest in the Gamblers, and thus would profit if the Gamblers were profitable, and would incur substantial personal liabilities should the Gamblers not be financially successful. Since this showing has been made, fraud on Argovitz's part is presumed and the Gamblers' contract must be rescinded unless Argovitz has shown by a preponderance of evidence that he informed Sims of every material fact that might have influenced Sims' decision whether or not to sign the Gamblers' contract. The careless fashion in which Argovitz went about ascertaining the highest price for Sims' service convinces us of the wisdom of the maxim: no man can faithfully serve two masters whose interests are in conflict. Judgment will be entered for the plaintiffs rescinding the Gamblers' contract with Sims.

Detroit Lions, Inc. v. Argovitz, 580 F.Supp. 542 (D. Mich. 1982).

2. Obedience and Performance The contractual relationship between the principal and the agent may be an ongoing process creating a variety of instructions the agent is obligated to follow. An agent generally is obligated to comply with the principal's reasonable instructions. If *A* violates the instructions, causing harm to *P*, even if acting in good faith, *A* is liable to *P*. Accordingly, if *A*, acting in good faith, sells to an unauthorized company in violation of *P*'s instructions, *A* is liable to *P* for any resulting injury to *P*.

The agent is never obligated to perform illegal or unethical acts. Codes of trade practice and professional responsibility will determine whether the principal's instructions are reasonable. For example, a stockbroker may engage in proper customary trade practice in the sale of stock without objection by the principal/customer.

The following case illustrates a real estate agent's liability for carrying out his principal's illegal instructions in refusing to sell property for racial motivations.

FACTS

A real estate development corporation (AFBIC) owned and subdivided a parcel of land and appointed another corporation (RSI) as its exclusive agent to sell the unimproved lots to home builders, who in turn appointed RSI as their agent to sell the homes built by the builders.

Warren and Jean Dillon, a black couple, wished to buy one of the homes. Jean delivered a written offer to an RSI salesman who delivered the offer to Smith, its vice president, telling him that Jean was black. Smith delivered the offer to Greene, owner of Bay City, who rejected the offer and refused to sell to the Dillons because they were black. Smith knew this reason for Greene's refusal but misrepresented to the Dillons that Greene's refusal was for other reasons. Plaintiffs sued, claiming that their wrongful refusal to sell the home to them was in violation of federal laws.

Was Smith, RSI's agent, liable for carrying out RSI's racially motivated refusal to sell the home to the plaintiffs?

DECISION

Yes.... Under the Fair Housing Act it is unlawful "to refuse to negotiate for the sale or rental of, or otherwise make unavailable or deny, a dwelling to any person because of race, color, religion, or national origin."

Smith's participation in the refusal to sell renders both RSI and Smith liable under the Fair Housing Act. An agent has no obligation to carry out his principal's order to do an illegal act. "... an agent who assists his principal in committing a tort is himself liable as a joint tortfeasor." [Restatement (Second) of Agency sec. 411 (1958), Comment d.] Smith knew that Greene's decisions to refuse to sell to the plaintiffs were racially motivated. In these circumstances, Smith's own conduct violated the federal antidiscrimination statutes. It is equally clear that RSI is vicariously (in place of) liable for the statutory violations of Smith, the company's vice president and sole shareholder.

AFBIC is not responsible for the discriminatory acts of Smith and RSI because it had no legal authority to control their efforts to market the lot and home and it made no effort to exercise such control.

Dillon v. AFBIC Development Corp., et al., 597 F.2d 556 (1979).

3. Reasonable Care An agent is subject to not only the express and implied contract terms with the principal (as well as the fiduciary obligations imposed by the common law) but also the tort law of negligence as it applies to the transaction. The agent has a duty to exercise proper care in acting as an agent. Under Section 379 of the Restatement (Second) of Agency: "Unless otherwise agreed, a paid agent is subject to a duty to the principal to act with standard care and skill . . . in the locality for the kind of work which he is employed to perform and . . . to exercise any special skill that he has."

For example, if *A*, a real estate agent, does not advertise an exclusive listing, *A* may be liable to *P* for not complying with the local trade practice.

4. Accounting Whatever an agent receives during and as a result of the agency, the agent holds in trust for the principal. He cannot secretly keep profits from the agency;

they belong to the principal. For example, if *T* owes *P* money and *T* pays *P*'s agent, *A*, who has authority to receive such payments, *A* holds the money in trust for *P* and cannot secretly keep it for himself. One of the implied fiduciary duties requires the agent to keep an account of all the property and money belonging to the principal. This is a serious obligation and need not be expressed in the agency contract. Unless otherwise provided in the agency contract, the agent may render an account within a reasonable time after receipt or disbursement of funds. The agent must present an account upon termination of the agency.

If the agent is sued by the principal for failure to properly account, the agent has the burden of proving that he or she paid the principal. For example, if *A* should deposit corporate funds in *A*'s personal checking account, the corporation could claim the funds in *A*'s account.

The agent has a duty to keep a separate account of the principal's funds. The agent will be held personally liable for the loss of any commingled funds.

5. Information An agent has a duty to communicate information to the principal even though not instructed to do so under the express terms of the contract. For example, a counteroffer made to a real estate agent by *T*, the prospect, must be communicated to *P*, the home owner.

In the following case the court found that an import agent does not have a duty to inform unless the agent knew the principal would want to have the information in question.

FACTS

Hunter Farms contracted with Petrolia, a Canadian company, to purchase a farm herbicide called Sencor for resale. Petrolia learned from the U.S. Customs Service that the import duty for the Sencor would be 5 percent but that the final rate could only be determined upon an examination of the herbicide at the time of importation. This information was forwarded to Hunter. Hunter retained F.W. Myers & Company, an import broker, to assist in moving the herbicide through customs. Customs later determined that certain chemicals in the herbicide, not listed on its label, would increase the duty from approximately $30,000 to $128,000. Myers paid the additional amount under protest and sought for indemnification from Hunter. Hunter refused to pay Myers, arguing that Myers breached its duty of care as an import broker in failing to advise Hunter that the 5 percent duty rate was subject to being increased. Myers brought an action against Hunter, arguing that it was not retained to give advice to Hunter on matters of importation.

DECISION

An agent is required to exercise such skill as is required to accomplish the object of his employment. If he fails to exercise reasonable care, diligence, and judgment under the circumstances, he is liable to his principal for any loss or damage resulting. Evidence was presented that the standard of care for import brokers did not include a special duty to rend advice to the importer unless requested to do so. Myers was never informed of the need to convey this information to Hunter which, it could reasonably presume, possessed the fundamental knowledge of an importer. Myers was never advised of Hunter's lack of experience in the business, nor was it aware of the problem in labeling the herbicide which caused the increase in the duty charged. Absent knowledge of Hunter's special need for advice and of the circumstances which might give rise to the additional importation fees, there was no special duty on Myers to advise Hunter of the tentative nature of the assessment.

F.W. Myers & Co. v. Hunter Farms, 319 N.W.2d 186 (Iowa 1982).

► Principal to Agent

The contract between the principal and agent creates the duties that the principal owes to the agent.[5] The implied terms of the contract common to this relationship may create duties of the principal to pay the agent for the performance of services, to reimburse the agent for authorized advances and expenses, and to indemnify the agent against liability to third parties. In general, the principal has four duties to the agent.

1. Duty of Compensation An agent is entitled to the agreed compensation or the fair value of the agent's services. If the agent is hired by the principal, the resulting employment contract will determine the compensation and duration of the agency. For example, if a stockbroker is hired without an agreed commission rate, the stockbroker is entitled to the customary trade commission.

2. Duty to Comply with the Agency Contract The principal has a duty to comply with the terms of the agency contract and to allow the agent to perform under the contract. If a real estate agent is given an "exclusive agency" to list the principal's house for sale for ninety days, the principal cannot terminate the agency before that time nor employ another agent for the same purpose. Under an "exclusive sale contract," only the agent may make the sale.

3. Duty of Reimbursement The intent of the principal and the agent as expressed in their contract determines the right of the agent to recover expenses incurred while authorizedly performing the agency contract.

If the principal requests the agent to expend the agent's own money in the performance of the agency, the agent has the authority to do so and the principal has a duty to **reimburse** the agent for such expense. The principal's request may be express, or implied from performance pursuant to the agent's authority that required the agent to incur expense. A typical example is a principal's request that the agent is to do something that will require the agent to travel and incur travel expense.

reimbursement
One person's right against another to be repaid money paid on the other's behalf for which the latter was responsible

indemnity
An absolute obligation to pay for another's loss

4. Duty of Indemnity **Indemnity** is an obligation to pay for another's loss. A principal has the duty, unless a contract provides otherwise, to indemnify the agent for the agent's payment of damages to third persons because of the proper performance of the agency contract or a resulting tort. A principal has an implied duty to indemnify the agent for the payment of damages the agent was required to make for loss the agent sustained without the agent's fault while acting pursuant to the agent's authority.

Summary Statement

1. *Express authority* occurs when the principal specifies, either orally or in writing, what the agent is authorized to do.
2. *Implied authority* is customary or incidental, and consent for the agent to perform occurs when the agent reasonably believes that it is necessary to carry out the express authority.

[5] See Restatement (Second) of Agency secs. 432–41 (1958) for a discussion of the duties a principal owes to the agent.

3. *Incidental authority* occurs from the circumstances allowing the agent to perform those acts that are incidental to perform the agent's express authority.
4. *Customary authority* is found when the trade or professional practice in which the agent acts creates an implied authorization to conform with the general custom.
5. *Emergency authority* occurs when the agent is confronted with circumstances that the agent reasonably can believe the principal did not foresee would occur and that require action which the agent reasonably believes is what the principal would do if aware of the circumstances.
6. *Apparent authority* occurs when the principal's words or other conduct addressed to a third party reasonably cause the third party to believe that someone is the principal's agent with authority. Under this theory, it is sometimes said that the principal is "estopped" from denying such agency and authority.
7. The third party is under a duty to determine the extent of the agent's authority.
8. A third party is not bound by secret limitations on the agent's authority. However, as between the principal and the agent, any express limitations on the scope of the agent's authority are valid.
9. Generally, an agent cannot delegate to another the agent's authority to act for the principal. However, if the agent's special skill, discretion, or judgment are not involved, the agent may delegate under the following instances:
    a) When duties are ministerial or mechanical
    b) When there is an established custom to employ subagents
    c) If an unforeseen emergency arises, making it impracticable to communicate with the principal
    d) If it is reasonably inferred from the principal's business that the parties contemplated the appointment of subagents
10. As a result of the fiduciary relationship, an agent owes to the principal the following duties:
    a) Loyalty
    b) Obedience and performance
    c) Reasonable care
    d) Accounting for agency funds
    e) Keeping the principal informed
11. The principal owes to the agent the following duties:
    a) Compensating the agent
    b) Complying with the agency contract
    c) Reimbursing the agent for expenses authorizedly incurred
    d) Indemnifying the agent for losses caused to the agent by the agency relationship through no fault of the agent
12. The agency relationship creates a fiduciary obligation on the agent toward the principal. A fiduciary is a person with a duty to act primarily for the benefit of another. The law imposes special duties to perform with a high degree of care.

The following case illustrates the doctrine of *respondeat superior* and when an employer is exempted from liability for its negligent employee.

HARRIS v. TROJAN FIREWORKS COMPANY, 174 Cal. Rptr. 452 (1981).

Anthony Barajas was an employee of Trojan Fireworks Company. On Friday, December 21, at the Trojan manufacturing plant, commencing at noon and continuing until 4 P.M., Trojan held a Christmas party for its employees at which they drank large quantities of alcoholic beverages. Barajas attended the party and became intoxicated to the extent that it impaired his ability to drive an automobile. In his attempt to drive home he was involved in the accident which resulted in the death of James Harris and injury to Dawn and Steven Griffin. Harris and the Griffins contend that Barajas' intoxication occurred in the course and scope of his employment so that under the doctrine of respondeat superior his employer, Trojan, is liable for the resulting injuries and wrongful death. Trojan contends that the respondeat superior doctrine is not applicable here because the accident did not occur until after Barajas had left the defendant's plant and was on his way home.

As a general rule, a principal is responsible for the acts of his agent; however, an employer is often exempted from liability for injury caused to or by the employee while the employee is traveling to or from work. This exemption of employer liability is often referred to as the "going and coming" rule. In third-party liability cases, the negligent employee's employer is often excused from liability under the "going and coming" rule on the rationale that the employer should not be liable for acts of the employee which occur when the employee is not rendering service to his employer. It may be argued that the purpose of the party was to improve employer/employee relations or to increase the continuity of employment by providing employees with the fringe benefit of a party, or to improve relations between the employees by providing them with this opportunity for social contact. That Trojan intended for Barajas to attend the party is indicated by the fact that the party was held at work during work hours and Barajas was paid to attend. That Trojan intended for Barajas to consume alcohol is implied from the fact that the employer furnished the alcoholic beverages and it is further alleged that Trojan, its agents and employees caused him to imbibe large quantities of alcoholic beverages. It is further alleged that he became intoxicated at the party, to such an extent that his ability to operate a motor vehicle was substantially impaired. We hold that plaintiffs have pleaded sufficient facts, which, if proved, would support a jury's determination that Barajas' intoxication occurred at the party and that his attendance at the party as well as his state of intoxication occurred within the scope of his employment. That he would attempt to drive home while still intoxicated and might have an accident was foreseeable.

Questions and Case Problems

1. Bromber, the general manager of a hotel, offered a $1,000 reward in a newspaper for information leading to the arrest and conviction of the person who killed the hotel clerk during a hotel robbery. Plaintiff, Jackson, claimed the reward, and the defendant, hotel owner Goodman, denied that Bromber had the authority to make the reward offer. Was there sufficient evidence to present a jury question that Bromber, as the hotel manager, had apparent authority to make the reward offer? The jury returned a finding in favor of Jackson, but the judge set aside the jury's finding and entered judgment for the defendant as a matter of law. Plaintiff appealed. What judgment on appeal? [*Jackson v. Goodman,* 244 N.W.2d 423 (Mich. 1976).]
2. Glen Wood, an executive vice-president of SAR Manufacturing Co., checked into the Holiday Inn facility at Phenix City, Alabama, and tendered payment for his room by using his Gulf Oil Company credit card. Goynes, the "night auditor" of the Phenix City Holiday Inn, called National Data in Atlanta on a toll-free number provided by Gulf in order to confirm the plaintiff's credit card number and receive an

authorization to extend credit on the basis of the card. He received a communication from National Data advising him: "Do not honor this sale. Pick up the credit card and send it in for reward." Goynes then telephoned Wood's room at 7:00 A.M. and advised him that he was unable to obtain credit authorization and requested Wood to surrender the card. Goynes said that Wood voluntarily complied. Goynes was offensive, abusive, and insulting to Wood. Wood then paid in cash and left the motel. Upon returning home, Wood called Gulf and complained that his account was current, and his credit was immediately reinstated. Wood sued the Gulf Oil Corporation, Holiday Inns, Inc., Interstate Inns, Inc. (the owner of the Phenix City Holiday Inn), and Goynes. Interstate and Goynes denied any negligence or wrongful conduct and asserted by way of cross-claim that they were acting under the direction of Gulf and were therefore entitled to indemnification by Gulf. (a) Was the Holiday Inn clerk the agent of the Gulf Oil Company? (b) Is Gulf liable for the clerk's tortious conduct? (c) Is Gulf required to indemnify the Holiday Inn for its clerk's negligence? [*Wood v. Holiday Inns, Inc.,* 508 F.2d 167 (Ala. 1975).]

3. Must a third party who paid a traveling salesperson, authorized to solicit orders for the salesperson's principal, who never turned the money over to the principal, pay the money again to the principal?
4. The owner of land appointed a real estate agent to sell his land. The real estate agent owned 80 percent of the stock in a company to whom he sold the land at its appraised fair market value. When the seller discovered the real estate agent's interest in the company that bought the land he sued the company demanding it return the land to the seller. Did the real estate agent violate any duty owed to the seller?
5. Davis was a salaried outside salesperson of defendant, International Playtex Corporation. His duties included selling Playtex products to retail stores. He worked out of his home and was required to own and operate a motor vehicle for business use. He had no set hours of employment and was urged by Playtex's district manager to work evenings and weekends. While traveling to his girlfriend's home to do paperwork for Playtex, Davis was involved in a collision with Barnum, who died from his injuries. Rappaport, the plaintiff, the executor of Barnum's estate, brought this suit against Playtex. Was Davis acting within the scope of his employment at the time of the accident? [*Rappaport v. Int'l Playtex Corp.,* 352 N.Y.S.2d 241 (N.Y. 1974).]
6. Rushing, King, and Kenney, defendants, are the owners of an undivided three-fourths interest in the real property in question. Garrett, plaintiff, the owner of the remaining one-fourth undivided interest, filed suit in the Circuit Court for **partition** and for specific performance of an alleged contract of sale to him of their interests in the real property. The court found that a series of letters written by counsel for the plaintiff and the defendants during the course of the partition suit constituted a written binding contract for the sale of defendants' interest in the property to plaintiff. There was no proof that defendants had given to their attorney any express authority to contract for the sale of their interests in the property. Does an attorney employed by a party in litigation such as in the instant case, have implied authority to execute a written agreement for the conveyance of property? [*Rushing, King and Kenney v. Garrett, Jr.* 375 So.2d 903 (Fla. 1979).]
7. Anglo-American Clothing Corporation brought an action against Marjorie's of Tiburon, Inc., d/b/a/ under the trade name of Rebel Jeans, alleging that Rebel Jeans was indebted to Anglo-American Clothing, by virtue of a contract of sale in which Rebel Jeans purchased from plaintiff 132 jackets at a total purchase price of $2,739. Rebel Jeans defended on the basis that approximately 40 jackets were defective and

partition
A division of property between joint owners

that they had attempted a proper rejection of said items upon the grounds that the transaction was a sale or return transaction. The evidence clearly established that the transaction constituted a "sale or return." Seller, Anglo-American Clothing, introduced uncontroverted evidence that their agent did not have authority to enter into a "sale or return" type of contract. Although Anglo-American's agents do not have actual authority to enter into such type of transactions, both witnesses testifying for Rebel Jeans indicated that statements made to them by Anglo-American's agent led them to believe that he had such authority by virtue of owning an interest in the business. The testimony disclosed that Anglo-American's agent did not however own any interest in the business. Did Anglo-American's agent have implied or apparent authority to enter into a sale or return contract? [*Anglo-American Clothing Corp. v. Marjorie's of Tiburon, Inc.*, 571 P.2d 427 (Okla. 1977).]

8. Ford, a black, visited the "Bud" Orth Real Estate Agency. Ford asked Ken Orth, a licensed salesperson on duty at the agency, to show him a particular piece of property as advertised for sale. Orth informed Ford that the owner did not want to show the property to black persons and therefore he could not see it. Ford told Ken Orth that he was discriminating and left the agency. Ford filed a complaint with the Wisconsin Real Estate Examining Board, alleging in substance that E. C. "Bud" Orth, a licensed broker, was guilty of racial discrimination. Was Ken Orth, acting as an agent under the explicit instructions of his principal, the seller, guilty of discrimination? [*Ford v. Wisconsin Real Estate Examining Board,* 179 N.W.2d 786 (Wis. 1970).]

9. At the beginning of 1976, the Hagues listed land with Hilgendorf for sale at a stated price. This listing gave Hilgendorf the exclusive right to sell the land for a period of twelve months. The Hagues sent Hilgendorf a letter on August 13, 1976 purporting to terminate the listing on the 160 acre parcel. Hilgendorf did not acquiesce in Hagues' termination of the listing of the 160 acres and insisted he had the right to sell the land. In August and September 1976, Hilgendorf produced several buyers who were willing and able to buy the 160 acres on the terms indicated by the Hagues, but the Hagues ignored their offers. The Hagues secured another real estate broker who, later in 1976, sold the 160 acres. Hilgendorf sued the Hagues for damages for breach of the listing contract, the damages being measured by the commission. Did the Hagues have the right to terminate the listing contract? [*Hilgendorf v. Hague,* 293 N.W.2d 272 (Iowa 1980).]

10. In *Harris v. Trojan Fireworks Company,* excerpted at the beginning of this section, the court held that if the facts alleged by the plaintiff were proved, a jury could find that the employee's intoxication occurred within the scope of his employment and hence the "going and coming rule" would not apply. How could an employer avoid liability for its intoxicated employees at a company party?

CHAPTER 17

AGENCY AND THE LAW OF CONTRACTS AND TORTS

After you have read this chapter, you should be able to:

1. Explain the three things an agent must do to be protected from personal liability on a breach of contract suit.
2. Know the application of the parol evidence rule to:
   a) Simple (informal) agency contracts with a third party and an agent
   b) Formal contracts with a third party and an agent
3. Understand when an agent may agree to be held personally liable to a contract with a third party.
4. Explain an implied warranty of authorization.
5. Explain an implied warranty of the principal's capacity.
6. Define a disclosed principal and a partially disclosed principal, and explain when these principals are personally liable under the agent's contract.
7. Define an undisclosed principal, and explain when the undisclosed principal is and is not personally liable under the agent's contract.
8. Explain when a third party's payment to the agent will bind the principal, and when it will not bind the principal.
9. Distinguish a servant from a nonservant agent, and explain the reason for and the importance of this difference.
10. Explain when the principal is liable or not liable for the torts of its agent, and when the principal is not liable.
11. Determine a public accountant's liability.
12. Determine the status and liability of independent auditors.

BUSINESS DECISIONS and the LAW

Helen, owner of Specialty Clothing, Ltd., employed Sam as a sales associate. Realizing that she needed office supplies, she sent Sam, as her agent, to pick up the stationery. Since it was a beautiful day, Sam decided to go to the driving range and hit golf balls. While there, he and another patron, Fred, began arguing and Sam hit him with a golf club. Fred sustained serious injuries and sued both Helen and Sam. What outcome?

Sam was out on an errand as Helen's agent in our case. The general rule is that the principal is liable for the agent's actions provided that the agent is acting within the scope of the agency. The law of agency would therefore hold that Helen is not liable to Fred for injuries inflicted on him by agent Sam. Sam was not at a place, nor acting in a way which was in furtherance of the agency. Sam was merely on a frolic and detour of his own and thus stands alone in defending his actions.

Fred can look only to Sam for damages. Meanwhile, Helen fired Sam because of the tort he committed during the agency. Sam will no doubt stick to business in the future.

Introduction

In the preceding chapters of this part we discussed the concept of agency, the authority and apparent authority of an agent, and the duties of the principal and the agent to each other. In this chapter we will discuss the impact on third persons of an agent's conduct resulting in contractual and tort liability of the agent and of a disclosed and an undisclosed principal.

Agency relationships are not created to be static. Rather, what is expected is action that will change relationships between two persons, namely the principal and a third party.

Most often it is the law of contracts with which people are concerned in their business dealings. However, while attempting to create contracts, during the operation of the agency, the law of **torts** may come into the situation.

tort
A civil (private) noncontractual wrong for which a court will give a remedy

Agents can protect themselves from assuming duties and giving rights to the principal or to third parties if they conduct themselves properly in the operation of the agency.

This chapter is important because it gives you insight into how increased exposure to risk in the legal environment brought about by agency can be limited.

Basically, two substantive areas of law are impacted significantly by the agency relationship: contracts and torts.

Contract Liability of Agents

▶ Liability of Agent As a Party to a Contract

The agent must do the following three things to be protected from contractual liability:

1. Disclose the principal. The disclosure of the agent's capacity and the fact that the agent is acting on behalf of a particular principal may be expressed in any manner. The third party must be aware that the agent is acting on behalf of another.
2. Have authority to act. The agent must be authorized by the principal to act on the principal's behalf. The authority may be express or implied, or there may be apparent authority.[1]
3. Have any written contracts properly executed. If an agent signs a written contract with the third party, the agent must disclose his or her representative capacity on the contract. For example, if Jane Arnold is acting for Peter Powers, a proper signature would be, "Peter Powers by Jane Arnold." If the agent simply signed "Jane Arnold," even though the third party knew she was acting for her principal, the parol evidence rule may apply and prevent verbal testimony to explain the agent's capacity.

The parol evidence rule[2] has the following applications:

simple contract
A contract that need not be in any particular form

1. *Simple contracts* If the written contract is simple (i.e., not under seal, or not a negotiable instrument such as a promissory note or a check), the agent may testify concerning the fact that the third party knew he or she was acting on behalf of the principal, although the written contract does not disclose this.

[1]See pp. 310–11, for discussion of authority and apparent authority.

[2]See p. 227, for discussion of the parol evidence rule.

2. *Formal contracts* If the contract was under seal or negotiable commercial paper (e.g., a check), the parol evidence rule will prevent the agent from giving testimony concerning the third party's knowledge that the agent was acting on behalf of the principal.

formal contract
A contract that must be in a certain form

► Agent May Agree to Personal Liability

The agent may agree to be held personally liable at the request of the third party. For example, if *T* requests *A* to stand behind a sales contract, the agent *(A)*, in order to effect a sale and receive a commission, may agree to be held personally liable in the event of a breach.

► Agent's Implied Warranties

An agent makes two implied **warranties** on the contract made by the agent for the principal with third persons: (1) implied warranty of authorization, and (2) implied warranty of the principal's capacity to contract. The agent will be held personally liable if the agent breaches either warranty even though acting in good faith.

warranty
An express or implied assurance that certain facts exist

Implied Warranty of Authorization When an agent contracts with a third party, the agent impliedly warrants having the authority to contract for the principal. If the agent does not have this authority, or exceeds the scope of such authority, the agent is liable to the third party for **damages** for breach of implied warranty of authority.

damages
The money judicially awarded to an injured party for another's wrongful conduct

In the following case a corporate president made an offer to sell corporation property without the approval of the board of directors or stockholders. The court held he was in breach of an agent's implied warranty of authorization.

FACTS

Husky Industries, Inc., sued defendant Craig Industries, Inc. for specific performance of an alleged contract for the sale of the Craig Industries' Mountain View charcoal plant, or, in the alternative, damages for breach of the agreement. Husky Industries also sued D. C. Craig, as president of Craig Industries, for breach of warranty of authority. On September 19, 1977, Mr. Craig telephoned Mr. Gideon, of Husky Industries, to inquire if the plaintiff corporation was interested in buying the Mountain View plant. Mr. Gideon gave Mr. Craig his $25,000 check as a down payment on the transaction. The check was made payable to "Craig Industries, Inc."

On September 27, 1977, the attorneys for Craig Industries wrote Husky Industries' lawyer that the corporation's board of directors had met that date and "voted to reject the offer." Mr. Gideon's uncashed $25,000 check was returned with the letter. Plaintiff thereafter commenced suit. Judgment was rendered against both defendants, and Mr. Craig appealed. Did Mr. Craig breach his implied warranty of authority?

DECISION

Yes. Judgment affirmed for the plaintiff, Husky Industries, Inc., against Mr. Craig only. Having represented himself as an agent of a disclosed principal, an individual who purports to contract in the name of his principal without or in excess of his authority to do so, becomes personally subject to liability to the other contracting party. The individual liability of the agent is fixed unless he manifests that he does not make a warranty of authority or the other contracting party knows the agent is not so authorized. The agent is personally liable even if he acts in the utmost good faith and honestly believes he was authorized and regardless of whether he has falsely represented his authority with intent to deceive.

Mr. Craig at no time, either before or after revealing his principal was a corporation, said or indicated anything to the effect that he possessed or did not possess authority to make an agreement binding on the corporation. In short, nothing was mentioned or discussed regarding the apparent authority Mr. Craig was using to contract on behalf of the corporation. Mr. Craig, representing himself as an agent, undertook to contract in the name of his disclosed principal without or in excess of his authority to do so; plaintiff's agents were unaware of such lack of authority; and plaintiff was damaged by defendant Mr. Craig's breach of his express or implied covenant or warranty of authority.

Husky Indus., Inc. v. Craig Indus., Inc. and D. C. Craig, 618 S.W.2d 458 (Mo. 1981).

Implied Warranty of Principal's Capacity The agent impliedly warrants to the third party that the principal has capacity to be contractually bound. For example, if the agent acts for a dissolved corporation, the former corporation will not be liable under any contract, but the agent can be held liable for breach of the agent's implied warranty of the principal's capacity. However, if the agent acts on behalf of a minor/principal and does not represent that the principal has full capacity, the agent is not liable if the minor avoids the contract.

Contract Liability of Principals

Whether a principal is disclosed, undisclosed, or partially disclosed to the third person depends upon the third person's knowledge of a person as a principal and the principal's identity. When the third person knows that the agent is acting for a principal but the third person does not know the principal's identity, the latter is a **partially disclosed principal.** In this book, unless otherwise indicated, reference to a disclosed principal includes a partially disclosed principal, because the third person intends to contract with the principal whoever it may be and the agent.

partially disclosed principal
A person whose identity is not disclosed to a third person who knows, or reasonably should know, that an agent is, or may be acting as, an agent for that principal whoever it may be

► Liability of Disclosed Principal or Partially Disclosed Principal As Party to a Contract

Once the agent has **disclosed** to the third party the identity of the **principal** for whom the agent is authorized to contract, or the third person reasonably should be aware of the principal's identity, the principal becomes liable on the subsequently made contract.[3] However, if the agent is not authorized, or if the agent exceeds the scope of his or her authority, the principal may ratify[4] the contract and thus become liable on the contract with the effect as though it were initially authorized. Accordingly, if there is a principal with contractual capacity, and the agent with authority properly executed the contract with the third party, a contract exists only between *P* and *T*. If the principal is partially disclosed, both the principal and the agent are parties to the contract with the third person.

disclosed principal
A person known, or who reasonably should be known, by a third party to be a principal for an agent

► Liability of Undisclosed Principal As Party to a Contract

If the third party is not aware and reasonably should not be aware that the agent is acting for anyone, the principal is called an **undisclosed principal.** The parties to the contract

undisclosed principal
A person not known, or who is not reasonably known, to be a principal for an agent by a third party

[3]See Restatement (Second) of Agency sec. 4 (1958) for a general discussion of a disclosed, partially disclosed, and undisclosed principal.

[4]See pp. 301–03 on the rules of ratification in agency.

are the agent and the third party. However, if the third party breaches the contract, the assets of the third party are available to satisfy a judgment obtained by the agent against the third party. Because the agent then holds such assets in trust for the benefit of the principal, the law causes the undisclosed principal also, along with the agent, to be a party to the contract authorizedly made by the agent so that the principal's assets are available to the third party if the agent breaches the contract. So there are three parties to the contract—namely the agent, principal, and third party—unless the undisclosed principal is excluded from being a party to the contract either (1) expressly by the contract, (2) by the contract being under seal, or (3) if the contract is a negotiable instrument in which the principal's name does not appear. Each of the three parties is liable as a contracting party.

The following case illustrates how the court found a travel bureau (agent) liable to a customer because of its undisclosed principal.

FACTS

Rosen purchased a package tour for an African safari from Deporter-Butterworth Tours, Inc. Rosen had direct contact with the travel bureau but never with the tour sponsor, World Trek. World Trek was an undisclosed principal. Rosen told the travel bureau where he could be contacted in Europe and in Egypt prior to the start of the tour. The travel bureau failed to contact Rosen overseas, leaving him stranded in Egypt for a week. Rosen sued the travel bureau for damages. The travel bureau claimed that it was not liable because it was merely an agent for World Trek and that World Trek was the proper party to the lawsuit. The trial court held for Rosen, and the travel bureau appealed.

DECISION

Judgment for Rosen. The traditional relationship between a travel bureau and the tour sponsors of the various tours sold has been categorized as one of agent and principal particularly in the field of tort liability of the travel bureau for injuries that occur to the traveler. No sound reason exists for not finding the same principal/agent relationship between a tour sponsor and a travel bureau in the case of alleged liability for breach of an agreement involving the ultimate sale of the tour to an ordinary member of the traveling public, such as Rosen. If an agent does not disclose the existence of an agency relationship and the identity of his principal, he binds himself to the third party with whom he acts as if he himself were the principal. The fact that Rosen knew that World Trek and not Deporter-Butterworth Tours was the tour sponsor does not satisfy the necessary disclosure to prevent it from becoming liable as principal.

Rosen v. Deporter-Butterworth Tours, Inc., 379 N.E.2d 407 (Ill. 1978).

The important point is that the agent was authorizedly acting on behalf of the undisclosed principal when the agent contracted with the third party, and the latter should stand behind the contract. When *P* authorizes *A* to purchase property on *P*'s behalf without disclosing that *A* is representing anyone and *A*, intending to act for *P*, authorizedly contracts with *T* to purchase the property in *A*'s own name, *P* (as well as *A*) is liable on the contract.

► Effect of Agent's Improper Purpose

If an agent makes a contract for the disclosed or undisclosed principal as the agent is authorized to do, but with an improper purpose of which the third party does not have notice, the principal is bound on the contract as though the agent had a proper purpose. For example, payment by the third party to the agent of funds due to the principal, the agent having authority to receive such funds, will bind the principal even if the agent never remits the payment. This rule applies only if the third party acted in good faith and did not know that the agent would act improperly. For example, *P* appoints *A* to collect rents on *P*'s behalf. *T*, a tenant, paid the rent to *A*, who kept the money. *P* would have to give credit to *T* for the monthly rent.

The reasons for this rule are that *T* cannot ascertain *A*'s improper purpose, and public policy requires *P* to select the agent carefully for loyalty to *P*.

► Effect of Agent's Unauthorized Misrepresentation of What the Agent Was Authorized to Represent Truthfully

If an agent makes a contract for the disclosed or partially disclosed principal as the agent is authorized to do, but misrepresents matters in connection with the contract of which the third party does not have notice, the principal is liable on the contract and also for such misrepresentations. For example, a salesperson misrepresents the fabric content of a sweater sold to an innocent store customer third party. The store owner principal is liable to the customer for the agent's untruthful statement.

Tort Liability

The three-party relationship created by an agency contract frequently involves an injury arising from tort liability. If the principal directs its agent to commit a wrongful act, the *principal* is liable in tort to the injured third party. The principal is also liable for all other tortious acts committed by the agent while acting within the scope of the agent's authority.

Even though the agent may injure the third party while acting for the principal, the agent may also be held liable. An agent is liable to third parties for the agent's torts irrespective of whether or not his principal is also liable and whether or not the agent was acting within the scope of the agent's authority. The injured third party may select the principal or the agent as liable for the agent's torts committed within the course and scope of the agent's authority. Also, it is possible that the third person may be liable to the agent for torts caused by the third person's improper conduct.

misfeasance
Misdoing

nonfeasance
Not doing

Although an agent is liable to a third party for the agent's misdoing, called **misfeasance,** the agent is not liable for not doing anything, called **nonfeasance,** in the absence of any legal obligation to act. The agent has no duty to the third party and so has no liability for nonfeasance. But once an agent begins to act, the law imposes a duty upon the agent to act carefully, as it does for everyone, and also imposes liability for misfeasance.

► Principal's Liability for Torts of the Agent while Acting within the Scope of the Agent's Authority

servant
An agent whose physical conduct his or her master (principal) has the right to control or controls

master
A principal who has the right to control, or controls, the physical conduct of his or her servant agent

Let us briefly examine the *principal's* tort liability within the three-party relationship.

An agent may be a **servant** or a nonservant agent. We have defined an agent as a person authorized to act on behalf of another and subject to the other's control. The principal's degree of control over the conduct of the agent may vary. If the principal has the right to control, or exercises control over, the physical conduct of its agent, the agent is called a servant and the principal is called a **master.** Often courts refer to them as principal and agent. Most agents are servants.

The reason for distinguishing between servants and nonservant agents is that the principal's liability varies as the degree of the principal's control over the conduct of the agent. Thus a master is liable for the tortious physical harm (or loss) to third persons caused by the servant while acting within the scope of the servant's employment (servants are usually called employees). A principal is liable for the nonphysical torts of its nonservant agent while acting within the scope of the agent's authority.

For example, independent contractors who become special agents (e.g., brokers, lawyers) are nonservant agents, and because the principal does not control their physical conduct, the principal is not liable for their tortious physical harm to third persons. (*P* retains *A*, a real estate broker, to produce a prospective buyer of *P*'s land. While *A* is driving *A*'s auto showing the land to a customer, *A* drives negligently and injures the customer. *P* is not liable for *A*'s tortious physical harm to the customer because *A* is a nonservant agent.) (*A, P*'s truck driver, while delivering *P*'s goods, negligently injures a pedestrian. *P* is a master and liable for the tortious physical harm to the pedestrian caused by *A, P*'s servant.) Accordingly, let us first consider torts by servants and then torts by nonservant agents.

A principal or master is not liable to third persons for **punitive damages** for the acts of the agent unless (1) the act was previously authorized by the principal, (2) the act was later ratified or approved by the principal, (3) the principal was reckless in employing an unfit agent, or (4) the act occurred while the agent was acting in the scope of the agent's employment in a managerial capacity.[5]

punitive (exemplary) damages
The money judicially awarded to an injured party in excess of compensatory damages to punish for malicious, wanton, or intentional wrongful conduct

Torts by Servants The doctrine of a master's liability for the torts of the servant committed while acting within the scope of the servant's employment is called **respondeat superior.** "Scope of employment" is a broad phrase, but in general it means in furtherance of the master's business. In certain instances a master is liable even when the servant has *not* acted within the scope of the servant's employment.

respondeat superior
Let the master (superior) be responsible for the torts of his or her servant committed while acting within the scope of the servant's employment

1. *Torts committed within the scope of employment.* Once tortious physical harm has occurred, the first step is to determine if the wrongdoer is an agent. If the wrongdoer is, the next step is to decide if the wrongdoer is a servant. If the agent is, then the last step is to see if the servant was acting within the scope of the servant's employment when the tort was committed. Section 228(1) of the Restatement (Second) of Agency establishes the following criteria to ascertain whether the conduct of a servant is within the scope of employment:

- **a)** It is of the kind of conduct the servant is employed to perform.
- **b)** It occurs substantially within the authorized time and space limits.
- **c)** It is activated, at least in part, by a purpose to serve the master.
- **d)** If force is intentionally used by the servant against another, the use of force is not unexpectable by the master.

The court in the following case held an employer was not responsible for its employee's act causing injury to another because the employee was not discharging his duty owed to the employer at the time of its occurrence. The employee was not acting within the scope of his employment.

FACTS

The plaintiff, who was working for Harrison Electrical Constructors, alleges that a welder, an employee of one of the Natkin companies, contractors, stuffed paper into the ends of a pipe the plaintiff was welding, filled the pipe with acetylene gas from his welding rig and

[5]See Restatement (Second) of Agency sec. 217C.

caused the gas to explode. This action was, according to the plaintiff, either a practical joke or harassment directed at him for not being a union member. Plaintiff claims that the explosion caused him to contract a rash, ringing and deafness in both ears, nausea, and dizziness. The defendants filed motions for summary judgment on the grounds that no Natkin employee was authorized to use acetylene gas for any purpose other than the cutting of steel, nor did Natkin have any interest in any union activity of its employees. The lower court allowed the motion and plaintiff appealed.

DECISION

Motion for summary judgment affirmed. The employee setting off the explosion with acetylene gas, had temporarily abandoned the interests of his employer and was acting in a purely personal manner and contrary to the policy and instructions of his employer. The act of that individual in no way could be construed as having been in the discharge of a duty owed to the employer nor incident to such duty. Therefore, there is no genuine issue as to any material fact, and the defendants are entitled to summary judgment as a matter of law.

Williams v. Natkin and Co. et al. 508 F.Supp. 1017 (D. Ark. 1981).

In what is known as the "independent frolic" or "detour" cases, the chief question is whether the servant's deviation from the servant's authority is sufficient to cause the servant's conduct not to be within the scope of the servant's employment. Thus the following examples of a servant's conduct at variance with the servant's authority have been held to be within the servant's scope of employment: the servant's unauthorized use of equipment that was not that much substantially different from what was authorized; the negligence and traffic violation of a servant truck driver when the master had instructed the servant to drive carefully; the servant salesperson keeping a store open a little longer than the established closing time; and the servant truck driver paying a social call requiring a slight deviation from the servant's established service route. The latter is an illustration of a "detour" case where the servant *temporarily* deviates and then resumes activity within the authorized scope of employment. Any injury to a third person at the point of "detour" will subject the employer/master to liability for the servant's tort.

2. *Torts committed beyond the scope of the servant's authority.* The master is not liable to the third party for torts committed by the servant when the servant acts beyond the scope of the servant's employment. If the servant is no longer acting for the benefit of the master and has dealings with the third party outside the servant's employment relationship with the master, the injured third party generally has no recourse against the master. When a servant engages in an independent frolic or detour that is not within the servant's scope of employment, there is much difficulty and difference among the cases in determining at what point in time and space the servant returns into the employ of the master.

FACTS

White, an employee of Inter-City Auto Freight, Inc., while driving a large tractor-trailer truck attempted to pass Kuehn, a motorist. After Kuehn had moved to the next lane, he motioned with his fist for White to pull over. After Kuehn regained control of his car, both parties stopped on the highway. White got out of his cab carrying a metal pipe and as he approached Kuehn, swung the pipe. It grazed the side of Kuehn's face and knocked Kuehn's glasses to the ground. As Kuehn bent over to pick up his glasses, White hit him twice more. Kuehn sued both White and his employer, Inter-City.

DECISION

A master is responsible for the servant's acts under the doctrine of respondeat superior when the servant acts within the scope of his employment and in furtherance of the master's business. When a servant steps aside from the master's business in order to effect some purpose of his own, the master is not liable. When the servant's intentionally tortious or criminal acts are not performed in furtherance of the master's business, the master will not be held liable as a matter of law, even though the employment situation provided the opportunity for the servant's wrongful acts or the means for carrying them out. White assaulted Kuehn because of his anger toward Kuehn, not because of any intent to serve Inter-City.

Kuehn v. White & Inter-City Auto Freight, Inc., 600 P.2d 679 (Wash. 1979).

Torts by Nonservant Agents The principal is not liable for tortious physical harm committed by a nonservant agent because the principal has no control over the agent's physical conduct. However, the principal is liable for the agent's nonphysical torts committed while acting within the agent's authority or apparent authority. For example, if the agent intentionally misrepresents to a customer third party regarding the subject matter authorized or apparently authorized to be sold by the agent, the principal may be liable for the tort of **deceit.**

deceit
Briefly, a tort consisting of contractual fraud causing loss (for a full definition, see the Glossary)

It should be noted that an agent is not liable for the torts or breach of contract committed by the principal in connection with a transaction authorizedly made by the agent. The following case is an example.

FACTS

The plaintiffs, Mr. and Mrs. Dorkin, contracted with the defendant, American Express Company, for a European tour. While being transported from Antwerp to Amsterdam in Holland, Mrs. Dorkin sustained personal injuries when the tour bus in which she and her husband were riding braked abruptly, causing her to be thrown to the floor. The plaintiffs claimed that the negligence of the defendant was a failure to exercise reasonable and prudent care in providing safe equipment and careful personnel in the discharge of its contractual obligation to supply a safe, entertaining European vacation. The plaintiffs contend that the defendant was the agent of the various hotels and transportation companies as principals who supplied the services abroad and that the defendant as agent is liable for their tortious conduct. Defendant denies that it is so liable. Was American Express liable for the injury of Mrs. Dorkin?

DECISION

No. Judgment for American Express. In the absence of agreement or acts indicating an intention of the contracting parties to superadd the responsibility of the agent, there is no such responsibility of the agent to third parties for tortious acts of the principal. Similarly, there is no liability on the part of the agent for breach of contract by the principal. In the instant case there was no breach of contract, either between the plaintiffs and the defendant agent or between plaintiffs and the bus company on whose vehicle the accident happened. American Express contracted on behalf of its principals, hotels and transportation companies, if we regard the defendant as an agent (which I do not, although I recognize that the nomenclature "travel agent" is used to designate or describe the nature of defendant's business), to provide for a planned, structured trip to Europe with a designated place of beginning and a point of termination covering a stated number of days and to provide for food and lodging and transportation between points to be visited within the context of the total trip. Defendant performed its contract with plaintiffs and, as an agent, is not liable for the tortious conduct of its principals. Further the defendant is really an independent contractor and not an agent.

Dorkin v. Am. Express Co., 74 Misc.2d 673 (N.Y. 1974).

The Status and Liability of Public Accountants

▶ Status

independent contractor
A person who contracts independently for him- or herself to render a result, and who is not acting on behalf of another nor subject to another's control

We have learned that a public accountant is an **independent contractor.** A public accountant certified by the state is called a *certified public accountant* (CPA). However, a public accountant may become an agent for a principal if the principal controls or has the right to control the accountant, or the accountant has authority to contract for a principal. If the accountant becomes an agent, then the law of agency is applicable and determines the liability of the accountant to the principal and to third persons in contract and in tort.

▶ Liability

To the Client The public accountant is a professional person, either an individual or a firm of accountants, with the overall responsibility and duty, pursuant to contract, to exercise reasonable care in the examination of the recorded business affairs of the client and, as a result, to disclose all material relevant financial information in a manner that is not misleading. This responsibility does not include the discovery of irregularities—for example, defalcations (defection, misappropriation of money)—unless otherwise agreed. However, if the accountant discovers suspicious circumstances, the accountant then has the responsibility to investigate further. Also, the accountant may be liable if the accountant's negligence prevents such discovery.

breach of contract
Wrongful nonperformance of a contractual promise

lien
A legal right in another's property as security for the performance of an obligation

possessory lien
A lien that includes the right to possession of the property that is subject to the lien

privileged communication
A communication between certain persons which, because of their relationship, is inadmissible in evidence without a waiver of the privilege

The accountant's disclosure to the client must be made in terms and manner that the particular client reasonably can understand. Failure to provide the agreed-upon careful quality of work is a **breach of contract** by the accountant with the client. An illustration of such a breach is the accountant's failure to render the services contracted for within the express, or if not express then within a reasonable, time. The accountant's material breach of contract precludes any right to compensation for services that have been rendered.

The accountant does not have a common law **possessory lien** on the client's materials possessed by the accountant as security for payment for services rendered. However, some states provide for a statutory lien on such materials. The accountant's working papers and own copies of data belong to the accountant.

The personal relationship between the accountant and the client causes their contract to be a personal contract and, therefore, nonassignable and nondelegable. Also, because of this personal relationship, the communications between the accountant and the client are confidential, and are not to be disclosed without the client's express or implied permission. The common law did not cause **communications** between accountant and client to be **privileged,** although this privilege existed between doctor and patient and between lawyer and client. Today no such privilege exists between accountant and client, except by statute in a minority of the states. It does not exist by federal statute. The client can always waive confidentiality and privileged communications.

To Third Persons We have stressed the accountant's responsibility and liability to the client for negligent misrepresentation and resulting breach of contract; but is the accountant responsible and liable to third persons for the accountant's services to the client? Because there is no contract between the accountant and third persons, there is no **privity** between them. However, if the accountant has reason to believe that, through the client, the accountant's product (e.g., financial statement, other materials) will be made available to third persons, a duty of care by the accountant toward such third persons springs into being, and the accountant is liable to the third person for negligent misrepresentation in the accountant's product that proximately causes harm to that third person.

privity
A mutuality of relationship between persons or between persons and a particular transaction

The extent of such duty of care by the accountant to the third person depends upon whether or not the accountant knows the identity of the particular third person and that the third person may rely on the accountant's product. If the third person's identity is known by the accountant, then the accountant's duty of care toward such known third person is for simple **negligence** producing misrepresentation in the accountant's product—that is, failure to exercise ordinary reasonable prudent care. This is the same duty of care that the accountant owes to the client. However, if the third person's identity is not known to the accountant, then the accountant is liable for damage proximately caused by the accountant's **fraud,** or gross negligence amounting to "actual" or "constructive" fraud. If the accountant intends to mislead (called "scienter"), then there is actual fraud. Constructive fraud exists if there is reckless disregard for the truth.

negligence
Regarding conduct, failure to use the degree of care demanded by the circumstances

fraud
In contracts, a misrepresentation of fact, known to be false, intentionally made to induce another person to make or refrain from making a contract, and reasonably relied on by the other person

It should be carefully noted that it is the accountant's negligent or fraudulent misrepresentation in the accountant's product which subjects the accountant to liability to the client for breach of contract, and to liability to certain third persons who have relied on such misrepresentation.

The Status and Liability of Auditors

A certified public accountant in providing the audit function reviews financial statements and reports to determine whether they are in accordance with generally accepted accounting principles. This obligation is one of ten generally accepted auditing standards. As auditors are often professional agents, the preceding material on the status and liability of public accountants applies to the CPA as an agent engaged in auditing.

The auditor's special function is to assist management by providing it with verifiable reports to be used by third parties. Hence, to a great extent auditor's liability involves claims by the third party as the primary beneficiary of the auditor's report.[6] For example, a person about to sell her business retains an auditor to prepare financial statements for a known potential buyer. The buyer is a foreseen third party that can hold an auditor liable for ordinary negligence in preparing the report. Courts have held auditors liable for negligent misrepresentations reasonably relied on by the foreseen third parties.[7] The Restatement (Second) of the Law of Torts, Section 552, provides a basis for auditor's liability by stating in part ". . . One who, in the course of his . . . profession . . . supplies false information for the guidance of others in their business transactions, is subject to liability . . . if he fails to exercise reasonable care of competency in obtaining or

[6]See O'Brien, "The Legal Environment of the Accounting Profession," 25 *Duq. L. Rev.* 283 (1987).

[7]*Rusch Factors, Inc. v. Levin,* 284 F.Supp. 85 (D.R.I. 1968); *Citizens State Bank v. Timm, Schmidt & Co. and General Casualty Co. of Wisconsin,* 335 N.W.2d 361 (Wis. 1983).

communicating the information." Hence, an auditor's liability extends to all third parties whom the auditor should reasonably foresee as recipients. An auditor's risk of liability includes those third parties who commonly use auditors' reports such as buyers of a business, bankers, and investors.

The following case considers the common law standards governing the liability of independent auditors for failing to detect fraud by the management of the audited company.

FACTS

Between 1970 and 1975, managerial employees of Cenco, Inc. engaged in a massive fraud. The fraud began in Cenco's Medical/Health Division but eventually spread to the top management of Cenco, and by the time it was unmasked the chairman and president of Cenco plus a number of vice-presidents and other top managers were deeply involved. The fraud was eventually discovered by a newly hired financial officer at Cenco who reported his suspicions to the Securities and Exchange Commission. Cenco's independent auditor throughout the period of the fraud, the accounting partnership of Seidman & Seidman (Seidman), either never discovered the fraud or if it did it failed to report it. The fraud primarily involved the inflating of inventories in the Medical/Health Division far above their actual value. This increased the apparent worth of Cenco and greatly increased the market price of its stock (when the fraud was unmasked, the market price of its stock plummeted by more than 75 percent).

Cenco's evidence tended to show in the early stages of the fraud: that Seidman had been careless in checking Cenco's inventory figures and its carelessness had prevented the fraud from being nipped in the bud; that as the fraud expanded, Seidman's auditors became suspicious, but, perhaps to protect the very high fees that Seidman was getting from Cenco, they concealed their suspicions and kept giving Cenco a clean bill of health in their audit reports; that one partner in Seidman, asked by Cenco's general counsel (who was not in on the fraud) whether Seidman suspected anything, answered: "No one suspects fraud." Was Seidman entitled to use the wrongdoing of Cenco's managers as a defense against the charges of breach of contract, negligence and fraud?

DECISION

Yes. Cenco's cross-claim against the auditors, Seidman, dismissed.

Auditors are not detectives hired to ferret out fraud, but if they chance on signs of fraud they may not avert their eyes—they must investigate. The references to keeping an eye out for fraud that appear in the accounting standards incorporated (by reference) in the retention letters between Cenco and Seidman would have little point if not interpreted to impose a duty on auditors to follow up any signs of fraud that come to their attention. In any action by a corporation against its auditors an employee's fraud intended to benefit the company rather than the employee at the company's expense will be attributed to the corporation.

We think it premature as well as unnecessary to decide that an auditor is never liable for the frauds of loyal but misguided company employees that he could have prevented by taking care. But here the uncontested facts show fraud permeating the top management of Cenco. In such a case the corporation should not be allowed to shift the entire responsibility for the fraud to its auditors.

Cenco Inc. v. Seidman & Seidman, 686 F.2d 449 (7th Cir. 1982).

Summary Statement

1. To be protected from personal liability, an agent must:

- **a)** Disclose the principal
- **b)** Be authorized by the principal to act on its behalf
- **c)** Have any written contract with a third party properly executed by the agent

2. The parol evidence rule will allow an agent who signed a *simple* contract to testify that the third party with whom the agent contracted knew the agent was acting on behalf of a principal. A simple contract, as contrasted with a formal contract, is not in any required form.
3. If the agent signed a *formal* contract, the parol evidence rule will prevent the agent from giving testimony concerning the third party's knowledge that the agent was acting on behalf of the principal.
4. If requested by the third party, the agent may agree to become personally liable on the contract.
5. The circumstances surrounding an agent's contract for a principal with a third person create an implied warranty of authorization. This means that the agent warrants he or she has authority and has not exceeded its scope.
6. Also, the agent impliedly warrants that the principal has capacity to be contractually bound.
7. An *undisclosed principal* is a principal not known to the third party who is unaware of any agency. The undisclosed principal has authorized the agent to act for the principal's benefit and on the principal's behalf. The undisclosed principal is liable to the third party on a simple contract, as is the agent also.
8. A *disclosed principal* is a principal that is known to the third party. The principal is liable to the third party if the principal has capacity to contract and if the agent was authorized or apparently authorized to act on the principal's behalf or if the contract was ratified by the principal.
9. If the agent makes an authorized contract for the disclosed or partially disclosed principal but with an improper purpose, of which the third party does not have notice, the principal is bound on the contract.
10. If the agent makes an authorized contract for the disclosed or partially disclosed principal and misrepresents matters in connection with the contract, of which the third party did not have notice, the principal is liable on the contract and for such misrepresentations.
11. A principal is liable for the nonphysical torts of its nonservant agent when they are committed within the course and scope of the agent's authority or apparent authority. The principal (master) is also liable for the tortious physical harm to third persons committed by the principal's servant while acting within the scope of the servant's employment. This rule is based on the theory that the servant, although acting wrongfully, is acting for the benefit of the principal (master). It is known as the doctrine of respondeat superior.
12. A public accountant may be liable to the client for breach of contract and, to certain third persons, for negligent or fraudulent misrepresentation in connection with the accountant's examination of the client's business.
13. An independent auditor is liable to all third persons who the auditor can reasonably forsee will be recipients of the auditor's false information if the auditor fails to exercise reasonable care or competency in obtaining or communicating the information.

The following case illustrates the doctrine of *respondeat superior* when a tort was committed by an employee engaged in his employer's service.

GOLDEN WEST BROADCASTERS v. BALL
171 Cal. Rptr. 95 (1981)

Prudden was employed by Golden West Broadcasters, Inc., owners of television station KTLA. One evening after work, he and some fellow employees drove to the bar at the Gene Autry Hotel in a station wagon supplied to him by Golden West. During the several hours at the bar, Prudden spent some time with his former wife, Barbara Matson. Dean Ball, a patron of the bar, objected to Prudden's treatment of Barbara. A fight ensued and Ball was injured. After the fight Prudden was observed driving away in a station wagon with a KTLA insignia painted on it. Ball sued Golden West for damages on the theory of respondeat superior, claiming that Prudden was acting in the scope of his employment at the time of the fight.

Generally, liability of an employer under the doctrine of respondeat superior extends to torts of an employee committed within the scope of his employment. Many of the cases arising in this area involve, as here, assaults on the plaintiff by an employee of defendant. In such instances the imputation of liability follows where the employment in some way involves the risk of force being used against the plaintiff, i.e. where the act is connected with the employment. Where the question is one of vicarious liability, the inquiry should be whether the risk was one "that may fairly be regarded as typical of or broadly incidental" to the enterprise undertaken by the employer. If a tort is committed for the employee's own purposes, or as the result of a personal quarrel, the employer need not be liable even though at the time the employee is yet engaged in his employer's service. In the case before us we have reached that point. Conceding as fact all of the items urged by Ball as demonstrating that Prudden was acting in the scope of his employment when he beat up Ball in the parking lot at the hotel, we hold as a matter of law that the beating was not inflicted in the scope of Prudden's employment. To invoke the doctrine of respondeat superior here would be to sanction a rule which would impose the liability of an insurer on all employers for every willful tortious act of their employees committed while off duty. Merely to state such a proposition is enough to discredit it, and we do.... [Motion for summary judgment granted.]

Questions and Case Problems

1. Claude I. Bennett, a partner in Bennett Dairy, a partnership, pursuant to his authority, executed a contract in Claude's name with Putney, who was to erect a silo on the Bennett farm and build a foundation on which the silo could be placed. Putney built the foundation but never erected the silo. Bennett Dairy alleges that it is the undisclosed principal of Claude, and it sued Putney for damages for breach of contract. May the partnership as the undisclosed principal sue on the agent Claude's contract? [*Bennett Dairy v. Putney,* 362 N.Y.S.2d 93 (1974).]
2. This action arose out of a traffic collision involving a vehicle owned by the Arkansas Highway and Transportation Department and a vehicle owned by Martin Mittlesteadt and driven by Edna Mittlesteadt, the plaintiffs. At the time of the occurrence defendants were part of a crew engaged in the repair of the Arkansas State Highway. On April 23, 1976 Edna Mittlesteadt was driving the Mittlesteadt vehicle in a westerly direction on Arkansas State Highway when a dump truck suddenly backed from the shoulder of the road into her path of travel. It was admitted that no flagman was present on the highway giving warning to oncoming traffic. It was also admitted that it was the responsibility of the crew team leader to make sure a flagman was in position. The plaintiffs claim damages to their motor vehicle of $1,113.68 and $61 in medical expenses incurred by Edna Mittlesteadt. Upon a trial to a jury, judgment in the amount of $1,174.68 was entered in behalf of the plaintiffs. After the entry of the judgment, defendants filed a motion for a new trial that was overruled by the trial

court. The defendants argue that the trial court was without jurisdiction. They contend that this suit was against the State of Arkansas and constituted a matter that should be filed with the State Claims Commission. Plaintiffs claim that the case was filed against the defendants as individuals and does not attempt to subject the State to any liability whatsoever. May a State employee, while acting within the scope of employment, be held personally responsible for his or her negligence occurring upon a highway? [*Ralls, et al. v. Mittlesteadt, et al.,* 596 S.W.2d 349 (Ark. 1980).]

3. Jerry and JoAnn Cameron, plaintiffs, sought to purchase a home. They contacted a real estate salesperson who showed them several homes. In the process of showing homes to the Camerons, this agent allowed them to look at a multiple listing book that contained a description of the property they ultimately bought. That description stated that the home was 2,400 square feet. After the purchase the Camerons learned in fact that there were only 2,245 square feet. The Camerons filed suit against Terrell & Garrett, defendants, the real estate agents of the seller, who had submitted the information for the multiple listing book. Terrell & Garrett had obtained the square footage information from the seller and were unaware of the misrepresentation. Judgment for whom? [*Cameron v. Terrell & Garrett, Inc.,* 599 S.W.2d 680 (Tex. 1980).]
4. A 10-year-old boy got into a fight with an 11-year-old neighbor. Must the 11-year-old's father pay for the medical bills incurred as a result of this fight?
5. Donald Riviello, a patron of the Pot Belly Pub, a Bronx bar and grill operated by Raybele Tavern, Inc., lost the use of an eye because of what was found to be negligence on the part of Joseph Waldron, also a defendant, a Raybele employee as chef.

   Living nearby, Riviello had frequented the establishment regularly for some years. One night Riviello gravitated to the end of the bar near the kitchen, where, during an interval when Waldron had no food orders to fill, Waldron and another patron and mutual friend were chatting. Riviello joined in the discussion which turned to street crime in the neighborhood. In the course of the conversation, Waldron exhibited a knife containing a small blade and screwdriver attachment, which he said he carried for protection. At this point Waldron went to the kitchen to fill a food order. Several minutes later, while Waldron was returning from his chore to rejoin Riviello, Riviello suddenly turned and, as he did so, his eye unexpectedly came in contact with the blade of the knife which Waldron still had in his hand while demonstrating self-defense. Riviello sued Waldron and the Tavern. Judgment for whom? [*Riviello v. Waldron and Raybele Tavern, Inc.,* 391 N.E.2d 1278 (N.Y. 1979).]
6. David Hall engaged Wagner Company Realtors to sell Hall's house. Mrs. Silva was the sales agent for Wagner. Hall alleges that Silva received $1,000 earnest money from Flores, a prospective, ready, able, and willing buyer; that Silva converted $900 of the earnest money to her own use by keeping it; that the earnest money receipt and contract of sale reflected only $100 as the earnest money paid, and for this reason Flores rescinded the contract. Hall further alleged that, because of this, Hall's property was not sold to Flores and had to be sold to another person at a reduced price causing loss to Hall. Hall sued Wagner Company Realtors for such loss and punitive damages caused by the alleged Silva conversion of $900. Is the Wagner Company Realtors liable in punitive damages for the **conversion** of its sales agent, Mrs. Silva? [*Wagner v. Hall,* 519 S.W.2d 488 (Tex. 1975).]

conversion
The tort of intentional interference with another's right to possession, control, and dominion of a chattel

7. Bruce Advertising supplied services to Crane-Maier on a contractual basis for development of realty. Bruce Advertising was not aware that the Sherrill Trust owned the property that Crane-Maier was developing as its agent. Suit was brought by Bruce Advertising against Crane-Maier, defendant, for the services rendered by Bruce

Advertising when payment was not forthcoming. After suit was instituted, Crane-Maier informed Bruce Advertising that the Sherrill Trust was owner of the property that Crane-Maier was developing. The trial court entered judgment against both Crane-Maier and the Sherrill Trust, holding them jointly and severally liable for the services rendered by Bruce Advertising. The Sherrill Trust appealed. Can Bruce Advertising recover a judgment against both the principal, Sherrill Trust, and the agent, Crane-Maier? [*M. A. Sherrill, trustee of the William W. Sherrill Trust v. Bruce Advertising, Inc., et al.*, 538 S.W.2d 865 (Tex. 1976).]

8. A principal hired an agent to drive his truck and deliver goods for his business. On the agent's return from a delivery he stopped at his house to attend his daughter's birthday party. The children at the party jumped into the truck for a ride, and one child—while riding on the truck fender—fell under the truck wheel and was injured. May the child's parent sue the principal for the agent's negligence?

9. Leo Joiner employed Carter to make an application of pesticide by means of an aircraft in flight to his crops in the immediate vicinity of the fish pond of the plaintiffs. The plaintiffs' lake was stocked with game fish and used as a recreation area for fishing and water pleasure and added to the value of the adjoining real estate. Large numbers of fish started dying in the plaintiffs' pond as well as in another pond in the vicinity of plaintiffs' pond, and the fish continued to die until all of the fish in the pond were dead. Scientific tests conducted on the fish and water established that the fish kill was caused by the pesticide. Plaintiffs' complaint charged that spraying the pesticide permitted it to escape or drift onto the property of plaintiffs and into plaintiffs' fish pond and, as a proximate consequence, the lake was contaminated and the fish died and the value of the plaintiffs' land was depreciated. The complaint also alleged that Carter was an independent contractor employed by Joiner to do this spraying. Was Joiner responsible for the negligent acts of his independent contractor? [*Boroughs et al. v. Joiner*, 337 So.2d 340 (Ala. 1976).]

10. *Golden West Broadcasters v. Ball,* excerpted at the beginning of this section, established that the imputation of liability to an employer follows where the employee's wrongful act is connected with his employment. Why was Prudden, the employee, not acting within the scope of his employment at the time of the fight?

C H A P T E R

18

TERMINATION OF AGENCY

After you have read this chapter, you should be able to:

1. List and explain the five methods by which agency is terminated by acts of the parties.
2. List and explain the six methods by which agency is terminated by operation of law.
3. Distinguish agency coupled with an interest in the subject matter of the agency from agency given as security.
4. Explain the effect of the principal terminating the agency without giving notice to third parties.
5. Explain the effect of terminating the agency between the principal and agent when notice is not given to third parties.

BUSINESS DECISIONS and the LAW

Joan and Bert lived in a stunning Tudor-style house in the estate section of Brookline. It featured among other things, an indoor pool, formal grounds, and stables. Although they enjoyed the home, Joan's international business venture required the couple to relocate in Brussels. They knew they had to sell the house and contacted Gail, owner of Better Homes Realty.

Gail was thrilled to receive their call, as a 6 percent commission on a sale of this magnitude meant well over one year's salary. The parties quickly completed an agency agreement, whereby Gail possessed the exclusive right for three months to sell the house. (Gail figured that this guaranteed a handsome commission.) Gail had trouble finding buyers for the $5 million home, and Joan and Bert became anxious. Needing the money to relocate, Bert began looking for buyers in spite of the agency agreement.

George, a newly transferred Raytheon executive, decided to buy the house as soon as Bert showed it to him. Although Gail still had the exclusive right to sell the house, Joan and Bert decided they did not want to wait until the agreement expired and risk losing George. The couple sold the house for $5.2 million, and Gail sued in the amount of a 6 percent commission despite the fact that she did nothing in furtherance of the sale of the house. Will Gail succeed?

In agency law, the principal always retains the power to terminate an agent's authority. Therefore, in our case, Joan and Bert possessed the power to revoke Gail's authority to sell their house. Gail is not out of luck, however, because the principal is liable to the agent for wrongful revocation. Gail therefore may collect a commission since the sale occurred during the time in which she had an exclusive right to sell the house. It may just be the easiest $312,000 that Gail ever made.

Introduction

Once agency with its express, implied, and apparent authority has been created, how is the agency and such kinds of authority terminated? Basically, how is an agent's power to act for a principal terminated so that the principal cannot be made liable any longer by an agent's conduct?

If the agent knows, or reasonably should know, that if the principal knew of changed circumstances the principal would not want the agent to act, then the agent's power is terminated. In the case of apparent authority, the same is true, if the third party so knew or reasonably should know this.

Our concern here is under what circumstances does agency, the agent's authority, and apparent authority terminate. Just as it is important for you to know how an agency relationship is created, it is also important to know how it ends.

Termination by Acts of the Parties

There are five ways by which agency power may be terminated by acts of the principal and agent: expiration, mutual agreement, option, revocation, and renunciation.

► Expiration of the Agency Contract

The contract between the principal and the agent may specify that it will terminate upon the happening of a certain event or at the end of a time period—for instance, a contract with a real estate broker that creates an exclusive agency to list the principal's house for sale for ninety days. At the expiration of the ninety-day period, the contract is terminated, even though the purpose of the contract has not been accomplished.

► Termination by Mutual Agreement

The common law principles of the law of contracts relative to termination of a contract are applicable to terminating an agency contract. (See p. 245.) Hence, the parties by mutual consent may terminate an agency contract.

► Option of a Party

An agency contract, by its terms, may allow either the principal or the agent to terminate by giving advance notice to the other. Exercising this option will have the effect of a termination. For example, a life insurance agent may, under the employment contract with the insurance company, have the option to terminate by giving the company thirty days notice.

Revocation by the Principal

Once the principal has authorized the agent to perform on the principal's behalf, the principal always retains the power to "revoke" (terminate) the authority. Even though the principal may be liable to the agent for damages sustained due to wrongful revocation, the principal nevertheless has the power to revoke. For example, the agency contract may provide that it cannot be terminated by either party. The contract can still be revoked, although revocation will subject the principal to damages for its breach.

Unless the parties have otherwise agreed, the principal's revocation is ineffective to terminate the agency unless the agent has actually received notice of the principal's intent so to terminate, or other facts reasonably cause the agent to believe that revocation has occurred. (*P* mails a letter to *A*, *P*'s agent, stating that the agency is at an end. Before *A* received the letter he made a contract in *P*'s name with *T* pursuant to *A*'s authority. *P* is bound on the contract.)

In the following case a licensed real estate broker sued his client for the agreed commission when the client terminated the agency relationship because of financial difficulties.

FACTS

Hilgendorf was a licensed real estate broker acting as the agent of the Hagues in the sale of their farmland. The Hagues terminated Hilgendorf's agency when they encountered financial difficulties before the expiration of the listing contract. Hilgendorf brought this action for breach of the listing contract. The Hagues maintain that Hilgendorf's duty of loyalty requires him to give up the listing contract.

DECISION

A principal has the power to terminate an agency that is not coupled with an interest although the agency contract has not yet expired. Absent some legal ground, the principal does not have the right to terminate an unexpired agency contract and may subject himself to damages for doing so. Although an agent's duty of loyalty does require him to place the principal's interests first in dealing with third parties, in the contract of agency itself between the agent and the principal each is acting in his own behalf. The Hagues' financial difficulties did not give them the legal right to terminate the agency relationship, and Hilgendorf was under no duty to relinquish his role as their agent simply because the principal had financial problems. Hence Hilgendorf may recover damages for breach of the listing contract before its agreed termination date.

Hilgendorf v. Hague, 293 N.W. 2d 272 (Iowa 1980)

Renunciation by the Agent

The agent maintains the same power as the principal to terminate the agency contract, regardless of its terms. This is called a power to "renunciate" or "renounce."

If under the terms of the agency contract the agency is terminable at the will of the agent, the agent can renounce at any time without incurring damages for breach of the agency contract. If the principal's instructions are illegal, the agent has the right to renunciate.

The agent will be liable for damages for breach of the agency contract. An example is when the agency contract is for a stated period of time and the agent wrongfully renounces the contract. Thus an exclusive ninety-day real estate listing will terminate when *A* notifies *P* two weeks after accepting the listing that the agent is listing the house with other brokers.

Unless the parties have otherwise agreed, the agent's renunciation is ineffective to terminate the agency unless the principal has notice, or other facts reasonably cause the principal to believe, that renunciation has occurred.

The following case illustrates how an "indefinite duration agency" may be terminated at the will of either the principal or the agent; however, the agent may be entitled to damages.

FACTS

The parties agreed that plaintiff was to work for defendant to obtain for defendant prior customers of plaintiff; that plaintiff would have "as long as he wanted," "whatever time was necessary," and "no deadline was placed thereon"; and "when plaintiff succeeded in said efforts," he would get a five percent commission on the business he brought to defendant . . .

Plaintiff performed his obligations for seven months, brought to defendant a monthly average of $10,000 in business, and spent $3,600 in expenses. After seven months, defendant discharged plaintiff without good cause. Was this a rightful termination of the agency?

DECISION

No. Judgment for plaintiff. Agreements between principal and agent for an indefinite time generally may be terminated at will of either party. The agreement between plaintiff and defendant was "for an indefinite period of time, its duration was not fixed expressly or impliedly, and its expiration did not depend on the completion of a given undertaking." The agreement was therefore terminable at the will of either party, but there is a limitation on the power to terminate an agency, namely, that the principal is liable to the agent for the value of services and reasonable expenses incurred up to the time of revocation.

Want v. Century Supply Company, 508 S.W.2d 515 (Mo. 1974).

The following case illustrates that a power of attorney will terminate upon the death of the principal.

FACTS

Mary Long was the executrix of the estate of the decedent, Ethel Mae Schull, who entered the hospital in early March, 1975, for an ailment diagnosed as terminal cancer. On March 31, 1975, the decedent executed a power of attorney in favor of her stepson, Andrea C. Schull. After she executed the power of attorney, she told her stepson where she had hidden her will and several savings account passbooks and instructed him to retrieve them. Her stepson obtained possession of these items and, after his stepmother's death, with the power of attorney, withdrew the funds from the savings accounts, depositing the money in accounts in his name, his wife's name, or both. The total sum of money involved amounted to $25,001.64 the executor which the plaintiff now seeks to recover from the stepson and his wife.

Did the agency relationship created by the power of attorney survive the death of the stepmother, Ethel Mae Schull?

DECISION

No. Judgment for the Executrix of the estate. The power of attorney was a formal contract of agency, creating a principal-agent relationship between the decedent and her stepson. Unless the agency is coupled with an interest, which is not the case here, the well-settled rule is that the agency relation created by this power of attorney terminated at the death of the principal.

A legal power of attorney was executed and within the authority of that instrument the power of attorney terminated with the author's death and the balance of the monies disbursed by the stepson and his wife belong to the estate.

Mary Long, Executrix v. Schull, et al. 439 A.2d 975 (Conn. 1981).

Termination by Operation of Law

When an agency contract is terminated by operation of law, it ends, regardless of the parties' consent. The law brings about the result even though the principal or the agent may have another intent.

There are six ways by which agency power may be terminated by operation of law: death, insanity, bankruptcy, war, destruction of the agency subject matter, and change of law or other circumstances.

► Death

Since agency is a personal service contract (see p. 262), because the agent is a fiduciary acting primarily on behalf of the principal, the authority given to the agent terminates without any notice to the agent upon the principal's death. The agent cannot act for a nonexistent person. An ordinary contract, however, will not terminate upon the obligor's death, but rather becomes an estate obligation.[1] In the following case a customer's death revoked the bank's authority to pay a check because the bank knew of the death and had a reasonable opportunity to act.

FACTS

Rose Mary McCoy Sturgill, Administratix, attempted to recover from Virginia Citizens Bank (Bank) the $13,748.58 balance of R. V. McCoy, Jr.'s bank account which the Bank, after McCoy's death, had transferred to a third party. On March 28, 1975, McCoy opened an individual checking account with the Bank. Eighteen months later, McCoy telephoned Jimmy Vanover, the Bank president, stating that he had remarried and desired to change his account to a joint account. On October 11, 1976, he and "Kaye Stanley McCoy" appeared at the Bank. They added "Kaye McCoy's" signature to the account card and requested new checks issued bearing both their names.

Vanover's office lies next door to the apartment complex where McCoy lived. On December 4, 1975, Vanover was working in his office when he noticed an ambulance. Upon investigation, he learned of McCoy's death: The Administratrix testified that she called Vanover on December 6, 1976, between 9:00 and 9:05 a.m. and instructed him not to honor any checks drawn on McCoy's account. According to Vanover, the Administratrix did not call him until 10:30 a.m., after "Kaye McCoy" had cashed a check for $13,478.58. The Administratrix offered into evidence a cancelled check in the amount of $13,478.58, dated December 6, 1976, and drawn by "Kaye McCoy" on McCoy's account payable to the Bank to close the account.

DECISION

Because death of a principal terminates an agent's authority . . . "Kaye McCoy" had no authority to write checks on the account after December 4, 1976. Simply put, a "power ceases with the life of the person who gives it." Of course, a customer's death will not revoke a bank's authority to pay a check until the bank knows of the death and has had a reasonable opportunity to act on it. In this case, the Bank had immediate, actual knowledge of McCoy's death and a reasonable opportunity to act on this knowledge. It could have refused payment easily on the December 6 check. The court concluded that "Kaye McCoy" had the authority to sign checks on McCoy's account, that her authority ended at his death, and that the Bank knew of McCoy's death with a reasonable time to act on such knowledge. The court entered final judgment for the Administratrix in the amount of $13,478.58.

Sturgill v. Virginia Citizens Bank, 291 S.E.2d 207 (Va. 1982).

---

[1] *Commercial Nursery Co. v. Ivey*, 51 S.W.2d 238 (Tenn. 1932).

However, some state statutes and a few courts take the position that the agent has power to bind the deceased principal's estate until the agent receives notice of death. Examples are statutes that relate to principals who are in the armed forces and banks that have authority to pay checks drawn by the principal or the agent before the principal's death. (See p. 345.)

► Insanity

The principal who appointed the agent to act on the principal's behalf must be capable of maintaining supervision over the agent. Therefore the insanity of the principal will terminate the agency, as is illustrated by the following case.

FACTS

The decedent, Margaret Berry, was admitted to the hospital in February 1970. On March 26, 1970, she executed a power of attorney designating her niece, Irene Montanye, as her agent. Thereafter, the decedent was discharged from the hospital. On April 29, 1970, the decedent suffered a stroke and was readmitted to the hospital. She remained in a comatose or semicomatose condition until her death on June 30, 1971. On April 30, 1971, Mrs. Montanye, acting under the power of attorney, transferred some $109,000 of the decedent's funds into a trust account in the name of the decedent in trust for Ann R. Scully, administratrix of this estate.

Distributees of the decedent and their assignees objected that the alleged agency created by the power of attorney was void for the following reasons: the decedent did not understand what she was doing; the transfer of the funds to the trust was void as being beyond the scope of any agency created; and the transfer of the funds was void because at the time of the transfer and thereafter the decedent was mentally incompetent by reason of being in a comatose or semicomatose state and, therefore, the agency was suspended or revoked. Can an agency be terminated by the mental incompetency of the principal?

DECISION

Yes. Permission is given to distributees to file verified objections to prove decedent's mental incompetency.

If the objectors prove that, at the time of the agent's transfer of the funds, and thereafter, the decedent was mentally incompetent or incapacitated by reason of her alleged comatose or semicomatose state, then the agency would have been suspended or revoked. The court finds that the proposed amended objections raised valid issues of law and fact and granted permission to file amended objections.

In re *Estate of Berry,* 329 N.Y.S.2d 915 (1972).

The agent's insanity that occurs after the agent's appointment will terminate the agency as a matter of law. Some courts have held that, once the incapacity has been removed, the agency relationship can be restored.

► Bankruptcy

The bankruptcy of the principal will terminate the authority of the agent to act with respect to property related to the bankruptcy if the agent reasonably can believe that, because of the bankruptcy, the principal would no longer want the agent to have such authority.

The agent's bankruptcy will also, generally, terminate the relationship. The credit of the agent is frequently related to the principal's reputation in the business community. Thus the agent's authority to act will terminate if the agent reasonably can believe that, if the principal knew the facts, the principal would not want the agent's authority to continue.

► War

The outbreak of a war in the country where the agent has been authorized to transact the principal's business will terminate the agent's authority if the agent reasonably can believe that, if the principal knew the facts, the principal would not want the agent's authority to continue. The large number of multinational corporations and international trade could be affected by this rule. For example, if a U.S. corporation is selling its equipment in country *X*, and a war unexpectedly breaks out in *X*, the corporate agent's authority to sell in *X* may terminate.

► Impossibility by Supervening Destruction of the Agency Subject Matter

If performance by the agency becomes impossible, the agent's authority is terminated. For example, a marine broker who is authorized to sell *P*'s boat would lose his authority if the boat were destroyed by a storm.

► Impossibility by Supervening Change of Law or Other Circumstances

The agent's authority is terminated by a change in law or other circumstances that would make performance impossible. For instance, if *A*, a construction contractor, must substantially change his contract because an amended building code requires fireproof material, his authority to act on behalf of *P* is terminated without *P*'s specific consent.

Irrevocable Agency

► Termination of Authority Coupled with an Agent's Security Interest

We have learned that agency and authority can be terminated by either the principal or the agent, and that if the termination of the agency contract is wrongful the terminating party is liable for breach of the contract. However, there are two situations when the principal cannot terminate the power of the agent to act and affect the principal. These are often called "irrevocable agency" situations, meaning that the power of the agent cannot be terminated by the principal, as distinguished from termination of agency and authority, which the principal can do at any time.

These two situations occur when the power given to the agent is security to assure the agent that the principal will perform his or her promise to the agent. In one situation "authority" or power is given as security, and in the other the authority or power is coupled with an interest in the subject matter of the agency.

Authority Given As Security When the principal gives authority as security to the agent in exchange for consideration then given by the agent, there is a contract between them and the principal cannot revoke that authority. (On January 6, *P* requests a $200 loan from *A, P* promising to repay the loan on January 24 and that, on his default, *A* has authority to sell *P*'s electric typewriter. The loan is made and there is now a contract between *P* and *A. P* defaults and informs *A* that his authority to sell is terminated. *A*'s power to sell is not terminated and *A* can sell the typewriter. *P*'s authority to *A* was given in exchange for the new consideration of a loan of $200 made to *P* by *A,* creating a contract between them. However, if *P* already owes money to *A* and *P* later gives *A* authority to sell *P*'s typewriter on *P*'s default, *P*'s authority was not given to *A* in exchange for any new consideration from *A;* since there is no contract between them, *P* can terminate *A*'s authority because it is not given as security. For there to be a contract, the authority must be given as security in exchange for consideration then given by *A.*) In many states, death of the principal will not terminate this power.

Authority Coupled with an Interest in the Subject Matter of the Agency An agent has an irrevocable, vested security interest in and power over property transferred to the agent by the principal with authority to dispose of the property if the principal should default on an obligation owing by the principal to the agent. (*P* owes *A* $200. On February 6, *P* promises to repay the loan on February 24 and that, on default, *A* has authority to sell *P*'s calculator. *P* delivers the calculator to *A. A*'s power to sell on *P*'s default is irrevocable by *P.*) A contract is not required here to make the agency irrevocable. Death of the principal will not terminate this power.

Effect of Termination of Agency and Authority

The principal's termination of agency or of the agent's authority is immediately effective between them when the agent actually received notice of the principal's intent so to terminate. But what is the effect of such termination on third parties? We have learned that third parties have the duty to determine whether agency exists and the extent of the agent's authority.

If the principal (*P*) has represented to third persons (*T*) that someone (*A*) is *P*'s agent, *A* has apparent authority to act for *P* within the scope of *A*'s apparent authority with the same effect as though *A* had authority so to act. If *P* wishes to terminate such apparent authority, he must give proper notice of termination of authority to those third persons to whom *P* had so represented creating the apparent authority.

The extent of such notice varies. If *A* is a special agent, *P* need not give any notice to such third persons, with certain exceptions when notice is required: (1) *A* is a specially accredited agent, specially accredited to deal with *T* on a continuing basis; or (2) *P* has notice that *A* has begun to deal with *T;* or (3) *A* has a written authorization to be exhibited to *T;* or (4) *P* knows of the termination of an event on the continuance of which *A*'s authority depends. If *A* is a general agent, *P* must give notice of termination to such third persons. For example, *P* appointed *A* as *P*'s agent for the purpose of selling and handling fire insurance for *P. A* sold a fire insurance policy of *P* to *T.* A few months later, *P* informed *A* that the agency was terminated. Subsequently *T* has a fire and reported it to *A.* Since *A* still has apparent authority to act as *P*'s agent, which includes authority to receive fire reports from insured third persons, *T*'s report to *A* was made to *P.*

The kind of such notice varies. If *T* has dealt with *P* on credit, *T* must receive actual notice of termination of authority; otherwise reasonable notice is sufficient by either: "(a) advertising the fact in a newspaper of general circulation in the place where the agency is regularly carried on; or (b) giving publicity by some other method reasonably adapted to give the information to such third person."[2]

Summary Statement

1. An agency may be terminated by acts of the parties. There are five methods for so doing:
   - **a)** Expiration of the contract
   - **b)** Mutual agreement
   - **c)** Option of a party in giving advance notice to the other
   - **d)** Revocation by the principal
   - **e)** Renunciation by the agent
2. An agency may be terminated by operation of law, which will end the relationship regardless of the parties' consent. There are six methods for doing this:
   - **a)** Death of either the principal or the agent
   - **b)** Insanity of either the principal or the agent
   - **c)** Bankruptcy
   - **d)** War
   - **e)** Impossibility by supervening destruction of the agency subject matter
   - **f)** Impossibility by supervening change of law or other circumstances
3. When the principal gives authority as security to the agent in exchange for consideration then given by the agent, there is a contract between them and the principal cannot revoke that authority.
4. An agent with authority coupled with an interest in the subject matter of the agency has an irrevocable vested security interest in and power over the property transferred to the agent, with authority to dispose of the property if the principal should default on an obligation owing to the agent.
5. As between the principal and agent, the question of notice to third parties of termination of the agent's authority is of no consequence. The agent may have the power but not the right to act on behalf of the principal.
6. The principal's termination of agency or of the agent's authority is immediately effective between them when the agent actually receives notice of the principal's intent so to terminate.
7. If the principal wishes to terminate apparent authority, he or she must give proper notice to those third persons to whom *P* has represented and thereby created apparent authority.
8. If the agent is a general agent, the principal must give notice of termination to third persons to whom the principal has represented that a person is an agent in order to terminate the agent's apparent authority.
9. If the agent is a special agent, the principal need not give any notice to such third persons unless:
   - **a)** *A* is specially accredited to deal with *T* on a continuing basis; or
   - **b)** *P* has notice that *A* has begun to deal with *T;* or
   - **c)** *A* has a written authorization to be exhibited to *T;* or
   - **d)** *T* knows of the termination of an event on the continuance of which *A*'s authority depends.

---

[2]See Restatement (Second) of Agency sec.136(3a, b) (1958).

10. If T has dealt with P on credit, T must receive actual notice of termination; otherwise reasonable notice is sufficient.

In the following case, the court found a trust agreement was validly ratified regardless of the mental competency of its creator.

In re ESTATE OF HEAD
615 P.2d 271 (N.M. 1980)

William Grady Head signed a general power of attorney that appointed his wife, Emma, to act on his behalf. While he was mentally competent, Mr. Head along with Mrs. Head created a revocable trust for the benefit of their two daughters and a third woman (Esther Taute) they had raised. Each daughter's interest in the trust assets was 40 percent, and Esther Taute's interest was 20 percent. Six days after the trust agreement was signed, Mr. Head signed an amended trust document which removed Taute's 20 percent interest. Mr. Head was not mentally competent when this amendment was signed. Three weeks later, Mrs. Head acting for herself and as Mr. Head's attorney-in-fact, ratified the amended trust document. After both Mr. and Mrs. Head had died, the beneficiaries of this trust sought a declaration of their respective interests. The trial court ruled that the trust was valid as originally written. The natural daughters appealed, arguing their mother's ratification of the amendment removed Esther Taute's interest....

...A power of attorney is revoked by operation of law upon an adjudication of insanity. If the agent's authority is "coupled with an interest" the principal's insanity does not terminate the agency.... "Coupled with an interest" means that the agent must have a present interest in the property upon which the power is to operate. There must be a beneficial interest in the thing itself which is the subject of the power. As a trustor, Mrs. Head had a present existing interest in the trust estate and in the distribution of the property held in trust. It was independent of the power conferred. It was of primary importance that she determine the beneficiaries of the trust. If she desired to restore her ... property interest, she could have revoked the trust. She had an interest in the subject upon which the power was to be exercised. She had a power of attorney coupled with an interest. Mrs. Head sought to exercise her power of attorney with reference to the trust agreement. A "trust" is the beneficial ownership of property which the legal title is in another. Mr. and Mrs. Head were the joint beneficial owners of the trust property. Mrs. Head was a trustor along with her husband. She had the right at any time during his lifetime to amend or revoke the trust. Her power of attorney was "coupled with an interest" in the trust estate and was irrevocable. The trust agreement was validly ratified regardless of the mental competency of Mr. Head.

Questions and Case Problems

1. Clinkenbeard responded to Central Southwest Oil Corporation's (Central) advertisement in Argosy Magazine, which described the possibilities for individuals to win valuable oil leases in the monthly leasings of federal land by the Department of the Interior. Central offered to select valuable tracts coming up for leasing, handle the paper work involved in entering the individual's name in the running for the leasing of such tracts, and notify the entrant if he had won a lease. Clinkenbeard accepted the offer and sent in approximately $40 per month from September, 1971, to October, 1972. His lucky day arrived on June 5, 1972, when he received a call from

Tom Allen, President of Central, informing him that he had won a lease. Although, according to Allen, the lease was not a particularly valuable one on which there had been few filings, Central offered Clinkenbeard $5,020 for it. In fact the lease was one of the most heavily filed upon in the lottery and there was evidence that, at least as of the time of trial, it was worth several times what Central had offered. Did the fiduciary duty owed by Central to Clinkenbeard exist at the time of the assignment? [*Clinkenbeard v. Central Southwest Oil Corp.,* 526 F.2d 649 (5th Cir. 1976).]

2. Nathan Francis, a co-lessee with defendant, Ted Bartlett, managed a gravel mining operation. Bartlett gave a power of attorney to Francis as the manager authorizing Francis to pay Bartlett his portion of the royalties from the operation. Bartlett claims that the royalty due him for the past two years was five cents per cubic yard of gravel instead of two-and-a-half cents, at which rate he was paid. Bartlett accepted such reduced payments during the past two years without complaint. Bartlett then sued Francis for the additional amount of royalty allegedly due him. Was Bartlett correct? [*Francis v. Bartlett,* 121 So.2d 18 (La. 1960).]

3. A principal gave her agent a power of attorney to sell her building that stated "the agency shall continue for ninety days and will not be revoked during that period." A month later the principal gave her agent notice that the agency was revoked. The agent later made a contract with a buyer, who knew the agency was revoked, to sell the land. May the buyer eject the principal from the building and purchase the land?

4. *P* owned a building and authorized *A,* a real estate broker, to keep it rented and deduct a 6 percent commission on the amount collected and send the balance to *P.* *A,* in *P*'s name, leased to *T,* who paid rent to *A* for several years. *P* died but *T* had no notice or knowledge of *P*'s death. For the next year *T* continued to pay *A* the rent, with which *A* absconded. The executor of *P*'s estate sued *T* for the year's rent due from the time of *P*'s death. *T* claimed that *T*'s payment to *A* even after *P*'s death is a defense. Is *T* correct?

5. *A* was the general manager of a hardware store owned by *P,* who was declared insane by a court. *G,* appointed by the court to be *P*'s guardian, immediately terminated *A* as the manager and agent of *P.* Did *G* have the right to do so?

6. The sole proprietor of a restaurant hired an agent to manage the business. The sole proprietor later filed voluntary bankruptcy. The bankruptcy court appointed a trustee in bankruptcy to manage the sole proprietor's assets. Does the agent continue to have authority to manage the restaurant?

7. William Mubi, husband of Sharon Mubi, commenced a civil suit against Walter W. Tribble for personal injuries and property damage resulting from a motor vehicle collision. On August 5, 1970 Tribble through his attorney filed an Offer of Judgment in the amount of $3,150. Under the Rules of Civil Procedure, this offer had to be accepted within ten days or it was deemed withdrawn. William Mubi died at approximately 9:00 a.m. on August 11, 1970, six days after the offer was made. Prior to his death he had requested his wife, Sharon Mubi, plaintiff, to accept the Offer of Judgment of $3,150, and she, in turn, advised William Mubi's attorney. Although the decision to accept the Offer was communicated to decedent's attorney before he died, the attorney's written acceptance, as procedurally required, was not made until after William Mubi's death. Did the power of attorney, given by William Mubi (through his wife) to his attorney, Spillman, to answer on his behalf, terminate at his death? [*Mubi v. Broomfield,* 492 P.2d 700 (Ariz. 1972).]

8. *P,* a casualty insurance company, made *A* its general agent to write casualty insurance in *P*'s name. *A* wrote *T*'s casualty insurance on *T*'s business. Thereafter, and without notifying *T,* the general agency of *A* was revoked by *P.* *T* later incurred a loss and promptly notified *A.* *T* had neither notice nor knowledge of the revocation of *A*'s authority by *P*. *A* notified *P* one year later and *P* refused to honor the claim because *P* was not notified by the insured, *T*, within a reasonable time after the loss. *T* sued *P* on the policy issued by *A*. Can *T* recover?

9. Decedent was the widow of the late Arnold Friedman, an artist of some repute. In 1961 she transferred almost the entire collection of her late husband's art works to an art dealer, for exhibition and sale. The dealer was to retain one-half of any purchase price realized as his "commission." In a later written agreement decedent was to "sell, transfer, and assign all of the works of the late Arnold Friedman, now in her possession . . . absolutely and forever" to the art dealer. In consideration for same the art dealer agreed to accept these art works; prepare them for sale and exhibition; "put forth his best efforts to sell," and pay over to the decedent one-half of the sale price as these art works were sold. The petitioner brought this action to recover the art works claiming that title never passed to the art dealer. Did the written agreement constitute a sales contract or a consignment creating an agency relationship? [*Estate of Wilhelmina Friedman, Deceased,* 397 N.Y.S.2d 561 (1977).]

10. In *In re Estate of Head*, excerpted at the beginning of this section, why did the court find that Mrs. Head had a power of attorney *coupled* with an interest?

CHAPTER 19

EMPLOYMENT

After you have read this chapter, you should be able to:

1. Recognize the limitations on employment contracts-at-will.
2. Indicate what kind of discrimination in employment is prohibited by the federal Equal Employment Opportunity Act.
3. State those circumstances when discrimination in employment is not prohibited under the Act.
4. Recognize the age groups of employees that are, or are not, protected from age discrimination in employment under the federal Age Discrimination in Employment Act.
5. Explain how the federal Wage-Hour Law applies to:
   a) Child labor
   b) Maximum daily and weekly hours of employment
   c) Wages
6. Discuss the employer's liability for injury experienced by employees under the common law and under state workers' compensation statutes.
7. Explain the purpose of the federal Occupational Safety and Health Act and how business is affected by the Act.
8. Describe how the following federal programs operate under the Social Security Act:
   a) Old age, survivors, and disability insurance
   b) Medicare
   c) Unemployment insurance
   d) Employee pension plans controls
9. Recognize the increasing use by employers of lie, drug, and alcohol detection devices.
10. Discuss the current status and rights of women in the work force.

BUSINESS DECISIONS and the LAW

Carl Forbes is a newly appointed vice president in charge of personnel for a fairly large manufacturer of computers and electronic technology. He has encountered many personnel problems, three of which are the following:

Jane, an employee of the company for ten years, is a very capable and attractive woman who works on assembling parts for electronic products. A number of Jane's male coworkers have been whistling at her, making obscene gestures to her, and using obscene language to and about her. Jane has complained several times to Carl's predecessor, who assured her that he would take care of the matter, but he has done nothing. As a result, Jane has become very unhappy in her job and her performance is now declining. When a vacancy develops in another section of the plant for an associate supervisor on assembly of parts, she applies for the position, for which she is unusually well qualified. The company has an affirmative action program with a provision for testing and evaluation for promotion, one of the factors being the sex of the applicant. The percentage of men in this section and this job category is overwhelming, far outnumbering the few women in that section and category. Four men also apply for the vacancy position. On the test, Jane scores below two of the men by the exceedingly small fraction of 1 1/2 points out of a possible 100. Carl appoints Jane to the position and the two men complain of the discrimination factor of sex being unfair and illegal and they threaten legal action.

Carl suspects that some of the personnel are addicted to drug or alcohol abuse that affects their job performance. The company has no program for testing for such abuse. Carl confers with the firm's president and, with his consent, decides to institute a testing program for such abuse among employees and job candidates. This involves many issues, such as random or periodic testing; use of the urinalysis test; retesting and a rehabilitation program for individuals who initially tested positive, or summary dismissal if they tested positive. Carl and the company are much concerned about liability for testing as an infringement of various employee constitutional rights.

Carl is also wondering what to do about an employee who now has AIDS.

All these problems are discussed in this chapter.

Introduction

Society is concerned that people have proper and equal opportunity to obtain employment, and that the terms of employment are reasonable and do not constitute an invasion of any employee's legal rights, particularly that employment be lawfully nondiscriminatory and that fair labor standards apply. This area will be discussed under the heading "The Employment Contract."

Another concern of society is that proper reasonable standards are established to ensure the safety and health of employees while engaged in their work, and that reasonable compensation is provided for any injury they may sustain in their work. This area will be discussed under the heading "Protection and Compensation for Injury."

Society is also concerned about the financial status of employees on their retirement, disability, hospitalization, and unemployment. This area will be discussed under the heading "Social Security."

Lastly, society is concerned with employer use of detection tests to determine employee lying and use of drugs and alcohol, and with unfair discrimination against women in the work force.

The term **employee** as generally used in statutes (e.g., employers' liability acts and workers' compensation acts) and in court decisions means a servant agent, although some statutes (e.g., social security, unemployment insurance, minimum age, and fair labor statutes) are interpreted to give the term employee a wider meaning. The term **employer** is a principal, or more specifically a master.

employee

As generally used, a servant agent, although some statutes are interpreted to give it a wider meaning

employer

A principal, or more specifically a master

The Employment Contract

▶ The Employment "Contract-at-Will"

Under the common law right of freedom of contract, an employer may make a "contract-at-will." Unless the understanding between the employer and the employee **(agent** or **servant)** is that service to be rendered is for a fixed and definite period, the contract of employment is for an indefinite hiring, terminable at the will of either party for any reason without notice, and whose termination does not give rise to a cause of action. This is called an "at-will" relationship and the contract is one at-will.

agent

A person authorized to act on behalf of another and subject to his or her control

servant

An agent whose physical conduct his or her master (principal) has the right to control or controls

Exception Today there are exceptions to the at-will rule.

The implied contract of good faith and fair dealing exception. Some courts have declared that an underlying principle of good faith and fair dealing is implicit in the employment contract, which requires the contracting parties to deal fairly with each other and which prohibits either party from so acting as to injure the rights of the other to receive the benefits of the agreement between them, namely that *all* employees be treated alike. This concept is a limitation on the employer's right to fire without cause.

The express or implied contract exception. Although there is conflict among the courts, a large number of courts have declared that, consistent with contract law, an employer's unilateral representations to its employees with respect to the employment contract become part of the contract, unless they clearly and conspicuously tell the employees that such representations are not part of the contract. Illustrations are the employer's handbook, policy and personnel manuals, practices, and oral promises that limit the employer's right to discharge, except for cause. Most courts *require knowledge by the employee* of the handbook or manual on which the employee *relied* as a part of the employment contract in order to alter the at-will contract so as to preclude the employer from terminating the contract without cause. There *must* be an oral or written agreement between the employer and employee specifically adopting the handbook or manual, or a course of conduct between them, treating it as a part of the at-will contract. This exception was the issue in the following case.

FACTS

Joan Leikvold was hired by Valley View Community Hospital as its Operating Room Supervisor. Nothing was disclosed regarding job security. She did not have a contract for a specific duration, nor was she specifically told that the hospital would not discharge her except for cause. She did receive a policies manual and was told that the policies therein were to be followed in employee relationships with the hospital. Later she became Director of Nursing. The next year she requested a transfer to her former position in the operating room. The hospital's Chief Executive refused her request. Joan withdrew her transfer request, but a few days later she was fired, her personnel record showing insubordination as the reason for her discharge. Her request for a "grievance hearing" as provided for in the hospital's Administrative and Personnel Policies Manual was denied.

She sued the hospital for breach of contract, alleging that the manual was a part of her employment-at-will contract and the hospital did not comply with the grievance procedure in the manual. The trial court granted the hospital's motion for summary judgment, which was reversed on her appeal. The hospital petitioned the state Supreme Court for review, which was granted.

DECISION

The trial court's entry of summary judgment is reversed and the case remanded to the trial court for further proceedings. [Although some courts have held otherwise], we hold that an employer's representations in a personnel manual can become terms of the [at-will] employment contract and can limit an employer's ability to discharge his or her employees. Whether any particular personnel manual modifies any particular employment-at-will relationship and becomes part of the particular employment contract is a question of fact. Evidence relevant to this factual decision includes the language used in the personnel manual as well as the employer's course of conduct and oral representations regarding it. Because a material question—whether the policies manual was incorporated into and became part of the terms of the employment contract—remains in dispute, summary judgment is improper here [and a decision on this issue is for the trial court.]

Leikvold v. Valley View Community Hosp., 688 P.2d 170 (Ariz. 1984).

The independent consideration exception. If the employer's promise is for a bargained consideration by the employee that is independent of the services to be rendered by the employee, or if the employer's representation was made in such a way as to arouse the employee's reasonable expectation of job security on which the employee claimed he or she relied, the employer's promise will be enforced. Probably the most familiar example is the employer's promise of permanent employment until retirement if the employee would not accept another firm's competing offer for the employee's services. Such an employer's promise is interpreted to be a promise *not* to terminate the employee without just cause.

The public policy exception. This exception of public policy on at-will contracts must be clearly identified, as for example in federal or state constitutions, legislation, administrative rules and regulations, and judicial decisions. Also, an employer is liable for employee discharge because of the employee's refusal to act contrary to law, as to engage in criminal or tortious conduct, refusal to refrain from reporting illegal or unethical conduct of the employer or a fellow employee (for example, whistleblowing), or insisting on serving on a jury. Public policy here imposes employer liability for employee discharge without just cause.

The following federal and state legislation establishes public policy and its enforcement as a limitation on the employer's business conduct including freedom of contract in *all* kinds of contracts, the right to discharge an employee, and consideration for employee welfare. The judicial interpretation and enforcement of such legislation become very important to you as a present or future employer or employee.

► Nondiscriminatory Employment

The two major pieces of federal legislation amending the federal Civil Rights Act of 1964 to ensure equal nondiscriminatory opportunity for employment are the Equal Employment Opportunity Act of 1972 and the Age Discrimination in Employment Act of 1967, with their later amendments.

Equal Employment Opportunity Act (EEOA) This federal Act applies to persons as employers engaged in an industry in or affecting interstate commerce with fifteen or more employees for each working day in each of twenty or more calendar weeks in the current or preceding calendar year, and any agent of such person. It also applies to state and local governments; government agencies; political subdivisions; the District of Columbia department and agencies; employment agencies; labor organizations; apprenticeship programs; and in advertising.

Title VII of the Civil Rights Act of 1964 prohibits employers from *unlawfully* discriminating in employment and makes it

> an unlawful employment practice for an employer (1) to fail or refuse to hire or to discharge any individual, or otherwise to discriminate against any individual with respect to his compensation, terms, conditions, or privileges of employment, *because of* such individual's race, color, religion, sex, or national origin; or (2) to limit, segregate, or classify his employees or applicants for employment in any way which would deprive or tend to deprive any individual of employment opportunities or otherwise adversely affect his status as an employee *because of* such individual's race, color, religion, sex, or national origin.

In the following case, the first of its kind to be decided by the U.S. Supreme Court, the court had to decide whether the difference in longevity between men and women employees could justify a valid difference in the contributions to a pension fund required to be made by those employees.

FACTS

Based on a study of mortality tables and its own experience, the Los Angeles Department of Water and Power, defendant, determined that its female employees would, as a class, outlive its male employees. Accordingly, the Department required its female employees to make significantly larger pension fund contributions than the males, with the result that each female employee took home less pay than a male earning the same salary.

A class action suit was brought by Marie Manhart, a woman employee in the Department, on behalf of all women employed and formerly employed by the Department, plaintiffs, seeking an injunction against this action by the Department and retroactive relief. The federal district court and, on appeal, the federal court of appeals, decided in favor of the plaintiffs, except that retroactive relief was denied. The Department, defendant, brought this matter before the Supreme Court of the United States.

DECISION

Affirmed, for plaintiffs, without retroactive relief, and sent back for further proceedings. The Equal Employment Opportunity Act makes it unlawful "to discriminate against any *individual* with respect to his compensation, terms, conditions, or privileges of employment, because of such *individual's* race, color, religion, sex, or national origin." An employment practice that requires 2,000 individuals to contribute more money into a fund than 10,000 other employees simply because each of them is a woman rather than a man is in direct conflict with both the language and the policy of the Act. It constitutes discrimination against every individual woman employed by the Department, and is unlawful unless exempted by the Equal Pay Act of 1963 or some other affirmative justifiction.

City of Los Angeles Dep't of Water and Power et al. v. Manhart et al., 435 U.S. 702 (1978).

In another decision the U.S. Supreme Court further implemented the concept in the above case. The court held that it is unlawful discrimination on the basis of sex in violation of Title VII of the Civil Rights Act of 1964 for an employer to offer its employees the option of receiving retirement benefits from one of several companies selected by the employer, all of which pay a woman lower monthly benefits than a man who has made the same contributions. The court also held that all retirement benefits derived from contributions made after its decision must be calculated without regard to the sex of the beneficiary, that its decision is not retroactive, and that, under the Arizona deferred compensation plan involved, benefits derived from contributions made *prior* to its decision may be calculated as provided by the existing terms of the Arizona plan. [*Arizona Governing Comm. for Tax Deferred Annuity and Deferred Compensation Plans v. Norris*, 463 U.S. 1073 (1983).]

In still another decision of importance to employers and employees, the U.S. Supreme Court held that it is unlawful sex discrimination based on pregnancy in violation of Title VII of the Civil Rights Act of 1964 as amended by the Pregnancy Discrimination Act of 1978: (1) for an employer to exclude pregnancy coverage from an otherwise inclusive employee health insurance benefits plan; and (2) for an employer's employee health insurance benefit plan to provide hospitalization benefits for pregnancy-related conditions to its female employees but less extensive pregnancy benefits for spouses of male employees, such being discrimination against female spouses of male employees and therefore also discrimination against male employees. [*Newport News Shipbuilding and Drydock Co. v. EEOC*, 462 U.S. 669 (1983).]

The U.S. Supreme Court has recently made it clear in *Ward's Cove Packing Co., Inc., et al. v. Antonio, et al.*, (see p. 378) that, in cases of alleged unlawful discrimination in employment on the basis of an individual's race, color, religion, sex, or national origin, there are two steps to be considered:

prima facie
At first sight

1. A *disparate* (unequal) *impact* (effect) *case* (nonintentional discrimination) is concerned with causation of the discrimination or impact. The plaintiff has the burden of establishing a **prima facie** case by identifying and challenging each specific employer practice that causes the statistical disparity. A mere showing of statistical disparities is not enough. Proof of the element of causation is vital and *always* remains with the plaintiff and, if proved, there is unlawful discrimination, rebuttable by the employer in Step 2. If not so proved, there is no unlawful discrimination.
2. If the plaintiff establishes such a prima facie case, the burden then shifts to the employer to produce evidence of business justification for the practice. The employer need not *prove* that the challenged practice is "essential" or "indispensable" to the employer's business. If the employer's challenged business practice is not justified, then the discrimination is *unlawful*. If justified, then there is no unlawful discrimination. If a challenged employer's business practice is justified, then the plaintiff has an opportunity to show that other tests or selection devices without a similar discriminating effect would serve the employer's legitimate goals in light of the alternatives' costs and other burdens. If the plaintiff can show this, then the discrimination is *unlawful* and must be corrected by the employer.

A discriminatory impact together with a discriminatory intent is called *disparate treatment* and results in unlawful discrimination. However, it is *not* unlawful under the EEOA:

bona fide
In good faith

1. for an employer to employ an employee on the basis of religion, sex, or national origin in those certain instances where religion, sex, or national origin is a **bona fide** occupational qualification reasonably necessary to the normal operation of that particular business or enterprise;
2. for any educational institution of learning to employ employees of a particular religion if such institution is, in whole or in substantial part, owned, supported, controlled, or managed by a particular religion or by a particular religious corporation, association, or society, or if the curriculum of the institution is directed toward the propagation of a particular religion; and
3. for an employer to apply different standards of compensation, or different terms, conditions, or privileges of employment pursuant to a bona fide seniority or merit system, or to a system that measures earnings by quantity or quality of production, or to employees who work in different locations—so long as such differences are not the result of an intention to discriminate because of race, color, religion, sex, or national origin. The employer may give and act upon the results of any professionally developed ability test so long as the test, its administration, or action upon the results is not designed, intended, or used to discriminate because of race, color, religion, sex, or national origin. However, the test must be job related in order not to be unlawfully discriminatory. Also, the employer may legally discriminate in determining the amount of wages or compensation if it is authorized by the federal Fair Labor Standards Act of 1938, as amended in 1974.[1]

---

[1]See sec. 703(e) and (h) of Title VII, 78 Stat. 256–57; see also Equal Pay Amendment, discussed on p. 364.

The EEOA further provides that nothing in the Act shall be interpreted to *require* any employer to grant preferential treatment to any individual or group because of the race, color, religion, sex, or national origin of such individual or group on account of an imbalance which may exist with respect to the total number or percentage of qualified persons of any race, color, religion, sex, or national origin employed by any employer in comparison with the total number or percentage of qualified persons of such race, color, religion, sex, or national origin in any community, state, section, or other area or available work force there. The fact that an employer has no minority people among the employees does not of itself mean that illegal discrimination has occurred. However, it raises a strong inference of such illegality. In order to dispel such an inference, many employers employ only a few minority employees so as to create an impression of nondiscrimination when, in fact, their intention is to discriminate illegally.

Of great importance to employers and employees is a dramatic change in the law permitting, as lawful, racial prejudicial discrimination under the limited circumstances of a bona fide affirmative action plan. This change occurred by the decision of the U.S. Supreme Court in the 1979 landmark case of *United Steelworkers of America, et al. v. Weber, et al.*[2] The court's majority decision was that the federal Act did not "forbid private employers and unions from voluntarily agreeing upon bona fide affirmative action plans that accord racial prejudices in the manner and for the purpose provided in the Kaiser-USWA plan" (p. 200). "Had Congress meant to prohibit all race-conscious affirmative action ... it easily could ... [have provided] that Title VII would not require or permit racially preferential integration efforts. But Congress did not choose such a course.... [The section 703(j)] does not state that 'nothing in Title VII shall be interpreted to permit' voluntary affirmative efforts to correct racial imbalances. The natural inference is that Congress chose not to forbid all voluntary race-conscious affirmative action" (pp. 205–6). "We need not today define in detail the line of demarcation between permissible and impermissible affirmative action plans. It suffices to hold that the challenged Kaiser-USWA affirmative action plan falls on the permissible side of the line. The purposes of the plan mirror those of the statute. Both were designed to break down old patterns of racial segregation and hierarchy. Both were structured to 'open employment opportunities for Negroes in occupations which have been traditionally closed to them' " (p. 208).

A later case that follows the guidelines set down in the Weber case permitting discrimination under an affirmative action plan is *Johnson v. Transp. Agency, Santa Clara County, Cal., et al.*, 107 S.Ct. 1442 (1987). Santa Clara County Transit District Board of Supervisors adopted an affirmative action plan for the County Transportation Agency. The plan provided that, in making promotions to positions within a traditionally segregated job classification in which women have been significantly underrepresented, the Agency is authorized to consider as one factor the sex of a qualified applicant. A woman with a very slightly lower test score than a man was selected to fill a vacancy of road dispatcher. The U.S. Supreme Court held that the plan was valid and that the woman's selection was proper. It stated that consideration of the sex of applicants for skilled craft jobs was, in this case, justified by the existence of a "manifest imbalance" that reflected underrepresentation of women in "traditional segregated job categories." The plan was intended to *attain* a balanced workforce, not to *maintain* a permanent racial and sexual balance, and was fully consistent with Title VII.

[2]*United Steelworkers of America, et al. v. Weber, et al.*, 443 U.S. 193 (1979), *petition for rehearing denied* 444 U.S. 889 (1979).

The Civil Rights Act establishes an Equal Employment Opportunity Commission (EEOC), appointed by the president, to administer the Act. This federal commission has power to bring civil actions in federal courts against employers where there is reasonable cause to believe that an unlawful employment practice has occurred and attempts to conciliate the matter have failed. Usually states and cities have fair employment practices agencies, and employees who have complaints about illegal discrimination must apply to the latter agencies before the federal commission will consider the matter. In the case of illegal discrimination against *federal* employees, enforcement of the law is done by the EEOC.

Sexual Harassment Illegal sexual harassment in the workplace has increasingly become of public concern and has led to a multitude of civil lawsuits alleging such conduct.[3] The EEOC has adopted Federal Regulation 29 [Sexual Harassment, 29 C.F.R. sec. 1604.11 (1987)] concerning sexual harassment in the workplace. Two subdivisions are of particular importance:

> (a) Harassment on the basis of sex is a violation of Sec. 703 of Title VII. Unwelcome sexual advances, requests for sexual favors, and other verbal or physical conduct of a sexual nature constitute sexual harassment when (1) submission to such conduct is made either explicitly or implicitly a term or condition of an individual's employment, (2) submission to or rejection of such conduct by an individual is used as the basis for employment decisions affecting such individual, or (3) such conduct has the purpose or effect of unreasonably interfering with an individual's work performance or creating an intimidating, hostile, or offensive working environment.
>
> (b) In determining whether alleged conduct constitutes sexual harassment, the Commission will look at the record as a whole and at the totality of the circumstances, such as the nature of the sexual advances and the context in which the alleged incidents occurred. The determination of the legality of a particular action will be made from the facts, on a case by case basis.

Subdivisions (c), (d), and (e) prescribe employer responsibility for sexual harassment, of which employers should be especially aware.

Age Discrimination in Employment Act (ADIEA) This federal Act of 1967 as amended in 1978 and 1986 has for its purpose "to promote employment of older persons based on their ability rather than age; to prohibit arbitrary age discrimination in employment; to help employers and workers find ways of meeting problems arising from the impact of age on employment."

The Act applies to employers with at least 20 employees. It provides in section 623(a)(1)(2) that it is unlawful for an employer engaged in an industry in or affecting interstate commerce

> (1) to fail or refuse to hire or to discharge any individual or otherwise discriminate against any individual with respect to his compensation, terms, conditions, or privileges of employment, because of such individual's age;
>
> (2) to limit, segregate, or classify his employees in any way which would deprive or tend to deprive any individual of employment opportunities or otherwise adversely affect his status as an employee, because of such individual's age.

---

[3]See the excellent discussion by John R. Wells, "Recent Developments in the Law of Sexual Harassment," 18 *Colo. Law.* 2 (Feb. 1989): 263–66.

The prohibition of age discrimination applies to nonfederal employees who are at least forty years of age. This prohibition applies to tenured faculty at institutions of higher learning. Under certain conditions, the prohibition does not apply to bona fide executives or high policymakers who have been employed for a two-year period immediately before retirement. The Act also provides that employees of the federal government who are at least forty years of age are free of any discrimination based on age. With certain exceptions, there is no maximum seventy years of age limit for federal employees. The EEOC is responsible for administering the federal part of the Act.

In the following case the court established the test "of function and not of pay" in determining whether the employee was in the bona fide executive or high policymaking position exemption under ADIEA, 29 U.S.C. sec. 631(c)(1).

FACTS

Whittlesey, 65 years of age and the Chief Labor Counsel of Union Carbide Corporation, was compulsorily retired by Union Carbide after having been employed by Union Carbide as an attorney since 1953. Whittlesey brought an age discrimination action against Union Carbide in the United States District Court of New York for violation of the federal Age Discrimination in Employment Act. Union Carbide claimed that Whittlesey was in a bona fide executive or a high policymaking position and therefore exempt under the Act. The Court found in favor of Whittlesey, and Union Carbide appealed to the United States Court of Appeals.

DECISION

Affirmed for Whittlesey. This case is among the first to test the scope of the exemption. The central liability issue was whether Whittlesey was exempt from ADIEA protection as a "bona fide executive or high policymaking employee" under 29 U.S.C. sec. 631(c)(1). Judge Leval correctly rejected the argument that Whittlesey's high salary and title of chief labor counsel automatically removed him from coverage. After analyzing the statute, regulations, and case law, he determined that congress intended the test for the exemption to be "one of function, not of pay." 567 F.Supp. at 1326. From the evidence concerning Whittlesey's duties at Union Carbide, Judge Leval found that Whittlesey was not a "bona fide executive," but "was primarily an attorney doing legal work, giving legal advice, giving attention to the effect of statutes, regulations and administrative action upon company practices and attending to litigation." *Id.* at 1323. While Whittlesey had "some administrative or executive responsibility over the functioning of this small [labor law] section", his supervisory duties nevertheless "were quite minimal and occupied a very small portion of his time." *Id.*

Nor did Whittlesey lose his ADIEA protection under the "high policymaking employee" prong of the exemption, for Judge Leval found that "Union Carbide did not encourage or invite its house lawyers to play a dynamic policy-creating role" and that "they were employed to do legal work." *Id.* at 1324. He further found that when Whittlesey did contribute to corporate policy, his "role in connection with policy formulation was minor" and did not rise to the exemption level contemplated by the statute and regulations. *Id.* at 1325. Since these findings by Judge Leval are amply supported by the record, we affirm his determination that Whittlesey was not exempt from ADIEA protection by sec. 631(c)(1).

Whittlesey v. Union Carbide Corp., 742 F.2d 724 (2nd Cir. 1984).

The Act contains one general exception to this prohibition: When age is shown to be "a bona fide occupational qualification [BFOQ] reasonably necessary to the normal operation of the particular business," sec. 623(f)(1), an employee may be terminated on the basis of his age before reaching age seventy.

In a recent case, *Johnson et al. v. Mayor and City of Baltimore et al.*, 472 U.S. 353 (1985), the U.S. Supreme Court held that a federal statute generally requiring federal firefighters to retire at age fifty-five does not establish, as a matter of law, that age fifty-five is a BFOQ for nonfederal firefighters within the meaning of the ADIEA. The City of Baltimore's municipal code provisions established a mandatory retirement age of lower than seventy for firefighters and police personnel. Six city firefighters claimed that those provisions violated the ADIEA. The city contended that the federal BFOQ provisions were applicable to the city and state local firefighters as a matter of law, and that the city did not have to factually prove a BFOQ. Since the city failed to prove that age was a BFOQ for its firefighters, and the federal BFOQ did not apply to nonfederal (City of Baltimore) firefighters,[4] the Supreme Court reversed the holding of the U.S. Court of Appeals that "the federal retirement provision at issue in this case provides an absolute defense in an ADIEA action."

AIDS in the Workplace AIDS (acquired immunodeficiency syndrome) is a lethal contagious disease of developing epidemic proportions in the United States. It is caused by the retrovirus called HIV which, as is now known, can be transmitted only through (1) sexual contact; (2) injection into the bloodstream either by intravenous drug needles or by transfusion of contaminated blood or blood products; (3) or by an infected mother to her unborn child or through her breast-milk to her infant. It cannot be transmitted by casual contact. In the early stages of the AIDS epidemic, there was what amounted to a national hysteria about possible transmission of HIV by HIV carriers.

Employers have become greatly concerned because of their potential liability in ascertaining whether their employees or job applicants have AIDS, their legal duty to provide safe working conditions for their employees under federal and state laws, and their lack of knowledge about how to cope with the presence of AIDS in their work force. An employer is confronted with various issues: (1) the ability of an employee with AIDS to perform his or her job physically and mentally; (2) the reaction of coworkers on learning that a coworker has AIDS; (3) customer or client reaction regarding the business of the firm when informed that an employee in that firm has AIDS if the business is directly dealing with the public (for example, a restaurant or hotel). There is also the matter of the infected employee's concern to continue to be employed as long as he or she is "qualified" to perform that job. Job performance will vary with the stage of the disease.

Federal laws and many state laws prohibit employers from discriminating against otherwise "qualified handicapped individuals" *solely by reason of their handicaps.* State laws, with exceptions, in general have wording similar to that of the federal Rehabilitation Act of 1973 (as amended), which defines a handicapped individual as "any person who (i) has a physical or mental impairment which substantially limits one or more of such person's major life activities, (ii) has a record of such an impairment, or (iii) is regarded as having such an impairment." Department of Health and Human Services (HHS) regulations define "physical impairment" to mean, among other things, any physiological disorder affecting the respiratory system; they define "major life activities" to include working. The Act also prohibits discrimination based *solely on handicap* against any "otherwise qualified handicapped individual" in any program that is conducted by the federal government or that receives federal financial assistance. Although the Act does not mention AIDS, it is now recognized that a person with AIDS is a "handicapped individual."

[4]In October 1986, the ADIEA was amended exempting state and local firefighters and law enforcement officers from the Act.

Many legal experts believe that the following U.S. Supreme Court case, concerned with a discharged teacher with tuberculosis, would be equally applicable to a person with AIDS.

FACTS

Gene Arline was hospitalized for tuberculosis in 1957. The disease went into remission for the next 20 years, during which time she began teaching elementary school in Florida. In 1977, March 1978, and November 1978, she had relapses. At the end of the 1978–1979 school year, the School Board discharged her after a hearing because of the continued recurrence of tuberculosis. After she was denied relief in state administrative proceedings, she brought suit in Federal District Court, alleging a violation of sec. 504. The District Court held that she was *not* a "handicapped person" under the Act, but that, even assuming she were, she was *not* "qualified" to teach elementary school. The Court of Appeals reversed, holding that persons with contagious diseases are within sec. 504's coverage, and remanded for further findings as to whether respondent was "otherwise qualified" for her job. Section 504 of the Rehabilitation Act of 1973, 29 U.S.C. sec. 794 (Act), provides, *inter alia,* that no "otherwise qualified handicapped individual," as defined in 29 U.S.C. sec. 706(7), shall, solely by reason of his handicap, be excluded from participation in any program receiving federal financial assistance. Section 706(7)(B) defines "handicapped individual" to mean any person who "(i) has a physical . . . impairment which substantially limits one or more of [his] major life activities, (ii) has a record of such an impairment, or (iii) is regarded as having such an impairment." Department of Health and Human Services (HHS) regulations define "physical impairment" to mean, *inter alia,* any physiological disorder affecting the respiratory system, and define "major life activities" to include working.

DECISION

1. A person afflicted with the contagious disease of tuberculosis may be a "handicapped individual" within the meaning of sec. 504.

(a) Arline is a "handicapped individual" as defined in sec. 706 (7)(B) and the HHS regulations. Her hospitalization in 1957 for a disease that affected her respiratory system and that substantially limited "one or more of [her] major life activities" establishes that she has a "record of . . . impairment."

(b) The fact that a person with a record of impairment is also contagious does not remove that person from sec. 504's coverage. To allow an employer to justify discrimination by distinguishing between a disease's contagious effects on others and its physical effects on a patient would be unfair, would be contrary to sec. 706(7)(B)(iii) and the legislative history, which demonstrate Congress' concern about an impairment's effect on others, and would be inconsistent with sec. 504's basic purpose to ensure that handicapped individuals are not denied jobs because of the prejudice or ignorance of others. The Act replaces such fearful, reflexive reactions with actions based on reasoned and medically sound judgments as to whether contagious handicapped persons are "otherwise qualified" to do the job.

2. In most cases, in order to determine whether a person handicapped by contagious disease is "otherwise qualified" under sec. 504, the District Court must conduct an individualized inquiry and make appropriate findings of fact, based on reasonable medical judgments given the state of medical knowledge, about (a) the nature of the risk (*e. g.,* how the disease is transmitted), (b) the duration of the risk (how long is the carrier infectious), (c) the severity of the risk (what is the potential harm to third parties), and (d) the probabilities the disease will be transmitted and will cause varying degrees of harm. In making these findings, courts normally should defer to the reasonable medical judgments of public health officials. Courts must then determine, in light of these findings, whether any "reasonable accommodation" can be made by the employer under the established standards for that inquiry.

3. Because the District Court did not make appropriate findings, it is impossible for this Court to determine whether respondent is "otherwise qualified" for the job of elementary school teacher. The judgment of the Court of Appeals is affirmed, and the case is remanded for additional findings of fact.

School Board of Nassau County of Fla., et al. v. Arline, 480 U.S. 273 (1987).

Fair Labor Standards Act

This federal Act of 1938 as amended, also known as the Wage-Hour Law, has for its purpose "the establishment of fair labor standards in employment in and affecting interstate and foreign commerce, and for other purposes." For example, if you are an employee of a manufacturer of goods that are shipped outside the state of manufacture for the purpose of doing interstate business, you are covered under the Act. It is administered by the secretary of labor. We are generally concerned here with the Act's provisions for child labor, minimum wages, and maximum hours of employment. Many states have laws in these areas.

Child Labor The Act prohibits "oppressive child labor" as the employment of an employee under the age of sixteen years, other than by a parent under certain circumstances; or the employment of an employee between the ages of sixteen and eighteen in an occupation particularly hazardous to, or detrimental to the health and well-being of, such persons in that age group. Many states require persons below eighteen years of age to obtain a work permit.

Maximum Hours An employer can compel an employee to work more than the usual forty hours per week. If the employee works more than forty hours per week, the employer must pay the employee no less than one and one-half times the regular rate at which the individual is employed. However, exceptions are made in special situations, such as for employees under the terms of a collective bargaining agreement, and for wages at piece goods rates.

Many states limit the hours of work permitted for persons under sixteen years of age, with a maximum of eight hours per day and forty hours per week, although other states vary concerning the maximum weekly hours of labor.

Minimum Wages The Act establishes a minimum hourly wage which must be paid to an employee; this amount is periodically revised by Congress. Under the Equal Pay Act amendment, wage discrimination on the basis of sex is prohibited except when such pay is made pursuant to a seniority system, a merit system, a system that measures earnings by quantity or quality of production, or a differential based on any other factor other than sex.

The term "wages" includes the reasonable cost to the employer of furnishing such employee with board, lodging, or other facilities, if they are customarily furnished by such employer to the employees. However, such cost is not included in wages to the extent that a collective bargaining agreement applicable to that particular employee excludes it as a part of wages.

Exemptions from the Above Provisions The above maximum hourly and minimum wage provisions of the Act do *not* apply in many instances (with certain exceptions), some of which would involve the following employees:

1. An employee in a bona fide executive, administrative, or professional capacity, or generally as an outside salesperson.
2. Generally an employee in a retail or service establishment if more than 50 percent of such establishment's annual dollar volume of sales of goods or services is made within the state in which the establishment is located.

3. Generally an employee in an amusement or recreational establishment not operating for more than seven months in a calendar year.
4. An employee generally employed in agriculture. (See Title 29 U.S. Code, sec. 213, as amended.)

▶ Unions and Collective Bargaining

This subject is discussed in detail in Chapter 36, Labor Law. Beginning with the Norris–La Guardia Act of 1932, the movement to recognize and strengthen unions of employees started as an important part of the labor-management process. Subsequent federal labor legislation, discussed in Chapter 36, attempted to attain a just and legal balance regarding the rights, duties, and conduct of labor and management, respectively. The various unfair labor practices by employees and unions as well as by employers are listed and discussed in that chapter.

Protection and Compensation for Injury

▶ State Workers' Compensation Statutes

Common law established various duties of employers toward their employees regarding their work. Generally, they were: (1) to provide reasonably safe working conditions, which included reasonably safe tools and equipment; (2) to exercise reasonable care in the selection of competent and adequate number of fellow servant employees; and (3) to exercise reasonable care in operating the business and in the establishment of reasonable operating rules.

common law
Principles of nonstatutory law reflecting the customs and usages of society and found in judicial decisions

Employers were liable to their employees for injury caused to them by their negligence, with three exceptions. The first exception was the *fellow-servant rule,* when the injury to an employee was caused not by the employer's negligence but, rather, by the negligence of a fellow-servant employee. The second exception was the *servant's contributory negligence rule,* when the injury to an employee was caused by the injured employee's contributory negligence. The third exception was the *servant's assumption-of-risk rule,* when the injured employee knew of the risks of injury from the job and assumed them by entering upon the employment with such risks.

The law is different today as a result of public policy that the risks of injury to employees arising out of, and in the course of, employment should be those of the employer. The cost of paying for such injury should be a part of the operating expense of the business. An employee's contributory negligence and noncompliance with his or her employer's rules will not preclude the employee from recovering for any injury that *arose out of and in the course of the employment.* (The company policy required workers using a lathe to wear protective eye goggles supplied by the company. Ann, an employee working over a lathe, did not wear any goggles, and *Ann's* eyes were injured by sparks from the lathe. Ann can recover for the injury.)

There has been much concern among businesses and some conflict among state courts on the meaning and application of the phrases "arising out of" and "in the course of" employment. In the following well reasoned and often cited case, the phrases "arising out of" and "in the course of" employment were interpreted and determined to be not synonymous but, rather, two separate elements both of which are necessary for recovery of workers' compensation. Once it is determined that "*arising* in the course of employment" means "*originating* in the course of employment," then we look to see whether the employee's injury had its *genesis* or origin at the workplace in order to determine if "course of employment" is present. The case is concerned primarily with course of employment.

FACTS

The Florida statute defines injury, for purposes of the workers' compensation act, as "personal injury or death by accident arising out of and in the course of employment, and such diseases or infection as naturally or unavoidably result from such injury." Strother, a cashier at Morrison's Cafeteria, defendant, was charged with the responsibility of handling the payment of food bills from customers from mid-afternoon to closing at nine each night. Although not a part of her regular employment, on two occasions she drove the cafeteria's manager to the bank to deposit the day's receipts. On the two days preceding the incident which resulted in the injury for which she now seeks workers' compensation, Strother observed two men in the cafeteria who were not customers or employees. On the evening of the incident, she noticed the same two men enter the cafeteria in the same manner as they had entered on the two previous days. This evening, she left work and drove directly home (some fifteen or twenty minutes' drive from the cafeteria) where she was assaulted by, and her purse was taken by, the men whom she had observed in the cafeteria. They thought she was carrying the cafeteria's money since they demanded "the money or deposits."

Plaintiff filed a claim with the Florida Commission for workers' compensation under the Florida statute. The Commission's judge of industrial claims ordered workers' compensation to the plaintiff on the basis that the circumstances of the plaintiff's employment exposed her to a greater risk than that of a regular cashier and that the assault arose out of and in the course of her employment. However, the Industrial Relations Commission reversed the order of the judge of industrial claims and denied workers' compensation on the basis that, while the plaintiff's injuries did arise out of her employment, they were not sustained in the course of her employment. The plaintiff petitioned the Supreme Court of Florida claiming that she sustained the injuries in the course of her employment.

DECISION

The Commission's decision is quashed [void], and the order of the judge of industrial claims reinstated. The plaintiff's injuries from the assault had their origin and cause entirely within the course of her employment and arose out of her employment. The "arising out of" requirement refers to causation, only incidentally related to considerations of time and space, and must be satisfied by a showing of causal connection between work and "injury." The "course of" requirement, on the other hand, refers to continuity of time, space and circumstances, only incidentally related to causation. This requirement must be satisfied by a showing of an unbroken course beginning with work and ending with work and ending with injury under such circumstances that the beginning and the end are connected parts of a single work-related incident.

We hold that, to be compensable, an injury must arise out of employment in the sense of causation and be in the course of employment in the sense of continuity of time, space, and circumstances. This latter factor may be proved by showing that the causative factors occurred during the time and space limits of employment. Plaintiff's injuries resulting from the assault had their genesis at the place of employment since the assailants were actually on the business premises, casing it so to speak, and, then when the plaintiff left, they followed her to her home and there assaulted her and robbed her of her purse which they thought contained the cafeteria's cash receipts. The time bomb began ticking while she was on the business premises and during working hours and went off at a time and place remote from the place of employment.

Strother v. Morrison Cafeteria et al., 383 So.2d 623 (Fla. 1980).

There must be a *substantial* causal relationship between the employment and the injury experienced by the employee. Also, if the injury arises out of or in the course of employment, any new injury that flows from and is a consequence of the initial injury is covered by workers' compensation.

In order to ensure that there is proper and adequate financial security to cover this risk—i.e., to indemnify the injured employee—employers must comply with state workers' compensation laws. Usually employers are required either to take out insurance through a state insurance fund or a private insurance company, or to deposit adequate securities with the state workers' compensation committee. Employees who are domestic servants or farm laborers usually are not covered by workers' compensation statutes. Also, an employer is not liable for injury self-inflicted by the employee or resulting from the employee's intoxication. Since workers' compensation coverage must be provided by the employer, an employee cannot waive such coverage. Also, since the employee is covered by workers' compensation, in many states the employee cannot sue the employer, although in states that permit such suit the common law defenses become available to the employer if sued by an employee. The employee can sue a third person who wrongfully injured the employee. For example, the employee can sue the driver of a vehicle for the driver's negligence causing injury to the employee while the driver was transporting the employer's goods. The state laws have detailed schedules specifying the limited money amounts payable for various injuries.

► Health and Safety Laws

Society is concerned about the health and safety of employees while on the job. Various state and federal laws and administrative rules and regulations have as their purpose to set standards to reduce preventable hazards to employees in the place of work and to provide for safe and healthful working conditions.

On the state level, there are departments of labor or of health that have the responsibility for determining whether an employer is complying with the state health and safety statute and administrative rules and regulations.

On the federal level, there is the Occupational Safety and Health Act (OSHA) of 1970 as amended, administered by the secretary of labor. The Act provides for and directs the secretary of labor to establish and publish specific mandatory and occupational safety and health standards with which employers in a business in or affecting interstate commerce must comply. The specification of standards does not relieve an employer, in the absence of a specific standard, from the duty to furnish a place of employment that will not expose employees to a recognized risk of death or serious bodily harm. The Act provides for employer record keeping of illness, injury, and death experienced by employees and for employer reports to the secretary of labor under certain conditions.

The OSHA division of the Department of Labor is responsible for making inspections of an employer's business premises and working conditions and for issuing citations for alleged violation of OSHA. Employers may appeal from such citations to the OSHA Review Commission and, after exhausting their administrative remedies, they may seek judicial relief in the U.S. Court of Appeals. At the present time, there is much public concern about allegedly lessened governmental enforcement of OSHA. Illustrative of this cause for concern are the numerous lawsuits for large amounts of money brought by present and former employees as asbestosis sufferers.

Pursuant to the purpose of the Act to reduce safety hazards and improve working conditions, 29 U.S.C. Sec. 654 provides:

(a) Each employer—
 (1) shall furnish to each of his employees employment and a place of employment which are free from *recognized* hazards that are causing or are likely to cause death or serious physical harm to his employees;
 (2) shall comply with occupational safety and health standards **promulgated** under this chapter.

(b) Each employee shall comply with occupational safety and health standards and all rules, regulations, and orders issued pursuant to this chapter which are applicable to his own actions and conduct. [Emphasis added]

promulgate
Proclaim

This section is called the "general duty" provision of the Act, and is intended as a catchall provision to cover dangerous conditions of employment *not specifically covered* by existing health and safety standards promulgated by the secretary.

Section 660 (29 U.S.C.) provides for civil and criminal penalties for serious and nonserious violations of Section 654 and of occupational safety and health standards promulgated by the secretary. Subsection (j) defines a *serious* violation:

(j) For purposes of this section, a serious violation shall be deemed to exist in a place of employment if there is a substantial probability that death or serious physical harm could result from a condition which exists, or from one or more practices, means, methods, operations, or processes which have been adopted or are in use, in such place of employment unless the employer did not, and could not with the exercise of reasonable diligence, know of the presence of the violation.

In the following case the court had to decide whether there was a violation of the standard published in the rule of the secretary of labor and therefore a violation of the general duty provision (Section 654), and, if there was a violation, whether it was a serious one. Notice the careful analysis of an administrative regulation made by the parties.

FACTS

Petitioner, Everglades Sugar Refinery, Inc. (company), engages in the refining, packaging, and shipping of cane sugar. Decedent Carter, and Sauls, company employees, were assigned one weekend to do routine maintenance and cleanup operations, which included cleaning up "mud" from the syrup process. They could do this by using a small pickup truck and shovels. They knew that a particular payloader vehicle needed repair and was inoperable because of a disconnected throttle linkage and that they were not authorized to use or attempt to repair it. They felt they could do the cleaning up faster if they could repair the payloader and use it. They had mechanical ability. While trying to make the payloader work, Sauls accidentally bumped the boom release and the heavy bucket with a 300-pound load fell upon Carter who was underneath trying to make repairs and killed him.

A regulation promulgated by the Secretary of Labor stated as a standard "Any power-operated industrial truck not in safe operating condition shall be removed from service. All repairs shall be made by authorized personnel." The Secretary issued a citation to the company for violation of the regulation and of section 654 (29 U.S.C.). The matter was heard by an Administrative Law Judge, and on appeal, by the Occupational Safety and Health Review Commission, both affirming the Secretary's citation. The company appeals.

The issues and the contentions of the parties are as follows: 1. Was there a violation of the regulation and, therefore, of section 654? The company contends that the regulation applies only to industrial trucks not in safe operating condition, that there was nothing unsafe about the payloader in its state of disrepair at the time of the accident, that the regulation applies only to unsafe trucks, that the second sentence of the regulation with respect to repairs would be applicable only to unsafe trucks, and therefore there was no violation of the regulation and of section 654. The Secretary interprets the regulation to mean that a repair made by unauthorized personnel on an inoperable industrial truck constitutes a violation without the truck being initially in an unsafe operating condition, provided the attempted repair may result in creating an unsafe condition. Also, that the second sentence of the regulation applies to the repair of all power-operated trucks, whether or not the truck is in a safe or unsafe condition under the circumstances.

2. If there is a violation of the regulation and, of section 654, is the violation a serious one? The company contends that the violation is not serious because the accident could not have happened but for Carter's **negligence,** and since there was not a substantial probability that death or serious injury could result from an employee's repairing the throttle linkage the company could not have reasonably foreseen that death or serious injury could result because Carter's own negligence caused the injury. The Secretary contends the company reasonably could foresee that what happened could occur irrespective of whether or not negligence might occur.

negligence
In conduct, failure to use the degree of care demanded by the circumstances

DECISION

Affirmed, for the Secretary and the Commission. The Secretary's interpretation of its own regulation should be upheld. The Secretary's interpretation of an OSHA regulation is entitled to great deference. [The court quoted from another case], "We have held that the promulgator's interpretation is controlling as long as it is one of several reasonable interpretations, although it may not appear as reasonable as some other." In this case the Secretary's interpretation of the regulation was a reasonable interpretation governing unauthorized repairs. The company violated the regulation and, therefore, section 654. The violation was a serious one. The company cannot avoid its responsibility to adhere to the regulations because Carter himself was negligent in what he did. Further, under the circumstances the company could conceive that an employee could injure himself in repairing the loader. Foreseeability is an expectation which a person, experienced in the circumstances, could conceive would happen.

Everglades Sugar Refinery, Inc. v. Raymond J. Donovan, Secretary of Labor, and Occupational Safety and Health Review Comm'n, 658 F.2d 1076 (5th Cir. 1981).

Social Security

Society is further concerned about the *financial* impact upon employees by reason of their retirement, disability, death, hospitalization, and unemployment. These are areas of grave financial risk to an employee, and the federal and state governments participate in a program of insurance to cover this risk. The key federal law on this subject is the Social Security Act of 1935, as amended.

Employees who are included under the Act are employees of private business; new federal employees hired in 1984 and thereafter; employees of nonprofit organizations; and employees of only those states that are currently under Social Security. Nonfederal employers currently under Social Security cannot withdraw from its coverage.

► Old-age, Survivors, and Disability Insurance (OASDI)

Both the employer and the employee contribute, as taxes, under the Federal Insurance Contributions Act (FICA) to help pay for the loss of income benefits on retirement at age sixty-five, or earlier at age sixty-two at a reduced benefit if early retirement is chosen by the employee; survivor benefits on death of the employee; and financial benefits to employees under sixty-five years of age who are physically disabled. Persons who are self-employed must financially contribute to this insurance program and thereby participate in the insurance coverage.

Congress enacted legislation in 1983 that increases the current retirement age of sixty-five to sixty-seven in two steps. Beginning in the year 2000, the retirement age will advance by two months each year until it reaches sixty-six in the year 2005. Then beginning in 2017, the retirement age will resume its advance by two months each year until it reaches sixty-seven in 2022.

Tax of Employee and Employer An employer is required to withhold the necessary contributions from the employee's wages as he or she is paid, and the employer also makes a similar contribution and makes deposit and payment of both such funds as required by law. This involves the employee's annual wage base and the percentage of tax on that base.

1. *Employee's Annual Wage Base.* The basis for the employee's contribution is called the employee's annual wage base, which is the maximum amount of an employee's wages that are subject to the tax. For example, Ann's annual wage is $54,000. For the calendar year 1990, the first $51,300 is taxable as the annual wage base. The Secretary of the Treasury has the authority to adjust the maximum contribution by the percentage of increase in "average wages," as measured by the Department of Labor in its annual review of hourly wages paid nationally.
2. *Percentage of Tax on That Base.* The percentage of tax on the employee's annual wage base is fixed by the statute. The OASDI and Hospital Insurance Taxes on the annual wage base are: for 1990 and thereafter, 6.20 percent (OASDI) + 1.45 percent (Medicare) = 7.65 percent (total). When any employee has more than one job and is paid wages by two different employers, the tax on both wages is withheld from each employer and the *employee* is entitled to a refund for the excess tax paid by him or her; neither employer is entitled to any refund. Also, the employee's tax is not a deductible item on the employee's annual federal income tax return. The employer's contribution will be in the same amount as that of its employee.

Self-Employment Tax The self-employment tax percentage (before tax credits) will be the same as the above combined employee and employer tax percentages. For example, the rate of tax for 1990 and thereafter is 15.30 percent. But the *amount* of the tax will increase as the amount of the above employee's annual wage base increases. However, only for the self-employed, there is a special *deduction*—not a tax credit—for the taxable year of an amount equal to one-half of the taxes imposed for 1990 and each year thereafter.

Benefits Old-age, survivors, and disability benefits are fixed by the statute, and the extent of such benefits depends on various factors. Benefits increase automatically, subject to limitations, with an increase in the cost-of-living (or COLA, a "cost of living adjustment") of a statutorily prescribed percent as indicated by the consumer price index. Delayed retirement adds an increase in benefits by statutorily specified percentages.

Recipients of benefits are subject to tax on their Social Security benefits. Up to one-half of the benefits will be taxed if a recipient's adjusted gross income exclusive of Social Security benefits, plus one-half of his or her Social Security benefits, exceeds a certain base amount—$25,000 for single retirees, and $32,000 total for a married couple filing a joint return.

On retirement, the employee's *earnings beyond a certain maximum,* which is indexed annually, reduce retirement benefits until age seventy. As of 1990, benefits have been reduced $1 for every $3 of *"earned* income" *above* the 1990 base of $9,360 for any person sixty-five years of age or older but not yet seventy who is entitled to Social Security benefits, and $1 for every $2 earned *above* $6,840 for such entitled persons under sixty-five. Earned income means *work income* earned in the form of wages or by self-employment. It does not include other income such as (but not limited to) retirement pay, investment income (other than by a dealer in securities), interest from savings accounts and from loans (unless your business is lending money), capital gains, rental income from owned real estate (other than a real estate dealer), income from a limited partnership as a limited partner, payments from certain trust funds and annuity plans, royalties from patent or copyright. Statewide federal social security offices are available to provide all social security information to the public.

► Hospital Insurance (Medicare)

Medicare is a federal health insurance program for people sixty-five or older, and some under sixty-five who have been disabled. It is administered by the Health Care Financing Administration. Medicare has two parts: Part A, called *hospital insurance,* and Part B, called *medical insurance,* which assists the patient in his or her payment of doctor's expenses. Most people who have Medicare hospital insurance do not have to make monthly payments for this protection. They have hospital insurance because of credits for work under social security. Persons who have Medicare hospital insurance are eligible to obtain federal medical insurance on payment of relatively small monthly premiums, payable quarterly, while working but then withheld monthly from benefit checks when not working, but which rise as the cost of medical care rises.

► Unemployment Insurance

The purpose of the Federal Unemployment Tax Act (FUTA) is to provide temporary financial assistance to a former employee with a sufficient number of credits from former employment during a period of unemployment, provided he or she is ready, able, and willing to take a suitable full-time job that becomes available. Refusal to take such a job that the state employment office indicates is available may well disqualify the unemployed person from receiving unemployment insurance benefits. The cost of the operation of the unemployment insurance program is administered by the federal government out of part of the tax collected, but each state and the District of Columbia administers the program in its own area.

Under FUTA, employers who are within the provisions of the Act and not exempt are taxed annually by the federal government. Each state also taxes the employer, the state tax being at least 5.4 percent in most states. The employer can receive an offset credit against the federal tax up to 5.4 percent of the state unemployment tax. While the federal government does not require that an employee pay a tax while he or she is employed, a few states do impose a tax on the employee when the state has a supplemental program. Taxes are collected by the employer and submitted to the state, which deposits them with the federal government, where an Unemployment Insurance Fund is maintained with an account for each state and subject to withdrawal by the particular state solely for the payment of benefits. The federal tax is based on a percentage of a wage-base amount. A tax of 6.2 percent (before tax credits) is imposed on the first $7,000 of wages paid to a covered employee by such an employer. An employer with a low rate of unemployment may benefit by having a good experience rating and thereby further reduce the employer's *state* tax and still retain the federal offset against the federal tax of 5.4 percent.

► Employee Pension Plans Controls

Pension plans for employees have been established by many private employers. It has become very apparent that there was a need for close governmental supervision over such plans in order to ensure greater protection of the beneficial interests of employees covered by such plans. The federal Employee Retirement Income Security Act (ERISA) of 1974, as amended by the Retirement Equity Act of 1984 and the Tax Reform Act of 1986, serves this purpose. More than 50 million workers are protected by ERISA. The secretary of labor has the responsibility for operation and supervision of such pension plans and the secretary of the treasury has the authority to issue regulations pertaining to funding.

ERISA does not require any employer to establish a pension plan; it requires only that pension plans comply with certain standards. While ERISA provides for pension and welfare plans, our discussion is concerned only with pension plans.

Eligibility for Pension Plan Participation ERISA imposes rules on employee pension plans regarding eligibility for participation. Most pension plans require employees to meet age and service requirements before they are permitted to become plan "participants." Eligibility for participation generally may not be denied if the employee attains the age of twenty-one or has one year of service, whichever is later. Years of service before age eighteen may be disregarded. Plans that provide for immediate 100 percent vesting after not more than two years of service may require the employee to be twenty-one years of age with two years of service.

Pension plans may not exclude an employee solely on the basis of seasonal employment if the employee has a "year of service." Generally, a year of service is 1,000 hours of service during a calendar year. In the case of a seasonable industry where the customary period of employment is less than 1,000 hours during the calendar year, a year of service is defined by regulations.

Accrual of Benefits Participants in a pension plan *accrue* benefits, which is the benefit accumulated to a particular point in time. Funds are accumulated in the individual's pension account. An employee's accrued benefits are based on his or her years of participation in the plan as provided in the plan.

Vesting An employee may accrue retirement benefits but until they are *vested,* he or she has no *right* to these benefits on retirement. A vested benefit is a *nonforfeitable* immediate or deferred benefit that the employee has gained. Usually, if the employee leaves the job before retirement, his or her accrued benefits based on employer contributions become vested only if the employee has worked for the required period of time. If the plan requires contributions from both the employer and employee, the accrued benefits derived from the participant's own contributions must be fully and immediately vested. ERISA requires a single-employer plan to provide that accrued benefits based on employer contributions vest at least as rapidly as one of the two following schedules:

1. Vest participants fully (100 percent) upon completion of five years of service.
2. Vest 20 percent after three years of service and then 20 percent per year thereafter until 100 percent vested after seven years of service.

Payment Under the Plan Unless the participant elects a later date, payment of a participant's benefits must begin no later than the sixtieth day after the close of the plan year in which the *latest* of these events occurs:

1. The employee reaches sixty-five or, if it is earlier, when he or she reaches the normal retirement age specified under the plan; or
2. The employee reaches the tenth year after the employee began participation in the plan; or
3. The employee terminates his or her service with the employer.

If the plan provides for early retirement benefits, employers are generally free to establish eligibility standards for the payment of early retirement benefits. However, early retirement benefits must be at least the actuarial equivalent of the normal retirement benefits. The plan must permit terminated employees who have completed the required period of service but had not reached the required age at the time of termination to elect to receive vested benefits when they do reach the required age.

Management and Protection of the Plan ERISA's fiduciary provisions protect the plan from financial losses caused by mismanagement and misuse of assets. The administrator is a fiduciary with the duty to protect the interests of the participants in the plan. He or she is to exercise the "prudent person" standard of care, for breach of which he or she may be personally liable for loss caused to the plan. ERISA also establishes rules for funding and monitoring pension plans, and rules for joint and survivor provisions in pension plans.

Employer Use of Lie, Drug, and Alcohol Detection Devices

▶ Use of Lie Detection Devices

Employer use of lie detection (polygraph) devices on their employees is a subject of much current public discussion and controversy. A number of states, by statute, prohibit employers from using lie detection tests as a condition of employment or of continuing employment. But law enforcement, government agencies, and drug dispensing firms often are exempted from such prohibition. The purpose of these polygraph examinations in the workplace is to predict and prevent employee theft. In the public area, the test is given to law enforcement applicants and employees to predict criminal and otherwise unacceptable behavior, and as an aid in internal investigations in cases of alleged employee wrongdoing and sexual harassment.

Under the federal Employee Polygraph Protection Act of 1988, most private employers are prohibited from using lie detector tests to screen job applicants or to test current employees unless the employer *reasonably suspects* that the employee was involved in a workplace theft or other incident causing economic loss to the employer. The Act exempts federal, state, and local governments. However, it permits private security firms and drug companies to continue to administer polygraph tests to job applicants and employees under certain conditions. Employers are prohibited from disciplining, discharging, discriminating against, or denying employment and promotion to prospective or current workers *solely* on the basis of polygraph test results. The Act sets forth detailed procedures that an employer must follow during any legally permitted lie detector test, and it specifies detailed qualifications for any individual examiner who conducts a lie detector test. It also prohibits employees and job applicants from waiving their rights under the Act. The Act does not pre-empt more stringent or more restrictive state or local laws or collective bargaining agreements. The National Labor Relations Board has ruled that private employers must bargain with a union before imposing a lie detector test as a condition of employment.

The Act also authorizes civil lawsuits by the secretary of labor, employees, and job applicants and gives federal courts the power to award back pay and benefits, employment and reinstatement, as well as civil fines up to $10,000 against employers. The signal to all employers is to know the law and be extremely careful in complying with it.

▶ Use of Drug and Alcohol Detection Devices

Employee use of drugs and alcohol and its probable cause of impairment on the job has led to widespread reaction from employers and federal and state governments in the form of tests to detect such use. Often opposition to the use of such tests is based on alleged invasion of the federal constitutional right of privacy and the right against unreasonable searches and seizures. Testing may be pre-employment, random, or screening of employee use. Drug testing involves urine testing and analyses, and it is challenged as a violation of the U.S. Constitution's Fourth Amendment ban on *unreasonable* searches and seizures (urinalysis testing involves a search); the Fifth Amendment's privilege against self-incrimination; the Fourteenth Amendment's rights to due process of law and equal protection of the laws; and the right to privacy which, as enunciated by the U.S. Supreme Court,[5] is found "in specific guarantees in the Bill of Rights [that] have penumbras [shadows] formed by emanations from those guarantees."

In the private sector, private employers are tired of paying the enormously high bill for substance (drug) abuse in the workplace, reflected for example in high absenteeism, accident rates and medical expenditures, increased theft, and lower productivity. The National Institute on Drug Abuse estimates that a substantial number of major corporations in the United States currently screen prospective employees for drug abuse. Many employers are encouraging employees to use Employee Assistance Programs—company-sponsored efforts that offer a host of medical and counseling services to troubled employees.

The current trend in the private (and public-governmental) sectors is to test for illegal drug and alcohol abuse. A number of large companies test only *pre-employment applicants* so as to deter habitual users of drugs or alcohol from applying and avoid hiring them. Applicants who refuse to take the test are rejected. However, mandatory testing of employees in a private firm for illegal drug or alcohol abuse has been under attack with differing results in the federal district and circuit courts. Generally, a private firm's policy of announcing a reasonable standard, such as testing on *suspicion* of employee illegal drug or alcohol abuse with due regard for privacy during the test, with competent testers, is upheld as constitutionally valid by the courts. The courts have stated that the reasonableness of a test will be determined by balancing the need for the test (for example, based on the nature of the industry, the job in question, and any evidence of an existing drug problem) against the resulting privacy intrusion. Then the courts will examine whether the testing process is reasonably related in scope to the circumstances that may have justified the test. However, in a union shop, the NLRB has issued two

[5]*Griswold v. Connecticut,* 381 U.S. 479, 485 (1965).

important decisions on employer drug/alcohol testing. "Drug/alcohol testing of employees is germane to the working environment, . . . and thus, to that extent, is a mandatory subject of bargaining."[6] For applicants for employment, the test "is *not* a mandatory subject of bargaining."[7]

The U.S. General Accounting Office prepared a report dated March 2, 1988, on its findings from surveys it made on employee drug testing in the private sector in the United States.[8] Among other statistical data are the following:

1. Firms with large numbers of employees were more likely to have drug-testing programs. One-half of the Fortune 100 firms conducted some type of employee testing.
2. More firms test job applicants than test current employees.
3. To a certain extent, firms used random or periodic testing for employees.
4. Most firms use independent laboratories to perform the testing.
5. The majority of survey respondents reported urinalysis as the test used.
6. The majority of firms perform some kinds of retest on individuals who initially tested positive. This practice is less common with respect to applicants than to employees.
7. Among the reasons for drug testing were improving workplace safety, increasing productivity, curbing illegal drug traffic, and reducing employee medical costs.
8. The majority of firms referred employees to drug rehabilitation programs. Firms did not necessarily dismiss employees who failed the test.

In the public sector, the federal government is engaged in a determined effort to combat drug abuse. The President's Commission on Organized Crime, after more than two years of study, prescribed widespread drug testing of public and private employees whose employers are engaged in government contract work as an important weapon in the war against drugs. The President's Executive Order of September 15, 1986, requires each federal agency chief to create a random testing program of federal employees in "sensitive positions." Because the railroad industry has been wracked in the past several years by a series of drug- and alcohol-influenced accidents, the Federal Railroad Administration promulgated rules that include post-accident toxicological testing of railroad employees; authorization to "test for cause" if on-the-job impairment is suspected; and pre-employment screening.[9] The rules establish "minimum federal safety standards for alcohol and drug abuse" as applied to railroads. The U.S. Supreme Court upheld these rules as valid.[10]

In *National Treasury Employees Union et al. v. Von Raab, Commissioner, United States Customs Serv.,* 109 S.Ct. 1384 (1989), the U.S. Supreme Court held constitutionally valid as reasonable a commissioner of customs *mandatory* drug testing program

---

[6]*Johson-Bateman Co. and Int'l Ass'n of Machinists and Aerospace Workers,* 295 N.L.R.B. No. 26, Case Nos. 31-CA-16299, 16578 (June 15, 1989).

[7]*Star Tribune, Div. of Cowles Media Co., and Newspaper Guild of the Twin Cities,* 295 N.L.R.B. No. 63, Case Nos. 18-CA-9938-10296 (June 15, 1989).

[8]Report by L. Nye Stevens to U.S. Representative Charles Shumer, "GAO Reports on Private Sector Drug Testing," Employment Practices Guide [1985–1989 Transfer Binder] *Lab. L. Rep.* (CCH) ¶ 5123 (March 2, 1988).

[9]Control of Alcohol and Drug Use, 49 C.F.R. Part 219 (1988). For other federal government drug abuse testing programs, see C.F.R. Index under "Drug Testing."

[10]*Skinner, Secretary of Transp. v. Railway Labor Executives Ass'n,* 109 S.Ct. 1402 (1989).

providing that drug tests were a condition of placement or enforcement for positions that involve direct involvement in drug interdiction, without a requirement of individualized suspicion of drug abuse and without the issuance of a warrant for the test. The Court held that the program did not violate the U.S. Constitution's Fourth Amendment prohibition of unreasonable searches and seizures nor the individual right to privacy. The Court also stated that "where a Fourth Amendment intrusion serves special government needs, beyond the normal need for law enforcement, it is necessary to balance the individual's privacy expectations against the Government's interests to determine whether it is impracticable to require a warrant or some level of individualized suspicion in the particular text. . . . Against these valid public interests we must weigh the interference with individual liberty that results from requiring these classes of individuals to undergo a urine test."

Women's Rights

It seems appropriate that in discussing employment a comment be made on the subject of the current status and rights of women in the work force as they overcome unfair discrimination against them because of their sex.

During the last several years, a long overdue recognition of women's rights, particularly in freedom from unfair discrimination solely because of sex, has emerged in federal and state legislation and in judicial decisions as well as in general business and societal acceptance. Difficulty lies in wide business acceptance and in greater governmental and legal enforcement, and particularly in greater opportunity for advancement to higher paying jobs and positions of greater responsibility.

Some statistics concerning the number and status of women in the work force would probably surprise many people and businesses.[11] For example:

1. Women accounted for more than three-fifths (62 percent) of the increase in the civilian labor force since 1977 (13 million women, 7.8 million men).
2. Sixty-seven percent of all women eighteen to sixty-four years of age, or 50.8 million women, were in the civilian labor force in 1987. Most women work because of economic need.
3. Women accounted for 44.8 percent of all persons in the civilian labor force in 1987. Among these, half of all black workers were women (6.5 million); 44.1 percent of all white workers were women (45.5 million); and 39.5 percent of all Hispanic workers were women (3.4 million).
4. Women continue to constitute large proportions of workers in traditionally female occupations. In 1987, they were 80 percent of all administrative support (including clerical) workers but only 9 percent of precision production, craft, and repair workers; and 69 percent of retail and personal sales workers but only 38 percent of managers, administrators, and executives.
5. Married-couple families with the wife in the paid labor force rose from about 40 percent, to 56 percent between 1972 and 1987.
6. The more education a woman has the greater the likelihood she will seek paid employment. Among women twenty-five to fifty-four years of age with four or more

[11]See U.S. Department of Labor, "Facts on Women Workers," *Fact Sheet No. 88-2* (1988) and "A Working Woman's Guide to Her Job Rights," (June 1988).

years of college in March 1987, 82 percent were in the labor force. Among women of the same age group with less than four years of high school, 70 percent were in the labor force in March 1987.

7. More women are choosing to be entrepreneurs.
8. About 64.7 percent of all mothers with children under eighteen years of age (33 million women) were in the labor force, and 57 percent of mothers with preschool children (8.9 million women) were labor force participants in March 1987.

One of the major issues for women is that of equal pay for different work of *comparable worth,* that is, equal remuneration for different work of equal value performed by men and women. This concept is presently the subject of much controversy. The EEOC, in its first decision on this subject (Decision No. 85–8, June 17, 1985), decided that the theory of comparable worth is not within the scope of Title VII of the Civil Rights Act of 1964. "We find that sole reliance on a comparison of the intrinsic value of dissimilar jobs—which command different wages in the market place—does not provide a violation of Title VII. . . . We are convinced that Congress never authorized the government to take on wholesale restructuring of wages that were set by non-sex based decisions of employers—by collective bargaining—or by the marketplace." In that case the municipal employer's administrative staff (predominantly female) had claimed that they were being paid less than the employer's maintenance staff (predominantly male) even though the duties performed by the female employees in the administrative staff required equal or more skill, effort, and responsibility than the duties performed by employees in the maintenance classification.

Summary Statement

1. There are various exceptions to the common law employment contract-at-will limiting the employer's right to fire an employee without cause.
2. The federal Equal Employment Opportunity Act (EEOA) specifies what is and what is not an unlawful employment discriminatory practice by an employer on the basis of an individual's race, color, religion, sex, or national origin. There are two steps necessary to determine when there is unlawful discrimination in employment because of an individual's race, color, religion, sex, or national origin under EEOA.
3. The federal Age Discrimination in Employment Act (ADIEA) prohibits arbitrary age discrimination in employment mainly with respect to nonfederal employees between the ages of forty and seventy years, with certain exceptions.
4. The increasing presence of AIDS and HIV in the workplace has created problems for employers regarding how to treat their infected employees as handicapped individuals.
5. The federal Fair Labor Standards Act (FLSA), also known as the Wage-Hour Law, establishes fair standards for the employment of child labor, maximum hours of employment, and minimum wages. Oppressive child labor is prohibited.
6. State workers' compensation statutes changed the common law basis for employer liability for injury to employees arising out of and in the course of employment.
7. The federal Occupational Safety and Health Act (OSHA) provides for promulgation by the Secretary of Labor of specific mandatory occupational safety and health standards for employers in the workplace. Sections 654 (general duty provision) and 660 (29 U.S.C.) are particularly applicable.

8. Irrespective of OSHA's specific standards, an employer has a duty to so maintain the workplace as not to expose employees to a recognized risk of death or serious bodily harm.
9. The broad federal Social Security Act includes in its coverage the following:
   a) Old-Age, Survivors, and Disability Insurance (OASDI): Provision is made for financial assistance to employees on their retirement, benefits to the survivors of employees, and benefits in the event of disability.
   b) Employee Retirement Income Security Act (ERISA): This Act serves to provide needed federal governmental supervision over private pension plans for the benefit of employees.
   c) Hospital insurance (Medicare): a health program providing coverage for eligible persons sixty-five years of age or older, and some under sixty-five who are disabled.
   d) Federal Unemployment Tax Act (FUTA): This Act provides temporary financial assistance to former employees who are eligible, with sufficient credits from former employment, and who are unemployed and are ready, able, and willing to take a suitable full-time job.
10. Widespread employee abuse of drugs and alcohol has triggered a variety of employer tests aimed at detecting their use and relieving their disruptive economic effect in the marketplace.
11. Women's rights, particularly in freedom from unfair discrimination solely on the basis of sex, is now the subject of increasing favorable legislation and judicial decisions, as well as of general business and societal acceptance.

In the following case, the U.S. Supreme Court clearly explained the process by which *illegal* discrimination in violation of the federal Civil Rights Act is determined. Observe carefully the court's approach to the question of illegal discrimination: How the burden of proof of disparate impact is on the employee initially; then the burden of producing evidence of (but not proving) business justification for the disparate impact becomes that of the employer; and finally, the employee's opportunity to show that alternate satisfactory employer practices are available.

WARD'S COVE PACKING COMPANY, INC., et al. v. ANTONIA
109 S.Ct. 2115 (1989).

White, J. for the divided court. Title VII of the Civil Rights Act of 1964 makes it an unfair employment practice for an employer to discriminate against any individual with respect to hiring or the terms and condition of employment because of such individual's race, color, religion, sex, or national origin; or to limit, segregate or classify his employees in ways that would adversely affect any employee because of the employee's race, color, religion, sex, or national origin. . . . [We previously] construed Title VII to proscribe "not only overt discrimination but also *practices that are fair in form but discriminatory in practice.*" Under this basis for liability, which is known as the "*disparate-impact*" theory and which is involved in this case, a facially neutral employment practice may be deemed violative of Title VII without evidence of the employer's subjective intent to discriminate that is required in a "disparate treatment" case. [Emphasis added]

I

The claims before us are disparate-impact claims, involving the employment practices of petitioners, two companies that operate salmon canneries in remote . . . areas of Alaska. The canneries operate only during the salmon runs in the summer months. . . . When salmon runs are about to begin, the workers who will operate the cannery lines arrive, remain as long as there are fish to can, and then depart. . . .

Jobs at the canneries are of two types: "cannery jobs" on the cannery line, which are unskilled positions; and "noncannery jobs," which fall into a variety of classifications. Cannery jobs are filled predominantly by nonwhites, Filipinos and Alaska Natives. . . . Noncannery jobs are filled with predominantly white workers, who are hired during the winter months from the companies' offices in Washington and Oregon. Virtually all of the noncannery jobs pay more than cannery positions. . . .

In 1974, respondents, a class of nonwhite cannery workers who were (or had been) employed at the canneries, brought this Title VII action against petitioners. Respondents alleged that a variety of petitioners' hiring/promotion practices . . . were responsible for the racial stratification of the work force, and had denied them and other nonwhites employment as noncannery workers on the basis of race. . . .

The District Court held . . . for petitioners. On appeal . . . the Ninth Circuit reversed [holding] . . . that respondents had made out a *prima facie case of disparate-impact* in hiring for both skilled and unskilled noncannery positions. . . . [Emphasis added]

Petitioners sought review . . . we granted certiorari. . . .

II

In holding that respondents had made out a prima facie case of disparate impact, the Court of Appeals relied *solely on respondents' statistics* showing a high percentage of nonwhite workers in the cannery jobs and a low percentage of such workers in the noncannery positions. . . . the Court of Appeals' ruling here misapprehends our precedents and the purposes of Title VII, and we therefore reverse.

It is . . . a comparison—between the racial composition of the qualified persons in the labor market and the persons holding at-issue jobs—that generally forms the proper basis for the initial inquiry in a disparate impact case. . . .

It is clear to us that the Court of Appeals' acceptance of the comparison between the racial composition of the cannery work force and that of the noncannery work force, as probative of a prima facie case of disparate impact in the selection of the latter group of workers, was flawed. . . .

The Court of Appeals also erred with respect to the unskilled noncannery positions. *Racial imbalance in one segment of an employer's work force does not, without more, establish a prima facie case of disparate impact with respect to the selection of workers for the employer's other positions.* . . . [Emphasis added]

Consequently, we reverse the Court of Appeals' ruling. . . .

III

. . . [w]e address two other challenges petitioners have made to the decision of the Court of Appeals.

A

First is the question of *causation* in a disparate-impact case. . . . "[t]he plaintiff's burden in establishing a prima facie case goes beyond the need to show that there are statistical disparities in the employer's work force. The plaintiff must begin by identifying the specific employment practice that is challenged. . . ."

Our disparate-impact cases have always focused on the impact of particular hiring practices on employment opportunities for minorities. . . . a Title VII plaintiff does not make out a case of disparate impact simply by showing that . . . there is racial imbalance in the work force. As a general matter, a plaintiff must demonstrate that it is the *application of a specific or particular employment practice* that has created the disparate impact under attack. [Emphasis added]

Consequently, on remand, the courts below are instructed to require, as part of respondents' prima facie case, a demonstration that specific elements of the petitioners' hiring process have a significantly disparate impact on nonwhites.

B

If, on remand, respondents meet the proof burdens outlined above . . . the case will shift to any business justification petitioners offer for the use of these practices. This phase of the disparate-impact case contains two components: first, a consideration of the justifications an employer offers for his use of these practices; and second, the availability of alternate practices to achieve the same business ends, with less racial impact.

(1)

. . .[i]t is generally well-established that at the justification stage of such a disparate impact case, the dispositive issue is whether a challenged practice serves, in a significant way, the legitimate employment goals of the employer. . . . The touchstone of this inquiry is a reasoned review of the employer's justification for his use of the challenged practice. . . .

In this phase, the employer carries the burden of producing evidence of a business justification for his employment practice. The burden of persuasion, however, remains with the disparate-impact plaintiff. To the extent that the Ninth Circuit held otherwise . . . suggesting that the persuasion burden should shift to the petitioners once the respondents established a prima facie case of disparate impact—its decisions were erroneous. . . . "*[T]he ultimate burden of proving that discrimination against a protected group has been caused by a specific employment practice remains with the plaintiff at all times.*" [Emphasis added]

(2)

Finally, if . . . respondents cannot persuade the trier of fact on the question of petitioners' business necessity defense, respondents may still be able to prevail. To do so, respondents will have to persuade the factfinder that "other tests or selection devices, without a similarly undesirable racial effect, would also serve the employer's legitimate [hiring] interests;" by so demonstrating, respondents would prove that "[petitioners were] using [their] tests merely as a 'pretext' for discrimination." . . .

Of course, any alternative practices which respondents offer up in this respect must be equally effective as petitioners' chosen hiring procedures in achieving petitioners' legitimate employment goals. Moreover, "[f]actors such as the cost or other burdens of proposed alternative selection devices are relevant in determining whether they would be equally as effective as the challenged practice in serving the employer's legitimate business goals." . . .

IV

[T]he judgment of the Court of Appeals is reversed and the case is remanded for further proceedings consistent with this opinion. It is so ordered.

Questions and Case Problems

1. Mark Glagola was hired August 10, 1984 as a mechanic for an indefinite term by North Texas Municipal Water District, which did not give any reason when it terminated Glagola's employment approximately one year later. The Water District has a Personnel Policy Manual that provides:

> Probation—All appointments and promotions shall be made to a probationary status for a period of six (6) months. During the probationary period the employee should evaluate the job and the supervisor should evaluate the employee to determine if this is a compatible relationship. At the end of the probation period an employee will be considered to be of permanent status as long as he continues to perform his job in a satisfactory manner.

The second provision, Section 11.A, provides in part:

> Disciplinary action shall include demotion, suspension and dismissal. Any employee is subject to disciplinary action for proper cause. . . .

Glagola was unaware of the contents of the manual while he was employed, and he had no oral or written agreement with the Water District to adopt any manual as part of his employment. Glagola sued the Water District in the U.S. District Court for wrongful discharge. He claimed that he was a tenured employee mechanic with a property interest in his continued employment and that, solely on the basis of the manual, he could be terminated only for cause. Indicate for whom you would render judgment and explain why. [*Glagola v. North Tex. Mun. Water Dist.*, 705 F.Supp. 1220 (E.D. Tex. 1989).]

2. Michael Hauck was hired in Texas as a deckhand for an indefinite term by Sabine Pilot Services, Inc. One of his duties each day was to pump into the water the bilges of the boat on which he worked. He observed a placard posted on the boat that stated it was illegal to pump the bilges into the water. He called the U.S. Coast Guard, which confirmed that pumping bilges into the water was illegal. Hauck refused to pump the bilges into the water because it was illegal to do this, and he was fired for his refusal. Hauck sued his employer for wrongful discharge. The trial court granted the Services' motion for summary judgment. Hauck appealed to the Court of Appeals and the judgment was reversed. The Service then appealed to the Supreme Court of Texas. Indicate for whom you would render judgment and explain why. [*Sabine Pilot Services, Inc. v. Hauck,* 687 S.W.2d 733 (Tex. 1985).]

3. Professor Scott, a black faculty member of the University of Delaware, who does not have a Ph.D. degree, brought a class action against the university, alleging illegal employment discrimination in violation of the federal Civil Rights Act of 1964, resulting in the university's failure to renew his contract. Among the various reasons for his assertion of illegal discrimination was that the university's requirement that an individual have a Ph.D. degree or equivalent to attain an assistant professorship had a disparate (unequal) impact upon blacks in the areas of hiring, contract renewal, promotion, and tenure. There was insufficient evidence to prove any intent by the university to discriminate against blacks by this requirement. He asserted that this requirement is not justified by the legitimate needs of the university. The university emphasized scholarship and the advancement of knowledge and sought people for its faculty who had "the capabilities of making significant contribution to scholarship that would bring recognition to the University." Was the Ph.D. degree or equivalent requirement related to job performance and justified by the legitimate interest of the university? [*Scott v. Univ. of Delaware,* 455 F.Supp. 1102 (D. Del. 1978).]

4. In 1974 Michelle Vinson was hired by Sidney Taylor, vice president and branch manager, for the position of teller-trainee at Meritor Savings Bank, with Taylor as her supervisor. Based on merit alone, she advanced over four years through various positions to assistant branch manager. In September 1978 she notified Taylor that she was taking sick leave for an indefinite period and on November 1 the bank discharged her for excessive use of that leave. During the four years, Vinson claimed that, beginning at the end of her probationary period as a teller-trainee, she was constantly subjected to sexual harassment by Taylor. For fear of losing her job, she agreed to his demands for sexual relations with him. He made repeated demands upon her for sexual favors, usually at the branch, both during and after hours, and during the next several years she had numerous occasions of sexual intercourse with him. He fondled her in front of other employees, followed her into the women's restroom when she went there alone, exposed himself to her, and even forcibly raped her on several occasions. She claimed that Taylor touched and fondled other women bank employees. Vinson did not avail herself of the grievance procedure in the bank whose policy was against discrimination but not against sexual harassment in particular. Under that procedure, Vinson would have had to complain first to her supervisor, who was Taylor. Vinson sued Taylor and the bank in the U.S. District Court for damages for violation of Title VII of the Civil Rights Act of 1964.

The District Court held that if they did have a sexual relationship, it was voluntary and had nothing to do with her continued employment at the bank and therefore Vinson was not the victim of sexual harassment. Also, since the bank was without notice, it could not be held liable for the supervisor's alleged sexual harassment. The U.S. Circuit Court of Appeals reversed and remanded the case to the District Court. The U.S. Supreme Court granted certiorari. Did these circumstances establish a basis for a claim against Taylor and the bank under the Title VII employment discrimination statute? Explain fully the reasons for your answer. [*Meritor Sav. Bank v. Vinson, et al.,* 106 S.Ct. 2399 (1986).]

5. Connie Cunico, a white, non-Hispanic female, was employed as a salaried, probationary social worker for Pueblo School District No. 60 for three years through the 1981–82 school year. Faced with a severe financial exigency during 1981 and 1982, the Colorado State Board of Education cancelled various contracts for teachers and other employees around the state. Cancellations and reassignments were accomplished by seniority. Cunico and five other discharged social workers, of which she was the senior, requested and had a hearing before Mr. Martinez, the hearing officer. A few days later, Mr. Hunter, who is the only black social worker of the six, filed a written complaint of racial discrimination with the board alleging an "obvious pattern of the exclusion of blacks from every administrative level position," and contending that the "District has not worked in 'good faith' toward achieving parity among administrators with regard to black employees and their distribution throughout the School system." This complaint was investigated and no evidence was found of discrimination in the decision to reduce the number of social workers, although it was regrettable that losing Hunter as the only black administrator was a step backward in terms of affirmative action. Martinez reported that he interpreted the policy of the board regarding minority teachers to mean that they should protect with special consideration the only black administrator in the district. By a split vote the board rescinded the cancellation of Hunter's contract. The decision to retain a black administrator was not controlled by any provision in the affirmative action plan. There was no evidence that anything other than the seniority of blacks in the relevant work force was responsible for racial imbalance.

At a later date an Hispanic male social worker whose contract was cancelled was rehired as a social worker, even though he had less seniority than Cunico. The district said that this was done because he could speak Spanish and, therefore, could better communicate with families of Hispanic children. The job description for the social worker position did not include proficiency in Spanish as a job requirement.

Cunico was rehired in 1984, and she now sued Pueblo School District for back pay for the period of her termination. Should she receive back pay? Explain fully your reasons for your decision. [*Cunico v. Pueblo School Dist. No. 60,* 693 F.Supp. 954 (D. Colo. 1988).

6. Cactus Craft of Arizona is a firm that manufactures and distributes novelty and souvenir gift items, including cactus lamps, jewelry, and numerous other items. An employee between the ages of 16 and 18 years of age operated a power tool for drilling part of the time under supervision, which included shaping and forming of pieces of wood so that they could be used for lamps. The secretary of labor issued a regulation prohibiting employment of minors between 16 and 18 years of age in the operation of power-driven wood-working machines, which are defined as "all fixed or portable machines or tools driven by power and used or designed for cutting, shaping, forming (or) surfacing wood." A power tool for drilling is not specifically mentioned in the regulation. The secretary of labor contends that the defendant violated the Fair Labor Standards Act concerning child labor. Was this oppressive child labor under that Act? [*Hodgson v. Cactus Craft of Ariz.*, 481 F.2d 464 (9th Cir. 1973).]

7. Sam Dell's Dodge Corp. is an automobile dealership. Salespersons received a base pay and commissions on sales of cars, trucks, accessories, etc. The company furnished many of the salespersons with demonstrator cars. These cars were used primarily in connection with the salespersons' duties at the company. The cars were parked on the lot during the day. Salespersons used them for demonstration rides for their customers. Occasionally the cars would be lent to other salespersons for the same use. Salespersons were permitted to drive the cars for personal use when not working; however, they were specifically told that the cars were not for their families. For each week that a car was provided to a salesperson, the company deducted money from that salesperson's earnings for insurance. The value of the use of the cars was not included on the salesperson's W-2 tax statements or the company's pay records. The mileage accumulated by the salespersons when driving for personal use apparently was significant when compared with business use. The secretary of labor claims that the company employer violated the minimum wage requirements of the Fair Labor Standards Act. Were the demonstration cars furnished for salespersons' use "wages" under the Act? [*Marshall v. Sam Dell's Dodge Corp.*, F.Supp. 294 (N.D.N.Y. 1978).]

8. Reese was employed by Gas Engineering and Construction Company as a pipeline welder. While working under a large pipe, the scaffolding collapsed and the pipe fell, crushing Reese's left knee. This type of injury is included in the Kansas Workers' Compensation Statute schedule of injuries for which compensation will be paid. As a result of this injury, Reese favored his left leg and now has a sore back strain and pain and shin splints on his right leg. Reese filed a claim under the Kansas Workers' Compensation Statute, and the examiner awarded 50 weeks of temporary total disability and 40 percent permanent partial general disability. The company appealed. Should workers' compensation for general bodily disability be awarded, such disability being a separate and distinct injury resulting from the scheduled injury under the state's workers' compensation Act? [*Reese v. Gas Eng'g and Constr. Co.*, 532 P.2d 1044 (Kan. 1975).]

9. Davis, the decedent, was a new employee working his fourth day with Republic Creosoting Co. He was hired to sort and stack railroad wood ties after completion of the unloading process of getting the ties off the delivery trucks. The unloader (fork lift) operator suggested to Davis that he come to the unloading so that he could help sort the ties after they had been unloaded. Davis had never witnessed the unloading operation before nor had it been described to him. However, the field superintendent, when hiring Davis, told Davis not to get around the trucks and that the unloader did all the unloading. During the entire operation of unloading, all the company's employees, other than the unloader operator, remained a safe distance from the truck, as did Davis on this occasion. The usual unloading process began with the removal of the chains holding the packages of ties onto the truck. The unloader operator then would move the unloader into position so that it supported a package of steel banded ties holding 25 to 45 ties. Only after the unloader was supporting a package did the truckdriver cut the band of the package to be unloaded.

Under no circumstances would the band be cut before the unloader was in position. The unloader then removed the loosened ties from the truck.

On the day of the accident, the chains had been removed from the truck but the unloader had not yet been moved into position. Without being ordered to do so and without informing anyone of what he intended to do, Davis went up to the truck and, while standing on the ground next to the truck, cut the steel band on a package of ties with an axe. As a result, five of the ties fell on Davis, killing him.

The Secretary of Labor claimed that the company had violated the Occupational Safety and Health Act general duty clause by failing to instruct and supervise properly an untrained employee regarding the hazards of unloading railroad ties. The Occupational Safety and Health Review Commission decided that there was no violation. The secretary, Brennan, appealed. Did the company commit such a violation with respect to Davis? [*Brennan v. Occupational Safety and Health Review Commission,* 501 F.2d 1196 (7th Cir. 1974).]

10. In the case of *Wards Cove Packing Company, Inc. et al. v. Antonia, et al.,* excerpted at the beginning of this section, explain fully why the U.S. Supreme Court reversed and held that the Circuit Court of Appeals had erred in:

a) holding that the cannery workers (respondents) made out a prima facie case of disparate impact;

b) its test of causation of disparate impact by the employer's hiring practices on employment of minorities.

PART 3 AGENCY AND EMPLOYMENT

ETHICS AND BUSINESS LAW

Introduction

This end-of-part discussion, like the others in this book, is designed to encourage you to begin forming personal beliefs about what is right or wrong conduct in business. The discussion here builds on the material in the first end-of-part discussion; you may find it helpful to review that.

This material has several goals. The overview section is designed to help you see the range of ethical issues associated with this area of the law. The in-depth discussion is intended to provide you with a background for forming your own beliefs about a single very important ethical issue in business. The problems at the end of this part are designed to build your skill in ethical analysis while exploring further the in-depth issue.

Overview of Ethical Issues in Agency and Employment

► Agency

Agency law raises a variety of ethical issues for persons in business. Many arise from the existence of the *fiduciary relationship*. Because the agent's fiduciary duties are owed to the principal, the principal can reasonably expect that the agent will look out for the principal's best interests. Occasions arise, however, when the agent may be tempted to place his or her best interests above those of the principal. There is no ethical standard, except egoism, which could justify this.

Because the fiduciary duty of loyalty compels the agent to place the interests of the principal above that of the third party, other ethical issues arise. Sometimes, the agent must assess the principal's ethical conduct. For example, if the third party is being legally injured by the principal, what ought the agent to do? One alternative is to withdraw from the agency relationship. Of course, this raises the risk of liability for breach of an agency contract. Which, in your view, is the lesser evil: being a party to an unfair transaction or breaching an agency contract?

When a professional agent such as an attorney is appointed, the agent is legally obligated to perform in accordance with external ethical standards of a profession. These may prevent the agent from withdrawing from the agency relationship. In these situations then, the professions decide what actions are generally ethical rather than leaving it to the individual agent.

Confidential information can create an issue for agents when they are tempted to use the information for their own benefit. While use of such information would probably violate the agent's fiduciary duties, it is often possible to do this without detection.

Employment

The doctrine of respondeat superior makes the employer liable for the physical harm caused by the torts of employees who are acting within the scope of their employment. Is this always an ethical outcome? Suppose the employer is completely faultless? Also, do you think it is ethical for an employee to disclose trade secrets of a former employer to a new employer if this might well result in a promotion for the employee? Can you see how tempted to do this a new employee might be? Can you see that the new employee might be pressured to do this by a new boss?

As you have read in this part, society feels that it is morally unjust to subject workers to discrimination in employment based on an individual's race, color, religion, sex, national origin, and age. One ethically intense issue is affirmative action. In practical effect this legal doctrine sometimes results in preferential treatment to one group, over another, in order to remedy prior discrimination. Employers are experiencing extensive economic loss because of employee use of drugs and alcohol, as well as from employee theft. Explosive ethical issues arise currently concerning employer use of lie, drug, and alcohol detection processes. The employer's need for such information is countered by employee arguments concerning invasion of privacy.

In-Depth Discussion of a Basic Issue: Ethical Treatment of Coworkers

The purpose of this in-depth discussion is to give you an opportunity to begin deciding for yourself what you believe ought to be your style of relating to those with whom you work—superiors, subordinates, and other coworkers.

Notice that agency law, particularly the agent's fiduciary duties described in Chapter 16, creates a legal system that allows one party to wisely trust another in a business transaction. The basis for this trust is the force of law; if parties who are required by law to be trustworthy are not, they can be legally liable. In a sense, agency law describes a distinctive moral style for relating to certain coworkers—a style based on *trust*.

In contrast with agency or fiduciary relationships, most commercial relationships are said to be *at arm's length*. This means that the law assumes that the parties to a transaction will look out for their own self-interests. The law described in Part 2, contract law, describes the way arm's-length relationships work. In general, this body of law does not recognize the importance of trust in anywhere near the same way as agency law. Thus a used-car dealer might sell a five-year-old Volkswagen for 25 percent more than its fair market value, and, as long as there has been no misrepresentation or deception, the courts will enforce the agreement because the parties must look out for their own self-interests.

Perspective

Recall that in the first end-of-part discussion we made a distinction between ethical views that seek a good for *one's self*, such as egoism, and views that seek the good of *others*, such as utilitarianism, Kantian philosophy, and religious ethics. We labeled this attribute "perspective." This idea of perspective also distinguishes arm's-length from fiduciary relations. The fiduciary relationship is, from the agent's perspective, "other" oriented while the arm's-length relationship is basically self-oriented.

► Styles of Ethical Reasoning

Egoistic Egoists might have a preference for the arm's-length way of relating to coworkers because this allows them to exploit others and thereby increase their material or psychological well-being. Of course some sophisticated egoists might modify their appearance and project themselves as other-oriented if that would suit their purpose. For example, a common egoist strategy is to adopt an apparent fiduciary relationship with superiors while openly treating peers and subordinates in an arm's-length fashion.

Utilitarianism This style of reasoning illustrates an important difference between the results of legal analysis and personal ethical analysis. Notice that the law classifies most business relationships as arm's-length. That is, the majority of business relationships are assumed by the law not to be based on trust. Why does the law do this? Probably for utilitarian reasons such as the following.

If persons were legally required to look out for the interests of others in the majority of business transactions, then there would likely be a great deal more litigation over business transactions thereby burdening the courts. Reasoning in a similar way, if persons left it to the legal system to look out for their self-interests, they might become lax, perhaps more vulnerable, and become easy prey for the ruthless in society. For these reasons, the *legal system* can justify encouragement of arm's-length relationships.

But the reasoning that is valid for the legal system may not be valid for an individual embracing utilitarianism. On the individual level, it is likely that the greatest good for the greatest number arises when you treat others in ways more similar to the fiduciary style.

Kantian Philosophy and Religious Ethics These views both stress great respect for individual human dignity. This aspect of both styles of moral reasoning makes it very unlikely that they could justify the extreme version of arm's-length relations. Both would require that we be open and honest, make full disclosure, and respect the informed choices of our coworkers.

► The Law As a Constraint on Relating to Coworkers

As you think about fiduciary and employment relationships, perhaps you can see that while they articulate an other-oriented perspective they also compel, as the other side of the coin, a self-oriented perspective. Thus, in the fiduciary relationship, the agent's way of relating to the third party is definitely not aimed at aiding the third party. In fact, the reverse is closer to the truth. Thus if the agent advances the interests of the third party in ways that are adverse to the interest of the principal, that would be a breach of the agent's fiduciary duty of loyalty. Accordingly, agents and employees may be more constrained in their conduct than those who act independent of these legal relationships. Can you see that being an agent may compel you to treat *third parties* in ways that you may think are unfair?

Solving Ethics Problems

Like the other end-of-part discussions in this book, this one presents problems for you to consider. These problems have three goals. The first is to give you the opportunity to further explore the in-depth issue. The second goal is to give you experience in ethical reasoning about the law and about related management problems. The third goal is to let you see how thinking critically about the law can increase your ability to make ethical decisions. To facilitate this, the problems begin by asking you to analyze the law for its ethical content and then shift to looking at related problems in managerial ethics.

For a discussion of the ethical roles of markets and the law and examples of the four styles of ethical reasoning—egoism, utilitarianism, Kantian philosophy, and religious ethics—read the business ethics material at the end of Part 1.

▶ Problems

1. In Chapter 19 (p. 366), you read the case of *Strother v. Morrison Cafeteria et al.* In case a cashier working in a cafeteria was followed home from work by criminals who intended to steal from her the receipts of the cafeteria. At her home she was assaulted and her purse stolen. She filed for workers' compensation. On appeal the claim was denied after a careful interpretation of the statutory language that defines when an injury *arises* in, and *originates* in, the course of employment. Assume that you owned the cafeteria. Would you feel that your duty to this employee had been extinguished because her legal claim had been denied? Is this a case where legal analysis and ethical analysis reach opposite conclusions? If you viewed your ethical relationship with employees as more fiduciary than arm's-length, what would this imply for your treatment of the cashier?
2. A highly talented subordinate of yours is doing an outstanding job and making you look like an excellent manager, but your boss does not know about this superstar. Suppose your boss indicated that one of your peers—a manager on the same level as you—is leaving and that your boss is looking for a replacement. Would you recommend the superstar for the other management position? Note that if this subordinate leaves your department, its performance will decline. Also note that by elevating the star you will make *your* relative performance look worse. Assume there would be a promotion available to you or one of your peers in the next 18 months and that, if you recommended the star for the immediate promotion, in all likelihood the star would get the next promotion too. Would you recommend the star to your boss? In other words, would you relate to this subordinate as a fiduciary or at arm's-length? What do you think the law requires you to do in this situation? Do you think the legal requirement is one that is likely to be litigated if it is not met?
3. Assume that you have learned that one of your employees has contracted AIDS. There is no risk that anyone else can contract this deadly disease from this person. However, staff morale and customer relations are likely to suffer if you allow this person to continue working for your organization. What ought you to do and why?
4. You are the supervisor of an engineering group for a large aerospace organization. One of your key subordinates, a Ph.D. chemist, approached you with the news that he has a job offer from a competing firm. To help him in making a decision, he is asking you about his future with the company. You ask for time to discuss the matter with your boss. Your boss informs you that the project that the subordinate is working on will be concluded in three months. At that time, all the people on that project, including the subordinate, will be laid off. You know that this subordinate is critical to the successful conclusion of the project. The boss therefore tells you to inform the subordinate that he is highly regarded by the management, but to say nothing to him about the project, its termination, and layoff of persons working on the project. The fact that the subordinate is highly regarded by top management is technically true and, without the information about the project's upcoming termination and consequent personnel layoffs, will lead him to the wrong conclusion about his future with the company. In this circumstance, should you treat the

subordinate as though you were his fiduciary or at arm's length? How does your boss want to treat him? What will you do? Why?

INTERNATIONAL DIMENSIONS

Economic interdependence among the nations of the world has given rise to greater emphasis on the necessity for transnational business with its elements of exporting and importing of goods and technologies. The competing forces of the economies of the United States, Japan, and Western European countries are readily apparent today, especially in the marketplace where the names of products reflect the many different countries involved in their production. Some day you may well become involved in this lucrative and challenging whirlwind of transnational business—as an exporter or the employee of an exporter, or as an importer of foreign goods for sale or for inclusion as parts in American products.

The export of American products requires a business mechanism or procedure for making arrangements for importation into a foreign country. Although an American exporter can deal directly with the foreign importing buyer, many exporters also want some form of representation or contact abroad to coordinate with the foreign buyer. That representative is usually an agent, distributor/independent contractor, and either a subsidiary corporation or branch of the corporate exporter, each with its own employees. This means that contractual relationships must be made between the exporter and one or more of these persons or firms. Of course, American firms are also importers of foreign products as well as being exporters. The American exporter's exposure to the law of contracts, agency, and employment becomes a necessity, and it is partly for this reason that Parts 2 and 3 of this book discuss these subjects.

Anyone who engages in transnational business must consider many things. Among them are the following issues:

1. An orientation into the meaning and legal significance of the legal status of the various kinds of representatives just mentioned;
2. How and when title to a product is to pass from the exporter to the buyer;
3. How and when the purchase price is to be paid, and whether there are any foreign country restrictions on the flow of its currency out of the country;
4. A keen awareness of that part of the foreign country's law relevant to the sales transaction that must be complied with;
5. In the event of irreconcilable disputes between the contracting parties, the method of resolution by arbitration, or by a lawsuit involving questions of what country courts will have jurisdiction over the controversy and which law of what country will be applicable.

These are only a few of the many factors that a potential exporter (or importer) or its employees will have to consider. Part 12 of this book on Business Law in the International Marketplace should provide helpful information and guidance. You should also become aware of the European Communities (E.C.), formerly called the European Economic Community. In 1992 twelve European countries will terminate trade barriers among themselves, an event that will have important implications for Americans doing transnational business with importers and exporters of those countries.

PART 4

PERSONAL PROPERTY AND BAILMENTS

20 PERSONAL PROPERTY

A description of personal property, how it is distinguished from real property, how it is acquired, and the various kinds of ownership of property.

21 BAILMENTS

The meaning of bailment, how the law of bailments applies in business and other transactions, and the rights and duties of the parties to a bailment. Lost, misplaced, and abandoned personal property are also discussed.

22 CARRIERS, DOCUMENTS OF TITLE, AND INNKEEPERS

The use of carriers of goods—particularly the common carrier—their liability, and the documents of title (e.g., bills of lading and warehouse receipts) issued by carriers and warehousemen. Innkeepers (e.g., hotel and motel operators) are also considered.

PREVIEW

Property is something that is the subject of ownership. Personal property consists of movable things and interests in those things, which can be transferred from one person to another in many types of business transactions.

One method of transfer is to deliver only *possession* of the goods, with the goods to be returned to the owner later. This creates a "bailment" of the goods. *Title* to the goods may be transferred in various ways, as by gift or sale.

The goods may be added to, as when a muffler is placed on an automobile; or the goods may produce something, as when an animal produces offspring. This is a form of "accession." The goods may also be permanently affixed to land, in which case they become a part of the realty and are called "fixtures."

Warehousemen and carriers as "bailees" issue paper, called "documents of title," which acknowledge receipt of goods and contain the contract terms. This paper is personal property and capable of transfer by sale, as security, or in other ways. All bailees have duties of care with respect to the bailed goods and have varying levels of liability.

Business ethics as it relates to the text material in these chapters is considered at the end of the part.

CHAPTER 20

PERSONAL PROPERTY

After you have read this chapter, you should be able to:

1. Define real property, personal property, and fixtures.
2. Explain why property distinctions are legally important.
3. List the methods by which property is acquired.
4. Define and distinguish accession and confusion.
5. Define gifts inter vivos and gifts causa mortis.
6. Describe the methods by which gifts are made to minors.
7. List the cases in which a purchaser will acquire good title from a nonowner.
8. List and define the different types of common ownership of property.

BUSINESS DECISIONS and the LAW

Susan, a recent college graduate, made a list of the property she owned: (1) ten shares of corporate stock in Widgets International Corporation; (2) an antique dresser; (3) a valuable bookcase that Susan had attached to the wall in her apartment; and (4) an acre of farmland that Susan used for organic farming. Susan now wonders how this property would be legally classified and whether the classification would affect her rights to use or transfer the property.

If Susan acquires additional property with her husband or with another person, additional questions will be raised. Susan might question the different methods of acquiring property. For example, is it safe to purchase goods from a merchant who might not own them? May Susan transfer property to her sister, who is a minor? What are the tax consequences of making a gift? Susan also might question the form of ownership. What is the nature of joint ownership of property? What are the special joint ownership rules in states such as California? Is joint ownership a good substitute for a will?

Susan's questions are important in our society because the answers will determine whether Susan may keep the property when her ownership is challenged by other individuals or by the government. Property classifications are especially important in determining Susan's right to use the property, to transfer the property to other persons, or to pass the property on to her loved ones when she dies. In this chapter we will discuss what is meant by property, the different kinds of property, the methods of acquiring property, and the various forms of property ownership.

Introduction

Property is difficult to classify because the concept of property has a number of meanings. On a broad philosophical level, property is a concept that is the cornerstone of law, for the law developed to protect property rights. According to the English philosopher Jeremy Bentham, "Property and law are born together, and die together. Before laws were made there was no property; take away laws, and property ceases."

On a more practical level, **property** means a thing or any interest or right in a thing that is capable of being owned. The owner of an interest or right in a thing is entitled to use, enjoy, or dispose of such interest or right, subject only to governmental regulations. The owner has "property."

Property Classifications

property
A thing; also an interest or right in a thing

real property (realty)
Land and immovable things attached to land, along with interests and rights in the land; also a freehold interest in land

personal property (personalty)
A movable thing, along with interests and rights in the thing

chattel
A tangible, movable thing

► Real and Personal Property

Real property is land or an interest or right in land and other immovable things fixed to the land, including structures on the land. Land is a tangible, immovable thing. The owner of the surface of land owns the soil beneath the surface and the air above the surface, subject to reasonable use by aircraft. Susan's acre of land is classified as real property.

Personal property is a movable thing or an interest or right in the thing. It moves with the person, thus becoming "personal" property. Personal property is considered to be tangible if it can be touched. The word **chattel** means tangible personal property. Intangible property is property that cannot be touched. Susan's antique dresser would be considered tangible personal property. Her shares of stock would be intangible personal property because, while the certificate is tangible, the shares are interests in the corporation and cannot be touched. Another illustration of intangible personal property is an account receivable. (Dan owes Charlie $100. Charlie has an account receivable—an intangible claim—against Dan for $100.)

fixture
A chattel that, under real estate law, has become permanently attached to realty and thus ceases to be a chattel and becomes part of the realty; it still can be used as collateral for a **security interest**

security interest
"an interest in personal property or fixtures which secures payment or performance of an obligation" UCC 1–201(37)

► Fixtures

The remaining item on Susan's list, the bookcase, is difficult to classify as real or personal property because it once was movable but now it is immovable, having been attached to the wall. The bookcase is considered to be a **fixture,** which is defined as a chattel which has become attached to real estate in such a way that it is considered to be real property, but is still available for chattel financing.[1]

[1]The fixture still retains sufficient character as a chattel. For example, a bathtub fixed in a house can be used as security for a loan. However, the brick, lumber, tile, and glass in a building are not fixtures; they are a part of the structure.

Three tests are used to decide whether a chattel has become a fixture. *First,* is the chattel annexed to the real estate by nails, screws, glue, or other methods? It is possible that even where the property is not physically annexed, the annexation test will be met because of the weight of the object, as is illustrated by the following nineteenth century case.

FACTS

A statue weighing three to four tons was erected in a courtyard in front of a house. The statue was not fastened to the real estate with clamps, cement, or by any other device. Snedeker bought the owner's personal property; Warring bought the owner's real property. Snedeker sued Warring for the value of the statue contending that it was not a fixture.

DECISION

Judgment for Warring. The statue is a fixture and therefore part of the real estate. A chattel may be annexed to real estate as much by weight as by any other device.

Snedeker v. Warring, 12 N.Y. 170 (1854).

The *second* fixture test is *adaptation*—is the article adapted to, and necessary for, the use of the real estate? A furnace installed in a house is necessary for the use of the house and would meet this test. In some cases, where the article is closely adapted to the use of the real estate, it will be considered a fixture even though there is no physical annexation. Examples include garage door openers and television antenna dials.

The *third* and most important test used by courts is *intention*—do the actions, words, purposes, and relationships of the parties show that they intended to make the property fixtures? In determining intention, the courts are not interested in the hidden or secret intention of the parties, as is illustrated by the following case.

FACTS

Green sold his house to Strain, but after the sale Green removed a chandelier from the dining room. The chandelier had been in Green's family for fifteen years and he had moved it from house to house whenever he moved. Strain sued Green for the chandelier, contending that it was a fixture.

DECISION

Judgment for Strain. The chandelier was a fixture and should not have been moved by Green. Even though Green always intended to take the chandelier with him, the intention was never disclosed. The court will not consider the secret intention of a party.

Strain v. Green, 172 P.2d 216 (Wash. 1946).

Reasons for Property Distinctions

Now that Susan has classified her property, she faces the question of why the classification is important. There are four reasons why property distinctions are legally important.

Transfer During Life If Susan wants to transfer her *real property* and fixtures attached to the real property during her lifetime, she will use a deed. A **deed** is a written document that must be in a form required by law. When Susan transfers her *personal*

deed
A formal document used to transfer title to real estate

FIGURE 20.1 **Bill of Sale**

BILL OF SALE

I, John H. Doe, in consideration of the sum of $5000 paid by Tom J. Smith, the receipt whereof is hereby acknowledged, do grant and convey to Tom J. Smith, his executors, administrators or assigns, my Eversharp Riding Lawn Mower, serial #1007, to have and to hold forever.

In witness whereof, I have set my hand and seal this 12th day of April, 1990.

WITNESSES:

____________________ ____________________
John H. Doe

____

State of ______________] ss
County of ______________]

John H. Doe, being duly sworn, deposes and says that he is the vendor named in the within Bill of Sale, that he has knowledge of the facts, and that the consideration of said instrument was actual and adequate, and that the same was given in good faith for the purpose therein set forth, and not for the purpose of security, or for defrauding creditors of the vendor or subsequent purchasers.

____

Subscribed and sworn to before me this 12th day of
April 1990.
Notary Public, County of ______________
State of ______________
My commission expires ______________ 19__

property, however, it is unlikely that she will use a document to transfer title; although in cases involving a substantial transfer of personal property, a document called a **bill of sale** is often used. A bill of sale is somewhat similar in form to a deed. (See Figure 20.1.)

bill of sale
A formal document used to transfer title to personal property

Transfer at Death The distinction between real and personal property is important in determining the transfer of property at death. Susan might have a **will,** a document that governs the transfer of her property at her death. Unlike a deed, a will has no legal significance until a person's death and can be revoked at any time before death. If Susan has a will, it probably includes separate provisions covering transfer of her real property and her personal property.

will
A formal document that governs the transfer of property at death

If Susan dies without a will, she is said to have died **intestate.** In such cases, state law determines the disposal of her property, and the law usually distinguishes between real and personal property. For example, if Susan died leaving a husband and one child, state law might provide that the husband will inherit one-third of Susan's real property and one-half of her personal property while the child will inherit two-thirds of the real property and one-half of the personal property. However, the law varies from state to state.

intestate
(noun) A person who dies without a will

Source of the Law The source of the law will vary, depending on whether property is classified as real or personal. For instance, when personal property is sold, the sale is governed by the provisions of the Uniform Commercial Code, a statute that has been enacted in all states except Louisiana, where parts of it have been enacted. The law relating to the sale of real property, on the other hand, will usually be found in case decisions or in statutes other than the Uniform Commercial Code.

Taxation The taxation of property varies, depending on whether the property is real or personal. Real property is normally taxed by a local governmental body, such as a city or township. Personal property is often not subject to taxation, or is taxed locally or by the state at a different rate than real property.

Methods of Acquiring Ownership

A number of methods may be used to acquire personal property. For example, an artist may acquire personal property by creating it—through painting or sculpture. A creditor may acquire personal property by obtaining a court judgment against a debtor. A person may acquire personal property by finding it, as discussed in the following chapter. And the state may acquire personal property through **escheat,** whereby property passes to the state when a person dies leaving no one to inherit the property. Four methods of acquisition, however, have special legal significance: accession, confusion, gifts, purchase.

escheat
The transfer of property to the state when a person dies without heirs

► Accession

Susan has decided to replace the shelving in her antique dresser. She takes the dresser to a furniture repair shop, where the new shelving is built into the dresser. This is an example of **accession**—the increase in property by what it produces or by the addition of other property to it. Examples are adding a muffler to an automobile or a mare producing a foal. Here, the shelving as property is added to other property in the form of the dresser. In such cases, Susan, as owner of the dresser, becomes owner of the shelving as well.

accession
The increase in property by what it produces or by the addition of other property to it

The situation becomes more complicated when the new shelving is installed by an innocent third party to whom the shopowner has wrongfully sold Susan's dresser or by a thief who steals the dresser from Susan. If the shelving cannot be removed without damaging the dresser, the general rule is that Susan may recover from the thief either the dresser or damages based on the value of the dresser as repaired. The result would be the same if Susan sued the innocent third party, with two major qualifications. First, Susan would not be allowed to recover the dresser if the innocent purchaser substantially altered the dresser to such an extent that it is in reality a different and more valuable dresser than the one which Susan originally owned. Second, in a suit for damages against the innocent purchaser, value would be based upon the value of the dresser when Susan owned it rather than its value with the new shelves.

Whether or not property has become an accession is an important issue when the property is used by creditors as collateral for a loan (see Chapter 50). This issue is illustrated by the following case.

FACTS

A debtor's telephone equipment was used as collateral for a loan from a creditor. Another creditor, the Internal Revenue Service (IRS), had a claim on the debtor's car. The debtor installed a mobile phone in the car. Which creditor has first rights to the phone?

DECISION

The creditor who used the debtor's telephone equipment as collateral wins. Mobile phones are not accessions because they are easy to install and remove from cars without damaging the car or the phone. The IRS loses because the phone is not an accession to the car which it claimed.

Bucci v. Internal Revenue Serv., 653 F.Supp. 479 (D.R.I. 1987).

► Confusion

confusion

The mixing of chattels of like kind of different persons so that the chattels of one person cannot be distinguished from the chattels of the other persons

Confusion occurs when chattels of different persons are mixed so that the chattels of one person cannot be distinguished from the chattels of the other persons. Confusion of personal property generally is not complicated in legal terms. For instance, assume that Susan grows wheat on her real estate and stores her wheat at a local grain elevator, where it is mixed with the wheat of the elevator operator. If the wheat is of the same quality, it can easily be divided when Susan decides to sell her share of the wheat.

The problem becomes more complex, however, when Susan's high-grade, expensive wheat is mixed with the owner's low-grade, cheap wheat. If Susan consented to the mixture of the two grades of wheat, she would have no cause to complain and would be entitled to remove only her proportionate share of the mixture. However, if the owner of the elevator intentionally mixed Susan's high-grade wheat with his low-grade wheat without Susan's knowledge and it is impossible to divide, Susan might be entitled to all the wheat.

The question of whether or not confusion has occurred can be vital in determining a creditor's rights, as illustrated by the following case.

FACTS

A farmer gave a bank an interest in part of his corn as collateral for a loan. The farmer allegedly mixed the corn with other corn and delivered it to a grain elevator for sale. After the mixture was sold, the bank sued the grain elevator for conversion—the wrongful exercise of dominion over another person's property. The grain elevator asserted that it was liable only for the percentage of corn that represented collateral for the bank's loan. Is the elevator operator correct?

DECISION

Yes. If confusion has occurred, the grain elevator must pay only a portion of the sale proceeds to the bank. If on the other hand there had been no confusion, all of the corn sold would be subject to the bank's interest, and all of the sale proceeds would go to the bank.

Dakota Bank and Trust Co. of Fargo v. Brakke, 404 N.W.2d 438 (N.D. 1987).

► Gifts

gift

A voluntary transfer of personal or real property by someone who is not to receive anything in return

donor

The person who makes a gift

donee

The recipient of a gift

Gift Inter Vivos While a gift may be made of personal or real property, here we are concerned with only personal property, particularly chattels. Accordingly, a **gift** is a voluntary transfer of a chattel by a **donor** who is not to receive anything in exchange from the **donee,** the person receiving the chattel. As discussed below under Estate

Planning, a gift after the death of a person is accomplished by the use of a will. A gift during life—an **inter vivos** gift—is somewhat more complicated than after-death gifts because two requirements must be met: (1) the donor must have intended to make a gift, and (2) there must be delivery of the chattel to the donee.

inter vivos
Among living persons

The *intent* requirement means that the donee needs to prove more than mere possession of the chattel to prove a gift. In many cases, the intent of the donor is clearly spelled out in a letter or other writing. In other cases, courts will infer intent to make a gift because of factors such as the relationship between the parties and the size of the gift.

The *delivery* requirement is met when the donor transfers the chattel to the donee in such a manner that the donor relinquishes all right to and control over the chattel. Delivery may be actual, as when the donor delivers a new automobile to the donee, or symbolic, as when the donor delivers the keys to the car to the donee instead of delivering the car itself. Additionally, the delivery may be made to a third party who is to hold the property for the donee, or to a person already in possession of the chattel who is to keep it as a gift.

Acceptance by the donee is frequently mentioned as an additional requirement for a valid inter vivos gift. However, this requirement is rarely important to the outcome of a case because courts presume that acceptance is present when the gift benefits the donee.

The requirements of donor intent, delivery, and donee's acceptance for a valid gift to occur are illustrated by the following case:

FACTS

Alfred opened a joint savings account in his name and in the name of a friend, Mary. He later delivered the account passbook to Mary. After Alfred's death, his executor claimed that Alfred had not made a gift because, when he opened the account, he signed Mary's name on the signature card. Mary claimed that a gift had been made to her.

DECISION

Judgment for Mary. This was a valid gift. Alfred clearly intended to make a gift when he opened the account, even though he signed Mary's name. Delivery occurred when Alfred delivered the passbook to Mary, and the acceptance requirement was met when Mary received the passbook, although acceptance is also presumed.

In re Estate of Sipe, 422 A.2d 826 (Pa. 1980).

Gift Causa Mortis Gift cases are not difficult to resolve when the required intent and delivery exist and when the donor makes an *unconditional* gift to the donee. The cases are more difficult when the donor places a condition on the gift, such as, "This stereo is yours if I do not return from my trip to Boulder." In this case there is not a valid gift because it is not a present gift but, instead, an attempted future gift. This is true even if the condition is met.

The major exception to the conditional gift rule is the case where a donor facing imminent death from a present illness or impending peril makes a conditional gift to a donee that is to be *effective immediately.* The donor may revoke the conditional gift anytime before the donor's death from that illness or peril, and revocation occurs automatically if either the donor recovers or the donee predeceases the donor. However, the gift is valid if not revoked. This is a **gift causa mortis.**

gift causa mortis
A conditional, revocable gift by someone facing imminent death from a present illness or impending peril

Gift to a Minor Susan wants to make a gift of $100 to her sister Sally, aged ten, but feels that Sally is too young to manage the property. How should Susan make the gift? Each state has adopted either the Uniform Gifts to Minors Act or the Uniform Transfers to Minors Act. These laws allow Susan to open a bank account under her own name "as custodian for Sally." Any money deposited in the account represents a completed gift to Sally, who is given control of the account when she reaches the age of eighteen, twenty-one or twenty-five (depending on state law).

Gift Tax The federal government imposes a gift tax on a donor and an estate tax on an estate at death. At one time it was advantageous for a person to give away property before death because the gift tax was three-fourths of the estate tax. However, the Tax Reform Act of 1976, which became effective on January 1, 1977, created a unified tax schedule for gift and estate taxes. Even after the tax reform, gifts are popular because no tax is levied for gifts that do not exceed $10,000 per year for each donee. Thus by combining their gift tax exclusions, a husband and wife could jointly give a child $20,000 per year tax free.

Purchase

The last method of acquiring property is by purchase. The sale and purchase of *goods* under the Uniform Commercial Code is the subject of Part 5, Sales. The most troublesome area in the purchase and sale of chattels in general is the case where a nonowner sells the chattel.

Assume, for example, that a thief, Clyde, steals Susan's bookcase and sells it to an innocent third party, Rudolph. If Susan sues Rudolph to recover the dresser, the difficult question the law faces is deciding which innocent party, Susan or Rudolph, must suffer the loss. The cases generally fall into one of the following four categories.

Void Title If the person selling property had *void title,* which is no title at all, the purchaser acquires no title. Thus, in our example, Susan would win the case because the thief, Clyde, having no title of his own, had no title to transfer to Rudolph.

Voidable Title In many cases a person will acquire title to goods that may be avoided by the seller. For instance, if Susan were a minor and sold the bookcase to Clyde, Clyde would have *voidable title.* Susan could avoid her contract with Clyde any time before reaching the age of majority. In such cases, however, Rudolph would win if sued by Susan because, under Section 2–403(1) of the Uniform Commercial Code, a person with a voidable title to goods, such as Clyde, has the power to transfer a good title to a good faith purchaser who pays value.

Entrustment Whenever an owner entrusts goods to a merchant who deals in similar goods, the merchant has the power to sell the goods to a "buyer in the ordinary course of business." If Susan delivered a valuable antique necklace to a dealer in jewelry for repairs, and the jeweler sold the necklace to Rudolph, Rudolph would be the owner of the necklace. Susan's only recourse would be to sue the jeweler either for **damages** for breach of the bailment contract, or for the tort of **conversion** for the value of the necklace.

damages
The money judicially awarded to an injured party for another's wrongful conduct

conversion
The tort of intentional interference with another's right to possession, control, and dominion of a chattel

Estoppel If the owner of goods indicates to a third party that someone else owns the goods, and the third party, in reliance on the statement, buys the goods from the nonowner, the third party may keep the goods under the principle of law called **estoppel.** This principle prevents a person from denying what he or she had represented (held out) previously to another person if, meanwhile, the other person had changed his or her position materially in reasonable reliance on the representation.

estoppel
A principle of law stating that when one person "holds out" (represents) a material fact to another person, who changes his or her position materially to his or her prejudice in reasonable reliance on the holding out, the first person is "estopped" (prohibited) to deny what he or she asserted previously

In the following case the court held that allowing a nonowner to act as if he or she were the owner is a holding out resulting in an estoppel.

FACTS

Harry Winston, Inc., a diamond merchant, owned a diamond ring. Winston delivered the ring to Brand who, with the knowledge and approval of Winston, offered the ring for sale. Brand, acting as the owner, sold the ring to Zendman for $12,500; but, before paying Winston, Brand declared bankruptcy. Zendman now sues Winston to determine ownership of the ring.

DECISION

Judgment for Zendman. Winston is estopped from asserting ownership. Winston allowed the nonowner, Brand, to act as if he were the owner of the ring, and Zendman relied on the apparent ownership of Brand.

Zendman v. Harry Winston, Inc., 111 N.E.2d 871 (N.Y. 1953).

(Note that this case occurred before enactment of the Uniform Commercial Code.)

Forms of Ownership

Ralph and Betty are engaged to be married. Before the marriage they decide to purchase personal property (a car) and real property (a summer cottage on a lake). If either Ralph or Betty purchases the property as individuals, the form of ownership would not be complicated in legal terms because the title would be in the name of only one of the two. However, whenever two or more persons join together to purchase property, they must decide whether to purchase the property as joint tenants, tenants by entirety (or the entireties), or tenants in common. Each of these methods will result in different legal consequences.

► Joint Tenancy

Ownership in **joint tenancy** is ownership of property by more than one person with the right of survivorship. When one person dies, the other surviving person or persons automatically becomes the sole owner or owners because this is what the parties intended in using joint tenancy. If Ralph and Betty purchased the car and cottage as *joint tenants,* on Betty's death the property would be owned by Ralph alone without the necessity of probate (proof of a will) court proceedings, which are usually necessary when a person dies.

joint tenancy
A form of ownership of property by more than one person with the right of survivorship

Four requirements must be met if there is to be a joint tenancy between two or more persons such as Ralph and Betty. (1) Ralph and Betty must acquire their interests at the *same time;* (2) they must acquire their interests in the *same conveyance*—that is, their title must be the same; (3) they must have an *equal interest* in the property; and (4) they must have the right to *equal possession* of the property.

If any one of these requirements is missing, most courts will decide that there is a "tenancy in common" (discussed later) rather than a joint tenancy. For example, if Ralph owned the cottage and deeded it "to Ralph and Betty as joint tenants" a joint tenancy would not be created because Ralph originally acquired his interest at an earlier time and in an earlier conveyance than Betty. In order to create a joint tenancy, Ralph would have to deed the cottage to a third party, usually Ralph's attorney, who would then deed the cottage to Ralph and Betty. In recent years, however, many states have decided that this procedure should not be required and, therefore, as an exception to the first requirement, allow a direct conveyance to Ralph and Betty.

Severance A joint tenancy will be *severed,* that is, the interest of the parties will be separated, whenever one of the four requirements is destroyed. A joint tenancy interest, however, cannot be severed or transferred by a will. There are four common methods of severance: conveyance, divorce or dissolution of marriage, partition, and murder.

Conveyance A conveyance by one of the joint tenants will sever the joint tenancy. For instance, if Ralph and Betty own the cottage as joint tenants and Betty sells her interest to Steve, Ralph and Steve would own the property as tenants in common, not as joint tenants. The same result is reached in cases of involuntary conveyance where a sheriff sells Betty's interest in order to pay her creditors. If *three* persons—Alice, Bill, and Carl—own as joint tenants and Carl sells his interest to Dick, the relationship between Alice and Bill is still a joint tenancy but, with respect to Dick, they are tenants in common.

Divorce or Dissolution of Marriage If Ralph and Betty own property as joint tenants as a married couple, severance occurs when they are divorced. In some states, however, the divorce judgment must specifically order severance; and, if the property is not specifically mentioned in the divorce judgment, the joint tenancy continues after the divorce.

partition
A division of property between joint owners

Partition A **partition** takes place when Ralph and Betty divide their property either voluntarily or by court order. If a court handles the partition, a physical division of the property is preferred. It is not possible, however, to physically divide a cottage or a car, and in such cases a court will order that the property be sold and the proceeds divided between Ralph and Betty.

Murder Assume that Ralph murders Betty while they hold property as joint tenants. Should Ralph be allowed to take the property as the survivor? This has been a difficult question for the courts, and three different approaches have developed. The first approach is to decide that Ralph receives the property as survivor despite the murder. The second approach would be that the property passes to Betty's estate, with Ralph receiving nothing. The third approach would be to give Ralph half the property and Betty's estate the other half.

► Tenancy by Entirety

A **tenancy by entirety** (or by the entireties) is identical to a joint tenancy with the following three qualifications.

tenancy by entirety
A form of co-ownership between husband and wife with the right of survivorship

Husband and Wife A tenancy by entirety can be created only between a husband and wife, and the couple must have been husband and wife at the time the property was acquired, as the following case illustrates.

FACTS

Al married Sally. Later, before divorcing Sally, he married Helen. With Helen he purchased real estate as "tenants by the entireties." Al then divorced Sally and remarried Helen. Do Al and Helen own the real estate as tenants by the entireties?

DECISION

They do not own the real estate as tenants by the entireties because they were not legally married at the time they acquired the property. The court in this case held that they held the property as joint tenants rather than as tenants by the entireties.

Lopez v. Lopez, 243 A.2d 588 (Md. 1968).

Severance A joint tenancy can be severed when *one* of the owners sells his or her interest. However, a tenancy by entirety can be terminated only when *both* husband and wife agree to the sale. We might assume that Ralph and Betty, now married, purchase a house as tenants by entirety. After the purchase, Ralph leaves Betty and moves to a different state. A few years later, Ralph's creditors contact Betty and tell her that if she does not pay Ralph's debts they will ask the sheriff to sell the house and use the proceeds to pay the debts. The creditors will not be allowed to force a sale of the house for the reason that the debts were Ralph's alone, and one party's interest in a tenancy by entirety cannot be conveyed.

Control The husband and the wife have equal right to control and possess the property held as tenants by entirety.

▶ Tenancy in Common

A **tenancy in common** is distinguished from the joint tenancy and tenancy by entirety by the fact that in a tenancy in common, when one person dies, the decedent's interest passes to the decedent's estate rather than to the surviving tenant. A tenant in common is free to convey his or her interest or seek a partition by agreement or by court proceedings.

tenancy in common
A form of ownership of property by more than one person without survivorship

▶ Community Property

If Ralph and Betty settle in one of nine states, much of their property would be considered **community property.** These states are Arizona, California, Idaho, Louisiana, New Mexico, Nevada, Texas, Washington, and Wisconsin.

community property
A form of ownership by husband and wife of property acquired by their efforts during their marriage

Although community property laws often vary from state to state, the law generally provides that all property acquired through the efforts of the husband and wife during their marriage is considered to be community property. All other property—property acquired before marriage, by gift, or by inheritance during marriage—is the separate property of the husband or wife.

As a general rule, the husband and wife have equal control of community property, and both husband and wife must sign the deed when community real property is sold. When one spouse dies, the decedent's one-half interest will pass according to the terms of the will or, if there is no will, according to state law. The surviving spouse retains a one-half interest in the property.

► Joint Ownership and Estate Planning

trust

A legal device whereby legal title to property is held by one person (a trustee) for the benefit of a beneficiary

beneficiary

A person who is to receive a benefit

probate court

A court that has jurisdiction over the estate of a deceased person

executor (executrix)

A court-appointed man (woman) designated in a decedent's will as the decedent's personal representative

guardian

A person legally entrusted with the custody and/or the property of another

A person establishes an *estate plan* in order to arrange for the orderly transfer of property to loved ones after death. Most estate plans include the use of a will and a trust. The **trust** involves the transfer of property before or after death to a *trustee,* often a bank, which will hold and invest the property for the trust **beneficiaries.**

In recent years it has become popular to avoid the use of a will and trust by placing property in joint tenancy or tenancy by entirety. The reasons for not using a will is that wills must be "probated"—that is, proven to be legally valid in a **probate court**—and probate court proceedings often are time-consuming and expensive. If property is held jointly, the survivor automatically becomes the sole owner without the approval of probate court.

While joint ownership is a useful estate planning device, it should not be used exclusively, but, instead, should be used along with a will and a trust. For example, Ralph and Betty have two young children and own assets worth $100,000, all of which are held in joint ownership. When Ralph dies, Betty automatically becomes the sole owner of the property without probate court proceedings. However, what will happen if Ralph and Betty die together in an automobile accident? Who would receive their property? Who would be named guardian for their children? Do they want their children to receive all of the property when they become adults, which in most states would be at the age of eighteen? Who will manage the property until the children are to receive it? In order to resolve these questions, Ralph and Betty should execute wills which name an **executor** who will manage the property and which name a **guardian** for the children. Additionally, if they do not want the children to receive the property at age eighteen, they should enter into a trust agreement with a bank or a friend and provide in the agreement that the property is to pass to the children at a specified age.

The need for a will and a trust becomes more important later in life after Ralph and Betty have accumulated substantial assets. By setting up the trust in the proper manner, thousands of dollars in estate taxes will be saved at their deaths.

Summary Statement

1. The distinctions of real property, personal property, and fixtures are important in matters such as transfer of property and taxation.
2. Accession involves the addition of property; confusion involves the mixing of chattels of different owners.
3. Gifts may be made during life if there is intention and delivery. A conditional gift, such as a gift causa mortis, may be made during life.
4. In making a gift to a minor, the donor must meet the requirements of either the Uniform Gifts to Minors Act or the Uniform Transfers to Minors Act.
5. A good faith purchaser for value will acquire good title from a nonowner if the nonowner (1) has voidable title; (2) is a merchant dealer of goods to whom similar goods have been entrusted; or (3) has been held out as the owner by the real owner under the principle of estoppel.
6. When property is acquired by more than one person, it may be held in (1) tenancy in common, (2) joint tenancy, or (3) tenancy by entirety.
7. Community property represents another form of ownership of property in certain states.

The following well-known case illustrates the difficult decision courts face when one joint tenant murders another.

BRADLEY v. FOX
129 N.E.2d 699 (Ill. 1955)

Lawrence Fox murdered his wife, Matilda, with whom he owned property in joint tenancy. After the murder, in a case brought by the administrator of Matilda's estate (Rolland Bradley), a question arose concerning ownership of the property.

Davis, J. In this category of cases the courts have differed as to whether the murderer should be allowed his survivorship rights. Those courts which hold that he is entitled to the entire property as surviving joint tenant predicate their conclusion on the legal fiction incident to the concept of joint tenancy, whereby each tenant is deemed to hold the entire estate from the time of the original investiture, and reason that the murderer acquired no additional interest by virtue of the felonious destruction of his joint tenant, of which he can be deprived.... Other courts, however, concerned with the equitable principles prohibiting a person from profiting from his own wrong, and with the realities of the situation, have abandoned the Common Law fictions, and have either divested the killer of the entire estate ... or have deprived him of half the property ... or have imposed a constructive trust on the entire estate held by the murderer for the benefit of the heirs of the victim ... or a constructive trust modified by a life interest in half the property.

In joint tenancy the contract that the survivors will take the whole necessarily presupposes that the death of either will be in the natural course of events and that it will not be generated by either tenant murdering the other. One of the implied conditions of the contract is that neither party will acquire the interest of the other by murder. It is fundamental that four coexisting unities are necessary and requisite to the creation and continuance of a joint tenancy; namely, unity of interest, unity of title, unity of time, and unity of possession. Any act of a joint tenant which destroys any of these unities operates as a severance of the joint tenancy and extinguishes the right of survivorship.... It is our opinion, therefore, that it would be unconscionable for defendant Fox, as murderer of his joint tenant, and for defendant Downey, as transferee [of the property from Fox] with full knowledge of how Fox acquired the sole legal title to the property and of the fact that the conveyance was in fraud of creditors' claims, to retain and enjoy the beneficial interest in the property. It is our conclusion that Fox, by his felonious act, destroyed all rights of survivorship and lawfully retained only the title to his undivided one-half interest in the property in dispute as a tenant in common with the heir-at-law of Matilda Fox, deceased.

Questions and Case Problems

1. The Premonstratensian Fathers purchased a supermarket and leased it back to the prior owners. The building contained five coolers, valued at over $23,000. The cooler walls constituted the walls of other rooms, and the coolers were attached to a hardwood floor that was attached to concrete. When the coolers were destroyed by fire, the insurance company refused to pay on the grounds that they were not fixtures and therefore were not covered by fire insurance on the building. Is the company correct? [*Premonstratensian Fathers v. Badger Mut. Ins. Co.,* 175 N.W.2d 237 (Wis. 1970).]
2. Emma decided to assign certain property rights to her children. Her attorney prepared an assignment and his secretary took it to Emma's house. After the secretary read the assignment, Emma signed it and gave it to the secretary with the intent that it be delivered to her children. Three days later, Emma changed her mind

and asked the attorney to return the assignment. Did Emma make a valid gift? [*In the matter of the Estate of Saathoff,* 295 N.W.2d 290 (Neb. 1980).]

3. Sligo Furnace Co. owned timberland. Hobart-Lee Tie Co. trespassed on the land, cut down timber, and used it to make railroad ties. Sligo sues Hobart-Lee to recover the value of the ties, claiming that, under the law of accession, a willful trespasser is liable for the value of the timber as improved. Decision? [*Sligo Furnace Co. v. Hobart-Lee Tie Co.,* 134 S.W. 585 (Mo. 1911).]
4. A mother, using her own money, purchased securities in her name and the name of her daughter as joint tenants with the right of survivorship. The mother retained possession of the certificates. A dispute arose regarding dividends, and the mother brought suit against the daughter claiming that the daughter had no interest in the securities. Decision? [*Kinney v. Ewing,* 492 P.2d 636 (N.M. 1972).]
5. Closter lived in the same rooming house with his friend Schutz. Closter owned a note for a debt owed him by a third party. One day Closter went to his room, indorsed the note to Schutz, placed the note on a table and shot himself. Schutz entered the room and took the note while Closter was unconscious but before death. Did Closter make a valid gift to Schutz? [*Liebe v. Battman,* 54 P. 179 (Or. 1898).]
6. Montgomery, a career soldier, had a savings account in a bank. Before going to Germany, he delivered the savings account passbook to his first cousin, Mrs. Stone, and stated: "If I happen to crap out, it is all yours." Montgomery died in Germany. Does Mrs. Stone own the savings account? [*Guest v. Stone,* 56 S.E.2d 247 (Ga. 1949).]
7. Moseley purchased a car from a used car dealer and installed a sun visor, gasoline tank, and seat cover. The car had been stolen from Grunwell and the thief had installed a new engine. Grunwell's insurance company now sues to recover the car from Moseley. Decision? [*Farm Bureau Mut. Auto. Ins. Co. v. Moseley,* 90 A.2d 485 (Del. 1952).]
8. Charles and Julia lived together but were not married. They purchased a house as tenants by the entireties. After Julia's death, her sisters claimed that the tenancy by the entireties was not valid. Were they correct? [*Thurmond v. McGrath,* 344 N.Y.S.2d 917 (N.Y. 1972).]
9. A husband and wife lived in a community property state. Husband owned two restaurants as separate property. Through the husband's efforts during the marriage, the restaurants were income-producing. Is this income community property? [*Steward v. Torrey,* 95 P.2d 990 (Ariz. 1939).]
10. In *Bradley v. Fox,* excerpted at the beginning of this section, the court held that it would be unconscionable for Fox to profit from his criminal conduct by taking, as a joint tenant, property by surviving his victim. How does this decision evidence the complementary nature of the various areas of the law and a limit to the concept of property?

CHAPTER

21

BAILMENTS

After you have read this chapter, you should be able to:

1. List at least five situations where bailment law personally affects you.
2. Define a bailment.
3. Discuss some of the applications of bailment principles.
4. Describe the duties of a bailee in the three types of bailment.
5. Decide whether a bailee may disclaim liability.
6. Determine who bears expenses that arise when the bailee uses goods.
7. Describe the rights of a person who finds lost or mislaid goods.

BUSINESS DECISIONS and the LAW

Harry recently purchased a new suit that he planned to wear while interviewing with companies visiting campus. A week before his first interview he delivered the suit to Quick'n Clean Dry Cleaners to have the suit dry-cleaned. Quick'n Clean gave Harry a receipt for the suit and told him the suit would be ready within one week. The morning of his first job interview Harry went to Quick'n Clean, presented his receipt, but was told by the owner: "I'm sorry, I can't seem to find your suit." When Harry demanded that the owner pay for the suit, he refused, claiming that he and his employees were always careful with customers' property and that the loss could not have been their fault.

Harry at first might think that his dispute would be classified as a contract or tort problem. However, because of historical reasons and because in many bailments the elements of a contract such as mutual assent or consideration are not present, the principles of contract law do not govern this situation. For example, one person may hold goods as a favor to the owner. And tort law, while relevant to the solution, does not control because the cleaners may have a greater duty of care than would normally be the case and, additionally, the law might impose a stronger burden of proof on the cleaners. As a result this case falls within the law of bailments, which is concerned with the transfer of *possession* of *goods*, the goods to be returned on the accomplishment of a particular purpose.

Introduction

The law of bailments is obviously important to individuals such as Harry. In one day Harry may park his car in a parking lot, deposit his books in a locker at the entrance to a bookstore, hang his coat in a restaurant cloakroom, lend his stereo to a friend for a party, and ask another friend to watch his belongings in the library while he takes a study break. In each situation it is possible that Harry has created a bailment.

Bailment law is also of extreme importance to persons in business, especially when, unaware of potential liability, they fail to purchase adequate insurance to cover losses. For instance, a person who owns a hotel should be aware of the consequences when his employees park guests' cars in the hotel lot, hang guests' coats in the cloakroom of the hotel restaurant, and store guests' valuables in the hotel safe.

Bailment Defined

bailment
A delivery of goods by a bailor to a bailee which are to be returned to the bailor or as the bailor directs, in accordance with the bailment agreement

bailor
The person who bails goods

bailee
The person to whom goods are bailed

lease
Of goods, a form of contract giving the lessee the exclusive right to use or possess the goods of the lessor for a stated period

sale
The transfer of title from seller to purchaser for a price

A **bailment** may be defined generally as the delivery of goods (or chattels) by one person, the **bailor,** to another person, the **bailee,** for a particular purpose, with the understanding that at a future time the goods are to be redelivered to the bailor or delivered to a third person as directed by the bailor in accordance with the bailment agreement. For example, a seller (bailor) delivers goods to a railroad (bailee) for delivery to a buyer. Another example is the commercial bailment (for hire)—e.g., the rental of office furniture, equipment, or machines, which are to be returned at the end of the rental period.

The word bailment is derived from the French word *bailler* meaning "to deliver." The key to the creation of any bailment is *delivery* of goods and their *return*. The courts interpret delivery as a combination of a voluntary transfer of physical possession coupled with the bailee's intention to control the property. This combination will be further explored in the applications that follow.

Using the general definition of a bailment, two related transactions may be distinguished: a **lease** of space and a sale. When a person leases a locker or a parking space and deposits goods in the locker or parks a car in the space, a bailment is not created because the goods have not been delivered to the lessor. Instead, the owner of the goods has retained possession and control of the goods. However, a lease of goods creates a bailment.

A **sale** is distinguished from a bailment in that the purchaser acquires title to the goods and is under no duty to return the goods, although it is possible that the purchaser will deliver other goods to the seller as payment. For example, if Nick leases his farm and the cows on his farm to Alexandra for one year, and if the lease provides that Alexandra is to return cows of equal quality at the end of the year, there has been a sale of the cows to Alexandra. As a result, she is free to dispose of the cows as she pleases, and her creditors may force a sale of the cows to satisfy her debts.

Applications

To illustrate the application of bailment principles, we will examine three situations where bailment law has been especially troublesome to courts.

► The Cloakroom

A common bailment issue arises when a person hangs his or her coat in a cloakroom in a theater, restaurant, or store. To illustrate the application of bailment law to such a setting, we might assume that three students—Tom, Dick, and Harry—visit a clothing store to shop for sweaters. Tom takes off his coat, lays it across a clothes rack, and begins to try on sweaters. A clerk helps Dick remove his coat and lays it next to Tom's coat. Harry leaves his coat on a hook in a changing room before trying on the sweaters. A thief steals all three coats, and the question arises whether the store is liable for the coats as a bailee.

In all three cases the coats were left on the store's property, and consequently the store potentially had the power to physically control the coats. But was the other requirement met? Did the store show an intention to control the coats? Most courts would agree that there was no intention to control Tom's coat. There is no proof that the store even knew that Tom had laid down his coat. A clerk physically removed Dick's coat, however, and this act implies an intention to control. Thus the store would be a bailee of Dick's coat but not of Tom's coat.

Harry's coat presents the greatest legal difficulty. On the one hand, it is generally held that a store does not become a bailee merely because there are hooks on the wall for customers' garments, for the reason that the store offers this as a service to the public and makes no attempt to supervise the clothing. On the other hand, a bailment would exist if a coat is checked with a person in a restaurant cloakroom, or if the coat is left in a private room or office, as is illustrated in the following case concerning a clothes closet in a doctor's office used for patients' clothing.

FACTS

A woman visited her psychiatrist wearing a fur coat worth $1,725. Upon entering the office, she deposited her coat in a clothes closet in the reception room. After her consultation with the psychiatrist she discovered that her coat was missing, and she sued the psychiatrist, claiming that he was liable as a bailee. Is the psychiatrist a bailee?

DECISION

The psychiatrist is a bailee. By maintaining the closet, the psychiatrist was impliedly inviting his patients to leave their coats there under his control. He also should know that patients normally must remove their coats before their consultation.

Laval v. Leopold, 47 Misc. 2d 624 (N.Y. 1965).

► The Parking Lot

Let us assume that upon leaving the store without their coats Tom, Dick, and Harry proceeded to their respective cars. Tom had parked his car in an unfenced, unguarded lot. He had paid the attendant upon entering the lot, kept the keys to the car, and was free to pick up his car and to leave at any time. Dick had parked his car in a lot where an attendant had taken the key to his car, had parked it for him, and had retained the key. Harry parked his car in the type of lot commonly found at airports. He entered the lot by removing a ticket from a machine and, in order to leave the lot, he must produce the ticket and pay an attendant. Upon arriving at the three lots from the store, Tom, Dick, and Harry discover that thieves have stolen their cars and, once more, they question whether a bailment has been created.

In Tom's case, clearly a bailment has not resulted, because Tom has retained control of the car. Dick clearly has created a bailment because, in delivering the key to the attendant, he also delivered physical possession, and the attendant, by taking the key, showed the required intent to control the car. In other words, in many cases the key to determining whether a bailment exists is the possession of the key!

Harry's case is more difficult. In cases involving airport lots, most courts hold that a bailment relationship is not created because the parking lot owner does not control vehicles parked in the lot. The following case is illustrative.

FACTS

At the parking lot at O'Hare Airport in Chicago motorists enter through automatic gates and receive a ticket that notes the time and date of arrival. They then park their own cars and retain the keys. When they are ready to leave, they pick up their own cars and, at an exit, give the ticket to an attendant who collects the parking charges. An automobile was stolen from the lot, and the parking lot company was sued as a bailee. Is the parking lot company a bailee?

DECISION

The parking lot company is not a bailee. The company never accepted control of the vehicle. Motorists retained actual control by locking their cars and taking the keys.

Wall v. Airport Parking Co. of Chicago, 244 N.E.2d 190 (Ill. 1969).

closed container rule
A bailee is not responsible for the contents of a closed container unless the bailee knows or should know the contents

If we assume that Dick can recover the value of his car because of the bailment relationship, can he also recover the value of a CB radio that he had installed in the car and the value of a tennis racket that was in the trunk of the car? Under the **closed container rule**, the bailment of the automobile includes only those items of which the parking lot attendant has actual notice or which the parking lot attendant should have known were in the car. Thus if Dick did not give the attendant actual notice that the CB and the racket were in the car, the bailment would cover only the CB, because the attendant should have seen the CB when he parked the car. The bailment would not include items in the "closed container," the trunk, such as the tennis racket, but would include the spare tire, the jack, and other ordinary accessories, because people generally are aware of their presence in a car truck.

▶ The Safe Deposit Box

Joan has rented a safe deposit box at a local bank. In order to gain access to the box, Joan must sign a signature card and produce a key to the box. A bank employee will then produce a second key and proceed to the vault with Joan to open the box. After entering the vault, the safe deposit box can be opened only by using both keys. One day Joan discovered that some valuable coins had been removed from the box. Is the bank liable as a bailee?

The bank, of course, will argue that, if there is a bailment relationship, it is the bailee only of the box itself and not of the contents because of the "closed container" rule. Courts have generally decided, however, that the bank is also bailee of the contents of the box because banks should know that customers use the boxes to store valuable possessions. In many states court decisions have been overturned by statutes that provide that the rental of the box is a lease of the box but not a bailment of its contents, and which allow a bank to limit its liability to a certain amount.

Rights and Duties

▶ Bailee's Duty to Return Identical Property to Bailor

fungible goods
Every unit of goods is the equivalent of any other like unit, either actually or by contract

At the conclusion of the bailment, the bailee must return the identical property to the bailor, or to a third person, as directed by the bailor or as previously agreed. If there is no duty to return identical property, the transaction is a sale rather than a bailment. A major exception to this rule exists when the goods are **fungible,** that is, goods that are the equivalent of other goods. For instance, Farmer Brown and Farmer Green might each store 10,000 bushels of wheat in a local grain elevator. Since the wheat will be mixed together, it will be impossible for the elevator operator, the bailee, to return the identical wheat to each farmer. However, because of the commercial importance of such transactions, coupled with the intentions of the parties, a bailment has been created; and, while the wheat is in the elevator, both farmers are considered to be bailor tenants in common and the elevator operator becomes the bailee. If the elevator operator becomes insolvent, the farmers are entitled to the return of their wheat unless the court concludes that the transaction is a sale by the farmer to the elevator operator.

In a recent highly publicized case,[1] the U.S. District Court, on appeal from the U.S. Bankruptcy Court, held that, while the defendant farmer depositor of grain in the bankrupt debtors' grain elevators is the owner of his stored grain and the relationship between these parties is that of bailor/bailee, nevertheless the farmer depositor was a "tenant in common with other [grain] depositors and legally bound by the [Bankruptcy] Code to leave his claimed portion in possession of the [bankruptcy] trustee until some proper method of disbursement and apportionment could be effected." The District Court also held that the Bankruptcy Court was without authority to cite the defendant grain depositor for civil contempt for removing from the trustee's possession 31,000 bushels of grain deposited in the debtors' grain elevators even though removal was made in disobedience of an order of the Court of Appeals giving the trustee jurisdiction over the grain, because the power of civil contempt vested in the bankruptcy judge under the 1978 Bankruptcy Act was unconstitutional.

► Bailee's Duty to Return to Bailor

In most cases the bailee must return the goods to the bailor, even if the bailor is not the owner. However, in the following two situations the bailee is excused from this duty.

First, the bailee might be under a court order to deliver the goods to a legal officer who has a **writ of execution** that authorizes the officer to take possession of and sell the goods to satisfy a judgment. Although the bailee must deliver the goods to the officer, the bailee should make every effort to contact the bailor so that the bailor may take appropriate action to recover the goods.

writ of execution
A court order authorizing a sheriff or other proper legal officer to seize tangible property to satisfy a court judgment

Second, a situation might arise where the bailor is not the owner of the goods or, at least, the bailor's rights to possession are subordinate (inferior) to those of a third person. If the real owner or the person with a superior right to possession appears and claims the goods, the bailee must deliver the goods to that person. However, any action by the bailee is risky. For example, assume that Tinkers, the bailor, delivers her car to a repair shop run by Evers, the bailee. A few days later Chance contacts Evers and states that he, not Tinkers, owns the car and demands that Evers return it to Chance. *If Chance is telling the truth,* then Evers must deliver the car to him; if, instead, Evers returns it to the bailor, Evers must pay damages to Chance. *If Chance is not telling the truth,* or if he does not have the right to possession, having previously loaned the car to Tinkers, then Evers must return the car to Tinkers or pay damages to her for not doing so. In such cases the safe approach would be for Evers to commence a court action against both Tinkers and Chance so that the court could determine to whom the car belongs. This remedy is called **interpleader.**

interpleader
An equitable remedy of a person who has some thing but does not claim any interest in it, requesting the court to decide who, as between two or more claimants, is entitled to the thing

[1] *In re Cox Cotton Co.,* 24 Bankr. 930 (D.C. 1982)

► Bailee's Duty of Care

A bailee is not liable as an insurer of the goods. That is, a bailee is not liable in all cases when goods within the bailee's control are damaged or destroyed. Instead, the bailee is responsible only when he or she is *negligent* by failing to exercise the proper degree of care, which will vary depending on the facts of each case. However, in all cases the burden of proving that the requisite degree of care was met is on the bailee since, because of his or her possession and control of the goods, the bailee is in the best position to explain why the goods were damaged or destroyed.[2]

To illustrate the different degrees of care required of a bailee, we might assume that Jimmy owns a pair of tennis shoes, a tennis racket, and a can of tennis balls. In preparation for a trip, Jimmy asks his good friend Able to do him a favor and keep his tennis shoes for him, which Jimmy then delivers to Able. Jimmy then delivers his tennis racket to Susan who is to restring the racket for $10. And Chance borrows Jimmy's tennis balls for use in a local tournament. Three different types of bailment have been created. The bailment of the tennis shoes is a bailment for the sole benefit of the bailor, Jimmy, and the bailee owes only a duty of minimal care in looking after the shoes. The bailment of the tennis racket is a bailment for mutual benefit in that Jimmy benefits by having his racket restrung and Susan benefits by being paid. In such cases the bailee owes a duty of ordinary care. The bailment of the tennis balls is for the sole benefit of the bailee, Chance, who must exercise extraordinary care in looking after them. (See Figure 21.1.)

A bailee who uses the goods for his own purposes without the permission of the bailor is liable for any loss. For example, if Susan, after stringing Jimmy's racket, had used it in a tournament and, during the tournament, an armed robber stole the racket, Susan would be liable for the loss even though she exercised reasonable care under the circumstances.

► Contractual Modification of the Duty

The bailor and the bailee may decide to modify the legal duty of care of the bailee when they negotiate the bailment contract. In some cases the bailee will assume a greater duty. For example, the contract might provide that the bailee is an insurer of the goods, or that

FIGURE 21.1 **Types of Ordinary (Private) Bailments and Bailee's Duty of Care**

Type of Ordinary Bailments	Bailee's Degree of Care
Sole benefit of bailor	Minimal
Mutual benefit	Reasonable, ordinary
Sole benefit of bailee	Extraordinary

[2]There is an additional reason for the element of the bailee's negligence in bailments. A bailee has the duty to return the goods in proper condition to the bailor. The bailee's failure to do this subjects him or her to liability for breach of their agreement, usually a contract, unless the bailee can prove that such failure was not due to his or her negligence. If the bailee is not negligent, then the failure is excused. If the bailee is negligent, the failure is not excused.

the bailee has a duty either to return or to pay for the goods. This agreement is legally valid.

A more common type of contractual modification is a **disclaimer** of liability by the bailee. For example, when you deliver a car to a garage for repairs, a sign on the wall might provide: "The garage is not responsible for loss or damage to cars"; or when you deliver your coat to a restaurant cloakroom attendant, there might be a provision on the back of the claim check: "The restaurant is not responsible for any loss or damage to articles."

disclaimer
Denial of an obligation or a claim

A bailee using these disclaimers faces two major legal problems. First, since the disclaimer involves a contractual agreement, the bailee must prove that the bailor agreed to the terms of the contract. A bailor who was unaware of the sign or the language on the back of the claim check will not be bound by the disclaimer. Furthermore, courts generally do not favor disclaimers and will not uphold them unless the language is clear. In the following case the disclaimer did not specifically cover negligence.

FACTS

A corporation, which was engaged in commercial photography, purchased several rolls of Kodak film that it used to shoot movies in Alaska. After the movies were taken, the film was sent to Eastman Kodak Company for processing. However, as a result of Kodak's negligence, a substantial portion of the film was damaged. The corporation sued Kodak for over $1,500, representing expenses incurred in refilming. Kodak's defense was that the box containing the film noted that, except for replacement of film, the sale "is without warranty or other liability of any kind."

DECISION

Kodak is liable. Judgment for the corporation. The law disfavors disclaimers of liability especially when, as in this case, the disclaimer does not specifically cover negligence.

Willard Van Dyke Productions v. Eastman Kodak Co., 189 N.E.2d 693 (N.Y. 1963).

The second problem is that many courts have decided that, on the grounds of public policy, a bailee may not disclaim liability for his or her own negligence. The public policy reasons are especially strong when the person receiving the goods is in the bailment business and when the bailor has little bargaining power. For instance, Waldo wanted to park his car in a major city, and all of the parking lots had signs disclaiming liability for damage to cars. (See Figure 21.2.) When Waldo tried to negotiate with the lots by offering to pay more if they would remove the disclaimer, they all refused and, in effect, told him, "Take it or leave it." Many courts would hold that Waldo would not be bound by the disclaimer because it was forced on him by the party offering an essential service. However, the result would be different when the bailor is a large corporation with strong bargaining power of its own or when Waldo is negotiating with a friend who wants to rent his stereo. In such cases the disclaimer will probably be upheld because the bargaining power is equal.

► Compensation and Expenses

In most cases involving a bailment for mutual benefit, one of the parties must compensate the other, and the amount of the compensation will normally be decided in advance. For example, if Clyde, the bailee, rents a moving van from Do-It-Yourself Van Company, the contract will provide the compensation due the company. If the compensation is not agreed upon in advance, then reasonable compensation must be paid. Thus if Susan takes her car to a garage for a new transmission, she must pay reasonable compensation if the cost of the service is not determined in advance. If the goods are

FIGURE 21.2 **Parking Ticket with Disclaimer**

FAIL-SAFE PARKING LOT
TICKET #10567
Company is not responsible for any loss or damage to the automobile or its contents.

destroyed through no fault of the bailee after the service has been performed, the bailee is still entitled to compensation. That is, if the transmission were installed and the car destroyed by lightning before Susan could pick it up, she would still have to pay for the transmission.

In addition to compensation, one of the parties to a bailment contract will be liable for expenses that arise in using the goods. If Clarence rents a car for two weeks from We-Try-Harder Rentals, and during the two weeks the car needs a quart of oil and a new transmission, who is liable for these expenses? The general rule is that the bailee is responsible for ordinary maintenance, in this case for the oil, while the bailor must pay for extraordinary expenses—e.g., the transmission work.

► Bailor's Liability

In the most common bailment situation, the *bailment for mutual benefit,* the bailor traditionally was required to exercise reasonable care in checking the goods for defects and in warning the bailee of potential damages. However, this traditional rule has changed in recent years, and now a bailor will be liable even when he or she exercises the greatest degree of care in attempting to protect the bailee. The bailor's liability is based upon two theories. First, under the UCC, bailors give the same express warranties that are included in a sales contract. Second, courts have applied the tort theory of strict liability to bailors,[3] as illustrated by the following case involving a defective ladder.

FACTS

An airline company leased from Shell Oil Company a gasoline tank with a movable ladder mounted on the tank for use in refueling airplanes. An aircraft mechanic employed by the airline company was seriously injured while climbing the ladder when both of the ladder's legs split. He sued Shell for damages.

DECISION

Judgment for the mechanic. Shell is liable on the theory of strict liability. The purpose of strict liability is to require manufacturers who put products on the market to bear the cost of injuries caused by the products rather than place this burden on innocent consumers. The purpose applies equally to bailors who put goods on the market by means of a lease.

Price v. Shell Oil Co. 466 P.2d 722 (Cal. 1970).

[3]For a discussion of both warranties and strict liability, see Chapters 27 and 28.

Lost, Mislaid, and Abandoned Personal Property

► Finder's Rights

In leaving class one day Ray discovered someone's business law book. Ray is legally considered a *finder,* and his rights depend upon the legal status of the book.

The book might be considered **abandoned property,** discarded goods in which the owner has voluntarily relinquished all interest. If the book was found in a wastebasket, it is likely that the book would be considered *abandoned,* and Ray, the finder, would now own the book.

abandoned property
Discarded goods in which the owner has voluntarily relinquished all interest

But the book might also be classified as **lost property,** goods in a place where they were not intentionally put by the owner, who does not know where they are. If the book were accidentally dropped in the hall by the owner, it would be considered *lost* property. The book might also be considered **mislaid property,** goods that the owner has voluntarily laid down and forgotten where they were laid. If the owner laid the book on a windowsill and then forgot where it was laid, it would be considered *mislaid* property. With both lost and mislaid property, the owner retains the right to the goods.

lost property
Goods in a place where they were not put by the owner, who does not know where they are

mislaid property
Goods that the owner has voluntarily laid down and forgotten where they were laid

However, the finder, as an *involuntary* bailee,[4] has a right to the goods that is superior to everyone in the world except that of the owner. If the owner never reclaims the goods, the finder may keep them. In other words, the rule is "finders keepers," although the losers are not weepers if the losers reclaim the goods! In the following classic case from the eighteenth century, the finder of jewelry prevailed over a person to whom the finder bailed the goods and who refused to return the goods to the finder.

FACTS

A chimney sweep found a piece of jewelry. He delivered it to a jeweler to have it appraised. The jeweler's apprentice removed the jewels and refused to return them to the chimney sweep. The chimney sweep sued the jeweler for the value of the jewels.

DECISION

Judgment for the chimney sweep. A finder has superior rights of ownership against everyone but the real owner.

Armory v. Delamire, 1 Strange 505, 93 Eng. Rep. 664 (1722).

► Owner of the Locus in Quo

Although as a general rule the finder's rights to the goods are superior to all but the owner, the rule often has no effect when the goods are discovered on *private* property. The owner of the private property is called the owner of the **locus in quo,** which means the "place in which" the goods are found. If the owner of the *locus* can prove any one of the following five tests, he or she will be considered the *involuntary* bailee and, if the owner never appears, will keep the goods.

locus in quo
The place in which

1. The owner of the *locus* will prevail if the goods are found in a private area on the property. The reason for this rule is that the owner of the *locus* is considered to have taken constructive possession of the goods in the private area. For example, if goods are found in a bank in a private room used to open safe deposit boxes, the bank has the better right to possession of the goods. But if the goods are found in an area

[4]Although a finder is not a bailee because the goods have not been delivered to the finder and there is no understanding with the owner, the law, nevertheless, imposes a duty upon the finder involuntarily to exercise the care of a bailee.

open to the public, such as the bank lobby, the finder has the better right to possession.

2. If the finder is an employee with a duty to turn goods over to the employer, the employer will have the superior right to possession, as is illustrated by the following case.

FACTS

A chambermaid in a hotel discovered eight \$100 bills hidden beneath the paper lining of a dresser drawer. She turned the bills over to the owner of the hotel. When the owner of the money could not be located, the chambermaid asked the hotel owner to return the bills to her and, when he refused, she sued him.

DECISION

Judgment for the hotel owner. The chambermaid, as an employee of the owner of the *locus,* was simply performing her duties in turning the money over to her employer. She had been expressly instructed to take such property to the desk clerk.

Jackson v. Steinberg, 200 P.2d 376 (Or. 1948).

3. Courts generally hold for the owner of the *locus* if the goods are mislaid. The reason for this rule is that the owner of the goods is likely to remember where the mislaid property was left and to return to that spot. If the true owner does, the owner of the locus would be holding it for the true owner. This principle could have been used to decide the *Jackson* case above.

4. Courts will hold for the owner of the *locus* if the property has been buried in the ground. In some states, however, if the property is **treasure trove,** the finder will have the superior right to possession. Treasure trove is defined as found buried treasure such as gold, silver, or money. The following case involving buried property was decided in favor of the owner of the *locus.*

treasure trove
Found buried treasure

FACTS

Allred, while swimming in the Chariton River, discovered a twenty-seven-foot prehistoric Indian canoe, one-third of which was embedded in the soil. He sued the owner of the *locus in quo* to recover possession of the canoe.

DECISION

Judgment for the owner of the *locus in quo.* The canoe is considered to be property embedded in the soil. In such cases the finder has no rights in the property; it belongs to the owner of the *locus in quo.*

Allred v. Biegel, 219 S.W.2d 665 (Mo. 1949).

5. Courts will hold for the owner of the *locus* if the finders are trespassers. This rule is discussed in the *Bishop v. Ellsworth* case excerpted below.

Summary Statement

1. Bailment law is important both to business and the consumer. Bailment questions often arise when you park a car in a parking lot, leave goods in a safe deposit box, or hang your coat in a store or restaurant.
2. A bailment is a delivery of goods by a bailor to a bailee, with the understanding that the bailee is to return the goods to the bailor or deliver them to a third person, as directed by the bailor or as previously agreed.
3. If a bailment is for the sole benefit of the bailor, the bailee owes a duty of minimal care of the goods. A bailee in a bailment for mutual benefit owes a duty of ordinary care. In a bailment for the sole benefit of the bailee, the bailee must exercise extraordinary care.
4. A bailee may disclaim liability only if the bailor agreed to the disclaimer, the language of the disclaimer is clear, and the disclaimer does not violate public policy.
5. A bailee must bear the cost of ordinary expenses while the bailor must pay for extraordinary expenses, unless the contract provides otherwise.
6. The finder of lost or mislaid goods has superior right to the goods against everyone but the true owner. However, if the goods are found on someone else's property, the owner of the property will usually have rights superior to the finder.

In the following well-reasoned case, the court discussed several of the issues noted in the text regarding the right to lost property. The court also summarized a typical state statute that can often be used by a finder to obtain rights superior to those of the person who lost the property.

BISHOP v. ELLSWORTH
234 N.E.2d 49 (Ill. 1968)

The plaintiff, Bishop, owned a salvage yard. He claimed that the defendants, three small boys, entered the salvage yard without his permission and found a bottle that was partially embedded in loose soil. In the bottle was $12,590, which the boys delivered to the local police chief, who deposited it in the Canton State Bank (another defendant).

Stouder, J. It is defendants' contention that the provisions of Ill. Rev. Stat., Chap. 50, Subsections 27 and 28 govern this case. The relevant portions of this statute are as follows:

> 27. Lost goods. . . . If any person or persons find any lost goods, money, bank notes, or other choses in action, of any description whatever, such person or persons shall inform the owner thereof, if known, and shall make restitution of the same, without any compensation whatever, except the same shall be voluntarily given on the part of the owner. If the owner be unknown, and if such property found is of the value of $15 or upwards, the finder . . . shall, within five days after such finding . . . appear before some judge or magistrate . . . and make affidavit of the description thereof, the time and place when and where the same was found, that no alteration has been made in the appearance thereof since the finding of the same, that the owner thereof is unknown to him and that he has not secreted, withheld or disposed of any part thereof. The judge or magistrate shall enter the value of the property found as near as he can ascertain in his estray book together with the affidavit of the finder, and shall also, within ten days after the proceedings have been entered on his estray book, transmit to the county clerk a certified copy thereof, to be by him recorded in his estray book

and to file the same in his office. . . .
28. Advertisement. . . . If the value thereof exceeds the sum of $15, the county clerk, within twenty days after receiving the certified copy of the judge or magistrate's estray record shall cause an advertisement to be set up on the court house door, and in three other of the most public places in the county, and also a notice thereof to be published for three weeks successively in some public newspaper printed in this state and if the owner of such goods, money, bank notes, or other choses in action does not appear and claim the same and pay the finder's charges and expenses within one year after the advertisement thereof as aforesaid, the ownership of such property shall vest in the finder.

Defendants assert that their initiation of proceedings in accord with the foregoing statute, which is admitted in the complaint, establishes the superiority of their claim, as a matter of law. Defendants also argue that the common law and majority of jurisdictions adhere to the rule which favors the finder of personal property against all others but the real owner.

We think it apparent that the statute to which defendants make reference provides a means of vesting title to lost property in the finder where the prescribed search for the owner proves fruitless. This statute does not purport to provide for the disposition of property deemed mislaid or abandoned nor does it purport to describe or determine the right to possession against any party other than the true owner. . . .

There is a presumption that the owner or occupant of land or premises has custody of property found on it or actually embedded in the land. . . . The ownership or possession of the locus in quo is related to the right to possession of property discovered thereon or embedded therein in two respects. First, if the premises on which the property is discovered are private, it is deemed that the property discovered thereon is and always has been in the constructive possession of the owner of said premises, and in a legal sense the property can be neither mislaid nor lost. . . . Second, the question of whether the property is mislaid or lost in a legal sense depends upon the intent of the true owner. The ownership or possession of the premises is an important factor in determining such intent. If the property be determined to be mislaid, the owner of the premises is entitled to the possession thereof against the discoverer. It would also appear that if the discoverer is a trespasser, such trespasser can have no claim to possession of such property even if it might otherwise be considered lost. . . .

. . . The facts as alleged in substance are that the plaintiff was the owner and in possession of real estate, that the money was discovered in a private area of said premises in a bottle partially embedded in the soil, and that such property was removed from the premises by the finders without any right or authority and in effect as trespassers. We believe the averment of facts in the complaint substantially informs the defendants of the nature of and basis for the claim and is sufficient to state a cause of action.

The judgment of the Circuit Court of Fulton County is reversed and the cause is remanded with directions to proceed in accordance with this opinion.

Judgment reversed and remanded with directions.

Questions and Case Problems

1. The plaintiff left his car with the defendant parking lot, a bailee. The plaintiff's golf clubs were in the trunk of the car but plaintiff did not tell defendant of their presence. The car was stolen and later recovered but the golf clubs were missing. Is the defendant bailee liable for the clubs? [*Allen v. Houserman,* 250 A.2d 389 (Del. 1969).]
2. Baer shipped merchandise to Slater, a salesperson, who was to sell the merchandise. Baer later directed Slater to return the merchandise to Baer. Slater delivered the merchandise to a person dressed in an American Railway Express uniform who gave

Slater a receipt and who was to deliver the goods to Baer. The person was an imposter who left with the goods and has not been seen again. Is Slater liable to Baer for the goods? [*Baer v. Slater,* 158 N.E. 328 (Mass. 1927).]

3. The Freeds delivered their household furniture to Barrett for storage at 618 I Street, Washington, D.C. Barrett later moved the goods to another address, where they were destroyed by fire. Barrett was in no way negligent. The warehouse receipt that Barrett gave the Freeds stated that he would not be liable for loss by fire. Is he liable for the loss? [*Barrett v. Freed,* 35 A.2d 180 (D.C. 1943).]

4. The plaintiff delivered his registered Tennessee Walking mare, a show horse, to the defendant's stables for breeding. The defendant was warned that the mare was skittish and would kick. The defendant placed the mare in a stall next to a stall that held defendant's stallion. After she was left unattended for 18 minutes, the mare was found with a broken leg and had to be destroyed. No one knew how the injury occurred. If we assume that the defendant exercised minimal care but failed to exercise ordinary care, would he be liable? [*David v. Lose,* 218 N.E.2d 442 (Ohio 1966).]

5. Healy checked his handbag in the parcel room of a railroad company. He was given a receipt that stated that the company would not be liable for any loss or damage in excess of $10. The wording on the receipt was not pointed out to Healy, and he put the receipt in his pocket without reading it. The clerk later mistakenly gave Healy's handbag, which was worth $70, to another person and it was not recovered. Is the railroad liable for $70? [*Healy v. New York Cent. & H.R.R.,* 138 N.Y.S. 287 (1912), aff'd 105 N.E. 1086 (1914).]

6. A motorist parked her car in a parking lot and was instructed by an attendant to leave her keys in the car so that it could be moved. The motorist was given a ticket that stated that the parking lot company would not be liable for any loss, regardless of the cause. The motorist was not warned of the printed condition on the parking ticket. The car was stolen and was later recovered in a damaged condition. Is the parking lot company liable for the damages? [*Agricultural Ins. Co. v. Constantine,* 58 N.E.2d 658 (Ohio 1944).]

7. A student enrolled in a flight school. While on a practice flight at 900 feet, the student discovered that a rudder was stuck and that he could not straighten the plane. The plane struck the ground at a 45-degree angle and the student was seriously injured. It was later discovered that a screwdriver had been left in the plane below the floorboard and had caused the rudder to stick. Is the flight school liable? [*Aircraft Sales & Serv., Inc. v. Gantt,* 52 So.2d 388 (Ala. 1951).]

8. Mr. and Mrs. Smiley delivered household goods to a bailee. Later, when they became involved in divorce proceedings, Mrs. Smiley notified the bailee that the goods were not to be delivered to either her or her husband until further instructions were given. Despite the notice, the bailee delivered the goods to Mr. Smiley. Is the bailee liable? [*Bishop v. Allied Van Lines, Inc.,* 399 N.E.2d 698 (Ill. 1980).]

9. Singer stored air conditioning units in Stoda warehouses. A fire in one of the warehouses totally destroyed Singer's units. Singer sued Stoda for damages and at trial showed that the sprinkler system in the warehouse did not operate (which Stoda knew), the fire alarm would not automatically activate, and no watchmen were present. Should Stoda be held liable? [*Singer Co. v. Stoda Corp.,* 436 N.Y.S.2d 508 (N.Y. 1981).]

10. In *Bishop v. Ellsworth,* excerpted at the beginning of this section, the court refused to give ownership of found property to trespassers. How does this result illustrate the complementary nature of substantive areas of law?

C H A P T E R

22

CARRIERS, DOCUMENTS OF TITLE, AND INNKEEPERS

After you have read this chapter, you should be able to:

1. Distinguish a common carrier from a private carrier, and discuss the liability of each.
2. List five exceptions to the general rule governing liability of the common carrier.
3. Determine when the exceptional liability of the common carrier begins.
4. Define the term "document of title."
5. Discuss the rights of a purchaser of a document of title after due negotiation.
6. Summarize the liability of a common carrier to passengers.
7. Compare the liability of a common carrier to that of an innkeeper.

BUSINESS DECISIONS and the LAW

Rachel recently graduated from a large state university and accepted a position with a major manufacturing firm in Chicago. On her first day on the job, Rachel's supervisor asked her to make arrangements to ship a large quantity of the firm's products to Atlanta. The supervisor also asked Rachel to handle negotiation of the bill of lading provided by the carrier. Finally, the supervisor wanted Rachel to travel to Atlanta to deliver in person several valuable designs used in specially manufacturing the products to meet the buyer's specifications.

In handling this transaction, Rachel will be involved with several special bailment situations. First, in shipping the goods, she will contract with a common carrier who faces a unique type of bailment liability if the company's products are lost or damaged. Second, in handling the bill of lading, she will be dealing with a document of title that represents far more than the common carrier's receipt for the goods. Documents of title are of special legal importance because they represent the contract between the bailor and bailee, and often the purchaser of the document obtains greater rights than the seller. Finally, bailment questions will arise if the designs are stolen from Rachel's hotel room in Atlanta before she has a chance to deliver them to the buyer.

Introduction

In this chapter we will examine the special bailment situations illustrated by Rachel's transaction. These situations, which involve common carriers of goods, documents of title, and innkeepers, are especially important to the person in business.

Common Carrier of Goods

Defined

Rollo decided to move to a different town and began to make arrangements for moving his personal belongings. Eventually Rollo discovered that he had two options for moving his goods: (1) He could hire a professional moving company, or (2) his friend Sam could move the goods in his pickup truck for free.

common carrier
A carrier that offers its services to the general public for a fee

private carrier
A carrier that does not offer its services to the general public

In legal terms, Rollo must choose between a **common carrier** and a **private carrier,** and his choice will become important if the goods are lost or destroyed en route. A common carrier is a carrier that offers its services to the public and charges a fee; if either of those two elements is missing, the carrier is considered to be a private carrier. Thus Rollo's friend would be classified as a private carrier, while the moving company would be considered a common carrier.

Liability

There are two reasons why the distinction between common and private carriers is important. First, a common carrier must accept and deliver goods of the type it normally ships from any member of the public, while a private carrier is free to pick and choose its customers. Second, and more important, a private carrier is liable only for loss caused by its negligence, as an ordinary bailee. The common carrier, however, is said to be absolutely liable as an insurer of the goods and will be held liable for any loss unless it can prove one of the five exceptions to liability, as the following case illustrates.

FACTS

Frosty Land Foods delivered beef in good condition to Refrigerated Transport, a common carrier, in Alabama for shipment to California. The meat was delivered six days later in damaged condition and as a result Frosty incurred a loss of $13,529. Frosty sued the carrier for the loss.

DECISIONS

Judgment for the shipper, Frosty. Once a shipper has shown delivery of goods to a carrier in good condition and delivery by the carrier to the consignee in bad condition, it is presumed that the carrier is liable. The carrier must then show that damages resulted solely from one of five traditional causes, which were not present in this case.

Frosty Land Foods Int'l v. Refrigerated Transp. Co., Inc., 613 F.2d 1344 (5th Cir. 1980).

There are five exceptions to the absolute liability of a common carrier: act of God, act of public enemy, act of the shipper, inherent nature of the goods, and act of public authorities.

Act of God If the goods are destroyed by an act of God, the carrier will not be liable. An **act of God** is generally defined as un unexpected force of nature, such as an earthquake or lightning, which cannot be prevented or avoided. However, if the loss resulted from a combination of an act of God and *human* error, the carrier remains liable as an insurer.

act of God
An unexpected force of nature

Act of a Public Enemy A carrier is not liable for the acts of a public enemy. The term *public enemy* is defined narrowly to include only a foreign nation at war with the United States, pirates on the high seas, and in some cases rebels in insurrection against the government. Today piracy would probably include piracy by aircraft. The following case held that domestic criminals are not public enemies.

FACTS

A shipper delivered goods to a common carrier. While the goods were being shipped, the truck on which they were loaded was hijacked on the streets of New York City. The shipper sued the carrier, claiming that the carrier is liable for the loss. The carrier's defense is that the loss resulted from the act of a public enemy.

DECISION

Judgment for the shipper. Domestic criminals are not public enemies under the exception to common carrier liability, even when they have been designated "public enemies" by the F.B.I.

David Crystal, Inc. v. Ehrlich-Newmark Trucking Co., 64 Misc. 2d 325 (N.Y. 1970).

Act of the Shipper Widget Corporation has just received an order for 1000 crystal widgets, which are to be shipped by railroad. An employee of Widget carelessly packs the crystal widgets so that they all are shattered while being shipped by the railroad. Widget Corporation now claims that the railroad is liable as an insurer on the **consignment.**

consignment
The shipment of goods from one person to another

As a general rule a common carrier (the railroad) is not liable for losses caused by the acts of the shipper (the **consignor**). However, there are two long-recognized exceptions to this rule. First, if the loss was caused in part by the negligence of the common carrier, the carrier must bear the full loss. The fact that the shipper was contributorily negligent is irrelevant because the carrier is not being sued for committing the tort of negligence but, instead, as an insurer. In our case, if the engineer accidentally stopped the train too quickly and, as a result, the poorly packed widgets were damaged, the carrier would be liable. A common carrier is liable for loss caused by its negligence as well as for loss as an insurer.

consignor
One who ships goods to another

Second, common carriers are liable as insurers in cases when they know that the shipper has been careless in packing or loading the goods. Thus if the railroad has inspected the boxes and knew that they were packed defectively or if the railroad knew that Widget Corporation was careless in loading the boxes, the carrier would be absolutely liable for resulting losses.

Inherent Nature of the Goods In many cases the inherent nature of the goods will result in damage or destruction while the goods are being shipped. For instance, goods such as molasses will be damaged through natural fermentation, certain metals will become rusted or corroded, perishable fruits will deteriorate, and animals will die during shipment. In each of these cases the common carrier will not be liable unless the carrier's own negligence was a contributing factor. In the following case the damage to goods was not caused by the inherent nature of the goods.

FACTS

A shipper shipped crates of honeydew melons from Rio Grande City, Texas, to Chicago, Illinois. The melons were in good condition when they were delivered to the common carrier, but 640 crates of melons were damaged upon arrival in Chicago even though the carrier was not negligent. The shipper now sues the carrier, claiming that the carrier is liable for the loss.

DECISION

Judgment for the shipper. The carrier bears the burden of proving the cause of the loss. In this case, the carrier did not prove that the loss resulted from the inherent nature of the goods.

Missouri Pacific R.R. v. Elmore and Stahl, 377 U.S. 134 (1964).

writ of execution
A court order authorizing a sheriff or other proper legal officer to seize tangible property to satisfy a court judgment

Act of Public Authorities A common carrier is not liable for failure to deliver the goods because of the act of a public authority. For example, a **writ of execution** is a court order that authorizes a sheriff or other proper legal officer to seize tangible property in order to satisfy a court judgment. If a sheriff seizes property from the carrier because the shipper has failed to pay a court judgment, the carrier would not be liable. However, the carrier should notify the shipper of the execution so that the shipper may take appropriate legal action to defend itself.

Impact of Deregulation

At one time, carriers were subject to heavy government regulation. However, beginning in the late 1970s, Congress began to deregulate the transportation industry in an attempt to make it more competitive and economically viable. For carriers that have become deregulated, an important legal question arises: Are they still subject to traditional common carrier liability? It is likely that deregulation will not change their traditional liability because—as Sorkin points out in *Goods in Transit* (New York: Matthew Bender, 1989)—this liability is a product of the common law, rather than statute.

Scope of Carriage

warehouseman
A person in the business of storing goods for a fee

Beginning of Carriage A **warehouseman** is a person in the business of storing goods in a warehouse in return for compensation. When goods are stored in a warehouse, a bailment for mutual benefit is created. As discussed in greater detail in the previous chapter, in a bailment for mutual benefit the bailee—the warehouseman—owes a duty of ordinary care. This common law rule is incorporated into Section 7–204 of the Uniform Commercial Code, which provides: "A warehouseman is liable for damages for loss of or injury to the goods caused by his failure to exercise such care in regard to them as a reasonably careful man would exercise under like circumstances."

In many cases a common carrier will act as a warehouseman in storing goods either before or after shipment and, as such, will be liable as a bailee rather than as an insurer.

To illustrate, Mary works for a banana company and wants to ship 1000 crates of bananas from Tampa to a buyer, Tom, in Phoenix. She delivers 600 crates to the common carrier, a railroad, and asks the carrier to delay shipment until she delivers the other 400 crates. Before she completes the delivery, the 600 crates are stolen by thieves. If the railroad proves that it exercised ordinary care, is it still liable as an insurer?

The test to be applied in such cases is: Must the shipper do something else before the goods can be shipped? If so, the carrier is liable only as a bailee. But if the shipper has done everything necessary for shipment, the carrier is liable as an insurer. Thus where the shipper has not yet told the carrier where the goods are to be shipped or, as in Mary's case, the shipper has not yet completed delivery of the goods to the carrier, the carrier is a warehouseman-bailee and is liable only for not exercising ordinary care. When goods are delivered to a common carrier for *immediate shipment*, there is a **shipper-carrier** relationship between the shipper and the carrier, who is now liable as an insurer.

shipper-carrier
A legal relationship between the shipper and the common carrier when goods have been delivered to the carrier for immediate shipment

Termination of Carriage A similar problem exists after the goods have arrived at the destination point. If the 1000 crates of bananas arrived in Phoenix but, before the buyer, Tom, could pick them up, they were stolen from the carrier by thieves, would the railroad be considered an insurer or a warehouseman-bailee?

The answer usually depends on the contract in each case. If the contract is silent, or if the contract specifies that delivery is to be made to Tom's company, the railroad would be liable as a carrier until the goods are delivered to Tom or, at least, until the carrier has made reasonable efforts to deliver the bananas to Tom.

However, if the contract or the local business custom dictates that Tom is to pick up the goods at the station, the carrier must unload the crates in the depot so that they are ready to be picked up by Tom. In a few states, once this has been done, the railroad's liability is that of a bailee. However, most state courts have decided that the railroad does not achieve bailee status until the **consignee** has had a reasonable chance to pick them up or until the railroad notifies the consignee that the goods have arrived and the consignee has had an opportunity to pick them up.

consignee
One to whom goods are shipped

► Limitation of Liability

If goods are shipped *interstate*, the *federal* Interstate Commerce Act governs attempts by the common carrier to limit its liability. Under this Act, carriers generally may not limit their liability. However, there are exceptions to this rule. For instance, liability may be limited for damage to *baggage* carried on passenger trains and boats. In another situation a carrier may establish rates that are dependent upon the value of the goods being shipped. The second exception has the effect of limiting liability because the shipper will be allowed to recover only up to the value declared by the shipper if the goods are lost or damaged.

If the goods are not shipped interstate, Section 7–309 of the Uniform Commercial Code provides that a common or private carrier who issues a bill of lading—which will be discussed below under Documents of Title—must at least act with reasonable care. However, as under federal law, the carrier may limit damages by providing that its liability is limited to the value stated by the shipper, provided that rates are dependent on value and that the shipper is given the chance to declare a higher value.

Under both federal and state law, carriers who want to limit their liability to a declared value must show that the shipper actually agreed to the valuation placed on the property. This important principle of law is illustrated by the following case.

FACTS

The owner of a mobile home hired a carrier to transport the home from Pratt to Lavant, Kansas. The carrier's driver gave the owner a bill of lading, which included a low valuation of the home, but gave the owner no time to read the document before signing it. During shipment, the home became disconnected from the truck and was severely damaged, as were its contents. Is the owner bound by the valuation in the document?

DECISION

The owner is not bound under these circumstances. This is an intrastate shipment governed by the state law, which provides that a shipper must agree to the valuation. Furthermore, state law is similar to federal law which also requires an agreement as to valuation.

Bailey v. Morgan Drive-Away, Inc., 647 F.Supp. 648 (D. Kan. 1986).

FIGURE 22.1 Non-negotiable Warehouse Receipt (Front)

Weicker Transfer and Storage Company
P.O. BOX 5207 • DENVER, COLORADO • 80217

PAGE:

NON-NEGOTIABLE WAREHOUSE RECEIPT / INVOICE

DATE OF RECEIPT:

WAREHOUSE BUILDING NO.:

IN ALL CORRESPONDENCE KINDLY REFER TO THIS INVOICE NO.:

RECEIVED FOR ACCOUNT OF

INVOICE DATE

STORER CONSIGNMENT NO.:
DELIVERING CARRIER
CAR INITIALS & NO.:

INBOUND SEALS:
OUTBOUND SEALS:
RECEIPT TYPE:

WAYBILL NO.:

QUANTITY RECEIVED	ITEM CODE / LOT NO.	SAID TO BE OR CONTAIN	OSD	WEIGHT	RATE	CHARGES		
						HANDLING	STORAGE	OTHER

RECEIVED FROM

* Denotes minimum billing

PLEASE PAY THIS AMOUNT $

These goods are not insured by this warehouse for the benefit of the depositor against fire or any other casualty.

The goods listed hereon were received in apparent good order, except as noted hereon (contents, condition and quality unknown) subject to all the terms and conditions contained herein and on the reverse hereof, such property to be delivered to the depositor upon the payment of all storage, handling and other charges.

Liability for other loss or damage shall be limited to the actual value of the goods stored; Liability Sec. 10, (a) and in no case shall the liability exceed 250 times the base storage rate unless an excess value is declared by the storer in writing at the time the goods are stored. There will be a charge of 4/10 of 1 per cent per month on the excess valuation in addition to the base storage rate.

WEICKER TRANSFER AND STORAGE COMPANY claims a lien for all lawful charges for storage and preservation of the goods, also for all lawful claims for money advanced, interest, insurance, transportation, labor, weighing, coopering, and other charges and expenses, in relation to such goods; and for the balance on any account that may be due.

No Delivery Will Be Made On This Receipt Except On Written Order Of Authorized Agent.

WAREHOUSE RECEIPT / INVOICE ORIGINAL

WEICKER TRANSFER AND STORAGE COMPANY

By

This Receipt is valid only when signed by an officer of the company, or an authorized agent.

warehouse receipt
A document issued to the bailor by a warehouseman

bill of lading
A document issued to the shipper by a carrier of goods

document of title
A document evidencing that the person possessing it "is entitled to receive, hold, and dispose of the document and the goods it covers" UCC 1-201(15)

Documents of Title

▶ Definition

If Herman delivers his furniture to a warehouseman for storage, the warehouseman will give him a receipt for the furniture called a **warehouse receipt** (see Figure 22.1). If Herman delivered the goods to a carrier for shipment, he would receive a receipt called a **bill of lading** (see Figure 22.2). Both the warehouse receipt and the bill of lading are **documents of title** and, as such, are more than mere receipts. Documents of title

FIGURE 22.2 **Negotiable Bill of Lading (Front)**

UNION PACIFIC RAILROAD

FORM 1585

(Uniform Domestic Order Bill of Lading, adopted by Carriers in Official, Southern, Western and Illinois Classification Territories, March 15, 1922, as amended August 1, 1930, and June 15, 1941.)

9-66— 15M Sets
1st SHEET

UNIFORM ORDER BILL OF LADING
ORIGINAL

Shipper's No. ________
Agent's No. ________

UNION PACIFIC RAILROAD COMPANY

RECEIVED, subject to the classifications and tariffs in effect on the date of the issue of this Bill of Lading,

at ________ 19 ____

from ________
the property described below, in apparent good order, except as noted (contents and condition of contents of packages unknown), marked, consigned, and destined as indicated below, which said company (the word company being understood throughout this contract as meaning any person or corporation in possession of the property under the contract) agrees to carry to its usual place of delivery at said destination, if on its own road or its own water line, otherwise to deliver to another carrier on the route to said destination. It is mutually agreed, as to each carrier of all or any of said property over all or any portion of said route to destination, and as to each party at any time interested in all or any of said property, that every service to be performed hereunder shall be subject to all the conditions not prohibited by law, whether printed or written, herein contained, including the conditions on back hereof, which are hereby agreed to by the shipper and accepted for himself and his assigns.

The surrender of this Original ORDER Bill of Lading properly indorsed shall be required before the delivery of the property. Inspection of property covered by this Bill of Lading will not be permitted unless provided by law or unless permission is indorsed on this Original Bill of Lading or given in writing by the shipper.

Consigned to ORDER OF ________

Destination ________ State of ________ County of ________

Notify ________

At ________ State of ________ County of ________

Route ________

Delivering Carrier ________ Car Initial ________ Car No. ________

No. Packages	DESCRIPTION OF ARTICLES, SPECIAL MARKS, AND EXCEPTIONS	*WEIGHT (Subject to Correction)	CLASS OR RATE	CHECK COLUMN

Subject to Section 7 of conditions, if this shipment is to be delivered to the consignee without recourse on the consignor, the consignor shall sign the following statement:

The carrier shall not make delivery of this shipment without payment of freight and all other lawful charges.

____
(Signature of Consignor)

If charges are to be prepaid, write or stamp here, "To be Prepaid."

Received $ ________
to apply in prepayment of the charges on the property described hereon.

____
Agent or Cashier.

Per ________
(The signature here acknowledges only the amount prepaid.)

Charges Advanced:

$ ________

*If the shipment moves between two ports by a carrier by water, the law requires that the bill of lading shall state whether it is "carrier's or shipper's weight."

NOTE—Where the rate is dependent on value, shippers are required to state specifically in writing the agreed or declared value of the property.

The agreed or declared value of the property is hereby specifically stated by the shipper to be not exceeding

per

________ Shipper. ________ Agent

Per ________ Per ________

Permanent postoffice address of shipper ________

COURTESY, SAFETY AND RELIABLE SERVICE

normally spell out the terms of the contract between Herman and the bailee. In many cases, a person who has possession of the document is the only one entitled to recover the goods from the bailee.

► Source of Law

State law governing documents of title is found in Article 7 of the Uniform Commercial Code. If goods are shipped interstate, federal treaties and statutes take precedence over state law. The Uniform Commercial Code also provides that Article 7 is subject to the provisions of state regulatory statutes.

► Negotiation

In Chapter 29, we discuss commercial paper generally and the distinction between negotiable and nonnegotiable commercial paper. A document of title is a type of commercial paper that is referred to as "commodity paper" in order to distinguish it from the "money paper" (for example, checks and notes) discussed in Part 6. The tests to determine whether a document of title is negotiable differ from the "money paper" tests to be discussed in Chapter 29.

negotiable document
A document of title stating that the goods covered by the document are to be delivered to bearer or to the order of someone

A document of title is considered to be a **negotiable document** if it states that the goods are to be delivered either to bearer, meaning any person in possession of the document, or to the order of someone. If neither of these requirements is met, the document is nonnegotiable. Thus if the warehouse receipt states that the goods are to be delivered "to the order of Herman," it is negotiable. If it states that the goods are to be delivered "to Herman," it is nonnegotiable.

The difference between a negotiable and a nonnegotiable document of title has an important consequence for the bailee. If the document is negotiable, the goods must be delivered to the holder of the document—namely, the person who has possession of the document that flows to that person either originally or by indorsement. If the document is nonnegotiable, the goods must usually be delivered to the person named in the document.

bearer
The person in possession of an instrument, document of title, or certificated security payable or deliverable to bearer or indorsed in blank (a signature without additional words)

due negotiation
Delivery of a negotiable document of title to a holder who purchases it for value, in good faith, and without notice of any claim or defense to the document

Furthermore, if Herman's document of title is negotiable, Herman must follow certain procedures to duly negotiate it to his friend Fred. If the document is **bearer** paper, it is negotiated by simple delivery to Fred. If the document is order paper, Herman must first indorse the document and then deliver it to Fred. In either case, Fred must purchase the document as a holder in good faith without notice of any claim or defense to the document and must pay value in order to claim **due negotiation.** If Fred were to purchase the document as payment for a past money debt owing to him by Herman, Fred would not be giving value. Fred must also purchase the document in the regular course of business or financing.

If there is due negotiation, the holder usually takes the document, and the goods, free of claims and defenses raised by the bailee or third persons. However, there are two major exceptions to the protection given to the purchaser of a document of title. First, the bailee is entitled to compensation for transportation or storage charges, which is usually specified on the document or in tariffs filed by the carrier. Second, the holder will not be entitled to the goods in cases where the bailor had no authority to deliver the goods to the bailee carrier or warehouseman. For example, if a thief stole Herman's furniture, delivered it to a warehouseman, and then duly negotiated the warehouse receipt to Fred, Herman would still have a right to the furniture superior to that of Fred. The reason is that Herman never put the goods in the stream of commerce. The second exception does not apply in cases where Herman delivered the goods to the warehouse and received a warehouse receipt that a thief then stole from Herman and duly negotiated to Fred. Under the Uniform Commercial Code, Section 7–502 (2), rights acquired by a holder after due negotiation are not impaired even though a prior "person has been deprived of possession of the document by misrepresentation, fraud, accident, mistake, duress, loss, theft or conversion."

Nonconformity of Goods to the Receipt

Clara has just purchased a bill of lading from the consignee, the person to whom goods are shipped. The bill of lading describes the goods being shipped as "five packages of class B Widgets." When Clara delivers the bill of lading to the carrier, she is advised that only four packages were shipped. May Clara recover damages from the carrier for the value of the missing package?

The answer to this question will vary, depending on the circumstances. In most cases, a good faith purchaser for value may recover damages from the carrier. However, if the document indicates that the carrier does not know whether the goods were received or conform to the description, the carrier will not be liable for damages. Consequently, Clara could not recover if the bill of lading states "contents unknown" or "said to contain" or "shipper's load, weight and count" if these statements were, in fact, true. The following case illustrates the rule that the common carrier is not liable for damage to goods on a shipper's load and count movement.

FACTS

A shipper delivered goods to a common carrier for shipment to a buyer. This was a "shipper's load, weight and count" shipment. The goods arrived in a damaged condition. Is the carrier liable for the damage?

DECISION

The carrier is not liable. Because this was a "shipper's load, weight and count" shipment, the carrier had no knowledge of the contents or condition of the goods.

United Steel & Strip v. Monex Corp., 310 So.2d 339 (Fla. 1975).

If a bill of lading is filled in or otherwise altered without authority, the carrier is liable only according to the original terms of the document, irrespective of whether it is negotiable or nonnegotiable. The same rule is true for warehouse receipts except that when a blank is filled in on a negotiable warehouse receipt, a purchaser for value may enforce the receipt as completed, even though it was completed without authority.

Sale by the Bailee

Suppose that Herman delivers his furniture to a warehouse and the warehouseman, without permission, sells Herman's furniture to Claude and then leaves the country. May Herman recover his furniture from Claude? In most cases, the bailor, Herman, will win because the bailee had no title to convey to Claude. There is one exception to the rule under the Uniform Commercial Code, Section 7–205, which provides that, when a buyer in the ordinary course of business purchases fungible goods from a warehouseman who is in the business of buying and selling such goods, the buyer takes free and clear of all claims under a warehouse receipt.[1] Thus if Herman had delivered grain for storage to a

[1]Under UCC 2 on Sales, the same result occurs with respect to *any* goods (whether or not fungible) entrusted to a merchant who deals in goods of that kind. (See Chapter 24.)

warehouseman who deals in grain and Claude had purchased Herman's grain from the warehouseman, Claude would prevail even against a person to whom the warehouse receipt has been duly negotiated. The dealer has been given the appearance of being an owner, and the dealer's sale to the innocent purchaser transfers the title.

Liens

lien
A legal right in another's property as security for the performance of an obligation

A **lien** is a legal right in another's property as security for the performance of an obligation. It includes the right of a creditor to have a debt paid from the proceeds of the sale of the property. A carrier is given a *specific possessory lien* on the goods described in the bill of lading as security to assure payment for storage and transportation charges. A warehouseman has a similar lien on the goods described in the warehouse receipt as security to assure payment for storage and transportation charges as well as insurance and labor expenses. A *possessory lien* is a lien that includes the right to possession of the property subject to the lien. A *specific lien* is a lien only on *specific* property for services rendered to that property.

Under Sections 7–210 and 7–308 of the Uniform Commercial Code, both the carrier and the warehouseman may enforce the lien by public or private sale of the goods in a commercially reasonable manner after notifying all persons known to claim an interest in the goods. Additionally, in cases where the bailor is not a merchant, the warehouseman must also publish an advertisement of the sale once a week for two consecutive weeks in a newspaper in the place where the sale is to be held, and the sale must take place at least fifteen days after the first publication. If the sale of goods brings more than the amount due the bailee, the bailee must hold the balance for the person who was to have received the goods.

Warranties

When a person sells a document of title, by law the seller gives the purchaser the usual warranties made when someone sells goods, discussed in Part 5, Sales and Consumer Law. But additionally, the seller warrants that (1) the document is genuine; (2) the seller knows of no fact that impairs its validity or worth; and (3) the negotiation is rightful and effective. However, an intermediary entrusted with a document of title, such as a collecting bank, warrants only that it is acting in good faith with authority.

Common Carrier of Passengers

The common carrier of passengers faces two main legal concerns. First, the carrier faces possible liability for injuries to passengers during the course of the journey. The general rule is that the carrier is not liable as an insurer for every injury suffered by passengers, but the carrier does owe the highest degree of care to passengers.

An increasingly common question is whether a common carrier should be held liable when one passenger assaults another. And, if a carrier does owe a duty to protect its passengers from assaults, what measures must be taken to meet its duty? For instance, must the carrier provide armed security guards or are less expensive measures sufficient? These questions are addressed by the court in the following case.

FACTS

A group of juveniles harassed passengers on a rapid transit bus. The bus driver was notified but took no action and eventually a fight broke out. During the fight, several innocent passengers were injured and sued the rapid transit corporation. Does the corporation owe a duty to protect passengers from assaults by other passengers?

DECISION

Yes. In virtually every state, courts have held that common carriers must protect passengers from assaults. Most courts in these cases impose the same high duty of care that common carriers owe generally to passengers. In meeting this duty, carriers do not necessarily have to place an armed guard on every bus. Other actions might be sufficient to meet the duty. Those actions include warnings to unruly passengers by the driver, summoning the police, ejecting unruly passengers, alarm lights on buses to alert police, special training for drivers, and radio communication to bus headquarters.

Lopez v. Southern Cal. Rapid Transit, 710 P.2d 907 (Cal. 1985).

Second, the common carrier faces liability as an insurer in cases where a passenger's baggage is lost or damaged. However, in order to recover, the passenger must prove that there was a bailment of the baggage. If the passenger retained possession of the baggage during the trip, there would be no bailment because the delivery requirement is missing. Furthermore, even when there is delivery to the carrier, the carrier is normally not liable for the contents of the baggage unless the contents were for the personal use and convenience of the passenger. This rule prevents unexpected liability on the part of the carrier when a passenger attempts to ship valuables, such as paintings or rare china, as baggage without paying the customary rates for goods of higher value and greater risk to the carrier.

Innkeepers

An **innkeeper** is an operator of a hotel, inn, motel, or any other establishment engaged in making lodging accommodations available to travelers.

innkeeper
Operator of an establishment engaged in making lodging accommodations available to travelers

At common law, the liability of an innkeeper for lost or damaged goods was similar to that of the common carrier; the innkeeper was liable as an insurer of the goods, unless an exception applied, such as loss resulting from an act of God, an act of a public enemy, an act of a public authority, or the inherent nature of the goods.

In most states the common law rule has been changed by statute. Although the statutes vary from state to state, the Florida statute provides one example of a statutory modification of the innkeeper's duty. Under the Florida statute, Section 509.111, an innkeeper is not obliged to accept a guest's valuables and an innkeeper who does accept them is only liable if negligence is proven. But even in cases of negligence, the innkeeper's liability is limited to $1,000 if it provides the guest with a receipt that states the $1,000 limit. The innkeeper's limitation of liability and a copy of the statute must be posted in the hotel office, lobby, or other prominent place.

In order to limit its liability, a hotel must strictly comply with the statute, as the following case illustrates.

FACTS

A guest staying in a Florida hotel deposited $85,000 in jewelry in the hotel's safe deposit box. A hotel employee who had recently been hired as a desk clerk stole the jewelry. The hotel posted a limitation of liability and a copy of the Florida statute described above in each guests' bathroom but not in any other prominent place. The guest was not given a receipt for the jewelry. Is the hotel's liability limited to $1,000?

DECISION

No. The hotel did not comply with two requirements of the Florida statute and thus is not entitled to limitation of its liability. First, the hotel did not post its limitation of liability and a copy of the statute in the office, lobby, or other prominent place. Second, the hotel did not give the guest a receipt.

Florida Sonesta Corp. v. Aniballi, 463 So.2d 1203 (Fla. 1985).

Summary Statement

1. The liability of a common carrier is unique in bailment law in that the carrier is liable in most cases as an insurer of the goods.
2. A common carrier is not liable for (a) an act of God, (b) an act of a public enemy, (c) an act of the shipper, (d) a loss resulting from the inherent nature of the goods, and (e) an act of public authorities.
3. A common carrier is liable as an ordinary bailee until the shipper has done everything necessary to make the goods ready for shipment (thereby creating a *shipper-carrier relationship*), the carrier then becoming liable as an insurer.
4. A document of title is a receipt given by a warehouseman or common carrier that also serves as the contract between the bailor and the bailee.
5. In most cases, when a document of title has been duly negotiated, the purchaser takes the document free and clear of defenses that could have been raised by the bailee against the bailor, and also free and clear of claims to the document and to the goods by third persons.
6. A common carrier is not liable as an insurer of the safety of passengers; however, the carrier does owe passengers the highest degree of care.
7. Under the common law, an innkeeper was liable as an insurer for guests' belongings that were damaged or destroyed. Today this liability has been changed by statute in most states.

In the following case the court discusses the common law liability of the innkeeper and problems that arise in interpreting modern statutes.

FEDERAL INSURANCE COMPANY v. WALDORF-ASTORIA HOTEL
60 Misc.2d 996 (N.Y. 1969)

Guests staying in the Waldorf-Astoria Hotel discovered that a night table in their hotel room had been opened and that a pair of gold cufflinks, with a pearl in each, had been stolen. The cufflinks were worth $175. The guests' insurance company sued the hotel for the value of the cufflinks.

Schwartz, J. . . . Section 200 of the General Business Law . . . provides that the proprietor of a hotel is relieved from liability for loss to a guest of his money, jewels, ornaments, bank notes, bonds, negotiable securities or precious stones, if the hotel provides a place of safekeeping and patrons do not avail themselves of it. Defendant argues that the gold cufflinks . . . satisfied the definition of "jewels" under Sec. 200.

Plaintiff [argues] that the articles lost were not "jewels," "ornaments" or "precious stones" within the meaning of Sec. 200, but were articles of ordinary wear carried for use and convenience and not for ornamentation. Plaintiff refers to Sec. 201, General Business Law, which places certain limits, not applicable here, on the common law liability of a hotel keeper for loss of his guests' property.

Both parties agree that . . . the sole question to be determined is whether the missing cufflinks come within the meaning of the words "jewels," "ornaments" or "precious stones" in the statute. . . .

At common law, an innkeeper was liable as an insurer of the property of his guests unless the loss was occasioned by the negligence or fault of the guest. . . .

The purpose of Sec. 200, in providing that the hotelkeeper shall not be liable for money, jewels, ornaments, and precious stones if they are not deposited in the hotel safe provided, is to protect the hotel from an undisclosed excessive liability. . . .

Section 200 of the General Business Law, being in derogation of the common law relative to the liability of innkeepers, is strictly construed. . . . The exemption is limited to the particular species of property named and, being strictly construed, cannot be extended in its application by doubtful construction so as to include property not fairly within its terms. "Property . . . which is useful or necessary to the comfort and convenience of the guest, that which is usually carried and worn as a part of the ordinary apparel and outfit . . . is left, as before the statute, at the risk of the innkeeper." . . .

In *Kennedy v. Bowman Biltmore Hotel Corporation*, . . . the article lost from the hotel guest's room was a wrist watch ornamented with diamonds. The court said, "The watch involved while ornamented with diamonds was primarily an article of daily use and not a jewel, ornament or precious stone within the meaning of Section 200 of the General Business Law. . . . Nor would the fact that a broken clasp made it unsafe to wear the watch on the day of its loss change the nature of the article." . . .

By analogy, the cufflinks in suit, even though fashioned of gold and ornamented with a pearl in each, cannot be considered as jewels or ornaments, as these terms are used and understood in common parlance. Black's Law Dictionary defines "jewels" as "an ornament of the person, such as earrings, pearls, diamonds, etc. prepared to be worn . . . , an ornament made of precious metal or a precious stone." Cufflinks are not used as jewels or ornaments but to close the cuffs, otherwise buttonless, of shirts. They are articles of utilitarian and ordinary wear in daily use, on all occasions, with business clothes as well as clothes designed for leisure, in the daytime as well as the evening. They are carried principally for use and convenience and not for ornament. Cufflinks, as with watches and other articles of ordinary wear, may be made of precious metals, and even made more elaborate with precious stones, but these do not change their essential description as articles of ordinary wear.

Section 200 of the General Business Law has modified the hotelkeeper's liability only as to the articles named. Cufflinks, even though made of gold and decorated with a pearl, are articles of use and are not jewels or ornaments within the meaning of Section 200. The defendant hotel is therefore not relieved of liability for their loss despite the failure of the guests to deposit them in the hotel safe provided.

Questions and Case Problems

1. A shipper shipped packaged jewelry from Dallas to New York City on Delta Air Lines. The shipper told Delta that the package contained "printed matter," and the package was not wrapped in accordance with Delta's regulations covering jewelry shipments. The jewelry was lost during shipment, but Delta claims it is not liable because of the shipper's misdescription and improper packaging. Is Delta liable? [*Travelers Ins. Co. v. Delta Air Lines, Inc.*, 498 S.W.2d 443 (Tex. 1973).]

2. Karmely delivered 22 precious rubies to a warehouseman for storage in a warehouse. It was later discovered that the rubies were missing. The warehouseman claimed that the rubies had been stolen, but offered no details to back up this claim. Is the warehouseman liable for the rubies? [*Karmely v. Alitalia-Linee Aerre, S.p.A.*, 18 U.C.C. Rep. Serv. (Callaghan) 479 (N.Y. Sup.Ct. 1975).]
3. A common carrier contracted with a shipper to ship 100 bales of cotton. The shipper delivered 29 bales to the shipping platform and advised the carrier that the remaining 71 bales would be delivered within a few days. A fire destroyed the 29 bales on the platform. Is the carrier absolutely liable for the cotton? [*Rio Grande City Ry. Co. v. Guerra*, 26 S.W.2d 360 (Tex. 1930).]
4. A 17-year-old desk clerk gave a pass key to all rooms in the motel where he worked to two strangers. The strangers unlocked a room, broke the chain, entered the room, and assaulted and robbed a husband and wife staying in the room. A statute provides that innkeepers are not responsible for property stolen by force or extraordinary violence. Is the motel liable for damages to the couple? [*Kraaz v. La Quinta Motor Inns, Inc.* 410 So.2d 1048 (La. 1982).]
5. A passenger checked a bag and contents worth $2,190 at a room in the railroad station at Portland, Oregon. A railroad employee gave him a receipt that limited the railroad's liability to $25, unless the passenger paid a higher rate. The passenger was unaware of the limitation. When the passenger returned, the bag could not be found. The railroad claimed that the limitation of liability was valid because the rules and regulations governing carriers allowed such contracts. Is the carrier correct? [*Allen v. Southern Pac. Co.*, 213 P.2d 667 (Utah 1950).]
6. A construction company entered into a contract with a railroad to build a section of track. The railroad agreed to ship materials needed for construction to the company at a special rate, but their contract also provided that the common carrier would not be liable for any losses. Is the exemption from liability valid? [*Santa Fe, P. & P. Ry. Co. v. Grant Bros. Const. Co.*, 228 U.S. 177 (1913).]
7. A 70-year-old passenger was riding on a streetcar. The motorman of the streetcar, in driving through an intersection, had to stop quickly because of an approaching vehicle. The passenger fell to the floor and fractured two vertebrae. Is the streetcar owner liable? [*Dolan v. New Orleans Pub. Serv., Inc.*, 317 So.2d 688 (La. 1975).]
8. A seaman was riding on a bus. Four drunken youths entered the bus and sat behind the seaman. They tried to pick his pocket and asked him for money. When he refused, they began to punch and kick him. The driver then stopped the bus, called the police, and ordered the youths off the bus. Is the bus company liable for the seaman's injuries? [*Orr v. New Orleans Pub. Serv., Inc.*, 349 So.2d 417 (La. 1977).]
9. Two guests, each traveling with jewelry collections worth $1 million, were staying at a Manhattan luxury hotel. They deposited the jewelry in the hotel's safe-deposit boxes, which were in a plasterboard room, controlled by two hollow core wood doors, one of which had an ordinary residential lock. The rooms allegedly were unguarded and open to the general public. Thieves broke into the safe-deposit boxes and stole the jewelry. The hotel argues that its liability is limited by the New York law discussed in the *Federal Insurance Co. v. Waldorf-Astoria Hotel*, excerpted at the beginning of this section. What counter-argument should the guests make? [*Goncalves v. Regent Intern. Hotels, Inc.*, 447 N.E.2d 693 (N.Y. 1983).]

10. In the *Federal Insurance Co.* case, the court indicated that the statute is in derogation of the common law and must be strictly construed. How does this approach provide flexibility to meet the needs of commerce?

PART 4 PERSONAL PROPERTY AND BAILMENTS

ETHICS AND BUSINESS LAW

Introduction

This end-of-part discussion, like the others in this book, is designed to encourage you to begin forming personal beliefs about what is right or wrong conduct in business. The discussion here builds on the material in the first end-of-part discussion; you may find it helpful to review that.

This material has several goals. The overview section is designed to help you see the range of ethical issues associated with this area of the law. The in-depth discussion is intended to provide you with a background for forming your own beliefs about a single very important ethical issue in business. The problems at the end of this part are designed to build your skill in ethical analysis while exploring further the in-depth issue.

Overview of Ethical Issues in Personal Property and Bailments

The rapid development of technology in recent years has raised many ethical issues related to infringing and pirating of intangible industrial property interests, such as patents, copyrights, trademarks, computer programs, and videocassette recordings. Such conduct occurs not only in the United States but also worldwide in national and international trade. Creative innovation of original works is encouraged, protected, and rewarded by the law. But often these laws are difficult to enforce. Society depends to a large extent on the personal ethics of individuals to make this law work.

In reading about the liability of hotels for the loss of guests' property, you were learning about how our legal system resolves the conflict between guests and hotels. Recall that at common law the innkeeper acted as the insurer of a guest's goods. However, most states have, by statute, changed the common law. Now, even if the innkeeper is negligent, the innkeeper's liability is generally limited to $100.

Most likely, the hotel industry lobbied their state legislatures to get the common law modified. They did this probably because they suffered repeated financial losses, so lobbying was an understandable worthwhile effort. Guests, however, were not highly motivated; it wasn't worth their time to lobby. In this instance the more active hotel lobbyist prevailed over the more numerous but less active guest. Thus the law makes the individual's interest secondary to the interests of the hotels.

The legislative process is the law-making mechanism that most often reflects the desires of a group—usually a majority on an issue. On the other hand, constitutions and the courts most often protect the desires of a minority such as a solitary individual. Notice that the courts fashioned the protection for the guests while the legislatures took that protection away.

In-Depth Discussion of a Basic Issue: Private Ownership of Property

The ethical basis for the law of personal property and bailments is the right to ownership of property by private parties. Because this is such a basic attribute of our society and our legal system, as well as an essential element of personal and economic liberty, it is important for you to develop mature beliefs about it.

► Groups and Individuals

Generally, when you, as an individual, join a *group*, it is because your desires coincide with those of the group. Occasions often arise, however, when the desires of the individual differ from, or conflict with, those of the group.

This conflict between the individual and the group occurs frequently on several levels in all societies. The way it is resolved accounts for basic differences between economic systems such as capitalism and socialism, between political systems such as democracy and communism, between philosophical systems such as egoism and utilitarianism, and between styles of managing and interacting with others.

► Alternative Paths to the Common Good

Nearly all societies try to advance "the common good"; that is, they try to improve the welfare of the society. While most societies share this goal, they differ dramatically on the extent to which they emphasize the individual good and the collective good as a means for achieving the common good. In some societies, most decisions are made by asking whether the decision will directly advance the interests of the group or collective. In other societies, there is more of a willingness to see the individual as a vehicle for improving the welfare of the group. Thus there are different conceptions of the relative rights of the individual and the rights of the group.

A nation's property law usually reflects its basic attitude about individual and group rights. For example, the property law of socialist countries is based on the idea that property should be held for the benefit of all citizens rather than for the benefit of particular individuals. In these countries, only the government can own the "means of production." In capitalist societies, however, the means of production are owned by individuals. Capitalists generally believe that the common good is advanced when individual self-interest is channeled, perhaps somewhat indirectly, toward the common good.

In some socialist societies, property cannot be willed from one private party to another, it must go to the state on death. In contrast, our property law goes to great length to benefit the individual. Our law of intestacy causes your property to go to your relatives even if you die without a will. Only if you die both without a will and without surviving relatives will the property *escheat*, that is go to the state.

► Philosophic Views

Karl Marx articulated the strongest opposition to the institution of private property and the role of the individual versus that of the group. His view is that working for others undermines our humanity and that private property stimulates greed. He wrote:

> Private property has made us so stupid and partial that an object is only *ours* when we have it, when it exists for us as capital or when it is directly eaten, drunk, worn, inhabited, etc., in short, *utilized* in some way.

> The suppression of private property is, therefore, the complete *emancipation* of all the human qualities and senses.

The most widely recognized justification for private ownership of property was articulated by John Locke. Locke's argument is grounded largely on natural law and religion. He wrote:

> Whether we consider natural reasons . . . or revelation . . . it is very clear that God . . . 'has given the earth to the children of men,' given it to mankind in common. Though the earth and all inferior creatures be common to all men, yet every man has a property in his own person; this nobody has any right to but himself. Whatsoever then he removes out of the state that nature has provided . . . , he has mixed his labor with, and joined to it, something that is his own, and thereby makes it his property.

A more modern—and clearly utilitarian—justification for private ownership has been articulated by Richard Posner:

> Imagine a society in which all property rights have been abolished. A farmer plants corn, fertilizes it, and erects scarecrows, but when the corn is ripe his neighbor reaps and sells it. The farmer has no legal remedy against his neighbor's conduct since he owns neither the land that he sowed nor the crop. After a few such incidents the cultivation of land will be abandoned and the society will shift to methods of subsistence (such as hunting) that involve less preparatory investment.
>
> This example suggests that the legal protection of property rights has an important economic function: to create incentives to use resources efficiently. . . .
>
> The creation of exclusive rights is a necessary rather than sufficient condition for the efficient use of resources. The rights must be transferable. Suppose the farmer in our example owns the land that he sows but is a bad farmer; his land would be more productive in someone else's hands. The maximization of value requires a mechanism by which the farmer can be induced to transfer rights in the property to someone who can work it more productively. A transferable right is such a mechanism. . . .
>
> The foregoing discussion suggests three criteria of an efficient system of property rights. The first is universality. Ideally, all resources should be owned, or ownable, by someone, except resources so plentiful that everybody can consume as much of them as he wants without reducing consumption by anyone else.
>
> The second criterion—is exclusivity. We have assumed so far that either the farmer can exclude no one or he can exclude everyone, but of course there are intermediate stages: the farmer may be entitled to exclude private individuals from reaping his crop, but not the government in time of war. It might appear that the more exclusive the property right, the greater the incentive to invest the right amount of resources in the development of the property.
>
> The third criterion of an efficient system of property rights is transferability. If a property right cannot be transferred, there is no way of shifting a resource from a less productive to a more productive use through voluntary exchange. The costs of transfer may be high to begin with; a legal prohibition against transferring may, depending on the penalties for violation, make the costs utterly prohibitive.

In 1864, Abraham Lincoln addressed the issue of *unequal* distribution of property in the following words:

> Property is the fruit of labor; property is desirable; it is a positive good in the world. That some should be rich shows that others may become rich, and hence is just encouragement to industry and enterprise.

> Let not him who is houseless pull down the house of another, but let him work diligently and build one for himself, thus by example assuring that his own shall be safe from violence when built.

As you can see, the views of these thinkers vary dramatically. In order to function effectively in the business world, and make high-quality ethical decisions, you need to develop your own views on private ownership of property. Is Marx right, or are Locke, Posner, and Lincoln correct?

Solving Ethics Problems

Like the other end-of-part discussions in this book, this one presents problems for you to consider. These problems have three goals. The first is to give you the opportunity to further explore the in-depth issue. The second goal is to give you experience in ethical reasoning about the law and about related management problems. The third goal is to let you see how thinking critically about the law can increase your ability to make ethical decisions. To facilitate this, the problems begin by asking you to analyze the law for its ethical content and then shift to looking at related problems in managerial ethics.

For a discussion of the ethical roles of markets and the law, and examples of the four styles of ethical reasoning—egoism, utilitarianism, Kantian philosophy, and religious ethics—read the business ethics material at the end of Part 1.

▶ Problems

1. In *Bishop v. Ellsworth* (see p. 419–20), you read about a dispute over lost property—some money in a bottle that had been found. The case tried to resolve the claims of the finders and the claims of the party on whose property the bottle had been found. In a moral sense, neither has a very strong claim to ownership. These claims are morally quite weak, especially when compared to the claims of the party who owned the money but lost it. Isn't it possible to assume that society has a stronger claim to the found money than either the finder or owner of the land? Do you think the laws of communist countries would differ in their approach to this problem? Try to make persuasive arguments that justify allowing one of the private parties to keep the money. Do you believe this law is the best law?
2. In Chapter 20 you learned about the concept of *escheat*. This is the legal requirement that when individuals die without heirs, their property goes to the state. Can you make a persuasive argument justifying the transfer of property to heirs, when they exist? Do you think property should escheat even when there are heirs? Or do you think property should be passed on death from one individual to another? Which goals of the marketplace are advanced or retarded by the inheritability of property?
3. Frequently in business discussions, people toss out ideas to be evaluated by a group. Suppose you are brainstorming a problem with a group of your subordinates and one of them comes up with an idea that you judge to be quite useful to your company. Further assume that you could appropriate this idea as your own, in your discussions with your boss, without any risk of adverse consequences to yourself. If you think there might be a substantial benefit to you, perhaps a significant raise, should you do so? Why or why not? Do you think you would?

4. Suppose you were the manager of a programming group for a software firm. One of your star programmers has approached you with a request for 15 percent release time and tuition reimbursement of $4,000 for attending evening classes reading the "great books" of Western literature. He believes this will broaden his perspective and allow him to generate more creative ideas for the firm. Do you think that such an investment in him (an individual) can be justified by its indirect benefit to the firm (the group)? Why or why not?

PART 5

SALES AND CONSUMER LAW

PREVIEW

This part covers Article 2 on the sale of goods, which is a portion of the Uniform Commercial Code; consumer legislation, both federal and state; and federal and state judicial decisions interpreting and applying the Code. The Code establishes guidelines and rules of interpretation for merchants and consumers in their sales transactions in the absence of their agreement to the contrary. In some instances the Code does not permit variation and establishes fixed rules. The first four chapters discuss the history and objectives of the Code, and the formation, performance, breach, and remedies in connection with the sales contract for goods. Many changes in the common law of contracts are made by the Code.

However, Article 2 is not enough to reflect the protection needed by the consumer when dealing with merchants, and particularly in establishing manufacturer liability for defective products. A whole new body of consumer law has evolved, making a startling change in relationships among consumers, retailers, and manufacturers. Chapters 27 and 28 discuss this breakthrough in consumer protection, particularly with respect to the area called "products liability."

Business ethics as it relates to sales and consumer law is considered at the end of the part.

CHAPTER 23

INTRODUCTION TO THE UNIFORM COMMERCIAL CODE

After you have read this chapter, you should be able to:

1. Give the reasons for having the Uniform Commercial Code (UCC).
2. Define a code.
3. State the purposes of the UCC.
4. Define the term "merchant."
5. Describe briefly:
   a) The contributions of Karl Llewellyn to the formulation of the UCC.
   b) "Goods" and distinguish goods from items or commercial circumstances not covered by Article 2.
   c) The standard of conduct required by Article 2 and explain how this standard of conduct is to be "found" in many cases.
6. Define the statute of frauds and the parol evidence rule under Article 2, and then explain how they apply in real-life situations.

BUSINESS DECISIONS and the LAW

A large portion of our economy depends on the design, production, marketing, and distribution from state to state of tangible, movable things we call goods. An automobile, for example, may be assembled in Michigan from parts made in Ohio and Indiana, and shipped to California to be sold. Today our nationwide distribution system for goods is the envy of other potentially strong economic units—from Western Europe to Eastern Europe, to the Pacific Rim. These loosely created economic trading units lack a crucial central social control device that makes our country what it is today—that is, a nationwide system of commercial law that provides uniformity and predictability in the commercial practices involving the movement and sale of goods from sovereign state to sovereign state. In this country, the law that applies to the sale of goods is essentially the same in all states. But, how do we create a nationwide system of uniform law when our country has fifty separate, independent states, and our contract law is a matter of state, not federal, law?

The answer is that our separate, autonomous states have seen it in their best interests to each adopt the same code that applies to the commercial sale of goods. This code is called the Uniform Commercial Code and has been adopted by all the states except Louisiana.* This code may become a model for all of the other sovereign trading nations that wish to form a more integrated economic market.

*Louisiana has adopted only Articles 1, 3, 4, and 5 of the UCC.

Introduction

personal property (personalty)
A movable thing, along with interests and rights in the thing

Our Uniform Commercial Code (UCC) is concerned with certain commercial transactions in, or regarding, **personal property,** and contracts and other documents concerning them. It has nine substantive articles. Part 5 of this book will focus primarily upon Article 2, Sales, and will include some explanation of Article 1, General Provisions, and Article 6, Bulk Transfers.

The Concept of a Code

code
A comprehensive, systematic collection of statutes in a particular legal area

There is a distinct difference between a code and other statutory enactments. A **code** is a comprehensive, systematic collection of statutes in a particular legal area. The Uniform Commercial Code contains and governs much of the law applicable to ordinary commercial transactions. A code, because of its comprehensive and integrated character, is its own best reference for interpretation. Noncode enactments are often fragmentary, and interpretation of them varies widely.

The purposes of the Uniform Commercial Code are set out in one of its initial passages as follows:

> **(a)** to simplify, clarify and modernize the law governing commercial transactions;
> **(b)** to permit the continued expansion of commercial practices through custom, usage and agreement of the parties; [and]
> **(c)** to make uniform the law among the various jurisdictions.[1]

History of the UCC

Proposals for uniform legislation for sales of goods have been made since the nineteenth century. One of the UCC's sponsors, the National Conference of Commissioners on Uniform State Laws, has been in existence since 1892 and has drafted approximately 170 Uniform Acts.[2] In 1940 this commission adopted a resolution to create a nationwide Uniform Commercial Code. The American Law Institute—an organization composed of over 1,500 law professors, judges, and leading attorneys—joined the National Conference in this endeavor, and between 1945 and 1952 numerous drafts and redrafts of the UCC were debated. In 1952 the first official edition of the Code was published. Today all states (except Louisiana) have adopted most of its articles. Many of the states have made a few small changes when adopting the Code, but it is essentially the same Code. The Code has been amended only four times. References in this text are to the 1978 Official Text and its **Comments.**

Comments to the UCC
Comments that appear at the end of the Code sections; they are not part of the official Code, but they are provided by the drafters to help explain and interpret the Code

The Legal Philosophy of Karl Llewellyn

Perhaps the single most influential person in the drafting of the UCC was its "chief reporter," Karl Llewellyn, a law professor at the University of Chicago Law School. He determined which subjects the UCC would cover and in what order. He was the principal

---

[1]UCC 1–102(2).

[2]For a fine but short history of the UCC, see W. D. Malcolm, "The Uniform Commercial Code," reprinted in *Uniform Commercial Code Handbook* (Chicago: American Bar Association, 1964), 1–19.

draftsman of Articles 1 and 2. Of greater importance, however, was the fact that much of the language of Articles 1 and 2 reflected notions Llewellyn held as a result of his commitment to "legal realism." Legal realism is a phrase used to designate a school of jurisprudential thought that maintains that the "law" *should reflect what is socially desirable in "reality."* Thus when one applies this notion to the development of a commercial code for the sale of goods, as Llewellyn did, one should appreciate the fact that the rules are an attempt to state simply and make uniform much of the changing current commercial practices. Llewellyn believed that commercial law should reflect the most desirable practices of business people.[3]

In our study of Articles 1 and 2, be mindful of the fact that the *words* of these Articles are but a starting point for our study. In many key instances the words direct us to current commercial practice to establish the standards for a transaction. No better example of this manifestation of Llewellyn's legal philosophy can be found than in the official comments to Section 2–302 on **unconscionable** contracts, one of the most important sections of Article 2, which provides in part:

unconscionable
Offensive to the conscience; immoderate, too one-sided

> The basic test [for unconscionability] is whether, *in the light of the general commercial background and the commercial needs of the particular trade or case,* the clauses involved are so one-sided as to be unconscionable under the circumstances . . . [Emphasis added]

This approach tells a court to look to current commercial needs to define an unconscionable clause in a contract. The genius of this approach to law accommodates the seemingly inconsistent needs of our commercial society. On the one hand, our commercial society demands consistency, regularity, and stability in its rules. On the other hand, because our commercial society is very dynamic, we must provide for change and development of the rules. The required measure of stability is provided by the fact that so many state legislatures have adopted the UCC and the fact that these state legislatures are discouraged from amending the Code. However, a means for growth is provided by the fact that in interpreting and applying the words of the UCC, especially Articles 1 and 2, attorneys and courts are directed to current commercial standards of performance to decide a case.[4] As the standards change, so do the meanings of some of the key words of the Sales Article.

Evaluation of the UCC

In general, has the Code been successful? A few legal scholars lament the soft structure and loose wording of the Code,[5] but because of its wide adoption and the growing amount of litigation (especially involving the provisions on warranties and unconscion-

[3]See Danzig, "A Comment on the Jurisprudence of the Uniform Commercial Code," 27 *Stan. L. Rev.* 621–35 (1975).

[4]The words "reasonable" and "unreasonable" appear at least 97 times in Article 2. See Bonsignore, "Existentialism, The Rule of Law and Article 2 of the Uniform Commercial Code," 8 *Am. Bus. L.J.* 133 (1970), 147.

[5]See Mellinkoff, "The Language of the Uniform Commercial Code," 77 *Yale L. Rev.* 185 (1967).

ability[6]), indicating developing definitions of key words, many scholars believe the Code has been successful in achieving its objectives. Indeed, one well respected authority has called the UCC "the most spectacular success story in the history of American law."[7]

As we move into the final years of this century, we know that international business and contracts with firms in foreign countries will become much more important, so our American law may change even though it has been successful. We can see the beginnings of this change in Chapter 57, which discusses business law in the international marketplace.

Introduction to Article 2: Transactions Covered

sale
The transfer "of title from seller to purchaser for a price" UCC 2–106(1)

security interest
"An interest in personal property or fixtures which secures payment or performance of an obligation" UCC 1–201(37)

gift
A voluntary transfer of personal or real property by someone who is not to receive anything in return

lease
Of goods, a form of contract giving the lessee the exclusive right to use or possess the goods of the lessor for a stated period

goods
Tangible, movable things

Article 2 applies (1) to commercial transactions (2) in goods.[8] A commercial transaction is usually interpreted to mean a **sale** of goods and does not include transactions where only a **security interest** is transferred or where a **gift** or a **lease** of goods is involved. In the following case the court did not use Article 2 directly, but referred to it indirectly when a lease was entered into.

FACTS

Plaintiff was a passenger in a truck rented by his employer from Hertz. It was alleged that the truck had defective brakes and the plaintiff was injured as a result. Should the plaintiff's claim against the defendant, Hertz, be determined by Article 2?

DECISION

The court held that no "sale" was involved, so Article 2 was not to be applied directly. However, the appellate court did find in the plaintiff's favor by relying both on the common law and the general policy embedded in the warranty provisions of the UCC. It held that the offering to the public of trucks and pleasure vehicles for hire necessarily carries with it a representation or implied warranty that they are fit for operation.

Cintrone v. Hertz Truck Leasing & Rental Serv., 212 A.2d 769 (N.J. 1965).

You will notice that the case above makes two important points. The first is that the UCC does not apply to leases of **goods.** The second is that just because the UCC is not directly applicable does not mean it cannot be used as a general reference to shape the rights and duties of parties to nonsales transactions. A central point of this chapter is that the UCC and Article 2 are more than an isolated grouping of statutes; they are a comprehensive treatment of commercial law enacted by almost all the states and represent the major policy statements regarding commercial transactions. The impact of the UCC in shaping commercial law may go far beyond its "technical" applications.[9] In

---

[6]See White, "Evaluating Article 2 of the Uniform Commercial Code: A Preliminary Empirical Expedition," 75 *Mich. L. Rev.* 1262 (1977).

[7]White and Summers, *Handbook of the Law Under the Uniform Commercial Code* (St. Paul: West Publishing, 1972), 5; and see White and Summers, *Uniform Commercial Code* 3d ed. (St Paul: West Publishing, 1988), 21.

[8]UCC 2–102.

[9]Nordstrom, *Handbook of the Law of Sales* (St. Paul: West Publishing, 1970), 43–44.

fact, as of 1988, one state, Oklahoma, had adopted the new Article 2A of the UCC, which applies to leases; most states though would still abide by the *Cintrone* case, holding that a lease is not covered by Article 2.

While the distinction between a sale and a lease of goods may appear somewhat artificial, the distinction between goods (tangible movable things that can be identified), on the one hand, and services and nonmovable things, on the other, is not. Goods are those things that must be dealt with *uniformly* by the states, or the value they have because they can be shipped and used elsewhere will be impaired. **Services**—such as those rendered by an accountant, a doctor, an architect, or a plumber—are peculiarly local in nature, and the necessity for uniform treatment by states is not as apparent. Also land and things so fastened to the land that they cannot be moved are not goods either because land is not movable. Of course, what is movable and what is not movable depends on the effort someone is willing to exert.[10] Even London Bridge was moved! Generally, however, Article 2 was intended to apply not to items of an extraordinary character, like London Bridge, but to things that normally can flow in commerce and can be reasonably identified.

service
Usually labor rendered by one person for another

Growing crops and timber are goods (2–105); and so are minerals (including oil and gas) and other substances or structures in the land if they are to be mined, extracted, or severed by the seller.[11] If minerals or structures in the land (not crops or timber) are to be mined or severed by the buyer, then the contract is viewed as a sale of an interest in land and is not covered by Article 2. The reason that minerals, etc. to be severed by the buyer are not covered by Article 2 is not explained clearly in the Code, but it seems that this is the traditional distinction recognized by the common law. That is, a lease of land to an oil company to extract oil and gas has always been treated as a lease of real property; a sale of coal to be mined by the seller has always been treated as a sale of goods and not a sale of an interest in land. The UCC maintains this distinction.

Investment securities such as stocks and bonds traditionally have been regulated separately (separately, that is, from goods), so they are excluded from Article 2. They are discussed in Chapter 45.

The most difficult distinction to make, however, is whether Article 2 applies to transactions involving *both* the sale of goods and the sale of services or labor. The "test" used to determine the applicability of Article 2 in this circumstance is clearly defined in the following case.

FACTS

The Cox brothers had operated a bowling alley for twenty years in Missouri Valley, Iowa. In February 1968 it was gutted by fire and they contracted with the plaintiff, Simek, to "rebuild" the bowling alley with "used" equipment. Some of the used equipment furnished did not operate properly, and, before the job was completed and the liabilities for the faulty equipment established, Simek died. The Cox brothers hired someone else to complete the work, and the representative of Simek's estate sued them for breach of contract. Should the obligations of the parties be determined by Article 2 of the UCC?

DECISION

The court held that Article 2 did apply even though the contract involved "substantial amounts" of labor. The test, it held, is not whether the contract involves a service too, but, granting that it does, "whether the pre-

---

[10]Nordstrom, 45.

[11]UCC 2–107.

DECISIONS (cont.)

dominant factor, the thrust, the purpose, reasonably stated, is the rendition of service with goods incidentally involved (e.g., a contract with an artist for a painting...) or is a transaction of sale, with labor incidentally involved (e.g., installation of a water heater in a bathroom....)"

Bonebrake v. Cox, 499 F.2d 951 (1974).

By applying the test in the *Bonebrake v. Cox* case to other cases, the courts have held that an operation requiring the transfusion of blood and a beauty parlor treatment requiring the sale of hair dye did not involve the sale of goods. These transactions involved a service as the predominant factor with the sale of goods incidental to the service.

An example of the need for commercial law to change and adapt to current commercial realities is highlighted by the question, "Is Article 2 applicable to the sale of data processing programs?" By applying the above test we can provide the answer. If the predominant factor in the transaction is the sale of data processing *services*, then Article 2 does not apply. However, the more the transaction involves data processing *equipment* such as mainframe computers, software, and various kinds of programs, the more likely the court will say the transaction is one involving the sale of goods. Although contracts for the exchange of pure ideas are not contracts for goods, once the idea takes the form of a computer program—in the form of a tape or otherwise—it becomes a good.[12]

future goods
"Goods which are not both existing and identified" to the contract UCC 2–105(2)

If a transaction in goods exists, then Article 2 applies whether or not the goods are in existence at the time the contract is made. In a later chapter we will discuss the consequences of distinguishing between "existing" and **"future" goods.** For the present, it is important just to note that if the predominant factor in a transaction is the sale of goods, then Article 2 applies even though the goods are to be made in the future.[13]

Standard of Conduct Under Article 2

► Good Faith

Article 2 preserves our fundamental American notions about freedom of contract by allowing the parties to vary the effect of Code provisions or determine standards of performance by their agreement. These standards of performance will be upheld as long as they are not "manifestly unreasonable."[14] One standard of performance that may not be waived or altered by agreement because it would be unreasonable is the requirement that "every contract" covered by the Code must be entered into and conducted in good faith.[15] *Good faith* is defined as "honesty in fact in the conduct or transaction concerned."[16] When **merchants** are involved, good faith also means "the observance of reasonable commercial standards of fair dealing in the trade." Almost every contract involves the exercise of some discretion. It is these discretionary elements that must be governed by the concept of good faith. The court found bad faith in the following case.

merchant
"A person who deals in goods of the kind or otherwise by his occupation holds himself out as having knowledge or skill peculiar to the practices or goods involved in the transaction" UCC 2–104(1)

[12]See, "Computer Programs as Goods Under the UCC," 77 *Mich. L. Rev.* 1149 (1979).

[13]UCC 2–105(2), 2–106(1).

[14]UCC 1–102(3).

[15]UCC 1–203.

[16]UCC 1–201(19).

FACTS

The plaintiff, seller, contracted to plant and cultivate 28 acres of beans. The defendant, buyer, was to use its own judgment as to when the beans would be ripe and was then to send its crew in to pick the beans. A severe drought in the area made the time for picking the beans very critical. The plaintiff notified the defendant that they should be picked by Tuesday, July 1. An agent for the buyer inspected the crops on June 30 and indicated they would be picked after Ennis's crop, which had been planted earlier than plaintiff's. The pickers finished Ennis's crop on July 2 but were directed by defendant to go elsewhere because the crops were of better quality. Defendant began picking plaintiff's crops on July 4, but stopped after a short while because the beans were of "unacceptable" quality. Did the defendant fail to meet its standard of performance?

DECISION

The trial court found for the plaintiff, and the appellate court affirmed this. The court held that matters of judgment in contractual understandings must be exercised honestly and in good faith. In this case, there was evidence which could demonstrate that the buyer's decision to delay harvesting the crop was not made in good faith. "To begin with there was testimony that the effect of hot temperatures and drought on any snap beans is not only to accelerate the maturing process but also to dehydrate the crop. . . . Since this type of crop, even under normal weather conditions, must be harvested within a few days of when it ripens, a three-day delay during a drought is evidence from which a jury may conclude bad faith was exhibited."

Dorsey Bros., Inc. v. Anderson, 287 A.2d 270, at 272 (Md. 1972).

The court decision above illustrates an interesting problem for the law and for an understanding of Article 2 in particular. Exactly how do you define "good faith"? Are there positive elements to the standard of good faith, or is good faith usually defined only in the negative. For example, the presence of bad faith shows the absence of good faith, thus an important standard under Article 2 has not been satisfied. As you can see from the above case, the court concludes that bad faith was present, thus there was an absence of good faith. Legal scholars have agreed with this approach and have said that the good faith requirement of Article 2 has no independent meaning of its own. It was intended as a device for courts to use to exclude certain types of conduct that they would label "bad faith" conduct.[17]

► Merchants

In the remaining chapters of Part 5 we will see that in some instances Article 2 imposes on merchants more rigid standards of performance than on nonmerchants. The common law of contracts did not recognize a difference between someone who sells goods only occasionally (e.g., selling a lawnmower at a garage sale) and someone who sells goods of a particular kind for a living (e.g., retailer). However, it seems obvious that someone who holds himself or herself out as a seller of goods of a particular kind should have a certain "expertise" in the sale of those items. Thus a "professional" seller or merchant should be held to a higher standard of care in some instances. This is a "realistic" view of some sales transactions.

One of the more troublesome applications of the term "merchants" involves farmers. Many people have gardens and grow all varieties of vegetables, fruits and flowers. Many such people have small, roadside structures from which they sell their produce or they sell it to neighbors or friends. Is such a seller a merchant? As one's business grows from

[17]Summers, " 'Good Faith' in General Contract Law and the Sales Provisions of the Uniform Commercial Code," 54 *Va. L. Rev.* 195 (1968).

a single sale to a friend to a more elaborate sales effort, at what point does one become a merchant? Courts have provided inconsistent answers to this question. Some courts have said that farmers are not merchants. But a more reasoned approach is that provided by the long case at the end of this chapter. Legal scholars have suggested that courts consider these questions in making their decision: How long has the person been in farming? What was the quantity sold? Did the contract involve a special planting? Did the seller belong to a trade association? Were there extensive negotiations involved?[18] If the answers to these questions tend to show the seller in question was representing that it had knowledge or skill particular to the goods sold, then the seller is a merchant.

Article 2 and the Common Law of Contracts

common law
Principles of nonstatutory law reflecting the customs and usages of society and found in judicial decisions

The fact that Article 2 imposes more rigid standards of performance on merchants than on nonmerchants when the **common law** did not do this highlights the fact that Article 2 does change some of the contract law you studied in Part 2. In general, the purpose of the Code changes was to recognize circumstances of current commercial practice not recognized by the common law of contracts. More specifically, Article 2 differs from "contract" law and embodies notions of current commercial practice in the following important areas (in addition to the distinction made for merchants noted above):

1. Statute of frauds
2. Firm offers
3. Additional terms in acceptance
4. Modification
5. Unconscionable contracts

Some of these changes were noted in Chapters 6 through 14, on contract law. However, here in Part 5 we will go into greater detail on these changes. Of course, in those areas of commercial law not covered by Article 2 (lease of goods, sale of an interest in land, contracts for services, etc.), the common law of contracts still controls.

It is impossible in such a complex area as the commercial sale of goods to enact a code that will stand alone in its application to appropriate factual situations. The Code was intended not to be read in isolation but together with and relying upon other areas of the law. It is very important to observe that other areas of the law—for example, the common law of contracts—*supplement* the Code that governs these areas. For example, to make a sale, we have to make a contract, and the common law of contracts applies, except as the Code changes the law of contracts or adds to it.[19]

Statute of Frauds

In Chapter 12, on the common law of contracts, we observed that an enactment by the English Parliament in 1677 called the Statute of Frauds stated that promises had to be evidenced by a writing before they would be *enforced* by a court. Both the present-day

---

[18]See Henkel and Shedd, "Article 2 of the Uniform Commercial Code: Is A Farmer A 'Merchant' or a 'Tiller of the Soil'?" 18 *Am. Bus. L.J.* 323 (1980).

[19]UCC 1–103.

law of contracts and the UCC retain the use of the phrase **statute of frauds** to designate those enforceable promises that must be evidenced by a writing.

statute of frauds

A statute requiring that certain kinds of contracts be proved only by a proper writing

Article 2 adds to the list of transactions under the law of contracts, to which the statute of frauds applies. It provides that a contract for the sale of goods for the price of $500 or more is not enforceable unless there is some writing (1) recognizing the contract, (2) stating the quantity of goods involved, and (3) signed by the party against whom enforcement is sought.[20] There is a distinction between saying the contract must be in writing and stating that the promises must be evidenced by a writing. Article 2 requires only written evidence of the contract. For example, *S* orally agrees to sell his car to *P* for $1,000 and *S* then refers to this fact in his letter to *Q*, *P*'s sister. *S* may not assert the statute of frauds as a defense if *P* should sue *S* for breach of *S*'s promise because the letter, if signed by *S*, is sufficient evidence of *S*'s promise to sell. This would be true even if the letter incorrectly stated one of the terms, but the promise would not be enforceable beyond the quantity of the goods referred to in the letter. Office memos, minutes of a board of directors' meeting, and the like may also be used.

▶ Purpose of the Statute of Frauds

The purpose of the statute of frauds is to protect an innocent party against others who might fraudulently assert that the innocent party had promised to perform. The opportunity for fraud is minimized when there is some evidence that a party who made an oral promise has begun to perform. Article 2 recognizes this and provides that an oral promise is enforceable without a writing when: (1) goods are to be specially manufactured for the buyer, and they are not suitable for sale to others in the ordinary course of the seller's business, and the seller has made either a substantial beginning of their manufacture or commitments for their procurement;[21] or, (2) if the party being charged admits in its pleadings or testimony in court that a contract was made;[22] or, (3) if the party being charged has either paid for the goods in question or accepted the goods.[23] It should be obvious that, in these three circumstances, the *actions* of the party being charged with having made a contract have themselves minimized the chance for fraud: the party has either begun work on the goods requested, admitted the contract, or paid for or accepted the goods.

FACTS

Frank Adams and Company (Adams) alleged that Baker telephoned an order for 1,514 steel reinforcing rods to be delivered to Baker's construction site. The rods were delivered and some of them were cut to various lengths specified in Baker's drawings which an agent of Adams had allegedly seen. Also, some of the rods were bent to the shape of an "L" with a hook at the tip of the base, also complying with Baker's drawings. Baker alleged he never visited the construction site and denied he ordered the steel rods. Adams sued for the purchase price. There is no writing signed by Baker. Does the statute of frauds bar Adams' claim?

DECISION

The court held that the statute of frauds does not bar Adams' claim because UCC 2–201

[20] UCC 2–201(1).

[21] UCC 2–201(3)(a).

[22] UCC 2–201(3)(b).

[23] UCC 2–201(3)(c).

DECISION (cont.)

(3)(a) and (c) both apply. The statute of frauds does not bar an assertion that there is an oral contract when the goods are to be specially manufactured and are not suitable for sale to others in the ordinary course of business. The court said there was evidence which established the rods were bent to comply with the drawings of Baker and because some were cut and some bent they were not suitable for sale to others in the ordinary course of business. Moreover, Baker made no attempt to reject the goods within a reasonable time after delivery since he admitted he never did visit the construction site.

Frank Adams and Co. v. Baker, 439 N.E.2d 953 (Ohio, 1981)

Merchants and the Statute of Frauds

confirmation
An assuring expression of understanding

Finally, Article 2's version of the statute of frauds recognizes a different standard of performance for merchants and in so doing substantially changes the older common law interpretations. It provides that, if a *written* **confirmation** of the contract is sent by one merchant to another merchant within a reasonable time of the exchange of oral promises and the receiver has reason to know its contents, it satisfies the writing requirement for both the sender and the receiver even though not signed by the receiver, unless the receiver objects to its contents within ten days of receipt.[24] Since much of today's business is conducted by one merchant's merely filling in a few blanks on a form and sending it off to another merchant, this section of the statute puts a duty on merchants to read their mail! If the merchant receiving the form or confirmation has no intent to contract with the sending merchant and has reason to know the contents of the form, then the receiving merchant must reject the form within ten days. If this is not done, the receiving merchant may be bound by the terms on the form of the sending party.

Contents of the Writing

In general, Article 2 is fairly liberal in allowing evidence of an oral contract. The Code Comments to the statute of frauds section make it clear that, when a writing is required, it need not state the price, time, or place of payment or delivery, nor the general quality of the goods. Business people frequently base their agreement as to price on a price list or catalogue known to both of them. Therefore the only three essential ingredients of the required evidence of a writing are that (1) it must refer to a contract for the *sale of goods* between the parties, (2) it must specify the *quantity* of goods, and (3) it must be *signed by the party* to be charged with performance of the contract. A diagram of Article 2's statute of frauds (2–201) might appear as in Figure 23.1.

Applying the Statute of Frauds

In applying Section 2–201 to a factual situation, we must keep the position of the parties in mind. In a case where the plaintiff alleges that the defendant orally promised to sell or buy goods, it is most likely that the plaintiff's claim is true. *Usually* the plaintiff is asserting the existence of an agreement with the defendant and the fact that the defendant did not perform in some respect. The plaintiff, then, is met with a defense. It is a defense that does not go to the merits of the case but is intended to clarify preliminary matters about precisely what was agreed upon, if anything, and to minimize

[24]UCC 2–201(2).

FIGURE 23.1 **Diagram of Article 2's Statute of Frauds**

Exchange of Oral Promises for the Sale of Goods Between:	A	B	C
Nonmerchant	No written evidence of promises required if: (1) goods are to be specially manufactured and are not suitable for sale to others in the ordinary course of the seller's business, and there has been a substantial beginning on their manufacture or a commitment for their procurement; or (2) party against whom enforcement is sought admits in court that the contract was made; or (3) part or full payment was received and accepted, or part or all of the goods was received and accepted.	If transaction does not qualify in ***A*** and price of goods is $500 or over, then ⇒	Written evidence of the promises is required and must be signed by the party to be charged and must state the quantity of the goods sold.
Merchant	No written evidence of promises signed by party to be charged if within a reasonable time of the exchange of oral promises one of the merchants sends a written confirmation stating the quantity of the goods *and* the receiver has reason to know its contents *and* does not object in writing within 10 days of its receipt.	If transaction does not qualify in ***A*** and price of goods is $500 or over, then ⇒	Written evidence of the promises is required and must be signed by the party to be charged and must state the quantity of the goods sold.

the chances of fraud.[25] The defense asserts that the statute of frauds requires a signed writing (unless the parties are merchants) sufficient to allow the plaintiff to continue with the proof, and no such writing exists. At this point the court focuses upon the sufficiency of the writings, if any, or other facts required by the statute of frauds. If these requirements are not met, the court will hold that a good defense exists and dismiss the case for lack of proof that a required signed writing was made by the defendant. However, if the requirements are met, then this simply means the plaintiff must proceed with proof of the contents of the contract, its breach, and loss. Because the defense of the statute of frauds is overcome, do not assume that the plaintiff has won. Substantial problems of proof may remain. The plaintiff must still prove that there was an offer and acceptance, consideration, breach, damage, etc.

► Evaluating the Statute of Frauds

In recent years the statute of frauds has been criticized because, despite its avowed purpose of eliminating fraud, it also offers the possibility for creating fraud. Consider this example. *D* orally agreed to build and stock a store for *P*. *P* sold a bakery business and

[25]Nordstrom, p. 54.

purchased a site for the new store. Then, the deal fell through before there was any writing. *P* sued *D* on *D*'s promise to build and stock the store.[26] A literal application of the statute of frauds would defeat *P*'s action. In this case, the court applied **equitable estoppel** to *D* and allowed *P* to state a good claim. However, if equitable estoppel were not used in this case and the court applied the statute of frauds, then *P* would clearly be unfairly treated. Some commentators have said that the commercial realities of today reveal there is a great reliance on oral promises and thus, oral promises deserve legal protection. Moreover, some have said that the statute of frauds is an anachronistic device that results in such a probability concerning *P*, that it will be used to perpetuate a fraud, and that it outweighs any utility that it may possess as a method for fraud protection.[27] However, the statute still exists in all states, but there is an increasing use of equitable estoppel to mitigate its harsher applications.[28]

equitable estoppel
A doctrine that operates to prevent a person from denying anything to the contrary of that which, by the person's own deeds, acts, or representations, has been set forward as the truth

Parol or Extrinsic Evidence

An issue often perceived as closely related to the application of the statute of frauds—but, in reality, quite different—is the use of oral testimony **(parol evidence)** or written evidence to clarify a *written* understanding. The usual position of the parties when we see the **parol evidence rule** asserted is that the plaintiff has introduced as evidence a *writing* that purports to be "the understanding" between the parties. The defendant admits the existence and signing of the document but counters with an assertion that one of the terms of the writing was varied or modified by a *prior* oral understanding or other evidence. For example,[29] buyer and seller exchange memoranda confirming a telephone conversation in which the buyer agreed to purchase goods for "$35 per hundredweight." The seller ships the goods, and the buyer now claims that, during the initial phone conversation, the seller agreed to give the buyer a 2 percent discount if payments were made within ten days of the invoice date. The seller claims that the parol evidence should not be admitted because it would vary or contradict their memoranda. Should the parol evidence be admitted?

parol evidence
Oral testimony

parol evidence rule
A rule of law providing that, when there is a written contract, it cannot be contradicted (added to or varied) by any prior or contemporaneous oral agreement, or by a prior written agreement

Article 2 attempts to cover this rather common situation by providing:

> Terms with respect to which confirmatory memoranda of the parties agree or which are otherwise set forth in writing intended by the parties as a final expression of their agreement with respect to such terms . . . may not be contradicted by evidence of any prior agreement or of a contemporaneous oral agreement but may be explained or supplemented:
>
> **(a)** by course of dealing or usage of trade . . . or by course of performance . . .; and
>
> **(b)** by evidence of consistent additional terms unless the court finds the writing to have been intended also as a complete and exclusive statement of the terms of the agreement.[30]

---

[26]See *Hoffman v. Red Owl Stores, Inc.*, 133 N.W.2d 267 (Wisc. 1965).

[27]Metzger and Phillips, "Promissory Estoppel and Section 2–201 of the Uniform Commercial Code," 26 *Vill. L. Rev.* 63 (1981).

[28]Ibid.

[29]Nordstrom, p. 164.

[30]UCC 2–202.

▶ Application of the Parol Evidence Rule

The key features of this section direct a court first to find whether the parties intended their writing, namely the memoranda in question, to be a "final" expression of their agreement with respect to the "term" in question. If a court so finds, then any oral (parol) or other evidence of an agreement between the parties which occurred *before,* and any oral agreement which occurred *contemporaneously* with, the writing will not be admitted if it contradicts the writing. Please note that oral agreements made *after* the confirmatory memoranda will be admissible as evidence unless the statute of frauds requires their exclusion.

In our example above, if a court finds from the evidence that the parties intended their memoranda as a final expression of their agreement, then it must decide if the evidence of a discount contradicts the price term or not. Whether it does so in our example is not perfectly clear. The UCC definition of the word *term* is "that portion of an agreement which relates to a particular matter."[31] If the words "particular matter" are interpreted to mean "price," then a court could exclude the oral testimony about the discount. Perhaps this is the best result, because "discounts" are very directly related to "price." However, if a court recognizes that within a given industry discounts are customarily given, and have been given between the two parties in the past, then it might decide to admit the oral evidence on the basis that there is no contradiction but a mere explanation of the term. Evidence that *explains* and does not contradict will be admissible. The parol evidence rule will not be applied in situations where one of the parties is alleging that contractual capacity was lacking, or that the agreement was procured through fraud, duress, or illegality. The following case is an example of the application of the parol evidence rule, Section 2–202 of Article 2.

FACTS

Philipp Brothers Division of Engelhard Minerals and Chemicals Corporation, buyer, plaintiff, agreed to buy sugar from the defendant, El Salto, S. A., seller, in five written contracts made in the months of September, October and November, 1979. The contracts were expressed on a standard written form. From September 1979, through March 1980, there were extensive communications between the parties by letter, telephone and personal visits. The defendant seller contends that during this period (after some of the contracts in question had been made) the parties had orally agreed that Philipp would furnish $750,000 in cash advances on the contract so that the El Salto could purchase sugar cane for processing. Philipp, buyer, did not make such advances and the defendant declared the contracts void as of February 19, 1980. The buyer sues the seller for breach of contract. The defendant argued that oral evidence about the cash advance should be admitted.

DECISION

The court held for the plaintiff, buyer. The defendant argued that the oral evidence of the cash advance should be admitted because the parties did not intend the written form contracts to be a final expression of their agreement. The court said that this issue is to be resolved by measuring the completeness of the written instrument itself and not on the basis of evidence of the subjective beliefs of the parties. The language relating to payment makes no provision for advance payments. "We thus conclude that the law of New York (section 2–202 of Article 2) forbids the admissibility of oral evidence to prove the alleged requirement for a cash advance. Admissibility of such evidence would altogether vary the complete and clear terms of the contract.

Philipp Bros. Div. of Engelhard Minerals & Chemicals Corp. v. El Salto, S. A., 487 F.Supp. 91 (1980).

---

[31] UCC 1–201(42).

We can see from our study of both the statute of frauds and the parol evidence sections how Article 2 attempts to achieve the main objectives of the UCC. Both sections require merchants and others to meet certain minimum standards in the statement and modification of their agreement for the sale of goods. Yet, in defining these standards, the parties are allowed a large measure of flexibility. This flexibility is intended to reflect changes in custom and commercial usage of documents dictated by an ever-changing commercial world.

Summary Statement

1. The purposes of the Uniform Commercial Code are to simplify, clarify, and modernize the law governing commercial transactions; to permit the growth of commercial law; and to make uniform the commercial law of the various states.
2. Article 2 of the UCC was drafted by Karl Llewellyn, who believed that the best commercial rules were those that reflected the best parts of current commercial practice. Article 2 uses such words as "reasonable" and "good faith" so that courts may update the Article by continuing to focus on the best commercial conduct as defining what is "reasonable" and so forth.
3. Article 2 applies to transactions in *goods* and does not apply to leases, gifts, the sale of an interest in land (and other nonmovables), investment securities, and services.
4. Every transaction for the sale of goods covered by Article 2 must be conducted in good faith.
5. Even though Article 2 changes some of the rules of the common law of contracts, the latter still supplements the UCC and is applicable in cases where Article 2 or the UCC do not provide the answer to a legal question.
6. Article 2's statute of frauds provision provides that a contract for the sale of goods for the price of $500 or more is not enforceable unless there is some writing recognizing the contract and stating the quantity of goods involved, and it is signed by the party against whom enforcement of the contract is sought. No writing is needed under the following circumstances:
   - **a)** The goods are to be specially manufactured for the buyer, they are not suitable for sale to others in the ordinary course of the seller's business, and the seller has made either a substantial beginning of their manufacture or commitments for their procurement.
   - **b)** The party being charged admits in court that a contract was made.
   - **c)** The party being charged with performance of the contract has paid for or accepted the goods.
7. If a written confirmation of the contract is sent by one merchant to another merchant within a reasonable time of the exchange of oral promises, and the receiver has reason to know its contents, it satisfies the writing requirement for both the sender and receiver even though not signed by the receiver, unless the receiver objects to its contents within ten days of receipt.
8. The parol evidence rule is a rule of evidence that excludes testimony of an oral agreement made prior to, or contemporaneously with, a written agreement, or a prior written agreement, which would contradict the written agreement.

The following case is a good example of how the Code's statute of frauds is applied to merchants.

CAMPBELL v. YOKEL
313 N.E.2d 628 (Ill. 1974)

Crebs, J. The plaintiffs, owners and operators of the Campbell Grain and Seed Company, alleged that they had reached an oral agreement on February 7, 1973 with the defendant group of farmers to purchase 6,800 to 7,200 bushels of yellow soybeans at a price of $5.30 per bushel. After the conversation between the plaintiffs and the defendants on February 7, the plaintiffs signed and mailed a written confirmation of the oral agreement. Defendants received the written confirmation but did not sign it or give any notice of objection to its contents to the plaintiffs. The defendants refused to deliver any soybeans to the plaintiffs and, on April 30, 1973, informed the plaintiffs that, since the defendants did not sign the written confirmation, they were not bound by it. They also stated that it was their understanding that the agreement was tentative and was not to be binding unless a written contract was signed.

The plaintiffs rely on UCC 2–201(2), the Statute of Frauds, which provides that there is no writing required if:

> Between merchants if within a reasonable time a writing in confirmation of the contract and sufficient against the sender is received and the party receiving it has reason to know its contents, it satisfies the requirements of subsection (1) against such parties unless notice of objection to its contents is given within 10 days after it is received.

The first issue the court had to decide was whether the defendants were merchants. The court noted that some state courts have held that farmers were not merchants but that the better reasoned opinions held that farmers were merchants, especially with regard to an agreement to sell growing crops. UCC 2–104(1) defines a merchant as

> a person who deals in goods of the kind or otherwise by his occupation holds himself out as having knowledge or skill peculiar to the practices or goods involved in the transaction or to whom such knowledge or skill may be attributed by his employment. . . .

The defendants admitted in discovery depositions that they had grown and sold soybeans and other grains for several years. The court concluded that "we believe that a farmer who regularly sells his crops is a person who 'deals in goods of that kind.' " Holding that farmers are merchants and applying Section 2–201(2) of the Statute of Frauds to these defendants lessens the possibility that the Statute of Frauds would be used as an instrument of fraud. For example, assuming that an oral agreement had been reached, . . . that the farmers had received written confirmation signed by the plaintiffs, and that the farmers were not "merchants," the farmers would be in a position to speculate on a contract to which the grain company was bound. If the market price fell after the agreement had been reached, the farmers could produce the written confirmation and enforce the contract. If the market price rose, the farmers could claim the protection of the Statute of Frauds and sell their crops on the open market.

The court concluded, "Our decision is not tantamount to a finding that a contract did exist between plaintiffs and defendants. We hold merely that since the defendants were merchants Section 2–201(2) operates to bar the defendants from asserting the defense of the Statute of Frauds. The burden of persuading the trier of fact that an oral contract was in fact made prior to the written confirmation is unaffected."

Questions and Case Problems

1. In your own words, write a short but complete paragraph describing the need for a uniform commercial code, the purposes of the UCC, and the basic philosophy underlying many of Article 2's key provisions.
2. The plaintiff, a manufacturer of textiles, contracted with the defendant, a large processor of textiles, to "finish" and dye a large quantity of unfinished textiles. The

defendant accepted a large shipment of textiles from the plaintiff and "finished" and dyed the material and then sent it on to the plaintiff's customer. The defendant billed the plaintiff, but the plaintiff refuses to pay because it maintains that the defendant improperly performed the finishing and dyeing and this was a breach of warranty. The plaintiff sues the defendant for breach of implied warranty; but before the parties can reach the issue of the breach of warranty, the defendant moves to dismiss the case because it is not governed by the UCC. The plaintiff maintains that the UCC applies. How would a court decide this issue? Is the defendant right? [*Manes Org., Inc. v. Standard Dyeing and Finishing Co.,* 472 F.Supp. 687 (D.C.S.D.N.Y. 1979).]

3. Contractors Equipment and Supply Co. (CESCO) leased a forklift to McCrory and it was delivered together with a signed lease from CESCO. McCrory used the forklift for a while and then asserted that at the time of the lease agreement, the president of CESCO promised McCrory an option to buy the forklift for $40,000 and, against this purchase price, McCrory would also receive a credit of 90 percent of the past rental payments. The president of CESCO died and McCrory refused to make rental payments, alleging that he was exercising his agreement to buy the forklift. CESCO sues for back lease payments and McCrory asserts a valid oral contract for the sale of the forklift and says any amounts to be paid must be credited toward the purchase price. The signed lease agreement said nothing about the purchase arrangement. Will CESCO be successful in asserting the statute of frauds against McCrory's claim? [*W. H. McCrory & Co. v. Contractors Equip. & Supply Co.,* 691 S.W.2d 717 (Tex. 1985).]

4. The plaintiffs allege that they entered into a contract with the defendants for the purchase of a Falcon Jet, Model 50, for a total consideration of $9.4 million. The defendants allege that the series of meetings held with the plaintiffs did include discussions of the sale of the aircraft but no final terms were agreed to and no written agreement existed that could satisfy the statute of frauds. The plaintiffs counter and prove that a check for $250,000 had been accepted by the defendants as a deposit on the aircraft. The defendants allege that the check was payment as an option and all defendants were obligated to do was hold the plane off the market. With regard to the defendant's claim that the statute of frauds applied in this case, since there was no writing should a court enter judgment for them on these facts? [*Songbird Jet Ltd., Inc. v. Amax, Inc.,* 581 F.Supp. 912 (S.D.N.Y. 1984).]

5. A printing company, the plaintiff, accepted typed and edited pages and other material from the defendant, publisher of a magazine, sufficient for the printing company to print the magazine. Fifteen thousand copies of the magazine were printed based on the publisher's original copy as submitted to the printer. After the printing, the printer submits a bill for more than the publisher says they agreed upon. The printer argues that under the UCC no new consideration is needed for a modification of the original agreement. The defendant argues that the UCC is not applicable. Make this argument for the publisher. Do you think a court would agree? State why or why not. [*Gross Valentino Printing Co. v. Clarke,* 458 N.E.2d 1027 (Ill. 1983).]

6. Indicate which, if any, of the following transactions and legal disputes arising therefrom would be governed by sections of Articles 1 and 2 of the UCC:

a) A written contract in which *S* agrees to manufacture special parts for *P*, which are not currently in existence

b) An oral contract for the sale of a used car from one neighbor to another for $450

c) An oral contract to paint your neighbor's house for $800

d) A contract to sell an **easement** over your farm, so a neighbor may water cattle in your stream

easement
An irrevocable right to the limited use of another's land

e) A written contract to sell your house and lot
f) A written agreement to buy a TV set from Sears
g) An agreement made with an oil drilling company to drill for oil on your land
h) A written agreement to sell your fall crop of apples, which will be picked by you
i) An agreement to lease your sailboat to a friend for the summer
j) An oral agreement you make to purchase, cut, and haul away all of the dead trees in a large forest owned by a farmer for $600

7. The plaintiff bought a used car from the defendant, a car dealer. The plaintiff signed a contract that clearly stated there were no warranties made by the seller beyond the manufacturer's new car warranty insofar as it may be applicable. Several weeks after the purchase, the plaintiff alleges, the paint on the car developed "defects." The plaintiff sues the defendant for the value of a new paint job and attempts to state at the trial that the defendant's agent made certain oral representations about the condition of the car (and paint) at the time of the sale. Should oral testimony of the representations or warranties of the seller's agent be admissible? [*Tracy v. Vinton Motors, Inc.*, 296 A.2d 269 (Vt. 1972).]

8. The plaintiff, Lipschutz, a large New York wholesaler of diamonds, sends a **consignment** of diamonds to the defendant, Linz, a retailer of diamonds. The defendant acknowledges receipt of the diamonds by sending the following "all risk" memorandum to the wholesaler:

consignment
The shipment of goods from one person to another

> Received on consignment from Lipschutz & Gartwirth Co., 630 Fifth Avenue, New York City, the following goods pursuant to the following agreement: "The goods described and valued as below are delivered to undersigned Linz Bros. for examination, . . . and shall be at once returned to you on demand. The undersigned assumes full and unqualified responsibility for the absolute return of the said property, or the cash proceeds to you on demand, without any excuse or defense whatsoever. . . ."

After receipt of the diamonds, there was a robbery at Linz in which merchandise valued at $1.5 million (retail value) was taken; of this amount, Lipschutz owned $700,000. The insurance policy of Linz did not cover the entire *retail* value of the loss. The plaintiff asserts the defendant Linz is liable for the full retail market value of its diamonds, $700,000. The defense argues that custom and trade usage in the diamond business establish that, where the loss is the result of a robbery and there is insufficient insurance, the consignee is liable not for the retail value of the diamonds, but the consignor's actual cost plus a small percentage to cover the costs of handling the diamonds. Should oral and other evidence be admitted to substantiate the defendant's arguments? [*Lipschutz v. Gordon Jewelry Corp.*, 373 F.Supp. 375 (S.D. Tex. 1974).]

9. *P*, a store owner, entered into a written contract with *S*, an air conditioning company, to purchase an air conditioning system and to have it installed in the store. The contract referred to a sale and installation of an "air conditioning apparatus." The total contract price was $1,200. The contract contained this statement: "This contract contains the entire agreement of the parties, and no representations or promises or warranties of any kind and no other agreements written or oral exist except as contained in this written agreement."

a) In a dispute between *P* and *S* that centers on the sufficiency of the "air conditioning apparatus," will *S* be allowed to introduce oral or extrinsic testimony to prove that it was the parties' intent to have installed a G.E. air conditioning unit #L.B. 4 and not a larger model as *P* argues? How will this dispute be resolved?

b) Disregard 9(a) and assume that, three days after *P* receives the written contract, *P* decides to purchase the unit and have the employees of *P* install it. *P* telephones *S* and *S* agrees to sell an air conditioning unit to *P* for $900 and not to provide the installation. A dispute between *P* and *S* develops, and *P* sues *S*. May *S* successfully assert the parol evidence rule to defeat *P*'s attempt to introduce evidence of the oral modification? Does *S* have another defense?

10. In the case of *Campbell v. Yokel,* excerpted at the beginning of this section, a farmer was held to be a merchant. Discuss how a farmer may not be a merchant.

CHAPTER

24

FORMATION AND INTERPRETATION OF THE SALES CONTRACT

After you have read this chapter, you should be able to:

1. Describe the general circumstances in which merchants contract.
2. State how the UCC altered the common law of offer and acceptance in the creation of a sales contract.
3. Describe how Section 2–207 resolves some of the problems created by the fact that most merchants do business by exchanging forms.
4. Define course of performance, course of dealing, and usage of trade and then clearly state how these terms are used by courts to help them ascertain the parties' intended meanings of words used by them.
5. State how the UCC allows merchants to modify a contractual agreement and state the circumstances in which a court might decide that a party has waived a contractual provision.
6. Define an insurable interest; describe when an insurable interest is created in a buyer; then define when the "risk of loss" for damage to or destruction of goods passes to the buyer; and, finally, be able to differentiate between the creation of an insurable interest and passage of the risk of loss.

BUSINESS DECISIONS and the LAW

When corporate giant Bethlehem Steel Corporation wanted five ships constructed to carry iron ore and manufactured products, it contacted Litton Industries, one of the largest builders of ships in this country. The total value of the construction contract for the five ships exceeded $100 million. The construction of these ships, ranging in value from $18.4 million to $22.4 million, was the subject of long negotiations with perhaps hundreds of phone calls, letters, documents such as technical design plans, and complex financing arrangements involving dozens of employees. In this mass of very complicated communications, where is "The Contract"? Can the understanding of the parties ever be reduced to one single document that covers everything? What laws apply to such a transaction?

The answer to the last question is the simplest. Article 2 of the Uniform Commercial Code applies and can be used to help the parties and, if need be, a court will decide what the contractual understanding of the parties is. A complex transaction such as this one can probably not be covered in one document but must be understood to involve many levels of understanding that only a commitment to deal in good faith can accomplish so that the parties are satisfied. But the challenge for the law in this instance is substantial. We see two very large merchants working for their own benefit and their conduct is controlled by the agreements they make and by Article 2. This Article sets the outlines of permissible behavior, it sets the context in which these parties negotiate and, when their understandings are not clear, it provides the means by which conflicts will be resolved.

Introduction

In this chapter we focus on the law of the sale of goods as applied to exchanges between two merchants. We will be concerned with many issues: When does a negotiation become a binding contract? What happens when provisions in form contracts conflict? Who suffers loss when goods are destroyed? We will also examine other parts of the law that give merchants the confidence to make contracts such as the proposed Bethlehem-Litton agreement.

Well regarded social commentators such as John Kenneth Galbraith and Kenneth Boulding[1] emphasize that the abstract images we use to interpret reality change much more slowly than does reality. In order to understand today's rapidly changing world, we must modify our collective and individual images of reality. The conventional wisdom about the law, its rules, its functions, and its value lags behind the fast-moving sociological and economic events of our day. A good illustration of this can be found by pointing out that it is a common belief (the conventional wisdom) that consumers "contract" in the traditional sense when they purchase consumer goods from a merchant. At the heart of our conventional wisdom about "contracting" is the notion that the parties **bargain** or **negotiate.** This implies that they are each aware of all unfavorable and favorable terms, and they consciously select those that best serve their interests.

bargain/negotiate
Terms used to indicate that both parties to a sales contract are aware of all the terms of the contract and that both parties exchanged value to establish the terms

Yet this image does not reflect reality, and it misleads us in our study of the law. When was the last time you made a "bargain" or "negotiated" the terms of a sale as a consumer? The belief that one "bargains" with Standard Oil, Sears, General Motors, a McDonald's restaurant, the Adidas sports shop, or a utility such as your local electric or gas company and almost all merchant-sellers of goods persists today despite the fact that many of the notions you have learned about "contracting" are not applicable.[2] You may shop around and choose from several alternatives, but when the "bargain" is struck, you as a consumer take what is *given*!

The disparity between how one imagines contracting is done and how it is, in fact, done is greatest with regard to the sale of goods from a merchant to a consumer. The standardized contract produced by the thousands or, in the case of very large merchants, by the millions, is the rule of the day. Moreover, it is reasonable to expect that such contracts are more favorable to their authors than to the other party to the transaction. Add to this the realization that when the UCC was adopted in most of the states, the interests of merchants dominated those of consumers, so some commentators believed the UCC was biased toward merchants.

---

[1]Galbraith, *The Affluent Society* (Boston: Houghton Mifflin, 1958); Boulding, *The Image* (Ann Arbor: University of Michigan Press, 1956).

[2]On the diminished role of contract law and doctrine generally, see Friedman, *Contract Law in America: A Social and Economic Study* (Madison: University of Wisconsin Press, 1965), and Gilmore, *The Death of Contract* (Columbus, Ohio: State University Press, 1974).

We only wish to emphasize at this point that it is useful to imagine at least two general patterns of commercial conduct (with numerous variations) and, consequently, two broad categories of commercial law. On the one hand, we have commercial activity in large economically concentrated markets in which, generally, *merchants deal with merchants*. On the other hand, we have the retail level of markets for goods in which large, *powerful merchants contract with consumers*.

Since the reality is that we have at least these two general commercial patterns and two categories of legal principles, we have separated the remaining material in this Part on the UCC into two broad categories. This chapter and Chapters 25 and 26 are largely based on an image of the parties involved both being merchants. Chapters 27 and 28 are on consumer law and the image here should be one of a consumer contracting with a merchant.

► A General Pattern of Commercial Conduct

Today, dealings between merchants, especially the large corporate merchants, are often conducted by employees at a low level in the corporate organization who use standardized forms provided by their legal departments or management. These employees do not think of themselves as "contracting," but they do realize that they place and receive "orders" or "confirmations," using "order forms," "quotation forms," or any of a series of forms provided for use.

Very often a supplier will provide a catalogue with prices and descriptions of goods, and the first response from a merchant purchaser may be by telephone, asking for clarifications of price or credit terms. If the response is satisfactory, the purchaser's employee will take a form from a drawer and, in the blank spaces, either write or type the price, description of the goods, quantity, delivery time and means of transportation, and credit terms. When the seller receives the form, an employee will usually transfer the crucial information from the filled-in blanks (after perhaps varying some terms) to the seller company's "confirmation" form and send it back to the purchaser. (See Figure 24.1.) If the "contract" is a complex one, as for the construction of a large machine or the sale of complex goods over a period of years, it is highly likely that the exchange of forms was preceded by "negotiations" at several levels within the two corporate organizations.

Moreover, after the exchange of forms, there may be numerous further changes or modifications as the economic, technological, or political environment changes. In addition to the forms, there may be telephone calls, letters, resolutions from the board of directors, intracorporate communications, standard operating procedures, and other similar pieces of evidence, all of which reflect the understanding of the parties.

If one were to attempt to apply the common law contract rules of offer and acceptance to this typical situation, then a court would be compelled to hold that no contract existed because a few essential terms in the offer or acceptance varied. Under the common law, an acceptance was effective only if it "mirrored" the offer by completely complying with the offer, the terms of the acceptance being identical to the terms of the offer. Given the common actual pattern of commercial activity as sketched above, this result would be absurd, especially when one considers that it was the terms and not the general intent which had been varied. The authors of the UCC recognized this and drafted Article 2 to reflect reality.

The remaining portion of this chapter will focus upon contract formation and interpretation and the various ways that both large and small merchants may protect themselves from loss caused by damage or destruction to the goods. We will use the above general factual pattern to establish an image of current commercial realities.

FIGURE 24.1 A General Pattern of Commercial Conduct

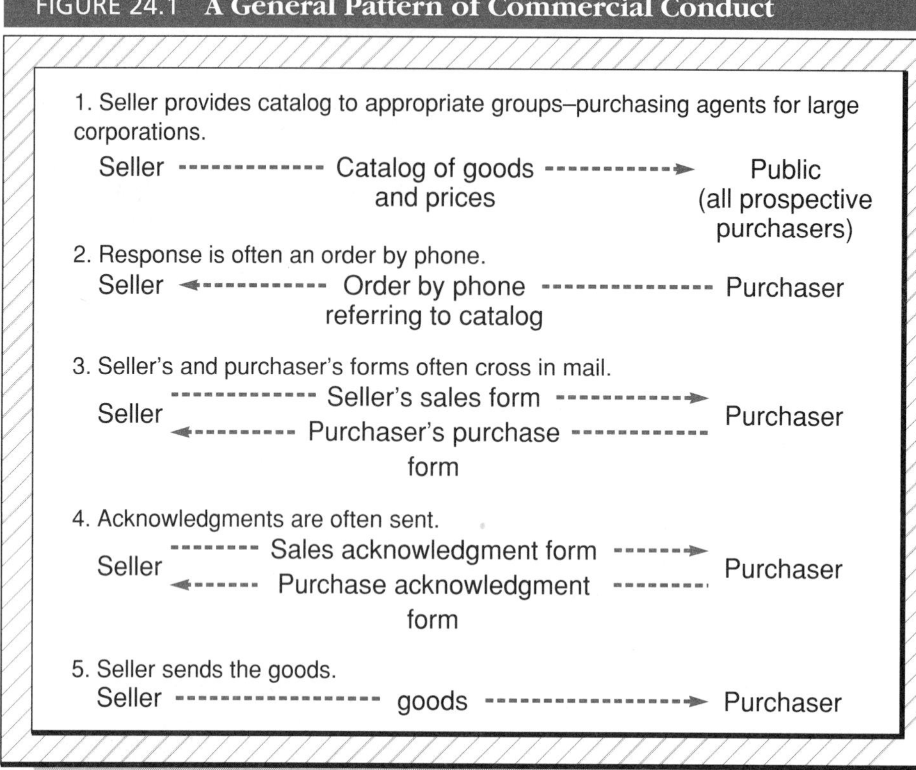
1. Seller provides catalog to appropriate groups–purchasing agents for large corporations.
Seller
Catalog of goods and prices
Public (all prospective purchasers)
2. Response is often an order by phone.
Seller
Order by phone referring to catalog
Purchaser
3. Seller's and purchaser's forms often cross in mail.
Seller
Seller's sales form
Purchaser's purchase form
Purchaser
4. Acknowledgments are often sent.
Seller
Sales acknowledgment form
Purchase acknowledgment form
Purchaser
5. Seller sends the goods.
Seller
goods
Purchaser

Contract Formation—Offer and Acceptance

How is a sales contract made? Article 2 substantially changes the common law doctrines of contract formation. It provides that a contract for the sale of goods may be made in *any* manner sufficient to show *agreement* by the parties.[3] This includes conduct by both parties that recognizes the existence of a contract. Moreover, it states that a contract for the sale of goods may be found to exist even though the moment of its making is undetermined or one or more terms are left open, so long as a court could find the general intent to contract and there is a reasonably certain basis for giving an appropriate remedy for its breach.[4] The Official Comments to Section 2–204 add that commercial standards on the degree of "indefiniteness" should be applied and that, generally, the more terms the parties leave open, the less likely it is they have intended to be bound. In many instances a party's actions may be frequently conclusive on the matter despite the omissions. This is illustrated by the following case.

[3]UCC 2–204(1).

[4]UCC 2–204(3).

FACTS

The plaintiff, Admiral Plastics Corporation, ordered three specially designed machines from the defendant, Trueblood, Inc. The chief engineer for the plaintiff, Paul Marcus, was told by the defendant at the time of the initial contact that the defendant had never made machines of the type ordered but would consider doing so if Admiral would provide the specifications. Based upon preliminary specifications and Marcus' oral discussions with the defendant, the defendant quoted a price to the plaintiff on May 24, 1966 of $39,750 per machine. At this point Marcus orally ordered three machines and promised that a down payment, a written order form, and the specifications would be sent.

Not until July 20, 1966 did the defendant receive from Admiral a check for $29,812.50 as a partial payment as well as a set of specifications and a purchase order. The purchase order provided that the delivery dates for the three machines were to be November 1, November 15, and December 1, 1966. In late August, Marcus visited the defendant's plant and expressed concern that the construction had not started. Marcus was informed that there were discrepancies between the specifications as submitted and Marcus' earlier discussions and that revised specifications were needed. On September 9, 1966 revised specifications were received by the defendant, but they were inadequate in some respects. On November 11, 1966 and again on December 1, 1966 an agent of Admiral visited the defendant's plant to observe the machines in operation and found that the basic welding on only one machine had been done. The defendant never did sign the purchase order form. On December 8, 1966 the plaintiff informed the defendant that there was a default and the plaintiff was initiating suit. No machines were ever delivered, and the defendant did not return the $29,812.50 paid, stating that this did not even cover its expenses. Was there a contract?

DECISION

The trial court found that there was a contract followed by mutual rescission. The appellate court affirmed this. The court relied upon UCC 2–204 and said, in part, that "a contract for sale of goods may be made in any manner sufficient to show agreement, including conduct by both parties which recognizes the existence of such a contract [and] . . . a contract for sale does not fail for indefiniteness if the parties have intended to make a contract and there is a reasonably certain basis for giving an appropriate remedy." In the designing and producing of special machines, it is understandable that certain terms were to be left unspecified and that difficulties would be encountered.

The court emphasized that the nature of the contract made it imperative that both parties cooperate to the fullest extent in order for the machines to be successfully designed and built. Both parties failed to act in good faith and failed to cooperate. There was evidence that Admiral was delinquent in furnishing the specifications, as was the defendant in failing to pursue its obligations.

The court concludes by noting that the UCC does not provide a remedy for the specific situation of a mutual breaching of contract, so it turns to "other . . . principles of law and equity." The court dismissed the defendant's counterclaim and ordered the return of the plaintiff's down payment.

Admiral Plastics Corp. v. Trueblood, Inc., 436 F.2d 1335 (6th Cir. 1971).

The above case reveals that in complex commercial transactions not all details of the transaction can be spelled out at the time the parties become bound. Article 2 clearly accounts for this reality and rejects many of the technical requirements of contract formation developed by the common law. However, while such common law formalities as the effect of a seal on a document today have no legal effect under Article 2 (2–203), the method of analysis for finding the existence of an agreement that courts will enforce remains intact. That is, courts still search for an offer and a response thereto, indicating an intent to be bound, called an acceptance. Also, the promise of the parties must manifest a desired exchange of value. This exchange of value was defined as "consideration" in the chapters on the common law of contracts, and, generally, this concept retains its vitality in Article 2.[5]

It is interesting to note that Article 2 does not *expressly* require an offer or consideration in a contract for the sale of goods but, obviously, they are required by implication, and the supplementary nonconflicting common law of contracts becomes applicable in this regard. This was not an oversight on the part of the drafters. As we pointed out in this last chapter, many of the fundamental, nontechnical rules developed over several centuries of mercantile conduct are applicable to Article 2 by Section 1–103, which provides:

> Unless displaced by the particular provisions of this Act, the principles of law and equity, including the . . . law relative to capacity to contract . . . estoppel, fraud, misrepresentation, duress, coercion, mistake . . . shall *supplement* its provisions. [Italics added.]

► At What Moment Are the Parties Bound by Their Promises?

mail box rule

The rule in *Adams v. Lindsell:* An acceptance is effective when it is sent if the means of sending it were impliedly authorized by, for example, the offeror's use of the mails to send the offer

Generally, offers may be made in any way that reveals an intent to be bound by the promises contained in the offer, and an acceptance shall be made in any manner and by any medium reasonable in the circumstances.[6] What did the drafters of Article 2 do to the famous **mail box rule?**[7] At what point does an acceptance become effective? This very question was not of great importance to the drafters. In one sense they minimized its importance by providing that a court could find that a contract existed even though the time of its "making" was uncertain, and by adding that acceptance could be by any reasonable means. Moreover, in the Comments to Section 2–206, they provide that "former technical rules as to acceptance, such as requiring that telegraphic offers be accepted by telegraphic acceptance, etc., are rejected and a criterion that the acceptance be, 'in any manner and by any medium reasonable under the circumstances,' is substituted." Of course, if the offer requires a specific medium for acceptance, an acceptance is to occur only by that medium.

There persists in some cases, nevertheless, a search for the time of contracting, compelled by the conventional assumption that an agreement must arise at some point in time. The better authorities suggest that, if the circumstances demand it, courts are still free to use the mail box test even when applying Section 2–206.[8] In short, under the UCC an acceptance is effective, binding both parties, when it is *sent* if the means of sending it are *reasonable under the circumstances,* in the absence of requirements specified in the offer.

---

[5]An exception is UCC 2–205, which provides that a signed, firm offer by a merchant will remain open for a reasonable time even though no consideration is given.

[6]UCC 2–206(1)(a) and (b).

[7]Under the common law of contracts, if *A* mailed an offer to *B* and *B* received it on September 15 and then sent an acceptance by mail the same day, a contract was formed as of the time *B* posted the letter of acceptance. A later attempt by *A* to revoke his offer and a later attempt by *B* to revoke his acceptance are not effective.

[8]R. J. Nordstrom, *Handbook of the Law of Sales* (St. Paul: West Publishing, 1970).

► Bilateral and Unilateral Promises

Article 2 recognizes the distinction between bilateral promises and unilateral promises by providing that an order or other offer to buy goods for prompt shipment shall be construed as inviting acceptance either by a prompt promise to ship (forming a bilateral contract) or by the prompt shipment of conforming goods (forming a unilateral contract). If the offer requests prompt shipment, then a contract for sale is formed upon the prompt shipment by the seller even though the goods shipped are nonconforming.[9] The drafters thought it would expedite commerce by recognizing that the shipment of nonconforming goods was an acceptance. In this case, although technically a contract exists upon shipment of nonconforming goods, the contract has been breached, and the purchaser has a remedy for the breach (paradoxically, the act of shipping nonconforming goods may be both an acceptance and a breach).

► "Accommodating" the Buyer

If a seller realizes that the goods shipped are nonconforming and ships them anyway to "accommodate" the buyer, then the act of shipment may not be an acceptance so long as the seller notifies the buyer that the goods are being shipped only as an "accommodation." For example, assume that *P* Co. orders for prompt shipment a large quantity of #10 *aluminum* wood screws from *S* Co. Upon receiving the order, the agent for *S* Co. realizes that it has no #10 aluminum wood screws but can ship immediately #10 *steel* wood screws. If *S* Co. ships the steel wood screws, there is an acceptance of the offer and a contract results, but *P* Co. may have a remedy for breach of the contract. However, the proper response here would have been for *S* Co. to notify *P* Co. that it was out of the aluminum screws and, if the steel screws would suffice, they would be sent as an accommodation to *P* Co.[10] In this case, no contract for the sale of aluminum wood screws would result and, therefore, there could be no breach of contract. If *P* Co. assents, there would be a contract for the sale of #10 steel wood screws.

► Performance As Acceptance

Finally, Section 2–206 protects the offeror by adding that where the beginning of a requested performance is a reasonable mode of acceptance, the offeree must notify the offeror that performance has begun. If the offeror is not notified within a reasonable time, the offeror may treat the offer as having lapsed before acceptance.[11] This section of the Code recognizes a basic fact of commercial life: both buyers and sellers are looking forward to performance, and usually the sooner the better. If an "offer" form or "order" form requests prompt shipment, then, to protect the offeree, an acceptance occurs when the requested performance begins so long as some notification is sent to the offeror. This notice must be sent within a reasonable time or the offeror may treat the offer as having lapsed. What is a reasonable time? When a merchant makes such an offer, it is usually to some other merchant from whom goods have been received in the past. It is the past conduct or, in the absence of this conduct, current commercial practice that will establish whether or not the notice of the beginning of performance was sent within a reasonable time.

---

[9]UCC 2–206(1)(b).

[10]Nordstrom, p. 88.

[11]UCC 2–206(2).

The Battle of the Forms and Section 2–207

Recall now the fact pattern we discussed at the beginning of this chapter to show how many commercial contracts are formed. We have an exchange of forms together with prior and subsequent agreements. What is "the contract"? Before we begin our analysis of the contract, we should reemphasize that any statute of frauds or parol evidence problems should first be evaluated. They have been treated in Chapter 23, Introduction to the Uniform Commercial Code. With this out of the way, we then proceed to the key section, 2–207. Following our discussion of this section and a case to reveal its application, we will discuss two more aspects of the problem created by the battle of the forms: first, how "course of performance" is used to interpret contracts; and second, modification, rescission, and waiver of the contract.

Section 2–207 provides:

> **(1)** A definite and seasonable expression of acceptance or a written confirmation which is sent within a reasonable time operates as an acceptance even though it states terms additional to or different from those offered or agreed upon, unless acceptance is expressly made conditional on assent to the additional or different terms.
>
> **(2)** The additional terms are to be construed as proposals for addition to the contract. Between merchants such terms become part of the contract unless:
>
> **(a)** the offer expressly limits acceptance to the terms of the offer;
>
> **(b)** they materially alter it; or
>
> **(c)** notification of the objection to them has already been given or is given within a reasonable time after notice of them is received.
>
> **(3)** Conduct by both parties that recognizes the existence of a contract is sufficient to establish a contract for sale although the writings of the parties do not otherwise establish a contract. In such case the terms of the particular contract consist of those terms on which the writings of the parties agree, together with any supplementary terms incorporated under any other provisions of this Act.

It should be obvious from the first paragraph above that Section 2–207 shatters the mirror-image requirement of an acceptance that prevails at common law. Section 2–207 reflects this approach of the Code: *Is there a bargain between the parties;* do their forms agree on *anything?* If they do, then there is a contract on what they agree upon, unless the offer clearly indicates that acceptance can be *only* in compliance with the offer's terms. The Code is saying: speak up clearly to indicate your intent, for if you do not do so, this is how the UCC will interpret your expression or silence or conduct in order to determine your intent and its legal effect.

In the battle of forms context, then, the starting point is that there is a contract that consists of the *terms on which the forms agree,* unless it is expressly stated in the acceptance that the acceptance is a counteroffer.

With regard to terms in the forms that *vary,* Section 2–207 provides two lines for analysis depending upon the character of the parties. If one or both of the parties are not merchants, then the additional terms are to be construed as proposals for additions to the contract. This means they are not part of the contract unless the offeror agrees to them. However, Section 2–207 contemplates our given factual pattern involving merchants and provides a second and more significant line of analysis. If both the parties are merchants and the acceptance does not expressly state it is a counteroffer, then the added terms of the offeree in the acceptance become part of the contract unless (1) the offer form expressly limits acceptance to its terms, or (2) the added terms materially alter the offeror's form, or (3) notification of objection to the added terms is given within a reasonable time after notice of them is received.[12]

Although neither of the merchants in our factual pattern may have read the other's form, the law properly assumes that they should. Section 2–207 seems to favor the merchant offeror by making its document controlling if it limits acceptance to its terms only. If the offering form does not so limit acceptance, then the offeree's additions become part of the contract (again, on the assumption that the acceptance cannot be termed a counteroffer) unless the offeror objects to them within a reasonable time after notice of them is received or they materially alter the offeror's form.

This brings us to the crucial question of what is a material alteration? The Comments to Section 2–207 state that a **material alteration** is one that would result in unreasonable surprise or hardship to the other party. Comment 4 gives (in part) the following general examples of additions that would materially alter an offer:

material alteration
"Any alteration of an instrument is material which changes the contract of any party thereto in any respect" UCC 3–407(1)

1. "A clause negating . . . standard warranties"; and
2. "A clause reserving to the seller the power to cancel upon the buyer's failure to meet any invoice when due."

Another example is a clause requiring one of the parties to meet a much higher standard of performance than is accepted in the trade generally.

Comment 5 suggests alterations that would not materially alter an offer. They are (in part):

1. "A clause setting forth and perhaps enlarging slightly upon the seller's exemption [from liability] due to supervening causes beyond his control";
2. "A clause fixing a reasonable time for complaints within customary limits";
3. "A clause providing for interest on overdue invoices . . . where they are within the range of trade practice".

By comparing the above suggestions on defining materiality, we see the central policy of this section. It is, stated briefly: *Where either of the parties attempts to vary standard or accepted commercial usage, they should bring this to the attention of the other party and make it a subject of negotiation.* If such a variation is not negotiated, then a court may find that such a provision is not part of the contract.

A simple approach to the complexities created by doing business through standardized forms is to provide large spaces for the parties either to write or type in all key features of the understanding. Where trade usage is being varied (not merely clarified), this should be typed or written in and the offeror's approval of it should be sought. The UCC provides that, where express terms in a contract conflict with a course of performance or usage of trade, the express terms will control.[13] In the following case there was no express consent to a disclaimer of consequential damages, so the disclaimer did not become part of the contract.

[12]For a thorough review and analysis of Section 2–207, see Barron and Dunfee, "Two Decades of 2–207: Review, Reflection and Revision," 24 *Clev. St. L. Rev.* 171, 182 (1975).

[13]UCC 1–205(4) and 2–208(2).

FACTS

The plaintiff, Air Products and Chemicals, Inc., purchased from the defendant, Fairbanks Morse, Inc., ten large electric motors ranging from 800 to 1700 horsepower. The negotiations formally began on April 15, 1964 when the plaintiff orally ordered some of the motors which were to become the subject of this controversy. On April 21, 1964 the plaintiff sent its "purchase order" confirming its verbal order of April 15. On April 30, 1964 the defendant returned an executed copy of the plaintiff's purchase order together with the defendant's "Acknowledgment of Order" form. After the motors were constructed, shipped, and installed, the plaintiff alleged that they failed to perform as promised and sued the defendant for more than $31,000.

In this case there were numerous issues of law and fact to be decided, and just one of them was whether the plaintiff could sue for damages beyond what it cost to have the motors repaired to perform properly. These damages, called consequential damages, may be awarded if they are a foreseeable event at the time the contract is made and the other party is aware of them. In this case the plaintiff was asking for consequential damages because of work stoppage and lost profits.

The plaintiff's purchase order form stated, in part:

> Seller recognizes that failure to make delivery of . . . equipment conforming to the requirements of this purchase order . . . will subject buyer to substantial damages due to delay and disruption of work schedules, inefficient use of manpower and other reasons. . . .

In response to the purchase order, the defendant sent its "Acknowledgment of Order" form, which read, in part:

> We thank you for your order as copied hereon, which will receive prompt attention and shall be governed by the provisions on the reverse side hereof unless you notify us to the contrary within 10 days or before shipment whichever is earlier. . . .

On the reverse side of the acknowledgment form it stated, in part:

> The Company nowise assumes any responsibility or liability with respect to use, purpose, or suitability, and shall not be liable for damages of any character, whether direct or consequential, for defect, delay, or otherwise. . . .

Was there a "contract"? If so, which contract provision controls the question of whether the plaintiff may seek damages for the delay caused by the improper performance of the motors?

DECISION

The appellate court held that the plaintiff could sue for consequential damages caused by the delay. The court said that a contract existed because the "Acknowledgment of Order" form stated that the provisions contained there "form part of the order acknowledged and accepted on the face hereof," and, this form contained no express provision making assent to its different or additional terms necessary. The remaining issue was whether the additional or different terms of the "Acknowledgment of Order" form were material. On this point the court held that a disclaimer for consequential loss that has the effect of eliminating millions of dollars in damages is sufficiently material to require that a waiver or alteration of it be expressly consented to by the party affected, which did not occur here, so the plaintiff may sue for consequential damages.

Air Products & Chemicals, Inc., v. Fairbanks Morse, Inc., 206 N.W.2d 414 (Wis. 1973).

Section 2–207 should not be viewed as a rigid mechanistic legal rule. It cannot be understood in isolation. This section must be thought of as part of a general effort in Article 2 to free up the courts to search for an agreement in fact between the parties. If the intention of the parties is ambiguous, courts are to refer to current commercial usage to reach a resolution of the conflict. Again we see the impact of Article 2—let us fit the law to business rather than fit business to the law.

Interpretation of the Sales Contract

▶ The Significance of Course of Performance, Course of Dealing, and Usage of Trade

Interpreting the intent of parties by focusing on their exchange of *words* may not be a good way to arrive at the parties' understanding. Words, although used precisely, lack precision. Yet they are the single best starting point for an analysis of the parties' "contract."

The UCC read with the common law of contracts helps to determine what evidence can be used by a court to give meaning to words. One of these rules of evidence, the parol evidence rule, which prefers written words over spoken words, was presented in Chapter 23, the first chapter on sales, because it is a general guide for courts to use in ascertaining the parties' intent.

The UCC provides us with two more lines of analysis to help us in arriving at a fair interpretation of the parties' contractual intent. One is on course of performance, course of dealing, and usage of trade; the other is on modification, rescission, and waiver.

Comment 1 to Section 1–205 sets out the general rule that "the meaning of the agreement of the parties is to be determined by the language used by them and by their action, read and interpreted in the light of commercial practices and other surrounding circumstances." Of course, the terms of the agreement and any **course of performance, course of dealing** and **usage of trade** are to be construed as consistent with each other whenever reasonable.[14]

When there is conflict between events such as those just mentioned, the UCC provides this order of priority of controlling events:

1. Express terms of an agreement;[15]
2. Course of performance;[16]
3. Course of dealing
4. Usage of trade

The distinction between course of performance and course of dealing is directly related to the time in the transaction when the conduct occurs. Conduct after the particular agreement is made and which is a result of the agreement is a *course of performance;* conduct of the parties prior to the particular agreement is a *course of dealing.*[17]

Usage of trade is defined by the conduct of "the great majority of decent dealers, even though dissidents ready to cut corners do not agree" and is not defined solely by the

course of performance
"Where the contract for sale involves repeated occasions for performance by either party with knowledge of the nature of the performance and opportunity for objection to it by the other, any course of performance accepted or acquiesed in without objection shall be relevant to determine the meaning of the agreement" UCC 2–208(1)

course of dealing
"A sequence of previous conduct between the parties to a particular transaction which is fairly to be regarded as establishing a common basis of understanding for interpreting their expressions and other conduct" UCC 1–205(1)

usage of trade
"Any practice or method of dealing having such regularity of observance in a place, vocation or trade as to justify an expectation that it will be observed with respect to the transaction in question" UCC 1–205(2)

---

[14]UCC 1–205(4), 2–208(2).

[15]UCC 1–205(4).

[16]UCC 2–208(2).

[17]R. J. Nordstrom, p. 152.

parties themselves.[18] The following case is concerned with an industry-wide practice as a usage of trade.

FACTS

During February 1973 a general contractor, defendant, telephoned a supplier of concrete, plaintiff, and inquired about the price and terms for the sale of concrete. The supplier said that the stated price would be "adhered to for the year." The supplier provided concrete for the general contractor from February 1973 through March 1974. The price remained the same from February 1973 until December 30, 1973. These deliveries were paid for by the general contractor. The general contractor was notified of a price increase effective January 1, 1974 but believed that since "the contract" was for "the year" they would not be effective regarding him until the end of February 1974. Deliveries were made by the supplier to the general contractor during January and February 1974. When billed for these at the increased price, the general contractor offered to pay only at the 1973 price. Plaintiff sued defendant for the additional amount under the new price contending that the contract price was only for the 1973 calendar year. Was the initial oral contract, neither of which the parties deny, for the delivery of concrete at a stated price for "the year" to run for one year from the date of its making or to run until the end of the calendar year?

DECISION

The court held the price was for the calendar year. The court relied on the fact that both parties agreed the words were "the" year and not "a" year. Seeing no circumstances surrounding the contract formation or the subsequent conduct of the parties which would lead it to believe the parties intended anything other than the normal and natural meaning, the court concluded that when one uses the words "the year," the calendar year is contemplated.

Secondly, the court noted that it was an industry-wide practice to make price increases effective on January 1, and the general contractor could be charged with notice of this.

Finally, the court said that, in fact, the general contractor had actual notice of the price increase.

Loizeaux Builders Supply Co. v. Donald B. Ludwig Co., 366 A.2d 721 (N.J. 1976).

▶ Contract Modification, Rescission, and Waiver

If an offeree agrees to most of the terms in an offer but conspicuously notes additional terms in its form and makes acceptance conditional upon them and they are agreed to by the offeror, then, technically, there is a contract on the first set of terms and a modification of the contract by the offeree's terms. Such a modification needs no consideration to be binding.[19] Again, the UCC de-emphasizes the technical requirements of the common law and makes the manifested intent of the parties controlling. Certain "adjustments" to contractual understandings are inevitable, and these are recognized and given effect—as long as they are done in good faith. Comment to 2–209 expressly provides that a "modification" without legitimate commercial reason is ineffective as a violation of the duty of good faith.

There are two potential problems with modification that were contemplated by the drafters of the UCC. The first is that they recognized the commercial necessity for modification, but they perceived that many merchants would attempt to protect

[18]UCC 1–205, comment 5.

[19]UCC 2–209(1).

themselves against fraudulent oral modifications[20] by putting in their forms that no modification will be effective unless it is signed by the parties. If such a provision is in a merchant's form, then Section 2–209(2) states that a requirement compelling a written modification must be separately signed by the merchant party not supplying the form. For example, if a merchant-seller's form states that it cannot be modified or rescinded except by a signed writing, then, to be effective, the merchant purchaser must separately sign or initial this requirement. The UCC requires the merchant who is not the author of the form to sign separately this provision in the form because such a provision may vary trade usage with regard to modification.

A second and related problem may involve the application of the statute of frauds. If the contract as modified (a change of price from $600 to $550, for example) is the type that originally had to be evidenced by a signed writing, then a signed writing by the party to be charged is needed for the modification to be effective.

The UCC does not define waiver but does recognize that waivers may exist where modifications or rescissions do not. Section 2–209(4) states that, although an attempt at modification or rescission does not satisfy the signed writing requirements of a modification or of the statute of frauds, the attempt may be effective if the party having the right to insist upon a writing does not do so but acquieses to behavior that substantiates the modification.

In conclusion, Section 2–209 cautions both the parties to a contract and the courts about the need for a writing to support *oral* modifications of written contracts, but the section allows a court the flexibility to find that a party has waived a right if the court is convinced the party knowingly relinquished it and the other party has relied upon this.

The Exchange of Property Interests in a Sales Transaction

The nature of property merits our attention as another dimension to our image of a typical sales transaction between merchants. **Property,** as the word is conventionally used, refers to things, such as goods or land, that are tangible, and rights of action (e.g., accounts receivable) that are intangible. However, the law and the UCC in particular recognize numerous different legal rights in property often called **property interests.** This accumulation of property interests, usually likened to a bundle of sticks, should be the object of our attention together with the physical item that is the object of the contract. In other words, we are talking about a thing and an interest in that thing. For example, if you own a typewriter, the typewriter is the thing and your title is evidence of the interest in the thing. The contract of sale is merely the legal device by which these property interests are shifted—sometimes one at a time, sometimes in bunches—from one party to another.

property
A thing; also an interest or right in a thing

property interest
A legally recognized and protected right in property

The UCC recognizes many different property interests. Article 3, for example, sets out the law on commercial paper, the use of which, among other things, shifts property interests in checking accounts. Also, all of Article 9 is devoted to the creation, transfer, enforcement, and destruction of a property interest called a "security interest." This property interest allows the holder of it to claim possession of goods under certain

[20]The circumstance contemplated here is when the seller tells the buyer after a substantial down payment has been made, "I cannot possibly produce for the contract price, I must have ten percent more." Understandably, purchasers desire protection when it is asserted fraudulently by the seller that they agreed to the modification. See J. White and R. Summers, *Handbook of the Law Under the Uniform Commercial Code* (St. Paul: West Publishing, 1972), 40; and see discussion in J. White and R. Summers, *Uniform Commercial Code* 3d ed. (St. Paul: West Publishing, 1988), 53.

circumstances—usually when a buyer defaults in payment of the purchase price to the holder of the interest.

In this part of the chapter we analyze a very important property interest recognized by Article 2, the insurable interest. We then analyze a related notion, risk of loss of the goods, and finally we discuss the concept of title under Article 2.

insurable interest
In sales, a person's interest in property that can be insured against loss

► Insurable Interest

One of the most important things in the minds of contracting merchants is how to protect themselves from some unforeseeable event that might cause damage or destruction to goods that are the subject of the contract. Section 2–501 was drafted specifically to cover this concern of the parties. It is one of the least complicated sections of Article 2, so spelling it out is the best way to begin our analysis of it. It provides:

> **(1)** The buyer obtains a special property and an insurable interest in goods by identification of existing goods as goods to which the contract refers even though the goods so identified are nonconforming and he has an option to return or reject them. Such identification can be made at any time and in any manner explicitly agreed to by the parties. In the absence of explicit agreement identification occurs
> **(a)** when the contract is made if it is for the sale of goods already existing and identified;
> **(b)** if the contract is for the sale of future goods . . . when goods are shipped, marked or otherwise designated by the seller as goods to which the contract refers. . .
>
> **(2)** The seller retains an insurable interest in goods so long as title to or any security interest in the goods remains in him and where the identification is by the seller alone he may until default or insolvency or notification to the buyer that the identification is final substitute other goods for those identified.
>
> **(3)** Nothing in this section impairs any insurable interest recognized under any other statute or rule of law.

Possession of an insurable interest in goods enables the possessor to obtain insurance on the goods to cover the risks of damage to, or loss of his interest in, the goods. An insurable interest exists independently of which party has title, and of which party has the risk of loss; and, it may exist in duplicate so that both the seller and buyer may have insurable interests in the same goods.[21]

The crucial inquiry is: when is the earliest possible moment that a buyer can acquire an insurable property interest in goods for which the buyer may have already made a substantial payment? The answer is: as soon as the seller (or in some cases the buyer) *identifies* the goods—designates those goods for that contract. The act of identification may be defined by the agreement of the parties and, if it is not, then it occurs according to subsections (a) and (b) above. The following case illustrates that an insurable interest passed to the purchaser when the contract was made since the goods were existing and could be identified then.

FACTS

The Missouri Pacific Railroad sold to the firm of Carrow and McGee all of its equipment located in five buildings in DeSoto, Missouri, on April 21, 1966. Carrow and McGee were to remove all of the equipment, and the best reading of the contract for sale was that title to the equipment was to pass when the equipment was removed. Before removal of the equipment, Carrow and McGee sold a large compressor on the property to Davis, who

[21]Nordstrom, pp. 383, 387.

some weeks later sold it to the National Compressor Corporation for $12,000, which was paid. A fire destroyed the compressor before its removal.

National Compressor sued numerous parties alleging that its compressor was destroyed by the fire which was negligently caused by the various parties involved in cleaning up the property. The defendants moved to have the plaintiff, National Compressor, dismissed from the suit because it had no property interest in the compressor because title was to pass upon removal.

DECISION

Judgment for the plaintiff. The court held for the plaintiff and reasoned that the passage of title to the compressor was *not* controlling because the plaintiff had a "special property" or insurable interest in the compressor. This property interest passed at the time the contract for sale was made because the compressor was existing and had been identified at that time.

National Compressor Corp. v. Carrow and McGee, 417 F.2d 97 (1969).

If the contract is for the sale of future goods, then an insurable interest passes to the buyer when the "goods are shipped, marked or otherwise designated by the seller as goods to which the contract refers." This "designation" by the seller requires some overt act by the seller which comes at a time when those goods are so far assembled that they would be considered "existing" in the common understanding of those in commerce.[22] Under Section 2–501 most doubts about identification are to be resolved in favor of identification. Providing for early identification by resolving all doubts in favor of identification does not give the buyer a windfall because only the loss suffered can be recovered from an insurance company.

Fungible goods are goods (such as grain or oil) in which every part of the goods is perfectly substitutable, or is so treated by the sales contract. Under Section 2–501(1)(a), the mere making of a contract for the sale of existing fungible goods is sufficient identification to effect an identification.

fungible goods
Every unit of goods is the equivalent of any other like unit, either actually or by contract

Risk of Loss

Article 2 has two sections directly applicable in determining which party has the risk of loss. The underlying theory of both of these sections is that the risk of loss should shift according to the agreement of the parties. If the agreement is silent, then the point at which the risk shifts depends upon whether the seller has completed its performance and whether the seller breaches the agreement by tendering nonconforming goods. That is, the drafters of Article 2 did not think it fair that the seller, who is assumed to have the risk of loss, could shift the risk to the buyer by tendering goods that failed to conform to the contract. So, two sections were devised: one to operate in the absence of a breach, the other to operate when there has been a breach by either party.

First, in the absence of a breach by the seller and in the absence of a contractual provision to the contrary, the risk of loss shifts, generally speaking, when the seller completes its performance with regard to the goods. So, where the contract requires the seller to ship the goods by carrier, the risk of loss passes to the buyer when the goods

[22]Nordstrom, p. 386.

are duly delivered[23] to the carrier[24] or, if the contract requires delivery at a particular destination, the risk of loss passes at the destination when the goods are so tendered to enable the buyer to take delivery.[25] In the following case the seller was to ship the goods by carrier and so the risk of loss shifted to the buyer when the seller completed its performance with regard to the goods.

FACTS

The plaintiff, Amar, contracted to buy some watches from the defendant, Karinol Corporation. The watches were to be shipped to Amar in Chetumal, Mexico. Amar made a deposit and the watches were shipped but were lost in transit. Amar asked for a refund of the deposit. The defendant claimed that the risk of loss was on the purchaser and that the balance of the purchase price should be paid. The plaintiff, sues for the deposit and the trial court held for the defendant seller. The plaintiff was ordered to pay the balance of the purchase price. The plaintiff appeals.

DECISION

The appellate court held for the defendant, seller, reasoning that where the contract has no explicit provisions allocating the risk of loss while the goods are in the possession of the carrier, then such a contract constitutes a shipment contract wherein the risk of loss passes to the buyer when the seller duly delivers the goods to the carrier. Thus, where the risk of loss falls on the buyer at the time the goods are lost or destroyed, the purchaser is liable to the seller for the purchase price of the goods sold if payment has not been made in full.

Pestana v. Karinol Corp., et al., 367 So.2d 1096 (Fla. 1979).

bailee
The person to whom goods are bailed

When the goods are in the possession of a **bailee**—a warehouseman for example—and they are to be delivered without being moved, then the risk of loss again passes when the seller completes its performance under the contract by passing the right to control the goods to the buyer. This may occur (a) when the seller delivers a negotiable document of title to the buyer for the goods; or (b) when the bailee acknowledges the buyer's right to possession of the goods; or (c) after the buyer receives, and does not object to, an nonnegotiable document of title or written direction of the seller for the bailee to deliver the goods.[26] The buyer is entitled to (a) or (b) above; the buyer does not have to accept (c).

Finally, in circumstances in which the seller is not required to ship and the goods are not in the possession of a bailee, the risk of loss passes to the buyer on receipt of the

[23]The words "duly delivered" are meant to incorporate the tender requirements of a shipment contract (set out in 2–504) which are that the seller must (1) put the goods in the possession of such a carrier as is reasonable; (2) make a reasonable contract for their transportation; and (3) obtain and promptly deliver the necessary documents and notify the buyer of shipment. See Comment 2 in Section 2–509.

[24]UCC 2–509(1)(a).

[25]UCC 2–509(1)(b).

[26]UCC 2–509(2).

goods if the seller is a merchant; otherwise the risk passes on tender of delivery of the goods.[27]

Second, obviously, the seller should not be able to shift the risk of loss to the buyer when the seller has breached the contract, as by tendering nonconforming goods or otherwise failing to fulfill its obligations. This result is reached by Section 2–510, which provides that the risk does not shift when the goods fail to conform until the seller **cures** the defect or the buyer accepts the goods. If the goods have been accepted by the buyer and then the buyer discovers a defect that would be a breach of contract by the seller, or if the buyer breaches the contract while the goods are still in the possession of the seller and the goods are damaged or loss occurs, then the one suffering the loss may recover any amounts not covered by its insurance from the other party.[28] For example, if the buyer repudiates the contract *after* the seller has identified conforming goods to the contract but *before* shipment, and the goods are damaged through no fault of the seller, the seller may collect the loss not covered by its insurance from the buyer. In short, the wrongdoer suffers the loss.

cure
A seller's correction of his or her failure to deliver conforming goods under a contract for sale before the due date has expired

In conclusion, insurable interests and the risk of loss, are special property interests that may exist independently, although there are circumstances in which both will pass to the buyer at the same time. One example of an insurable interest in the buyer being significant—without risk of loss passing—exists when the buyer contracts for the construction and delivery of a large, complex machine. After the machine has been identified to the contract in the seller's plant, it is destroyed by fire that consumed the entire plant. The buyer, let us assume, had paid $10,000 at the time the contract was formed on a total price of $50,000. Further, let us assume the seller is now insolvent and had not carried sufficient insurance to cover the loss of the machine. The risk of loss may still be on the seller because the machine had not been delivered; but if the buyer had been prudent, it should have insured its interest in the machine, which would have been at least $10,000. The buyer could have done so because an insurable interest (its contract right to the machine) passed to the buyer when the machine was identified to the contract.

Basically, the party with an insurable interest can obtain insurance against damage or destruction to the goods, while the party with the risk of loss will suffer such loss as between the contracting parties. The creation and recognition of these two property interests is a major contribution of Article 2. Persons in business recognized these two important circumstances (being able to identify when an insurable interest and the risk of loss passed from one party to the other) before the commercial law did. Sections 2–501 (Insurable Interest) and 2–509 and 2–510 (Risk of Loss) clarified the law and made it conform to the common expectations of merchants. Moreover, based on what little data there is, these sections seem to be working very well.[29]

▶ Transfer of Title Under Article 2

In pre-UCC law, the predominant property interests in goods were all linked to the concept of title to the goods. Title to goods was and is today often represented by a piece

[27]UCC 2–509(3).

[28]UCC 2–510(2)(3), Comment 3.

[29]Student Note, "Risk of Loss in Commercial Transactions: Efficiency Thrown into the Breach," 65 *V. L. Rev.* 557 (1979).

of paper identifying the goods, for example, a bill of lading, or a warehouse receipt. Possession of the piece of paper usually gave the possessor the legally enforceable right to get the goods, if the paper flowed to the possessor either originally or by indorsement as a "holder." But the abstract notion of who had title became confusing as merchants entered into increasingly complex commercial transactions. The drafters of the UCC realized that what the parties were essentially interested in when they referred to title, was who could get insurance on the goods and who would suffer damage due to loss if the goods were destroyed. Therefore they drafted Article 2 to deal specifically with these circumstances, which were discussed above.

Although many of the rights of the parties to a contract should not depend on a single concept such as title,[30] the matter of title is still very important in other areas of the Code and in business. For example, in Article 9 of the Code on Secured Transactions, discussed in Chapters 50 and 51, you will learn that the matter of who has title to the goods becomes vitally important because only the owner of the title having rights in the goods can give a security interest in the goods. Also, in business, for example, accountants auditing clients' books must ascertain whether the client has title to the goods inventory and whether there is a valid security interest in those goods. Also, today, one of the most important reasons for establishing which party has title to goods is to determine which party may be subject to various forms of state taxation. Inventory taxes, sales taxes, personal property taxes, and the like may be assessed depending on which party has title.

Before we proceed to an examination of ownership or title problems created by a "faulty title" or entrusting goods to another, we will consider when and how title is transferred to a buyer.

When Title Can Pass Under Article 2 Title to goods cannot pass prior to the time goods exist and are identified to the contract. If the goods exist and are identified to the contract at the time the contract is made, then the passage of title will depend upon the express or implied intention of the parties. If the agreement expresses when title is to pass, it will pass at that time. However, if the agreement contains no expression of intent, then title will pass at the moment the seller commits those goods to the contract.[31] Under the Code, committing goods to the contract depends on whether delivery is to be made by moving the goods. When delivery is to be made, without moving the goods (seller says, pick up the goods at my warehouse or from a third party), then:

(a) if the seller is to deliver a document of title, title passes at the time when and the place where he delivers such documents; or
(b) if the goods are at the time of contracting already identified and no documents are be delivered, title passes at the time and place of contracting.[32]

When delivery is to be made by moving the goods, title passes at the time and place at which the seller completes its performance with reference to the physical delivery of

---

[30]UCC 2–401, opening paragraph.

[31]UCC 2–401.

[32]UCC 2–401(3)(a), (b).

the goods.[33] Determining when this performance has been completed is aided by using certain shipment abbreviations.

If the seller is to ship the goods, then when the title passes depends on whether the seller is to "send" the goods—namely, "**F.O.B.** shipping point"—or the seller is to "deliver" the goods at a destination—namely, "F.O.B. destination." If F.O.B. shipping point, then there is no expense to the buyer until the goods are delivered to the carrier. If F.O.B. destination, then there is no expense to the buyer until the goods are tendered at the destination point. If F.O.B. shipping point, title passes at the time and place the goods are delivered to the carrier. If F.O.B. destination, title passes when the goods are tendered at the destination (See Figure 24.2) Delivery may be of the actual goods, or of a negotiable bill of lading covering them. The form of the bill of lading, whether negotiable or nonnegotiable, and irrespective of who the consignee is, has no effect on the transfer of title.

F.O.B.
Free on board

When, pursuant to the contract, goods are shipped **C.O.D.,** meaning "collect on delivery," the carrier is to collect the purchase price before delivering the goods. C.O.D. has no effect on the transfer of title. It defers the buyer's right to inspect the goods before accepting them.

C.O.D.
Collect on delivery

Also, please note that, in a "sale on approval," neither title nor risk of loss passes until the buyer approves. However, in a "sale or return," title and risk of loss pass to the buyer subject to the buyer's right to return the goods instead of paying the purchase price. If

FIGURE 24.2 **Shipping Terms**

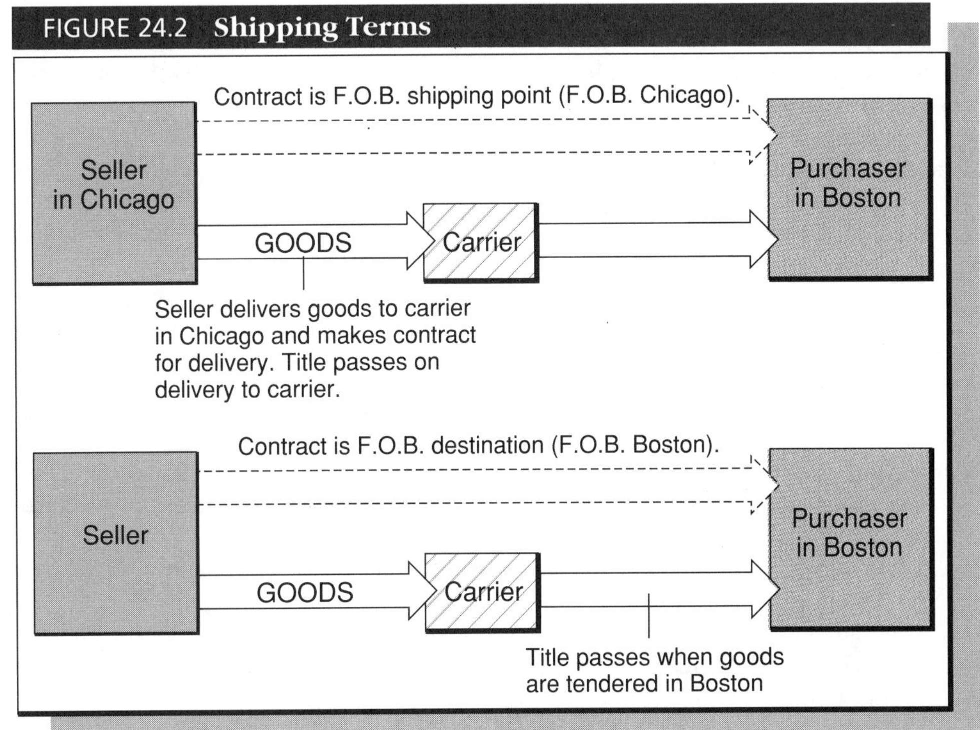
Contract is F.O.B. shipping point (F.O.B. Chicago).
Seller in Chicago
Purchaser in Boston
GOODS
Carrier
Seller delivers goods to carrier in Chicago and makes contract for delivery. Title passes on delivery to carrier.
Contract is F.O.B. destination (F.O.B. Boston).
Seller
Purchaser in Boston
GOODS
Carrier
Title passes when goods are tendered in Boston

[33]UCC 2–401(2).

the intention of the parties is unclear as to which of these it is, the following applies: if the goods are acquired *primarily for use,* it is a sale on approval; if *primarily for resale,* it is a sale or return.[34]

The above discussion of when title could pass under Article 2 was premised on the fact that the goods existed and were identified at the time the contract was made. If the goods do not exist and are therefore not identified to the contract (for example, a contract to sell a machine to be built), they are "future goods." A contract for future goods is enforceable, but title cannot pass until the goods are identified to the contract in accordance with the intention of the parties.

How Title Can Be Transferred Under Article 2 The general rule is that a person can transfer only what he or she has. So a seller cannot pass to a buyer a "better" title than the seller had. (*T* steals *O*'s goods and sells them to *B,* a **good faith** purchaser for value. *B* got what *T* had and, since *T* got nothing from *O,* then *O* still owns the goods.) To facilitate trade, Article 2 recognizes situations in which a seller may transfer a "better" title than the seller has. Perhaps the most important of these involves "entrusting" goods. UCC 2–403(2) provides:

good faith
"Honesty in fact in the conduct or transaction concerned" UCC 1–201(19)

> Any entrusting of possession of goods to a *merchant* who deals in goods of that kind gives him power to transfer all rights of the entruster to a buyer in ordinary course of business. [Emphasis added.]

When the owner of goods "entrusts" (delivers) them to a merchant who deals in goods of that kind, the owner clothes the merchant with the appearance of being the owner of the goods. The merchant's unauthorized sale of the goods to a **buyer in ordinary course of business** transfers a good title to such buyer. (You deliver your watch for repair to a jeweler, *J,* who sells watches. *J* sells your watch for $100 to *B,* who believes *J* owns the watch. *B* gets title to your watch. You may recover the reasonable value of the watch from *J* because of his tort of **conversion** by his unauthorizedly exercising control and dominion over your watch as the owner without authority to do so, but *B* will have title to the watch.)

buyer in ordinary course of business
"A person who, in good faith and without knowledge that the sale to him is in violation of the ownership rights or security interest of a third party in the goods, buys in ordinary course from a person in the business of selling goods of that kind" UCC 1-201(9)

conversion
The tort of intentional interference with another's right to possession, control, and dominion of a chattel

In this chapter we have seen that Article 2 has a policy bias and this bias is one that favors the free flow of commerce over technical rule interpretations.

Summary Statement

1. In your study of this chapter and the next two chapters, imagine two corporate merchants doing business; usually they "contract" by exchanging various form documents.
2. A contract for the sale of goods may be made in any manner sufficient to show agreement.
3. Generally, offers may be made in any way that reveals an intent to be bound, and an acceptance shall be made in any manner and by any medium reasonable in the circumstances.

---

[34]UCC 2–326(1). But, with one exception, if the goods are delivered for sale to a person who has a place of business under a name other than that of the person selling him or her the goods, then, solely with respect to the buyer's creditors, the transaction can be only a sale or return and not a sale on approval irrespective of the intentions of the parties. UCC 2–326(3).

4. A shipment of nonconforming goods may be an acceptance, and so may the beginning of a requested performance if it is a reasonable mode of acceptance.
5. An acceptance sent within a reasonable time is effective even though it includes additional or different terms from those offered unless the acceptance is expressly made conditional on assent to the additional or different terms. Additional terms are to be construed as proposals for additions to the contract and, as between merchants, they become part of the contract unless:
    - **a)** the offer expressly limits acceptance to the terms of the offer;
    - **b)** the added terms materially alter the offer; or
    - **c)** notification of the objection to the added terms has been given or is given within a reasonable time after notice of them is received.
6. Express terms of an agreement together with course of performance, course of dealing, and usage of trade are all used to ascertain the parties' contractual intent.
7. The parties to a sales contract may modify their contractual understanding without consideration.
8. An insurable interest in the goods may pass to the buyer independently of the passage of the risk of loss or title to the goods; it passes when goods are identified to the contract. If the goods are existing, then identification occurs when the contract is made; if the contract is for the sale of future goods, then they are identified when they are shipped or otherwise designated by the seller as goods to which the contract refers.
9. The risk of loss for the goods passes from seller to buyer when the parties agree it will pass. If they have not so agreed, then the risk of loss shifts when the seller completes its performance with regard to the goods. But if the seller tenders nonconforming goods, then the risk shifts when the seller cures the defect or the buyer accepts the goods.
10. Goods must exist and be identified to the contract before title can pass, depending on the intention of the parties. If no intent is expressed, then the Code establishes the rules for the implied intent.
11. Generally, a seller cannot pass to a buyer a better title than the one that the seller has. However, the doctrine of the entrusting of goods section of Article 2 makes it possible for a seller to have the power to transfer a better title than the seller has.

The following appellate case presents a typical, complex commercial dispute and its resolution by Article 2. The court's opinion is very clear and educational, tying together the common law of contracts concerning offer and acceptance and the need for Article 2, particularly Section 2–207. The case is well worth reading, even though it is long.

DORTON & CASTLE v. COLLINS & AIKMAN CORPORATION
453 F.2d 1161 (6th Cir. 1972)

Celebrezze, Circuit J. The plaintiff, a carpet dealer doing business under the name of The Carpet Mart, sued the defendant, Collins & Aikman, a carpet manufacturer. Between 1968 and 1970 the plaintiff and defendant entered into more than 55 transactions involving the purchase and sale, respectively, of substantial quantities of carpeting. In 1970 the plaintiff learned that some of the carpeting purchased from the defendant was not 100 percent

Kodel polyester fiber, as ordered, but was made of cheaper carpet fiber. The plaintiff sued for $450,000 based upon fraud and misrepresentation. Before the trial court could reach the merits of the case, the defendant moved to stay [stop] the proceedings based upon the allegation that its printed "sales acknowledgment" form *compelled* the parties to arbitrate their agreement if a dispute should arise. Before proceeding to an account of how the court resolved the issue about whether the parties were compelled to arbitrate, it is instructive to consider this factual background recounted by the court because it serves as an excellent explanation of the pattern of much merchant-to-merchant contracting today.

> In each of the more than 55 transactions, one of the partners in The Carpet Mart, or on some occasions, Collins & Aikman's visiting salesman, telephoned Collins & Aikman's order department in Dalton, Georgia, and ordered certain quantities of carpets listed in Collins & Aikman's catalog. There is some dispute as to what, if any, agreements were reached through the telephone calls and through the visits by Collins & Aikman's salesman. After each oral order was placed, the price, if any, quoted by the buyer was checked against Collins & Aikman's price list, and the credit department was consulted to determine if The Carpet Mart had paid for all previous shipments. After it was found that everything was in order, Collins & Aikman's order department typed the information concerning the particular order on one of its printed acknowledgment forms. Each acknowledgment form bore one of three legends: "Acknowledgment," "Customer Acknowledgment," or "Sales Contract." The following provision was printed on the face of the forms bearing the "Acknowledgment" legend: "The acceptance of your order is subject to all of the terms and conditions on the face and reverse side hereof, including arbitration, all of which are accepted by buyer; it supersedes buyer's order form, if any. . . ."

The small print on the reverse side of the forms provided, among other things, that all claims arising out of the contract would be submitted to arbitration in New York City. Each acknowledgment form was signed by an employee of Collins & Aikman's order department and mailed to The Carpet Mart on the day the telephone order was received or, at the latest, on the following day. The carpets were thereafter shipped to The Carpet Mart, with the interval between the mailing of the acknowledgment form and shipment of the carpets varying from a brief interval to a period of several weeks or months. Absent a delay in the mails, however, The Carpet Mart always received the acknowledgment forms prior to receiving the carpets. In all cases The Carpet Mart took delivery of and paid for the carpets without objecting to any terms contained in the acknowledgment form.

Before the court reached the application of section 2–207 to these facts, it stated the following about the intended purpose of section 2–207:

> [I]t is clear that section 2–207, and specifically subsection 2–207(1), was intended to alter the . . . "mirror" rule of common law, under which the terms of an acceptance or confirmation were required to be identical to the terms of the offer or oral agreement. . . . Under the common law, an acceptance or a confirmation that contained terms additional to or different from those of the offer or oral agreement constituted a rejection of the offer or agreement and thus became a counteroffer. The terms of the counteroffer were said to have been accepted by the original offeror when he proceeded to perform under the contract without objecting to the counteroffer. Thus, a buyer was deemed to have accepted the seller's counteroffer if he took receipt of the goods and paid for them without objection.
>
> Under section 2–207 the result is different. This section of the Code recognizes that in current commercial transactions, the terms of the offer and those of the acceptance will seldom be identical. Rather, under the current "battle of the forms," each party typically has a printed form drafted by his attorney, containing as many terms as could be envisioned to favor that party in his sales transactions. Whereas under common law the disparity between the fineprint terms in the parties' forms would have prevented the consum-

mation of a contract when these forms are exchanged, section 2–207 recognizes that in many, but not all, cases the parties do not impart such significance to the terms on the printed forms.... [U]nder subsection (1), a contract is recognized notwithstanding the fact that an acceptance or confirmation contains terms additional to or different from those of the offer or prior agreement, provided that the offeree's intent to accept the offer is definitely expressed... and provided that the offeree's acceptance is not expressly conditioned on the offeror's assent to the additional or different terms. When a contract is recognized under subsection (1), the additional terms are treated as "proposals for addition to the contract," under subsection (2), which contains special provisions... such additional terms are deemed to have been accepted when the transaction is between merchants. Conversely, when no contract is recognized under subsection 2–207(1)—either because no definite expression of acceptance exists or, more specifically, because the offeree's acceptance is expressly conditioned on the offeror's assent to the additional or different terms—the entire transaction aborts (stops) at this point. If, however, the subsequent conduct of the parties—particularly, performance by both parties under what they apparently believe to be a contract—recognizes the existence of a contract, under subsection 2–207(3) such conduct by both parties is sufficient to establish a contract, notwithstanding the fact that no contract would have been recognized on the basis of their writings alone.

The appellate court remanded this case back to the trial court for further findings of fact and suggested a method for resolving the issue of whether the parties had "agreed" to arbitrate the dispute. First, it said the court should find if the agreement was composed of the plaintiff's oral order and the defendant's acknowledgment. Second, if it was, was the arbitration provision an addition to or a term different from the offer? Third, if the arbitration provision was additional or different from the offer, was the acceptance expressly made conditional on assent to the additional terms so that 2–207(1) would be applicable? On this point the court advised that merely stating that the acceptance was "subject to all of the terms and conditions on the face and reverse side hereof including arbitration, all of which are accepted by the buyer," might not be sufficient to meet the requirement of 2–207(1). It suggested: "In order to fall within this proviso (2–207(1)), it is not enough that an acceptance is expressly conditional on additional or different terms; rather an acceptance must be *expressly* conditional on the offeror's assent to those terms."

Fourth, if on remand the trial court were to find that the acceptance was not expressly made conditional on assent to the additional terms, then the court must find there was a contract and, finally, the term compelling arbitration would bind both of the parties unless it materially altered the parties' understanding. This finding of materiality was the final point demanding the trial court's opinion.

[Authors' note: in most cases, a provision requiring arbitration would be a material alteration, unless requiring arbitration was a well established practice in that particular business.]

Questions and Case Problems

1. The plaintiff, general contractor, relied on a bid from a subcontractor to build over 400 wardrobes, to be used in refurbishing a state institution for the mentally retarded in New York. The plaintiff was awarded the bid and then it began correspondence with the defendant subcontractor about some of the details of the work. In one exchange of letters, the general contractor said the wardrobes must meet state standards and the general contractor agreed to pay an extra $17,375 to cover extra work done by the subcontractor. The subcontractor replied by letter three days later that the $17,375 was for "additional costs for amending specifica-

tions, method of assembly, and construction of wardrobes to meet (state) requirements." The subcontractor failed to perform and the general contractor sued. The subcontractor argues that it never (subjectively) intended to accept the offer for additional work and $17,375, and the letter in response to the general contractor's offer to pay the extra money was a mere acknowledgment of receipt of that letter. Do you believe there was an acceptance based on the language used? [*J. Baranello & Sons v. Hausman Indus., Inc.* 571 F.Supp 333 (E.D.N.Y. 1983).]

2. In April of 1968, Litton Industries wrote a letter that was not quite two pages long to Bethlehem Steel Corporation stating that it was "extending to (Bethlehem) an option to purchase . . . 'vessels' " . . . of 1,000 feet in length. In the letter the prices of 5 vessels were set out and these ranged from $22.4 million to $18.4 million each. If all 5 vessels were to be built, the total value of the contract would exceed $100 million. No ship construction contracts setting out all the specifications of design and the like were ever finalized and when Bethlehem attempted to order the first vessel mentioned in the letter, Litton refused. Litton argued that the two-page letter was merely an agreement to agree on the construction of from one to five vessels. The letters exchanged showed only the price of each vessel and its length. Is such a writing sufficient for a court to conclude that the parties manifested an intent to contract? [*Bethlehem Steel Corp. v. Litton Indus., Inc.*, 468 A.2d 748 (Pa. 1983).]
3. Courts often must go beyond the terms of a written contract to give the words used some meaning. Clearly state what items of evidence or circumstances they may use in this inquiry and which bits of evidence are to control over others when there is a conflict.
4. An item of great importance to any sales contract is the question of which party is to bear the risk of loss for damage or destruction of the goods. Describe the point at which the risk of loss passes from the seller to the buyer, and how and when buyers can protect themselves from suffering loss due to damage or destruction of goods.
5. Roto-Lith, Ltd. is a corporation engaged in manufacturing cellophane bags for packaging vegetables. It ordered a drum of N-132-C emulsion from F. P. Bartlett & Co. on October 23, 1969 for the stated purpose of making wet pack spinach bags. In response to Roto-Lith's order form, the seller sent its "acknowledgment" form and the goods were shipped. The acknowledgment form and the invoice accompanying the goods both stated in conspicuous language, "all goods sold without warranties, express or implied. . . ." Further, on the back of the acknowledgment there was this statement, "If these terms are not acceptable, buyer must so notify seller at once."

   Roto-Lith did not protest the waiver of the warranties; it received, paid for, and used the emulsion. The emulsion was defective and Roto-Lith sued F. P. Bartlett for breach of contract (warranties). Article 2 states that, in every contract for the sale of goods, the seller makes a warranty that the goods sold were fit for the use for which the goods were sold. These "implied" warranties exist unless the contract between the parties waives these warranties. What was the contractual understanding between these parties with regard to the warranties? [*Roto-Lith Ltd. v. F. P. Bartlett & Co.*, 297 F.2d 497 (1st Cir. 1962).]
6. Blue Rock Industries, a seller of sand, contracted with Raymond International to deliver large quantities of sand for road construction in Maine. The initial contract between the two stated that Blue Rock's price was to be as follows:

   > For truck measured sand delivered to the job site as you require: $2.75 per cubic yard delivered to the north side of the project; and $2.60 per cubic yard delivered to the south side of the project.

Assume that the sand delivered may be measured in at least two ways. One way is to fill a five-yard dump truck up to the top; another is to figure what one yard of sand weighs, then weigh the sand (in the truck) and compute the price on this basis. That is, one method is to price the sand by volume, and one by weight.

a) Looking at the contract, which method was contemplated?

b) If a dispute arose between the two parties over these two varying methods of measuring sand, how would a court resolve it?

7. The firm of Bowman Hydro-Vat owned an airplane that they agreed to sell to Hemmer on December 12, 1970 for a price of $18,500. On that date $15,000 was paid down and the balance of $3,500 was to be paid later. Both parties agreed that title was to pass when "the necessary paperwork" was completed. A formal document of title was requested from the Federal Aviation Administration (FAA), and meanwhile Hemmer began using the airplane. The formal document was received by the seller on December 18, 1970 and was put in the mail on that date to Hemmer. On that same day, while Hemmer was piloting the aircraft, the tip of the wing caught a snow bank on takeoff, resulting in extensive damage. According to FAA regulations, the purchaser of an aircraft had to sign the title document received from the seller and then send it to the FAA, which would issue a title to the purchaser.

a) Can the seller, Bowman Hydro-Vat, recover for the damage from its insurance company, provided that premiums were paid and the policy had not been cancelled?

b) Could the purchaser have purchased insurance on the aircraft on December 12, 1970?

[*Bowman v. American Home Assurance Co.*, 213 N.W.2d 446 (Neb. 1973).]

8. Purchaser orders $10,000 worth of goods from seller and pays $5,000 down. The contract said that the seller was "to ship" the goods to the purchaser's plant. The parties did not otherwise agree on who was to bear the risk of loss, and the contract did not state that the shipment was to be F.O.B.

a) When does the purchaser have an insurable interest?

b) If the goods are placed on board a carrier by the seller and the goods conform to the contract and a reasonable contract for their shipment is made and the goods are destroyed in transit, which party bears the loss?

c) Would the result in (b) change if the goods placed on board the carrier by the seller were nonconforming? If so, how?

9. *F* fraudulently induced *O*, the owner of goods, to sell and deliver certain goods to *F*. *F* then sold and delivered the goods to *G*, a good faith purchaser for value without notice of the fraud. *G* made a gift of the goods to *D*, who also is innocent of the fraud. *O* now discovers the fraud and demands the goods from *D*. Who gets the goods?

10. In the case of *Dorton & Castle v. Collins & Aikman Corp.*, excerpted at the beginning of this section, the court discussed the impact of UCC 2–207 on that part of the law of contracts concerned with offer and acceptance. How would you explain that impact?

CHAPTER 25

PERFORMANCE OF THE SALES CONTRACT

After you have read this chapter, you should be able to:

1. Define how performance obligations of the parties are determined.
2. List and define the performance obligations of the seller and buyer in a typical sales transaction and be able to define the terms F.O.B., F.A.S., C.I.F., C.F., and C.&F. and state the legal consequences of using them.
3. State what is meant by "perfect tender" of goods and documents and then state two circumstances in which the requirement of perfect tender is lessened.
4. Define what is meant by payment and state when and under what circumstances it is due.
5. Describe two special circumstances in which both the seller and buyer have performance obligations to one another and, in one case, obligations to creditors of the seller.
6. Define and explain three exceptions to the general rule that the parties must perform as promised.

BUSINESS DECISIONS and the LAW

Vince Cardi inherited his father's furniture-making business in Chicago and wanted to expand it beyond the state of Illinois. His catalog was mailed to decorators of commercial buildings in most major cities of the country and soon orders were coming in for the merchandise his firm designed and manufactured. When an order for $10,000 worth of desks came from a firm he had not heard of in Los Angeles, how could he assure himself that once he shipped the desks, he would be paid the purchase price? Also, who was to perform first and how was payment to be made?

These questions raise the central issues of this chapter: What provisions does the law make for the performance obligations of a sales contract once the contract has been made? Sales contracts usually provide the outlines of the performance expected by each party. However, sometimes the intent of the parties and, hence, these outlines are not clear and the exact performances must be established either by Article 2 or by trade practice and custom. Vince Cardi and his agents can rely on Article 2 to express reasonable requirements for each party in the performance of the contract for the delivery and payment for the desks. The best way, though, for him to understand the performance required of him is to clearly express his intended wishes for performance in the sales contract that binds him to the buyer.

Introduction

In this chapter we will examine the performance obligations of the parties to a contract for the sale of goods. In many cases the sales contract will set forth these obligations. The sales contract will control disputes about performance, but Article 2 will apply if the sales contract is ambiguous or does not cover the dispute.

An overview of Article 2's provisions on performance will give you a good idea of how buyers and sellers are expected to perform.

Performance Obligations of the Seller

► Tender Obligations of the Seller

tender
(Verb) To proffer, make available

The general obligations of both parties to a sales contract are set out clearly in Section 2–301. It provides: "The obligation of the seller is to transfer and deliver and that of the buyer is to accept and pay in accordance with the contract."

condition
An uncertain event on the occurrence of which a contractual obligation is made contingent or dependent

concurrent condition
A condition that must occur at the same time as another condition

This section creates a set of **concurrent conditions—conditions** that must occur at the same time unless otherwise agreed. The seller must duly tender the goods as a condition to the buyer's duty to accept and pay,[1] and the buyer must offer payment as a condition to the seller's duty to tender and complete delivery of the goods.[2] One of the parties must manifest an intent to perform (by either tendering the goods or payment) before the other party can be put in default. To put a buyer in default, the seller must tender the goods in accordance with the contract, and, if the buyer does not respond with payment, then a breach exists.

Conversely, to put the seller in default, the buyer must tender payment. Theoretically, if a substantial period of time passes after the date for performance and neither party comes forward to put the other in default by tendering performance, then courts may conclude that the parties have treated the contract as having expired. What usually happens, however, is that one of the parties will tender.

conforming goods
Those goods that are produced and tendered in accordance with the obligations under the contract

Remember that both parties are under a fundamental duty to perform in good faith. We must proceed then on the assumption that, unless otherwise agreed, the parties will begin their performance after the agreement is made, by the seller making plans for delivery of goods and the buyer making plans for payment.

Let us first examine what is meant by the seller's performance and start with the seller's obligation to tender. Under Section 2–503 (in part):

> **(1)** Tender of delivery requires that the seller put and hold **conforming goods** at the buyer's disposition and give the buyer any notification reasonably necessary to enable him to take delivery. The manner, time and place for tender are determined by the agreement and this Article, and in particular
>
> **(a)** tender must be at a reasonable hour, and if it is of goods they must be kept available for the period reasonably necessary to enable the buyer to take possession; but
>
> **(b)** unless otherwise agreed the buyer must furnish facilities reasonably suited to the receipt of the goods.

The section above provides that the seller is to "put and hold conforming goods at the buyer's disposition," but it does not state *where* this is to take place. Usually the

---

[1]UCC 2–507(1).

[2]UCC 2–511.

contract of the parties will state either where the seller is to ship the goods or where tender is to take place. There are three common arrangements that are made for tendering the goods: "destination" sales contracts, "delivery" sales contracts, and sales contracts with no delivery or pricing terms.

"Destination" Sales Contracts The first common circumstance concerned with tender is where the contract provides that the goods are to be shipped **F.O.B.** or **F.A.S.** destination. If, for example, a seller in Chicago agrees to tender the goods in Los Angeles, or at any particular destination not in the seller's town, then the seller must make all shipment arrangements and tender, through an agent of some sort, at that destination. This obligation is *usually* imposed upon the seller by the use of the term F.O.B. (e.g., "F.O.B. Los Angeles" and the seller is in Chicago), or F.A.S. followed by the name of a vessel and a port.

F.O.B.
Free on board

F.A.S.
Free alongside

In the first instance (F.O.B. Los Angeles), tender is to take place in Los Angeles and the seller must, at its own expense and risk, transport the goods there to an address provided by the purchaser and there tender the goods.[3] If the term used is "F.O.B. Los Angeles"and the port and a vessel are named, then the seller must, again at its own expense and risk, transport the goods to Los Angeles and load the goods on board the vessel.[4]

If the term F.A.S. followed by a named port and vessel is used, the seller must deliver the goods at its own expense and risk alongside the vessel and there tender documents to an agent of the buyer.[5]

"Delivery" Sales Contracts A second common circumstance concerned with tender is that the contract will state F.O.B. "place of shipment," "seller's town," or "seller's factory" (e.g., "F.O.B. Chicago" if the seller is in Chicago), or will merely state that the seller is "to ship" the goods. In this case the seller must, in its town or place of business, put the goods in the possession of such a carrier and make such a contract for its shipment as may be reasonable, having regard for the nature of the goods, and then promptly notify the buyer of the shipment.[6] The seller will obtain from the carrier a document, e.g., **bill of lading,** which is sufficient to enable the buyer to obtain possession of the goods, and the seller must then deliver or tender this document to the buyer.[7]

bill of lading
A document issued to the shipper by a carrier of goods

Pricing Terms The terms F.O.B. and F.A.S. are not intended to be used in pricing goods, but are intended to be used to determine performance with regard to delivery and tender. However, merchants often use the term **C.I.F.** when they do not use the terms F.O.B. or F.A.S. When they use the term C.I.F., they intend that the price quoted is a lump sum which includes the cost, insurance, and freight to a named destination. If they use the term **C.&F.** or C.F., it means that the price includes the cost of the goods plus freight to the named destination. The obligations imposed on the seller when the term "C.I.F. destination" is used are to load the goods onto a carrier, make a contract for their shipment, and pay for the freight and insurance. (The insurance is purchased for the

C.I.F.
Cost, insurance, freight

C.&F.
Cost plus freight

---

[3]UCC 2–319(1)(b).

[4]UCC 2–319(1)(c).

[5]UCC 2–319(2)(a).

[6]UCC 2–504(a)(c).

[7]UCC 2–504(b).

benefit of the buyer since the risk of loss passes upon the loading of the goods.) Finally, the seller must obtain a document enabling the buyer to obtain possession of the goods from the carrier and must deliver it or tender it to the buyer.[8] Under the terms C.&F. or C.F., the seller is obligated to do the same except that insurance is not purchased.

The main distinction between using F.O.B. or F.A.S., on the one hand, and C.I.F. or C.&F. or C.F., on the other, will be discussed later in this chapter. The important point to remember here is that the terms F.O.B., or "F.A.S. vessel," followed by either the town of the point of shipment or the town of destination indicate where the seller is to tender the goods and, consequently, where the risk of loss passes from the seller to the buyer.

Sales Contracts with No Delivery or Pricing Terms A third circumstance establishing the seller's obligation to tender at a specific place occurs when the agreement states nothing about delivery—the terms F.O.B., F.A.S., C.I.F., etc. are not used. When this occurs, the place for delivery is the seller's place of business,[9] if that is where the goods are located. If the goods are located at some other place at the time of the contract and if the goods are identified, then the delivery is presumed to be wherever the goods are located.[10]

In summary, we think of three different circumstances in which the seller meets its obligation of tendering. Two of them involve moving the goods—either to a carrier in its town to be shipped or to some other destination where the seller is to tender. One does not involve moving the goods—the seller must simply inform the buyer how and where to pick up the goods. Also, remember that the risk of loss usually passes on tender of delivery;[11] and when no specific place of tendering is stated, it is assumed to be the seller's place of business.[12]

Moving the goods—or not, as the case may be—is not the final event of tendering. When the goods are to be shipped from the seller's town or when the goods are in the possession of a bailee, the seller must send to the buyer the proper documents enabling the buyer legally to gain possession of the goods.[13] But is the seller required to tender the goods *and* send the documents entitling the other party to possession without first being paid? The answer is yes! Unless the agreement provides otherwise, payment must be made when the obligations of tender are met. But does this not put the seller at a slight disadvantage? The seller does not want to give up possession of the goods until it is paid, nor, really, does the buyer want to pay until the goods have been properly shipped and tendered. How is this difficulty of both parties dealt with in practice?

A Typical Sales Transaction—Tendering the Goods and Payment Although there are many ways of dealing with this circumstance, a usual one might be as follows. (See Fig. 25.1.) Let us assume that a manufacturer of steel desks near Chicago, Illinois, contracts to sell 100 of them "F.O.B. Los Angeles, California" for a total price of $10,000.

---

[8]UCC 2–320.

[9]UCC 2–308(a).

[10]UCC 2–308(b).

[11]UCC 2–509(3).

[12]UCC 2–308.

[13]UCC 2–503(3)(4)(5).

FIGURE 25.1 A Typical Sales Transaction

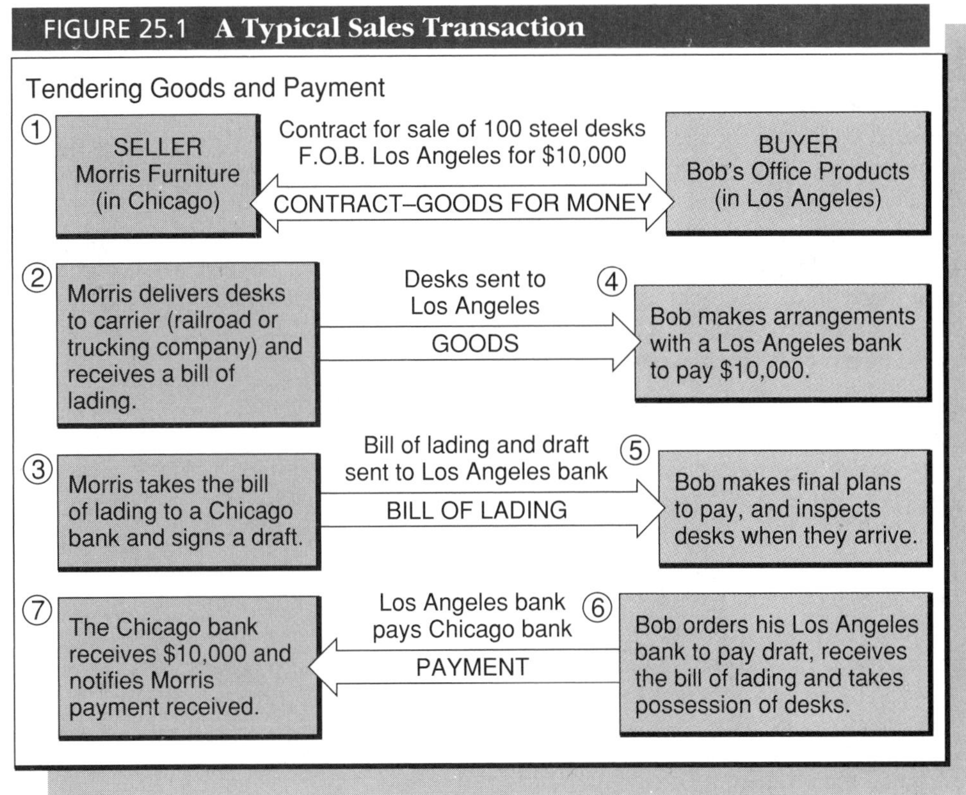

The seller has the duty to deliver them to Los Angeles, California, and, unless the agreement specifies otherwise, the seller is to tender, usually at the carrier's terminal in Los Angeles, in accordance with the terms set out in Section 2–503, already discussed. The seller crates the desks and delivers them to the railroad and receives a bill of lading from the railroad. For purposes of this discussion, a bill of lading is a document issued by the carrier entitling the holder of it to the physical possession of the goods. The seller takes the bill of lading to his bank in Chicago and there signs a money instrument called a "draft." A draft is simply an instrument drawn by the seller ordering the buyer to pay the sum of $10,000 to the Chicago bank. The seller then usually indorses (signs) the bill of lading over to the buyer and asks his Chicago bank to send the bill of lading and the draft to a Los Angeles bank, which the Chicago bank knows and trusts. The Chicago bank then indorses the draft, stating thereon, "Pay to the order of any bank." What has happened so far is that the seller has asked his bank to be a collecting agent, and the bank has, by its indorsement, empowered a bank in Los Angeles to be the bank's collecting agent. Both the draft and the bill of lading are then mailed to a Los Angeles bank. The two items together are called a **documentary draft.**

documentary draft
"Any negotiable or nonnegotiable draft with accompanying documents, securities or other papers to be delivered against honor of the draft" UCC 4–104(f)

When the documentary draft arrives in Los Angeles (before, we assume, the goods arrive), the buyer is notified and an employee of the buyer will go to the Los Angeles bank and make arrangements for payment. Before the actual payment is made, the buyer has a right to inspect the goods. After the goods arrive and while they are still in the possession of the carrier, they are inspected, and then the employee goes to the bank to complete the transaction. The employee pays at the bank and then receives the bill of lading. The employee delivers the indorsed bill of lading to the carrier and receives the desks. The $10,000, through various bank transfers, will be credited to the seller's account in the Chicago bank. This use of banks as agents enables both the seller and buyer to be more comfortable with the transaction. The seller was able to retain control of the goods until the price was paid (its agents had the bill of lading), and the buyer was not required to pay until it was assured that the goods were on the carrier, shipped to it, and inspection had been completed.[14]

The mechanics of tender, then, usually involve two separate events. One is the tendering of the goods, and a second is tendering the proper documents to the buyer. These mechanics are greatly simplified if tender is to be at the seller's plant.

► Standard of Performance by the Seller

We have just discussed the mechanics of *where* and *how* the seller is to tender. *What* the seller is obligated to tender are the exact goods required by the agreement of the parties.

Under the common law of contracts, the seller was required "substantially" to perform its obligations before triggering the buyer's obligation to pay. Article 2 has changed this and now requires that the seller perform in *every respect.* More particularly, Article 2 provides that if either the goods or the tender of delivery fail in any respect to conform to the contract, then the buyer may reject the whole, accept the whole, or accept any **commercial unit** or units and reject the rest.[15] This section imposes on the seller the requirement of a perfect tender[16] of both the goods and any documents needed to make the mechanics of tender good.[17] At first, this requirement may seem burdensome. Certainly it would have been burdensome in the late nineteenth and early twentieth centuries before our manufacturing processes could produce uniform quality of a single line of products. Today, however, when a large merchant seller represents that goods will be exactly as they appear in either a catalog or a sales presentation where models are used, the seller is not unduly burdened by a requirement that the goods tendered be exactly like those originally represented to the buyer. In the following case the court held that the buyer could reject nonconforming goods.

commercial unit
"Such a unit of goods as by commercial usage is a single whole for purposes of sale and division of which materially impairs its character or value on the market or in use" UCC 2–105 (6)

FACTS

Maas, a large commercial grower of wheat and corn, agreed to purchase a large silo and other needed equipment for the storage of grain. The contract stated that there was a "one year warranty of customer satisfaction." There was some evidence that the equipment and the construction of the silo were not exactly as they should be. From time to time the equipment would fail and, it was alleged, several hundred bushels of corn out of 3,000-plus spoiled within a year of delivery of the equipment. Maas wrote the seller saying it was rejecting the silo and the equipment. Rather than ask for damages, Maas requested the seller simply to remove all of the items provided from his property. To what standard of performance should the seller be held in this case?

---

[14]See R. J. Nordstrom, *Handbook of the Law of Sales* (St. Paul: West Publishing, 1970).

[15]UCC 2–601.

[16]Nordstrom, p. 308; see also Comment 2, Section 2–106, defining "conforming goods" wherein it is stated it is the policy of Article 2 to require "exact performance" by the seller.

[17]This discussion assumes that the goods sold are *new* and not used. When used goods are sold, the term "as is" is usually used to describe them, and the use of such a term requires the seller to deliver the goods in the used condition as they exist.

DECISION

The appellate court found in favor of Maas. The court held that the one-year warranty of customer satisfaction gave the buyer, Maas, the right to reject the goods one year from the date of installation. With regard to the standard of performance, the court recognized that courts follow one of two rules. The first is that the test of the buyer's satisfaction is his own personal judgment (which must be exercised in good faith). The second is that the purchaser is bound to be satisfied with the goods if a reasonable person would be satisfied with them. Since section 2–601 states, "If the goods or the tender of delivery fail in any respect to conform to the contract. . .", the first standard must be used. The court concluded that so long as the rejection was done in good faith and not capriciously, the jury in the trial court could have properly found for Maas. The seller was required to remove all of the equipment and the silo.

Maas v. Scoboda, 195 N.W.2d 491 (Neb. 1972).

Exceptions to the Perfect Tender Rule There are two important instances in which the impact of this requirement of a perfect tender on the seller's obligations may be *lessened.*

The first instance (Section 2–508) gives the seller, following an initial defective tender, an opportunity to tender again, or to **cure** the original defective tender of goods or documents when there is time or when the seller believed the original defective tender would be accepted. Assume that a contract calls for delivery on September 1. If there is a tender *before* that date and it is rightfully rejected, and there is time remaining in which to perform, the seller is given the opportunity to do so as long as reasonable notice is given to the buyer.

cure
A seller's correction of his or her failure to deliver conforming goods under a contract for sale before the due date has expired

Section 2–508 attempts to protect the seller from a surprise rejection.[18] The surprise rejection may arise from a rejection of goods or documents which the seller had reasonable grounds to believe would be acceptable. For example, assume that a seller agrees to sell 1,000 mini-calculators, model A-500, for $50 each. Only 950 of model A-500 can be conveniently located, so the seller decides to send along, for the same price, 50 of his newest model, A-502, which has two more functions than the A-500 and which would normally sell for $60. It seems that the seller should be given an opportunity to cure and tender the remaining 50 of model A-500 if the buyer objects to the imperfect tender.[19]

The second instance in which the impact of perfect tender on the seller's obligations is lessened occurs when the parties have agreed to an **installment contract.** If the goods are to arrive in separate lots, then the buyer may reject any such lot only if it substantially impairs the value of that installment and cannot be cured.[20] The Uniform Commercial Code generally favors any reasonable legal standard that attempts to keep goods moving in commerce. When parties contract for a one-time sale, the standard of the seller's performance, as we have seen, is that it must tender precisely what the contract calls for. When, however, the parties have contracted for a series of deliveries over a period of some months or years, Article 2 lessens the perfect tender requirement and allows the buyer to reject the goods only if the nonconformity substantially impairs the value of that installment and cannot be cured. This is true even if the contract states

installment contract
"One which requires or authorizes the delivery of goods in separate lots to be separately accepted" UCC 2–612 (1)

[18] UCC 2–508, Comment 2.

[19] UCC 2–508, Comment 2.

[20] UCC 2–612(2).

that "each delivery is a separate contract." The drafters apparently intended to provide some flexibility for the parties in installment contracts.

We assume that if the tender of an installment did not exactly meet the standards of the contract but the defect did not substantially impair its value, there would be some adjustment in price. If the defect in tender does substantially impair the value of that installment, the seller is given the opportunity to cure. If the seller cannot cure within a reasonable time and if the defect would substantially impair the value of the whole contract, there may then be a breach of the *whole* contract.[21] This is illustrated by the following case.

FACTS

Hans Holterbosch, Inc., was an American importer and distributor of Lowenbrau beer. It applied for and received permission to operate a Lowenbrau Pavilion at the 1964 New York World's Fair. It contracted with Graulich Caterer, Inc. to provide quality food for the pavilion. The quality of the food was to be equal to that presented to the agents of Holterbosch at a meeting on March 17, 1964 in which eight different platters of food were displayed and sampled. The initial contract was for about 1,000,000 units of food to be delivered over a one-year period. The first delivery of food on April 23, 1964 did not, according to Holterbosch's employees, in any way match the contract samples presented on March 17. The first 955 unit installment was rejected as unacceptable. Holterbosch agreed that it would allow Graulich to tender another batch of food. On April 25, 1964, 2520 units were delivered. Out of this number, between 500 and 700 were distributed among employees of Holterbosch and patrons at the exhibit. The complaints in response to this food were numerous. Generally, Holterbosch complained that the food was not German in character and was of such inferior quality that it could not be served. Holterbosch cancelled the contract.

Graulich sued Holterbosch for out-of-pocket loss of $29,937 spent on platters, trays, and doilies, and for the amount of profit lost, $35,950. Was Holterbosch liable for cancelling the entire contract?

DECISION

No. The appellate court found in favor of Holterbosch. The appellate court relied on the trial court's conclusion that the tenders of food on April 23 and 25 did not conform to the samples provided on March 17. This conclusion was reached by the jury, who observed the testimony and demeanor of the witnesses for both sides.

The key question was, however, did the nonconforming tenders substantially impair the value of the whole contract? The court said that the failure of the second delivery to be acceptable left Holterbosch without food for one week. Time was critical, and Graulich knew that platters of maximum quality German food were required on a daily basis. So, because of Holterbosch's immediate need for quality food and the failure of Graulich to cure and the nonconformity of the second delivery, the court found a substantial impairment of the value of the whole contract and allowed the buyer, Holterbosch, to cancel.

Graulich Caterer, Inc. v. Hans Holterbosch, Inc., 243 A.2d 253 (N.J. 1968).

Do the Goods in Fact Conform to the Contract? Whether the goods provided are in "accordance with the contract"[22] is itself an issue often as complex as the nature of the goods sold. For example, ascertaining whether a carload of construction lumber is in accordance with the contract is easy compared to ascertaining whether a Boeing 747, a

[21] UCC 2–612(3).

[22] UCC 2–106(2).

supertanker, or a new model computer is in accordance with the contract. In many instances, issues involving the failure of such complex goods are resolved by a breach of warranty analysis. We point this out here simply to illustrate that the seller's performance obligations to tender goods exactly as they were promised are subject to at least two methods of analysis. The first—whether the goods conformed to the contract at the time of delivery—is relatively easy. Only obvious defects will be revealed at this point. However, failure of goods during the time of its use requires a second method of analyzing a seller's obligation to provide the quality of goods promised. This second method relies on a breach of warranty analysis and will be found in Chapter 27.

Performance Obligations of the Buyer

The performance obligations of the buyer, not as complex as those of the seller, may be divided into two classifications. The first classification of performance obligations of the buyer is technical and exists only if the contract for sale does not establish the order for performance by the buyer and seller. Recall that we said that the seller's and the buyer's obligations are, technically, *concurrent*. This means that the seller must tender the goods in order to trigger the buyer's obligation to pay, and the buyer must tender payment in order to trigger the seller's obligation to deliver the goods.

The effect of this approach is to make it relatively easy for a court to determine when a breach of the sales agreement has taken place. In order to maintain a lawsuit based on a breach of a sales agreement, the complaining party must allege and prove that it was willing and able to discharge its performance obligations but the other party was not. Therefore, unless the agreement provides another order of performance, and if the buyer wishes to put the seller in default, the buyer must perform first by tendering payment.[23] This, then, is the first classification of performance obligations for the buyer.

► Payment by the Buyer

Obviously the buyer is to pay, but what are the specifics of this obligation? What is payment? When and where must it (usually) be made? Tender of payment is sufficient when it is made by any means current in the ordinary course of business.[24] Unless the agreement provides otherwise, this means that the full price must be tendered in cash or check. If the payment tendered is by check and the seller demands cash, the buyer will be allowed an extension of time reasonably necessary to procure the cash.[25] Credit or a delay in payment is available only if the parties have agreed to it.

Also, the parties may agree to exchange something other than cash for goods. Goods, for example, may be exchanged for goods,[26] and such a "barter" transaction is a sale for purposes of Article 2. The parties need not have agreed upon a price or payment, but as long as there is evidence that the parties intend to be bound, a court may find that an enforceable agreement exists. In this case the amount of the price is to be a reasonable

---

[23]UCC 2–511(1).

[24]UCC 2–511(2).

[25]UCC 2–511(2).

[26]UCC 2–304(1).

one.[27] In the following case the court found from the evidence that the parties intended to be bound even though they had not reached agreement on payment.

FACTS

Southwest Engineering Company, Inc., plaintiff, was engaged in general contracting work and wanted to bid on the construction of runway lighting facilities, for which they needed large electrical generators. They asked Martin Tractor Company (Martin), defendant, for a bid on the type of generator needed, and this bid was received in the amount of $18,500 on April 13, 1966 over the phone. Southwest relied on the price of $18,500 for the generator in making its bid on the runway lighting job, and, on April 14, Southwest's bid was accepted. When the parties met on April 28 to "firm up" the deal, the price was renegotiated to $21,500 and the detailed specifications of the generator were discussed and a "memorandum" satisfying the statute of frauds was signed by Martin. Toward the end of the meeting Martin's agents testified that they said they wanted payment as follows: 10 percent with the order, 50 percent on delivery, and the balance upon acceptance. Southwest's agents testified that they thought payment was to be 20 percent down and the balance on delivery, while there was testimony that the way payment was usually made was 90 percent on the 10th of the month following delivery and the balance on final acceptance.

No payment was made when the order was placed; and when Southwest demanded performance, Martin denied that there was an enforceable agreement because, among other things, the parties had never agreed on the terms of payment. Southwest sued Martin for breach of contract. The signed memorandum did not mention a specific term of payment. Was there an enforceable contract?

DECISION

Yes. The appellate court affirmed a decision for Southwest. The court concluded from the conflicting testimony that the parties had reached no agreement on payment. They found from other evidence, however, that the parties intended to contract and that there was a reasonably certain basis for giving an appropriate remedy. The time for payment is supplied by section 2–310, which states, "Unless otherwise agreed (a) payment is due at the time and place at which the buyer is to receive the goods. . . ." The buyer was ready and willing to perform at this point, and so the court found for it.

Southwest Eng'g Co., Inc. v. Martin Tractor Co. 473 P.2d 18 (Kan. 1970).

When and where must the tender of payment be made? Generally, the buyer is to tender payment at the time and place at which the buyer is to receive the goods.[28] This clearly means that the seller must complete all obligations of shipment and delivery and must wait until the buyer has received the goods before payment can be expected. In the absence of the need for the buyer to establish a breach of the agreement, the delivery and receipt of the goods is a precondition and not a concurrent condition.[29]

► Inspection by the Buyer

A second significant precondition to payment is the buyer's right to inspect the goods. The buyer has a right to inspect the goods after they have been identified to the contract

---

[27]UCC 2–305(1).

[28]UCC 2–310(a).

[29]White and Summers, *Handbook of the Law Under the Uniform Commercial Code* (St. Paul: West Publishing, 1972).

for sale or after tender or delivery (or whenever the seller completes performance) and *before* payment.[30] The time, place, and manner of inspection must be reasonable, and the expenses of inspection must be borne by the buyer but may be recovered from the seller if the goods do not conform and are rejected.[31]

► Acceptance by the Buyer

Finally, Article 2 requires that the buyer accept the goods. This is a technical performance obligation and occurs when the buyer

> **(a)** after a reasonable opportunity to inspect the goods signifies to the seller that the goods are conforming or that he will take or retain them in spite of their non-conformity; or
> **(b)** fails to make an effective rejection ... but such acceptance does not occur until the buyer has had a reasonable opportunity to inspect them; or
> **(c)** does any act inconsistent with the seller's ownership.[32]

Acceptance is important because, once it occurs, the seller is given an additional remedy in the case of a breach of the sales contract. Generally, before acceptance the seller's chief remedy upon the breach by a buyer is to stop shipment, recover the goods, or sue for lost profit. After acceptance, the buyer may not reject the goods[33] and the seller has the additional remedy of suing for the entire purchase price.[34]

In summary, the buyer's obligations, generally speaking, follow those of the seller to ship or deliver the goods. Upon receipt of the goods, the buyer is to inspect, pay, and accept them.

Performance Obligations in Special Circumstances

Article 2 has more performance obligations of the parties than we present here. However, this text on commercial law is intended to be as thorough as possible given space constraints. Of necessity, some of the provisions of Article 2 must be left for explanation and analysis in later courses on commercial law. Two sets of performance obligations are so important, however, that they merit special attention. The first set arises from Article 2 itself. The second arises from Article 6, Bulk Transfers. First we present the additional performance obligations of Article 2.

► The Obligation to Provide Adequate Assurance of Performance When Demanded

The parties to a contract for the sale of goods contemplate performance and not breach or the right to sue. So, "if either the willingness or the ability of a party to perform declines

---

[30]UCC 2–513(1).

[31]UCC 2–513(2).

[32]UCC 2–606.

[33]UCC 2–607(2).

[34]UCC 2–709.

insolvency

When the debtor "either has ceased to pay his debts in the ordinary course of business or cannot pay his debts as they become due or is insolvent within the meaning of the federal bankruptcy law" (assets are less than liabilities) UCC 1–201(23)

materially between the time of contracting and the time for performance, the other party is threatened with the loss of a substantial part of what has been bargained for."[35]

From the seller's point of view—and this is especially true if the seller is selling on credit—any information that the buyer is **insolvent** or in financial difficulty should cause the seller to demand in writing that the buyer's financial condition be clarified. A mere rumor of insolvency is not sufficient grounds upon which the seller may refuse to perform;[36] however, if the rumor is true, or if the seller learns by inquiring from the buyer that there are reasonable grounds to believe that the buyer may be insolvent, the seller may refuse to deliver except for cash.[37]

If either party receives a written demand reasonable under the circumstances for adequate assurance of performance and does not respond with an adequate assurance within a reasonable time—in any event, not longer than thirty days—then the demanding party may treat this as a repudiation of the contract.[38] In short, if reasonable grounds for insecurity exist, the party owing the obligation to perform may: (1) suspend performance; (2) demand in writing an adequate assurance of performance from the other party; (3) await a reply for a reasonable time, which is not over thirty days; and (4) if there is not an adequate reply, view the contract as repudiated by the other party. In the following case since adequate assurance was demanded by the seller and not given, there was justifiable ground for the seller's suspended performance.

FACTS

Gestetner, defendant, sold goods on credit to Turntables, Inc., plaintiff. After delivery of some of the goods, Gestetner found out that Turntables' "Fifth Avenue Showroom" address was a telephone answering service, that its "Island Park factory" was someone else's premises and Turntables had no leased space, and that they had a "bad" reputation for performance. Gestetner demanded adequate assurance for future performance (payment on delivery, we assume) even though the sales were to be on credit. Turntables was not insolvent at the time even though Gestetner believed it to be so. Adequate assurance was not given, so Gestetner refused to make more deliveries required by the contract. Turntables, Inc. sued Gestetner for failure to perform.

DECISION

The facts of the case, not disputed by Turntables, do reveal reasonable grounds for insecurity, and section 2–609 allows such a party having reasonable grounds for insecurity to suspend performance for which he has not already received an agreed exchange.

Turntables, Inc. v. Gestetner, 382 N.Y.S.2d 798 (1976).

► Performance Obligations Imposed When Bulk Sales Are the Subject of the Contract

The image of a complex commercial sale of goods we suggested in the last chapter was based upon the assumption that the seller was a manufacturer of some kind. Most manufacturers buy materials, usually on credit, and then add value to the materials by

[35]UCC 2–609, Comment 1.

[36]Nordstrom, p. 495.

[37]Ibid.

[38]UCC 2–609(4).

constructing either a final product or one that is not completely finished but is used by another manufacturer. Many of the suppliers who sell raw materials to the seller in our typical example rely on the fact that they will be paid out of the proceeds of what our seller transfers to others.

Article 2 is premised on the notion that a seller is offering goods in the ordinary course of its business. When a seller of goods decides either to exchange the nature of its business or to sell out completely by selling a major part of all of its materials, supplies, or other inventory, then there is a potential for commercial injury to those who normally rely on the fact that the seller will continue in operation. Those persons who could be commercially injured are the creditors of the seller.

For example, assume that for a merchant seller of goods insolvency seems imminent. Such a seller might desire to sell its inventory to a friend for less than it is worth, pay the creditors less than is owed them, and some time later reenter the business by getting a loan from the friend. Or the seller might simply sell the inventory, pocket the proceeds, and disappear.[39] So, to protect the creditors of the seller, Article 6 of the Uniform Commercial Code was drafted and has now been adopted by most of the states. However, Article 6 does provide the same general type of protection as the Uniform Fraudulent Conveyance Act, so some states have not adopted Article 6; or if they have adopted it, they may have substantially changed some of its provisions.[40] Nevertheless, it is important to realize that in many states the sellers and buyers involved in bulk transfers have certain performance obligations that run to the creditors of the seller.

Article 6 defines a **bulk transfer** as one that is a transfer, not in the ordinary course of the **transferor's** business, of a *major part* of the materials, supplies, merchandise, or other inventory. The Article does not clearly define what is a *major part* of the materials, supplies, etc. It has been suggested by prominent authorities that a major part refers to value and not quantity of the materials or inventory, and that certainly a transfer of 45 percent of the total value should be a "major part."[41] Some courts have recognized a sale of 25 percent of a merchant's inventory as a major part.[42]

bulk transfer
"Any transfer in bulk and not in the ordinary course of the transferor's business of a major part of the materials, supplies, merchandise or other inventory of an enterprise subject to Article 6" UCC 6–102(1)

Generally, there are several performance obligations required of the transferor (seller) and the transferee (buyer). The first is that, before the actual transfer takes place, the intended **transferee** must demand and receive a sworn list of creditors of the transferor together with a schedule of the property sufficient to identify it. The transferee must preserve the schedule for six months after the transfer and permit inspection of it by any creditor of the transferor during this period.[43]

transferor
One who has transferred some thing to another

transferee
One to whom another has transferred some thing

Second, at least ten days before the transferee is to take possession of the goods or is to pay for them (whichever happens first), the transferee must give notice of the transfer to creditors of the transferor.[44] This notice must be either delivered personally or sent by registered or certified mail to all persons shown on the list provided by the

[39]See UCC 6–101, Comment 2.

[40]For example, less than half of the states had adopted Section 6–106 of the Article as of 1989.

[41]White and Summers, *Handbook of the Law Under the Uniform Commercial Code,* p. 646.

[42]See *Danning v. Daylin, Inc.,* 488 F.2d 185 (1973).

[43]UCC 6–104.

[44]UCC 6–105.

transferor, and to all other persons who, the transferee knows, hold or assert claims against the transferor.[45]

The failure to comply with the above obligations renders the bulk transfer ineffective as against any creditor.[46] In such cases, the creditor of the seller will be able to assert whatever legal rights it has in the goods. The purpose of Article 6 is not to protect the creditors of a transferor in all cases in which a bulk transfer occurs; the purpose is to alert these creditors that a bulk transfer of goods in which they may have some property interest is about to take place. If their interests are not legally jeopardized by the proposed transfer, then the creditors cannot object.

The central point to remember is that, in certain cases, a buyer of a major part of a seller's inventory may have to relinquish possession of the goods if the performance obligations of Article 6 are not met. In the following case the buyer did not comply with the notice requirements, and the bulk sale was declared ineffective.

pro rata distribution
Distribution in proportion to one's contribution, loan or advance

FACTS

Pastimes Publishing Company was a publisher of books and on August 23, 1968 sold its entire inventory of books to Saalfield for $27,000. At this time Pastimes owed Midland Paper Company $34,000 and owed other unsecured creditors substantial sums. No notice of the sale was sent to the creditors of Pastimes. The entire proceeds of the sale were credited to Midland. The other creditors of Pastimes objected, and litigation resulted. What are the remedies of the unsecured creditors of Pastimes against Saalfield and Midland?

DECISION

The court held that a bulk sale was made and that the failure to meet the notice requirements of Article 6 resulted in a violation. Article 6 itself provides no specific remedies for unsecured creditors of bulk-sale sellers except to provide that the sale is ineffective. Under Illinois law, the unsecured creditors of Pastimes could recover the inventory sold or, at their option, divide the proceeds of the sale. The creditors opted to divide the proceeds and this had to be done on a **pro rata** basis. The credit of the entire proceeds to Midland was inappropriate since the amount credited arose from an ineffective transfer.

Pastimes Publishing Co. v. Advertising Displays, 286 N.E.2d 19 (Ill. 1972).

Most courts would allow judgment creditors of a bulk-sale seller to recover possession of the goods sold, but there would be little value in this if the goods were sold at a fair market price. The easiest remedy would be to attempt to recover the sales price as the creditors did in the case above.

Circumstances Excusing Performance of the Parties

Almost the entire body of our commercial law is built upon the assumption that parties to a commercial agreement intended and contemplated performance. The strength and value of our contract and commercial law are directly dependent upon the extent to which the law facilitates the parties' intent to perform pursuant to their agreement. Even when there is a failure of performance or a breach of the agreement, the law responds

---

[45]UCC 6–107(3).

[46]UCC 6–105.

by providing a measure of damages calculated to put the injured party in the same position it would have been in had there been performance.

In a sense, the commercial law is weakened in each instance in which the law recognizes an exception to the general rule that parties must perform when they have promised to do so. In some circumstances, however, there are good reasons for such exceptions. Generally, the reasons for excusing one or both of the parties from their agreement are based upon the occurrence of events that neither party could reasonably foresee, given the current commercial realities.

Article 2 recognizes four important circumstances in which a court will excuse performance. Three of these will now be considered. A fourth, involving "unconscionable contracts," will be discussed in Chapter 27. As you read the final part of this chapter, remember that, generally speaking, exceptions to the fundamental obligations of performance are narrowly defined and are recognized only where our notions of fairness override the necessary emphasis on performance. Note also that, since the seller usually has the first obligation to perform, it is generally the seller who is excused from performance.

► First: Excuse by Casualty to Identified Goods

A contract for the sale of goods contemplates the delivery of specific, identifiable goods, so their *total* destruction through no fault of either party will excuse *both* parties from their performance obligations. (Section 2–613)

There are four important conditions though that must be satisfied before the seller is excused from performance because of casualty to the goods:

1. The first condition is that the goods must be "identified when the contract is made." The precise meaning of this phrase is not made clear in Article 2 but most authorities believe it means that they could be reasonably specified or described at the time of the contract. Specification or description means that the goods can be separated from others when made or when the contract is formed; e.g., that one generator and no other, or that machine to be built and no other.[47]
2. The goods must be *totally* destroyed. If the goods are only partially damaged, the seller should notify the buyer and, if the buyer desires, the buyer may demand tender and inspection and may accept the goods with an allowance in price for the diminution of value. If the buyer chooses this option, however, the seller may not be sued for failure to deliver conforming goods.
3. The casualty must not have been caused by either party.
4. The risk of loss must not have passed to the buyer.

While these four conditions are necessary to excuse the seller *and* buyer from their performance obligations, which one will suffer the loss? If the casualty to the goods occurs before the risk of loss passes to the buyer, although the seller is excused from any performance obligation, the seller will suffer the loss. The seller is excused from having to tender new goods or a set of goods. If the casualty occurs *after* the risk passes to the buyer, the parties are not excused from their performance obligations, and the buyer suffers the loss.

[47]Nordstrom, p. 327.

► Second: Excuse by Failure of the Manner of Delivery, or Failure of the Means or Manner of Payment

Failure of the Manner of Delivery When neither party is at fault and the agreed manner of delivery becomes commercially impracticable, if there is a reasonable substitute, it must be tendered and accepted.[48] The "excuse" provided by this section is not a total one. From the seller's point of view, the excuse is from the agreed manner of delivery. Delivery is still required, but a reasonable substitute for the agreed manner of delivery may be used. The words "commercially impracticable" are not defined in Article 2, although Section 2–614(1) gives the following illustrations: "the agreed berthing, loading, or unloading facilities fail or an agreed type of carrier becomes unavailable." Generally, "commercially impracticable" means something more than simply "more expensive." If the agreed means of delivery becomes tremendously more expensive, then the seller will probably seek application of the next section below for "excuse by failure of presupposed conditions."

Failure of the Means or Manner of Payment The buyer is also protected by this section. If the agreed means or manner of payment fails because of a domestic or foreign governmental regulation, then the buyer may provide payment by a means that is a substantial equivalent.[49]

► Third: Excuse by Failure of Presupposed Conditions

At a very basic level, the law of contracts and Article 2 of the UCC are intended to protect and enforce the intention of parties to an agreement when they consciously allocate business risks. Simply put, if a seller agrees on January 1 to deliver 100 cases of tennis balls, "F.O.B. Buyer's City" on May 30 for $80 per case, then the seller has assumed the risk that on May 30 the same tennis balls could be sold for the higher price of $100 per case. Any time an agreement calls for future performance (and most do), there are certain price, delivery, and product risks. An important reason for our commercial law is to enforce the allocations of these risks. So, if the price of tennis balls in the buyer's city is $100 per case on the date of delivery, our seller has lost $20 per case because the same balls could have been sold there for the higher price. The law, however, requires the seller to perform or pay damages, because the seller assumed this risk.

The buyer also assumed some risks back in January. It assumed the risk that the price for the tennis balls in its city would be at least $80 per case. If it were less (say, $50 per case) on the date of delivery, then the buyer would lose $30 per case, but would be required to perform its obligations to the seller at $80 per case on that date or pay damages. The general rule is that the law will not excuse performance merely because a transaction may have become unprofitable. A rise or a collapse in the market for goods is not in itself a justification for excuse of performance; that is exactly the type of business risk that business contracts made at set prices are intended to cover.[50] There are thousands, perhaps millions, of transactions each day that result in losses to one of the parties. There is no excuse from such performance unless a court can be convinced that the parties did not consciously allocate the risk of an event that occurred.

---

[48]UCC 2–614(1).

[49]UCC 2–614(2).

[50]See UCC 2–615, Comment 4.

We emphasize that increased cost to the seller does not by itself excuse performance so long as the increased cost reflects only *normal* business risks. Some of the basic assumptions made by parties when they contract are that there will be not catastrophic storms, crop failures, unforeseen bankruptcies of major suppliers, unforeseen embargoes or wars, and so forth. When one of these events does occur, causing a drastic or unusual change in price, then the seller must first give notice to the buyer that there will be a delay or nondelivery[51] and may then attempt to "renegotiate" the contract with the buyer. However, if the parties cannot agree, the final arbiter will be a court. Whether the court will classify the event as a normal business risk, or a totally unforeseen contingency altering the essential nature of the performance obligation, is not certain. In the following case the court found a normal business risk and imposed liability for nonperformance by the seller.

FACTS

Wegematic Corporation, defendant, designed and produced a small computer known as the ALWAC III-E, which enjoyed considerable success. Wegematic designed in a preliminary way the ALWAC 800, which was characterized as a "truly revolutionary system," and submitted a proposal to the Federal Reserve Board for the production of the ALWAC 800 computer. The proposal was submitted as a competitive bid and was selected by the Federal Reserve Board. The parties agreed that the ALWAC 800 would be delivered on June 30, 1957 at a cost of $231,000. The board emphasized the importance of delivery on time, and the parties agreed that Wegematic would pay the board $100 per day for each day the delivery was late.

In March of 1957 Wegematic requested a postponement of the delivery date to late summer. In April they requested an October 30 delivery date because of design difficulties. And in mid-October Wegematic announced that it had become impracticable to deliver the ALWAC 800 due to engineering difficulties. They requested a cancellation of the contract with the board and a waiver of damage claims.

In October, 1957 the Federal Reserve Board set out to purchase comparable equipment and then the United States sued Wegematic for a total of $235,806, which included damages for delay and the increased price they had to pay another computer firm for substantially similar goods. Wegematic argued that to produce the ALWAC 800 would have taken an additional $1 million to $1.5 million and between one or two years full-time research. It argued that the agreement had become commercially impracticable because of the occurrence of events it could not predict in the fields of electronic engineering and rapidly developing computer technology.

Should the seller be excused from performance and the payment of damages because it was involved in a high risk field where developing new products was uncertain and hazardous?

DECISION

No. The court awarded judgment to the government for $235,806 plus interest. If one of the parties expressly assumed the risk attendant to some promised performance, then it must suffer the consequences. The court stated, "We see no basis for thinking that when an electronics system is promoted by its manufacturers as a revolutionary breakthrough, the risk of the revolution's occurrence falls on the purchaser." Even in fields of new and rapidly developing technology, a seller of a product should not be able to transfer the risks accompanying development to the purchaser. Sellers should not be free to gamble on mere probabilities of development without any risk of liability.

United States v. Wegematic Corp., 360 F.2d 674 (1966).

---

[51]UCC 2–615(c).

► Concluding Ideas About Risk Allocation

The best method for determining which of the parties assumed which risks is to read the agreement, or, where there is no written agreement, ascertain the oral understanding of the parties. Course of performance, course of dealing, and usage of trade are also important in ascertaining which risks the parties allocated in the absence of an expressed statement in the agreement.

Also, it is important to determine whether the seller owns the goods at the time of the contract. For example, if a seller agreed to deliver oranges from groves located in two Florida counties and then could not deliver because an unanticipated freeze destroyed the crop, the first issue a court would have to determine would be whether the oranges were the seller's and could be identified when the contract was made. If this were so, Section 2–613 (on casualty to identified goods) would excuse performance. However, if the seller could not identify the oranges at the time of the contract and was merely to buy oranges from growers to meet its own performance obligation, then the seller would be under a duty to buy whatever oranges were available in the two counties and supply them to the buyer on the date for delivery even though the seller would suffer a loss. If there were no oranges available in the two counties and the agreement or surrounding circumstances revealed that the seller assumed the risks of a freeze, the seller would be required to pay damages. If it did not assume such a risk, the seller could then attempt to assert Section 2–615.[52]

► Mistake by One of the Parties

There are no specific Article 2 sections directly applicable to circumstances in which one or both of the parties makes a mistake of calculation, typing, or the like. However, the common law rules on mistake are to supplement Article 2 (1–103), so the rules you learned in Part 2, Contracts, on mistake are applicable in appropriate circumstances and may be argued.

Finally, we must emphasize that the defenses of mistake, excuse of performance, duress, coercion—or the existence of an unconscionable provision or contract (discussed in Chapter 27)—are recognized and have legal significance only when courts declare them to be applicable. An assertion by one of the contracting parties that these circumstances excuse performance is not effective until and unless a court or the other party agrees.

Summary Statement

1. Generally, it is the parties' intent as expressed in their contractual documents that will determine the performance obligations of the parties.
2. The obligation of the seller is to transfer and deliver the goods and that of the buyer is to accept and pay for them in accordance with the contract.
3. The seller must tender the goods to the buyer in a manner and at the time and place as set in the agreement. The use of the terms F.O.B. or F.A.S. followed by a destination (e.g., the name of a distant town) require the seller at its own expense and risk to transport the goods *there* and tender them. If the terms used are F.O.B. or F.A.S. seller's town, or if the seller is to ship the goods, then the seller must put the goods

---

[52]See *Holly Hill Fruit Products Co. v. Bob Staton, Inc.*, 275 So.2d 583 (Fla. 1973).

in the possession of a carrier in its town and make a reasonable contract for their shipment and then notify the buyer.

4. If the term C.I.F. is used (e.g., C.I.F. Austin, Texas, when the seller is in Lansing, Michigan), the seller is to load the goods onto a carrier, make a contract for their shipment, and pay for the freight and insurance.
5. If the agreement states nothing about the place for delivery, the place for delivery is the seller's place of business, but if the goods are somewhere else, then delivery is where the goods are located.
6. The goods tendered by the seller must conform to the contract in every respect; if they do not, the buyer may reject them but the seller may cure its tender if there is time or if the seller reasonably thought the goods would be accepted.
7. The obligations of the buyer are to inspect, pay for, and accept the goods. The buyer is to tender payment at the time and place at which the buyer is to receive the goods.
8. A party has an obligation to provide an adequate assurance of performance when demanded if there are reasonable grounds for insecurity with respect to the party's performance.
9. In some states the sellers and buyers involved in bulk transfers have performance obligations to inform the creditors of the seller of the transfer.
10. The parties to a sales agreement may be excused from their performance obligations under the following circumstances:
    - **a)** The goods are totally destroyed through no fault of either party before the risk of loss passes to the buyer.
    - **b)** The manner of delivery or the manner of payment fails; however, a reasonable substitute must be tendered.
    - **c)** An event occurs that neither party could foresee and the risk for which was not allocated between the parties.

In the following case the question of who was to bear the risk of loss was determined by the seller's typing-in certain words on its form.

NATIONAL HEATER COMPANY, INC. v. CORRIGAN COMPANY MECHANICAL CONTRACTORS, INC.
482 F.2d 87 (1973)

Stephenson, Circuit J. National Heater, the seller, offered on March 1, 1969 to sell certain heating units to be used in the construction of the Chrysler automobile plant in Fenton, Missouri. The original offer of the seller stated that the price quoted was for the merchandise "F.O.B., St. Paul, Minnesota." The buyer, Corrigan Company, sent its "purchase order" back to the seller with the statement that the price was "$275,640—Delivered." The seller then mailed to the buyer an "Acknowledgment of Purchase Order" bearing the printed words "Sale Price Total" followed by typed-in wording "$275,640, Total Delivered to Rail Siding." In another of the seller's acknowledgment forms were the printed words "delivery of equipment hereunder shall be made F.O.B. point of shipment unless otherwise stated."

The heating units were shipped by the seller but were damaged in transit. The buyer received the goods and accepted them subject to a reduction in the sales price. The full contract price was not paid and the seller sued the buyer for the balance. The buyer counterclaimed, arguing that the risk of loss due to shipment damage was on the seller until delivery to the construction site in Missouri. The seller argued that the risk of loss was on the buyer once a reasonable contract for the delivery of the heaters was made in St. Paul. At the trial it was shown that both parties contemplated a Fenton, Missouri "rail siding" when the words "rail siding" were used.

When did the agreement of the parties state that the risk of loss was to pass? Judgment for the buyer, Corrigan Company. Seller appeals.

The intention of the parties is to control in determining the allocation of the risk of loss. When a written contract is partly written or typewritten and partly printed, any conflict between the printed portion and the typewritten portion will be resolved in favor of the latter. Also, any ambiguity in a party's form will be construed against that party since they drafted it and should not be allowed to take advantage of their own ambiguous draftsmanship. The seller's form stated in print that delivery was to be F.O.B., point of shipment, unless otherwise stated. It was "otherwise stated." The seller had typed in the words "$275,640, Total Delivered to Rail Siding." There was uncontradicted evidence that the rail siding referred to was the one at the construction site in Fenton, Missouri. The seller's obligations were to deliver to that point, and there the risk of loss would pass to the buyer.

Affirmed for the buyer, Corrigan Company.

Questions and Case Problems

1. Explain how banks are sometimes used in commercial transactions to facilitate the surrendering of possession of goods, the inspection of the goods by the buyer, and payment.
2. The plaintiff, Joc Oil USA, Inc., contracted to sell fuel oil to the defendant, Consolidated Edison, Inc. The contract described the oil as .50 percent maximum sulfur content. The contract included a clause that provided for a price adjustment between the parties under certain circumstances. The refinery certificate indicated a sulfur content of .52 percent and another test measured the sulfur content at .92 percent. The defendant rejected the shipment. Plaintiff then offered to reduce its price but this offer was rejected. Then the plaintiff made an offer to cure by providing oil to arrive seven days after the contract date. Time was not a factor. The defendant rejected this offer. In addition, the evidence showed the defendant was legally authorized to burn oil with up to 1.0 percent sulfur content, was in fact using and mixing oils with up to between .6 percent and .8 percent sulfur content with a few of the oils burned in excess of 1.0 percent. Did the defendant act reasonably in rejecting the plaintiff's shipment and the plaintiff's offer to cure? [*Joc Oil USA, Inc. v. Consolidated Edison Co. of N.Y.*, 434 N.Y.S.2d 623 (N.Y. 1980).]
3. *S*, seller, has just sold $14,000 worth of chains, sprockets, and steel tubing to *B*, buyer, on credit. *B* has a business in which he manufactures bicycles for the retail market. You are interested in starting a bicycle manufacturing operation and agree with *B* to buy 40 percent of *B*'s inventory of parts. Explain the performance obligations imposed on your transaction with *B* by Article 6 of the UCC (Bulk Transfers). If these obligations are not met, what are the remedies available to *S* if *S* is not paid?
4. The seller, plaintiff, agreed to custom-manufacture metal siding for the buyer, defendant. The exact shipping date was not agreed upon but, through correspondence, it was clear that the defendant needed the siding by May 1. It appeared from the evidence that this was a commercially reasonable time and that the defendant was relying on delivery on or before this date. The doors had not arrived by June and the buyer cancelled the contract. The seller alleges that this was a breach of contract and had it not been for strikes and faulty material received from its suppliers it

would have performed on time. Do the strikes and faulty material excuse the seller from its failure to deliver on time so that it may now maintain an action against the buyer? [*Morin Building Products, Co., Inc. v. Volk Const., Inc.*, 500 F.Supp. 82 (Mont. 1980)].

5. *S* agreed to sell to *B* 50 crates of machine parts for $300 per crate. The agreement stated nothing about the place of delivery nor the place or manner of payment. Several months after the agreement, *B* demanded that *S* deliver the machine parts to *B*'s place of business in a town 150 miles from *S*'s place of business. *S* countered by demanding that *B* pay for and pick up the crates of machine parts which had been identified and were at *S*'s warehouse. How is this dispute resolved by Article 2? Where is delivery and tender to take place? What must both parties do to place the other in default?

6. *S* contracted to sell to *B* 1,000 bushels of apples at $6 per bushel, "to be shipped in September" to *B* in *B*'s city. On September 20, 850 bushels were shipped to *B* and they arrived on September 25, when the price of apples in *B*'s city was $5 per bushel. The usual time of shipment was three to seven days. *B* refused the delivery after inspection because *B* found there were only 850 bushels. On September 26, *S* was notified and on that date shipped the remaining 150 bushels. What are the rights and obligations of the parties?

7. *A* agreed to sell and *B* agreed to purchase 1,000 small electric motors for $85 each, "F.O.B., Lansing, Michigan," the buyer's place of business. Nothing else in the agreement defined the delivery or payment obligations. The seller's place of business is Mobile, Alabama. What are the performance obligations of *A* and *B?*

8. In the fact pattern of question 7, assume that after *B* took possession of the motors, it is discovered that 20 percent of the motors would not perform according to the specifications supplied to *A* by *B*. What should *B* do? If there is sufficient time, what course should *A* follow? How would the performance obligations differ if the parties had negotiated an "installment contract?"

9. Neal-Cooper, buyer, was engaged in the business of selling grain and fertilizer. Neal-Cooper used large quantities of phosphates and potash, most of which were supplied by Texas Gulf Sulphur Co., seller. For several years prior to 1969 these two parties conducted business on an order basis without written contracts. Usually a phone call was made by the buyer stating the quantity needed; the seller stated a price and when and where the shipment would arrive. On November 20, 1969 the buyer received from the seller some printed form contracts which they were to use in making future orders. Two of the forms already bore the signature of the *seller's* general sales manager. The buyer was asked to fill in the quantities needed, sign the forms, and return them to the seller.

The buyer's agent agreed to buy 10,000 tons of coarse potash and 2,000 tons of granular potash for the period November 1, 1969 through June 30, 1970. All deliveries were to be "F.O.B. cars seller's plant, Potash, Utah." The printed form stated that the price was to be in accordance with the "seller's attached price list." No price list was attached but at the bottom of the agreement were the typed words:

Coarse at 21¢ per unit through January 31, 1970
Granular at 23¢ per unit through January 31,1970

Furthermore, the printed form stated that the contract would not be binding upon the seller until duly accepted at its New York office. The seller's form also had a provision enabling the seller to institute a price increase during the life of the

exculpatory clause
A clause that relieves a party from liability

contract effective 15 days after receipt by the buyer of a "revised TGS price list." Finally, the form contained an **exculpatory clause** excusing the parties from performance caused by, among other things, the operation of statutes or law.

Between November 12 and December 4, 1969 the seller shipped three shipments of potash to the buyer at the price stated in the form contract. On December 2, 1969 the buyer placed a large order for potash to be delivered in January. The seller refused to fill the order because (among other things): (1) the original contract was never formally accepted in New York so there was no "enforceable" agreement; (2) the Canadian government passed regulations that controlled the seller's production and price of potash so they were unable to promise any fixed tonnage for shipment in the future. (The Canadian regulations were intended to limit the production of potash and to set a minimum price of 33.75 Canadian cents per unit.) The seller argued that the agreement, if there was one, was thus rendered commercially impracticable, thereby excusing performance under Section 2–615 of the UCC.

At the trial there was testimony that the Canadian source was the primary source of the seller's potash but not the only source. The seller did have potash mines in the United States.

a) Was there an enforceable agreement? Why?
b) What was the price? Could the seller change its price during the life of the agreement?
c) Was the seller excused from performance?
d) If the buyer had ordered all 10,000 tons of coarse and 2,000 tons of granular potash for January delivery, would the seller have an excuse for not shipping all of it at that time?

[*Neal-Cooper Grain Co. v. Texas Gulf Sulphur Co.*, 508 F.2d 283 (1974).]

10. In the case of *National Heater Company, Inc. v. Corrigan Co. Mechanical Contractors, Inc.*, excerpted at the beginning of this section, if you were the seller, what would you have done to avoid the risk of loss that the seller had in that case?

CHAPTER 26

BREACH OF THE SALES CONTRACT, COURSES OF ACTION, AND REMEDIES

After you have read this chapter, you should be able to:

1. Describe the buyer's courses of action if the seller defaults before the seller is required to perform; then describe the seller's courses of action if the buyer defaults before the buyer is required to perform.
2. List and then define the various monetary remedies available to buyers and sellers upon the breach by the other party.
3. Describe the differences between incidental and consequential damages, give an example of each, and state the circumstances in which the court will award consequential damages.
4. List and then describe the circumstances in which the buyer may recover the goods contracted for from the seller and the circumstances in which the seller may recover the goods it has delivered to the buyer.
5. Discuss the circumstances in which the parties may limit the damage recovery of the opposing party.
6. Define what is meant by a statute of limitations and describe when the time period of this statute usually begins and ends in sales transactions.

BUSINESS DECISIONS and the LAW

It is human nature to be optimistic. Most merchants enter commercial contracts for the sale of goods with a clear expectation of performance, and most of them are not disappointed. The experienced merchant, however, also knows that commercial life can be unpredictable and that even the most "ironclad" agreement may be breached. So, a discussion of remedies for breach of a sales contract including the measures of damages is inevitable.

For example, is it enough to think about giving a seller its out-of-pocket losses when the buyer decides not to perform and breaches the sales agreement? It is not. The policy of our commercial law favors performance and providing a remedy that essentially puts the parties back where they were when the contract was made is not sufficient to meet this policy in favor of performance. Somehow we need a set of remedies that looks forward to performance. We need measures of damages that are given to the damaged parties that compensate them by putting them in the same position they would have been in had there been performance. In some cases, this may involve some speculation about the amount of damages awarded, but this is more desirable than opting for certainty and a policy that does not hold out performance by both parties as its central objective.

The fact that a remedy is available does not mean that the party receiving it is fully compensated. In general, there is no substitute for full performance. Lawsuits are costly to both parties in terms of money spent for lawyers and in the time and energy demanded from management during trial. So, performance is always preferable even though at times it may be not as profitable as originally thought.

Introduction

Courts and "the law" must attempt to put the nonbreaching party in the same position it would have been in had there been full performance.[1] If the remedy sections do not achieve this objective, the value of all other sections is diminished. It is for this reason that the principles of breach and remedies are so important. This chapter presents an analysis of both the buyer's and seller's courses of action once they have learned of a breach by the other party and their various remedies. The material is best read based upon the central image of two corporate merchants who have entered into an enforceable sales agreement.

Breach of the Sales Contract by the Seller

▶ Buyer's Courses of Action Without Bringing a Lawsuit

One of the most difficult problems that arise from commercial conduct is the judgment about the other party's anticipated performance. When a doubt about the seller's performance is created in the mind of the buyer, for example, what should the buyer do? Below we consider first the possible courses of action of the buyer; then we analyze the remedies and measures of damage available to the buyer when the seller breaches. We start with the buyer's courses of conduct and remedies because, generally, the buyer faces a tougher problem in assessing the nature of the seller's performance than does the seller in assessing whether the buyer has paid or will pay.

The discussion of the various courses of action analyzed below is based on the assumption that the opposing party is *not* perfectly clear about repudiating its performance obligations. If a party is clear about repudiating, then the course of conduct is clear. For example, if the seller writes to the buyer that the seller has no intention of performing at all, this is called an **anticipatory repudiation,** and the buyer may select one of two courses of action. (1) The buyer may, for a commercially reasonable time, await performance (to see if the seller changes its mind), or (2) the buyer may suspend its performance obligations and resort to any of the remedies for breach discussed below.[2]

anticipatory repudiation
A party's manifestation of an intent not to perform contractual obligation, made before his or her performance is due

Also, remember that the *buyer's* actions in response to a seller's actions indicating breach should be clear and free from doubt. Article 2 (2–301) imposes on the parties *mutual* obligations of performance. Until the buyer is convinced of the seller's intent not to perform, or to perform partially, the buyer should remain ready to accept and pay for the goods.

Buyer's Right to Adequate Assurance of Performance If reasonable grounds appear that cause the buyer (or seller) to feel insecure about the seller's (or buyer's) performance, then the buyer (seller) should (1) suspend performance, (2) demand in

[1] UCC 1–106(1).

[2] UCC 2–610.

writing an adequate assurance of performance, and (3) await a reply for a reasonable time, which is not over thirty days. If there is no adequate reply, then the buyer (seller) may treat the contract as repudiated by the seller (buyer).[3] Section 2–609 was intended to provide a course of action to a party when the other party's actions were ambiguous or cast doubt on its ability to perform. Obviously, it was intended to apply to circumstances *before* the date of performance of either party. This section was discussed more fully in Chapter 25, Performance of the Sales Contract.

Buyer's Right to Reject or Accept the Goods Generally, at the time of the seller's tender of the goods, it is the obligation of the buyer to inspect the goods and either accept or **reject** them. The buyer *must* accept and pay for them if they conform to the contract. If, however, the goods fail *in any respect,*[4] then the buyer may reject the whole, or accept the whole (with, we assume, an allowance in the price for the defect), or accept any **commercial unit** or units and reject the rest.[5] The definition of a commercial unit may vary depending upon the type of goods in question and the practices of merchants in the market for the goods. The importance of the definition of a commercial unit is illustrated by the following case.

rejection
In sales, the buyer's refusal to accept goods provided by the seller under a contract for sale

commercial unit
"Such a unit of goods as by commercial usage is a single whole for purposes of sale, and division of which materially impairs its character or value on the market or in use" UCC 2–105(6)

FACTS

The seller, Salinas Lettuce Farmers Cooperative located in Salinas, California, sold a truckload of various kinds of vegetables to the buyer, Larry Ober Company, Inc., a produce broker located in Pompano Beach, Florida. The load contained 115 cartons of green cabbage, 4 cartons of broccoli and 10 cartons of romaine. When it arrived the cabbage and broccoli were badly discolored and the romaine was decaying. The buyer accepted all of the good vegetables and rejected the cabbage, broccoli and romaine. The seller sued the buyer. The court hearing the case said that the question in this case is the treatment of a mixed load of vegetables in the perishable agricultural commodities industry and whether the industry considers *each lot* of distinct vegetables to be a commercial unit or whether it considers the *entire truckload* to constitute a commercial unit?

DECISION

The court held that the entire truckload was a commercial unit. The court reasoned that in the market for perishable agricultural commodities, the seller lacks the ability to control what happens to its goods if they are rejected, and particularly so when a portion is accepted while another portion is not. Thus there has arisen in the industry the practice of accepting or rejecting whole truckloads. So, the court concluded that whenever there is a shipment of several perishable agricultural commodities the entire truckload (or carload) is the commercial unit. A buyer may not accept some commodities and reject others. Rather, its appropriate course of action if it accepts the goods is to accept the *entire* shipment and seek damages for breach of warranty on the inferior or spoiled goods. In this case, the purchaser became liable for the entire contract price less damages resulting from any breach of warranty by the seller. The burden is on the purchaser to establish the breach and the resulting damages.

Salinas Lettuce Farmers Coop. v. Larry Ober Co., Inc., 28 U.C.C.Rep. 684 (1980).

---

[3]UCC 2–609.

[4]This is the language of the Code creating the requirement of a "perfect" tender discussed in Chapter 25. Although the Code itself states that "exact performance" is required (see sec. 2–106, Comment 2), some legal scholars have concluded that "substantial" performance is all that is required. See J. White and R. Summers, *Uniform Commercial Code* (St. Paul: West Publishing Company, 1972), p. 256. This view seems to contradict the expressed intent of the drafters.

[5]UCC 2–601.

Rejection of the Goods Let us assume that the buyer has ordered one shipment of goods and it has arrived and the buyer desires to *reject* the entire shipment. How is an effective rejection made?

1. It must be made within a reasonable time after the delivery or tender of the goods (but before acceptance).
2. It is effective when the buyer seasonably notifies the seller of the rejection.[6]

These requirements of an effective rejection demand that the buyer act promptly. The words "reasonable" and "seasonably" are not defined in this section, so a court is left free to define them in relation to the circumstances of the case. The buyer's actions must be precise when rejecting goods. Any exercise of ownership of the goods by the buyer is wrongful against the seller and may cause a court to conclude that the buyer has waived rejection.

After notice of rejection is sent, the buyer's course of action will depend on whether the buyer has paid anything for the goods received. If the buyer has not paid anything for the goods, it is under a duty to hold them with reasonable care for disposition by the seller.[7] If the seller has no agent or place of business at the place where the rejection takes place, then a *merchant* buyer must follow any reasonable instructions from the seller. In the absence of such instructions, and if the goods are perishable or will quickly decline in value if not sold, the buyer must make reasonable efforts to sell the goods for the account of the seller, deducting from the sales price the buyer's reasonable expenses for caring for and selling the goods.[8]

If the buyer has paid something for them, whether it is the full price or just a partial payment, the buyer has a property interest in the goods in its possession or control, called a **security interest,** for the amount paid *and* expenses reasonably incurred in their inspection, receipt, transportation, care, and custody.[9] This property interest in the goods enables the buyer to sell the goods in good faith and in a commercially reasonable manner. The buyer must account to the seller for any excess money received over the amount of the security interest.[10]

security interest
"An interest in personal property or fixtures which secures payment or performance of an obligation" UCC 1–201(37)

Acceptance of the Goods The alternative to rejecting the goods is to accept them. Acceptance occurs (1) after a reasonable opportunity to inspect and when the buyer signifies to the seller that the goods are conforming or that the buyer will take them in spite of their nonconformity; or (2) if the buyer fails to make an effective rejection (after a reasonable opportunity to inspect); or (3) if the buyer does any act inconsistent with the seller's ownership.[11] Acceptance of a part of any commercial unit is acceptance of that entire unit.[12]

---

[6]UCC 2–602(1).

[7]UCC 2–602(2)(b).

[8]UCC 2–603(1)(2).

[9]UCC 2–711(3).

[10]UCC 2–706(6).

[11]UCC 2–606(1).

[12]UCC 2–606(2).

Acceptance of the goods has three important consequences. (1) Acceptance obligates the buyer to pay for the goods at the contract rate.[13] (2) Acceptance gives the seller an additional remedy for a breach by the buyer. (3) Of more importance to our inquiry into breach and damages, acceptance shifts the burden of proof for establishing nonconformity from the seller to the buyer. Whereas rejection of the goods by the buyer results in the *seller* bearing the burden of proving that the goods were conforming, if acceptance has taken place and then an alleged nonconformity is detected, it is the burden of the *buyer* to establish the nature of the seller's breach.[14]

Buyer's Right to Revoke Its Acceptance We must assume that many, if not most, of the breaches by a seller for tendering nonconforming goods are discovered after acceptance. The complexity of goods manufactured today makes it difficult to discover whether goods tendered are nonconforming by mere visual inspection or even sampling their performance. The Code recognizes this and provides a course of action for the buyer when it discovers a nonconformity after acceptance. Section 2–608 allows a buyer to revoke acceptance. It provides:

> **(1)** The buyer may revoke his acceptance of a lot or commercial unit whose nonconformity *substantially impairs* its value to him if he has accepted it
>
> > **(a)** on the reasonable assumption that its nonconformity would be cured and it has not been seasonably cured; or
> >
> > **(b)** without discovery of such nonconformity if his acceptance was *reasonably induced* either by the difficulty of discovery before acceptance or by the seller's assurances.
>
> **(2)** Revocation of acceptance must occur *within a reasonable time* after the buyer discovers or should have discovered the ground for it and before any substantial change in condition of the goods.... It is not effective until the buyer notifies the seller of it.
>
> **(3)** A buyer who so revokes has the same rights and duties with regard to the goods involved as if he had rejected them. [Emphasis added.]

Rejection and revocation of acceptance have some similarities and some substantial differences. If the revocation is effective, then, as in rejection, the goods will be treated as if they were the seller's, and the buyer has the same courses of action open to it, including the right to sell the goods it possesses. Unlike a rejection, which is available in single delivery contracts for any nonconformity, a revocation of acceptance is permitted only where the nonconformity substantially impairs the value of the goods to the buyer. This substantial impairment of value can be asserted by the buyer only where the buyer noted an earlier nonconformity that was not reasonably cured, or where detection of the nonconformity was reasonably induced either by difficulty in discovery or by the seller's assurances. The right to revoke acceptance may be lost unless it is asserted within a reasonable time after the discovery of the nonconformity (or the passage of time within which the buyer should have discovered it). If the buyer uses the goods after an attempted revocation, the courts will most likely hold that such use bars the assertion of the revocation, with the result that the buyer would retain the goods.[15]

In the following case, the nonconformity of the goods did not substantially impair the value of the goods to the buyer, who was not permitted to revoke its acceptance.

---

[13]UCC 2–607(1).

[14]UCC 2–607(4).

[15]R. J. Nordstrom, *Handbook of the Law of Sales* (St. Paul: West Publishing, 1970).

counterclaim
A claim asserted by the defendant against the plaintiff's claim in a civil action

FACTS

The plaintiff, Kearney & Trecker Corp., was the seller of sophisticated industrial equipment used to make metal parts. On July 1, 1970 Kearney & Trecker agreed to sell to Fargo Machine & Tool Co., defendant, for $153,725 a metal-shaping machine with additional parts that made the machine adaptable for a number of tasks. Delivery and installation were completed in September, 1971. The machine did not operate to the full satisfaction of the buyer, and numerous service calls followed. As of January, 1972 Fargo Machine had paid $75,000 on the machine and was not content with the machine's performance but agreed to pay an additional $28,868, reducing the balance to $50,000 in return for Kearney's promise to correct specified deficiencies. In June of 1972 Kearney advised Fargo that the deficiencies had been remedied and requested prompt payment of the balance. Fargo refused to pay, stating that new deficiencies were noticed all the time. In April of 1973 the seller, Kearney & Trecker, filed suit for the balance. The buyer, Fargo Machine & Tool Company, **counterclaimed** by asserting that they wished to revoke their acceptance of the machine. Can the buyer revoke its acceptance?

DECISION

The court held that the buyer could not revoke its acceptance but did allow the buyer to offset specified items of damage against the seller's claim for the balance.

The court relied on UCC Section 2–608 and the requirement that a nonconformity must substantially impair the value of the goods to the buyer before revocation of acceptance will be ordered. The court stated that although the impairment in value is a subjective issue requiring the court to focus on the impairment of value to the particular buyer before the court, it is to be resolved based upon the objective facts of the case and not based upon personal beliefs of the buyer. The "facts" the court found persuasive were: (1) the buyer made a $28,000-plus payment after acceptance and had a reasonable opportunity to use the machine; (2) in the first two years of operation there was only one period when the machine went down, and there were no incidents where a work piece was defectively machined or finished late; and (3) in the nearly 5½ years that Fargo operated it, the machine was used to at least the same productive extent as is normally expected of such a machine. The court concluded that Fargo's extensive use of the machine is a clear indication that the effect of the malfunctions on the user was not substantially adverse. The court awarded the plaintiff $46,260, allowing the defendant to offset over $4,000 of damages for lost profits and repairs.

Fargo Machine & Tool Co. v. Kearney & Trecker Corp., 428 F.Supp. 364 (E. D. Mich. 1977).

In most situations where goods do not conform to the contract, the buyer and the seller, guided by their own notions of good faith action, and perhaps by the thought of doing business with one another in the future, will attempt to work out an adjustment of the price for the nonconformity. If such an adjustment is not possible and the buyer has followed one of the courses of action just described and, further, desires a legal remedy for breach, then the buyer *must notify* the seller that the buyer is claiming a breach of the agreement.[16] Upon breach of the sales agreement by the seller, the buyer may select one or more of the court-awarded remedies discussed next.

► Buyer's Resort to the Courts

Valuing the Expectation, Reliance, and Restitution Interests of the Injured Party

The law must attempt to compensate the nonbreaching party so that it is put as close as possible to the position it would have been in had there been performance. Courts, as

[16] UCC 2–607(3)(a).

a general guide to awarding remedies, recognize three basic principles that are usually phrased in terms of the nonbreaching party's interests in the transaction. They are, in order of importance, the *expectation, reliance,* and *restitution* interests.

No single legal principle will provide a guide for action in every situation involving a breaching party. However, given the general objective of compensation, the best principle to begin with is that courts should give the nonbreaching party what it *expected* from the other party's performance. In some cases an award of money damages will do this, and in other cases an order to the seller to convey the goods will do this. The fundamental notion, though, is to give the buyer the *gain* that it had expected. When such a gain is given to the nonbreaching party, a court is protecting the expectation interest of that party.

In some circumstances, however, a buyer may have incurred expenses in reliance upon the expected performance that exceed the gain from the particular breached performance. For example, a manufacturer of small steel products may have spent $1,000 for cement footings and supporting structures for a large steel stamping machine it ordered from the seller. Assume that the seller repudiates the contract and the buyer finds that it can purchase a similar machine for the same price it was to pay the first seller. However, the new machine required new cement footings, which cost another $1,000, and the old ones had to be removed at a cost of $500. This buyer incurred expenses of $1,500 in reliance on the first seller's promise and should be able to recover that amount even though the measurable gain to the buyer had there been no breach may have been less.

In a few cases the anticipated gain may be too speculative to measure and there may be no amounts expended by the nonbreaching party in reliance on the breached promise, but the breaching party may have experienced a gain as a result of the transaction. In this case the courts will measure the amount of loss to the nonbreaching party by allowing it to recover the breaching party's gain. Courts are protecting the **restitution** interest of the buyer in this instance. The best example of this measure of damage is a case in which the buyer pays $3,000 down on a $5,000 contract and there is a breach by the seller. For a number of reasons, the buyer is unable to prove its gain had there been performance and cannot show damage caused by reliance on the breached promise. (Assume, for example, that a mountain ski resort had ordered a large snow-making machine the fall before a winter in which there were record snowfalls.) Courts would order the return of the $3,000.

restitution
A legal remedy restoring a party to his or her original position prior to the particular transaction

Buyer's Remedies in the Courts Protecting the expectation, reliance, and restitution interests of the nonbreaching party is accomplished by the law's recognizing one or more of the following remedies of the buyer: (1) the right to cover (buying substitute goods); (2) the right to sue for damages for nondelivery or repudiation; (3) the right to accept the goods and either deduct damages from the price or sue for damages resulting from the accepted goods; and (4) the right to require the seller to deliver the goods. In this section we analyze the different types of the buyer's monetary recovery (the first three listed remedies). In the next major section we analyze the fourth category of remedies, the right to the goods.

Before the buyer claims one of the first two remedies discussed below, it must give the breaching seller notice that it is claiming a breach, and the buyer may also demand the return of any money paid the seller under the breached contract. If this money paid is not returned, the money may be made part of the damage claim.

1. Buyer's Right to Cover (Procure Substitute Goods) One of the innovations in Article 2 is the buyer's remedy of **covering.** After a breach (nondelivery of the

cover
To seek a substitute performance of a contract

goods) by the seller and notice to the seller that the buyer is claiming such a breach, the buyer may, in good faith and without unreasonable delay, make a reasonable purchase of goods in substitution for those due from the seller.[17] If the goods cost more than the buyer had agreed to pay, the buyer may sue the seller for this added cost plus any incidental or consequential damages, but less any expenses saved in consequence of the seller's breach.[18] The section on "covering" was intended by the drafters of the Code to be the primary remedy of the buyer, but the buyer is not "forced" to cover (it may select any appropriate remedy). In the following case the buyer chose to cover.

FACTS

The plaintiff, Owens, agreed to buy 143,500 feet of 6-inch pipe and 103,000 feet of 3-inch pipe from the defendant, Clow Corporation. The defendant did not make several deliveries on time, and the plaintiff suffered some damage as a result. When it appeared that the defendant would not be able to make future deliveries on time, the plaintiff "cancelled" the contract with Clow, bought the required pipe elsewhere for more than it was required to pay Clow, and sued Clow for the difference. Clow admitted that it could not fully perform the contract but argued that Owens was required to buy all the pipe Clow had before buying the pipe from another source. Was the defendant correct?

DECISION

No. The appellate court affirmed a trial court finding in favor of the plaintiff, Owens. In reviewing Owens' action in claiming a breach and covering, the court noted that whether it was reasonable for Owens to purchase elsewhere, after his agreement with Clow caused him damaging delays, was a classic jury issue. The court affirmed the charge to the jury on the law and quoted it as follows:

> [I]f you are reasonably satisfied from the evidence that defendant, Clow, . . . failed to furnish the materials as agreed or within a reasonable time, then Owens would be entitled to cancel the contract with Clow and purchase other materials from another supplier and set off the difference in cost against. . . Clow, provided such purchase was reasonably necessary and was made in good faith without any unreasonable delay.

Owens v. Clow Corp., 491 F.2d 101, 104 (5th Cir. 1974).

Note that the court did not say that the law required Owens to purchase the supply of pipe Clow had on hand before covering.

The Code provision for covering reads simply, but applying its provisions to a factual pattern may be complicated by the nature of the goods contracted for and the buyer's plans for the goods when received. Let us start with a simple example. Assume that *B* contracted to buy a quantity of apples for $5,000, payment due on delivery. *S*, seller, breaches and the buyer buys elsewhere the same quantity and quality apples for $4,500. This is one of those rare situations where there has been a breach but no **damage.** In such cases the court would award **nominal damages** of $1 to *B* should *B* desire to sue. The more realistic situation is one in which *B* must pay $6,000 for the same apples (or reasonable substitutes). In this case *B* could buy the apples and sue *S* for $1,000.

damage
Loss or harm

nominal damages
The money judicially awarded to an injured party when no damage has occurred from another's wrongful conduct

[17] UCC 2–712(1).

[18] UCC 2–712(2).

Now let us change from apples to a complex piece of machinery and assume that there are very few sellers of such machinery. If there is only one seller of such machinery, then *B* would attempt to get the machine itself (if it had been constructed) and would not have opted to cover. If there are a few sellers, good commercial practice would dictate that *B* get price quotes from them for the machinery. The identical machine need not be ordered, but the Code requires that the substitute be "commercially usable as a reasonable substitute under the circumstances of the particular case."[19] What is meant by "commercially usable as a reasonable substitute" cannot be defined without the facts of a particular case. Ultimately who defines such terms is the trier of fact (either the jury or the judge sitting without a jury). If *B* finds a machine that is commercially usable as a reasonable substitute, *B* may buy it and sue *S* for any added cost.

Another factor (besides the nature of the goods) that complicates the calculation of monetary damages for the buyer is what the buyer intended to do with the goods. At this point we are going to emphasize a basic distinction in the types of monetary damages. This distinction is between incidental and consequential damages. The discussion below relates to *both* buyers' and sellers' money damages.

a. Incidental Damages Obviously, the buyer should be able to recover all of its expenses resulting from the seller's breach. So, if there are added expenses in covering for inspection, receipt, transportation, care or custody of the goods rejected or later purchased, these may be recovered. Article 2 calls "reasonable expenses" associated with breach **incidental damages.**[20] These are essentially reliance losses and they must be *caused* by the seller's breach. In our apple example above, if *B* had agreed to send *B*'s truck (at a cost of $100) for the apples, and *S* refused to deliver the apples when the truck arrived, and it cost *B* an *additional* $75 to get substitute apples, then *B* should be able to recover the $75. *B* should not be able to recover as incidental damages the $100 it had planned to spend to get the first load. The breach did not cause the $100 expenditure; it did cause the $75 expenditure.[21] If *B* decided not to purchase substitutes, then the $100 may be recovered because this amount was spent by the buyer with no realization of value for it. The truck made the trip to *S*'s place.

incidental damages
The money judicially awarded to a nonbreaching party for expenses reasonably incurred by the nonbreaching party on the other party's breach

b. Consequential Damages However, *B* may have incurred an additional item of damage. If *B* had one contract to purchase apples for $5,000 before *S* breached and then made another contract to sell them for $5,800, *B* was expecting an $800 gain from the two transactions. This gain is an item of **consequential damages** and may be recovered from *S* so long as *S* knew or had reason to know that the apples were being purchased for resale at the time *B* and *S* contracted. Consequential damages are those resulting from the breach and the buyer's inability to fulfill general or particular requirements for which the goods were needed. Usually in a sales contract case,

consequential damages
The money judicially awarded to an injured party for loss that the breaching party reasonably could foresee would be a result of his or her breach

[19]UCC 2–712, comment 2.

[20]UCC 2–715(1).

[21]See Nordstrom pp. 464–65. Is there a conflict between this example and the one mentioned earlier in the chapter where a buyer was allowed to recover $1,500 for cement footings prepared for a machine not delivered? No! In the latter case the buyer was willing to spend $1,000 to properly seat the machine. As a result of the breach it spent $500 to remove unsuitable footings and $1,000 more to create new ones. The recovery should be for $1,500 because these were the expenses *caused by the breach*.

consequential damages refer to the lost gain or lost expectation of the parties.[22] Recovery of this gain in proper circumstances is important, and it is for this reason we said that what the buyer of goods plans to do with the goods is a complicating factor in our analysis of monetary damages.

When persons assert that they are entitled to consequential damages, they face a relatively tough matter of proof. First they must prove that it is more probable than not that the breaching party knew, or had reason to know, at the time the contract was formed the general or particular requirements for the goods that were not fulfilled. This is relatively easy to do where the buyer is a known "middleman" whose sole purpose for being in business is to purchase and resell goods. It is also relatively easy to do where the contract states that the goods are for resale. But what test should be applied by a court where these circumstances are not present? How much and what kind of "knowledge" must the seller possess to make it liable for consequential damages?

The majority of courts seem to be utilizing the same test announced in the classic case of *Hadley v. Baxendale*,[23] summarized by Corbin in his classic treatise on contract law. He stated that a plaintiff may recover consequential damages if it can prove that "it is one that ordinarily follows the breach of such a contract in the usual course of events, or [is one] that reasonable men in the position of the parties would have foreseen as a probable result of breach."[24]

Another troublesome part of proving consequential damages is proving that it is more probable than not that the exact amount asserted by the plaintiff would have been gained had there been performance. While the Code does not require "mathematical precision" in the proof of loss,[25] it does require that the buyer prove with 51 percent certainty that the amount lost and claimed as consequential damages would have been gained had the other party performed as promised. Like so many other issues, this one must be left for the jury or a judge sitting as a fact finder. The following case illustrates that the plaintiff suffered damages but was unable to prove the exact amount or that the defendant knew about circumstances necessary for the award of consequential damages.

FACTS

The plaintiff, Great American Music Machine, Inc., contracted with the defendant, Mid-South Record Pressing Company, to press some record albums from a tape made by Ralph Harrison, an unknown songwriter and singer. The plaintiff planned to have Harrison's records distributed and promoted and at the same time planned to raise additional capital through a public offering of its stock. On April 3, 1972 the plaintiff received the first shipment of records and, upon inspection, discovered that they were warped, pitted, and blistered and produced excessive surface noise. The plaintiff immediately contacted the defendant but was told that 8,000 of the records had already been distributed. In the meantime the plaintiff had contacted a brokerage firm to underwrite some of its stock. The brokerage

[22]In a breach of *warranty* case, consequential damages also refer to damages to persons or property proximately resulting from the breach.

[23]156 Eng. Rep. 145 (Ex. 1854).

[24]A. Corbin, "Corbin on Contracts," in J. White and R. Summers, *Handbook of the Law Under the Uniform Commercial Code*, p. 316.

[25]UCC 2–715, comment 4.

firm agreed to underwrite $500,000 worth of the plaintiff's securities if it could get the Harrison record album "up and going." The plaintiff alleged that the defective pressing of the records virtually destroyed the market for Harrison's records and caused the failure of the brokerage firm to underwrite its stock. Can the plaintiff recover the capital lost from the projected underwriting as a measure of damages for the defendant's breach?

DECISION

No. On the issue of the consequential damages, the court found for the defendant. The court says that although there was "some mention" between the plaintiff and defendant of the stock offering, it does not appear from the proof that this matter was discussed in sufficient detail so that the defendant had *any* idea it might be held liable for the failure of the underwriting. Also, the court rejected the $500,000 claim because the proof was not sufficient to establish that the underwriting failed as a result of the defective record pressing.

Great American Music Machine, Inc. v. Mid-South Record Pressing Co., 393 F.Supp. 877 (M. D. Tenn. 1975).

c. Mitigation of Damages We have explained incidental and consequential damages because they are available in almost all cases where either party is claiming monetary damages. We should emphasize that many merchant-seller's form agreements attempt to limit recovery for consequential damages. This attempted limitation of damages will be discussed near the end of this chapter.

The common law required the parties to mitigate (reduce, limit) their damages. This means that a nonbreaching party had to choose a course of action upon breach that would limit rather than compound the damages. This policy of the law is continued in Article 2.[26]

In summary, the buyer's primary monetary remedy is to "cover" by making a good faith purchase of substitute goods and then to sue the seller for the difference between the cost of cover and the contract price plus incidental and consequential damages less expenses saved when covering.

2. Buyer's Right to Sue for Damages for Nondelivery or Repudiation The buyer is free to choose between the cover remedy just discussed and suit for damages for nondelivery under section 2–713.[27] It may not, however, "cover" *and* sue for damages under section 2–713.[28] Section 2–713 permits a buyer who has not accepted or received the goods to sue a repudiating seller for an amount of money determined by the difference between the market price of the goods at the time the buyer learned of the breach and the contract price, together with any incidental or consequential damages and less expenses saved. The place where market price is to be determined is the place where the goods were to be tendered; or, in cases of rejection or revocation of acceptance, at the place of arrival.[29]

[26]UCC 2–715(2)(a).

[27]See UCC 2–712, comment 3.

[28]See UCC 2–713, comment 5.

[29]UCC 2–713(2).

Assume that on April 10, *B* agreed to pay $5,000 to *S* for a quantity of apples, "F.O.B. *S*'s orchard" in Holland, Michigan, for delivery September 10. On August 10, *S* repudiates the contract. Further, assume that on August 10 the price for the same quantity and quality apples in Holland, Michigan (a noted apple-growing region) is $6,000. *B* may sue *S* for $1,000 plus any incidental or consequential damages, less expenses saved in consequence of the breach.

3. Buyer's Right to Accept the Goods and Either Deduct Damages from the Price or Sue for Damages As a last remedy for monetary recovery, the buyer may accept the goods and either (a) notify the seller of the breach within a reasonable time after the buyer discovers or should have discovered the breach, and recover damages for loss as well as incidental and consequential damages; or (b) notify the seller of his or her intention to deduct from the purchase price due to the seller the damages resulting from the seller's breach.

4. Buyer's Right to Recovery of the Goods

specific performance
The exact performance of a contract by a party as ordered by a court

(a) Buyer's Right to Specific Performance Section 2–716(1) directs a court to award **specific performance** "where the goods are unique or in other proper circumstances." Specific performance is an order from a court decreeing that a party to a contract should perform as promised or face contempt of court charges. The old common law of contracts provided that specific performance should be decreed only where the remedy at law (usually the award of money damages) was inadequate. Recall that contracts for the sale of land were assumed to be contracts of such a special type that the remedy at law was deemed inadequate and specific performance was awarded in almost every case.

Contracts for the sale of priceless works of art or heirlooms were, at common law, and remain under Article 2, appropriate cases for the award of specific performance.[30] However, the drafters wanted Section 2–716 to be read more broadly and they admonished that "this Article seeks to further a more liberal attitude than some courts have shown in connection with the specific performance of contracts of sale."[31] The only requirement is that the goods be "unique." Certainly this means that the goods could not be purchased in a reasonable fashion or for a reasonable price elsewhere.

Where one merchant agrees to buy all of its requirements for goods for a stated period of time from a "peculiarly available source," then Article 2 provides that a court may award specific performance.[32] The court may also order such payment of damages or other relief for the nonbreaching party as it may deem just.[33]

In the following case the court found that the circumstances merited a decree of specific performance.

---

[30]UCC 2–716, comment 2.

[31]UCC 2–716, comment 1.

[32]UCC 2–716, comment 2.

[33]UCC 2–716(2).

FACTS

The plaintiff, Mitchell-Huntley Cotton Company, agreed to buy from a group of merchant-farmers all of the cotton planted, produced, and ginned by the defendants through December 15, 1973. The plaintiff was engaged in the business of buying cotton from large commercial growers and selling and delivering it to textile mills and others. The contract was made on February 15, 1973 and the basic price to be paid for the cotton was $.30 per pound. Shortly after the contract was made, a drastic shortage of cotton developed, and the price for cotton increased to over $.80 per pound by the late summer of 1973. The defendants claimed that the contract was unenforceable since, by the terms of the contract, they could wait until after December 15, 1973 to have their cotton ginned and were thus not required to perform. The plaintiff sued the defendants for breach of the contract and requested the court to order the defendants to specifically perform. Should the plaintiff be awarded the remedy of specific performance?

DECISION

Yes. The court entered judgment for the plaintiff. The court found that since the tradition and trade custom was to gin cotton promptly upon its maturity, the defendants were under an obligation of good faith performance to so gin all their cotton which matured prior to December 15, 1973. The court further found that, as of the fall of 1973, the "majority" of all cotton to be produced in the U.S. for 1973 had been sold, and that there were no merchantable grades of cotton in storage in the U.S. So, as of February 25, 1974 the court ordered the defendants to harvest their cotton, have it ginned and deliver it to the plaintiffs.

Mitchell-Huntley Cotton Co., Inc. v. Waldrep, 377 F.Supp. 1215 (N. D. Ala. 1974).

b. Buyer's Right to the Goods When the Seller Becomes Insolvent The buyer may attempt to get the goods contracted for under the authority of two more Code sections in addition to the specific performance action. We will examine first the one that is more likely to be used.

The buyer is very much interested in receiving the goods from the seller when the buyer has made a substantial prepayment to the seller and then finds out that the seller is insolvent. In this case any later court judgment for money damages against the seller will probably remain unpaid (or the buyer will be paid just a fraction of what its judgment is worth). Section 2–502 allows the buyer to recover the goods contracted for if the following conditions are met:

1. The goods must have been identified to the contract so that a "special property" interest in them passes to the buyer. (This happens when the contract is made, if the goods are existing and can be identified at the time the contract is made. If the goods are not existing, it happens when the seller designates which goods are for the particular contract. You may want to review Section 2–501 here.)
2. The buyer must have paid all or a part of the purchase price.
3. The buyer must remain willing to pay any balance owing.
4. The seller must become insolvent within ten days after receipt of the first installment payment.

There are other sections of Article 2 that provide remedies for buyers when a seller breaches, but their use is so unusual that covering them demands too much time and space. In conclusion, we emphasize that in almost all cases performance is preferred over a breach and remedy. In very few instances do the remedies provided by this Code or any other *really* put the nonbreaching party in the *same* position it would have been in had there been performance. This, however, is the appropriate aim of the remedies of the buyer. The primary remedies of "cover" and suit for damages for nondelivery should be the first alternatives explored by a buyer. The buyer's other remedies discussed above are of less significance but may be awarded by a court when the proper conditions are satisfied.

Breach of the Sales Contract by the Buyer

▶ Seller's Courses of Action Without Bringing a Lawsuit

In most instances when a buyer's performance becomes doubtful, the seller's courses of action are going to depend upon an assessment of the buyer's solvency. The seller has contracted for *payment,* and potential insolvency threatens this promised performance. In many commercial transactions it is the tradition to pay sometime after receipt of the goods. Often the seller will have lost control of the goods when the seller learns of the buyer's insolvency or other breach. Therefore we can imagine at least three courses of conduct based upon who has the goods: the seller, the buyer, or perhaps a third party to whom the buyer has transferred the goods. *The courses of action discussed below assume that the seller still has control of the goods.* Generally, a seller who has relinquished control of the goods must seek assistance of a court order (a remedy) to regain them.

Seller's Right to Adequate Assurance of Performance If the seller still has the goods and if reasonable grounds for insecurity exist, then the seller may (1) suspend performance, (2) demand in writing an adequate assurance of performance, and (3) await a reply for a reasonable time, which is not over thirty days.[34] If the assurance—the reasonableness of which is to be determined according to prevailing commercial standards—is not adequate under the circumstances, then the buyer has repudiated the contract, and the seller may choose one of the remedies discussed below.[35]

Seller's Right to Receive Cash Payment Upon Discovery of the Buyer's Insolvency If the seller should discover that the buyer is insolvent, then, even if the buyer is not required by the sales contract to pay cash, the seller may refuse delivery unless payment is made in cash. The seller may also ask for cash for goods already delivered and, if the goods are in transit, stop the delivery of them unless payment is made in cash.[36] A buyer who refuses to pay cash is in default.

Seller's Right to Withhold Goods and Stop Delivery of Goods in Transit or Otherwise If the buyer repudiates the contract before delivery, or fails to make a payment due on or before delivery, or wrongfully rejects or revokes acceptance of the goods, or becomes insolvent before performance is due, the seller may withhold the goods.[37] If the goods

---

[34]UCC 2–609.

[35]UCC 2–609(4).

[36]UCC 2–702(1).

[37]UCC 2–703(a).

are in the possession of *any* carrier or bailee, the seller may order the goods withheld when the seller discovers the buyer to be insolvent; in other instances of breach such as a repudiation or failure to make a payment due, the seller may withhold or stop delivery only if the goods are shipped by the carload, truckload, planeload, or are in larger shipments of express or freight.[38] Stoppage of a shipment is a burden to carriers. However, it is permitted in all cases of the buyer's insolvency—a crucial event for the seller because, if the goods are tendered to the buyer and the buyer accepts, creditors of the buyer may have a claim for the goods. In other cases of breach by the buyer, stoppage is allowed only if the shipment is large. Stoppage is effected by notifying the carrier (a bailee) with reasonable diligence.[39] Once the goods are stopped, the seller may direct the carrier to deliver them to any destination.

On stoppage, the seller then pays the cost of transporting the goods in another direction other than to the buyer. However, if a *negotiable* bill of lading is outstanding (see Chapter 22), *the carrier is not obligated to stop the goods in transit without surrender of the negotiable bill.*

► Seller's Remedies in the Courts

Seller's Monetary Recovery Some of the courses of action discussed above may be thought of as "remedies" in that they are attempts to minimize the seller's damages and thus, to a limited degree, compensate the seller. However, usually more is needed to compensate the seller. In this section we present the causes of action that a court would recognize in attempting to put the damaged seller in the same position that party would have been in had there been performance. These remedies are presented in two broad classifications: the seller's right to monetary recovery; and the seller's right to reclaim the goods under certain conditions, discussed in the next section. The Code recognizes that there may be instances in which more than one remedy would be appropriate and specifically sanctions this by rejecting any doctrine requiring the seller to "elect" one remedy to the exclusion of another.[40]

In applying the remedies discussed below, courts will attempt to protect the *expectation* interest of the seller, and, where this is not adequate, the *reliance* interest and the *restitution* interest. Before focusing on these general guides to a remedy, a court must find that the buyer has defaulted. A default may be established by proving that the buyer: (1) wrongfully rejected the goods; or (2) wrongfully revoked acceptance; or (3) failed to make payment that was due on or before delivery; or (4) repudiated with respect to a part or the whole of the contract.[41] A "wrongful" rejection or a "wrongful revocation of acceptance" establishes a breach by the buyer and is proved by showing that the buyer has refused to accept or retain conforming goods properly tendered.[42] This is illustrated by the following case of a wrongful rejection by the buyer.

---

[38]UCC 2–705(1).

[39]UCC 2–705(3)(a).

[40]UCC 2–703, comment 1.

[41]UCC 2–703.

[42]See UCC 2–602, comment 3.

FACTS

The plaintiff, E. H. Thrift Air Conditioning, Inc., contracted on October 13, 1967 with the defendant subcontractor, R. R. Waites Company, to construct large air ducts for installation in a Ramada Inn. The plaintiff was given the detailed plans for the air ducts and fabricated them exactly as the plans indicated. In December of 1968 the goods were received by the defendant, and a few days later the defendant informed the plaintiff that the goods could not be used because there was an error in the defendant's construction plans. The defendant said that it was shipping the goods back. The plaintiff informed the defendant that it should keep the goods, pay the price, and the plaintiff would help the defendant resell the goods. In May 1969 the defendant shipped the goods back to the plaintiff and refused to pay for them. The plaintiff claimed that the goods conformed to the contract and brought an action for the full price. Should it recover?

DECISION

Yes. The appellate court affirmed a decision for the plaintiff for the full price. An agent of the defendant corporation testified that the delivered air ducts conformed in all respects to the plans given to the plaintiff. A tender by the seller of goods which conform to the contract in all respects gives rise to a positive duty on the buyer to accept and pay in accordance with the contract. If the goods conform to the contract, the buyer has no other option than to pay. A failure to do so gives rise to a wrongful rejection, which gives the seller immediate remedies for breach. The court allowed the plaintiff to recover the full contract price and said nothing about the plaintiff returning the goods to the defendant, purchaser. [We must assume, therefore, that their market value was zero.]

R. R. Waites Co., Inc. v. E. H. Thrift Air Conditioning, Inc., 510 S.W.2d 759 (Mo. 1974).

1. Seller's Right to Resell and Recover the Difference Between Resale Price and Contract Price When the buyer wrongfully rejects or revokes acceptance or fails to make a payment due, the seller may resell the goods and, if the sale is made in good faith *and* in a commercially reasonable manner, recover the difference between the resale price and the contract price together with incidental damages, but less expenses saved.[43] In our simple example involving the sale of apples for $5,000, if we assume a breach by the buyer before delivery, and a resale price of $4,200 and an added expense of $50, the seller should be able to recover $850 from the buyer. If the apples were resold for $5,500, then the seller suffered no damage and may keep the profit.[44]

Today's commercial transactions are rarely this simple, however. Assume that the seller of the apples could prove reasonable expenses of $4,200 in growing the apples and a profit of $800 in the transaction. Assume further there were some apples of the seller that were not yet identified to any contract for sale at the time of breach. Therefore the "resale" remedy would not be adequate because the purchaser of the "resale" apples would have purchased apples originally intended to be sold to the breaching buyer, and the seller would have made $1,600 on the two transactions ($800 on the sale to the breaching buyer and $800 from the resale buyer). So the "resale" remedy will not give the seller's expectation value where the seller has a relatively limitless inventory of goods to sell.[45] The loss profit may be recovered under Section 2–708(2). The point is that the appropriateness of Section 2–706's applicability may be determined by an evaluation of

[43]UCC 2–706(1).

[44]UCC 706(6).

[45]Such a seller has been labeled a "lost volume seller." See Harris, "A Radical Restatement of the Law of Seller's Damages: Sales Act and Commerce Code Results Compared," 18 *Stan. L. Rev.* 66 (1965); Harris' analysis is summarized and supported in White and Summers, pp. 226–27.

appropriateness of Section 2–706's applicability may be determined by an evaluation of the seller's potential to sell other goods on hand (the seller's inventory) and the market conditions (could two sales really have been made?) together with the nature of the product (is it unique or standard?).

Other complicating circumstances are the nature of the goods and the time of breach. Assume that the buyer repudiates just as the seller is assembling the parts to a complex, specially designed machine. In this case Article 2 provides the seller great flexibility. If the goods are not identified to the contract but are finished, the seller may identify such goods and then resell them. If the goods are not finished, the seller may, in the exercise of reasonable commercial judgment, do either of the following: complete the goods, identify them to the contract, and then resell them; or it may cease manufacture of them and resell the pieces for scrap or salvage value and sue for the contract price less the resale price; or it may proceed in any other reasonable manner.[46]

Article 2 has rather lengthy provisions governing the *resale* of goods. For our purposes, however, it is sufficient to point out that the remedy of resale[47] is premised on the assumption that the resale will be in good faith and will minimize (not maximize) the seller's losses. The resale price is assumed to be a reflection of the reasonable value of the goods in the seller's possession.

2. Seller's Right to Sue for Damages for Nonacceptance or Repudiation

The seller may desire not to resell the goods identified to the contract and is not compelled to do so. For example, if the seller has agreed to sell apples in March but finds that, after a buyer breaches in September, the seller can make more money by converting the apples to applesauce or apple cider, then the seller may do so. In this instance, and in any instance where the buyer does not accept the goods or repudiates, the seller may sue the buyer for the difference between the market price at the time and place for tender and the unpaid contract price, together with any incidental damages but less expenses saved in consequence of the buyer's breach.[48]

The most obvious problem with this remedy is with the seller's burden of proving what the market price of the goods was at the time and place for tender. This is not so troublesome if the contract is for common agricultural products, typical consumer goods, or other standardized products for which there often are daily or weekly quoted prices in various geographical locations. In the case of nonstandardized products, a market price may be established by evidence which in the commercial judgment or the usage of trade of those in the market for the goods would serve as a reasonable substitute.[49] As is so often the case, what is a reasonable market price or a reasonable substitute for it is a matter for the finder of fact.

If the buyer repudiates and the seller wishes to sue before the date of tender, the seller may do so. In this instance the market price for the goods will be determined at the time when the seller learned of the repudiation.[50]

---

[46]UCC 2–704.

[47]UCC 2–706.

[48]UCC 2–708(1).

[49]UCC 2–723(2).

[50]UCC 2–723(1).

If the measure of damages as calculated by the contract-price-minus-market-price formula is inadequate to compensate the seller for the seller's expected gain, it may sue for the lost profits it would have made from full performance plus incidental damages.[51] The calculation of "lost profits" is usually measured by taking the seller's cost from the seller's list price or contract price. Utilization of this measure is appropriate only to put the seller in the same position it would have been in had there been performance. It cannot put the seller in a better position. For example, if a seller had constructed a machine at a cost of $7,000 and contracted to sell it for $8,000 and, following a breach by the buyer, realized $7,800 on resale of it, the seller's recovery is limited to $200 (plus incidental damages). The seller may not recover $1,000 unless the seller proves that it is more probable than not that the seller could have sold two machines (one to the breaching buyer and one to the resale buyer).

3. Seller's Right to Sue for the Full Contract Price The seller's right to sue for the full contract price can be viewed as a parallel remedy to the buyer's cause of action for specific performance. Like the buyer's cause of action for specific performance, this right of the seller is limited rather substantially. It is available in only three circumstances. If the buyer has failed to pay the price as it becomes due, the seller may recover the price, together with any incidental damages, where:

1) the goods have been delivered and accepted by the buyer;[52] or
2) conforming goods were lost or damaged within a commercially reasonable time after risk of their loss has passed to the buyer;[53] or
3) the seller is unable, after a reasonable effort, to resell goods identified to the contract at a reasonable price, or the circumstances reasonably indicate that such effort will be unavailing.[54]

The first and second circumstances above, are so clear they need no explanation. The third circumstance may at first seem complex, but ask yourself, how many instances are there in which the goods cannot be resold after a reasonable effort? These relatively rare instances may occur when the seller is in a specialty market of some sort (for example, making silverware heavily embossed with a unique family crest).[55] When this alternative is selected, the seller must hold the goods for the buyer if they are identified to the contract and within the seller's control. If an opportunity to resell develops while the seller still has the goods, the seller may resell the goods any time before judgment, crediting the buyer with the proceeds.[56]

---

[51]UCC 2–708(2).

[52]UCC 2–709(1)(a).

[53]UCC 2–709(1)(a).

[54]UCC 2–709(1)(b).

[55]Nordstrom, p. 545.

[56]UCC 2–709(2).

Seller's Recovery of the Goods from an Insolvent Buyer In most commercial transactions between merchants, at least three Articles of the UCC may apply. This is especially true in the common situation where a seller sells goods on credit. Depending upon the nature of the breach and the damages sought, Article 2 (Sales) may control or Article 3 (Commercial Paper) may control or Article 9 (Secured Transactions) may control.

When a seller delivers goods and demands payment and payment is made by a check that is later dishonored, the seller may use one of the remedies provided in Article 3 and bring suit "on the check." These remedies are discussed in Part 6 of this book.

When contracting to sell goods, the seller may agree to deliver the goods with payment in thirty, sixty, or ninety days after delivery. To protect itself, the seller may create an enforceable security interest by complying with the requirements of Article 9. Such a seller is a "secured" party and may recover (upon breach of the **security agreement**) the goods delivered to the buyer by following the procedures outlined in Article 9. Article 9 is the subject of Chapters 50 and 51 and will not be discussed here.

security agreement
"An agreement which creates or provides for a security interest"
UCC 9–105(1)(l)

This section focuses upon "unsecured" sellers and the right to *reclaim* goods under Article 2. An unsecured seller is one who has no agreement with the buyer creating a **security interest** in the goods sold. Such a seller has merely a promise to pay for the goods delivered, either upon acceptance or sometime thereafter. Except for instances in which the buyer is insolvent, Article 2 contains no section that gives the unsecured seller a right to reclaim the goods. In circumstances in which the buyer was insolvent, Section 2–702(2) provides:

security interest
"An interest in personal property or fixtures which secures payment or performance of an obligation"
UCC 1–201(37)

> Where the seller discovers that the buyer has received goods on credit while insolvent he may reclaim the goods upon demand made within ten days after the receipt, but if misrepresentation of solvency has been made to the particular seller in writing within three months before delivery the ten day limitation does not apply.

The applicability of the first part of this section is limited substantially. Recall that if the seller knows of the buyer's insolvency before delivery, it may refuse to deliver unless it is paid in cash.[57] So the section above would probably apply only if the seller did not know of the buyer's insolvency upon delivery but found out within ten days of the receipt of the goods. In such a case the seller may reclaim the goods. This ten-day limitation does not apply, however, if the seller has received during the three months before delivery, in writing, a representation by the buyer that the buyer is solvent. Just how long the seller has to reclaim the goods if the seller has received a writing that makes representations about solvency dated within three months of the delivery is not mentioned in Article 2.

Finally, the unsecured-credit seller always runs the risk that the buyer will sell the goods delivered, or transfer a security interest in them, to someone else. If the buyer sells the goods to a buyer in the ordinary course of business or to some other good faith purchaser, then the seller may not reclaim the goods.[58] If, however, the buyer has transferred a security interest in the goods that are subject to reclamation by a third party, the judgment as to which party gets the goods will be made by a court or a trustee in bankruptcy applying the appropriate state or federal law.

---

[57] UCC 2–702(1).

[58] UCC 2–702(3).

It should be obvious that unsecured-credit sellers take substantial risks. Usually such sales are made only to buyers who are well known and trusted by the sellers.

Limitation of Remedies and Damages

liquidated damages
The money judicially awarded in the amount as agreed to by the parties in their contract at the time it was made as reasonable compensation for damage that may be caused by the wrongful conduct of one of the parties in the future

Courts have long respected attempts by the parties to agree in advance what the damages will be upon breach. Where such a limitation is attempted in "the contract," the amount of damages stated is called **liquidated damages.** These liquidated damages will be awarded to a nonbreaching party only if they are reasonable. An attempt to fix unreasonably large liquidated damages may be declared void as a penalty.[59] (For example, seller sells the buyer a fire detection system for $498. The contract provided that one-third of the contract price is to be paid in the event the buyer cancels the contract. The day after the contract is signed, the buyer cancels the contract before the seller does anything in respect to the work seller is to perform. The seller cannot recover the one-third of the purchase price because, since no actual damage was suffered by the seller, the stipulated sum is unreasonably and grossly disproportionate to any real damage, and enforcing it would be a penalty against the buyer.) The reasonableness of the amount is to be determined as of the time the contract is made. Courts also will consider (1) the anticipated or actual harm caused by the breach; (2) the difficulties of proof of loss; and (3) the inconvenience or nonfeasibility of otherwise obtaining an adequate remedy. In the following case the court held that the agreement for liquidated damages is to be considered as of the time the agreement was made.

FACTS

The plaintiff, Bethlehem Steel Company, agreed on December 21, 1961 to furnish steel and construction crews to erect part of the defendant's (the City of Chicago) "South Route Superhighway." The contract price was for $1,734,200. The critical clause of the contract provided for $1,000 "liquidated damages" for each day of delay. The work was to have been completed on or before July 29, 1962, but that date was later extended to September 20, 1962. The work was actually completed 52 days late, on November 21, 1962, thus creating an alleged breach of the agreement. The defendant withheld $52,000 as its liquidated damages from the final payment due the plaintiff, and the plaintiff sued for this and other amounts allegedly due from the city. The plaintiff alleged that the city *actually* sustained no damage, that the highway was completed "substantially on time" (even though the contract said "time was of the essence"), and that the $52,000 withheld amounted to a penalty. Should the plaintiff recover the $52,000?

DECISION

No. The court found in favor of the defendant, City of Chicago, thus enforcing the liquidated damages provision of the contract. The court stated that it made no difference whether or not actual loss followed from the breach because the validity of the liquidated damages stipulation must be judged as of the time when the contract was entered into. At the time the contract was entered into the damages resulting from the plaintiff's breach were difficult if not impossible to ascertain. Moreover, the court emphasized that the law should look with favor "upon such provisions in contracts when deliberately entered into between parties who have equality of opportunity for understanding (because such provisions promote) . . . prompt performance of contracts and . . . adjust . . . in advance, and amicably, matters the settlement of which through courts would often involve difficulty, uncertainty, delay, and expense."

Bethlehem Steel Co. v. City of Chicago, 234 F.Supp. 726, 730 (N. D. Ill. 1964).

[59] UCC 2–718(1).

The parties may also agree that remedies in addition to, or in substitution for, those in Article 2 (arbitration, for example) are to be utilized in the case of breach.[60] In this area, Article 2 expressly provides that both of the parties are to have some "minimum adequate remedy"[61] and that courts should police attempts at waiver of remedies by using their power to declare such a waiver unconscionable. As between bargaining merchants, a limitation of consequential damages may be binding. But where a merchant attempts to limit a consumer to suing for damages for defective consumer goods (and excluding damages for personal injury), a court may declare the limitation unconscionable.[62]

Statute of Limitations

statute of limitations
A statute limiting the time in which a claim may be asserted in court; expiration bars enforcement of the claim

A **statute of limitations** exists for all areas of the law—for example, criminal law, tort law, contract law, and sales law. These statutes express a policy judgment by state legislatures that for the "efficient" administration of justice, plaintiffs should bring their claims to court as soon as it is reasonably possible to do so. They achieve this by simply stating in a "statute of limitations" that if the particular action is not commenced within a specified number of years, the action is barred; the legal cause of action is thus extinguished.

The heart of Article 2's statute of limitations in contracts for sale, Section 2–725,[63] provides:

> An action for breach of any contract for sale must be commenced within four years after the cause of action has accrued. By the original agreement the parties may reduce the period of limitation to not less than one year but may not extend it.[64]

In most cases the four-year period begins to run from the date when a breach is *announced* by a party or the date the breaching party fails to perform.[65] For a breaching seller, this is the date of tender; for a breaching buyer, the date payment is due. But what happens when there is a breach of warranty after both parties have performed? The Code attempts to deal with this difficult problem by providing:

> A breach of warranty occurs when tender of delivery is made, except that where a warranty explicitly extends to future performance of the goods and discovery of the breach must await the time of such performance the *cause of action accrues* when the breach is or should have been discovered.[66] [Emphasis added.]

---

[60]UCC 2–719(1)(a).

[61]See UCC 2–719, comment 1.

[62]UCC 2–719(3).

[63]The subject litigated most in the reported appellate cases was attempted disclaimers of warranties. White, "Evaluating Article 2 of the Uniform Commercial Code: A Preliminary Empirical Expedition," 75 *Mich. L. Rev.* 1262 (1977).

[64]UCC 2–725(1).

[65]UCC 2–725(5).

[66]UCC 2–725(2).

The words "cause of action accrues" mean that the four-year period begins to run for a breach of warranties on the date of tender of the goods. However, if a seller "explicitly extends a warranty to future performance (for example, a merchant seller gives a "lifetime guaranty" or promises that a machine will last for 10,000 hours), then it seems that if a breach occurs during this period, the buyer has four years to bring suit from the date of that breach.[67]

In Chapters 27 and 28 on consumer law, the final chapters of this part, we lift our focus from Article 2 of the UCC and examine the broad range of remedies available to consumers when they have been financially damaged or personally injured from defective consumer goods.

Summary Statement

1. Generally, the damage remedies of buyers and sellers must attempt to put the nonbreaching party in the same position that party would have been in had there been full performance.
2. The following courses of action are available to a buyer who learns of a breach or potential breach:
   - **a)** Demand an adequate assurance of performance if the goods have not been delivered.
   - **b)** Reject nonconforming goods.
   - **c)** Accept the goods.
   - **d)** Revoke acceptance of a lot or commercial unit whose nonconformity substantially impairs its value to the buyer.
   - **e)** *In all cases,* the buyer who wishes to pursue legal remedies for damages must notify the seller that a breach of the agreement is being claimed.
3. In awarding damages to a nonbreaching party, a court will attempt to protect the party's expectation, reliance, or restitution interests.
4. The buyer's possible remedies for breach of the sales agreement by the seller are as follows:
   - **a)** The right to cover.
   - **b)** The right to sue for damages for nondelivery or repudiation.
   - **c)** The right to accept the goods and either deduct damages from the price or sue for damages resulting from the accepted goods.
   - **d)** The right to require the seller to convey the goods contracted for (specific performance).
   - **e)** The right to the goods when the seller becomes insolvent and replevin.
5. Incidental damages are money amounts awarded by a court for *expenses* reasonably *incurred* by the nonbreaching party; consequential damages are money amounts awarded by a court for loss which a breaching party reasonably could *foresee* would result from its breach.
6. A seller who learns of a potential breach or an actual breach may pursue the following courses of action:
   - **a)** Demand an adequate assurance of performance.
   - **b)** Demand and receive cash payment upon the discovery of the buyer's insolvency.
   - **c)** Withhold the goods or stop delivery of goods in transit.

[67]White & Summers, *Handbook of the Law Under the Uniform Commercial Code,* p. 342.

7. The seller's possible remedies for breach of the sales agreement by the buyer are as follows:
   a) The right to resell the goods and recover the difference between the resale price and the contract price; but, if this is inadequate, to put the seller in as good a position as performance would have; then the measure of damages is the profit that the seller would have made from full performance by the buyer together with any incidental damages.
   b) The right to sue the buyer for damages for nonacceptance or repudiation.
   c) The right to sue for the full contract price.
   d) The right to recover the goods from an insolvent buyer.
8. The buyer and seller may, in their agreement, limit the remedies available to the other party and the damages they may be liable for. Such limitations are enforceable so long as they are reasonable.
9. An action for breach of any contract for sale must be commenced within four years after the cause of action has accrued.
10. The time when a breach of warranty occurs is when tender of delivery is made, except that where a warranty explicitly extends to future performance, and discovery of the breach must await the time of such performance, the cause of action accrues when the breach is or should have been discovered.

In the following case involving two large corporations, the court first examined the nature of a "requirements contract" and then passed judgment on the claim for specific performance and the defense of commercial impracticability.

EASTERN AIR LINES, INC. v. GULF OIL CORPORATION
415 F.Supp. 429 (S.D. Fla. 1975)

King, J. The plaintiff, Eastern Air Lines, Inc. (Eastern), had been purchasing some of its aviation fuel in the south from the defendant, Gulf Oil Corporation (Gulf), for over thirty years. On June 27, 1972 Eastern and Gulf agreed that Gulf would furnish jet fuel to Eastern at certain specific cities in the Eastern system until January 31, 1977. The contract was one of Gulf's "standard form aviation fuel contracts," which was similar to contracts in general use in the aviation fuel trade. It was signed after "substantial arm's length negotiation" between the parties and considered to be favorable to both. The agreement was a "requirements contract," which provided Eastern the opportunity to demand and receive aviation fuel as their requirements dictated at the various sites. Eastern gave up the right to buy fuel from other suppliers at these locations. The "requirements" agreement provided Gulf with a long-term outlet for their jet fuel, which was needed because of the construction of a new refinery. Gulf had to be prepared to supply Eastern's reasonable good faith demands at these locations. The price of the fuel was to be set according to an indicator which was directly dependent upon the price of *domestic* crude oil. Both parties knew at the time of contract negotiations that increases in crude oil prices would be expected and were "a way of life."

The major Arabian countries producing oil (OPEC) increased their crude oil prices 400 percent between September 1973 and January 1974. The price of a portion of the U.S. domestic production also increased by this amount, but much of the domestic production was covered by a U.S. government pricing system which kept the price relatively low. The contract price of the Eastern-Gulf agreement was set by the government pricing system. As the price of aviation fuel began to climb dramatically, Eastern began buying more and more fuel from Gulf. In a requirements contract there almost always is a large measure of discretion exercised by the purchaser. In this case Eastern could fill its planes from several different suppliers, each at a different location. As the terms of the Gulf agreement became more favorable to Eastern, it ordered that more of its planes fill up at the cities served by Gulf. This practice was called "fuel freighting."

On March 8, 1974 Gulf informed Eastern that it was increasing its price for aviation fuel beyond that provided for by the price indicator in their agreement, and that if Eastern would not agree to this, Gulf would shut off Eastern's supply of jet fuel within fifteen days. Eastern responded by filing a complaint in court alleging that Gulf had breached its contract and requesting the court to enter an order of specific performance. Gulf replied by arguing three major points. (1) Eastern's practice of fuel freighting was not performance in good faith and was a breach of the agreement. (2) If the court found against it on the first point, then Gulf argued that the agreement was unenforceable because it had become commercially impracticable within the meaning of the UCC. (3) An order for specific performance was not appropriate.

The court stated that the UCC specifically approves requirements contracts. Section 2–306 (1) states:

> A term which measures the quantity by the output of the seller [called an "output" contract] or the requirements of the buyer [called a "requirements" contract] means such actual output or requirements as may occur in good faith, except that no quantity unreasonably disproportionate to any stated estimate or in the absence of a stated estimate to any normal or otherwise comparable prior output or requirements may be tendered or demanded.

Was Eastern's practice of "fuel freighting" performance in good faith? The court found that it was because it was consistent with established commercial practice. The fuel taken on by a plane depends upon the price, the weather, schedule changes, aircraft load, ground time, and many other factors. The court found these factors have been known to oil companies and have been taken into account by them in drafting their fuel contracts. "Fuel freighting" is an established industry practice inherent in the nature of the business and is not performance in bad faith.

The court responded to Gulf's second argument by pointing out that the UCC states that increases in price alone do not excuse performance unless the rise in cost is due to some unforeseen contingency which alters the essential nature of the performance. Both parties knew that the price of fuel was going to rise, and they agreed on a formula to account for this. The court used these words to find for Eastern on this issue:

> *We will not allow a party to a contract to escape a bad bargain merely because it is burdensome.* The buyer has a right to rely on the party to the contract to supply him with goods regardless of what happens to the market price. That is the purpose for which such contracts are made. [Emphasis added.]

In addition, the court stated that it could not approve the defense of commercial impracticability where Gulf had tendered no evidence, on how much it cost Gulf to produce jet fuel. For all the court knew from the evidence, Gulf might still be selling jet fuel to Eastern at a profit. Indeed, the court noted that in 1973, the year in which the "energy crisis" began, Gulf had its best year ever, recording $800 million in net profits after taxes.

Finally, the court awarded specific performance to Eastern because the UCC directed courts to take a more liberal attitude toward this remedy. A party was no longer required to prove that the money damage remedy would be inadequate. In this case the issues were squarely framed and clearly resolved in Eastern's favor, and it would be a "vain, useless and potentially harmful exercise" to declare that Eastern had a valid contract but then leave it to bring another suit to determine its past and future damages.

The court found in favor of Eastern and entered an order for specific performance of the agreement.

Questions and Case Problems

1. *B,* buyer, has just received a large metal-working machine from *S,* seller. *B* has visually inspected the machine but it will not be ready for operation until it is installed. If *B* detects a defect in the machine upon visual inspection at the time of installation (assume that there is a crack in the metal casing), what should *B* do? If *B* installs the machine and it does not appear to work properly, what may *B* attempt to do? In what circumstances will *B* be successful in choosing a course of action?
2. In question 1 above, assume that *B* lost 20 days' production because the machine did not function properly. In what circumstances may *B* recover consequential damages?
3. If *B,* buyer, buys from *S,* seller, 10 dozen electronic staplers for *B*'s business-supply company to resell, and *S* phones *B* before delivery that it will not perform, carefully describe at least two of the remedies available to *B.*
   - **a)** In what circumstances can *B* "force" *S* to deliver the staplers?
   - **b)** Assume that *B* properly accepted the staplers once they were delivered but discovered later that they were defective. What is the measure of *B*'s damages?
4. *S,* seller, has contracted with *B,* buyer, to sell 100 finished picture frames of various sizes and made from various kinds of rare hardwood. Describe the courses of conduct and/or remedies of *S* in each of the circumstances below:
   - **a)** *S* has received word that *B* is insolvent.
   - **b)** *S* has completed some and has shipped some (which are in the possession of a carrier) when it is informed by *B* that *B* is repudiating the contract.
   - **c)** *S* can prove that it would have spent $2,500 to make the frames, and the contract price was $3,700. In what circumstances may it recover the lost profit?
5. *M,* manufacturer, manufactures small tent-campers. These are nothing but aluminum boxes placed on wheels and towed by car owners. When the owners wish to stop and camp, they unfold a tent, which springs up from the aluminum box. *M* contracted to sell 15 of these units for $800 each to *R,* retailer. *M* produced the units for $675 each and usually kept such a large supply of these tent-campers on hand that it could fill any order. Five days before *M* was to deliver the tent-campers, *R* telephoned *M* and explained that it was having trouble moving its inventory and was "reconsidering" its order.
   - **a)** What should *M* do?
   - **b)** On the date for *M*'s performance, it tenders the goods and *R* refuses, saying that it is "cancelling" the order. What are *M*'s remedies and measures of damage?
   - **c)** Assume that *M* resells the very tent-camper units it had identified for the contract with *R* for $800 each. Has *M* suffered any damage? If so, what amount?
6. Burk, seller, contracted to sell about 950 head of yearling steers to Emmick, buyer. The steers were delivered and payment was made by a negotiable instrument that was dishonored when it was presented to the buyer's bank. Burk reclaimed the cattle and then resold them for less than the contract price. Burk sues Emmick for the difference between the contract price and the resale price. The buyer argues that once the cattle were reclaimed, the seller's position was as good as it had been before the contract so the seller was not entitled to a money judgment in addition to reclaiming the cattle. What is your response to this argument? Explain your answer in detail. [*Burk v. Emmick,* 637 F.2d 1172, (8th Cir. 1980).]

7. *S* agreed to manufacture and deliver 12 snowmobiles to *P* on November 1, 1982. They were delivered on that date, inspected, and paid for by *P*. On the packaging, in the sales contract, and in the instructions for the snowmobiles, *S* stated that he would warrant that the snowmobiles would perform properly for one year from the date of delivery to *P*. In December 1982 *P* sold three of the snowmobiles to *A, B,* and *C,* individually, who received the same warranty from *S*. The snowmobiles of *A, B,* and *C* all malfunctioned within one year of delivery, and *S* denied any liability. *A* filed a lawsuit against *S* on October 30, 1986, *B* filed suit exactly one year later, and *C* filed one year after that (October 30, 1988). Can these legal actions be maintained? Why or why not?
8. For purposes of review, this question and the one that follows contain some fundamental legal issues discussed in Chapters 23 to 25.

   W, an oil well drilling company, contracted with *S,* a southwest oil company, to explore a small region of Texas for oil formations and to drill if the formations appeared to be of the type that might yield oil. The "contract" which was made was oral and provided that *W* would be paid expenses for exploring, would be paid $10 per foot for drilling, and would be paid what it cost *W* for the piping needed. *W* and *S* were to share the profits if any oil was found. *W* explored for oil for three weeks and found a promising location and began drilling. After it had been drilling for a week and reached a depth of 500 feet, *S* informed *W* that as far as it was concerned no contract was ever formed and it did not intend to pay *W* for exploration and drilling expenses. *W* had received several letters from *S* during the one month of its operation referring to their agreement. What legal problems does *W* have?
9. The *L* Corporation was engaged in the business of building lobster boats. The Maine Lobstermens' Cooperative Association, Inc. (*M*) ordered three lobster boats from *L*. *M*'s order form stated a price of $50,000 per boat, a delivery date of April 1, 1990, and other technical information relating to the specifications and performance capabilities of the boats. *L*'s acknowledgment form agreed in all important particulars with *M*'s except that printed on it in large letters were the words "The parties hereby expressly agree that *L* will not be liable for consequential damages." Agents of *M* had signed *L*'s form and returned a copy of it to *M*. The boats were delivered on time and, during one of the first voyages of one of the boats, the engine malfunctioned because it was not properly installed in the boat. It was out of line, and the shaft and bearing overheated and broke. The boat was swept upon the rocks and destroyed. Miraculously, the crew of the boat was saved, but there were injuries. *M* sued *L* for the value of the destroyed boat, and the injured crew sued for their injuries. What arguments would you expect from *L,* and do you think they will be successful?
10. In the case of *Eastern Air Lines, Inc. v. Gulf Oil Corporation,* excerpted at the beginning of this section, why was the court reluctant to consider the commercial impractability defense of Gulf? Why was an order for specific performance more appropriate than a remedy for money damages?

CHAPTER

27

CONSUMER LAW

A. SELLER'S WARRANTIES AND THEIR WAIVER, MODIFICATION, AND BREACH

After you have read this chapter, you should be able to:

1. Define the various possible types of warranty that can be made by a seller in a sales transaction and list the elements of each or the conditions in which each is made.
2. Describe the circumstances in which each of the warranties made by a seller or merchant may be excluded or modified.
3. Outline the main purpose and the major provisions of the Magnuson-Moss Warranty Act.
4. Write a paragraph explaining the reasons for the doctrine of unconscionability and then describe the circumstances in which this legal principle is usually applied.
5. Make a list of all the major defenses that can be asserted by a manufacturer in a case by an injured consumer-plaintiff based on a breach of warranty, and briefly describe each.
6. Explain horizontal and vertical privity.

BUSINESS DECISIONS and the LAW

Our modern business enterprises operate in an environment in which management must be constantly aware of the needs and opinions of numerous constituencies or groups of interests that make the business enterprise possible. One such group is the suppliers who contract with the business enterprises to provide the raw materials needed in the business. These suppliers are themselves merchants, as are the managers in our business enterprises. Another group, perhaps the most important, is the consumers who buy finished products for their own use. Article 2 of the Uniform Commercial Code (UCC) applies to contracts for the sale of goods from and to both of these groups.

What happens when either the raw materials we buy as merchants or the goods we buy as consumers do not operate as expected, with their failure causing destruction of the good itself and personal injury to the person using it? Liability and compensation for the injury are usually established through the court system by using legal arguments based on breach of a warranty created by Article 2 or legal principles from the area of tort law. Much of the material we refer to as "consumer law" refers to the body of law that establishes liability for compensation when a product causes injury to a consumer.

How "successful" is our consumer law? To merchants who have to pay the judgments against them for defective products, the system of consumer law we have does not appear to be very efficient or, in some cases, fair. To the consumer, having to bring a lawsuit to establish compensation for a serious injury also appears burdensome and, in some cases, unfair. For example, in 1986 the Institute for Civil Justice, a division of the Rand Corporation that collects data on numbers of lawsuits and sizes of awards, published a report, "Costs and Compensation Paid in Tort Litigation," in which it concluded that between $29 and $36 billion was expended nationwide on tort lawsuits in 1985. Between $16 and $19 billion of that represented costs ($5,400 to $6,600 per lawsuit) such as fees to lawyers, insurance company costs, the time expended by witnesses, and the like with the net compensation paid out between $14 and $16 billion. Plaintiffs thus received between 52 percent (in auto cases) and 43 percent (in nonauto cases) of the money awards.

We can generalize and say that a lawsuit is very time consuming, expensive, and emotionally burdensome for all the parties involved. These figures also show that we support a tremendous system of lawyers, insurance company investigators, court personnel and the like to process these lawsuits. In short, our consumer law, which we will examine in this chapter and the next, is not perfect. Yet, it appears to be the best in the world.

In Pacific Rim countries such as Japan and Korea and in the countries of the European communities, policy planners are studying our system of consumer-related legal principles to learn how to handle the problem of defective goods. We live in a society in which the design, production, marketing and sale of consumer goods is the dominant economic activity. Just one consumer product, the automobile, which is directly or indirectly responsible for one out of six jobs in this country, generates about half of the lawsuits in the area of consumer law. Because not every person injured when an automobile is defective is a **purchaser** of the defective car, we will see in this chapter and the next that consumer-related lawsuits may rely on a number of differing legal principles. Because the law in this area is complex and changing as rapidly as the nature of our consumer products change, we have devoted two chapters to this topic.

purchaser
One who makes a contract to buy goods

Introduction

In this chapter, we shift our focus from the situation in which a merchant contracts with a merchant to a merchant contracting with a consumer. The word "merchant" refers to one "who deals in goods of the kind [sold] or otherwise by his occupation holds himself out as having knowledge or skill peculiar to the practices or goods involved in the transaction. . . ."[1]

A **consumer** is a person who buys goods to use primarily for personal, family, or household purposes.[2] In short, a merchant is a person who is in business to sell goods or leads others to believe he or she has special knowledge about the goods sold, and a consumer is the one who buys goods for use (but not for resale).

consumer
A person who buys goods for use primarily for personal, family, or household purposes

A key to understanding the legal principles used today to resolve a merchant-consumer dispute is to realize that this transaction probably evidenced by a form contract drafted by the merchant-seller. We emphasized in this part that consumers no longer

[1]UCC 2–104(1).

[2]UCC 9–109(1).

bargain in the traditional sense. They may choose from a limited variety of alternatives offered by a few merchant-sellers, but when it comes time to transact the sale, the terms are spelled out by the seller on its form, drafted, we must assume, to benefit it. This reality aids us in understanding why some of the consumer remedies discussed in the next chapter were imposed by state or federal legislation and not left to consumers to work out with merchants.

Today the words *consumer law* denote a wide variety of consumer remedies based upon state and federal statutory law and common law. These remedies may be divided into two broad categories depending upon the circumstances of the case and the nature of the damage suffered by the consumer. The first and probably the most important category of consumer remedies are those available to a consumer who suffers economic loss or personal injury caused by a *defective product*. The second category of remedies are those available to a consumer who suffers economic loss caused by an *illegal credit transaction*. Personal injuries from defective products are more serious and thus more important than damage from an illegal credit transaction, so we will emphasize the remedies of a consumer when injured by a defective product.

The remedies available to a consumer for economic loss or personal injury caused by a defective product may be divided into three very broad classifications. First, there are those remedies based upon a suit for a *breach of warranty* (a promise, either expressed or implied) made in the sales transaction. Since the topic of the creation of warranties, their waiver, modification and breach is important to any discussion of sales law, we have devoted this entire chapter to this topic. Please do not forget, though, that this discussion of warranties applies to both merchant-consumer transactions and merchant-merchant transactions. The second category of remedies—a category becoming very important, if not already the most important area of law when one discusses consumer law—is that of the **tort** remedies for negligent manufacture and negligent design of products plus the tort remedy based on the theory of strict liability. The third category is those remedies created by state and federal law. These last two categories are the subject of Chapter 28.

tort
A civil (private) noncontractual wrong for which a court will give a remedy

Excluded from this discussion is an analysis of liability for the sale of a service. Although the service segment of our economy is growing more rapidly than the industrial segment, space simply does not permit a presentation of, for example, the liability of doctors, attorneys, accountants, and related service-oriented professions. In very general terms, the liability of a seller of a service is based upon negligence principles and these cases are often referred to as "malpractice" suits.

In a particular circumstance, an injured consumer-plaintiff may argue theories of relief from all of the categories just mentioned. There is no inconsistency in arguing that, for example, liability may be based upon one or more of the warranties provided for in Article 2 of the UCC, upon negligent design, and also upon strict liability. The circumstances will usually favor one theory over another, however. We will explain these circumstances in the sections that follow.

The Warranties of Article 2 of the UCC

Using **warranty** theories, there are five elements essential to establish a claim for damages caused by a defective product: (1) establishing the existence of a warranty; (2) establishing the fact that the goods did not conform to the warranty at the time the sale was made; (3) establishing that the nonconformity (the breach of warranty) caused the **injury**; (4) establishing the amount of damage suffered as a result of the breach of warranty; and (5) establishing facts that may be needed to overcome any defenses

warranty
An express or implied assurance that certain facts exist; in sales of goods, generally, an affirmation of fact or an express promise made by a seller or manufacturer of goods, or a promise implied in a sales transaction by law, that the goods sold are of a certain quality or will perform in a certain manner

injury
The wrongful invasion of another person's interest

asserted. Items (2), (3), and (4) are matters of proof and vary with each case, so they will not be explained here. In this section we will first explain how and what types of warranties are made by sellers and/or merchants and then examine some of the possible defenses.

Since warranties are essentially based upon our notions of contract law, it has long been held that the parties to a sales transaction may bargain away, waive, disclaim, or modify warranties. The questions arising from whether a warranty was so changed by the "bargaining" of the parties present the chief defenses or challenges to a warranty claim. If it is established that a warranty was so waived or modified as to affect the plaintiff's case, then, in appropriate circumstances, the plaintiff may argue that the waiver or modification was "unconscionable." Because the issue of whether an "agreement" was unconscionable usually is litigated in this circumstance,[3] we will analyze unconscionability at the end of this section.

There are three classifications of warranties made by sellers or merchants: express warranties, implied warranties, and warranties of title and against infringement of **patent** or **copyright.**[4] Express and implied warranties are much more significant than warranties of title and against infringement, so they will be analyzed first.

patent
A governmental grant of protection of an invention

copyright
A governmental grant of protection of original works in a tangible medium of expression

express warranty
A warranty expressed by a party

► Express Warranties

As stated in the UCC, a seller makes **express warranties** through the following:

> **a)** Any affirmation of fact or promise made . . . to the buyer which relates to the goods and becomes part of the basis of the bargain. . . .
> **b)** Any description of the goods which is made part of the basis of the bargain. . . .
> **c)** Any sample or model which is made part of the basis of the bargain. . . .[5]

This warranty must, simply put, be *expressed*—that is, *outwardly stated*—by the seller as an affirmation of fact or promise, or by the seller's providing a description, model, or sample. It is not necessary that the words "warrant" or "guarantee" be used or that the seller have an intention to make a warranty.[6]

The expression that the seller must make may be found in the sales agreement, in advertising, in plans or instructions furnished with the goods, in packaging, or it may be made orally. This expression, however, must be more than a statement of opinion. The statement that "this car is tuned like an orchestra and will provide good service and will get 32 miles per gallon when driven at 50 miles per hour" contains just one expressed warranty—the mileage-per-gallon phrase. However, sometimes the distinction is hard to make. Consider these assertions made by a merchant in an actual case: (1) the parts are of high quality; (2) experiences and testing have shown that the frequency of repairs was very low and would remain so; (3) the purchase of machines by the buyer and leasing of them to customers probably would return a substantial profit to the buyer; (4) replacement parts are readily available; and (5) the goods sold will not cause fires, and the machines have been tested and they are ready. The court held only the fourth and fifth assertions were statements of fact.[7]

---

[3]J. White and R. Summers, *Uniform Commercial Code,* (St. Paul: West Publishing Company, 1972), 114.

[4]For a discussion of patents and copyrights, see pp. 91, 1198, 1205–6.

[5]UCC 2–313(1).

[6]UCC 2–313(2).

[7]*Royal Business Machines, Inc. v. Lorraine Corp.,* 633 F.2d 34 (7th Cir. 1980).

The opinion portion of an assertion made by a seller is labeled "puffing" by the courts and creates no liability for the seller. One of the vestiges of the doctrine of caveat emptor is that a buyer should be able to tell the difference between fact and opinion and is allowed to rely only on the former.

Section 2–313 also requires that the statement of the seller creating the express warranty become part of the *basis of the bargain*. The basis of the bargain phrase is not defined in the UCC, and its definition has not been clarified by case law. The comments to Section 2–313 state that "no particular reliance on such statements (affirmations of fact) need be shown in order to weave them into the fabric of the agreement."[8] In all probability, in a case involving a consumer plaintiff and a merchant defendant, all the plaintiff need do is allege that he or she relied on an express warranty in making a purchase, and this should be sufficient to submit the issue of the existence of the express warranty to the jury.[9] The facts in the following case were such that the court held there was no express warranty.

FACTS

The plaintiff, Myrtle Carpenter, purchased some hair dye from a local drug store. When she used the hair dye, she suffered an adverse skin reaction and sued both the local drug store and the manufacturer of the hair dye, Alberto Culver Company. She alleged that while she was viewing the various hair-dyeing products in the store she was offered assistance by one of the sales clerks. She claims the clerk indicated that several of her friends had used the hair-dyeing product in question and that her own hair came out "very nice" and "very natural." Also, the plaintiff stated that the clerk told her she "would get very fine results."

The package containing the solution and the bottle had cautionary instructions. They instructed the user to first make a preliminary skin test (called a patch test) to determine if the buyer would be unusually susceptible to the product. The plaintiff claimed that she did this and suffered no adverse reaction but did admit that she had suffered adverse reactions from other hair dyes in the past. Does the evidence presented indicate that the seller made an express warranty?

DECISION

The appellate court held that the trial court properly refused to submit the express warranty issue to the jury. As a matter of law, no express warranty was made. The appellate court stated that, in determining whether a statement of the seller is to be deemed a warranty, it is important to consider whether, in the statement, the seller asserts a fact of which the buyer is ignorant or merely states an opinion or judgment upon a matter of which the seller has no special knowledge and on which the buyer may be expected also to have an opinion and to exercise her judgment. Representations which merely express the seller's opinion, belief, judgment, or estimate do not constitute a warranty. From the context in which the statements were made in this case, coupled with the cautionary instructions, no express warranty existed.

Carpenter v. Alberto Culver Co., 184 N.W.2d 547 (Mich. 1970).

► Implied Warranties

Implied warranties are those imposed on a sales transaction by statute or court decision. If certain circumstances exist, there is a tradition in our legal system that

implied warranty
A warranty imposed by law

[8] UCC 2–313, comment 3.

[9] R. J. Nordstrom, *Law of Sales* (St. Paul: West Publishing Company, 1970), 204.

compels courts to assert that a seller has made implied warranties whether the seller intended them or not. Article 2 creates two types of implied warranties: the implied warranties of merchantability and of fitness for a particular purpose.

Implied Warranty of Merchantability This warranty, imposed on all merchants, implies a promise by the selling merchant that the goods are fit for the ordinary purposes for which such goods are used.[10] This warranty may be excluded or modified by the agreement as discussed below.

If a consumer buys a TV set, a camera, a washing machine, an automobile, or whatever from a merchant, there is imposed on the sales transaction, unless waived or modified, a warranty that the goods are of a quality comparable to that generally acceptable in that line of trade. Certainly the goods must perform for the purposes for which they were intended. A TV set must show a picture, a camera must take a picture, etc.

There are no "technical" requirements to proving the existence of this warranty other than proving that the seller is a merchant with respect to goods of the kind sold. The sale of food items not to be consumed on the premises (from, say, a grocery store) has traditionally been thought of as a sale of goods, hence subject to the imposition of implied warranties for the sale of goods. However, under the pre-Code law, the sale of food to be consumed *on the premises* (from a restaurant, for example) was held to be the sale of a service and thus the transaction was not subject to the imposition of implied warranties for the sale of goods. Article 2 changed this by providing that, "the serving for value of food or drink to be consumed either on the premises or elsewhere is a sale."[11]

There is a substantial problem with the remedy when an implied warranty is breached. The buyer is entitled to a new good or a return of money paid if the breach of warranty damages the whole contract. If less than the whole contract is affected, the buyer must keep the goods and sue for an amount that covers the loss from the breach of warranty.

FACTS

Wallace purchased a new, 1978 Lincoln Continental for $13,812 from Royal Lincoln-Mercury Sales (Royal). Two weeks after the auto was delivered, the engine hesitated, the chrome rattled and the vinyl roof peeled. After repair, the air conditioning failed, and the car began to leak oil. Again, after repair, the arm rests came unsewn, the paint began to fade, wire protruded through the upholstery, the oil leak appeared again, and the air conditioning would not work properly. At 2,200 miles, Wallace returned the car and demanded a new one or his money back. There was no dispute that the car needed a new top and a new paint job and, probably, a new engine. Royal said that the car could be driven and that they would continue to make repairs as required. Was there a breach of the warranty of merchantability in that the auto was not fit for the ordinary purpose for which it was purchased? And, what remedy is Wallace entitled to?

DECISION

The court held for Wallace, affirming a jury decision that the auto was not fit for the ordinary purpose for which it was purchased. He was entitled to a recovery of the purchase price less the auto's ordinary and reasonable depreciation. He did not have to keep the car because the extent of the damage caused by the various breaches of warranty did go to the value of the whole purchase contract.

Royal Lincoln-Mercury Sales, Inc. v. Wallace, 425 So.2d 1024 (Miss. 1982).

---

[10]UCC 2–314(2)(c).

[11]UCC 2–314(1).

Implied Warranty of Fitness for a Particular Purpose Section 2–315 states:

> Where the seller at the time of contracting has reason to know any particular purpose for which the goods are required and that the buyer is relying on the seller's skill or judgment to select or furnish suitable goods, there is unless excluded or modified ... an implied warranty that the goods shall be fit for such purpose.

This implied warranty is imposed on any seller (not just merchants) but requires two elements of proof: (1) that the seller knew the particular purpose for which the goods were bought, and (2) the buyer relied on the seller to select the goods. Actual knowledge of the particular purpose is not required so long as the circumstances of the purchase are such that the seller should have reason to know the purpose.[12] This implied warranty usually arises when a consumer asks a merchant seller to provide goods for a specific task that is beyond the consumer's general knowledge. For example, a consumer may hire a heating and cooling firm to air-condition his or her home to 72 degrees during the summer months. If the equipment fails to cool the home as provided in the contract, then this warranty is breached. Note that the air-conditioning system installed may work properly and therefore be "merchantable" but does not fulfill the particular purpose for which it was purchased.

Also, this implied warranty is significant in a large commercial transaction between merchants when the buyer submits some rough plans or basic specifications and relies on the seller to design and then manufacture an item. In the following case the two elements necessary for an implied warranty of fitness for a particular purpose were present.

FACTS

The plaintiff, Michael Catania, entered the defendant's retail paint business and asked the defendant to recommend a paint to cover the exterior stucco walls of the plaintiff's house. The defendant was told that the stucco was in a "chalky" and "powdery" condition. The defendant advised the plaintiff to "wire brush" any loose particles which were "flaky" or "scaly" before applying any paint. The defendant recommended and sold to the plaintiff a paint known as Pierce's shingle and shake paint and told him to mix two or three gallons of the paint in a container and to add a thinner. The plaintiff followed the instructions, and five months after the date of the purchase, the paint on the exterior walls of the plaintiff's house began to peel, flake, and blister. Did an implied warranty of fitness for a particular purpose exist?

DECISION

Yes. The appellate court affirmed a decision by the trial court that such a warranty existed. In creating an implied warranty of fitness for a particular purpose, the court acknowledged that two requirements must be met: (a) the buyer must rely on the seller's skill or judgment to select or furnish suitable goods; and (b) the seller at the time of contracting must have reason to know the buyer's purpose. In every case it is a matter of fact whether these requirements are met. In this case the jury found that these facts existed, so a decision in the plaintiff's favor was proper.

Catania v. Brown, 231 A.2d 668 (Conn. 1967).

[12]See UCC 2–315, comment 1.

One factual pattern or circumstance may create all three of the warranties discussed thus far. If a buyer informs a seller of a purpose for the purchased goods and relies on the seller to select it and the seller goes on to say, "These goods will fit your needs," or similar language, the statement may be an express warranty.[13] If the intended use of the goods was an *ordinary* use of the goods and the product failed to operate for this use, both the express warranty and the warranty of merchantability may have been breached. If the intended use was not an "ordinary" one and the product failed to perform, then a breach of the warranty of fitness may be argued. Article 2 recognizes that more than one of the warranties may exist and states that they may be cumulative so long as they can be construed as consistent with each other.[14] If there is an inconsistency in cumulating the warranties such that it appears unreasonable, then the intention of the parties is to prevail over the implied warranties created by Article 2. For example, express warranties will be favored over implied warranties of merchantability.[15]

► Warranty of Title

encumbrance
A person's right in another person's property

When a seller contracts to sell goods, Article 2 provides that there is a warranty that the title to the goods shall be good and its transfer rightful and that the goods shall be delivered free from any security interest or other **encumbrance** of which the buyer at the time of contracting has no knowledge.[16] This provision requires the seller to defend any lawsuit against the purchaser that involves claims of ownership of the goods sold. The seller must also defend against any claims that it, the seller, infringed any patent or trademark in producing or selling the goods if it is a dealer in those goods.[17]

► Exclusion or Modification of Warranties and Limitation of Damages for Breach of Warranty

Perhaps the most fundamental notion in American contract law is that there should be "freedom of contract." Generally, this means that the parties to a contract should be free to work out the terms of their agreement and courts should not interfere with the bargaining process or the terms of the contract. The function of courts should be to enforce the parties' contractual intent. As we have seen, ascertaining that intent is not always an easy task. However, if the parties intend, as evidenced by their written agreement or otherwise, to waive warranties implied by Article 2, then courts should enforce this intent unless the waiver violates the Magnuson-Moss Warranty Act described below. One place we find this freedom-of-contract notion in Article 2 is in Section 2–316, which permits the parties to exclude altogether or modify the warranties just explained above. First we will describe how each of the warranties above may be waived or

---

[13]Nordstrom, p. 243.

[14]UCC 2–317.

[15]UCC 2–317(c).

[16]UCC 2–312.

[17]See UCC 2–312, comment 3.

modified, and then we will examine some circumstances that reveal how merchants seek to waive or modify warranties. Next, we will explain how the exclusion and modification of warranties was treated by the Magnuson-Moss Warranty Act.

Express warranties are supposed to arise from the negotiated or dickered terms of the parties. Words or conduct which create express warranties and words or conduct tending to limit such warranties are to be construed as consistent with one another. When the words or conduct of limitation are unreasonable, they are inoperative as a waiver of modification.[18] So a seller may describe goods in one clause of an advertisement or contract and then state elsewhere that no express warranties are made. A reasonable interpretation of this would be that the disclaimer was intended to apply to qualities of the goods not stated or implicit in the description.[19] The attempted disclaimer could not be read to waive the express warranty created by the description. In short, any attempt by a seller to first make an express warranty and then later deny making it should be labeled as unreasonable conduct and will be inoperative. The way around this for the merchant is, of course, to make no express warranties but to rely on the seller's right to "puff" to make a sale.

The implied warranty of merchantability may be excluded or modified by a writing that uses conspicuous language and mentions the word "merchantability."[20] Language is conspicuous if it is so written that a reasonable person against whom it is to operate ought to have noticed it. If the language is in the text of a form contract, it is conspicuous if it is in larger or contrasting type or color.[21]

The implied warranty of fitness for a particular purpose may be waived or modified (1) by a writing and (2) by conspicuous language of waiver or modification in the writing. This warranty may be waived by, for example, conspicuous language that states that "there are no warranties which extend beyond the description on the face hereof."[22]

In addition, both implied warranties may be excluded if the goods are said to be sold "as is" or "with all faults" or if other language calls the buyer's attention to the exclusion of warranties and makes plain that there is no implied warranty.[23] Also, when the buyer has examined the goods *before* entering into the contract or has refused the seller's demand to examine the goods if given an opportunity, there is no implied warranty with regard to defects that such an examination ought (in the circumstances) to have revealed.[24] In some cases where the intent of the parties is not clear,[25] course of dealing or course of performance or usage of trade may result in a waiver or modification of an implied warranty.[26]

---

[18]UCC 2–316(1).

[19]Nordstrom, p. 286.

[20]UCC 2–316(2).

[21]UCC 1–201(10).

[22]UCC 2–316(2).

[23]UCC 2–316(3)(a).

[24]UCC 2–316(3)(b).

[25]Nordstrom, p. 271.

[26]UCC 2–316(3)(c).

The warranty of title may be excluded or modified by specific language of waiver or modification or by circumstances that give the buyer reason to know that the person selling does not claim title.[27]

► Exclusion or Modification in Practice

There can be no doubt that the sections of Article 2 providing for waiver or modification of warranties are powerful and significant when a merchant sells to a consumer. When merchants deal with one another, the warranty provisions in the sales contract, or the attempted waiver or modification of implied warranties, usually will be the subject of close scrutiny and negotiation. But when *you* as a consumer make a purchase from a merchant, how often do you read the seller's agreement for warranty provisions? If you did read the agreement, what would you find? And if you found conspicuous language that waived or modified the implied warranties, what could you do about it?

It is impossible here to review the content of many merchants' sales contracts to determine how they attempt to waive or modify warranties. We will, however, single out just a few for analysis to illustrate how merchants use Section 2–316, Exclusion or Modification of Warranties. The fact that many merchants do take advantage of Section 2–316 and the fact they are successful helps to explain why so many different remedies for damage caused by defective products have developed *outside* the context of contract law.

Some form contracts of merchants first state clearly which warranties are made and then state that all other warranties are excluded. Some, in addition, attempt to limit liability for a breach of the warranty. Recall that in Chapter 26 we explained that damages may be limited by agreement of the parties.

Consider, for example, the warranty and limitation of damages provided for on the package of Sears "Early One" Smoke and Fire Detector. This is a typical smoke and fire alarm that sells for under $20 and is intended for home installation. On the box there is the language:

> FULL ONE YEAR WARRANTY ON SMOKE DETECTOR
>
> For one year from the date of purchase, Sears will repair or replace this smoke detector free of charge, if defective in material or workmanship. This warranty shall not apply to the batteries, which are expendable. To obtain warranty service, simply return the smoke detector to your nearest Sears store throughout the United States.

In heavy black letters there follows this language:

> LIMITATION ON LIABILITY
>
> Sears will not be liable for loss or damage to property or any incidental or consequential loss or expense from property damage due directly or indirectly to occurrences which the smoke detector is designed to detect.

Sears makes a rather generous warranty on the detector! But what would happen if the alarm failed to operate and, as a result, a home was destroyed by fire and, in addition, persons suffered injury? Damage to the property and persons in this case would be consequential damage, and a court would have to judge whether the limitation on the damages found on the box and other sales material was effective. In some states there are

[27] UCC 2–312(2).

statutes prohibiting this, or courts have held that such a limitation is "unconscionable" and have not enforced the limitation provision. Sears does note this on the box by adding:

> Some states do not allow the exclusion or limitation of incidental or consequential damages, so the ... limitation or exclusion may not apply to you.

Before we begin our explanation of the Magnuson-Moss Warranty Act and the legal doctrine of unconscionability, let us set out another typical but more complex example of merchant language that attempts to waive or modify warranties and limit damages. All automobiles and most trucks are sold, technically, by manufacturers to dealers, who then sell to the public. A few years ago, a "retail order" for a new van that was purchased from a dealer read as follows:

> All warranties, if any, by a manufacturer or supplier other than dealer are theirs, *not* dealer's, and only such manufacturer or other supplier shall be liable for performance under such warranties. Unless dealer furnishes buyer with a separate written warranty or service contract made by dealer on its own behalf, dealer hereby disclaims all warranties, express or implied, including any implied warranties of merchantability or fitness for a particular purpose: (A) on all goods and services sold by dealer, and (B) on all used vehicles which are hereby sold "as is—not expressly warranted or guaranteed."

And, on the back of the "retail order," under the heading "Additional Terms and Conditions," there is this language:

> Purchaser shall not be entitled to recover from dealer any consequential damages, damages to property, damages for loss of use, loss of time, loss of profits, or income, or any other incidental damages.

It is clear that the dealer is attempting to exempt itself entirely from any warranty liability or damage claims—unless, of course, a consumer could prove that a salesperson made an oral express warranty or, as the language reveals, the dealer provides a separate written warranty contract. In the package of materials a consumer receives from the dealer at the time of purchase there is a manufacturer's "Warranty Facts Booklet." In this booklet we find this statement:

> Manufacturer warrants for its ... cars and light trucks operated under normal use in the U.S. or Canada that the Selling Dealer will repair, replace, or adjust free any parts, except tires, found to be defective in factory materials or workmanship within the earlier of 12 months or 12,000 miles from either first use or retail delivery.

In larger and bolder type it further provides:

> There is no other express warranty on this vehicle. To the extent allowed by law:
>
> **1.** Any implied warranty of merchantability or fitness is limited to the 12-month or 12,000 mile duration of this written warranty.
> **2.** Neither manufacturer nor the selling dealer shall have any responsibility for loss of use of the vehicle, loss of time, inconvenience, commercial loss or consequential damages.

> Some states do not allow limitations on how long an implied warranty lasts or the exclusion or limitation of incidental or consequential damages so the above limitations may not apply to you.

If the language above were applied literally, then a consumer who suffered injury to his or her person because a new car failed to stop due to defective brakes could not sue the manufacturer of the car based on a contract or sales theory of liability and recover damages for the personal injury. Fortunately for the consumer, the law has responded in at least two ways that are of importance here. Congress passed legislation to help consumers cope with warranty abuse, and the courts expanded the definition of unconscionability to apply to warranty waivers and exclusions. We will first explain the federal legislation.

The Magnuson-Moss Warranty Act

The Consumer Product Warranty and Federal Trade Commission Improvement Act (also called the Magnuson-Moss Warranty—Federal Trade Commission Improvement Act),[28] which became law on July 4, 1975, was prompted in part because consumers were dissatisfied with their "protection" afforded by the UCC warranties. "Warranty abuse" was a phenomenon substantiated in 1974 when a congressional subcommittee reviewed 200 warranties from fifty-one major companies and found only one which offered a warranty free of ambiguous phrases, exemptions, and disclaimers.[29] This Act seeks to make warranty enforcement a reality by providing to the consumer the information needed to pursue a claim for a breach. The Act does not alter the warranties of merchantability or fitness for a particular purpose, and the provisions of the Act do not compel a merchant to make a warranty.

The general provisions of the Act do apply when a *written* warranty is made *and* the cost of the item purchased exceeds $15. This $15 requirement, as well as many of the other standards and procedures under the Act, are established by Federal Trade Commission regulation. The one who makes a warranty (called a "warrantor") is required by the Act to fully and conspicuously disclose the terms and limitations of the warranty to the consumer *before* the sale. Some of the items that warrantors should disclose are:

1. The names and addresses of the warrantors.
2. The product or parts covered.
3. A statement of what the warrantor will do upon breach of the warranty, at whose expense the work will be done, and the period of time the warranty will last.
4. The step-by-step procedure consumers must take in order to obtain performance of any obligation under the warranty.
5. A brief summary of the legal remedies available to the consumer upon breach.

The Act requires that when a warranty is made, it be *conspicuously* designed either (1) a full (statement of duration) warranty (for example, "full one year warranty") or (2)

---

[28] 15 U.S.C.A. sec. 2301.

[29] W. Haemmel, B. George, and J. Bliss, *Consumer Law* (St. Paul: West Publishing, 1975), 285.

a limited warranty. If a warranty is labeled a *full* warranty then, unless the warrantor is exempted from the requirements by FTC rules, it must meet four standards:

1. A warrantor must remedy a defective consumer product within a reasonable time and without charge.
2. A warrantor may not impose any limitation on the duration of any implied warranty.
3. A warrantor may not exclude or limit consequential damages for breach of an implied warranty unless the exclusion or limitation conspicuously appears on the face of the warranty.
4. If the product (or a component part) contains a defect or malfunction after a reasonable number of attempts by the warrantor to remedy the defect, a warrantor must permit the consumer to elect either a refund or replacement—without charge.[30]

A consumer product may be sold with both full and limited warranties so long as they are clearly and conspicuously differentiated.

Perhaps the most significant provision of the Act limits the use of written warranties to disclaim the implied warranties created in a sales transaction by the UCC by superceding the UCC in this area of waiver and modification of implied warranties. Under this Act, a supplier may not disclaim or modify implied warranties if the supplier makes any written warranty or if the supplier either at the time of sale or within ninety days thereafter enters into a service contract with the consumer. This provision applies to both full and limited warranties. However, if a limited warranty is provided, then the duration of the warranty may be limited so long as it is limited to a reasonable time and it is set forth in clear and unmistakable language.[31]

Finally, this Act creates a private cause of action for an injured consumer and provides that the consumer may sue for an amount equal to the aggregate amount of cost and expenses (including attorney's fees) determined by the court to have been reasonably incurred by the consumer.[32] So, subject to some qualifications that are not that important here, damaged consumers may sue for both attorney's fees and costs (to be awarded to the attorney) plus an amount of damage as determined generally by these costs. The Act also provides for class actions.

The Unconscionable Contract or Clause

Certainly the most potent weapon a consumer plaintiff has to support an assertion that a clause of a contract or an entire contract with a merchant is basically unfair is Section 2–302, which describes an **unconscionable contract** or clause. It provides:

unconscionable contract
A contract in which one of the parties is in too unequal or one-sided a bargaining position at the time the contract is made

> If the court as a matter of law finds the contract or any clause of the contract to have been unconscionable at the time it was made the court may refuse to enforce the contract, or it

---

[30] 15 U.S.C.A. sec. 2304.

[31] 15 U.S.C.A. sec. 2308.

[32] 15 U.S.C.A. sec. 2310.

> may enforce the remainder of the contract without the unconscionable clause, or it may so limit the application of any unconscionable clause as to avoid any unconscionable result.[33]

This section gives the judge, not the jury, the right to "police" sales contracts for fundamental fairness. According to one legal scholar, what Karl Llewellyn had in mind when he first drafted Section 2–302 was the development of an open and direct attack upon one-sided, unbargained-for, small-print clauses in standardized form contracts.[34]

The official comments to this section state that the basic test or definition is whether "in the light of the general commercial background and the commercial needs of the particular trade or case, the clauses involved are so one-sided as to be unconscionable under the circumstances existing at the time of the making of the contract."[35] Section 2–719(3) provides that limitation in a contract "of consequential damages for injury to the person in the case of consumer goods is prima facie unconscionable."

Section 2–302 is one of those sections, similar to those which use the words "reasonable" or "unreasonable," which permit courts to change the meaning of the written words of the law as our commercial society changes. Courts have traditionally had the power to declare sales agreements unenforceable because they were fundamentally unfair, but they did this by varying the definition of such concepts as "misrepresentation," "illegality," "consideration," or by declaring an agreement "void" because it violated "public policy." In fact, one state (California) that adopted other sections of the Code did not adopt Section 2–302. Apparently the courts in this state still rely on their traditional equity powers to police sales agreements.

We can best understand the notion of unconscionability by reexamining how courts respond to what could be labeled "unfair" sales agreements between a merchant seller and a merchant buyer on the one hand, and a merchant seller and a consumer on the other hand.

A sales agreement between merchants is intended to shift certain business risks. If a court is convinced that the merchants "bargained" for the provisions of the sales agreement, the provisions will be enforced even if the result is to cause severe economic loss. In the following case the court held that a price rise of goods did not, of itself, make the enforceability of a contract unconscionable.

FACTS

The plaintiff, a textile manufacturer, agreed in the spring of 1973 to buy all of the cotton produced by the seller for $.32 a pound. In the fall of 1973 on the date when the seller's performance was due, the market price of cotton was over $.80 a pound. The seller refused to perform, and the buyer sued it, seeking specific performance. The seller asserted as a defense that the contract for the sale of its cotton is now unconscionable and should not be enforced by the court. The seller further argued that the plaintiff had a "peculiar knowledge" that the price of cotton would spectacularly rise even though it admitted that the contract price was not substantially out of line with the market price of cotton at the time the contract was made. Was the contract unconscionable?

DECISION

The court found in favor of the plaintiff and as a matter of law would not allow the defendant to argue unconscionability. The court said that

---

[33]UCC 2–302(1).

[34]W. Zelermyer, "The Unconscionable Contract," paper read at the American Business Law Association Annual Meeting, College Park, Md. (August 18, 1978).

[35]UCC 2–302, comment 1.

"unconscionability" must be defined as an absence of meaningful choice on the part of one of the parties together with contract terms which are unreasonably favorable to the other party. The presence of a meaningful choice can only be determined by consideration of all the circumstances surrounding the transaction. Such circumstances as gross inequality of bargaining power, the education of each party, and the nature of the language used are usually significant. The general rule that one who signs an agreement is bound by its terms should be followed unless one or more of these circumstances existed at the time the contract was made. In this case, there was no issue of fact which could be used to establish unconscionability.

West Point-Pepperell, Inc. v. O. W. Bradshaw, 377 F.Supp. 154 (M.D.Ala. 1974).

Almost all instances in which there has been a successful assertion at the appellate level that a contract or clause of a contract is unconscionable involve consumers and merchants as the two parties.[36] The following case is such a successful assertion. This case is a classic example of how the courts use the principle of unconscionability to protect consumers against those merchants who are overzealous in their use of standard form contracts.

FACTS

Mr. Henningsen purchased a new Plymouth automobile from Bloomfield Motors, Inc., as a Mother's Day gift for his wife. Ten days after getting the car, Mrs. Henningsen was driving when she heard a "crack" under the hood of the car, the steering wheel spun in her hands and the car veered 90 degrees from its path into a brick wall. The car, with 468 miles on it, was totally destroyed and Mrs. Henningsen was injured. Mr. and Mrs. Henningsen sued Bloomfield Motors, Inc., and Chrysler Corporation, manufacturer of Plymouths, for personal and property damage based, among other things, on a breach of warranty theory.

The purchase order signed by Mr. Henningsen contained this language (in part):

> The manufacturer warrants each new motor vehicle ... chassis or parts ... to be free from defects in material or workmanship under normal use and service. Its obligation under this warranty being limited to making good at its factory any part or parts thereof which shall within ninety (90) days after delivery ... or before such vehicle has been driven 4,000 miles, whichever event shall first occur, be returned to it with transportation charges prepaid and which its examination shall disclose to its satisfaction to have been thus defective; this warranty being expressly in lieu of all other warranties expressed or implied and all other obligations or liabilities on its part....

The auto dealer and manufacturer argued that the last clause of the above "warranty" barred the plaintiff, Mrs. Henningsen, from asserting a claim for personal injuries. The jury returned a verdict for the plaintiffs and the defendants appealed. Should the "warranty" language apparently modifying or limiting the plaintiffs' right to sue for personal injuries be a bar to the plaintiffs' claim?

DECISION

No. The appellate court agreed with the trial court and affirmed the verdict for the plaintiffs. The court said that the terms of the warranty are a "sad commentary" upon the automobile manufacturers' marketing practices [in the late 1950s]. The manufacturer agrees to replace defective parts for 90 days or 4,000 miles, whichever occurs first, if the part is sent to the factory, transportation charges prepaid, and if examination discloses to its satisfaction that the part is defective. It is difficult to imagine a greater burden on the consumer or a less satisfactory remedy, said the court. It added that, aside from imposing on the buyer the trouble of removing and shipping the part, the manufacturer has sought to retain the un-

[36]White and Summers, p. 114.

controlled discretion to decide the issue of defectiveness. The court called the security provided to the buyer by the warranty illusory in character and then concluded that the warranty, even though apparently agreed to by the parties, should not be enforced. It said:

> The status of the automobile industry is unique. Manufacturers are few in number and strong in bargaining position. In the matter of warranties on the sales of their products, the Automotive Manufacturers Association has enrolled them to present a united front. From the standpoint of the purchaser, there can be no arms length negotiating on the subject. Because his capacity for bargaining is so grossly unequal, the inexorable conclusion which follows is that he is not permitted to bargain at all. He must take or leave the automobile on the warranty terms dictated by the maker. He cannot turn to a competitor for better security.
>
> The attempted exclusion of all obligations except those specifically assumed by the express warranty are a studied effort to frustrate the protection given to consumers by the warranties created by law. The attempted disclaimer is so inimical to the public good as to compel an adjudication of its invalidity.
>
> *Henningsen v. Bloomfield Motors, Inc. and Chrysler Corp.*, 161 A.2d 69, 94 (N.J. 1960).

The above case was decided in 1960 before the UCC was adopted in New Jersey and before the passage of the Magnuson-Moss Warranty Act. However, the court's reasoning is a classic statement of the need for the doctrine of unconscionability.

Although the above case makes clear the "policy" reasons for the doctrine of unconscionability, it does not clearly define the doctrine itself. Such a definition is difficult and varies from state to state and case to case. Generally, in finding that a contract or clause is unconscionable, courts consider these circumstances important: (1) the background of the party asserting unconscionability—such facts as age, education, economic status, etc.; (2) the "hidden" or complex nature of the language used; (3) the degree of inequality in bargaining position; and (4) the number of "meaningful choices" available to the party asserting unconscionability.

Privity Under Article 2—Defenses to a Products Liability Claim Based on a Breach of Warranty

▶ Privity Under Article 2

privity
A mutuality of relationship between persons or between persons and a particular transaction

The liability of a seller of goods for economic loss or personal injury caused by a defective product is still limited by **privity** in many jurisdictions today. This limitation can best be described by dividing privity issues into two major classifications: horizontal privity and vertical privity.

Horizontal Privity Cases involving the question of who is a proper plaintiff are labeled horizontal privity cases. These cases involve the question "to whom is the warranty made?" Typically, a consumer buys goods and either takes them home or gives them as a gift and someone else is then injured as a result of a defect. Should this injured person recover? Article 2 provides some guidance in answering this question. The 1978 Official Text of Article 2 provides three alternative sections which may be adopted by states. The alternative adopted by most of the states provides:[37]

[37]Four states have adopted a more liberal version, Alternative B, and at least eight states have adopted the most liberal version, Alternative C. See White and Summers, *Handbook of the Law Under the Uniform Commercial Code*, p. 331.

> A seller's warranty whether express or implied extends to any natural person who is in the family or household of his buyer or who is a guest in his home if it is reasonable to expect that such person may use, consume or be affected by the goods and who is injured in person by breach of the warranty. A seller may not exclude or limit the operation of this section.[38]

Thus the UCC has expanded the traditional definition of privity, but there is still confusion resulting from courts applying this section. Some have held that this section states once and for all the *entire* group of plaintiffs who may be allowed to recover for a breach of warranty. Other courts—and this view is preferred by some scholars—have held that Section 2–318 was intended to set the *minimum* boundaries on the class of those who could sue for a breach of warranty.[39]

Horizontal privity, then, is a legal defense that is of varying vitality depending upon what the supreme court of the state in which the suit is brought has held on this issue.

Vertical Privity There seems to be more agreement in state appellate decisions about vertical privity. This class of issues refers to which party in the chain of distribution—the manufacturer, the wholesaler, the distributor, or the retailer—is the *proper defendant* when facing a plaintiff injured by defective goods and who is relying on a breach of warranty theory. In most cases where a consumer is suing a manufacturer, there is no technical privity. Usually, the plaintiff is in privity only with a retailer. In most of the recent cases, the need for this privity has been discarded when a defendant higher up in the chain of distribution is sued by a consumer. There are several reasons for this. (1) It is usually the manufacturer who, through mass advertising campaigns, has created the demand for the goods, thus, it is "fair" that it be liable for injury caused by a defect. (2) If such privity were required, it might result in hardship to the plaintiff if the retailer were insolvent. (3) Requiring this technical privity would result in a multiplicity of lawsuits where the consumer sues a retailer, the retailer sues the wholesaler, etc.

► Statute of Limitations and Notice of Breach of Warranties

Finally, recall that Section 2–725(1)(2) requires that any claim for a breach of warranty be brought within, usually, four years from the date of tender of delivery unless there is a warranty explicitly extending this period. Many injured plaintiffs must use a tort theory of liability because their sales-theory claim has been barred by this statute of limitations.

A closely related notion is that Article 2 imposes on a buyer the obligation to notify the seller of any breach within a reasonable time after it discovers or should have discovered the breach.[40] If a buyer fails to give this notice, it is barred from any remedy. This provision is applied liberally to the merchant-consumer transaction, but there are cases denying a consumer-plaintiff recovery because of failure to give notice of breach so that a merchant-defendant may act to preserve evidence essential for its defense.

Conclusion

This chapter has presented only a part of the material that is usually thought of as "consumer law." As you can see from the examples and some of the cases, some of this

---

[38]UCC 2–318, Alternative A.

[39]Nordstrom, p. 280.

[40]UCC 2–607(3)(a).

law was illusory in that it really did not help the consumer in a claim against a manufacturer for a defective product. Often, manufacturers were able to waive or modify the various warranties provided for by Article 2. Also, to some extent, the defenses of privity, based on our older notions of contract law, were used to defeat consumer claims. In response to a demand for increased consumer protection, Congress passed the Magnuson-Moss Warranty Act, and the court system relied more heavily on the notion of unconscionability to strike down unfair and burdensome contract clauses that waived or modified seller warranties. However, these were only part of the approach to this significant problem. In the next chapter we explore other approaches.

Summary Statement

1. Briefly, merchants deal in goods or by their occupation hold themselves out as having knowledge or skill peculiar to the sale of goods. Consumers buy goods to use primarily for personal, family, or household purposes.
2. The doctrines of privity and caveat emptor kept our law from developing remedies for consumers injured by defective products until the midpoint of this century and after.
3. In Article 2 there are provisions for the creation of three kinds of sales warranties. Each serves a different purpose and is made in different circumstances. These warranties are express warranties, implied warranties of merchantability, implied warranties of fitness for a particular purpose, and warranties of title including warranties against infringement of patent or copyright.
4. Each of the four kinds of warranty may be modified or waived by the agreement of the parties. Like the creation of these warranties, their modification and waiver each requires different circumstances.
5. In many instances, when a large merchant seller attempts to modify or waive warranties or consumer remedies in a sales contract with a consumer, a court may declare such an attempt "unconscionable" and refuse to enforce it. An unconscionable clause or contract is one that, in light of the general commercial background and the commercial needs of the particular trade or case, appears so one-sided at the time the contract was made that a court in good conscience cannot enforce it.
6. The Magnuson-Moss Warranty Act was passed by Congress to protect consumers against merchants who took unfair advantage of the waiver and modification of warranty sections of Article 2. It provides for full and limited warranties and prohibits merchants from waiving implied warranties under some conditions.
7. Major legal defenses used by merchant sellers in a defective products liability claim based on a breach of warranty may include the lack of horizontal privity, failure to give notice of breach, and the running of the statute of limitations.

The following case will probably make history in the area of products liability law. The litigation involving this case is very long and complex and we present here just a portion of the various court holdings in this matter. On the face of it, the claims of the plaintiff seem rather simple. The estate of the plaintiff is claiming (among other things) that the defendant cigarette companies made certain express warranties about the purity and safety of their products in advertising, that the deceased plaintiff relied on these assertions, and developed lung cancer and died as a result. The decision below holds that the plaintiff has stated a good case in breach of warranty (one of the first such cases to hold this way) and that the jury may decide the damage claims. This case did not decide the value of the damage claims, just that there may possibly be such damages awarded. This matter is still in the courts and probably will be for some time to come because it presents a substantial threat to the future of an entire industry.

CIPOLLONE v. LIGGETT GROUP, INC.
Prod. Liab. Rep. (CCH) para. 11,768 (1988)

Rose De Francesco Cippolone was born in 1925 and began to smoke at age 16 . . . while she was still in high school. She testified that she began to smoke because she saw people smoking in the movies, in advertisements and looked upon it as something "cool, glamorous and grown-up" to do. She began smoking Chesterfields (manufactured by defendant Liggett . . .) primarily because of advertisements of "pretty girls and movie stars" and because Chesterfields were described in the advertisements as "mild." By the end of 1943, she was smoking a pack a day. . . . In 1955 she switched from Chesterfields to L&M cigarettes . . . because L&M cigaretes were filtered, and she believed that the filter would trap whatever was "bad" for her. . . . She relied upon advertisements which supported that contention. She continued to smoke approximately a pack and one-half a day until 1968, when she switched to Virginia Slims. In this instance, she changed because the cigarettes were glamorous and long, and were associated with beautiful women—and the liberated woman. In this period she smoked between one and two packs a day.

She testified that she believed that the "tobacco companies wouldn't do anything that was really going to kill you," and she read and relied upon statements from the industry in the media that indicated that there was no specific proof that cigarette smoking caused cancer.

In 1981 her cancer was diagnosed, and even though her doctors advised her to stop, she was unable to do so. She even told her doctors and her husband that she had quit when she had not, and she continued to smoke until June of 1982 when her lung was removed. Even thereafter she smoked occasionally—in hiding. She stopped smoking in 1983 when her cancer had metastasized and she was diagnosed as fatally ill. Mrs. Cipollone eventually died on October 21, 1984.

There has been overwhelming evidence presented to the jury from which they could conclude . . . that smoking caused lung cancer in Mrs. Cipollone, and that lung cancer was the cause of her eventual death.

Plaintiff presented expert testimony that Mrs. Cipollone was heavily dependent on tobacco and would grasp at any rationalization to continue, and that the cigarette companies provided that rationalization on a steady basis. The defendants and others in the industry repeatedly and publicly questioned the scientific and medical literature which linked smoking with cancer and other diseases. Furthermore, plaintiff offered expert testimony which demonstrated that even after the companies ceased making specific health claims, the vast advertising of the industry created a consistent message of purity, health, safety, reduced tars and nicotine, etc. This campaign . . . played on the weakness of those who were either addicted and/or dependent.

Plaintiff presented testimony that $250,000 is spent per hour, 24 hours a day, 7 days a week, 365 days a year on cigarette advertising . . . Recognizing that smokers would look to their doctors for advice and that many doctors were smokers themselves, the industry created a magazine entitled Tobacco and Health (Research) and mailed it free to practically every doctor in the country, ... The publication was a blatant and biased account of the smoking "controversy". It had one purpose—to convince doctors that the claimed risks were unfounded, unsupported, or refuted.

Plaintiff has presented evidence that Liggett made "affirmations of fact," within the meaning of UCC 2–313(1)(a), concerning the health risks of smoking..... [And] Plaintiff has presented evidence from which the jury could conclude that Liggett's advertisements were the basis of the bargain for Mrs. Cipollone's purchase of Liggett's cigarettes.

[In] connection with plaintiff's express warranty and failure to warn claims, Mrs. Cipollone's continued smoking after the appearance of the congressionally mandated warning in 1966 does not, as a matter of law, relieve defendants of liability. The court denies Liggett's motion for a directed verdict on the express warranty claims.

This court holds that a jury may find that the defendant did make express warranties in cigarette advertising about health, and whether these warranties were breached is a matter for the jury.

Questions and Case Problems

1. Plaintiff, manufacturer of plastic bottle caps sold to major distillers of liquor, ordered plastic liners for the bottle caps from the defendant. Before a contract was made, the defendant had supplied the plaintiff with brochures, bulletins, and other materials that made certain factual representations about the defendant's product. The contract itself did not contain these representations. The defendant shipped an order of bottle cap liners to the plaintiff and the plaintiff alleges they were not in conformance with the specifications and representations made in the brochures and bulletins. Do you believe the seller has made an express warranty in these bulletins and brochures? [*AFA Corp. v. Phoenix Closures, Inc.,* 501 F.Supp 224 (D.C. Ill. 1980).]
2. Buyer purchased a round hay baler from John Deere Co., seller, defendant, in May of 1976. About one month later, the buyer's arm was severed when it became caught in the baler. The buyer, plaintiff, sues defendant based on a breach of an express warranty that the baler was especially designed to be safe. The operator's manual stated:

   > The safety of the operator was one of the prime considerations in the minds of John Deere engineers when this baler was designed. Shielding, simple adjustments and other safety features were built into the baler wherever possible.

   Defendant, by means of conspicuous language in both the purchase order and in the attached warranty materials, disclaimed all express warranties. Do you believe that John Deere made an express warranty and, if so, was it properly disclaimed? [*Schlenz v. John Deere Co.,* 511 F.Supp. 224 (D.C. Mont. 1981).]
3. John wanted to buy a new electric drill. He saw an advertisement in the local newspaper which said that Sears was having a special sale on "half-inch electric drills, reduced 20% to $15." John went to Sears to buy the drill but was very interested in whether or not the drill was double-insulated. This meant that the drill had special wiring in it so that if a short developed the drill would not shock the user. John was interested in this feature because he often worked in his basement, where the floor was damp as a result of leaky plumbing, and there was a substantial risk of electrocution. John asked the saleswoman at Sears, "Do you have double-insulated drills?" The saleswoman replied, "We have just what you want," and got for John one of the drills on sale. She said, "This drill is double-insulated." John then said, "Fine, I'll take it," and handed her his Sears credit card. The saleswoman made out the appropriate sales slip and John left with the drill.

   Did Sears make any of the warranties listed below? Explain your answer briefly.

a) An express warranty
b) An implied warranty of merchantability
c) An implied warranty of fitness for a particular purpose
d) Any other warranties

4. Based on the information in question 3, assume that John took the drill home and one day his daughter used it in the basement and was injured because the drill was not double-insulated. If Sears were sued for the injuries based upon a warranty theory, what might Sears argue? Would Sears be successful? Assume that John, before using the drill, had sold it to a friend visiting from another state and the friend was injured in his (the friend's) home because the drill was not double-insulated. What would Sears argue in response to a claim for injury based upon warranty theories? Would Sears be successful this time?

5. In questions 3 and 4 above, the packaging for the drill that John purchased and the instructions said in plain and conspicuous language:

> For one year from the date of purchase, Sears will repair or replace this drill free of charge if defective in material or workmanship.

And, in larger type, it added:

> Sears will not be liable for loss or damage to property or any incidental or consequential loss or expense from property damage due directly to defects in the drill.

Assume that all of the information in question 3 is true, and that after John purchased the drill, he was severely injured when using the drill in his basement, which at the time was dry. You may also assume that the drill was not properly double-insulated. As a result of this defect, the drill exploded and caused John's basement to catch fire, resulting in $5,000 damage to the basement and personal injury to John. Does the above language on the packaging and directions limit John's measure of recovery to the value of the drill? What additional circumstances might help John's case?

6. Walker-Thomas Furniture Co. operated a retail furniture store in the District of Columbia. From 1957 to 1962 it contracted with Williams for the "purchase" of household items. The "agreement" of the parties read in such a way that Walker-Thomas was supposedly leasing each item to Williams for a stipulated monthly rent. It also provided that title to the goods would remain in Walker-Thomas until the total of all the monthly payments had been made on all items purchased. Also, an obscure provision added that all payments now and hereafter made shall be credited pro rata on all outstanding "leases," bills, and accounts. The effect of this last provision was to keep a balance due on every item purchased until the balance due on all items, whenever purchased, had been fully paid. This resulted in the debt created by any new credit purchase being secured by the right to repossess all items previously purchased by that purchaser. On April 17, 1962 Williams bought a stereo set for a stated value of $514.95, but she soon defaulted in her payments. Walker-Thomas seeks to repossess all items purchased by her since December 1957. What legal argument would you expect Williams to make in her defense? What circumstances might be important in establishing this defense? [*Williams v. Walker-Thomas Furniture Co.,* 350 F.2d 445 (D.C. Cir. 1965).]

7. Robert Jones owned a small business providing amusement rides at shopping centers. In the course of Jones' operation he had on occasion made trades of his equipment with manufacturers of the rides and with other ride operators. He believed new or different rides attracted more people. He sold one of these rides, a "pony cart" ride, to Nicole, Inc. The ride was defective and injured one of Nicole's patrons, and now Nicole sues Jones because of the defect, alleging that the sale from Jones to Nicole breached the implied warranty of merchantability. Can Nicole recover from Jones on this theory? [See *Allen v. Nicole, Inc.,* 412 A.2d 824 (N. J. 1980).]

8. Plaintiff, a dairy farmer, bought four milking machines from the defendant for his dairy herd. The machines were delivered on Feb. 19, 1973 and installed by March 1, 1973. In 1976, the buyer's herd suffered a severe epidemic of mastitis, an udder infection, and he maintains that the cause of the epidemic was a defect in the milking machines. The plaintiff filed suit for breach of warranty on March 11, 1977. There is a four-year statute of limitations. The defendant claims the suit is barred by the statute of limitations, and the plaintiff argues that the claim arose upon discovery of the defect in 1976. Is the plaintiff's claim barred by the four-year statute of limitations? [*Clark v. De Laval Separator Corp.,* 639 F.2d 1320 (5th Cir. 1981).]

9. In 1989, *C* purchased a 1955 Chevrolet Corvette from *S* for $2,800. Some time later *C* learned that a prior owner had placed a $3,600 lien on the Corvette. Describe the remedy that *C* has against *S,* if any.

10. Using the case of *Cipollone v. Liggett Group,* excerpted at the beginning of this section, explain how you would try to prove today the defendant's cigarettes to be a breach of expressed warranty in view of the movement toward decreased nicotine content and the required labeling of cigarette smoking as dangerous to health, yet in view of increased print advertising.

C H A P T E R

28

CONSUMER LAW

B. MANUFACTURER'S LIABILITY AND CONSUMER PROTECTION LEGISLATION

After you have read this chapter, you should be able to:

1. Define the two general categories of tort law that provide remedies for injured consumers, and explain how the legal device of "res ipsa loquitur" is used in a products liability case.
2. Write a paragraph on the need for the tort theory of strict liability by emphasizing the limitations on the use of warranty-based and negligence-based theories of seller liability.
3. Define in some detail what a "defect" is and what "unreasonably dangerous" means for purposes of applying section 402A of the Restatement of Torts.
4. Briefly discuss three defenses to products liability claims.
5. Explain how market share liability provides a remedy to an injured consumer.
6. Outline the key features of the Model Uniform Products Liability Act and state the purpose of statutes of repose.
7. Explain briefly the purpose and function of the Consumer Product Safety Commission and the Federal Trade Commission, and describe how they operate.
8. Explain the purpose of the Consumer Credit Protection Act, Fair Credit Reporting Act and Equal Credit Opportunity Act; give an example of a violation of the last two acts.

BUSINESS DECISIONS and the LAW

Today there is a virtual explosion in not only the number of product related injuries and cases but in the legal theories and mechanisms available to compensate injured consumers. It is no overstatement to say that coping with the phenomenon of dangerous and defective products is one of the most challenging problems facing our commercial society and consumers today.

Let us consider just two examples that are modern product liability catastrophies. By the close of the 1980s more than 14,000 American women who had worn the intrauterine birth control device called the Dalkon Shield had filed product liability lawsuits against the manufacturer, the A. H. Robins Company.* The terrible damage caused by the distribution of over 4.5 million of these devices in eighty countries has resulted in the A. H. Robins Company agreeing to set aside several billion dollars to help pay for the pain and suffering.** Both consumers and the manufacturer had suffered tremendously, and the solution for this catastrophe was sought in the application of the legal theories discussed in this chapter.

The readily available insulation material asbestos, however, has caused wider damage. Manville Corporation, once the world's largest asbestos company with twenty-five thousand employees and more than fifty factories and mines in the United States and Canada, filed for bankruptcy in August 1982. It did so because it estimated that it would be named as defendant in at least 52,000 asbestos-disease lawsuits in the foreseeable future. The total value of the law suits was predicted to exceed $2 billion and management decided that, rather than continue in business, they would let the courts establish an effective system for handling the asbestos claims under the bankruptcy code.†

These two examples show that the issues raised by the design, production, and consumption of consumer goods is at once tragic for the consumer, a challenge for our legal system, and a most serious problem for corporate management. As you will see from the discussions below, the court system and the state and federal legislatures have attempted to deal with this challenging problem. To begin our discussion of the law that is applicable to the kinds of cases that resolve the Dalkon Shield and asbestos liability issues, we present a brief overview of the growth of products liability law.

*See Mintz, *At Any Cost* (New York: Pantheon, 1985).
**See Perry and Dawson, *Nightmare: Women and the Dalkon Shield*, (New York: Macmillan Publishing, 1985).
†Brodeur, *Outrageous Misconduct*, (New York: Pantheon, 1986), p. 3.

Introduction

privity
A mutuality of relationship between persons or between persons and a particular transaction

Liability for defective products in the mid-to-late 1800s was almost unknown. There are two reasons for this. The first is that such liability was conceived of as a "commercial circumstance"; thus the principles creating liability should arise from contract law, not from other areas of civil liability such as negligence. Many of the appellate cases from this period held that an injured person could not even bring an action against a producer or seller unless it was in **privity** with that producer or seller. Thus an injured consumer could not sue a manufacturer unless he or she was the one who had contracted to buy the defective good. Family members, friends, and bystanders were all unable to sue for a consumer-product related injury. The notion that privity was needed to maintain an action served the industrial interests of the period and most probably eliminated numerous suits. However, under an exception to the general rule requiring privity, one could recover (if there were no privity) if the goods causing the injury were "inherently dangerous." The goods that were "inherently dangerous" in the mid-to-late 1800s and early 1900s included mislabeled poison, a defective scaffold ninety feet high, and a defective bottle of aerated water.

The severe result of invoking the requirement of privity was lessened shortly after the turn of the century when an appellate court[1] held that a Buick automobile was negligently manufactured and, therefore, allowed an injured plaintiff consumer to maintain an action for personal injury against a defendant corporate manufacturer with whom the plaintiff had *not* contracted. We learn in this chapter how the classification of "inherently dangerous" goods grew into a significant element of one of the major theories of products liability today: strict liability in tort.

caveat emptor
A Latin phrase meaning "let the buyer beware"

A second reason for the relatively slow development of products liability law in the late 1800s and early 1900s was the doctrine in our law of **caveat emptor.** This phrase expresses a general policy recognized by courts that the one who buys a defective product should, as against the producer or seller, suffer the loss. This is a less precise

[1]*MacPherson v. Buick Motor Co.*, 111 N.E. 1050 (N.Y. 1916).

notion than privity and arose from the social and economic climate of the times. Caveat emptor denotes a general behavior of courts rather than a precise legal principle.

At a time when manufactured goods were relatively simple, it was judged best to let the consumer choose the appropriate product—even try it out—and if a purchase of a product were made, then the consumer should be stuck with it even if it were defective. This was good policy because, in an economic system that encouraged the presence of numerous sellers in the market for goods, over time the producer of faulty products would go out of business as word spread about the quality of its product. However, with the increasing complexity of goods and with the trend toward concentration (fewer producers) in almost all major industrial markets, the doctrines of privity and caveat emptor were perceived as increasingly unjust.

The response of the law has been literally explosive. Today, in most jurisdictions, privity is no longer referred to, and many legal scholars would characterize products liability law as based on the premise of "*seller* beware." The predominance of these doctrines for decades, though, shaped the legal environment of today's products liability law.

The remedies available to an injured consumer today may come from one of three general areas: from the *warranties* provided for in Article 2 of the UCC previously discussed in Chapter 27; from the *common law of torts* (here there are two chief theories of remedies based upon "negligence theory" and "strict liability theory"); and, from miscellaneous *federal and state statutory provisions* creating liability for sellers who sell defective products or deceive consumers. The last two areas are discussed in this chapter.

Tort Theories of Products Liability

Our American "civil" law may be divided into the two broad categories of contract law and tort law. **Tort** law may be further divided into three categories: intentional torts, negligence, and strict liability. Establishing liability based upon an intentional tort theory requires proof of the defendant's *intent* to commit a wrongful act. This theory is almost never used in products liability cases because manufacturers and sellers *intend* no harm by the sale of their product. Negligence and strict liability are today, however, widely accepted theories of products liability.

tort
A civil (private) noncontractual wrong for which a court will give a remedy

This has not always been true. As we pointed out above, until the second or third decade of this century, most courts would bar a plaintiff from asserting a claim against the manufacturer or seller unless the plaintiff could prove privity with the defendant. An exception to this general rule allowed an injured plaintiff to recover on a negligence theory if the defective goods were "inherently or unreasonably dangerous." During the 1960s, courts so expanded the classification of goods that were "inherently or unreasonably dangerous" that today these words do not mean exceptionally or especially dangerous but mean "capable of causing harm" if the good is defective. However, some courts may not have freed themselves entirely from this requirement and thus demand that the plaintiff at least allege that the defective goods were "unreasonably dangerous."

Today *negligence* and *strict liability* are two independent legal theories upon which an injured plaintiff may base its product liability claim. They may be alleged and proved in the same case in which a breach of warranty theory is argued or they may serve as the sole basis for liability. Obviously these theories cannot be defeated by an assertion that there was no privity. Nor are any arguments based upon a waiver or modification of a warranty relevant.

A chief reason for using tort theories of liability is that although the statute of limitations for personal injury is usually shorter—most jurisdictions have a three-year statute of limitations on personal *injury* claims—the time period begins to run from the date of injury, not the date of delivery of the good. A disadvantage of using these theories is that most courts will not permit recovery for economic loss alone, such as lost profits or damage to the goods. To recover for economic loss, the plaintiff must also show personal injury.[2] Providing a remedy in the form of money damages to one who has suffered personal injury is the real purpose of our tort law.

Negligence

negligence
In conduct, failure to use the degree of care demanded by the circumstances; in tort, negligent conduct proximately causing injury to another person's interest

To establish **negligence** in a products liability case, the plaintiff must prove that the defendant's conduct in either manufacturing or designing goods produced a risk of harm greater than society is willing to accept in light of the benefits to be derived from that activity. Simply put, the risk of harm must be unreasonable in the circumstances.[3] In almost all negligence cases the issue of the "reasonableness" of the defendant's conduct is an issue for the jury to decide. That is, most of these cases present problems of proof rather than issues of substantive law.

res ipsa loquitur
The thing speaks for itself

Proving that goods were negligently manufactured or designed is no easy task. Without the help of an additional legal device, it would be impossible to prove if the goods were destroyed as a result of a defect. This legal device is designated by the Latin phrase **res ipsa loquitur,** which, literally translated, means "the thing speaks for itself." This device is properly used where there is a gap in the plaintiff's proof of negligence caused simply by the circumstances of the case. If the plaintiff can show that (1) the injury complained of does not normally happen in the absence of negligence, and (2) at the time of the alleged negligent act—the time of the manufacture of the goods, not the time of injury—the defendant had exclusive control of the thing that later caused the injury, than an application of res ipsa loquitur will cause the judge to state that the plaintiff has filled the gap in its evidence, and an inference of negligence will be created. It is then up to the defendant to rebut that inference. The following classic case illustrates the use of res ipsa loquitur.

FACTS

The plaintiff, a waitress in a restaurant, was severely injured when a bottle of Coca Cola exploded in her hand. She sued the bottler and alleged that it either negligently bottled the Coke (put it under too much pressure) or negligently manufactured the bottle. She was unable to show any specific acts of negligence. The bottler defended by introducing evidence that it bottled Coke in a manner all bottlers used and was therefore not acting unreasonably—that is, was not negligent. The defendant also argued that it was the plaintiff who must have mishandled the bottle. The jury returned a verdict for the plaintiff. On appeal, the defendant argued there was not sufficient evidence of negligence to submit the issue to the jury. Should the plaintiff's verdict be reversed?

DECISION

No. The appellate court found in favor of the plaintiff. The appellate court held that the doctrine of res ipsa loquitur applies in a negligence case when the alleged defective good has been destroyed and the plaintiff alleges, and the evidence could reasonably show, that (1) the defendant had exclusive control of the thing causing the injury and (2) the injury is of such a nature that it ordinarily would not occur in the absence of negligence by the defendant. The plaintiff also alleged that the bottle had not changed since it left the defen-

---

[2]See D. Noel and J. Phillips, *Products Liability in a Nutshell* (St. Paul: West Publishing, 1974), 10.

[3]J. Henderson and R. Pearson, *The Tort Process* (Boston: Little, Brown, 1975), 268.

dant's possession and that she was using due care at the time the bottle exploded. The court concluded that the evidence was sufficient to support a reasonable inference that the bottle was in some manner defective at the time it left the defendant's possession. The jury could properly rely on this inference in finding for the plaintiff.

Escola v. Coca Cola Bottling Co., 150 P.2d 436 (Cal. 1944).

The above case represents one of the early approaches by courts to search for and apply legal principles that could be used to provide remedies for injured consumers. Today, many of the products liability cases rely on a negligence theory to provide a remedy when the design of a product may have caused injury. In many of these cases there is no defect in the goods in that they operate as they are intended to operate. The conduct that is "unreasonable" is the failure to design a safe product when injury of the type complained of occurs and is foreseeable by the manufacturer. Below is an early case that is typical of the law's approach in this area.

FACTS

The plaintiff was driving a 1963 Chevrolet Corvair when the car was struck head-on by another car. The plaintiff was severely injured when the steering column was thrust into his head. The car was so designed that the steering column was one piece of steel all the way from a position directly in front of the driver to a point 2.7 inches in front of the leading surface of the front tire. The plaintiff did not contend that the design caused the accident but that, because of the design, he received injuries he would not otherwise have received. The defendant, General Motors Corporation, the designer and manufacturer of the car, argued that it has no legal duty to produce a vehicle in which it is safe to collide or which is accident-proof. The trial court dismissed the plaintiff's claim, and the plaintiff appealed. Did the plaintiff state a proper case based upon negligent design?

DECISION

Yes. The appellate court reversed the trial court and held that the plaintiff did state a good cause of action based upon negligent design. The court reasoned that an automobile manufacturer is under no duty to design an accident-proof vehicle, but such manufacturer is under a duty to use reasonable care in the design of its vehicle to avoid subjecting the user to an unreasonable risk of injury in the event of collision. Collisions with or without fault of the user are clearly foreseeable by the manufacturer and are statistically inevitable. The injury of the type complained of in this case was foreseeable as an incident to the normal and expected use of an automobile, given the fact that the steering column was designed as it was. The normal risk of driving must be accepted by the user, but there is no need to further penalize the user by subjecting him to an unreasonable risk of injury.

Larsen v. General Motors Corp., 391 F.2d 495 (1968).

The defendant may meet the plaintiff's case with proof that its conduct is not unreasonable because it conforms to the generally accepted standards of performance in the particular area of conduct. For example, Coca Cola attempted to counter the plaintiff's case in Escola by introducing evidence that the industry standard of taking a sample bottle every three hours from the manufacturing mold (this is approximately one out of every 600 bottles) and subjecting it to an internal pressure of 450 pounds per square inch, sustained for one minute, is "pretty near" infallible in guarding against defectively manufactured bottles. The Escola case presented some difficult factual issues for the jury. It was a very close case. The original fact finder in that case simply believed the plaintiff's evidence, but many negligence cases on similar evidence result in verdicts for the defendant.

► Strict Liability

strict liability
Absolute liability irrespective of the absence of negligence or fault

Strict liability as a tort theory used in products liability cases is of recent and increasing significance. It is probably the dominant theory in products liability cases. A manufacturer may be strictly liable when it:[4]

> ... sells any product in a defective condition unreasonably dangerous to the user or consumer or to his property and is subject to liability for physical harm thereby caused to the ultimate user or consumer, or to his property, if
> **a)** the seller is engaged in the business of selling such a product and
> **b)** it is expected to and does reach the user or consumer without substantial change in the condition in which it is sold.

The basic reason for the increasing use of this theory is that there are fewer well-established legal defenses to such claims. For the reasons already stated, warranty theory and negligence theory still permit the successful assertion of defenses when a plaintiff may be injured by a product through no fault of the plaintiff. Strict liability is based on the notion that, as between an innocent injured plaintiff and a merchant, the latter should pay for an injury caused by a defect.

The Escola case discussed above was so close on the negligence issue that Judge Traynor, a famous California jurist, could have applied the theory of strict liability in that case. In a concurring opinion, he clearly stated the policy reasons for strict liability as follows:

> Even if there is no negligence, ... public policy demands that responsibility be fixed wherever it will most effectively reduce the hazards to life and health inherent in defective products that reach the market. It is evident that the manufacturer can anticipate some hazards and guard against the recurrence of others as the public cannot. Those who suffer injury from defective products are unprepared to meet its consequences. The cost of an injury and the loss of time or health may be an overwhelming misfortune to the person injured, and a needless one, for the risk of injury can be insured by the manufacturer and distributed among the public as a cost of doing business. It is to the public interest to discourage the marketing of products having defects that are a menace to the public. If such products nevertheless find their way into the market it is to the public interest to place the responsibility for whatever injury they may cause upon the manufacturer, who, even if he is not negligent in the manufacture of the product, is responsible for its reaching the market. However intermittently such injuries may occur and however haphazardly they may strike, the risk of their occurrence is a constant risk and a general one. Against such a risk there should be general and constant protection and the manufacturer is best situated to afford such protection.[5]

There are two key concepts in the application of strict liability. The first is the definition and application of the term "defect" and the second is the term "unreasonably dangerous." We will first explain the current thinking of courts about the term defect.

---

[4]RESTATEMENT (SECOND) OF TORTS sec. 402A (1965).

[5]*Escola v. Coca Cola Bottling Co.,* 150 P.2d 436, 440–41 (Cal. 1944).

Defect The term defect is also used in both negligent manufacture and negligent design cases in that if a product is negligently manufactured it has a defect in it; and if a good is negligently designed it may also be said to be "defective." But, the term defect when used in a strict liability case has a slightly different meaning.

In a strict liability case there are two fairly well-established definitions of the term defect. That is, state supreme courts that have defined the word defect for use in a strict liability case have adopted, generally speaking, one of the following two definitions:

1. A product may be found defective if it fails to perform as safely as an ordinary consumer would expect.
2. A product may be defective if the risk of danger inherent in the challenged design outweighs the benefits of the design.[6]

As you can see, the first definition of defect takes a rather individualistic point of view. That is, it focuses on the individual and then asks, "what would an ordinary consumer expect?" The second or alternative definition of the term focuses more on the value of the product to society. This second definition appears to represent an emerging consensus.[7] In very general terms, the second definition requires a judge or jury to engage in a form of cost-benefit analysis. If the dangerousness of the product outweighs its benefit to society, then the decision-maker may conclude it was defectively designed. For example, is an ordinary butcher's knife defectively designed? Most people would say "no" even though they are inherently very dangerous. The reason is that the benefit to our society of having them outweighs the costs associated with the inherent design. The following case is an application of the above first definition of defect.

FACTS

Benjamin E. Dunham, the plaintiff, was using a hammer manufactured by Vaughan & Bushnell Manufacturing Co., defendant, to drive a pin into the connector between his tractor and a manure spreader. A chip from the beveled edge of the hammer broke off and struck him in the right eye, resulting in the permanent loss of sight in that eye. The hammer was about eleven months old and had been used for ordinary tasks around the plaintiff's farm. The defendant argued that the plaintiff's reliance on strict liability was not appropriate because the evidence did not show that there was a defect in the hammer when it left the manufacturer's control. The defendant also argued that everyone knows metal "tires" with age and use and is subject to failure. No manufacturer should be expected to produce a hammer which would last forever. The trial court found in favor of the plaintiff, and the defendant argued, on appeal, that strict liability was not proved in the trial court.

DECISION

The appellate court affirmed a verdict for the plaintiff. The court acknowledged that there must have been a defect in the goods and it must have existed when the goods left the custody of the manufacturer; this does not mean, however, that the defect must manifest itself at once. On this issue the court relied on another case in which a defective brake linkage bracket on a tractor broke over three years after it was installed in the tractor. The court also concluded that the jury could find that a defect existed because the definition of a defect rests on the premise that those products

[6]Note, "Strict Products Liability: Giving Content to the Term 'Defect' in Design Cases," 40 *Ohio St. L. J.* 209 (1979).

[7]Henderson, "Reviewed Judicial Controversy over Defective Product Design: Toward the Preservation of an Emerging Consensus," 63 *Minn. L. Rev.* 773, 775 (1979).

are defective which are dangerous because they fail to perform in the manner reasonably to be expected in light of their nature and intended function. A defect may be a "condition" not contemplated by the ultimate consumer, which would be unreasonably dangerous to him.

Dunham v. Vaughan & Bushnell Mfg. Co., 247 N.E.2d 401 (Ill. 1969).

Unreasonably Dangerous A second circumstance that must be alleged and proved in a products liability case based on strict liability is that the product was "unreasonably dangerous." Like the term, "defect," the definition of the term "unreasonably dangerous" may differ from state to state and some courts confuse the requirements of a defect with those requiring unreasonably dangerous products and state only one need be proved. The supreme courts of some states define an unreasonably dangerous product as one that is dangerous to an extent beyond that contemplated by the ordinary consumer who purchases it.[8] Since this definition of unreasonably dangerous would defeat a plaintiff's claim if the product were not dangerous beyond that contemplated by the ordinary consumer, some courts have taken a different approach. A second definition of unreasonably dangerous is found in the following case.

FACTS

A four-year-old boy, plaintiff, was badly burned while playing with matches when his T-shirt caught fire. He brought suit, through his father acting as his representative, against the manufacturer and seller of the T-shirt, defendant. The basis of the suit was strict liability, and the central arguments were that the T-shirt was designed defectively and that it was unreasonably dangerous. The T-shirt was later found to have been manufactured in conformity with applicable federal standards for flammability. The jury returned a verdict for the defendant, Union Underwear Co., and this verdict was affirmed on appeal. The plaintiff now appealed to the state Supreme Court. The issues on appeal centered on the appropriate definition of "unreasonably dangerous." The plaintiff had argued that the flammability of the fabric made it unreasonably dangerous, and objected to that portion of the trial court's instruction to the jury defining "unreasonably dangerous."

DECISION

The Supreme Court of Kentucky reversed the decision for the manufacturer, and held that it was an error for the trial court to define an unreasonably dangerous product as one that is dangerous to an extent beyond that contemplated by the ordinary consumer who purchases it. The court said that a careful reading of section 402A reveals that, as a condition precedent to strict liability becoming operative in a particular case, the product sold must be "unreasonably dangerous" to the user or consumer or to his property. The court held that, defining this important term by finding that a product is unreasonably dangerous if, and only if, it is more dangerous than an ordinary adult would expect it to be, is too restrictive. The effect of this test is to insulate a manufacturer from liability unless a product is patently or obviously dangerous. The court stated that the form of an instruction to the jury on the definition of "unreasonably dangerous" in the state of Kentucky was to be applied in this manner:

> You will find for the plaintiff only if you are satisfied from the evidence that the material of which the T-shirt was made created such a risk of its being accidentally set on fire by a child wearing it that an ordinary prudent company engaged in the manufacture of clothing, being fully aware of the risk, would not have put it on the market; otherwise, you will find for the defendant.

Nichols v. Union Underwear Co., Inc. 602 S.W.2d 429 (Ky. 1980).

[8] RESTATEMENT (SECOND) OF TORTS sec. 402A comment i (1958).

The definition of "unreasonably dangerous" adopted by the court in the above case differs substantially from the definition discussed before the case. The difference is that the definition in this case focuses on the expectations and observations of the *manufacturer* and not those of the consumer.

Defenses to Products Liability Cases

It is beyond the scope of this material to explain in detail all of the possible legal defenses of a merchant to a claim for damage caused by a defective product. We will just briefly and generally define each.

A significant category of defenses is directed at what may be called the plaintiff's misbehavior in using the product. These defenses are **contributory negligence** of the plaintiff, **assumption of a known risk,** misuse, hypersensitivity, and lack of **proximate causation.** These defenses may be used by a manufacturer or seller in either a breach of warranty case, or negligence or strict liability cases. Moreover, the use and application of these defenses varies so widely from state to state that generalization about them is almost impossible. Some states, for example, have adopted the position that contributory negligence is *not* a defense to a claim for damage based upon a breach of warranty theory, while some other state supreme courts have held that it is an absolute defense.[9] Moreover, courts in some states could hold that, where a woman uses a hair dye when she knows she experiences severe skin reactions to hair dyes, a doctrine of "hypersensitivity" would preclude her recovery for damage. Some courts could hold that similar "misconduct" tended to prove a lack of proximate causation in that it was the plaintiff's own acts which were the primary cause, not the product. Whatever the label used, where an injured plaintiff voluntarily and unreasonably proceeds to encounter a known danger or a danger that would be known to a reasonable person, or where the plaintiff uses a product in a manner for which it was not intended, the plaintiff will most probably encounter some form of defense. The "reasonableness" of the plaintiff's conduct ultimately will be decided by the jury.

contributory negligence
Plaintiff's conduct that falls below the standard to which he or she should conform for his or her own protection and that is a legally contributing cause with the defendant's negligence causing the plaintiff's harm

assumption of risk
Voluntarily assuming a known risk of harm

proximate cause
The cause of an injury without which the injury would not have occurred

Recently, we have learned that some products we once believed were safe were really very dangerous. Asbestos, a substance made of tiny fibers used widely as insulation and fire retardant material, was found to be carcinogenic to some people exposed to it. When the manufacturers were sued by plaintiffs damaged by this substance, they pleaded that they used the most advanced technology of the time to discover the product's dangerous qualities and thus did all that could be required of them. This is called the "state of the art defense."

A majority of jurisdictions do allow a state of the art defense. This means that in a strict liability case, the courts will allow the jury to consider evidence on whether a defendant used technology that was available at the time a "defective" product was manufactured. However, in one recent development, the New Jersey Supreme Court held that state of the art evidence was not admissible in a strict liability suit.[10] This case, like the one discussed below involving DES, may point to areas that will represent the law of a majority of jurisdictions in the near future.

---

[9] White and Summers, *Uniform Commercial Code* (St. Paul: West Publishing, 1972), p. 336.

[10] *Beshada et al. v. Johns-Manville Products Corp.*, 447 A.2d 539 (N.J. 1982).

Developments in Products Liability Law

► Liability without Causation

An essential element of any plaintiff's cause of action in tort law is that there be some reasonable connection between the alleged negligence or defect, and the damage that the plaintiff suffered. In short, the defendant must have caused the damage.

The DES Cases Several cases, however, have indicated the establishment of a significant trend away from a strict application of the causation requirement. These cases involved the chemical diethylstilbestrol (DES).

DES was first introduced to the drug market in the late 1940s to prevent miscarriages in pregnant women. It was banned by the Food and Drug Administration in 1971, but as of that date about 200 companies had manufactured it. The drug was banned because of a high incidence of cancer contracted by the daughters of DES users. These daughters were plaintiffs in about one thousand products liability cases against the former DES manufacturers.

Let us consider a typical case in order to understand this trend of liability without causation. Assume that a daughter of a DES user is informed that she has cancer. She is obviously severely damaged and she elects to sue a manufacturer. But, which one? Because of the passage of time it is impossible to identify which manufacturer made the DES consumed by her mother. Prescriptions and the bottles they came in were discarded long ago. So, under conventional tort theories the plaintiff could not state a good case because she could not identify with reasonable certainty, the defendant that caused the injury. In the leading case, *Sindell v. Abbott Laboratories,*[11] the California Supreme Court held that an injured plaintiff is relieved of the burden of proving causation of a specific defendant so long as: (1) identification of the manufacturer is impossible through no fault of the plaintiff; and (2) the product is **fungible;** and (3) a plaintiff joined enough defendants so that a "substantial percentage" of the market for the product is represented. In addition the court held that, once the elements of the case are established, a defendant could be held liable for the proportion of the judgment represented by its share of sales in that market, unless it demonstrates that it could not have made the product that caused the plaintiff's injury. So, if a particular defendant had 10 percent of the sales in the market for DES, it would pay 10 percent of the judgment. This theory does give the plaintiff a chance to state a good case, and it supposedly prevents unfairness to defendants by directly tying likelihood of causation with the percentage of sales in the market.[12]

fungible goods
Every unit of goods is the equivalent of any other like unit, either actually or contract

This fairly new theory of "market share" liability has not yet gained wide use for other products. Some writers have suggested that some of the cigarette companies will be joined by plaintiffs in asbestos and other industrial pollutants cases because smoking cigarettes greatly enhances the lung damage resulting from the inhalation of asbestos, and many of these plaintiffs cannot remember which brand of cigarettes they were smoking twenty years ago or so.[13]

Other Legal Theories There are three other legal theories that have been proposed by scholars for use when plaintiffs cannot establish causation. In our commercial society

---

[11] 607 P.2d 924 (Cal. 1980).

[12] "The DES Cases and Liability Without Causation," 19 *Am. Bus. L. J.* 511 (1982).

[13] Ibid., 519.

dominated by three or more sellers or manufacturers in a market, these theories will become more prominent in years to come. Briefly stated, these theories all result in lessening the burden of proving causation when it would be impossible or unfair to the plaintiff to have this burden.

1. *Alternative liability*. This theory was first used when a plaintiff was shot by one of two other hunters and he could not prove which one. The court reasoned that it would be fair to shift the burden of causation to the defendants because they were in a far better position to identify the real wrongdoer than was the injured plaintiff.[14] For example, if a machine part fails due to a defect and causes injury, and two suppliers may have made the part and it is not possible to tell which may have made the specific part, then this theory may be used.
2. *Concert of action*. Under this theory, multiple defendants may be held liable for the acts or omissions of one of the defendants if there is a common design among the defendants creating an unreasonable risk. The usual example given is that of an illegal drag race between two cars and one of the cars causes injury to a third party. All of the racers may be held liable.[15] For example, applying this theory to a business context, you would first have to find a violation of a standard, such as the production of a drug that was not approved for sale by the proper authorities, then there must be the sale of the drug by several drug companies, and then there must be damage caused by the drug and an inability to find which drug company caused which injury.
3. *Enterprise liability*. This theory is very similar to the concert of action theory but lessens the burden of the plaintiffs in proving a common design. The common design of the defendant is inferred because of the defendants' mutual adherence to an industry-wide standard relating to the production of the injury-producing product.

We conclude here the material on the law applicable to defective goods that enables an injured consumer (or merchant) to sue the manufacturer for injury. Recall that the costs of litigation for attorneys and witnesses, and the costs of the court system may take as much as 40 percent of the amount recovered. So, being able to sue for injury caused by a defective product is a very imperfect remedy. Many lawyers will not even take such a case unless the award could exceed $10,000 to $15,000. It is just not worth their time to take a case in which a toe may have been severed or a finger severely mangled or broken. So, the legal system has responded with an array of approaches that involve the legislative and executive functions of government. The remainder of the chapter is devoted to an explanation of the "government regulation" applicable to consumer law and the problem of defective goods and services.

Federal And State Consumer Product Safety Legislation—Products

▶ Proposed Legislation

In this section we first discuss legislation that has been proposed, not passed, to help deal more efficiently with what some people have described as a products-liability crisis. Following this discussion we provide an explanation of legislation that has been passed.

---

[14]See *Summers v. Tice,* 199 P.2d 1 (Cal. 1948) and RESTATEMENT (SECOND) OF TORTS, sec. 433B(3) (1965).

[15]RESTATEMENT (SECOND) OF TORTS, sec. 876 comment on clause (a), illustration 2 (1965).

The proposed legislation that is of the most significance exists in two areas. The first is the attempt by the federal government to bring about a measure of uniformity and consistent treatment to products liability claims by promoting a Model Uniform Product Liability Act (MUPLA). The second is the adoption in about seventeen states of "statutes of repose."

Model Uniform Product Liability Act The MUPLA was published by the Department of Commerce on October 31, 1979.[16] It was the result of a process begun by President Ford in 1976 to clarify and stabilize the proliferation of the law applicable to products liability. The Commerce Department provides the Act so that state legislatures may use it as a model for refining their own approach to products liability law.

The MUPLA preempts the UCC and common law theories discussed above for products liability: breach of warranty, negligence, and strict liability. It replaces these principles with a single "product liability claim." This claim may be asserted by injured consumers, bystanders, or their estates and does not depend on a contractual relationship with a seller. So, the Act opts for more of a negligence approach than one based on contract. The essence of the cause of action is liability created because of *defective construction, defective design, or inadequate warnings or instructions.* The term "defect" is the heart of this cause of action and it is not defined. Rather, factors are listed that the jury or judge as a fact finder will consider.

The defenses available to a defendant center on comparative responsibility of the plaintiff. The fact finder may determine the total amount of damages and then deduct from this an amount equal to what the plaintiff contributed to his or her own injury because of conduct that was not similar to that which would have been used by a prudent person. That is, the Act allows recovery for injury from a defective product reduced by the amount of money that approximates the percentage of injury caused by the plaintiff by not using the product as a prudent person would.

This Act has caused much discussion and debate. The concepts of a type of unified products liability claim and the use of comparative fault are new to this area of the law, and it is too early to judge whether the MUPLA will be of lasting value.

Statutes of Repose Another legislative solution that is at the proposal stage in many state legislatures is the passage of "statutes of repose." Statutes of repose are urged by insurance companies and manufacturers to help them assess the possible losses due to defective products. These statutes create a time period after which a product goes into repose (a period of permanent rest). Any injury caused by that product after the period has ended is not actionable. The time period would be measured from either the date of manufacture or the date of sale for use, and not from the time of infliction of the actual harm. The statutes actually favor merchants and the insurance industry and do not favor injured plaintiffs whose injury falls outside the period. Nevertheless, some have argued that such acts favor all consumers since it is guessed that products liability insurance premiums will fall if these acts are passed, thus resulting in lower consumer prices.

The major item of debate is the length of the time period. It must be sufficiently long to allow a reasonable time for aggrieved parties to discover a product's defects, and sufficiently short to eliminate uncertainty concerning exposure to liability. Proposed time

---

[16]Model Uniform Product Liability Act, reprinted in 44 Fed. Reg. 62,714 (1979); and see Dworkin, "Product Liability Reform and the Model Uniform Product Liability Act," 60 *Neb. L. Rev.* 50 (1981).

periods range from five to twelve years, with most proposals in the range from eight to ten years.[17]

► Existing Consumer Product Safety Legislation

Since 1966 Congress has passed six acts that govern some aspect of product safety or product design.

Consumer Product Safety Act of 1972 The Consumer Product Safety Act of 1972[18] created the Consumer Product Safety Commission (CPSC). This commission has jurisdiction over every consumer product *except* automobiles, food, and a few other items regulated by older agencies of government. The basic idea behind the creation of the CPSC was to bring order to an increasingly confusing mishmash of federal and state consumer regulatory bodies. The commission is to collect and disseminate information relating to injuries and to conduct investigations and tests on consumer products and their use. When a consumer product creates a hazard of injury or illness, the CPSC may develop consumer product safety standards. These standards must be set forth in performance requirements. If the CPSC finds that an unreasonable risk exists and that no standard will provide protection, it may ban a product. It has banned such products as garments containing asbestos, some baby cribs, some drain cleaners, assorted types of fireworks, furniture painted with lead paint, some kinds of lawn darts, and self-pressurized products containing vinyl chloride.[19] The basic idea of the CPSC was to disseminate information about product safety and attempt to get products redesigned in light of the consumer's foreseeable ignorance and consumer misbehavior or misuse. While these objectives are commendable, the performance of the CPSC unfortunately has been less than spectacular. After a few years of operation, one source reported that there has been no notable reduction in consumer-product related injuries.[20] This judgment may be offered too soon. The long case at the end of this chapter should give you some idea of how the CPSC operates. From a reading of this case, judge for yourself the value of the CPSC.

Motor Vehicle Safety Legislation Motor vehicle safety legislation has been on the books since 1966, but only recently have the various enforcement activities established the legislation as noteworthy. Although the National Traffic and Motor Vehicle Safety Act of 1966[21] and the Highway Safety Act[22] have been amended or altered by legislation or executive order almost every year since their adoption, they are some of the more successful attempts to regulate product safety. It has been estimated that 150,000 lives

---

[17]"Limiting Liability: Products Liability and a Statute of Repose," 32 *Baylor L. Rev.* 137, 145 (1980).

[18]15 U.S.C.A. sec. 2051.

[19]U.S. Consumer Product Safety Commission, *1979 Annual Report,* Appendix L.

[20]"The Hazards of Trying to Make Consumer Products Safer," *Fortune,* July 1975, pp. 103–4.

[21]15 U.S.C.A. sec. 1381.

[22]23 U.S.C.A. sec. 401.

have been saved between 1967 and 1977 due to automobile safety legislation and the reduced speed limit necessitated by the oil shortage of 1973.[23]

The National Traffic and Motor Vehicle Safety Act of 1966 created the National Highway Traffic Safety Administration. It has the authority to promulgate rules for traffic safety, conduct research, disseminate information about vehicle safety, and, if a manufacturer will not voluntarily comply, initiate procedures resulting in the recall of automobiles that pose a threat to the public.

Federal Trade Commission Act and Related Legislation The Federal Trade Commission (FTC) was created in 1914 to deal with anticompetitive practices in business. Gradually its powers have expanded and today one of its major functions is to regulate in the area of deceptive trade practices. This regulation primarily focuses on advertising methods and claims of businesses where the common law remedies of misrepresentation and deceit are not thought to be effective. This regulation is made possible not only by the Federal Trade Commission Act itself and its various amendments, but also by a succession of other acts that add to the powers of the commission. A list of just some of these acts includes the Export Trade Act, the Fair Packaging and Labeling Act, the Lanham Trademark Act, the Trans-Alaska Pipeline Authorization Act, the Truth-in-Lending Act, the Fair Credit Reporting Act and the Magnuson-Moss Warranty Act.

Generally, the FTC gathers information concerning the "competitiveness" and "fairness" of the businesses in our economy. These reports provide the basis for major legislation by highlighting uneconomic or objectionable trade practices. The FTC can act to create its own rules and regulations, and it can investigate and then judge a competitor in violation of one of these rules and regulations.[24] It can also enforce these rules and regulations by one of two primary means. The first is that it can issue "trade regulation rules" and then enforce these rules by demanding that an alleged offender appear before the commission for a hearing. The result of this hearing is usually the issuance of a cease and desist order that can be enforced by a court or a federal marshall. The following is an example of a trade regulation rule.

> Trade Regulation Rule Concerning Retail Food Store Advertising and Marketing Practices
>
> 16 C.F.R. Part 424 (1972)
>
> § 424.1 The Rule
>
> **(a)** The Commission, . . . hereby promulgates as a trade regulation rule its determination that:
>
> **(b)** In connection with sale or offering for sale by retail food stores of food and grocery products or other merchandise, . . . it is an unfair method of competition and an unfair or deceptive act or practice to:
>
> **(1)(i)** Offer any such products for sale at a stated price, by means of any advertisement disseminated in an area served by any of its stores which are covered by the advertisement which do not have such products in stock, and readily available to customers during the effective period of the advertisement. (If not readily available, clear and adequate notice shall be provided that the items are in stock and may be obtained upon request.)
>
> **(ii)** *Provided, however,* That it shall constitute a defense to a charge under subdivision i. of this subparagraph if the retailer maintains records sufficient to

---

[23]U.S. Department of Transportation, "Motor Vehicle Safety," *1977 Annual Report.*

[24]For administrative procedures of the FTC, see 742–745.

show that the advertised products were ordered in adequate time for delivery and delivered to the stores in quantities sufficient to meet reasonably anticipated demands.

(2) Fail to make the advertised items conspicuously and readily available for sale at or below the advertised prices.

Unless, in each of the above cases, there is clear and conspicuous disclosure in all such advertisements as to all exceptions and/or limitations or restrictions with respect to stores, products or prices otherwise included within the advertisements.

A second method the FTC has of enforcing the powers given to it is to give a firm notice that they are engaged in a deceptive trade practice and then ask them to stop. Many times the firms dispute these assertions and the issue is taken before a court.[25] Although the category of deceptive trade practices is very broad, the case below is fairly typical of the kind of cases and the kind of powers that the FTC has.

FACTS

The FTC ordered Fedders to stop advertising that its air conditioners were unique because they had "reserve cooling power," a term which was intended to imply an unusual ability to produce cold air under extreme conditions of heat and humidity. In fact, the FTC found, the Fedders conditioners had no technical advantage over the equipment of its competitors. The FTC determined that Fedders was engaged in a violation of the FTC Act because it misrepresented what its product could do. Fedders petitioned the court for a review of the FTC order. Is the cease and desist order proper?

DECISION

The court dismissed the petition of Fedders thus leaving the original cease and desist order in force. The order challenged by Fedders prohibits Fedders from making, directly or indirectly, any statement or representation in any advertisement as to the air cooling capacity or capabilities of any air conditioner, unless at the time of such representation Fedders has a reasonable basis for such statement or evidence which shall consist of competent scientific, engineering or other similar objective material or industry-wide standards based on such material. Fedders argues that the part of the order requiring a reasonable scientific or engineering basis for their advertising claim is overly broad.

The court held that there is broad language in the FTC order and that this is proper because the FTC must have wide discretion in its choice of a remedy to cope with deceptive trade practices. So long as the remedial order is reasonably related to the unlawful practices found to exist, the FTC order should be upheld.

Fedders Corp. v. Fed. Trade Comm'n, 529 F.2d 1398 (2d Cir. 1976).

Food Quality and Packaging Legislation Under the Fair Packaging and Labeling Act,[26] passed in 1966, often called the Truth-in-Packaging Act, the Federal Trade Commission and the Food and Drug Administration were to establish and regulate standards regarding contents information to be shown on packages and to encourage the voluntary development of standards for package sizes. The Wholesale Meat Act[27] passed in 1967

[25]For FTC adjudicative proceedings and judicial review, see pp. 744–746.

[26]15 U.S.C.A. sec. 1451.

[27]21 U.S.C.A. sec. 610.

strengthened and updated the federal standards of meat inspection and provided states with assistance so that local standards might be "at least equal" to federal standards.

Related Federal and State Legislation Attempts by the federal government to legislate standards for merchants and products performance have been, at best, mildly successful. It now appears that because of two related developments at the state level, a remedy of value is beginning to emerge for consumers who are damaged by merchant misconduct. Now about four-fifths of the states[28] have legislation that provides a remedy to consumers who are not dealt with in an ethical or fair way. This legislation, plus the fact that many states allow consumer-related complaints to be filed without an attorney's help in small claims courts, provide remedies within the reach of many consumers. For example, Michigan law provides that "unfair, unconscionable or deceptive methods, acts or practices in the conduct of trade or commerce are unlawful."[29] The legislation defines twenty-nine unlawful acts. A partial listing of these specific acts is as follows:

> **(i)** Making false or misleading statements of fact concerning the reasons for, existence of, or amounts of, price reductions.
>
> **(j)** Representing that a part, replacement, or repair service is needed when it is not.
>
> **(n)** Causing a probability of confusion or of misunderstanding as to the legal rights, obligations, or remedies of a party to a transaction.
>
> **(o)** Causing a probability of confusion or of misunderstanding as to the terms or conditions of credit if credit is extended in a transaction.
>
> **(r)** Representing that a consumer will receive goods or services "free," "without charge," or words of similar import without clearly and conspicuously disclosing with equal prominence in immediate conjunction with the use of those words the conditions, terms, or prerequisites to the use or retention of the goods or services advertised.
>
> **(s)** Failing to reveal a material fact, the omission of which tends to mislead or deceive the consumer, and which fact could not reasonably be known to the consumer.
>
> **(bb)** Making a representation of fact or statement of fact material to the transaction such that a person reasonably believes the represented or suggested state of affairs to be other than it actually is.
>
> **(cc)** Failing to reveal facts which are material to the transaction in light of representations of fact made in a positive manner.

This Michigan legislation also provides that a person who suffers loss as a result of a violation of one of the twenty-nine listed acts may bring an action to recover actual damages or $250, whichever is greater. The legislation does not provide a remedy for the recovery of substantial amounts for personal injury as a result of a defective product but does allow recovery for minor amounts. For example, a student at Michigan State University was awarded $250 when he showed in the local small claims court that he was told by a merchant that his defective stereo speaker was covered by warranty and would be repaired without charge. When he went to pick up the speaker from the merchant, he was told that it would cost him $60. He paid the amount under protest and then filed his claim.

About thirty states have passed legislation dealing with a very specific area of consumer complaints. This legislation applies to *new* cars that cannot be repaired properly and are thus the proverbial "lemon." These "Lemon Laws" vary from state to

---

[28] W. Haemmel, B. George, J. Bliss, *Consumer Law* (St. Paul: West Publishing, 1975), p. 36.

[29] 14 MICH. STAT. ANN. secs. 19.418(3).

state but usually provide that: (1) if a new car is under warranty and it has a defect that significantly affects its value or use, and (2) if the dealer is unable to fix the defect in a stated number of tries (usually four), the owner is entitled to a new car or the return of the purchase price. Most of these laws require that an informal jury established by Better Business Bureaus in cooperation with auto dealers find facts supporting the consumer's claim.

A few states such as New York (in 1984) passed legislation to provide consumer protection for buyers of *used* cars. The New York law requires a dealer in used cars (defined as a person who sells three or more used vehicles a year) to provide a written warranty for certain parts for a period of from thirty days or 1,000 miles if the car has over 36,000 miles, to sixty days or 3,000 miles if the car has 36,000 miles or less. Such law applies to used car sales for $1,000 or more.[30]

Product Liability Risk Retention Act Finally, we explain briefly here another approach to the products liability crisis. Many manufacturers are doubtless aware and regret that their products cause the damage that they do. Also, what they are very concerned about is the uncertainty of the amount of liability. A large recovery by just one plaintiff can jeopardize the existence of a firm. Products liability insurance has gained wide acceptance, but the premiums for this insurance also reflect both the uncertainty involved and the necessary profit of an insurance company. Since manufacturers are closer to the products liability cases than the insurers, Congress thought it prudent to let the manufacturers *jointly* form "captive" or wholly owned insurance companies to cover the risks involved. On September 25, 1981, the Product Liability Risk Retention Act was passed.[31] This Act allows manufacturers, distributors, and retailers of products to form insurance companies that they own together. The Act exempts these insurance companies from antitrust investigation (the antitrust laws prohibit activities that might look like conspiracies or combinations of competitors that might unreasonably restrain competition) so long as the insurance companies are regulated by state law. The insurance companies must be established according to state not federal law.

It is believed that this Act will result in manufacturers better evaluating their risks of liability than the underwriting staff of a distant insurer. The Act should also reduce consumer product prices because, it is assumed, the profit of a unrelated insurance company should be eliminated. Also, the owners of the insurance company can better spread the risks of the products' dangerous properties among themselves.[32]

Federal and State Consumer Protection Legislation—Credit

A substantial amount of consumer protection legislation involves the regulation of credit transactions. Closely related to the actual sale of goods (or real property) is the manner in which the buyer pays. Quite often the buyer pays a small portion of the purchase price in cash and then promises to pay the balance plus interest on this outstanding balance until the full amount is paid. When a seller relies on a buyer's promise to pay in the future, it is extending credit to the buyer.

---

[30]N.Y. General Business Law, Sec. 198-b, 1984.

[31]15 U.S.C. sec. 3901.

[32]Shea, "The Product Liability Risk Retention Act of 1981," 28 *Prac. Law.* (March 3, 1982): 9.

Often it is difficult for a consumer to assess the exact amount that will be paid for goods when credit is involved, and just as difficult is the computation of the cost of credit itself. Recently both Congress and state legislatures passed statutes to provide the consumer with knowledge about his or her credit transactions.

The Consumer Credit Protection Act

The Consumer Credit Protection Act (CCPA),[33] also called the Truth-in-Lending Act, is administered by the Federal Reserve System and has been in force since 1969, when the Federal Reserve Board adopted regulations for conduct. These regulations reach all extensions of credit for personal, family, household, or agricultural purposes. The applicability of the Act is suspended if there is state legislation covering similar transactions and the requirements for disclosure are substantially similar to those imposed by the Act.

Under the 1969 regulations, the lender must furnish to the borrower, before the credit is extended, a written disclosure statement that sets forth (1) the cash price, (2) the down payment, (3) the total amount financed, (4) the dollar amount the loan will cost, (5) the approximate amount of the true annual interest rate, and (6) an explanation of the delinquency and default charges. The Act does not set any ceiling on finance charges or interest rates, nor does it affect state **usury** laws. A violator of the Act may incur both civil and criminal liability.

usury
Charging a rate of interest on a loan higher than that permitted by statute

Today the Act is enforced by a number of federal agencies, such as the Director of the Bureau of Federal Credit Unions and the Federal Home Loan Bank Board. Also, the coverage of the Act has been extended by enactment of the Fair Credit Reporting Act of 1970,[34] which covers credit-card transactions. This amendment limits the liability of new credit-card holders to $50 if this liability is incurred by someone using the owner's lost or stolen credit card.

The Fair Credit Reporting Act

The Fair Credit Reporting Act became law in 1970.[35] Its purpose is to make available to consumers requesting credit the information relied upon by the merchant or the one extending the credit. This is done so that the consumer may check the accuracy of this information. The Act covers credit information supplied to potential creditors, insurers, or employers of that person. A less important goal is to help protect consumers against the discharge of such confidential information to persons who may have no legitimate use for it.

The Act focuses on the disclosure by the merchant to the consumer of the name and address of the credit reporting agency or credit bureau that made the report. If the consumer asks, the user of the information must disclose free of charge the information in the report. The consumer may require the credit reporting agency to delete any

[33] 15 U.S.C.A. sec. 1601.

[34] 15 U.S.C.A. sec. 1642, 1643, 1644.

[35] 15 U.S.C.A. sec. 1681.

inaccurate or obsolete information from the file. If a dispute develops, the consumer may give his or her version of the dispute to the credit agency and they must put it in the file.

The consumer can require that a credit report be withheld from anyone who under the law does not have a legitimate business need for the information. Generally, the users of this information are businesses extending credit or employing the consumer. If there is a violation of the Act, the consumer may sue for damages plus punitive damages and attorney's fees.

► The Equal Credit Opportunity Act

The Equal Credit Opportunity Act (ECOA)[36] was passed in 1977 to help prevent discrimination against any applicant for credit on the basis of race, color, religion, national origin, sex, or marital status. One of the strongest provisions of this Act requires the party extending credit to provide each applicant who is denied credit or whose account is terminated, the reasons for such action if the applicant requests. The Act applies to banks, finance companies, retail stores, credit card issuers, and other firms that usually extend credit. The Act does not guarantee credit to any applicant. The creditors may still set the standards, but the standards may not discriminate against one of the classes mentioned above. The case below involves an application of both the Fair Credit Reporting Act and the Equal Credit Opportunity Act.

FACTS

Kathleen Carroll, plaintiff, a single working woman, applied to Exxon Company, U.S.A., defendant, for a credit card in August of 1976. She was informed about one month later that her application for credit had been denied, but no specific reasons were given for this. A short time later she requested Exxon to furnish her with the specific reasons for the credit denial. Exxon apparently had written to a credit bureau, which supplied the information relied upon by Exxon, but the evidence introduced in court indicated there was insufficient information in the files of the credit bureau to establish her credit. So, Exxon apparently denied her credit because of lack of information about her. The letter from Exxon to Carroll did not contain the name of the credit bureau nor was it dated. Carroll filed a law suit on October 26, 1976, and on November 2, 1976, Exxon sent another letter to the plaintiff that also did not contain the name of the credit bureau which had been relied on by Exxon in denying the plaintiff's application. Do these facts constitute a violation of either the Fair Credit Reporting Act or the Equal Credit Opportunity Act?

DECISION

Both Acts have been violated. The Fair Credit Reporting Act (FCRA) requires that whenever credit for personal purposes is denied either wholly or partially because of information contained in a consumer report from a consumer reporting agency, the user of the consumer report shall so advise the consumer against whom such action has been taken and supply the name and address of the consumer reporting agency making the report. A mere cursory reading of Exxon's undated letter to the plaintiff reveals that the credit denial was, in fact, based on a credit report and Exxon failed to supply the name of it. The court concluded, "We find that Exxon's failure to properly identify the consumer reporting agency in its letters under the facts and circumstances of

[36]15 U.S.C.A. sec. 1691.

this case, constitutes a willful non-compliance with the requirements of the FCRA." On this issue the court referred the matter to a referee for a determination of the amount of damages, both actual and punitive, plus attorney's fees.

The court also found a violation of the ECOA Act. This Act also requires each applicant who is denied credit a statement of the reasons for such action if the applicant so requests. Exxon argued that its correspondence satisfied the requirements of the Act. The Act provides that a statement of reasons meets the requirements of the Act only if it contains the specific reasons for the adverse action. The only reason given by Exxon was that the credit bureau contacted could furnish little or no definitive information regarding plaintiff's establishment of credit. This was not specific enough. The requirement that creditors give reasons for adverse action is a strong and necessary adjunct to the anti-discrimination purpose of the legislation, for only if creditors know they must explain their decisions will they effectively be discouraged from discriminatory activities. This requirement also fulfills a broader need: rejected credit applicants will be able to learn where and how their credit status is deficient, and this information should have a pervasive and valuable educational benefit. Instead of being told only that they do not meet a particular creditor's standards, consumers particularly should benefit from knowing that it is their short residence in the area, or their recent change of employment, that are the reasons.

Carroll v. Exxon Co., U.S.A., 434 F. Supp. 557 (D.N.D. 1977).

► The Fair Debt Collection Practices Act

The Fair Debt Collection Practices Act was passed in 1977 by Congress as an amendment to the CCPA discussed above in order to provide a remedy to consumers who are harassed by debt collectors.[37] The Act can be enforced by the FTC or by damaged consumers and it applies only where there are no similar state laws applicable to the abuses of debt collectors. There are about forty states with such laws, so this federal law applies in only a minority of the states. Generally, this law and the state laws similar to it, make it illegal to contact a consumer at unusual or inconvenient times and to use misleading tactics such as posing as an attorney or police officer. A debt collector who violates this Act may be liable for actual damages caused to the plaintiff; in addition, the plaintiff may be awarded punitive damages not to exceed $1,000, courts costs and reasonable attorneys' fees.

► The Uniform Consumer Credit Code

The Uniform Consumer Credit Code (UCCC), like the Uniform Commercial Code, was drafted by the National Conference of Commissioners on Uniform State Laws and was published in 1974 for adoption by the states. This legislation has been controversial; only a handful of states have adopted it.[38]

As in the Truth-in-Lending Act, the annual percentage rate for the credit and the difference between the cash price and the credit price must be disclosed in every transaction involving retail installment sales, consumer credit, or small loans. This act was intended to thwart the practice of some unscrupulous sellers of taking the buyer's negotiable promissory note for worthless goods, negotiating the note to a good faith

---

[37] 15 U.S.C.A. sec. 1692.

[38] Uniform Consumer Credit Code, 74 U.L.A. 17 (1974).

"holder in due course," and leaving town.[39] The Act also prohibits "balloon" payment provisions that require a debtor to pay the full amount due plus a penalty if the debtor misses just one payment, and other unfair abuses of consumers.

Summary Statement

1. A consumer injured by a defective product may use the tort theories of negligence (negligent manufacture and negligent design of a product) and strict liability to state a good claim against a manufacturer.
2. The doctrine of *res ipsa loquitur* may help the plaintiff establish a prima facie case of negligence.
3. The theory of strict liability depends on a court's definition of "defect" and "unreasonably dangerous" as those terms are applied to products.
4. The defenses to a products liability claim based upon negligence, strict liability, and in some cases breach of warranty, include those related to the misuse of the product by the plaintiff. These defenses are contributory negligence of the plaintiff, assumption of a known risk, misuse, hypersensitivity, and lack of proximate causation.
5. The courts have developed the legal principles of market share liability, alternative liability, concert of action, and enterprise liability. These are used to shift the burden of causation from the plaintiff to the defendant in circumstances in which the plaintiff cannot prove with reasonable certainty which of several defendants caused the injury.
6. The Model Uniform Product Liability Act has been proposed by the Department of Commerce to simplify and make uniform the trial of cases involving products liability claims. It establishes a "product liability claim" that is based on defective construction, defective design, or inadequate warnings.
7. Statutes of repose have been adopted in some states to put a time limit on claims brought by injured consumers.
8. The Consumer Product Safety Commission was created to help collect data on defective products and related consumer injuries, and to help prevent consumer injury by the adoption of product safety standards.
9. The Federal Trade Commission can issue trade regulations and cease and desist orders to help prevent deceptive trade practices.
10. Consumer law also includes the federal and state regulation of credit. Three important federal statutes that regulate credit are the Consumer Credit Protection Act, Fair Credit Reporting Act, and Equal Credit Opportunity Act.

The following case shows how the federal government is reacting to the products liability crisis. Generally, it does this by creating product safety standards.

[39]For an explanation of the rights of a holder in due course (HIDC) against a consumer/maker of a negotiable promissory note if the UCCC had not provided protection to the consumer in a credit sale of goods, see pp. 669, 676–677.

SOUTHLAND MOWER CO. v. CONSUMER PRODUCT SAFETY COMMISSION
619 F.2d 499 (5th Cir. 1980)

Gee, Circuit J. Approximately 77,000 people are injured each year in the United States by contacting the blades of walk-behind power mowers. Of these injuries, an estimated 9,900 involve the amputation of at least one finger or toe, 11,400 involve fractures, 2,400 involve the tearing of flesh, there are 2,300 severe cuts and 51,400 other lesser cuts and lacerations requiring emergency room treatment. The annual economic cost inflicted by the 77,000 yearly blade-contact injuries has been estimated to be about $253 million and this figure does not include an amount for pain and suffering or for lost use of amputated fingers and toes.

To reduce these blade-contact injuries, the Consumer Product Safety Commission (CPSC) promulgated a safety standard for walk-behind power mowers. The standard consisted of three provisions: (1) a requirement that rotary walk-behind mowers pass a foot-probe test; (2) a requirement that rotary machines have a blade-control system that will stop the mower blade within three seconds after the operator's hands leave their normal operating position; and (3) a requirement, applicable to both rotary and reel-type mowers, that the product have a label of specified design to warn of the danger of blade contact. There were a few other standards not here important.

These standards were challenged by the Outdoor Power Equipment Institute (OPEI) as being too strict, severe, or inappropriate (for reasons discussed below), and by an interested consumer as being too lax. The arguments of OPEI, representing the manufacturers of power mowers, are, in part, that: the standard does include some non-consumer products within its scope; there was not substantial evidence on the record to support the foot-probe and shielding requirements; the blade-stopping requirement is a design restriction rather than a performance requirement; the technology required is currently unsafe and unreliable; and the three-second stopping time is not justified by the evidence.

Are the standards proposed by the CPSC within the jurisdiction of the Commission and are they appropriate and enforceable?

The Court held that some of the standards are appropriate and enforceable while others are not, so it affirmed the CPSC standards in some respects and vacated a few of the standards.

A response to each one of the issues argued by OPEI is here presented in order.

1. The standards apply to ordinary power mowers as well as "unique" power mowers, such as high-wheel and three-wheel or five-wheel mowers that do differ significantly from the typical mower used by consumers. The CPSC can only create and enforce safety standards that are applicable to consumer products. For purposes of the Consumer Product Safety Act, a consumer product is an article or component thereof:

    > produced or distributed 1) for sale to a consumer for use in or around a permanent or temporary household or residence, a school, in recreation, or otherwise, or 2) for the personal use, consumption or enjoyment of a consumer in or around a permanent or temporary household or residence, a school . . . but not . . . a) any article which is not customarily produced or distributed for sale to, for use or consumption by, or enjoyment of a consumer. . . .

    The court said that in the present case no evidence was introduced to show that the "unique" design or specialty mowers were significantly dissimilar in function or risk characteristics from the typical walk-behind power lawn mower studied by the CPSC. The unique design machines are part of the general product category of walk-behind power mowers, and, in the absence of any evidence pointing to features differentiating their risk or function characteristics for purposes of protecting consumers from blade-contact injuries, the standard was proper.
2. The legislation creating the CPSC requires that safety standards be supported by substantial evidence on the record as a whole. The foot-probe provision can be

sustained only if the record contains such relevant evidence as a reasonable mind might accept as adequate to support a conclusion that an unreasonable risk of foot injury exists from blade contact at the discharge chute, that the foot-probe will lessen it, and that the benefits of this proposed reform make it reasonable in light of the burdens it imposes on product manufacturers and consumers. The determination of whether an unreasonable risk of discharge-chute injury exists involves a balancing test like that familiar in tort law: The regulation is enforceable if the severity of the injury that may result from the product, factored by the likelihood of the injury, offsets the harm the regulation imposes upon manufacturers and consumers. Under this test, even a very remote possibility that a product would inflict an extremely severe injury could pose an unreasonable risk of injury if the proposed safety standard promised to reduce the risk effectively without unduly increasing the product's price or decreasing its availability or usefulness. Conversely, if the potential injury is less severe, its occurrence must be proven more likely in order to render the risk unreasonable and the safety standard warranted. The court said that its examination of the record has failed to reveal substantial evidence that injury at the discharge-chute was sufficiently provable or likely that it made the risk addressed by the foot-probe of this area unreasonable. In a study of 36 blade-contact foot injuries conducted for CPSC, only one occurred when the operator inserted his foot into the blade path at the discharge-chute. So, this standard is unenforceable.

3. The blade-control system is intended to protect the operator against blade-contact injuries to both hands and feet by stopping the blade before the operator can contact it after he or she leaves the normal operating position and thus releases the deadman's control. The CPSC estimates that the blade-control provisions will eliminate approximately 46,500 operator blade-contact injuries a year. This figure represents approximately 60 percent of all blade-contact injuries and nearly 80 percent of all injuries claimed to be reduced by the standard. OPEI asserts that the standard is expressed as a design requirement rather than a performance requirement, and the Act creating the CPSC directs that a safety standard's provisions shall, whenever feasible, be expressed in terms of performance requirements. The court found that the blade-stop provisions are performance requirements. While the standard does mandate that the mower blades stop within a specified time period, it does not dictate a specific means of fulfilling this condition. Manufacturers are neither formally or practically restricted to employing a particular design, since two existing and different mechanisms are capable of passing the blade-stop test.
4. Is there substantial evidence to support the selection of three seconds as the time limit within which blades must stop? The CPSC commissioned at least three studies to determine the length of time it took for a person to reach the blades after letting go of the handle. These times ranged from about .6 seconds to 4.9 seconds. In setting the blade-stop time, the CPSC considered not only the time in which an operator could reach the blade after releasing the deadman's control but also the incremental cost of successively faster blade-stop times. The record contains substantial evidence that the cost of the blade-stop mechanism varies inversely with the length of time in which the device stops the blade. The three-second requirement is not arbitrary and is supported by substantial evidence and is therefore valid.

[*Note:* The above case is a good illustration of how the federal government through one of its agencies, the CPSC, is attempting to reduce consumer-product related injuries. These types of injury are particularly difficult for the legal system to deal with because, in most cases, the injury is severe, but not severe enough to make it feasible to hire an attorney and sue the manufacturer under a rather vague and difficult cause of action of negligent design.]

Questions and Case Problems

1. Remington Arms, defendant, has sold approximately 3 million model 870 shotguns, primarily to hunters. It has sold 75,000 model 870P shotguns to police departments. About 80 percent of all law enforcement agencies in the United States use this gun, including the FBI and the U.S. secret service. Officer Paton was unloading his model 870P at the scene of a disturbance when the gun discharged killing officer DeRosa. Officer Paton does not recall firing the weapon, but admits that he was holding it when it discharged. In subsequent laboratory tests, the gun was found to have been in good working order. The trigger pull and safety devices on the gun were set exactly as they had been designed to be. The family of officer DeRosa sues Remington. State what argument you believe they made in their attempt to state a claim and whether you believe they would be successful. [*DeRosa v. Remington Arms Co., Inc.,* 509 F.Supp. 762 (D.Ct. N.Y. 1981).]
2. Let's refer once again to question 3 in Chapter 27. John wanted to buy a new electric drill. He saw an advertisement in the local newspaper which said that Sears was having a special sale on "half inch electric drills, reduced 20% to $15." John went to Sears to buy the drill but was very interested in whether the drill was double-insulated. This meant that the drill had special wiring in it so that if a short developed the drill would not shock the user. John was interested in this feature because he often worked in his basement, where the floor was damp as a result of leaky plumbing, and there was a substantial risk of electrocution. John asked the saleswoman at Sears, "Do you have double-insulated drills?" The saleswoman replied, "We have just what you want," and got for John one of the drills on sale. She said, "This drill is double-insulated." John then said, "Fine, I'll take it," and handed her his Sears credit card. The saleswoman made out the appropriate sales slip and John left with the drill.

   Assume that, after John purchased the drill, he was severely injured when using the drill in his basement, which was dry. You may also assume that the drill was not properly double-insulated. As a result of this defect, the drill exploded and caused John's basement to catch fire, resulting in $5,000 damage to the basement and personal injury to John. Also, assume that the drill was destroyed.

   In a series of short paragraphs, first *define* and then *apply* the tort theories that John may use to help him state a good case against Sears for the injuries received.
3. The plaintiff, Philip Schemel, was a passenger in a car that was being driven within the 55 mph speed limit when it was struck from behind by a 1960 Chevrolet Impala traveling at a speed of about 115 mph. The plaintiff was injured and sues General Motors Corp., the manufacturer of the Impala, defendant, alleging the following items:

   a) The defendant knew, or should have known, that there was no useful purpose in designing an automobile that could be driven at excessive speed.

   b) The defendant should have foreseen that the automobile would, in fact, be driven by someone at an excessive and unlawful speed, to the risk of the public in general.

   c) The defendant advertised the speed at which its automobile could be driven, thereby encouraging irresponsible persons to exceed lawful and reasonable speed limits.

   d) The defendant has a duty basically the same as that of any member of our society—the duty to act with reasonable care.

e) Therefore, General Motors should be liable because they designed an automobile that they knew was capable of violating, and in fact would probably violate, the expressed social policy of traveling no faster than 55 mph; and the injury of the kind complained of was therefore reasonably foreseeable, given the design features of the Impala.

The driver of the speeding car is not a party to the lawsuit, and nowhere does the plaintiff argue that the Impala was defective. Based on the material you read in this chapter, should a court dismiss the plaintiff's claim for failure to state a legally recognizable claim? [*Schemel v. Gen. Motors Corp.*, 384 F.2d 802 (7th Cir. 1967).]

4. The plaintiff was burned severely when his General Motors pickup truck rolled over. He sued General Motors and Corbin, Ltd. Corbin manufactured the pants worn by the plaintiff at the time of the accident. The complaint against Corbin alleged that the "burn characteristics" of the pants enhanced the severity of the plaintiff's injuries. He alleged that the pants melted and stuck to flesh when they burned instead of disintegrating and falling away. The defendant, Corbin, has asked the court to join Burlington Industries, Inc., since Burlington manufactured all the fabric used by Corbin. Further, Corbin pleads that if they are found liable on a strict liability theory, then Burlington should pay the judgment. From what you know about strict liability law, do you think the plaintiff's complaint against Corbin based on a strict liability theory would be dismissed or do you think the case would be heard? Do you think a court would require the plaintiff to prove its case against Burlington, or against the seller of the pants, Corbin? [See, *Kelly v. Gen. Motors Corp.*, 487 F.Supp. 1041 (D.C. Mont. 1980).]

5. The plaintiff filed a wrongful death action against Velcro USA, Inc., the defendant. The defendant makes Velcro, a type of closing device used on coats, pants, and other garments. It consists of one pad of plastic loops that attaches to another pad of hooks. The plaintiff's husband was killed when, it was alleged, the Velcro closure installed on the deflation panel of his Raven S-55 hot air balloon failed and the balloon fell to the ground. Velcro never participated in the design, manufacture, sale or servicing of hot air balloons. Velcro alleges that, when it found out about Velcro's use on hot air balloons, they attempted to bring to the attention of the aviation community the inherent dangers of such usage. Velcro tried to have the Federal Aviation Administration issue a directive about the dangers in the use of Velcro in aviation devices, but the agency refused. In addition, Velcro sent a direct warning to all registered owners of balloons known to use Velcro. There is evidence the deceased received the warning but failed to pay attention to it.

   The plaintiff attempts to state a claim based on breach of express and implied warranties, negligence and strict liability. Do you think evidence of Velcro's attempt to warn users of its product should be admitted as evidence of a valid defense? [*Temple v. Velcro USA., Inc.*, 196 Cal.Rptr. 531 (Cal. 1983).]

6. *P* had taken a common medicine used to relieve the symptoms of the flu. Following repeated use of the medicine, *P* developed cataracts in her eyes. The doctors said, and subsequent tests proved, that there was a link between the cataracts and the medicine. *P* cannot recall the manufacturer or brand name of the medicine, and the place where she bought it sells many such medicines. Can *P* state a claim in court against a manufacturer of the medicine? What is the legal issue in this case and how would *P* respond to the arguments of the defendant?

7. In your own words and from a consumer's perspective, list some of the shortcomings of using the two major tort theories of products liability. Aside from the loss of money, what objections would a manufacturer who distributes nationwide have to

these theories? How does the Model Uniform Product Liability Act propose to deal with these shortcomings and objections?

8. What is the function of the Federal Trade Commission? How does it carry out its tasks with regard to protecting consumers?

9. Jose Valdez, a Puerto Rican–born American male, applied to Standard Oil Co. for a credit card. He did own a home and a car but was planning to buy a new VW convertible. He had no debts out of the ordinary for a person who bought some of his consumer items on credit. Standard denied him a credit card and gave no reason for this. What are his remedies, if any, and how might Standard respond to avoid liability?

10. In the case of *Southland Mower Co. v. Consumer Product Safety Commission,* excerpted at the beginning of this section, what arguments did the petitioners (OPEI) use to attack the safety standards of the CPSC? In your opinion is such federal regulation worthwhile?

PART 5 SALES AND CONSUMER LAW

ETHICS AND BUSINESS LAW

Introduction

This end-of-part discussion, like the others in this book, is designed to encourage you to begin forming personal beliefs about what is right or wrong conduct in business. The discussion here builds on the material in the first end-of-part section; you may find it helpful to review that.

More specifically, the section immediately following is designed to help you see the range of ethical issues associated with this area of the law. The in-depth discussion is intended to provide you with a background for forming your own beliefs about a single very important ethical issue in business.

A Sampling of Ethical Issues in Sales and Consumer Law

In many ways, the ethical issues in the law of sales are similar to those discussed for the law of contracts. Thus promise keeping is again a critical issue that arises when a promise does not constitute a contract. The statute of frauds, or the statute of limitations, may make the promise unenforceable in court. But does this eliminate your ethical duty to fulfill your promise?

Products liability law raises another classic ethical issue. If both the manufacturer and the buyer of a product are without fault, who ought to pay for an injury? If the buyer pays for the injury, this reduces the manufacturer's costs, perhaps allowing lower prices. Since that lowers prices, it benefits more people. So utilitarians prefer this outcome. On the other hand, Kant's philosophy is likely to condemn this approach because it uses the injured buyer exclusively as a means to an end (lower prices).

Another ethics issue is associated with the extent of the manufacturer's obligation to make products safe. For example, how much money should auto makers be required to spend to make their cars safe? If they can save one life by spending an additional $10,000 should they be required to do so? Most of us would say yes. But what if the cost to save the one life rose to $50,000, or $250,000, or $10,000,000? Can we attach a financial value to a human life?

Warranty law and freedom of contract also raise ethical issues. Since merchants can waive warranties such as the warranty of merchantability, many do. Consumers often purchase certain products without an awareness of the presence or absence of a warranty. Does the fact that consumers are not paying attention to this part of the transaction justify merchants in modifying the implied warranties?

Section 2–302 of the UCC makes clauses or contracts unenforceable if they are unconscionable. This is an attempt to give judges flexibility and the opportunity to assess particular transactions against an uncertain, but clearly ethical, standard as opposed to the usually clear legal standard. Notice that the uncertain standard here in the law creates social costs because many people cannot determine whether their agreements are enforceable. Is it better to have a legal system with clear, precise rules that may produce some unfair results, or is it better to have uncertain rules that produce fairer results?

In-Depth Discussion of a Basic Issue: Is Legal Always Ethical?

Does the legality of an act always make it ethical? To illustrate, your study of both sales and contract law has equipped you to determine when the courts will enforce one of your promises. This discussion is designed to hep you decide whether you believe, for example, that you are bound to your promises even when they do not constitute a contract and thus are not enforceable in court. In a sense, we are asking whether or not conduct that may be unethical by some standards, can be justified because it is legal. The following section describes alternative ethics views of this issue.

► The Egoist Views

Many who believe that there is not an ethical obligation in business, beyond obeying the law, justify this conclusion with egoistic reasoning. Thus this group simply asks what course of conduct generates for them the greatest benefit. They often see that there are great benefits associated with ignoring the effect of their conduct on others and seeking only their own self-interest. For example, persons in this group would be willing to deceive others as long as it does not constitute fraud. The reality is that in many business situations, deception—which does not necessarily constitute fraud—is often profitable. Similarly, when dealing with a naive person this group might *orally* contract to sell wheat at the market price when delivery is to take place sixty days later. If during the sixty days the price goes down, these egoists would assert the statute of frauds, making the contract unprovable and therefore unenforceable. If the price goes up, they would not assert the statute and would enforce the wheat contract. For convenience we will refer to this group as "open egoists."

Another group of egoists follow typical ethical standards in business because they conclude that this conduct makes good business sense. This group has decided that—in a practical sense—you always "reap as you shall sow" or that "what goes around, comes around." That is, you maximize your self-interest by always appearing to be ethical. This group would not assert the defense of the statute of frauds on the wheat transaction because they believe this would injure their business reputation. We can call this group "timid egoists."

Other egoists reject the views described above. They believe that they must generally appear to be ethical but that they can profitably act very self-interestedly in some situations. The focus here is on the careful evaluation of each situation to determine whether it is profitable to appear clearly self-interested. If a transaction is public, then one acts with apparent ethics. On the other hand, if a transaction is not visible and the other party is one not likely to be a source of future business, then it makes sense for the egoist to do things such as asserting the statue of frauds in the wheat transaction. We will refer to this group as "disguised egoists."

► Utilitarian Views

Some utilitarians reach the same conclusions about conduct as many kinds of egoists, but for different reasons. They believe that ethics ought not to play a role in business decision making; that it is the role of the legal system to ensure that profitable and legal conduct benefits society. These persons sometimes assert that they are unable to decide what is best for society and, therefore, they should only try to decide what is best for themselves. They justify self-centered action on the basis that the legal system functions with sufficient perfection so that society's interests and their self-interests are the same. When legal imperfections are obvious, this group often concludes that self-centered action that exploits the imperfection leads to its cure. That is, by engaging in acts that appear to be unethical, these utilitarians draw attention to the flaws in the legal system and thereby promote reforms that make such future conduct illegal. This group of utilitarians clearly acknowledges that there are imperfections in our legal system. But they see no need to evaluate obligations beyond obeying the law because they see self-interest and the utilitarian interests as the same. We can call this group "quasi-utilitarians."

"Pure utilitarians" reject the line of reasoning that is used to purportedly justify exploitation of legal imperfections. This reasoning is condemned as a form of rationalizing—a way to espouse utilitarian views while acting as an egoist. Pure utilitarians believe that each individual must try to forecast the consequences of each act and only do those things which will generate the greatest good for the greatest number. For these utilitarians, it is clear that the law is only one of many ethical constraints on business behavior.

► Kantian and Religious Views

In general the Kantian and religious views, like that of the pure utilitarian, clearly conclude that there are duties in business beyond simply obeying the law. These groups derive their ethical obligations from sources independent of the law. For Kantians, the source is duty, identified by making acts or rules universal. For religious persons, the source is usually a sacred writing or the teachings of a prophet or church. For these groups, compliance with the law is only one part of a much broader range of ethical duties.

► To Which Group Do You Belong?

One way to begin thinking about your beliefs about whether there is a duty beyond simply obeying the law is to assess how you would react to working for supervisors who are religious, or who are open egoists, timid egoists, disguised egoists, quasi-utilitarians, pure utilitarians, or Kantians. Do you find some of these ethical orientations more appealing in a supervisor than others? Similarly, you might ask yourself whom you would want to be doing business with on a regular basis? Do you think it is all right to want to work with others who are pure utilitarians when you are a disguised egoist? What would Kant say about this?

Solving Ethics Problems

Like the other end-of-part discussions in this book, this one presents problems for you to consider. These problems have three goals. The first is to give you the opportunity to further explore the in-depth issue. The second goal is to give you experience in ethical reasoning about the law and about related management problems. The third goal is to let you see how thinking critically about the law can increase your ability to make ethical decisions. To facilitate this, the problems begin by asking you to analyze the law for its ethical content and then shift to looking at related problems in managerial ethics.

For a discussion of the ethical roles of markets and the law, and examples of the four styles of ethical reasoning—egoism, utilitarianism, Kantian philosophy, and religious ethics—read the business ethics material at the end of Part 1.

▶ Problems

1. Review the case of *Philipp Brothers v. El Salto, S.A.,* (see p. 459). Assume that El Salto's statements are true, that there was an oral agreement whereby Philipp would advance the $750,000. Do you think it is ethical, making these assumptions, for Philipp to assert the parol evidence rule?
2. Suppose someone decided to buy a used car and began following the want ads for a particular model in the *New York Times.* After following the ads for two months and inspecting many of the cars, he became very aware of the values of these models. One day an ad appeared offering a car for sale for $2,100. After looking at it, the buyer decided that it was worth $4,400. The seller was a bright college student who was just unaware of the market for this car. The buyer bargained with the student and agreed on a purchase price of $1,750. Later the student discovered the true value of the car and sued, claiming lack of consideration. Who prevails in the lawsuit? Assess the buyer's conduct in the context of our imperfect legal and economic systems using the four styles of ethical reasoning. Do you believe the conduct of the buyer was ethical?
3. Assume that you have entered into a contract for the purchase of a year's supply of exterior base paint for your painting business that you operate part time during the school year and full time during summers. The contract price is $6.75 per gallon, about fair market value for a large wholesale purchase. You know that the seller's profit on the transaction is about 75 cents per gallon. Further, you know that the paint has been ordered, delivered, and is in storage at the wholesaler's warehouse. Later, you learn that another paint supplier is on the verge of bankruptcy and is willing to sell the same paint for $3.75 per gallon. What is the amount of your legal liability if you breach your contract? What is the amount of your savings if you breach and purchase from the near bankrupt supplier? Evaluate this conduct using the four basic styles of ethical reasoning. Which style of ethical reasoning do you find most appealing?
4. Suppose you were the owner of a mail-order house specializing in small farm implements such as shovels, hoes, spades, and brooms. A buyer outside your target market, a manufacturer, ordered 144 specialized shovels that he intended to use in his firm's production process. After he received the shovels, it took him almost six months to try them out and discover that they would not do what he had hoped they would. As a result he is now asking to return the shovels and get his money back. You have discussed the matter with your lawyer and he informs you that you have no legal liability to do anything. Your profit on the transaction is about $1,000. If you refund the whole amount, you would lose all of your profit on the transaction, but you could resell the shovels in a year. Since the manufacturer has no use for specialized shovels, you can probably buy them back for about half what you sold them for. If you do that, you can resell them and earn a total profit of $1,500. How would a disguised egoist analyze this transaction? How would a religious person analyze it? What do you think is the right thing to do? Why?

PART 6

COMMERCIAL PAPER

29 INTRODUCTION TO COMMERCIAL PAPER AND BANKING OPERATIONS

The concept of the negotiable instrument and how its creation is dependent upon matters of form. Relationships and duties assumed by parties associated with negotiable instruments are explored. You will see how these instruments are processed by the banking industry.

30 TRANSFER AND NEGOTIATION

How rights existing in negotiable instruments can be transferred to third persons and how additional rights by warranty become associated with the instrument.

31 HOLDER, HOLDER IN DUE COURSE, AND DEFENSES

The concept of the holder in due course, the most favored status with regard to rights associated with negotiable instruments, and the limitations placed upon the holder in due course status by personal and real defenses.

32 BANKS, CHECKS, AND CUSTOMER RELATIONS

The relationship of a bank to its customer, especially the bank's liability to its customer. Transactions involving checks are viewed from all dimensions and special cases are examined.

33 DEADLINES AND DISCHARGE

The establishment of duties that the parties owe on negotiable instruments, and discussion of how these duties are discharged.

PREVIEW

Over the centuries it was recognized that it was much more convenient, and in many ways safer, to use paper that could transfer *rights to payment* than to use money. If the paper qualified as "negotiable" as opposed to "nonnegotiable," it could pass to an innocent purchaser *greater rights* than are normally transferred to another by assignment. "Commercial paper" under Article 3 of the Uniform Commercial Code may be either negotiable or nonnegotiable. Our main concern in Part 6 is with that kind of commercial paper called the "negotiable instrument."

Negotiable instruments are in the form of checks, drafts, promissory notes, and certificates of deposit. Some instruments—payable to bearer in form—can be "negotiated" by their delivery to a "holder." Other instruments—payable to order in form—require for their negotiation an indorsement coupled with delivery.

Banks have an important role in the collection of checks. They have rights and duties toward each other and toward their customers.

An understanding of Article 3 of the Uniform Commercial Code is essential to learning the law of commercial paper.

Business ethics as it relates to the text material in these chapters is considered at the end of the part.

CHAPTER 29

INTRODUCTION TO COMMERCIAL PAPER AND BANKING OPERATIONS

After you have read this chapter, you should be able to:

1. Understand the concept of negotiability.
2. Recognize practical applications of negotiable instruments.
3. Relate the flow of commercial paper to banking operations.
4. Identify the various types of negotiable instruments.
5. Discuss the formal requirements of negotiable instruments.

BUSINESS DECISIONS and the LAW

Two and one-half years ago, Rachel Webb was promoted from chief cashier to loan officer of the Holly Hills Bank. She worked hard for the promotion and feels that experience she gained in the cashier division, and the jobs she held in other phases of the bank's operations, prepared her well for the position she is now occupying.

Given a recent management shake-up at Holly Hills, and some unexpected retirements, she finds herself somewhat ahead of her own career schedule. She discovers, quite by accident, that she is being considered for an early promotion to vice president for real estate loans, but she is in some tough competition with a man with somewhat more banking experience than she has, but not with Holly Hills, and not in real estate loans.

Her "competitor," Dan Vela, is congenial and has, in fact, become an office favorite on the strength of his keen sense of humor and the thoughtfulness he shows toward his coworkers. Nevertheless, Rachel believes him to be ill-equipped for the job. For one thing, he has been in real estate loans for only eight months. Beyond that, when Dan and Rachel were talking "shop" in the coffee room, he showed her a file on a customer to whom he had just spoken. The $10,000 loan had yet to be approved by the current vice president, but Dan had assured the customer this procedure was merely a formality. As security for this loan, Dan had taken a note for $15,000, backed up by a real estate mortgage. The note had been issued to this customer by a real estate developer, but it was not due for four years. Dan's customer needed working capital now.

As they discussed the matter, Dan handed Rachel a copy of the $15,000 note his customer was using as security. It read in part as follows:

> This note is secured by mortgage on real estate made by the maker hereof in favor of payee (Dan's customer), and shall be construed and enforced according to the laws of this state. The terms of said mortgage are by this reference made a part hereof.

Upon reading this, Rachel struggled to hide her surprise. If the vice president sees this in conjunction with Dan's recommendation, she thought to herself, he is "out the door." What does she see that makes her think that? And what does she do about it? After all, she owes Dan nothing. And in the long run, Dan could do the bank a lot of financial harm if he does not know Article 3 of the Uniform Commercial Code well enough to spot a problem with negotiability.

What's happening here?

Introduction

negotiable instrument
A writing signed by the maker or drawer containing an unconditional promise or order to pay a sum certain in money payable on demand or at a definite time to order or to bearer

formal contract
A contract that must be in a certain form

Most people take negotiable instruments for granted, and there are very good reasons for this. Each time someone writes a check for the purchase of goods and services, or signs a promissory note for a loan or for a purchase on credit, in all likelihood that person has created a negotiable instrument.

The **negotiable instrument** is a **formal written contract** used extensively in everyday business transactions. It is a means by which a person called a "holder in due course" can get "greater rights" against the party who made or drew the instrument than would be the case if liability depended simply on the law of contracts. Accordingly, it becomes extremely important to learn about negotiable instruments as a kind of commercial paper.

► Negotiation and Assignment Compared

A familiar illustration can quickly identify and compare the qualities of negotiation with an *assignment,* a legal concept that was introduced in Part 2, Contracts. Suppose that Mary buys for business use a $600 electric typewriter from Pete on credit. The sales contract may allow her a period of time—six months, for example—before she is required to pay the purchase price. Prior to the due date, however, Pete is entitled to sell or assign his rights in the contract to a third party.

Assume that Pete sells his rights in the $600 contract to Community Bank for $500 cash—a $100 discount. In this event, Community, the assignee, simply steps into the shoes of Pete, assignor. Community receives all of Pete's rights, but it is also subject to all of the defenses against Pete that Mary might raise under the original contract. If, for example, Pete had warranted the typewriter and the warranty is breached, Mary's defense in refusing to pay under the original contract will be valid against Community just as it would have been against Pete if he had never made the assignment. Community may then recover from Pete under the terms of the assignment contract or on the basis of an implied warranty.

Now, consider the difference in outcome if the credit terms of the sale to Mary are embodied in the form of a negotiable promissory note[1] payable to the order of Pete. Mary would be the "maker"[2] of the note and Pete the "payee" to whom it was payable. He could then indorse and transfer the note in a manner that would create in the Community Bank the rights of a **holder in due course (HIDC)**.[3]

holder in due course (HIDC)
The holder of a negotiable instrument who takes it for value, in good faith, and without notice that the instrument is overdue or has been dishonored or of any defense against, or claim to, the instrument by any person

If the note was not voluntarily paid at maturity, Community could enforce it against Mary despite the breach of warranty defense mentioned above and most other defenses that she could raise.[4] Mary would then be compelled to bring a warranty action against Pete to rescind the contract or to recover money damages for getting the typewriter fixed.

In either event, notice that the responsibility for the breach ultimately falls on Pete, as it should. However, when a negotiable promissory note is used as a credit instrument, HIDCs like the bank can be confident of getting a judgment against the primary party-maker, Mary, or, as will be discussed later, against the secondary party-indorser, Pete.[5]

► The HIDC Concept

From the point of view of HIDCs then, negotiable instruments are a great advantage over mere assignment. Greater rights can be obtained by an HIDC of a negotiable instrument than by an assignee of a contract right. Indirectly they benefit debtors too, because many sales would not be made unless the seller-payee could depend on negotiating the instrument for cash to some third party, typically a bank or finance company.

This transaction is known as *discounting*. The seller-payee will normally receive less than face value for the note—for example, a $1,000 note may sell for $980 (a low discount) or for $800 or less (a high discount).

The difference between face value and the discount price is the margin or yield. The purpose of this margin is to compensate the third party for its risk. This margin will vary, depending on the credit rating of the debtor, the length of time until maturity, and the security or collateral that stands behind the instrument in the event of default.

► Negotiable Instruments As a Substitute for Money

Negotiable instruments can be used as substitutes for money just as, in the previous example, a promissory note was used as a credit device. The *check,* which is a form of

---

[1]UCC 3–104(1).

[2]UCC 3–413(1).

[3]UCC 3–302.

[4]UCC 3–305.

[5]UCC 3–414(1).

FIGURE 29.1 **Check Flow Chart**

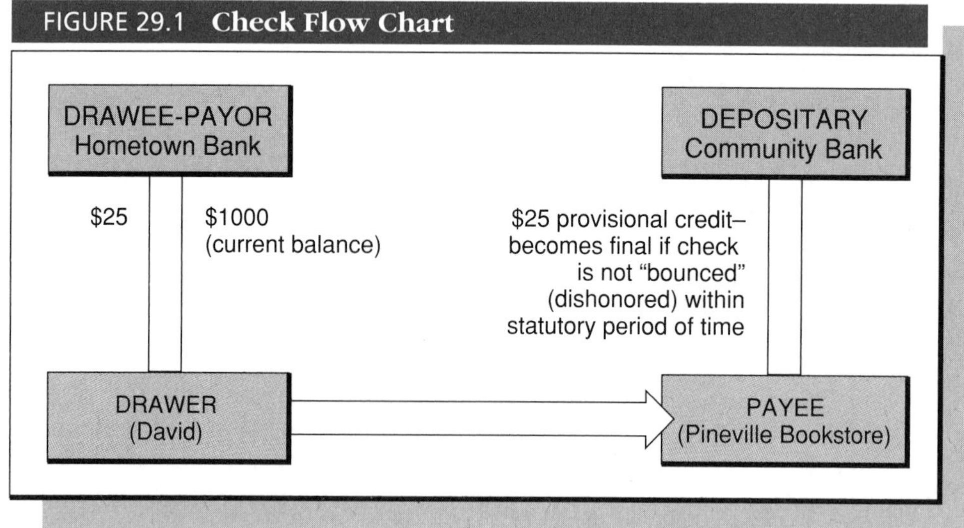

FIGURE 29.2 **Sample Check**

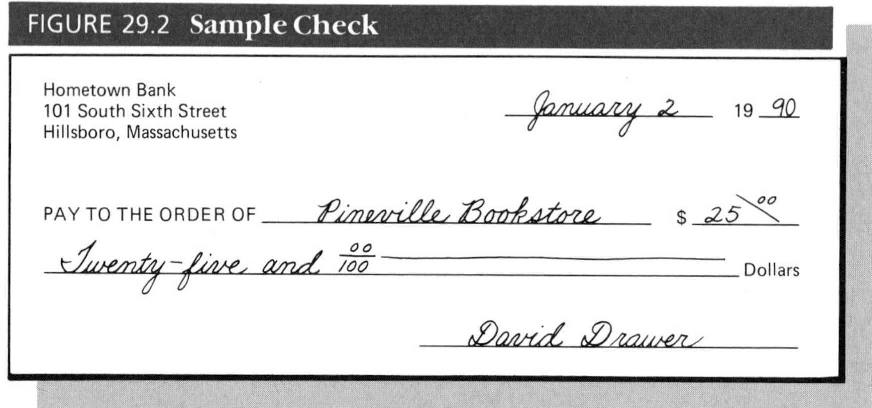

draft
A negotiable instrument containing an unconditional order (e.g., "pay")

check
A negotiable "draft drawn on a bank and payable on demand" UCC 3–104(2)(b)

a **draft** drawn on a bank and payable on demand, is the most familiar illustration.[6] (See Figures 29.1, 29.2, and 29.3.)

Assume that David, who has money on deposit in a checking account with Hometown Bank, draws a $25 **check** payable to the order of Pineville Bookstore, payee, for the purchase of textbooks. An authorized agent of the bookstore, usually the cashier who handles the transaction, will indorse on the back of the check with a rubber stamp: "Pay to Community Bank, For Deposit, Pineville Bookstore."[7]

[6]UCC 3–104(2)(b).

[7]This indorsement is "special," UCC 3–204(1), because it names the person to whom it is indorsed; it is also "restrictive," 3–205(c), because it limits the things that the indorsee Community Bank can do with it. The bank can place this for deposit only in the Pineville Bookstore's account and forward the check for collection.

FIGURE 29.3 Deposit Stamp on Back of Check

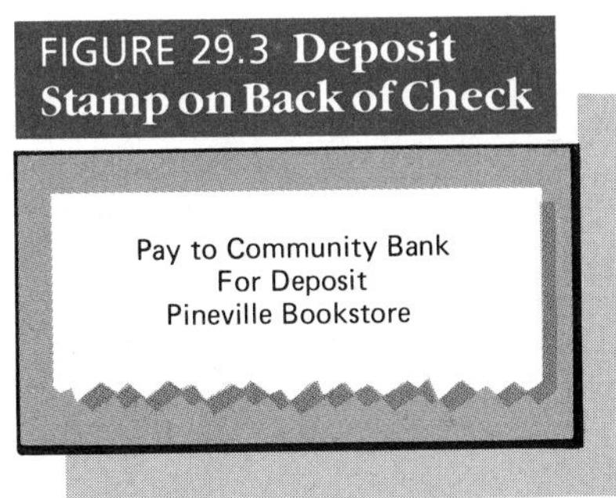

As a routine matter, this check, along with other items,[8] will be placed in Pineville's depositary bank,[9] Community. Pineville Bookstore will be given a $25 provisional credit[10] in its checking account, and the check will be forwarded through bank channels to David's Hometown Bank, known as the **drawee,** payor bank.[11]

drawee
The person on whom a draft is drawn and ordered to pay

If there are sufficient funds on deposit in **drawer** David's checking account, the item will be debited, or charged, against his balance. Periodically, David will receive through the mail a statement of his account and often his cancelled checks.

drawer
The person who initially draws or creates and signs a draft

The provisional credit that **payee** Pineville Bookstore received at Community becomes final since the check was paid from David's account by Hometown. Pineville Bookstore can now draw on that account as it wishes—for example, to pay its bills, replenish its inventory, or expand its operations.

payee
The person to whose order the instrument is originally written

If David did not have sufficient funds on deposit with Hometown, the drawee-payor bank, or if for some reason David stopped payment on his check,[12] the check would be returned through channels to Community. Community would then reverse the provisional credit with an offsetting debit entry and return the check to Pineville Bookstore.

At this stage Pineville would have to collect on the check from David, perhaps resulting in a lawsuit. Keep in mind that the payment of debts with checks or notes is conditional payment only—conditioned on the instrument being paid.[13]

You can see that an assignment of contract rights would be very awkward in this situation. Checks, however, are tailor-made for such transactions. With very little change, if Community Bank permitted Pineville to withdraw the funds represented by David's check prior to its being "bounced," or returned, Community Bank may become an HIDC of the check since it paid value for it by advancing money to Pineville. In that capacity, Community could proceed against David, the drawer, on the check, and most defenses that David could raise would be ineffective against Community as an HIDC. The HIDC

[8]UCC 4–104(1)(g).

[9]UCC 4–105(a).

[10]UCC 4–201(1).

[11]UCC 4–105(b).

[12]UCC 4–403.

[13]UCC 3–802(1)(b).

Community Bank could, and probably would, first make every effort to collect from its customer Pineville, the payee-indorser; but the status of HIDC is very valuable because it practically assures Community of a judgment against David.

▶ Types of Negotiable Instrument—Notes and Drafts

Many new terms were introduced during the previous discussion of the concept of negotiability. In this part of the chapter we will elaborate on these terms and observe further the importance of negotiability as we discuss the following.

1. Types of instrument
2. Parties and banks that deal with them
3. Form that all instruments must have in order to be negotiable

All instruments are either notes or drafts.[14] Notes promise payment and are promissory instruments, while drafts order payment and are order instruments. Notes are two-party instruments in which a maker, such as a credit purchaser or borrower, promises to pay money to a payee. A certificate of deposit, shown in Figure 29.4, is a

FIGURE 29.4 **Certificate of Deposit**

CERTIFICATE OF DEPOSIT

NO INTEREST PAID AFTER DUE DATE INVESTMENT—SAVINGS **No. 2382**

HILLSBORO, MASSACHUSETTS ____________

THIS CERTIFIES THAT ____________

HAS DEPOSITED WITH

Hometown State Bank HILLSBORO, MASSACHUSETTS $ ________

____________ DOLLARS

PAYABLE ________ DAYS-MONTHS AFTER DATE IN CURRENT FUNDS ON RETURN OF THIS CERTIFICATE PROPERLY ENDORSED WITH INTEREST

AT THE RATE OF ________ PER CENT PER ANNUM.

THIS CERTIFICATE SHALL BE CONSIDERED RENEWED AUTOMATICALLY FOR THE SAME LENGTH OF TIME AND INTEREST RATE FROM ITS ORIGINAL MATURITY AND THEREAFTER FOR SUCCESSIVE PERIODS OF TIME OF THE SAME LENGTH, UNLESS PRESENTED FOR REDEMPTION WITHIN TEN (10) DAYS AFTER THE END OF THE ORIGINAL TERM OR ANY SUBSEQUENT TERM. THE BANK MAY REDEEM THIS CERTIFICATE AT ANY ORIGINAL OR SUBSEQUENT MATURITY DATE BY TEN (10) DAYS WRITTEN NOTICE TO THE PAYEE AT HIS ADDRESS SHOWN BY THE BANK'S RECORDS. IF SUCH NOTICE IS GIVEN, THIS DEPOSIT WILL NOT BEAR INTEREST AFTER THE REDEMPTION DATE. SUBJECT TO THE FOREGOING, THIS CERTIFICATE IS CONTINUOUS; NO RENEWAL NECESSARY.

TAX I.D. NO. ADDRESS

☐ DEPOSIT INTEREST TO ACCOUNT

☐ ADD INTEREST TO PRINCIPAL UPON RENEWAL

____
EXEC. ASSISTANT CASHIER—VICE PRESIDENT

NOT SUBJECT TO CHECK

[14] UCC 3–104(2).

particular kind of note in which a bank acknowledges receipt of money and engages to repay it.

Drafts are three-party instruments in which a drawer orders the drawee to pay to a payee. A check is a special form of a draft that is drawn on a bank, the drawee. The drawee bank is ordered to pay the money on demand.

Notes and drafts may or may not be negotiable. If not negotiable, they are still legal and enforceable as contracts, and they may be transferred by assignment; but they cannot be negotiated.

► Negotiability Is a Matter of Form

The form that notes and drafts must assume in order to qualify as negotiable will be discussed in detail later; but to aid in understanding the various types of commercial paper, notice that all negotiable instruments must comply with *all* of the following requirements:

1. The instrument must be in writing and signed by the maker or drawer.
2. Each instrument must contain an unconditional promise or order to pay a sum certain in money.
3. The time of payment must be on demand or at a definite time.
4. Each instrument must be payable to order or to bearer.[15]

► Negotiable Promissory Notes

Recall the previous hypothetical situation in which Mary purchased a typewriter on credit and financed the unpaid balance by creating a $600 negotiable promissory note to the order of Pete, payee. The note had two parties, **maker** and *payee,* and a promise to pay. The instrument gave a definite time before the maker, Mary, was required to pay.

maker
The person who initially makes and signs a promissory note

This illustrated the use of a negotiable note as a credit device.[16] If the terms had called for payment on demand,[17] Pete could have required payment at any time after the note was issued to him.[18] This would not have suited the needs of the parties quite as well, but on some occasions the only way a maker can induce the payee to lend money or to sell on credit is by promising to pay on demand.

Mary, the maker of the note, is undertaking a direct and personal obligation to pay Pete the $600 at maturity. No one else is being ordered to pay on her behalf. Since the maker is absolutely liable, she is described as a "primary party."[19] (Figure 29.5 shows an example of a promissory note.)

---

[15] UCC 3–104(1).

[16] UCC 3–109.

[17] UCC 3–108.

[18] UCC 3–122(1)(b).

[19] UCC 3–413(1).

FIGURE 29.5 **Promissory Note**

PROMISSORY NOTE

NAME John Robinson NO. 471-00-3322 $ 1000.00

DUE Demand SECURITY Signature HILLSBORO, MASSACHUSETTS Current Date ,19 ____

On demand, or if no demand is made, then Six Months *after date, without grace,*

I, we or either of us, as principals, promise to pay to the order of Hillsboro State Bank, Hillsboro, Massachusetts,

the sum of One Thousand Dollars & 00/100 ——————————— *Dollars*

with interest at the rate of 10% *percent per annum from date until paid, at its offices in Hillsboro, Massachusetts.*

And in the event default is made in the payment of this note at maturity and it is placed in the hands of an attorney for collection, or suit is brought on same, then a reasonable additional amount shall be added as attorney's and collection fees.

The makers and endorsers hereof hereby severally waive all notices, demands for payment, presentation hereof for payment, protest in case this note is not paid at maturity, and agree to all extensions and partial payments before or after maturity without prejudice to holder, and further agree that any one of them, acting individually, may renew this note and thereby extend the time for payment of any portion of the principal and accumulated interest due and agree to pay an interest rate to be determined at the time of such renewal. Makers agree that each of them shall be and remain obligated as principals during any such extended period for payment. The death or loss of capacity of any of the makers hereof shall not revoke or terminate, as to the other makers, the authority of each to renew and extend this note for and on behalf of all other surviving or non-incapacitated makers.

(signed) John Robinson *Address* Hillsboro, Mass.

(signed) Larry Cox *Address* Hillsboro, Mass.

(signed) Richard Nelson *Address* Hillsboro, Mass.

Form 77B Revised

Promissory Note

1. Which party or parties occupy a position analogous to that of Mary in the textbook example?
2. Which party most closely resembles Pete, the person who sold Mary the car?
3. If John Robinson receives the entire $1000, what function do the signatures of Cox and Nelson serve?
4. What is an acceleration clause? Does this instrument have an acceleration clause?
5. Since three parties have signed this note payable to the order of the bank, does that fit the definition of a note as a TWO PARTY instrument and a PROMISE to pay?

▶ Negotiable Drafts

If the terms of an instrument include three parties—a *drawer* who orders a *drawee* to pay money to a *payee*—the instrument is a draft. (Figure 29.6 shows an envelope draft.) Suppose that a draft is used to finance the credit sale of $1,000 worth of goods. The seller may draw a six-month time-draft on the *buyer-drawee* ordering the buyer to pay $1,000 to a payee. The payee may be the seller, the seller's bank, or any person designated by the seller.

acceptor
The drawee on a draft who has assented in writing on the draft to pay it

This type of draft is known as a *trade acceptance.* When the instrument is drawn by the seller ordering the buyer to pay and it is signed as accepted by the *buyer,* the buyer becomes an **acceptor,** and now is a *primary party* with liability on the instrument similar to that of the maker of a note.[20] Primary parties are directly liable on the instrument they sign; unlike secondary parties, they do not expect someone else to pay on their behalf.

[20]UCC 3–413(1).

FIGURE 29.6 **Envelope Draft**

Customer's Draft

Hillsboro State Bank

On Demand/at Sight HILLSBORO, MASSACHUSETTS Current Date 19

PAY TO THE ORDER OF Payee-Seller $ 1,000.00

One Thousand Dollars and No/100 DOLLARS

VALUE RECEIVED AND CHARGE TO ACCOUNT OF WITH EXCHANGE

ENCLOSURES Invoice in triplicate airway bill of lading; marine and war risk insurance; non-negotiable airway bill of lading.

TO Drawee-Buyer

THROUGH Seller's Bank

Drawer-Seller

FORM 163

Envelope Draft

1. This draft is in the form of an envelope that will enclose the invoice, insurance policies, and bill of lading. The drawee-buyer is entitled to examine these documents before paying the $1000.
2. This draft is payable *on demand* or *at sight*. While the buyer can examine the enclosed documents to see that they are in proper order, the buyer must not use them to pick up the goods at the carrier's depot until the buyer has paid the draft.
3. A trade acceptance is a draft that would have given the buyer a *credit period* after his signature or acceptance of the draft. The time period would be, for example, six months after date. There is no place for the drawee-buyer's signature on this draft, but on the typical trade acceptance there will be a designated line.
4. A bank acceptance is a draft resembling a trade acceptance, except, by prior arrangement, the buyer's bank agrees to become the drawee-acceptor and to sign or accept on behalf of its customer.

If the bank accepts the draft—usually by prior arrangement between the buyer and his bank—the instrument is known as a *banker's acceptance*.

The importance of this distinction becomes apparent if you visualize a situation in which the payee needs cash before the instrument matures in six months. If the payee should decide to **negotiate** the instrument—i.e., indorse and discount the draft for as much cash as it will bring on the market—do you suppose the payee will receive a higher price (low discount from face value) if the instrument has been accepted by a bank rather than accepted by the buyer alone? Chances are that a purchaser of the paper will pay more for a banker's acceptance. Other things being equal, the bank's financial status and reputation will make this instrument more desirable than a trade acceptance.

negotiate
To deliver a negotiable instrument to a holder

Of course, most buyer-drawees will discharge their liability at maturity by full payment, but the financial reputation of the party who accepts can make an important difference. If a seller-payee wants to be assured of a ready and willing market for the draft, and also of a high price (low discount), a banker's acceptance normally is preferable.

Not all drafts are time drafts with a definite maturity date. Some are sight drafts payable "at sight" or "on demand" when presented to the drawee.

A check is the most common example of a draft payable on demand. Remember that a check is a special form of draft that is always drawn on a bank.[21] In the normal course of events it is expected that the drawee bank will pay on demand the amount designated in the check. Then the bank will charge or reduce the drawer-depositor's account by that amount.

cashier's check
A check drawn by a bank on itself and payable to the order of a payee

Other forms are the **cashier's check** and the *traveller's check.* A cashier's check is drawn by a bank officer (cashier) on the bank itself as drawee and payable to the order of a payee. It resembles a note since the one drawing the draft (the drawer) and the one expected to pay (the drawee) are the same party. The bank drawer of a cashier's check cannot stop payment on it, as is illustrated by the following case.

FACTS

Reinhard purchased goods from the plaintiff, Moon Over the Mountain Ltd. He paid for them by delivering to the plaintiff's agent a cashier's check which he had purchased from the defendant, Marine Midland Bank, where he was a customer. The check was drawn by the defendant payable to the plaintiff's agent, who indorsed and delivered it to the plaintiff. It was then deposited for collection in the bank where plaintiff had its account. Meanwhile, Reinhard decided to stop payment on the check and directed the defendant to do so. The check was returned to plaintiff's bank marked "Payment Stopped." Plaintiff sued the defendant on the check and obtained a judgment. Defendant appealed.

DECISION

Affirmed for plaintiff. Since under UCC 3–802(1)(a) the payee loses its right against its debtor when a cashier's check is taken in payment of an underlying debt, the bank drawer cannot refuse payment on the instrument. The bank here has drawn and issued the cashier's check; it is primarily liable thereon and cannot stop payment.

Moon Over the Mountain Ltd. v. Marine Midland Bank, 87 Misc.2d 918 (N.Y. 1976).

A traveller's check may name as drawee a financial institution that is not a bank. Strictly speaking, then, it is not a check at all but a draft.

In its original form, the traveller's check does not name a payee. The payee will be specified later when the owner or "traveller" decides to use or cash the check; the owner will then insert the name of the payee. The "traveller" will also be required to sign the instrument when it is used. This gives the recipient payee, perhaps a hotel or airline, an opportunity to verify the owner's written signature at that time by comparing it with the owner's written signature on the instrument as it was originally issued.

A *letter of credit* (shown in Figure 29.7) is neither a draft nor a note. It is a promise by a bank or other person to honor or to pay drafts drawn in accordance with its terms. For example, a Texas merchant who is not well known beyond the borders of his home state may bargain with his bank to guarantee payment of drafts drawn upon it by Mexican or Japanese exporters. This will allow the Texas businessperson to make purchases of goods that would not have been sold to him on the strength of his credit alone.

[21] UCC 3–104(2)(b).

FIGURE 29.7 **Letter of Credit**

CABLE ADDRESS
HILLSBANK

HILLSBORO STATE BANK
HILLSBORO, MASSACHUSETTS

IRREVOCABLE
COMMERCIAL CREDIT

HILLSBORO,
MASSACHUSETTS

NO. A-524
UP TO $10,186.50

SELLER'S NAME Po Lung-Yu
Tachibana Bldg., 1083 Ikebukuro,
2-chome, Toshima-ku, Tokyo, Japan

DATE OF ISSUE

GENTLEMEN:

WE HEREBY AUTHORIZE YOU TO DRAW ON HILLSBORO STATE BANK

FOR ACCOUNT OF NAME OF BUYER-CUSTOMER OF HILLSBORO STATE BANK, HILLSBORO, MASS. 86543

UP TO AN AGGREGATE AMOUNT OF **TEN THOUSAND ONE HUNDRED EIGHTY SIX AND 50/100***

AVAILABLE BY YOUR DRAFTS AT Sight

ACCOMPANIED BY Airbill, marked Freight Prepaid; Commercial Invoice, signed in triplicate; Packing List in Triplicate; Insurance policy or certificate endorsed in blank, for 110% of the invoice cost including: The Institute War Clauses, and the Institute Cargo Clauses (All Risks) and the Institute Strikes, Riots and Civil Commotions Clauses. Claims to be payable in the United States of America in the currency of drafts. Airbill should be made out to order and blank endorsed and marked "Notify the above mentioned applicant."

No partial shipments allowed.

Shipping Expiration: 60 days.

Document Negotiation: 90 days.

Bank: Dai-Ichi Kangyo Bank, Tokyo, Shinbashi Branch

Reference: Attached copy of Refiners & Producers Marketing, Inc. purchase order which becomes a part of this Letter of Credit.

DRAFTS MUST BE DRAWN AND NEGOTIATED NOT LATER THAN Expiration Date of Letter . EACH DRAFT MUST BE MARKED "DRAWN UNDER LETTER OF CREDIT NO. A-524 OF HILLSBORO STATE BANK, HILLSBORO, DATED Date of Issue " AND THE AMOUNT OF EACH DRAFT SO DRAWN ENDORSED BY THE NEGOTIATING BANK ON THE REVERSE SIDE HEREOF. WHEN PRESENTED BY THE MAKER DIRECT TO THE DRAWEE BANK, THE DRAFTS MUST BE ACCOMPANIED BY THIS LETTER OF CREDIT FOR THE PURPOSE OF SUCH ENDORSEMENTS BEING MADE THEREON.

WE HEREBY AGREE WITH THE DRAWERS, ENDORSERS AND BONA FIDE HOLDERS OF DRAFTS DRAWN UNDER AND IN COMPLIANCE WITH THIS CREDIT THAT SAME SHALL BE DULY HONORED UPON PRESENTATION TO THE DRAWEE BANK AS SPECIFIED ABOVE.

YOURS VERY TRULY

SIGNATURE OF BANK OFFICIAL

AUTHORIZED SIGNATURE

Parties

By this time most of the parties and banks that deal with negotiable instruments have been introduced. To review and reenforce your knowledge of this material, it will be discussed in more detail in the following three sections.

► Primary Parties

primary parties
Parties (maker and acceptor) on a negotiable instrument who are absolutely liable for its payment according to the terms at the time they sign

Primary parties are makers of notes and acceptors of drafts.[22] The party or parties who purchase on credit or borrow money and sign promissory notes as makers are primary parties. Acceptors of drafts—such as drawee banks that certify checks[23] or buyer-drawees that agree to be bound on trade acceptances by signing and accepting them[24]—are primary parties also.

These parties promise to pay the instrument according to its tenor or terms at the time the instrument is created or the time of acceptance. If the instrument is incomplete at the time of acceptance, a person takes a risk in accepting it. If the instrument is later filled in properly, there is no problem.[25] For example, if a buyer-drawee on a trade acceptance accepts it with his or her signature and authorizes the seller to fill in the blank space with the amount of the purchase price, the acceptor has no ground for complaint when the correct amount is inserted as authorized. If an excessive, unauthorized amount is filled in, however, the acceptor will be liable for that sum to a subsequent HIDC.[26] The acceptor is responsible for the incompleteness since the acceptor gives the wrongdoer a golden opportunity to materially alter the instrument. After paying the HIDC, the acceptor has a right of recovery against the wrongdoer.

Keep in mind that neither primary parties nor secondary parties, which you will study in the next section, are liable on the instrument forever. They may be discharged from liability based on the state statute of limitations that controls the original transaction between the parties. Our chapter-ending case, *Tepper v. Citizens Federal Savings and Loan Association* will explain this in greater detail.

► Secondary Parties

secondary parties
Parties on a negotiable instrument who are liable on the instrument only if certain conditions occur

If a person's signature on a negotiable instrument is other than as maker or acceptor, that person is a **secondary party.** The drawer and indorser are secondary parties.

Drawer It is easy to be trapped by the comparison of a secondary party-drawer who initiates a draft with a primary party-maker who initiates a note. Be careful—the analogy is misleading.

In the normal course of events, the *drawer* of a draft or check expects the drawee to pay. When a person writes a check, it is an order from the drawer to the drawee bank to pay out of the money on deposit in the drawer's checking account. When the maker of

[22]UCC 3–413.

[23]UCC 3–411.

[24]UCC 3–410.

[25]UCC 3–115(1).

[26]UCC 3–407(3). For material alteration of incomplete instruments, see pp. 674–676.

a note borrows money, however, or purchases on credit, the maker does not order someone else to pay,[27] he himself promises or undertakes to pay.

A drawer does not obligate him- or herself to pay the instrument if the holder takes the proper three steps:

1. *Presentment.* The instrument is properly **presented** to the drawee for payment.
2. *Dishonor.* The instrument is **dishonored** by the maker's or drawee's refusal to pay it.
3. *Notice.* The drawer is given proper notice of nonpayment or dishonor.[28]

presentment
"A demand for acceptance or payment made upon the maker, acceptor, drawee or other payor by or on behalf of the holder" UCC 3–504(1)

The drawer may avoid or disclaim this liability by drawing the draft "without recourse."[29] However, it is difficult to find people who are willing to do business with a drawer on this basis because they do not have recourse—i.e., they do not have the right of recovery—against the drawer on his or her signature if the draft is dishonored by the drawee.

dishonor
The refusal of the drawee to accept the draft, or of the drawee, acceptor, or maker to pay the draft or note

Indorser **Indorsers** are secondary parties who sign notes and drafts in the process of negotiation. They do not sign as makers or acceptors. Generally speaking, every indorser makes a conditional or secondary promise to pay the holder of the instrument if the usual three steps of presentment, dishonor, and notice are followed. Qualified indorsers ("without recourse" indorsers)[30] disclaim their signature as indorsements with secondary liability if the instrument is dishonored, but they are exceptions to the rule.

indorser
The person who signs on an instrument (or on a paper attached to it) other than as a maker, drawer, or acceptor

Discharge of Secondary Parties for Failure to Observe the Conditions of Presentment, Dishonor, and Notice of Dishonor These preliminary three steps are conditions for holding an indorser secondarily liable. They are the same as those for holding a drawer secondarily liable, but there is a very important difference. If these conditions do not occur, the indorser is completely discharged, but the drawer is discharged only if the drawee becomes insolvent during the delay in presentment for payment or notice of dishonor.[31]

If the drawee does become **insolvent,** the drawer is discharged to the extent that his or her claim against the drawee is reduced. For example, assume that a $100 check would have been paid by the drawee if the instrument had been properly presented. However, if the holder of the check is late in presenting it to the drawee for payment, and the drawee becomes insolvent during the delay, then the drawer is discharged from any further liability by assigning all of the drawer's rights to the holder. The holder may be able to recover a fraction of the $100 check from the insolvent drawee. Thus if the drawee's creditors eventually receive twenty cents on the dollar, the holder of the check will be entitled to collect $20.

insolvent
"A person is insolvent who either has ceased to pay his debts in the ordinary course of business or cannot pay his debts as they become due or is insolvent within the meaning of the federal bankruptcy law" UCC 1–201(23)

[27]Some states have adopted UCC 3–121, Alternative A, which makes a note payable at a bank "the equivalent of a draft drawn on the bank payable when it falls due out of any funds of the maker or acceptor for such payment."

[28]UCC 3–501.

[29]UCC 3–413(2).

[30]UCC 3–414(1).

[31]UCC 3–502(1).

Study carefully *Tepper v. Citizens Federal Savings and Loan Association* at the conclusion of this chapter for the effect of the state statute of limitations on the liability of secondary parties, and of primary parties as well.

► Other Parties

Payee The payee is the person to whose order the instrument is originally written. This person must be identified with reasonable certainty.[32] The payee normally becomes an indorser-secondary party when the payee signs on the instrument so that it can be negotiated to some other person.

indorsee
The person named by an indorser on an instrument to whom it is to be paid

indorsement
The indorser's signature on an instrument (or on a paper attached to it)

Indorsee The **indorsee** is the person named in the **indorsement**—for example, "Pay to *A* [indorsee], [signed] *B* [indorser]"; or "Pay to Community Bank [indorsee], [signed] Pineville Bookstore [indorser]."[33]

For the time being, please note that these indorsements which name the indorsee are called *special indorsements*—the indorsement is to a "special" person. If the last or only indorsement of an instrument is a special indorsement, the instrument is *order paper*. This means that the indorsee *must* indorse before the paper can be further negotiated.[34]

An additional point to observe here is that the word "order" does not necessarily have to appear in the special indorsement. If not present, it is simply assumed to be there—that is, the indorsement is read as if the word *order* appeared in it as follows: "Pay to [the order of] *A*, [signed] *B*."

Remember that we are speaking here of an *indorsement*. If words of negotiability—that is, "order" or "bearer" or their equivalents—do not appear on the *face* or front of the instrument, it is not negotiable to begin with.

holder
"A person who is in possession of a document of title or an instrument or a certificated investment security drawn, issued, or indorsed to him or his order or to bearer or in blank" UCC 1–201(20)

bearer
The person in possession of an instrument, document of title, or certificated security payable or deliverable to bearer or indorsed in blank (a signature without additional words)

Holder A **holder** is a person who is in possession of an instrument that has been originally drawn or issued to the person or his or her order, or later specially indorsed to him or her.[35] Merely naming someone as payee or indorsee is not sufficient to make the person a holder. That person must be *in possession* of the instrument as well.

Further, a holder may be a person who is in possession of an instrument that is **bearer** paper originally, e.g., on the face of the paper it reads "Pay to the order of *Bearer*," or "Pay to the order of *Cash*." Another possibility is that the holder may be in possession of an instrument that was originally order paper, but which has become bearer paper because the last or only indorsement is a *blank* indorsement—e.g., the indorser simply signs his name, "Jarrett Hudnall," but does not name an indorsee. A blank indorsement is an indorsement without any accompanying words. Because of the risk of a bearer instrument being lost or stolen and getting into the hands of a holder who can then collect on the instrument, one should be very careful when indorsing an instrument in blank.

---

[32]UCC 3–110(1).

[33]UCC 3–204(1).

[34]UCC 3–204(1).

[35]UCC 1–201(20).

Bearer A bearer[36] is a holder who is in possession of an instrument that is bearer paper on its face—i.e., it is made out to "Bearer," or to "Cash," or to the equivalent of these, discussed later. A bearer may also be a person who is in possession of an instrument on which the last or only indorsement is a blank indorsement.

Holder in Due Course (HIDC) An HIDC must first qualify as a holder. In addition, this holder must acquire the instrument "in due course," which means purchase for value, in good faith, and without notice that the instrument is overdue, has been dishonored, or that there is an outstanding claim of ownership on or defense against the instrument.[37] Any holder—a natural person, a business firm, or a bank—may become a HIDC. In the following case, a bank became a HIDC because it met all the requirements prior to receipt of notice of a stop payment order.

holder in due course (HIDC)
The holder of a negotiable instrument who takes it for value, in good faith, and without notice that the instrument is overdue or has been dishonored or of any defense against, or claim to, the instrument by any person

FACTS

Acting through its treasurer, J. M. Cook, Arizona Auto Auction, Inc., drew three checks payable to the order of Central Motors. Arizona Auto Auction's corporate name appeared twice on the printed checks: at the top-face of the checks in bold print, and again, in small print, just above the line for a signature. J. M. Cook signed each of these checks on the designated line without expressly disclosing his representative capacity.

Central Motors deposited the checks in its bank, Valley National, and withdrew the funds. Valley National initiated collection procedures, but a stop-payment order was placed on the checks by Arizona Auto, and the checks were returned to Valley National. Valley National initiated this lawsuit because it was unable to collect from its customer, Central Motors. In its capacity as a HIDC, it got a judgment against Arizona Auto, but not against J. M. Cook personally. It appealed from the trial judgment in favor of Cook.

DECISION

Examining the instrument as a whole, and especially in view of the face (1) that the corporate principal was named, (2) that Cook did not make any personal guarantee, and (3) that this officer, authorized to sign by corporate by-laws and resolutions, issued the check on a company account for a company debt, the appellate court concluded that Cook had no personal liability.

The decision turned in part on "business expectations." Distinguishing between notes and checks, the court related that it would be in keeping with common practice for creditors of small firms to demand that their officers incur a personal obligation on credit instruments like promissory notes, but that the business community would not have the same expectations on corporate checks.

Valley Nat'l Bank v. Cook, 665 P.2d 576 (Ariz. App. 1983)

► Special Relationships

Accommodation Party An **accommodation party** may be primarily or secondarily liable. This depends on whether the party signs as an accommodation maker, accommodation drawer, accommodation acceptor, or accommodation indorser.[38] The purpose of such a signature is to lend the name and financial resources of the accommodation

accommodation party
A person who signs commercial paper as an accommodation to another person whose signature is on the instrument for the purpose of assisting the latter to obtain credit

[36]UCC 1–201(5).

[37]UCC 3–302.

[38]UCC 3–415(2).

party to the instrument. The accommodation maker and acceptor are primarily liable. The accommodation drawer and indorser are secondarily liable.

An accommodation *maker,* for example, signs as an inducement to a third person to make a loan or to sell on credit to the one who is actually receiving the benefit of the transaction. The signature of an accommodation maker is part of the consideration received by the third person to encourage the third person to enter into the transaction. There are many variations on this theme. Suppose *D* wishes to buy goods on credit from *C,* but *D*'s credit is poor. *A*'s credit is good. *C* wishes to have *A* liable on the note as an accommodation maker for *D,* and to have *D* liable as the payee indorser as well. So *A* signs as an accommodation maker of a note with *D* as the payee. *D* indorses and delivers the note to *C,* who now sells the goods on credit to *D.*

The instrument may be signed by an accommodation *indorser* along with a payee who indorses, or along with a subsequent indorser. The purpose of the accommodation indorsement is to promote the acceptability or marketability of the instrument because of the accommodation indorser's liability on the instrument. Other things being equal, an instrument with an accommodation indorsement is more attractive to potential purchasers than one without such an indorsement. It supplies an additional secondary party to whom the holder may turn following presentment, dishonor, and notice.

The accommodation party is never liable to the party accommodated.[39] In the event an accommodation maker is required to pay the instrument, the accommodation maker can recover from the *accommodated* party.

The same is true of an accommodation indorser. The accommodation indorser who is required to pay the instrument, has a right to recover such payment from the accommodated indorser or from any prior person who has become liable as a secondary party.

Guarantor A person who uses the words "payment guaranteed" or an equivalent phrase with that person's signature is bound according to the terms of the instrument if it is not voluntarily paid at maturity. There is no need for the holder to pursue or to give notice to any other party.[40]

A person may undertake a less demanding guaranty obligation by merely guaranteeing collection. "Collection guaranteed" obligates the signer only if the primary party is insolvent or if the holder has gone into court and received a judgment on the instrument and is now unable to collect on the judgment.[41]

Words of guaranty will be interpreted to mean that *payment* is guaranteed unless collection is specified. Any words of guaranty make unnecessary presentment, dishonor, and notice, which are normally required before secondary parties become liable on their indorsement contracts.[42]

---

[39]UCC 3–415(5).

[40]UCC 3–416(1).

[41]UCC 3–416(2).

[42]UCC 3–416(5).

The Banking Process

▶ Depositary Bank

The first bank in which one deposits a check to begin the collection process is the **depositary bank.**[43] (Figure 29.8 diagrams the entire collection process.) The first bank may also be the drawee-payor bank. The depositor will receive a provisional or temporary credit in his or her checking account, and the item will be forwarded to the next bank for collection. If the check does not bounce within a prescribed deadline—i.e., if it is not returned to the depositary bank or if notice is not sent to the depositary bank

depositary bank
"The first bank to which an item is transferred for collection even though it is also the payor bank" UCC 4–105(a)

FIGURE 29.8 **Diagram of Check Collection Process**

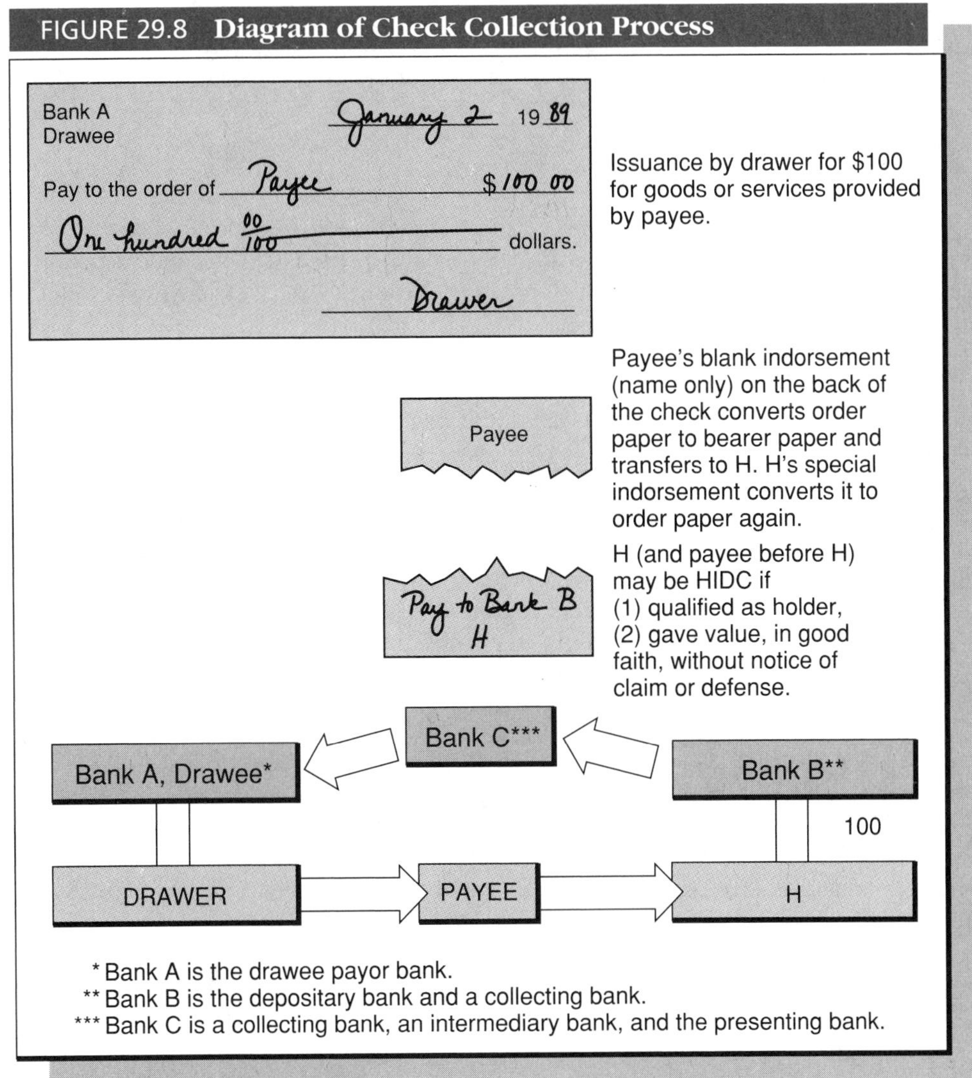
Bank A
Drawee
January 2 19 89
Pay to the order of Payee $100 00
One hundred 00/100 dollars.
Drawer
Issuance by drawer for $100 for goods or services provided by payee.
Payee
Payee's blank indorsement (name only) on the back of the check converts order paper to bearer paper and transfers to H. H's special indorsement converts it to order paper again.
Pay to Bank B
H
H (and payee before H) may be HIDC if
(1) qualified as holder,
(2) gave value, in good faith, without notice of claim or defense.
Bank C***
Bank A, Drawee*
Bank B**
100
DRAWER
PAYEE
H
* Bank A is the drawee payor bank.
** Bank B is the depositary bank and a collecting bank.
*** Bank C is a collecting bank, an intermediary bank, and the presenting bank.

[43] UCC 4–105(a).

that there are "not sufficient funds" to pay the check or that payment has been "stopped"—the provisional credit will be made final. If the check is properly returned or if notice is sent within the deadline, the depositary bank will reverse the provisional credit.

Remember, from the depositor's point of view, the depositary bank in which the depositor has an account is the drawee bank. Whenever this depositor writes a check, he or she will be drawing on this account and ordering the depositor's drawee bank to pay money to a payee.

The depositary bank could give value and perhaps become an HIDC if it allowed its customer-depositor to cash another person's check or to withdraw funds represented by another's check before the collection process was completed. Of course, the depositary bank would have to meet all the requirements for becoming an HIDC in addition to giving value. This could become very important if the other person's check bounced and, instead of proceeding against its own depositor-customer, the bank chose to pursue the drawer.

► Payor Bank

payor bank
"A bank by which an item is payable as drawn or accepted" UCC 4–105(b)

In the check collection process, items are transferred from the depositary bank through intermediary banks to the **payor bank.** The payor bank holds the checking account of the drawer. From the point of view of the drawer, the payor bank is synonymous with the drawee,[44] as is illustrated in Figure 29.8.

Assuming that there are sufficient funds on deposit in the drawer's account, the item will be paid and the depositor's account will be debited or charged. If funds are not sufficient or if payment has been stopped, the item will be returned to the depositary bank.

When a check reaches the payor bank through collection channels, it has until the midnight deadline[45]—midnight on the next banking day following receipt of an item—to decide whether to pay or to return the check. If the payor bank fails to examine its customer's account within the allotted time, and it discovers after the midnight deadline has passed that there are not sufficient funds to pay the check, the payor bank will be accountable for the amount of the item to the collecting banks.[46] It is penalized for failing to act within the prescribed time limits established by law. The payor bank then has recourse against its customer, the person who overdrew his or her account.[47]

Keep in mind that some drafts are not drawn on bank-drawees—e.g., a trade acceptance. In that case the payor may be an individual or a business firm.

► Collecting Banks

collecting bank
"Any bank handling the item for collection except the payor bank" UCC 4–105(d)

This term includes all banks, even the depositary bank, forwarding a check for collection to a payor bank.[48] It does not include the payor bank.

---

[44]UCC 4–105(b).

[45]UCC 4–104(h).

[46]UCC 4–302(a).

[47]UCC 4–401(1).

[48]UCC 4–105(d).

Presenting Bank

This is the last bank in the collection process. It turns the check over to a payor bank for final disposition.[49]

presenting bank
"Any bank presenting an item except a payor bank"
UCC 4–105(e)

Intermediary Bank

Intermediary banks are "in between" the depositary and the payor banks. Neither the depositary nor the payor bank is included, but the presenting bank does fall within the definition.[50]

intermediary bank
"Any bank to which an item is transferred in course of collection except the depositary or payor bank" UCC 4–105(c)

Formal Requisites of Negotiable Instruments

"Commercial paper" may be negotiable or nonnegotiable. We are primarily interested in the negotiable instrument. If the instrument is not negotiable, it is still valid and enforceable as a contract, but no one can become an HIDC.

The basic elements that are common to all negotiable instruments were introduced briefly in the discussion of the various types of instrument. The final portion of this chapter will deal with each of these components in detail:

1. *Written and signed.* The instrument must be in writing and signed by the maker or drawer.
2. *Unconditional promise or order—sum certain in money.* Each instrument must contain an unconditional promise or order to pay a sum certain in money.
3. *Demand or definite time.* The time of payment must be on demand or at a definite time.
4. *Order or bearer.* Each instrument must be payable to order or to bearer.[51]

Written

Oral contracts to pay money may or may not be enforceable, depending on the statute of frauds and its exceptions. Negotiable instruments, however, must be in writing.

Writing includes printing, typewriting, handwriting, or any other method of committing words to paper. The UCC permits the writing to be on anything, but as a practical matter, the writing will be on a convenient-to-handle printed form. Writing in pencil is permissible, but most prudent people will guard against that because of the opportunities for fraudulent material alteration of the instrument.

Signed

The signature of the maker or drawer may be written at any place on the instrument. Usually it appears at the bottom-right of the paper, but it may be incorporated in the language of the instrument itself. For example, a *handwritten* negotiable note may recite that "I, Jane Rhymes, promise to pay $100 to bearer on demand." Here Rhymes is clearly identified as the maker who engages or undertakes to pay. Unless clearly identified as a

---

[49] UCC 4–105(e).

[50] UCC 4–105(c).

[51] UCC 3–104(1).

maker, drawer, or acceptor, the person who signs will be treated as a secondary party indorser.[52]

The signature may consist of any mark, stamp, or symbol adopted by a party with a present intention to authenticate the writing.[53] It could be an X mark, for example, if it is the genuine intention of the signer to use such a symbol for this purpose.

Marks and symbols present practical problems. All X marks are basically alike, whereas a signature is a highly individualized symbol associated and identified with only one person. A payee of a note or draft may be quite satisfied upon witnessing Wayne Mondy, as maker or drawer, authenticate an instrument with an X. However, if the payee attempts to negotiate such an instrument to a third party, particularly one who was not present at the original transaction, that party may decline to pay out hard-earned cash for an instrument signed with an X.[54] If you were the third party, would you have any reluctance?

Signature by Authorized Agent or Representative A person's signature may be placed on the instrument by an authorized agent in a manner that obligates only the principal. If it is the intention of an agent operating within the scope of the agent's authority to obligate the principal alone, the agent should do one of the following:

1. Sign the name of the principal, but not the agent's own name.
2. Disclose the principal and clearly show that the agent is signing in a representative capacity.[55]

For example, if Lane Feazel is the authorized agent of World Services, Inc., he can obligate *only* his employer by signing in these examples:

1. "World Services, Inc."
2. "World Services, Inc., by Lane Feazel, Secretary-Treasurer," or "Lane Feazel, Secretary-Treasurer for World Services, Inc."[56]

One can feel confident that personal liability is avoided by following alternative 1 above because a person cannot be held liable on the instrument unless his or her signature appears on it.[57]

If a signature appears, even though it may be forged or unauthorized, the actual signer is personally liable. Forgers and unauthorized signers are, thus, personally liable even though their *real* signatures do not appear at all;[58] the improper signature becomes

---

[52]UCC 3–402.

[53]UCC 1–201(39).

[54]Some states require that a person who is capable of signing place his or her signature on the instrument as a witness.

[55]UCC 3–403(2)(b).

[56]UCC 3–403(3).

[57]UCC 3–401(1).

[58]UCC 3–404(1).

that of the person who wrongfully signed. For example, if the payee is Jones, and Smith forged Jones' signature as indorser, Smith is now liable as an indorser.

If the authorized agent follows alternative 2 above, the agent can obligate the principal only by disclosing the name of the principal before or after the name and office of the agent. For example, when agent *A* puts his own name on an instrument, he simply invites problems upon himself unless he both (a) discloses the principal and (b) clearly shows his representative capacity. In the event he does only one of these things, the agent may prove his representative capacity by parol evidence if he is being sued by an "immediate party"—for example, a payee.[59]

No such opportunity for defense will be available against one who is not an immediate party. The reason for this rule is that these parties, who were not present at the original transaction, are entitled to assume that there are two parties liable on the instrument—the principal, and the agent who did not take appropriate steps to show that he or she is operating in a representative capacity.

As a practical matter, it makes a great deal of sense to take precautionary measures that can avoid a lawsuit in the first place. Even those suits that are eventually won involve the expenditure of a great deal of time, money, and anxiety in the process.

► The Promise or Order

The Promise The promise contained on the face of a note to pay money simply discloses an intention to be bound or an engagement to pay. Synonyms such as "undertake" or "obligate" or "engage" would do just as well,[60] but when important sums of money are in the balance, why invite litigation by using such unusual terms?

Since most of the instruments that you will be called upon to sign are printed forms anyway, this does not present much of a problem. The word "promise" is typically used, and there is no necessity to discuss the matter.

Remember, however, that a mere acknowledgment of a sum due or payable in the future—"IOU $100, [signed] John Bonhomme"—while legal, enforceable, and assignable under the law of contracts, is not a sufficient promise under the Code and cannot be a negotiable instrument.

The Order An order is an instruction or direction to pay, issued by the drawer to the drawee.[61] For example, in every check the drawer orders the drawee bank to pay money. The drawer is entitled to do this because the relationship between the depositor and the drawee bank is creditor/debtor. The drawee is the drawer's debtor to the extent of the drawer's checking account balance. The contractual arrangement was agreed to when the drawer-depositor first opened that checking account.

The instruction, direction, or order must be more than a mere request or authorization. In other words, it must leave nothing to the discretion of the drawee. For example, on a check the first word addressed to the drawee bank is "Pay." The drawee must be identified with reasonable certainty, and may be addressed with words of courtesy—for example, "Please pay." The instrument in the following case was not payable to order or to bearer and, therefore, the holder could not be an HIDC.

[59]UCC 3–403(2)(b).

[60]UCC 3–104, comment 5.

[61]UCC 3–102(1)(b).

FACTS

Plaintiff, a law partnership, claims to be an HIDC of a negotiable instrument in the form of a letter given to it by a former client. The letter read in part as follows: "I agree to pay to your firm as attorney's fees for representing me in obtaining property settlement (and other matters), the sum of $2,760 (payable in installments). [signed] Barbara Hall Hodge." The defendant responded with defenses that are effective against plaintiff unless (a) the instrument is negotiable and (b) the plaintiff is an HIDC.

DECISION

Judgment for defendant. "One of the requirements of a negotiable instrument is that it contain the time honored 'words of negotiability,' such as pay to the order of or pay to bearer. This was inherent in our law prior to the enactment of the Commercial Code. . . . The Commercial Code continues this practice by now stating: 'Any writing to be a negotiable instrument within this Article must . . . be payable to order or to bearer.' 3–104(1)(d). . . . In the absence of such language, [the letter] would not be a negotiable instrument. . . .

"Furthermore, even a holder in due course takes the instrument free of all defenses *only* 'of any party to the instrument with whom the holder has not dealt.' 3–305(2). . . . Here, the plaintiffs failed to show they occupied the status of a holder in due course, or to establish they were not a party with whom the defendant dealt in this transaction."

Hall v. Westmoreland, Hall & Bryan, 182 S.E.2d 539 (Ga. 1971).

Unconditional The promise or order must be absolute, unconditional, and ironclad. It must be a general and unreserved commitment on the maker's or drawer's resources—no condition, escape clauses, or cop-outs.

Anything less than a full and total dedication of the maker's or drawer's financial strength would destroy the instrument's unique capacity to function as a substitute for money or as a credit device. It is obvious that potential purchasers of commercial paper would be less willing to spend their money on instruments that are hedged with excuses and alibis than on instruments that are not so limited.

FACTS

Radec, a general contractor on a construction project, became aware that one of its subcontractors, Carpet Center, was in financial trouble. To assist Carpet Center, and to assure that the job was completed on schedule, Radec advanced Carpet Center an $8700 check on the strength of certain oral promises and conditions agreed to between them. On the check itself, in the lower left-hand corner following the printed word "Memo," Radec wrote the following: "Payee must prove clear title to material."

Carpet Center deposited the check and was paid, despite the fact that the promises and conditions alluded to in the memo were not met. Radec stopped payment when it learned of this breach, and the check was returned to the Western Bank. By this time, Carpet Center had become insolvent, so Western instituted suit against Radec claiming to be a HIDC of a negotiable instrument. It was successful in the trial court despite Radec's defense that the memo rendered the check nonnegotiable.

DECISION

Radec's written memo did not insert a condition on the order to pay, and did not render the check nonnegotiable. In affirming the decision in favor of Western Bank, the court concluded that the memo was "nothing more than a self-serving declaration by Radec for its own benefit and recordkeeping. . . . An otherwise unconditional instrument cannot be rendered conditional by such a device."

Western Bank v. Radec Constr. Co., Inc., 42 UCC Rep. 1340 (S.D. 1986).

Only *express* conditions destroy negotiability. Implied conditions do not. Nor is negotiability affected by the mere mention of, or reference to, the underlying consideration which supports the original contract.[62] For example, "I promise to pay $1,000 to the order of J. T. Bain on demand, subject to his faithful performance of Contract #61382. [signed] Merrill Goodwyn." The express condition, "subject to his faithful performance of Contract #61382," makes the promise conditional and destroys negotiability.

One must be able to determine from the face of the instrument whether the commitment to pay is absolute and unconditional.[63] The above promise does not measure up to the standard of negotiability because the maker is entitled to avoid payment if the contract is not performed, and whether or not performance has occurred cannot be determined from the face of the instrument. The fact that Bain may have actually performed the contract does not make the instrument negotiable because that fact cannot be determined by examining the instrument.

Consider, however, a modification of the above note that simply mentioned that it was given in return for, or in consideration of, or in reference to, Contract #61382. One might say there was an implied condition that the maker not be liable contractually if Bain failed to perform, but this does not destroy negotiability.

If Bain does not perform the underlying transaction referred to, that is a matter to be taken up *outside* the scope of the negotiable instrument. The maker or drawer is absolutely committed on the instrument despite the implied condition that the payee may not perform and the maker or drawer may later have to sue the payee for breach of contract.

A statement in an instrument that it is secured—by a mortgage or in some other way—does not destroy negotiability.[64] This operates to the creditor-holder's benefit and simply adds to the salability or marketability of the instrument.

If, for purposes of bookkeeping convenience, the instrument mentions a particular fund to be debited or charged, negotiability is not affected.[65] This rule favoring negotiability holds true for commercial paper that is limited to a particular fund backed by a governmental unit or limited to payment from the entire assets of a partnership, unincorporated association, trust, or estate.[66] It is assumed that instruments issued by these entities will carry sufficient assurance of payment to encourage their acceptability.

Keep in mind that instruments expressly made subject to, or governed by, some other agreement—e.g., subject to Contract #61382—are not negotiable. Neither are instruments that are strictly limited to payment out of a particular fund.[67]

To illustrate: if Jack Sorenson limits or restricts payment of his note to "the proceeds from next year's corn crop," the instrument would be nonnegotiable. His general credit is not committed to payment, and no one can tell from examining the face of the note

---

[62]UCC 3–105(1)(b)(c).

[63]If an instrument states that it is void if drawn for more than a particular amount or void if presented for payment after a particular date, negotiability is *not* destroyed because that condition can be determined from the face of the instrument.

[64]UCC 3–105(e).

[65]UCC 3–105(f).

[66]UCC 3–105(h).

[67]UCC 3–105(2).

whether "next year's corn crop" will even be planted, much less whether it will be sufficient to pay the note.

A governmental unit can limit its obligation to payment out of a particular fund without affecting negotiability because it is assumed that tax revenues will always be sufficient. A similar exception is made in favor of instruments by partnerships, unincorporated associations, trusts, and estates when all their assets are committed.

► Sum Certain in Money

Sum Certain No serious buyer or investor wants to play guessing games on the amount of money involved. As a general rule, the sum is sufficiently certain if, at the time of payment, it can be computed from the information that appears on the face of the instrument.[68] This means that the sum certain is *unaffected* by the following:

1. Payment with interest or in installments.
2. Payment with interest at different rates before and after default.
3. Payment with a discount before a fixed date or with an addition afterward.
4. Payment with (or less) foreign exchange rates to protect the constant value of an instrument.
5. Payment with collection or attorney's fees in the event of default in payment.[69]

Keep in mind that the crucial time is the time of payment, and the computations must be made from what appears on the face of the instrument. It cannot be known at the time of issuance whether there will be a default, whether payment will be accelerated, or whether an attorney or collection agency will be needed; but these facts will be available at the time of payment.

An instrument with interest payable at the legal rate or judgment rate, as fixed by state law, is negotiable even though the actual rate of interest is not specified. An interest term that calls for application of the bank rate or current rate, however, does not satisfy the requirement of sum certain, as the next case illustrates.

FACTS

Olde Towne Investment Corporation issued a promissory note to VMC Mortgage Company in return for a real estate loan. The terms of the note required repayment of the principal amount plus interest of "3% over Chase Manhattan Prime to be adjusted monthly." VMC used this note as security for a loan it received from a pension fund, but Olde Towne had no knowledge of this transaction or of the transfer of the note. At maturity, Olde Towne paid the full amount to VMC. It was then entitled to a return of the note marked cancelled, but this was not done. Later, VMC went bankrupt, and the pension fund, through its representative Roeder, sought to exercise the rights of a HIDC and compel Olde Towne to pay the note a second time.

DECISION

Roeder, on behalf of the pension fund, cannot exert HIDC status because the instrument is not negotiable. While variable interest rates are becoming more and more common, and may make a great deal of business sense, such rates prevent the computation of the amount pay-

[68] UCC 3–106, comment 1.

[69] UCC 3–106(1).

able from the information available on the face of the instrument. Reference to an outside source to determine the amount due at maturity makes this note nonnegotiable, therefore Olde Towne's payment to VMC is a valid defense against Roeder.

Taylor v. Roeder, 360 S.E.2d 191 (Va. 1987)

However, statutes in thirteen states overrule this case; there a sum certain includes a rate of interest established by a named financial institution.

Money Money means a medium of exchange authorized or adopted by any government as part of its currency.[70] The medium of exchange must qualify as money at the time the instrument is issued. The reason for this, of course, is to give assurance to a potential purchaser right from the start that the instrument will be paid in the currency of a recognized government.

Keep in mind that for certainty of sum, the important time is the maturity date. For the purpose of qualifying as money, however, the important time is when the instrument is issued.

Note here as well that negotiable instruments are not the equivalent of money, and that a person cannot compel another to take commercial paper in payment of debts. Generally speaking, negotiable instruments are conditional payment contingent upon being honored at maturity. The obligation on the basis of which the instrument was given is suspended pending payment of the instrument on the due date. If not paid when due, then suit may be based on the instrument or on the obligation for which the instrument was given.[71]

Unless the instrument requires otherwise, a promise or order to pay in foreign currency may be satisfied by payment at maturity of the dollar amount that the foreign currency will buy at the exchange rate. For example, an instrument payable in Belgian francs, Japanese yen, or Chilean pesos may be satisfied with the number of U.S. dollars that the foreign currency could buy at current exchange rates. If the instrument requires payment in the foreign currency, an attempt to discharge one's obligation in U.S. dollars will not be sufficient.[72]

No other promise or order except payment of money is sufficient to establish negotiability. Promises or orders of payment in seal skins, wampum, or gold dust destroy negotiability because they are not money; the money value is not readily apparent on the face of the paper. Certain other promises are permitted, without affecting negotiability, because of one thing in common—they promote acceptability and marketability of the paper.

As an example, some instruments include a term that allows the holder or creditor to **confess judgment** against the debtor when an instrument is not paid at maturity.[73] This strengthens the creditor's position by expediting enforcement of the paper upon default. The creditor can get a judgment on the unpaid instrument without giving notice of the proceedings to the debtor. Whether or not a confession of judgment is illegal has no effect on the negotiability of the instrument.

confession of judgment
A party's consent to jurisdiction and judgment of a court without a trial in a civil case

Promises that give collateral security to an instrument, promises to protect or increase collateral should it decline in value, and promises that relinquish the benefit of

[70]UCC 3–107(1).

[71]UCC 3–802(1)(b).

[72]UCC 3–107(2).

[73]UCC 3–112(d). A note with such a term is called a "cognovit note."

debtor protection laws—all add to the advantage of the holder.[74] Since they encourage and promote the flow of negotiable paper rather than impede it, the law permits these extra promises to be made.

Time of Payment

If a prospective user of a negotiable instrument cannot tell from the face of the paper when it is due, this naturally will diminish its acceptability. To encourage a ready and open market for commercial paper then, a negotiable instrument must be made payable on demand or at a definite time.

On Demand An instrument is payable on demand if it expressly states that it is payable on demand, if it calls for payment at sight or presentation, or if no time for payment is stated.[75]

A check falls into the last category—no time for payment is stated. It normally contains the date of issue but no maturity date. It is the absence of a maturity date that makes it payable on demand.

From the point of view of the maker or drawer of an instrument, the time of payment is not certain, but that is not the controlling factor. The prospective buyer or holder is the one that the law wants to encourage, and it seeks to do that by allowing that person to collect on demand. It was held in the following case that blank spaces for installment payments on a note did not cause the note to be nonnegotiable for failure to state a definite time when it was payable; it was payable on demand.

FACTS

Defendants executed four negotiable promissory notes to plaintiffs totalling $21,000. The notes specified neither time nor place of payment. The notes contained the date of issue, but each had an unfilled blank after the printed word "Due". Defendants argued that the notes were due only when they were financially able to repay the loans. Plaintiffs contended that the notes were payable on demand.

DECISION

Judgment for plaintiffs. Instruments payable upon demand include those in which no time for payment is stated. A cause of action against the maker of a demand instrument accrues upon the instrument's date, or if no date is stated, on the date of issue. A written condition that a note is payable "if and when able to pay" creates an obligation to pay it within a reasonable time.

A promissory note executed without a maturity date is deemed to be a completed demand instrument, so testimony about a contemporaneous oral condition cannot vary that term of the instrument.

Ranieri et al. v. Terzano, et al., 457 N.E.2d 906 (Ohio 1983).

Definite Time The common link among each of the following requirements for definite time is the *face of the paper*. Time of payment is definite if it can be determined from the terms appearing on the instrument itself.

The requirement of definite time is met if the instrument is payable on a fixed date, before a fixed date (frequently these are combined as "on or before 31 December 1999,"

---

[74]UCC 3–112(b)(c)(e).

[75]UCC 3–108.

for example), or a fixed period after a fixed date (one year from the date of the instrument).[76] A term that recites that the paper is payable "on or before the expiration of one year from the date of issue" sets a maximum length of time but allows the maker or drawer to make payment before the end of a full year and thereby save money on interest.

The requirement for certainty of time is also satisfied if the instrument is payable "a fixed period after sight" or "a fixed period after acceptance."[77] This can be very useful in a sales transaction that allows an extended credit period to the buyer—i.e., the drawee on a trade acceptance drawn by the seller. The draft will be presented to the buyer-drawee by the seller or the seller's agent; if the buyer properly "accepts" the instrument by signing it and returning it to the seller, the goods will be delivered to the buyer. The seller keeps possession of the negotiable instrument; then, when the fixed period after sight or acceptance expires, the seller presents the instrument to the buyer for payment.

If maturity of an instrument is made to depend on an act or event uncertain as to time of occurrence, the time requirement is not satisfied even though the event later occurs.[78] Examples are promises to pay when a person attains a stated age, when a certain building is built, or on the death or marriage of a certain person. The standard, once more, is the *face* of the paper. If time is not certain on the face of the instrument, then time is not certain for purposes of negotiability, as the following case illustrates.

FACTS

The Faulkners executed a $25,000 promissory note to Miller and Rotert. Installments on the note were to become due "one month after Miller's death." In return for services rendered to Miller, he wrote "Paid in Full" on the face of the note. Rotert claims that the Faulkners owe him the full face value plus interest since 3–116 (b) of the UCC permits a discharge of debtors, such as the Faulkners, only by all of the payee/creditors (Miller and Rotert, not Miller alone).

DECISION

Judgment of the trial court favoring Rotert for full value of the note plus interest was reduced to one-half of that amount. This note was not negotiable because the due date could not be determined from its face, UCC 3–109 (2). Since UCC 3–116 requiring both payees to join in discharge applies to *negotiable instruments only,* the lower court should have given the Faulkners credit for having discharged one-half of their obligation on this nonnegotiable note.

Rotert v. Faulkner, 660 S.W.2d 463 (Mo. App. 1983).

Acceleration Clauses The Code approves of a definite time subject to any acceleration.[79] Normally the holder of an instrument is given the option of accelerating time of payment if the debtor defaults on an installment. The reason behind this rule is that the debtor "brings it upon him- or herself" by not living up to the agreement and

---

[76]UCC 3–109(1)(a).

[77]UCC 3–109(1)(b).

[78]UCC 3–109(2).

[79]UCC 3–109(c).

this is a reasonable way of assuring the creditor that appropriate protective action can be taken.

Other acceleration clauses allow the holder to declare the full amount to be due and payable at any time the holder in good faith feels insecure.[80] This term is not particularly advantageous to the debtor, but the debtor may not be given any choice in the matter—"take it or leave it" is the only option. For purposes of negotiability, such acceleration clauses do not destroy certainty of time.

Extension Clauses Clauses that give the debtor an additional period of time for payment are extension clauses and are just the opposite of acceleration clauses. They are permitted on the following terms:

1. At the option of the holder (this simply means that the creditor-holder can give the debtor more time to pay if the holder so chooses).
2. At the option of the maker or acceptor to a further definite time (except for this limitation, enforceability of the paper could be frustrated indefinitely).
3. Automatically upon the happening of a specified event (for example, "maturity shall be extended by one year, if crop yields fall below eighty bushels per acre").[81]

► The Words of Negotiability: To Order or To Bearer

Unless an instrument contains one of the "magic words" of negotiability—"to order of," "to bearer," or the equivalent—it is not negotiable and can be transferred only by assignment. "Pay to the order of *A*" is different from "Pay to *A*," the latter phrase causing the instrument to be nonnegotiable.

FACTS

Donna and Robert Andersen signed and delivered two promissory notes to Great Lakes Nursery Corporation as part of a franchise agreement. The notes read, in part, that the Andersens "promise to pay Great Lakes Nursery" $6400 in monthly installments. The nursery transferred the note to First Investment Company. Later, the Andersens stopped making installment payments on grounds of an alleged breach of the franchise contract by Great Lakes. First Investment argues that the breach of contract defense is not valid because it is a HIDC.

DECISION

In order to qualify as negotiable, "words of negotiability" such as "pay to the order" or "pay to bearer" must be used. Since these formalities were not observed, the instrument is not negotiable and may be transferred by assignment only. No one, including First Investment, can be a HIDC if the note is nonnegotiable. The Andersens' defense against the Nursery is valid against First Investment also.

First Investment Corp. v. Andersen, 621 P.2d 683 (Utah 1980).

To Bearer An instrument is payable to bearer when the terms specify "bearer," or "the order of bearer."[82] The latter phrase, "the order of bearer," normally occurs on a form that is printed to read "Pay to the order of ______," and the word "bearer" is inserted

---

[80] UCC 1–208.

[81] UCC 3–109(1)(d).

[82] UCC 3–111(a).

in the blank space. Until the space is filled in, the paper is incomplete in a necessary respect and, therefore, is nonnegotiable and unenforceable.[83]

The instrument is payable to bearer if the paper reads "Pay to Cash," or "Pay to the order of Cash," or any other word besides "cash" that does not designate a payee capable of making a signature.[84] An instrument that reads "Pay to the order of One Keg of Beer" or "Pay to Two Crates of Pop" shows that the maker or drawer is not interested in having a "payee" indorse! If the "payee" or the object designated instead of a payee is not capable of indorsing, then the instrument becomes payable to bearer.

Another illustration of bearer paper is one that names "a specified person or bearer" as payee.[85] The bearer provision takes precedence, and it is a bearer instrument—for example, "Pay to the order of John Jones or bearer."

When an instrument is order paper either on its face, or because of a special indorsement—for example, "Pay to *A,* [signed] Payee"—a subsequent blank indorsement, which consists only of the signature of the indorser—for example, "*A*" changes the instrument to bearer paper.[86]

To Order An instrument meets this requirement when it is payable to the order, or to the assigns, of any person reasonably identified, or to that person or that person's order[87]—for example, "Pay to the order of *A,*" or "Pay to *A* or *A*'s order." This indicates that the maker of the note or drawer of the draft intends that the payee be able to negotiate the instrument to some other party. An instrument on its face reading "Pay to Lee Young" is nonnegotiable; the words "order of" or "bearer" are missing.

On all drafts, the drawer first orders the drawee to pay money. To take the process a second step, the drawee may be ordered to pay "to the order of Rich Soland"—i.e., to the named payee Rich Soland or to whomever the payee may indicate in his indorsement.

If Rich Soland to whom the instrument flows indorses in blank with only his name, then the drawee will be directed to pay the bearer—i.e., the holder, of the instrument. If he indorses specifically, "Pay to Fran Zappa, [signed] Rich Soland," the drawee will be directed to pay the named indorsee.

Instruments may be made payable to the order of the following payees:

1. The maker or drawer; for example, the seller who is the drawer of a trade acceptance may name him- or herself as payee, or the drawer of a check may name him- or herself as payee.
2. The drawee; for example, the drawer of a check in paying a debt that the drawer owes to the drawee bank will name the drawee bank as payee.
3. A payee who is not a maker, drawer, or drawee (this covers the great majority of transactions).
4. Two or more payees *jointly*—for example, *A and B*—or two or more payees in the alternative—for example, *A or B.*

[83]UCC 3–805.

[84]UCC 3–111(c).

[85]UCC 3–111(b).

[86]UCC 3–204(2).

[87]UCC 3–110(1).

5. An estate, trust, or fund (in this event, the instrument is payable to the order of the representative—for example, a check payable to the order of United Fund would be treated as payable to the order of its authorized agent, perhaps the treasurer, who would indorse on behalf of the fund).
6. An office or officer by his title, in which event it is payable to the incumbent officer or his successor; for example, Travis County Tax Collector.
7. A partnership or unincorporated association.[88]

An instrument made payable both to order *and* to bearer is payable to order unless the "bearer" word is handwritten or typewritten. The reason for this is that on a printed form, "Pay to the order of ______ or bearer," the word "bearer" is likely to be overlooked when the name of a payee is inserted. To avoid an unintended result, the paper will be bearer paper only if the drawer or maker has shown that that is the desired objective by writing in the word "bearer."[89]

Summary Statement

1. Negotiable instruments are either notes or drafts. Notes are two-party instruments in which a maker-primary party promises to pay money to a payee. Drafts are three-party instruments in which the party who creates the draft (the drawer) orders the drawee to pay money to a payee.
2. A certificate of deposit is a special kind of note in which a bank borrows money from a customer, acknowledges receipt of it, and promises to repay. This is a reversal of the norm because usually the customer is borrowing from the bank.
3. A check is a special kind of draft that is drawn on a bank and payable on demand.
4. Frequently you come across a trade acceptance and a banker's acceptance in the financing of sales transactions. These are simply drafts drawn by the seller on the drawee, who is either the buyer or the buyer's bank, payable to the order of a payee. These drafts usually give the buyer some time or credit period in which to pay. Typically, the buyer or the buyer's bank will accept by signing the draft and returning it to the seller; the goods being sold on credit will be turned over to the buyer at that point, and at the end of the credit period the instrument will be presented to the acceptor for payment.
5. Notice that the drawee becomes a primary party when the drawee accepts the instrument by signing it. A check will have the drawee bank as a primary party only if the bank certifies the check.
6. Primary parties are makers of negotiable notes and acceptors of drafts. As a general rule, everyone else who signs an instrument is a secondary party.
7. Watch out for accommodation parties, however. An accommodation party may be an accommodation *maker* or an accommodation *acceptor,* in which event the accommodation party would be a primary party; or the accommodation party may be an accommodation *drawer* or *indorser,* and thus be a secondary party.

[88]UCC 3–110(1).

[89]UCC 3–110(3).

8. Primary parties are absolutely liable on the instrument according to its terms. Secondary parties expect to be called upon to pay only if, at maturity, the instrument is properly presented, dishonored, and notice of dishonor is given to the secondary party.
9. Other important parties are the *bearer* (a person in possession of bearer paper) and the *holder* (a person who must be in possession of an instrument that has been drawn, issued, or indorsed to him or her, or who is in possession of bearer paper). HIDCs are holders who have, in addition, given value, in good faith, and without (a) notice of a claim or defense, or (b) notice that the instrument is overdue or has been dishonored.
10. In the collection process, the banks with which one most frequently comes in contact are depositary banks—the first bank to receive a check and initiate the bank collection process—and the payor-drawee bank. The payor-drawee is the bank at the end of the line. It pays the check if its customer-depositor has sufficient funds on account and has not issued a stop-payment order; otherwise it returns the check by its midnight deadline to avoid being held accountable for it.
11. It is important to remember that any kind of writing will do—pen, pencil, typewriter, or some other form. The signatures can be written by an authorized representative as well as by the person who actually becomes a party on the instrument. It is crucial, however, that the signature, whether it be in the form of an X mark or a written name, actually be intended to validate the paper.
12. The instrument must not have any express conditions to the liability of the person creating it. Otherwise no one is likely to be willing to accept it as a credit device or as a substitute for money. Keep in mind that the holder must be able to determine from the *face* of the instrument that the person who issued it has absolutely committed his or her general credit to payment at maturity.
13. The money that is designated on the draft or note must be backed up by a recognized government, and the amount must be certain. The reason for this is to assure the prospective purchaser that he or she is receiving something of value.
14. From the *holder's* point of view, the time of payment must be certain. This requirement can be satisfied by maturity on a fixed date, before that date, a fixed time after a fixed date, a fixed date subject to *any* acceleration, and a fixed date with *some* extensions of time. It may be a bit confusing that demand instruments satisfy the time requirement; but remember, it is the holder who must be induced to accept these instruments. From that perspective, time is certain, and the person who issued the instrument must simply contend with this feature.
15. Every negotiable instrument must contain the "magic" words of negotiability—"to order," "to bearer," or their equivalents. This permits the payee or the holder to whom the instrument is first issued to negotiate it to some other party. That party may subsequently hold the instrument to maturity or further negotiate it to someone else.

In the following case a check was wrongfully dishonored by the drawee bank and the court had to decide when the statute of limitations began to run against the drawer.

TEPPER v. CITIZENS FEDERAL SAVINGS AND LOAN ASSOCIATION
448 So.2d 1138 (Fla. 1984)

Ferguson J. The sole question presented is when does the statute of limitations begin to run against a drawer in an action for wrongful dishonor of a check—on the date of issuance of the check or the date of presentment and dishonor?

Rose Tepper (appellant) was adjudicated an incompetent in December, 1982. On examination of her personal effects, a court-appointed guardian discovered a check for the sum of $6,068, dated January 4, 1974. The check was drawn to Rose Tepper by Citizens Federal Savings and Loan Association against its account with Jefferson National Bank.

On December 20, 1982, appellant's representative presented the check to the drawee bank, Jefferson National (not a party to this action), which refused payment. The representative then advised the drawer, Citizens Federal (appellee), of the dishonor. Citizens Federal orally notified appellant's representative that it would neither honor nor refund the instrument. The guardian instituted this action against the drawer on July 12, 1983.

The trial court dismissed the guardian's complaint on appellee's motion, holding that "the statute of limitations began to run on the date of issuance of the check herein sued upon, [so the] action is barred by the applicable five year statue of limitations." We reverse upon a holding that the statute of limitations begins to run against a drawer of a check on the date of presentment and dishonor.

A draft is a three-party instrument whereby the drawer orders the drawee to pay money to the payee. A draft is also called a check when the drawee is a bank and the instrument is payable on demand. A drawee is not liable on the instrument until there has been an acceptance. The drawee may, by accepting in writing on the instrument, agree to honor it as presented. By contrast, a drawee may reject the instrument, as by stamping insufficient funds on a check where the drawer's deposited funds are less than the amount of the instrument. The act of accepting the instrument renders the drawee primarily liable as an acceptor. Because there are no conditions precedent to its liability, a cause of action accrues against an acceptor in the case of a demand instrument on the date of the instrument or date of issue.

The drawer, on the other hand, is only secondarily liable on the instrument, in that there are conditions precedent to liability. The normal conditions precedent include presentment to the drawee, dishonor, and notice of dishonor. Therefore, a cause of action against the drawer of a draft accrues only upon demand following dishonor of the instrument. Notice of dishonor constitutes a demand. This latter section is clearly dispositive of the issue presented, as a cause of action against the drawer herein, Citizens Federal, thus did not accrue until appellant's representative received notice of dishonor from the drawee, Jefferson National Bank.

A cashier's check is a check on which the issuing bank acts as both the drawer and the drawee. Its own act of issuance renders the bank a drawee who has accepted the draft; thus the issuing bank becomes primarily liable as an acceptor. Presentment of a negotiable instrument is not necessary in order to establish liability against parties who are primarily liable. In such a case the statute of limitations begins to run on a demand instrument at the moment of issuance. As to parties secondarily liable, however, such as the drawer herein, there is no instant liability and thus no cause of action until demand following presentment and dishonor.

The distinction between a cashier's check where the issuing bank is primarily liable and other drafts, where the drawer is secondarily liable, is stated:

> [U]nder the Code, a cause of action against a certifying bank or a bank issuing a cashier's check accrues on the date of the check (or date of issue if the check is undated). This means that the statute of limitations begins to run at that time and suit against the bank will be barred after the statute of limitations has run. But a cause of action against a drawer of a check does not accrue until demand following dishonor. This theoretically means that the time for bringing action against the drawer may be deferred indefinitely if there is no presentment for payment.

Under Florida law an action may not be deferred indefinitely in all instances; instead, a drawer will be discharged from its liability if presentment is unreasonably delayed and the drawee bank becomes insolvent during the delay.

In that appellee herein was the drawer of the instrument which is the subject of this action, and therefore only secondarily liable, a cause of action did not accrue against it until after demand following presentment and dishonor on December 20, 1982. The action for wrongful dishonor of the instrument was commenced timely.

[Reversed, for appellant's representative.]

Questions and Case Problems

1. Defendant, McManus, signed a note of the corporation that employed him. His signature and that of another officer followed the stamped name of the corporation, but there was no designation of a representative capacity. McManus is being sued personally by the payee. Discuss the outcome. Would your answer be the same if McManus were being sued by an HIDC who took the instrument by negotiation from the payee? What if the payee negotiated the note to someone who did not qualify as an HIDC? Could that person get a judgment against McManus? [*Leahy v. McManus,* 206 A.2d 688 (Md. 1965).]

2. Assume that Jessica Taylor sees a $100 coat that she wants to purchase at Foxy Fashions. When she opens her personalized check book supplied by her bank, Capital State, she discovers that there are no more blank checks left in the book. Before the sales clerk can object, Jessica simply writes on a piece of scratch paper, as illustrated in Figure 29.9. The sales clerk consults the manager, who refuses to accept Jessica's "check."

a) Is this really a check?
b) Is it negotiable?
c) Is it enforceable—on the assumption that someone will take it—even if it is not negotiable?

FIGURE 29.9 "Handmade" Instrument

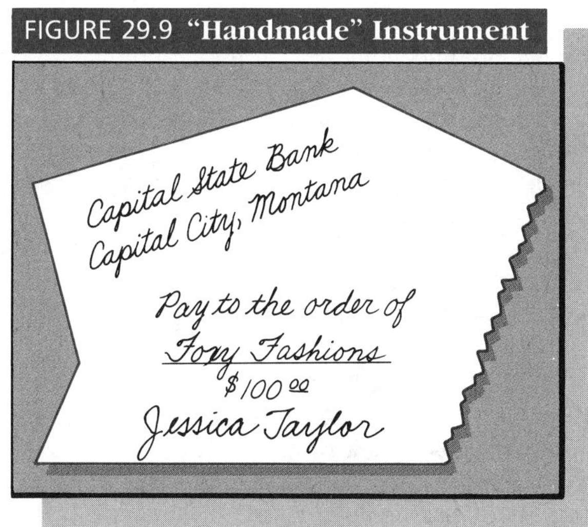

d) What is the effect on negotiability of the omission of a date on it?
e) When is the instrument payable?
f) What is the effect on negotiability of Jessica's failure to spell out $100 in words in addition to putting it into figures?
g) If the instrument is negotiable, can Jessica legally compel Foxy to take the instrument in payment for the coat?
h) If the instrument is negotiable, is it really a check or a draft?
i) On the assumption that this instrument is negotiable, will Foxy Fashions' indorsement be necessary to negotiate it?
j) Is Capital State properly classified as a depositary, presenting, drawee, or payor bank?

3. A note was drafted in duplicate. The original was signed by the maker and, with the use of carbon paper, the maker's signature was impressed on the duplicate copy. Since the original cannot be found, can the payee enforce the duplicate with a carbon copy of the maker's signature as a negotiable instrument? [*Chrismer v. Chrismer,* 144 N.E.2d 494 (Ohio 1956).]
4. The City of Concord acquired certain real property in the city by tax sale and wanted to auction it off to the highest bidder. The municipal ordinance and the announced terms of the auction sale require the bid to be accompanied by "cash or certified check." The newspaper advertisements required that all bids be accompanied by "cash or certified check in an amount to at least 10% of the bid price." Perry's high bid was accompanied by a bank draft of the New Hampshire Savings drawn on the Mechanics National Bank and payable to George West, Tax Collector. The second high bid, submitted by Henry J. Love, was accompanied by a cashier's check of Concord National Bank payable to the City of Concord. The third highest bid was submitted by Pasquale Alosa and accompanied by U.S. currency. Lockwood Realty Co. submitted the fourth highest bid accompanied by its check certified by the Mechanics National Bank. Who is the highest bidder that conformed to the terms of the auction and is, therefore, entitled to the property upon full payment of his bid price? [*Perry v. West,* 266 A.2d 849 (N.H. 1970).]
5. Defendant, Samuel Feinberg, signed a promissory note personally and as the representative of Sain Builders, Inc., which is now involved in bankruptcy proceedings. Feinberg argues that the phrase "as per contract" contained in the note destroys the requirement of an unconditional promise and that the plaintiff-indorsee, D'Andrea, is not an HIDC because he must have been aware of the underlying contract between Sain Builders and payee. Judgment for whom and why? [*D'Andrea v. Feinberg,* 45 Misc.2d 270 (N.Y. 1965).]
6. An instrument in all other respects negotiable related in part as follows: "It is agreed that this note is to be paid in Elks Club #8 Second Mortgage real estate bonds." Does this sentence render the entire note nonnegotiable? Why or why not? [*Moore v. Clines,* 57 S.W.2d 509 (Ky. 1932).]
7. A note provides that it is payable in 60 days, or sooner if certain property is sold. Is the note negotiable or does this acceleration provision destroy certainty of time? [*Fox v. Morris,* 496 P.2d 158 (Nev. 1972).]
8. A note with a definite maturity date provided that the holder could accelerate payment at any time the holder felt insecure. When the holder accelerated on the basis of this term, the maker of the note defended on grounds that there was no reason for the holder to feel insecure. Result?
9. Defendant, South Sea Apartments, Inc., issued a note to the order of payee in return for services that were to be performed by payee in the future. At the time payee

negotiated the note to plaintiff it was not disputed that plaintiff knew of this agreement. Since the agreement was later breached by payee, defendant refuses to pay at maturity and claims that the plaintiff's knowledge of the agreement imports a condition which destroys negotiability of the note. In the alternative, defendant asserts that plaintiff's knowledge of the agreement either destroys its good faith or puts it on notice of a defense, and as a result plaintiff is a mere holder, not an HIDC. Evaluate these defenses. [*Gordon Supply Co. v. South Sea Apts., Inc.,* 257 N.Y.S.2d 237 (1965).]

10. Among other things, *Tepper v. Citizens Federal Savings and Loan Association,* excerpted at the beginning of this section, discussed the importance of the state statute of limitations to negotiable instrument law. When does the statute of limitations begin to run against primary parties? Against secondary parties?

CHAPTER 30

TRANSFER AND NEGOTIATION

After you have read this chapter, you should be able to:

1. Speak confidently of the meaning and importance of "negotiation."
2. Be familiar with the methods of negotiating a negotiable instrument.
3. Recognize the types of indorsements, their common features, and the legal consequences of each.
4. Illustrate the "shelter provision" and its exceptions.
5. Explain the legal effect of reacquisition of an instrument by a prior owner.
6. Understand the importance of warranty liability and its relationship to indorsement liability.
7. Determine the legal effect of forged instruments, forged indorsements, and the signatures of impostors.
8. Discover when payment of an instrument is "final."

BUSINESS DECISIONS and the LAW

Margot is stunned. Normally, reading her mail at the end of a busy day is a pleasant experience. But after returning to her apartment this evening, she found a letter from USA Finance, holder of a security interest in her almost brand new car, containing a threat to sue her. The June payment was not received, they claim, and unless the default is cleared within thirty days, their lawyers will institute legal action and repossess her car.

"Oh, no you won't," she mutters. "Not my car. Not *the car*."

Immediately Margot examines her checkbook. Yes, she confirms, she wrote them a $450 check dated June 1 and mailed the next day. What could have gone wrong?

She begins to examine closely the cancelled checks she received earlier with her June bank statement. On June 12, $450 had been charged against her account. This was about the normal length of time it took for a check mailed to USA Finance to clear. It created no overdraft because she had enough money in the account—just barely enough—to clear the check and to cover her other expenses.

"Maybe the finance company is trying to pull something," she thinks. "They'd better not!"

She then examines the indorsements on the back of the check.

Pay to Apple Valley Bank,
For Deposit,
[signed] Peter Boch
Comptroller, USA Finance

Following that endorsement, she reads:

[signed] Mary Jameson-Boch
[signed] James W. Boch

In addition to that, there appear some barely legible print length-wise on the same side of the check that read, as best as she can decipher it:

Pay any bank, banker, or trust co.,
PEG
Apple Valley Bank

"I wonder what all this means," Margot wonders. "I wish I'd taken a business law course, just as my father said I should."

Introduction

We noted in Chapter 29, Introduction to Commercial Paper and Banking Operations, that a negotiable instrument, which is a type of formal contract, has the potential of conferring upon another "greater rights" than could be obtained under a simple contract by assignment. This chapter is important because it tells you *how* these greater rights become vested in another. It is not enough to know that these greater rights exist. If you are to derive the benefits or avoid the burdens associated with commercial paper, you must know how to use the law of commercial paper effectively.

Negotiation

negotiation
The delivery of negotiable paper to a person who thereby becomes a holder

At the outset of this inquiry it is important to fix firmly in mind that "order" paper requires an indorsement and delivery for a **negotiation.**[1] However, no indorsement is necessary for the negotiation of "bearer" paper; it can be negotiated by delivery alone.[2]

Order and Bearer Paper

▶ Identification of Order Paper

An instrument can be identified as order paper under the following circumstances:

[1]UCC 3–204(1).

[2]UCC 3–204(2).

1. It names a payee that is capable of indorsing—for example, "Pay to the order of Greenery USA."[3]
2. The last or only indorsement is a special indorsement (one that names an indorsee)—for example, "Pay to Ruston State Bank, [signed] Charles Ogden."[4]

In each of these illustrations the named party, Greenery USA or Ruston State Bank, must indorse and deliver the instrument before it can be further negotiated by the holder.

Identification of Bearer Paper

Bearer paper expressly states that it is payable to bearer, to the order of bearer, or it names no payee that is capable of making an indorsement—for example, "Pay to Bearer," "Pay to the order of Bearer," or "Pay to the order of Cash."[5] Order paper may even be converted into bearer paper if the last or only indorsement is in blank (blank indorsements consist of the signature of the indorser only; no indorsee is named).[6]

While the holder of bearer paper can legally negotiate it without further indorsement, people who are willing to receive negotiable paper normally require an indorsement. This will facilitate recovery against the indorser on the instrument in the event of later dishonor of the instrument. Also, a person who negotiates without an indorsement makes certain transfer warranties, but only to the *immediate recipient.* If the recipient indorses and transfers the instrument, he or she then incurs indorsement liability as well as warranty liability.[7]

Order and Bearer Paper in Action

To put this in a realistic focus, assume that Dorothy Adams, owner of a landscape firm, purchases a selection of plants from Greenery USA. By way of payment, she draws and issues a $4,800 check on her drawee bank, Pinnacle State, payable to the order of Greenery, the payee-supplier (Figure 30.1).

Greenery may either deposit the check for credit in its account, use the check to pay off its trade creditors, or discharge an obligation on a loan. The possibilities are far too numerous to pursue, but, for purposes of illustration, suppose that an authorized representative of Greenery indorses it "Without Recourse, Greenery USA, by Jack Ingram, President" and donates it to United Fund. "Without recourse" is discussed later; briefly, it means that the indorser will not be liable as an indorser if the instrument is not paid when due.

In all likelihood United Fund will indorse the check for deposit in its bank—for example, "For deposit, Pay to Ruston State Bank, [signed] United Fund, by Tamila Jackson, V.P." (Figure 30.2)—and the bank will then forward the check through collection channels to Pinnacle State. If funds are sufficient and no stop-payment order has been issued by Dorothy Adams, the check will be paid by the drawee-payor bank, Pinnacle State Bank.

---

[3]UCC 3–110.

[4]UCC 3–204(1).

[5]UCC 3–111(2)(6).

[6]UCC 3–111(c), 204(2).

[7]UCC 3–417(2).

FIGURE 30.1 Check

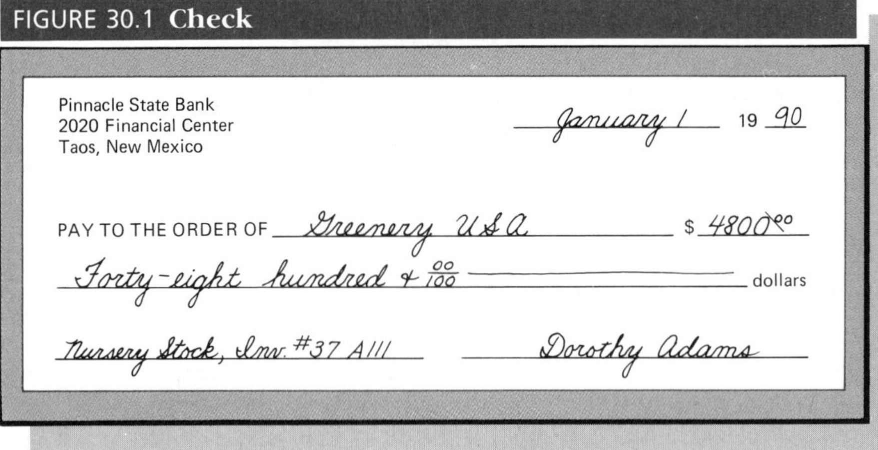

Pinnacle State Bank
2020 Financial Center
Taos, New Mexico
January 1 19 90
PAY TO THE ORDER OF Greenery USA
$ 4800.00
Forty-eight hundred & 00/100
dollars
Nursery Stock, Inv. #37 A111
Dorothy Adams

FIGURE 30.2 Indorsements on Check

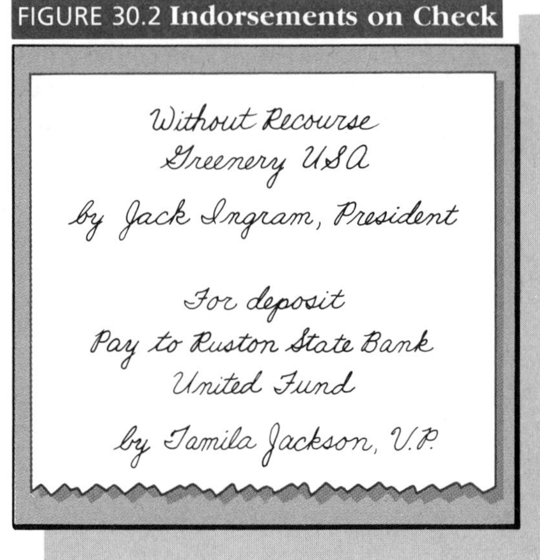

Indorsements

▶ Multifaceted (Many-Sided) Indorsements

Dorothy Adams' first delivery ("issue")[8] of her check to Greenery makes Greenery a holder.[9] A close look at the indorsements placed on the instrument by Greenery and United Fund will be helpful in illustrating certain elements that are common to all indorsements.

All indorsements, from the simplest to the most complex, are multifaceted (many-sided or mixed) in nature and may be analyzed on the following basis:

---

[8]UCC 3–102(1)(2).

[9]UCC 1–201(20).

1. *Blank or special:* determines the method to be used in subsequent negotiations
2. *Restrictive or nonrestrictive:* determines the type of interest being transferred
3. *Qualified or unqualified:* determines the liability of the indorser

► Blank Indorsement

A **blank indorsement** consists simply of the indorser's signature.[10] For example, in Figure 30.3 the payee's signature, Greenery USA, appears on the instrument without naming an indorsee. Since a business firm can act only through its agents, the fact that Greenery's signature was placed there by Jack Ingram does not change things in the least. Nor, for that matter, does the qualifying phrase "Without Recourse" (see the discussion below on qualified indorsements).

blank indorsement
An indorsement that does not specify any particular indorsee

The instrument is now bearer paper because the last or only indorsement is in blank. United Fund is the bearer and can negotiate it by delivery alone. Since a bearer instrument that is lost or stolen may get into the hands of an **HIDC,** a cautious party will be well advised to write above the signature of Greenery any contract or instructions consistent with the character of the indorsement.[11]

holder in due course (HIDC)
The holder of a negotiable instrument who takes it for value, in good faith, and without notice that the instrument is overdue or has been dishonored or of any defense against, or claim to, the instrument by any person

To illustrate, United Fund may write above Greenery's blank signature "Pay to United Fund." This converts Greenery's blank indorsement into a "special" one because it now names a special indorsee, namely, United Fund. If the instrument then is lost or stolen, it can never get into the hands of an HIDC because nobody can be a holder without the indorsee's indorsement. The instrument cannot *flow* to anyone as a holder without such indorsement.

No title or ownership can be transferred by a forgery of a required indorsement. Although *C,* an innocent party, may purchase an instrument in good faith and without notice of a forgery of a required indorsement, *C* cannot be an HIDC because *C* is not, first, a holder. To qualify as a holder, *C* would have to be in possession of an instrument indorsed to *C* or in blank—that means a genuine indorsement, not a forgery. (*P* is the

FIGURE 30.3 **Bank (and Qualified) Indorsement**

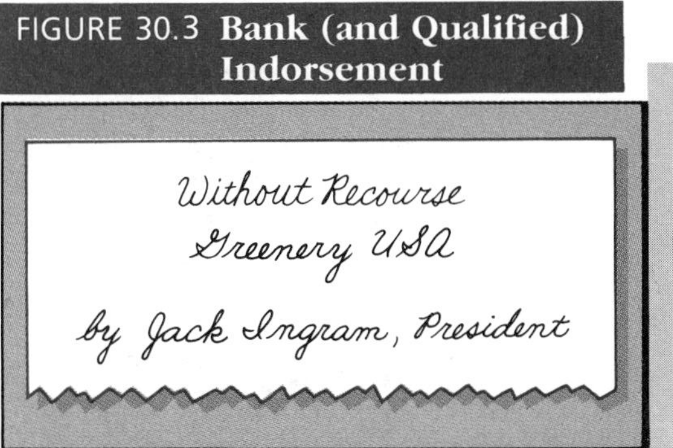

[10] UCC 3–204(2).

[11] UCC 3–204(3).

payee of a check. *T* stole it, forged *P*'s blank indorsement, and delivered it to you. Although you possess the check, ownership cannot flow to you without *P*'s indorsement.)

Usually an indorsement (or other signature) by a mark—such as an "X"—must be witnessed by two or more people and signed by them as witnesses.

Special Indorsement

special indorsement
An indorsement that specifies a particular indorsee

A **special indorsement** names the indorsee.[12] For example, when United Fund indorsed "Pay to Ruston State Bank," it named the bank an indorsee and, therefore, the indorsement is special (Figure 30.4). A special indorsement need not use the word "order"; it will be implied.[13]

The fact that the "For Deposit" language limits or restricts the use of the instrument has no bearing on the issue of special versus blank indorsements. Nor is it relevant to special or blank indorsements that the signature was made by an agent, Tamila Jackson, Vice President.

Before the instrument can be further negotiated, the special indorsee must indorse. If joint payees or indorsees are named ("*A* and *B*"), both must indorse; if payees or indorsees are named in the alternative ("*A* or *B*"), either may indorse.[14]

Blank and Special Indorsements: A Summary

All indorsements are either blank or special. If an indorsement consists of the indorser's name without designating an indorsee, it is a blank indorsement.

Do not be in the least bit surprised to find that the blank or special characteristics of an indorsement exist alongside the restrictive/nonrestrictive and qualified/unqualified elements of the same indorsement. An analysis of any indorsement will reveal each of these components, which will now be discussed.

FIGURE 30.4 Special (and Restrictive) Indorsement

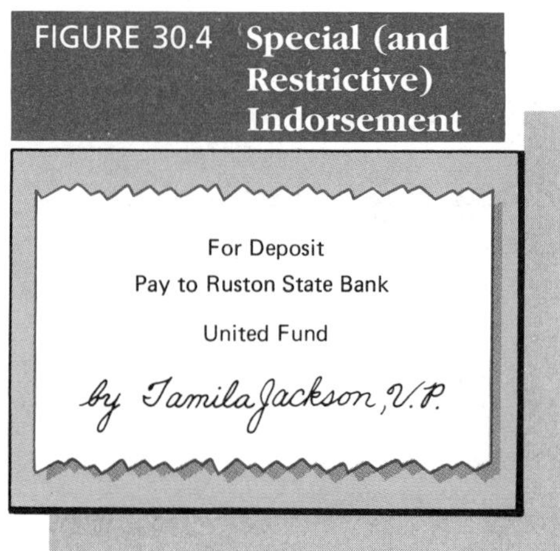

For Deposit
Pay to Ruston State Bank
United Fund
by Tamila Jackson, V.P.

[12]UCC 3–204(1).

[13]UCC 3–204(1).

[14]UCC 3–116.

▶ Restrictive Indorsement

Keep in mind that a **restrictive indorsement** determines the type of interest being transferred. It will either *condition* the indorser's liability on the instrument (transfer a conditional interest) or *regulate* the things that the recipient, who may be an agent or trustee, can do with the instrument (transfer a limited interest).[15]

restrictive indorsement
An indorsement that determines the type of interest in the instrument being transferred

Restrictive Indorsements That Impose Conditions It is important to point out that *no* indorsement destroys the negotiable character of a negotiable instrument. While the original promise or order on the *face* of a negotiable instrument must be absolute and unconditional, an indorser may make his or her indorsement contract depend on the performance of an express condition.[16] The right to impose a condition makes the instrument more adaptable to the indorser's needs. For example, the payee may indorse "Pay to Del Wells upon performance of contract #61387, [signed] David Reitzel."

Notice that the indorsement is special as well as restrictive, so Del Wells must indorse before the instrument can be further negotiated. The fact that the indorsement is both special and restrictive simply reenforces the earlier observation that all indorsements are hybrid (mixed) in nature. All parties including depositary banks (but not intermediary or drawee-payor banks)[17] must recognize the existence of the condition.

In order to become an HIDC, the person who receives such an instrument must pay in accordance with its terms.[18] In other words, you could not become a holder *for value*—one of the requirements of an HIDC—if you do not pay consistent with this indorsement.

An exception was noted above for nondepositary intermediary and drawee-payor banks.[19] These banks simply handle too many thousands of checks daily in the clearing-house or collection process to be responsible for this type of indorsement. They must, however, obey the terms of the indorsement of the bank that forwarded the item for collection.

To make certain that payment at maturity discharges the person who pays from further liability on the instrument, the condition must be obeyed. If the instrument that the payee, Reitzel, indorsed restrictively to Wells was a $1,000 *note* that you had issued, you could discharge your liability on the instrument only by paying the holder, Wells, in a manner "consistent with the terms of such restrictive indorsement."[20]

This restrictive indorsement should be a warning signal to you, the maker-primary party. If you expect to be fully discharged by your payment to Wells, you should inquire of the payee, Reitzel, to determine whether contract #61387 has been performed. If it has not been performed, payment should be withheld. Otherwise you may be compelled by the payee, Reitzel, to pay a second time.[21]

---

[15]UCC 3–205.

[16]UCC 3–205.

[17]UCC 3–206(2), 4–205(2). See pp. 611–13 for definitions of these banks.

[18]UCC 3–206(3).

[19]UCC 3–206(2), 4–205(2), 4–105(a)(c).

[20]UCC 3–603(1)(6).

[21]UCC 3–603(1).

Restrictive Indorsements That Purport to Prohibit Further Negotiation The indorsement "Pay *A* only, [signed] Indorser" *purports* to prohibit further transfer or negotiation of the instrument, but the UCC does not give it that legal effect.[22] It is treated as if it were a special *and* nonrestrictive indorsement instead.

By way of justification of this rule, you may keep in mind that it is really none of the indorser's business what the indorsee, *A*, does with this instrument. It may be convenient for *A* to collect it directly from the maker, drawee, or acceptor. But what if *A* is in Maine and the maker of the note is in California? Why shouldn't *A* be permitted to put the instrument in the hands of an agent for collection, or do anything else that *A* might want to with it? The UCC gives *A* that freedom despite the word "only" in the indorsement.

Restrictive Indorsements for Deposit and Collection The most frequent type of restrictive indorsement is one which reads "For Deposit" or "For Collection" along with the indorser's signature.[23] That is what the agent of United Fund did with the check received from Greenery USA, illustrated in Figure 30.4.

If you will consult the back of the cancelled checks your drawee-payor bank may send to you each month with a statement of your account, you will find another common form of restrictive indorsement: "Pay any bank" or "Pay any bank, banker, or trust co."[24] These are placed on the check by depositary and collecting banks, and they are the only indorsements to which banks in the collection process have to pay any attention.[25]

Once these indorsements have locked an instrument into bank collection channels, "outsiders" are put on notice. No one can become a holder for value unless payment for the instrument is applied consistent with this indorsement, i.e., the money is deposited into the account of the indorser.[26] In the following case the depositary bank failed to comply with the restrictive indorsement that it placed on the check on behalf of its customer.

FACTS

Price, Miller, defendants, issued check to Proctor as "progress payments" in connection with a construction contract. An employee of Proctor brought these checks, unindorsed, to Marine Midland and asked that the funds be telegraphed to a Proctor account in an Oklahoma bank. Based on UCC 4–405, a depositary bank (Marine Midland) taking a check for collection "may supply any indorsement of the customer which is necessary to title. . ." A bank employee then affixed a restrictive indorsement, "Credited to the account of payee herein named, [signed] Marine Midland," and transferred the funds to the Oklahoma account as directed by Proctor.

Proctor defaulted on the construction contracts, Price, Miller stopped payment, and the checks were returned to Marine Midland. It was unable to collect from Proctor because of a petition in bankruptcy, hence this suit against Price-Miller.

DECISION

Marine Midland is a holder in virtue of being in possession of a properly indorsed instrument. This would normally entitle it to a judgment against Price-Miller, but Proctor's

[22]UCC 3–205(b), 3–206(1), and comment 2.

[23]UCC 3–205(c).

[24]UCC 3–205(c).

[25]UCC 3–206(2) and 4–205(2).

[26]UCC 3–206(c) and 4–201(2).

default on the construction contract operates as a defense against Marine Midland unless it can establish that it gave value (and met the other requirements of an HIDC).

The plaintiff, Marine Midland, did not apply the funds represented by the check consistently with the restrictive indorsement. The indorsement was essentially "For Deposit and Collection." Instead of putting the funds on deposit, however, the bank paid cash. Since there was a discrepancy between the indorsement and the manner in which the checks were actually paid, Marine Midland did not give value within the meaning of the UCC, and it lost its suit against Price, Miller.

Marine Midland Bank v. Price, Miller, Evans & Flowers, 455 N.Y.S.2d 565 (1982).

Restrictive Indorsements in Trust A restrictive indorsement may establish a trust for the use or benefit of the indorser or some other person.[27] For example, the indorsements "Pay to *T* for the use of *P,* [signed] *P*" and "Pay to *T* in trust for *M,* [signed] *P*" establish *T* as the trustee for a beneficiary, who is either the indorser, *P,* in the first instance, or some other person, *M,* perhaps a minor child, in the second instance.

The party who receives the instrument from *T*—that is, the "first taker" following such an indorsement—must pay or apply the money consistent with the indorsement. If this is done, and if all of the other requirements are met, the first taker may qualify as an HIDC. Subsequent parties are not in any way affected or given notice by such an indorsement, unless they have actual knowledge that the trustee, *T,* has violated his or her duty in negotiating the instrument.[28]

▶ Qualified Indorsements or Indorsement Without Recourse

qualified indorsement
An indorsement that disclaims or qualifies the liability of the indorser on the instrument

Whenever a person transfers an instrument for consideration, the transferor makes certain implied transfer warranties,[29] discussed later. If the transfer is made with an indorsement, the holder receives, in addition to the implied warranties, a right of recourse against the indorser if the following steps are taken:

1. *Presentment:* the instrument is properly presented for payment or acceptance.
2. *Dishonor:* payment or acceptance is refused.
3. *Notice of dishonor:* the indorser is given timely notice of dishonor.[30]

It is possible for the indorser to avoid this conditional liability under the indorsement contract if the indorser so indicates expressly on the instrument. The use of the phrase "without recourse" along with the indorser's signature has this effect.[31] The phrase means that, in the event of dishonor, no recourse can be made against that indorser because of such dishonor. The implied transfer warranties of such an indorser are now comparable to those of an assignor under the common law.

[27]UCC 3–205(d).

[28]UCC 3–206(4), 3–304(2).

[29]UCC 3–417(2).

[30]UCC 3–414(1).

[31]UCC 3–414(1).

From the indorser's point of view, "without recourse" is an excellent way of escaping the normal liability that accompanies one's signature as an indorser on a negotiable instrument. The difficulty is in finding someone who will take such an indorsement.

You should be cautious in receiving instruments indorsed in this manner. If the holder is not able to collect from the debtor at maturity, the holder must rely on breach of implied warranty by the transferor.

Assume that *P* receives a check from *D* in return for the sale of merchandise. *P* indorses "without recourse" to *H* and delivers the check to *H*. Then *D* notifies the drawee bank to stop payment on the check (a stop-payment order). *H* will be able to recover from *P* only if *H* can prove some breach of the implied transfer warranties by *P*.

If *H* sues *P* on the basis of *P*'s transfer warranties to *H*, *H* would attempt to prove the following:

1. *P* did not have good title to the instrument. (But he did!)
2. Signatures were not genuine or authorized. (But they were!)
3. The instrument has been materially altered. (But it was not!)
4. *P* had knowledge of some defense. (Assume that *P* did not.)
5. *P* had knowledge of *D*'s insolvency. (Assume that *D* was not insolvent or that *P* had no knowledge of it.)[32]

In many situations *H* will simply be unable to recover a single penny from *P*. However, *H* may proceed against *D*. The stop-payment order does not mean that *D* is certain to be successful in a suit by *H*. In the following case a qualified "without recourse" indorsement did not prevent the qualified indorser from being liable for breach of warranty of no knowledge of any defense good against him.

FACTS

Prior litigations before this court invalidated a loan entered into in violation of the District of Columbia Loan Shark Law provisions against usury. The effect of the decision was to render uncollectible the unpaid balance of approximately $79,000. The present case involves a dispute as to bearing the loss.

Walker & Dunlop, Inc. loaned Suburban Motors a sum of $100,000. The loan, evidenced by a promissory note, was secured by a deed of trust on real property owned by Suburban. Walker & Dunlop, Inc. transferred the note and deed of trust to Hartford Life Insurance Co., indorsing the note "without recourse." Since the note was later invalidated, Hartford sued Walker & Dunlop, Inc. for $79,000.

DECISION

For Hartford Life Insurance Co. A "without recourse" indorsement is a qualified indorsement but it does not eliminate all obligation owed by the transferor of an instrument to his transferee. By the term "without recourse," Walker & Dunlop, Inc. warranted to Hartford that it had no knowledge of any fact which would establish the existence of a good defense against the note. Walker & Dunlop, Inc. breached the warranty. At all times it was fully aware that the note was unenforceable because of the illegality of the underlying loan. Walker & Dunlop, Inc.'s ignorance of the law was no excuse. Although Hartford had full knowledge of the same facts as Walker & Dunlop, Inc. and made the same "mistake" of law, it did not know when it accepted the note that a good defense existed against it. Therefore, it is entitled to coverage of warranty.

Hartford Life Ins. Co. v. Walker & Dunlop, Inc., 520 F.2d 1170 (D.C. Cir. 1975).

[32]UCC 3–417(2)(3).

FIGURE 30.5 **Qualified Indorsement**

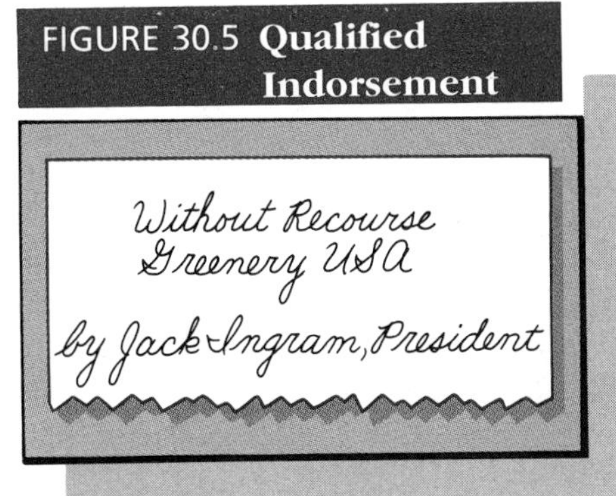

Without Recourse
Greenery USA
by Jack Ingram, President

FIGURE 30.6 **Irregular Indorsement**

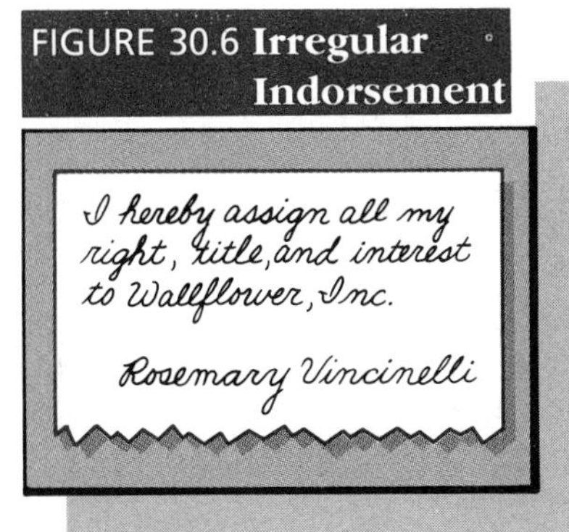

I hereby assign all my right, title, and interest to Wallflower, Inc.
Rosemary Vincinelli

Qualified indorsements are most likely to be used when the indorser has no personal interest in the instrument—e.g., the instrument has been made payable to an agent rather than to the principal (the agent's employer) and the agent simply indorses it over to the principal—or when the recipient has no bargaining power—e.g., the instrument is conveyed as a gift, such as the one by Greenery USA to United Fund (Figure 30.5).

▶ Irregular Indorsements

A bit of confusion can arise when a negotiable instrument is "assigned" (Figure 30.6). Beware of the obvious temptation to consider Rosemary's indorsement as having the same legal effect as either of the following:

1. The assignment of a nonnegotiable contract.
2. The indorsement of a negotiable instrument without recourse.

If Rosemary's indorsement were considered as being either 1 or 2, then Wallflower would have no recourse against her except for breach of implied transfer warranties. That is not the result, however. Wallflower has recourse against Rosemary as an *indorser* as well as a *warrantor*.

Words of assignment do not affect the character of Rosemary's signature as an indorsement.[33] The language that prefaces Rosemary's indorsement to Wallflower is not sufficient to warn the indorsee or to put it on notice that it is receiving something less than full recourse against Rosemary.

Transfers

▶ Transfers Without a Required Indorsement

By way of review, recall the manner in which negotiable paper is negotiated: bearer paper by delivery; order paper by indorsement and delivery. On some occasions, and normally because of forgetfulness, order paper will be transferred without an indorsement. For example, you may rush into a familiar store on the way to school or work to cash a payroll check or pay a bill and forget to indorse the instrument. In situations like

[33]UCC 3–202(4).

these, the transferee or recipient is entitled to your unqualified indorsement.[34] The negotiation takes place when you finally indorse. At that time the store becomes a holder and, if all the other requirements are met, an HIDC.

► Transfers for Less Than the Full Amount

An indorsement can be effective as a negotiation only if it conveys the full amount of the instrument or the unpaid balance. A $1,000 instrument indorsed $400 to *A* and $600 to *B* is quite legal and enforceable, but neither of the parties would qualify as a holder. They would be treated instead as assignees of the indorser's interest.[35]

shelter provision
Obtaining rights by claiming "through" or "under"

Shelter Provision

The transfer of a negotiable instrument conveys to the recipient-transferee all the rights of the transferor.[36] If, for example, the transferor was an HIDC, the transferee would receive all the rights of an HIDC; the transferee can claim through the HIDC using the HIDC as a shelter. This result will follow even though the transferee could not meet all the requirements for being an HIDC.

When Greenery USA donated a check to United Fund, United Fund could not qualify as an HIDC because it did not give value. Nevertheless, United Fund received the rights of Greenery, and, if Greenery qualified as an HIDC, United Fund would be entitled to exercise those rights as well.

The same result follows despite the fact that the transferee takes the instrument:

1. after it is overdue;
2. with notice of its previous dishonor;
3. with notice of a claim to it; or
4. with notice of a defense against it.

For example, if a draft or note payable to the order of *P*, payee, is negotiated to an HIDC, the rights of the HIDC pass to the transferee, *X*, even though:

1. *X* gave no value; or
2. *X* received the instrument after it was overdue; or
3. *X* had notice of a defense against the instrument, such as fraud by the payee on the maker or drawer of the instrument; or
4. *X* had notice that the instrument had been previously dishonored, such as by the drawee-payor or maker refusing to honor the instrument.

There are two easily recognized exceptions to this shelter provision. The transferee does not receive the transferor's rights:

1. where the transferee was a *party* to fraud or illegality affecting the instrument, or
2. where the transferee as a *prior holder* had notice of a claim or defense.

---

[34]UCC 3–201(3).

[35]UCC 3–202(3).

[36]UCC 3–201(1).

The justification for these exceptions is readily apparent.

1. A wrongdoer should not benefit from his wrongdoing. Therefore, if *X* collaborated with *P* in the fraud illustration above, *X* should not subsequently profit from the shelter provision by claiming through the HIDC.
2. If *X* was a prior holder before the HIDC—e.g., if the instrument went from *M* to *P* to *X* (assume that *X* knew of *P*'s fraud or illegality with regard to *M* although *X* played no part in it), and then from *X* to an HIDC before coming back to *X*—*X* cannot improve his status as a mere holder and he cannot claim through the HIDC. In other words, a reacquirer cannot "whitewash" or "launder" the instrument by running it through the hands of an HIDC.

Reacquirers

Generally speaking, when a party reacquires an instrument that he or she formerly held, that party may reissue or further negotiate it.[37] For example, a negotiable note issued by Mackey, the maker, to Peterson, the payee, could be negotiated initially to Arturo and then back to Arturo with the indorsements shown in Figure 30.7.

Arturo is a reacquirer. Even if the note is now overdue, he can still negotiate it. On the assumption in the above example that he further indorses and negotiates it to *X*, the liability of Bingham and of Carlin is discharged (1) against Arturo, the reacquiring party, and (2) against subsequent holders *not* in due course.[38] It would be foolish not to discharge Bingham and Carlin because, if Arturo or a subsequent holder *not* in due course collected from one of them, the one who paid would in turn proceed back against Arturo, as diagrammed in Figure 30.8.

The reacquiring party can cancel any indorsement that is not necessary to that party's title or ownership.[39] If so inclined, Arturo could mark out the special indorsements of

FIGURE 30.7 **Reacquired Instrument by Arturo**

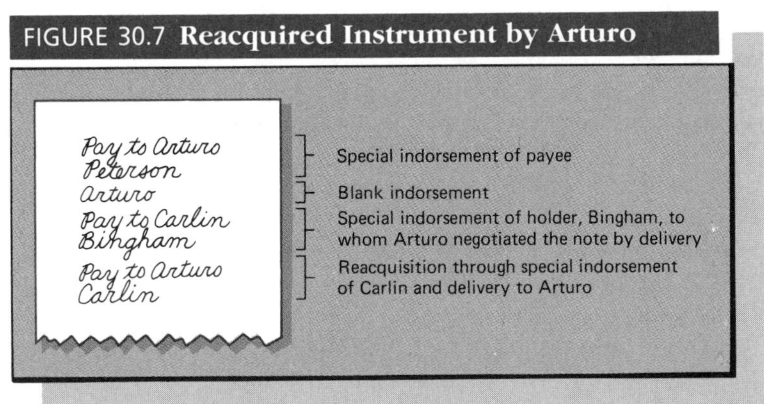

[37]UCC 3–208.

[38]UCC 3–601(3)(a).

[39]UCC 3–208.

FIGURE 30.8 **Instrument Renegotiated to Arturo**

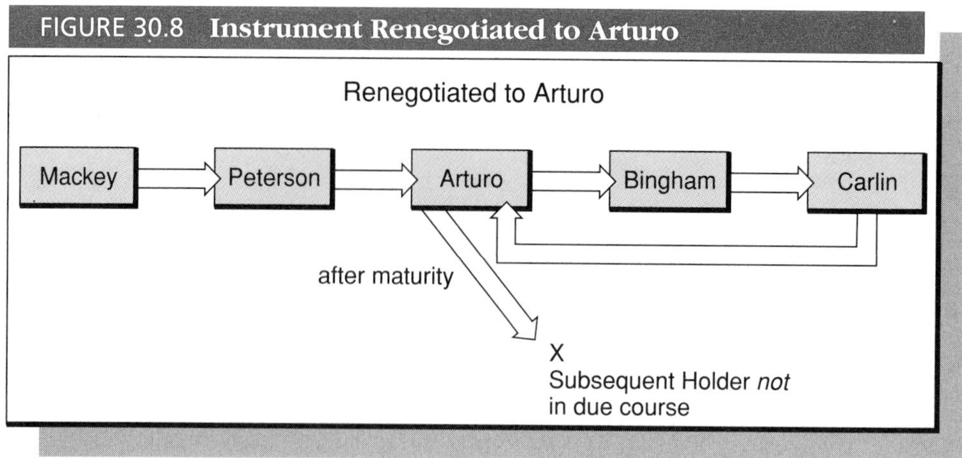

Bingham and Carlin. This would leave only Peterson's special indorsement and Arturo's blank one. If Arturo then negotiated the instrument to anyone who qualified as an HIDC, Bingham and Carlin would not be liable as indorsers. In effect, Arturo has made a gift to Bingham and Carlin by discharging them from further liability.[40]

Forgeries and Unauthorized Signatures

forgery
The unauthorized act of imitating or altering a writing with the intent to defraud and impose liability

No one is liable on a negotiable instrument unless his or her signature is on the instrument. The **forgery** of a signature or the unauthorized use of a signature (by an agent, for example) does not obligate the party whose name is wrongly used unless:

1. the party ratifies the transaction (after learning all the facts, the party OK's the transaction by word or other conduct); or
2. the party is precluded or estopped from denying it (engaged in conduct that makes it unfair to permit the party to avoid or disown the transaction).[41]

To illustrate each of the above, (1) a mother might ratify the forgeries of her signature on checks by a daughter, and (2) an employer might be precluded or estopped by its negligent supervision of a check-writing machine from disclaiming the conduct of an agent who abused his or her position and wrongfully placed the employer's signature on a company blank check.

In the following case the court held that the negligence of the payee of checks substantially contributed to the payee's agent unauthorizedly making the payee's indorsements on the checks.

---

[40]UCC 3–605(1)(a).

[41]UCC 3–404 and 3–406.

FACTS

Payee's general credit manager, Curie, took six checks payable to payee (Dunham-Bush), indorsed the name of the payee, and then indorsed them for deposit into his personal account at the Connecticut Bank and Trust Company (CBT), defendant. As general credit manager, Curie was responsible for handling accounts receivable, posting those accounts, and for issuance of reminder billing statements. Annual audits by Haskins and Sells for the year of these events, and for three previous years, recommended separation of the function of handling receivables, posting, and issuing reminders. These recommendations were not implemented.

Hartford Accident and Indemnity Company, surety of payee Dunham-Bush, reimbursed payee for its losses and proceeded, as plaintiff, against depositary bank, CBT. Since CBT took the check on the forged or unauthorized indorsement of payee, it will be liable to payee (or, in this case, payee's surety, Hartford) unless it can prove that payee's negligence substantially contributed to the forgery and that it acted in good faith and in accordance with reasonable commercial standards of the banking industry. Judgment was rendered for defendant, and plaintiff appealed.

DECISION

Judgment affirmed for defendant, Connecticut Bank and Trust Company. On the facts found, CBT has carried its burden of proof. Dunham-Bush's daily office procedure for handling receipts of its receivables at the time the defalcations occurred, the concentration in one person of authority for dealing at three levels with receivables, and the failure to act on the auditor's recommendations, which specifically addressed the procedures under which the defalcations took place, constituted that degree of negligence which substantially contributed to the making of the unauthorized indorsements. The procedure followed by CBT in the handling of its deposits is reasonable in the context of modern banking where checks have taken on a new importance as an accepted exchange medium. A multiplicity of teller stations have evolved to handle this volume and the evolution has led us into an electronic mode operation. As a result, banking procedure at the teller level focuses on the last indorser. This is the one who has received the proceeds of the check and to whom the electronic trail will lead. Modern banking practice considers the available safeguards and has structured its procedures accordingly.

Hartford Accident and Indem. Company v. Conn. Bank and Trust Co., 476 A.2d 1083 (Conn. Super. 1982).

You will want to make a distinction between two types of forgeries: (a) instruments that are completely forged from the very outset—for example, *X* forges *D*'s signature as drawer on a check; and (b) forged indorsements—for example, *X* steals a check drawn originally by *D* to the order of *P* and *X* forges *P*'s blank indorsement. The first of these forged instruments (a) can be negotiated to innocent HIDCs. Forgery of a drawer's signature does not prevent the otherwise negotiable instrument from being negotiable. The instrument is signed, although the drawer whose signature is forged is not liable thereon. However, following a forged required indorsement (b), no title passes, and no one can become a holder or an HIDC.

At maturity, *M* will refuse to pay *A*, an HIDC, because *M*'s signature does not appear on the instrument and, indeed, *M* did not know of its existence prior to the HIDC's demand for payment. No contract has ever existed between *M*, on the one hand, and either *X*, *P*, or *A*, on the other hand; therefore, *M* is not liable on the instrument and has a "real" defense that is valid against anyone, including an HIDC. (See Figure 30.9.)

M would be liable if *M* ratified *X*'s forgery or if *M* negligently supervised *X*'s use of a check-writing machine. However, as matters stand, *A*, the HIDC, must seek recovery

FIGURE 30.9 **Forged Instrument**

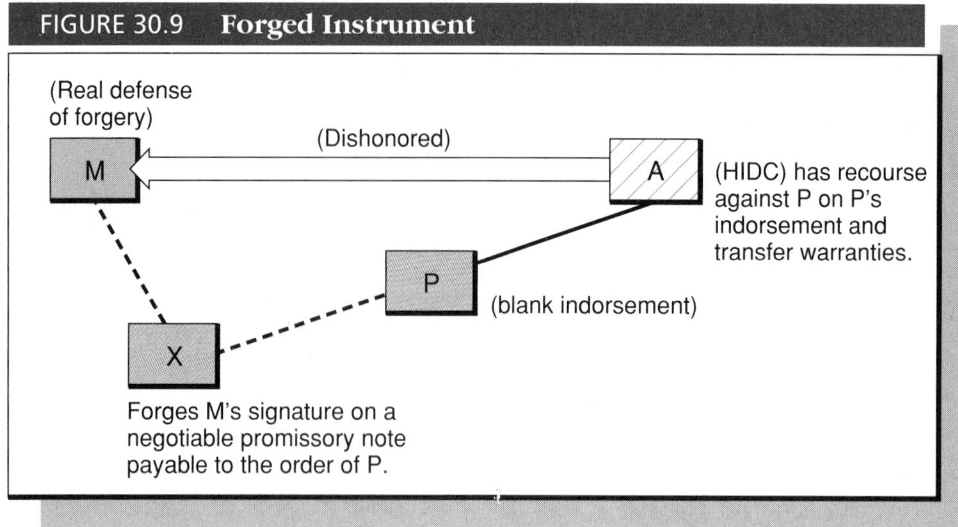

against *P* or *X*; but since *M* did not sign the instrument, *M* is not liable on the instrument. As a rule, the loss will fall upon the person who dealt with the forger unless the forger can be found and made to pay.

An unauthorized signature operates as the signature of the unauthorized signer; the latter did sign it. So *X*'s forgery of *M*'s signature causes *X* to be liable as the maker; if *X* had forged *P*'s indorsement, *X* would also be liable as an indorser.[42]

The fact that *A* is an HIDC does not assist him in these collection efforts. He will be pursuing *X* on his liability as a maker, and *P* as an indorser and as a warrantor. Accordingly, while *X*'s real name does not appear on the instrument, the forgery obligates him nevertheless. In the following case the court held that the drawee bank cannot charge its depositor drawer's account when the latter's signature was forged on the check.

FACTS

Plaintiff, Mortimer Agency, Inc., a depositor in Underwriters Trust Company (drawee), sued to recover $4,000 paid out of plaintiff's account by Underwriters on a forged check. The plaintiff's signature as drawer was forged. Underwriters in turn proceeded against both Chemical Bank and Rego Trading Company, asserting: (1) that the signature of the payee as indorser was also forged; and (2) that Chemical as the collecting bank, and Rego as a purchaser of the check, violated their respective warranties with regard to the forged indorsement of the payee and should be held ultimately responsible if Underwriters is found liable in the original action.

Some unknown individual forged a check in the name of the plaintiff by a rubber stamp and submitted a letter to Underwriters requesting that the check be certified. The letter was of suspicious appearance, and also misspelled the plaintiff's name. The check was certified by Underwriters. Rego bought the check for cash, and deposited the check for collection with its bank, Chemical. Chemical forwarded the check for collection to Underwriters, which honored the check and remitted

[42] UCC 3–404(1).

the money to Chemical. Mortimer, on receiving its bank statement, informed Underwriters of the forgery of its signature.

DECISION

For plaintiff, Mortimer, against Underwriters. Action of Underwriters against Chemical and Rego dismissed. The court found that Mortimer was not negligent because the forgery scheme (involving theft of check blanks) was too complicated for its security control. However, it found Underwriters negligent for not making further inquiries into the peculiar appearance of the check—rubber stamped signature, misspellings, and an uncommonly large sum.

A drawee, such as Underwriters, that certifies or pays an instrument on which the signature of the drawer is forged is bound on its acceptance and cannot recover its payment, according to UCC 3–418. Normally persons who obtain payment (both Chemical and Rego obtained payment) or acceptance, and any prior transferors, warrant to a drawee who in good faith pays or accepts that all previous indorsements are authentic. However, these checks were never at any time valid subsisting orders; they were fakes or forgeries right from the very beginning. Furthermore, the forged indorsement put the defendant in no worse position that it would be in if the indorsements were genuine. Why? Because Underwriters was supposed to recognize the signature of its depositor Mortimer and failed to do so. Finally, the defendant's certification set these events in motion and had much to do with Rego's decision to take the instrument. It would be anomalous now to hold Rego responsible to a party (Underwriters) whose conduct induced it to receive the check to begin with.

Mortimer Agency, Inc. v. Underwriters Trust Co., 341 N.Y.S.2d 75 (1973).

As shown in Figure 30.10, *M* signs a negotiable promissory note with *P* as the payee. *X* steals the note, forges *P*'s blank indorsement, and transfers the note to *A*, who, except for the forgery, meets the requirements for being an HIDC. At maturity, *M* refuses to honor the note, asserting *P*'s claim to the note.[43]

FIGURE 30.10 **Forged Indorsement**

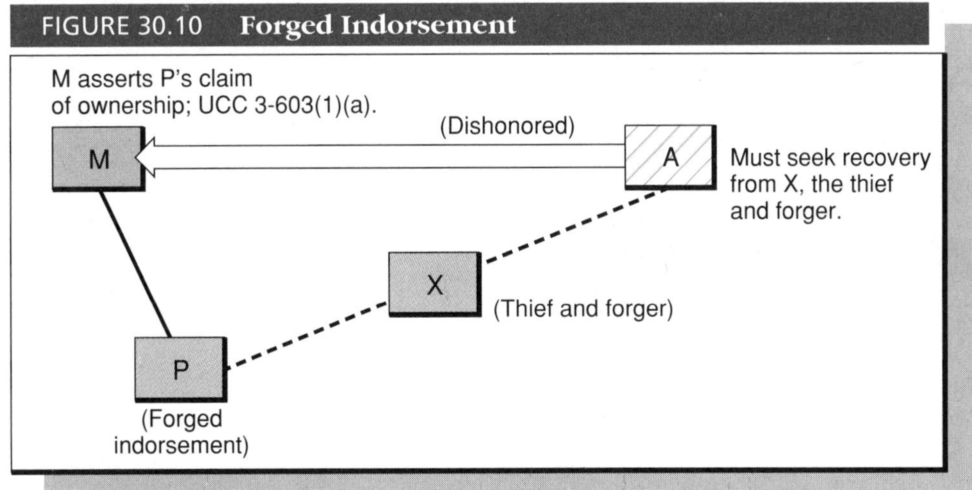

[43]UCC 3–603(1)(a).

In this situation, *A* is neither a holder nor an HIDC. *A* is in possession of an instrument, but it has not been properly indorsed so as to flow to him so he cannot become a holder nor an HIDC even if he met all of the other requirements. *A* can proceed against *X* on the forged indorsement and on the breach of transfer warranty, but *P* still owns the instrument.

If *P* is sued as an indorser by *A* or a subsequent party that has received the instrument through *A*, the forgery operates as a real defense for *P*, if we assume no ratification or estoppel by *P*. On the other hand, if *P* decides to take the initiative, *P* could assert a claim of ownership against *A* or anyone else to recover possession of the instrument.

Impostors

impostor (impersonator) A person who misrepresents himself or herself as another person

When an **impostor** payee induces issuance of an instrument, anyone can indorse in the payee's name. Thus if *X* impersonates *P* and induces *M* to issue a negotiable instrument to the order of *P* (the person who is being impersonated), *anyone* can indorse in *P*'s name. *X*'s indorsement of *P*'s name is not treated as a forgery. In other words, *X* can indorse *P*'s name and negotiate such an instrument to *A*, who may qualify as an HIDC. (See Figures 30.11 and 30.12.) The HIDC as a plaintiff will prevail against *M* if *M* refuses to pay the instrument at maturity.[44] While *M* is guilty of no wrongdoing, *M* nevertheless intended to create a negotiable instrument despite the trickery of *X*. This led to the purchase of the instrument by a completely innocent person (*A*) who had no opportunity

FIGURE 30.11 **Impersonator Receives an Instrument**

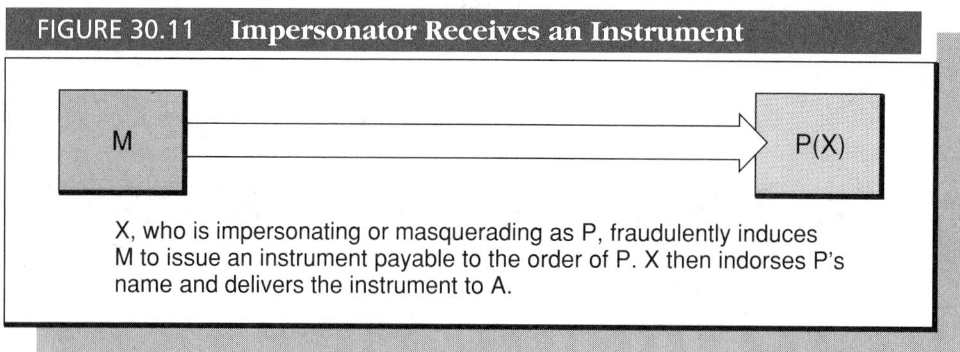

M
P(X)
X, who is impersonating or masquerading as P, fraudulently induces M to issue an instrument payable to the order of P. X then indorses P's name and delivers the instrument to A.

FIGURE 30.12 **Indorsement by Impersonator**

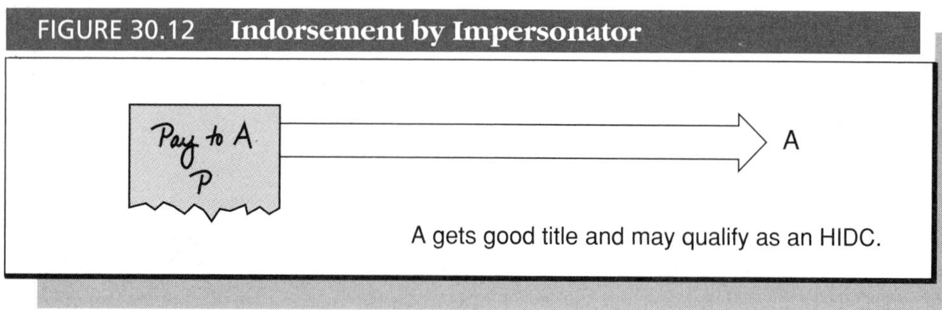

[44]UCC 3–405(1)(a).

to prevent or detect the original fraud. By way of justification of this rule, it can be said that, when one of two innocent persons must suffer (*M* or *A*), the loss falls on the one who had an opportunity to detect the wrongdoing or the opportunity to insure against it. Furthermore, *A* has the right to proceed against the wrongdoer, *X*. *A* cannot collect from *P*, the party who has been impersonated, because *P*'s signature never really appeared on the instrument.

This same result will follow: (1) if an employee supplies the maker or drawer with the name of a real or fictitious payee that the employee does not intend should have any interest in the instrument; or (2) if an agent with authority to sign does sign on behalf of the agent's employer but with the intention that the real or fictitious payee have no interest.[45]

What the employee or agent really intends is to take the instrument that has now been made out to a phony supplier-creditor or to a fictitious name added to the payroll list, indorse the payee's name, and pocket the cash. The innocent purchaser of such an instrument is protected, and once again the loss falls on the person who had an opportunity to prevent the deception, or to insure against it. Here, that person would be the employer. However, if the person who deals with the impersonator acts negligently in cashing the checks, that person may be liable instead of the employer.

The following case is illustrative of the general *impostor* or *fictitious payee* rule.

FACTS

Weilbacher Builder, Inc., sued Kirby State Bank to recover $22,000 on checks paid by Kirby but drawn by Weilbacher's bookkeeper, Norma Wilson. Upon Wilson's request, the checks were signed by Weilbacher in favor of payees to whom Weilbacher owed no debts and who were not entitled to the money. Wilson then signed the payees' names on the checks, deposited them in her personal account, and withdrew the funds. In accordance with banking practice, when the checks reached Kirby, they were paid and charged to Weilbacher's account.

DECISION

Weilbacher's attempt to recover is barred by UCC 3–405 (a)(3): "An indorsement by any person in the name of a named payee is effective if . . . an agent or employee of the maker or drawer has supplied him with the name of the payee intending the latter to have no such interest." Losses caused by a "faithless employee" are placed by the UCC on the employer rather than on the bank. This is simply a risk the business enterprise must bear because it is normally in a better position to prevent such conduct by reasonable care in the selection or supervision of employees. Failing that, the employer should cover these losses by fidelity insurance.

The appellate court affirmed summary judgment for Kirby State Bank. A summary judgment, you recall, is brief and uncomplicated compared to a jury trial. It is only appropriate when, as here, the facts are not in dispute (reasonable minds could not differ on the facts), and, as a matter of law, one of the parties is clearly entitled to judgment.

Clinton Weilbacher Builder, Inc., v. Kirby State Bank, 643 S.W.2d 473 (Tex. App. 1982).

Warranties

Various **warranties** implied by law under the Code are made by persons transferring a negotiable instrument and by persons who obtain payment or acceptance of the instrument.

warranty
An express or implied assurance that certain facts exist

[45] UCC 3–405(1)(b)(c).

► Transfer Warranties

If *M* issues a negotiable instrument payable to the order of *P, P* may indorse and deliver it to a holder, *A,* in payment for goods or services. In this situation, *P* becomes conditionally or secondarily liable on his indorsement contract to the holder, *A. P* impliedly agrees that the instrument will be honored. If *M* refuses to pay the note at maturity and *A* gives timely notice of dishonor or nonpayment, *P* is liable to *A* for the face amount. This is the liability of an indorser as a secondary party.

P may be liable to *A* for breach of implied transfer warranties as well. When a person transfers an instrument and receives a consideration, certain implied transfer warranties are created automatically or by operation of law. If the transferor has indorsed the instrument, these warranties extend to all subsequent transferees. However, if bearer paper is negotiated by delivery alone, transfer warranties are made to the immediate recipient only[46]—in other words, for the situation diagrammed in Figure 30.13:

1. *P*'s transfer warranties extend to *A, B,* and *H.*
2. *A*'s transfer warranties extend *only* to *B,* not to *H.*

Transferors warrant as follows:

1. The transferor has good title or is authorized by the owner to collect.
2. All signatures are genuine or authorized.
3. There are no material alterations of the instrument.
4. No defense of any party is valid against the transferor.
5. There is no knowledge of insolvency proceedings against the drawer of an unaccepted instrument (secondary party) or against the maker or acceptor (primary party).[47]

In the following case the depositary collecting bank fulfilled its warranty of good title and authority.

FIGURE 30.13 **Negotiable Promissory Note Indorsed in Blank by P, Payee, and Delivered to A, to B, to H**

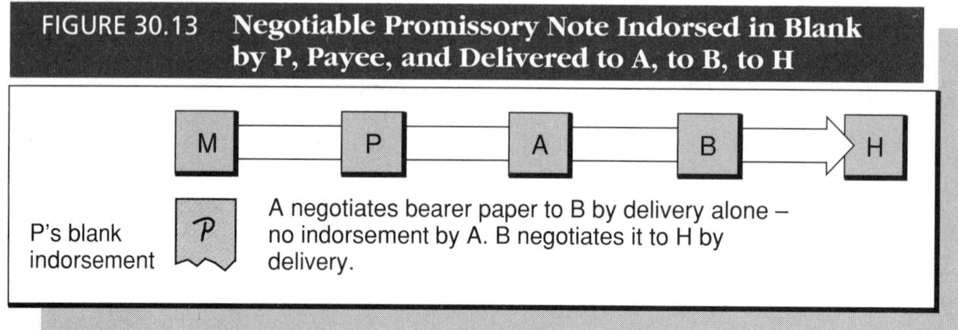
M
P
A
B
H
P's blank indorsement
P
A negotiates bearer paper to B by delivery alone – no indorsement by A. B negotiates it to H by delivery.

[46]UCC 3–417(2).

[47]UCC 3–417(2) (a)–(e).

FACTS

Pan American World Airways (Pan Am) is a member of the Air Transport Association of America. One of the functions of the Association is to appoint travel agents for its member carriers and to provide these travel agents with printed forms for flight tickets and other documents connected with air travel and related services. Travel agents then issue drafts drawn on member airlines (in this case Pan American), payable to themselves, in return for services that travel agents render to the member carriers. These services are for other than air transportation, e.g., promotional efforts, bookkeeping and so forth.

The Air Transport Association authorized a unique way of drawing these drafts—by the use of special embossing or validating plates. Eight drafts bearing the proper validating plates were issued by defunct travel agents and delivered to Roadway International. That company deposited them in its account at Continental National Bank of Miami (Continental Bank), defendant. The bank initiated the collection process against Pan Am. Proceeds in excess of $82,000 were paid by Pan Am to the account of Roadway.

Pan Am sued Continental Bank for the return of that sum. Judgment was rendered for Continental Bank and Pan Am appealed.

DECISION

Affirmed for defendant Continental Bank. Continental Bank's warranty of good title is limited to a finding that the draft was presented for payment with no forged indorsements. Even if issue of these drafts was unauthorized, Pan Am or Air Transport Association allowed that to happen. Continental played no role in the selection or supervision of these agents and is not responsible for their lack of authority.

Pan American World Airways, Inc. v. Continental Nat'l Bank of Miami, 444 So.2d 1073 (Fla. 1984).

Typically, a party's indorsement liability and warranty liability will overlap, as shown in Figure 30.14. Suppose that *X* forged *M*'s signature as maker of a negotiable promissory note with *X* as the payee; *X* then indorsed and negotiated the note to *A*, and *A* subsequently indorsed and delivered the note to *H*. *M* is justifiably entitled to refuse payment to *H* (assuming no ratification or estoppel by *M*). Given timely notice of dishonor by *H*, *A* is liable to *H* on his indorsement contract. *A* would be liable also as warrantor because *M*'s signature is not genuine.

If *A* negotiated bearer paper by delivery alone, or if *A* indorsed but *H* failed to properly present for payment or give notice of dishonor following *A*'s indorsement, *H*

FIGURE 30.14 **Overlap of Indorsement Liability and Warranty Liability**

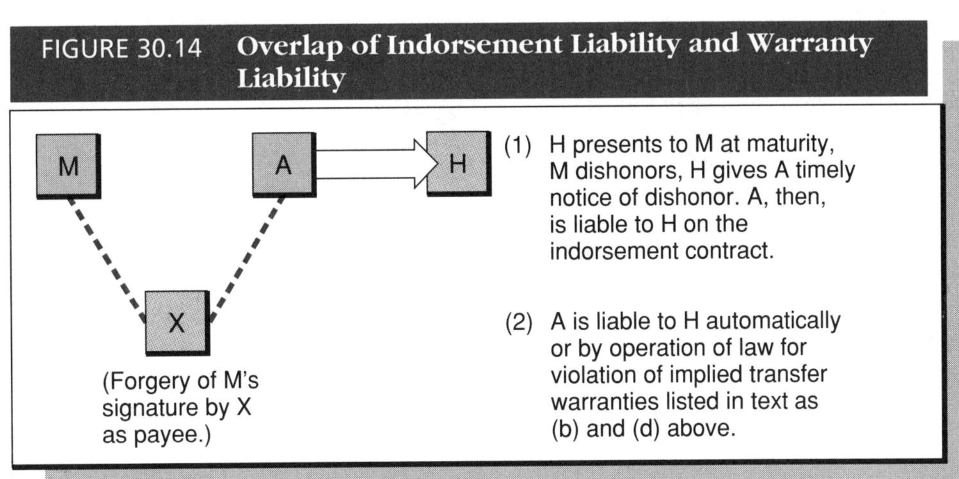
M
A
H
X
(Forgery of M's signature by X as payee.)
(1) H presents to M at maturity, M dishonors, H gives A timely notice of dishonor. A, then, is liable to H on the indorsement contract.
(2) A is liable to H automatically or by operation of law for violation of implied transfer warranties listed in text as (b) and (d) above.

would have to rely solely on breach of implied transfer warranty. Warranty liability, therefore, has a value over and above indorsement liability.

Keep in mind also that, if *A* indorses "Without Recourse," he is not liable as an indorser but he is liable on transfer warranties. In that case the transfer warranties are modified somewhat. The qualified indorser warrants that he or she has *no knowledge* of a defense that is valid against him or her.[48] All other indorsers warrant against valid defenses rather than no knowledge of defenses.

Presentment Warranties

When an instrument is presented to the proper party at maturity for payment or acceptance (certification), the person presenting warrants:

1. He or she has good title or is authorized to collect for the owner.
2. He or she has *no knowledge* that the signature of the maker or drawer is forged or unauthorized.
3. The instrument has not been materially altered.[49]

The general rules are basically straightforward and easily justified. For example, *M* makes a promissory note. *X* steals it from the payee *(P)* forges the payee's blank indorsement, and sells and delivers it to *A*. *A* does not have good title to the note. If *M* innocently pays *A*, then *M* should be able to recover from *A*.[50] After all, *A* is not the holder nor the owner of the instrument. The payee is still the owner and is entitled to payment from *M*.

The instrument has been "converted"[51] (a term to be explained later) if *M* pays following a forged indorsement. *M* is liable to *P*, so *M* should be entitled to recover from *A* any mistaken payment that *M* has made to *A*. The following case illustrates, in the case of a check, the liability of a depositary collecting bank on its warranty of title to the payor bank.

FACTS

Defendant, Zions First National Bank, presented two cashier's checks for $12,500 to plaintiff Valley Bank & Trust Company and received payment. These cashier's checks, on which Valley Bank was drawer and drawee, were payable to "Peck & Shaw Fine Cars" and to an individual joint payee, Steven J. Gibbs on one check and Jeffrey Olson on the other. When paid by Valley Bank, each check was indorsed with the name of both joint payees and also bore Zions Bank's notation, "PEG" (prior endorsements guaranteed). After Valley Bank learned that the Peck & Shaw indorsements were forgeries, it brought this action against Zions Bank to recover on Zions' guaranty of valid indorsements or for breach of Zions' warranty of good title as provided in UCC 3–417(1)(a) and 4–207(1)(a). Trial court held for Valley Bank. Zions Bank appealed.

DECISION

Affirmed for Valley Bank. It is settled beyond argument that a collecting bank obtaining payment on a cashier's check bearing a forged

---

[48] UCC 3–417(3).

[49] UCC 3–417(1).

[50] UCC 3–417(1)(a).

[51] UCC 3–419(1)(c).

indorsement is liable upon its warranty of good title and its guaranty of indorsements to the payor bank. This statutory liability under UCC sections 3–417(1) and 4–207(1) duplicates the liability incurred by the PEG guaranty of prior indorsements which Zions Bank entered upon these cashier's checks.

Valley Bank & Trust Co. v. Zions First Nat'l Bank, 656 P.2d 425 (Utah 1982).

Implicit in the second presentment warranty—no knowledge of a forged maker's or drawer's signature—is the thought that the one who is paying (the maker, acceptor, or drawee) is in a better position to recognize a forgery than the presenter.[52] If the maker's signature has been forged on a note but that person does not recognize the forgery when the instrument is presented at maturity for payment, the money cannot be recovered from the innocent HIDC who received payment. Similarly, the drawee or acceptor who pays a check or draft on the drawer's behalf, despite the forgery of the drawer's signature, is penalized because of this negligence or carelessness. Such persons do have the right to pursue the wrongdoer, however.

Material alteration,[53] which will be discussed in a later chapter, is a "real" or "universal" defense that is valid even against a holder in due course. The thought behind this rule is that a contracting party on an instrument should not be liable for more money than he or she has originally agreed to pay.

Carefully note the exceptions to presentment warranty rules—(1) no knowledge, and (2) material alterations—in favor of an HIDC acting in good faith. To summarize these exceptions, an HIDC who is acting in good faith—i.e., one who continues to be innocent of any knowledge of a forged maker's or drawer's signature or a material alteration when the HIDC presents for payment or acceptance—does not always make these warranties. Therefore, the HIDC is entitled to keep the money—the one who pays has recourse against the wrongdoer.

Finality of Payment or Acceptance

Payment or acceptance of an instrument is "final" in favor of an HIDC or one who in good faith changes his or her position in reliance on payment.[54] This rule is easily enough understood in its protection of an HIDC. However, if a person has not given value or does not otherwise qualify as an HIDC but has made some irrevocable commitment on the strength of this payment, then it is made final in that person's favor as well.

There are two exceptions to this rule. Payment may be recovered if a presentment warranty has been breached,[55] and if certain provisions of the Article on Bank Deposits and Collections are violated.[56]

---

[52]UCC 3–417(1)(b)(i)–(iii).

[53]UCC 3–417(1)(c).

[54]UCC 3–418.

[55]UCC 3–417(1).

[56]UCC 4–213, 4–301.

Conversion

conversion
The tort of intentional interference with another's right to possession, control, and dominion of a chattel

chattel
A tangible, movable thing

An instrument is **converted**—controlled by someone other than the rightful owner—when it is cashed on a forged indorsement.[57] If *X* steals from *P* a $1,000 check drawn payable to the order of *P*, forges *P*'s indorsement, and passes it to an innocent party, *A*, who collects on it from the drawee, the drawee has converted *P*'s instrument. If *P* acts within the time limits, *P* can assert his claim of ownership against the drawee for $1,000.[58] *P* can proceed against *X* and *A* as well in order to obtain a full recovery.

Since the drawee did not know what the payee's signature looked like (it has a copy of the drawer-customer's signature, which it is supposed to recognize, but not the payee's), it is entitled to charge back against collecting banks for breach of the presentment warranty of good title.[59]

If a forged signature of a drawer-customer is not detected, the bank is not likely to recover on grounds of a presentment warranty. It is penalized for its negligence or oversight, and as a rule, the drawee can recover from the wrongdoer only.[60]

Agents or representatives, including depositary and collecting banks, may advance checks through bank channels following a forged indorsement of the true owner's signature. If they have acted in good faith and in accordance with reasonable business standards, they are not liable to the true owner beyond the amount that remains in their hands.[61] For example, if *X* steals *P*'s $1,000 check, forges *P*'s indorsement, and transfers the check to *A*, *A* may indorse it for collection to the depositary bank (not the payor-drawee bank) and withdraw $500 before *P* discovers the theft and forgery. In such an event, the depositary bank is liable to *P* for the remaining $500. It may also have to account to the drawee bank for breach of the presentment warranty of good title.[62] (See *Pan American World Airways, Inc. v. Continental National Bank of Miami* (p. 651) in which the drawee could not recover against the collecting bank; no indorsements were forged.)

Summary Statement

1. Bearer paper is negotiated by delivery alone. Order paper is negotiated by indorsement and delivery.
2. To identify bearer paper, examine its face. If the face of the paper expressly states that it is payable "to Bearer" or "to Order of Bearer," or it names no payee capable of making a signature—e.g., "Cash"—then it is bearer paper. Don't stop there, however. If the instrument has been indorsed, examine the last (or only) indorsement. A blank indorsement means that the instrument is still bearer paper. A special indorsement converts it to order paper.
3. Order paper will name as payee on the face of the instrument a natural person—e.g., Willie Nelson—or some legal entity that is capable of making a signature through an

---

[57]UCC 3–419(1)(c).

[58]UCC 4–406(4).

[59]UCC 3–417(1)(a), 4–207(1)(2).

[60]UCC 3–417(1)(b), 4–207(1)(b).

[61]UCC 3–419(3).

[62]See UCC 3–419, comment 6.

agent—e.g., Ruston State Bank. Examine the reverse side of the instrument as well as the face, however. If the last or only indorsement is special, the instrument continues to be order paper. If the last or only indorsement is in blank, the instrument becomes bearer paper. If it was bearer to begin with, the special indorsement converts it into order paper.

4. All indorsements are hybrid in nature. Each one will contain elements of the following:
   a) *Blank or special.* These indorsements determine the method to be used in subsequent negotiations. (Delivery alone if the last or only indorsement is blank; indorsement plus delivery if the last or only indorsement is special.)
   b) *Restrictive or nonrestrictive.* These indorsements determine whether the interest conveyed is conditional or limited. One form of restrictive indorsement contains an express condition—e.g., "Pay to *A* when he finishes painting my house, [signed] *P.*" The other important form makes the indorsee an agent or trustee—e.g., "Pay to ABC Bank for deposit, [signed] *P,*" or "Pay to *T* in trust for *M,* [signed] *P.*"
   c) *Qualified or unqualified.* These indorsements determine the liability of the indorser. A party who indorses qualifiedly or without recourse and transfers for a consideration, he makes certain warranties but is not liable as an indorser.
5. The "shelter provision" transfers to the recipient of the instrument all the rights that the transferor had to convey. If the transferor was an HIDC, the transferee gets the rights of an HIDC. This rule opens up the market for commercial paper and makes it easier to sell. However, where the transferee was a party to fraud or illegality affecting the instrument, or where the transferee as a holder prior to the HIDC had notice of a claim or defense, the shelter provision rule is ineffective.
6. Forgeries and unauthorized signatures do not obligate the party whose name was wrongly used, unless that party ratifies the signature or is precluded or estopped from denying it. Forged instruments can get into the hands of HIDCs, but the forger and all indorsers incur signature liability as well as warranty liability. If a required indorsement is forged, no subsequent party can become a holder or an HIDC. The forger and all indorsers that follow do incur signature and warranty liability, however, and the true owner of the instrument will have a valid claim against the person in possession of the instrument.
7. An impersonator's signature of the name of the individual being impersonated is not a forgery. It operates as a valid signature and subsequent holders can qualify as HIDCs. The wrongdoer is responsible for his or her conduct but, if recovery against the wrongdoer is not practicable, the party who issued the instrument to the impersonator is liable for it.
8. Each time an instrument is transferred for a consideration, and each time one is presented and payment or acceptance is obtained, certain warranties are made. If the instrument is indorsed by the transferor, the warranties run in favor of all subsequent parties; if the instrument is negotiated by delivery alone, the transfer warranties extend only to the immediate recipient.
9. Warranty liability is different from indorsement liability but is compatible with it. Indorsement liability is discharged if the instrument is not presented for payment at the proper time or if timely notice of dishonor is not given. Warrantors continue to be liable, however. Their obligation is not conditioned on presentment, dishonor, and notice of dishonor.
10. A bank is supposed to know the status of its customers' accounts. When it honors a check—even one creating an overdraft—payment is, generally speaking, final in

favor of an HIDC or one who in good faith changes his or her position in reliance on payment.

11. If an indorsement has been forged, the drawee bank that pays the check is liable to the true owner. Then it may proceed against a collecting bank for violation of a presentment warranty. If a customer-drawer's signature is forged, the bank should detect it. Payment of such a forged instrument makes the payor bank liable to its customer. The bank may then proceed against the wrongdoer, but not against collecting banks.

This chapter has emphasized the various rights and duties that can arise when commercial paper is negotiated. The following case presents us with an example of how the principles of law (one is that a bank is required to know its depositor's signature) can be modified by equitable considerations (contributory negligence by one innocent party causing another innocent party to suffer loss).

NEELY ENTERPRISES, INC. v. AMERICAN NATIONAL BANK OF HUNTSVILLE
403 So.2d 887 (Ala. 1981)

Adams, J. Mr. and Mrs. Neely, the owners and operators of J. Gordon Neely Enterprises, Inc., [(Neeley), plaintiff,] are doing business as Midas Muffler. Mrs. Neely became acquainted with Bradshaw [a defendant] in 1976 when, as a Kelly Girl, [Bradshaw] was hired by the company's stockholder accountant to assist him with their account. Mrs. Neely became friendly with Bradshaw and hired her parttime to teach [Bradshaw] how to keep the corporate books. Since 1960, Mrs. Neely had performed all of the in-house bookkeeping duties by herself.

• • • • •

On Bradshaw's recommendation, Neely opened an account for payroll in American National Bank of Huntsville, a defendant, where Bradshaw kept her personal checking. Neely maintained its corporate account at First Alabama Bank of Huntsville where it had banked for a number of years. Mr. and Mrs. Neely signed the bank signature card and the [firm's] corporate resolution, which stated, among other things, that American National was authorized to pay out funds, on either bearer or order paper, to any of the signatories. Bradshaw was entrusted with these documents to return them to the bank, and without the knowledge or authorization of the Neelys, signed the signature card and added her name in a noticeably different type.

Bradshaw filled out checks drawn on the First Alabama account, except for two drawn on the American National account, made payable to American National and with a large space to the left of the amount written on the designated lines. Mrs. Neely signed these checks being fully aware of these large gaps. She admitted that she never left spaces like that on her personal or corporate checks because it could facilitate alterations, but Mrs. Neely never questioned Bradshaw's practice of doing so because she yielded to Bradshaw's superior knowledge.

Bradshaw altered the checks either by adding a digit or two to the left of the original amount, or by raising the first digit after using liquid erasure. She then made a split deposit by depositing the original amount into Neely's American National payroll account, and depositing to her [own] account the difference between the original and altered amounts. On some occasions she took the difference in cash without depositing it to her account. On those checks that were not raised, she either cashed them and kept the money, or deposited them to her account, or deposited part of the check into the Neely account and kept the rest.

• • • • •

After Bradshaw picked up the [firm's] monthly statements and items, she realtered them to reflect the original amounts by using liquid erasure. Together, the two women reconciled the statements with Mrs. Neely calling out the information from her journal entry and with Bradshaw responding from the bank statements and items. Consequently, Mrs. Neely never saw the altered checks or the statements. Even when the statements were mailed, Mrs. Neely never opened them and she never reconciled the statements without Bradshaw. A new accountant hired in the latter part of 1977 discovered the defalcations, totalling $17,005.18.

Neely filed a complaint against Bradshaw and American National for [the tort of] conversion. The trial court entered a judgment in favor of American National from which Neely appeals.

• • • • •

First, Neely contends that the bank converted its funds because it paid out proceeds to Bradshaw when she was not named as payee. We disagree. The checks at issue were made payable to the order of American National as opposed to being drawn to J. Gordon Neely Enterprises, and none of them was indorsed restrictively "For Deposit Only" into Neely's specially designated and numbered account.

• • • • •

Neely also relies heavily upon the proposition that

> It is generally held that a check or draft drawn to the order of a bank precludes the diversion of the proceeds of it to a use other than that of the drawer, and that such diversion can be justified only by proof of authority from drawer. 10 Am.Jur.2d Banks § 560 (1963).

However, overlooked by Neely, cited within the same paragraph from which it quotes, is the following:

> [B]ut . . . if the drawer has clothed his agent with apparent authority to receive the proceeds of such check, the bank is not negligent in, and is not liable to the drawer for, paying, in reliance upon such apparent authority, the proceeds of such check to such agent contrary to his actual authority, if the agent should misappropriate such proceeds. 10 Am.Jur.2d Banks § 560 (1963).

• • • • •

Next, Neely alleges that American National is liable for paying out on altered instruments. Both parties rely upon Code § 3–406.

• • • • •

Neely argues that American National did not pay the instruments according to commercially reasonable standards because the checks allegedly bore visible marks of alteration. American National contends that Neely is precluded from asserting the material alterations as a basis for liability because Neely's negligence substantially contributed to the alterations by leaving large spaces to the left of the amount designation, and by entrusting the same employee with writing the checks and reconciling the bank statements without the protection of internal corporate controls.

We must first resolve whether American National acted in a commercially reasonable manner, because unless the bank acted reasonably it cannot assert the defense that Neely's negligence substantially contributed to the alterations. American National produced expert witnesses testifying that although some of the words and numbers on the amount designation lines were slightly misaligned, and although a few checks visibly contained liquid erasure, the bank did not violate reasonable commercial standards when it paid out on these particular checks to Bradshaw. It was stated that the decision of whether to pay a particular check that may have appeared to be somewhat irregular on its face was based entirely upon a judgment call under the particular circumstances of that check. Based upon the judgment call surrounding the decision to pay each check, and after examining the checks exhibited, the trial court concluded that American National had acted in a commercially reasonable fashion under the circumstances. Inasmuch as this fact issue was found in favor of American National, the nonjury finding will stand on appeal because it was not plainly and palpably erroneous.

After resolving the threshold question of the commercial reasonableness of the bank's actions, we must next determine whether Neely, by its negligence, substantially contributed to the facilitation of the alterations. The Uniform Commercial Code does not define the negligence which will support the defense of § 3–406, and instructs that it is an issue strictly left to the fact-finder on a case by case approach. The official comment does advise, however, that "[n]egligence usually has been found where spaces are left in the body of the instrument in which words or figures may be inserted." It is undisputed that Mrs. Neely signed the checks fully aware of the large gaps in front of the amount.

Similarly, two other examples of negligence are supported by the record: no inquiry was made into Bradshaw's veracity, although it was rumored that previously she had been in trouble with embezzlement in Tennessee, and Neely failed to maintain internal controls so that the employee writing the checks was not also the principal person reconciling the bank statements.

Affirmed for American National Bank of Huntsville.

Questions and Case Problems

1. A negotiable instrument was indorsed in blank by *P,* the payee, and negotiated to *A.* The indorsement of *A* was placed on the instrument by an unauthorized party and then the instrument was transferred to *P.* Does *P* qualify as a holder? [*Westerly Hosp. v. Higgins,* 256 A.2d 506 (R.I. 1969).]
2. Jensen Movers drew a check on Union Bank payable to the order of Lewittes Furniture Enterprises, Inc., plaintiff, and delivered it to plaintiff. A thief, Joel Simpson, stole the check, forged Lewittes' indorsement, and transferred it to Margaret Marino. She deposited the check, containing plaintiff's forged indorsement, into her joint account with Peter Marino at Bankers Trust, defendant. Bankers presented the check to Union and it was paid. Plaintiff sued the defendant for recovery of the proceeds of the check. The plaintiff's case was based on its rights as assignee of the drawee bank to go against defendant collecting bank for breach of its implied (statutory) and express warranties of the genuineness of prior indorsements. Decision? [*Lewittes Furniture Enter., Inc. v. Bankers Trust of Suffolk,* 372 N.Y. S.2d 830 (N.Y. 1975).]
3. Cole drew a check on Buffalo Bank payable to the order of Wyoming Homes. An agent for Wyoming Homes deposited it in a Gillette bank without an indorsement. The bank stamped the check "First National Bank, Gillette, Wyoming, For Deposit Only" and collected it for the payee, Wyoming Homes. Buffalo Bank charged Cole's account. Cole then proceeded against the First National Bank of Gillette, contending that it was only a transferee of the check (not a holder or an HIDC) and that it took the check subject to Cole's defenses of fraud and failure of consideration against Wyoming Homes. Decision? [*Cole v. First Nat'l Bank of Gillette,* 433 P.2d 837 (Wyo. 1967).]
4. A negotiable note was created by the defendant-maker payable to the order of "Greenlaw & Sons Roofing & Siding Co." and indorsed in blank "Greenlaw & Sons by George M. Greenlaw." The plaintiff, a later indorsee of the note for value, is confronted with the defense that, since the note was not properly indorsed, the plaintiff cannot be a holder or a holder in due course. If the defendant is correct—he points to UCC 3–203 and 3–307 to substantiate his argument—any defense will be sufficient to defeat plaintiff's claim. Discuss. [*Watertown Fed. Sav. & Loan Ass'n v. Spanks,* 193 N.E.2d 333 (Mass. 1963).]
5. Plaintiffs, partners in a Tacoma barber shop, have maintained a partnership checking account with the defendant, Puget Sound National Bank, since October 1964. The signatures of both partners were required for withdrawal from the account. Mr. Nash, a longtime employee of the plaintiffs, was occasionally left alone and in charge of the barber shop. He had no formal managerial responsibilities and no authority to write

partnership checks. Between September 16, 1968 and January 3, 1969, Mr. Nash forged plaintiffs' signatures on numerous checks. Defendant bank honored these checks. In early January of 1969, plaintiffs discovered the forgeries. This action was then commenced to recover the monies paid. Are plaintiffs entitled to recover? [*Terry v. Puget Sound Nat'l Bank,* 492 P.2d 534 (Wash. 1972).]

6. A check was made payable to the order of payees *A* and *B*. After the check was certified by the drawee bank, it was indorsed by *B* only and cashed. When the check was eventually presented to the drawee bank, it refused payment because *A* did not indorse. Was the bank justified in its refusal to pay? [*Clinger v. Continental Nat'l Bank et al.,* 503 P.2d 363 (Colo. 1972).]

7. Feldman Construction Co. drew a check on Union Bank (defendant-drawee) payable to the order of "A Corp. and B Supply." A Corp. indorsed and cashed the check at Union Bank without B Supply's indorsement. Since B Supply was not paid, it filed a lien against Feldman's property. Feldman satisfied B Supply's lien and then proceeded against Union on the ground that the check had not been properly indorsed. Decision? [*Feldman Const. Co. v. Union Bank,* 104 Cal.Rptr. 912 (Cal. 1972).]

8. *D* issues a $100 check to *P*. *P* raises the check to $1,000 (a material alteration) and has it certified by the drawee bank. *P* then indorses the check "Pay to *H*, [signed] *P*" and negotiates it to *H*. *H*, an HIDC, cashes the check for $1,000. When *D* discovers these facts (immediately upon examining his monthly bank statement and cancelled checks), he compels the drawee to reinstate his account for $900.[63] UCC 4–401(2)(a). Can the drawee bank recover the $900 from *H*? If not, can it recover from *P*? Discuss the application of UCC 3–417 to this fact situation.

9. *D* draws a $1,000 check on *D*-Bank payable to the order of *P*. *X* steals the check and forges *P*'s blank indorsement. *A* receives the check from *X* for value, before maturity, and without knowledge of the forgery. *A* deposits the check in *A*-Bank, which forwards it to *D*-Bank for collection. *D*-Bank pays the check and returns it to *D* at the end of the month. *P* then discovers the wrongdoing and notifies *D*. Discuss *P*'s rights against *D*, *D*-Bank, *A*-Bank, *A*, and *X*.

10. In *Neely Enterprises, Inc. v. American National Bank of Huntsville,* excerpted at the beginning of this section, the court related that unless American National acted in a commercially reasonable manner, it could not assert as a defense that Neely's negligence substantially contributed to the alterations. How was the issue of the bank's conduct resolved?

---

[63]UCC 4–401(2)(a).

CHAPTER 31

HOLDER, HOLDER IN DUE COURSE, AND DEFENSES

After you have read this chapter, you should be able to answer the following questions:

1. What is a holder? What are the rights of a holder?
2. What is a holder in due course? What are the rights of a holder in due course?
3. What is "value"? Is value the same thing as consideration?
4. Is "notice" of a claim or a defense the same thing as "knowledge" of a claim or defense?
5. What does the phrase "good faith" mean? Can a person be in good faith if he or she has notice of a claim or a defense?
6. What is the difference between a claim and a defense?
7. What claims or defenses are valid against a holder? Are these valid against a holder in due course as well?

BUSINESS DECISIONS and the LAW

Leslie Leigh returned home worn out, but feeling deeply satisfied that her full month of four successive weekends had netted her just under $820. Leigh felt that she was quite lucky to have latched on to a part-time dispatcher's job so early in the school year. She was employed by Zapata, a large trucking firm, and while it could get a little boring, the people were nice, and she could study on the job.

With the sound turned down on the TV, she sipped her beer and made a mental list of the things she was going to do with her "loot." After the rent and school expenses, there wouldn't be a lot, but it was pleasant to think about. So pleasant, in fact, she drifted off to sleep while a Letterman re-run was getting into stupid pet tricks.

Monday morning found her running late for her class, so there would be no time to stop at College Lane Bank to make a deposit. "Better indorse the thing before I start," she thought, "in case anything happens to it." And she did. "For Deposit, [signed] Leslie Leigh." Too bad she couldn't find her ballpoint pen. It might have saved a lot of trouble down the line.

Leslie enjoyed her lit class. When class was over she made it through the sugar-doughnut-and-coffee line at the student union before noticing something "funny" about her bookbag. One of its zippered compartments was open. "Oh, damn!" exclaimed Leslie. "My check." That drew a few stares. She raced out of the building then to retrace her steps. No luck. What now? "Call your bank. Stop payment." That was the advice of her friends Alex and Nick.

She made a phone call to College Lane Bank. "Only the drawer can stop payment," she announced after reaching the bank. "What do we know," Nick responded. "Call your boss."

The payroll department at Zapata was quick to stop payment. "But we can't issue you a new check, Leslie, until this one turns up safe, or unless you post bond in case we have to pay the old one after we issue you a new one."

"Thanks." She hung up the phone then and related the news to Alex and Nick.

"So, what's the problem?" Alex responded. "Payment's been stopped. Someone will probably find your check and return it today. And even if they try to cash it, they'll have to forge your signature, and then they'll get caught."

Nick agreed. "Yeah," he said. "Don't worry, be happy."

Leslie's check was not found and returned that day. Zapata was trying to assist her in the paperwork involved in getting a new check issued when she received a registered letter. She signed for it fully expecting to see her check inside. Instead she found a printed letter from a bank in a neighboring city notifying her that it was in possession of a returned Zapata payroll check, and that as an indorser she was expected to be responsible on her indorsement.

"I'm not paying anything," she was murmuring as Nick and Alex came up the stairs. As she handed Alex the letter, a machine copy of the check, printed front and back, fell out of the envelope. "Look," she said as she examined the indorsements. "Someone must have erased the 'For Deposit' I put in front of my signature."

"What do you mean 'erased?' " Nick blurted out. "You weren't dumb enough to sign the check with a pencil, were you?"

Introduction

Chapters 29 and 30 illustrate the possibility of obtaining "greater rights" in a negotiable instrument by its negotiation. This chapter centers on the person who occupies the most favored position, namely, the *holder in due course* (HIDC). Therefore, since the negotiable instrument is used so commonly in business as *the* means of payment, and since many defenses cannot be asserted against a person who is an HIDC, it becomes necessary to understand fully how you can become an HIDC. HIDC status gives you as much protection as possible in being able to enforce payment on the instrument.

holder

"A person who is in possession of a document of title or an instrument or a certificated investment security drawn, issued, or indorsed to him or his order or to bearer or in blank" UCC 1–201(20)

Holder and Holder in Due Course

A **holder** is a person in possession of a negotiable instrument "drawn, issued, or indorsed to him or to his order, or to bearer, or in blank."[1] The holder may qualify as an **HIDC** if the instrument is taken (1) for value, (2) in good faith, and (3) without notice of any claim or defense or that it is overdue or has been dishonored.[2]

holder in due course (HIDC)

The holder of a negotiable instrument who takes it for value, in good faith, and without notice that the instrument is overdue or has been dishonored or of any defense against, or claim to, the instrument by any person

[1]UCC 1–201(20).

[2]UCC 3–302(1).

A payee may qualify as an HIDC,[3] but, if there is any defense on the instrument, normally the payee will know about it. For example, a retailer-payee who has sold defective merchandise to a consumer probably will not qualify as an HIDC because of bad faith and notice of a defense—e.g., breach of contract, failure of consideration.

Even on the assumption that the payee did meet all the requirements of an HIDC, HIDCs are subject to the *assertion* of defenses—real or personal—of those parties with whom they have dealt.[4] While a seller-payee may be in good faith and quite innocent of any notice of a defense at the time of the sale, the purchaser-drawer could still assert that defense against the seller-payee at a later time.

As a practical matter, the payee can benefit from the HIDC status only if the payee is somehow insulated from the transaction which gives rise to the defense of the maker or drawer of the instrument. Assume that *D* draws a $1,000 check without inserting the name of a payee. If *D* entrusts the check to his agent *A* to deliver it to *XYZ* Corporation, but instead *A* inserts the name of one of his personal creditors (*P*), *P* may become an HIDC if *P* meets all of the requirements.[5] The following case is an illustration.

FACTS

The plaintiff imported steel coil from Japan. It was damaged on arrival, and the plaintiff's insurer advertised and sold it "as is, where is." The defendant steel company purchased the coil and, as part of the purchase price, named the plaintiff importer as payee of a negotiable promissory note. Later the defendant complained that it was the victim of a fraudulent switch or substitution of inferior goods. It asserts this fraud as a defense against the plaintiff, who claimed to be an HIDC.

DECISION

For the plaintiff-payee (HIDC). There is no suggestion that plaintiff played any knowing role in the fraud. The insurer took over matters instantly on complaint by the plaintiff and arranged for the salvage sale without any participation by the plaintiff. As a technical matter, the insurance company and its surveyor were acting as agents of the plaintiff in arranging for the plaintiff to receive a negotiable promissory note from the defendant, but this was solely for the purpose of implementing the transfer and makes no difference in the outcome.

Saale v. Interstate Steel Co., Inc., 228 N.E.2d 397 (N.Y. 1967).

► Status of Holder Fixed at Time of Becoming Holder

If *H* becomes a holder in due course and later learns of facts which, if known before *H* became a holder, would have prevented him from becoming an HIDC, *H continues* as an HIDC.

► Value

Consideration is a "bargained for" exchange—a legal detriment that a promisee gives or promises to give in return for the promisor's promise. If *A* has promised to sell *B* a $400

[3] UCC 3–302(2).

[4] UCC 3–305(2).

[5] See UCC 3–302, comment 2(g).

Honda on credit, and *B* accepts, then *B*'s consideration is his promise to pay. Until *B* has actually paid, his promise is executory, i.e., it has not been executed or fulfilled.

value

Any consideration sufficient to support a contract, a commitment to extend credit, or a past debt UCC 1–201(44)

When the word **value** is used in connection with the law of negotiable instruments, it means consideration that has been performed,[6] and also a past debt. In the illustration above, if a negotiable promissory note is substituted for the Honda and is sold by *A* to *B*, *B* becomes a holder for value when *B* pays *A* the $400. If *B* makes only partial payment, *B* becomes a holder for value to the extent actually paid.

If the $400 note was being sold by *A* to *B* at a discount—say, for the price of $387—*B* would be a holder for full face value upon payment to *A* of the agreed sum, $387. On the assumption that all the other requirements were met, *B* would qualify as an HIDC as well.

However, if *B* has paid *A* only $200 of the $387 discount price, and then receives notice of a defense of the maker to payment on the note, *B* could not qualify as an HIDC for the remainder. *B* would be limited in his HIDC status to $200. *B* is not required to pay the additional $187 because he is not getting what he originally bargained for.

security interest

"An interest in personal property or fixtures which secures payment or performance of an obligation" UCC 1–201(37)

One who acquires a **security interest** in an instrument may become a holder for value.[7] For example, *P*, the payee of a $1,000 note due in one year, may need cash immediately. Instead of selling the note at a steep discount, the payee may pledge it as collateral security for a $600 loan. In that event, the one who advances the $600 on the security of *P*'s $1,000 note is a holder for value to the extent of the loan.

cancellation

The nullification of a contractual obligation

A holder may give value if an instrument is taken for an antecedent or preexisting claim whether the claim is due and matured or not. An easy illustration of this is the payment of a debt with a check. The **cancellation** of the debt in return for the check constitutes value.[8]

Keep in mind that "payment" with negotiable instruments is really only "conditional" payment. That is, the debt is considered paid only if the instrument is honored or paid. If the check "bounces" (is dishonored and returned) or the note is not paid at maturity, the debt is now enforceable in the courts.[9] A full discharge from an obligation occurs only in those situations where a bank is a maker, drawer, or acceptor of an instrument and the party who uses it to satisfy the obligation does not indorse.[10] For example, if Bert Jones purchased athletic equipment from Spaulding Company and paid for it with a cashier's check issued by Baltimore Trust Company payable to the order of Spaulding, Jones would not be liable on the instrument if he did not indorse it. The debt is solely that of Baltimore Trust, the primary party.

Value is given if negotiable instruments are exchanged—for example, if a check is given in purchase of a note, or if an irrevocable commitment is made to a third party in return for an instrument.[11] The latter is illustrated by the issuance of a letter of credit by a bank in return for a note or check of its customer.

---

[6]UCC 3–303(a).

[7]UCC 3–303(a), 4–209.

[8]UCC 3–303(b).

[9]UCC 3–802(1)(b).

[10]UCC 3–802(1)(a).

[11]UCC 3–303(c).

Banks give value, and may become HIDCs upon meeting the other requirements, to the extent they acquire a security interest.[12] Security interests arise to the extent that the credit given for an item has been withdrawn.[13] For example, if a bank that is in the process of collecting a $1,000 item for its customer-depositor allows the immediate withdrawal of $500, it will be a holder for value for $500 if the check later bounces.

A bank may give its customer an unreserved right of withdrawal prior to the time an item is collected. In this event, the bank is an HIDC for the full amount even if none of the credit has been drawn upon[14] because of the customer's right of immediate withdrawal and contingent liability of the bank. This is illustrated in the following case.

FACTS

Mr. Maisto purchased a "cashier's check" from the defendant, City Bank, for $3,446 making payment with two checks plus cash. One check was for $2,585.50 drawn on account no. 0–41190–6 (Tony's Sunoco) maintained with Laurel Bank, the plaintiff. Upon the issuance of the "cashier's check," an officer of the defendant, City Bank, phoned the plaintiff, Laurel, and was told by some unidentified person in bookkeeping that the check "was good at this time."

On the same day, Mr. Maisto deposited the cashier's check for $3,446 with other items for a total deposit of $9,501 in account no. 0–41233–3 (B & D Automotive), which was also maintained with plaintiff Laurel Bank. This account, at time of deposit, was overdrawn by $21,079.43. The deposit was provisionally credited by plaintiff to the B & D Automotive account and the overdrawn balance was reduced by that amount. The plaintiff later "bounced" (dishonored) the $2,585.50 check—returned it to the defendant, City Bank, because of insufficient funds. When the plaintiff, Laurel, then presented the cashier's check for $3,446 to the defendant, City Bank, it was dishonored.

The trial court concluded (1) that the plaintiff was a mere holder of the cashier's check because it did not establish that it took the check for value, and (2) that the defendant, City Bank, established a defense of want of consideration because the $2,585.50 check, which was one of the items used to purchase the cashier's check, was subsequently dishonored. The court rendered judgment for the plaintiff in the amount of only $860.50, the difference between the checks. The plaintiff then appealed.

DECISION

For the plaintiff; new trial. Defendant established want of consideration, which is a valid defense against a holder but not against an HIDC. The trial court held that no value was given because credit against the Maisto account was not irrevocable. Since Maisto's account B & D was overdrawn, the plaintiff, Laurel Bank, did give value through an antecedent claim. The provisional basis of credit in no way hinders the value given to determine one's HIDC status. The plaintiff's action in provisionally crediting a $9,501 deposit to the antecedent debt of Maisto was an exercise of its common law right of set-off. The plaintiff was an HIDC as far as value given is concerned. The judgment of the lower court is set aside and the matter remanded for trial limited to the issue of whether the plaintiff took the cashier's check in good faith and without notice of its being overdue, of dishonor, defect, or defense.

Laurel Bank and Trust Co. v. The City Nat'l Bank of Conn., 365 A.2d 1222 (Conn. 1976).

---

[12]UCC 4–209.

[13]UCC 4–208(1)(a).

[14]UCC 4–208(1)(b).

good faith

"Honesty in fact in the conduct or transaction concerned" UCC 1–201(19)

► Good Faith

There is a simply stated test for the good faith of a holder—"honesty in fact in the conduct or transaction concerned."[15] The test is entirely *subjective* in nature, i.e., the holder is not judged by an objective standard of reasonableness or anything else. Even though a reasonable person would or should have suspected some defense or claim, if the holder honestly did not, the holder can satisfy the good faith test.

The good faith test, sometimes characterized as "empty head—honest heart," means that a holder can meet this criterion even though the holder negligently or carelessly turns a deaf ear to facts and circumstances that would put a reasonable person on notice of a defense. Such disregard for suspicious circumstances, however, may cause one to flunk the "notice"[16] test. In the following case, the defendant could advance no reasons sufficient to overcome the presumed good faith of the plaintiff.

FACTS

Money Mart Check Cashing Center, Inc., cashed a payroll check for payee John Cronin that had been issued to him by defendant Epicycle Corporation. Epicycle, defendant, stopped payment on the check because one of its employees had written it for an amount in excess of the authorized amount. Money Mart, alleging to be an HIDC, sued Epicycle for the full sum of the instrument. Epicycle challenged Money Mart's good faith.

DECISION

Drafters of the UCC intended that the good faith standard be a subjective one. Hence the principal issue is whether the plaintiff is in good faith, however stupid and negligent his behavior might have been.

It is true that Money Mart cashed the check without knowing whether a stop order had been issued, and, further, it did not inquire into that point. But absence of such knowledge is not the equivalent of bad faith. Money Mart is an HIDC and is entitled to a judgment.

Money Mart Check Cashing Center, Inc. v. Epicycle Corp., 667 P.2d 1373 (Colo. 1983).

► The Notice Requirement

If a holder takes an instrument with notice that there is a claim or defense against it, or that it is overdue or has been dishonored, then the holder cannot qualify as an HIDC.[17] A holder has notice of one of these facts if:

1. the holder has actual knowledge of it; or
2. the holder has received[18] a notice or notification of it; or
3. from all the facts and circumstances known to the holder at the time in question, he or she has reason to know that it exists.[19]

---

[15]UCC 1–201(19).

[16]UCC 1–201(25).

[17]UCC 3–302(1)(c).

[18]UCC 1–201(25).

[19]Ibid.

Effective notice must allow a reasonable time to act.[20] To illustrate, assume that *H* is in good faith—i.e., that he honestly does not know that *M*, the maker of a note, has a defense of fraud against *P*, the payee. If *H* has received notification of this defense through the mail, and, while it has not actually come to his attention, the letter has been delivered to his business address in ample time for receipt of such communications,[21] then *H* has legal notice of the defense and cannot qualify as an HIDC.

Next—and still on the assumption that *H* is in good faith—suppose that two days before maturity he pays $100 for a $1,000 note that has been in circulation, with interest compounded, for ten years. The reason *P*, the payee, is willing to sell the instrument so cheaply is that *P* has defrauded the maker. Since *H* honestly does not know of the fraud, will he qualify as an HIDC? Not likely. The sale of this instrument at *such a large discount* is a fact "known to him at the time in question" and will probably be sufficient to give *H* "reason to know" that some defense exists.[22]

Claims exist when the owner has been wrongfully deprived of the instrument. In the above illustration, *H* would not qualify as an HIDC if, at the time he became a holder, he had notice of a *claim* rather than notice of a *defense*. The owner of an instrument would have a claim if it were stolen by someone and transferred to *H*. On the assumption that the instrument was *bearer* in form at the time it was stolen, *H* could be an HIDC if he had no notice of the owner's claim, and if all the other requirements were met.

If the instrument was order in form, however, the thief would have to forge the owner's indorsement, and in that event, *H* could not become an HIDC because he would not be a holder—the instrument did not flow to him by indorsement. Even in those situations where *H* is in good faith and has no notice of the forgery, title does not pass to him through the unauthorized indorsement of the forger.[23]

Notice of a Claim or Defense The following are illustrative of those events that will give notice of a claim or defense and prevent a holder from becoming an HIDC:[24]

1. Visible evidence of forgery, alteration, or other irregularity (such as wholesale incompleteness) that calls into question the validity, terms, or ownership of the instrument.
2. Information that the obligation of some party is voidable—e.g., the party was induced by fraud or mistake to sign the instrument—or, information that all parties have been discharged—e.g., all signatures have been cancelled or the instrument has been paid.
3. Knowledge that the **fiduciary** has negotiated in breach of duty—e.g., an instrument indorsed "Pay to *T* in trust for *P*, [signed] *P*" was negotiated by *T* to *H* in payment of *T*'s personal debt.

fiduciary
A person with a duty to act primarily for the benefit of another

[20]UCC 3–304(6).

[21]UCC 1–201(26).

[22]UCC 1–201(25)(c).

[23]UCC 3–404.

[24]UCC 3–304(1)(2).

In following case, the plaintiff bank was found to have notice of a defense in virtue of an irregularity appearing on the face of the note.

FACTS

Plaintiff Hessler made a negotiable promissory note payable to a grain company and, at the grain company's request, signed as co-maker his wife's name. Her name was followed by his initials to designate that he had signed it on her behalf; he affixed his signature to the note as well. The grain company negotiated the note to a holder, Arcanum National Bank, that alleges to be an HIDC.

DECISION

The plaintiff bank cannot qualify as an HIDC because it took the note with knowledge of an irregularity on its face. Since the Arcanum National Bank handled the Hessler's personal finances, it should have noticed that the note was not signed by Mrs. Hessler's authentic signature and that her name was followed by her husband's initials. This irregularity called into question the validity and terms of the note, and created an ambiguity regarding liability on the note.

Arcanum Nat'l Bank v. Hessler, 433 N.E.2d 204 (Ohio 1982).

Notice That the Instrument Is Overdue or Dishonored A purchaser is given notice that an instrument is overdue or dishonored if the purchaser has reason to know:

principal
In money, the capital sum of a money debt

default
A failure to perform a legal duty

1. that the **principal,** or any part of it, is overdue, or that there is an uncured **default** in payment of another instrument of the same series; or
2. that acceleration of the instrument has been made; or
3. that a demand instrument is being taken after a previous unsuccessful demand for payment, or after an unreasonable length of time following issuance (a reasonable period of time for an uncertified check drawn and payable in the United States is presumed to be thirty days).[25]

There are some events that do not convey notice. The public filing or recording of a document that relates to a negotiable instrument does not give notice sufficient to prevent a purchaser from becoming an HIDC.[26] Nor does knowledge of the following facts give notice of a claim or defense:[27]

1. The instrument was antedated or postdated.
2. The instrument was issued in exchange for an executory (unperformed) promise.
3. The instrument has an accommodation signature.
4. Completion of an incomplete instrument, without notice of impropriety.
5. Negotiation by a fiduciary but without knowledge that the fiduciary is breaching a duty.
6. Default in payment of interest on the instrument or in payment of another instrument (except a default on an instrument of the same series).

---

[25]UCC 3–304(3).

[26]UCC 3–304(5).

[27]UCC 3–304(4).

Rights of a Holder in Due Course

A holder who qualifies as an HIDC takes the instrument

1. free of all claims—e.g., the true owner of lost or stolen bearer paper cannot reclaim it from an HIDC;
2. free of all defenses, except real or universal defenses and defenses of those parties who dealt with the HIDC.[28]

Real or Universal Defenses

While a negotiable instrument is, for all appearances, a formal written contract, it may not be *contractually* binding on various parties because either they do not have the capacity to contract, or they assert other defenses that preclude or relieve them of contractual liability on the instrument.[29] Defenses to contractual liability on an instrument are called **real** or **universal defenses.** The following are examples of real defenses.

real or **universal defense**
A defense to *contractual* liability on an instrument

► Minority

This defense is allowed against an HIDC to the same extent that state law will allow it against anyone else.[30] For example, in most states a minor has the option to disaffirm any contract made with an adult. If the minor disaffirms the purchase of a *necessary* item, he or she is liable for the reasonable value. For *nonnecessaries,* the minor simply returns or offers to return what is left of the item (if anything) and is entitled to receive back all of the money he or she paid for the item. The adult is generally not permitted to retain any part of the money for wear and tear, damage, or depreciation.

Those states that follow the majority view outlined above would allow the minor a full defense against an HIDC if the minor purchased nonnecessaries. The HIDC would have to recover from other parties to the instrument on their indorsement contracts or their transfer warranties.

If the minor purchased a necessary item, he or she would be liable to the HIDC for an amount equaling the reasonable value of the item. For the amount between the reasonable value and the larger amount on the face of the instrument, the HIDC would have to pursue other parties to the instrument.

► Insanity or Duress Precluding Contractual Liability

A person who has been judicially committed to a mental institution has been **adjudicated** not to have capacity to contract, and, therefore, cannot be contractually liable as a party to a negotiable instrument. Such a person who made or drew a negotiable instrument, which was later negotiated to an HIDC, could assert the real defense of lack of capacity.

adjudicate
To determine by judicial authority

The effect of **duress** (coercion) in influencing someone to sign a negotiable instrument depends upon the law in each particular state. In some instances the duress

duress
Wrongful inducement to do that which a reasonable person would have been unable to resist

[28]UCC 3–305.

[29]UCC 3–305(2)(a)–(e).

[30]UCC 3–305(2)(a).

causes the contract to be voidable, in which case duress is a "personal defense" (discussed later) not assertable successfully against an HIDC. In other instances the duress prevents the transaction from being a contract, in which case it is a real defense assertable successfully against all parties. For example, *T* threatens *D* that, if *D* doesn't sign the check as drawer, *T* will urge the district attorney to prosecute *D*'s wife for the commission of an alleged crime. *D* signs the check. *D* is liable on the check as a voidable contract, which he can avoid; he has a "personal defense." However, if *T* pointed a loaded gun at *D*'s head, compelling *D* to sign the check, while the instrument is negotiable on its face, it is *not a contract* binding *D* as a party to it because *D* did not intentionally or voluntarily create it. This is a form of duress precluding contractual liability; it is a real defense, and *D* is protected from any liability on the check. But the instrument can be negotiated by *P* to an HIDC, and *P* would be liable thereon as a contracting party. The *HIDC* will have to recover from the wrongdoer or some indorser or transferor subsequent to the wrongdoer.

► Illegality

null
Of no legal effect

usury
Charging a rate of interest on a loan higher than that permitted by statute

Illegality also may be a real defense. For example, some states prohibit the enforcement of any contract or instrument given in connection with a gambling transaction. These obligations are treated as **null** and void because gambling is thought to be inimical to the public interest and, therefore, contrary to public policy. In such a state, an HIDC would be confronted with a real defense if the maker or drawer of an instrument can prove that it was issued in payment of a gambling debt.

Another common illustration of illegality as a real defense is **usury.** Some states penalize the charging of an excessive rate of interest on a loan by absolutely denying the enforcement of usurious instruments. The remedy of an HIDC in such cases is against the indorser or warrantor.

In each of these examples the nature of the defense—whether or not it is a real defense—depends on state law. In some states—Nevada for instance—gambling may be no defense at all. In some states illegality merely makes the contract voidable. Accordingly, where illegality makes the transaction *void,* it is a *real defense.* When illegality makes the transaction *voidable,* it is a *personal defense.*

In the following case the maker of a negotiable promissory note issued it pursuant to a transaction declared illegal by statute and therefore the maker had a real defense on the ground of illegality.

FACTS

Gateway Financial Service, a defendant, a corporation licensed to deal in secondary mortgages, made a loan to plaintiffs that was secured by a mortgage on their home. The transaction was governed by the New Jersey Secondary Mortgage Loan Act. Gateway sold the note and mortgage to Security Pacific Finance Corp., a defendant, also a corporation licensed to deal in secondary mortgages. At the closing of the loan by Gateway to the plaintiffs, a $3,000 deduction was made for credit life insurance; however, Gateway never acquired a policy of insurance because Gateway never caused the premium to be submitted to the insurance company. In addition, plaintiffs assert that they were forced to buy the insurance. They also say that the $800 attorney's fee charged at the closing was unlawfully high. In these ways, argue plaintiffs, the loan transaction violated various provisions of the Act.

Plaintiffs' suit against Gateway and Security Pacific seeks a judgment declaring that their note and mortgage are void and unenforceable by defendants. They also seek return from Security Pacific of all periodic payments plaintiffs made to it since the filing of the complaint, and a judgment against Gateway for the amount of the deducted insurance premium.

The N.J. Secondary Mortgage Loan Act of 1979 was adopted in response to numerous abuses in the secondary mortgage market. It provides, in part, as follows: Any obligation on the part of the borrower arising out of a secondary mortgage loan shall be void and unenforceable unless such secondary mortgage was executed in full compliance with the provisions of this Act.

DECISION

For plaintiffs. Assuming that Security Pacific is a holder in due course of plaintiffs' note and mortgage, what are its rights if, because of noncompliance with the Act's requirements, the note and mortgage are "void and unenforceable"? The answer lies in the policy of the Act and in the words of the Uniform Commercial Code as adopted in New Jersey. It is plain that the policy of the Act is to give generous protection to borrowers in regulated transactions. The Act recognizes that second mortgagors are frequently persons seeking loans of last resort, that they are usually in no position to bargain over the terms of the loan or to have any real idea what they might bargain about. The Act recognizes that lenders of last resort are frequently persons whose methods ought to attract careful scrutiny and that their customers are peculiarly unfit to perform that function. Thus, the Act not only creates monetary penalties for persons violating its terms, but it also authorizes the Commissioner of Banking to suspend or revoke the license of violators. The Act goes further and makes noncomplying loans void and unenforceable.

What does "void and unenforceable" mean to a holder in due course? UCC Section 3–305(2) says that a holder in due course takes the instrument free of all defenses of any party with whom he has not dealt except. . . .

(b) such other incapacity, or duress, or illegality of the transaction, as renders the obligation of the party a nullity.

Therefore, when the legislature decided that a noncomplying loan should be void and unenforceable, it must have had its eye on the Code provision that subjects even holders in due course to the defenses of "such . . . illegality of the transaction, as renders the obligation . . . a nullity." It is inconceivable that the legislature thought there was some difference between "void and unenforceable" in the Act and "a nullity" in the Code. The words are interchangeable. Surely, the legislature meant to say that a noncomplying secondary mortgage would be a nullity as the word is used in UCC 3–305(2).

Westervelt v. Gateway Fin. Serv., et al., 464 A.2d 1203 (N.J. 1983).

Surely, the legislature was conscious in 1970 of the need to harmonize the terms of the new Act with the already existing Code.

► Fraud in the Procurement (Fraud in the "Factum," "Execution," or "Essence")

Assume *A* has signed an instrument and that *A* has a real defense if *A* has been deceived to the extent that

1. *A* does not know that he signed an instrument, or *A* knows that he signed an instrument, but is completely tricked and deceived regarding its essential terms; and
2. *A* has not acted negligently or carelessly.[31]

If a country-western music fan rushes up to Willie Nelson to get his autograph, Willie will have a real or universal defense against a subsequent HIDC if that signature was placed on a negotiable note cleverly hidden in an autograph pad. It is clear that Willie did not intend to create the note, and, on the assumption that under these circumstances he was not negligent, he will be protected if the "fan" negotiates the instrument to an HIDC.

This defense would arise as well if the person who knowingly and intentionally signed an instrument did not have knowledge or reasonable opportunity to obtain

[31]UCC 3–305(2)(c).

knowledge of its essential terms. For example, assume that *M* is given one note to read and become familiar with while the salesperson is filling in the blanks of a supposedly identical note. Actually there are new and unfavorable terms in the salesperson's note, but *M* has been told that they are identical. Finally, the salesperson switches notes with *M,* and *M* innocently signs the one with the unfavorable terms. This will give *M* a real defense even if the salesperson negotiates the note to an HIDC.

The common features in these two examples of the real defense of fraud—sometimes called fraud in the *procurement, factum, execution,* or *essence*—are as follows:

1. There was no intent to create a negotiable instrument, or no knowledge of the terms, and
2. There was no negligence.

In effect, no contract has been created, so there is no legal ground for liability.

If, on the other hand, a person really intends to create a negotiable instrument but has been *induced* to do so by *P*'s fraud and deceit—e.g., *P* has lied to *M* regarding some essential component of a stereo unit—*M* would have only a personal or limited defense, which would not be valid against an HIDC. Such a defense of fraud in the inducement would be successful against a mere holder or assignee but not against an HIDC, who could get a judgment against *M. M* would then have to seek recovery against *P,* the person who defrauded *M.* This "personal" or "limited" defense of fraud—where *M* really intends to create the instrument and is not so defrauded that he does not know what he is signing—is known as *fraud in the inducement.* In the following case, the defendant tried unsuccessfully to establish a defense of fraud. Since the action was initiated by the payee, even a personal defense—fraud in the inducement—would have been sufficient.

FACTS

Prior to their divorce, Betty and W. G. Ellis executed a $2800 negotiable promissory note to Standard Finance Co. Nothing was paid on the note, and Standard brought this action against Betty. She appealed the judgment against her on the basis of fraud.

DECISION

Prior to the execution of this note, Betty related that her ex-husband gave her constant assurances that her "signature was a formality and that he alone was liable and that the debt would be repaid without any participation by her." She further insisted that these misrepresentations induced her to sign the note without an understanding of its essential terms and, therefore, her signature was not a manifestation of her real or actual consent.

If, indeed, the misrepresentations of W. G. were such that Betty neither knew nor had reasonable opportunity to know the character or the essential terms of the note, then the law would treat it as a void, or a void contract, and that would be a full defense. But in this case no representation was made to Betty that this note was anything other than a note. In fact the finance company representative explained the terms and conditions of the note to Betty and W. G. prior to their execution of the note.

Judgment for the finance company was affirmed; Betty's only recourse is against her ex-husband.

Standard Fin. Co., Ltd. v. Ellis, 657 P.2d 1056 (Haw. Ct. App. 1983).

► Unauthorized Signatures

A forgery or unauthorized signature does not obligate the person whose name has been wrongfully used, unless that person ratifies the signature or is precluded by his or her negligence from denying the signature.[32] The rationale for this rule is obvious. Since the person whose name has been forged had no intention of creating the instrument or parting with ownership, he or she is not obligated by the forgery. The person has not agreed to any contract, and is not liable on the instrument because his or her signature does not appear thereon. If the real owner's *indorsement* has been forged, the owner still has a claim to the instrument. The recipient of such an instrument, which is later reclaimed by the true owner, can attempt to recover from the wrongdoer on the forged indorsement[33] or on the transfer warranties.[34] In the following case the drawer/drawee was held liable on its draft to one of the payees whose indorsement was forged.

FACTS

The plaintiff, Naoma Lee, appealed from an order dismissing her complaint against the American National Life Insurance Company. The plaintiff had sued the insurance company for a fire loss covering the premises which she and another had contracted to sell to Murl and Adeline Skidmore. In her complaint, the plaintiff alleged that a contract of insurance was procured from the defendant by the parties pursuant to a land contract. The Skidmores and Naoma Lee were the named insureds.

On September 10, 1974 the property covered by the policy was partially destroyed by fire. The plaintiff maintained that the defendant company was notified of the fire but failed to indemnify her for the loss, which she alleges was $2,500. The company contended that it issued a draft on October 14, 1974 in the sum of $2,125 in the name of the land contract buyers (Skidmores) and plaintiff Lee to cover the fire damage. It maintained that, by issuing this instrument, which was apparently cashed by the Skidmores over plaintiff's forged indorsement, it has satisfied its obligation to plaintiff. Lee never got any of the money.

DECISION

Judgment for plaintiff. "Under the Ohio statute, an instrument payable to the order of two or more persons ... if not in the alternative is payable to all of them and may be negotiated, discharged, or enforced only by all of them." The draft in question was not payable in the alternative, and therefore it could not be properly negotiated nor discharged following the unauthorized and forged indorsement. As the defendant was both the drawer and drawee of the draft, it was obligated to make payment to the named payees therein, or other proper holders.

The payment of the draft through a forged indorsement failed to discharge the instrument as to the plaintiff, and such a payment by the drawer-drawee constitutes a conversion of that instrument for which it must respond in damages.

Lee v. Skidmore, 361 N.E.2d 499 (Ohio 1976).

Remember to distinguish *forgery* from the signature of an *impostor*, because the signature of an impostor does pass good title to the holder. The holder may even qualify as an HIDC, but there can never be a holder or an HIDC following a required indorsement that has been forged.[35]

---

[32]UCC 3–404, 406.

[33]UCC 3–404(1).

[34]UCC 3–417(2).

[35]For examples and discussion of these distinctions, see pp. 644–648.

► Material Alteration

material alteration

"Any alteration of an instrument is material which changes the contract of any party thereto in any respect" UCC 3–407(1)

The real or universal defense of **material alteration** can best be understood by considering, first, its definition, then its general effect, and finally its effect on an HIDC.[36] Keep in mind, however, that a defendant's negligence can deprive the defendant of this defense just as it can deprive one of the defense of forgery,[37] and further that any party may assent to or ratify a material alteration.

Any change in the contract of any party to the instrument in *any* respect is a material alteration. It may be only a slight change, such as the addition of one cent to the amount payable or an advance of one day in the date of payment.[38] This definition includes, but is not limited to, unauthorized filling in the blanks on an incomplete instrument as well as adding to or deleting from the instrument.

For example, an incomplete instrument may be issued to a payee-creditor with instructions to fill in the amount with the balance due. If this holder fills in an excessive amount, that would be a material alteration. It would be a material alteration as well if this person added, changed, deleted, or in any way modified terms of a complete instrument to which the issuer previously had become bound. In the following case the unauthorized completion of an incomplete instrument in the amount payable was a material alteration not assertable against the HIDC.

FACTS

Elias Saka, defendant, gave Weaver Levy a signed check that was blank regarding the amount. Levy was instructed to complete it for $800 and make payment to the payee, Sahara Hotel, plaintiff, on a $3,046.03 bill charged to Affinity Pictures, Inc. Instead, Levy completed the check for the full amount of $3,046.03 and delivered it to the Sahara. Saka stopped payment on the check, and this suit was instituted by Sahara for the full amount. Saka alleges by way of defense (1) that the payee Sahara is not an HIDC because it had notice that the charges were disputed and (2) that the completion of the check by Levy in a different handwriting from that of the drawer, Saka, was sufficient to put Sahara on notice of irregularity.

DECISION

Judgment for Sahara. A payee may be an HIDC, UCC 3–302(2), but, as a practical matter, this is the exception rather than the rule. Since the payee is an immediate party to the underlying transaction, under normal circumstances he cannot claim this status because he necessarily knows of any defenses to the contract. However, Saka's evidence was not sufficient to raise the issue that the hotel had notice of a dispute.

The fact that the body of the check was completed in a different handwriting from that of the drawer's signature did not impose on Sahara the duty to make further inquiries, nor did it destroy Sahara's good faith because UCC 3–304(4)(d) provides that knowledge that an incomplete instrument has been completed by another does not of itself give the purchaser notice of a claim or defense unless the purchaser has notice of any improper completion.

Elias Saka v. Sahara-Nevada Corp., 558 P.2d 535 (Nev. 1976).

---

[36] UCC 3–407.

[37] UCC 3–406.

[38] See UCC 3–407, comment 1.

The next inquiry concerns the effect of a material alteration. If a holder makes a material alteration and if it is made with a fraudulent purpose, any party whose contract is thereby changed receives a discharge from any further liability on the instrument. This means that, if the payee of an instrument raised the amount from $100 to $1,000, the maker or drawer is fully discharged.

If this instrument was issued by a buyer for merchandise, the buyer could retain the goods without making further payment to the seller payee-creditor. The payee-creditor is penalized for his fraud. To carry this example one step further, the payee and the issuer would be discharged if the material alteration was made by a subsequent holder. Those persons on the instrument prior to the material alteration are the ones whose contract and liability on the instrument are so affected.

Alterations that are not made by holders, or alterations that are made by holders without any fraudulent intent, do not discharge anyone. To illustrate: if a holder extended the time of payment with the purpose and effect of benefiting the debtor, there would be no fraudulent material alteration, and the debtor would not be discharged. Nor would anyone be discharged if the change was made by a person who did not qualify as a holder.

In the following case it was held that the alteration was not material nor fraudulently made.

FACTS

The plaintiff, William C. Thomas, filed suit alleging that the defendants, Mr. and Mrs. Osborn, as makers of a note payable to the plaintiff, refused to pay the note when due. After the note was signed, the plaintiff had a notary public who had seen James Osborn sign the note, but had not witnessed Mrs. Osborn's signature, add an acknowledgment and notarize the signature of James. The defendants denied the plaintiff's claim and asserted that the note was obtained by misrepresentation. They also counterclaimed for damages claimed to have resulted when the plaintiff added an acknowledgment to the note and when the note was recorded. The court entered judgment for the plaintiff.

The defendants challenged the decision of the trial court. They claimed that the acknowledgment, notarization, and recording of the note was fraudulent and a material alteration under UCC 3–407.

DECISION

Affirmed, for plaintiff. The Osborns contended that the recording of the note added the relationship of mortgagor-mortgagee to that of maker-payee and, therefore, there was a material alteration of the note. However, the note cannot be taken as a mortgage, for it does not contain the expression of an intent to impose a lien upon the property. The note includes the legal description of the real property because the terms of the note provide for payment in full on sale of the property and not because of the granting of a security interest which might be looked to in case of default. According to UCC 3–407, an alteration may be material if it involves a change in "the number or relations of the parties." In this case, the instrument could not be construed as a mortgage, and thus it did not change the relations of the parties.

The Code says that "alteration by a holder which is both fraudulent and material discharges any party whose contract is thereby changed . . ." 3–407(2)(a). Neither the recording of the instrument nor the addendum changed the relationships of the parties, or materially affected the form of the document, the time of payment, or the sum payable. Thus the change is not material. Finally, the plaintiff did not act fraudulently. The plaintiff's purpose for recording the note was to achieve security for payment of the debt; his intent was "misguided" rather than fraudulent.

Thomas v. Osborn, 536 P.2d 8 (Wash. 1975).

Material alterations do not deprive a subsequent HIDC of the right to enforce the instrument for the original amount, or for the amount that was fraudulently inserted on an incomplete instrument. If a payee raised a $100 instrument to $1,000 or improperly filled in the amount of $1,000 on an incomplete instrument, the issuer would be liable to an HIDC for $100 on the *raised* instrument, and for $1,000 on the improperly completed one.

► Discharge

If at the time the instrument is received the HIDC has notice that a party has been discharged, the discharge will operate as a real defense against the HIDC. Discharge in insolvency proceedings is a real defense even if the HIDC has no notice of it.

Personal or Limited Defenses

personal or **limited defense**
A defense that is not to *contractual* liability on an instrument but, rather, is to *avoid* liability on an instrument; any defense that is not a real defense

Defenses that seek to avoid liability on the instrument (*voidable* contract) are called **personal** or **limited defenses.** Such defenses cannot be asserted successfully against an HIDC. The following are examples:

1. Fraud inducing the making of an instrument
2. Failure of consideration
3. Want of consideration
4. Defenses to liability on a contract, a valid claim to the instrument by anyone
5. Nonperformance of any condition precedent
6. Nondelivery of the instrument
7. Delivery for a special purpose that has not occurred; the instrument is unauthorizedly delivered
8. Generally other defenses that are not the real defenses just discussed.

To illustrate: suppose *D* issues his check to *P* to pay for goods that *P* promises to deliver to *D*. *P* never delivers the goods and never intends to do so. *D* has the personal defenses of fraud and failure of consideration, which *D* can assert successfully against *P* and later holders but not against a subsequent HIDC. If *D* issues a check to *P* as a gift, there is a *want* of consideration.

HIDC and the Federal Trade Commission

The FTC issued a rule in 1976 that has the effect of denying the rights of an HIDC to a holder who receives an instrument given in a consumer credit transaction. The rule declares that it is an unfair and deceptive practice within Section 5 of the Federal Trade Commission Act for the credit-seller of personal, family, or household goods or services to natural persons to use any method of financing that separates the seller's duty to perform from the buyer's duty to pay.

In at least ten-point boldface type, the seller must include the following: Notice #1 in any consumer credit contract executed by the buyer and Notice #2 in any direct loan financing agreement that the seller arranges for the buyer.

Notice #1

ANY HOLDER OF THIS CONSUMER CREDIT CONTRACT IS SUBJECT TO ALL CLAIMS AND DEFENSES WHICH THE DEBTOR COULD ASSERT AGAINST THE SELLER OF GOODS OR SERVICES OBTAINED PURSUANT HERETO OR WITH THE PROCEEDS HEREOF. RECOVERY HEREUNDER BY THE DEBTOR SHALL NOT EXCEED AMOUNTS PAID BY THE DEBTOR HEREUNDER.

Notice #2

ANY HOLDER OF THIS CONSUMER CREDIT CONTRACT IS SUBJECT TO ALL CLAIMS AND DEFENSES WHICH THE DEBTOR COULD ASSERT AGAINST THE SELLER OF GOODS OR SERVICES OBTAINED WITH THE PROCEEDS HEREOF. RECOVERY HEREUNDER BY THE DEBTOR SHALL NOT EXCEED AMOUNTS PAID BY THE DEBTOR HEREUNDER.

The rule covers sellers who in the ordinary course of business sell or lease goods or services to consumers. It does *not* include the following:

1. Sales for industrial or commercial uses
2. Transactions by legal entities other than natural persons
3. Purchases of realty, commodities, securities, farm equipment, or services of public utilities
4. Consumer goods or services where the purchase price is more than $25,000

To illustrate: assume that a consumer enters into a credit purchase of a stereo with a local retailer. Prior to the FTC rule, the consumer may have been required to sign a negotiable promissory note for the unpaid balance, and the note may have been negotiated to an HIDC. If so, the HIDC could get a judgment against the consumer who defaulted upon payments even though the stereo never functioned properly.

Today the consumer preserves all his or her defenses, and these defenses may be asserted against the retailer or against a third party who, except for the FTC rule, would have had the rights of an HIDC. The third party is treated as an assignee of the retailer-assignor's rights. The third party assignee or transferee simply stands in the shoes of the retailer and is subject to all the consumer's defenses that are available against the retailer.

Summary Statement

1. An HIDC is a holder who has given value for a negotiable instrument in good faith and without notice of a claim or defense to the instrument or that the instrument is overdue or has been previously dishonored. A payee may qualify as an HIDC. Personal defenses cannot be asserted successfully against an HIDC, but real defenses can be asserted against the HIDC. However, even an HIDC is subject to the defenses (real or personal) of a party with whom the HIDC has dealt.
2. *Value* means that the consideration promised in exchange for an instrument has been executed or performed. It may also consist of an antecedent (preexisting) claim (past debt), whether the claim is due or not, or of a security interest acquired by any party (including a bank). Value is given when negotiable instruments are exchanged and when one party makes an irrevocable commitment to another in reliance on a negotiable instrument.
3. The good faith required of an HIDC simply means that the HIDC must have acted honestly in fact in the transaction in which he or she purchased the instrument. This standard is completely subjective and is applied on a case-by-case basis.
4. Notice of a claim or defense to the instrument, or that the instrument is overdue or previously dishonored, is a more rigid or objective standard than good faith. A

holder has notice of one of these and is prevented from becoming an HIDC: (a) if holder has actual knowledge; or (b) if holder has received notice even though he or she has not actually read it within a reasonable time after receipt; or (c) if from all the facts and circumstances known to the holder at the time in question, he or she has reason to know that one of these defects exists.

5. One may be confronted with notice of a claim or a defense, or that an instrument is overdue or dishonored, by information which appears on the face of the instrument or from outside sources. However, no notice is conveyed (a) by the filing of a document that affects the instrument; (b) by antedating or postdating; (c) by issuance of the instrument for an executory promise; (d) by knowledge of accommodation signatures; (e) by completion of an incomplete instrument; (f) by the negotiation of a fiduciary (*T* negotiates to you an instrument previously indorsed restrictively, "Pay to *T* in trust for *X*, [signed] William Carter," and you are without knowledge of any breach of trust by *T*); or (g) by default in payment of interest or in payment of another instrument.
6. Basically, a mere holder takes an instrument subject to all claims and defenses that may exist, but an HIDC is free from all claims and free from all defenses except real defenses and defenses of parties with whom the HIDC has dealt. Real defenses arise when the basic obligation for which the instrument was originally issued is null and void. This may be because the initial transaction—e.g., gambling "contracts" in some states—was completely illegal and prohibited by statute, or because a "contract" never really existed in the first place—e.g., extreme duress or other lack of capacity, fraud in the procurement or factum, forgery, or fraudulent material alteration. A discharge in insolvency proceedings is a real defense, and the same is true of any other discharge that the HIDC has notice of when taking the instrument.
7. The Federal Trade Commission has adopted a rule that has the effect of eliminating HIDCs from consumer credit transactions. Those parties who would normally qualify as HIDCs under the UCC are subjected to the same defenses as a retailer who has made a credit sale of personal, family, or household goods or services to a consumer.

This chapter has emphasized the benefits of the status of a holder in due course. The following case illustrates how the requirement of good faith can be undermined by a close working relationship between a bank and its customer.

ARCANUM NATIONAL BANK v. HESSLER
433 N.E. 2d 204 (Ohio 1982)

Appellant, Kenneth Hessler, was in the business of raising hogs for the John Smith Grain Company. John Smith Grain or J & J Farms, Inc., would deliver hogs to appellant and require appellant to sign a promissory note payable to John Smith Grain to cover the cost of the hogs and feed. Without the knowledge or consent of appellant, John Smith Grain would then sell the note to appellee, Arcanum National Bank. Appellee would credit John Smith Grain with the face amount of the note and open a commercial loan account for appellant. The first such transaction, according to the bank's records, was August 28, 1974. The hogs were usually sold by J & J Farms to Producer's Livestock Association, and a portion of the proceeds were applied to satisfy appellant's note and loan account. Appellant received a flat fee and a share of the net profits.

On January 4, 1977, appellant signed a promissory note payable to John Smith Grain for hogs delivered on that date. J & J Farms had previously mortgaged the hogs to Producer's Livestock Association. Accordingly, in its separate findings of fact and conclusions of law, the trial court found appellant received no consideration for the note.

In early 1977, Producer's Livestock Association took the hogs from appellant's farm because of the serious financial difficulties of John Smith Grain. John Smith Grain was later placed in receivership, and no funds were available to pay appellee bank for appellant's note.

In the separate findings of fact and conclusions of law, the trial court found the relationship between appellee bank, John Smith Grain, and J & J Farms was not an arm's length relationship. Appellee bank supplied John Smith Grain with blank note forms, provided the company with the interest rate to be charged, and customarily purchased the company's commercial paper. At the time it purchased appellant's first note, appellee bank ran its own credit check on appellant. The president of John Smith Grain, H. K. Smith, was also one of appellee bank's directors. An officer and director of John Smith Grain, C. North, Jr., was also an officer and director of J & J Farms. During the period between November 1976 and January 1977, at the time appellant signed the note, the executive vice-president of appellee bank, H. Henninger, was visiting John Smith Grain several times a week to advise the officers on business practices. During that time, John Smith Grain's financial condition was failing.

The trial court held appellee was a holder in due course of the note, and appellant's defense of want of consideration could not be asserted against appellee. The Court of Appeals affirmed.

Krupansky, J. The sole issue in this case is whether appellee is a holder in due course who takes the note free from appellant's defense of want of consideration.

In a suit by the holder of a note against the maker, the holder obtains a great advantage if granted the status of holder in due course. A holder in due course takes the instrument free from most defenses and claims. One such defense which is of no avail when raised against a holder in due course is want of consideration, the defense raised by appellant.

Whether one is a holder in due course is an issue which does not arise unless it is shown a defense exists. Once it is established a defense exists, the holder has the full burden of proving holder in due course status in all respects.

Appellant contends that appellee bank failed in its burden of proving holder in due course status because appellee failed to establish it took the note in good faith.

"Good faith" is defined as "honest in fact in the conduct or transaction concerned." Under the "close connectedness" doctrine a transferee does not take an instrument in good faith when the transferee is so closely connected with the transferor that the transferee may be charged with knowledge of an infirmity in the underlying transaction. The rationale for the close connectedness doctrine is as follows:

> In the field of negotiable instruments, good faith is a broad concept. The basic philosophy of the holder in due course status is to encourage free negotiability of commercial paper by removing certain anxieties of one who takes the paper as an innocent purchaser knowing no reason why the paper is not sound as its face would indicate. It would seem to follow, therefore, that the more the holder knows about the underlying transaction, and particularly the more he controls or participates or becomes involved in it, the less he fits the role of a good faith purchaser for value; the closer his relationship to the underlying agreement which is the source of the note, the less need there is for giving him the tension-free rights considered necessary in a fast-moving credit-extending world.

According to White and Summers, noted authorities on the Uniform Commercial Code, the following five factors are indicative of a close connection between the transferee and transferor:

> (1) Drafting by the transferee of forms for the transferor; (2) approval or establishment or both of the transferor's procedures by the transferee (e.g., setting the interest rate, approval of a referral sales plan); (3) an independent check by the transferee on the credit of the debtor

> or some other direct contact between the transferee and the debtor; (4) heavy reliance by the transferor upon the transferee (e.g., transfer by the transferor of all or substantial part of his paper to the transferee) and; (5) common or connected ownership or management of the transferor and transferee. White & Summers, Uniform Commercial Code 481 (1972).

An analysis of the above factors in relation to the facts of this case, as set forth in the trial court's findings, reveals an unusually close relationship between appellee bank (the transferee), John Smith Grain (the transferor payee) and J & J Farms.

The facts of this case clearly indicate such close connections between appellee bank and John Smith Grain as to impute knowledge by appellee bank of infirmities in the underlying transaction. The trial court specifically found, in its separate findings of fact and conclusions of law, the relationship between appellee bank and J & J Farms was not an arm's length relationship. In spite of this finding, the trial court erroneously concluded "the facts do not permit the court to void the holder in due course protections under these circumstances."

One cannot conclude with absolute certainty that appellee bank had actual knowledge of the failure of consideration. As appellant correctly states in his brief, however, the doctrine of close connectedness was developed in part because of difficulty of proving the transferee's actual knowledge of problems in the underlying transaction. The doctrine allows the court to imply knowledge by the transferee when the relationship between the transferee and transferor is sufficiently close to warrant such an implication.

Under the circumstances of this case, we find the relationship between appellee bank and John Smith Grain was so entwined that it was error for the trial court not to apply the doctrine of close connectedness to find appellee bank failed to carry its burden of proving good faith.

Judgment reversed; rendered in favor of Hessler.

Questions and Case Problems

1. Defendant, Arena Auto Auction, Inc., created a problem by twice mailing checks to the wrong payee. After the wrong payee received the first check, he indorsed it in the name of the named payee and cashed it with the plaintiff, Park State Bank. Park State knew the wrong payee, had cashed his checks and loaned him money in the past, and allowed him to withdraw the money before the check cleared.

   Payment on the check was stopped, but, instead of correcting its error, the drawer-defendant (Arena Auto Auction) innocently issued another check to the same wrong payee. He attempted to cash it as well, but when Park State refused to cooperate, he hastily left town.

   Is Park State liable for the amount of the first check because it dealt with a forger, or not? Discuss.
2. Temple drew a draft payable to the order of Yin-Li. Yin-Li indorsed in blank and lost it. The draft was found by Vasquez, who indorsed specially to Robel and negotiated it to Robel who gave value, in good faith, before maturity, and without knowledge of the preceding facts.
   - **a)** Does Robel qualify as an HIDC?
   - **b)** If Robel is an HIDC, is he subject to any valid claims or real defenses?
   - **c)** If Vasquez retained the instrument, would he be a holder, HIDC, and subject to any claims or defenses?
   - **d)** If Vasquez stole the instrument instead of finding it, discuss Robel's rights against Temple. All other facts remain as stated.
3. The Berenyis, defendants, bought carpeting from Kroyden Industries. The sales representative offered to give the Berenyis the carpeting, valued in the contract at $44 per square yard, without making any payments on their $1,520 note as long as

they referred prospective customers to Kroyden. At the time of this offer, Kroyden was under an injunction to refrain from making such offers. The Berenyis signed a negotiable promissory note for $1,520, which was later negotiated to the plaintiff, New Jersey Mortgage and Investment Corp., who sued the defendants on the note. Result? [*New Jersey Mortgage and Inv. Corp. v. Andrew and Anna Berenyi,* 356 A.2d 421 (N.J. 1976).]

4. Holler sold stolen goods to the unsuspecting defendant company, which gave Holler a check. The check was eventually negotiated to plaintiff company, an HIDC. When plaintiff sued defendant for nonpayment of the check, defendant raised the defense that the goods had been previously stolen. Result? [*Star Provision Co. v. Sears, Roebuck & Company,* 92 S.E.2d 835 (Ga. 1956).]
5. Defendant drew a check and payee indorsed it to plaintiff. Defendant stopped payment on the check and plaintiff sued defendant. Defendant raised the defense of failure of consideration and plaintiff replied that it was an HIDC. Defendant claimed that plaintiff was not an HIDC because it learned of a defense before it deposited the check in the bank. Discuss. [*Kemp Motor Sales Inc. v. Statham,* 171 S.E.2d 389 (Ga. 1969).]
6. A drawee bank was sued by one of its depositors on a check originally drawn in payment for services in the amount of $1.25. Actually, the depositor allowed the payee to fill out the amount of the check for her signature. Given this opportunity, the payee wrote the figures of $1.25 far to the right side so that the number 684 could be added to the left of $1.25, and the words "One 25/100" were written close to the printed word "dollars" on the check blank so that "six thousand eight hundred forty" could be inserted ahead of the words, causing the check to read $6,841.25. The drawee honored the check for $6,841.25. Must the drawee reimburse the customer's account for the full (or any) amount? Discuss. [*Williams v. Mont. Nat'l Bank of Bozeman,* 534 P.2d 1247 (Mont. 1975).]
7. A corporation drew a check for $1,400 payable to the order of a customer of plaintiff bank. The customer deposited the check in his account and plaintiff gave him provisional credit. The bank also allowed the customer to withdraw $140 before it discovered that the corporation had stopped payment on the check and then the check was dishonored. Meanwhile, the customer had "skipped," leaving no credits in his account on which to charge the $140. The bank sued the corporation, after it refused to pay. Result? [*Falls Church Bank v. Wesley Heights Realty, Inc.,* 256 A.2d 915 (D.C.App. 1969).]
8. Carolyn Brazil entered into a contract with the payee of her check to make certain home improvements. The payee made false representations to her regarding the purchase of construction materials for the job and cashed the check that same day. When she discovered the deception, she stopped payment by the drawee. The plaintiff-depositary bank, Citizens National, which is acknowledged to be an HIDC, instituted this action against Brazil. Result? [*Citizens Nat'l Bank of Quitman v. Brazil,* 233 S.E.2d 482 (Ga. 1977).]
9. Defendant Blackburn issued a check to Vanella for the purchase of a used car. Vanella deposited the check in plaintiff bank and received cash and credit. Blackburn stopped payment when he learned that Vanella misrepresented that the automobile was free of liens. Plaintiff received partial repayment of the value it advanced to Vanella and brings this action against Blackburn to recover the balance. It is conceded that the plaintiff bank is an HIDC. Discuss. [*Marine Midland Trust Co. of Rochester v. Blackburn,* 50 Misc.2d 954 (N.Y. 1966).]
10. In *Arcanum National Bank v. Hessler,* excerpted at the beginning of this section, what role did the doctrine of "close connectedness" play in Hessler's defense against the plaintiff bank?

C H A P T E R

32

BANKS, CHECKS, AND CUSTOMER RELATIONS

After you have read this chapter, you should be able to:

1. Recognize the contractual relationship between the bank and its customers.
2. Assess a bank's liability for the wrongful dishonor of an item.
3. Determine when a bank may charge a customer's account.
4. Understand the importance and effectiveness of stop-payment orders.
5. Appreciate the customer's duty to examine cancelled checks and the risk involved in failing to do so.
6. Explain the bank's alternatives when confronted with stale checks and checks issued by customers who later become deceased.
7. Compare certified with uncertified checks.
8. Examine bank collection indorsements and checks with missing indorsements.

BUSINESS DECISIONS and the LAW

Wanda and John-Boy Blake have just received some bad news. Their RV had been billowing oily exhaust fumes longer than they wanted to remember, and Jacob Vasnoskavich (Jake) from Jake's Garage has just called to tell them that the engine needs a complete overhaul.

"That'll be about $2200," Jake informed Wanda over the phone.

"OK, Jake." Wanda replied. "Go ahead and fix it."

The next afternoon Wanda and John-Boy took the RV for a test drive. It ran like new and has been running perfectly since. That has never been a problem.

Jake has been having the problems, and those problems started with the $2200 draft Wanda gave him in payment. She received it in settlement of an insurance claim. North American Accident Insurance Company drew the draft naming Wanda as payee, and routed the draft through its Chicago Bank, Illinois Savings and Trust. Wanda simply forgot to indorse it.

Jake didn't think anything about it. In fact, he didn't even notice. He stamped the instrument on the back, "For deposit only, Jake's Garage," just as he always did, deposited it in his bank, Guaranty Federal, and received full credit. Then, in the course of doing business, he began writing checks on the assumption that the credit with Guaranty was final.

Unfortunately for Jake, the draft was returned by Illinois Savings for violation of a title warranty: Wanda's missing indorsement. Guaranty notified Jake that its credit entry was provisional, not final, reversed the $2200 deposit, and created a significant amount in overdrafts—$2180 to be exact.

What should Jake do next? Can he sue his bank?

Introduction—The Nature of a Check

As individuals conducting personal business and transacting business for proprietorships, partnerships, and corporations, we will write checks and deal with banks. It is important to recognize that there is a body of law that governs banks and that has its impact on negotiable instruments. Our study of commercial paper would be incomplete, therefore, without an examination of the law of banking to the extent that it relates to checks and drafts.

The relationship between a drawee bank and its customer is debtor/creditor. The customer's check is a draft on the bank for the amount the bank owes the customer. A check is simply a "draft drawn on a bank and payable on demand."[1] It is assumed that there are sufficient funds on deposit with the drawee bank to cover any check that is issued; no such assumption is made with other drafts.

The demand nature of a check may be altered by postdating, but this does not affect its negotiability.[2] Since the drawee bank is under contract to follow orders of the depositor-drawer, it must not pay the check until the date arrives. The effect, then, of postdating is to change a check into a time draft.

A check does not operate as an assignment of funds in the hands of the drawee for payment of the holder. In fact, the holder has no rights against the drawee at all unless the drawee has accepted or certified the instrument.[3] If the drawee wrongfully dishonors an uncertified instrument, the holder can only pursue prior parties on their indorsements and warranties.

The Contract between a Bank and Its Customer

When a check is deposited for collection, the bank becomes the agent or subagent of the owner; any settlement given for the item is provisional and may be charged back until the check is finally honored by the payor bank.[4] The bank must use ordinary care in forwarding any item for collection.[5] If it does, the bank will not be liable for the insolvency, neglect, misconduct, mistake, or default of another bank or person or for loss or destruction of an item in transit or in the possession of others.[6]

These and all other provisions of UCC Article 4, Bank Deposits and Collections, can be changed by agreement of the bank and its customer. However, no agreement can disclaim the bank's liability for its lack of good faith or failure to exercise ordinary care;

---

[1]UCC 3–104(2)(b).

[2]UCC 3–114(1).

[3]UCC 3–409(1). No one is liable on a negotiable instrument unless his signature is on it. UCC 3–401.

[4]UCC 4–201(1), 4–212.

[5]UCC 4–202(1).

[6]UCC 4–202(3).

nor can an agreement limit the measure of damages for such lack of good faith or failure to exercise ordinary care. The bank and its customer may agree on reasonable **standards** of responsibility by which the conduct of the bank is to be judged.[7] In the following case the court used the common law principle of estoppel as supplementary to the Code provisions in establishing a standard of responsibility.

standard
An established measure

FACTS

Mr. Ulibarri operated a retail jewelry business in Denver and conducted his banking business with the First National Bank of Denver. He called the bank to inquire about the validity of a check issued to him by a customer in the amount of $3,500 and drawn on the First National for the purchase of a diamond ring. The reason for Mr. Ulibarri's call was to confirm the check's validity before releasing the ring to the customer. After talking to an officer of the bank and being assured that the check was genuine and the account sufficient to cover the amount, Mr. Ulibarri released the ring. However, when the check was presented for payment, the bank returned it marked, "No Account." Mr. Ulibarri contacted the bank but could not receive an adequate explanation, so he refused to repay the proceeds which the bank had advanced him on the check. The First National Bank of Denver then instituted the action against Ulibarri.

DECISION

For Ulibarri. Since Mr. Ulibarri suffered a loss by relying on the bank's assurances, the First National Bank of Denver was **estopped** from charging back the amount of the check against him. The Code states that, unless displaced by a particular section, the principles of law and equity including the law relative to estoppel shall supplement its provisions. UCC 1–103.

"The effect of the provisions of this Article may be varied by an agreement except that no agreement can disclaim a bank's responsibility for its own lack of good faith or failure to exercise ordinary care or can limit the measure of damages for such lack or failure . . ." UCC 4–103(1).

First Nat'l Bank of Denver v. Ulibarri, 557 P.2d 1221 (Colo. 1976).

estoppel
A principle of law stating that when one person "holds out" (represents) a material fact to another person, who changes his or her position materially to his or her prejudice in reasonable reliance on the holding out, the first person is "estopped" (prohibited) to deny what was asserted previously

Banks that participate in the collection process are supposed to take proper action on an item before the midnight deadline.[8] A bank acts seasonably or within the midnight deadline if it does so by midnight on the banking day following the one on which it receives the item.[9] *Failure to act within this time limit can make the bank accountable for the face amount of an item.*[10]

FACTS

Meeker sold a large tract of land to Brewer and received from Brewer a $204,000 check drawn on the C.T.S. Farms' account in the defendant, State and Savings Bank. The next day, Meeker deposited the check in his bank, and it was forwarded through banking channels for collection. On March 4, the check was presented to State and Savings and marked paid. One week later, C.T.S. Farms' (Brewer's) account was depleted because of a returned or dishonored check that Brewer had counted on to keep his balance sufficient.

Since Meeker never received payment on the $204,000 check, he instituted foreclosure

[7]UCC 4–103(1).

[8]UCC 4–202(2).

[9]UCC 4–104(h).

[10]UCC 4–302.

proceedings against Brewer and recovered the property. Now Meeker brings action against State and Savings Bank seeking to hold it strictly liable for failing to "pay or return the item or send notice of dishonor until after its midnight deadline."

DECISION

The only exception to this rule is circumstances beyond the control of the banking institution, and, even then, only if the bank has exercised all due diligence. Here the sole reason for the mistake was that the bank thought that the C.T.S. Farms' account was sufficient to cover the check. Through the exercise of due diligence, the bank could have avoided this mistake.

The bank will not be liable for the full face value of the check, however, if, upon remand, it is determined that the foreclosure and return of the property to Meeker has mitigated his damages.

State and Sav. Bank of Monticello v. Meeker, 469 N.E.2d 55 (Ind. App. 1984).

When an item has been finally paid or honored by the payor bank,[11] the relationship between the depositary bank and its customer becomes that of a debtor to its creditor. The bank is the debtor of its depositor to the extent of the money held on account. This is the basis of the customer's right to "order" its bank to pay one person or another.

Wrongful Dishonor

A bank is not liable on a check or other draft unless it certifies or accepts the item.[12] At that time it becomes a *primary* party and agrees to pay a holder according to the terms of the instrument.[13] Holders cannot compel the drawee bank to honor an uncertified or unaccepted instrument; their recourse is against prior parties on the instrument.

If the drawee bank does refuse to honor a properly payable item—i.e., that is, if it refuses to pay a check that has not been stopped, that is regular in form, and one for which there are sufficient funds on deposit—then the customer is entitled to recover from the drawee bank for damage proximately caused to the customer by the wrongful dishonor.[14]

The customer must prove the extent of the customer's damage, just as he or she must prove the other facts of his or her case. This may include an amount for the customer's arrest or prosecution or other consequential (indirect) damages. To illustrate: the direct damages proximately caused by wrongful dishonor might be the loss of profit on a transaction; consequential damages could be the permanent loss of that customer or damage to one's reputation.

When a Bank May Charge a Customer's Account

A bank may charge against its customer's account any item that is *properly payable*. This is true even though the charge creates an overdraft, because the issuance of the check itself carries authority to pay and the implied promise to reimburse the bank.[15]

---

[11]UCC 4–213.

[12]UCC 3–410, 4–411.

[13]UCC 3–413(1).

[14]UCC 4–402.

[15]UCC 4–401(1).

Since the bank is under a contract with its depositor, it is supposed to know and record the status of each account and to follow its depositor's orders. When an overdraft is paid, the recipient is protected and the drawee is repaid by its customer. Except for recovery of bank payments[16] and for violation of presentment warranties,[17] the rule to remember is that payment is final in favor of an HIDC and those who have in good faith substantially changed their position in reliance on the payment.[18] This is illustrated by the following case where, because of such reliance, the real defense of forgery cannot be asserted.

FACTS

A customer of the defendant-depositary bank forged the signature of one of the drawers of a check on the plaintiff-drawee bank. The depositary bank had no notice of suspicious circumstances when it received the check from the customer and it initiated collection. After the depositary bank received final payment from the drawee bank, it allowed its depositor (the forger) to withdraw the amount of the check. Drawee bank seeks to recover from the depositary bank the amount paid under the forged drawer's signature.

DECISION

For defendant-depositary bank. Under UCC 3–418, payment or acceptance of an instrument is final in favor of a holder in due course or a person who has in good faith changed his position in reliance on the payment.

Fireman's Fund Ins. Co. v. Security Pacific Nat'l Bank, 85 Cal.App.3d 797 (Cal. 1978).

In keeping with the protection of an HIDC (see the discussion of real or universal defenses on p. 669 in Chapter 31), a bank which in *good faith* makes payment to a *holder* may charge its customer's account for

1. the original **tenor** or amount of a materially altered item, or
2. the final or completed tenor of an item that was originally issued incomplete, unless the bank has notice that completion of the item was improper.[19]

tenor
What is stated as meant

To give an example, if the drawee-payor bank innocently charges a customer's account with an uncertified check that has been materially altered from $100 to $1,000, the customer can compel the bank to reimburse the account for $900. Material alteration is a real defense against an HIDC to the extent of the $900 alteration.[20] Since banks in the collection channel make transfer and presentment warranties, the drawee-payor bank would then be entitled to charge back against the presenting bank $900 for breach of material alteration warranty.[21]

---

[16]UCC 4–213, 4–301.

[17]UCC 3–417(1), 4–207(1).

[18]UCC 3–418.

[19]UCC 4–401(2).

[20]UCC 3–407.

[21]UCC 3–417, 4–207.

If the bank in good faith pays an item that was originally issued incomplete, it can charge the customer for the full amount. In the absence of notice to the bank of improper completion, the customer takes responsibility for these instruments.

Stop-Payment Orders

A customer may order its bank to stop payment on a check, but the bank must be given a reasonable time to put the order into effect.[22] A matter of hours may be a reasonable period of time. However, the drawer will be liable to an HIDC on a stopped check.

An oral stop order is effective for fourteen calendar days. Written orders, or written confirmations of oral orders, are valid for six months and may be renewed.[23] A slight error in the information given to the bank may not defeat the customer's right of recovery, as is illustrated in the following case.

FACTS

FJS Electronics, Inc., plaintiff, brought this action to recover the amount of a check drawn on defendant-appellant Fidelity Bank. The president of FJS phoned Fidelity and requested that payment be stopped on the check. The amount given in the phone conversation was $1,844.48; the actual amount was $1,844.98.

A written confirmation from defendant of plaintiff's oral stop payment containing the incorrect information was received in the mail by FJS. The confirmation included the following language: "PLEASE ENSURE AMOUNT IS CORRECT." FJS did not correct the information. The trial court concluded that defendant Fidelity Bank had a reasonable opportunity to stop payment and rendered judgment for plaintiff. Defendant appealed.

DECISION

Affirmed for FJS Electronics, plaintiff. It is clear that the order here was timely received. The court below determined that even though it contained an error, the order was given in such manner as to give the bank a reasonable opportunity to act. Fidelity, in essence, asserts that the UCC 4–403(1) should be read to require compliance with the procedures of a particular bank, regardless of what they are and regardless of whether the customer has been made aware of them. Fidelity argues that since its technique for ascertaining whether payment had been stopped required absolute accuracy as to the amount of a stopped check, this section would require absolute precision in order for the notice to be reasonable. Such a narrow view is not consistent with the intent of Section 4–403, expressed in Comment 2 following the section:

> The position taken by this section is that stopping payment is a service which depositors expect and are entitled to receive from banks notwithstanding its difficulty, inconvenience and expense. The inevitable occasional losses through failure to stop should be borne by the banks as a cost of the business of banking.

FJS Electronics, Inc. v. The Fidelity Bank, 431 A.2d 326 (Pa. 1981).

If the bank pays despite a valid stop order, the customer can compel the bank to reimburse the account by proof of the fact and amount of the loss.[24] The bank is then

[22]UCC 4–403(1).

[23]UCC 4–403(2).

[24]UCC 4–403(3).

subrogated to the customer's rights against the payee or any other holder of the check.[25] If this approach does not prevent unjust enrichment of the drawer-customer at the expense of the bank, the bank is subrogated to the rights of an HIDC, holder, or payee against the drawer.

subrogation
The substitution of one person for another with reference to a claim or a right

Assume that *D* purchases merchandise from *P* and issues a $45 check on ABC Bank (drawee) in payment. If, without any legitimate reason, *D* simply decides not to pay and issues a valid stop order to ABC Bank, *P* would be successful in a lawsuit against *D*. *D* has made a contract with *P* and has no legal grounds to avoid payment.

If ABC Bank paid the check despite the stop order, its customer, the drawer, could not compel ABC Bank to reimburse his account because he has suffered no loss. Even if the bank initially reimbursed the account to appease its customer, it could subsequently charge back. Remember that the bank is subrogated to the rights of an HIDC, holder, or payee against the drawer to avoid a loss and prevent the drawer from being unjustly enriched. After all, there is no good reason to allow *D* to keep the merchandise and, simply at his whim, stop payment on the check issued to pay for it.

On the assumption that *D* has legal grounds for stopping payment—e.g., *P* never delivered the merchandise to *D*—the bank's negligence in paying despite the order will cause *D* a loss. In this event, *D* can compel ABC Bank to reimburse his account, and ABC will be subrogated to *D*'s rights against *P*.

However, if *P* negotiated to an HIDC, the bank's conduct (negligent or not) in paying the check would not be the cause of *D*'s loss. *D* had a personal defense only—failure of consideration—and an HIDC would have succeeded in an action against *D* in spite of this defense. Thus the bank would be subrogated to the HIDC's rights and could charge *D*'s account. On the other hand, if *D* could prove a real defense, the bank's conduct in paying the check would cause *D* to suffer a loss, so it would have to reimburse *D*'s account.

Stale Checks

When an uncertified check has been in circulation more than six months, the drawee is not obligated to pay it. Normally the drawee will consult the drawee's depositor on such checks, but the drawee has the option to pay them without consultation if acting in good faith.[26] For example, the check may be issued in payment of dividends by one of the bank's corporate customers and held by one of the stockholders for more than six months. This check could be paid in good faith without consultation with the corporate issuer. In the following case it was held to be proper for the drawee bank to honor a check, in good faith, without consulting the drawer, fourteen months after the date of the check.

FACTS

Advanced Alloys, Inc., plaintiff, wrote a check payable to Sergeant Steel Corp. For some reason, this check was not presented for payment until fourteen months later. The drawee, Chase Manhattan Bank, honored this stale check, and

[25]UCC 4–407(c).

[26]UCC 4–404.

Advanced Alloys sued the bank, contending that it should have inquired of its depositor before honoring such an instrument, especially since the plaintiff had issued a written stop-payment order.

DECISION

For the bank. According to UCC 4–404, the bank, while not obligated to do so, may pay a stale check so long as it does so in good faith, and it is under no duty to make any inquiry of the depositor before doing so. The written stop-payment order was good only for six months and the plaintiff had not renewed it. The question the court had to decide was whether or not the bank had acted in good faith as required by UCC 4–404. UCC 1–201(19) defines "good faith" as "honesty in fact in the conduct of the transaction concerned." Under this definition, it appears that the payment of a stale check, even without making inquiry, constitutes a payment "in good faith."

Advanced Alloys, Inc. v. Sergeant Steel Corp., 72 Misc.2d 614 (N.Y. 1973).

Death or Incompetence of a Customer

Neither death nor adjudication of incompetence of a customer of either a collecting or payor bank affects that bank's authority to accept, pay, or collect an item or to account for its proceeds until the bank *knows* of the death or adjudication and has a *reasonable opportunity* to act on it.[27] Even with knowledge of the death of a customer, a bank may certify or pay checks (but not other items) for a period of *ten days after death*.[28] A person claiming an interest in the account—e.g., a relative or the executor of the decedent's will—may order the bank to stop further payment. The reason for this exception is that "there is almost never any reason why they should not be paid, and that filing in probate is a useless formality, burdensome to the holder, the executor, the court and the bank."[29]

Customer's Duty to Examine Cancelled Checks

Periodically the bank will send to each customer a statement of account supported by the cancelled or paid items that have been charged (debited) to the account. The customer must then exercise reasonable care and promptness in examining the materials for unauthorized signatures and for alterations. The bank is entitled to prompt notice if any irregularities are discovered.[30]

The bank is protected, and the customer must pursue other means of recovery, when an item bearing the customer's unauthorized signature or an alteration is paid if *all* of the three following conditions are satisfactorily proved:

1. The bank establishes that the customer failed in his or her duty to examine the checks and report unauthorized signatures or alterations.[31]

---

[27] UCC 4–405(1).

[28] UCC 4–405(2).

[29] UCC 4–405, comment 3.

[30] UCC 4–406(1).

[31] UCC 4–406(1).

2. The bank establishes that it suffered a loss because of the customer's breach of duty.[32]
3. The customer is not able to show that the bank failed to exercise ordinary care in the payment of these items.[33]

If the bank fails to establish either 1 or 2 above, or if the customer is able to establish the bank's failure in 3, then the bank is liable for the unauthorized signature or the altered item. This is exactly what one would expect. After all, the bank is under contract with its customer, it has a copy of the customer's signature, and it is supposed to follow the customer's orders—no forgeries or alterations, please. Since a certain number of these are bound to occur, the bank must train its employees to detect as many of these items as possible, and it must absorb the loss or losses that do materialize or insure against them.

If the same wrongdoer undertakes subsequent forgeries, unauthorized signatures, or alterations that the bank pays in good faith after the first check (or "first batch," if two or more items are involved) has been forwarded to its customer, the bank is once more protected. The customer must pursue other means of recovery if the customer failed within a reasonable period of time (not exceeding fourteen calendar days) to detect the "first batch" of irregularities and notify the bank. In this way the customer is penalized for his or her breach of duty in not promptly examining his or her checks and reporting irregularities.[34] The bank is not protected, however, and the customer may recover if the bank did not exercise ordinary care in paying the "second batch."[35]

Without regard to the exercise of reasonable care by either the customer or the bank, there is a statute of limitations on the customer's right to assert these irregularities against the bank. For unauthorized customer-drawer signatures and for alterations, the period is one year from the time the statement of account and supporting items are made available to the customer. Since the customer is not likely to recognize the forged or unauthorized signature of an indorser, the statute of limitations is three years, rather than one, from the time the materials are made available to the customer.[36] In the following case the court held that the drawee bank's limit of ten days in which the drawer is to notify the drawee of an alteration on the check was unreasonably short.

FACTS

A check was drawn upon an account by the state for $54. The bank of the payee improperly encoded the check for $10,000 more than the actual amount. The drawee bank's computer paid the overstated amount. The bank's statement in which the check was sent stated that, if not notified otherwise within ten days, the statement would be assumed to be correct. Seven and a half months later, during a routine audit, the mistake was found, the bank was notified, and a claim for the overstatement was made.

DECISION

For the state. While it is the customer's duty to examine the bank statement, violation of

[32]UCC 4–406(2)(a).

[33]UCC 4–406(3).

[34]UCC 4–406(2)(b).

[35]UCC 4–406(2)(b), (3).

[36]UCC 4–406(4).

the ten-day limit contained in the statement will not absolutely discharge the bank. Discharge of the bank's liability is a question to be determined upon the circumstances in each case. The check was mailed to the right person, it was the payee's bank that improperly encoded the check, and then the drawee bank improperly charged the improper amount.

The time frame set out by the Code to discover the error is one year, which is longer than the state took and much longer than the bank demanded. The loss was not due to the negligence of the state, and it has not been shown that an earlier notice would have prevented or reduced the amount of loss. Under UCC 4–406 a customer must exercise reasonable care and promptness to examine the statement to discover any alteration and then must promptly notify the bank of the error. If notice comes within one year, however, and if the bank suffers no loss on account of the delay, the account must be reimbursed.

The State ex. rel. Gabalac v. Firestone Bank, 346 N.E.2d 326 (Ohio 1975).

Certified Checks

There are no primary parties on a check as it is normally issued. The drawer is a party secondarily liable, and the drawee and payee are not liable until their signatures are on the item. The check is not an assignment of funds for the benefit of the payee or any subsequent holder,[37] and for this reason the bank cannot be compelled to pay by a holder. It is, however, liable to customers for wrongful dishonor of checks and other items.[38]

When a bank certifies a check, it becomes a primary party analogous to a maker of a note.[39] The certification or acceptance will be written or stamped on the instrument and signed by an authorized officer of the bank.[40] The bank is not obligated to provide this service,[41] so it will normally charge a fee when certification is requested.

Certification obtained by a *holder* has the effect of discharging the drawer and all indorsers *prior to the holder* who is having the check certified.[42] For example, if *D* issued a check to *P,* who indorsed to *A* and so on to *H,* a certification by the drawee bank at the request of *H* would discharge *D, P,* and *A* from further liability on the check. The reason for this is that the instrument is now the primary debt and responsibility of the certifying bank. Certification is analogous to cashing the check; and it is easy to see that if the drawee had paid *H* cash, all parties prior to *H* would be discharged. Anyone who indorses it following the certification, however, will incur the usual secondary liability.

When a *drawer* has an instrument certified, no one is discharged. Obviously there is no one prior to the drawer to be discharged.

---

[37]UCC 3–409.

[38]UCC 4–402.

[39]UCC 3–413(1).

[40]UCC 3–410(1).

[41]UCC 3–411(2).

[42]UCC 3–411(1). Their contract that the instrument would be honored is performed by the certification.

Missing Indorsements and Bank Collection Indorsements

In an effort to speed up the collection process and make it more efficient, depositary banks may supply any necessary indorsement of a customer, unless the item expressly requires the *payee's* indorsement. Generally, the bank's written statement on the instrument that it was deposited to the customer's account is sufficient.[43] Also, the drawee/payor bank may charge its customer's account for any item that is properly payable from that account even if the charge creates an overdraft.[44] This is illustrated in the following case.

FACTS

The plaintiffs, Barretts, are husband and wife. Mr. Barrett made a check payable to Aquatic Industries on July 19, 1975 for $1,500 drawn on their joint checking account at the drawee defendant bank. Aquatic Industries did not indorse the check when it deposited the check in its account at the Rosewell Bank. The Rosewell Bank, failing to add Aquatic's indorsement as it was authorized to do by UCC 4–205(1), sent the check through banking channels to the defendant bank. Upon receiving the check, the bank debited plaintiffs' account and returned it to them. Plaintiffs contended that the check should not have been paid because it was never indorsed.

DECISION

For the drawee bank. The check was properly payable. Since it was properly payable, a bank may charge against its customer's account any item which is otherwise properly payable from that account even though the charge creates an overdraft. UCC 4–401(1). The absence of the payee's indorsement and the failure of the collecting Rosewell Bank to supply the missing indorsement as it was authorized to do did not affect the payor bank's right to pay this check and to debit the plaintiffs' account. In absence of the indorsement of the payee, the instrument was not transferred by negotiation, and any subsequent transferee of the instrument could not acquire the status of a holder in due course. UCC 3–201(1).

First Nat'l Bank of Gwinnett v. Gerald Barrett, 233 S.E.2d. 24 (Ga. 1977).

Intermediary banks and nondepositary payor banks are not in any way given notice or affected by any restrictive indorsement except that of its immediate transferor. For example, if *P* indorses restrictively in trust for *M,* "Pay to *T* for the benefit of *M,* [signed] *P,*" the depositary bank must exercise due care in receiving this instrument from *T,* but subsequent banks in the collection channel need not pay any attention to it. They need only obey the instructions contained in the restrictive indorsement of the bank which transfers the check to them.[45]

Lost, Destroyed, or Stolen Instruments

If an instrument has been lost, stolen, or destroyed, the owner may still sue on it and recover from any party who is liable. This person, now a plaintiff in a lawsuit, will have

---

[43]UCC 4–205(1).

[44]UCC 4–401(1).

[45]UCC 3–206(2)(3)(4), 4–205(2).

to prove his or her ownership, the facts that prevent his or her production of the instrument (e.g., if it was destroyed by fire, this would have to be proven), and the terms of the instrument.[46]

Keep in mind that a contract is really more than the paper on which it is written. Even if the paper is destroyed, the contract, with its rights and duties agreed upon by the parties, continues to exist. It is now much harder to prove, but witnesses can be called and the owner's own testimony is admissible.

In order to protect the one who pays from having to pay a second time (assuming that the instrument eventually surfaces in the hands of a legitimate party), the court may require security. This protection against fraud or mistake could be in the form of a bond or insurance policy that the owner would have to post before the court will allow the owner to collect.

NOW Accounts and the Consumer Checking Account Equity Act

NOW
A negotiable order of withdrawal, as in a NOW account

Since 1980 U.S. financial institutions have been able to offer the practical equivalent of interest-paying checking accounts at rates as high as 5¼ percent. Congress authorized depositary institutions to permit their savers to make withdrawals **(NOWs)** by means of negotiable check-like instruments.[47] Savings and loan associations, mutual savings associations, credit unions as well as commercial banks can treat NOW drafts in the same manner as checks under the Uniform Commercial Code.[48]

NOW accounts are available only to individuals and to nonprofit religious, philanthropic, charitable, and educational organizations. This means that individuals who operate sole proprietorships are entitled to hold NOW accounts, but partnerships, corporations, and any other type of for-profit organizations are not. In an effort to clarify this important area of the law, the Federal Reserve Board supplied a listing of those eligible to maintain NOW accounts at member banks:

1. Individuals
2. Sole proprietors
3. Husband and wife operating unincorporated businesses
4. Local housing authority
5. Residential tenants' security deposits
6. Independent school districts
7. Redevelopment authority
8. Escrow funds (provided entire beneficial interest is held by individuals or qualifying organizations)
9. Labor unions
10. Trust and other fiduciary accounts (provided entire beneficial interest is held by individuals or qualifying organizations)
11. Pension funds
12. Trade associations

---

[46]UCC 3–804.

[47]Consumer Checking Account Equity Act of 1980, sec. 303, 12 U.S.C. sec. 1832 (1980).

[48]45 Fed. Reg. 64,164 (1980).

In sum, the changes made by Congress in the Consumer Checking Account Equity Act do not introduce any significant new problems for those engaged in the study of the Uniform Commercial Code.

Summary Statement

1. Checks are demand drafts drawn on banks. The drawer is entitled to order the drawee bank to pay money from the checking account because of the contractual relationship that exists between them. The bank is the debtor of its customer, the drawer, to the extent of the checking account balance.
2. A bank becomes an agent of its customer in the check clearing process. It will forward checks through bank channels to the drawee-payor for collection. Each bank that participates in the process must take proper action on the check before its midnight deadline—midnight of the next banking day following receipt of an item—or be held accountable for the amount of the check.
3. A holder cannot compel a drawee bank to honor a check, but if the drawee wrongfully dishonors, it is liable to the customer for actual damage, direct and consequential, proximately caused by such dishonor. The drawee may honor an item even though it creates an overdraft, and, generally speaking, payment of a check (whether it creates an overdraft or not) is final in favor of an HIDC and those who have in good faith substantially changed their position in reliance on payment. A drawee bank may charge its customer for the original tenor of a materially altered item or for the completed tenor of an item that was issued incomplete.
4. Once a check has been issued, the drawer may (for any reason) direct the bank to stop payment. Oral stop orders are valid for fourteen calendar days; written orders for six months. When the check "bounces" back into the hands of the holder or HIDC, the drawer must be ready to prove a personal or real defense; otherwise a judgment may be entered against the drawer.
5. If the drawee overlooks the stop order and through negligence pays the check anyway, the drawer-customer may recover from the drawee upon proof of the amount of loss caused by the drawee's negligence.
6. A drawee bank is not obligated to honor uncertified checks that have been in circulation more than six months, but it may do so in good faith. Death of a customer does not automatically terminate the drawee's right to pay checks that were drawn previously. Even with knowledge of death and an opportunity to act on it, the drawee may for ten days after date of death pay or certify such checks unless ordered to stop by a person claiming an interest in the account.
7. When the drawee periodically mails its customer a statement of account along with the customer's cancelled checks, the customer has a duty to examine the checks promptly and put the bank on notice of irregularities. If the customer does not act reasonably and promptly in the performance of this duty, and if such negligence or breach of duty causes the bank to suffer a loss, the customer will be responsible for the loss. However, if the drawee bank itself has been negligent, then the customer will *not* be responsible for the loss.
8. There are no primary parties on a check as originally issued, and the check does not operate as an assignment of funds for the payee or anyone else. When a check is certified, the drawee becomes a primary party-acceptor analogous to the maker of a note. All parties *prior* to the one having the check certified are discharged from further liability on the instrument.

9. An intermediary or a nondepositary payor bank is not in any way affected by a restrictive indorsement *except* that of its immediate transferor. Depositary banks are entitled to indorse for deposit on behalf of their customers unless the item expressly requires the payee's signature.
10. The owner of a lost, stolen, or destroyed instrument may still recover on it with proof of ownership, of the facts which prevent its production, and the terms of the instrument. To protect the payor against the possibility of a second payment, the court may require the owner to provide security for the payor's benefit.

In the following case the court held that the drawers' negligence in not detecting forgeries of their signatures on their checks relieved the drawee bank from liability for paying some of the forged checks.

K & K MANUFACTURING, INC., AND KNIGHT v. UNION BANK
628 P.2d 44 (Ariz. 1981)

Hathaway, C. J. In this case we must apply Articles three and four of the Uniform Commercial Code to determine who should bear the risk of loss when a dishonest employee forges her employer's name as drawer on a number of checks on his business and personal checking accounts, then appropriates the proceeds for her personal use.

Appellant Bill J. Knight is the president and majority stockholder of both K & K Manufacturing, Inc. and Knight Foundry & Manufacturing, Inc. Knight Foundry employed about 80 people at the time of trial, while K & K Manufacturing, appellant, which was formed to accomplish the contracting, buying and selling for the foundry business, employed only two persons when the events which form the basis of this action occurred. These two employees were Knight and a bookkeeper, Eleanor Garza. The bookkeeper's duties at K & K Manufacturing were very broad, including picking up the company mail and Knight's personal mail from a common post office box, preparing checks for Knight's signature to pay both company and personal bills, and making entries in a cash disbursement journal reflecting the expenses for which the checks were written. Most importantly, it was her responsibility to reconcile the monthly statements prepared and sent by appellee Union Bank, where Knight kept both his business and personal checking and savings accounts. No one shared these duties with Miss Garza.

Between March 1977 and January 1978, Miss Garza forged Knight's signature on some 66 separate checks drawn on his personal or business accounts at Union Bank. The majority of these checks were made payable to her. The total amount of the forgeries on the K & K Manufacturing account was $49,859.31. The total on Knight's personal account was $11,350. The bank paid each such check and Miss Garza received or was credited with the proceeds.

We need not concentrate on the details of the fraud, except to comment that it proved to be effective for nearly one year.

• • • • •

Eventually, an in-house audit showed the discrepancies in the 1977 disbursements. Appellants brought this action against appellee for breach of contract, seeking repayment of the funds the bank paid out on checks with unauthorized signatures. After a court trial, judgment was entered in favor of appellant Knight for $5,500, representing the amount paid out of his personal account on forged checks from March 28 to May 20, 1977. This figure included eight forged checks paid by the bank prior to the mailing of its monthly statement containing a record of the payments and the checks themselves to Knight on May 6, plus a 14-day period. Since no forged checks on the K & K Manufacturing account were paid prior to May 20, judgment was entered [for Union Bank].

• • • • •

The concept of which party bears the loss in a forgery situation such as the one presented here is addressed in Articles three and four of the Uniform Commercial Code, covering commercial paper and bank deposits and collections. [UCC 3–406, 4–406]

• • • • •

These provisions impose a duty on the depositor to check his monthly statement for unauthorized signatures or alterations on checks. If the depositor fails to do so, after the first forged check and statement relating thereto is sent to him, plus a reasonable period not exceeding 14 days, he is precluded from asserting the unauthorized signature or alteration against the bank. UCC Sec. 4–406, comment 3. The burden of proof of depositor's negligence is on the bank. Even if the bank succeeds in establishing the depositor's negligence, if the customer establishes that the bank failed to exercise ordinary care in paying the bad checks, the preclusion rule . . . does not apply. UCC Sec. 4–406, comment 4.

We first address the issue of whether appellee met its burden of proof of showing that appellants "substantially contributed" to the forgeries or failed to exercise "reasonable care and promptness" in examining the monthly statements. The record shows that appellants trusted Miss Garza completely with both writing checks and reconciling the monthly statements. No spot checks were made by Knight or the controller at Knight Foundry, both of whom had access to the banking records. Knight was informed by a bank officer that his personal account was overdrawn on 12 occasions in 1977, yet did nothing to discover the reasons therefor. Knight testified he was aware Miss Garza's work was often inaccurate as well as tardy in 1977 and 1978.

• • • • •

We adopt the majority view that the depositor is chargeable with the knowledge of all facts a reasonable and prudent examination of his bank statement would have disclosed if made by an honest employee. . . .

Secondly, we turn to the question of whether appellants met their burden of proof of demonstrating appellee did not exercise ordinary care in paying the bad checks, and did not act in good faith and in accordance with reasonable commercial standards. There appears to be no dispute regarding the good faith of appellee in paying the forgeries. The issue is whether its method of ascertaining unauthorized signatures on its depositor's checks met the standard of care under the circumstances.

Implied in the debtor/creditor relationship between a bank and its checking account depositor is the contractual undertaking on the part of the bank that it will only discharge its obligations to the depositor upon his authorized signature. The mere fact that the bank has paid a forged check does not mean the bank has breached its duty of ordinary care, however.

At trial, an operations officer for appellee testified as to the methods employed during the period the forgeries occurred to discover unauthorized signatures on depositor's checks. She testified that checks were organized so that a bundle from the same account could be compared with the authorized signature on the bank's signature card. A staff of five filing clerks handled an average of approximately 1,000 checks each per hour in this manner. She testified it was common for a file clerk to become familiar with the drawer's signature in large accounts such as appellants'. An official of a large Arizona bank testified that tellers and file clerks are not trained to be handwriting experts. He testified that in his opinion, because most large banks have completely abandoned physical comparison of checks with the signature card, the system employed by appellee was better than the norm of the banking community in Southern Arizona.

In view of this and other evidence, we conclude that there was sufficient evidence to support findings 13 and 14 and the judgment entered below. Similar methods of comparing drawer's signatures have been upheld as constituting ordinary care and being within reasonable commercial standards across the country. . . . Appellant Knight and his controller admitted the forgeries were quite good. Appellants also argue that because the bank tellers recognized Miss Garza was cashing large checks made to herself and her boyfriend and that she was driving an expensive sports car, they had a further duty to check the validity of the drawer's signature. This evidence was balanced by testimony that Miss Garza thoroughly explained the reasons for the large checks as increased salary, bonuses, and payment of Knight's expenses while he was out of town. Knight and Miss Garza were in the bank together on a regular basis and the tellers knew Miss Garza was authorized to handle large amounts of Knight's money.

Finally, there was evidence that some K & K Manufacturing checks were forged with a rubber stamp facsimile of Knight's signature, which was only authorized for use with the Knight Foundry account. Appellants argue appellee fell below the standard of ordinary care in honoring these checks. The trial court personally examined appellee's expert witness on this subject. There was testimony that if facsimile signatures appear "all of a sudden" on the checks, the depositor may be contacted, but there was sufficient evidence that the piecemeal use of the stamp here, which was at times authorized by appellants, was not such that appellee should be held to bring it to their attention. The finding of fact that appellee's acts, including those regarding the facsimile signature, did not fall below ordinary care or reasonable commercial standards was not clearly erroneous.

Affirmed.

Questions and Case Problems

1. *D* purchased inventory from *P* with a $5,000 check. Drawee Bank wrongfully dishonored *D*'s check, and *P* repossessed the inventory. This caused *D* much embarrassment and at least $1,000 in good will. In addition, *D* lost a $2,000 breach-of-contract suit to *X* for failure to deliver merchandise. If *D*'s inventory had not been repossessed, *D* could have fulfilled the contract with *X*. *D* then sued Drawee Bank. Result?
2. *D* issued a $100 check on Drawee Bank payable to the order of *P*. *P* materially altered the amount (words and figures) to $1,000 and negotiated it to an HIDC. The HIDC forwarded it to Drawee Bank for collection and received $1,000. When these facts were revealed by *D*'s examination of her monthly statement and cancelled checks, she proceeded against Drawee Bank to reinstate her account. Result?
3. Faye Zappacosta, bookkeeper for Arrow Builders, drew checks on defendant-drawee (Royal National Bank) purportedly representing social security and income taxes withheld from the wages of Arrow's employees. For 23 months she drew 54 such checks. Twenty-three were properly applied and the others were presented individually by Zappacosta and honored by the defendant-drawee (Royal National). This scheme could have been detected by Arrow's chief accountant after the first month's embezzlement if Zappacosta's work had been properly supervised. Arrow proceeded against defendant Royal National after these facts came to light. Result? [*Arrow Builders Supply Corp. v. Royal Nat'l Bank,* 288 N.Y. S.2d 609 (N.Y. 1968).]
4. The plaintiff, Tusso, delivered a check to the payee for the sum of $600 on July 24, 1972. The following morning at 9:00 A.M. the plaintiff appeared and placed a stop-payment order on the check. The same morning at 10:30 A.M. the payee appeared at the defendant Security National Bank, drawee, the same bank where the plaintiff had placed the stop order, and had the check certified. The bank charged the plaintiff's account immediately. Plaintiff sued to have the defendant Security National Bank reimburse his account. Result? [*Tusso v. Security Nat'l Bank,* 76 Misc.2d 12 (N.Y. 1973).]
5. Granite filed a written stop order with the drawee Hempstead Bank on a check issued to Overseas Equipment Co. Granite then delivered a new check to Overseas. More than a year later the first check was presented to Hempstead and paid. Granite claimed that the drawee bank is liable to it for paying the first check. Result? [*Granite Equip. Leasing Corp. v. Hempstead Bank,* 326 N.Y. S.2d 881 (N.Y. 1971).]

6. Depositor, Palmer, brought action against his bank to recover for the alleged wrongful dishonor of several checks. Jury found for the plaintiff and awarded actual and punitive damages, and the defendant appealed.

   The trial court jury answered several issues, which were: (1) that someone forged Palmer's signature as an indorser on a $275 check; (2) that thereafter the bank intentionally refused payment of checks written by Palmer; (3) that the bank attempted to collect an overdraft resulting from the chargeback against the account of the $275 check, and for insufficient check fund charges resulting from its dishonor of Palmer's checks after it knew or should have known that the indorsement was a forgery; (4) that Palmer had suffered actual damages of $2,000; (5) that Palmer was entitled to punitive damages of $3,500; and (6) that the dishonor of the checks was not the result of a mistake. Result? [*Northshore Bank v. Palmer,* 525 S.W.2d 718 (Tex. 1975).]

7. Atlantic Telec, Inc., drawer, recovered on a $13,000 check that its drawee bank, Southeast First National Bank, failed to stop on an oral order. The check had been given by Atlantic to the payee pursuant to a contract between Atlantic and the payee. Atlantic presented testimony to show that the payee had breached its contract with Atlantic. The bank did not object to the oral order. It appealed, arguing instead that Atlantic failed to show it had a right to stop payment. Result? [*Southeast First Nat'l Bank of Satellite Beach v. Atlantic Telec, Inc.,* 389 So.2d 1032 (Fla. 1980).]

8. Empire Packing Co., Inc. drew a check on its bank (Illinois National Bank and Trust Co., the drawee-payor) to the order of the plaintiff, Rock Island Auction Sales, Inc. in payment for cattle. The drawee-payor bank, Illinois National, received the check through clearinghouse channels for collection but held it for five days on assurance from Empire that funds would soon be deposited to cover it. Shortly afterward, the check was returned by the drawee-payor marked "Insufficient Funds." A petition in bankruptcy was filed against Empire. The plaintiff, Rock Island, was successful against Illinois National in the District Court, and Illinois National appeals.

   Plaintiff argues "that [as] the payor bank [Illinois National] became liable for the amount of the check because it held the check without payment, return or notice of dishonor, beyond the time limit fixed in UCC 4–302. . . ." Result? [*Rock Island Auction Sales, Inc. v. Empire Packing Co., Inc.,* 204 N.E.2d 721 (Ill. 1965).]

9. Plaintiff drew and delivered to Santo his check for $3,000 drawn on the defendant bank payable to the order of Santo on November 10, 1964. On December 10, 1964, plaintiff gave written notice to defendant to stop payment on the check. On December 24, 1964, defendant ignored the stop payment order and made payment of the check. Plaintiff sued defendant for the amount of the check and the bank raised the defense that plaintiff had not shown that he was damaged by the payment of the check. Discuss. [*Cicci v. Lincoln Nat'l Bank and Trust Co. of Central N.Y.,* 46 Misc.2d 465 (N.Y. 1965).]

10. In *K & K Manufacturing, Inc. v. Union Bank,* excerpted at the beginning of this chapter, why was Bill Knight, President of K & K, entitled to recover on the first eight forged checks ($5,500) his bookkeeper drew, but neither he nor the corporation was entitled to recover on subsequent forgeries?

CHAPTER

33

DEADLINES AND DISCHARGE

After you have read this chapter, you should be able to:

1. Distinguish between presentment for payment and presentment for acceptance.
2. Learn when presentment is necessary.
3. Become familiar with the mechanics of presentment—how it is made, to whom, and the length of time allowed.
4. Recognize the importance of giving notice of dishonor, and find how such notice is to be given.
5. Review the methods of discharging one's liability on an instrument.

BUSINESS DECISIONS and the LAW

Clint and Jinny, owners of a plumbing supply business, were feeling the "heat" from a highly competitive firm that had expanded into their community three years ago. They were determined to fight back, and were doing so successfully.

They experienced their fill of frustrations along the way, however, and many of these sidetracks drained their energies from more useful pursuits. One of the most anxiety-producing events involved a dispute with the son of a long-time friend.

Jim Evert was a high school drop-out, but an extremely talented carpenter and woodworker. Jinny first approached him about doing some interior work in the main display room of their firm. He looked the place over thoroughly, made a few suggestions, and later submitted some drawings and a bid. In no time, they had a deal.

The contract was for $87,000, and the work Jim did was excellent in every way. Clint and Jinny made monthly "progress payments," but, towards the end, it was not clear to them that they were getting credit for each of their payments. It was one of those embarrassing situations where you know the other party is honest, but just a little vague, or, in reality, slovenly, about bookkeeping procedures. Jim was more of an artisan than an accountant. In addition, there were several complicating factors: Clint and Jinny had made a number of payments in cash (and received no receipts); Jim had held down his expenses in a number of ways to save them money; and, finally, Clint and Jinny had authorized a number of changes and additions to the initial plan, but no written agreement was ever made regarding these changes.

Because Jim was next to impossible to sit down and talk to, Clint and Jinny, consulting between themselves, decided that in order to be fair, they would draw up a final payment check and submit it to Jim as full payment of their best estimate of what remained owing. They concluded that the amount of $2750 was correct insofar as that was determinable, and, in fact, that such a payment was generous to Jim.

By way of protecting themselves, however, and bringing the matter to a conclusion, they wrote on the line designated "Memo" (in the lower-left corner of the front side), "Full Settlement/Final Payment." On the back side, just above the space where Jim would indorse, they wrote: "By indorsement, Jim Evert accepts this check in full satisfaction of all claims against Clint and Jinny Curtis for interior construction work, 619 South Bonner, Ruston, La." Clint and Jinny expected the matter to end there to everyone's satisfaction.

In the next month's bank statement, however, Jinny found among their cancelled checks the following: "This check is accepted under protest and with full reservation of rights to collect the unpaid balance of $5575 on the debt for which this check was offered in settlement. [Signed] Jim Evert."

What now?

Introduction

The duties one assumes and the rights brought into existence by the creation of a negotiable instrument do not last forever. The same law that provided for the creation of commercial paper also provides for its ending. It was important for you to know how to create a formal contract, and it is equally important to know how to discharge (end) the formal contract.

Once an instrument has been created negotiable in form and issued to a payee under some contractual arrangement, it may be further negotiated to a holder or an HIDC. At maturity, the holder will expect to be paid, so the holder will take the very practical step of "presenting" it to the maker, acceptor, or, if it is a nonacceptable draft, to the drawee.

When a holder of an instrument is finally paid according to its terms by one of these parties, the holder is satisfied and the liability of all parties to the instrument is discharged. If it is not paid—if the instrument is dishonored—then the holder may institute a lawsuit and be faced with an array of real or personal defenses.

Instead of bringing suit immediately and undergoing the expense and anxiety that it entails, the holder may seek other avenues of recovery. After all, the holder had no part of the potential defendant's dispute with the payee.

At this stage, the holder will think of the secondary or conditional liability of the drawer or indorsers. These secondary parties, or any one of them, will be liable on the instrument if the holder takes the preliminary steps of timely presentment for payment and, if the instrument is not paid, notice of dishonor.

This chapter deals with the procedures that must be followed to bind primary and secondary parties, and with the ways in which a party can discharge his or her liability on an instrument.

Presentment, Dishonor, and Notice—In General

Presentment of an instrument for payment[1] at the proper time[2] and, under some circumstances, presentment for acceptance prior to payment,[3] is the first step a holder must take to preserve the liability of secondary parties—drawers and indorsers. Once *any* presentment has been made (whether presentment for acceptance or for payment, and whether presentment is necessary or optional), the instrument is **dishonored**[4] if the responsible party does not accept or pay within certain time deadlines.[5] Secondary parties engage to be liable only if the instrument is *duly presented* for acceptance or payment to the drawee, acceptor, or maker. Therefore it is essential that presentment be made if, on dishonor of the instrument, they are to be held liable by the holder.

Finally, the holder must give notice of dishonor to secondary parties,[6] and this notice must be sent prior to midnight of the third business day following dishonor or receipt of notice of dishonor.[7] For banks, the deadline is midnight of the next banking day following dishonor or receipt of notice of dishonor.[8]

presentment
"A demand for acceptance or payment made upon the maker, acceptor, drawee or other payor by or on behalf of the holder" UCC 3–504(1)

dishonor
The refusal of the drawee to accept the draft, or of the drawee, acceptor, or maker to pay the draft or note

Presentment

► How Made

Presentment—that is, the demand for payment or acceptance—is made upon the maker, acceptor, or drawee by or on behalf of the holder. It may be made by mail, through a clearinghouse, or personally at the place designated in the instrument. If no place is specified, then the business address or residence is acceptable. Presentment is excused if no one can be located at any of these places to accept or pay the instrument.[9]

► Rights of the Party to Whom Presentment Is Made

The maker, acceptor, or drawee (or their authorized agent) may require the following things without dishonoring the instrument:

1. Exhibition or physical display of the note or draft
2. Reasonable proof of identification and, if the presenter is an agent, reasonable proof of the agent's authority

---

[1]UCC 3–501(1)(b).

[2]UCC 3–503.

[3]UCC 3–501(1)(a), 3–503(1)(a).

[4]UCC 3–507(1)(a).

[5]UCC 3–506.

[6]UCC 3–501(2).

[7]UCC 3–508(2)(4).

[8]UCC 4–104(h).

[9]UCC 3–504.

3. Presentment at the specified place, or, if none is specified, at a place reasonable in the circumstances
4. A signed receipt on the instrument for full or partial payment, and surrender of the instrument if paid in full.[10]

Failure to comply with any of these requirements invalidates the presentment. However, the presenter must be given a reasonable time to comply—for example, the presenter who is an agent may need some time to produce proof of this authority to act on behalf of the owner.[11]

► Time Allowed for Acceptance or Payment

The instrument is not dishonored if acceptance is deferred until the close of the next business day following presentment. Even beyond that, the holder may allow postponement for an additional business day in a good faith effort to obtain acceptance.[12] As a general rule, payment may be deferred while reasonable steps are taken to determine whether the instrument is properly payable; but payment must be made before the close of business on the day of presentment to avoid dishonor.[13]

► Time of Presentment

When an instrument contains a due date, presentment for payment should be made on that date.[14] If payments have been accelerated, presentment for payment is due within a reasonable time after acceleration.[15] Any presentment for acceptance must be made on or before the date when payment is due.[16]

Presentment for payment or acceptance of all other instruments—i.e., those without due dates—is due within a reasonable time after date or issue or after the secondary party becomes liable.[17] Otherwise the secondary party is discharged.

A reasonable period of time is determined from the nature of the instrument, banking or **trade usage,** and the facts of the particular case. For uncertified checks drawn and payable in the United States a reasonable period of time for presentment or for the initiation of the bank collection process is presumed to be as follows:

usage of trade
"Any practice or method of dealing having such regularity of observance in a place, vocation or trade as to justify an expectation that it will be observed with respect to the transaction in question" UCC 1–205(2)

1. Thirty days after date or issue (whichever is later) with respect to the drawer's liability
2. Seven days after indorsement with respect to an indorser's liability[18]

---

[10]UCC 3–505(1).

[11]UCC 3–505(2).

[12]UCC 3–506(1).

[13]UCC 3–506(2).

[14]UCC 3–503(1)(c).

[15]UCC 3–503(1)(d).

[16]UCC 3–503(1)(a)(b).

[17]UCC 3–503(1)(e).

[18]UCC 3–503(2).

► Effect of Late Presentment

The holder's failure to make a proper and timely presentment,[19] as well as the holder's failure to give proper and timely notice of dishonor,[20] has the effect of discharging secondary parties. Indorsers will be fully discharged under these circumstances; drawers may be fully or partially discharged.

The drawer of a domiciled instrument—one payable at a particular bank—will not automatically receive a full discharge. The discharge is limited to the extent that funds placed on deposit in that bank and intended for payment of a domiciled instrument have "shrunk" because of the bank's insolvency during the delay—that is, the period of time beyond thirty days. To qualify for this discharge, the drawer must make a written assignment to the holder of all the rights the drawer has against the now insolvent bank.[21]

To illustrate, suppose that the drawee originally held sufficient funds to pay a customer-drawer's $1,000 check but that the payee or subsequent party held the check for more than thirty days before presenting it or initiating the bank collection process. If the drawee bank becomes insolvent during the delay (the period in excess of thirty days) and only $500 are ultimately available to pay the check, the drawer may discharge his liability by written assignment to the holder of his rights against the bank for $500. In the following case the drawee bank did not become insolvent; thus the drawer's obligation was not discharged because of the payee's delay in presentment.

FACTS

At issue is whether the defendant drawer's obligation to pay dishonored uncertified checks is discharged by failure of the plaintiff payee to demand payment within a reasonable amount of time. The district court ruled that the obligation was not discharged and entered a judgment for the payee. The checks were held by the payee for over thirty days after date of issue. When they were finally presented for payment, they were returned due to a lack of sufficient funds.

DECISION

On appeal, for the payee. Presentment does not in itself discharge the drawer since the record does not show that the drawee bank became insolvent during the delay, thereby depriving the drawer of funds with which to cover the checks. UCC 3–502(1) states: "Where without excuse any necessary presentment or notice of dishonor is delayed beyond the time when it is due (a) any indorser is discharged; and (b) any drawer or the acceptor of a draft payable at a bank or the maker of a note payable at a bank who, because the drawee or payor bank becomes insolvent during the delay, is deprived of funds maintained with the drawee of payor bank to cover the instrument may discharge his liability by written assignment to the holder of his rights against the drawee or payor bank in respect of such funds, but such drawer, acceptor or maker is not otherwise discharged."

Grist v. Osgood, 521 P.2d 368 (Nev. 1974).

Indorsers of uncertified checks are fully discharged if the instrument is presented or the collection process begun more than seven days after their indorsement. In essence,

[19]UCC 3–503(1)(e), 3–502(1), 3–501(b)(c).

[20]UCC 3–501(2), 3–502(1).

[21]UCC 3–503(1)(b).

the payee or holder is being penalized because of the failure to make a timely presentment.

Notice of Dishonor

Notice of dishonor may be given by the holder or by his or her bank or agent to anyone who may be liable on the instrument.[22] Notice to one partner is notice to all partners. To be effective, any notice of dishonor must be given by a bank before its one-day midnight deadline (midnight on its next banking day following the banking day on which it receives the item or notice of its dishonor), and by all other persons before the three-day midnight deadline (midnight of the third business day after dishonor or notice of dishonor).[23]

Failure to give timely notice of dishonor will result in the discharge of secondary parties in the same manner as a failure to make a timely presentment.[24] Although memorizing dates and deadlines can be quite a chore, it could be very beneficial to a person in the long run to remain familiar with these.

Notice may be given in any reasonable manner, written or oral. It must be sufficient to identify the dishonored instrument. A misdescription that is not misleading will still be effective as a notice.[25]

Notice operates for the benefit of all who have rights against the party notified.[26] For example, if *H* presents an instrument at maturity and it is dishonored, one notice by *H* to indorsers *A* and *B* is all that is needed. If *H* recovers from *B, B* can pursue *A* without giving further notice to *A.* If *H* gives notice to *B* only, then *B* has a full three-day period to notify *A.*

Written notice is given when sent although it is never received.[27] It may consist of the instrument itself with the stamped or written statement that acceptance or payment has been refused.[28] Accommodation indorsers are entitled to the same notice that other indorsers receive, as the following case illustrates.

FACTS

P&S Trailer Sales, Inc., was the payee of a negotiable promissory note received from the maker, Estep, in partial satisfaction for the sale of merchandise. P&S sold the note to the First National Bank of Ceredo under terms as follows:

WITH RECOURSE

Seller guarantees payment of the amount due on said contract as and when the same

---

[22]UCC 3–508(1).

[23]UCC 3–508(2), 4–104(h).

[24]UCC 3–501(2), 3–502(1).

[25]UCC 3–508(3).

[26]UCC 3–508(8).

[27]UCC 3–508(4).

[28]UCC 3–508(3).

shall become due, waiving any extension of time made by Lender and agrees to repurchase said contract at any time upon demand after any default by Buyer. Seller waives notice of acceptance of this guaranty and notices of nonpayment and nonperformance.

P&S Trailer Sales, Inc.
Seller
By/s/George Linn
President
/s/George Linn
/s/Harry F. Thompson, Jr.

Estep, the maker of the note, defaulted. Linn and Thompson were not given timely notice of this default because, the bank alleges, they are liable as guarantors to whom no notice is necessary. Since P&S Trailer Sales has gone out of business, the action against Linn and Thompson is First National's only realistic chance of recovery.

DECISION

Linn and Thompson are not guarantors because the contract of guaranty plainly applies to the seller only, P&S Trailer Sales, and because of the presumption established by UCC 3–402: "Unless the instrument clearly indicates that a signature is made in some other capacity, it is an indorsement."

As indorsers Linn and Thompson were entitled to notice of dishonor, and that requirement is not altered by their capacity as accommodation indorsers. UCC 3–415 (4): "An indorsement which shows that it is not in the chain of title is notice of its accommodation character." With notice of dishonor and demand for payment, Linn and Thompson could have proceeded to make the monthly payments instead of being confronted, as here, with the entire unpaid obligation.

First Nat'l Bank of Ceredo v. Linn, 282 S.E.2d 52 (W.Va. 1981).

▶ Protest

Protest is a formal method of preserving proof that presentment was made and that the instrument was dishonored.

protest
A formal certificate, issued by a properly authorized person, certifying that a foreign or international draft was duly presented for acceptance or payment and that it was dishonored

Protest is required for drafts that, on their face, appear to be drawn or payable outside the states and territories of the United States and the District of Columbia.[29] Such drafts at times are called "international" or "foreign" drafts. On all other drafts, protest is optional. It is a certificate of dishonor made by a U.S. consul, vice consul, notary public, or other authorized person according to the law of the place of dishonor. The protest must identify the instrument, and it may certify that some or all of the parties have been notified.[30]

Delayed, Waived, or Excused Presentment, Protest, or Notice

▶ Delay

Delay in presentment, protest, or notice of dishonor is excused if the party does not know that it is due—e.g., the holder received it after acceleration by a prior party but without notice of the acceleration.[31] Delay is also excused if it is caused by circumstances beyond the party's control and the party exercises reasonable diligence after the cause of the delay ceases.[32]

[29] UCC 3–501(3).

[30] UCC 3–509.

[31] UCC 3–511(1).

[32] UCC 3–511(1).

Waiver or Excuse

Presentment, protest, or notice of dishonor is completely excused if:

1. it has been expressly or impliedly waived;
2. the party has dishonored or countermanded (stopped) payment or otherwise has no reason to expect or right to require that the instrument be accepted or paid; or
3. presentment, protest, or notice cannot be given by the exercise of reasonable diligence.[33]

Presentment alone is excused if the maker, acceptor, or drawee is dead or insolvent. If payment or acceptance is refused for reasons other than the want of a proper presentment—e.g., the holder is told by the maker that he will not pay at maturity because the payee defrauded him—then presentment is excused because it would simply be useless.[34]

Waiver of protest is a waiver of presentment and notice of dishonor as well, even though protest is not required. Waiver of presentment, notice, or protest embodied in the instrument itself is binding on all parties. If it is written above the signature of one or more indorsers, it binds those only.[35]

Discharge

discharge
In contracts, termination of a contractual duty to perform a promise

A party is **discharged** from liability on an instrument by any act or agreement with the other party that would discharge a simple contract for the payment of money.[36] It is sometimes said that payment discharges the instrument, as is illustrated in the following case.

FACTS

Bruce Small, minor son of the defendant, Genevieve, purchased an automobile from the plaintiff, George Allen, for $225. He paid $100 down, and a note for the balance was signed by Bruce and Genevieve. Bruce paid the note, and it was marked "Paid in full, George S. Allen" and delivered to Bruce Small, who had the lien on the automobile discharged of record. Later Bruce Small, still a minor, by written notice rescinded his contract with the plaintiff. He assigned his ownership to the plaintiff by transferring the ownership using the form provided on the registration certificate. He then returned the car to the plaintiff's garage and demanded that the plaintiff return the $225, which plaintiff refused to do. Bruce Small successfully sued the plaintiff, who then returned the $225 to him. Plaintiff later sued Genevieve on the note, contending that Genevieve is liable to him on the note to the extent of its face amount. He argued that since Bruce rescinded his contract with the plaintiff, the lien note was restored to its former status as far as the defendant was concerned, she being an accommodation maker.

DECISION

For defendant, Genevieve Small. There is no question that the note was fully paid according to its terms and tenor, and the court so found.

[33] UCC 3–511(2).

[34] UCC 3–511(3).

[35] UCC 3–511(5)(6).

[36] UCC 3–601(2).

Payment is the final act which extinguishes a negotiable instrument and transmits it into a cancelled voucher. There is no longer a holder of the instrument and no suit may thereafter be maintained.

The findings establish that the defendant signed the note to insure its payment. The full payment was made. The surrender of a note by the holder to the maker, with intent thereby to discharge it, does discharge it. Whatever acts Bruce Small took on his own behalf, as a minor, were between him and the plaintiff and could not affect the rights of the defendant.

Allen v. Small, 271 A.2d 840 (Vt. 1970).

The following methods of discharge are exclusive insofar as the provisions of UCC Article 3 are concerned, but the Article does not prevent or affect discharge arising from other rules of law, such as bankruptcy:

1. Payment or **satisfaction** (Section 3–603); or
2. Tender of payment (Section 3–604); or
3. Cancellation or **renunciation** (Section 3–605); or
4. Impairment of right of recourse or of collateral (Section 3–606); or
5. Reacquisition of the instrument by a prior party (Section 3–208); or
6. Fraudulent and material alteration (Section 3–407); or
7. Certification of a check (Section 3–411); or
8. Acceptance varying a draft (Section 3–412); or
9. Unexcused delay in presentment or notice of dishonor or protest (Section 3–502).[37]

satisfaction

The discharge of an obligation by paying what is due

renunciation

The abandonment of a right by a person

The liability of all parties is discharged when one who has no right of action—i.e., no recourse against anyone on the instrument—reacquires it or is himself discharged.[38] For example, a note issued from *M* to *P* and negotiated from *P* to *A* to *H* may be reacquired by *M* prior to maturity or paid by *M* at maturity. Both reacquisition and payment discharge all parties to the instrument at that time.

If *M* chooses to reissue the note he purchased before maturity, he will of course be liable to subsequent parties. Intervening parties, *P, A,* and *H,* are discharged with respect to *M* and subsequent holders not in due course. If their indorsements are cancelled, they will not be liable even to an HIDC.[39]

► Effect of a Discharge

No discharge provided by Article 3 is effective against a subsequent HIDC unless the HIDC has notice of the discharge when he or she takes the instrument.[40] Discharges provided by other rules of law, such as, bankruptcy, are effective despite lack of notice.

► Payment or Satisfaction

In order to receive the benefit of a discharge, payment or satisfaction must be made to a holder or the holder's authorized agent. Payment offered in full settlement may, in some

[37] UCC 3–601(1).

[38] UCC 3–601(3).

[39] UCC 3–208.

[40] UCC 3–602.

states, be accepted in partial settlement only. However, it is best to proceed with caution and to always consult state law. In the following case the payee crossed out and protested the drawer's "Final Payment/Full Satisfaction" language prior to cashing the check. The payee was trying to lock on to the small amount represented by the check and proceed against the drawer for the remaining amount. See the result. For your own well being, look into your state law before leaping into such a controversy.

accord and satisfaction
A new contract (accord) that discharges a party from a previous contractual obligation; the old contract is discharged (satisfied)

FACTS

Wooding, defendant, issued to his creditor, County Fire Door Corporation, a $416 check that bore two warnings: (1) the face of the check read "Final Payment," and (2) the reverse side stated "By its endorsement, the payee accepts this check in full satisfaction of all claims against the C. F. Wooding Co. arising out of or relating to the Upjohn Project." Wooding blamed County Fire Door for late deliveries that caused it losses on the Upjohn project. County Fire Door denied any such responsibility and billed Wooding $2618. County Fire Door crossed out Wooding's language on the back of the check and added the following: "This check is accepted under protest and with full reservation of rights to collect the unpaid balance for which this check is offered in settlement." The plaintiff County Fire Door then indorsed and deposited the check.

DECISION

Contrary to the expectations raised by the language of UCC 1–207 that a party such as payee County Fire Door could "protest" a debtor's offer and reserve rights to the full amount of the debt, the court concluded that acceptance of the check by indorsement and deposit was an **"accord and satisfaction."** Whatever may have been County Fire Door's express intention by knowingly cashing such an instrument, it could not disown the terms upon which it had been tendered. This rule prevails in the majority of states if the dispute is unliquidated, that is, where both parties contend in good faith for different amounts due and owing.

County Fire Door Corporation v. C. F. Wooding Co., 520 A.2d 1028 (Conn. 1987).

jus tertii
The right of a third party

► Jus Tertii: The Law of the Third Party

The maker, acceptor, or drawee is discharged even though payment is made with knowledge that some other party has a claim of ownership on the instrument unless, prior to payment, the party with the claim either (1) secures or indemnifies the one seeking a discharge, or (2) gets a court order (injunction) against payment.[41]

To illustrate: suppose that the payee, *P*, is fraudulently induced to negotiate a note to *A*; or, if *P* is a minor, simply assume that *P* indorses the paper to *A* in a transaction for goods. In either case, *P* will have a claim on the instrument. Knowledge of this claim, however, will not affect the right of *M* (the maker) to pay *A* or a subsequent holder at maturity and receive a full discharge. After all, the maker has no defense of his or her own against the payee or the holder. The maker expects at maturity to be able to pay a holder and receive a discharge, and the maker does not want to be drawn into a dispute between *P* and *A*. Payment and discharge can be prevented only if *P*, the party with the claim, (1) posts security or **indemnity** for *M*, or (2) gets an injunction against payment.[42]

indemnity
An absolute obligation to pay for another's loss

Payment at maturity does *not* result in a discharge if it is made in bad faith or with knowledge that the holder acquired by theft or acquired through a thief. However, bearer paper could be stolen and still be negotiated to an HIDC. If this happens, payment

[41] UCC 3–603(1).

[42] UCC 3–306(d).

to an HIDC who innocently acquired through a thief is a discharge even though this fact is known to the payor at the time of payment.[43]

Finally, no discharge results if payment is inconsistent with the terms of a restrictive indorsement.[44] Assume that *P* indorses a note issued by *M* as follows: "Pay to *A* upon completion of contract #61384, [signed] *P*." If *A* presents this instrument to *M* for payment at maturity, *M* must take reasonable steps to determine that the contract has been completed. If it has not been completed, payment to *A* will not discharge *M* from liability to *P*.

You will recall, however, that intermediary banks and payor banks that are not also depositaries are only affected by the restrictive indorsement of their transferor. In the situation described above, these banks would not have to be concerned with *P*'s restrictive indorsement.[45]

▶ Tender of Payment

tender
(Verb) To proffer, make available

Tender or offer of full payment at maturity or at a later time discharges the tendering party only to the extent of all subsequent liability for interest, costs, and attorney's fees.[46] A tender before maturity has no effect, unless the terms permit a party who is liable on the instrument to accelerate payment and avoid the running of interest. For example, a note may provide that the maker promises to pay "on or before" the due date.

If the holder refuses tender of payment by a party (*M*, maker, for example), any party on the instrument who has a right of recourse against the tendering party (*M*) is fully discharged.[47] On an instrument issued by *M* and indorsed from *P* to *A* to *H*, *H*'s refusal of *M*'s tender completely discharges *P* and *A* because *H* had a chance to get his money and refused to take it.

The primary party on a time instrument makes tender if he or she is ready and able to pay at every place designated at maturity. Tender of payment of a domiciled note or draft—one payable at a bank—can be made at maturity if funds are available at that bank and instructions have been given to pay.[48]

▶ Cancellation and Renunciation

A holder may discharge the liability of any party on the instrument in any manner apparent on the face of the paper or the indorsements.[49] Since this discharge is in the nature of a gift, no consideration is necessary.

The holder who is discharging a party from further liability may do so by intentionally cancelling the instrument or the party's signature.[50] The holder may

---

[43]UCC 3–603(1)(a).

[44]UCC 3–603(1)(b).

[45]UCC 3–206(2), 4–205(2). See pp. 637–639.

[46]UCC 3–604(1).

[47]UCC 3–604(2).

[48]UCC 3–604(3).

[49]UCC 3–605(1)(a).

[50]UCC 3–605(1)(a).

renounce his or her rights either in a signed writing that is delivered to the party being discharged or by surrender of the instrument to that party.[51] Neither cancellation nor renunciation affects the title to the instrument unless it is surrendered.[52]

recourse

A right to resort to a person or to a thing

collateral

Property subject to a security interest UCC 9–105(1)(c)

pledge

The possessory security interest in bailed goods acquired by the bailee when there is a bailment for the purpose of security

► Impairment of Recourse or of Collateral

Assume that *M* issued *P* a $1,000 note that was subsequently indorsed to *A* and, finally, to *H*. If *M* dishonored at maturity and *A* was held secondarily liable to *H* on the indorsement contract, *A* could normally expect to seek reimbursement from *P*. After all, *P* was the one who got him into this fix to begin with.

This principle holds true in situations where *H* releases collateral security that *A* was depending on as well. Modify the *M* to *P* to *A* to *H* hypothetical to the extent that *M* pledges valuable goods, jewels, stocks, or commodities (or mortgages property) as security for the note. If *H* releases this security without the consent of *A*, or of *P*, they are discharged to the extent of their injury or loss. If $500 worth of security was **pledged** or mortgaged to strengthened the note, *A* or *P* would be discharged to that extent if *H* released or surrendered the security. Once again, the reason for this rule is that *H* cannot unilaterally inflict harm or alter the contract of those parties who precede him.

► Reacquisition of the Instrument by a Prior Party

Suppose that *D* drew a check payable to the order of *P*. The check was then negotiated by the indorsement of *A*, *B*, and *C* to *P*. *A*, *B*, and *C* are discharged because, on dishonor, they are liable to *P*, the holder, who as payee is, in turn, liable to them. In this way, persons who are liable to another, who then becomes liable to them, are spared the problem of circuity of action.

However, what if *H* released or discharged *P*? Is *A* left to seek recovery against *M* alone? *M*, remember, already refused to pay once, and he is likely to refuse again. Does it seem fair then for *H*, acting unilaterally and without *A*'s consent, to defeat *A*'s initial expectation of falling back on *P*?

No! One's gut reaction is that this is not fair, and the Code reinforces this conclusion.[53] *A* is fully discharged if *H* releases *P*. However, if *H* released *P* and reserved his rights against *A* at the time *P* was discharged, *A* would remain liable to *H* but *A* would be entitled to recourse against *P*.[54] The basic thought to keep in mind is that *A*'s right to seek reimbursement from prior parties cannot be jeopardized or destroyed by the unilateral conduct of *H*. In the following case the holder's undue extension of time of payment on a note discharged the nonconsenting accommodation co-maker on the note.

FACTS

Adamson, defendant, was an accommodation co-maker of a $13,000 negotiable promissory note that was in default. The loan was for the mushroom business of Wick, Adamson's son-in-law. Originally the Holcomb State Bank, plaintiff, would not make the loan to Wick.

---

[51] UCC 3–605(1)(b).

[52] UCC 3–605(2).

[53] UCC 3–606(1)(a).

[54] UCC 3–606(2)(c).

Then the Bank president suggested that Adamson sign as co-maker, which he did. On the note was handwritten, "For use in Wick's Mushroom Business," and "This is Wick's Note & Adamson is co-signer." The Bank credited the money to the mushroom company account. Adamson did not receive any of the proceeds from the loan.

When the note came due, Wick paid the interest but not the principal. Later, Wick entered into an agreement with the bank on a four month extension of the note, but Adamson refused to sign the extension form. On the note's default, plaintiff bank sued the defendant on the note. The trial court gave judgment for plaintiff bank, and defendant appealed.

DECISION

Reversed, for the defendant Adamson.
Under UCC 3–601(a)(1), an agreement by the holder bank to suspend the right to enforce a promissory note against the maker, without the consent of the accommodation co-maker, defendant, and without an express reservation of rights against him, discharges the accommodation co-maker from liability.

Holcomb State Bank v. Adamson, 438 N.E.2d 635 (Ill. 1982).

Summary Statement

1. When an instrument is presented by a holder to a maker, acceptor, or drawee for payment at maturity, or for acceptance at or prior to maturity, the instrument is dishonored if it is not paid or accepted within the deadline. Presentment for payment should be made on the due date or, if the instrument has been accelerated, within a reasonable time after acceleration. Presentment for acceptance must be made on or before maturity. Any other presentment—i.e., presentment of an instrument without a due date—must be made within a reasonable time after date or issue or after a secondary party becomes liable.
2. A reasonable period of time depends on the type of instrument, usage of trade, and the facts of the particular case. For an uncertified check drawn and payable in the United States, a reasonable period of time is presumed to be thirty days from issue with respect to the drawer's liability and seven days from indorsement for a secondary party's liability. Failure to make a proper presentment, unless excused, will fully discharge indorsers. The drawer, acceptor, or maker of an instrument payable at a bank may be fully or partially discharged if the drawee-payor bank becomes insolvent during the delay, depending on the extent of such insolvency.
3. Once an instrument has been dishonored, the holder must send notice of dishonor to secondary parties by midnight of the third business day following dishonor; for banks, the period is trimmed to midnight of the next banking day. Notice may be given in any reasonable manner, written or oral, which sufficiently identifies the instrument. It is effective if sent within the deadline even though it is never received. Failure to give proper notice, unless excused, will fully discharge indorsers; the drawer, maker, or acceptor of an instrument payable at a bank may be fully or partially discharged if the drawee-payor bank becomes insolvent during the delay, depending on the extent of such insolvency.
4. Protest, made in the presence of an authorized official, is a formal way of preserving proof of presentment, dishonor, and notice of dishonor. It is required on international or foreign drafts.
5. A party is discharged from all liability on an instrument by any act or agreement that would discharge a simple contract, e.g., payment to a holder at maturity. If a person reacquires an instrument, all intervening parties are discharged from liability to the

reacquirer; intervening parties will not be liable to subsequent holders, but they will be liable to subsequent HIDCs unless their indorsements are cancelled.

6. No discharge under Article 3 is effective against a subsequent HIDC unless the HIDC has notice of it at the time he takes the instrument. To be effective, payment or satisfaction must be made to a holder or the holder's authorized agent. The discharge is available even though payment is made with knowledge that some party has a claim of ownership on the instrument unless, prior to payment, the party with the claim either (a) secures or indemnifies the one seeking a discharge, or (b) gets an injunction against payment. Payment at maturity will not result in a discharge if it is made with knowledge that the holder acquired by theft or through a thief (unless the holder has the right of an HIDC). Neither will payment at maturity amount to a discharge if it is inconsistent with the terms of a restrictive indorsement.
7. Tender of full payment at or after maturity discharges the tendering party from liability for interest, costs, and attorney's fees. If the holder refuses a proper tender, all parties who had a right of recourse against the one making tender are discharged.
8. A holder may discharge the liability of any party by intentionally cancelling the instrument or the party's signature. If the holder releases a previous signatory against whom some intervening party has a right of recourse, the release will have the effect of discharging the intervening party as well, unless the holder reserves rights against the intervening party. In the event that the holder does reserve such right of recourse against the intervening party, the intervening party retains his or her original right to seek recovery against the one that the holder discharged. Similarly, if the holder releases collateral that a party on the instrument had access to as security for the party's original obligation on the instrument, that party will be discharged to the extent of injury or loss caused by such release.

In the following case note how the court held that, when the holder of a note impaired the collateral security for the note without the consent of the co-makers of the note, since the note did not indicate that either of them was an accommodation co-maker surety for the other, the impairment did not discharge them from their liability as co-makers—primary parties absolutely liable on the note.

UNITED STATES v. UNUM, INC.
658 F.2d 300 (5th Cir. 1981).

Politz, Circuit Judge. The Small Business Administration (SBA) filed suit to collect the balance due on a promissory note executed by Unum, Inc., and Lance W. Dreyer. Defendants-appellants admitted the obligation, but claimed a discharge from liability because the SBA had unjustifiably impaired the collateral securing the debt by releasing its lien to a third-party purchaser for $1,000. The district court rejected the defense of unjustifiable impairment, and this judgment was affirmed on appeal.

Unum and Dreyer purchased three Lockheed Constellations from the SBA that it had acquired in a foreclosure sale. The sale was financed by a $61,000 note that Unum and Dreyer issued to SBA, and secured by chattel mortgages on the planes. One of these planes was eventually seized and auctioned off by the Anchorage International Airport to pay for delinquent space rental and tie-down fees.

Aviation Specialties was high bidder at the airport auction sale. It purchased the plane for $3,670.00, the amount of the fees, subject to SBA's chattel mortgage. Later, for payment of $1,000.00, the SBA released its mortgage on the plane and credited the money to the original note. Aviation Specialties, meanwhile, made $20,000.00 improvements to the plane.

The United States filed suit on the note. Unum and Dreyer admitted the debt but advanced an affirmative defense claiming discharge from the obligation to the extent of the fair market value of the sold airplane. They predicated their defense on UCC Section 3–606, arguing that the SBA's release of its lien for $1,000 unjustifiably impaired the collateral:

> (1) The holder discharges any party to the instrument to the extent that without such party's consent the holder (b) unjustifiably impairs any collateral for the instrument given by or on behalf of the party or any person against whom he has a right of recourse.

At first blush, this section appears to provide a defense. However, a maker of a note, as opposed to a surety, is not entitled to invoke this defense.

This interpretation of 3–606 is soundly based. The maker of a note is always primarily responsible for the debt with no recourse except against co-makers. Sureties, whether accommodation makers or indorsers, are only secondarily liable; they retain a right of recourse against the primary obligor. Fairness dictates that if the risk a surety has agreed to undertake is increased through impairment of the securing collateral by the person to whom payment is due, the surety should be discharged to the extent of the impairment.

In the present case, the face of the note reflects that Dreyer and Unum are both makers. There is no evidence that Dreyer was an accommodation maker. Consequently, they may not seek relief under Section 3–606.

Affirmed for the Small Business Administration.

Questions and Case Problems

1. Bermes was required by state law to file his accident claim with the Industrial Commission within one year after final payment for his injuries under an insurance policy. The insurance company drew a draft to the order of Bermes which he received on May 3 and which was honored or paid in cash on May 6. He filed his claim with the Industrial Commission on May 4 of the next year. Did he file in time? [*Consol. Freightways v. Industrial Comm'n,* 269 N.E.2d 291 (Ill. 1971).]
2. The defendant, New House Products, Inc., offered to make part payment at maturity of a promissory note that it had issued to the payee, Commercial Plastics. The offer was rejected. Commercial then instituted this suit for the entire amount of the principal, interest, and attorney's fees. What was the effect of New House's tender? [*New House Products, Inc. v. Commercial Plastics and Supply Corp.,* 233 S.E.2d 45 (Ga. 1977).]
3. Two promissory notes payable to Beermann "Quality" Fertilizers, defendant, were executed on October 2, 1967 by the maker, David Vavra. Each of the notes provided on the face that "the makers, sureties, and guarantors of this note hereby severally waive presentment for payment, notice of nonpayment, protest, and notice of protest, and diligence in bringing suit against any party thereto and consent that time of payment may be extended without notice thereof." The notes were indorsed in blank by the defendant and transferred before maturity by the payee to the plaintiff bank for their full value. The payee, Beermann Brothers, is a defendant. Payment was not made at maturity, and Vavra executed two extension notes to the plaintiff which set maturity 21 days longer than the original period.

   Does this extension have any effect on the liability of defendant-payee, Beermann Brothers? [*Citizens State Bank v. Beermann Bros.,* 198 N.W.2d 458 (Neb. 1972).]
4. Glover and Ferguson, partners, signed a 90-day $20,000 note to the plaintiff-payee bank, National Bank of Commerce of The Pine Bluff. Before the note was due,

Ferguson bought Glover's partnership interest. Glover informed the bank that Ferguson was assuming all partnership obligations. Glover further related that he did not want the note extended nor would he sign a renewal.

Five months later Ferguson was discharged in bankruptcy, and the bank proceeded against Glover for the balance. Glover alleged that the bank agreed not to sue Ferguson and that this had the effect of discharging him (Glover) from any further liability under UCC 3–606(1)(a). Glover further alleged that the bank was estopped from pursuing him because Ferguson's checking account on several occasions exceeded the overdue and unpaid balance and the bank failed to off-set against it. Result? [*Glover v. Nat'l Bank of Commerce of the Pine Bluff,* 529 S.W.2d 333 (Ark. 1975).]

5. Security Pacific National Bank (Security), plaintiff-depositary bank, brought this action against Associated Motor Sales (A.M.S.), payee, to recover on overdrafts of $188,000 caused by the dishonor of $312,000 in checks by various payor banks which A.M.S. had deposited with Security. A.M.S. defends on the basis that the checks were not timely dishonored.

Security's evidence of dishonor consisted of copies of returned checks with payor bank stamps of dishonor, of the deposit ticket accompanying each deposit, and of Security's written notice of dishonor to payee A.M.S. Security's assistant cashier Olga Skoro also declared that she was present when Mr. Levine, president of A.M.S., was advised of the returned checks within one day after they were "bounced" back to Security. Has Security given proper notice within the prescribed time? [*Security Pac. Nat'l Bank v. Associated Motor Sales,* 106 Cal. Rptr. App.3rd 171 (Cal. 1980).]

6. The plaintiff secured a judgment on a promissory note executed by the defendants, Paul W. McAtee and McAtee Builders, Inc. and the defendant, Paul McAtee, appealed. The note was secured by a mortgage executed by the defendant, McAtee Builders, Inc., on real property owned by McAtee Builders, Inc. Paul McAtee's defense was that he was discharged from his obligation because the plaintiff, without Paul McAtee's consent, released the mortgage given by McAtee Builders. The relevant statutory authority, UCC 3–606 provides as follows:

> (1) The holder discharges any party to the instrument to the extent that without such party's consent the holder (b) unjustifiably impairs any collateral for the instrument given by or on behalf of the party or any person against whom he has a right of recourse.

Result? [*Christensen v. McAtee,* 473 P.2d 659 (Or. 1970).]

7. Mrs. Fischer indorsed a $2,000 check payable to the drawer and drawn on Clayton Bank. Nevada State Bank cashed the check for the payee/drawer and initiated collection through Valley Bank the same day. Ninety days later Valley Bank notified Nevada Bank that the check had been dishonored because the original was lost in transit. Nevada Bank immediately debited Mrs. Fischer's account by $2,000 and notified her of the payor bank's dishonor. It was apparent that one of the several banks in the collection process had violated its midnight deadline in giving notice of the dishonor. Had that bank acted timely, Mrs. Fischer would have learned in a reasonable time that the check had been dishonored. Is Mrs. Fischer liable as an indorser? [*Nevada State Bank v. Fischer,* 565 P.2d 332 (Nev. 1977).]

8. *M* issued a negotiable instrument to *P* for $100. *P* raised the amount to $200 and presented it to *M* for payment at maturity. *M* detected the alteration and refused to pay any amount. Is *M* liable to *P* for the original $100?

9. *M* issued a negotiable promissory note payable to the order of *P* for $800. *P* negotiated to *A*, and the instrument was subsequently negotiated to *B*, to *C*, then back to *A*, and finally to *H*. *H* did not qualify as an HIDC, however, because he received the instrument as a gift. At maturity, *M* refused to pay, and *H* gave timely notice to all indorsers. *B* and *C* claim that they have been discharged by *A*'s reacquisition. Result? Would your response be the same if *H* qualified as an HIDC?
10. In *United States v. Unum, Inc.*, excerpted at the beginning of this section, why did the court conclude that release or impairment of the collateral did not relieve defendants of liability on the note?

PART 6 COMMERCIAL PAPER

ETHICS AND BUSINESS LAW

Introduction

This end-of-part discussion, like the others in this book, is designed to encourage you to begin forming personal beliefs about what is right or wrong conduct in business. The discussion here builds on the material in the first end-of-part discussion; you may find it helpful to review that.

This material has several goals. The section below is designed to help you see the range of ethical issues associated with this area of the law. The in-depth discussion is intended to provide you with a background for forming your own beliefs about a single very important ethical issue in business. The problems at the end of this part are designed to build your skill in ethical analysis while exploring further the in-depth issue.

A Sampling of Ethical Issues in Commercial Paper

► Holder in Due Course Doctrine

The holder in due course (HIDC) doctrine is a core concept of commercial paper law. At first glance, the ethical character of this doctrine appears mysterious, difficult to perceive. In effect, this doctrine deprives a maker or drawer of commercial paper of the ability to assert personal defenses against a holder in due course. For example, if you issued a check to a local retailer as payment for living-room furniture, and the retailer negotiated the check to its wholesaler who is an HIDC, you would have to pay the check even if you did not receive the furniture from the retailer. This is because nondelivery of the furniture is "failure of consideration," which is only a personal defense. This may appear very unfair.

But notice that both you and the wholesaler have done nothing wrong. It is the retailer who has broken a promise. Therefore, regarding you and the wholesaler, the moral weight of the claims is about equal. The effect of the holder in due course doctrine is to shift the burden to one of these innocent parties, the maker or drawer of the instrument. In doing this, the law advances the interests of the majority by making commercial paper similar to currency, by making it easy to collect on the note or draft, so people will more readily accept commercial paper. This benefits almost everyone by making it easier for transactions to occur. In effect, the maker or drawer is required to first pay the note or draft, and then sue persons like the retailer for breach of contract.

But sometimes the innocent maker or drawer gets stuck. If the retailer has gone into bankruptcy, or disappeared, or died, the innocent drawer or maker may never see the furniture and never get the money back. Thus this party pays a price to benefit everyone else who enters into commercial paper transactions. Do you think it is ethical for our legal system to cause injury to innocent makers or drawers so that the whole system works better? Is there any other realistic alternative?

► Commercial Paper Time Limits

Another ethical issue in commercial paper law is associated with the *time* requirements for certain actions. If commercial paper is to play a role similar to currency, then the delays associated with the paper must be minimized. Therefore an unexcused delay in presenting an instrument will discharge any indorser thereon. Similarly, payment or acceptance of a check by a bank must occur within one business day or the instrument is deemed to be dishonored. Notice of dishonor must be given by the holder of the instrument within three business days or indorsers are discharged. Similarly, banks are not required to honor checks more than six months old.

These rules in effect punish those who are tardy in the performance of their commercial paper obligations. Sometimes the punishment is significant. Clearly, the goal is to speed the flow of commercial paper and make it more like currency. But in order to do this the law sometimes imposes time limit penalties on parties who are innocent of any wrongdoing except tardy action. In an ethical sense, these persons are sometimes sacrificed so that the whole system can operate more effectively. Do you think it is ethical to impose disproportionate penalties on a few individuals to benefit the many others who participate in the commercial paper system? Do you think it is ethical to punish for time delays those who are unaware of these time requirements?

In-Depth Discussion of a Basic Issue: Order and Ethics

While *negotiable* paper is often made "to the order of," here we use the word "order" in a different sense. In the following discussion, "order" refers to that characteristic of the law that produces stability, predictability, and consistency. Order is the idea that societies need peace, stability, and predictability in important legal, business, and political matters.

► Order and Arbitrariness

In many instances laws designed to create order also create some amount of arbitrariness. Thus, to achieve order, we have created the arbitrary rule that we must drive on the right side of the road. Laws aimed at creating order sometimes seem designed only to develop a predictable procedure, and usually one that is easily enforceable. For example, the law that oral stop orders are good for only fourteen calendar days seems quite arbitrary. Anyone would have a difficult time arguing that fourteen days is good while thirteen or fifteen days are bad or wrong. What is needed is an arbitrary standard, one which is easily enforced. For many persons, the arbitrary attribute of this and similar laws deprives them of their legitimacy and thus they don't comply. The fifty-five mile per hour speed limit is another example of a law with an arbitrary component.

► Positive Law: Legitimacy Based on Order or Power

In the first end-of-part discussion, we stated that positive law has as its philosophic goal the creation of order. However, not all thinkers seek to justify positive law by the fact that it usually generates order.

Some positive law thinkers believe that natural law and historical law do not provide bases for judging the legitimacy of laws. In this view, the only standard for judging legitimacy is whether or not a law has gone through the law-making process of the government in power. Sometimes this jurisprudence is expressed as "might makes right." Because the government has the power to put you in jail, you must obey its laws. And under this jurisprudence, the laws that promote slavery, apartheid, and Hitler's holocaust are entirely just. To a very large extent, this is a view of the law as divorced from morals. Because this positive law, justified only by power, is arbitrary, it is easy to confuse it with positive law justified by order. Arbitrariness is an attribute common to both.

► Natural Law: Order As an Ethical Principle

Order itself is definitely a moral good, something essential to organized society and civilization itself. Unless we are able to understand when the law seeks order, the law can seem to us unfair, harsh, arbitrary, and not deserving of our loyalty and compliance. To think about the law in philosophical ways, we need to be able to weigh the importance of order in various legal situations. Sometimes we need to compare order with other principles of justice and with the desires of those governed. Unless we develop this skill we can misunderstand the law and not see what it is really trying to accomplish.

If we see that order is essential to society, then it is very easy to assert that order is a part of the natural law, resting on the moral ideas that we ought to treat others equally, and in predictable ways.

Order can also flow from other ethical principles. For example, the requirement that we not harm others can lead us to require that everyone drive safely. And this may result in a law like the fifty-five mile per hour speed limit. As we think about such a law, it is important to see its constituent parts. Thus the basic thrust of this law is aimed at avoiding harm while another part identifies an exact speed (fifty-five miles per hour). This latter part is clearly arbitrary but it allows the law to be easily enforced. Thus while a small part of this law is arbitrary, the major thrust of it is aimed at creating order and promoting safety.

In a similar way, the UCC requires that commercial paper, to be negotiable, must identify a "sum certain." Without this requirement, parties would be uncertain of their obligations and courts would be entangled in prolonged disputes over the intent of the parties. Therefore the requirement promotes order.

The requirement that we drive on the right side of the road is often cited as a law that is completely arbitrary and is only justified because it produces only order. Hans Kelsen, an important legal philosopher, has articulated the idea that arbitrariness, used to achieve order, can be justified by nonpositivist thinking. Kelsen used the Kantian procedure of making a rule universal to evaluate whether we are obligated to obey laws that appear arbitrary. He concluded that not obeying cannot be made universal; if everyone disobeyed every arbitrary law, the result would be an irrational state of affairs.

Order and Other Legal Goals

► Legal Imperfections and Order

Because laws that promote order often must be arbitrary, they sometimes create opportunities for injustice. People can sometimes take advantage of an arbitrary law to gain unfair advantage. Recall that the statute of frauds makes some contracts unenforceable because they cannot be proved by a writing. If one party to a transaction knows this and the other does not, then for practical purposes one party thinks the contract can be enforced against each party, while the other party knows that the contract is unenforceable against either party. Thus the arbitrary character of this law allows it to be used in some instances to obstruct justice.

Solving Ethics Problems

Like the other end-of-part discussions in this book, this one presents problems for you to consider. These problems have three goals. The first is to give you the opportunity to further explore the in-depth issue. The second goal is to give you experience in ethical reasoning about the law and about related management problems. The third goal is to let you see how thinking critically about the law can increase your ability to make ethical decisions. To facilitate this, the problems begin by asking you to analyze the law for its ethical content and then shift to looking at related problems in managerial ethics.

For a discussion of the ethical roles of markets and the law, and examples of the four styles of ethical reasoning—egoism, utilitarianism, Kantian philosophy, and religious ethics—read the business ethics material at the end of Part 1.

► Problems

1. Review the case of *K & K Manufacturing, Inc. and Knight v. Union Bank* (p. 696). Is this case really about the negligence of Knight in failing to discover that his trusted bookkeeper, Garza, was forging his signature? Or is it more about creating an arbitrary rule for determining who shall bear a loss, the bank or the customer, when there has been a forgery and both parties are innocent? What style of ethical reasoning can be used to justify this law?
2. Suppose you are a banker with two customers, one large and one small. The small customer is more of a nuisance to the bank than the valued customer. A conflict arises between the two customers, and the small customer places an oral stop payment order on a check for $15,000 he issued to the large customer just before leaving for a three week vacation in Europe. You know that the large important customer will be appreciative if you do not tell the small customer that the oral stop order is only good for 14 calendar days. Ought you to tell the small customer about the effect of the oral stop order? Do you think it is ethical to use to your own advantage laws that promote order by using arbitrariness?
3. Suppose someone is negotiating to you a check that you intend to negotiate to another party. Because you are familiar with commercial paper law, you know you can avoid liability for some indorsement warranties by asking that the check be indorsed in blank so that your indorsement is not required for further negotiation of the check. Do you think this conduct is ethical? What ethical reasoning supports this conduct?
4. If you were the manager of a large work crew of 65 laborers who were required to punch a time clock each morning, would you be justified in creating a rule that stated that those more than six minutes late would be docked an hour's pay? Would such a managerial policy be justified by a desire to create order? What ethical reasoning can you articulate that justifies such a managerial policy?

PART 7

GOVERNMENT REGULATION OF BUSINESS

PREVIEW

The purpose of federal governmental regulation of business is fundamentally to protect our freedom to do business by curbing and preventing abuses. The government regulation discussed in Chapter 34 is intended to protect free enterprise and fair competition. Administrative agencies, as discussed in Chapter 35, have the responsibility to monitor business and establish rules and regulations to carry out the federal laws. In Chapter 36 the laws that identify and protect the rights of labor to organize and of management to manage are discussed. Laws to protect the human and physical environment from private and public abuse and unnecessary waste are discussed in Chapter 37.

Business ethics as it relates to the text material in these chapters is considered at the end of the part.

C H A P T E R

34

ANTITRUST LAW

After you have read this chapter, you should be able to:

1. Define pure monopoly and pure competition.
2. Explain the reason for the Sherman Act of 1890.
3. Explain why group boycotts are illegal.
4. Explain why Congress passed the Clayton Act.
5. Explain exclusive dealing contracts, tying arrangements, stock acquisitions designed to lessen competition, and horizontal versus vertical constraints.
6. Identify the Federal Trade Commission and its primary functions.
7. Understand the Robinson-Patman Act of 1936.
8. Understand the major defenses against the Robinson-Patman Act of 1936.

BUSINESS DECISIONS and the LAW

For many people today, and for many people throughout much of our history, the less that government is involved in regulating business the better. But many firms in today's advanced industrialized society are extremely large and hold the potential to completely control a market, even to the extent of eliminating all competition and harming the public health or safety. Because our business environment has this potential, most of us want to have the government intervene to the extent necessary to protect the public well-being.

Yet an appropriate balance between the regulation of business and the free exercise of the market is difficult to find. No area more dramatically illustrates this debate than antitrust law. Almost all economists would agree that a conscious decision to collude to exert market power in order to eliminate competition is illegal. But any number of questions exist about where to draw the line actively between appropriate and inappropriate business. For example, a merger is illegal if its effect would be to substantially lessen competition. But we exist in a time when there is worldwide competition. What is the appropriate measure of bigness? What is a large merger? Is the competition a local market or a regional, national, or worldwide market?

Many of us are familiar with the government's successful attempt to break up AT&T because of their large size and market control. By contrast, even more recently the government has been very lenient in its attitude toward mergers. The merger between Time, Inc. and Warner Communications has been approved. Should this have been considered an illegal merger?

Consider the value and power of Time, Inc. A recent article said that Time, Inc. was composed of at least the following assets: magazines worth $4.1 billion (including *Time* and *Sports Illustrated*); cable television programming (including HBO) worth $1.7 billion; books (including such publishers as Scott Foresman and Time-Life Books) worth $2.1 billion; and cable television operations worth $6.7 billion. The company that they plan to merge with is Warner Brothers, which is another very valuable and powerful media enterprise.*

Antitrust investigations may also extend to colleges and universities. As recently as September 1989, the U.S. Justice Department began an investigation of possible collusion to fix prices at various elite private colleges. The Justice Department was concerned that private schools were meeting periodically to compare tuition charges and to establish financial aid practices. Of course, the fact that the Justice Department is investigating a case does not mean that anything unlawful has been done. However, one might consider whether antitrust law should be used to control the activities of universities. Perhaps this is an area that should not concern the government. Perhaps it is an area where the free market should be allowed to prevail.

Various government administrations establish different attitudes toward big business. The Reagan and Bush administrations have generally been concerned with encouraging bigness as a way to deal with foreign competition and to increase productivity. Thus they have de-emphasized antitrust enforcement.

*"The Counterattack," *Newsweek*, June 26, 1989, p. 50.

Introduction

Imagine that you are an entrepreneur in a small midwestern town. Your company sells oil to consumers within a forty-mile radius and has been expanding rapidly since you began it ten years ago. You are finally making a decent living from the business. Suddenly you discover that your competitors are involved in a scheme that will allow them not only to control the industry but to wipe out your firm.

The stockholders of your larger competitors are turning their power to vote in corporate matters over to a select group of people called trustees. These trustees thereby gain enormous power in many firms at once and can control the supply (and so the price) of oil for the entire nation, including the area in which you have traditionally done business. By raising the price of oil in one state and making a great deal of profit, they can lower the price in another area, even to the point of taking a loss for a while, to drive out competition—including your firm. How would you feel?

This scheme is far more than a story. During the late 1800s and early 1900s, such business trusts were common. People like John D. Rockefeller and Cornelius Vanderbilt made their fortunes using schemes just like this one. The public became greatly concerned as business power became more and more concentrated in the hands of a few individuals. They therefore turned to law for help.

Freedom to compete is a healthy concept and goes hand in hand with the principles of freedom and liberty on which the United States was founded. The early governmental policy of laissez faire (governmental noninterference with business) made it possible for such freedoms to be abused as business sought to increase its power. The policy had to be modified by federal statute to check the increasing tide of unreasonable restraint of trade that interfered with free enterprise and fair competition.

Accordingly, the issue became how to balance free enterprise and fair competition on the one hand with governmental regulation of business on the other. The same issue exists today. This chapter analyzes the strains of public and private interests and the government's current reaction to them in controlling monopolies, combinations, and unfair restraints in business.

We shall see in this chapter the purposes of the various major antitrust statutes, how these statutes have worked, the type of business activities restrained, and the impact of the federal courts in interpreting and enforcing these statutes.

The Response of Law to Undue Concentration of Business Power

The United States was created with the intention of providing maximum opportunity for free competition in business. The doctrine of **laissez-faire**—that is, to let business alone—was dominant and worked well, at least until the industrial expansion after the Civil War. Then, with business growing by leaps and bounds, it became necessary to monitor the activities of some firms.

laissez-faire
A government policy of not interfering with business

The amount and type of government regulation of business has always been hotly debated in the world of work, but such regulation does exist. In this chapter we will examine the major federal antitrust laws: the Sherman Act of 1890; the Clayton Act of 1914; the Federal Trade Commission Act of 1914; and the Robinson-Patman Act of 1936 amending the Clayton Act. Students should be aware that a number of other laws also regulate business, but they are somewhat less important.

What is it we want to regulate? Anyone who has followed a winning baseball team knows that things tend to get exciting when the competition is a little too close for comfort. When your team is leading by four or five runs the game can become boring, but when the lead is cut to one and the opposition has a tying run on third base with no outs, the situation is entirely different. For many people, the world of business provides the same kind of excitement. Competition forces firms to do their best to stay ahead, and by and large this is a good thing for all of us. Firms come up with new products, increase their sales, and improve current products—all to be the leader of the industry. Once in a while, however, a firm becomes as strong or stronger than its competitors and can drive its rivals completely out of business. If this happens, the leader becomes the *only* one with a particular product and can establish any price it wants, no matter how exorbitant.

The difficulty for the government is to determine *when* the law should exert control over competition. When there are many firms of equal strength, control may not be needed. When there is but one firm, and that firm is in a position to hurt the public, control is clearly needed. But what about the case in the middle, where a few firms control an industry? And, what about the case of an industry where one firm rather than many would be desirable? For example, it would be useless to have thirty or forty different electric utilities competing in the same city. Think of all the wires the electric company now puts up. Can you imagine thirty times as many wires? As you can see, finding an answer is not easy. The government has set down some guidelines on when they will exert control and when they will not.

These guidelines are outlined in the chapter that follows. You should be aware of the fact that these laws are based on economic theory designed to enhance our country's competitive position. But not all economists have the same theoretical perspective. This means that antitrust law is a particularly dynamic and changing area. For example, one premise of antitrust law is the notion that small business should be preserved, as this enhances competition. Another premise is that managers react not only to competition but to other factors as well. They argue that bigness is not badness and that principles of efficiency are also very important. Antitrust efforts to break up large firms have greatly diminished in recent years as theoretical perspectives on what is best for our economy have shifted. Before we can examine antitrust laws, you need to understand two terms: pure monopoly and pure competition.

Pure Monopoly Versus Pure Competition

On rare occasions a firm discovers that it has no competitors. For example, most utility companies are unlikely to have competition in a given town. One gas company or one electric company satisfies the needs of the entire community; duplication is simply unnecessary. In a small community, one barber shop may be enough to cut everyone's hair. In these cases, it is either impossible for a competitor to enter the market or merely improbable or unlikely. The more improbable or unlikely competition is, the closer the market is to a **pure monopoly**—a market situation where only one firm is producing a product or providing a service. A market that is controlled by a small number of companies, but by more than one, is called an **oligopoly.**

pure monopoly
A market in which there is a single firm with no competitors

oligopoly
A market in which there is a small number of sellers

pure competition
A market in which many firms compete and no one firm has very much power

More often, however, a number of firms compete with each other for business. On occasion, the products are so similar that consumers cannot distinguish between the goods of different firms. There may also be so many sellers that the size of the market for each firm is small, and an individual company cannot have any meaningful influence over the price of the goods. If both things happen at the same time, we approach **pure competition.**

The market for wheat is an example of nearly pure competition. Many farmers produce wheat, and there is little if any difference between their end products. Furthermore, no individual farmer can influence the price very much because the market is so large. If one farmer tries to get $.10 more per bushel, buyers will merely move on to the next farmer. Thus we can say that there is pure competition for wheat.

Controlling Monopolies, Combinations, and Unfair Restraints

As you can imagine, monopolies in key industries can become enormous and wield tremendous power. Unfortunately, this power is not always used to benefit consumers. The first example in this chapter pointed out how some firms try to drive out competition in the hope of ultimately forming a monopoly. The practice of giving controlling blocks of stock to trustees was the first target of federal regulation and the genesis of today's **antitrust laws.**

antitrust laws
Laws that limit monopolies, combinations, and unfair restraints to help prevent the undue concentration of economic power

► Sherman Act of 1890

In order to prevent absolute monopolies, the U.S. government had to develop a law to control situations that were *approaching* monopolistic competition. The first law to do this was the Sherman Act of 1890. The two major sections of this law are:

> Section 1: Every contract, combination in the form of trust or otherwise, or conspiracy, in restraint of trade or commerce among the several States, or with foreign nations, is hereby declared to be illegal. . . .

> Section 2: Every person who shall monopolize, or attempt to monopolize, or combine or conspire with any other person or persons, to monopolize any part of the trade or commerce among the several States, or with foreign nations, shall be deemed guilty of a felony. . . .[1]

Section 1, as later interpreted by the U.S. Supreme Court, makes *unreasonable* restraint of trade illegal. Section 2 goes on to explain that individuals who engage in such restraint can be prosecuted for their actions.

The U.S. Supreme Court recently held that agreement among competing physicians setting, by majority vote, maximum fees for payment from participants in specified insurance plans was per se unlawful under Section 1 of the Sherman Act.[2]

Boycotts Part of the Sherman Act has been interpreted by the courts to limit the opportunity for firms to join in not doing business with another company. Although any company can decide with whom it will or will not deal, if many firms get together in a concerted effort to boycott one firm, they are participating in a **group boycott,** which is a violation per se (of itself) of the Sherman Act. This is illustrated by the following case.

group boycott
A concerted effort by a number of firms to avoid doing business with a particular individual or firm

FACTS

Klor's Inc., plaintiff, was a San Francisco retail store, and Broadway-Hale Stores, Inc., defendant, was its principal competitor. The owners of Klor's accused Broadway-Hale of trying to get the manufacturers of household appliances to agree not to sell to Klor's or to discriminate against Klor's by the method of offering Klor's goods at unreasonably high prices. Judgment for plaintiff. Defendant appealed.

DECISION

Affirmed, for plaintiff, Klor's. The plaintiff's contention that this concerted effort on the part of Broadway-Hale, and others violated the Sherman Act was sustained. Mr. Justice Black wrote: "Group boycotts . . . have long been held to be in the forbidden category. . . . Plainly the allegations of this complaint disclose such a boycott. This is not a case of a single trader refusing to deal with another, nor even of a manufacturer and a dealer agreeing to an exclusive distributorship. Alleged in this complaint is a wide combination consisting of manufacturers, distributors and a retailer. It deprives the manufacturers and distributors of their freedom to sell to Klor's at the same prices . . . made available to Broadway-Hale. . . . It clearly has, by its nature and character, a monopolistic tendency." [Emphasis added.]

Klor's Inc. v. Broadway-Hale Stores, Inc., 359 U.S. 207 (1959).

Violations of the Sherman Act may be punished by a jail sentence or a fine or both. Over the years, Congress has increased the fine by amending the Act.[3] Today, a corporate violator can be required to pay $1 million, and individuals to pay as much as $100,000. The government also has the power to enjoin violators from further action. Finally, individuals whose businesses have been injured by a violation of the Act can sue for treble (triple) the amount of injury sustained, plus related court costs.

---

[1]See Sherman Act, 15 U.S.C.A., secs. 1–7.

[2]*Arizona v. Maricopa County Medical Society, et al.*, 457 U.S. 332 (1982).

[3]Amendments to Sherman Act, sec. 2.

Clayton Act of 1914

The Sherman Act did not succeed in halting all of the abuses that Congress had hoped it would cover. As a result, Congress passed the Clayton Act of 1914. Among the more important parts of the Act are provisions dealing with exclusive-dealing contracts, tying sales, and stock acquisition designed to substantially lessen competition or tending to create a monopoly, discussed below.

Exclusive-Dealing Contracts If you were a manufacturer, you might want to get retailers to agree not to sell the products of your competitors. Some retailers might even find the arrangement beneficial. The retailer would get to know your product very well and could depend on you for a constant supply. If enough retailers agreed to such an arrangement, you could effectively wipe out your competition. If your firm were powerful enough to exert some influence on the retailer, you might consider forcing the retailer into such an arrangement. Whatever its effect on the retailer, such an arrangement might substantially decrease competition. The Clayton Act prohibits this kind of activity and labels it an **exclusive-dealing contract.**

exclusive-dealing contract
An agreement between a seller or lessor and a purchaser or lessee that the latter shall not use or deal in the products of a competing seller or lessor

Tying Arrangements A **tying arrangement** is another technique to substantially lessen competition or that tends to create a monopoly. Here is how a tying contract works. Suppose you are the owner of a medium-size manufacturing plant. You decide to purchase 1,000 fountain pens from Ajax Pen Company. Ajax gives you a good deal on the fountain pens, but as part of that deal makes you sign a contract agreeing to purchase only Ajax *ink* for those pens. Clearly, if Ajax has a monopoly on pens and can get its customers to sign such agreements, it soon will have a monopoly on ink as well. Tying contracts are regulated by Section 3 of the Clayton Act. They have been declared illegal where the contract will "*substantially* lessen competition or *tend* to create a monopoly in any line of commerce." [Emphasis added.] In the following case the court details the elements of a tying arrangement.

tying arrangement
An agreement between a seller or lessor and a purchaser or lessee that a sale or lease of a product to the latter is contingent upon the latter's purchase or lease of another product of the seller or lessor

FACTS

The government brings this suit against Mercedes-Benz of North America for an alleged violation of the Sherman Act under a theory of a per se tying violation based on the dealer agreements between Mercedes-Benz of North America and each of its franchised dealers. The government argues that the following provision of that agreement relating to customer service is a per se violation of the Sherman Act: "Dealer shall neither sell or offer to sell for use in connection with Mercedes-Benz cars nor use in the repair or servicing of . . . cars . . . any parts other than genuine Mercedes-Benz parts or parts expressly approved. . . . Mercedes argues that tying standards are inapplicable and that a rule of reason is the appropriate standard for determining a restraint of trade. Mercedes asks for a summary judgment.

DECISION

A summary judgment is denied. Plaintiff must demonstrate three elements to establish a per se illegal tying arrangement. (1) Two separate products with the sale of one conditioned on the purchase of the other. (2) A seller with sufficient economic leverage in the tying market to appreciably restrain competition in the tied product market and (3) a tie in affecting a not insubstantial amount of interstate commerce. The motion for a summary judgment was denied because significant questions existed about whether the defendant had sufficient economic leverage in the tying product market to appreciably restrain competition.

U.S. v. Mercedes-Benz of North America, 517 F. Supp. 1369 (N. D. Cal. 1981).

The law does not require that there be a monopoly in an industry before it will step in to regulate the firms involved. It merely requires that the action substantially lessen competition by foreclosing competitors from a substantial volume of the tied market. In the case above, Ajax would be lessening competition by limiting the ability of other ink companies to sell their products. But how large a volume of tied sales is necessary to effectively limit competition? In a landmark case, the court decided that tied sales should amount to at least $500,000 to require regulatory action.[4]

Stock Acquisitions Designed to Lessen Competition It was suggested earlier in this chapter that the courts often face difficult questions as to *when* a firm becomes large enough to wield a great deal of power. One problem that has been particularly perplexing is whether the sheer size of the firm should dictate governmental control, or whether the firm must actually use that power to restrain trade in some way. The government's answer came in Section 7 of the Clayton Act as amended by the Cellar-Kefauver Act of 1950:

> No corporation shall acquire, directly or indirectly, the whole or any part of the stock or other share capital and no corporation subject to the jurisdiction of the Federal Trade Commission shall acquire the whole or any part of the assets of one or more corporations engaged in commerce, where in any line of commerce in any section of the country, the effect of such acquisition, of such stocks or assets, or of the use of such stock by the voting or granting of proxies or otherwise, *may* be substantially to lessen competition, or *tend* to create a monopoly. [Emphasis added.]

Notice that such acquisition need not result in substantially lessening competition or creating a monopoly in order to be unlawful. All that is required is that it "may" or "tend to" produce the unlawful result.

Corporate acquisition of stock may result in a horizontal or vertical merger, and if it *may* substantially lessen competition or *tend* to create a monopoly, it is unlawful. The following example illustrates the concept of horizontal and vertical mergers. Stop Time, Inc. is a firm that manufactures and sells pocket watches. To manufacture these watches, Stop Time must purchase the raw materials, put them together as pocket watches, and sell the watches to retailers, who sell to the public. Stop Time probably competes with companies such as Timex, Westclox, and Benrus, to name a few. Stop Time's competitive situation would probably look like the diagram in Figure 34.1.

If Stop Time purchased stock in Timex, Benrus, or Westclox, that would be a **horizontal merger;** Stop Time would be combining forces with its competitors. On the other hand, if Stop Time bought a controlling interest in all retailers of pocket watches or in all sources of raw materials, that would be a **vertical merger.**

horizontal merger
A merger of competing firms

vertical merger
A merger between a firm and one of its major suppliers or customers

According to Section 7 of the Clayton Act, horizontal mergers were illegal; vertical ones were not. Today, because of complex case law and vast and overlapping administrative rules and regulations, students are advised to see a legal specialist if their problem seems to extend beyond this brief description. Although both types of combinations could cause problems, the Act limited only horizontal mergers. This was an important weakness in the law.

In the following case the court held that the proposed **merger** of the two firms "may be to substantially lessen competition" and, therefore, would violate the Clayton Act.

merger
In corporations, the absorption of one corporation by another corporation

[4]*International Salt Co., Inc. v. United States,* 332 U.S. 392 (1947).

FIGURE 34.1 **Diagrammatic Representation of Stop Time, Inc.'s Competitive Situation**

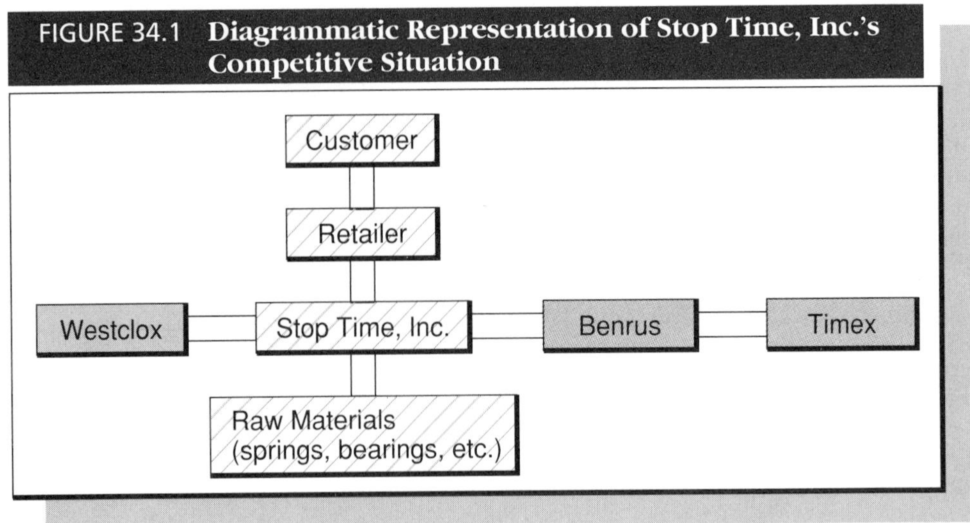

FACTS

The plaintiff, Brown Shoe Co., Inc., initiated a suit against the United States government, defendant, in November 1955, when the government tried to stop Brown from merging with G. R. Kinney Co., Inc. through an exchange of stock. By dollar volume, Brown was the third largest seller of shoes in the United States, and Kinney was the eighth largest. Judgment for the United States government. Plaintiff appealed.

DECISION

Affirmed, for the United States government. "[T]he government contended that the effect of the merger of Brown . . . and Kinney . . . 'may be substantially to lessen competition or to tend to create a monopoly' by eliminating actual or potential competition in the production of shoes for the national wholesale market and in the sale of shoes at retail in the nation." In deciding whether this merger would violate Section 7 of the Clayton Act as amended, the court examined both the vertical and horizontal aspects of the contemplated merger. It also examined congressional intent in amending Section 7 of the Clayton Act:

"Congress sought to assure the Federal Trade Commission and the courts the power to brake this [merger] force at its outset and before it gathered momentum."

"Congress indicated plainly that a merger had to be functionally viewed, in the context of its particular industry."

"Congress used the words *may be* to substantially lessen competition."

". . . On the basis of the record before us, we believe that the Government sustained the burden of proof. . . . The judgment is affirmed."

Brown Shoe Co., Inc. v. United States, 370 U.S. 294 (1962).

A third kind of merger occasionally ends up in litigation. It is called a *conglomerate merger*. A conglomerate merger is one in which there is little or no distinguishing connection between the output or industry of the firms that are brought together. An example of a conglomerate merger would be the union of a book publisher with a manufacturer of canned pineapple. As with other types of mergers, the court looks at the merger and asks what the impact is likely to be. If an unfair advantage is likely to result, the merger will probably be declared illegal.

Federal Trade Commission Act

Federal Trade Commission
A government body that monitors unfair competition and commercial practices

The **Federal Trade Commission** was created in 1914 when Congress passed the Federal Trade Commission Act. Congress intended the FTC to monitor two areas: (1) unfair methods of competition, and (2) unfair or deceptive acts or practices in or affecting commerce.

Implications of the Federal Trade Commission Act for Other Laws Congress gave the FTC power to enforce antitrust laws. Specifically, the FTC monitors the performance of firms to see that they meet the criteria established in both the Sherman Act and the Clayton Act. The FTC also monitors other less well-known laws. For example, it may move to cancel deceptive trademarks under the Lanham Act of 1946, or monitor the kinds of fiber in wool products under the Wool Products Labeling Act of 1939. The following case came under the Lanham Act and held that there was trademark infringement.

FACTS

Plaintiff, Ye Olde Tavern Cheese Products, Inc., registered its trademark properly in 1957. Commencing at least as early as 1957, plaintiff has been packaging and distributing various snacks, including nuts in individual cellophane bags stapled to large cards. The bags bore the label "Ye Olde Tavern."

In 1964, Planters Peanuts Division of Standard Brands, Inc., defendant, placed on sale a product which it identified as "Planters Ye Olde Tavern Nuts." [This product consisted of nuts and was displayed in a way similar to the plaintiff's product.] After receiving notice of plaintiff's objections, defendant immediately removed its product from the market. However, three months later the defendant reintroduced the same product in the same form as "Planters Tavern Nuts."

This is a suit by the plaintiff for trademark infringement, unfair competition, trademark dilution, and injury to business reputation, taken under the Lanham Act.

DECISION

Judgment for the plaintiff, Ye Olde Tavern Cheese Products, Inc. The court stated that a plaintiff in a trademark infringement suit has an easier burden of proof, in that the prior use of the trademark gives rise to a presumption of exclusive right to it, and renders proof of an actual intent to defraud unnecessary.

Ye Olde Tavern Cheese Products, Inc. v. Planters Peanuts Division of Standard Brands, Inc., 261 F.Supp. 200 (N.D.Ill., E.D. 1966), *aff'd* 394 F.2d 833 (7th Cir. 1967).

Federal Trade Commission May Act on Its Own Initiative If the Federal Trade Commission believed that a firm is using some unfair method of competition, it would probably try to prosecute the firm under an appropriate section of one of the major antitrust laws.[5] However, on many occasions the FTC has moved on its own to stop deceptive acts in commerce, as in the following case.

FACTS

The case arose out of Colgate's attempt to prove on television that its shaving cream, Rapid Shave, outshaves them all. Colgate had three one-minute commercials designed to show that Rapid Shave could soften even the toughness of sandpaper. The announcer informed the audience that "to prove Rapid Shave's super-moisturizing power, we put it right from the can onto tough, dry sandpaper. Apply . . . soak . . . off in a stroke." It appeared that sandpaper was being used, but it was re-

[5]For FTC administrative procedures and techniques for dispute resolution, see pp. 742–744.

ally a "simulated sandpaper" made of plexiglass to which sand had been applied. The Federal Trade Commission found that the commercial was a material deceptive device. Colgate appealed.

DECISION

Affirmed, for the Federal Trade Commission. The court had to decide whether it was a deceptive practice under Section 5 of the FTC Act to represent falsely that a televised test, experiment, or demonstration provides a viewer with visual proof of a product claim. The court held: "We agree with the Commission that the undisclosed use of plexiglass in the present commercials was a material deceptive practice, independent and separate from the other misrepresentations found. We find unpersuasive Colgate's other objections to this conclusion. They claim that it will be impractical to inform the viewing public that it is not seeing an actual test . . . but we think . . . that the ingenious advertising would well be able . . . , if it so desires, to conform to the Commission's insistence that the public not be misinformed."

Federal Trade Comm'n v. Colgate-Palmolive Co., 380 U.S. 374 (1965).

If a firm is found to be violating the law, a number of punishments are available, ranging from civil penalties to criminal prosecution. The FTC has generally used a combination of consent decrees and orders. These are similar to settlements with the offending firm and are not nearly as severe as criminal prosecution.

Robinson-Patman Act of 1936

price discrimination
The practice of offering the same product to different competing customers at different prices

Section 2(a) of the Clayton Act was difficult for both courts and businesses to understand. In an attempt to clear the air, Congress passed the Robinson-Patman Act of 1936, amending Section 2(a). This Act was specifically designed to deal with **price discrimination.** Experts today contend that the Robinson-Patman Act has not actually clarified the issue to the satisfaction of all interested parties. It does, however, state that it shall be "unlawful to discriminate in price between different purchasers of commodities of like grade and quality, where . . . the effect of such discrimination may be (a) to substantially lessen competition, or (b) to tend to create a monopoly in any line of commerce or (c) to injure, destroy, or prevent competition with any person who either grants or knowingly receives the benefit of such discrimination, or with customers of either of them."[6]

Uses of the Robinson-Patman Act The Act is used to eliminate a number of unfair practices. One of these is to lower the price of goods in a geographical area to drive out the competition. A second practice is to give discounts on goods to one seller but not to another, where the only reasonable explanation of the discount is an intent to destroy competition or create a monopoly. A third practice is to discriminate against purchasers by charging inordinately high freight costs with the intent to destroy competition. In the following case the FTC held that the firm's charging lower prices for its product in certain geographical areas drove out competition and was violative of the Clayton Act.

FACTS

"Dean Milk Co. maintain [ed] its executive offices in Franklin Park, Illinois, and [was] engaged in the processing and sale of fluid milk . . . in a number of states. . . . Its prices in Evansville, Indiana, . . . and Lexington, Kentucky, all of which are served by the Louisville processing plant, were lower than prices in Louisville." The FTC had to decide whether the

[6]Robinson-Patman Act, 15 U.S.C. sec. 13 (1936).

price difference reflected a violation of Section 2(a) of the Clayton Act.

DECISION

Dean's price difference was such a violation. The dairy argued that evidence of a "reasonable possibility" of adverse competition effects on competition is not enough to issue an order to cease. The FTC disagreed, "Congress clearly intended to prevent in their incipiency practices which might harm the competitive process and thus explicitly provided that a showing of actual injury was not necessary. [Here] we think the conditions . . . in the market—the low profit margins and the high mortality rate in the smaller dairies—support a conclusion that there is a reasonable possibility that continued sales . . . where they cannot realize a reasonable profit . . . will cause the demise of other small dairies.

Respondent [Dean Milk Co.] will be ordered to cease charging lower prices . . ."

In re Dean Milk Co., 68 F.T.C. 710 (1965).

Resale Price Fixing Resale price fixing occurs when the price is fixed at which the purchased product is to be resold by the buyer. When two or more competing suppliers agree to so fix the price, there is *horizontal* price fixing. When the supplier so agrees with his or her buyer, there is *vertical* price fixing. Both are illegal today. Some manufacturers try to avoid the consequences of vertical price fixing by merely *suggesting* retail prices to buyers rather than entering into an agreement (conspiracy to restrain trade) with the buyers concerning prices.

Defenses Against a Charge Under the Robinson-Patman Act Not all price differences or discounts are violations per se of the Robinson-Patman Act. If a buyer purchases such a large quantity of goods that the manufacturer can save money on production or on purchase of raw materials, a discount may be offered. If a change in conditions makes the goods sell for more (or less), this would not be a violation. If you can demonstrate that you did not attempt to lessen competition, but merely acted in good faith to challenge your competitors, you will be safe. This was the point of the following case, which held that there was no violation of the Robinson-Patman Act.

FACTS

The Beam Brothers allege that the Monsanto Company violated the Robinson-Patman Act. The Beams claim that they were contractors whose primary business was repairing and refacing highways in Arkansas. They claimed that Monsanto damaged them by reason of direct overcharges for materials purchased and that they were forced out of business because of these actions. The Beams showed two instances of F.O.B. invoice price differences to Arkansas Rock and Gravel showing lower prices to that firm. Is this a sufficient showing to satisfy the requirements of Robinson-Putnam?

DECISION

No. Monsanto agrees that there are numerous invoices in its files which show different F.O.B. prices paid for the same product at about the same time. There is nothing in the law that prohibits different prices in noncompetitive geographic areas or with respect to noncompetitive projects on jobs, or merely because differing supply conditions suggest to seller that the market will bear a higher or lower price at one time or another.

Beam v. Monsanto, 414 F. Supp. 570 (W.D. Ark. 1976)

Cost-price comparisons are not conclusive as to predatory pricing. The U.S. Court of Appeals[7] has well stated that "the ultimate question is 'Did the justification for the

[7]*William Inglis & Sons Baking Co.*, 504 Trade Reg. Rep. (CCH) para. 64,229 (Aug. 25, 1981); see also *Matsushita Elec. Indus. Co. Ltd., et al. v. Zenith Radio Corp.*, 106 Sup. Ct. 1348 (1986).

defendant's price depend upon its anticipated destructive effect on competition, or was the price justified as a reasonably calculated means of maximizing profits, minimizing losses, or achieving some other legitimate end?' This is the standard analysis of alleged predatory pricing, not rigid adherence to a particular cost-based rule."

Summary Statement

1. With a stated belief in free competition, the United States has grown from an agrarian economy to the world's foremost industrialized nation. Sometimes competition becomes extremely stiff, and weak, ineffective firms are driven out of the market. This may lead to a monopoly. Not all monopolies are evil and not all require governmental regulation. In some circumstances, however, the government may wish to intervene.
2. The major federal antitrust laws are the Sherman Act of 1890; the Clayton Act of 1914 with the Cellar-Kefauver Amendment; the Federal Trade Commission Act of 1914; and the Robinson-Patman Act of 1936, which amended Section 2(a) of the Clayton Act. Some defenses against the Robinson-Patman Act were noted in order to emphasize that firms sometimes discriminate among their customers for good commercial reasons, with the apparent result of hurting competitors. The government is not trying to eliminate competition; it is trying to regulate abuses.
3. The Federal Trade Commission has an important role in today's antitrust regulations. The Commission monitors performance of companies around the criteria of the Sherman and Clayton Acts.
4. The Robinson-Patman Act is used to eliminate unfair practices such as unfair discounts or discrimination in pricing.
5. Under the Robinson-Patman Act, there are certain violations that can be defended against by showing that the actions taken were just good business and not designed to lessen competition.

In the following well-known case the court found a tying arrangement in violation of the Sherman Act.

SIEGEL v. CHICKEN DELIGHT, INC.
448 F.2d 43 (1971), cert. denied 405 U.S. 955 (1972)

Before Madden, Judge of the United States Court of Claims, and Merrill and Hufstedler, Circuit Judges.

Merrill, J. This antitrust suit is a class action in which certain franchisees of Chicken Delight seek treble damages for injuries allegedly resulting from illegal restraints imposed by Chicken Delight's standard form franchise agreements. The restraints in question are Chicken Delight's contractual requirements that franchisees purchase certain essential cooking equipment, dry-mix food items, and trademark bearing packaging exclusively from Chicken Delight as a condition of obtaining a Chicken Delight trademark license. These requirements are asserted to constitute a tying arrangement, unlawful per se under Section 1 of the Sherman Act. . . .

• • • • •

II. The Existence of an Unlawful Tying Arrangement

In order to establish that there exists an unlawful tying arrangement plaintiffs must demonstrate: First that the scheme in question involves two distinct items and provides that one (the tying product) may not be obtained unless the other (the tied product) is also purchased.... Second, that the tying product possesses sufficient economic power appreciably to restrain competition in the tied product market.... Third, that a "not insubstantial" amount of commerce is affected by the arrangement.... Chicken Delight concedes that the third requirement has been satisfied. It disputes the existence of the first two. Further it asserts that... there is a fourth issue: whether there exists a special justification for the particular tying arrangement in question....

A. Two Products

The District Court ruled that the license to use the Chicken Delight name, trademark, and method of operations was "a tying item in the traditional sense," the tied items being the cookers and fryers, packaging products, and mixes.

The hallmark of a tie-in is that it denies competitors free access to the tied product market, not because the party imposing the arrangement has a superior product in that market, but because of the power or leverage exerted by the tying product.

Sale of a franchise license, with the attendant rights to operate a business in the prescribed manner and to benefit from the goodwill of the tradename, in no way requires the forced sale by the franchisor of some or all of the component articles....

... The relevant question is not whether the items are essential to the franchise, but whether it is essential to the franchise that the items be purchased from Chicken Delight. This raises not the issue of whether there is a tie-in but rather the issue of whether the tie-in is justifiable, a subject to be discussed below.

We conclude that the District Court was not in error.

B. Economic Power

Under the per se theory of illegality, plaintiffs are required to establish not only the existence of a tying arrangement but also that the tying product possesses sufficient economic power to appreciably restrain free competition in the tied product markets.

... It is not the nature of the public interest that has caused the legal barrier to be erected that is the basis for the presumption, but the fact that such a barrier does exist. Accordingly we see no reason why the presumption that exists in the case of the patent and copyright does not equally apply to the trademark.

C. Justification

Chicken Delight maintains that, even if its contractual arrangements are held to constitute a tying arrangement, it was not an unreasonable restraint under the Sherman Act. Three different bases for justification are urged.

First, Chicken Delight contends that the arrangement was a reasonable device for measuring and collecting revenue.

Second, Chicken Delight advances as justification the fact that when it first entered the fast food field in 1952 it was a new business and was then entitled to the protection afforded by *United States v. Jerrold Electronics Corp.*...

The third justification Chicken Delight offers is the "marketing identity" purpose, the franchisor's preservation of the distinctiveness, uniformity and quality of its product.

We conclude that the District Court was not in error in holding as matter of law (and upon the limited jury verdict) that Chicken Delight's contractual requirements constituted a tying arrangement in violation of Section 1 of the Sherman Act.... [J]udgment is affirmed.

The District Court judgment was reversed and remanded for limited trial on several damage questions.

Questions and Case Problems

1. Soft Top Ice Cream, Inc., sells franchises that allow the purchaser of the franchise to sell several different flavors of soft ice cream. However, Soft Top demands that retailers purchase a special machine from them to make the product. They explain that only the combination of their special machine and special mix will produce the product which is sold as "Soft Top Ice Cream." Is this a violation of the Clayton Act? [*Engbrecht v. Dairy Queen Co. of Mexico, Mo.*, 203 F.Supp. 714 (D. Kan. 1962).]

2. Car Carriers, Inc., is in the car transport business. The company and other related enterprises brought antitrust action against Ford Motors Co. which had terminated

Car Carriers contract in favor of a second car transport company. Among all the firms in the area, Car Carriers could prove injury only to themselves. Given these facts, does Ford Motor Co. participate in wrongful monopolization? Explain. [*Car Carriers, Inc., et al. v. Ford Motor Co.,* 745 F.2d 1101 (7th Cir. 1984).]

3. Assume that, in the question above, the consumers of the car transport business were injured because of diminishing competition resulting from Ford Motor Co.'s action. Would this be considered when deciding whether Ford is engaging in anticompetitive acts? [*Car Carriers, Inc. v. Ford Motor Co.,* 745 F.2d 1101 (7th Cir. 1984).]

4. Lynch Business Machines, Inc., filed a complaint based on antitrust action. The defendant, manufacturer of office products, had acquired stock in a company manufacturing cosmetics. This acquisition enhanced competition in this particular market. Plaintiff claims that defendant's acquisition of the stock violates the Clayton Act. Do you agree or disagree with plaintiff's claim? Explain. [*Lynch Business Machines, Inc., v. A. B. Dick Company,* 594 F.Supp. 59 (N.D. Ohio, E.D. 1984).]

5. The Federal Trade Commission decided to stop a cigarette manufacturer from advertising its cigarettes as "1 mg. tar" because it believed that the manufacturer's advertisements were misleading to consumers. Does the FTC have the power to act on its own to enforce the law or must it wait for a private complaint? [*FTC v. Brown* & Williamson Tobacco, 778 F.2d 35 (D.C. Cir. 1985).]

6. Bristol-Myers Co. is the manufacturer of the nonprescription product Bufferin. In advertising for Bufferin, Bristol-Myers referred to the results of scientific tests or studies claiming that Bufferin is twice as fast and twice as strong as aspirin in relieving pain in addition to implying that "Doctors specify Bufferin for minor pain more than any leading brand of pain reliever you can buy." However, Bufferin's faster-action claim has not been established. Is this legal? Explain. [*In re Bristol-Myers Co., et al.,* 102 F.T.C. 21 (1983).]

7. Borden Inc., a producer of processed lemon juice, chose to price this product below its variable cost in order to promote sales. Why may this be considered as wrongful pricing? [*In re Borden, Inc.,* 102 F.T.C. 1147 (1983).]

8. Borden had monopoly power in the market for processed lemon juice. However, it argued that it was only a small part of the overall market for lemon juice when one adds the processed lemon juice and natural lemon juice markets together. If the FTC can demonstrate that processed juice was not reasonably interchangeable with fresh lemons, can it succeed in bringing a case against Borden under Section 1 of the Sherman Act? [*Borden v. FTC,* 674 F.2d 498 (6th Cir. 1982).]

9. The Federal Trade Commission found that members of a dental association were meeting to agree to withhold X rays requested by dental insurers for use in evaluating claims. Is this a violation of the Sherman Act? [*FTC v. Indiana Fed'n of Dentists,* 106 Sup. Ct. 2009 (1986).]

10. In the case of *Siegel v. Chicken Delight, Inc.,* excerpted at the beginning of this section, the court said that "the relevant question is not whether the items are essential to the franchise, but whether it is essential to the franchise that the items be purchased from Chicken Delight. This raises not the issue of whether there is a tie-in but rather the issue of whether the tie-in is justifiable." Discuss this statement by the court and explain how a business may so operate as to avoid violation of this part of the Sherman Act.

C H A P T E R

35

ADMINISTRATIVE LAW

After reading this chapter, you should be able to identify all of the following terms:

1. Administrative Procedures Act of 1946
2. Administrative investigations
3. Informal settlements
4. Adjudicative procedures
5. Judicial review
6. Substantial evidence test
7. Administrative reparations
8. License

BUSINESS DECISIONS and the LAW

The cost of medical care in the United States continues to climb each year. Diseases such as acquired immunodeficiency syndrome (AIDS) have increasingly come to the public's attention. The number of cases of AIDS worldwide jumped 56 percent in just one year. Such catastrophic increases in disease are not the only reason for increased medical costs. People are living longer and medical science is uncovering new methods for treating many life-threatening diseases. One way that the public has found to contain costs is to permit pharmacists to prescribe generic drugs in place of brand names.

Many physicians will recommend a drug by its brand name. But a so-called generic drug has exactly the same chemical composition and effect as the brand-name product. Producers of generic drugs may not have to pay the cost of advertising or promotion. One concern that we all share is that the drugs that we take for our health are safe. We all want to be assured that brand name or not, the drug we ingest will do the proper job. We rely on professionals in the health care industry to reassure us about drug safety. For example, a recent statement by the American Academy of Family Physicians suggested that great caution be used before prescribing generic drugs for diseases such as asthma and diabetes. But our primary resource for regulation of the drug industry is the federal Food and Drug Administration, a division of the Department of Health and Human Services. This large administrative agency has established procedures for new products. Within the FDA, the center for Drug Evaluation and Research carries on an elaborate program with regard to establishing policy for the safety and effectiveness and labeling of all drug products. It also must develop and implement programs "to monitor the quality of marketed drugs through product testing and surveillance."

Recently the FDA began testing thirty of the leading generic drug firms for safety in producing drugs. An FDA spokesperson said that these firms were selected "in large part because of their large numbers of approved applications for generic drugs." He went on to say that the FDA requires the agency to "inspect pharmaceutical companies at least every two years." He hoped that this recent decision to inspect this group of firms would help people have confidence in the value of generic drugs.

Our nation produces many different goods and services. We all value our health and safety. One way of ensuring good health and safety is to ask our government to monitor the workings of manufacturers. Drug companies are monitored by the FDA. Television stations and radio stations are monitored by the Federal Communications Commission (FCC). Airlines are monitored by the Federal Aviation Authority (FAA). The rules and procedures followed by these agencies is known as administrative law.

Sources: *New York Times*, August 29, 1989, p. D. 2; *USA Today*, August 22, 1989, p. 1

Introduction

Congress provided for the creation of federal administrative agencies because it needed help to implement legislation it enacted. These agencies have the following responsibilities: (1) creating administrative rules and regulations; (2) establishing administrative procedures necessary for administrative action; (3) monitoring and providing for administrative investigation of industries for violations of antitrust laws and for consumer protection; and (4) adjudicating violation of such laws and administrative rules and regulations.

In this chapter we will consider the establishment and growth of federal administrative agencies, and observe how they operate. We will note again the problem of how far government, through its administrative agencies in the fulfillment of their responsibilities, should interfere in our daily business and private life. As you read this chapter, you should keep in mind the fact that every state has administrative agencies that may affect a particular business. However, as the wide diversity of these state agencies makes summary in this text impossible, we will be concerned only with federal administrative law.

The Response of the Law

Administrative agencies are so numerous today that just listing them with a brief description of the function of each would take up the rest of this book and a major portion of another. A more manageable task for us is to present an overview of the growth of administrative agencies and provide some idea of how they operate. We will therefore examine the foundation upon which administrative law has grown from the federal Administrative Procedures Act of 1946.

Administrative agencies do far more than set standards. Once standards are set in the form of rules, these rules are law and must be enforced. Note that administrative agencies establish rules, not statutory laws, which are made only by Congress as a legislative body authorized by the U.S. Constitution. Agencies monitor performance. If persons do not meet their standards, the agencies often have the power to levy fines or revoke previously granted privileges. These powers are not unlimited and, on occasion, agency decisions are overturned by courts of law through a process known as "judicial review."

Both the number and the domain of concern of administrative agencies have grown rapidly in the past twenty years. In reading the materials that follow, students should recall the question asked at the beginning of Part 7: How great an involvement do we, as managers of major industries and as private citizens, want the government to have in our lives?

Delegation

► The Problem of Time

Elementary civics texts have traditionally told students that legislators make laws, but this has not always been the case. Administrative agencies also have the power to create law in the form of rules and regulations, which all of us must obey. Where does that power come from? Article I, Section 1 of the U.S. Constitution states: "All legislative powers herein granted shall be vested in a Congress of the United States, which shall consist of a Senate and a House of Representatives." Reading on, you simply never come across a section stating that there shall be a Federal Trade Commission.

The power comes from a concept familiar to management students known as "delegation." Suppose you were to start a small business, perhaps a gas station. At first you might be able to handle all of the issues that come up during the day. You can pump gas, change the tires, and fix all of the engines that need fixing. As the business grows, however, you may be faced with growing lines of customers demanding gasoline. As you spend more and more time at the pumps, you get further and further behind on your repairs. You might throw up your hands in disgust and shout, "There aren't enough hours in a day to do all of the things I would like to do." So you might hire an assistant to pump gas—i.e., you delegate the responsibility to someone else, thus freeing you to do the more enjoyable task of repairing Mercedes and Jaguars.

Congress did the same thing when it delegated the responsibility for rule-making to administrative agencies. It simply did not have the *time* to create all the rules necessary for the smooth operation of our nation. It may not lack the interest, but it very well may have far too many other things to do.

► The Problem of Expertise

If we go back to our gas station example: suppose the assistant gas pumper works out well, and you go back to the job of fixing engines. Then a customer approaches you with a Classic 19XX Stutz Bearcat. If you have never been trained in making repairs on classic automobiles and if you thought that such repairs might become a significant part of your business, you would consider delegating the responsibility for repairs. Certainly you would want to keep your role as owner and manager of the work of your assistants, but, if others have expertise that you lack, you delegate to them the responsibility for getting the job done.

Once again, Congress sought to delegate its responsibility when it discovered that it did not have nearly as much collective specialized knowledge about particular areas as could be marshalled in an administrative agency. This combination of pressures on Congress—too little time and insufficient expertise—led to the creation of the huge number of federal administrative agencies. At first, some people considered this delegation a potential violation of the Constitution. But the power to delegate responsibility downward from Congress to administrative agencies has long been guaranteed. The case that follows is a classic because it is one of the very few instances of a delegation downward from Congress being held *invalid*. It has come to be known as the *Hot Oil* case.

FACTS

In 1933, the United States was in the midst of a great depression. However, in the state of Texas, huge oil reserves were discovered. This led to a vast oversupply of oil in the marketplace. Through the National Industrial Recovery Act, section 9(c), President Roosevelt was authorized to prohibit transportation in interstate commerce of petroleum and the products thereof . . . [48 Stat. 200 (1933)]. The Panama Refining Company sued (ultimately to the Supreme Court), claiming that section 9(c), and therefore the President's Executive Order implementing it, and the Regulations of the Secretary of the Interior were unconstitutional delegations of power, notwithstanding sections of the law which declared this to be a national emergency and saying that action had to be taken to conserve national resources. Were they unconstitutional and, therefore, void?

DECISION

Yes. Judgment for Panama Refining Co. "Thus, in every case in which the question has been raised, the court has recognized that there are limits of delegation which there is no constitutional authority to transcend. We think that section 9(c) goes beyond these limits. . . . The power sought to be delegated is legislative power, and nowhere in the statute has Congress declared or indicated any policy or standard to guide or limit the President when acting under such delegation. . . . There is such a breadth of authorized action as essentially to commit to the President the functions of a legislature rather than those of an executive or administrative officer executing a declared legislative policy."

Panama Refining Co. v. Ryan, 293 U.S. 388 (1935).

Administrative Procedures

While agencies vary somewhat in the procedures they use, it is still possible to create a composite picture of what happens when it is necessary for an agency to take action against a business firm for violation of a rule. In the next few pages we shall examine some typical administrative techniques for dispute resolution. The agency we shall examine is the Federal Trade Commission (FTC).

You will recall that, in the previous chapter, the FTC was identified as the agency responsible for monitoring industries for violation of antitrust laws. In addition to having that responsibility, the FTC is actively involved in consumer protection. For example, the FTC has consistently prosecuted individuals involved in false advertising or those who make deceptive claims, as is illustrated in the following case.

FACTS

Charles of the Ritz Distributors Corporation, a manufacturer, produced a cream designed for cosmetic use. According to its own claims, the cream "restores natural moisture necessary for a live, healthy skin"; "your face need know no drought years"; and the preparation brings to the user's "skin quickly the clear radiance . . . the petal-like quality and texture of youth." The cream is called "Rejuvenescence Cream." The Federal Trade Commission sued to stop the use of the name "Rejuvenescence Cream." Is the name deceptive in that it would lead people to believe that the cream would actually rejuvenate skin?

DECISION

Judgment for the Federal Trade Commission. Representations merely having the capacity to deceive are unlawful. The Federal Trade Commission had produced an expert who testified that the average woman, conditioned by talk in magazines and over the radio . . . might take rejuvenescence to mean that "this is one of the modern miracles" and is something which would actually cause her youth to be restored.

Charles of the Ritz Distrib. Corp. v. FTC, 143 F.2d 676 (2nd Cir. 1944).

► Investigations

In order to do its job effectively, administrative agencies need to have the power to investigate instances in which they believe rules have been violated. The FTC has that power. Typically, federal agencies have large groups of staff members who spend their time continuously collecting data on the industry or industries being monitored. Therefore it is likely that instances of deviation from the rules would rapidly come to the attention of the agency staff. If the problem becomes acute, the enforcement arm of the agency can initiate some action.

The FTC, like most other agencies, has the power to compel people to testify before it. To accomplish this task, it may issue what is known as a **subpoena.** Subpoenas are designed to elicit testimony from particular witnesses, but they may be insufficient and unrealistic as a technique for gathering the quantity of information constantly needed for monitoring purposes. Therefore administrative agencies also have the power to demand the periodic filing of reports. While some businesspeople complain about the volume of paperwork, the advantage of these reporting procedures is that a wide range of activities can be carefully monitored at once.

subpoena
An order to appear before a judicial or proper administrative body for the purpose of giving testimony

► Informal Settlements

In Chapter 2, Organization of the United States Legal System, we mentioned that, when a dispute arises, lawyers rarely try to bring the case to court immediately. Rather, they try to discuss the problem with the adversary in the hope of arriving at some mutually satisfactory settlement. The FTC and most other agencies have mechanisms that facilitate informal enforcement of standards.

Needless to say, the degree to which the agency is willing to settle informally depends upon the nature of the infraction (Is it a major offense?) and the number of infractions which that firm has been involved in previously. If a company refuses to voluntarily cease the offensive activity, the administrative agency can issue a formal letter giving the firm a fixed period of time to cease and desist. The company can agree at this point to stop its actions without admitting that it was acting incorrectly. It has to sign an agreement to that effect known as a *consent decree.* If an agreement is struck between the parties, the FTC requires that a formal affidavit be filed detailing the nature of the complaint and providing the agency with written assurance that there will be no further violations of the rules.

▶ Adjudicative Proceedings

Certainly not all matters can be settled informally. Therefore agencies have established adjudicative procedures designed to formally decide cases of alleged violations of administrative rules.

Complaint An administrative agency issues a complaint. This is a document designed to serve as notice to the business involved that the agency believes that the business has violated a particular standard. The FTC, for example, issues an "adjudicative complaint." (This is also known as a Part III complaint since it is issued pursuant to Part III of the FTC's rules.)

Hearings At first glance, administrative hearings appear to be much like any courtroom trial. However, closer examination reveals several significant differences. Just as in formal courts, administrative hearings are presided over by a judge. The judges are called "administrative law judges," and they are employees of the agency. They are *not* members of the state or federal judiciary.

At the hearing, the administrative law judge allows each side to present evidence. In FTC proceedings, parties may cross-examine witnesses and make motions and objections. In fact, in the case of an indigent (poor person), the FTC can make arrangements to have counsel appointed to represent the indigent. Once all of the evidence has been presented, the judge issues an opinion. As we will see shortly, this opinion may be appealed to a higher authority if deemed necessary.

Evidence One major difference between formal state and federal courts, on the one hand, and administrative agencies, on the other, is in the kind of evidence that they will find acceptable. Formal court systems tend to be more restrictive about the kinds of evidence they will receive. The formal courts have grown up with a system that is based upon exclusionary rules of evidence. That is, the courts have rather rigorously tended to exclude evidence if it may in any way be undependable—the classic example being the courts' reluctance to accept **hearsay.**

hearsay
A matter not personally known but heard from others

Administrative hearings are conducted less formally than state or federal court hearings. They also allow evidence of a much broader scope. The federal Administrative Procedures Act defines the scope of acceptable evidence in Section 7(c):

> Any oral or documentary evidence may be received, but every agency shall as a matter of policy provide for the exclusion of irrelevant immaterial or unduly repetitious evidence and no sanction shall be imposed or rule or order be issued except upon consideration of the whole record or such portions thereof as may be cited by any party and as supported by and in accordance with the reliable, probative and substantial evidence.

This means that evidence that would otherwise be unacceptable in a court may be included as part of an administrative hearing for its probative value, as is illustrated in the following case.

FACTS

Plaintiff was acting tour II superintendent at an office of the U.S. Post Office. He was responsible for supervising several postal clerks engaged in compiling and reporting information on the volume of mail handled by various distribution operations. He was charged with the falsification of mail volume records, or with directing his subordinates to falsify the records. During an administrative hearing, certain statements were made which could be considered hearsay. These statements would be damaging to plaintiff's case if they are admitted. Can the plaintiff have hearsay evidence excluded?

DECISION

No. We begin with a recognition that strict rules of evidence do not apply in the administrative context. Indeed the Administrative Procedures Act provides that "any oral or documentary evidence may be received, but every agency shall as a matter of policy provide for the exclusion of irrelevant, immaterial, or unduly repetitious evidence. Thus it is not the hearsay nature per se of the evidence that is significant, it is its probative value, reliability, and fairness of its use that is determinative.

Calhoun v. Bailer, 626 F.2d 145 (9th Cir. 1980).

Decision The administrative judge considers all of the evidence and issues an opinion. This opinion is usually subject to review by the entire administrative agency and they may either accept the opinion or reject it. However, notice that the original decision is made by the administrative judge and that there is no right to a jury trial. The opinion may contain a recommendation for a sanction. For example, the FTC judge may decide that a particular business advertising practice should not continue, and therefore a cease and desist order may be issued.

Judicial Review

Decisions made by administrative agencies are reviewable. By this we mean that if you, as an aggrieved party, are not satisfied with a decision made by an agency, you may appeal the decision to a court of law. However, courts do not automatically have to hear your case. First, in order to have judicial review of an agency's actions you must demonstrate that you have suffered some direct injury because of the agency action. Generally, a party will show an economic injury resulting from the agency's activities. This is called establishing *standing.* Next you must show that you have gone through all of the steps for reviewing your case within the agency itself. That is, you must fully complete the agency's own procedures for appealing your case. This is known as the concept of *exhaustion of remedies.*

The standard that the courts use in deciding whether or not to review an administrative agency's decision is the *substantial evidence* test. This test declares that courts will review issues that involve questions of law. However, questions of fact are reviewed only if the decision violates a test of reasonableness. While this is the dominant view today, there are some *state* statutes that give the courts the right to have a *trial de novo* (new trial).[1] The argument in favor of allowing de novo trials is that this assures that the courts will have an opportunity to provide a somewhat stronger check on arbitrary administrative action. Finally, the Administrative Procedures Act, Section 706, provides useful guidance on the scope of judicial review. The following case illustrates the reasons courts examine agency decisions.

---

[1]See 82 AM. JUR. 2d *Workers Compensation,* Section 618 (1962); and Ohio Rev. Code, Title 41, *Labor and Industry,* Section 4123.519.

FACTS

Krause, an employee of the Small Business Administration, asked for a court review of a seven-day suspension from his position as a Loan Specialist on the grounds that there was no substantial evidence to support the suspension and the failure to provide him with a trial type evidentiary hearing upon his appeal to the merit Systems Protection Board. Was it reasonable for the SBA to impose a seven-day suspension where the employed allegedly falsified records of one loan application in violation of an administrative rule?

DECISION

Judicial review of an agency's action is based on the administrative record, and the court's role is to address, not the wisdom or good judgement of the agency's decision, but only whether the agency complied with applicable procedures and whether its actions were arbitrary or capricious. In this case the agency was neither arbitrary nor capricious.

Krause v. SBA, 502 F.Supp. 1332 (S.D.N.Y. 1980).

In a recent case, the U.S. Supreme Court considered whether a federal administrative agency was arbitrary in its action. The Court held that, before federal administrative agencies can rescind their regulations, the agencies must have evidence to show that the regulations are no longer carrying out the intent of Congress for which they were issued initially, in other words the same standards apply to rescinding rules as govern issuing them. Specifically, the Court held that the National Highway Traffic Safety Administration failed to justify its 1981 decision to scrap its 1977 air-bag and nondetachable-belt rule that required installation, beginning in 1982-model cars, of either air-bags, which inflate on impact to protect a vehicle's occupants in a crash, or automatic safety belts, which move into place when a car door is closed.[2] While federal administrative agencies must give sufficient reasons justifying their issuance of regulations and courts can nullify such regulations if they are arbitrary or capricious, under the decision in this case an agency must give equally sufficient reasons for rescinding its previously issued regulations, which did not occur here.

In another recent case, the U.S. Supreme Court had to consider the validity of a federal administrative regulation concerning tax exemption of an educational institution that engaged in racial discrimination. Section 501(c)(3) of the Internal Revenue Code of 1954 provides that "organizations . . . organized and operated exclusively for religious, charitable . . . or educational purposes" are entitled to tax exemption. In 1970, the Internal Revenue Service (IRS) changed its previous policy and refused to continue the tax exempt status under this Code section to private schools that practiced racial discrimination, and issued a Revenue Policy 71–447, which provided that a private school not having a racially nondiscriminating policy as to students is not "charitable" within the common law concepts reflected in the Code. Two private educational institutions engaged in racial discrimination as to students challenged the IRS interpretation of the Code, the IRS Revenue Policy, and the IRS refusal to continue their tax exempt status. The Court held that the IRS interpretation was correct, and that racial discrimination in education is contrary to public policy and does not confer a public benefit within the "charitable" concept.[3]

[2] *Motor Vehicle Mfr. Ass'n of the United States, Inc., et al. v. State Farm Mut. Auto. Ins. Co. et al.*, 463 U.S. 29 (1983).

[3] *Bob Jones Univ., and Goldsboro Christian Schools, Inc. v. United States*, 461 U.S. 574 (1983).

Types of Powers Held by Administrative Agencies

Administrative agencies have several different ways in which to exert control over their respective companies. It is, of course, possible for an administrative agency to simply use the power of moral persuasion to obtain compliance with its rules. However, the chances of this technique working satisfactorily are quite limited. Perhaps the most common technique used is to fine rule-breakers. Another form of sanction is to force the regulated party to pay *reparations* to the injured party. Finally, a third technique employed by administrative agencies is the granting, revocation, and withholding of a license.

At the state level, one example of a licensing requirement is the license you must earn to drive your car. A driver's license is a privilege granted to you after you have demonstrated a rudimentary understanding of automobile safety and handling. If you violate too many driving laws, your license can be suspended or revoked.

Summary Statement

1. Federal administrative agencies are a creation born of necessity. Although the federal Constitution specifies that legislators make laws, reality dictates that rule-making procedures be delegated to administrative agencies.
2. While it is impossible to outline all of the different structures of the many administrative agencies that exist, there is a substantial body of federal laws guiding their actions. The most important of these laws is the Administrative Procedures Act.
3. Administrative agencies investigate violations of rules and may take informal action to settle disputes. However, there are more formal alternatives available. Agencies may hold hearings, complete with elaborate procedures (formal or informal), and may issue decisions that the regulated groups must follow.
4. The decisions of administrative agencies may be appealed to courts of law, but courts are reluctant to use their power of judicial review.
5. Finally, agencies vary in their strength. Some agencies can fine, and impose reparations upon, rule violators; others have the power to grant, withhold, and revoke licenses.

As was discussed earlier, decisions made by administrative agencies are reviewable, but the courts understand that administrative agencies are competent to review even complex administrative matters. The following case illustrates the judiciary's appropriate use of an administrative law judge.

GULL v. WEINBERGER
694 F.2d 838 (D.C. Cir. 1982)

In October, 1977 the United States Navy granted a contract to Consolidated Airborne Systems, Inc. (CAS), for the procurement of certain fuel quantity test sets and data. Following several attempts to obtain administrative relief, appellant, Gull Airborne Instruments, Inc. (Gull), the second low bidder on the contract, filed suit in federal district court, alleging that both the Navy's award and its administration of the contract were illegal and asking that further performance be enjoined.

In September 1976 the U.S. Navy's Aviation Supply Office (ASO) invited bids for "capacitance-type, tank-unit, fuel quantity test sets and data." Bids were opened in January 1977. Of the three that had been entered, CAS' was the low bid on the contract and Gull's was the second low bid.

[1] Gull contends here that it is entitled, as an injured party, to seek review of both the contract award to CAS and the Navy's subsequent administration of the contract as actions in violation of the regulations governing the issuance and administration of government contracts. We agree with the district court that Gull has standing to contest the award of the contract but not its administration.

[2] Section 702 of the APA gives a right to judicial review to any person "adversely affected or aggrieved by agency action within the meaning of a relevant statute." *Control Data Corp. v. Baldrige*, 665 F.2d 283, 288–89 (D.C. Cir.), cert. denied, 454 U.S. 881, 102 S. Ct. 363, 70 L.Ed.2d 190 (1981), sets out a three-part test for standing to obtain review of administrative action: (1) the complainant must allege injury in fact; (2) the complainant must assert that arbitrary or capricious agency action injured an interest arguably within the zone of interests to be protected or regulated by the statute or constitutional guarantee in question; and (3) there must be no "clear and convincing" indication of a legislative intent to withhold judicial review.

[3] Gull contends that it has standing under 702 as a disappointed bidder on the Navy's contract to protest both its award to CAS and its subsequent maladministration. We agree with both Gull and the district court that disappointed bidders have standing to challenge the failure of an administering agency to follow the applicable statutes and regulations regarding contract awards.

Gull also contends that it has standing to seek review of the Navy's alleged maladministration of the contract. To be accorded such standing, Gull must satisfy the Control Data test. We agree with the government and the district court that it has been unable to do so.

The first two parts of the test require that the complainant allege injury to an interest arguably within a statute's or regulation's zone of interests. Here, Gull alleges that it suffered economic loss from the illegal entry of a government-funded competitor into its own line of business. It also alleges that it suffered economic loss because it was denied an opportunity to bid on reprocurement of the contract. The government, on the other hand, argues that the only economic injury Gull suffered was the original failure to win the contract. Once a contract is in place, it contends, disappointed bidders on the contract revert to the status of ordinary citizens who have no generalized standing to object to government actions. In addition, the government argues, any economic loss sustained through denial of an opportunity to Gull to bid on the reprocurement is conjectural since Gull may not have been the low bidder on that second contract.

Even were we to assume, however, that the Navy's award of the contract to CAS, its novation of the contract to Bendix, and its decision to extend the contractual delivery date conferred cognizable injury on Gull by illegally allowing CAS and Bendix to become its competitors and by preventing Gull from bidding on the reprocurement of the contract, that injury alone would be insufficient to confer standing on Gull to contest the administration of the contract. Gull must also demonstrate that the regulatory or statutory requirements it seeks to enforce were intended to protect it against such competitive injury.

[4] Unlike the regulations governing the award of contracts, the regulations governing termination of contracts for default are not designed to foster competition or to protect unsuccessful bidders from illegal injury to their economic interests. The default regulations, see 32 C.F.R. 8–600 to 8–602 (1981), are intended to protect the government against injury from the contractor's inability to perform the contract and the contracting party from the government's premature or unjustified cancellation. As a result, Gull must rely on its protest against the original award of the contract to CAS, not its subsequent administration, to establish that the government has illegally injured its economic interests.

Questions and Case Problems

1. Congress gave the FCC the power to determine reasonable rates for cable service. A trade association representing a group of community antenna television systems petitions the U.S. Supreme Court for review of a revised fee schedule set by the FCC. They set the annual fee at $.30 per subscriber. May Congress delegate its job of lawmaking to an administrative agency? [*Nat'l Cable Television Ass'n., Inc. v. United States,* 415 U.S. 336 (1974).]
2. Must all agencies attempt to resolve disputes informally before moving to a hearing?
3. Bergen Pines County Hospital is challenging the validity of the Department of Human Services' regulations. These regulations are prescribing how the hospital should fix the rates paid to it for caring for medicaid patients in its long-term medical care facility. The hospital is arguing that the administrative agency is not qualified to make such rules. What qualifies administrative agencies to make rules? Why shouldn't the legislature do it? [*Bergen Pines County Hosp. v. N.J. Dep't of Human Services,* 476 A.2d 784 (N.J. 1984).]
4. Petitioner challenges a final decision of the District of Columbia Department of Employment Services (DOES) disqualifying him from unemployment compensation benefits for a ten week period on the ground that he was discharged from his most recent job because of "dishonesty" amounting to "misconduct." Having reviewed the record, the judge observed that the formal rules of evidence were not closely followed. Does this mean the decision may be reversed? Explain. [*Jadallah v. D.C. Dep't of Employment,* 476 A.2d 671 (D.C. 1984).]
5. Describe the purpose of a complaint issued by an administrative agency.
6. The Kentucky State Racing Commission disqualified a horse from winning the Kentucky Derby. Tests performed after the race had shown the presence of a prohibited medication and the commission had ruled the horse was disqualified. The commissioner's ruling was appealed to court. Assume that the commission properly followed its own procedures. Should a court reexamine and possibly overturn the commission's finding? [*Kentucky State Racing Comm'r v. Fuller,* 481 S.W.2d 298 (Ky. 1972).]
7. William Pector, a liquor law enforcement agent, testified that although he was not a member he entered the Yacht Club and purchased a "VO and Coke." He claims that he placed a sample of the drink in a vial, which sample was later sent to the state chemist for testing. Based on Pector's testimony and the toxicology report, the Utah Liquor Control Commission suspended the Club's liquor license and operations for thirty days because the Club had made an unlawful sale of an alcoholic beverage to a nonmember. The state chemist's toxicology report on the alcoholic content of a specimen drink allegedly sold to nonmembers of the Club was admissible under exception to the hearsay rule for reports and findings of public officials. Is hearsay evidence admissible in an administrative agency hearing? Explain. [*Yacht Club v. Utah Liquor Control Comm'n,* 681 P.2d 1224 (Utah 1984).]
8. An action is brought seeking review of a decision made by Secretary of Health, Education and Welfare denying claimant's social security benefits. The claim is made that the evidence in the case would be inadmissable under the rules of evidence which control judicial hearings. Can such evidence be accepted at an administrative hearing? [*Garcia v. Califano,* 463 F.Supp. 1098 (N.D. Ill., E.D. 1979).]
9. The Funeral Directors and Embalmers Examining Board appeals from the trial court's order vacating the Board's decision suspending Calvin Monroe's license to

practice as a funeral director and embalmer. The Board concluded him to be of unprofessional conduct, obnoxious behavior, and gross negligence. On judicial review, how much weight should be given to the decision rendered by the agency? [*Monroe v. Funeral Directors and Embalmers Examining Bd.,* 349 N.W.2d 746 (Wis. 1984).]

10. In the case of *Gull v. Weinberger,* excerpted at the beginning of this section, it is argued that the unsuccessful bidder did not have standing to contest the alleged administration of the contract. What rationale does the court use to establish whether a party has standing to sue?

CHAPTER 36

LABOR LAW

After reading this chapter, you should be able to identify all of the following terms:

1. Craft union
2. Industrial union
3. Knights of Labor
4. AFL-CIO
5. Criminal conspiracy
6. Injunction
7. Yellow dog contract
8. Norris–La Guardia Act
9. Wagner Act
10. Taft-Hartley Act
11. Unfair labor practices
12. Bargaining unit
13. Boulwarism
14. Executive Orders 10988 and 11491
15. Hot Cargo

BUSINESS DECISIONS and the LAW

Labor unions play an important role in the U.S. economy. Unions are essentially groups of employees who have gathered together to collectively determine the terms and conditions of their employment in conjunction with their employer. But long before a union ever negotiates a contract on behalf of their members, several issues must be resolved.

Employees must first decide if they want to join a union. Experts in labor management relations have analyzed the reasons why people join unions. Perhaps the main reason is that any single employee in a large organization has a small voice. However, collectively employees can exert a good deal of pressure on an employer. Of course, other reasons may exist as well. For example, some people come from a long family tradition of union membership and find unions to be useful in the workplace. They also use unions as a social or community activity. Another important decision that workers face is which union to affiliate with. Several unions may compete for the privilege of representing a group of employees.

Overall, the union attempts to establish a good working relationship with the employer. It tries to enhance the quality of work life for the employees. Some employers also make an effort to establish a high quality of work life. Part of the reason that employers are concerned with the quality of work life is because they are concerned with increasing corporate productivity. One personnel expert has defined quality of work life as a "process by which all members of the organization, through appropriate and open channels of communication, have some say in decisions that affect their jobs in particular and the work environment in general, resulting in greater work job involvement and satisfaction."*

Labor law in the United States establishes a framework for mutual decision making with regard to wages, hours, and terms and conditions of employment. The Wagner Act is a major component of the law. One problem that it was attempting to rectify was employer-dominated unions. The law declares it is "illegal for an employer to dominate or interfere with the formation of any labor organization or to contribute financial support." But how do quality of work life programs fit this model? The brief answer is they do not fit the original mold of the Wagner Act. But the courts recognize quality of work programs as an important element of progressive labor management relations.

For example, the Scott & Fetzer Company of Westlake, Ohio, formed a committee that was part of the company's program to "develop more readily accessible channels of communications within manufacturing operations and to . . . provide an informal yet orderly process for communicating company plans and programs; define . . . problem areas and eliciting suggestions and ideas for improving operations."** The union challenged this committee as a company-dominated labor organization that violated labor law. The problem found its way to court, and ultimately the U.S. Court of Appeals said, "The committee was not, under any enlightened view of the act, a labor organization."

There are many examples of quality of work life programs. They can be a very valuable managerial tool. But managers must be very careful to adhere to labor law and the work with union groups to provide a decent workplace.

*R. Schuler, *Personnel and Human Resources Management*, 3rd ed. (St. Paul: West Publishing, 1987), 437.
**NLRB v. Streamway*, 691 F.2d 288 (6th Cir. 1982).

Sources: Ibid., and D. Beach, *Personnel*, 5th ed. (New York: Macmillan, 1985), 388.

Introduction

sole proprietorship
A business owned and operated by one person

partnership
(general partnership) "An association of two or more persons to carry on as co-owners of a business for profit" UPA, sec. 6

corporation
A legal entity created by statute authorizing an association of persons to carry on an enterprise

If you were to work for a small firm, such as a **sole proprietorship,** there is an excellent chance that you would know the owner personally. If you had a problem concerning your wages, hours, or the conditions of employment, it would be relatively easy to bring your concern to the proper authority. Further, in a small organization, since your labor is a significant part of the whole, management has a great deal of interest in your well-being.

In a larger organization, such as a **partnership,** there may be a division of work among the partners such that one partner manages the firm while the other participates largely through investment of capital. As an employee, you may rarely see one of the partners. **Corporations** are incorporated firms and have the potential of growing to be huge organizations. Examples of organizations in this category abound—Ford, General Motors, IBM, and General Mills. It is highly unlikely that people working on the assembly line will know anyone in top management. If problems arise concerning wages, hours, line will know anyone in top management. If problems arise concerning wages, hours, or conditions of employment, an employee might raise his or her concern with a foreman and perhaps with the personnel department, but the employee's voice is just one among the crowd. Unlike the situation in a sole proprietorship, one employee rarely makes up a significant part of the work force.

The question of how an employee can be heard in a large organization has been answered in the United States by labor unions. Labor organizations such as the American Federation of Teachers, the United Auto Workers, and the American Federation of State, County, and Municipal Employees have flourished in the past several decades in response to employees' needs for representation in the workplace.

Not only have these unions pressed employers for better labor contracts, but they have also been instrumental in pressing legislators to pass legislation that has improved our lives immeasurably.

The Response of the Law

Unions were not always welcome additions to the world of work. Indeed, at first they were strenuously resisted by employers. Today, unions are generally accepted as part of the work environment, but many employers resist union organizing efforts because they believe unions will drive up wages or take away management prerogatives. This book does not take any position on the impact of unions in the workplace. Its purpose is to present, educationally, the labor union as a present-day factor in business, except to note that the issue is certainly unresolved. This chapter presents an overview of the major federal laws that govern labor-management relations.

At first, employers resisted unions by dismissing employees who exhibited pro-union tendencies, and the courts were supportive of employers' actions for many years. Gradually, as we shall see, the courts and the legislators have sought to strike a balance between the unions' right to organize employees and the employers' right to manage the business free from outside interference. Laws such as the Wagner Act, Taft-Hartley, and Landrum-Griffin Acts are frequently referred to by contemporary labor relations specialists as they attempt to discern the best course of action in resolving a labor dispute.

The law has also attempted to provide benefits to employees of the federal government. For example, the following pieces of federal legislation are all part of the domain of Labor Law: (a) Executive Order 10988 and (b) Executive Order 11491, discussed later.

In this chapter we will examine some of these laws in order to understand their impact on employees and management.

A Brief History of Unions

▶ The Origin of Craft Unionism

As we all learned in history courses, the United States was largely an agricultural nation during its early years. Unions were virtually nonexistent then. However, even in colonial America, farmers could not produce all of the items they needed to survive, and gradually craftsmen and their stores began to flourish. These craftsmen hired employees to assist in filling orders, and they often trained these employees in the skilled crafts.

Craftsmen would often join with others to discuss their trade and to socialize. Their primary motive was not to induce an employer to increase their wages or improve their working conditions; rather, their common bond was that they shared a skill. In fact, often the craftsmen were independent employers. These groups represented the beginnings of craft style unions in our country.

As our country continued to grow, the craft unions began to do more than just socialize. In an attempt to maintain high quality workmanship, they began to set standards for entrance into their trade. People interested in joining a particular craft union were given **apprentice** status for a period of time. If they succeeded as an apprentice, they ultimately were given the rank of **journeyman** and were allowed to work on their own.

apprentice
A student learning a particular craft

journeyman
A skilled craftsman

Some historians have made the point that these unions were designed not only to maintain high quality standards, but also to keep out "undesirables." In the early years of our nation, almost any newcomer was viewed suspiciously and as potentially undesirable competition. In fact, these early unions were attempting to limit competition. Apprentice groups were one technique they employed. Another technique designed to limit competition was the creation of a **closed shop.** A closed shop means that an employer may hire only union workers to perform a particular task. Failure to do so did not usually result in any sort of retribution during these early years, but employers risked having lower quality products produced.

closed shop
An employer who, by agreement with a union, will employ only union members

► The Origins of Industrial Unions

As our nation developed, it moved from an agrarian economy to an industrial nation and, as corporations began to grow, the workplace became increasingly less personal. Furthermore, technological change began to alter the nature of work. Companies needed fewer and fewer skilled craftsmen. The very work which these craftsmen once did slowly and painstakingly was gradually usurped by a machine and some unskilled laborers working at low wages. Who would organize these people? At first, nobody. Employees had to protect themselves, if they could, from those employers who cared little about their employees' well-being.

The Civil War marked the point in our history when industrialization began to move at a pace unparalleled in the history of any other nation in the world. While our nation produced goods at rates previously unheard of, the employees producing those goods were often locked into poverty by well-to-do employers and were unable to take part in the great society of which they were a part. When they finally realized that they were in an untenable position, they began to organize for collective action.

One of the first unions to gain national recognition was the Knights of Labor. The Knights were led in their quest by Uriah Stephens, and upon his retirement by the Grand Master Workman Terrance Powderly. Powderly did not succeed for long, however. One of the major difficulties faced by the Knights was that they were organized to accept any person who worked for a living. Thus craftsmen and unskilled laborers formed mixed assemblies, which often led to internal quarrels. This organizational strategy, plus a disastrous and violent demonstration at Haymarket Square in Chicago, ultimately led to the downfall of the union.

Workers did not enjoy being part of violent unions. Just as the Knights of Labor failed, so too did the International Workers of the World (I.W.W., or Wobblies). Although this group also grew to national size, it never established a firm hold on the workers because it was associated with violence and radical behavior. Other early unions grew for a while and then died. Many—such as the socialist labor unions—died because American workers separated their political life from their "bread and butter" (wage and hour) concerns.

► Contemporary Unions

Out of these early unions grew today's powerful union groups. The American Federation of Labor (AFL) grew under the early leadership of Samuel Gompers. Gompers was concerned about representing the skilled craftsmen. The AFL craft locals represent craft autonomy, that is, for each particular skill there is a union group that represents their interests. Gompers, for example, was a member of the cigar-makers. Other craft-oriented unions include the carpenters, the plumbers, and the electricians.

Industrial unions were formed because people like John L. Lewis, of the coal miners union, believed that the AFL was ineffective in representing the interests of workers who were semiskilled or unskilled in mass production industries. In the 1930s people were able to join with others in massive organizing campaigns that resulted in large numbers of people joining labor unions. The AFL and the CIO were not always joined in one organization, as they are today. In fact, for many years a bitter rivalry existed between the two groups. At first, the CIO was called the Committee (later Congress) of Industrial Organizations and was a branch of the AFL. Internal disputes and rivalries over organizing strategies led to a split that lasted until 1955, when new leaders of each organization were brought together by a man named Arthur Goldberg. (Goldberg subsequently was a member of the U.S. Supreme Court and then U.S. Ambassador to the United Nations.)

Today unions within the AFL-CIO and independent unions are rivals for control of a major group of largely unorganized employees. These are white-collar workers, professionals, and government employees. As we shall see, the law has had a significant impact upon the growth of unions in our country, and we can expect further growth of unions among government employees to be shaped by social control exerted through law.

Early Attempts to Control Labor Unions

► Criminal Conspiracy

Employers have traditionally resisted union organizing attempts. The earliest strategy adopted by employers to quash a union was to accuse the union of having unlawfully combined into a **criminal conspiracy** to control wages. The logic of this argument was that, if wages were driven up, eventually the consuming public would suffer, since prices would rise. Thus any time a worker joined with others to ask for a wage increase the worker was risking a court action. During the first half of the nineteenth century this doctrine was quite effective.

criminal conspiracy
A combination of persons for the purpose of committing an unlawful act

Then, in a landmark decision, the courts of the state of Massachusetts decided the following case.

FACTS

The defendants were bootmakers who were organized into a union group. They were accused by the Commonwealth of Massachusetts of having committed the crime of unlawfully attempting to extort great sums of money from the employer by means of organizing a union. Was the formation of a union an unlawful conspiracy?

DECISION

No. Judgment for the defendants. The intent of the association is to induce all those engaged in the same occupation to become members of it. Such a purpose is not unlawful.... An association may be formed, the declared object of which is innocent and laudable. If the plaintiff wanted to demonstrate that this union was formed for criminal purpose, it should have brought this forward as part of the evidence.

Commonwealth v. Hunt, 4 Metcalf 111 (Mass. 1842), 44 Mass. Reports.

The criminal conspiracy doctrine, which began with an incident involving shoemakers in Philadelphia in 1806, ended following the *Hunt* case just noted. It was a powerful weapon for its time but finally yielded to the injunction.

Injunction

injunction
A court order requiring a person to do or not to do something

Another early weapon used against employees was the **injunction.** An injunction is an order issued by a court ordering that a person do or not do something. For example, if students decided to march and perhaps take violent action against a professor's decision to give an entire class failing grades, it would be possible for the university to obtain a stop order, an injunction. In the case of a labor dispute, if a union embarked on a course of action that seemed likely to injure the employer in any way, the employer would request an injunction. Needless to say, in the late 1800s such an order was relatively easy to obtain, the potential damage to the employer would be minimal, and the injunction would still be issued.

In 1894, the U.S. Supreme Court affirmed the use of injunctions in labor disputes when it heard *In re Debs,* 158 U.S. 564 (1895). Since that time injunctions have been used in labor disputes. However, courts are much more careful about the circumstances under which they issue a stop order.

yellow dog contract
An agreement between an employer and employee that the employee will not be, nor continue to be, a member of a union

Associated with the injunction was a tactic used by employers called the **yellow dog contract.** Under these contracts, employees had to promise their employer not to join a union. If they did join, they were automatically fired for violating a condition of employment. Such contracts are illegal because they unfairly hinder union members' ability to organize for collective action. The reason a yellow dog contract is associated with the injunction is that employers would seek an injunction from the courts to stop unions from attempting to organize workers who had previously signed yellow dog agreements. Yellow dog contracts have been declared illegal.

Sherman Act of 1890

In Chapter 34, Antitrust Law, we mentioned that the first attempt to regulate monopolistic competition by business was a federal enactment called the Sherman Act. This law not only made monopolies illegal, but it also said that combinations or conspiracies to restrain trade were illegal. The sections of the Sherman Act that should provide us with guidance about whether Congress intended unions to be covered by the Act were, in fact, silent on the issue. Thus the case of the *Danbury Hatters,* which brought the issue to the Supreme Court, was an important decision.

FACTS

A union group composed of hatmakers in Danbury, Connecticut, attempted to organize Loewe and Company. One of its tactics was to initiate a boycott of Loewe hats. This strategy caused the managers of Loewe to bring an action against the union under the Sherman

Act. Was the union activity a combination in restraint of trade as contemplated by the Sherman Act?

DECISION

Yes. Judgment for Loewe and Company. The hatters union members violated the Sherman Act by their actions. The boycott of plaintiff's goods was ordered for the purpose of obstructing the flow of commerce. Thus, Loewe and Company would not be able to engage in business as effectively as they might have. This is the kind of action that Congress intended to restrain through antitrust legislation.

Lawlor v. Loewe, 235 U.S. 522 (1915).

Thus the impact of the *Danbury Hatters* case was to bring unions within the domain of the antitrust statutes. Employers used this decision as a weapon until Congress acted to change the state of affairs in the Clayton Act of 1914. Section 6 of the Clayton Act specifically held that neither labor organizations nor "the members thereof . . . be held or construed to be illegal combinations or conspiracies in restraint of trade, under the antitrust laws."

Unfortunately for labor unions, Section 6 of the Clayton Act has suffered at the hands of the courts. In a series of Supreme Court decisions, the justices claimed the power to determine whether the unions were carrying out "legitimate objects." This posture was clearly adhered to in *Bedford Cut Stone Co. v. Journeymen Stone Cutters Association,* 274 U.S. 37 (1927).

Contemporary Federal Labor Legislation

▶ Norris–La Guardia Act

Until the 1930s, labor unions were at the mercy of employers. Early in the 1930s, when the United States was in the midst of a severe depression, President Hoover attempted to deal with the extremely high rate of unemployment and low wages by offering workers a piece of legislation designed to give employees an advantage in the labor-management relations arena that they had not previously enjoyed. It was the Norris–La Guardia Act of 1932, and it had several noteworthy provisions. First, it declared yellow dog contracts to be illegal. Second, it guaranteed employees the right to organize into unions and to bargain collectively with their employers. This principle remains an important part of our federal labor laws today.

▶ Wagner Act

In 1933, the Roosevelt administration was attempting to do what the Hoover administration had failed to do—that is, bring our country out of the depression. One attempt to move in this direction was the National Industrial Recovery Act. The critical section with respect to labor relations was 7(a), which specifically endorsed employees' rights "to bargain collectively through representatives of their own choosing." The Supreme Court held that the NIRA was unconstitutional.

Within two years Congress acted again to protect labor's interests. In 1935, it passed the National Labor Relations Act. The NLRA is usually referred to as the Wagner Act. It remains today as one of the most important pieces of federal labor legislation. The following case illustrates its purpose to safeguard the rights of employees.

FACTS

Jones & Laughlin Steel produced steel in Pennsylvania and sold their goods throughout the United States. One of the elements defined by the Wagner Act as an unfair labor practice is the discharge of employees for union activity. Jones & Laughlin had committed this act and so were charged by the NLRB with an unfair labor practice. Jones & Laughlin fought the NLRB by arguing that the Wagner Act was unconstitutional and that their manufacturing business was not in the "stream of commerce." Is the Wagner Act unconstitutional and is Jones & Laughlin in commerce?

DECISION

Judgment for NLRB. We think it clear that the National Labor Relations Act may be construed to operate within the sphere of constitutional authority. The statute goes no further than to safeguard the rights of employees. Further, Jones & Laughlin clearly fits as in the stream of commerce and so is subject to federal regulations.

NLRB v. Jones & Laughlin Steel Corp., 301 U.S. 1 (1937).

unfair labor practices
Tactics by an employer or a union that are legally prohibited as unfair

As referred to in the *Jones & Laughlin* case, the Wagner Act defined some practices were designed to give employees more rights to organize for labor action. These were called **unfair labor practices** by *employers*. Later the Taft-Hartley Act defined unfair labor practices by a *union*.

There are five unfair labor practices by employers. Employers may *not:*

1. refuse to bargain with employee representatives;
2. discharge an employee for filing a complaint under the Wagner Act;
3. encourage or discourage union membership or discriminate when hiring or retaining employees just because of their union leanings;
4. interfere with employees in any way in their right to determine who shall represent them; and
5. dominate or interfere with any labor organization or contribute to its support in any way.

Needless to say, such a powerful Act would not be effective unless it had some administrative support. Thus Congress created the National Labor Relations Board to handle disputes as they arose. In addition to the unfair labor practices as enumerated, the NLRB also was charged with the task of setting up union election procedures and defining the appropriate **bargaining unit.**

bargaining unit
A group of employees appropriately joined together for the purpose of collective bargaining

The bargaining unit is a group of employees appropriately joined together for the purpose of collective bargaining. In an industrial setting, for example, the bargaining unit might be all of the employees within a particular department, or all employees doing essentially the same job. The NLRB enters the scene if there is a dispute concerning whether or not particular employees should be in the unit. Disputes often arise in this regard. For example, employers may argue that particular employees, such as first line foremen, have managerial responsibility, while the union argues that they are members of the unit.

► Taft-Hartley Act

Some labor law experts argue that labor laws and labor sentiment in our country move in pendulum swings. That is, strongly pro-labor laws are passed, then strongly pro-management laws are enacted. Since the Wagner Act was clearly pro-labor, protecting employees' rights to organize, the Taft-Hartley Act would be pro-management. Indeed, it was precisely that. Passed in 1947, it was designed to redress an imbalance that Congress and the American people perceived in the labor area. It is not difficult to imagine why they believed there was a need for a law controlling labor. In the period just prior to passage of Taft-Hartley our nation was embroiled in strikes. Not only was there a nationwide coal strike, but telephone company, steel, oil, textile, and maritime workers also had work stoppages, and many other unions were involved in labor disputes of one kind or another.

State Right-to-Work Provisions One of the most controversial sections of the Taft-Hartley Act is Section 14(b), the "right-to-work" section. This portion of the Act allows states to pass right-to-work laws. These laws allow companies to make contracts that have very weak union security clauses. In effect, they permit people to work in a union plant without joining the union. The merits of right-to-work laws have been argued for a number of years.

Free Speech Taft-Hartley made several important changes in the state of labor law in the United States. First, it allowed employers to comment more freely on union organizing activities than they had been able to do in the past. Prior to Taft-Hartley, employers had to be extremely careful about what they said to employees about the union. Taft-Hartley directly addresses the subject of free speech in Section 8(c), where it says that employers would not commit an unfair labor practice to speak to employees, unless they threaten reprisal or promise some benefit to employees. This is the so-called "free speech" amendment.

Unfair Labor Practices Another important part of the Taft-Hartley Act is its section on unfair labor practices. This time the unfair practices were aimed at labor rather than at management. There are a number of such unfair labor practices by unions. First, it is an unfair labor practice for the union to try to coerce employees to join unions. In other words, no harsh tactics can be used to get an employee to join. Second, certain kinds of strikes and boycotts are unfair labor practices. Strikes or boycotts designed to make an employer assign work to a particular craft group, strikes or boycotts designed to force an employer to recognize a union without NLRB precertification, and secondary boycotts are all held to be unfair labor practices.

Secondary Boycott A **secondary boycott** is a union attempt to place *concerted pressure* on an otherwise *uninvolved party* in order to get that party to pressure the union's real adversary into capitulating. The following case held that there was activity amounting to a secondary boycott.

secondary boycott
The bringing of pressure by a union on a neutral party who will then pressure the employer with whom the union has a dispute

FACTS

The project site superintendent anticipated labor problems because both union and nonunion contractors were working on the site. Signs were posted at each of the two entrances to the job site and the union placed a picket line at the main gate. The picketers carried placards stating that one of the nonunion subcontractors, R-B & Sons Electric, was paying less than the prevailing wage rate. The union did not picket the entrance designated for use by R-B and other nonunion employers but instead continued to picket at the main gate. Is this a violation of secondary boycott laws?

DECISION

Yes, the controlling factor in determining the legality of picketing is not its effect but its object. If the object of picketing is to bring pressure upon a neutral employer, then the activity is secondary and unlawful. The union could have communicated its dissatisfaction with R-B by using the entrance assigned to nonunion workers.

NLRB v. Local 58 IBEW, 638 F.2d 36 (6th Cir. 1980).

Other unfair labor practices defined by this Act include:

featherbedding
Make-work arrangements for employees when there is no work for them to perform or their services are not required

1. union attempts to charge excessive dues;
2. a prohibition against **featherbedding** (Featherbedding is forcing an employer to keep unneeded employees—such as, keeping workers on jobs that no longer exist. An example is forcing a newspaper to continue to employ people to set type even though modern typesetting technology eliminates the need for this work.);
3. union refusal to bargain in good faith;
4. union attempts to force employers to discriminate against employees who are not interested in the union, in an attempt to influence union membership.

The duty to bargain in *good faith* is now shouldered regularly by both the union and management, as part of the collective bargaining process. An interesting case emerged in 1964 which tested the principle of good faith bargaining. General Electric instituted a policy that has come to be known as *Boulwarism,* named after Mr. Boulware, an executive at General Electric. The case is as follows:

FACTS

General Electric negotiated a contract with the International Union of Electrical Workers (I.U.E.). G.E.'s strategy involved making considerable efforts prior to negotiation to determine what was right and fair for the employees. They then presented the package to the union and made it clear that it would not make any changes which it did not consider "correct" merely because of an actual or threatened strike. The NLRB decided that G.E.'s conduct was not bargaining in good faith. G.E. petitioned for review.

DECISION

Petition denied. G.E.'s bargaining technique, its campaign among employees, and its conduct at the bargaining table, all complementing each other, were calculated to disparage the union. This is not bargaining in good faith.

NLRB v. General Electric Co., 418 F.2d 736 (2nd. Cir. 1969).

National Emergency Strikes Under Taft-Hartley Because of all the strikes that had occurred in the period immediately preceding the Taft-Hartley Act, Congress decided to build in a provision that would give the government power to act when a vital industry was adversely affected by a labor action. In the event that a dispute in an industry (or in a substantial part thereof) "imperils the nation's health or safety," the president may appoint a Board of Inquiry to report on the dispute. This can result in an order by the court to stop the strike for sixty days and then again for another twenty days, if needed. During the second period, an election is conducted among the workers to see whether they would accept the last offer of the employer. If no progress results, the president then reports to Congress about the state of affairs and makes recommendations that the president believes to be appropriate.

► Landrum-Griffin Act

The technical name for the Landrum-Griffin Act is the Labor Management Reporting and Disclosure Act of 1959. The reason for this Act was largely to clean up the internal affairs of unions. In the mid-1950s Senator McClellan began an investigation into the activities of unions and uncovered massive amounts of corruption and violence. The public was sufficiently alarmed to push for strong reform legislation, and in 1959 that is precisely what the public received in the form of the Landrum-Griffin Act.

For our purposes, the most important part of the Landrum-Griffin Act is Title I, which is also known as a "bill of rights" for union members. This is because it assures that all union members will have an opportunity to participate in the internal affairs of their organization in some meaningful way. For example, Landrum-Griffin Title I guarantees members the right to vote in union elections. Titles II–VI contain other provisions to deal with internal union problems, such as the election of officers and the prohibition of certain kinds of people (for example, certain convicted offenders) from holding union office. In the following case labor's bill of rights is demonstrated in action.

FACTS

Mr. Pless campaigned for office in a union. For several hours he greeted incoming members of the union and passed out cards espousing his candidacy. Then another candidate for a different office in the union came in and in an angry and foul manner began to heckle him. After this episode with Mr. Moore, Mr. Pless testified that he had lost his earlier spirit in campaigning and was of the opinion that this improper interference had denied him his right to support his candidacy. Were Mr. Moore's comments a violation of the Landrum-Griffin Act?

DECISION

No, everything Mr. Moore said in his angry and profane way, related to and grew out of incidents relating to the union. No other topic was discussed. Labor's "bill of rights" guaranteed Mr. Moore his right to meet with other members and express any views, arguments or opinions. Moore's remarks may not have been gentlemanly but they cannot be deemed improper.

Marshall v. Local 815 of the United Textile Workers, 479 F.Supp. 613 (E.D. Tenn. 1979).

Title VII of Landrum-Griffin contains amendments to Taft-Hartley. Perhaps the most important amendment was to make it an unfair labor practice to become involved in a **hot cargo agreement.** Hot cargo agreements generally were union decisions not to handle items that were produced by, or were going to support, an anti-union company.

hot cargo agreement
An agreement between an employer and a union that the employer is not to handle or otherwise deal with goods of another employer

► Government Employees

The federal government has always been rather slow in managing its own labor-management relations. Although there are examples of some concerted labor activity in the federal government in the 1800s, union-management relations in the public service were virtually dead until President Kennedy enacted Executive Order 10988 in 1962. The thrust of this Order was to have three kinds of union recognition in the federal sector. "Informal recognition" allowed employees to gather together but management did not have to consult the group before acting. "Exclusive recognition" meant that a union represented at least 10 percent of the number of the employees in question. The union was then entitled to bargain a contract for all employees in the unit, and management had to meet with the representatives. "Formal recognition" was an intermediate step that obligated the managers to speak with the union only prior to acting.

President Nixon substantially altered labor relations in the public sector by issuing Executive Order 11491 in October 1969 and did away with all but the exclusive form of recognition. This change, in addition to other amendments, has marked a period of rapid expansion of interest of federal employees in union groups. Today, there are well over a million government employees represented by union organizations, such as the American Federation of Government Employees.

However, the range of items and the power of federal government union groups is still rather limited.

► The Strike: Public versus Private Sector

Almost all of us take for granted the right of employees to strike for higher wages. In fact, we are often surprised to learn that the courts can sometimes stop groups from striking.

In the *private* sector, the right to strike is so much a part of labor relations that it is rarely interfered with by the courts. The only time the courts will stop a private sector strike is in the event of violence.

In the *public* sector, the right to strike is much more restricted. The courts have repeatedly ruled that strikes in the public sector are illegal. The reason given by the courts is that if government employees strike they threaten the well-being of the entire community. However, there is some debate about this argument, and we may one day see legal public sector strikes.

In both the public and private sectors, management has a limited arsenal of weapons to fight the strike. These weapons include the *lockout* and the *injunction*. By the injunction, the court is ordering a group to "stop" a certain kind of behavior that may cause damage. A lockout is, as its name suggests, a closing of a plant before the union strikes.

Summary Statement

1. The origins of craft unionism and industrial unions are quite different. Industrial unions exist as a response to technological change.
2. Various methods have been used to control labor unions. Early attempts at labeling unions as criminal conspiracies gave way to attempts to use antitrust laws, followed by a regularized pattern of laws.
3. Today's labor laws have their roots in the Norris–La Guardia Act. However, the three major contemporary laws are the Wagner Act, the Taft-Hartley Act, and the Landrum-Griffin Act.
4. Government employees represent an ever-increasing number of potential union members. Special executive orders regulate labor-management relations between government and its employees. Supervisors and managerial employees are normally

excluded from the categories of employees entitled to the benefits of collective bargaining.

The following case addresses the question of whether faculty members should be excluded from the categories of employees entitled to the benefit of collective bargaining. The decision was made by a closely divided court.

NLRB v. YESHIVA UNIVERSITY
444 U.S. 672 (1979)

I

Powell, J. Yeshiva is a private university. . . . On October 30, 1974, the Yeshiva University Faculty Association (Union) filed a representation petition with the National Labor Relations Board (Board). The Union sought certification as bargaining agent for the full-time faculty members at 10 of the 13 schools. The University opposed the petition on the ground that all of its faculty members are managerial or supervisory personnel and hence not employees within the meaning of the National Labor Relations Act (Act).

Faculty power at Yeshiva's schools extends beyond strictly academic concerns. The faculty at each school make recommendations to the dean or director in every case of faculty hiring, tenure, sabbaticals, termination, and promotion. Although the final decision is reached by the central administration on the advice of the dean or director, the overwhelming majority of faculty recommendations are implemented.

II

A three-member panel of the Board granted the Union's petition in December, 1975, and directed an election in a bargaining unit consisting of all full-time faculty members at the affected schools.

The Union won the election and was certified by the Board. The University refused to bargain, reasserting its view that the faculty are managerial. In the subsequent unfair labor practice proceeding, the Board refused to reconsider its holding in the representation proceeding and ordered the University to bargain with the Union. . . . When the University still refused to sit down at the negotiating table, the Board sought enforcement in the Court of Appeals for the Second Circuit, which denied the petition. . . .

The Court concluded that such [faculty] power is not an exercise of individual professional expertise. Rather, the faculty are, "in effect, substantially and pervasively operating the enterprise." Accordingly, the court held that the faculty are endowed with "managerial status" sufficient to remove them from the coverage of the Act. We granted certiorari, 440 U.S. 906 (1979), and now affirm.

III

There is no evidence that Congress has considered whether a university faculty may organize for collective bargaining under the Act. . . . The Board has recognized that principles developed for use in the industrial setting cannot be "imposed blindly on the academic world." *Syracuse University*, 204 N.L.R.B. 641, 643 (1973).

IV

The status of such employees, in the Board's view, must be determined by reference to the "alignment with management" criterion. The Board argues that the Yeshiva faculty are not aligned with management because they are expected to exercise "independent professional judgment" while participating in academic governance, and because they are neither "expected to conform to management policies [nor] judged according to their effectiveness in carrying out those policies." Because of this independence, the Board contends there is no danger of divided loyalty and no need for the managerial exclusion. In its view, union pressure cannot divert the faculty from adhering to the interests of the university, because the university itself expects its faculty to pursue professional values rather than institutional interests. The Board concludes that application of the managerial exclusion to such employees would frustrate the national labor policy in favor of collective bargaining.

This "independent professional judgment" test was not applied in the decision we are asked to uphold. The Board's opinion relies exclusively on its previous faculty decisions for both legal and factual analysis.

V

The controlling consideration in this case is that the faculty of Yeshiva University exercise authority which in any other context unquestionably would be managerial. Their authority in academic matters is absolute. They decide what courses will be offered, when they will be scheduled, and to whom they will be taught. They debate and determine teaching methods, grading policies, and matriculation standards. They effectively decide which students will be admitted, retained, and graduated. On occasion their views have determined the size of the student body, the tuition to be charged, and the location of a school. When one considers the function of a university, it is difficult to imagine decisions more managerial than these. To the extent the industrial analogy applies, the faculty determines within each school the product to be produced, the terms upon which it will be offered, and the customers who will be served.

The Board nevertheless insists that these decisions are not managerial because they require the exercise of independent professional judgment. We are not persuaded by this argument. There may be some tension between the Act's exclusion of managerial employees and its inclusion of professionals, since most professionals in managerial positions continue to draw on their special skills and training. But we have been directed to no authority suggesting that that tension be resolved by reference to the "independent professional judgment" criterion proposed in this case.

VI

The question we decide today is a mixed one of fact and law. But the Board's opinion may be searched in vain for relevant findings of fact. The absence of factual analysis apparently reflects the Board's view that the managerial status of particular faculties may be decided on the basis of conclusory rationale rather than examination of the facts of each case. The Court of Appeals took a different view, and determined that the faculty of Yeshiva University "in effect, substantially and pervasively operate the enterprise." 582 F.2d at 698. We find no reason to reject this conclusion. As our decisions consistently show, we accord great respect to the expertise of the Board when its conclusions are rationally based on articulated facts and consistent with the Act. . . . In this case, we hold that the Board's decision satisfies neither criterion.

Affirmed.

Questions and Case Problems

1. Distinguish between a craft and an industrial union.
2. Can employers still request an injunction against a union group, even though we live in an age of enlightened human resource management?
3. The Mine Workers Union was trying to obtain and enforce a collective bargaining contract's clause. This clause would limit the coal operators to subcontracting coal hauling to "contractors employing union members." In their attempt to obtain this clause, the union forced the coal operators and coal haulers to sign a contract containing the clause in question. Is this clause legal? What would you call this clause? Explain. [*Feather v. Mine Workers,* 113 L.R.R.M. (BNA) 3367 (1983).]
4. The employer told employees that the company preferred that they supported and voted for the incumbent union rather than the outside union. In return, the

employees were promised wage increases, bonuses, and other improvements in their working conditions. Are these promises legal? Explain. [*New York Tel. Co. v. Communication Workers, Local 1108, AFL-CIO,* 112 L.R.R.M. (BNA) 1416 (1983).]

5. In the question above, the employer laid off one employee due to the worker's support for the outside union rather than the incumbent union. This layoff occurred after the employer had received a telegram stating that the worker was one of the outside union's supporters. Since the worker's duties still were essential and there was still a need for him in the factory, did the employer violate any laws by laying off this worker? Explain. [*New York Telephone Co. v. Communication Workers, Local 1108, AFL-CIO,* 112 L.R.R.M. (BNA) 1416 (1983).]
6. Four employees wore hats that specifically distinguished them from laborers. Their pay scale was twice that of the laborers and their job functions were supervisory. Is this a sufficient amount of evidence for the NLRB to exclude them from a bargaining unit with the laborers? [*Justak Bros. v. NLRB,* 664 F.2d 1074 (7th Cir. 1981).]
7. A local beverage manufacturer's union petitions to allow it to continue to picket in front of a neutral employer. They were hoping to influence consumers to buy only locally manufactured soda. In the absence of a conventional labor dispute, is the union's secondary boycott against a neutral employer a violation of labor law? [*Soft Drink Workers v. NLRB,* 657 F.2d 1252 (D.C. Cir. 1980).]
8. A union group of employees of Allis-Chalmers Mfg. Co. decides to engage in a lawful strike against Allis-Chalmers. Some employee members of the union decide they do not want to participate in the strike and so they cross the picket line. The union fines them. The employees claim their rights under Landrum-Griffin have been violated. Do they have a case? [*NLRB v. Allis-Chalmers Mfg. Co.,* 388 U.S. 175 (1967).]
9. A group of retired workers were concerned about their benefits. They requested that the union bargain with the employer about the benefit issue. Is an employer obliged to bargain about benefits for retired employees? [*Allied Chemical Workers Local v. Pittsburg Plate Glass,* 404 U.S. 157 (1971).]
10. In connection with the case of *NLRB v. Yeshiva University,* excerpted at the beginning of this section, the University refused to bargain with its faculty members, claiming that they were managerial employees. Do you consider faculty members to be managerial employees? What are the legal criteria for such a decision?

CHAPTER 37

ENVIRONMENTAL LAW

After you have read this chapter, you should be able to:

1. Understand the purpose and function of the National Environmental Protection Agency.
2. Discuss the major components of the National Environmental Policy Act.
3. Trace the development of the Clean Air Act and the Clean Water Act as recently amended.
4. Introduce the main concepts of the Toxic Substances Control Act, the Resource Conservation and Recovery Act, and the federal Environmental Pesticide Control Act.
5. Examine the four principal components of the Superfund Act and its imposition of "joint and several" liability.
6. Analyze the Noise Control Act and compare its strategy with that of the air and water Acts.
7. Highlight the provisions of the Endangered Species Act and its recent amendments.
8. Distinguish state from federal land use powers.

BUSINESS DECISIONS and the LAW

No one could ever accuse Eve and Martin Beebe of lacking an environmental conscience. As Midwesterners reared on small family farms, they were both "born" with a land ethic. At the small state university they attended in the late sixties, they were active in agricultural and environmental groups. After graduating with agriculture degrees and getting married, they joined the Peace Corps and were sent to a remote area of the Sudan, where they assisted in the development of an agricultural cooperative.

As a result of their background and experiences, the Beebes were influenced deeply by the traditional wisdom of cultivating "native" crops—crops that thrived under conditions of natural soil nutrition and rainfall. Although they were willing to adopt scientific agricultural methods, including pesticides and fertilizers, that appeared to be compatible with their beliefs and common sense, they never expanded these practices to the same degree as their toughest competitors—the modern agricorporations. Most of these farm complexes were mere operating divisions under the "umbrella" of multinational firms. Consequently, they were more capable than most farmers of surviving a bad year or two.

Today the Beebes were suffering economically. They had always taken great pride in carving out for their family a life that was challenging and rewarding, while at the same time showing immense respect for the land and its natural resources. They felt a kind of a "calling" to protect and preserve their land for future generations. Yet the Beebes' goal was being threatened more seriously than either of them wanted to acknowledge. One year of failing crops—brought on by a drought that had devastated the Midwest—and three years of marginal production had brought them to the brink of losing everything.

The Beebes were being offered a chance to solve their problems by devoting their entire acreage to a crop that got mixed reviews from the Department of Agriculture experimental station and from the state university. If the crop were a success, it would clear their accumulated debts and would distinguish them as truly innovative farmers—real "pioneers." By being willing to take risks with relatively untested crops and by using the latest agricultural technology, they could revitalize the farm economy in that region of the country. Raising this crop would, however, bring about a devastating change. They would have to clear the land of most other crops and concentrate on their experimental acreage.

Eve and Martin spent many hours formulating their decision. They searched through their old textbooks, looking for information about the environment and the controls that the government had placed on the production and use of agriculture-related chemicals. Some facts were promising, but there were no assurances that the intensive use of modern technology would not "foul the nest" for years.

As they walked on their land one particularly beautiful evening, Eve said to Martin, "I never expected it to come to anything like this. Did you?"

"No," he replied. "No matter what we do, things are going to be very different for us next year."

Introduction

One student defined the *environment* as "the universe, and all that surrounds it." This droll and provocative description, while accurate, is somewhat broad for our purposes. The focus of our present inquiry is the *ecosphere*—that intricate web of the earth's living things and the thin global skin of air, water, and soil that supports its existence. The *human environment* is still more complex because it does not consist merely of our physical surroundings—it encompasses the vast interplay of our emotional, intellectual, and cultural life as well.

A study of environmental law, then, is the study of humankind's efforts to regulate intrusions on the ecosphere, particularly those intrusions that stress the environment beyond its natural capacity to adjust. In the broadest sense, this includes worldwide and peaceful attempts to enhance the human environment as well. The efforts include measures designed to:

1. control population growth and minimize pollution;
2. encourage food production and an equitable distribution of the world's material goods;
3. regulate the extraction of nonrenewable resources and promote alternative energy technologies; and
4. bring the economic system into a harmonious relationship with the ecosystem.

As a practical matter, this chapter will be limited to an examination of environmental protective measures within the United States and how they interrelate to form a national strategy for maintaining the integrity of the ecosphere.

Federal Regulation—The Environmental Protection Agency

The Environmental Protection Agency (EPA) was established by a 1970 executive reorganization plan designed to consolidate federal environmental activities into a single agency.[1] The objective was to structure a coordinated response to a broad range of pollutants—air, water, noise, solid wastes, toxic chemicals, pesticides, and radiation. Generally speaking, Congress conferred upon EPA a twofold task: (a) creating national pollution standards, and (b) enforcement of these standards (normally in conjunction with the states).

The problems have been enormous, however. First, within each area, millions of dollars in research are needed to make way for enlightened regulation. Second, environmentally sound solutions often run into opposition from energy and production-minded interests—for example, emission control limits on automobiles sometimes frustrate fuel economy and production schedules. Finally, progress in one area may provoke difficulties in another area. To illustrate, cleaner air and water require the removal of solid and chemical wastes. Disposal of these wastes creates land-use problems that are not entirely within the jurisdiction of EPA. The cooperative efforts of federal, state, regional, and local governmental agencies are frequently essential to progress toward an environmentally acceptable solution. Such problems are not respecters of political boundaries.

The National Environmental Policy Act

The National Environmental Policy Act (NEPA)[2] is the kingpin of U.S. environmental laws. Contrary to popular belief, it does not set a single pollution standard for air, water, noise, radiation, hazardous substances, or solid wastes. Neither does it establish a veto over harmful environmental projects. The Council on Environmental Quality (CEQ), which was chartered by NEPA, merely serves as the president's policy advisor. It has issued regulations to all federal agencies on the implementation of NEPA,[3] but it does not have enforcement powers.

On the other hand, NEPA does firmly command a rigorous decision-making process for all agencies of the federal government. Federal agencies are required to implement these procedures to the fullest extent possible in order to achieve the environmental standards or goals set forth in Section 101:

1. Safe, healthful, productive, and esthetically and culturally pleasing surroundings.
2. Preserve important historic, cultural, and natural aspects of our natural heritage.

---

[1]Reorganization Plan #3 of 1970, 35 Fed. Reg. 15,623, 84 Stat. 2086 (1970).

[2]42 U.S.C. secs. 4321–4347, 83 Stat. 852, Pub. L. No. 91–190 (1970) as amended by Pub. L. No. 94–52 (1975), and Pub. L. No. 94–83 (1975).

[3]40 C.F.R. secs. 1500–1508.

3. Achieve a balance between population and resource use.
4. Enhance the quality of renewable resources and promote recycling of depletable resources.

Congress directed that all laws, policies, and regulations of the United States be interpreted and administered in accordance with NEPA. Federal agencies were ordered to utilize an interdisciplinary approach to decision making and to give environmental values appropriate consideration along with economic and technical factors.

► Environmental Impact Statements

The most dramatic innovation introduced by NEPA is the Section 102 requirement for Environmental Impact Statements (EIS). These statements must accompany every proposal for legislation and other major federal actions significantly affecting the quality of the human environment. CEQ regulations require the following format:

1. A statement of the purpose and need for the project.
2. A rigorous comparison of the reasonable alternatives.
3. A succinct description of the environment of the area to be affected by the proposed project.
4. A discussion of the environmental consequences of the proposal and of alternatives (including direct and indirect effects, energy requirements and conservation potential, mitigation measures, depletable resource requirements, impacts on urban quality and historic and cultural resources, and possible conflicts with state or local land-use plans, policies, and controls).
5. A list of the names and qualifications of the people primarily responsible for preparing the EIS and of the agencies to which the EIS was sent.
6. An appendix.

Purpose The genius of this approach is the early alert it gives federal agencies. Since Congress has established as a national policy that environmental values be integrated into the decision-making process to assure an overall balance, the EIS is designed to give *advance warning* of harmful environmental consequences. Full disclosure of all the environmental, technological, and economic pros and cons should avoid wasteful expenditures on projects and proposals that have not been well thought out. In short, NEPA simply requires the federal bureaucracy to do what conscientious citizens and taxpayers had every reason to expect in the first place. The CEQ regulations introduced a "scoping process," which requires prompt and full administrative analysis of important issues. The regulations also demand a written record that documents the reasonable alternatives, the steps taken to mitigate environmental harm, and the justification for the agency's decision.

Theory and Practice That, at least, is the way things are supposed to work. However, as everyone knows, there is frequently a big gap between theory and practice—and that is precisely the case with NEPA.

In the first place, NEPA, like the U.S. Constitution, is not self-executing. It relies upon the integrity of government bureaucracies, the alertness of concerned citizens, and the supervision of federal courts to carry out its mandate.

For example, when a federal agency undertakes a project, it must first determine whether the EIS process has been triggered—i.e., whether there is a major federal action significantly affecting the quality of the human environment. If, contrary to your own analysis, the agency decides that an impact statement is not necessary, there is no one except you or other concerned citizens to step in and do something about it. The Council on Environmental Quality is not authorized to stop the project; neither is the Environmental Protection Agency. Congress and the president have the power to influence an administrative decision, but NEPA does not supply an automatic stop on environmentally harmful projects. *People* have to make it work.

▶ NEPA and the Courts

Once an agency has prepared an EIS—and we will assume that the statement is a fair, adequate, and objective evaluation of the pros and cons—what happens if the agency decides to proceed with a project despite protests that it is environmentally disastrous? Does NEPA make demands beyond mere procedural compliance? Once the formalities of NEPA are satisfied, can the federal agency proceed with business as usual?

In *Vermont Yankee Nuclear Power Corp. v. Natural Resources Defense Council,* 435 U.S. 519 (1978), the Supreme Court overturned an appellate court case that found a Nuclear Regulatory Commission decision to be "arbitrary and capricious." In issuing Yankee Vermont a construction permit for a nuclear-fired electrical generated plant, the appellate court concluded that the NRC failed to consider all the relevant factors (energy conservation) and made a clear error of judgment (permitting an unnecessary plant).

In reversing this decision, the Supreme Court said that "NEPA does set forth significant substantive goals for the Nation, but its mandate to the agencies is *essentially procedural.*" This could mean that a certain amount of paper shuffling within federal bureaucracies is capable of meeting minimal procedural requirements without really doing anything to protect the environment. Alternatively, one could assume that federal civil servants have the kind of professional integrity that taxpayers are entitled to expect of them, and that they go beyond the bare minimum. In any event, there is an important role for concerned citizens here. NEPA allows citizens to intervene through appropriate legal measures and bring questionable governmental conduct into judicial focus.

In *Strycker's Bay Neighborhood Council, Inc., v. Karlen,* 444 U.S. 223 (1980), the Supreme Court held that environmental considerations were not necessarily "determinative" or "decisive" with regard to administrative projects that affect the quality of the human environment. A federal appellate court advanced the opposite view and concluded that HUD's mandate to consider environmental factors meant more than merely considering them in the sense of acknowledging their presence or discussing them. The appellate court believed that HUD (and, by implication, other federal agencies) should give environmental factors an overriding importance.

Citing the *Vermont Yankee* case for the proposition that a federal agency's NEPA duties are essentially procedural, the Supreme Court reversed the appellate decision:

> The National Environmental Policy Act cuts sharply against the Court of Appeals' conclusion that an agency, in selecting a course of action, must elevate environmental concerns over other appropriate considerations. On the contrary, once an agency has made a decision subject to NEPA's procedural requirements, the only role for a court is to insure that the agency has considered the environmental consequences.

▶ Citizen Suits

Citizens may file lawsuits to compel other persons, firms, or even governmental agencies to obey environmental protection statutes. These suits are specifically authorized by some statutes, but even when they are not, federal district courts have the jurisdiction, or power, to hear citizen actions if the citizen-plaintiff has standing to sue.

"Standing to sue" is legal jargon that encompasses two elements: (1) "injury in fact," meaning that the plaintiff must allege in the petition or pleadings filed in the trial court that some sort of environmental, conservational, aesthetic or other noneconomic injury has been suffered (for example, that the federal government has permitted a private construction company to build a bridge and that the construction will cause visual and other types of environmental pollution), and (2) "zone of interest," meaning that the injury is arguably within the scope or zone of protection that the law was designed to achieve (for example, that the bridge construction permit was granted without the preparation of an EIS required by NEPA).

Quite aside from this method of getting into court—a method analogous to "kicking down the door"—a number of federal environmental laws "invite" citizens to participate in the enforcement process by a specific grant of standing. The idea here is not only to make citizens feel like they are full partners in the effort to protect our environment but to encourage individual citizens and environmental groups to stand guard over the illegal pollution of private industry and over the ineptness or lack of enforcement zeal of governmental agencies.

The Clean Air Act, which we are about to examine, authorized citizen suits against *any person, including the U.S. government,* if they are in violation of an air pollution standard, or if they have ignored an enforcement order that had previously been issued by a federal or state agency. For example, a coal-fired electric generating plant owned by the Tennessee Valley Authority could be sued by a citizen if the plant was not in compliance with the law. Citizen-plaintiffs must give a sixty-day notice before bringing suit, and they cannot recover damages for personal injuries. However, these actions are so important to the efficient working of the enforcement process that they may be brought against the administrator of EPA if that person is not performing one or more mandatory duties that have been spelled out by Congress in the Act.

The Clean Water Act has comparable provisions that allow citizens to sue violators of water pollution standards, or EPA for not enforcing those standards, if the citizens' water-related interests are adversely affected. Again, damages for personal injuries are not recoverable, but attorney and expert witness fees are. Here, as under the Clean Air Act, the evidence used to establish these violations is based on the monitoring and record-keeping requirements of the law. These records are public information, meaning that they cannot be withheld as "trade secrets."

Citizen-suit provisions in other federal environmental protection statutes are basically variations on the theme established in the Clean Air Act and the Clean Water Act. The Resource Conservation and Recovery Act (RCRA) authorizes these suits against any person, including EPA, where past or present management or disposal of hazardous wastes has contributed to a situation that may present an imminent or substantial endangerment to human health or the environment. The notice or waiting period prior to filing suit under RCRA is ninety days, but that drops back down to sixty under the Toxic Substance Control Act (TSCA). Federal trial courts are empowered to hear citizen suits against the administrator of EPA alleging that the administrator has permitted some "unreasonable risk of injury to health or the environment" or has failed to perform some congressionally mandated duty. These suits may be initiated against private parties if they are in violation of any of the rules that EPA has published on the basis of TSCA. Finally, under Superfund, discussed on page 779, citizens who have expended their own funds in responding to a hazardous waste clean-up effort may bring suit in federal court for recovery of their costs. This provision reinforces the basic mission of the Superfund act, which was to make available an amount of money sufficient to clean up abandoned hazardous waste sites.

The Clean Air Act

▶ Introduction

The Clean Air Act Amendments of 1977 continue the impressive but difficult task that Congress undertook in 1970.[4] Implementation of the Act necessitated separate treatment of emissions from stationary sources (factories, utilities) and from mobile sources (automobiles, trucks). Control of both types was expected to lead to the achievement of ambient (surrounding) air quality standards by certain target dates. Figure 37.1 summarizes the chief pollutants by source and health effects.

▶ Stationary Sources

EPA was authorized by the 1970 Act to formulate *primary standards* to protect *public health,* and *secondary standards* to protect *public welfare*—visibility, vegetation, animal

FIGURE 37.1 Air Pollutants, by Sources and Health Effects

Pollutant	Source	Health Effect
1. Sulphur dioxide (SO_2)	Power plants; automotive emissions	Causes and aggravates respiratory ailments
2. Particulates	Power plants; oil and coal combustion; agricultural operations	Injury to lungs; throat and eye irritation
3. Carbon monoxide (CO)	Automotive emissions	Decreases blood oxygen; impairs heart functions; impairs visual perception and alertness
4. Photochemical oxidants (ozone)	Refineries; petrochemical plants; automotive emissions	Aggravates respiratory ailments; causes eye irritation
5. Nitrogen dioxide (NO_2)	Power plants; oil and coal combustion	Combines with hydrocarbons to form photochemical oxidants (ozone)
6. Hydrocarbons	Petroleum products, refineries, automobiles	Combines with nitrogen oxides to form photochemical oxidants (ozone)

[4] 42 U.S.C. secs. 1857–1858(a), 84 Stat. 1676, Pub. L. No. 91–604 (1970), as amended by 42 U.S.C. secs. 7401–7642, 91 Stat. 685, Pub. L. No. 95–96 (1977).

life. States were expected first to inventory their air quality and then to subdivide their geographical area into manageable air quality control regions (AQCR). Next, the states were required to hold public hearings and to formulate state implementation plans (SIPs) that described the means and methods of achieving those standards within each AQCR.

Each state was given three years following EPA approval of its SIP to reach the primary standard. A reasonable period of time was allotted for the secondary standard.

► Mobile Sources

Congress dealt with emissions from automobiles by requiring that carbon monoxide and hydrocarbons be reduced by 90 percent between 1970 and 1975 and nitrogen dioxides by 90 percent between 1971 and 1976. The EPA awarded automakers a two-year delay on these deadlines.

With regard to both stationary and mobile sources, great strides were made toward ambient air quality standards. None of them was achieved on the national level, however. This gave rise to the 1977 Clean Air Act Amendments.

► The 1977 Clean Air Act Amendments

Congress extended the basic strategy of the 1970 Act in its 1977 amendments. New SIPs were required to be submitted to EPA by January 1, 1979. The EPA then had six months to approve, disapprove, or seek state modification of the SIP. Attainment under these new plans was targeted for December 31, 1982. EPA regulations allow states to treat a plant as if it had a bubble over the top—the "bubble" concept—and to reduce high cost controls for a pollutant in exchange for an equal increase in the control of that pollutant in the same plant where abatement is less expensive.

For states that are seriously affected by automobile emissions and that had not attained the standards by 1982, revised plans to meet the standards by 1987 were required to be submitted. This meant that the 1977 amendments extended the deadline for most pollutants until 1982 and for automobile-related pollutants until 1987.

New SIPs begin with an air quality index of each AQCR. Next, the states detail their approach to *nonattainment* (dirty air) regions and *nondeterioration* (clean air) regions. Nonattainment regions include those AQCRs within the state that were not reaching the ambient air quality standards for one or more pollutants. Nondeterioration areas contain air of higher quality than the law demands. This may sound confusing, but a single AQCR could be classified nonattainment for one pollutant (a dirty air region for SO_2, for example) and nondeterioration for another (a clean air region for CO). It all depends on that region's mix of stationary and mobile sources.

► Nonattainment Areas

applicant
An individual or a firm seeking governmental permission to engage in some activity

If a SIP submitted by January 1, 1979 met EPA's approval within six months, then the air quality control board could begin evaluating permit **applicants** on July 1, 1979. After that date new or modified major stationary source applicants in nonattainment areas would be issued permits under the following conditions:

1. The net effect is reduced emissions (existing sources are retrofitted so that they will more than offset new or modified sources within the area).

2. The source meets lowest achievable emission rate.
3. All other facilities of the applicant within the state are in compliance.

If EPA rejects the SIP, then, until a new plan meets its approval, there can be no new industrial construction within the state. Additionally, EPA and Department of Transportation funds will be withheld, except funds for safety, mass transit, and air quality improvement projects.

▶ Prevention of Significant Deterioration

In those parts of the country where the air is cleaner than it is required to be under national standards, Congress established three air quality categories. Within these categories emission limitations have been established for particulates and sulfur dioxide. In 1980, EPA limitations for hydrocarbons, carbon monoxide, photochemical oxidants, and nitrogen oxides became effective.

In Class I, very little air pollution is tolerated. It includes international parks as well as national parks and wilderness areas in excess of 5,000 or more acres. (There are occasions, however, when a plant may receive a limited variance for sulfur dioxide emissions). Class II areas are susceptible to moderate amounts of air quality deterioration. In Class III areas, degradation is permissible to the limits of national primary standards. Except for certain federal lands discussed above, procedures are available to redesignate land from Class II to Class III so that industrial expansion may be accommodated.

▶ Enforcement

Congress placed at the disposal of EPA a variety of criminal and civil enforcement measures. The most innovative contribution of the 1977 amendments was an economic penalty that eliminated any cost advantage of being out of compliance. States can enforce their own air pollution laws if they do not substantially burden interstate commerce and if they have not been preempted by Congress. The following case illustrates this point.

FACTS

Illinois passed a law prohibiting the movement, from out of state, of any spent nuclear fuel for disposal or storage in Illinois. The Nuclear Regulatory Commission (NRC), however, was given comprehensive regulatory powers over such matters when Congress passed the Atomic Energy Act. With regard to the shipment and storage of spent nuclear fuel, inter- and intrastate, it appears that the federal government has totally pre-empted, or excluded, state legislation.

Nevertheless, Illinois argues, the Clean Air Act (CAA) authorizes it to nullify NRC authority: Section 116 provides that "nothing in this Act shall preclude or deny the right of any state . . . to adopt or enforce . . . any requirement respecting control or abatement of air pollution." Air pollution includes "radioactive substance or matter which is emitted into or otherwise enters the ambient air."

Is General Electric entitled to move spent nuclear fuel into Illinois despite this state statute?

DECISION

Yes. For General Electric. The Clean Air Act, Section 116, qualifies federal power under that Act only. It does not limit federal power under other statutes such as the Atomic Energy Act.

People of the State of Ill. v. General Electric Co., 683 F.2d 206 (7th Cir. 1982).

▶ Proposed Amendments to the Clean Air Act

In April 1990, the Senate passed and sent to the House of Representatives the first comprehensive set of amendments to the Clean Air Act since 1977. It is too early yet to predict the outcome of the House amendments, the adjustments that may be expected from a conference committee, and the impact of a threatened White House veto, or actual veto, but the main outlines are as follows. Automakers, chemical manufacturers, steelmakers, and coal-fired utility companies will be the hardest hit. The White House estimates that the cost to industry will be $20 billion a year over the next decade.

Both the Senate package and the expected House amendments address the problems of acid rain, smog, and toxic chemicals. Two stages of controls are being required to reduce tailpipe emissions from automobiles and to reduce emissions from plants that manufacture hazardous chemicals. The House version, but not the Senate's, would require the EPA to step in and enforce a plan to reduce urban smog and other pollution where the states are unwilling to act.

At this stage, the House is showing particular sensitivity to provisions that would reduce acid rain, but without causing economic hardship in coal-mining states. The hardship would be felt equally in Midwestern states because it is principally the coal-fired plants located in the Midwest that produce the emissions that are precipitated as acid rain over New England and Canada. Both versions of the bill will require sulfur dioxide emissions to be reduced by 10 million tons annually through the year 2000.

The 1977 Clean Water Act

▶ Background

The 1977 Clean Water Act (CWA) amended the 1972 Federal Water Pollution Control Act (FWPCA).[5] The announced goals of the 1972 Act were (1) no effluent discharges by 1985 and (2) water clean enough for swimming and other recreational values by 1983.

These goals were to be accomplished in stages—first, by establishing quality standards based on water use, such as human consumption, recreation, and industrial purposes; next, by treating effluents that are discharged into waters of the United States from *point* sources (e.g., ditches, pipers, defined channels). These effluents are controlled by EPA-specified technology. *Nonpoint,* or undefined, sources are dealt with through a planning process somewhat resembling SIPs under the Clean Air Act.

Industrial discharges were required to install the best practicable control technology by July 1, 1977, and the best available technology economically achievable by July 1, 1983. Municipalities were subjected to less stringent demands. Secondary treatment was required by 1977, and best practicable by 1983. For a fee, industrial dischargers could use municipal facilities if the effectiveness of these publicly owned treatment works was not jeopardized.

Both industrial and municipal discharges were required to obtain National Pollutant Discharge Elimination System (NPDES) permits prior to commencing operations. The permit system was designed to bolster the monitoring and enforcement provisions of the Act.

[5]33 U.S.C. secs. 1251–1376, 86 Stat. 816, Pub. L. No. 92–500 (1977), as amended by 91 Stat. 1567, 1575, Pub. L. No. 95–217 (1977).

▶ New Developments Under the 1977 CWA

Funding A *Buy America* provision requires funds to be spent on domestic construction materials. This section of the Act does not apply if EPA finds it to be inconsistent with the public interest, if costs are unreasonable, or if the materials are not available in satisfactory quality and quantity.

Effluent Requirements The 1977 CWA classified pollutants as conventional (sanitary waste), toxic (65 designated chemicals), and nonconventional (all other). Regarding conventional pollutants, EPA had to publish regulations and set effluent limitations requiring best conventional technology (BCT). Industrial compliance was targeted for July 1, 1984.

For toxic chemicals, the July 1, 1984 deadline was applicable as well. However, industry was required to comply with more stringent effluent limitation requirements —best available technology economically achievable (BAT). Nonconventional pollutants were to be controlled by BAT not later than July 1, 1984, with the possibility of a variance until July 1, 1987.

An evaluation of BCT and BAT performance since July 1, 1984, was undertaken in 1990. On the basis of this evaluation, the EPA is expected to make recommendations to the House and Senate following the passage of the 1990 Clean Air Act amendment.

▶ Enforcement

The civil and criminal enforcement sections of the Act substantially parallel those of the Clean Air Act. While there is no provision that deprives a firm of the economic advantage of noncompliance, it resembles the Clean Air Act in that states retain some flexibility in enforcing their own statutes. The following case illustrates this flexibility.

FACTS

The City of Chicago, defendant, adopted an ordinance providing that the sale of detergents containing any phosphorus constituted a criminal offense. The plaintiff, Proctor & Gamble, sought declaratory and injunctive relief, alleging that the ordinance violated the commerce clause of the U.S. Constitution in that it constituted an unconstitutional burden on interstate commerce.

DECISION

For the City of Chicago. The Proctor & Gamble Company could not prove convincingly that the Chicago City Council was wrong in its conclusion that limiting phosphorus in waters under its jurisdiction could someday be the key to clean water. The ordinance will not solve the problem, but it is a significant first step. Since interstate commerce is only slightly affected, and since states (and cities through their state-granted city charters) have Tenth Amendment powers to protect the public health, this ordinance is valid.

Proctor & Gamble Co. v. City of Chicago, 509 F.2d 69 (1975), cert. denied, 421 U.S. 978 (1975).

The Toxic Substances Control Act

Prior to the 1976 Toxic Substances Control Act (TSCA),[6] national policy addressed to the production and sale of toxic chemical substances was one of reaction from crisis to crisis.

[6] 15 U.S.C. secs. 2601–2629, 90 Stat. 2003, Pub. L. No. 94–469 (1976).

Toxicity and environmental studies were generally undertaken only after the damage had been done.

The 1976 Act revamped this essentially "wait and see" approach. The TSCA expanded, systematized, and exploited information on production, use, and toxicity to prevent hazardous environmental and human exposure.

Congress charted a course between affirmative clearance of new chemicals by EPA before sale and no premarket notification at all. The federal government can now control and stop the production or use of chemical substances that may present an unreasonable risk of injury to health or the environment. Manufacturers of new chemicals and chemicals for new uses must notify EPA ninety days prior to beginning production.

Manufacturers may also be required to test selected chemicals or to report production quantities, use, biological properties, and other information necessary for hazard assessment. The following criteria are used to pinpoint those substances that must undergo the rigorous testing procedures mandated by the Act:

1. Does substantial exposure to the chemical imply an unreasonable risk to health or the environment?
2. If data for predicting health and environmental effects are inadequate, testing is necessary to develop data.

The EPA was authorized to require reports on the name and identity of each chemical, proposed uses, production level, by-products, adverse effects, and number of workers exposed. Trade secrets and financial data required by the Act are confidential, but health and safety information is subject to public disclosure. Records of significant adverse health effects must be kept for thirty years; information regarding environmental damage must be kept for five years.

The Resource Conservation and Recovery Act of 1976

Within six months of enactment, the Resource Conservation and Recovery Act[7] required EPA to identify areas with common solid waste management problems and appropriate planning units. Not later than eighteen months following enactment, EPA was required to publish guidelines to aid state development of solid waste management plans. Ambient air standards, groundwater quality, waste collection, open dumps, resource recovery, and markets for recovered materials are the chief considerations of these management plans. Before EPA will approve the state plan:

1. state, local, and regional responsibilities must be identified;
2. strategy for coordinating regional planning must be specified;
3. establishment of new open dumps must be prohibited and old ones must be improved or phased out; and
4. nonhazardous wastes must be disposed of in sanitary landfills or used for resource recovery.

[7]42 U.S.C. secs. 6901–6987, 90 Stat. 2796, Pub. L. No. 89–272, as added Pub. L. No 94–580 (1976).

There are a number of incentives embodied in the plan—economic, technical assistance, and personnel training. While its success is largely contingent upon the states' voluntary acceptance of responsibility, there are certain coercive measures. If a state does not present a plan that meets EPA's approval, or if it does not revise the plan to accommodate EPA's objections, EPA can impose upon the state a plan of its own. The real effectiveness of such an alternative is open to question, however, because EPA simply does not have the resources to enforce it.

▶ Hazardous Wastes

One of the more significant features of the Act directs EPA to identify hazardous wastes that threaten the human environment. Once these wastes have been identified, owners and operators of hazardous waste treatment and storage facilities must apply for EPA permits (or state permits under EPA approved plans). Applications must detail composition, quantity, location, and the method and rate of disposal.

Essentially hazardous wastes are to be tracked from the manufacturing stage through transportation, treatment, storage, and disposal. A *manifest system* designed along a pathways approach is the chief component of this strategy. It is enforced with civil *and* criminal penalties, both with a maximum of $25,000 per day. Imprisonment for not more than one year is also a possibility.

The Superfund

The "superfund," created by the Comprehensive Environmental Response, Compensation, and Liability Act of 1980 (CERCLA),[8] was designed to eliminate threats to public health and to the environment from uncontrolled hazardous waste sites. The owners and operators of these hazardous waste sites, or the generators and transporters of the hazardous materials, are primarily responsible for the clean-up. If they do not do so voluntarily, or respond to EPA orders, EPA is authorized to get the job done. EPA's expenditures will be financed from the $9 billion Hazardous Substance Response Trust Fund, and the responsible parties will be "jointly and severally" liable for reimbursing EPA for the clean-up cost.

In a landmark case,[9] the U.S. sued 24 defendants who were allegedly responsible for the hazardous substances at the Ohio Chem-Dyne treatment facility. CERCLA does not specify "joint and several" liability, perhaps because that was a politically sensitive issue that Congress left for the courts to resolve, but the position of the Department of Justice was that the liability provisions of the Act allowed full recovery for the entire cost of clean-up from one, some, or all of the defendants.

The defendants moved for a summary judgment, which means that in the absence of a factual controversy, the law is sufficiently clear to permit a dismissal of the government's suit based on the pleadings alone. In other words, granting the motion would end this phase of the lawsuit—there would be no introduction of evidence nor would there be any further trial-level proceedings because the suit would be resolved "as a matter of law."

---

[8]42 U.S.C. sec. 9601 et seq. (1980).

[9]*United States v. Chem-Dyne Corp.*, 572 F.Supp. 802 (S.C. Ohio 1983).

The judge denied the defendants' motion and had the following to say about the recovery of clean-up costs:

> This recovery task may prove difficult when several companies used a site, when dumped chemicals react with others to form new or more toxic substances, or when records are unavailable. Nevertheless, those responsible for the problems caused by the hazardous wastes were intended to bear the costs and responsibilities for remedying the condition. The House sponsor, Representative Florio, commented at length:
>
>> The liability provisions of this bill do not refer to the terms strict, joint and several liability, terms which were contained in the version of H.R. 7020 passed earlier by this body. The standard of liability in these amendments is intended to be . . . strict liability . . . . I have concluded that despite the absence of these specific terms, the strict liability standard already approved by this body is preserved. Issues of joint and several liability not resolved by this bill shall be governed by traditional and evolving principles of common law. The terms "joint and several" have been deleted with the intent that the liability of joint tortfeasors be determined under common or previous statutory law.
>
> Typically, as in this case, there will be numerous hazardous substance generators or transporters who have disposed of wastes at a particular site. The term joint and several liability was deleted from the express language of the statute in order to avoid its universal application to inappropriate circumstances. An examination of the common law reveals that when two or more persons acting independently cause a distinct or single harm for which there is a reasonable basis for division according to the contribution of each, each is subject to liability only for the portion of the total harm that he has himself caused.
>
> But where two or more persons cause a single and indivisible harm, each is subject to liability for the entire harm. Restatement (Second) of Torts, sec. 875. Furthermore, where the conduct of two or more persons liable under CERCLA has combined to violate the statute, and one or more of the defendants seek to limit their liability on the ground that the entire harm is capable of apportionment, the burden of proof as to apportionment is upon each defendant.
>
> The question of whether the defendants are jointly or severally liable for the clean-up costs turns on a fairly complex factual determination. Read in the light most favorable to the United States, the following facts illustrate the nature of the problem. The Chem-Dyne facility contains a variety of hazardous waste from 289 generators or transporters, consisting of about 608,000 pounds of material. Some of the wastes have been commingled, but the identities of the sources of these wastes remain unascertained. The fact of the mixing of the wastes raises an issue as to the divisibility of the harm. Further, a dispute exists over which of the wastes have contaminated the groundwater, the degree of their migration, and the concomitant health hazard. Finally, the volume of waste of a particular generator is not an accurate predictor of the risk associated with the waste because the toxicity or migratory potential of a particular hazardous substance generally varies independently with the volume of the waste.
>
> This case, as do most pollution cases, turns on the issue of whether the harm caused at Chem-Dyne is "divisible" or "indivisible." If the harm is divisible and if there is a reasonable basis for apportionment of damages, each defendant is liable only for the portion of harm he himself caused. In this situation, the burden of proof as to apportionment is upon each defendant. On the other hand, if the defendants caused an indivisible harm, each is subject to liability for the entire harm. The defendants have not carried their burden of demonstrating the divisibility of the harm and the degrees to which each defendant is responsible.

The 1980 Act was built around four basic elements, which were extended, and reinforced, by amendments to the Act in 1986:

1. Owners of the hazardous waste site are required to notify EPA of the types of wastes buried there. The 1986 amendments require notification to state and municipal authorities, and to the general public as well.
2. The Act authorizes EPA to clean up hazardous spills in those cases where the responsible parties do not act. In accordance with this authorization, EPA has developed a National Contingency Plan that includes a National Priorities List of more than 400 sites that are given top priority consideration.
3. The original $1.6 billion trust fund has been increased to $9 billion.
4. Liability for the cost of clean-up is imposed on site owners, generators, and transporters. Congress left intact the decision in *United States v. Chem-Dyne,* which imposes joint and several liability on these parties. Under certain circumstances, these actions will be permitted to "pierce the corporate veil" and proceed against the responsible corporate officer individually and personally. Suits to recover compensation for death or personal injuries, however, are not covered by the Act. Plaintiffs must pursue those actions under state tort law.

The Noise Control Act of 1972

Both the Clean Air Act and the Clean Water Act begin with national quality standards. These standards, you recall, are to be achieved mainly through the application of appropriate technology.

The Noise Control Act[10] differs from this approach in that Congress did not establish a national standard of quietness. It focused instead on a technology-based strategy that required EPA to identify the principal sources of noise. Newly manufactured products so identified became subject to noise emission regulations set by EPA. These regulations are expected to be tough enough to protect public health, safety, and welfare while taking into consideration the following:

1. Conditions of product use
2. Amount of noise reduction achievable through the most modern technology available
3. Cost

The federal Act preempts state rules and regulations that are different from the required noise-suppressant technology of EPA-designated products. States can address the problem through their zoning authority, however, and may further limit the sound level by restricting the movement and operation of such products.

Products that do not conform to the requirements of the Act cannot be imported, nor can they be distributed in interstate commerce. In addition to this, manufacturers are not permitted to remove any noise-suppressant devices, notices, or labels required to be affixed to the product prior to its sale to the ultimate consumer. Any use of a product following the removal (or rendering inoperative) of its muffler system is forbidden as well.

[10]42 U.S.C. sec. 4901–4915 (1972).

Manufacturers must warrant the noise-emission components of each product against defects in materials and workmanship during useful product life (assuming normal maintenance and operation). EPA can require manufacturers to affix appropriate labels, maintain records, supply information, and conduct tests necessary to ascertain full compliance with the Act.

The principal incentive to encourage compliance is the requirement that federal agencies purchase EPA-designated low-noise-emission products if their cost does not exceed 125 percent of the retail price for a "reasonably substitutable" commodity. Civil and criminal sanctions are available to reinforce this and other provisions of the Act.

Pesticide Regulation

The federal Insecticide, Fungicide, and Rodenticide Act of 1947 and the federal Environmental Pesticide Control Act of 1972[11] require registration and labeling of agricultural pesticides. The objective is to prevent unreasonable risk to human life and health and to the environment, with the social, environmental, and economic costs and benefits being taken into account.

Pesticides must be classified for "general" or "restricted" use. Those within the latter category may be used only by or under the supervision of state-certified and EPA-approved applicators.

The use of any registered pesticide in a manner contrary to labeling instructions is prohibited. EPA may issue a "stop sale, use and removal" order when a pesticide is found to be in violation of federal statutes. Such pesticides may also be seized.

Manufacturing plants must be registered with EPA, and they must furnish information on the types and amounts of pesticides produced, distributed, and sold. Federal inspectors with appropriate warrants are entitled to enter and inspect such establishments and take samples.

Criminal sanctions for knowing violations ranging up to $1,000 or thirty days imprisonment (or both) can be imposed on farmers and private applicators. Registered manufacturers, commercial applicators, wholesalers, distributors, and retailers who knowingly violate the law face the possibility of a maximum $25,000 criminal fine or one year imprisonment (or both).

The Endangered Species Act

Most people never heard of the Endangered Species Act[12] until the now-famous snail darter was discovered in the waters of the Little Tennessee River. Approximately $102 million had been sunk into the Tellico Dam by this time and there was strong pressure for completion. *TVA v. Hill*[13] provides the U.S. Supreme Court's analysis of the Act, but Congress has since modified it to exclude the Tellico Dam from its coverage.[14]

---

[11]7 U.S.C. secs. 136–136y, 86 Stat. 975, Pub. L. No. 92–516 (1972), as amended by 87 Stat. 903, Pub. L. No. 93–205 (1973), 89 Stat. 754, Pub. L. No. 94–140 (1975).

[12]16 U.S.C. secs. 1531–43, 87 Stat. 884, Pub. L. No. 93–205 (1973), as amended.

[13]*Tennessee Valley Authority v. Hill,* 437 U.S 153 (1978).

[14]Pub. L. No. 96–69 (1979).

The Endangered Species Act authorizes the secretary of the interior, in consultation with representatives from the states, to designate species of fish, wildlife, and plants threatened with extinction and those that might become endangered in the foreseeable future. Federal agencies must avoid jeopardizing endangered species. Fines ranging from $1,000 to $10,000 can be imposed on private citizens who buy, sell, transport in interstate commerce, import, or export in violation of the Act.

Congress created a three-member review panel to examine controversial federal projects. The review is not undertaken, however, until all alternatives to the project have been pursued in good faith. After the review panel has compiled a detailed report on the merits of granting an exemption, the report is considered by a seven-person cabinet-level committee. The committee may then finally exempt a project on the basis of the following criteria:

1. The benefits of the project clearly outweigh benefits of alternative action consistent with conserving the species or its critical habitat.
2. The project is in the public interest.
3. There are no reasonable and prudent alternatives.

If the committee does not grant an exemption, the project cannot be continued. In the case of Tellico Dam, the statute remains intact, but the dam was removed from the committee's jurisdiction.

Land Use

In the final analysis, all pollution problems come down to decisions regarding land use. If property is zoned for industrial purposes or devoted to highway or automobile-related uses, air pollution is a likely result. With less land available for food production, demands for increased yields per acre require the application of chemical fertilizers, insecticides, and pesticides—and therefore invite their related problems. Land dedicated to airport and other transportation uses will likely raise complaints about excessive noise. Sanitary landfills frequently evoke criticism based on aesthetics, odor, and, perhaps, contamination of groundwater. The following examples document the relationship between pollution and land use, and include illustrations on the state and federal level.

► Zoning

zoning
The division of a geographical area by legislative regulation into districts, and the prescription and application of regulations concerning use and design of structures within those districts

Zoning of real property is discussed in detail in Chapter 47, Real Property and Its Ownership.

Zoning ordinances are exercises of local police powers—powers reserved under the Tenth Amendment to the U.S. Constitution, designed to protect the public health, morals, and safety. If zoning regulations exceed a certain degree, they amount to a taking, and the owner must be paid a reasonable value for the property so condemned. While no clear and unmistakable lines are drawn between regulation and taking, the prohibition of some uses merely amounts to regulation. If all uses are forbidden, or if title to the property is transferred to someone else, then a compensable taking has occurred.[15]

[15] *South Terminal Corp. v. EPA*, 504 F.2d 646 (1974).

Translated to environmental terms, this means that a state or the District of Columbia may take private property for the purpose of devoting it to a better balanced and more attractive community.

> Miserable and disreputable housing conditions may do more than spread disease and crime and immorality. They may also suffocate the spirit by reducing the people who live there to the status of cattle. They may indeed make living an almost insufferable burden. They may also be an ugly sore, a blight on the community which robs it of charm, which makes it a place from which men turn. The misery of housing may despoil a community as an open sewer may ruin a river.[16]

Private property may be *regulated* without payment of compensation to the owner. For example, the U.S. Supreme Court has upheld a zoning ordinance limiting to two the number of unrelated, unmarried persons forming a household. This caused certain landlords the loss of tenants—hence, an economic loss.

> It is said, however, that if two unmarried people can constitute a "family," there is no reason why three or four may not. But every line drawn by a legislature leaves some out that might well have been included. That exercise of discretion, however, is a legislative, not a judicial, function. . . . A quiet place where yards are wide, people few, and motor vehicles restricted are legitimate guidelines in a land-use project addressed to family needs. This goal is a permissible one. . . . The police power is not confined to elimination of filth, stench, and unhealthy places. It is ample to lay out zones where family values, youth values, and the blessings of quiet seclusion and clean air make the area a sanctuary for people.[17]

► Solar Zoning

A special application of zoning regulation—and one that you may fully expect to have an immense social impact in years to come—is solar zoning. In a sense, this means parceling out the sun's rays in a manner that accommodates both public and private interests.

Suppose, for example, that you and your spouse plan to build a home utilizing solar energy for heating and cooling. Typically, this will entail the installation of solar collectors on the roof and the use of a liquid or gaseous medium to transfer the heat for direct use (hot water tank, radiator, heat pump) or indirect use (storage as chemical energy in a battery).

The technology for these systems has been available for years and is relatively simple. Depending on the part of the country you are in (the sunny Southwest versus the cold Northeast) and the size of your house (currently solar collectors occupy roofspace that is the equivalent of 30 to 60 percent of floorspace), the system may cost from $4,000 to $14,000 and more with inflation. In any event, the investment necessary for solar heating is sufficiently large to make you think twice. At a minimum, you will expect certain assurances that the solar panels will not be shielded from the sunlight by obstructions on neighboring lands. The issue is simply this—are you entitled to the uninterrupted flow

---

[16] *Berman v. Parker,* 348 U.S. 26, 32–33 (1954).

[17] *Village of Belle Terre v. Boraas,* 416 U.S. 1 (1974).

of sunlight across adjacent property? Could you expect to win a lawsuit against an offending property owner if he caused obstruction of sunlight that would otherwise fall on your solar collectors? The following landmark case, which arose in Wisconsin a number of years ago, addresses a similar issue and reflects a movement among some courts to change the common law rule denying such relief.

FACTS

Plaintiff Prah's home was the first residence built in the subdivision, and although plaintiff did not build his house in the center of the lot, it was built in accordance with applicable restrictions. Plaintiff advised defendant, Maretti, that if the defendant's home were built at the proposed site it would cause a shadowing effect on the solar collectors on Prah's home, which would reduce the efficiency of the system and possibly damage the system. To avoid these adverse effects, plaintiff requested defendant to locate his home an additional several feet away from the plaintiff's lot line, the exact number being disputed. Plaintiff and defendant failed to reach an agreement on the location of defendant's home before defendant started construction. The Architectural Control Committee of the subdivision and the Planning Commission of the City of Muskego approved the defendant's plans for his home, including its location on the lot. Prah's appeal presents an issue of first impression whether the owner of a solar-heated residence states a claim upon which relief can be granted when he asserts that his neighbor's proposed residence (which conforms to existing deed restrictions and local ordinances) interferes with his access to an unobstructed path for sunlight across defendant-neighbor's property.

DECISION

For plaintiff-appellant Prah. The common law doctrine of private nuisance limits a landowner's right to use his property in a way that injures the rights of others. Property owners' rights are relative, not absolute; the uses by one must not unreasonably impair the uses or enjoyment of the other.

Defendant asserts that his right to develop his property in accordance with statutes, ordinances, and private covenants, without regard for the effects of such development on plaintiff's access to sunlight, stems from three fundamental public policy considerations: (1) such rights are limited only by the potential for causing physical damage; (2) loss of sunlight for aesthetic or illumination value is relatively unimportant; and (3) land development should not be restricted.

The court found these policy considerations no longer to be binding, however, and in reaching its decision for the plaintiff, concluded as follows:

> Courts should not implement obsolete policies that have lost their vigor over the course of the years. The law of private nuisance is better suited to resolve landowners' disputes about property development in the 1980s than is a rigid rule which does not recognize a landowner's interest in access to sunlight.

Prah v. Maretti, 321 N.W.2d 182 (Wis. 1982).

Despite the outcome in the Prah case, local zoning ordinances offer a more likely solution to solar zoning problems. For highly developed areas, zoning regulations in the form of building restrictions offer no easy answers. Many structures already existing would be characterized as nonconforming uses, and no controls could be installed until new ones take their place.

Zoning offers greater promise for newly developing rural and suburban areas, however. Restrictive covenants can be useful as well.[18] Height limitations placed on houses and other buildings will assure neighboring property owners of uninterrupted, direct sunlight.

Such restrictions are quite in line with traditional measures to promote open spaces and an aesthetically pleasing community. There are no constitutional or other prohibitions that would frustrate this approach. Of course, it is not an overnight solution. Local governing bodies prodded by thoughtful citizens will need to phase in these controls in anticipation of expanded use. This pattern of development is illustrative of the adaptability and flexibility of our legal system when confronted with a new and exciting challenge.

► Federal Land Use—Surface Mining

There is no single comprehensive piece of federal legislation that controls land use. About one-third of the nation's land is federally owned, and it ranges from wilderness areas to multiple-use lands that may be leased for minerals, timber, and grazing. In addition to the federal antipollution laws discussed so far, tax laws, federally guaranteed loan programs, and agricultural subsidies influence the use of privately owned land that is within the jurisdiction of state and local zoning authorities.

The Surface Mining Control and Reclamation Act of 1977,[19] based on Congress' commerce power, regulates the use of privately owned land. In line with the Clean Air Act and Clean Water Act, the regulatory functions will be carried out by the states if permanent regulatory programs meeting minimum federal standards are enacted by state legislatures. Otherwise, the program will be administered by the Department of the Interior.

As a prerequisite for eligibility to administer its own regulatory program, each state must establish a mechanism for designating certain lands as unsuitable for mining. As for the land that is appropriate for development, mine operators are required to restore topsoil and revegetate after mining, and treat harmful minerals so that groundwater and surface water will not be contaminated.

Prime farmlands cannot be mined unless the operator has the technological capacity to restore the area to equivalent or higher levels of yield. Alluvial valley floors cannot be mined if the mining would damage farming in the valleys or the quantity or quality of waters that supply the valley floors.

Reclamation plans must be filed by the mine operator as part of the permit application, and a $10,000 performance bond must be posted as well. Where federal coal lies beneath privately owned land, the consent of the owner is necessary before operations can begin. There is no legal maximum that can be demanded by the surface owner for this privilege.

A citizen-suit provision allows any person who is or may be adversely affected by some failure to comply with this Act to file suit against the responsible regulatory body. Finally, the Act created an abandoned mine reclamation fund to repair land from

---

[18] In Colorado, a sun state, some lending institutions require easements as a condition of making a loan for a solar system.

[19] 30 U.S.C. secs. 1201–1328, 91 Stat. 447, Pub. L. No. 95–87 (1977).

previous strip operations, and it established within the Department of the Interior the Office of Surface Mining Reclamation and Enforcement to administer the Act's provisions.

Summary Statement

1. The National Environmental Policy Act (NEPA) established high goals of environmental protection to be achieved through vigorous decision-making procedures.
2. Environmental Impact Statements (EISs) guide proposals for legislation and other major federal actions that significantly affect the quality of the human environment.
3. NEPA created the Council on Environmental Quality (CEQ) as a policy advisor to the president, and by Executive Order the president organized the Environmental Protection Agency (EPA) to exercise certain important standard setting and enforcement functions.
4. The proposed amendments to the 1977 Clean Air Act attack the problem of acid rain by requiring a significant reduction in sulfur dioxide emissions and the problem of urban air pollution by strengthening automobile tailpipe emissions standards.
5. The 1977 Clean Water Act continues to focus chiefly on *point* sources of pollution. It requires the application of the *best conventional technology* (BCT) for most pollutants and the *best available technology economically achievable* (BAT) for toxic and nonconventional wastes. The National Pollutant Discharge Elimination System requires the installation of this technology before permits are granted to dischargers of conventional, toxic, or nonconventional effluents. Industrial compliance was targeted for 1984, and a 1990 EPA evaluation was expected to contribute to pending legislation.
6. EPA was empowered by the 1976 Toxic Substances Control Act to control and stop the manufacture or use of chemicals that may present unreasonable risk of injury to health or the environment. Manufacturers may be required to test chemicals, and their reports to EPA are public information.
7. Solid waste management problems are the subject of the 1976 Resource Conservation and Recovery Act. It embodies economic, technical, and other incentives, but success depends upon full state cooperation. Hazardous wastes are given special treatment by the Act—they are literally tracked by a permit system from manufacture through disposal.
8. The Superfund Act requires owners of hazardous waste sites to notify EPA, state, and municipal authorities of the types of waste buried there, authorizes EPA to clean up hazardous spills if the owners do not act, imposes liability for clean up costs on site owners, generators, and transporters of hazardous waste, and, in the event that responsible parties cannot be located or are insolvent, authorizes reimbursement of EPA for clean up expenditures out of a $9 billion trust fund.
9. The 1972 Noise Control Act authorized EPA to identify newly manufactured products that are principal sources of noise and to require the application of noise-suppressant technology. EPA regulations are intended to protect public health, safety, and welfare while taking into consideration product use, noise-reduction technology, and cost.
10. The 1972 Federal Environmental Pesticide Control Act—amending earlier legislation—controls registration, labeling, and application of pesticides. Its objective is to prevent unreasonable risk to human life and health and to the environment,

while taking into account the social, environmental, and economic costs and benefits.

11. The Endangered Species Act as amended authorizes the secretary of the interior to protect certain plants, fish, and wildlife (including their habitat) from extinction. If federal projects jeopardize the life or habitat of endangered species, a seven-person cabinet-level panel must determine the outcome.

12. State and federal governments formulate land-use policies. Whether a state is proceeding on its U.S. Constitution Tenth Amendment reserved powers, or the federal government on its Article I legislative powers, a just compensation must be paid to the private landowner for property that is taken for a public purpose. If the private property is merely regulated, for example, through local zoning ordinances or federal strip-mining controls, the landowner is not entitled to compensation.

The Metropolitan Edison case will communicate a sense of the complexity involved in deciding whether the National Environmental Policy Act requires the Nuclear Regulatory Commission to consider potential psychological harm in evaluating Metropolitan Edison's petition to resume operations at Three Mile Island.

METROPOLITAN EDISON COMPANY v. PEOPLE AGAINST NUCLEAR ENERGY
103 S. Ct. 1556 (1983)

Rehnquist, Justice. The issue in these cases is whether petitioner Nuclear Regulatory Commission (NRC) complied with the National Environmental Policy Act, 42 U.S.C. Section 4321 *et seq.* (NEPA), when it decided to permit petitioner Metropolitan Edison Co. to resume operation of the Three Mile Island Unit 1 nuclear power plant (TMI-1). The Court of Appeals for the District of Columbia Circuit held that the NRC improperly failed to consider whether the risk of an accident at TMI-1 might cause harm to the psychological health and community well-being of residents of the surrounding area. . . . We reverse.

. . . . .

Petitioner People Against Nuclear Energy (PANE), intervened and responded to this invitation. PANE is an association of residents of the Harrisburg area who are opposed to further operation of either TMI reactor. PANE contended that restarting TMI-1 would cause both severe psychological health damage to persons living in the vicinity, and serious damage to the stability, cohesiveness, and well being of the neighboring communities.

. . . . .

The Court of Appeals concluded that the Atomic Energy Act does not require the NRC to address PANE's contentions. . . . It did find, however, that NEPA requires the NRC to evaluate "the potential psychological health effects of operating" TMI-1 which have arisen since the original EIS was prepared. . . . It also held that, if the NRC finds that significant new circumstances or information exist on this subject, it shall prepare a "supplemental [EIS] which considers not only the effects on psychological health but also effects on the well being of the communities surrounding Three Mile Island." We granted certiorari.

All the parties agree that effects on human health can be cognizable under NEPA, and that human health may include psychological health. The Court of Appeals thought these propositions were enough to complete a syllogism that disposes of the case: NEPA requires agencies to consider effects on health. An effect on psychological health is an effect on health. Therefore, NEPA requires agencies to consider the effects on psychological health asserted by PANE.

• • • • •

PANE, using similar reasoning, contends that because the psychological health damage to its members would be caused by a change in the environment (renewed operation of TMI-1). NEPA requires the NRC to consider that damage. . . . Although these arguments are appealing at first glance, we believe they skip over an essential step in the analysis. They do not consider the closeness of the relationship between the change in the environment and the "effect" at issue.

Section 102(C) of NEPA directs all federal agencies to

> include in every recommendation or report on proposals for legislation and other major Federal actions significantly affecting the quality of the human environment, a detailed statement by the responsible official on—
> (i) the environmental impact of the proposed action, [and]
> (ii) any adverse environmental effects which cannot be avoided should the proposal be implemented. . . .

To paraphrase the statutory language in light of the facts of this case, where an agency action significantly affects the quality of the human environment, the agency must evaluate the "environmental impact" and any unavoidable adverse environmental effects of its proposal. The theme of Section 102 is sounded by the adjective "environmental": NEPA does not require the agency to assess *every* impact or effect of its proposed action, but only the impact or effect on the environment. If we were to seize the word "environmental" out of its context and give it the broadest possible definition, the words "adverse environmental effects" might embrace virtually any consequence of a governmental action that some one thought "adverse." But we think the context of the statute shows that Congress was talking about the physical environment—the world around us, so to speak. NEPA was designed to promote human welfare by alerting governmental actors to the effect of their proposed actions on the physical environment.

• • • • •

. . . Thus, although NEPA states its goals in sweeping terms of human health and welfare, these goals are *ends* that Congress has chosen to pursue by *means* of protecting the physical environment.

To determine whether Section 102 requires consideration of a particular effect, we must look at the relationship between that effect and the change in the physical environment caused by the major federal action at issue.

• • • • •

Some effects that are "caused by" a change in the physical environment in the sense of "but for" causation, will nonetheless not fall within Section 102 because the causal chain is too attenuated. For example, residents of the Harrisburg area have relatives in other parts of the country. Renewed operation of TMI-1 may well cause psychological health problems for these people. They may suffer "anxiety, tension and fear, a sense of helplessness," and accompanying physical disorders . . . because of the risk that their relatives may be harmed in a nuclear accident. However, this harm is simply too remote from the physical environment to justify requiring the NRC to evaluate the psychological health damage to these people that may be caused by renewed operation of TMI-1.

Our understanding of the congressional concerns that led to the enactment of NEPA suggests that the terms "environmental effect" and "environmental impact" in Section 102 be read to include a requirement of a reasonably close causal relationship between a change in the physical environment and the effect at issue. This requirement is like the familiar doctrine of proximate cause from tort law. See generally W. Prosser, Law of Torts ch. 7 (4th ed. 1971). The issue before us, then, is how to give content to this requirement. This is a question of first impression in this Court.

• • • • •

PANE argues that the psychological health damage it alleges "will flow directly from the risk of [a nuclear] accident." But a *risk* of an accident is not an effect on the physical environment. A risk is, by definition, unrealized in the physical world. In a causal chain from renewed operation of TMI-1 to psychological health damage, the element of risk and its perception by PANE's members are necessary middle links. We believe that the element of risk lengthens the causal chain beyond the reach of NEPA.

• • • • •

We do not mean to denigrate the fears of PANE's members, or to suggest that the psychological health damage they fear could not, in fact, occur. Nonetheless, it is difficult for us to see the differences between someone who dislikes a government decision so much that he suffers anxiety and stress, someone who fears the effects of that decision so much that he suffers similar anxiety and stress, and someone who suffers anxiety and stress that "flow directly" from the risks associated with the same decision. It would be extraordinarily difficult for agencies to differentiate between "genuine" claims of psychological health damage and claims that are grounded solely in disagreement with a democratically adopted policy. Until Congress provides a more explicit statutory instruction than NEPA now contains, we do not think agencies are obliged to undertake the inquiry.

Questions and Case Problems

1. Congress designed Environmental Impact Statements to give an "early alert" regarding the environmental consequences of certain federal actions. How is this early alert system implemented?
2. Among the purposes of the Clean Air Act of 1970, Congress established the following:

   > To protect and enhance the quality of the Nation's air resources so as to promote the public health and welfare and the productive capacity of its population

   Following EPA approval of State Implementation Plans that allowed industrial expansion in previously undeveloped and underdeveloped regions, the Sierra Club brought suit alleging that this section of the Clean Air Act had been violated. EPA argued that the plans it approved promoted industrial growth and protected against air pollution below the national standards. Result? [*Sierra Club v. Ruckelshaus,* 344 F.Supp. 253 (1972), aff'd 412 U.S. 541 (1973).]
3. Discuss the strategy established by Congress in the 1970 Clean Air Act. What is the relationship between the approach to stationary and mobile sources?
4. Discuss the approach Congress took to clean air areas and dirty air areas under the 1977 Clean Air Act Amendments.
5. New York City, defendant, enacted an ordinance requiring exhaust emission controls for licensed taxicabs. The plaintiffs, fifteen licensed taxicab companies, sought an injunction prohibiting enforcement of the ordinance and a declaratory judgment that it was null and void. The cab companies argued that the New York City ordinance both conflicted with the Clean Air Act and was pre-empted by it. Result? [*Allway Taxi, Inc. v. City of New York,* 340 F.Supp. 1120 (S.D.N.Y. 1972) aff'd per curiam 468 F.2d 624 (1973).]
6. The Eden Roc Hotel, plaintiff, in Miami Beach, Florida, objected to a fourteen-story addition by a competitor, the Fontainebleau Hotel Corp., defendant, because it shaded portions of Eden Roc's pool and beach. Plaintiff petitioned the court for an injunction restraining the defendant's construction. Eden Roc based its suit on the doctrine of Ancient Lights, an English common law concept that the uninterrupted use of light through a window for twenty years or more gave the recipient an easement that the adjoining landowner cannot terminate. Result? [*Fontainebleau Hotel Corp. v. Forty-five Twenty-five, Inc.,* 114 S.2d 357 (Fla. 1959).]

7. Since the 1972 federal Water Pollution Control Act, the United States no longer pins its clean-up efforts exclusively on water quality standards. It requires effluent-control technology as well. What is the difference between these two approaches? Discuss.
8. The Toxic Substances Control Act may require manufacturers to test selected chemicals. What are the criteria that are used to determine those substances that must undergo the testing procedures mandated by the Act?
9. Compare the approach Congress took in establishing national uniform clean air standards with its approach in establishing noise standards under the Noise Control Act of 1972.
10. In *Metropolitan Edison Company v. People Against Nuclear Energy,* excerpted at the beginning of this section, the Supreme Court reversed a Court of Appeals decision that would have required the Nuclear Regulatory Commission to prepare an Environmental Impact Statement prior to the resumption of operations at a Three Mile Island plant. The Supreme Court agreed with the appeals court that human health effects were covered by NEPA, and that human health may include psychological health. Nevertheless, the Supreme Court concluded that the "logic" of the appeals court's decision was faulty. Explain the defect in the appeals court's logic as expressed by Chief Justice Rehnquist.

PART 7: GOVERNMENT REGULATION OF BUSINESS

ETHICS AND BUSINESS LAW

Introduction

This end-of-part discussion, like the others in this book, is designed to encourage students to begin forming personal beliefs about what is right or wrong conduct in business. The discussion here builds on the material in the first end-of-part discussion; you may find it helpful to review that.

This material has several goals. The "sampling of ethical issues" section immediately following is designed to help you see the range of ethical issues associated with this area of the law. The in-depth discussion is intended to provide you with a background for forming your own beliefs about a single very important ethical issue in business. The problems at the end of this part are designed to build your skill in ethical analysis while exploring further the in-depth issue.

A Sampling of Ethical Issues in Government Regulation of Business

Antitrust law is designed in large part to reduce the power which businesses have over one another and over consumers. Most basically, it raises the issue of when, and to what extent, one may ethically exercise power over another. Managers have a great deal of power over their subordinates and they must often decide when, and to what extent, they are justified in exercising that power. Under what circumstances do you think you are justified in exercising power over those with whom you do business?

Administrative law raises interesting ethical issues. One is associated with the delegation of legislative powers. Legislatures seek to advance the will of those governed. When authority is delegated to an administrative agency, the agency is not subject to the same pressures as elected representatives. Also, their technical expertise tends to give them a certain degree of freedom to do what they judge is ethically right. Do you think an administrative agency is ever justified in, for example, ignoring the desires of the electorate and doing what it thinks is ethically right? Would you ever be ethically justified in ignoring the desires of your superiors and doing what you think is ethically right? Would you ever be ethically justified in ignoring the desires of your subordinates and doing what you think is ethically right?

Administrative hearings are generally conducted with different procedures from those used in court trials. One difference is that hearsay evidence is admissible in an administrative hearing and often inadmissible in trials. What procedures do you think lead to more ethical decisions, those which completely exclude hearsay evidence or those which allow it?

Labor law is one of the most ethically intense areas of business law. A fundamental ethical issue of this body of law is its adversarial nature. Labor law creates a structure which often causes employers and employees to perceive each other as in hostile, instead of in collaborative, ways. Other countries, such as Japan and Germany, have approached labor relations law in ways which are not as adversarial and which do not create as much conflict. But doing this sometimes deprives workers of the power to shape the nature of their working lives through the threat of strikes. And some employers would certainly take advantage of workers who were less powerful. Which style of relationship do you find most ethically appealing, one of respect based on fear of a strike, or one based on trust which could be easily betrayed?

Environmental law also raises interesting ethical issues of great concern to society. There is conflict between those who advocate preservation of natural conditions of land, water, and air in the environment and those who would consume some of these resources without paying society for them for their own self-interest. For example, a company may pollute the water in a stream, river, or harbor by the discharge of the by-products of its manufacturing process.

In-Depth Discussion of a Basic Issue: Market Power

▶ Market Failures

In studying antitrust law, labor law, and environmental law you have been examining the way the legal system addresses problems in the operation of the marketplace, or what are sometimes called "market failures." In a sense, antitrust law is concerned with keeping either sellers or buyers from escaping the forces of the marketplace. In large part, labor law arises out of the economic reality that there are very many workers and, in some locations at least, few employers; therefore employers have a large amount of power over those whom they hire. Environmental law is concerned with the problem of avoiding costs by shifting them to others such as those who breathe the polluted air or use the contaminated rivers.

The law has been quite effective in dealing with these major problems of market failure. However, there are in business many opportunities to exploit other, unregulated, market failures to our own benefit. Because there are opportunities, we must make decisions about whether it is ethical for us to exploit them. In order to have mature views in this area, you need a refined understanding of market power. This concept is the key to sophisticated resolution of many of the ethical dilemmas in business.

▶ Historical Views

Many important moralists have given substantial thought to the practices of businesses and the operations of markets.

Aristotle, Aquinas, and Luther These persons all wrote about market power. In general, their major concern has been with "extortion" and "exploitation" of poor or powerless persons in the marketplace. For some time this concern was expressed in the condemnation of what was called "usury," the charging of interest on money loaned. This condemnation occurred before people realized that there was a time value associated with the possession of money—that one dollar today is worth more to almost everyone than one dollar twenty-five years from today. Because these moralists did not clearly perceive this time value concept, they viewed the charging of interest as a manifestation of market power in which the party with money to lend was able to "unjustly extort" interest from a desperate borrower. Careful reading of their works reveals that it was the exercise of market power that they condemned rather than simply the collection of interest.

Adam Smith's View In his 1776 treatise on economics entitled *The Wealth of Nations,* Adam Smith originated the now well-known phrase "the invisible hand" to describe in summary fashion one moral characteristic of free markets. In his words:

> As every individual . . . endeavors as much as he can both to employ his capital in the support of domestic industry, and so to direct industry that its produce may be of greatest value; every individual necessarily labors to render the annual revenue of the society as great as he can. He generally, indeed, neither intends to promote the public interest, nor knows how much he is promoting it . . . he intends only his own gain, and he is in this, as in many other cases, led by an invisible hand to promote an end which was no part of his intention.

Smith's ideas can be stated more directly and in more modern language as follows: Market competition among individuals pursuing self-interest, yields a socially optimal allocation of society's scarce resources. The marketplace exists when independent parties, acting freely, buy and sell from one another. If you sold this book to another student, the transaction would be viewed as occurring in a marketplace—the one for used books.

► Philosophic Goals and Markets

Persons with different philosophical perspectives have differing views of the role of marketplaces. However, it is reasonably clear that the marketplaces are primarily utilitarian in character. They are means to some end. While we may not all agree on what that end is, or ought to be, most people in this country agree that the marketplace achieves some ends that they find desirable. To a large extent, business persons define their moral character by the marketplace ends that they elect to emphasize.

The major philosophic goals or ends are the following:

1. Personal pleasure: markets allow us to get rich or spend our earnings to buy things which give us pleasure.
2. Personal liberty: markets are created by decisions made by large numbers of producers and consumers. Thus, no person or organization has very much power over anyone else.
3. Social wealth: markets allocate resources in ways which maximize the material well-being of society.
4. Service: markets are viewed by many religious persons as vehicles for satisfying the material needs of society.

Certainly egoists would embrace the view that markets ought to maximize personal pleasure. And religious persons would see services as the market's main legitimate purpose. Personal liberty and social wealth might be a desired goal for all four groups: egoists, utilitarians, Kantians and religious persons.

▶ Market Imperfections

As we said in end-of-part 1, when markets work perfectly, they often cause persons with differing philosophical perspectives to behave in the marketplace in about the same way. Thus, an egoist and a religious person might act the same way in a perfect market. On the other hand, when markets work imperfectly, they often force persons to elect one of the competing philosophical perspectives over the others. Accordingly, it is important that every business person know clearly what his or her personal philosophical perspective is and that he or she be able to determine when markets are operating imperfectly.

We have identified the following imperfections:

1. Too few sellers or too few buyers;
2. Barriers to entry, which keep either new buyers or new sellers from entering a particular market;
3. Imperfect knowledge by either a buyer or a seller;
4. Externalities, that is, costs such as pollution, which are not borne by the appropriate buyer or seller;
5. Agency costs, that is, a cost created to benefit the agent rather than the principal.

These imperfections can also be classified as those that create market power and those that create externalities. The first three imperfections cause one party in a marketplace transaction to have market power.

▶ When Market Power Exists

Market power exists when someone operating in the marketplace has, because of imperfections in a particular market, more power than he or she would have in a perfectly functioning marketplace. Market power exits when one party—buyer or seller—has more influence over the terms of the transaction than the other party. An extreme example of market power can be easily seen in a situation in which there is a single firm selling a product that cures cancer. Even if the firm's cost of research, production, marketing and distribution were only $1.00 per unit, it could set a much higher price. If, however, there were ten firms selling this product, the competition among them would drive down the price. Thus, with only one firm its market power allows it to control the price, but with ten firms the marketplace determines price.

▶ The Exercise of Market Power

An individual who achieves market power must decide whether or not to exercise it. If one views personal pleasure as the basic goal of the marketplace, then it is logical to use the market power to enhance your wealth and pleasure. Suppose, for example, that you owned the only electrical generator for sale in a small town affected by a power outage. This creates an imperfection because there is only one seller and many potential buyers. You might, if egoistic pleasure were your basic goal, auction off the generator to the highest cash bidder—perhaps the wealthiest person in town.

If your view of the market is that its basic function is the reduction of power of people over each other, and the associated increase in individual liberty, you might decline to auction the generator and perhaps allow the group to draw lots to determine how to use it.

If your view of the market is that its basic function is material service to society, you might logically decline to auction off the generator out of a sensitivity to the fact that the imperfection in this situation—one seller—prevents the market mechanism from maximizing service to society. You might, in trying to maximize service, make a gift of the generator, perhaps to a local hospital.

If you consider the market's greatest goal to be maximization of social wealth, you might again recognize the imperfections in the marketplace and negotiate a fair sale of the generator, instead of auctioning it, to the largest employer in the community so jobs would be preserved.

Solving Ethics Problems

Like the other end-of-part discussions in this book, this one presents problems for you to consider. These problems have three goals. The first is to give you the opportunity to further explore the in-depth issue. The second goal is to give you experience in ethical reasoning about the law and about related management problems. The third goal is to let you see how thinking critically about the law can increase your ability to make ethical decisions. To facilitate this, the problems begin by asking you to analyze the law for its ethical content and then shift to looking at related problems in managerial ethics.

For a discussion of the ethical roles of markets and the law, and examples of the four styles of ethical reasoning—egoism, utilitarianism, Kant's philosophy, and religious ethics—read the business ethics material at the end of part 1.

► Problems

1. Recall the case of *In re Dean Milk Company* on page 734. There Dean Milk Co. was one of the larger milk sellers in the region and smaller dairies were often going out of business. Dean charged lower prices in some markets than in others. As a result, small dairies in an area where Dean's prices were low had a difficult time operating profitably. The FTC held that this conduct violated section 2(a) of the Clayton Act which prohibits price discrimination. What is the ethical goal of this statute? If there were no law against price discrimination, do you think it would be ethical to engage in the same conduct as Dean?
2. Suppose you owned the only gasoline station in a rural town. Since there is only one station, you have substantial market power. Assume that many residents would gladly pay an additional fifteen cents per gallon rather than drive the fifty miles to the next town. You know that such a price increase is perfectly legal. Would you raise your price as high as you possibly, and profitably, could, or would you decline to completely exploit your market power? What styles of reasoning support your decision?
3. Suppose you are the chief purchasing agent for a large aerospace firm. One of your responsibilities is arranging for the janitorial services for the firm's local offices. The firm currently doing the work is going out of business. Three other local firms do janitorial work. After receiving sealed bids from these firms, you have the opportunity to "whipsaw" the firms, playing one against the other in the bidding process. You could call one firm and disclose the amount of the lowest bid and ask if it would be willing to do the work for at least 10 percent less than that bid. If that firm says yes, you could call a second firm and ask if it will go even lower. This process can be continued in some situations until you have driven almost all of the profit (often

even much of the overhead) out of the supplying firms' bids. Will you accept the first bids or will you "whipsaw?" Why or why not?

4. Suppose you are the marketing manager of a profit-making firm that has discovered a way to collect whole blood, process it into plasma, and store it for long periods of time. As a result the firm always has on hand a large inventory of blood plasma. The market for plasma is usually very stable because the rate of consumption is—most of the time—relatively uniform across the country. Occasionally there is a major disaster, such as an earthquake or a hurricane, which dramatically increases the demand by hospitals for plasma. If, as marketing manager, you carefully price your product to reflect market conditions, charging one normal price and another much higher price during emergencies, you can substantially increase the profitability of the firm. Would you recommend to your firm that it use such pricing policies? Why or why not?

PART 8

BUSINESS ORGANIZATIONS
A. General Partnerships and Special Ventures

PREVIEW

The oldest known form of business organization is the partnership. Although partnerships are easy to create, their structure is complex with consequent exposure to liability. If you ever become a partner, these chapters will help you understand the managerial problems you can expect to encounter. As a partner you will have many legal rights and duties to your co-partners as well as to third persons dealing with your firm. These chapters explain the resulting rights and duties.

Chapter 41, Special Ventures, will acquaint you with various types of noncorporate business ventures, such as the limited partnership, joint venture, mining partnership, business trust, unincorporated association, joint-stock company, and the franchise.

Business ethics as it relates to the text material in these chapters is considered at the end of Part 8B. The international dimensions of partnerships are discussed at the end of this part.

CHAPTER

38

CREATION AND TERMINATION OF GENERAL PARTNERSHIPS

BUSINESS DECISIONS and the LAW

It is a partnership aimed at those Japanese consumers "who drive Mercedes and BMW autos" explained Lief Johansson, head of Electrolux's Appliance Division. Recently Sweden's AB Electrolux and Japan's Sharp Corporation announced a partnership whereby Sharp will offer Electrolux appliances to customers at approximately 1,000 of its stores.

This agreement represents the start of the effort to open the coveted Japanese markets to foreign manufacturing concerns. The agreement was in the making for quite some time. The two companies collaborated on a venture in the 1970s and the negotiations for this partnership began one year ago.

Mr. Johansson recalls that it took a lot of convincing on his part to create a consensus within Sharp. The agreement calls for Sharp to market, and for Electrolux to supply, the appliances. The partnership, Electrolux estimates, will generate revenue of about "$70 million in a couple of years." Sharp, in turn, will generate revenue from each sale that it makes. Not a bad deal between the two former competitors.

Sources: Stephen D. Moore, "Electrolux to Sell its Appliances at Sharp's Retail Stores in Japan," *Wall Street Journal*, August 31, 1979, p. A 12, and Michael Berger, "Breaking All the Rules (Electrolux Marketing Strategy in Japan," *International Management*, February 1990, p. 58.

After you have read this chapter, you should be able to:

1. Identify the source of partnership law.
2. Define a general partnership.
3. Explain the legal distinction between the aggregate and entity theories of partnership.
4. List and explain the classifications of partnerships.
5. List and explain the classifications of partners.
6. Explain what is necessary to create a partnership.
7. Explain what is generally found in the articles of partnership.
8. Explain who may be partners.
9. Explain and define partnership by estoppel.
10. Discuss what is meant by partnership property.
11. List and explain the five characteristics of tenancy in partnership.
12. Discuss partnership dissolution.
13. List and explain the three methods of dissolution by acts of the partners.
14. List and explain the two methods of dissolution by operation of law.
15. List and explain the five instances when a partnership can be dissolved by decree of the court.
16. Explain when and why notice of dissolution must be given to partners and to third parties.
17. Discuss the winding up of partnership affairs.
18. Explain the order of distributing partnership assets after dissolution.

Introduction

Partnership is one of the oldest forms of business organization. Hammurabi, a king of Babylon, made reference to the regulation of partnerships in 2000 B.C. The development of ancient partnership law has its origin with the Italian merchants of the late Middle Ages.

> Under the name of La Société en commandite, it has existed in France from the time of the Middle Ages; mention being made of it in the most ancient commercial records, and in the early mercantile regulations of Marseilles and Montpelier. . . . In the statutes of Pisa and Florence, it is recognized so far back as the year 1166. . . . In the Middle Ages it was one of the most frequent combinations of trade, and was the basis of the ancient and widely extended commerce of the opulent maritime cities of Italy.[1]

However, modern partnership law, as it exists in the United States, evolved from the English law. The civil law, the law merchant, the common law, and equity all contributed to a confused state that demanded a statutory body of partnership law. The result in England was the adoption of the Partnership Act of 1890. In the United States the Uniform Partnership Act (UPA) was approved by the Conference of Commissioners on Uniform States Laws in 1914 and has been adopted by most states.[2]

general partnership
A partnership as defined by the UPA

The purpose of the UPA is to codify the principles of partnership law for **general partnerships,** as distinguished from limited partnerships, which are discussed in Chapter 41, Special Ventures. *Unless stated otherwise, reference to "partnership" is to the general partnership.* Unless the Act provides otherwise, the common law rules of contract and agency will govern partnership transactions.[3] The law governing partnerships is essentially the *state* statutory law of the Uniform Partnership Act. The Uniform Partnership Act is reproduced as Appendix C of this book.

The Nature of Partnership

partnership
(general partnership) "An association of two or more persons to carry on as co-owners of a business for profit" UPA, sec. 6

A **partnership** has been defined in UPA, Section 6, as "an association of two or more persons to carry on as co-owners a business for profit." It is a contractual agreement between competent parties to pool their capital and/or services in a business and to share the profits and losses. The definition for *tax* purposes is considerably broader. The Internal Revenue Code, Section 761 (a), defines a partnership as "a syndicate, group, pool, joint venture, or other unincorporated organization through . . . which any business . . . is carried on, and which is not . . . a corporation or a trust or estate."

Our concern will be limited to the legal relationships between the partners and between the partnership and third parties. The Uniform Partnership Act will be cited as the applicable law throughout the text. You may refer to it in Appendix C.

In the following case, a family partnership brought suit alleging an "oral" partnership with a previous partner of their family firm. The court found that the oral partnership was not proved by "clear, unequivocal and decisive evidence." Notice that the money

---

[1]*Ames v. Downing,* 1 Brad. 321, 329 (N.Y. Surr. Ct. 1850).

[2]The UPA has been adopted by all states except Louisiana and Georgia.

[3]UPA, sec. 4.

received by the previous partner was viewed as an investment in the partnership rather than as a sharing in the net profits.

FACTS

The Singer family formed an oil production partnership in the late 1930s. The original partnership was called Joseline Production Co. and was made up of the following partners: Josepn B. Singer, Joe L. Singer, Alex Singer, the Trachtnberg Brothers, and the Singer Brothers. In 1947 the partnership was dissolved and the Trachtnberg Brothers received 17 percent of the assets. The Singer family continued to operate as a partnership after the Trachtnbergs were excluded. In 1962 a revised partnership consisted of essentially the same partners, except for the Trachtnbergs.

After 1947 the Trachtnbergs continued to hold a 17 percent undivided co-ownership in the oil and gas properties that had been distributed when they were dismissed from the partnership. Josaline continued to do business. As opportunities arose, in many cases, the Trachtnbergs were permitted to invest in Josaline projects to the same extent (17 percent) as their original holdings. It is important to note that profit from each of the oil and gas properties was distributed to the Trachtnbergs as royalty owners, or as working interest co-owners, and not as distributions from the Josaline partnership. In other words, since 1947, the Trachtnbergs were treated as co-tenants and participating investors in most of the projects in which the Josaline partnership was involved.

The suit was brought on behalf of Josaline and its partners. The case was tried on the theory that the Josaline partners had been simultaneously engaged in an "oral" partnership within the Josaline partnership. This "oral" partnership included the Trachtnbergs and affected the partners' business dealings.

DECISION

We observe the manner of dealing between these highly sophisticated investors, partners and family members completely belies a casual business relationship. It is noted that the various businesses owned by the parties all were family partnerships and each was carefully reduced to writing. It is inconsistent that men of such sound business tradition would be party to an oral business relationship as extensive and pervasive as that claimed by plaintiffs without also reducing it to writing.

For their common profit and convenience, they did business together. All such business was conducted through the Josaline partnership. However, outside the Josaline partnership, any interest offered to outsiders was treated as an *ad hoc* co-investment opportunity. These outside investors included the Trachtnbergs, who retained the privilege of whether to accept or reject the investment opportunity. In other words, the parties outside Josaline were simply investors with a common area of interest. Investment in oil and gas leases as co-tenants or co-owners gives no presumption of the existence of partnership. It is well settled that the relationship of co-tenancy is not a [partnership] relationship.

Singer v. Singer, 624 F.2d 766 (10th Cir. 1981).

► Aggregate and Entity Theories of Partnership

You, as an individual, are endowed by the law with a legal personality. In that capacity your personal rights and property are protected. You can make contracts on your own behalf, sue and be sued; you are a legal entity. State legislatures and the Congress can create a legal entity such as a business corporation. The **common law** regarded the partnership as a group of individuals and not as a legal group entity. The **law merchant** took the view that a partnership was a legal entity having a legal personality of its own, apart from the individual partners. The Uniform Partnership Act appears not to have solved the problem as to whether a partnership is an aggregate of persons or a legal

common law
Principles of nonstatutory law reflecting the customs and usages of society and found in judicial decisions

law merchant
A body of law that developed by the customs and usages of merchants and that later became part of the common law

property

A thing; also an interest or right in a thing

entity.[4] There are, however, functional operations of a partnership that support the *legal entity theory*. For example, the partnership can own and convey **property,** both real and personal, in the firm name;[5] the partnership is the principal of the partners who are its agents;[6] each partner is accountable to the firm as a fiduciary;[7] books and records are kept for the firm;[8] contributions and advances are made to the firm and are returnable by it;[9] and a partnership is defined as an association—a person.[10]

Torts committed by a partner within the scope of the partner's authority are based upon the *aggregate theory* (of persons) and hence the unlimited liability of partnerships for the acts of those persons. For instance, each partner and the partnership could be held liable to satisfy the claims of an injured party.

The Internal Revenue Code requires the partnership to file an information return, and each partner must report and pay his or her share of partnership income in their individual tax returns, hence, treating the partnership as an aggregate of persons.

Notice the reasoning in the following case in which the partnership was found to be a legal entity.

FACTS

Plaintiff, Horn's Crane Service, sold supplies and services to a partnership comprised of the two defendants, Wendell H. Prior and Orie Cook. There is no allegation that the partnership property is insufficient to satisfy its debts. This action seeks a personal judgment against the individual members of the partnership for supplies sold and not paid for. Are the partners personally liable for the partnership's debt?

DECISION

No. Judgment for defendants. The partnership relationship is such that the separate property of a partner cannot be subjected to the payment of partnership debts until the property of the firm is exhausted. Firm property must also be subjected to the payment of the firm debts before it can be applied to the debts of the individual members of the firm. The partners are personally, jointly, and severally responsible for partnership liabilities. But the benefits and liabilities of a partner arise from and are the result of the partnership relationship. Therefore in this state a partnership is an entity, distinct and apart from the members composing it, for the purpose for which the partnership exists. There are several reasons for the rule. One of the most obvious is that credit having been extended to the partnership or firm, the members ought to have a right to insist that the partnership property be exhausted first. To permit a firm creditor to bypass the partnership property and exhaust the assets of an individual member leaving the partnership property extant, would be an obvious injustice, permit the other partners to profit at his expense, and place him in an adverse position with relation to his co-partners.

Horn's Crane Serv. v. Prior, 152 N.W.2d 421 (Neb. 1967).

[4]See Jensen, "Is a Partnership Under the Uniform Partnership Act an Aggregate or an Entity?" 16 *V and L. Rev.* 377 (1963).

[5]UPA, secs. 8, 25.

[6]UPA, sec. 9(1).

[7]UPA, sec. 21.

[8]UPA, sec. 19.

[9]UPA, secs. 18(a), 38(1).

[10]UPA, sec. 2.

Kinds of Partnership

Partnerships have been divided into several classes regarding their extent of business activity and the nature of their employment. This classification is helpful in determining whether a partner has customary authority as an agent to bind the partnership with third parties, as discussed in Chapter 39.

A partnership is a **trading partnership** when it *buys and sells property*. Some trading partnerships—e.g., plumbing contractors or TV repair shops—combine the sale of goods with the furnishing of services.

trading partnership
A partnership in the business of buying and selling property

A **nontrading partnership** engages in providing only services, generally on a fee-for-services basis, such as one of lawyers, physicians, and accountants.

nontrading partnership
A partnership in the business of selling only services

This classification shows that the customary authority of a partner in a trading partnership will be substantially broader than in a nontrading partnership. The implied authority of partners in trading and nontrading partnerships is discussed in Chapter 39.

Kinds of Partners[11]

Dormant partners are those who are not active in the business and are not known to the public as partners. An example would be a retired accountant still sharing in the firm profits after having sold his or her practice.

Nominal partners are not partners but hold themselves out as partners or allow others to hold them out as partners—for example, a partner may permit his name to appear on firm stationery as a member of the partnership. To illustrate, if a partnership is purchased, it may be helpful to retain the name of the selling partner. He is not a partner. Because he is held out to be a partner, he may be held liable as such by "estoppel."

Secret partners take an active part in firm management but are not known to the public as partners.

Ostensible or *public partners* hold themselves out, or permit themselves to be held out, as partners and actively engage in the partnership business. If they do not actively so engage, they are silent partners.

General partners are *ordinary* partners in a general partnership or in a limited partnership.

Limited partners are partners in a limited partnership who are not general partners. They are sometimes called "special partners."[12]

Creation of the Partnership

A partnership is generally created by the express or implied contractual agreement of the parties. If the parties intended to create a partnership, and they comply with the UPA requisites, as between each other there is a partnership. However, when the question concerns the firm's liability to third parties, a partnership may be implied in law by the courts, regardless of the parties' intent to form a partnership.

[11]See A. Bromberg, *Crane and Bromberg on Partnership*, (St. Paul: West Publishing, 1968), 141–42, for a general discussion on the many kinds of partners.

[12]See pp. 848–854 for a discussion of limited partnership.

Form

Unless the state statutory law requires a writing, no particular form is required to create a partnership agreement. If it falls within the statute of frauds,[13] there must be written evidence of the partners' contract. For example, an accounting partnership agreement should be in writing under the statute of frauds, as it will normally exist for a specified time of more than one year. It is always desirable to have a written partnership agreement to avoid a misunderstanding regarding its terms. (See Figure 38.1.)

Articles of Partnership

The partnership contract is called the *articles of partnership*. The agreement generally includes the date of formation, the names and addresses of the partners and the partnership, its purpose and duration, the capital contribution of each partner, the proportions by which the partners share in the profits and losses, salaries and drawing accounts, the duties and restrictions on managing the firm, the method of accounting and the fiscal year, rights and duties on voluntary termination, disability, retirement, death of a partner, and dissolution procedures.

Firm Name

The partnership may select any name it desires provided it complies with state statutory law. It may use a fictitious trade name or the names of the partners. The name cannot be *deceptively similar* to an existing business. State statutes usually require the partnership to file a *business certificate* in a local government office (e.g., city hall, county clerk's office), where the firm is located, indicating the name and location of the partnership and the names and addresses of the partners. The purpose of this is to allow a party who wants to sue the firm to discover who the partners are who own the business.

Illegality

A partnership agreement must comply with contract law concerning the legality of its operation. If the agreement is illegal under statutory law or court decision for public policy reasons, it is a void agreement. The courts will attempt to separate the legal portion of the partnership agreement from its illegal part and allow the partnership to exist only for its legal purpose.

UPA As Part of the Partnership Agreement

Unless the parties agree to change the effect of the UPA where allowed, the UPA becomes part of the partnership agreement. For instance, *unless the partnership agreement provides otherwise,* all partners have equal rights in the management and conduct of the partnership business regardless of their capital contribution.[14]

---

[13]See pp. 218–224 for a discussion of the statute of frauds.

[14]UPA, sec. 18(e).

Figure 38.1 General Partnership Agreement (Short Form)

GENERAL PARTNERSHIP AGREEMENT (Short Form)

Agreement, made this ________ day of ______________ , 19 ____ , by and between John Doe, of ____________________ , and Richard Roe, of ________________________ .

Whereas, Richard Roe has acquired an undivided one-half interest in the real estate and insurance business heretofore owned and conducted by John Doe, with office and place of business located at ____ ;

It is agreed as follows:

1. **Name and Duration.** The parties hereby agree to continue the operation of said business as partners under the name of __________________________ , the partnership to continue for an indefinite time and until terminated as herein provided or as may be mutually agreed upon.

2. **Capital.** The amount of capital contributed to the partnership by the parties is hereby agreed to be the sum of $__________ each, and is represented by the following personal property: [*here describe*].

3. **Reserve Fund.** An additional sum of__________dollars ($ ________) shall be set up and reserved from the profits of the partnership business, and shall become and be a part of the invested capital, it being agreed that not less than____% of the net earnings shall be so reserved until said amount is accumulated.

4. **Banking.** The funds of the partnership shall be deposited in its name in the Bank of _____________ , and all trust funds shall be deposited in such bank in a separate account. All such funds, partnership or trust, shall be subject to withdrawal only by check made in the name of the partnership and signed by either partner.

5. **Duties.** Each partner shall devote all his time and attention to the business of the partnership, and shall not, directly or indirectly, engage in any other business without the consent of the other partner.

6. **Books.** Full and accurate accounts of the transactions of the partnership shall be kept in proper books, and each partner shall cause to be entered therein full and accurate accounts of all his transactions in behalf of the partnership. Such books shall be kept at the place of business of the partnership, and each party shall at all times have access to and may inspect and copy any of them.

7. **Drawings.** Each party shall be entitled to withdraw such amounts and at such times, from the partnership earnings, as shall from time to time be fixed and agreed upon.

8. **Profits and Losses.** At the end of each calendar year, a full and accurate inventory shall be prepared, and the assets, liabilities, and income, both gross and net, shall be ascertained, and the net profits or net losses of the partnership shall be fixed and determined. The net profits or net losses shall be divided equally between the parties, and the account of each shall be credited or debited with his proportionate share thereof.

9. **Limitations.** Neither party shall, without the written consent of the other, make, execute, deliver, indorse or guaranty any commercial paper, nor agree to answer for, or indemnify against, any act, debt, default or miscarriage of any person, partnership, association or corporation, other than that of the parties hereto.

10. **Termination.** The partnership may be terminated by either party upon giving 60 days notice to the other party of his desire to withdraw, in which event an accounting shall be had and a division of the partnership assets made, provided, however, that the party to whom notice is given shall have the right to acquire the whole interest of the partnership at a price not to exceed the book value thereof, on such terms as may be agreed upon, and to continue the partnership business under the same name.

In Witness Whereof, the parties have signed this agreement.

______________________________ ______________________________

[Signatures]

Source: Reprinted with permission from Edmund O. Belsheim's "Modern Legal Forms." Copyright © 1971 by West Publishing Co.

► An Association

You recall that Section 6 of the UPA defined a partnership "as an association of two or more persons." An association as partners is not a master/servant or employer/employee relationship. It is a relationship that makes each member a coprincipal and a general agent for the firm in transacting partnership business. Although it does not pay tax itself, a partnership is a unique entity for tax purposes and is required to calculate its income or loss and file an information return. This taxable income or loss is then passed through to the partners,[15] who show it on their individual tax returns.

Two or More Persons The "two or more persons" requirement immediately will distinguish the partnership from the sole proprietorship, where one person earns the profits and bears all losses. The "person" under UPA, Section 2, "includes individuals, partnerships, corporations, and other associations." However, the *person* must have the *capacity to contract.*

Infants or Minors Under most state laws, a minor may be a partner with partnership rights. The minor's agreement is voidable by the minor during minority or a reasonable time thereafter. The minor can disaffirm and withdraw during that time without incurring liability for breach of contract. The minor may also disaffirm his or her individual liability on partnership contracts with third parties, although some states will not allow a minor of an insolvent partnership to withdraw the minor's capital contribution.

Insane Persons The state law governing competency of the mentally ill to contract will determine their ability to be partners. Generally, their contracts will be voidable, unless they have been adjudicated to be insane, in which case they have no capacity to contract and cannot be partners.[16]

Corporations Modern corporate law and the UPA, Sections 2 and 6(1), permit corporations to become partners.[17]

► Carrying on a Business for Profit

Partners must "carry on as co-owners a business for profit." To illustrate, if *X* and *Z* invest in an apartment building and agree to share the rental income, this in itself will not create a partnership;[18] it is not a business. A business must carry on a number of *continuous commercial transactions* as an enterprise. A fraternity or sorority or other nonprofit organization cannot be a partnership.

► Co-owners of a Business

Section 7(2) of the UPA lists a number of forms of co-owned property that do not, in themselves, establish a partnership. Joint tenancy, tenancy in common, tenancy by the entirety, joint property, or part ownership—even if the co-owners share profits made by use of the property—are not partnerships.

Sharing Profits The sharing of profits is prima facie evidence that a person is a partner in a business. However, under UPA, Section 7(4), no such inference may be

---

[15]See I.R.C. (1954) ch. 1, subch. K (26 U.S.C.A.) for the tax effect of partnership transactions.

[16]See pp. 190, 194 on capacity to contract.

[17]See Revised Model Business Corporation Act sec. 3.02(10).

[18]UPA, sec. 7(3).

drawn when profits are received in payment: (a) as a debt, by installments or otherwise; (b) as wages of an employee or rent to a landlord; (c) as an annuity to a widow or representative of a deceased partner; (d) as interest on a loan; or (e) as the consideration for the sale of the goodwill of a business. However, in any of these instances, if the recipient of the profits also has the right to participate in the management of the business, there is a co-ownership and a resulting partnership.

In order for there to be a partnership, the business enterprise, subject to the partnership agreement, must merge the individual rights and liabilities of each member as well as the control of the partnership property.

Fixed payment is not evidence of a partnership. The partner must have an interest in the profits granting him or her the *control* of an owner. For instance, if *X*, a doctor, is to receive a fixed percentage of the profits from *X*'s associate without any control over the medical practice, *X* is not a partner. As is illustrated in the following case, sharing in the *gross* profits is insufficient to prove that a partnership existed; the persons must share in the *net* profits.

FACTS

Jenkins, defendant, transported cattle and leased the truck-tractors to pull the trailers from various individuals, including Joe Lewis, under a written lease agreement. The gross income from the operation was divided, with Jenkins receiving 30 percent and Lewis 70 percent. Under the terms of the agreement, Jenkins had exclusive control over the entire operation. Jenkins kept books on the operation and collected all money due for the hauling. After the parties operated under this agreement for about a year, Lewis commenced negotiating with Brodnax White Truck Company, plaintiff, to trade for a new truck. Brodnax required a down payment of approximately $2,500 and advised him that he would have to have a cosigner on the chattel mortgage. Lewis and a representative of Brodnax called on Jenkins to see if he would cosign the chattel mortgage. Jenkins signed. Subsequently the truck was involved in a collision, and Lewis returned it to Brodnax for repairs, which forms the basis of this suit. When the repairs were completed, Brodnax presented Lewis a bill for $1,304.48. He was unable to pay the account, and Brodnax sued Jenkins upon the theory that Lewis contracted the repairs as his partner. Does the sharing of gross income constitute a partnership?

DECISION

No. Judgment for defendant, Jenkins. The mere participation of two persons in the gross receipts of an enterprise in which their capital, skill, and labor may be combined cannot of itself make them partners. To constitute a partnership, the parties in the business or transaction must be entitled to share in the net profits. It is not sufficient that they participate in the "gross profits."

It is apparent that neither Lewis nor Jenkins contemplated joint ownership of the profits as such. They merely intended to share in the gross receipts and used such division as a guide to determine the compensation due each of them.

Jenkins v. Brodnax White Truck Co., 437 S.W.2d 922 (Tex. 1969).

Partner by Estoppel

A person who is not a member of a partnership may incur partnership liability to a third party as though the person were a partner under the doctrine of partnership by **estoppel.** This occurs when persons who are not partners by words or conduct represent themselves, or permit themselves to be represented, to anyone as partners and

estoppel
A principle of law stating that when one person "holds out" (represents) a material fact to another person, who changes his or her position materially to his or her prejudice in reasonable reliance on the holding out, the first person is "estopped" (prohibited) to deny what he or she had asserted previously

a third party *relies* on that representation[19] and *extends credit* to the partnership in reasonable reliance on the holding out. The person is really not a partner and does not become a firm member but is a nominal partner and cannot deny liability. By estoppel, he or she is liable to third persons as a partner. For example, Jones permits Moran to inform Peters that Jones and Moran are partners when, in fact, they are not partners. Moran tells Peters that Jones is his partner, and Peters, in reliance on Moran's statement, extends credit through Moran to the apparent Jones/Moran partnership. Jones is estopped to assert that she and Moran are not partners, and Jones is liable as a partner to Peters.

In the following case, the court refused to find a partnership by estoppel because there was not evidence of a misleading representation that the defendant was a partner.

FACTS

Plaintiffs entered into contracts with Mike Norman, d/b/a Norman Construction Company, for the construction of new homes. Construction on both homes was begun, but neither home was completed. Plaintiffs filed a contract action against Mike Norman and his father Max Norman, individually and as partners doing business as Norman Construction Company. The plaintiffs' case against Max Norman is based upon an estoppel theory. The plaintiffs contend that Norman led them to believe he was a partner with his son Mike in Norman Construction Company. They argued that during the construction work on their homes, they made payments to Mike Norman in reliance on Max Norman's representations that he was a partner in the business. Because of this alleged reliance, they assert that Max Norman, although he was in actuality not a partner of his son, should be estopped from denying liability for the losses sustained by the plaintiffs from the alleged poor workmanship and failure to complete their homes.

DECISION

The undisputed facts in this case do not support a cause of action against the defendant based upon the doctrine of equitable estoppel. The plaintiffs bore the burden of proving that they relied to their detriment on the defendant's alleged representations. They did not meet this burden.

. . . In this case, there is not a scintilla of evidence that the plaintiffs entered into their contracts with Mike Norman based upon any conduct or declaration by his father. Plaintiff Glenn Smith testified that when he entered into the contract with Mike Norman, he did not think Max Norman was a partner in Mike Norman's business. Plaintiff David Wright testified that he likewise dealt only with Mike Norman and knew of no involvement by Max Norman in the business. Although the plaintiffs allege that there was detrimental reliance in that they made payments to Mike Norman based upon Max Norman's alleged representations, their existing contracts clearly obligated them to make those payments. Had the alleged representations by Max Norman been made prior to or at the time the plaintiffs entered into their contracts with Mike Norman, the decision in this case might be different. Because the alleged representations came after the plaintiffs had obligated themselves to make the payments, however, it cannot be said that they relied upon those alleged representations to their detriment.

Judgment for defendant.

Smith v. Norman, 495 So.2d 536 (Ala. 1986).

Partnership Property

The assets of a partnership consist of the partnership property and the contributions of the partners necessary for the payment of the partnership liabilities. UPA, Section 8(1)

[19]UPA, sec. 16(1).

defines partnership property as "all property originally brought into the partnership stock or subsequently acquired by purchase or otherwise, on account of the partnership."

Creditors

Firm Creditors The issue of partnership property is important when the firm is insolvent and its creditors are seeking satisfaction of their claims.

Individual Creditors The partners of a firm in their individual capacity may incur personal debts. A partner's personal creditors, in that instance, may reach that partner's interest in the firm by means of a *charging order*.[20]

For example, a personal creditor of a partner must first reduce the claim to a judgment, and then request the court (1) to charge the interest of the debtor partner in a share of the partnership profits and any other money due the debtor from the partnership; and (2) to appoint a **receiver** and direct the receiver to collect such moneys from the partnership and pay them to the judgment creditor until the judgment is satisfied. It then becomes necessary to determine what is firm property.

receiver
A person appointed by a court to receive, preserve, and manage property that is involved in litigation

Title to Partnership Property

A partnership may hold title to **personal property,** and under UPA, Section 8(3) to **real property,** in the firm name. A majority of states allow the partnership to hold title to real property under a fictitious name.

personal property (personalty)
A movable thing, along with interests and rights in the thing

real property (realty)
Land and immovable things attached to land, along with interests and rights in the land; also a freehold interest in land

Transfer of the Partnership Property

Personal Property Any partner with express, implied, or apparent authority may transfer personal property owned by the firm to another party. For example, *X,* a partner in a construction firm, may sell a truck owned by the partnership to *Z* without the actual authority of the co-partners if there is **customary authority** in that business to sell equipment.

customary authority
Implied authority to do those acts that conform to the general custom or usage

Real Property If title to the real property is in the name of the partnership on the deed, the title can be transferred by any partner executing the deed in the partnership name. The partner must have authority or **apparent authority** to make the conveyance. If the partner does not, the partnership can recover the property.

apparent authority
The power of a person (*A*) to act as though *A* were an agent, created by another's (*P*'s) manifestation to a third person (*T*) that *A* is *P*'s agent

Title to Partnership Property Held in the Name of an Individual Partner An individual partner may have the title to partnership property in that partner's own name. For example, the partner may have owned property before the partnership was formed and contributed that property to the firm but failed to transfer record title to the partnership. The partner holds the title as a trustee, in constructive trust, for the benefit of the co-partners.

[20]UPA, sec. 28.

Tenancy in Partnership

Each partner has a property interest in firm property and is a co-owner in such property. Title to firm property is held by the partners as a *tenancy in partnership*.[21]

tenancy in common
A form of ownership of property by more than one person without survivorship

joint tenancy
A form of ownership of property by more than one person with the right of survivorship

This concurrent ownership has characteristics that distinguish it from a **tenancy in common** and a **joint tenancy**. For example, a joint tenant has full survivorship rights upon the death of a co-tenant; a surviving partner does not.

The characteristics of a tenancy in partnership are as follows:

1. A partner, subject to any agreement between them, has an equal right with the other partners to use specific partnership property for partnership purposes.
2. A partner's right in specific partnership property cannot be transferred by the partner (sold, assigned, or mortgaged) without the consent of all the other partners.
3. A partner's right in specific partnership property is not subject to attachment by the partner's personal creditors.
4. On the death of a partner, the decedent partner's right in specific partnership property vests in the surviving partners; except that when the deceased is the last surviving partner, then the decedent's right in such property vests in the legal representative of the decedent,[22] who holds it in trust for partnership purposes.
5. A partner's right in specific partnership property is not subject to any interest of the partner's surviving spouse.

The following case illustrates that a personal creditor of a partner with a "charging order" may reach only a partner's interest in the firm and not the assets of the partnership.

FACTS

Amerco secured a judgment against Bohonus, and sought to enforce that judgment by judicial sale of Bohonus' interest in a partnership by having partnership assets sold. Amerco, after it secured a judgment against Bohonus, sought a charging order from the court. The court granted the request for a charging order and as a part of that order mandated the sale of Bohonus' interest in the assets and property of the partnership business. Bohonus appealed. May the trial court order the sale of partnership property to satisfy the individual debt of a partner?

DECISION

No, only the partner's interest. Reversed, for Bohonus. We now look at the Partnership Statute. "A partner's right in specific partnership property is not subject to attachment or execution, except on a claim against the partnership.... The property rights of a partner are: 1. his rights in specific partnership property; 2. his interest in the partnership; 3. his right to participate in the management. A partner's interest in the partnership is his share of the profits and surplus, and the same is personal property. On due application to a competent court by any judgment creditor of a partner, the court which entered the judgment may charge the interest of the debtor partner with payment of the unsatisfied amount of such judgment debt with interest theron." Only the "interest in the partnership" may be charged and we find no provision therein for sale of assets or property of the partnership.

Bohonus v. Amerco, et al., 602 P.2d 469 (Ariz. 1979).

---

[21] UPA, sec. 28.

[22] UPA, sec. 25(d).

We have seen what a partnership is and how it comes into existence. The operation of a partnership may be interrupted by any number of events resulting in its *dissolution* or in *termination* of its legal entity as a partnership. These are now to be discussed.

Dissolution, Winding up, and Termination

The termination of the partnership is a process involving the sale of its assets, the payment of its liabilities, ultimate distribution of cash to the partners, and ending with the termination of the partnership entity. Termination is preceded by *dissolution* and *winding up,* which occur in that order.

► Dissolution

Dissolution is defined by UPA, Section 29 as follows:

> The dissolution of a partnership is the change in the relation of the partners caused by any partner ceasing to be associated in the carrying on as distinguished from the winding up of the business.

The "change in the relation of the partners" may be the result of a partner leaving the firm, or of a partner's disability, retirement, or death. The well-designed partnership agreement will provide for the continuance of the partnership business, giving the remaining partners the right to purchase the leaving partner's interest and a pay-off of his or her distributive share of the profits.

The legal effect of dissolution is to terminate all authority of any partner to act for the partnership[23] except to wind up the partnership business. After dissolution, the partnership remains obligated to pay its liabilities. For instance, a deceased partner's estate is liable for the deceased partner's share of the partnership debts.

It is important to recognize that the partnership entity is *not* terminated by dissolution. The partnership will continue in accordance with the partnership agreement during the winding up of its affairs.

In the following case the court held that a partnership may be sued in its own name following dissolution but prior to termination.

FACTS

Commonwealth Capital Investment Corporation brought an action against Leland R. McElmurry. McElmurry was a general partner of MHS Enterprises, a dissolved partnership, which had guaranteed performance on a promissory note and loan agreement. The court granted the plaintiff summary judgment against McElmurry in his capacity as a general partner of MHS. McElmurry appeals, alleging that because MHS had been dissolved prior to suit no judgment could be rendered against it and he could not, therefore, be held liable on the void judgment.

DECISION

Judgment for Commonwealth Capital Investment Corporation affirmed. A partnership is not terminated upon dissolution. It continues on until the winding up of partnership affairs is completed. The winding up includes the satisfaction of debts against the partnership. Therefore, a partnership may be sued in its own name following dissolution but prior to

---

[23]UPA, sec. 33.

termination. The judgment against MHS was not void and McElmurry, as a former general partner, could properly be held liable.

The terms "dissolution" and "termination," as employed in the Partnership Act are not synonyms and, as used, have different meanings. Dissolution does not terminate the partnership and does not end completely the authority of the partners. The order of events is: (1) dissolution; (2) winding up; and (3) termination. Termination extinguishes their authority. It is the ultimate result of the winding up and it occurs at the conclusion of the winding up. The "winding up of partnership affairs" includes the satisfaction of debts against it. Consequently, it is our opinion that a partnership may be sued in its own name following dissolution, but prior to termination.... Consequently, the judgment entered against the partnership was not void, and McElmurry could be held liable as a general partner of the partnership.

Commonwealth Capital Inv. Corp. v. McElmurry, 302 N.W.2d 222 (Mich. 1980).

Causes for Dissolution Dissolution is effected by the acts of the partners, by operation of law, and by decree of court.

1. By Acts of the Partners

a. Agreement. The partnership agreement may provide for its dissolution upon a specified period of time or the occurrence of an event.[24] For example, a partnership may have been created for the purpose of buying, developing, and selling a condominium. When the dissolution occurs in accordance with the partnership agreement, there is no further liability for any partner.

b. Withdrawal. For any number of reasons, a partner may decide to withdraw from the firm in violation of the partnership agreement. Although the partner has the power to withdraw, by doing so the partner may thereby incur damages for breach of the partnership agreement. Usually the partnership agreement will provide for a partner's withdrawal by giving proper advance notice to the associates. UPA, Section 31(b), states: "Dissolution is caused by the express will of any partner when no definite term or particular undertaking is specified."

c. Expulsion. A partner may be expelled by the co-partners for cause. The partnership agreement may specify certain reasons for dismissal. A partnership is dissolved by the expulsion of any partner for cause.[25]

2. By Operation of Law

a. Death. UPA, Section 31(4) provides for the automatic dissolution of the partnership upon the death of a partner.

b. Bankruptcy. Bankruptcy of any partner or of the partnership will cause the firm to dissolve.[26] The partner or firm in bankruptcy cannot carry on the partnership business.

3. By Decree of Court An individual partner may petition the court to obtain its dissolution under certain circumstances. The issue before the court is whether or not the firm can continue to carry on partnership business. UPA, Section

[24]UPA, sec. 31(1)(a).

[25]UPA, sec. 31(1)(d).

[26]UPA, sec. 31(5). As noted in Chapter 52, a partnership is not entitled to a discharge in bankruptcy.

32 provides upon petition that the court shall decree a dissolution whenever any of the following occur:

a. Insanity. A partner has been declared a lunatic in any judicial proceeding or is shown to be of unsound mind.

b. Incapacity. A partner becomes in any way incapable of performing part of the partnership contract. For example, if a partner suffered a physical disability that prevented the partner from providing services, that fact would allow the court to dissolve the partnership even over the disabled partner's objections.

c. Misconduct. The conduct of a partner that tends to affect prejudicially the carrying on of the business is ground for another partner to petition for a dissolution. For instance, the conduct of a partner who continues to cause a disruption in the working relationship affecting the carrying on of the business is ground for dissolution.

d. Operation Only at a Loss. The statutory definition of a partnership (UPA, Section 6) is to carry on the business for a profit. When the business of the partnership can be carried on only at a loss, a partner may petition the court for dissolution.

e. Equitable Necessity. The UPA provides a "catch all" provision in Section 32(f), which allows dissolution "whenever other circumstances render a dissolution equitable." An example is, when a person is fraudulently induced to enter a partnership based on a misrepresentation in its financial statements.

Notice of Dissolution The legal effect of dissolution is to terminate all authority of any partner to act for the partnership, except so far as may be necessary to wind up the partnership affairs.[27]

Notice to Partners When dissolution is caused by an act of a partner (for instance, a partner who became disabled and could not continue working), the partner must give notice to the other partners of intent to withdraw from the firm. If the partner fails to give notice of withdrawal, the partner is liable to the other partners for his or her share of any liability created by any partner acting for the partnership as if the partnership had not been dissolved.

Notice to Third Parties While dissolution terminates the authority of partners to continue to act for the partnership and continue the partnership business, nevertheless third persons who know of the partnership may not know that the partnership has been dissolved. As to them, the partners have apparent authority to continue the partnership business.

Also, with respect to the winding up process there is an apparent authority problem. The winding up process may be done only by partners who have not wrongfully caused a dissolution. They have implied authority to sell the partnership assets and pay off the various firm creditors with the proceeds. A partner who has wrongfully caused a dissolution (for example, by a withdrawal in violation of the partnership agreement) may have apparent authority to engage in the winding up process with third parties who knew of the partnership's dissolution but did not know which of the partners were ineligible to engage in the winding up process.

In order to eliminate the above instances of such apparent authority, notice must be given to those third parties of dissolution and partner ineligibility, except that no notice

[27]UPA, sec. 33.

of dissolution is required when the dissolution is caused by operation of law (e.g., a partner's death or bankruptcy). There may be "actual notice" or "constructive notice."

1. Actual Notice. Third parties who have extended credit to the partnership (for example, past creditors) must be given actual notice; that is, they must actually receive notice that the firm has been dissolved and of partner ineligibility. This will destroy the apparent authority.

2. Constructive Notice. To third parties who knew of the partnership but never had extended credit to the firm, general notice, such as by local newspaper publication, is sufficient to eliminate the apparent authority. A third party is held to have notice without ever having read the notice.

In the following case the partnership creditor had notice of the dissolution of the partnership and, therefore, could not hold the partners liable for new partnership obligations sought to be imposed on the partnership after the dissolution.

FACTS

Wieladt and Teschendorf had been partners doing business under the firm name of Belmont Upholstering Company and as partners they signed a five-year lease. LaHood was the lessor. Belmont Upholstering Company ceased doing business as a partnership, though they filed no certificate of dissolution, and formed a corporation, the Belmont Furniture Company, Inc. Sometime prior to the lease expiration, LaHood, the landlord, tendered to Teschendorf, a new five-year written lease, at a higher rental, naming the same partnership and partners as lessees. Teschendorf objected to its rent provisions and refused to sign. LaHood thereafter went to Wieladt, a partner of the dissolved partnership, who did sign the lease which, as later changed, was solely in the name of Wieladt and did not purport to be a partnership lease. The corporation continued for a number of months to deliver to LaHood checks for the rent. These checks, as had been true for the previous year, no longer named the partnership "Belmont, Wieladt and Teschendorf, Upholstering Company" as payor, but instead "Belmont Furniture Company," the name of the corporation. This is an action by the landlord against all the members of the former partnership for the due rent. Could the landlord, LaHood, rely upon Wieladt's apparent authority to bind the dissolved partnership?

DECISION

No. Judgment for defendants, former partners. One partner may bind another, but here there was no partnership when the second lease was signed by Wieladt. The lease, by its terms, did not purport to be a partnership lease, but one between LaHood and Wieladt, and the rental payments were not out of Teschendorf's or partnership funds, but were payments by the corporation.

LaHood v. Wieladt, 105 N.W.2d 39 (Mich. 1960).

► Winding up Partnership Affairs

The winding up of partnership affairs is the orderly liquidation of partnership assets and the distribution of proceeds to partnership creditors and then to the partners themselves. Throughout the winding up process the partners continue to owe a fiduciary duty to each other. They are prevented from taking on new partnership business. In the following case the court held that responsibility for any delay in winding up the partnership that causes expenses must be shared equally by the partners.

FACTS

On May 15, 1971, Chaim and Sheila Ben-Dashan, plaintiffs, and Plitt, defendant, entered into a written partnership agreement for the breeding and management of cattle and standardbred horses. In October 1973 plaintiffs brought an action for dissolution of the partnership, seeking appointment of a receiver and sale of the remaining assets. Plaintiffs argue that, at the time of dissolution of the partnership defendant assumed the role of liquidating partner and that it was his responsibility to dispose of the horses in a reasonable time and effect a final termination of the partnership. They further assert that defendant delayed almost fourteen months in selling the horses and winding up the business at an average expense to the partnership in excess of $1,000 a month. Therefore, plaintiffs contend that they should not be held liable for one-half of the expenses incurred by defendant during that time, particularly in light of the fact that they offered to purchase the horses from defendant in March of 1973 for $5,200.

DECISION

The expenses for the delay in winding up will be shared equally by the partners. A partnership is not terminated upon dissolution, but rather continues until the winding up of the partnership affairs is completed. There was never any agreement reached with respect to who would take it upon himself to liquidate the remaining assets, i.e., sell the remaining horses, nor did the partnership agreement provide for a liquidation process. Both parties, plaintiffs on the one hand and defendant on the other, procrastinated in winding up the partnership until such time as plaintiffs initiated an action in October, 1973 for its dissolution and appointment of a referee to complete the liquidation. Therefore, responsibility for any delay in winding up the partnership must be shared by both parties, as well as any expenses generated by the delay, which in this case is the cost to the partnership of the caring for and feeding of the horses from March 1973 to their sale.

Ben-Dashan v. Plitt, 396 N.Y.S.2d 542 (N.Y. 1977).

Right to Wind Up Partnership Affairs Section 37 of the UPA provides that "unless otherwise agreed the partners who have not wrongfully dissolved the partnership or the legal representative of the last surviving partner, not bankrupt, have the right to wind up the partnership affairs." A court-appointed receiver will wind up the partnership if the dissolution is by court decree. A surviving partner is entitled to reasonable compensation for services rendered in winding up the partnership affairs.

Upon dissolution, each partner has the right to be paid his or her interest in the partnership. To prevent a liquidation, partners commonly enter into a "buy and sell" agreement that provides for a method to evaluate and pay the partners' interests.

In the following case the court was bound by the buy-sell provision of the partnership agreement that did not mention discounts in determining the value of a deceased partner's interest.

FACTS

On July 1, 1950, Burt Marshall, Roy Marshall and Blanche Olsen executed a partnership agreement forming the M & M Investment Company.... Blanche Olsen died October 29, 1971. Seattle-First National Bank (Seattle-First) was named executor of her will.

In valuing Olsen's partnership interest as part of her estate, Seattle-First valued the partnership's land only, without taking into account other assets or any liabilities. The partnership agreement contains a buy-sell provision: in the event of the death of one of the partners, the surviving partners would purchase the interest of the deceased partner.

Seattle-First offered to sell Olsen's interest to Burt Marshall, the only surviving partner, for $151,000. In a letter dated September 30, 1974 Marshall strenuously objected, stating that the interest was overpriced because Seattle-First improperly computed the net worth of the partnership. Marshall contends that the value of the partnership interest should have been discounted by sales costs, minority interest, and capital gains taxes to be paid upon sale of the partnership interest. Although these discount factors are not mentioned in the partnership agreement, Marshall's position is that these discounts are inherent in the concept of "current market value."

The trial court stated it was bound by the partnership agreement which does not mention such discounts in determining the value of a deceased partner's interest and found for Seattle-First, the plaintiff. Defendant appealed.

DECISION

Judgment of the trial court affirmed, for plaintiff Seattle-First. A buy-sell provision in a partnership agreement represents an effort to resolve the conflicts likely to arise upon the death of a partner. It is not unreasonable to conclude that the parties to the M & M Investment Company partnership agreement intended an outgoing partner's interest to be valued as indicated, without discounts. Discounts might be appropriate if the partnership agreement called for the reasonable or current market value of the partnership interest without further definition of such value. However, the transaction is governed by the partnership agreement, rather than what might be appropriate in sales of other interests. Because the partnership agreement setting forth the method of valuing a deceased partner's interest makes no allowance for discount factors, the trial court properly refused to discount the value of Olsen's partnership interest.

Seattle-First Nat'l Bank as Executor v. Marshall, et al., 641 P.2d 1194 (Wash. 1982).

Distribution of Assets Section 40 of the UPA establishes the rules for settling accounts between the partners after dissolution as a part of the winding up process. The partners may by their own agreement change the statutory order of payments *among themselves*. Under 40(b), distribution of partnership assets is made (1) to creditors who are not partners; (2) to partners for their advances to the partnership; (3) to partners of their capital contributions; and (4) to partners of their respective shares of the profits.

Insolvent Partnership with Solvent Partners Assume you are *X*, an equal partner in *XYZ* partnership. Your partnership agreement states "all partners are to share equally in the profits." The partnership has assets of $35,000 consisting of partners' capital contributions, and liabilities of $95,000, hence a partnership loss of $60,000. You and your partners are solvent; how will firm creditors be paid? To what extent may firm creditors reach your personal assets? Assume you, as Partner *X*, made a capital contribution of $20,000; *Y* contributed $10,000; and *Z*, $5,000. Firm creditors will be paid from partnership assets. Section 40(a) of the UPA defines partnership assets as partnership property and the contributions of the partners necessary for the payment of partnership liabilities. Keep in mind that each partner must contribute toward the partnership losses according to his or her share in the profits.[28] From your personal assets you as partner *X* would pay firm creditors nothing; *Y* must pay $10,000; and *Z* $15,000, as illustrated by the following:

[28]UPA, sec. 18(a); on dissolution, see sec. 40(d).

XYZ Partnership

	Partner X	Partner Y	Partner Z
Partnership loss = $60,000			
Capital contribution	$20,000	$10,000	$ 5,000
Personal payment to creditors	-0-	$10,000	$15,000
	$20,000	$20,000	$20,000

Insolvent Partnership with a Personally Insolvent Partner If Partner *Z* and your *XYZ* firm are insolvent, as between the firm creditors and personal creditors of Partner *Z*, who will be given preference on firm assets? A court with equity powers will segregate the assets and liabilities of the partnership and of the individual partners. The court will apply the **doctrine of marshaling of assets.** Under UPA, Section 40(i), the partnership creditors of the insolvent firm are entitled to be paid first from partnership property. The Bankruptcy Code, in Section 723(a), provides that if there is a deficiency of partnership assets to pay in full the partnership creditors, then each general partner is personally liable for the full amount of such deficiency. The individual personal creditors of an insolvent partner are entitled to be paid first from the property of their debtor/partner. An insolvent partner must distribute his or her personal property in the following order: (1) personal creditors are to be paid first; (2) partnership creditors second; and (3) then partners who paid partnership creditors an amount in excess of their share of partnership liabilities. Personal creditors have no claim against the personal property of the other partners.

marshaling of assets
An equitable doctrine that, when there are two classes of creditors, one class having recourse to more than one asset while the other class has recourse to only some but not all of those assets, creditors of the first class are to resort first to those assets not available to other creditors and then to the other assets available to the other creditors

Summary Statement

1. A partnership is an association of two or more persons to carry on as co-owners a business for profit. Each element in this definition must be satisfied for there to be a partnership.
2. With the exception of Louisiana and Georgia, the Uniform Partnership Act is the statutory source of partnership law.
3. Under the aggregate theory of partnerships, each partner is personally liable for partnership claims; the partnership is legally viewed as a group of individual persons. Under the legal entity theory, the partnership has a legal status of its own apart from the individual partners.
4. Partnerships are classified as trading and nontrading.
5. General partners are classified as dormant, nominal, secret, and general.
6. The articles of partnership or partnership agreement generally include many items so that there is no uncertainty about the terms of the partners' relationship.
7. Any person competent to contract may be a partner; another partnership or a corporation may also become a partner.
8. A partnership is a contractual relationship; hence the parties must agree to its creation.
9. A partnership by estoppel occurs when individuals by words or conduct represent themselves, or permit themselves to be represented, as partners, and a third party in reasonable reliance on that holding out extends credit to the partnership.

10. Partnership property is held as a *tenancy in partnership* with the following characteristics:
    a) Any partner may use it for partnership purposes.
    b) A partner may not, without the consent of the other partners, transfer his or her interest in it.
    c) Personal creditors of a partner may not attach that partner's right in it.
    d) Upon a partner's death, the decedent partner's right in partnership property vests in the surviving partners.
    e) The surviving spouse of a partner has no interest in the deceased partner's property.
11. Dissolution is the change in the relation of the partners caused by any partner ceasing to be associated in the carrying on of the business. Upon dissolution, no partner is authorized to act for the partnership except to wind up partnership business.
12. Dissolution does not terminate the partnership entity.
13. Dissolution may be caused by the acts of the partners or by operation of law.
14. Actual notice of dissolution, and ineligibility to participate in the winding up process, must be given to third parties who had extended credit to the partnership, and constructive notice (e.g., newspaper publication) to third parties who knew of the partnership but had never extended credit to the firm.
15. Winding up of a partnership is the liquidation of partnership assets and distribution of proceeds to partnership creditors and then to the partners themselves.
16. After dissolution, partnership assets are distributed as follows:
    a) Firm creditors who are not partners
    b) Partners' advances
    c) Partners' capital contributions
    d) Remaining assets, distributed as profits.

In the following case, notice how the court distinguished between the sharing of income of the business and sharing of profits.

CHAIKEN v. EMPLOYMENT SECURITY COMMISSION
274 A.2d 707 (Del. 1971)

Storey, Justice. Richard Chaiken and two others ran a barber shop. The State of Delaware claimed that the other two persons were employees of Chaiken and that Chaiken failed to pay the unemployment compensation tax assessed against employers. He defended on the ground that they were not his employees but rather partners.

...Chaiken contends that he and his "partners":

1. properly registered the partnership name and names of partners in the Prothonotary's office...
2. properly filed federal partnership information returns and paid federal taxes quarterly on an estimated basis, and
3. duly executed partnership agreements.

Of the three factors, the last is most important. Agreements of "partnership" were executed between Chaiken and Mr. Strazella, a barber in the shop, and between Chaiken and Mr. Spitzer, similarly situated. The agreements were nearly identical. The first paragraph declared the creation of a partnership and the location of business. The second provided that Chaiken would provide barber chair, supplies, and licenses, while the other partner would provide tools of the trade. The paragraph also declared that upon dissolution of the partnership, ownership of items would revert to the party providing them. The third paragraph declared that the income of the partnership would be divided 30% for Chaiken, 70% for Strazella; 20% for Chaiken and 80% for Spitzer. The fourth paragraph declared that all partnership policy would be decided by Chaiken, whose decision was final. The fifth paragraph forbade assignment of the agreement without permission of Chaiken. The sixth paragraph required Chaiken to hold and distribute all receipts. The final paragraph stated hours of work for Strazella and Spitzer and holidays.

The mere existence of an agreement labelled "partnership" agreement and the characterization of signatories as "partners" does not conclusively prove the existence of a partnership. Rather, the intention of the parties, as explained by the wording of the agreement, is paramount.

A partnership is defined as an association of two or more persons to carry on as co-owners a business for profit.... As co-owners of a business, partners have an equal right in the decision-making process. But this right may be abrogated by agreement of the parties without destroying the partnership concept, provided other partnership elements are present.

Thus, while paragraph four reserves for Chaiken all right to determine partnership policy, it is not standing alone, fatal to the partnership concept. Co-owners should also contribute valuable consideration for the creation of the business. Under paragraph two, however, Chaiken provides the barber chair (and implicitly the barber shop itself), mirror, licenses and linen, while the other partners merely provide their tools and labor—nothing more than any barber-employee would furnish. Standing alone, however, mere contribution of work and skill can be valuable consideration for a partnership agreement.

Most importantly, co-owners carry on "a business for profit." The phrase has been interpreted to mean that partners share in the profits and the losses of the business. The intent to divide the profits is an indispensable requisite of partnership.... Paragraph three of the agreement declares that each partner shall share in the income of the business. There is no sharing of the profits, and as the agreement is drafted, there are no profits....

It is the conclusion of this Court that Chaiken did not carry the burden of proving the existence of partnerships with Spitzer and Strazella.... Since... no partnership at law exists, the facts support the commission's finding.

Questions and Case Problems

1. In late February or early March of 1977 Gregory Walsh contacted Ellingson at the Ellingson Agency, a real estate corporation to purchase a parcel of real estate. Ellingson showed Walsh a lot that he thought might meet Walsh's needs. Ellingson told Walsh that he owned the property with "some partners" and that it was for sale for $30,000. Walsh returned to the Ellingson Agency and told Ellingson that he wished to buy the property for $29,000 cash. A buy-sell agreement was drafted and signed by both parties, and Walsh gave Ellingson $1,000 in earnest money. A closing date of April 5, 1977 was set. Prior to March 17 the other owners of the property had not been disclosed. Shortly after March 17, 1977 Walsh received a title insurance policy that revealed that the property was owned by the Ellingson Agency and Four Seasons Motor Inn as tenants in common. This is the first time that Walsh learned who the other "partners" were. On April 5, 1977, Walsh went to the Ellingson Agency and told Ellingson that he was ready to write a check pursuant to the buy-sell agreement. Ellingson told Walsh that he could not get his partners to sell, and he offered to return the $1,000. Walsh would not accept the return of his earnest money. Ellingson testified that he had no authority to act for the Four Seasons but that he thought the sale would be acceptable to the Four Seasons. Walsh filed a complaint against Ellingson Agency and Four Seasons Motor Inn seeking the execution and

delivery of a deed to the subject property and actual damages as reimbursement for expenses occasioned as a result of the defendants' refusal to perform. Walsh alleged that Ellingson represented that he was a partner and agent of the other partners, and was authorized to contract to sell the property. Was there a partnership between the Ellingson Agency and the Four Seasons Motor Inn, and if so, are defendants bound by the buy-sell agreement? [*Walsh v. Ellingson Agency and Four Seasons Motor Inn,* 613 P.2d 1381 (Mont. 1980).]

2. In 1959 plaintiff met Philip Miller. Later, Mr. Miller asked plaintiff to marry him, to move to Jackson, and to help him run the nursery business. Plaintiff gave up her well-paying job to move to Jackson. The business was close to failing at the time of their marriage. By 1974, the time of Mr. Miller's death, the business was prosperous. Plaintiff did not make any capital contribution to the partnership, although she held a management position in the nursery business and did physical labor. She kept all the books and hired and fired employees. In 1960 a business registration certificate was filed for the nursery listing it as a partnership. Annual tax forms listed the business as a sole proprietorship and plaintiff's occupation as a housewife. There never was any formal written partnership agreement. Mrs. Miller, the plaintiff, sued defendant bank, her husband's executor, claiming that she was a partner in the nursery business with her deceased husband. Was there a partnership? [*Miller v. City Bank and Trust Co.,* 266 N.W.2d 687 (Mich. 1978).]
3. *X* owns a building with a restaurant rented to *Z*. *Z* is the manager of the restaurant and is authorized by *X* to make all food purchases in *X*'s name. In addition to rental payments, *Z* pays *X* 15 percent of the monthly net profits. *Y*, a creditor of the restaurant, sued *X* and *Z* as partners. Are they partners?
4. A claim was filed in court on behalf of, and in the name of, a law partnership, Horton, Davis & McCaleb. One of the partners was deceased. The claim was signed by a surviving member of the firm. The claim was for the balance due on an outstanding bill for legal services rendered to decedent by the claimant law firm. The claim recited that the claimant law partnership had rendered legal services on behalf of decedent during his lifetime; that decedent had acknowledged the debt and had paid part of it before his death. Claimant alleged that the balance was $24,750. The claim was signed and verified by Malcolm McCaleb, who was described as a partner in the claimant law firm. The court stated that since claimant was not in existence, it could not file a claim. Claimant contends that the trial court erred in dismissing the partnership's claim based upon an asserted lack of legal existence. Claimant maintains that in dismissing the claim the court failed to perceive the distinction between dissolution and termination of a partnership. Did the court err in dismissing the claim? [*Horton, Davis & McCaleb v. Howe* 85 Ill.App.3d 970 (1980).]
5. Juanita Bailes and Fred Bailes were married in 1953. They began operation of a business, Bailes Best Made Dog Food, as a partnership in 1958, and continued such operation until Fred Bailes died intestate (without a will) in 1969. Surviving him were Juanita, his wife, and an only son Fred, Jr., by a previous marriage. Plaintiff, Fred, Jr., claims that all the assets of the business should become part of the estate of his father and should be distributed according to the law of descent and distribution. Juanita Bailes, defendant, objects. Is plaintiff entitled to his father's interest in the partnership? [*Bailes v. Bailes,* 549 S.W.2d 69 (Ark. 1977).]
6. *X*, *Y*, and *Z* were doctors who owned their medical building as partners. The building was owned free and clear of any mortgage debt. *Z* died and his widow sued *X* and *Y* for her husband's interest in the medical building. Decide.

7. Plaintiff, a judgment creditor of defendant partner, seeks to impose and foreclose (enforce) a lien on defendant's undivided interest in partnership real estate. The court held that foreclosing on real estate of a partnership to satisfy the judgment debt of an individual partner was legal. Plaintiff appealed. You decide. [*Buckman v. Goldblatt,* 314 N.E.2d 188 (Ohio 1974).]
8. Jebeles and Costellos entered into an oral partnership agreement on September 2, 1977 under the business name of "Dino's Hot Dogs." A rift was created between Jebeles and Costellos, who ceased to remit any sums to Jebeles as his share of the profits of the partnership. He changed the locks on the doors to the establishment and has failed or refused to furnish Jebeles with an accounting of the partnership business. It is evident that these two men cannot engage in a business undertaking in a manner that would continue the contracts that normally exist between partners in an active business. On November 19, 1979, Jebeles filed his complaint seeking a dissolution of the partnership and a full and complete accounting by Costellos for all profits received since December 3, 1978. Costellos counterclaimed that there was no partnership agreement, but that, if there was one, Jebeles breached it. The court ordered an accounting, but refused to dissolve the partnership. Should the court have dissolved the partnership? [*Jebeles v. Costellos* and *Costellos v. Jebeles,* 391 So.2d 1024 (Ala. 1980).]
9. An agent for Marvil Properties, plaintiff, a general partnership, entered into a contract in the name of the partnership with Fripp Island Development Corporation, defendant, for the sale by Fripp to Marvil of certain real estate. This action for specific performance of the sales agreement was brought by Marvil in the partnership's name without naming the partners. Demurrer was interposed to the complaint on the ground, among others, that the plaintiff does not have legal capacity to sue. Does a general partnership have the capacity to sue in its name? [*Marvil Properties v. Fripp Island Dev. Corp.,* 258 S.E.2d 106 (S.C. 1979).]
10. In *Chaiken v. Employment Security Commission,* excerpted at the beginning of this section, what should Chaiken have done to assure the formation and operation of a partnership?

C H A P T E R

39

PARTNERSHIP MANAGEMENT AND THE AUTHORITY OF PARTNERS

After you have read this chapter, you should be able to:

1. Identify the source of law regarding the management of a partnership.
2. Identify trading and nontrading partnerships.
3. Explain the source of a partner's implied authority.
4. Explain what is meant by the implied authority of a partner, and list and give examples.
5. Discuss the express authority of a partner.
6. List and explain the five prohibited transactions under the UPA on a partner's implied authority to bind the firm.
7. Explain what is meant by a partner's apparent authority.
8. Explain when a majority is required to effect a partnership decision; explain when a unanimous vote is required.

BUSINESS DECISIONS and the LAW

Lillian and Miles Cahn started out like many other couples who are business partners. In 1960, they purchased a factory in New York City and began manufacturing low margin, private-label billfolds. The Cahns, in a management decision, decided to expand their product line and developed classic premium-priced handbags bearing the name Coach.

By the 1980s the Cahns had to ration the Coach bags to stores. The demand for these handsome well-made bags far outstripped supply and again the Cahns were faced with management decisions. They could expand, but that meant they would spend more time on administration and risk diluting the quality as well as lessening the cachet of Coach bags. Or, they could maintain the size of the company and continue to manufacture quality products by a skilled work force with whom they were on a first-name basis. The Cahns, who are both in their sixties, opted for the latter. They decided that the latter option allowed them to slow down somewhat and enjoy outside interests. Still the business grew at an astounding pace and in 1986 the partners decided to sell out to Sara Lee for an estimated $30 million. The Cahns express no regret that sale of Coach bags have since increased five-fold to $100 million.

What has this entrepreneurial couple done for an encore? The partners now produce goat cheese on a 300-acre dairy farm north of New York City. Already

Coach Farm cheese is featured in gourmet shops and chic restaurants. Sara Lee is probably working on a purchase agreement already.

Source: P. Berman, "Goat Cheese, Anyone?" Excerpted by permission of *Forbes* magazine, September 18, 1989, p. 220-21. © Forbes, Inc., 1989.

Introduction

Partnerships engage in a broad spectrum of business activities ranging from the small hardware store to Wall Street law offices. The management problems and contractual relationships encountered by each partnership will vary, depending upon the size and nature of the partnership.

This chapter examines the legal procedures established by the Uniform Partnership Act to manage the partnership and engage in contracts with third parties. The law of **agency** as discussed in Part 3, Agency and Employment, will apply.[1]

agency
A legal relationship between two persons who agree that one is to act on behalf of the other, subject to the other's control

agent
A person authorized to act on behalf of another and subject to the other's control

actual authority
Express and implied authority

express authority
An agent's authority specifically expressed in the principal's manifestation to the agent

implied authority
An agent's authority that the agent reasonably can understand he or she has from the principal's manifestation to the agent but not expressed therein

Actual Authority of Partners

Each partner is an **agent** of the partnership for the purpose of carrying on, in the usual way, the partnership business.[2] Hence, all partners have **actual authority** to bind the firm with third parties unless prohibited by the partnership agreement. The partners also have equal voice in the internal management of the business, unless denied by the agreement.[3] In addition to the actual authority, a partner may have apparent authority to bind the firm with third parties as that partner carries on the partnership business in the usual and customary manner.

► Express Authority

Partners have, by virtue of their agreement, **express authority** to act on behalf of the partnership. Thus a managing partner of a retail department store has *express authority* to purchase inventory on credit and thereby obligate the firm. The partnership agreement will determine the extent of the individual partners' express authority but not their apparent authority.

► Implied Authority

A partner may have **implied authority** to bind the firm with third parties. This may occur even if the partnership agreement or the partners do not give him or her any authority. The extent of the partner's implied authority will depend upon the scope of the firm's business and its character as a "trading" or "nontrading" partnership.[4] A *trading* partnership is engaged in buying and selling *property*. A *nontrading* partnership is

[1]UPA, sec. 4(3), and *Rice v. Jackson,* 171 Pa. 89 (1895).

[2]UPA, sec. 9(1).

[3]UPA, sec. 18(e).

[4]See p. 805 for classification of partnerships.

engaged in selling *services*. The following are common examples of a partner's implied authority to contract with third persons on behalf of the partnership.[5]

Contracts to Buy and Sell The authority of a partner to buy or sell the firm's assets depends upon whether the firm is a trading or nontrading partnership. A partnership engaged in manufacturing, wholesaling, or retailing is a trading partnership. Partnerships of lawyers, doctors, and accountants are nontrading partnerships.

In the following case the defendant contends that since he did not authorize his co-partner in writing to enter into a real estate contract, the contract was binding only on his co-partner and not on the partnership. Notice how the court applies the law of agency to the facts of the case.

FACTS

Kenneth C. Ball and Theresa A. Ball brought this action against Dennis Carlson, Charles Edward Ishmael, and Stephen M. Teegardin, individually and doing business as C.I.T. Construction Company (C.I.T.) to recover damages resulting from the alleged breach of a contract for the sale of a lot and the construction of a home thereon. The Balls commenced this action for damages, alleging that C.I.T. had breached its contractual duty to construct and sell the house. Teegardin contended that since he did not authorize Carlson in writing to enter into the real estate contract, the contract was only binding on Carlson individually. The district court entered judgment for the plaintiffs. One of the defendants, Teegardin, appealed.

DECISION

Every partner is an agent of the partnership for the purpose of its business, and every act of every partner, including the execution in the partnership name of any instrument for apparently carrying on in the usual way the business of the partnership of which he is a member, binds the partnership. The status of a partner, as both principal and agent of the partnership, serves as complete authority with respect to acts which are apparently within the usual course of the partnership's particular business, unless the other party knows that he has no such authority. This obviates the necessity of a specific written authorization from the other partners. Thus, the act of a partner in selling real estate, when in the apparent scope of the partnership, is binding upon the partnership and the other partners without obtaining their written consent, notwithstanding the statute of frauds requirement, that the authority of an agent to sell real estate must be in writing. C.I.T. was engaged in the business of real estate development and sale. Therefore, Carlson bound each partner by signing the contract in C.I.T.'s name.

Ball v. Carlson, 641 P.2d 303 (Colo. 1981).

To Borrow Money and Execute Commercial Paper A trading partnership that is buying and selling inventory will have frequent needs to borrow money and execute promissory notes in the firm name. A partner in such a firm has implied authority to do both and to pledge partnership property, provided that it is reasonably necessary to carry on the partnership business. A partner in a nontrading partnership does not have this implied authority unless an emergency requires it or it is customary for that business to borrow money and sign notes.

[5]See A. Bromberg, *Crane and Bromberg on Partnership*, (St. Paul: West Publishing, 1968), 280, for a discussion of trading and nontrading partnerships.

Employment Partners have implied authority to employ personnel whose services are necessary to carry on the partnership business.

Firm Debts A partner has implied authority to pay the partnership's creditors with partnership funds. However, a partner may not pay his or her personal creditors with firm funds.

Settle and Compromise Claims A partner has implied authority to settle and compromise a claim of a partnership creditor.

Representations and Admissions A partner has implied authority to make representations and admissions that may bind the firm, provided that they are made in the ordinary and usual course of firm business. For example, *X,* a partner, admitted to *Z,* a firm creditor, that *Z*'s claim was owed. *X*'s admission will bind the firm.[6]

Notice to a Partner A partner has implied authority to receive notice on any matter relating to partnership affairs, and such notice will bind the partnership, except in the case of fraud.[7] To illustrate, if a landlord gave notice of an increase in the partnership rent to a partner, the notice will bind the firm.

Limitation on Authority

Partners have no implied authority to perform acts that are not customary and usual in the carrying on of the partnership business. The partnership agreement, however, may give a partner express authority to do acts not for the carrying on of usual partnership business. However, certain transactions are prohibited under UPA, Section 9(3).

1. *A partner may not assign the partnership property for the benefit of creditors.* If a partner made such an assignment, it would prevent the firm from conducting its usual business. The UPA allows an assignment if authorized by the other partners.[8]
2. *A partner may not dispose of the goodwill of the business.* A partner has no implied authority to sell the partnership goodwill, because this would cause a discontinuance of firm business. Partnership authorization would be required from all the other partners.[9]
3. *A partner may not do any act that would make it impossible to carry on the ordinary business of the partnership.* For example, an individual partner has no implied authority to sell an office computer that is required to process its monthly billings.[10]
4. *A partner may not* **confess a judgment**. An individual partner has no implied authority to admit that a claim is due, because the partners have the right to defend

confession of judgment
A party's consent to jurisdiction and judgment of a court without a trial in a civil case

[6]UPA, sec. 11.

[7]UPA, sec. 12.

[8]UPA, sec. 9(3)(a).

[9]UPA, sec. 9(3)(b).

[10]UPA, sec. 9(3)(c).

the claim in court.[11] For example, in a malpractice claim against a medical partnership, an admission of liability by a doctor partner who treated the patient will not bind the firm.

5. *A partner may not submit a partnership claim to arbitration.* A partner cannot submit a firm dispute to arbitration without the consent of the other partners unless the firm has ceased doing business.[12] Since arbitration is becoming a common method of resolving disputes[13] and is found in many contracts, third persons dealing with a partnership should insist on unanimous consent in a contract that provides for arbitration.

Apparent Authority

Partners have apparent authority[14] to carry on in the usual way the partnership business, and third persons who reasonably rely on such authority can bind the firm.[15] A partner without actual or apparent authority cannot bind the firm with third parties. If the third person knows of the lack of authority, he cannot bind the firm for the partner's unauthorized acts.

Firm Management

The internal management of the partnership is accomplished by the partners' vote in the decision-making process.

▶ Ordinary Business

At a partnership meeting, the decision of the majority will govern, provided that it is an ordinary business matter and the vote does not contradict an agreement between the parties. Hence, the majority may decide those business affairs that are normal and customary in carrying on the firm's business.[16] For example, in a construction firm, the majority may decide to rent construction equipment over the objection of the minority. All of the partners will be bound under the equipment lease. Half of the partners is not a majority.

▶ Extraordinary Business

A *unanimous vote* by the partners is necessary for a business decision that would change the partnership agreement.[17] Thus changing the location of the firm is a matter all the partners must agree to, unless the partnership agreement provides otherwise.

---

[11]UPA, sec. 9(3)(d).

[12]UPA, sec. 9(3)(e).

[13]See pp. 20–21 for a discussion of arbitration.

[14]For the concept of apparent authority, see p. 311.

[15]UPA, sec. 9(1).

[16]UPA, sec. 18(h).

[17]UPA, sec. 18(h).

In the following case the partners incorporated part of the business without the consent of one partner, who brought suit to reach his partnership interest in the corporation.

FACTS

Fortugno, plaintiff, a member of a family partnership that was organized to collect and sell manure, brought an action for its dissolution. The partnership, Hudson Manure Company, sold its manure to mushroom growers in southeastern Pennsylvania. In the course of its operation, the partnership found it convenient to put certain of its activities in corporate form in order to limit the liability of the individual partners. Fortugno refused to authorize the corporate division of the partnership and claimed that the enterprises constitute a single integrated partnership, whether or not any phase of the business was conducted in corporate form. He sought to be paid in cash for his partnership interest in both the partnership and the corporation and requested the court to order the sale of the corporate assets. May the partnership property be traced into the corporation?

DECISION

Yes. Judgment for Fortugno. Less than all the partners may not bind the partnership by an act not performed for the purpose of carrying on the usual partnership business, unless authorized by the other partners. Because Fortugno never ratified the act of incorporating part of the partnership, no assets of the partnership may remain in the corporation.

Fortugno v. Hudson Manure Co., 144 A.2d 207 (N.J. 1958).

Summary Statement

1. Partnership management is governed by the Uniform Partnership Act and agency law. The partners by agreement may change the effect of the UPA, which states in Section 18(e) that "all partners have equal rights in the management and operation of the partnership business."
2. The extent of a partner's contribution to the firm does not affect that partner's equal voice in management.
3. The partnership agreement grants to each partner *express authority* to act as an agent on behalf of the partnership.
4. *Implied authority* of a partner to act on behalf of the firm depends upon whether it is a trading or nontrading firm.
5. The implied authority of a partner depends on the nature of the firm; some common examples of a partner's implied authority are authority to do the following:
    - **a)** Buy and sell inventory in a trading partnership
    - **b)** Borrow money and execute commercial paper in a trading partnership
    - **c)** Employ personnel
    - **d)** Pay firm debts with partnership funds
    - **e)** Settle and compromise claims
    - **f)** Make admissions that will bind the firm if made in the ordinary and usual course of firm business
    - **g)** Receive notice on any matter relating to partnership affairs
6. Unless authorized by *all* the other partners, or unless they have abandoned the business, a partner may not do the following:
    - **a)** Assign the partnership property in trust for creditors
    - **b)** Dispose of the partnership's goodwill

c) Do any other act that would make it impossible to carry on the ordinary partnership business
d) Confess a judgment
e) Submit a partnership claim to arbitration

7. A majority vote is required to effect *ordinary* business decisions connected with the partnership business.
8. A unanimous vote of the partners is required to change the partnership agreement or any material agreement between the partners.

In the following case the court held that a partner had actual authority to execute notes for partnership obligations that bind the partnership and its individual partners.

WOMACK v. FIRST NATIONAL BANK OF SAN AUGUSTINE
613 S.W.2d 548 (Tex. 1981)

J. W. Summers, Chief Justice. The First National Bank of San Augustine, Texas, (bank), plaintiff, sued Charles C. McClanahan (Charles) and his brother, Dr. H. Lane McClanahan (Lane), to recover upon five promissory notes. The bank alleged that the notes represented individual obligations of each of the brothers or, alternatively, were partnership obligations executed by Charles on behalf of a partnership composed of the two brothers named McClanahan Brothers. Charles answered, admitting liability and claiming that the notes were partnership notes. Dr. H. Lane McClanahan filed a general denial. Prior to trial, Lane died, and Leo Womack was appointed as Temporary Administrator of the decedent's estate and substituted as a party defendant. The case was tried before a jury which found that the notes were partnership obligations and judgment was rendered for the First National Bank of San Augustine, from which Womack appeals.

On August 4, 1972, the McClanahan brothers executed a partnership agreement for the express purpose of engaging in the operation of a hog farm. By this agreement, which consisted of only four provisions and covered only a half page, the brothers agreed that Charles was to devote his time to the business and in return, receive 75% of the profits and share 50% of the losses while Lane would receive 25% of the profits and share 50% of the losses. Additionally, the agreement provided that the partnership funds would be kept in a joint account and Charles agreed "to keep a complete record of the business, and shall be subject to inspection by Lane at any time." The agreement does not contain any provision relative to the partners' authority, nothing limiting their authority nor defining it. No partnership name is indicated in the agreement and there is testimony that the partnership operated under the names "McClanahan Farms," "C. C. McClanahan Farms," "McClanahan Brothers" and "Sugar Bush Farms" interchangeably.

Following formation of the partnership, Lane and Charles began executing a series of notes with appellee-bank as payee. All notes reflect on their face that they were executed in contemplation of investment in the partnership business, each containing notations that they are secured by either livestock, feeding equipment or hogs. The notes are signed "Charles McClanahan" or "C. C. McClanahan" and "H. Lane McClanahan, M.D."

In full recognition of that rule (that one is not liable on an instrument unless he signs it), our supreme court has stated that there are several instances in which a non-signing partner may be liable upon a note signed by another partner. A partner's authority to bind the partnership and his partners is governed by the Texas version of the Uniform Partnership Act unless expanded or limited by the partnership agreement.

Section 9 of the UPA provides that: "(1) Every partner is an agent of the partnership for the purpose of its business, and the act of every partner, including the execution in the partnership name of any instrument, for apparently carrying on in the usual way the business of the partnership of which he is a member binds the partnership, unless the partner so acting has in fact no authority to act for the partnership in the particular matter, and the person with whom he is dealing has knowledge of the fact that he has no such authority." As we construe this section, Dr. McClanahan may be held liable on the notes as a partner if they were executed for "apparently carrying on in the usual way the business of the partnership." Thus, since the partnership agreement was silent as to Charles McClanahan's authority to issue negotiable paper in the partnership name, he had the actual or express authority to do so under Sec. 9 if such acts were for the purpose of "apparently carrying on" the business of the partnership in the way other firms engaged in the same business in the locality usually transact business, or in the way in which the particular partnership usually transacts its business. Whether Dr. McClanahan was aware that Charles was executing the notes has no effect upon his authority to do so, "for it is familiar law that each partner of a partnership has, as agent, power to bind all members of his firm for an indebtedness incurred in the prosecution of his firm's business; and this is true even though members other than the acting one is (sic) without knowledge of the obligatory act." Stated another way, it has been said that an agent's authority is presumed to be co-extensive with the business entrusted to his care. He is limited in his authority to such acts as are incident to the management of the particular business with which he is entrusted. Thus, the inquiry becomes whether Charles McClanahan executed the notes in order to conduct the business which Dr. McClanahan testified had been entrusted to his care, in its ordinary and normal manner, there being no evidence in the record as to the normal business transactions of other hog farms in San Augustine County.

We believe that there was ample evidence to support the jury's finding that Charles McClanahan had the authority to execute the notes and bind the partnership thereto. The notes themselves reflect that the monies loaned upon the notes were invested in the partnership business; the farm was initially financed over an eight month period by the execution and payment of a series of notes; the partnership agreement did not attempt, in any manner, to limit Charles McClanahan's authority. This conclusion is further buttressed by the fact that partners normally have the right to execute negotiable paper for commercial purposes consistent with the object of the partnership and for the benefit of the partnership. Where the partnership business contemplates periodical or continuous or frequent purchasing, not as incidental to an occupation, but for the purpose of selling again the thing purchased, it is usual and customary to purchase on credit and to execute paper evidencing the existence of the partnership debt. Both Charles McClanahan and Ray Neal McEachern testified that Charles would execute a note, buy hogs and feed them on the proceeds thereof, sell them and pay on the notes. Such was the customary business of the partnership. We must therefore conclude that Charles McClanahan had the actual authority to execute the notes in question as partnership obligations.

Judgment affirmed.

Questions and Case Problems

1. Voeller, the managing partner of the Pay-Out Drive-In Theatre, signed a contract with Hodge, plaintiff, for the sale of a small parcel of land belonging to the partnership. That parcel, although adjacent to the theater, was not used in theater operations. The agreement for the sale of land stated that it was between Hodge and the Pay-Out Drive-In Theatre, a partnership. Plaintiff sued the defendants, partners of the Theatre, for specific performance of the contract. The trial court found that Voeller had apparent authority to execute the contract on behalf of the partnership, and that the contract should be specifically enforced against the defendant partners. Defendants appeal arguing that Voeller did not have apparent authority to sell the property. The other partners have maintained from the inception of this controversy that Voeller did not have apparent authority to sell this property. Did Voeller have apparent authority to sell the property? [*Hodge v. Garrett, Voeller et al.*, 614 P.2d 420 (Idaho 1980).]

2. Oswald, plaintiff, and Leckey, defendant, signed a partnership agreement to conduct an accounting practice. The partnership was not harmonious and was terminated. Plaintiff seeks an accounting and claims defendant had no authority to write off uncollectible accounts without plaintiff's consent while winding up the partnership affairs. Defendant claimed he acted in good faith and has the power to compromise claims. You decide. [*Oswald v. Leckey*, 572 P.2d 1316 (Or. 1977).]
3. *X*, *Y*, and *Z* ran a college bookstore as partners. At a partnership meeting they agreed that *X* and *Y* would work in the store but *Z* would be the only partner authorized to order textbooks. A salesperson who knew that *X* was a partner but did not know that she was without authority to order textbooks, took an order from her for 1,000 books. The partnership refused to accept or pay for the books. Can the textbook company collect?
4. *X* and *Z* were partners in a medical practice. *Y*, a patient of *Z*, was billed $600 for an operation. *Y* claimed that the bill was unfair, and *Z* agreed to compromise by accepting $300 as payment in full. *X* told *Z* that *Z* had no authority to accept less than the original bill and told *Y* that the partnership was going to sue for the additional $300. *Y* claimed that partner *X* was bound by the compromise. Decide.
5. A client owed an accounting partnership $200 for services rendered to her. She paid the money to a partner who used it to pay off a personal home improvement loan. Must she repay the fee to the partnership?
6. A Boston partnership engaged in the antique business desired to move the firm to Vermont. At a partnership meeting, one of the three partners objected to the move. Is a majority vote sufficient to move the firm to Vermont?
7. *X* and *Y* operated a construction business as partners. *Z*, a customer, complained to *X* that the construction of his apartment building was defective. *X* found *Z* to be unreasonable but agreed to submit the dispute to arbitration. *Y* protested the arbitration procedure and claimed that the partnership is not bound to arbitrate. Is *Y* correct?
8. *X*, *Y*, and *Z* are partners in an accounting firm. *X* and *Y* want to rent additional space on the floor where they always operated the firm. *Z* feels it is too expensive to do so and votes against it. *X* and *Y* sign the lease and rent the new space. Is *Z* liable as a partner on the lease?
9. Feingold, plaintiff, sued William and Charlotte Davis, husband and wife and owners of Davis Nursing Home as a partnership. Mr. Davis signed a purchase and sale agreement to sell the nursing home to Feingold, including its assets and goodwill. Mrs. Davis, his co-partner, never signed nor consented to the agreement and refused to convey the property. Feingold sought specific performance of the purchase and sale agreement. Decide. [*Feingold v. Davis*, 282 A.2d 291 (Pa. 1971).]
10. After reading the case of *Womack v. First National Bank of San Augustine*, excerpted at the beginning of this section, what specific provision should have been in the partnership agreement to have protected Dr. McClanahan and his estate from this lawsuit by the payee/bank?

CHAPTER 40

RIGHTS, DUTIES, AND REMEDIES OF PARTNERS AMONG THEMSELVES

After you have read this chapter, you should be able to:

1. List and explain the nine rights of a partner as an owner of the firm.
2. Explain the remedies of a partner.
3. List and explain the five duties of partners to each other.
4. Analyze and discuss the nature of a partner's liability on firm contracts and torts committed by a partner or an employee of the firm.
5. Explain the liability of an incoming partner entering an existing firm.
6. Explain the nature and extent of a partner's liability.
7. Explain the effect of dissolution of the firm on a partner's existing liability.
8. List and explain the three property rights a partner has in the partnership.

BUSINESS DECISIONS and the LAW

The renowned partnership of Kohlberg, Kravis, Roberts & Company, (KKR), pioneers of modern leveraged buyouts, has begun to show signs of strain. The partnership which, among other things, invests in companies, is best known for its $25 billion buyout of RJR Nabisco, Inc.

The partners began working together at Bear Stearns & Co., and left to form their own firm. According to the partnership agreement, each partner received a stake in KKR investment properties.

Jerome Kohlberg, Jr. left KKR in 1987 after reportedly becoming alienated from the firm by his partners' aggressive strategy. After he left the firm, he remained a partner in four properties. According to a lawsuit Mr. Kohlberg just filed, KKR unilaterally refinanced these properties subsequent to Mr. Kohlberg's departure, which had the effect of cutting his ownership interest. Mr. Kohlberg charges that this action breached their fiduciary duty to him.

Meanwhile, KKR maintains that Mr. Kohlberg is mistaken in his interpretation of the partnership agreement. It looks to be a lengthy legal battle over the proper interpretation of the parties' partnership agreement. The outcome, as you may guess, involves millions of dollars.

Sources: "Kohlberg Kravis Sued By Founding Partner Over His Holdings," *Wall Street Journal*, Aug. 31, 1989, p. A3, and Richard Satran, "Kohlberg Sues Ex-Partners; Says His Stake Unfairly Cut," *The Boston Globe*, Aug. 31, 1989, p. 59.

Introduction

Many students will some day be partners and will be dealing with partners, in business. They should be carefully aware of the nature of their duties and rights, just as they should be aware of those of partners in other firms that are dealing with them. The liability of a partner to the other partners and, particularly, to third persons is great.

This chapter explains the rights and duties of the partners among themselves as well as the partnership's liability to third persons who have dealt with the firm. The UPA, Section 18, establishes the rules that determine the rights and duties of the partners, unless their partnership agreement provides otherwise. Also, since partners are general agents of the partnership, the law of agency applies[1] and spells out the common law agent duties of each partner, unless the partnership agreement provides otherwise.

The Rights of Partners

Each partner, as a co-owner of the partnership, has, unless otherwise agreed, the following statutory rights under the UPA, Section 18.

► Share Equally in Profits and Losses

Unless otherwise agreed, each partner has the right to share in the profits and surplus equally.[2] This rule is not affected by a disproportionate amount of capital and contributions or the amount of services rendered by a partner. Thus, if *A* contributes $10,000 and *B* $5,000 and *C* services only, they each will share the profits equally unless otherwise agreed. Unless otherwise agreed, losses are shared as profits are shared.

► Equal Rights in Management

Each partner has an equal right in the management of the firm.[3] Thus a partner who provides only services has the same voice in management as the partner who made a substantial capital contribution.

► Payment of Interest

Loans A partner who makes a loan to the firm shall be paid interest from the date of the loan. An advance by a partner, beyond the amount of capital that the partnership agreement obligated the partner to contribute, is a loan to the partnership. The lending partner is entitled to interest from the date of advance and to repayment when the loan is due. If partnership funds are insufficient to pay the note on its due date, the co-partners must contribute their share of the amount due.

Capital Contributions A partner who makes a capital contribution shall receive interest from the date when repayment should be made. The contribution used in the business should be returned upon dissolution after partnership debts have been paid. If the contribution is then not returned to the partner, unless otherwise agreed the partner

---

[1]UPA, sec. 4(3).

[2]UPA, secs. 26 and 18(a).

[3]UPA, sec. 18(e).

is entitled to interest on the amount due. In the following case a partner's skill and labor on behalf of the partnership were determined to be a part of the partner's capital contribution to the firm to which the partner was entitled on dissolution, as well as interest thereon, when the other partner refused to make payment.

FACTS

Thompson was a partner with defendant, Beth, in a business organized to erect and operate a resort area. Thompson was a skilled cabinet maker and electrician who invested $400 and contributed 2,000 hours of labor in building the lake resort. Upon dissolution of the partnership, Thompson made demand for an accounting and payment of his share of the proceeds from the sale of the property. Beth refused. Thompson claimed he was entitled to compensation for his 2,000 hours of labor as a capital investment and to interest on his share from the date of the sale of the partnership assets.

DECISION

Judgment for Thompson. A partner who has been active in contributing his skill and labor on a day-to-day basis is compensated by a share in the partnership profits. This rule does not apply where the skill and labor of the partner are his contribution to the capital assets of the partnership. Here, Thompson's return of his contribution on liquidation is not remuneration, but a return on capital investment, and he is entitled to interest from the date of sale of the partnership assets.

Thompson v. Beth, 111 N.W.2d 171 (Wis. 1961).

► Partnership Books

The partnership books and records shall be kept at the principal place of business of the partnership. Each partner has the right to inspect and copy the books at any time. However, the partnership agreement may prevent a partner from inspecting the books and using the information for other than partnership purposes. In the following case the court ordered that, pursuant to the request of one of the partners, there should be a dissolution and an accounting even though the partnership books were poorly kept.

FACTS

Luchs formed a partnership with Ormsby to service government contracts for specialized construction work. Luchs brought this action for a dissolution and an accounting. The lower court entered a judgment against Ormsby and he appealed. Ormsby stated at the trial that he would accept the accountants' report, and that any incompleteness in their report was through negligent bookkeeping of the partnership. Ormsby then claimed that the accountants' report was inadequate and demanded a new audit.

DECISION

Judgment for Luchs. Any incompleteness in the accountants' report was due to the negligent bookkeeping of the partnership, and a better job could not have been done under the circumstances.

Luchs v. Ormsby, 340 P.2d 702 (Cal. 1959).

► New Partners

A new partner may be admitted only with the consent of *all* the partners unless the partnership agreement provides otherwise. Recall that a partnership is a contractual relationship, and the admission of a new member is a material change in the agreement. The new incoming partner is liable for partnership obligations before and after becoming a partner. However, the incoming partner's personal assets cannot be reached to satisfy partnership creditors whose claims existed *before* he or she became a partner.

If a new partner promises the co-partners that he or she will pay old partnership creditors, the latter will generally be entitled to enforce the new partner's promise as third party creditor beneficiaries.[4]

If the incoming partner buys a partnership interest from a retiring partner, the transaction is not within the bulk sales law because the new partner is bound to pay the old partner's debts from partnership property. However, the incoming partner must give public notice of the purchase.[5]

► Partnership Assets

Partnership *property* is what the partnership has accumulated. It is a part of the assets of the partnership, which consist of (1) the partnership property and (2) the contributions of each of the partners necessary for payment of all partnership liabilities.

► Reimbursement and Indemnity

reimbursement

One person's right against another to be repaid money paid on the other's behalf for which the latter was responsible

indemnity

An absolute obligation to pay for another's loss

Provided that a partner is acting reasonably and in good faith, a partner is entitled to be **reimbursed** for payments made and reasonable personal debts incurred by the partner in properly carrying on the partnership business. For example, an accountant who paid for office supplies with a personal check, is entitled to be reimbursed by the firm. The accountant is also entitled to be **indemnified** for damage to the accountant's property while used in the partnership business, as is illustrated by the following case.

FACTS

Smith is one of the eight partners who owned and operated a coal mine with a fleet of thirty trucks. Smith sued the partnership to recover damages for the value of his personally owned truck which was damaged as the result of the negligence of an employee of the partnership while acting for the partnership. Is Smith entitled to reimbursement for his loss?

DECISION

Yes. Judgment for Smith. If the negligence of the partnership caused damage to the property of a stranger, the partnership would be liable. There is no reason to deny recovery where the damaged property is that of a partner. The negligence was that of a firm employee acting within the scope of his employment. The partners are jointly and severally liable for the loss.

Smith v. Hensley, 354 S.W.2d 744 (Ky. 1962).

► Compensation

No partner is entitled to extra compensation for services rendered in carrying on partnership business. It is important for the partnership agreement to provide for salaries to be paid to the partners because sharing the profits is considered adequate compensation, unless the parties otherwise agree. It is not unusual in a professional partnership for one partner to be authorized as a general manager. For example, a law firm may

[4]See pp. 264–267 for a discussion of third party beneficiaries.

[5]UCC 6–103(6); see pp. 502–504 for a discussion of the bulk sales law.

designate a partner who will expend additional time in managing the law practice. Unless the partnership agreement entitles a partner to additional compensation for additional services, there is no extra compensation. The UPA does provide for reasonable compensation for a *surviving* partner's services in winding up the partnership affairs.[6]

In the following case the court held that, to be awarded compensation, a partner must show that his services extended beyond normal partnership functions, in the absence of an agreement to the contrary.

FACTS

From 1952 to 1973, Sydney Altman and Ashley Altman operated a number of partnerships engaged in real estate construction and management in southeastern Pennsylvania. During this period the two brothers shared equally in the management and control of the partnerships, and through their joint efforts they built the business into very profitable and substantial enterprises. Sydney and Ashley received identical salaries, and each brother was permitted to charge certain personal expenses to the partnerships.

Sydney told Ashley in November 1973 that he was considering retiring from the Altman businesses.

When a satisfactory retirement agreement could not be reached, Sydney brought this action in the district court seeking judicial dissolution of the partnerships. Judgment was rendered for Sydney and Ashley appealed. Ashley challenged the district court's holding that he is not entitled to compensation beyond his share of partnership profits for managing the partnerships between August 1973 and June 1977.

DECISION

Affirmed, judgment for plaintiff, Sydney Altman. In the absence of an agreement to the contrary, a partner is not entitled to compensation beyond his share of the profits, for services rendered by him in performing partnership matters. A right to compensation arises only where the services rendered extend beyond normal partnership functions. Ashley, however, does not expressly contend that the services he performed went beyond normal partnership functions. Ashley must show more than the fact that a failure to award compensation would be highly inequitable; he must also show that his services extended beyond normal partnership functions.

The district court's factual finding that Ashley's services did not warrant compensation beyond his share of the partnership profits was not clearly erroneous.

Altman v. Altman, 653 F.2d 755 (3rd Cir. 1981).

► Accounting

A partner may, under limited circumstances as provided by the UPA Section 22 require a *formal* accounting during the ordinary operation of the partnership. This right should be distinguished from the informal process of inspecting and copying the books and records. The right to a formal accounting occurs:

1. when the partner is wrongfully excluded from the partnership business, or
2. when the right to a formal accounting exists under the partnership agreement, or
3. when a partner has acquired secret profits without the consent of the other partners from any transaction connected with the firm, or
4. whenever other circumstances render it just and reasonable.

[6]UPA, sec. 18(f).

Remedies of Partners

► Contracts

The partnership is liable for the contracts of its partners as agents of the firm. According to UPA Section 2, "Every partner is an agent of the partnership for the purpose of its business." Hence, contract liability of the partners in carrying out partnership business is the responsibility of the firm. As to third persons, the partners are liable jointly (collectively) for partnership contracts.[7]

A breach of the partnership agreement subjects the wrongdoer to contract liability. Generally, the usual common law remedies for breach of contract are available to partners among themselves.[8] A partner has the remedy of an accounting if the partner sues the partnership.

► Torts

tort
A civil (private) noncontractual wrong for which a court will give a remedy

All partners are jointly and severally (individually) liable to third persons for **torts** committed in the ordinary course of the partnership business.

> Where, by any wrongful act or omission of any partner acting in the ordinary course of the business of the partnership . . . loss or injury is caused to any person, not being a partner in the partnership . . . the partnership is liable therefor to the same extent as the partner so acting or omitting to act.[9] All partners are liable (a) Jointly and severally for everything chargeable to the partnership under sections 13 and 14.[10].

To illustrate, if Doctor *X* is a partner in a medical partnership and negligently treats a patient, the malpractice negligence claim may be brought against Doctor *X* and the partnership.

The following case illustrates the joint and several liability of partners in a medical partnership for a malpractice claim.

FACTS

Daniel Zuckerman, an infant, by his mother and natural guardian, Elaine Zuckerman, and Elaine Zuckerman, individually, brought a medical malpractice action against Dr. Joseph Antenucci and Dr. Jose Pena. Both had treated the mother during pregnancy. Although the summons did not state that the two defendants were partners, the undisputed, unopposed, and uncontradicted evidence at the trial established that relationship and that the alleged acts of malpractice were done in the course of partnership business. The jury returned a verdict finding that defendant Pena was guilty of malpractice. The amount of the verdict totalled $4 million.

DECISION

The issue is whether this court has jurisdiction to render a judgment against defendant Antenucci on the basis of a tort committed by his partner, even though the summons served did not designate defendant Antenucci as a partner. A party may be sued individually and directly for the tort of his partner. A partnership is liable for the tortious act of a partner,

---

[7]UPA, sec. 15(b).

[8]See pp. 269–274 for remedies on breach of contract.

[9]UPA, sec. 13.

[10]UPA, sec. 15.

and a partner is jointly and severally liable for tortious acts chargeable to the partnership. It may thus be seen that the plaintiffs herein did not have to sue a partnership entity and did not have to write "Joseph Antenucci, a partner" on the summons in order to hold him liable on a partnership theory for the act of defendant Pena. Jurisdiction over defendant Antenucci individually is sufficient for a judgment against him based on a tort committed by his partner. Therefore, even though the jury found that defendant Antenucci was not guilty of any malpractice in his treatment of the patient, they were then both jointly and severally liable for the malpractice committed by defendant Pena by operation of law.

Zuckerman v. Antenucci, 478 N.Y.S. 2d 578 (N.Y. 1984).

Of course, partners are liable to each other and to the partnership for their torts committed on each other and on the partnership.

The Duties of Partners

► Partnership Agreement

A partnership is created by a contract between the parties. Thus each partner has a duty to comply with the terms of the partnership agreement. A partner is liable for any loss caused to the firm for violation of his or her duties.

► Information

Each partner has the statutory duty to render full information of partnership matters to any partner. A similar duty is owed by agents to their principals. The duty is based on the *fiduciary status* of partners who act on behalf of the partnership. This duty to render information "on demand" extends to the legal representative of a partner.

► Reasonable Care

Each partner is under a common law duty to exercise reasonable care and skill in transacting partnership business. A partner is personally liable to the partnership for any loss proximately caused by the partner's negligence. However, a partner is *not* liable for honest mistakes or errors of judgment.

► Good Faith

A partner's **fiduciary** status obligates a partner to act with complete loyalty to the firm. This fiduciary duty prohibits a partner from making a secret profit. A partner holds all profits in trust for the partnership.

fiduciary
A person with a duty to act primarily for the benefit of another

Each partner is under the fiduciary duty not to compete with the firm. This obligates the partner to devote full time and effort to the partnership. The co-partners may, however, agree to a partner engaging in a competing business.

In the following case the court held that members of a leasing partnership who elected to compete with the firm, breached their duty owed to the partnership.

FACTS

Whittier Leasing Company was a general partnership formed to assist Whittier Hospital in its remodeling program and general financial well-being.

The partnership's success was due entirely to the fact that partners Frischling, Taylor,

Kraushaar, Akin, Hanten, Kurz and Springer were members of the "governing Board of Directors" of Whittier Hospital.

Defendants, Frischling, Taylor, Kraushaar B. and Kraushaar I. Akin, Hanten, Kurz, Springer and Jackson formed a competing partnership known as Friendly Hills Leasing Company (Friendly Hills). Together, these nine constituted the total Board of Directors of the hospital. Thereafter, Whittier Hospital, acting through its board, concluded all of its transactions with Friendly Hills, to the total exclusion of Whittier Leasing Company. Plaintiffs sought dissolution of the Whittier partnership, as well as an accounting, and recovery of damages, i.e., profits lost to Friendly Hills Leasing Company.

DECISION

Judgment for plaintiffs. It is well settled that a partner who agrees to give his personal attention to the partnership business may not engage in any other business which gives him an interest adverse to that of the firm, or which prevents him from giving to the firm business all the attention which would be advantageous to it.

Clearly, the facts here alleged reflect that certain of the partners of Whittier Leasing have elected to compete with the firm itself and to thus breach one of the partnership's basic underlying tenets. We think it therefore indisputable that plaintiffs, should they be able to prove their allegations, would be entitled to a court-ordered dissolution of Whittier Leasing.

Olivet, et al. v. Frischling, et al., 164 Cal. Rptr. 87 (Cal. 1980).

► Keeping Accounts

Each partner has a fiduciary duty to keep accounts of the partnership business. Usually a managing partner assumes this duty on behalf of the firm.

Summary Statement

1. Unless the partners otherwise agree, each partner as an owner has the following rights:

a) to share equally in profits and losses, UPA, sec. 4(3);
b) to have equal rights in the management of the firm, UPA, sec. 18(e);
c) to be paid interest from the date of partnership loans made to the firm;
d) to be paid interest from the date when repayment should be made on capital contributions made to the firm, UPA, sec. 18(d);
e) to inspect the firm books, UPA, sec. 19;
f) to vote on the admission of new partners, UPA, sec. 18(g);
g) to be indemnified for payments made and reimbursed for reasonable personal debts incurred in carrying on the partnership business, UPA, sec. 18(b);
h) in limited circumstances, to require a formal accounting during the ordinary operation of the partnership, UPA, sec. 22.
i) to vote on the admission of new partners, UPA, sec. 18(g).

2. Each partner, as an agent and a fiduciary, owes to his or her co-partners the following duties:

a) to obey the partnership agreement;
b) to render information to his co-partners on all important matters affecting the firm;
c) to act with reasonable care in transacting firm business;

d) good faith and loyalty;
e) to keep an account and record of his partnership business, UPA, sec. 21;
f) unless otherwise agreed, to share in the losses in the same ratio as they share in the profits.

3. Each partner is liable jointly with the other partners on partnership contracts made in its name and within the scope of the acting partner's actual or apparent authority.
4. Each partner is liable jointly and severally for the torts of other partners and firm employees acting in the ordinary course of the business or with the authority of the co-partners (UPA, sec. 13).
5. A partner admitted into an existing partnership is liable for all previously incurred firm obligations, and this liability is satisfied only out of partnership property (UPA, sec. 17).
6. Dissolution of the firm does not discharge the liability of the partners, unless the firm creditors agree.
7. The partnership assets are the partnership property and the contributions of the partners necessary for the payment of all partnership liabilities.

In the following case a suit was brought by a husband against a medical partnership for the alienation of his wife's affections by one of the physician partners. Section 13 of the UPA provides for partnership liability where any partner acting in the ordinary course of the business caused loss or injury to any person not being a partner.

KELSEY-SEYBOLD CLINIC v. MACLAY
466 S.W.2d 716 (Tex. 1971)

Walker, J. This is a suit for alienation of affections in which the trial court rendered summary judgment for the defendant, Kelsey-Seybold Clinic, a medical partnership. [Plaintiff appealed, and the appellate court reversed and sent the case back for trial. Defendant medical partnership now appeals to this Supreme Court claiming there is no issue of fact and, therefore, summary judgment is proper.] The question to be decided is whether the Clinic established conclusively that it is not liable for the damages alleged to have been caused by the acts of one of the partners.

Plaintiff alleged that Dr. Brewer and the Clinic had treated him, his wife, and their children for several years; that Dr. Brewer, who is a pediatrician and one of the partners in the Clinic, was the doctor to whom his wife had taken their children; that beginning in late 1966, Dr. Brewer conceived and entered into a scheme to alienate the affections of plaintiff's wife, Mrs. Maria Maclay; that he showered his attentions and gifts upon her until April or May, 1967, when her affections were alienated as a direct result of his actions, causing her to separate from plaintiff on or about July 25, 1967.

Plaintiff further alleged that Dr. Brewer's actions designed to alienate Mrs. Maclay's affections occurred while he was acting as a medical doctor for plaintiff's family and in the course and scope of his employment as a partner in the Clinic; that various acts of undue familiarity occurred both on and off the premises of the Clinic; that prior to April, 1967, the Clinic, through Dr. Mavis Kelsey, one of the senior partners, had knowledge of Dr. Brewer's actions; that at the time this knowledge was acquired, the Clinic was providing medical treatment for plaintiff and his entire family; and that the "partnership approved of, consented to, and ratified and condoned such conduct of its partner, Brewer, and refused to come to the aid of your plaintiff or in any way attempt to halt or disapprove the actions of Brewer." Plaintiff prayed for the recovery of damages both actual and exemplary, from Dr. Brewer and the Clinic, jointly and severally.

Where a partner proposes to do, in the name or for the benefit of the partnership, some act that is not in the ordinary course of the business, consent by the other partners may constitute his authority to do the act for the partnership. We also recognize that even a willful or malicious act outside the ordinary scope of the partnership business may be so related to the business that tacit consent of the other partners could fairly be regarded as a grant of authority. In this instance, however, Dr. Brewer was acting solely for his own personal gratification. His conduct could not benefit the Clinic in any way, and no one would have supposed that he was acting for the partnership. It is our opinion that in these circumstances the "consent" that might be inferred from the silence or inaction of the Clinic after learning of his conduct does not render the Clinic vicariously liable for the damages claimed by the plaintiff.

We are also of the opinion that the Clinic owed a duty to the families of its patients to exercise ordinary care to prevent a tortious interference with family relations. It was not required to maintain constant surveillance over personnel on duty or to inquire into and regulate the personal conduct of partners and employees while engaged in their private affairs. But if and when the partnership received information from which it knew or should have known that there might be a need to take action, it was under a duty to use reasonable means at its disposal to prevent any partner or employee from improperly using his position with the Clinic to work a tortious invasion of legally protected family interests.

The rather meager information in the present record does not necessarily indicate that the Clinic was under a duty to act or that it could have done anything to prevent the damage when Dr. Kelsey first learned of the situation. On the other hand, it does not affirmatively and clearly appear that the Clinic could or should have done nothing. Mrs. Maclay's affections may have been alienated from her husband before anyone talked with Dr. Kelsey, but the facts in that respect are not fully developed. There is no proof as to when, where, or under what circumstances the misconduct, if any, on Dr. Brewer's part occurred. Dr. Kelsey testified that he did not believe anything improper occurred at the Clinic, but the proofs do not establish as a matter of law that he was justified in not making further inquiry after his conversations with plaintiff and Mrs. Maclay's uncle. The record does not show whether there is a partnership agreement that might have a bearing on the case, and we have no way of knowing the extent to which the Clinic might have determined which patients were to be seen by Dr. Brewer or controlled his actions while on duty. Dr. Kelsey's testimony suggests that the partners might have been in a position to prevent improper conduct by one of their number on the premises of the Clinic. In our opinion the Clinic has failed to discharge the heavy, and in the case of this character virtually impossible, burden of establishing as a matter of law at the summary judgment stage that it is not liable under any theory fairly presented by the allegations of the petition. [The court held that there was an issue of fact as to whether the medical partnership breached its duty to use reasonable means at its disposal to prevent Dr. Brewer from improperly using his position with the Clinic to work a tortious invasion of legally protected family interests, thus precluding summary judgment. The decision of the appellate court was affirmed.]

Questions and Case Problems

1. Appellant sought compensatory relief for petitioner's violation of his fiduciary obligation as a partner in a law firm contending that petitioner, while a partner, willfully solicited clients for his own individual purpose and willfully interfered with the relationship between the firm and its clients. May a partner solicit partnership clients for his own purposes while a partner? [*In re Silverberg and Schwartz,* 438 N.Y.S.2d 143 (N.Y. 1981).]

2. *X* and *Z* operated a collection agency as partners. While attempting to collect a debt for the firm, *Y*, a firm employee, committed an assault and battery on *W*. When *W* sued the firm, *C*, a new partner, who was not a partner at the time the assault and battery was committed, was joined as a party defendant. Is *C* personally liable along with the other partners?
3. Plaintiff, Bovy, was a partner with the defendants, Graham, Cohen, and Wampold in a law partnership. The written partnership agreement did not provide for the distribution of fees upon dissolution. The partners entered into a subsequent agreement that specified how fees should be divided upon dissolution. The partnership was dissolved, and Bovy brought this suit to compel compliance with the subsequent agreement regarding the division of fees. The defendants claim that, during the negotiations for the new agreement, Bovy had not fully disclosed the number of cases in which he claimed a contingent fee. Was Bovy subject to a fiduciary duty of disclosure to divulge the number of cases and value of their contingent fees during the negotiation of the subsequent partnership agreement? [*Bovy v. Graham, Cohen & Wampold,* 564 P.2d 1175 (Wash. 1977).]
4. The defendants loaned money to Dalton Waldrop in 1974. In mid-1975, Dalton Waldrop and Thomas Waldrop, his brother, formed a partnership for the drilling of wells. In January 1976, this partnership was incorporated as Waldrop Drilling & Pipe Co., Inc., plaintiff. In August 1976, defendants employed Waldrop Drilling & Pipe Co., Inc., to repair one of their pumps. This repair work was completed on August 24, 1976, at a reasonable cost of $2,873.75. On November 4, 1976, at the request of defendants, plaintiff performed additional repair services in the reasonable amount of $710.54. Neither of these bills was paid. Plaintiff brought this action to collect the amount due. Defendants sought to offset these amounts against the balance owed to them by Dalton Waldrop. It is defendants' position that because Dalton Waldrop, the original debtor, used the loan proceeds to purchase well-drilling equipment that later became an asset of the partnership between Dalton and Thomas Waldrop, and later a corporate asset, the partnership and the corporation are liable for the original loan. Consequently, defendants contend that the repair cost should have been offset against the balance owed to them by Dalton Waldrop. Did the partnership assume the original loan obligation of Dalton Waldrop? [*Waldrop v. Holland,* 558 P.2d 1237 (Wash. 1979).]
5. Plaintiff, Koenig, and defendant, Huber, were partners engaged in a plumbing and heating business. They signed a partnership agreement that provided that the parties were to employ themselves diligently in the business; that each partner was to contribute equally to the capital of the firm in the form of equipment and machinery; and that all debts and obligations of the partnership would be shared equally and all profits would be distributed equally. Koenig filed suit for the dissolution of the partnership and an accounting. The lower court failed to consider "extra time" spent by Koenig in the partnership business while the defendant, Huber, was operating an oil station. Is a partner entitled to be paid for "extra time" spent in a partnership business? [*Koenig v. Huber,* 210 N.W.2d 825 (S.D. 1973).]
6. Weiss was one of the partners in Pike Associates that was formed to build and operate a shopping center. Weiss put up all his right, title, and interest in the shopping center as security for a personal loan made by the defendant to Weiss. Plaintiff bank also loaned Weiss money some years earlier. Defendant attempted to foreclose on its interest in the shopping center partnership after Weiss was in default on his note to the defendant. Plaintiff seeks to enjoin the foreclosure and to establish that its interest has priority because a partner cannot pledge specific partnership property

for a personal loan. May a partner pledge as security an interest in the partnership assets? [*Madison Nat'l Bank v. Newrath,* 275 A.2d 495 (Md. 1971).]

7. *X, Y,* and *Z* own a partnership engaged in the collection of corporate debts. *X,* while attempting to collect a debt, violated a federal law on unfair debt collection practices. The debtor sued the firm. *Y* and *Z* claim that only *X* is liable for his unauthorized conduct. Decide.
8. A dentist was a member of a dental partnership who signed a partnership agreement that provided for a fixed annual salary. She was an ambitious person who worked evenings, weekends and gave up her summer vacation to care for the partnership patients. Is she entitled to be paid for her extra time spent in performing partnership business?
9. Harris, the president of defendant company, International Realty Ltd., formed a partnership with a group of physicians to purchase an apartment house under construction as a good "tax shelter." Harris stated the purchase price as $1,010,000 but failed to disclose that it could have been purchased for $907,500. Harris also did not disclose to his partners that the defendant, of which he was the president and major stockholder, would receive a $100,000 commission. The doctors, plaintiffs, brought this suit to require Harris to account to the partnership for the commission received by him without their consent. Harris claims that the doctors knew someone was going to make a commission and, therefore, no disclosure was required. You decide. [*Starr v. Int'l Realty Ltd.,* 533 P.2d 165 (Or. 1975).]
10. In light of *Kelsey-Seybold Clinic v. Maclay,* excerpted at the beginning of this section, if you were a partner in a partnership, what basic guidelines would you help to establish and observe so that matters of partner impropriety could be so handled as to minimize the risk of partnership liability for such impropriety?

CHAPTER

41

SPECIAL VENTURES

After you have read this chapter, you should be able to:

1. Define a limited partnership.
2. Explain the liability of a
   a) General partner
   b) Limited partner
3. Explain how a limited partnership is formed.
4. Define a joint venture.
5. Define a mining partnership.
6. Explain a business trust.
7. Explain an unincorporated association.
8. Define a joint-stock company.
9. Define and explain a franchise.
10. Explain the relationship of a trademark to a franchise; define a trademark.

BUSINESS DECISIONS and the LAW

Who could imagine a better product: one that combines legendary Japanese manufacturing technology with the marketing expertise of America's premier computer maker? Recently International Business Machines Corporation (IBM) and Toshiba Corporation announced the formation of a joint venture known as Display Technologies, Inc., to produce computer screens. The IBM-Toshiba venture will make color liquid crystal displays for use in the increasingly popular portable computers that must be small and lightweight. This new technology offers a remarkably high resolution picture that is not currently possible with the existing large screen standard.

Production will start in 1991, with each company owning 50 percent of the venture and controlling half of the board of directors. The president will come from Toshiba, and the vice president from IBM. Display Technologies is expected to produce about 1 million units by 1991—a goal that should not be difficult to attain given the track records of both companies thus far.

Source: "IBM, Toshiba to Produce Screens Jointly," *Wall Street Journal*, August 31, 1989, p. B5; reprinted by permission of *Wall Street Journal*,

Introduction

When you enter business, you will find that there are many different kinds of business all operating within some kind of formal or loose business structure. We have just discussed the general partnership, and in Chapters 42 through 46 we will study the corporation. There are still other forms of business organization that are likely to have importance for you, either as a participant in one or more of them, or because you have dealings with them. It is therefore important for you to have an opportunity to learn about them and their character, legal status, and liability.

Special Venture Organizations

► Limited Partnership

limited partnership
A partnership of one or more general partners and one or more limited partners formed in compliance with the Revised Uniform Limited Partnership Act (1976) with the 1985 amendments

The *limited partnership* is a noncorporate business organization that protects the capital investor (limited partner (s)) from liability for firm losses beyond the investment. It is a form of partnership created by statute in the thirteen states that have adopted the Uniform Limited Partnership Act of 1916 and the thirty-seven states that adopted the Revised Act of 1976 with the 1985 amendments (1985 Act). This text will deal with the 1985 Act. Appendices D and E contain the entire 1916 Act and the 1976 Act as amended in 1985.

The limited partnership is comprised of one or more limited partners and one or more general partners. The limited partners, often called "special partners," share in the profits without sharing losses beyond their investment. The general partners manage the firm. Each limited partnership must have at least one general partner with unlimited liability.

Formation The partners must sign and swear to a limited partnership *certificate* that states the firm name, character, location, names and addresses of general and limited partners and their investment and share of the profits, and other information. The certificate must be filed with the "designated official" as required by each state (usually in the office of the secretary of state). A limited partnership can be formed only by complete or substantial compliance in good faith with the statutory requisites. (See Figure 41.1, which illustrates a form of certificate.)

In the following case, decided under the 1916 Act, limited partners were held not to be liable as general partners because of minor defects in the partnership certificate and in not filing proof of publication since the creditor seeking recovery was not misled by such errors. The 1985 Act would not change the result of this case.

FACTS

Micheli Contracting Corporation, a contractor, brought this suit to recover the sum of $192,268.27 for work, labor, and material provided and furnished for the construction of an apartment project known as the Fairwood Apartments in the Town of Guilderland, County of Albany, owned by Fairwood Associates, a limited partnership. In addition to Fairwood Associates, the complaint names each individual partner as a defendant. Harold V. Gleason,

FIGURE 41.1 **Form of Limited Partnership Certificate***

FORM OF LIMITED PARTNERSHIP CERTIFICATE

We, the undersigned, for the purpose of forming a limited partnership pursuant to the Uniform Limited Partnership Act as set forth in Sections_________of the_________Code, hereby certify:

1. **Name.** The name of the partnership is ____.
2. **Character of Business.** The character of the business to be carried on is to engage in the business of____________.
3. **Place of Business.** The location of the principal place of business of the partnership is ______________________.
4. **General Partners.** The name and place of residence of each general partner are:

__________________________ __________________________

__________________________ __________________________

Limited Partners. The name and place of residence of each limited partner are:

__________________________ __________________________

__________________________ __________________________

5. **Term.** The term for which the partnership is to exist is indefinite [*or* from __________ , 19__, to the close of business on__________, 19__, and thereafter from year to year].

6. **Initial Contribution of Each Limited Partner.** The amount of cash and a description of and the agreed value of the other property contributed by each limited partner are:

Name	Cash	Description of Other Property	Agreed Value of Other Property
____________	____________	____________	____________
____________	____________	____________	____________

7. **Additional Contributions of Each Limited Partner.** Each limited partner may (but shall not be obliged to) make such additional contributions to the capital of the partnership as may from time to time be agreed upon by the general partners.

8. **Return of Contribution to Each Limited Partner.** The contribution of each limited partner is to be returned to him as may from time to time be agreed upon by the general partners.

9. **Profit Shares of Each Limited Partner.** The share of the profits or other compensation by way of income which each limited partner shall receive by reason of his contribution is:

__________________________ __________________________%

__________________________ __________________________%

10. **Assignment of Limited Partner's Interest.** 'Each limited partner is given the right to substitute an assignee as contributor in his place, provided that the assignment is approved by all the general partners.

11. **Admission of Additional Limited Partners.** The general partners are given the right to admit additional limited partners, provided that the admissions are approved by all the general partners, but in no event other than upon a cash contribution to the partnership and upon the same terms as herein expressed.

12. **Death, Retirement or Insanity of General Partner.** In the event of the death, retirement or insanity of a general partner, the remaining general partners shall have the right to continue the business of the partnership under the same name by themselves or in conjunction with any other person or persons they may select.

13. **Right of Limited Partner to Receive Property Other Than Cash.** Each limited partner is given the right to demand and receive property other than cash in return for his contribution, and the value of such property shall be that shown on the books of the partnership.

Signed the ____________________day of____________, 19___.

[*Signatures of general and limited partners*]

Subscribed and sworn to before me this_____________ day of ______________________, 19_____.

____

Notary Public

*The limited partner's name and contribution are not necessary under the 1985 Act.

Herbert Pearlman, and Abraham Portnoy, each of whom, by a motion to dismiss, claims that they are limited partners and, thus, not liable for partnership debts. Fairwood Associates was created by an agreement, dated October 31, 1972, with each of the partners signing the agreement. As part of the agreement, the limited partners expressly agreed to designate each and all of the general partners as the attorney(s)-in-fact for the purpose of filing the certificate of limited partnership. Micheli Contracting claims that the limited partnership was not formed in substantial compliance with the partnership law, and that, thus, the defendants, Gleason, Pearlman, and Portnoy are general partners of Fairwood Associates. It further contends that the certificate of limited partnership was not properly subscribed pursuant to a valid power of attorney, and further, that the signature of the general partner did not disclose his authority for signing. In addition, plaintiff states that proof of publication as required by statute was not filed in the clerk's office.

DECISION

Judgment for the defendants, Gleason, Pearlman, Portnoy. A certificate of limited partnership may be executed by a general partner or some other person on behalf of a limited partner pursuant to a power of attorney. Although publication of the certificate is an essential element of the proper formation of a limited partnership, the failure to file the affidavits of publication is not a fatal defect. In view of the fact that the certificate of limited partnership omitted nothing of substance required to be contained therein by the statute, and there is no claim that anything contained therein is false, or that the defects complained of misled and injured respondent, it would appear that there was substantial compliance with the statute, and the limited partnership was validly formed.

Micheli Contracting Corp. v. Fairwood Assoc., 418 N.Y.S.2d 164 (N.Y. 1979).

Under the 1985 Act, a limited partner's *capital* contribution can be cash, other property, or services. The limited partner may be *employed* by the firm to render services and be paid for such work just as anyone else would be.

Liability of a Limited Partner The limited partners are not personally liable for firm debts *provided that they do not participate in the control or management* of the firm. They are nonparticipating investors. The *general* partners have the duty to control and manage the firm and, therefore, are personally liable for the firm's obligations. If the limited partner participates in the control of the business, he or she is liable to a firm creditor who reasonably believes that, based on the limited partner's conduct, the limited partner is a general partner.

Under section 303(b) of the Act of 1985 an expanded "safe harbor" list incorporates case decisions and recent state statutory development regarding when a limited partner does not participate in the control of the business. It is generally no longer considered sound public policy to hold a limited partner who is not also a general partner liable for partnership obligations. An exception would be a partnership creditor who reasonably believed, based on the limited partner's conduct, that the limited partner was in fact a general partner. The 1985 Act, which specifies exactly what does not constitute participation in the control of the business, should be of enormous help to investors and to courts in adopting states, namely:

(1) being a contractor for or an agent or employee of the limited partnership or of a general partner or being an officer, director, or shareholder of a general partner that is a corporation;

(2) consulting with and advising a general partner with respect to the business of the limited partnership;
(3) acting as surety for the limited partnership or guaranteeing or assuming one or more specific obligations of the limited partnership;
(4) taking any action required or permitted by law to bring or pursue a derivative action in the right of the limited partnership;
(5) requesting or attending a meeting of partners;
(6) proposing, approving, or disapproving, by voting or otherwise, one or more of the following matters:
  (i) the dissolution and winding up of the limited partnership;
  (ii) the sale, exchange, lease, mortgage, pledge, or other transfer of all or substantially all of the assets of the limited partnership;
  (iii) the incurrence of indebtedness by the limited partnership other than in the ordinary course of its business;
  (iv) a change in the nature of the business;
  (v) the admission or removal of a general partner;
  (vi) the admission or removal of a limited partner;
  (vii) a transaction involving an actual or potential conflict of interest between a general partner and the limited partnership or the limited partners;
  (viii) an amendment to the partnership agreement or certificate of limited partnership; or
  (ix) matters related to the business of the limited partnership not otherwise enumerated in this subsection (b), which the partnership agreement states in writing may be subject to the approval or disapproval of limited partners;
(7) winding up the limited partnership pursuant to Section 803; or
(8) exercising any right or power permitted to limited partners under this [Act] and not specifically enumerated in this subsection (b).[1]

The 1985 Act, Section 102, generally prohibits the use of a limited partner's surname (last name) as part of the firm name, unless it is the same as that of a general partner or it appeared in the partnership name before he or she became a limited partner. Under Section 502(a) of the 1985 Act, a limited partner is liable to the partnership for capital contributions to the firm that the limited partner agreed in the agreement of partnership would be made but had not yet been made. When creditors have a claim against the firm, a limited partner cannot withdraw his or her capital contribution.

A managing general partner may desire to invest in the limited partnership and thereby become a limited partner. The ULPA, Section 12(2), provides for this and grants to that partner all the rights and duties of a general partner.

In order to allow general partners to have limited liability, some states permit the general partners to incorporate. In such an instance, the general partners are employees and stockholders of the general partner corporation and are exempt from personal liability. The firm's creditors can reach only its business assets.

Keep in mind as you read the following case that not all state corporate laws allow a corporation to be a general partner of a limited partnership. The 1985 Act, Section 101(11), defines a "person" as including a corporation, thereby allowing a corporation to be a general partner under the limited partnership law. Hence, the court's decision would be the same under the 1985 Act. Pay attention to the court's reasoning in placing

[1](Revised) Uniform Limited Partnership Act As Amended (1985), sec. 303 (b).

the burden on Frigidaire to obtain personal guarantees from the stockholders of a general partner corporation in order to hold them personally liable, which Frigidaire did not do.

FACTS

Frigidaire Sales Corporation entered into a contract with Commercial Investors (Commercial), a limited partnership. Leonard Mannon and Raleigh Baxter were limited partners of Commercial and were also officers, directors, and shareholders of Union Properties, Inc., the only general partner of Commercial. Mannon and Baxter controlled Union Properties, and through their control of Union Properties they exercised the day-to-day control and management of Commercial. Commercial breached the contract with Frigidaire, and Frigidaire brought suit against Union Properties and against Mannon and Baxter individually.

Frigidaire's sole contention was that Mannon and Baxter should incur general liability for the limited partnership's obligations because they exercised the day-to-day control and management of Commercial. Mannon and Baxter, on the other hand, argued that Commercial was controlled by Union Properties, a separate legal entity, and not by them in their individual capacities.

DECISION

Judgment for Mannon and Baxter. When the shareholders of a corporation, who are also the corporation's officers and directors, conscientiously keep the affairs of the corporation separate from their personal affairs, and no fraud or manifest injustice is perpetrated upon third persons who deal with the corporation, the corporation's separate entity should be respected.

Mannon and Baxter scrupulously separated their actions on behalf of the corporation from their personal actions. Frigidaire never mistakenly assumed that Mannon and Baxter were general partners with general liability. Frigidaire knew Union Properties was the sole general partner and did not rely on Mannon and Baxter's control by assuming that they were also general partners. If Frigidaire had not wished to rely on the solvency of Union Properties as the only general partner, it could have insisted that Mannon and Baxter personally guarantee contractual performance.

Frigidaire Sales Corp. v. Union Properties, Inc., 562 P.2d 244 (Wash. 1977).

Rights of a Limited Partner The 1985 Act, Section 305, provides that a limited partner shall have the following rights:

1. to inspect and copy partnership records;
2. to have on demand true and full information of all things affecting the partnership, and a formal account of partnership affairs whenever circumstances render it just and reasonable, including a copy of the limited partnership's federal, state, and local income tax returns;
3. to receive a share of the profits or other compensation by way of income, and to the return of his or her contribution as provided in the partnership agreement.

Liquidation Upon liquidation, each limited partner has priority over general partners in net assets. After payment to outside partnership creditors and to limited partners who have made loans to the firm, the limited partners receive their share of profits and then their capital contribution. General partners are then paid back their loans, share of profits, and, lastly, their capital contributions.[2]

Use of Limited Partnership The popularity of the limited partnership today is questionable in a venture where investors seek both no liability (although there is the risk of loss of capital investment), and the right to deduct expenses and losses against their other income. For example, *X* is a high-income earner who wants to invest in a project with high risk and high earning potential. If the project should fail, *X* as a limited partner may not be able to claim *X*'s loss of capital as a deduction against *X*'s income.[3]

Research and Development Limited Partnership Suppose you are a majority stockholder of a corporation that requires capital for a new product it desires to produce and sell. This kind of high risk venture is not attractive to equity (stock sale) or bank financing. However, if an investor has no liability exposure and could deduct any loss incurred in that taxable year as an offset against earned income with the potential of earning royalty income on the sale of the product, it would be an attractive tax shelter.

R & D limited partnership
A special kind of limited partnership allowing a limited partner to invest and claim a deduction on the investment as an expense in his or her business, although the limited partnership engages only in research and development and not sales

The Internal Revenue Code, Section 174(a)(1), provides for a taxpayer to treat research and development expenditures paid or incurred during the taxable year in connection with his or her trade or business as deductible expenses. Consistent with this you could form a limited partnership for the purpose of developing a new venture. The investors (limited partners) would contribute the capital to finance the research and development of the technology. The general partners may contract with an outside firm to perform the research and development with the cash provided by the limited partners.

The following Supreme Court landmark case allowed the limited partner to offset his other income with his share of the limited partnership expense although the limited partnership had not even offered the product for sale in the year of deduction. The Commissioner of Internal Revenue disallowed the deduction claimed by the limited partner taxpayer as a business expense, and the Tax Court sustained the Commissioner since there had been no sales in the limited partnership during the tax year of the limited partner. The Court of Appeals affirmed the Tax Court, and the limited partner appealed to the U.S. Supreme Court.

FACTS

Edwin A. Snow was disallowed as a deduction his distributive share of the net operating loss of a limited partnership, Burns Investment Company, for the taxable year 1966. Snow claimed the deduction under Section 174(a)(1) of the Internal Revenue Code of 1954 that allows a taxpayer to take as a deduction "experimental expenditures which are paid or incurred during the taxable year in connection with his trade or business as expenses which are not chargeable to capital accounts." Snow was a limited partner who contributed $10,000 for a four percent interest in Burns, the limited partnership, that was formed to

[2](Revised) Uniform Limited Partnership Act As Amended (1985), sec. 804.

[3]Tax Reform Act of 1986.

develop a "special purpose incinerator for the consumer and industrial markets."

During 1966 Burns reported no sales of the incinerator or any other product. May Snow claim as a deduction the $10,000 contribution in the limited partnership?

DECISION

Yes. Judgment for Snow. Section 174 was enacted in 1954 to dilute some of the conceptions of "ordinary and necessary" business expenses. Established firms with ongoing business had continuous programs of research quite unlike small or pioneering business enterprises. Mr. Reed of New York, Chairman of the House Committee on Ways and Means, made the point even more explicit when he addressed the House on the bill: "Present law contains no statutory provision dealing expressly with the deduction of these expenses. The result has been confusion and uncertainty. Very often, under present law small businesses which are developing new products and do not have established research departments are not allowed to deduct these expenses despite the fact that their large and well-established competitors can obtain the deduction. . . . This provision will greatly stimulate the search for new products and new inventions upon which the future economic and military strength of our Nation depends. It will be particularly valuable to small and growing businesses." Congress may at times in its wisdom discriminate taxwise between various kinds of business, between old and oncoming business and the like. But we would defeat the congressional purpose somewhat to equalize the tax benefits of the ongoing companies and those that are upcoming and about to reach the market by perpetuating the discrimination created below and urged upon us here. We read Section 174 to encourage expenditure for research and experimentation.

Reversed.

Snow v. Comm'r of Internal Revenue, 416 U.S. 500 (1974).

► Joint Venture

joint venture
An association of two or more persons as co-owners to engage in a limited business transaction for a profit

A **joint venture,** sometimes referred to as a joint adventure, has many characteristics similar to a partnership but is generally organized for a single transaction. Hence, it does not meet the statutory definition of a partnership under Section 6 of the UPA, which requires the partners to "carry on" a business. It can be defined as an association of two or more persons as co-owners to form a limited business transaction for a profit. Generally, it is a single undertaking for a limited duration. For example, *X* and *Z* purchase recreational property for investment purposes. They agree to share the rental income and expenses. When the property is sold, they will share the "profits" or "gains." Both *X* and *Z* have other full-time jobs.

In the above example, *X* as a joint venturer has authority to bind *X*'s associate *Z* and the joint venture within the actual or apparent scope of *X*'s authority. Due to the narrow scope of the business, a joint venturer's authority is limited to a greater extent than that of a general partner.

The negligence of one joint associate is imputed to the others in a joint venture. Any associate may be held liable to injured third persons caused by the negligence of another associate.[4]

Because of the close similarity of a joint venture to a partnership, it is commonly held that their rights and duties are governed by the UPA. Hence, the joint members have the

[4]*Keiswetter v. Rubenstein*, 209 N.W. 154 (Mich. 1926).

consequent fiduciary duties to account for profits. Similar to a partnership, profits of the joint venture are taxable when earned, whether or not distributed.[5]

► Joint-Stock Company

The joint-stock company or association is generally a nonstatutory business organization with many characteristics of a corporation. Its articles of association, which need not be filed with a government office, provide for centralization of management in a board of trustees, continuity of existence, and transferability of shares. It is a form of partnership in which the members have shares that are transferable. The members have power to control the conduct of their trustee representatives and, therefore, they are personally liable for company debts.

The popularity of the joint-stock company occurred in the early nineteenth century when free enterprise was rapidly expanding. Obtaining a corporate charter from the state was a difficult process. The joint-stock company, like a general partnership, required only a private contract for its existence. However, it never attained limited liability, unless a third party business creditor by contract agreed to look only to company assets. It was always liable for tort claims.

Today with the relative ease of forming a corporation, there is no need to seek corporate attributes in another business organization.

► Business Trust

The business trust, sometimes called a Massachusetts trust, is similar to a common law trust with the trustees acting as business managers and the beneficiaries as capital investors and holders of transferable shares. The trust is formed by a trust instrument that describes the nature of the business, a description of the trust property, the trustees and their powers, the beneficiaries' interests, and the rights of creditors dealing with the trustees. (See Fig. 41.2 for an illustration of a business trust.)

Early statutory law in Massachusetts did not allow corporations to deal in real property, and this was the reason for the common use of the name "business trust" and for its popularity. At one time it was not regulated nor subject to corporate taxation, and its members were free from personal liability. Legislation has gradually subjected the business trust to the same federal income taxation as corporations, and has imposed personal liability on the trustees, and also on its beneficiaries only if they have the power to control.

Generally, the beneficiaries will be held personally liable for trust obligations if they have power to control the trust management. For example, if they retain powers to instruct the trustees or to alter, amend, or terminate the trust, they are held to be principals and, hence, liable to the trust creditors.

Although the trust instrument will probably state that the trustees and beneficiaries cannot be held personally liable for trust debts, it has no effect against creditors who do not assent to it. For instance, if a tenant is injured due to defective stairs in a building owned and managed by a business trust, the trustees are personally liable for the

[5] I.R.C. sec. 761(a) (1954).

Figure 41.2 **Declaration of Trust**

BUSINESS TRUST

1. *Declaration of Trust.* Made on ________, 19___ by ______________________________ [*insert names of five individuals*] as Trustees and __________________ (stockholders).

2. *Purpose.* The purpose of this Trust is that the Trustees shall acquire and manage properly the earnings, the proceeds of which will be divided into shares whose certificates are to be held by the shareholders.

3. *Name.* This Trust is to be named ______________ Company Unincorporated. It shall conduct all business under this name.

4. *Term of Office.* Of the five Trustees ______________, ________________, and ________________ will hold office until the first annual meeting of stockholders. ________________ and ________________ will hold office until the second annual meeting of stockholders.

Should a Trustee prove unable to fulfill his term of office, the remaining Trustees shall fill the vacancy for the unexpired term.

5. *Election of Trustees.* The Trustees are to be elected b the stockholders. Three are to be elected at the first annual meeting and two are to be elected at the second annual meeting. The election of Trustees shall follow this same pattern in alternative years thereafter.

6. *Trust Property.* Trust property is to be held by the Trustees in joint tenancy, with survivorship among the remaining Trustees upon the death, resignation, or removal of any of them.

The Trustees hold legal title to all property belonging to the Trust and have absolute control thereof.

7. *Powers.* The Trustees may engage in any business, including sale, exportation, manufacture, production purchase, or transportation of ____________________________ [*describe nature of Business Trust*]. The Trustees may enter into any contracts necessary to conduct the business, loan and borrow money, indemnify each other, and employ counsel and initiate suits at law, equity, or arbitration. ____________________ [*List other powers.*]

8. *Officers.* The Trustees will elect annually a President, Vice-President, Treasurer, and Secretary from their ranks. These Officers will have the authority and perform the duties usually incident to officers in a corporation. The Secretary shall keep a record of all stockholder, Trustee, and Officer's meetings.

9. *Certificates.* The beneficial interest in the Business Trust shall be held by the shareholders in the form of Certificates having a par value of $______ (dollars). These are to be considered personal property, to be passed on in such manner upon the death of a stockholder.

10. *Duration.* This Trust shall continue for a term of ___________ years, at which time the then Trustees shall wind up its affairs, liquidate its assets, and distribute them among the stockholders.

11. *Compensation.* The Trustees are to be compensated as follows: _______________

____

____

12. *Amendments.* The stockholders may amend this Declaration of Trust by a two-thirds vote, at an annual or special meeting. However, the fact that Trustees, Officers, employees and stockholders are exempt from personal liability may not be amended.

____

____

____

Signatures of Trustees

Source: Reprinted by permission from Basic Legal Forms by Marvin Hyman, 1981.

damages resulting from the tort of negligence. In the following case, the U.S. Supreme Court explains the nature of a business trust.

FACTS

The trustees brought suit in the Federal District Court to recover damages for breach of a promissory note held in their name as trustees. The defendant, Navarro Savings Association, was a Texas firm. Some of the trust's beneficial shareholders were also Texas residents. Because federal court jurisdiction is based on diversity of citizenship, the District Court dismissed the action for want of subject matter jurisdiction and claimed a business trust is a citizen of every State in which its shareholders reside. The U.S. Court of Appeals reversed and the trustees appealed to the U.S. Supreme Court. Notice how the court examines the written trust instrument to determine the trustees' powers and their authority over the trust property.

DECISION

Navarro contends that Fidelity's trust form masks an unincorporated association of individuals who make joint real estate investments. Navarro observes that certain features of the trust's operations also characterize the operations of a corporation, centralized management, continuity of enterprise, and unlimited duration. Arguing that this trust is in substance a corporation, Navarro reasons that the real parties to the lawsuit are Fidelity's beneficial shareholders. We need not reject the argument that Fidelity shares some attributes of a corporation. In certain respects, a business trust also resembles a corporation. Fidelity is an express trust, and the question is whether its trustees are real parties to this controversy for purposes of a federal court's diversity jurisdiction. A trustee is a real party to the controversy for purposes of diversity jurisdiction when he possesses certain customary powers to hold, manage, and dispose of assets for the benefit of others. The trustees in this case have such powers. At all relevant times, Fidelity operated under a declaration of trust that authorized the trustees to take legal title to trust assets, to invest those assets for the benefit of the shareholders, and to sue and be sued in their capacity as trustees. Trustees filed this lawsuit in that capacity. The trustees have legal title; they manage the assets; they control the litigation. In short, they are real parties to the controversy. For more than 150 years, the law has permitted trustees who meet this standard to sue in their own right without regard to the citizenship of the trust beneficiaries. The judgment of the Court of Appeals is affirmed.

Navarro Savings Ass'n. v. Lee et al., 446 U.S. 458 (1980).

► Mining Partnership

The development of oil and gas by co-owners who share the profits and losses of the operation in some states creates a distinct form of association called a mining partnership.[6] Some states have enacted statutory law that recognizes the mining partnership.[7]

---

[6] *McAnally v. Cochran*, 46 P.2d 955 (Okla. 1935); mining partnership recognized by judicial decision in California, Colorado, Kansas, Kentucky, Michigan, Montana, Oklahoma, Texas, Utah, West Virginia, and Wyoming.

[7] Alabama, California, Idaho, and Montana all require a written document to create a mining partnership.

Differences with Partnership Unlike a general partnership, a mining partnership is not dissolved by the bankruptcy or death of a partner. A mining partner has limited authority to bind the co-partners and implied authority to charge them for necessary business expenses. Each partner is personally liable for such an expense. In the following case the partners in a mining partnership were held to be jointly and severally liable for tortious conduct.

FACTS

Dunkin acquired a three-year agricultural lease on 240 acres of land in Oklahoma. Thereafter, Mikel Drilling Co., a mining partnership, acquired oil and gas leases on a portion of the 240 acres. Dunkin claimed that the mining partners commenced drilling on his cropland and they cut his fence and left his gates down, causing injury to Dunkin's cattle when drinking oil and salt water that had flowed over and across the surface of plaintiff's land. Dunkin claimed that the defendants are jointly and severally liable for the damage caused to his cattle. Are partners of a mining partnership subject to joint and several liability?

DECISION

Yes. Judgment for Dunkin. By virtue of the joint control and management of a mining partnership, every general partner is liable to third persons for all the obligations of the partnership, jointly with his co-partners.

Mikel Drilling Co. v. Dunkin, 318 P.2d 435 (Okla. 1957).

Franchising

franchise

A business relationship between a franchisor, who markets goods or services through a franchisee, who has the right to use the franchisor's trade name, trademark, and methods of operation

Franchising is a composition of marketing, management, finance, and law. The marketing development of the chain store that slowly replaced the individual entrepreneur in the late 1940s initiated the phenomenal growth of franchising. The small-business owner simply could not compete with the purchasing power and advertising of the postwar chain store giants. Franchising outlets for goods and services created a new method of distribution that has affected the lives of everyone. (See Figure 41.3 for an illustration of a Franchise Agreement.)

► Definition

Franchising is a business relationship between a *franchisor,* who markets goods or services through a *franchisee,* who has the right to use the franchisor's trade name, trademark, and methods of operation. In return, the franchisee agrees to sell the services or products under the control of the franchisor.

Why franchise? Any company that has established a sound business may consider the advantages of becoming a franchisor. The franchisor has a controlled outlet enabling it to maintain its reputation and goodwill for its merchandise. The distribution takes place over a large geographic area. The franchisor will sell a franchise for a fee that provides it with a source of capital for further expansion. Other advantages allow the franchisor to have independent operators run the various franchises and purchase merchandise from their designated suppliers.

The court in the following case upheld the right of a franchisor to compel their franchisees to buy only from designated suppliers and sell only approved products.

FIGURE 41.3 **Form of Franchise Agreement**

FRANCHISE AGREEMENT – SALE OF FRANCHISOR'S PRODUCTS – USE OF FRANCHISOR'S TRADEMARK

1. *Introduction.* Agreement made on . . . . , 19 . . . . . . between . . . . , Inc., with offices at . . . . (Franchisor), and . . . . , residing at . . . . (Franchisee).

2. *Purpose of Agreement.* Franchisor is engaged in the business of manufacturing and distributing . . . . , similar products, and products used in conjunction with Franchisor's principal products (the Products), all under the tradename and mark of ". . . . ." Franchisee wishes to distribute the products and operate a business under the Tradename and Trademark.

3. *Grant of Franchise.* Franchisor grants to Franchisee an exclusive franchise during the term of this Agreement to sell the Products and use Franchisor's Tradename in the territory bounded as follows: . . . . (the Territory). Franchisor also grants to Franchisee a nontransferable license to use the Trademark in connection with the franchise granted, but only in the Territory and during the term of this Agreement.

4. *Term of Agreement – Extensions.* The term of this Agreement shall be . . . . years commencing with . . . . , 19 . . . . The term will be extended automatically for an additional . . . . years unless either party notifies the other of its intention not to continue the Agreement in force for the extended term. This notice must be in writing, addressed to the address given above for the party to be notified, mailed by certified or registered mail, and posted no later than . . . . months before the end of the original term of this Agreement.

5. *Early Termination of Agreement.* If Franchisee breaches or violates any provision of this Agreement or of the Franchisor's Manual, described in Paragraph 9, and fails to remedy the breach or violation within . . . . days following notice by Franchisor, Franchisor may terminate this Agreement at once and without any further notice to Franchisee.

6. *Sale of Franchisor's Products to Franchisee.* Franchisor will sell to Franchisee all of the Products ordered by Franchisee and which are listed in Franchisor's current catalog. Franchisor may discontinue any of the Products without notice to Franchisee. The purchase price for any of the Products shall be the wholesale price then current as established by the wholesale price lists furnished by Franchisor to all of its franchisees from time to time, exclusive of shipping charges and insurance, if any.

7. *Franchisee to Deal in Franchisor's Products Exclusively – No Sales Outside of Territory.* Franchisee shall not sell or distribute or offer for sale in the Territory any products, goods, or services that are not manufactured or distributed by Franchisor or that Franchisee has not purchased from Franchisor. Franchisee shall not sell or distribute the Products outside of the Territory.

8. *Royalty for Use of Tradename and Trademark.* Franchisee acknowledges that Franchisor by long usage of its Tradename and Mark, by continual advertising in all media at great expense to Franchisor, and by the maintenance of quality standards of the highest order for the Products sold under the Tradename and Mark, has created great demand for the Products and has developed substantial value in the Tradename and Mark. Franchisee will pay Franchisor a royalty of . . . . . . percent of Franchisee's gross sales as compensation for the license to use Franchisor's Tradename and Mark. The royalty is payable quarterly, no later than . . . . days following the end of each calendar quarter, and shall be accompanied by an accounting on the form furnished by Franchisor.

9. *Franchisee to Comply With Franchisor's Standards.* The standards to which Franchisee must conform in the sale and distribution of Franchisor's Products are set out in Franchisor's Manual for Franchisees (the Manual), which is made a part of this Agreement by reference. Franchisee acknowledges receipt of a copy of the Manual and acknowledges that he has read it and is familiar with its provisions. Franchisor reserves the right to amend or revise the Manual from time to time. Any amendment or revision shall be deemed a part of this Agreement upon a receipt of a copy of the amendment or revision by Franchisee. Franchisee acknowledges that adherence to the standards set out in the Manual is essential for the maintenance of Franchisor's Tradename and Mark, the demand for the Products, and the continued success of Franchisor and all of Franchisor's franchisees. Therefore, any breach of any provision of the Manual can result in the early termination of this Agreement in accordance with Paragraph 5 of this Agreement.

10. *Prohibited Use of Trademark.* Franchisor's Tradename and Trademark will be used only in the manner provided in the Manual. It will not be used by Franchisee in any form of advertising unless Franchisee has first obtained Franchisor's written consent to the specific use.

FIGURE 41.3 (Continued)

11. *Franchisee's Maintenance of Inventory and Service Facilities.* Franchisee will maintain an inventory of Franchisor's Products and one or more service facilities in the Territory sufficient to properly exploit the franchise. Franchisor's determination of the sufficiency of Franchisee's inventory and service facilities shall be conclusive on Franchisee.

12. *Insurance.* Franchisee will obtain and keep in force insurance protecting Franchisee and Franchisor from loss resulting from any third party's death, injury, property damage, or loss, regardless of where the transaction or occurrence giving rise to the loss occurs, or whether it is the result of Franchisee's or Franchisor's acts. The insurance in force at any time shall not be less than $ . . . . for personal injury per person and $ . . . . for any accident and $ . . . . for property damage for any accident. Franchisee shall not be relieved of this obligation even if Franchisor maintains overlapping insurance.

13. *Franchisor May Inspect Franchisee's Records and Premises.* Franchisor or its representatives may inspect Franchisee's books of account and business records during business hours and upon . . . . days written notice to confirm the accuracy of the accountings furnished by Franchisee in accordance with Paragraph 8 and to determine whether Franchisor is in compliance with the provisions of this Agreement and the Manual. Franchisor or its representatives may visit and inspect any premises maintained by Francishee in connection with the franchise to determine whether Franchisee is in compliance with the provisions of this Agreement and the Manual.

14. *Effect of Termination of Agreement – Repurchase of Franchisee's Inventory by Franchisor.* Upon the termination of this Agreement for any reason, Franchisee will immediately stop the sale and distribution of Franchisor's products. Within . . . . days following the termination of this Agreement, Franchisor and Franchisee or their representatives will take an inventory of Franchisor's products on hand on Franchisee's premises. Franchisor will repurchase these Products from Franchisee at the price paid for them by Franchisee, less . . . . percent. From the total purchase price, Franchisor may deduct any sums owed to it by Franchisee. Upon delivery to Franchisee of Franchisor's check for the net sum due, Franchisee will deliver to Franchisor a fully executed bill of sale for the Products resold together with all documents that may be required to comply with the Bulk Sales provisions (Article 6) of the Uniform Commercial Code of the State of . . . .

15. *Effect of Termination of Agreement – Franchisee's License and Grant Ends.* Upon the termination of this Agreement for any reason, Franchisee's right and license to sell or distribute Franchisor's products and to use and exploit Franchisor's Tradename and Trademark shall cease at once. Any such sale, distribution, use, or exploitation following the termination of this Agreement shall be deemed an infringement of Franchisor's Tradename and Trademark for which Franchisor may seek relief in equity and law.

16. *Restrictive Covenant.* For a period of . . . . years from the date of termination of this Agreement, Franchisee will not engage in any business in the territory similar to or competitive with Franchisor's business, directly or indirectly, either as principal, partner, agent, manager, employee, stockholder, director, officer, or in any other capacity.

17. *Parties Not Partners, Joint Venturers, Etc.* This Agreement shall not be construed to constitute a partnership, joint venture, or agency between the parties nor to create an employer-employee relationship between Franchisor and Franchisee. Franchisee acknowledges that he is an independent contractor, that his business is his own and entirely separate from that of Franchisor, and that he will not deal with or represent himself to the public in any other way.

18. *Agreement Not Assignable by Franchisee – Assignable by Franchisor.* This Agreement shall inure to the benefit of Franchisor, its successors and assigns. The franchise granted by this Agreement is personal to Franchisee and cannot be assigned or transferred by him through his act or by operation of law without Franchisor's written consent. Upon Franchisee's death, insolvency, or bankruptcy this Agreement shall terminate.

. . . ., Inc.

by . . . .
Franchisor

. . . .
Franchisee

FACTS

Thomas Carvel, president of Carvel Corporation, defendant, went into the ice cream business in 1934. In 1948 the business issued franchises and sold freezers for the operation of soft ice cream stores under the Carvel name. This is an action by franchise operators under franchise agreements with Carvel Corporation claiming that the supplier, H.P. Hood & Sons, and Carvel Corporation violated the antitrust laws by their refusal to deal directly with them. The franchisees allege that they have the right to purchase Carvel Mix ice cream, made pursuant to Carvel's secret formula, other than on the terms Carvel Corporation prescribed in the franchise agreement. Did Carvel Corporation violate the antitrust laws by requiring its franchise operators to deal only with its supplier of ice cream, H.P. Hood & Sons?

DECISION

No. Judgment for defendant, Carvel Corporation. Carvel Corporation had the right to bind the dairy companies to manufacture this secret formula mix solely for its own use or for persons whom it might designate. No outsider, without Carvel Corporation's approval, had the right to require the dairy companies to sell them this special formula mix. The plaintiff did not contend that Carvel Corporation engaged in any common conspiracy with the supplier, H.P. Hood & Sons.

Susser v. Carvel Corp., 206 F.Supp. 636 (S. D. N. Y. 1962).

► Trademark

trademark
An identifying designation differentiating one's goods from those of another

A company that desires to franchise should acquire federal registration in the United States Patent Office of its trademark and trade name. The Lanham Act, Section 5, defines a trademark as "any word, name, symbol, or device, or any combination thereof adopted and used by manufacturer or merchant to identify his goods and distinguish them from those manufactured by others." Once the trademark is registered, the owner may grant to another (the franchisee) the right to use it in accordance with the franchise contract. Well-known trademarks include McDonald's, Shell, and Holiday Inn.

► Exclusivity

The franchise contract includes a provision that designates a geographical area where the franchisee can operate. The court in the following case found no antitrust violation in an exclusive dealership franchise.

FACTS

Hudson Sales Corporation urged Schwing Motor Company, a Ford dealer in Baltimore, to establish a Hudson agency in the Baltimore area. Schwing agreed to become a master franchise dealer for Hudson upon assurance that Schwing would receive an annual quota of 150 Hudson automobiles. Thereafter Bankert was granted an exclusive dealership franchise with Hudson and opened in Baltimore. Schwing's dealership was not renewed. Schwing Motor Company claims that the purpose of the nonrenewal was to eliminate him from competition with Bankert and thereby create a monopoly in the Baltimore area to the end that higher prices might be obtained from the public. May Hudson grant an exclusive dealership and thereby give a dealer an actual monopoly?

DECISION

Yes. Judgment Hudson Sales Corporation. Every manufacturer has a natural and complete monopoly on his particular product, especially when sold under his own brand or trade name. A manufacturer may prefer to deal with one person rather than another, and may grant exclusive dealership to sell in a particular territory. An exclusive dealership to sell in a particular area is not invalid. The public was not injured since the automobile market remained in its normal competitive state. Unless the manufacturer dominates the market, he has the right to give a dealer an actual monopoly.

Schwing Motor Co. v. Hudson Sales Corp., 138 F.Supp. 899 (D.Md. 1956).

tying arrangement
An agreement between a seller or lessor and a purchaser or lessee that a sale or lease of a product to the latter is contingent upon the latter's purchase or lease of another product of the seller or lessor

Tying Arrangement Many franchisors recognize the importance of a location. Hence they purchase the buildings and lease the premises to a franchisee. To ensure a standardized image and decor, the layout, design, and equipment are considered part of the trademark image. The items in the "franchise package" must all interrelate as part of the franchise outlet in order to justify its anticompetitive effect; otherwise the franchise arrangement will be held to be illegal.

► Service or Product Control

The franchisor has an interest in maintaining the goodwill of the business that the purchasing public has come to associate with its trade name. Hence a common provision found in a franchising contract obligates the franchisee to purchase *all* its products from the franchisor or its authorized suppliers. Since this is "full-line" forcing—that is, a *full* line of products must be taken by the franchisee in order to obtain *any* of the franchisor's products—such an arrangement is *not* an unlawful tying under the Clayton Antitrust Act.

► Federal and State Regulation of Franchising

In an attempt to remedy misrepresentations by franchisors to promote the sale of franchises, the Federal Trade Commission promulgated (published) a Trade Regulation Rule on franchising.[8] In addition, various states require the franchisor to register its franchise prospectus before offering its franchise for sale to the public.[9]

The FTC Rule requires in the advertising, offering, licensing, contracting, sale, or other promotion of any franchise in interstate commerce, an extensive disclosure of information, including:

1. The trademark, place of business of the franchisor, and the parent firm or holding company of the franchisor, if any
2. A factual description of the franchise offered
3. Names of directors and stockholders owning more than 10 percent of the franchisor's stock, and executive officers for the past ten years
4. The business and financial experience of the franchisor including balance sheets and profit and loss statements for the most recent five-year period
5. A description of the franchise fee, how it was determined if it is not the same in all cases, and the conditions on when all or part may be returned

---

[8]16 C.F.R. Part 436 (1980).

[9]As of May 1985, fourteen states have statutes requiring franchisors to register their franchise offerings by filing a prospectus: California, Hawaii, Illinois, Indiana, Maryland, Michigan, Minnesota, New York, North Dakota, Rhode Island, South Dakota, Virginia, Washington, and Wisconsin.

6. The number of franchises presently operating and how many are company owned
7. A statement that the franchisee may inspect the profit and loss statements of all existing franchises

In the following case the court had to determine if a franchise agreement created a fiduciary relationship.

FACTS

In September of 1971, Picture Lake Campground, Inc., plaintiff, applied to Holiday Inns, Inc., defendant, for a franchise in the Holiday Inn Trav-L-Park system, a franchised recreational vehicle campground system offering camper rental spaces, recreation, food, and other accommodations, and using Holiday Inns' trade names, trademarks, and service marks. In July 1972 the parties executed a written License Agreement. (There was another plaintiff in the lower court who is not involved in the appeal of this case.) Picture Lake Campground alleges that Holiday Inns has breached the License Agreement and has effectively discontinued the development of the Trav-L-Park franchise system, thus destroying its value, in violation of representations made by Holiday Inns to plaintiff, thereby causing plaintiff considerable damage. The complaint alleges that, during several meetings between representatives of Holiday Inns and the owners of the Picture Lake property, various representations were made by Holiday Inns concerning, among other things: the favorable market conditions for recreational vehicle campgrounds; Holiday Inns' concept of a high quality, expanding system of franchise campgrounds, with developmental, promotional and maintenance support provided by the experienced Holiday Inns corporation; the suitability of Picture Lake as a site for such a campground; and the substantial income potential of the Picture Lake property as a part of the system developed under the guidance and control of Holiday Inns.

The plaintiff alleges in its complaint that these representations were made with the intent to deceive and defraud plaintiff, that such representations were false and were known by Holiday Inns to be false. Plaintiff's complaint alleges that Holiday Inns has breached its fiduciary duties of good faith, loyalty, and honesty owed to Picture Lake. It is plaintiff's contention that such a fiduciary duty may exist in a franchise relationship and, when violated, is actionable under Virginia law. Holiday Inns' motion to dismiss the complaint was granted, and the plaintiff appealed. Does a franchise agreement create a fiduciary relationship?

DECISION

No. Affirmed for the defendant, Holiday Inns. The application of a fiduciary duty to a franchisor-franchisee relationship is inappropriate. A franchise relationship is inherently a business relationship, not a fiduciary relationship. While Holiday Inns had a duty to deal fairly with Picture Lake, it did not have the duty of a fiduciary with all of the obligations and responsibilities pertaining thereto. Each party served the interest of the other, but each also quite properly sought its own interest.

Picture Lake Campground, Inc. v. Holiday Inns, Inc., 497 F.Supp. 858 (D. Va. 1980).

► Termination

In the following case Mobil Oil Corporation attempted to terminate a one-year trial franchise without providing any reason for doing so.

FACTS

Plaintiff, the operator of a Mobil Gasoline Service Station, seeks injunctive relief to prevent defendant, Mobil Oil Corporation, from terminating or nonrenewing his one-year trial franchise. After successfully completing a three-week course of instruction in defendant's dealer training school, plaintiff was granted a one-year trial franchise beginning May 14, 1979 and ending May 13, 1980. On February 7, 1980, defendant mailed to plaintiff by certified mail, a notice that defendant "hereby elects not to renew its franchise relationship with [plaintiff] and that relationship will terminate on May 13, 1980." Section 2803 of the Petroleum Marketing Practices Act provides that "(if) the notification requirements of Section 2803 . . . are met" the franchisor may fail to renew the franchise relationship under a trial franchise at the conclusion of the initial term thereof. Section 2804 (c)(3) mandates that the notification of nonrenewal "shall contain . . . a statement of intention to terminate the franchise or not to renew the franchise relationship, together with the reasons therefor." The notice which defendant gave to plaintiff in this case stated, "The reason or reasons for our non-renewal decision are that Mobil has determined that it does not wish to continue its franchise relationship with you." Did this notice effectively terminate the franchise?

DECISION

No. Judgment for the plaintiff. The notice in question wholly fails to provide any reason and so does not conform to the notification requirements of Section 2804(c). And since the statute explicitly permits a franchisor to fail to renew a trial franchise only if the notification requirements of Section 2804 have been met, it follows that plaintiff is entitled to relief.

Clark v. Mobil Oil Corp., 496 F.Supp. 132 (D. Miss. 1980).

Summary Statement

1. A limited partnership is a partnership formed by two or more persons having as members one or more general partners and one or more limited partners. A limited partner shall not become liable as a general partner unless he or she takes part in the control of the business.
2. (a) The general partners in a limited partnership are personally liable for partnership debts. (b) The limited partners are liable to the partnership for capital contributions to the firm that they agreed in the certificate of partnership that they would make but had not yet made.
3. A limited partnership must be formed by a signed and sworn certificate, which is filed as required by each state, usually in the county clerk's office or the registry of deeds where the firm business is carried on.
4. A joint venture is an association of two or more persons organized as co-owners to engage in a *limited* business transaction for a profit.
5. A mining partnership is an association of co-owners organized to develop oil and gas production and share the profits and losses. It is not dissolved by the death or bankruptcy of a partner.
6. A business trust is formed by a trust instrument with the trustees acting as business managers and the beneficiaries as capital investors and holders of transferable shares. The beneficiaries will be held personally liable for trust obligations only if they have power to control the trust management.
7. A joint-stock company is a nonstatutory business organization created by contract that provides for centralized management and transferability of shares. The shareholder members are personally liable for company debts.
8. Franchising is a contractual arrangement whereby one party, the franchisor, allows another party, the franchisee, to use its trade name, trademark, supplied products,

equipment, and managerial expertise. The franchisee agrees to sell the services or products under the control and supervision of the franchisor.

The court in the following case reviewed the plaintiff's allegation of an illegal tying arrangement to determine if the tied products were integral components of the business method being franchised.

PRINCIPE et al. v. McDONALD'S CORPORATION
631 F.2d 303 (4th Cir. 1980)

Harry Phillips, Senior Circuit Judge. Plaintiffs, Frank A. Principe, Ann Principe, and Frankie, Inc., a family owned corporation, plaintiffs, are franchisees of McDonald's System, Inc. At the time this suit was filed, McDonald's consisted of at least four separate corporate entities. McDonald's Systems, Inc. controlled franchise rights and licensed franchisees to sell hamburgers under the McDonald's name. Franchise Realty Interstate Corporation (Franchise Realty) acquires real estate, either by purchase or long term lease, builds McDonald's hamburger restaurants, and leases them either to franchisees or to a third corporation, McOp Co. Straddling this triad is McDonald's Corporation, the parent, defendant, who owns all the stock of the other defendants. Because the various defendants have substantially similar corporate hierarchies and operate in conjunction under the direction and control of the corporate parent, we shall refer to them collectively as McDonald's, defendant.

The McDonald's system of restaurants included some 4,465 stores in 1978, 99% of which were owned by Franchise Realty. McDonald's is not primarily a fast food retailer. While it does operate over a thousand stores itself, the vast majority of the stores in its system are operated by franchisees. Nor does McDonald's sell equipment or supplies to its licensees. Instead its primary business is developing and collecting royalties from limited menu fast food restaurants operated by independent business people. McDonald's develops new restaurants according to master plans that originate at the regional level and must be approved by upper management. Regional administrative staffs meet at least annually to consider new areas into which McDonald's can expand. Once the decision is made to expand into a particular geographic area, specialists begin to search for appropriate restaurant sites. McDonald's uses demographic data generated by the most recent census and its own research in evaluating potential sites.

The Principes argue McDonald's is selling not one but three distinct products, the franchise, the lease, and the security deposit note. The alleged antitrust violation stems from the fact that a prospective franchisee must buy all three in order to obtain the franchise. As evidence that this is an illegal tying arrangement, the Principes point to the unfavorable terms on which franchisees are required to lease their stores. Not only are franchisees denied the opportunity to build equity and depreciate their property, but they must maintain the building, pay for improvements and taxes, and remit 8.5 percent of their gross sales as rents. McDonald's responds that it is not in the business of licensing use of its name, improving real estate for lease or selling long term notes. Its only business is developing a system of hamburger restaurants and collecting royalties from their sales. The allegedly tied products are but parts of the overall bundle of franchise benefits and obligations. According to McDonald's, the Principes are asking the court to invalidate the way McDonald's does business and to require it to adopt the licensing procedures of its less successful competitors. Federal antitrust laws do not compel such a result, McDonald's contends. Judgment in the lower court was for the defendant franchisor, and the plaintiffs franchisees appeal.

There is at the outset of every tie-in case the problem of determining whether two separate products are in fact involved. Because we agree with McDonald's that the lease, note, and license are not separate products but component parts of the overall franchise package, we hold on the facts of this case there was no illegal tie-in. Given the realities of modern franchising, we think the proper inquiry is not whether the allegedly tied products are associated in the public mind with the franchisor's trademark, but whether they are integral components of the business method being franchised. Where the challenged aggregation is an essential ingredient of the franchised system's formula for success, there is but a single product and no tie-in exists as a matter of law. Applying this standard to the present case, we hold the lease is not separable from the McDonald's franchise to which it pertains. McDonald's practice of developing a system of company owned restaurants operated by franchisees has substantial advantages, both for the company and for franchisees. It is part of what makes a McDonald franchise uniquely attractive to franchisees. To characterize the franchise as an unnecessary aggregation of separate products tied to the McDonald's name is to miss the point entirely. Among would be franchisees, the McDonald's name has come to stand for the formula, including all that it entails. We decline to find that it is an illegal tie-in.

Affirmed, for defendant franchisor.

Question and Case Problems

1. Since November of 1960, Tappan Motors, Inc. (Tappan), has been a regularly franchised Volvo dealer. The franchise agreement provided for its termination by the distributor upon 30 days' written notice to the dealer in the event that the dealer fails to correct any default in performance of its responsibilities under the foregoing provisions within 60 days after written notice of such default. A New York statute prohibits termination by a distributor of contracts for sales of new motor vehicles to a dealer except for cause.

The evidence presented at trial shows: that Tappan had repeatedly experienced problems in servicing Volvo automobiles; Tappan's facilities were neither as large nor as clean as Volvo required; some of the specialized tools required for servicing Volvos were missing from Tappan's premises; certain of Volvo's factory service manuals were also missing; Volvo customers at Tappan were subjected to inconvenience and excessive waiting times for repairs; Tappan failed or refused to keep an adequate inventory of Volvo parts; Tappan delayed installation of a computer system for the control of its parts inventory until after its termination was scheduled to take effect; and Tappan repeatedly complained about its allocation of automobiles and threatened to dissuade customers from purchasing a Volvo elsewhere if Tappan could not supply them with the Volvo model of their choice. Was this evidence sufficient to justify Volvo's decision to terminate Tappan's franchise? [*Tappan Motors, Inc. v. Volvo of America Corp. et al.,* 444 N.Y. S. 2d 938 (N.Y. 1981).]

2. H. C. Blackwell Co., Inc. (Blackwell), instituted this action against Kenworth Truck Co. (Kenworth), under the Automobile Dealers' Franchise Act, seeking damages for claimed wrongful termination and/or nonrenewal of its franchise. On February 4, 1976, Kenworth advised Blackwell by letter that the then existing "informal arrangement" would terminate in 90 days, but that Kenworth would then offer Blackwell a dealer agreement if Blackwell met 12 specified demands within that period of 90 days. These demands included substantial capital improvements, increased sales, and a better bookkeeping system. Kenworth's regional sales manager testified that it would have taken Blackwell at least one year to meet the demands delineated in that letter. Blackwell attempted to meet these requirements, spending approximately $90,000 in the process. Although Blackwell was unable to accomplish everything required by Kenworth within the designated 90-day time limit, it made substantial progress toward compliance with the conditions. On June 24, 1976, Blackwell received a letter from Kenworth stating that the franchise would not be renewed because the May inspection report was "not favorable." Did Kenworth legally, in good faith, terminate the franchise? [*H. C. Blackwell Co., Inc. v. Kenworth Truck Co.,* 620 F.2d 104 (5th Cir. 1980).]

3. Polikoff and Levy, with others, formed a joint venture known as the State House Inn. The members, over the objection of Polikoff, caused all of the assets to be transferred to a new corporation, the State House Inn, Inc. Polikoff brought this suit claiming that co-venturers cannot arbitrarily dispose of the assets of the venture over the objection of one co-venturer. He asked the court to have the assets disposed of by a judicial sale. You decide. [*Polikoff v. Levy,* 270 N.E.2d 540 (Ill. 1971).]
4. Bailey Employment Systems, Inc. (Bailey), commenced this action seeking payment of a $10,000 note. The defendant, Clifford Hahn, admitting the existence and execution of the note, counterclaimed against Bailey, alleging misrepresentation and fraud by Bailey in connection with the sale of a franchise to Hahn. A Bailey brochure set forth "Projected Earnings" of different levels of Bailey franchises. The brochure was clearly meant to indicate to a potential purchaser what earnings he or she could expect from a Bailey franchise. The figures in the "Projected Earnings" table are unrepresentative, and in some instances, without any reasonable basis in fact for any of the three years prior to Hahn's purchase. Did Bailey act in a deceptive manner? [*Bailey Employment System, Inc. v. Clifford Hahn et al.,* 545 F.Supp. 62 (D. Conn. 1982).]
5. Fidelity Lease, Ltd., is a limited partnership organized to lease restaurant locations. It is composed of 22 limited partners and a corporate general partner, Interlease Corp. Interlease's officers, directors, and shareholders were Crombie, Kahn, and Sanders, who were also limited partners of Fidelity. Delaney is a building contractor who entered into an agreement with the limited partnership, Fidelity, acting by and through its corporate general partner, Interlease, to lease a fast-food restaurant to the partnership. Delaney built the restaurant, but Fidelity failed to take possession or pay rent. Delaney brought suit for damages for breach of the lease agreement, naming as defendants the limited partnership of Fidelity Lease, Ltd., its corporate general partner, Interlease Corp., and all of its limited partners individually. Are Crombie, Kahn, and Sanders—the officers, directors, and shareholders of Interlease—personally liable? [*Delaney v. Fidelity Lease, Ltd.,* 526 S.W.2d 543 (Tex. 1975).]
6. Thorson and defendant Bellamy are real estate agents. Thorson entered into a listing agreement with one Grafe to sell the real estate parcel in question. The agreement gave Thorson a right to a commission if he arranged a sale. Grafe offered Bellamy an exclusive listing on the property. Bellamy accepted the listing, but insisted that Thorson's name be included in the agreement as real estate broker. Bellamy also included at the bottom of the listing agreement: "This is a cooperative listing with Freeland Thorson of Weiser, Idaho." At the time they reached the agreement, Bellamy had told Grafe that he intended to act in a cooperative arrangement with Thorson. Concerning the commission for a sale, Bellamy testified that he intended Thorson to receive a share of the commission even if Thorson did not make the sale.

Bellamy actively sought a buyer for the Grafe property during the second listing; Thorson did not. Thorson's participation in the sale of the property consisted solely of visits to the home of Mrs. Madsen whose signature was later needed for certain papers to clear title. However, Bellamy did not complain to Thorson about Thorson's inactivity; neither did he seek to terminate the agreement. Bellamy eventually purchased the land himself from Grafe and immediately resold it to Harland Crawford. Thorson's sole participation in the sale of the property came in connection with arrangements for financing the transaction. When Bellamy refused to acknowledge the commission and to give Thorson his share, Thorson brought this proceeding claiming a joint venture existed and, because they never reached an agreement about how to split the commission, the two men should split the commission and expenses fifty-fifty. Bellamy argues that, because he included Thorson in the listing gratuitously, the agreement was not supported by consideration and, therefore, it is not a contract. Decide. [*Thorson v. Bellamy,* 635 P.2d 1048 (Or. 1981).]

7. Loomis Land & Cattle Co. brought suit to enjoin the sale of a shopping center. The right to have the sale enjoined was based upon the ground that Diversified Mortgage was a Massachusetts business trust and not a recognizable entity under the laws of Texas and was, therefore, without standing in court to pursue any of the remedies arising under the sales contract. Defendant argues that it has standing to sue in the Texas courts because a Massachusetts trust is to be treated as an unincorporated joint-stock company. May a state regard a Massachusetts business trust as a joint-stock company? [*Loomis Land & Cattle Co. v. Diversified Mortgage Investors,* 533 S.W.2d 420 (Tex. 1976).]

8. Richardson, the plaintiff and co-trustee of a business trust, brought this action to nullify two leases and a purchase and sale agreement executed by two of the three trustees. The Brattle Craigie Trust was created in 1913 by Joseph Clarke and two other individuals under a declaration of trust for the purpose of "purchasing, improving, holding, managing, disposing and otherwise dealing with real estate." In September 1942, by a unanimous vote of all the business trustees, including Richardson, the instrument creating the Brattle Craigie Trust was amended to permit the powers of the business trustees to be exercised by a majority. Richardson, the plaintiff, now contends that the amendment is invalid because it deprives the trustees of their power and duty to control the operation of the business trust. May a business trust be amended to provide for majority control of trust business? [*Richardson v. Clarke,* 364 N.E.2d 804 (Mass. 1977).]

9. Petitioner M.I.F. Securities Company (MIF), a limited partnership, and R. C. Stamm & Co. (Stamm), a general partnership, were engaged in the securities business. They entered into an agreement whereby Stamm was to operate as a division of MIF under certain limited profit and expense sharing provisions. MIF was a member firm of the American Stock Exchange (Amex), while Stamm was not a member of Amex or any other securities exchange. The agreement did not contain any provision for the arbitration of disputes between the parties.

   A few months after the agreement was executed, a dispute arose over Stamm's clearing charges. When Stamm thereafter served MIF with a demand for arbitration before Amex, MIF sought a stay (stop) on the ground that the parties had not agreed to arbitrate. Finding that the applicable arbitration provision of the Amex constitution was "broad enough to cover the parties herein and their disputes," since "[u]nder the terms of the [a]greement between the parties, [Stamm], as a 'division' of MIF, is essentially a partner of a member firm," the court denied MIF's petition for a stay and granted Stamm's motion to compel arbitration. Was Stamm a partner? [*M.I.F. Securities Co. v. R. C. Stamm & Co.*, 463 N.Y.S.2d 771 (N.Y. 1983).]

10. In the case of *Principe et al. v. McDonald's Corporation,* excerpted at the beginning of this section, the plaintiffs/franchisees alleged an antitrust violation and an illegal tying arrangement as the theory that McDonald's is selling three distinct products, the franchise, lease and note, rather than component parts of the overall franchise package. What standard did the court apply to determine there was a single product being franchised and no illegal tie-in?

PART 8A BUSINESS ORGANIZATIONS

A: General Partnerships and Special Ventures

INTERNATIONAL DIMENSIONS

Scores of companies every day are faced with the challenges of entering new markets and forming new businesses in order to remain competitive on a global basis. Scholars speculate that companies that go at it alone will not survive at the world-class level. Consequently, companies have begun to use joint ventures as a form of leverage in pursuit of new markets and companies.

Corning Glass Works, the glass and ceramics maker best known for its Steuben crystal and Pyrex housewares, is one company that has used joint ventures to its advantage. Corning has started thirty-eight joint ventures in a dozen countries and only six have failed. Joint ventures recently account for more than half of its operating income. Moreover, half of these joint ventures have existed for at least ten years. The average success rate for a joint venture is only 46 percent and the average life span is 3.5 years.

Corning's current joint venture is with Japan's Asahi Glass Company, the world's largest maker of glass bulbs. The venture, known as Corning Asahi Video Products, will produce large-sized and advanced high-resolution glass bulbs for televisions and computers. Corning will manage the venture and Asahi will initially own 67 percent of it, while Asahi will supply the technology and eventually own 49 percent of the company. Why did the companies need each other? Corning has found such alliances to be politically advantageous and the ventures give Corning access to the world-wide computer and television markets and to the Japanese manufactures. Asahi gains the management expertise of Corning and the font of Corning's reputation. (Corning is credited with helping Thomas Edison develop the light bulb.)

Corning's venture partners include both domestic and international companies. Corning and Dow Chemical became the leading producers of silicone. Corning and Owens-Illinois Corporation grew to become America's largest maker of glass fiber. After two years of negotiations, Corning and Ciba-Geigy agreed to start a firm to develop new blood and urine analyzers. Most recently, Corning formed a venture with Genetech and Kodak under the name of Genecore, Inc., which has successfully entered the lucrative industrial-enzymes market.

Its venture partners credit Corning's unassuming corporate culture as an essential ingredient of success. Joint ventures require compromise and flourish in an atmosphere of give and take. Egos, therefore, must take a back seat. Joint ventures with foreign companies entail other challenges, such as overcoming language barriers and even cultural stereotypes. When Corning and Ciba-Geigy began talks, Ciba at one point said that it preferred to buy Corning outright. Corning had to persuade Ciba that a joint venture rather than an outright purchase was in their best interest. Observes a Corning employee, "[Corning's Chairman James Houghton] didn't go in as a Wall Street dealmaker or a Texas gunslinger. He didn't fit any of the Swiss stereotypes about American businessmen." It certainly helped that Houghton was fluent in French and once lived in Switzerland.

Corning remains committed to the joint venture as a cheaper and quicker way to build a business instead of starting one from scratch. To be sure, Corning has had its failures. But usually that is because it failed to adhere to its five joint-venture rules: seek a compatible partner, share in it equally, set the venture apart from the parent companies, agree on goals, and select strong managers. Mr. Houghton also noted that both partners need to trust one another for the joint venture to really survive in this era of global markets.

PART 8

BUSINESS ORGANIZATIONS
B. Corporations

45 CORPORATE STOCK AND SHAREHOLDERS

The meaning of corporate stock owned by shareholders, the various kinds of shares, rights of shareholders, and transferability of shares; securities regulations; and foreign corrupt practices are also discussed.

46 CORPORATE MANAGEMENT

How a corporation actually operates; the functions of the board of directors and corporate officers who participate in that operation as managers, and their duties, powers, and liability; the managerial function of shareholders is also examined.

Note: Chapters 42 through 46 are keyed to the 1983 Revised Model Business Corporation Act (RMBCA). All references to the Act, and all quotations of selected sections from the Act are reproduced with the permission of the American Bar Foundation, which holds the copyright for the Act.

PREVIEW

The need for corporations in a government-regulated free-enterprise system is discussed, followed by a brief history and descriptions of the various kinds of corporations. You will see how a corporation is formed and dissolved. The powers granted to a corporation by the state are reviewed. The rights of stockholders are explained as well as the few instances when a shareholder may be held personally liable. Finally, the managerial functions of a corporation's officers and directors are discussed from a legal viewpoint.

Business ethics as it relates to the chapters in Parts 8A and 8B is considered at the end of the part. There is also a consideration of the international aspects of corporate law.

CHAPTER 42

NATURE AND CLASSES

After you have read this chapter, you should be able to:

1. Define a corporation.
2. Explain limited liability.
3. Identify the source of corporation law.
4. Explain the contribution to corporate law from the following:
   a) Roman law.
   b) Canon law.
   c) Civil law.
   d) Common law.
   e) Overseas trading companies.
   f) Revised Model Business Corporation Act.
5. List and explain the classification of corporations.
6. Explain what is meant by "doing business" in a foreign state.
7. List activities that generally do not constitute transacting business in a foreign state.
8. Explain the meaning and purpose of a registered agent.
9. Explain how private corporations are regulated by the government.
10. Explain the constitutional restrictions on government regulation of a corporation.
11. Explain what is meant by disregarding the corporate entity and when the court may do so.
12. List and explain the corporate attributes.
13. Define a (Subchapter) S corporation.
14. Explain what is meant by "piercing the corporate veil."

BUSINESS DECISIONS and the LAW

Suppose that you love island life and decide to start a moped rental business on Lost Island in order to support yourself. You have heard that by incorporating your business you can avoid personal liability for injuries or losses from the business. This sounds great—you get to keep the profits and at the same time limit your liability. Since money is scarce, you decide to do without insurance on the mopeds, your employees, and the building. Repairs on the bikes fall behind. Likewise, the mortgage payments on your house are behind, so you decide to take money from the business to pay for this personal expense.

The worst happens: a patron is injured on one of your bikes as a result of neglect on your part. The patron sues for millions and your response is that liability is limited, so your beachfront house and luxury automobile are safe. Right? Wrong! A court will disregard the corporate entity when it is effectively the alter ego of the individual. Thus you will be personally liable for all business and cannot hide behind the corporation.

While the law permits the incorporation of a business for the very purpose of enabling its proprietors to escape personal liability, this privilege is not without limits. Courts indeed take a harsh view of inadequacy of capitalization as measured by the nature and magnitude of the undertaking, as well as the commingling of personal and corporate funds. This piercing of the corporate veil is a vehicle to avoid the perpetration of a fraud on innocent persons. The lesson to be learned for all would-be incorporators? With the benefits of incorporation follow the burdens that must be adhered to without fail.

Introduction

You are one of five people who wish to engage in business together but who have two main problems: you need capital, the money to get the business started and operating; and you don't want to have the risk of your individual properties being available to pay creditors of the business. You also want to be able to transfer your shares or interests in the business easily to other persons without affecting the continuation of the business. The corporation came into being as a result of these and other needs.

Nature

corporation
A legal entity created by statute authorizing an association of persons to carry on an enterprise

shareholder (stockholder)
The owner of a unit of interest in a corporation

share of stock
A unit of interest in a corporation

A **corporation** is a legal entity created by statute authorizing an association of persons to carry on an enterprise. The corporation exists as a *legal person* with many powers. For example, it can own property, real and personal, in its own name; make contracts; incur debts; issue stocks and bonds; and sue and be sued. As a legal person, its owners, the **shareholders** or stockholders, are distinct from the legal entity and cannot be sued for corporate liabilities. This is known as *limited liability*—that is, the corporate investor's risk is limited to the loss of his or her investment. A shareholder cannot be held personally liable for corporate debts. For example, if you purchased **shares of stock** for $5,000, corporate creditors could not sue you personally, although your investment may be lost.

A corporation is granted its existence by the state or the federal government. The formation of a corporation, under modern statutory law, is accomplished by submitting to the secretary of state a document called the *articles of incorporation.* The articles, discussed in a later chapter, identify the name and location of the corporation, the nature of its business, the incorporators, sometimes the directors, and officers, and authorized capitalization.

Larger business organizations function as corporations because the corporate form affords them the many advantages of *corporate attributes.* These consist of:

1. the ability to raise substantial capital by dividing its ownership into shares of stock that may be sold to the general public;
2. the ability to continue in existence upon the death of an owner, called perpetual succession;
3. an easy method of transferring corporate stock;
4. the centralization of management by a board of directors;
5. the limited liability of its stock investors; and
6. the legal entity theory that creates an artificial person liable for its obligations.

Figure 42.1 illustrates the general composition and rights of the corporate officers, directors, and shareholders.

FIGURE 42.1 Structure of the Corporation

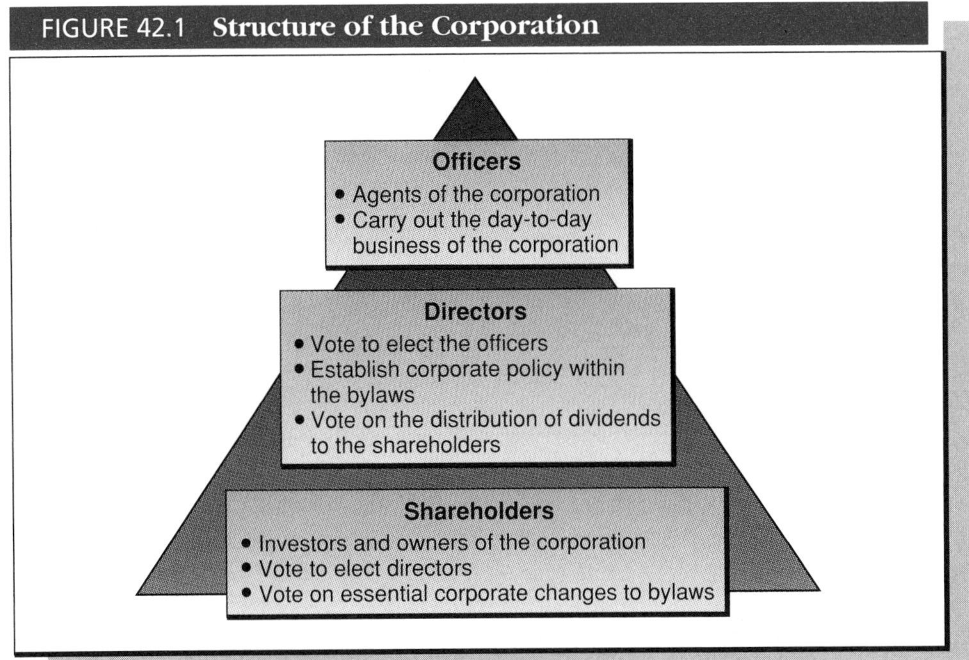

Officers
• Agents of the corporation
• Carry out the day-to-day business of the corporation
Directors
• Vote to elect the officers
• Establish corporate policy within the bylaws
• Vote on the distribution of dividends to the shareholders
Shareholders
• Investors and owners of the corporation
• Vote to elect directors
• Vote on essential corporate changes to bylaws

Historical Background

▶ Roman Law

The concept of the government creating an "artificial person" with certain characteristics having legal status has an ancient origin. During the early Roman republic various religious, educational, and governmental groups began to develop. The Roman Empire's rulers, desiring control over these groups, granted them legal authorization only by express approval. This created the origin of a business association requiring governmental authorization.

▶ Canon Law

The law of the Roman Catholic Church affected corporate law by regulating ecclesiastical property ownership. Pope Innocent IV (1243–1254) developed the concept of an "artificial person" that would own church property and permit its use without personal ownership by the clergy, thus creating the principle of a legal entity separate and distinct from its owners.

▶ Civil Law

A codified legal system based on the Roman law also recognizes the corporation as a separate entity. The codification of the civil law in some European countries adopted many characteristics of the Roman law.

Common Law

In England, as early as the fourteenth century, many ecclesiastical, charitable, and municipal corporations developed. Their most common trait was perpetual existence, which became a corporate characteristic.

Overseas Trading Companies

The British government granted powers to explore, trade with, and colonize foreign territory. The British East India Company (1600), the Virginia Company (1609)—which founded the Virginia Colony and brought the Pilgrims to America—and the South Sea Company (1711) are examples of business associations that were the prototypes of the modern business corporation.

Corporate Law in the United States

Corporate laws were enacted in the United States as early as 1795 in North Carolina. A twentieth century demand to incorporate created a need to modernize corporate law, which led to the development of the Model Business Corporation Act (MBCA) first published as a complete Act in 1950. The Act was last revised in 1984. Many states have amended their corporate law statutes substantially in accordance with the MBCA prior to its last revision. In most states today, filing the articles of incorporation, paying the necessary fee, and getting state approval cause the creation of an "artificial legal person"—the corporation.

Classification of Corporations

The needs of our society are commonly provided for by corporate institutions. For example, educational and health care needs are served by colleges and hospitals that may be *nonprofit corporations*. When the general public is served by the corporation—for example, a municipality—it is a *public corporation*. If substantial business is carried on in interstate commerce, it is a *foreign corporation* in other than its state of incorporation.

Public, Private, and Quasi-Public Corporations

A *public corporation* is one organized by the state or federal government to administer government affairs. An example is the Federal Deposit Insurance Corporation (FDIC). The government may then employ recognized business procedures in such matters as the purchase of property and management of its functions. For example, a city is a *municipal public corporation* granted authority to operate by the state.

Private corporations are created by private parties and may serve a profit or nonprofit purpose but not a governmental function. For instance, the national corporations that constitute our free-enterprise system are private corporations although their stock is sold to the public. They engage in business for a profit and to provide a return on the stockholders' investment by way of a dividend. Private corporations are now highly regulated by governmental agencies such as the Department of Labor and the Federal Trade Commission.[1] Most of our discussion in these chapters on corporations will be concerned with the private corporation organized for a profit and selling its stock

[1]See Chapters 34 through 37 on government regulation of business.

to the public. They are "business corporations" and sometimes referred to as "public" because of their stock ownership.

Quasi-public corporations are known as "public service corporations." They provide services that the general public has an interest in, such as supplying gas and electricity and operating railroads. Because of their public involvement, they are subjected to greater governmental regulation than are private corporations.

► Domestic and Foreign Corporations

A *domestic corporation* is a corporation formed and created under the laws of the state that granted its corporate charter. In all other states or countries it is a *foreign corporation*. For example, if you incorporate in Massachusetts but do extensive business in New York and Florida and all the stockholders reside in Connecticut, you are a domestic corporation in Massachusetts and a foreign corporation in New York and Florida.

It is not unusual for many large corporations to do business in several states. When a foreign corporation transacts business in a substantial and continuous manner as opposed to a casual transaction, it must obtain permission for this intrastate business in the foreign state. For example, if a corporate representative procured purchase orders in Texas that would be accepted by a Massachusetts corporation in Massachusetts, where its permanent corporate office was located, it would not be "doing business" in Texas.

> [T]he following activities, among others, do not constitute transacting business in a state:
>
> **(1)** maintaining, defending, or settling any proceedings;
> **(2)** holding directors' or shareholders' meetings or carrying on other activities concerning internal corporate affairs;
> **(3)** maintaining bank accounts;
> **(4)** maintaining offices or agencies for the transfer, exchange and registration of the corporation's own securities or maintaining trustees or depositories with respect to these securities;
> **(5)** selling through independent contractors;
> **(6)** soliciting or obtaining orders, whether by mail or through employees or agents or otherwise, if the orders require acceptance outside this state before they become contracts;
> **(7)** creating or acquiring indebtedness, mortgages, and security interests in real or personal property;
> **(8)** securing or collecting debts or enforcing mortgages and security interests in property securing the debts;
> **(9)** owning, without more, real or personal property;
> **(10)** conducting an isolated transaction that is completed within 30 days and that is not one in the course of repeated transactions of a like nature;
> **(11)** transacting business in interstate commerce; the list of activities is not exhaustive. [RMBCA, sec. 15.01.]

In the following case the court found a professional law association was not doing business in a foreign state based on an isolated transaction.

FACTS

Dr. Reisman is a medical doctor and general surgeon. The plaintiff is an Arizona professional association comprised of approximately 18 lawyers. In November of 1977 Dr. Reisman contacted Edwin Hendricks, a member of plaintiff, seeking legal advice and representation in a dispute between himself and Floyd County Medical Center (hospital) in Georgia.

Hendricks flew to Atlanta, Georgia, and associated local counsel, who was hired with Dr. Reisman's approval and was to be paid for his services directly by Dr. Reisman. A hearing was obtained before the hospital authority resulting in affirmance of the restrictions of Dr. Reisman's privileges. Dr. Reisman requested that the case be abandoned and a final bill presented. The total bill for Hendricks' services, including travel costs and professional services of several of Hendricks' associates who also worked on the case, was $21,438.14. Dr. Reisman had made advances of $15,000 but failed and refused to pay the balance. Plaintiff sued Dr. Reisman and judgment was rendered for the plaintiff. Dr. Reisman appealed, urging that the trial court erred in denying his motion for a directed verdict based upon appellee law association's failure to register as a foreign corporation in accordance with Georgia law for the purpose of maintaining this suit.

DECISION

The trial court properly denied Dr. Reisman's motion for a directed verdict.

The purpose of the Georgia statute is to require registration of foreign corporations which intend to conduct business in Georgia on a continuous basis, not as a temporary matter. Activity related to a single transaction or contract is thus not contemplated. The professional association's activities were concentrated in Arizona, although various attorneys in the firm had handled litigation outside the state of incorporation. Hendricks had represented clients in Georgia on two prior occasions, but these had nothing to do with his representation of Dr. Reisman. Under these circumstances, there is ample basis for the court's conclusion that the appellee had neither extended its business into Georgia on a continuous basis nor engaged "in a number of repeated transactions of like nature" within the state. Affirmed, for plaintiff.

Reisman v. Martori, Meyer, Hendricks & Victor, 271 S.E.2d 685 (Ga. 1980).

State corporate statutes require a foreign corporation that intends to do intrastate business to procure a certificate of authority. The application generally requires filing the foreign corporation's articles of incorporation with the secretary of state and paying the filing fee. Of most importance is the name and office address of the corporation's registered agent to receive service of process in the event the foreign corporation is sued.

In the following case the court reviewed the corporate activity in the foreign state and, although the corporation appeared to have only casual transactions, filing in the foreign state was nevertheless required to comply with the foreign state statute.

FACTS

Sinwellan Corporation, organized under the laws of Maryland, brought this action in a Delaware court against the Farmers Bank of the State of Delaware, alleging that Farmers wrongfully dishonored certain checks drawn on Sinwellan's checking account. Farmers Bank brought a motion to dismiss the complaint on the grounds that Sinwellan is a "foreign corporation" doing business in Delaware and it has not filed the appropriate certificate with the Secretary of State and hence has no right to sue in Delaware.

Sinwellan maintained a Delaware bank account in its corporate name, advertised in two Delaware newspapers, stored its financial records in Delaware, executed contracts with Delaware residents in Delaware, sold securities and engaged in credit transactions with Delaware residents, and provided a taxi service in Delaware.

The lower court applied the "doing business" test and found the activities inadequate to require filing and hence denied the defendant's motion to dismiss the complaint. Defendant appealed.

DECISION

Reversed. Judgment for defendant, Farmers Bank. The Delaware statute on foreign corporations requires a foreign corporation to file a certificate stating the name and address of its

> registered agent in Delaware. The primary object of the statute is to secure to the state and its people a way to serve process on a corporation which is organized elsewhere and which comes here to act through officers or agents. Given the scope of intrastate activities in which Sinwellan is engaged, the statute requires that it formalize its presence here through the nomination of a registered agent, the identification of an office, and by otherwise complying with the Delaware statute.
>
> *Farmers Bank of the State of Del. v. Sinwellan Corp.*, 367 A.2d 180 (Del. 1976).

Foreign corporations are subject to the foreign state regulating agencies and corporate state taxation.

► Close Corporations

It is a common misconception that the corporate organization with its many advantages is reserved for "big business." Many small companies desire to incorporate and thereby obtain limited liability. In a **close corporation** the stock is generally owned by one individual or his or her family. Hence, the managerial control of the corporation is in the owners. The closely held stock is not traded publicly, and the business is referred to as a close corporation. It has a separate corporate entity with all the corporate attributes of any corporation. Many state statutes authorize one person to incorporate, own all the stock, and serve as sole director and president.[2]

close corporation
A corporation in which managerial control is in the hands of the owners or shareholders

► Subchapter S Corporations

Profits earned by a corporation normally are taxed two times! First the corporation is taxed on the profits and then, on distribution of the profits as corporate dividends to shareholders, the shareholders must include such dividends as taxable income in their income tax returns.

Under the federal Internal Revenue Code, shareholders of certain closely held small business corporations may elect to be individually taxed as partners.[3] If the corporation qualifies, the individual shareholders are taxed on their shares of the corporation's income, or can deduct their proportionate share of its losses. The corporation, as an entity, pays no federal income tax. (It may have to pay a state corporate income tax.) Hence, the shareholders are relieved of the double-tax burden on corporate income—namely, a corporate tax on the profit when made and also a tax on the dividend when the profits are distributed.

The Subchapter S Revision Act of 1982 allows income deductions, losses and credits of the corporation to pass through to each of the shareholders the same way such items pass through to partners. To be eligible for Subchapter S treatment under the new Act, the following must be satisfied:

1. The number of permitted stockholders must not exceed 35.
2. Only one class of stock, voting as well as nonvoting common stock, is allowed.
3. All shareholders must consent to the election; however, a person who becomes a shareholder after the initial election of Subchapter S status will be bound by the initial election until the election is terminated.

---

[2]See, for example, Mass. Gen. Laws, ch. 156, A sec. 8 (1963).

[3]I.R.C., subch. S, secs. 1371–1377 (1958) as amended by the Subchapter S Revision Act of 1982.

4. Passive investment income (e.g., royalties or rental income) is now allowed for corporations that do not have accumulated earnings and profits at the close of the taxable year; for those that *do* have such accumulated earnings and profits, a corporate level tax of 46 percent will be imposed on the excess of passive investment income over 25 percent of gross receipts, and the election will be terminated when the corporation has excessive passive investment income for three consecutive years.
5. The election for Subchapter S may be revoked by those shareholders holding a majority of the corporation's voting stock.
6. Income and losses are passed through the corporation and allocated to shareholders on a per-share basis.

professional corporation
A corporation formed by professionals (those who render personal services to the public of a type that requires a license or other legal authorization)

Professional Corporations

As the result of professional groups attempting to obtain various corporate advantages by way of tax-sheltered qualified pension and profit-sharing plans and other employee fringe benefits, every state has enacted corporate legislation allowing professionals to incorporate their practice. Members of the professions have found themselves annually confronted with a substantial tax liability because of their status as employers or proprietorships or partnerships. By incorporating their practice, they become owner-employees and are thereby eligible to participate in employee fringe benefits such as pension and profit-sharing plans. Contributions to these plans are tax deductible by the professional corporation, and the trust income invested is tax free until distributed to the employees at retirement.

Creation of the corporation does not exempt the professional shareholder employees from liabilities that they otherwise would have had. That is, generally a shareholder individual who renders professional services as an employee of a professional corporation is liable for any negligence in which the individual personally participated to the same extent as if the individual were a sole practitioner. However, such individuals would not be liable for the conduct of other employees unless such individuals were at fault in appointing, supervising or cooperating with them. For example, doctors *X, Y,* and *Z* form a professional medical corporation. *X* engages in a malpractice procedure with patient *P*. *P* may sue the corporation and also *X* as an individual. Generally, *P* would not be allowed to recover personally from doctors *Y* and *Z*. The Revised Model Professional Corporation Act provides for alternative theories of stockholders' liability.[4] Generally, this diminution in liability is an advantage over the unlimited liability of a partnership. The following case illustrates this principle.

FACTS

Zagoria and Stoner were co-shareholders in a professional corporation, Zagoria and Stoner, P.C., all of whom are defendants. The corporation was organized for the practice of law under the Georgia Professional Corporation Act. At a real estate closing, Zagoria issued a check on the escrow account of Zagoria and Stoner, P.C., for $3,130 to the plaintiff, DuBose Enterprises, Inc., for commission as real estate broker. DuBose deposited the check that was subsequently returned unpaid.

DuBose sued the professional corporation and Zagoria and Stoner individually to recover on the check. DuBose contends that Stoner as

[4]See the Revised Model Professional Corporation Act, sec. 34 and official comment thereto that provide for three alternatives regarding shareholder's liability: (1) limited liability as in a business corporation; or (2) complete vicarious personal liability as in a partnership; or (3) personal liability limited in amount conditioned upon financial responsibility in the form of insurance or a surety bond established by the licensing authority for each profession as security required as a condition for limiting liability of shareholders.

a shareholder of the professional corporation should be individually liable for the dishonored check and should not be allowed the protection of the corporate shield from liability for the professional corporation's debts. Are Stoner and/or Zagoria personally liable for the corporation's debt? Is the corporation liable?

DECISION

No. Judgment for defendants. Stoner rendered no services in connection with the transaction in which the check was issued, and further, there was no evidence that DuBose was the client of the professional corporation in the real estate transaction. An attorney-shareholder of a professional corporation who does not participate in the rendering of the services out of which a claim arises will be free from personal liability for that claim. DuBose alleges that Zagoria is individually liable under the Georgia Professional Corporation Act. There was no evidence that DuBose was the client represented by Zagoria in the real estate closing. The law applicable to business corporations and professional corporations alike is that shareholders enjoy limited liability, but they will be liable individually for their own tortious or wrongful acts. Plaintiff DuBose presented no evidence to show that Zagoria issued the check with knowledge that it would be dishonored. DuBose alleged that the corporate escrow account on which the check was drawn was closed but presented no evidence on this point. However, DuBose also claimed that the professional corporation was liable. Any acts on the part of Zagoria which may have caused DuBose losses were ***ultra vires,*** unauthorized or beyond the scope of any authority to act for the professional corporation.

Zagoria v. DuBose Enter., Inc., 296 S.E.2d 353 (Ga. 1982).

ultra vires
Beyond the powers

Applicability of TEFRA Under the Tax Equity and Fiscal Responsibility Act of 1982 (TEFRA), the pension benefits for self-employed individuals and shareholder/employers participating in a **defined contribution plan** of a Subchapter S corporation are increased from the lesser of 15 percent of compensation or $15,000 to the lesser of 20 percent of compensation or $30,000. In a **defined benefit plan** for self-employed individuals, partners, and shareholder/employees of a Subchapter S corporation the new contribution is the lesser $90,000 or 100 percent of the average compensation for the three highest paid consecutive years, the same limits that apply for corporate plans. The above-referenced dollar limits in the Keogh Plan and the corporate pension plans are indexed for changes in the cost of living. Hence, the new law essentially makes pension plan contributions the same for corporations and individuals using a Keogh Plan.

defined contribution plan
A plan under which the employer is required to contribute a specific amount annually to the plan for the employee's retirement

defined benefit plan
A plan under which the employee contributes an annual payment to the plan based upon a benefit expected to be received upon retirement

Keogh Plan
A pension plan for self-employed individuals

However, contributions for life insurance and accident and health insurance for the benefit of its employees are deductible by a corporation and not by a self-employed individual or partnership.

The IRS is granted broad discretionary powers to disregard the corporate form of any professional corporation organized for the principal purpose of evading or avoiding federal income tax by obtaining significant tax benefits for any employee/owner that would not be otherwise available. In view of this, legal counsel and their clients must seriously consider whether it is appropriate and wise to incorporate a professional practice. The interpretations and IRS regulations of the new Act must be carefully complied with by the corporation's tax counsel.

▶ Nonprofit Corporations

A *nonprofit* (eleemosynary) corporation is organized for charitable purposes, examples being colleges and hospitals. Because they are given preferential tax treatment, special statutes govern their formation and operation.[5]

[5]See the Revenue Act of 1978, Pub. L. No. 95–600, sec. 341, and amendments thereunder.

Corporate Regulations

Our economy may be described today as a highly regulated free-enterprise system. If you were to incorporate, state statutory law would grant you various corporate powers. However, as a domestic corporation in the state of formation, your company would be subject to the state tax laws and state regulating agencies. For example, if you were manufacturing raw materials, the state environmental protection agency would regulate the extent of the allowed pollution caused by the company. If you were "doing business" in a foreign state, the company would be subject to the regulating agencies and tax law of that state also. Interstate business would require you to comply with the regulations of the federal agencies, such as the Federal Trade Commission.

Constitutional Restrictions

State and federal administrative agencies are subject to certain constitutional restrictions in regulating a corporation's activities.

► Corporation As a Legal Person

When a corporation comes into existence by filing the necessary documents with the appropriate state office, a legal entity is formed that exists independently of its owners. Today the corporation is highly regulated by various state and federal administrative agencies (e.g., the Internal Revenue Service) that have the right to review not only its books and records but also its operational procedures (e.g., the Department of Labor). As a legal person, the corporation has constitutional rights to protect itself from arbitrary governmental intervention. For example, an administrative summons issued by the IRS to review corporate books and records is subject to a court "show cause" hearing.

The U.S. Constitution allows the corporation the right of the "people" under the Fourth Amendment (to be secure against unreasonable searches and seizures), the Fifth Amendment (right not to be deprived of liberty or property without due process of law), and the Fourteenth Amendment (the right not to be denied the equal protection of the laws). State constitutions commonly have similar restrictions.

Disregard of Corporate Entity

The corporation as a legal entity distinct from its shareholders is the basis for limited liability. Notice the court's reasoning in the following case on why it would not pierce the corporate veil and disregard the corporate entity.

FACTS

Jones operated a sheet metal business as a sole proprietorship until it was incorporated in September of 1975. At that time, Jones transferred the assets of that business to the corporation in exchange for an equal amount of stock for himself and his wife. The building in which the business was located and which is a partial subject of this action was owned by Jones and was not transferred to the corporation.

Pierson was an employee of the corporation from July 1976 to December 1976, and in such capacity he had occasion to work with and check the business records of the corporation on a daily basis. During that period of time Pierson loaned the corporation $80,571.42.

The business began sustaining financial losses and on February 9, 1977, Pierson's attorney threatened suit against the corporation and Jones if a security interest for the Pierson debt was not obtained. On February 10, 1977, Jones assigned corporate accounts receivable of $34,000 to Pierson. The corporation filed bankruptcy on June 2, 1977, at which time it owed Pierson $33,187.64. This action was instituted by Pierson against Jones personally to recover that sum and obtain an equitable **lien** against the building owned by Jones. Judgment was rendered for Jones, and Pierson appeals.

Pierson contends that Jones did not have authority to borrow money for the corporation; that the trial court erred in not piercing the corporate veil, in not finding that Jones had personally guaranteed the corporate debt, in not imposing an equitable lien on the real property owned by Jones, and in awarding attorney fees against Pierson. Does the evidence justify piercing the corporate veil?

DECISION

No. Judgment for Jones, affirmed. To justify piercing the corporate veil, it must also be shown that there is such a unity of interest and ownership that the individuality of such corporation and such person has ceased; and it must further appear from the facts that the observance of the fiction of separate existence would, under the circumstances, sanction a fraud or promote injustice.

Pierson also asserts that the corporation was undercapitalized at the time he lent it money and that this is a justification for piercing the corporate veil. We disagree. Undercapitalization is one factor to be considered in determining whether or not to pierce the corporate veil. However, financial inadequacy is measured by the nature and magnitude of the corporate undertaking or the reasonableness of the cushion for creditors at the time of the inception of the corporation. Here the corporate accountant testified that at the time of its inception the corporation was not undercapitalized. Clearly, a corporation adequately capitalized at its inception can become undercapitalized at a later time for any of a variety of legitimate reasons.

Pierson v. Jones, 625 P.2d 1085 (Idaho 1981).

lien
A legal right in another's property as security for the performance of an obligation

The courts have the power, under certain circumstances, to treat the corporation and the shareholders as identical parties. In the following case the court held an individual shareholder who dissolved the corporation personally liable on a corporate debt.

FACTS

Daisy Lee Williams, the personal representative of the deceased Daisy Burrell, brought this suit against Philip F. Cohen, who was the only stockholder, director, and officer of the dissolved Mobile Roofing and Construction Company, Inc. Daisy Burrell obtained a judgment against the Mobile Roofing and Construction Company for damages resulting from a home construction contract. When the corporation went out of business, Williams sued Cohen, the only stockholder, personally on the corporate judgment. The lower court found for Williams and Cohen appealed. Is Cohen personally liable for the corporation's debt?

DECISION

Yes. Judgment for Williams. A corporation is a distinct and separate entity from the individuals who compose it as stockholders or who manage it as directors or officers. In a proper case, when the corporate form is being used to evade personal responsibility, the court can impose liability on the person controlling the corporation. When Cohen dissolved the corporation, there were no assets from which the judgment could be collected. He personally assumed liability for all corporate debts except the Burrell judgment. A corporation dissolved to evade creditors can enjoy no more standing as an entity separate and apart from its sole stockholder than a corporation formed to accomplish such evasion.

Cohen v. Williams, 318 So.2d 279 (Ala. 1975).

The corporation serves as a form of legal entity to answer the needs of business society. It serves small as well as large businesses. However, because it is formed with the permission of society, it is subject to societal constraints and cannot do what society condemns. When it attempts to do so, the courts will "pierce the corporate veil" that is, look behind the corporate legal entity to determine such impropriety. For example, if shareholders *X, Y,* and *Z* form a closely-held corporation without adequate capital to support its transactions, commingle corporate and their personal funds, and never hold director or stockholders' meetings, the corporation is vulnerable to the *doctrine of piercing the corporate veil.* When the doctrine is applied by a court, the shareholders' personal assets may be reached by a corporate business creditor, or by a tort claimant suing the shareholders for a personal injury that occurred on the corporate premises. Another example would be an undercapitalized **subsidiary corporation** owned by a parent corporation that is sued by a business creditor of the subsidiary. A court may hold the parent liable for the obligations of the subsidiary.

subsidiary corporation
A corporation owned by another corporation

In some instances in order to obtain credit, the shareholders may have to make themselves personally liable for the corporate debts. For example, a bank may ask them to individually sign a corporate note.

The courts will always pierce the corporate veil when the stockholders form the corporation to perpetuate a fraud or to accomplish an illegal purpose. The following case illustrates the reasons why a court will disregard the corporate entity and hold the owner/stockholders personally liable.

FACTS

The Kaisers formed a corporation to run a tennis club and entered into a contract with Stap to play professional tennis. Stap sued the Kaisers individually for breach of the contract. They raised the defense of the corporation being the contracting party. Stap attempted to "pierce the corporate veil" because the corporation was undercapitalized.

DECISION

Judgment for Stap. A corporate entity will be disregarded and the veil of limited liability pierced where it would otherwise present an obstacle to the protection of private rights or when the corporation is merely the alter ego or business conduit of a governing or dominating personality.

For the doctrine traditionally known as "piercing the corporate veil" to apply, two requirements must be met: (1) there must be such unity of interest and ownership that the separate personalities of the corporation and the individual no longer exist; and (2) circumstances must exist that adherence to the fiction of separate corporation existence would sanction a fraud or promote injustice.

The specific issue before us is whether the requirements of a cause of action founded upon a "piercing of the corporate veil" has been set forth.

It is alleged that plaintiff entered into an agreement with the Club to play tennis for a salary and bonuses; that the Kaisers owned 100 percent of the Club stock; that they had contributed 100 percent of the capital in Kaiser Investments, a partnership; that the Kaisers were majority shareholders in four other corporation—one of which was the owner of the facilities used by the Club; that the Kaisers, through Kaiser Investments, manipulated the funds between the Club and the other corporation in disregard of the entities of each; that the Club was undercapitalized and, as a result, was unable to pay its debts and did not pay the salary and bonuses earned by plaintiff; that the Kaisers, through Kaiser Investments, failed to carry out the business of the Club and other four corporations as separate interests; and that the observance of the fiction of separate corporate existence would sanction a fraud and permit injustice against Stap.

Stap v. Chicago Aces Tennis Team, Inc., 379 N.E. 2d 1298 (Ill. 1978).

► Subsidiaries

A subsidiary corporation has a majority of its outstanding and issued stock owned by a parent corporation. When the parent corporation owns all the stock it is a wholly owned subsidiary. For example, a new line of merchandise may involve such a substantial risk to a corporation that it desires to fragment its liability by forming a subsidiary to sell the new products. Generally, the officers and directors of the parent corporation will also serve in the subsidiary corporation. If the parent corporation exercises control over the wholly owned subsidiary, it will usually be liable for the contracts and torts of the subsidiary.

Figure 42.2 will help explain the distinguishing factors in the different kinds of business organizations.

FIGURE 42.2 **Comparison of Business Organizations**

	General Partnership	Limited Partnership	Business Trust	Franchise	Corporation
Creation	By agreement per UPA	In writing per RLPA with 1985 amendments	Filing business trust certificate per statute	By contract with the franchisee	Filing articles of organization per statute
Liability	Unlimited liability with respect to torts and contracts for all partners	Unlimited liability for general partners; limited partners are generally not liable for business torts and contracts	Trust beneficiaries may be personally liable if they have power to control the trust management; trustees may be held liable for business obligations	Franchisor may be liable for torts of franchisee if it maintains control over the business; generally not liable for its contracts	Shareholders are generally not liable for corporate obligations
Management	Unless changed by the partnership agreement, each partner has an equal vote per UPA	General partners manage with equal vote, unless changed by agreement; limited partners do not manage the business	Trustees manage the trust business in accordance with the trust agreement	Franchisee manages the franchise in accordance with the franchise contract	Officers carry out the management policy determined and authorized by the board of directors
Agency	Each partner is an agent of the partnership for partnership business per UPA	General partners are agents; limited partners are not	Trustees are agents for business trust purposes; beneficiaries are not	Franchisee is an agent of the franchise; franchisors are generally not	Officers are agents; directors and shareholders are not
Taxation	Not a taxable entity but files an information return	Taxed similar to a general partnership; limited partners have limited liability and are taxed as partners	Taxable entity; may be taxed as a corporation due to corporate attributes	Taxable entity; generally a corporation	Taxable entity; may qualify as an S corporation and avoid double taxation

Summary Statement

1. A corporation is a legal entity created by statute authorizing an association of persons to carry on an enterprise.
2. The corporation as a legal person is a distinct legal entity and hence the corporate stockholders cannot be sued for corporate liabilities. This is known as "limited liability." A stockholder's risk is limited to the loss of his or her investment.
3. Corporation law is found in state or federal statutory law. Each state has its own corporation laws, and many have modernized them to comply substantially with the former Model Business Corporation Act.
4. Roman law required government approval for a corporation.
5. Canon law developed the concept of an "artificial person" that could own property in its own name.
6. Civil law recognized the corporation as a separate entity.
7. Common law established the perpetual existence of a corporation.
8. Corporations may be classified as follows:
   - **a)** Public
   - **b)** Private
   - **c)** Quasi-public
   - **d)** Domestic
   - **e)** Foreign
9. A foreign corporation is one that is "doing business" in a substantial and continuous manner where it was not originally incorporated.
10. A foreign corporation must maintain a registered agent in the foreign state to receive service of process in the event the corporation is sued.
11. Private corporations are highly regulated by the state and federal governments. As a "legal person," a corporation is entitled to many constitutional rights.
12. The courts may disregard the corporate entity and "pierce the corporate veil" whenever necessary to prevent fraud.
13. A corporation that qualifies under the Internal Revenue Code may elect to be taxed similarly to a partnership. It is referred to as a Subchapter S corporation.
14. Corporations have numerous attributes that make them a very popular form of business, namely:
    - **a)** Perpetual succession
    - **b)** Centralization of management
    - **c)** No shareholder liability for corporate obligations
    - **d)** Power to sell their stock to raise capital
    - **e)** Ease of transferring corporate stock
    - **f)** Under the legal entity theory they are liable for their own obligations.

In the following case the court analyzed the factors involved in piercing the corporate veil.

UNITED STATES v. HEALTHWIN-MIDTOWN CONVALESCENT HOSPITAL AND REHABILITATION CENTER, INC., AND ISRAEL ZIDE

511 F.Supp. 416 (D. Cal. 1981)

Maletz, Judge. On September 14, 1971, the Healthwin Corporation was organized in California for the purpose of operating a health care facility. From that date, until November

30, 1974, it participated as a provider of services under the Medicare Act, and received periodic payments from the United States Department of Health, Education and Welfare (HEW). These payments, which were compensation for the services provided Medicare beneficiaries by Healthwin, were only approximations of the exact amount due; the exact amount was determined by periodic audits conducted by Blue Cross of Southern California, which was HEW's agent for the purpose of paying Healthwin and auditing its cost reports. It is undisputed that these audits showed that a series of overpayments had been made to Healthwin in 1972, 1973 and 1974 in the total amount of $30,481.55. It is this sum, plus interest, that the United States, plaintiff, seeks to recover here.

The issue here is whether defendant Zide, president and administrator of Healthwin Corporation, is personally liable for the Medicare overpayments to Healthwin. As a basis for such liability, plaintiff first argues that the corporate entity should be disregarded under the alter ego theory of liability. Plaintiff's alter ego claim must be analyzed in accordance with state law. Under California law, "issues of alter ego do not lend themselves to strict rules and prima facie cases. Whether the corporate veil should be pierced depends upon the innumerable individual equities of each case." Generally, however, the corporate veil may be pierced when it is shown that there . . . [is] such unity of interest and ownership that the separate personalities of the corporation and the individual no longer exist and that if the acts are treated as those of the corporation alone, an inequitable result will follow.

With regard to the "unity of interest and ownership" test, the evidence at trial showed that at all times relevant here, Zide was a fifty percent shareholder of the Healthwin corporation. In addition, Zide had a fifty percent interest in a partnership which owned both the realty in which Healthwin's health care facility was located and the furnishings used at that facility.

Other factors the courts consider in determining whether the corporate veil should be pierced include the inadequacy of the corporation's capitalization or its insolvency; the failure to observe corporate formalities; the absence of regular board meetings; the nonfunctioning of corporate directors; the commingling of corporate and noncorporate assets; the diversion of assets from the corporation to the detriment of creditors; and the failure of an individual to maintain an arm's length relationship with the corporation.

All these factors are present here. Zide himself testified that the corporation was undercapitalized. This testimony was confirmed by further evidence which established that, although Healthwin consistently had outstanding liabilities in excess of $150,000, its initial capitalization was only $10,000.

The evidence also established that Zide exercised his control over Healthwin so as to cause its finances to become inextricably intertwined with both his personal finances and his other business holdings. As noted earlier, Healthwin's health care facility was located in realty owned by a partnership in which Zide had a fifty percent interest. This partnership had made substantial loans to the corporation. The pattern of payments from Healthwin to the partnership and to Zide makes clear that neither payments to the partnership for use of the realty nor the repayment of the loans was handled in a regular arm's length business fashion.

The necessary conclusion from all this is that Zide handled Healthwin's finances so as to accommodate his own business interests. Treatment of corporate assets in this fashion has long been considered a significant factor supporting the piercing of the corporate veil.

Another factor present here is that the operations of Healthwin were marked by an essential disregard of corporate formalities. Thus board meetings were not regularly held and, with the exception of the first board meeting, Zide and his wife were the only directors or shareholders present.

There is the final consideration that the court should not pierce the corporation's veil unless necessary to prevent an inequitable result. As to this, it is not necessary that plaintiff prove actual fraud; it is enough if the failure to pierce the corporation's veil would result in an injustice. Given the situation present here, the court must conclude that it would be unjust not to pierce the corporate veil. For one thing, Healthwin's undercapitalization subjected all its creditors, including plaintiff, to inequitable risks regarding Healthwin's obligations to them.

In view of the foregoing considerations, the court holds that Healthwin's corporate entity should be disregarded under the alter ego theory of liability. Judgment for plaintiff.

Questions and Case Problems

1. Schaumburg Planet Project Corporation (Planet) was the beneficial owner of 66 acres of unimproved land located in Schaumburg, Illinois, held in trust, and Chicago Title and Trust Company (hereinafter CT&T) as trustee was the legal owner. In October of 1973, Planet borrowed $7,622,956.71 from Bankers Trust Company (Bankers) securing the loan by a first mortgage on that land. The loan was also personally guaranteed by Romano, the president and sole shareholder of Planet, and by his wife, Barbara, who owned no interest in Planet. In October of 1975, Planet defaulted on the loan, and Bankers instituted foreclosure proceedings against CT&T. Romano was neither a named defendant nor made a party to this action. On December 4, 1976, Hartenfeld filed his petition to intervene, asserting a $150,000 equitable lien on the land for the following reasons. On February 12, 1973, Hartenfeld and Romano entered into a written agreement drafted by Hartenfeld, attached to the petition, whereby Hartenfeld was to receive $200,000 for performing legal services for Romano. The contract provided that "whenever during 1973, you (Romano) successfully accomplish a new land loan on any of your parcels of real estate, I will be paid immediately all fees then owed me under this letter agreement. In any event, however, all fees owed to me under this letter agreement shall be paid to me by no later than the end of 1973." The petition concludes that the loan Planet received from Bankers in 1973 was in fact a loan to Romano covered by the above agreement; Hartenfeld was not paid from this loan, which entitled him to an equitable lien on the loan proceeds. On February 8, 1977, after notice to all interested parties, the subject land was sold at a sheriff's sale to Bankers, the sole bidder, for $7,622,956.71, the principal amount of the loan. On February 14, 1977, the trial court granted Hartenfeld's petition to intervene over Bankers' objections. Hartenfeld claims that the loan by Bankers to Planet must be construed as a loan to Romano under a "reverse" piercing of the corporate veil. The court allowed an imposition of an equitable lien in Hartenfeld's favor and Bankers appealed. May the court pierce the corporate veil of Planet and hold Romano personally liable to Hartenfeld? [*Bankers Trust Co. et al. v. Chicago Title & Trust Co. et al.*, 412 N.E.2d 660 (Ill. 1980).]
2. The Village Press, Inc., negotiated with Stephen Blum, as agent for the Stephen Edward Co., Inc., to prepare mail order catalogues for Pridecraft, Inc. Stephen Blum controlled both the Stephen Edward Co. and Pridecraft. The parties exchanged correspondence and entered into an agreement whereby Village Press would print the Pridecraft catalogues and bill Stephen Edward Co. Village Press delivered the catalogues, but due to a dispute over their quality, neither corporation tendered payment. Village Press then brought this action. No evidence was presented at trial that indicated that Blum suppressed the fact that his businesses were incorporated. In fact, the exhibits show that Blum mailed all of his correspondence on letterheads of the Stephen Edward Co., Inc. and signed them "Stephen Blum, President." Village Press, in turn, sent its correspondence to Stephen Blum at the Stephen Edward Co. Moreover, no evidence was offered that Blum ever made any agreement to hold himself personally responsible for his corporations' debts. Village Press argues that Blum personally controlled the corporations, making them, in effect, his alter egos. Village Press concludes therefrom that Blum is personally liable for their debts. Is Blum personally liable for the debts of the two corporations he controlled? [*Village Press, Inc. v. Stephen Edward Co., Inc. et al.*, 416 A.2d 1373 (N.H. 1980).]
3. Colin sought to evict a tenant under a rent control regulation. Altman, the rent commissioner, denied the request. The building was owned by 130 West 112th Street

Corp. and all the stock was owned by Colin. Colin claimed that he desired the apartment for his own personal use. The rent commissioner denied the application on the ground that Colin had no standing (no legal status in the case) because he was not the owner of the building, and the rental regulations do not recognize a corporation as having a necessity to occupy housing. Colin claimed, because he owned all the stock, the court should disregard the corporate entity. May the corporate veil be pierced for the benefit of the corporation or its stockholders? [*Colin v. Altman,* 333 N.Y.S.2d 432 (N.Y. 1972).]

4. This is an action filed by the Associated Press to collect for the breach of two contracts executed by the defendant, Briarcliff Communications Group, Inc., one a news service and membership contract and the other a wirephoto contract. The Associated Press is a nonprofit, New York corporation that is engaged in the business of gathering and disseminating news and literary property to its members. It has not registered with the Georgia Secretary of State to do business in Georgia. Does the interstate nature of the plaintiff's business render it exempt from the Georgia statutory registration requirement by virtue of the supremacy of the commerce clause of the U.S. Constitution? [*Briarcliff Comm. Group, Inc. v. Associated Press,* 268 S.E.2d 356 (Ga. 1980).]

5. Linton & Company, Inc., (Linton) is a consulting firm engaged primarily in urban planning and environmental studies, maintaining its principal office in Washington, D.C. R. L. Reid is an officer and shareholder of Robert Reid Engineers, Inc., (Engineers), defendant, that performs engineering services and maintains its principal offices in Houston, Texas. The present dispute between the parties related to work done incident to the planned construction of the Red Mountain Expressway in Birmingham, Alabama. Engineers entered into a subcontract on December 27, 1976, with Linton whereby Linton agreed to contribute to the preparation of the environmental impact statements. The subcontract was sent to Washington, D.C. where Linton executed it.

During the time of negotiating the subcontract as well as performing upon it, Linton had three or four employees who came to Alabama to collect data for the environmental impact statements for the proposed Red Mountain Expressway project. During the entire two and a half year period that Linton was involved in this project, which includes the time spent negotiating the contract, Linton's employees made approximately 12 trips to Alabama. The average duration of a trip was two or three days, with the employees staying in hotels while in Alabama and returning to Linton's Washington offices. At least 75 percent of Linton's work pursuant to the subcontract was performed in Linton's offices in Washington, D.C. The State of Alabama asserted that defendant failed to perform in a timely fashion and the Alabama Highway Director wrote Mr. Reid terminating the contract. On June 26, 1978, Mr. Reid wrote Linton terminating the subcontract.

Although Engineers was paid by the state on March 6, 1979, Engineers has refused to pay anything to Linton. Consequently, Linton initiated this suit to recover money for breach of contract and work and labor done. Plaintiff has never qualified to do business in Alabama. Defendant claims that this failure precludes plaintiff from bringing this action. Decide. [*Linton & Co., Inc., v. Robert Reid Engineers, Inc.,* 504 F.Supp. 1169 (D. Ala. 1981).]

6. S. & L. Painting Contractors, Inc., plaintiff, does virtually all its business in Mississippi and less than 1 percent of its business in Arkansas. It is not registered to do business in the State of Arkansas as is required by law; the company's officers did not know of the requirement. Its agents came to Arkansas and entered into a contract in Arkansas to do some work on a residence near Lake Village. Plaintiff was not paid for its work and filed an action to impose a lien against the Arkansas residence. The owners, J. D. Vickers and Susan Smith Vickers, as well as several mortgage holders were joined as parties defendants. May plaintiff, a foreign corporation, enforce its contract in Arkansas? [*S. & L. Painting Contractors, Inc. v. J. D. Vickers, et al.*, 589 S.W.2d 196 (Ark. 1979).]

7. *X, Y,* and *Z* are stockholders of a real estate business they operate as a corporation. They have purchased a building for office use and formed a separate corporation to own the building. The real estate office and other tenants will pay rent to the corporation that owns the building. *P,* a client, brought suit against the real estate corporation for return of her down payment and has attached the building owned by the separate corporation. May the court disregard the corporate entity that owns the building and allow *P*'s attachment?

8. *X* owned a small department store as a sole proprietor. *X* had many personal and business creditors. In an attempt to save his business, he incorporated the store and purchased all the stock. *X*'s personal creditors sought to reach the corporate assets to collect their claims. *X* claimed that the store as a corporation owned assets distinct from his personal assets. Decide.

9. Diversacon, Industries, Inc. (Diversacon), a Florida corporation with its principal place of business in that state is one of many wholly owned subsidiaries of United States Industries, Inc. (USI) a Delaware corporation. USI maintains an administrative office in Jackson, Mississippi at the headquarters of Con-Plex, one of its subdivisions. In 1972, USI administrative employees in Jackson traveled to Baton Rouge, Louisiana to bid on the construction of a portion of the interstate highway system to be built there. The bid was submitted in the name of Diversacon, listing Con-Plex post office address and telephone in Jackson. Diversacon was awarded the contract. Subsequently, all administrative support necessary to the Louisiana construction project was handled out of the Con-Plex office in Jackson by USI personnel. Diversacon brought suit against National Bank of Commerce of Mississippi for reimbursement of funds expended. The Mississippi Federal District Court found Diversacon's activities to constitute "doing business" in that state, which required it to qualify as a foreign corporation under Mississippi law in order to have access to its courts. Was Diversacon doing business in Mississippi? [*Diversacon Industries, Inc. v. Nat'l Bank of Commerce of Miss.*, 629 F.2d 1030 (5th Cir. 1980).]

10. In the case of *United States v. Healthwin-Midtown Convalescent Hospital and Rehabilitation Center, Inc. and Israel Zide,* excerpted at the beginning of this section, the court held the defendant Zide, a director/shareholder, personally liable for Medicare overpayments made to his corporation and pierced the corporate veil on the theory that he was the alter ego of the corporation. What should Zide have done to have prevented this result?

CHAPTER 43

CREATION AND TERMINATION

After you have read this chapter, you should be able to:

1. Define and explain the function of a promoter.
2. Explain why a promoter is a fiduciary.
3. Explain the information required in the articles of incorporation.
4. Define and explain a *de jure* corporation.
5. Define and explain a *de facto* corporation.
6. Define and explain a so-called "corporation by estoppel."
7. Explain involuntary dissolution by the state.
8. Explain when the incorporators may dissolve a corporation.
9. Explain when the shareholders may dissolve a corporation.
10. Distinguish a merger from a consolidation.
11. Explain the legal effect of a merger or a consolidation.
12. Explain the legal effect of a "stock exchange."

BUSINESS DECISIONS and the LAW

The pace towards a unified European market is quickening. With 1992 around the corner, many industries are striving to position themselves for this consolidation. By way of example, Europe's $170 billion dollar electronics industry has reshaped itself in readiness for 1992, and further international competition. One of the largest players, Britain's Plessey Company, is now one of the recent victims.

General Electric Company of Britain (no relation to the U.S.-based General Electric Company) and West Germany's Siemens AG through a partnership gained control of 62.1 percent of Plessey's shares, and Plessey thereby merged into the two companies. Plessey mounted a ferocious defense against the competitors by suing to block the bid. But the defense failed and the British government cleared the takeover attempt. Plessey shareholders rushed to tender their shares, and Plessey had no choice but to concede defeat.

Experts point to other industries facing a wave of mergers as well. Restructuring should start in defense electronics, data processing, appliance makers, semiconductor makers, and video technology firms. Mergers have transformed industries by shrinking the number of players and raising the specter of antitrust abuses. They also have the effect of pooling resources, expanding market share, and cutting costs. As markets increasingly become global, the push for mergers will continue.

Sources: "Plessey Takeover Isn't Expected to End String of Electronics Mergers in Europe," *Wall Street Journal*, September 11, 1989; P. Fletcher, "GEC-Siemens Bid for Plessey May Be Realized," *Electronics*, September 1989, p. 32 (H); "Corridors of Obfuscation (The Takeover of Plessey Co.)," *The Economist*, June 24, 1989, p. 69 (1).

Introduction

Assume that you have decided to join with other persons to form a corporation. Where would you look to determine how to form the corporation? What societal limitations may prevent you from doing so? You probably will want to retain an attorney to give you this advice. It may come as a surprise to learn that a corporation can be formed only by permission of the state and, therefore, only by compliance with the laws of the state. Also, only the state can terminate corporate existence. You and your associates are called *promoters*, and all of you assume certain duties and liabilities in connection with organizing the corporation and contracts made before the corporation came into existence. We will begin with a discussion of promoters.

Creation

► Promoters

If you were to plan the incorporation of a business venture, it would be necessary to consider whether contracts have to be signed *before* the corporation is formed. For example, will it own or lease its place of operation? Who will invest in the business? Or will it have to borrow funds from a bank? Planning the corporation and attending to its organization is the function of a **promoter.**

promoter
A person who organizes and brings a corporation into existence

The promoter is not always associated with the business after it obtains corporate existence. Modern statutes authorize corporate formation upon filing the articles of incorporation and paying the necessary fee. At that point, the corporate officers are capable of signing on behalf of the corporation and, hence, do not require the services of a promoter. If the officers sign in their respective capacities on behalf of the corporation, they are not personally liable. In a later chapter we will discuss the liability of corporate officers. This liability is based on the agency theory that a disclosed principal (the corporation) is liable for authorized contracts made on its behalf by an agent (the corporate officer) with third parties. Hence, once the corporation is formed, a promoter is no longer necessary because the corporation can contract on its own behalf through the corporate officers.

Promoter's Liability Because the promoter performs various functions *before* formation of the corporation, the promoter is not its agent. Accordingly, the promoter is personally liable on contracts made on behalf of the proposed corporation. For example, as a promoter, you would be personally liable if you signed an office lease on behalf of a nonexisting corporation. If the corporation later occupied the premises, it may also be liable; however, this would not relieve you, the promoter, from your liability to the landlord.

After incorporation, the corporation may become bound to the terms of the preincorporation contract, but the courts differ on how this may be accomplished. There are four theories: The first is *adoption,* whereby the corporation adopts or assumes the obligation of performing the preincorporation contract either by corporate resolution of its board of directors or impliedly by knowingly accepting the benefits of the contract. The promoter is still liable as a party to the contract. A second, and the most used, theory is **novation,**[1] whereby the nonpromoter party to the preincorporation contract agrees to discharge the contract and, by a new contract, take the corporation in place of the promoter. A third theory is *continuing offer,* whereby the preincorporation contract is construed to be a continuing offer to the corporation by the nonpromoter party, and the corporation on its creation can accept it and be bound. A fourth theory, not legally sound, is *ratification,* whereby the corporation seeks to authenticate the making of the contract on its behalf retroactively as of the time the preincorporation contract was made. The ratification theory is not sound because the corporation was not in existence at the time the preincorporation contract was made and, therefore, could not at that time appoint an agent nor authorize the contract to be made.

novation
A new contract in which one of the parties was not a party to the old contract and which immediately discharges the old contract

Although the promoter is not an agent for the proposed corporation, the promoter is under a duty to act for its benefit and hence is a **fiduciary.**[2] In that capacity the promoter owes the corporation being promoted and its stock subscribers a high degree of care. Upon incorporation, a promoter is obligated to make a full disclosure to the board of directors of any contract signed on its behalf. All transactions made by the promoter on behalf of the corporation must be accounted for. A promoter is personally liable for any secret profit made, and the corporation or the shareholders may sue the promoter for their damages.

fiduciary
A person with a duty to act primarily for the benefit of another

► Incorporators

State corporate laws require the **incorporator** to sign and file the articles of incorporation with the secretary of state. While some states insist on three incorporators, the modern trend requires only one. Generally, the statutes require the incorporators to be natural persons, and often citizens of the state or of the United States. Because incorporation is a contractual undertaking, the incorporators must not be minors, with their limited capacity to contract. The modern statutory trend is to allow a corporation to act as an incorporator.

incorporator
A person who signs the articles of incorporation

► Articles of Incorporation

State corporate statutes establish the procedures involved in incorporating a business. The **articles of incorporation** is the written application to the state for permission to incorporate. (See Figure 43.1.) It must be filed with the secretary of state and generally must have the following information.

articles of incorporation
The written application to the state for permission to incorporate

Name of the Corporation The incorporators must select a name that is distinguishable from other corporations upon the records of the secretary of state.[3] State statutes generally allow for the reservation of the corporate name (for three or four months) in

---

[1]See pp. 266–267 for a discussion of novation.

[2]See pp. 316–319 for an explanation of the implied duties of a fiduciary.

[3]RMBCA, sec. 4.01(b).

FIGURE 43.1 **Example of Articles of Incorporation**

The Commonwealth of Massachusetts

OFFICE OF THE MASSACHUSETTS SECRETARY OF STATE

MICHAEL JOSEPH CONNOLLY, Secretary

ONE ASHBURTON PLACE, BOSTON, MASS. 02108

ARTICLES OF ORGANIZATION

(Under G.L. Ch. 156B)

Incorporators

NAME POST OFFICE ADDRESS

Include given name in full in case of natural persons; in case of a corporation, give state of incorporation.

The above-named incorporator(s) do hereby associate (themselves) with the intention of forming a corporation under the provisions of General Laws, Chapter 156B and hereby state(s):

1. The name by which the corporation shall be known is:

2. The purpose for which the corporation is formed is as follows:

3. The total number of shares and the par value, if any, of each class of stock within the corporation is authorized as follows:

CLASS OF STOCK	WITHOUT PAR VALUE	WITH PAR VALUE		
	NUMBER OF SHARES	NUMBER OF SHARES	PAR VALUE	AMOUNT
Preferred				$
Common				

*4. If more than one class is authorized, a description of each of the different classes of stock with, if any, the preferences, voting powers, qualifications, special or relative rights or privileges as to each class thereof and any series now established:

*5. The restrictions, if any, imposed by the Articles of Organization upon the transfer of shares of stock of any class are as follows:

*6. Other lawful provisions, if any, for the conduct and regulation of business and affairs of the corporation, for its voluntary dissolution, or for limiting, defining, or regulating the powers of the corporation, or of its directors or stockholders, or of any class of stockholders:

advance of the filing date.[4] This may be a convenient way of assuring the organizing members that the selected name will qualify. The name must contain one of the following words or its abbreviation: "corporation," "company," "incorporated," or "limited."

[4]RMBCA, sec. 4.02.

FIGURE 43.1 **(Continued)**

7. By-laws of the corporation have been duly adopted and the initial directors, president, treasurer and clerk, whose names are set out below, have been duly elected.

8. The effective date of organization of the corporation shall be the date of filing with the Secretary of the Commonwealth or if later date is desired, specify date, (not more than 30 days after the date of filing.)

9. The following information shall not for any purpose be treated as a permanent part of the Articles of Organization of the corporation.

   a. The post office address of the initial principal office of the corporation of Massachusetts is:

   b. The name, residence, and post office address of each of the initial directors and following officers of the corporation are as follows:

	NAME	RESIDENCE	POST OFFICE ADDRESS
President:			
Treasurer:			
Clerk:			
Directors:			

   c. The date initially adopted on which the corporation's fiscal year ends is:

   d. The date initially fixed in the by-laws for the annual meeting of stockholders of the corporation is:

   e. The name and business address of the resident agent, if any, of the corporation is:

IN WITNESS WHEREOF and under the penalties of perjury the INCORPORATOR(S) sign(s) these Articles of Organization this day of 19

Purpose There must be a statement of the purpose for which the corporation is organized. As we previously discussed under the classification of corporations, the members may incorporate for a profit, nonprofit, professional, or charitable purpose. State statutes establish the rules to qualify as a special class of corporation. For example, separate laws exist for the incorporation of a professional medical practice because of its stock ownership by the licensed physicians and medical purpose to deliver health services.

Capital Stock Authorization The amount and class of shares the corporation shall have authority to issue is stated in the articles of incorporation. This is not the amount of stock the corporation must issue. For example, the corporation may initially issue 5,000 shares of stock although it is authorized 25,000 shares; the remaining 20,000 shares may be issued at a later date. The 5,000 are referred to as *issued and outstanding*.

Any restrictions placed on the transfer of shares of stock are also specified. For instance, closely held corporations commonly provide that a shareholder who desires to sell his or her stock must first notify the directors of the selling price and grant the corporation the option to redeem the shares at the same price. This method assures control of the voting stock by the owner-directors of the small corporation. The transfer of stock is discussed in a later chapter.

Place of Business The post office address of the *initial* principal office of the corporation must be listed. This establishes that it is doing business as a *domestic* corporation in that state.

Directors and Officers Most states require a listing of the names and addresses of the initial directors and officers of the corporation.

The directors need not be residents of the state of incorporation nor shareholders of the corporation. The directors may be one or more in number, and they may be increased or decreased by amending the articles of incorporation. The initial directors hold office until the organizational stockholders' meeting, when they are ratified or new directors are elected by the stockholders. Each director will hold office generally until the next annual stockholders' meeting or until a successor is elected. A director may resign prior to that time or be terminated by the stockholders for cause. After approval of the articles of incorporation by the state, which is now called the corporate **charter,** the directors named therein hold an organizational meeting for the purpose of adopting the bylaws, electing the corporate officers,[5] and transacting whatever other business comes before the meeting—for example, approving any previous contracts entered into by the promoters.

charter
Articles of incorporation approved by the state

The officers appointed by the board of directors generally consist of a president, one or more vice presidents, a secretary, and a treasurer. Many states allow the same person to be both secretary and treasurer. The directors and officers are discussed in a later chapter.

Incorporators The incorporator must sign and file the articles of incorporation under the penalties of **perjury,** stating that the information they contain is correct.

perjury
Knowingly falsely swearing under oath, or affirming, in a judicial or quasi-judicial proceeding

Registered Agent The name and address of the registered agent is placed in the articles to provide a claimant access to whom and where legal service can be made. The articles of incorporation are a matter of public information in the office of the secretary of state and may be viewed there by anyone. A person desirous of suing the corporation may send legal process to the registered agent or a corporate officer. Many states require a registered agent only when the applicant is a foreign corporation.

Bylaws The rules and regulations of a corporation for its internal management and operation are its **bylaws.** They implement the charter and must be reasonable and not

bylaws
In corporations, rules and regulations of a corporation for its internal management and operation

[5]RMBCA, sec. 2.05.

contrary to law. The shareholders have the right to enact bylaws, in the absence of statute and charter to the contrary. The Revised Model Business Corporation Act gives to the incorporators or initial directors the power to enact the initial bylaws[6] and also, in most states, the power to amend and repeal them in the absence of statute or charter to the contrary.

▶ Certificate of Incorporation

Upon the filing of the articles of incorporation and payment of the filing fee, a certificate of incorporation is issued by the secretary of state. In most states, and under the Revised Model Business Corporation Act, corporate existence then begins.[7] The approved articles of incorporation are now called the charter. At this stage, creditors deal with the corporation as an entity separate from its stockholders, and the officers may do business in their respective capacities to avoid personal liability. The first order of business will be an organizational meeting for the stockholders to elect the directors, who will appoint the officers. The directors then adopt the bylaws, open a corporate checking account, and commence the management of the business.

▶ Defective Incorporations

De Jure Corporation

Upon issuance of the corporate certificate, the corporate entity is formed. Although minor errors occur in attempting to comply with the statutory requirements for incorporation, a ***de jure*** (by law) **corporation** exists. For example, an incorporator may have failed to list a director's address in the articles of incorporation, or the seals required by statute to be next to the signatures of the incorporators may have been omitted. As most states follow typical procedures for the review by government officials of incorporation papers before issuance of the certificate, the chances of a defective filing are remote. If complete or substantial compliance with the mandatory requirements of the incorporation statute and the prerequisites for the organization of the corporation have occurred, a valid *de jure* corporation exists.

***de jure* corporation**
A corporation that has completely or substantially complied with the mandatory requirements of a valid state incorporation statute

De Facto Corporation

When a *de jure* corporation cannot be found, the courts will determine if a defective incorporation is in "sufficient compliance" with the mandatory provisions of the corporation law. If it finds (1) a colorable attempt (i.e., real effort) in good faith (2) to comply with the mandatory provisions (3) of a valid corporate law for its incorporation and (4) business use of the corporation beyond just the organizational meeting, a ***de facto*** (by fact) **corporation** has been formed. It exists in fact although not by law, and a *de facto* corporate debtor cannot avoid liability on the basis of its being defective. Although a *de facto* corporate defendant may not attack its legal existence for the reason stated, the state may do so. The certificate of incorporation is conclusive evidence of corporate existence. Often the phrase "colorable compliance" is used to describe "colorable attempt," and it means that some real effort has been made to comply, but the compliance is less than substantial, although getting close to it.

***de facto* corporation**
A corporation that has not complied substantially with the mandatory requirements of a valid state incorporation statute but has made a colorable attempt to do so, in good faith, and has begun to operate as a corporation

Corporate status, whether *de jure* or *de facto,* is very important with respect to the liability of the corporate members (shareholders) because, with the corporate status as a shield, the members are not liable for corporate obligations. Without corporate status,

---

[6]RMBCA, sec. 2.06.

[7]RMBCA, sec. 2.03.

they are personally liable for their contractual obligations. This is illustrated in the following case where the court held that there was no colorable attempt to comply with the state corporate statute and, therefore, since there was no *de facto* corporation, the members were personally liable.

FACTS

Conway entered into a contract with Trend Set Construction Corporation for remodeling work on Conway's home. Samet signed the contract as president of Trend Set. Conway subsequently learned that Trend Set had never filed a certificate of incorporation. Suit was then brought by Conway against Samet personally. Samet defended on the ground that her attorney was supposed to have incorporated the business. The attorney told Samet she was incorporated and gave her a corporate seal. Her attorney had all the necessary information to incorporate and was paid the incorporation fees. Samet claimed she had a *de facto* corporation. Was this a *de facto* corporation?

DECISION

No. Judgment for Conway. More is required to establish the *de facto* corporation defense than giving instructions to an attorney to incorporate. There must be a colorable attempt to comply with the statute governing incorporations made before the contract. Without any certificate of incorporation having been even prepared or acknowledged, there can be no *de facto* corporation.

Conway v. Samet, 300 N.Y.S.2d 243 (N.Y. 1969).

► Corporation by Estoppel

estoppel
A principle of law stating that when one person "holds out" (represents) a material fact to another person who changes his or her position materially to his or her prejudice in reasonable reliance on the holding out, the first person is "estopped" (prohibited) to deny what he or she asserted previously

The so-called "corporation by **estoppel**" occurs when business associates hold themselves out as being a corporation to third persons who materially changed their position in reasonable reliance on the misrepresentation. The estoppel prevents such associates from later denying corporate existence, but it does not create a corporation. There is an estoppel to deny corporate status.

Notice how the court in the following case decided that the doctrine of corporation by estoppel is distinct from a *de facto* corporation.

FACTS

Bukacek and three others were the incorporators of Pell City Farms, Inc. Pursuant to an agreement between the incorporators and Pell City Farms, Inc., Bukacek conveyed his 300-acre tract to Pell City Farms, Inc. Bukacek then claimed that Pell City was incapable of taking legal title to the property as a corporation because it had not filed its articles of incorporation. Bukacek executed the deed, transferring his interest in the land to the corporation; he was an incorporator, officer, director, and stockholder of the corporation and participated in the business activities of the corporation relating to the land after the articles of incorporation were filed. May Bukacek have the corporation's title to the land set aside?

DECISION

No. Judgment for defendant, Pell City Farms. The incidence of corporate existence may exist as between the parties by virtue of an estoppel. Corporations by estoppel are not based upon the same principles as corporations *de facto*. A *de facto* corporation cannot be created by estoppel. The only effect of an estoppel is to prevent the raising of the question of the existence of a corporation.

Bukacek was one of the incorporators who dealt with the corporation as a corporation both before and after the articles of incorporation were filed. Bukacek is estopped to deny the existence of the corporation at the time he voluntarily executed a deed transferring property to the corporation even though the articles of incorporation had not been filed at that time.

Bukacek v. Pell City Farms, Inc., 237 So.2d 851 (Ala. 1970).

Termination

The state creates corporate existence, and only the state can authorize its dissolution. Unlike a sole proprietorship or a partnership, a corporation will not terminate upon the death of an owner. When a stockholder dies, his or her shares, as personal property, become an asset of the decedent stockholder's estate. As previously discussed, this continuity of the corporation is called "perpetual succession." Our discussion will focus on methods of terminating a corporation either voluntarily by the incorporators or shareholders, or involuntarily by the state, shareholders, or creditors. By the term "dissolution" is meant the termination of the existence of a corporation as an entity.

► Voluntary Dissolution

A corporation has statutory power to voluntarily terminate, provided that it complies with the state corporate laws. In some instances the incorporators may dissolve the corporation; however, it is usually the shareholders. The directors have no power to dissolve without the stockholders' approval.

By Incorporators or Initial Directors After having filed the articles of incorporation and being granted the corporate charter by the state, the corporation may be unable to issue its stock and, therefore, may decide not to commence business. The incorporators or initial directors may file *articles of dissolution* stating the following:

1. The corporate name
2. The issuance date of the certificate of incorporation
3. That none of its shares was issued or that it has not commenced business
4. That any proceeds of the liquidation and winding up have been distributed to the shareholders, if shares were issued
5. That the corporation has no debts
6. That a majority of the incorporators or initial directors elect to dissolve.[8]

Upon approval, the secretary of state will issue a *certificate of dissolution,* and corporate existence will terminate.

By Shareholders The shareholders may, by following state corporate law, dissolve the corporation for any reason. The board of directors adopts a resolution recommending dissolution that is submitted to a vote at a shareholders' meeting. In most states, at least a majority vote is required. Articles of dissolution are then filed, and the certificate of dissolution will be issued by the secretary of state.

[8]RMBCA, sec. 14.01.

In most states and under Section 14.05 of the Revised Model Business Corporation Act the dissolved corporation may not carry on any business except that necessary to wind up and liquidate its business affairs. The corporation must notify and pay the creditors, pay any taxes due, collect the receivables, liquidate the assets, and distribute the remainder of the assets to the shareholders.

► Involuntary Dissolution

The court, on a petition brought by the shareholders or the state, may dissolve the corporation.

By Shareholders The shareholders may bring a petition to dissolve the corporation for gross mismanagement by the board of directors (e.g., voting for plant expansion with insufficient funds to finance the venture); on the ground of unfair advantage by the majority over the minority stockholders; or on the grounds of dissension and deadlock.

In the following case the court refused to dissolve a solvent corporation whose shareholders were deadlocked in electing a board of directors for two successive years.

FACTS

Cooper-George, Inc. was created in 1950 by J. L. Cooper, Henry George and John George, for the primary purpose of building an apartment house. The shares were divided evenly between the Cooper family and the George family. In April of 1979 Henry George & Sons initiated this suit for dissolution under RCW (Revised Code of Washington), which reads as follows: "The superior courts shall have full power to liquidate the assets and business of a corporation: (1) In an action by a shareholder when it is established: (a) that the directors are deadlocked in the management of the corporate affairs and the shareholders are unable to break the deadlock. . . ." Judgment was rendered for the plaintiff, and defendants Cooper-George, Inc. and various shareholders appealed.

The Cooper-George apartment house, a 13-story apartment building in downtown Spokane, is the sole asset of the corporation. The defendants contend that RCW does not require a dissolution when a company has been in business for 28 years, operates a major apartment building, is solvent, is not being mismanaged, is not deadlocked at the board of director level regarding transaction of business, is not denying to any shareholder requested information, and is not causing any shareholder to benefit to the financial detriment of another. Henry George & Sons maintains that the mere fact that the shareholders were deadlocked in electing a board of directors for two successive years is all that is required under RCW to dissolve a corporation.

DECISION

Reversed. Judgment for Cooper-George, Inc., and its appealing shareholders. At common law, many courts refused to intervene in shareholder disputes since the state licensed the corporation, and as such, the state and not the courts had the authority to dissolve the corporation. More recently, many states have adopted statutory provisions granting courts of equity power to dissolve corporations in suits brought by shareholders where irreparable injury to the shareholders or the corporation occurred or was threatened. We conclude that our present statute contemplates that the trial court, in its discretion, shall determine whether there exist equitable grounds for ordering dissolution of the corporation. In so ruling, the trial court should consider business profitability despite the deadlock. In this case, the trial court erroneously ruled that Cooper-George should be dissolved merely on the basis that the jurisdictional requirements were met. We remand the matter to the trial court to determine, after considering the best interests of all the shareholders, whether dissolution is warranted.

Henry George & Sons, Inc. v. Cooper-George, Inc., et al., 632 P.2d 512 (Wash. 1981).

By State The state, acting through the attorney general's office, may cause an involuntary dissolution for a corporation's failure to pay state taxes, for not filing annual reports, for fraudulently filing articles of incorporation, for the failure of a foreign corporation to appoint a resident agent, or for abuse of its corporate authority.

► Bankruptcy

A corporation may voluntarily elect to file for bankruptcy, or its creditors may commence involuntary bankruptcy proceedings by petitioning the bankruptcy court. The corporate assets will then be liquidated and applied to creditors' claims, or a repayment plan will be considered by the bankruptcy court, depending on the nature of the bankruptcy case. Once bankruptcy proceedings have commenced, a board of directors' resolution to dissolve adopted by a majority of the shareholders will effect a dissolution.[9]

Mergers, Consolidations, and Exchange of Stock

► Merger

In a **merger,** one corporation is absorbed by another corporation, which continues to exist as the surviving corporation while the other terminates. State corporate statutes have specific procedures that must be followed. Generally, each board of directors involved adopts a plan of merger that is approved by its stockholders that must set forth the following:

merger
In corporations, the absorption of one corporation by another corporation

1. The name of each corporation planning to merge and the name of the surviving corporation into which each plans to merge
2. The terms and conditions of the merger
3. The manner and basis of converting the shares of each corporation into shares, obligations or other securities of the surviving or any other corporation or into cash or other property in whole or part

The plan or merger may set forth the following:

1. Any amendments to the articles of incorporation of the surviving corporation;
2. Other provisions relating to the merger.[10]

In the following case, a shareholder contested a sale of the corporation on the grounds that it was, in fact, a merger and that the merger statute, which required a two-thirds shareholders' vote, was not followed.

FACTS

Applestein, a shareholder of United Board and Carton Corporation, sought to enjoin a proposed sale of 40 percent of the corporation's stock to Epstein, the sole shareholder of Interstate Corporation, in exchange for all of Interstate's stock. Interstate would then cease to exist, and United would then take over all its assets and liabilities. Applestein argued that

[9]See Chapter 52, Bankruptcy under the Bankruptcy Reform Act of 1978. A corporation is not entitled to a discharge in bankruptcy in a Chapter 7 case.

[10]RMBCA, sec. 11.01.

this was a merger rather than a sale and hence required a vote of approval of two-thirds of the stockholders. United claimed that it had the right to purchase stock without shareholders' approval.

DECISION

Judgment for Applestein. A merger of two corporations contemplates that one will be absorbed by the other and go out of existence but the absorbing company will remain. As a consequence of the legislative power to legalize mergers, the state can prescribe the terms and conditions for a valid merger. This is more than a simple purchase by United of the assets of Interstate. In substance, the transaction is a merger. Accordingly, the shareholders of United were entitled to be notified of their statutory rights of dissent. The failure of the corporate officers of United to take these steps to obtain stockholder approval of the agreement by the statutory two-thirds vote at a proper stockholders' meeting would render the proposed corporate action invalid.

Applestein v. United Board and Carton Corp., 159 A.2d 146 (N.J. 1960).

Figure 43.2 illustrates how acquiring corporation *X*, having acquired all of the assets and liabilities of acquired corporation *Y*, becomes the sole surviving corporation.

Consolidation

consolidation
In corporations, the combination of two or more corporations forming a new corporation

In a **consolidation,** two or more corporations combine together, forming a new corporation. In a merger, the corporations combine together, resulting in a surviving corporation rather than a new corporation that is formed under a plan of consolidation. Thus *X* and *Y* corporations combine with and merge into corporation *Z*, the surviving corporation; but when *X*, *Y*, and *Z* consolidate they form a new corporation, corporation *C*.

However, the legal effects of a merger, consolidation, and exchange of stock are similar. The following points, as found in the Revised Model Business Corporation Act, Section 11.06, are illustrative:

(1) Every other corporation party to the merger merges into the surviving corporation and the separate existence of every corporation except the surviving corporation ceases.

FIGURE 43.2 **Statutory Merger**

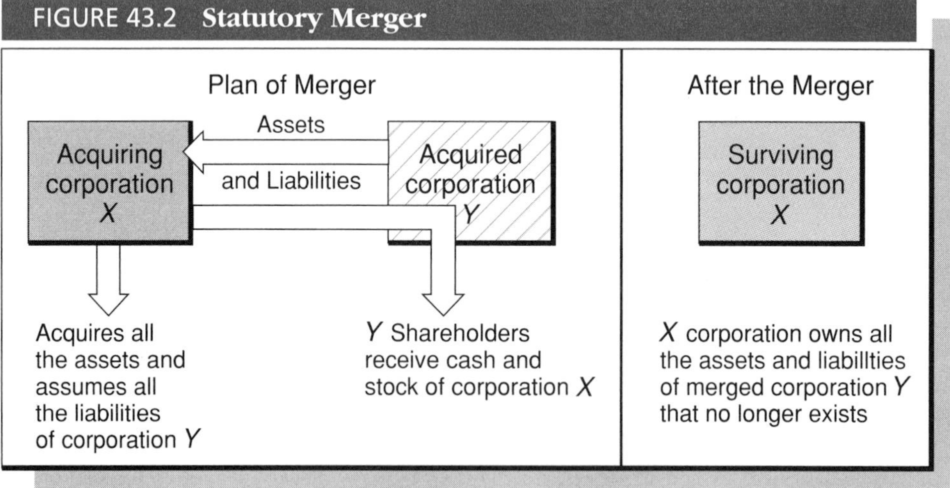
Plan of Merger
After the Merger
Acquiring corporation X
Assets
and Liabilities
Acquired corporation Y
Surviving corporation X
Acquires all the assets and assumes all the liabilities of corporation Y
Y Shareholders receive cash and stock of corporation X
X corporation owns all the assets and liabillties of merged corporation Y that no longer exists

(2) The title to all real estate owned by each corporation party to the merger is vested in the surviving corporation without reversion or impairment.
(3) The surviving corporation has all liabilities of each corporation party to the merger.
(4) A proceeding pending against any corporation party to the merger may be continued as if the merger did not occur or the surviving corporation may be substituted in the proceeding for the corporation whose existence ceased.
(5) The articles of incorporation of the surviving corporation are amended to the extent provided in the plan of merger.

When a share exchange takes effect, the shares of each acquired corporation are exchanged as provided in the plan, and the holders of the shares are entitled only to the exchange rights provided in the articles of share exchange.

Figure 43.3 illustrates the formation of a new corporation *Z*, which owns all the assets and liabilities of acquired corporation *X* and *Y*, which no longer exist.

► Exchange of Stock

All of the issued and outstanding shares of a corporation may be acquired through the exchange of these shares by another corporation pursuant to a plan adopted by the board of directors and approved by the stockholders of the acquired corporation.[11] For example, corporation *X* acquires the stock of corporation *Z*, both corporations maintaining their legal entity. Corporation *Z* becomes a subsidiary of corporation *X*, whose board of directors governs the operations of the acquired corporation *Z*. The tax consequences of a merger, consolidation or stock exchange are referred to as a

FIGURE 43.3 **Statutory Consolidation**

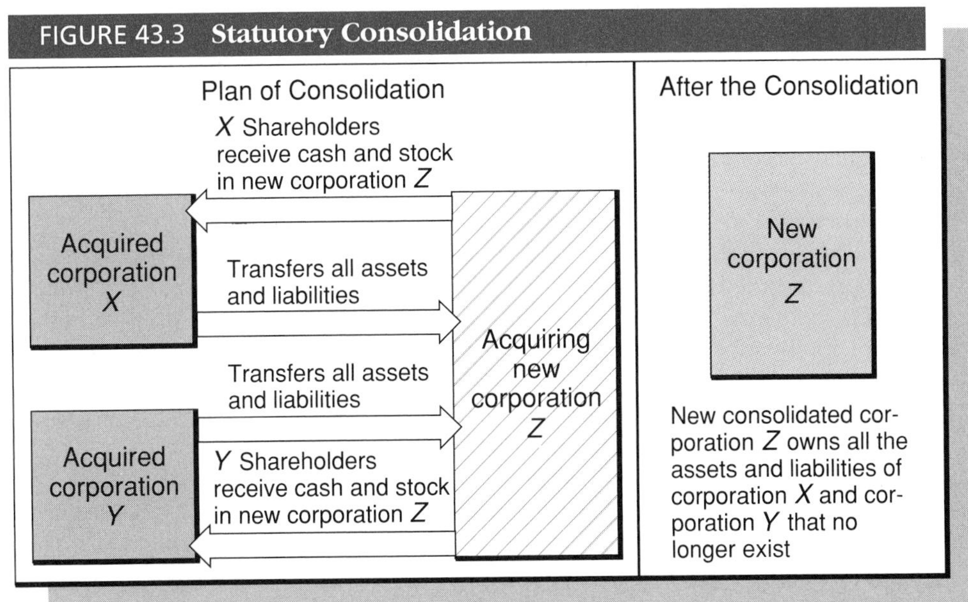
Plan of Consolidation
X Shareholders receive cash and stock in new corporation Z
Acquired corporation X
Transfers all assets and liabilities
Transfers all assets and liabilities
Acquiring new corporation Z
Acquired corporation Y
Y Shareholders receive cash and stock in new corporation Z
After the Consolidation
New corporation Z
New consolidated corporation Z owns all the assets and liabilities of corporation X and corporation Y that no longer exist

[11] Cf. RMBCA, sec. 11.02.

"reorganization" under the Internal Revenue Code[12] and would be carefully examined by tax counsel in any of these situations.

Some Reasons for Merger, Consolidation, or Exchange of Stock A corporation may wish to merge with another to acquire a related or unrelated line of merchandise in order to diversify and reduce some of its economic risks; or it may wish to invest accumulated income rather than pay a dividend or tax as it is. If the effect is to lessen interstate competition, it may violate a federal antitrust law. For example, a large computer corporation may acquire a smaller one for all of the above reasons. There are always significant tax consequences to any merger, consolidation, or exchange of stock.

Summary Statement

1. Promoters plan the corporation and attend to its organization. In doing so, they frequently sign preincorporation contracts, on which the promoter is personally liable to third parties thereon.
2. A promoter is a fiduciary because a promoter is under a duty to act for the benefit of the corporation. He or she is liable to the corporation for any secret profits made while acting as a promoter.
3. The articles of incorporation must be filed and approved by the secretary of state's office. The corporate name, purpose, capital stock authorization, place of business, names and addresses of directors and officers, fiscal year, and resident agent are listed in the articles of incorporation that are signed by the incorporators.
4. A defectively formed corporation may be given legal status in certain circumstances.
5. A *de jure* (by law) corporation exists by complete or substantial compliance with the statutory requirements for incorporation.
6. A *de facto* (by fact) corporation exists when there was a good faith colorable attempt to organize under a state corporation law and there is business use of the defectively formed corporation.
7. A corporation by estoppel does not create a corporation, but prevents the denial of corporate existence by associates who held themselves out as being a corporation to third parties who materially changed their position in reasonable reliance on the misrepresentation.
8. The state, acting through the attorney general's office, may dissolve a corporation that fails to act legally.
9. Shareholders may voluntarily dissolve the corporation by voting to adopt the board of directors' resolution to dissolve, or the corporation may be involuntarily dissolved with court approval.
10. A merger is the absorption of one corporation by another corporation, which continues to exist while the other terminates.
11. A consolidation is the combination of two or more corporations forming a new corporation.
12. The legal effect of a merger or consolidation is the termination of all corporations except the surviving corporation (merger) or new corporation (consolidation); the surviving or new corporation has all the rights and duties of a corporation, and the rights of creditors are not impaired.

---

[12] Cf. I.R.C. sec. 368(a)(1) (1954).

13. An exchange of stock is a legal process whereby, pursuant to the directors' plan being approved by the shareholders, all the issued and outstanding shares of a corporation are acquired through the exchange of shares in another corporation, the acquired corporation becoming a subsidiary of the acquiring corporation.

In the following case the court held a defective corporation was liable on a note that was executed by its officer when, after legal incorporation, the company accepted the benefits of the contract with the knowledge of its terms.

FRAMINGHAM SAVINGS BANK v. JOSEPH SZABO, TRUSTEE
617 F.2d 897 (1st Cir. 1980)

Coffin, Chief Judge. In February 1977, George Sulak purchased all of the assets of the Framingham Lumber Company for a new enterprise he was forming, to be entitled Framingham Lumber Company, Inc. The new company carried on a business essentially identical to that of the old company on the same site. The same month Sulak signed Articles of Incorporation for the new company in his role as president and treasurer. However, when the Articles were mailed to the Secretary of State of Massachusetts, they were rejected by the Secretary and returned to Sulak's attorney. More than one year later, in October, 1973, an employee of Sulak's attorney hand delivered the Articles to the office of the Secretary; they were again rejected because the name of the new company was too similar to that of the old, and the procedure was explained whereby the defect in incorporation could be cured. These procedures were never followed. However, the Articles were finally accepted and filed in October 1975, and Sulak's corporation commenced its legal existence at that time.

In August, 1974, Sulak's company purchased a 1974 White truck with purchase money furnished by plaintiff Framingham Savings Bank (bank). The bank took a promissory note and a security interest in the truck; Sulak signed the documents as an officer of the corporation. In July, 1975, the bank again advanced the corporation purchase money, on this occasion for a 1974 Audi automobile, taking a similar note and security interest in the vehicle. The corporation defaulted on its payments to the bank in June 1976, went bankrupt, and the bank repossessed the two vehicles and sold them for $25,675 and $3,450 respectively. The bank brought this action against the corporation's trustee in bankruptcy to establish its entitlement to these proceeds, based on its security interests in the vehicles. The trustee defended on a number of grounds, including the contention that the security interest was invalid because the corporation did not exist at the time the agreement was formed.

Most states hold that a corporation can be bound to a pre-incorporation agreement by knowing ratification or adoption of the contract. The rationale for the contrary Massachusetts rule stems from the premise that the individual executing the contract could not act as an agent for the not yet existing corporation. Therefore, the corporation could not become bound to the contract by ratification or adoption of the putative agent's bargain. Rather, to bind itself the corporation must introduce "into the transaction such an element as would be sufficient foundation for a new contract." The corporation can become liable on the terms of the original contract, but only if its post-incorporation acts are sufficient independently to bind it to a new contract. The bank made its offer to the corporation not Sulak. Indeed, the entire transaction was carried out by both parties on the assumption that the contract was between the bank and Framingham Lumber Co., Inc. The bank looked to the corporation, not to the individual, Sulak, to perform the obligations of the contract. The corporation's name appeared on the security agreement and the certificates of title for the vehicles; the checks used to pay loan installments were drawn on the corporation's bank account. Moreover, the corporation, after its legal status was secured, used the vehicles and paid installments with knowledge of the terms of the contract.

Thus, we hold that the agreement between the bank and Sulak, acting on behalf of the defectively incorporated firm, created a continuing offer to the putative corporation, and when the corporation entered into legal life and, with knowledge of the terms of the agreement, availed itself of the benefits of the bank's performance, it obligated itself to perform those terms just as if it had explicitly promised to do so. We hold the corporation in this case is bound and therefore reverse the judgment of the district court.

Questions and Case Problems

1. Emmick has been involved in the promotion of nursing homes and the management of various farming activities. Emmick approached J. B. Morris with a plan whereby Morris' ranch would be incorporated and through Emmick's managerial skills made to show a profit. At approximately the same time, Emmick approached Golden and proposed that Golden contribute some farm machinery and livestock to Oahe Enterprises, Inc., the corporation to be formed for the operation and management of the Morris ranch. At this meeting, it was concluded that Oahe shares would be given a $50 par value. As Emmick's payment for the Oahe's shares he transferred 6,514 shares of Colonial Manors, Inc., stock (CM stock) to Oahe Enterprises Inc. Golden's complaint is that Emmick was allowed to use as the value of his CM stock a value arbitrarily affixed by the CM board of directors for a strictly internal purpose—that of raising badly needed funds for CM by offering stock options at a desperate juncture in its corporate life. This value admittedly bore no relationship to the book value of CM stock. Emmick admitted that he used for his valuation of CM stock the internal stock option price set by the CM board of directors. Did Emmick, as a promoter of Oahe Enterprises, Inc. violate a fiduciary duty owed to Golden? [*Warren Golden v. Oahe Enterprises, Inc.*, 295 N.W.2d 160 (S.D. 1980).]
2. Neal was an incorporator for Main Street Electric Company, Inc. He filed the articles of incorporation with the Secretary of State in Texas. The articles were refused because there already existed a Main Street Electronic Company, Inc. in Texas. May the secretary of state refuse an application on these grounds?
3. On July 21, 1975, prior to the date the articles of incorporation were executed, a certificate or reservation of the name Roseberry Inn, Inc. was filed with the secretary of state by Harry Chudnofsky. On July 24, 1975, the Board of Directors of Roseberry Inn, Inc. executed a certificate of incorporation and passed a corporate borrowing resolution. On July 30, 1975, Roseberry Inn filed a certificate of incorporation with the secretary of state. On August 4, 1975, Roseberry Inn, Inc. applied for a liquor license using its corporate name. On March 2, 1976 the corporation entered into a lease agreement with Cable-Wiedemer, Inc. which lease was signed by Chudnofsky both in his individual capacity and as president of Roseberry Inn, Inc. Was Roseberry Inn Inc. a *de facto* corporation? [*Bankers Trust Co. of Western N.Y. v. Zecher et al.*, 103 Misc.2d 777 (N.Y. 1980).]
4. Defendant, Morgan, executed a note in Georgia on November 19, 1970 as president of Beefmastor, Inc. Beefmastor was subsequently incorporated on December 31, 1970. The note was in partial payment for a business located in Georgia and all payments on the note were to be made in Georgia. After making some payments, Beefmastor defaulted on the note. Can defendant be held personally liable on a note that he executed as president of a corporation that had not yet been formed, but

which was subsequently incorporated and that made payments on the note until default? [*Smith v. Morgan,* 50 N.C.App. 208 (N.C. 1980).]

5. Levin, an incorporator, filed the articles of incorporation and named the corporation "Levin's, Limited." The secretary of state's office refused to accept the articles because "limited" would not indicate to the public that the business is a corporation, and hence the name is improper. Decide.

6. Martin Stern, Jr., brought this action for architectural services rendered to Nathan Jacobson, in Jacobson's development of a hotel and casino, known as the Kings Castle, on the north shore of Lake Tahoe, Nevada. In January 1969 Jacobson contacted Stern and asked him to draw plans for Jacobson's new hotel/casino at Lake Tahoe. Stern immediately began preliminary work on the project and contracted soil engineers and surveyors in this regard. At this time Stern dealt directly with Jacobson, who referred to the project as "my hotel," and with Taylor of Nevada who was to be the general contractor. On February 18, 1969, Stern wrote to Jacobson detailing, among other things, the architect's services and the fee. A letter from Jacobson to Stern, written March 10, 1970, acknowledges that the parties entered into a contract in April 1969. At the same time as the plans for the building were being developed by Stern, Jacobson was negotiating financing and setting up business structures to own and manage the property.

On May 1, 1969, Jacobson acquired all of the stock of A.L.W., Inc., a corporation which had previously operated a casino on this site and which was to operate the Kings Castle. The business structure included the formation of Lake Enterprises, a corporation of which Jacobson was the sole stockholder and president. Kings Castle, Limited Partnership was formed with Lake Enterprises, Inc., as the general partner and Jacobson and others as limited partners. Jacobson was the most substantial investor in Kings Castle, Limited Partnership with investments in excess of $3 million. After May 9, 1969, A.L.W., Inc. operated the hotel and casino, and Kings Castle, Limited Partnership leased the land. All monies were subsequently paid and received through these two entities. Stern billed Jacobson beginning in June of 1969. All of the checks were drawn on the account of A.L.W., Inc.; only one of the checks was signed by Jacobson. The Kings Castle opened in July 1970. On February 3, 1972, A.L.W., Inc., as owner of Kings Castle and Casino, filed its petition for arrangements under Chapter 11 of the Bankruptcy Act. Jacobson contends that his obligations were adopted by A.L.W., Inc., and such adoption constitutes a novation and Jacobson was released from his obligation. Decide. [*Jacobson v. Stern,* 605 P.2d 198 (Nev. 1980).]

7. Colorado Indoor Trap Shoot, Inc., the plaintiff, sued Tucker, defendant, doing business as Consolidated Sales Co. Plaintiff was to purchase from defendant the necessary equipment to open and operate one of the indoor trap shoot establishments in Colorado. Plaintiff was to pay the defendant $2,100,000 for the exclusive rights to sell, lease, and distribute all such indoor trap shoot equipment in the State of Colorado for a maximum period of five years. Defendant claims that the contract was entered into on behalf of its company which was to be formed by him as a promoter, and this was known to the plaintiff. Is Tucker, as a promoter, personally liable on the preincorporation contract? [*Tucker v. Colorado Indoor Trap Shoot, Inc.,* 471 P.2d 912 (Okla. 1970).]

8. The plaintiff, Stephens Wholesale Bldg. Supply Co., sold merchandise to the defendant, Norman R. Harris, individually, and doing business as Bessemer Building and Improvement Company. Prior to the filing of incorporation papers by defendant Harris, on April 2, 1969, a corporate checking account was opened, a lease for corporate office space and a bid on a construction job were made in the name of the corporation. Harris opened his business relationship with Stephens in an individual capacity, although he subsequently operated as a corporation. Was Harris personally liable under contract with Stephens before he incorporated? [*Harris v. Stephens Wholesale Bldg. Supply Co., Inc.,* 309 So.2d 115 (Ala. 1975).]

9. Plaintiffs prepared the lease in the name of Sunshine Greenery, Inc., as the tenant, and it was signed by Brunetti as president. Mr. Cantor, acting for plaintiffs, knew that Brunetti was starting a new venture as a newly formed corporation known as Sunshine Greenery, Inc. Mr. Cantor knew and expected that the lease agreement was undertaken by the corporation and not by Brunetti individually. The lease was repudiated by a letter from counsel for Sunshine Greenery, dated December 17, 1974. On November 21, 1974, the corporate name of Sunshine Greenery had been reserved for Brunetti by the secretary of state and on December 3, 1974 a certificate of incorporation for that company was signed by Brunetti as incorporator. The certificate was forwarded by mail to the secretary of state on that same date with a check for the filing fee, but for some unexplained reason it was not officially filed until December 18, 1974, two days after the execution of the lease. Was Brunetti individually liable for the lease? [*Cantor v. Sunshine Greenery, Inc.,* 165 N.J.Super. 411 (N.J. 1979).]

10. In the case of *Framingham Savings Bank v. Joseph Szabo, Trustee,* excerpted at the beginning of this section, the court held the defectively organized corporation liable on a note rather than the officer who signed on its behalf. What should the bank have done if it intended the officer and the corporation to be liable on the note?

CHAPTER 44

CORPORATE POWERS

After you have read this chapter, you should be able to:

1. Explain the function of the purpose clause in the articles of incorporation.
2. Explain the source of the corporation's express powers.
3. Discuss the implied powers of a corporation.
4. List and explain the corporate statutory powers.
5. Explain the function of corporate bylaws.
6. Explain the doctrine of *ultra vires.*
7. Explain the remedies for *ultra vires* acts.

BUSINESS DECISIONS and the LAW

If a corporation may perform only those acts authorized by its express, implied, or statutory powers, what is the legal effect of the large donations made by Ben & Jerry's Homemade Ice Cream?

Co-founders Ben Cohen and Jerry Greenfield currently enjoy annual sales of $50 million for their premium ice cream, which is distributed through supermarkets and franchises around the country. This astonishing level of success has been reached after just eleven years in the business.

That the company is a maverick and quirky is well known: it offers eager consumers such flavors as "Cherry Garcia." But how far do corporate powers go? Shareholders and bankers, after all, are indirectly supporting Ben & Jerry's political messages, which appear on their ice cream containers, as well as their exceptionally high level of charitable donations. Ben & Jerry's donates 1 percent of its profits to a peace organization, and 7.5 percent to other charitable causes.

In another bold move, Mr. Cohen, with Mr. Greenfield as an investor, has started a new company to make nut brittle out of nuts harvested from the endangered Brazilian nut forest. He plans to hand over 40 percent of the profits to organizations working to preserve the rain forest.

While it is clear that Ben & Jerry's primary goal is to make money, the corporation has added new meaning to the corporate beneficence and continues to challenge the limits of corporate powers.

Source: Jonathan Kaufman, "Doing Good While Doing Well," *Boston Globe,* September 3, 1989, p. 74. (Reprinted courtesy of The Boston Globe).

Introduction

While the corporation may exist as a legal entity by permission of the state, it cannot function without authority or power. The state is the source of all corporate power and determines what a corporation may and may not do. Accordingly, it is necessary to consider the nature and extent of corporate powers.

The Nature of Corporate Powers

corporate express powers
Those powers specifically stated in the corporation's articles of incorporation and in the corporation statutes

corporate implied powers
Those powers reasonably necessary to carry out the express powers

In the planning stages of the corporation it is necessary to determine the purpose of its formation. This is described in the purpose clause of the articles of incorporation. Once authorized by the state to function as a corporation, it has the consequent **express powers** as stated in the articles of incorporation and the corporate statutes to carry out its business purpose. For instance, as an "artificial person" the corporation may, in its own name, own property, sell stock, borrow money, and hire employees. If the incorporators anticipate a new line of business, the purpose clause should be broadly descriptive of its express powers so as to avoid a later necessary amendment of the articles of incorporation, requiring stockholders' approval.

Many states, as well as the Revised Model Business Corporation Act (RMBCA) in Section 3.01(a), allow a purpose clause authorizing the corporation to engage in any lawful business transaction. For example, a typical purpose clause for a restaurant business may state that the purpose is "to engage in the restaurant business and any legal business transactions related thereto." The powers that are reasonably necessary to carry out the express powers are called **implied powers.** *Corporate officers have no authority to bind a corporation without express, implied, or statutory power.*

The following case illustrates that the power to issue stock is not among the incidental or implied powers of a corporation.

FACTS

The purported stockholders of a country club sued the club and claimed that the right to issue stock was an implied power of all corporations and expressly provided for in the articles of incorporation. The original laws of incorporation in Arkansas did not prohibit the issuance of stock for non-profit corporations but neither did they provide for issuance.

DECISION

The issuance of stock to its members was void. Much like the power to create the corporate status, the power to create corporate stock is a legislative function which must be exercised for such stock to have legal existence; the power to issue stock must be specifically granted by the statutes under which a corporation is formed, which results in the rule that the power to issue stock is not held to be among the incidental or implied powers of a corporation. As such we reject the purported stockholders' contention that the issuance of stock was incidental to the purpose of the club or that it was an implied power of the country club.

Allen v. Malvern Country Club, 746 S.W. 2d 546 (Ark. 1988).

► Corporate Statutory Powers

The state where the corporation is organized gives it various statutory powers. These powers are the reasons why the corporation is the most desirable way of operating a business. Under Section 3.02 of the RMBCA, "unless the articles of incorporation provide otherwise, every corporation has the same powers as an individual to do all things necessary or convenient to carry out its business and affairs, including without limitation power:"

1. ***Perpetual Succession.*** "To have perpetual duration and succession in its corporate name."

   You will recall that a partnership is dissolved by a change in the relationship among the partner-owners. This will not occur in a corporation as the death of a shareholder causes the stock to pass to the representative for the shareholder's estate. For example, the death of a shareholder or a change in management will not affect its perpetual existence. The stability provided by this attribute makes it the only proper business form for the larger corporations with many shareholders.
2. ***To Sue and Be Sued in Its Corporate Name.*** "To sue and be sued, complain and defend, in its corporate name."

   Sole proprietors and partners are sued and sue in their own names. The corporation as a distinct and independent legal person sues in its own name. This is a significant advantage because the owners and managers are not personally liable for corporate debts.
3. ***To Have a Corporate Seal.*** "To have a corporate seal."

   This right is consistent with the *legal person* aspect of the corporation. The seal is commonly used on important documents to evidence corporate authorization of the transaction. For example, banks generally require a corporate seal when a corporate checking account is opened, and the certificate of stock normally has the corporate seal on it.
4. ***To Make and Alter Bylaws.*** "To make and amend bylaws, not inconsistent with its articles of incorporation or with the laws of this state for managing the business and regulating the affairs of the corporation."

   Bylaws determine the policy of the corporation and establish the authority of the officers, directors and stockholders. They can grant extraordinary powers to the board of directors allowing them to make decisions that ordinarily would require stockholders' approval. The initial bylaws are usually adopted by the board of directors who have the power to alter or amend unless the articles of incorporation reserve that to the stockholders.[1]
5. ***To Acquire and Deal with Property.*** "To purchase, receive, lease, or otherwise acquire, and own, hold, improve, use, and otherwise deal with, real or personal property, or any legal or equitable interest in property, wherever located."

   A corporation may purchase property in its own name either as an investment or for its own use. The property then becomes a corporate asset, subject to the rights of creditors. For example, a corporate restaurant, that does not pay its debts and owns its own kitchen equipment, may have the equipment attached and liquidated by its creditors and the proceeds used to satisfy their claims.
6. ***To Dispose of Its Property.*** "To sell, convey, mortgage, pledge, lease, exchange, and otherwise dispose of all or part of its property."

   We will see in Chapter 46 that the decision to sell corporate property generally requires board authorization because of its effect on the stockholders' investment. Once authorized, it is the corporation, as a legal person, who sells the property, and not the board of directors or corporate officers who act for the corporation.

[1]RMBCA, sec. 2.06.

7. ***To Acquire, Dispose of, and Deal in Interests in Other Corporations.*** "To purchase, . . . or otherwise acquire; own, hold, vote, use, sell, mortgage, lend, pledge, or otherwise dispose of; and deal in and with shares or other interests in, or obligations of, other domestic or foreign corporations, associations, partnerships . . . , and individuals, the United States, a state, or a foreign government."

   This power clearly identifies the investment potential of the corporation beyond its own business purpose. A corporation may own, in its own name, stock or bonds in another business or government.

8. ***To Make Contracts, Incur and Secure Its Obligations.*** "To make contracts and guarantees, incur . . . obligations, and secure any of its obligations by mortgage or pledge of any of its property, franchises, or income."

   This corporate power to engage in debt financing is commonly used to meet cash flow demands. The ability to raise money by the issuance of bonds and notes is an essential statutory power.

9. ***To Lend and Invest.*** "To lend money, invest and reinvest its funds, and receive and hold real and personal property as security for repayment."

   Prudent investment of corporate profit is an obligation of the board of directors.

10. ***To Be a Member of Another Enterprise.*** "To be a promoter, partner, member, associate, or manager of any partnership, joint venture, trust, or other entity."

    This power permits a corporation to be a general partner in a general or limited partnership with unlimited liability for the partnership's obligations.[2]

11. ***To Engage in Intrastate and Interstate Business Activities.*** "To conduct its business, locate offices, and exercise the powers granted by this Act within or without this state."

    Many corporations carry on business activities, not only in their state of formation, but in many others. Our economy could not function without this power.

12. ***To Have Directors and Agents, and Financially Assist Its Employees.*** "To elect directors and appoint officers, employees, and agents of the corporation, define their duties, fix their compensation, and lend them money and credit."

    The corporation may use corporate funds for the benefit of its directors and employees who may wish to borrow. The corporation could assist in the establishment of corporate credit unions for its employees who can borrow from the credit union.

13. ***To Establish Incentive, Pension, and Other Benefit Plans.*** "To pay pensions and establish pension . . . plans, and benefit and incentive plans for any or all of its former or current directors, officers, employees, and agents."

    Planning for retirement is essential to the well-being of our labor force. The Employee Retirement Income Security Act[3] governs the procedure and tax advantages of the pension area. Many small business associations have elected to incorporate to obtain these benefits.

14. ***To Make Donations for the Public Good.*** "To make donations for the public welfare or for charitable, scientific, or educational purposes."

    This power allows the corporation to make tax deductible charitable contributions. Our society, with its numerous nonprofit organizations (e.g., colleges and hospitals), relies upon substantial corporate contributions for their funding.

---

[2]See Chapter 38 and pp. 848–854 for a discussion of both general and limited partnerships.

[3]29 U.S.C., ch. 18, and amendments thereto.

15. ***To Aid Public Policy.*** "To transact any lawful business that will aid governmental policy."

    The board of directors, as the principal governing body of the corporation, will be discussed in a later chapter. The directors are generally elected by the stockholders and their number is fixed by the bylaws.

16. ***To Have All Implied Powers to Effect Its Purposes.*** "To make payments or donations, or do any other act, not inconsistent with law, that furthers the business and affairs of the corporation."

    This is a broad statement of the corporation's implied power and authority.

The following early case illustrates how a court will extend the power to contract beyond the corporation's immediate expressed purpose, provided that the contract is within the corporation's implied powers and authority, is executed, and is not contrary to public policy.

FACTS

Miller sued Temple Lumber Company for breach of a contract to construct a dwelling house. Temple Lumber was to furnish all labor and materials in the construction of a house for Miller and was to do the construction according to a set of plans and specifications. Temple Lumber's corporate charter set out the purpose of the corporation as that of "manufacturing lumber and the purchase and sale of material used in such business and doing all things necessary and incident to such lumber business." Temple Lumber claimed it was not liable on the contract since construction of a building was not an act within its "purpose" clause and, therefore, was beyond the powers of the corporation.

DECISION

Judgment for Miller. An act of a corporation is *ultra vires* when it is beyond the scope either of the express or implied power of the charter. If the act is not one prohibited by law or public policy, and it enures to the direct benefit of the corporation, and is executed, it is not, strictly speaking, *ultra vires*. Acts which are not enumerated in the purpose clause of the charter of a corporation but are not prohibited and are appropriate, convenient, and suitable in carrying out the purposes for which the charter was expressly granted are the "implied powers and authority" of a corporation.

Temple Lumber Co. v. Miller, 169 S.W.2d 256 (Tex. 1943).

The corporate powers listed above are the *general* powers of a corporation. Section 303(d) of the RMBCA states the *emergency* powers of a corporation: "an emergency exists for the purposes of this section if a quorum of the corporation's directors cannot readily be assembled."

Unauthorized Corporate Acts

► *Ultra Vires* Acts

A corporation may perform only those acts that are authorized by its express, implied, or statutory powers. These powers are derived from the state of incorporation as established in corporate statutory law, the articles of incorporation, and its reasonably implied powers. If a corporation should engage in an unauthorized act, it is **ultra vires**—that is, beyond the powers of the corporation. For example, if the board of directors of a computer corporation were to authorize the expenditure of funds to purchase conservation land in order to protect the wildlife, although this may be socially desirable, it would be beyond the authority of a computer corporation and *ultra vires*.

ultra vires
Beyond the powers

Illegal Acts Distinguished from *Ultra Vires* Corporate action in excess of corporate authority is *ultra vires,* but it is not illegal unless it is contrary to statute or public policy as declared by the courts. For example, in the above illustration, while the board action was in excess of corporate authority, such action was not illegal as contrary to public law. However, if the board had bribed a congressman to vote in Congress to make the land available to the corporation, this would be contrary to federal statute and public policy, and it would be illegal and viewed as a crime.

Legal Effect of *Ultra Vires* Acts Under common law, *ultra vires* business transactions were void because they were performed without legal authorization. Under modern statutory law, the defense of *ultra vires* is abolished in a suit for breach of contract by or against a corporation. The official comment to Section 3.04 of the RMBCA states it is unnecessary for persons dealing with a corporation to inquire into limitations on its purposes or powers that may appear in its articles of incorporation. A person who is unaware of these limitations when dealing with the corporation is not bound by them.

The following case illustrates this when the defendant's corporate president acted beyond his authority.

FACTS

Southeastern Beverage & Ice Equipment Company, Inc., brought suit against the Free For All Missionary Baptist Church, Inc., for rent due under a lease for liquor dispensing equipment. The lease was signed by the president and secretary of the corporation. The church contends that the lease was *ultra vires* and unauthorized.

DECISION

Judgment for Southeastern Beverage. Incapacity or lack of power on the part of the church corporation does not make the lease invalid, and the defense of *ultra vires* is not available. The State Business Corporation Code abolished the doctrine of *ultra vires* as a means of avoiding a transaction which the corporation later claims is beyond its capacity or power. The corporation is not relieved of liability to any third persons for acts of its officers by reason of any limitation upon the power of the officers not known to such third persons. There is no evidence that Southeastern Beverage as lessor knew of any limitation upon the power of the Baptist Church president.

Free For All Missionary Baptist Church, Inc. v. Southeastern Beverage & Ice Equip. Co., Inc., 218 S.E.2d 169 (Ga. 1975).

Many courts will allow *ultra vires* as a defense where the contract is executory—that is, not yet performed. If the corporation or the other party has received full performance of the contract, they cannot avoid liability by the defense of *ultra vires*. This occurred in the following case.

FACTS

Total Automation, Inc., was a corporation with a checking account in the Illinois National Bank & Trust Co. The bank operated a travel department that was owed money by Total Automation. The bank deducted the amount owed to the travel department from Total's checking account. Total Automation claims that the bank had no right to setoff because the operation of a travel agency by a national bank is an *ultra vires* act.

DECISION

Judgment for Illinois National Bank & Trust Co. The defense of *ultra vires* is not favored by the courts where it is raised by a private party seeking to avoid payment for a benefit received. Total Automation is not aggrieved as a private person by having to pay for services it used, nor can it be heard to say it is aggrieved as a member of the public by a departure from sound policy relating to banking, since it voluntarily entered into the *ultra vires* transaction and reaped its benefits.

Total Automation, Inc. v. Ill. Nat'l Bank & Trust Co. of Rockford, 351 N.E.2d 879 (Ill. 1976).

Remedies for *Ultra Vires* Acts The corporation may be protected from *ultra vires* activity engaged in by the officers or directors. A corporation's lack of power to act may be challenged:

1. in a proceeding by a shareholder against the corporation to enjoin the act;
2. in a proceeding by the corporation, directly, derivatively, or through a receiver, trustee, or other legal representative, against an incumbent or former director, officer, employee, or agent of the corporation; or
3. in a proceeding by the Attorney General if it establishes that the corporation obtained its articles of incorporation through fraud or the corporation has continued to exceed or abuse the authority conferred upon it by law.[4]

Summary Statement

1. The purpose clause of the articles of incorporation give a corporation the express and implied powers to engage in the stated purpose.
2. The express powers of a corporation are found in the articles of incorporation and the corporate statutory law.
3. The implied powers grant to the corporation authority to perform those reasonably incidental acts in carrying on corporate business.
4. The corporate statutory powers give to a corporation the implied authority
    - **a)** to have perpetual duration and succession in its corporate name;
    - **b)** to sue and be sued in its corporate name;
    - **c)** to have a corporate seal;
    - **d)** to make and amend bylaws for managing the business and regulating the affairs of the corporation;
    - **e)** to acquire and deal with property;
    - **f)** to dispose of its property;
    - **g)** to purchase, . . . or otherwise acquire and deal in other interests or obligations of other corporations, associations or partnerships;
    - **h)** to make contracts, incur and secure its obligations;
    - **i)** to lend money, invest and reinvest its funds;
    - **j)** to be a member of another enterprise;
    - **k)** to engage in intrastate and interstate business activities;
    - **l)** to have directors and agents, and financially assist its employees;
    - **m)** to establish incentive, pension, and other benefit plans;
    - **n)** to make donations for the public good;

[4] RMBCA, sec. 3.04 and sec. 14.30.

o) to aid public policy;
p) to have all implied powers to effect its purposes.

5. The bylaws regulate the internal affairs of the corporation. They establish the authority of the directors, officers, and shareholders as well as the procedures for calling meetings.
6. The acts of the corporation outside the scope of the corporate authority are *ultra vires.* Executed corporate contracts are valid, and the creditor cannot use the defense of *ultra vires;* if executory, either party may use the *ultra vires* defense.
7. If officers or directors propose an *ultra vires* act, the shareholders may enjoin the act, the shareholders in a representative suit may sue the officers or directors personally, or the attorney general may bring a proceeding to dissolve the corporation.

Notice how the court in the following case examined the nature of the contract signed by the corporate president and found it to be "unusual and extraordinary," thus requiring express authority to execute.

GOLDENBERG v. BARTELL BROADCASTING CORPORATION
262 N.Y.S.2d 274 (N.Y. 1965)

Wilfred A. Waltemade, Justice. In the case on trial, the plaintiff sets forth two causes of action, both of which seek recovery of damages for an alleged breach of a written contract of employment. The first cause of action is against the defendant Bartell Broadcasting Corporation, an entity incorporated under the laws of the State of Delaware. It is alleged in substance that on or about March 16, 1961, the plaintiff and the defendant Bartell Broadcasting Corporation entered into a written contract wherein the plaintiff was engaged as an assistant to Gerald A. Bartell, the president of the defendant Bartell Broadcasting Corporation. The plaintiff's primary duties were to engage in corporate development in the field of pay television. The contract, which was for a period of three years, provided for (1) payment to the plaintiff of $1,933 per month; and (2) for the delivery to plaintiff of 12,000 shares of "Free Registered" stock of defendant Bartell Broadcasting Corporation, which stock was payable in three installments of 4,000 shares each in the months of January 1962, 1963, and 1964; and (3) the payment of plaintiff's traveling and living expenses in connection with the services to the employer; and (4) that the defendant Bartell Broadcasting Corporation would provide the plaintiff with a private office and proper office facilities; and (5) that the agreement would be binding on any successor corporation or any corporation with which defendant Bartell Broadcasting would merge.

This written contract was signed by the plaintiff and by Gerald A. Bartell in his capacity as the president of Bartell Broadcasting Corporation. It is further claimed that on or about May 1961, this contract was amended to increase plaintiff's monthly compensation from $1,933 to $2,400. It is further contended that the plaintiff was not paid his monthly compensation commencing with the month of November 1961; that the defendant Bartell Broadcasting Corporation failed to deliver 4,000 shares of stock allegedly due in January 1962; and that in July 1962, the defendant Bartell Broadcasting Corporation denied the validity of plaintiff's employment contract. . . .

The court will now turn its consideration to the first cause of action set forth in the complaint.

A corporation can only act through its directors, officers, and employees. They are the conduit by and through which the corporation is given being and from which its power to act and reason springs. Therefore in every action in which a person sues a corporation on a contract executed on behalf of the corporation by one of its officers, one of the issues to be determined is whether the officer had the express, implied, or apparent authority to execute the contract in question.

The authority of an officer to act on behalf of a corporation may be express, implied, or apparent. There has been no proof offered in this case indicating that Gerald A. Bartell, as president of the defendant Bartell Broadcasting Corporation, had express authority to enter into the agreement, dated March 16, 1961, which is the subject of the first cause of action.

Did Gerald A. Bartell then have either implied or apparent authority to execute the contract?

Implied authority is a species of actual authority, which gives an officer the power to do the necessary acts within the scope of his usual duties. Generally the president of a corporation has the implied authority to hire and fire corporate employees and to fix their compensation. However, the president of a corporation does not have the implied power to execute "unusual or extraordinary" contracts of employment. . . .

The agreement of March 16, 1961 not only provides for the payment of a substantial monthly compensation, but also requires the delivery of 12,000 shares of "free registered" stock of the defendant Bartell Broadcasting Corporation. While the payment of the monthly compensation would not make the contract of March 16, 1961 "unusual or extraordinary," the Court is of the opinion that the inclusion in the contract of the provision requiring the delivery to plaintiff of 12,000 shares of "free registered" stock does bring the agreement within the category of being an "unusual and extraordinary" contract.

With the varied and broad business experience acquired by the plaintiff in his wide business association as evidenced by his career resumé furnished to the defendants . . . and by plaintiff's own testimony, it can be truly said that he not only was presumed to have knowledge of the statutory provisions of the law pertaining to corporations, but that he apparently also had actual knowledge of such laws. It is reasonable to infer that the plaintiff was aware, or at the least had reason to be aware, that the authority for the issuance of corporate stock rests solely within the powers of the Board of Directors of the corporation, and that in the absence of express authority, the president of a corporation does not have the implied or apparent authority to enter into an employment contract which provides for the issuance of corporate stock as compensation.

The Court concludes, after a careful analysis of the evidence and the application of the law reviewed herein, that the plaintiff has not made out a prima facie case of express, implied, or apparent authority of the president of the defendant Bartell Broadcasting Corporation to execute the contract of employment.

Accordingly, the motion by the defendants to dismiss the complaint is granted.

Questions and Case Problems

1. The purpose clause of *Z* Corporation stated that it was organized to operate a sporting goods store. The directors authorized the corporate purchase of an apartment. *S*, a shareholder of *Z* Corporation, brought an action against the corporation, claiming that it was about to perform an *ultra vires* act. The directors claim they have the statutory power "to purchase real property wherever situated." Is the shareholder correct?

2. *X* Co., Inc. was a life insurance agency. *X* Co. purchased a carwash and began its operation. *X* Co. had 10 shareholders who knew of the car wash purchase and did not object although *X* Co. never amended its articles of incorporation. *X* Co. purchased various shop products from *S* on open account and owed it $5,000. When sued by *S*, *X* Co. defended on the ground that, as a life insurance agency, the entire carwash business was *ultra vires,* and hence it is not liable under any contract with *S*. Decide.

3. The plaintiff is a member in good standing of the defendant nonstock Connecticut corporation. Each of the individual defendants is a director of the corporation and together the individual defendants constitute the entire board of directors. The certificate of incorporation sets forth that the sole purpose of the corporation is to provide facilities for the serving of luncheon or other meals to members. Neither the certificate of incorporation nor the bylaws of the corporation contain any qualifications for membership, nor does either contain any restrictions on the guests members may bring to the club. The club is one of the principal luncheon clubs for business and professional people in the city, and is a gathering place where a great many of the civic, business, and professional affairs of the community are discussed in an atmosphere of social intercourse.

The plaintiff sought to bring a female to lunch with him, and both he and his guest were refused seating at the luncheon facility. Plaintiff wrote two times to the president of the corporation to protest this action, but he received no reply to either letter. On three different occasions plaintiff submitted applications for membership on behalf of a different female, and only on the third of those occasions did the board process the application, which was then rejected. Plaintiff's complaint is that the corporation's board of directors has refused to admit the plaintiff's proposed candidate as a member solely because she is a female, and likewise, that the board has refused to allow plaintiff to bring female guests to the corporation's facility. The plaintiff claims that the corporation and its directors have acted *ultra vires* in that they have exceeded the powers conferred upon them by the certificate of incorporation, the bylaws, and the state statutes regulating corporate powers and in so doing they have breached the plaintiff's rights as a member of the corporation. Decide. [*Cross v. The Midtown Club, Inc., et al.,* 365 A.2d 1227 (Conn. 1976).]

4. Legal Aid Services, Inc., plaintiff, brought an action against American Legal Aid, Inc., defendant, to enjoin it from using the term "Legal Aid" in defendant's business transactions on the grounds that it was deceptively similar to plaintiff's name. Legal Aid Services was organized in 1966 as a Wyoming nonprofit corporation for the purpose of rendering free legal services to persons of low income. The Natrona County Bar Association and members contribute through the plaintiff approximately 700 hours annually in free legal service to the poor. Plaintiff corporation was funded by a federal grant through the Office of Economic Opportunity. American Legal Aid was incorporated in 1970. It sold memberships to the general public for reimbursement of attorney's fees incurred in specified areas according to a schedule. There was considerable evidence that many people were confused about the two corporations. Defendant claims that it has the express statutory power to have its own corporate name. Decide. [*American Legal Aid, Inc. v. Legal Aid Services, Inc.,* 503 P.2d 1201 (Wyo. 1972).]
5. The president of a corporation was very friendly with the deceased vice president's family. Without approval of the corporate board of directors, he paid $5,000 per month to the family as a corporate benefit. When the shareholders discovered this, they sued the president for the corporate loss. Did the president have authority to make this charitable contribution?
6. Marsili and other shareholders, plaintiffs, brought a derivative action against Pacific Gas & Electric Co., defendant, and allege that a contribution to Citizens for San Francisco was *ultra vires* because neither defendant's articles of incorporation nor the state law permits a corporation to make political donations. The Citizens group was an association organized to defeat a local ballot proposition that would prohibit the construction of buildings exceeding 72 feet unless approved in advance by the voters. Did the board of directors have authority to make the contribution? [*Marsili v. Pacific Gas & Electric Co.,* 124 Cal.Rptr. 313 (Cal. 1975).]

7. A contract was made on December 1, 1975, between plaintiff American Heritage Investment Corp. (American) and defendant Nathan Hale Investment Corp. (Hale Investment). The latter agreed to transfer to American its shares in Nathan Hale Life Insurance Co. (Hale Life) in exchange for which American agreed to pay Hale Investment $750,000 or transfer to Hale Investment 500,000 of Hale Investment's own shares or make payment by both shares and cash with the shares valued at $1.50 each. On May 24, 1977, plaintiff filed suit seeking specific performance of the contract. Defendant Hale Investment answered the complaint setting forth as an affirmative defense the provisions of the Illinois Business Corporation Act, which prohibits a corporation from purchasing its own shares. Hale Investment counterclaimed, seeking a declaration that the contract was illegal to the extent that it required a transfer to it of its own shares. Plaintiff American replied that Hale Investment's defense was a plea of *ultra vires,* which could not be raised by the corporation. The Illinois Business Corporation Act provided in part that "No act of a corporation and no conveyance or transfer of real or personal property to or by a corporation shall be invalid by reason of the fact that the corporation was without capacity or power to do such act or to make or receive such conveyance or transfer." That section permits assertion of the corporation's lack of power only in certain types of proceedings brought (1) by shareholders against the corporation; (2) by the corporation against its officers; or (3) by the State against the corporation. May Hale Investment raise the defense of *ultra vires?* [*American Heritage Inv. Corp. v. Ill. Nat'l Bank of Springfield, et al.,* 68 Ill.App.3d 762 (Ill. 1979).]
8. National Organization for Women, Essex County Chapter, plaintiff, brought this action against Little League Baseball, Inc., to allow girls aged 8 to 12 to participate in local Little League baseball teams. Plaintiff claims that Congressional Charter of Little League Baseball, Inc., with a purpose clause "to promote, develop, supervise and voluntarily assist in all lawful ways to interest boys who will participate in Little League baseball" violates the New Jersey statutory policy of sex discrimination in places of public accommodation. Decide. [*Nat'l Org. for Women, Essex County Chapter v. Little League Baseball, Inc.,* 318 A.2d 33 (N.J. 1974).]
9. Alfalfa Electric Co-op, Inc., plaintiff, brought this action against First National Bank & Trust Co. of Oklahoma City, defendant, to determine if a loan granted by the bank to plaintiff was unlawful. Alfalfa claims that its board of directors had no authority to encumber a portion of its assets by pledging them as collateral for loans to a nonprofit development corporation created by the plaintiff. Alfalfa seeks a declaratory judgment to determine whether the loan was *ultra vires* and, if so, it requests return of the encumbered assets from defendant, First National Bank. Is pledging corporate assets as collateral for a corporate loan within the powers of the corporation? [*Alfalfa Electric Co-op, Inc. v. First Nat'l Bank & Trust Co. of Oklahoma City,* 525 P.2d 644 (Okla. 1974).]
10. In the case of *Goldenberg v. Bartell Broadcasting Corp.,* excerpted at the beginning of this section, the court held that the corporation had acted *ultra vires.* Discuss the court's holding and explain how the court reached this conclusion.

CHAPTER 45

CORPORATE STOCK AND SHAREHOLDERS

After you have read this chapter, you should be able to:

1. Define a share of stock.
2. List and explain the rights of a shareholder.
3. Distinguish the two basic kinds of stock.
4. Explain cumulative voting by shareholders.
5. Explain voting by proxy.
6. Define and explain a voting trust.
7. Define a dividend and explain a surplus for its payment.
8. Distinguish a certificated security from an uncertificated security and explain the transferring of each.
9. Explain the procedures for restricting the transfer of stock.
10. Explain a shareholders' derivative suit.
11. Give examples when a shareholder may be held personally liable to corporate creditors.
12. Explain the function of the state and federal regulation of stock issuance.
13. Define a wasting asset corporation.
14. Explain the purpose and function of the Foreign Corrupt Practices Act.
15. Explain the purpose of the Securities Act of 1933.
16. List and explain the statutory exemptions to the registration process required under the Securities Act of 1933.
17. Explain the purpose of the Securities Exchange Act of 1934.
18. Explain what is meant by an insider transaction.

BUSINESS DECISIONS and the LAW

A shareholder's remedy, known as a direct suit, is a claim for relief in favor of the investors. Two Wang shareholders have filed such class action suits in federal court, contending that the computer maker falsified information to inflate the price of its stock. The investors, claiming reliance on information supplied by Wang, contend that they would not have purchased its stock for as high as $10 per share if they had "been aware of the materially false and misleading nature of Wang's public statements." The shareholders further maintain that Wang's 1988 annual report portrayed a company that was turning around when, in fact, its position worsened.

The lawsuits claim that founder An Wang and his son, Frederick A. Wang, "knowingly or recklessly omitted material facts, misrepresented material facts to the investing public. . .including. . .the failure to disclose the extent and severity of the company's financial problems. . .and [that it] had the products and the management to achieve sustained profitability and growth."

If the court agrees with the investors, they will stand to make out handsomely for their troubles. If their suits do not succeed, however, they might have to sit back and root for Wang's recovery in order to just break even on their investment.

Source: Mary Sit, *"Investors Sue Wang for Misrepresentation," Boston Globe*, September 9, 1989 (Reprinted courtesy of The Boston Globe).

Introduction

We have learned that the corporation is a legal entity separate and distinct from its shareholders. As a result, shareholders are not liable for obligations of the corporation; the obligations are not obligations of the shareholders. The corporate stock is owned by the shareholders and, therefore, it becomes important to discuss what is meant by corporate stock and to understand the rights of the shareholders.

Corporate Stock

► Nature

share of stock
A unit of interest in a corporation

When you purchase shares of stock in a corporation, a stock certificate similar to that illustrated in Figures 45.1(a) and (b), is generally issued as evidence of your fractional ownership in the business.[1] "**Share** means the units into which the proprietary interests

FIGURE 45.1(a) **Example of a Stock Certificate (Front)**

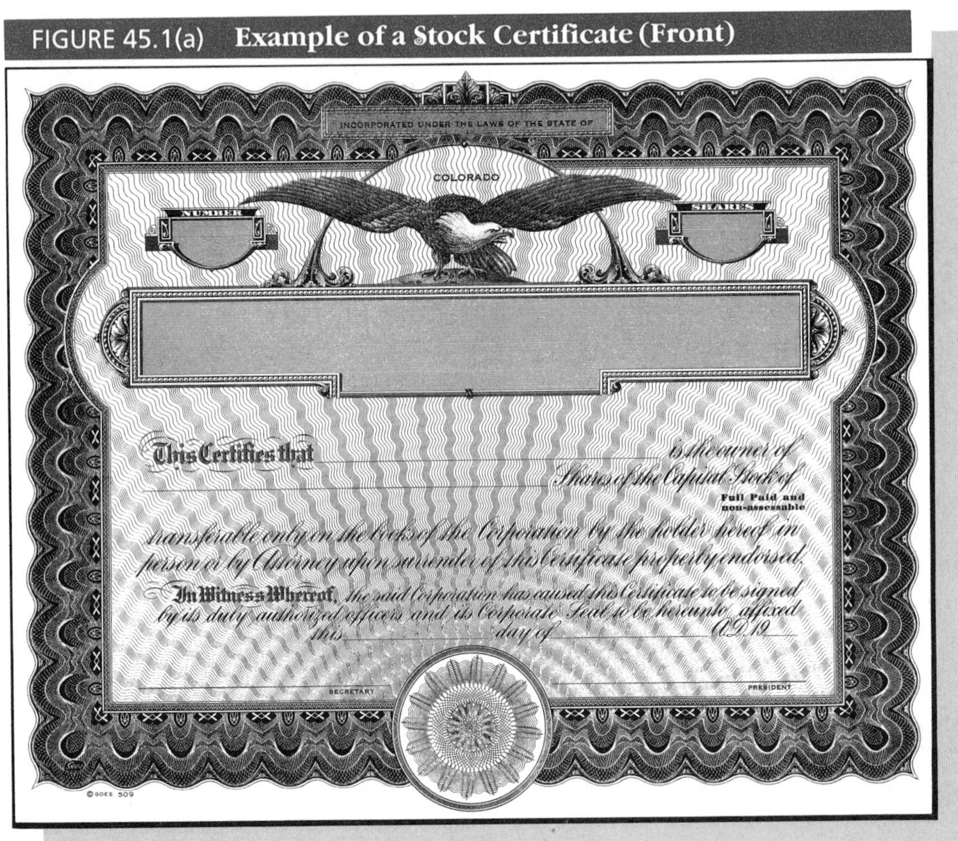

INCORPORATED UNDER THE LAWS OF THE STATE OF
COLORADO
NUMBER
SHARES
This Certifies that is the owner of Shares of the Capital Stock of
Full Paid and non-assessable
transferable only on the books of the Corporation by the holder hereof in person or by Attorney upon surrender of this Certificate properly endorsed.
In Witness Whereof, the said Corporation has caused this Certificate to be signed by its duly authorized officers and its Corporate Seal to be hereunto affixed this day of A.D. 19
SECRETARY
PRESIDENT
©GOES 509

[1]Revised art. 8 of the UCC (1977) covers a registered security interest not represented by a written instrument called an "uncertificated security." See pp. 935–936 for further discussion.

in a corporation are divided."[2] As an owner, you have numerous rights, depending on the kind of stock purchased. Generally, a **shareholder** (stockholder) has: (1) the right to share in the profits of the corporation by way of a dividend distribution; (2) the right to share in the surplus upon dissolution; (3) the right to vote at shareholders' meetings; and (4) the right to transfer his or her stock. However, because the corporation owns the assets in its own name, as a shareholder you do not have any interest in *specific* corporate property. A corporation's ability to raise substantial capital by dividing its ownership into shares of stock that may be sold to the general public is part of the foundation of our free enterprise system.

shareholder (stockholder)
The owner of a unit of interest in a corporation

► Purchase of Stock

While persons may purchase stock from shareholders, they may also subscribe to purchase stock from a corporation either to be formed or already in existence. The purchaser who signs a "preincorporation" subscription agreement, usually prepared by the promoter, is making an offer to purchase shares from the corporation when it comes

FIGURE 45.1(b) Example of a Stock Certificate (Back)

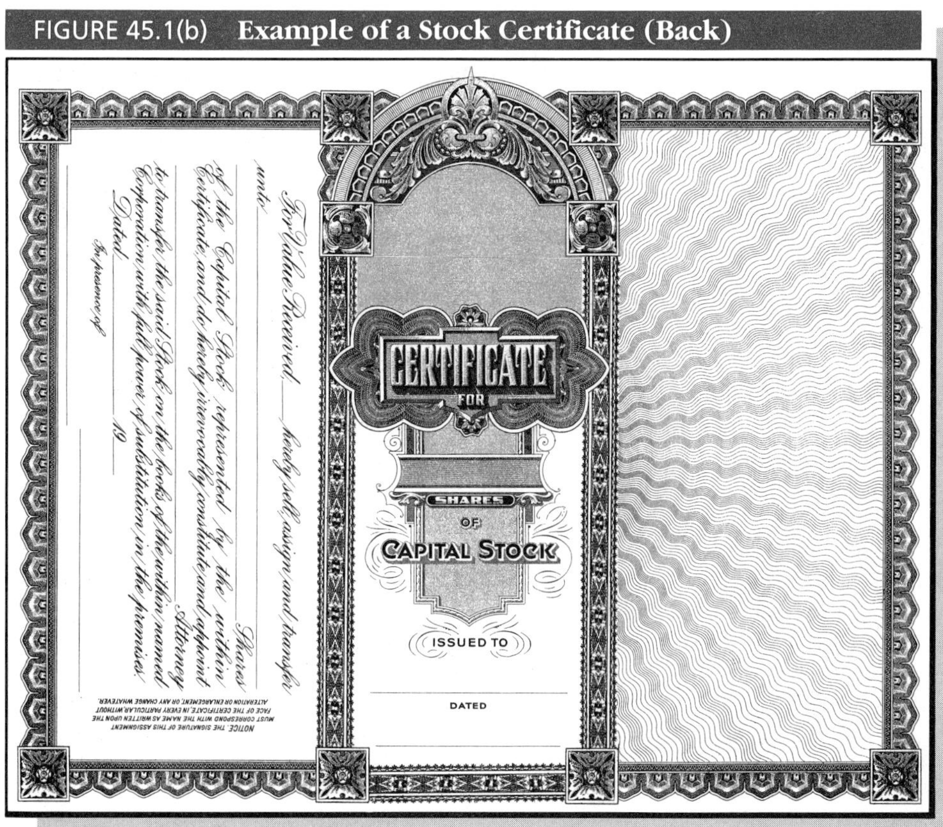

[2]RMBCA, sec. 1.40(22).

into existence. Under Section 6.20(a) of the RMBCA, the offer is irrevocable for six months unless otherwise provided in the subscription agreement. On incorporation, the purchaser immediately becomes a shareholder for the subscribed number of shares. The purchaser who signs a "postincorporation" subscription agreement, usually prepared by the existing corporation, thereby accepts the corporation's offer to sell to the purchaser the specified number of shares.

► Classes of Stock

The articles of incorporation require the incorporators to state the initial capitalization of the corporation—that is, the number of shares and the kind of stock the corporation will have the authority to issue. A selection of the kinds of stock will depend upon the nature of the business. The capitalization may subsequently be changed by amending the articles of incorporation with the stockholders' approval.

common stock
Corporate stock with the ordinary rights of participation in a corporation

Common Stock The two basic kinds of stock are *common* and *preferred*. **Common stock** has the ordinary rights of participation in a corporation, such as the right to vote at shareholders' meetings, share in the dividends, and share in the distribution of corporate assets on dissolution.

Par value stock is stock having a certain minimum dollar price when issued—for example, $1 par value means that each share is to be sold by the corporation at not less than $1 as determined by the board of directors, payable by the purchaser to the corporation. *No-par value stock* is stock issued for any price as determined by the board of directors, in the absence of charter provision to the contrary.

preferred stock
Corporate stock with a preference over the common stock

dividend
A portion of corporate net profits or surplus set aside for distribution to the shareholders

Preferred Stock A holder of **preferred stock** is given preferential rights over a holder of common stock. These rights make the stock more attractive to an investor. Generally, they give preference in the payment of **dividends** and in the distribution of assets upon dissolution. Although these rights do not have a promise of receiving a dividend, dividends will be paid to preferred shareholders before the holders of common stock. The articles of incorporation generally deny holders of preferred stock the right to vote.

Cumulative preferred stock entitles the holder to a certain dividend distribution each year, which, if not paid, accumulates over the years until funds become available. When a dividend is declared, it cannot be paid until all back accumulations are paid first. *Noncumulative preferred stock* does not have such an accumulation, but it does have priority over dividends declared on common stock. *Participating preferred stock* entitles the holder to participate with the holders of common stock in any dividend distribution remaining after dividends are first paid on the preferred stock. *Nonparticipating preferred stock* is not entitled to participate in the surplus that is distributed to the holders of common stock. Even preferred shareholders have no right to demand a dividend when the directors honestly decide not to declare one.

The Rights of Shareholders

A shareholder has a contractual relationship with the corporation whereby it agrees to give the shareholder certain rights for the consideration (selling price) of the stock. "Consideration for shares may consist of cash, promissory notes, services performed, contracts for services to be performed or any other tangible or intangible property. If shares are issued for other than cash, the board of directors shall determine the value of the consideration received as of the time the shares are issued."[3] The following case illustrates the requirement that the price must be paid before issuance of corporate shares.

FACTS

Manhart and others filed this suit individually and as major stockholders against United Steel Industries, Inc., Hurt and Griffitts, alleging that the corporation had issued Hurt 5,000 shares of its stock in consideration of Hurt agreeing to perform CPA and bookkeeping services for the corporation for one year in the future, and had issued Griffitts 4,000 shares of its stock in consideration for the promised conveyance of a five-acre tract of land to the corporation, which land was never conveyed. The lower court entered judgment, declaring the stock issued to Hurt and Griffitts void. United Steel Industries appealed.

DECISION

Affirmed, judgment for Manhart. Article 12, section 6, Texas Constitution, Vernon's Ann. St. provides: "No corporation shall issue stock . . . except for money paid, labor done, or property actually received." The 5,000 shares were issued to Hurt before the CPA services were rendered and hence were illegally issued and void. The 4,000 shares issued to Griffitts were issued for a promise to convey land in the future and were also illegally issued and void. The board of directors does not have authority to issue shares contrary to state statutory law for services to be performed in the future (as in the case of Hurt) or for property not received (as in the case of Griffitts).

United Steel Industries, Inc. v. Manhart 405 S.W.2d 231 (Tex. 1966).

However, Section 6.21(c) of the RMBCA permits promises of future services to serve as consideration for the issuance of shares.

As evidence of the contractual relationship, the shareholder may receive a stock certificate (certificated security) duly executed by the corporate officers, generally the president and secretary.

The shares of a corporation shall be represented by certificates or shall be uncertificated shares. Under Section 6.25 of the RMBCA, at a minimum each certificate representing shares shall state upon the face thereof:

(1) the name of the issuing corporation and that it is organized under the law of this state;
(2) the name of the person to whom issued; and
(3) the number and class of shares and the designation of the series, if any, the certificate represents. . . .

> **(c)** If the issuing corporation is authorized to issue different classes of shares or different series within a class, the designations, relative rights, preferences and limitations applicable to each class and the variations in rights, preferences, and limitations determined for each series (and the board's authority to determine variations for future series) must be summarized on the front or back of each certificate. Alternatively, each certificate may state conspicuously on its front or back that the corporation will furnish the shareholder on request and without charge a complete written explanation of this information.

[3] RMBCA, sec. 6.21(c).

(d) Each share certificate (1) must be signed (either manually or in facsimile) by two officers designated in the bylaws or by the board of directors and (2) may bear the corporate seal or its facsimile.

(e) If the person who signed (either manually or in facsimile) a share certificate no longer holds office when the certificate is issued, the certificate is nevertheless valid.

As an owner of the stock, the shareholder may generally sell it at any price, transfer the shareholder's title to another as a gift, or pledge it as security for a loan.

Shareholders usually have the following rights: (1) the right to vote at shareholders' meetings; (2) the right to receive a dividend; (3) the right to inspect the corporate books; (4) pre-emptive rights; (5) the right to transfer the stock; (6) the right to sue the corporation or third parties for improper action; and (7) the right to share in the profits upon dissolution.

► Right to Vote

Shareholders have the right to vote for the directors and on other appropriate matters at their annual meeting or at any duly called special stockholders' meeting. The right to vote may be denied to any class of stock in the articles of incorporation, in which event a stockholder has *nonvoting shares*. Changes in the articles of incorporation require directors' and stockholders' approval and the amended articles to be filed at the office of the secretary of state.[4] For example, a corporate name change or recapitalization generally requires approval by a majority of the stockholders. Treasury shares—i.e., its own shares reacquired by the corporation—do not have any voting rights. The corporation may reacquire its shares in various ways, such as by buying them.

Who May Vote The corporation maintains a stock transfer book that records the shareholders who are entitled to receive notice of all meetings. Generally only those recorded shareholders may vote.[5]

A shareholder may desire to **pledge** the stock to obtain a loan. In that event the shareholder retains the right to vote unless the shares are *transferred* to the pledgee.[6] For example, if a bank required you to pledge your IBM stock as security for a $5,000 loan, you would maintain voting rights during the term of the loan. If you defaulted and transferred the shares to the bank, it would have voting rights.

Nonvoting shareholders[7] may have the statutory right to vote as a class upon certain amendments to the articles of incorporation. Examples of such amendments are (1) an increase or decrease of the aggregate number of authorized shares of the nonvoting stock; (2) an increase in the number of authorized shares having superior rights to the nonvoting stock; and (3) a cancellation of accrued dividends of the nonvoting stock that have not been declared.

pledge

The possessory security interest in bailed goods acquired by the bailee when there is a **bailment** for the purpose of security

bailment

A delivery of goods by a bailor to a bailee, which are to be returned to the bailor or as the bailor directs, in accordance with the bailment agreement

---

[4]See RMBCA, sec. 10.01, 10.02, and 10.03 for procedures to amend articles of incorporation.

[5]UCC 8–207(1).

[6]UCC 8–207.

[7]The official comments to sec. 7.21 of the RMBCA state the articles of incorporation may provide that some classes of shares are nonvoting.

Number of Votes Under the common law, a shareholder was entitled to only one vote regardless of the number of shares the shareholder owned. Today by statute a stockholder may vote as many shares of voting stock as he or she owns.

State statutes generally provide for **cumulative voting** by shareholders in the election of directors. The articles of incorporation will grant this right that entitles a shareholder to as many votes as he or she has shares of voting stock multiplied by the number of directors to be elected. For example, if the corporate board consists of 10 directors and you have 100 shares of voting stock, you may have 1,000 votes that may be cast for any one director or in any other manner. The minority shareholders are thereby given an indirect voice in the management of the corporation that could otherwise be denied to them by 51 percent of the voting shareholders.

cumulative voting
A method of voting whereby a shareholder has as many votes as he or she has shares of voting stock multiplied by the number of directors to be elected

Voting by Proxy Many shareholders of large corporations do not desire to personally attend the annual shareholders' meeting and other special meetings but wish to exercise their voting right. The shareholder may, by written **proxy**, authorize another to vote for him or her.[8]

proxy
A shareholder's written authorization to another person to vote his or her shares at a corporate meeting; also the person with such authority

Minority shareholders of large corporations occasionally engage in a proxy fight in an attempt to vote as a block for a particular issue or to elect directors. Proxy solicitation is now regulated by the Securities and Exchange Commission, which requires that sufficient information be provided shareholders regarding the nature of the proxy fight.[9] In the following case notice the court's reasoning based on the ethical and social significance of the stockholder's proposal:

FACTS

Peter C. Lovenheim, owner of 200 shares of Iroquois Brands, Ltd. (IBL), seeks to prevent IBL from excluding his proposed resolution from the proxy materials prepared for a shareholders' meeting. Lovenheim's proposal relates to procedures used to forcefeed geese, and calls upon IBL to research the problem and report to the shareholders its findings. Lovenheim contends that the production methods amount to cruelty to animals and brought suit under Section 14(a) of the Securities Exchange Act of 1934 and the Securities Exchange Commission Rule 14a-8. IBL, relying on an exception to the general rule of proposal inclusion, contends that its position is legally justified. IBL argued that, as a securities issuer, it may omit such shareholder proposals since the proposal relates to operations accounting for less than 5 percent of total assets, net earnings, and gross sales. Indeed, IBL lost money the year before on its paté sales. Lovenheim contends that his proposal is includable notwithstanding its failure to reach the 5 percent threshold.

DECISION

The likelihood of Lovenheim prevailing in this litigation turns primarily on the applicability to his proposal of the exception to the shareholder proposal rule contained in Rule 14a-8(c)(5).

None of the company's net earnings and less than .05 percent of its assets are implicated by plaintiff's proposal.

Lovenheim does not contest that his proposed resolution relates to a matter of little economic significance to Iroquois/Delaware. Nevertheless he contends that the Rule 14a-8(c)(5) exception is not applicable. . . .

Iroquois/Delaware challenges plaintiff's view that ethical and social proposals cannot be excluded even if they do not meet the economic or five percent test. Instead

[8]RMBCA, sec. 7.22(c) states no proxy shall be valid after eleven months from the date of its execution unless otherwise provided in the proxy.

[9]Securities Exchange Act of 1934, sec. 14(a).

Iroquois/Delaware views the exception solely in economic terms as permitting omission of any proposals relating to a de minimis share of assets and profits. Iroquois/Delaware asserts that since corporations are economic entities, only an economic test is appropriate.

The court cannot ignore the history of the rule which reveals no decision by the Commission to limit the determination to the economic criteria relied on by Iroquois/Delaware. The court therefore holds that in light of the ethical and social significance of plaintiff's proposal and the fact that it implicates significant levels of sales, plaintiff has shown a likelihood of prevailing on the merits.

Lovenheim v. Iroquois Brands, Ltd. 618 F. Supp. 554 (D.D.C. 1985).

voting trust
A trust created by an agreement between the shareholders to transfer legal title to their voting stock to a party (trustee) who is authorized to vote the stock as a unit

fiduciary
A person with a duty to act primarily for the benefit of another

Voting Trust The shareholders may agree to pool their voting stock in an attempt to control the management of the corporation. Shareholders' voting agreements were valid under the common law. A **voting trust** is a trust created by an agreement among the shareholders to transfer legal title to their voting stock to a party serving as a trustee who is authorized by the trust to vote the stock as a unit.[10] The trustee is a **fiduciary** with implied duties owed to the shareholders to protect their interest and with limited powers to act in accordance with the voting trust agreement.

In the following case a voting trust agreement was held to be unenforceable because it was contrary to the state's voting trust statute.

FACTS

Plaintiffs, individually and as trustees, are the owners of 76 percent of the outstanding stock of the defendant Oceanic Exploration Company (Oceanic). On February 10, 1976, plaintiffs entered into a written agreement whereby 50% of the company's stock was placed into a "voting trust agreement" which gave their voting rights in the stock to others and an option in favor of the corporation which gave it the right for a period of five years to purchase "all or any part" of plaintiffs' stock. Plaintiffs attempted to have the "voting trust agreement and purchase option agreement" declared void so as to regain control of the corporation because it imposed an illegal restraint on their right to alienate their stock interests. The court found for the defendant and plaintiffs appealed.

DECISION

Reversed, judgment for plaintiffs. A voting trust as commonly understood is a device whereby two or more persons owning stock with voting powers, divorce the voting rights thereof from the ownership, retaining the ownership in themselves and transferring the voting rights to trustees in whom the voting rights of all the depositors in the trust are pooled.

While we do not suggest that the mere fact that the corporation is a party removes a trust from the statute, we do find that the final contract in issue here including a stock purchase option agreement running from an already unified majority shareholder group to the corporation may be so foreign. The main purpose of a voting trust statute is "to avoid secret, uncontrolled combinations of stockholders formed to acquire control of the corporation to the possible detriment of non-participating shareholders." We are faced with a "voting trust agreement" which may not fit into the situation contemplated by the language of the statute, and may have little, if any, connection with the purpose for which the statute was enacted. We conclude the court erred in holding the contract in this case to be, as a matter of law, a voting trust.

Oceanic Exploration Co. v. Grynberg, et al., 428 A.2d 1 (Del. 1980).

[10]RMBCA, sec. 7.30(b). Under the Act, a voting trust agreement may not be for a period exceeding ten years.

▶ Dividends

If you were to invest in a corporation as a shareholder, you would expect a return on your investment by way of a **dividend** and an increase in the market value of the stock. A dividend is a portion of the corporate net profits or surplus set aside for distribution to the shareholders. It is within the discretion of the directors to declare a dividend, but it is not to be declared when the corporation is insolvent. Until a dividend is declared by the board of directors, the shareholders have no right to receive one. If the directors refuse to declare a dividend and have clearly abused their discretion by continuously voting against a "declaration," a court may require the payment of a dividend. This is illustrated by the following well-known case.

dividend

A portion of corporate net profits or surplus set aside for distribution to the shareholders

FACTS

Shareholders in the Ford Motor Company brought an action to compel the company's board of directors to declare a special dividend. The company had made substantial profits over the years, and a regular quarterly dividend of 5 percent per month on its capital stock had been paid since 1911, with additional special dividends of from $1 million to $10 million per year from 1911 to 1915. In 1916 the board of directors decided to continue the regular 5 percent per month dividend but no longer to make any additional special dividends. At that time the company's surplus was $112 million, its yearly profits $60 million, its liabilities including capital stock less than $20 million, and its cash on hand $54 million. The company had planned improvements costing $24 million. Judgment was for the shareholders and the company appealed.

DECISION

Affirmed in part for shareholders and reversed in part for Ford Motor Company. Mr. Ford's testimony creates the impression that he thinks the Ford Motor Company has made too much money, has had too large profits, and that, although large profits might still be earned, a sharing of them with the public by reducing the price of the output of the company ought to be undertaken.

A business corporation is organized and carried on primarily for the benefit of its stockholders. The powers of the directors are to be exercised in the choice of means to attain that end and do not extend to a change in the end itself, to the reduction of profits or to the nondistribution of profits among stockholders in order to devote them to other purposes. It is not within the lawful powers of a board of directors to shape and conduct the affairs of a corporation for the merely incidental benefit of shareholders and for the primary purpose of benefiting others. There was a large daily, weekly, monthly receipt of cash. The output was practically continuous and was continuously, and within a few days, turned into cash. Moreover, the contemplated expenditures were not to be immediately made. It would appear that, accepting and approving the plan of the directors, it was their duty to distribute on or near the 1st of August 1916 a very large sum of money to stockholders.

Dodge v. Ford Motor Co., 170 N.W. 668 (Mich. 1919).

However, the courts are hesitant to substitute their judgment for the dividend policy of the directors who were elected by the shareholders to use their discretion in managing the corporation. This is illustrated by the following case.

FACTS

Gay was a minority shareholder in Gay's Super Markets, Inc. He brought this suit against the corporation and its directors, alleging that their refusal to declare a dividend was not done in good faith. Gay's Super Markets claimed that, although it had $125,000 in cash, the directors felt that due to the expansion commitments of the company, the funds could not be considered available for dividends. Is this an abuse of the directors' discretion?

DECISION

No. Judgment for Gay's Super Markets, Inc. To justify judicial intervention it must be shown that the decision not to declare a dividend amounted to fraud, bad faith, or an abuse of discretion on the part of the corporate officials authorized to make the determination. If there are plausible business decisions supportive of the board of directors' judgment not to declare a dividend, a court will not interfere. It is not our function to referee every corporate squabble or disagreement.

Gay v. Gay's Super Markets, Inc., 343 A.2d 577 (Me. 1975).

Fund for Declaration of Dividends A dividend is declared when the board of directors votes to approve a resolution on a dividend and announces its distribution. There must be a "surplus" for the payment—that is, an amount of assets that exceeds the liabilities and the issued and outstanding shares.

The shareholders entitled to the dividend then become *general creditors* of the corporation and may enforce the debt if the corporation should become insolvent prior to distributing the dividends. Once the dividend has been declared, announced, and set aside, the fund is held in trust for the benefit of the shareholders. Corporate creditors cannot reach the assets in this fund. If the stock is transferred to a new owner *after* the dividend is declared but *before* the announced record date for payment, the transferee is generally entitled to receive the dividend.

As an exception to the rules discussed regarding the need for a surplus before the directors can declare a dividend, a *wasting asset corporation* may pay dividends out of current net profits. For instance, an off-coast oil drilling venture is a wasting asset corporation because it is organized to exhaust or use up the assets (oil) of the corporation, in contrast to an industrial corporation organized to manufacture computers on a continuing basis.

Effective Date of Dividend Distribution As the owner of stock, you generally have the right to sell it at any time. If the directors declare a dividend, the question arises as to whom it should be paid if the holder transferred the stock after the declaration date. For example, the board may declare a dividend today (*declaration date*) to be effective in one month (*effective date*) and payable to the shareholders of record in two months (*payment date*). The vote to declare a dividend is irrevocable and the registered holder on the effective date will be sent the dividend on the payment date. If the corporation is not aware that a transfer took place and paid the registered holder who sold the stock to a transferee, the corporation is protected and the transferee must sue the transferor, *not the corporation*, for the money received.[11]

► Right to Inspect Corporate Books

As a shareholder in a corporation, you are an owner of a fractional interest. In that capacity you are entitled to exercise certain ownership rights over the stock, such as selling, pledging, or giving it to another, as well as the right to inspect the property held by the corporation. Other owners have the same rights and hence their property interests must also be protected. The common law, therefore, granted to a shareholder the right to inspect the corporate books and records at reasonable times for a proper purpose. It is the "proper purpose" aspect of this right that frequently causes a problem. Review of the books as a "fishing expedition" is not permitted. For example, may a public interest

[11]UCC 8–207.

group, such as the environmentalists, purchase a block of stock (100 shares) in a corporation and demand the right to review the minute book of the board of directors and shareholders? Generally no, because a shareholder does not demonstrate a "proper purpose" by disapproving of a corporate activity such as a manufacturing company causing a high rate of pollution. The federal Environmental Protection Agency has authority to regulate air standards; it would be the proper party to investigate the alleged illegal act.[12]

If the corporation improperly refuses an inspection of the records, the shareholder may seek court action. In the following case the court refused to require a corporation to permit inspection by a shareholder for an improper purpose.

FACTS

Pillsbury bought several shares of Honeywell, Inc., stock during the Vietnam War to give himself a voice in Honeywell's affairs so that he could persuade the company to cease munitions productions. He made formal demands that Honeywell permit him access to its shareholder ledger and all corporate records dealing with weapons manufacture. Honeywell rejected the demands and argued that a "proper purpose" for inspection must be one that involves an economic concern.

DECISION

Judgment for Honeywell. The right to inspect is based on the shareholder's economic concern. The shareholder must have a proper purpose to examine the corporate books. Pillsbury would have the right to inspect the records only if he were concerned with the long- or short-term effect of Honeywell's production of munitions. Pillsbury was not here interested even in Honeywell's long-term well-being or in the enhancement of the value of his shares. His sole purpose was to persuade the company to adopt his social and political concerns regardless of any economic benefit to himself or Honeywell.

State ex rel. Pillsbury v. Honeywell, Inc., 191 N.W.2d 406 (Minn. 1971).

In the following case plaintiff was allowed to see a breakdown list of stockholders for the purpose of soliciting their proxies.

FACTS

Hatleigh Corporation is the record holder of 1,000 shares of common stock of Lane Bryant, Inc. On November 5, 1980, Hatleigh requested Lane Bryant to provide Hatleigh with a stockholder list of Lane Bryant. It is conceded by Lane Bryant that Hatleigh's demand for the stated purpose of the solicitation of stockholder proxies is a proper purpose for the statute. Lane Bryant contends, however, that the demand was not bona fide because Hatleigh had not formed an intention to actually solicit proxies but was seeking the list of stockholders for a different purpose. A number of shares of Lane Bryant are listed on the books of the corporation as being held by "CEDE & CO." This denotes a recognized system whereby various brokerage firms hold stock that is actually owned by their customers in the name of CEDE & CO. or in the name of other similar firms organized to hold shares of stock for others. Hatleigh filed a demand with the court to inspect and copy a list of the stockholders of Lane Bryant.

[12]See pp. 767–791 for a discussion of administrative regulations.

DECISION

Judgment for Hatleigh Corporation. Hatleigh seeks this "breakdown" list as to CEDE in order that plaintiff too may get its proxy solicitation materials into the hands of the beneficial owners in ample time for the annual meeting. Such information should be made available to the plaintiff forthwith so that its list of stockholders for its proper purpose of soliciting their proxies is at least equivalent, in this aspect, with the list available to the corporation for the same purpose.

Hatleigh Corp. v. Lane Bryant, Inc., 428 A.2d 350 (Del. 1981).

Most states have statutory laws regulating the inspection right. Some give the shareholder the absolute right while others go beyond the "proper purpose" limitation of the common law. Section 1602 of the RMBCA grants the right only to shareholders of record to examine and copy at the shareholders' expense (1) excerpts from minutes of meetings of the board of directors and stockholders, (2) the accounting records of the corporation, and (3) if demand is made in good faith and with a proper purpose, a list of the corporate shareholders.

A shareholder may authorize an attorney or other agent to inspect the books on the shareholder's behalf.

In the following case the court held that stockholders could inspect corporate books only at reasonable times.

FACTS

Plaintiffs are minority shareholders in Schwartzman Packing Company, a closely held family corporation. They alleged that the majority shareholders of the company engaged in various willful acts of oppressive conduct toward the plaintiffs resulting in damages to the corporate entity and to themselves. The defendant corporation informed plaintiffs more than two months before trial that it would cooperate with plaintiffs and permit a reasonable inspection of corporate books and records. Plaintiffs delayed almost two months from the time this notice was given until the date they scheduled their examination to begin. After examination had begun, the corporation felt that the scope of examination being pursued by the plaintiffs was placing a severe burden upon the operations of the corporation because plaintiffs were sending teams of three to six accountants or bookkeepers to examine books and records of the corporation during normal business hours. Plaintiffs, appellants, contend that the trial court limited plaintiffs' request for inspection and review of the defendant's corporate records to such an extent that it constituted a violation of the law.

DECISION

Affirmed judgment for defendants. The right of a shareholder to examine books and records is not unlimited. Inspection must be made at "reasonable times." A trial court must of necessity have some discretion in determining when and in what manner the right of examination should be exercised. Under the facts in this case, it was not an abuse of discretion for the trial court to limit examination to regular business hours in addition to the 222 hours of examination which had previously been allowed.

Schwartzman, et al. v. Schwartzman Packing Co., 659 P.2d 888 (N.M. 1983).

► Financial Statements

An inspection of the corporate books may include the minutes of the directors' and stockholders' meetings, the stock transfer books, and the books of account. Due to their personal nature, we have seen most states require a "proper purpose" to inspect. There is generally no such limitation to the shareholders' right to receive financial statements showing the corporation's assets, liabilities, and operations.[13]

► Pre-emptive Rights

You will recall that the incorporators established the original *authorized* capitalization in the articles of incorporation filed with the secretary of state. The corporation then had the right to issue shares up to the authorized amount. If the corporation desires to exceed that initial authorization, it must amend the articles by the directors voting a resolution and having it approved by a majority of the voting shareholders. When the amended articles of incorporation are filed and approved by the state, new stock may be issued. A **pre-emptive right** is the right of the voting stockholders of record to purchase the new stock in proportion to their old stock interest before the new stock may be offered to the public. Hence a shareholder may maintain his or her relative voting power and dividend interest.

pre-emptive right
A shareholder's right to subscribe to a newly authorized issue of stock proportionate to his or her holdings in the corporation

Most states prohibit the pre-emptive right for an issuance of **treasury stock** or for an issuance to employees as a part of a stock purchase plan. The RMBCA is generally in accord with the modern trend of corporate law, which limits or abolishes the pre-emptive right.[14]

treasury stock
Corporate stock reacquired by the issuing corporation

The following early case shows how the common law viewed the nature of stock ownership to include pre-emptive rights.

FACTS

Stokes, a shareholder in defendant corporation, Continental Trust Co. of the City of New York, brought suit to compel Continental Trust to issue to him at par such a proportion of an increase made in its capital stock as the number of shares held by him before such increase bore to the number of all the shares originally issued. Continental Trust was a banking corporation organized in 1890 with a capital stock of $500,000 consisting of 5,000 shares of the par value of $100 each. Stokes was one of the original shareholders of the corporation. The directors of Continental Trust met and authorized a special stockholders' meeting for the purpose of voting on the increase of stock. The stockholders voted to increase the stock, and Stokes demanded from Continental Trust the right to subscribe for his proportionate increase of the new stock and offered to pay immediately for the same.

DECISION

Judgment for Stokes. The question presented for decision is whether, according to the facts found, Stokes had a legal right to subscribe for and take the same number of shares of the new stock that he held of the old.

The power of the individual stockholder to vote in proportion to the number of his stocks is vital and cannot be cut off or curtailed by the action of all the other stockholders even with the cooperation of the directors and officers.

Stokes v. Continental Trust Co. of the City of New York, 78 N.E. 1090 (N.Y. 1906).

► Transfer of Shares

The rights and duties of corporations and stockholders to transfer stock is governed by Article 8 of the Uniform Commercial Code. Article 8 was revised in 1977 to include a security investment not represented by a written certificate defined as an "uncertificated

[13]RMBCA, sec. 16.02.

[14]RMBCA, sec. 6.30.

security."[15] The issuance of an "uncertificated security" is registered upon the security transfer book maintained by the corporation. An *initial transaction statement* is then sent to the shareholder. The Official Comment to the UCC Section 8–101 states: "This Article does not purport to determine whether a particular issue of securities should be represented by certificates, in whole or in part. That determination is left to the parties involved, subject to federal and state law."

Transfer of Uncertificated Securities An uncertificated security is transferred by the transferor (seller) instructing the corporation to issue a transaction statement to the new owner (or pledgee) and register the transaction on its transfer ledger. Within two business days after the registration of a transferred uncertificated security, the corporation must send the new registered owner (or registered pledgee) and the transferor a transaction statement. The transaction statement serves as registration notice to the new owner and a reduction of interest notice to the transferor-seller.

A periodic statement must be sent at least annually to the registered owners describing the issuance of which the uncertificated security is a part.[16]

Transfer of Certificated Securities To effect a proper transfer of a certificated security (stock certificate), the transferor-seller must deliver the certificate and if necessary indorse it over to the purchaser. If the transfer is of a temporary nature (e.g., a pledge of the stock as security for a bank loan), the owner may make the assignment on a separate instrument that requires delivery of both the separate document pledging the stock and the stock certificate.[17]

bona fide purchaser
In corporations, a purchaser for value in good faith and without notice of any adverse claim, and who is either a holder of a certificated security or registered on the corporate books as the owner

Bona Fide Purchaser Article 8 of the UCC deals with "investment securities" that include stock and bonds. These securities may be transferred to a **bona fide purchaser** who may acquire greater rights than the transferor-holder.[18]

> A bona fide purchaser is a purchaser for value in good faith and without notice of any adverse claims.[19]

This is a change from the common law of assignments that limited the transferee's rights in the stock to those of the transferor. Article 8 allows the bona fide purchaser to defeat a claim by the owner of the stock that could be asserted against the transferor; for example, if the stock was acquired by fraud, deceit, or without consideration by the transferor from the owner.

Example 1: *A* fraudulently induces *O*, the owner of a stock certificate for 100 shares of *X* corporation, to indorse and deliver the certificate to *A*. *O* can avoid the transaction and reacquire the certificate. However, if *A* sells and delivers the certificate to *B*, a bona fide purchaser, *B* acquires the title to the certificate and the shares represented thereby.

---

[15]UCC 8–102(1)(b).

[16]UCC 8–408.

[17]UCC 8–309.

[18]Although a security is a negotiable instrument, its transfer is not governed by Article 3 on Commercial Paper but rather by Article 8 of the UCC.

[19]UCC 8–302.

Example 2: *T* steals *O*'s certificate of stock and sells and delivers it to *Z*, an innocent purchaser for value. Since *O* never indorsed the certificate, nobody can later become a **holder**. Therefore no later person can become a bona fide purchaser. However, if *O* indorses it (signs *O*'s name) making it a bearer certificate, and then *T* steals it and sells and delivers it to *Z*, *Z* will be a holder and become a bona fide purchaser with title to the certificate and the shares represented thereby.

holder
In corporations, the person in possession of a certificated security that flows to him or her either initially or by indorsement

Statute of Frauds If you orally contract to sell your stock, it would be unenforceable regardless of the selling price under UCC 8–319, a special statute of frauds provision. Under the Code, if the contract for sale of securities is in writing, it is enforceable. If it is oral, it is unenforceable unless proved in one of four ways. Reference should be made to Section 8–319 of the Code.

In the following case there was no contract for sale but, rather, an agency contract, and therefore the contract did not come under any statute of frauds and was enforceable even though oral.

FACTS

Reinhart was a stockholder who hired the defendant, Rauscher Pierce Securities Corp., to sell his stock. He orally instructed Rauscher Pierce to sell when its value decreased by more than 10 percent of the cost to Reinhart. Rauscher Pierce failed to sell, and Reinhart sued for damages. The defense was that there was no liability for an oral contract to sell stock. From a decision in favor of Rauscher Pierce, Reinhart appealed.

DECISION

Reversed, judgment for Reinhart. UCC Section 8–319 does not apply here because this is not a "sale of securities" but rather an agency relationship. Reinhart never said he wanted Rauscher Pierce to hold his stock for a year or more. He could terminate the agency within a year. Hence, the statute of frauds does not apply.

Reinhart v. Rauscher Pierce Securities Corp., 490 P.2d 240 (N.M. 1971).

Restrictions on Transfer The incorporators of a closely held corporation may decide to issue its stock to select shareholders. For instance, a family business may desire to keep control of its ownership and management. The articles of incorporation and the bylaws may state a restriction allowing the corporation or its shareholders the right to purchase the stock before it is offered to outsiders. The selling price may be established in accordance with a specified formula stated in the text of the restriction or it may be the current market price. Restrictions on the transfer of stock are generally valid if they are conspicuous and reasonable. Because a purchaser is generally not aware of restrictions in the articles of incorporation or bylaws, the stock certificate must conspicuously note the restriction, unless the buyer has actual knowledge of it, in order for it to be effective.

In order to be conspicuously noted, the Code requires it to be written so that a reasonable person ought to have noticed it, as a printing or heading in capitals or in larger or contrasting type or color.[20] The stock certificate need not state the terms of the

[20]UCC 1–201(10).

restriction, but the purchaser must have the right to read the full text that generally appears in the articles of incorporation or the bylaws.

If the security is uncertificated, the initial transaction statement sent to the registered owner must note the restriction.[21]

Shareholders' Remedies

As a shareholder, you own a fractional portion of the corporation with contractual rights. If the directors act wrongfully and deprive the shareholders of their rights, they may sue for breach of contract. For example, a shareholder may sue the directors for not being permitted to exercise any of his rights previously discussed, such as his right to a dividend when one should have been declared, to vote at meetings, to inspect the corporate books for a proper purpose, or to exercise his pre-emptive right. In any of these instances, more than one shareholder will be *individually* injured and any one, on behalf of the others, may bring a class or representative action against the corporation.

Shareholders' Derivative Suit As a shareholder, you may individually, or with other minority shareholders, bring an action on behalf of the corporation against the directors and officers on the basis of breach of their managerial fiduciary duties resulting in a depletion of corporate assets. You must procedurally first prove that, on proper demand, the corporation refused to bring suit against the officers and/or directors for mismanagement. This means you must first exhaust your internal corporate remedies. You do this by first requesting the board of directors to take proper action, unless it would be futile to do so (e.g., a majority of the board are involved in the wrong, or are prejudiced). If such a request is unsuccessful or futile, then you must request the shareholders at a corporate meeting to take proper action, unless it would be futile to do so (e.g., a majority are involved in the wrong, or a majority are biased). You may also bring an action on behalf of the corporation against an outside person if the corporation wrongfully refuses to do so. Such actions are called "derivative" actions. In both instances the right to sue and damages awarded belong to the corporation.

In the following long and well reasoned case the plaintiffs, stockholders of the defendant corporation, brought this individual class action rather than a stockholders' derivative suit. On appeal, the court reversed the certification of the suit as a class action.

FACTS

Donald J. Richardson, Grove L. Cook, and Wayne Weaver are stockholders of Major Oil Corporation (Major Oil) who brought this action individually and on behalf of all other stockholders of Major Oil. The original complaint named as defendants Arizona Fuels, Inc.; Eugene Dalton; and Deanna J. Dalton, the legal or beneficial owners of 47 percent of the issued and outstanding shares of stock of Major Oil. Eugene Dalton is alleged to be the controlling stockholder, officer and director of Arizona Fuels and the controlling officer and director of Major Oil. Deanna Dalton is alleged to be an officer and director of both Major Oil and Arizona Fuels. The issue is whether the district court erred in certifying this matter as a class action.

DECISION

Yes. Judgment for plaintiffs reversed. A class action and a derivative action rest upon fundamentally different principles of substantive law. A derivative action must necessarily be based on a claim for relief which is owned by the stockholders' corporation. The stockholder, as a nominal party, has no right, title or interest whatsoever in the claim itself—whether the

[21]UCC 8–204(b).

action is brought by the corporation or by the stockholder on behalf of the corporation. A recovery in a class action is a recovery which belongs directly to the shareholders. However, in a derivative action, the plaintiff shareholder recovers nothing and the judgment runs in favor of the corporation.

The claim for relief belongs to the corporation. The cause of actions then goes on to allege that the defendants "mismanaged the corporate and prudential affairs of Major Oil." The rule in Utah is that mismanagement of the corporation gives rise to a cause of action in the corporation, even if the mismanagement results in damage to stockholders by depreciating the value of the corporation's stock. Therefore, any compensatory damages, which may be recovered on account of any breach by defendants of their fiduciary duty as directors and officers or arising as a result of mismanagement of the corporation by defendants belong to the corporation and not to the stockholders individually.

Richardson et al. v. Arizona Fuels Corp., et al., 614 P.2d 636 (Utah 1980).

Stockholders' Direct Suit If as a shareholder you were deprived of a rightful incident of share ownership (e.g., the right to vote,[22] a claim to compel dividends wrongfully withheld,[23] a claim that a corporate action is *ultra vires*,[24] an action to inspect corporate books and records[25]) you would have a direct action claim against the corporation. Damages are awarded to you as an individual in a direct action suit. If such a wrong were perpetrated upon other shareholders as well as yourself, you could bring an action on behalf of yourself and the other shareholders against the corporation. This is called a "class" or "representative" action.

The Shareholder's Liability

Shareholders are not liable for corporate contracts or tort claims because the corporation, as a legal entity, is separate and distinct from its owners, the shareholders. However, shareholders contract with the corporation in the purchase of stock and are obligated to pay to the corporation the full consideration of the shares.

Corporate creditors who cannot satisfy their claims from corporate assets may bring a "bill in equity" against a stockholder who failed to pay his or her subscription price. In this way the price, or corporate right to the price, as an asset of the corporation becomes available through the corporation to the corporate creditors.

► Watered Stock

You recall that the consideration for stock issuance of shares may be paid in property or services actually performed or, under Section 6.21(c) of the RMBCA, to be performed for the corporation. If such property or services are overvalued and worth less than the par value of the share, the share is diluted; hence the term **watered stock**. Par value stock may also be issued for less than par value for (1) insufficient cash; (2) payment of a stock dividend without transferring the surplus to the capital account;[26] (3) a stock bonus; or (4) a gratuitous issue. In such events, both the corporation and the stockholders are

watered stock

Corporate stock reduced in value by the issuance of par value shares for less than their par value

[22]*Reifsnyder v. Pittsburgh Outdoor Advertising Co.*, 173 A.2d 319 (Pa. 1961).

[23]*Tankersley v. Albright*, 80 F.R.D. 441 (1978).

[24]*Eisenburg v. Flying Tiger Line, Inc.*, 451 F.2d 267 (2d Cir. 1971).

[25]*Kahn v. American Cone & Pretzel Co.*, 74 A.2d 160 (Pa. 1950).

[26]See p. 932, Fund for Declaration of Dividends.

liable in tort for deceiving the corporate creditors who relied upon the misrepresented outstanding par value capital stock as having been paid for in an amount of at least its par value. However, the innocent purchaser for value of watered stock, unaware of the previous watering, takes the shares free and clear of any liability for such watering.

Securities Regulations

▶ State Blue-Sky Laws

blue-sky laws
State laws regulating the sale and transfer of securities

Suppose a corporation in which you are a stockholder is in need of capital. The accountant for the corporation has prepared statements indicating its present financial status. If you, the other shareholders, and the corporate board desire to sell additional stock to state residents, the corporate attorney would have to assure compliance with the state **blue-sky laws**. The phrase "blue-sky" comes from persons praising the stock to the blue sky. Each state has enacted statutes established to ensure public protection from a fraudulent issuance of stock. A stock sale that intentionally violates the law can subject the corporate board, officers, and the corporation to criminal prosecution and an injunction against the corporation preventing future stock sales. A shareholder may rescind a stock sale made in violation of a blue-sky law. Generally, the corporation that desires to sell its stock (issuer) must file corporate information with the appropriate state official for registration. Keep in mind that the interstate sale of stock to the public requires compliance with the federal statutes, and state blue-sky laws relate only to an intrastate sale.

▶ Federal Securities Laws

Securities Act of 1933 The federal Securities Act of 1933, Section 5, requires registration with the Securities and Exchange Commission (SEC) of securities offered to the public through the use of the mails or any means of interstate commerce, unless there is a specific statutory exemption. The registration statement must disclose necessary financial and other information, which is also in a prospectus furnished to each prospective investor allowing the latter to make an intelligent investment decision based upon the merits of the security. The SEC does not approve or disapprove of the offering; it simply requires disclosure of relevant information about the corporation. The stock offered for sale may be worthless, but the prospectus information must be true. (See Figure 45.2.)

Registration Process The statute provides for a pre-filing, waiting, and post-effective period. During the pre-filing period, the corporation or an underwriter (a person who sells the stock on behalf of the issuer) may make an offer to sell its stock that complies with prospectus requirements, providing that acceptance is postponed. The waiting period is twenty days after the registration statement is filed before the registration statement becomes effective. During the post-effective period (after the twenty-day waiting period has expired), the stock may be sold by providing the investor with a prospectus that contains information in the registration statement. It is unlawful to sell the securities before the post-effective period.

Statutory Exemptions

1. Regulation D (Private Sales Offerings) In 1982 the SEC promulgated Regulation D composed of Rules 501 through 506 to simplify the exemptions for

FIGURE 45.2 **Announcement of a Stock Offering by Underwriters**

This announcement is neither an offer to sell nor a solicitation of an offer to buy these securities. The offer is made only by the Prospectus.

OXY

New Issue/February 1, 1990

23,000,000 Shares

Occidental Petroleum Corporation

Common Stock

($.20 Par Value)

Price $26.50 Per Share

Copies of the Prospectus may be obtained in any State in which this announcement is circulated only from such of the undersigned as may legally offer these securities in such State.

Salomon Brothers Inc

Donaldson, Lufkin & Jenrette
Securities Corporation

Merrill Lynch Capital Markets

Morgan Stanley & Co.
Incorporated

PaineWebber Incorporated

Dean Witter Reynolds Inc.

private sales of stock and eliminate the necessity of filing a formal registration statement with the SEC.

Rule 501 defines the terms of Regulation D.

Rule 502 establishes conditions that apply to all offerings under Regulation D. Of great importance are those that prohibit advertising to the general public, require the issuing corporation to "legend" the stock by stating on it they are *restricted securities* and can be resold only by a full registration or in an exempt registration transaction and making information about the offering available to certain investors.

Rule 503 requires notice of a Regulation D offering be filed with the SEC in Washington, regardless of the amount of the issuance.

Rule 504 allows the corporation to issue an aggregate sale of securities within twelve months that does not exceed $500,000 to any number of purchasers, without providing them with any information. Local state law may require a disclosure document concerning the corporation be furnished to the buyers. In that event the offering may be advertised and the stock need not be restricted as required under Rule 503.

Rule 505 allows a corporation to sell securities not in excess of $5,000,000 per issue, in any twelve-month period to any number of accredited investors, and up to thirty-five other purchasers. The accredited investors do not receive a formal registration statement describing the nature of the offering, however, any of the thirty-five other purchasers must.

The term *accredited investor* is defined in Rule 501 to include (1) any bank, insurance company, investment company, or employee benefit plan; (2) any business development company; (3) any charitable or educational institution with assets of more than $5 million; (4) any director, executive officer or general partner of the issuer; (5) any person who purchases at least $150,000 of the securities being offered, provided the purchase does not exceed 20 percent of his or her net worth; (6) any person with a net worth of more than $1 million; and (7) any person with an annual income of more than $200,000.

Rule 506 allows a corporation to offer any unlimited amount of securities to any number of accredited investors and up to thirty-five others provided they (the thirty-five nonaccredited investors) are capable of evaluating the risks involved. This rule will allow a large corporation to issue substantial numbers of stock to accredited investors without formally registering as a public offering. However, the corporation must be sure its purchases are from the group defined in Rule 501. Any purchaser outside the group places a burden on the corporation to persuade the SEC that the nonaccredited investors understand the risk involved.

2. Regulation A (Small Public Offerings) If a corporation wishes to offer up to $1.5 million of securities to the general public in any twelve-month period, it can do so as a *small public offering* without a full registration statement being filed with the SEC. The corporation, as the issuer, would have to file a "notification" and an "offering circular" to the investor and the SEC regional office disclosing relevant information. Regulation A filings are less detailed, are processed faster, and are less costly than full registration.

3. Short-term Commercial Paper If a corporation issues a promissory note, a draft, bill of exchange, or any other type of commercial paper, it will be exempt from registration with the SEC, provided the issuance arises out of a current business transaction and has a maturity date of not more than nine months. The paper may not be advertised for sale to the public.

4. Intrastate Issues If you are sure each purchaser of your securities is a resident of the state where your business is incorporated, there is another exemption from registration with the SEC. To qualify, at least 80 percent of your corporation's gross revenues must come from operations within the state of incorporation.

5. Nonprofit Organizations If a corporation is organized for educational, health, recreational, or charitable purposes, there is an exemption from registration in the sale of its securities. For example, a college that issues tax-exempt bonds need not file with the SEC.

Civil Liability If you (1) signed the registration statement, or (2) were a director of the corporation that issued the security, or (3) with your consent were named in the registration statement as a person about to become a director, or (4) served as an accountant who assisted in the certification or preparation of the statement, you could be held personally liable if the Registration Statement contained an untrue statement of a material fact or omitted necessary material information. However, a director may reasonably rely on statements made by the corporate CPA or legal counsel.

Criminal Liability Any *willful* violation of the Act will subject the wrongdoer to criminal liability of up to five years in prison and/or a fine of up to $10,000. Keep in mind that if the issuance must comply with the SEC registration, the corporation will also have to register in each state where it sells its securities.

Securities Exchange Act of 1934 In addition to creating the SEC, the 1934 Act regulates the trading by the stock exchanges of securities after a company has "gone public." Holders of securities listed on national stock exchanges are protected, as "public companies" must file periodic reports that update information in the original registration statement. Examples are the annual Form 10-K and the quarterly Form 10-Q. (See Figures 45.3 and 45.4.)

Insider Transactions If you were a director, officer, or the owner of 10 percent or more of the corporate stock listed on a national stock exchange, you are an "insider" and subject to special regulations under Section 16(b) of the 1934 Act. Suppose you purchased stock in the corporation as an officer or director and sold it within six months from the date of purchase, or sold the stock and then repurchased the stock within six months from the date of its sale; any profits you may have realized could be recovered by the corporation. The purpose of this rule is to prevent "short-swing" trading based upon inside information not made available to the public.

The 1934 Act imposes both criminal and civil liability for its violation similar to the 1933 Act.

SEC Rule 10b-5 (Full Disclosure Rule) The SEC issued Rule 10b-5 implementing Section 10(b) of the Act. There are no exceptions to compliance with SEC Rule 10b-5. The Rule makes unlawful an intentional material misstatement or an omission by a person buying or selling any security. The rule applies to *any* person and is not limited to officers, directors, or owners of 10 percent or more of the corporation's stock. For example, if you had "inside information" concerning a stock, you have a duty to disclose this information to buyers or sellers of the security. The U.S. Supreme Court ruled in the following case that the deception must be intentional under Section 10(b) and SEC Rule 10b-5.

FACTS

Ernst and Ernst, an accounting firm, was retained by First Securities Company of Chicago, a brokerage firm and member of the Midwest Stock Exchange, to perform audits of the firm's books and records. In connection therewith, Ernst and Ernst prepared for filing with the SEC the required annual reports. Hochfelder was a customer of First Securities who innocently invested in a fraudulent securities scheme perpetrated by Lester B. Noy, the president and owner of 92 percent of First Securities Company stock. In 1968 Noy committed suicide, leaving a note that described First Securities as bankrupt. Hochfelder filed this negligence action against Ernst and Ernst, contending that they failed to utilize appropriate auditing procedures thereby failing to discover internal practices of the firm and were in violation of section 10(b) and Rule 10b-5. Does violation of section 10(b) and Rule 10b-5 require intentional misconduct?

DECISION

Yes. Judgment for Ernst and Ernst. Section 10(b) of the 1934 Act makes it unlawful for any person to use or employ, in connection with the purchase or sale of any securities, any manipulative or deceptive devices. Courts and commentators long have differed with regard

FIGURE 45.3 **Form 10-K**

SECURITIES AND EXCHANGE COMMISSION
Washington, D.C. 20549

FORM 10-K

ANNUAL REPORT

PURSUANT TO SECTION 13 OR 15(d) OF THE SECURITIES EXCHANGE ACT OF 1934

For the fiscal year ended June 30, 1990 — Commission file number 1-9999

CHANDLERS, INC.
(Exact name of registrant as specified in its charter)

Delaware (State or other jurisdiction of incorporation or organization)	**13-1234567** (I.R.S. Employer Identification Number)
4444 Fourth Street, New York, N.Y. (Address of principal executive offices)	10099 (Zip Code)

(212) 555–4444
(Registrant's telephone number)

Securities registered pursuant to Section 12(b) of the Act:

Title of each class	**Name of each exchange on which registered**
Common Stock—Par Value $1 Per Share	New York Stock Exchange Pacific Coast Stock Exchange

Securities registered pursuant to Section 12(g) of the Act:

4% Convertible Subordinated Debentures due November 1, 1990
(Title of class)

9½% Sinking Fund Debentures originally due November 15, 1995
(Title of class)

Indicate by check mark whether the registrant (1) has filed all reports required to be filed by Section 13 or 15(d) of the Securities Exchange Act of 1934 during the preceding 12 months and (2) has been subject to such filing requirements for the past 90 days.

Yes X No —

Indicate by check mark whether the registrant has filed all documents and reports required to be filed by Sections 12, 13 or 15(d) of the Securities Exchange Act of 1934 subsequent to the distribution of securities under a plan confirmed by a court.

Yes X No —

The aggregate market value of Common Stock, Par Value $1 Per Share, held by non-affiliates (based upon the closing sale price of the New York Stock Exchange) on August 13, 1982 was approximately $38,998,000.

As of August 31, 1982, there were 7,799,584 shares of Common Stock, Par Value $1 Per Share, outstanding.

DOCUMENTS INCORPORATED BY REFERENCE

Portions of the definitive Proxy Statement for the Annual Meeting of Stockholders on November 12, 1982 are incorporated by reference into Part III.

to whether scienter (intent) is a necessary element of such a course of action, or whether negligent conduct alone is sufficient.

It is difficult to believe that any legislative draftsman would use the words of section 10(b) if the intent was to create liability for merely negligent acts or omissions. Neither the legislative history nor the briefs supporting plaintiff's arguments identify any usage or authority for construing manipulative or

FIGURE 45.4 **Form 10-Q**

SECURITIES AND EXCHANGE COMMISSION
Washington, D.C. 20549
FORM 10-Q

QUARTERLY REPORT UNDER SECTION 13 OR 15(d) OF THE SECURITIES EXCHANGE ACT of 1934

For Quarter Ended March 31, 1989 Commission File Number 1-2345

FORGE INDUSTRIES CORPORATION
(Exact name of registrant as specified in its charter)

DELAWARE
(State or other jurisdiction of incorporation or organization)

12-3456789
(I.R.S. Employer Identification No.)

FORGE BUILDING, HEAVY DRIVE, ANYTOWN, DELAWARE 99999
(address of principal executive offices and zip code)

Registrant's telephone number, including area code (777) 555–0000

Indicate by check mark whether the registrant (1) has filed all reports required to be filed by Section 13 or 15(d) of the Securities Exchange Act of 1934 during the preceding 12 months (or for such shorter period that the registrant was required to file such reports), and (2) has been subject to such filing requirements for the past 90 days. Yes X No ___

Indicate the number of shares outstanding of each of the issuer's classes of common stock, as of the latest practicable date.

Class	Outstanding at April 30, 1989
Common Stock, par value 66-2/3¢ per share	7,020,531

FORGE INDUSTRIES CORPORATION
INDEX

deceptive devices to include negligence. When a statute speaks so specifically in terms of manipulation and deception, the commonly understood terminology of intentional wrongdoing, we are quite unwilling to extend the scope of the statute to negligent conduct. Moreover, the scope of Rule 10b-5 cannot exceed the power granted the SEC under section 10(b).

Ernst and Ernst v. Hochfelder, 425 U.S. 185 (1976).

Proxy Solicitation Rules The SEC requires a registered company in advance of a stockholders' meeting to furnish each stockholder with a "proxy statement" and a form of a proxy where the stockholder can vote on each proposal that will be presented at the meeting. Rule 14a-3 requires the proxy statement be accompanied by the annual report when they are solicited for the election of directors at the annual stockholders' meeting.

Tender Offers A corporation that makes an offer to purchase the stock of another corporation is often opposed by the "target corporation's" management. Anyone that acquires more than 5 percent of a registered security must file an information statement with the SEC under Section 13(d). A tender offer is a public invitation to a corporation's shareholders to purchase their stock and does not include stock purchases on the open market.

The Insider Trading Sanctions Act of 1984

On August 10, 1984, President Reagan signed the Insider Trading Sanctions Act. Investors owning publicly traded securities are now protected by federal statutory law from traders who take advantage of material inside nonpublic information. It is an unethical practice for insiders to frustrate an investor's reasonable expectation that a fair securities market will make information available to all traders at the same time.

Under the Act, the SEC may seek an injunction against an inside trader and require the defendant to pay any profit made or loss avoided to the corporation. A federal district court has authority to require a defendant who traded a security with material nonpublic information to pay as damages up to three times the profit gained or loss avoided. There is a five-year statute of limitations on SEC claims seeking treble damages. Criminal liability may be imposed with fines of up to $100,000.

The Act extends liability to nontrading "tippers" who engage in "aiding and abetting" the violation of the "tippee." Hence, brokers and dealers who advise their customers to trade based on nonpublic material inside information may be liable under the Act. However, the Act eliminates the liability of a securities salesperson who executed a stock transaction for a customer knowing the customer had inside information.

The brokerage firm that employed the securities salesperson is not liable if its agent traded on inside information or disclosed it to a customer. This is a change from agency law that generally holds a principal (employer) liable for the negligence of its agents (employees). Section 21 (d)(2)(B) of the Securities Exchange Act of 1934 states that no person is liable under the Act "by reason of employing another person who is liable" for the new sanctions.

In the following lengthy, highly publicized, and important case notice the reason why the court found a "tippee" investment analyst was *not* under a duty to abstain from using inside information.

FACTS

In 1973, Dirks was an officer of a New York broker-dealer firm who specialized in providing investment analysis of insurance company securities to institutional investors. On March 6, Dirks received information from Ronald Secrist, a former officer of Equity Funding of America. Secrist alleged that the assets of Equity Funding, a diversified corporation primarily engaged in selling life insurance and mutual funds, were vastly overstated as the result of fraudulent corporate practices. Secrist also stated that various regulatory agencies had failed to act on similar charges made by Equity Funding employees. He urged Dirks to verify the fraud and disclose it publicly.

Dirks decided to investigate the allegations. The senior management denied any wrongdoing, but certain corporation employees corroborated the charges of fraud. Neither Dirks nor his firm owned or traded any Equity Funding stock, but throughout his investigation he openly discussed the information he had obtained with a number of clients and investors. Some of these persons sold their holdings of Equity Funding securities, including five investment advisers who liquidated holdings of more than $16 million. Recognizing, however, that Dirks "played an important role in bringing [Equity Funding's] massive fraud to light," the SEC only censured him. Dirks appealed the SEC's ruling but the U.S. Court of Appeals entered judgment against Dirks. The case is now before the U.S. Supreme Court.

DECISION

Reversed, judgment for Dirks. We find that there was no actionable violation by Dirks. It is undisputed that Dirks himself was a stranger to Equity Funding, with no preexisting fiduciary duty to its shareholders. He took no action, directly or indirectly, that induced the shareholders or officers of Equity Funding to repose trust or confidence in him. There was no expectation by Dirks' sources that he would keep their information in confidence. Nor did Dirks misappropriate or illegally obtain the information about Equity Funding.

The tippers received no monetary or personal benefit for revealing Equity Funding's secrets, nor was their purpose to make a gift of valuable information to Dirks. As the facts of this case clearly indicate, the tippers were motivated by a desire to expose the fraud. In the absence of a breach of duty to shareholders by the insiders, there was no derivative breach by Dirks.

We conclude that Dirks, in the circumstances of this case, had no duty to abstain from use of the inside information that he obtained.

Dirks v. Sec. and Exch. Comm'n., 463 U.S. 646 (1980).

The Foreign Corrupt Practices Act, As Amended in 1988

Investigations by the SEC disclosed corrupt foreign payments by over 300 U.S. corporations involving hundreds of millions of dollars. Congress responded to these corporate abuses by enacting the Foreign Corrupt Practices Act of 1977. The Act amends Section 13 (b) of the Securities Exchange Act of 1934 to require reporting corporations to comply with certain accounting standards. The Act also makes it unlawful for such reporting corporations or any domestic concern (i.e., any business association) not subject to the Securities Exchange Act to engage in corrupt practices with foreign officials. Finally, the Act further contains provisions on disclosure.

► Accounting Standards

The accounting standards provision applies only to reporting corporations subject to SEC jurisdiction. It requires them to keep books, records, and accounts which, in reasonable detail, accurately and fairly reflect the transactions and dispositions of corporate assets. Foreign bribery is often paid from off-the-books slush funds that are made illegal by the Act. Corporations subject to the SEC are also required to devise and maintain a system of internal accounting controls sufficient to provide reasonable assurance that transactions are executed in accordance with management's specific authorization and are recorded as necessary to permit preparation of financial statements in conformity with generally accepted accounting principles or other applicable criteria and to maintain accountability for its assets. Access to assets is permitted only in accordance with management authorization, and the recorded accountability for assets is compared with existing assets at reasonable intervals. The Act requires appropriate action to be taken with respect to any differences.[27]

► Foreign Corrupt Practices

This portion of the Act applies to reporting corporations subject to the SEC, their officers, directors, employees, agents (of the corporation), or stockholders, and to any individuals of a domestic concern (any business association), who make use of the mails or any means of interstate commerce to corruptly pay any official of a foreign government or a foreign political party for the purpose of influencing any decision in order to obtain or retain business.

► Disclosure

This portion of the Act may be cited as the Domestic and Foreign Investment Improved Disclosure Act of 1977. It supplements the Securities Exchange Act of 1934 relative to the requirement of disclosure in connection with filing periodic and other reports with the SEC. More detail is required to be disclosed by the same beneficial owners. The disclosure requirements are very detailed.

The Foreign Corrupt Practices Act places full responsibility on a firm's board of directors to ensure that there is compliance with the Act's requirements for proper record-keeping and a system of internal accounting controls, and to make provision for their continual review so as to detect illegal payments in violation of the Act.

► Amendments of 1988

In 1988 the Foreign Corrupt Practices Act was amended. The amendments allow facilitating payments to a foreign official, political party, or party official to expedite or secure the performance of a routine governmental action. It is a prohibited foreign trade practice to use the mails (or any instrumentality of interstate commerce) to offer, pay, or promise to pay money to a foreign official or foreign political party in order to obtain or retain business. Violation under the amended Act permits a corporation fine of not more than $2 million, a civil fine of not more than $10,000 and a criminal fine of not more than $100,000 and/or imprisonment of not more than five years against an officer, director, or shareholder acting on behalf of a corporation.

Summary Statement

1. Shareholders have a contractual relationship with the corporation with consequent rights.
2. Generally, a shareholder has the following rights:
    - **a)** the right to vote at shareholders' meetings;
    - **b)** the right to receive a dividend;
    - **c)** the right to inspect the corporate books;
    - **d)** pre-emptive rights;
    - **e)** the right to transfer the stock;
    - **f)** the right to sue the corporation or third parties for improper action; and
    - **g)** the right to share in the profits upon dissolution.

---

[27] 15 U.S.C., sec. 78q–1(b).

3. Common stock is the ordinary voting stock of the corporation.
4. Preferred stock has preference over other kinds of stock with respect to dividends and, generally, a priority on distribution of the profits upon dissolution. Preferred stock may be:
   a) cumulative,
   b) noncumulative,
   c) participating,
   d) nonparticipating.
5. Cumulative voting entitles a shareholder to as many votes as the shareholder has shares of voting stock multiplied by the number of directors to be elected.
6. Proxy vote is written authorization given to another to vote on behalf of a shareholder. The SEC regulates proxy solicitation.
7. A voting trust is a shareholders' agreement whereby title to their stock is transferred to a trustee who votes the stock as a unit.
8. A dividend is a portion of the corporate net profits or surplus set aside for distribution to the shareholders. It is declared by the directors.
9. An uncertificated security is not represented by a stock certificate. The shareholder receives a transaction statement from the corporation as evidence of his registered interest.
10. Stock transfer may be restricted if the terms are conspicuous and reasonable.
11. A shareholder may sue the directors if wrongfully deprived of his or her rights.
12. Shareholders may be held personally liable to corporate creditors if they fail to pay the full consideration of the purchased shares or for the purchase of "watered stock."
13. The Securities Act of 1933 requires registration with the SEC of securities offered to the public, unless there is a specific statutory exemption.
14. Some statutory exemptions for filing a registration statement with the SEC for the sale of stock are (a) a Regulation D private sale offering, (b) a Regulation A small public offering, (c) short-term commercial paper, (d) intrastate issues, and (e) nonprofit organizations.
15. Short-swing trading by insiders is prohibited by the Securities Exchange Act of 1934.
16. The Foreign Corrupt Practices Act of 1977 (amended in 1988) is an antibribery law concerned with corrupt payments to foreign government officials.

The following case illustrates how the Court construes the term "security" to include an offer to sell a condominium unit with an option to participate in a rental pool agreement.

HOCKING v. DUBOIS
839 F. 2d 560 (9th Cir. 1988)

Gerald Hocking visited Hawaii and became interested in buying a condominium there as an investment. When he returned to his home in Las Vegas, he made this known to a co-worker whose wife, Maylee Dubois, was a licensed real estate agent in Hawaii. A meeting was arranged between Hocking and Dubois.

Subsequently, Dubois agreed to help Hocking find a suitable unit. Dubois found a condominium unit owned by Tovik and Yaacov Liberman that was for sale. The unit was located in a resort complex developed by Aetna Life Insurance Company (Aetna). As a part of the original development, Aetna had offered purchasers an opportunity to participate in a rental pool arrangement (RPA). In arranging the sale of the Libermans' condominium, Dubois advised Hocking of the availability of the rental pool arrangement. Hocking purchased the condominium unit . . . [and] . . . entered into a rental management agreement with Hotel Corporation of the Pacific (HCP) and a rental pool agreement. It appears that HCP performed management services at the option of the condominium purchasers. Hocking subsequently filed suit alleging violations of the antifraud provisions of the Securities Exchange Act of 1934.

Reinhardt Circuit Judge. The term "security" is defined in section 2 of the Securities Act of 1933, and in section 3 of the Securities Exchange Act of 1934. The sections, which are substantially identical, define a security to include any "investment contract." However, the definition is not a static one. Congress cast it "in sufficiently broad and general terms so as to include within that definition the many types of instruments that in our commercial world fall within the ordinary concept of a security." It embodies a flexible principle "capable of adaptation to meet the countless and variable schemes devised by those who seek the use of the money of others on the promise of profits." Generally, simple transactions in real estate, without more, do not satisfy the [*SRC v. Hovey*] criteria. When a purchaser is motivated exclusively by a desire to occupy or develop the land personally, no security is involved. Real estate transactions may involve an offer to securities when an investor is offered both an interest in real estate and a collateral expectation of profits. However, drawing the line between the offering of land sales contracts and investment contracts has not been easy. To resolve this difficulty, at least in the area of condominiums, the Securities and Exchange Commission issued guidelines in 1973 on the applicability of federal securities laws to the burgeoning resort condominium market. In Release 5347, the Commission states unequivocally that it will view a condominium as a security if it is offered with the "offering of participation in a rental pool arrangement." . . . The offering of a condominium with an RPA automatically makes the investment a security. Even apart from the guidelines, we find that under the following criteria an offer of a condominium with an RPA constitutes an offer of an investment contract.

1. *Investment of Money.* Hocking invested money in the condominium.
2. *Common Enterprise.* We define common enterprise as a venture in which the "fortunes of the investor are interwoven with and dependent upon the efforts and success of those seeking the investment of third parties."
3. *Expectation of Profits Produced by Others' Efforts.* We conclude that this requisite is met whenever a condominium is sold with an RPA option. This is what the Commission has done in its guidelines for condominiums. The SEC and its advisory committee recognized the wisdom of having a rule that would make the sale of all the condominiums in a particular condominium development subject to the securities laws or would exclude the sale of all those units—regardless of the fortuity of the individual economic expectations of the particular buyer. A rule correctly notes that under some circumstances, a real estate offering can constitute an "investment contract" and thus a "security" within the meaning of the federal security laws.

Questions and Case Problems

1. When Blackhawk Holding Corp. was organized, it issued Class A common stock and Class B common stock. Owners of Class B stock were not entitled to dividends or to participate in the distribution of assets but did have the right to vote. Class B stock represented 28 percent of the total stock issuance. Stroh, a Class B shareholder, claimed that Class B stock was not valid because there was no economic interest in the corporation associated with its ownership. Is stock that only confers a right to vote valid? [*Stroh v. Blackhawk Holding Corp.*, 272 N.E.2d 1 (Ill. 1971).]

2. X Corporation had 50,000 shares of issued and outstanding Class A voting common stock and 10,000 shares of issued and outstanding Class B nonvoting stock. The board of directors voted to submit to the shareholders a plan to increase the aggregate number of authorized shares of the nonvoting stock. The Class A shareholders voted in favor of the increase. Class B shareholders were not permitted to vote, and they claim that the increase was not validly approved. Decide.
3. XYZ Corporation's board of directors never declared a dividend in its 15 years of business. The company always earned a profit, but the directors believed a large cash account was much safer than declaring dividends. The shareholders sued the company to force a dividend. Decide.
4. The Vista Fund (Vista) is a Minnesota partnerhip formed to invest in promising new enterprises. In December 1967, Vista purchased shares in RayGo, a Minnesota corporation. On March 26, 1974, RayGo entered into a plan of merger with Foster Wheeler Acquisition Corporation, a wholly owned subsidiary of Foster Wheeler. In a letter dated November 16, 1976, Vista's counsel made a demand on Foster Wheeler's board of directors to commence a shareholders' derivative suit against RayGo. Foster Wheeler decided to take no action as a result of the demand letter because, in its counsel's opinion and in the opinion of management, "Foster Wheeler Corporation had no claim against RayGo Inc., or its past or present officers and directors that Foster Wheeler Corporation might assert in a derivative action." On August 3, 1977, Vista Fund purchased 100 shares of Foster Wheeler stock. Must a plaintiff be a shareholder at the time he commences a stockholder's derivative action and, if so, must such ownership be continuous and uninterrrupted from the time of the alleged wrongs to the time suit is brought? [*Vista Fund v. Garis, et al.*, 277 N.W.2d 19 (Minn. 1979).]
5. Plaintiff's principal, George Delmarmo, a 13 percent shareholder of defendant, sought and was denied access to the list of shareholders prior to the commencement of this litigation. During oral argument, Delmarmo stated that he wanted the list of shareholders to show him the shareholders. According to defendant, Delmarmo's purpose was to solicit purchase of stock from other shareholders in order to gain control and assume management himself, to accomplish his employment by defendant as a consultant, to merge or sell defendant or initiate a public offering of its stock. Defendant is an industrial hardware corporation founded in 1895, an established, successful business. It is threatened with disruption by an outsider without business experience in industrial hardware, a self-proclaimed "wheeler dealer," according to the defendant. Was plaintiff entitled to the list of shareholders? [*Delmarmo Assoc. v. N.J. Eng'g & Supply Co.*, 424 A.2d 847 (N.J. 1980).]
6. Minority shareholders of a close corporation filed a shareholders' derivative action against the majority shareholders and the corporation alleging that the majority shareholders, acting as corporate directors and officers, purchased from themselves and for the corporation shares of capital stock of the corporation at a price in excess of its market value. The complaint alleged that, while the purchase was made from retained corporate earnings, it so financially depleted the corporation that the corporation was required to borrow $10,000 back from the majority shareholders. The trial court dismissed the complaint as failing to state a cause of action and the minority shareholders appealed. Decide. [*Tills, et al. v. United Parts, Inc., et al.*, 395 So.2d 618 (Fla. 1981).]
7. Wilkes, the plaintiff, and three individual defendants organized a corporation to run a nursing home. Each party was an equal shareholder and director. They all received $100 per week for services rendered to the nursing home. The business was

successful for 15 years, when the plaintiff and another shareholder had a misunderstanding. The relationship degenerated to the point where in January of 1967 plaintiff gave notice to sell his shares for their appraised value. At the board of directors' meeting in February 1967, plaintiff's salary was cancelled and at the annual shareholders' meeting in March he was not re-elected as a director or officer. Plaintiff sued the corporation and the individual defendants for damages for lost salary and for breach of the fiduciary duties owed to minority shareholders. Decide. [*Wilkes v. Springside Nursing Home, Inc.*, 353 N.E.2d 657 (Mass. 1976).]

8. Skoglund and Ackerly, plaintiffs, brought an action against Ormand Industries, Inc., to inspect their books. Ormand Industries is engaged in the outdoor advertising business in California. Skoglund had bought and sold several communication corporations engaged in the outdoor advertising business. Ackerly is the president of Ackerly Communications, Inc., a closely held Seattle outdoor advertising company in which Skoglund is a major shareholder. Skoglund and Ackerly are substantial shareholders of Ormand. They believed that Ormand was being mismanaged and requested an inspection of the corporate books and a list of the shareholders. Ormand refused because the plaintiffs failed to show a proper purpose, and because they are in a competitive position with Ormand because of their outdoor advertising interests in the Seattle area. Decide. [*Skoglund v. Ormand Indus., Inc.,* 372 A.2d 204 (Del. 1976).]

9. F.H.T. was formed by Feuerhelm, Hutton, and Thompson, who became the sole shareholders, directors, and officers of the corporation, with Thompson and Feuerhelm each receiving a 40 percent interest and Hutton owning the remaining 20 percent. At a shareholders' meeting a stock transfer restriction resolution was entered between Thompson and Feuerhelm. The minutes of that meeting reflect that the purpose of the resolution was to restrict "the sale or transfer of shares of the company both during the lifetime and at the death of any of the stockholders in order to assure the continuity of the ownership of the company." The first provision of the resolution consists of a lifetime stock transfer restriction requiring the shareholders to first offer their shares for sale to the company at a price equal to the book value at that time. The resolution also contains a buy-out provision to be effective upon the death of a shareholder. The resolution was endorsed by Thompson and Feuerhelm as both officers and shareholders of the corporation. Jerald Feuerhelm died on June 5, 1980.

This action arises from a dispute among the parties concerning their participation in the corporation, its capitalization, and the validity of the 1972 stock transfer. This action was brought on behalf of F.H.T., seeking an injunction to enforce the buy-out resolution. The Feuerhelm estate has refused to sell its shares back to F.H.T. and has counterclaimed on behalf of F.H.T., alleging the resolution as void, unenforceable as being an unreasonable restraint on alienation. The court found the stock transfer resolution to be valid and properly executed by Feuerhelm and Thompson. The court ordered specific performance of the resolution and ordered Duane Feuerhelm, administrator of the estate of the decedent, to comply with the resolution by delivering the stock to the corporation. Duane Feuerhelm appealed. What decision? [*F.H.T., Inc. v. Bailey, et al.*, 320 N.W.2d 772 (Neb. 1982).]

10. In the case of *Hocking v. Dubois*, excerpted at the beginning of this section, how did the court resolve the issue of whether an offer of a condominium with a rental pool agreement constitutes an offer of an investment contract?

C H A P T E R

46

CORPORATE MANAGEMENT

After you have read this chapter, you should be able to:

1. Explain the managerial function of a shareholder.
2. Explain when shareholders' approval is necessary for corporate management.
3. Define a quorum.
4. Explain the managerial role of the directors.
5. Explain how board action may be taken without a formal meeting.
6. Explain the significance of a director being a fiduciary.
7. Give an illustration of a director's breach of a fiduciary duty.
8. Explain how directors are elected and removed.
9. Explain what is meant by the indemnification of a corporate officer or director.
10. Explain the managerial role of the corporate officers.
11. Explain when a corporate officer may be held personally liable.
12. Explain the business judgment rule and the public policy for the rule.

BUSINESS DECISIONS and the LAW

It all began innocently enough: Time, Inc., planned to merge with Warner Communications, Inc., through a stock swap. But when threatened by a takeover from Paramount, Time decided to buy Warner instead, in a move costing Time about $14 billion. Had the board of directors decided differently, Time shareholders would have been free to collect $200 per share. Analysts speculate that a Time Warner merger could produce a price of only about $140 per share.

Does the business judgment rule protect such decisions by directors whereby they pass up a sizable profit in favor of incurring a massive debt? Delaware, the leading state in corporate law matters, answered in the affirmative. In this defeat for shareholders, there are lessons to be learned. First, the business judgment rule is alive and stronger than ever. Second, courts are generally deferential to directors' decisions, such that a decision must border on the irrational before a court will invalidate it. Third, courts are generally pro-management. This decision, while advantageous to managers, offers very little to investors.

Evidence showed that Time's board relied heavily upon data from management, and added little to the decision-making. The court then looked at this process and determined that the board's decision was not so outrageous that it should be overruled. Shareholders, while the actual owners of a corporation, necessarily delegate authority to the board to oversee its management. Time's shareholders meanwhile, have learned the hard lesson that Boards are not obligated to follow the wishes of a majority of shares.

Sources: "Time-Warner: This Close to Victory," *Bus. Wk.*, July 31, 1989; S. Taub, "Time Is On Your Side," *Financial World*, April 4, 1989, p. 12; "Investors Advised: Play Time-Warner Deal from the Warner Corner," *Television-Radio Age*, April 17, 1989, p. 59; "WCI Shareholders Rights Plan Puts Kibosh on Takeovers," *Variety*, March 15, 1985, p. 5.

Introduction

Society today, more than ever before, depends upon efficient management of its corporate institutions. You may serve as an employee for a corporation and depend upon it for your livelihood, well-being, and a dignified retirement. To administer to these needs, corporate policy must be clearly defined and implemented. State corporate laws, the articles of incorporation, and the corporate bylaws grant authority to the shareholders, the board of directors, and the corporate officers to effectively manage the corporation. Our discussion will focus on the managerial functions of each group and their respective roles therein. Figure 46.1 illustrates the general duties of the officers, directors, and shareholders.

Shareholders

Shareholders are given their authority from state corporate law, the articles of incorporation, and the bylaws. In the last chapter we discussed the rights of a shareholder as a fractional owner of the corporation and his or her concern with making a profit from the investment. This was generally accomplished by a dividend and an increase in the market value of the stock. The principal managerial function of the shareholder is to elect the board of directors at a legal shareholders' meeting. Hence the shareholder is not directly involved with policy decisions, which are reserved to the board of directors. A voting majority of shareholders dissatisfied with corporate policy may elect a new board of directors.

Managerial decisions that would substantially change the nature of the corporation—for example, changes in the articles of incorporation such as the corporate name, changes in its authorized stock, changes in corporate purpose, or a merger or a consolidation—require approval by the voting shareholders.

► Shareholders' Meetings

The shareholders may vote and act legally only at a duly called and properly held regular or special shareholders' meeting.[1]

Time The time of the annual shareholders' meeting is fixed in the articles of incorporation and the bylaws. Most state statutes require a regular annual meeting.[2] Notice to the shareholders of the annual meeting is often not required but is usually

[1]RMBCA, secs. 7.01 and 7.02.

[2]See, for example, Mass. Gen. Laws Ann., Chapter 156, Section 28.

FIGURE 46.1 **Corporate Management**

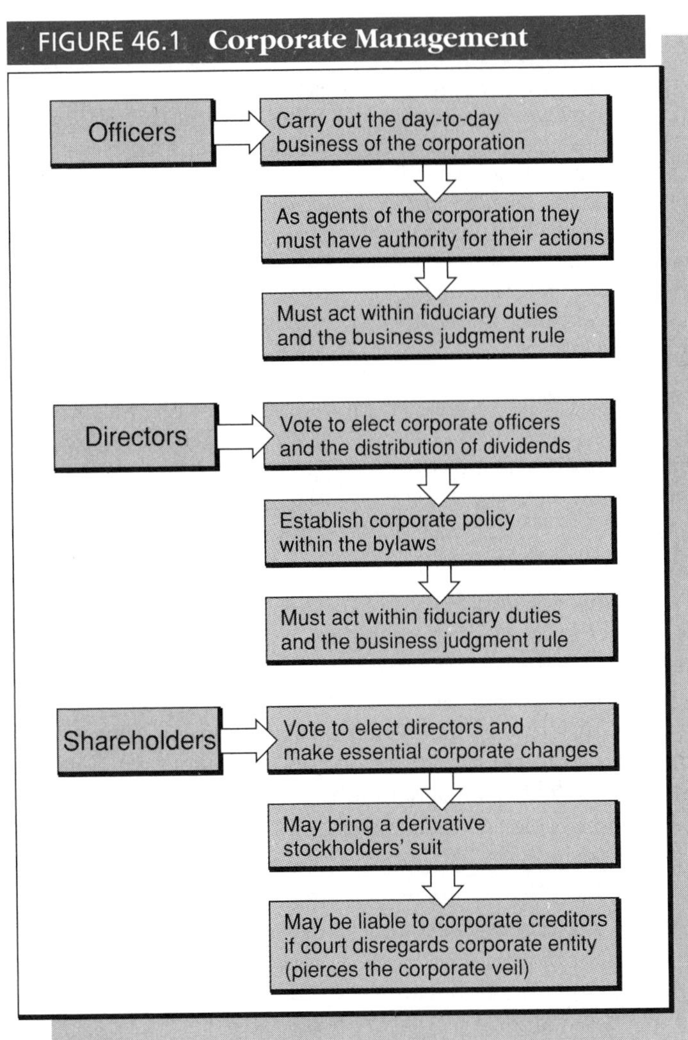

given. However, advance written notice of a special meeting is required. The notice must indicate the time, place, date, and purpose of the meeting. The bylaws generally allow a majority of the shareholders the right to call a special meeting of the shareholders. A closely held corporation may find it burdensome to give written notice of the meeting to its few shareholders. Most statutes allow a written *waiver of notice* signed by the shareholders either before or after the meeting.

Officers
Carry out the day-to-day business of the corporation
As agents of the corporation they must have authority for their actions
Must act within fiduciary duties and the business judgment rule
Directors
Vote to elect corporate officers and the distribution of dividends
Establish corporate policy within the bylaws
Must act within fiduciary duties and the business judgment rule
Shareholders
Vote to elect directors and make essential corporate changes
May bring a derivative stockholders' suit
May be liable to corporate creditors if court disregards corporate entity (pierces the corporate veil)

In the following case the court held that attendance at a shareholders' meeting will not waive proper notice.

FACTS

Darvin brought this action to set aside actions taken at the stockholders' meeting of Belmont Industries, Inc. Darvin and four other stockholders owned all of the shares in Belmont Industries. They were also directors and officers of the corporation. A dispute over corporate management arose between Darvin and the other directors, who no longer wanted Darvin in the corporation. Accordingly, a special meeting of the stockholders and directors was scheduled for September 12, 1969. Darvin received notice of the meeting on September 11. At the meeting Darvin was eliminated as a director and officer. The bylaws of the corporation provided that shareholders shall receive notice "at least ten days prior to any meeting." Darvin claims that the actions taken at the meeting are ineffective because he was given notice only one day in advance. Was Darvin's attendance at the meeting together with the nonvoting of his shares sufficient participation to waive the notice requirement?

DECISION

No. Judgment for Darvin. The purpose of the time-notice requirement is to provide a shareholder with sufficient opportunity to study contemplated action at the shareholders' meeting and the legality thereof. Although the notice given to Darvin was sufficient to obtain his physical presence at the meeting, it was not sufficient to allow him time to ascertain what action was to be taken at the special meeting. Darvin's mere attendance at the meeting coupled with the nonvoting of his shares was not sufficient participation to waive the notice requirement.

Darvin v. Belmont Indus., Inc., 199 N.W. 2d 542 (Mich. 1972).

quorum
The number of persons necessary to be present, or shares necessary to be represented, at a meeting in order to transact business

Quorum A legal shareholders' meeting requires a quorum to transact business. A **quorum** is a specified number of shareholders required to be present or a specified number of shares required to be represented before the shareholders' meeting can begin. State statutes, the articles of incorporation, and the bylaws determine the specific number, generally a majority of the voting shareholders or shares represented.[3] A shareholders' meeting that opens with a quorum may generally continue to transact corporate business even after a sufficient number of shareholders leave the meeting and break the quorum. This provides for a continuation of the meeting over the objection of dissident shareholders who have left.[4]

Shareholders' Action Without a Meeting Small closely held corporations may wish to transact business that requires shareholders' approval but decide not to call a special meeting. Most corporate statutes allow this if the shareholders sign their consent to the action taken without a meeting.

Directors

The directors elected by the shareholders manage the business and establish corporate policy. In that capacity they do not carry on the day-to-day business. The authority of the board to manage the corporation is derived from state statutes, the articles of incorporation, and the bylaws.[5]

[3]RMBCA, secs. 7.25 and 7.27.

[4]RMBCA, sec. 7.25.

[5]RMBCA, sec. 8.01(c), provides that a corporation having 50 or fewer shareholders may dispense with or limit the authority of a board of directors by describing in its articles of incorporation who will perform some or all of the duties of a board.

► Powers of Directors

The board of directors acts on behalf of the corporation. While acting within the scope of their authority the directors as a board have the power to bind the corporation with respect to corporate matters voted on by the board, but not with respect to contracts with outside parties because the board is not an agent of the corporation for such an operational or administrative purpose. The board delegates the administration of corporate policy to the officers authorizing them to carry out the day-to-day business. The board votes on policy and functions only as a body; individual members have no authority to act without board consent.

► Number of Directors

Most state corporate statutes require at least three board members. The articles of incorporation or the bylaws will fix the exact number. To accommodate the closely held corporation and the professional corporations, many states allow as few as one director.[6]

► Qualifications

Generally, any person may be a director, including a nonresident, minor, or nonshareholder. Corporate statutes, the articles of incorporation, or the bylaws may place restrictions on eligibility. It is not unusual for the bylaws to impose stock ownership requirements on the directors. Larger corporations encourage "outside directors" to serve as board members.

► Directors' Meetings

The directors may vote on corporate matters only at a legally held board meeting. A quorum is necessary for a meeting, and must continue for action to be taken. The bylaws may provide for regular board meetings to be held with or without notice. Special meetings require notice to the directors unless it is impracticable to do so. If proper notice was not sent and a director should attend a meeting, he or she may be deemed to have waived the notice requirement. Board action may be taken without a meeting when all the directors sign a *consent statement* that recites the action taken.[7] This is especially convenient in a closely held corporation where the directors and stockholders are the same parties. Bylaws may require the meetings to be held at a particular place, but most states allow meetings within or without the state of incorporation.

In the following case the court held that directors having a personal interest in the matter before the board could not be counted toward the quorum.

---

[6]RMBCA, sec. 8.03.

[7]RMBCA, sec. 8.21.

FACTS

Plaintiff, an Illinois corporation, is a medical clinic. Defendants are two physicians, Kim and Ladpli, licensed to practice medicine in Illinois. On October 10, 1972, and April 11, 1973, Kim and Ladpli, respectively entered into employment agreements with plaintiff containing restrictive covenants. There were twelve shareholders, of whom seven were elected directors. All seven directors were present at the meeting of the board of directors on February 3, 1977. Four of these directors, including Ladpli, had written employment contracts containing the restrictive covenant. The corporate minutes of the meeting read in relevant part: "After some discussion, to make it easier for physicians being 'eased out' of the clinic under the incentive system to leave and to make it easier for future physician recruitment, it was unanimously decided that the 'restrictive covenant' on all existing contracts be removed."

Plaintiff sued to enforce the restrictive covenant provision in the employment contracts of the two defendants, contending that their personal interest in the contract disqualified them to vote.

DECISION

Judgment for plaintiff. A quorum is composed of a majority of the number of directors fixed by the corporation's bylaws. The act of a majority of the directors at a meeting at which a quorum is present is the act of the board of directors. At the time of the resolution in issue, plaintiff's bylaws provided for thirteen directors; thus seven directors constituted a quorum. The four directors had a personal interest in the matter under consideration by the board. They were among the intended beneficiaries of the board's resolution. We conclude that the directors with restrictive covenants in their contracts were clearly disqualified to vote this benefit of removal to themselves.

In view of the personal interest of four board members, when the matter of restrictive covenants was considered, there were only three directors whose lack of personal interest entitled them to be counted towards a quorum. Consequently, no affirmative action on restrictive covenants was taken by a qualified majority of the board of directors. Although the action could have been ratified by the shareholders, the shareholders expressed objections at a meeting on June 6, 1977 and ratification was not achieved.

Weiss Medical Complex, Ltd. v. Sun C. Kim, M.D., et al., 408 N.E.2d 959 (Ill. 1980).

► Liability of Directors

Directors may be held personally liable to the corporation or to the shareholders in the management of the corporation if they violate a duty owed to either of them causing a financial loss. This duty is based upon the director being a fiduciary that manages the company on behalf of the corporation and the shareholders. A director's dissent to board action, made at the board meeting or by registered mail to the secretary immediately thereafter, protects the director from liability for such action.

Directors have a common law duty to exercise the standard of care of an ordinary prudent director in a similar business, and they are held liable for their negligent acts.[8] Directors are not liable for honest errors of judgment if they acted in good faith and with due diligence. For example, if the board of directors in exercising its discretion votes to adopt a new line of merchandise that results in a financial loss, the directors cannot be held personally liable.

[8] *Atherton v. Anderson*, 99 F.2d 883 (6th Cir. 1938) and *Murphy v. Hanlon*, 79 N.E.2d 292 (Mass. 1948).

Business Judgment Rule Corporate directors and officers have a duty of care that must be exercised in the performance of their corporate functions. They must perform in *the best interest of the corporation and with the care that an ordinary prudent person would reasonably be expected to exercise under similar circumstances.*[9] What are the functions of an officer or director and where are they found? The corporation itself may impose duties found in the certificate of incorporation, bylaws, or directors' and shareholders' resolutions. If a director or officer accepts a position on a corporate committee (for example, an audit committee), there is a consequent responsibility to perform those committee functions with a duty of care consistent with the reasonable prudent person standard. An employment contract between a corporation and corporate officer will also define corporate duties.

In all of these instances independent business judgments must be made by the officer or director involving risks. Public policy demands that, in exercising the duty of care in the performance of their functions as officers and/or directors, an independent business judgment must be made safe from hindsight review simply because the decision was unsuccessful. Case law has established what is known as the *business judgment rule* that allows a director or officer to make an honest and rational informed business decision that turns out to be wrong without being personally liable for its consequences.

The "safe harbor" provided by the business judgment rule is illustrated in the following case.

FACTS

Cramer brought a shareholder's derivative action stemming from the making of illegal overseas payments to foreign government officials and private persons. A committee that acted in good faith and with the full authority of the board of directors of General Telephone & Electronics Corporation (GTE) found no illegal activity on behalf of the corporation. The four directors, defendants, claim that the committee's determination was a business judgment of GTE's management and that the derivative suit should not proceed—a business judgment which is insulated from judicial review and which bars the maintenance of the derivative suit.

Plaintiff claims that defendant corporate directors so dominated the board as to make a demand futile.

DECISION

Judgment for defendant directors. The business judgment rule originated as a means of limiting the liability of corporate directors and officers for mistakes made while performing their duties. Absent bad faith or some other corrupt motive, directors are normally not liable to the corporation for mistakes of judgment, whether those mistakes are classified as mistakes of fact or mistakes of law.

At the time Cramer commenced this suit, there were fourteen individuals on GTE's board of directors. Only four of these were named as defendants in this action. The remaining ten directors had not been involved in the allegedly fraudulent activities. Indeed, several of the directors had not even been members of the board at the time the questionable transactions occurred. Under these circumstances, we cannot agree with Cramer that the four directors named as defendants in this instant case dominated the board to such an extent that the plaintiff should be excused from the mandatory requirement that he first make a demand on the directors.

Cramer v. General Tel. & Electronics Corp., 582 F.2d 259 (3rd Cir. 1978).

[9]See RMBCA, sec. 8.30, and Tentative Draft No. 1, *Principles of Corporate Governance and Structure: Restatement and Recommendations,* A.L.I. (1982), sec. 4.01.

State corporate statutes commonly provide duties that establish a director's liability with respect to an illegal declaration of dividends, purchase of treasury stock, or the illegal distribution of assets during corporate liquidation.

Director's Breach of Fiduciary Duties

A director, as a fiduciary, must account to the corporation for secret profits received in violation of the director's duty of loyalty as well as secret profits made by using inside information acquired at a board of directors' meeting. A director will be protected from suit for breach of a fiduciary duty if the director makes a full disclosure of any financial interest the director may have in the contract to the board of directors or to the voting shareholders, who approve. The corporation or the shareholders may sue the director for breach of a fiduciary duty and compel the director to pay any secret profits to the corporation. In the following case the corporation sued its former director for breach of his fiduciary duty to disclose material facts to the corporation.

FACTS

Aero Drapery of Ky., Inc., brought suit against Engdahl, an officer and treasurer of Aero. While employed by Aero, Engdahl entered into a contract with several of Aero's key employees to leave and form a new corporation in direct competition with it. Engdahl and the other employees then quit and began competing with Aero, who alleged breach of fiduciary duties against Engdahl.

DECISION

Judgment for Aero Drapery of Ky., Inc. Engdahl as a director and officer was a fiduciary of Aero. Whenever a fiduciary possesses information and the withholding of that information will damage the corporation, it is his duty to fully disclose these facts to the corporation. Engdahl should have terminated his duties as director and treasurer when he first began preparation to directly compete with Aero.

Aero Drapery of Ky., Inc. v. Engdahl, 507 S.W.2d 166 (Ky. 1974).

Removal of Directors

The shareholders may call a meeting to remove a director or the board of directors. State statutory law generally provides specific grounds for a director to be removed "for cause." Generally, a majority of the shareholders may remove a director "without cause."

Corporate Officers

State corporate statutes require corporations to have officers, elected and removed by a board of directors. These officers carry out, on a day-to-day basis, the policy established by the board. The kinds of officers, as well as the term of office and the duties of the officers, are stated in the bylaws. They usually consist of a president, secretary, and treasurer and as many vice-presidents as are required in the bylaws.

▶ Powers of Officers

The powers of corporate officers are determined by the law of agency because they are agents of the corporation. The board of directors, the articles of incorporation, and the bylaws delegate authority to the officers. An officer must not misuse his or her powers so as to breach the officer's duty of loyalty to the corporation, as is illustrated in the following case.

FACTS

Wilshire Oil Company of Texas sued Riffe, its former corporate officer, to recover profits made by Riffe by participating in competitive enterprises, and to recover compensation paid during the period he was involved in the competitive corporation. Riffe claims he is entitled to compensation because his services were properly performed.

DECISION

Judgment for Wilshire Oil Company of Texas. When a corporate officer engages in conduct which constitutes a breach of his duty of loyalty, or if it is a willful breach of his contract of employment, he is not entitled to compensation for services during such period of time although part of his services may have been properly performed. In the Restatement (Second) of Agency, sec. 469, the above doctrine is set forth:

> An agent who without the acquiescence of his principal, acts . . . in competition with the principal . . . is not entitled to compensation.

Wilshire Oil Co. of Tex. v. Riffe, 406 F.2d 1061 (10th Cir. 1969).

▶ Liability of Officers

The officers are acting on behalf of the corporation and, therefore, are fiduciaries. Similar to directors, the officers have a duty to exercise that degree of care that an ordinary prudent officer would exercise under the circumstances.

In the following case a corporate president is held personally liable for breach of his fiduciary duty of loyalty when he supplied a competitor with a list of the corporation's employees and their salaries.

FACTS

Bancroft-Whitney Co. brought this action against Glen, its past corporate president. Glen signed a contract with Bender Co. to become president of its division. Without resigning or giving notice to Bancroft-Whitney, he offered employees of Bancroft-Whitney a job at more favorable terms. Was Glen liable to Bancroft-Whitney for breach of his fiduciary duty?

DECISION

Yes. Judgment Bancroft-Whitney Co. Corporate officers and directors are not permitted to use their position of trust and confidence to further their private interests. The mere fact that the officer makes preparations to compete before he resigns his office is not sufficient to constitute a breach of duty. It is the nature of his preparation which is significant. A corporate officer breaches his fiduciary duties when, with the purpose of facilitating the recruiting of the corporation's employees by a competitor, he supplies the competitor with a selective list of the corporation's employees, together with the salary the competitor should offer in order to be successful in recruitment.

Bancroft-Whitney Co. v. Glen, 411 P.2d 921 (Cal. 1966).

► Indemnification of Officers, Directors, Employees, and Agents

Corporate officers or directors may believe that they are acting in good faith but still may be sued by shareholders or other aggrieved parties. The cost of defending the lawsuit and the risk of being found liable may discourage competent individuals from accepting such an office. Under the common law, the expenses involved in defending a director or officer in a suit were borne by them. Today many state statutes, following the Model Business Corporation Act, authorize the corporation to indemnify a corporate officer, director, or agent. Insurance companies will write indemnification policies to cover this loss. The articles of incorporation and bylaws should state the terms of indemnification, such as those specified under the Revised Model Business Corporation Act, Section 8.51:

> A corporation may indemnify an individual made a party to a proceeding because he is or was a director against liability incurred in the proceeding if . . . he conducted himself in good faith; and he reasonably believed . . . in the case of conduct in his official capacity with the corporation, that his conduct was in its best interests; and in all other cases, that his conduct was at least not opposed to its best interests; and in the case of any criminal proceeding, he had no reasonable cause to believe his conduct was unlawful.
>
> A director's conduct with respect to an employee benefit plan for a purpose he reasonably believed to be in the interests of the participants in and beneficiaries of the plan is conduct that satisfies the above stated requirements.
>
> The termination of a proceeding by judgment, order, settlement, conviction, or upon a plea of **nolo contendere** or its equivalent is not, of itself, determinative that the director did not meet the standard of conduct described in this section.
>
> A corporation may not indemnify a director under this section in connection with a proceeding by or in the right of the corporation in which the director was adjudged liable to the corporation; or . . . in connection with any other proceeding charging improper personal benefit to him, whether or not involving action in his official capacity in which he was adjudged liable on the basis that personal benefit was improperly received by him. Indemnification permitted under this section in connection with a proceeding by or in the right of the corporation is limited to reasonable expenses incurred in connection with the proceeding.

nolo contendere
No contest

Many states have enacted legislation similar to the Delaware Code (see Figure 46.2, which illustrates a Delaware law allowing limited liability of directors) to eliminate or limit the personal liability of the corporate directors for breach of a fiduciary duty as a director.

Although corporate debts and taxes are generally the obligation of the corporation, some state statutes impose personal liability on the officers and directors for corporate debts, wages, taxes, and crimes.

Summary Statement

1. Shareholders indirectly manage the corporation by voting to elect the board of directors at the shareholders' meeting.
2. Managerial decisions that substantially change the nature of the corporation require approval by the shareholders.

FIGURE 46.2 **Delaware Law Allowing the Elimination of Directors' Liability**

DEL. CODE ANN. § 102(b)(7) (1983 & Supp. 1986). In addition to the matters required to be set forth in the certificate of incorporation . . . the certificate of incorporation may also contain any or all of the following matters . . . a provision eliminating or limiting the personal liability of a director to the corporation or its stockholders for monetary damages for breach of fiduciary duty as a director, provided that such provision shall not eliminate or limit the liability of a director (i) for any breach of the director's duty of loyalty to the corporation or its stockholders, (ii) for acts or omissions not in good faith or which involve intentional misconduct or a knowing violation of law, (iii) under section 174 of the Title, or (iv) for any transaction from which the director derived an improper personal benefit. No such provision shall eliminate or limit the liability of a director for any act or omission occurring prior to the date when such provision becomes effective. All references in this subsection to a director shall also be deemed to refer to a member of the governing body of a corporation which is not authorized to issue capital stock.
The statute became effective on August 1, 1986.

3. A quorum is a specified number of shareholders or shares represented required to be present before the shareholders' meeting can begin.
4. Directors manage the business affairs and establish corporate policy.
5. Board action may be taken without a meeting when all directors sign a *consent statement* that recites the action taken.
6. A director is a fiduciary because a director manages the company on behalf of the shareholders. Directors are not liable for honest errors of judgment if they act in good faith.
7. A director, as a fiduciary, is liable for secret profits received in violation of a director's duty of loyalty.
8. The shareholders elect and may remove the directors.
9. A corporation may indemnify directors or officers for any loss incurred in connection with a suit, provided that they acted in good faith.
10. Corporate officers are elected by the directors to carry out the day-to-day business of the corporation.
11. Officers act on behalf of the corporation and are fiduciaries. They can be held liable for breach of a fiduciary duty of loyalty.
12. The business judgment rule allows an officer and/or a director to make an honest business decision that turns out to be wrong without being personally liable for its consequences. Public policy demands that officers and/or directors in performing their functions in good faith must be safe from lawsuits because their decisions were unsuccessful.

As you read the following case, notice how the Court reviews a director's duty to exercise an informed business judgment as required by the business judgment rule.

SMITH v. VAN GORKOM, 488 A.2d 858 (Del. 1985)

Horsey, J. Van Gorkom met with Jay A. Pritzker, a well known corporate takeover specialist, regarding the possibility of Pritzker acquiring TUC. Van Gorkom's actions relating to a fundamental corporate change took place without consulting the board of directors. Pritzker became interested in the merger proposal and moved swiftly. Van Gorkom failed to apprise TUC's legal staff of the merger proposal. He finally reported the negotiations to senior management, whose reaction was completely negative. Later, Van Gorkom presided over a special meeting of the board of directors. He provided no reports ahead of time, nor had he given advance notice to all members of the board as to the subject of the meeting. Van Gorkom did not invite Salomon Brothers, TUC's investment bankers, or TUC's Chicago-based partner.

At the special meeting, Van Gorkom announced Pritzker's interest in a merger agreement and the terms, but supplied neither a copy of the agreement nor the methodology used to compute the price. Further, he failed to disclose that he actually proposed the price to Pritzker. The board took only two hours to approve the proposed merger, based upon oral presentations, although the board claimed to have attached conditions to its acceptance. Van Gorkom signed the merger agreement at a formal social event, even though neither he nor any director read the agreement prior to its signing.

Subsequently, senior management's dissension forced Pritzker to accept modifications of the merger agreement. Again the TUC board approved of the modified agreement, sight unseen. The plaintiff shareholders commenced suit seeking to block the proposed merger; however, the board voted to proceed with it.

We turn to the issue of the application of the business judgment rule to the meeting of the Board. Under Delaware law, the business judgment rule is the offspring of the fundamental principle . . . that the business and affairs of a . . . corporation are managed by or under its board of directors.

[D]irectors are charged with an unyielding fiduciary duty to the corporation and its shareholders. The rule itself "is a presumption that in making a business decision, the directors of a corporation acted on an informed basis, in good faith and in the honest belief that the action taken was in the best interests of the company." Thus, the party attacking a board decision as uninformed must rebut the presumption that its business judgment was an informed one.

Under the business judgment rule, there is no protection for directors who have made "an unintelligent or unadvised judgment." A director's duty to inform himself in preparation for a decision derives from the fiduciary capacity in which he serves the corporation and its stockholders. [H]e must execute that duty with the recognition that he acts on behalf of others. Such obligation does not tolerate faithlessness or self-dealing. But fulfillment of the fiduciary function requires more than the mere absence of bad faith or fraud. Representation of the financial interests of others imposes on a director an affirmative duty to protect those interests and to proceed with a critical eye in assessing information of the type and under the circumstances present here.

Thus a director's duty to exercise an informed business judgment is in the nature of a duty of care, as distinguished from a duty of loyalty.

[D]irector liability is predicated upon concepts of gross negligence.

We think the concept of gross negligence is also the proper standard for determining whether a business judgment reached by a board of directors was an informed one.

In the specific context of a proposed merger of domestic corporations, a director has a duty . . . to act in an informed and deliberate manner in determining whether to approve an agreement of merger before submitting the proposal to the stockholders.

It is against those standards that the conduct of the directors of Trans Union must be tested. . .

On the record before us, we must conclude that the Board of Directors did not reach an informed business judgment. Our reasons, in summary, are as follows:

The directors (1) did not adequately inform themselves as to Van Gorkom's role in forcing the "sale" of the Company and in establishing the per share purchase price; (2)

were uninformed as to the intrinsic value of the Company; and (3) given these circumstances, at a minimum, were grossly negligent in approving the "sale" of the Company upon two hours' consideration, without prior notice, and without the exigency of a crisis or emergency.

For the foregoing reasons, we conclude that the director defendants breached their fiduciary duty of candor by their failure to make true and correct disclosures of all information they had, or should have had, material to the transaction submitted for stockholder approval.

Questions and Case Problems

1. Two creditors of an insolvent corporation sued its sole shareholder and chief officer to recover on their money judgments against the corporation. Defendant Robert J. Fleming was the president and sole shareholder of Fleming Sheet Metal Co. (Fleming Metals), a heating and ventilating business incorporated in 1965. Initially the corporation prospered, but by 1970 it was showing a loss and in 1973 it became insolvent. Plaintiff Snyder Electric Co. obtained a judgment against Fleming Metals in January 1977 for $15,500 for supplies and service purchased to June 1973, and plaintiff Ace Manufacturing, Inc., obtained a judgment for $17,000 for materials supplied. Rather than sell additional stock to finance the corporation, Fleming would advance money through loans, retained salary, or payment of corporate debts. These advances were reflected on an "officer's due" account from which Fleming was paid with corporate assets after 1973. Plaintiffs contend that Fleming breached a fiduciary duty by favoring himself over other creditors. Decide. [*Snyder Electric Co. v. Fleming,* 305 N.W.2d 863 (Minn. 1981).]
2. Barr, the plaintiff and shareholder of Talcott, a corporation, brought a derivative shareholders' suit against Wackman and other directors of Talcott. Because of the self-dealing and breach of fiduciary duties of Talcott's directors, First Capital, a subsidiary of Gulf and Western, had been able to obtain board approval of an unfair stock offer. Wackman claims that the derivative action cannot be maintained since no demand was made on the board to rescind the offer. Must demand be first made on the directors before the shareholders bring a derivative suit? [*Barr v. Wackman,* 329 N.E.2d 180 (N.Y. 1975).]
3. Smith, a director of XYZ Corp., attended a corporate board meeting when a dividend was declared. Due to an inadequate surplus, this was an illegal dividend. Smith did not vote against the dividend. The next day Smith decided she should vote against the declaration of the dividend and sent a registered letter to the secretary. Creditors of XYZ Corp. sued the directors, including Smith, for declaring an illegal dividend. Is Smith liable?
4. Jones, the president of XYZ Co., with the directors' approval, franchised a successful business throughout the east coast. As a result of this new franchising venture, the corporation overextended and became insolvent. A shareholders' suit was brought against Jones, alleging a breach of his fiduciary duty as the chief executive officer to transact business in a reasonable manner. Decide.
5. Segal and Martinez were two physicians who formed plaintiff corporation, Patient Care Services, to provide comprehensive health services to a hospital. Both physicians were directors, officers, and shareholders of Patient Care Services. The hospital that engaged its services did not renew the contract. A new medical corporation formed, owned, and managed by Segal was awarded the new contract.

Segal informed Martinez of his intent to negotiate with the hospital on behalf of his corporation. Was Segal liable for breach of his fiduciary duty of loyalty? [*Patient Care Services, S.C. v. Segal,* 337 N.E.2d 471 (Ill. 1975).]

6. Jones, the president of XYZ Corp., developed a competing corporation during his office as president. The directors knew of this but never attempted to stop Jones. XYZ Corp. became insolvent because of this competition. The shareholders brought suit against Jones and the directors for breach of their fiduciary duty of loyalty. The directors claim that they are not liable because they did not participate in the competing company. Decide.

7. Gimbel, plaintiff and shareholder of Signal Companies, Inc., defendant, sued to enjoin the sale of its stock in a subsidiary corporation. Gimbel represents a minority group of shareholders who object to a proposed sale of all the capital stock of Signal Oil, a wholly owned subsidiary of defendant corporation. A special meeting of the defendant's board of directors was called without notice of its purpose. Three of the four outside directors were unaware of the proposed sale prior to the meeting. A handwritten outline of the transaction was handed to the directors and an oral presentation was made supporting it. The tax consequences of the sale were discussed. The general financial status of Signal Oil, including its sales, income, cash flow, balance sheet, projected expenditures, and risks, were also reviewed. Gimbel attacked the proposed sale on the grounds that the directors recklessly authorized the sale without informed reasonable deliberations. Judgment for whom? [*Gimbel v. Signal Companies, Inc.,* 316 A.2d 599 (Del. 1974).]

8. The Pintura Corp. was engaged in the business of finishing and installing dry wall in construction projects. Nieto was its president and sole shareholder. Wille Building Materials Corp. (Wille) supplied Pintura with dry wall and other supplies. National Acceptance Company of America (NACA) was and is in the business of making commercial loans. On May 23, 1974, Pintura assigned to Wille the balance of all monies to become due to Pintura from Highland Construction Co., for work performed on a project. The assignment recites that it was given in consideration for Wille's continued extension of credit to Pintura. On September 27, 1974, in order to secure Wille's indebtedness to NACA, Wille assigned to NACA its right in the Pintura-Wille assignment. Subsequently, Highland issued five checks, payable jointly to Pintura and Wille. All checks were deposited in Pintura's corporate account. Defendant Nieto indorsed three checks in Pintura and Wille's names, and he directed an authorized indorsement and deposit of the other two checks in Pintura's behalf. May Nieto, a corporate officer, be held individually liable for conversion committed by him in behalf of and for the sole benefit of the corporation? [*Nat'l Acceptance Co. of America v. Pintura Corp., et al.,* 418 N.E.2d 1114 (Ill. 1981).]

9. McCrary Engineering Corp. (McCrary) is an Indiana corporation specializing in the planning, design, and supervision of construction of water and sewerage projects for municipalities, counties, and industry. McCrary has an office in Atlanta, Georgia, from which it operates throughout the state. Hood, whose office is in Atlanta, was employed by McCrary in 1971 and became its president in 1972. In April 1976, Hood caused Southeast Consultants, Inc. (Southeast) to be chartered, with Hood as principal shareholder and president. Unknown to McCrary's directors, Southeast used McCrary's Atlanta office as its office and used McCrary's equipment, supplies and personnel in its engineering operations. McCrary had no written employment contract and hence no covenant not to compete.

McCrary sued Hood and Southeast for damages and injunctive relief, alleging that Hood had breached his fiduciary duties to McCrary by forming a competing engineering firm without notice and by improperly using McCrary's resources to set up and operate the new firm. Decide. [*Southeast Consultants, Inc. v. McCrary Eng'g Corp.,* 273 S.E.2d 112 (Ga. 1980).]

10. In the case of *Smith v. Van Gorkom,* excerpted at the beginning of this section, the court carefully reviewed the duty the directors owe to a corporation. What were the reasons the court found that indicated the directors breached their fiduciary duty of care? What should directors do to avoid the consequences of this decision?

PART 8B BUSINESS ORGANIZATIONS

B: Corporations

INTERNATIONAL DIMENSIONS

It seems that even Mickey Mouse is feeling the pressure to expand and become ever more profitable. This era of globalization of business markets has caused companies to devise investment financing and investment strategies in order to remain competitive at the world level.

Walt Disney Company, with its usual fanfare, announced plans to open a "Euro Disneyland" twenty miles east of Paris. Disney purchased 4,800 acres of sugar-beet farmland for an undisclosed amount, and will transform it into a $3 billion fantasy land in just over two years. Scheduled to open in 1992, Disney has already spent approximately $300 million and it will be the company's biggest project thus far. Disney already operates theme parks in California, Florida, and Japan.

Although Disney has some experience in foreign markets, the financing and ownership of Euro Disneyland set it apart from its counterpart in Japan. The French government is requiring Disney to place more than half of the shares in Euro Disneyland with European community investors. Thus Disney will for the first time have a public offering of its shares. Disney will retain a 49 percent ownership in the theme park and sell 51 percent of its stake to European investors. Disney shares are to be offered simultaneously in all European Community countries and should raise about $900 million to be used in the construction of the park. Analysts expect that the shares will be snapped up quickly since theme parks are a proven concept and the Disney name has such a cachet to it. Disney has advertised the sale of its shares in thirty-five European newspapers and planned a ten-city media show to publicize the public offering. Although the French government required initial placement of the shares with European investors, these shareholders are free to transfer their shares to American investors ninety days after the initial public offering, which promises to be a great success.

Although Disney ventures have thus far enjoyed the Midas touch, this one faces uncertainties, both financial and cultural. Three other entertainment and theme parks have opened or are scheduled to be opened in France. Moreover, one of Disney's archrivals, MCA, Inc., is looking at France and Great Britain as potential sites for an entertainment park. Besides competition, another often cited problem is that of language. The French government has required Disney to make French the park's "official" language, although English will be included on signs as well. To make things even easier, universal signs will be posted whenever possible so that patrons will identify attractions by visual cues.

As for the uncertain weather in this region of France, Disney has planned more indoor attractions and covered waiting areas than the two other Disney parks in the fair-weather states of California and Florida.

Disney must also adapt to the varied currency used by the park's visitors. Possible solutions include leasing space to banks to perform a money exchange service, or for Disney to create such a business itself, which is known to be quite profitable.

Adapting products to foreign markets takes planning, vision, skill, and to some extent, timing and luck. Flexibility is important, too, as evidenced by the fact that in order to build the park in France, Disney must, for the first time, relinquish the majority of ownership shares. It will be interesting to find out who will end up owning, and possibly even controlling, Euro Disneyland.

In the meantime, the French and the French-bound tourists will enjoy choosing between visits to two fantasies: the Palace at Versailles and Disney's Magic Kingdom.

ETHICS AND BUSINESS LAW

Introduction

This end-of-part discussion, like the others in this book, is designed to encourage you to begin forming personal beliefs about what is right or wrong conduct in business. The discussion here builds on the material in the first end-of-part discussion; you may find it helpful to review that.

This material has several goals. The section that immediately follows is designed to help you see the range of ethical issues associated with this area of the law. The in-depth discussion is intended to provide you with a background for forming your own beliefs about a single very important ethical issue in business. The problems at the end are designed to build your skill in ethical analysis while exploring further the in-depth issue.

A Sampling of Ethical Issues in Business Organizations

► Partnerships

Partners owe fiduciary duties to the partnership. But this duty often conflicts with self-interest. For example, assume that you are one of ten partners and you come across

Sources: "Expansion set for Disneyland," *New York Times,* January 13, 1990, p. 12 (N), 37 (L); "Will Sneezy Be Making Cold Calls to Sell European Disneyland?" *Wall Street Journal,* September 13, 1989, p. C1; P. Lewis, "Disney Advances on Europe," *Maclean's,* July 8, 1985, p. 42; "Bonjour, Mickey (Disneyland International Plans Euro Disneyland Park in Paris," *Fortune,* January 20, 1986, p. 8 (1).

a business opportunity that should, by law, be turned over to the partnership, but which you could secretly take for yourself. Would this tempt you? Suppose the opportunity would generate for you a secret profit of $30,000, but only $3,000 if you turn it over to the partnership. Can you see how great the temptations can be in partnerships and, therefore, how important trust and ethical character are among partners?

Another ethical issue stems from the nature of partnership law. It makes partners *jointly and severally* liable for the torts of the partnership. Sometimes this may appear unjust. Suppose there are three partners each worth, respectively, $5,000, $10,000, and $1,000,000. If the partner worth $5,000 commits a partnership tort that results in a judgment of $500,000, practically all the money could be collected from the wealthiest partner. Do you think this result is just? Can you articulate a style of ethical reasoning that supports this aspect of partnership law?

In partnership law, partners share profits and losses equally unless the partnership agreement is to the contrary. This is true despite unequal capital contributions and unequal work for the partnership. Can you see that in a new two-person partnership, especially one without a written partnership agreement, it is possible for one partner to contribute 80 percent of the capital and the work yet be legally entitled only to 50 percent of the profits? Can you articulate a style of ethical reasoning that supports this aspect of partnership law?

► Special Ventures

Limited partners share in the profits of the partnership but are not personally liable, beyond their capital contributions, for the claims against the partnership. This is true as long as they do not participate in the management of the partnership. Do you think that nonparticipation in management is a strong enough ethical basis for limiting liability? If a *general* partner becomes inactive in the management of an accounting partnership, should this eliminate liability on his or her part?

► Corporations

The basic goal of corporate conduct is an important and controversial ethical concern. Some argue that maximizing shareholder wealth is the only ethical goal. Others claim corporations must be "socially responsible" to be ethical.

Social responsibility is the idea that we must evaluate the impact of corporate action, not just on shareholders, but on all parts of society—employees, suppliers, consumers, neighbors, even future generations.

The conflict between shareholder wealth maximization and social responsibility becomes very visible when large corporations engage in acts of charity, such as making gifts to hospitals or educational institutions. Some shareholders criticize this because they claim it reduces their dividends. Others criticize it because corporate managers are giving away money that is not theirs; charity decisions should be made by *owners* of property, such as shareholders, not by mere managers. In contrast, the social responsibility group argues that corporations are chartered by society to serve the public good. Often society, and even corporations, are benefitted more by using profits for charitable activities rather than just for dividends. What is your view on this issue?

Another ethics issue in corporation law centers on the duty of loyalty owed by officers to the corporation and thereby to shareholders. When mergers, buy-outs, or hostile takeovers are on the horizon, officers often fear losing their jobs. This fear sometimes causes them to place their own self-interest above that of the corporation.

"Golden parachutes" provide large severance payments to officers if their corporation is taken over and they are fired. Some argue that golden parachutes are necessary to keep talented officers with a firm that is vulnerable to a takeover. Others claim that golden parachutes are merely a way for officers to enrich themselves at the expense of shareholders. What do you think?

"Poison pills" are devices that make hostile takeovers more risky. They work by authorizing existing shareholders to purchase additional shares at a low price in the event a hostile purchaser acquires more than a specified percentage of the firm's stock. Since the hostile party cannot buy these new shares, they in effect dilute, and reduce the value of, the hostile party's investment. A poison pill reduces the risk of takeovers and thereby preserves the jobs of officers. But shareholders are injured when a poison pill is used because, in the typical takeover, shares increase in value 25 to 40 percent, a profit that is lost by the shareholders if there is no hostile takeover. Do you think poison pills are ethical?

In-Depth Discussion of a Basic Issue: What Moral Obligations Do We Owe Employing Organizations?

What *moral,* as opposed to *legal* obligations, do we owe to partnerships, corporations, and other business organizations? To a large extent, the answer turns on what we define organizations to be in a *moral* sense. If you conclude that business organizations are the same as persons, then you would conclude that you owe many obligations to the organization beyond mere contractual duties. For example, in an organizational emergency you might feel morally bound to work extra hours without pay. In contrast, if you conclude as many do, that business organizations do not exist in a moral sense, you owe the business organization no duties beyond your legal obligations. Thus in an organizational emergency you might try to extract a very high rate of pay for any extra work.

► Juristic Entities

Persons are considered "legal entities" in the sense that they are recognized by the law as able to assume legal rights and incur legal duties. They may be individuals, or in the eyes of the law nonhuman legal entities called "juristic entities." Many business organizations, such as corporations, are juristic entities. In many ways, the law treats corporations the same as it treats individuals. Thus it places individuals and corporations on the same legal level. This may imply that we owe similar moral duties to organizations as well as to individuals.

► The Historical View

Historically in western civilization, individuals have been the main moral entities. This flows out of our Judeo-Christian tradition, from the belief that individuals are made in the image of God and that the things of the earth have been given to humankind. As a consequence, we feel free to kill cows for food, cut down trees for housing, pick flowers to decorate a table, and in other ways destroy life. Whales can be harvested for their economic value and horses can be rendered into dog food. In contrast, it is wrong to do even minor injury to other human beings. Certainly we cannot eat them. And even if they ask us, we cannot help them take their own lives. In the Judeo-Christian tradition, and in most but not all major religions, persons and churches are the only moral entities besides God. Churches were among the first recognized juristic entities and corporation law has grown from this source. The following sections discuss the way the moral status of business organizations would be analyzed using the four styles of ethical reasoning.

► The Egoistic View

The egoist will not recognize business organizations as moral entities. For the egoist, even other human beings do not exist in an ethical sense. Employers, co-workers, even spouses, are solely means to the end of the egoist's self-satisfaction. Therefore an egoist who is a director of a corporation can justify taking a director's fee without exercising the due care required by law if there is no risk of liability.

► The Utilitarian View

Utilitarians generally recognize other persons as moral entities. They must weigh the impact of *their* ethical decisions on other persons. The act that benefits the *majority* of persons most is the act which the utilitarian is obligated to do.

Utilitarian views of organizations are sometimes articulated in terms of *mission*. That is, because we operate in an imperfect social system some organizations generate more social good than others and some utilitarians therefore accord them more moral stature. A hospital may be highly regarded while a firm manufacturing cigarettes might be viewed very negatively. A utilitarian nurse might work extra hours for free for the hospital while refusing to work for the cigarette company even for double the pay.

► The Kantian View

In Kant's thinking, human beings are entitled to distinctive moral treatment because they have the capacity to engage in moral reasoning. This is the attribute that distinguishes humans from other life forms. In Kant's view, we can eat hamburgers because cows cannot engage in moral reasoning. Since each individual has the potential to engage in moral reasoning, each is entitled to moral dignity.

A debate is now raging among serious philosophers about whether, in a Kantian sense, some organizations are able to engage in moral reasoning. If one concludes that they can, then by Kantian reasoning, these organizations would be entitled to treatment similar to that accorded to human beings. Some argue that organizations perceive, transmit information, evaluate the information, *and as an organization* make ethical decisions. They argue that an organization's decisions can have attributes different from the decisions made by individual persons in the organization. The sense that there is an ethical culture to an organization points to its Kantian existence. Perhaps you have seen an organization keep employed a disabled worker long after the person has become unable to carry on his or her share of the organization's responsibilities; this might suggest that the organization is engaging in moral reasoning and thus "exists" in a Kantian sense.

A Kantian who believes organizations are moral entities might be compelled to quit, or advocate that he be laid off, if he concluded that was the best thing for the organization.

► The Religious View

The religious view is that human beings are the only moral entities, other than churches and God. As a consequence, organizations are viewed as nonexisting and as simply a grouping of existing individuals. Thus an analysis of a problem confronting a college is resolved by analyzing its impact on students, faculty, alumni, staff, and administrators.

Kantians might reach a different conclusion than religious thinkers. For example, if all of the people associated with a college were given pay raises or reduced tuition, that might benefit these people yet do injury to the university by limiting its ability to transmit its ethical values in the future. Thus Kantians sometimes see organizations as entities to which they owe moral obligations while religious individuals sometimes see only other people.

► Conclusion

The way we think about organizations as moral entities greatly influences the types of ethical decisions we make about them. Some view organizations as nonexisting, others see their existence in their mission, some see existence in the ability to engage in moral reasoning, and some see organizations as simply groups of people. Which of these views of organizations—egoist, utilitarian, Kantian, or religious—do you find most appealing?

Solving Ethics Problems

Like the other end-of-part discussions in this book, this one presents problems for you to consider. These problems have three goals. The first is to give you the opportunity to further explore the in-depth issue. The second goal is to give you experience in ethical reasoning about the law and about related management problems. The third goal is to let you see how thinking critically about the law can increase your ability to make ethical decisions. To facilitate this, the problems begin by asking you to analyze the law for its ethical content and then shift to looking at related problems in managerial ethics.

For a discussion of the ethical roles of markets and the law, and examples of the four styles of ethical reasoning—egoism, utilitarianism, Kantian philosophy, and religious ethics—read the business ethics material at the end of Part 1.

► Problems

1. Review the case of Smith v. Van Gorkon, pp. 964–65. There, the court held that the defendant directors breached their fiduciary duty of care by failing to disclose all the information they had about the proposed merger of TVC corporation. How do you classify the director's liability law articulated in this case? Is it egoistic, utilitarian, Kantian, or religious in nature? Or is it some combination?
2. Seon Cab Corporation had one shareholder, Carlton. The only assets of this corporation were two taxicabs, which were operated in New York City. Carlton was also the principal shareholder in nine other corporations. Each of these also owned two taxicabs operated in New York City. A cab owned by Seon Cab was operated negligently and as a result ran over Walkovszky. Walkovszky sued only Seon. Do you think Seon Cab is a moral entity? Do you think Walkovszky should be allowed to recover from Carlton's other corporations if he had sued them? Why or why not?
3. Assume you are the business manager of a research hospital that does important work on finding cures for certain types of cancers. Because you have worked for them for a long time, you are quite effective and the work of the organization would be slowed down significantly for about a year if you were to leave. You make $60,000 per year. An auto parts chain has asked you to join their organization and is offering

you $85,000 per year. You know the hospital is unable to pay you any more. Is this hospital a moral entity? Ought you to take the new job? Why or why not? If you think you should take the new job, what styles of moral reasoning support your view? What styles conflict with it?

4. Suppose that you are the manager of marketing for a firm that makes high quality stereo sound systems for installation by automobile manufacturers. Your product is superior to that of any competitor. One of your subordinates has a serious drinking problem. As a result, your organization has lost an important customer and its profits will therefore be 3 percent lower this year. Your organization contributes to the March of Dimes, sponsors excellence in a local elementary school with low-income students, and employs an unusually high percentage of handicapped persons. Is this organization a moral entity? How do you weigh the rights of your organization in comparison to the needs of this alcoholic employee? Should you fire him? How would this situation be analyzed by an egoist, a utilitarian, a Kantian, and a religious individual?

PART 9

REAL PROPERTY

PREVIEW

The three chapters in this part discuss the law of real property. This law developed earlier than almost any other body of law discussed in this text. As a result, it sometimes reflects its age and the fact that it developed in a primarily agricultural society. As you read through the chapters, see if you can spot aspects of the law that reflect these ancient and rural roots.

Another feature of real property law is that it is enormously complex. Even so, there are a very large number of real property transactions handled each day in every area. The great complexity causes transfer costs to be fairly high. Thus real estate brokers typically charge 4 to 10 percent of the sale price for helping conclude transactions smoothly.

Finally, when reading the chapters think about strategies and tactics you could adopt as a prospective seller, buyer, landlord, or tenant. If you master the material in these chapters, and devise common-sense strategies, you can often dramatically improve your legal position in real estate transactions.

Business ethics as it relates to the text material in these chapters is considered at the end of the part.

C H A P T E R

47

REAL PROPERTY AND ITS OWNERSHIP

After you have read this chapter, you should be able to:

1. Identify the physical parts of real property and distinguish them from personal property.
2. Understand the legal relationship between persons who co-own real estate.
3. Identify the powers over realty possessed by owners.
4. Identify the rights that the government may take from owners of real estate.
5. Identify the rights that the owner may give to another without actually transferring ownership.

BUSINESS DECISIONS and the LAW

Gary and Gail are recent college graduates. They want to invest in an apartment house near campus together. Both will participate in the management of the building and both will share the profits and any losses that may flow from the ownership. They have agreed that Gail will own 60 percent of the building and Gary will own 40 percent. Gail is married and Gary is single. If either should die, they want the surviving partner to own the whole (100 percent) of the building. They wonder what legal arrangements will permit them to create such an ownership relationship between them. After reading this chapter, you will be able to answer this and similar questions.

Introduction

The law must frequently decide what is and what is not real property. For example, if a student leases certain "real property," has he also leased the stove and refrigerator on the premises? And if someone sells or wills "real property," exactly what passes by the sale or will? If a mother wills the family home to her daughter, will the daughter become the owner of the workbench in the garage when the mother dies?

realty
Real property

Once we know what real property is, then we can examine the ways that more than one person can own the same **realty.** Of course, that introduces problems concerning the relationships among the owners. For example, if a husband and wife own realty together, should either be allowed to sell his or her interest without the other spouse's consent?

Exactly what powers should the law give to owners? Should they be allowed to cause ownership to stay forever in their family? And can an owner sell some of the ownership rights and keep the others?

How much power should be given to the government to restrict an owner's use of his or her property? If the government does restrict the use, should the owner be compensated for any loss in value of the property?

As you read through this material on real property and its ownership, ask yourself whether the rules of law seem fair and just for *all* the parties. If you disagree with the law, can you propose an alternative that will work better?

The Physical Characteristics of Real Property and Rights Therein

▶ Surface Rights

The basic physical element of realty is land. The buyer of real property usually purchases the *surface rights* or the right to occupy the surface of a piece of land.

▶ Right to Air Space

The air space above the surface of the land is also part of the realty. Ownership of that space is called the *right to air space*. The ownership power, except for the right to exclude aircraft overflight,[1] extends to the upper atmosphere. Therefore if the branch of a neighbor's tree grew into your air space, you would have the right to force its removal. While surface rights and the right to air space are usually owned by the same party, it is sometimes the case that one party owns the surface rights and another owns the right to the air space. For example, in New York City the city has sold the air space over certain highways to developers. They then build a structure like an office building over the highway. The city then owns the surface rights and the developer owns the air space. Even if a party owns just the right to the air space, the law treats that right as realty.

▶ Mineral Rights

In General In addition to the surface area and the air space, realty also includes the earth beneath the surface. The right to dig or mine that earth is called a *mineral right*. In theory, ownership of mineral rights extends down from the land surface to the center of the earth. In practice, however, no one has been able to extract minerals from a depth

---

[1]See *United States v. Causby*, 328 U.S. 256 (1946).

of more than five miles. Ownership powers over minerals depend in part upon whether the minerals are *solid* or *fluid*.

Solid Minerals Ownership of solid minerals such as coal, iron ore, copper ore, or uranium usually extends downward from the perimeter of the surface right. The owner of the mineral right has the power to remove any mineral located within that area.

Fluid Minerals Ownership of minerals such as oil (a liquid) and natural gas (a vapor) also usually extends downward from the surface area. However, the *doctrine of capture* grants ownership of these fluid minerals to the party who extracts (or *captures*) them. Thus if a person drilled an oil well on a quarter-acre lot and began pumping from a pool of oil that extended beneath a twenty-five-acre area, all the oil could be removed under the doctrine of capture. This is so even though the oil was originally another's property and, because of the pumping, it flowed from one location to another. Note that the well shaft itself may not extend into realty owned by other persons.

▶ Right to Lateral and Subjacent Support

This right means that the physical support for the land surface cannot be removed by a neighbor or the owner of the mineral right.[2] Thus one could not excavate along the property line, thereby causing a neighbor's soil to slide into the trench. Similarly, the owner of the mineral right would be liable (to the owner of the surface right) if the support timbers for a coal mine were removed, allowing the tunnel system to cave in, causing deep depressions on the surface.

▶ Water Rights

In General Water on the surface or under the ground is a part of the realty. Control of that water is called a *water right*. In the United States there are two systems for regulating the exercise of water rights. The major system is the *riparian rights system*. A minority of states, primarily western, use the *prior appropriation system*.

Riparian Rights This system allows those who own land *abutting* a body of water to make use of it. Thus ownership of the adjoining land (or the land beneath the water) carries with it the right to use the water.

riparian
Relating to land abutting a body of water

The riparian system limits the amount of water that the landowner may use with one of two theories. The *natural flow theory* allows use of the water on the riparian land so long as the natural condition of the stream, river, or lake is maintained. In contrast, the *reasonable use theory* allows the riparian owner to use any amount of water so long as it does not interfere with uses being made by other riparian owners.

Prior Appropriation Rights This system does not connect the right to use the water with the adjoining land. Rather, it grants the first party to use the water (for a beneficial purpose) priority in subsequent years over other potential users. The extent of the initial beneficial use determines the amount of water that may be used in later years.

Water Subject to Private Water Rights. Both systems of water rights regulate the use of water in nonnavigable bodies. If a body of water is **navigable,** it

navigable water
A body of water that can support commerce between states

[2] *Empire Star Mines Co., Ltd. v. Butler,* 145 P.2d 49 (Cal. 1944).

is owned by the state or federal government and landowners may not use the water without the state's consent. A body of water is navigable if it can support commerce between states.

► Distinguishing Between Real and Personal Property

The ability to distinguish between real and personal property is critical to an understanding of real estate transactions. This is so because different bodies of law govern transfers of real and personal property. Thus the Uniform Commercial Code will generally govern the sale of personal property, while the common law of contracts will govern the sale of realty. Similarly, tax treatment of real and personal property varies greatly. Thus property tax rates established by local counties are different for real and personal property. Also, income tax treatment of real and personal property varies in important ways. For example, personal property can generally be depreciated much more rapidly than real property.

real property (realty)
Land and immovable things attached to land, along with interests and rights in the land

personal property (personalty)
A movable thing, along with interests and rights in the thing

In General The usual test is that **real property** is land and immovable things attached to the land. In contrast, **personal property** is a movable thing.

Sometimes real and personal property are very closely connected—for example, a stove (perhaps personal) and a house (real). In these situations the law uses finer tests than the general test of mobility. These are the tests of *attachment, intention,* and *annexation,* which were discussed in Chapter 20, Personal Property.

Attachment or Annexation In some cases the permanency of the attachment of a thing to realty will determine whether it is real or personal. Thus crops are sometimes part of the realty and sometimes personal property. When a crop is frequently harvested, as is corn, then it is treated as personal property even while in the ground, because it is not *permanently* attached to the land. On the other hand, if the crops are *infrequently harvested,* as are Christmas trees, they are a part of the realty until severed from the ground. Avocado trees, grape vines, and rose bushes would be real property. Avocados, grapes, and roses raised by a *florist* would be personal property.

Structures or buildings are part of the real property if they are permanently attached to the land. Thus office buildings and college classrooms are part of the realty. However, a house trailer sitting on its wheels is usually considered personal property. Mobile homes that are on rented foundations and are not permanently attached to the land are **personalty.** A small garden shed resting on top of the ground would be personalty. If the wheels of the house trailer were removed and it were set on a permanent foundation, it would be realty. If the garden shed were bolted to a cement pad, it would be realty.

personalty
Personal property

fixture
A chattel that, under real estate law, has become permanently attached to realty and thus ceases to be a chattel and becomes part of the realty; it still can be used as collateral for a **security interest**[3]

security interest
"An interest in personal property or fixtures which secures payment or performance of an obligation" UCC 1–201(37)

Personal property like stoves and dishwashers become a part of the realty if they are permanently attached. In most cases a free-standing stove is personalty, but a built-in stove is realty. Personal property that becomes realty by permanent attachment, but still can be used as collateral for a security interest, is called a **fixture.**

Intention Sometimes parties reach agreements about how property is to be classified. For example, a landlord and a tenant might agree that the dishwasher installed by the tenant could be removed at the end of the lease period. This would be an indication of an *intention* to treat the property as personal. Without this display of

---

[3]For security interests in secured transactions, see pp. 1054, 1070.

intention, the dishwasher would, if permanently attached, become realty and, therefore, the property of the landlord at the end of the lease.

The fixtures attached by business tenants are called **trade fixtures.** Unlike other fixtures, trade fixtures are treated as personalty because they are usually not intended to be permanent. Thus if a baker permanently attaches ovens to a *rented* bakery shop, they would still be treated as personalty because the landlord and tenant probably intended that they should be removed at the end of the lease period.

trade fixture
A chattel attached to leased realty by a business tenant; it is usually treated as personal property

Adaptation This test will cause certain items to be classed as realty because they are truly essential to the functioning of realty. Thus a toilet in a residence is usually attached with about the same degree of permanency as a free-standing stove (personalty). But since the toilet is more essential to the functioning of the residence, it is annexed to it and treated as realty. Similarly, the key to the front door is treated as real property in some states under the doctrine of annexation!

The following case illustrates the application of these concepts.

FACTS

Michigan National Bank, Lansing, installed night depository equipment, drive-up window equipment, vault doors, and remote transaction units in six of its branches. The City of Lansing sought to increase the bank's real estate taxation because of these improvements. The bank claims these improvements are personal property, and thus not subject to the City's tax on real estate.

DECISION

The test to be applied in order to ascertain whether or not an item is a fixture emphasizes three factors:

1. Annexation to the realty, either actual or constructive;
2. Adaptation or application to the use or purpose of that part of the realty to which it is connected or appropriated; and
3. Intention to make the article a permanent accession to the realty.

Applying these factors to the present case necessitates the conclusion that the items in question are fixtures. All four items are physically annexed to the realty. The night depository equipment, drive-up window equipment, and the vault doors are all cemented into place. Once installed, they are integrated with and become part of the wall in which they are mounted. The remote transaction units are also physically integrated with the land and the buildings. Such a unit consists of a roof-type canopy supported by pillars which extends from the building wall or roof over the customer unit. The customer unit is mounted with steel bolts to a specially constructed concrete island. A pneumatic tube system runs either up into the canopy or down into the ground and then into the building.

Furthermore, each item is adapted to the use of the realty. In fact, not only is the present use of these buildings dependent on the presence of these items, none of these items can be used unless they are affixed to a building or land.

Taken together, these factors establish the [bank's] intent to permanently affix these items to the realty.

Michigan Nat'l Bank, Lansing v. City of Lansing, 293 N.W.2d 626 (Mich. 1980).

Co-ownership

► Severalty and Co-ownership

When real estate is owned by one person alone, he or she is said to own the realty in *severalty*. Co-ownership exists when realty is owned by more than one person. Thus two persons together may buy a farm and become co-owners of the property.

There are several types of co-ownership.[4] The major types of co-ownership are tenancy in common, joint tenancy, tenancy by entirety, and community property. These names are labels defining four or five characteristics of the relationships among co-owners. The characteristics generally involved are the potential number of co-owners, the possible percentage of ownership, co-owners' rights to sell their portions of ownership, and the distribution of a co-owner's interest in the realty on the co-owner's death. In general, the use of such words as "tenancy in common" in a deed or a lease is sufficient to bind the co-owners to all of the characteristics of that particular form of co-ownership.

All methods of co-ownership have a common characteristic: It is that co-owners all have equal rights to occupy all the property. Thus one co-owner may not exclude any other co-owner from any portion of their co-owned property. (See Figure 47.1.)

tenancy in common
A form of ownership of property by more than one person without survivorship

heirs
Persons who, by statute, are entitled to property not disposed of by a decedent's will

joint tenancy
A form of ownership of property by more than one person with the right of survivorship

right of survivorship
A relationship among co-owners where death of one owner causes the decedent's interest to be transferred to the remaining owners

In **tenancy in common,** the interest of the co-owner passes on his or her death to the decedent's **heirs** or devisees (the persons named in the decedent's will to receive real property). Any number may co-own as tenants in common. They may have unequal percentage ownerships. For example, one may own 99 percent while the other co-owner owns 1 percent. Each of these co-owners may sell his or her interest without the other's consent unless there is a contract provision to the contrary.

In **joint tenancy,** on the death of a co-owner, the decedent's interest passes to, and is equally divided among, the remaining joint tenants. This is called the **right of survivorship.** Any number may own as joint tenants, but each must have an equal interest. Thus if there are four joint tenants, each must own 25 percent. Each joint tenancy owner may sell his or her interest without the consent of the other co-owners, unless there is a contract provision to the contrary.

FIGURE 47.1 **Characteristics of Co-ownership**

Type of Co-ownership	Legal Characteristics					
	Right to occupy all the realty	Ownership interests must be equal	Consent required from co-owners for sale of interest	*All* interest passes to co-owners on death	Interest willable, but if not willed passes to co-owners on death	Only available to married couples
Tenants in common	✓					
Joint tenants	✓	✓		✓		
Tenants by entirety	✓	✓	✓	✓		✓
Community property	✓	✓	✓		✓	✓

Tenancy by entirety is a form of co-ownership allowed only for married couples. This method of co-ownership has all the characteristics of joint tenancy—including survivorship—except that a party may *not* sell his or her interest without the consent of the spouse. Further, a divorce or separation usually transforms tenancy by entirety into tenancy in common.

tenancy by entirety
A form of co-ownership between husband and wife with the right of survivorship

Both joint tenancy and tenancy by entirety must be created with special language because judges fear that these names of co-ownership do not adequately communicate the nature of the relationship among the co-owners. The following case illustrates this idea.

FACTS

Fred and Patricia Gilbert were husband and wife living in Alaska. They bought a parcel of land and received a warranty deed which described them as, "Fred T. Gilbert and Patricia Gilbert, husband and wife . . . grantees." Patricia then died without a will. Later Fred sold the land to Carver. After the sale Mark, the son of Fred and Patricia, filed suit against Carver to recover a portion of the land as an inheritance from his mother. Mark claimed his parents owned the land as tenants in common, and Carver argued that they owned it as tenants by entirety.

DECISION

We . . . favor the view that tenancy by the entirety is but a species of joint tenancy, their incidents being identical.

This being the case, the statutory presumption favorable to tenancy in common "unless it is expressly declared" in the conveyance that the grantees shall take as joint tenants, must be taken to apply to tenants by the entirety. So, to overcome the presumption that a man and woman named as grantees in a conveyance and described therein as "husband and wife" shall take as tenants in common, the conveyance must declare that they shall take as tenants by the entirety with right of survivorship. [Tenancy in common existed, so Mark prevails.]

Carver v. Gilbert, 387 P.2d 928 (Alaska 1963).

Some states recognize **community property**[5] as a substitute for tenancy by entirety. Again, this method of co-ownership is only for married couples. In these states, property acquired during marriage is generally presumed to be community property. However, property owned by one spouse before marriage, or received during the marriage by gift or inheritance, is presumed to be that person's *separate property*. As such, it is not community property.

community property
A form of ownership by husband and wife of property acquired by their efforts during their marriage

Survivorship is treated differently in different community property states. Some provide that, on death, half the community property goes to the surviving spouse while the other half can pass to devisees. If the decedent's one half is not willed away, it also goes to the surviving spouse. Other states treat survivorship in the same way as in tenancy by entirety. Often both spouses must consent to any conveyance of community real property.

It is important for you to be aware of community property law even if you live in a state that does not recognize it. There are several reasons for this. First, it is possible that

[5]For a further discussion of community property, see p. 405. The "sharing" concept in community property law is now embodied in a new Uniform Marital Property Act (UMPA) of 1983, which is a proposed community property act being presently considered by state legislatures.

you will be transferred to a community property state sometime during your career. Second, it is very likely that you will do business with customers located in these states.

The Nature of Ownership

Ownership of realty is usually acquired by purchase, gift, or inheritance. But everyone does not receive the same powers of ownership. The powers of ownership are defined by the **estate** in land that the new owner receives. Each estate is composed of a certain bundle of ownership rights. The words used in the deed, will, lease, or other instrument transferring ownership determine which estate the new owner receives. The party who gives up ownership powers is called the **grantor.** The party who receives ownership powers is called the **grantee.** A grantor can transfer only those ownership powers that the grantor owns.

estate
In realty, a bundle of ownership rights in, or powers over, realty

grant
In realty, a conveyance by deed

grantor
The person who has made a grant

grantee
The person to whom a grant has been made

One parcel of land usually supports only a single estate. For example, most owner-occupied homes involve just one estate. Occasionally, however, two or more estates exist in the same parcel. Thus both the landlord and the tenant own estates in the rented apartment. The tenant's ownership rights include the right to occupy the property. The landlord's ownership rights include the powers to collect the rent and regain possession at the end of the lease.

When more than one estate with more than one owner exists in a single parcel, these owners do not co-own, for example, as in tenancy in common. Rather, each owns a *separate* estate with *separate* powers of ownership. Co-owners own *together* a single estate. The following paragraphs discuss the powers of ownership of the major estates in land.

► Fee Simple Absolute

Fee simple absolute is the estate with *all* the ownership rights. The owner of this estate exercises all the power allowed by law. If this estate is present, there can be no other estate in the same land. Most buyers of homes and farms and commercial property purchase the fee simple absolute estate.

fee simple absolute
The greatest bundle of ownership rights in, and powers over, realty

► Conditional Estates

Conditional estates make the ownership conditional on some act or event. For example, ownership may exist only "so long as no alcoholic beverages are served on the premises." If scotch were served, ownership would shift from the owner of the conditional estate to the one who conditionally sold the property.

conditional estate
An estate where ownership is dependent upon some act or event

Whenever there is a conditional estate there must also be another corresponding estate. This second estate is made up of the ownership power retained by the grantor of the conditional estate. The retained power permits the grantor to receive back all the ownership rights held by the owner of the conditional estate if the condition is violated. The grantor would then have a fee simple absolute because he or she would be the owner of the only estate in the property.

► Life Estates

A **life estate** is ownership only for the length of a life. This owner exercises all the ownership powers except the right to permanently dispose of the property. The length of the ownership period is generally measured by the life of the holder of the life estate.

life estate
An estate that lasts only for the length of a particular person's life

For example, a husband might convey "to my wife Julia, for life." Occasionally the period is measured by the life of someone else. When the life estate lasts for the life of one other than the owner, it is called a *life estate pur autre vie*. For example, a father may will a home to a nurse for her use during the life of his mentally ill son.

When the life ends, the possessory rights return to the original grantor of the life estate or to another party designated by that grantor. Fee simple absolute, conditional estates, and life estates are called *freehold estates*.

► Nonfreehold Estates

Nonfreehold estates, called **tenancies,** involve ownership for a limited period of time. *Tenants* own nonfreehold estates. The length of ownership is specified in a lease, or indicated by the payment period, or is only for so long as the landlord desires. These estates are discussed in detail in Chapter 49, Renting Realty.

tenancy
A form of nonfreehold ownership in realty

► Future Interests

Future interests are estates that usually give possession of the realty when a life or a conditional estate terminates. If the right of possession returns to the one who originally granted the life or conditional estate, the future interest is usually called a **reversion.** If the right of possession goes to another person, it is sometimes called a **remainder.** Thus if a hunting guide were to convey his mountain cabin "to my brother Albonzo for life, and then to his son Fredrico," the son would, on his father's death, receive a remainder. If the guide conveyed simply "to my brother Albonzo for life," the law would probably conclude that the guide intended to regain ownership on Albonzo's death. The guide would receive a reversion.

reversion
A future interest that will, or may, be returned to the grantor. In contrast, a remainder goes to one other than the grantor

remainder
That remaining part of an estate in land which, on the termination of a preceding estate, passes to someone other than the grantor

Future interests are also classified as *vested* and *contingent*. Vested interests arise when there is certainty that the estate will become possessory—that is, the grantee will acquire the possessory estate. For example, if a deed conveyed property to "my son, Al, for life, and then to my grandson, Mark, and his heirs," the future interest of Mark is *vested*. It is certain that he or his heirs will possess the estate. However, if the conveyance were from grandfather to son for life, and then to grandson provided that he shall then be unmarried, this grandson's future interest is *contingent*. It will not vest if the grandson is married when the son dies. One cannot be certain that the grandson or his heirs will ever possess the estate.

Rule against Perpetuities The distinction between vested and contingent future interests is especially important because the **rule against perpetuities** makes void certain contingent future interests. These are contingent future interests that do not vest within the length of a life in being at the time of the conveyance plus twenty-one years. To illustrate, suppose a successful business woman were to convey her estate "to my daughter, Alberta, for life, and then to my firstborn granddaughter twenty-five years after Alberta's death, provided she is then a registered Democrat, and if not. . . ." The conveyance is contingent on the granddaughter's survival and her political affiliation. And at least twenty-five years would be required for her interest to vest. This violates the requirement that the interest vest within "the length of a life in being plus twenty-one years." Thus the attempted conveyance to the granddaughter violates the rule. This rule is intended to ensure that property is not burdened for long periods of time when the identity of the ultimate owner is uncertain.

rule against perpetuities
The beneficiary of a trust, or of a contingent future interest in realty, must be identifiable at the time the trust or contingent future interest is created, or, in most states, within a period for the life of a person or persons in existence at the time the trust or contingent future interest is created and 21 years after the death of such person or persons

The Rights of Others in an Owner's Land

► Liens

lien
A legal right in another's property as security for the performance of an obligation

A **lien** is a legal right in another's property as security for the performance of an obligation. In a way it is a claim against the financial value of an estate in land. A "mortgage" is a lien; so is a "trust deed." (See pp. 1006–1008.) These are called *voluntary liens;* the owner of the realty consents to (or volunteers) the lien, usually because he or she receives money in return for granting the lien. These voluntary liens are discussed in more detail in Chapter 48, Transferring Ownership of Realty.

Involuntary liens arise without the consent of the owner. For example, if an owner does not pay property taxes when due, they often automatically become a lien against the property. This is called a *tax lien*. If the tax lien is not paid, the taxing authority can cause the property to be sold to pay the debt. This is called *foreclosure* and is discussed in more detail in Chapter 48.

Mechanic's liens are another example of involuntary liens. A mechanic is someone who supplies labor or material that is used to improve real property. A carpenter can be a mechanic; so can a plumber, a lumber yard, or the college student who installs lawn sprinklers. If mechanics who improve the realty are not paid, they can file with the county recorder or county clerk a mechanic's lien against the property. Usually the lien must be filed within a certain time period after the work is done—for example, within sixty or ninety days. If the lien is filed within the required time period, but it is not paid off, the mechanic can file suit, prove his or her claim, and cause the property to be foreclosed (i.e., sold) to pay the debt. The main feature of the mechanic's lien is that it is effective as of the date when the work was done, not when the lien was filed, or when the lawsuit was won. Thus, in foreclosure, the mechanic will generally have his or her lien paid *before* any other lien that arose *after* the work was done.

► Licenses

When someone owns a *possessory* estate in land, whether in severalty or as a co-owner, he or she controls all the ownership rights associated with that particular estate. Frequently the owner will give some right in the land to another. For example, a theatre owner may grant someone the privilege (right) to sit through one showing of a film. This kind of temporary, oral right to come upon the land of another is called a **license.** A license is a temporary, revocable right (privilege) to some limited use of another's land. It is personal, nontransferable, not inheritable, and not an estate in land. Stores grant implied licenses to their customers to enter the store to shop for goods. Dinner guests are on the host's property by right of a license.

license
In real property, a temporary, revocable right (privilege) to some limited use of another's land

Generally, oral licenses are revocable. Thus the theatre patron or the dinner guest would become *trespassers* if they failed to leave immediately when asked. The theatre patron may be entitled to a refund of money, but the patron cannot legally sit through the show when asked to leave. In many places trespass is a criminal offense and the police will assist in removing the trespasser. Usually an oral license is revoked automatically when the one who granted it sells the land.

► Easements

easement
An irrevocable right to the limited use of another's land

Easements are usually *irrevocable* rights to some limited use of another's land. In contrast with licenses, easements are generally given for substantial periods of time—for example, for five or for fifty years or forever. To comply with the statute of frauds, easements should be in writing. Easements may be granted to allow a neighbor to drive across your land, to bury a sewer pipe, to hang power lines over the land, or to make any other use that does not constitute exclusive possession. Easements may be *appurtenant* or *in gross*.

Easements Appurtenant When easements are given to neighboring landowners and the easement *benefits* the neighbor's land, then it is called an *easement appurtenant*. Appurtenant means attached to the land. Thus an easement to drive farm equipment across a neighbor's land in order to farm an otherwise inaccessible parcel would be an easement appurtenant. (See Figure 47.2.)

The land belonging to the person granting the appurtenant easement is called the **servient tenement.** That land is in a sense the servant of the benefited land. The servient tenement is burdened with the easement. The land benefited is named the **dominant tenement.**

servient tenement
Property in which someone has an easement appurtenant

dominant tenement
Property that is benefited by an easement appurtenant in nearby land

Easements for access roads or water ditches are easements appurtenant. These easements are transferred with the dominant tenement. However, the servient tenement is bound after its transfer only if the buyer of the servient tenement had notice of the easement prior to the purchase. Notice can come from a recorded document or from physical signs, such as a road rut.

The following case illustrates the issue of transferability of rights to the use of the land of another.

FACTS

In 1962 Offutt, defendant, sold a house to the Wynns. The house adjoined an apartment building owned by Offutt. In the apartment building was a swimming pool. In order to induce the Wynns to purchase the home Offutt agreed in the contract of sale that, "use of the apartment swimming pool to be available to purchaser and his family." No mention of the pool was made in Wynn's deed. In 1969 the Wynns sold the house to the Bunns and informed them that they had the right to use the pool. When the Bunns sought to use the pool, they were denied access. Accordingly they sued Offutt for the right to use the pool.

DECISION

Judgment for defendant. The Bunns did not have the right to use the pool. The use of the pool was personal in nature and was not essential to the beneficial enjoyment of the Bunns' property and thus it was not transferred with the land to the Bunns.

Bunn v. Offutt, 222 S.E.2d 522 (Va. 1976).

FIGURE 47.2 **Easement Appurtenant for the Benefit of Property A**

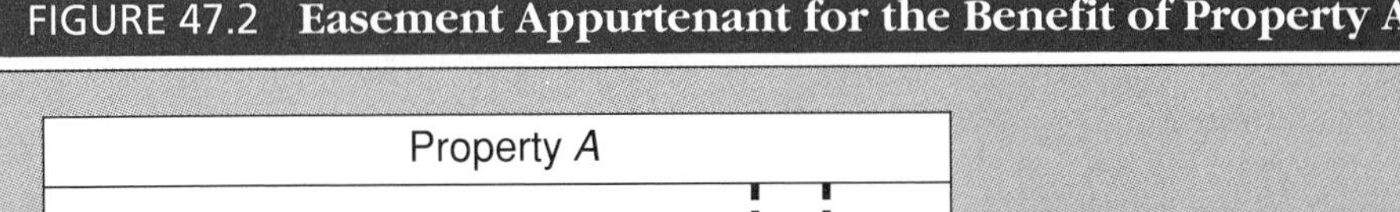

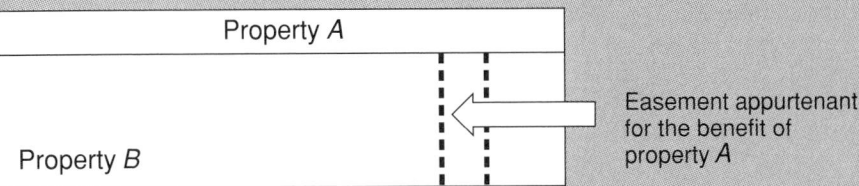

Property *A* is the dominant tenement, while property *B* is the servient tenement. *A* is benefited because the easement makes that land more accessible. Property *B* is burdened because someone other than the owner of *B* has a right to the use of the property.

Easements in Gross Easements that do not benefit neighboring land, like easements for access given to a nonneighbor, or for telegraph lines and poles, are called *easements in gross.* Easements in gross pass to the buyer when the burdened property is sold. However, the person benefited generally cannot transfer his or her rights.

There are two other important types of easements called *easements by prescription* and *easements by implication.* Easements by prescription are discussed in Chapter 48, Transferring Ownership of Realty. The following case discusses the law related to *easements by necessity.*

FACTS

Oscar and Martha Helms, are the owners of a forty-acre tract of land in DeKalb County. . . . Between the land owned by the Helmses and the nearest public road, . . . there is a one-acre lot . . . owned by the Tullises. The Helmses moved a house trailer onto their forty-acre tract, and sought to have electrical service furnished to their trailer by way of a power line to be run from the road over the one-acre tract owned by the Tullises. To accomplish this, Oscar Helms told a representative of the Sand Mountain Electric Cooperative that he owned the land all the way to the road. Relying on this representation, employees of the electric cooperative cut approximately twenty trees from the land owned by the Tullises in preparation for the power line to be run to the Helmses' trailer. When the Tullises became aware that trees were being cut on their land without their permission, they ordered the electric cooperative's employees to cease. The Helmses filed suit to enjoin the Tullises from further interference with the service of electrical power to the Helmses' property, and or damages. . . .

DECISION

The only possible theory upon which the Helmses would be entitled to restrain an adjoining landowner from preventing the cutting of trees from the landowner's own property would be that an easement existed across the adjoining lot for the purpose of running a power line. . . .

The only . . . possible ways an easement could have been created in the case before us are by necessity and by implication. Creation by necessity is actually a form of creation by implication, but is treated separately by some authors. . . .

The rationale for allowing an easement by necessity is that public policy demands that land not be rendered unusable. . . . Under Alabama law, however, there must be a genuine necessity; mere convenience is not enough. . . . The burden is on the one seeking to establish the easement to prove the easement is "reasonably necessary for the enjoyment" of the land. . . . Easements by necessity almost always involve access roads across the servient tenement connecting the dominant tenement to a public road or highway. . . . Original unity of ownership of the dominant and servient tenements is always required for an easement by necessity. . . .

Easements created by implication cover a variety of types of easements. Creation by this method requires not only original unity of ownership, . . . but also that the use be open, visible, continuous, and reasonably necessary to the estate granted. . . . The implication is that the parties implied such an easement because the grantee, having seen the use the grantor made of the property, can reasonably expect a continuance of the former manner of use. . . .

In the present case there is no easement created by either necessity or implication. The Helmses failed to show that there was no other route by which a power line could be brought to their property. Thus, there was no necessity. Furthermore, electrical service was not shown to be necessary to the reasonable enjoyment of the property, although it was shown to be necessary to one use of the property, i.e., as a site for a residence. There was no easement created by implication, since there had never been a power line run over that strip of land; thus there was no open, visible and continuous use. . . .

The judgment of the trial court is therefore affirmed.

Helms v. Tullis, 398 S.2d 253 (Ala. 1981).

► Zoning Ordinances

The owner's use of his or her realty can also be restricted by zoning ordinances. An **ordinance** is a municipal law or legislation. Zoning ordinances may be adopted by cities or counties to regulate the location of residential, business, and industrial districts. The purpose of zoning is to ensure fair use and orderly development of land within the community.

ordinance
Municipal legislation

The legal power to enact zoning ordinances comes from the U.S. Constitution, which recognizes the **police power** of the separate states. Generally the states cannot use police power except to promote the health, safety, morals, and general welfare of the community. State legislatures usually pass statutes that permit the cities and counties to enact the zoning ordinances.

police power
The power of a state or federal government to legislate reasonably for the general public welfare

The zoning power is very broad. Courts generally support the right of cities and counties to enforce community zoning goals at the expense of individual landowners. For example, a commercial area could be rezoned residential. If the zoning reduced the value of the owner's land, the owner would bear the loss and could not recover for the financial injury from the local government.

On the other hand, zoning cannot be used unreasonably to eliminate an *existing use*. Thus a zoning ordinance restricting use of an area to residential could not be used to eliminate an already existing cemetery.[6] The cemetery in a residential zone is called a nonconforming use. If the city wishes to eliminate the cemetery, it must go through **condemnation** procedures, which permit the city to take title to the property by paying the owners the reasonable value of the property. Recently, however, some states have begun to allow reasonable zoning ordinances that eliminate existing uses. Thus an ordinance requiring the elimination of billboard signs within five years would be enforceable in some states.

condemnation
Forcing a property owner to transfer property to a government in exchange for just compensation

The following case describes the law that applies to condemnations. The reader is asked to think about when the government should be required to compensate private parties when it takes from them some of their property.

FACTS

This case presents the question whether a minor but permanent physical occupation of an owner's property authorized by government constitutes a "taking" of property for which just compensation is due under the Fifth and Fourteenth Amendments of the Federal Constitution. New York law provides that a landlord must permit a cable television company to install its cable facilities upon his property.... In this case, the cable installation occupied portions of appellant's roof and the side of her building. The New York Court of Appeals ruled that this appropriation does not amount to a taking, but the U.S. Supreme Court reversed.

DECISION

The New York Court of Appeals described the installation as follows:

> On June 1, 1970 Teleprompter installed a cable slightly less than one-half inch in diameter and of approximately 30 feet in length along the length of the building about 18 inches above the roof top, and directional taps, approximately 4 inches by 4 inches by 4 inches, on the front and rear of the roof. By June 8, 1970 the cable had been extended another 4 to 6 feet and cable had been run from the directional taps to the adjoining building at 305 West 105th Street....

[6]See *Lockard v. City of Los Angeles,* 202 P.2d 38 (Cal. 1949).

Prior to 1973, Teleprompter routinely obtained authorization for its installation from property owners along the cable's route, compensating the owners at the standard rate of 5 percent of the gross revenues that Teleprompter realized from the particular property. To facilitate tenant access to CATV, the State of New York enacted Section 828 of the Executive Law, effective January 1, 1973. Section 828 provides that a landlord may not "interfere with the installation of cable television facilities upon his property or premises," and may not demand payment from any tenant for permitting CATV, or demand payment from any CATV company "in excess of any amount which the [State Commission on Cable Television] shall, by regulation, determine to be reasonable." . . . Pursuant to Section 828(1)(b), the State Commission has ruled that a one-time $1 payment is the normal fee to which a landlord is entitled. . . . The Commission ruled that this nominal fee, which the Commission concluded was equivalent to what the landlord would receive if the property were condemned . . . satisfied constitutional requirements "in the absence of a special showing of greater damages attributable to the taking." . . .

Appellant did not discover the existence of the cable until after she had purchased the building. She brought a class action against Teleprompter in 1976 on behalf of all owners of real property in the state on which Teleprompter has placed CATV components, alleging that Teleprompter's installation was a trespass and, insofar as it relied on Section 828, a taking without just compensation. She requested damages and injunctive relief. . . .

The Court of Appeals determined that Section 828 serves the legitimate public purpose of "rapid development of and maximum penetration by a means of communication which has important educational and community aspects," . . . and thus is within the State's police power. We have no reason to question that determination. It is a separate question, however, whether an otherwise valid regulation so frustrates property rights that compensation must be paid. . . . We conclude that a permanent physical occupation authorized by government is a taking without regard to the public interests that it may serve. Our constitutional history confirms the rule, recent cases do not question it, and the purposes of the Takings Clause compel its retention.

A "taking" may more readily be found when the interference with property can be characterized as a physical invasion by government, . . . than when interference arises from some public program adjusting the benefits and burdens of economic life to promote the common good." . . .

The Court has often upheld substantial regulation of an owner's use of his own property where deemed necessary to promote the public interest. At the same time, we have long considered a physical intrusion by government to be a property restriction of an unusually serious character for purposes of the Takings Clause. Our cases further establish that when the physical intrusion reaches the extreme form of a permanent physical occupation, a taking has occurred. In such a case, "the character of the government action" not only is an important factor in resolving whether the action works a taking but is determinative.

Our holding today is very narrow. We affirm the traditional rule that a permanent physical occupation of property is a taking. In such a case, the property owner entertains an historically rooted expectation of compensation, and the character of the invasion is qualitatively more intrusive than perhaps any other category of property regulation. We do not, however, question the equally substantial authority upholding a State's broad power to impose appropriate restrictions upon an owner's *use* of his property.

The judgment of the New York Court of Appeals is reversed and the case is remanded for further proceedings not inconsistent with this opinion.

Loretto v. Teleprompter Manhattan CATV Corp., et al., 458 U.S. 419 (1982).

Spot zoning is the treatment of a single property in a manner inconsistent with the treatment of similar properties in the area. It is usually prohibited.[7] Further, zoning will not be enforceable if it exceeds the police power of the state. This occurs when the

[7] *Smith v. County of Washington*, 406 P.2d 545 (Or. 1965).

ordinance is clearly arbitrary, unreasonable, and without substantial relation to the public health, safety, morals, and general welfare.

A *variance* may be granted by a city or county to allow a landowner to make some use of his or her land that is inconsistent with the general zoning ordinance. Usually the owner must appear before the variance board and establish hardship and lack of injury to others. For example, a particular zoning ordinance may prohibit fences taller than five feet. A property owner might obtain a variance allowing a six-foot fence by showing that all the neighbors consent and by arguing that the taller fence is needed to keep four large dogs in the yard. The following case illustrates the use of a variance.

FACTS

The City of Moline planned to build a firehouse on a corner lot. The lot was subject to country zoning ordinances which established "setback lines." These established a uniform distance from the street for buildings. The effect of the uniform distance is to make the area look neat and give each building equal visibility from the road.

Moline's plans placed the firehouse closer to the one street than the zoning ordinance allowed. Accordingly, the City of Moline filed for a variance with the Board of Zoning Adjustments. The Board granted the variance. The Conners owned adjoining property and appealed the decision of the Board to the courts.

DECISION

The property in question is on the northwest corner of Chambers Road and Clairmont Drive in an unincorporated portion of St. Louis County. Chambers Road is a major thoroughfare which was widened shortly before the application for variance. The land in question is owned by Moline and has been the site for its fire station since at least 1946. The old fire house complied with the Chambers Road setback line but not with the Clairmont Drive building line upon which it encroached approximately 4¼ feet as a pre-existing use.

The most efficient and satisfactory type of fire station for Moline's purposes is one where returning trucks can enter the back of the station from Clairmont Drive, remove the hoses and other equipment for cleaning, put clean equipment on the truck and move the truck into position for exit through the front onto Chambers Road for the next call. The lot in question is 165 feet in depth (after the widening of Chambers to 80 feet) and 80 feet in width. If the set-back line on Chambers Road, 80 feet, is adhered to there would not be enough room at the rear of the station (39 feet) for the large fire trucks to negotiate the turn from Clairmont Drive into the rear of the station. The entrance from Clairmont would also obviate the need for the trucks to back into the station from Chambers Road. There was also testimony that having the station located nearer the road than the old station would allow greater traffic safety in leaving the station in that both the dispatcher and the driver would have greater visibility along Chambers Road.

The Board could find here that in the absence of a variance Moline would be confronted with substantial additional expense, interruption of fire protection service during the period of construction, and unnecessary inconvenience if not outright danger to the residents of the district. The Board is not required to ignore the source of the funds available to the district (taxpayers) in determining that additional expense constitutes an unnecessary hardship. Under Rosedale-Skinker, there exist sufficient "practical difficulties" and "unnecessary hardships" to the district to permit a variance and these arise from the inadequate size of the lot to contain a fire station. This was the essence of the Board's finding "that because of the requirements, the proposed new building and facilities cannot be erected as the 80 foot set back line on Chambers Road and the thirty foot building line on Clairmont Drive are intended."

The effect on general welfare finding is supported by the evidence of the need for the new building to render adequate fire protection to the district and by the testimony on the beneficial effect of the proposed construction upon traffic safety on Chambers Road, including the installation of a traffic light on Chambers Road to be controlled by the dispatcher when trucks leave the station. [The action of the zoning board is affirmed.]

Conner v. Herd, 452 S.W.2d 272 (Mo. 1970).

Building codes specify the construction techniques and standards that must be used in the city or county.

Restrictive Covenants

covenant
A promise as a part of a contract

Even when there are no zoning restrictions, the owner may still be prohibited from certain uses. This occurs when a former owner created a restrictive **covenant** or when the nature of the neighborhood creates an *equitable servitude*. Equitable servitudes may arise when the general building plan or scheme of development in the area may give notice to a purchaser that his or her use of the property must conform with the general use. When this occurs, the purchaser is said to be bound by an equitable servitude. A restrictive covenant is a promise usually made by the buyer to the seller. It is often written in the deed or contract for sale or other recordable document. Usually the promise limits the use of the land in some way. For example, the buyer may contract with the seller, promising not to graze sheep on the land. This buyer is almost always bound by the restrictive covenant.

covenant running with the land
The promise of an owner of land that binds future owners of the same land

If the buyer who gave the covenant resells, the new owner is bound only if the covenant is the kind that **runs with the land**. Restrictive covenants run with the land when they meet all four of the following legal tests:

1. The original parties must have *intended* the covenant to run.
2. It must touch and concern the land. This means that the covenant must affect the use of the property or affect the title to the property.
3. The buyer must have had notice of the covenant at the time of purchase. Notice exists when the buyer is told about the restrictive covenant or when a copy of the restrictive covenant is recorded.
4. There must be a chain of ownership connections between the original promisee and the current owner. This is called *privity of estate*.

If one of the tests is not passed, then the restrictive covenant does not bind subsequent purchasers. For example, if the buyer promises not to buy a Chevrolet automobile while owning the land, then this restrictive covenant binds the buyer but not subsequent purchasers. This would be so because this particular promise does not touch and concern the land.

Note that sellers can extract the same promise from buyers by a restrictive covenant, or by transferring a conditional estate, or by separate contract. If the restrictive covenant is broken, the owner may be required to pay damages or may be enjoined from future breaches. In contrast, if the condition of conveyance is violated, the violator loses his or her ownership.

Possessor's Tort Duties

A possessor—a person who owns a possessory interest in land—may owe certain tort duties to other persons who come on the land. The extent of the duties depends upon whether the persons who come on the land are trespassers, licensees, or invitees.

Trespasser A *trespasser* is a person who is on the land without any right to be there. Thus when a neighbor walks upon your land without your consent, the neighbor is a trespasser. Generally, a trespasser takes the property as the trespasser finds it. The possessor does not have any duty to the trespasser to keep the land in a reasonably safe condition. However, the possessor cannot intentionally cause harm to the trespasser.

Further, if the possessor knows that the trespasser is on the land, or that persons constantly trespass on the land, then various tort duties are imposed upon the possessor with respect to the condition of the land. An **attractive nuisance** attracts children to **trespass** and broadens the possessor's responsibility.

attractive nuisance
A dangerous and attractive condition of realty that may lure children into trespassing

trespass
(verb) To wrongfully interfere with another's possession of land or chattels

Licensee A *licensee* is a person whom the possessor of land has permitted to be on that land. A social guest is an example. A licensee takes the premises for what they appear to be, and therefore the possessor has the duty to disclose to the licensee nonobvious dangers on the land known to the possessor and which the licensee would not be likely to discover.

Invitee An *invitee* is a person who is either a *public invitee*—that is, a member of the public invited to enter or remain on the land by its possessor for a public purpose—or a *business visitor*—one who is invited by the possessor to enter or remain on the land for the purpose of doing business with the possessor. A person becomes a public invitee when he or she is permitted to go upon the land of another for a public meeting. When a retail store invites prospective customers to enter the store and consider making purchases, the customers become business visitors. Thus a social guest is not an invitee because neither of the two purposes (public or business) is present. The possessor of land has the duty to keep the premises in a reasonably safe condition and to warn invitees of dangers on the land of which the possessor should, on reasonable examination, be aware and which are not reasonably discoverable by the invitee.

Summary Statement

1. The physical elements of real property include surface rights, air rights, mineral rights, and water rights.
2. Personal property becomes realty when that is what is intended, or when it is permanently attached to the realty, or when it is adapted to the realty. It is then a fixture. Trade fixtures, however, are usually personal property. Crops are classified as real or personal property according to their permanence in the ground.
3. Co-ownership can take the form of tenancy in common, joint tenancy, tenancy by entirety, or community property. All but tenancy in common have some right of survivorship.
4. The rights and powers of ownership are determined by the estate in land received by the purchaser. Fee simple absolute is the most common and greatest estate. Other major estates are conditional estates, life estates, nonfreehold estates, and future interests.
5. A license is a temporary, revocable right (privilege) to some limited use of another's land. Easements are rights to some use of another's land that cannot be revoked by the possessor. Easements may be appurtenant or in gross.
6. Zoning is an exercise of police power. Spot zoning, attempts to eliminate current uses, and arbitrary and unreasonable zoning are generally unenforceable.
7. Only those restrictive covenants that run with the land bind later purchasers.
8. Possessors of land owe tort duties to trespassers and greater duties to licensees and invitees.

The following older but well explained case confronts the problems associated with covenants that run with the land. The case is intended to illustrate the way a court will scrutinize the words creating the covenant. The reader is asked to think about whether or not prior owners should be allowed to control current use of realty.

PARRISH v. RICHARDS
336 P.2d 122 (Utah 1959)

McDonough, J. This is an action to enjoin maintenance of a tennis court and fence allegedly built in violation of a real property restrictive covenant.

The parties are contiguous owners of real property. . . . [The Richards'] residence is located between those of plaintiffs, Parrish and Peterson. Prior to the acquisition by any of the parties of any of the tracts of land here involved, there had been placed upon and against such lands certain restrictive covenants recorded in the office of the County Recorder of Salt Lake County, Utah. The covenant here involved reads as follows:

> Use of Land: Each lot is hereby designated as a residential lot, and none of said lots shall be improved, used or occupied for other than private residence purposes, and no flat or apartment house . . . shall be erected thereon, *and no structure shall be erected* . . . other than a one-, two-, or three-car garage, and one single family residence, not to exceed one story in height. . . . [Emphasis added.]

Prior to August 1, 1955 [the Richards] leveled their land on the south side and laid down a concrete apron in the southwest corner measuring 78 feet by 36 feet for a tennis court. Around and upon such concrete [the Richards] placed a six-foot wire fence. [The Richards] testified that they do not intend to put up any overhead lights or floodlights whatsoever over the tennis court.

Parrish brought suit, alleging that the described construction of the tennis court is a "structure" erected and placed upon the property in violation of the above-mentioned restrictive covenant. Parrish also alleged that the construction interfered with their view; that there had been no waiver of the covenant on their part; that the value of their property had diminished as a result of the construction; and they prayed for an injunction permanently enjoining the defendants from proceeding with the construction.

The trial court followed the correct doctrine that in the construction of uncertain or ambiguous restrictions, the courts will resolve all doubts in favor of the free and unrestricted use of property and that it will "have recourse to every aid, rule, or canon of construction to ascertain the intention of the parties." In applying that doctrine to the situation, the court concluded that the fence surrounding said tennis court does not violate the covenant. Garages and other similar buildings which are of solid construction are of a different character entirely. Structures of that kind, which are solid, obstruct the view for the neighborhood and crowd the area with buildings, which would reduce the beauty of it. It seems quite plain that the covenant was intended to prevent the blocking of the view and the crowding of the buildings which would reduce the beauty and utility and therefore depreciate the value of the property within the subdivision. But the objections which validly may be made against solid constructions do not exist in regard to a flat concrete slab for a tennis court. Nor does the wire fence around it obstruct the view. Based upon the foregoing, it is our opinion that the trial court was correct in its conclusion that the tennis court and fence are not the type of structure prohibited by the covenant.

Affirmed, for [the Richards].

Questions and Case Problems

1. In 1941 W. E. and Jennie Hutton executed a warranty deed conveying their interest in a parcel of land to the local school district. The words of conveyance stated: This land to be used for school purposes only; otherwise to revert to grantors herein.

The property was used for a school for the period from 1941 to 1973. After 1973 the property was used by the school district for storage purposes. When this occurred, the heirs of the Huttons filed suit to recover the property from the school district. Who owns the land? [*Mahrenholz v. County Board of School Trustees of Lawrence County,* 417 N.E.2d 138 (Ill. 1981).]

2. Wicks, a farmer, entered into an oral contract for the sale of four acres of uncut barley to Candle, a grocer, for $450. The parties agreed that the crop was to be severed three weeks after the agreement was made. Because the market price for barley rose nearly 60 percent, Wicks barred Candle from cutting the crop. Candle sues, and Wicks defends by citing that part of the statute of frauds requiring that a contract for the sale of an interest in land must be in writing. Who prevails?
3. In 1939 Cyrus M. Beachy conveyed real property to a trust for the benefit of his grandchildren, ages 11 and 15. Beachy required that the property pass from the trust to the children "when the youngest . . . shall have attained the age of forty (40) or would have attained such age had he survived."

   If either grandchild died before the property passed, his interest was to go to his children, if any, and to his heirs at law if no children were born.

   In 1945 Beachy died. His will left all his property to the grandchildren. The grandchildren claim that the conveyance to the trust violates the rule against perpetuities and is therefore void. If void, the property was part of the estate that passed through the will. Thus the grandchildren would have immediate possession. Must the grandchildren wait the remaining 23 years before receiving the property? [*McEwen v. Enoch,* 204 P.2d 736 (Kan. 1949).]
4. Consiglio owned a building in West Yarmouth, Mass. He rented it to Carey for summer seasons. Carey operated a restaurant in the building called Dorsie's Steak House and paid rent of $4,500 to $8,500 per month. After Consiglio and Carey discussed the possibility of Carey's purchase of the building. Consiglio raised the rent to $35,000 per month in an attempt to encourage Carey to conclude the purchase. Instead of purchasing, Carey prepared to move to another nearby building. Consiglio then brought suit to prevent Carey from removing certain items of restaurant equipment installed by Carey on the grounds that they were real property. The equipment pertinent here is a walk-in freezer, a compressor which supplies the cold air to the freezer, two air conditioners, and a bar. The two air conditioners were installed in two of the three window casings. They were large units, and their installation necessitated removal of the sash from each casing. The freezer, which is 12 feet high and too high to be brought into the building, was installed at the back wall of the building on an insulated concrete slab. A hole was cut in the rear wall of the building to provide access to the freezer door. The freezer is portable. The compressor is also located outside the building and is attached only to the freezer. The built-in bar is attached to the realty. Will the injunction be granted? [*Consiglio v. Carey,* 421 N.E.2d 1257 (Mass. 1981).]
5. Clarence sold to Delbert a parcel of land on which there was a home, a barn, unharvested crops, and a housetrailer. Delbert protested when Clarence removed the trailer and Delbert sues to recover it. Will he prevail?
6. Mr. Thomas and Mr. Sturgeon were elderly gentlemen with heart ailments living in a home owned by them in joint tenancy in Fresno, California. On September 2, 1947, at about 9:00 P.M., a neighbor heard Mr. Sturgeon yelling to a neighbor to call a doctor. After calling, the neighbor went over and saw Mr. Thomas lying on the ground. The neighbor thought Mr. Thomas' body was cold and felt for a pulse but none was present. At that same time he heard a thud in the house. On investigation

he found Mr. Sturgeon lying with his head on the piano pedals. Artificial respiration was administered. Within 30 minutes Mr Sturgeon stopped breathing.

Shortly thereafter, the fire chief arrived and observed that Mr. Thomas' body was discolored and cool while Mr. Sturgeon's body was still warm and had good color.

At the trial between the heirs of Mr. Thomas and Mr. Sturgeon, evidence was introduced that an autopsy could not establish who had died first.

Further, a physician testified that body temperature as felt at the scene would not be a good indication of who died first.

California has a provision in its Probate Code which states:

> Where there is no sufficient evidence that two joint tenants have died otherwise than simultaneously the property so held shall be distributed one-half as if one had survived and one-half as if the other had survived.

The trial court found that Thomas died first and his heirs appealed the case. What decision by the appellate court? [*Thomas v. Anderson,* 215 P.2d 478 (Cal. 1950).]

7. Purcey gave a written easement to her neighbor Pistol allowing Pistol to run a water ditch across Purcey's property to irrigate Pistol's land. Purcey sells her property to Rifle, who fills in the ditch because "it's dangerous for my kids." Pistol sues. Who prevails?
8. Holmes was engaged in the business of raising and processing chickens. In 1963 he bought property in Clackamas County, Oregon, on which he planned to erect a chicken-processing plant. To prepare for construction, he spent $33,000 to install a well system, plant special grass, and run soil tests to determine where drain fields for the plant's sewage should be located. In 1967 Clackamas County enacted an ordinance zoning the property Rural Agricultural-Single Family Residential. The zoning prohibited further construction of the chicken-processing plant. Holmes continued work and the county sued. The trial court enjoined defendant from further construction and he appealed. What result? [*Clackamas County v. Holmes,* 508 P.2d 190 (Or. 1973).]
9. The Davis family rented an apartment in a complex controlled by McDougall. The laundry room in the complex contained a Maytag washing machine with tub, agitator, and roller-type wringer. The roller wringer was designed to release automatically when misused. However, the release mechanism was defective. Jodi Davis, aged 3½, climbed up on a stool, started the washer and inserted her hand in the roller wringer, causing permanent injuries to her fingers, hand, and wrist. Her parents sued on her behalf, alleging that the landlord maintained an attractive nuisance. The trial court granted McDougall's motion for summary judgment and ruled that the washing machine was not an attractive nuisance. Jodi's parents appealed. What result? [*Davis v. McDougall,* 480 P.2d 907 (Idaho 1971).]
10. In the case of *Parrish v. Richards,* excerpted at the beginning of this section, is there anything that suggests the kind of attitude this court has toward restrictive covenants? Explain.

CHAPTER 48

TRANSFERRING OWNERSHIP OF REALTY

After you have read this chapter, you should be able to:

1. Describe the process of transferring ownership of realty with deeds.
2. Describe the major methods of financing ownership and indicate the advantages and disadvantages of each method.
3. Identify the consequences of recording a document associated with realty.
4. Describe the steps involved in the typical sales transaction.
5. Identify methods for transferring ownership other than by a sale.

BUSINESS DECISIONS and the LAW

Gail and Gary are about to invest in an apartment house near a college campus. They intend to rent to college students. However, they do not trust the seller of the building. So they have approached you and asked what steps they can take to protect themselves so they will not be cheated when they take title to the property. They want to know what type of deed they should get and what they should do with the deed after they receive it. They believe they should immediately place the deed in a safe-deposit box so that it cannot be stolen or lost. After reading this chapter, you should be able to tell them what they should do with respect to the deed in this transaction.

Introduction

In the previous chapter we discussed the meaning of real property, forms of ownership and co-ownership, and the various interests in land that may be owned. In this chapter we will discuss the ways that ownership in realty can be transferred.

Ownership of realty is most frequently transferred as a part of a *sales transaction*. Basically, the seller transfers ownership, through the *deeding process,* in return for the buyer's payment of the purchase price. Since most buyers do not have enough cash to pay the full price, they usually borrow most of the money from a lender such as a bank. The lender usually protects its interest by requiring the buyer to execute an *instrument of finance,* such as a mortgage or a trust deed. These instruments generally allow the lender to collect the loan by selling the realty if payments are not made as promised.

Ownership is often transferred without being part of a sales transaction. Further, the deeding process is not always needed to effectuate a transfer. For example, a city may condemn realty. In this process it forces a transfer of ownership without the consent of the private party.

This chapter examines ownership transfers by describing the deeding process and by evaluating the instruments of finance. Once these basic processes are developed, one can then examine the whole of the sales process. The nonsale transfers of ownership, such as condemnation, are discussed last.

As you read through this material, ask yourself whether the average college graduate who has successfully completed a course in business law can competently handle his or her own purchase or sale. How about the college graduate without a background in business law? Or the person who did not graduate from high school? If you conclude that the average consumer needs professional help, then think about the kind of background such a professional person ought to have.

The Deeding Process

► Historical Development

livery of seisin
An ancient ceremony used to transfer ownership of land

The law of deeds has its roots in the ancient rite of **livery of seisin.** That ceremony served as the forerunner of the modern deeding process at a time when very few persons could write. This method of transferring ownership required that the buyer and seller gather a group of local residents on the property to be sold. All the persons would march around the boundaries of the property and then assemble at its center. There the seller would dig up a chunk of sod and offer it to the buyer with the local residents as witnesses. While offering the sod, the seller would recite the terms of the transaction. Ownership was transferred when the buyer accepted the chunk of sod from the hands of the seller. While the modern deeding process has replaced the old rite of livery of seisin, it is easier to understand the modern process when it is compared with the old ceremony.

► Overview of the Modern Deeding Process

deed
A formal document used to transfer title to real estate

Today paper replaces the chunk of sod. Usually a **deed** is a single piece of paper. (See Figure 48.1.) Like the sod, a new deed is created each time there is a sale. Like the ancient ceremony of livery of seisin, it is the whole deeding process that transfers ownership. All the parts of the modern process must be completed before ownership is transferred. These elements of the modern deeding process are *execution, delivery,* and *acceptance.*

FIGURE 48.1 **Warranty Deed**

WARRANTY DEED

1 **THIS DEED**, Made this Eleventh day of July , 1990 , between Terry D. Alger and Kaye L. Alger, husband and wife

of the County of Jefferson , State of Colorado, grantor(s) and *

2 Edward J. Conry and Anne L. Conry, husband and wife, as joint tenants with full rights of survivorship whose legal address is

1475 Lawrence Street

of the City and County of Denver , State of Colorado, grantee(s):

3 **WITNESSETH**, That the grantor(s), for and in consideration of Two hundred fifty five thousand dollars ($255,000.00)------------------------------ DOLLARS,

4 the receipt and sufficiency of which is hereby acknowledged, have granted, bargained, sold and conveyed, and by these presents do / grant, bargain, sell, convey, and confirm, unto the grantee(s), and their heirs and assigns forever, all the real property together with improvements, if any, situate, lying and being in the City of Evergreen, County of Jefferson , State of Colorado, described as follows:

5 Lot 261 of the Hiwan First Filing as Filing No.372227 on July 4, 1976, in the Office of the Recorder for Jefferson County.

also known by street and number as: 1425 Iverness Street

6 **TOGETHER** with all and singular the hereditaments and appurtenances thereto belonging, or in anywise appertaining, and the reversion and reversions, remainder and remainders, rents, issues and profits thereof, and all the estate, right, title, interest, claim and demand whatsoever of the grantor(s), either in law or equity, of, in and to the above bargained premises, with the hereditaments and appurtenances.
TO HAVE AND TO HOLD the said premises above bargained and described with the appurtenances, unto the grantee(s), their heirs and assigns forever. And the grantor(s), for their heirs and personal representatives, do hereby covenant, grant, bargain, and agree to and with grantee(s), their heirs and assigns, that at the time of the ensealing and delivery of these presents, they are well seized of the premises above conveyed, have good, sure, perfect, absolute and indefeasible estate of inheritance, in law, in fee simple, and have good right, full power and authority to grant, bargain, sell and convey the same in manner and form as aforesaid, and that the same are free and clear from all former and other grants, bargains, sales, liens, taxes, assessments, encumbrances, and restrictions of whatever kind or nature soever, except

----- EASEMENTS OF RECORD AND NONE OTHER -----

and the above bargained premises in the quiet and peaceable possession of the grantee(s), their heirs and assigns against all and every person or persons lawfully claiming or to claim the whole or any part thereof, grantor(s) shall and will WARRANT AND FOREVER DEFEND.
IN WITNESS WHEREOF, the grantor(s) have executed this deed on the date set forth above.

7 Terry D. Alger
Kaye L. Alger

STATE OF COLORADO
} SS.
City and County of Denver

The foregoing instrument was acknowledged before me in the City and County of Denver , State of Colorado , this Eleventh day of July , 1990 by

My commission expires. 6-1-91
Witness my hand and official seal.

P. Notary

P. Notary
Notary Public
11253 E. Public St.
Address
Denver, Colorado

Key to Deed Sections

1. *Grantors' Names*
2. *Grantees' Names*
3. *Consideration Statement*
4. *Words of Conveyance*
5. *Property Description*
6. *Habendum*
7. *Signatures and Certification*

notarize

Verification by a proper public official of the authenticity of a signature

delivery

In realty, the voluntary transfer of a deed with the intent thereby to transfer ownership of the realty

Execution refers to the format, language, and signing of the deed document. Many states have enacted statutes that specify a form for short, simple deeds. These are called *statutory deeds.* While all deeds are essentially similar, there are slight variations from state to state. For example, while some states require that deeds be notarized to be valid, most states do not. **Notarizing** involves marking signed documents in a way indicating that an official of the state has determined that the signatures are valid.

By itself, execution of a valid deed does not transfer ownership. Delivery and acceptance are also required to complete the deeding process. **Delivery,** like transferring the chunk of sod, merely involves transferring possession of a properly executed deed with the *intention* of shifting ownership. The following case illustrates a situation where there was not a valid delivery because there was no intention to shift ownership.

FACTS

Mrs. Marshall was eighty-four years old and owned two parcels of real estate. Her son Ralph had great influence over her. One day Ralph asked Mrs. Marshall to go with him to an attorney's office, and she did. The attorney represented Ralph. After waiting for six hours in the attorney's office while Ralph and the attorney talked in another office, Mrs. Marshall was asked by Ralph to sign several documents. Her son, Ralph, urged Mrs. Marshall to sign. She did. Later she learned that she had signed deeds transferring title to her realty to her three sons. Later she died and other relatives sued for rescission of the deeds. The probate court granted rescission, and the sons appealed.

DECISION

The probate judge did not err in ordering rescission of the deeds by which the eighty-four-year-old woman decedent had conveyed her two parcels of real estate to her three sons, reserving a life estate in herself. He specifically found that Ralph took the plaintiff to the attorney's office; that she was highly susceptible to Ralph's influence; that Ralph "urged his mother to execute the aforesaid instruments and that such urging constituted undue influence in view of the age of the plaintiff, her susceptibility to [Ralph's] influence . . . , and her presence in the defendant's attorney's office"; and "after the plaintiff's execution of the deeds as aforesaid, [she] was chagrined to discover that she had caused the properties to be transferred to [her sons]"; that she later asserted repeatedly "that she never intended to convey the properties to [her sons]"; and that "the plaintiff did not know she had conveyed title to the properties to [her sons]." Affirmed, the deeds are invalid.

Marshall v. Marshall, 409 N.E.2d 1322 (Mass. 1980).

Delivery can be made to either the buyer or the buyer's agent. Thus if a mother executed a deed in favor of a daughter but the deed was left in the mother's safe-deposit box until her death, the deed would not transfer ownership because it was not delivered. Further, if a deed were delivered just as security for a debt, ownership would not be transferred because there was no *intent* to shift ownership.

Acceptance merely means that the buyer indicates a willingness to assume ownership. Retaining the deed after delivery usually constitutes acceptance.

Deed Document

Most deeds contain the information that was illustrated in Figure 48.1. The major sections of deeds include the following:

1. Name(s) of the grantor(s), often a seller
2. Names of the grantees, often a purchaser

3. Consideration statement
4. Words of conveyance
5. Property description
6. Habendum
7. Signatures and certifications

Each section communicates important information about the nature of the parties or the property or the transaction. Since the deed is the heart of most real estate transactions, it must be scrutinized carefully by both the buyer and the seller if they are to protect their interests.

Grantors' Names The person giving up ownership is the grantor. The person receiving the deed is the grantee. The names of those executing the deed as grantors appears first. These persons must be owners of the estate conveyed in order for that interest to pass.

Words of Conveyance The words of conveyance generally determine which promises or warranties the grantor makes to the grantee. When the words "warranty and convey" or "grant and convey" are used, this indicates that the grantor promises or warrants the following:

1. The grantor owns the estate transferred and will pay the grantee for his or her injury if it turns out that the grantee does not receive the estate described in the deed.
2. There are no liens, leases, easements, mortgages, or other **encumbrances** that bind the grantee other than those disclosed in the deed.

encumbrance
A person's right in another person's property

Deeds of this type are generally called **warranty deeds** or *grant deeds.* They are the kind most frequently used.

warranty deed
A deed conveying title and giving warranties to the grantee

The other major type of deed is called the **quitclaim deed.** The words of conveyance for it often include the word "quitclaim." This deed merely transfers the grantor's ownership, *if any. No promises or warranties are implied in the deed.* Thus if a professor gave a student a *warranty* deed to the school building in exchange for $10,000, the student could sue and recover the money if it turned out that the professor did not own the building. If, however, a *quitclaim* deed were given, the student could not recover the money.

quitclaim deed
A document used in transferring the grantor's interest in realty, if any, without any warranties

Quitclaim deeds are often used to remove "clouds on title." For example, if a divorced man sold property and then died and the buyer feared that the man's ex-wife might have a **dower** claim, the buyer could ask the ex-wife to execute a quitclaim deed. She might sign—perhaps in return for $75; but her lawyer would surely advise her *not* to execute a warranty deed because she is *not* certain that she owns any interest in the property.

dower
A widow's life estate in a portion of the land of her deceased husband; at common law but generally abolished by statute today

In many states there is a *special warranty deed* in addition to the warranty and quitclaim deeds. A special warranty deed reduces the grantor's legal risks because it warrants only that the title has not been impaired during the time when the grantor owned the property.

In the absence of other indications, the law generally presumes that the grantor and grantee intended the conveyance of the fee simple absolute estate. Conditional and life estates can usually be identified by examining the words of conveyance. For example, the words "warrant and convey so long as no sheep are grazed on the land" would transfer a conditional estate. The words "quitclaim for life" would convey only a life estate.

Grantees' Names Aside from identifying the grantees, this section indicates the form of co-ownership, if it exists, and each co-owner's percentage of ownership. In community property states, a statement that the grantees are husband and wife would create a presumption that community property is the form of co-ownership with each co-owning 50 percent. Tenancy by entirety would be presumed from the "husband and wife" designation in some, but not all, states that recognize that form of co-ownership.

Where no relationship is stated and the grantees are not married, the law in almost all states presumes that the parties co-own as tenants in common with equal percentage ownerships. Of course, when the ownership percentages are stated, they will govern. Thus one could convey to "Oliver Wendell Holmes as to ninety-nine percent (99 percent) and John Marshall as to one percent (1 percent)," and Marshall would own one percent, not fifty.

Generally, joint tenancy must be specifically identified. Some states demand extremely clear and emphatic language to create joint tenancy. Many lawyers use phrases such as *A* to *B* and *C* "as joint tenants, with full rights of survivorship, and not as tenants in common."

Consideration Generally, most deeds recite a fictitious amount like "ten dollars" as the stated consideration. This protects the privacy of the parties because then the actual consideration for the sale does not become a part of the public record when the deed is recorded. In many cases consideration is not required for effective deeding.

Description of the Property This section of the deed describes the physical boundaries of the parcel being conveyed. If the description is defective, the deed may be treated as invalid. The following case illustrates this.

FACTS

Penelope Overton and Alexander Badham held title to a tract of land in North Carolina through a deed that contained the following description:

> [T]he following real estate in Chowan County, to wit: A certain tract of Pocosin Land adjoining the lands of the late Henderson Luton & others, containing, by estimation, Three Hundred and Nineteen Acres.

A.C. Boyce also claimed ownership of the same tract. Because of this, Penelope and Alexander filed suit against Boyce to determine who was the true owner.

DECISION

The description in the deed under which the plaintiffs claim title is patently ambiguous. It refers to nothing extrinsic to which one may turn in order to identify with certainty the land intended to be conveyed. All that the deed tells us about the land is that it is "pocosin land," i.e., swamp land, in Chowan County, it adjoins the lands of the late Henderson Luton and contains, by estimation, 319 acres. It is a matter of common knowledge that there are numerous, extensive tracts of pocosin land in Chowan County. The deed leaves the reader of it in doubt as to each of the following things: (1) The exact area of the tract intended to be conveyed, (2) whether the tract intended to be conveyed is all or only part of a single pocosin area, (3) assuming the "Henderson Luton" tract can be located with certainty, on which side of it lies the land here intended to be conveyed, and (4) the length of the common boundary between the "Henderson Luton" tract and the land here intended to be conveyed. Furthermore, the record shows, and the Superior Court found, there were recorded in the office of the Register of Deeds of Chowan County three separate deeds conveying large tracts of land in Chowan County to Henderson Luton and another deed conveying a smaller tract to Henderson Luton and another. The descriptions of the three larger tracts conveyed to Henderson Luton alone show that each of these tracts had one or more boundary lines running along or through a swamp or along the Chowan River.

Since the description in the deed under with the plaintiffs claim is patently ambiguous, the deed is void and cannot be the basis for a valid claim of title to the land now claimed by Penelope Overton and Alexander Badham.

Overton v. Boyce, 221 S.E.2d 347 (N.C. 1976).

Frequently deeds must contain a legal description of the property to satisfy the execution requirement for deeding. Legal descriptions include subdivision lot descriptions, and meets and bounds descriptions. Street addresses and farm names often do not qualify as legal descriptions. Thus in some states a deed describing property as "1600 Pennsylvania Avenue" would not be recordable even though the city, county, and state were identified.

The description of the property can divide the air, surface, or mineral rights. The following case shows the way this is done. It also illustrates the difficulty sometimes associated with determining the intent of the parties to the deeding process.

FACTS

A grantor executed a deed to 86 1/2 acres of land in Cherobee County, Texas, to a grantee. The deed referred to "an undivided 1/2 interest in and to all the oil, gas and other minerals in and under, and that may be produced from," the 86 1/2 acre tract of land. Several years later the iron ore under the surface became valuable. Acker holds title to the land under the grantee. Guinn claims under the grantor. Both claimed ownership of the iron ore. Judgment was rendered for Acker and on appeal by Guinn, judgment was reversed in his favor. Acker appealed to this court.

DECISION

Affirmed, for Guinn. The iron ore did not pass to the grantee with the oil and gas and thus Guinn owns it.

A grant or reservation of minerals by the fee owner effects a horizontal severance and the creation of two separate and distinct estates: an estate in the surface and an estate in the mineral.... The parties to a mineral lease or deed usually think of the mineral estate as including valuable substances that are removed from the ground by means of wells or mine shafts ... a grant of "minerals" or "mineral rights" should not be construed to include a substance that must be removed by methods that will, in effect, consume or deplete the surface estate....

That is the rule to be applied in determining whether an interest in the iron ore was conveyed by the deed in this case. In terms of its location with respect to the surface, methods by which it must be mined, and the effect of production upon the surface, the ore is quite similar to gravel and limestone. Aside from the general reference to "other minerals," moreover, there is nothing in the deed even remotely suggesting an intention to vest in the grantee the right to destroy the surface. It is our opinion that in these circumstances the ore, like gravel and limestone, should be considered as belonging to the surface estate and not as part of the minerals. We accordingly hold that as a matter of law no interest in the ore passed by the deed.

Acker v. Guinn, 464 S.W.2d 348 (Tex. 1971).

Habendum That portion of the deed immediately below the property description is called the **habendum.** It is in this section of the deed that the grantor indicates the encumbrances that will affect the grantee's estate. Recall that in the words of conveyance of the warranty deed the grantor promises that there are no encumbrances except those listed on the deed. If an encumbrance, such as an easement or mortgage, exists but is not excepted (recited) in the habendum of a warranty deed, the grantor would be liable for

habendum
That portion of a deed indicating the encumbrances burdening the estate

any financial loss suffered by an innocent grantee because of the encumbrance. It is not necessary to recite encumbrances on a quitclaim deed because that deed does not warrant anything.

Signature and Notarizing Generally only the grantors sign the deed. Grantees usually need not sign although some grantors may require it as proof of acceptance. In some states the grantor's signature must be witnessed and the deed notarized.

The Instruments of Finance

Most buyers of realty do not have enough cash to pay the full purchase price. So buyers usually borrow part of the price. Lenders want to be very certain they will be repaid. So they almost always require that the borrower give the lender the legal right to force the sale of the property if loan payments are not made as promised. The lender then can use the money from the forced sale to pay off the loan. The three major instruments of finance used to protect lenders are the *mortgage, trust deed,* and *land sale contract.* Realty can also be transferred with the seller's existing financing.

► Mortgages

mortgagor
The person who has given a mortgage

mortgage
A security interest in realty; also the instrument giving lenders the power to sell the mortgaged realty and to repay the debt when the borrower defaults on the payments

mortgagee
The person to whom a mortgage has been given

foreclosure
The cutting off of an owner's interest in realty by sale pursuant to court decree

Mortgages are the most common instrument for financing the acquisition of realty. (See Figures 48.2 and 48.3.) Generally, the buyer **(mortgagor)** will give a **mortgage** to a lender **(mortgagee)** such as a bank or savings and loan association. The mortgage gives the lender the legal right to file suit in court to *foreclose* (cut off) the buyer's ownership rights in the property in the event loan payments are not made as promised. After the suit is initiated and the judge hears the evidence, the judge issues a decree of **foreclosure.** After the decree is issued, a *sheriff's sale* occurs and the property is auctioned off to the

FIGURE 48.2 **Minnesota Short Form Mortgage**

Minnesota Short Form Mortgage

This statutory mortgage, made this ________ day of ________________, 19______, between [give name and address] mortgagor, and [give name and address] mortgagee,

Witnesseth, that to secure the payment of [give description of indebtedness and instruments evidencing same], the mortgagor hereby mortgages to the mortgagee [give description of premises "subject to" any encumbrances thereon].

And the mortgagor covenants with the mortgagee the following statutory covenants:

1. To warrant the title to the premises.
2. To pay the indebtedness as herein provided.
3. To pay all taxes.
4. To keep the buildings insured against fire for ____________ dollars ($ _________), and against [give other hazards insured against and amount of such other insurance] for the protection of the mortgagee.
5. That the premises shall be kept in repair and no waste shall be committed.
6. That the whole of the principal sum shall become due after default in the payment of any instalment of principal or interest, or of any tax, or in the performance of any other covenant, at the option of the mortgagee.

If default be made in any payment or covenant herein, the mortgagee shall have the statutory power of sale, and on foreclosure may retain statutory costs and attorney's fees.

In witness whereof the mortgagor has duly executed this mortgage. [Or use other testimonium clause. Add signatures and other formalities of execution.]

Minnesota Statutes 1961, §507.15.

FIGURE 48.3 Mortgage "Closing"

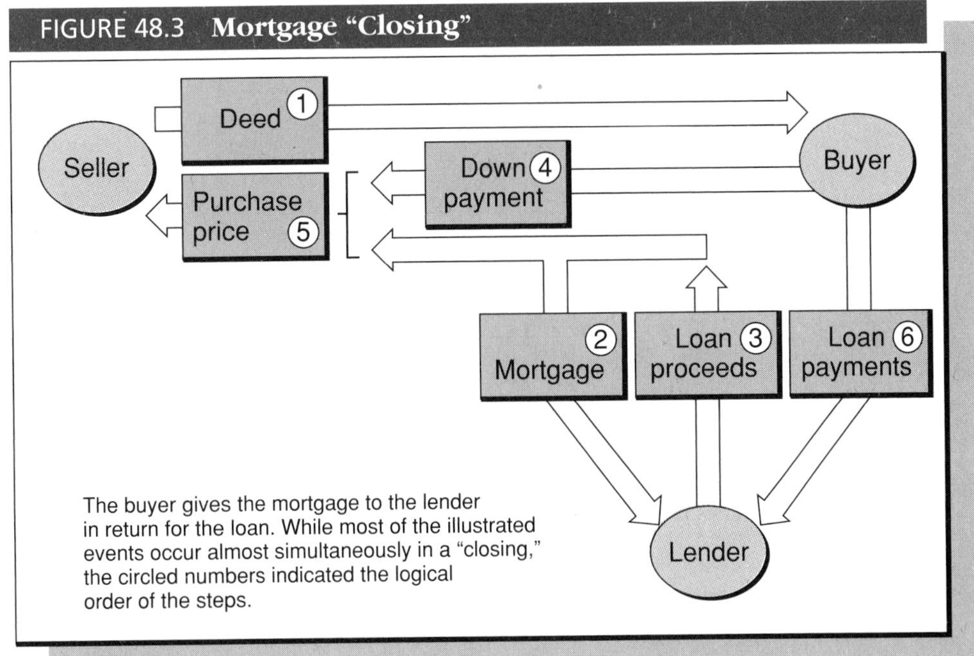

The buyer gives the mortgage to the lender in return for the loan. While most of the illustrated events occur almost simultaneously in a "closing," the circled numbers indicated the logical order of the steps.

highest bidder. The money received from the sheriff's sale is used to repay the debt owed the lender. If the money received exceeds the debt, the surplus goes to the mortgagor (the borrower). If the money is not sufficient to pay the debt, the lender can usually obtain a **deficiency judgment** against the borrower for the balance due.

deficiency judgment
A judgment after foreclosure, against the borrower, for the remaining unpaid balance of the mortgage loan

Mortgagors are protected in most states with rights of **redemption.** Prior to the decree of foreclosure, the mortgagor can sometimes stop the foreclosure process by simply paying all past-due installments along with those expenses incurred by the lender because of the default. This ability to stop foreclosure is generally called the "equity of redemption." After the decree of foreclosure is issued, the mortgagor is still protected in a majority of states by a redemption period—usually six months to a year—during which he or she can regain the property by paying off the *whole* amount of the mortgage along with the lender's default expenses. This is generally called the right of "statutory redemption." Mortgages sometimes contain clauses that waive rights of redemption. Generally these clauses cannot be enforced.

redemption
The reclaiming of a foreclosed ownership interest in realty

The process of mortgage foreclosure is usually very time consuming. The delays associated with the suit, sheriff's sale, and possible redemption can often delay the sale for one or two years.

► Trust Deeds

With this method of financing the buyer first obtains the deed from the seller. The buyer then gives a **trust deed** to a **trustee.** (See Figure 48.4.) The trustee holds the trust deed on behalf of the lender. The trust deed contains language that allows the trustee to sell the property if the buyer defaults on the loan payments. Note that a court order is not required to cause the sale, and that it is a sale conducted by the trustee rather than by the sheriff. In some states there are no redemption periods associated with trust deeds, or they are very short. For these reasons, sale after default often occurs more rapidly under

trust deed
A deed given to a trustee, in trust, with the power to sell the land on default of the secured obligation

trustee
In realty, the one who holds the trust deed for the benefit of the lender

FIGURE 48.4 Trust Deed "Closing"

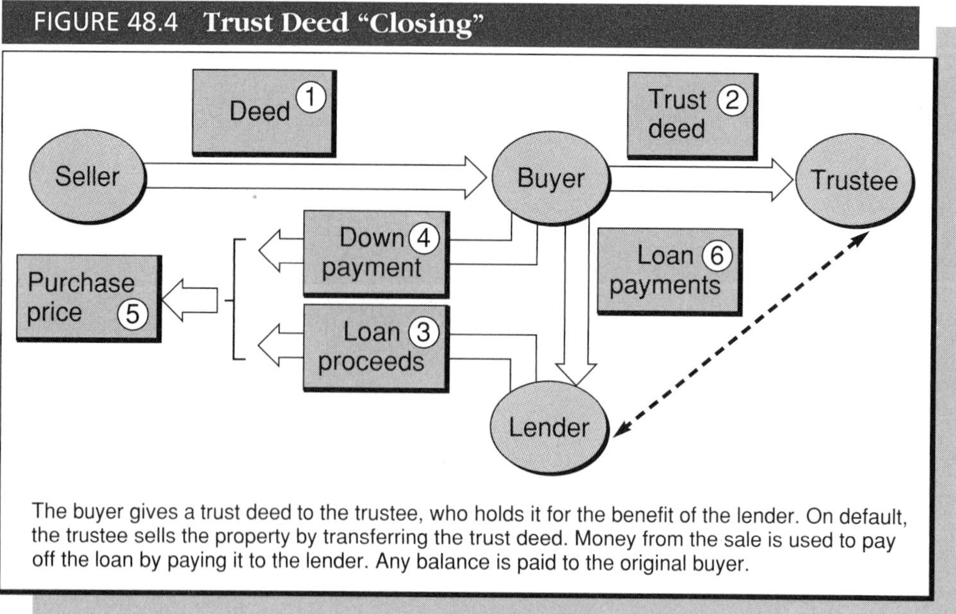

The buyer gives a trust deed to the trustee, who holds it for the benefit of the lender. On default, the trustee sells the property by transferring the trust deed. Money from the sale is used to pay off the loan by paying it to the lender. Any balance is paid to the original buyer.

a trust deed than under a mortgage. Therefore lenders frequently prefer trust deeds to mortgages.

A mortgage with "power of sale" is similar to a trust deed. No foreclosure suit is required, and a private sale occurs. This sale is conducted by the mortgagee. Some states do not permit mortgages with powers of sale, and those states that do permit them carefully regulate by statute the conduct of the lender after default.

► Land Sale Contracts

With this method of financing the lender—who often is also the seller—keeps the deed all the contracted payments have been made. Then the lender must deliver a deed. (See Figure 48.5.)

The land sale contract gives the buyer the right to occupy the realty and treat it as his or her own. The law refers to the buyer under a land sale contract as the *equitable owner* even though the buyer has not yet received the deed.

If the buyer defaults, the lender in some states can have the buyer removed from the property in about the same way a landlord evicts a tenant who has not paid the rent. This may involve a lawsuit, which is sometimes concluded much more rapidly than either a mortgage foreclosure or a sale by trustee. In these states the lender can sometimes treat the installment payments as though they were rental charges so that the defaulting buyer loses everything.

Most other states force the lender in the land sale contract to return to the defaulting buyer his or her equity in the property. The word "equity" as used here is a financial term meaning the difference between the value of something and the amount owed on it. Thus if a buyer purchases a home for $60,000 by making a $10,000 down payment and executing a land sale contract for $50,000, the buyer's equity would be $10,000. If after a few years the balance due on the land sale contract is $40,000, the buyer's equity will be $20,000. If the buyer defaults, most states will force the lender to return the $20,000

FIGURE 48.5 Performance of a Land Sale Contract

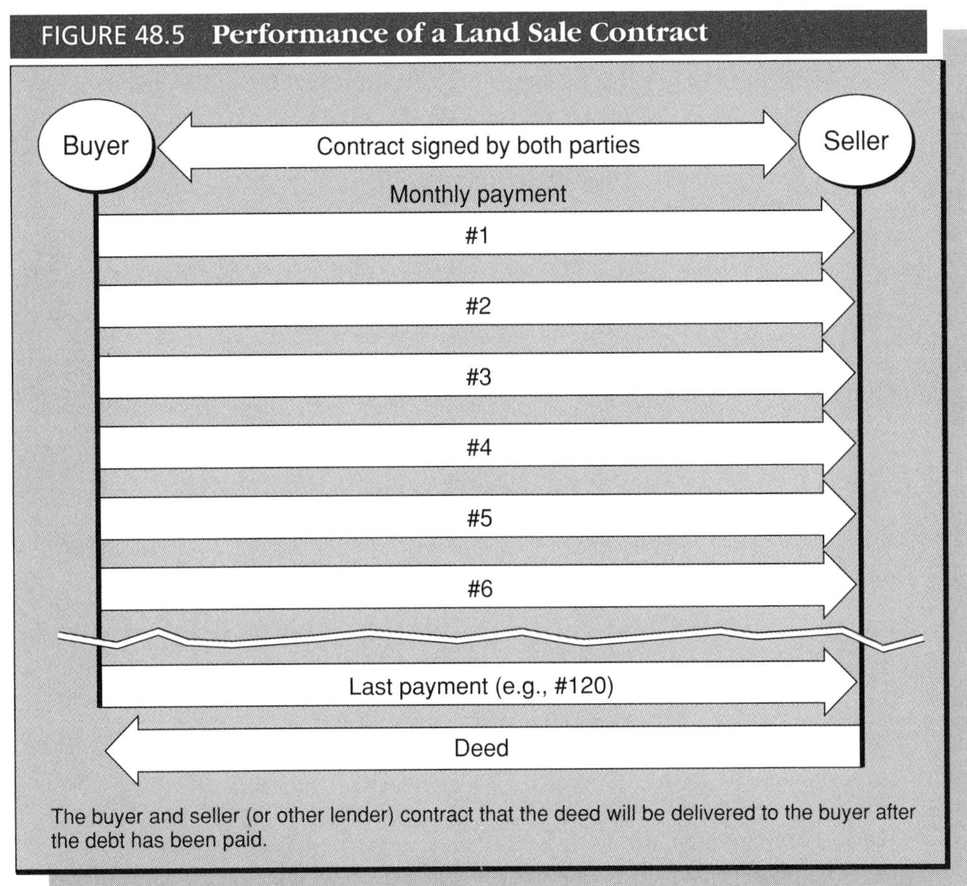

The buyer and seller (or other lender) contract that the deed will be delivered to the buyer after the debt has been paid.

equity, less the rental value of the property. These states generally treat the land sale contract in the way mortgages are handled, including the grant of redemption rights to the borrower.

Lenders prefer land sale contracts in those states where they allow rapid resolution of the problems associated with a debtor in default.

► Sale with Existing Financing

Another method of financing involves the sale of the property with the existing financing intact. Thus the seller may deed mortgaged property to the buyer. This mortgage should then be recited in the habendum of the deed as an encumbrance. The property can be transferred when encumbered by a mortgage, trust deed, or even a land sale contract.

Some lenders include clauses in their financial instruments that prohibit such sales without the lender's consent. Also, some such clauses provide that, if sale is made without such consent, the entire debt is accelerated (speeded up) and is due, on sale, to the lender (called "due on sale" clause). The U.S. Supreme Court has held that such clauses are enforceable if made by federally chartered lenders such as federal savings and loan associations.

A buyer of property with a mortgage on it takes the property "subject to the mortgage." While sellers remain personally liable to the mortgagee (lender) for the secured debt in sales with existing financing, the buyer may or may not be personally liable. Generally, the deed recites in the habendum that the property is conveyed "subject to" the mortgage. On default the property may be foreclosed, but the buyer has no personal liability to the foreclosing mortgagee. However, if the buyer also "assumes" the financing, then the buyer, as well as the seller, will be personally liable. Thus the habendum portion of a deed may state as follows:

> Grantee hereby assumes the mortgage against the above described property in favor of Wells Fargo Bank, N.A., in the amount of $283,219.00, as recorded in Book 218, page 21 of the records of the County Recorder for the County of Cache, State of Utah on January 1, 1901.

The use of the additional word "assumes," instead of just stating "Grantee takes subject to the mortgage . . . ," causes the grantee to be personally liable for the mortgage.

Recording

Recording is the process of filing a document related to realty with the county clerk or commissioner of deeds. Deeds, mortgages, land sale contracts, easements, and liens are among the many documents usually recorded. In general, the purpose of recording is to give notice to the world and to influence **priority** with respect to any other claims against the realty.

priority
In realty, the order in which claims against realty are satisfied

► Priority

Priority determines the *order* in which claims against real estate are satisfied. For example, if there are two mortgages against a property, their *priority* determines which will be paid first. Generally, the claim with first priority will be completely paid before any funds are applied to a claim with second priority. Similarly, a deed with first priority will be valid while a conflicting deed from the same grantor that does not have first priority will be completely invalid.

There are two basic approaches to determining priority in the United States: the *notice system* and the *race-notice system*. In states using the notice system there is enormous pressure to immediately record a deed or other instrument. If you receive the first deed and do not record, then anyone who receives a second deed to the same property will become the owner, as long as they did not know of the first deed.

In states using the race-notice system, there is still a lot of pressure to quickly record. If you receive the first deed but do not record, then anyone who receives a second deed, without knowledge of the first, *and who records this second deed before you record yours,* will become the owner. The following case illustrates the way the race-notice system works.

FACTS

The Garcias were involved in foreclosure proceedings. As a part of this process a *lis pendens* [Latin for: a suit is pending] was filed and the Garcias deeded their interest in property to Rizzo. At a later date, they executed a quitclaim deed to the same property naming Kordecki as the grantee. The property was located in Wisconsin, which is a race-notice state.

DECISION

Under the law of conveyancing (without considering the recording statute), because Garcia had already passed title to Rizzo as trustee, Garcia could convey no interest to Kordecki and Kordecki could acquire no interest in the land under the quitclaim deed. Hence under the law of conveyancing, Rizzo takes priority over Kordecki. . . . [However, Wisconsin] is a notice-race recording [state and this] changes the common law of conveyancing. When we consider the recording statue, we must recognize that since Rizzo did not record the Garcias' deed to him . . . Kordecki recorded his deed before Rizzo recorded his.

The recording statute is designed (1) to force the recording of all instruments so that the record will show a complete history of the title and (2) to protect purchasers who rely on the record and purchase in good faith and for value over those who have not recorded their interest in the real estate thereby possibly misleading others. In other words, the purpose of the recording statute is to render record title authoritative to protect a purchaser who relies on the record and is a purchaser in good faith and for a valuable consideration.

In determining rights under the recording statute, in contrast with determining rights under the common law of conveyancing, the initial question is not what the Garcias actually owned when they conveyed the property to Kordecki but what the record shows they owned. To claim the benefits of . . . a purchaser in good faith, Kordecki is deemed to have examined the record and to have notice of the contents of all instruments in the chain of title and of the contents of instruments referred to in an instrument in the chain of title. A purchaser in good faith is one without notice, constructive or actual, of a prior conveyance. . . .

Had Kordecki examined the record, which he did not, he would have found the lis pendens which would have led him to the Kenosha county circuit court file on the proceedings to foreclose the land contract. . . . Thus Kordecki is viewed as having constructive notice from the recorded instruments that Garcia had no power to sell the property on December 12, 1977, that there may be unrecorded conveyances and that the proffered deed might be a nullity. Despite Rizzo's failure to record, the record gave Kordecki notice of defects of his grantor's title and the possibility of unrecorded conveyances. . . .

Because Kordecki cannot claim sanctuary under the notice-race recording statute, we affirm the decision of the court of appeals.

Rizzo v. Kordecki, 317 N.W.2d 479 (Wis. 1982).

The Sale Process

▶ Overview

Deeding and financing are at the heart of most realty transactions. Once you understand these processes, they can be integrated into the typical sale process. By examining the total sale process, you can gain a perspective on the way many legally complex business transactions are structured. Such a perspective can also illustrate the way several bodies of law can merge in a single transaction.

The typical process for selling a single-family residence involves a sequence of steps by the seller, the real estate broker, and the buyer. Each step involves contract law or agency law or real property law. Some steps involve the application of all three bodies of law. Figure 48.6 depicts the structure of the typical residential transaction. The remaining part of this section provides an overview of the major steps involved in transferring ownership in the context of a *sale*.

listing
An agency contract between a broker and a seller of realty

special agent
"An agent authorized to conduct a single transaction or a series of transactions not involving continuity of service" (Restatement (Second) of Agency, sec. 3)

professional agent
A professional, independent contractor employed as a special agent

Listing Usually the owner of realty, such as a house, will sign a **listing** contract with a real estate broker. This contract makes the broker the **special** or **professional agent** and fiduciary of the seller, as illustrated by the following case.

FACTS

The Spragins signed a listing agreement with Taylor, a real estate broker, for the sale of four Arkansas farms. Eventually an offer for the purchase of the farms was submitted through Taylor to the Spragins. The offer was made by an organization called Huber Farm Services. In fact, Taylor owned a one-third interest in Huber but this was not disclosed to

FIGURE 48.6 The Legal Environment of Real Estate Sales

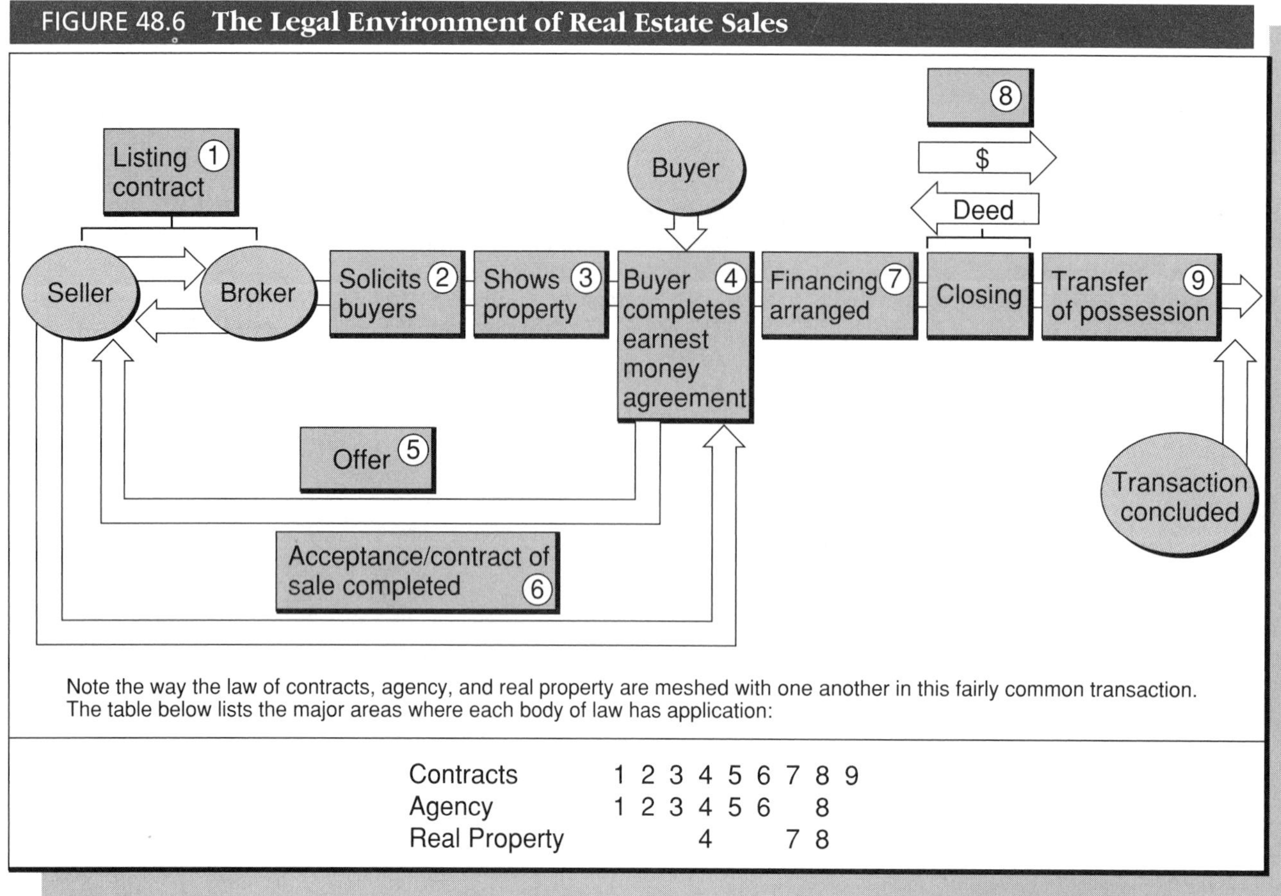

Note the way the law of contracts, agency, and real property are meshed with one another in this fairly common transaction. The table below lists the major areas where each body of law has application:

Contracts	1	2	3	4	5	6	7	8	9
Agency	1	2	3	4	5	6		8	
Real Property				4			7	8	

the Spragins. The contract for sale was executed, but when the Spragins failed to deliver a deed to Huber, both Huber and Taylor sued the Spragins for specific performance and for commissions. Judgment was rendered for Spragins, and Huber and Taylor appealed.

The facts in this case reveal that Taylor failed to disclose material information to the Spragins. We note that Taylor did not make any disclosure to the Spragins that she was a stockholder, director, and officer in Huber Farm Services or that the corporation might acquire the four farms. Spragins' testimony, if admitted, indicates that no such disclosure was ever made. Additionally, Taylor failed to inform the Spragins that Huber Farm Services planned to sell the properties for a profit.

As a broker, Taylor was obligated to reveal to her principals all information possessed by the broker concerning the value of the property. The broker must obtain for the principal the best available deal without any information the broker has which is adverse to the principal. The broker must reveal the source and amount of any profit she may make from the transaction, including any relationship she has with any other party to the transaction.

Secret profits are not allowable to the broker.

DECISION

Affirmed for the Spragins. Taylor violated her fiduciary duty to her client, the Spragins.

Spragins v. Louise Plantation, Inc., 391 So.2d 97 (Miss. 1980).

Usually the broker can collect the negotiated commission once the broker has produced a *ready, willing, and able buyer* who offers to purchase the property under the same terms as those indicated in the listing contract. Brokers cannot agree among themselves to fix commission rates. Commission rates must be determined through negotiation between the seller and the broker.

Sales Efforts and the Earnest Money Agreement The broker then must use reasonable efforts in finding prospective buyers. The prospective buyers are escorted around the property by the broker. The broker generally explains the terms under which the seller might be willing to sell. Then the broker persuades the prospect to make what is sometimes called an "earnest money offer." While the broker aids the buyer by filling in the blank spaces on this standard form, the broker is still the agent and fiduciary of the seller and represents the seller's best interests. The earnest money offer proposes a contract that generally specifies the following:

1. Buyer's name(s)
2. Amount of the earnest money (the amount of money given the seller, which the seller may keep if the buyer breaches the contract
3. Estate transferred and a description of the property
4. Sale price and method of financing (e.g., land sale contract)
5. Date of closing (when the final financing is to be concluded; for example, the date when the deed and money will be exchanged in a cash sale)
6. Date of possession (when the buyer may move into the property)
7. Date of proration (when the buyer assumes liability for property taxes, insurance obligations, utilities, etc.)
8. Buyer's form of co-ownership if any
9. Party who shall pay for the abstract of title or title insurance policy

Arranging Financing The buyer will frequently make an offer conditioned upon, or subject to, obtaining appropriate financing or obtaining an appraisal of the realty for a certain amount. The broker will usually assist the buyer in arranging the financing or the appraisal.

Closing After financing has been arranged, the closing can take place. The closing is the meeting where the remainder of the purchase price is usually paid, and arrangements are made for the proration of property taxes, insurance, and utilities. The deed can be delivered to the buyer at this time if the earnest money contract so provides.

Transfer of Possession Physical possession is transferred on the date specified in the earnest money contract.

► Escrow

Frequently the closing or settlement process is fairly complex and involves large amounts of money. The parties may then direct that the transaction be closed in **escrow.** This means that the buyer and seller execute a detailed contract with an escrow officer—someone other than the buyer or seller—which directs the officer as to the exact procedures to be used in closing. When an escrow is not used, the broker, lender, attorney, or title insurance company may close the transaction by relying on the earnest money agreement and the oral instructions of the buyer and seller.

escrow
The conditional delivery of property to a person who is to deal with it on the occurrence of specified conditions

When land sale contracts are used, the buyer will often require that the seller execute a deed and deliver it into escrow. The escrow officer then accepts the deed for the buyer and, following the instructions in the escrow contract, the officer will turn the deed over to the buyer after all the payments have been made.

Title Insurance

While warranties of title protect buyers of realty, the value of a warranty depends upon the financial strength of the seller. Thus if a seller conveys fee simple absolute by warranty deed, then loses all his or her money gambling in Atlantic City, the buyer has no effective remedy if the buyer discovers that the seller owned only a life estate.

A search of the chain of title would have revealed the problem, but most buyers do not know how to check the county recorder's records. Therefore buyers sometimes turn to an attorney for assistance. The attorney will ask a title abstract company to prepare a summary of all the recorded events that have had an effect on the title to the property. This is called an **abstract of title.** The attorney will examine the abstract and then give the buyer a written *title opinion.* If the buyer is injured by an undisclosed defect in the title, the buyer may be able to collect, in a suit for negligence, from the abstract company or the attorney.

abstract of title
A record of the history of the title to land as found in official records

Title insurance often can be purchased as a substitute for an abstract of title and a title opinion. The policy contracts to pay the buyer for injuries arising from undisclosed defects of title up to the face amount of the policy. Generally, such policies are limited to defects that could be identified from an examination of the recorded documents in the chain of title. Since most states have laws regulating the financial structure of title insurance companies, the injured buyer with title insurance is more likely to be able to recover from a financially stable party.

The Real Estate Settlement Procedures Act (RESPA)

The federal Real Estate Settlement Procedures Act of 1974 (RESPA) along with later amendments and regulations[1] is intended to educate consumers, reduce the costs associated with transferring ownership of realty, and eliminate abusive practices such as kickbacks.

The RESPA covers all transactions where the sale is financed by a *federally* related mortgage loan on residential structures other than large apartment buildings. In such transactions, the lender must provide the buyer with a copy of an information booklet and an opportunity to obtain estimates of settlement costs in advance of the closing. Further, the party conducting the closing or settlement must use a Uniform Settlement Statement. That federal document is intended to clearly identify settlement costs incurred by the buyer and seller.

Finally, the Act prohibits kickbacks and unearned fees. For example, brokers, lenders, sellers, or buyers cannot receive compensation for referring a buyer or seller to a particular bank, attorney, title insurance company, or fire insurance company. Such action can be criminal conduct. However, brokers can operate cooperative brokerage arrangements and multiple listing services.

Lenders have a limited exemption from this provision. They can require that the seller pay a prepayment penalty on the old mortgage if the new loan is not made with

[1] *HUD Regulations,* subtitle B, part 3500 et seq.

the same lender. Thus sellers will often ask buyers to borrow from the old lender. That tactic increases the lender's volume of business.

Sellers may not specify a particular title company to be used by the buyer even though there is no kickback. Lenders, however, may specify a title company since a second title policy is usually written for them in the amount of their loan.

Further, the Act requires that lenders who collect from the borrower advance payments (sometimes called "impounds") for expenses, such as property taxes and insurance, can collect only a reasonable amount.

Nonsale Transfers of Ownership

▶ Other Deed-Related Transfers

While the deeding process is generally associated with transactions involving the *sale* of realty, deeding is also involved with transfers of ownership through gifts and wills.

Ownership of realty is also transferred when one dies without a will. Decedents dying without a will are said to have died "intestate." In these cases the laws of descent and distribution will determine who among the surviving relatives will become the new owner or owners. Thus in many states if a man dies intestate without children, all of the property goes to his surviving wife. If there are no heirs of the person who dies intestate, then his or her property **escheats** to the state. This means the state becomes the owner.

escheat
The transfer of property to the state when a person dies without heirs

▶ Dedication

If a developer wants to give land to a local government—perhaps for use as public streets—then the developer can dedicate it. However, ownership is not transferred until the government accepts the transfer.

▶ Condemnation

When a government wants private property for a public use, it may exercise its power of **eminent domain** and take title through **condemnation** if it pays the owner the reasonable value of the property.

eminent domain
Government power to appropriate private land for public use on payment of just compensation without the owner's consent

condemnation
Forcing a property owner to transfer property to a government in exchange for just compensation

▶ Adverse Possession

The doctrine of **adverse possession** rests on the idea that owners of realty should be aware of the use being made of their lands. If an owner is careless, and someone comes upon the land and occupies it for a *substantial period of time,* and meets certain other technical legal requirements, the occupant may acquire title to the land. The occupant would receive title under the doctrine of adverse possession.

adverse possession
A method of acquiring title to land by actual, exclusive, and continuous possession of land under color of title adverse or hostile to the true owner in an open and notorious manner for a statutory period of time

Time Period The adverse occupier is required to be in possession of the land for a period of time specified by state statutes. The statutes vary dramatically from state to state. Usually it is from five to fifteen years.

Continuous Use Required The state statutes uniformly require that the time period be satisfied by *continuous* use. Thus an adverse possessor who occupied land, in a state requiring seven years of occupation, would not obtain title if the adverse possessor occupied for six years, left for a year, and then returned and occupied for another six years. On the other hand, if one adverse occupant possessed the land for five years, then immediately transferred possession to another adverse possessor, who occupied for three years, the law would view the occupancy as having been continuous for eight years. The process of adding the possession period of one occupant to the possession period of a subsequent occupant is called *tacking*.

Open, Notorious, and Exclusive Use Required Even if the time period and continuous use requirements have been met, the occupant will not obtain title unless the occupation has been *open and notorious*. This means that the possession could be easily observed, or seen, by a careful owner. In addition, the occupation must be exclusive. This means that the occupant must be the only party in possession. Thus if the general public uses land as a park, no one could adversely possess that land. However, it may become dedicated to the public after passage of the statutory time period. Private roads often become dedicated to the public after they have been used by the public continuously for the statutory period.

Color of Title Some states require that the occupant come upon the land under color of title. This means that the occupant would have, for example, come upon the land after receiving an invalid deed, or a deed from one who was not the true owner.

Other states do not require strict color of title and will allow the occupant to acquire true title even when the occupant knowingly comes upon the land of another with the intent of adversely possessing it.

Payment of Taxes Most states require that the adverse possessor pay property taxes during the period of possession.

Applications of Adverse Possession In every state, the doctrine can be used to acquire title to land without the use of other processes for transferring ownership. In many states the doctrine is also used to settle old problems or mistakes. For example, a fence might be built two feet inside the true boundary line; if it were not moved for the period of adverse possession, then in some states the neighbor with the extra land would acquire title to it under the doctrine of adverse possession. The following case illustrates the application of the doctrine of adverse possession.

FACTS

In 1958, Mrs. Dorothea Karell, defendant, purchased 18.9 acres of land in Tarrant County, Texas. A fence encompassed this land along with another parcel of about 3.7 acres. Mrs. Karell rented her property to tenants from 1958 until 1970. In 1970 she hired one Howe to remove the top soil from portions of the land including the 3.7 acre parcel. When West, plaintiff, owner of record of the 3.7 acre parcel discovered Howe's activities, he sued to quiet title and recover damages for the lost top soil. Mrs. Karell defended claiming title by adverse possession. Judgment was rendered for West and Mrs. Karell appealed.

DECISION

It is undisputed that the property in issue was enclosed by a fence. Such enclosure gives rise to a rebuttable presumption that an adverse claim is being made by the party in possession. . . . In any event, in order for the Karells to establish a title they are required to prove continuous cultivation, use, or enjoyment of the land as well as possession and adverse claims. It is uncontroverted that the Karells never lived on the disputed acreage nor did they personally use or cultivate it. Any claim of title made by them is through the tenants by whom the property was supposedly occupied. Both Mr. and Mrs. Karell testified as to a succession of tenants from 1958 through 1972. (The tenants actually occupied a house located on the 18.9 acre tract.) Neither could testify that for a continuous ten-year period each tenant used the disputed tract by cultivating crops, grazing livestock or by using the land in any manner so as to put the true owners on notice that an adverse claim of ownership of the property in issue was being made. Their testimony also shows that periods of nonoccupancy would sometimes last as long as two months. West produced witnesses who testified that not all of the tenants had livestock or crops. In fact, one witness testified that, other than a tenant named Davis who occupied the premises for two or three years, no other tenant had livestock.

The use to which the Karells put the land did not constitute an actual and visible appropriation of the land which was continuous and unbroken. Affirmed for West.

Karell v. West and Shobert, 616 S.W.2d 692 (Tex. 1981).

Prescription

The method for acquiring ownership by **prescription** is analogous to adverse possession. However, prescription applies to those "uses" that are associated with easements. Accordingly, property taxes need not be paid. In some cases where a claimant would not qualify as an adverse possessor because of failure to pay taxes, the claimant may prevail in a claim for prescription. For example, a person who reasonably believed that he or she was the owner of a pasture and grazed cattle there for thirty years, but whose property tax assessment did not include the pasture, might not qualify for adverse possession but could probably win the prescription right to continue grazing cattle because of the previous use of the pasture.

prescription
In real property, a method of obtaining the right to use of another's land as an easement by open and continuous possession and use of the land under a claim of right to such use for a statutory period of time

Accretion

When a boundary line is defined by a creek, river, stream, or shoreline, then the very *gradual change* in the location of the water will shift the location of the boundary. This method of acquiring ownership of the additional land caused by such gradual change is called **accretion.** When the shift is rapid and radical, the physical process is called *avulsion.* Avulsion does not change the boundary.

accretion
A method of obtaining title to another's land caused by gradual changes in the natural boundaries of such land

Summary Statement

1. The deeding process is the most common method use to transfer ownership of realty. It requires execution of the deed document, delivery, and acceptance.
2. Warranty deeds warrant (assure) transfer of the indicated estate free of all encumbrances except those stated in the deed. Quitclaim deeds transfer only the grantor's interest, if any. The grantor does not warrant that he or she has an interest to transfer or that all encumbrances have been disclosed in the deed.
3. The language used in deeds determines the estate transferred, the form of co-ownership, the physical boundaries of the estate, and the limitations on the ownership of the grantee, such as restrictive covenants and mortgages.
4. Financing the purchase of realty usually involves either a mortgage, trust deed, land sale contract, or a sale with existing financing.
5. Generally, the debtor in default can be removed from the property most rapidly under a land sale contract, less rapidly under a trust deed, and most slowly under a mortgage.
6. Recording influences the priority among competing claims and gives notice of the recorded document to the whole world.

7. Escrows are contracts that direct a person to perform specific acts in connection with property, such as recording a deed. They are often used in closing a real estate sale.
8. Title insurance and abstracts of title allow a buyer to collect from someone other than the grantor when the buyer is injured by a defect of title not disclosed in the insurance policy or in the title opinion.
9. RESPA requires distribution of a pamphlet and use of the Uniform Settlement Statement, prohibits most referral kickbacks, and limits amounts collected for lender's prepayment accounts for insurance and taxes.
10. Ownership can be transferred without using the deeding process. This can occur through condemnation, adverse possession, prescription, and accretion.

The following case illustrates the importance of the elements of the deeding process.

PARKER v. LAMB
567 S.W.2d 99 (Ark. 1978)

Smith, G. R., Justice. This suit to cancel two deeds is between brother and sister: . . . Robert J. Parker, Jr., and . . . Mary Louise Lamb. The single question is whether the Chancellor was right in holding that the deeds, executed by the parties' parents, were ineffective for want of delivery. We agreed with the Chancellor.

In 1971 the elder Parkers went to a trusted friend, who was an abstracter, for advice about the disposition of their property upon their death. The abstracter had an attorney prepare the two deeds in question, one conveying the city homeplace to the daughter and the other conveying a farm (which became quite valuable) to the son. The abstracter told the Parkers to put the deeds in envelopes, to be delivered after their death. He said that they could do anything they wanted to do with the property before they died, but if they still owned it at the time of their death it would go according to the deeds. Needless to say, the advice was erroneous.

Upon the elder Parker's death in 1974, the title passed to his widow as the surviving tenant by the entirety. Mrs. Parker kept the deeds, in a storm cellar behind her home in Conway. The son, to prove delivery of the deeds, relies upon two incidents that occurred during his mother's last illness in 1976. In the first incident, Mrs. Parker, during the last several days of her life, told her daughter that she could go down to the cellar, get the two envelopes, and tear them up if she wanted to. The daughter declined.

The second incident took place two days before Mrs. Parker's death. The son and daughter went together to the storm cellar upon another matter and noticed that the envelopes were not there. Knowing that their aunt, Mrs. Reidmatten, had another key to the storm cellar, they went next door to ask her about the envelopes. Mrs. Reidmatten had removed them, for safekeeping. She handed the envelopes to Robert, who kept them. He and his sister opened them just enough to be sure the deeds were there. When Robert told his mother the next day about how he had come into possession of the envelopes, she said in effect: "Good enough. Take care of them. And for goodness' sake put them is a safe place." It is now argued that those words amounted to a ratification of Mrs. Reidmaten's manual delivery of the deeds.

No effective delivery is shown. The law wisely requires the delivery of a deed, as a positive act bringing home to the grantor that he is definitely parting with the ownership of his land. An essential element of a valid delivery is the grantor's intention to pass the title *immediately.* [Emphasis added.]

No such intention to pass title immediately could have existed in this case because there is no suggestion whatever in the proof that Mrs. Parker did not still believe that the abstracter's advice—that the envelopes be delivered after her death—was sound. There is no possibility that Mrs. Parker, relying upon that advice, could have intended an *inter vivos* delivery of the deeds. In fact, the existence of any such intention is actually rebutted by her offer to let her daughter tear up the deeds and by her warning her son to put the envelopes in a safe place. Those statements imply that she thought that she still had control over her property and that the eventual delivery of the envelopes would carry out her wishes after her death.

Affirmed, for appellee, the deeds were ineffective.

Questions and Case Problems

1. Kruithoff leased seven and one-half acres of pasture land from Mrs. Sandy on November 27, 1970, for $15 per year. They entered into an oral agreement that allowed Kruithoff to erect a fence and take it down and keep it at the end of the lease. This agreement was not recorded. Before the end of the lease, Mrs. Sandy sold the land to Bailey and told him about the lease but not the oral agreement concerning the fence. When Kruithoff removed the fence at the end of the lease, Bailey sued him for the value of the fence. The fence was of four-strand barbed wire consisting of approximately 150 fence posts and an iron sucker rod gate. Only eight of the posts were imbedded in concrete. Who wins? [*Bailey v. Kruithoff,* 280 So.2d 262 (La. 1963).]

2. Arthur Glander received a deed to a small farm from his parents. A month after receiving that deed, Arthur executed a quitclaim deed for the property to his brother and his sister, Gladys. The deed was in proper form, signed and notarized. The deed was given to Arthur's father for him to hold. The father was to give the deed to the brother and sister if Arthur died. Gladys moved to New York. Thirteen years later, while visiting the father's home and rummaging through his papers, Gladys found the deed. She promptly recorded it. Arthur now sues, asking the court to determine who is the true owner in a quiet title action. Who prevails, Arthur or Gladys? [*Glander v. Glander,* 239 P.2d 254 (Ida. 1951).]

3. In 1919 Nix and Nix Co. purchased land for a substantial sum of money from Tooele County in Utah. Title was transferred with a quitclaim deed. The Nixes paid property taxes to the county for the property for 20 years. Then they discovered that an honest mutual mistake had been made because the county never owned any interest in the land. Nix and Nix Company now sue Tooele County to recover the purchase price. Who prevails? [*Nix v. Tooele County,* 118 P.2d 376 (Utah 1941).]

4. The Kendricks owned property in Snohomish County, Washington. In 1961 they sold two houses and lots for $18,500 with a down payment of $1,100 and monthly payments of $120 under a land sale contract. The land sale contract was recorded. The buyers were Millard C. Davis and his wife. They mortgaged this interest under the land sale contract to a finance company to secure a loan of $1,000. In 1965 the buyers defaulted on the land sale contract. The Kendricks (the sellers) recorded and sent a notice of declaration of forfeiture and cancellation of contract to the Davises. The Kendricks filed a *lis pendens,* which gives notice that a suit is pending, and initiated an **action to quiet title.** The finance company became a party to the suit and offered to pay off the balance of the land sale contract in return for acquiring ownership. The Kendricks, sellers, want clear title to the property free of the mortgage. Who prevails, the Kendricks or the finance company? [*Kendrick v. Davis,* 452 P.2d 222 (Wash. 1969).]

action to quiet title
A legal proceeding initiated by a claimant to title in land affording any adverse parties opportunity to prove a claim to interest in the land or thereafter be barred from doing so

5. Erasmus Wiley occupied an old house in a commercial area for about 20 years. On his sixtieth birthday he executed a warranty deed to his neighbor, Buster Blue, in return for $200,000 in cash. Erasmus retained the right to occupy the property for an additional three months. Buster did not record his deed. After two months Erasmus executed a quitclaim deed for $150,000 in favor of Jerry Green, a politician. Jerry had no knowledge of the prior deed, and he immediately recorded his quitclaim deed. Erasmus now resides in a Brazilian resort and is incommunicado. What are the rights of the parties?
6. Winnie Selsor, a full-blood Creek Indian, owned 160 acres of unimproved, unfenced, poorly wooded mountainous land. When she failed to pay the property taxes, the county sold the property to L. P. Kelley. Later Winnie deeded the property to Eddie Cox. Kelley asked Herman Johnson to take care of the land. Johnson ran 35 to 40 head of cattle on the property and came upon the land about 50 times a year to check on the cattle and the land. Cox claims that the tax deed is void. Kelley asserts title through adverse possession. Cox counters that, while other requirements may have been met, Kelley did not possess the land. Who prevails? [*Cox v. Kelley,* 295 P.2d 1061 (Okla. 1956).]
7. Able leased a room in a home from widow Wilma. The parties executed a written lease for two years so Able could complete graduate school. Able moved in. Six months later Wilma sold the house to Professor Pickey. When Pickey discovered Able, he told him to leave because Pickey intends to use the room to display his rodent collection. Able claims he has the right to rent the room for another one and one-half years. The lease was not recorded, and Pickey could not tell when he inspected the property that the one room had been rented out. Who prevails?
8. Frank Willett and George Miller owned lands on opposite shores of the Camarron River. From 1913 until 1930 the Camarron River moved about a half mile into Miller's property. Over 200 acres of Miller's former property are now on Willett's side of the river. The change was caused by several floods, each lasting about five days, which shifted the river's location as much as 300 feet. Willett and Miller now claim ownership of the property between the old location of the river and the new location. Who prevails? [*Willett v. Miller,* 55 P.2d 90 (Okla. 1936).]
9. Monte Bucks, the holder of a bachelor's degree in business administration, bought a large apartment house by putting $2,000 down and taking the property "subject to" an existing mortgage of about $750,000. He installed a former beauty queen as the manager in the hope that she would lure many of her friends into renting apartments in his building. The plan worked, and occupancy approached 100 percent. However, rental receipts declined dramatically because maintenance expenses rose significantly. Monte could not make the mortgage payments. The lender foreclosed on the mortgage and recovered $600,000 on the sale of the distressed apartment building. The lender now sues Monte for the other $150,000. Who prevails?
10. In the case of *Parker v. Lamb,* excerpted at the beginning of this section, were the Parkers exercising good judgment in the way they obtained legal advice? Explain.

CHAPTER 49

RENTING REALTY

After you have read this chapter, you should be able to:

1. Describe the kinds of rental relationships that landlords and tenants may create.
2. Describe the promises implied in most leases.
3. Describe the covenants and conditions that should be included in a residential lease.
4. Describe the rights and obligations of landlords and tenants on termination of a lease.
5. Explain the major provisions of the Uniform Residential Landlord Tenant Act (URLTA).

BUSINESS DECISIONS and the LAW

Phyllis has just been accepted at your college and plans to live off-campus in a rental unit beginning next fall. Her financial situation is a little uncertain and she is not sure she will have enough money to go to school the whole academic year. She may need to move back home after just one term. So she is looking for housing that will allow her to do that. She turns to you for advice on the type of lease she should get to accomplish her goals. After reading this chapter, you will be able to tell Phyllis what type of lease she needs.

Introduction

By the early 1700s, the common law of England had developed a fairly sophisticated body of case law defining the landlord-tenant relationship. That case law was transplanted to each of our states as they adopted the common law of England for their state law. After the initial adoption, and with the passage of time, the uniform body of law was transformed significantly by the statutory and case law of each state. Today, landlord-tenant law varies dramatically from state to state.

In the previous chapter we discussed the various ways that ownership in realty can be transferred. In this chapter we will discuss the law of landlord-tenant relationships involved in the renting of realty.

In 1972 a Uniform Residential Landlord Tenant Act (URLTA) was drafted. Since then it has been adopted by seventeen states. The last section of this chapter discusses the URLTA and contrasts it with the material discussed in the balance of the chapter.

The Basic Nature of the Landlord-Tenant Relationship

freehold estates
Fee simple absolute, conditional, and life estates

demise
In realty, to lease or rent

leasehold estate
The estate in realty owned by tenants

lease
Of realty, a form of contract giving one person, the tenant (or lessee), the exclusive right to occupy for a period the realty of another, the landlord (or lessor)

The landlord-tenant relationship arises when the owner of a **freehold estate** (e.g., fee simple absolute, a conditional estate, or a life estate) transfers to another the right to temporarily possess the realty. Generally, the right of *possession* is given in exchange for the payment of *rent.* The temporary transfer of the right of possession is referred to as **demising** or **leasing** the property. Since the transfer of possession is temporary, the owner of the freehold will eventually regain possession. This power to regain possession is called the *right of reversion.* The owner of the freehold is called the *landlord* or *lessor,* and the party receiving the temporary right of possession is called the *tenant* or *lessee.* After transfer, the tenant is said to own a **leasehold estate.** (See Figure 49.1).

When a written document evidences the relationship between the parties, the document is usually called the **lease** or *rental agreement.* Most leases constitute a blending of the law of *conveyancing* (i.e., transferring ownership of realty) and the law of contracts. The conveyancing aspect of the transaction is concerned with transferring a leasehold estate to the tenant. The contract aspects relate to the agreements between the parties on such issues as payment of the rent, who shall repair the realty, the amount of security or cleaning deposits and the conditions under which they can be returned, and limitation on uses of the property.

The law treats tenants as owners of *nonfreehold* estates. These estates do not occupy the same status in the law as freehold estates. The owners of freehold estates are said to be *seised* of the property. Owners of estates are seised when they acquire possession of a freehold with a deed. Tenants are not seised, though they do possess the realty. Because of this, the landlord retains some obligations of ownership, like the duty to pay the property taxes. Further, the tenant's estate will be treated as personalty. Thus if a tenant dies, the tenant's leasehold interest may pass via the tenant's will to those who receive the decedent's *personalty.*

Because leases are two-party contracts, the law assumes that the parties negotiate the terms of the lease at arm's length, with each party protecting his or her own self-interest. Accordingly, there is no standard lease document. Most printed lease documents have been prepared by the attorneys for landlords. If tenants are too shy or uninformed to negotiate changes in the printed forms, they may be severely injured.

FIGURE 49.1 **Creation and Termination of a One Year Leasehold Estate**

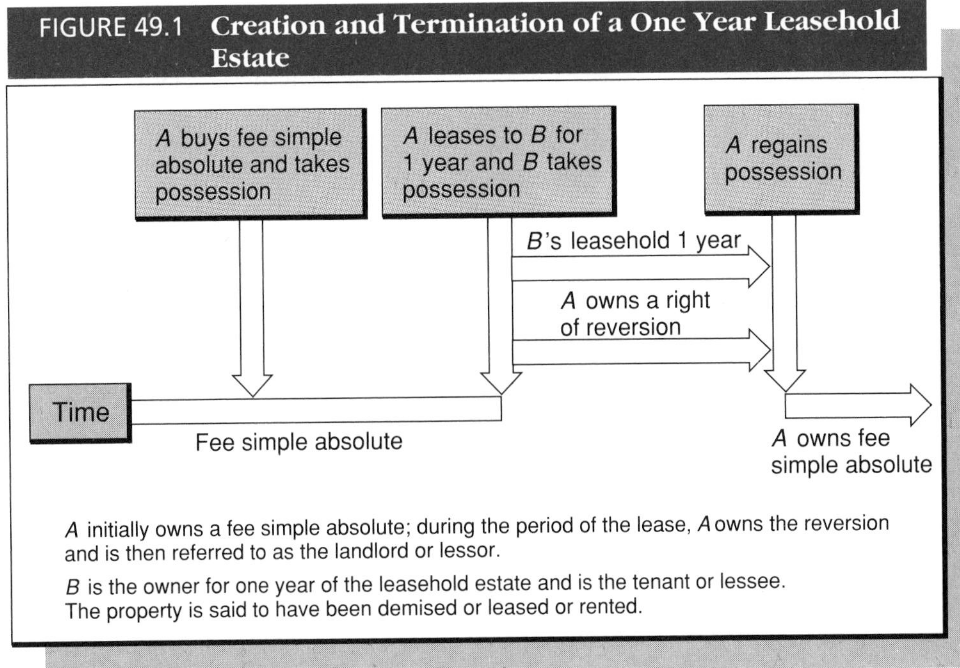
A buys fee simple absolute and takes possession
A leases to B for 1 year and B takes possession
A regains possession
B's leasehold 1 year
A owns a right of reversion
Time
Fee simple absolute
A owns fee simple absolute
A initially owns a fee simple absolute; during the period of the lease, A owns the reversion and is then referred to as the landlord or lessor.
B is the owner for one year of the leasehold estate and is the tenant or lessee.
The property is said to have been demised or leased or rented.

The Creation of the Rental Relationship

▶ Oral Leases

A lease may be created in a variety of ways. It can be created orally, and is then called a **parol lease;** or it can be created without words—by implication from the acts of the parties. While oral leases are often enforceable, every state requires that certain leases be placed in writing. Generally it is the statute of frauds[1] for each state that determines which leases must be written.

parol lease
A lease not reduced to writing

▶ Statute of Frauds

The states vary dramatically in defining when a lease falls *within* the **statute of frauds.** Most states require leases to be in writing only when they exceed a term specified by statute, usually one or three years. While most states do not treat leases as the sale of an "interest in land," a few do. In these states all leases must be written. In general, the consequence of failing to comply with the statute is that the lease is treated as terminable at the will of the lessor or lessee, either without notice or with minimal notice.

statute of frauds
A statute requiring that certain kinds of contracts be proved only by a proper writing

Generally, the statute of frauds requires that the writing be signed by the defendant and that it contain all the essential terms of the lease, so that a court need not hear oral

[1]See Chapter 12, Contractual Form—Requirement of a Writing for Enforceability, Statute of Frauds.

testimony to determine the rights of the parties. Even when a lease is within the statute of frauds and not in writing, the lease may still be enforced in an equity action if the plaintiff can establish that *part performance* has cured the defective creation. Generally, part performance occurs when there has been transfer of possession, payment of rent, and improvement of the property by the lessee. The following case illustrates the application of the statute of frauds to a lease.

FACTS

The Tovars, defendants, entered into a written lease for lot 2337 in Phoenix, Arizona. On this lease document a notation was made concerning lot 2339. The Tovars took possession of both lots and operated an adult bookstore and theater on these premises. William Henry Brophy College is a plaintiff and lessor of the land subject to these leases. The College sought to evict the Tovars claiming that the lease for lot 2339 was oral, outside the statute of frauds, and thus void.

DECISION

Basically the College asserts that the Tovars are in possession only as tenants from month to month; that the tenancy was properly terminated; and that the Tovars have no further right to possession. They also say that Tovars' claimed oral lease of 2339 is void under the Statute of Frauds, and that there is no memorandum thereof sufficient to comply with the statute.

. . . [W]e have no trouble agreeing with the trial court that the Statute of Frauds, A.R.S. Section 44–101, applies to the purported oral lease of 2339. That section provides in part as follows:

> No action shall be brought in any court in the following cases unless the promise or agreement . . . or some memorandum thereof, is in writing, and signed by the party to be charged. . . 5. Upon an agreement which is not to be performed within one year from the making thereof. 6. Upon an agreement for leasing for a longer period than one year.

The minimum essential terms that must appear in the memorandum itself in order to make it sufficient to establish a lease are identification of the property to be leased, the term of the lease, and the rental agreed on.

The only writing claimed to constitute any memorandum here is the series of handwritten notations which were added to the typed lease for [lot] 2337. Examination of these notations indicates that they do not in any sense unequivocally set forth the premises to be rented, the rent promised to be paid, or the term of the lease. . . .

In order to take an oral contract out of the Statute of Frauds under this doctrine, the part performance alleged must be unequivocally referable solely to the oral contract. Here, appellees relied on possession, payment of rent, and the making of improvements. Appellants claim that this part performance was not referable solely to the oral lease but instead was merely consistent with appellees' month to month tenancy. Appellees remained in possession and paid rent both before and after the claimed oral lease, and it is true that both of these acts are consistent with a month to month tenancy except for that period of about six to eight months when they continued to pay rent when not using the premises. Payment during that period, we believe, is inconsistent with a month to month tenancy and instead reinforces appellees' claim that they were in possession under a long-term lease. Also, their making of improvements of value approaching that of five months' rent is inconsistent with a monthly tenancy and referable, as we see it, to a longer term.

Affirmed, for the Tovars. The oral lease is valid and enforceable under the Statute of Frauds.

William Henry Brophy College v. Tovar, 619 P.2d 19 (Ariz. 1980).

Leasehold Estates

If a landlord-tenant relationship comes into being, the law will classify it as an estate at sufferance, an estate at will, a periodic estate, or an estate for years. The distinctions among the types of estates are important because the estates are terminated differently.

Estate at Sufferance This estate arises when one rightfully takes possession of property as a lessee but then remains in possession *after* termination of the lease. A few states allow landlords to use self-help eviction if no force is used. But most states require notice of termination of an estate at sufferance and permit eviction only by a police officer after a lawsuit.

Estate at Will When someone takes possession of the realty with the landlord's consent, but *without* entering into an oral or written lease, he or she owns an *estate at will*. This usually occurs when the parties agree that the prospective tenant can move in and that the lease will be negotiated later.

This landlord-tenant relationship can be terminated at any time by either party. Some states protect the lessee by requiring notice before eviction.

Periodic Estate This relationship arises when the parties agree on the terms and conditions of the lease but *do not specify its term (length)*. For example, the parties may agree that the rent is "five dollars per day payable monthly in advance." There is a clear implication in this language that the lease is intended to run for longer than one month, yet the lease specifies no ending date. The law allows this tenant a *periodic estate*. In general, this estate continues for the length of the payment period and is automatically renewed unless one party gives adequate notice of termination. Often the notice of termination must equal the length of the payment period. Thus where rent is paid every two months, most states would require a two-month notice to terminate.

The main characteristic of periodic leases is their flexibility. Since either the landlord or tenant can terminate, in most instances with a thirty-day notice, the terms of the lease are open to easy revision. For example, a landlord who wants to raise the rent 30 percent can submit a new lease to the tenant. For all practical purposes, the tenant must accept it or be forced to leave within about thirty days. On the other hand, the student who rented a periodic estate in the worst apartment in town on the first day of classes can easily move out in the middle of the semester when more attractive accommodations become available.

Estate for Years This estate arises when the parties *agree on the beginning date and ending date for the lease*. The term "estate for years" is misleading because it can be for any length of time, such as one week, or two months, or 340 days, or five years. Because the parties know the date when the lease ends, no notice is required to terminate. Further, neither the landlord nor the tenant may terminate the lease without cause before the agreed termination date. Thus if a student executed a nine-month lease and moved out after three months, he or she might be liable for six months' rent! That liability

FIGURE 49.2 **Methods of Terminating Leasehold Estates**

Estate	Self-Help Dispossession	Notice Required to Terminate	Termination on Death of Party	Termination When Landlord Sells
At sufferance	Yes*	No*	Yes	Yes
At will	No	No*	Yes	Yes
Periodic	No	Yes	No	No
Years	No	No	No	No

*Only in some states

arises only when the landlord has used reasonable efforts to rerent but has not found a new tenant. If a new tenant rerents after a vacancy of three months, the original tenant will be liable for the amount of rent for the three months' vacancy. (See Figure 49.2.)

The following case illustrates the risks of premature termination and the duty to rerent.

mitigation of damages
A doctrine that imposes on the injured party the duty to minimize his or her damages after injury has been inflicted on him or her

FACTS

Kridel, defendant, leased an apartment from Sommer, plaintiff, for two years for himself and his bride to be. Two weeks after Kridel was scheduled to move in, Sommer received the following letter:

> I was to be married on June 3, 1972. Unhappily the engagement was broken and the wedding plans cancelled. Both parents were to assume responsibility for the rent after our marriage. I was discharged from the U.S. Army in October 1971 and am now a student. I have no funds of my own, and am supported by my stepfather.
>
> In view of the above, I cannot take possession of the apartment and am surrendering all rights to it. Never having received a key, I cannot return same to you.
>
> I beg your understanding and compassion in releasing me from the lease, and will of course, in consideration thereof, forfeit the two months' rent already paid.
>
> Please notify me at your earliest convenience.

Sommers later had an opportunity to relet Kridel's apartment but declined to do so. He then sued Kridel for the whole two years' rent.

DECISION

While there is a split of authority over this question, the trend among the recent cases appears to be in favor of a **mitigation** requirement. . . . The older rule is based on principles of property law which equate a lease with a transfer of a property interest in the owner's estate. Yet the distinction between a lease for ordinary residential purposes and an ordinary contract can no longer be considered viable. Kridel is liable only for rent for the period of time from the beginning of the lease until the time when Sommers had an opportunity to relet.

Sommer v. Kridel, 378 A.2d 767 (N.J. 1977).

Holdover Tenants Frequently tenants remain in possession after termination of the estate. When this occurs, the landlord generally has a choice of several remedies.

The holdover tenant can be **evicted**—that is, forceably removed from the property by the sheriff. Further, the tenant is liable for reasonable rent for the holdover period. In some states the landlord can collect double or triple rent for the holdover period.

eviction
The dispossession of a tenant from the leased premises

If the tenant holds over, the landlord may elect to compel the tenant to remain. This is an alternative to eviction. In general, the tenant will thereby become liable for rent for a period equal to the length of the original term. Thus if Harvey Hardsnoz rented an apartment to Suzie Pillow for one year to terminate on January 1, and Suzie held over until January 3, Hardsnoz could, in some states, treat her as his tenant for the remainder of the second year. If, however, Suzie had a month-to-month tenancy and held over, she would be liable for only one month's rent.

Covenants and Conditions in Leases

When parties enter into a lease agreement, there are generally numerous promises flowing from both the landlord and the tenant. For example, the lessor may promise to deliver possession on a certain date, while the lessee may promise to pay $150 as a cleaning deposit before the end of the first month of occupancy. Promises in leases can be classified as covenants or conditions. Breach of a **condition** automatically gives the other party the legal right not to perform his or her obligations. In contrast, breach of a **covenant** does not eliminate the obligation of the injured party to perform. It merely gives the injured party the right to sue for damages caused by the breach of the covenant. Leases that have been well drafted by a landlord's lawyer will make all the tenant's promises conditions. Thus if the lease contains a condition prohibiting any pet of any kind in the residence, and the tenant kept a caged hamster, the landlord could evict the tenant. If, on the other hand, the lease did not make the tenant's promise a condition, the landlord could only sue for the damages resulting from keeping the hamster, if any can be proved. Some states have enacted statutes that cause all the tenant's promises to be treated as conditions.

condition
An uncertain event on the occurrence of which a contractual obligation is made contingent or dependent

covenant
A promise as a part of a contract

In general, the law assumes that the lessor and lessee will negotiate all the covenants and conditions needed to establish a workable relationship. In many cases, however, the parties agree only on the very basic terms of the transaction, such as the rental amount and the length of the lease. In these situations the law will recognize the existence of *implied* covenants and conditions.

Implied Covenants and Conditions

In general, these implied promises favor landlords rather than tenants. Thus most wise tenants will insist on executing a detailed written lease.

The following case addresses the landlord's tort liability for defects in the property.

FACTS

Agnes Rosebury, defendant, owned a rental unit and had a new roof installed. The roofers removed the gutters from the front of the house but failed to reinstall them. Later, Agnes leased the house to Rienecker.

One January, water ran off the front of the roof and accumulated as ice on the front steps of the house. Rienecker cleared the ice off the steps in the afternoon. Gary Borders, plaintiff, a social guest of Rienecker, arrived at 4:00 P.M. and stayed for dinner. At 9:00 P.M., while leaving, Borders slipped on a new accumulation of ice on the steps. Borders then sued Agnes Rosebury, the landlord.

DECISION

The landlord is liable for defective conditions of the leased property existing at the time the lease is executed only if the defect is unknown to the tenant, or the lessor maintains control of the area where the defect exists.

Borders v. Rosebury, 532 P.2d 1366 (Kan. 1975).

Habitability At common law, tenants leased property under the doctrine of *caveat tenant,* let the tenant beware. The recent trend in landlord tenant law is to recognize an implied warranty of *habitability* and *fitness for the use intended.* Thus if a tenant leased property unseen, and it turned out to be infested with vermin, the tenant's duties would be extinguished for the landlord's violation of the warranty of habitability.

Duty to Repair Unless the lease provides to the contrary, in the majority of states the *lessee* has the duty to make ordinary repairs to the rented property. This duty stems from the common law obligation imposed on all who temporarily occupy realty not to allow the property to *waste* (deteriorate). However, if the landlord's conduct *causes* the defect, the landlord may be obligated to repair. Further, if this landlord-caused defect makes the property unfit for the intended use, and the landlord refuses to repair, the tenant may, in some states, treat the situation as a **constructive eviction** by moving out and paying no further rent. For example, if the landlord failed to repair the heating system in a large apartment complex during the middle of a very cold winter, the tenants could move out and not be liable for rent even though six months of the lease period were remaining.

constructive eviction
A tenant's moving out of leased premises because the landlord caused the premises to become unfit for their intended use by the tenant

Tort Duties In the majority of states, lessees assume liability for tortious injuries to themselves and to others that occur on the leased property. An exception to this rule exists when the defective condition is known to the landlord but not disclosed to the tenant, and the tenant would not be able to identify the problem after a reasonable inspection. Further, the landlord is also liable for injuries occurring on portions of the property, such as hallways, which the landlord controls. In general, the landlord controls the common areas. These are areas used by all the tenants. Thus if a tenant's guest is injured because of a defective diving board in the pool area of an apartment complex, the landlord is likely to be liable.

Similar rules exist with respect to a landlord's liability when tenants are victims of crimes. When a crime becomes *reasonably foreseeable* from the landlord's breach of duty, then the landlord may be liable. Suppose a tenant in a high crime area repeatedly complained about failure to repair a broken deadbolt lock, which the landlord was under a duty to repair. The landlord would be liable for a loss by theft if a burglar entered through the unlocked door. The loss was foreseeable from the breach of the landlord's duty.

Knowledge of crimes against tenants may also subject the landlord to liability. Thus the landlord of a large apartment complex with knowledge of repeated criminal acts against tenants may become legally obligated to warn other tenants, or to take reasonable steps to protect them. The following case discusses a landlord's liability to warn tenants.

FACTS

Sophir owned an apartment complex and became aware that a rape had occurred in the parking lot of the building. C.S. was a female tenant. She was later a victim of sexual assault in the same parking lot. She sued Sophir, claiming that the landlord was under a duty to warn her of the earlier sexual assault.

DECISION

Under the facts as alleged in this case, it would be unfair to impose a duty upon the landlord based on a single prior assault at the complex.

First, landlords are not insurers that a tenant will be protected at all times.

Second, there is no duty to warn of a known danger. The ordinary, reasonable person is aware or should be aware that open parking lots provide an optimum place for crime to occur.

Third, there is no guarantee that if the duty to warn was imposed, a crime would be averted. As pointed out by the Illinois court in *Stelloh v. Cottage 83*, 52 Ill.App.2d 168, 201 N.E.2d 672 (1964), in affirming the dismissal of the plaintiff's case on facts similar to the present case, "[w]e doubt that the giving of [a] warning, under all the circumstances alleged, would have lessened the probability of the [rape], or that the failure so to notify plaintiff would have increased the hazard in any way."

Plaintiff asks the court to invoke the minority rule which imposes liability upon a landlord with notice of a prior criminal act on the premises. However, even in cases where such liability was imposed, there was a history of criminal activity at the leased premises sufficient to create in the landlord constructive notice of the foreseeability that such activity would recur in the future.

No cases were found which impose liability on a landlord based on a *single* prior criminal act perpetrated upon a tenant. . . . [I]n the present case, there would be no foreseeability, based on one prior assault, upon which to predicate liability. . . .

[Judgment affirmed]

C.S. v. Sophir, 368 N.W.2d 449 (Neb. App. 1985).

Quiet Enjoyment The landlord impliedly promises that the tenant will not be dispossessed by someone with title superior to the landlord's.

Fixtures Generally under *residential* leases, the personal property permanently affixed to leased realty becomes real property and, therefore, remains at the end of the lease as the landlord's property. Similarly, alterations and improvements of the realty accrue to the landlord, and the tenant is not entitled to compensation for their value. When the lease is for *commercial* property, the law presumes that the fixture may be removed by the tenant. However, the tenant must remove the fixture during the term of the lease; the tenant may not be able to remove it after the termination.

Emblements An emblement is what is sown and produced on the land. A corn crop can be an emblement. When *farm* property is leased and cultivated by the tenant, the law implies a right to harvest those crops. In some states the crop may be harvested by the tenant even after the lease expires.

emblements
What is sown and produced on the land

Taxes, Insurance, and Utilities The law implies, in the absence of a contrary agreement between the parties, that the landlord will pay the property taxes. However, neither party is obligated to insure the property. The tenant generally must pay for utilities such as garbage, electricity, gas, and water.

Use of the Property In the absence of a contrary agreement, the lessee may make any use of the property that is legal. Thus a tenant cannot be evicted for having pets, giving parties, installing a hot plate, or even playing loud country-rock music unless the lease so states.

Prohibition Against Discrimination Statute The federal Fair Housing Act of 1968, and its amendments, makes it unlawful to discriminate on the basis of race, color, religion, sex, or national origin in the rental or advertising of realty.

► Express Covenants and Conditions

Nearly all the *implied* promises discussed above can be negated by an *express* agreement between the lessor and the lessee. However, **exculpatory clauses,** which attempt to limit the lessor's tort liability, have been nullified by a few states. Of course, no agreement can give the lessor the right to discriminate on the basis of race, color, religion, sex, or national origin.

exculpatory clause
A clause that relieves a party from liability

Duty to Repair Most tenants will want an affirmative promise in writing from the landlord, phrased as a condition, whereby the duty to repair rests with the lessor.

Cleaning Deposits Most tenants should require a written promise stating that the cleaning deposit will be refunded if the premises are returned in the same condition as when leased, less normal wear and tear. The promise should also state that the landlord may only retain amounts actually paid others for cleaning prior to the rerenting of the premises.

Most cleaning deposit disputes arise because tenants do not plan their legal affairs intelligently. If they generate evidence of the condition of the premises before they move in and after they move out, their chances of recovering the full cleaning deposit are very high. For example, the lessee can walk through the property before and after occupancy with a respected mature person who would be a good witness in a small claims court. Then, if the issue is litigated, the tenant is likely to prevail even when the landlord lies. Note that, without the witness, it is the tenant's word against that of the landlord, and the tenant has the burden of proof. Therefore the landlord is likely to win.

Security Deposits Frequently lessors will require that tenants pay substantial rent in advance as security in the event that the leases are broken. For example, the lessee may be required to pay the first and last month's rent in advance.

Liquidated Damages Many tenants want to limit their risk under leases so they include **liquidated damages** clauses that limit the liability for rent. For example, a freshman student executing a nine-month lease on an apartment near campus might want to be able to terminate the lease if he or she flunks out, and pay only two months' additional rent, rather than risk greater liability.

liquidated damages
The money judicially awarded in the amount as agreed to by the parties in their contract at the time it was made as reasonable compensation for damage that may be caused by the wrongful conduct of one of the parties in the future

Joint and Several Liability In many instances there are several tenants of the same rental unit. Lessors often include a term in leases with these multiple tenants to protect the lessors. This term makes each tenant jointly and severally liable on the lease. This means that the lessor has a right to collect *all* the rent or damages from any one, or collectively from all, of the tenants.

The Transfer of the Lessee's Interest

In the absence of a contrary agreement between the lessor and the lessee, the lessee generally has the legal power to transfer his or her right of possession to another. If this power exists, the lessor has no control over the tenant's choice of a new occupant. Further, the new occupant is also allowed to transfer his or her possessory interest to another. Therefore landlords who want to carefully scrutinize tenants frequently include a clause in their leases prohibiting such transfers. These clauses are valid and enforceable. In addition, a few states have enacted statutes that prohibit such transfers without the lessor's consent.

While landlords dislike the lessee's power to transfer his or her interest, it can be very valuable to the tenant. When a tenant decides to vacate, the tenant can reduce his or her financial risk by rerenting the property to another. If a higher rent is obtained, the tenant can retain the surplus and thereby reap significant profits!

Such transfers can be either **assignments** or **sublettings.** The rights of the parties vary significantly, depending upon which method of transfer is used. They are so distinct that the courts will often permit an assignment when the lease document prohibits just subletting. The reverse is also true.

assignment
In realty, a transfer by the lessee of *all* the remaining term of the lease

sublet
A transfer by the lessee of a *part* of the remaining term of the lease

► Assignment

When assignment occurs, the original tenant is called the **assignor** and the new tenant is called the **assignee.** (See Figure 49.3.) In order for a tenant to *assign* his or her interest in realty, the tenant must transfer the interest for all the time remaining on the lease.

If all the remaining term of the lease has been transferred so that assignment has occurred, then one can determine the rights and liabilities of the parties (lessor, lessee, and assignee) by analyzing the concepts of **privity of contract** and **privity of estate.** In general, privity of contract means that parties are linked by legal rights and duties stemming from a *contract between them.* Similarly, privity of estate means that persons are legally connected by rights and duties flowing from *ownership or possession of the same realty.* For example, if Ms. Seller contracts to deed property to Ms. Buyer, they are said to be in privity of contract. If Ms. Seller recorded restrictive covenants during her ownership, they would bind Ms. Buyer because of privity of estate.

assignor
In realty, one who transfers *all* the remaining term of the lease

assignee
In realty, the person to whom *all* the remaining term of a lease is transferred

privity of contract
A legal relationship between two or more parties created by their contract

privity of estate
A legal relationship between two or more parties flowing from their ownership or possession of the same realty

In the landlord-tenant area, one can define the rights of the parties before and after assignments by referring to the following rules about privity:

1. Privity of *contract* always exists (before and after assignment) between the original lessor and the original lessee until the expiration of the lease.
2. Privity of *estate* exists only between the landlord and the tenant in possession (usually the most recent assignee).

These rules help us to define the relationships among the parties because certain rights and duties flow via privity of estate and certain other rights and duties flow via privity of contract. Generally, privity of contract is a conduit for *all* the obligations contained in a lease. Thus a landlord can enforce all the lease provisions against those

FIGURE 49.3 **Timing of Lease Assignment Events**

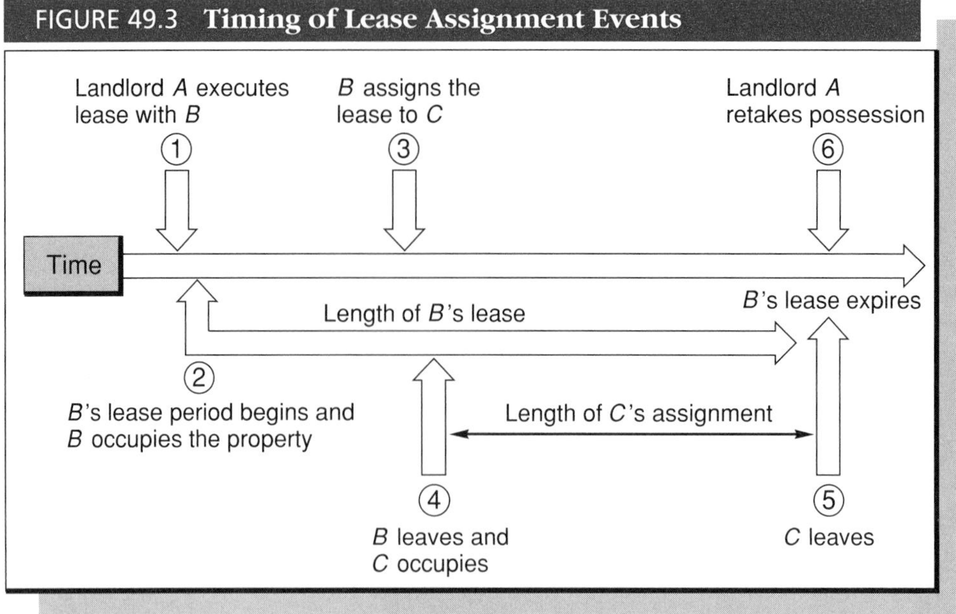

in privity of contract. However, most assignees are not in privity of contract with the lessor (because there is no contract directly between the lessor and assignee) and, therefore, the lessor may not be able to assert some provisions of the lease against them. But an assignee *will* become bound via privity of contract if the assignee assumes[2] the lease in addition to taking an assignment of it. **Assumption** occurs when an assignee agrees with the assignor to be bound by the terms in the original lease.

assumption of a lease
An agreement by an assignee with the assignor to become bound by all the terms and conditions in the original lease

The tenant in possession is in privity of estate with the landlord. Privity of estate is a conduit for only those terms of the lease that *run with the land.* Terms and conditions of leases run with the land when they touch and concern the land. Thus a covenant in a lease whereby the tenant promises to graze cattle on the land but not farm it would bind assignees in privity of estate with the landlord. In contrast, a covenant by the tenant promising not to drink alcohol on the premises does *not* touch and concern the land. It is called a **personal covenant.** The landlord can enforce this covenant against the original lessee (who is in privity of contract) but not against an assignee who is only in privity of estate. Covenants to pay rent, make repairs, extend the lease, or permit the tenant to option the realty are illustrations of covenants that generally touch and concern the land and, therefore, run with it to assignees.

personal covenant
A promise in a lease that does not touch and concern the realty

The relationship between the original tenant and his or her assignee is governed by the assignment contract. Since the original tenant is liable for the personal covenants contained in the lease, the original tenant should extract from the assignee a promise that no personal covenants will be breached. Otherwise the assignee may breach the covenant without liability, and the original tenant will be liable to the landlord for the breach!

Note that, when an assignee assigns his or her interest, the assignee is neither in privity of contract nor privity of estate with the landlord. The assignee's only liability stems from the assignment agreement made with the assignor. (See Figure 49.4.)

---

[2]A third party creditor beneficiary contract is created. (See p. 264.)

FIGURE 49.4 Lease Assignment Relationships

Before Assignment

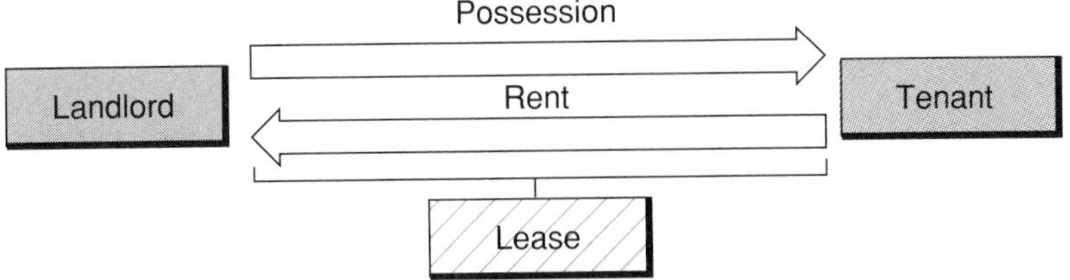

Possession places the tenant in privity of *estate* with the landlord.
The *lease* places the tenant in privity of *contract* with the landlord.

After Assignment

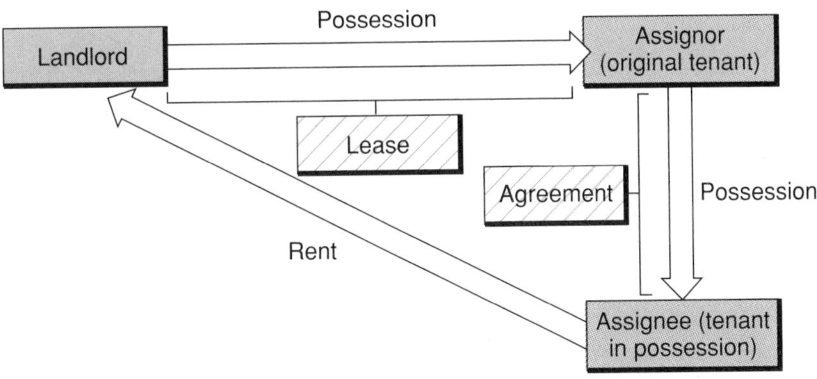

Possession places the assignee in privity of *estate* with the landlord.
The *lease* places the tenant/assignor in privity of *contract* with the landlord.

Further Assignment

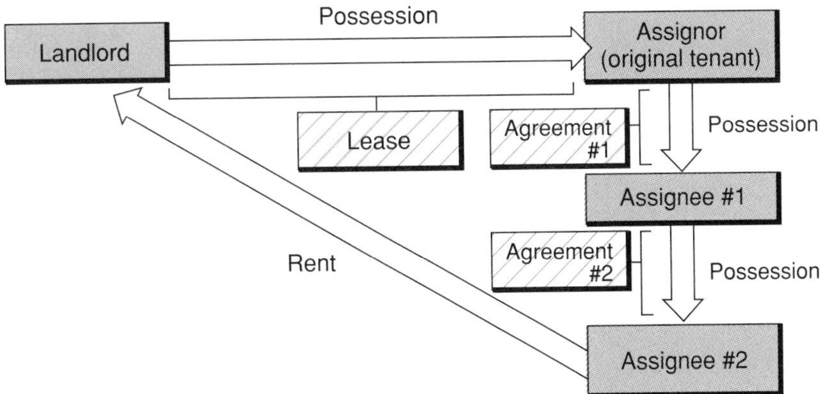

Possession places assignee #2 in privity of *estate* with the landlord.
The *lease* places the original tenant in privity of *contract* with the landlord.
Assignee #1 has *no* legal relationship with the landlord after the second assignment.

► Subletting

Subletting occurs when the tenant transfers the right of exclusive possession to another for a period *shorter than the remaining term of the lease.* The original tenant thereby retains a reversionary interest. Therefore at the end of the subletting period, the sublessor (the original tenant) regains possession for the remainder of the lease period. (See Figure 49.5.) Subletting creates a set of relationships among the parties that differ in important ways from those associated with assignments. In general, a sublessee is neither in privity of contract nor privity of estate with the original lessor.

It is the presence of the tenant's reversion that distinguishes assigning and subletting. The tenant's reversion may be for any period of time. If the owner in fee simple leases to a tenant for five years, and that tenant immediately transfers to another the right to exclusive possession for four years and 364 days, thereby retaining a reversion for one day, the tenant has sublet rather than assigned. Subletting does not affect the legal relationship between the original landlord and tenant. The landlord usually continues to collect the rent from the original tenant. The landlord may sue this tenant for breach of any term of the lease, even when the breach is caused by the sublessee.

Subletting establishes a landlord-tenant relationship between the sublessor and the sublessee. The sublessor is entitled to collect the rent, and the sublessee is entitled to the undisturbed use of the premises.

Subletting may be disadvantageous to the sublessee. His or her legal relationship with the *original lessor* is minimal and to some extent one-sided. Thus the sublessee cannot prevail in a suit against the original lessor to enforce provisions of the original

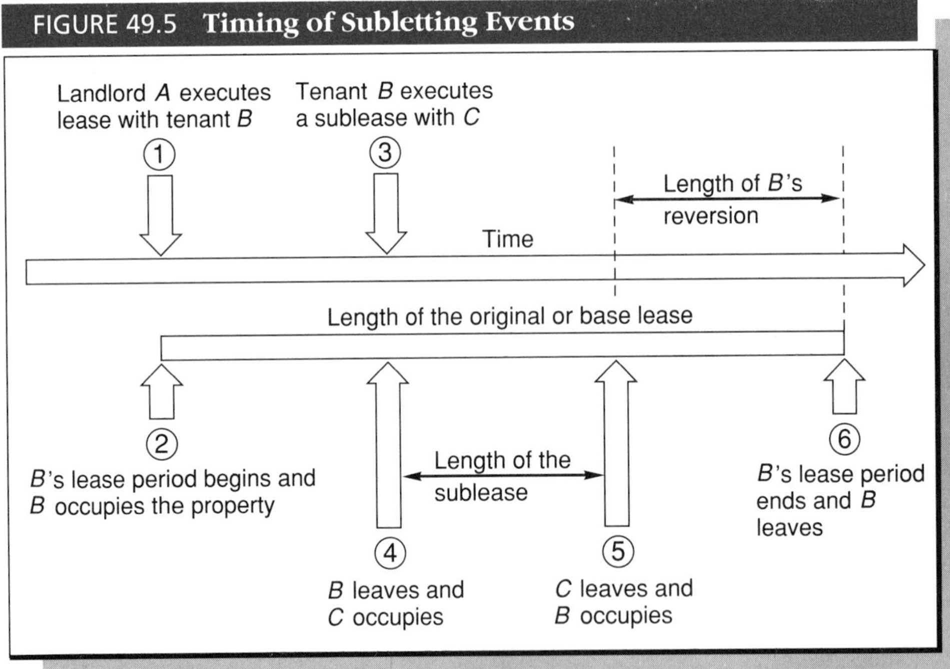

FIGURE 49.6 **Relationships in Lease Subletting**

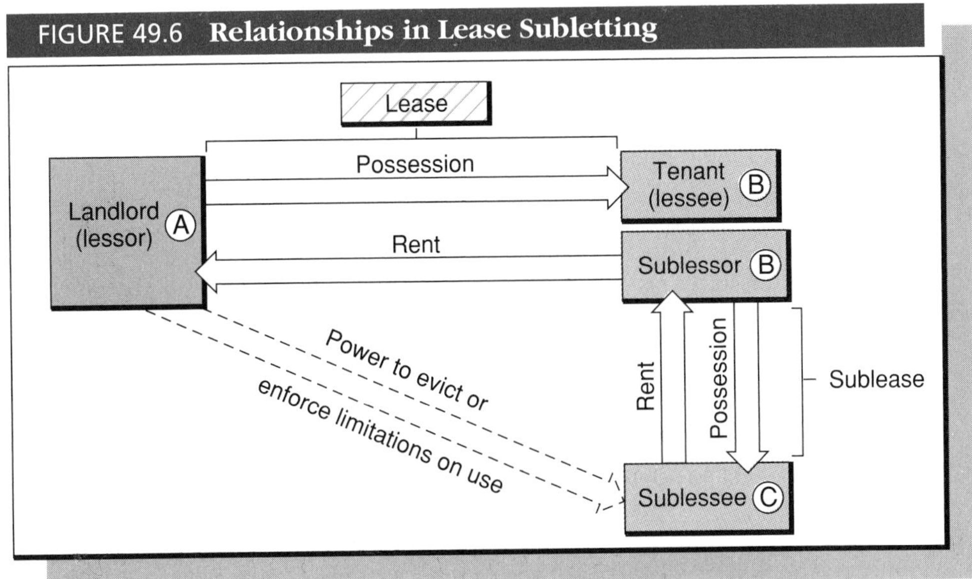

lease. On the other hand, the sublessee is bound by the provisions of the original lease that limit the use of the property. Thus if the original lease prohibits use of the property for anything except farming, the lessor would win a suit against a sublessee attempting to operate a gas station on the property. Further, while the sublessee is legally bound to pay rent to the sublessor and is *not* liable to the original lessor for the rent, the sublessee may be evicted if the original lessor is not paid. But eviction is the limit of the original lessor's remedy against the sublessee. If the original lessor is entitled to collect damages for past or future unpaid rent, the original lessor must collect from the original tenant. (See Figure 49.6.)

The Transfer of the Lessor's Interest

Landlords also have the legal power to transfer their interests in rented property. In general, the new owner takes the property subject to the rights of the tenants. Thus a tenant can assert the same rights against the new owner that the tenant could have asserted against the old owner. For example, a new owner of a student dormitory cannot raise rents if the student tenants leased with fixed rents for the remainder of the academic year with an estate for years.

The new owner is bound by the old leases because, in most cases, the new owner has knowledge of the leases from the presence of the tenants on the property. If the tenants are not on the property, and the buyer is not aware of the lease when he or she becomes the new owner, the buyer usually takes free of the lease.

Tenants who do not visibly occupy the realty can protect themselves by *recording* their leases. This gives **constructive notice** to all the world of the lessee's interest. Thus if a college freshman visited the college community in mid-July and found an apartment that was a great bargain close to campus, he or she could execute a lease at that time, with

constructive notice
Knowledge of a fact presumed or imputed by law

possession to begin when school started. To be protected from a buyer of the realty who might want to raise the rent, the student can *record* the lease. This establishes and protects the student's ownership priority.

The Termination of Leases

Leases can be terminated in a variety of ways by both the landlord and the tenant. But there must be some legal basis for termination or the lease continues to be effective. Thus if a landlord discovered that a tenant, occupying under an estate for years (which did not prohibit pets), kept a dog in the apartment and served the tenant with an impressive looking notarized legal document titled *Notice to Vacate or Be Evicted,* the tenant could continue occupying the property, with the dog! This landlord had no basis for terminating the relationship. The following paragraphs discuss the legal basis for termination of the rental relationship.

► Expiration of the Lease

Estates for years have well-defined ending dates. Periodic estates do not. The arrival of the ending date of the estate for years terminates the rental relationship without notice. If appropriate advance notice is given before the end of a periodic estate, the rental relationship will be terminated. The tenancy at will and tenancy at sufferance are terminated by the sale of the property or death of the landlord. No advance notice of termination is usually required.

► Surrender and Acceptance

If a lessee wants to terminate the lease before expiration of the term, the lessee can accomplish this by surrendering the lease to the landlord. However, to terminate the tenant's obligations, the landlord must *accept* the surrender. Surrender and acceptance are acts of the parties that clearly indicate that they both intend the obligations under the lease to be terminated. Thus if a tenant leased an apartment for five years, and, after two and one-half years was transferred to a new city, the tenant could tell the landlord that he or she wanted to terminate the lease. If the landlord assented and took possession of the apartment, the tenant's obligations might be terminated.

constructive eviction
A tenant's moving out of leased premises because the landlord caused the premises to become unfit for their intended use by the tenant

► Constructive Eviction

If after execution of the lease the landlord causes the leased premises to become unfit for their intended use by the tenant—as, for example, by refusing to provide water to an apartment—the tenant's obligations may be terminated if the tenant moves out because of the unfit condition.

► Breach of Condition

If either party breaches a *condition* (not a covenant) contained in the lease, that relieves the other party of his or her obligations under the lease. Thus if a tenant violates a condition prohibiting green plants on the premises, the landlord can deprive the tenant of possession through eviction. Conversely, a tenant can move out and not be liable for further rent if the landlord breaches an express *condition* promising to keep the premises in good repair.

► Eviction

eviction
The dispossession of a tenant from the leased premises

Generally, self-help eviction is available in only a few states. Landlords must almost always sue to evict. The proceedings are frequently called actions for unlawful detainer. As in all court actions, the defendant (in this situation the tenant) is given advance notice of the lawsuit. Courts try to handle this action speedily so that tenants can be dispossessed as rapidly as possible. If the landlord is, in fact, entitled to evict the tenant and the tenant fails to leave voluntarily, the sheriff will physically remove the tenant and the tenant's property from the premises.

In order to win the eviction proceedings the landlord must prove that the tenant's lease has been terminated.

The Uniform Residential Landlord Tenant Act

► In General

The Uniform Residential Landlord Tenant Act of 1972 has been adopted in a number of states including Alaska, Arizona, Connecticut, Florida, Hawaii, Iowa, Kansas, Kentucky, Michigan, Montana, Nebraska, New Mexico, Oklahoma, Oregon, Tennessee, Virginia, and Washington. The Act, as its title indicates, deals only with *residential* leases, which means that commercial, industrial, and agricultural leases do not come under its provisions. In general, the Act attempts to codify the existing court rulings on landlord-tenant law. In some areas it seeks to remove ambiguity, simplify, or adapt the law to both the modern environment and the realities of residential leases. While the Act is a complete codification of the law in this area, the following paragraphs point out just some of the areas where the Act conflicts with, clarifies, or adds to the existing case law on leases.

► Right to Inspect

The Act provides that the landlord may *not* enter the residence without the lessee's consent. However, the lessee may not *unreasonably* withhold consent for the lessor to enter to inspect or make repairs.

► Tenant's Conduct

The Act imposes relatively specific duties on tenants. Some are new duties while others are merely restatements of existing case law. The more interesting duties are as follows:

1. The tenant must comply with building codes affecting health and safety.
2. The tenant must dispose of all trash in a safe manner.

3. The tenant must not mistreat facilities, fixtures, or appliances, and plumbing fixtures must be kept clean.
4. The tenant, and his or her guests, must not disturb other tenants.

▶ Limitation to Residential Use Only

The Act limits the lessee's use of the realty to residential purposes.

▶ Duty to Repair

The Act places the duty to repair on the lessor and even limits, in some situations, the power of the lease agreement to shift that duty to the lessee.

Tenant's Right to Repair and Deduct The URLTA gives the tenant the right to make certain minor repairs when the lessor has failed to do so. However, the Act requires that the tenant give the landlord notice of the defect, and allow two weeks for the repair to be made. Then the tenant may make a minor repair and deduct the amount expended from the rent due. The amount may not be more than $100 or one-half the periodic rent, whichever is greater. Further, the tenant must provide the landlord with an itemized statement of the expenses at the time the reduced rent is paid.

▶ Retaliation

The Act formalized the definition of *retaliation* and expressly prohibits it. Retaliation is defined as raising rent, decreasing services, or eviction. If any of these events occur within one year after a conflict between the lessor and the lessee, the Act establishes a presumption that the lessor's action is illegal retaliation. A conflict is defined as: (1) a report by the lessee to a governmental authority of a violation of a housing or building code; or (2) a complaint to the lessor about the lessor's failure to maintain the property; or (3) organizing or joining a tenants union.

The following case illustrates the way states that have not adopted the URLTA handle claims of retaliatory eviction.

FACTS

Mrs. Goudzward entered into a lease for an apartment with Tom's Point Apartments. She held over after the expiration of her lease and eviction proceedings were begun. At the trial, she raised as a defense to eviction a claim of "retaliatory eviction." She testified that she previously had tried to organize a tenants' association and had complained to the State Attorney General that the landlord did not pay interest on security deposits.

DECISION

In order to establish retaliatory eviction the tenant must establish all of the following:

1. The tenant must have exercised a constitutional right in the action he undertook.
2. The grievance complained of by the tenant must be bona fide, reasonable, serious in nature, and have a foundation in fact. However, the grievance need not have

been adjudicated by the agency reviewing the complaint.

3. The tenant did not create the condition upon which the complaint is based.
4. The grievance complained of must be present at the time the landlord commences his proceeding.
5. The overriding reason the landlord is seeking the eviction is to retaliate against the tenant for exercising his constitutional rights.

Applying the facts in the present case to the above criteria, the Court finds that at the time the landlord commenced this action and, at the present time, none of the required grievances existed. The tenants' association sought by the tenant never came into being; the tenants had collected interest due them on rent security deposits; and the tenant had no current complaint against the landlord. Tenant failed to prove the elements necessary to sustain the alleged retaliatory eviction defense. Since the grievance had been resolved before the eviction process began, this is not a retaliatory eviction. Therefore, respondent may be evicted.

Tom's Point Apartments v. Goudzward, 339 N.Y.S.2d 281 (N.Y. 1972).

Holding Over

The Act provides that a tenant who, in bad faith, holds over will be liable for three months rent or treble the lessor's damages, whichever is greater.

Summary Statement

1. Real property law is very old and reflects the agrarian society in which it developed.
2. The basic nature of the rental relationship involves a temporary transfer of possession in return for the payment of rent.
3. Oral leases are generally enforceable only if they are for a short period.
4. The rental relationships recognized by law are estates at will, estates at sufferance, periodic estates, and estates for years.
5. There are express and implied covenants and conditions in leases.
6. If one party breaches a covenant, the injured party must still perform his or her duties under the lease. If, however, a condition is breached, the injured party need not perform.
7. An assignment is the transfer of all the remaining term of a lease. A subletting is the transfer of just a part of the remaining term.
8. Buyers of realty generally are bound by the leases executed by the seller.
9. A holdover tenant may be liable for all the rent for an additional lease period.
10. A lease may be terminated by expiration of the term, surrender and acceptance, constructive eviction, and breach of condition.
11. The Uniform Residential Landlord Tenant Act (URLTA), adopted in many states, attempts to codify existing court rulings on landlord-tenant law.

The following case illustrates the legal concepts of constructive eviction, implied covenants, and the nature of the landlord's duty to repair.

CHERBERG v. PEOPLES NATIONAL BANK OF WASHINGTON
564 P.2d 1137 (Wash. 1977)

Utter, Associate Justice. James Cherberg and his wife brought a claim based in part upon the tort of intentional interference with business expectancies arising from the willful refusal of the Joshua Green Corporation, as their landlord, to perform duties owed them under a commercial lease. A jury verdict for $42,000 was entered in favor of the Cherbergs. . . .

In 1967, James and Arlene Cherberg leased a portion of the Lewis Building on Fifth Avenue in downtown Seattle and invested some $80,000 in the establishment and operation of a restaurant business at that location. Joshua Green Corporation acquired the Lewis Building in February of 1972, subject to the [Cherberg] lease. . . . In April of 1972 Peoples National Bank of Washington, the owner of the property abutting the Lewis Building on the south, commenced demolition of the existing buildings on its property for the purpose of constructing a high-rise office tower. The demolition work resulted in the exposure of the south wall of the Lewis Building. It was found to be structurally unsafe and in need of substantial repairs to satisfy requirements of the City of Seattle Building Department. The . . . premises here at issue were located within the Lewis Building but did not abut the south wall.

The lease between the parties required the lessee to make necessary repairs to maintain the . . . premises, excepting the outside walls and other structural components of the building, and reserved to the lessor the use of the roof and outside walls of the building. The lease does not contain an express covenant concerning the responsibility to maintain the structural components of the building.

Upon learning of the problems with the south wall, the lessor contracted the Cherbergs, . . . indicating that the Green Corporation would probably elect not to repair the wall and that the City might order the building closed. The Cherbergs responded that the lessor was obligated under the lease to make repairs and that they would suffer substantial damage should their tenancy be disrupted.

Thereafter, the lessor terminated the lease and informed the Cherbergs of its intention to post the building as unsafe. The Cherbergs closed their business for approximately one week. An independent consultant then informed the Cherbergs that repair of the wall was, in fact, feasible. The Cherbergs reopened their business when the Green Corporation failed to actually post the building and at that time reiterated their demands. . . . The bank, not wishing to be delayed further in its construction plans, eventually repaired the wall at its own expense (estimated at $30,000 to $50,000).

This action was brought against the bank and the Green Corporation, alleging breach of the lessor's duty to repair, negligent demolition by the bank, and that the defendants had engaged in a conspiracy to destroy petitioners' business. Undisputed evidence was presented demonstrating that there were close ties between Joshua Green, III, the Green Corporation, and Peoples National Bank of Washington. The evidence disclosed that the Green Corporation viewed the Lewis Building as an adequately profitable investment under the circumstances existing at the time of purchase, but that it was the Corporation's desire to regain control of the premises as soon as possible in order to demolish the existing structure on the property and erect a new building which they felt might be more profitable. Demolition of the Lewis Building during the course of the new construction would have been of substantial economic benefit both to the Green Corporation and to the bank. In early 1972 both the bank and the Green Corporation had requested the same agent to engage in efforts to negotiate a sale of the Cherberg's leasehold in order that the Green Corporation might regain control of the premises.

The trial court, at the conclusion of testimony, dismissed the bank from the suit and also dismissed the negligence and conspiracy claims. [Green Corporation's] other motions pertinent to this appeal were denied. The jury was instructed that [Green Corporation] was liable for damages caused by the failure to repair the outside wall. It further instructed the jury with regard to the elements of the tort of intentional interference with business expectations and that, if the jury concluded that the defendant's actions were willful, damages for mental suffering, inconvenience, and discomfort would be compensable. The jury made a special finding of willful action and returned a verdict of $42,000. The only evidence of economic loss due to the temporary closure and attendant disruption of business was in the amount of $3,100.

The Court of Appeals held that the lessor did have a duty to make repairs to the wall on the basis of a mandate so to do from competent government authority. However, it reversed and remanded, holding that the Green Corporation was entitled to a directed verdict on the claim of interference with business expectations and the assessment of damages for inconvenience, discomfort, and mental distress.

The first issue is the rights and duties of the parties with regard to the unsafe condition of the south wall of the building. We agree with the holding of the Court of Appeals that an implied duty on the part of the lessor exists to make those repairs mandated by competent government authority where, as here, the appropriate authority determines that, in the interest of the public welfare, a defective condition of a building must be remedied. We also agree that the evidence presented established that the refusal of the respondent to take action to fulfill this duty, within a reasonable time after notification from the City, breached an implied covenant of quiet employment and resulted in an actionable constructive eviction.

In addition, however, even absent a mandate from government authority, the lessor was under a duty to make the repairs here in question. The general rule is that a landlord has no duty to make repairs to the demised premises absent an express covenant requiring such action. . . . While it is true that this lease did not contain an express covenant abrogating this common law rule, the area requiring repair was not a part of the demised premises but was an area of the building over which the landlord had expressly retained control.

A landlord has a duty to maintain, control, and preserve retained portions of the premises subject to a leasehold in a manner rendering the demised premises adequate to the tenant's use and safe for occupancy by both the tenant and his invitees. . . . Failure to fulfill this duty results in liability on the part of the lessor for injury caused thereby, . . . and failure to fulfill this duty, by omission to repair, can in a proper case constitute an actionable constructive eviction. . . .

The willful refusal to adequately maintain retained portions of a building so as to allow the tenant to enjoy the beneficial use of the demised portion of the building is a breach of an implied duty owed by the landlord to the tenant under Washington law. On these facts, this breach of duty was sufficient to constitute an actionable constructive eviction and provides a basis for the conclusion that the landlord was liable for any damages stemming from that breach, . . . independent of any directive to repair issued by the City of Seattle. . . .

The decision of the Court of Appeals is reversed and the judgment in favor of the [Cherbergs] is reinstated. It is so ordered.

Questions and Case Problems

1. Mr. Lemle leased, in 1965, a villa in the Diamond Head area of Honolulu for $800 per month. On the first night on the property Lemle, his wife and four children, slept together to protect themselves from rats that infested the main dwelling and particularly the thatched roof made of coconut leaves. After attempts to trap and exterminate the rats, Lemle and his family left and Mr. Lemle sued for the return of their prepaid rent. Will he prevail? [*Lemle v. Breeden,* 462 P.2d 470 (Haw. 1969).]
2. Industrial Investment Co. was the lessee of certain real property in the State of Hawaii. Industrial then, with the lessor's consent, sublet to Mr. and Mrs. Hayashi. Later Industrial assigned its interest in the lease to Broida Properties who agreed to perform the lease and pay the rent to the lessor. The Hayashis then, with the consent of Broida, assigned their leasehold estate to Mr. and Mrs. Hanuna who, in turn, assigned the leasehold estate to Mrs. Park who agreed to pay the rent to Broida. She did not pay. Broida sues the Hayashis for the rent. The Hayashis, sublessees, assert that they are not liable to Broida for the rent because there is no longer any privity

of contract between the lessee, Industrial, and the lessor because of the lessee's assignment of its interest to Broida. Is there still privity of contract between the lessor and Industrial, the lessee, and must the Hayashis pay Broida? (Note: You may find it helpful to diagram the relations among the parties in this problem.) [*Broida v. Hayashi,* 464 P.2d 285 (Haw. 1970).]

3. Garcia leased an apartment in the East Harlem section of Manhattan. The lead-based paint on the walls was peeling and flaking off. Garcia's two children were eating the lead-based paint. Consumption of this paint can cause mental retardation and death. Garcia complained to the landlord without effect. Then he bought the necessary supplies and repainted, and brought suit against the landlord for his expenses. Will he recover? [*Garcia v. Freeland Realty, Inc.,* 314 N.Y.S.2d 215 (N.Y. 1970).]
4. Fidel rented property from De Baca. The lease agreement contained a covenant against assignments. Fidel sublet a portion of the property for a period shorter than the unexpired term of the lease. De Baca sues to evict Fidel. Who prevails?
5. Dr. Eldredge leased a 45-acre farm located in Gem County, Idaho, to Joseph W. Jensen and Rhea Bell Jensen for five years. After the first year, the Jensens defaulted in their rental payments but remained in possession. At the beginning of the fourth year, Dr. Eldredge sold the property to third parties. The Jensens elected to treat the sale as constructive eviction and abandoned the premises. Dr. Eldredge sued for unpaid rent of $1,200. The Jensens defended, claiming damages of $5,000 for early termination of the lease. Who prevails? [*Eldredge v. Jensen,* 404 P.2d 624 (Ida. 1965).]
6. Betty Reiman, a 14-year-old girl, went to the apartment of Mrs. Green, who had been ill, to assist in preparations for Mrs. Green's return from the hospital. Betty helped with the washing and drying of Mrs. Green's linen. The linen was dried by hanging it on a clothes line located on the roof of the apartment building. A skylight was also on the roof near the door giving tenants access to the clothes line area. Betty's cousin, Leah, helped her collect the clothes off the line, stacking them in Betty's arms. After stripping the line, Leah went ahead to open the door for Betty. When Leah pulled the door part way open, Betty stepped back to allow it to swing completely open. In so doing, her heel struck an object, causing her to fall backward through the skylight to the floor below. She now sues for the injuries sustained. The owner of the building, Moore, denies responsibility for the injuries. Who prevails? [*Reiman v. Moore,* 108 P.2d 452 (Cal. 1940).]
7. Sharon Fitzgerald leased, on a month to month basis, a house from Roger Parkin. At the time the lease was created, Roger promised to make certain repairs. After repeated demands by Sharon, and the passage of three and one-half months, Roger had not made the repairs. Sharon obtained an inspection from city authorities, which resulted in a citation of Roger for eight violations. One month later, Roger served Sharon with a 30-day notice to quit the premises. About a month and half later, Roger initiated an unlawful detainer action against Sharon. Sharon defended the action on the ground that Roger was engaged in retaliatory eviction. Roger claims that his reason for evicting Sharon is that one of Sharon's rent checks bounced, another rent check had been late, and that she had kept a dog on the premises in violation of the lease, which prohibited having dogs on the premises. Who prevails? [*Parkin v. Fitzgerald,* 240 N.W.2d 828 (Minn. 1976).]
8. Peterson leased property from Platt for a 10-year period. Peterson operated an Arctic Circle Drive Inn on the property. When Peterson fell two months behind in the rent, Platt waited until everyone was gone, took possession of the premises, changed the locks, and denied entry to Peterson and his employees. As a consequence, certain tasty goods perished. Peterson sued Platt, claiming that Platt took possession illegally

and, therefore, Platt should be liable for Peterson's injuries. Who prevails? [*Peterson v. Platt,* 400 P.2d 507 (Utah 1965).]

9. Sid Scholar leased an apartment near his girlfriend's dorm for a nine-month period. The lease agreement did not indicate who was to be responsible for repairs. When the toilet broke, Sid asked the landlord to repair it. He refused. Sid moved out five months before the end of the lease. The landlord sues Sid for the cost of repairing the toilet and for five months' rent. Who prevails?

10. In the case of *Cherberg v. Peoples National Bank of Washington,* excerpted at the beginning of this section, describe what motivated the landlord to refuse to make the repairs.

PART 9 REAL PROPERTY

ETHICS AND BUSINESS LAW

Introduction

This end-of-part discussion, like the others in this book, is designed to encourage you to begin forming personal beliefs about what is right or wrong conduct in business. The discussion here builds on the material in the first end-of-part discussion, which you may find helpful to review.

This material has several goals. The section immediately following is designed to help you see the range of ethical issues associated with this area of the law. The in-depth discussion is intended to provide you with a background for forming your own beliefs about a single very important ethical issue in business. The problems at the end of this part are designed to build your skill in ethical analysis while exploring further the in-depth issue.

A Sampling of Ethical Issues in Real Property Law

Real property law incorporates the ongoing conflict that inevitably arises between the interests of the individual and the needs of society.

► Individual Rights Versus the Needs of Society

Governments have the constitutional power to condemn and rezone property. Both of these activities bring the needs of society into conflict with the interests of individual landowners. A government agency can condemn private property for a public purpose. Of course, this advances the public need over the individual's interest. But since the government must pay the reasonable value of condemned property, the individual's injury is reduced. Do you think this is a reasonable balance between private interests and the public good? Can you think of situations where this process would produce an *unjust* result?

Zoning powers allow cities and counties to regulate the ways real property is used. There are, of course, limitations on this power. For example, a city could not engage in spot zoning. But zoning sometimes creates very large costs for individuals. Suppose you owned undeveloped land zoned for commercial use worth $400,000. If the land were rezoned to single family residences, its value could fall to $100,000. Of course, you would bear the loss rather than all the persons benefited by the rezoning. Do you think this is just? Can you articulate a justification for this law using one of the four styles of ethical reasoning? Can you decide why the law treats rezoning and condemnation in different ways?

Recording statutes also raise ethical issues. Recall that if a grantor issues two deeds to the same estate, the first to record will generally own all while the second to record will own nothing. This second party will undoubtedly try to sue the grantor. But if the grantor is bankrupt or has fled the jurisdiction, it is likely that the second grantee will recover nothing. Can you analyze this law from a utilitarian perspective? How do you think Kant would assess this law? Do you think this law is ethical?

Conditional estates and restrictive covenants also reflect the recurring conflict between individual desires and the needs of society. Our law allows owners to use restrictive covenants and conditional estates to control future use of the property. Many believe that individuals should not be able to control the use of realty that they do not have the legal right to possess. On this issue our law favors the individual. At one time such restraints were used to prevent realty from being owned by Catholics, Jews, Negroes, Asians, and/or Baptists. Today, of course, such restraints are invalid. Do you think it is ethical for a former owner of realty to be able to control its use?

► Exploitation of the Vulnerable

Real property law raises several issues where one party is able to gain an unfair advantage over another. For example, lessors often use their superior knowledge of landlord/tenant law to obtain a legal advantage over a naive tenant. One of the common tactics is for the lessor to have his attorney prepare a lease favorable to the lessor, then it is typeset and presented to tenants as a "standard" lease. If conflicts arise, the lessor is often coached by an attorney while the tenant often lacks the financial resources to protect his or her legal rights. If you were a landlord would you engage in such tactics? Why or why not?

Another example of exploitation occurs when a tenant moves to another part of the country. Lessors can delay inspecting the apartment until the tenant is gone, then unfairly withhold the cleaning deposit. For many tenants, it is just too expensive to come back and sue the lessor, so they just forget the loss. Can you see how tempted some lessors would be in this situation? Do you think you could be tempted enough to engage in this conduct?

In-Depth Discussion of a Basic Issue: Unequal Wealth

This issue asks whether it is ethical to encourage the unequal distribution of wealth. Because many business ethics decisions involve this issue, mature businesspersons need clear beliefs about it.

► Egoistic Views

A self-centered analysis leads to differing conclusions, depending on who does the analysis. If the egoist is a wealthy person, then economic systems that allow for unequal wealth are good because they help this person.

Frequently, wealthy or talented persons argue that merit justifies unequal wealth. One form of this argument says that there is an *entitlement* for those with the most talent and energy. This argument assumes that individual differences in persons justify different treatment by society.

This view is often attacked on the ground that talent and perhaps even energy are distributed to individuals by forces over which they have no control. That is, the highly talented individual is not necessarily highly talented because of his or her own efforts. Rather it is the "roll of the genetic dice" that determines talent. And since the individual is not responsible for this attribute, the individual should not be rewarded for it. This critique of merit concludes that talent ought not to entitle one to different treatment.

The egoistic analysis from the perspective of the poor person can reach the opposite conclusion of that of the rich person. Thus economic systems that encourage unequal wealth may be viewed as bad by the poor person because they may be seen as reducing the share of the poor person's wealth.

As you can see, egoism provides little guidance for assessing this issue because it leads to differing conclusions, depending on the status of the party who does the analysis.

► Utilitarian Analysis

This line of analysis asks what generates the greatest good for the greatest number. For example in real property law, those injured by rezoning are generally not entitled to compensation for their losses—they must bear the loss themselves. This law generates the greatest good for the greatest number because the loss is borne by only one party instead of many.

It is fairly clear that unequal distribution of wealth benefits the majority. This is because our economic system creates incentives that encourage everyone to contribute as much as possible to society in order to achieve personal rewards. Also, by placing more of society's wealth in the hands of the most talented, we increase the chance that it will be used most productively, thereby increasing total social wealth. Notice that the rewards are not justified as entitlements, but rather by contribution, which causes the total pie of wealth in society to increase. There is substantial evidence that the financial incentives that produce the unequal wealth do in fact increase total wealth.

The objection to this line of analysis is that what benefits the majority—the increase in total wealth—may come at the expense of the minority of persons with either little talent or little opportunity to exercise their talent. While this argument may be powerful to some, it carries little weight for the utilitarian, who tests right or wrong by looking for the greatest good for the greatest number.

► Kantian and Judeo-Christian Analysis

This line of reasoning generally focuses on duty or obligation. Since individuals may not be used exclusively as means to the ends of others, Kant would likely reject the rezoning law, seeing it as a way to use the landowner as a means to the ends of all the other taxpayers in the community. The real property law right to reasonable compensation for condemnation is more consistent with Kantian and religious ethics. While the majority benefit, it is not because they are able to impose the cost on a solitary landowner.

In the Kantian style of reasoning, duty is identified by the use of the three tests described in the first end-of-part discussion: (1) persons are moral entities and cannot be used exclusively as means; (2) we may not act, or create rules (or economic systems), where different rules apply to the sovereign (the rule maker) than to the subject (those ruled by the sovereign); and (3) the acts or rules must be able to be made universal without logical inconsistency.

Religions identify duty in large part by looking at scriptures. In general, nearly every religion imposes a duty on believers to accord special treatment to the poor. This is clearly true in the Judeo-Christian tradition and in most of the major religions of the world. The scriptural statement, "What you do unto the least of my brothers, you do unto me," exemplifies this view.

The religious view of the poor, and the Kantian requirement that we not use individuals exclusively as means, call into question the utilitarian analysis of economic systems. While utilitarians can justify unequal wealth by concluding that the majority are benefited, the special concern of religious and Kantian thinkers for members of society who are in minority positions prevents them from accepting the utilitarian argument. They conclude that those in economic minority positions cannot be exploited even if it benefits the majority.

John Rawls, a philosopher at Harvard, has articulated a system that justifies unequal distribution of wealth for religious and Kantian thinkers. Rawls concludes that the test of the rightness or wrongness of an economic system is its impact on the least advantaged members of society. If the consequence of the unequal wealth is that these least advantaged members are better off, then the system is good. If the consequence of the unequal wealth is that this group is worse off, then the system is not morally justified. Capitalism creates unequal wealth. But if it causes the total economy to grow rapidly, so that the least advantaged members of the capitalist society are better off than with equal division of wealth, the unequal wealth is, according to Rawls, justified.

► Conclusion

Can you see that egoism tests rightness or wrongness by looking at the impact on one individual, utilitarianism judges by looking at the impact on the majority, and Kantian and religious thinking on this issue look at the impact on the minority? Which line of reasoning do you find most persuasive?

Solving Ethics Problems

Like the other end-of-part discussions in this book, this one presents problems for you to consider. These problems have three goals. The first is to give you the opportunity to further explore the in-depth issue. The second goal is to give you experience in ethical reasoning about the law and about related management problems. The third goal is to let you see how thinking critically about the law can increase your ability to make ethical decisions. To facilitate this, the problems begin by asking you to analyze the law for its ethical content and then shift to looking at related problems in managerial ethics.

For a discussion of the ethical roles of markets and the law, and examples of the four styles of ethical reasoning—egoism, utilitarianism, Kantian philosophy, and religious ethics—read the business ethics material at the end of Part 1.

► Problems

1. Review the case of *Loretto v. Teleprompter Manhattan CATV Corp.*, p. 991. There, the state of New York enacted a statute that in effect made $1.00 the maximum fee a landlord could charge a cable TV company for installing cable in common areas in order to serve tenants. One landlord sued in federal court and the statute was declared unconstitutional as a violation of the "Taking Clause." Evaluate the ethical character of both the New York statute and the "Taking Clause."
2. Review the case of *Karell v. West and Shobert*, p. 1016. There, Mrs. Karell sought to assert ownership of a 3.7 acre parcel of land because it had been enclosed with her property by a fence for a substantial period of time. Her claim was denied because of insufficient proof that her use was continuous for the required period of time. Do you think this law seeks to allocate the land on the basis of merit (or social contribution), or the greatest good for the greatest number, or with concern for the

interests of the weakest members of society, or a combination of these? Does order play a role in this case?

3. You are the president of a large conglomerate with five major lines of business. Four are highly profitable and one is losing money for the corporation. This weak division is located in a part of the country undergoing economic difficulties. If you close down this division, about 1,000 people will be thrown out of work with little chance of finding other employment unless they relocate to more prosperous areas of the nation. If you do not close this division, profits will decline by about 30 percent. What ought you to do and why?
4. Your firm allocates bonus money to each department head for distribution to subordinates as he or she judges best. You have received a pot of $10,000 to be allocated among your five subordinates. One is a highly talented person who accounts for about 40 percent of the department's productivity. Two others carry their share, each contributing about 20 percent to the department's productivity. The remaining two contribute about 10 percent each. Of these latter two, one is not very bright and the other is bright but going through some personal problems at this time. How will you allocate this bonus money—by ability, by contribution, by dividing the bonus money equally, or by using a combination of these methods? How do you justify your distribution method?

PART 10

SECURED TRANSACTIONS, BANKRUPTCY, AND INSURANCE

PREVIEW

In this part we will examine four legal topics that are important to most individuals and businesses—secured transactions involving personal property, suretyship, bankruptcy, and insurance. A secured transaction is one in which an interest in personal property, such as a car, is given as collateral for a loan.

While we hope that bankruptcy law will not affect you individually, the law is extremely important to businesses forced to write off many thousands of dollars worth of debts discharged in bankruptcy.

Insurance involves the shifting of risks from one party (the insured) to another party (the insurer). Insurance has become so important that it has an impact on virtually every personal or business transaction, from birth (which is covered by health insurance) to death (which is covered by "life" insurance).

Business ethics as it relates to the text material in these chapters is considered at the end of this part.

C H A P T E R

50

CREATION OF SECURITY INTERESTS IN PERSONAL PROPERTY

After you have read this chapter, you should be able to:

1. Describe a secured transaction.
2. List the three major types of collateral.
3. Define after-acquired property and future advances.
4. Describe the floating lien.
5. List two methods used to create a security interest.
6. Describe the four methods used to perfect a security interest.
7. Discuss the rules regarding perfection that apply to multicounty and multistate transactions.

BUSINESS DECISIONS and the LAW

After graduating from college, Sue began working for a large corporation in a major city. She had $4,000 in her bank account and had to repay a large educational loan. Sue needed a car to travel to and from work. The car that Sue wanted to purchase cost $11,000. Consequently, Sue went to First Bank to borrow the remaining $7,000. The lending officer at the bank advised Sue that the bank would make the loan, but Sue would first have to sign documents giving the bank a security interest in her car. In borrowing the money and signing these documents, Sue entered into a secured transaction.

Introduction

As consumers such as Sue increase their use of credit in making purchases, the law of secured transactions becomes especially important. In most consumer transactions the creditor will want something more than the mere promise of the consumer to repay the debt. Many creditors will require the consumer to give the creditor a security interest in property that the consumer owns. Some creditors will require, additionally, the promise of another person, a surety, to pay the debt on the consumer's default. In this chapter and the next we will discuss these two credit transactions: the personal property secured transaction, and suretyship.

Although secured transactions are important for the consumer, they are especially important for the person in business. This is because a person in business will often enter into a secured transaction as a debtor in acquiring goods and will enter into a second secured transaction as a creditor in selling goods to a consumer.

The law of secured transactions is at times technical and complicated. However, it is important to keep in mind as you read these chapters that this material is especially important to the person who is not an attorney. This is because, in most cases, the person entering into a secured transaction does not retain an attorney but, instead, acts as his or her own attorney. While this practice is not recommended, it is often necessary because secured transactions are so common that it would usually be impractical and expensive to retain an attorney.

security interest
"An interest in personal property or fixtures which secures payment or performance of an obligation" UCC 1–201(37)

secured party
A creditor with a security interest

secured transaction
A transaction used to create a security interest

collateral
Property subject to a security interest UCC 9–105(1)(C)

purchase money security interest
"A security interest is a 'purchase money security interest' to the extent that it is (a) taken or retained by the seller of the collateral to secure all or part of its price; or (b) taken by a person who by making advances or incurring an obligation gives value to enable the debtor to acquire rights in or the use of collateral if such value is in fact so used." UCC 9–107

Definitions

In Sue's case, Sue is a *debtor* and First Bank is a *creditor*. The bank's **security interest** gives it the right to repossess Sue's property if she fails to make her loan payments. Because it possesses this right, the bank is called a **secured party** and the whole transaction is described as a **secured transaction.**

In many cases the creditor extends credit in order that the debtor may purchase the property that is then used as **collateral** for the loan. This is called a **purchase money security interest.** In Sue's case, she has given the bank a purchase money security interest in the car because she used the loan to purchase the car. If she had borrowed money to buy the car but had given the bank a security interest in only her speedboat, the security would not be a purchase money security interest.

The Source of Law

The law of secured transactions is found in Article 9 of the Uniform Commercial Code. Because the UCC has been adopted in all states but Louisiana, the law of secured transactions is generally uniform throughout the United States.

The UCC provides that Article 9 applies "to any transaction (regardless of its form) which is intended to create a security interest in personal property or fixtures. . . ."[1] This statement has two major consequences. First, if the creditor asks for real estate as security instead of personal property, the transaction is not a secured transaction but, instead, is a *mortgage*. Mortgage law is derived from real estate cases and statutes and has been discussed in Part 9, Real Property.

[1]UCC 9–102(1)(a).

The second consequence is that, regardless of what a transaction is called by the debtor and the creditor, it is a secured transaction if the parties intend to create a security interest in personal property or fixtures. Even a lease might be treated as a secured transaction, as the following case illustrates.

FACTS

Franklin National Bank of Minneapolis, defendant, leased three dump trucks and other equipment to Noyes Paving Company. Under the terms of the leases, Noyes was given the option to purchase the leased goods at the end of the term for $1. The bank did not comply with the law of secured transactions in that the bank did not make a timely filing within ten days after Noyes received possession of the leased goods. Noyes also gave a security interest in its "Construction Equipment, Motor Vehicles" to James Talcott, Inc. Talcott had perfected its security interest by filing a financing statement before the bank entered into the lease agreements. Noyes later defaulted in its payments to the bank and to Talcott, and both parties claimed the collateral. The bank repossessed and sold the collateral. Talcott sued for the proceeds claiming that its security interest had priority since the bank had not made a timely filing. The bank contended that the lease was not a secured transaction and, therefore, timely filing was unnecessary. Judgment was reached for the bank and Talcott appealed.

DECISION

Judgment reversed, for Talcott. The policy of the UCC is look to the substance of the agreement rather than the form. The bank's lease for a nominal consideration was, in substance, really a secured transaction, and the bank should have treated it as such, which it did not do. Thus, because Talcott filed its financing statement first and the bank did not file its financing statement within ten days after Noyes received the goods, Talcott's security interest has priority.

James Talcott, Inc. v. Franklin Nat'l Bank of Minneapolis, 194 N.W.2d 775 (Minn. 1972).

The Types of Collateral

The personal property that is subject to a security interest is called *collateral*. The types of personal property that may be used as security are either *tangible* (e.g., goods) or *intangible* (e.g., accounts receivable) and may be broken down into three major categories: tangible goods, intangibles, and paper. These categories will become important later when we discuss methods of "perfecting" a security interest and priorities among several secured parties.

▶ Tangible Goods

Goods are generally defined as tangible things that are movable when the security interest is created or that are fixtures. Specifically, there are four types of goods.

goods
Tangible, movable things

Consumer Goods **Consumer goods** are goods that are used or bought for use primarily for personal, family, or household purposes.[2] If Sue purchased her car primarily for a personal or family purpose, the car would be considered a consumer good.

consumer goods
Goods that "are used or bought for use primarily for personal, family, or household purposes" UCC 9–109(1)

[2]UCC 9–109(1).

equipment
Goods that "are used or bought for use primarily in business (including farming or a profession) UCC 9–109(2)

Equipment Goods that are used or bought for use primarily in business (including farming or a profession) are classified as **equipment**.[3] If Sue were a travelling sales representative and used the car primarily for travelling to customers, the car would be equipment.

inventory
Goods that are held for sale or lease

Inventory Goods that are held for sale or lease are considered to be **inventory.** If Sue were a car dealer and bought her car for purposes of resale, the car would be inventory.

farm products
"Crops or livestock or supplies used or produced in farming operations . . . in the possession of a debtor engaged in . . . farming operations" UCC 9–109(3)

Farm Products Crops, livestock, and supplies used or produced in farming operations that are in the possession of a debtor engaged in farming fall under the heading of **farm products.**

▶ Intangibles

account
A right to payment under a contract

Account Two types of intangibles, one specific and one general, can be used as security. The specific type of intangible is the **account.** Accounts include the *account receivable,* a right to payment for goods that have been sold or leased or for services rendered. Accounts also include a right to payment under a contract even where the right has not yet been earned by performance.[4]

assignment
The transfer of a contract right

Because of the increasing use of accounts as security for loans, the UCC allows accounts to be assigned freely. The UCC policy is reflected in UCC 9–318(4), which permits **assignment** even when the contract between the debtor and creditor prohibits assignment.

assignee
The person to whom a contract right is transferred

The **assignee** must bear in mind two factors that will affect the ability to collect an account. First, unless the debtor has made an enforceable agreement not to assert claims or defenses, the rights of the assignee are subject to such claims and defenses. Second, the debtor is authorized to make payments to the creditor until receiving notification of the assignment and notice that payment is to be made to the assignee. Unlike the common law discussed in Chapter 14, the UCC provides that notice of assignment alone is not enough to change the debtor's obligation to pay the creditor; such notice must include a demand that future payments be made to the assignee.

general intangibles
A catchall category covering a variety of personal property

General Intangibles The other type of intangibles are **general intangibles**, which include all personal property other than the property that we specifically list in this section. For example, goodwill, copyrights, patents, and trademarks would be considered general intangibles because they do not fall within the other categories.

▶ Paper

In many cases a right is evidenced by a piece of paper, and the paper may be used as a security. The UCC specifically provides that a security interest may be created in the following three types of paper.

chattel paper
A writing or writings that evidence both a monetary obligation and a security interest in or lease of specific goods UCC 9–105(1)(b)

Chattel Paper **Chattel paper** is defined as a writing or writings that evidence both a monetary obligation and a security interest in or lease of specific goods.[5] Suppose, for

---

[3]UCC 9–109(2).

[4]UCC 9–106.

[5]UCC 9–105(1)(b).

example, that Sue, instead of financing her car at the bank, had financed the purchase at the dealership under the type of security arrangement called a **conditional sale**, whereby the seller reserves title to the car until the buyer completes making payments. Under this arrangement Sue would sign both a note and a contract, and these writings together are chattel paper.

conditional sale
A sale in which the seller reserves title until the buyer completes payments; now called a secured transaction under Article 9 of the Uniform Commercial Code

In many cases the dealership cannot wait three or four years for Sue to pay because the dealership needs cash to purchase more automobiles. Consequently, the dealer might go to a bank, borrow money, and give the bank a security interest in the chattel paper. The bank would then have a security interest in the dealership's security interest, and, if the dealer defaulted in his payments to the bank, the bank would then begin receiving payments from Sue.

Instruments An **instrument** is any writing, apart from a security agreement or lease, that evidences a right to payment of money. One common type of instrument is the *negotiable instrument* (covered in Part 6, Commercial Paper), which includes drafts, checks, and notes. Another instrument is the *certificated security,* which is a share or other interest in property or in an enterprise of the issuer that is represented by an instrument in bearer or registered form and is commonly dealt in on securities exchanges or commonly recognized as a medium for investment.[6]

instrument
A writing that evidences a right to payment of money, including negotiable instruments, and also certificated securities

Documents of Title A **document of title** is a document that entitles the person in possession of it to hold and dispose of the document or the goods it covers as the person sees fit. Common examples are the *bill of lading,* a document issued by a carrier that evidences receipt of goods, and a *warehouse receipt,* a receipt issued by a person in the business of storing goods.

document of title
A document evidencing that the person possessing it "is entitled to receive, hold, and dispose of the document and the goods it covers" UCC 1–201(15)

Proceeds and After-Acquired Property

In addition to the categories of goods, the security interest might also cover proceeds and after-acquired property. **Proceeds** cover whatever the debtor receives upon selling, exchanging, or otherwise disposing of the collateral. Although there are a number of specific rules governing proceeds, the general rule is that a security interest in collateral also covers identifiable proceeds when the debtor disposes of the collateral. For utmost protection, however, a secured party should file a financing statement, described below, which specifically covers proceeds.

proceeds
What the debtor receives when he or she disposes of collateral

After-acquired property refers to property acquired after the debtor and creditor have entered into a security agreement. UCC 9–204 specifically provides that the security agreement may cover after-acquired collateral. The section also provides that the security agreement may include future loans made by the secured party. The combination of these two provisions allows a secured party to create a **floating lien** to cover present and future advances and acquisitions with the agreement.

after-acquired property
In security, property acquired after the security agreement is made

floating lien
A security device that covers after-acquired property and future advances

The floating lien is especially useful when the collateral is inventory. Suppose, for example, that Alpha Appliance Store borrows cash from First Bank and gives to the bank a security interest in present and future inventory. The security agreement also covers future advances by the bank and proceeds. One day Alpha sells a new stove to a customer in exchange for cash and an old stove is taken as a trade-in. Alpha then borrows money from the bank and purchases another new stove from a manufacturer. There is no need for the bank to create a new security interest because, under the floating lien concept, the

[6]UCC 8–102(1)(a).

original agreement covers the old stove (proceeds), the new stove (after-acquired property), and the new loan (future advances).

The Creation of Security Interests

In order to acquire rights in the debtor's property, the creditor must create a valid security interest. However, in order to create rights that are superior to those of other creditors and to ensure that he or she is paid first when the property is sold, the creditor must *perfect* the security interest. We will first discuss *creation* of the security interest and then *perfection* of the security interest.

► Form

security agreement
"An agreement which creates or provides for a security interest" UCC 9–105(1)(l)

Two methods are used to create a security interest. By the first method, the creditor and debtor might enter into a **security agreement,** an agreement that must, under the Code,[7] (1) be in writing, (2) be signed by the debtor, and (3) contain a description of the collateral.

The following excerpt from a security agreement has been taken from a Massachusetts case:

> [The debtor does] hereby grant, sell, assign, transfer and deliver to Grantee the following goods, chattels, and automobiles, namely: The business located at and numbered 574 Washington Street, Canton, Mass. together with all its goodwill, fixtures, equipment and merchandise. The fixtures specifically consist of the following: *All contents of luncheonette including equipment such as: booths and tables; stand and counter; tables; chairs; booths; steam tables; salad unit; potato peeler, a U.S. Slicer; range; case; fryer; compressor; bobtail; milk dispenser; silex; 100 Class air conditioner; signs; pastry case; mixer; dishes; silverware; tables; hot fudge; Haven Ex.; 2-door stationwagon 1957 Ford A57R107215* together with all property and articles now and which may hereafter be, used or mixed with, added or attached to, and/or substituted for, any of the foregoing described property.

The most common legal question regarding such agreements involves the question of whether the description of the collateral is sufficient, as is illustrated in the following case.

FACTS

On November 18, 1960, Firestone & Company made a loan to Kozy Kitchen, and Kozy Kitchen signed the security agreement quoted above, giving Firestone a security interest, of which Firestone filed notice the same day. On November 19, 1960, National Cash Register (NCR) delivered a cash register to Kozy Kitchen under a conditional sales contract, and a month later NCR filed notice of its security interest. Kozy defaulted on its loan and on its sales contract. Firestone then took possession of the cash register and sold it. NCR sued Firestone for the tort of conversion (intentional interference with its right to the cash register), claiming that it should receive the proceeds from the sale because Firestone's security agreement does not mention the cash register. Judgment was rendered for NCR in the trial and appellate courts, and Firestone appealed.

---

[7]UCC 9–203(1)(a).

DECISION

Judgment for Firestone. This case is one of first impression for this court under the UCC. Firestone's security agreement was broad enough to cover the cash register. "All contents of luncheonette" includes the cash register. Also, at the end of the agreement there is reference to after-acquired property, which would include the cash register.

National Cash Register Co. v. Firestone & Co., Inc., 191 N.E.2d 471 (Mass. 1963).

The second method used to create a security interest is the **pledge,** whereby the secured party actually takes *possession* of the collateral.[8] In most cases the pledge is not used, because the debtor wants to keep possession of the property for the debtor's own use and enjoyment. However, the pledge is the preferred method of creating a security interest when paper is used as collateral. In the following case a security agreement was not signed by the debtor and, since the lender did not have possession of any collateral, the court held that the lender did not have a security interest in anything.

pledge
The possessory security interest in bailed goods acquired by the bailee when there is a bailment for the purpose of security

FACTS

M. Rutkin Electric Supply Company, Inc. lent money to Burdette Electric, Inc. As security for the loan, Burdette assigned to Rutkin an account receivable owed by B. J. Builders, Inc. However, Burdette never signed a security agreement. Burdette became insolvent and a receiver was appointed. The receiver petitioned to have the assignment declared null and void because Burdette never signed a security agreement. Rutkin claims that it is entitled to the account.

DECISION

Judgment for the receiver. The assignment is null and void. A security interest is created by either a written agreement or by taking possession of the collateral. As an intangible, an account receivable cannot be possessed, and there was no written agreement.

M. Rutkin Electric Supply Co., Inc., v. Burdette Electric, Inc., 237 A.2d 500 (N.Y. 1967).

► Requirements

Regardless of whether the security agreement or pledge is used, the UCC imposes three requirements that must be met if the security interest is to *attach* to the collateral—that is, if it is to be enforceable by the creditor. First, the debtor and creditor must agree that it will attach. This requirement would automatically be met if a security agreement was used. Second, the creditor must give value**. Value**, generally, means any consideration sufficient under contract law. Under the UCC, value is also specifically defined[9] to include a creditor's binding commitment to extend credit and a creditor's taking security for a pre-existing claim. Third, the debtor must have rights in the collateral although, as we discussed above, the security interest may attach to after-acquired property.[10]

value
Any consideration sufficient to support a contract, a commitment to extend credit, or a past debt UCC 1–201(44)

[8]UCC 9–203(1)(a).

[9]UCC 1–201(44).

[10]UCC 9–204(1)(2).

The Perfection of Security Interests

When the three requirements for attachment have been met, the secured party may enforce his or her interest against the debtor. But often another party besides the debtor may claim an interest in the collateral. Suppose, for example, that Heidi purchases a refrigerator under a conditional sales contract from Bill's Appliance Store and that Bill's security interest attaches to the refrigerator. Heidi uses the refrigerator in her grocery store, thus making the refrigerator *equipment*. In each of the following three cases a third party might claim an interest in the collateral. (1) Heidi might sell the refrigerator to a friend who had no knowledge of Bill's security interest. (2) Another creditor might obtain a lien on the refrigerator, that is, a legal right in the refrigerator as security for the debt. (3) Heidi might go into bankruptcy and the trustee in bankruptcy would claim that the value of the refrigerator should be divided evenly among all her creditors.

In each of the three cases Bill's interest would be subordinate to that of the third party, even though the interest would be enforceable against Heidi alone. In order for Bill to gain rights superior to such third parties, he must give **constructive notice** (notice by law) to them that he has a security interest. This is called **perfection of a security interest.** Four common methods are used to perfect security interests.

constructive notice
Knowledge of a fact presumed or imputed by law

perfection of a security interest
When the creditor complies with Article 9 of the UCC's requirements for perfection, giving priority over other claims

financing statement
A document filed by the secured party to give public notice of the security interest in personal property

▶ Financing Statement

The first and the most common method used commercially to perfect security interests is to file a short document called a **financing statement** either locally in a county office, such as the registrar's office, or centrally with the secretary of state. The place of filing depends on the type of collateral and on the law in each particular state. For instance, in some states if an automobile is used as collateral, the financing statement should be filed locally unless the automobile is considered to be inventory, in which case there must be a central filing. Regardless of the place of filing, the financing statement is effective for five years from the date of filing; and after that time it lapses, unless a *continuation statement* is filed before the lapse.

The formal requirements for the financing statement are simple. The statement must (1) list the names and addresses of the debtor and of the secured party; (2) be signed by the debtor; and (3) contain a statement describing or indicating the types of the collateral. The example of a financing statement shown here is taken from the Pennsylvania case that follows below.

15110 of 1955
Financing Statement

This financing statement is presented to a filing officer for filing pursuant to the Uniform Commercial Code.

1. Debtor (or assignor)—Fort Pitt Packaging Co., Inc., 5615 Butler Street, Pittsburgh 1, Pa.
2. Secured Party (or assignee)—Provident Trust Co., 900 East Ohio St., Pittsburgh 1, Pa.
3. Maturity date of obligation ______________.
4. The financing statement covers the following types of property: All present and future accounts receivable submitted.

Fort Pitt Packaging Co., Inc. Leo A. Levy, Treas.	Provident Trust Company A. W. Charlton Executive Vice Pres.

In most cases where the validity of the financing statement is at issue, the major legal question relates to the third requirement: Does the financing statement adequately describe the collateral? This was the question in the following case.

FACTS

Provident Trust Company filed the above financing statement locally in Allegheny County on August 18, 1955 and centrally with the Secretary of the Commonwealth on August 19, 1955. In March, 1957 Fort Pitt assigned to Provident Trust, which was acting as an agent for another company, its accounts under a contract with the U.S. government. Fort Pitt was later placed in receivership. The receiver instituted this proceeding for an order declaring the assignment null and void because the financing statement did not specifically describe the U.S. government account. The lower court entered orders adverse to the receiver, who now appeals.

DECISION

Judgment for Provident. Under Section 9–110 of the UCC, "Any description is sufficient whether or not it is specific if it reasonably identifies the thing described." The UCC also allows the security agreement to cover after-acquired property.

Industrial Packaging Products Co. v. Fort Pitt Packaging Int'l Inc., 161 A.2d 19 (Pa. 1960).

Today, the fairly well accepted Uniform Commercial Code form of financing statement illustrated in Figure 50.1 is recognized nationwide, with the name of the particular state indicated at the top of the form.

Secured parties often, through ignorance of the law or laziness, attempt to use a security agreement as a financing statement or the financing statement as a security agreement. Two different documents should be used because the requirements differ. For instance, a security agreement cannot be used as a financing statement because the financing statement contains the additional requirement that the addresses of the parties be indicated. And the financing statement does not meet the requirements for a security agreement, as illustrated by the following case.

FACTS

On February 21, 1962 American Card Company executed a note for $12,373 payable to H.M.H. Company. American Card and H.M.H. both signed a financing statement which was properly filed. However, a written security agreement was never signed. Receivers for American Card contend that the claim of H.M.H. is not a valid security interest because the financing statement did not contain a grant of a security interest by American Card. H.M.H. claims that the financing statement may serve as the security agreement.

DECISION

Judgment for the receivers. While it is possible for one document to serve as both the financing statement and the security agreement, the separate requirements for each must be met by the document. The financing statement in question did not contain the required agreement by the debtor that H.M.H. be granted a security interest.

American Card Co. v. H.M.H. Co., 196 A.2d 150 (R.I. 1963).

Going back to our original example of Bill's sale of a refrigerator to Heidi, if Bill had filed a financing statement covering Heidi's refrigerator, Bill would be giving construc-

FIGURE 50.1 State of Colorado, Uniform Commercial Code, Financing Statement

STATE OF COLORADO
UNIFORM COMMERCIAL CODE — FINANCING STATEMENT - COLORADO U.C.C.-1 (Rev. 1-78)

INSTRUCTIONS

1. PLEASE TYPE this form. Do not write in Box 3.
2. If collateral is CROPS, state in Box 4, "The above described crops are growing or are to be grown on: (Describe Real Estate concerned)."
3. If collateral is or will become FIXTURES, or is TIMBER TO BE CUT, or is MINERALS OR OTHER SUBSTANCES OF VALUE WHICH MAY BE EXTRACTED FROM THE EARTH OR ACCOUNTS RESULTING FROM THE SALE THEREOF AT THE WELLHEAD OR MINEHEAD, CHECK ☒ "This Financing Statement is to be filed for record in the Real Estate records," in Box 4 and state if applicable. "The above goods are, or are to become, fixtures on (describe real estate)," or where appropriate, substitute either, "The above timber is standing on (describe real estate)," or, "The above minerals or other substances of value which may be extracted from the earth or accounts resulting from the sale thereof at the wellhead or minehead of the well or mine located on (describe real estate)." Describe real estate concerned sufficient as if it were contained in a mortgage of the real estate to give constructive notice of the mortgage under the law of this State. If the debtor does not have an interest of record in the realty, give the name of a record owner of the real estate concerned in Box 4.
4. If the space provided for any item on the form is inadequate, the item should be continued on additional sheets, that are 8½x11. Please do not staple or tape additional sheets directly on this form.
5. Remove Secured Party and Debtor copies, and send 3 copies with interleaved carbon paper still intact to the filing officer.
6. At the time of original filing, the filing officer will return third copy as an acknowledgment. If acknowledgment copy is to be returned to other than the Secured Party, please enclose a self-addressed envelope.

IMPORTANT— Read instructions before filling out form

This FINANCING STATEMENT is presented for filing pursuant to the Uniform Commercial Code.

3. For Filing Officer (Date, Time, Number and Filing Office)

1. Debtor(s) Name and Mailing Address:

2. Secured Party(ies) Name and Address:

4. This Financing Statement covers the following types (or items) of property:
(WARNING: If collateral is crops, fixtures, timber, or minerals or other substances to be extracted or accounts resulting from the sale thereof, read instructions above.)

5. Name and address of Assignee of Secured Party:

Check only if applicable
☐ This Statement is to be filed for record in the real estate records.
☐ Products of collateral are also covered.

6. This statement is signed by the Secured Party instead of the Debtor to perfect a security interest in collateral
(Please check appropriate box)
☐ already subject to a security interest in another jurisdiction when it was brought into this state, or when the debtor's location was changed to this state;
☐ which is proceeds of the original collateral described above in which a security interest was perfected;
☐ as to which the filing has lapsed; or
☐ acquired after a change of name, identity or corporate structure of the debtor.

7. Check only if applicable: ☐ The Debtor is a transmitting utility.

Use whichever signature line is applicable.

Signature(s) of Debtor(s) Signature(s) of Secured Party(ies)

tive notice to the world of his security interest in the refrigerator. It is important to note the practical implication of this rule: when you purchase property from someone outside the normal course of business, you should first check to determine whether the property is subject to a security interest. If there is a perfected security interest, the secured party of the seller may repossess the property from you, an innocent buyer. However, the secured party will be protected only when the financing statement is filed and indexed properly. In the following case the financing statement was filed under the wrong name.

FACTS

Kenston Corporation sold dry cleaning equipment under a conditional sales agreement to Matthew R. Leichter, who did business under the name Landman Dry Cleaners. Leichter signed a financing statement "Landman Dry Cleaners, By: Matthew R. Leichter." Kenston filed the financing statement under the name of Landman Dry Cleaners, not under Leichter's name. When Leichter went into bankruptcy, the trustee in bankruptcy claimed that the security interest was not properly perfected.

DECISION

Judgment for the trustee. Filing under a trade name alone is a major error. Later creditors looking under "Leichter" would not find the financing statement filed under "Landman."

In re Leichter, 471 F.2d 785 (1972).

► Pledge

A second method of perfection is the pledge, whereby the secured party takes possession of the goods. The **pledge** gives clear notice to the world of the security interest by virtue of the secured party's possession.

pledge
The possessory security interest in bailed goods acquired by the bailee when there is a bailment for the purpose of security

The pledge obviously cannot be used when one of the three types of collateral, namely intangibles, is used as security because by its very nature there is nothing to physically possess. On the other hand, the pledge in most cases must be used when the collateral is paper because of long-standing commercial practices. For instance, the UCC provides that, with few exceptions, a security interest in instruments can be perfected only by the secured party taking possession. A security interest in the other two types of paper—namely, chattel paper and negotiable documents—may be perfected by filing; but to be absolutely safe, the creditor should still take possession because certain purchasers are given priority over the secured party who has perfected by filing.

When it is difficult for the creditor to acquire a pledge by obtaining possession of the collateral by removing it from the debtor's possession (e.g., equipment or a large amount of the debtor's inventory in the debtor's place of business, or inventory stored in a warehouse), a pledge may be made by transferring to the creditor possession of the collateral in the place where it is located without actual removal of the collateral. This may be done by two devices: *field pledge* and *field warehousing.*

The "field" is the specific place where the particular collateral to be subjected to a security interest is located. With the *field pledge,* the creditor sends its agent to the debtor's business location where, with the debtor's approval, the agent takes control of the collateral, in place, without removal. With *field warehousing,* however, a special **warehouseman** or guard is hired by the creditor to take control of the collateral at the warehouse where the collateral is stored, usually by placing a fence around the specific area (the "field") where the collateral is stored and posting proper informative signs. The warehouseman guard then issues a warehouse receipt to the creditor, and the security interest is thereby perfected by the creditor having possession of the pledged warehouse receipt.

warehouseman
A person in the business of storing goods for a fee

Field warehousing is a popular and useful alternative to field pledge, and is obviously created for financing purposes. When the debtor wishes to obtain any of the pledged collateral so as to sell it and thereby use the proceeds to pay the creditor on the debt, the debtor will request the creditor to release the amount of the collateral needed, and the creditor will issue a written authorization to the guard/warehouseman to release possession of the collateral to the debtor. When release occurs, the collateral is no longer subject to the pledge because the creditor has voluntarily surrendered its possession, terminating the pledge.

► Automatic Perfection

In cases where a person purchases consumer goods and gives a creditor a purchase money security interest in those goods, the secured party's security interest will be perfected automatically. However, it is still a safe practice for the secured party to perfect the security interest by filing a financing statement because, if the statement is not filed, a buyer from the consumer takes the goods free of the security interest if: (1) the buyer buys without knowledge of the interest; (2) the buyer pays value; and (3) the buyer buys for his personal use. For example, in the situation where Bill sells the refrigerator to Heidi, Bill's security interest will be automatically perfected if, instead of equipment, the refrigerator were a consumer good bought for Heidi's personal use. Since there is perfection, Bill's security interest will prevail over other creditors and the trustee in bankruptcy. But if Heidi sells the refrigerator to a friend who has no notice of Bill's security interest and who buys for the buyer's own personal, family, or household purposes, the friend will take the refrigerator free and clear of the security interest.

The following case illustrates the general principle that a purchase money security interest in consumer goods is perfected automatically and prevails over a buyer who does not meet the three requirements discussed above.

FACTS

Rike-Kumber sold a diamond ring to Nicolosi on July 7, 1964. Nicolosi signed a purchase money security agreement, but a financing statement was not filed. Nicolosi gave the ring to his fiancee and later declared bankruptcy. Now Rike-Kumber claims the ring.

DECISION

Judgment for Rike-Kumber. Rike-Kumber has a purchase money security interest in consumer goods, which is perfected automatically. The fiancee did not take the ring free of the security interest because she did not give value for the ring and thus failed to meet the second of the three requirements.

In re Nicolosi, 4 U.C.C. Rep. Serv. (Callaghan) III (Ohio 1966).

► Certificate of Title Laws

In most states there are certificate of title laws that cover automobiles and may also cover other vehicles such as trailers, mobile homes, boats, and farm tractors. If goods are subject to such laws, filing a financing statement is not effective to perfect a security interest; instead, the security interest is perfected by notation on the certificate of title.

Multicounty and Multistate Transactions

In our mobile society it is common for debtors to move from one county to another or from one state to another, taking with them the property that is subject to a perfected security interest. When such a move takes place, does the security interest continue to be perfected? When the move is *from one county to another in the same state,* the states follow two different approaches. In some states if the financing statement was originally filed properly, it continues to be effective in the new county to which the debtor moves. In other states the secured party must file a copy of the financing statement within four months in the new county; otherwise the security interest becomes unperfected.

When the move is *from one state to another state,* there are two general UCC rules that apply, although these rules are subject to a number of exceptions. First, under Section 1–105, the parties may agree that the laws of a particular state or nation are to govern their rights and duties if the transaction bears a reasonable relation to such state or nation. Second, there is a provision governing perfection to the effect that perfection is governed by the law of the state where the collateral is located upon the occurrence of the *last* event that is necessary to perfect the interest. This event will usually be filing the financing statement. If the security interest in the collateral is perfected under the law of that state and then the collateral is moved to another state, it will remain perfected if, *within four months,* the secured party perfects the interest in the *new* state. The UCC also has detailed rules governing: accounts (e.g., accounts receivable); general intangibles (e.g., patents, copyrights); mobile goods of a type that are equipment, or inventory for lease by the debtor to others, that are normally used in more than one jurisdiction (e.g., trucks, rolling stock, airplanes, commercial harvesting machinery); goods covered by a certificate of title (e.g., automobiles); chattel paper; and minerals. With respect to accounts, general intangibles, and such mobile goods, the law applicable is the law of the state where the debtor is "located," which is the debtor's place of business if the debtor has one, or at the debtor's chief executive office if the debtor has more than one place of business, otherwise at the debtor's residence. Ascertaining the applicable law is important when you, as a secured creditor, must file a financing statement or when you must determine whether a previous secured creditor has filed one.

Summary Statement

1. A secured transaction is one in which a debtor gives to a creditor an interest in property owned by the debtor.
2. There are three major classifications of collateral: (a) tangible goods, (b) intangibles, and (c) paper.
3. The UCC specifically provides that the security agreement may cover after-acquired property and future advances. This allows a secured party to create a floating lien with one security agreement.
4. A security interest may be created by (a) security agreement or (b) pledge.
5. The most common methods used to perfect a security interest are the pledge and the filing of a financing statement.

In the following case the court discusses the general policy of the UCC regarding description of collateral in a security agreement.

In re AMEX-PROTEIN DEVELOPMENT CORPORATION
504 F.2d 1056 (9th Cir. 1974)

Plant Reclamation claimed a security interest in personal property held by Amex-Protein, which was in bankruptcy. Plant Reclamation claimed that the security interest was created by a promissory note which included the following language: "This note is secured by a Security Interest in subject personal property as per invoices." The invoices referred to in the note were submitted by Plant Reclamation when it sold equipment to Amex-Protein. Plant Reclamation also filed a financing statement listing the equipment.

I. Did the Promissory Note "Create or Provide for" a Security Interest?

No magic words or precise form are necessary to create or provide for a security interest so long as the minimum formal requirements of the Code are met.... This liberal approach is mandated by an expressed purpose of the secured transaction provisions of the Code:

"The aim of this Article is to provide a simple and unified structure within which the immense variety of present-day secured financing transactions can go forward with less cost and with greater certainty....

"The Article's flexibility and simplified formalities should make it possible for new forms of secured financing, as they develop, to fit comfortably under its provisions...." Comment to UCC and Cal. Com. C. section 9101.

Accordingly, the promissory note herein qualifies as a security agreement which by its terms "creates or provides for" a security interest.

II. Adequacy of Description of the Collateral

• • • • •

There is nothing in the Uniform Commercial Code to prevent reference in the security agreement to another writing for particular terms and conditions of the transaction. There is also nothing in the Uniform Commercial Code to prevent reference in the Security Agreement to another writing for a description of the collateral, so long as the reference in the security agreement is sufficient to identify reasonably what it described. In other words, it will at times be expedient to give a general description of the collateral in the security agreement and refer to a list or other writing for more exact description. In addition, the security agreement could itself consist of separate parts, one a general description of the obligation secured and the rights and duties of the parties, and the other a description of the collateral, both such writings being signed by the debtor and stated to comprise a single security agreement or referring to each other. [Footnotes omitted.] Id. section 109 at 387–388.... [The judgment is affirmed.]

Questions and Case Problems

1. The comptroller of Fibre Glass Boat Corp. sent the following letter to a creditor, Teleflex: "Pursuant to our telephone conversation, please find a duly executed copy of a financing statement received from your company, wherein the Fibre Glass Boat Corp. agrees to guarantee all inventory used in the production of boats, limited in the amount of fifteen thousand dollars, in order to cover all merchandise that may be purchased from your company." Teleflex later claimed that this letter created a security interest. Is Teleflex correct? [*In re Fibre Glass Boat Corp.,* 324 F.Supp. 1054 (S.D.Fla. 1971).]
2. Alpha purchased a pair of skis from her roommate Beta. Alpha agreed to make monthly payments on the skis over a period of six months and entered into an oral agreement with Beta that, in the event of a default on any payment, Beta could repossess the skis. Alpha later defaulted. May Beta legally repossess under their security agreement? Why?
3. Willard signed a security agreement giving Popular Finance Co. (PFC) a security interest in "1 2-pc. living room suite, wine; 1 5-pc. chrome dinette set, yellow; 1 3-pc. panel bedroom suite, lime oak, matt. & spgs." The agreement provided that this property was to be kept at Willard's residence and the address was stated in the agreement. When Willard later declared bankruptcy, it was claimed that the security interest was invalid because the description of the property was insufficient. Is the description sufficient? [*In re Drane,* 202 F.Supp. 221 (W.D.Ky. 1962).]

4. Elmer borrowed money from Friendly Finance (FF) and gave FF a security interest in all of his lawn equipment. FF filed a financing statement covering the equipment. Later Elmer sold his lawn mower to his next door neighbor, Rufus, who bought the mower in good faith, paid value, and was unaware of FF's security interest. If Elmer defaults in his loan payments, may FF repossess the mower from Rufus? Why?
5. Mitchell and Donelson were partners operating a clothing store under the name of Marby's Fashions. Marby's borrowed $25,000 from a bank and signed a security agreement covering the store's equipment. Marby's also signed a financing statement that covered equipment, inventory, and accounts receivable, and the bank filed the statement. Does the bank have a perfected security interest in Marby's equipment, inventory, and accounts receivable? [*Mitchell v. Shepherd Mall State Bank,* 458 F.2d 700 (10th Cir. 1972).]
6. A creditor took a security interest in the crops of a farmer. The security agreement included the kind of crops, the names of the farms where the crops were grown, and legal descriptions of the farms. A financing statement was filed that covered the farmer's crops "which are now growing or are hereafter planted, grown, and produced on land owned or leased by debtor in Cherokee County, Kansas." Later the farmer sold the crops to a third party, who claimed that the financing statement was insufficient to perfect a security interest in the crops and, therefore, the creditor had no lien on the crops. Is the third party correct? [*Chanute Production Credit Ass'n v. Wier Grain & Supply, Inc.,* 499 P.2d 517 (Kan. 1972).]
7. Excel Stores, Inc., a Connecticut corporation engaged in the business of selling toys and other merchandise, purchased six cash registers on credit from National Cash Register Company (NCR). NCR took a security interest in the cash registers. However, in signing the security agreement, the treasurer of Excel Stores inadvertently used the name "Excel Department Stores," and this name was also used on the financing statement. Does NCR have a perfected security interest? [*In re Excel Stores, Inc.,* 341 F.2d 961 (2d Cir. 1965).]
8. A bank agreed to lend money to a company, and the company signed a security agreement covering all existing and future accounts receivable. The bank filed a financing statement that described the collateral as "Accounts Receivable." The company later went into receivership, and the receiver claimed that the security interest was unperfected as to accounts receivable that arose after the date of the financing statement because the financing statement did not mention *future* accounts receivable. Is the receiver correct? [*South County Sand & Gravel Co. v. Bituminous Pavers Co.,* 256 A.2d 514 (R.I. 1969).]
9. The United Bank of Denver loaned $2,400,000 to Smith Enterprises and took a security interest in Smith's "inventory, accounts, contract rights, equipment and machinery." Later, when a bankruptcy petition was filed against Smith, the bank claimed that the security interest covered Smith's eggs and chickens. Is the bank correct? [*In re K. L. Smith Enterprises, Ltd., Debtor,*] 2 B.R. 280, 28 UCC Rptr. 534 (Colo. 1980).]
10. In the case of *In re Amex-Protein Development Corporation,* excerpted at the beginning of this section, the court concluded that a promissory note could be used to create a security interest. What Code policy is served by this liberal approach?

CHAPTER 51

ENFORCEMENT OF PERSONAL PROPERTY SECURITY INTERESTS; SURETYSHIP

After you have read this chapter, you should be able to:

1. Determine which of two secured parties has priority when both have perfected by filing a financing statement.
2. Discuss the rights of a secured party against a mortgagee who claims a fixture.
3. List the procedure that a secured party will follow after the debtor's default.
4. Define the three parties involved in a suretyship arrangement.
5. Explain the distinction between strict surety and guarantor, and the importance of this distinction under the statute of frauds.
6. Describe how the suretyship contract is created.
7. Explain the types of defense that are available to a surety.
8. Discuss the three options available to a surety after paying the creditor.

BUSINESS DECISIONS and the LAW

George owned a $1,000 stereo system. In need of cash, he borrowed $2,000 from Andy and gave Andy a security interest in the stereo. Later, having spent the $2,000, George borrowed another $2,000 from Kay and gave Kay a security interest in the same stereo. George then defaulted on both of his loan payments and the two creditors, Andy and Kay, each claim the stereo.

Introduction

We begin this chapter with a discussion of the rules that determine which creditor has priority upon a debtor's (George's) default. These rules are litigated frequently and are very important because a creditor can lose thousands of dollars in collateral if a court determines that the creditor does not have priority. Once a determination is made as to which creditor has priority, there is an additional question left to consider. What right does the creditor with priority have to repossess and to sell the collateral?

After concluding our examination of the law of secured transactions, we will look at another type of security arrangement, suretyship. This arrangement—under which the creditor obtains the promise of another person (a surety) to repay the obligor's debt (or to perform some other obligation of the obligor)—requires an understanding of the law of suretyship.

Priorities

As noted in Chapter 50, a secured party with a perfected security interest has priority over unperfected security interests. Thus, in the example involving creditors Kay and Andy, if Kay had perfected her security interest and Andy did not perfect, Kay would in most cases be entitled to the stereo. Many cases, however, cannot be resolved this easily, and the decision will depend on additional factors. Eight common fact situations that raise priority questions will be discussed below.

► Creditors Perfect by Filing

If both creditors have perfected their security interests by filing a financing statement, the first secured party to file has priority.[1] This rule illustrates the importance of filing the financing statement as soon as possible, even before the loan is made. For example, on June 1 Andy promised to lend George $2,000, took a security interest in the stereo, and filed a financing statement. On July 1 Kay loaned Andy $2,000, took a security interest in the stereo, and filed a financing statement. On August 1 Andy made his promised loan. Who has priority? The answer under the above rule is that Andy has priority because he filed his financing statement first, even though he did not lend the money until after Kay's loan. Before extending credit on July 1, Kay should have checked the public records and, if she had done so, would have discovered that the stereo was already subject to a security interest.

► Creditors Perfect by Using Different Methods

If each creditor uses a different method of perfection, the creditor who has either filed a financing statement or perfected first has priority.[2] Suppose that on June 1 Andy loaned $2,000 to George and took a security interest in George's stereo. On July 1 Kay loaned George $2,000, took a security interest in the stereo, and perfected by taking possession—that is, by pledge. On August 1 Andy filed a financing statement covering the stereo. Kay would have priority because her interest was *perfected* first, even though her

---

[1]UCC 9–312(5)(a).

[2]UCC 9–312(5)(a).

security interest was not the first to attach. Andy's security interest had *attached* on June 1, but his *perfection* did not occur until August 1.

► Neither Creditor Perfected

If neither Andy nor Kay perfect his or her security interest, the secured party who first created a security interest will prevail.[3] This rule will be rarely used because as soon as a secured party realizes that other security interests exist, he or she will immediately attempt to perfect his or her security interest, thus making the case subject to the above rules.

► Fixtures

A **fixture** is property that, although at one time personal property, has been attached to real estate in such a way that it is legally considered to be part of the real estate, although it still may be used as collateral in a secured transaction. Because it is legally part of the real estate, a new type of creditor now enters the picture: a creditor with a mortgage covering the real estate. To illustrate, we might assume that our debtor, George, lives in a house that he has mortgaged to First Bank. If he builds his stereo system into a wall in such a way that it is considered to be a fixture, the stereo, as part of the real estate, becomes subject to the mortgage of First Bank. If the mortgage is foreclosed, First Bank can claim not only the house and land but also the stereo.

fixture
A chattel that, under real estate law, has become permanently attached to realty and thus ceases to be a chattel and becomes part of the realty; it still can be used as collateral for a security interest

The situation becomes complicated when George gives a creditor, Second Bank, a security interest in the stereo to secure another loan. If George defaults on both loans, who has priority: the creditor with a mortgage or the secured party? Although the rules governing this situation are very complex and subject to exception, it may be generally stated that to gain priority over a creditor with a recorded mortgage, the secured party must have a purchase money security interest, and the security interest must be perfected by a fixture filing *before* the goods become fixtures or *within ten days after* they become fixtures. A **fixture filing** is a filing of the financing statement in the office where mortgages are recorded.[4]

fixture filing
Filing a financing statement in the office where mortgages are recorded

► Noninventory Financing

Noninventory financing is especially important to a person in business and to creditors who lend to businesses. To illustrate a typical situation, we might assume that George runs a business—a restaurant—and that he borrows $2,000 from First Bank, giving First Bank a perfected security interest in all of the *equipment* that he now owns or may acquire later. As discussed in Chapter 50, after-acquired property may be included in a security agreement. George then buys a stereo on credit from a local store, Loud Sounds, and gives Loud Sounds a security interest in the stereo. George uses the stereo to play music to customers. If George defaults on his payments to First Bank and to Loud Sounds, who has priority with regard to the stereo? In most cases, First Bank, with its prior, perfected security interest, prevails. However, there is a major exception that protects secured parties with a purchase money security interest such as that of Loud Sounds. If there is a purchase money security interest, the purchase money creditor has priority if

---

[3]UCC 9–312(5)(b).

[4]UCC 9–313.

it perfects within ten days after the debtor receives possession of the collateral.[5] In many cases an issue is raised concerning the meaning of possession, as is illustrated in the following case.

FACTS

National Acceptance Company loaned $692,000 to Ultra Precision Industries, Inc., and took a perfected security interest in Ultra's present and after-acquired equipment on March 7, 1967. In June, 1968 Ultra ordered a machine from Wolf, subject to the condition that Ultra obtain satisfactory financing and that Ultra have a reasonable time to test the machine. The machine was delivered to Ultra on August 7, 1968. Satisfactory financing was obtained, satisfactory testing was accomplished, and a security agreement was executed by Ultra and Wolf on October 23, 1968. The security interest was perfected on October 30, 1968. Wolf contends that: (1) Ultra became a debtor in "possession" of the collateral only when the contract terms had been met and a security agreement signed by Ultra and Wolf on October 23; and (2) perfection occurred on October 30, which is within the ten-day period required by the UCC. National contends "possession" occurred on August 7, and Wolf's filing of a financing statement on October 30 was untimely. Which secured party's interest has priority?

DECISION

Wolf's security interest has priority. Wolf's interest was perfected within ten days after Ultra received possession of the machine. Possession means more than physical delivery; in this case, possession occurred when Ultra became obligated to pay for the machine—that is, when the security agreement was signed after satisfactory financing was obtained and testing was completed.

In re Ultra Precision Indust., Inc., 503 F.2d 414 (9th Cir. 1974).

Inventory Financing

One might think initially that inventory financing should be treated in the same manner as equipment financing; that is, the secured party with an interest in after-acquired property should have priority over all other creditors except for the purchase money security interest. However, in practice, inventory financing differs from equipment financing in that inventory is bought and sold more frequently than equipment and, to finance the continuing purchase of new inventory, lenders often will automatically make periodic loans to a business. Loans made under this arrangement are secured by a security agreement covering both future advances and after-acquired inventory, as noted in our discussion of the floating lien in Chapter 50. A secured party with such a perfected security interest will have priority over later security interests in after-acquired inventory, except a subsequent secured party who (1) acquired a purchase money security interest in the same after-acquired inventory; (2) perfected the security interest before the debtor receives possession; and (3) gave written notice, within certain specified times, to the holder of the prior conflicting security interest if that holder had previously filed a financing statement, that he or she has, or expects to acquire, a purchase money security interest in the after-acquired inventory of the debtor.[6] Since the earlier secured party now has notice, the latter will not make the usual periodic advance, knowing that the loan is not required since the purchase has been financed under the purchase money arrangement.

[5] UCC 9–312(4).

[6] UCC 9–312(3).

To illustrate, George now operates a stereo store and has given First Bank a perfected security interest covering all present and future inventory. George later purchased a truckload of RCA stereos on credit, giving RCA a purchase money security interest in the stereos. In order to gain priority over the earlier perfected security interest of First Bank, RCA must do two things before delivering the stereos: (1) give notice to First Bank of its intention to acquire a security interest in the stereos, and (2) perfect its security interest in the stereos.

▶ Buyers in the Ordinary Course of Business

If a customer, Mary, visits George's stereo store, she might be unaware that the RCA stereos in the store are subject to the security interests of both First Bank and RCA. Does this mean that, if Mary buys a stereo, it might be repossessed by one of the creditors if George defaults on his payments? Such a result would have a detrimental effect on commerce, so the UCC specifically provides that a **buyer in the ordinary course of business,** such as Mary, buys free and clear of security interests created by the seller. This protection extends even to a case where the security interest is perfected or the buyer knows of the security interest.[7] The buyer prevailed in the following case.

buyer in ordinary course of business
"A person who, in good faith, . . . buys in ordinary course from a person in the business of selling goods of that kind. . . ." UCC 1–201(9)

FACTS

Newell was in the retail chemical business. First Bank had a perfected security interest in Newell's inventory. Newell sold chemicals to Herman, who paid for them although the chemicals were not to be delivered until a later date. Before delivery, Newell defaulted on its loan payments to the bank. Who is entitled to the chemicals sold to Herman—the bank or Herman?

DECISION

Judgment for Herman. Herman is a buyer in the ordinary course of business and therefore bought the fertilizer free and clear of the security interest. The fact that the chemicals had not yet been delivered does not affect Herman's status as a buyer in the ordinary course of business.

Herman v. First Farmers State Bank of Minier, 392 N.E.2d 344 (Ill. 1979).

▶ Bailee's Liens

In many cases the interest of a secured party will conflict with that of a **bailee** who has repaired or improved the collateral and who claims a **bailee's lien** in order to secure payment for services rendered and for materials supplied to the collateral. In such cases, a bailee *in possession* of the collateral and with a valid bailee's lien under the relevant state law, takes priority over a previously perfected security interest,[8] as is illustrated in the following case.

bailment
A delivery of goods by a bailor to a bailee, which are to be returned to the bailor or as the bailor directs, in accordance with the bailment agreement

bailee
The person to whom goods are bailed

bailee's lien
The bailee's legal right to retain possession of the bailed goods as security for the obligation owing to the bailee, usually payment for the bailee's services and for materials supplied to the bailed goods

[7]UCC 9–307(1).

[8]UCC 9–310.

FACTS

Nelms borrowed money from the Gulf Coast State Bank in order to purchase a car, and the bank took a perfected security interest in the car. Later the car was damaged in an automobile accident and taken to an auto repair shop. After the car was repaired, Nelms did not pay the repair bill, and the repair shop claimed a bailee's lien on the car. Since Nelms' car payments were in arrears, the bank claimed possession of the car from the repair shop, which refused, asserting that it had priority over the bank's perfected security interest under the UCC. The bank claimed that its perfected security interest had priority.

DECISION

Judgment for the repair shop. A bailee with a lien upon goods in its possession has priority unless the state lien law expressly provides otherwise. The Texas lien law did not change the UCC rule.

Gulf Coast State Bank v. Nelms, 525 S.W.2d 866 (Tex. 1975).

The Rights of Secured Party on Default

When a debtor defaults in making payments, the secured party with priority will normally take two courses of action: (1) repossess the collateral and (2) either retain or sell the collateral.

► Repossession

Dolly obtained financing from First Bank to purchase a new car and gave the bank a security interest in the car. Dolly parked the car every night in her driveway, which was her private property. One morning she discovered that the car was gone and, after calling the police, learned that the bank had repossessed the car during the night because she had missed two payments. Are such repossessions legal?

The answer is to be found in UCC 9–503, which provides: "Unless otherwise agreed a secured party has on default the right to take possession of the collateral . . . without judicial process if this can be done without breach of the peace." As interpreted by the courts, this allows a secured party to trespass secretly onto the debtor's property in the middle of the night in order to remove the collateral so long as there is no breach of the peace.

A **breach of the peace,** as defined by most courts, results from an act of violence or an act likely to produce violence. Using this definition, secured parties have been allowed to remove a car from a private driveway and an airplane from an open hangar. No breach of the peace occurred in the following case.

breach of the peace
A disturbance of public order by an act of violence, or by an act likely to produce violence, or which, by causing consternation and alarm, disturbs the peace and quiet of the community

FACTS

The Bank of Babylon entered into a security agreement covering property owned by Elwood Auto Parts, the debtor. The agreement gave the bank the right, on the debtor's default, to enter the debtor's premises and take away the property with or without legal process. After Elwood's default, the bank entered the premises, using a key obtained from a locksmith, and removed the property. Cherno, representing creditors of the debtor, sued the bank contending that the bank committed a breach of the peace when it removed the property.

DECISION

This was not a breach of the peace. Even though the bank might have committed a "breaking" into the premises, the bank did not commit an act of violence and did nothing to disturb the peace and quiet of the community. Also, in this situation the use of the key was not likely to result in violence.

Cherno v. Bank of Babylon, 282 N.Y.S.2d 114 (1967).

In addition to self-help repossession, a secured party might also commence an action to obtain a court order that the debtor turn over collateral. Because court proceedings involve state action, the due process clause of the federal Constitution requires that the debtor be given notice of the court hearing and an opportunity to present a defense before the property is seized. In a few states, courts have decided that even self-help repossession involves state action, and these courts require a court hearing before the collateral is seized.

After Repossession

A secured party who has possession of the collateral through self-help or a court order has two options. First, the secured party may sell the collateral at a public or private sale. The sale must be commercially reasonable with regard to the method, manner, terms, place, and time of sale. Furthermore, although subject to specific exceptions, such as a sale of perishable goods, the secured party must give reasonable notification of the sale to the debtor and to other secured parties who have sent written notice (to the repossessing secured party) claiming an interest in the collateral. If the sale of the collateral results in a surplus after secured parties have been paid, the debtor is entitled to the surplus. But if the proceeds are not sufficient to cover the secured debt, the debtor is liable for any deficiency.

The other option is for the secured party to keep the collateral in full satisfaction of the debt. This option will be used most frequently by a secured party when the collateral is worth more than the unpaid debt. In order to protect the debtor and prevent unfair enrichment of the secured party, the UCC provides that in most cases the secured party must send written notice to the debtor, and to other secured parties claiming an interest in the collateral, proposing to keep the collateral in satisfaction of the debt. If the debtor or another secured party objects within twenty-one days after the notice was sent, the repossessing secured party must sell the collateral. If no objection is raised, the secured party may keep the collateral in satisfaction of the debt.

The UCC provides special protection for the debtor where the collateral is *consumer goods* and the debtor has paid 60 percent of the loan or of the price. In such cases, the creditor must obtain from the debtor a written, signed statement under which the debtor allows the creditor to retain the collateral. A creditor without this statement must sell or dispose of the collateral within ninety days after taking possession.

Introduction to Suretyship

On the day when Junior reached the age of eighteen and legally became an adult, he decided to purchase a used car from Dealer. Junior selected a car and signed a conditional sales contract whereby he was to make monthly payments to Dealer for two years. But Dealer decided that he wanted more than Junior's promise to repay the debt; he wanted some type of security to protect him in the event of Junior's default.

There are two common types of security arrangements used in business. One type is the secured transaction discussed above where the debtor gives the creditor a security interest in certain collateral. The other security arrangement, which may be used separately or in conjunction with the secured transaction, is **suretyship.** Under this arrangement another person—for example, Junior's father—would also sign Junior's note and promise to pay the debt.

suretyship
A legal relationship in which one person (surety) and another person (principal, the debtor) are obligated to perform the same obligation to a third person (creditor) who is entitled to only one performance, and as between the surety and the principal the latter is to perform the obligation and is ultimately liable therefor

Definitions

principal
In suretyship, the debtor in a suretyship arrangement

surety
A person who promises the creditor to pay the principal's debt or to perform his or her obligation on the principal's nonperformance

surety bond
A promise by a professional surety to pay if the principal defaults or commits a wrongful act

guarantor
A type of surety

guaranty
A type of suretyship

In security arrangements using a surety, there are typically three parties. The **principal** or *principal debtor* is the debtor, in our case Junior. The principal is indebted to the *creditor* (Dealer). The **surety** (Junior's father in our example) is a third party who agrees to become liable on the debt of the principal (Junior).

A very common business arrangement is the **surety bond** under which a professional surety promises to make payment if a principal defaults or commits a wrongful act. In many cases surety bonds are required by contract. For example, a person building a new office building might require the contractor to furnish a construction bond to cover a possible failure of the contractor to complete the contract or to pay the subcontractors. Other bonds are required by statute. These include bonds required of public officials, bonds required of fiduciaries such as the executor of an estate, and bail bonds.

In some states a distinction is made between two categories of surety: one is the *strict surety* and the other is the **guarantor.** The strict surety is a *co-debtor* with the principal. For example, a son wants to buy an automobile on credit, but the seller will not sell to the son without the father as surety. Accordingly, the father and son sign the contract and promissory note for their purchase, on credit, of an automobile for the son, with the agreement between them that the son is to pay for the automobile. As to the creditor seller, the father and son are the co-debtor purchasers; as between the father and son, the son is the principal and the father is the strict surety. However, if the automobile had been sold to the son as the purchaser and the father agreed with the seller to be responsible for the son's payment and liable on his default, the father would be a guarantor, liable only on the son's default.

A guarantor is liable only in accordance with the terms of the suretyship contract. There are various types of **guaranty,** differing only in their contract terms, two of which will be considered here.

The *absolute guaranty* is a contract that the guarantor will perform only on the principal's default. A common example is the "guaranty of payment," such as Betty's written statement to Linda: "Extend credit to Al, and if Al does not pay, I will." At the maturity date, if Al does not pay, Linda can recover from Betty.

The *conditional guaranty* states a condition that must occur before the surety is liable to the creditor. A commonly used example is the "guaranty of collection," when the guarantor must pay only if the debt is *uncollectible*—that is, the creditor cannot collect it from the principal. It is uncollectible when the creditor has sued the principal, the resulting judgment cannot be paid, and the surety is notified of this within a reasonable time.

The Statute of Frauds

The distinction between a strict surety and a guarantor is important under the statute of frauds. The contract of a strict surety is not within that portion of the statute of frauds providing that a promise to answer for the duty (debt, default, or miscarriage—e. g., an employee's embezzlement of a firm's cash) of another is unenforceable without a proper writing. Since the strict surety is a co-debtor with the principal, as to the creditor they are both co-debtors and co-principals. The co-debtor strict surety does not condition its liability on the default by the other co-debtor principal. They are both liable to the creditor as co-debtor principals.

In contrast, the guarantor promises to pay or perform the principal's obligation *only on the principal's nonperformance* and, therefore, a contract of guaranty is within the statute and unenforceable without a proper writing. (Sara requests Cal to extend credit to Dan, stating that if Dan doesn't pay Cal then Sara will pay Cal. Cal then extends credit to Dan, who later defaults. Sara's contract with Cal is within the statute of frauds and is unenforceable unless there is a proper writing.[9]) The writing may be the signed contract itself, or a note or memorandum of an oral contract signed by the party to be charged with performance (the guarantor) or by that party's lawfully authorized agent.

The Suretyship Contract

A suretyship contract is created in the same manner as other contracts and must in addition to the statute of frauds, meet basic contractual requirements such as offer and acceptance, consideration, and legality. For example, we have learned under the law of contracts that, when an offer is made for a unilateral contract, unless otherwise agreed, the offeree's performance is the acceptance and a contract is *then* formed; the offeree has *no* duty to notify the offeror of the offeree's performance. However, *if* the offeree reasonably can believe that the offeror will not learn of the offeree's performance in the ordinary course of affairs and within a reasonable time, the law requires the offeree to notify the offeror of the performance. The offeree's failure to do so discharges the offeror. This is also the law of suretyship.[10] However, a number of courts have taken the view that there is no contract until notice of performance (acceptance) is given to the guarantor (offeror), unless circumstances excuse it. The following case illustrates this view.

FACTS

On July 30, 1960, Milo Black sent the following letter to the Electric Storage Battery Company: "In regard to credit rating for Gerald Black, I will guarantee payment of material purchased." Gerald is the defendant's son engaged in the rebuilt battery business. Gerald made purchases from August 29, 1960 to December 29, 1961. Electric Storage did not acknowledge Milo's letter but finally, in 1962, wrote him demanding payment because of Gerald's failure to pay for the purchases. Milo refused to pay, contending that there was no contract of guaranty. Electric Storage sued Milo.

DECISION

Judgment for Milo. There was no contract because Electric Storage never notified Milo that it had accepted his offer.

Electric Storage Battery Co., v. Black, 134 N.W.2d 481 (Wis. 1965).

Because of these conflicting views, the creditor (offeree), in order to be safe, should notify the guarantor (offeror) *promptly* of the creditor's performance by its extension of credit.

The Surety's Defenses

▶ Complete Defenses

Both the principal and the surety may have defenses against the creditor when the creditor seeks to enforce their contracts with him or her. There are the usual contract

---

[9]For the requirements of a proper writing, see Chapter 12.

[10]See Restatement of Security sec.86 (1941).

defenses (discussed in Part 2, Contracts) such as fraud, duress, coercion, and undue influence, which the principal and surety may assert against the creditor in their respective contracts. If Junior's father is a *strict surety* with the principal Junior on a note signed by them for the purchase of a car from Dealer but Dealer never delivers the car, neither will be liable on the note because of failure of consideration—Dealer's failure to render the agreed consideration, namely, delivery of the car. If the father is a *guarantor*, he can also assert Junior principal's defenses in a suit against him by Dealer.

It must be emphasized that all of the principal's defenses that are not personal to the principal are also available to the surety (guarantor). For example, assume that Dealer fraudulently induces Junior to buy the car. On Junior's default by his nonpayment, the father surety (guarantor) can assert the fraud if he is sued by Dealer.

There are a few contract defenses, however, that are personal to the principal and cannot be raised by the surety. These include the principal's discharge in bankruptcy, the principal's power of avoidance resulting from the principal's infancy or insanity, and the running of the statute of limitations on the principal's obligation. The last is illustrated in the following case.

FACTS

Yockey purchased oil well supplies on credit from Bomud Company under an oral agreement. The agreement was guaranteed in writing by Osborn. Yockey later defaulted, but was not liable because the statute of limitations is very short for oral agreements. Bomud then sued Osborn, the statute of limitations not having run on Osborn's written agreement. Osborn claims that, since the principal is not liable, he should not be liable either. Bomud appealed.

DECISION

Reversed, for Bomud Company. Osborn, as a guarantor, made a separate written agreement to perform Yockey's contract. The fact that Bomud cannot collect from Yockey is of no consequence with regard to this separate agreement.

Bomud Co. v. Yockey Oil Co. and Osborn, 299 P.2d 72 (Kan. 1956).

There are special defenses unique to the suretyship arrangements. When the creditor and the principal agree to a modification of their contract without the consent of the surety, if the modification agreement is binding on them (e. g., there is consideration), *and* it would increase the possibility of the surety's risk, the surety is discharged from the suretyship obligation.

The surety will also be discharged in cases where the creditor does not perform the suretyship contract—for example, by failing to mail copies of the principal's bills to the surety. Furthermore, the surety will be discharged when the principal's debt is paid or when a proper tender of payment is rejected by the creditor.

► Partial Defenses

We have considered the surety's defenses that *completely discharge* the surety. However, there are some defenses that only partially discharge the surety. A few are considered here.

Surrender or Impairment of Property Security When the creditor has property as security as well as a surety and the creditor surrenders the property to the principal or wrongfully impairs its value, the surety is discharged to the extent of the value of the surrendered property or of its impairment. The following case illustrates this rule.

FACTS

L.R.Z.H. Corporation borrowed $57,500 from Langeveld and gave him a real estate mortgage as security for the loan. Jones agreed to guarantee the loan. Langeveld failed to record the mortgage and, as a result, several other creditors had first claim to the real estate. When the corporation defaulted on the loan, Langeveld sued Jones. Is Jones liable?

DECISION

Jones is not liable for the entire debt. By failing to record the mortgage, Langeveld impaired the value of the security. Thus Jones should be discharged from the debt to the extent of the value of the mortgage.

Langeveld v. L.R.Z.H. Corp., 376 A.2d 931 (N.J. 1977).

Release of a Co-Surety There may be more than one surety on the same obligation of the principal. They are called *co-sureties.* When the creditor releases one of various co-sureties without the consent of the others, thereby causing them to lose their contributive shares from the released co-surety in the event the principal defaults, the other co-sureties are discharged to the extent of the loss of such contributive shares. For example, Paul owes Clara $900 and Karen, Tim, and Kevin are equal co-sureties as guarantors on the debt. Clara releases Kevin without the consent of Karen and Tim, and without reserving Clara's rights against Kevin.[11] Paul defaults and has no assets, and Karen, Tim, and Kevin individually are solvent with sufficient assets to pay the debt. Clara can collect only $600 from Karen and Tim because, by Clara's release of Kevin, Clara prevented Karen and Tim from recovering Kevin's contributive share on the $900 debt.

Guaranty of Collection When there is a guaranty of collection, if the creditor delays in collecting from the principal or delays in giving notice of uncollectibility to the surety so as to cause loss to the surety in the surety's effort to be reimbursed by the principal, the surety is discharged to the extent of such loss.

The Surety's Rights

In cases where the surety has no defense or only a partial defense and must pay the creditor on the principal's default, there are four options available to the surety. First, the surety has the right of **exoneration.** The debtor may induce a person to become a surety for him or her by express or implied promise to the surety that the debtor will perform his or her obligation to the creditor and, if the debtor should fail to do so, the debtor will make the surety whole for the surety's performance of his or her suretyship obligation. Should the debtor so promise and, on the debtor's nonperformance, the creditor legally seek to enforce the surety's obligation to him or her, the surety can obtain a court order compelling the debtor to perform his or her promise to the surety to the extent of the debtor's available assets. The surety is still liable to the creditor on his or her suretyship contract but, to the extent of the debtor's available assets, the surety can be exonerated, that is spared loss and inconvenience in the performance of his or her suretyship obligation. For example, John requests Frank to be surety on the purchase that John is to make from Henry, Frank becomes a surety, and then John defaults on his debt. When Henry sues Frank as a surety, Frank can obtain a court order making John's assets available to pay his debt to Henry.

exoneration
In suretyship, the surety's right to have a court compel the debtor to perform his or her promise to the surety to perform the debtor's obligation to his or her creditor to the extent of the debtor's available assets.

[11]If Clara had reserved Clara's rights against Kevin, the courts would construe Clara's reservation of those rights against Kevin as meaning that Clara is promising not to sue Kevin rather than discharging Kevin from Kevin's obligation to Clara.

reimbursement
In suretyship, the surety's right to recover from the principal

Second, the surety is entitled to **reimbursement** from the principal for expenditures made by the surety in performance of the debtor's obligation. For instance, if Junior's father as surety paid Dealer on Junior's failure to pay Dealer, Junior would be liable to his father for those payments.

subrogation
In suretyship, the surety succeeds to the creditor's rights against the principal

Third, the surety is entitled to be subrogated to the rights of the creditor. With a **subrogation,** the surety steps into the shoes of the creditor and takes over all the creditor's rights to collect the debt. We might assume, for example, that Junior had given Dealer a security interest in his car. If Junior defaulted and his father paid off Dealer, his father would succeed to Dealer's rights, in this case the right to collect the debt and to repossess the collateral.

contribution
In suretyship, the right of sureties who have paid the creditor to collect part of the payment from other sureties

Finally, in cases where there are several sureties (co-sureties) for the same debt, the liability of the co-sureties is joint and several; that is, a creditor may collect from all co-sureties jointly, or may decide to sue and collect from only one of the co-sureties. If the creditor collects from less than all of the co-sureties, those who pay are entitled to **contribution** from the other co-sureties. If the co-sureties have contracted together to be co-sureties, their contract will provide how their respective contributive shares will be determined. If they have not contracted together, the contributive share of each co-surety is determined by the maximum liability of each co-surety. In the latter event, if each of the co-sureties is liable for the same maximum amount, then their contributive shares are equal. If each of the co-sureties is not liable for the same maximum amount, then the contributive share of each co-surety is determined by the proportion which that co-surety's maximum liability bears to the total maximum liability of *all* the co-sureties. (Andy is a co-surety with a maximum liability of $5,000, Brad for $10,000, Cindy for $15,000. On the principal's default of her $10,000 debt, Brad paid the creditor $10,000. Andy's share of the liability is 5,000/30,000, Brad's is 10,000/30,000, and Cindy's is 15,000/30,000 of the $10,000 paid by Brad. Thus, Andy's contributive share is 1/6 of $10,000, Brad's is 1/3 of $10,000, and Cindy's is 1/2 of $10,000.)

Summary Statement

► Enforcement of Personal Property Security Interests

1. When two or more creditors claim an interest in the same collateral and all creditors have perfected by filing a financing statement, the first creditor to file has priority.
2. A secured party will prevail over a mortgagee who claims a fixture if the secured party has a purchase money security interest and has perfected by a fixture filing either before the goods become fixtures or within ten days after the goods become fixtures.
3. A perfected security interest in *equipment* is subject to the priority of a purchase money security interest that has been perfected within ten days after the debtor receives the collateral.
4. A perfected security interest in *after-acquired inventory* has priority over later security interests, except as against a secured party with a purchase money security interest in the same after-acquired inventory, who has perfected the security interest before the debtor obtains possession, and who has given proper notice to the holder of the conflicting security interest.
5. Buyers in the ordinary course of business take property free from a previously perfected security interest in the property created by the seller.

6. Generally a bailee's lien has priority over a previously perfected security interest in the bailed goods.
7. After a debtor defaults, a secured party will (a) repossess the collateral through self-help or court order and (b) sell the collateral or, subject to certain limitations, keep the collateral in full payment of the debt.

Suretyship

8. Three parties are involved in a suretyship relationship: (a) a principal, who is the debtor; (b) a creditor; and (c) a surety who promises the creditor to pay the debt either as a co-debtor with the principal or as a guarantor on the principal's default.
9. A strict surety is a co-debtor with the principal on their contract with the creditor and the surety's contract is not within the statute of frauds. A guarantor's contract is within the statute.
10. A guaranty of collection is enforceable only when the debt is uncollectible.
11. All of the principal's defenses that are not personal to the principal may be asserted by the surety against the creditor on the principal's default.
12. Defenses personal to the principal are (a) the principal's discharge in bankruptcy; (b) the principal's power of avoidance resulting from the principal's infancy or insanity; and (c) the running of the statute of limitations on the principal's obligation.
13. Binding modification of the principal's contract by the principal and the creditor without the surety's consent, which increases the possibility of the surety's risk, discharges the surety.
14. The surety has partial defenses and is partially discharged by the creditor's (a) surrendering or impairing property security held by the creditor; (b) releasing a solvent and available co-surety without a reservation of rights; and (c) delaying either collection or in giving notice of uncollectibility to the surety on a guaranty of collection causing loss to the surety.
15. A surety who has paid the creditor is entitled to (a) reimbursement from the principal; (b) subrogation to the creditor's rights; and (c) contribution from other co-sureties.

In the following case the court considers the constitutionality of self-help repossession under the Uniform Commercial Code.

FROST v. MOHAWK NATIONAL BANK
74 Misc.2d 912 (N.Y. 1973)

Frost purchased a Fiat automobile. The purchase was financed by Mohawk National Bank. When Frost missed two monthly payments, the bank repossessed the car by removing it from where it was parked on a street. Frost brought suit to recover the car.

Conway, J. . . .There is no longer any question but that where repossession is obtained through judicial process under the replevin [an action to regain possession of personal property] statutes, a person must be afforded notice and an opportunity to be heard prior to any taking, except in extraordinary circumstances. . . .

In the opinion of this Court, the rationale of the Sniadach and Fuentes cases is that in the exercise of "due process" by the state, notice and an opportunity to be heard must be given where the object of the action is the taking of property in which the possessor has a significant property interest, except in extraordinary circumstances.

The Court has examined the retail installment contract in the instant case and finds that there is a clause which allows the seller, in the event of a default, the right without notice or demand, to enter upon any premises where the vehicle may be found and take possession of and remove the vehicle without process of law.

Section 9–503 of the Uniform Commercial Code provides in part:

> Unless otherwise agreed a secured party has on default the right to take possession of the collateral. In taking possession a secured party may proceed without judicial process if this can be done without breach of the peace or may proceed by action. . . .

Many text writers on the Uniform Commercial Code have expressed opinions that "self-help" under Section 9–503 of the Code may very well be struck down under the rationale of *Sniadach v. Family Finance Corp.*, . . . and *Fuentes v. Shevin*. . . . However, they all make a distinction between "self-help" and replevin prior to a hearing even though both involve a "taking" of the debtor's property before any judicial determination of the validity of the taking. Most of them make a distinction when self-help repossession is authorized by a private contract and the consumer has contracted for the security interest.

It is the opinion of this Court that an agreement entered into in compliance with Section 9–503 of the Uniform Commercial Code must be held to be legal, especially where the debtor has expressly authorized the "self-help" provisions of the contract. Such an agreement cannot be held to be unconscionable when such terms are expressly authorized by statute. To stretch the rationale of the Sniadach case and later cases following it to include a prohibition of "self-help" under a security agreement would require this Court to go beyond the point permitted by good reason under the circumstances of this case.

[Frost's motion for an order directing the bank to return the car is denied.]

Questions and Case Problems

► Enforcement of Personal Property Security Interests

1. Burrows purchased livestock from Bailey on an installment sale arrangement. Burrows later borrowed $80,000 from Walker Bank, which took a perfected security interest in the livestock Burrows was purchasing. Bailey then filed a financing statement covering the livestock being sold to Burrows. Does the bank have a security interest that is prior to Bailey's interest? [*Walker Bank and Trust Co. v. Burrows,* 507 P.2d 384 (Utah 1973).]
2. Central Bank had a perfected security interest in "equipment now owned or hereafter acquired" by Galleon. Lewyn sold a machine to Galleon on credit, keeping title to the machine until Galleon made payment. The machine was delivered to Galleon, and Lewyn did not file a financing statement. Who has priority to the machine—Lewyn or Central Bank? Why? [*Galleon Industries, Inc. v. Lewyn Machinery Co., Inc.,* 279 So.2d 137 (Ala. 1973).]
3. Carol works for First Bank as a lending officer. Carol is considering making a loan to Disco Duds Clothing Store (DD) to enable the store to purchase a new stock of inventory, in which First Bank will take a security interest. However, Carol learns that Second Bank already has a perfected security interest in Disco's present and future inventory. Can First Bank gain priority over Second Bank's interest? If so, how?
4. National Shawmut Bank had a perfected security interest in a car owned by Wever. Wever sold the car to Hanson-Rock, an automobile dealer, who resold the car to

Jones. Now National Shawmut wants to repossess Jones' car. May it do so? [*National Shawmut Bank of Boston v. Jones,* 236 A.2d 484 (N.H. 1967).]

5. Corbin Deposit Bank had a perfected security interest in Foreman's car. Foreman took his car to King, who was in the business of repairing cars, for repair work. Foreman did not pay King for the repair work, and King claimed a lien on the car, which was still in his possession. Foreman also failed to pay his debt to the bank. The car was sold. Who is entitled to the proceeds? [*Corbin Deposit Bank v. King,* 384 S.W.2d 302 (Ky. 1964).]
6. Walter signed two combination notes and security agreements giving Citizens State Bank a security interest in his automobile and boat. After Walter defaulted on his payments on both notes, the bank repossessed the collateral and sent Walter a notice that the automobile would be sold. The bank then sold the automobile and boat, and sued Walter for a deficiency judgment. Is the bank entitled to the deficiency? [*Citizens State Bank v. Hewitt,* 279 S.E.2d 531 (Ga. 1981).]
7. Moody gave Sherman County Bank a perfected security interest in property used in his farming operation, including after-acquired property. Moody later bought equipment from an implement company on an installment basis. The company took a security interest in the equipment and later filed financing statements. When Moody defaulted on his payments, the bank claimed that it was entitled to the equipment Moody purchased from the implement company because, in fact, the implement company did not file the financing statements within 10 days after the installment contract was signed. Is the bank correct? [*Sherman County Bank v. Kallhoff,* 288 N.W.2d 24 (Neb. 1980).]

► Suretyship

8. Kennedy agreed with Exxon to guarantee the account of Plastifax, Inc. When Plastifax filed for bankruptcy, Exxon sued Kennedy on the guaranty. Does the Plastifax bankruptcy discharge the guarantor Kennedy? [*Exxon Chemical Americas v. Kennedy,* 295 S.E.2d 770 (N.C. 1982).]
9. Cardwell guaranteed purchases by McPeters from Failing. The guaranty provided that Failing would promptly mail copies of all invoices to Cardwell. Failing waited seven months after one purchase before mailing the invoice. If McPeters fails to pay the invoice, is Cardwell liable? [*George E. Failing Co. v. Cardwell Investment Co.,* 376 P.2d 892 (Kan. 1962).]
10. In 1933, Keyes signed a note promising to pay a debt to Laney. Dyer was a surety on the note. When Keyes failed to pay the note, Dyer paid Laney in 1946 and sued Keyes for reimbursement in 1948. Keyes defended by claiming that Dyer could not bring suit on the 1933 note in 1948 because the statute of limitations requires lawsuits to be brought within three years after the cause of action arises. Is Keyes correct? [*Keyes v. Dyer,* 243 P. 2d 710 (Okla. 1952).]

C H A P T E R

52

BANKRUPTCY UNDER THE BANKRUPTCY REFORM ACT OF 1978

After you have read this chapter, you should be able to:

1. Discuss the source of bankruptcy law.
2. Describe the bankruptcy administrative framework.
3. Distinguish between voluntary and involuntary bankruptcy.
4. Describe the property in the debtor's estate.
5. Discuss the distribution of the estate after liquidation.
6. Suggest two alternatives to bankruptcy.

BUSINESS DECISIONS and the LAW

John has extensive debts, including unpaid federal taxes and alimony payments owed to his ex-wife. He has few assets: a guitar, a car, his clothing, and some personal mementos that have no market value. Unable to pay his debts, John is considering bankruptcy but has many questions about how the process works. He wonders, for example, whether he must file for bankruptcy or whether his creditors will begin the process. He is unsure whether bankruptcy is a federal matter or can be handled by state courts. He does not know whether he will be entitled to keep his personal belongings once the process is complete and is also unclear about whether bankruptcy eliminates all of his debt obligations. He also wants to develop a plan to repay his creditors, if this is possible.

Introduction

John's questions are becoming increasingly common. In recent years the use of credit to finance the purchase of property and services has become extremely popular with both consumers and businesses. The popularity of credit purchases, however, has resulted in an unfortunate and unexpected consequence for many borrowers—a trip to bankruptcy court. In a typical year, hundreds of thousands of Americans file for bankruptcy. Bankruptcy is not a crime; it is a legal remedy affecting debtors who are experiencing financial difficulty.

In this chapter we will examine what happens when an individual files for "liquidation" bankruptcy and the effect of the bankruptcy on the debtor and the creditors. We will also examine two alternative courses of action available under the bankruptcy law: wage earner plans for individuals with regular income and reorganization plans for businesses.

The Source of Bankruptcy Law

The U.S. Constitution, Article I, Section 8, provides that "the Congress shall have power ... to establish ... uniform laws on the subject of Bankruptcies throughout the United States." This means that bankruptcy is a *federal* matter and that the states do not have the power to enact bankruptcy laws.

bankruptcy
A federal procedure whereby a debtor's nonexempt assets are gathered together and used to discharge the debtor from most of his or her debts

Congress has used its power to enact **bankruptcy** acts five times—in 1800, 1841, 1867, 1898, and 1978. The current Act, the Bankruptcy Reform Act of 1978 (effective on October 1, 1979) repealed the 1898 Act and made a number of changes in bankruptcy law. These reforms include: (1) a change in the list of property that is exempt from liquidation; (2) a clarification of the law governing the debtor's reaffirmation of discharged debts; (3) simplification of the method for commencing a bankruptcy case; (4) changes in the law allowing trustees to avoid certain property transfers made by the debtor; and (5) a consolidation of the chapters in the prior law covering business reorganization. The Bankruptcy Reform Act of 1978, as amended in 1984 and 1986, will be the primary source for the following discussion of bankruptcy law. Many attorneys refer to the Act as the "Bankruptcy Code" in order to distinguish it from the old 1898 Act.

The Administrative Framework

Under the 1978 Act, a new bankruptcy system was created. Bankruptcy courts were established as adjuncts for each federal district court. As originally enacted, the law provided that bankruptcy judges were to be appointed by the president for fourteen-year terms. Bankruptcy courts were given exclusive jurisdiction over the debtor's property, could handle all proceedings relating to bankruptcy cases, and had most powers of any court of law or equity.

In *Northern Pipeline Construction Company v. Marathon Pipe Line Company,* 102 S.Ct. 2858 (1982), however, the Supreme Court decided that this part of the law violated Article III of the U.S. Constitution because it gave bankruptcy judges powers that may be exercised only by judges appointed for life. In 1984 Congress amended the law to provide that (1) U.S. Courts of Appeals are to appoint bankruptcy judges, and (2) bankruptcy judges are not, absent agreement of the parties, to decide matters going beyond bankruptcy issues.

In addition to jurisdictional limitations resulting from the 1984 amendments, bankruptcy judges are not allowed to administer the debtor's estate. For example, the bankruptcy judge may not preside at—and cannot even attend—the first meeting of creditors to plan for the administration of the debtor's estate because the judge might learn something at the meeting that would bias the judge's later judicial decisions. Consequently, the administration of the estate is handled by a separate officer, the **trustee** in bankruptcy.

trustee
In bankruptcy, the officer responsible for administering the debtor's estate

Trustees are initially appointed by the bankruptcy judge from a panel of private trustees. However, at the first meeting of creditors, a new trustee may be elected if the election is requested by creditors holding at least 20 percent of the unsecured claims. The trustee generally serves as the representative of the debtor's estate and handles a wide range of administrative duties, such as collecting and selling the debtor's property, investigating the financial affairs of the debtor, and making a final report and accounting to the court.

Title 11 of the U.S. Code containing the 1978 Act originally had eight chapters. We will discuss three chapters of primary concern to individuals and businesses. Chapter 7 has the title "Liquidation," Chapter 11 "Reorganization," and Chapter 13 "Adjustment of Debts of an Individual with Regular Income." Chapter 7, often called "straight bankruptcy," involves the collection, liquidation, and distribution of the debtor's **estate.** Chapters 11 and 13 are concerned with plans for full or part payment of creditors. The person who is the subject of a "bankruptcy case" is called a "debtor," not a "bankrupt." A debtor may be an individual or a business, and each of Chapters 7, 11, and 13 is concerned with various kinds of debtors.

estate
In bankruptcy, the debtor's legal or equitable interest in property on the date the case commences

Before 1986, it was difficult for family farmers to use Chapter 13 because of the low debt requirements. (See p. 1093.) Chapter 11 was also unattractive because it was often time-consuming and expensive. As a result, a 1986 law created Chapter 12, entitled "Adjustment of Debts of a Family Farmer with Regular Annual Income." To qualify for Chapter 12, a family farmer's debts must not exceed $1,500,000.

Chapter 7 Liquidation

To illustrate the procedure followed in a typical bankruptcy case, let us assume that Micawber, a young college graduate, has made a number of purchases on credit and suddenly discovers that he has $10,000 in debts and only $2,000 worth of assets. Micawber is unable to make the installment payments on his debts as they become due and he is afraid that his wages will be subject to **garnishment.** He is now considering filing for bankruptcy.

garnishment
A statutory proceeding begun by a judgment creditor to reach the intangible assets of the judgment debtor—e.g., the debtor's right to his or her salary—by writ of garnishment

► Commencement of the Case

A bankruptcy case is commenced with the filing of a petition by a *debtor,* which is called a **voluntary case,** or by the debtor's creditors, which is called an **involuntary case.** The term "debtor" includes "persons" who are individuals, corporations, or partnerships that reside, or have a domicile, a place of business, or property in the United States.

voluntary case
A bankruptcy case in which the petition is filed by the debtor

involuntary case
A bankruptcy case in which the petition is filed by the creditors

In a *voluntary case,* the debtor may be any person except, primarily, a railroad, bank, insurance company, savings and loan association, or building and loan association. Insolvency of the debtor is not required. The petition may be filed by husband and wife jointly. The voluntary filing of a petition automatically acts as an *order for relief* under the bankruptcy law—that is, an order adjudicating bankruptcy of the debtor. The court is permitted, however, to dismiss the petition where the debts are mainly consumer debts and granting relief would constitute a "substantial abuse" of bankruptcy law. The following case illustrates the substantial abuse test.

FACTS

A debtor filed for bankruptcy. The debtor's consumer debts exceeded $46,000 and his nonconsumer debts totaled $40,248. The debtor's family income was $41,400. The debtor filed for bankruptcy simply to eliminate his debts, not because he was unable to pay them. The bankruptcy petition contained fraudulent omissions and the expense statement was padded. The debtor sought to maintain a "relatively exorbitant" lifestyle while seeking protection under the bankruptcy law. Should the bankruptcy be allowed?

DECISION

The court dismissed the case. First, the case involved primarily consumer debt. Second, the case represents substantial abuse of bankruptcy law. Bankruptcy courts originated in the Courts of Equity and the debtor in this case did not act in a equitable manner.

In re Bryant, 47 Bankr. 21 (W.D.N.C. 1984).

In an *involuntary case,* the debtor may be any person except the above five types of organization excluded in a voluntary case as well as a farmer or a charitable corporation. If the debtor has twelve or more creditors, the petition may be filed by three or more creditors whose *unsecured* claims total at least $5,000. If there are fewer than twelve creditors, the petition may be filed by one or more of such creditors whose total claims amount to at least $5,000. The debtor, Micawber in our case, may choose not to contest the petition, in which case the court will order the relief requested in the petition. If the debtor does contest the petition, the court will order relief only if, after a trial, it is determined that the debtor is not paying his or her debts as they become due, or that a custodian was appointed or took possession of the debtor's property within 120 days before the filing of the petition. If the court dismisses the petition, it may award the debtor costs, attorney's fees, and damages, including, in some cases, **punitive damages.**

punitive (exemplary) damages
The money judicially awarded to an injured party in excess of compensatory damages to punish for malicious, wanton, or intentional wrongful conduct

The filing of the petition acts as an automatic **stay** of (1) judicial, administrative, or other proceedings against the debtor; (2) the enforcement of a judgment against the debtor; and (3) the creation or enforcement of any lien against the debtor's estate. Thus Micawber's creditors could not start a suit or enforce their judgments by garnishment or otherwise after a petition is filed. There are, however, certain actions that are excluded from the operation of the stay, including criminal proceedings, the collection of alimony or support, and an action of the Department of Housing and Urban Development to foreclose a mortgage insured under the National Housing Act. Also, under Section 361 of the Bankruptcy Code, certain measures, such as requiring cash payments to creditors, may be taken to provide adequate protection for creditors harmed by the stay.

stay
A halt

► Creditors' Claims

Within a reasonable time after the order for relief, there will be a meeting of the creditors. The debtor, here Micawber, is required to appear at this meeting and to testify under oath if any creditor wants to question him. As previously noted, the judge is not allowed to attend this meeting and the creditors in certain cases may elect a trustee to replace the one appointed by the court. The creditors may also elect a **creditor's committee** that may consult with, and make recommendations to, the trustee and submit questions to the court regarding administration of the case.

creditors' committee
In bankruptcy, a committee elec[illegible] the creditors to advise in bankruptcy

Each creditor may file a **proof of claim,** which is automatically allowed unless an objection is raised by a party affected by the bankruptcy. If there is an objection, the court will allow the claim unless it determines that the claim falls within a specified list of claims that are not allowed, such as claims that are unenforceable against the debtor, claims for unmatured interest, and unmatured alimony and support that is not discharged by the bankruptcy.

proof of claim
The claim filed by a creditor in a bankruptcy case

If a **claim** is **contingent** or unliquidated, the court may estimate the value of the claim to determine the amount of the allowance. And when a creditor has a claim secured by a security interest or other lien on the debtor's property, the allowance is treated as a secured claim to the extent of the value of the property and an unsecured claim to the extent that the claim exceeds the property value. For example, Cory has a $10,000 claim against Dave and has Dave's office furniture worth $6,000 as security. Cory's unsecured claim is for $4,000.

contingent claim
A claim not certain of occurring, depending on a possible future event

The Estate

The trustee is responsible for collecting the property of the debtor's estate, reducing the property to money, and closing the estate in a manner that serves the best interests of the parties. The estate generally includes all legal or equitable interests that the debtor has in property *as of the date the case was commenced.* There are, however, three ways in which additional property might be added to the estate even though the debtor had no interest in the property on commencement of the case.

First, the estate includes property acquired by the debtor within 180 days after the petition was filed (1) by inheritance, bequest, or devise; (2) as a beneficiary on a life insurance policy; or (3) as the result of a property settlement agreement with a spouse for a divorce.

Second, if the debtor, while insolvent, made a preferential transfer of the debtor's property before the bankruptcy petition was filed, called a "voidable preference," the trustee has the right to avoid the transfer and reacquire the property for the estate. A **preference** is a transfer of property to a creditor for a debt owed before the transfer was made. The transfer must have been made while the debtor was **insolvent** (defined as a financial condition where the debts are greater than the assets, exclusive of fraudulent transfers and exempted property) and within ninety days before the petition was filed; however, there are special rules governing transfer to insiders such as a relative of an individual debtor or a director of a corporation. It also must be shown that the transfer enabled the creditor to receive preferential treatment. Additionally, the trustee may avoid fraudulent transfers made by the debtor within a year before the petition was filed and also transfers voidable under state law. The following case illustrates the preferential treatment requirement.

preference
In bankruptcy, a debtor's transfer of his or her property, made when insolvent and within 90 days before a petition in bankruptcy was filed, which gives a creditor preferential treatment

insolvency
In bankruptcy, when a debtor's assets are less than his or her liabilities

FACTS

The debtors borrowed $10,000 from a bank to purchase crates for use on their hog farm. The bank took a security interest in the crates but did not perfect the security interest (see Chapter 50) until eight months later, at a time when the debtor was insolvent. Within ninety days after the bank perfected its interest, the debtors filed for bankruptcy. Is the bank's perfected security interest a voidable preference?

DECISION

The bank's perfected security interest is voidable. When the bank perfected its security interest, it received a transfer of property for an earlier debt. This transfer took place when the debtor was insolvent and within ninety days before the bankruptcy.

In re Meritt, 7 Bankr. 876 (W.D.Mo. 1980).

There are several important exceptions to the rules allowing the trustee to avoid preferences. For example, the trustee may not avoid a transfer (1) that was a contemporaneous exchange for new value given to the debtor; (2) that was in payment of a debt incurred in the ordinary course of business and made according to ordinary business terms (e.g., payment of monthly utility bills); (3) that created a purchase money security interest in property acquired by the debtor that secured new value that is perfected within ten days after the debtor received the property; (4) to a creditor to the extent that, after the transfer, the creditor gave new value not secured by an unavoidable security interest; (5) that created a perfected security interest in inventory or receivables or the proceeds of either; or (6) in a case involving an individual with primarily consumer debts if the total value of the property transferred is less than $600.

lien creditor
A creditor with a judicial lien or a writ of execution

The third possibility for adding property to the estate is for the trustee to use his or her rights as a **lien creditor** to avoid certain transfers by the debtor. The trustee's rights include the power of (1) a creditor who has a judicial lien; (2) a creditor who has obtained a writ of execution that was returned unsatisfied; and (3) a bona fide purchaser of real property from the debtor. To illustrate the trustee's rights, we must assume that our debtor, Micawber, gave an unperfected security interest in his boat to a creditor, Heep. Because Heep's security interest in the boat is not perfected, a lien creditor would have priority with regard to the boat. Thus the trustee, with the powers of a lien creditor, can avoid Heep's interest in the boat. Heep's only recourse is to file a claim as an unsecured creditor and share Micawber's assets with other unsecured creditors.

exemption
In bankruptcy, a debtor's property that is not liquidated and not distributed to creditors in bankruptcy

Although the trustee may make additions to the estate by avoiding preferences and by exercising his or her rights as a lien creditor, certain property is exempt and will not be included in the estate. A debtor may choose to use the **exemptions** listed in the federal bankruptcy statute or, alternatively, may elect the exemptions available under state law, although the states have the right to require the debtor to use the state exemptions. At this date, over half the states have decided to require the use of their own exemptions. Property exempt under the federal law is very extensive and includes the following: (1) the debtor's residence up to a maximum interest of $7,500; (2) one motor vehicle up to $1,200 in value; (3) household furnishings, wearing apparel, appliances, books, animals, crops, or musical instruments held for personal, family, or household use up to a maximum $200 value for *each* item and a total value of $4,000; (4) up to $500 in jewelry; (5) implements, professional books, tools of the debtor's trade up to $750 in value; (6) an unmatured life insurance contract owned by the debtor other than credit life insurance; (7) prescribed health aids; (8) various state and federal benefits including social security, unemployment compensation, local public assistance, veterans' and disability benefits; (9) private benefits including the debtor's right to alimony and support payments, pension, profit-sharing and other plans, to the extent reasonably necessary for the support of the debtor; and (10) the debtor's right to receive certain payments such as an award under a law compensating victims of a crime, a payment under a life insurance policy on a person of whom the debtor was a dependent, and a payment of up to $7,500 on account of personal injury. The debtor is also entitled to exempt any other property up to a value of $400, plus any unused amount under (1) above up to $3,750. Thus, under this last provision, a debtor who is not a homeowner may exempt $4,150 in any property.

The state exemption laws are not uniform and, if the debtor elects the state exemptions, the debtor's rights will vary considerably, depending on the state of the debtor's residence. Additionally, many of the state laws were drafted many years ago and the exemptions are not as useful today as they once were. For instance, the Michigan law exempts, among other property, ten sheep, two cows, five swine, one hundred hens, five roosters, and enough hay and grain to feed the animals and poultry for six months!

► Distribution of the Estate

After the trustee has collected and liquidated the debtor's property, the property will be distributed according to the following **priorities:** (1) administrative expenses and specified fees and charges; (2) unsecured claims, in an involuntary case, arising in the ordinary course of business after the case was commenced but before the order for relief or the appointment of trustees; (3) unsecured claims up to $2,000 for wages, salaries, or commissions earned by an individual within ninety days before the filing of the petition or the cessation of the debtor's business; (4) unsecured claims for contributions to employee benefit plans arising from services rendered within 180 days before the petition was filed or the debtor ceased doing business, but only to the extent of $2,000 per employee less amounts paid for wage claims and to other employee benefit plans; (5) unsecured claims (up to $2,000 per individual) of grain producers and fishermen against grain and fish storage businesses; (6) unsecured claims up to $900 owed to individuals who have deposited money for the purchase of consumer goods or services that were not delivered or provided; and (7) unsecured tax claims of governmental units. Any property remaining after priority claims and expenses have been paid will be distributed on a pro rata basis to unsecured creditors who have filed a proof of claim.

priorities
In bankruptcy, claims that are paid first after the estate has been liquidated

► Discharge

After the estate has been liquidated and distributed, the court will order a **discharge.** However, a discharge will not be allowed if the case falls within one of seven main categories.

discharge
In bankruptcy, a court order releasing the individual debtor from his or her debts after the estate has been liquidated and distributed

1. Discharges are allowed only to *individuals,* not to corporations or partnerships (in order to avoid what a U.S. House of Representatives report referred to as "trafficking in corporate shells and bankrupt partnerships"). However, corporations and partnerships may utilize Chapter 11 of the Code on business reorganization or they may liquidate under state law.
2. A discharge is not allowed if the debtor has transferred, destroyed, or concealed property within one year before, or any time after, the petition was filed with the intent to hinder, delay, or defraud creditors.
3. A debtor who has concealed, destroyed, falsified, or failed to preserve recorded information relating to the debtor's financial condition or business transactions will not be granted a discharge unless the act was justified.
4. A debtor who fraudulently makes a false oath, presents a false claim, gives or receives property for acting or failing to act, or withholds recorded information from officials is not entitled to a discharge.
5. A discharge is not allowed when the debtor has failed to explain satisfactorily a loss or deficiency of assets.
6. A debtor who refuses to obey a lawful order of the court will not be discharged.
7. A discharge will not be allowed if the debtor has been granted a discharge in an earlier bankruptcy case commenced within six years before the petition in the current case was filed.

The following case illustrates the discharge provisions.

FACTS

A husband and wife filed for bankruptcy. Four days before filing their petition, they obtained a mortgage on their residence. They did not disclose the mortgage in their bankruptcy schedules. Are they entitled to a discharge?

DECISION

They are not entitled to a discharge. The mortgage on the residence represents an attempt by the debtors to keep their equity in the property away from general creditors. The transfer represented by the mortgage was made to hinder, delay, and defraud general creditors, while preferring creditors who received the mortgage.

In re Carroll, 70 Bankr. 143 (W.D.Mo. 1986).

If these exceptions do not apply and the *discharge* is granted, it serves to release the debtor from debts that arose before the date of the order for relief. The discharge also voids judgments relating to such debts and operates as an injunction against the collection of the debts.

However, even after a discharge, certain types of debts must still be paid by the debtor. These include: (1) certain taxes—e.g., taxes for which the debtor failed to file a return or filed a fraudulent return; (2) debts incurred in obtaining property or services by false pretenses or false financial statements reasonably relied on by creditors; (3) debts owed to creditors whose names were not given to the court by the debtor; (4) debts resulting from breach of fiduciary duty, larceny, or embezzlement; (5) debts owed for alimony or support; (6) debts resulting from a willfull and malicious injury caused by the debtor; (7) certain debts owed to a governmental unit, including educational loans owed to a governmental unit or nonprofit institution that became due within five years of the bankruptcy petition filing, unless that debt is causing undue hardship on the debtor; and (8) debts owed for injuries resulting from the debtor's drunk driving. The following case illustrates the type of debt that is not dischargeable.

FACTS

A doctor filed for bankruptcy. A question arose as to whether a $180,000 debt that the doctor agreed to pay as a result of improper medical treatment should be discharged in bankruptcy. The court considered the doctor's treatment of his patient (which included failure to perform timely tests, ignoring the results of belated tests, and failure to hospitalize patient) to be absolutely appalling. If the court considers that the treatment constituted a willful and malicious injury, should the debt be discharged?

DECISION

The debt is not dischargeable. Debts resulting from willful and malicious injuries are not dischargeable in bankruptcy. In this case the doctor's treatment was willful and malicious because it was an intentional act that resulted in injury.

Perkins v. Scharffe, 817 F.2d 392 (6th Cir. 1987).

In addition to the eight types of debts listed above, certain debts are presumed to be nondischargeable, in order to prevent a debtor from buying luxury goods immediately before the bankruptcy. These are: (1) debts totalling more than $500 for luxury goods and services purchased within forty days before the filing and certain cash advances totalling more than $1,000 obtained within twenty days before the filing.

Prior to the 1978 Act, debtors who were previously discharged were subjected to much pressure from former creditors to reaffirm (promise to pay) discharged debts. In order to correct this abuse, Congress made it more difficult for former creditors to obtain such promises to resume liability. Reaffirmation can occur no later than the time when a discharge is granted in bankruptcy proceedings. In cases where an individual wants to reaffirm a debt, the bankruptcy court must inform the debtor at a hearing that the reaffirmation is not required under law and of the legal effect of the reaffirmation. Unless an individual is represented by an attorney, the court must also determine that the reaffirmation does not impose undue hardship on the debtor and is in the debtor's best interest. If the debtor is represented by an attorney, the attorney must file an affidavit stating that the agreement does not impose undue hardship. Even when these requirements are met, the debtor is entitled to rescind the agreement within sixty days after it is filed with the court.

Governmental units are prohibited from discriminating against a person who has gone through bankruptcy. Debtors are also protected from discrimination by private employers; for example, a private employer may not fire a person because of the bankruptcy.

Chapter 13 Adjustment of Debts of Individual

As an alternative to the straight bankruptcy procedure described above, which leads to liquidation and distribution of the debtor's estate, it is possible for a debtor to propose a plan for the payment of debts under Chapter 13 of the Code. A **Chapter 13** case, commonly called a "wage earner's plan," is commenced by the filing of a *voluntary petition,* which operates as an automatic stay of proceedings in the same manner as a straight bankruptcy petition. Only individuals (except a stock broker or a commodity broker) with *regular income,* and with less than $100,000 in unsecured debt and less than $350,000 in secured debt, are eligible for Chapter 13 proceedings.

Chapter 13 plan
A plan for the payment of debts proposed by an individual as an alternative to a straight bankruptcy

The debtor then proposes a plan that provides for the submission of future income to the control of the trustee and provides for payments to creditors, including full payment of the claims entitled to priority discussed above. Chapter 13 contains a number of provisions that may be included in the plan, including the modification of the claims of secured creditors. The plan may not provide for payments over a period exceeding three years unless the court feels that there is cause to extend the plan an additional two years. The debtor retains title to, and possession of, the property unless the plan provides otherwise.

After the debtor has filed the plan, the court will schedule a **confirmation hearing,** at which time creditors may object to the plan. The plan must be accepted by each secured creditor unless an exception applies, such as when the property subject to the security interest is surrendered to the creditors or the claims are paid in full. The plan must be accepted by unsecured creditors unless the plan provides for payment of the claims in full or unless all of the debtor's disposable income is to be applied to payments. The court will decide whether or not to confirm the plan after considering various requirements set forth in Section 1325 of the Code. Especially important is a requirement that the debtor must propose the plan in good faith. If the plan is confirmed and the debtor makes all payments promised under the plan, the debtor will be discharged of the debts provided for by the plan, although there are certain exceptions, such as alimony and support payments.

confirmation hearing
The hearing at which a Chapter 13 plan is considered by the court

The following case illustrates the good faith test that must be met before the court will confirm a plan.

FACTS

The debtor filed a Chapter 13 plan proposing to pay 19 percent of her unsecured debt. Most of the debt (81 percent) represented student loan obligations. The debtor filed her Chapter 13 petition six weeks before completing graduate school, at a time when the loans had not yet become due. The debtor made no attempt to repay the educational loans, even though they enabled her to obtain a job that paid well. Should the court confirm the debtor's plan?

DECISION

The plan should not be confirmed. The good faith test requires that the court examine the totality of the debtor's conduct on a case-by-case basis. The facts in this case indicate that the debtor filed the plan in bad faith.

In re Doersam, 849 F.2d 237 (6th Cir. 1988).

Chapter 11 Business Reorganization

Chapter 11 plan
A plan for the reorganization of a business

As an alternative to bankruptcy, a business may choose to reorganize under **Chapter 11** of the Code. A Chapter 11 proceeding may be commenced by the filing of either an involuntary petition, or a voluntary petition by a debtor as defined in a Chapter 7 proceeding (but not a stockbroker or a commodity broker) or by a debtor railroad. Once a petition is filed, only the debtor may file a plan for 120 days after the order for relief unless a trustee has been appointed, in which case any party in interest may file a plan. The court may order the appointment of a trustee for cause (including fraud, dishonesty, incompetence, or gross mismanagement) or if the appointment is in the interest of creditors, security holders, or other interests of the estate.

In addition to the possible appointment of a trustee, the court is also required to appoint a creditors' committee as soon as possible after the order for relief. The creditors' committee consults with the debtor or trustee concerning administration of the estate, investigates all matters relevant to the formulation of a plan, participates in the formulation of a plan, and performs other services as representative of other creditors.

The contents of the plan are set forth in Section 1123 of the Code. This section requires that the plan (1) designate classes of claims; (2) specify which claims or interests are not impaired by the plan; (3) specify the treatment given claims or interests that are impaired by the plan; (4) provide the same treatment for claims within a particular class; and (5) provide adequate means for executing the plan.

After the plan is formulated, it will be transmitted, along with a written disclosure statement approved by the court, to holders of claims, who may accept or reject the plan. The court will then schedule as hearing and will confirm the plan if it complies with Chapter 11. If the plan is fair and equitable, it may be confirmed even though all classes of claims have not accepted the plan; once confirmed, it binds all interested parties.

Amendments to the Act in 1984 resolved a very controversial issue of whether, and to what extent, a court can *reject* a collective (union) bargaining agreement between a union and the debtor. The Act provides that the debtor or the trustee must make a proposal to the union for modification of the collective bargaining agreement *before* applying to the court for rejection of the agreement. The debtor or the trustee must meet, at reasonable times, with the union representative to confer in good faith in attempting to reach mutually satisfactory modifications of the labor contract.

The debtor's proposal for modification of the collective bargaining agreement must include protections that are necessary to allow the debtor to reorganize and that treat all parties fairly and equitably. These important requirements are at issue in the following case.

FACTS

Wheeling-Pittsburgh (WP) filed for bankruptcy under Chapter 11 on April 16, 1985. On May 9, WP proposed to its union a modification of their collective bargaining agreement. The proposal did not include a "snap back" provision that would increase employees' wages if the company's performance was better than anticipated. "Snap back" provisions were included in prior collective bargaining agreements, and WP offered no explanation as to why one was not included in the proposal. When the union did not respond to the proposal, WP asked the court on May 31 for permission to reject the collective bargaining agreement. The district court allowed rejection, without discussing whether it was necessary for the company to exclude the "snap back" provision. Was this a good decision?

DECISION

No. Bankruptcy law requires courts to consider whether the absence of a "snap back" provision is necessary. Furthermore, the court should determine whether the proposal is fair and equitable to WP's employees.

Wheeling-Pittsburgh Steel v. United Steelworkers, 791 F.2d 1074 (3rd Cir. 1986).

Summary Statement

1. Under the U.S. Constitution, bankruptcy is a federal matter; states do not have the power to enact bankruptcy laws.
2. Under Chapter 7, in a voluntary bankruptcy the petition is filed by the debtor, while in an involuntary bankruptcy the petition is filed by creditors. If the debtor contests the petition in an involuntary bankruptcy, the court will order relief if it determines that the debtor is not paying his or her debts as they become due.
3. The debtor's estate includes all legal or equitable interests that the debtor has in property as of the date the case was commenced.
4. After liquidation under Chapter 7, the estate will be distributed first to creditors with priority and then to unsecured creditors.
5. As an alternative to Chapter 7, an individual might file a plan under Chapter 13, and a business might file a reorganization plan under Chapter 11.

In the following case the court discusses the question of whether student loans are dischargeable in bankruptcy.

In re CONARD, DEBTOR
6 B.R. 151 (Ky. 1980)

The debtor Conard, aged 31, lost his job as a full-time teacher in April 1979, and filed for bankruptcy in October 1979. In his filing he listed $25 in assets and debts totalling $37,354. The debts included a business loan connected with the debtor's business venture (Double Dip Ice Cream), credit card debt, and a student loan. The United States argued that the student loan should not be discharged, while the debtor asserted that it should be discharged because it was imposing undue hardship.

Merritt, J. . . . The following facts were developed at the trial, at which Conard was the only witness:

Upon being discharged from military service, Conard used the G.I. Bill of Rights to obtain a college education. His thirst for knowledge led him through five different colleges.

At some point in his academic travels the wellspring of benefits from the G.I. Bill was depleted, and Conard applied for and obtained a series of three federally guaranteed, long-term, low-interest loans with which he could complete his collegiate journey. He obtained a bachelor's degree in education at Western Kentucky University, and there studied toward, but did not obtain, a postgraduate degree.

Conard, unmarried with no dependents, lives at the home of his 75-year-old mother. Having no car of his own, he drives her van.

Accurately describing himself as "overweight," Conard testified that his physical appearance "turns off a lot of people," including potential employers. The weight problem—and it is a severe one—has not been diagnosed as having any medical origin. Conard attributes it to "a different metabolic rate."

Conard has unsuccessfully sought sales jobs. He has *not* applied for employment at any private schools in Jefferson County, nor has he applied at any schools, public or private, in surrounding counties. He apparently is content to await recall by the county board of education, and he ranks low on the recall roster.

With his elderly mother as a guarantor, Conard obtained a $5,000 loan from Union Trust Bank this summer, some months after filing bankruptcy. Curiously, he is using the loan proceeds only to retire as they become due the $150 monthly payments on that same loan.

. . . . .

This claim of undue hardship rests upon two asserted facts: (1) Conard must support and provide for his elderly mother, and (2) he is unable to obtain employment because of his physical appearance.

Upon the first point, we have some question as to who is supporting whom. The mother, who gave birth to this healthy young man while in her 44th year, and who fancies a mode of transportation generally associated with drivers two generations her junior, may be a vital woman indeed. Although the record does not indicate the extent of her income or financial substance, it is at least clear that the Union Trust Bank would not extend credit to the son without the mother's hand being put to the note.

Upon the second point we must observe with neither cynicism nor cruelty, that corpulence is a condition which may swiftly diminish with continued impecuniosity.

This unemployed former president of the Double Dip Ice Cream Company, having double-dipped the available federal subsidies to obtain a superior education, should consider some alternatives. Enlightened self-interest would seem to suggest the virtue of a vigorous and energetic search for a proper workshop in which to use those intellectual tools which have been well honed at federal expense. Productivity is preferable to living off the substance of the land. In order to stimulate some reflection upon such heretical theories of individual enterprise, it is hereby ordered, that the indebtedness of Paul George Conard to the Department of Health, Education and Welfare, United States of America, is not dischargeable in bankruptcy. This is a final order. Judgment shall be entered accordingly.

Questions and Case Problems

1. A debtor had net take-home pay of approximately $432 per month and also received help in paying his expenses from his fiancee, with whom he shared an apartment. He was trained as a diesel mechanic and had worked as a hypnotist, but his future employment prospects were clouded because he was a convicted felon. Should his student loan, which he owes to the Wisconsin Higher Education Aids Board, be discharged in the debtor's bankruptcy? [*In re Tobin, Bankrupt,* 18 Bankr. 560 (Wisc. 1982).]

2. Pauline paid a sum of money to the Wyatts in return for their promise to support her. They used the money to purchase a house, where Pauline resided temporarily. The Wyatts later stopped supporting Pauline and filed a Chapter 13 petition. Under state law, the Wyatts hold legal title to the property while Pauline holds equitable title. Should the house be included in the debtors' estate? [*Collomb v. Wyatt,* 6 Bankr. 947 (N.Y. 1980).]
3. Robert, who was granted bankruptcy discharges in 1960 and 1967, petitioned for a third bankruptcy in 1973. He kept few records of his financial transactions because he dealt almost exclusively in cash and because he did not like banks. Should the court grant Robert's discharge? [*In re Horton, Bankrupt,* 621 F.2d 968 (9th Cir. 1980).]
4. Sam, who operated a fencing company as a sole proprietor, filed a Chapter 7 bankruptcy petition on April 11, 1980. During January and February, 1980, Sam drew checks totalling $4,300 from the business, made payable to his wife. Sam was unable to explain what happened to these funds beyond stating that they were used for "personal expenses." He claimed monthly recreational expenses of $720. He also failed to provide a satisfactory explanation for the loss of cash drawn from his business in January and February of 1980. Should Sam's discharge in bankruptcy be allowed? [*In re Ramos, Debtor,* 8 Bankr. 490 (Wisc. 1981.)]
5. Clara had two elderly aunts, Millie and Tillie. Under Millie's will, Clara was to receive all of Millie's property. Tillie named Clara as the beneficiary in her life insurance policy. Clara was deeply in debt and decided to file bankruptcy under Chapter 7 in order to discharge her debts and avoid using the inheritance and insurance money to pay her creditors. A petition under Chapter 7 was filed on January 15. Aunt Tillie died the following May 15 and Aunt Millie died the following November 15. Are the inheritance and the insurance proceeds included in Clara's estate and thus available to creditors? Why?
6. Kermit filed a voluntary bankruptcy petition under Chapter 7. Sixty days before filing the petition, Kermit had given a security interest in his boat to First Bank, at which time First Bank made a $1,000 loan to Kermit. At the time of this transaction, Kermit was not insolvent. The trustee now wants to avoid the security interest. First Bank claims that the trustee cannot avoid the interest because (1) Kermit was not insolvent and (2) the bank gave new value to Kermit. Who wins? Why?
7. A medical student obtained a grant from the Physician Shortage Area Scholarship Program to help pay for his medical education. The scholarship required him to practice for a limited time in an area where there was a shortage of physicians. He agreed to repay the grant with interest if this requirement were not met. After completing his residency, he did not practice in a physician shortage area and did not repay the grant. When he later filed for bankruptcy, a question arose as to whether this obligation was dischargeable. Is it? [*U.S. Dept. of Health and Human Services v. Smith,* 807 F.2d 122 (8th Cir. 1986).]
8. A jury entered a verdict against Joseph in the amount of $86,704. After the verdict Joseph transferred notes worth $93,337 to his father-in-law in exchange for $54,400. He then transferred $40,000 to a corporation owned by his children in exchange for a $40,000 note which was to be repaid over a 36-year period. During the same year an involuntary Chapter 7 petition was filed against Joseph. Can the trustee recover the property transferred by Joseph? [*In re Newman, Debtor,* 6 Bankr. 798 (N.Y. 1980).]
9. A lumber company furnished lumber to a contractor for home construction. When the contractor later filed for bankruptcy, the lumber company claimed that its debt

was not dischargeable. The company argued that the contractor's promise to pay for the lumber constituted obtaining property by false pretenses. Is this a valid argument? [*In re Martin,* 70 Bankr. 146 (M.D.Ala. 1986).]

10. An attorney specializing in bankruptcy law granted Shell Oil an option to purchase a parcel of land. In order to back out of the option agreement, the attorney later filed a Chapter 13 petition in bankruptcy. At the time of the filing, the attorney owed no debts, owned a $125,000 home, and had an impressive stock portfolio. Should the court allow the attorney to use bankruptcy to avoid his option agreement? [*In re Waldron,* 785 F.2d 936 (11th Cir. 1986).]

CHAPTER 53

GENERAL PRINCIPLES OF INSURANCE LAW

After you have read this chapter, you should be able to:

1. List the major types of insurance.
2. Define insurance.
3. Describe the regulation of insurance transactions.
4. Explain what is meant by an insurable interest and indicate when the insurable interest must exist.
5. Explain why warranties, representation, and concealment are important and how they are used as defenses by insurance companies.
6. Indicate what is meant by subrogation and when it is applicable.

BUSINESS DECISIONS and the LAW

Fred, a recent college graduate, is married, and has one child. He owns a house and a car and has recently purchased a small clothing store. In talking with their personal financial planning advisor, Fred and his wife recognize the importance of various types of insurance such as homeowner's, life, health, disability, automobile, and title insurance. Through reading business publications, Fred also realizes that special insurance is necessary for his business. This special insurance includes business interruption, liability and workers' compensation insurance. In discussing his insurance needs with an agent, Fred is confused by the different types of insurance and by a number of insurance concepts such as insurable interest, warranties, and subrogation.

Introduction

Fred's situation illustrates the importance of insurance to every individual on both a personal and a business level. Like death and taxes, insurance is certain to affect you at some time during your life. If you own an automobile, a house, or a business, or wish to provide financial security for your family, insurance represents a key element in personal, business, and estate planning.

In this chapter we will examine the general principles of the law relating to insurance contracts. In Chapter 54 we will examine closely the three most common types of insurance: (1) life insurance, (2) homeowner's insurance, and (3) automobile insurance.

The Types of Insurance

► Homeowner's Insurance

In the situation described above, Fred and his wife should purchase a homeowner's policy that will provide coverage for losses due to damage or destruction of their home. As discussed in Chapter 54, the policy should also protect them in the event they are sued by someone whom they accidentally injure or who is injured while on their property.

► Life Insurance

Fred and his wife should create an estate plan that includes a will and life insurance, and possibly also a trust and lifetime gifts. The types and form of life insurance policies will be discussed in Chapter 54.

► Health Insurance

Health care costs are rising faster than the costs of most products and services. In some communities the charge for spending one night in the hospital runs into hundreds of dollars, not including medical treatment and other services. Consequently, it is extremely important that Fred obtain insurance covering hospital expenses, medical and surgical fees, and other services such as X rays, radiological treatment, and laboratory tests. It is common for individuals to supplement their health insurance with a major medical insurance policy that provides coverage for extended illness, which might cost more than the coverage provided by the primary insurance policy.

► Disability Insurance

If Fred should become ill, his health insurance will pay for hospital and medical treatment, but a source of income will be needed to support the family until his recovery. A disability insurance policy can be purchased that will provide a monthly income for Fred until he recovers.

► Annuity

annuity
An insurance policy that pays the insured a designated amount periodically, beginning at a date set in the policy

In planning for his eventual retirement, Fred might decide to purchase an **annuity** policy. An annuity is a type of insurance policy that will pay Fred a designated amount periodically, the payments to begin at a date set in the policy. Fred might choose to purchase a fixed dollar annuity that pays a set amount—e.g., $10,000 per year. Alternatively, he might choose a variable annuity where the annuity premiums are invested in stocks or bonds and the benefit rises or falls, depending on the current value of the portfolio.

▶ Automobile Insurance

Fred and his wife will need either regular or no-fault automobile insurance for their car. Both types of insurance will be discussed in Chapter 54.

▶ Title Insurance

When Fred and his wife purchased their home, it is likely that they purchased **title insurance,** which protects them in the event that the person who sold them the house did not have clear title to the property. For instance, there might be a deed on record with a hidden defect, such as a voidable deed signed by a minor. Title insurance will protect Fred and his wife for as long as they own the property. With title insurance, only one premium is paid—at the closing—although if the owner or owners mortgage the house, the bank usually will require the purchase of a second policy to protect the bank's interest.

title insurance
Insurance that covers the title to real estate

▶ Social Insurance

Today approximately 90 percent of workers are covered by social security,[1] even when they are self-employed; and almost all of our country's population over sixty-five years of age is covered by Medicare, which is provided by the federal government. During their working years, employees covered by social security make contributions that are automatically deducted from wages; the employer matches the amount of the deduction and forwards the total to the Internal Revenue Service. Workers who are self-employed will pay the social security contribution when they file an annual income tax return. The social security contributions are used (1) to pay workers a retirement income when they retire at age sixty-two or later, (2) to pay disability income to workers who are unable to work because of a disability, and (3) to pay survivors of a deceased worker.

Medicare provides hospital and medical insurance for persons sixty-five or older and for disabled persons who have been receiving social security benefits for at least two years. Everyone sixty-five or older who is entitled to receive social security payments automatically receives hospital insurance. Medical insurance, to cover doctor's fees and other services, is available for a modest monthly premium.

▶ Workers' Compensation Insurance

Workers' compensation laws protect workers who are injured on the job. In almost every state these laws provide that employers, such as Fred in his role as the owner of a clothing store, must pay for all accidental injuries occurring on the job. For instance, if one of Fred's employees carelessly leaves a coat hanger on the floor and later trips on the hanger and is injured, Fred is liable for damages resulting from the injury. Most employers purchase a workers' compensation insurance policy from a private company, or purchase coverage through a state workers' compensation fund. A few employers use self-insurance; that is, they pay injured workers from company assets.

---

[1]For discussion of social security and workers' compensation, see Chapter 19.

► Business Insurance

business interruption insurance
Insurance that covers lost revenues when a business is closed as the result of property damage

inland marine insurance
Insurance that covers goods that are being shipped

crime insurance
Insurance that protects the insured from losses due to criminal acts, such as burglary, against the insured

malpractice insurance
Liability insurance that protects professional people (doctors, lawyers, accountants) against claims brought against them

In addition to workers' compensation insurance, there are several types of insurance that Fred will need for his business. Fred should purchase fire and liability insurance for his business as well as automobile insurance if automobiles are used in the business. Fred might purchase **business interruption insurance,** which will reimburse him for lost revenues in the event he has to close his business temporarily because of property damage. If Fred ships his clothing in the ordinary course of business, he will want to purchase **inland marine insurance** to cover against loss while the goods are in transit. **Crime insurance** can be purchased to protect Fred from dishonesty of his employees or theft by outsiders. A number of the personal insurance coverages discussed above can be purchased by the employer as a fringe benefit for the employees, including group life, medical disability, and retirement insurance. Finally, if Fred is considered the key person in his business, the business should purchase key employee life insurance coverage to cover financial losses suffered by the company in the event that Fred dies.

Malpractice Insurance If Fred were engaged in a profession such as medicine, law, or accounting, he would also need **malpractice** (also called professional liability) **insurance,** which would provide liability coverage in the event he is sued by a patient or client for failing to meet the duty of care demanded by the profession. In the professions that have been deeply involved in malpractice litigation, notably medicine and accounting, insurance is difficult to obtain and very expensive.

► Excess Liablilty Insurance

Damage awards to injured persons have increased greatly in recent years, and liability coverage under standard homeowner's automobile and business policies is often inadequate. For instance, homeowner's insurance usually provides liability coverage for $50,000; if Fred injures someone—for example, by accidentally hitting someone in the eye with a golf ball—the damages could easily run over $100,000. Consequently, it is wise to purchase an excess liability policy, sometimes called an "umbrella" policy, which will provide liability coverage for at least $1 million.

► Self-Insurance

When insurance coverage becomes too expensive, many businesses and organizations use some type of self-insurance mechanism. Some companies simply "go bare"; they purchase no insurance and use company assets to pay losses. Some companies self-insure for most losses but purchase supplementary catastrophic loss insurance. Other companies or organizations group together to form insurance "pools" and thus spread their losses among the group. Finally, many companies in recent years have formed subsidiaries, called "captive" insurance companies, and then purchase coverage from the captives, thus avoiding brokerage commissions and other costs.

insurance
A contract in which the insurer agrees to pay the insured for losses affecting the insured's interests

insurer
The person who assumes another's risk (in the insurance contract)

insured
The person whose risk has been assumed by another (in the insurance contract)

Definition of Insurance

Before we proceed further, it will be useful to define insurance. There are two different types of insurance definitions. First, most courts have adopted a very general definition: **insurance** is a contract, usually called an insurance policy, where one party (called the **insurer** or underwriter) agrees to pay another party (the **insured**) for losses affecting the insured's interests (the insurable interest). The consideration that the insurer receives for contracting to pay for such losses is called the *premium*.

Second, state insurance commissioners are guided by specific statutory definitions of insurance, which they use in deciding whether a particular acitvity is subject to insurance regulation. For example, Section 22 of the California Insurance Code defines insurance as a "contract whereby one undertakes to indemnify another against loss, damage, or liability arising from a contingent or unknown event." Certain companies in California offered home buyers a "homeowner's protection plan" that required the companies to repair plumbing, electrical, and heating systems that become defective within one year after the home was purchased. The California Attorney General, in an opinion dated May 3, 1978, advised those companies that, under the statutory definition of insurance, the companies were engaged in the insurance business and were thus subject to insurance regulation. In the following case the court held that plans for prepaid legal services were not insurance.

FACTS

The New York County Lawyer's Association and a Teamsters Union local created two experimental plans for prepaid legal services. The New York statutes define insurance as an agreement whereby one party (the insurer) is obligated to pay another party (the insured) upon the happening of a fortuitous event. A fortuitous event is an occurrence which is beyond the control of either party. As required by state statute, the Association and the Union applied to the lower court for approval of these plans. Approval was denied on the ground that the plans were in the nature of insurance. The Association and Union appealed.

Do the prepaid legal services plans constitute insurance?

DECISION

No. Reversed, for the Association and Union. These prepaid legal services plans do not constitute insurance. Many of the events covered by the legal services plans are not fortuitous. These services include legal assistance in estate planning, divorce, and the purchase of real estate.

Feinstein v. Attorney General of the State of New York, 326 N.E.2d 288 (N.Y. 1976).

Organization of Insurers

Many insurance companies, especially those that write fire and casualty insurance, are organized as typical business corporations. That is, they authorize, issue, and sell stock to shareholders, who own the business and receive dividends. However, two other methods of organization are also commonly used by insurance companies.

First, a substantial amount of insurance at the international level is underwritten by Lloyd's of London. Lloyd's is not a company but, instead, is a society with thousands of members who join together to form syndicates, each of which specializes in a certain type of insurance. A person who purchases insurance from Lloyd's is really purchasing insurance from one or more of these individual syndicates. In an effort to make American insurers more competitive with Lloyd's, the state of New York enacted legislation in 1978 that provides for the creation of the New York Insurance Exchange, which is modeled after Lloyd's.

Second, many American insurers—especially those that underwrite life insurance—are mutual companies. A **mutual company** is one that is owned by the insureds, with the result that the insureds are purchasing insurance at cost since there are no shareholders to be paid. A few mutual companies sell assessable policies, which means

mutual company
A company owned by the insureds

that the policyholders must pay an amount in addition to the premium if the company suffers losses. For example, after a Colorado insurance company failed in 1975, the policyholders, many of whom were unaware that their policies were assessable, were charged an average of $500 to cover the company's losses.

Another way of classifying insurance companies is by the type of insurance they sell. At one time an insurance company could sell only one type of insurance—fire, life, or casualty. Today, however, all states allow multiple-line underwriting under which a nonlife insurer can sell all types of insurance except for life insurance. Most states today have gone one step further and allow all-line companies to sell all types of insurance.

Insurance Regulation

Unlike most contracts, the contract of insurance is closely regulated by the government. Insurance regulations govern the financial condition of insurers, policy premiums, policy forms, and the licensing of insurers and their agents. The overriding legal question with regard to insurance regulation has been whether the individual states or the federal government should be primarily responsible for regulating insurance. The question arises because the commerce clause of the U.S. Constitution, Article I, Section 8, provides that Congress has the power to regulate *interstate* commerce. But in the 1868 case of *Paul v. Virginia,*[2] the Supreme Court ruled that issuing an insurance policy is not an act of commerce and, therefore, the states have the right to regulate insurance contracts. This case was followed until 1944, when the Supreme Court ruled in *United States v. South-Eastern Underwriters Association*[3] that an insurance company that conducts business across state lines is engaged in interstate commerce and subject to regulation by Congress. However, Congress reacted to this decision by enacting the McCarran-Ferguson Act, which became effective in 1945. The McCarran-Ferguson Act recognized that state regulation of insurance should continue unless a federal law is specifically directed toward the insurance industry. The Act also provided that federal antitrust acts would not apply to the insurance industry if states established their own regulations. Most states have developed their own regulations and, consequently, today insurance is regulated chiefly by the states.

However, state regulation of insurance is still a live issue today because Congress periodically considers the question of whether the federal government could regulate the insurance industry better than state governments. Furthermore, even with our present system of regulation, questions of federal versus state regulation are frequently raised in the courts, as is illustrated in the following case.

FACTS

Seasongood, an insurance agent, handled the insurance for Sports Car Club of America (SCCA), which required its members across the country to purchase SCCA-approved coverage. After several years, SCCA hired another agency to handle its insurance plan. Under federal law, a business of insurance regulated by state law is exempt from federal antitrust laws. Nevertheless, Seasongood filed suit for treble damages, claiming that SCCA's plan violated federal antitrust statutes. The trial court dismissed the complaint because the state where the agent resided, Missouri, had a statute regulating the business of insurance. Seasongood appealed.

[2]Wall. 168 (1868).

[3]322 U.S. 533 (1944).

DECISION

Reversed, and the case was remanded to the District Court for further proceedings. The agent's complaint alleged a nationwide conspiracy. Consequently, the trial court should have determined whether the other states involved also regulate insurance, thereby exempting the defendant's activity from federal law.

Seasongood v. K & K Ins. Agency, 548 F.2d 729 (8th Cir. 1977).

Insurable Interest

One of the key distinctions between an insurance contract and other types of contract is the requirement that the insured have some type of interest, called an **insurable interest,** in the risk covered by the insurance contract. There are three reasons why the law requires the insured to have an insurable interest. First, insurance is usually considered to be a contract of indemnity; that is, the purpose of insurance is to provide compensation for losses suffered by the insured. Without the requirement of insurable interest, a person could insure property he or she does not own and thus be overindemnified for a loss.

insurable interest
An interest the insured has in the risk covered by the insurance contract

Second, the insurable interest requirement is designed to prevent gambling contracts, which are void in most states. For example, if Jack insures something in which he has an interest (as when he purchases collision insurance on his own car), he is not gambling but, instead, is merely shifting an existing risk to the insurer in exchange for his payment of premiums. However, if Jack purchases collision insurance on Sam's car, a car in which he has no interest, the insurance "contract" will be a wager; Jack will be betting the company that Sam's car will be damaged in a collision.

Third, an insurable interest is required because of the moral risks that would be created by allowing a person to insure a risk in which the person has no interest. For instance, if we allow Jack to insure Sam's life or car when Jack has no interest in either, Jack will be tempted to destroy the car or even to murder Sam in order to collect on the policies.

Although these reasons underlie insurable interest theory, in practice the theory is applied differently for life and property insurance. With life insurance, insurable interest means that the insured has a reasonable expectation of economic benefit or a legal interest in the life being insured. To illustrate, if Clyde took in a young orphan with the intention of caring for and supporting him, the orphan would have an insurable interest in Clyde's life based on the reasonable expectation of economic benefit provided by Clyde, even though the orphan was not legally adopted. If Clyde legally adopted the orphan, the orphan would have an even better case because of his legal relationship to Clyde under which Clyde is required to provide support. Thus the orphan could take out a policy of life insurance on Clyde's life.

With life insurance, the insurable interest must exist when the policy is purchased, but it is not required that there be an interest at the time of the loss. Once an insurable interest is established, the insured may purchase any amount of life insurance on the insured which the insurer is willing to sell. In the following case the insurable interest in life existed when the policy was purchased but not at the time of death.

FACTS

Jack, the decedent, was employed by Pioneer Foundry Co., Inc., for nine years. During Jack's employment, the company had an insurable interest in Jack's life, and it purchased a $50,000 policy on his life, the company being named as beneficiary on the policy. When Jack later left the company, the company continued to pay the premiums on the policy until Jack's death, when the insurance proceeds were paid to Pioneer. Jack's widow sued Pioneer for the proceeds, contending that Pioneer's insurable interest in Jack's life ceased at the time he left Pioneer and, therefore, the proceeds belong to Jack's estate. Is the company, which had no insurable interest at the time of Jack's death, entitled to recover $50,000 on the policy?

DECISION

Yes. The company is entitled to keep the proceeds. If the insurable interest requirement is met when the policy is issued, the policy proceeds must be paid even if there is no insurable interest at death. The company is not limited in its recovery to the amount of its financial loss, which in this case was nothing.

Secor v. Pioneer Foundry Co., Inc. 173 N.W.2d 780 (Mich. 1970).

There are two views as to what constitutes an insurable interest in property. In some states the insured must actually have some type of legal or equitable interest in the insured property. For instance, Jack obviously has an insurable interest in his own car if he is the legal owner of the car. In other states an insurable interest exists if a person expects to suffer an economic loss if the property is destroyed. Under this theory, if Jack owns a pizza shop and often borrows his friend Sue's car to make deliveries, Jack would have an insurable interest in Sue's car because Jack would suffer an economic loss if Sue's car were destroyed (a loss of sales because he would be unable to make deliveries).

The following case illustrates the economic loss test.

FACTS

Linda and Eddie, a married couple, purchased a home. They later divorced and Linda deeded her interest in the home to Eddie. When Eddie died, the home passed to the couple's two minor children, and Linda and the children moved into the home. Linda assumed a mortgage on the property. She also maintained the property and purchased fire insurance. When the home was later totally destroyed by fire, the insurance company refused to pay, claiming that Linda had no insurable interest. Did she have an insurable interest?

DECISION

Yes. Even though Linda did not have legal title to the property, she had an insurable interest as a result of her extensive economic investment in the residence. Consequently, she is entitled to payment from the insurance company.

Motorists Mut. Ins. v. Richmond, 676 S.W.2d 478 (Ky. 1984).

Unlike life insurance, with property insurance the insurable interest must *exist at the time of loss,* and the insured may recover *only up to the value of his or her interest* at the time of loss. For instance, if Jack purchased automobile insurance on his car but later sold the car, his insurable interest would cease at the time of sale. He could recover nothing if the car were destroyed after the sale.

Insurance Company Defenses

It is common belief that insurance companies often refuse to make payment on their policies because of fine print provisions in the policies—or, stated another way, "the large print giveth and the fine print taketh away!" While this is, of course, an exaggeration, there are many cases where a company has a legitimate defense in its refusal to pay. Most of these defenses fall within one of three categories.

Warranties

A **warranty** is a statement of fact or a promise made by the insured which is part of the insurance contract and which must be true if the insurer is to be liable on the contract. Under the common law, the insurance company would be justified in rescinding the policy if the warranty were untrue. For example, if Jack purchased insurance on his frame house and warranted in the policy that the house was brown when it actually was pink, under the common law rule he could not recover for fire losses because his statement was untrue. This harsh rule has been changed in most states by statutes providing that, unless the contract provides otherwise, statements of fact or promises made by the insured are interpreted to be representations.

warranty
In insurance, a statement of fact or a promise made by the insured that is part of the insurance contract and that must be true if the insurer is to be liable on the contract

Representations

A **representation** is a statement of fact made by the insured *during negotiations* with the insurer before the policy is issued. It is *not a part of the insurance contract* and normally is made in the application for insurance. For instance, when Jack applied for fire insurance, he might have stated that his house was brown, but the statement might not be incorporated into the policy. If Jack's representation is not true—i.e., if the house is pink—may the company avoid liability on the policy? In the absence of fraud, the general rule is that the company may not avoid liability unless the representation was material to its decision whether to issue the policy. In other words, the question is whether the company would have issued the policy even if the representation had not been made. The color of Jack's house would not be material and, therefore, Jack's misrepresentation would be no defense. However, if Jack had represented that the house was made of stone when in fact it was a frame house, the company could avoid liability because of the misrepresentation of a material fact. The following case illustrates this.

representation
In insurance, a statement of fact made by the insured that is not a part of the insurance contract but, during negotiation, is made to induce formation of the contract

FACTS

In applying to Countryside Casualty Co. for automobile insurance, Orr stated in his application that he had no arrests for offenses other than traffic violations, that he had not been fined or convicted for a moving violation, and that he did not use alcoholic beverages. In fact Orr had a number of convictions for traffic violations, forgery, and drunkenness. The company issued the policy, and Orr's car was later involved in an accident. Orr was not driving the car at the time of the accident. The company instituted an action to have the policy declared void because of Orr's misrepresentations, and to be relieved of any liability for the automobile accident. May the company cancel the policy and avoid liability because of Orr's false statement?

DECISION

Yes. Orr's misrepresentations were material to the risk. Consequently, the policy was void and the company is not liable.

Countryside Casualty Co. v. Orr, 523 F.2d 870 (8th Cir. 1975).

Concealment

Concealment occurs when the insured intentionally fails to disclose a *material fact* to the insurer. Generally the insured must disclose material facts and may not recover on the policy if such facts were concealed with the intention of defrauding the company. In

concealment
In insurance, the insured's intentional failure to disclose a material fact to the insurer

the following case the information not disclosed by the insured was material to the insurer's decision to insure.

FACTS

Tate was listed as the beneficiary in a $25,000 life insurance policy on his wife, issued by the Massachusetts Life Insurance Co. When the policy was originally issued, the wife failed to disclose "that she had received advice from or attendance or treatment by physicians, other practitioners or psychologists" as requested by the application form. She had consulted a psychiatrist, who had treated her for depression, psychiatric disorder, and alcohol addiction. Shortly after applying for the insurance, she was hospitalized for severe depression and died of pneumonia two years after the policy was issued. The company then instituted an action to rescind the policy because of the wife's misrepresentations. Tate, in turn, asserted a claim against the company.

DECISION

Judgment for the company. The insured (wife's) intentional material misrepresentation by nondisclosure of her consultation with a psychiatrist concerning her condition and his treatment of her depression and alcoholism justified rescission of the policy. The fact that the wife died from another cause does not disprove the increase of risk.

Massachusetts Mutual Life Ins. Co. v. Tate, 369 N.E.2d 767 (N.Y. 1977).

Subrogation

subrogation
The substitution of one person for another with reference to a claim or a right

Subrogation is generally defined as the substitution of one person for another with reference to claim or a right. In insurance law, subrogation is the substitution of the insurance company for the insured (after the company has paid the loss) with reference to the insured's rights or claims against the party who caused the loss.

Insurance companies generally have the right of subrogation in property insurance policies but not in life insurance policies. For example, let us assume that Jane purchased an automobile policy from No-Dent Insurance Company and that she was named as the beneficiary on her husband's life insurance policy, which was issued by Deep Pockets Insurance Company. If her husband was killed and her car damaged in an accident caused by Leroy, Jane would collect under both policies. No-Dent would then be subrogated to Jane's rights against Leroy, but Deep Pockets would have no right of subrogation.

Summary Statement

1. There are several types of insurance that directly affect the average person. Among the most important types are life insurance, homeowner's insurance, and automobile insurance.
2. Insurance is generally defined as a contract where one party agrees to pay another party for specified losses.
3. Under the federal McCarran-Ferguson Act, the regulation of the insurance business is primarily a matter for individual states.
4. An insured person must have an insurable interest in the risk covered by the contract to acquire insurance.
5. For life insurance, the insured must have an insurable interest in the insured life at the time the contract is formed; for property insurance, the insured must have an insurable interest in the property at the time of property loss.

6. In most cases an insurance company cannot raise a warranty or representation as a defense unless the statement was material to its decision whether to issue the policy.
7. Insurance companies generally have the right to subrogation in property insurance policies but not in life insurance policies.

The following case illustrates the application of the legal rules regarding misrepresentation by an applicant for insurance.

VAUGHN v. AMERICAN NATIONAL INSURANCE COMPANY
543 P.2d 1404 (Okla. 1975)

Vaughn was named as the beneficiary on a life insurance policy obtained by her son Marvin. After Marvin's death in an automobile accident, the company refused coverage on the basis of misrepresentations in the application for insurance. Vaughn sued the insurance company and the company, in turn, sought to rescind the policy. The trial court held for the company, while the next higher court (Court of Appeals) held for Vaughn.

Lavender, J. . . . The application for insurance was taken from Marvin Vaughn October 19, 1971. American's agent filled in the application from information and answers to the questions given to the agent by Marvin Vaughn. Vaughn then signed the application. Material to this action are the following questions and answers. . . .

> 15. State name and address of family physician, specialist or clinic for principal proposed insured:
> Name: Dr. D.R.
> Address: 1217 N. Shartel, Oklahoma City
> Date last seen: May 1968
> Reason: Penicillin shot—flu . . .
> 19. Has any proposed insured . . .
> (f) Ever been under observation or treatment in any hospital, sanitarium, clinic, or rest home?
>
> Yes ( ) No (X)
>
> . . .
>
> (j) Consulted or been treated or examined by any physician or practitioner for any cause not previously mentioned in this application?
>
> Yes ( ) No (X)
>
> . . .

As a part of the application, a medical authorization (to receive any and all information about the applicant with reference to health and medical history and as to any hospitalization, advice, diagnosis, treatment, disease or ailment) was given by the applicant to the insurance company.

In an investigation by the insurer upon the filing of a claim under the policy by the beneficiary after her son's death, it was determined:

> The family physician, Dr. R., hospitalized deceased in Deaconess Hospital for "post natural gas inhalation" complications on June 6, 1967. That physician consulted with Dr. W., a psychiatrist. Deceased was transferred to the psychiatric ward at Baptist Hospital, where he was treated for depression until discharged by Dr. W. on June 24, 1967.

Because of these established facts, both the trial court and the Court of Appeals found the answers to questions 19(f) and (j) were false.

The Court of Appeals holds the insurer should be charged with knowledge of applicant's mental and emotional problems for it (1) knew the applicant had a family physician, (2) knew that physician's identity, and (3) had authority from the applicant to secure his medical information. That court excused the false answers because applicant had freely given his family physician's name in the application. The false answers are excused because the applicant was not familiar with the underwriting requirement of the defendant. He did not know what to reveal and what to conceal.

Under 36 O.S. 1971, section 3609 misrepresentations, omissions, concealment of facts, and incorrect statements in the application for insurance prevent recovery under the policy if (1) fraudulent; or (2) material to the acceptance of the risk; or (3) the insurer in good faith would not have issued the policy, or in as large an amount, if the true facts had been made known as required by the application.

In *Massachusetts Mutual Life Ins. Co. v. Allen* . . . (1965) this court said:

> A "misrepresentation" in negotiations for a life insurance policy under 36 O.S. 1961, section 3609, is a statement as a fact of something which is untrue, and which the insured knows or should know is untrue . . . and which has a tendency to mislead, where such misrepresentation is material to the risk.

The false information given by the applicant in the application of his not being hospitalized and of no consultation or treatment by a physician, except for flu, concealed from the insurer true facts. These true facts, if revealed, would have given the insurer knowledge requiring a prudent insurer to investigate and would have led to the discovery of applicant's prior emotional problems.

We hold that false information was a misrepresentation. That misrepresentation was material to the acceptance of the risk on the life of the applicant. The insurer is entitled to a judgment of rescission.

Questions and Case Problems

1. A home appliance service company sold plans to homeowners who were planning to sell their homes. Under the plans the company performed a check on the appliances in the home and agreed to repair the appliances during a one-year period if the home buyer experienced problems with them. Is this plan a contract of insurance? [78–20 Op. N.M. Att'y Gen. (October 4, 1978).]
2. Baum discussed forming a corporation with Cook and extended over $16,000 worth of credit to Cook. Baum purchased key man life insurance on Cook from New York Life Insurance Co. Shortly after issuance of the policy, Cook formed a corporation with someone else. Does Baum, who was not included in the corporation, have an insurable interest in Cook's life? [*New York Life Ins. Co. v. Baum,* 700 F.2d 928 (5th Cir. 1983).]
3. Because of poor health, Stefan and Justina transferred title to their residence to their son Stephen. They continued to reside in the house and insured the property with Excelsior Insurance Co. of New York. Stephen was not named in the insurance policy. When the house was damaged by fire, Excelsior claimed it was not liable because the parents had no insurable interest in the property. Is Excelsior correct? [*Etterle v. Excelsior Ins. Co. of N.Y.,* 428 N.Y.S.2d 95 (1980).]
4. Mary purchased an insurance policy on the life of her husband, Steve, in the amount of $600,000. Mary and Steve were later divorced, but Mary continued to pay premiums on the insurance policy. Later, when Steve died, the company refused to pay Mary on the grounds that (1) she had no insurable interest in Steve's life because of the divorce or (2) if she did have an insurable interest, its value was only $300,000 as determined by the size of Steve's alimony payments and his life expectancy. Is the company correct on either of these grounds? Why?
5. A husband and wife purchased a lot in a beach subdivision for $12,500. A street bordering the property gave the couple access to the lot. When they bought the property, the couple also obtained title insurance. After the purchase, they learned that their lot and the adjoining street are covered by high tide water every spring and

fall. Does title insurance cover their loss? Why? [*Title & Trust Co. of Fla. v. Barrows,* 381 So.2d 1088 (Fla. 1979).]

6. An automobile that had been stolen in Ohio was sold to an innocent purchaser in Alabama. The purchaser bought an automobile insurance policy on the car, including fire and theft coverage. The car was later stolen from the purchaser and was destroyed by fire. The insurance company claimed that the purchaser was not entitled to collect on the policy because he had no insurable interest in the car. Is the company correct? Why? [*Ex parte Granite State Ins. Co. v. Lowe,* 362 So.2d 240 (Ala. 1978).]
7. A couple acquired a residence. The deed to the property was in the husband's name. After his death, the widow purchased fire insurance on the residence, paid all taxes, and made necessary repairs. When the residence was destroyed by fire, the insurance company denied coverage on the grounds that the widow did not have an insurable interest in the property. Does the widow have an insurable interest? [*McElrath v. State Capital Ins. Co.,* 184 S.E.2d 912 (N.C. 1971).]
8. An insurance company issued a life insurance policy to a man who lied about his smoking in order to obtain lower premiums that were available to nonsmokers. After the insured's death, the company discovered the misrepresentation. May the company rescind the policy? [*Mutual Benefit Ins. Co. v. JMR Electronics Corp.,* 848 F.2d 30 (2d Cir. 1988).]
9. Arthur, in completing an insurance application, answered "no" to the following question: "Have you ever had or been told by a physician or other practitioner that you had . . . heart trouble?" In fact, Arthur had been told—and had been treated for a heart condition. When Arthur died, the company refused to pay the insurance proceeds to Arthur's widow. May the widow recover the proceeds? Why? [*Weeser v. Provident Mut. Life Ins. Co.,* 322 So.2d 230 (La. 1975).]
10. In the case of *Vaughn v. American National Insurance Company,* excerpted at the beginning of this section, would the decision have been different if the court had concluded that the applicant's answers in the application were warranties rather than representations? Why?

CHAPTER

54

LIFE, FIRE, AND AUTOMOBILE INSURANCE LAW

After you have read this chapter, you should be able to:

1. Describe the three most common types of life insurance and explain their coverages.
2. Discuss the legal effect of a conditional receipt.
3. Define the term "incontestability" as it is used in an insurance contract.
4. List the types of homeowner's insurance policy forms and explain their coverages.
5. Compare traditional and no-fault automobile insurance.

BUSINESS DECISIONS and the LAW

In discussing his insurance needs with an agent, Fred realizes that the three most important types of insurance are life insurance, fire insurance (which is purchased as part of a package known as homeowner's insurance), and automobile insurance. In reviewing his life, fire, and automobile coverage, Fred is confused by a number of concepts. For example, what is the difference between whole life and term insurance? What are the general rights of the beneficiaries named in his life insurance policies? What form of homeowner's insurance is best suited to Fred's needs? Is the liability coverage in his homeowner's policy adequate? Has he met the policy's coinsurance requirements? Should he include no-fault coverage in his automobile coverage? Why is it necessary for him to purchase uninsured motorist coverage? The answers to these and related questions are discussed in this chapter.

Life Insurance

► Types of Life Insurance

term insurance
Insurance sold for a specified time period, with no cash value

whole life insurance
Insurance for the entire life of the insured, with cash values that increase through the years

endowment insurance
Insurance that pays the policyholder a lump sum at a specified date

There are three general types of life insurance policies: term, whole life, and endowment. **Term insurance** is insurance sold for a specified time period. If the policyholder dies within the time period, the company will pay the face value of the policy. If the insured does not die within the term, the insurance terminates and the company usually has the right to keep all premiums—i.e., there is no cash value. Term policies are "level term" when the policy value remains the same throughout the life of the policy; they are "decreasing term" when the face value decreases as the policy termination date approaches. Term policies may also be convertible to whole life insurance or may include a right to renew the policy without proof of insurability. Term life insurance is especially popular with young married couples. It is the cheapest type of insurance and can provide insurance for a term long enough to cover the family in the event the breadwinner dies before the mortgage on the family home is paid off or before the children graduate from college or otherwise get started in life.

Whole life insurance (sometimes called straight life, ordinary life, or permanent life insurance) provides coverage throughout the life of the insured. Whole life insurance includes cash values that build up through the years. The policyholder is entitled to borrow money from the company up to the cash value or to turn in the policy to the insurance company for cash.

Endowment insurance is insurance that pays the policyholder a lump sum of money at a date specified in the policy. If the insured person dies before that date, the money is paid to the beneficiary at death. This typé of policy is popular with persons who will need a large sum of money at a future date—e.g., for college expenses or retirement. However, because of inflation, the money eventually received by the insured or the beneficiary may be inadequate to buy what it was originally expected to be able to buy.

An insurance policy might be a combination of some of the above three types of insurance. For instance, in recent years companies have developed "adjustable life" insurance that combines term and whole life insurance. With adjustable life, the amount of coverage and the premiums can be raised or lowered to meet changes in insurance needs resulting from births, deaths, marriages, and other events. For example, if a policyholder becomes a father, he might want to increase his term coverage but shorten the length of the term to reduce expenses. Or if the policyholder receives a substantial raise, he might want to convert his term policy to whole life which, although more expensive, can be cashed in at a later date.

► Settlement Options

When the insured party dies, the beneficiary might decide to receive a lump sum payment. However, most policies give the beneficiary at least three optional methods of settling with the company. First, the lump sum might be left on deposit, with the company to pay a specified annual interest rate. Second, the beneficiary might elect to receive periodic income from the proceeds for a specified number of years. Third, the beneficiary may elect to receive equal monthly payments for life.

► Conditional Receipts

There is often a time gap between the application for life insurance and the approval of the application by the insurer. This is because life insurance represents a long-term, potentially costly commitment on the part of the insurer, and the insurer will normally require the applicant to undergo a medical examination before approving the policy. However, most applicants want coverage during this time gap in the event that something should happen after the application date. And it is to the company's advantage to provide coverage during the gap as a means of preventing the applicant from having a change of mind. The **conditional receipt** has been developed to meet these needs.

conditional receipt

A receipt that provides an applicant for life insurance with temporary coverage until the application is approved by the company

Although conditional receipts vary in form,[1] the most common type of receipt provides that coverage is effective on the date of application unless the company determines that the applicant was not an acceptable or insurable risk according to company rules and standards on that date. If, under company rules and standards, the applicant is considered insurable, there is coverage even when the applicant dies before company approval of the policy.

Incontestability

Let us assume that Clyde purchased a life insurance policy naming his wife as beneficiary. Clyde died after the policy had been in effect for nine years. After his death the company refused coverage, claiming that Clyde had lied about his health on the application. The company's refusal obviously puts the beneficiary in a difficult position; it will be hard to prove what Clyde's health was nine years ago, and the person best able to testify, Clyde, is dead. To avoid undue burden on beneficiaries, state law usually requires insurance companies to include an **incontestability clause** in life insurance policies. This clause provides that the company may not contest the coverage, except for nonpayment of premiums, after the policy has been in effect for a stated time period, usually one or two years.

incontestability clause

A clause in a life insurance policy providing that the company may not contest coverage after the policy has been in effect for a stated time period

Suicide

Life insurance policies usually contain a clause stating that if the insured commits suicide within a certain period (e.g., two years) from the date the policy was issued, the company is not liable. Such clauses are upheld by the courts, which have decided that the public policy of enforcing the contract and providing for the beneficiary outweighs the public policy of discouraging suicide. Furthermore, when death occurs within the two-year period, there is a presumption that the death was not a suicide. In the following case it was held that suicide did not occur because the death was not intentional.

FACTS

A twenty-year-old Marine served in a fighter squadron as a radar technician. He was familiar with .45 calibre automatic pistols and had given instructions on their use. The Marine was a happy-go-lucky, cheerful person who sometimes tried to "shake up" his friends by placing a .45 to his head and pulling the trigger. One day when the Marine was apparently in good spirits, he suddenly put a pistol to his head, said "Here's to it" to a friend, and pulled the trigger. The gun fired, killing the Marine. Government Personnel Life Insurance Company, which insured him, claimed this was a suicide and refused to pay on the policy. The Marine's mother, the beneficiary under the policy, sued for the policy proceeds.

DECISION

Judgment for the beneficiary. The death is not a suicide. The company must prove that the death was intentional. The burden of proof was not met here.

Angelus v. Government Personnel Life Ins. Co., 321 P.2d 545 (Wash. 1958).

---

[1]See p. 1122, the Decision in *Prudential Ins. Co. of America v. Lamme* for a discussion of an "insurability" type receipt, which provides that coverage is effective as of a specified date provided that the company is satisfied that on that date the applicant was an insurable risk under the company's underwriting rules.

Beneficiaries

beneficiary
In insurance, the person designated in a life insurance policy to receive the death benefit

The **beneficiary** in an insurance policy is the person designated to receive the death benefit after the insured dies. Most policies provide for the designation of second beneficiaries, who will take the death benefit if the first beneficiary is not alive when the insured dies.

Although, as a general rule, contract rights of a third party beneficiary cannot be altered,[2] the insurance contract is an exception to this rule. In most policies the contract stipulates that the policy owner reserves the right to change the beneficiary and can do so by following a procedure set forth in the policy. The change of beneficiary is usually not effective unless the company records the change at its home office.

As a general rule under common law, a person will not be allowed to benefit from his or her own wrongful act. As applied to the insurance contract, this rule means that a beneficiary who murders the insured cannot recover on the insurance policy. If the killing is justifiable, however, such as when the beneficiary is acting in self defense, recovery will be allowed. This principle is illustrated by the following case.

FACTS

A wife was named as beneficiary on her husband's life insurance policy. One evening the husband arrived home drunk and proceeded to slap and kick her. She was afraid to leave because the couple's two young children were in the house and she was concerned about their safety. When the husband threatened to pistol whip and kill her, the wife shot and killed him. Is she entitled to the proceeds of the life insurance policy?

DECISION

The wife is entitled to the proceeds. In this case the beneficiary was acting in self-defense when she killed the insured.

Calaway v. Southern Farm Bureau Ins. Co., 619 S.W.2d 301 (Ark. 1981).

Homeowner's Insurance

The purchase of a house represents the largest investment ever made by most individuals. Consequently, it is extremely important that this investment is protected with the proper insurance coverage. Most homeowner's policies today represent a package of property and liability coverages.

Policy Forms

Four types of policy forms are commonly used today. The *Basic Form* provides protection for eleven types of perils, including fire,[3] windstorm, hail, explosion, and vandalism. The *Broad Form* policy, probably the most popular policy, adds coverage for five additional perils: (1) the weight of ice and snow, (2) the collapse of a building, (3) accidents from

[2]See Chapter 14.

[3]The term "fire" applies to a "hostile" fire, which is a fire burning in a place where it was *not* intended to burn. A fire in a place where it was intended to burn is a "friendly" fire (e.g., a fire set in a fireplace), which is not covered by the insurance policy.

steam or water systems, (4) accidents from electrical equipment, and (5) falling objects such as trees. The *Comprehensive Form* is "all-risk" coverage—that is, all perils are covered with very few exceptions, such as earthquake, tidal waves, war, and nuclear radiation. Finally, a *Special Form* provides Comprehensive Form coverage on the real estate and Broad Form coverage on personal property.

► Property Coverage

Three types of property are covered by a homeowner's policy. First, of course, the *dwelling* itself is protected from loss by the above perils. Second, *appurtenant structures* such as a garage or storage sheds are normally covered for an amount equal to ten percent of the coverage on the dwelling. Third, *personal property* such as furniture, clothing, and jewelry is normally covered up to an amount equal to 50 percent of the coverage on the dwelling.

In addition to these property coverages, the standard policy will provide an **additional living expense** in an amount up to 20 percent of the coverage on the dwelling. This is used to cover living expenses incurred by a homeowner who is forced to leave the home while repairs are being made.

additional living expense
A homeowner's insurance policy provision that covers living expenses incurred by a homeowner forced to leave the home while repairs are being made

► Liability Coverage

The standard homeowner's policy includes comprehensive **personal liability coverage.** Most individuals are protected under their automobile insurance policies if they injure someone while driving a car. However, many accidents are not caused by the use of an automobile. For example, if Sam is playing golf and hits another player with a ball, or if a visitor slips on the carpet in Sam's house, Sam might be liable for substantial damages. The personal liability coverage protects the homeowner in the event such claims are made.

personal liability coverage
A homeowner's insurance policy provision covering liability for accidents on or away from the insured property

As additional protection, the standard homeowner's policy will pay reasonable medical expenses to persons injured in the house or as a result of the insured's activities away from the house. For example, if Gloria slipped on the sidewalk when visiting Sam's house, the policy would pay Gloria's medical expenses up to a certain amount, even though Sam was not legally responsible for the accident.

There are important limitations on the liability coverage provided in most homeowner's policies. For example, liability coverage is limited to accidents. Thus there is no coverage when the insured intentionally injures someone. Another limitation is that there is generally no coverage for business pursuits. These limitations are illustrated by the following case.

FACTS

A lawyer and other members of his firm were sued for sexual harassment. The company that provided the lawyer's homeowner's insurance refused to defend him. Does the company owe a duty to defend the lawyer?

DECISION

There is no duty to defend. In this case the victim is alleging sexual harassment, which is not an "accident" but an intentional act that is not covered by the policy. Furthermore, the injury arose out of a business pursuit—the law practice.

Greenman v. Michigan Mutual Ins. Co., 433 N.W.2d 346 (Mich. 1988).

Exclusions

The standard homeowner's policy contains certain express exclusions from both property and liability coverage. Examples of exclusions from *property coverage* are losses resulting from volcanic eruptions, earthquakes, landslides, floods, and water that backs up through sewers. Exclusions from *liability coverage* include losses covered by workers' compensation laws; liability resulting from the use of aircraft, motor vehicles, and watercraft; and liability resulting from business pursuits.

In addition to the express exclusions from coverage, certain exceptions from coverage will be implied by the courts. A "friendly fire" exception occurred in the following case.

FACTS

Youse wrapped her star sapphire ring in a handkerchief and placed it on her dresser with some Kleenex tissue. Her maid later inadvertently threw the Kleenex and the handkerchief into a wastebasket. Another servant then emptied the wastebasket into a trash burner and burned the trash. The ring, which was later discovered in the trash burner, was damaged to the extent of $900. Youse claimed that her homeowner's policy, issued by Employers Fire Insurance Company, covered the loss because personal property was insured "against all direct loss or damage by fire." Judgment was rendered for Youse in the lower court, and the company appealed.

DECISION

Reversed, for the company. This loss is not covered. The policy's clause covering loss by fire means by a hostile fire. There is an implied exception in homeowner's policies for "friendly fires." Friendly fires are those lighted and contained in a usual place for fire such as a fireplace, an incinerator, or a trash burner. Here, the loss was caused by a friendly fire.

Youse v. Employers Fire Ins. Co., 238 P.2d 472 (Kan. 1951).

Replacement Cost or Coinsurance

Many homeowner's policies contain a provision that may trap an unsuspecting homeowner and result in a loss of thousands of dollars in coverage. This is a provision that requires a homeowner to carry insurance equal to a certain percentage (usually 80 percent) of the full replacement cost of the house. An owner who meets the 80 percent requirement is covered for the full cost of the replacement *up to the amount of coverage.* If the coverage is less than 80 percent, then the homeowner receives the larger of (1) the actual cash value of the part of the building damaged, or (2) the proportion of the replacement cost that the amount of insurance coverage bears to the required 80 percent of the full replacement cost.

To illustrate, assume that Betty purchases for $100,000 an old Victorian home that would cost $150,000 to replace. In order to save premiums, Betty purchased only $60,000 in coverage. If the roof of the house, which had an actual cash value of $1,000 but which would cost $4,000 to replace, is destroyed by fire, how much can Betty collect? Betty obviously has coverage less than 80 percent of the full replacement cost ($150,000) of the house. Therefore she can only recover the larger of (1) the actual cash value of the roof ($1,000), or (2) the proportion of the replacement cost ($4,000) that the insurance bears to 80 percent of the full replacement cost ($120,000). Thus Betty would recover only

$2,000, figured as follows: 60,000/120,000 × 4,000 = $2,000. She would have to pay the other $2,000 required to replace the roof out of her own pocket—i.e., she would become a "co-insurer" for part of the loss.

Automobile Insurance

Thousands of Americans are disabled or die in motor vehicle accidents each year. There are two basic automobile insurance mechanisms in our country to cover injuries and property damage resulting from such accidents: traditional automobile insurance and no-fault automobile insurance.

Traditional Automobile Insurance

Traditional automobile insurance is a package of four basic types of coverages. First, and probably most important, the policy provides **liability insurance,** which covers you for damages you might have to pay if you injure someone or damage someone's property in an automobile accident. In several states, financial responsibility laws require owners of automobiles to purchase liability insurance. The purpose of such laws is to protect the public from losses caused by motorists who are not financially responsible. Liability coverage insures not only the named insured and residents of the insured's household but also other persons using the automobile with the permission of the named insured. This coverage for "permittees" extends, in most states, to deviations from the permission granted, as illustrated by the following case.

automobile liability insurance
Insurance that covers a driver who injures someone, or damages someone's property, in an automobile accident

FACTS

Davis gave Self permission to drive the insured car. While driving the car on a highway, Self caused an accident. Davis's insurance company argued that Self had no coverage because Davis had given him permission to drive only a short distance on a country road, not on a highway. Is this a good argument?

DECISION

No. The insurance company is liable. Under the "initial permission" rule followed by most courts, if Self had permission to use the car initially, he is covered by the owner's policy regardless of how he later used the car.

Commercial Union Ins. Co. v. Johnson, 745 S.W.2d 589 (Ark. 1988).

The second basic coverage is for *medical payments,* including all reasonable expenses for medical, surgical, and hospital services incurred within one year from the date of the accident. Covered persons include the named insured, relatives, and guests riding in the automobile.

The third basic coverage provides insurance for *physical damage to the automobile.* Most automobile owners purchase two types of property insurance. **Collision insurance** pays for damage to the insured automobile when it is involved in a collision. **Comprehensive insurance** covers damage to the insured automobile resulting from causes other than collision, such as falling objects, fire, theft, explosion, earthquake, windstorm, hail, flood, or riot. Both collision and comprehensive insurance are often sold with a deductible for a specified amount, such as $100. This means that if there is

collision insurance
Insurance covering damage to the insured automobile resulting from a collision

comprehensive insurance
Insurance covering damage to the insured automobile resulting from causes other than collision

physical damage to the automobile, the owner pays the first $100 and the company pays losses above that amount.

uninsured motorist coverage
Insurance that pays all sums that the insured is entitled to recover when he or she is injured by an uninsured or a "hit and run" driver

The fourth and last type of basic coverage is **uninsured motorist coverage.** It is possible that the insured owner of an automobile, member of the insured's family, or guests in the automobile might be injured in an accident caused by a person who does not have liability insurance as required by law or who is a "hit and run" driver. In such cases uninsured motorist coverage pays all sums which the insured is entitled to recover for bodily injury caused by the accident. A "hit and run" accident is defined as one in which there is physical contact between the automobiles at the time of the accident and the identity of the other driver cannot be determined. In the following case no such physical contact occurred.

FACTS

An unidentified car stopped suddenly at an intersection. This caused the following car to stop abruptly and a motorcycle to run into the following car. The motorcycle was driven by Hensley, who claimed that he was entitled to recover under the uninsured motorist coverage in his insurance policy issued by Government Employees Insurance Company.

DECISION

Judgment for the insurance company. This was not a hit and run accident, and consequently the motorcyclist is not covered. There was no physical contact between the motorcycle and the unidentified first vehicle.

Hensley v. Government Employees Ins. Co., 340 So.2d 603 (La. 1976).

► No-Fault Automobile Insurance

No-fault automobile insurance has been enacted in one form or another in approximately half of the states and now covers over half the population of the United States. Since the first no-fault statute was enacted in Massachusetts, effective January 1, 1971, appellate courts in a number of states have approved the no-fault concept and have declared it to be constitutional.

The basic no-fault concept is simple, although the details may vary, depending on the state. No-fault, in essence, gives victims of automobile accidents the right to be paid by their own insurance policies for *personal injury,* no matter who caused the loss (personal injury protection). But no-fault laws also take away the right to sue the person who caused the accident. The net result is that to recover under no-fault you no longer must prove that another person is "at fault."

To illustrate no-fault, we might assume that twins, Jack and Jill, are involved in similar automobile accidents. In both cases the cars driven by Jack and Jill are rear-ended by careless drivers and their cars, each worth $10,000, are totally destroyed. Both Jack and Jill suffer broken right legs and their out-of-pocket losses total $4,000 for medical care and $3,000 in lost wages. The only difference is that Jack is injured in Detroit and, as a Michigan resident, is covered by the most liberal no-fault law in the United States. Jill, an Ohio resident, is injured a few miles south of Detroit in Toledo and is not covered by no-fault.

Under the Michigan no-fault system, victims of automobile accidents are entitled to recover from their own insurance companies all charges for medical and hospital care and lost wages for up to three years. In addition to this *required* coverage, drivers have the option, also available in states without no-fault, of purchasing collision coverage for their cars. In our case, Jack would immediately collect from his company $4,000 for medical care, $3,000 for lost wages and, if he had purchased enough optional collision coverage, $10,000 for the car.

But in no-fault states like Michigan, a victim cannot sue the person who caused the accident unless the damages are greater than the benefits provided under the law (or unless the victim dies, has bodily functions seriously impaired, or is seriously disfigured). Thus, in our case, Jack cannot sue the other driver and will receive no compensation for his pain and suffering. Also, if he has no collision coverage, he will recover nothing from the other driver for the damage to his car.

Jill, living in a state without no-fault, could recover the value of her car and at least part of the cost of medical care from her own insurance company if she had elected to include these coverages. But even if she had no insurance coverage, she could sue the other driver and might recover not only her out-of-pocket losses, but also a substantial amount for pain and suffering. According to one study, the amount paid in the average settlement is 2.4 times the amount of actual loss, or in this case $40,800.

Consequently, if neither Jack nor Jill had purchased collision coverage, Jack would be limited to a total of $7,000 under no-fault, which he can collect only from his own company, while Jill might recover $40,800 from the person who caused the accident.

However, is Jill really in a better position than Jack? Under the fault system, in order to recover from the other driver, Jill must prove that the other driver is at fault. If we assume that this can be proven, in many states Jill will still recover nothing if the other driver proves that Jill's own carelessness contributed in even a small way to the accident. Regardless of the final outcome, Jill will have to wait more than five years in some metropolitan areas for her case to come to trial, and in the meantime must pay her own bills. And, if Jill wins the case, it is possible that as much as 50 percent of her recovery will be used for attorney's fees and related costs. Considerations such as these have caused Congress and the states without no-fault to continue to debate as to whether no-fault systems should be adopted.

Some Trends in Insurance

In the business world there exists the potential for large, powerful organizations to take advantage of relatively powerless individuals. In these situations the law often serves as an equalizer and thus prevents, to a large extent, unethical behavior. For example, three trends have developed in recent years to protect insureds from companies that might attempt to insert "fine print" clauses in insurance contracts or that are tempted to act unfairly in paying claims and establishing rates.

First, state insurance commissioners in several states have adopted regulations requiring certain types of policies to be readable. For example, the purpose of the Pennsylvania regulation, Section 64.1, "is an auto insurance policy that is understandable to a person of average intelligence and education." To carry out this purpose, the regulations require the use of a certain size type, short sentences, and simple words.

Second, courts in several states have developed the doctrine of "reasonable expectations" to protect the insurance consumer. Under this rule, persons who have reasonable expectations that they are covered by an insurance policy will, in fact, be covered—even though they did not read the policy and the fine print of the policy denies coverage. This is illustrated in the following case.

FACTS

Richard applied for a $25,000 life insurance policy from Prudential Insurance Company of America. He completed the Part I non-medical portion of the application form and sent it, together with the first quarterly premium, to the company, which accepted them. The company then gave Richard a conditional receipt. Richard never completed the Part II medical information portion of the application to be supplied by the examining physician, and he did not appear for a required physical examination. He died from a heart attack about seven weeks after applying for the insurance. Prudential denied recovery on the grounds that the conditional receipt covered Richard only if he was an insurable risk, and he could not be considered insurable without a physical examination. Richard's widow sued the company for the policy proceeds.

DECISION

Judgment for the widow. Richard is covered. Although Prudential is correct under normal principles of contract law, the insurance contract (including the conditional receipt) is unique. Here Richard was covered because he had reason to believe that he was insured. If nothing is said about the complicated and legalistic phrasing of the receipt, and the agent accepts an application for insurance together with the first premium payment, the applicant has reason to believe that he is insured. Otherwise, he is deceived.

Prudential Ins. Co. of America v. Lamme, 425 P.2d 346 (Nev. 1967).

Third, courts in many states, led by California, have decided that insurance companies have a duty to act in good faith when dealing with insureds. Insurance companies that breach this duty are often required to pay millions of dollars in punitive damages.

Apart from these trends, many individuals and organizations today are discovering that liability insurance is unavailable or unaffordable. For several years, doctors and other professionals have had difficulty in obtaining insurance at affordable prices. Recently, however, insurance has also become a problem for many organizations in our society, ranging from large corporations to day care centers. For instance, with the erosion of the doctrine of sovereign immunity the number of lawsuits against government units (e.g., municipalities) and their insurance premiums have increased substantially. Individuals, likewise, have been affected by increasing insurance costs, notably in automobile insurance rates.

The cause of these insurance problems is uncertain. Some observers blame the insurance industry for manufacturing a crisis. Others blame the operation of the legal system, pointing especially to the contingent fee system and large punitive damage awards. Still others feel that the legal system is a positive factor in forcing defendants to exercise greater care. As some lawyers have put it, the cause of the malpractice insurance crisis is malpractice. Whatever the cause, it is likely that, in the long run, the solution will be political (legislative) rather than judicial in nature. For example, consumer groups in many states, following the lead of California, are advocating new laws that would require a reduction in automobile insurance rates. In 1989, the California Supreme Court upheld Proposition 103, a law that forced California automobile insurers to cut their rates by 20 percent.

Summary Statement

1. The three most common types of life insurance are term insurance, whole life insurance, and endowment insurance.
2. A conditional receipt is used to provide insurance coverage between the date of application and the date the company approves the policy, provided that the applicant was insurable on the application date.

3. The incontestability clause in life insurance policies prevents the company from contesting coverage after the policy has been in effect for a specified time, normally one or two years.
4. There are four common types of homeowner's insurance. The most popular type is the Broad Form, which provides coverage for sixteen specific perils.
5. Traditional automobile insurance is a package of four coverages: liability, medical payments, property, and uninsured motorist.
6. With no-fault automobile insurance, persons injured in automobile accidents are compensated by their own insurance companies and, in most cases, cannot sue the person who caused the accident.

The following case illustrates the problems faced by a person who is injured by an uninsured motorist—even when there is uninsured motorist coverage.

TAFT v. SWEENEY
373 A.2d 712 (N.J. 1977)

Taft was injured when his car collided with an automobile driven by Sweeney, who was negligent and driving under the influence of alcohol. Sweeney's liability policy provided only the minimal coverage required by law, $30,000. The value of Taft's injuries exceeded Sweeney's liability coverage. Taft claimed that he was entitled to use his uninsured motorists coverage for the excess.

Fundamental to the issue raised in this appeal is the meaning to be attributed to the word "uninsured" in N.J.S.A. 17:28–1.1 which sets forth the requirement for uninsured motorists coverage. It reads as follows:

> No automobile liability policy . . . of insurance . . . shall be issued in this State . . . unless it includes coverage, in limits for bodily injury or death as follows:
>
> a. an amount or limit of $15,000, exclusive of interest and costs, on account of injury to, or death of, one person, in any one accident . . .
>
> . . . for payment of all or part of the sums which the insured . . . shall be legally entitled to recover as damages from the operator or owner of an uninsured automobile, or hit and run automobile. . . . [Emphasis added.]

The coverage afforded by the policy in question is consistent with the foregoing statutory requirements. Hence, it is clear that coverage afforded is triggered by the insured's accident with an "uninsured" automobile.

This essential element of uninsured motorists coverage is not tainted by ambiguity. Such coverage becomes available only when the insured is injured by an uninsured motor vehicle or a hit and run automobile. Neither is involved in this case.

Defendant Sweeney was insured to the statutory minimum. Nothing in N.J.S.A. 17:28–1.1 suggests that UM coverage is to be made available as excess insurance whenever a liability policy, meeting the statutory minimum limits of coverage, proves an inadequate source of compensation to the injured insured. The essential requirement for such coverage is lack of insurance, not inadequate insurance.

Neither of the two cases cited by plaintiff supports his contentions. *Motor Club of America Ins. Co. v. Phillips* . . . held that a person injured by an uninsured motorist is entitled to UM coverage under more than one policy affording him such coverage. Basic to that holding, however, is the fact that the insured was injured by an uninsured motorist. In this case plaintiff's injuries were caused by an insured motorist. *Gorton v. Reliance Ins. Co.* . . . held that each of several injured plaintiffs could recover under his own uninsured motorists coverage the difference between the amounts received under the defendant['s] liability policy and the existing statutory limit for bodily injury or death. In this case, however, plaintiff has received the full statutory limit from Sweeney's liability carrier. Gorton has no application to this case.

The statutory scheme is clear. The Legislature intended . . . to guarantee to each person injured by an automobile in this State an available source of reparation for the injuries received up to the statutory minimum. . . . That goal has been achieved in this case.

[Judgment for the insurance company.]

Questions and Case Problems

1. Tom and Mary, a young married couple, have just purchased their first home after obtaining a 20-year mortgage from First Bank. Tom and Mary both work and need their incomes to make the mortgage payments. However, they are afraid that if one of them should die, the other would be unable to make the payments. What type of insurance protection would you recommend for Tom and Mary? Why?
2. An attorney represented an engineering company for a fee of $300 a month and was provided coverage under the company's group life insurance plan. Although the engineering company did not withhold taxes for the attorney and she was not listed on the payroll, the company did send a letter to the insurer listing her as an employee. However, the attorney did not meet the definition of employee within the policy because she was not employed on a full-time basis. The attorney died after the policy had been in effect for two years, and the insurer refused to pay the beneficiary. Must the insurer pay? Why? [*Bonitz v. Travelers Ins. Co.,* 372 N.E.2d 254 (Mass. 1978).]
3. Patch, as a hobby, repaired bicycles in his garage. He had never taken courses on repairing bicycles and did not stock bicycle parts or equipment. A person was injured on a bicycle repaired by Patch. Is Patch covered by his personal liability coverage or does this case fall within the "business pursuit" exclusion? [*Reinsurance Ass'n of Minnesota v. Patch,* 383 N.W.2d 708 (Minn. 1986).]
4. An insured owned a life insurance policy that named certain beneficiaries. The insured executed a will in which he provided that persons other than the named beneficiaries were to receive the insurance proceeds. He died the day after signing the will. Who should receive the proceeds—the beneficiaries named in the will or the beneficiaries named in the policy? [*Pena v. Salinas,* 536 S.W.2d 671 (Tex. 1976).]
5. A homeowner (with homeowner's liability insurance coverage) worked at a research center. One of his duties at the center was to take care of a wolf named Sophie and, in order to fulfill this duty, he kept Sophie at his home. One day while at the home Sophie bit a child. The insurance company claimed that the homeowner had no liability coverage for the bite. Is the company correct? Why? [*North River Ins. Co. v. Poos,* 553 S.W.2d 500 (Mo. 1977).]
6. Charlie's car would not start. He borrowed his friend Evelyn's car in order to charge the battery. While Charlie's battery was being charged through jumper cables attached to Evelyn's vehicle, the battery exploded and injured Charlie. Evelyn's insurance provides coverage for liability resulting from "ownership, maintenance and use" of her vehicle. Is Charlie entitled to recover damages from Evelyn's insurer? [*McNeill v. Maryland Ins. Guaranty Ass'n,* 427 A.2d 1056 (Md. 1981).]
7. William and Donald were guests at a party. William made a crude and insulting remark about Donald's wife. Donald struck William near his left eye, causing extensive damage that resulted in two sensitive eye operations and loss of vision. Is

Donald covered by his homeowner's policy for these injuries? [*Hartford Fire Ins. Co. v. Spreen,* 343 So.2d 649 (Fla. 1977).]

8. Sarchett was insured by Blue Shield of California. Blue Shield refused to pay for Sarchett's three-day stay in a hospital, claiming it was not medically necessary. When Sarchett protested, Blue Cross did not tell him that he had the right to arbitration, a right that was included in the insurance policy. Did Blue Cross violate its duty of good faith to Sarchett? [*Sarchett v. Blue Shield of Cal.,* 233 Cal. Rptr. 76 (Cal. 1987).]

9. Suzanne was driving her car west on a highway when an approaching car crossed the center line and forced her off the highway. She crashed into several trees and another automobile. The approaching car, which did not strike her car, did not stop and was not identified. Suzanne now claims that her own insurer must pay the damages, which she claimed were $27,500, under her uninsured motorist coverage. Is she correct? Why? [*Jett v. Doe,* 551 S.W.2d 221 (Ky. 1977).]

10. In the case of *Taft v. Sweeney,* excerpted at the beginning of this section, assume that four passengers riding with Taft were seriously injured in the accident along with Taft. Would Taft and the passengers be entitled to collect under Taft's uninsured motorist coverage? Why?

PART 10 SECURED TRANSACTIONS, BANKRUPTCY, AND INSURANCE

ETHICS AND BUSINESS LAW

Introduction

This end-of-part discussion, like the others in this book, is designed to encourage you to begin forming personal beliefs about what is right or wrong conduct in business. The discussion here builds on the material in the first end-of-part discussion; you may find it helpful to review that.

This material has several goals. The section that immediately follows is designed to help you see the range of ethical issues associated with this area of the law. The in-depth discussion is intended to provide you with a background for forming your own beliefs about a single very important ethical issue in business. The problems at the end of this part are designed to build your skill in ethical analysis while exploring further the in-depth issue.

A Sampling of Ethical Issues in Secured Transactions, Insurance, and Bankruptcy

One ethical issue is the extent to which unethical conduct by one party may justify another party in also engaging in unethical conduct. Often in business, one firm feels justified in engaging in unethical conduct because a competitor does it and failure to respond in kind will result in a loss of business. The right to repossess raises this same issue. UCC 9–503 allows creditors to repossess property without going to court if they do so without a "breach of peace." If repossession places persons in danger of physical harm, this would impose a burden on them that far exceeds the benefit to the repossessor and therefore would be illegal. But many repossessions involve some form of trickery. Often cars are repossessed late at night, by breaking into them and using a master key to start them and drive them away. In one case a "repo man" tricked the debtor into driving his car into a dealership to determine whether he was behind in his monthly payments. While the debtor was inside a dealership office, the car was taken and locked up in a storage area.

When the debtor sued the creditor for the tort of conversion, the judge concluded that the repossession had been in violation of UCC 9–503, stating that "to allow repossession in these circumstances would be to encourage practices abhorrent to society: fraud, trickery, chicanery, and subterfuge. . . ." Do you think unethical conduct on the part of someone else (such as a debtor failing to pay a just debt) is valid justification for you to engage in questionable conduct (such as repossessing with the use of trickery)?

Insurance raises a basic ethical issue: Should individuals be able to escape responsibility for their own behavior? Some forms of insurance have this effect. For example, workers' compensation insurance shifts the responsibility for a safe workplace away from the employer. When an injury occurs, the insurance pays rather than a negligent employer. Do you think it is right to allow people and organizations to escape personal responsibility through insurance?

Another insurance issue involves the ethics of adjusting rates for differing classes of risk. Thus most nondrinkers and nonsmokers can purchase life insurance at a discount because they have a lower risk of early death. Smoking and drinking are factors over which most potential insureds *have control.* And the lower insurance rates provide an incentive for healthy conduct. You probably think this type of rating is ethical.

In many other instances, individuals are rated on the basis of factors over which they have no control. Thus, if you applied for life insurance and disclosed that both of your parents and one brother died before age fifty, you would likely be declined or charged a very high rate. Do you think this type of rating is ethical?

A recent case in bankruptcy illustrates an ethical dilemma for the legal system. In the case *In re Graham, Debtor,* 21 B.R. 235 (Iowa, 1982), a radiologist, aged fifty-nine, who earned over $200,000 per year filed for voluntary bankruptcy under Chapter 7, showing debts of over $1,000,000. His nonexempt property was worth about $97,000. One of the unsecured creditors petitioned to convert the case from Chapter 7 to Chapter 11 to allow for repayment of the debts. The court denied the petition stating that Dr. Graham was entitled to make a fresh start and that society was better off by encouraging him to work rather than discouraging him by using his wages to fund a Chapter 11 plan. Do you think Chapter 7 was intended to help persons in Dr. Graham's position? Or do you think Dr. Graham was exploiting the legal system? If you were in Dr. Graham's position would you seek Chapter 7 or Chapter 11 protection?

In-Depth Discussion of a Basic Issue: Are People Only Economic Entities?

The issue addressed here is the moral status of other human beings and what this implies for the way the law and managers treat them. Stated another way, is it ethically right to treat others as exclusively economic entities?

► What the Law Implies

Clearly, the law recognizes that individuals are, at least in part, economic entities. Thus the law allows them to contract, to be financially liable for breach of contract, and to be obligated to financially compensate those whom they tortiously injure. In allowing individuals to give security interests in their property, and allowing that property to be repossessed and sold to satisfy the debt, the law again acknowledges that people are at least in part economic entities.

On the other hand, the law imposes limits on the economic injury that persons can be compelled to endure. For example, there are substantial procedural obstacles to collecting an unsecured debt. Thus the debtor must be sued and the debt proved in court before the available property can be seized and sold. Even when the unsecured debt has been proven in court, there are some items of the debtor's property, called *exempt property,* which are not available to satisfy the unpaid debt. The existence of the exempt property category suggests that the legal system places limits on the extent to which individuals can be treated as economic entities.

The whole idea of allowing an individual's debts to be forgiven without repayment (bankruptcy) again illustrates the law's conclusion that there are limits to the economic entity idea. The presence of an exempt property category for bankruptcy further reinforces this idea. In effect, the general thrust of this body of law is to allow persons to escape their economic obligation in order to preserve their human dignity.

In the following paragraphs we examine these concepts of exempt property and bankruptcy using the four styles of ethical reasoning. Our objective is to see the way these styles of ethical reasoning lead to differing conclusions about the ethical character of individuals.

► Egoism

For egoists, the moral worth of exempt property and forgiveness of legitimate debts varies, depending on the status of the individual egoist. Debtors evaluate these legal concepts as ethically good while creditors evaluate them as ethically bad.

Most fundamentally however, an egoist views all others as entities that only have value in proportion to the pleasure they generate for the egoist. This is almost the same as viewing persons exclusively as economic entities.

► Utilitarianism

At some times in history, debtors could be jailed for failure to repay their obligations. If such a severe penalty were to exist today, default on a debt would be a more rare event. Because of its rarity, the risks and expenses of lending money would be reduced. This is likely to lead to lower interest rates which affect the majority of persons positively. Consequently, a utilitarian could justify treating individuals as exclusively economic entities.

► Kantian Philosophy

This style of ethical reasoning accords distinctive status to individuals. Kant sees people as unique because of their capacity to engage in ethical reasoning. Therefore he concludes that we may never use persons "exclusively as a means to an end." Therefore the exclusively utilitarian approach to people—which, for example, treats the individual only as an economic entity—is in Kant's view ethically wrong.

► Religious Ethics

Religious persons reach a conclusion similar to Kant's, but for different reasons. This ethic generally sees humans as made in the image of God, possessing an eternal soul, and with God-given dominion over the other forms of life on the earth. Further, in many religious traditions, the poor occupy a status that entitles them to special treatment. Certainly this orientation would reject the conclusion that individuals can be exclusively economic entities.

Solving Ethics Problems

Like the other end-of-part discussions in this book, this one presents problems for you to consider. These problems have three goals. The first is to give you the opportunity to further explore the in-depth issue. The second goal is to give you experience in ethical reasoning about the law and about related management problems. The third goal is to let you see how thinking critically about the law can increase your ability to make ethical decisions. To facilitate this, the problems begin by asking you to analyze the law for its ethical content and then shift to looking at related problems in managerial ethics.

For a discussion of the ethical roles of markets and the law, and examples of the four styles of ethical reasoning—egoism, utilitarianism, Kant's philosophy, and religious ethics—read the business ethics material at the end of Part 1.

► Problems

1. Review the case of *In re Conard, Debtor* on p. 1095. There Conard filed for bankruptcy and sought relief from a student loan on the grounds of undue hardship. Try to assess the style of ethical reasoning implicit in portions of the Bankruptcy Code that exempt student loans from discharge and the section that allows discharge for undue hardship. Also try to compare the judge's style of reasoning along with that of Paul Conard.
2. You are a student just completing an undergraduate degree in business. You have a job offer from your father's firm for $24,000 per year, to begin in six months. During your years as a student, you incurred personal debts that require monthly payments of $750 per month. If you file bankruptcy, all of these debts will be forgiven. Ought you to do this? Why or why not?
3. Suppose you are a loan officer of a small bank in charge of small business loans. One of your borrowers is encountering severe financial difficulty. This person bought a franchised computer store in the mid-1980s and competition has, through no fault of the franchisee, made this business much less profitable than in the past. You have a security interest in all the store's inventory. The franchisee is in default and asking you for extra time to make up the past due amount. You judge that if you repossess the inventory and drive him out of business you will recover about 80 cents for every dollar loaned. On the other hand, if you wait you judge that there is a 25 percent chance he will turn the business around and you will collect both principal and interest; however there is a corresponding risk of 75 percent that he will still go under. If he does, you will collect only 60 cents on the dollar. In making your decision, should you consider the impact of this decision on the franchisee's personal life? If you think you should, how much weight should this be given? What would you do?
4. Suppose you have a subordinate who has worked for you for two years and has usually done a very good job. Currently this employee is going through a protracted, emotionally draining, divorce. As a consequence, his productivity has fallen dramatically. In thinking carefully you conclude that your department would be substantially ahead financially if you fired this employee and hired someone whose life is more stable. Should you fire and rehire? Why or why not?

PART 11

WILLS AND DECEDENTS' ESTATES, AND TRUSTS

55 WILLS AND DECEDENTS' ESTATES

General state statutory law concerning the transfer of property on death by will and by intestacy (without a will).

56 TRUSTS

The various kinds of trusts, particularly the express trust that is so widely used as a means of transferring property either during lifetime or by a will.

PREVIEW

The event of death has an immediate legal effect on the ownership of the decedent's property. In Chapter 55, the importance of making a will, the formal requisites of a will, beneficiaries, revocation of a will, proof of a will's validity (probate), and administration of the decedent's estate with and without a will are discussed.

Chapter 56 considers the trust as a legal device for the transfer of property, made either during lifetime or on death, to be administered for the benefit of a beneficiary. Various kinds of trusts are examined, especially the express trust, and their creation, administration, modification, and termination are discussed.

Business ethics as it relates to the text material in these chapters is considered at the end of the part.

C H A P T E R

55

WILLS AND DECEDENTS' ESTATES

After you have read this chapter, you should be able to:

1. Explain why a will is desirable.
2. Briefly discuss the Uniform Probate Code and where it differs from the non-Code general law.
3. Indicate which state has jurisdiction over a decedent's will and estate.
4. Enumerate and explain the usual requisites for making a will.
5. Describe who may be the beneficiary of a will.
6. Explain how a will may be revoked by the testator/testatrix and by operation of law.
7. Discuss what is meant by a codicil and its effect.
8. Briefly discuss the legal procedure to probate a will.
9. Explain the meaning and effect of intestacy on the transfer of a decedent's estate.
10. Explain how a decedent's estate is administered.

BUSINESS DECISIONS and the LAW

Peter Sterling is a forty-five-year-old businessman, married, with two children aged ten and twelve born of the marriage, and one adopted child aged eleven. Peter is deliberating on how his property would be distributed on his death in the event that he does or does not make a will. Consider the following possible scenarios and the legal effect of each one.

Peter decides to make a will. In order to save expense, he handwrites and signs a paper providing for the distribution of his house and personal property on his death. There are no witnesses to the signed writing. Will this be a valid will?

Peter consults with his lawyer and signs a writing prepared by the lawyer as his will. Can Peter's lawyer properly be one of the witnesses to Peter's will? Can Peter's wife properly be one of the witnesses to Peter's will and with what legal effect? Peter provides in his will that his wife and ten year-old child will not get any of Peter's property; what is the legal effect of this provision on Peter's death? Peter's cousin, Susan, urges Peter, while he is in failing health, to show his deep affection for Susan by making a new will, providing in it that all of his property is to go to Susan on Peter's death. He so provides in his new will; what is the legal effect of this provision on Peter's death? Peter later reflects on what he had done, and, his conscience hurting him, he tells his wife to go to his attorney's office and there obtain and destroy his new will, which she then does; what is the legal effect of this event?

Peter makes a valid will but later decides to leave certain items of furniture and personal jewelry to various people; he had not made any provision for these specific items in his will. He types and signs a paper expressing to whom those specific items should go on his death, and staples the paper to his will. On Peter's death are those named people entitled to the various articles referred to in the paper?

Peter and his wife make their separate wills, each leaving his or her property to the other. Both die simultaneously in an automobile accident. How will this circumstance affect distribution of their individual properties under their wills?

Peter wants to travel, so he executes a power of attorney naming his wife therein as the power-holder. Subsequently Peter becomes so physically ill that he is unable to administer his own affairs. Can his wife exercise this power? In addition, Peter decides that if he becomes terminally ill, he does not want any life-sustaining treatment. What should he do?

Peter decides not to make a will but, rather, to let the members of his family decide on the distribution of his property among themselves on his death. Peter dies. What legal rights does each member have to Peter's property?

Peter's wife dies, and Peter is named in her will as her personal representative. What should Peter do, and how quickly should he do it, as his wife's personal representative?

These are only some of the problems and questions that Peter may have to consider. Answers to many of them are discussed in this chapter.

Introduction

▶ Background

Like most persons, you desire to acquire and enjoy property during your lifetime, whether acquired by your own efforts or by inheriting from your parents or other persons. You also would probably like to leave some of your property to other persons on your death. Accordingly, it is of importance that you acquire some knowledge of the law by which your property will transfer on your death.

Persons may own **property** and dispose of it as they wish either during their lifetime (inter vivos—among living persons) or at the time of their death. Nevertheless the state is concerned and interested in seeing that, to a certain extent, various persons closely related to the decedent must not be overlooked (disinherited) by the decedent in the distribution of his or her property at the time of death. For example, states generally prohibit the decedent's disinheritance of his or her spouse. Accordingly, state **statutory** law governs the validity of the decedent's will and the distribution of the decedent's property.

property
A thing; also an interest or right in a thing

decedent
One who is dead

statute
Law created by a legislative body and approved by the executive

will
A formal document that governs the transfer of property at death

testator (testatrix)
A man (woman) who executes a will

Transfer of Property on Death A **will** is a formal document that governs the transfer of property at death. It is a testament to the decedent's intent to transfer the decedent's property on his or her death, often called a "testamentary disposition." The person executing a will is called a **testator** if a man and a **testatrix** if a woman. A person who executes a will dies "testate," and a person who dies without a will dies "intestate." A will provides not only for the transfer of property on death but for other matters that must be attended to, such as a designation of who is to represent the decedent in the administration of the decedent's estate or who is to be the **guardian** of the decedent's minor children. Also, the will may provide for a **trust,** called a "testamentary trust" because of its inclusion in the will, which is a legal device whereby legal title to property is held by one person (a trustee) for the benefit of a beneficiary. Unless otherwise indicated, use of the word "testator" or "testatrix" includes the other.

guardian
A person legally entrusted with the custody and/or the property of another

trust
A legal device whereby legal title to property is held by one person (a trustee) for the benefit of a beneficiary

► Uniform Probate Code

The Uniform Probate Code (UPC) was approved by the National Conference of Commissioners on Uniform State Laws and the American Bar Association in 1969. By 1989, the UPC was adopted by only fifteen states: Alaska, Arizona, Colorado, Florida, Hawaii, Kentucky, Idaho, Maine, Michigan, Minnesota, Montana, Nebraska, New Mexico, North Dakota, and Utah. Kentucky adopted only Article VII, Part 1. Because of such limited adoption, limited reference to the UPC will be made as the general non-UPC state law is discussed in this chapter. Its underlying purposes and policies are:[1]

1. to simplify and clarify the law concerning the affairs of decedents, missing persons, protected persons, minors, and incapacitated persons;
2. to discover and make effective the intent of a decedent in distribution of his property;
3. to promote a speedy and efficient system for liquidating the estate of the decedent and making distribution to his successors;
4. to facilitate use and enforcement of certain trusts;
5. to make uniform the law among the various jurisdictions.

The Will

► Formal Requisites

Generally, seven elements must be considered in making a will: the law applicable to wills; testamentary capacity; testamentary intent; the writing; the signature; attestation; and publication. There are also special types of will to be considered.

Law Applicable to Wills The statutory law of the state where the testator was **domiciled** at the time of death governs the making of his will. However, if the testator has a legal interest in land located in another state, then the law of the state where the land is located governs the validity of the will regarding the disposition of the land located there. Only the state's statutes determine the validity of the will and exact compliance with the statutes is necessary. UPC 2–506 makes an important change providing for a choice of law as to execution.[2]

domicile
The state in which a person has his or her permanent home, not merely a residence

---

[1]UPC 1–102(b).

[2]"A written will is valid if executed in compliance with Section 2–502 or 2–503 or if its execution complies with the law at the time of execution of the place where the will is executed, or of the law of the place where at the time of execution or at the time of death the testator is domiciled, has a place of abode or is a national." UPC 2–506.

Testamentary Capacity The testator must be of a minimum statutory age and must have testamentary capacity to make a will. In most states and under UPC 2–501, the legal age is eighteen years and the testator must be of "sound mind" *at the time the will is executed.* Generally, by sound mind is meant that the testator has sufficient mental capacity to make a will if he has the ability to know: that he is making a will to dispose of his property on his death; the nature and extent of his property; and the "natural objects of his bounty," namely members of his immediate family (e.g., spouse, children), and persons for whom he has affection. There is a legal presumption of testamentary capacity. Contestants who question the testator's testamentary capacity have the burden of proving that it did not exist *at the time of the will's execution.* A careful examination of all the facts becomes very important. In the following case, the court decided that the decedent had lucid moments when he had testamentary capacity.

FACTS

Ralph Mangan died August 22, 1972 at age 72, a widower with no children. On November 16, 1971 Ralph sustained a gunshot wound and was hospitalized until December 22, 1971 when he was removed to a nursing home. On February 26, 1972 he resided with his brother, Edward, the petitioner, until April 5, 1972 when he was hospitalized with a bleeding ulcer, arteriosclerotic cardiovascular disease and other secondary ailments. On May 9, 1972 Ralph returned to the nursing home, on June 6, 1972 he was adjudicated an incompetent, and he died while in the nursing home.

While in the nursing home from December 1971 to February 26, 1972, he executed a will on February 23, 1972. The will was filed for probate and is contested by the petitioner as invalid on the ground that Ralph lacked testamentary capacity, alleging that Ralph was thoroughly disoriented because of his advanced age, arteriosclerosis, and the trauma of the gunshot wound; and had devised property to a person he named as his nephew when there was no such nephew.

Witnesses testified that during Ralph's first stay in the hospital and later at the nursing home he was self-reliant and attended to all his business affairs even after the will was executed. At Ralph's request, his attorney had gone over the will in detail with Ralph. The attorney testified that Ralph was of sound and disposing mind, knew what he wanted and what the objects of his bounty were, mentioned dollar amounts and street addresses, and went over various names mentioning a number of nephews, cousins, and others.

Two physicians testified that at times Ralph was confused and disoriented as a result of cerebral arteriosclerosis and medication. They also testified that patients suffering from cerebral arteriosclerosis enjoy periods of lucidity, that Ralph was given a drug to improve his cerebral circulation, but they were unable to state with reasonable certainty that Ralph lacked testamentary capacity on February 23, 1972.

The lower court found that Ralph had testamentary capacity on February 23, 1972 and that the will was valid. Petitioner appealed.

DECISION

On appeal, affirmed. The physicians stated that patients suffering from cerebral arteriosclerosis enjoy periods of lucidity, that Ralph was given a drug to improve his cerebral circulation, and that they were unable to state with reasonable certainty that Ralph lacked testamentary capacity on February 23, 1972. Ralph's attorney gave evidence of Ralph's testamentary capacity at the time he executed the will. Ralph had many kinsmen, and he could have testamentary capacity without knowing whether all of them were alive and without remembering the names of all of his nephews.

Mangan v. Mangan, et al., 554 S.W.2d 418 (Mo. 1977).

Testamentary Intent The "will" is an expression of the testator's testamentary *intent* (will) to dispose of his property on his death. Testamentary capacity (ability) must be accompanied by this intent. The will must manifest in writing the testator's intent to make the writing his will in order to transfer his property as indicated in the writing. However, in case of ambiguity, extrinsic evidence is admissible to explain the intent of the testator. **Undue influence**[3] or fraud practiced on the testator, and sometimes the testator's mistake, invalidates the writing as an intent to make it his will. In the following case, the court held that there was no undue influence, because an illicit relationship did not constitute such undue activity as to unduly influence the testator in making his will.

undue influence
Unfair persuasion by one who, because of his or her relationship with another, dominates the other

FACTS

Mack Reed was a bachelor who died at age 74. He executed a will on June 30, 1964 leaving his real estate to Mary Shipp, as trustee, in trust for, and apportioned by description among, her three minor children; his household furnishings to his unmarried sisters, Lula and Bertha, with whom he lived; and the residue equally and directly to Mary's three children. Lula and her sister, Fannie, petitioners, contest the will, asserting that it is invalid because of undue influence exercised by Mary on Mack by being unduly active in and about the execution and preparation of the will. The lower court directed a verdict that there was no undue activity amounting to undue influence by Mary on Mack and that the will was valid. Petitioners claim that the will is invalid and appeal.

There was evidence that Mary and her husband, Cary, were neighbors of Mack while he was living with Lula and Bertha and they worked for Mack during the last 25 years of his life. Cary was usually not around. A neighbor witnessed Mary and Mack having sexual relations in the barn. They were together daily in the fields, in the truck going and coming from town, and at the livestock shows in towns nearby. Mack spent considerable time with Mary's children, carrying them in his arms when they were small, playing with them, buying for them, and referring to them as his children. Another witness testified that anybody who didn't know them would have thought that it was a man and wife and their children. Additional evidence was that Mary employed the attorney who drew Mack's will, she excluded persons from Mack during a trip with Mary to Andalusia that she arranged, and she concealed the making of the will.

DECISION

On appeal, affirmed. In order to raise a question of fact for the jury of undue influence affecting the validity of the will, the contestants must prove: (1) a confidential relationship; (2) a person must have been favored under the will or must have done something which causes people close to her (Mary) to be favored under the will; *and* (3) the favored beneficiary or someone else must have done and performed some undue activity in and about the procurement of the will....

There was sufficient evidence regarding (1) and (2). The only question is with regard to (3) as to whether an inference is raised by the evidence that Mary was "active" in and about the execution and preparation of the will, as undue activity is legally defined. The illicit relationship between the testator and Mary is insufficient of itself to prove undue influence. Additional evidence of the testator having made an unnatural disposition of his property as a result of restraint on the testator is evidence of undue influence. Undue influence must be such as, in some manner, to destroy the free agency of the testator, and to prevent the exercise of that discretion which the law requires a party should possess as essential to a valid testamentary disposition of his property.

---

[3]"A presumption of undue influence arises when it is shown that (1) a confidential or fiduciary relationship existed between the testator and the beneficiaries; (2) the beneficiary or beneficiaries were given a substantial bequest or devise; (3) the beneficiary or beneficiaries were active in procuring the execution of the will.... Nevertheless, the law does not ban as undue the natural influence of affection or attachment or the desire to gratify the wishes of one beloved or trusted by the testator,... and the fact that the testator made an unequal or even unjust distribution of his property does not of itself support an inference of undue influence. A man has the right to will his property to whomever he chooses, and the beneficiary in his will is not bound to account for the choice...." *Mangan v. Mangan et al.,* 554 S.W.2d 418 (Mo. 1977).

> No presumption of undue activity in the procurement of a will amounting to undue influence arises from the mere disposition by the testator of his property to these children whom he loved and treated as his own. This may have influenced him to provide for them; but *unduly influenced*, as that term is legally understood, is entirely another matter.
>
> *Reed and Simmons v. Shipp et al.*, 308 So.2d 705 (Ala. 1975).

nuncupative will
An oral will as permitted by statute

personal property (personalty)
A movable thing, along with interests and rights in the thing

holographic will
A will that is entirely in the testator's handwriting

The Writing The will need not be formal, as long as it substantially complies with the statutory requirements. Statutes require that, with one exception, the will must be in writing. The exception is the **nuncupative** (oral) **will,** which is subject to certain limitations. The testator's spoken words manifesting his intent to make them his will must be made during the testator's last sickness in his home or in the place where he died, his words must be published (spoken) to the requisite number of witnesses present as such at his request who must commit the testator's words to writing within a specified number of days thereafter. In this way, by the statute, soldiers in military service and sailors at sea can make nuncupative wills. Only **personal property** can be transferred by a nuncupative will.

If a will and its signature are entirely handwritten by the testator, it is called a **holographic will.** UPC 2–503 requires that the holographic will's "material provisions" and signature be made by the testator.

The will may be handwritten, typed, printed, in ink or pencil, or be a combination of these. It may consist of one or more pages as long as they are clearly designated as being part of the single instrument. Figure 55.1 shows an example of a will (short form). Also, in most states written papers not attached to the will and without the formal requisites of a will may be included as a part of the will if the will clearly and unambiguously identifies them and indicates an intention that they are to be a part of the will; and they are in existence at the time the will is executed. This doctrine is called "incorporation by reference."

However, under UPC 2–513, if the separate writing referred to in the will identifies certain *tangible personal property,* it may be "prepared before or after the execution of the will; it may be altered by the testator after its preparation." For example, the separate writing may list various items of property designating which items—for example, furniture, china, silverware, pictures—are to go to the various named persons. This is *not* incorporation by reference, which requires that a separate document *be in existence* at the time the will is executed and the document is not to identify certain tangible personal property. The following case involved a list of personal property referred to in the will.

FACTS

Marion Bentley Wall created a living trust which provided for the conveyances of certain personal property to trustees. The trust document referred to a list of personal assets to be attached to the trust document to effectuate the conveyance. The list was never attached. Marion also left a will which contained a provision disposing of assets by a separate writing. After Marion's death, a list disposing of personal property was found in the decedent's safe with both the trust and the will. When the will was probated, the question arose of whether the items in the list became assets of the trust or became assets of the estate under the will. The trial court held that they were assets of the estate under the separate writing provision of the will.

DECISION

On appeal, affirmed. The personal property passed under the separate writing provision of the will and became part of the decedent's estate.

Flagship Nat'l Bank of Boynton Beach v. Kelly, 516 So.2d 1067 (Fla. Dist. Ct. App. 1987).

FIGURE 55.1 **Will (Short Form)**

WILL

OF

PETER L. STERLING

I, Peter L. Sterling, of the County of Boulder and State of Colorado, make this my Will and revoke all previous Wills and Codicils made by me.

ARTICLE I

Statement of Family

My wife is Jane E. Sterling. Any reference in this Will to "my wife" is to her.

My children now living are:

Oscar E. Sterling	Born July 5, 1957
Ona E. Sterling	Born March 10, 1959
Rose E. Sterling	Born March 15, 1961

My Personal Representative may rely on such information above stated for any purpose. I intend the provisions of this Will to apply to such children as well as their descendants.

ARTICLE II

Payment of Charges

My Personal Representative shall pay all death taxes and other governmental charges payable by reason of my death on any property included in my estate for tax purposes, without contribution from any person and without apportionment. Further, my Personal Representative shall pay all expenses of my last illness, funeral expenses, expenses of administration of my estate and all of my legal debts and obligations from the assets of my estate.

(Continued)

The Signature The will must be "signed" by the testator, although in most states the testator's signature may be made for him by another person at the testator's request and direction and in his presence. The word "sign" is different from "subscribe," the latter word meaning that the signature must appear at the end of an instrument. In most states and under the UPC 2–502, the testator's signature may appear anywhere in the will; subscribing is not required. Any writing, initials, mark, print, or impression that the testator intends to be his signature is such.

FIGURE 55.1 (Continued)

ARTICLE III

Personal Representative

I appoint Oscar E. Sterling , as the Personal Representative of this Will and direct that he be permitted to qualify and serve as such Personal Representative without giving bond or surety on bond in such capacity. In the event said Oscar E. Sterling shall die, decline to serve, ceases to serve, refuses to serve for any reason whatsoever, or shall resign, then I appoint Jane E. Sterling as the successor Personal Representative of this Will and direct that she be permitted to qualify and serve as such successor Personal Representative without giving bond or surety on bond in such capacity.

ARTICLE IV

Disposition of Personal Effects

I give all my personal and household effects, including automobiles, and any insurance policies and claims under such policies covering such property, to my said wife , Jane E. Sterling , if she survives me by thirty (30) days, to be hers absolutely. In the event my said wife shall predecease me, then I give such property in substantially equal shares to my said children who so survive me. In the event a child shall predecease me leaving issue surviving me, then the share that would have been taken by such deceased child shall be distributed to his or her then living descendants, by representation. If a child shall predecease me leaving no issue, then the share that would have been taken by such deceased child shall be distributed in substantially equal shares to my then living descendants, by representation.

ARTICLE V

Disposition of Remainder of Estate

I hereby give the rest, residue and remainder of my estate to my said wife , Jane E. Sterling , if she survives me by thirty (30) days, to be hers absolutely. In the event my said wife shall not so survive me, then I give the rest, residue and remainder of my estate, in substantially equal shares, to my said children who so survive me. In the event a child shall predecease me leaving issue surviving me, then the share that would have been taken by such deceased child shall be distributed to his or her then living descendants, by representation. If a child shall predecease me leaving no issue, then the share that would have been taken by such deceased child shall be distributed in substantially equal shares to my then living descendants, by representation.

ARTICLE VI

Powers of Personal Representative

Whether or not I die a resident of Colorado, my Personal Representative shall have all the powers conferred upon fiduciaries by the Colorado Fiduciaries' Powers Act, as it exists at the time of the execution of this Will, which Act is incorporated in this Will by reference and notwithstanding the fact that the Act may subsequently be repealed or held to be invalid.

(Continued)

attest
To witness

Attestation and Publication In order to authenticate the signature as that of the testator, either made by him or acknowledged by him as his signature, the making of the signature must be witnessed (**attested**) by the required number of people at the testator's request, usually two and sometimes three depending on the state. UPC 2–502

FIGURE 55.1 **(Continued)**

ARTICLE VII

Unsupervised Administration

It is my intent that my estate not be subject to supervised administration and I, therefore, direct that such intent be followed unless changed circumstances occur which I could not have anticipated and which would require a supervised administration to protect the interests of my estate and its beneficiaries.

IN WITNESS WHEREOF, I, Peter L. Sterling, the Testator, sign my name to this instrument, consisting of four typewritten pages, this 3rd day of August, 1990, and being first duly sworn, do hereby declare [to the undersigned authority]* that I sign and execute this instrument as my last Will and that I sign it willingly, that I execute it as my free and voluntary act for the purposes therein expressed, and that I am eighteen years of age or older, of sound mind and under no constraint or undue influence.

Peter L. Sterling
TESTATOR

We, John Able, Joseph Byrnes and Susan Chadwick, the Witnesses, sign our names to this instrument, first being duly sworn, and do hereby declare [to the undersigned authority]* that the Testator signs and executes this instrument as his last Will and that he signs it willingly and that he executes this instrument as his free and voluntary act for the purposes therein expressed, and that each of us, at his request, in the presence and hearing of the Testator, hereby signs this Will as witness to the Testator signing, and that to the best of his/her knowledge, the Testator is eighteen years of age or older, of sound mind and under no constraint or undue influence, this 3rd day of August, 1990.

John Able
Witness
400-16th Street, Boulder, Colorado
Address

Joseph Byrnes
Witness
600 Cherry Lane, Boulder, Colorado
Address

Susan Chadwick
Witness
86 Baseline Road, Boulder, Colorado
Address

(*Continued*)

requires at least two witnesses. The witnesses must be competent to testify later to the occasion of the signing—that is, the circumstances at the time—the testamentary capacity, and the testamentary intent of the testator. They are to "sign" as witnesses, although their signatures usually occur at the end of the will. Generally, all of them do not have to be

FIGURE 55.1 **(Continued)**

STATE OF COLORADO)
) ss
COUNTY OF BOULDER)

Subscribed, sworn to and acknowledged before me by Peter L. Sterling, the Testator, and subscribed and sworn to before me by John Able, Joseph Byrnes, and Susan Chadwick, the Witnesses, this 3rd day of August, 1990.

WITNESS MY HAND AND OFFICIAL SEAL.

MY COMMISSION EXPIRES: ______________________

[SEAL] ______________________
NOTARY PUBLIC

***Note:** These words and phrases, and the notary form at the end, may be used in states which have adopted the Uniform Probate Code. The Code requires at least two witnesses. Examination should be made of the statutes in a particular state, whether or not it has adopted the Code, to see if an established statutory form of attestation clause is required.

present at the same time nor to sign as witnesses in each other's presence, although they usually do. While an attestation clause of what occurred is not required in most states nor under the UPC, it nevertheless usually appears in most wills. In most states and under the UPC 2–503, a holographic will does not require any witnesses. The testator is not required to make a "publication" (declaration) that the instrument is his will nor is he required to disclose the contents of the will to the witnesses.

In most states the fact that a person is an "interested party" under the will, namely a *direct* beneficiary, does not disqualify that person from being an attesting witness to the will. However, if that person's testimony as a witness is necessary to prove the will, in many if not most states that person loses his or her interest as a beneficiary *under the will,* but still has a right to any statutory intestate share due him or her as though there were no will at all. For example, if the testator's daughter is named as a beneficiary in the will and, as one of the two required witnesses her testimony is necessary to prove the will, the daughter will lose her beneficial share under the will but she may now inherit a statutory intestate share of her father's estate as though there were no will. A person with an *indirect* beneficial interest under a will is not an interested party,—for example, a member of an association that has been named as a beneficiary in a will. Under the UPC 2–505, any person may serve as an attesting witness without thereby invalidating the instrument as a will and without loss of his or her beneficial interest under the will.

Beneficiaries

A person who acquires as a gift property of a decedent on death is a "beneficiary." Personal property is "given" or "bequeathed" by a will to a beneficiary called a **legatee.** Real property is "devised" by a will to a beneficiary called a **devisee,** although under the UPC 1–201(7)(8), a **devise** and devisee are concerned with real *and* personal property. A "general legacy" is a gift out of the general assets of the estate; no specific property is indicated. For example, "I give and bequeath to my friend, John Smith, if he survives me, the sum of $10,000." A "specific legacy" is a gift of specific personal property. For example, "I give and bequeath to my husband, Peter Sterling, if he survives me, the Hammersmith shelf clock which I inherited from my mother."

legatee
The beneficiary of a testamentary gift of personal property

devise
A testamentary gift of real property

devisee
The beneficiary of a testamentary gift of real property

legacy
A testamentary gift of personal property

A named beneficiary may renounce his or her beneficial interest under the will, often either for tax purposes or in order to receive a greater share of the estate, sometimes called a "forced share." An example is a surviving spouse's election against the will. An illustration is if a surviving wife renounces a $10,000 **legacy** to her and demands one-half the $300,000 estate as her statutory forced share. Because of the state's concern that certain persons—for example, the spouse or a child of the decedent—not be disinherited by the decedent, statutes provide for limitations on such disinheritance and require that such persons have a right to a specified minimal share in the estate. Generally, a beneficiary who murders the decedent cannot receive any of the decedent's property under the will or by intestacy.

The beneficiary must survive the testator in order to take under the will on the testator's death. However, if the beneficiary predeceases the testator, under the common law the legacy "lapsed" or failed and the beneficiary did not receive the gift. But today, in states having "antilapse" statutes and under the UPC 2–605, the legacy does not lapse and the gift is distributed as provided by the statute.

If the beneficiary and the testator should die simultaneously because it cannot be determined who died first, under Section 1 of the Uniform Simultaneous Death Act as amended in 1953, each decedent is treated as having survived the other and the property of each is so distributed. However, under Section 2, if the will provided that the beneficiary *must* survive the testator and there is insufficient evidence that they died other than simultaneously, then the beneficiary is not presumed to have survived the testator. Illustrative of Section 1 is the following case.

FACTS

Roy and June Villwock, husband and wife, were critically injured but alive and conscious after an automobile accident on July 25, 1985, and were transported together to a hospital. June died in the hospital at 8:23 p.m. Dr. Kotila was in the ambulance where cardiopulmonary resuscitation (CPR) was administered to both. Upon arrival at the hospital, CPR begun by Dr. Kotila in the ambulance was continued and after an hour Dr. Kotila pronounced Roy dead at 8:34 p.m. At a probate hearing to determine the time of Roy's death, Dr. Kotila testified that Roy's heart and lung failure in the ambulance was irreversible despite efforts to revive him. By state statute such a condition meant the person was dead and hence that Roy died in the ambulance.

Hintz, Roy's daughter, contends that Dr. Kotila's testimony is contradictory and speculative and that, under the Uniform Simultaneous Death Act there is no sufficient evidence that Roy and June have died otherwise than simultaneously. Dr. Kotila has nine years experience in emergency room practice. The trial court accepted Dr. Kotila's testimony and found that Roy died in the ambulance while June was still alive. Hintz appealed.

DECISION

The deaths of Roy and June did not occur at the same time; June died at 8:23 p.m. and Roy at 8:34 p.m. Therefore the Simultaneous Death Act is inapplicable. Dr. Kotila offered explanations for the conflicts in his testimony. He said that his "original death pronouncement was not intended to preclude a reevaluation to establish death at an earlier time." Given the demands upon an emergency room physician in a time of crisis, it is not difficult to accept his explanation. Dr. Kotila also explained that CPR was continued for an hour or more to preclude any possibility of an erroneous judgment of death made in haste. This explanation is not incredible as a matter of law. The determination of credibility is the sole province of the trial court. Given the few minutes between Roy's cardiopulmonary failure and that suffered by June, the margin for error, when measured by time, is admittedly narrow. The narrow margin for error is no reason to reject the trial court's fact finding.

In re Estate of Roy Villwock, 418 N.W.2d 1 (Wis. Ct. App. 1987).

joint tenancy

A form of ownership of property by more than one person with the right of survivorship

testamentary trust

A trust created by the will of a decedent

Under Section 6 of the Act, the Act does not apply where, in the will, "provision is made for distribution of property different from the provisions of this Act, or where provision is made for a presumption as to survivorship that results in a distribution of property different from that here provided." Also, under Section 3 of the Act, if the parties hold title to property as **joint tenants** with the right of survivorship,—for example, husband and wife as joint tenants of their home—and there is insufficient evidence that they died other than simultaneously, then each party receives a pro rata share of the property. Thus if husband and wife are joint tenants, each receives one-half of the property as if the other spouse had survived.

If the will provides for a **testamentary trust,** the trust beneficiary must be definitely identified or can be identified within the period of the rule against perpetuities.[4]

► Revocation

Since a will speaks and is effective as of the time of the testator's death, it can be revoked (terminated) at any time prior to his death. Revocation may occur in two ways: by act of the testator or by operation of law.

By Act of the Testator The testator revokes his will when he properly expresses an intent that, from that moment, he no longer wants the instrument to be his will. State statutes prescribe the two ways by which such an intention of revocation can be

[4]See pp. 1060–61. For the rule against perpetuities, see pp. 1166.

expressed: (1) by the testator's subsequent writing expressly or impliedly manifesting an intent thereby to revoke his will; *and* (2) by the testator's physical act to the instrument with the intent thereby to revoke it as his will.

1. By a Subsequent Writing. In most states, the testator's subsequent written manifestation of revocation must have the same formality as that required for the execution of his will. A subsequent nuncupative will does not revoke a prior written will. The subsequent writing may be a new will. If the new will expressly states that it revokes a prior will, then the prior will is revoked. For example, "I hereby revoke all prior wills." The new will without such express words of revocation may impliedly revoke a prior will when its terms are contrary to those of a prior will.

   A subsequent writing may also be a **codicil,** which is a writing executed with the same formality as a will, expressly referring to a prior will, by its terms either partially revoking or adding to the prior will by making changes or additions to the will and thereby becoming a supplemental part of the will to the extent of such changes or additions, or entirely revoking the prior will. The codicil's wording determines its legal effect. Any proper subsequent writing of revocation may revoke a prior will and its later codicils.
2. By Act to the Instrument. Again, the testator's physical act of mutilating the will must be in exact compliance with the statute in order to effect a total or partial revocation of his will. The testator's act must be done with the intent thereby to revoke the will. The physical act may be by burning, tearing, cancelling, obliterating, or destroying the will. In the following unusual older case, selected for its excellent simplicity and directness, the court held that an attempt to destroy a will was not the same as actual destruction as required by the state statute.

codicil
A writing executed with the same formality as a will, expressly referring to a prior will, by its terms either partially revoking or adding to the prior will by making changes or additions to the will and thereby becoming a supplemental part of the will to the extent of such changes or additions, or entirely revoking the prior will

FACTS

J. T. Payne, the testator, executed his will on June 29, 1934, which was offered for probate after his death. A witness testified that: she, the testator and his wife were in a room in the testator's home during July 1934; the testator told his wife "I am going to get rid of this damn will right now"; he then threw the will into the fireplace where there were some live coals and he immediately turned around and walked out; the testator's wife jerked the will out of the fireplace; only one end of the will landed in the fire and the will was smoking on one end when the wife removed it from the fireplace; the wife put the will in her apron pocket and immediately left the room. Except for slight singeing of the edges of the will, not a single word was destroyed, obliterated, or even rendered obscure in the slightest degree.

The New York State statute provides that revocation of a will may be expressly effected by destruction or obliteration of it by the testator, or by someone else at his direction, with an intention to revoke it. The will is contested as invalid on the ground that the testator revoked the will offered for probate by throwing it into the fire with the intent thereby to revoke it. The lower court held that the will had been destroyed and, therefore, revoked. The proponent of the will made a motion for a new trial, which was denied. The proponent appealed.

DECISION

On appeal, judgment reversed, new trial ordered.

The will was never destroyed and, therefore, never revoked. The statute clearly requires two things for a testator's revocation of a will by his act to the document, namely his intent to revoke the will and actual destruction or obliteration of the will. Here, while the testator intended to revoke his will, no revocation occurred by his attempt to destroy it. An attempt to destroy would open wide the gate to fraud and defeat the wholesome purpose of the statute requiring these two things.

Payne v. Payne, 100 S.E.2d 450 (Ga. 1957).

The physical act may be performed by the testator or by someone *in his presence* and *by his direction*. In the absence of proof of the testator's intent to the contrary, it is presumed that the testator's physical act revoking the will was made with the intent thereby to revoke any codicils. Some states permit partial revocation of a will by the testator's physical act to the will, as by crossing out words or provisions in the will as long as the rest of the will makes sense and complies with the statute. However, nothing can be *added* without compliance with the formal requisites for making a will.

By Operation of Law After a testator has made his will, his circumstances may so change as to create a presumption that he impliedly no longer has an intention to have the entire instrument be his will or that a portion of his will no longer continue because of such change. The states and the UPC 2–508 differ on many points regarding the legal effect of some of these circumstances. A few of the more important circumstances and their legal effect will be briefly considered.

By statute in many states, the testator's marriage subsequent to his making his will revokes the will, unless the will expressed that it was made in contemplation of the subsequent marriage or the will made provision for the surviving spouse. Under the UPC 2–508, the subsequent marriage does not revoke the will; but if the testator, by will, does not make provision for his surviving spouse, under the UPC 2–301 the surviving spouse would take her *intestate share* as though the decedent had died without a will. Under that section, no change of circumstances other than a divorce or annulment revokes a will.

By statute in most states, the testator's divorce or annulment of his marriage occurring subsequent to his making his will does not revoke either his will or any provision therein for his surviving spouse. However, if the divorce or annulment provided for a property settlement, such provision would impliedly revoke only that portion of the will that made a gift for the surviving spouse.

By statute in most states and under the UPC 2–302, the birth of the married testator's child subsequent to his making a will does not revoke his will. By marriage a testator generally contemplates having a child from the marriage and, therefore, if his will does not provide for a later-born child it is implied that he did not intend to disinherit and exclude the child from sharing in his estate. Accordingly, the later-born child is not such a change in circumstances as to imply an intent by the testator to revoke his previous will when it did not provide for the child subsequently born of the marriage. However, public policy against disinheriting a later-born child because of the testator's failure to provide for the child in his will has caused the UPC 2–302 and most states by statute to provide that a later-born child will receive its intestate share as if there were no will. The testator can disinherit a later-born child, and if the will expressly so states or if it merely makes mention of a possible later-born child, this indicates that the testator contemplated such possible event and his implied intention, therefore, is to preclude any intestate share for the later-born child.

Probate, and Administration of the Decedent's Estate

probate

The procedure of proving to a proper court that an instrument is the will of a decedent

A decedent dies either with a will (testate) or without a will (intestate). If the decedent had executed an instrument that is alleged to be the decedent's will, then its validity as a will must be proved. This involves **probate** (proof). Whether the decedent died testate or intestate, the decedent's estate must be administered under the authority of a proper state court. Accordingly, we will first consider probate if the decedent died testate, then the effect of intestacy, and finally the administration of the decedent's estate.

Probate

Procedure Probate is the procedure of proving to a proper court that an instrument is the will of a decedent. An instrument can be effective as a will *only on the testator's death.* The instrument is submitted to the proper state court where it is subject to probate. This court is usually called a **probate court** or "surrogate court." The state in which the decedent was domiciled has jurisdiction over the will of the decedent and the decedent's property, except that if any of the decedent's real property is located in another state then the latter state has jurisdiction to determine the validity of the will to the extent of such real property. The will is probated in the probate court in the county where the decedent was domiciled (his or her permanent home). Once it is probated and found valid there, the probate is effective in all other states, except for real property in another state.

probate court
A court that has jurisdiction over the estate of a deceased person

The probate proceeding is begun by the filing of a petition for probate with the proper court by any interested party, usually the person who is named in the will as the personal representative desired by the decedent. All interested parties are notified of the proceeding.

The attesting (testifying) witnesses to the will testify under oath as to the execution of the will. If they are not available, or if the original of the will is lost or destroyed by other than the testator, statutes make special provision for probate under these circumstances by other evidence,—for example, the testimony of other people and proof of a copy of the alleged lost or destroyed will. When the instrument is approved by the court as being the last will and testament of the decedent, "letters of administration" or "letters testamentary" are issued by the court to the person named in the will as desired by the testator to be appointed by the court to represent the testator and administer his estate. The instrument can be contested as not being the will of the decedent, and if it is found to be invalid as a will and there is no other instrument proved as a valid will, then the decedent has died intestate.

In states where the UPC has been adopted, reference should be made to it because of its provision for flexibility in handling probate of decedents' estates.

Intestacy

Death without a will causes the decedent to die intestate. State statutes of "descent and distribution" specifically provide for the distribution of intestate property to persons according to their marital or blood relationship to the intestate. Persons who, by statute, are entitled to property not disposed of by a decedent's will are called **heirs.** The meaning is the same under the UPC 1–201(17).

heirs
Persons who, by statute, are entitled to property not disposed of by a decedent's will

With respect to a person's *marital* relationship with the intestate (as husband or wife), state statutes on descent and distribution differ. Generally, they provide that a surviving spouse will receive a fractional share of the intestate property, the extent of the share depending on whether or not there are surviving children and their number. If there are no surviving children, the surviving spouse usually takes the entire estate. The law in community property states[5] recognizes differences in the ownership and distribution on death of property of each spouse acquired before and after the marriage of the spouses.

With respect to a person's *blood* relationship with the intestate, the statutes of descent and distribution in the various states usually have a pattern of *first* applying a *descending*

[5]See pp. 405, 985–86.

line of inheritance and *then* an *ascending* line of inheritance for the purpose of intestate succession. Children of the intestate, irrespective of sex or age, are primary beneficiaries. If there is no surviving spouse and only one child and it survives the intestate, the child takes the entire estate. If there is no surviving spouse and more than one child and they all survive the intestate, they share equally. If there is no surviving spouse and more than one child but not all the children survive the intestate, then usually the children of those who predeceased the intestate share "by representation" taking the share of their deceased parent. For example, *A* has three children, *X, Y,* and *Z,* each having three children. *X* has *B, C,* and *D; Y* has *E, F,* and *G; Z* has *H, J,* and *K. A* dies and surviving are *X* and all his children, *Y* and all her children, and *H, J,* and *K. A*'s estate will be distributed one-third to *X,* one-third to *Y,* and one-ninth to each of *H, J, K.* If *X, Y,* and *Z* do not survive *A,* but all of their children survive *A,* in most states all of *A*'s grandchildren share **per capita** (by heads), and in other states they share **per stirpes** (by stocks, or by roots). Per capita means that all persons who stand in the same degree of relationship to the intestate share equally in the estate without consideration of any right of representation. Per stirpes means that the survivors of their parent represent their parent and take the parent's share in an intestate's estate by such representation for division among themselves.

per capita
"By heads"; all persons who stand in the same degree of relationship to the intestate share equally in the estate without consideration of any right of representation

per stirpes
"By stocks, or by roots"; the survivors of their parent represent their parent and take the parent's share in an intestate's estate by such representation for division among themselves

If there is no surviving spouse or children and no children of children, the line of succession cannot descend and it then ascends, usually beginning with surviving parents, then brothers and sisters, etc. Reference should be made to the particular state statutes for details.

▶ Administration of the Decedent's Estate

The Personal Representative

personal representative
A court-appointed person to represent a decedent and administer his or her estate

executor (executrix)
A court-appointed man (woman) designated in a decedent's will as the decedent's personal representative

administrator (administratrix) with the will annexed
A court-appointed man (woman), who was not designated in a decedent's will, who acts as the decedent's personal representative

administrator (administratrix)
A court-appointed man (woman) who acts as the intestate's personal representative

1. Appointment. The probate court will appoint a person to represent the decedent and to administer the decedent's estate, called the **personal representative.** This person has a variety of names in the absence of statute to the contrary depending on various circumstances. If the decedent died testate and designated such a person in his will, the court usually will appoint that person the **executor** (man) or **executrix** (woman) who therefore becomes the personal representative. If the will does not so designate any such person, or the person so designated is unavailable (for example, if that person has died, or refuses or is unqualified to be the personal representative), the court will appoint someone else as the personal representative, to be called an **administrator** (man) or **administratrix** (woman) **with the will annexed.** If the decedent died intestate, the court will appoint an **administrator** (man) or **administratrix** (woman). If the personal representative cannot complete his (her) duties, the court will appoint a new personal representative called an "administrator or administratrix de bonis non." While these terms refer to men and women, nevertheless often a legal entity other than an individual—for example, a bank—may become a personal representative, known as an "executor." Under the UPC 1–201(30) each of these persons is called a "personal representative." The UPC 1–201(29) defines a person as "an individual, a corporation, an organization, or other legal entity."
2. Responsibilities. The responsibility of the personal representative is to "administer" the decedent's estate in accordance with the legally valid directions as expressed by the testator in his will, or in accordance with the statute of descent and distribution with respect to an intestate estate. Briefly, this involves the collection of the decedent's property that forms the decedent's "estate", payment of claims against the

estate, and expeditious distribution of the remaining property as provided in the will or pursuant to the statute on descent and distribution. The personal representative must post a bond to assure that he or she properly carries out his or her responsibility, unless the will expressly waives the requirement of a bond. In the following case, the court held that executors will be surcharged (penalty charged) for their breach of duty for not distributing the estate promptly.

FACTS

Mrs. Katherine McCrea died testate on March 24, 1961. Her will divided her estate among six children: Katherine, William, Sarah, Elizabeth, Margaret, and John. Her will named as executors John, William and Sarah, all of whom were law school graduates. At her death Mrs. McCrea owned several farms. Some structures on the property were rental units, and others were converted into rental units by the executors. The will contains no authority to continue the operation of either the farms or the rental units, and the executors did not request permission to do so as required by state statute. Following Mrs. McCrea's death in 1961, John and William continued operation of the properties. Their law partnership used one building on the property as an office, and William lived in another building.

The executors made no attempt to file an account and wind up the estate for twelve years when, in late 1973, William filed his First Account. Katherine petitioned and the court removed the executors and substituted Farmers Trust Company. The Company filed its First Account requiring the law firm to pay rent for the premises occupied and requesting the imposition on the previous executors of a surcharge of 3.5 percent per year on the value of the property. The lower court approved of this Account and imposed the surcharge, except as to Sarah who relied solely on the advice of her brothers. Appeal is from the court's approval of this Account. Margaret died before these proceedings were begun.

The former executors claim that the lower court improperly imposed the surcharge, asserting that there was no loss to the estate and its beneficiaries since the real estate had appreciated in value since Mrs. McCrea's death from $39,000 to $218,000.

DECISION

On appeal, affirmed. An executor is required to exercise the same degree of judgment that a reasonable person would exercise in the management of his own estate. This duty includes the responsibility to distribute the estate promptly. If the executor breaches this duty, he may properly be surcharged for interest on the assets not expeditiously distributed.

The former executors, through their position of trust, took control of the farm operations and all the accompanying realty. They made no effort to distribute the estate promptly. They never petitioned the lower court to allow continued operation of the farming business. Instead they delayed the final settlement of the estate for twelve years, and allowed the property to remain unproductive. This delay is inexcusable, particularly in view of their legal training. This breach of duty has deprived one devisee, Margaret, who died before the proceedings began, of all benefits; it has deprived the others of their benefits until now. The increase in the value of real estate is not surprising. Nonetheless, the beneficiaries have been denied its beneficial enjoyment by this unwarranted delay.

In re McCrea, Deceased, 380 A.2d 773 (Pa. 1977).

In order to carry out this responsibility, the personal representative has many duties, a few of which are the following. The personal representative must exercise that degree of prudent care that a person in such a position is expected to exercise. Careful and accurate records of receipts and disbursements must be kept; all estate funds collected and placed in a safe depository; all proper claims against the estate paid; and the estate dealt with pursuant to the will's directions or as ordered by the court. The personal representative is personally liable for any contracts made in his or her own name as a contracting party that concern the administration of the estate. The personal representative has a right of reimbursement out of the estate for expenditures and of indemnity for loss sustained. In most states, in paying debts of the estate, the personal representative is to use first the estate personal property and then, if necessary, the estate real property as required by the will or pursuant to statute or court order.

When the statutory time has expired in which claims against the estate may be presented and after they have been paid, the personal representative must file with the court a final account of the administration of the estate. Proper notice of such filing must be given to all interested parties. After a court hearing, if all is proper the court will approve of the "final account," issue a "decree of final settlement," and order distribution of the property in the estate to the proper persons. After such distribution, the personal representative is discharged and the estate "closed."

The Living Will and the Durable Power of Attorney

State courts and legislatures throughout the United States are grappling with the highly controversial and complex problem of whether to permit termination of the use of extraordinary life support medical procedures and new technology to prolong the lives of persons who are either terminally ill or in a persistent comatose or vegetative state. An examination of various judicial decisions, medical journals, law reviews, and the *Report of the President's Commission for the Study of Ethical Problems in Medicine and Biomedical and Behavioral Research, Deciding to Forego Life-Sustaining Treatment* (1983), discloses that the courts, as well as society, are in conflict. The courts often distinguish between persons who are either terminally ill, or not terminally ill but in a persistent comatose vegetative state, who can continue to live temporarily or permanently by the use of such sustaining medical support systems and technology.

The basic problem is to ascertain the patient's intent as to health care concerning his or her person, particularly to reject such medical procedures and technology to sustain the patient's life. Preferably, the patient's manifestation of intent should be in writing either in the form of a so-called "living will" or a durable power of attorney for the patient's health care. The living will is the patient's instrument or declaration of his or her intent. However, the patient's durable power of attorney for health care is most preferred, as recommended by the 1983 President's Commission. A durable power of attorney is defined in the UPC 5–501 as a writing that "contains the words 'this Power of Attorney shall not be affected by the subsequent disability or incapacity of the principal' or similar words showing the intent of the principal that the authority conferred shall . . . continue beyond the principal's incapacity."

Taxes

Federal and state laws provide for the imposition of taxes on the transfer of property. Accordingly, the transfer of the property in a decedent's estate becomes subject to these tax laws. A federal "estate tax" is imposed *on the estate* depending on the net value of the estate. In contrast, in addition to the federal estate tax, most states impose an "inheritance tax" on the inheriting recipient measured by the value of the property inherited or by the recipient's blood or other relationship with the decedent. State inheritance tax statutes vary widely. The federal law provides for certain exemptions and tax credits to soften the estate tax bite.

Summary Statement

1. State statutory law governs the validity of a decedent's will and the distribution of a decedent's property.
2. The Uniform Probate Code has been adopted in a minority of states and seeks to simplify and make more effective the law concerning decedents' estates.
3. A testator (testatrix) must be of a minimum statutory age, and must have testamentary capacity to make a will, meaning he (she) must be of sound mind having the ability to know what he (she) is doing.
4. A will is an expression of the testator's testamentary intent to dispose of his property on his death.
5. A will must be in writing, except for nuncupative wills which can be made only under certain conditions and can dispose of only personal property.
6. A holographic will is entirely handwritten by the testator.
7. "Sign" is different from "subscribe"; in most states a will must be "signed."
8. A will must have the proper number of attesting witnesses, except for a holographic will for which attesting witnesses are not required.
9. A "direct" beneficiary is not disqualified from being an attesting witness, but the beneficiary *may* lose his or her beneficial interest under the will if the beneficiary's testimony is necessary to prove the will.
10. A beneficiary under a will may be a legatee of personal property and/or a devisee of real property.
11. A written will may be revoked by the act of the testator in a subsequent writing such as a new will or codicil, by his act to the instrument, by his subsequent marriage. A subsequent divorce or annulment of the marriage and a later-born child of the marriage do not revoke a prior will.
12. Probate of a will occurs in the state and county where the decedent was domiciled, except that the state where a decedent's real property is located has jurisdiction to determine the validity of a will regarding the disposition of the real property located there.
13. State statutes of descent and distribution govern the distribution of a decedent's intestate property according to a recipient's marital relationship to the decedent, or according to the recipient's blood relationship to the decedent per capita or per stirpes.
14. The personal representative appointed by the court may be an executor/executrix, administrator/administratrix, administrator/administratrix with the will annexed, or administrator/administratrix de bonis non. A legal entity other than an individual may become a personal representative.
15. The responsibility of the personal representative is to administer the decedent's estate, which involves the collection of the decedent's property, payment of claims against the estate, and proper distribution of the remaining property.
16. A decedent's estate is subject to the laws on federal estate taxes and state inheritance taxes.
17. The living will/durable power of attorney is used to determine a patient's intent concerning his or her health care to sustain life.

In this chapter we observed how important it is that a person have testamentary capacity in order to make a will. The following case illustrates the problem of three courts in determining whether the evidence established that the decedent lacked mental capacity to make a will.

HELLAMS v. ROSS
233 S.E.2d 98 (S.C. 1977)

Lewis, C. J. The issues involve the validity of the will of the late Marvin Robert Bass and, particularly, his testamentary capacity at the time he executed the instrument.

The testator died on March 9, 1975, leaving a will dated May 2, 1974 under which he devised all of his property to the Rabon Creek Baptist Church to the exclusion of his wife. He had no children.

The widow objected to the probate of the will upon the grounds that the testator lacked testamentary capacity to make it.... The Probate Court... admitted it to probate. However, upon appeal to the Circuit Court, a jury found that ... he did not have sufficient mental capacity to make a will on May 2, 1974....

At the trial the executor took the position that there was no evidence to sustain the conclusion that the deceased was mentally incompetent... at the time of the execution of the will and, accordingly, moved for a directed verdict in favor of the will upon that ground. This motion was refused.... This appeal by the executor is from the denial of the foregoing motion[s]. The charge that the lower court erred in denying the motion[s] for a directed verdict present[s] the sole issue of whether there was any evidence to support the finding of the jury that the testator lacked mental capacity to make a will....

It is conceded that the will was properly executed. The charge of testamentary incapacity was based upon allegations that the excessive use of alcohol and drugs had affected the testator's mental faculties. The testimony showed that the testator had been a heavy consumer of alcoholic beverages for a number of years. In fact, it is inferable that his consumption of intoxicating beverages had reached a point that he was an habitual drunkard; but the testimony shows conclusively that the testator was not under the influence of intoxicants on the date of execution of the will. The issue then is whether there was any evidence from which a reasonable inference could be drawn that the testator's intemperance had so affected his mental faculties as to render him incompetent to make a will even though he was not actually intoxicated at the time he executed it.

The burden of proof was upon the widow, as the contestant, to show a lack of mental capacity. This principle was more fully stated in...:

> It is the settled law of this state that when the formal execution of a will is admitted or proved, a prima facie case in favor of the will is made out, and that, as a general rule, the burden is then on the contestants to prove undue influence, incapacity or other basis of invalidation, and such burden remains upon the contestants throughout. In determining whether the contestants sustained such burden, the evidence has to be viewed in the light most favorable to the contestants.

The general principles governing the determination of testamentary capacity apply in cases where it is charged that the testator was affected by the use of alcohol or drugs. *Therefore, the capacity of the testator to make a will is tested by whether he (1) knew his estate, (2) knew the objects of his affections, and (3) knew to whom he wished to give his property....*

Since intoxication is a temporary condition, even an habitual drunkard is presumed to be competent, when sober, to make a will; and the person, who asserts that the excessive use of intoxicants rendered a testator incompetent to make a valid will, must affirmatively show either (1) that at the time the will was made the testator's use of intoxicants had so impaired or deranged his mind that he lacked testamentary capacity even when he was not under the immediate influence of intoxicants or (2) that he was in fact incompetent due to intoxication existing at the time of the making and execution of the will....

A careful review of the record convinces us that the evidence failed to show mental incapacity of the testator at the time the will was made.... There was no evidence of probative value that his drinking had produced a derangement of his mental faculties when he was not under the influence of intoxicants.

One of the witnesses to the will was dead, but the other two testified. One was the attorney who prepared and supervised the execution of the will and the other was the attorney's secretary. Both certified that the testator came to the attorney's office and requested that the will be prepared, giving directions as to the disposition to be made of his estate. These witnesses were positive in their testimony that the testator was sober, normal in his actions, and possessed of testamentary capacity when he signed the will.

We find no evidence of probative value to counter the positive testimony of the attesting witnesses that the testator was possessed of testamentary capacity when he signed the instrument. The lower court was therefore in error in refusing to grant appellant's motion for a directed verdict.

[The widow] argues, however, that the testimony of the lay or nonexpert witnesses, that testator was "unbalanced" and did not know "what he was doing" when he signed the will, presented a factual issue concerning the testator's mental competency and supports the jury's finding of incompetency. We disagree.

We follow the general rule which permits a nonexpert to "give his opinion concerning the mental condition of a testator when a proper foundation for such testimony is laid by proof of opportunity on his part to observe the testator and of the facts and circumstances upon which the opinion reasonably may be based." . . .

The nonexpert or lay testimony in this case was merely a general conclusion that the testator was "unbalanced" and did not know "what he was doing" based, not upon his condition at the time of the execution of the will, but, mainly, on the fact that he left the family no part of his estate. . . .

The fact alone that the testator disposed of property contrary to what others usually consider fair is not sufficient to declare his will void. "In the case of . . . we find: 'That a will is unjust to one's relations is no legal reason that it should be considered an irrational act. . . .' "

The judgment is accordingly reversed and the cause remanded to the lower court for entry of judgment in favor of the validity of the will.

Questions and Case Problems

1. Darrell Gentry served in the United States Army from 1952 to 1954, and again from 1956 to 1958, when he was discharged after six months' confinement in the psychiatric ward at Walter Reed Hospital. He was admitted to the Roseburg Veterans Administration Hospital in 1959.

In 1965 Darrell, while still a patient at this facility, was adjudicated incompetent to manage his own affairs by the circuit court of Douglas County, Oregon, and placed under guardianship, with Pioneer Trust Company named as guardian.

Dr. Esperson, the ward physician under whose care Darrell was placed while Darrell was at the Veterans Administration Hospital from 1967 to 1973, testified that Darrell suffered from a psychosis diagnosed as schizophrenia; that his mental illness was largely controllable by psychiatric medication; that he was generally lucid so long as he took his prescribed medication, but when allowed to leave the hospital for any extended period would stop taking his medicines and would shortly become psychotic and sometimes obstreperous; that he would then have to be returned to the hospital. The record shows that this pattern of behavior was repeated again and again almost from the beginning of Darrell's hospitalization at Roseburg until his death. Not infrequently Darrell would go AWOL from the hospital. Dr. Esperson expressed the opinion, however, that Darrell was mentally competent to execute a will if not in one of his deranged intervals, and that he was capable of executing the instant will.

In a letter received by Pioneer Trust Company September 29, 1969, three days before the challenged will was executed, Darrell wrote to Mr. E. E. Smith, a trust officer who was handling his financial affairs at Pioneer Trust Company, stating in part that "I want my mother to inherit my four or five thousand." This was reiterated by Darrell on other occasions, including in a letter to his mother postmarked October 6, 1969. In a letter dated September 30, 1969, apparently in response to the letter received from Darrell, Trust Officer Smith wrote Darrell informing him that if he was serious about having his estate go to his mother he should go to some attorney in Roseburg and have him prepare a valid will, taking care to inform the attorney that he was "living currently at the Veterans Administration Hospital at Roseburg."

The attorney who drafted the will, and who was an attesting witness, testified that Darrell came to him on October 2, 1969 apparently bearing the above described letter from Smith; that he, the attorney, spent approximately 25 to 30 minutes discussing the details with Darrell, including the nature and extent of his property, the persons who were the natural objects of his bounty and the effect of his will prior to drafting the will; that he, the attorney, was fully aware that Darrell was under guardianship; that notwithstanding Darrell appeared to be mentally competent when the will was executed. The attorney's secretary, however, had no specific recollection of Darrell or the circumstances.

The sole beneficiary under Darrell's will was his mother who, when requested by Darrell, came to his assistance when he had psychiatric or financial difficulties while out of the hospital or on furlough or AWOL. Darrell was divorced and the petitioner is Darrell's 22-year-old daughter who, after age 15, lived with her maternal grandparents. She rarely saw her father as she was growing up. Darrell's will was executed by him October 2, 1969. He died February 2, 1978.

The will is filed for probate and the petitioner contested the will on the ground that it was invalid because Darrell was mentally incompetent to make a will. You decide, explaining the reasons for your decision. [*In re Gentry, Deceased,* 573 P.2d 322 (Or. 1978).]

2. Victor and Agnes were very happily married and lived together for many years until Agnes died. They were childless, but Agnes had six brothers and sisters and many nieces and nephews. They owned two houses and a farm. Sandra Cook was Agnes' great niece, and Sandra and her family lived next door to Victor and Agnes in a house rented from them. In late 1974 or early 1975 Victor and Agnes gave a parcel of land to Sandra and they also loaned Sandra $20,000 for her to build a new house. Sandra was to pay $200 per month to Victor and Agnes on the loan.

When Agnes died May 2, 1976, Victor was in very poor health. Two weeks after Agnes' death Sandra and her family moved into Victor's home. A month later Victor's furniture was sold, and Victor, Sandra and her family moved into Sandra's new home on the farm now owned by Victor. While Victor was living with Sandra, it was agreed that Sandra would not make payments on the $20,000 loan and she discontinued these payments two months after Agnes' death. In late 1976 Sandra bought a new car and a Jeep with Victor's funds. She said Victor gave her the money because her Volkswagen was too small and the road to the house was impassable in the winter.

On December 22, 1976 Victor consulted an attorney about making a will, and a few days later he returned to the attorney's office and signed the will. Sandra accompanied Victor both times. On the second visit, she read the will to Victor, and he went into another room with two witnesses to sign it. The new will left his entire estate to Sandra. Victor and Agnes had executed previous wills on January 23, 1975, each will having the same provisions, each leaving his and her property to each other unless either predeceased the other, in which event the estate was to go to various individuals including some of Agnes' relatives. On leaving the attorney's office, Victor took home both the 1975 and 1976 wills and tore up the 1975 will before throwing it into the trash. He told Sandra that he was upset with his other relatives for trying to put him in a nursing home. Several parties testified that both Victor and Agnes had a severe aversion to living in a nursing home. Sandra admitted that she told Victor that others were going to put him in a nursing home; however, witnesses testified that they did not know of anyone who planned to do so.

In February of 1977, a guardianship hearing for Victor was held. At this hearing, Victor expressed his belief that the hearing was to put him into a nursing home. Dr. Jefferson Streepy admitted that he had told Sandra on September 30, 1977 that Victor should be put into a nursing home, but he did not recall any earlier conversations on the subject. Victor died February 2, 1978.

The 1976 will was filed for probate and the petitioners, interested parties, contested the will on the ground that it was invalid because of undue influence. You decide, explaining the reasons for your decision. [*Cook v. Loftus et al.,* 414 N.E.2d 581 (Ind. 1981).]

3. Hendrick Baarslag, Sr., executed his will in 1968 and died in 1972. The fourth paragraph of the will provided that the testator gave "the bulk of my property" to seven named "devisee-trustees" in an "unlimited trust" to be used "for certain purposes which are dear to my heart, and which are known to my Executor and the devisees-trustees hereinafter named, in accordance with oral and written directions that I have given to them. . . . [They] shall execute the wishes and purposes which I have in mind and with respect to which I have given written and oral instructions as guide lines to them." An undated document written in the testator's handwriting entitled "Guidelines for some persons named in My last will and testament" was found with the testator's will. The handwritten guidelines were in existence at the time the will was executed. The will was filed for probate and was valid, except that the fourth paragraph was challenged as being invalid and not admissible to probate. Does the fourth paragraph of the will incorporate by reference the handwritten guidelines and should that paragraph be admitted to probate? You decide, explaining the reasons for your decision. [*Baarslag, Jr., et al. v. Hawkins et al.,* 531 P.2d 1283 (Wash. 1975).]

4. Mrs. Bottoms died December 21, 1944. At her request an officer at the bank which was holding her securities prepared for her a living trust agreement and her will. The residuary clause in the will reads as follows: "I give, bequeath and devise to Texarkana National Bank of Texarkana, Texas, to be added to and become a part of, and subject to all the terms and conditions of living trust created by me under date of January 27th, 1944, all of my estate remaining after paying all debts legally chargeable to same, including fees to my executors." On January 27, 1944 Mrs. Bottoms appeared at the bank to sign both documents which were already prepared and on a table. She signed them in the presence of two witnesses, who were unable to say which document she signed first.

   The will of Mrs. Bottoms and the trust agreement were filed for probate. There is no objection to the validity of the will, but there is objection to the trust agreement being admitted to probate as a part of the will. You decide, explaining the reasons for your decision. [*Montgomery et al. v. Blankenship et al.,* 230 S.W.2d 51 (Ark. 1950).] (This older case is authoritative, highly respected by the courts, and cited in many of their case opinions.)

5. At his request, a will was prepared for Joseph McCready who was blind and a resident of a home for the blind. The occasion for his execution of the will at the home was supervised by an attorney who was an attesting witness. The attorney first read the will aloud to Joseph McCready in the presence of the two additional attesting witnesses. Joseph stated that the said will met with his approval and declared the instrument to be his will. With the assistance of one of the attesting witnesses, Joseph made a cross mark for his signature. This witness wrote on the instrument after the cross mark "(Joseph McCready) his mark by Lillian T. MacKinnon." At the request of Joseph and after the reading aloud of the attestation clause of the will (which recites the facts just stated) the three attesting witnesses signed their names in the presence of Joseph. Was the will duly executed? You decide, explaining the reasons for your decision. [*In re McCready, Deceased,* 369 N.Y.S.2d 325 (1975).]

6. Alvin L. Cooledge died April 22, 1984 leaving a will executed November 3, 1983. The portions of the will dealing with the disposition of assets consists of "FIRST," "SECOND," and "THIRD". The FIRST and SECOND portions gave and devised certain described property to named beneficiaries. The THIRD portion had detailed provisions with respect to how the University of Georgia would award scholarships but contained no words of conveyance to establish an intention to transfer property to the university in trust from which scholarships could be awarded. Subparagraphs (b) through (f) of paragraph THIRD set forth guidelines for granting the scholarships based on need and ability. Also, the will did not contain a residuary clause.

First Florida Bank, as personal representative of the estate, filed a petition for construction of the will. The testator's sister responded by contending that there was a partial intestacy because paragraph THIRD included no words of conveyance to establish an intention to transfer property and the will did not contain a valid residuary clause. The University of Georgia maintained that in construing the will as a whole, paragraph THIRD was a valid testamentary disposition of the residue of the testator's estate to the university for purposes of a scholarship fund.

Should the following testimony be admitted or excluded by the probate court?

An attorney testified that he had drawn a prior will which Mr. Cooledge had executed on December 14, 1982. The prior will was identical to the subject will except that it contained an additional $1,000 bequest in the second paragraph and limited the University of Georgia scholarships to the testator's relatives. The attorney testified that Mr. Cooledge intended for the gift to the university to be of the residue of his estate. A vice president of the university testified that Mr. Cooledge mailed him a copy of the prior will and told him that the trust would be funded with the "residual" of his estate and that such amount should be significant. In a letter to the university, the testator indicated his intention to "eliminate so-called 'family' in that he had hassles with a cousin and '[his]' sister." Several friends also testified that the testator had indicated that he wanted his estate which was not designated in the will to individual people to go to the University of Georgia. Numerous witnesses explained how Mr. Cooledge's lifestyle evidenced his unwavering support of the University of Georgia and its football program. Also, should the university be a beneficiary under paragraph THIRD? Explain the reasons for your two decisions. [*Wilson v. First Fla. Bank,* 498 So.2d 1290 (Fla. Dist. Ct. App. 1986).]

7. Explain what a codicil is and the reasons for making one.

8. H. Eugene Kraus, testator, executed two valid wills, one on August 11, 1964 and the other on November 7, 1973. On December 10, 1975 Eugene telephoned his attorney who had possession of the 1973 will and directed him to destroy the 1973 will immediately by tearing and discarding it. This was done. Eugene had told the attorney that he wanted a new will drawn by another attorney. Eugene died April 3, 1976 without making another will.

The 1964 will and a conformed copy of the 1973 will were filed for probate. Which of these two documents is Eugene's will? You decide, explaining the reasons for your decision. [*In re Kraus, Deceased,* 385 N.Y.S.2d 933 (1976).]

9. A. P. Allen's will devised the residue of his estate to his wife, Lucy K. Allen, "if she shall survive me" but "in the event my wife . . . dies prior to distribution of my estate, my estate shall be distributed to the persons named in Paragraph Fourth." A. P. Allen died on May 11, 1975 and Lucy was appointed as personal representative. The will was probated November 5, 1975, and on February 11, 1976, Lucy filed an inventory of assets, federal estate tax return, and Idaho Inheritance Tax Return. The federal tax return was audited in early 1977 and Lucy had extended negotiations with the IRS, a compromise being reached January 18, 1979 which resulted in the estate paying approximately $16,000 less in taxes than those initially incurred. Five days after the compromise, but before payment of interest on the tax deficiency was submitted to the IRS, Lucy died on January 23, 1979. The estate could not be properly closed until the federal and state taxes and interest thereon were paid. Lucy had refused to make distribution until those taxes were determined and paid. Distribution was made after Lucy's death. Boyd Allen, son and principal heir to Lucy's estate, claims that Lucy unreasonably delayed distribution pending the federal tax audit. Did she? You decide, explaining the reasons for your decision. [*Allen v. Shea,* 665 P.2d 1041 (Idaho 1983).]

10. The case of *Hellams v. Ross,* excerpted at the beginning of this section, dealt with a determination of whether or not the decedent had testamentary capacity under particular circumstances to make a will. Explain what you learned about testamentary capacity from the facts in that case.

CHAPTER 56

TRUSTS

After you have read this chapter, you should be able to:

1. Explain the trust concept.
2. Distinguish a trust from bailment, agency, and sale.
3. Enumerate the methods by which an express trust can be created.
4. Explain the importance and form of the settlor's manifestation in order to create an express trust.
5. Discuss the testamentary trust.
6. Explain the significance of the trust purpose.
7. Indicate what is meant by trust property and discuss the importance of its transfer to the trust.
8. Discuss who may be a trustee and who a beneficiary.
9. Explain the trustee's various duties to the beneficiary.
10. Discuss the trustee's powers.
11. Discuss the liability of the trustee and indicate how the beneficiary may limit or remove such liability.
12. Explain how a trust may be modified and terminated.
13. Describe a charitable trust.
14. Distinguish the express trust from resulting and constructive trusts.

BUSINESS DECISIONS and the LAW

Mary Todd, 58 years old and married, is a wealthy and very successful businesswoman. She lives with John, her invalid husband. Their two children are now adults and do not live with Mary and John. Mary is concerned about John's health and about her children's future. She wonders how she can safely invest a substantial part of her own property for their benefit. The following scenarios illustrate events that frequently occur in real life; each of these scenarios raises the question of whether a valid *inter vivos* trust has been created.

John suggested that Mary consider creating a trust of $400,000 of her funds for his benefit. Mary, feeling she could take care of John while she was alive, transferred $400,000 to her sister Dorothy to be held by her, invested, and accumulated for the benefit of John, effective on Mary's death when distribution was to be made to John as needed according to Dorothy's discretion.

Mary was also very much concerned about her older sister, Jane. Mary orally promised her brother, Frank, to create a trust of $100,000 for the benefit of Jane if Frank would be the trustee, manage the trust for Jane's benefit—services for which Mary would pay Frank $1,000 now and $3,000 a year for as long as the trust existed. Frank so promised, and Mary paid him $1,000. A week later, Mary learned that Jane planned to marry a man whom Mary despised, so Mary told Frank that she had changed her mind and did not want to create any such trust for Jane.

Mary also desired to create an inter vivos trust for their two children. She transferred to Chestnut Bank $200,000 and various promissory notes of third persons payable to her and indorsed by her together with a document signed by her which provided that the funds and notes were delivered to the bank in trust for their named children, the trust funds to be distributed pursuant to the terms in the document. Because Mary was concerned about the future behavior of their two children, she provided in the document that she reserved the power to revoke, modify, participate with the bank in the administration of the trust, and to retake the trust property, all within her sole and personal discretion.

The legal effects of Mary's actions are discussed in this chapter.

---

property
In trusts, an interest or right in a thing; not the thing itself

sale
The transfer "of title from seller to purchaser for a price" UCC 2–106(1)

bailment
A delivery of goods by a bailor to a bailee, which are to be returned to the bailor or as the bailor directs, in accordance with the bailment agreement

trust
A legal device whereby legal title to property is held by one person (a trustee) for the benefit of a beneficiary

trustee
A person who holds title to property in trust for the benefit of someone

beneficiary
A person who is to receive a benefit

fiduciary
A person with a duty to act primarily for the benefit of another

trust property
The property held in trust, sometimes called the "trust res"

Introduction

► Background

In the law of trusts, **property** is an interest or right in a thing; not the thing itself. For example, you may have title to, or the right to possess, a truck. Your title or right is property in the truck. Property may be transferred in many ways and for different purposes, as has been discussed in previous chapters in this book. In some instances you may wish to transfer the title to your property without any limitations on its use and on its later transferability, as by a **sale** of goods. On the other hand, you may wish to transfer only the right to possession, as by a **bailment.**

However, there are occasions when you would want to transfer the title to your property to a person to hold and administer the property for the benefit of someone who either is incapable of managing the property or who does not want to take the responsibility for managing it, as in the case possibly of your spouse or child. For example, *X* delivers property to *Y* to hold in trust for the benefit of *Z*, to distribute the income from the property to *Z* during *Z*'s lifetime and on *Z*'s death to transfer the property to *D*.

This is the trust concept, namely the transfer of the legal title to property to a person to hold for the benefit of someone who thereby acquires an "equitable interest"[1] in the property for what it produces or for its use in any other way. Possibly the outstanding characteristic of a trust is its flexibility of suitability for a variety of purposes. It is necessary that *both* the legal title to the property *and* the beneficial interest in the property be transferred to create a trust.

A **trust** is a legal device whereby legal title to property is held by one person (a **trustee**) for the benefit of a **beneficiary,** usually another person. A beneficiary is a person who is to receive a benefit. A **fiduciary** relationship exists between the trustee and the beneficiary in that the trustee has the duty to administer the trust property solely for the benefit of the beneficiary. The trustee has the power to transfer the **trust property** (the property held in trust) in order to carry out the requirements of the trust. The trust is a legal entity administered by the trustee. It is for this reason that a trust is often created in order to shift property out of the owner into a trust when the tax on the income from the trust property will be less than if the property had remained in the original owner.

---

[1]Principles of equity are applicable to an interest in trust property.

Trust Distinguished A trust is easily distinguished from other legal relationships by considering the various characteristics of a trust. A trust may be of real or personal property. Legal title to the trust property passes to the trustee. The trustee is not subject to anyone's control. Death of the trustee or beneficiary ordinarily does not terminate the trust. There is a fiduciary relationship between the trustee and the beneficiary. The trustee cannot subject the beneficiary to liability to third persons. The beneficiary has an equitable interest in the trust property in that the property is to be administered in accordance with the terms of the trust solely for the benefit of the beneficiary. The trustee is governed by the terms of the trust.

In contrast, a bailment involves only goods, and only the right to possession is transferred to the bailee. There is no separation of the legal (e.g., title) and equitable interests. In agency, the agent usually has only possession of some thing for the principal, is subject to the control of the principal, can subject the principal to liability to third persons, and the agent's death terminates the agency relationship. A sale may be of real or personal property. However, in a sale of either kind of property the legal title is transferred from the seller to the buyer without any responsibility in the buyer to hold the property for anyone else's benefit. There are other legal relationships from which a trust can be easily distinguished.[2]

The subject of trusts deals with various kinds of trust, which can be classified as the express trust, the resulting trust, and the constructive trust. Although the charitable trust is very much like the express trust, it will be considered separately. We will first consider the commonly used express trust, and conclude with a brief examination of the charitable trust, the resulting trust, and the constructive trust, in that order.

The Express Trust

► Creation of an Express Trust

Methods of Creation The Restatement (Second) of Trusts, Section 17, describes various ways by which an **express trust** may be created:

express trust
A fiduciary relationship between persons in connection with property whereby one person called the "settlor" by his or her manifestation of intention causes property to be held by a person called the "trustee" for the benefit of a person called a "beneficiary" or *"cestui que trust,"* the trustee being under a duty so to deal with the property

> A trust may be created by
>
> **(a)** a declaration by the owner of property that he holds it as trustee for another person; or
> **(b)** a transfer *inter vivos* by the owner of property to another person as trustee for the transferor or for a third person; or
> **(c)** a transfer by will by the owner of property to another person as trustee for a third person; or
> **(d)** an appointment by one person having a power of appointment to another person as trustee for the donee of the power or for a third person;[3] or
> **(e)** a promise by one person to another person whose rights thereunder are to be held in trust for a third person.

---

[2]See Restatement (Second) of Trusts, 1959, secs. 5–16C.

[3]For example, *W* conveys land to *X* for *X*'s life, the remainder to be determined by *X*. *X* creates a trust of the remainder for the benefit of *Z*, naming *Y* as trustee.

settlor
The person who has created an express trust

inter vivos
Among living persons

Settlor's Capacity An express trust is created by a **settlor**—the person who settles the trust. While a trust may be created in the above five ways, the settlor must have the legal capacity to create the trust. With respect to (a) and (b) above, the settlor must have legal capacity to transfer the property to another living person (**inter vivos**). With respect to (c) above, the settlor must have legal capacity to transfer the property by will, which means that the settlor must have testamentary capacity, discussed previously in Chapter 55, under Wills and Decedents' Estates. (See p. 1136.) With respect to (d) above, the person with the power of appointment must have the legal capacity to make the appointment. For example, *X* transfers property to *Y* in trust for *Y* to receive the income therefrom for *Y*'s life, with power in *Y* to appoint how the property is to go on *Y*'s death. *Y* has legal capacity and can appoint *Z* as trustee of a trust for the benefit of beneficiaries designated by *Y*. With respect to (e) above, the contracting promisor must have the legal capacity to make a contract so that his or her promise to transfer property in trust is enforceable by the promisee who holds this contract right in trust for the benefit of the beneficiary. For example, *X* is contractually bound to *Y* on *X*'s promise to pay *Y* $25,000 as trustee for *Z*. *Y* holds this contract right against *X* in trust for *Z*.

The settlor must not be under any disability, such as incompetency or intoxication. Also, the inducement to create a trust by illegal or improper conduct (e.g., duress, fraud, undue influence) on the part of the trustee, beneficiary, or anyone else may prevent creation of a trust because the transaction then was made involuntarily.

Usually, a person is presumed to be competent with mental capacity to create a trust, and persons who assert incompetency have the burden of proving it. Once incompetency is established, the burden of proving competency shifts to those persons who assert competency during a brief interval by clear and convincing evidence and that a trust was created during that brief, lucid interval. Mental capacity is best determined by a person's spoken words, acts, and conduct at a particular point in time. It has long been basic law that persons who challenge the presumed mental competency of a settlor to create an inter vivos trust have the burden of proving that the settlor was incompetent at the time he or she executed the inter vivos trust instruments.[4]

Settlor's Intent The settlor must manifest an intention to create a trust. The express, inter vivos trust *must come into existence at the time of the manifestation,* not in the future. The manifestation must indicate an intent to impose legally enforceable duties on the trustee. Words suggesting, hoping, or wishing that the transferee of the property to be held in trust will use the property for the benefit of someone, leaving it to the discretion of the transferee, do not impose legally enforceable duties on the transferee. Such words are called "precatory" words.

Form of the Settlor's Manifestation The settlor's manifestation of an intent thereby to create a trust may be by the settlor's spoken or written words or conduct and may be in any form, in the absence of statute to the contrary. The word "trust" need not be used, although use of the word does not of itself establish a trust; other elements are necessary—for example, the transfer of trust property and identifiable beneficiaries. This is illustrated in the following case.

[4]See *American Trust Co. v. Dixon, et al.*, 78 P.2d 449 (Cal. 1938).

FACTS

Thorvald K. Laursen (T.K.) by deed conveyed real property to his son, Orville, who on the same day signed and delivered to T.K.'s attorney his following affidavit:

> The undersigned acknowledges that as of this date his father, T. K. Laursen, did by written Deed convey certain property to him to be held by him in Trust for the said T. K. Laursen (a copy of said Deed is attached hereto). Undersigned covenants and agrees that all income from such properties shall belong to T. K. Laursen and that he, the **affiant**, will re-convey the property to T. K. Laursen at any time the said T. K. Laursen requests and that if the said T. K. Laursen should die while the property is still in the name of affiant such property shall be considered as an asset of T. K. Laursen's estate and be disposed of in accordance with T. K. Laursen's Will.

McCaffrey, as conservator of T.K.'s estate, contended that Orville was trustee of T.K.'s property and sued to recover from Orville title to the real property and to obtain an accounting for the income from the property. Orville contended that there is not evidence that a trust existed and testified: that he believed T.K. deeded the property to him because T.K. wanted someone to take care of the property and to take care of him; that T.K. wanted to make it more difficult for his wife to get the property in T.K.'s upcoming divorce action; and that T.K. deeded the property to him for estate planning purposes. The trial court held that the property was held in trust and ordered accounting and reconveyance of the property. Orville appealed.

DECISION

Affirmed on appeal. Orville is a trustee. He was entrusted with the property of T.K. Orville's affidavit proves that Orville accepted the deed from his father with the intent of holding the property for the benefit of his father. He promised to convey the property to T.K. on request or to T.K.'s estate if T.K. should die without demanding its return. These promises show Orville's intent to act as trustee for his father's property. His testimony is consistent with the affidavit. The Montana statute on creation of a trust has been complied with by T.K.'s *act* indicating with reasonable certainty his intention to create a trust, and Orville's acts indicating with reasonable certainty his acceptance of the trust.

McCaffrey v. Laursen, 697 P.2d 103 (Mont. 1985).

affiant
The person who makes and signs an affidavit

A statute may require the settlor's manifestation of intent to be proved by a proper writing because the trust property is an interest in land or the trust is being created by a will. Most states have a statute of frauds, which is a statute requiring such written proof in these instances. Without such written proof there is no trust.

With respect to an interest in land, the owner of the interest can create a trust by transferring the interest to another person as trustee, or the owner may name himself or herself as trustee. If the owner transfers the interest inter vivos to another person in trust, the memorandum evidencing and thereby proving the trust must be signed either by the *owner* at or prior to the transfer, or by the *transferee* at or prior to the transfer or after the transfer but before he or she has transferred the interest to a third person. If the owner of the interest declares himself or herself the trustee of the interest, the memorandum evidencing and thereby proving the trust must be signed by the *owner* either prior to or at the time of the owner's declaration (i.e., manifestation) of trust, or after the declaration but before he or she has transferred his or her interest. A lease of land is an interest in land.

A will is a testamentary disposition and may provide for a trust, called a **testamentary trust.** (See Chapter 55 for a discussion of wills.) Inasmuch as a will is ineffective until the death of the testator (the person who made the will), the trust cannot come into existence until the death of the testator. Since the trust is provided for in the will, the will

testamentary trust
A trust created by the will of a decedent

must be a valid will complying with the law of the testator's domicile, or with the law in the state where the testator's real property is located.

A will creating a trust must be in writing, signed by the testator, and attested to by witnesses, effective on the testator's death. An inter vivos trust can take effect only *prior* to the settlor's death. If property is transferred in trust by the transferor during his or her lifetime but the trust is to *take effect* only on the transferor's death, there is no trust inter vivos nor any trust on his or her death because it is an attempted testamentary disposition that has not complied with the requirements of being a will. To have a testamentary trust, the testator must have manifested *in the will* his intent to create a trust in the will and designated the trust property; and the beneficiaries and the trust purposes must be capable of being identified from the will. The testator may, by his will, add ("pour over") property into an inter vivos trust created by the testator prior to his death.

Under the law of wills, in many states written papers not attached to the will and without the formal requisites of a will may be included as a part of the will if the will identifies them and indicates an intention that they are to be a part of the will. This doctrine is called "incorporation by reference." In some states the testamentary trust may be included in such papers under this doctrine.

illegal
Contrary to law

crime
An act, committed or omitted, in violation of a public law governing it

tort
A civil (private) noncontractual wrong for which a court will give a remedy

Purposes of the Trust The settlor's manifestation of an intent to create a trust must indicate the definite purposes of the trust. The purposes must not be **illegal,** i.e., contrary to law. If the trust purpose is illegal, then the intended trust is void. If only a trust provision is void for illegality, the otherwise valid trust may exist as a trust if separation of the illegal provision would not defeat the valid purpose for which the trust was created. Otherwise the intended trust would be void. If the trust purpose is to commit a **crime** or a **tort,** the intended trust is void. If a trust provision in a valid trust requires the trustee to perform an act that was valid when the trust was created but the performance of which would later become a tort, the provision, but not necessarily the trust, becomes unenforceable. If the carrying out of the trust purpose or of a trust provision would be against public policy other than a crime or tort, the intended trust or provision would be void for illegality. The comments to Section 62 of the Restatement (Second) of Trusts, indicate various illustrations of purposes that are against public policy, some of which are inducing the commission of a crime or tort; encouraging immorality, divorce or separation, and neglect of parental duties; restraining religious freedom. Also, if the intended trust is for a fraudulent purpose, e.g., to defraud third persons, it is invalid as a trust.

No Consideration Required Consideration is not required in order to create a trust. The settlor may declare himself or herself trustee, or deliver trust property to a person, gratuitously. However, if a promise is made to create a trust, it is not binding as a contract unless it is supported by consideration. If legal consideration is rendered for the promise and the law of contracts is complied with, the promise to create a trust is specifically enforceable.

chattel
A tangible, movable thing

chose in action
Intangible personal property, such as an account receivable

Transfer of Property A trust establishes a beneficial interest in property, and a trust cannot be created until property is transferred. In the law of trusts, property is an interest (e.g., title) or right in a thing; property is not the thing itself. The thing may be tangible (land or **chattels**) or intangible (a **chose in action,** such as a contract right or an account receivable). Thus transferable *interests* in life insurance, patents, and copyrights can be trust property. The interest in property must be definite and existing, and capable of being transferred, at the time the trust is created. For example, a declaration of trust of corporate shares in a corporation to be formed fails to create a trust because the corporate shares and the declarant's interest in them have not yet come into existence and the declarant cannot transfer the shares as yet. When the corporation is formed and the declarant becomes the owner of the shares, the declarant then can create a trust of the shares. However, a general power of appointment of property, although not transferable by the holder of the power since it can be exercised only by the holder, can be held in trust. The settlor's reservation of a power to revoke or modify the trust or to participate in the administration of the trust does not prevent the settlor from creating a trust, provided the power does not include retaking the trust property or controlling the trustee in his or her use of the property.

Notice to, and Acceptance by, the Trustee and the Beneficiary A trust may be created without any notice to the trustee or the beneficiary that a trust has been created, and without their acceptance. If the named trustee refuses to accept transfer of trust property to him or her *directly,* there is no trust. However, if trust property has been transferred to the trustee in trust and the trustee later **disclaims** the title to the property, the title goes back to the transferor who holds it in a constructive trust[5] for the intended beneficiary with a duty to transfer the title to a new trustee. Similarly, if disclaimer is by a testamentary trustee, the property will be held in constructive trust by the testator's executor who must transfer the property to a new trustee. If the beneficiary disclaims any beneficial interest in the trust, the trust terminates.

disclaimer
Denial of an obligation or a claim

The Trustee Property must be transferred to a person in trust, called a trustee, in order to create a trust. A settlor can name himself or herself as trustee without any transfer. However, if a transfer is ineffective *only* because a trustee is not named in the instrument of conveyance of the property (e.g., deed of real property) or, if named, the intended trustee is dead or not capable of taking the title to the property, such lack of name, death, or incapability does not prevent the creation of a trust.

All persons who have legal capacity to take, hold, *and* administer property for themselves can be trustees. They have capacity to administer if they can transfer, and make contracts concerning, the trust property. A beneficiary can be an individual, including a married man or woman, a minor, a **juristic** person (e.g., corporation), a state, the federal government, the settlor. However, a person cannot be the sole beneficiary and at the same time the sole trustee. The reason why the sole beneficiary cannot be the sole trustee is because there is no separation of the legal and the beneficial (equitable) interests, and the beneficiary can do anything the beneficiary wishes with the property.

juristic
By law

The Beneficiary A trust involves the transfer of property to a trustee for the benefit of someone and, therefore, the trust requires a beneficiary, sometimes called a **cestui que trust.** The beneficiary is indicated in the settlor's manifestation of an intent to create a trust for the benefit of *that* beneficiary. Anyone not indicated in the manifestation who may incidentally benefit from the performance of the trust is an incidental beneficiary and is not a beneficiary of the trust. For example, *X* delivers money to *Y* in trust to pay *X*'s debts. *X* is the beneficiary of the trust, not *X*'s creditors, because *X* is primarily benefiting from the payment of his debts. Any person with the legal capacity to take legal title to property can be a beneficiary, although if subsequently that person no longer has

cestui que trust
The beneficiary of a trust

[5]For constructive trust, see p. 1176.

such capacity he or she can no longer be a beneficiary. A trust may have more than one beneficiary.

rule against perpetuities

The beneficiary of a trust must be identifiable at the time the trust is created or, in most states, within a period for the life of a person or persons in existence at the time the trust is created and 21 years after the death of such person or persons

A trust cannot be created unless, from the settlor's manifestation, the beneficiary is definitely identified or can be identified within the period of the **rule against perpetuities.** The beneficiary may be specifically named in the settlor's manifestation, or can be ascertained from facts in existence at the time the trust is to be created or which come into existence within the period of the rule against perpetuities. In most states the rule against perpetuities means a period of time measured by the life of a person or persons in existence at the time the trust is created *and* twenty-one years after the death of such person or persons. For example, *X* delivers money to *Y* in trust to pay the income therefrom to *Z* during *Z*'s life and, on *Z*'s death, to pay the principal to *Z*'s children who are then living at the time of *Z*'s death. A trust has been created irrespective of whether or not *Z* has any children at the time of the settlor's manifestation creating the trust. The members of a definite class of persons can be the beneficiaries of a trust. The settlor may be the beneficiary or one of the beneficiaries of the trust. For example, *X* delivers money to *Y* in trust for *X*.

If the trust property is personal property the beneficiary's interest is personal property, and if the trust property is real property the beneficiary's interest is real property. There is an exception—the doctrine of "equitable conversion." Under that doctrine, if the terms of the trust require the trustee to sell trust *real property* and either hold the proceeds in trust or distribute them, the beneficiary's interest is *personal property;* while if the terms of the trust require the trustee to sell trust *personal property* and use the proceeds *to buy real property,* the beneficiary's interest is *real property.*

► Administration of an Express Trust

The trustee has various duties to the beneficiary and powers in the administration of the trust. These are determined by the terms of the trust contained in the settlor's manifestation of intent to create the trust, subject to the settlor's exercise of any power reserved by him or her in connection with the trust; and by implication from the trustee's relationship to the beneficiary of the trust in the absence of trust terms to the contrary.

However, there are some instances when the trustee has no duty to the beneficiary to comply with the terms of the trust and may deviate from the trust terms. If the trust terms are, or reasonably appear to the trustee to be, impossible of performance, the trustee has no duty to comply with the trust terms, although for the trustee's own protection the trustee may ask for a court's guidance if the trustee is uncertain as to whether or not performance is possible. Similarly, the trustee has no duty to perform trust terms that the trustee reasonably should know are illegal or the performance of which would be either illegal or materially detrimental to the interest of the beneficiary.

Also, a change in circumstances not considered or anticipated by the settlor may cause performance of the trust terms to defeat or substantially impair the purpose of the trust. In such an event, the trustee can apply to a court and, by court order, deviate from the trust terms to the extent that the trust does not prohibit such deviation. Examples of such a change in circumstances would be a change in law making performance of a trust term illegal or an economic depression causing the sale of trust property as required by the trust to be ruinous. Another instance of action by a court ordering a trustee not to comply with the trust terms is when the financial plight of the beneficiary may justify payment to the beneficiary before the time prescribed in the trust.

Duties of the Trustee to the Beneficiary The trustee has the following duties to the beneficiary:

1. The trustee's duty to the beneficiary is to properly administer the trust.
2. The trustee is a fiduciary toward the beneficiary with the duty of loyalty to the beneficiary to administer the trust property for the sole benefit of the beneficiary's interest. If the trustee deals with the beneficiary for the trustee's benefit, the trustee has the duty to make full disclosure to the beneficiary of all material facts of which the trustee should be aware.
3. Because of the trustee's personal fiduciary relationship with the beneficiary, unless the trust provides otherwise, the trustee has the duty not to delegate to third persons the performance of trust terms that the trustee personally can perform.

Thus acts that require the trustee's discretion cannot be delegated.

Administrative Duties of the Trustee The trustee has many other duties.

1. The trustee has the duty to keep accurate accounts of his or her administration, make them available to the beneficiary, and, on the beneficiary's request, provide full information concerning the trust property.
2. The trustee is to exercise the same care that an ordinary prudent person would exercise regarding that person's own property, and if, when appointed as trustee, the trustee represented having a greater skill, there is a duty to exercise such greater skill.
3. The trustee must take and retain control of the trust property and use reasonable care to preserve it, designate it as trust property of that particular trust unless the trust provides otherwise, and carefully select a bank for the deposit of trust funds designated as such.
4. The trustee must act reasonably to enforce any claims held as trustee and to defend in any action which, if successful, could cause loss to the trust estate.
5. The trustee has a duty, unless the trust provides otherwise, to make the trust property productive, which means the trustee must use reasonable care in the retention, transfer, and investment of the trust property. This is illustrated in the following case.

FACTS

Henry F. Nussbaum, testator, made a residual bequest and devise of his estate in his will to his niece, Jane Ann Blair, as trustee, "in Trust however, for the education of my grandchildren (children of my daughter, Dorothy Janice Witmer) living at the time of my decease, or born within a period of nine months thereafter."

Henry died in 1960. The trust estate came into the hands of the trustee in 1961, consisting of $1,905 in checking and savings accounts, $5,700 in certificates of deposit and a house valued at $6,000.00. The house was sold in 1962, netting $4,467 to the trust estate. That amount was deposited in a trust checking account. In 1963, $2,000 in certificates of deposit were acquired by the trust and $500 was so invested in 1964. As of December 31, 1970, the trust fund assets consisted of $5,847 in checking account, $506 in savings account and $8,200 in certificates of deposit. In 1971 and 1972, the checking account balance was reduced by transfers to the savings account and on December 31, 1975 the trust assets consisted of $2,741 checking account, $5,474 savings account and $8,200 certificates of deposit.

Marguerite Janice Witmer was the only grandchild of the testator who became a beneficiary of the trust. She was born September 3, 1953. At the time of the trial, she was

23 years of age. She had not attended a college or university. However, various sums of money had been expended from the trust for her benefit, including a typewriter, clothes, glasses, modeling school tuition and expenses, and a tonsillectomy. These expenditures totalled some $1,225.00. The trust also provided $350 for dentures for the mother, Dorothy Witmer.

The trustee kept no books for the trust, which she handled rather informally. An accountant who testified calculated that between the opening of the trust and 1971, when college for Marguerite would have been a realistic possibility, had the trust funds, in excess of $100 checking account and approximately $800 to $1,000 in a savings account, been invested in one-year certificates of deposit, the trust would have earned additional interest of $2,840.

Marguerite brought an action seeking an accounting, removal of the trustee, and actual and punitive damages for breach of fiduciary duties. After trial to the court, the court ordered an accounting and removal of Jane as trustee and entered judgment against Jane for $309 for unaccounted for funds but found against Marguerite on her claim for damages for breach of fiduciary duties. Marguerite appeals from this portion of the decree.

DECISION

Judgment reversed insofar as it denied Marguerite's claim for actual damages. Remanded with directions to enter judgment for Marguerite for $2,840 actual damages.

The court quoted from Restatement (Second) of Trusts (1959), sec. 181, Comment c: "*Money.* In the case of money, it is normally the duty of the trustee to invest it so that it will produce an income. The trustee is liable if he fails to invest trust funds which it is his duty to invest for a period which is under all the circumstances unreasonably long. If, however, the delay is not unreasonable, he is not liable." The court also quoted from sec. 201: "A breach of trust is a violation by the trustee of any duty which as trustee he owes to the beneficiary."

Under the above rules, there has been a breach of trust by the trustee in this case and her good faith is not a defense to Marguerite's claim. When Jane came into possession of the trust estate in 1962, Marguerite was some nine years of age. Jane was acquainted with her and was aware of her age. Obviously there was no prospect of the beneficiary's attending college for a number of years. Jane's failure to invest a large portion of the trust corpus during such time may not be justified on the grounds that during such time she acceded to requests of Marguerite's mother to provide small sums for Marguerite or her mother. Jane acknowledges that such expenditures were not authorized under the trust. A breach of duty by the trustee in that regard cannot justify her further breach of duty to invest the trust corpus.

In view of the trustee's transfer of a substantial portion of the checking account balance to savings in 1971 and 1972 and in view of the relatively small difference between the return from savings and what might have been earned from certificates of deposit (½% to 1½%), no damages should be assessed against the trustee for the handling of the estate during that period. However, the trustee should be held liable for the $2,840 which, according to the measure of damages, invoked by Marguerite, might have been earned by investment of the trust between 1962 and 1971.

Witmer et al. v. Blair, 588 S.W.2d 222 (Mo. 1979).

Unproductive trust property and wasting trust property—that is, property such as patents or copyrights subject to depletion—should be disposed of. Investments should be diversified in order to reduce or distribute risk of loss, proper investments should be retained and improper investments disposed of. In most states the trustee may invest in U.S. securities and, subject to limitations, in bonds of states, cities, and counties, as well as in corporate shares. In many states, a trustee may invest in "common trust funds" whereby trust property of different, usually small, trusts is put into a common pool for investment. Courts differ on whether or not a trustee has a duty to amortize the depreciation or obsolescence of a building.

Principal and Income Accounts One of the troublesome areas for a trustee is compliance with the duty to make proper allocations and charges to the principal and income accounts. Under the 1962 Revised Uniform Principal and Income Act, Section 3(a, b), "income is the return in money or property derived from the use of principal," while "principal is the property that has been set aside by the owner or the person legally empowered so that it is held in trust eventually to be delivered to the remainderman while the return or use of the principal is in the meantime taken or received by or held for accumulation for the income beneficiary." *Ordinary and current* administrative and operative expense is chargeable to income (e.g., insurance on the trust property, trustee insurance bond premiums, ordinary repairs to trust property). Expense that is *not ordinary and current* is chargeable to principal (e.g., expense in setting up the trust, the cost of purchasing and selling investments). Prepaid rent by tenants of trust real property is allocated to income. Proceeds from insurance for loss to trust property (e.g., fire insurance) are allocated to principal.

Often investments are purchased at a premium. If the *trustee* makes such a purchase, the trustee must amortize the premium out of the income from the investment and the amortization fund is principal. If the *settlor* had made such a purchase, the trustee has no duty to amortize the premium, unless the trust provides otherwise, and all income from the investment is income available to the income beneficiary. If the investment was made at a discount, the benefit of the discount usually is principal and available to the principal beneficiary. But when treasury bills are redeemed at a discount, the amount of the discount is income.

The Restatement (Second) of Trusts, Section 236, states the rules for determining whether *receipts from shares of stock* are principal or income:

> Except as otherwise provided by the terms of the trust, if shares of stock of a corporation are held in trust to pay the income to a beneficiary for a designated period and thereafter to pay the principal to another beneficiary, the following rules are applicable:
>
> **(a)** Except as stated in Clauses (e) and (f), dividends payable in cash or in property other than in shares of the declaring corporation, including ordinary and extraordinary dividends, are income, if payable to shareholders of record on a designated date which is within the period; or, if no such date is designated, if declared at a date within the period.
> **(b)** Dividends payable in shares of the declaring corporation are principal.
> **(c)** If the trustee has the option of receiving a dividend either in cash or in shares of the declaring corporation, the dividend is income irrespective of the choice made by the trustee.
> **(d)** Rights to subscribe to the shares or other securities of the declaring corporation and the proceeds of any sale of such rights are principal, but rights to subscribe to the shares of other corporations are income.
> **(e)** Upon the total or partial liquidation of the corporation during the period, amounts paid as cash dividends declared before such liquidation occurred or as arrears of preferred or guaranteed dividends are income; all other amounts paid upon corporate shares on distribution of the corporate assets to the shareholders are principal.
> **(f)** A distribution by a corporation which is a return of capital and not a distribution of earnings is principal.
> **(g)** The earnings of a corporation not distributed by the corporation during the period are not income.

Powers of the Trustee The powers of the trustee not in violation of the trustee's duties to the beneficiary are either expressly stated in the trust terms, or are implied in order to carry out the trust purposes unless the trust provides otherwise. Previous text discussion of the meaning of the phrase "trust terms," and of instances when the trustee had no duty to the beneficiary to comply with the trust terms thereby permitting the trustee to deviate from the trust terms, are applicable here. (See p. 1166.) The duties of the trustee to the beneficiary, just discussed, indicate, in part, the trustee's powers, which the trustee must exercise in order to carry out the trustee's duties. The trustee also has the power:

1. to incur expenses (e.g., for managing and making repairs and improvements to the trust property);
2. to lease the trust property on reasonable terms and conditions;
3. to sell the trust property;
4. to settle claims affecting the trust; and
5. to exercise the powers of a holder of securities with respect to trust securities.

Except when the trust terms or a change in circumstances permits (see p. 1166) or state law permits, the trustee normally cannot mortgage or pledge trust property. When there is more than one trustee, they must agree unanimously, unless the law or trust terms provide otherwise.

By the trust terms and in order to carry out his or her duties, the trustee may have discretionary powers, such as whether or not, when, and how to exercise the trustee's powers. While the trustee's *proper* exercise of the trustee's discretionary powers is not subject to a court's substitution of its preference in its exercise, the court nevertheless serves as a control mechanism to assure that there is no abuse of this power. The court will act if it is necessary to control the trustee in the trustee's dishonest use of the power, as when acting with an improper motive, or when acting arbitrarily by failing to use his or her judgment.

Liability of the Trustee The trustee has the duty to the beneficiary to properly administer the trust and, as discussed previously on p. 1167, has many duties to the beneficiary in this regard. The trustee's violation of any trust duty owing to the beneficiary is a **breach of trust** for which the trustee is liable to the beneficiary. Only the beneficiary or the beneficiary's representative can sue the trustee for equitable relief for the trustee's breach. If there is more than one beneficiary, any beneficiary can sue the trustee for relief to that beneficiary.

breach of trust
A trustee's violation of a trust duty

The beneficiary may be precluded from holding the trustee liable for the trustee's breach of trust. The beneficiary is precluded if, prior to or at the time of the trustee's breach, the beneficiary consented to the wrongful conduct of the trustee, with the following exceptions. Such consent is ineffective if (a) the beneficiary was fraudulently induced to give consent, or (b) the beneficiary did not know of his or her rights and of material facts of which the trustee should reasonably have known, or (c) the beneficiary lacked capacity to consent, i.e., the beneficiary had no legal capacity to contract. Similarly, a beneficiary's release of the trustee or of the beneficiary's contract to discharge the trustee is effective unless at the time of such release or discharge (a), (b), or (c) above with respect to such release or discharge occurred, or (d) the trustee did not act fairly and reasonably in a transaction. Also, if a beneficiary with the option to reject or affirm (ratify) a transaction by the trustee that is a breach of trust subsequently affirmed the transaction and is thereby precluded from holding the trustee liable, nevertheless such affirmance is ineffective if, at the time the beneficiary affirmed, (a), (b), (c), or (d) above with respect to his or her affirmance occurred.

An **exculpatory clause** in the trust terms will relieve the trustee of liability for the trustee's breach of trust, except that it is ineffective if the trustee committed the breach in **bad faith,** intentionally, indifferent to the beneficiary's interest, or for any profit the trustee acquired from the breach.

exculpatory clause
A clause that relieves a party from liability

bad faith
Dishonesty in fact in the conduct or transaction concerned

If there is more than one trustee, no trustee is liable for a breach by a co-trustee unless he or she participated in the breach, was negligent in not preventing it, or neglected to obtain redress from the wrongful trustee.

For properly administering the trust, the trustee is entitled to be compensated out of the trust estate for services rendered, unless the trust terms are to the contrary or the court denies compensation because of the trustee's breach of trust. Also, while properly administering the trust, the trustee may become personally liable to third persons. The trustee is personally liable for contracts made by the trustee with third persons, and has a right to **indemnity** from the trust estate for the trustee's expenditures and loss sustained while acting properly in administering the trust. If the trustee has breached the trust, the court may reduce or deny compensation for acting as trustee.

indemnity
An absolute obligation to pay for another's loss

Modification and Termination of the Trust

Modification A settlor may modify or revoke a trust only if the settlor reserved powers to do so in the trust terms. If the trust terms do not have such a reservation, but at the time the trust was created the settlor intended to include these powers that were omitted by mistake, the settlor can show sufficient circumstances evidencing such mistake and obtain a court order reforming the trust terms so as to include these powers. A circumstance creating an inference that the settlor intended to reserve the power to revoke is when the settlor declares himself or herself trustee and deposits money in a bank account in his or her own name as trustee for another person. If the settlor received consideration for transferring property in trust, the law of contracts regarding mistake becomes applicable and the mistake is insufficient to set aside the transfer.

The settlor's reservation of the power to revoke ordinarily is interpreted to include the power to modify, and the settlor's reservation of the power to modify without any limitations includes the power to revoke.

If fraud, duress, undue influence, or mistake have induced the settlor to create the trust, the settlor can rescind the trust or have it reformed as in the case of other transfers of property so induced.

Totten Trust and Payable on Death Accounts Both of these devices are in current use today to accomplish the same result, to create a *revocable,* tentative transfer of an interest in funds, usually by the deposit of funds in a bank account. A Totten Trust is illustrated by a bank deposit by *"X,* in trust for *Y",* which is revocable by *X* until his death when the beneficiary (*Y*) can acquire the account funds. The beneficiary does not own the account but has an *equitable interest* in it and cannot make a withdrawal from the account until the depositor's death. While this device is not a true formal express trust (nor is it a will) and some states refuse to recognize it as a trust, other states by statute or by judicial decision recognize it as a so-called tentative trust.

Quite different is the "payable on death" account (POD). For example, *X* deposits money in a bank account "payable on death of *X* to *Y*". This is a *third-party contract*[6] between the bank and its customer depositor for the benefit of the named beneficiary.[7]

Termination The trust may terminate in various ways. The trust terms may specify a period of time for its duration, or that it is to end on the occurrence of a particular event. Also, a trust may terminate if, under the circumstances, a particular trust purpose no longer needs to be carried out. The expiration of the period or the occurrence of the event terminates the trust. If the entire purpose of the trust cannot be carried out because of supervening (later) impossibility or illegality, the court will order termination of the entire trust. However, if only some of the purposes cannot be carried out because of such supervening impossibility or illegality, the court will, when possible, permit the trustee to deviate from such purposes.

Destruction of the trust property terminates the trust, with two exceptions. The destruction may be caused by the fault of the trustee, in which event the trustee will have to pay the amount of the loss and hold such amount in trust as trust property. The destruction may be caused by the wrongful act of a third person, in which event the trustee will hold the claim against the wrongdoer as trust property.

Circumstances not known to the settlor and not anticipated by the settlor at the time the trust was created may occur, which would cause performance of the trust terms to defeat or substantially impair compliance with the trust's purpose. In this event the court will order the trust to terminate.

All the beneficiaries may consent to termination of the trust and compel its termination, unless termination would violate a material purpose of the trust. An example of a material purpose is a "spendthrift trust," when the trust terms prohibit a beneficiary from voluntarily or involuntarily being deprived of his or her beneficial interest by the beneficiary or by creditors of the beneficiary. If the settlor and all the beneficiaries consent to termination of the trust, the trust can be terminated irrespective of the nonaccomplishment of the trust's material purpose. Merger of the beneficial interest with the legal title to the trust property in one person terminates the trust.

If the trustee named in the trust terms no longer continues as trustee, the trust does not terminate and another trustee will be appointed. But if the settlor's manifestation of intent was that the trust was to continue only so long as the named trustee continues as such, that trustee's discontinuance terminates the trust.

The Charitable Trust

charitable trust
A trust created for a charitable purpose

A **charitable trust** is created for a charitable purpose. Much of the law applicable to an express trust is applicable to a charitable trust, but there are major differences. Because of such differences, and solely to distinguish the express trust from the charitable trust, the express trust is often called a "private trust."

The methods of creating an express trust[8] are the same for a charitable trust, except that the purpose is charitable. Purposes are charitable if they are beneficial to the

[6]For third party contracts, see pp. 264–65, 267–68.

[7]*In re Estate of Nona E. Morton, Deceased,* 733 P.2d 834 (Kan. App. 1987).

[8]See p. 1161.

community. The Restatement (Second) of Trusts, Section 368 states *specific* charitable purposes:

(a) the relief of poverty;
(b) the advancement of education;
(c) the advancement of religion;
(d) the promotion of health;
(e) governmental or municipal purposes;
(f) other purposes the accomplishment of which is beneficial to the community.

Under Section 373: "A trust for the erection or maintenance of public buildings, bridges, streets, highways, parks or other public works or for other governmental or municipal purposes is charitable." Many foundations are formed for a charitable purpose.

Examples of other specific charitable purposes beneficial to a community are the promotion of temperance; relief of animals; protection of national security; various patriotic purposes; community purposes (e.g., city beautification, community swimming facilities); aid for persons of limited opportunities; erection and maintenance of tombs or monuments to commemorate notable persons; and to change existing law by legal means.[9] If the property or its income intended for a charitable trust is to be for a private use, there cannot be a charitable trust.

The trust terms *must specify a particular charitable purpose* for the creation of a charitable trust. However, it is sufficient if the trust terms leave to the trustee the power to select any unnamed charitable purpose. Also, unlike the express trust, a charitable trust cannot have a named beneficiary in the sense of being a particular *person*. The trust states only a purpose that must be for the benefit of a *community*. When the settlor had manifested *both* a *general* charitable purpose and a *particular* charitable purpose and the particular charitable purpose *cannot* be carried out, under the doctrine of **cy pres,** meaning "as near as possible," the court will order that the trust property be applied to a charitable purpose within the general charitable purpose as nearly as possible in accordance with the settlor's intent. However, if there is no general charitable purpose, or if the settlor's manifestation provides that, if the particular charitable purpose cannot be accomplished then the trust is to end, on failure of the particular purpose cy pres will not be applied. Cy pres will not be applied to defeat the settlor's intent. If the purpose of a charitable trust is accomplished and some trust property remains, the court will apply the remaining property to a charitable purpose within the settlor's general charitable intention. In the following case the court held that cy pres could not be applied and the trust had terminated.

cy pres
An equitable trust doctrine applicable particularly in charitable trusts whereby, by court order, the general trust purpose will be carried out as nearly as possible in accordance with the settlor's intent when the particular trust purpose cannot be carried out

FACTS

The testator created a testamentary trust in his will in 1969 under the terms of which he devised and bequeathed money to Drake University and Parsons College, in equal shares, for scholarship purposes only, only the income therefrom to be used to assist needy students to receive a college education, and if either or both of these institutions failed to carry out these trust provisions then the trust or trusts shall fail and shall be cancelled and revoked, the principal to go to the testator's heirs at law. Testator died in 1974. After the execution of the will but prior to the testator's death, Parsons College became bankrupt and no longer operated as an educational institution. Drake University urges that the court should apply cy pres and that Drake University serve as trustee for the entire fund. Dorothy Sim-

[9]See Restatement (Second) of Trusts, 1959, comments to sec. 374.

mons, executor of the testator's estate, brought an action to have the court construe the will as it relates to these two trusts for Drake University and Parsons College. Parsons College, Drake University, and the testator's heirs at law are the defendants. The lower court held for the heirs at law and Drake University appealed.

DECISION

Affirmed, for the heirs at law. The bequest to Parsons College in trust for the purposes set out in the testator's will has failed because Parsons College is unable to administer the trust. It is of no import that the trust failed at the outset rather than after it had been under administration for some time. Cy pres will not apply here. Courts may not ignore the testator's intent in order to give effect to doubtful trust provisions by invoking the doctrine of cy pres. Cy pres is simply a liberal rule of construction used to carry out, not defeat, the testator's intent. The cy pres doctrine is inapplicable when the testator has anticipated the possible failure of the trust and has made alternative disposition of his property to meet that contingency. Under such circumstances the testamentary intent may be ascertained without such extrinsic help. This is the case here where the testator stated unequivocally that the assets which would have gone to the trust should then go to his heirs at law.

Simmons v. Parsons College et al., 256 N.W.2d 225 (Iowa 1977).

State statutes govern charitable trusts, and the states vary in their restrictions concerning charitable trusts, such as how much property can be owned by a charitable trust, how much property a decedent may transfer by will to a charitable trust, and to what extent a charitable trust is exempt from taxation. Since the community receives the beneficial interest, usually the state attorney general or another public officer is responsible for the enforcement of charitable trusts. A co-trustee also can enforce the charitable trust.

Two Trusts Implied by Law

An express or charitable trust is created by (1) the settlor's manifestation of an intent to create a trust; (2) transfer of the settlor's legal title to property to a trustee; and (3) the transfer of the beneficial interest in the property either to a named beneficiary in the case of an express trust, or for the purpose of benefiting a community in the case of a charitable trust. However, two trusts are implied by law where all three of these elements are *not* present. They are the "resulting trust" and the "constructive trust."

► Resulting Trust

In an express trust, the trustee to whom the property is transferred normally is not intended to have the beneficial interest in the trust property. The settlor's manifestation intended the beneficial interest to go to a third person as the beneficiary. If the beneficial interest in transferred property is not transferred, the *result* is that there is no trust, and the person to whom the property was transferred holds the property in trust for the person who transferred or caused the transfer of the property and who still retains the beneficial interest in the property. Thus we have the "resulting trust." While no manifested intent to create a trust has been made, it is nevertheless *presumed by law* that the parties intended to create a trust for the benefit of the person retaining the beneficial interest.

A resulting trust can arise in various ways. One way is where the express or charitable trust fails. Since the beneficial interest in the property transferred has not been transferred to anyone and the person holding the property is not intended to have the beneficial interest in it, the result is that the person holding the property is intended to hold it in trust for the original owner.

Another way for the resulting trust to arise is where an express or charitable trust has been performed but some of the trust property remains undisposed of. Since there no longer is any beneficial interest of the intended beneficiary in the remaining trust property and the trustee is not intended to have a beneficial interest in the property, the *result* is that the trustee is presumed by law to be intended to hold the property in a resulting trust for the settlor who has the remaining beneficial interest in the property. This is illustrated in the following case.

FACTS

Norma and Paul Petro were husband and wife. They owned real property as community property and a joint savings account with right of survivorship. Norma became seriously ill and she and her sister, Gladys Uriarte, went to the bank and Norma withdrew $15,000 which she turned over to Gladys only to take care of Norma and Paul. Norma also executed and delivered a deed of their real property to Gladys for the purpose of taking care of Norma. No consideration was given to Norma and Paul for the transfer of the savings account money nor for the conveyance of the real property even though consideration was recited in the deed. Gladys testified that were her sister living today she would return the property to her because she really owns it. Norma had no children. Norma died. Paul sued to compel Gladys to return to him the balance of $5,592.99 remaining from the $15,000 handed to Gladys by Norma, and the real property. After Norma died, Gladys sold the real property and, because of this trial, the proceeds are held in escrow pending the outcome of the litigation. The trial court held that Gladys held both the $5,592.99 and the proceeds from the sale of the real estate as trustee under a resulting trust in favor of Paul for which Gladys must account and distribute to Paul. Gladys appeals on an issue of community property law concerning property rights involved.

DECISION

Affirmed on appeal. The court held that the community property law was without merit here. Since the purpose of the trust funds was fulfilled on Norma's death with funds remaining, the remainder reverted to Norma's estate and consequently to her husband, Paul, and Gladys held the remainder in a resulting trust for Paul. "A resulting trust is an 'intent trust' and the trust and the trust property must have been taken in trust for some special purpose, which purpose subsequently fails or is frustrated, so that consequently the law will imply a trust for the equitable owner of the property, rather than the legal title holder."

Uriarte v. Petro, Tex. Cir. App., 606 S.W.2d 25 (Tex. 1980).

A third and very common way for the resulting trust to arise is in connection with the purchase of property. When property is sold, the buyer pays the purchase price to the seller, and at the direction of the buyer the legal title is transferred to a third person. Unless circumstances are to the contrary, it is *presumed* that the buyer had no intent that the transferee holder of the title was to have the beneficial interest in the property. Rather, it is *presumed by law* that the intention of the parties was that the transferee holder of the property was to hold the property in trust for the buyer. Thus a resulting trust has been created. This type of resulting trust is often called a "purchase money trust."

The presumption of intending a purchase money resulting trust may be rebutted by evidence showing that the person paying the money intended to lend the money to the holder of the property so that the holder might acquire the property, or to make a gift to the holder of the property. The presumption of a resulting trust is also *rebutted* if, in the absence of a contrary intent, the property is transferred to a close relative (e.g., spouse, child) of the payor, or if the transfer was intended to satisfy a debt of the payor to the transferee holder.

Constructive Trust

The "constructive trust" created by law does not arise, like the resulting trust, by any legal presumption of an intention to create a trust. Rather, it is created to impose an equitable duty upon a person to hold and transfer property to another because the holder's retention of the property for himself or herself would be wrongful and the holder would be unjustly enriched. The constructive trust usually is employed to remedy a wrong committed by a person in the acquisition of another's property, e.g., by fraud, duress, undue influence. For example, *Y* fraudulently or unduly influenced *X* to transfer *X*'s property to *Y*. *Y* holds the property in constructive trust for *X*. This is illustrated by the following case.

FACTS

John F. Tufts, Sr. (Senior), mentally infirm but not incompetent, executed two **powers of attorney** to his son, John F. Tufts, Jr. (Junior). One was a special power to sell Senior's 45.9 acre realty, and the other was a general power. Junior, Rick L. Mai, and Clifford A. Johnson formed TMJ Joint Venture (TMJ). Mai and Johnson had met Senior, knew of his mental infirmity, and knew of Junior's fiduciary responsibilities to his father. Junior, pursuant to his powers of attorney, sold the realty to TMJ for $1,837,104. Johnson stated that the price was more than that shown by four appraisals obtained by him. The appointed guardian of Senior made a motion to the probate court for court approval of the sale based on Johnson's appraisals. However, a subsequent appraisal showed that, at the time of the sale, the property had a market value of $6,500,000, and the guardian then withdrew his motion.

Mary F. Smiley, Senior's daughter, complained to the probate court of Junior's self-dealing and requested that the property be reclaimed. The probate court held that Junior had breached his fiduciary duty to Senior by selling Senior's property to TMJ, in which Junior has a one-third interest, but found that the terms of the sale were fair and reasonable and approved it. The court imposed a constructive trust in favor of Senior's estate on Junior's one-third interest in the property through his ownership of TMJ, but not on any interests of Mai and Johnson in the property or TMJ. The court then ordered Senior's estate to sell to Mai and Johnson the constructive trust interest it had awarded and decreed that the estate take nothing from them. Smiley appealed.

power of attorney
Written authority by a principal to an agent

DECISION

Reversed on appeal. Junior's sale to TMJ was a breach of his fiduciary duties to Senior. Also, the terms of the sale were unfair and unreasonable. Mai and Johnson having participated fully with Junior and with his knowledge of Senior and having shared the benefits of the sale, must share with Junior his liability for breach of his fiduciary duties. For complete redress of the wrong suffered, the estate was entitled to a constructive trust of the interests of Junior, Mai, and Johnson in the property.

Smiley v. Johnson, 763 S.W.2d 1 (Tex. Ct. App. 1988).

Summary Statement

1. A trust is a legal device whereby legal title to property is held by one person (a trustee) for the benefit of a beneficiary.
2. A trust is distinguished from a bailment, agency, and sale.

3. There are five ways to create an express trust, as set out under the Restatement (Second) of Trusts, on page 1169.
4. The settlor must have legal capacity to create an inter vivos or testamentary trust.
5. A person is presumed to be competent with mental capacity to create a trust. Persons who assert incompetency have the burden of proving it.
6. Mental capacity is best determined by a person's spoken words, acts, and conduct *at a particular point in time.*
7. The settlor of an express inter vivos trust must manifest an intention to create a trust, *effective at the time of the manifestation.* It may be in any form, unless the statute of frauds is applicable, as when the trust property is an interest in land.
8. A testamentary trust is a trust in a will, and it cannot come into existence until the death of the testator.
9. The settlor's manifestation of intent to create a trust must indicate the definite, legal purposes of the trust.
10. A trust cannot be created without a transfer of property.
11. Notice to, and acceptance by, the trustee and the beneficiary are not required in order to create a trust.
12. Any person who has legal capacity to take, hold, and administer property for himself or herself can be a trustee.
13. A trust must have a beneficiary definitely identified or identifiable under the rule against perpetuities.
14. The trustee has many trust duties to the beneficiary and, as a fiduciary, the trustee is to act *solely* for the benefit of the beneficiary's interest in administering the trust.
15. The trustee is to exercise the same care that an ordinary, prudent person would exercise regarding his or her own property.
16. The trustee is to make proper allocations and charges to the principal and income accounts.
17. The trustee is liable to the beneficiary for breach of trust.
18. A settlor may modify or revoke a trust only if the settlor reserved powers to do so in the trust terms.
19. A trust may terminate in various ways: expiration; supervening impossibility or illegality; destruction of the trust property; and merger in one person of the beneficial interest in, with the legal title to, the trust property.
20. A charitable trust is created for a *particular* charitable purpose for the benefit of a community.
21. Cy pres means "as near as possible," and may be applied to further the *general* charitable purpose indicated in the trust terms if the specified particular charitable purpose fails.
22. A resulting trust may occur when the title to property is transferred but the beneficial interest in the property has not been transferred.
23. A constructive trust usually is employed to remedy a wrong committed by a person in the acquisition of another's property.

The following long case, frequently cited in later cases, illustrates the careful consideration given by the court to all the facts and the shifting of the burden of proof in determining whether or not there was a lucid period of competency when capacity was present to execute a written trust agreement.

In re MEYERS
189 A.2d 852 (Pa. 1963)

Jones, J. This proceeding seeks to rescind an inter vivos deed of trust wherein Miriam H. Girsh [appellant] and Myers L. Girsh [Mr. Girsh], *then* husband and wife, were the settlors, appellant the principal beneficiary, and Joseph Goldstein, appellant's father, was the sole trustee. The vital, although not the sole, issue is the mental competency of appellant on June 29, 1950, the date upon which she executed the trust deed.

In 1947, appellant became mentally ill, her illness being diagnosed as "paranoid schizophrenia," . . . With the *possible* exception of a comparatively short period of time beginning March 5, 1948 when, as a result of forty insulin shock treatments, appellant regained mental competency and returned to her home, it seems clear that, during the latter part of 1947 and throughout 1948 and 1949, appellant was mentally incompetent and a patient in mental institutions. . . .

Appellant remained at . . . Pennsylvania Hospital until April 23, 1950 when she was permitted to "go out on visit," in the company of two nurses specially trained in psychiatry, to a hotel in New York . . . "to determine whether a change in environment would result in an improvement in her mental illness. . . ."

On five occasions—April 29, May 6, May 13, May 20 and May 27—Dr. Hughes visited appellant in New York and on five occasions—May 2, June 1, June 8, June 24, and June 27—appellant, accompanied by one of her nurses, went to Philadelphia and consulted with Dr. Hughes. . . .

On June 28, 1950 Mr. Goldstein in New York City presented [a] written [trust] agreement to appellant for execution. . . . The trust agreement, although dated June 28, 1950, was executed by appellant on June 29, 1950 and witnessed by Mr. and Mrs. Goldstein. The validity of the execution of this trust agreement is herein attacked. . . .

On June 30, 1950, appellant, accompanied by Mrs. Goldstein and a graduate nurse, went to Johnstown, appellant's hometown and the place of abode of her father and stepmother, where she remained until November 3, 1950. During this period appellant remained under the care of Dr. Hughes and, on at least one occasion, July 14, 1950, went to Philadelphia for an examination by Dr. Hughes.

On November 3, 1950 appellant was admitted, under Dr. Hughes' care, to Roseneath Sanitorium near Philadelphia, an institution which cared for mentally ill patients. Appellant's condition deteriorated and in January, 1951 she was readmitted, as a patient of Dr. Alpers, to the Institute where she remained continuously until May 23, 1955, a period of four and one-quarter years, at which time she was discharged. *It is undisputed that since May 23, 1955 appellant has been mentally competent and has made a remarkable recovery.* [Emphasis added.]

Under the trust agreement, Mr. Joseph Goldstein was named as the sole trustee but . . . Mr. Meyers now serves in that capacity. Mr. Meyers, as trustee, has filed three accounts, . . . the third account on June 28, 1960. At the audit of the third account, appellant filed this petition to rescind the trust and to have the balance in the hands of the trustee awarded to her on the ground that she was mentally incompetent at the time she signed the trust agreement on June 29, 1950. . . .

After hearings . . . , the Orphans' Court of Cambria County concluded: (1) that, on June 28, and on June 29, 1950, when appellant executed . . . the trust agreement, she was mentally competent; (2) . . . ; (3) . . . ; (4) that the . . . trust agreement [is] valid; (5) that the petition to rescind the trust must be dismissed. Appellant [appealed.]. . . .

On this appeal five questions are raised: (1) on the evidence of record, did the court err in finding that appellant on June 29, 1950 was mentally competent to execute this trust agreement?. . . .

The mental competency of a person is a fact but the existence of that fact must be determined by inferences or deductions from other facts such as the spoken words, the acts, and the conduct of the person and thus the finding of mental capacity is reviewable on appeal.

In proof of her mental incompetency on June 28 and June 29, 1950, appellant presented her own testimony and that of.... Appellant's initial contention is three-fold: (a) on the posture of this record, the *ultimate* burden of proving that, on June 29, 1950, appellant possessed sufficient mental competency to execute this trust agreement rested on appellees; (b) that to sustain this burden required proof of mental competency not by a *preponderance* of, but by *clear* and *convincing*, evidence; (c) that appellees have not met this burden.

First, as to the burden of proof. *Ordinarily, the mental competency of a person who executes an instrument is presumed and the burden of proof is upon the person who alleges incompetency....* [Emphasis added.]

Therefore, in the case at bar, the *initial* burden of proof of incompetency was upon appellant. In assumption of that burden, the appellant proved that, prior to June 28 and June 29, 1950, she had been confined in mental institutions for approximately 21½ months out of 32½ months and that as late as June 10 and June 11, 1950, although there was reason to hope for a remission in her condition, appellant's condition was "such that she could not enter into any legal contract or relationship," and that, *subsequent* to June 28 and 29, 1950, (beginning *at the latest* in November, 1950) appellant was hospitalized in one or another mental institution for the next four and one-quarter years. The record is clear that appellant was suffering from "schizophrenia, paranoid" which has been defined as a "disintegration of the individual's mind and personality, characterized by disturbances of thinking,... hallucinations and similar manifestations." ... Under such circumstances, did the burden of proof shift to the appellees to prove the mental competency of appellant? In ... it was said: "If however general or habitual unsoundness of mind be once established, the burden of proving a lucid interval or a restoration, at any particular time, is thrust upon those who allege the fact."...

On the state of the instant record, it is clear beyond question that, very shortly before the date upon which this trust agreement was executed, appellant suffered from the "most serious form of mental illness known to psychiatry," an illness which had existed for upwards of two years; that, prior to, at the time of, and subsequent to the time of execution of the trust agreement, appellant was under the care of psychiatric nursing; that, for a period of over four years thereafter, appellant was continuously a patient in mental institutions. In its adjudication the court below stated: "There is no doubt that [appellant] was incompetent before this period and relapsed into incompetency some time later." The record not only fully supports this statement but indicates that the time interval between the date of execution of the trust agreement and the previous and succeeding incompetency was short in duration. Under such circumstances, appellant's previous and subsequent mental incompetency was of such recent and *serious* nature and *apparent* permanence as to *impose upon appellees the burden of proving that, on the date the trust agreement was executed, appellant possessed mental competency....*

Under the instant circumstances, it being definitely appellees' burden to prove that, on the date of execution of the trust agreement, appellant possessed mental competency, i.e., the ability to understand and appreciate the nature and effect of the trust agreement, to sustain such burden required the production not of a preponderance of evidence but of proof clear and convincing in nature....

The critical or crucial time at which appellant's mental competency must be determined [is] June 29, 1950—when the trust agreement was executed....

To that which transpired on June 28 and June 29 the sole witnesses were Mrs. Goldstein, who witnessed [the] agreement, and Misses Warwick and Hunt, the nurses. All three witnesses testified to the events which transpired on both dates; Mr. Goldstein's arrival at the hotel apartment with the agreement, the discussion, sometimes in loud tones, between appellant and Mr. Goldstein of the contents of the agreement, the reading at length of the agreement by appellant,... the deletion by appellant from the trust agreement of references therein to a certain law firm and her refusal to execute the trust agreement until such references were deleted in a redrafted agreement, the execution on June 29 of the trust agreement redrafted to suit appellant's wishes, appellant's actions on both dates subsequent to Mr. Goldstein's departure, etc.

We have said that a person's "mental capacity is best determined by his spoken words, his acts and conduct." . . . These witnesses did outline and describe the words, acts, and conduct of the appellant and, from their observation of such words, acts, and conduct, they all concluded that the appellant *on those dates* did possess sufficient mental capacity to understand and appreciate the meaning and nature of the agreements which she executed. . . .

Appellees produced the testimony of Dr. Joseph Hughes [that] . . . during the latter part of June, 1950 and July, 1950, appellant entered a period of remission to the extent that she had regained full mental competency to execute this agreement. Dr. Hughes gave his opinion that, both on the dates when the agreement [was] executed as well as on July 14, 1950, appellant was mentally competent.

Appellees also called Morton Meyers, Esq., . . . [a] member of the bar. Mr. Meyers . . . on April 11, 1950 visited appellant in the Institute, found her then unable to discuss business matters and urged her father to have a guardian appointed for her which the father hesitated to do. On June 3, 1950 Mr. Meyers visited appellant in her hotel apartment in New York and found her very confused, hallucinating and engaged in bizarre behavior. However, on June 25, 1950, . . . Mr. Meyers again visited appellant in New York. On the occasion of that visit, Mr. Meyers found appellant "indeed improved," "pleasant," and she "talked intelligently" to him; he discussed with her the pending agreement. . . . While he would not express any "psychiatric opinion" as to her competency, he did testify: "She talked to me. She knew me. She appeared to understand what I was telling her." . . .

A review of this record clearly indicates, as found by the court below, that shortly *before* and *after* June 29 appellant was mentally incompetent. Our task is to ascertain from this record whether the evidence clearly demonstrates that in the *interim* period appellant was in such a state of remission and was experiencing such a lucid interval that she was then mentally competent. . . . Appellees have sustained their burden of showing that on June 29 appellant was mentally competent. . . .

. . . Our conclusion [is] that appellant did have sufficient mental capacity to execute this trust agreement. . . .

[Decree affirmed]

Questions and Case Problems

1. On Friday, Dr. Charles Cabaniss (decedent) told Stephanie Cabaniss, his sister-in-law, that he had been putting away some checks he received as payment for medical services for Carla Cabaniss, his incompetent adult daughter. On Saturday in Stephanie's home, he endorsed the checks telling her that she was to open a checking account for Carla's benefit, and that she was to be Carla's trustee for the money, to which Stephanie agreed. He then wrote two letters to his attorney authorizing Stephanie to deposit the checks in an account to be opened by Stephanie for the various needs of Carla and that she was to act as trustee, with withdrawals to be used only for the benefit of Carla. Stephanie told decedent that he would probably have to accompany her to the bank to make the deposits. Decedent then wrapped up the checks in the letters, handed them to Stephanie who placed them in her file cabinet for safekeeping, so that he could get them if he wanted them or needed them. He had a key to Stephanie's home and later the same day he left the key on the rug inside the door. On Sunday the decedent committed suicide. On Monday, without knowing of the suicide, Stephanie opened, and deposited the checks in, a trustee savings account at a savings and loan association.

Lorena Cabaniss, decedent's widow, sued to obtain the money from the checks, alleging that the decedent did not sufficiently manifest an unambiguous firm intention to create a present trust. The court held that the decedent had created an inter vivos trust. Lorena appealed. Did the decedent's oral and written declarations and conduct create an inter vivos trust? Explain the reasons for your decision. [*Cabaniss v. Cabaniss,* 484 A.2d 87 (D.C. App. 1983).]

2. Albert A. Berges, the decedent, provided in part in his will: "I do hereby give, devise and bequeath to Jim Feliz, as trustee, the sum of $600 for each of his children, and I do hereby give, devise and bequeath to Josephine Feliz Dawson, as trustee, the sum of $600 for each of her children at the time of my **demise.** Said trusts shall terminate when each of said children, attain the age of 18 years." Do these words create a testamentary trust on Berges' death? Give reasons for your decision. [*In re Berges,* 142 Cal.Rptr. 635 (1977).]

demise
Death

3. In 1952 Ann B. duPont made a gift of her home, later called "Memorial House," to The Executive Council of the Protestant Episcopal Church in the Diocese of Delaware, a Delaware corporation. She died in 1963. Her will provided in part:

> I give and bequeath to The Executive Council of the Protestant Episcopal Church of the Diocese of Delaware the sum of five hundred thousand dollars ($500,000) for the maintenance and care of, and the operations carried on in, the property known as 'Memorial House,' at 56 Oak Avenue, Rehoboth, Delaware, which I have heretofore given to said Executive Council, the expenditures for such maintenance, care, and operation to be as the Bishop and Standing Committee of said Diocese shall determine in their discretion.

Is there a testamentary trust? Give reasons for your decision. [*The Executive Council of the Protestant Episcopal Church in the Diocese of Delaware, Inc. v. Moss, et al.,* 231 A.2d 463 (Del. 1967).]

4. Aaron E. Rentz named his sister, Myrtis R. Polk, as executrix and trustee in his will, which provides in part:

> V. I give, devise, and bequeath all the rest and residue of the property of which I may die possessed, including, but not limited to bank accounts, real estate, mortgages, choses in action, growing crops, money, and life insurance policy benefits unto Myrtis R. Polk, IN TRUST, nevertheless, under the following terms and conditions: . . . VI. Upon the death of my Mother-in-law, Danna H. Kinard, my Trustee shall turn over the corpus of the trust to my beloved wife, Lennis, in its entirety. Should my beloved wife predecease her Mother then, and in that event, my Trustee shall turn over the corpus of the trust to my son, Danny, ten (10) years after my death.

Is there a testamentary trust here? Give the reasons for your decision. [*Rentz and Rentz v. Polk,* 228 S.E.2d 106 (S.C. 1976).]

5. Public Service Co. of Colorado (PSCC) appointed Chase Manhattan Bank (Chase) on July 1, 1952 as a professional trustee of PSCC's pension fund to make investments for the fund. On January 29, 1964, as trustee for 17 pension funds, Chase made a $4.7 million 15-year loan to Glassmanor apartments. PSCC's share was $300,000. Security for the loan was a mortgage on Glassmanor, a 13-year-old complex of 30 buildings and 771 apartments located near downtown Washington, D.C. At the time the loan was made, an independent appraiser found the apartments in generally good condition valued at $6.8 million, and that income was more than adequate to pay debt services.

Chase, in violation of its own policies, failed to review the loan in 1971 and 1972 and after 1970 failed to conduct its regularly scheduled inspections for five years.

This is contrary to the accepted practice in mortgage management of inspection every 18 months. Chase's superficial inspection and appraisal reports were few and inadequate to report the deteriorating condition of Glassmanor. Specifically, a steadily increasing process of poor maintenance and hundreds of annual housing code violations beginning in 1967 caused the loan to become an improper trust investment by the fall of 1973. The reports had too little detail to permit Chase officials to form an intelligent opinion as to the condition of the property. In fact, a note on one stated that "the property is in satisfactory condition." Also, beginning in 1966, apartment vacancies kept increasing; in April 1981, six out of seven were vacant. Chase failed to react in any way to outside reports by the owner and others that the property was not being properly maintained.

Chase never offered sale of the loan at a discount that reflected the deteriorated condition of the property. In 1971 a New York bank bought and then returned the loan because of its inadequate security, and in 1976 again declined to buy after visiting the property. In 1976 and 1977, Chase declined the offers of Glassmanor's owner to buy the loan at a 20 percent discount. By mid-1975, the loan could have been sold for 80 cents on the dollar. In May 1983, Chase sold the mortgage loan for $1.1 million, with a consequent substantial monetary loss to PSCC, who then sued Chase for its loss. Judgment for whom? Explain fully your reasons. [*Public Serv. Co. of Colo. v. Chase Manhattan Bank,* 577 F.Supp. 92 (S.D.N.Y. 1983).]

6. The testatrix's will, executed October 18, 1941, devised a specific parcel of improved real property to her trustees in trust "to furnish my daughter, Anna . . . with one of the apartments in said premises . . . rent free during her lifetime," and to pay the balance of the net income therefrom in equal shares to Anna and Daniel, with Daniel's share of the income payable to his issue if he predeceased Anna. The will nominated them as co-executors and trustees, but Daniel renounced his appointment and Anna has acted in both capacities. The language in the will indicates clearly that the primary and dominant purpose of the testatrix was to furnish Anna with an apartment in the family home rent free for life. Testatrix died September 13, 1954. In 1964 Anna vacated the apartment provided her by the will, and in 1965, because of the continued vacancy of the building and the general deterioration of the surrounding area, the trust realty was sold with the consent of the interested parties.

Anna petitions that the testamentary part of the will be construed, contending that the trust has been terminated and that the proceeds should be distributed to the beneficiaries named in the will. You decide, giving reasons for your decision. [*In re Frank's Will,* 57 Misc.2d 446 (N.Y. 1968).] (This older case was selected for its excellent simplicity and directness.)

7. The testator had constructed George M. Hoffman Memorial Hospital in 1916 in his name. His will created a testamentary trust under the terms of which trust income was to be paid to the trustees solely for maintenance of the hospital, and if the hospital failed to operate as a hospital for one year the trust fund with accumulated interest or income from the fund was to be distributed to, and become the absolute property of, the testator's friend, George Green, if living, otherwise to his friend's heirs. Testator died in 1931. By 1972 the hospital building could no longer be licensed as a hospital and the Hoffman Memorial Hospital ceased to operate. In 1975 the trustees of the Hoffman trust asked the court to construe the will as it relates to this testamentary trust and to determine ownership of the assets held in the testamentary trust. Is the cy pres doctrine applicable? Give reasons for your decision. [*Nelson and Sharpe v. Kring,* 592 P.2d 438 (Kan. 1979).]

8. Distinguish a resulting trust from a constructive trust.

9. A & M Records, Inc., is a California corporation that commercially manufactures and sells recorded musical performances in the form of disc phonograph records and prerecorded magnetic tapes. Heilman has admitted advertising and selling record and tape "albums" which included performances of songs duplicated from recordings owned and manufactured by A & M Records without making payments to A & M Records or to any of the musicians involved. Gross receipts from the sale of pirated A & M Records' performances totaled at least $80,000. On what legal basis does A & M Records have a claim against Heilman? Explain. [*A & M Records, Inc. v. Heilman,* 142 Cal.Rptr. 390 (1978).]

10. In the case of *In re Meyers,* excerpted at the beginning of this section, the court discussed the shifting of various burdens of proof in establishing incompetency and competency in the execution of the written trust agreement. Explain how the court did this.

PART 11 WILLS AND DECEDENTS' ESTATES, AND TRUSTS

ETHICS AND BUSINESS LAW

Introduction

This end-of-part discussion, like the others in this book, is designed to encourage you to begin forming personal beliefs about what is right or wrong conduct in business. The discussion here builds on the material in the first end-of-part discussion; you may find it helpful to review that.

This material has several goals. The section that immediately follows is designed to help you see the range of ethical issues associated with this area of the law. The in-depth discussion is intended to provide you with a background for forming your own beliefs about a single very important ethical issue in business. The problems at the end are designed to build your skill in ethical analysis while exploring further the in-depth issue.

A Sampling of Ethical Issues in Wills and Trusts

All of the law you have studied so far in this book has been the product of elaborate legal decision-making processes. The case law mechanism, in particular, is uniquely rigorous in making the *process* as utterly fair, impartial, and free of emotion as possible. In contrast, the study of wills and trusts is the examination of topics where individual decision making is loaded with emotion. Because this decision-making process is often vulnerable to emotion, it is quite easy to make the wrong decisions. This accounts for the formal requirements for creating a will. The general requirement for a writing, a signature, and attestation are, at least in part, designed to ensure that the testator has the appropriate mental capacity or free will. Similarly, many business ethics issues must be decided in contexts that make high quality decision making difficult. Can you see that in some ethically intense situations you may need to use different procedures to ensure that you make a quality decision?

Sometimes it is impossible to ensure an ethical outcome. In these instances we often are compelled to rely just on *procedures* that are ethical. In a sense this is what the law does in the area of wills and trusts. The law prescribes formal procedures to ensure that the process is as fair as possible because there is no practical way to ensure that the disposition by will of a decedent's property is ethical. Can you see that managers must sometimes rely on just an ethical procedure because they cannot compel an ethical result?

Can you see that the selection of beneficiaries for one's estate is an activity that reflects an ethical orientation? Some take a purely egoistic approach and leave their property to persons who have given them the most pleasure. Sometimes pets are recipients of the benefits of estates of egoists. Utilitarians might leave everything to a college, university, or research institute in the hope of generating the greatest good for the greatest number. Kant's philosophy might suggest that we have a duty to help take care of those whom we have produced, namely our offspring. Religious ethics might require that we leave our estate to a church or a charitable organization which helps the poor.

In-Depth Discussion of a Basic Issue: Mental Capacity and Free Will

This body of law addresses the issue of mental capacity directly. To make a will or create a trust, a person must have mental capacity and be free of undue influence. Mental ability is also a prerequisite to the creation of ethical decisions. An understanding of modern psychology can help us avoid pitfalls and make quality decisions so that our ethical desires translate into ethical conduct.

Business ethics is played out in markets. And markets allow individuals to seek their own self-interest and at the same time to advance the common good. But when markets and other social systems, such as the law, function imperfectly, morally sensitive businesspersons often must elect between advancing their self-interest or advancing the common good. For many, alternating their perspective from self to others is an insurmountable psychological challenge. The need to alternate perspectives can trigger several processes that cause us to misperceive, or misthink, so that our actions do not match our beliefs about what is right or wrong.

► Rationalization

This process has its roots in the idea that we have difficulty simultaneously maintaining two psychologically conflicting ideas. When our minds try to resolve the conflicts, they sometimes ignore reality. For example, car buyers typically collect information about various models and, prior to the purchase, accurately absorb information about each car's strengths and weaknesses. After a purchase, they see their purchase behavior as psychologically inconsistent with the fact that their car has weaknesses. To resolve the conflict, many respond by ignoring their car's weaknesses. Thus the decision maker rationalizes and devises after the fact self-satisfying but incorrect reasons for the purchase—the Cadillac becomes the perfect car rather than what it is, in reality, a compromise between good comfort and poor mileage. It is a form of self-deception. Similarly, the father who decides to leave all of his wealth to a poor daughter thereby disinheriting a financially successful son may suffer from psychological conflict over this action. One potential way to reconcile the treatment of the son is to decide that he has been disinherited for other reasons. In the search for other reasons, the father may incorrectly conclude that he has not been a good son.

Business ethics decisions can be plagued by rationalization. Since the ideas of concern for one's self and concern for others are, for some, psychologically inconsistent, they rationalize their moral behavior. Some rationalize self-interested behavior as "other" oriented. For example, radar detector users and manufacturers often declare that the detectors reduce highway speed by causing users to slow down when the buzzer goes off. But most of us recognize that their motivation is not to slow down but, rather, to be able to speed without getting a traffic ticket.

Rationalization can push some people in the opposite direction. They engage in conduct that is other oriented but describe it to themselves as self-oriented. When contributing to a relief fund for Mexico City after the earthquake in 1985, the contributors say, "What goes around comes around." But we know they will not receive any financial return on this investment. Their impulse is fundamentally other oriented, but they have a hard time seeing themselves in this way. These people need to come to grips with the idea that they are impelled by strong concerns for others and, therefore, they sometimes suppress their self-interest.

► Selective Perception

This is a process similar to rationalization in that it allows us to maintain our ego, or self image, by altering the way we perceive reality. In a famous experiment, college students who heard many classmates falsely describe line *A* as longer than line *B*, came to perceive the lines in the way their classmates described them rather than the way they actually were. Similarly, a son or daughter left out of a will may wrongly recall that the testator lacked testamentary capacity at the time the will was executed.

Sometimes subordinates are judged with selective perception. Only the mistakes are noticed and contributions do not seem to capture the supervisor's attention. Often, a stereotype based on race, sex, accent, appearance or education causes one to view another negatively. So the negative image must be reconciled with the good work performance. Selective perception solves this psychological problem by causing us to see only the negative. As a result a good worker can be unfairly evaluated.

In part, the doctrine of undue influence derives from this reality of human nature. If an elderly person is being cared for by a close relative, the elderly person frequently appreciates the person so much as to stop seeing reality clearly. If there are conflicts between the close relative and other family members, the dependent elderly party often favors the relative on whom she or he is most dependent. Often wills leave a high percentage of an estate to the person who took care of the decedent last.

► Groupthink

This is a phenomenon where close-knit groups lose their ability to objectively evaluate reality. The group pressures its members to conform to its beliefs in the face of evidence that the group is wrong. Dissent is suppressed and members protect the group from "unpleasant" information that conflicts with the group views. Maintaining membership and group cohesion seem to be more important than perceiving reality. In business, competitors are sometimes seen as subhuman "sharks." Unhappy consumers are "the crazies." When the group uses these labels, its members are able to reconcile treating the ones labeled in ways they would not treat "real persons." Families sometimes feud and this can create camps where groupthink prevails.

Solving Ethics Problems

Like the other end-of-part discussions in this book, this one presents problems for you to consider. These problems have three goals. The first is to give you the opportunity to further explore the in-depth issue. The second goal is to give you experience in ethical reasoning about the law and about related management problems. The third goal is to let you see how thinking critically about the law can increase your ability to make ethical decisions. To facilitate this, the problems begin by asking you to analyze the law for its ethical content and then shift to looking at related problems in managerial ethics.

For a discussion of the ethical roles of markets and the law, and examples of the four styles of ethical reasoning—egoism, utilitarianism, Kantian philosophy, and religious ethics—read the business ethics material at the end of Part 1.

▶ Problems

1. Review the case of *Reed and Simmons v. Shipp,* p. 1137. Try to determine who, among the parties to this case, was most likely to have misthought or misperceived. Was it Mack, or Mary or Lula and Fannie? If there was misperception, what type was it?
2. Review the case of *Hellams v. Ross,* pp. 1152–53. There the will of the late Marvin Ross was contested on the basis that he was a drunkard. The will was upheld on the ground that the party attempting to break a will has the burden of proving the lack of testamentary capacity. Ross had entered into bad business transactions, expressed the view that he could buy his way into heaven, and left nothing to his family. What is the philosophic purpose of this law?
3. Suppose you have a strong belief requiring compliance with the law. Also assume you are aware that copying applications software without permission is illegal because it violates the copyright laws. If you were a new employee in an organization that made a practice of buying one copy of applications software then illegally duplicating it for use by 20 to 30 other people, what would you do? Can you see how intense the pressure on you would be to rationalize, or selectively perceive, or engage in groupthink? Suppose you were asked to do the illegal duplication. How do you think you would respond? Can you devise any strategies to keep from getting into such situations?
4. Assume you had worked for IBM for 10 years in its new product development laboratory. One of its competitors has tried to lure you away. While you know many trade secrets that it would be illegal to disclose to the competitor, they give you assurances that they are not hiring you for that information and that they would not pressure you to disclose such information if you came to work for them in their research laboratory. If you accept their offer, do you think you would suffer any dissonance in the new job? Do you think you might lose touch with ethical reality and begin disclosing IBM's trade secrets after inventing some false justification for doing so? How could you protect yourself from such psychological traps?

PART 12

BUSINESS LAW IN THE INTERNATIONAL MARKETPLACE

PREVIEW

Part 12 of this text is an exposure to that part of private international law concerned with transnational business, that is the transfer of property among persons across national boundary lines. International export and import of property is a necessity for a healthy, progressive national economy. It is subject to the business law and governmental regulations of various countries. You will, in all probability, be in a business that directly or indirectly handles property for export or property that has been imported, or both.

Part 12 opens with an introduction to the subject, followed by a discussion of: methods of operating transnational business abroad; the contract between the parties in a transnational business transaction; protection of industrial property interests located abroad; antitrust laws applicable to transnational business; foreign-trade zones; international gift-giving and social courtesies protocol; and the *United Nations Convention on Contracts for the International Sale of Goods*.

Business ethics as it relates to the text material in this part is considered at the end of the part.

57 BUSINESS LAW IN THE INTERNATIONAL MARKETPLACE

Transnational business done by persons (firms and individuals) in the United States and abroad; including the new United Nations Convention on Contracts for the International Sale of Goods, in force since 1988.

CHAPTER

57

BUSINESS LAW IN THE INTERNATIONAL MARKETPLACE

After you have read this chapter, you should be able to:

1. Explain how a letter of credit is used to assure contract performance of payment and delivery of goods.
2. Describe the nature of a foreign agent.
3. Distinguish a foreign distributor from a foreign agent.
4. Understand the use of a turn-key operation.
5. Recognize the legal significance of a parent firm establishing a branch or a subsidiary abroad.
6. Understand what is meant by technology.
7. Discuss the impact of foreign law on domestic (U.S.) technology exported abroad.
8. Explain the significance and importance of the various clauses that should be considered for inclusion in a transnational business contract.
9. Understand the meaning of industrial property interests and the need and means for their protection.
10. Discuss the impact of U.S. and foreign antitrust laws applicable to transnational business.
11. Explain the origins, structure, and operation of the European Economic Community.
12. Understand the meaning of the Foreign Sales Corporation.
13. Explain the importance of a foreign-trade zone (FTZ)
14. Realize the importance of the new United Nations Convention on Contracts for the International Sale of Goods.

BUSINESS DECISIONS and the LAW

If you would like to take advantage of the burgeoning opportunity to engage in transnational business, this chapter is must reading for you.

A global whirlwind of transnational business has been building up in recent years, offering great export (and import) opportunities for small and large American businesses. In Europe for example, an economic community of at least twelve nations, called the European Communities (E.C.), will tear down its internal trade barriers in 1992. This historic event will create a tremendous new consumer market not only for those nations but also for the United States.

Legal expertise in the field of international business is in such great demand that some U.S. law firms with 500 or more lawyers are finding it necessary to station some of their lawyers abroad and to open branches in European and Asian countries. Such firms are also establishing alliances with foreign local law firms, and in some cases even merging with them. Prime Minister Margaret Thatcher's government has proposed a sweeping change in the British legal system that would allow English solicitors to work in international legal partnerships of United States and United Kingdom law firms. In addition, approximately fifteen American law firms have now opened offices in Tokyo under the new Foreign Lawyers Legal Consultants Act; sixteen firms have offices in Hong Kong, and five have branch offices in Singapore.

We are only now beginning to realize how many components of American-made products, such as automobiles, come from abroad, and how many American products are bought by people and firms in foreign nations. The steadily increasing international exchange of trade is enormous and affects both small and large American businesses.

Let's assume you have been hired as a consultant for Olympia Company, an American corporation doing business in the United States. Olympia has discovered an opportunity to engage profitably in the manufacture and sale of a food product whose food supplies are needed throughout the world, particularly in those countries deficient in proper nutrition. The product is a simple, compact pill consisting of various natural, easily grown agricultural items that when combined together according to a secret formula will produce a concentrated food product high in vitamins and protein. Olympia wants to manufacture and export this product for sale abroad. What should the company consider doing, apart from obtaining whatever necessary approval is required from the U.S. Food and Drug Administration?

There are many things to be done. First, an intensive market survey must be made. Since the goods are to be exported, you must determine to what extent the United States and foreign countries limit the exportation and foreign importation of specific kinds of goods. This involves some knowledge of the laws of the countries concerned—the laws of foreign countries as well as those in the United States. It is readily apparent that Olympia needs expert governmental and legal advice.

Does the company know that professional, inexpensive help can be made available to it through the U.S. Government? How can the company prevent unauthorized imitation of its products? In distributing its goods abroad, will it make any difference if Olympia has a foreign sales agent, a foreign distributor, a subsidiary, or a branch corporation located abroad? What if it engages in a joint venture with a foreign firm, or engages in a turn-key operation whereby the company would establish the foreign business enterprise and then turn it over to a foreign firm? Would it be best to manufacture abroad or to manufacture in the United States, considering cost of manufacture, international transportation, and taxes in the countries involved? Should Olympia operate on an account receivable basis? Sell for cash only? Use a letter-of-credit method to further assure payment by the buyer? Will the foreign country permit the purchase money currency to leave the country without governmental permission? Can Olympia legally set the resale price of the goods and limit their foreign territorial distribution without violating antitrust laws and other laws at home and abroad? What contract clauses should be used to assure clarity and completeness of the contract terms and an accurate expression of the intention of the contracting parties? In the event of a dispute between Olympia and the foreign buyer, can the contract of sale effectively establish the place of a lawsuit and governing law? Would a contract provision for international arbitration be desirable? Finally, is the foreign state of the importing company a signatory to the United Nations Convention on Contracts for the International Sale of Goods?

These are only some of the problems and questions that Olympia must consider in the big business of exporting.

Introduction

The relevant curriculum standards of the American Assembly of Collegiate Schools of Business provide: "The purpose of the curriculum shall be to provide for a broad education preparing the student for imaginative and responsible citizenship and leadership roles in business and society—domestic and world-wide. . . . There is no intention that any single approach is required to satisfy the world-wide dimension of the Curriculum Standard, but every student should be exposed to the international dimension through one or more elements of the curriculum."

Persons have a "freedom to contract," subject to the legal limitations imposed by the State as sovereign. In this chapter, unless otherwise indicated, the word "State" is used to describe a nation in the international family of nations and not one of the fifty states in the United States of America. This entire book is a discussion on the various legal areas of limitations on that freedom to contract which, internationally, differ widely from one country to another.

The law in the various nations limiting this freedom takes on differing forms. In the United States we have the **common law,** statutory, administrative, constitutional, and **case law** in each state and in the federal government. This is true also in other countries with a common law background, e.g., Canada, England, Australia. Most other nations have the same forms of law but with one very important exception, namely, code law or civil law based on Roman law instead of the common law. Code law is an all-inclusive system of law stated in each national code, quite different from the common law that consists of principles of law evolving from judicial decisions rendered in the absence of any statutory (legislative or constitutional) provision. Since the common law and the civil law spring from different historical, cultural, political, economic, and philosophical backgrounds, it is not surprising therefore to find among the nations different concepts of freedom to contract to do business and in the enforcement of their laws.

common law
Principles of nonstatutory law reflecting the customs and usages of society and found in judicial decisions

case law
The law that comes from decided cases

These differences become extremely important when American business firms contemplate doing business abroad. The conclusion is obvious that, in order to avoid unnecessary risk of financial loss and to ensure knowledge of the law of the nation in which one desires to engage in business, *competent legal advice and business expertise are absolutely necessary*. Further, these must be supplemented with foreign legal advice and foreign business expertise available in the particular country. Yet it is surprising how often American business is transacted abroad without observing these necessary factors. Also, American business firms are surprised at the great extent of legal and business know-how that is necessary and their high cost. Expert knowledge and experience are not acquired easily, and they command a price.

At this point, you should begin to understand the great impact of the law on transnational business which, basically, is business law in the international marketplace of whatever is being sold. The subject is receiving increasingly greater attention in the United States and throughout the world because of national and business and industrial interest in a healthy and profitable exporting and importing economy. In the United States, particular attention should be given to the impact of the antitrust laws,[1] federal (and state) securities laws,[2] the Foreign Corrupt Practices Act of 1977[3] and anti-boycott

[1]See pp. 725–36.

[2]See pp. 940–47.

[3]See pp. 947–48.

regulations.[4] Domestic and foreign taxation is always a major factor for consideration in transnational business.[5] The world has become smaller in terms of accessibility and interchange among people and nations, providing opportunity for mutually beneficial relationships.

Only a limited exposure to the subject of this chapter is possible because of shortage of space. Our approach to the subject will be to consider the following selected areas and, as each area is discussed, to deal with the legal ramifications affecting each of them:

1. Methods of operating transnational business abroad
2. Contract between the parties in a transnational business transaction
3. Protection of industrial property interests located abroad
4. Antitrust laws applicable to transnational business
5. Foreign Sales Corporation and Shared Foreign Sales Corporation
6. Foreign-Trade Zones
7. United Nations Convention on Contracts for the International Sale of Goods

Methods of Operating Transnational Business Abroad

property
A thing; also an interest or right in a thing

goods
Tangible, movable things

technology
A particular kind of property concerned with material things

Transnational business is concerned with the transfer of **property** among persons across national boundary lines. Property consists of things that are either tangible or intangible. Tangibles are those things that can be touched, such as land and **goods.** Intangibles are things that cannot be touched, that is rights, such as a contract right, an account receivable for money owed, or a copyright or patented right in some thing. Technology is concerned with both intangibles such as ideas and processes related to material things, and tangible material things such as machines and tools resulting from those ideas and processes. **Technology** is owned by the originator. Our main concern here is with the international business transfer of goods and technology, not land.

There are various methods of operating abroad in the transfer of property. We will consider first the sale of goods and then the licensing of technology.

► Sale of Goods

Whether to produce goods in the United States for sale abroad, or to arrange for their foreign manufacture and sale, are decisions to be made only after considering established commercial procedures; cost, which includes domestic and foreign taxes; risks; and foreign laws.

---

[4]United States antiboycott regulations prohibit and make illegal activities by U.S. (domestic) "persons" (which includes those persons who control others, e.g., controlled subsidiaries) in interstate and foreign commerce of the United States that have the effect of furthering or supporting certain international boycotts by one or more foreign countries of another foreign country. Any request to participate in such a boycott or for information about that domestic person's business interest that is boycott related, made to that domestic person, *must* be reported by that domestic person to the U.S. Department of Commerce and the Treasury Department.

[5]Reference should be made to two alternative provisions in the federal Tax Code that are concerned with the exemption and deferment of federal tax on income resulting from doing transnational business. One is concerned with a Domestic International Sales Corporation (DISC), and the other with a Foreign Sales Corporation (FSA). Both are designed to further and encourage American transnational business. See pp. 1216–17.

Domestic Production ***Direct Export Sales*** If the product is to be made in the United States for direct sale to a foreign customer, the domestic seller has the same concerns of how and when to ship the goods and of definite and prompt payment of the purchase price as are in a sale made to a customer in the United States. Unless the seller has absolute trust in the foreign buyer's unsecured credit, the normal and safe procedure is that the parties will require two intermediaries for their mutual protection to assure shipment of the goods and definite prompt payment—one bank acting for the buyer and one bank acting for the seller. The seller will not part with possession or title to the goods, nor the buyer with payment, without such assurances.

The sales agreement between the domestic seller and the foreign buyer will provide for the following procedure. The buyer is to obtain a **letter of credit** issued by a bank in the buyer's country. A letter of credit is an agreement by that bank (the issuing bank) to pay a stated amount of money on presentation to it of a **document of title** (e.g., a **bill of lading**) that itemizes the goods that have been shipped, such itemization of goods being the same as in the letter of credit. Also, the buyer is to arrange with a bank in the United States, satisfactory to the seller, which is to confirm the letter of credit—this means that the "confirming" bank will honor the letter of credit and pay the seller on delivery to it of a bill of lading with the same itemization of products as in the letter of credit. In this way, the seller ships the goods, obtains a bill of lading and delivers it to the confirming bank, which immediately pays the seller the agreed sales price. The confirming bank then delivers the bill of lading to the issuing bank, which immediately reimburses the confirming bank and delivers the bill of lading to the buyer.

letter of credit
"An engagement by a bank or other person made at the request of a customer and of a kind within the scope of UCC 5–102 that the issuer will honor drafts or other demands for payment upon compliance with the conditions specified in the" letter of credit UCC 5–103 (1)(a): see also UCC 2–325(3)

document of title
A document evidencing that the person possessing it "is entitled to receive, hold, and dispose of the document and the goods it covers" UCC 1–201(15)

bill of lading
A document issued to the shipper by a carrier of goods

Suppose the buyer complains that the goods are not as agreed. The intermediate banks have no responsibility for any loss sustained by the buyer. Their only responsibilities were for the confirming bank to pay the seller and the issuing bank to reimburse the confirming bank on the basis of the bill of lading having the same itemization of goods as in the letter of credit. The buyer will have to negotiate with the seller and, possibly, resort to legal proceedings against the seller.

Sale by a Foreign Agent It is normal business practice for a foreign commercial agent to be appointed by an American manufacturing firm (principal) to assist in the sale of its products abroad. The agency law in foreign countries is different in many respects from that in the United States.[6] Foreign laws, particularly in civil or code law countries, often provide for different kinds of agents and define their authority in their commercial codes. The agency agreement must be carefully drawn; stating that there is an agency relationship is not enough.[7] An explanation of what the agent is to do must not include functions that preclude an agency relationship. A knowledge of the legal concept of agency is very important here. Generally, sales are made by the American firm as the principal and the agent is paid a commission on those *sales resulting from the agent's efforts*. The agent does not buy the goods and does not have title to the goods. Agents generally do not have this authority. In some countries, an agent for a foreign principal with authority to make contracts of sale for the principal or to accept orders for its goods is considered to be "doing business" in that country with various legal effects, one of which is to subject the principal to local taxes.

---

[6]For the American law of agency, see Chapters 15–18.

[7]See *Lamb v. Goring*, [1932] 1 K.B. 710 for an excellent discussion of "agency" in that case.

There are other important differences in foreign agency law. In some countries the law requires that only their own nationals may be agents for foreign principals, while in other countries goods may be imported only through their governmental agencies. Many American firms might be surprised to learn that in many countries agency contracts with foreign principals must be registered with the proper foreign governmental agency and, in some countries, the law limits the amount of commission that an agent may receive under the agency contract. Payment by the principal of a higher commission, irrespective of how disguised, may constitute a violation of the U.S. Foreign Corrupt Practices Act of 1977.[8]

In some countries, the national interest to protect their people who represent foreign principals is shown in various labor laws. Some host countries have laws that require that commercial agents for foreign principals must have *exclusive* rights to represent the principal in that country. Such agents often are treated as employees with the many legal effects of such status. There are also laws regarding the termination of such agency relationships, such as requiring advance notice before termination, and providing for an indemnity payment to be made by the principal to the agent either in the form of a lump sum or in an amount reflecting the amount of business brought to the principal by the agent's efforts.

distributor
An independent contractor who sells on his or her own account, independent of the seller of goods to him or her

independent contractor
A person who contracts independently for himself or herself to render a result, and who is not acting on behalf of another nor subject to another's control

Sale by a Foreign Distributor A foreign **distributor** is an **independent contractor.**[9] The agreement establishing this relationship must be very carefully drawn to clearly establish the status of distributorship and to preclude an agency relationship. A distributor, rather than an agent, is appointed usually when the American manufacturer wishes to engage extensively in business in the foreign country. This often involves considerable American expense because the distributor, *in acquiring title to the goods,* will need to establish an inventory and often need training for its employees if the product is technological (e.g., machines and technical equipment). The American firm may prefer appointing a distributor in order not to make a large foreign investment by establishing a foreign branch or subsidiary, and to avoid foreign labor laws applicable to commercial agents for foreign firm principals. Also, as an independent contractor with title to the goods, the foreign distributor, not the American firm, shoulders the risk of establishing good business relationships in the foreign country and of reselling the goods at a profit. The distributor is an independent legal entity with an independent business, and the American firm is not a party to any contracts made by the distributor.

In order for the foreign distributor to have maximum opportunity for resale and for its protection, the appointment of a foreign distributor normally grants the right to *exclusive* distribution of the goods in *one specific country,* and gives protection to the distributor against the American firm establishing substantial future price increases of the goods. Exclusivity of distribution may well raise antitrust problems in some countries. An agreement that the American firm can fix the resale price of the goods to be resold by a *foreign* distributor apparently is not a violation of U.S. antitrust law, but it is a violation of the antitrust laws in some countries. There is a danger that the right to fix the resale price may be deemed such a "control over" the distributor under foreign law as to cause the status of distributor to become one of agency. Further, in order to provide for mutual

---

[8]See pp. 947–48.

[9]For a discussion of an independent contractor, see pp. 294–95.

protection against difficult and burdensome foreign laws concerning termination of the distributor relationship, as is the case with agency, the agreement should provide for a *specified* distributorship period during which, except for *specified* cause, the relationship cannot be terminated by the American firm.

In order to avoid problems of foreign labor law regarding the possible status of an agent or a distributor *as an employee,* it should help considerably if the American manufacturer could induce its representative to incorporate. However, the foreign labor law should be examined carefully to be certain that such corporate status for the purpose of selling the manufactured goods is excluded from that law.

Other Organizational Methods for Transnational Sale of Goods Domestically Produced In addition to sale by direct export, foreign commercial agents, and foreign distributors, there are other organizational methods for transnational sales of goods. One method is a "turn-key" operation, whereby an American firm provides what is necessary in establishing a foreign business enterprise, e.g., manufacturing, supplying equipment, management and personnel training, and licensing of technology, and the firm then "turns" over to a foreign firm the operation of the enterprise. Another method increasingly used is the creation of a **joint venture** between American and foreign firms for a business purpose in a foreign (host) country. In still another method, an American firm may enter into an arrangement to operate a foreign production extraction business,—for example, for oil or minerals—in return for a share in the production.

joint venture
An association of two or more persons as co-owners to engage in a limited business transaction for a profit

The extent of the American seller's activity or of the application of foreign tax laws may justify consideration of establishing either a branch or a **subsidiary** of the American firm in the host country. This means the establishment of a foreign presence in the host country and, therefore, consequent possible submission of itself to foreign jurisdiction and its problems. An important element in establishing jurisdiction is the *degree* of co-ownership between the domestic and foreign corporations. The following well-known, leading case is an illustration of an American court's jurisdiction over a parent foreign corporation with a subsidiary corporation in the United States.

subsidiary corporation
A corporation owned by another corporation

FACTS

Rolls-Royce of England, Ltd. (Ltd.) is a British corporation which manufactures and sells motor cars and airplane engines, and sells parts and gives services to its customers. These products are sold world-wide and customers get service at many places. Ltd. owns all the stock of Rolls-Royce of Canada, a Canadian corporation, and this Canadian company owns all the stock of Rolls-Royce, Inc. (Inc.) which operates in New York State.

The business of Inc. is solely in the sale of products manufactured by Ltd. and in the servicing of the products for purchasers. All sales literature used by Inc. is written and published by Ltd. All three companies have some directors in common, and key executive personnel in Inc. were former executives of either Ltd. or the Canadian company and were assigned to their positions by Ltd., the parent English company. There are frequent conferences among executives of the three companies at which the policies of Inc. are determined. Inc. employees who require technical training are given it by Ltd. in England. Inc. owns no automobiles, and when a car sale is made to a customer, Inc. buys a car from Ltd. in England and imports it. As to airplane engines, compensation for service is paid to Inc. by the Canadian company. All net income of Inc. goes to the Canadian company and appears on the company's balance sheet, and ultimately on the balance sheet of Ltd.

Taca International Airlines (Taca), a corporation of San Salvador, sued Ltd. and served a summons on Inc. as being a part of Ltd. Taca's suit is for damage to its airplane allegedly caused by the negligence of Ltd. and Inc. Ltd. made a motion to dismiss the suit, alleging that Inc. is a distinctly separate corporate entity and that service of a summons on Inc. is not service on Ltd. Ltd. contends that Inc. is a mere incorporated division or arm of Ltd. and a subsidiary of Ltd. Is Inc. an independent entity, or a subsidiary and a mere department of Ltd.?

DECISION

Judgment for Taca; Ltd.'s motion denied. Inc. is Ltd.'s wholly owned subsubsidiary which sold and serviced Ltd.'s products in New York, is a mere sales agent department of Ltd. rather than an independent entity, and service of a summons on Inc. was sufficient service on Ltd. Ltd. was doing extensive business in New York through its local department separately incorporated as Inc.

Taca Int'l Airlines v. Rolls-Royce of England, Ltd. 204 N.E. 329 (N.Y. 1965).

Such foreign jurisdiction includes the American firm's required compliance with the host's laws, resolution of disputes in the host's courts, and taxation problems, to mention only a few of its features. Branches or subsidiaries may be established only with the permission, or at the request, of the host country. It is important that a firm consider the tax consequences in the United States and abroad before deciding whether to have branches or subsidiaries.

Transnational Transfer of Technology

Technology is a particular kind of property concerned with material things. It signifies that *tangible* material thing that is the result of innovation (e.g., machine, computer, factory); and also that which is the *intangible* innovative process itself, sometimes called "intellectual property" (e.g., ideas, processes, inventions). As property, technology can be transferred. We have already discussed the *sale* of goods, which includes the sale of tangible technology. Here, we will briefly consider a few other methods by which a transfer of technology may be made together with legal restrictions on such transfer.

In both kinds of technology (tangible and intangible) governmental legal restrictions are applied to their transnational business transfer because of their international importance, national security, and need in foreign countries. Legal restrictions on, or affecting the export or import of, technology in the United States and foreign countries are either in the form of domestic or foreign statutory or administrative law, or in international accords such as treaties and agreements. For example, in the United States the Export Administration Act of 1969, as amended, and the Department of Commerce Export Regulations restrict the export of technology. Some technology can be exported under the general **license** provisions of the Department of Commerce without applying for any license, while the export of other technology is prohibited without application for and issuance of a validated license. For the most part, national interest in the various countries determines the extent of licensing or the registration of the export and import of technology.

license
Permission to do something

Technology such as patents and trademarks is subject to protection from infringement abroad.[10] Many foreign national laws and international accords (agreements, treaties) provide a certain amount of protection, but opportunity for violation is always present. However, in some countries certain items are not patentable (e.g., medical

[10]For patents, trademarks, and copyrights, see pp. 91–92, 542, 861, 1205–06.

devices, food, energy controls), and owners' rights are limited. Many countries require that governmental agencies must approve technology transfer agreements, and some have the power to modify such agreements. A suggested method of owner protection is to provide in the agreement that such modification will, at the election of the owner, void the agreement.

A careful examination should be made of the antitrust laws of the United States and of the foreign country where the recipient of the technology transfer is located. For example, the owner's restriction on the foreign recipient's use of the technology, substantial effect of the technology on American export or import, and contracts and combinations abroad intending and accomplishing restraint of foreign commerce with the United States may well be subject to U.S. antitrust law. Clearance with proper foreign and U.S. governmental agencies should be obtained in advance in order to plan properly and be legally safe. A type of activity fraught with possible violation of foreign antitrust laws, as it is in the United States, is the **tying** or "tie-in" **arrangement** whereby a seller's agreement with a buyer for the sale of a particular product makes such sale contingent on the buyer's agreement to purchase another of the seller's products. The development of technology products abroad causes foreign countries to view license agreements for product use in their countries with a careful eye, and often to require that local nationals be employed by the licensee or that local materials be used by the licensee in the development of the technology.

tying arrangement
An agreement between a seller or lessor and a purchaser or lessee that a sale or lease of a product to the latter is contingent upon the latter's purchase or lease of another product of the seller or lessor

The Contract Between the Parties in a Transnational Business Transaction

The transnational business contract between the parties should use plain language and be as simple, clear, and precise as possible so that the parties can operate under it without outside legal help. This is necessary for two main reasons. First, it is surprising to the uninformed how different the foreign political climate and concepts of doing business are from those of the United States. These must be considered carefully and in detail *before* preparing the contract. Second, there is a wide difference in the meaning of business terms as used in the United States and abroad. The contract must meet these problems to the greatest extent possible. A few items will be considered in the sections that follow.

But first, unlike the Uniform Commercial Code in the United States, which fills gaps in the agreement of the contracting parties in a contract for the sale of goods by provisions reflecting realistic common business understanding and practices concerning intention and interpretation, until 1988 there apparently was no such similar help abroad among nations. It should be realized that transnational business contracts may be judged on the basis of the civil code or religiously based law of conduct in various countries. Accordingly, the contract must reflect a balance between conciseness and completeness. Fortunately, as of January 1, 1988, there is now the United Nations Convention on Contracts for the International Sale of Goods (CISG), ratified by the United States and a relatively small number of sovereign States. At the end of this chapter, there is a brief analysis of some of the sections of CISG.

► A Writing

The contract should be in writing. If the contract is oral as a result of oral or written communications, e.g., telephone or written correspondence, a written confirmation of the oral contract and its terms should be made and approved by the parties.

Language There should be only one official draft in only one official language, and the contract should so specifically provide. If at all possible, the language should be English. However, if a foreign language is to be used, and a foreign country by law may require only its own language or that a translation copy accompany the English version, then local foreign co-counsel should be retained to assure that the intended understanding of the parties is reflected in the writing. The contract should provide for a written "official" translation to be ratified by the parties for guidance and reliance in their contractual performance. Where it is necessary to have a foreign language *in addition* to English, *both* language versions should be made "official," if at all possible.

Definition of Terms Because of differences in the meaning of words, particularly in the use of different languages and in differing business concepts, the contract should provide its own definitions of terms. To the extent necessary, it should provide that, as a part of the contract, standard terms used in a specified outside reference shall control. Probably the most complete and widely used international reference set of standard terms is *Incoterms* by the International Chamber of Commerce.

Price and Legal Compliance In addition to these terms, there are some other matters that require attention and inclusion in the contract. There should be carefully drafted clauses concerning how payment is to be made, the kind of currency, how price is to be determined, and the responsibility for compliance with local foreign law concerning the contemplated business transaction. Some countries will not permit their currency to leave the country without governmental permission, with the result that the outside party to receive payment may never be able to use it as intended.

A way out of this dilemma is to provide in the contract that the foreign party in such country will have the responsibility to procure governmental permission and to make arrangements with an agreed outside financial institution (e.g., a bank), and that the domestic party to receive payment has no obligation to perform under the contract until all this is done. That same foreign party should also have the specified responsibility to comply with that country's laws: for registration, and procurement of governmental approval, of the contract; for obtaining a license for the business to be done, where such is required; and for the payment of necessary government taxes and fees in that connection. It should not be forgotten that U.S. law also requires contract approval in specified instances.

"Force Majeure" Every contract should have a "force majeure" clause, which in French means an "irresistible or impossible force." This suggests the phrase "act of God" but its international business meaning is much more extensive. The clause should provide for those specified occasions beyond the control of the parties when a party will not be liable for failure to perform the contract. A few examples are war, embargo, governmental prohibition of export or import of goods or technology covered by the contract, governmental expropriation, accident, fire, flood, and interruption of transportation. The clause should be detailed and complete.

jurisdiction
The power of a court to hear and decide a case involving a person or subject matter properly brought before the court

Jurisdiction—Clauses for Choice-of-Law and Choice-of-Forum Disputes may occur among the parties to a transnational business contract requiring resolution by a court. The law of the place where the legal proceedings occur (the forum) has **jurisdiction**

over the matter to be adjudicated. However, what substantive law is the court to apply? We are in the legal area called "conflict of laws."

If the contracting parties provide in their contract a *choice-of-law* clause specifying the law of which State shall apply, the court of the forum usually will apply that specified law, unless it is contrary to the fundamental policy of the forum State. In the absence of such a clause, the court may apply the law of either the State where the contract was made or where contractual performance was to occur. A similar problem arises with respect to which State courts shall be the *forum* for the adjudication of the matter in dispute. Here, again, the parties can provide a *choice-of-forum* clause in their contract specifying which State shall be the forum. Various international and regional conventions approve of the validity and enforceability of such clauses. Contracting parties should examine their contracts carefully and be especially cognizant of these clauses and their meaning.

In the United States United States law on choice-of-law clauses is reflected in the Restatement (Second) of Conflict of Laws, Section 187, and the Uniform Commercial Code, Section 1–105(1). For choice-of-forum clauses, it is the same Restatement, Section 80, supplemented by Sections 81–90. United States courts generally recognize such clauses as valid and enforceable.

1. Choice-of-Law The choice-of-law clause should be drafted carefully after an examination of Section 187 of the Restatement and the facts surrounding the transnational business contract. The clause by itself is not sufficient for validity and enforceability. Figure 57.1 states the provision of Section 187.

In the following case the court found a choice-of-law clause in a contract to be valid and enforceable after a careful application of Section 187.

FIGURE 57.1 **Section 187 of the Restatement (Second) Conflict of Laws**

§ **187. Law of the State Chosen by the Parties**

(1) The law of the state chosen by the parties to govern their contractual rights and duties will be applied if the particular issue is one which the parties could have resolved by an explicit provision in their agreement directed to that issue.

(2) The law of the state chosen by the parties to govern their contractual rights and duties will be applied, even if the particular issue is one which the parties could not have resolved by an explicit provision in their agreement directed to that issue, unless either

(a) the chosen state has no substantial relationship to the parties or the transaction and there is no other reasonable basis for the parties' choice, or

(b) application of the law of the chosen state would be contrary to a fundamental policy of a state which has a materially greater interest than the chosen state in the determination of the particular issue and which, under the rule of § 188, would be the state of the applicable law in the absence of an effective choice of law by the parties.

(3) In the absence of a contrary indication of intention, the reference is to the local law of the state of the chosen law.

adhesion contract
A standard form contract in which the weaker party has no realistic choice or opportunity to bargain

FACTS

Dr. Pirkey, a Colorado physician, was employed by Hospital Corporation of America (Hospital), an international recruiting and hospital management company, to render medical services at the King Faisal Hospital in Saudi Arabia. The written contract provided "This agreement shall be construed in accordance with the Laws and Regulations of the Kingdom of Saudi Arabia." Before Dr. Pirkey was to leave for Saudi Arabia, the Hospital learned that Dr. Pirkey did not include in his employment application information regarding his 1974 criminal conviction for shoplifting. The Hospital then terminated his employment. Dr. Pirkey sues the Hospital in Colorado federal district court for damages for breach of contract, alleging that the choice-of-law clause is part of an **adhesion contract** and should not be respected. The Hospital contends it is not an adhesion contract and the clause is valid and enforceable. Is the clause valid and enforceable?

DECISION

Yes. Judgment for the Hospital. The court referred to Section 187 of the Restatement (Second) of Conflict of Laws. The forum should apply the law chosen by the parties unless there is no reasonable basis for the choice. Saudi Arabia bears enough of a relationship to this transaction to remove doubts that there was not a reasonable basis for the parties' choice. Dr. Pirkey's services were to be rendered in Saudi Arabia. Choice-of-law provisions such as the one contained in this employment agreement are ordinarily given effect; they are a clear manifestation of the parties' intentions.

This is not an adhesion contract. Although the agreement is a printed form apparently prepared by the King Faisal Hospital, this alone does not define adhesion contracts. Dr. Pirkey does not show that there was no opportunity for negotiation. Further this is not a case involving a party with superior bargaining power attempting to take advantage of a weaker party who is incapable of fully understanding the contract provisions. Dr. Pirkey signed the contract with full knowledge of its contents; he did not protest the inclusion of this choice-of-law provision in the contract at the time he signed it or subsequently prior to this action. Since Dr. Pirkey did not lack any opportunity to negotiate the provision, nor is the provision oppressive or offensive, this is not an adhesion contract.

Finally, application of the Saudi Arabian law chosen by the parties to determine their rights and duties under the contract will not be contrary to a fundamental policy of Colorado. A fundamental policy must be a substantial one, which is not the case here.

Pirkey v. Hospital Corp. of America, 483 F.Supp 770 (D. Colo. 1980).

2. Choice-of-Forum Section 80 of the Restatement provides "The parties agreement as to the place of the action cannot oust a State of judicial jurisdiction, but such an agreement will be given effect unless it is unfair or unreasonable." This is illustrated in the following leading U.S. Supreme Court case when this court first departed from the rigid common law doctrine that refused to honor choice-of-forum clauses.

exculpate
To relieve from liability

FACTS

Unterweser, a German corporation, entered into an international towage contract with Zapata Off-Shore Co., a Texas corporation, to tow Zapata's ocean-going drilling rig from Louisiana to a point off Italy in the Adriatic Sea. The contract, submitted by Unterweser with changes subsequently negotiated by the parties, contained the provision "Any dispute arising must be treated before the London Court of Justice." The contract also contained two clauses to **exculpate** Unterweser from liability for damage to the towed rig. The rig while being towed by Unterweser's tug, the Bremen, was seriously damaged in a storm in the Gulf of Mexico, and the Bremen towed the damaged rig to Tampa, Florida, the nearest port of refuge.

Zapata sued Unterweser in the federal District Court in Tampa for $3,500,000 damages for alleged negligent towage and for breach of the towage contract. Unterweser invoked the forum clause of the contract, and made a motion to dismiss the case for lack of jurisdiction or on grounds of inconvenience. Before the District Court acted on the motion, Unterweser sued Zapata in the High Court of Justice in London for damages for breach of the towage contract as the contract provided. The High Court held that the forum clause conferred jurisdiction on the High Court and would be enforced, absent a showing that it would not be fair and right to do so. The federal District Court then denied Unterweser's motion to dismiss and, on appeal, the decision was affirmed, following the traditional American judicially established view that "agreements in advance of controversy whose object is to oust the jurisdiction of the courts are contrary to public policy and will not be enforced." Unterweser petitioned the United States Supreme Court for review.

DECISION

Reversed, for Unterweser. Remanded to the District Court for further proceedings consistent with the Supreme Court's opinion.

Forum selection clauses are **prima facie** valid and should be enforced unless enforcement is shown by the resisting party to be "unreasonable" under the circumstances. The approach substantially followed in other common-law countries including England is "that parties to a contract may agree in advance to submit to the jurisdiction of a given court, to permit notice to be served by the opposing party, or even to waive notice altogether." It is the view adopted by the *Restatement (Second) of Conflict of Laws*, Section 80. It accords with ancient concepts of freedom of contract. The language of the forum clause is clearly mandatory and all-encompassing, and the courts of England plainly meet the standards of neutrality and long experience in admiralty litigation. The choice of that forum was made in an arms-length negotiation by experienced and sophisticated businessmen, and absent some countervailing reason it should be honored by the parties and enforced by the courts. A freely negotiated private international agreement, unaffected by fraud, undue influence, or overwhelming bargaining power, as is the one here, should be given full effect.

Nevertheless, to allow Zapata opportunity to carry its heavy burden of showing not only that the balance of convenience is strongly in favor of trial in Tampa (that is, that it will be far more inconvenient for Zapata to litigate in London than it will be for Unterweser to litigate in Tampa), but also that a London trial will be so manifestly and gravely inconvenient for Zapata that it would be effectively deprived of a meaningful day in court, we remand for further proceedings.

prima facie
At first sight

The Bremen v. Zapata Off-Shore Co., 407 U.S. 1 (1972).

Section 82 of the Restatement provides that a State will not exercise jurisdiction, which has been obtained by fraud or unlawful force, over a defendant or his or her property. Also, Section 84 provides that a State will not exercise jurisdiction if it is a seriously inconvenient forum for the trial of the action.

In Foreign States Regional and international conventions recognize choice-of-law and choice-of-forum clauses as valid and enforceable.

Transnational Commercial Arbitration **Arbitration** is a process of resolving a dispute by using a third party chosen for his or her neutrality and expertise to decide the disputed issue or issues. The parties must agree to be bound by the decision of the intermediary. It is a method of resolving disputes without the necessity of court proceedings, although judicial appeal from arbitration decisions is available. This method of resolving disputes relating to transnational business contracts is used increasingly and widely because of many factors: convenience; reduction in expense; timeliness; arbitrators with expertise in the subject of the dispute and with experience in

arbitration
A method for deciding disputes outside of the court by persons called arbitrators, appointed by the disputing parties

arbitration; reduced adversary confrontation with increased preservation of amicable business relations between the parties; and continued performance of the contract during arbitration proceedings. However, the cost of arbitration must be considered.

Commercial arbitration clauses often are included in transnational business contracts. However, the choice of arbitration clause and the provisions to be included in it are most important. A poor clause can do more harm than good. The clause should have exact language and, among other items, probably should cover the following: provide a choice-of-forum clause and possibly a choice-of-law clause; specify the particular kind of arbitrator expertise required; and, where necessary, specify the issues which are *not* subject to arbitration.

Since the rules and procedures to be used in transnational commercial arbitration are important, examination should be made of the formal rules and procedures, as well as commercial arbitration clauses and associated costs, available from some of the existing arbitration groups. Some of these groups are regional, such as the Inter-American Commercial Arbitration Commission. Others are world-wide, such as the American Arbitration Association (AAA) and the International Chamber of Commerce (ICC) with its Court of Arbitration. Each has its own formal rules and procedures. In particular, the AAA and the ICC are very good.

Most countries recognize transnational commercial arbitration clauses as valid and enforceable, and they will enforce valid transnational commercial arbitration awards in their courts. The United Nations 1958 Convention on the Recognition and Enforcement of Foreign Arbitration Awards, to which the United States is a party and which is widely adopted, recognizes the validity and enforceability of arbitration clauses in transnational business contracts, and provides for the enforcement of valid arbitration awards with the same effect as local judicial judgments. It should be noted that, in the United States, actions in violation of U.S. antitrust laws are not subject to arbitration. Also, some countries refuse to enforce transnational business arbitration awards unless the arbitration clause requires that arbitration is to occur only in those particular countries.

Protection of Industrial Property Interests Located Abroad

A State has sovereign jurisdiction over all persons, property, and actions that occur within its geographical borders. Transnational business investment in a foreign State subjects the firm's industrial property interests to that State's jurisdiction. Risk of loss to such interests always exists, principally from three sources: (1) foreign governmental action, as by **expropriation** or other change in law having an adverse effect on such interest; (2) damaging conduct by the foreign contracting party, as by its breach of the transnational business contract; and (3) by other foreign persons, as by their improper, unauthorized use of the owner's inventions, patents, and trademarks.

expropriation
The taking of an owner's property by the government

Foreign Expropriation

The possibility of foreign State expropriation of physical and other property of the investing firm suggests that the political and economic stability of the foreign country should be considered before making an investment. If expropriation does occur without adequate compensation, the investing firm has only three sources of relief.

The first is the Overseas Private Investment Corporation (OPIC), established by the U.S. government to encourage U.S. private investment and private skills in the economic and social development of certain specified less developed friendly countries. It issues insurance to eligible investors, assuring a certain amount of protection against various enumerated risks with respect to projects that OPIC has approved. Among the enumerated risks are partial or complete loss by expropriation by a foreign government. A low rate of premium is charged for this insurance. It is essential that this insurance be obtained *before* the investment is made; it is not available afterwards. On the occurrence of such loss, OPIC will pay the investing firm, and the U.S. government will then seek repayment from the foreign country.

A second source of relief consists of the various insurance programs of the Export Import Bank of the United States, available through its agent the Foreign Credit Insurance Association (FCIA). Foreign political actions, such as foreign expropriation, which result in a loss to the U.S. exporter are insurable through FCIA. Additional information about these programs is available from many sources, including state export finance agencies, FCIA regional offices, and specialty private insurance brokers.

The third source of relief is to use the investing firm's State courts, sue the foreign country, and enforce the judgment against the foreign country's assets located in the local country where the judgment was obtained. (*X* country expropriates *Y* Company's assets located in *X*. *Y* can sue *X* in a U.S. federal court, obtain judgment against *X*, and levy upon *X*'s assets in the United States.) This can occur only if the forum court has jurisdiction over the matter and the power to enforce its judgment. Use of this remedy presents problems because of the judicially created "act of state doctrine" and the U.S. Foreign Sovereign Immunities Act.

Under the act of state doctrine, U.S. courts presume the *validity* of *public* acts committed by a foreign sovereign state *in its own territory* and will not examine such acts for validity, even if the acts are violations of international law. The reasoning is that such acts are a matter of political and not judicial concern. When the expropriated or confiscated property is located *within the United States* at the time of the attempted expropriation or confiscation, the U.S. courts will give effect to the acts of a foreign state only if the acts are consistent with the policy and law of the United States. In the leading case of *Banco Nacional De Cuba v. Sabbatino*, 376 U.S. 398 (1964), the U.S. Supreme Court applied this doctrine, refusing to inquire into the validity of Cuba's expropriation of an American's sugar *in Cuba*, and permitting a Cuban bank instrumentality to sue an American broker in New York for sugar money proceeds owing to it.

The Foreign Sovereign Immunities Act (FSIA) recognizes the sovereign immunity of a foreign state, with exceptions of the extent to which a legal action may be brought against a foreign state in the United States and levy made upon the property of the foreign state *located in the United States*. If the foreign state is engaged in a "commercial activity" in the United States, generally it no longer has sovereign immunity.

Intangible Industrial Property Interests (Rights)

The association in the consumer's mind of goods with a trademark or brand name can be of great value in the marketing of such goods. The same is true of processes, **patents, copyrights,** and other kinds of intangible industrial property interests. The pirating or use of such property without a license from the owner is world-wide. Improper use may be made by the previous licensee after the license has expired. It may also be made by other persons who never had a license and who wish to profit at the owner's expense without having incurred the often considerable investment expense to produce the product with its trademark, brand name, patent, process, or other industrial property interest.

patent
A governmental grant of protection of an invention

copyright
A governmental grant of protection of original works in a tangible medium of expression

Under the common law, the *first user* of industrial property interests becomes their owner. Often there is difficulty in establishing priority of use. In a transnational business contract where industrial property interests are involved, there could be inserted a provision to the effect that the parties agree that, as between them, the industrial firm is the first user and owner of the property. An antipiracy provision should also be included. However, the law is different in many foreign code countries where the law requires registration of trademarks, brand names, patents, and other industrial property interests, the *first to register* becoming the owner.[11] However, various regional and international conventions provide recognition and protection of ownership of industrial property interests by compliance with the convention requirements. Of particular interest is the International Convention for the Protection of Industrial Property, of which the United States is a member, under which a single registration in the home country assures recognition of the registering party's ownership and protection of the registered property interests by all the member States without the necessity of repeated registrations in those States.

Antitrust Laws Applicable to Transnational Business

The U.S. antitrust laws have been discussed previously in Chapter 34.[12] Reference should be made to that material at this time to provide background and avoid unnecessary repetition. There the main thrust was the application of such laws to *domestic* business transactions. Here we will relate those laws to *transnational* business transactions. First we will see antitrust law in operation in the United States, and then we will briefly consider foreign antitrust law particularly as it is applied and enforced in the European Economic Community (EEC).

► Antitrust in the United States

The philosophy of the United States is that free competition is the best means to stimulate progress and to achieve higher living standards. Antitrust laws are designed to eliminate the abuses that militate against this philosophy.

The Sherman Act provides in Section 1 that every contract, combination, or conspiracy in [unreasonable] restraint of trade or commerce among the several states or with foreign nations is illegal. In Section 2, it is illegal for any person to monopolize, atempt to monopolize, or combine or conspire with any other person or persons, to monopolize any part of the trade or commerce among the several states or with foreign nations. The Clayton Act states that certain specific business practices that produce the prohibited results are illegal. Section 4 provides, "Any person who shall be injured in his business or property by reason of anything forbidden in the antitrust laws may sue therefor in any district court of the United States in which the defendant resides or is found or has an agent, with respect to the amount in controversy, and shall recover threefold the damages by him sustained, and the cost of suit, including a reasonable attorney's fee." The word "person" has been construed to include a foreign nation, as well as a natural person and a **juristic person,** such as a corporation. Foreign governments can be sued for violation of U.S. antitrust laws.

juristic person
An artificial person created by law

"A conspiracy to monopolize or restrain the domestic or foreign commerce of the United States is not outside the reach of the Sherman Act just because the conduct

[11]For patents, trademarks, and copyrights, see pp. 91–92, 542, 861, 1205–06.

[12]See pp. 725–36.

complained of occurs in foreign countries."[13] Similarly, if a U.S. person improperly uses its advantages in a particular product domestic market to attempt to restrain competition of that same product in the international market, the U.S. antitrust laws are applicable. This is illustrated by the following case.

FACTS

Plaintiffs, three subsidiaries of the International Telephone and Telegraph Company, allege that Western Union Telegraph Company (WU), defendant, has violated and continues to violate Sections 1 and 2 of the Sherman Act by: (1) refusing to interconnect with plaintiffs' domestic and international telex transmission lines; (2) using its monopoly over domestic telex service to gain a competitive advantage in the provision of international service; and (3) entering into a contract with TRT, an international telex carrier, assuring TRT at least 50,000,000 minutes of outbound international telex traffic from the WU network and gaining TRT's assistance in WU's provision of international telex service. WU made a motion to dismiss some portions of the complaint relating to WU's provision of international telex service on the ground that the allegations fail to state a claim upon which relief can be granted.

DECISION

WU's motion is denied. First, the complaint alleges WU's entry into the international telex service market as part of a more general scheme by WU to restrain competition in both the domestic and international telex markets. Even if WU's international telex service and contracts with TRT were in themselves legal, "they lose that character when they become constituent elements of an unlawful scheme." Second, the complaint alleges that WU used its domestic telex monopoly to gain a competitive advantage in the provision of international telex service. "The use of monopoly power attained in one market to gain a competitive advantage in another is a violation of Section 2, even if there has not been an attempt to monopolize the second market." A competitor in the market in which another company is unfairly using its monopoly power to gain a competitive advantage has standing to sue. Third, the complaint alleges that WU and TRT agreed that WU would guarantee 50,000,000 minutes of outbound international traffic and that TRT would assist WU's entry into the international telex market, thereby foreclosing plaintiffs from competing for that portion of the market. It is established that, if a contract effects an unreasonable restraint of trade, a company foreclosed by that contract may bring an antitrust action under Section 1 of the Sherman Act.

ITT World Communications Inc., et al. v. Western Union Telegraph Co., 524 F.Supp. 702 (S.D.N.Y. 1981).

In the absence of specified **per se** illegal conduct in violation of antitrust law, conspiring by a person in a foreign country with an American person to restrain trade subjects both parties and the matter to the jurisdiction of the U.S. courts.[14] Alleged antitrust violation for unreasonable restraint of trade must have *substantial effect* on U.S. commerce before U.S. courts will exercise jurisdiction and apply U.S. antitrust law. The fact that illegal antitrust acts occur *abroad* does not preclude U.S. courts from taking jurisdiction *so long as there is a significant or substantial effect on the foreign or interstate commerce of the United States*. Also, the line of product to be monopolized illegally may include a product imported into the United States.

per se
In and of itself

[13] *Continental Ore Co. v. Union Carbide & Carbon Corp.*, 370 U.S. 704 (1962).

[14] *National Bank of Canada v. Interbank Card Ass'n* 507 F.Supp. 1113 (S.D.N.Y. 1980).

Among the frequent instances of per se antitrust violations are resale price fixing and tying contracts. Attempts to restrain when and how a customer disposes of a product often are antitrust violations. There are also cases where a domestic firm's restraint on a U.S. distributor not to export in order to prevent competition with an exclusive foreign distributor is an antitrust violation. However, if substantial restraint by a domestic firm was *essential* in conducting business abroad, it may be reasonable and not an antitrust violation. But it would be a violation if the domestic firm joined in a foreign **cartel** with a substantial restraining effect on commerce in the United States, such as causing an increase in the price of imports or excluding products from the American market.

cartel
A combination of private enterprises or states to control production, price, or distribution of like commodities or services

An agreement between manufacturers and potential competitors to allocate and divide world markets is illegal antitrust conduct. However, a parent corporation's allocation of territorial markets and setting prices for its subdivisions, if the parent really *controls* the subsidiary, is not a violation of U.S. antitrust laws.

Persons in foreign countries are included among those persons protected by, and also subject to, U.S. antitrust laws. Foreign competitors and foreign consumers are protected under U.S. antitrust laws from violations of such laws committed by U.S. persons. Foreign persons, including foreign governments, have the right to sue for treble damages under U.S. antitrust laws. Also, a foreign person can sue another foreign person in U.S. courts for violations of U.S. antitrust laws. In *Joseph Muller Corp. Zurich v. Société Anonyme de Gerance et D' Armement,* 451 F.2d 727 (2d Cir. 1971), *cert. denied,* a Swiss corporation sued a French corporation, both with offices in the United States and carrying on foreign and domestic commerce in the same commodities, for alleged conspiracy to fix prices for and to monopolize the transportation of various chemical commodities from the United States to other countries. The presence of a U.S. person with a foreign person in a conspiracy to restrain trade involves such contact with U.S. commerce as will subject both persons to U.S. jurisdiction under its antitrust laws.

Export Trading Company Act of 1982 The federal Export Trading Company Act became law in October 1982. The purpose of the Act is "to increase United States exports of products and services by encouraging more efficient provision of export trade services to United States producers and suppliers."

The Act provided for the establishment of the Office of Export Trade in the Department of Commerce under the secretary of commerce to "promote and encourage to the greatest possible extent feasible the formation of export trade associations and export trade companies." [Sec. 102(b).] An export trading company (ETC) is an individual, association, or organization operated for profit or nonprofit, doing business under the laws of the United States or any of its states, and for the principal purposes of "exporting goods or services produced in the United States; or facilitating the exportation of goods or services produced in the United States by unaffiliated persons by providing one or more export trade services." [Sec. 103(4).]

Under the Act, the secretary of commerce is to promulgate regulations implementing the Act's policy. The Federal Reserve Board is made responsible for assisting in the financing and development of export trading companies in the United States.

Export Trade Certificates of Review Title III of the Act provides that persons who wish to establish an ETC can apply to the secretary of commerce for a "certificate of review," which in effect is a *certificate of antitrust immunity*. The certificate will be issued, after concurrence of the U.S. attorney general, if the applicant establishes that its specified export trade, export trade activities, and methods of operation will:

(1) result in neither a substantial lessening of competition or restraint of trade within the United States nor a substantial restraint of the export trade of any competitor of the applicant;
(2) not unreasonably enhance, stabilize, or depress prices within the United States of the goods, wares, merchandise, or services of the class exported by the applicant;
(3) not constitute unfair methods of competition against competitors engaged in the export of goods, wares, merchandise, or services of the class exported by the applicant; and
(4) not include any act that may reasonably be expected to result in the sale for consumption or resale within the United States of the goods, wares, merchandise, or services exported by the applicant. [Sec. 303(a).]

The effect of this certificate is to confer the following antitrust protection upon the recipient of the certificate:

> Sec. 306. (a) Except as provided in subsection (b), no criminal or civil action may be brought under the antitrust laws against a person to whom a certificate of review is issued which is based on conduct which is specified in, and complies with the terms of, a certificate issued under section 303 which certificate was in effect when the conduct occurred.
>
> **(b)(1)** Any person who has been injured as a result of conduct engaged in under a certificate of review may bring a civil action for injunctive relief, actual damages, the loss of interest on actual damages, and the cost of suit (including a reasonable attorney's fee) for the failure to comply with the standards of section 303(a). Any action commenced under this title shall proceed as if it were an action commenced under section 4 or section 16 of the Clayton Act, except that the standards of section 303(a) of this title and the remedies provided in this paragraph shall be the exclusive standards and remedies applicable to such action.
> **(2)** Any action brought under paragraph (1) shall be filed within two years of the date the plaintiff has notice of the failure to comply with the standards of section 303(a) but in any event within four years after the cause of action accrues.
> **(3)** In any action brought under paragraph (1), there shall be a presumption that conduct which is specified in and complies with a certificate of review does comply with the standards of section 303(a).
> **(4)** In any action brought under paragraph (1), if the court finds that the conduct does comply with the standards of section 303(a), the court shall award to the person against whom the claim is brought the cost of suit attributable to defending against the claim (including a reasonable attorney's fee).
> **(5)** The Attorney General may file suit pursuant to section 15 of the Clayton Act (15 U.S.C. 25) to enjoin conduct threatening clear and irreparable harm to the national interest.

The recipient of a certificate of review must submit annual reports to the secretary of commerce.

Amendments to the Sherman Act and to the Federal Trade Commission Act Title III amends the Sherman Act and the Federal Trade Commission Act (FTC) by providing that the Sherman Act shall not apply to conduct, and the FTC shall not apply to unfair methods of competition, involving U.S. export trade or commerce with foreign nations unless such conduct or methods of unfair competition "have a direct, substantial, and reasonably foreseeable effect" on domestic commerce and domestic competition that gives rise to a claim for damages thereunder. (Secs. 402, 403.)

Accordingly, ETCs have a choice of utilizing either (1) the certificate of review process under Title III, with its advantages of a specific detailed set of four standards and no treble damages for violation, as opposed to the disadvantages of cost, and the required extensive disclosure of detailed financial and marketing information that competitors could use to their advantage; or (2) the much broader standard of no "direct, substantial, and reasonably foreseeable effect" on domestic commerce and domestic competition, but with the disadvantage of treble damages for violation.

The Export Trading Company Act of 1982 will undoubtedly be important in future litigation involving antitrust matters.

► Antitrust in the European Common Market

Background We should be aware, initially, that individual nations and groups of nations differ among themselves and from the United States concerning their economic and political conditions, goals, and methods used to accomplish those goals. For example, while the more advanced industrial nations seek protection by monopoly of their industrial property interests (e.g., patents, licensing, processes of production), the less developed countries (LDCs) are opposed to this concept and will disregard foreign national or international treaties because of their need for such property to further their goal of national development. It is not surprising, therefore, that these latter countries pay particular attention to transnational business agreements that may militate against their goal.

After World War II, the Western European nations decided that it was necessary to integrate themselves economically by creating a single integrated system for the purpose of eliminating the public (e.g., tariffs) and private (e.g., restrictive agreements by and among business firms in those nations) barriers, and create an agreed *common* market for its members without internal frontiers. The concept reflected what has always been the case among European nations—protection of local business and industry from foreign competition. This concept is quite different from the U.S. policy of free trade. Business conduct permitted among themselves may well be prohibited to outsiders whose conduct may interfere with such economic unity. The result was the Treaty Establishing the European Economic Community signed in Rome in 1957. This economic group consisting of twelve countries is often called the Common Market or EEC. The EEC is only one of other common markets such as the Central American Common Market (CACM) and the Caribbean Community (CARICOM) and others.

Since 1957, the EEC has made great progress toward freeing trade within the community for the benefits of its members, accompanied by much regulation. The hope is that by the end of 1992, there will be a genuine common market, with goods, labor, and capital crossing national barriers without hindrance. An example is the European monetary system, which sets limits on how much each member country's currency can rise or fall against the others.

Structure This treaty established the Commission of the European Communities (Commission) located in Brussels. It is the body to enforce Articles 85 and 86 of the treaty, which are probably the most important and frequently used sections on prohibited business restraint of trade. Complaints of violation are made to the Commission which, either as a result of such complaints or on its own initiative, under its very broad powers investigates and determines whether a violation has occurred. The Commission has power to order cessation of continued illegal violations and to impose fines for violations. Appeal and review from the Commission's decisions is to the European Court of Justice in Luxembourg. This court is now assisted by the new 1990 Court of First Instance. It is possible for private persons in the member countries to bring actions for violations of Articles 85 and 86 in their national courts, as is done by private persons in the United States, but this is not a usually desirable method.

Article 85 Articles 85 and 86 differ in their thrust and coverage. Article 85 is concerned with a statement of the *policy regarding prohibited business conduct,* and Article 86 with *abuse by a dominant enterprise position.*

Article 85 is reproduced in Figure 57.2. You will observe that Paragraph 1 has two parts. The first part is an overall statement of prohibited business practices followed by an (a) through (e) enumeration of particular, but not exclusive, prohibited business practices. This structure is similar to the overall prohibition stated in Section 1 of the Sherman Act, and the particularity of the Clayton Act as amended by the Robinson-Patman Act.[15] The specific prohibited conduct in the second part of Paragraph 1 is, in effect, per se violations, as are those enumerated in the Clayton Act. The word "undertakings" is a synonym for "enterprises" (businesses) and signifies that the Article applies to subsidiaries that are *independent* of their parent, and not to dependent subsidiaries. Agreements between parent and subsidiaries reflecting duties and functions of the subsidiaries are normal for dependent subsidiaries. Paragraph 2 declares null and void agreements and decisions prohibited by Section 1.

Paragraph 3 reflects a policy of making exceptions to conduct that otherwise would be prohibited under Paragraph 1 if the excepted business agreement, decision, or practice would, without eliminating competition *substantially, benefit* the member countries and their nationals by the improvement of production or distribution of goods or promote technical or economic progress. This policy is a reason for encouragement to new or small developing enterprises. The Commission will issue such a statement of inapplicability of Paragraph 1 where appropriate when *notified* by the interested party

FIGURE 57.2 **Article 85 of the EEC Treaty**

Article 85 states:

"1. The following practices shall be prohibited as incompatible with the Common Market: all agreements between undertakings, all decisions by associations of undertakings and all concerted practices which are liable to affect trade between Member States and which are designed to prevent, restrict or distort competition within the Common Market or which have this effect. This shall, in particular, include:

(*a*) the direct or indirect fixing of purchase or selling prices or of any other trading conditions;
(*b*) the limitation or control of production, markets, technical development or investment;
(*c*) market-sharing or the sharing of sources of supply;
(*d*) the application of unequal conditions to parties undertaking equivalent engagements in commercial transactions, thereby placing them at a competitive disadvantage;
(*e*) making the conclusion of a contract subject to the acceptance by the other party to the contract of additional obligations, which, by their nature or according to commercial practice, have no connection with the subject of such contract.

"2. Any agreements or decisions prohibited pursuant to this Article shall automatically be null and void.

"3. The provisions of paragraph 1 may, however, be declared inapplicable in the case of:

– any agreement or type of agreement between undertakings,
– any decision or type of decision by associations of undertakings, and
– any concerted practice or type of concerted practice which helps to improve the production or distribution of goods or to promote technical or economic progress, while allowing consumers a fair share of the resulting profit and which does not:

(*a*) subject the concerns in question to any restrictions which are not indispensable to the achievement of the above objectives;
(*b*) enable such concerns to eliminate competition in respect of a substantial part of the goods concerned."

before the occurrence of the particular business activity under consideration. Subsequent notification is too late.

Notice the "effect" principle at the heart of paragraph 1 "which are liable to affect . . . or have this effect." We are reminded of the "substantial effect" principle of U.S. antitrust law. Note Paragraph 1(a)'s prohibition of direct or indirect fixing of purchase or selling prices as having such a prohibited effect. The European Court of Justice has held that selective distribution systems for the sale of products that are capable of affecting trade between member States and have, as their object or effect, the prevention, restriction, or destruction of competition, are violative of Article 85, Paragraph 1. The following case by the Commission is illustrative of Commission case decisions. It is the first case in which the Commission made a decision on the anticompetitive application of a previously approved selective distribution system, finding it violative of Article 85, Paragraph 1.

FACTS

The Allgemeine Elektricitäts-Gesellschaft AEG-Telefunken (AEG) is a German corporation. It is a major firm engaged in, among other things, developing, manufacturing and marketing consumer electronics. It has a significant share of the market in such equipment. Since January 1, 1970, this sector of AEG's business has been entrusted to the AEG subsidiary TFR, which has been an independent division of AEG since June 1, 1979. TFR manufactures and markets these products, and in marketing them uses the AEG marketing organization—in Germany the AEG sales offices or branches and in the Community Member States the AEG subsidiaries responsible for marketing. The subsidiaries here involved are in France (ATF) and in Belgium (ATBG), and they receive instructions from TFR. The goods are distributed through wholesalers and retailers who generally are supplied directly by the AEG sales offices.

AEG notified the Commission of its distribution agreement (European Community Agreement). Under this Agreement its products could be sold within the Community only by wholesalers and retailers approved in advance on the basis of a list of conditions of admission, and any dealer who satisfied these conditions would be admitted. The legal basis of this distribution system consists of standard contracts with selected resellers at the various marketing stages. The Director-General for Competition informed AEG that he had no objections under Article 85(1) of the EEC Treaty to the wording of the "European Community Agreement" submitted by AEG.

In practice, AEG applied a completely different distribution system. In order to obtain as high a price as possible, admission to the system was refused, rendered difficult or made subject to further conditions in the case of certain distributor organizations and certain dealers whose pricing threatened AEG's price policy, even though they satisfied the conditions laid down in the distribution agreement. AEG also directly and indirectly exercised a substantial influence on the setting of retail prices by dealers.

This case came before the Commission of the European Communities on whether AEG had violated Article 85(1) of the EEC treaty.

DECISION

Article 1. The Allgemeine Elektricitäts-Gesellschaft AEG-Telefunken has infringed Article 85(1) of the Treaty establishing the European Economic Community by applying the distribution agreement for Telefunken products, which was introduced in the European Community on November 1, 1973, in such a way that:

(a) dealers, although satisfying the conditions for authorization, could not obtain the contract goods; and
(b) the selling prices of contracted dealers were directly or indirectly determined by AEG.

Article 2. AEG is hereby required to terminate the infringements found without delay.

Article 3. A fine of 1,000,000 (one million) ECU, or DM 2,445,780 (two million, four hundred and forty-five thousand, seven hundred and eighty Deutsch Marks), is hereby imposed on AEG. . . .

Article 4. This decision shall be enforceable in accordance with Article 192 of the Treaty establishing the European Economic Community.

Decisions of the Court of Justice concerning selective distribution systems

Selective distribution systems may constitute an aspect of competition, which accords with Article 85(1), provided that resellers are chosen on the basis of objective criteria of a qualitative nature relating to the technical qualifications of the reseller and his staff and the suitability of his trading premises, and that such conditions are laid down uniformly for all potential resellers and are not applied in a discriminatory fashion.... Agreements laying down a system of selective distribution based on criteria for admission which go beyond a simple objective selection of a qualitative nature are in principle caught by the prohibition in Article 85(1), particularly where they are based on quantitative selection criteria.... It is important for the appreciation of selective distribution systems whether these agreements, either individually or together with others, in the economic and legal context in which they are concluded and on the basis of a body of objective features of law and fact, are capable of affecting trade between Member States and have, as either their object or effect, the prevention, restriction or distortion of competition....

The above decisions of the Court of Justice show that the distribution system applied by AEG can escape the prohibition provided for in Article 85(1) only if it is clear from the economic and legal context within which the distribution agreement is operated and from all the attendant circumstances:

—that all resellers who meet the technical qualifications necessary for selling the products covered by the distribution agreement have, in principle, access to the goods,

—that dealers are not automatically excluded from the distribution network because they might jeopardize the pricing policy pursued by AEG, and

—that authorized contracted dealers are free to set their resale prices on their own initiative without direct or indirect interference from AEG.

Furthermore, the Commission has already pointed out [in a previous decision] that, in the case of selective distribution systems, competition must be ensured by allowing authorized dealers to determine their selling prices at their own discretion.

• • • • •

Infringements committed

AEG has intentionally infringed Article 85(1). It has knowingly and deliberately applied a distribution system under which suitable applicant retailers were not authorized or were authorized only after satisfying additional conditions not evident from the distribution contract, and under which authorized dealers were prevented from determining their resale prices freely and without interference from AEG or other dealers. In so doing, AEG intended to obstruct competition involving its products within the common market. AEG must also bear the blame for this discriminatory selection and influencing of prices, it being immaterial that these infringements were largely committed by its subsidiaries. Until the end of 1978 AEG concluded contracts directly with dealers. Since January 1, 1979, distribution contracts have been concluded by TFR or marketing firms in other Member States on behalf and for the account of AEG. The distribution agreement was applied in the interests of AEG which, in the final analysis, was itself responsible for introducing and implementing it. AEG used its subsidiaries to market its products as described above and even, in individual cases, played a direct part by giving instructions to its subsidiaries. AEG is therefore responsible for the infringements committed by the divisions and subsidiaries which it used to conclude the distribution contracts.

Allegemeine Elektricitäts-Gesellschaft AEG-Telefunken (AEG), Common Mkt. Rep. (CCH) para. 10,366 (1982).

Article 86 Article 86 (Figure 57.3) is concerned basically with *enterprise market or geographical dominance and prohibited abuse by the exercise of such dominance*. The Article has two parts, the first paragraph establishing the *prohibitive policy of improper exploitation through dominance,* and subdivisions (a) through (d) enumerating, without

FIGURE 57.3 **Article 86 of the EEC Treaty**

Article 86 states:

"Any improper exploitation by one or more undertakings of a dominant position within the Common Market or within a substantial part of it shall be deemed to be incompatible with the Common Market and shall be prohibited, in so far as trade between Member States could be affected by it. The following practices, in particular, shall be deemed to amount to improper exploitation:

(*a*) the direct or indirect imposition of any unfair purchase or selling prices or of any other unfair trading conditions;

(*b*) the limitation of production, markets or technical development to the prejudice of consumers;

(*c*) the application of unequal conditions to parties undertaking equivalent engagements in commercial transactions, thereby placing them at a commercial disadvantage;

(*d*) making the conclusion of a contract subject to the acceptance by the other party to the contract of additional obligations which by their nature or according to commercial practice have no connection with the subject of such contract."

exclusion, *forms of abuse constituting improper exploitation which are prohibited*. It should be noted that the prohibited anticompetitive conduct enumerated in Article 85(1)—for example, improper price fixing, improper control over distributors, tying, by dominant enterprise—is such an abuse.

Several important terms and phrases in Article 86 need clarification. The phrase "dominant position" is not defined. Decisions of the Commission and of the European Court of Justice have provided some guidelines. Among the many factors considered in determining dominant position are: percent of product (at least 30 percent) and geographical market share; extent of trademark, technological, and patent recognition and consumer acceptance; production and marketing strength; financial strength and sources; vertical and horizontal integration; independence of the enterprise; know-how; and the effect of combinations of enterprises, such as joint ventures. Monopoly of property industrial rights are not per se a violation of Article 86—for example, exclusivity of trademarks, patents, and licenses; it is their abuse constituting "improper exploitation" that causes the conduct to be prohibited.

The Commission's Regulation 17 pursuant to its power to regulate trade permits parties who are uncertain of the validity of their business agreement to request the Commission, on the basis of presented facts, for a "negative clearance." If granted, such clearance confirms that the agreement and the projected activity are not a violation of Articles 85 or 86, and that the Commission will not "intervene." If not granted, there is still the opportunity to request an exemption under Article 85(3), previously discussed.

The Commission is concerned with the preservation of free trade among the EEC members, and with conduct within as well as outside the Community which affects the free movement of goods in the Community. It is an "effects" approach again between conduct and result. With respect to Article 86, it is a question of whether there is abuse by dominance causing the prohibited result or effect.

The "Effect" and "Single Enterprise" Theories in the United States and the EEC

We have seen in this chapter that the United States and the EEC are concerned about transnational business operation that has a prohibited restraining "effect" on commerce.

The local firm in the United States and the local firm in the EEC causing this effect were subject to the jurisdiction of the federal courts in the United States and the Commission and the Court of Justice in the EEC. However, a jurisdictional problem arose if the local firm in the United States and the local firm in the EEC were subsidiaries of foreign parents. How could the foreign parent come within the jurisdiction of the United States and the EEC?

In the United States, where the law places great responsibility on persons for *control* of an activity, we have seen that the United States acquired jurisdiction over the foreign parent as well as the local subsidiary as separate legal entities for the purpose of jurisdiction, *if the parent has control over its subsidiary*. The parent and its subsidiary were then really one person. *If there was no control* and the subsidiary were an "independent" legal entity, then the parent was not subject to federal jurisdiction; jurisdiction was *only over the subsidiary*. Accordingly, the concept of a "single entity" arose whereby, *if there were control,* the subsidiary was but a part of the parent, they were treated as a single entity, a single firm. Thus the foreign parent was locally present *in the form of its controlled subsidiary* and, therefore, completely subject to federal jurisdiction. Service of process on the subsidiary was service upon the parent. Touching the corporate arm was touching the corporate body. But the element of control still was of crucial importance to establish the "single entity."

The EEC was faced with the same problem of control. If the foreign parent did not have control over the subsidiary located in the Community, then the parent was not subject to the jurisdiction of the Commission and the Court of Justice for the prohibited restraint of trade effect caused by the subsidiary. In the early cases the Commission sought for the control element. Because of the difficult burden of establishing the necessary control, the Commission later sought for the margin of 51 percent share control by a parent over the subsidiary rather than trying to prove as a fact, as was being done in U.S. courts, that actual control was being exercised over the subsidiary. If control existed, then, as in the United States, the foreign parent *and* its local subsidiary were considered to be a single entity or "enterprise" and, therefore, the subsidiary's prohibited conduct was the parent's conduct and the parent, *not* the subsidiary, was the legal enterprise within the jurisdiction of the Commission. It was but a short step, therefore, for the Commission to assert jurisdiction over a foreign parent merely by showing that the prohibited conduct performed by the local subsidiary *was really the act of the foreign parent without attempting to prove any control at all. The burden was placed on the foreign parent to prove absence of control,* and not only is it almost impossible to bear this burden but often the foreign parent defendant does not even challenge the Commission on the matter of control!

The concept of "effect" on trade is very much used by the Commission, but gradually *the concept of a "single enterprise" is assuming a greater basis for Commission jurisdiction over the foreign parent.* However, the single enterprise theory has its limitations. One limitation is that, by using this concept, there is no competition between the parent and the subsidiary since there is a single entity, and Article 85 does not apply because there is *no agreement* between individual enterprises causing the prohibited conduct of restraint of trade in the Community. However, the single enterprise concept assists in establishing "dominance" for purposes of Article 86. But, because of *dominance*, the Commission would probably issue a "negative clearance" since only one enterprise is involved. The Commission still can disregard the single enterprise concept and, by considering the parent and its subsidiary as separate legal enterprises, proceed under Article 85(1).

dictum
That portion of a judge's opinion in a case that is not necessary to the decision of the case

It can readily be seen that great strides have been taken by the United States and the EEC following the omniscient **dictum**[16] of the great American judge Benjamin Cardozo. He suggested that, while a corporate subsidiary as a legal entity may be separate from its corporate parent thereby absolving the parent from responsibility for the conduct of its subsidiary, this fiction of a "corporate veil" should nevertheless, be pierced when public policy so requires, and both the subsidiary and the parent be considered as a unity. Let us not mistakenly conclude that our earlier discussion of distributorships is applicable here, because an *independent distributor is an independent contractor and not a subsidiary nor a part of the foreign firm or "enterprise."*

International Gift-giving and Social Courtesies Protocol

International gift-giving customs and social courtesies reflecting different cultures should be carefully observed in doing business abroad. Gift exchange in international business protocol is very important. For an American to ignore ritual would make him or her appear as either ignorant of the culture or insensitive to cultural preferences, which could lead to loss of respect, business opportunities, and even violation of local or American law.

There is no substitute for local advice. The advice of a native resident or the local U.S. consulate should be sought if you have any doubt about the proper protocol. In general[17] avoid giving the impression of bribery by spending too much on a gift. Get to know the recipient's preferences if possible. Gift-giving should be thoughtful, sincere, spontaneous and not ceremonial. Do not give a more expensive return gift.

Foreign Sales Corporation

The Foreign Sales Corporation (FSC) was created by Congress in 1984 to provide a tax incentive for corporations to engage in transnational business. Certain foreign trade income, as defined in Sections 923 and 924, is treated as foreign source income and exempt from tax. Under 26 USCA Section 922, FSC means any corporation:

(1) which—
 (A) was created or organized—
  (i) under the laws of any foreign country which meets the requirements of section 927(e)(3), or
  (ii) under the laws applicable to any possession of the United States,
 (B) has no more than 25 shareholders at any time during the taxable year,
 (C) does not have any preferred stock outstanding at any time during the taxable year,
 (D) during the taxable year—
  (i) maintains an office located outside the United States in a foreign country which meets the requirements of section 927(e)(3) or in any possession of the United States,
  (ii) maintains a set of the permanent books of account (including invoices) of such corporation at such office, and

[16]*Berkey v. Third Avenue R. R. Co.*, 155 N.E. 58, 61 (N.Y. 1926).

[17]For details, see the booklet *International Business Gift-Giving Customs* published by the Parker Pen Company.

(iii) maintains at a location within the United States the records which such corporation is required to keep under section 6001,

(E) at all times during the taxable year, has a board of directors which includes at least one individual who is not a resident of the United States, and

(F) is not a member, at any time during the taxable year, of any controlled group of corporations of which a DISC is a member, and

(2) which has made an election (at the time and in the manner provided in section 927(f)(1)) which is in effect for the taxable year to be treated as a FSC.

In 1988, a new export vehicle called a Shared Foreign Sales Corporation" (SFSC) was created by Congress,[18] particularly for the benefit of small corporations. SFSC means any corporation if:

(A) such corporation maintains a separate account for transactions with each shareholder (and persons related to such shareholder),
(B) distributions to each shareholder are based on the amounts in the separate account maintained with respect to such shareholder, and
(C) such corporation meets such other requirements as the Secretary may by regulations prescribe.

Each separate account maintained by a SFSC is treated as a separate corporation. The accounting rules and procedures are complex, and it is advisable to retain an accounting firm with expertise about FSCs and SFSCs.[19]

The Foreign-Trade Zone

In the United States, many state governments, seeking foreign markets for products of local firms and encouraging foreign firms to establish facilities in states, encourage the establishment of Foreign-Trade Zones (FTZs) in their states. FTZs, also known as "free zones" and "free ports," are established, operated, and maintained as public utilities by public corporations, meaning a state, its political subdivision, and a municipality, or by a private chartered corporation, for the purpose of promoting international trade. The U.S. Foreign-Trade Zone Board reviews applications to become FTZs adjacent to ports of entry, approves them if they are in the public interest, and monitors all FTZ operations.

FTZs encourage international trade by offering cost-saving facilities to U.S. importers and exporters. They are large enclosed areas, used for temporary storage of goods in warehouses or other buildings of varying size, which are considered by the U.S. government to be outside of the customs territory of the United States. American firms *importing foreign goods into a FTZ* do not pay customs duties or federal excise taxes until the goods are shipped out of the zone *to U.S. markets.* If the imported foreign goods are shipped *from a FTZ to a foreign country,* no U.S. import duty is imposed on the goods. Also, the imported foreign goods stored in the FTZ may be manufactured or processed while in the FTZ without incurring U.S. duties or taxes. For example, you, an American firm, import foreign machine parts into a FTZ, assemble them into a machine made by you, and then sell and deliver the finished product to a buyer in a foreign

---

[18]26 U.S.C.A sec. 927(g)(3).

[19]For excellent general and specialized reading lists see A.B.A. J., (September 1989): 80.

country without having to pay U.S. customs and excise taxes on the imported foreign parts. You thereby avoid manufacture in a foreign country because customs duty is not paid on American labor, overhead, and profit; make substantial financial savings; save time in the distribution of your goods; and the state and local community in which the FTZ is located benefit by increased employment and taxable income.

International Franchising

International franchising should be mentioned because of its impact on transnational business and the relevance of much of the previous discussion in this chapter. Primarily because of the advantages of international franchising and the American franchise market becoming oversaturated for large franchising companies, there is now an increasing American movement for international franchising.[20] A few familiar examples are McDonald's and Coca-Cola. (The subject of franchises has been discussed previously on pp. 858–61.)

United Nations Convention on Contracts for the International Sale of Goods

► Introduction

When we think of the many differences among States in their law, economy, culture, and level of development, we can readily understand the great need for international uniformity in the business or commercial law governing transnational business contracts, particularly for the sale of goods. A notable achievement has been made in accomplishing much uniformity by the new United Nations Convention on Contracts for the International Sale of Goods (CISG), effective in 1988. The United States ratified it in 1986 with one reservation or "declaration." Pursuant to Article 95, the United States "declared" that it would not be bound by Article 1(1)(b). "Declaration" means the reservation or objection by a State to a CISG provision or to the CISG itself.

A thorough analysis of CISG is not possible in our book. However, a relatively brief consideration of some of its particularly important provisions will be made. At the outset, notice the very close parallels with, and some of the differences from, Article 2 on sales of goods under the Uniform Commercial Code (UCC), and the common law of contracts as stated in Restatement (Second) of Contracts, both of which are the law in almost all U.S. states.

The preface to the content of the Convention expresses its purpose:

> *The states parties to this Convention:*
>
> Bearing in mind the broad objectives in the resolutions adopted by the sixth special session of the General Assembly of the United Nations on the establishment of a New International Economic Order,
>
> Considering that the development of international trade on the basis of equality and mutual benefit is an important element in promoting friendly relations among States,
>
> Being of the Opinion that the adoption of uniform rules which govern contracts for the international sale of goods and take into account the different social, economic and legal

---

[20]For a good, brief overview of international franchising with a reference reading list, see Litka, *An International Franchise*, University of Akron, College of Business Administration, Working Paper Series (Akron, Ohio).

systems would contribute to the removal of legal barriers in international trade and promote the development of international trade,

Have agreed as follows:

► Part I—Sphere of Application and General Provisions

CISG *covers only contracts for the international sale of goods.* It has four parts with various chapters and articles in each part. Part I has 13 articles. Under Article 1, "This Convention applies to contracts of sale of goods between parties whose places of business are in different States: (a) When the States are Contracting States [meaning those States who have ratified the Convention]; or (b) When the rules of private international law lead to the application of the law of a Contracting State [the United States declared against, and is not bound by, 1(1)(b)]." Article 95 provides: "Any State may declare at the time of... [its] ratification that it will not be bound by [Article 1(1)(b)]." Because the United States is not bound by Article 1(1)(b), if the other State is not a ratifying State under Article 1(1)(a), then both States are *not* Contracting States, 1(1)(a) does not apply, the Convention is not applicable to them, and in the event of dispute between the parties to an international contract for the sale of goods the conflicts of laws rules (private international law) of those States will govern. This means that the UCC Article 2 on sales of goods could be applicable and utilized by U.S. courts where the judicial proceeding occurs. However, if both States *are* Contracting States, CISG governs the sales contract in U.S. courts. In addition, if either of the contracting parties has more than one place of business, under Article 10(a) the relevant place of business "is that which has the closest relationship to the contract and its performance."

Article 2, as well as Article 1, indicates the contracts that are, and are not, subject to the Convention. Inasmuch as the main impact of CISG is on *commercial* sales, meaning sales between merchants, under Article 2(a) the CISG does not apply to sales of *consumer* goods, "unless the seller, at any time before or at the conclusion of the contract, neither knew nor ought to have known that the goods were bought for such use." Also excluded are sales "of stocks, shares, investment securities, negotiable instruments, money, ships, vessels, hovercraft or aircraft, electricity." The CISG does not define "goods."

Under Article 3, two transactions are excluded from CISG: (1) if the party who *orders* the goods is to supply a substantial part of the materials necessary for the other party's manufacture or production of such goods, the transaction is not considered to be a sale within CISG; (2) a *service* contract "in which the preponderant part of the obligations of the party who furnishes the goods consists in the supply of labor or other services."

Article 4 provides that CISG "governs only the formation of the contract for sale [Part II], and the rights and obligations of the *seller and the buyer* arising from such contract [Part III]. . . . [CISG] is not concerned with: (a) the validity of the contract or any of its provisions or of any usage; (b) the effect which the contract may have on the property in the goods sold [title]." Property interests of third parties in the goods are not considered by CISG. Also, Article 5 excludes coverage for products liability "for death or personal injury caused by the goods" in order to avoid collision with rules of applicable domestic law.

Article 6 emphasizes the concept of freedom to contract and a Contracting State's preservation of its privilege to preserve its domestic requirements by providing: "The parties may exclude the application of this Convention or, subject to Article 12, derogate from or vary the effect of any of its provisions." Reflecting this, Article 12 deals with the problem raised by Article 11, which reflects modern commercial practice not to require a writing to prove the existence of a contract for the sale of goods—the cessation of the familiar domestic sales of goods statute of frauds. Article 11 provides "A contract of sale need not be concluded in or evidenced by writing and is not subject to any other requirement as to form. It may be proved by any means, including witnesses." Since some States still require proof by writing, Article 12 provides:

> Any provision of Article 11, Article 29, or Part II of the Convention that allows a contract of sale or its modification or termination by agreement or any offer, acceptance, or other indication of intention to be made in any form other than in writing does not apply where any party has his place of business in a Contracting State which has made a declaration under Article 96 of this Convention. . . .

Also reflecting freedom to contract, Article 29 provides:

> **(1)** A contract may be modified or terminated by the mere agreement of the parties.
> **(2)** A contract in writing which contains a provision requiring any modification or termination by agreement to be in writing may not be otherwise modified or terminated by agreement. However, a party may be precluded by his conduct from asserting such a provision to the extent that the other party has relied on that conduct.

► Part II—Formation of the Contract

Let us begin with Article 92, which provides that a Contracting State may "declare" that it will not be bound by Part II, or by Part III which deals with the obligations of the seller and buyer.

The Offer Articles 14 through 17 are concerned with the offer. Under Article 16(2), an offer is irrevocable "(a) If it indicates, whether by stating a fixed time for acceptance or otherwise, that it is irrevocable; or (b) If it was reasonable for the offeree to rely on the offer as being irrevocable and the offeree has acted in reliance on the offer."

The Acceptance Articles 18 through 24 are concerned with acceptance of the offer, which under Article 23 creates a contract. Under Article 18:

> **(2)** An acceptance of an offer becomes effective at the moment the indication of assent reaches [Article 24] the offeror. . . .
> **(3)** However, if, by virtue of the offer or as a result of practices which the parties have established between themselves or of usage, the offeree may indicate assent by performing an act, such as one relating to the dispatch of the goods or payment of the price, without notice to the offeror, the acceptance is effective at the moment the act is performed, provided that the act is performed within the period of time laid down in the preceding paragraph.

Article 19 is concerned with an offeree's reply to an offer *purporting to be an acceptance* which *modifies* the offer. This occurs frequently from the exchange of the buyer's printed purchase order and the seller's printed acknowledgement of sale form. As you recall, under the common law of contracts "mirror image rule" the acceptance must be a "mirror image" of the offer, and its variation of the offer's terms caused the offer to be rejected and the purported acceptance to be a counter-offer. However, under the UCC 2–207, if the transaction was between merchants, the additional terms become part of the contract unless "(a) the offer expressly limits acceptance to the terms of the offer; (b) they materially alter it; or (c) notification of the objection to them has already been given or is given within a reasonable time after notice of them is received."

The CISG contract being between merchants provides in Article 19:

> **(1)** A reply to an offer which purports to be an acceptance but contains additions, limitations, or other modifications is a *rejection* of the offer and constitutes a counter-offer;
> **(2)** However, a reply to an offer which purports to be an acceptance but contains additional or different terms which *do not materially alter* the terms of the offer constitutes an acceptance, unless the offeror, without undue delay, objects orally to the discrepancy or dispatches a notice to that effect. If he does not so object, the terms of the contract are the terms of the offer *with the modifications* contained in the acceptance;
> **(3)** Additional or different terms relating, among other things, to the price, payment, quality and quantity of the goods, place and time of delivery, extent of one party's liability to the other or the settlement of disputes are considered to alter the terms of the offer *materially* [Emphasis added].

This substantially avoids the "battle of the forms" problem under UCC 2–207. It should be recalled that the offeree's reply to the offer may not purport to be acceptance. For example, the offeree may request further information concerning the offer's terms or suggest negotiation of those terms.

► Part III—Sale of Goods

If you find that an enforceable international contract for the sale of goods has been formed under Articles 1 and 2 of Part I, then Part III becomes important in establishing and governing the obligations of the seller and the buyer, their performance and nonperformance, their breach of the contract, and their remedies for the breach.

Two terms are introduced by Article 25, "avoidance" and "fundamental breach". Under domestic U.S. law, breach by either the seller or the buyer creates remedies of the seller to refuse delivery of the goods, and of the buyer to reject the goods. A party's right not to perform the contract because of such breach is called "avoidance of the contract" rather than the terms "rejection," "revocation of acceptance," "avoidance," "termination," and "cancellation" under our domestic sales of goods and contract law.

Also, avoidance is not available for every breach; under Articles 49(1)(a) and 64(1)(a), it must be a "fundamental breach." If one party has committed a fundamental breach, then the other party may avoid the contract. This is similar to the UCC and contract law terms of "substantial" breach.[21] Article 25 defines a breach as "fundamental" if the breach "results in such detriment to the other party as substantially to deprive him of what he is entitled to expect under the contract, unless the party in breach did not foresee and a reasonable person of the same kind in the same circumstances would not have foreseen such a result."

However, as in UCC 2–602(1) on notice of rejection and UCC 2–608(2) on notice of revocation of acceptance, Article 26 provides "A declaration of avoidance of the contract is effective only if made by notice to the other party." This prevents the other party from continuing to perform ignorant of the injured declaring party's decision to refuse to perform the contract. Under Article 27's general rule, "any notice, request, or other communication is given or made by a party . . . by means appropriate in the circum-

[21]But UCC 2–601 provides that the buyer may reject delivery of the goods if they "fail in any respect to conform to the contract."

stances. . . ." Exceptions to this rule are found in Articles 47(2), 48(4), 63(2), 65(1) and (2), and 79(4), where "receipt" of notice is required.

Reflecting the Convention's intent not to interfere with provisions of a member State's domestic law which are singularly important to, and better accommodated by, that State, Article 28 provides with respect to the remedy of specific performance of a contract that:

> If, in accordance with the provisions of the Convention, one party is entitled to require performance of any obligation by the other party, a court is not bound to enter a judgment for specific performance unless the court would do so under its own law in respect of similar contracts of sale not governed by this Convention.

Since limited space here does not permit examination of the remaining articles under Part III, only a descriptive enumeration of such articles is provided.

Chapter II: **Obligations of the Seller**
- Section I (Articles 30–34) Delivery of the Goods and Handing Over of Documents
- Section II (Articles 35–44) Conformity of the Goods and Third Party Claims
- Section III (Articles 45–52) Remedies for Breach of Contract by the Seller

Chapter III: **Obligations of the Buyer**
- Section I (Articles 54–59) Payment of the Price
- Section II (Article 60) Taking Delivery
- Section III (Articles 61–65) Remedies for Breach of Contract by the Buyer

Chapter IV: Articles 66–70: **Risk** of the parties for loss or damage to the goods

Chapter V: **Provisions Common to the Obligations of the Seller and of the Buyer**
- Section I (Articles 71–73) Anticipatory Breach and Installment Contracts
- Section II (Articles 74–77) Damages
- Section III (Article 78) Interest
- Section IV (Articles 79–80) Exemptions
- Section V (Articles 81–84) Effects of Avoidance
- Section VI (Articles 85–88) Preservation of the Goods

► Part IV—Final Provisions

Many of the provisions in Part IV are ministerial in nature and concerned with ratification of the Convention. Some provisions involve reservations or "declarations" by a Contracting State that it will not be bound by Part II or Part III. A Contracting State's declaration concerning the statute of frauds concept relating to the sale of goods has already been discussed. Article 93 deals with a Contracting State which "has two or more territorial units in which, according to its constitution, different systems of law are applicable in relation to the matters dealt with in the Convention." This does not include the United States.

Summary Statement

1. Common law is very different from code law.
2. One of the methods of operating abroad in the sale of goods is by domestic production and direct export sales by a foreign agent.

3. The letter of credit is used for the purpose of assuring the domestic seller and the foreign buyer of goods that payment and delivery will be made.
4. The status of a person as a foreign agent must be carefully defined in the agency contract, and the foreign law examined for different effects of an agency status.
5. A foreign distributor is an independent contractor for whose conduct the domestic principal firm is not liable abroad.
6. The establishment of a foreign branch of a firm possibly submits the firm to the jurisdiction of the State in which the branch is located, depending on whether the parent firm has "control" over the branch.
7. Technology is a particular kind of property concerned with material things. It may be intangible or tangible. Its transfer abroad is subject to careful examination by foreign governments and may be a violation of foreign antitrust laws.
8. Transnational business contracts should be in writing, be in only one official language, provide for carefully defined terms, ensure compliance with the foreign law concerning pricing and currency payment, and include the following clauses: force majeure, choice-of-law and forum, and commercial arbitration.
9. Industrial property interests transferred abroad are subject to many risks and all means should be used to protect such interests. Some risks are foreign expropriation, and the infringement and pirating of intangible property interests.
10. Under the common law, the first user of industrial property interests is the owner. Under the code law in many foreign countries requiring registration of such interests—particularly trademarks, brand names, and patents—the first to register becomes the owner. However, various regional and international conventions provide recognition and protection.
11. The U.S. Sherman and Clayton antitrust laws, and the Federal Trade Commission Act, are designed to eliminate the abuses that militate against the American philosophy of free competition.
12. Under the Sherman Act, violations are basically for unreasonable restraint of trade and for monopolies. The Clayton Act specifies per se antitrust violations. The Federal Trade Commission Act prohibits unfair methods of competition.
13. The Export Trading Company Act of 1982 establishes a basis for eligibility of export trading companies for exemption from U.S. antitrust laws, and provides for federal certification of such exemptions.
14. Foreign firms are subject to U.S. antitrust laws for their antitrust conduct abroad having a substantial effect on U.S. commerce. Also, foreign firms and their governments can sue in U.S. courts for antitrust violations by American firms adversely affecting their trade.
15. The European Economic Community was created by the Treaty of Rome in 1957. Its primary purpose was the economic integration of the member States into a single integrated system to eliminate trade barriers and restrictive trade agreements by having a common market, and to protect local business and industry from foreign competition.
16. EEC Treaty Article 85 is concerned with policy of what constitutes prohibited business conduct. Article 86 is concerned with abuse by a dominant enterprise position.
17. The Commission of European Communities (Commission) is the enforcing body of the Treaty, and appeals from its decisions are to the European Court of Justice (Court).
18. The EEC Court has held that selective distribution systems for the sale of products that are capable of affecting trade between member States and have, as their object

or effect, the prevention, restriction, or destruction of competition, are violative of Article 85, paragraph 1.

19. The "Effect" and "Single Enterprise" theories have been developed by the EEC Commission and Court in order to obtain jurisdiction over foreign parent firms doing business in the EEC through their subsidiaries. Control by the parent is now presumed, the parent having a most difficult burden to overcome this presumption. In the United States, the emphasis on proof of parental control still exists as a fact to be proved by the party asserting control and instigating the legal proceeding.

20. International business gift-giving customs and social courtesies reflecting differing cultures should be carefully observed in doing business abroad.

21. The Foreign Sales Corporation and the Shared Foreign Sales Corporation are trade vehicles providing excellent tax benefits and very helpful operational and professional administration to a transnational business firm.

22. Foreign-Trade Zones (FTZs) are public utilities, approved by the U.S. Foreign-Trade Zone Board for the purpose of promoting international trade. They encourage international trade by offering cost savings to U.S. importers and exporters.

23. The United Nations Convention on Contracts for the International Sale of Goods establishes uniform rules governing contracts for the international sale of goods, thereby removing legal barriers to, and prompting the development of, international trade among ratifying States. It does not apply to sales of consumer goods.

In the following leading case the U.S. District Court held that there was a tying arrangement that affected a not insubstantial amount of interstate commerce. However, the arrangement would be illegal as a violation of Section 1 of the Sherman Act only if the evidence at a trial to be held established that the arrangement appreciably restrained competition in the tied product market; *and* the defendant did not demonstrate legitimate business justification for the tying arrangement. The court denied motions for summary judgment made by both parties so that these issues may be resolved in a trial.

UNITED STATES OF AMERICA v. MERCEDES-BENZ OF NORTH AMERICA, INC.
517 F.Supp. 1369 (N.D. Cal. 1981)

Patel, District Judge. This action is before the court on cross-motions for summary judgment. The government brings suit for an alleged violation of Section 1 of the Sherman Act under a theory of a per se tying violation based on the Dealer Agreement between Mercedes-Benz of North America, Inc. (MBNA) and each Mercedes-Benz franchised dealer. Defendant strenuously objects to the application of a per se rule and argues that a rule of reason should apply under which MBNA has demonstrated that in fact its Dealer Agreement and actual practice do not constitute a restraint of trade. [T]he court finds it necessary to deny both motions for summary judgment. *The parties must proceed to trial on the issue of defendant's economic power and, if that be established, whether defendant can demonstrate sufficient business justification for a tying arrangement.*[22] [Emphasis added.]

---

[22][Notice the similarity of approach here with Article 86 of the EEC Treaty, above, p. 1214. First, here—defendant's economic power, 1st paragraph of 86–dominant position. Second, here and under 86(d), tying arrangement, also in Article 85(1)(e), above, p. 1211.]

I
BACKGROUND

Defendant MBNA has been the exclusive United States distributor of Mercedes-Benz automobiles since 1965. Its company, Daimler-Benz AG [DBAG] of Stuttgart, Germany, is one of the oldest automobile manufacturers in the world. [T]he Mercedes-Benz trademark, a three-pointed star in a circle, is recognized worldwide for its representation of automotive luxury, performance and technology.

Daimler-Benz assembles Mercedes-Benz autos in its German factory and ships them through its exclusive importer Daimler-Benz of North America [DBNA] to MBNA for resale to Mercedes-Benz dealers. Parts for these autos can come from several sources:

1. DBAG manufactures certain parts for use in the assembly process and to be used for replacement of used parts;
2. Original parts may come from independent automotive parts manufacturers, called "original equipment manufacturers" (OEMs). Some of these OEMs manufacture parts for several automobile manufacturers.

There are approximately 400 Mercedes dealers in the United States. Once approved by MBNA, each dealer becomes party to a standardized written Dealer Agreement with MBNA to sell and service Mercedes passenger cars and parts.

The government rests its claim of a per se illegal tying arrangement on "Standard Provisions" subpart 9C of the Dealer Agreement. Part 9 sets out various requirements relating to customer service. Subpart 9C reads:

> Dealer shall neither sell nor offer to sell for use in connection with MB passenger cars nor use in the repair or servicing of MB passenger cars any parts other than genuine MB parts or parts expressly approved by DBAG if such parts are necessary to the mechanical operation of such MB passenger cars.

"MB parts" are defined in part one of the Dealer Agreement as "parts, accessories, components, assemblies, and optional equipment for MB passenger cars supplied by MBNA, DBAG, or by DBNA."

II
THE APPLICABLE STANDARD

[P]urchasing auto replacement parts only from a limited number of sources does not have as its primary purpose increasing competition for the franchised automobile. The direct result of such a requirement is to reduce the opportunity for Mercedes-Benz dealers in exercising their independent judgment in choosing parts to consider such factors as price and availability. Restricting the source of dealer replacement parts may serve to increase the price of these parts and thereby restrain the dealers' ability to compete with independent distributors.

A per se rule long has been applied to tying arrangements because of "their pernicious effect on competition and lack of any redeeming virtue."

III
PER SE TYING STANDARD

The rule of per se restraint of trade has been applied in a number of diverse business settings under section 1 of the Sherman Act.

Essentially a tying arrangement exists where a seller with some market leverage over a (tying) product conditions the sale of that product on the purchaser also agreeing to buy a different (tied) product from the seller or foregoing such a purchase from any other source.

". . . Where tying conditions are successfully exacted competition on the merits with respect to the tied product is inevitably curbed. Indeed, 'tying agreements serve hardly any purpose beyond the suppression of competition.' They deny competitors free access to the market for the tied product, not because the party imposing the tying requirements has a better product or a lower price but because of his power or leverage in another market. At the same time buyers are forced to forego their free choice between competing products. For these reasons 'tying agreements fare harshly under the laws forbidding restraints of trade.' "

Plaintiff must demonstrate the existence of three elements to establish a per se illegal tying agreement:

1. Two separate products with the sale of one conditioned on the purchase of the other;

2. A seller with sufficient economic leverage in the tying market to appreciably restrain competition in the tied product market; and
3. A tie-in affecting a not insubstantial amount of interstate commerce.

Once the above elements have been shown, a defendant engaged in a per se tying arrangement may defend itself by an affirmative showing of business justification.

A. Separate Products Tied Together

Two Separate Products

In the present case, it is undisputed that MBNA has separate personnel and price lists for new car and replacement part sales. Many replacement (as well as original) parts are manufactured by outside suppliers.

MBNA argues that the purchase of MBNA replacement parts is an "integral component" of its franchised business method. The essence of the Mercedes-Benz franchise is the sale of trademarked automobiles. . . . The court rejects defendant's argument that no difference may be noticed between original parts in a new automobile and parts purchased at a later date for repair or renewal for purposes of determining whether they are separate products. ". . . [T]he relevant inquiry is not whether the two items must be used together but whether they must come from the same seller." . . . While the use of DBAG-approved parts in the assembly of a Mercedes-Benz automobile is an important factor in producing the trademarked product, the use of trademarked Mercedes-Benz replacement parts is not necessary to carry out the essence of the franchise, that is, the sale of new Mercedes-Benz automobiles.

In the light of the foregoing discussion and in light of the actual practice of Mercedes-Benz and the industry in maintaining a separate parts division, separate prices, separate personnel and, occasionally, separate manufacturers, *the court finds that the Mercedes-Benz passenger car and its replacement parts are indeed separate products.* [Emphasis added.]

Products Tied Together

In addition to a showing that two products are separate, it must be demonstrated that the purchase of one product is conditioned on the purchase of the other. Plaintiff relies on the express wording of the Dealer Agreement to demonstrate the tie-in. . . . The existence of the language still acts as a powerful lever in restraint of trade. . . . [T]he language of subpart 9C expressly refers to parts "necessary to the mechanical operation" of Mercedes-Benz cars. . . . The wording of subpart 9C allows dealers to purchase parts "expressly approved by DBAG." An 'approved source' clause may negate a finding of an illegal tying arrangement.

This is not a case where the allegedly tied product may be obtained only from an approved source; there is no express provision in the Dealer Agreement setting forth a procedure for dealers seeking to request additional approval.

In the present case, plaintiff has presented uncontroverted evidence that no formal system for approval of non-MBNA parts exists in the DBAG/MBNA network and that crucial MBNA officers are unaware of an established procedure for testing the quality of non-MBNA supplied parts upon dealer request for DBAG approval. The evidence discloses that the approved source provision exists on paper only and does not represent a true alternative for dealers wishing to avoid the effects of tie-in.

For the foregoing reasons, *the court finds that the Mercedes-Benz passenger car and its replacement parts are separate products tied together by the use of the MBNA Dealer Agreement.* [Emphasis added.]

B. Sufficient Economic Power

The second factor in determining a per se illegal tying arrangement is that the seller must have "sufficient economic power to impose an appreciable restraint on free competition in the product. . . ." This standard can be met in one of three ways:

1. The seller occupies a dominant position in the tying product market. . . .
2. A product is sufficiently unique that the seller has some advantage not shared by competitors in the market for the tying product. . . .
3. A substantial number of customers have accepted the tie-in and there are no explanations other than the seller's economic power for their willingness to do so.

Looking at the third factor first, plaintiff argues that this standard is easily met because each of 400 Mercedes-Benz dealers has signed the Dealer Agreement agreeing to buy replacement parts from MBNA under subpart 9C.

In the present case, there is no identified population against which to compare the 400 Mercedes dealers. Plaintiff might argue that 400 represents an appreciable number of buyers from a total population of import car dealers or of import luxury car dealers. Plaintiff has not attempted such a showing.

The essence of any showing under this test is that defendant has leverage within the market sufficient to compel buyers to accept a tying arrangement. If plaintiff is able to show that a significant number of customers in the market have accepted the tie-in, it still must show that there are no explanations for the acceptance other than the seller's economic power. Plaintiff has failed on each of these counts.

Alternatively, plaintiff may satisfy the second factor, sufficient economic power, if it can show that the alleged tying product, the Mercedes-Benz automobile, is sufficiently unique to give defendant a competitive advantage in the tying product market. If the tying product is sufficiently desirable to consumers or is a product not easily replicated or commonly available, then the producer of the tying product is likely to have sufficient leverage to restrain the tied product market. Monopoly power is not the test for uniqueness and defendant's own authorities show themselves distinguishable. [O]wnership of a trademark is not conclusive of economic power.

In the present case, Mercedes-Benz' trademark may be a factor in determining its market leverage, but alone it is not sufficient. While Mercedes-Benz may be well-known and its products highly respected, it is not one of the industry's largest competitors. Plaintiff has failed to support its claim of uniqueness with information bearing on market characteristics. For instance, does plaintiff argue that Mercedes-Benz is an automobile unique as to other luxury cars or to other imported cars? If Mercedes is a unique automobile, would not every trademarked auto also be unique? Or all luxury/import cars?

A finding of economic power based on uniqueness of a tying product is one that must be based largely on objective market factors and partially on subjective impression. Such a result cannot be determined in the present action as a matter of law.

The court finds that there is substantial factual dispute on the question of sufficient economic power and declines to resolve the matter on summary judgment. [Emphasis added.]

C. Effect on Interstate Commerce

The third required element of a per se tying violation is that the tie-in affect a not insubstantial amount of interstate commerce. The 'not insubstantial' test is interpreted broadly. "[T]he controlling consideration is 'whether a total amount of business, substantial enough in terms of dollar-volume so as not to be merely *de minimis* is foreclosed to competitors.' "

From 1974 through 1979, the total dollar volume of MBNA replacement part sales to dealers increased from $50 million to $110 million. A determination of amount of commerce affected is based on the volume of sales *allegedly* foreclosed.

Therefore the court finds that the volume sales of mechanically necessary replacement parts to be not insubstantial and that as a matter of law, plaintiff has satisfied this third requirement. [Emphasis added.]

It has thus far been established that per se tying principles are applicable to the present action. The court has found, as a matter of law, that (1) the Mercedes-Benz automobile and MBNA replacement parts are separate products tied together by language in the Dealer Agreement, and (2) the tie-in affects a not insubstantial amount of interstate commerce. However a per se illegal tying violation is not shown unless plaintiff prevails at trial on the issue of defendant's economic power.

IV
BUSINESS JUSTIFICATION

In certain circumstances, defendant may demonstrate a business justification to excuse an otherwise per se illegal tying agreement.... The issue before the court is narrowed to whether defendant is justified in requiring the purchase of only mechanically necessary "MB parts" for replacement after the warranty period.

The government and the public has a legitimate interest in encouraging unrestrained trade in automotive parts, yet defendant has an important legitimate interest in protecting its trademarked automobile and public confidence in the quality and safety of the product. If parts of like quality and design are available from other sources of supply, defendant's sole justification for requiring a tie-in becomes the impermissible desire to restrict trade and maintain artificially inflated prices.

At this time, the court is unable to make a finding regarding defendant's business justification defense. If plaintiff is able to establish the final element of a per se tying violation, it remains for defendant to demonstrate the necessity for its quality control procedures and the unavailability of comparable mechanically necessary replacement parts from non-MBNA sources.

V
CONCLUSION

Based on the foregoing discussion, the court finds a genuine dispute of material fact within plaintiff's motion for summary judgment and its motion is HEREBY DENIED. In accord with this court's determination that a per se standard is applicable to MBNA's alleged tying violation, defendant's cross-motion for summary judgment is also HEREBY DENIED.

Pursuant to F.R.Civ.P. 54(d), the court finds that the following material facts exist without substantial controversy:

1. The Mercedes-Benz automobile and MBNA mechanically necessary replacement parts are separate products tied together by the terms of the MBNA Dealer Agreement; and
2. The tie-in affects a not insubstantial amount of interstate commerce.

Genuine controversy exists as to:

1. Whether MBNA has sufficient economic leverage in the tying product market to appreciably restrain competition in the tied product market; and
2. Whether MBNA has demonstrated a legitimate business justification for tying the sale of its replacement parts to that of its trademarked automobile.

IT IS SO ORDERED.

Questions and Case Problems

1. Volkswagenwerk Aktiengesellschaft (VW), a German corporation, purchased an airplane manufactured by Beech Aircraft Corporation (Beech). The airplane crashed on landing at Bremen, West Germany. VW claimed that the landing gear was defectively designed and/or manufactured by Beech. VW sued Beech in the federal District Court in New York by serving a summons on East, a wholly owned subsidiary of Beech, a dealer doing business in New York marketing only Beech's products. Beech has its headquarters and manufacturing facilities in Kansas and markets its aircraft primarily through a network of independent and wholly owned dealers, of which East is one. Beech made a motion to dismiss the complaint, claiming that Beech was not within the jurisdiction of the court in New York because service of process on East was not service on Beech.

   Beech owns 100 percent of East's shares of stock. East is wholly dependent upon Beech's financial support to stay in business. Unlike Beech's independent distributors, East is required to operate on a cash on delivery basis. Also, Beech includes East in Beech's product liability policy but does not extend the same courtesy to its independent dealers. East's five-member board of directors consists of the president, treasurer, and a vice president of Beech, who occupy the same positions at East, and two officers of Beech. Beech pays the entire salaries of officers serving in those positions for Beech and East. Formal directors meetings were never held by East, although the general managers of the marketing subsidiaries report quarterly as a group to a marketing vice president of Beech. Beech prescribes minimum inventory levels, accounting systems, insurance policies, and advertising campaigns. Distributors are not permitted to change ownership or management without prior Beech approval. Beech trains distributors' salesmen at Beech headquarters and sends management consultants to instruct them. What is your decision on Beech's motion?

Explain the reasons for your decision. [*Volkswagenwerk Aktiengesellschaft v. Beech Aircraft Corp.*, 751 F.2d 117 (2nd Cir. 1984).]

2. Connelly sued Uniroyal Englebert Belgique, S. A. (Englebert), a Belgian tire manufacturer, and Uniroyal, Inc. (Uniroyal), in an Illinois court for personal injuries he suffered when a tire manufactured by Englebert and bearing Uniroyal's trademark failed while his 1969 Opel Kadett was being operated on a highway in Colorado. Connelly purchased the car in 1969 from a dealer in Evanston, Illinois. The tire bore the name "Uniroyal" and the legend "made in Belgium," was manufactured by Englebert, sold in Belgium to General Motors, and subsequently installed on the Opel when it was assembled at a General Motors plant in Belgium. The car was shipped to the United States for distribution by General Motors.

   Uniroyal's wholly owned subsidiary owns approximately 96 percent of the outstanding shares of Englebert corporation. Uniroyal gave Englebert the nonexclusive license to use its registered trade name "Uniroyal" on the tires manufactured by Englebert. Uniroyal also gave Englebert detailed information as to the methods, processes, and formulas used in the manufacture of tires and tubes and other products manufactured by Uniroyal. Uniroyal supplied technical services and instruction to Englebert, who was required to permit Uniroyal's representatives to have knowledge at all times of the goods and manufacturing operations. Englebert maintained its own books and accounts separate and distinct from Uniroyal, had its own banking sources and line of credit, and did not share common manufacturing facilities, offices, addresses, telephone numbers or employees with Uniroyal. There were no employees of Uniroyal at Englebert's plant in Belgium, and Uniroyal had no control or direction over production at that plant. Englebert's liability insurance policy was separate and distinct from Uniroyal's insurance. There never had been any joint meetings of the separate boards of the directors of Uniroyal and Englebert. Can liability be imposed upon Uniroyal for the torts of Englebert in its manufacture of tires? Explain the reasons for your decision. [*Connelly v. Uniroyal, Inc., et al.*, 389 N.E.2d 155 (Ill. 1979).]

3. Nakhleh, a Syrian lawyer and business broker, sued Chemical Construction Corp. (Chemical), an American corporation doing business in New York, in a federal court in New York to recover a finder's fee for breach of an alleged oral contract to help Chemical obtain a contract to build a large fertilizer plant in Saudi Arabia. Assume that, as Nakhleh alleges, the oral contract included an agreement that the contract was to be governed by Saudi Arabian law. New York has recognized the choice-of-law principle that the parties to a contract have a right to choose the law to be applied to their contract. New York Obligations Law prohibits enforcement of oral finders' contracts. The purpose of this law is to avoid the possibility of frequent perjury caused by employees seeking to recover from their employers for nonperformed or fictitious finders' services. Chemical contends that the federal court in New York does not have jurisdiction. Does this statute of frauds provision against finders' contracts being oral represent such a fundamental New York policy that its courts will not honor the intentions of the parties regarding the law they intended to apply? Explain the reasons for your decision. [*Nakhleh v. Chem. Constr. Corp., et al.*, 359 F.Supp. 357 (S.D.N.Y. 1973).]

4. Copperweld Steel Company (Copperweld), a Pennsylvania corporation, sued DeMag-Mannesmann-Boehler (DeMag), a German engineering corporation doing business in the United States, for failure to perform satisfactorily a written contract between them. The case was brought in the federal court in Pennsylvania. The contract provided that DeMag design in Germany a four strand continuous casting

plant to be built for Copperweld in Ohio. The contract contained the following clause: "Any disputes arising out of the terms of the contract shall be brought before the court of justice having jurisdiction in the area where the supplier has its main offices." All records regarding the operation of the plant, and all Copperweld's personnel who operated the plant and who engaged in the negotiation of the contract are in Ohio. Certain of DeMag's personnel involved in the sale are located in the United States. Practically everything done in connection with the transaction has been done in the English language. Almost all witnesses are English speaking. Can this federal Pennsylvania court exercise jurisdiction over this case? Explain the reasons for your decision. [*Copperweld Steel Co. v. DeMag-Mannesmann-Boehler, et al.*, 54 F.R.D. 539 (1972), reh'g, 347 F.Supp.53 (W.D. Pa. 1972), reh'g, 354 F.Supp. 571 (W.D. Pa. 1973), aff'd., 578 F.2d 953 (3rd Cir. 1978).]

5. Stumm Handel Gmbh (Stumm), is a German firm doing business in New York under the name of Stumm Trading Company. Gaskin was employed by Stumm as manager in charge of the New York operation. The written employment contract signed by Gaskin was fairly negotiated at arm's length and in a businesslike fashion between the parties and voluntarily entered into by Gaskin. The contract provided that: "Any controversies arising out of this contract shall be settled by means of negotiations with the Management and, if necessary, with the remaining partners. In case of failure of such negotiations it is agreed that Essen [the Republic of West Germany] shall be the forum to which any controversy must be submitted." The contract was written in German, a language which Gaskin neither speaks nor understands. A literal translation of the contract was conveyed to Gaskin by a representative of Stumm. Gaskin asserts that he was never informed that by executing the contract he was consenting to the Republic of West Germany as the forum within which he must submit all controversies, and that if he had known this he would not have agreed to this provision because it is onerous and unconscionable, and a deterrent to bringing any actions whatsoever. Gaskin sued Stumm in the federal District Court in New York for $306,260.40 he claimed was owing to him by Stumm. Stumm moved to dismiss the action on the ground that the choice-of-forum clause required litigation under the contract in the courts of West Germany. What decision on Stumm's motion? Explain the reasons for your decision. [*Gaskin v. Stumm Handel Gmbh*, 390 F.Supp. 361 (S.D.N.Y. 1975).]
6. Montreal Trading Ltd., plaintiff, is a Canadian corporation that trades commodities in the international market. It has never traded potash. The defendants are U.S. companies that produce potash. Plaintiff sued the defendants for treble damages under U.S. antitrust laws, alleging that plaintiff was unable to sell potash to its customers because the defendants were engaged in a concerted refusal to deal with plaintiff and had deliberately limited potash production to drive up prices. Plaintiff alleged that the concerted refusal was by the defendants' Canadian subsidiaries whom the plaintiff contacted and who refused to sell potash for delivery in Canada. Plaintiff had never contacted the defendants for potash. The defendants were acquitted in previous federal antitrust criminal proceedings. The plaintiff has not sustained any injury in its property or business, and cannot show that it could have resold any potash that it might have purchased. Judgment for whom? Explain the reasons for your decision. [*Montreal Trading Ltd. v. Amax, Inc., et al.*, 661 F.2d 864 (1981), *cert. denied*, 455 U.S. 1001 (10th Cir. 1982).]
7. Eastman Kodak Co. (Eastman) of New York, is a corporation engaged in the manufacture and sale of photographic apparatus and supplies. Over the years, Eastman acquired property and business of competing firms and secured control of

from 75 to 80 percent of the entire interstate trade in the articles in which it dealt. Eastman also, by contract with the makers, obtained entire control in the United States of the imported raw paper that was recognized as the only standard paper for the manufacture of photographic printing-out paper. Eastman's refusal to sell the imported raw paper to other manufacturers compelled several competing companies to sell or go out of business. All photographic supplies manufactured by Eastman were sold with the conditions that dealers carry only such materials for sale to customers as were sold to them by Eastman at listed prices; no articles were to be consigned by them to others without first obtaining the permission of Eastman; and the articles sold to dealers should not be sold by them to other dealers.

The United States brought an antitrust action in the federal District Court in New York to restrain Eastman from violating the Sherman Act, charging that Eastman and others entered into contracts and combinations in restraint of interstate trade and commerce, and with monopolizing a part of such trade. Judgment for whom? Explain the reasons for your decision. [*United States v. Eastman Kodak Co., et. al.*, 226 F. 62 (W.D.N.Y. 1915).] (This is a well-known leading case.)

8. United Brands Co. (UBC) of New York, applicant, is the largest group in the world banana market and accounted for 35 percent of world exports in 1974. Its European subsidiary (UBCBV) is responsible for coordinating banana sales in all the Member States of the EEC except for the United Kingdom and Italy. UBC has 40 to 50 percent of the market in Denmark, West Germany, Ireland, The Netherlands, Belgium, and Luxembourg. UBC also controls both the growing and shipping of bananas because of its vertical integration in the control of sources of bananas in the banana producer countries. Because of UBC's extensive advertising, a consumer preference for its "Chiquita" brand has been created. The bananas are shipped to Europe at two ports with little cost difference and are sold to distributors at prices varying as much as 50 percent. Since bananas are imported while still green and are later ripened, UBC required its distributors/ripeners not to sell bananas while still green, to whom UBC applied differing prices, the difference sometimes amounting to 138 percent. In order to maintain its scheme to control the pricing and conduct of its distributors, UBC terminated its long-standing Danish distributor, Olsen, because it had participated in the advertising campaign of a competitor (Dole). Olsen and others complained to the Commission of the European Communities, which initiated a procedure for infringement of Article 86 of the EEC Treaty against UBC and UBCBV. The Commission decided that UBC and UBCBV had infringed Article 86. UBC and UBCBV then applied to the Court of Justice of the European Communities to have the Commission's decision annulled. Should it be annulled? Explain the reasons for your decision. [*United Brands Co. and United Brands Continental B.V., v. Commission of the European Communities*, Common Mkt. Rep. (CCH) para. 8429 (1978).]

9. Without enumeration, explain the overall EEC policy of prohibited conduct stated in the first portion of:
   a) Article 85
   b) Article 86

10. In the case of *United States of America v. Mercedes-Benz of North America*, excerpted at the beginning of this section, the court stated three elements were necessary to establish a per se illegal tying arrangement. What are those elements?

PART 12 BUSINESS LAW IN THE INTERNATIONAL MARKETPLACE

ETHICS AND BUSINESS LAW

Introduction

This end-of-part discussion, like the others in this book, is designed to encourage students to begin forming personal beliefs about what is right or wrong conduct in business. The discussion here builds on the material in the first end-of-part discussion; you may find it helpful to review that.

This material has several goals. The section that immediately follows is designed to help you see the range of ethical issues associated with this area of the law. The in-depth discussion is intended to provide you with a background for forming your own beliefs about a single very important ethical issue in business. The problems at the end of this part are designed to build your skill in ethical analysis while exploring further the in-depth issue.

A Sampling of Ethical Issues in International Law

International law raises distinctive ethical issues. One stems from the fact that, as we travel from one culture to another, the laws and their ethical underpinnings can change significantly. As a consequence, international business is an area where we are most likely to discover ourselves in fundamental disagreement with the laws of a country that has power over us. When this occurs, the nature of one's ethical duty to comply with the law becomes critically important. Is one ever justified in violating the law of another country? Is one ever justified in violating the law of one's own country?

Another issue is associated with business practices that in this country are viewed as unethical but are common in another country. Bribery is the best example. In many cultures everyone engages in bribery. It doesn't carry the strong negative ethical connotation that it does in the United States. Rather, people often see it as a cost of doing business with government officials who are underpaid. Persons in these cultures see the officials as justified in accepting bribes because they are trying to earn a decent living. The reality is that, if you don't engage in bribery on the same terms as your competitors, you often cannot win new business, or obtain important government help on a timely basis. In a sense, our Foreign Corrupt Practices Act imposes a handicap on American firms doing business in different cultures. Do you think your beliefs about business ethics should change depending upon the country in which you are doing business? Do you think you are justified in engaging in practices such as bribery because others do it? Does it make a difference if the others are your competitors?

Another issue is associated with foreign laws that conflict with your ethical standards. Child labor laws are a common example. Apartheid is another. Apartheid is a form of pervasive racial discrimination practiced in the Republic of South Africa and incorporated in its laws. For some time, many serious thinkers urged businesses not to comply with these laws when operating in the Republic of South Africa. Rather, they urged that American business follow the ethical standards of our nation. More recently these thinkers have concluded that apartheid is such a moral evil that it is wrong for this country, and wrong for its businesses, to support a government that enforces apartheid laws. As a consequence they have urged economic sanctions, some of which would involve the withdrawal of American firms from South Africa.

Some argue that economic sanctions against the Republic of South Africa would themselves be unethical. They claim that the persons injured by sanctions would be employed or unemployed poor black persons there rather than those who enforce racist policies. Further, they claim, it would be wrong to impose sanctions without the consent of the black population.

Do you think it is wrong to do business in a country that adopts policies you judge to be fundamentally unethical? Or do you think this is not an issue with which business should concern itself?

Another fundamental ethical issue in international business is trade protection. Can you see that low wage rates in poor countries would attract labor intensive industries? When this occurs, wealthier countries with higher wage rates lose jobs. One response by the wealthy is to impose tariffs so that products manufactured in the low wage country cannot be imported. This keeps jobs at home. But it also takes jobs away from the poor. Can you see the way that capitalism tends to benefit the most poor in international trade and is, in this aspect, consistent with Kant's philosophy and religious ethics? And can you see the way the tariffs thwart this process? Can you articulate assessments of protectionist tariffs using the four styles of ethical reasoning?

In-Depth Discussion of a Basic Issue: The Duty to Comply with the Law

Every person in business needs mature views on what they believe about the duty to comply with the law. Business affords many opportunities to sidestep the law, to avoid being detected, and to profit from the violation.

In this country, an ethically mature view on our duty to comply with the law must reflect the fact that we have the opportunity to change the law. If we were to conclude that a law is ethically wrong, then we would become obligated to try to change it. In most moral systems this responsibility to try changing the law is the first step required before one can morally justify disobeying any law.

► Kant's Philosophy

While the following historical incident is true, and reflects many attributes of Kant's style of ethical reasoning, it is not purely Kantian.

One view on *compliance* is illustrated by the life of a man who was charged with violating the laws of his country. At his trial, the man was sentenced to death. The man and his friends believed the law he was charged with violating was wrong, and that his trial had not been fair. Because of this, while the man was awaiting execution, his friends arranged an opportunity for him to escape. When told about this opportunity, the man turned to his personal ethics to decide whether it would be right or wrong to violate the law of his country and escape the unjust sentence. In reaching his decision he weighed three arguments. First he said, we should never harm others, and by escaping he would harm the state by violating its laws. Second he reasoned, each citizen impliedly agrees to obey the laws of his or her country and by escaping he would be breaking his promise—his implied agreement to obey the law. A third reason was that one's country is like a teacher or parent and we ought, therefore, to obey our country by following its laws. The man concluded that it would be ethically wrong for him to escape; accordingly he declined the chance and was put to death. The man's name was Socrates. His style of reasoning about compliance with the law was based on promises, consent, and duty; its perspective is clearly "other" oriented and, in important ways, it is similar to Kant's.

The ethical belief which Socrates possessed about compliance with the law is inspiring. But it was the result of a long life devoted to reasoning about ethical issues. Most students are at the beginning of their lives and less able to reason with such assurance and commitment about ethical issues.

► Egoistic Analysis

Others, such as egoists, adopt a radically different view toward compliance with the law. For an egoist, the decision to comply or not usually turns on the *risks versus the rewards*. Thus an egoist is mainly concerned with whether or not the violation of the law could be detected, and, if so, what the penalties would be in comparison to the potential profits. For example, an egoist would weigh the decision to cheat on tax returns in this way. By claiming three extra dependent exemptions for cats (illegal conduct) there could be an after tax savings of about \$1,500. On the other hand, the risk of being caught by an audit is only about 2 percent. If caught, there would probably be a penalty assessed at 50 percent of the unpaid tax for *civil* fraud and the possibility of conviction and imprisonment for *criminal* fraud. In a statistical sense, the reward for cheating (\$1,500) would be compared with the potential civil risk (\$1,500 + \$750 = \$2,250 × .02 = \$45!). Since the civil reward exceeds the civil risk, the egoist would probably take exemptions for his or her cats, unless deterred by the risk of criminal prosecution.

► Utilitarian Analysis

Utilitarians would be likely to conclude that *the greatest good for the greatest number* occurs when everyone obeys the law. This is especially true in this country where there are a variety of mechanisms for changing laws. Electing different legislators and initiating constitutional amendments are mechanisms for changing a law which is judged, by any philosophic standard, to be wrong.

► Religious Analysis

Persons with religious orientations are generally compelled by their religion to obey the laws of the country where they live. Again, in our country, if there is a conflict between the beliefs of a religion and the law of our country, the law changing mechanisms are available to try to modify the law.

Sometimes utilitarians, Kantians, and persons with religious ethics conclude that a law is, by their particular ethical standard, very wrong or unjust. Political efforts to change such a law are sometimes unsuccessful. Since persons of these ethical views are generally committed to complying with law, an important law which they believe to be unethical presents them with a real dilemma, to comply with the unethical law or, by its violation, to betray their general commitment to compliance. In these situations, some resolve the matter by engaging in civil disobedience.

Civil Disobedience

Civil disobedience is another way of attempting to induce a change in the law. It is very important, however, to distinguish conduct which is egoistic from that which constitutes valid civil disobedience. Mohandas Ghandi of India and Martin Luther King in the United States are among the persons most widely recognized as serious philosophers and practitioners of civil disobedience. You may understand civil disobedience better by studying an incident in the life of Martin Luther King.

In early 1963, King, as leader of the Southern Christian Leadership Conference, was organizing activities to protest racial segregation in the city of Birmingham, Alabama. A judge issued an injunction prohibiting marches and other kinds of protests. In defiance of the injunction, King continued to march and was arrested. While in the Birmingham jail he wrote a now famous letter in which he explained *his* justification for *his* civil disobedience. An edited version of the letter is reproduced below.

> My dear Fellow Clergymen,
> While confined here in the Birmingham City Jail, I came across your recent statement calling our present activities "unwise and untimely."
>
> . . . . .
>
> I think I should give the reason for my being in Birmingham, since you have been influenced by the argument of "outsiders coming in."
>
> . . . . .
>
> I am in Birmingham because injustice is here. Just as the eighth-century prophets left their little villages and carried their "thus saith the Lord" far beyond the boundaries of their home towns; and just as the Apostle Paul left his little village of Tarsus and carried the gospel of Jesus Christ to practically every hamlet and city of the Graeco-Roman world, I too am compelled to carry the gospel of freedom beyond my particular home town. Like Paul, I must constantly respond to the Macedonian call for aid.
>
> Moreover, I am cognizant of the interrelatedness of all communities and states. I cannot sit idly by in Atlanta and not be concerned about what happens in Birmingham. Injustice anywhere is a threat to justice everywhere. We are caught in an inescapable network of mutuality, tied in a single garment of destiny. Whatever affects one directly affects all indirectly. Never again can we afford to live with the narrow, provincial "outside agitator" idea. Anyone who lives inside the United States can never be considered an outsider anywhere in this country.
>
> Birmingham is probably the most thoroughly segregated city in the United States. Its ugly record of police brutality is known in every section of this country. Its injust treatment of Negroes in the courts is a notorious reality. There have been more unsolved bombings of

Negro homes and churches in Birmingham than any city in this nation. These are the hard, brutal and unbelievable facts. On the basis of these conditions Negro leaders sought to negotiate with the city fathers. But the political leaders consistently refused to engage in good faith negotiation.

• • • • •

You may well ask, "Why direct action? Why sit-ins, marches, etc.? Isn't negotiation a better path?" You are exactly right in your call for negotiation. Indeed, this is the purpose of direct action. Nonviolent direct action seeks to create such a crisis and establish such creative tension that a community that has constantly refused to negotiate is forced to confront the issue. It seeks so to dramatize the issue that it can no longer be ignored. I just referred to the creation of tension as a part of the work of the nonviolent resister. This may sound rather shocking. But I must confess that I am not afraid of the word tension. I have earnestly worked and preached against violent tension, but there is a type of constructive nonviolent tension that is necessary for growth. Just as Socrates felt that it was necessary to create a tension in the mind so that individuals could rise from the bondage of myths and half-truths to the unfettered realm of creative analysis and objective appraisal, we must see the need of having nonviolent gadflies to create the kind of tension in society that will help men to rise from the dark depths of prejudice and racism to the majestic heights of understanding and brotherhood. So the purpose of the direct action is to create a situation so crisis-packed that it will inevitably open the door to negotiation. We, therefore, concur with you in your call for negotiation. Too long has our beloved Southland been bogged down in the tragic attempt to live in monologue rather than dialogue.

• • • • •

My friends, I must say to you that we have not made a single gain in civil rights without determined legal and nonviolent pressure. History is the long and tragic story of the fact that privileged groups seldom give up their privileges voluntarily. Individuals may see the moral light and voluntarily give up their unjust posture; but as Reinhold Niebuhr has reminded us, groups are more immoral than individuals.

We know through painful experience that freedom is never voluntarily given by the oppressor; it must be demanded by the oppressed. Frankly, I have never yet engaged in a direct action movement that was "well timed," according to the timetable of those who have not suffered unduly from the disease of segregation. For years now I have heard the words "Wait!" It rings in the ear of every Negro with a piercing familiarity. This "Wait" has almost always meant "Never." It has been a tranquilizing thalidomide, relieving the emotional stress for a moment, only to give birth to an ill-formed infant of frustration. We must come to see with the distinguished jurist of yesterday that "justice too long delayed is justice denied." We have waited for more than three hundred and forty years for our constitutional and God-given rights. The nations of Asia and Africa are moving with jet-like speed toward the goal of political independence, and we still creep at horse and buggy pace toward the gaining of a cup of coffee at a lunch counter. I guess it is easy for those who have never felt the stinging darts of segregation to say, "Wait." But when you have seen vicious mobs lynch your mothers and fathers at will and drown your sisters and brothers at whim; when you have seen hate-filled policemen curse, kick, brutalize and even kill your black brothers and sisters with impunity; when you see the vast majority of your twenty million Negro brothers smothering in an air-tight cage of poverty in the midst of an affluent society; when you suddenly find your tongue twisted and your speech stammering as you seek to explain to your six-year-old daughter why she can't go to the public amusement park that has just been advertised on television, and see tears welling up in her little eyes when she is told that Funtown is closed to colored children, and see the depressing clouds of inferiority begin to form in her little mental sky, and see her begin to distort her little personality by unconsciously developing a bitterness toward white people; when you have to concoct an answer for a five-year-old son asking in agonizing pathos: "Daddy, why do white people treat colored people so mean?"; when you take a cross country drive and find it necessary to sleep night after night in the uncomfortable corners of your automobile because no motel will accept you; when you are humiliated day in and day out by nagging signs reading "white" and "colored"; when your first name becomes "nigger" and your middle name becomes "boy" (however old you are) and your last name becomes "John," and when your wife and mother are never given the respected title "Mrs."; when you are harried by day and haunted at night by the fact that you are a Negro, living constantly at tip-toe stance never quite knowing what to expect next, and plagued with inner fears and outer resentments; when you are forever fighting a degenerating sense of "nobodiness"; then you will understand why we find it difficult to wait. There comes a time when the cup of endurance runs over, and men are no longer willing to be plunged into an abyss of injustice where they experience the blackness of corroding despair. I hope, sirs, you can understand our legitimate and unavoidable impatience.

You express a great deal of anxiety over our willingness to break laws. This is certainly a legitimate concern. Since we so diligently urge people to obey the Supreme Court's decision of 1954 outlawing segregation in the public schools, it is rather strange and paradoxical to find us consciously breaking laws. One may well ask, "How can you advocate breaking some laws and obeying others?" The answer is found in the fact that there are two types of laws: There are just and there are unjust laws. I would agree with Saint Augustine that "An unjust law is no law at all."

Now what is the difference between the two? How does one determine when a law is just or unjust? A just law is a man-made code that squares with the moral law or the law of God. An unjust law is a code that is out of harmony with the moral law. To put it in the terms of Saint Thomas Aquinas, as unjust law is a human law that is not rooted in eternal and natural law. Any law that uplifts human personality is just. Any law that degrades human personality is unjust. All segregation statutes are unjust because segregation distorts the soul and damages the personality. It gives the segregator a false sense of superiority, and the segregated a false sense of inferiority. To use the words of Martin Buber, the great Jewish philosopher, segregation substitutes an "I-it" relationship for the "I-thou" relationship, and ends up relegating persons to the status of things. So segregation is not only politically, economically and sociologically unsound, but it is morally wrong and sinful. Paul Tillich has said that sin is separation. Isn't segregation an existential expression of man's tragic separation, an expression of his awful estrangement, his terrible sinfulness? So I can urge men to disobey segregation ordinances because they are morally wrong.

Let us turn to a more concrete example of just and unjust laws. An unjust law is a code that a majority inflicts on a minority that is not binding on itself. This is difference made legal. On the other hand a just law is a code that a majority compels a minority to follow that it is willing to follow itself. This is sameness made legal.

Let me give another explanation. An unjust law is a code inflicted upon a minority which that minority had no part in enacting or creating because they did not have the unhampered right to vote. Who can say that the legislature of Alabama which set up the segregation laws was democratically elected? Throughout the state of Alabama all types of conniving methods are used to prevent Negroes from becoming registered voters and there are some counties without a single Negro registered to vote despite the fact that the Negro constitutes a majority of the population. Can any law set up in such a state be considered democratically structured?

These are just a few examples of unjust and just laws. There are some instances when a law is just on its face and unjust in its application. For instance, I was arrested Friday on a charge of parading without a permit. Now there is nothing wrong with an ordinance which requires a permit for a parade, but when the ordinance is used to preserve segregation and to deny citizens the First Amendment privilege of peaceful assembly and peaceful protest, then it becomes unjust.

I hope you can see the distinction I am trying to point out. In no sense do I advocate evading or defying the law as the rabid segregationist would do. This would lead to anarchy.

One who breaks an unjust law must do it *openly, lovingly* (not hatefully as the white mothers did in New Orleans when they were seen on television screaming "nigger, nigger, nigger"), and with a willingness to accept the penalty. I submit that an individual who breaks a law that conscience tells him is unjust, and willingly accepts the penalty by staying in jail to arouse the conscience of the community over its injustice, is in reality expressing the very highest respect for law.

Of course, there is nothing new about this kind of civil disobedience. It was seen sublimely in the refusal of Shadrach, Meshach and Abednego to obey the laws of Nebuchadnezzar because a higher moral law was involved. It was practiced superbly by the early Christians who were willing to face hungry lions and the excruciating pain of chopping blocks, before submitting to certain unjust laws of the Roman empire. To a degree academic freedom is a reality today because Socrates practiced civil disobedience.

We can never forget that everything Hitler did in Germany was "legal" and everything the Hungarian freedom fighters did in Hungary was "illegal." It was "illegal" to aid and comfort a Jew in Hitler's Germany. But I am sure that if I had lived in Germany during that time I would have aided and comforted my Jewish brothers even though it was illegal. If I lived in a Communist country today where certain principles dear to the Christian faith are suppressed, I believe I would openly advocate disobeying these anti-religious laws.

• • • • •

In your statement you asserted that our actions, even though peaceful, must be condemned because they precipitate violence. But can this assertion be logically made? Isn't this like condemning the robbed man because his possession of money precipitated the evil act of robbery? Isn't this like condemning Socrates because his unswerving commitment to truth and his philosophical delvings precipitated the misguided popular mind to make him drink the hemlock? Isn't this like condemning Jesus because His unique God-Consciousness and never-ceasing devotion to His will precipitated the evil act of crucifixion? We must come to see, as federal courts have consistently affirmed, that it is immoral to urge an individual to withdraw his efforts to gain his basic constitutional rights because the quest precipitates violence. Society must protect the robbed and punish the robber.

You spoke of our activity in Birmingham as extreme. At first I was rather disappointed that fellow clergymen would see my nonviolent efforts as those of the extremist. I started thinking about the fact that I stand in the middle of two opposing forces in the Negro community. One is a force of complacency made up of Negroes who, as a result of long years of oppression, have been so completely drained of self-respect and a sense of "somebodiness" that they have adjusted to segregation, and, of a few Negroes in the middle class who, because of a degree of academic and economic security, and because at points they profit by segregation, have unconsciously become insensitive to the problems of the masses. The other force is one of bitterness and hatred, and comes perilously close to advocating violence. It is expressed in the various black nationalist groups that are springing up over the nation, the largest and best known being Elijah Muhammad's Muslim movement. This movement is nourished by the contemporary frustration over the continued existence of racial discrimination. It is made up of people who have lost faith in America, who have absolutely repudiated Christianity, and who have concluded that the white man is an incurable "devil." I have tried to stand between these two forces, saying that we need not follow the "donothingism" of the complacent or the hatred and despair of the black nationalist. There is the more excellent way of love and nonviolent protest. I'm grateful to God that, through the Negro church, the dimension of nonviolence entered our struggle. If this philosophy had not emerged, I am convinced that by now many streets of the South would be flowing with floods of blood. And I am further convinced that if our white brothers dismiss as "rabble rousers" and "outside agitators" those of use who are working through the channels of nonviolent direct action and refuse to support our nonviolent efforts, millions of Negroes, out of frustration and despair, will seek solace and security in black nationalist ideologies, a development that will lead inevitably to a frightening racial nightmare.

• • • • •

Now this approach is being dismissed as extremist. I must admit that I was initially disappointed in being so categorized.

But as I continued to think about the matter I gradually gained a bit of satisfaction from being considered an extremist. Was not Jesus an extremist in love—"Love your enemies, bless them that curse you, pray for them that despitefully use you." Was not Amos an extremist for justice—"Let justice roll down like waters and righteousness like a mighty stream." Was not Paul an extremist for the gospel of Jesus Christ—"I bear in my body the marks of the Lord Jesus." Was not Martin Luther an extremist—"Here I stand; I can do none other so help me God." Was not John Bunyan an extremist—"I will stay in jail to the end of my days before I make a butchery of my conscience." Was not Abraham Lincoln an extremist—"This nation cannot survive half slave and half free." Was not Thomas Jefferson an extremist—"We hold these truths to be self-evident, that all men are created equal." So the question is not whether we will be extremist but what kind of extremist will we be. Will we be extremists for hate or will we be extremists for love? Will we be extremists for the preservation of injustice—or will we be extremists for the cause of justice? In that dramatic scene on Calvary's hill, three men were crucified. We must not forget that all three were crucified for the same crime—the crime of extremism. Two were extremists for immorality, and thusly fell below their environment. The other, Jesus Christ, was an extremist for love, truth and goodness, and thereby rose above his environment. So, after all, maybe the South, the nation and the world are in dire need of creative extremists.

• • • • •

I must close now. But before closing I am impelled to mention one other point in your statement that troubled me profoundly. You warmly commended the Birmingham police force for keeping "order" and "preventing violence." I don't believe you would have so warmly commended the police force if you had seen its angry violent dogs literally biting six unarmed, nonviolent Negroes. I don't believe you would so quickly commend the policemen if you would observe their ugly and inhuman treatment of Negroes here in the city jail; if you would watch them push and curse old Negro women and young Negro girls; if you would see them slap and kick old Negro men and young boys; if you will observe them, as they did on two occasions, refuse to give us food because we wanted to sing our grace together. I'm sorry that I can't join you in your praise for the police department.

It is true that they have been rather disciplined in their public handling of the demonstrators. In this sense they have been rather publicly "nonviolent." But for what purpose? To preserve the evil system of segregation. Over the last few years I have consistently preached that nonviolence demands that the means we use must be as pure as the ends we seek. So I have tried to make it clear that it is wrong to use immoral means to attain moral ends. But now I must affirm that it is just as wrong, or even more so, to use moral means to preserve immoral ends. Maybe Mr. Conner and his policemen have been rather publicly nonviolent, as Chief Pritchett was in Albany, Georgia, but they have used the moral means of nonviolence to maintain the immoral end of flagrant racial injustice. T. S. Eliot has said that there is no greater treason than to do the right deed for the wrong reason.

I wish you had commended the Negro sit-inners and demonstrators of Birmingham for their sublime courage, their willingness to suffer and their amazing discipline in the midst of the most inhuman provocation. One day the South will recognize its real heroes. They will be the James Merediths, courageously and with a majestic sense of purpose facing jeering and hostile mobs and the agonizing loneliness that characterizes the life of the pioneer. They will be old, oppressed, battered Negro women, symbolized in a seventy-two year old woman of Montgomery, Alabama, who rose up with a sense of dignity and with her people decided not to ride the segregated buses, and responded to one who inquired about her tiredness with ungrammatical profundity: "My feet is tired, but my soul is rested." They will be the young high school and college students, young ministers of the Gospel and a host of their elders courageously and nonviolently sitting-in at lunch counters and willingly going to jail for conscience's sake. One day the South will know that when these disinherited children of God sat down at lunch counters they were in reality standing up for the best in the American dream and the most sacred values in our Judeo-Christian heritage, and thusly, carrying our whole nation back to those great wells of democracy which were dug deep by the founding fathers in the formulation of the Constitution and the Declaration of Independence.

Never before have I written a letter this long (or should I say a book?). I'm afraid that it is much too long to take your precious time. I can assure you that it would have been much shorter if I had been writing from a comfortable desk, but what else is there to do when you are alone for days in the dull monotony of a narrow jail cell other than write long letters, think strange thoughts, and pray long prayers?

Yours for the cause of Peace and Brotherhood,
Martin Luther King, Jr.

Non-violent civil disobedience, lead by Martin Luther King, resulted in the passage of the Civil Rights Act of 1964. But Dr. King, like Socrates, was put to death. In his case it was by a lawless, violent, assassin who sought to conceal his conduct and avoid the prescribed punishment.

Solving Ethics Problems

Like the other end-of-part discussions in this book, this one presents problems for you to consider. These problems have three goals. The first is to give you the opportunity to further explore the in-depth issue. The second goal is to give you experience in ethical reasoning about the law and about related management problems. The third goal is to let you see how thinking critically about the law can increase your ability to make ethical decisions. To facilitate this, the problems begin by asking you to analyze the law for its ethical content and then shift to looking at related problems in managerial ethics.

For a discussion of the ethical roles of markets and the law, and examples of the four styles of ethical reasoning—egoism, utilitarianism, Kantian philosophy, and religious ethics—read the business ethics material at the end of Part 1.

► Problems

1. Review *Pirkey v. Hospital Corporation of America*, p. 1202. Can you see that the choice-of-law issue is likely to determine the outcome of this case? We might surmise that if the case were tried under Colorado law, Dr. Pirkey would prevail while under the law of Saudi Arabia he would lose. Since these two bodies of law apparently conflict, the battle over the choice of law is really the battle over who will win the case. Can you see that this is a conflict between the need for order and the need to resolve the case based on other ethical principles? Is exploiting this need for order to try to win the case a form of civil disobedience? If it is a form of civil disobedience, would Dr. King judge it to be ethical?
2. Union Carbide operated plants that manufacture the pesticide methyl isocyanate. One plant located in West Virginia was subject to stringent U.S. safety and environmental laws. This plant had a computerized safety system. Another plant was located in Bhopol, India, where safety and environmental standards were lax; this

plant did not have the computerized system. In December 1984, the Bhopol plant leaked about 25 tons of the gaseous pesticide. As a result, 2,000 died and 100,000 were injured. Is it ethical to build plants outside the United States if the sole motivation is to escape more stringent safety and environmental laws? Is complying with a lax safety law a valid moral defense to a disaster like Bhopol? Was Union Carbide under a moral obligation to use the same safety standards in both countries?

3. If you were the manager of international marketing for an American firm, would you do business in South Africa, a country that uses the law to achieve racial segregation? If you did elect to do business in that country, would you comply with all of its laws?
4. If you learn that you can invest $10,000 in a company that manufactures radar detectors for use by speeding drivers and receive a 25 percent return on your investment each year, will you do so? Why or why not?

APPENDIX A

AN EXPLANATION OF THE CIVIL TRIAL PROCESS

Introduction

The judicial system and its courts deal with the interpretation, validity, declaration, and application of legal rules to the factual situations it confronts. It is through this process that law is made, indicating what is legal now and, therefore, as case precedent, what applies for the future. The court acts only on matters brought before it by parties who want judicial action. It has only the jurisdiction and powers given to it by federal or state statutes.

Some court cases involve the federal and state constitutions, and administrative rules and regulations, while other cases involve the common law and equity in the absence of constitutional or legislative guidance. In any event, the decisions of the courts are law, providing guidance to society as to what is legal. It is therefore important to understand the meaning of these decisions by reading and analyzing them. All too often members of the public have no concept of how their judicial system works. An explanation here of the civil trial process will be helpful.

One of the most important ways law is made is by the published opinions of appellate courts. Most of the abbreviated court decisions in this text are edited versions of these appellate court opinions. The opinions of the courts in deciding cases are often contained in reports of those cases, which are available in the libraries of courthouses, law schools, and other public places. Reference to a court opinion is called a *case citation.* For example, *Vigil v. Lamm,* 190 Colo. 180, 544 P.2d 631 (1976), refers to a Colorado case report found in volume 190 of the Colorado Reports at page 180, which may also be found in the regional Pacific Reporter in volume 544, second series at page 631. The date of the case is 1976. In this textbook we will always use case citations so that you may look up the original version if you are interested.

To understand how the parties to a legal dispute get to an appellate court to have their case heard, we offer here a brief overview of the civil trial process. The process described may vary slightly from state to state, but the definitions of the terms used are widely accepted.

The Trial of a Civil Case

plaintiff

The party who initiates a civil suit by filing a compliant in the proper court

complaint

The first pleading in a civil action

A civil suit is initiated by the **plaintiff,** who files several documents in a trial court of general jurisdiction (usually a county court located in the county government building).[1] The document of greatest importance is called the **complaint,** which is filed by the plaintiff. The complaint must contain the following information:

1. The names of the parties to the case, the plaintiff(s) and defendant(s)
2. A statement sufficient to show that the court has jurisdiction to hear the matter; and
3. A short and plain statement of the facts, indicating
   (a) the existence of a legal duty and
   (b) the breach of this duty and
   (c) a claim for relief in the form of a request for a given amount of money damages and/or a claim for equitable relief, such as a request for an injunction or an order for specific performance of a contract.

summons

A writ or process served on the defendant in a civil action notifying him or her of the action and summoning him or her to appear and plead

defendant

The party against whom a civil suit (or criminal action) is brought

The complaint normally is filed together with a **summons,** which directs the server of the papers (usually a county sheriff if the case is filed in a county court, or a federal marshall if filed in a federal court) to the last known address of the **defendant.** Usually a copy of the complaint is included for the purpose of this *service.* When the server of the papers locates the defendant(s) or, in some states, when the server locates the permanent residence of the defending party(ies), the papers are left with someone of suitable age and discretion residing therein. The server then files a sworn statement with the court, often called a *return,* in which the server swears that the defendant(s) was (were) served.

The defendant may file a document with the court responding to the complaint, called an *answer,* within a given time period, usually twenty to thirty days. A copy of the answer is given to the plaintiff. The answer may

[1]Some of this material is from Wolfe and Naffzinger, *The Law of American Business Organizations* (New York: John Wiley & Sons, 1984).

FIGURE A.1 **Trial and Appeal of a Civil Suit**

I. PRETRIAL
   A. Plaintiff: contacts lawyer and lawyer files complaint with proper trial court.
   B. Defendant: receives copy of complaint and must file an answer and any counterclaim within 20 days.
   C. Preliminary motions by either party—for example, motion to dismiss for failure to state a claim.
   D. Discovery process: deposition, interrogatories.
   E. Preliminary motions by either party—for example, a judgment on the pleadings or a summary judgment.
   F. Jury trial demanded by either party if appropriate.

II. TRIAL
   A. Qualifying the jury: voir dire, if needed.
   B. Evidence introduced: plaintiff first, then defendant attempt to establish facts by introducing evidence for jury to see and listen to; jury (or court) finds facts by watching demeanor of witnesses, by listening to direct and cross examination, and by viewing physical evidence, documents, and related circumstances.
   C. Trial motions: party may request directed verdict.
   D. Judge instructs jury on application of proper rules to the evidence.
   E. Verdict and final motions: judgment notwithstanding the verdict.

III. APPEALS—EITHER PARTY MAY APPEAL MATTERS OF LAW APPLICATION
   A. Appellant files petition for review with intermediate appellate court.
   B. Appellee answers petition.
   C. Decision by intermediate appellate court based on trial transcripts and written briefs of parties.
   D. Final appeal to highest state appellate court or federal supreme court.

---

admit all, part, or none of the facts as alleged in the complaint, and may admit or deny any or all of the legal consequences. In addition, the answer may include a claim for relief against the plaintiff, called a **counterclaim,** if the grounds exist.

counterclaim

A claim asserted by the defendant against the plaintiff's claim in a civil action

The general rule defining those persons who may be plaintiffs or defendants is that they must have a direct interest in the subject matter of the suit; that is, these persons must be directly affected by the outcome. This rule has been expanded somewhat recently by permitting *class action* suits.

Class action suits were first widely used on the federal level, but gradually states have been adopting procedures that provide for this type of litigation. The class action procedural rules provide that one or more members of a class may sue or be sued as representatives of a class of persons if: (1) the class is so numerous that joinder of all members of the class is not practicable; (2) there are questions of law or fact that are common to all members of the class; (3) the claims or defenses of the parties representing the class are typical of the claims or defenses of the class; (4) the representatives of the class will fairly protect the interests of the class; and (5) all the members of the class must be identifiable (within reason). In addition to these prerequisites, the court must find that the class action is superior to other available methods for the fair and efficient adjudication of the controversy.

If a party is properly served with the complaint and fails to file an answer within the time period provided by law, then the plaintiff may ask the court to enter a *default* judgment. If such is entered, the court is making a judgment that the plaintiff is entitled to the relief claimed in the complaint.

As stated earlier, a defendant may *answer,* or the defendant may challenge the plaintiff's case by **motion** before the issue is formally tried. There are several motions the parties may use to challenge the legal arguments of the other party asserted through the **pleadings** filed with the court. The first such opportunity to present such a motion is presented by the defendant, who may make a motion to the court to dismiss the complaint for failure to state a claim upon which relief may be granted. In this case the motion is made by filing a document labeled "Motion" with the court.

motion

A procedural device asking the court to take some action

pleadings

The formal documents filed with a court that usually include the complaint, answer, and motions regarding them

The filing of the "Motion to Dismiss for Failure to State a Claim" by the defendant requires the judge to rule on whether or not the plaintiff has stated the existence and breach of a legal duty. The judge must consider the complaint and the facts stated therein and resolve every inference created by the facts in favor of the plaintiff. When this is done, the court will grant or deny the motion to dismiss.

Discovery

If the defendant files an answer, then the litigation moves into a phase of the process generally called the *discovery* stage. Generally the objectives of this *pre-trial* procedure are to: (1) simplify the issues; (2) obtain admissions of fact to avoid unnecessary arguments and avoid surprise; (3) limit the number of expert witnesses; and (4) cover any other matters that would expedite the trial.

deposition

A written statement made by a person under oath or affirmation in a judicial proceeding where there is opportunity for cross-examination before trial

interrogatory

A written question

privileged communication

A communication between certain persons which, because of their relationship, is inadmissible in evidence without a waiver of the privilege

summary judgment

A judgment rendered on a motion by a party in a civil action that, solely on the basis of the pleadings and affidavits there is no genuine issue as to any material fact and that the moving party is entitled to judgment as a matter of law without the necessity of a trial on the facts

jury

Trial jury, a group of people selected to decide the facts in a trial

voir dire

The examination before trial of a prospective juror or witness in which he or she is to answer the questions truthfully

The following legal devices permit an adverse party to discover almost all information relevant to the trial of a civil suit. The best known discovery device is the **deposition.** A deposition is a sworn statement of any person, including a party to the action (the plaintiff or defendant) or any witness, which is made in response to questions from the attorneys for the opposing sides. The deposition is used to discover physical evidence, to discover what a witness will say at trial, or to discover any other matter relevant to the subject of the case. A deposition is taken under oath or affirmation, usually in front of attorneys for both parties, and is transcribed by a court reporter. The final copy is signed as a true statement by the one being deposed and is filed with the court. This signed statement may be used at the trial if the witness is unavailable, or it may be used at the trial to challenge the oral testimony of the deposing witness if such testimony varies from that in the deposition.

If the party or witness cannot be interviewed in person, then a series of written questions may be sent and must be answered under oath. These written questions are called **interrogatories.**

In addition to depositions and interrogatories, a party may ask the court to order another party, if good cause is shown, to produce documents and other items of evidence for inspection, copying, or photographing. The subject of this order may be books, papers, accounts, letters, photographs, objects or tangible things, or other items that constitute evidence relating to the subject of the suit. If the mental or physical condition of the party is in controversy, the court may order the party to submit to a physical or mental examination by a physician if good cause is shown. This latter method of discovery is used in many cases where personal injury is the subject of the case.

Courts in the various states adopted many of these discovery procedures in the 1960s so they are viewed as relatively new. This adoption has resulted in many more cases being settled out of court because the procedures allow a party to discover almost all of the relevant evidence of the opposing party. The only evidence that is not obtainable by an opposing party are those materials that are **privileged.** Generally, such materials include an attorney's work product (thoughts and research on a case) and communications between the client and his attorney or the patient and his doctor.

If the parties decide to *settle* the case out of court, the attorneys ask the permission of the judge to dismiss the case. If this dismissal is done *with prejudice,* it means that a party will be barred from filing the suit again. If the pretrial procedures do not result in settlement, then the parties usually ask the judge to rule on another series of motions challenging the legal assertions of the adverse parties. After the pleadings are all filed, either party may make a motion to dismiss the claims of an adverse party and enter judgment for the moving party by asking for a *judgment on the pleadings* or **summary judgment.** Some procedural systems make a distinction between these two motions but, in essence, they are the same. Like the initial motion to dismiss described above, these motions require the judge to consider the arguments made in all of the pleadings, resolve every reasonable inference against the moving party, and make a finding as to whether or not the arguments made and facts asserted warrant submission of the case to the jury in a trial on the facts. Generally, if the judge finds that the legal arguments and facts presented could lead to but one reasonable conclusion, and that is in favor of the moving party, then the motion must be granted. If there are issues of fact present that would lead reasonable minds to differ, then the motion should be overruled.

A matter may be tried before a **jury** or a judge alone. If a party in a civil suit desires a jury trial, it must be demanded, usually during the initial pleading phase. In federal courts, the U.S. Constitution guarantees a trial by jury in all civil actions at common law where the value of the controversy exceeds twenty dollars. The U.S. Constitution does not guarantee the right of a trial by jury in civil cases in state courts. However, the constitutions of the states usually provide that there is such a right in cases similar to those where the common law gave such a right at the time the constitution was adopted. Practically speaking, this means that almost all matters involving judgments of fact and requests for money damages may be tried before a jury. Usually negligence cases, and other personal injury cases, are tried before a jury. On the other hand, cases involving the equity powers of the court or those involving very complex issues such as antitrust suits or breaches of industrial contracts and other cases where evaluation of the evidence requires rigorous analysis and expertise are usually tried before the judge alone. In very exceptional cases, the judge may appoint a *master* or *referee* to hear some of the evidence and make findings of fact.

The process of questioning prospective jurors to determine which of them will be permitted to sit on the jury is called **voir dire.** This phrase is French in origin and means "to speak the truth." The voir dire procedure allows the court and parties to reject a prospective juror if, after questioning, it is revealed that the person is barred by statute to serve in that case (for example, if the person is the spouse of the plaintiff) or might be prejudiced or unable to render an impartial judgment. Usually each party is given three challenges to use for *any* reason—called *peremptory challenges*[2] additional; challenges can be made for sufficient cause (statutory cause)—called *challenge for cause.*

---

[2]See the important criminal case of *Batson v. Kentucky,* 106 S. Ct. 1712 (1986), discussed on page 32.

Trial

At the trial, the plaintiff, through the attorney representing the plaintiff's interests, presents its side of the **evidence.** After each witness is sworn and "directly" examined by the plaintiff's attorney, the defendant's attorney may "cross-examine" the witness on matters brought out on direct examination. It must be emphasized at this point that, since most of the cases that proceed to trial do involve disputes of fact, the process by which the facts are "found" is the process of *direct examination* of a witness by the attorney who initially uses the witness followed by *cross-examination* by the attorney for the other side. The jury or the judge, by watching the witnesses respond to the questions asked, must determine whether they are telling the truth or accurately recalling an event. The answers that are given by the witness are considered by the fact-finder (jury or judge) together with the witness's demeanor (facial expressions and hand movements).

evidence

A fact from which an inference can be drawn of another fact

Following the plaintiff's version of the facts in the case, the defendant presents the evidence relevant to its side.

During the trial itself, a party may challenge the entire case of an adverse party by moving for a **directed verdict.** Either party may move this, and it requires the judge to rule on whether or not there are still issues of fact present that warrant the continuation of the trial. If reasonable minds could differ about the interpretation or existence of certain crucial facts, or the inferences to be drawn from the facts, then the court will overrule the motion and the trial will proceed.

directed verdict

A jury verdict as directed by the judge

verdict

A jury's finding of fact

At the close of the defendant's case, both sides make summary arguments emphasizing the aspects of the testimony and other evidence they believe most pertinent to their arguments. Before the jury retires to make its finding of fact, the judge instructs the jury on the appropriate rules of law that the jurors are to apply to the facts as determined by them. Below is an example of the type of "instruction" the judge may give to the jury in a negligence case:

> Negligence is lack of ordinary care. It is a failure to exercise that degree of care which a reasonably prudent person would have exercised under the same circumstances. It may arise from doing an act which a reasonably prudent person would not have done under the same circumstances, or, on the other hand, from failing to do an act which a reasonably prudent person would have done under the circumstances.[3]

In applying this statement of the law, each juror must decide by using his or her own life experience as a guide whether or not the defendant acted as a "reasonably prudent person" would have, given the circumstances.

The judge gives the jury instructions on each matter of law argued in the case. After the instructions, the jury retires to the jury room, where it applies all the rules stated by the judge to the facts as presented to them at the trial by the parties, witnesses, attorneys, and other evidence and reaches a verdict both as to liability (was the defendant legally at fault for a breach of a rule?) and **damages** (if the defendant was liable, what is the appropriate amount of damages that will compensate the plaintiff for the breach of the rule?).

damages

The money judicially awarded to an injured party for another's wrongful conduct

A motion for *judgment notwithstanding the verdict* may be made by an aggrieved party against whom the verdict has been announced after the trial of the issues. This motion requires the judge to rule on whether the jury could reasonably have reached the verdict it did, given the evidence and the court's instructions. This motion is granted only when the judge believes that the jury reached a verdict by ignoring the instructions, or where, after hearing and seeing all of the evidence, the jury could not logically have reached the verdict it did. This motion, like the one for summary judgment or the one for a directed verdict, essentially challenges the legal sufficiency of a party's case. It must not be confused with a motion for a new trial, which may be made after a verdict is reached but is granted only where substantial errors in the trial process occurred.

The Appellate Process

If either of the parties believes that there was an error during the trial and that this error caused an unfavorable verdict, the party may appeal. The error must be one in the process of introducing evidence or in the statement of the law or in the application of the rule to the facts. *Parties usually cannot appeal the finding of a fact.* For example, if the jury finds that, as a matter of fact, the defendant did *sign* an agreement in question on a given date, then this may not be appealed. However, a party may appeal the issue of whether or not signing the agreement did legally *bind* the party. This latter conclusion is one which is a mixture of fact-finding and law application and is appropriate for appeal. The reasons for this are that a party should get only one chance to introduce the evidence the party deems appropriate. Therefore the trial courts are set up to take evidence; all the procedures at this level are adopted to ensure the fairness of the evidence-producing process. The right to cross-examination, the right to demand and examine other evidence, and the right to object to the introduction of irrelevant or excessively prejudicial evidence all exist at the trial level.

---

[3]New York Pattern Jury Instructions—Civil, Committee on Pattern Jury Instructions, Assoc. of Supreme Court Justices, vol. 1, 2d ed. (Rochester: The Lawyers Co-operative Pub. Co., 1974), p. 126.

appellant

A party who appeals a case decision against him or her

appelle (respondent)

A party against whom an appeal is taken

Appellate courts are not equipped to hear testimony or inspect evidence. Appellate courts are composed of three or more judges who hear the arguments of the appealing parties as to why the statements of the rules in the trial court were erroneous or why the process of rule application was erroneous.

An appeal may be initiated by either party. The one appealing is called the **appellant** or, in some courts, the *petitioner*. The one answering the appeal is the **appellee** or the *respondent*. At the trial stage, the case is given a name or "style" (in legal language); almost always this is done by putting the name of the plaintiff first, followed by the name of the defendant. However, on appeal, some courts, but not all, put the name of the appellant first when reporting the case. So if the defendant appeals, the defendant's name goes first in the official report. Please note that the appellate case's style does not reveal who is the plaintiff or defendant in the original trial of the matter. This may be determined only by reading the appellate opinion.

The appellant must file with the appellate court at least two documents. One is the transcribed version of what occurred in the trial. During the trial a court reporter took down all of the testimony, all objections and motions, and other relevant happenings in a special form of shorthand. This shorthand version of the trial is not transcribed into prose unless it is requested and paid for by one of the parties. Together with this transcript, the appellant files a legal brief which contains the appellant's legal arguments. The appellate court considers the trial transcript, the written legal arguments (briefs) of both parties, and in many cases allows attorneys for the parties to appear before it to orally answer questions asked by the appellate court and, in general, to argue the merits of the issues advanced. For the reasons stated above, the appellate court does not consider additional evidence, cannot call new or recall the old witnesses, or, generally, view the evidence again. The *facts* as found by the trial court must be taken as given.

The appellate court then takes the matter under consideration, does considerable legal research on the matter, votes, and writes its opinion. If some of the judges do not agree with the majority of the court, they may write dissenting opinions stating their reasons. This appellate opinion is usually published and is available to all persons.

If either party is still of the belief that a substantial error in the statement of the rule or in the application of the rule to the facts was made by either the trial or intermediate appellate court, the party may appeal the case to the next higher level, the supreme court of the state or federal system, which is usually the highest level. Again, the party appealing this time is called the appellant or petitioner and the answering party is the appellee or respondent. The name of the appellant is usually placed first. The same general practice is followed in filing the appeals papers and hearing the arguments, except that additional arguments are made either supporting or attacking the decision of the first appellate court.

An appellate court (either intermediate or supreme court) may do one of the three things with the case before it. It may *affirm* the holding of the court immediately below it and state its reasons for affirming the holding. If it affirms the decision, the same party who won the case in the court below wins again.

The appellate court may *reverse* the decision being appealed and enter its own judgment, giving the reasons. The third option is to order all or part of the case *tried again* using the interpretation of the law as stated by the appellate court. In this case, if the parties so desire, the case will be tried again. The same trial judge may preside again, but a new jury will be chosen.

This concludes our presentation of material on the trial and appeal of a civil case. The terms defined above and the process outlined are crucial to our understanding of how to study law because the published opinions of appellate judges are the best source available to indicate how the law is applied. For this reason we have used in this book excerpts of mostly appellate cases to illustrate the application of important legal principles discussed in this book. We have made an attempt to edit the irrelevant portions out of these opinions but to leave in enough information so that you may discern the complete outlines of how the dispute developed and how the legal rules were applied to solve the dispute.

Briefing Appellate Cases

Some of the appellate cases excerpted in the text, especially the longer ones at the end of the chapters, are very complex and will require some effort on your part to fully understand them. We suggest that you keep notes on these cases. These notes are called "briefs" by students of the law. The briefs usually have the following components:

1. A statement of the "facts" of the case as found by the trial court and restated by the appellate court.
2. A statement of the "legal" arguments advanced by both the plaintiff and the defendant.
3. A precise statement of the legal issue or legal problem facing the court; this usually involves an application of a legal principle (rule) or principles (rules) to the facts.
4. A summary of the court's reasoning used to reach its conclusion; this is best accomplished by stating in your own words which facts the court finds are "legally operative" and then summarizing how the legal principle or rule applies to these facts.

APPENDIX B

THE CONSTITUTION OF THE UNITED STATES OF AMERICA

Preamble

We the people of the United States, in order to form a more perfect union, establish justice, insure domestic tranquillity, provide for the common defense, promote the general welfare, and secure the blessings of liberty to ourselves and our posterity, do ordain and establish this Constitution for the United States of America.

Article I

Section 1. All legislative powers herein granted shall be vested in a Congress of the United States, which shall consist of a Senate and House of Representatives.

Section 2. 1. The House of Representatives shall be composed of members chosen every second year by the people of the several States, and the electors in each State shall have the qualifications requisite for electors of the most numerous branch of the State legislature.

2. No person shall be a representative who shall not have attained to the age of twenty-five years, and been seven years a citizen of the United States, and who shall not, when elected, be an inhabitant of that State in which he shall be chosen.

3. Representatives and direct taxes shall be apportioned among the several States which may be included within this Union, according to their respective numbers, which shall be determined by adding to the whole number of free persons, including those bound to service for a term of years, and excluding Indians not taxed, three fifths of all other persons. The actual enumeration shall be made within three years after the first meeting of the Congress of the United States, and within every subsequent term of ten years, in such manner as they shall by law direct. The number of representatives shall not exceed one for every thirty thousand, but each State shall have at least one representative; and until such enumeration shall be made, the State of New Hampshire shall be entitled to choose three, Massachusetts eight, Rhode Island and Providence Plantations one, Connecticut five, New York six, New Jersey four, Pennsylvania eight, Delaware one, Maryland six, Virginia ten, North Carolina five, South Carolina five, and Georgia three.

4. When vacancies happen in the representation from any State, the executive authority thereof shall issue writs of election to fill such vacancies.

5. The House of Representatives shall choose their speaker and other officers; and shall have the sole power of impeachment.

Section 3. 1. The Senate of the United States shall be composed of two senators from each State, *chosen by the legislature thereof,* for six years; and each senator shall have one vote.

2. Immediately after they shall be assembled in consequence of the first election, they shall be divided as equally as may be into three classes. The seats of the senators of the first class shall be vacated at the expiration of the second year, of the second class at the expiration of the fourth year, and of the third class at the expiration of the sixth year, so that one third may be chosen every second year; and if vacancies happen by resignation, or otherwise, during the recess of the legislature of any State, the executive thereof may make temporary appointments until the next meeting of the legislature, which shall then fill such vacancies.

3. No person shall be a senator who shall not have attained to the age of thirty years, and been nine years a citizen of the United States, and who shall not, when elected, be an inhabitant of that State for which he shall be chosen.

4. The Vice President of the United States shall be President of the Senate, but shall have no vote, unless they be equally divided.

5. The Senate shall choose their other officers, and also a president *pro tempore,* in the absence of the Vice President, or when he shall exercise the office of the President of the United States.

6. The Senate shall have the sole power to try all impeachments. When sitting for that purpose, they shall be on oath or affirmation. When the President of the United States is tried, the chief justice shall preside: and no person shall be convicted without the concurrence of two thirds of the members present.

7. Judgment in cases of impeachment shall not extend further than to removal from office, and disqualifications to hold and enjoy any office of honor, trust or profit under the United States: but the party convicted shall nevertheless be liable and subject to indictment, trial, judgment and punishment, according to law.

Section 4. 1. The times, places, and manner of holding elections for senators and representatives, shall be prescribed in each State by the legislature thereof; but the Congress may at any time by law make or alter such regulations, except as to the places of choosing senators.

2. The Congress shall assemble at least once in every year, and such meeting shall be on the first Monday in December, unless they shall by law appoint a different day.

Section 5. 1. Each House shall be the judge of the elections, returns and qualifications of its own members, and a majority of each shall constitute a quorum to do business; but a smaller number may adjourn from day to day, and may be authorized to compel the attendance of absent members, in such manner, and under such penalties as each House may provide.

2. Each House may determine the rules of its proceedings, punish its members for disorderly behavior, and, with the concurrence of two thirds, expel a member.

3. Each House shall keep a journal of its proceedings, and from time to time publish the same, excepting such parts as may in their judgment

require secrecy; and the yeas and nays of the members of either House on any question shall, at the desire of one fifth of those present, be entered on the journal.

4. Neither House, during the session of Congress, shall, without the consent of the other, adjourn for more than three days, nor to any other place than that in which the two Houses shall be sitting.

Section 6. 1. The senators and representatives shall receive a compensation for their services, to be ascertained by law, and paid out of the Treasury of the United States. They shall in all cases, except treason, felony, and breach of the peace, be privileged from arrest during their attendance at the session of their respective Houses, and in going to and returning from the same; and for any speech or debate in either House, they shall not be questioned in any other place.

2. No senator or representative shall, during the time for which he was elected, be appointed to any civil office under the authority of the United States, which shall have been created, or the emoluments whereof shall have been increased during such time; and no person holding any office under the United States shall be a member of either House during his continuance in office.

Section 7. 1. All bills for raising revenue shall originate in the House of Representatives; but the Senate may propose or concur with amendments as on other bills.

2. Every bill which shall have passed the House of Representatives and the Senate, shall, before it becomes a law, be presented to the President of the United States; if he approves he shall sign it, but if not he shall return it, with his objections to that House in which it shall have originated, who shall enter the objections at large on their journal, and proceed to reconsider it. If after such reconsideration two thirds of that House shall agree to pass the bill, it shall be sent, together with the objections, to the other House, by which it shall likewise be reconsidered, and if approved by two thirds of that House, it shall become a law. But in all such cases the votes of both Houses shall be determined by yeas and nays, and the names of the persons voting for and against the bill shall be entered on the journal of each House respectively. If any bill shall not be returned by the President within ten days (Sundays excepted) after it shall have been presented to him, the same shall be a law, in like manner as if he had signed it, unless the Congress by their adjournment prevent its return, in which case it shall not be a law.

3. Every order, resolution, or vote to which the concurrence of the Senate and the House of Representatives may be necessary (except on a question of adjournment) shall be presented to the President of the United States; and before the same shall take effect, shall be approved by him, or being disapproved by him, shall be repassed by two thirds of the Senate and House of Representatives, according to the rules and limitations prescribed in the case of a bill.

Section 8. The Congress shall have the power

1. To lay and collect taxes, duties, imposts, and excises, to pay the debts and provide for the common defense and general welfare of the United States; but all duties, imposts, and excises shall be uniform throughout the United States;

2. To borrow money on the credit of the United States;

3. To regulate commerce with foreign nations, and among the several States, and with the Indian tribes;

4. To establish a uniform rule of naturalization, and uniform laws on the subject of bankruptcies throughout the United States;

5. To coin money, regulate the value thereof, and of foreign coin, and fix the standard of weights and measures;

6. To provide for the punishment of counterfeiting the securities and current coin of the United States;

7. To establish post offices and post roads;

8. To promote the progress of science and useful arts, by securing for limited times to authors and inventors the exclusive right to their respective writings and discoveries;

9. To constitute tribunals inferior to the Supreme Court;

10. To define and punish piracies and felonies committed on the high seas, and offenses against the law of nations;

11. To declare war, grant letters of marque and reprisal, and make rules concerning captures on land and water;

12. To raise and support armies, but no appropriation of money to that use shall be for a longer term than two years;

13. To provide and maintain a navy;

14. To make rules for the government and regulation of the land and naval forces;

15. To provide for calling forth the militia to execute the laws of the Union, suppress insurrections and repel invasions;

16. To provide for organizing, arming, and disciplining the militia, and for governing such part of them as may be employed in the service of the United States, reserving to the States respectively, the appointment of the officers, and the authority of training the militia according to the discipline prescribed by Congress.

17. To exercise exclusive legislation in all cases whatsoever, over such district (not exceeding ten miles square) as may, by cession of particular States, and the acceptance of Congress, become the seat of the government of the United States, and to exercise like authority over all places purchased by the consent of the legislature of the State in which the same shall be, for the erection of forts, magazines, arsenals, dock-yards, and other needful buildings; and

18. To make all laws which shall be necessary and proper for carrying into execution the foregoing powers, and all other powers vested by this Constitution in the government of the United States, or in any department or officer thereof.

Section 9. 1. The migration or importation of such persons as any of the States now existing shall think proper to admit, shall not be prohibited by the Congress prior to the year one thousand eight hundred and eight, but a tax or duty may be imposed on such importation, not exceeding ten dollars for each person.

2. The privilege of the writ of *habeas corpus* shall not be suspended, unless when in cases of rebellion or invasion the public safety may require it.

3. No bill of attainder or *ex post facto* law shall be passed.

4. No capitation, or other direct, tax shall be laid, unless in proportion to the census or enumeration hereinbefore directed to be taken.

5. No tax or duty shall be laid on articles exported from any State.

6. No preference shall be given by any regulation of commerce or revenue to the ports of one State over those of another: nor shall vessels bound to, or from, one State be obliged to enter, clear, or pay duties in another.

7. No money shall be drawn from the treasury, but in consequence of appropriations made by law; and a regular statement and account of the receipts and expenditures of all public money shall be published from time to time.

8. No title of nobility shall be granted by the United States: and no person holding any office of profit or trust under them, shall, without the consent of the Congress, accept of any present, emolument, office, or title, of any kind whatever, from any king, prince, or foreign State.

Section 10. 1. No State shall enter into any treaty, alliance, or confederation; grant letters of marque and reprisal; coin money; emit bills of credit; make anything but gold and silver coin a tender in payment of debts; pass any bill of attainder, *ex post facto* law, or law impairing the obligation of contracts, or grant any title of nobility.

2. No State shall, without the consent of the Congress, lay any imposts or duties on imports or exports, except what may be absolutely necessary for executing its inspection laws: and the net produce of all duties and imposts laid by any State on imports or exports, shall be for the use of the treasury of the United States; and all such laws shall be subject to the revision and control of the Congress.

3. No State shall, without the consent of the Congress, lay any duty of tonnage, keep troops, or ships of war in time of peace, enter into any agreement or compact with another State, or with a foreign power, or engage in war, unless actually invaded, or in such imminent danger as will not admit of delay.

Article II

Section 1. 1. The executive power shall be vested in a President of the United States of America. He shall hold his office during the term of four years, and, together with the Vice President, chosen for the same term, be elected as follows:

2. Each State shall appoint, in such manner as the legislature thereof may direct, a number of electors, equal to the whole number of senators and representatives to which the State may be entitled in the Congress: but no senator or representative, or person holding an office of trust or profit under the United States, shall be appointed an elector.

The electors shall meet in their respective States, and vote by ballot for two persons, of whom one at least shall not be an inhabitant of the same State with themselves. And they shall make a list of all the persons voted for, and of the number of votes for each; which list they shall sign and certify, and transmit sealed to the seat of the government of the United States, directed to the president of the Senate. The president of the Senate shall, in the presence of the Senate and House of Representatives, open all the certificates, and the votes shall then be counted. The person having the greatest number of votes shall be the President, if such number be a majority of the whole number of electors appointed; and if there be more than one who have such majority, and have an equal number of votes, then the House of Representatives shall immediately choose by ballot one of them for President; and if no person have a majority, then from the five highest on the list the said House shall in like manner choose the President. But in choosing the President, the votes shall be taken by States, the representation from each State having one vote; a quorum for this purpose shall consist of a member or members from two thirds of the States, and a majority of all the States shall be necessary to a choice. In every case, after the choice of the President, the person having the greatest number of votes of the electors shall be the Vice President. But if there should remain two or more who have equal votes, the Senate shall choose from them by ballot the Vice President.

3. The Congress may determine the time of choosing the electors, and the day on which they shall give their votes; which day shall be the same throughout the United States.

4. No person except a natural born citizen, or a citizen of the United States, at the time of the adoption of this Constitution, shall be eligible to the office of President; neither shall any person be eligible to that office who shall not have attained to the age of thirty-five years, and been fourteen years a resident within the United States.

5. In case of the removal of the President from office, or of his death, resignation, or inability to discharge the powers and duties of the said office, the same shall devolve on the Vice President, and the Congress may by law provide for the case of removal, death, resignation, or inability, both of the President and Vice President, declaring what officer shall then act as President, and such officer shall act accordingly, until the disability be removed, or a President shall be elected.

6. The President shall, at stated times, receive for his services a compensation, which shall neither be increased nor diminished during the period for which he shall have been elected, and he shall not receive within that period any other emolument from the United States, or any of them.

7. Before he enter on the execution of his office, he shall take the following oath or affirmation:—"I do solemnly swear (or affirm) that I will faithfully execute the office of President of the United States, and will to the best of my ability, preserve, protect and defend the Constitution of the United States."

Section 2. 1. The President shall be commander in chief of the army and navy of the United States, and of the militia of the several States, when called into the actual service of the United States; he may require the opinion, in writing, of the principal officer in each of the executive departments, upon any subject relating to the duties of their respective office, and he shall have power to grant reprieves and pardons for offenses against the United States, except in cases of impeachment.

2. He shall have power, by and with the advice and consent of the Senate, to make treaties, provided two thirds of the senators present concur; and he shall nominate, and by and with the advice and consent of the Senate, shall appoint ambassadors, other public ministers and consuls, judges of the Supreme Court, and all other officers of the United States, whose appointments are not herein otherwise provided for, and which shall be established by law: but the Congress may by law vest the appointment of such inferior officers, as they think proper, in the President alone, in the courts of law, or in the heads of departments.

3. The President shall have power to fill up all vacancies that may happen during the recess of the Senate, by granting commissions which shall expire at the end of their next session.

Section 3. He shall from time to time give to the Congress information of the state of the Union, and recommend to their consideration such measures as he shall judge necessary and expedient; he may, on extraordinary occasions, convene both Houses, or either of them, and in case of disagreement between them with respect to the time of adjournment, he may adjourn them to such time as he shall think proper; he shall receive ambassadors and other public ministers; he shall take care that the laws be faithfully executed, and shall commission all the officers of the United States.

Section 4. The President, Vice President, and all civil officers of the United States, shall be removed from office on impeachment for, and conviction of, treason, bribery, or other high crimes and misdemeanors.

Article III

Section 1. The judicial power of the United States shall be vested in one Supreme Court, and in such inferior courts as the Congress may from time to time ordain and establish. The judges, both of the Supreme and inferior courts, shall hold their offices during good behavior, and shall, at stated times, receive for their services, a compensation, which shall not be diminished during their continuance in office.

Section 2. 1. The judicial power shall extend to all cases, in law and equity, arising under this Constitution, the laws of the United States, and treaties made, or which shall be made, under their authority;—to all cases affecting ambassadors, other public ministers and consuls;—to all cases of admiralty and maritime jurisdiction;—to controversies to which the United States shall be a party;—to controversies between two or more States; between a State and citizens of another State;—between citizens of different States;—between citizens of the same State claiming lands under grants of different States, and between a State, or the citizens thereof, and foreign States citizens or subjects.

2. In all cases affecting ambassadors, other public ministers and consuls, and those in which a State shall be party, the Supreme Court shall have original jurisdiction. In all the other cases before mentioned, the Supreme Court shall have appellate jurisdiction, both as to law and to fact, with such exceptions, and under such regulations as the Congress shall make.

3. The trial of all crimes, except in cases of impeachment, shall be by jury; and such trial shall be held in the State where the said crimes shall have been committed; but when not committed within any State, the trial shall be at such place or places as the Congress may by law have directed.

Section 3. 1. Treason against the United States shall consist only in levying war against them, or in adhering to their enemies, giving them aid and comfort. No person shall be convicted of treason unless on the testimony of two witnesses to the same overt act, or on confession in open court.

2. The Congress shall have power to declare the punishment of treason, but no attainder of treason shall work corruption of blood, or forfeiture except during the life of the person attained.

Article IV

Section 1. Full faith and credit shall be given in each State to the public acts, records, and judicial proceedings of every other State. And the Congress may by general laws prescribe the manner in which such acts, records and proceedings shall be proved, and the effect thereof.

Section 2. 1. The citizens of each State shall be entitled to all privileges and immunities of citizens in the several States.

2. A person charged in any State with treason, felony, or other crime, who shall flee from justice, and be found in another State, shall on demand of the executive authority of the State from which he fled, be delivered up to be removed to the State having jurisdiction of the crime.

3. No person held to service or labor in one State under the laws thereof, escaping into another, shall in consequence of any law or regulation therein, be discharged from such service or labor, but shall be delivered up on claim of the party to whom such service or labor may be due.

Section 3. 1. New States may be admitted by the Congress into this Union; but no new State shall be formed or erected within the jurisdiction of any other State, nor any State be formed by the junction of two or more States, or parts of States, without the consent of the legislatures of the States concerned as well as of the Congress.

2. The Congress shall have power to dispose of and make all needful rules and regulations respecting the territory or other property belonging to the United States; and nothing in this Constitution shall be so construed as to prejudice any claims of the United States, or of any particular State.

Section 4. The United States shall guarantee to every State in this Union a republican form of government, and shall protect each of them against invasion; and on application of the legislature, or of the executive (when the legislature cannot be convened) against domestic violence.

Article V

The Congress, whenever two thirds of both Houses shall deem it necessary, shall propose amendments to this Constitution, or, on the application of the legislature of two thirds of the several States, shall call a convention for proposing amendments, which in either case, shall be valid to all intents and purposes, as part of this Constitution when ratified by the legislatures of three fourths of the several States, or by conventions in three fourths thereof, as the one or the other mode of ratification may be proposed by the Congress; Provided that no amendment which may be made prior to the year one thousand eight hundred and eight shall in any manner affect the first and fourth clauses in the ninth section of the first article; and that no State, without its consent, shall be deprived of its equal suffrage in the Senate.

Article VI

1. All debts contracted and engagements entered into, before the adoption of this Constitution, shall be as valid against the United States under this Constitution, as under the Confederation.

2. This Constitution, and the laws of the United States which shall be made in pursuance thereof; and all treaties made, or which shall be made, under the authority of the United States, shall be the supreme law of the land; and the Judges in every State shall be bound thereby, anything in the Constitution or laws of any State to the contrary notwithstanding.

3. The senators and representatives before mentioned, and the members of the several State legislatures, and all executive and judicial officers, both of the United States and of the several States, shall be bound by oath or affirmation to support this Constitution; but no religious test shall ever be required as a qualification to any office or public trust under the United States.

Article VII

The ratification of the conventions of nine States shall be sufficient for the establishment of this Constitution between the States so ratifying the same.

Done in Convention by the unanimous consent of the States present the seventeenth day of September in the year of our Lord one thousand seven hundred and eighty-seven, and of the independence of the United States of America the twelfth. In witness whereof we have hereunto subscribed our names.

Amendments

[First Ten Amendments, called the Bill of Rights, were ratified in 1791]

Article I

Congress shall make no law respecting an establishment of religion, or prohibiting the free exercise thereof; or abridging the freedom of speech, or of the press; or the right of the people peaceably to assemble, and to petition the government for a redress of grievances.

Article II

A well regulated militia, being necessary to the security of a free State, the right of the people to keep and bear arms, shall not be infringed.

Article III

No soldier shall, in time of peace be quartered in any house, without the consent of the owner, nor in time of war, but in a manner to be prescribed by law.

Article IV

The right of the people to be secure in their persons, houses, papers, and effects, against unreasonable searches and seizures, shall not be violated, and no warrants shall issue, but upon probable cause, supported by oath or affirmation, and particularly describing the place to be searched, and the persons or things to be seized.

Article V

No person shall be held to answer for a capital, or otherwise infamous crime, unless on a presentment or indictment of a grand jury, except in cases arising in the land or naval forces, or in the militia, when in actual service in time of war or public danger; nor shall any person be subject for the same offense to be twice put in jeopardy of life or limb; nor shall be compelled in any criminal case to be a witness against himself, nor be deprived of life, liberty, or property, without due process of law; nor shall private property be taken for public use without just compensation.

Article VI

In all criminal prosecutions, the accused shall enjoy the right to a speedy and public trial, by an impartial jury of the State and district wherein the crime shall have been committed, which district shall have been previously ascertained by law, and to be informed of the nature and cause of the accusation; to be confronted with the witnesses against him; to have compulsory process for obtaining witnesses in his favor, and to have the assistance of counsel for his defense.

Article VII

In suits at common law, where the value in controversy shall exceed twenty dollars, the right of trial by jury shall be preserved, and no fact tried by a jury shall be otherwise reexamined in any court of the United States, than according to the rules of the common law.

Article VIII

Excessive bail shall not be required, nor excessive fines imposed, nor cruel and unusual punishments inflicted.

Article IX

The enumeration in the Constitution of certain rights shall not be construed to deny or disparage others retained by the people.

Article X

The powers not delegated to the United States by the Constitution, nor prohibited by it to the States, are reserved to the States respectively, or to the people.

Article XI [1798]

The judicial power of the United States shall not be construed to extend to any suit in law or equity, commenced or prosecuted against one of the United States by citizens of another State, or by citizens or subjects of any foreign State.

Article XII [1804]

The electors shall meet in their respective States, and vote by ballot for President and Vice President, one of whom, at least, shall not be an inhabitant of the same State with themselves; they shall name in their ballots the person voted for as President, and in distinct ballots, the person voted for as Vice President, and they shall make distinct lists of all persons voted for as President and of all persons voted for as Vice President, and of the number of votes for each, which lists they shall sign and certify, and transmit sealed to the seat of the government of the United States, directed to the President of the Senate;—The President of the Senate shall, in the presence of the Senate and House of Representatives, open all the certificates and the votes shall then be counted;—The person having the greatest number of votes for President, shall be the President, if such number be a majority of the whole number of electors appointed; and if no person have such majority, then from the persons having the highest numbers not exceeding three on the list of those voted for as President, the House of Representatives shall choose immediately, by ballot, the President. But in choosing the President, the votes shall be taken by States, the representation from each State having one vote; a quorum for this purpose shall consist of a member or members from two thirds of the States, and a majority of all the States shall be necessary to a choice. And if the House of Representatives shall not choose a President whenever the right of choice shall devolve upon them, before the fourth day of March next following, then the Vice President shall act as President, as in the case of the death or other constitutional disability of the President. The person having the greatest number of votes as Vice President shall be the Vice President, if such number be a majority of the whole number of electors appointed, and if no person have a majority, then from the two highest numbers on the list, the Senate shall choose the Vice President; a quorum for the purpose shall consist of two thirds of the whole number of Senators, and a majority of the whole number shall be necessary to a choice. But no person constitutionally ineligible to the office of President shall be eligible to that of Vice President of the United States.

Article XIII [1865]

Section 1. Neither slavery nor involuntary servitude, except as punishment for crime whereof the party shall have been duly convicted, shall exist within the United States, or any place subject to their jurisdiction.

Section 2. Congress shall have power to enforce this article by appropriate legislation.

Article XIV [1868]

Section 1. All persons born or naturalized in the United States, and subject to the jurisdiction thereof, are citizens of the United States and of the State wherein they reside. No State shall make or enforce any law which shall abridge the privileges or immunities of citizens of the United States; nor shall any State deprive any person of life, liberty, or property, without due process of law; nor deny to any person within its jurisdiction the equal protection of the laws.

Section 2. Representatives shall be apportioned among the several States according to their respective numbers, counting the whole number of persons in each State, excluding Indians not taxed. But when the right to vote at any election for the choice of electors for President and Vice President of the United States, representatives in Congress, the executive and judicial officers of a State, or the members of the legislature thereof, is denied to any of the male inhabitants of such State, being twenty-one years of age, and citizens of the United States, or in any way abridged, except for participation in rebellion, or other crime, the basis of representation therein shall be reduced in the proportion which the number of such male citizens shall bear to the whole number of male citizens twenty-one years of age in such State.

Section 3. No person shall be a senator or representative in Congress, or elector of President and Vice President, or hold any office, civil or military, under the United States, or under any State, who having previously taken an oath, as a member of Congress, or as an officer of the United States, or as a member of any State legislature, or as an executive or judicial officer of any State, to support the Constitution of the United States, shall have engaged in insurrection or rebellion against the same, or given aid or comfort to the enemies thereof. But Congress may by a vote of two thirds of each House, remove such disability.

Section 4. The validity of the public debt of the United States, authorized by law, including debts incurred for payment of pensions and bounties for services in suppressing insurrection or rebellion, shall not be questioned. But neither the United States nor any State shall assume or pay any debt or obligation incurred in aid of insurrection or rebellion against the United States, or any claim for the loss or emancipation of any slave; but all such debts, obligations, and claims shall be held illegal and void.

Section 5. The Congress shall have power to enforce, by appropriate legislation, the provisions of this article.

Article XV [1870]

Section 1. The right of citizens of the United States to vote shall not be denied or abridged by the United States or by any State on account of race, color, or previous condition of servitude.

Section 2. The Congress shall have power to enforce this article by appropriate legislation.

Article XVI [1913]

The Congress shall have power to lay and collect taxes on incomes, from whatever source derived, without apportionment among the several States, and without regard to any census or enumeration.

Article XVII [1913]

The Senate of the United States shall be composed of two senators from each state, elected by the people thereof, for six years; and each senator shall have one vote. The electors in each State shall have the qualifications requisite for electors of the most numerous branch of the State legislature.

When vacancies happen in the representation of any State in the Senate, the executive authority of such State shall issue writs of election to fill such vacancies: *Provided,* That the legislature of any State may empower the executive thereof to make temporary appointments until the people fill the vacancies by election as the legislature may direct.

This amendment shall not be so construed as to affect the election or term of any senator chosen before it becomes valid as part of the Constitution.

Article XVIII [1919; repealed by the 21st Amendment]

After one year from the ratification of this article, the manufacture, sale, or transportation of intoxicating liquors within, the importation thereof into, or the exportation thereof from the United States and all territory subject to the jurisdiction thereof for beverage purposes is hereby prohibited.

The Congress and the several States shall have concurrent power to enforce this article by appropriate legislation.

This article shall be inoperative unless it shall have been ratified as an amendment to the Constitution by the legislatures of the several States, as provided in the Constitution, within seven years from the date of the submission hereof to the states by Congress.

Article XIX [1920]

The right of citizens of the United States to vote shall not be denied or abridged by the United States or by any State on account of sex.

The Congress shall have power by appropriate legislation to enforce the provisions of this article.

Article XX [1933]

Section 1. The terms of the President and Vice President shall end at noon on the 20th day of January, and the terms of Senators and Representatives at noon on the 3d day of January, of the years in which such terms would have ended if this article had not been ratified; and the terms of their successors shall then begin.

Section 2. The Congress shall assemble at least once in every year, and such meeting shall begin at noon on the 3d day of January, unless they shall by law appoint a different day.

Section 3. If, at the time fixed for the beginning of the term of the President, the President-elect shall have died, the Vice President-elect shall become President. If a President shall not have been chosen before the time fixed for the beginning of his term, or if the President-elect shall have failed to qualify, then the Vice President-elect shall act as President until a President shall have qualified; and the Congress may by law provide for the case wherein neither a President-elect nor a Vice President-elect shall have qualified, declaring who shall then act as President, or the manner in which one who is to act shall be selected, and such person shall act accordingly until a President or Vice President shall have qualified.

Section 4. The Congress may by law provide for the case of the death of any of the persons from whom the House of Representatives may choose a President whenever the right of choice shall have devolved upon them, and for the case of the death of any of the persons from whom the Senate may choose a Vice President whenever the right of choice shall have devolved upon them.

Section 5. Sections 1 and 2 shall take effect on the 15th day of October following the ratification of this article.

Section 6. This article shall be inoperative unless it shall have been ratified as an amendment to the Constitution by the legislatures of three-fourths of the several States within seven years from the date of its submission.

Article XXI [1933]

Section 1. The Eighteenth Article of amendment to the Constitution of the United States is hereby repealed.

Section 2. The transportation or importation into any State, Territory, or possession of the United States for delivery or use therein of intoxicating liquors in violation of the laws thereof, is hereby prohibited.

Section 3. This article shall be inoperative unless it shall have been ratified as an amendment to the Constitution by conventions in the several States, as provided in the Constitution, within seven years from the date of the submission thereof to the States by the Congress.

Article XXII [1951]

Section 1. No person shall be elected to the office of the President more than twice, and no person who has held the office of President, or acted as President, for more than two years of a term to which some other person was elected President shall be elected to the office of the President more than once. But this article shall not apply to any person holding the office of President when this article was proposed by the Congress, and shall not prevent any person who may be holding the office of President, or acting as President, during the term within which this article becomes operative from holding the office of President or acting as President during the remainder of such term.

Section 2. This article shall be inoperative unless it shall have been ratified as an amendment to the Constitution by the legislatures of three-fourths of the several States within seven years from the date of its submission to the States by the Congress.

Amendment XXIII [1961]

Section 1. The District constituting the seat of Government of the United States shall appoint in such manner as the Congress may direct:

A number of electors of President and Vice President equal to the whole number of Senators and Representatives in Congress to which the District would be entitled if it were a State, but in no event more than the least populous State; they shall be in addition to those appointed by the States, but they shall be considered, for the purposes of the election of President and Vice President, to be electors appointed by a State; and they shall meet in the District and perform such duties as provided by the twelfth article of amendment.

Section 2. The Congress shall have power to enforce this article by appropriate legislation.

Amendment XXIV [1964]

Section 1. The right of citizens of the United States to vote in any primary or other election for President or Vice President, for electors for President or Vice President, or for Senator or Representative in Congress, shall not be denied or abridged by the United States or any State by reason of failure to pay any poll tax or other tax.

Section 2. The Congress shall have power to enforce this article by appropriate legislation.

Amendment XXV [1967]

Section 1. In case of the removal of the President from office or of his death or resignation, the Vice President shall become President.

Section 2. Whenever there is a vacancy in the office of the Vice President, the President shall nominate a Vice President who shall take office upon confirmation by a majority vote of both Houses of Congress.

Section 3. Whenever the President transmits to the President pro tempore of the Senate and the Speaker of the House of Representatives has written declaration that he is unable to discharge the powers and duties of his office, and until he transmits to them a written declaration to the contrary, such powers and duties shall be discharged by the Vice President as Acting President.

Section 4. Whenever the Vice President and a majority of either the principal officers of the executive departments or of such other body as Congress may by law provide, transmit to the President pro tempore of the Senate and the Speaker of the House of Representatives their written declaration that the President is unable to discharge the powers and duties of his office, the Vice President shall immediately assume the powers and duties of the office as Acting President.

Thereafter, when the President transmits to the President pro tempore of the Senate and the Speaker of the House of Representatives his written declaration that no inability exists, he shall resume the powers and duties of his office unless the Vice President and a majority of either the principal officers of the executive department or of such other body as Congress may by law provide, transmit within four days to the President pro tempore of the Senate and the Speaker of the House of Representatives their written declaration that the President is unable to discharge the powers and duties of his office. Thereupon Congress shall decide the issue, assembling within forty-eight hours for that purpose if not in session. If the Congress, within twenty-one days after receipt of the latter written declaration, or, if Congress is not in session, within twenty-one days after Congress is required to assemble, determines by two-thirds vote of both Houses that the President is unable to discharge the powers and duties of his office, the Vice President shall continue to discharge the same as Acting President; otherwise, the President shall resume the powers and duties of his office.

Amendment XXVI [1971]

Section 1. The right of citizens of the United States, who are eighteen years of age or older, to vote shall not be denied or abridged by the United States or by any State on account of age.

APPENDIX C

UNIFORM PARTNERSHIP ACT (1914)

Part I Preliminary Provisions

Section 1. Name of Act

This act may be cited as Uniform Partnership Act.

Section 2. Definition of Terms

In this act, "Court" includes every court and judge having jurisdiction in the case.

"Business" includes every trade, occupation, or profession.

"Person" includes individuals, partnerships, corporations, and other associations.

"Bankrupt" includes bankrupt under the Federal Bankruptcy Act or insolvent under any state insolvent act.

"Conveyance" includes every assignment, lease, mortgage, or encumbrance.

"Real property" includes land and any interest or estate in land.

Section 3. Interpretation of Knowledge and Notice

(1) A person has "knowledge" of a fact within the meaning of this act not only when he has actual knowledge thereof, but also when he has knowledge of such other facts as in the circumstances shows bad faith.

(2) A person has "notice" of a fact within the meaning of this act when the person who claims the benefit of the notice:

(a) States the fact to such person, or

(b) Delivers through the mail, or by other means of communication, a written statement of the fact to such person or to a proper person at his place of business or residence.

Section 4. Rules of Construction

(1) The rule that statutes in derogation of the common law are to be strictly construed shall have no application to this act.

(2) The law of estoppel shall apply under this act.

(3) The law of agency shall apply under this act.

(4) This act shall be so interpreted and construed as to effect its general purpose to make uniform the law of those states which enact it.

(5) This act shall not be construed so as to impair the obligations of any contract existing when the act goes into effect, nor to affect any action or proceedings begun or right accrued before this act takes effect.

Section 5. Rules for Cases Not Provided for in This Act

In any case not provided for in this act the rules of law and equity, including the law merchant, shall govern.

Part II Nature of Partnership

Section 6. Partnership Defined

(1) A partnership is an association of two or more persons to carry on as co-owners a business for profit.

(2) But any association formed under any other statute of this state, or any statute adopted by authority, other than the authority of this state, is not a partnership under this act, unless such association would have been a partnership in this state prior to the adoption of this act; but this act shall apply to limited partnerships except in so far as the statutes relating to such partnerships are inconsistent herewith.

Section 7. Rules for Determining the Existence of a Partnership

In determining whether a partnership exists, these rules shall apply:

(1) Except as provided by section 16 persons who are not partners as to each other are not partners as to third persons.

(2) Joint tenancy, tenancy in common, tenancy by the entireties, joint property, common property, or part ownership does not of itself establish a partnership, whether such co-owners do or do not share any profits made by the use of the property.

(3) The sharing of gross returns does not of itself establish a partnership, whether or not the persons sharing them have a joint or common right or interest in any property from which the returns are derived.

(4) The receipt by a person of a share of the profits of a business is prima facie evidence that he is a partner in the business, but no such inference shall be drawn if such profits were received in payment:

(a) As a debt by installments or otherwise,

(b) As wages of an employee or rent to a landlord,

(c) As an annuity to a widow or representative of a deceased partner,

(d) As interest on a loan, though the amount of payment vary with the profits of the business,

(e) As the consideration for the sale of a good-will of a business or other property by installments or otherwise.

Section 8. Partnership Property

(1) All property originally brought into the partnership stock or subsequently acquired by purchase or otherwise, on account of the partnership, is partnership property.

(2) Unless the contrary intention appears, property acquired with partnership funds is partnership property.

(3) Any estate in real property may be acquired in the partnership name. Title so acquired can be conveyed only in the partnership name.

(4) A conveyance to a partnership in the partnership name, though without words of inheritance, passes the entire estate of the grantor unless a contrary intent appears.

Part III Relations of Partners to Persons Dealing with the Partnership

Section 9. Partner Agent of Partnership as to Partnership Business

(1) Every partner is an agent of the partnership for the purpose of its business, and the act of every partner, including the execution in the partnership name of any instrument, for apparently carrying on in the usual way the business of the partnership of which he is a member binds the partnership, unless the partner so acting has in fact no authority to act for the partnership in the particular matter, and the person with whom he is dealing has knowledge of the fact that he has no such authority.

(2) An act of a partner which is not apparently for the carrying on of the business of the partnership in the usual way does not bind the partnership unless authorized by the other partners.

(3) Unless authorized by the other partners or unless they have abandoned the business, one or more but less than all the partners have no authority to:

- (a) Assign the partnership property in trust for creditors or on the assignee's promise to pay the debts of the partnership,
- (b) Dispose of the good-will of the business,
- (c) Do any other act which would make it impossible to carry on the ordinary business of a partnership,
- (d) Confess a judgment,
- (e) Submit a partnership claim or liability to arbitration or reference.

(4) No act of a partner in contravention of a restriction on authority shall bind the partnership to persons having knowledge of the restriction.

Section 10. Conveyance of Real Property of the Partnership

(1) Where title to real property is in the partnership name, any partner may convey title to such property by a conveyance executed in the partnership name; but the partnership may recover such property unless the partner's act binds the partnership under the provisions of paragraph (1) of section 9, or unless such property has been conveyed by the grantee or a person claiming through such grantee to a holder for value without knowledge that the partner, in making the conveyance, has exceeded his authority.

(2) Where title to real property is in the name of the partnership, a conveyance executed by a partner, in his own name, passes the equitable interest of the partnership, provided the act is one within the authority of the partner under the provisions of paragraph (1) of section 9.

(3) Where title to real property is in the name of one or more but not all the partners, and the record does not disclose the right of the partnership, the partners in whose name the title stands may convey title to such property, but the partnership may recover such property if the partners' act does not bind the partnership under the provisions of paragraph (1) of section 9, unless the purchaser or his assignee, is a holder for value, without knowledge.

(4) Where the title to real property is in the name of one or more or all the partners, or in a third person in trust for the partnership, a conveyance executed by a partner in the partnership name, or in his own name, passes the equitable interest of the partnership, provided the act is one within the authority of the partner under the provisions of paragraph (1) of section 9.

(5) Where the title to real property is in the names of all the partners a conveyance executed by all the partners passes all their rights in such property.

Section 11. Partnership Bound by Admission of Partner

An admission or representation made by any partner concerning partnership affairs within the scope of his authority as conferred by this act is evidence against the partnership.

Section 12. Partnership Charged with Knowledge of or Notice to Partner

Notice to any partner of any matter relating to partnership affairs, and the knowledge of the partner acting in the particular matter, acquired while a partner or then present to his mind, and the knowledge of any other partner who reasonably could and should have communicated it to the acting partner, operate as notice to or knowledge of the partnership, except in the case of a fraud on the partnership committed by or with the consent of that partner.

Section 13. Partnership Bound by Partner's Wrongful Act

Where, by any wrongful act or omission of any partner acting in the ordinary course of the business of the partnership or with the authority of his co-partners, loss or injury is caused to any person, not being a partner in the partnership, or any penalty is incurred, the partnership is liable therefor to the same extent as the partner so acting or omitting to act.

Section 14. Partnership Bound by Partner's Breach of Trust

The partnership is bound to make good the loss:

- (a) Where one partner acting within the scope of his apparent authority receives money or property of a third person and misapplies it; and
- (b) Where the partnership in the course of its business receives money or property of a third person and the money or property so received is misapplied by any partner while it is in the custody of the partnership.

Section 15. Nature of Partner's Liability

All partners are liable

- (a) Jointly and severally for everything chargeable to the partnership under sections 13 and 14.
- (b) Jointly for all other debts and obligations of the partnership; but any partner may enter into a separate obligation to perform a partnership contract.

Section 16. Partner by Estoppel

(1) When a person, by words spoken or written or by conduct, represents himself, or consents to another representing him to any one, as a partner in an existing partnership or with one or more persons not actual partners, he is liable to any such person to whom such representation has been made, who has, on the faith of such representation, given credit to the actual or apparent partnership, and if he has made such representation or consented to its being made in a public manner he is liable to such person, whether the representation has or has not been made or communicated to such person so giving credit by or with the knowledge of the apparent partner making the representation or consenting to its being made.

(a) When a partnership liability results, he is liable as though he were an actual member of the partnership.

(b) When no partnership liability results, he is liable jointly with the other persons, if any, so consenting to the contract or representation as to incur liability, otherwise separately.

(2) When a person has been thus represented to be a partner in an existing partnership, or with one or more persons not actual partners, he is an agent of the persons consenting to such representation to bind them to the same extent and in the same manner as though he were a partner in fact, with respect to persons who rely upon the representation. Where all the members of the existing partnership consent to the representation, a partnership act or obligation results; but in all other cases it is the joint act or obligation of the person acting and the persons consenting to the representation.

Section 17. Liability of Incoming Partner

A person admitted as a partner into an existing partnership is liable for all the obligations of the partnership arising before his admission as though he had been a partner when such obligations were incurred, except that this liability shall be satisfied only out of partnership property.

Part IV Relations of Partners to One Another

Section 18. Rules Determining Rights and Duties of Partners

The rights and duties of the partners in relation to the partnership shall be determined, subject to any agreement between them, by the following rules:

(a) Each partner shall be repaid his contributions, whether by way of capital or advances to the partnership property and share equally in the profits and surplus remaining after all liabilities, including those to partners, are satisfied; and must contribute towards the losses, whether of capital or otherwise, sustained by the partnership according to his share in the profits.

(b) The partnership must indemnify every partner in respect of payments made and personal liabilities reasonably incurred by him in the ordinary and proper conduct of its business, or for the preservation of its business or property.

(c) A partner, who in aid of the partnership makes any payment or advance beyond the amount of capital which he agreed to contribute, shall be paid interest from the date of the payment or advance.

(d) A partner shall receive interest on the capital contributed by him only from the date when repayment should be made.

(e) All partners have equal rights in the management and conduct of the partnership business.

(f) No partner is entitled to remuneration for acting in the partnership business, except that a surviving partner is entitled to reasonable compensation for his services in winding up the partnership affairs.

(g) No person can become a member of a partnership without the consent of all the partners.

(h) Any difference arising as to ordinary matters connected with the partnership business may be decided by a majority of the partners; but no act in contravention of any agreement between the partners may be done rightfully without the consent of all the partners.

Section 19. Partnership Books

The partnership books shall be kept, subject to any agreement between the partners, at the principal place of business of the partnership, and every partner shall at all times have access to and may inspect and copy any of them.

Section 20. Duty of Partners to Render Information

Partners shall render on demand true and full information of all things affecting the partnership to any partner or the legal representative of any deceased partner or partner under legal disability.

Section 21. Partner Accountable as a Fiduciary

(1) Every partner must account to the partnership for any benefit, and hold as trustee for it any profits derived by him without the consent of the other partners from any transaction connected with the formation, conduct, or liquidation of the partnership or from any use by him of its property.

(2) This section applies also to the representatives of a deceased partner engaged in the liquidation of the affairs of the partnership as the personal representatives of the last surviving partner.

Section 22. Right to an Account

Any partner shall have the right to a formal account as to partnership affairs:

(a) If he is wrongfully excluded from the partnership business or possession of its property by his co-partners,

(b) If the right exists under the terms of any agreement,

(c) As provided by section 21,

(d) Whenever other circumstances render it just and reasonable.

Section 23. Continuation of Partnership Beyond Fixed Term

(1) When a partnership for a fixed term or particular undertaking is continued after the termination of such term or particular undertaking without any express agreement, the rights and duties of the partners remain the same as they were at such termination, so far as is consistent with a partnership at will.

(2) A continuation of the business by the partners or such of them as habitually acted therein during the term, without any settlement or liquidation of the partnership affairs, is prima facie evidence of a continuation of the partnership.

Part V Property Rights of a Partner

Section 24. Extent of Property Rights of a Partner

The property rights of a partner are (1) his rights in specific partnership property, (2) his interest in the partnership, and (3) his right to participate in the management.

Section 25. Nature of a Partner's Right in Specific Partnership Property

(1) A partner is co-owner with his partners of specific partnership property holding as a tenant in partnership.

(2) The incidents of this tenancy are such that:

(a) A partner, subject to the provisions of this act and to any agreement between the partners, has an equal right with his partners to possess specific partnership property for partnership purposes; but he has no right to possess such property for any other purpose without the consent of his partners.

(b) A partner's right in specific partnership property is not assignable except in connection with the assignment of rights of all the partners in the same property.

(c) A partner's right in specific partnership property is not subject to attachment or execution, except on a claim against the partnership. When partnership property is attached for a partnership debt the partners, or any of them, or the representatives of a deceased partner, cannot claim any right under the homestead or exemption laws.

(d) On the death of a partner his right in specific partnership property vests in the surviving partner or partners, except where the deceased was the last surviving partner, when his right in such property vests in his legal representative. Such surviving partner or partners, or the legal representative of the last surviving partner, has no right to possess the partnership property for any but a partnership purpose.

(e) A partner's right in specific partnership property is not subject to dower, curtesy, or allowances to widows, heirs, or next of kin.

Section 26. Nature of Partner's Interest in the Partnership

A partner's interest in the partnership is his share of the profits and surplus, and the same is personal property.

Section 27. Assignment of Partner's Interest

(1) A conveyance by a partner of his interest in the partnership does not of itself dissolve the partnership, nor, as against the other partners in the absence of agreement, entitle the assignee, during the continuance of the partnership, to interfere in the management or administration of the partnership business or affairs, or to require any information or account of partnership transactions, or to inspect the partnership books; but it merely entitles the assignee to receive in accordance with his contract the profits to which the assigning partner would otherwise be entitled.

(2) In case of a dissolution of the partnership, the assignee is entitled to receive his assignor's interest and may require an account from the date only of the last account agreed to by all the partners.

Section 28. Partner's Interest Subject to Charging Order

(1) On due application to a competent court by any judgment creditor of a partner, the court which entered the judgment, order, or decree, or any other court, may charge the interest of the debtor partner with payment of the unsatisfied amount of such judgment debt with interest thereon; and may then or later appoint a receiver of his share of the profits, and of any other money due or to fall due to him in respect of the partnership, and make all other orders, directions, accounts and inquiries which the debtor partner might have made, or which the circumstances of the case may require.

(2) The interest charged may be redeemed at any time before foreclosure, or in case of a sale being directed by the court may be purchased without thereby causing a dissolution:

(a) With separate property, by any one or more of the partners, or

(b) With partnership property, by any one or more of the partners with the consent of all the partners whose interests are not so charged or sold.

(3) Nothing in this act shall be held to deprive a partner of his right, if any, under the exemption laws, as regards his interest in the partnership.

Part VI Dissolution and Winding Up

Section 29. Dissolution Defined

The dissolution of a partnership is the change in the relation of the partners caused by any partner ceasing to be associated in the carrying on as distinguished from the winding up of the business.

Section 30. Partnership not Terminated by Dissolution

On dissolution the partnership is not terminated, but continues until the winding up of partnership affairs is completed.

Section 31. Causes of Dissolution

Dissolution is caused:

(1) Without violation of the agreement between the partners,

(a) By the termination of the definite term or particular undertaking specified in the agreement,

(b) By the express will of any partner when no definite term or particular undertaking is specified,

(c) By the express will of all the partners who have not assigned their interests or suffered them to be charged for their separate debts, either before or after the termination of any specified term or particular undertaking,

(d) By the expulsion of any partner from the business bona fide in accordance with such a power conferred by the agreement between the partners;

(2) In contravention of the agreement between the partners, where the circumstances do not permit a dissolution under any other provision of this section, by the express will of any partner at any time;

(3) By any event which makes it unlawful for the business of the partnership to be carried on or for the members to carry it on in partnership;

(4) By the death of any partner;

(5) By the bankruptcy of any partner or the partnership;

(6) By decree of court under section 32.

Section 32. Dissolution by Decree of Court

(1) On application by or for a partner the court shall decree a dissolution whenever:

(a) A partner has been declared a lunatic in any judicial proceeding or is shown to be of unsound mind,

(b) A partner becomes in any other way incapable of performing his part of the partnership contract,

(c) A partner has been guilty of such conduct as tends to affect prejudicially the carrying on of the business,

(d) A partner wilfully or persistently commits a breach of the partnership agreement, or otherwise so conducts himself in matters relating to the partnership business that it is not reasonably practicable to carry on the business in partnership with him,

(e) The business of the partnership can only be carried on at a loss,

(f) Other circumstances render a dissolution equitable.

(2) On the application of the purchaser of a partner's interest under sections 28 or 29;

(a) After the termination of the specified term or particular undertaking,

(b) At any time if the partnership was a partnership at will when the interest was assigned or when the charging order was issued.

Section 33. General Effect of Dissolution on Authority of Partner

Except so far as may be necessary to wind up partnership affairs or to complete transactions begun but not then finished, dissolution terminates all authority of any partner to act for the partnership,

(1) With respect to the partners,

(a) When the dissolution is not by the act, bankruptcy or death of a partner; or

(b) When the dissolution is by such act, bankruptcy or death of a partner, in cases where section 34 so requires.

(2) With respect to persons not partners, as declared in section 35.

Section 34. Right of Partner to Contribution from Co-partners after Dissolution

Where the dissolution is caused by the act, death or bankruptcy of a partner, each partner is liable to his co-partners for his share of any liability created by any partner acting for the partnership as if the partnership had not been dissolved unless

(a) The dissolution being by act of any partner, the partner acting for the partnership had knowledge of the dissolution, or

(b) The dissolution being by the death or bankruptcy of a partner, the partner acting for the partnership had knowledge or notice of the death or bankruptcy.

Section 35. Power of Partner to Bind Partnership to Third Persons after Dissolution

(1) After dissolution a partner can bind the partnership except as provided in Paragraph (3).

(a) By any act appropriate for winding up partnership affairs or completing transactions unfinished at dissolution;

(b) By any transaction which would bind the partnership if dissolution had not taken place, provided the other party to the transaction

(I) Had extended credit to the partnership prior to dissolution and had no knowledge or notice of the dissolution; or

(II) Though he had not so extended credit, had nevertheless known of the partnership prior to dissolution, and, having no knowledge or notice of dissolution, the fact of dissolution had not been advertised in a newspaper of general circulation in the place (or in each place if more than one) at which the partnership business was regularly carried on.

(2) The liability of a partner under Paragraph (1b) shall be satisfied out of partnership assets alone when such partner had been prior to dissolution

(a) Unknown as a partner to the person with whom the contract is made; and

(b) So far unknown and inactive in partnership affairs that the business reputation of the partnership could not be said to have been in any degree due to his connection with it.

(3) The partnership is in no case bound by any act of a partner after dissolution

(a) Where the partnership is dissolved because it is unlawful to carry on the business, unless the act is appropriate for winding up partnership affairs; or

(b) Where the partner has become bankrupt; or

(c) Where the partner has no authority to wind up partnership affairs; except by a transaction with one who

(I) Had extended credit to the partnership prior to dissolution and had no knowledge or notice of his want of authority; or

(II) Had not extended credit to the partnership prior to dissolution, and, having no knowledge or notice of his want of authority, the fact of his want of authority has not been advertised in the manner provided for advertising the fact of dissolution in Paragraph (1b II).

(4) Nothing in this section shall affect the liability under Section 16 of any person who after dissolution represents himself or consents to another representing him as a partner in a partnership engaged in carrying on business.

Section 36. Effect of Dissolution on Partner's Existing Liability

(1) The dissolution of the partnership does not of itself discharge the existing liability of any partner.

(2) A partner is discharged from any existing liability upon dissolution of the partnership by an agreement to that effect between himself, the partnership creditor and the person or partnership continuing the business; and such agreement may be inferred from the course of dealing between the creditor having knowledge of the dissolution and the person or partnership continuing the business.

(3) Where a person agrees to assume the existing obligations of a dissolved partnership, the partners whose obligations have been assumed shall be discharged from any liability to any creditor of the partnership who, knowing of the agreement, consents to a material alteration in the nature or time of payment of such obligations.

(4) The individual property of a deceased partner shall be liable for all obligations of the partnership incurred while he was a partner but subject to the prior payment of his separate debts.

Section 37. Right to Wind Up

Unless otherwise agreed the partners who have not wrongfully dissolved the partnership or the legal representative of the last surviving partner, not bankrupt, has the right to wind up the partnership affairs; provided, however, that any partner, his legal representative or his assignee, upon cause shown, may obtain winding up by the court.

Section 38. Rights of Partners to Application of Partnership Property

(1) When dissolution is caused in any way, except in contravention of the partnership agreement, each partner, as against his co-partners and all persons claiming through them in respect of their interests in the partnership, unless otherwise agreed, may have the partnership property applied to discharge its liabilities, and the surplus applied to pay in cash the net amount owing to the respective partners. But if dissolution is

caused by expulsion of a partner, bona fide under the partnership agreement and if the expelled partner is discharged from all partnership liabilities, either by payment or agreement under section 36(2), he shall receive in cash only the net amount due him from the partnership.

(2) When dissolution is caused in contravention of the partnership agreement the rights of the partners shall be as follows:

(a) Each partner who has not caused dissolution wrongfully shall have,

(I) All the rights specified in paragraph (1) of this section, and

(II) The right, as against each partner who has caused the dissolution wrongfully, to damages for breach of the agreement.

(b) The partners who have not caused the dissolution wrongfully, if they all desire to continue the business in the same name, either by themselves or jointly with others, may do so, during the agreed term for the partnership and for that purpose may possess the partnership property, provided they secure the payment by bond approved by the court, or pay to any partner who has caused the dissolution wrongfully, the value of his interest in the partnership at the dissolution, less any damages recoverable under clause (2a II) of this section, and in like manner indemnify him against all present or future partnership liabilities.

(c) A partner who has caused the dissolution wrongfully shall have:

(I) If the business is not continued under the provisions of paragraph (2b) all the rights of a partner under paragraph (1), subject to clause (2a II), of this section,

(II) If the business is continued under paragraph (2b) of this section the right as against his co-partners and all claiming through them in respect of their interests in the partnership, to have the value of his interest in the partnership, less any damages caused to his co-partners by the dissolution, ascertained and paid to him in cash, or the payment secured by bond approved by the court, and to be released from all existing liabilities of the partnership; but in ascertaining the value of the partner's interest the value of the good-will of the business shall not be considered.

Section 39. Rights Where Partnership Is Dissolved for Fraud or Misrepresentation

Where a partnership contract is rescinded on the ground of the fraud or misrepresentation of one of the parties thereto, the party entitled to rescind is, without prejudice to any other right, entitled,

(a) To a lien on, or a right of retention of, the surplus of the partnership property after satisfying the partnership liabilities to third persons for any sum of money paid by him for the purchase of an interest in the partnership and for any capital or advances contributed by him; and

(b) To stand, after all liabilities to third persons have been satisfied, in the place of the creditors of the partnership for any payments made by him in respect of the partnership liabilities; and

(c) To be indemnified by the person guilty of the fraud or making the representation against all debts and liabilities of the partnership.

Section 40. Rules for Distribution

In settling accounts between the partners after dissolution, the following rules shall be observed, subject to any agreement to the contrary:

(a) The assets of the partnership are:

(I) The partnership property,

(II) The contributions of the partners necessary for the payment of all the liabilities specified in clause (b) of this paragraph.

(b) The liabilities of the partnership shall rank in order of payment, as follows:

(I) Those owing to creditors other than partners,

(II) Those owing to partners other than for capital and profits,

(III) Those owing to partners in respect of capital,

(IV) Those owing to partners in respect of profits.

(c) The assets shall be applied in the order of their declaration in clause (a) of this paragraph to the satisfaction of the liabilities.

(d) The partners shall contribute, as provided by section 18 (a) the amount necessary to satisfy the liabilities; but if any, but not all, of the partners are insolvent, or, not being subject to process, refuse to contribute, the other partners shall contribute their share of the liabilities, and, in the relative proportions in which they share the profits, the additional amount necessary to pay the liabilities.

(e) An assignee for the benefit of creditors or any person appointed by the court shall have the right to enforce the contributions specified in clause (d) of this paragraph.

(f) Any partner or his legal representative shall have the right to enforce the contributions specified in clause (d) of this paragraph, to the extent of the amount which he has paid in excess of his share of the liability.

(g) The individual property of a deceased partner shall be liable for the contributions specified in clause (d) of this paragraph.

(h) When partnership property and the individual properties of the partners are in possession of a court for distribution, partnership creditors shall have priority on partnership property and separate creditors on individual property, saving the rights of lien or secured creditors as heretofore.

(i) Where a partner has become bankrupt or his estate is insolvent the claims against his separate property shall rank in the following order:

(I) Those owing to separate creditors,

(II) Those owing to partnership creditors,

(III) Those owing to partners by way of contribution.

Section 41. Liability of Persons Continuing the Business in Certain Cases

(1) When any new partner is admitted into an existing partnership, or when any partner retires and assigns (or the representative of the deceased partner assigns) his rights in partnership property to two or more of the partners, or to one or more of the partners and one or more third persons, if the business is continued without liquidation of the

partnership affairs, creditors of the first or dissolved partnership are also creditors of the partnership so continuing the business.

(2) When all but one partner retire and assign (or the representative of a deceased partner assigns) their rights in partnership property to the remaining partner, who continues the business without liquidation of partnership affairs, either alone or with others, creditors of the dissolved partnership are also creditors of the person or partnership so continuing the business.

(3) When any partner retires or dies and the business of the dissolved partnership is continued as set forth in paragraphs (1) and (2) of this section, with the consent of the retired partners or the representative of the deceased partner, but without any assignment of his right in partnership property, rights of creditors of the dissolved partnership and of the creditors of the person or partnership continuing the business shall be as if such assignment had been made.

(4) When all the partners or their representatives assign their rights in partnership property to one or more third persons who promise to pay the debts and who continue the business of the dissolved partnership, creditors of the dissolved partnership are also creditors of the person or partnership continuing the business.

(5) When any partner wrongfully causes a dissolution and the remaining partners continue the business under the provisions of section 38(2b), either alone or with others, and without liquidation of the partnership affairs, creditors of the dissolved partnership are also creditors of the person or partnership continuing the business.

(6) When a partner is expelled and the remaining partners continue the business either alone or with others, without liquidation of the partnership affairs, creditors of the dissolved partnership are also creditors of the person or partnership continuing the business.

(7) The liability of a third person becoming a partner in the partnership continuing the business, under this section, to the creditors of the dissolved partnership shall be satisfied out of partnership property only.

(8) When the business of a partnership after dissolution is continued under any conditions set forth in this section the creditors of the dissolved partnership, as against the separate creditors of the retiring or deceased partner or the representative of the deceased partner, have a prior right to any claim of the retired partner or the representative of the deceased partner against the person or partnership continuing the business, on account of the retired or deceased partner's interest in the dissolved partnership or on account of any consideration promised for such interest or for his right in partnership property.

(9) Nothing in this section shall be held to modify any right of creditors to set aside any assignment on the ground of fraud.

(10) The use by the person or partnership continuing the business of the partnership name, or the name of a deceased partner as part thereof, shall not of itself make the individual property of the deceased partner liable for any debts contracted by such person or partnership.

Section 42. Rights of Retiring or Estate of Deceased Partner When the Business is Continued

When any partner retires or dies, and the business is continued under any of the conditions set forth in section 41 (1, 2, 3, 5, 6), or section 38(2b) without any settlement of accounts as between him or his estate and the person or partnership continuing the business, unless otherwise agreed, he or his legal representative as against such persons or partnership may have the value of his interest at the date of dissolution ascertained, and shall receive as an ordinary creditor an amount equal to the value of his interest in the dissolved partnership with interest, or, at his option or at the option of his legal representative, in lieu of interest, the profits attributable to the use of his right in the property of the dissolved partnership; provided that the creditors of the dissolved partnership as against the separate creditors, or the representative of the retired or deceased partner, shall have priority on any claim arising under this section, as provided by section 41(8) of this act.

Section 43. Accrual of Actions

The right to an account of his interest shall accrue to any partner, or his legal representative, as against the winding up partners or the surviving partners or the person or partnership continuing the business, at the date of dissolution, in the absence of any agreement to the contrary.

Part VII Miscellaneous Provisions

Section 44. When Act Takes Effect

This act shall take effect on the .... day of .... one thousand nine hundred and ....

Section 45. Legislation Repealed

All acts or parts of acts inconsistent with this act are hereby repealed.

APPENDIX D

UNIFORM LIMITED PARTNERSHIP ACT (1916)

Section 1. Limited Partnership Defined

A limited partnership is a partnership formed by two or more persons under the provisions of section 2, having as members one or more general partners and one or more limited partners. The limited partners as such shall not be bound by the obligations of the partnership.

Section 2. Formation

(1) Two or more persons desiring to form a limited partnership shall

(a) Sign and swear to a certificate, which shall state

I. The name of the partnership,

II. The character of the business,

III. The location of the principal place of business,

IV. The name and place of residence of each member; general and limited partners being respectively designated,

V. The term for which the partnership is to exist,

VI. The amount of cash and a description of and the agreed value of the other property contributed by each limited partner,

VII. The additional contributions, if any, agreed to be made by each limited partner and the times at which or events on the happening of which they shall be made,

VIII. The time, if agreed upon, when the contribution of each limited partner is to be returned,

IX. The share of the profits or the other compensation by way of income which each limited partner shall receive by reason of his contribution,

X. The right, if given, of a limited partner to substitute an assignee as contributor in his place, and the terms and conditions of the substitution,

XI. The right, if given, of the partners to admit additional limited partners,

XII. The right, if given, of one or more of the limited partners to priority over other limited partners, as to contributions or as to compensation by way of income, and the nature of such priority,

XIII. The right, if given, of the remaining general partner or partners to continue the business on the death, retirement or insanity of a general partner, and

XIV. The right, if given, of a limited partner to demand and receive property other than cash in return for his contribution.

(b) File for record the certificate in the office of [here designate the proper office].

(2) A limited partnership is formed if there has been substantial compliance in good faith with the requirements of paragraph (1).

Section 3. Business Which May Be Carried On

A limited partnership may carry on any business which a partnership without limited partners may carry on, except [here designate the business to be prohibited].

Section 4. Character of Limited Partner's Contribution

The contributions of a limited partner may be cash or other property, but not services.

Section 5. A Name Not to Contain Surname of Limited Partner; Exceptions

(1) The surname of a limited partner shall not appear in the partnership name, unless

(a) It is also the surname of a general partner, or

(b) Prior to the time when the limited partner became such the business had been carried on under a name in which his surname appeared.

(2) A limited partner whose name appears in a partnership name contrary to the provisions of paragraph (1) is liable as a general partner to partnership creditors who extend credit to the partnership without actual knowledge that he is not a general partner.

Section 6. Liability for False Statements in Certificate

If the certificate contains a false statement, one who suffers loss by reliance on such statement may hold liable any party to the certificate who knew the statement to be false

(a) At the time he signed the certificate, or

(b) Subsequently, but within a sufficient time before the statement was relied upon to enable him to cancel or amend the certificate, or to file a petition for its cancellation or amendment as provided in section 25 (3).

Section 7. Limited Partner Not Liable to Creditors

A limited partner shall not become liable as a general partner unless, in addition to the exercise of his rights and powers as a limited partner, he takes part in the control of the business.

Section 8. Admission of Additional Limited Partners

After the formation of a limited partnership, additional limited partners may be admitted upon filing an amendment to the original certificate in accordance with the requirements of section 25.

Section 9. Rights, Powers and Liabilities of a General Partner

(1) A general partner shall have all the rights and powers and be subject to all the restrictions and liabilities of a partner in a partnership without limited partners, except that without the written consent or ratification of

the specific act by all the limited partners, a general partner or all of the general partners have no authority to

(a) Do any act in contravention of the certificate,

(b) Do any act which would make it impossible to carry on the ordinary business of the partnership,

(c) Confess a judgment against the partnership,

(d) Possess partnership property, or assign their rights in specific partnership property, for other than a partnership purpose,

(e) Admit a person as a general partner,

(f) Admit a person as a limited partner, unless the right so to do is given in the certificate,

(g) Continue the business with partnership property on the death, retirement or insanity of a general partner, unless the right so to do is given in the certificate.

Section 10. Rights of a Limited Partner

(1) A limited partner shall have the same rights as a general partner to

(a) Have the partnership books kept at the principal place of business of the partnership, and at all times to inspect and copy any of them.

(b) Have on demand true and full information of all things affecting the partnership, and a formal account of partnership affairs whenever circumstances render it just and reasonable, and

(c) Have dissolution and winding up by decree of court.

(2) A limited partner shall have the right to receive a share of the profits or other compensation by way of income, and to the return of his contribution as provided in sections 15 and 16.

Section 11. Status of Person Erroneously Believing Himself a Limited Partner

A person who has contributed to the capital of a business conducted by a person or partnership erroneously believing that he has become a limited partner in a limited partnership, is not, by reason of his exercise of the rights of a limited partner, a general partner with the person or in the partnership carrying on the business, or bound by the obligations of such person or partnership; provided that on ascertaining the mistake he promptly renounces his interest in the profits of the business, or other compensation by way of income.

Section 12. One Person Both General and Limited Partner

(1) A person may be a general partner and a limited partner in the same partnership at the same time.

(2) A person who is a general, and also at the same time a limited partner, shall have all the rights and powers and be subject to all the restrictions of a general partner; except that, in respect to his contribution, he shall have the rights against the other members which he would have had if he were not also a general partner.

Section 13. Loans and Other Business Transactions with Limited Partner

(1) A limited partner also may loan money to and transact other business with the partnership, and, unless he is also a general partner, receive on account of resulting claims against the partnership, with general creditors, a pro rata share of the assets. No limited partner shall in respect to any such claim

(a) Receive or hold as collateral security any partnership property, or

(b) Receive from a general partner or the partnership any payment, conveyance, or release from liability, if at the time the assets of the partnership are not sufficient to discharge partnership liabilities to persons not claiming as general or limited partners.

(2) The receiving of collateral security, or a payment, conveyance, or release in violation of the provisions of paragraph (1) is a fraud on the creditors of the partnership.

Section 14. Relation of Limited Partners Inter Se

Where there are several limited partners the members may agree that one or more of the limited partners shall have a priority over other limited partners as to the return of their contributions, as to their compensation by way of income, or as to any other matter. If such an agreement is made it shall be stated in the certificate, and in the absence of such a statement all the limited partners shall stand upon equal footing.

Section 15. Compensation of Limited Partner

A limited partner may receive from the partnership the share of the profits or the compensation by way of income stipulated for in the certificate; provided, that after such payment is made, whether from the property of the partnership or that of a general partner, the partnership assets are in excess of all liabilities of the partnership except liabilities to limited partners on account of their contributions and to general partners.

Section 16. Withdrawal or Reduction of Limited Partner's Contribution

(1) A limited partner shall not receive from a general partner or out of partnership property any part of his contribution until

(a) All liabilities of the partnership, except liabilities to general partners and to limited partners on account of their contributions, have been paid or there remains property of the partnership sufficient to pay them,

(b) The consent of all members is had, unless the return of the contribution may be rightfully demanded under the provisions of paragraph (2), and

(c) The certificate is cancelled or so amended as to set forth the withdrawal or reduction.

(2) Subject to the provisions of paragraph (1) a limited partner may rightfully demand the return of his contribution

(a) On the dissolution of a partnership, or

(b) When the date specified in the certificate for its return has arrived, or

(c) After he has given six months' notice in writing to all other members, if no time is specified in the certificate either for the return of the contribution or for the dissolution of the partnership.

(3) In the absence of any statement in the certificate to the contrary or the consent of all members, a limited partner, irrespective of the nature of his contribution, has only the right to demand and receive cash in return for his contribution.

(4) A limited partner may have the partnership dissolved and its affairs wound up when

(a) He rightfully but unsuccessfully demands the return of his contribution, or

(b) The other liabilities of the partnership have not been paid, or the partnership property is insufficient for their payment as required by paragraph (1a) and the limited partner would otherwise be entitled to the return of his contribution.

Section 17. Liability of Limited Partner to Partnership

A limited partner is liable to the partnership

(a) For the difference between his contribution as actually made and that stated in the certificate as having been made, and

(b) For any unpaid contribution which he agreed in the certificate to make in the future at the time and on the conditions stated in the certificate.

(2) A limited partner holds as trustee for the partnership

(a) Specific property stated in the certificate as contributed by him, but which was not contributed or which has been wrongfully returned, and

(b) Money or other property wrongfully paid or conveyed to him on account of his contribution.

(3) The liabilities of a limited partner as set forth in this section can be waived or compromised only by the consent of all members; but a waiver or compromise shall not affect the right of a creditor of a partnership who extended credit or whose claim arose after the filing and before a cancellation or amendment of the certificate, to enforce such liabilities.

(4) When a contributor has rightfully received the return in whole or in part of the capital of his contribution, he is nevertheless liable to the partnership for any sum, not in excess of such return with interest, necessary to discharge its liabilities to all creditors who extended credit or whose claims arose before such return.

Section 18. Nature of Limited Partner's Interest in Partnership

A limited partner's interest in the partnership is personal property.

Section 19. Assignment of Limited Partner's Interest

(1) A limited partner's interest is assignable.

(2) A substituted limited partner is a person admitted to all the rights of a limited partner who has died or has assigned his interest in a partnership.

(3) An assignee, who does not become a substituted limited partner, has no right to require any information or account of the partnership transactions or to inspect the partnership books; he is only entitled to receive the share of the profits or other compensation by way of income, or the return of his contribution, to which his assignor would otherwise be entitled.

(4) An assignee shall have the right to become a substituted limited partner if all the members (except the assignor) consent thereto or if the assignor, being thereunto empowered by the certificate, gives the assignee that right.

(5) An assignee becomes a substituted limited partner when the certificate is appropriately amended in accordance with section 25.

(6) The substituted limited partner has all the rights and powers, and is subject to all the restrictions and liabilities of his assignor, except those liabilities of which he was ignorant at the time he became a limited partner and which could not be ascertained from the certificate.

(7) The substitution of the assignee as a limited partner does not release the assignor from liability to the partnership under sections 6 and 17.

Section 20. Effect of Retirement, Death or Insanity of a General Partner

The retirement, death or insanity of a general partner dissolves the partnership, unless the business is continued by the remaining general partners

(a) Under a right so to do stated in the certificate, or

(b) With the consent of all members.

Section 21. Death of Limited Partner

(1) On the death of a limited partner his executor or administrator shall have all the rights of a limited partner for the purpose of settling his estate and such power as the deceased had to constitute his assignee a substituted limited partner.

(2) The estate of a deceased limited partner shall be liable for all his liabilities as a limited partner.

Section 22. Rights of Creditors of Limited Partner

(1) On due application to a court of competent jurisdiction by any judgment creditor of a limited partner, the court may charge the interest of the indebted limited partner with payment of the unsatisfied amount of the judgment debt; and may appoint a receiver, and make all other orders, directions, and inquiries which the circumstances of the case may require.

(Commissioners' Note: In those states where a creditor on beginning an action can attach debts due the defendant before he has obtained a judgment against the defendant it is recommended that paragraph (1) of this section read as follows:

"On due application to a court of competent jurisdiction by any creditor of a limited partner, the court may charge the interest of the indebted limited partner with payment of the unsatisfied amount of such claim; and may appoint a receiver, and make all other orders, directions, and inquiries which the circumstances of the case may require.")

(2) The interest may be redeemed with the separate property of any general partner, but may not be redeemed with partnership property.

(3) The remedies conferred by paragraph (1) shall not be deemed exclusive of others which may exist.

(4) Nothing in this act shall be held to deprive a limited partner of his statutory exemption.

Section 23. Distribution of Assets

(1) In settling accounts after dissolution the liabilities of the partnership shall be entitled to payment in the following order:

(a) Those to creditors, in the order of priority as provided by law, except those to limited partners on account of their contributions, and to general partners,

(b) Those to limited partners in respect to their share of the profits and other compensation by way of income on their contributions,

(c) Those to limited partners in respect to the capital of their contributions,

(d) Those to general partners other than for capital and profits,

(e) Those to general partners in respect to profits,

(f) Those to general partners in respect to capital.

(2) Subject to any statement in the certificate or to subsequent agreement, limited partners share in the partnership assets in respect to their

claims for capital, and in respect to their claims for profits or for compensation by way of income on their contributions respectively, in proportion to the respective amounts of such claims.

Section 24. When Certificate Shall Be Cancelled or Amended

(1) The certificate shall be cancelled when the partnership is dissolved or all limited partners cease to be such.

(2) A certificate shall be amended when

- (a) There is a change in the name of the partnership or in the amount or character of the contribution of any limited partner,
- (b) A person is substituted as a limited partner,
- (c) An additional limited partner is admitted,
- (d) A person is admitted as a general partner,
- (e) A general partner retires, dies or becomes insane, and the business is continued under section 20,
- (f) There is a change in the character of the business of the partnership,
- (g) There is a false or erroneous statement in the certificate,
- (h) There is a change in the time as stated in the certificate for the dissolution of the partnership or for the return of a contribution,
- (i) A time is fixed for the dissolution of the partnership, or the return of a contribution, no time having been specified in the certificate, or
- (j) The members desire to make a change in any other statement in the certificate in order that it shall accurately represent the agreement between them.

Section 25. Requirements for Amendment and for Cancellation of Certificate

(1) The writing to amend a certificate shall

- (a) Conform to the requirements of section 2 (1a) as far as necessary to set forth clearly the change in the certificate which it is desired to make, and
- (b) Be signed and sworn to by all members, and an amendment substituting a limited partner or adding a limited or general partner shall be signed also by the member to be substituted or added, and when a limited partner is to be substituted, the amendment shall also be signed by the assigning limited partner.

(2) The writing to cancel a certificate shall be signed by all members.

(3) A person desiring the cancellation or amendment of a certificate, if any person designated in paragraphs (1) and (2) as a person who must execute the writing refuses to do so, may petition the [here designate the proper court] to direct a cancellation or amendment thereof.

(4) If the court finds that the petitioner has a right to have the writing executed by a person who refuses to do so, it shall order the [here designate the responsible official in the office designated in section 2] in the office where the certificate is recorded to record the cancellation or amendment of the certificate; and where the certificate is to be amended, the court shall also cause to be filed for record in said office a certified copy of its decree setting forth the amendment.

(5) A certificate is amended or cancelled when there is filed for record in the office [here designate the office designated in section 2] where the certificate is recorded

- (a) A writing in accordance with the provisions of paragraph (1), or (2) or
- (b) A certified copy of the order of court in accordance with the provisions of paragraph (4).

(6) After the certificate is duly amended in accordance with this section, the amended certificate shall thereafter be for all purposes the certificate provided for by this act.

Section 26. Parties to Actions

A contributor, unless he is a general partner, is not a proper party to proceedings by or against a partnership, except where the object is to enforce a limited partner's right against or liability to the partnership.

Section 27. Name of Act

This act may be cited as The Uniform Limited Partnership Act.

Section 28. Rules of Construction

(1) The rule that statutes in derogation of the common law are to be strictly construed shall have no application to this act.

(2) This act shall be so interpreted and construed as to effect its general purpose to make uniform the law of those states which enact it.

(3) This act shall not be so construed as to impair the obligations of any contract existing when the act goes into effect, nor to affect any action or proceedings begun or right accrued before this act takes effect.

Section 29. Rules for Cases Not Provided for in This Act

In any case not provided for in this act the rules of law and equity, including the law merchant, shall govern.

Section 30. Provisions for Existing Limited Partnerships

(1) A limited partnership formed under any statute of this state prior to the adoption of this act, may become a limited partnership under this act by complying with the provisions of section 2; provided the certificate sets forth

- (a) The amount of the original contribution of each limited partner, and the time when the contribution was made, and
- (b) That the property of the partnership exceeds the amount sufficient to discharge its liabilities to persons not claiming as general or limited partners by an amount greater than the sum of the contributions of its limited partners.

(2) A limited partnership formed under any statute of this state prior to the adoption of this act, until or unless it becomes a limited partnership under this act, shall continue to be governed by the provisions of [here insert proper reference to the existing limited partnership act or acts], except that such partnership shall not be renewed unless so provided in the original agreement.

(Commissioners' Note: Sections 30, 31, will be omitted in any state which has not a limited partnership act.)

Section 31. Act (Acts) Repealed

Except as affecting existing limited partnerships to the extent set forth in section 30, the act (acts) of [here designate the existing limited partnership act or acts] is (are) hereby repealed.

(Commissioners' Note: Sections 30, 31, will be omitted in any state which has not a limited partnership act.)

APPENDIX E

(REVISED) UNIFORM LIMITED PARTNERSHIP ACT, AS AMENDED (1985)

Article 1 General Provisions

Section 101. [Definitions]

As used in this Act, unless the context otherwise requires:

(1) "Certificate of limited partnership" means the certificate referred to in Section 201, and the certificate as amended or restated.

(2) "Contribution" means any cash, property, services rendered, or a promissory note or other binding obligation to contribute cash or property or to perform services, which a partner contributes to a limited partnership in his capacity as a partner.

(3) "Event of withdrawal of a general partner" means an event that causes a person to cease to be a general partner as provided in Section 402.

(4) "Foreign limited partnership" means a partnership formed under the laws of any state other than this State and having as partners one or more general partners and one or more limited partners.

(5) "General partner" means a person who has been admitted to a limited partnership as a general partner in accordance with the partnership agreement and named in the certificate of limited partnership as a general partner.

(6) "Limited partner" means a person who has been admitted to a limited partnership as a limited partner in accordance with the partnership agreement.

(7) "Limited partnership" and "domestic limited partnership" mean a partnership formed by 2 or more persons under the laws of this State and having one or more general partners and one or more limited partners.

(8) "Partner" means a limited or general partner.

(9) "Partnership agreement" means any valid agreement, written or oral, of the partners as to the affairs of a limited partnership and the conduct of its business.

(10) "Partnership interest" means a partner's share of the profits and losses of a limited partnership and the right to receive distributions of partnership assets.

(11) "Person" means a natural person, partnership, limited partnership (domestic or foreign), trust, estate, association, or corporation.

(12) "State" means a state, territory, or possession of the United States, the District of Columbia, or the Commonwealth of Puerto Rico.

Section 102. [Name]

The name of each limited partnership as set forth in its certificate of limited partnership:

(1) shall contain without abbreviation the words "limited partnership";

(2) may not contain the name of a limited partner unless (i) it is also the name of a general partner or the corporate name of a corporate general partner, or (ii) the business of the limited partnership had been carried on under that name before the admission of that limited partner;

(3) may not be the same as, or deceptively similar to, the name of any corporation or limited partnership organized under the laws of this State or licensed or registered as a foreign corporation or limited partnership in this State; and

(4) may not contain the following words [here insert prohibited words].

Section 103. [Reservation of Name]

(a) The exclusive right to the use of a name may be reserved by:

(1) any person intending to organize a limited partnership under this Act and to adopt that name;

(2) any domestic limited partnership or any foreign limited partnership registered in this State which, in either case, intends to adopt that name;

(3) any foreign limited partnership intending to register in this State and adopt that name; and

(4) any person intending to organize a foreign limited partnership and intending to have it register in this State and adopt that name.

(b) The reservation shall be made by filing with the Secretary of State an application, executed by the applicant, to reserve a specified name. If the Secretary of State finds that the name is available for use by a domestic or foreign limited partnership, he shall reserve the name for the exclusive use of the applicant for a period of 120 days. Once having so reserved a name, the same applicant may not again reserve the same name until more than 60 days after the expiration of the last 120-day period for which that applicant reserved that name. The right to the exclusive use of a reserved name may be transferred to any other person by filing in the office of the Secretary of State a notice of the transfer, executed by the applicant for whom the name was reserved and specifying the name and address of the transferee.

Section 104. [Specified Office and Agent]

Each limited partnership shall continuously maintain in this State:

(1) an office, which may but need not be a place of its business in this State, at which shall be kept the records required by Section 105 to be maintained; and

(2) an agent for service of process on the limited partnership, which agent must be an individual resident of this State, a domestic corporation, or a foreign corporation authorized to do business in this State.

Section 105. [Records to Be Kept]

(a) Each limited partnership shall keep at the office referred to in Section 104(1) the following:

(1) a current list of the full name and last known business address of each partner, separately identifying the general partners (in alphabetical order) and the limited partners (in alphabetical order);

(2) a copy of the certificate of limited partnership and all certificates of amendment thereto, together with executed copies of any powers of attorney pursuant to which any certificate has been executed;

(3) copies of the limited partnership's federal, state and local income tax returns and reports, if any, for the three most recent years;

(4) copies of any then effective written partnership agreements and of any financial statements of the limited partnership for the three most recent years; and

(5) unless contained in a written partnership agreement, a writing setting out:

(i) the amount of cash and a description and statement of the agreed value of the other property or services contributed by each partner and which each partner has agreed to contribute;

(ii) the times at which or events on the happening of which any additional contributions agreed to be made by each partner are to be made;

(iii) any right of a partner to receive, or of a general partner to make, distributions to a partner which include a return of all or any part of the partner's contribution; and

(iv) any events upon the happening of which the limited partnership is to be dissolved and its affairs wound up.

(b) Records kept under this section are subject to inspection and copying at the reasonable request and at the expense of any partner during ordinary business hours.

Section 106. [Nature of Business]

A limited partnership may carry on any business that a partnership without limited partners may carry on except [here designate prohibited activities].

Section 107. [Business Transactions of Partner with Partnership]

Except as provided in the partnership agreement, a partner may lend money to and transact other business with the limited partnership and, subject to other applicable law, has the same rights and obligations with respect thereto as a person who is not a partner.

Article 2 Formation: Certificate of Limited Partnership

Section 201. [Certificate of Limited Partnership]

(a) In order to form a limited partnership a certificate of limited partnership must be executed and filed in the office of the Secretary of State. The certificate shall set forth:

(1) the name of the limited partnership;

(2) the address of the office and the name and address of the agent for service of process required to be maintained by Section 104;

(3) the name and the business address of each general partner;

(4) the latest date upon which the limited partnership is to dissolve; and

(5) any other matters the general partners determine to include therein.

(b) A limited partnership is formed at the time of the filing of the certificate of limited partnership in the office of the Secretary of State or at any later time specified in the certificate of limited partnership if, in either case, there has been substantial compliance with the requirements of this section.

Section 202. [Amendment to Certificate]

(a) A certificate of limited partnership is amended by filing a certificate of amendment thereto in the office of the Secretary of State. The certificate shall set forth:

(1) the name of the limited partnership;

(2) the date of filing the certificate; and

(3) the amendment to the certificate.

(b) Within 30 days after the happening of any of the following events, an amendment to a certificate of limited partnership reflecting the occurrence of the event or events shall be filed:

(1) the admission of a new general partner;

(2) the withdrawal of a general partner; or

(3) the continuation of the business under Section 801 after an event of withdrawal of a general partner.

(c) A general partner who becomes aware that any statement in a certificate of limited partnership was false when made or that any arrangements or other facts described have changed, making the certificate inaccurate in any respect, shall promptly amend the certificate.

(d) A certificate of limited partnership may be amended at any time for any other proper purpose the general partners determine.

(e) No person has any liability because an amendment to a certificate of limited partnership has not been filed to reflect the occurence of any event referred to in subsection (b) of this Section if the amendment is filed within the 30-day period specified in subsection (b).

(f) A restated certificate of limited partnership may be executed and filed in the same manner as a certificate of amendment.

Section 203. [Cancellation of Certificate]

A certificate of limited partnership shall be cancelled upon the dissolution and the commencement of winding up of the partnership or at any other time there are no limited partners. A certificate of cancellation shall be filed in the office of the Secretary of State and set forth:

(1) the name of the limited partnership;

(2) the date of filing of its certificate of limited partnership;

(3) the reason for filing the certificate of cancellation;

(4) the effective date (which shall be a date certain) of cancellation if it is not to be effective upon the filing of the certificate; and

(5) any other information the general partners filing the certificate determine.

Section 204. [Execution of Certificates]

(a) Each certificate required by this Article to be filed in the office of the Secretary of State shall be executed in the following manner:

(1) an original certificate of limited partnership must be signed by all general partners;

(2) a certificate of amendment must be signed by at least one general partner and by each other general partner designated in the certificate as a general partner; and

(3) a certificate of cancellation must be signed by all general partners.

(b) Any person may sign a certificate by an attorney-in-fact, but a power of attorney to sign a certificate relating to the admission, of a general partner must specifically describe the admission.

(c) The execution of a certificate by a general partner constitutes an affirmation under the penalties of perjury that the facts stated therein are true.

Section 205. [Execution by Judicial Act]

If a person required by Section 204 to execute any certificate fails or refuses to do so, any other person who is adversely affected by the failure or refusal may petition the [here designate the proper court] to direct the execution of the certificate. If the court finds that it is proper for the certificate to be executed and that any person so designated has failed or refused to execute the certificate, it shall order the Secretary of State to record an appropriate certificate.

Section 206. [Filing in Office of Secretary of State]

(a) Two signed copies of the certificate of limited partnership and of any certificates of amendment or cancellation (or of any judicial decree of amendment or cancellation) shall be delivered to the Secretary of State. A person who executes a certificate as an agent or fiduciary need not exhibit evidence of his authority as a prerequisite to filing. Unless the Secretary of State finds that any certificate does not conform to law, upon receipt of all filing fees required by law he shall:

(1) endorse on each duplicate original the word "Filed" and the day, month and year of the filing thereof;

(2) file one duplicate original in his office; and

(3) return the other duplicate original to the person who filed it or his representative.

(b) Upon the filing of a certificate of amendment (or judicial decree of amendment) in the office of the Secretary of State, the certificate of limited partnership shall be amended as set forth therein, and upon the effective date of a certificate of cancellation (or a judicial decree thereof), the certificate of limited partnership is cancelled.

Section 207. [Liability for False Statement in Certificate]

If any certificate of limited partnership or certificate of amendment or cancellation contains a false statement, one who suffers loss by reliance on the statement may recover damages for the loss from:

(1) any person who executes the certificate, or causes another to execute it on his behalf, and knew, and any general partner who knew or should have known, the statement to be false at the time the certificate was executed; and

(2) any general partner who thereafter knows or should have known that any arrangement or other fact described in the certificate has changed, making the statement inaccurate in any respect within a sufficient time before the statement was relied upon reasonably to have enabled that general partner to cancel or amend the certificate, or to file a petition for its cancellation or amendment under Section 205.

Section 208. [Scope of Notice]

The fact that a certificate of limited partnership is on file in the office of the Secretary of State is notice that the partnership is a limited partnership and the persons designated therein as general partners are general partners, but it is not notice of any other fact.

Section 209. [Delivery of Certificates to Limited Partners]

Upon the return by the Secretary of State pursuant to Section 206 of a certificate marked "Filed", the general partners shall promptly deliver or mail a copy of the certificate of limited partnership and each certificate to each limited partner unless the partnership agreement provides otherwise.

Article 3 Limited Partners

Section 301. Admission of Limited Partners.

(a) A person becomes a limited partner:

(1) at the time the limited partnership is formed; or

(2) at any later time specified in the records of the limited partnership for becoming a limited partner.

(b) After the filing of a limited partnership's original certificate of limited partnership, a person may be admitted as an additional limited partner:

(1) in the case of a person acquiring a partnership interest directly from the limited partnership, upon compliance with the partnership agreement or, if the partnership agreement does not so provide, upon the written consent of all partners; and

(2) in the case of an assignee of a partnership interest of a partner who has the power, as provided in Section 704, to grant the assignee the right to become a limited partner, upon the exercise of that power and compliance with any conditions limiting the grant or exercise of the power.

Section 302. [Voting]

Subject to Section 303, the partnership agreement may grant to all or a specified group of the limited partners the right to vote (on a per capita or other basis) upon any matter.

Section 303. [Liability to Third Parties]

(a) Except as provided in subsection (d), a limited partner is not liable for the obligations of a limited partnership unless he is also a general partner or, in addition to the exercise of his rights and powers as a limited partner, he participates in the control of the business. However, if the limited partner participates in the control of the business, he is liable only to persons who transact business with the limited partnership reasonably believing, based upon the limited partner's conduct, that the limited partner is a general partner.

(b) A limited partner does not participate in the control of the business within the meaning of subsection (a) solely by doing one or more of the following:

(1) being a contractor for or an agent or employee of the limited partnership or of a general partner or being an officer director, or shareholder of a general partner that is a corporation;

(2) consulting with and advising a general partner with respect to the business of the limited partnership;

(3) acting as surety for the limited partnership or guaranteeing or assuming one or more specific obligations of the limited partnership;

(4) taking any action required or permitted by law to bring or pursue a derivative action in the right of the limited partnership;

(5) requesting or attending a meeting of partners;

(6) proposing, approving, or disapproving, by voting or otherwise, one or more of the following matters:

(i) the dissolution and winding up of the limited partnership;

(ii) the sale, exchange, lease, mortgage, pledge, or other transfer of all or substantially all of the assets of the limited partnership;

(iii) the incurrence of indebtedness by the limited partnership other than in the ordinary course of its business;

(iv) a change in the nature of the business;

(v) the admission or removal of a general partner;

(vi) the admission or removal of a limited partner;

(vii) a transaction involving an actual or potential conflict of interest between a general partner and the limited partnership or the limited partners;

(viii) an amendment to the partnership agreement or certificate of limited partnership; or

(ix) matters related to the business of the limited partnership not otherwise enumerated in this subsection (b), which the partnership agreement states in writing may be subject to the approval or disapproval of the limited partners;

(7) winding up the limited partnership pursuant to Section 803; or

(8) exercising any right or power permitted to limited partners under this [Act] and not specifically enumerated in this subsection (b).

(c) The enumeration in subsection (b) does not mean that the possession or exercise of any other powers by a limited partner constitutes participation by him in the business of the limited partnership.

(d) A limited partner who knowingly permits his name to be used in the name of the limited partnership, except under circumstances permitted by Section 102(2)(i), is liable to creditors who extend credit to the limited partnership without actual knowledge that the limited partner is not a general partner.

Section 304. [Person Erroneously Believing Himself Limited Partner]

(a) Except as provided in subsection (b), a person who makes a contribution to a business enterprise and erroneously but in good faith believes that he has become a limited partner in the enterprise is not a general partner in the enterprise and is not bound by its obligations by reason of making the contribution, receiving distributions from the enterprise, or exercising any rights of a limited partner, if, on ascertaining the mistake, he:

(1) causes an appropriate certificate of limited partnership or a certificate of amendment to be executed and filed; or

(2) withdraws from future equity participation in the enterprise.

(b) A person who makes a contribution of the kind described in subsection (a) is liable as a general partner to any third party who transacts business with the enterprise (i) before the person withdraws and an appropriate certificate is filed to show withdrawal, or (ii) before an appropriate certificate is filed to show that he is not a general partner but in either case only if the third party actually believed in good faith that the person was a general partner at the time of the transaction.

Section 305. [Information]

Each limited partner has the right to:

(1) inspect and copy any of the partnership records required to be maintained by Section 105; and

(2) obtain from the general partners from time to time upon reasonable demand (i) true and full information regarding the state of the business and financial condition of the limited partnership, (ii) promptly after becoming available, a copy of the limited partnership's federal, state and local income tax returns for each year, and (iii) other information regarding the affairs of the limited partnership as is just and reasonable.

Article 4 General Partners

Section 401. [Admission of Additional General Partners]

After the filing of a limited partnership's original certificate of limited partnership, additional general partners may be admitted as provided in writing in the partnership agreement, or if the partnership agreement does not provide in writing for the admission of additional general partners, with the written consent of all partners.

Section 402. [Events of Withdrawal]

Except as approved by the specific written consent of all partners at the time, a person ceases to be a general partner of a limited partnership upon the happening of any of the following events:

(1) the general partner withdraws from the limited partnership as provided in Section 602;

(2) the general partner ceases to be a member of the limited partnership as provided in Section 702;

(3) the general partner is removed as a general partner in accordance with the partnership agreement;

(4) unless otherwise provided in writing in the partnership agreement the general partner: (i) makes an assignment for the benefit of creditors; (ii) files a voluntary petition in bankruptcy; (iii) is adjudicated a bankrupt or insolvent; (iv) files a petition or answer seeking for himself any reorganization, arrangement, composition, readjustment, liquidation, dissolution or similar relief under any statute, law, or regulation; (v) files an answer or other pleading admitting or failing to contest the material allegations of a petition filed against him in any proceeding of this nature; or (vi) seeks, consents to, or acquiesces in the appointment of a trustee, receiver, or liquidator of the general partner or of all or any substantial part of his properties;

(5) unless otherwise provided in writing in the partnership agreement [120] days after the commencement of any proceeding against the general partner seeking reorganization, arrangement composition, readjustment, liquidation, dissolution or similar relief under any statute, law or regulation, the proceeding has not been dismissed, or if within [90] days after the appointment without his consent or acquiescence of a trustee, receiver, or liquidator of the general partner or of all or any substantial part of his properties, the appointment is not vacated or stayed or within

[90] days after the expiration of any such stay, the appointment is not vacated;

(6) in the case of a general partner who is a natural person,

(i) his death; or

(ii) the entry by a court of Competent jurisdiction adjicating him incompetent to manage his person or his estate;

(7) in the case of a general partner who is acting as a general partner by virtue of being a trustee of a trust, the termination of the trust (but not merely the substitution of a new trustee);

(8) in the case of a general partner that is a separate partnership, the dissolution and commencement of winding up of the separate partnership;

(9) in the case of a general partner that is a corporation, the filing of a certificate of dissolution, or its equivalent, for the corporation or the revocation of its charter; or

(10) in the case of an estate, the distribution by the fiduciary of the estate's entire interest in the partnership.

Section 403. [General Powers and Liabilities]

Except as provided in this Act or in the partnership agreement, a general partner of a limited partnership has the rights and powers and is subject to the restrictions and liabilities of a partner in a partnership without limited partners.

Section 404. [Contributions by General Partner]

A general partner of a limited partnership may make contributions to the partnership and share in the profits and losses of, and in distributions from, the limited partnership as a general partner. A general partner also may make contributions to and share in profits, losses, and distributions as a limited partner. A person who is both a general partner and a limited partner has the rights and powers, and is subject to the restrictions and liabilities, of a general partner and, except as provided in the partnership agreement, also has the powers, and is subject to the restrictions, of a limited partner to the extent of his participation in the partnership as a limited partner.

Section 405. [Voting]

The partnership agreement may grant to all or certain identified general partners the right to vote (on a per capita or any other basis), separately or with all or any class of the limited partners, on any matter.

Article 5 Finance

Section 501. [Form of Contribution]

The contribution of a partner may be in cash, property, or services rendered, or a promissory note or other obligation to contribute cash or property or to perform services.

Section 502. [Liability for Contribution]

(a) A promise by a limited partner to contribute to the limited partnership is not enforceable unless set out in a writing signed by the limited partner.

(b) Except as provided in the partnership agreement, a partner is obligated to the limited partnership to perform any enforceable promise to contribute cash or property or to perform services, even if he is unable to perform because of death, disability or any other reason. If a partner does not make the required contribution of property or services, he is obligated at the option of the limited partnership to contribute cash equal to that portion of the value (as stated in the partnership records required to be kept pursuant to Section 105, of the stated contribution that has not been made.

(c) Unless otherwise provided in the partnership agreement, the obligation of a partner to make a contribution or return money or other property paid or distributed in violation of this Act may be compromised only by consent of all the partners. Notwithstanding the compromise, a creditor of a limited partnership who extends credit, or otherwise acts in reliance on that obligation after the partner signs a writing which reflects the obligation, and before the amendment or cancellation thereof to reflect the compromise, may enforce the original obligation.

Section 503. [Sharing of Profits and Losses]

The profits and losses of a limited partnership shall be allocated among the partners, and among classes of partners, in the manner provided in writing in the partnership agreement. If the partnership agreement does not so provide in writing, profits and losses shall be allocated on the basis of the value as stated in the partnership records required to be kept pursuant to Section 105, of the contributions made by each partner to the extent they have been received by the partnership and have not been returned.

Section 504. [Sharing of Distributions]

Distributions of cash or other assets of a limited partnership shall be allocated among the partners, and among classes of partners, in the manner provided in writing in the partnership agreement. If the partnership agreement does not so provide in writing, distributions shall be made on the basis of the value, as stated in the partnership records required to be kept pursuant to Section 105, of the contributions made by each partner to the extent they have been received by the partnership and have not been returned.

Article 6 Distributions and Withdrawal

Section 601. [Interim Distributions]

Except as provided in this Article, a partner is entitled to receive distributions from a limited partnership before his withdrawal from the limited partnership and before the dissolution and winding up thereof to the extent and at the times or upon the happening of the events specified in the partnership agreement.

Section 602. [Withdrawal of General Partner]

A general partner may withdraw from a limited partnership at any time by giving written notice to the other partners, but if the withdrawal violates the partnership agreement, the limited partnership may recover from the withdrawing general partner damages for breach of the partnership agreement and offset the damages against the amount otherwise distributable to him.

Section 603. [Withdrawal of Limited Partner]

A limited partner may withdraw from a limited partnership at the time or upon the happening of events specified in writing in the partnership agreement. If the agreement does not specify in writing the time or the events upon the happening of which a limited partner may withdraw or a definite time for the dissolution and winding up of the limited partnership, a limited partner may withdraw upon not less than 6 months' prior written notice to each general partner at his address on the books of the limited partnership at its office in this State.

Section 604. [Distribution Upon Withdrawal]

Except as provided in this Article, upon withdrawal any withdrawing partner is entitled to receive any distribution to which he is entitled under the partnership agreement and, if not otherwise provided in the agreement, he is entitled to receive, within a reasonable time after withdrawal, the fair value of his interest in the limited partnership as of the date of withdrawal based upon his right to share in distributions from the limited partnership.

Section 605. [Distribution in Kind]

Except as provided in writing in the partnership agreement, a partner, regardless of the nature of his contribution, has no right to demand and receive any distribution from a limited partnership in any form other than cash. Except as provided in writing in the partnership agreement, a partner may not be compelled to accept a distribution of any asset in kind from a limited partnership to the extent that the percentage of the asset distributed to him exceeds a percentage of that asset which is equal to the percentage in which he shares in distributions from the limited partnership.

Section 606. [Right to Distribution]

At the time a partner becomes entitled to receive a distribution, he has the status of, and is entitled to all remedies available to, a creditor of the limited partnership with respect to the distribution.

Section 607. [Limitations on Distribution]

A partner may not receive a distribution from a limited partnership to the extent that, after giving effect to the distribution, all liabilities of the limited partnership, other than liabilities to partners on account of their partnership interests, exceed the fair value of the partnership assets.

Section 608. [Liability Upon Return of Contribution]

(a) If a partner has received the return of any part of his contribution without violation of the partnership agreement or this Act, he is liable to the limited partnership for a period of one year thereafter for the amount of the returned contribution, but only to the extent necessary to discharge the limited partnership's liabilities to creditors who extended credit to the limited partnership during the period the contribution was held by the partnership.

(b) If a partner has received the return of any part of his contribution in violation of the partnership agreement or this Act, he is liable to the limited partnership for a period of 6 years thereafter for the amount of the contribution wrongfully returned.

(c) A partner receives a return of his contribution to the extent that a distribution to him reduces his share of the fair value of the net assets of the limited partnership below the value, as set forth in the partnership records to be kept pursuant to Section 105, of his contribution which has not been distributed to him.

Article 7 Assignment of Partnership Interests

Section 701. [Nature of Partnership Interest]

A partnership interest is personal property.

Section 702. [Assignment of Partnership Interest]

Except as provided in the partnership agreement, a partnership interest is assignable in whole or in part. An assignment of a partnership interest does not dissolve a limited partnership or entitle the assignee to become or to exercise any rights of a partner. An assignment entitles the assignee to receive, to the extent assigned, only the distribution to which the assignor would be entitled. Except as provided in the partnership agreement, a partner ceases to be a partner upon assignment of all his partnership interest.

Section 703. [Rights of Creditor]

On application to a court of competent jurisdiction by any judgment creditor of a partner, the court may charge the partnership interest of the partner with payment of the unsatisfied amount of the judgment with interest. To the extent so charged, the judgment creditor has only the rights of an assignee of the partnership interest. This Act does not deprive any partner of the benefit of any exemption laws applicable to his partnership interest.

Section 704. [Right of Assignee to Become Limited Partner]

(a) An assignee of a partnership interest, including an assignee of a general partner, may become a limited partner if and to the extent that (i) the assignor gives the assignee that right in accordance with authority described in the partnership agreement or (ii) all other partners consent.

(b) An assignee who has become a limited partner has, to the extent assigned, the rights and powers, and is subject to the restrictions and liabilities, of a limited partner under the partnership agreement and this Act. An assignee who becomes a limited partner also is liable for the obligations of his assignor to make and return contributions as provided in Articles 5 and 6. However, the assignee is not obligated for liabilities unknown to the assignee at the time he became a limited partner.

(c) If an assignee of a partnership interest becomes a limited partner, the assignor is not released from his liability to the limited partnership under Sections 207 and 502.

Section 705. [Power of Estate of Deceased or Incompetent Partner]

If a partner who is an individual dies or a court of competent jurisdiction adjudges him to be incompetent to manage his person or his property, the partner's executor, administrator guardian, conservator, or other legal representative may exercise all the partner's rights for the purpose of settling his estate or administering his property, including any power the partner had to give an assignee the right to become a limited partner. If a partner is a corporation, trust, or other entity and is dissolved or terminated, the powers of that partner may be exercised by its legal representative or successor.

Article 8 Dissolution

Section 801. [Nonjudicial Dissolution]

A limited partnership is dissolved and its affairs shall be wound up upon the happening of the first to occur of the following:

(1) at the time specified in the certificate of limited partnership;

(2) upon the happenings of events specified in writing in the partnership agreement;

(3) written consent of all partners;

(4) an event of withdrawal of a general partner unless at the time there is at least one other general partner and the written provisions of the partnership agreement permit the business of the limited partnership to be carried on by the remaining general partner and that partner does so, but the limited partnership is not dissolved and is not required to be wound up by reason of any event of withdrawal, if, within 90 days after the withdrawal, all partners agree in writing to continue the business of the limited partnership and to the appointment of one or more additional general partners if necessary or desired; or

(5) entry of a decree of judicial dissolution under Section 802.

Section 802. [Judicial Dissolution]

On application by or for a partner the [designate the proper court] court may decree dissolution of a limited partnership whenever it is not reasonably practicable to carry on the business in conformity with the partnership agreement.

Section 803. [Winding Up]

Except as provided in the partnership agreement, the general partners who have not wrongfully dissolved a limited partnership or, if none, the limited partners, may wind up the limited partnership's affairs; but the [here designate the proper court] court may wind up the limited partnership's affairs upon application of any partner, his legal representative, or assignee.

Section 804. [Distribution of Assets]

Upon the winding up of a limited partnership, the assets shall be distributed as follows:

(1) to creditors, including partners who are creditors, to the extent permitted by law, in satisfaction of liabilities of the limited partnership other than liabilities for distributions to partners under Section 601 or 604;

(2) except as provided in the partnership agreement, to partners and former partners in satisfaction of liabilities for distributions under Section 601 or 604; and

(3) except as provided in the partnership agreement, to partners *first* for the return of their contributions and *secondly* respecting their partnership interests, in the proportions in which the partners share in distributions.

Article 9 Foreign Limited Partnerships

Section 901. [Law Governing]

Subject to the Constitution of this State, (1) the laws of the state under which a foreign limited partnership is organized govern its organization and internal affairs and the liability of its limited partners, and (2) a foreign limited partnership may not be denied registration by reason of any difference between those laws and the laws of this State.

Section 902. [Registration]

Before transacting business in this State, a foreign limited partnership shall register with the Secretary of State. In order to register, a foreign limited partnership shall submit to the Secretary of State, in duplicate, an application for registration as a foreign limited partnership, signed and sworn to by a general partner and setting forth:

(1) the name of the foreign limited partnership and, if different, the name under which it proposes to register and transact business in this State;

(2) the State and date of its formation;

(3) the name and address of any agent for service of process on the foreign limited partnership whom the foreign limited partnership elects to appoint; the agent must be an individual resident of this State, a domestic corporation, or a foreign corporation having a place of business in, and authorized to do business in, this State;

(4) a statement that the Secretary of State is appointed the agent of the foreign limited partnership for service of process if no agent has been appointed under paragraph (3) or, if appointed, the agent's authority has been revoked or if the agent cannot be found or served with the exercise of reasonable diligence;

(5) the address of the office required to be maintained in the state of its organization by the laws of that state or, if not so required, of the principal office of the foreign limited partnership;

(6) the name and business address of each general partner; and

(7) the address of the office at which is kept a list of the names and addresses of the limited partners and their capital contributions, together with an undertaking by the foreign limited partnership to keep those records until the foreign limited partnership's registration in this State is cancelled or withdrawn.

Section 903. [Issuance of Registration]

(a) If the Secretary of State finds that an application for registration conforms to law and all requisite fees have been paid, he shall:

(1) endorse on the application the word "Filed", and the month, day and year of the filing thereof;

(2) file in his office a duplicate original of the application; and

(3) issue a certificate of registration to transact business in this State.

(b) The certificate of registration, together with a duplicate original of the application, shall be returned to the person who filed the application or his representative.

Section 904. [Name]

A foreign limited partnership may register with the Secretary of State under any name (whether or not it is the name under which it is registered in its state of organization) that includes without abbreviation the words "limited partnership" and that could be registered by a domestic limited partnership.

Section 905. [Changes and Amendments]

If any statement in the application for registration of a foreign limited partnership was false when made or any arrangements or other facts described have changed, making the application inaccurate in any respect, the foreign limited partnership shall promptly file in the office of the Secretary of State a certificate, signed and sworn to by a general partner, correcting such statement.

Section 906. [Cancellation of Registration]

A foreign limited partnership may cancel its registration by filing with the Secretary of State a certificate of cancellation signed and sworn to by a general partner. A cancellation does not terminate the authority of the Secretary of State to accept service of process on the foreign limited partnership with respect to [claims for relief] [causes of action] arising out of the transactions of business in this State.

Section 907. [Transaction of Business Without Registration]

(a) A foreign limited partnership transacting business in this State may not maintain any action, suit, or proceeding in any court of this State until it has registered in this State.

(b) The failure of a foreign limited partnership to register in this State does not impair the validity of any contract or act of the foreign limited partnership or prevent the foreign limited partnership from defending any action, suit, or proceeding in any court of this State.

(c) A limited partner of a foreign limited partnership is not liable as a general partner of the foreign limited partnership solely by reason of having transacted business in this State without registration.

(d) A foreign limited partnership, by transacting business in this State without registration, appoints the Secretary of State as its agent for service of process with respect to [claims for relief] [causes of action] arising out of the transactions of business in this State.

Section 908. [Action by [Appropriate Official]]

The [appropriate official] may bring an action to restrain a foreign limited partnership from transacting business in this State in violation of this Article.

Article 10 Derivative Actions

Section 1001. [Right of Action]

A limited partner may bring an action in the right of a limited partnership to recover a judgment in its favor if general partners with authority to do so have refused to bring the action or if an effort to cause those general partners to bring the action is not likely to succeed.

Section 1002. [Proper Plaintiff]

In a derivative action, the plaintiff must be a partner at the time of bringing the action and (i) must have been a partner at the time of the transaction of which he complains or (ii) his status as a partner must have devolved upon him by operation of law or pursuant to the terms of the partnership agreement from a person who was a partner at the time of the transaction.

Section 1003. [Pleading]

In a derivative action, the complaint shall set forth with particularity the effort of the plaintiff to secure initiation of the action by a general partner or the reasons for not making the effort.

Section 1004. [Expenses]

If a derivative action is successful, in whole or in part, or if anything is received by the plaintiff as a result of a judgment, compromise or settlement of an action or claim, the court may award the plaintiff reasonable expenses, including reasonable attorney's fees, and shall direct him to remit to the limited partnership the remainder of those proceeds received by him.

Article 11 Miscellaneous

Section 1101. [Construction and Application]

This Act shall be so applied and construed to effectuate its general purpose to make uniform the law with respect to the subject of this Act among states enacting it.

Section 1102. [Short Title]

This Act may be cited as the Uniform Limited Partnership Act.

Section 1103. [Severability]

If any provision of this Act or its application to any person or circumstance is held invalid, the invalidity does not affect other provisions or applications of the Act which can be given effect without the invalid provision or application, and to this end the provisions of this Act are severable.

Section 1104. [Effective Date, Extended Effective Date and Repeal]

Except as set forth below, the effective date of this Act is ____________ and the following acts [list existing limited partnership acts] are hereby repealed:

(1) The existing provisions for execution and filing of certificates of limited partnerships and amendments thereunder and cancellations thereof continue in effect until [specify time required to create central filing system], the extended effective date, and Sections 102, 103, 104, 105, 201, 202, 203, 204 and 206 are not effective until the extended effective date.

(2) Section 402, specifying the conditions under which a general partner ceases to be a member of a limited partnership, is not effective until the extended effective date, and the applicable provisions of existing law continue to govern until the extended effective date.

(3) Sections 501, 502 and 608 apply only to contributions and distributions made after the effective date of this Act.

(4) Section 704 applies only to assignments made after the effective date of this Act.

(5) Article 9, dealing with registration of foreign limited partnerships, is not effective until the extended effective date.

(6) Unless otherwise agreed by the partners, the applicable provisions of existing law governing allocation of profits and losses (rather than the provisions of Section 503), distributions to a withdrawing partner (rather than the provisions of Section 604), and distribution of assets upon the winding up of a limited partnership (rather than the provisions of Section 804) govern limited partnerships formed before the effective date of this [Act].

Section 1105. [Rules for Cases Not Provided for in This Act]

In any case not provided for in this Act the provisions of the Uniform Partnership Act govern.

Section 1106. [Savings Clause]

The repeal of any statutory provision by this [Act] does not impair, or otherwise affect, the organization or the continued existence of a limited partnership existing at the effective date of this [Act], nor does the repeal of any existing statutory provision by this [Act] impair any contract or affect any right accrued before the effective date of this [Act].

APPENDIX F

UNIFORM COMMERCIAL CODE (1978 TEXT)

Title

An Act

To be known as the Uniform Commercial Code, Relating to Certain Commercial Transactions in or regarding Personal Property and Contracts and other Documents concerning them, including Sales, Commercial Paper, Bank Deposits and Collections, Letters of Credit, Bulk Transfers, Warehouse Receipts, Bills of Lading, other Documents of Title, Investment Securities, and Secured Transactions, including certain Sales of Accounts, Chattel Paper, and Contract Rights; Providing for Public Notice to Third Parties in Certain Circumstances; Regulating Procedure, Evidence and Damages in Certain Court Actions Involving such Transactions, Contracts or Documents; to Make Uniform the Law with Respect Thereto; and Repealing Inconsistent Legislation.

Article 1 General Provisions

Part 1 Short Title, Construction, Application and Subject Matter of the Act

Section 1–101. Short Title

This Act shall be known and may be cited as Uniform Commercial Code.

Section 1–102. Purposes; Rules of Construction; Variation by Agreement

(1) This Act shall be literally construed and applied to promote its underlying purposes and policies.

(2) Underlying purposes and policies of this Act are

- (a) to simplify, clarify and modernize the law governing commercial transactions;
- (b) to permit the continued expansion of commercial practices through custom, usage and agreement of the parties;
- (c) to make uniform the law among the various jurisdictions.

(3) The effect of provisions of this Act may be varied by agreement, except as otherwise provided in this Act and except that the obligations of good faith, diligence, reasonableness and care prescribed by this Act may not be disclaimed by agreement but the parties may by agreement determine the standards by which the performance of such obligations is to be measured if such standards are not manifestly unreasonable.

(4) The presence in certain provisions of this Act of the word "unless otherwise agreed" or words of similar import does not imply that the effect of other provisions may not be varied by agreement under subsection (3).

(5) In this Act unless the context otherwise requires

- (a) words in the singular number include the plural, and in the plural include the singular;
- (b) words of the masculine gender include the feminine and the neuter, and when the sense so indicates words of the neuter gender may refer to any gender.

Section 1–103. Supplementary General Principles of Law Applicable

Unless displaced by the particular provisions of this Act, the principles of law and equity, including the law merchant and the law relative to capacity to contract, principal and agent, estoppel, fraud, misrepresentation, duress, coercion, mistake, bankruptcy, or other validating or invalidating cause shall supplement its provisions.

Section 1–104. Construction Against Implicit Repeal

This Act being a general act intended as a unified coverage of its subject matter, no part of it shall be deemed to be impliedly repealed by subsequent legislation if such construction can reasonably be avoided.

Section 1–105. Territorial Application of the Act; Parties' Power to Choose Applicable Law

(1) Except as provided hereafter in this section, when a transaction bears a reasonable relation to this state and also to another state or nation the parties may agree that the law either of this state or of such other state or nation shall govern their rights and duties. Failing such agreement this Act applies to transactions bearing an appropriate relation to this state.

(2) Where one of the following provisions of this Act specifies the applicable law, that provision governs and a contrary agreement is effective only to the extent permitted by the law (including the conflict of laws rules) so specified:

Rights of creditors against sold goods. Section 2–402.

Applicability of the Article on Leases. Sections 2A–105 and 2A–106.

Applicability of the Article on Bank Deposits and Collections. Section 4–102.

Bulk transfers subject to the Article on Bulk Transfers. Section 6–102.

Applicability of the Article on Investment Securities. Section 8–106.

Perfection provisions of the Article on Secured Transactions. Section 9–103.

Section 1–106. Remedies to Be Liberally Administered

(1) The remedies provided by this Act shall be liberally administered to the end that the aggrieved party may be put in as good a position as if the

other party had fully performed but neither consequential or special nor penal damages may be had except as specifically provided in this Act or by other rule of law.

(2) Any right or obligation declared by this Act is enforceable by action unless the provision declaring it specifies a different and limited effect.

Section 1–107. Waiver or Renunciation of Claim or Right After Breach

Any claim or right arising out of an alleged breach can be discharged in whole or in part without consideration by a written waiver or renunciation signed and delivered by the aggrieved party.

Section 1–108. Severability

If any provision or clause of this Act or application thereof to any person or circumstances is held invalid, such invalidity shall not affect other provisions or applications of the Act which can be given effect without the invalid provision or application, and to this end the provisions of this Act are declared to be severable.

Section 1–109. Section Captions

Section captions are parts of this Act.

Part 2 General Definitions and Principles of Interpretation

Section 1–201. General Definitions

Subject to additional definitions contained in the subsequent Articles of this Act which are applicable to specific Articles or Parts thereof, and unless the context otherwise requires, in this Act:

(1) "Action" in the sense of a judicial proceeding includes recoupment, counterclaim, set-off, suit in equity and any other proceedings in which rights are determined.

(2) "Aggrieved party" means a party entitled to resort to a remedy.

(3) "Agreement" means the bargain of the parties in fact as found in their language or by implication from other circumstances including course of dealing or usage of trade or course of performance as provided in this Act (Sections 1–205 and 2–208). Whether an agreement has legal consequences is determined by the provisions of this Act, if applicable; otherwise by the law of contracts (Section 1–103). (Compare "Contract".)

(4) "Bank" means any person engaged in the business of banking.

(5) "Bearer" means the person in possession of an instrument, document of title, or certificated security payable to bearer or indorsed in blank.

(6) "Bill of lading" means a document evidencing the receipt of goods for shipment issued by a person engaged in the business of transporting or forwarding goods, and includes an airbill. "Airbill" means a document serving for air transportation as a bill of lading does for marine or rail transportation, and includes an air consignment note or air waybill.

(7) "Branch" includes a separately incorporated foreign branch of a bank.

(8) "Burden of establishing" a fact means the burden of persuading the triers of fact that the existence of the fact is more probable than its non-existence.

(9) "Buyer in ordinary course of business" means a person who in good faith and without knowledge that the sale to him is in violation of the ownership rights or security interest of a third party in the goods buys in ordinary course from a person in the business of selling goods buys of that kind but does not include a pawnbroker. All persons who sell minerals or the like (including oil and gas) at wellhead or minehead shall be deemed to be persons in the business of selling goods of that kind. "Buying" may be for cash or by exchange of other property or on secured or unsecured credit and includes receiving goods or documents of title under a pre-existing contract for sale but does not include a transfer in bulk or as security for or in total or partial satisfaction of a money debt.

(10) "Conspicuous": A term or clause is conspicuous when it is so written that a reasonable person against whom it is to operate ought to have noticed it. A printed heading in capitals (as NON-NEGOTIABLE BILL OF LADING) is conspicuous. Language in the body of a form is "conspicuous" if it is in larger or other contrasting type or color. But in a telegram any stated term is "conspicuous." Whether a term or clause is "conspicuous" or not is for decision by the court.

(11) "Contract" means the total legal obligation which results from the parties' agreement as affected by this Act and any other applicable rules of law. (Compare "Agreement.")

(12) "Creditor" includes a general creditor, a secured creditor, a lien creditor and any representative of creditors, including an assignee for the benefit of creditors, a trustee in bankruptcy, a receiver in equity and an executor or administrator of an insolvent debtor's or assignor's estate.

(13) "Defendant" includes a person in the position of defendant in a cross-action or counterclaim.

(14) "Delivery" with respect to instruments, documents of title, chattel paper, or certificated securities means voluntary transfer of possession.

(15) "Document of title" includes bill of lading, dock warrant, dock receipt, warehouse receipt or order for the delivery of goods, and also any other document which in the regular course of business or financing is treated as adequately evidencing that the person in possession of it is entitled to receive, hold and dispose of the document and the goods it covers. To be a document of title, a document must purport to be issued by or addressed to a bailee and purport to cover goods in the bailee's possession which are either identified or are fungible portions of an identified mass.

(16) "Fault" means wrongful act, omission or breach.

(17) "Fungible" with respect to goods or securities means goods or securities of which any unit is, by nature or usage of trade, the equivalent of any other like unit. Goods which are not fungible shall be deemed fungible for the purposes of this Act to the extent that under a particular agreement or document unlike units are treated as equivalents.

(18) "Genuine" means free of forgery or counterfeiting.

(19) "Good faith" means honesty in fact in the conduct or transaction concerned.

(20) "Holder" means a person who is in possession of a document of title or an instrument or a certificated investment security drawn, issued, or indorsed to him or his order or to bearer or in blank.

(21) To "honor" is to pay or to accept and pay, or where a credit so engages to purchase or discount a draft complying with the terms of the credit.

(22) "Insolvency proceedings" includes any assignment for the benefit of creditors or other proceedings intended to liquidate or rehabilitate the estate of the person involved.

(23) A person is "insolvent" who either has ceased to pay his debts in the ordinary course of business or cannot pay his debts as they become due or is insolvent within the meaning of the federal bankruptcy law.

(24) "Money" means a medium of exchange authorized or adopted by a domestic or foreign government as a part of its currency.

(25) A person has "notice" of a fact when

(a) he has actual knowledge of it; or

(b) he has received a notice or notification of it; or

(c) from all the facts and circumstances known to him at the time in question he has reason to know that it exists.

A person "knows" or has "knowledge" of a fact when he has actual knowledge of it. "Discover" or "learn" or a word or phrase of similar import refers to knowledge rather than to reason to know. The time and circumstances under which a notice or notification may cease to be effective are not determined by this Act.

(26) A person "notifies" or "gives" a notice or notification to another by taking such steps as may be reasonably required to inform the other in ordinary course whether or not such other actually comes to know of it. A person "receives" a notice or notification when

(a) it comes to his attention; or

(b) it is duly delivered at the place of business through which the contract was made or at any other place held out by him as the place for receipt of such communications.

(27) Notice, knowledge or a notice or notification received by an organization is effective for a particular transaction from the time when it is brought to the attention of the individual conducting that transaction, and in any event from the time when it would have been brought to his attention if the organization had exercised due diligence. An organization exercises due diligence if it maintains reasonable routines for communicating significant information to the person conducting the transaction and there is reasonable compliance with the routines. Due diligence does not require an individual acting for the organization to communicate information unless such communication is part of his regular duties or unless he has reason to know of the transaction and that the transaction would be materially affected by the information.

(28) "Organization" includes a corporation, government or governmental subdivision or agency, business trust, estate, trust, partnership or association, two or more persons having a joint or common interest, or any other legal or commercial entity.

(29) "Party," as distinct from "third party," means a person who has engaged in a transaction or made an agreement within this Act.

(30) "Person" includes an individual or an organization (See Section 1–102).

(31) "Presumption" or "presumed" means that the trier of fact must find the existence of the fact presumed unless and until evidence is introduced which would support a finding of its non-existence.

(32) "Purchase" includes taking by sale, discount, negotiation, mortgage, pledge, lien, issue or re-issue, gift or any other voluntary transaction creating an interest in property.

(33) "Purchaser" means a person who takes by purchase.

(34) "Remedy" means any remedial right to which an aggrieved party is entitled with or without resort to a tribunal.

(35) "Representative" includes an agent, an officer of a corporation or association, and a trustee, executor or administrator of an estate, or any other person empowered to act for another.

(36) "Rights" includes remedies.

(37) "Security interest" means an interest in personal property or fixtures which secures payment or performance of an obligation. The retention or reservation of title by a seller of goods notwithstanding shipment or delivery to the buyer (Section 2–401) is limited in effect to a reservation of a "security interest". The term also includes any interest of a buyer of accounts or chattel paper which is subject to Article 9. The special property interest of a buyer of goods on identification of those goods to a contract for sale under Section 2–401 is not a "security interest", but a buyer may also acquire a "security interest" by complying with Article 9. Unless a consignment is intended as security, reservation of title thereunder is not a "security interest", but a consignment in any event is subject to the provisions on consignment sales (Section 2–326).

Whether a transaction creates a lease or security interest is determined by the facts of each case; however, a transaction creates a security interest if the consideration the lessee is to pay the lessor for the right to possession and use of the goods is an obligation for the term of the lease not subject to termination by the lessee, and

(a) the original term of the lease is equal to or greater than the remaining economic life of the goods,

(b) the lessee is bound to renew the lease for the remaining economic life of the goods or is bound to become the owner of the goods,

(c) the lessee has an option to renew the lease for the remaining economic life of the goods for no additional consideration or nominal additional consideration upon compliance with the lease agreement, or

(d) the lessee has an option to become the owner of the goods for no additional consideration or nominal additional consideration upon compliance with the lease agreement.

A transaction does not create a security interest merely because it provides that

(a) the present value of the consideration the lessee is obligated to pay the lessor for the right to possession and use of the goods is substantially equal to or is greater than the fair market value of the goods at the time the lease is entered into,

(b) the lessee assumes risk of loss of the goods, or agrees to pay taxes, insurance, filing, recording, or registration fees, or service or maintenance costs with respect to the goods,

(c) the lessee has an option to renew the lease or to become the owner of the goods,

(d) the lessee has an option to renew the lease for a fixed rent that is equal to or greater than the reasonably predictable fair market rent for the use of the goods for the term of the renewal at the time the option is to be performed, or

(e) the lessee has an option to become the owner of the goods for a fixed price that is equal to or greater than the reasonably predictable fair market value of the goods at the time the option is to be performed.

For purposes of this subsection (37):

(x) Additional consideration is not nominal if (i) when the option to renew the lease is granted to the lessee the rent is stated to be the fair market rent for the use of the goods for the term of the renewal determined at the time the option is to be performed, or (ii) when the option to become the owner of the goods is granted to the lessee the price is stated to be the fair market value of the goods determined at the time the option is to be performed. Additional consideration is nominal if it is less than the lessee's reasonably predictable cost of performing under the lease agreement if the option is not exercised;

(y) "Reasonably predictable" and "remaining economic life of the goods" are to be determined with reference to the facts and circumstances at the time the transaction is entered into; and

(z) "Present value" means the amount as of a date certain of one or more sums payable in the future, discounted to the date certain. The discount is determined by the interest rate specified by the parties if the rate is not manifestly unreasonable at the time the transaction is entered into; otherwise, the discount is determined by a commercially reasonable rate that takes into account the facts and circumstances of each case at the time the transaction was entered into.

(38) "Send" in connection with any writing or notice means to deposit in the mail or deliver for transmission by any other usual means of communication with postage or cost of transmission provided for and properly addressed and in the case of an instrument to an address specified thereon or otherwise agreed, or if there be none to any address reasonable under the circumstances. The receipt of any writing or notice within the time at which it would have arrived if properly sent has the effect of a proper sending.

(39) "Signed" includes any symbol executed or adopted by a party with present intention to authenticate a writing.

(40) "Surety" includes guarantor.

(41) "Telegram" includes a message transmitted by radio, teletype, cable, any mechanical method of transmission, or the like.

(42) "Term" means that portion of an agreement which relates to a particular matter.

(43) "Unauthorized" signature or indorsement means one made without actual, implied or apparent authority and includes a forgery.

(44) "Value." Except as otherwise provided with respect to negotiable instruments and bank collections (Sections 3–303, 4–208 and 4–209) a person gives "value" for rights if he acquires them

(a) in return for a binding commitment to extend credit or for the extension of immediately available credit whether or not drawn upon and whether or not a chargeback is provided for in the event of difficulties in collection; or

(b) as security for or in total or partial satisfaction of a preexisting claim; or

(c) by accepting delivery pursuant to a pre-existing contract for purchase; or

(d) generally, in return for any consideration sufficient to support a simple contract.

(45) "Warehouse receipt" means a receipt issued by a person engaged in the business of storing goods for hire.

(46) "Written" or "writing" includes printing, typewriting or any other intentional reduction to tangible form.

Section 1–202. Prima Facie Evidence by Third Party Documents

A document in due form purporting to be a bill of lading, policy or certificate of insurance, official weigher's or inspector's certificate, consular invoice, or any other document authorized or required by the contract to be issued by a third party shall be prima facie evidence of its own authenticity and genuineness and of the facts stated in the document by the third party.

Section 1–203. Obligation of Good Faith

Every contract or duty within this Act imposes an obligation of good faith in its performance or enforcement.

Section 1–204. Time; Reasonable Time; "Seasonably"

(1) Whenever this Act requires any action to be taken within a reasonable time, any time which is not manifestly unreasonable may be fixed by agreement.

(2) What is a reasonable time for taking any action depends on the nature, purpose and circumstances of such action.

(3) An action is taken "seasonably" when it is taken at or within the time agreed or if no time is agreed at or within a reasonable time.

Section 1–205. Course of Dealing and Usage of Trade

(1) A course of dealing is a sequence of previous conduct between the parties to a particular transaction which is fairly to be regarded as establishing a common basis of understanding for interpreting their expressions and other conduct.

(2) A usage of trade is any practice or method of dealing having such regularity of observance in a place, vocation or trade as to justify an expectation that it will be observed with respect to the transaction in question. The existence and scope of such a usage are to be proved as facts. If it is established that such a usage is embodied in a written trade code or similar writing the interpretation of the writing is for the court.

(3) A course of dealing between parties and any usage of trade in the vocation or trade in which they are engaged or of which they are or should be aware give particular meaning to and supplement or qualify terms of an agreement.

(4) The express terms of an agreement and an applicable course of dealing or usage of trade shall be construed wherever reasonable as consistent with each other; but when such construction is unreasonable express terms control both course of dealing and usage of trade and course of dealing controls usage of trade.

(5) An applicable usage of trade in the place where any part of performance is to occur shall be used in interpreting the agreement as to that part of the performance.

(6) Evidence of a relevant usage of trade offered by one party is not admissible unless and until he has given the other party such notice as the court finds sufficient to prevent unfair surprise to the latter.

Section 1–206. Statute of Frauds for Kinds of Personal Property Not Otherwise Covered

(1) Except in the cases described in subsection (2) of this section a contract for the sale of personal property is not enforceable by way of action or defense beyond five thousand dollars in amount or value of remedy unless there is some writing which indicates that a contract for sale has been made between the parties at a defined or stated price, reasonably identifies the subject matter, and is signed by the party against whom enforcement is sought or by his authorized agent.

(2) Subsection (1) of this section does not apply to contracts for the sale of goods (Section 2–201) nor of securities (Section 8–319) nor to security agreements (Section 9–203).

Section 1–207. Performance or Acceptance Under Reservation of Rights

A party who with explicit reservation of rights performs or promises performance or assents to performance in a manner demanded or offered by the other party does not thereby prejudice the rights reserved. Such words as "without prejudice," "under protest" or the like are sufficient.

Section 1–208. Option to Accelerate at Will

A term providing that one party or his successor in interest may accelerate payment or performance or require collateral or additional collateral "at will" or "when he deems himself insecure" or in words of similar import shall be construed to mean that he shall have power to do so only if he in good faith believes that the prospect of payment or performance is impaired. The burden of establishing lack of good faith is on the party against whom the power has been exercised.

Section 1–209. Subordinated Obligations

An obligation may be issued as subordinated to payment of another obligation of the person obligated, or a creditor may subordinate his right to payment of an obligation by agreement with either the person obligated or another creditor of the person obligated. Such a subordination does not create a security interest as against either the common debtor or a subordinated creditor. This section shall be construed as declaring the law as it existed prior to the enactment of this section and not as modifying it.

Note: *This section is proposed as an optional provision to make it clear that a subordination agreement does not create a security interest unless so intended.*

Article 2 Sales

Part 1 Short Title, General Construction and Subject Matter

Section 2–101. Short Title

This Article shall be known and may be cited as Uniform Commercial Code—Sales.

Section 2–102. Scope; Certain Security and Other Transactions Excluded From This Article

Unless the context otherwise requires, this Article applies to transactions in goods; it does not apply to any transaction which although in the form of an unconditional contract to sell or present sale is intended to operate only as a security transaction nor does this Article impair or repeal any statute regulating sales to consumers, farmers or other specified classes of buyers.

Section 2–103. Definitions and Index of Definitions

(1) In this Article unless the context otherwise requires

(a) "Buyer" means a person who buys or contracts to buy goods.

(b) "Good faith" in the case of a merchant means honesty in fact and the observance of reasonable commercial standards of fair dealing in the trade.

(c) "Receipt" of goods means taking physical possession of them.

(d) "Seller" means a person who sells or contracts to sell goods.

(2) Other definitions applying to this Article or to specified Parts thereof, and the sections in which they appear are:

"Acceptance." Section 2–606.

"Banker's credit." Section 2–325.

"Between merchants." Section 2–104.

"Cancellation." Section 2–106(4).

"Commercial unit." Section 2–105.

"Confirmed credit." Section 2–325.

"Conforming to contract." Section 2–106.

"Contract for sale." Section 2–106.

"Cover." Section 2–712.

"Entrusting." Section 2–403.

"Financing agency." Section 2–104.

"Future goods." Section 2–105.

"Goods." Section 2–105.

"Identification." Section 2–501.

"Installment contract." Section 2–612.

"Letter of Credit." Section 2–325.

"Lot." Section 2–105.

"Merchant." Section 2–104.

"Overseas." Section 2–323.

"Person in position of seller." Section 2–707.

"Present sale." Section 2–106.

"Sale." Section 2–106.

"Sale on approval." Section 2–326.

"Sale or return." Section 2–326.

Termination." Section 2–106.

(3) The following definitions in other Articles apply to this Article:

"Check." Section 3–104.

"Consignee." Section 7–102.

"Consignor." Section 7–102.

"Consumer goods." Section 9–109.

"Dishonor." Section 3–507.

"Draft." Section 3–104.

(4) In addition Article 1 contains general definitions and principles of construction and interpretation applicable throughout this Article.

Section 2–104. Definitions: "Merchant"; "Between Merchants"; "Financing Agency"

(1) "Merchant" means a person who deals in goods of the kind or otherwise by his occupation holds himself out as having knowledge or skill peculiar to the practices or goods involved in the transaction or to whom such knowledge or skill may be attributed by his employment of an agent or broker or other intermediary who by his occupation holds himself out as having such knowledge or skill.

(2) "Financing agency" means a bank, finance company or other person who in the ordinary course of business makes advances against goods or documents of title or who by arrangement with either the seller or the buyer intervenes in ordinary course to make or collect payment due or claimed under the contract for sale, as by purchasing or paying the seller's

draft or making advances against it or by merely taking it for collection whether or not documents of title accompany the draft. "Financing agency" includes also a bank or other person who similarly intervenes between persons who are in the position of seller and buyer in respect to the goods (Section 2–707).

(3) "Between merchants" means in any transaction with respect to which both parties are chargeable with the knowledge or skill of merchants.

Section 2–105. Definitions: Transferability; "Goods"; "Future" Goods; "Lot"; "Commercial Unit"

(1) "Goods" means all things (including specially manufactured goods) which are movable at the time of identification to the contract for sale other than the money in which the price is to be paid, investment securities (Article 8) and things in action. "Goods" also includes the unborn young of animals and growing crops and other identified things attached to realty as described in the section on goods to be severed from realty (Section 2–107).

(2) Goods must be both existing and identified before any interest in them can pass. Goods which are not both existing and identified are "future" goods. A purported present sale of future goods or of any interest therein operates as a contract to sell.

(3) There may be a sale of a part interest in existing identified goods.

(4) An undivided share in an identified bulk of fungible goods is sufficiently identified to be sold although the quantity of the bulk is not determined. Any agreed proportion of such a bulk or any quantity thereof agreed upon by number, weight or other measure may to the extent of the seller's interest in the bulk be sold to the buyer who then becomes an owner in common.

(5) "Lot" means a parcel or a single article which is the subject matter of a separate sale or delivery, whether or not it is sufficient to perform the contract.

(6) "Commercial unit" means such a unit of goods as by commercial usage is a single whole for purposes of sale and division of which materially impairs its character or value on the market or in use. A commercial unit may be a single article (as a machine) or a set or articles (as a suite of furniture or an assortment of sizes) or a quantity (as a bale, gross, or carload) or any other unit treated in use or in the relevant market as a single whole.

Section 2–106. Definitions: "Contract"; "Agreement"; "Contract for Sale"; "Sale"; "Present Sale" "Conforming" to Contract; "Termination"; "Cancellation"

(1) In this Article unless the context otherwise requires "contract" and "agreement" are limited to those relating to the present or future sale of goods. "Contract for sale" includes both a present sale of goods and a contract to sell goods at a future time. A "sale" consists in the passing of title from the seller to the buyer for a price (Section 2–401). A "present sale" means a sale which is accomplished by the making of the contract.

(2) Goods or conduct including any part of a performance are "conforming" or conform to the contract when they are in accordance with the obligations under the contract.

(3) "Termination" occurs when either party pursuant to a power created by agreement or law puts an end to the contract otherwise than for its breach. On "termination" all obligations which are still executory on both sides are discharged but any right based on prior breach or performance survives.

(4) "Cancellation" occurs when either party puts an end to the contract for breach by the other and its effect is the same as that of "termination" except that the cancelling party also retains any remedy for breach of the whole contract or any unperformed balance.

Section 2–107. Goods to Be Severed From Realty: Recording

(1) A contract for the sale of minerals or the like (including oil and gas) or a structure or its materials to be removed from realty is a contract for the sale of goods within this Article if they are to be severed by the seller but until severance a purported present sale thereof which is not effective as a transfer of an interest in land is effective only as a contract to sell.

(2) A contract for the sale apart from the land of growing crops or other things attached to realty and capable of severance without material harm thereto but not described in subsection (1) or of timber to be cut is a contract for the sale of goods within this Article whether the subject matter is to be severed by the buyer or by the seller even though it forms part of the realty at the time of contracting, and the parties can by identification effect a present sale before severance.

(3) The provisions of this section are subject to any third party rights provided by the law relating to realty records, and the contract for sale may be executed and recorded as a document transferring an interest in land and shall then constitute notice to third parties of the buyer's rights under the contract for sale.

Part 2 Form, Formation and Readjustment of Contract

Section 2–201. Formal Requirements; Statute of Frauds

(1) Except as otherwise provided in this section a contract for the sale of goods for the price of $500 or more is not enforceable by way of action or defense unless there is some writing sufficient to indicate that a contract for sale has been made between the parties and signed by the party against whom enforcement is sought or by his authorized agent or broker. A writing is not insufficient because it omits or incorrectly states a term agreed upon but the contract is not enforceable under this paragraph beyond the quantity of goods shown in such writing.

(2) Between merchants if within a reasonable time a writing in confirmation of the contract and sufficient against the sender is received and the party receiving it has reason to know its contents, it satisfies the requirements of subsection (1) against such party unless written notice of objection to its contents is given within 10 days after it is received.

(3) A contract which does not satisfy the requirements of subsection (1) but which is valid in other respects is enforceable

(a) if the goods are to be specially manufactured for the buyer and are not suitable for sale to others in the ordinary course of the seller's business and the seller, before notice of repudiation is received and under circumstances which reasonably indicate that the goods are for the buyer, has made either a substantial beginning of their manufacture or commitments for their procurement; or

(b) if the party against whom enforcement is sought admits in his pleading, testimony or otherwise in court that a contract for sale was made, but the contract is not enforceable under this provision beyond the quantity of goods admitted; or

(c) with respect to goods for which payment has been made and accepted or which have been received and accepted (Section 2–606).

Section 2–202. Final Written Expression: Parol or Extrinsic Evidence

Terms with respect to which the confirmatory memoranda of the parties agree or which are otherwise set forth in a writing intended by the parties as a final expression of their agreement with respect to such terms as are included therein may not be contradicted by evidence of any prior agreement or of a contemporaneous oral agreement but may be explained or supplemented

(a) by course of dealing or usage of trade (Section 1–205) or by course of performance (Section 2–208); and

(b) by evidence of consistent additional terms unless the court finds the writing to have been intended also as a complete and exclusive statement of the terms of the agreement.

Section 2–203. Seals Inoperative

The affixing of a seal to a writing evidencing a contract for sale or an offer to buy or sell goods does not constitute the writing a sealed instrument and the law with respect to sealed instruments does not apply to such a contract or offer.

Section 2–204. Formation in General

(1) A contract for sale of goods may be made in any manner sufficient to show agreement, including conduct by both parties which recognizes the existence of such a contract.

(2) An agreement sufficient to constitute a contract for sale may be found even though the moment of its making is undetermined.

(3) Even though one or more terms are left open a contract for sale does not fail for indefiniteness if the parties have intended to make a contract and there is a reasonably certain basis for giving an appropriate remedy.

Section 2–205. Firm Offers

An offer by a merchant to buy or sell goods in a signed writing which by its terms give assurance that it will be held open is not revocable, for lack of consideration, during the time stated or if no time is stated for a reasonable time, but in no event may such period of irrevocability exceed three months; but any such term of assurance on a form supplied by the offeree must be separately signed by the offeror.

Section 2–206. Offer and Acceptance in Formation of Contract

(1) Unless otherwise unambiguously indicated by the language or circumstances

(a) an offer to make a contract shall be construed as inviting acceptance in any manner and by any medium reasonable in the circumstances;

(b) an order or other offer to buy goods for prompt or current shipment shall be construed as inviting acceptance either by a prompt promise to ship or by the prompt or current shipment of conforming or non-conforming goods, but such a shipment of non-conforming goods does not constitute an acceptance if the seller seasonably notifies the buyer that the shipment is offered only as an accommodation to the buyer.

(2) Where the beginning of a requested performance is a reasonable mode of acceptance an offeror who is not notified of acceptance within a reasonable time may treat the offer as having lapsed before acceptance.

Section 2–207. Additional Terms in Acceptance or Confirmation

(1) A definite and seasonable expression of acceptance or a written confirmation which is sent within a reasonable time operates as an acceptance even though it states terms additional to or different from those offered or agreed upon, unless acceptance is expressly made conditional on assent to the additional or different terms.

(2) The additional terms are to be construed as proposals for addition to the contract. Between merchants such terms become part of the contract unless:

(a) the offer expressly limits acceptance to the terms of the offer;

(b) they materially alter it; or

(c) notification of objection to them has already been given or is given within a reasonable time after notice of them is received.

(3) Conduct by both parties which recognizes the existence of a contract is sufficient to establish a contract for sale although the writings of the parties do not otherwise establish a contract. In such case the terms of the particular contract consist of those terms on which the writings of the parties agree, together with any supplementary terms incorporated under any other provisions of this Act.

Section 2–208. Course of Performance or Practical Construction

(1) Where the contract for sale involves repeated occasions for performance by either party with knowledge of the nature of the performance and opportunity for objection to it by the other, any course of performance accepted or acquiesced in without objection shall be relevant to determine the meaning of the agreement.

(2) The express terms of the agreement and any such course of performance, as well as any course of dealing and usage of trade, shall be construed whenever reasonable as consistent with each other; but when such construction is unreasonable, express terms shall control course of performance and course of performance shall control both course of dealing and usage of trade (Section 1–205).

(3) Subject to the provisions of the next section on modification and waiver, such course of performance shall be relevant to show a waiver or modification of any term inconsistent with such course of performance.

Section 2–209. Modification, Rescission and Waiver

(1) An agreement modifying a contract within this Article needs no consideration to be binding.

(2) A signed agreement which excludes modification or rescission except by a signed writing cannot be otherwise modified or rescinded, but except as between merchants such a requirement on a form supplied by the merchant must be separately signed by the other party.

(3) The requirements of the statute of frauds section of this Article (Section 2–201) must be satisfied if the contract as modified is within its provisions.

(4) Although an attempt at modification or rescission does not satisfy the requirements of subsection (2) or (3) it can operate as a waiver.

(5) A party who has made a waiver affecting an executory portion of the contract may retract the waiver by reasonable notification received by the other party that strict performance will be required of any term waived, unless the retraction would be unjust in view of a material change of position in reliance on the waiver.

Section 2–210. Delegation of Performance: Assignment of Rights

(1) A party may perform his duty through a delegate unless otherwise agreed or unless the other party has a substantial interest in having his original promisor perform or control the acts required by the contract. No delegation of performance relieves the party delegating of any duty to perform or any liability for breach.

(2) Unless otherwise agreed all rights of either seller or buyer can be assigned except where the assignment would materially change the duty of the other party, or increase materially the burden or risk imposed on him by his contract, or impair materially his chance of obtaining return performance. A right to damages for breach of the whole contract or a right arising out of the assignor's due performance of his entire obligation can be assigned despite agreement otherwise.

(3) Unless the circumstances indicate the contrary a prohibition of assignment of "the contract" is to be construed as barring only the delegation to the assignee of the assignor's performance.

(4) An assignment of "the contract" or of "all my rights under the contract" or an assignment in similar general terms is an assignment of rights and unless the language or the circumstances (as in an assignment for security) indicate the contrary, it is a delegation of performance of the duties of the assignor and its acceptance by the assignee constitutes a promise by him to perform those duties. This promise is enforceable by either the assignor or the other party to the original contract.

(5) The other party may treat any assignment which delegates performance as creating reasonable grounds for insecurity and may without prejudice to his rights against the assignor demand assurances from the assignee (Section 2–609).

Part 3 General Obligation and Construction of Contract

Section 2–301. General Obligations of Parties

The obligation of the seller is to transfer and deliver and that of the buyer is to accept and pay in accordance with the contract.

Section 2–302. Unconscionable Contract or Clause

(1) If the court as a matter of law finds the contract or any clause of the contract to have been unconscionable at the time it was made the court may refuse to enforce the contract, or it may enforce the remainder of the contract without the unconscionable clause, or it may so limit the application of any unconscionable clause as to avoid any unconscionable result.

(2) When it is claimed or appears to the court that the contract or any clause thereof may be unconscionable the parties shall be afforded a reasonable opportunity to present evidence as to its commercial setting, purpose and effect to aid the court in making the determination.

Section 2–303. Allocation or Division of Risks

Where this Article allocates a risk or a burden as between the parties "unless otherwise agreed," the agreement may not only shift the allocation but may also divide the risk or burden.

Section 2–304. Price Payable in Money, Goods, Realty, or Otherwise

(1) The price can be made payable in money or otherwise. If it is payable in whole or in part in goods each party is a seller of the goods which he is to transfer.

(2) Even though all or part of the price is payable in an interest in realty the transfer of the goods and the seller's obligations with reference to them are subject to this Article, but not the transfer of the interest in realty or the transferor's obligations in connection therewith.

Section 2–305. Open Price Term

(1) The parties if they so intend can conclude a contract for sale even though the price is not settled. In such a case the price is a reasonable price at the time for delivery if

(a) nothing is said as to price; or

(b) the price is left to be agreed by the parties and they fail to agree; or

(c) the price is to be fixed in terms of some agreed market or other standard as set or recorded by a third person or agency and it is not so set or recorded.

(2) A price to be fixed by the seller or by the buyer means a price for him to fix in good faith.

(3) When a price left to be fixed otherwise than by agreement of the parties fails to be fixed through fault of one party the other may at his option treat the contract as cancelled or himself fix a reasonable price.

(4) Where, however, the parties intend not to be bound unless the price be fixed or agreed and it is not fixed or agreed there is no contract. In such a case the buyer must return any goods already received or if unable so to do must pay their reasonable value at the time of delivery and the seller must return any portion of the price paid on account.

Section 2—306. Output, Requirements and Exclusive Dealings

(1) A term which measures the quantity by the output of the seller or the requirements of the buyer means such actual output or requirements as may occur in good faith, except that no quantity unreasonably disproportionate to any stated estimate or in the absence of a stated estimate to any normal or otherwise comparable prior output or requirements may be tendered or demanded.

(2) A lawful agreement by either the seller or the buyer for exclusive dealing in the kind of goods concerned imposes unless otherwise agreed an obligation by the seller to use best efforts to supply the goods and by the buyer to use best efforts to promote their sale.

Section 2–307. Delivery in Single Lot or Several Lots

Unless otherwise agreed all goods called for by a contract for sale must be tendered in a single delivery and payment is due only on such tender but where the circumstances give either party the right to make or demand delivery in lots the price if it can be apportioned may be demanded for each lot.

Section 2–308. Absence of Specified Place for Delivery

Unless otherwise agreed

(a) the place for delivery of goods is the seller's place of business or if he has none his residence; but

(b) in a contract for sale of identified goods which to the knowledge of the parties at the time of contracting are in some other place, that place is the place for their delivery; and

(c) documents of title may be delivered through customary banking channels.

Section 2–309. Absence of Specific Time Provisions; Notice of Termination

(1) The time for shipment or delivery or any other action under a contract if not provided in this Article or agreed upon shall be a reasonable time.

(2) Where the contract provides for successive performances but is indefinite in duration it is valid for a reasonable time but unless otherwise agreed may be terminated at any time by either party.

(3) Termination of a contract by one party except on the happening of an agreed event requires that reasonable notification be received by the other party and an agreement dispensing with notification is invalid if its operation would be unconscionable.

Section 2–310. Open Time for Payment or Running of Credit; Authority to Ship Under Reservation

Unless otherwise agreed

(a) payment is due at the time and place at which the buyer is to receive the goods even though the place of shipment is the place of delivery; and

(b) if the seller is authorized to send the goods he may ship them under reservation, and may tender the documents of title, but the buyer may inspect the goods after their arrival before payment is due unless such inspection is inconsistent with the terms of the contract (Section 2–513); and

(c) if delivery is authorized and made by way of documents of title otherwise than by subsection (b) then payment is due at the time and place at which the buyer is to receive the documents regardless of where the goods are to be received; and

(d) where the seller is required or authorized to ship the goods on credit the credit period runs from the time of shipment but post-dating the invoice or delaying its dispatch will correspondingly delay the starting of the credit period.

Section 2–311. Options and Cooperation Respecting Performance

(1) An agreement for sale which is otherwise sufficiently definite (subsection (3) of Section 2–204) to be a contract is not made invalid by the fact that it leaves particulars of performance to be specified by one of the parties. Any such specification must be made in good faith and within limits set by commercial reasonableness.

(2) Unless otherwise agreed specifications relating to assortment of the goods are at the buyer's option and except as otherwise provided in subsections (1) (c) and (3) of Section 2–319 specifications or arrangements relating to shipment are at the seller's option.

(3) Where such specification would materially affect the other party's performance but is not seasonably made or where one party's cooperation is necessary to the agreed performance of the other but is not seasonably forthcoming, the other party in addition to all other remedies

(a) is excused for any resulting delay in his own performance; and

(b) may also either proceed to perform in any reasonable manner or after the time for a material part of his own performance treat the failure to specify or to cooperate as a breach by failure to deliver or accept the goods.

Section 2–312. Warranty of Title and Against Infringement; Buyer's Obligation Against Infringement

(1) Subject to subsection (2) there is in a contract for sale a warranty by the seller that

(a) the title conveyed shall be good, and its transfer rightful; and

(b) the goods shall be delivered free from any security interest or other lien or encumbrance of which the buyer at the time of contracting has no knowledge.

(2) A warranty under subsection (1) will be excluded or modified only by specific language or by circumstances which give the buyer reason to know that the person selling does not claim title in himself or that he is purporting to sell only such right or title as he or a third person may have.

(3) Unless otherwise agreed a seller who is a merchant regularly dealing in goods of the kind warrants that the goods shall be delivered free of the rightful claim of any third person by way of infringement or the like but a buyer who furnishes specifications to the seller must hold the seller harmless against any such claim which arises out of compliance with the specifications.

Section 2–313. Express Warranties by Affirmation, Promise, Description, Sample

(1) Express warranties by the seller are created as follows:

(a) Any affirmation of fact or promise made by the seller to the buyer which relates to the goods and becomes part of the basis of the bargain creates an express warranty that the goods shall conform to the affirmation or promise.

(b) Any description of the goods which is made part of the basis of the bargain creates an express warranty that the goods shall conform to the description.

(c) Any sample or model which is made part of the basis of the bargain creates an express warranty that the whole of the goods shall conform to the sample or model.

(2) It is not necessary to the creation of an express warranty that the seller use formal words such as "warrant" or "guarantee" or that he have a specific intention to make a warranty, but an affirmation merely of the value of the goods or a statement purporting to be merely the seller's opinion or commendation of the goods does not create a warranty.

Section 2–314. Implied Warranty: Merchantability; Usage of Trade

(1) Unless excluded or modified (Section 2–316), a warranty that the goods shall be merchantable is implied in a contract for their sale if the seller is a merchant with respect to goods of that kind. Under this section the serving for value of food or drink to be consumed either on the premises or elsewhere is a sale.

(2) Goods to be merchantable must be at least such as

(a) pass without objection in the trade under the contract description; and

(b) in the case of fungible goods, are of fair average quality within the description; and

(c) are fit for the ordinary purposes for which such goods are used; and

(d) run, within the variations permitted by the agreement, of even kind, quality and quantity within each unit and among all units involved; and

(e) are adequately contained, packaged, and labeled as the agreement may require; and

(f) conform to the promises or affirmations of fact made on the container or label if any.

(3) Unless excluded or modified (Section 2–316) other implied warranties may arise from course of dealing or usage of trade.

Section 2–315. Implied Warranty: Fitness for Particular Purpose

Where the seller at the time of contracting has reason to know any particular purpose for which the goods are required and that the buyer is relying on the seller's skill or judgment to select or furnish suitable goods, there is unless excluded or modified under the next section an implied warranty that the goods shall be fit for such purpose.

Section 2–316. Exclusion or Modification of Warranties

(1) Words or conduct relevant to the creation of an express warranty and words or conduct tending to negate or limit warranty shall be construed wherever reasonable as consistent with each other; but subject to the provisions of this Article on parol or extrinsic evidence (Section 2–202) negation or limitation is inoperative to the extent that such construction is unreasonable.

(2) Subject to subsection (3), to exclude or modify the implied warranty or merchantability or any part of it the language must mention merchantability and in case of a writing must be conspicuous, and to exclude or modify any implied warranty of fitness the exclusion must be by a writing and conspicuous. Language to exclude all implied warranties of fitness is sufficient if it states, for example, that "There are no warranties which extend beyond the description on the face hereof."

(3) Notwithstanding subsection (2)

(a) unless the circumstances indicate otherwise, all implied warranties are excluded by expressions like "as is," "with all faults" or other languages which in common understanding calls the buyer's attention to the exclusion of warranties and makes plain that there is no implied warranty; and

(b) when the buyer before entering into the contract has examined the goods or the sample or model as fully as he desired or has refused to examine the goods there is no implied warranty with regard to defects which an examination ought in the circumstances to have revealed to him; and

(c) an implied warranty can also be excluded or modified by course of dealing or course of performance or usage of trade.

(4) Remedies for breach of warranty can be limited in accordance with the provisions of this Article on liquidation or limitation of damages and on contractual modification of remedy (Sections 2–718 and 2–719).

Section 2–317. Cumulation and Conflict of Warranties Express or Implied

Warranties whether express or implied shall be construed as consistent with each other and as cumulative, but if such construction is unreasonable the intention of the parties shall determine which warranty is dominant. In ascertaining that intention the following rules apply:

(a) Exact or technical specifications displace an inconsistent sample or model or general language of description.

(b) A sample from an existing bulk displaces inconsistent general language of description.

(c) Express warranties displace inconsistent implied warranties other than an implied warranty of fitness for a particular purpose.

Section 2–318. Third Party Beneficiaries of Warranties Express or Implied

Note: *If this Act is introduced in the Congress of the United States this section should be omitted. (States to select one alternative.)*

Alternative A

A seller's warranty whether express or implied extends to any natural person who is in the family or household of his buyer or who is a guest in his home if it is reasonable to expect that such person may use, consume or be affected by the goods and who is injured in person by breach of the warranty. A seller may not exclude or limit the operation of this section.

Alternative B

A seller's warranty whether express or implied extends to any natural person who may reasonably be expected to use, consume or be affected by the goods and who is injured in person by breach of the warranty. A seller may not exclude or limit the operation of this section.

Alternative C

A seller's warranty whether express or implied extends to any person who may reasonably be expected to use, consume or be affected by the goods and who is injured by breach of the warranty. A seller may not exclude or limit the operation of this section with respect to injury to the person of an individual to whom the warranty extends.

Section 2–319. F.O.B. and F.A.S. Terms

(1) Unless otherwise agreed the term F.O.B. (which means "free on board") at a named place, even though used only in connection with the stated price, is a delivery term under which

(a) when the term is F.O.B. the place of shipment, the seller must at that place ship the goods in the manner provided in this Article (Section 2–504) and bear the expense and risk of putting them into the possession of the carrier; or

(b) when the term is F.O.B. the place of destination, the seller must at his own expense and risk transport the goods to that place and there tender delivery of them in the manner provided in this Article (Section 2–503);

(c) when under either (a) or (b) the term is also F.O.B. vessel, car or other vehicle, the seller must in addition at his own expense and risk load the goods on board. If the term is F.O.B. vessel the buyer must name the vessel and in an appropriate case the seller must comply with the provisions of this Article on the form of bill of lading (Section 2–323).

(2) Unless otherwise agreed the term F.A.S. vessel (which means "free alongside") at a named port, even though used only in connection with the stated price, is a delivery term under which the seller must

(a) at his own expense and risk deliver the goods alongside the vessel in the manner usual in that port or on a dock designated and provided by the buyer; and

(b) obtain and tender a receipt for the goods in exchange for which the carrier is under a duty to issue a bill of lading.

(3) Unless otherwise agreed in any case falling within subsection (1) (a) or (c) or subsection (2) the buyer must seasonably give any needed instructions for making delivery, including when the term is F.A.S. or F.O.B. the loading berth of the vessel and in an appropriate case its name and sailing date. The seller may treat the failure of needed instructions as a failure of cooperation under this Article (Section 2–311). He may also at his option move the goods in any reasonable manner preparatory to delivery or shipment.

(4) Under the term F.O.B. vessel or F.A.S. unless otherwise agreed the buyer must make payment against tender of the required documents and the seller may not tender nor the buyer demand delivery of the goods in substitution for the documents.

Section 2–320. C.I.F. and C. & F. Terms

(1) The term C.I.F. means that the price includes in a lump sum the cost of the goods and the insurance and freight to the named destination. The term C. & F. or C.F. means that the price so includes cost and freight to the named destination.

(2) Unless otherwise agreed and even though used only in connection with the stated price and destination, the term C.I.F. destination or its equivalent requires the seller at his own expense and risk to

(a) put the goods into the possession of a carrier at the port for shipment and obtain a negotiable bill or bills of lading covering the entire transportation to the named destination; and

(b) load the goods and obtain a receipt from the carrier (which may be contained in the bill of lading) showing that the freight has been paid or provided for; and

(c) obtain a policy or certificate of insurance, including any war risk insurance, of a kind and on terms then current at the port of shipment in the usual amount, in the currency of the contract, shown to cover the same goods covered by the bill of lading and providing for payment of loss to the order of the buyer or for the account of whom it may concern; but the seller may add to the price the amount of the premium for any such war risk insurance; and

(d) prepare an invoice of the goods and procure any other documents required to effect shipment or to comply with the contract; and

(e) forward and tender with commercial promptness all the documents in due form and with any indorsement necessary to perfect the buyer's rights.

(3) Unless otherwise agreed the term C. & F. or its equivalent has the same effect and imposes upon the seller the same obligations and risks as a C.I.F. term except the obligation as to insurance.

(4) Under the term C.I.F. or C. & F. unless otherwise agreed the buyer must make payment against tender of the required documents and the seller may not tender nor the buyer demand delivery of the goods in substitution for the documents.

Section 2–321. C.I.F. or C. & F.: "Net Landed Weights"; "Payment on Arrival"; Warranty of Condition on Arrival

Under a contract containing a term C.I.F. or C. & F.

(1) Where the price is based on or is to be adjusted according to "net landed weights," "delivered weights," "out turn" quantity or quality or the like, unless otherwise agreed the seller must reasonably estimate the price. The payment due on tender of the documents called for by the contract is the amount so estimated, but after final adjustment of the price a settlement must be made with commercial promptness.

(2) An agreement described in subsection (1) or any warranty of quality or condition of the goods on arrival places upon the seller the risk of ordinary deterioration, shrinkage and the like in transportation but has no effect on the place or time of identification to the contract for sale or delivery or on the passing of the risk of loss.

(3) Unless otherwise agreed where the contract provides for payment on or after arrival of the goods the seller must before payment allow such preliminary inspection as is feasible; but if the goods are lost delivery of the documents and payment are due when the goods should have arrived.

Section 2–322. Delivery "Ex-Ship"

(1) Unless otherwise agreed a term for delivery of goods "ex- ship" (which means from the carrying vessel) or in equivalent language is not restricted to a particular ship and requires delivery from a ship which has reached a place at the named port of destination where goods of the kind are usually discharged.

(2) Under such a term unless otherwise agreed

(a) the seller must discharge all liens arising out of the carriage and furnish the buyer with a direction which puts the carrier under a duty to deliver the goods; and

(b) the risk of loss does not pass to the buyer until the goods leave the ship's tackle or are otherwise properly unloaded.

Section 2–323. Form of Bill of Lading Required in Overseas Shipment; "Overseas"

(1) Where the contract contemplates overseas shipment and contains a term C.I.F. or C. & F. or F.O.B. vessel, the seller unless otherwise agreed must obtain a negotiable bill of lading stating that the goods have been loaded on board or, in the case of a term C.I.F. or C. & F., received for shipment.

(2) Where in a case within subsection (1) a bill of lading has been issued in a set of parts, unless otherwise agreed if the documents are not to be sent from abroad the buyer may demand tender of the full set; otherwise only one part of the bill of lading need be tendered. Even if the agreement expressly requires a full set

(a) due tender of a single part is acceptable within the provisions of this Article on cure of improper delivery (subsection (1) of Section 2–508); and

(b) even though the full set is demanded, if the documents are sent from abroad the person tendering an incomplete set may nevertheless require payment upon furnishing an indemnity which the buyer in good faith deems adequate.

(3) A shipment by water or by air or a contract contemplating such shipment is "overseas" insofar as by usage of trade or agreement it is subject to the commercial, financing or shipping practices characteristic of international deep water commerce.

Section 2–324. "No Arrival, No Sale" Term

Under a term "no arrival, no sale" or terms of like meaning, unless otherwise agreed,

(a) the seller must properly ship conforming goods and if they arrive by any means he must tender them on arrival but he assumes no obligation that the goods will arrive unless he has caused the non-arrival; and

(b) where without fault of the seller the goods are in part lost or have so deteriorated as no longer to conform to the contract or arrive after the contract time, the buyer may proceed as if there had been casualty to identified goods (Section 2–613).

Section 2–325. "Letter of Credit" Term; "Confirmed Credit"

(1) Failure of the buyer seasonably to furnish an agreed letter of credit is a breach of the contract for sale.

(2) The delivery to seller of a proper letter of credit suspends the buyer's obligation to pay. If the letter of credit is dishonored, the seller may on seasonable notification to the buyer require payment directly from him.

(3) Unless otherwise agreed the term "letter of credit" or "banker's credit" in a contract for sale means an irrevocable credit issued by a financing agency of good repute and, where the shipment is overseas, of good international repute. The term "confirmed credit" means that the credit must also carry the direct obligation of such an agency which does business in the seller's financial market.

Section 2–326. Sale on Approval and Sale or Return; Consignment Sales and Rights of Creditors

(1) Unless otherwise agreed, if delivered goods may be returned by the buyer even though they conform to the contract, the transaction is

(a) a "sale on approval" if the goods are delivered primarily for use, and

(b) a "sale or return" if the goods are delivered primarily for resale.

(2) Except as provided in subsection (3), goods held on approval are not subject to the claims of the buyer's creditors until acceptance; goods held on sale or return are subject to such claims while in the buyer's possession.

(3) Where goods are delivered to a person for sale and such person maintains a place of business at which he deals in goods of the kind involved, under a name other than the name of the person making delivery, then with respect to claims of creditors of the person conducting the business the goods are deemed to be on sale or return. The provisions of this subsection are applicable even though an agreement purports to reserve title to the person making delivery until payment or resale or uses such words as "on consignment" or "on memorandum." However, this subsection is not applicable if the person making delivery

(a) complies with an applicable law providing for a consignor's interest or the like to be evidenced by a sign, or

(b) establishes that the person conducting the business is generally known by his creditors to be substantially engaged in selling the goods of others, or

(c) complies with the filing provisions of the Article on Secured Transactions (Article 9).

(4) Any "or return" term of a contract for sale is to be treated as a separate contract for sale within the statute of frauds section of this Article (Section 2–201) and as contradicting the sale aspect of the contract within the provisions of this Article on parol or extrinsic evidence (Section 2–202).

Section 2–327. Special Incidents of Sale on Approval and Sale or Return

(1) Under a sale on approval unless otherwise agreed

(a) although the goods are identified to the contract the risk of loss and the title do not pass to the buyer until acceptance; and

(b) use of the goods consistent with the purpose of trial is not acceptance but failure seasonably to notify the seller of election to return the goods is acceptance, and if the goods conform to the contract acceptance of any part is acceptance of the whole; and

(c) after due notification of election to return, the return is at the seller's risk and expense but a merchant buyer must follow any reasonable instructions.

(2) Under a sale or return unless otherwise agreed

(a) the option to return extends to the whole or any commercial unit of the goods while in substantially their original condition, but must be exercised seasonably; and

(b) the return is at the buyer's risk and expense.

Section 2–328. Sale by Auction

(1) In a sale by auction if goods are put up in lots each lot is the subject of a separate sale.

(2) A sale by auction is complete when the auctioneer so announces by the fall of the hammer or in other customary manner. Where a bid is made while the hammer is falling in acceptance of a prior bid the auctioneer may in his discretion reopen the bidding or declare the goods sold under the bid on which the hammer was falling.

(3) Such a sale is with reserve unless the goods are in explicit terms put up without reserve. In an auction with reserve the auctioneer may withdraw the goods at any time until he announces completion of the sale. In an auction without reserve, after the auctioneer calls for bids on an article or lot, that article or lot cannot be withdrawn unless no bid is made within a reasonable time. In either case a bidder may retract his bid until the auctioneer's announcement of completion of the sale, but a bidder's retraction does not revive any previous bid.

(4) If the auctioneer knowingly receives a bid on the seller's behalf or the seller makes or procures such a bid, and notice has not been given that liberty for such bidding is reserved, the buyer may at his option avoid the sale or take the goods at the price of the last good faith bid prior to the completion of the sale. This subsection shall not apply to any bid at a forced sale.

Part 4 Title, Creditors and Good Faith Purchasers

Section 2–401. Passing of Title; Reservation for Security; Limited Application of This Section

Each provision of this Article with regard to the rights, obligations and remedies of the seller, the buyer, purchasers or other third parties applies irrespective of title to the goods except where the provision refers to such title. Insofar as situations are not covered by the other provisions of this Article and matters concerning title become material the following rules apply:

(1) Title to goods cannot pass under a contract for sale prior to their identification to the contract (Section 2–501), and unless otherwise

explicitly agreed the buyer acquires by their identification a special property as limited by this Act. Any retention or reservation by the seller of the title (property) in goods shipped or delivered to the buyer is limited in effect to a reservation of a security interest. Subject to these provisions and to the provisions of the Article on Secured Transactions (Article 9), title to goods passes from the seller to the buyer in any manner and on any conditions explicitly agreed on by the parties.

(2) Unless otherwise explicitly agreed title passes to the buyer at the time and place at which the seller completes his performance with reference to the physical delivery of the goods, despite any reservation of a security interest and even though a document of title is to be delivered at a different time or place; and in particular and despite any reservation of a security interest by the bill of lading

(a) if the contract requires or authorizes the seller to send the goods to the buyer but does not require him to deliver them at destination, title passes to the buyer at the time and place of shipment; but

(b) if the contract requires delivery at destination, title passes on tender there.

(3) Unless otherwise explicitly agreed where delivery is to be made without moving the goods,

(a) if the seller is to deliver a document of title, title passes at the time when and the place where he delivers such documents; or

(b) if the goods are at the time of contracting already identified and no documents are to be delivered, title passes at the time and place of contracting.

(4) A rejection or other refusal by the buyer to receive or retain the goods, whether or not justified, or a justified revocation of acceptance revests title to the goods in the seller. Such revesting occurs by operation of law and is not a "sale."

Section 2–402. Rights of Seller's Creditors Against Sold Goods

(1) Except as provided in subsections (2) and (3), rights of unsecured creditors of the seller with respect to goods which have been identified to a contract for sale are subject to the buyer's rights to recover the goods under this Article (Sections 2–502 and 2–716).

(2) A creditor of the seller may treat a sale or an identification of goods to a contract for sale as void if as against him a retention of possession by the seller is fraudulent under any rule of law of the state where the goods are situated, except that retention of possession in good faith and current course of trade by a merchant-seller for a commercially reasonable time after a sale or identification is not fraudulent.

(3) Nothing in this Article shall be deemed to impair the rights of creditors of the seller

(a) under the provisions of the Article on Secured Transactions (Article 9); or

(b) where identification to the contract or delivery is made not in current course of trade but in satisfaction of or as security for a pre-existing claim for money, security or the like and is made under circumstances which under any rule of law of the state where the goods are situated would apart from this Article constitute the transaction a fraudulent transfer or voidable preference.

Section 2–403. Power to Transfer; Good Faith Purchase of Goods; "Entrusting"

(1) A purchaser of goods acquires all title which his transferor had or had power to transfer except that a purchaser of a limited interest acquires rights only to the extent of the interest purchased. A person with voidable title has power to transfer a good title to a good faith purchaser for value. When goods have been delivered under a transaction of purchase the purchaser has such power even though

(a) the transferor was deceived as to the identity of the purchaser, or

(b) the delivery was in exchange for a check which is later dishonored, or

(c) it was agreed that the transaction was to be a "cash sale," or

(d) the delivery was procured through fraud punishable as larcenous under the criminal law.

(2) Any entrusting of possession of goods to a merchant who deals in goods of that kind gives him power to transfer all rights of the entruster to a buyer in ordinary course of business.

(3) "Entrusting" includes any delivery and any acquiescence in retention of possession regardless of any condition expressed between the parties to the delivery or acquiescence and regardless of whether the procurement of the entrusting or the possessor's disposition of the goods have been such as to be larcenous under the criminal law.

(4) The rights of other purchasers of goods and of lien creditors are governed by the Articles on Secured Transactions (Article 9), Bulk Transfers (Article 6) and Documents of Title (Article 7).

Part 5 Performance

Section 2–501. Insurable Interest in Goods; Manner of Identification of Goods

(1) The buyer obtains a special property and an insurable interest in goods by identification of existing goods as goods to which the contract refers even though the goods so identified are nonconforming and he has an option to return or reject them. Such identification can be made at any time and in any manner explicitly agreed to by the parties. In the absence of explicit agreement identification occurs.

(a) when the contract is made if it is for the sale of goods already existing and identified;

(b) if the contract is for the sale of future goods other than those described in paragraph (c), when goods are shipped, marked or otherwise designated by the seller as goods to which the contract refers;

(c) when the crops are planted or otherwise become growing crops or the young are conceived if the contract is for the sale of unborn young to be born within twelve months after contracting or for the sale of crops to be harvested within twelve months or the next normal harvest season after contracting whichever is longer.

(2) The seller retains an insurable interest in goods so long as title to or any security interest in the goods remains in him and where the identification is by the seller alone he may until default or insolvency or notification to the buyer that the identification is final substitute other goods for those identified.

(3) Nothing in this section impairs any insurable interest recognized under any other statute or rule of law.

Section 2–502. Buyer's Right to Goods on Seller's Insolvency

(1) Subject to subsection (2) and even though the goods have not been shipped a buyer who has paid a part or all of the price of goods in which he has a special property under the provisions of the immediately preceding section may on making and keeping good a tender of any unpaid portion of their price recover them from the seller if the seller becomes insolvent within ten days after receipt of the first installment on their price.

(2) If the identification creating his special property has been made by the buyer he acquires the right to recover the goods only if they conform to the contract for sale.

Section 2–503. Manner of Seller's Tender of Delivery

(1) Tender of delivery requires that the seller put and hold conforming goods at the buyer's disposition and give the buyer any notification reasonably necessary to enable him to take delivery. The manner, time and place for tender are determined by the agreement and this Article, and in particular

- (a) tender must be at a reasonable hour, and if it is of goods they must be kept available for the period reasonably necessary to enable the buyer to take possession; but
- (b) unless otherwise agreed the buyer must furnish facilities reasonably suited to the receipt of the goods.

(2) Where the case is within the next section respecting shipment tender requires that the seller comply with its provisions.

(3) Where the seller is required to deliver at a particular destination tender requires that he comply with subsection (1) and also in any appropriate case tender documents as described in subsections (4) and (5) of this section.

(4) Where goods are in the possession of a bailee and are to be delivered without being moved

- (a) tender requires that the seller either tender a negotiable document of title covering such goods or procure acknowledgment by the bailee of the buyer's right to possession of the goods; but
- (b) tender to the buyer of a non-negotiable document of title or of a written direction to the bailee to deliver is sufficient tender unless the buyer seasonably objects, and receipt by the bailee of notification of the buyer's rights fixes those rights as against the bailee and all third persons; but risk of loss of the goods and of any failure by the bailee to honor the non-negotiable document of title or to obey the direction remains on the seller until the buyer has had a reasonable time to present the document or direction, and a refusal by the bailee to honor the document or to obey the direction defeats the tender.

(5) Where the contract requires the seller to deliver documents

- (a) he must tender all such documents in correct form, except as provided in this Article with respect to bills of lading in a set (subsection (2) of Section 2–323); and
- (b) tender through customary banking channels is sufficient and dishonor of a draft accompanying the documents constitutes non-acceptance or rejection.

Section 2–504. Shipment by Seller

Where the seller is required or authorized to send the goods to the buyer and the contract does not require him to deliver them at a particular destination, then unless otherwise agreed he must

- (a) put the goods in the possession of such a carrier and make such a contract for their transportation as may be reasonable having regard to the nature of the goods and other circumstances of the case; and
- (b) obtain and promptly deliver or tender in due form any document necessary to enable the buyer to obtain possession of the goods or otherwise required by the agreement or by usage of trade; and
- (c) promptly notify the buyer of the shipment.

Failure to notify the buyer under paragraph (c) or to make a proper contract under paragraph (a) is a ground for rejection only if material delay or loss ensues.

Section 2–505. Seller's Shipment Under Reservation

(1) Where the seller has identified goods to the contract by or before shipment:

- (a) his procurement of a negotiable bill of lading to his own order or otherwise reserves in him a security interest in the goods. His procurement of the bill to the order of a financing agency or of the buyer indicates in addition only the seller's expectation of transferring that interest to the person named.
- (b) a non-negotiable bill of lading to himself or his nominee reserves possession of the goods as security but except in a case of conditional delivery (subsection (2) of Section 2–507) a non-negotiable bill of lading naming the buyer as consignee reserves no security interest even though the seller retains possession of the bill of lading.

(2) When shipment by the seller with reservation of a security interest is in violation of the contract for sale it constitutes an improper contract for transportation within the preceding section but impairs neither the rights given to the buyer by shipment and identification of the goods to the contract nor the seller's powers as a holder of a negotiable document.

Section 2–506. Rights of Financing Agency

(1) A financing agency by paying or purchasing for value a draft which relates to a shipment of goods acquires to the extent of the payment or purchase and in addition to its own rights under the draft and any document of title securing it any rights of the shipper in the goods including the right to stop delivery and the shipper's right to have the draft honored by the buyer.

(2) The right to reimbursement of a financing agency which has in good faith honored or purchased the draft under commitment to or authority from the buyer is not impaired by subsequent discovery of defects with reference to any relevant document which was apparently regular on its face.

Section 2–507. Effect of Seller's Tender; Delivery on Condition

(1) Tender of delivery is a condition to the buyer's duty to accept the goods and, unless otherwise agreed, to his duty to pay for them. Tender entitles the seller to acceptance of the goods and to payment according to the contract.

(2) Where payment is due and demanded on the delivery to the buyer of goods or documents of title, his right as against the seller to retain or dispose of them is conditional upon him making the payment due.

Section 2–508. Cure by Seller of Improper Tender or Delivery; Replacement

(1) Where any tender or delivery by the seller is rejected because non-conforming and the time for performance has not yet expired, the seller may seasonably notify the buyer of his intention to cure and may then within the contract time make a conforming delivery.

(2) Where the buyer rejects a non-conforming tender which the seller had reasonable grounds to believe would be acceptable with or without money allowance the seller may if he seasonably notifies the buyer have a further reasonable time to substitute a conforming tender.

Section 2–509. Risk of Loss in the Absence of Breach

(1) Where the contract requires or authorizes the seller to ship the goods by carrier

(a) if it does not require him to deliver them at a particular destination, the risk of loss passes to the buyer when the goods are duly delivered to the carrier even though the shipment is under reservation (Section 2–505); but

(b) if it does require him to deliver them at a particular destination and the goods are there duly tendered while in the possession of the carrier, the risk of loss passes to the buyer when the goods are there duly so tendered as to enable the buyer to take delivery.

(2) Where the goods are held by a bailee to be delivered without being moved, the risk of loss passes to the buyer

(a) on his receipt of a negotiable document of title covering the goods; or

(b) on acknowledgment by the bailee of the buyer's right to possession of the goods; or

(c) after his receipt of a non-negotiable document of title or other written direction to deliver, as provided in subsection (4) (b) of Section 2–503.

(3) In any case not within subsection (1) or (2), the risk of loss passes to the buyer on his receipt of the goods if the seller is a merchant; otherwise the risk passes to the buyer on tender of delivery.

(4) The provisions of this section are subject to contrary agreement of the parties and to the provisions of this Article on sale on approval (Section 2–327) and on effect of breach on risk of loss (Section 2–510).

Section 2–510. Effect of Breach on Risk of Loss

(1) Where a tender or delivery of goods so fails to conform to the contract as to give a right of rejection the risk of their loss remains on the seller until cure or acceptance.

(2) Where the buyer rightfully revokes acceptance he may to the extent of any deficiency in his effective insurance coverage treat the risk of loss as having rested on the seller from the beginning.

(3) Where the buyer as to conforming goods already identified to the contract for sale repudiates or is otherwise in breach before risk of their loss has passed to him, the seller may to the extent of any deficiency in his effective insurance coverage treat the risk of loss as resting on the buyer for a commercially reasonable time.

Section 2–511. Tender of Payment by Buyer; Payment by Check

(1) Unless otherwise agreed tender of payment is a condition to the seller's duty to tender and complete any delivery.

(2) Tender of payment is sufficient when made by any means or in any manner current in the ordinary course of business unless the seller demands payment in legal tender and gives any extension of time reasonably necessary to procure it.

(3) Subject to the provisions of this Act on the effect of an instrument on an obligation (Section 3–802), payment by check is conditional and is defeated as between the parties by dishonor of the check on due presentment.

Section 2–512. Payment by Buyer Before Inspection

(1) Where the contract requires payment before inspection nonconformity of the goods does not excuse the buyer from so making payment unless

(a) the non-conformity appears without inspection; or

(b) despite tender of the required documents the circumstances would justify injunction against honor under the provisions of this Act (Section 5–114).

(2) Payment pursuant to subsection (1) does not constitute an acceptance of goods or impair the buyer's right to inspect or any of his remedies.

Section 2–513. Buyer's Right to Inspection of Goods

(1) Unless otherwise agreed and subject to subsection (3), where goods are tendered or delivered or identified to the contract for sale, the buyer has a right before payment or acceptance to inspect them at any reasonable place and time and in any reasonable manner. When the seller is required or authorized to send the goods to the buyer, the inspection may be after their arrival.

(2) Expenses of inspection must be borne by the buyer but may be recovered from the seller if the goods do not conform and are rejected.

(3) Unless otherwise agreed and subject to the provisions of this Article on C.I.F. contracts (subsection (3) of Section 2–321), the buyer is not entitled to inspect the goods before payment of the price when the contract provides

(a) for delivery "C.O.D." or on other like terms; or

(b) for payment against documents of title, except where such payment is due only after the goods are to become available for inspection.

(4) A place or method of inspection fixed by the parties is presumed to be exclusive but unless otherwise expressly agreed it does not postpone identification or shift the place for delivery or for passing the risk of loss. If compliance becomes impossible, inspection shall be as provided in this section unless the place or method fixed was clearly intended as an indispensable condition failure of which avoids the contract.

Section 2–514. When Documents Deliverable on Acceptance; When on Payment

Unless otherwise agreed documents against which a draft is drawn are to be delivered to the drawee on acceptance of the draft if it is payable more than three days after presentment; otherwise, only on payment.

Section 2–515. Preserving Evidence of Goods in Dispute

In furtherance of the adjustment of any claim or dispute

(a) either party on reasonable notification to the other and for the purpose of ascertaining the facts and preserving evidence has the right to inspect, test and sample the goods including such of them as may be in the possession or control of the other; and

(b) the parties may agree to a third party inspection or survey to determine the conformity or condition of the goods and may agree that the findings shall be binding upon them in any subsequent litigation or adjustment.

Part 6 Breach, Repudiation and Excuse

Section 2–601. Buyer's Rights on Improper Delivery

Subject to the provisions of this Article on breach in installment contracts (Section 2–612) and unless otherwise agreed under the sections on contractual limitations of remedy (Sections 2–718 and 2–719), if the goods or the tender of delivery fail in any respect to conform to the contract, the buyer may

(a) reject the whole; or

(b) accept the whole; or

(c) accept any commercial unit or units and reject the rest.

Section 2–602. Manner and Effect of Rightful Rejection

(1) Rejection of goods must be within a reasonable time after their delivery or tender. It is ineffective unless the buyer seasonably notifies the seller.

(2) Subject to the provisions of the two following sections on rejected goods (Sections 2–603 and 2–604),

(a) after rejection any exercise of ownership by the buyer with respect to any commercial unit is wrongful as against the seller; and

(b) if the buyer has before rejection taken physical possession of goods in which he does not have a security interest under the provisions of this Article (subsection (3) of Section 2–711), he is under a duty after rejection to hold them with reasonable care at the seller's disposition for a time sufficient to permit the seller to remove them; but

(c) the buyer has no further obligations with regard to goods rightfully rejected.

(3) The seller's rights with respect to goods wrongfully rejected are governed by the provisions of this Article on Seller's remedies in general (Section 2–703).

Section 2–603. Merchant Buyer's Duties as to Rightfully Rejected Goods

(1) Subject to any security interest in the buyer (subsection (3) of Section 2–711), when the seller has no agent or place of business at the market of rejection a merchant buyer is under a duty after rejection of goods in his possession or control to follow any reasonable instructions received from the seller with respect to the goods and in the absence of such instructions to make reasonable efforts to sell them for the seller's account if they are perishable or threaten to decline in value speedily. Instructions are not reasonable if on demand indemnity for expenses is not forthcoming.

(2) When the buyer sells goods under subsection (1), he is entitled to reimbursement from the seller or out of the proceeds for reasonable expenses of caring for and selling them, and if the expenses include no selling commission then to such commission as is usual in the trade or if there is none to a reasonable sum not exceeding ten per cent on the gross proceeds.

(3) In complying with this section the buyer is held only to good faith and good faith conduct hereunder is neither acceptance nor conversion nor the basis of an action for damages.

Section 2–604. Buyer's Options as to Salvage of Rightfully Rejected Goods

Subject to the provisions of the immediately preceding section on perishables if the seller gives no instructions within a reasonable time after notification of rejection the buyer may store the rejected goods for the seller's account or reship them to him or resell them for the seller's account with reimbursement as provided in the preceding section. Such action is not acceptance or conversion.

Section 2–605. Waiver of Buyer's Objections by Failure to Particularize

(1) The buyer's failure to state in connection with rejection a particular defect which is ascertainable by reasonable inspection precludes him from relying on the unstated defect to justify rejection or to establish breach

(a) where the seller could have cured it if stated seasonably; or

(b) between merchants when the seller has after rejection made a request in writing for a full and final written statement of all defects on which the buyer proposes to rely.

(2) Payment against documents made without reservation of rights precludes recovery of the payment for defects apparent on the face of the documents.

Section 2–606. What Constitutes Acceptance of Goods

(1) Acceptance of goods occurs when the buyer

(a) after a reasonable opportunity to inspect the goods signifies to the seller that the goods are conforming or that he will take or retain them in spite of their non-conformity; or

(b) fails to make an effective rejection (subsection (1) of Section 2–602), but such acceptance does not occur until the buyer has had a reasonable opportunity to inspect them; or

(c) does any act inconsistent with the seller's ownership; but if such act is wrongful as against the seller it is an acceptance only if ratified by him.

(2) Acceptance of a part of any commercial unit is acceptance of that entire unit.

Section 2–607. Effect of Acceptance; Notice of Breach; Burden of Establishing Breach After Acceptance; Notice of Claim or Litigation to Person Answerable Over

(1) The buyer must pay at the contract rate for any goods accepted.

(2) Acceptance of goods by the buyer precludes rejection of the goods accepted and if made with knowledge of a non-conformity cannot be revoked because of it unless the acceptance was on the reasonable assumption that the non-conformity would be seasonably cured but

acceptance does not of itself impair any other remedy provided by this Article for non-conformity.

(3) Where a tender has been accepted

(a) the buyer must within a reasonable time after he discovers or should have discovered any breach notify the seller of breach or be barred from any remedy; and

(b) if the claim is one for infringement or the like (subsection (3) of Section 2–312) and the buyer is sued as a result of such a breach he must so notify the seller within a reasonable time after he receives notice of the litigation or be barred from any remedy over for liability established by the litigation.

(4) The burden is on the buyer to establish any breach with respect to the goods accepted.

(5) Where the buyer is sued for breach of a warranty or other obligation for which his seller is answerable over

(a) he may give his seller written notice of the litigation. If the notice states that the seller may come in and defend and that if the seller does not do so he will be bound in any action against him by his buyer by any determination of fact common to the two litigations, then unless the seller after seasonable receipt of the notice does come in and defend he is so bound.

(b) if the claim is one for infringement or the like (subsection (3) of Section 2–312) the original seller may demand in writing that his buyer turn over to him control of the litigation including settlement or else be barred from any remedy over and if he also agrees to bear all expense and to satisfy any adverse judgment, then unless the buyer after seasonable receipt of the demand does turn over control the buyer is so barred.

(6) The provisions of subsections (3), (4) and (5) apply to any obligation of a buyer to hold the seller harmless against infringement or the like (subsection (3) of Section 2–312).

Section 2–608. Revocation of Acceptance in Whole or in Part

(1) The buyer may revoke his acceptance of a lot or commercial unit whose non-conformity substantially impairs its value to him if he has accepted it

(a) on the reasonable assumption that its non-conformity would be cured and it has not been seasonably cured; or

(b) without discovery of such non-conformity if his acceptance was reasonably induced either by the difficulty of discovery before acceptance or by the seller's assurances.

(2) Revocation of acceptance must occur within a reasonable time after the buyer discovers or should have discovered the ground for it and before any substantial change in condition of the goods which is not caused by their own defects. It is not effective until the buyer notifies the seller of it

(3) A buyer who so revokes has the same rights and duties with regard to the goods involved as if he had rejected them.

Section 2–609. Right to Adequate Assurance of Performance

(1) A contract for sale imposes an obligation on each party that the other's expectation of receiving due performance will not be impaired. When reasonable grounds for insecurity arise with respect to the performance of either party the other may in writing demand adequate assurance of due performance and until he receives such assurance may if commercially reasonable suspend any performance for which he has not already received the agreed return.

(2) Between merchants the reasonableness of grounds for insecurity and the adequacy of any assurance offered shall be determined according to commercial standards.

(3) Acceptance of any improper delivery or payment does not prejudice the aggrieved party's right to demand adequate assurance of future performance.

(4) After receipt of a justified demand failure to provide within a reasonable time not exceeding thirty days such assurance of due performance as is adequate under the circumstances of the particular case is a repudiation of the contract.

Section 2–610. Anticipatory Repudiation

When either party repudiates the contract with respect to a performance not yet due the loss of which will substantially impair the value of the contract to the other, the aggrieved party may

(a) for a commercially reasonable time await performance by the repudiating party; or

(b) resort to any remedy for breach (Section 2–703 or Section 2–711), even though he has notified the repudiating party that he would await the latter's performance and has urged retraction; and

(c) in either case suspend his own performance or proceed in accordance with the provisions of this Article on the seller's right to identify goods to the contract notwithstanding breach or to salvage unfinished goods (Section 2–704).

Section 2–611. Retraction of Anticipatory Repudiation

(1) Until the repudiating party's next performance is due he can retract his repudiation unless the aggrieved party has since the repudiation cancelled or materially changed his position or otherwise indicated that he considers the repudiation final.

(2) Retraction may be by any method which clearly indicates to the aggrieved party that the repudiating party intends to perform, but must include any assurance justifiably demanded under the provisions of this Article (Section 2–609).

(3) Retraction reinstates the repudiating party's rights under the contract with due excuse and allowance to the aggrieved party for any delay occasioned by the repudiation.

Section 2–612. "Installment Contract"; Breach

(1) An "installment contract" is one which requires or authorizes the delivery of goods in separate lots to be separately accepted, even though the contract contains a clause "each delivery is a separate contract" or its equivalent.

(2) The buyer may reject any installment which is non-conforming if the non-conformity substantially impairs the value of that installment and cannot be cured or if the non-conformity is a defect in the required documents; but if the non-conformity does not fall within subsection (3) and the seller gives adequate assurance of its cure the buyer must accept that installment.

(3) Whenever non-conformity or default with respect to one or more installments substantial impairs the value of the whole contract there is a breach of the whole. But the aggrieved party reinstates the contract if he

accepts a non-conforming installment without seasonably notifying of cancellation or if he brings an action with respect only to past installments or demands performance as to future installments.

Section 2–613. Casualty to Identified Goods

Where the contract requires for its performance goods identified when the contract is made, and the goods suffer casualty without fault of either party before the risk of loss passes to the buyer, or in a proper case under a "no arrival, no sale" term (Section 2–324) then

(a) if the loss is total the contract is avoided; and

(b) if the loss is partial or the goods have so deteriorated as no longer to conform to the contract the buyer may nevertheless demand inspection and at his option either treat the contract as avoided or accept the goods with due allowance from the contract price for the deterioration or the deficiency in quantity but without further right against the seller.

Section 2–614. Substituted Performance

(1) Where without fault of either party the agreed berthing, loading, or unloading facilities fail or an agreed type of carrier becomes unavailable or the agreed manner of delivery otherwise becomes commercially impracticable but a commercially reasonable substitute is available, such substitute performance must be tendered and accepted.

(2) If the agreed means or manner of payment fails because of domestic or foreign governmental regulation, the seller may withhold or stop delivery unless the buyer provides a means or manner of payment which is commercially a substantial equivalent. If delivery has already been taken, payment by the means or in the manner provided by the regulation discharges the buyer's obligation unless the regulation is discriminatory, oppressive or predatory.

Section 2–615. Excuse by Failure of Presupposed Conditions

Except so far as a seller may have assumed a greater obligation and subject to the preceding section on substituted performance:

(a) Delay in delivery or non-delivery in whole or in part by a seller who complies with paragraphs (b) and (c) is not a breach of his duty under a contract for sale if performance as agreed has been made impracticable by the occurrence of a contingency the non-occurrence of which was a basic assumption on which the contract was made or by compliance in good faith with any applicable foreign or domestic governmental regulation or order whether or not it later proves to be invalid.

(b) Where the causes mentioned in paragraph (a) affect only a part of the seller's capacity to perform, he must allocate production and deliveries among his customers but may at his option include regular customers not then under contract as well as his own requirements for further manufacture. He may so allocate in any manner which is fair and reasonable.

(c) The seller must notify the buyer seasonably that there will be delay or non-delivery and, when allocation is required under paragraph (b), of the estimated quota thus made available for the buyer.

Section 2–616. Procedure on Notice Claiming Excuse

(1) Where the buyer receives notification of a material or indefinite delay or an allocation justified under the preceding section he may by written notification to the seller as to any delivery concerned, and where the prospective deficiency substantially impairs the value of the whole contract under the provisions of this Article relating to breach of installment contracts (Section 2–612), then also as to the whole,

(a) terminate and thereby discharge any unexecuted portion of the contract; or

(b) modify the contract by agreeing to take his available quota in substitution.

(2) If after receipt of such notification from the seller the buyer fails so to modify the contract within a reasonable time not exceeding thirty days the contract lapses with respect to any deliveries affected.

(3) The provisions of this section may not be negated by agreement except in so far as the seller has assumed a greater obligation under the preceding section.

Part 7 Remedies

Section 2–701. Remedies for Breach of Collateral Contracts Not Impaired

Remedies for breach of any obligation or promise collateral or ancillary to a contract for sale are not impaired by the provisions of this Article.

Section 2–702. Seller's Remedies on Discovery of Buyer's Insolvency

(1) Where the seller discovers the buyer to be insolvent he may refuse delivery except for cash including payment for all goods theretofore delivered under the contract, and stop delivery under this Article (Section 2–705).

(2) Where the seller discovers that the buyer has received goods on credit while insolvent he may reclaim the goods upon demand made within ten days after the receipt, but if misrepresentation of solvency has been made to the particular seller in writing within three months before delivery the ten day limitation does not apply. Except as provided in this subsection the seller may not base a right to reclaim goods on the buyer's fraudulent or innocent misrepresentation of solvency or of intent to pay.

(3) The seller's right to reclaim under subsection (2) is subject to the rights of a buyer in ordinary course or other good faith purchaser under this Article (Section 2–403). Successful reclamation of goods excludes all other remedies with respect to them.

Section 2–703. Seller's Remedies in General

Where the buyer wrongfully rejects or revokes acceptance of goods or fails to make a payment due on or before delivery or repudiates with respect to a part or the whole, then with respect to any goods directly affected and, if the breach is of the whole contract (Section 2–612), then also with respect to the whole undelivered balance, the aggrieved seller may

(a) withhold delivery of such goods;

(b) stop delivery by any bailee as hereafter provided (Section 2–705);

(c) proceed under the next section respecting goods still unidentified to the contract;

(d) resell and recover damages as hereafter provided (Section 2–706);

(e) recover damages for non-acceptance (Section 2–708) or in a proper case the price (Section 2–709);

(f) cancel.

Section 2–704. Seller's Right to Identify Goods to the Contract Notwithstanding Breach or to Salvage Unfinished Goods

(1) An aggrieved seller under the preceding section may

(a) identify to the contract conforming goods not already identified if at the time he learned of the breach they are in his possession or control;

(b) treat as the subject of resale goods which have demonstrably been intended for the particular contract even though those goods are unfinished.

(2) Where the goods are unfinished an aggrieved seller may in the exercise of reasonable commercial judgment for the purposes of avoiding loss and of effective realization either complete the manufacture and wholly identify the goods to the contract or cease manufacture and resell for scrap or salvage value or proceed in any other reasonable manner.

Section 2–705. Seller's Stoppage of Delivery in Transit or Otherwise

(1) The seller may stop delivery of goods in the possession of a carrier or other bailee when he discovers the buyer to be insolvent (Section 2–702) and may stop delivery of carload, truckload, planeload or larger shipments of express or freight when the buyer repudiates or fails to make a payment due before delivery or if for any other reason the seller has a right to withhold or reclaim the goods.

(2) As against such buyer the seller may stop delivery until

(a) receipt of the goods by the buyer; or

(b) acknowledgment to the buyer by any bailee of the goods except a carrier that the bailee holds the goods for the buyer; or

(c) such acknowledgment to the buyer by a carrier by reshipment or as warehouseman; or

(d) negotiation to the buyer of any negotiable document of title covering the goods.

(3) (a) To stop delivery the seller must so notify as to enable the bailee by reasonable diligence to prevent delivery of the goods.

(b) After such notification the bailee must hold and deliver the goods according to the directions of the seller but the seller is liable to the bailee for any ensuing charges or damages.

(c) If a negotiable document of title has been issued for goods the bailee is not obliged to obey a notification to stop until surrender of the document.

(d) A carrier who has issued a non-negotiable bill of lading is not obliged to obey a notification to stop received from a person other than the consignor.

Section 2–706. Seller's Resale Including Contract for Resale

(1) Under the conditions stated in Section 2–703 on seller's remedies, the seller may resell the goods concerned or the undelivered balance thereof. Where the resale is made in good faith and in a commercially reasonable manner the seller may recover the difference between the resale price and the contract price together with any incidental damages allowed under the provisions of this Article (Section 2–710), but less expenses saved in consequence of the buyer's breach.

(2) Except as otherwise provided in subsection (3) or unless otherwise agreed resale may be at public or private sale including sale by way of one or more contracts to sell or of identification to an existing contract of the seller. Sale may be as a unit or in parcels and at any time and place and on any terms but every aspect of the sale including the method, manner, time, place and terms must be commercially reasonable. The resale must be reasonably identified as referring to the broken contract, but it is not necessary that the goods be in existence or that any or all of them have been identified to the contract before the breach.

(3) Where the resale is at private sale the seller must give the buyer reasonable notification of his intention to resell.

(4) Where the resale is at public sale

(a) only identified goods can be sold except where there is a recognized market for a public sale of futures in goods of the kind; and

(b) it must be made at a usual place or market for public sale if one is reasonably available and except in the case of goods which are perishable or threaten to decline in value speedily the seller must give the buyer reasonable notice of the time and place of the resale; and

(c) if the goods are not to be within the view of those attending the sale the notification of sale must state the place where the goods are located and provide for their reasonable inspection by prospective bidders; and

(d) the seller may buy.

(5) A purchaser who buys in good faith at a resale take the goods free of any rights of the original buyer even though the seller fails to comply with one or more of the requirements of this section.

(6) The seller is not accountable to the buyer for any profit made on any resale. A person in the position of a seller (Section 2–707) or a buyer who has rightfully rejected or justifiably revoked acceptance must account for any excess over the amount of his security interest, as hereinafter defined (subsection (3) of Section 2–711).

Section 2–707. "Person in the Position of a Seller"

(1) A "person in the position of a seller" includes as against a principal an agent who has paid or become responsible for the price of goods on behalf of his principal or anyone who otherwise holds a security interest or other right in goods similar to that of a seller.

(2) A person in the positions of a seller may as provided in this Article withhold or stop delivery (Section 2–705) and resell (Section 2–706) and recover incidental damages (Section 2–710).

Section 2–708. Seller's Damages for Non-acceptance or Repudiation

(1) Subject to subsection (2) and to the provisions of this Article with respect to proof of market price (Section 2–723), the measure of damages for non-acceptance or repudiation by the buyer is the difference between the market price at the time and place for tender and the unpaid contract price together with any incidental damages provided in this Article (Section 2–710), but less expenses saved in consequence of the buyer's breach.

(2) If the measure of damages provided in subsection (1) is inadequate to put the seller in as good a position as performance would have done then the measure of damages is the profit (including reasonable overhead) which the seller would have made from full performance by the buyer, together with any incidental damages provided in this Article (Section 2–710), due allowance for costs reasonably incurred and due credit for payments or proceeds of resale.

Section 2–709. Action for the Price

(1) When the buyer fails to pay the price as it becomes due the seller may recover, together with any incidental damages under the next section, the price

(a) of goods accepted or of conforming goods lost or damaged within a commercially reasonable time after risk of their loss has passed to the buyer; and

(b) of goods identified to the contract if the seller is unable after reasonable effort to resell them at a reasonable price or the circumstances reasonably indicate that such effort will be unavailing.

(2) Where the seller sues for the price he must hold for the buyer any goods which have been identified to the contract and are still in his control except that if resale becomes possible he may resell them at any time prior to the collection of the judgment. The net proceeds of any such resale must be credited to the buyer and payment of the judgment entitles him to any goods not resold.

(3) After the buyer has wrongfully rejected or revoked acceptance of the goods or has failed to make a payment due or has repudiated (Section 2–610), a seller who is held not entitled to the price under this section shall nevertheless be awarded damages for non-acceptance under the preceding section.

Section 2–710. Seller's Incidental Damages

Incidental damages to an aggrieved seller include any commercially reasonable charges, expenses or commissions incurred in stopping delivery, in the transportation, care and custody of goods after the buyer's breach, in connection with return or resale of the goods or otherwise resulting from the breach.

Section 2–711. Buyer's Remedies in General; Buyer's Security Interest in Rejected Goods

(1) Where the seller fails to make delivery or repudiates or the buyer rightfully rejects or justifiably revokes acceptance then with respect to any goods involved, and with respect to the whole if the breach goes to the whole contract (Section 2–612), the buyer may cancel and whether or not he has done so may in addition to recovering so much of the price as has been paid

(a) "cover" and have damages under the next section as to all the goods affected whether or not they have been identified to the contract; or

(b) recover damages for non-delivery as provided in this Article (Section 2–713).

(2) Where the seller fails to deliver or repudiates the buyer may also

(a) if the goods have been identified recover them as provided in this Article (Section 2–502); or

(b) in a proper case obtain specific performance or replevy the goods as provided in this Article (Section 2–716).

(3) On rightful rejection or justifiable revocation of acceptance a buyer has a security interest in goods in his possession or control for any payments made on their price and any expenses reasonably incurred in their inspection, receipt, transportation, care and custody and may hold such goods and resell them in like manner as an aggrieved seller (Section 2–706).

Section 2–712. "Cover"; Buyer's Procurement of Substitute Goods

(1) After a breach within the preceding section the buyer may "cover" by making in good faith and without unreasonable delay any reasonable purchase of or contract to purchase goods in substitution for those due from the seller.

(2) The buyer may recover from the seller as damages the difference between the cost of cover and the contract price together with any incidental or consequential damages as hereinafter defined (Section 2–715), but less expenses saved in consequence of the seller's breach.

(3) Failure of the buyer to effect cover within this section does not bar him from any other remedy.

Section 2–713. Buyer's Damages for Non-Delivery or Repudiation

(1) Subject to the provisions of this Article with respect to proof of market price (Section 2–723), the measure of damages for nondelivery or repudiation by the seller is the difference between the market price at the time when the buyer learned of the breach and the contract price together with any incidental and consequential damages provided in this Article (Section 2–715), but less expenses saved in consequence of the seller's breach.

(2) Market price is to be determined as of the place for tender or, in cases of rejection after arrival or revocation of acceptance, as of the place of arrival.

Section 2–714. Buyer's Damages for Breach in Regard to Accepted Goods

(1) Where the buyer has accepted goods and given notification (subsection (3) of Section 2–607) he may recover as damages for any non-conformity of tender the loss resulting in the ordinary course of events from the seller's breach as determined in any manner which is reasonable.

(2) The measure of damages for breach of warranty is the difference at the time and place of acceptance between the value of the goods accepted and the value they would have had if they had been as warranted, unless special circumstances show proximate damages of a different amount.

(3) In a proper case any incidental and consequential damages under the next section may also be recovered.

Section 2–715. Buyer's Incidental and Consequential Damages

(1) Incidental damages resulting from the seller's breach include expenses reasonably incurred in inspection, receipt, transportation and care and custody of goods rightfully rejected, any commercially reasonable charges, expenses or commissions in connection with effecting cover and any other reasonable expense incident to the delay or other breach.

(2) Consequential damages resulting from the seller's breach include

(a) any loss resulting from general or particular requirements and needs of which the seller at the time of contracting had reason to know and which could not reasonably be prevented by cover or otherwise; and

(b) injury to person or property proximately resulting from any breach of warranty.

Section 2–716. Buyer's Right to Specific Performance or Replevin

(1) Specific performance may be decreed where the goods are unique or in other proper circumstances.

(2) The decree for specific performance may include such terms and conditions as to payment of the price, damages, or other relief as the court may deem just.

(3) The buyer has a right to replevin for goods identified to the contract if after reasonable effort he is unable to effect cover for such goods or the circumstances reasonably indicate that such effort will be unavailing or if the goods have been shipped under reservation and satisfaction of the security interest in them has been made or tendered.

Section 2–717. Deduction of Damages From the Price

The buyer on notifying the seller of his intention to do so may deduct all or any part of the damages resulting from any breach of the contract from any part of the price still due under the same contract.

Section 2–718. Liquidation or Limitation of Damages; Deposits

(1) Damages for breach by either party may be liquidated in the agreement but only at an amount which is reasonable in the light of the anticipated or actual harm caused by the breach, the difficulties of proof of loss, and the inconvenience or nonfeasibility of otherwise obtaining an adequate remedy. A term fixing unreasonably large liquidated damages is void as a penalty.

(2) Where the seller justifiably withholds delivery of goods because of the buyer's breach, the buyer is entitled to restitution of any amount by which the sum of his payments exceeds

- (a) the amount to which the seller is entitled by virtue of terms liquidating the seller's damages in accordance with subsection (1), or
- (b) in the absence of such terms, twenty per cent of the value of the total performance for which the buyer is obligated under the contract or $500, whichever is smaller.

(3) The buyer's right to restitution under subsection (2) is subject to offset to the extent that the seller establishes

- (a) a right to recover damages under the provisions of this Article other than subsection (1), and
- (b) the amount or value of any benefits received by the buyer directly or indirectly by reason of the contract.

(4) Where a seller has received payment in goods their reasonable value or the proceeds of their resale shall be treated as payments for the purposes of subsection (2); but if the seller has notice of the buyer's breach before reselling goods received in part performance, his resale is subject to the conditions laid down in this Article on resale by an aggrieved seller (Section 2–706).

Section 2–719. Contractual Modification or Limitation of Remedy

(1) Subject to the provisions of subsections (2) and (3) of this section and of the preceding section on liquidation and limitation of damages,

- (a) the agreement may provide for remedies in addition to or in substitution for those provided in this Article and may limit or alter the measure of damages recoverable under this Article, as by limiting the buyer's remedies to return of the goods and repayment of the price or to repair and replacement of non-conforming goods or parts; and
- (b) resort to a remedy as provided is optional unless the remedy is expressly agreed to be exclusive, in which case it is the sole remedy.

(2) Where circumstances cause an exclusive or limited remedy to fail of its essential purpose, remedy may be had as provided in this Act.

(3) Consequential damages may be limited or excluded unless the limitation or exclusion is unconscionable. Limitation of consequential damages for injury to the person in the case of consumer goods is prima facie unconscionable but limitation of damages where the loss is commercial is not.

Section 2–720. Effect of "Cancellation" or "Rescission" on Claims for Antecedent Breach

Unless the contrary intention clearly appears, expressions of "cancellation" or "rescission" of the contract or the like shall not be construed as a renunciation or discharge of any claim in damages for an antecedent breach.

Section 2–721. Remedies for Fraud

Remedies for material misrepresentation or fraud include all remedies available under this Article for non-fraudulent breach. Neither rescission or a claim for rescission of the contract for sale nor rejection or return of the goods shall bar or be deemed inconsistent with a claim for damages or other remedy.

Section 2–722. Who Can Sue Third Parties for Injury to Goods

Where a third party so deals with goods which have been identified to a contract for sale as to cause actionable injury to a party to that contract

- (a) a right of action against the third party is in either party to the contract for sale who has title to or a security interest or a special property or an insurable interest in the goods; and if the goods have been destroyed or converted a right of action is also in the party who either bore the risk of loss under the contract for sale or has since the injury assumed that risk as against the other;
- (b) if at the time of the injury the party plaintiff did not bear the risk of loss as against the other party to the contract for sale and there is no arrangement between them for disposition of the recovery, his suit or settlement is, subject to his own interest, as a fiduciary for the other party to the contract;
- (c) either party may with the consent of the other sue for the benefit of whom it may concern.

Section 2–723. Proof of Market Price: Time and Place

(1) If an action based on anticipatory repudiation comes to trial before the time for performance with respite to some or all of the goods, any damages based on market price (Section 2–708 or Section 2–713) shall be determined according to the price of such goods prevailing at the time when the aggrieved party learned of the repudiation.

(2) If evidence of a price prevailing at the times or places described in this Article is not readily available the price prevailing within any reasonable time before or after the time described or at any other place which in commercial judgment or under usage of trade would serve as a reasonable substitute for the one described may be used, making any proper allowance for the cost of transporting the goods to or from such other place.

(3) Evidence of a relevant price prevailing at a time or place other than the one described in this Article offered by one party is not admissible unless and until he has given the other party such notice as the court finds sufficient to prevent unfair surprise.

Section 2–724. Admissibility of Market Quotations

Whenever the prevailing price or value of any goods regularly bought and sold in any established commodity market is in issue, reports in official publications or trade journals or in newspapers or periodicals of general circulation published as the reports of such market shall be admissible in evidence. The circumstances of the preparation of such a report may be shown to affect its weight but not its admissibility.

Section 2–725. Statute of Limitations in Contracts for Sale

(1) An action for breach of any contract for sale must be commenced within four years after the cause of action has accrued. By the original agreement the parties may reduce the period of limitation to not less than one year but may not extend it.

(2) A cause of action accrues when the breach occurs, regardless of the aggrieved party's lack of knowledge of the breach. A breach of warranty occurs when tender of delivery is made, except that where a warranty explicitly extends to future performance of the goods and discovery of the breach must await the time of such performance the cause of action accrues when the breach is or should have been discovered.

(3) Where an action commenced within the time limited by subsection (1) is so terminated as to leave available a remedy by another action for the same breach such other action may be commenced after the expiration of the time limited and within six months after the termination of the first action unless the termination resulted from voluntary discontinuance or from dismissal for failure or neglect to prosecute.

(4) This section does not alter the law on tolling of the statute of limitations nor does it apply to causes of action which have accrued before this Act becomes effective.

[Article 2A on Leases is omitted.]

Article 3 Commercial Paper

Part 1 Short Title, Form and Interpretation

Section 3–101. Short Title

This Article shall be known and may be cited as Uniform Commercial Code—Commercial Paper.

Section 3–102. Definitions and Index of Definitions

(1) In this Article unless the context otherwise requires

- (a) "Issue" means the first delivery of an instrument to a holder or a remitter.
- (b) An "order" is a direction to pay and must be more than an authorization or request. It must identify the person to pay with reasonable certainty. It may be addressed to one or more such persons jointly or in the alternative but not in succession.
- (c) A "promise" is an undertaking to pay and must be more than an acknowledgment of an obligation.
- (d) "Secondary party" means a drawer or indorser.
- (e) "Instrument" means a negotiable instrument.

(2) Other definitions applying to this Article and the sections in which they appear are:

"Acceptance." Section 3–410.

"Accommodation party." Section 3–415.

"Alteration." Section 3–407.

"Certificate of deposit." Section 3–104.

"Certification." Section 3–411.

"Check." Section 3–104.

"Definite time." Section 3–109.

"Dishonor." Section 3–507.

"Draft." Section 3–104.

"Holder in due course." Section 3–302.

"Negotiation." Section 3–202.

"Note." Section 3–104.

"Notice of dishonor." Section 3–508.

"On demand." Section 3–108.

"Presentment." Section 3–504.

"Protest." Section 3–509.

"Restrictive Indorsement." Section 3–205.

"Signature." Section 3–401.

(3) The following definitions in other Articles apply to this Article:

"Account." Section 4–104.

"Banking Day." Section 4–104.

"Clearing house." Section 4–104.

"Collecting bank." Section 4–105.

"Customer." Section 4–104.

"Depositary Bank." Section 4–105.

"Documentary Draft." Section 4–104.

"Intermediary Bank." Section 4–105.

"Item." Section 4–104.

"Midnight deadline." Section 4–104.

"Payor bank." Section 4–105.

(4) In addition Article 1 contains general definitions and principles of construction and interpretation applicable throughout this Article.

Section 3–103. Limitations on Scope of Article

(1) This Article does not apply to money, documents of title or investment securities.

(2) The provisions of this Article are subject to the provisions of the Article on Bank Deposits and Collections (Article 4) and Secured Transactions (Article 9).

Section 3–104. Form of Negotiable Instruments; "Draft"; "Check"; "Certificate of Deposit"; "Note"

(1) Any writing to be a negotiable instrument within this Article must

- (a) be signed by the maker or drawer; and
- (b) contain an unconditional promise or order to pay a sum certain in money and no other promise, order, obligation or power given by the maker or drawer except as authorized by this Article; and

(c) be payable on demand or at a definite time; and

(d) be payable to order or to bearer.

(2) A writing which complies with the requirements of this section is

(a) a "draft" ("bill of exchange") if it is an order;

(b) a "check" if it is a draft drawn on a bank and payable on demand;

(c) a "certificate of deposit" if it is an acknowledgment by a bank of receipt of money with an engagement to repay it;

(d) a "note" if it is a promise other than a certificate of deposit.

(3) As used in other Articles of this Act, and as the context may require, the terms "draft," "check," "certificate of deposit" and "note" may refer to instruments which are not negotiable within this Article as well as to instruments which are so negotiable.

Section 3–105. When Promise or Order Unconditional

(1) A promise or order otherwise unconditional is not made conditional by the fact that the instrument

(a) is subject to implied or constructive conditions; or

(b) states its consideration, whether performed or promised, or the transaction which gave rise to the instrument, or that the promise or order is made or the instrument matures in accordance with or "as per" such transaction; or

(c) refers to or states that it arises out of a separate agreement or refers to a separate agreement for rights as to prepayment or acceleration; or

(d) states that it is drawn under a letter of credit; or

(e) states that it is secured, whether by mortgage, reservation of title or otherwise; or

(f) indicates a particular account to be debited or any other fund or source from which reimbursement is expected; or

(g) is limited to payment out of a particular fund or the proceeds of a particular source, if the instrument is issued by a government or governmental agency or unit; or

(h) is limited to payment out of the entire assets of a partnership, unincorporated association, trust or estate by or on behalf of which the instrument is issued.

(2) A promise or order is not unconditional if the instrument

(a) states that it is subject to or governed by any other agreement; or

(b) states that it is to be paid only out of a particular fund or source except as provided in this section. As amended 1962.

Section 3–106. Sum Certain

(1) The sum payable is a sum certain even though it is to be paid

(a) with stated interest or by stated installments; or

(b) with stated different rates of interest before and after default or a specified date; or

(c) with a stated discount or addition if paid before or after the date fixed for payment; or

(d) with exchange or less exchange, whether at a fixed rate or at the current rate; or

(e) with costs of collection or an attorney's fee or both upon default.

(2) Nothing in this section shall validate any term which is otherwise illegal.

Section 3–107. Money

(1) An instrument is payable in money if the medium of exchange in which it is payable is money at the time the instrument is made. An instrument payable in "currency" or "current funds" is payable in money.

(2) A promise or order to pay a sum stated in a foreign currency is for a sum certain in money and, unless a different medium of payment is specified in the instrument, may be satisfied by payment of that number of dollars which the stated foreign currency will purchase at the buying sight rate for that currency on the day on which the instrument is payable or, if payable on demand, on the day of demand. If such an instrument specifies a foreign currency as the medium of payment the instrument is payable in that currency.

Section 3–108. Payable on Demand

Instruments payable on demand include those payable at sight or on presentation and those in which no time for payment is stated.

Section 3–109. Definite Time

(1) An instrument is payable at a definite time if by its terms it is payable

(a) on or before a stated date or at a fixed period after a stated date; or

(b) at a fixed period after sight; or

(c) at a definite time subject to any acceleration; or

(d) at a definite time subject to extension at the option of the holder, or to extension to a further definite time at the option of the maker or acceptor or automatically upon or after a specified act or event.

(2) An instrument which by its terms is otherwise payable only upon an act or event uncertain as to time of occurrence is not payable at a definite time even though the act or event has occurred.

Section 3–110. Payable to Order

(1) An instrument is payable to order when by its terms it is payable to the order or assigns of any person therein specified with reasonable certainty, or to him or his order, or when it is conspicuously designated on its face as "exchange" or the like and names a payee. It may be payable to the order of

(a) the maker or drawer; or

(b) the drawee; or

(c) a payee who is not maker, drawer or drawee; or

(d) two or more payees together or in the alternative; or

(e) an estate, trust or fund, in which case it is payable to the order of the representative of such estate, trust or fund or his successors; or

(f) an office, or an officer by his title as such in which case it is payable to the principal but the incumbent of the office or his successors may act as if he or they were the holder; or

(g) a partnership or unincorporated association, in which case it is payable to the partnership or association and may be indorsed or transferred by any person thereto authorized.

(2) An instrument not payable to order is not made so payable by such words as "payable upon return of this instrument properly indorsed."

(3) An instrument made payable both to order and to bearer is payable to order unless the bearer words are handwritten or typewritten.

Section 3–111. Payable to Bearer

An instrument is payable to bearer when by its terms it is payable to

(a) bearer or the order of bearer; or

(b) a specified person or bearer; or

(c) "cash" or the order of "cash," or any other indication which does not purport to designate a specific payee.

Section 3–112. Terms and Omissions Not Affecting Negotiability

(1) The negotiability of an instrument is not affected by

(a) the omission of a statement of any consideration or of the place where the instrument is drawn or payable; or

(b) a statement that collateral has been given to secure obligations either on the instrument or otherwise of an obligor on the instrument or that in case of default on those obligations the holder may realize on or dispose of the collateral; or

(c) a promise or power to maintain or protect collateral or to give additional collateral; or

(d) a term authorizing a confession of judgment on the instrument if it is not paid when due; or

(e) a term purporting to waive the benefit of any law intended for the advantage or protection of any obligor; or

(f) a term in a draft providing that the payee by indorsing or cashing it acknowledges full satisfaction of an obligation of the drawer; or

(g) A statement in a draft drawn in a set of parts (Section 3–801) to the effect that the order is effective only if no other part has been honored.

(2) Nothing in this section shall validate any term which is otherwise illegal.

Section 3–113. Seal

An instrument otherwise negotiable is within this Article even though it is under a seal.

Section 3–114. Date, Antedating, Postdating

(1) The negotiability of an instrument is not affected by the fact that it is undated, antedated or postdated.

(2) Where an instrument is antedated or postdated the time when it is payable is determined by the stated date if the instrument is payable on demand or at a fixed period after date.

(3) Where the instrument or any signature thereon is dated, the date is presumed to be correct.

Section 3–115. Incomplete Instruments

(1) When a paper whose contents at the time of signing show that it is intended to become an instrument is signed while still incomplete in any necessary respect it cannot be enforced until completed, but when it is completed in accordance with authority given it is effective as completed.

(2) If the completion is unauthorized the rules as to material alteration apply (Section 3–407), even though the paper was not delivered by the maker or drawer; but the burden of establishing that any completion is unauthorized is on the party so asserting.

Section 3–116. Instruments Payable to Two or More Persons

An instrument payable to the order of two or more persons

(a) if in the alternative is payable to any one of them and may be negotiated, discharged or enforced by any of them who has possession of it;

(b) if not in the alternative is payable to all of them and may be negotiated, discharged or enforced only by all of them.

Section 3–117. Instruments Payable With Words of Description

An instrument made payable to a named person with the addition of words describing him

(a) as agent or officer of a specified person is payable to his principal but the agent or officer may act as if he were the holder;

(b) as any other fiduciary for a specified person or purpose is payable to the payee and may be negotiated, discharged or enforced by him;

(c) in any other manner is payable to the payee unconditionally and the additional words are without effect on subsequent parties.

Section 3–118. Ambiguous Terms and Rules of Construction

The following rules apply to every instrument:

(a) Where there is doubt whether the instrument is a draft or a note the holder may treat it as either. A draft drawn on the drawer is effective as a note.

(b) Handwritten terms control typewritten and printed terms, and typewritten control printed.

(c) Words control figures except that if the words are ambiguous figures control.

(d) Unless otherwise specified a provision for interest means interest at the judgment rate at the place of payment from the date of the instrument, or if it is undated from the date of issue.

(e) Unless the instrument otherwise specifies two or more persons who sign as maker, acceptor or drawer or indorser and as a part of the same transaction are jointly and severally liable even though the instrument contains such words as "I promise to pay."

(f) Unless otherwise specified consent to extension authorizes a single extension for not longer than the original period. A consent to extension, expressed in the instrument, is binding on secondary parties and accommodation makers. A holder may not exercise his option to extend an instrument over the objection of a maker or acceptor or other party who in accordance with Section 3–604 tenders full payment when the instrument is due.

Section 3–119. Other Writings Affecting Instrument

(1) As between the obligor and his immediate obligee or any transferee the terms of an instrument may be modified or affected by any other written agreement executed as a part of the same transaction, except that a holder in due course is not affected by any limitation of his rights arising out of the separate written agreement if he had no notice of the limitation when he took the instrument.

(2) A separate agreement does not affect the negotiability of an instrument.

Section 3–120. Instruments "Payable Through" Bank

An instrument which states that it is "payable through" a bank or the like designates that bank as a collecting bank to make presentment but does not of itself authorize the bank to pay the instrument.

Section 3–121. Instruments Payable at Bank

Note: *If this Article is introduced in the Congress of the United States this section should be omitted. (States to select either alternative)*

Alternative A

A note or acceptance which states that it is payable at a bank is the equivalent of a draft drawn on the bank payable when it falls due out of any funds of the maker or acceptor in current account or otherwise available for such payment.

Alternative B

A note or acceptance which states that it is payable at a bank is not of itself an order or authorization to the bank to pay it.

Section 3–122. Accrual of Cause of Action

(1) A cause of action against a maker or an acceptor accrues

- (a) in the case of a time instrument on the day after maturity;
- (b) in the case of a demand instrument upon its date or, if no date is stated, on the date of issue.

(2) A cause of action against the obligor of a demand or time certificate of deposit accrues upon demand, but demand on a time certificate may not be made until on or after the date of maturity.

(3) A cause of action against a drawer of a draft or an indorser of any instrument accrues upon demand following dishonor of the instrument. Notice of dishonor is a demand.

(4) Unless an instrument provides otherwise, interest runs at the rate provided by law for a judgment

- (a) in the case of a maker, acceptor or other primary obligor of a demand instrument, from the date of demand;
- (b) in all other cases from the date of accrual of the cause of action.

Part 2 Transfer and Negotiation

Section 3–201. Transfer: Right to Indorsement

(1) Transfer of an instrument vests in the transferee such rights as the transferor has therein, except that a transferee who has himself been a party to any fraud or illegality affecting the instrument or who as a prior holder had notice of a defense or claim against it cannot improve his position by taking from a later holder in due course.

(2) A transfer of a security interest in an instrument vests the foregoing rights in the transferee to the extent of the interest transferred.

(3) Unless otherwise agreed any transfer for value of an instrument not then payable to bearer gives the transferee the specifically enforceable right to have the unqualified indorsement of the transferor. Negotiation takes effect only when the indorsement is made and until that time there is no presumption that the transferee is the owner.

Section 3–202. Negotiation

(1) Negotiation is the transfer of an instrument in such form that the transferee becomes a holder. If the instrument is payable to order it is negotiated by delivery with any necessary indorsement; if payable to bearer it is negotiated by delivery.

(2) An indorsement must be written by or on behalf of the holder and on the instrument or on a paper so firmly affixed thereto as to become a part thereof.

(3) An indorsement is effective for negotiation only when it conveys the entire instrument or any unpaid residue. If it purports to be of less it operates only as a partial assignment.

(4) Words of assignment, condition, waiver, guaranty, limitation or disclaimer of liability and the like accompanying an indorsement do not affect its character as an indorsement.

Section 3–203. Wrong or Misspelled Name

Where an instrument is made payable to a person under a misspelled name or one other than his own he may indorse in that name or his own or both; but signature in both names may be required by a person paying or giving value for the instrument.

Section 3–204. Special Indorsement; Blank Indorsement

(1) A special indorsement specifies the person to whom or to whose order it makes the instrument payable. Any instrument specially indorsed becomes payable to the order of the special indorsee and may be further negotiated only by his indorsement.

(2) An indorsement in blank specifies no particular indorsee and may consist of a mere signature. An instrument payable to order and indorsed in blank becomes payable to bearer and may be negotiated by delivery alone until specially indorsed.

(3) The holder may convert a blank indorsement into a special indorsement by writing over the signature of the indorser in blank any contract consistent with the character of the indorsement.

Section 3–205. Restrictive Indorsements

An indorsement is restrictive which either

- (a) is conditional; or
- (b) purports to prohibit further transfer of the instrument; or
- (c) includes the words "for collection," "for deposit," "pay any bank," or like terms signifying a purpose of deposit or collection; or
- (d) otherwise states that it is for the benefit or use of the indorser or of another person.

Section 3–206. Effect of Restrictive Indorsement

(1) No restrictive indorsement prevents further transfer or negotiation of the instrument.

(2) An intermediary bank, or a payor bank which is not the depositary bank, is neither given notice nor otherwise affected by a restrictive indorsement of any person except the bank's immediate transferor or the person presenting for payment.

(3) Except for an intermediary bank, any transferee under an indorsement which is conditional or includes the words "for collection," "for deposit," "pay any bank," or like terms (subparagraphs (a) and (c) of Section 3–205) must pay or apply any value given by him for or on the

security of the instrument consistently with the indorsement and to the extent that he does so he becomes a holder for value. In addition such transferee is a holder in due course if he otherwise complies with the requirements of Section 3–302 on what constitutes a holder in due course.

(4) The first taker under an indorsement for the benefit of the indorser or another person (subparagraph (d) of Section 3–205) must pay or apply any value given by him for or on the security of the instrument consistently with the indorsement and to the extent that he does so he becomes a holder for value. In addition such taker is a holder in due course if he otherwise complies with the requirements of Section 3–302 on what constitutes a holder in due course. A later holder for value is neither given notice nor otherwise affected by such restrictive indorsement unless he has knowledge that a fiduciary or other person has negotiated the instrument in any transaction for his own benefit or otherwise in breach of duty (subsection (2) of Section 3–304).

Section 3–207. Negotiation Effective Although It May Be Rescinded

(1) Negotiation is effective to transfer the instrument although the negotiation is

- (a) made by an infant, a corporation exceeding its powers, or any other person without capacity; or
- (b) obtained by fraud, duress or mistake of any kind; or
- (c) part of an illegal transaction; or
- (d) made in breach of duty.

(2) Except as against a subsequent holder in due course such negotiation is in an appropriate case subject to rescission, the declaration of a constructive trust or any other remedy permitted by law.

Section 3–208. Reacquisition

Where an instrument is returned to or reacquired by a prior party he may cancel any indorsement which is not necessary to his title and reissue or further negotiate the instrument, but any intervening party is discharged as against the reacquiring party and subsequent holders not in due course and if his indorsement has been cancelled is discharged as against subsequent holders in due course as well.

Part 3 Rights of a Holder

Section 3–301. Rights of a Holder

The holder of an instrument whether or not he is the owner may transfer or negotiate it and, except as otherwise provided in Section 3–603 on payment or satisfaction, discharge it or enforce payment in his own name.

Section 3–302. Holder in Due Course

(1) A holder in due course is a holder who takes the instrument

- (a) for value, and
- (b) in good faith; and
- (c) without notice that it is overdue or has been dishonored or of any defense against or claim to it on the part of any person.

(2) A payee may be a holder in due course.

(3) A holder does not become a holder in due course of an instrument:

- (a) by purchase of it at judicial sale or by taking it under legal process; or
- (b) by acquiring it in taking over an estate; or
- (c) by purchasing it as part of a bulk transaction not in regular course of business of the transferor.

(4) A purchaser of a limited interest can be a holder in due course only to the extent of the interest purchased.

Section 3–303. Taking for Value

A holder takes the instrument for value

- (a) to the extent that the agreed consideration has been performed or that he acquires a security interest in or a lien on the instrument otherwise than by legal process; or
- (b) when he takes the instrument in payment of or as security for an antecedent claim against any person whether or not the claim is due; or
- (c) when he gives a negotiable instrument for it or makes an irrevocable commitment to a third person.

Section 3–304. Notice to Purchaser

(1) The purchaser has notice of a claim or defense if

- (a) the instrument is so incomplete, bears such visible evidence of forgery or alteration, or is otherwise so irregular as to call into question its validity, terms or ownership or to create an ambiguity as to the party to pay; or
- (b) the purchaser has notice that the obligation of any party is voidable in whole or in part, or that all parties have been discharged.

(2) The purchaser has notice of a claim against the instrument when he has knowledge that a fiduciary has negotiated the instrument in payment of or as security for his own debt or in any transaction for his own benefit or otherwise in breach of duty.

(3) The purchaser has notice that an instrument is overdue if he has reason to know

- (a) that any part of the principal amount is overdue or that there is an uncured default in payment of another instrument of the same series; or
- (b) that acceleration of the instrument has been made; or
- (c) that he is taking a demand instrument after demand has been made or more than a reasonable length of time after its issue. A reasonable time for a check drawn and payable within the states and territories of the United States and the District of Columbia is presumed to be thirty days.

(4) Knowledge of the following facts does not of itself give the purchaser notice of a defense or claim

- (a) that the instrument is antedated or postdated;
- (b) that it was issued or negotiated in return for an executory promise or accompanied by a separate agreement, unless the purchaser has notice that a defense or claim has arisen from the terms thereof;
- (c) that any party has signed for accommodation;
- (d) that an incomplete instrument has been completed, unless the purchaser has notice of any improper completion;
- (e) that any person negotiating the instrument is or was a fiduciary;

(f) that there has been default in payment of interest on the instrument or in payment of any other instrument, except one of the same series.

(5) The filing or recording of a document does not of itself constitute notice within the provisions of this Article to a person who would otherwise be a holder in due course.

(6) To be effective notice must be received at such time and in such manner as to give a reasonable opportunity to act on it.

Section 3–305. Rights of a Holder in Due Course

To the extent that a holder in due course he takes the instrument free from

(1) all claims to it on the part of any person; and

(2) all defenses of any party to the instrument with whom the holder has not dealt except

(a) infancy, to the extent that it is a defense to a simple contract; and

(b) such other incapacity, or duress, or illegality of the transaction, as renders the obligation of the party a nullity; and

(c) such misrepresentation as has induced the party to sign the instrument with neither knowledge nor reasonable opportunity to obtain knowledge of its character or its essential terms; and

(d) discharge in insolvency proceedings; and

(e) any other discharge of which the holder has notice when he takes the instrument.

Section 3–306. Rights of One Not Holder in Due Course

Unless he has the rights of a holder in due course any person takes the instrument subject to

(a) all valid claims to it on the part of any person; and

(b) all defenses of any party which would be available in an action on a simple contract; and

(c) the defenses of want or failure of consideration, non-performance of any condition precedent, non-delivery, or delivery for a special purpose (Section 3–408); and

(d) the defense that he or a person through whom he holds the instrument acquired it by theft, or that payment or satisfaction to such holder would be inconsistent with the terms of a restrictive indorsement. The claim of any third person to the instrument is not otherwise available as a defense to any party liable thereon unless the third person himself defends the action for such party.

Section 3–307. Burden of Establishing Signatures, Defenses and Due Course

(1) Unless specifically denied in the pleadings each signature on an instrument is admitted. When the effectiveness of a signature is put in issue

(a) the burden of establishing it is on the party claiming under the signature; but

(b) the signature is presumed to be genuine or authorized except where the action is to enforce the obligation of a purported signer who has died or become incompetent before proof is required.

(2) When signatures are admitted or established, production of the instrument entitles a holder to recover on it unless the defendant establishes a defense.

(3) After it is shown that a defense exists a person claiming the rights of a holder in due course has the burden of establishing that he or some person under whom he claims is in all respects a holder in due course.

Part 4 Liability of Parties

Section 3–401. Signature

(1) No person is liable on an instrument unless his signature appears thereon.

(2) A signature is made by use of any name, including any trade or assumed name, upon an instrument, or by any word or mark used in lieu of a written signature.

Section 3–402. Signature in Ambiguous Capacity

Unless the instrument clearly indicates that a signature is made in some other capacity it is an indorsement.

Section 3–403. Signature by Authorized Representative

(1) A signature may be made by an agent or other representative, and his authority to make it may be established as in other cases of representation. No particular form of appointment is necessary to establish such authority.

(2) An authorized representative who signs his own name to an instrument

(a) is personally obligated if the instrument neither names the person represented nor shows that the representative signed in a representative capacity;

(b) except as otherwise established between the immediate parties, is personally obligated if the instrument names the person represented but does not show that the representative signed in a representative capacity, or if the instrument does not name the person represented but does show that the representative signed in a representative capacity.

(3) Except as otherwise established the name of an organization preceded or followed by the name and office of an authorized individual is a signature made in a representative capacity.

Section 3–404. Unauthorized Signatures

(1) Any unauthorized signature is wholly inoperative as that of the person whose name is signed unless he ratifies it or is precluded from denying it; but it operates as the signature of the unauthorized signer in favor of any person who in good faith pays the instrument or takes it for value.

(2) Any unauthorized signature may be ratified for all purposes of this Article. Such ratification does not of itself affect any rights of the person ratifying against the actual signer.

Section 3–405. Imposters; Signature in Name of Payee

(1) An indorsement by any person in the name of a named payee is effective if

(a) an imposter by use of the mails or otherwise has induced the maker or drawer to issue the instrument to him or his confederate in the name of the payee; or

(b) a person signing as or on behalf of a maker or drawer intends the payee to have no interest in the instrument; or

(c) an agent or employee of the maker or drawer has supplied him with the name of the payee intending the latter to have no such interest.

(2) Nothing in this section shall affect the criminal or civil liability of the person so indorsing.

Section 3–406. Negligence Contributing to Alteration or Unauthorized Signature

Any person who by his negligence substantially contributes to a material alteration of the instrument or to the making of an unauthorized signature is precluded from asserting the alteration or lack of authority against a holder in due course or against a drawee or other payor who pays the instrument in good faith and in accordance with the reasonable commercial standards of the drawee's or payor's business.

Section 3–407. Alteration

(1) Any alteration of an instrument is material which changes the contract of any party thereto in any respect, including any such change in

(a) the number of relations of the parties; or

(b) an incomplete instrument, by completing it otherwise than as authorized; or

(c) the writing as signed, by adding to it or by removing any part of it.

(2) As against any person other than a subsequent holder in due course.

(a) alteration by the holder which is both fraudulent and material discharges any party whose contract is thereby changed unless that party assents or is precluded from asserting the defense;

(b) no other alteration discharges any party and the instrument may be enforced according to its original tenor, or as to incomplete instruments according to the authority given.

(3) A subsequent holder in due course may in all cases enforce the instrument according to its original tenor, and when an incomplete instrument has been completed, he may enforce it as completed.

Section 3–408. Consideration

Want or failure of consideration is a defense as against any person not having the rights of a holder in due course (Section 3–305), except that no consideration is necessary for an instrument or obligation thereon given in payment of or as security for an antecedent obligation of any kind. Nothing in this section shall be taken to displace any statute outside this Act under which a promise is enforceable notwithstanding lack or failure of consideration. Partial failure of consideration is a defense pro tanto whether or not the failure is in an ascertained or liquidated amount.

Section 3–409. Draft Not an Assignment

(1) A check or other draft does not of itself operate as an assignment of any funds in the hands of the drawee available for its payment, and the drawee is not liable on the instrument until he accepts it.

(2) Nothing in this section shall affect any liability in contract, tort or otherwise arising from any letter of credit or other obligation or representation which is not an acceptance.

Section 3–410. Definition and Operation of Acceptance

(1) Acceptance is the drawee's signed engagement to honor the draft as presented. It must be written on the draft, and may consist of his signature alone. It becomes operative when completed by delivery or notification.

(2) A draft may be accepted although it has not been signed by the drawer or is otherwise incomplete or is overdue or has been dishonored.

(3) Where the draft is payable at a fixed period after sight and the acceptor fails to date his acceptance the holder may complete it by supplying a date in good faith.

Section 3–411. Certification of a Check

(1) Certification of a check is acceptance. Where a holder procures certification the drawer and all prior indorsers are discharged.

(2) Unless otherwise agreed a bank has no obligation to certify a check.

(3) A bank may certify a check before returning it for lack of proper indorsement. If it does so the drawer is discharged.

Section 3–412. Acceptance Varying Draft

(1) Where the drawee's proffered acceptance in any manner varies the draft as presented the holder may refuse the acceptance and treat the draft as dishonored in which case the drawee is entitled to have his acceptance cancelled.

(2) The terms of the draft are not varied by an acceptance to pay at any particular bank or place in the United States, unless the acceptance states that the draft is to be paid only at such bank or place.

(3) Where the holder assents to an acceptance varying the terms of the draft each drawer and indorser who does not affirmatively assent is discharged.

Section 3–413. Contract of Maker, Drawer and Acceptor

(1) The maker or acceptor engages that he will pay the instrument according to its tenor at the time of his engagement or as completed pursuant to Section 3–115 on incomplete instruments.

(2) The drawer engages that upon dishonor of the draft and any necessary notice of dishonor or protest he will pay the amount of the draft to the holder or to any indorser who takes it up. The drawer may disclaim this liability by drawing without recourse.

(3) By making, drawing or accepting the party admits as against all subsequent parties including the drawee the existence of the payee and his then capacity to indorse.

Section 3–414. Contract of Indorser; Order of Liability

(1) Unless the indorsement otherwise specifies (as by such words as "without recourse") every indorser engages that upon dishonor and any necessary notice of dishonor and protest he will pay the instrument according to its tenor at the time of his indorsement to the holder or to any subsequent indorser who takes it up, even though the indorser who takes it up was not obligated to do so.

(2) Unless they otherwise agree indorsers are liable to one another in the order in which they indorse, which is presumed to be the order in which their signatures appear on the instrument.

Section 3–415. Contract of Accommodation Party

(1) An accommodation party is one who signs the instrument in any capacity for the purpose of lending his name to another party to it.

(2) When the instrument has been taken for value before it is due the accommodation party is liable in the capacity in which he has signed even though the taker knows of the accommodation.

(3) As against a holder in due course and without notice of the accommodation oral proof of the accommodation is not admissible to give the accommodation party the benefit of discharges dependent on his character as such. In other cases the accommodation character may be shown by oral proof.

(4) An indorsement which shows that it is not in the chain of title is notice of its accommodation character.

(5) An accommodation party is not liable to the party accommodated, and if he pays the instrument has a right of recourse on the instrument against such party.

Section 3–416. Contract of Guarantor

(1) "Payment guaranteed" or equivalent words added to a signature mean that the signer engages that if the instrument is not paid when due he will pay it according to its tenor without resort by the holder to any other party.

(2) "Collection guaranteed" or equivalent words added to a signature mean that the signer engages that if the instrument is not paid when due he will pay it according to its tenor, but only after the holder has reduced his claim against the maker or acceptor to judgment and execution has been returned unsatisfied, or after the maker or acceptor has become insolvent or it is otherwise apparent that it is useless to proceed against him.

(3) Words of guaranty which do not otherwise specify guarantee payment.

(4) No words of guaranty added to the signature of a sole maker or acceptor affect his liability on the instrument. Such words added to the signature of one of two or more makers or acceptors create a presumption that the signature is for the accommodation of the others.

(5) When words of guaranty are used presentment, notice of dishonor and protest are not necessary to charge the user.

(6) Any guaranty written on the instrument is enforcible notwithstanding any statute of frauds.

Section 3–417. Warranties on Presentment and Transfer

(1) Any person who obtains payment or acceptance and any prior transferor warrants to a person who in good faith pays or accepts that

- (a) he has a good title to the instrument or is authorized to obtain payment or acceptance on behalf of one who has a good title; and
- (b) he has no knowledge that the signature of the maker or drawer is unauthorized, except that this warranty is not given by a holder in due course acting in good faith
    - (i) to a maker with respect to the maker's own signature; or
    - (ii) to a drawer with respect to the drawer's own signature, whether or not the drawer is also the drawee; or
    - (iii) to an acceptor of a draft if the holder in due course took the draft after the acceptance or obtained the acceptance without knowledge that the drawer's signature was unauthorized; and
- (c) the instrument has not been materially altered, except that this warranty is not given by a holder in due course acting in good faith
    - (i) to the maker of a note; or
    - (ii) to the drawer of a draft whether or not the drawer is also the drawee; or
    - (iii) to the acceptor of a draft with respect to an alteration made prior to the acceptance if the holder in due course took the draft after the acceptance, even though the acceptance provided "payable as originally drawn" or equivalent terms; or
    - (iv) to the acceptor of a draft with respect to an alteration made after the acceptance.

(2) Any person who transfers an instrument and receives consideration warrants to his transferee and if the transfer is by indorsement to any subsequent holder who takes the instrument in good faith that

- (a) he has a good title to the instrument or is authorized to obtain payment or acceptance on behalf of one who has a good title and the transfer is otherwise rightful; and
- (b) all signatures are genuine or authorized; and
- (c) the instrument has not been materially altered; and
- (d) no defense of any party is good against him; and
- (e) he has no knowledge of any insolvency proceeding instituted with respect to the maker or acceptor or the drawer of an unaccepted instrument.

(3) By transferring "without recourse" the transferor limits the obligation stated in subsection (2)(d) to a warranty that he has no knowledge of such a defense.

(4) A selling agent or broker who does not disclose the fact that he is acting only as such gives the warranties provided in this section, but if he makes such disclosure warrants only his good faith and authority.

Section 3–418. Finality of Payment or Acceptance

Except for recovery of bank payments as provided in the Article on Bank Deposits and Collections (Article 4) and except for liability for breach of warranty on presentment under the preceding section, payment or acceptance of any instrument is final in favor of a holder in due course, or a person who has in good faith changed his position in reliance on the payment.

Section 3–419. Conversion of Instrument; Innocent Representative

(1) An instrument is converted when

- (a) a drawee to whom it is delivered for acceptance refuses to return it on demand; or
- (b) any person to whom it is delivered for payment refuses on demand either to pay or to return it; or
- (c) it is paid on a forged indorsement.

(2) In an action against a drawee under subsection (1) the measure of the drawee's liability is the face amount of the instrument. In any other action under subsection (1) the measure of liability is presumed to be the face amount of the instrument.

(3) Subject to the provisions of this Act concerning restrictive indorsements a representative, including a depositary or collecting bank, who has in good faith and in accordance with the reasonable commercial standards applicable to the business of such representative dealt with an instrument or its proceeds on behalf of one who was not the true owner is not liable in conversion or otherwise to the true owner beyond the amount of any proceeds remaining in his hands.

(4) An intermediary bank or payor bank which is not a depositary bank is not liable in conversion solely by reason of the fact that proceeds of an item indorsed restrictively (Section 3–205 and 3–206) are not paid or applied consistently with the restrictive indorsement of an indorser other than its immediate transferor.

Part 5 Presentment, Notice of Dishonor and Protest

Section 3–501. When Presentment, Notice of Dishonor, and Protest Necessary or Permissible

(1) Unless excused (Section 3–511) presentment is necessary to charge secondary parties as follows:

- (a) presentment for acceptance is necessary to charge the drawer and indorsers of a draft where the draft so provides, or is payable elsewhere than at the residence or place of business of the drawee, or its date of payment depends upon such presentment. The holder may at his option present for acceptance any other draft payable at a stated date;
- (b) presentment for payment is necessary to charge any indorser;
- (c) in the case of any drawer, the acceptor of a draft payable at a bank or the maker of a note payable at a bank, presentment for payment is necessary, but failure to make presentment discharges such drawer, acceptor or maker only as stated in Section 3–502(1) (b).

(2) Unless excused (Section 3–511)

- (a) notice of any dishonor is necessary to charge any indorser;
- (b) in the case of any drawer, the acceptor of a draft payable at a bank or the maker of a note payable at a bank, notice of any dishonor is necessary, but failure to give such notice discharges such drawer, acceptor or maker only as stated in Section 3–502(1) (b).

(3) Unless excused (Section 3–511) protest of any dishonor is necessary to charge the drawer and indorsers of any draft which on its face appears to be drawn or payable outside of the states, territories, dependencies and possessions of the United States, the District of Columbia and the Commonwealth of Puerto Rico. The holder may at his option make protest of any dishonor of any other instrument and in the case of a foreign draft may on insolvency of the acceptor before maturity make protest for better security.

(4) Notwithstanding any provision of this section, neither presentment nor notice of dishonor nor protest is necessary to charge an indorser who has indorsed an instrument after maturity.

Section 3–502. Unexcused Delay; Discharge

(1) Where without excuse any necessary presentment or notice of dishonor is delayed beyond the time when it is due

- (a) any indorser is discharged; and
- (b) any drawer or the acceptor of a draft payable at a bank or the maker of a note payable at a bank who because the drawee or payor bank becomes insolvent during the delay is deprived of funds maintained with the drawee or payor bank to cover the instrument may discharge his liability by written assignment to the holder of his rights against the drawee or payor bank in respect of such funds, but such drawer, acceptor or maker is not otherwise discharged.

(2) Where without excuse a necessary protest is delayed beyond the time when it is due any drawer or indorser is discharged.

Section 3–503. Time of Presentment

(1) Unless a different time is expressed in the instrument the time for any presentment is determined as follows:

- (a) where an instrument is payable at or a fixed period after a stated date any presentment for acceptance must be made on or before the date it is payable;
- (b) where an instrument is payable after sight it must either be presented for acceptance or negotiated within a reasonable time after date or issue whichever is later;
- (c) where an instrument shows the date on which it is payable presentment for payment is due on that date;
- (d) where an instrument is accelerated presentment for payment is due within a reasonable time after the acceleration;
- (e) with respect to the liability of any secondary party presentment for acceptance or payment of any other instrument is due within a reasonable time after such party becomes liable thereon.

(2) A reasonable time for presentment is determined by the nature of the instrument, any usage of banking or trade and the facts of the particular case. In the case of an uncertified check which is drawn and payable within the United States and which is not a draft drawn by a bank the following are presumed to be reasonable periods within which to present for payment or to initiate bank collection:

- (a) with respect to the liability of the drawer, thirty days after date or issue whichever is later; and
- (b) with respect to the liability of an indorser, seven days after his indorsement.

(3) Where any presentment is due on a day which is not a full business day for either the person making presentment or the party to pay or accept, presentment is due on the next following day which is a full business day for both parties.

(4) Presentment to be sufficient must be made at a reasonable hour, and if at a bank during its banking day.

Section 3–504. How Presentment Made

(1) Presentment is a demand for acceptance or payment made upon the maker, acceptor, drawee or other payor by or on behalf of the holder.

(2) Presentment may be made

- (a) by mail, in which event the time of presentment is determined by the time of receipt of the mail; or
- (b) through a clearing house; or
- (c) at the place of acceptance or payment specified in the instrument or if there be none at the place of business or residence of the party to accept or pay. If neither the party to accept or pay nor anyone authorized to act for him is present or accessible at such place presentment is excused.

(3) It may be made

- (a) to any one of two or more makers, acceptors, drawees or other payors; or
- (b) to any person who has authority to make or refuse the acceptance or payment.

(4) A draft accepted or a note made payable at a bank in the United States must be presented at such bank.

(5) In the cases described in Section 4–210 presentment may be made in the manner and with the result stated in that section.

Section 3–505. Rights of Party to Whom Presentment Is Made

(1) The party to whom presentment is made may without dishonor require

(a) exhibition of the instrument; and

(b) reasonable identification of the person making presentment and evidence of his authority to make it if made for another; and

(c) that the instrument be produced for acceptance or payment at a place specified in it, or if there be none at any place reasonable in the circumstances; and

(d) a signed receipt on the instrument for any partial or full payment and its surrender upon full payment.

(2) Failure to comply with any such requirement invalidates the presentment but the person presenting has a reasonable time in which to comply and the time for acceptance or payment runs from the time of compliance.

Section 3–506. Time Allowed for Acceptance or Payment

(1) Acceptance may be deferred without dishonor until the close of the next business day following presentment. The holder may also in a good faith effort to obtain acceptance and without either dishonor of the instrument or discharge of secondary parties allow postponement of acceptance for an additional business day.

(2) Except as a longer time is allowed in the case of documentary drafts drawn under a letter of credit, and unless an earlier time is agreed to by the party to pay, payment of an instrument may be deferred without dishonor pending reasonable examination to determine whether it is properly payable, but payment must be made in any event before the close of business on the day of presentment.

Section 3–507. Dishonor; Holder's Right of Recourse; Term Allowing Re-Presentment

(1) An instrument is dishonored when

(a) a necessary or optional presentment is duly made and due acceptance or payment is refused or cannot be obtained within the prescribed time or in case of bank collections the instrument is seasonably returned by the midnight deadline (Section 4–301); or

(b) presentment is excused and the instrument is not duly accepted or paid.

(2) Subject to any necessary notice of dishonor and protest, the holder has upon dishonor an immediate right of recourse against the drawers and indorsers.

(3) Return of an instrument for lack of proper indorsement is not dishonor.

(4) A term in a draft or an indorsement thereof allowing a stated time for re-presentment in the event of any dishonor of the draft by nonacceptance if a time draft or by nonpayment if a sight draft gives the holder as against any secondary party bound by the term an option to waive the dishonor without affecting the liability of the secondary party and he may present again up to the end of the stated time.

Section 3–508. Notice of Dishonor

(1) Notice of dishonor may be given to any person who may be liable on the instrument by or on behalf of the holder or any party who has himself received notice, or any other party who can be compelled to pay the instrument. In addition an agent or bank in whose hands the instrument is dishonored may give notice to his principal or customer or to another agent or bank from which the instrument was received.

(2) Any necessary notice must be given by a bank before its midnight deadline and by any other person before midnight of the third business day after dishonor or receipt of notice of dishonor.

(3) Notice may be given in any reasonable manner. It may be oral or written and in any terms which identify the instrument and state that it has been dishonored. A misdescription which does not mislead the party notified does not vitiate the notice. Sending the instrument bearing a stamp, ticket or writing stating that acceptance or payment has been refused or sending a notice of debit with respect to the instrument is sufficient.

(4) Written notice is given when sent although it is not received.

(5) Notice to one partner is notice to each although the firm has been dissolved.

(6) When any party is in insolvency proceedings instituted after the issue of the instrument notice may be given either to the party or to the representative of his estate.

(7) When any party is dead or incompetent notice may be sent to his last known address or given to his personal representative.

(8) Notice operates for the benefit of all parties who have rights on the instrument against the party notified.

Section 3–509. Protest; Noting for Protest

(1) A protest is a certificate of dishonor made under the hand and seal of a United States consul or vice consul or a notary public or other person authorized to certify dishonor by the law of the place where dishonor occurs. It may be made upon information satisfactory to such person.

(2) The protest must identify the instrument and certify either that due presentment has been made or the reason why it is excused and that the instrument has been dishonored by nonacceptance or nonpayment.

(3) The protest may also certify that notice of dishonor has been given to all parties or to specified parties.

(4) Subject to subsection (5) any necessary protest is due by the time that notice of dishonor is due.

(5) If, before protest is due, an instrument has been noted for protest by the officer to make protest, the protest may be made at any time thereafter as of the date of noting.

Section 3–510. Evidence of Dishonor and Notice of Dishonor

The following are admissible as evidence and create a presumption of dishonor and of any notice of dishonor therein shown:

(a) a document regular in form as provided in the preceding section which purports to be a protest;

(b) the purported stamp or writing of the drawee; payor bank or presenting bank on the instrument or accompanying it stating that acceptance or payment has been refused for reasons consistent with dishonor;

(c) any book or record of the drawee, payor bank, or any collecting bank kept in the usual course of business which shows dishonor, even though there is no evidence of who made the entry.

Section 3–511. Waived or Excused Presentment, Protest or Notice of Dishonor or Delay Therein

(1) Delay in presentment, protest or notice of dishonor is excused when the party is without notice that it is due or when the delay is caused by circumstances beyond his control and he exercises reasonable diligence after the cause of the delay ceases to operate.

(2) Presentment or notice or protest as the case may be is entirely excused when

(a) the party to be charged has waived it expressly or by implication either before or after it is due; or

(b) such party has himself dishonored the instrument or has countermanded payment or otherwise has no reason to expect or right to require that the instrument be accepted or paid; or

(c) by reasonable diligence the presentment or protest cannot be made or the notice given.

(3) Presentment is also entirely excused when

(a) the maker, acceptor, or drawee of any instrument except a documentary draft is dead or in insolvency proceedings instituted after the issue of the instrument; or

(b) acceptance or payment is refused but not for want of proper presentment.

(4) Where a draft has been dishonored by nonacceptance a later presentment for payment and any notice of dishonor and protest for nonpayment are excused unless in the meantime the instrument has been accepted.

(5) A waiver of protest is also a waiver of presentment and of notice of dishonor even though protest is not required.

(6) Where a waiver of presentment or notice or protest is embodied in the instrument itself it is binding upon all parties; but where it is written above the signature of an indorser it binds him only.

Part 6 Discharge

Section 3–601. Discharge of Parties

(1) The extent of the discharge of any party from liability on an instrument is governed by the sections on

(a) payment or satisfaction (Section 3–603); or

(b) tender of payment (Section 3–604); or

(c) cancellation or renunciation (Section 3–605); or

(d) impairment of right of recourse or of collateral (Section 3–606); or

(e) reacquisition of the instrument by a prior party (Section 3–208); or

(f) fraudulent and material alteration (Section 3–407); or

(g) certification of a check (Section 3–411); or

(h) acceptance varying a draft (Section 3–412); or

(i) unexcused delay in presentment or notice of dishonor or protest (Section 3–502).

(2) Any party is also discharged from his liability on an instrument to another party by any other act or agreement with such party which would discharge his simple contract for the payment of money.

(3) The liability of all parties is discharged when any party who has himself no right of action or recourse on the instrument

(a) reacquires the instrument in his own right; or

(b) is discharged under any provision of this Article, except as otherwise provided with respect to discharge for impairment of recourse or of collateral (Section 3–606).

Section 3–602. Effect of Discharge Against Holder in Due Course

No discharge of any party provided by this Article is effective against a subsequent holder in due course unless he has notice thereof when he takes the instrument.

Section 3–603. Payment or Satisfaction

(1) The liability of any party is discharged to the extent of his payment or satisfaction to the holder even though it is made with knowledge of a claim of another person to the instrument unless prior to such payment or satisfaction the person making the claim either supplies indemnity deemed adequate by the party seeking the discharge or enjoins payment or satisfaction by order of a court of competent jurisdiction in an action in which the adverse claimant and the holder are parties. This subsection does not, however, result in the discharge of the liability

(a) of a party who in bad faith pays or satisfies a holder who acquired the instrument by theft or who (unless having the rights of a holder in due course) holds through one who so acquired it; or

(b) of a party (other than an intermediary bank or a payor bank which is not a depositary bank) who pays or satisfies the holder of an instrument which has been restrictively indorsed in a manner not consistent with the terms of such restrictive indorsement.

(2) Payment or satisfaction may be made with the consent of the holder by any person including a stranger to the instrument. Surrender of the instrument to such a person gives him the rights of a transferee (Section 3–201).

Section 3–604. Tender of Payment

(1) Any party making tender of full payment to a holder when or after it is due is discharged to the extent of all subsequent liability for interest, costs and attorney's fees.

(2) The holder's refusal of such tender wholly discharges any party who has a right of recourse against the party making the tender.

(3) Where the maker or acceptor of an instrument payable otherwise than on demand is able and ready to pay at every place of payment specified in the instrument when it is due, it is equivalent to tender.

Section 3–605. Cancellation and Renunciation

(1) The holder of an instrument may even without consideration discharge any party

(a) in any manner apparent on the face of the instrument or the endorsement, as by intentionally cancelling the instrument or the party's signature by destruction or mutilation, or by striking out the party's signature; or

(b) by renouncing his rights by a writing signed and delivered or by surrender of the instrument to the party to be discharged.

(2) Neither cancellation nor renunciation without surrender of the instrument affects the title thereto.

Section 3–606. Impairment of Recourse or of Collateral

(1) The holder discharges any party to the instrument to the extent that without such party's consent the holder

(a) without express reservation of rights releases or agrees not to sue any person against whom the party has to the knowledge of the holder a right of recourse or agrees to suspend the right to enforce against such person the instrument or collateral or otherwise discharges such person, except that failure or delay in effecting any required presentment, protest or notice of dishonor with respect to any such person does not discharge any party as to whom presentment, protest or notice of dishonor is effective or unnecessary; or

(b) unjustifiably impairs any collateral for the instrument given by or on behalf of the party or any person against whom he has a right of recourse.

(2) By express reservation of rights against a party with a right of recourse the holder preserves

(a) all his rights against such party as of the time when the instrument was originally due; and

(b) the right of the party to pay the instrument as of that time; and

(c) all rights of such party to recourse against others.

Part 7 Advice of International Sight Draft

Section 3–701. Letter of Advice of International Sight Draft

(1) A "letter of advice" is a drawer's communication to the drawee that a described draft has been drawn.

(2) Unless otherwise agreed when a bank receives from another bank a letter of advice of an international sight draft the drawee bank may immediately debit the drawer's account and stop the running of interest pro tanto. Such a debit and any resulting credit to any account covering outstanding drafts leaves in the drawer full power to stop payment or otherwise dispose of the amount and creates no trust or interest in favor of the holder.

(3) Unless otherwise agreed and except where a draft is drawn under a credit issued by the drawee, the drawee of an international sight draft owes the drawer no duty to pay an unadvised draft but if it does so and the draft is genuine, may appropriately debit the drawer's account.

Part 8 Miscellaneous

Section 3–801. Drafts in a Set

(1) Where a draft is drawn in a set of parts, each of which is numbered and expressed to be an order only if no other part has been honored, the whole of the parts constitutes one draft but a taker of any part may become a holder in due course of the draft.

(2) Any person who negotiates, indorses or accepts a single part of a draft drawn in a set thereby becomes liable to any holder in due course of that part as if it were the whole set, but as between different holders in due course to whom different parts have been negotiated the holder whose title first accrues has all rights to the draft and its proceeds.

(3) As against the drawee the first presented part of a draft drawn in a set is the part entitled to payment, or if a time draft to acceptance and payment. Acceptance of any subsequently presented part renders the drawee liable thereon under subsection (2). With respect both to a holder and to the drawer payment of a subsequently presented part of a draft payable at sight has the same effect as payment of a check notwithstanding an effective stop order (Section 4–407).

(4) Except as otherwise provided in this section, where any part of a draft in a set is discharged by payment or otherwise the whole draft is discharged.

Section 3–802. Effect of Instrument on Obligation for Which It Is Given

(1) Unless otherwise agreed where an instrument is taken for an underlying obligation

(a) the obligation is pro tanto discharged if a bank is drawer, maker or acceptor of the instrument and there is no recourse on the instrument against the underlying obligor; and

(b) in any other case the obligation is suspended pro tanto until the instrument is due or if it is payable on demand until its presentment. If the instrument is dishonored action may be maintained on either the instrument or the obligation; discharge of the underlying obligor on the instrument also discharges him on the obligation.

(2) The taking in good faith of a check which is not postdated does not of itself so extend the time on the original obligation as to discharge a surety.

Section 3–803. Notice to Third Party

Where a defendant is sued for breach of an obligation for which a third person is answerable over under this Article he may give the third person written notice of the litigation, and the person notified may then give similar notice to any other person who is answerable over to him under this Article. If the notice states that the person notified may come in and defend and that if the person notified does not do so he will in any action against him by the person giving the notice be bound by any determination of fact common to the two litigations, then unless after seasonable receipt of the notice the person notified does come in and defend he is so bound.

Section 3–804. Lost, Destroyed or Stolen Instruments

The owner of an instrument which is lost, whether by destruction, theft or otherwise, may maintain an action in his own name and recover from any party liable thereon upon due proof of his ownership, the facts which prevent his production of the instrument and its terms. The court may require security indemnifying the defendant against loss by reason of further claims on the instrument.

Section 3–805. Instruments Not Payable to Order or to Bearer

This Article applies to any instrument whose terms do not preclude transfer and which is otherwise negotiable within this Article but which is not payable to order or to bearer, except that there can be no holder in due course of such an instrument.

Article 4 Bank Deposits and Collections

Part 1 General Provisions and Definitions

Section 4–101. Short Title

This Article shall be known and may be cited as Uniform Commercial Code—Bank Deposits and Collections.

Section 4–102. Applicability

(1) To the extent that items within this Article are also within the scope of Articles 3 and 8, they are subject to the provisions of those Articles. In the event of conflict the provisions of this Article govern those of Article 3 but the provisions of Article 8 govern those of this Article.

(2) The liability of a bank for action or non-action with respect to any item handled by it for purposes of presentment, payment or collection is governed by the law of the place where the bank is located. In the case of action or non-action by or at a branch or separate office of a bank, its liability is governed by the law of the place where the branch or separate office is located.

Section 4–103. Variation by Agreement; Measure of Damages; Certain Action Constituting Ordinary Care

(1) The effect of the provisions of this Article may be varied by agreement except that no agreement can disclaim a bank's responsibility for its own lack of good faith or failure to exercise ordinary care or can limit the measure of damages for such lack or failure; but the parties may by agreement determine the standards by which such responsibility is to be measured if such standards are not manifestly unreasonable.

(2) Federal Reserve regulations and operating letters, clearing house rules, and the like, have the effect of agreements under subsection (1), whether or not specifically assented to by all parties interested in items handled.

(3) Action or non-action approved by this Article or pursuant to Federal Reserve regulations or operating letters constitutes the exercise of ordinary care and, in the absence of special instructions, action or non-action consistent with clearing house rules and the like or with a general banking usage not disapproved by this Article, prima facie constitutes the exercise of ordinary care.

(4) The specification or approval of certain procedures by this Article does not constitute disapproval of other procedures which may be reasonable under the circumstances.

(5) The measure of damages for failure to exercise ordinary care in handling an item is the amount of the item reduced by an amount which could not have been realized by the use of ordinary care, and where there is bad faith it includes other damages, if any, suffered by the party as a proximate consequence.

Section 4–104. Definitions and Index of Definitions

(1) In this Article unless the context otherwise requires

- (a) "Account" means any account with a bank and includes a checking, time, interest or savings account;
- (b) "Afternoon" means the period of a day between noon and midnight;
- (c) "Banking day" means that part of any day on which a bank is open to the public for carrying on substantially all of its banking functions;
- (d) "Clearing house" means any association of banks or other payors regularly clearing items;
- (e) "Customer" means any person having an account with a bank or for whom a bank has agreed to collect items and includes a bank carrying an account with another bank;
- (f) "Documentary draft" means any negotiable or non-negotiable draft with accompanying documents, securities or other papers to be delivered against honor of the draft;
- (g) "Item" means any instrument for the payment of money even though it is not negotiable but does not include money;
- (h) "Midnight deadline" with respect to a bank is midnight on its next banking day following the banking day on which it receives the relevant item or notice or from which the time for taking action commences to run, whichever is later;
- (i) "Properly payable" includes the availability of funds for payment at the time of decision to pay or dishonor;
- (j) "Settle" means to pay in cash, by clearing house settlement, in a charge or credit or by remittance, or otherwise as instructed. A settlement may be either provisional or final;
- (k) "Suspends payments" with respect to a bank means that it has been closed by order of the supervisory authorities, that a public officer has been appointed to take it over or that it ceases or refuses to make payments in the ordinary course of business.

(2) Other definitions applying to this Article and the sections in which they appear are:

"Collecting bank." Section 4–105.

"Depositary bank." Section 4–105.

"Intermediary bank." Section 4–105.

"Payor bank." Section 4–105.

"Presenting bank." Section 4–105.

"Remitting bank." Section 4–105.

(3) The following definitions in other Articles apply to this Article:

"Acceptance." Section 3–410.

"Certificate of deposit." Section 3–104.

"Certification." Section 3–411.

"Check." Section 3–104.

"Draft." Section 3–104.

"Holder in due course." Section 3–302.

"Notice of dishonor." Section 3–508.

"Presentment." Section 3–504.

"Protest." Section 3–509.

"Secondary party." Section 3–102.

(4) In addition Article 1 contains general definitions and principles of construction and interpretation applicable throughout this Article.

Section 4–105. "Depositary Bank"; "Intermediary Bank"; "Collecting Bank"; "Payor Bank"; "Presenting Bank"; "Remitting Bank"

In this Article unless the context otherwise requires:

(a) "Depositary bank" means the first bank to which an item is transferred for collection even though it is also the payor bank;

(b) "Payor bank" means a bank by which an item is payable as drawn or accepted;

(c) "Intermediary bank" means any bank to which an item is transferred in course of collection except the depositary or payor bank;

(d) "Collecting bank" means any bank handling the item for collection except the payor bank;

(e) "Presenting bank" means any bank presenting an item except a payor bank;

(f) "Remitting bank" means any payor or intermediary bank remitting for an item.

Section 4–106. Separate Office of a Bank

A branch or separate office of a bank [maintaining its own deposit ledgers] is a separate bank for the purpose of computing the time within which and determining the place at or to which action may be taken or notices or orders shall be given under this Article and under Article 3.

Note: *The brackets are to make it optional with the several states whether to require a branch to maintain its own deposit ledgers in order to be considered to be a separate bank for certain purposes under Article 4. In some states "maintaining its own deposit ledgers" is a satisfactory test. In others branch banking practices are such that this test would not be suitable.*

Section 4–107. Time of Receipt of Items

(1) For the purpose of allowing time to process items, prove balances and make the necessary entries on its books to determine its position for the day, a bank may fix an afternoon hour of 2 P.M. or later as a cut-off hour for the handling of money and items and the making of entries on its books.

(2) Any item or deposit of money received on any day after a cut-off hour so fixed or after the close of the banking day may be treated as being received at the opening of the next banking day.

Section 4–108. Delays

(1) Unless otherwise instructed, a collecting bank in a good faith effort to secure payment may, in the case of specific items and with or without the approval of any person involved, waive, modify or extend time limits imposed or permitted by this Act for a period not in excess of an additional banking day without discharge of secondary parties and without liability to its transferor or any prior party.

(2) Delay by a collecting bank or payor bank beyond time limits prescribed or permitted by this Act or by instructions is excused if caused by interruption of communication facilities, suspension of payments by another bank, war, emergency conditions or other circumstances beyond the control of the bank provided it exercises such diligence as the circumstances require.

Section 4–109. Process of Posting

The "process of posting" means the usual procedure followed by a payor bank in determining to pay an item and in recording the payment including one or more of the following or other steps as determined by the bank:

(a) verification of any signature;

(b) ascertaining that sufficient funds are available;

(c) affixing a "paid" or other stamp;

(d) entering a charge or entry to a customer's account;

(e) correcting or reversing an entry or erroneous action with respect to the item.

Part 2 Collection of Items: Depositary and Collecting Banks

Section 4–201. Presumption and Duration of Agency Status of Collecting Banks and Provisional Status of Credits; Applicability of Article; Item Indorsed "Pay Any Bank"

(1) Unless a contrary intent clearly appears and prior to the time that a settlement given by a collecting bank for an item is or becomes final (subsection (3) of Section 4–211 and Sections 4–212 and 4–213) the bank is an agent or sub-agent of the owner of the item and any settlement given for the item is provisional. This provision applies regardless of the form of indorsement or lack of indorsement and even though credit given for the item is subject to immediate withdrawal as of right or is in fact withdrawn; but the continuance of ownership of an item by its owner and any rights of the owner to proceeds of the item are subject to rights of a collecting bank such as those resulting from outstanding advances on the item and valid rights of set-off. When an item is handled by banks for purposes of presentment, payment and collection, the relevant provisions of this Article apply even though action of parties clearly establishes that a particular bank has purchased the item and is the owner of it.

(2) After an item has been indorsed with the words "pay any bank" or the like, only a bank may acquire the rights of a holder

(a) until the item has been returned to the customer initiating collection; or

(b) until the item has been specially indorsed by a bank to a person who is not a bank.

Section 4–202. Responsibility for Collection; When Action Seasonable

(1) A collecting bank must use ordinary care in

(a) presenting an item or sending it for presentment; and

(b) sending notice of dishonor or non-payment or returning an item other than a documentary draft to the bank's transferor [or directly to the depositary bank under subsection (2) of Section 4–212] (*see note to Section 4–212*) after learning that the item has not been paid or accepted, as the case may be; and

(c) settling for an item when the bank receives final settlement; and

(d) making or providing for any necessary protest; and

(e) notifying its transferor of any loss or delay in transit within a reasonable time after discovery thereof.

(2) A collecting bank taking proper action before its midnight deadline following receipt of an item, notice or payment acts seasonably; taking proper action within a reasonably longer time may be seasonable but the bank has the burden of so establishing.

(3) Subject to subsection (1) (a), a bank is not liable for the insolvency, neglect, misconduct, mistake or default of another bank or person or for loss or destruction of an item in transit or in the possession of others.

Section 4–203. Effect of Instructions

Subject to the provisions of Article 3 concerning conversion of instruments (Section 3–419) and the provisions of both Article 3 and this Article concerning restrictive indorsements only a collecting bank's transferor can give instructions which affect the bank or constitute notice to it and a collecting bank is not liable to prior parties for any action taken pursuant to such instructions or in accordance with any agreement with its transferor.

Section 4–204. Methods of Sending and Presenting; Sending Direct to Payor Bank

(1) A collecting bank must send items by reasonably prompt method taking into consideration any relevant instructions, the nature of the item, the number of such items on hand, and the cost of collection involved and the method generally used by it or others to present such items.

(2) A collecting bank may send

(a) any item direct to the payor bank;

(b) any item to any non-bank payor if authorized by its transferor; and

(c) any item other than documentary drafts to any non-bank payor, if authorized by Federal Reserve regulation or operating letter, clearing house rule or the like.

(3) Presentment may be made by a presenting bank at a place where the payor bank has requested that presentment be made.

Section 4–205. Supplying Missing Indorsement; No Notice from Prior Indorsement

(1) A depositary bank which has taken an item for collection may supply any indorsement of the customer which is necessary to title unless the item contains the words "payee's indorsement required" or the like. In the absence of such a requirement a statement placed on the item by the depositary bank to the effect that the item was deposited by a customer or credited to his account is effective as the customer's indorsement.

(2) An intermediary bank, or payor bank which is not a depositary bank, is neither given notice nor otherwise affected by a restrictive indorsement of any person except the bank's immediate transferor.

Section 4–206. Transfer Between Banks

Any agreed method which identifies the transferor bank is sufficient for the item's further transfer to another bank.

Section 4–207. Warranties of Customer and Collecting Bank on Transfer or Presentment of Items; Time for Claims

(1) Each customer or collecting bank who obtains payment or acceptance of an item and each prior customer and collecting bank warrants to the payor bank or other payor who in good faith pays or accepts the item that

(a) he has a good title to the item or is authorized to obtain payment or acceptance on behalf of one who has a good title; and

(b) he has no knowledge that the signature of the maker or drawer is unauthorized, except that this warranty is not given by any customer or collecting bank that is a holder in due course and acts in good faith

(i) to a maker with respect to the maker's own signature; or

(ii) to a drawer with respect to the drawer's own signature, whether or not the drawer is also the drawee; or

(iii) to an acceptor of an item if the holder in due course took the item after the acceptance or obtained the acceptance without knowledge that the drawer's signature was unauthorized; and

(c) the item has not been materially altered, except that this warranty is not given by any customer or collecting bank that is a holder in due course and acts in good faith

(i) to the maker of a note; or

(ii) to the drawer of a draft whether or not the drawer is also the drawee; or

(iii) to the acceptor of an item with respect to an alteration made prior to the acceptance if the holder in due course took the item after the acceptance, even though the acceptance provided "payable as originally drawn" or equivalent terms; or

(iv) to the acceptor of an item with respect to an alteration made after the acceptance.

(2) Each customer and collecting bank who transfers an item and receives a settlement or other consideration for it warrants to his transferee and to any subsequent collecting bank who takes the item in good faith that

(a) he has a good title to the item or is authorized to obtain payment or acceptance on behalf of one who has a good title and the transfer is otherwise rightful; and

(b) all signatures are genuine or authorized; and

(c) the item has not been materially altered; and

(d) no defense of any party is good against him; and

(e) he has no knowledge of any insolvency proceeding instituted with respect to the maker or acceptor or the drawer of an unaccepted item.

In addition each customer and collecting bank so transferring an item and receiving a settlement or other consideration engages that upon dishonor and any necessary notice of dishonor and protest he will take up the item.

(3) The warranties and the engagement to honor set forth in the two preceding subsections arise notwithstanding the absence of indorsement or words of guaranty or warranty in the transfer or presentment and a collecting bank remains liable for their breach despite remittance to its transferor. Damages for breach of such warranties or engagement to honor shall not exceed the consideration received by the customer or collecting bank responsible plus finance charges and expenses related to the item, if any.

(4) Unless a claim for breach of warranty under this section is made within a reasonable time after the person claiming learns of the breach, the person liable is discharged to the extent of any loss caused by the delay in making claim.

Section 4–208. Security Interest of Collecting Bank in Items, Accompanying Documents and Proceeds

(1) A bank has a security interest in an item and any accompanying documents or the proceeds of either

(a) in case of an item deposited in an account to the extent to which credit given for the item has been withdrawn or applied;

(b) in case of an item for which it has given credit available for withdrawal as of right, to the extent of the credit given whether or not the credit is drawn upon and whether or not there is a right of charge-back; or

(c) if it makes an advance on or against the item.

(2) When credit which has been given for several items received at one time or pursuant to a single agreement is withdrawn or applied in part the security interest remains upon all the items, any accompanying documents or the proceeds of either. For the purpose of this section, credits first given are first withdrawn.

(3) Receipt by a collecting bank of a final settlement for an item is a realization on its security interest in the item, accompanying documents and proceeds. To the extent and so long as the bank does not receive final settlement for the item or give up possession of the item or accompanying documents for purposes other than collection, the security interest continues and is subject to the provisions of Article 9 except that

(a) no security agreement is necessary to make the security interest enforceable (subsection (1) (a) of Section 9–203); and

(b) no filing is required to perfect the security interest; and

(c) the security interest has priority over conflicting perfected security interests in the item, accompanying documents or proceeds.

Section 4–209. When Bank Gives Value for Purposes of Holder in Due Course

For purposes of determining its status as a holder in due course, the bank has given value to the extent that it has a security interest in an item provided that the bank otherwise complies with the requirements of Section 3–302 on what constitutes a holder in due course.

Section 4–210. Presentment by Notice of Item Not Payable by, Through or at a Bank; Liability of Secondary Parties

(1) Unless otherwise instructed, a collecting bank may present an item not payable by, through or at a bank by sending to the party to accept or pay a written notice that the bank holds the item for acceptance or payment. The notice must be sent in time to be received on or before the day when presentation is due and the bank must meet any requirement of the party to accept or pay under Section 3–505 by the close of the bank's next banking day after it knows of the requirement.

(2) Where presentment is made by notice and neither honor nor request for compliance with a requirement under Section 3–505 is received by the close of business on the day after maturity or in the case of demand items by the close of business on the third banking day after notice was sent, the presenting bank may treat the item as dishonored and charge any secondary party by sending him notice of the facts.

Section 4–211. Media of Remittance; Provisional and Final Settlement in Remittance Cases

(1) A collecting bank may take in settlement of an item

(a) a check of the remitting bank or of another bank except the remitting bank; or

(b) a cashier's check or similar primary obligation of a remitting bank which is a member of or clears through a member of the same clearing house or group as the collecting bank; or

(c) appropriate authority to charge an account of the remitting bank or of another bank with the collecting bank; or

(d) if the item is drawn upon or payable by a person other than a bank, a cashier's check, certified check or other bank check or obligation.

(2) If before its midnight deadline the collecting bank properly dishonors a remittance check or authorization to charge on itself or presents or forwards for collection a remittance instrument of or on another bank which is of a kind approved by subsection (1) or has not been authorized by it, the collecting bank is not liable to prior parties in the event of the dishonor of such check, instrument or authorization.

(3) A settlement for an item by means of a remittance instrument or authorization to charge is or becomes a final settlement as to both the person making and the person receiving the settlement

(a) if the remittance instrument or authorization to charge is of a kind approved by subsection (1) or has not been authorized by the person receiving the settlement and in either case the person receiving the settlement acts seasonably before its midnight deadline in presenting, forwarding for collection or paying the instrument or authorization,—at the time the remittance instrument or authorization is finally paid by the payor by which it is payable;

(b) if the person receiving the settlement has authorized remittance by a non-bank check or obligation or by a cashier's check or similar primary obligation of or a check upon the payor or other remitting bank which is not of a kind approved by subsection (1) (b),—at the time of the receipt of such remittance check or obligation; or

(c) if in a case not covered by sub-paragraphs (a) or (b) the person receiving the settlement fails to seasonably present, forward for collection, pay or return a remittance instrument or authorization to it to charge before its midnight deadline,—at such midnight deadline.

Section 4–212. Right of Charge-Back or Refund

(1) If a collecting bank has made provisional settlement with its customer for an item and itself fails by reason of dishonor, suspension of payments by a bank or otherwise to receive a settlement for the item which is or becomes final, the bank may revoke the settlement given by it, charge-back the amount of any credit given for the item to its customers' account or obtain refund from its customer whether or not it is able to return the items if by its midnight deadline or within a longer reasonable time after it learns the facts it returns the item or sends notification of the facts. These rights to revoke, charge-back and obtain refund terminate if and when a settlement for the item received by the bank is or becomes final (subsection (3) of Section 4–211 and subsections (2) and (3) of Section 4–213).

[(2) Within the time and manner prescribed by this section and Section 4–301, an intermediary or payor bank, as the case may be, may return an unpaid item directly to the depositary bank and may send for collection a draft on the depositary bank and obtain reimbursement. In such case, if the depositary bank has received provisional settlement for the item, it must reimburse the bank drawing the draft and any provisional credits for the item between banks shall become and remain final.]

Note: *Direct returns is recognized as an innovation that is not yet established bank practice, and therefore, Paragraph 2 has been bracketed. Some lawyers have doubts whether it should be included in legislation or left to development by agreement.*

(3) A depositary bank which is also the payor may charge-back the amount of an item to its customer's account or obtain refund in accordance with the section governing return of an item received by a payor bank for credit on its books (Section 4–301).

(4) The right to charge-back is not affected by

(a) prior use of the credit given for the item; or

(b) failure by any bank to exercise ordinary care with respect to the item but any bank so failing remains liable.

(5) A failure to charge-back or claim refund does not affect other rights of the bank against the customer or any other party.

(6) If credit is given in dollars as the equivalent of the value of an item payable in a foreign currency the dollar amount of any charge-back or refund shall be calculated on the basis of the buying sight rate for the foreign currency prevailing on the day when the person entitled to the charge-back or refund learns that it will not receive payment in ordinary course.

Section 4–213. Final Payment of Item by Payor Bank; When Provisional Debits and Credits Become Final; When Certain Credits Become Available for Withdrawal

(1) An item is finally paid by a payor bank when the bank has done any of the following, whichever happens first:

(a) paid the item in cash; or

(b) settled for the item without reserving a right to revoke the settlement and without having such right under statute, clearing house rule or agreement; or

(c) completed the process of posting the item to the indicated account of the drawer, maker or other person to be charged therewith; or

(d) made a provisional settlement for the item and failed to revoke the settlement in the time and manner permitted by statute, clearing house rule or agreement.

Upon a final payment under subparagraphs (b), (c) or (d) the payor bank shall be accountable for the amount of the item.

(2) If provisional settlement for an item between the presenting and payor banks is made through a clearing house or by debits or credits in an account between them, then to the extent that provisional debits or credits for the item are entered in accounts between the presenting and payor banks or between the presenting and successive prior collecting banks seriatim, they become final upon final payment of the item by the payor bank.

(3) If a collecting bank receives a settlement for an item which is or becomes final (subsection (3) of Section 4–211, subsection (2) of Section 4–213) the bank is accountable to its customer for the amount of the item and any provisional credit given for the item in an account with its customer becomes final.

(4) Subject to any right of the bank to apply the credit to an obligation of the customer, credit given by a bank for an item in an account with its customer becomes available for withdrawal as of right

(a) in any case where the bank has received a provisional settlement for the item,—when such settlement becomes final and the bank has had a reasonable time to learn that the settlement is final;

(b) in any case where the bank is both a depositary bank and a payor bank and the item is finally paid,—at the opening of the bank's second banking day following receipt of the item.

(5) A deposit of money in a bank is final when made but, subject to any right of the bank to apply the deposit to an obligation of the customer, the deposit becomes available for withdrawal as of right at the opening of the bank's next banking day following receipt of the deposit.

Section 4–214. Insolvency and Preference

(1) Any item in or coming into the possession of a payor or collecting bank which suspends payment and which item is not finally paid shall be returned by the receiver, trustee or agent in charge of the closed bank to the presenting bank or the closed bank's customer.

(2) If a payor bank finally pays an item and suspends payments without making a settlement for the item with its customer or the presenting bank which settlement is or becomes final, the owner of the item has a preferred claim against the payor bank.

(3) If a payor bank gives or a collecting bank gives or receives a provisional settlement for an item and thereafter suspends payments, the suspension does not prevent or interfere with the settlement becoming final if such finality occurs automatically upon the lapse of certain time or the happening of certain events (subsection (3) of Section 4–211, subsections (1) (d), (2) and (3) of Section 4–213).

(4) If a collecting bank receives from subsequent parties settlement for an item which settlement is or becomes final and suspends payments without making a settlement for the item with its customer which is or becomes final, the owner of the item has a preferred claim against such collecting bank.

Part 3 Collection of Items; Payor Banks

Section 4–301. Deferred Posting; Recovery of Payment by Return of Items; Time of Dishonor

(1) Where an authorized settlement for a demand item (other than a documentary draft) received by a payor bank otherwise than for immediate payment over the counter has been made before midnight of the banking day of receipt the payor bank may revoke the settlement and recover any payment if before it has made final payment (subsection (1) of Section 4–213) and before its midnight deadline it

(a) returns the item; or

(b) sends written notice of dishonor or nonpayment if the item is held for protest or is otherwise unavailable for return.

(2) If a demand item is received by a payor bank for credit on its books it may return such item or send notice of dishonor and may revoke any credit given or recover the amount thereof withdrawn by its customer, if

it acts within the time limit and in the manner specified in the preceding subsection.

(3) Unless previous notice of dishonor has been sent an item is dishonored at the time when for purposes of dishonor it is returned or notice sent in accordance with this section.

(4) An item is returned:

(a) as to an item received through a clearing house, when it is delivered to the presenting or last collecting bank or to the clearing house or is sent or delivered in accordance with its rules; or

(b) in all other cases, when it is sent or delivered to the bank's customer or transferor or pursuant to his instructions.

Section 4–302. Payor Bank's Responsibility for Late Return of Item

In the absence of a valid defense such as breach of a presentment warranty (subsection (1) of Section 4–207), settlement effected or the like, if an item is presented on and received by a payor bank the bank is accountable for the amount of

(a) a demand item other than a documentary draft whether properly payable or not if the bank, in any case where it is not also the depositary bank, retains the item beyond midnight of the banking day of receipt without settling for it or, regardless of whether it is also the depositary bank, does not pay or return the item or send notice of dishonor until after its midnight deadline; or

(b) any other properly payable item unless within the time allowed for acceptance or payment of that item the bank either accepts or pays the item or returns it and accompanying documents.

Section 4–303. When Items Subject to Notice, Stop-Order, Legal Process or Setoff; Order in Which Items May be Charged or Certified

(1) Any knowledge, notice or stop-order received by, legal process served upon or setoff exercised by a payor bank, whether or not effective under other rules of law to terminate, suspend or modify the bank's right or duty to pay an item or to charge its customer's account for the item, comes too late to so terminate, suspend or modify such right or duty if the knowledge, notice, stop-order or legal process is received or served and a reasonable time for the bank to act thereon expires or the setoff is exercised after the bank has done any of the following:

(a) accepted or certified the item;

(b) paid the item in cash;

(c) settled for the item without reserving a right to revoke the settlement and without having such right under statute, clearing house rule or agreement;

(d) completed the process of posting the item to the indicated account of the drawer, maker or other person to be charged therewith or otherwise has evidenced by examination of such indicated account and by action its decision to pay the item; or

(e) become accountable for the amount of the item under subsection (1)(d) of Section 4–213 and Section 4–302 dealing with the payor bank's responsibility for late return of items.

(2) Subject to the provisions of subsection (1) items may be accepted, paid, certified or charged to the indicated account of its customer in any order convenient to the bank.

Part 4 Relationship Between Payor Bank and Its Customer

Section 4–401. When Bank May Charge Customer's Account

(1) As against its customer, a bank may charge against his account any item which is otherwise properly payable from that account even though the charge creates an overdraft.

(2) A bank which in good faith makes payment to a holder may charge the indicated account of its customer according to

(a) the original tenor of his altered item; or

(b) the tenor of his completed item, even though the bank knows the item has been completed unless the bank has notice that the completion was improper.

Section 4–402. Bank's Liability to Customer for Wrongful Dishonor

A payor bank is liable to its customer for damages proximately caused by the wrongful dishonor of an item. When the dishonor occurs through mistake liability is limited to actual damages proved. If so proximately caused and proved damages may include damages for an arrest or prosecution of the customer or other consequential damages. Whether any consequential damages are proximately caused by the wrongful dishonor is a question of fact to be determined in each case.

Section 4–403. Customer's Right to Stop Payment; Burden of Proof of Loss

(1) A customer may by order to his bank stop payment of any item payable for his account but the order must be received at such time and in such manner as to afford the bank a reasonable opportunity to act on it prior to any action by the bank with respect to the item described in Section 4–303.

(2) An oral order is binding upon the bank only for fourteen calendar days unless confirmed in writing within that period. A written order is effective for only six months unless renewed in writing.

(3) The burden of establishing the fact and amount of loss resulting from the payment of an item contrary to a binding stop payment order is on the customer.

Section 4–404. Bank Not Obligated to Pay Check More Than Six Months Old

A bank is under no obligation to a customer having a checking account to pay a check, other than a certified check, which is presented more than six months after its date, but it may charge its customer's account for a payment made thereafter in good faith.

Section 4–405. Death or Incompetence of Customer

(1) A payor or collecting bank's authority to accept, pay or collect an item or to account for proceeds of its collection if otherwise effective is not rendered ineffective by incompetence of a customer of either bank existing at the time the item is issued or its collection is undertaken if the bank does not know of an adjudication of incompetence. Neither death nor incompetence of a customer revokes such authority to accept, pay, collect or account until the bank knows of the fact of death or of an adjudication of incompetence and has reasonable opportunity to act on it.

(2) Even with knowledge a bank may for 10 days after the date of death pay or certify checks drawn on or prior to that date unless ordered to stop payment by a person claiming an interest in the account.

Section 4–406. Customer's Duty to Discover and Report Unauthorized Signature or Alteration

(1) When a bank sends to its customer a statement of account accompanied by items paid in good faith in support of the debit entries or holds the statement and items pursuant to a request or instructions of its customer or otherwise in a reasonable manner makes the statement and items available to the customer, the customer must exercise reasonable care and promptness to examine the statement and items to discover his unauthorized signature or any alteration on an item and must notify the bank promptly after discovery thereof.

(2) If the bank establishes that the customer failed with respect to an item to comply with the duties imposed on the customer by subsection (1) the customer is precluded from asserting against the bank

(a) his unauthorized signature or any alteration on the item if the bank also establishes that it suffered a loss by reason of such failure; and

(b) an unauthorized signature or alteration by the same wrongdoer on any other item paid in good faith by the bank after the first item and statement was available to the customer for a reasonable period not exceeding fourteen calendar days and before the bank receives notification from the customer of any such unauthorized signature or alteration.

(3) The preclusion under subsection (2) does not apply if the customer establishes lack of ordinary care on the part of the bank in paying the item(s).

(4) Without regard to care or lack of care of either the customer or the bank a customer who does not within one year from the time the statement and items are made available to the customer (subsection (1)) discover and report his unauthorized signature or any alteration on the face or back of the item or does not within 3 years from that time discover and report any unauthorized indorsement in precluded from asserting against the bank such unauthorized signature or indorsement or such alteration.

(5) If under this section a payor bank has a valid defense against a claim of a customer upon or resulting from payment of an item and waives or fails upon request to assert the defense the bank may not assert against any collecting bank or other prior party presenting or transferring the item a claim based upon the unauthorized signature or alteration giving rise to the customer's claim.

Section 4–407. Payor Bank's Right to Subrogation on Improper Payment

If a payor bank has paid an item over the stop payment order of the drawer or maker or otherwise under circumstances giving a basis for objection by the drawer or maker, to prevent unjust enrichment and only to the extent necessary to prevent loss to the bank by reason of its payment of the item, the payor bank shall be subrogated to the rights

(a) of any holder in due course on the item against the drawer or maker; and

(b) of the payee or any other holder of the item against the drawer or maker either on the item or under the transaction out of which the item arose; and

(c) of the drawer or maker against the payee or any other holder of the item with respect to the transaction out of which the item arose.

Part 5 Collection of Documentary Drafts

Section 4–501. Handling of Documentary Drafts; Duty to Send for Presentment and to Notify Customer of Dishonor

A bank which takes a documentary draft for collection must present or send the draft and accompanying documents for presentment and upon learning that the draft has not been paid or accepted in due course must seasonably notify its customer of such fact even though it may have discounted or bought the draft or extended credit available for withdrawal as of right.

Section 4–502. Presentment of "On Arrival" Drafts

When a draft or the relevant instructions require presentment "on arrival," "when goods arrive" or the like, the collecting bank need not present until in its judgment a reasonable time for arrival of the goods has expired. Refusal to pay or accept because the goods have not arrived is not dishonor; the bank must notify its transferor of such refusal but need not present the draft again until it is instructed to do so or learns of the arrival of the goods.

Section 4–503. Responsibility of Presenting Bank for Documents and Goods; Report of Reasons for Dishonor; Referee in Case of Need

Unless otherwise instructed and except as provided in Article 5 a bank presenting a documentary draft

(a) must deliver the documents to the drawee on acceptance of the draft if it is payable more than three days after presentment; otherwise, only on payment; and

(b) upon dishonor, either in the case of presentment for acceptance or presentment for payment, may seek and follow instructions from any referee in case of need designated in the draft or if the presenting bank does not choose to utilize his services it must use diligence and good faith to ascertain the reason for dishonor, must notify its transferor of the dishonor and of the results of its effort to ascertain the reasons therefor and must request instructions.

But the presenting bank is under no obligation with respect to goods represented by the documents except to follow any reasonable instructions seasonably received; it has a right to reimbursement for any expense incurred in following instructions and to prepayment of or indemnity for such expenses.

Section 4–504. Privilege of Presenting Bank to Deal with Goods; Security Interest for Expenses

(1) A presenting bank which, following the dishonor of a documentary draft, has seasonably requested instructions but does not receive them within a reasonable time may store, sell, or otherwise deal with the goods in any reasonable manner.

(2) For its reasonable expenses incurred by action under subsection (1) the presenting bank has a lien upon the goods or their proceeds, which may be foreclosed in the same manner as an unpaid seller's lien.

[The new Article 4A "Uniform Commercial Code—Funds Transfers," approved in 1989, is omitted because of its length and complexity. It is concerned primarily with *wire* transfers between banks of customers' funds. Article 4A–104(a) defines a funds transfer as "the series of transactions, beginning with the originator's payment order, made for the purpose of making payment to the beneficiary of the order."]

Article 5 Letters of Credit

Section 5–101. Short Title

This Article shall be known and may be cited as Uniform Commercial Code—Letters of Credit.

Section 5–102. Scope

(1) This Article applies

(a) to a credit issued by a bank if the credit requires a documentary draft or a documentary demand for payment; and

(b) to a credit issued by a person other than a bank if the credit requires that the draft or demand for payment be accompanied by a document of title; and

(c) to a credit issued by a bank or other person if the credit is not within subparagraphs (a) or (b) but conspicuously states that it is a letter of credit or is conspicuously so entitled.

(2) Unless the engagement meets the requirements of subsection (1), this Article does not apply to engagements to make advances or to honor drafts or demands for payment, to authorities to pay or purchase, to guarantees or to general agreements.

(3) This Article deals with some but not all of the rules and concepts of letters of credit as such rules or concepts have developed prior to this act or may hereafter develop. The fact that this Article states a rule does not by itself require, imply or negate application of the same or a converse rule to a situation not provided for or to a person not specified by this Article.

Section 5–103. Definitions

(1) In this Article unless the context otherwise requires

(a) "Credit" or "letter of credit" means an engagement by a bank or other person made at the request of a customer and of a kind within the scope of this Article (Section 5–102) that the issuer will honor drafts or other demands for payment upon compliance with the conditions specified in the credit. A credit may be either revocable or irrevocable. The engagement may be either an agreement to honor or a statement that the bank or other person is authorized to honor.

(b) A "documentary draft" or a "documentary demand for payment" is one honor of which is conditioned upon the presentation of a document or documents. "Document" means any paper including document of title, security, invoice, certificate, notice of default and the like.

(c) An "issuer" is a bank or other person issuing a credit.

(d) A "beneficiary" of a credit is a person who is entitled under its terms to draw or demand payment.

(e) An "advising bank" is a bank which gives notification of the issuance of a credit by another bank.

(f) A "confirming bank" is a bank which engages either that it will itself honor a credit already issued by another bank or that such a credit will be honored by the issuer or a third bank.

(g) A "customer" is a buyer or other person who causes an issuer to issue a credit. The term also includes a bank which procures issuance or confirmation on behalf of that bank's customer.

(2) Other definitions applying to this Article and the sections in which they appear are:

"Notation of Credit." Section 5–108.

"Presenter." Section 5–112(3).

(3) Definitions in other Articles applying to this Article and the sections in which they appear are:

"Accept" or "Acceptance." Section 3–410.

"Contract for sale." Section 2–106.

"Draft." Section 3–104.

"Holder in due course." Section 3–302.

"Midnight deadline." Section 4–104.

"Security." Section 8–102.

(4) In addition, Article I contains general definitions and principles of construction and interpretation applicable throughout this Article.

Section 5–104. Formal Requirements; Signing

(1) Except as otherwise required in subsection (1) (c) of Section 5–102 on scope, no particular form of phrasing is required for a credit. A credit must be in writing and signed by the issuer and a confirmation must be in writing and signed by the confirming bank. A modification of the terms of a credit or confirmation must be signed by the issuer or confirming bank.

(2) A telegram may be a sufficient signed writing if it identifies its sender by an authorized authentication. The authentication may be in code and the authorized naming of the issuer in an advice of credit is a sufficient signing.

Section 5–105. Consideration

No consideration is necessary to establish a credit or to enlarge or otherwise modify its terms.

Section 5–106. Time and Effect of Establishment of Credit

(1) Unless otherwise agreed a credit is established

(a) as regards the customer as soon as a letter of credit is sent to him or the letter of credit or an authorized written advice of its issuance is sent to the beneficiary; and

(b) as regards the beneficiary when he receives a letter of credit or an authorized written advice of its issuance.

(2) Unless otherwise agreed once an irrevocable credit is established as regards the customer it can be modified or revoked only with the consent of the customer and once it is established as regards the beneficiary it can be modified or revoked only with his consent.

(3) Unless otherwise agreed after a revocable credit is established it may be modified or revoked by the issuer without notice to or consent from the customer or beneficiary.

(4) Notwithstanding any modification or revocation of a revocable credit any person authorized to honor or negotiate under the terms of the original credit is entitled to reimbursement for or honor of any draft or demand for payment duly honored or negotiated before receipt of notice of

the modification or revocation and the issuer in turn is entitled to reimbursement from its customer.

Section 5–107. Advice of Credit; Confirmation; Error in Statement of Terms

(1) Unless otherwise specified an advising bank by advising a credit issued by another bank does not assume any obligation to honor drafts drawn or demands for payment made under the credit but it does assume obligation for the accuracy of its own statement.

(2) A confirming bank by confirming a credit becomes directly obligated on the credit to the extent of its confirmation as though it were its issuer and acquires the rights of an issuer.

(3) Even though an advising bank incorrectly advises the terms of a credit it has been authorized to advise the credit is established as against the issuer to the extent of its original terms.

(4) Unless otherwise specified the customer bears as against the issuer all risks of transmission and reasonable translation or interpretation of any message relating to a credit.

Section 5–108. "Notation Credit"; Exhaustion of Credit

(1) A credit which specifies that any person purchasing or paying drafts drawn or demands for payment made under it must note the amount of the draft or demand on the letter or advice of credit is a "notation credit."

(2) Under a notation credit

- (a) a person paying the beneficiary or purchasing a draft or demand for payment from him acquires a right to honor only if the appropriate notation is made and by transferring or forwarding for honor the documents under the credit such a person warrants to the issuer that the notation has been made; and
- (b) unless the credit or a signed statement that an appropriate notation has been made accompanies the draft or demand for payment the issuer may delay honor until evidence of notation has been procured which is satisfactory to it but its obligation and that of its customer continue for a reasonable time not exceeding thirty days to obtain such evidence.

(3) If the credit is not a notation credit

- (a) the issuer may honor complying drafts or demands for payment presented to it in the order in which they are presented and is discharged pro tanto by honor of any such draft or demand;
- (b) as between competing good faith purchasers of complying drafts or demands the person first purchasing has priority over a subsequent purchaser even though the later purchased draft or demand has been first honored.

Section 5–109. Issuer's Obligation to Its Customer

(1) An issuer's obligation to its customer includes good faith and observance of any general banking usage but unless otherwise agreed does not include liability or responsibility

- (a) for performance of the underlying contract for sale or other transaction between the customer and the beneficiary; or
- (b) for any act or omission of any person other than itself or its own branch or for loss or destruction of a draft, demand or document in transit or in the possession of others; or
- (c) based on knowledge or lack of knowledge of any usage of any particular trade.

(2) An issuer must examine documents with care so as to ascertain that on their face they appear to comply with the terms of the credit but unless otherwise agreed assumes no liability of responsibility for the genuineness, falsification or effect of any document which appears on such examination to be regular on its face.

(3) A non-bank issuer is not bound by any banking usage of which it has no knowledge.

Section 5–110. Availability of Credit in Portions; Presenter's Reservation of Lien or Claim

(1) Unless otherwise specified a credit may be used in portions in the discretion of the beneficiary.

(2) Unless otherwise specified a person by presenting a documentary draft or demand for payment under a credit relinquishes upon its honor all claims to the documents and a person by transferring such draft or demand or causing such presentment authorizes such relinquishment. An explicit reservation of claim makes the draft or demand non-complying.

Section 5–111. Warranties on Transfer and Presentment

(1) Unless otherwise agreed the beneficiary by transferring or presenting a documentary draft or demand for payment warrants to all interested parties that the necessary conditions of the credit have been complied with. This is in addition to any warranties arising under Articles 3, 4, 7 and 8.

(2) Unless otherwise agreed a negotiating, advising, confirming, collecting or issuing bank presenting or transferring a draft or demand for payment under a credit warrants only the matters warranted by a collecting bank under Article 4 and any such bank transferring a document warrants only the matters warranted by an intermediary under Articles 7 and 8.

Section 5–112. Time Allowed for Honor or Rejection; Withholding Honor or Rejection by Consent; "Presenter"

(1) A bank to which a documentary draft or demand for payment is presented under a credit may without dishonor of the draft, demand or credit

- (a) defer honor until the close of the third banking day following receipt of the documents; and
- (b) further defer honor if the presenter has expressly or impliedly consented thereto.

Failure to honor within the time here specified constitutes dishonor of the draft or demand and of the credit [except as otherwise provided in subsection (4) of Section 5–114 on conditional payment].

Note: *The bracketed language in the last sentence of subsection (1) should be included only if the optional provisions of Section 5–114(4) and (5) are included.*

(2) Upon dishonor the bank may unless otherwise instructed fulfill its duty to return the draft or demand and the documents by holding them at the disposal of the presenter and sending him an advice to that effect.

(3) "Presenter" means any person presenting a draft or demand for payment for honor under a credit even though that person is a

confirming bank or other correspondent which is acting under an issuer's authorization.

Section 5–113. Indemnities

(1) A bank seeking to obtain (whether for itself or another) honor, negotiation or reimbursement under a credit may give an indemnity to induce such honor, negotiation or reimbursement.

(2) An indemnity agreement inducing honor, negotiation or reimbursement

(a) unless otherwise explicitly agreed applies to defects in the documents but not in the goods; and

(b) unless a longer time is explicitly agreed expires at the end of ten business days following receipt of the documents by the ultimate customer unless notice of objection is sent before such expiration date. The ultimate customer may send notice of objection to the person from whom he received the documents and any bank receiving such notice is under a duty to send notice to its transferor before its midnight deadline.

Section 5–114. Issuer's Duty and Privilege to Honor; Right to Reimbursement

(1) An issuer must honor a draft or demand for payment which complies with the terms of the relevant credit regardless of whether the goods or documents conform to the underlying contract for sale or other contract between the customer and the beneficiary. The issuer is not excused from honor of such a draft or demand by reason of an additional general term that all documents must be satisfactory to the issuer, but an issuer may require that specified documents must be satisfactory to it.

(2) Unless otherwise agreed when documents appear on their face to comply with the terms of a credit but a required document does not in fact conform to the warranties made on negotiation or transfer of a document of title (Section 7–507) or of a certificated security (Section 8–306) or is forged or fraudulent or there is fraud in the transaction:

(a) the issuer must honor the draft or demand for payment if honor is demanded by a negotiating bank or other holder of the draft or demand which has taken the draft or demand under the credit and under circumstances which would make it a holder in due course (Section 3–302) and in an appropriate case would make it a person to whom a document of title has been duly negotiated (Section 7–502) or a bona fide purchaser of a certificated security (Section 8–302); and

(b) in all other cases as against its customer, an issuer acting in good faith may honor the draft or demand for payment despite notification from the customer of fraud, forgery or other defect not apparent on the face of the documents but a court of appropriate jurisdiction may enjoin such honor.

(3) Unless otherwise agreed an issuer which has duly honored a draft or demand for payment is entitled to immediate reimbursement of any payment made under the credit and to be put in effectively available funds not later than the day before maturity of any acceptance made under the credit.

[(4) When a credit provides for payment by the issuer on receipt of notice that the required documents are in the possession of a correspondent or other agent of the issuer

(a) any payment made on receipt of such notice is conditional; and

(b) the issuer may reject documents which do not comply with the credit if it does so within three banking days following its receipt of the documents; and

(c) in the event of such rejection, the issuer is entitled by charge back or otherwise to return of the payment made.]

[(5) In the case covered by subsection (4) failure to reject documents within the time specified in sub-paragraph (b) constitutes acceptance of the documents and makes the payment final in favor of the beneficiary.]

Note: *Subsections (4) and (5) are bracketed as optional. If they are included the bracketed language in the last sentence of Section 5–112(1) should also be included.*

Section 5–115. Remedy for Improper Dishonor or Anticipatory Repudiation

(1) When an issuer wrongfully dishonors a draft or demand for payment presented under a credit the person entitled to honor has with respect to any documents the rights of a person in the position of a seller (Section 2–707) and may recover from the issuer the face amount of the draft or demand together with incidental damages under Section 2–710 on seller's incidental damages and interest but less any amount realized by resale or other use or disposition of the subject matter of the transaction. In the event no resale or other utilization is made the documents, goods or other subject matter involved in the transaction must be turned over to the issuer on payment of judgment.

(2) When an issuer wrongfully cancels or otherwise repudiates a credit before presentment of draft or demand for payment drawn under it the beneficiary has the rights of a seller after anticipatory repudiation by the buyer under Section 2–610 if he learns of the repudiation in time reasonably to avoid procurement of the required documents. Otherwise the beneficiary has an immediate right of action for wrongful dishonor.

Section 5–116. Transfer and Assignment

(1) The right to draw under a credit can be transferred or assigned only when the credit is expressly designated as transferable or assignable.

(2) Even though the credit specifically states that it is nontransferable or nonassignable the beneficiary may before performance of the conditions of the credit assign his right to proceeds. Such an assignment is an assignment of an account under Article 9 on Secured Transactions and is governed by that Article except that

(a) the assignment is ineffective until the letter of credit or advice of credit is delivered to the assignee which delivery constitutes perfection of the security interest under Article 9; and

(b) the issuer may honor drafts or demands for payment drawn under the credit until it receives a notification of the assignment signed by the beneficiary which reasonably identifies the credit involved in the assignment and contains a request to pay the assignee; and

(c) after what reasonably appears to be such a notification has been received the issuer may without dishonor refuse to accept or pay even to a person otherwise entitled to honor until the letter of credit or advice of credit is exhibited to the issuer.

(3) Except where the beneficiary has effectively assigned his right to draw or his right to proceeds, nothing in this section limits his right to transfer or negotiate drafts or demands drawn under the credit.

Section 5–117. Insolvency of Bank Holding Funds for Documentary Credit

(1) Where an issuer or an advising or confirming bank or a bank which has for a customer procured issuance of a credit by another bank becomes insolvent before final payment under the credit and the credit is one to which this Article is made applicable by paragraphs (a) or (b) of Section 5–102(1) on scope, the receipt or allocation of funds or collateral to secure or meet obligations under the credit shall have the following results:

(a) to the extent of any funds or collateral turned over after or before the insolvency as indemnity against or specifically for the purpose of payment of drafts or demands for payment drawn under the designated credit, the drafts or demands are entitled to payment in preference over depositors or other general creditors of the issuer or bank; and

(b) on expiration of the credit or surrender of the beneficiary's rights under it unused any person who has given such funds or collateral is similarly entitled to return thereof; and

(c) a charge to a general or current account with a bank if specifically consented to for the purpose of indemnity against or payment of drafts or demands for payment drawn under the designated credit falls under the same rules as if the funds had been drawn out in cash and then turned over with specific instructions.

(2) After honor or reimbursement under this section the customer or other person for whose account the insolvent bank has acted is entitled to receive the documents involved.

Article 6 Bulk Transfers

Section 6–101. Short Title

This Article shall be known and may be cited as Uniform Commercial Code—Bulk Transfers.

Section 6–102. "Bulk Transfers"; Transfers of Equipment; Enterprises Subject to This Article; Bulk Transfers Subject to This Article

(1) A "bulk transfer" is any transfer in bulk and not in the ordinary course of the transferor's business of a major part of the materials, supplies, merchandise or other inventory (Section 9–109) of an enterprise subject to this Article.

(2) A transfer of a substantial part of the equipment (Section 9–109) of such an enterprise is a bulk transfer if it is made in connection with a bulk transfer of inventory, but not otherwise.

(3) The enterprises subject to this Article are all those whose principal business is the sale of merchandise from stock, including those who manufacture what they sell.

(4) Except as limited by the following section all bulk transfers of goods located within this state are subject to this Article.

Section 6–103. Transfers Excepted From This Article

The following transfers are not subject to this Article:

(1) Those made to give security for the performance of an obligation;

(2) General assignments for the benefit of all the creditors of the transferor, and subsequent transfers by the assignee thereunder;

(3) Transfers in settlement or realization of a lien or other security interests;

(4) Sales by executors, administrators, receivers, trustees in bankruptcy, or any public officer under judicial process;

(5) Sales made in the course of judicial or administrative proceedings for the dissolution or reorganization of a corporation and of which notice is sent to the creditors of the corporation pursuant to order of the court or administrative agency;

(6) Transfers to a person maintaining a known place of business in this State who becomes bound to pay the debts of the transferor in full and gives public notice of that fact, and who is solvent after becoming so bound;

(7) A transfer to a new business enterprise organized to take over and continue the business, if public notice of the transaction is given and the new enterprise assumes the debts of the transferor and he receives nothing from the transaction except an interest in the new enterprise junior to the claims of creditors;

(8) Transfers of property which is exempt from execution.

Public notice under subsection (6) or subsection (7) may be given by publishing once a week for two consecutive weeks in a newspaper of general circulation where the transferor had its principal place of business in this state an advertisement including the names and addresses of the transferor and transferee and the effective date of the transfer.

Section 6–104. Schedule of Property, List of Creditors

(1) Except as provided with respect to auction sales (Section 6–108), a bulk transfer subject to this Article is ineffective against any creditor of the transferor unless:

(a) The transferee requires the transferor to furnish a list of his existing creditors prepared as stated in this section; and

(b) The parties prepare a schedule of the property transferred sufficient to identify it; and

(c) The transferee preserves the list and schedule for six months next following the transfer and permits inspection of either or both and copying therefrom at all reasonable hours by any creditor of the transferor, or files the list and schedule in (a public office to be here identified).

(2) The list of creditors must be signed and sworn to or affirmed by the transferor or his agent. It must contain the names and business addresses of all creditors of the transferor, with the amounts when known, and also the names of all persons who are known to the transferor to assert claims against him even though such claims are disputed. If the transferor is the obligor of an outstanding issue of bonds, debentures or the like as to which there is an indenture trustee, the list of creditors need include only the name and address of the indenture trustee and the aggregate outstanding principal amount of the issue.

(3) Responsibility for the completeness and accuracy of the list of creditors rests on the transferor, and the transfer is not rendered ineffective by errors or omissions therein unless the transferee is shown to have had knowledge.

Section 6–105. Notice to Creditors

In addition to the requirements of the preceding section, any bulk transfer subject to this Article except one made by auction sale (Section 6–108) is ineffective against any creditor of the transferor unless at least ten days before he takes possession of the goods or pays for them, whichever happens first, the transferee gives notice of the transfer in the manner and to the persons hereafter provided (Section 6–107).

[Section 6–106. Application of the Proceeds

In addition to the requirements of the two preceding sections:

(1) Upon every bulk transfer subject to this Article for which new consideration becomes payable except those made by sale at auction it is the duty of the transferee to assure that such consideration is applied so far as necessary to pay those debts of the transferor which are either shown on the list furnished by the transferor (Section 6–104) or filed in writing in the place stated in the notice (Section 6–107) within thirty days after the mailing of such notice. This duty of the transferee runs to all the holders of such debts, and may be enforced by any of them for the benefit of all.

(2) If any of said debts are in dispute the necessary sum may be withheld from distribution until the dispute is settled or adjudicated.

(3) If the consideration payable is not enough to pay all of the said debts in full distribution shall be made pro rata.]

Note: *This section is bracketed to indicate division of opinion as to whether or not it is a wise provision, and to suggest that this is a point on which State enactments may differ without serious damage to the principle of uniformity. In any State where this section is omitted, the following parts of sections, also bracketed in the text, should also be omitted, namely:*

Section 6–107(2)(e)
6–108(3)(c)
6–109(2)

In any State where this section is enacted, these other provisions should be also.

Optional Subsection (4)

[(4) The transferee may within ten days after he takes possession of the goods pay the consideration into the (specify court) in the county where the transferor had its principal place of business in this state and thereafter may discharge his duty under this section by giving notice by registered or certified mail to all the persons to whom the duty runs that the consideration has been paid into that court and that they should file their claims there. On motion of any interested party, the court may order the distribution of the consideration to the persons entitled to it.]

Note: *Optional subsection (4) is recommended for those states which do not have a general statute providing for payment of money into court.*

Section 6–107. The Notice

(1) The notice to creditors (Section 6–105) shall state:

(a) that a bulk transfer is about to be made; and

(b) the names and business addresses of the transferor and transferee, and all other business names and addresses used by the transferor within three years last past so far as known to the transferee; and

(c) whether or not all the debts of the transferor are to be paid in full as they fall due as a result of the transaction, and if so, the address to which creditors should send their bills.

(2) If the debts of the transferor are not to be paid in full as they fall due or if the transferee is in doubt on that point then the notice shall state further:

(a) the location and general description of the property to be transferred and the estimated total of the transferor's debts;

(b) the address where the schedule of property and list of creditors (Section 6–104) may be inspected;

(c) whether the transfer is to pay existing debts and if so the amount of such debts and to whom owing;

(d) whether the transfer is for new consideration and if so the amount of such consideration and the time and place of payment; [and]

[(e) if for new consideration the time and place where creditors of the transferor are to file their claims.]

(3) The notice in any case shall be delivered personally or sent by registered or certified mail to all the persons shown on the list of creditors furnished by the transferor (Section 6–104) and to all other persons who are known to the transferee to hold or assert claims against the transferor.

Note: *The words in brackets are optional. See Note under Section 6–106.*

Section 6–108. Auction Sales; "Auctioneer"

(1) A bulk transfer is subject to this Article even though it is by sale at auction, but only in the manner and with the results stated in this section.

(2) The transferor shall furnish a list of his creditors and assist in the preparation of a schedule of the property to be sold, both prepared as before stated (Section 6–104).

(3) The person or persons other than the transferor who direct, control or are responsible for the auction are collectively called the "auctioneer." The auctioneer shall:

(a) receive and retain the list of creditors and prepare and retain the schedule of property for the period stated in this Article (Section 6–104);

(b) give notice of the auction personally or by registered or certified mail at least ten days before it occurs to all persons shown on the list of creditors and to all other persons who are known to him to hold or assert claims against the transferor; [and]

[(c) assure that the net proceeds of the auction are applied as provided in this Article (Section 6–106).]

(4) Failure of the auctioneer to perform any of these duties does not affect the validity of the sale or the title of the purchasers, but if the auctioneer knows that the auction constitutes a bulk transfer such failure renders the auctioneer liable to the creditors of the transferor as a class for the sums owing to them from the transferor up to but not exceeding the net proceeds of the auction. If the auctioneer consists of several persons their liability is joint and several.

Note: *The words in brackets are optional. See Note under Section 6–106.*

Section 6–109. What Creditors Protected; [Credit for Payment to Particular Creditors]

(1) The creditors of the transferor mentioned in this Article are those holding claims based on transactions or events occurring before the bulk transfer, but creditors who become such after notice to creditors is given (Sections 6–105 and 6–107) are not entitled to notice.

[(2) Against the aggregate obligation imposed by the provisions of this Article concerning the application of the proceeds (Section 6–106 and subsection (3) (c) of 6–108) the transferee or auctioneer is entitled to credit for sums paid to particular creditors of the transferor, not exceeding the sums believed in good faith at the time of the payment to be properly payable to such creditors.]

Note: *The words in brackets are optional. See Note under Section 6–106.*

Section 6–110. Subsequent Transfers

When the title of a transferee to property is subject to a defect by reason of his non-compliance with the requirements of this Article, then:

(1) A purchaser of any of such property from such transferee who pays no value or who takes with notice of such non-compliance takes subject to such defect, but

(2) A purchaser for value in good faith and without such notice takes free of such defect.

Section 6–111. Limitation of Actions and Levies

No action under this Article shall be brought nor levy made more than six months after the date on which the transferee took possession of the goods unless the transfer has been concealed. If the transfer has been concealed, actions may be brought or levies made within six months after its discovery.

Note to Article 6: *Section 6–106 is bracketed to indicate division of opinion as to whether or not it is a wise provision, and to suggest that this is a point on which State enactments may differ without serious damage to the principle of uniformity. In any State where Section 6–106 is not enacted, the following parts of sections, also bracketed in the text, should also be omitted, namely:*

Sec. 6–107(2) (e).

6–108(3) (c).

6–109(2).

In any State where Section 6–106 is enacted, these other provisions should be also.

Article 7 Warehouse Receipts, Bills of Lading and Other Documents of Title

Part 1 General

Section 7–101. Short Title

This Article shall be known and may be cited as Uniform Commercial Code—Documents of Title.

Section 7–102. Definitions and Index of Definitions

(1) In this Article, unless the context otherwise requires:

(a) "Bailee" means the person who by a warehouse receipt, bill of lading or other document of title acknowledges possession of goods and contracts to deliver them.

(b) "Consignee" means the person named in a bill to whom or to whose order the bill promises delivery.

(c) "Consignor" means the person named in a bill as the person from whom the goods have been received for shipment.

(d) "Delivery order" means a written order to deliver goods directed to a warehouseman, carrier or other person who in the ordinary course of business issues warehouse receipts or bills of lading.

(e) "Document" means document of title as defined in the general definitions in Article 1 (Section 1–201).

(f) "Goods" means all things which are treated as movable for the purposes of a contract of storage or transportation.

(g) "Issuer" means a bailee who issues a document except that in relation to an unaccepted delivery order it means the person who orders the possessor of goods to deliver. Issuer includes any person for whom an agent or employee purports to act in issuing a document if the agent or employee has real or apparent authority to issue documents, notwithstanding that the issuer received no goods or that the goods were misdescribed or that in any other respect the agent or employee violated his instructions.

(h) "Warehouseman" is a person engaged in the business of storing goods for hire.

(2) Other definitions applying to this Article or to specified Parts thereof, and the sections in which they appear are:

"Duly negotiate." Section 7–501.

"Person entitled under the document." Section 7–403(4).

(3) Definitions in other Articles applying to this Article and the sections in which they appear are:

"Contract for sale." Section 2–106.

"Overseas." Section 2–323.

"Receipt" of goods. Section 2–103.

(4) In addition Article 1 contains general definitions and principles of construction and interpretation applicable throughout this Article.

Section 7–103. Relation of Article to Treaty, Statute, Tariff, Classification or Regulation

To the extent that any treaty or statute of the United States, regulatory statute of this State or tariff, classification or regulation filed or issued pursuant thereto is applicable, the provisions of this Article are subject thereto.

Section 7–104. Negotiable and Non-Negotiable Warehouse Receipt, Bill of Lading or Other Document of Title

(1) A warehouse receipt, bill of lading or other document of title is negotiable

(a) if by its terms the goods are to be delivered to bearer or to the order of a named person; or

(b) where recognized in overseas trade, if it runs to a named person or assigns.

(2) Any other document is non-negotiable. A bill of lading in which it is stated that the goods are consigned to a named person is not made negotiable by a provision that the goods are to be delivered only against a written order signed by the same or another named person.

Section 7–105. Construction Against Negative Implication

The omission from either Part 2 or Part 3 of this Article of a provision corresponding to a provision made in the other Part does not imply that a corresponding rule of law is not applicable.

Part 2 Warehouse Receipts: Special Provisions

Section 7–201. Who May Issue a Warehouse Receipt; Storage Under Government Bond

(1) A warehouse receipt may be issued by any warehouseman.

(2) Where goods including distilled spirits and agricultural commodities are stored under a statute requiring a bond against withdrawal or a license for the issuance of receipts in the nature of warehouse receipts, a receipt issued for the goods has like effect as a warehouse receipt even though issued by a person who is the owner of the goods and is not a warehouseman.

Section 7–202. Form of Warehouse Receipt; Essential Terms; Optional Terms

(1) A warehouse receipt need not be in any particular form.

(2) Unless a warehouse receipt embodies within its written or printed terms each of the following, the warehouseman is liable for damages caused by the omission to a person injured thereby:

(a) the location of the warehouse where the goods are stored;

(b) the date of issue of the receipt;

(c) the consecutive number of the receipt;

(d) a statement whether the goods received will be delivered to the bearer, to a specified person, or to a specified person or his order;

(e) the rate of storage and handling charges, except that where goods are stored under a field warehousing arrangement a statement of that fact is sufficient on a nonnegotiable receipt;

(f) a description of the goods or of the packages containing them;

(g) the signature of the warehouseman, which may be made by his authorized agent;

(h) if the receipt is issued for goods of which the warehouseman is owner, either solely or jointly or in common with others, the fact of such ownership; and

(i) a statement of the amount of advances made and of liabilities incurred for which the warehouseman claims a lien or security interest (Section 7–209). If the precise amount of such advances made or of such liabilities incurred is, at the time of the issue of the receipt, unknown to the warehouseman or to his agent who issues it, a statement of the fact that advances have been made or liabilities incurred and the purpose thereof is sufficient.

(3) A warehouseman may insert in his receipt any other terms which are not contrary to the provisions of this Act and do not impair his obligation of delivery (Section 7–403) or his duty of care (Section 7–204). Any contrary provisions shall be ineffective.

Section 7–203. Liability for Non-Receipt or Misdescription

A party to or purchaser for value in good faith of a document of title other than a bill of lading relying in either case upon the description therein of the goods may recover from the issuer damages caused by the non-receipt or misdescription of the goods, except to the extent that the document conspicuously indicates that the issuer does not know whether any part or all of the goods in fact were received or conform to the description, as where the description is in terms of marks or labels or kind, quantity or condition, or the receipt or description is qualified by "contents, condition and quality unknown," "said to contain" or the like, if such indication be true, or the party or purchaser otherwise has notice.

Section 7–204. Duty of Care; Contractual Limitation of Warehouseman's Liability

(1) A warehouseman is liable for damages for loss of or injury to the goods caused by his failure to exercise such care in regard to them as a reasonably careful man would exercise under like circumstances but unless otherwise agreed he is not liable for damages which could not have been avoided by the exercise of such care.

(2) Damages may be limited by a term in the warehouse receipt or storage agreement limiting the amount of liability in case of loss or damage, and setting forth a specific liability per article or item, or value per unit of weight, beyond which the warehouseman shall not be liable; provided, however, that such liability may on written request of the bailor at the time of signing such storage agreement or within a reasonable time after receipt of the warehouse receipt be increased on part or all of the goods thereunder, in which event increased rates may be charged based on such increased valuation, but that no such increase shall be permitted contrary to a lawful limitation of liability contained in the warehouseman's tariff, if any. No such limitation is effective with respect to the warehouseman's liability for conversion to his own use.

(3) Reasonable provisions as to the time and manner of presenting claims and instituting actions based on the bailment may be included in the warehouse receipt or tariff.

(4) This section does not impair or repeal . . .

Note: *Insert in subsection (4) a reference to any statute which imposes a higher responsibility upon the warehouseman or invalidates contractual limitations which would be permissible under this Article.*

Section 7–205. Title Under Warehouse Receipt Defeated in Certain Cases

A buyer in the ordinary course of business of fungible goods sold and delivered by a warehouseman who is also in the business of buying and selling such goods takes free of any claim under a warehouse receipt even though it has been duly negotiated.

Section 7–206. Termination of Storage at Warehouseman's Option

(1) A warehouseman may on notifying the person on whose account the goods are held and any other person known to claim an interest in the goods require payment of any charges and removal of the goods from the warehouse at the termination of the period of storage fixed by the document, or, if no period is fixed, within a stated period not less than thirty days after the notification. If the goods are not removed before the date specified in the notification, the warehouseman may sell them in accordance with the provisions of the section on enforcement of a warehouseman's lien (Section 7–210).

(2) If a warehouseman in good faith believes that the goods are about to deteriorate or decline in value to less than the amount of his lien within the time prescribed in subsection (1) for notification, advertisement and sale, the warehouseman may specify in the notification any reasonable shorter time for removal of the goods and in case the goods are not removed, may sell them at public sale held not less than one week after a single advertisement or posting.

(3) If as a result of a quality or condition of the goods of which the warehouseman had no notice at the time of deposit the goods are a hazard to other property or to the warehouse or to persons, the

warehouseman may sell the goods at public or private sale without advertisement on reasonable notification to all persons known to claim an interest in the goods. If the warehouseman after a reasonable effort is unable to sell the goods he may dispose of them in any lawful manner and shall incur no liability by reason of such disposition.

(4) The warehouseman must deliver the goods to any person entitled to them under this Article upon due demand made at any time prior to sale or other disposition under this section.

(5) The warehouseman may satisfy his lien from the proceeds of any sale or disposition under this section but must hold the balance for delivery on the demand of any person to whom he would have been bound to deliver the goods.

Section 7–207. Goods Must Be Kept Separate; Fungible Goods

(1) Unless the warehouse receipt otherwise provides, a warehouseman must keep separate the goods covered by each receipt so as to permit at all times identification and delivery of those goods except that different lots of fungible goods may be commingled.

(2) Fungible goods so commingled are owned in common by the persons entitled thereto and the warehouseman is severally liable to each owner for that owner's share. Where because of overissue a mass of fungible goods is insufficient to meet all the receipts which the warehouseman has issued against it, the persons entitled include all holders to whom overissued receipts have been duly negotiated.

Section 7–208. Altered Warehouse Receipts

Where a blank in a negotiable warehouse receipt has been filled in without authority, a purchaser for value and without notice of the want of authority may treat the insertion as authorized. Any other unauthorized alteration leaves any receipt enforceable against the issuer according to its original tenor.

Section 7–209. Lien of Warehouseman

(1) A warehouseman has a lien against the bailor on the goods covered by a warehouse receipt or on the proceeds thereof in his possession for charges for storage or transportation (including demurrage and terminal charges), insurance, labor, or charges present or future in relation to the goods, and for expenses necessary for preservation of the goods or reasonably incurred in their sale pursuant to law. If the person on whose account the goods are held is liable for like charges or expenses in relation to other goods whenever deposited and it is stated in the receipt that a lien is claimed for charges and expenses in relation to other goods, the warehouseman also has a lien against him for such charges and expenses whether or not the other goods have been delivered by the warehouseman. But against a person to whom a negotiable warehouse receipt is duly negotiated a warehouseman's lien is limited to charges in an amount or at a rate specified on the receipt or if no charges are so specified then to a reasonable charge for storage of the goods covered by the receipt subsequent to the date of the receipt.

(2) The warehouseman may also reserve a security interest against the bailor for a maximum amount specified on the receipt for charges other than those specified in subsection (1), such as for money advanced and interest. Such a security interest is governed by the Article on Secured Transactions (Article 9).

(3) (a) A warehouseman's lien for charges and expenses under subsection (1) or a security interest under subsection (2) is also effective against any person who so entrusted the bailor with possession of the goods that a pledge of them by him to a good faith purchaser for value would have been valid but is not effective against a person as to whom the document confers no right in the goods covered by it under Section 7–503.

(b) A warehouseman's lien on household goods for charges and expenses in relation to the goods under subsection (1) is also effective against all persons if the depositor was the legal possessor of the goods at the time of deposit. "Household goods" means furniture, furnishings, and personal effects used by the depositor in a dwelling.

(4) A warehouseman loses his lien on any goods which he voluntarily delivers or which he unjustifiably refuses to deliver.

Section 7–210. Enforcement of Warehouseman's Lien

(1) Except as provided in subsection (2), a warehouseman's lien may be enforced by public or private sale of the goods in block or in parcels, at any time or place and on any terms which are commercially reasonable, after notifying all persons known to claim an interest in the goods. Such notification must include a statement of the amount due, the nature of the proposed sale and the time and place of any public sale. The fact that a better price could have been obtained by a sale at a different time or in a different method from that selected by the warehouseman is not of itself sufficient to establish that the sale was not made in a commercially reasonable manner. If the warehouseman either sells the goods in the usual manner in any recognized market therefor, or if he sells at the price current in such market at the time of his sale, or if he has otherwise sold in conformity with commercially reasonable practices among dealers in the type of goods sold, he has sold in a commercially reasonable manner. A sale of more goods than apparently necessary to be offered to insure satisfaction of the obligation is not commercially reasonable except in cases covered by the preceding sentence.

(2) A warehouseman's lien on goods other than goods stored by a merchant in the course of his business may be enforced only as follows:

(a) All persons known to claim an interest in the goods must be notified.

(b) The notification must be delivered in person or sent by registered or certified letter to the last known address of any person to be notified.

(c) The notification must include an itemized statement of the claim, a description of the goods subject to the lien, a demand for payment within a specified time not less than ten days after receipt of the notification, and a conspicuous statement that unless the claim is paid within that time the goods will be advertised for sale and sold by auction at a specified time and place.

(d) The sale must conform to the terms of the notification.

(e) The sale must be held at the nearest suitable place to that where the goods are held or stored.

(f) After the expiration of the time given in the notification, an advertisement of the sale must be published once a week for two weeks consecutively in a newspaper of general circulation where the sale is to be held. The advertisement must include a description of the goods, the name of the person on whose account they are being held, and the time and place of the sale. The sale must take place at least fifteen days after the first publication. If there is no newspaper of general circulation where the sale is to be held, the advertisement must be posted at least ten days before the sale in not less than six conspicuous places in the neighborhood of the proposed sale.

(3) Before any sale pursuant to this section any person claiming a right in the goods may pay the amount necessary to satisfy the lien and the reasonable expenses incurred under this section. In that event the goods must not be sold, but must be retained by the warehouseman subject to the terms of the receipt and this Article.

(4) The warehouseman may buy at any public sale pursuant to this section.

(5) A purchaser in good faith of goods sold to enforce a warehouseman's lien takes the goods free of any rights of persons against whom the lien was valid, despite noncompliance by the warehouseman with the requirements of this section.

(6) The warehouseman may satisfy his lien from the proceeds of any sale pursuant to this section but must hold the balance, if any, for delivery on demand to any person to whom he would have been bound to deliver the goods.

(7) The rights provided by this section shall be in addition to all other rights allowed by law to a creditor against his debtor.

(8) Where a lien is on goods stored by a merchant in the course of his business the lien may be enforced in accordance with either subsection (1) or (2).

(9) The warehouseman is liable for damages caused by failure to comply with the requirements for sale under this section and in case of willful violation is liable for conversion.

Part 3 Bills of Lading: Special Provisions

Section 7–301. Liability for Non-Receipt or Misdescription; "Said to Contain"; "Shipper's Load and Count"; Improper Handling

(1) A consignee of a non-negotiable bill who has given value in good faith or a holder to whom a negotiable bill has been duly negotiated relying in either case upon the description therein of the goods, or upon the date therein shown, may recover from the issuer damages caused by the misdating of the bill or the non-receipt or misdescription of the goods, except to the extent that the document indicates that the issuer does not know whether any part or all of the goods in fact were received or conform to the description, as where the description is in terms of marks or labels or kind, quantity, or condition or the receipt or description is qualified by "contents or condition of contents of packages unknown," "said to contain," "shipper's weight, load and count" or the like, if such indication be true.

(2) When goods are loaded by an issuer who is a common carrier, the issuer must count the packages of goods if package freight and ascertain the kind and quantity if bulk freight. In such cases "shipper's weight, load and count" or other words indicating that the description was made by the shipper are ineffective except as to freight concealed by packages.

(3) When bulk freight is loaded by a shipper who makes available to the issuer adequate facilities for weighing such freight, an issuer who is a common carrier must ascertain the kind and quantity within a reasonable time after receiving the written request of the shipper to do so. In such cases "shipper's weight" or other words of like purport are ineffective.

(4) The issuer may by inserting in the bill the words "shipper's weight, load and count" or other words of like purport indicate that the goods were loaded by the shipper; and if such statement be true the issuer shall not be liable for damages caused by the improper loading. But their omission does not imply liability for such damages.

(5) The shipper shall be deemed to have guaranteed to the issuer the accuracy at the time of shipment of the description, marks, labels, number, kind, quantity, condition and weight, as furnished by him; and the shipper shall indemnify the issuer against damage caused by inaccuracies in such particulars. The right of the issuer to such indemnity shall in no way limit his responsibility and liability under the contract of carriage to any person other than the shipper.

Section 7–302. Through Bills of Lading and Similar Documents

(1) The issuer of a through bill of lading or other document embodying an undertaking to be performed in part by persons acting as its agents or by connecting carriers is liable to anyone entitled to recover on the document for any breach by such other persons or by a connecting carrier of its obligation under the document but to the extent that the bill covers an undertaking to be performed overseas or in territory not contiguous to the continental United States or an undertaking including matters other than transportation this liability may be varied by agreement of the parties.

(2) Where goods covered by a through bill of lading or other document embodying an undertaking to be performed in part by persons other than the issuer are received by any such person, he is subject with respect to his own performance while the goods are in his possession to the obligation of the issuer. His obligation is discharged by delivery of the goods to another such person pursuant to the document, and does not include liability of breach by any other such persons or by the issuer.

(3) The issuer of such through bill of lading or other document shall be entitled to recover from the connecting carrier or such other person in possession of the goods when the breach of the obligation under the document occurred, the amount it may be required to pay to anyone entitled to recover on the document therefor, as may be evidenced by any receipt, judgment, or transcript thereof, and the amount of any expense reasonably incurred by it in defending any action brought by anyone entitled to recover on the document therefor.

Section 7–303. Diversion; Reconsignment; Change of Instructions

(1) Unless the bill of lading otherwise provides, the carrier may deliver the goods to a person or destination other than that stated in the bill or may otherwise dispose of the goods on instructions from

- (a) the holder of a negotiable bill; or
- (b) the consignor on a non-negotiable bill notwithstanding contrary instructions from the consignee; or
- (c) the consignee on a non-negotiable bill in the absence of contrary instructions from the consignor, if the goods have arrived at the billed destination or if the consignee is in possession of the bill; or
- (d) the consignee on a non-negotiable bill if he is entitled as against the consignor to dispose of them.

(2) Unless such instructions are noted on a negotiable bill of lading, a person to whom the bill is duly negotiated can hold the bailee according to the original terms.

Section 7–304. Bills of Lading in a Set

(1) Except where customary in overseas transportation, a bill of lading must not be issued in a set of parts. The issuer is liable for damages caused by violation of this subsection.

(2) Where a bill of lading is lawfully drawn in a set of parts, each of which is numbered and expressed to be valid only if the goods have not been delivered against any other part, the whole of the parts constitute one bill.

(3) Where a bill of lading is lawfully issued in a set of parts and different parts are negotiated to different persons, the title of the holder to whom the first due negotiation is made prevails as to both the document and the goods even though any later holder may have received the goods from the carrier in good faith and discharged the carrier's obligation by surrender of his part.

(4) Any person who negotiates or transfers a single part of a bill of lading drawn in a set is liable to holders of that part as if it were the whole set.

(5) The bailee is obliged to deliver in accordance with Part 4 of this Article against the first presented part of a bill of lading lawfully drawn in a set. Such delivery discharges the bailee's obligation on the whole bill.

Section 7–305. Destination Bills

(1) Instead of issuing a bill of lading to the consignor at the place of shipment a carrier may at the request of the consignor procure the bill to be issued at destination or at any other place designated in the request.

(2) Upon request of anyone entitled as against the carrier to control the goods while in transit and on surrender of any outstanding bill of lading or other receipt covering such goods, the issuer may procure a substitute bill to be issued at any place designated in the request.

Section 7–306. Altered Bills of Lading

An unauthorized alteration or filling in of a blank in a bill of lading leaves the bill enforceable according to its original tenor.

Section 7–307. Lien of Carrier

(1) A carrier has a lien on the goods covered by a bill of lading for charges subsequent to the date of its receipt of the goods for storage or transportation (including demurrage and terminal charges) and for expenses necessary for preservation of the goods incident to their transportation or reasonably incurred in their sale pursuant to law. But against a purchaser for value of a negotiable bill of lading a carrier's lien is limited to charges stated in the bill or the applicable tariffs, or if no charges are stated then to a reasonable charge.

(2) A lien for charges and expenses under subsection (1) on goods which the carrier was required by law to receive for transportation is effective against the consignor or any person entitled to the goods unless the carrier had notice that the consignor lacked authority to subject the goods to such charges and expenses. Any other lien under subsection (1) is effective against the consignor and any person who permitted the bailor to have control or possession of the goods unless the carrier had notice that the bailor lacked such authority.

(3) A carrier loses his lien on any goods which he voluntarily delivers or which he unjustifiably refuses to deliver.

Section 7–308. Enforcement of Carrier's Lien

(1) A carrier's lien may be enforced by public or private sale of the goods, in block or in parcels, at any time or place and on any terms which are commercially reasonable, after notifying all persons known to claim an interest in the goods. Such notification must include a statement of the amount due, the nature of the proposed sale and the time and place of any public sale. The fact that a better price could have been obtained by a sale at a different time or in a different method from that selected by the carrier is not of itself sufficient to establish that the sale was not made in a commercially reasonable manner. If the carrier either sells the goods in the usual manner in any recognized market therefor or if he sells at the price current in such market at the time of his sale or if he has otherwise sold in conformity with commercially reasonable practices among dealers in the type of goods sold he has sold in a commercially reasonable manner. A sale of more goods than apparently necessary to be offered to ensure satisfaction of the obligation is not commercially reasonable except in cases covered by the preceding sentence.

(2) Before any sale pursuant to this section any person claiming a right in the goods may pay the amount necessary to satisfy the lien and the reasonable expenses incurred under this section. In that event the goods must not be sold, but must be retained by the carrier subject to the terms of the bill and this Article.

(3) The carrier may buy at any public sale pursuant to this section.

(4) A purchaser in good faith of goods sold to enforce a carrier's lien takes the goods free of any rights of persons against whom the lien was valid, despite noncompliance by the carrier with the requirements of this section.

(5) The carrier may satisfy his lien from the proceeds of any sale pursuant to this section but must hold the balance, if any, for delivery on demand to any person to whom he would have been bound to deliver the goods.

(6) The rights provided by this section shall be in addition to all other rights allowed by law to a creditor against his debtor.

(7) A carrier's lien may be enforced in accordance with either subsection (1) or the procedure set forth in subsection (2) of Section 7–210.

(8) The carrier is liable for damages caused by failure to comply with the requirements for sale under this section and in case of willful violation is liable for conversion.

Section 7–309. Duty of Care; Contractual Limitation of Carrier's Liability

(1) A carrier who issues a bill of lading whether negotiable or non-negotiable must exercise the degree of care in relation to the goods which a reasonably careful man would exercise under like circumstances. This subsection does not repeal or change any law or rule of law which imposes liability upon a common carrier for damages not caused by its negligence.

(2) Damages may be limited by a provision that the carrier's liability shall not exceed a value stated in the document if the carrier's rates are dependent upon value and the consignor by the carrier's tariff is afforded an opportunity to declare a higher value or a value as lawfully provided in the tariff, or where no tariff is filed he is otherwise advised of such opportunity; but no such limitation is effective with respect to the carrier's liability for conversion to its own use.

(3) Reasonable provisions as to the time and manner of presenting claims and instituting actions based on the shipment may be included in a bill of lading or tariff.

Part 4 Warehouse Receipts and Bills of Lading: General Obligations

Section 7–401. Irregularities in Issue of Receipt or Bill or Conduct of Issuer

The obligations imposed by this Article on an issuer apply to a document of title regardless of the fact that

(a) the document may not comply with the requirements of this Article or of any other law or regulation regarding its issue, form or content; or

(b) the issuer may have violated laws regulating the conduct of his business; or

(c) the goods covered by the document were owned by the bailee at the time the document was issued; or

(d) the person issuing the document does not come within the definition of warehouseman if it purports to be a warehouse receipt.

Section 7–402. Duplicate Receipt or Bill; Overissue

Neither a duplicate nor any other document of title purporting to cover goods already represented by an outstanding document of the same issuer confers any right in the goods, except as provided in the case of bills in a set, overissue of documents for fungible goods and substitutes for lost, stolen or destroyed documents. But the issuer is liable for damages caused by his overissue or failure to identify a duplicate document as such by conspicuous notation on its face.

Section 7–403. Obligation of Warehouseman or Carrier to Deliver; Excuse

(1) The bailee must deliver the goods to a person entitled under the document who complies with subsections (2) and (3), unless and to the extent that the bailee establishes any of the following:

(a) delivery of the goods to a person whose receipt was rightful as against the claimant;

(b) damage to or delay, loss or destruction of the goods for which the bailee is not liable [, but the burden of establishing negligence in such cases is on the person entitled under the document];

Note: *The brackets in (1) (b) indicate that State enactments may differ on this point without serious damage to the principle of uniformity.*

(c) previous sale or other disposition of the goods in lawful enforcement of a lien or on a warehouseman's lawful termination of storage;

(d) the exercise by a seller of his right to stop delivery pursuant to the provisions of the Article on Sales (Section 2–705);

(e) a diversion, reconsignment or other disposition pursuant to the provisions of this Article (Section 7–303) or tariff regulating such right;

(f) release, satisfaction or any other fact affording a personal defense against the claimant;

(g) any other lawful excuse.

(2) A person claiming goods covered by a document of title must satisfy the bailee's lien where the bailee so requests or where the bailee is prohibited by law from delivering the goods until the charges are paid.

(3) Unless the person claiming is one against whom the document confers no right under Sec. 7–503(1), he must surrender for cancellation or notation of partial deliveries any outstanding negotiable document covering the goods, and the bailee must cancel the document or conspicuously note the partial delivery thereon or be liable to any person to whom the document is duly negotiated.

(4) "Person entitled under the document" means holder in the case of a negotiable document, or the person to whom delivery is to be made by the terms of or pursuant to written instructions under a non-negotiable document.

Section 7–404. No Liability for Good Faith Delivery Pursuant to Receipt or Bill

A bailee who in good faith including observance of reasonable commercial standards has received goods and delivered or otherwise disposed of them according to the terms of the document of title or pursuant to this Article is not liable therefor. This rule applies even though the person from whom he received the goods had no authority to procure the document or to dispose of the goods and even though the person to whom he delivered the goods had no authority to receive them.

Part 5 Warehouse Receipts and Bills of Lading: Negotiation and Transfer

Section 7–501. Form of Negotiation and Requirements of "Due Negotiation"

(1) A negotiable document of title running to the order of a named person is negotiated by his indorsement and delivery. After his indorsement in blank or to bearer any person can negotiate it by delivery alone.

(2) (a) A negotiable document of title is also negotiated by delivery alone when by its original terms it runs to bearer.

(b) When a document running to the order of a named person is delivered to him the effect is the same as if the document had been negotiated.

(3) Negotiation of a negotiable document of title after it has been indorsed to a specified person requires indorsement by the special indorsee as well as delivery.

(4) A negotiable document of title is "duly negotiated" when it is negotiated in the manner stated in this section to a holder who purchases it in good faith without notice of any defense against or claim to it on the part of any person and for value, unless it is established that the negotiation is not in the regular course of business or financing or involves receiving the document in settlement or payment of a money obligation.

(5) Indorsement of a non-negotiable document neither makes it negotiable nor adds to the transferee's rights.

(6) The naming in a negotiable bill of a person to be notified of the arrival of the goods does not limit the negotiability of the bill nor constitute notice to a purchaser thereof of any interest of such person in the goods.

Section 7–502. Rights Acquired by Due Negotiation

(1) Subject to the following section and to the provisions of Section 7–205 on fungible goods, a holder to whom a negotiable document of title has been duly negotiated acquires thereby:

(a) title to the document;

(b) title to the goods;

(c) all rights accruing under the law of agency or estoppel, including rights to goods delivered to the bailee after the document was issued; and

(d) the direct obligation of the issuer to hold or deliver the goods according to the terms of the document free of any defense or claim by him except those arising under the terms of the document or under this Article. In the case of a delivery order the bailee's obligation accrues only upon acceptance and the obligation acquired by the holder is that the issuer and any indorser will procure the acceptance of the bailee.

(2) Subject to the following section, title and rights so acquired are not defeated by any stoppage of the goods represented by the document or by surrender of such goods by the bailee, and are not impaired even though the negotiation or any prior negotiation constituted a breach of duty or even though any person has been deprived of possession of the document by misrepresentation, fraud, accident, mistake, duress, loss, theft or conversion, or even though a previous sale or other transfer of the goods or document has been made to a third person.

Section 7–503. Document of Title to Goods Defeated in Certain Cases

(1) A document of title confers no right in goods against a person who before issuance of the document had a legal interest or a perfected security interest in them and who neither

- (a) delivered or entrusted them or any document of title covering them to the bailor or his nominee with actual or apparent authority to ship, store or sell or with power to obtain delivery under this Article (Section 7–403) or with power of disposition under this Act (Sections 2–403 and 9–307) or other statute or rule of law; nor
- (b) acquiesced in the procurement by the bailor or his nominee of any document of title.

(2) Title to goods based upon an unaccepted delivery order is subject to the rights of anyone to whom a negotiable warehouse receipt or bill of lading covering the goods has been duly negotiated. Such a title may be defeated under the next section to the same extent as the rights of the issuer or a transferee from the issuer.

(3) Title to goods based upon a bill of lading issued to a freight forwarder is subject to the rights of anyone to whom a bill issued by the freight forwarder is duly negotiated; but delivery by the carrier in accordance with Part 4 of this Article pursuant to its own bill of lading discharges the carrier's obligation to deliver.

Section 7–504. Rights Acquired in the Absence of Due Negotiation; Effect of Diversion; Seller's Stoppage of Delivery

(1) A transferee of a document, whether negotiable or non-negotiable, to whom the document has been delivered but not duly negotiated, acquires the title and rights which his transferor had or had actual authority to convey.

(2) In the case of a non-negotiable document, until but not after the bailee receives notification of the transfer, the rights of the transferee may be defeated

- (a) by those creditors of the transferor who could treat the sale as void under Section 2–402; or
- (b) by a buyer from the transferor in ordinary course of business if the bailee has delivered the goods to the buyer or received notification of his rights; or
- (c) as against the bailee by good faith dealings of the bailee with the transferor.

(3) A diversion or other change of shipping instructions by the consignor in a non-negotiable bill of lading which causes the bailee not to deliver to the consignee defeats the consignee's title to the goods if they have been delivered to a buyer in ordinary course of business and in any event defeats the consignee's rights against the bailee.

(4) Delivery pursuant to a non-negotiable document may be stopped by a seller under Section 2–705, and subject to the requirement of due notification there provided. A bailee honoring the seller's instructions is entitled to be indemnified by the seller against any resulting loss or expense.

Section 7–505. Indorser Not a Guarantor for Other Parties

The indorsement of a document of title issued by a bailee does not make the indorser liable for any default by the bailee or by previous indorsers.

Section 7–506. Delivery Without Indorsement: Right to Compel Indorsement

The transferee of a negotiable document of title has a specifically enforceable right to have his transferor supply any necessary indorsement but the transfer becomes a negotiation only as of the time the indorsement is supplied.

Section 7–507. Warranties on Negotiation or Transfer of Receipt or Bill

Where a person negotiates or transfers a document of title for value otherwise than as a mere intermediary under the next following section, then unless otherwise agreed he warrants to his immediate purchaser only in addition to any warranty made in selling the goods

- (a) that the document is genuine; and
- (b) that he has no knowledge of any fact which would impair its validity or worth; and
- (c) that his negotiation or transfer is rightful and fully effective with respect to the title to the document and the goods it represents.

Section 7–508. Warranties of Collecting Bank as to Documents

A collecting bank or other intermediary known to be entrusted with documents on behalf of another or with collection of a draft or other claim against delivery of documents warrants by such delivery of the documents only its own good faith and authority. This rule applies even though the intermediary has purchased or made advances against the claim or draft to be collected.

Part 6 Warehouse Receipts and Bills of Lading: Miscellaneous Provisions

Section 7–601. Lost and Missing Documents

(1) If a document has been lost, stolen or destroyed, a court may order delivery of the goods or issuance of a substitute document and the bailee may without liability to any person comply with such order. If the document was negotiable the claimant must post security approved by the court to indemnify any person who may suffer loss as a result of non-surrender of the document. If the document was not negotiable, such security may be required at the discretion of the court. The court may also in its discretion order payment of the bailee's reasonable costs and counsel fees.

(2) A bailee who without court order delivers goods to a person claiming under a missing negotiable document is liable to any person injured

thereby, and if the delivery is not in good faith becomes liable for conversion. Delivery in good faith is not conversion if made in accordance with a filed classification or tariff or, where no classification or tariff is filed, if the claimant posts security with the bailee in an amount at least double the value of the goods at the time of posting to indemnify any person injured by the delivery who files a notice of claim within one year after the delivery.

Section 7–602. Attachment of Goods Covered by a Negotiable Document

Except where the document was originally issued upon delivery of the goods by a person who had no power to dispose of them, no lien attaches by virtue of any judicial process to goods in the possession of a bailee for which a negotiable document of title is outstanding unless the document be first surrendered to the bailee or its negotiation enjoined, and the bailee shall not be compelled to deliver the goods pursuant to process until the document is surrendered to him or impounded by the court. One who purchases the document for value without notice of the process or injunction takes free of the lien imposed by judicial process.

Section 7–603. Conflicting Claims; Interpleader

If more than one person claims title or possession of the goods, the bailee is excused from delivery until he has had a reasonable time to ascertain the validity of the adverse claims or to bring an action to compel all claimants to interplead and may compel such interpleader, either in defending an action for non-delivery of the goods, or by original action, whichever is appropriate.

Article 8 Investment Securities

Part 1 Short Title and General Matters

Section 8–101. Short Title

This Article shall be known and may be cited as Uniform Commercial Code—Investment Securities.

Section 8–102. Definitions and Index of Definitions

(1) In this Article, unless the context otherwise requires:

- (a) A "certificated security" is a share, participation, or other interest in property of or an enterprise of the issuer or an obligation of the issuer which is
  - (i) represented by an instrument issued in bearer or registered form;
  - (ii) of a type commonly dealt in on securities exchanges or markets or commonly recognized in any area in which it is issued or dealt in as a medium for investment; and
  - (iii) either one of a class or series or by its terms divisible into a class or series of shares, participations, interests, or obligations.
- (b) An "uncertificated security" is a share, participation, or other interest in property or an enterprise of the issuer or an obligation of the issuer which is
  - (i) not represented by an instrument and the transfer of which is registered upon books maintained for that purpose by or on behalf of the issuer;
  - (ii) of a type commonly dealt in on securities exchanges or markets; and
  - (iii) either one of a class or series or by its terms divisible into a class or series of shares, participations, interests, or obligations.
- (c) A "security" is either a certificated or an uncertificated security. If a security is certificated, the terms "security" and "certificated security" may mean either the intangible interest, the instrument representing that interest, or both, as the context requires. A writing that is a certificated security is governed by this Article and not by Article 3, even though it also meets the requirements of that Article. This Article does not apply to money. If a certificated security has been retained by or surrendered to the issuer or its transfer agent for reasons other than registration of transfer, other temporary purpose, payment, exchange, or acquisition by the issuer, that security shall be treated as an uncertificated security for purposes of this Article.
- (d) A certificated security is in "registered form" if
  - (i) it specifies a person entitled to the security or the rights it represents; and
  - (ii) its transfer may be registered upon books maintained for that purpose by or on behalf of the issuer, or the security so states.
- (e) A certificated security is in "bearer form" if it runs to bearer according to its terms and not by reason of any indorsement.

(2) A "subsequent purchaser" is a person who takes other than by original issue.

(3) A "clearing corporation" is a corporation registered as a "clearing agency" under the federal securities laws or a corporation:

- (a) at least 90 percent of whose capital stock is held by or for one or more organizations, none of which, other than a national securities exchange or association, holds in excess of 20 percent of the capital stock of the corporation, and each of which is
  - (i) subject to supervision or regulation pursuant to the provisions of federal or state banking laws or state insurance laws,
  - (ii) a broker or dealer or investment company registered under the federal securities laws, or
  - (iii) a national securities exchange or association registered under the federal securities laws; and
- (b) any remaining capital stock of which is held by individuals who have purchased it at or prior to the time of their taking office as directors of the corporation and who have purchased only so much of the capital stock as is necessary to permit them to qualify as directors.

(4) A "custodian bank" is a bank or trust company that is supervised and examined by state or federal authority having supervision over banks and is acting as custodian for a clearing corporation.

(5) Other definitions applying to this Article or to specified Parts thereof and the sections in which they appear are:

"Adverse claim." Section 8–302.

"Bona fide purchaser." Section 8–302.

"Broker." Section 8–303.

"Debtor." Section 9–105.

"Financial intermediary." Section 8–313.

"Guarantee of the signature." Section 8–402.

"Initial transaction statement." Section 8–408.

"Instruction." Section 8–308.

"Intermediary bank." Section 4–105.

"Issuer." Section 8–201.

"Overissue." Section 8–104.

"Secured Party." Section 9–105.

"Security Agreement." Section 9–105.

(6) In addition, Article I contains general definitions and principles of construction and interpretation applicable throughout this Article.

Section 8–103. Issuer's Lien

A lien upon a security in favor of an issuer thereof is valid against a purchaser only if:

(a) the security is certificated and the right of the issuer to the lien is noted conspicuously thereon; or

(b) the security is uncertificated and a notation of the right of the issuer to the lien is contained in the initial transaction statement sent to the purchaser or, if his interest is transferred to him other than by registration of transfer, pledge, or release, the initial transaction statement sent to the registered owner or the registered pledgee.

Section 8–104. Effect of Overissue; "Overissue"

(1) The provisions of this Article which validate a security or compel its issue or reissue do not apply to the extent that validation, issue, or reissue would result in overissue; but if:

(a) an identical security which does not constitute an overissue is reasonably available for purchase, the person entitled to issue or validation may compel the issuer to purchase the security for him and either to deliver a certificated security or to register the transfer of an uncertificated security to him, against surrender any certificated security he holds; or

(b) a security is not so available for purchase, the person entitled to issue or validation may recover from the issuer the price he or the last purchaser for value paid for it with interest from the date of his demand.

(2) "Overissue" means the issue of securities in excess of the amount the issuer has corporate power to issue.

Section 8–105. Certificated Securities Negotiable; Statements and Instructions Not Negotiable; Presumptions

(1) Certificated securities governed by this Article are negotiable instruments.

(2) Statements (Section 8–408), notices, or the like, sent by the issuer of uncertificated securities and instructions (Section 8–308) are neither negotiable instruments nor certificated securities.

(3) In any action on a security:

(a) unless specifically denied in the pleadings, each signature on a certificated security, in a necessary indorsement, on an initial transaction statement, or on an instruction, is admitted;

(b) if the effectiveness of a signature is put in issue, the burden of establishing it is on the party claiming under the signature, but the signature is presumed to be genuine or authorized;

(c) if signatures on a certificated security are admitted or established, production of the security entitles a holder to recover on it unless the defendant establishes a defense or a defect going to the validity of the security;

(d) if signatures on an initial transaction statement are admitted or established, the facts stated in the statement are presumed to be true as of the time of its issuance; and

(e) after it is shown that a defense or defect exists, the plaintiff has the burden of establishing that he or some person under whom he claims is a person against whom the defense or defect is ineffective (Section 8–202).

Section 8–106. Applicability

The law (including the conflict of laws rules) of the jurisdiction of organization of the issuer governs the validity of a security, the effectiveness of registration by the issuer, and the rights and duties of the issuer with respect to:

(a) registration of transfer of a certificated security;

(b) registration of transfer, pledge, or release of an uncertificated security; and

(c) sending of statements of uncertificated securities.

Section 8–107. Securities Transferable; Action for Price

(1) Unless otherwise agreed and subject to any applicable law or regulation respecting short sales, a person obligated to transfer securities may transfer any certificated security of the specified issue in bearer form or registered in the name of the transferee, or indorsed to him or in blank, or he may transfer an equivalent uncertificated security to the transferee or a person designated by the transferee.

(2) If the buyer fails to pay the price as it comes due under a contract of sale, the seller may recover the price of:

(a) certificated securities accepted by the buyer;

(b) uncertificated securities that have been transferred to the buyer or a person designated by the buyer; and

(c) other securities if efforts at their resale would be unduly burdensome or if there is no readily available market for their resale.

Section 8–108. Registration of Pledge and Release of Uncertificated Securities

A security interest in an uncertificated security may be evidenced by the registration of pledge to the secured party or a person designated by him. There can be no more than one registered pledge of an uncertificated security at any time. The registered owner of an uncertificated security is the person in whose name the security is registered, even if the security is subject to a registered pledge. The rights of a registered pledgee of an uncertificated security under this Article are terminated by the registration of release.

Part 2 Issue—Issuer

Section 8–201. "Issuer"

(1) With respect to obligations on or defenses to a security, "issuer" includes a person who:

(a) places or authorizes the placing of his name on a certificated security (otherwise than as authenticating trustee, registrar, transfer agent, or the like) to evidence that it represents a share, participation, or other interest in his property or in an enterprise, or to evidence his duty to perform an obligation represented by the certificated security;

(b) creates shares, participations, or other interests in his property or in an enterprise or undertakes obligations, which shares, participations, interests, or obligations are uncertificated securities;

(c) directly or indirectly creates fractional interests in his rights or property, which fractional interests are represented by certificated securities; or

(d) becomes responsible for or in place of any other person described as an issuer in this section.

(2) With respect to obligations on or defenses to a security, a guarantor is an issuer to the extent of his guaranty, whether or not his obligation is noted on a certificated security or on statements of uncertificated securities sent pursuant to Section 8–408.

(3) With respect to registration of transfer, pledge, or release (Part 4 of this Article), "issuer" means a person on whose behalf transfer books are maintained.

Section 8–202. Issuer's Responsibility and Defenses; Notice of Defect or Defense

(1) Even against a purchaser for value and without notice, the terms of a security include:

(a) if the security is certificated, those stated on the security;

(b) if the security is uncertificated, those contained in the initial transaction statement sent to such purchaser, or, if his interest is transferred to him other than by registration of transfer, pledge, or release, the initial transaction statement sent to the registered owner or registered pledgee; and

(c) those made part of the security by reference, on the certificated security or in the initial transaction statement, to another instrument, indenture, or document or to a constitution, statute, ordinance, rule, regulation, order or the like, to the extent that the terms referred to do not conflict with the terms stated on the certificated security or contained in the statement. A reference under this paragraph does not of itself charge a purchaser for value with notice of a defect going to the validity of the security, even though the certificated security or statement expressly states that a person accepting it admits notice.

(2) A certificated security in the hands of a purchaser for value or an uncertificated security as to which an initial transaction statement has been sent to a purchaser for value, other than a security issued by a government or governmental agency or unit, even though issued with a defect going to its validity, is valid with respect to the purchaser if he is without notice of the particular defect unless the defect involves a violation of constitutional provisions, in which case the security is valid with respect to a subsequent purchaser for value and without notice of the defect. This subsection applies to an issuer that is a government or governmental agency or unit only if either there has been substantial compliance with the legal requirements governing the issue or the issuer has received a substantial consideration for the issue as a whole or for the particular security and a stated purpose of the issue is one for which the issuer has power to borrow money or issue the security.

(3) Except as provided in the case of certain unauthorized signatures (Section 8–205), lack of genuineness of a certificated security or an initial transaction statement is a complete defense, even against a purchaser for value and without notice.

(4) All other defenses of the issuer of a certificated or uncertificated security, including nondelivery and conditional delivery of a certificated security, are ineffective against a purchaser for value who has taken without notice of the particular defense.

(5) Nothing in this section shall be construed to affect the right of a party to a "when, as and if issued" or a "when distributed" contract to cancel the contract in the event of a material change in the character of the security that is the subject of the contract or in the plan or arrangement pursuant to which the security is to be issued or distributed.

Section 8–203. Staleness as Notice of Defects or Defenses

(1) After an act or event creating a right to immediate performance of the principal obligation represented by a certificated security or that sets a date on or after which the security is to be presented or surrendered for redemption or exchange, a purchaser is charged with notice of any defect in its issue or defense of the issuer if:

(a) the act or event is one requiring the payment of money, the delivery of certificated securities, the registration of transfer of uncertificated securities, or any of these on presentation or surrender of the certificated security, the funds or securities are available on the date set for payment or exchange, and he takes the security more than one year after that date; and

(b) the act or event is not covered by paragraph (a) and he takes the security more than 2 years after the date set for surrender or presentation or the date on which performance became due.

(2) A call that has been revoked is not within subsection (1).

Section 8–204. Effect of Issuer's Restrictions on Transfer

A restriction on transfer of a security imposed by the issuer, even if otherwise lawful, is ineffective against any person without actual knowledge of it unless:

(a) the security is certificated and the restriction is noted conspicuously thereon; or

(b) the security is uncertificated and a notation of the restriction is contained in the initial transaction statement sent to the person or, if his interest is transferred to him other than by registration of transfer, pledge, or release, the initial transaction statement sent to the registered owner or the registered pledgee.

Section 8–205. Effect of Unauthorized Signature on Certificated Security or Initial Transaction Statement

An unauthorized signature placed on a certificated security prior to or in the course of issue or placed on an initial transaction statement is ineffective, but the signature is effective in favor of a purchaser for value of the certificated security or a purchaser for value of an uncertificated security to whom the initial transaction statement has been sent, if the purchaser is without notice of the lack of authority and the signing has been done by:

(a) an authenticating trustee, registrar, transfer agent, or other person entrusted by the issuer with the signing of the security, of similar securities, or of initial transaction statements or the immediate preparation for signing of any of them; or

(b) an employee of the issuer, or of any of the foregoing, entrusted with responsible handling of the security or initial transaction statement.

Section 8–206. Completion or Alteration of Certificated Security or Initial Transaction Statement

(1) If a certificated security contains the signatures necessary to its issue or transfer but is incomplete in any other respect:

(a) any person may complete it by filling in the blanks as authorized; and

(b) even though the blanks are incorrectly filled in, the security as completed is enforceable by a purchaser who took it for value and without notice of the incorrectness.

(2) A complete certificated security that has been improperly altered, even though fraudulently, remains enforceable, but only according to its original terms.

(3) If an initial transaction statement contains the signatures necessary to its validity, but is incomplete in any other respect:

(a) any person may complete it by filling in the blanks as authorized; and

(b) even though the blanks are incorrectly filled in, the statement as completed is effective in favor of the person to whom it is sent if he purchased the security referred to therein for value and without notice of the incorrectness.

(4) A complete initial transaction statement that has been improperly altered, even though fraudulently, is effective in favor of a purchaser to whom it has been sent, but only according to its original terms.

Section 8–207. Rights and Duties of Issuer With Respect to Registered Owners and Registered Pledgees

(1) Prior to due presentment for registration of transfer of a certificated security in registered form, the issuer or indenture trustee may treat the registered owner as the person exclusively entitled to vote, to receive notifications, and otherwise to exercise all rights and powers of an owner.

(2) Subject to the provisions of subsections (3), (4), and (6), the issuer or indenture trustee may treat the registered owner of an uncertificated security as the person exclusively entitled to vote, to receive notifications, and otherwise to exercise all the rights and powers of an owner.

(3) The registered owner of an uncertificated security that is subject to a registered pledge is not entitled to registration of transfer prior to the due presentment to the issuer of a release instruction. The exercise of conversion rights with respect to a convertible uncertificated security is a transfer within the meaning of this section.

(4) Upon due presentment of a transfer instruction from the registered pledgee of an uncertificated security, the issuer shall:

(a) register the transfer of the security to the new owner free of pledge, if the instruction specifies a new owner (who may be the registered pledgee) and does not specify a pledgee;

(b) register the transfer of the security to the new owner subject to the interest of the existing pledgee, if the instruction specifies a new owner and the existing pledgee; or

(c) register the release of the security from the existing pledge and register the pledge of the security to the other pledgee, if the instruction specifies the existing owner and another pledgee.

(5) Continuity of perfection of a security interest is not broken by registration of transfer under subsection (4) (b) or by registration of release and pledge under subsection (4)(c), if the security interest is assigned.

(6) If an uncertificated security is subject to a registered pledge:

(a) any uncertificated securities issued in exchange for or distributed with respect to the pledged security shall be registered subject to the pledge;

(b) any certificated securities issued in exchange for or distributed with respect to the pledged security shall be delivered to the registered pledgee; and

(c) any money paid in exchange for or in redemption of part or all of the security shall be paid to the registered pledgee.

(7) Nothing in this Article shall be construed to affect the liability of the registered owner of a security for calls, assessments, or the like.

Section 8–208. Effect of Signature of Authenticating Trustee, Registrar, or Transfer Agent

(1) A person placing his signature upon a certificated security or an initial transaction statement as authenticating trustee, registrar, transfer agent, or the like, warrants to a purchaser for value of the certificated security or a purchaser for value of an uncertificated security to whom the initial transaction statement has been sent, if the purchaser is without notice of the particular defect, that:

(a) the certificated security or initial transaction statement is genuine;

(b) his own participation in the issue or registration of the transfer, pledge, or release of the security is within his capacity and within the scope of the authority received by him from the issuer; and

(c) he has reasonable grounds to believe the security is in the form and within the amount the issuer is authorized to issue.

(2) Unless otherwise agreed, a person by so placing his signature does not assume responsibility for the validity of the security in other respects.

Part 3 Transfer

Section 8–301. Rights Acquired by Purchaser

(1) Upon transfer of a security to a purchaser (Section 8–313), the purchaser acquires the rights in the security which his transferor had or had actual authority to convey unless the purchaser's rights are limited by Section 8–302(4).

(2) A transferee of a limited interest acquires rights only to the extent of the interest transferred. The creation or release of a security interest in a security is the transfer of a limited interest in that security.

Section 8–302. "Bona Fide Purchaser"; "Adverse Claim"; Title Acquired by Bona Fide Purchaser

(1) A "bona fide purchaser" is a purchaser for value in good faith and without notice of any adverse claim:

(a) who takes delivery of a certificated security in bearer form or in registered form, issued or indorsed to him or in blank;

(b) to whom the transfer, pledge, or release of an uncertificated security is registered on the books of the issuer; or

(c) to whom a security is transferred under the provisions of paragraph (c), (d), (i), or (g) of Section 8–313(1).

(2) "Adverse claim" includes a claim that a transfer was or would be wrongful or that a particular adverse person is the owner of or has an interest in the security.

(3) A bona fide purchaser in addition to acquiring the rights of a purchaser (Section 8–301) also acquires his interest in the security free of any adverse claim.

(4) Notwithstanding Section 8–301(1), the transferee of a particular certificated security who has been a party to any fraud or illegality affecting the security, or who as a prior holder of that certificated security had notice of an adverse claim, cannot improve his position by taking from a bona fide purchaser.

Section 8–303. "Broker"

"Broker" means a person engaged for all or part of his time in the business of buying and selling securities, who in the transaction concerned acts for, buys a security from, or sells a security to, a customer. Nothing in this Article determines the capacity in which a person acts for purposes of any other statute or rule to which the person is subject.

Section 8–304. Notice to Purchaser of Adverse Claims

(1) A purchaser (including a broker for the seller or buyer, but excluding an intermediary bank) of a certificated security is charged with notice of adverse claims if:

(a) the security, whether in bearer or registered form, has been indorsed "for collection" or "for surrender" or for some other purpose not involving transfer; or

(b) the security is in bearer form and has on it an unambiguous statement that it is the property of a person other than the transferor. The mere writing of a name on a security is not such a statement.

(2) A purchaser (including a broker for the seller or buyer, but excluding an intermediary bank) to whom the transfer, pledge, or release of an uncertificated security is registered is charged with notice of adverse claims as to which the issuer has a duty under Section 8–403(4) at the time of registration and which are noted in the initial transaction statement sent to the purchaser or, if his interest is transferred to him other than by registration of transfer, pledge, or release, the initial transaction statement sent to the registered owner or the registered pledgee.

(3) The fact that the purchaser (including a broker for the seller or buyer) of a certificated or uncertificated security has notice that the security is held for a third person or is registered in the name of or indorsed by a fiduciary does not create a duty of inquiry into the rightfulness of the transfer or constitute constructive notice of adverse claims. However, if the purchaser (excluding an intermediary bank) has knowledge that the proceeds are being used or that the transaction is for the individual benefit of the fiduciary or otherwise in breach of duty, the purchaser is charged with notice of adverse claims.

Section 8–305. Staleness as Notice of Adverse Claims

An act or event that creates a right to immediate performance of the principal obligation represented by a certificated security or sets a date on or after which a certificated security is to be presented or surrendered for redemption or exchange does not itself constitute any notice of adverse claims except in the case of a transfer:

(a) after one year from any date set for presentment or surrender for redemption or exchange; or

(b) after 6 months from any date set for payment of money against presentation or surrender of the security if funds are available for payment on that date.

Section 8–306. Warranties on Presentment and Transfer of Certificated Securities; Warranties of Originators of Instructions

(1) A person who presents a certificated security for registration of transfer or for payment or exchange warrants to the issuer that he is entitled to the registration, payment, or exchange. But, a purchaser for value and without notice of adverse claims who receives a new, reissued, or re-registered certificated security on registration of transfer or receives an initial transaction statement confirming the registration of transfer of an equivalent uncertificated security to him warrants only that he has no knowledge of any unauthorized signature (Section 8–311) in a necessary indorsement.

(2) A person by transferring a certificated security to a purchaser for value warrants only that:

(a) his transfer is effective and rightful;

(b) the security is genuine and has not been materially altered; and

(c) he knows of no fact which might impair the validity of the security.

(3) If a certificated security is delivered by an intermediary known to be entrusted with delivery of the security on behalf of another or with collection of a draft or other claim against delivery, the intermediary by delivery warrants only his own good faith and authority, even though he has purchased or made advances against the claim to be collected against the delivery.

(4) A pledgee or other holder for security who redelivers a certificated security received, or after payment and on order of the debtor delivers that security to a third person, makes only the warranties of an intermediary under subsection (3).

(5) A person who originates an instruction warrants to the issuer that:

(a) he is an appropriate person to originate the instruction; and

(b) at the time the instruction is presented to the issuer he will be entitled to the registration of transfer, pledge, or release.

(6) A person who originates an instruction warrants to any person specially guaranteeing his signature (subsection 8–312(3)) that:

(a) he is an appropriate person to originate the instruction; and

(b) at the time the instruction is presented to the issuer

(i) he will be entitled to the registration of transfer, pledge, or release; and

(ii) the transfer, pledge, or release requested in the instruction will be registered by the issuer free from all liens, security interests, restrictions, and claims other than those specified in the instruction.

(7) A person who originates an instruction warrants to a purchaser for value and to any person guaranteeing the instruction (Section 8–312(6)) that:

(a) he is an appropriate person to originate the instruction;

(b) the uncertificated security referred to therein is valid; and

(c) at the time the instruction is presented to the issuer

(i) the transferor will be entitled to the registration of transfer, pledge, or release;

(ii) the transfer, pledge, or release requested in the instruction will be registered by the issuer free from all liens, security interests, restrictions, and claims other than those specified in the instruction; and

(iii) the requested transfer, pledge, or release will be rightful.

(8) If a secured party is the registered pledgee or the registered owner of an uncertificated security, a person who originates an instruction of release or transfer to the debtor or, after payment and on order of the debtor, a transfer instruction to a third person, warrants to the debtor or the third person only that he is an appropriate person to originate the instruction and, at the time the instruction is presented to the issuer, the transferor will be entitled to the registration of release or transfer. If a transfer instruction to a third person who is a purchaser for value is originated on order of the debtor, the debtor makes to the purchaser the warranties of paragraphs (b), (c)(ii) and (c)(iii) of subsection (7).

(9) A person who transfers an uncertificated security to a purchaser for value and does not originate an instruction in connection with the transfer warrants only that:

(a) his transfer is effective and rightful; and

(b) the uncertificated security is valid.

(10) A broker gives to his customer and to the issuer and a purchaser the applicable warranties provided in this section and has the rights and privileges of a purchaser under this section. The warranties of and in favor of the broker, acting as an agent are in addition to applicable warranties given by and in favor of his customer.

Section 8–307. Effect of Delivery Without Indorsement; Right to Compel Indorsement

If a certificated security in registered form has been delivered to a purchaser without a necessary indorsement he may become a bona fide purchaser only as of the time the indorsement is supplied; but against the transferor, the transfer is complete upon delivery and the purchaser has a specifically enforceable right to have any necessary indorsement supplied.

Section 8–308. Indorsements; Instructions

(1) An indorsement of a certificated security in registered form is made when an appropriate person signs on it or on a separate document an assignment or transfer of the security or a power to assign or transfer it or his signature is written without more upon the back of the security.

(2) An indorsement may be in blank or special. An indorsement in blank includes an indorsement to bearer. A special indorsement specifies to whom the security is to be transferred, or who has power to transfer it. A holder may convert a blank indorsement into a special indorsement.

(3) An indorsement purporting to be only of part of a certificated security representing units intended by the issuer to be separately transferable is effective to the extent of the indorsement.

(4) An "instruction" is an order to the issuer of an uncertificated security requesting that the transfer, pledge, or release from pledge of the uncertificated security specified therein be registered.

(5) An instruction originated by an appropriate person is:

(a) a writing signed by an appropriate person; or

(b) a communication to the issuer in any form agreed upon in a writing signed by the issuer and an appropriate person.

If an instruction has been originated by an appropriate person but is incomplete in any other respect, any person may complete it as authorized and the issuer may rely on it as completed even though it has been completed incorrectly.

(6) "An appropriate person" in subsection (1) means the person specified by the certificated security or by special indorsement to be entitled to the security.

(7) "An appropriate person" in subsection (5) means:

(a) for an instruction to transfer or pledge an uncertificated security which is then not subject to a registered pledge, the registered owner; or

(b) for an instruction to transfer or release an uncertificated security which is then subject to a registered pledge, the registered pledgee.

(8) In addition to the persons designated in subsections (6) and (7), "an appropriate person" in subsections (1) and (5) includes:

(a) if the person designated is described as a fiduciary but is no longer serving in the described capacity, either that person or his successor;

(b) if the persons designated are described as more than one person as fiduciaries and one or more are no longer serving in the described capacity, the remaining fiduciary or fiduciaries, whether or not a successor has been appointed or qualified;

(c) if the person designated is an individual and is without capacity to act by virtue of death, incompetence, infancy, or otherwise, his executor, administrator, guardian, or like fiduciary;

(d) if the persons designated are described as more than one person as tenants by the entirety or with right of survivorship and by reason of death all cannot sign, the survivor or survivors;

(e) a person having power to sign under applicable law or controlling instrument; and

(f) to the extent that the person designated or any of the foregoing persons may act through an agent, his authorized agent.

(9) Unless otherwise agreed, the indorser of a certificated security by his indorsement or the originator of an instruction by his origination assumes no obligation that the security will be honored by the issuer but only the obligations provided in Section 8–306.

(10) Whether the person signing is appropriate is determined as of the date of signing and an indorsement made by or an instruction originated by him does not become unauthorized for the purposes of this Article by virtue of any subsequent change of circumstances.

(11) Failure of a fiduciary to comply with a controlling instrument or with the law of the state having jurisdiction of the fiduciary relationship, including any law requiring the fiduciary to obtain court approval of the transfer, pledge, or release, does not render his indorsement or an instruction originated by him unauthorized for the purposes of this Article.

Section 8–309. Effect of Indorsement Without Delivery

An indorsement of a certificated security, whether special or in blank, does not constitute a transfer until delivery of the certificated security on which it appears or, if the indorsement is on a separate document, until delivery of both the document and the certificated security.

Section 8–310. Indorsement of Certificated Security in Bearer Form

An indorsement of a certificated security in bearer form may give notice of adverse claims (Section 8–304) but does not otherwise affect any right to registration the holder possesses.

Section 8–311. Effect of Unauthorized Indorsement or Instruction

Unless the owner or pledgee has ratified an unauthorized indorsement or instruction or is otherwise precluded from asserting its ineffectiveness:

(a) he may asset its ineffectiveness against the issuer or any purchaser, other than a purchaser for value and without notice of adverse claims, who has in good faith received a new, reissued, or re-registered certificated security on registration of transfer or received an initial transaction statement confirming the registration of transfer, pledge, or release of an equivalent uncertificated security to him; and

(b) an issuer who registers the transfer of a certificated security upon the unauthorized indorsement or who registers the transfer, pledge, or release of an uncertificated security upon the unauthorized instruction is subject to liability for improper registration (Section 8–404).

Section 8–312. Effect of Guaranteeing Signature, Indorsement or Instruction

(1) Any person guaranteeing a signature of an indorser of a certificated security warrants that at the time of signing:

(a) the signature was genuine;

(b) the signer was an appropriate person to indorse (Section 8–308); and

(c) the signer had legal capacity to sign.

(2) Any person guaranteeing a signature of the originator of an instruction warrants that at the time of signing:

(a) the signature was genuine;

(b) the signer was an appropriate person to originate the instruction (Section 8–308) if the person specified in the instruction as the registered owner or registered pledgee of the uncertificated security was, in fact, the registered owner or registered pledgee of the security, as to which fact the signature guarantor makes no warranty;

(c) the signer had legal capacity to sign; and

(d) the taxpayer identification number, if any, appearing on the instruction as that of the registered owner or registered pledgee was the taxpayer identification number of the signer or of the owner or pledgee for whom the signer was acting.

(3) Any person specially guaranteeing the signature of the originator of an instruction makes not only the warranties of a signature guarantor (subsection (2)) but also warrants that at the time the instruction is presented to the issuer:

(a) the person specified in the instruction as the registered owner or registered pledgee of the uncertificated security will be the registered owner or registered pledgee; and

(b) the transfer, pledge, or release of the uncertificated security requested in the instruction will be registered by the issuer free from all liens, security interests, restrictions, and claims other than those specified in the instruction.

(4) The guarantor under subsections (1) and (2) or the special guarantor under subsection (3) does not otherwise warrant the rightfulness of the particular transfer, pledge, or release.

(5) Any person guaranteeing an indorsement of a certificated security makes not only the warranties of a signature guarantor under subsection (1) but also warrants the rightfulness of the particular transfer in all respects.

(6) Any person guaranteeing an instruction requesting the transfer, pledge, or release of an uncertificated security makes not only the warranties of a special signature guarantor under subsection (3) but also warrants the rightfulness of the particular transfer, pledge, or release in all respects.

(7) No issuer may require a special guarantee of signature (subsection (3)), a guarantee of indorsement (subsection (5)), or a guarantee of instruction (subsection (6)) as a condition to registration of transfer, pledge, or release.

(8) The foregoing warranties are made to any person taking or dealing with the security in reliance on the guarantee, and the guarantor is liable to the person for any loss resulting from breach of the warranties.

Section 8–313. When Transfer to Purchaser Occurs; Financial Intermediary as Bona Fide Purchaser; "Financial Intermediary"

(1) Transfer of a security or a limited interest (including a security interest) therein to a purchaser occurs only:

(a) at the time he or a person designated by him acquires possession of a certificated security;

(b) at the time the transfer, pledge, or release of an uncertificated security is registered to him or a person designated by him;

(c) at the time his financial intermediary acquires possession of a certificated security specially indorsed to or issued in the name of the purchaser;

(d) at the time a financial intermediary, not a clearing corporation, sends him confirmation of the purchase and also by book entry or otherwise identifies as belonging to the purchaser

(i) a specific certificated security in the financial intermediary's possession;

(ii) a quantity of securities that constitute or are part of a fungible bulk of certificated securities in the financial intermediary's possession or of uncertificated securities registered in the name of the financial intermediary; or

(iii) a quantity of securities that constitute or are part of a fungible bulk of securities shown on the account of the financial intermediary on the books of another financial intermediary;

(e) with respect to an identified certificated security to be delivered while still in the possession of a third person, not a financial intermediary, at the time that person acknowledges that he holds for the purchaser;

(f) with respect to a specific uncertificated security the pledge or transfer of which has been registered to a third person, not a financial intermediary, at the time that person acknowledges that he holds for the purchaser;

(g) at the time appropriate entries to the account of the purchaser or a person designated by him on the books of a clearing corporation are made under Section 8–320;

(h) with respect to the transfer of a security interest where the debtor has signed a security agreement containing a description of the security, at the time a written notification, which, in the case of the creation of the security interest, is signed by the debtor (which may be a copy of the security agreement) or which, in the case of the release or assignment of the security interest created pursuant to this paragraph, is signed by the secured party, is received by

(i) a financial intermediary on whose books the interest of the transferor in the security appears;

(ii) a third person, not a financial intermediary, in possession of the security, if it is certificated;

(iii) a third person, not a financial intermediary, who is the registered owner of the security, if it is uncertificated and not subject to a registered pledge; or

(iv) a third person, not a financial intermediary, who is the registered pledgee of the security, if it is uncertificated and subject to a registered pledge;

(i) with respect to the transfer of a security interest where the transferor has signed a security agreement containing a description of the security, at the time new value is given by the secured party; or

(j) with respect to the transfer of a security interest where the secured party is a financial intermediary and the security has already been transferred to the financial intermediary under paragraphs (a), (b), (c), (d), or (g), at the time the transferor has signed a security agreement containing a description of the security and value is given by the secured party.

(2) The purchaser is the owner of a security held for him by a financial intermediary, but cannot be a bona fide purchaser of a security so held except in the circumstances specified in paragraphs (c), (d)(i), and (g) of subsection (1). If a security so held is part of a fungible bulk, as in the circumstances specified in paragraphs (d)(ii) and (d)(iii) of subsection (1), the purchaser is the owner of a proportionate property interest in the fungible bulk.

(3) Notice of an adverse claim received by the financial intermediary or by the purchaser after the financial intermediary takes delivery of a certificated security as a holder for value or after the transfer, pledge, or release of an uncertificated security has been registered free of the claim to a financial intermediary who has given value is not effective either as to the financial intermediary or as to the purchaser. However, as between the financial intermediary and the purchaser the purchaser may demand transfer of an equivalent security as to which no notice of adverse claim has been received.

(4) A "financial intermediary" is a bank, broker, clearing corporation, or other person (or the nominee of any of them) which in the ordinary course of its business maintains security accounts for its customers and is acting in that capacity. A financial intermediary may have a security interest in securities held in account for its customer.

Section 8–314. Duty to Transfer, When Completed

(1) Unless otherwise agreed, if a sale of a security is made on an exchange or otherwise through brokers:

(a) the selling customer fulfills his duty to transfer at the time he:

(i) places a certificated security in the possession of the selling broker or a person designated by the broker;

(ii) causes an uncertificated security to be registered in the name of the selling broker or a person designated by the broker;

(iii) if requested, causes an acknowledgment to be made to the selling broker that a certificated or uncertificated security is held for the broker; or

(iv) places in the possession of the selling broker or of a person designated by the broker a transfer instruction for an uncertificated security, providing the issuer does not refuse to register the requested transfer if the instruction is presented to the issuer for registration within 30 days thereafter; and

(b) the selling broker, including a correspondent broker acting for a selling customer, fulfills his duty to transfer at the time he:

(i) places a certificated security in the possession of the buying broker or a person designated by the buying broker;

(ii) causes an uncertificated security to be registered in the name of the buying broker or a person designated by the buying broker;

(iii) places in the possession of the buying broker or of a person designated by the buying broker a transfer instruction for an uncertificated security, providing the issuer does not refuse to register the requested transfer if the instruction is presented to the issuer for registration within 30 days thereafter; or

(iv) effects clearance of the sale in accordance with the rules of the exchange on which the transaction took place.

(2) Except as provided in this section or unless otherwise agreed, a transferor's duty to transfer a security under a contract of purchase is not fulfilled until he:

(a) places a certificated security in form to be negotiated by the purchaser in the possession of the purchaser or of a person designated by the purchaser;

(b) causes an uncertificated security to be registered in the name of the purchaser or a person designated by the purchaser; or

(c) if the purchaser requests, causes an acknowledgment to be made to the purchaser that a certificated or uncertificated security is held for the purchaser.

(3) Unless made on an exchange, a sale to a broker purchasing for his own account is within subsection (2) and not within subsection (1).

Section 8–315. Action Against Transferee Based Upon Wrongful Transfer

(1) Any person against whom the transfer of a security is wrongful for any reason, including his incapacity, as against anyone except a bona fide purchaser, may:

(a) reclaim possession of the certificated security wrongfully transferred;

(b) obtain possession of any new certificated security representing all or part of the same rights;

(c) compel the origination of an instruction to transfer to him or a person designated by him an uncertificated security constituting all or part of the same rights; or

(d) have damages.

(2) If the transfer is wrongful because of an unauthorized indorsement of a certificated security, the owner may also reclaim or obtain possession of the security or a new certificated security, even from a bona fide purchaser, if the ineffectiveness of the purported indorsement can be asserted against him under the provisions of this Article on unauthorized indorsements (Section 8–311).

(3) The right to obtain or reclaim possession of a certificated security or to compel the origination of a transfer instruction may be specifically enforced and the transfer of a certificated or uncertificated security enjoined and a certificated security impounded pending the litigation.

Section 8–316. Purchaser's Right to Requisites for Registration of Transfer, Pledge, or Release on Books

Unless otherwise agreed, the transferor of a certificated security or the transferor, pledgor, or pledgee of an uncertificated security on due demand must supply his purchaser with any proof of his authority to transfer, pledge, or release or with any other requisite necessary to obtain registration of the transfer, pledge, or release of the security; but if the transfer, pledge, or release is not for value, a transferor, pledgor, or pledgee need not do so unless the purchaser furnishes the necessary expenses. Failure within a reasonable time to comply with a demand made gives the purchaser the right to reject or rescind the transfer, pledge, or release.

Section 8–317. Creditors' Rights

(1) Subject to the exceptions in subsections (3) and (4), no attachment or levy upon a certificated security or any share or other interest represented thereby which is outstanding is valid until the security is actually seized by the officer making the attachment or levy, but a certificated security which has been surrendered to the issuer may be reached by a creditor by legal process at the issuer's chief executive office in the United States.

(2) An uncertificated security registered in the name of the debtor may not be reached by a creditor except by legal process at the issuer's chief executive office in the United States.

(3) The interest of a debtor in a certificated security that is in the possession of a secured party not a financial intermediary or in an uncertificated security registered in the name of a secured party not a financial intermediary (or in the name of a nominee of the secured party) may be reached by a creditor by legal process upon the secured party.

(4) The interest of a debtor in a certificated security that is in the possession of or registered in the name of a financial intermediary or in an uncertificated security registered in the name of a financial intermediary may be reached by a creditor by legal process upon the financial intermediary on whose books the interest of the debtor appears.

(5) Unless otherwise provided by law, a creditor's lien upon the interest of a debtor in a security obtained pursuant to subsection (3) or (4) is not a restraint on the transfer of the security, free of the lien, to a third party for new value; but in the event of a transfer, the lien applies to the proceeds of the transfer in the hands of the secured party or financial intermediary, subject to any claims having priority.

(6) A creditor whose debtor is the owner of a security is entitled to aid from courts of appropriate jurisdiction, by injunction or otherwise, in reaching the security or in satisfying the claim by means allowed at law or in equity in regard to property that cannot readily be reached by ordinary legal process.

Section 8–318. No Conversion by Good Faith Conduct

An agent or bailee who in good faith (including observance of reasonable commercial standards if he is in the business of buying, selling, or otherwise dealing with securities) has received certificated securities and sold, pledged, or delivered them or has sold or caused the transfer or pledge of uncertificated securities over which he had control according to the instructions of his principal, is not liable for conversion or for participation in breach of fiduciary duty although the principal had no right so to deal with the securities.

Section 8–319. Statute of Frauds

A contract for the sale of securities is not enforceable by way of action or defense unless:

(a) there is some writing signed by the party against whom enforcement is sought or by his authorized agent or broker, sufficient to indicate that a contract has been made for sale of a stated quantity of described securities at a defined or stated price;

(b) delivery of a certificated security or transfer instruction has been accepted, or transfer of an uncertificated security has been registered and the transferee has failed to send written objection to the issuer within 10 days after receipt of the initial transaction statement confirming the registration, or payment has been made, but the contract is enforceable under this provision only to the extent of the delivery, registration, or payment;

(c) within a reasonable time a writing in confirmation of the sale or purchase and sufficient against the sender under paragraph (a) has been received by the party against whom enforcement is sought and he has failed to send written objection to its contents within 10 days after its receipt; or

(d) the party against whom enforcement is sought admits in his pleading, testimony, or otherwise in court that a contract was made for the sale of a stated quantity of described securities at a defined or stated price.

Section 8–320. Transfer or Pledge Within Central Depository System

(1) In addition to other methods, a transfer, pledge, or release of a security or any interest therein may be effected by the making of appropriate entries on the books of a clearing corporation reducing the account of the transferor, pledgor, or pledgee and increasing the account of the transferee, pledgee, or pledgor by the amount of the obligation or the number of shares or rights transferred, pledged, or released, if the security is shown on the account of a transferor, pledgor, or pledgee on the books of the clearing corporation; is subject to the control of the clearing corporation; and

- (a) if certificated,
  - (i) is in the custody of the clearing corporation, another clearing corporation, a custodian bank, or a nominee of any of them; and
  - (ii) is in bearer form or indorsed in blank by an appropriate person or registered in the name of the clearing corporation, a custodian bank, or a nominee of any of them; or
- (b) if uncertificated, is registered in the name of the clearing corporation, another clearing corporation, a custodian bank, or a nominee of any of them.

(2) Under this section entries may be made with respect to like securities or interests therein as a part of a fungible bulk and may refer merely to a quantity of a particular security without reference to the name of the registered owner, certificate or bond number, or the like, and, in appropriate cases, may be on a net basis taking into account other transfers, pledges, or releases of the same security.

(3) A transfer under this section is effective (Section 8–313) and the purchaser acquires the rights of the transferor (Section 8–301). A pledge or release under this section is the transfer of a limited interest. If a pledge or the creation of a security interest is intended, the security interest is perfected at the time when both value is given by the pledgee and the appropriate entries are made (Section 8–321). A transferee or pledgee under this section may be a bona fide purchaser (Section 8–302).

(4) A transfer or pledge under this section is not a registration of transfer under Part 4.

(5) That entries made on the books of the clearing corporation as provided in subsection (1) are not appropriate does not affect the validity or effect of the entries or the liabilities or obligations of the clearing corporation to any person adversely affected thereby.

Section 8–321. Enforceability, Attachment, Perfection and Termination of Security Interests

(1) A security interest in a security is enforceable and can attach only if it is transferred to the secured party or a person designated by him pursuant to a provision of Section 8–313(1).

(2) A security interest so transferred pursuant to agreement by a transferor who has rights in the security to a transferee who has given value is a perfected security interest, but a security interest that has been transferred solely under paragraph (i) of Section 8–313(1) becomes unperfected after 21 days unless, within that time, the requirements for transfer under any other provision of Section 8–313(1) are satisfied.

(3) A security interest in a security is subject to the provisions of Article 9, but:

- (a) no filing is required to perfect the security interest; and
- (b) no written security agreement signed by the debtor is necessary to make the security interest enforceable, except as provided in paragraph (h), (i), or (j) of Section 8–313(1). The secured party has the rights and duties provided under Section 9–207, to the extent they are applicable, whether or not the security is certificated, and, if certificated, whether or not it is in his possession.

(4) Unless otherwise agreed, a security interest in a security is terminated by transfer to the debtor or a person designated by him pursuant to a provision of Section 8–313(1). If a security is thus transferred, the security interest, if not terminated, becomes unperfected unless the security is certificated and is delivered to the debtor for the purpose of ultimate sale or exchange or presentation, collection, renewal, or registration of transfer. In that case, the security interest becomes unperfected after 21 days unless, within that time, the security (or securities for which it has been exchanged) is transferred to the secured party or a person designated by him pursuant to a provision of Section 8–313(1).

Part 4 Registration

Section 8–401. Duty of Issuer to Register Transfer, Pledge, or Release

(1) If a certificated security in registered form is presented to the issuer with a request to register transfer or an instruction is presented to the issuer with a request to register transfer, pledge, or release, the issuer shall register the transfer, pledge, or release as requested if:

- (a) the security is indorsed or the instruction was originated by the appropriate person or persons (Section 8–308);
- (b) reasonable assurance is given that those indorsements or instructions are genuine and effective (Section 8–402);
- (c) the issuer has no duty as to adverse claims or has discharged the duty (Section 8–403);
- (d) any applicable law relating to the collection of taxes has been complied with; and
- (e) the transfer, pledge, or release is in fact rightful or is to a bona fide purchaser.

(2) If an issuer is under a duty to register a transfer, pledge, or release of a security, the issuer is also liable to the person presenting a certificated security or an instruction for registration or his principal for loss resulting from any unreasonable delay in registration or from failure or refusal to register the transfer, pledge, or release.

Section 8–402. Assurance that Indorsements and Instructions Are Effective

(1) The issuer may require the following assurance that each necessary indorsement of a certificated security or each instruction (Section 8–308) is genuine and effective:

- (a) in all cases, a guarantee of the signature (Section 8–312(1) or (2)) of the person indorsing a certificated security or originating an instruction including, in the case of an instruction, a warranty of the taxpayer identification number or, in the absence thereof, other reasonable assurance of identity;
- (b) if the indorsement is made or the instruction is originated by an agent, appropriate assurance of authority to sign;

(c) if the indorsement is made or the instruction is originated by a fiduciary, appropriate evidence of appointment or incumbency;

(d) if there is more than one fiduciary, reasonable assurance that all who are required to sign have done so; and

(e) if the indorsement is made or the instruction is originated by a person not covered by any of the foregoing, assurance appropriate to the case corresponding as nearly as may be to the foregoing.

(2) A "guarantee of the signature" in subsection (1) means a guarantee signed by or on behalf of a person reasonably believed by the issuer to be responsible. The issuer may adopt standards with respect to responsibility if they are not manifestly unreasonable.

(3) "Appropriate evidence of appointment or incumbency" in subsection (1) means:

(a) in the case of a fiduciary appointed or qualified by a court, a certificate issued by or under the direction or supervision of that court or an officer thereof and dated within 60 days before the date of presentation for transfer, pledge, or release; or

(b) in any other case, a copy of a document showing the appointment or a certificate issued by or on behalf of a person reasonably believed by the issuer to be responsible or, in the absence of that document or certificate, other evidence reasonably deemed by the issuer to be appropriate. The issuer may adopt standards with respect to the evidence if they are not manifestly unreasonable. The issuer is not charged with notice of the contents of any document obtained pursuant to this paragraph (b) except to the extent that the contents relate directly to the appointment or incumbency.

(4) The issuer may elect to require reasonable assurance beyond that specified in this section, but if it does so and, for a purpose other than that specified in subsection (3)(b), both requires and obtains a copy of a will, trust, indenture, articles of co-partnership, by-laws, or other controlling instrument, it is charged with notice of all matters contained therein affecting the transfer, pledge, or release.

Section 8–403. Issuer's Duty as to Adverse Claims

(1) An issuer to whom a certificated security is presented for registration shall inquire into adverse claims if:

(a) a written notification of an adverse claim is received at a time and in a manner affording the issuer a reasonable opportunity to act on it prior to the issuance of a new, reissued, or re-registered certificated security, and the notification identifies the claimant, the registered owner, and the issue of which the security is a part, and provides an address for communications directed to the claimant; or

(b) the issuer is charged with notice of an adverse claim from a controlling instrument it has elected to require under Section 8–402(4).

(2) The issuer may discharge any duty of inquiry by any reasonable means, including notifying an adverse claimant by registered or certified mail at the address furnished by him or, if there be no such address, at his residence or regular place of business that the certificated security has been presented for registration of transfer by a named person, and that the transfer will be registered unless within 30 days from the date of mailing the notification, either:

(a) an appropriate restraining order, injunction, or other process issues from a court of competent jurisdiction; or

(b) there is filed with the issuer an indemnity bond, sufficient in the issuer's judgment to protect the issuer and any transfer agent, registrar, or other agent of the issuer involved from any loss it or they may suffer by complying with the adverse claim.

(3) Unless an issuer is charged with notice of an adverse claim from a controlling instrument which it has elected to require under Section 8–402(4) or receives notification of an adverse claim under subsection (1), if a certificated security presented for registration is indorsed by the appropriate person or persons the issuer is under no duty to inquire into adverse claims. In particular:

(a) an issuer registering a certificated security in the name of a person who is a fiduciary or who is described as a fiduciary is not bound to inquire into the existence, extent, or correct description of the fiduciary relationship; and thereafter the issuer may assume without inquiry that the newly registered owner continues to be the fiduciary until the issuer receives written notice that the fiduciary is no longer acting as such with respect to the particular security;

(b) an issuer registering transfer on an indorsement by a fiduciary is not bound to inquire whether the transfer is made in compliance with a controlling instrument or with the law of the state having jurisdiction of the fiduciary relationship, including any law requiring the fiduciary to obtain court approval of the transfer; and

(c) the issuer is not charged with notice of the contents of any court record or file or other recorded or unrecorded document even though the document is in its possession and even though the transfer is made on the indorsement of a fiduciary to the fiduciary himself or to his nominee.

(4) An issuer is under no duty as to adverse claims with respect to an uncertificated security except:

(a) claims embodied in a restraining order, injunction, or other legal process served upon the issuer if the process was served at a time and in a manner affording the issuer a reasonable opportunity to act on it in accordance with the requirements of subsection (5);

(b) claims of which the issuer has received a written notification from the registered owner or the registered pledgee if the notification was received at a time and in a manner affording the issuer a reasonable opportunity to act on it in accordance with the requirements of subsection (5);

(c) claims (including restrictions on transfer not imposed by the issuer) to which the registration of transfer to the present registered owner was subject and were so noted in the initial transaction statement sent to him; and

(d) claims as to which an issuer is charged with notice from a controlling instrument it has elected to require under Section 8–402(4).

(5) If the issuer of an uncertificated security is under a duty as to an adverse claim, he discharges that duty by:

(a) including a notation of the claim in any statements sent with respect to the security under Sections 8–408(3), (6), and (7); and

(b) refusing to register the transfer or pledge of the security unless the nature of the claim does not preclude transfer or pledge subject thereto.

(6) If the transfer or pledge of the security is registered subject to an adverse claim, a notation of the claim must be included in the initial transaction statement and all subsequent statements sent to the transferee and pledgee under Section 8–408.

(7) Notwithstanding subsections (4) and (5), if an uncertificated security was subject to a registered pledge at the time the issuer first came under a duty as to a particular adverse claim, the issuer has no duty as to that claim if transfer of the security is requested by the registered pledgee or an appropriate person acting for the registered pledgee unless:

(a) the claim was embodied in legal process which expressly provides otherwise;

(b) the claim was asserted in a written notification from the registered pledgee;

(c) the claim was one as to which the issuer was charged with notice from a controlling instrument it required under Section 8–402(4) in connection with the pledgee's request for transfer; or

(d) the transfer requested is to the registered owner.

Section 8–404. Liability and Non-Liability for Registration

(1) Except as provided in any law relating to the collection of taxes, the issuer is not liable to the owner, pledgee, or any other person suffering loss as a result of the registration of a transfer, pledge, or release of a security if:

(a) there were on or with a certificated security the necessary indorsements or the issuer had received an instruction originated by an appropriate person (Section 8–308); and

(b) the issuer had no duty as to adverse claims or has discharged the duty (Section 8–403).

(2) If an issuer has registered a transfer of a certificated security to a person not entitled to it, the issuer on demand shall deliver a like security to the true owner unless:

(a) the registration was pursuant to subsection (1);

(b) the owner is precluded from asserting any claim for registering the transfer under Section 8–405(1); or

(c) the delivery would result in overissue, in which case the issuer's liability is governed by Section 8–104.

(3) If an issuer has improperly registered a transfer, pledge, or release of an uncertificated security, the issuer on demand from the injured party shall restore the records as to the injured party to the condition that would have obtained if the improper registration had not been made unless:

(a) the registration was pursuant to subsection (1); or

(b) the registration would result in overissue, in which case the issuer's liability is governed by Section 8–104.

Section 8–405. Lost, Destroyed, and Stolen Certificated Securities

(1) If a certificated security has been lost, apparently destroyed, or wrongfully taken, and the owner fails to notify the issuer of that fact within a reasonable time after he has notice of it and the issuer registers a transfer of the security before receiving notification, the owner is precluded from asserting against the issuer any claim for registering the transfer under Section 8–404 or any claim to a new security under this section.

(2) If the owner of a certificated security claims that the security has been lost, destroyed, or wrongfully taken, the issuer shall issue a new certificated security or, at the option of the issuer, an equivalent uncertificated security in place of the original security if the owner:

(a) so requests before the issuer has notice that the security has been acquired by a bona fide purchaser.

(b) files with the issuer a sufficient indemnity bond; and

(c) satisfies any other reasonable requirements imposed by the issuer.

(3) If, after the issue of a new certificated or uncertificated security, a bona fide purchaser of the original certificated security presents it for registration of transfer, the issuer shall register the transfer unless registration would result in overissue, in which event the issuer's liability is governed by Section 8–104. In addition to any rights on the indemnity bond, the issuer may recover the new certificated security from the person to whom it was issued or any person taking under him except a bona fide purchaser or may cancel the uncertificated security unless a bona fide purchaser or any person taking under a bona fide purchaser is then the registered owner or registered pledgee thereof.

Section 8–406. Duty of Authenticating Trustee, Transfer Agent, or Registrar

(1) If a person acts as authenticating trustee, transfer agent, registrar, or other agent for an issuer in the registration of transfers of its certificated securities or in the registration of transfers, pledges, and releases of its uncertificated securities, in the issue of new securities, or in the cancellation of surrendered securities:

(a) he is under a duty to the issuer to exercise good faith and due diligence in performing his functions; and

(b) with regard to the particular functions he performs, he has the same obligation to the holder or owner of a certificated security or to the owner or pledgee of an uncertificated security and has the same rights and privileges as the issuer has in regard to those functions.

(2) Notice to an authenticating trustee, transfer agent, registrar or other agent is notice to the issuer with respect to the functions performed by the agent.

Section 8–407. Exchangeability of Securities

(1) No issuer is subject to the requirements of this section unless it regularly maintains a system for issuing the class of securities involved under which both certificated and uncertificated securities are regularly issued to the category of owners, which includes the person in whose name the new security is to be registered.

(2) Upon surrender of a certificated security with all necessary indorsements and presentation of a written request by the person surrendering the security, the issuer, if he has no duty as to adverse claims or has discharged the duty (Section 8–403), shall issue to the person or a person designated by him an equivalent uncertificated security subject to all liens, restrictions, and claims that were noted on the certificated security.

(3) Upon receipt of a transfer instruction originated by an appropriate person who so requests, the issuer of an uncertificated security shall cancel the uncertificated security and issue an equivalent certificated security on which must be noted conspicuously any liens and restrictions of the issuer and any adverse claims (as to which the issuer has a duty under Section 8–403(4)) to which the uncertificated security was subject. The certificated security shall be registered in the name of and delivered to:

(a) the registered owner, if the uncertificated security was not subject to a registered pledge; or

(b) the registered pledgee, if the uncertificated security was subject to a registered pledge.

Section 8–408. Statements of Uncertificated Securities

(1) Within 2 business days after the transfer of an uncertificated security has been registered, the issuer shall send to the new registered owner and, if the security has been transferred subject to a registered pledge, to the registered pledgee a written statement containing:

(a) a description of the issue of which the uncertificated security is a part;

(b) the number of shares or units transferred;

(c) the name and address and any taxpayer identification number of the new registered owner and, if the security has been transferred subject to a registered pledge, the name and address and any taxpayer identification number of the registered pledgee;

(d) a notation of any liens and restrictions of the issuer and any adverse claims (as to which the issuer has a duty under Section 8–403(4)) to which the uncertificated security is or may be subject at the time of registration or a statement that there are none of those liens, restrictions, or adverse claims; and

(e) the date the transfer was registered.

(2) Within 2 business days after the pledge of an uncertificated security has been registered, the issuer shall send to the registered owner and the registered pledgee a written statement containing:

(a) a description of the issue of which the uncertificated security is a part;

(b) the number of shares or units pledged;

(c) the name and address and any taxpayer identification number of the registered owner and the registered pledgee;

(d) a notation of any liens and restrictions of the issuer and any adverse claims (as to which the issuer has a duty under Section 8–403(4)) to which the uncertificated security is or may be subject at the time of registration or a statement that there are none of those liens, restrictions, or adverse claims; and

(e) the date the pledge was registered.

(3) Within 2 business days after the release from pledge of an uncertificated security has been registered, the issuer shall send to the registered owner and the pledgee whose interest was released a written statement containing:

(a) a description of the issue of which the uncertificated security is a part;

(b) the number of shares or units released from pledge;

(c) the name and address and any taxpayer identification number of the registered owner and the pledgee whose interest was released;

(d) a notation of any liens and restrictions of the issuer and any adverse claims (as to which the issuer has a duty under Section 8–403(4)) to which the uncertificated security is or may be subject at the time of registration or a statement that there are none of those liens, restrictions, or adverse claims; and

(e) the date the release was registered.

(4) An "initial transaction statement" is the statement sent to:

(a) the new registered owner and, if applicable, to the registered pledgee pursuant to subsection (1);

(b) the registered pledgee pursuant to subsection (2); or

(c) the registered owner pursuant to subsection (3).

Each initial transaction statement shall be signed by or on behalf of the issuer and must be identified as "Initial Transaction Statement."

(5) Within 2 business days after the transfer of an uncertificated security has been registered, the issuer shall send to the former registered owner and the former registered pledgee, if any, a written statement containing:

(a) a description of the issue of which the uncertificated security is a part;

(b) the number of shares or units transferred;

(c) the name and address and any taxpayer identification number of the former registered owner and of any former registered pledgee; and

(d) the date the transfer was registered.

(6) At periodic intervals no less frequent than annually and at any time upon the reasonable written request of the registered owner, the issuer shall send to the registered owner of each uncertificated security a dated written statement containing:

(a) a description of the issue of which the uncertificated security is a part;

(b) the name and address and any taxpayer identification number of the registered owner;

(c) the number of shares or units of the uncertificated security registered in the name of the registered owner on the date of the statement;

(d) the name and address and any taxpayer identification number of any registered pledgee and the number of shares of units subject to the pledge; and

(e) a notation of any liens and restrictions of the issuer and any adverse claims (as to which the issuer has a duty under Section 8–403(4)) to which the uncertificated security is or may be subject or a statement that there are none of those liens, restrictions, or adverse claims.

(7) At periodic intervals no less frequent than annually and at any time upon the reasonable written request of the registered pledgee, the issuer shall send to the registered pledgee of each uncertificated security a dated written statement containing:

(a) a description of the issue of which the uncertificated security is a part;

(b) the name and address and any taxpayer identification number of the registered owner;

(c) the name and address and any taxpayer identification number of the registered pledgee;

(d) the number of shares or units subject to the pledge; and

(e) a notation of any liens and restrictions of the issuer and any adverse claims (as to which the issuer has a duty under Section 8–403(4)) to which the uncertificated security is or may be subject or a statement that there are none of those liens, restrictions, or adverse claims.

(8) If the issuer sends the statements described in subsections (6) and (7) at periodic intervals no less frequent than quarterly, the issuer is not obliged to send additional statements upon request unless the owner or pledgee requesting them pays to the issuer the reasonable cost of furnishing them.

(9) Each statement sent pursuant to this section must bear a conspicuous legend reading substantially as follows: "This statement is merely a record of the rights of the addressee as of the time of its issuance. Delivery of this statement, of itself, confers no rights on the recipient. This statement is neither a negotiable instrument nor a security."

Article 9 Secured Transactions; Sales of Accounts and Chattel Paper

Part I Short Title, Applicability and Definitions

Section 9–101. Short Title

This Article shall be known and may be cited as Uniform Commercial Code—Secured Transactions.

Section 9–102. Policy and Subject Matter of Article

(1) Except as otherwise provided in Section 9–104 on excluded transactions, this Article applies

(a) to any transaction (regardless of its form) which is intended to create a security interest in personal property or fixtures including goods, documents, instruments, general intangibles, chattel paper or accounts; and also

(b) to any sale of accounts or chattel paper.

(2) This Article applies to security interests created by contract including pledge, assignment, chattel mortgage, chattel trust, trust deed, factor's lien, equipment trust, conditional sale, trust receipt, other lien or title retention contract and lease or consignment intended as security. This Article does not apply to statutory liens except as provided in Section 9–310.

(3) The application of this Article to a security interest in a secured obligation is not affected by the fact that the obligation is itself secured by a transaction or interest to which this Article does not apply.

Note: *The adoption of this Article should be accompanied by the repeal of existing statutes dealing with conditional sales, trust receipts, factor's liens where the factor is given a non-possessory lien, chattel mortgages, crop mortgages, mortgages on railroad equipment, assignment of accounts and generally statutes regulating security interests in personal property.*

Where the state has a retail installment selling act or small loan act, that legislation should be carefully examined to determine what changes in those acts are needed to conform them to this Article. This Article primarily sets out rules defining rights of a secured party against persons dealing with the debtor; it does not prescribe regulations and controls which may be necessary to curb abuses arising in the small loan business or in the financing of consumer purchases on credit. Accordingly there is no intention to repeal existing regulatory acts in those fields by enactment or re-enactment of Article 9. See Section 9–203(4) and the Note thereto.

Section 9–103. Perfection of Security Interest in Multiple State Transactions

(1) Documents, instruments and ordinary goods.

(a) This subsection applies to documents and instruments and to goods other than those covered by a certificate of title described in subsection (2), mobile goods described in subsection (3), and minerals described in subsection (5).

(b) Except as otherwise provided in this subsection, perfection and the effect of perfection or non-perfection of a security interest in collateral are governed by the law of the jurisdiction where the collateral is when the last event occurs on which is based the assertion that the security interest is perfected or unperfected.

(c) If the parties to a transaction creating a purchase money security interest in goods in one jurisdiction understand at the time that the security interest attaches that the goods will be kept in another jurisdiction, then the law of the other jurisdiction governs the perfection and the effect of perfection or non-perfection of the security interest from the time it attaches until thirty days after the debtor receives possession of the goods and thereafter if the goods are taken to the other jurisdiction before the end of the thirty-day period.

(d) When collateral is brought into and kept in this state while subject to a security interest perfected under the law of the jurisdiction from which the collateral was removed, the security interest remains perfected, but if action is required by Part 3 of this Article to perfect the security interest,

(i) if the action is not taken before the expiration of the period of perfection in the other jurisdiction or the end of four months after the collateral is brought into this state, whichever period first expires, the security interest becomes unperfected at the end of that period and is thereafter deemed to have been unperfected as against a person who became a purchaser after removal;

(ii) if the action is taken before the expiration of the period specified in subparagraph (i), the security interest continues perfected thereafter;

(iii) for the purpose of priority over a buyer of consumer goods (subsection (2) of Section 9–307), the period of the effectiveness of a filing in the jurisdiction from which the collateral is removed is governed by the rules with respect to perfection in subparagraphs (i) and (ii).

(2) Certificate of title.

(a) This subsection applies to goods covered by a certificate of title issued under a statute of this state or of another jurisdiction under the law of which indication of a security interest on the certificate is required as a condition of perfection.

(b) Except as otherwise provided in this subsection, perfection and the effect of perfection or non-perfection of the security interest are governed by the law (including the conflict of laws rules) of the jurisdiction issuing the certificate until four months after the goods are removed from that jurisdiction and thereafter until the goods are registered in another jurisdiction, but in any event not beyond surrender of the certificate. After the expiration of that period, the goods are not covered by the certificate of title within the meaning of this section.

(c) Except with respect to the rights of a buyer described in the next paragraph, a security interest, perfected in another jurisdiction otherwise than by notation on a certificate of title, in goods brought into this state and thereafter covered by a certificate of title issued by this state is subject to the rules stated in paragraph (d) of subsection (1).

(d) If goods are brought into this state while a security interest therein is perfected in any manner under the law of the jurisdiction from which the goods are removed and a certificate of title is issued by this state and the certificate does not show that the goods are subject to the security interest or that they may be subject to security interests not shown on the certificate, the security interest is subordinate to the rights of a buyer of the goods who is not in the business of selling goods of that kind to the extent that he gives value and receives delivery of the goods after issuance of the certificate and without knowledge of the security interest.

(3) Accounts, general intangibles and mobile goods.

(a) This subsection applies to accounts (other than an account described in subsection (5) on minerals) and general intangibles (other than uncertificated securities) and to goods which are mobile and which are of a type normally used in more than one jurisdiction, such as motor vehicles, trailers, rolling stock, airplanes, shipping containers, road building and construction machinery and commercial harvesting machinery and the like, if the goods are equipment or are inventory leased or held for lease by the debtor to others, and are not covered by a certificate of title described in subsection (2).

(b) The law (including the conflict of laws rules) of the jurisdiction in which the debtor is located governs the perfection and the effect of perfection or non-perfection of the security interest.

(c) If, however, the debtor is located in a jurisdiction which is not a part of the United States, and which does not provide for perfection of the security interest by filing or recording in that jurisdiction, the law of the jurisdiction in the United States in which the debtor has its major executive office governs the perfection and the effect of perfection or non-perfection of the security interest through filing. In the alternative, if the debtor is located in a jurisdiction which is not a part of the United States or Canada and the collateral is accounts or general intangibles for money due or to become due, the security interest may be perfected by notification to the account debtor. As used in this paragraph, "United States" includes its territories and possessions and the Commonwealth of Puerto Rico.

(d) A debtor shall be deemed located at his place of business if he has one, at his chief executive office if he has more than one place of business, otherwise at his residence. If, however, the debtor is a foreign air carrier under the Federal Aviation Act of 1958, as amended, it shall be deemed located at the designated office of the agent upon whom service of process may be made on behalf of the foreign air carrier.

(e) A security interest perfected under the law of the jurisdiction of the location of the debtor is perfected until the expiration of four months after a change of the debtor's location to another jurisdiction, or until perfection would have ceased by the law of the first jurisdiction, whichever period first expires. Unless perfected in the new jurisdiction before the end of that period, it becomes unperfected thereafter and is deemed to have been unperfected as against a person who became a purchaser after the change.

(4) Chattel paper. The rules stated for goods in subsection (1) apply to a possessory security interest in chattel paper. The rules stated for accounts in subsection (3) apply to a non-possessory security interest in chattel paper, but the security interest may not be perfected by notification to the account debtor.

(5) Minerals. Perfection and the effect of perfection or non-perfection of a security interest which is created by a debtor who has an interest in minerals or the like (including oil and gas) before extraction and which attaches thereto as extracted, or which attaches to an account resulting from the sale thereof at the wellhead or minehead are governed by the law (including the conflict of laws rules) of the jurisdiction wherein the wellhead or minehead is located.

(6) Uncertificated securities. The law (including the conflict of laws rules) of the jurisdiction of organization of the issuer governs the perfection and the effect of perfection or non-perfection of a security interest in uncertificated securities.

Section 9–104. Transactions Excluded From Article

This Article does not apply

(a) to a security interest subject to any statute of the United States, to the extent that such statute governs the rights of parties to and third parties affected by transactions in particular types of property; or

(b) to a landlord's lien; or

(c) to a lien given by statute or other rule of law for services or materials except as provided in Section 9–310 on priority of such liens; or

(d) to a transfer of a claim for wages, salary or other compensation of an employee; or

(e) to a transfer by a government or governmental subdivision or agency; or

(f) to a sale of accounts or chattel paper as part of a sale of the business out of which they arose, or an assignment of accounts or chattel paper which is for the purpose of collection only, or a transfer of a right to payment under a contract to an assignee who is also to do the performance under the contract or a transfer of a single account to an assignee in whole or partial satisfaction of a preexisting indebtedness; or

(g) to a transfer of an interest in or claim in or under any policy of insurance, except as provided with respect to proceeds (Section 9–306) and priorities in proceeds (Section 9–312); or

(h) to a right represented by a judgment (other than a judgment taken on a right to payment which was collateral); or

(i) to any right of set-off; or

(j) except to the extent that provision is made for fixtures in Section 9–313, to the creation or transfer of an interest in or lien on real estate, including a lease or rents thereunder; or

(k) to a transfer in whole or in part of any claim arising out of tort; or

(l) to a transfer of an interest in any deposit account (subsection (1) of Section 9–105), except as provided with respect to proceeds (Section 9–306) and priorities in proceeds (Section 9–312).

Section 9–105. Definitions and Index of Definitions

(1) In this Article unless the context otherwise requires:

(a) "Account debtor" means the person who is obligated on an account, chattel paper or general intangible;

(b) "Chattel paper" means a writing or writings which evidence both a monetary obligation and a security interest in or a lease of specific goods, but a charter or other contract involving the use or hire of a vessel is not chattel paper. When a transaction is evidenced both by such a security agreement or a lease and by an instrument or a series of instruments, the group of writings taken together constitutes chattel paper;

(c) "Collateral" means the property subject to a security interest, and includes accounts and chattel paper which have been sold;

(d) "Debtor" means the person who owes payment or other performance of the obligation secured, whether or not he owns or has rights in the collateral, and includes the seller of accounts or chattel paper. Where the debtor and the owner of the collateral are not the same person, the term "debtor" means the owner of the collateral in any provision of the Article dealing with the collateral, the obligor in any provision dealing with the obligation, and may include both where the context so requires;

(e) "Deposit account" means a demand, time, savings, passbook or like account maintained with a bank, savings and loan association, credit union or like organization, other than an account evidenced by a certificate of deposit;

(f) "Document" means document of title as defined in the general definitions of Article 1 (Section 1–201), and a receipt of the kind described in subsection (2) of Section 7–201;

(g) "Encumbrance" includes real estate mortgages and other liens on real estate and all other rights in real estate that are not ownership interests;

(h) "Goods" includes all things which are movable at the time the security interest attaches or which are fixtures (Section 9–313), but does not include money, documents, instruments, accounts, chattel paper, general intangibles, or minerals or the like (including oil and gas) before extraction. "Goods" also includes standing timber which is to be cut and removed under a conveyance or contract for sale, the unborn young of animals, and growing crops;

(i) "Instrument" means a negotiable instrument (defined in Section 3–104), or a certificated security (defined in Section 8–102) or any other writing which evidences a right to the payment of money and is not itself a security agreement or lease and is of a type which is in ordinary course of business transferred by delivery with any necessary indorsement or assignment;

(j) "Mortgage" means a consensual interest created by a real estate mortgage, a trust deed on real estate, or the like;

(k) An advance is made "pursuant to commitment" if the secured party has bound himself to make it, whether or not a subsequent event of default or other event not within his control has relieved or may relieve him from his obligation;

(l) "Security agreement" means an agreement which creates or provides for a security interest;

(m) "Secured party" means a lender, seller or other person in whose favor there is a security interest, including a person to whom accounts or chattel paper have been sold. When the holders of obligations issued under an indenture of trust, equipment trust agreement or the like are represented by a trustee or other person, the representative is the secured party;

(n) "Transmitting utility" means any person primarily engaged in the railroad, street railway or trolley bus business, the electric or electronics communications transmission business, the transmission of goods by pipeline, or the transmission or the production and transmission of electricity, steam, gas or water, or the provision of sewer service.

(2) Other definitions applying to this Article and the sections in which they appear are:

"Account." Section 9–106.

"Attach." Section 9–203.

"Construction mortgage." Section 9–313(1).

"Consumer goods." Section 9–109(1).

"Equipment." Section 9–109(2).

"Farm products." Section 9–109(3).

"Fixture." Section 9–313(1).

"Fixture filing." Section 9–313(1).

"General intangibles." Section 9–106.

"Inventory." Section 9–109(4).

"Lien creditor." Section 9–301(3).

"Proceeds." Section 9–306(1).

"Purchase money security interest." Section 9–107.

"United States." Section 9–103.

(3) The following definitions in other Articles apply to this Article:

"Check." Section 3–104.

"Contract for sale." Section 2–106.

"Holder in due course." Section 3–302.

"Note." Section 3–104.

"Sale." Section 2–106.

(4) In addition Article 1 contains general definitions and principles of construction and interpretation applicable throughout this Article.

Section 9–106. Definitions: "Account"; "General Intangibles"

"Account" means any right to payment for goods sold or leased or for services rendered which is not evidenced by an instrument or chattel paper, whether or not it has been earned by performance. "General intangibles" means any personal property (including things in action) other than goods, accounts, chattel paper, documents, instruments, and money. All rights to payment earned or unearned under a charter or other contract involving the use or hire of a vessel and all rights incident to the chart or contract are accounts.

Section 9–107. Definitions: "Purchase Money Security Interest"

A security interest is a "purchase money security interest" to the extent that it is

(a) taken or retained by the seller of the collateral to secure all or part of its price; or

(b) taken by a person who by making advances or incurring an obligation gives value to enable the debtor to acquire rights in or the use of collateral if such value is in fact so used.

Section 9–108. When After-Acquired Collateral Not Security for Antecedent Debt

Where a secured party makes an advance, incurs an obligation, releases a perfected security interest, or otherwise gives new value which is to be secured in whole or in part by after-acquired property his security interest in the after-acquired collateral shall be deemed to be taken for new value and not as security for an antecedent debt if the debtor acquires his rights in such collateral either in the ordinary course of his business or under a contract of purchase made pursuant to the security agreement within a reasonable time after new value is given.

Section 9–109. Classification of Goods; "Consumer Goods"; "Equipment"; "Farm Products"; "Inventory"

Goods are

(1) "consumer goods" if they are used or bought for use primarily for personal, family or household purposes;

(2) "equipment" if they are used or bought for use primarily in business (including farming or a profession) or by a debtor who is a non-profit organization or a governmental subdivision or agency or if the goods are not included in the definitions of inventory, farm products or consumer goods;

(3) "farm products" if they are crops or livestock or supplies used or produced in farming operations or if they are products of crops or livestock in their unmanufactured states (such as ginned cotton, wool-clip, maple syrup, milk and eggs), and if they are in the possession of a debtor engaged in raising, fattening, grazing or other farming operations. If goods are farm products they are neither equipment nor inventory;

(4) "inventory" if they are held by a person who holds them for sale or lease or to be furnished under contracts of service or if he has so furnished them, or if they are raw materials, work in process or materials used or consumed in a business. Inventory of a person is not to be classified as his equipment.

Section 9–110. Sufficiency of Description

For the purposes of this Article any description of personal property or real estate is sufficient whether or not it is specific if it reasonably identifies what is described.

Section 9–111. Applicability of Bulk Transfer Laws

The creation of a security interest is not a bulk transfer under Article 6 (see Section 6–103).

Section 9–112. Where Collateral Is Not Owned by Debtor

Unless otherwise agreed, when a secured party knows that collateral is owned by a person who is not the debtor, the owner of the collateral is entitled to receive from the secured party any surplus under Section 9–502(2) or under Section 9–504(1), and is not liable for the debt or for any deficiency after resale, and he has the same right as the debtor

(a) to receive statements under Section 9–208;

(b) to receive notice of and to object to a secured party's proposal to retain the collateral in satisfaction of the indebtedness under Section 9–505;

(c) to redeem the collateral under Section 9–506;

(d) to obtain injunctive or other relief under Section 9–507(1); and

(e) to recover losses caused to him under Section 9–208(2).

Section 9–113. Security Interests Arising Under Article on Sales or Under Article on Leases.

A security interest arising solely under the Article on Sales (Article 2) or the Article on Leases (Article 2A) is subject to the provisions of this Article except that to the extent that and so long as the debtor does not have or does not lawfully obtain possession of the goods

(a) no security agreement is necessary to make the security interest enforceable; and

(b) no filing is required to perfect the security interest; and

(c) the rights of the secured party on default by the debtor are governed (i) by the Article on Sales (Article 2) in the case of a security interest arising solely under such Article or (ii) by the Article on Leases (Article 2A) in the case of a security interest arising solely under such Article.

Section 9–114. Consignment

(1) A person who delivers goods under a consignment which is not a security interest and who would be required to file under this Article by paragraph (3)(c) of Section 2–326 has priority over a secured party who is or becomes a creditor of the consignee and who would have a perfected security interest in the goods if they were the property of the consignee, and also has priority with respect to identifiable cash proceeds received on or before delivery of the goods to a buyer, if

(a) the consignor complies with the filing provision of the Article on Sales with respect to consignments (paragraph (3)(c) of Section 2–326) before the consignee receives possession of the goods; and

(b) the consignor gives notification in writing to the holder of the security interest if the holder has filed a financing statement covering the same types of goods before the date of the filing made by the consignor; and

(c) the holder of the security interest receives the notification within five years before the consignee receives possession of the goods; and

(d) the notification states that the consignor expects to deliver goods on consignment to the consignee, describing the goods by item or type.

(2) In the case of a consignment which is not a security interest and in which the requirements of the preceding subsection have not been met, a person who delivers goods to another is subordinate to a person who would have a perfected security interest in the goods if they were the property of the debtor.

Part 2 Validity of Security Agreement and Rights of Parties Thereto

Section 9–201. General Validity of Security Agreement

Except as otherwise provided by this Act a security agreement is effective according to its terms between the parties, against purchasers of the collateral and against creditors. Nothing in this Article validates any charge or practice illegal under any statute or regulation thereunder governing usury, small loans, retail installment sales, or the like, or extends the application of any such statute or regulation to any transaction not otherwise subject thereto.

Section 9–202. Title to Collateral Immaterial

Each provision of this Article with regard to rights, obligations and remedies applies whether title to collateral is in the secured party or in the debtor.

Section 9–203. Attachment and Enforceability of Security Interest; Proceeds; Formal Requisites

(1) Subject to the provisions of Section 4–208 on the security interest of a collecting bank, Section 8–321 on security interests in securities and Section 9–113 on a security interest arising under the Article on Sales, a security interest is not enforceable against the debtor or third parties with respect to the collateral and does not attach unless:

(a) the collateral is in the possession of the secured party pursuant to agreement, or the debtor has signed a security agreement which contains a description of the collateral and in addition, when the security interest covers crops growing or to be grown or timber to be cut, a description of the land concerned;

(b) value has been given; and

(c) the debtor has rights in the collateral.

(2) A security interest attaches when it becomes enforceable against the debtor with respect to the collateral. Attachment occurs as soon as all of the events specified in subsection (1) have taken place unless explicit agreement postpones the time of attaching.

(3) Unless otherwise agreed a security agreement gives the secured party the rights to proceeds provided by Section 9–306.

(4) A transaction, although subject to this Article, is also subject to .... *, and in the case of conflict between the provisions of this Article and any such statute, the provisions of such statute control. Failure to comply with any applicable statute has only the effect which is specified therein.

Note: *At * in subsection (4) insert reference to any local statute regulating small loans, retail installment sales and the like.*

The foregoing subsection (4) is designed to make it clear that certain transactions, although subject to this Article, must also comply with other applicable legislation.

This Article is designed to regulate all the "security" aspects of transactions within its scope. There is, however, much regulatory legislation, particularly in the consumer field, which supplements this Article and should not be repealed by its enactment. Examples are small loan acts, retail installment selling acts and the like. Such acts may provide for licensing and rate regulation and may prescribe particular forms of contract. Such provisions should remain in force despite the enactment of this Article. On the other hand if a retail installment selling act contains provisions on filing, rights on default, etc., such provisions should be repealed as inconsistent with this Article except that inconsistent provisions as to deficiencies, penalties, etc., in the Uniform Consumer Credit Code and other recent related legislation should remain because those statutes were drafted after the substantial enactment of the Article and with the intention of modifying certain provisions of this Article as to consumer credit.

Section 9–204. After-Acquired Property; Future Advances

(1) Except as provided in subsection (2), a security agreement may provide that any or all obligations covered by the security agreement are to be secured by after-acquired collateral.

(2) No security interest attaches under an after-acquired property clause to consumer goods other than accessions (Section 9–314) when given as additional security unless the debtor acquires rights in them within ten days after the secured party gives value.

(3) Obligations covered by a security agreement may include future advances or other value whether or not the advances or value are given pursuant to commitment (subsection (1) of Section 9–105).

Section 9–205. Use or Disposition of Collateral Without Accounting Permissible

A security interest is not invalid or fraudulent against creditors by reason of liberty in the debtor to use, commingle or dispose of all or part of the collateral (including returned or repossessed goods) or to collect or compromise accounts or chattel paper, or to accept the return of goods or make repossessions, or to use, commingle or dispose of proceeds, or by reason of the failure of the secured party to require the debtor to account for proceeds or replace collateral. This section does not relax the requirements of possession where perfection of a security interest depends upon possession of the collateral by the secured party or by a bailee.

Section 9–206. Agreement Not to Assert Defenses Against Assignee; Modification of Sales Warranties Where Security Agreement Exists

(1) Subject to any statute or decision which establishes a different rule for buyers or lessees of consumer goods, an agreement by a buyer or lessee that he will not assert against an assignee any claim or defense which he may have against the seller or lessor is enforceable by an assignee who takes his assignment for value, in good faith and without notice of a claim or defense, except as to defenses of a type which may be asserted against a holder in due course of a negotiable instrument under the Article on Commercial Paper (Article 3). A buyer who as part of one transaction signs both a negotiable instrument and a security agreement makes such an agreement.

(2) When a seller retains a purchase money security interest in goods the Article on Sales (Article 2) governs the sale and any disclaimer, limitation or modification of the seller's warranties.

Section 9–207. Rights and Duties When Collateral is in Secured Party's Possession

(1) A secured party must use reasonable care in the custody and preservation of collateral in his possession. In the case of an instrument or chattel paper reasonable care includes taking necessary steps to preserve rights against prior parties unless otherwise agreed.

(2) Unless otherwise agreed, when collateral is in the secured party's possession

(a) reasonable expenses (including the cost of any insurance and payment of taxes or other charges) incurred in the custody, preservation, use or operation of the collateral are chargeable to the debtor and are secured by the collateral;

(b) the risk of accidental loss or damage is on the debtor to the extent of any deficiency in any effective insurance coverage;

(c) the secured party may hold as additional security any increase or profits (except money) received from the collateral, but money so received, unless remitted to the debtor, shall be applied in reduction of the secured obligation;

(d) the secured party must keep the collateral identifiable but fungible collateral may be commingled;

(e) the secured party may repledge the collateral upon terms which do not impair the debtor's right to redeem it.

(3) A secured party is liable for any loss caused by his failure to meet any obligation imposed by the preceding subsections but does not lose his security interest.

(4) A secured party may use or operate the collateral for the purpose of preserving the collateral or its value or pursuant to the order of a court of appropriate jurisdiction or, except in the case of consumer goods, in the manner and to the extent provided in the security agreement.

Section 9–208. Request for Statement of Account or List of Collateral

(1) A debtor may sign a statement indicating what he believes to be the aggregate amount of unpaid indebtedness as of a specified date and may send it to the secured party with a request that the statement be approved or corrected and returned to the debtor. When the security agreement or any other record kept by the secured party identifies the collateral a debtor may similarly request the secured party to approve or correct a list of the collateral.

(2) The secured party must comply with such a request within two weeks after receipt by sending a written correction or approval. If the secured party claims a security interest in all of a particular type of collateral owned by the debtor he may indicate that fact in his reply and need not approve or correct an itemized list of such collateral. If the secured party without reasonable excuse fails to comply he is liable for any loss caused to the debtor thereby; and if the debtor has properly included in his request a good faith statement of the obligation or a list of the collateral or both the secured party may claim a security interest only as shown in the statement against persons misled by his failure to comply. If he no longer has an interest in the obligation or collateral at the time the request is received he must disclose the name and address of any successor in interest known to him and he is liable for any loss caused to the debtor as a result of failure to disclose. A successor in interest is not subject to this section until a request is received by him.

(3) A debtor is entitled to such a statement once every six months without charge. The secured party may require payment of a charge not exceeding $10 for each additional statement furnished.

Part 3 Rights of Third Parties; Perfected and Unperfected Security Interests; Rules of Priority

Section 9–301. Persons Who Take Priority Over Unperfected Security Interests; Rights of "Lien Creditor"

(1) Except as otherwise provided in subsection (2), an unperfected security interest is subordinate to the rights of

(a) persons entitled to priority under Section 9–312;

(b) a person who becomes a lien creditor before the security interest is perfected;

(c) in the case of goods, instruments, documents, and chattel paper, a person who is not a secured party and who is a transferee in bulk or other buyer not in ordinary course of business or is a buyer of farm products in ordinary course of business, to the extent that he gives value and receives delivery of the collateral without knowledge of the security interest and before it is perfected;

(d) in the case of accounts and general intangibles, a person who is not a secured party and who is a transferee to the extent that he gives value without knowledge of the security interest and before it is perfected.

(2) If the secured party files with respect to a purchase money security interest before or within ten days after the debtor receives possession of the collateral, he takes priority over the rights of a transferee in bulk or of a lien creditor which arise between the time the security interest attaches and the time of filing.

(3) A "lien creditor" means a creditor who has acquired a lien on the property involved by attachment, levy or the like and includes an assignee for benefit of creditors from the time of assignment, and a trustee in bankruptcy from the date of the filing of the petition or a receiver in equity from the time of appointment.

(4) A person who becomes a lien creditor while a security interest is perfected takes subject to the security interest only to the extent that it secures advances made before he becomes a lien creditor or within 45 days thereafter or made without knowledge of the lien or pursuant to a commitment entered into without knowledge of the lien.

Section 9–302. When Filing Is Required to Perfect Security Interest; Security Interests to Which Filing Provisions of This Article Do Not Apply

(1) A financing statement must be filed to perfect all security interests except the following:

(a) a security interest in collateral in possession of the secured party under Section 9–305;

(b) a security interest temporarily perfected in instruments or documents without delivery under Section 9–304 or in proceeds for a 10 day period under Section 9–306;

(c) a security interest created by an assignment of a beneficial interest in a trust or a decedent's estate;

(d) a purchase money security interest in consumer goods; but filing is required for a motor vehicle required to be registered; and fixture filing is required for priority over conflicting interests in fixtures to the extent provided in Section 9–313;

(e) an assignment of accounts which does not alone or in conjunction with other assignments to the same assignee transfer a significant part of the outstanding accounts of the assignor;

(f) a security interest of a collecting bank (Section 4–208) or in securities (Section 8–321) or arising under the Article on Sales (see Section 9–113) or covered in subsection (3) of this section;

(g) an assignment for the benefit of all the creditors of the transferor, and subsequent transfers by the assignee thereunder.

(2) If a secured party assigns a perfected security interest, no filing under this Article is required in order to continue the perfected status of the security interest against creditors of and transferees from the original debtor.

(3) The filing of a financing statement otherwise required by this Article is not necessary or effective to perfect a security interest in property subject to

(a) a statute or treaty of the United States which provides for a national or international registration or a national or international certificate of title or which specifies a place of filing different from that specified in this Article for filing of the security interest; or

(b) the following statutes of this state; [list any certificate of title statute covering automobiles, trailers, mobile homes, boats, farm tractors, or the like, and any central filing statute*.]; but during any period in which collateral is inventory held for sale by a person who is in the business of selling goods of that kind, the filing provisions of this Article (Part 4) apply to a security interest in that collateral created by him as debtor; or

(c) a certificate of title statute of another jurisdiction under the law of which indication of a security interest on the certificate is required as a condition of perfection (subsection (2) of Section 9–103).

(4) Compliance with a statute or treaty described in subsection (3) is equivalent to the filing of a financing statement under this Article, and a security interest in property subject to the statute or treaty can be perfected only by compliance therewith except as provided in Section 9–103 on multiple state transactions. Duration and renewal of perfection of a security interest perfected by compliance with the statute or treaty are governed by the provisions of the statute or treaty; in other respects the security interest is subject to this Article.

***Note:** *It is recommended that the provisions of certificate of title acts for perfection of security interests by notation on the certificates should be amended to exclude coverage of inventory held for sale.*

Section 9–303. When Security Interest Is Perfected; Continuity of Perfection

(1) A security interest is perfected when it has attached and when all of the applicable steps required for perfection have been taken. Such steps are specified in Sections 9–302, 9–304, 9–305 and 9–306. If such steps are taken before the security interest attaches, it is perfected at the time when it attaches.

(2) If a security interest is originally perfected in any way permitted under this Article and is subsequently perfected in some other way under this Article, without an intermediate period when it was unperfected, the security interest shall be deemed to be perfected continuously for the purposes of this Article.

Section 9–304. Perfection of Security Interest in Instruments, Documents, and Goods Covered by Documents; Perfection by Permissive Filing; Temporary Perfection Without Filing or Transfer of Possession

(1) A security interest in chattel paper or negotiable documents may be perfected by filing. A security interest in money or instruments (other than certificated securities or instruments which constitute part of chattel paper) can be perfected only by the secured party's taking possession, except as provided in subsections (4) and (5) of this section and subsections (2) and (3) of Section 9–306 on proceeds.

(2) During the period that goods are in the possession of the issuer of a negotiable document therefor, a security interest in the goods is perfected by perfecting a security interest in the document, and any security interest in the goods otherwise perfected during such period is subject thereto.

(3) A security interest in goods in the possession of a bailee other than one who has issued a negotiable document therefor is perfected by issuance of a document in the name of the secured party or by the bailee's receipt of notification of the secured party's interest or by filing as to the goods.

(4) A security interest in instruments (other than certificated securities) or negotiable documents is perfected without filing or the taking of possession for a period of 21 days from the time it attaches to the extent that it arises for new value given under a written security agreement.

(5) A security interest remains perfected for a period of 21 days without filing where a secured party having a perfected security interest in an instrument (other than a certificated security), a negotiable document or goods in possession of a bailee other than one who has issued a negotiable document therefor

(a) makes available to the debtor the goods or documents representing the goods for the purpose of ultimate sale or exchange or for the purpose of loading, unloading, storing, shipping, transshipping, manufacturing, processing or otherwise dealing with them in a manner preliminary to their sale or exchange, but priority between conflicting security interests in the goods is subject to subsection (3) of Section 9–312; or

(b) delivers the instrument to the debtor for the purpose of ultimate sale or exchange or of presentation, collection, renewal or registration of transfer.

(6) After the 21 day period in subsections (4) and (5) perfection depends upon compliance with applicable provisions of this Article.

Section 9–305. When Possession by Secured Party Perfects Security Interest Without Filing

A security interest in letters of credit and advices of credit (subsection (2)(a) of Section 5–116), goods, instruments (other than certificated securities), money, negotiable documents, or chattel paper may be perfected by the secured party's taking possession of the collateral. If such collateral other than goods covered by a negotiable document is held by a bailee, the secured party is deemed to have possession from the time the bailee receives notification of the secured party's interest. A security interest is perfected by possession from the time possession is taken without a relation back and continues only so long as possession is retained, unless otherwise specified in this Article. The security interest may be otherwise perfected as provided in this Article before or after the period of possession by the secured party.

Section 9–306. "Proceeds"; Secured Party's Rights on Disposition of Collateral

(1) "Proceeds" includes whatever is received upon the sale, exchange, collection or other disposition of collateral or proceeds. Insurance payable by reason of loss or damage to the collateral is proceeds, except to the extent that it is payable to a person other than a party to the security agreement. Money, checks, deposit accounts, and the like are "cash proceeds." All other proceeds are "non-cash proceeds."

(2) Except where this Article otherwise provides, a security interest continues in collateral notwithstanding sale, exchange or other disposition thereof unless the disposition was authorized by the secured party in the security agreement or otherwise, and also continues in any identifiable proceeds including collections received by the debtor.

(3) The security interest in proceeds is a continuously perfected security interest if the interest in the original collateral was perfected but it ceases to be a perfected security interest and becomes unperfected ten days after receipt of the proceeds by the debtor unless

(a) a filed financing statement covers the original collateral and the proceeds are collateral in which a security interest may be perfected by filing in the office or offices where the financing statement has been filed and, if the proceeds are acquired with cash proceeds, the description of collateral in the financing statement indicates the types of property constituting the proceeds; or

(b) a filed financing statement covers the original collateral and the proceeds are identifiable cash proceeds; or

(c) the security interest in the proceeds is perfected before the expiration of the ten day period.

Except as provided in this section, a security interest in proceeds can be perfected only by the methods or under the circumstances permitted in this Article for original collateral of the same type.

(4) In the event of insolvency proceedings instituted by or against a debtor, a secured party with a perfected security interest in proceeds has a perfected security interest only in the following proceeds:

(a) in identifiable non-cash proceeds and in separate deposit accounts containing only proceeds;

(b) in identifiable cash proceeds in the form of money which is neither commingled with other money nor deposited in a deposit account prior to the insolvency proceedings;

(c) in identifiable cash proceeds in the form of checks and the like which are not deposited in a deposit account prior to the insolvency proceedings; and

(d) in all cash and deposit accounts of the debtor in which proceeds have been commingled with other funds, but the perfected security interest under this paragraph (d) is

(i) subject to any right to set-off; and

(ii) limited to an amount not greater than the amount of any cash proceeds received by the debtor within ten days before the institution of the insolvency proceedings less the sum of (I) the payments to the secured party on account of cash proceeds received by the debtor during such period and (II) the cash proceeds received by the debtor during such period to which the secured party is entitled under paragraphs (a) through (c) of this subsection (4).

(5) If a sale of goods results in an account or chattel paper which is transferred by the seller to a secured party, and if the goods are returned to or are repossessed by the seller or the secured party, the following rules determine priorities:

(a) If the goods were collateral at the time of sale, for an indebtedness of the seller which is still unpaid, the original security interest attaches again to the goods and continues as a perfected security interest if it was perfected at the time when the goods were sold. If the security interest was originally perfected by a filing which is still effective, nothing further is required to continue the perfected status; in any other case, the secured party must take possession of the returned or repossessed goods or must file.

(b) An unpaid transferee of the chattel paper has a security interest in the goods against the transferor. Such security interest is prior to a security interest asserted under paragraph (a) to the extent that the transferee of the chattel paper was entitled to priority under Section 9–308.

(c) An unpaid transferee of the account has a security interest in the goods against the transferor. Such security interest is subordinate to a security interest asserted under paragraph (a).

(d) A security interest of an unpaid transferee asserted under paragraph (b) or (c) must be perfected for protection against creditors of the transferor and purchasers of the returned or repossessed goods.

Section 9–307. Protection of Buyers of Goods

(1) A buyer in ordinary course of business (subsection (9) of Section 1–201) other than a person buying farm products from a person engaged in farming operations takes free of a security interest created by his seller even though the security interest is perfected and even though the buyer knows of its existence.

(2) In the case of consumer goods, a buyer takes free of a security interest even though perfected if he buys without knowledge of the security interest, for value and for his own personal, family or household purposes unless prior to the purchase the secured party has filed a financing statement covering such goods.

(3) A buyer other than a buyer in ordinary course of business (subsection (1) of this section) takes free of a security interest to the extent that it secures future advances made after the secured party acquires knowledge of the purchase, or more than 45 days after the purchase, whichever first occurs, unless made pursuant to a commitment entered into without knowledge of the purchase and before the expiration of the 45 day period.

Section 9–308. Purchase of Chattel Paper and Instruments

A purchaser of chattel paper or an instrument who gives new value and takes possession of it in the ordinary course of his business has priority over a security interest in the chattel paper or instrument

(a) which is perfected under Section 9–304 (permissive filing and temporary perfection) or under Section 9–306 (perfection as to proceeds) if he acts without knowledge that the specific paper or instrument is subject to a security interest; or

(b) which is claimed merely as proceeds of inventory subject to a security interest (Section 9–306) even though he knows that the specific paper or instrument is subject to the security interest.

Section 9–309. Protection of Purchasers of Instruments, Documents and Securities

Nothing in this Article limits the rights of a holder in due course of a negotiable instrument (Section 3–302) or a holder to whom a negotiable document of title has been duly negotiated (Section 7–501) or a bona fide purchaser of a security (Section 8–302) and the holders or purchasers take priority over an earlier security interest even though perfected. Filing under this Article does not constitute notice of the security interest to such holders or purchasers.

Section 9–310. Priority of Certain Liens Arising by Operation of Law

When a person in the ordinary course of his business furnishes services or materials with respect to goods subject to a security interest, a lien upon goods in the possession of such person given by statute or rule of law for such materials or services takes priority over a perfected security interest unless the lien is statutory and the statute expressly provides otherwise.

Section 9–311. Alienability of Debtor's Rights: Judicial Process

The debtor's rights in collateral may be voluntarily or involuntarily transferred (by way of sale, creation of a security interest, attachment, levy, garnishment or other judicial process) notwithstanding a provision in the security agreement prohibiting any transfer or making the transfer constitute a default.

Section 9–312. Priorities Among Conflicting Security Interests in the Same Collateral

(1) The rules of priority stated in other sections of this Part and in the following sections shall govern when applicable: Section 4–208 with respect to the security interests of collecting banks in items being collected, accompanying documents and proceeds; Section 9–103 on security interests related to other jurisdictions; Section 9–114 on consignments.

(2) A perfected security interest in crops for new value given to enable the debtor to produce the crops during the production season and given not more than three months before the crops become growing crops by planting or otherwise takes priority over an earlier perfected security interest to the extent that such earlier interest secures obligations due more than six months before the crops become growing crops by planting or otherwise, even though the person giving new value had knowledge of the earlier security interest.

(3) A perfected purchase money security interest in inventory has priority over a conflicting security interest in the same inventory and also has priority in identifiable cash proceeds received on or before the delivery of the inventory to a buyer if

- (a) the purchase money security interest is perfected at the time the debtor receives possession of the inventory; and
- (b) the purchase money secured party gives notification in writing to the holder of the conflicting security interest if the holder had filed a financing statement covering the same types of inventory (i) before the date of the filing made by the purchase money secured party, or (ii) before the beginning of the 21 day period where the purchase money security interest is temporarily perfected without filing or possession (subsection (5) of Section 9–304); and
- (c) the holder of the conflicting security interest receives the notification within five years before the debtor receives possession of the inventory; and
- (d) the notification states that the person giving the notice has or expects to acquire a purchase money security interest in inventory of the debtor, describing such inventory by item or type.

(4) A purchase money security interest in collateral other than inventory has priority over a conflicting security interest in the same collateral or its proceeds if the purchase money security interest is perfected at the time the debtor receives possession of the collateral or within ten days thereafter.

(5) In all cases not governed by other rules stated in this section (including cases of purchase money security interests which do not qualify for the special priorities set forth in subsections (3) and (4) of this section), priority between conflicting security interests in the same collateral shall be determined according to the following rules:

- (a) Conflicting security interests rank according to priority in time of filing or perfection. Priority dates from the time a filing is first made covering the collateral or the time the security interest is first perfected, whichever is earlier, provided that there is no period thereafter when there is neither filing nor perfection.
- (b) So long as conflicting security interests are unperfected, the first to attach has priority.

(6) For the purposes of subsection (5) a date of filing or perfection as to collateral is also a date of filing or perfection as to proceeds.

(7) If future advances are made while a security interest is perfected by filing, the taking of possession, or under Section 8–321 on securities, the security interest has the same priority for the purposes of subsection (5) with respect to the future advances as it does with respect to the first advance. If a commitment is made before or while the security interest is so perfected, the security interest has the same priority with respect to advances made pursuant thereto. In other cases a perfected security interest has priority from the date the advance is made.

Section 9–313. Priority of Security Interests in Fixtures

(1) In this section and in the provisions of Part 4 of this Article referring to fixture filing, unless the context otherwise requires

- (a) goods are "fixtures" when they become so related to particular real estate that an interest in them arises under real estate law
- (b) a "fixture filing" is the filing in the office where a mortgage on the real estate would be filed or recorded of a financing statement covering goods which are or are to become fixtures and conforming to the requirements of subsection (5) of Section 9–402
- (c) a mortgage is a "construction mortgage" to the extent that it secures an obligation incurred for the construction of an improvement on land including the acquisition cost of the land, if the recorded writing so indicates.

(2) A security interest under this Article may be created in goods which are fixtures or may continue in goods which become fixtures, but no security interest exists under this Article in ordinary building materials incorporated into an improvement on land.

(3) This Article does not prevent creation of an encumbrance upon fixtures pursuant to real estate law.

(4) A perfected security interest in fixtures has priority over the conflicting interest of an encumbrancer or owner of the real estate where

- (a) the security interest is a purchase money security interest, the interest of the encumbrancer or owner arises before the goods become fixtures, the security interest is perfected by a fixture filing before the goods become fixtures or within ten days thereafter, and the debtor has an interest of record in the real estate or is in possession of the real estate; or

(b) the security interest is perfected by a fixture filing before the interest of the encumbrancer or owner is of record, the security interest has priority over any conflicting interest of a predecessor in title of the encumbrancer or owner, and the debtor has an interest of record in the real estate or is in possession of the real estate; or

(c) the fixtures are readily removable factory or office machines or readily removable replacements of domestic appliances which are consumer goods, and before the goods become fixtures the security interest is perfected by any method permitted by this Article; or

(d) the conflicting interest is a lien on the real estate obtained by legal or equitable proceedings after the security interest was perfected by any method permitted by this Article.

(5) A security interest in fixtures, whether or not perfected, has priority over the conflicting interest of an encumbrancer or owner of the real estate where

(a) the encumbrancer or owner has consented in writing to the security interest or has disclaimed an interest in the goods as fixtures; or

(b) the debtor has a right to remove the goods as against the encumbrancer or owner. If the debtor's right terminates, the priority of the security interest continues for a reasonable time.

(6) Notwithstanding paragraph (a) of subsection (4) but otherwise subject to subsections (4) and (5), a security interest in fixtures is subordinate to a construction mortgage recorded before the goods become fixtures if the goods become fixtures before the completion of the construction. To the extent that it is given to refinance a construction mortgage, a mortgage has this priority to the same extent as the construction mortgage.

(7) In cases not within the preceding subsections, a security interest in fixtures is subordinate to the conflicting interest of an encumbrancer or owner of the related real estate who is not the debtor.

(8) When the secured party has priority over all owners and encumbrancers of the real estate, he may, on default, subject to the provisions of Part 5, remove his collateral from the real estate but he must reimburse any encumbrancer or owner of the real estate who is not the debtor and who has not otherwise agreed for the cost of repair of any physical injury, but not for any diminution in value of the real estate caused by the absence of the goods removed or by any necessity of replacing them. A person entitled to reimbursement may refuse permission to remove until the secured party gives adequate security for the performance of this obligation.

Section 9–314. Accessions

(1) A security interest in goods which attaches before they are installed in or affixed to other goods takes priority as to the goods installed or affixed (called in this section "accessions") over the claims of all persons to the whole except as stated in subsection (3) and subject to Section 9–315(1).

(2) A security interest which attaches to goods after they become part of a whole is valid against all persons subsequently acquiring interests in the whole except as stated in subsection (3) but is invalid against any person with an interest in the whole at the time the security interest attaches to the goods who has not in writing consented to the security interest or disclaimed an interest in the goods as part of the whole.

(3) The security interests described in subsections (1) and (2) do not take priority over

(a) a subsequent purchaser for value of any interest in the whole; or

(b) a creditor with a lien on the whole subsequently obtained by judicial proceedings; or

(c) a creditor with a prior perfected security interest in the whole to the extent that he makes subsequent advances

if the subsequent purchase is made, the lien by judicial proceedings obtained or the subsequent advance under the prior perfected security interest is made or contracted for without knowledge of the security interest and before it is perfected. A purchaser of the whole at a foreclosure sale other than the holder of a perfected security interest purchasing at his own foreclosure sale is a subsequent purchaser within this section.

(4) When under subsections (1) or (2) and (3) a secured party has an interest in accessions which has priority over the claims of all persons who have interests in the whole, he may on default subject to the provisions of Part 5 remove his collateral from the whole but he must reimburse any encumbrancer or owner of the whole who is not the debtor and who has not otherwise agreed for the cost of repair of any physical injury but not for any diminution in value of the whole caused by the absence of the goods removed or by any necessity for replacing them. A person entitled to reimbursement may refuse permission to remove until the secured party gives adequate security for the performance of this obligation.

Section 9–315. Priority When Goods Are Commingled or Processed

(1) If a security interest in goods was perfected and subsequently the goods or a part thereof have become part of a product or mass, the security interest continues in the product or mass if

(a) the goods are so manufactured, processed, assembled or commingled that their identity is lost in the product or mass; or

(b) a financing statement covering the original goods also covers the product into which the goods have been manufactured, processed or assembled.

In a case to which paragraph (b) applies, no separate security interest in that part of the original goods which have been manufactured, processed or assembled into the product may be claimed under Section 9–314.

(2) When under subsection (1) more than one security interest attaches to the product or mass, they rank equally according to the ratio that the cost of the goods to which each interest originally attached bears to the cost of the total product or mass.

Section 9–316. Priority Subject to Subordination

Nothing in this Article prevents subordination by agreement by any person entitled to priority.

Section 9–317. Secured Party Not Obligated on Contract of Debtor

The mere existence of a security interest or authority given to the debtor to dispose of or use collateral does not impose contract or tort liability upon the secured party for the debtor's acts or omissions.

Section 9–318. Defenses Against Assignee; Modification of Contract After Notification of Assignment; Term Prohibiting Assignment Ineffective; Identification and Proof of Assignment

(1) Unless an account debtor has made an enforceable agreement not to assert defenses or claims arising out of a sale as provided in Section 9–206 the rights of an assignee are subject to

(a) all the terms of the contract between the account debtor and assignor and any defense or claim arising therefrom; and

(b) any other defense or claim of the account debtor against the assignor which accrues before the account debtor receives notification of the assignment.

(2) So far as the right to payment or a part thereof under an assigned contract has not been fully earned by performance, and notwithstanding notification of the assignment, any modification of or substitution for the contract made in good faith and in accordance with reasonable commercial standards is effective against an assignee unless the account debtor has otherwise agreed but the assignee acquires corresponding rights under the modified or substituted contract. The assignment may provide that such modification or substitution is a breach by the assignor.

(3) The account debtor is authorized to pay the assignor until the account debtor receives notification that the amount due or to become due has been assigned and that payment is to be made to the assignee. A notification which does not reasonably identify the rights assigned is ineffective. If requested by the account debtor, the assignee must seasonably furnish reasonable proof that the assignment has been made and unless he does so the account debtor may pay the assignor.

(4) A term in any contract between an account debtor and an assignor is ineffective if it prohibits assignment of an account or prohibits creation of a security interest in a general intangible for money due or to become due or requires the account debtor's consent to such assignment or security interest.

Part 4 Filing

Section 9–401. Place of Filing; Erroneous Filing; Removal of Collateral

First Alternative Subsection (1)

(1) The proper place to file in order to perfect a security interest is as follows:

(a) when the collateral is timber to be cut or is minerals or the like (including oil and gas) or accounts subject to subsection (5) of Section 9–103, or when the financing statement is filed as a fixture filing (Section 9–313) and the collateral is goods which are or are to become fixtures, then in the office where a mortgage on the real estate would be filed or recorded;

(b) in all other cases, in the office of the [Secretary of State].

Second Alternative Subsection (1)

(1) The proper place to file in order to perfect a security interest is as follows:

(a) when the collateral is equipment used in farming operations, or farm products, or accounts or general intangibles arising from or relating to the sale of farm products by a farmer, or consumer goods, then in the office of the .... in the county of the debtor's residence or if the debtor is not a resident of this state then in the office of the .... in the county where the goods are kept, and in addition when the collateral is crops growing or to be grown in the office of the .... in the county where the land is located;

(b) when the collateral is timber to be cut or is minerals or the like (including oil and gas) or accounts subject to subsection (5) of Section 9–103, or when the financing statement is filed as a fixture filing (Section 9–313) and the collateral is goods which are or are to become fixtures, then in the office where a mortgage on the real estate would be filed or recorded;

(c) in all other cases, in the office of the [Secretary of State].

Third Alternative Subsection (1)

(1) The proper place to file in order to perfect a security interest is as follows:

(a) when the collateral is equipment used in farming operations, or farm products, or accounts or general intangibles arising from or relating to the sale of farm products by a farmer, or consumer goods, then in the office of the ...... in the county of the debtor's residence or if the debtor is not a resident of this state then in the office of the .... in the county where the goods are kept, and in addition when the collateral is crops growing or to be grown in the office of the ...... in the county where the land is located;

(b) when the collateral is timber to be cut or is minerals or the like (including oil and gas) or accounts subject to subsection (5) of Section 9–103, or when the financing statement is filed as a fixture filing (Section 9–313) and the collateral is goods which are or are to become fixtures, then in the office where a mortgage on the real estate would be filed or recorded;

(c) in all other cases, in the office of the [Secretary of State] and in addition, if the debtor has a place of business in only one county of this state, also in the office of ...... of such county, or, if the debtor has no place of business in this state, but resides in the state, also in the office of ...... of the county in which he resides.

Note: *One of the three alternatives should be selected as subsection (1).*

(2) A filing which is made in good faith in an improper place or not in all of the places required by this section is nevertheless effective with regard to any collateral as to which the filing complied with the requirements of this Article and is also effective with regard to collateral covered by the financing statement against any person who has knowledge of the contents of such financing statement.

(3) A filing which is made in the proper place in this state continues effective even though the debtor's residence or place of business or the location of the collateral or its use, whichever controlled the original filing, is thereafter changed.

Alternative Subsection (3)

[(3) A filing which is made in the proper county continues effective for four months after a change to another county of the debtor's residence or place of business or the location of the collateral, whichever controlled the original filing. It becomes ineffective thereafter unless a copy of the financing statement signed by the secured party is filed in the new county within said period. The security interest may also be perfected in the new county after the expiration of the four-month period; in such case perfection dates from the time of perfection in the new county. A change in the use of the collateral does not impair the effectiveness of the original filing.]

(4) The rules stated in Section 9–103 determine whether filing is necessary in this state.

(5) Notwithstanding the preceding subsections, and subject to subsection (3) of Section 9–302, the proper place to file in order to perfect a security interest in collateral, including fixtures, of a transmitting utility is the office of the [Secretary of State]. This filing constitutes a fixture filing (Section 9–313) as to the collateral described therein which is or is to become fixtures.

(6) For the purposes of this section, the residence of an organization is its place of business if it has one or its chief executive office if it has more than one place of business.

Note: *Subsection (6) should be used only if the state chooses the Second or Third Alternative Subsection (1).*

Section 9–402. Formal Requisites of Financing Statement; Amendments; Mortgage as Financing Statement

(1) A financing statement is sufficient if it gives the names of the debtor and the secured party, is signed by the debtor, gives an address of the secured party from which information concerning the security interest may be obtained, gives a mailing address of the debtor and contains a statement indicating the types, or describing the items, of collateral. A financing statement may be filed before a security agreement is made or a security interest otherwise attaches. When the financing statement covers crops growing or to be grown, the statement must also contain a description of the real estate concerned. When the financing statement covers timber to be cut or covers minerals or the like (including oil and gas) or accounts subject to subsection (5) of Section 9–103, or when the financing statement is filed as a fixture filing (Section 9–313) and the collateral is goods which are or are to become fixtures, the statement must also comply with subsection (5). A copy of the security agreement is sufficient as a financing statement if it contains the above information and is signed by the debtor. A carbon, photographic or other reproduction of a security agreement or a financing statement is sufficient as a financing statement if the security agreement so provides or if the original has been filed in this state.

(2) A financing statement which otherwise complies with subsection (1) is sufficient when it is signed by the secured party instead of the debtor if it is filed to perfect a security interest in

(a) collateral already subject to a security interest in another jurisdiction when it is brought into this state, or when the debtor's location is changed to this state. Such a financing statement must state that the collateral was brought into this state or that the debtor's location was changed to this state under such circumstances; or

(b) proceeds under Section 9–306 if the security interest in the original collateral was perfected. Such a financing statement must describe the original collateral; or

(c) collateral as to which the filing has lapsed; or

(d) collateral acquired after a change of name, identity or corporate structure of the debtor (subsection (7)).

(3) A form substantially as follows is sufficient to comply with subsection (1):

Name of debtor (or assignor) ____________________
Address ____________________
Name of secured party (or assignee) ____________________
Address ____________________

1. This financing statement covers the following types (or items) of property:
   (Describe) ____________________
2. (If collateral is crops) The above described crops are growing or are to be grown on:
   (Describe Real Estate) ____________________
3. (If applicable) The above goods are to become fixtures on*
   (Describe Real Estate) ____________________
   and this financing statement is to be filed [for record] in the real estate records. (If the debtor does not have an interest of record) The name of a record owner is ____________________
4. (If products of collateral are claimed) Products of the collateral are also covered.

(use whichever is applicable)

____
Signature of Debtor (or Assignor)

____
Signature of Secured Party (or Assignee)

(4) A financing statement may be amended by filing a writing signed by both the debtor and the secured party. An amendment does not extend the period of effectiveness of a financing statement. If any amendment adds collateral, it is effective as to the added collateral only from the filing date of the amendment. In this Article, unless the context otherwise requires, the term "financing statement" means the original financing statement and any amendments.

(5) A financing statement covering timber to be cut or covering minerals or the like (including oil and gas) or accounts subject to subsection (5) of Section 9–103, or a financing statement filed as a fixture filing (Section 9–313) where the debtor is not a transmitting utility, must show that it covers this type of collateral, must recite that it is to be filed [for record] in the real estate records, and the financing statement must contain a description of the real estate [sufficient if it were contained in a mortgage of the real estate to give constructive notice of the mortgage under the law of this state]. If the debtor does not have an interest of record in the real estate, the financing statement must show the name of a record owner.

(6) A mortgage is effective as a financing statement filed as a fixture filing from the date of its recording if

(a) the goods are described in the mortgage by item or type; and

(b) the goods are or are to become fixtures related to the real estate described in the mortgage; and

(c) the mortgage complies with the requirements for a financing statement in this section other than a recital that it is to be filed in the real estate records; and

(d) the mortgage is duly recorded.

No fee with reference to the financing statement is required other than the regular recording and satisfaction fees with respect to the mortgage.

(7) A financing statement sufficiently shows the name of the debtor if it gives the individual, partnership or corporate name of the debtor, whether or not it adds other trade names or names of partners. Where

**Where appropriate substitute either "The above timber is standing on . . . ." or "The above minerals or the like (including oil and gas) or accounts will be financed at the wellhead or minehead of the well or mine located on . . . ."*

the debtor so changes his name or in the case of an organization its name, identity or corporate structure that a filed financing statement becomes seriously misleading, the filing is not effective to perfect a security interest in collateral acquired by the debtor more than four months after the change, unless a new appropriate financing statement is filed before the expiration of that time. A filed financing statement remains effective with respect to collateral transferred by the debtor even though the secured party knows of or consents to the transfer.

(8) A financing statement substantially complying with the requirements of this section is effective even though it contains minor errors which are not seriously misleading.

Note: *Language in brackets is optional.*

Note: *Where the state has any special recording system for real estate other than the usual grantor-grantee index (as, for instance, a tract system or a title registration or Torrens system) local adaptations of subsection (5) and Section 9–403(7) may be necessary. See Mass. Gen. Laws Chapter 106, Section 9–409.*

Section 9–403. What Constitutes Filing; Duration of Filing; Effect of Lapsed Filing; Duties of Filing Officer

(1) Presentation for filing of a financing statement and tender of the filing fee or acceptance of the statement by the filing officer constitutes filing under this Article.

(2) Except as provided in subsection (6) a filed financing statement is effective for a period of five years from the date of filing. The effectiveness of a filed financing statement lapses on the expiration of the five year period unless a continuation statement is filed prior to the lapse. If a security interest perfected by filing exists at the time insolvency proceedings are commenced by or against the debtor, the security interest remains perfected until termination of the insolvency proceedings and thereafter for a period of sixty days or until expiration of the five year period, whichever occurs later. Upon lapse the security interest becomes unperfected, unless it is perfected without filing. If the security interest becomes unperfected upon lapse, it is deemed to have been unperfected as against a person who became a purchaser or lien creditor before lapse.

(3) A continuation statement may be filed by the secured party within six months prior to the expiration of the five year period specified in subsection (2). Any such continuation statement must be signed by the secured party, identify the original statement by file number and state that the original statement is still effective. A continuation statement signed by a person other than the secured party of record must be accompanied by a separate written statement of assignment signed by the secured party of record and complying with subsection (2) of Section 9–405, including payment of the required fee. Upon timely filing of the continuation statement, the effectiveness of the original statement is continued for five years after the last date to which the filing was effective whereupon it lapses in the same manner as provided in subsection (2) unless another continuation statement is filed prior to such lapse. Succeeding continuation statements may be filed in the same manner to continue the effectiveness of the original statement. Unless a statute on disposition of public records provides otherwise, the filing officer may remove a lapsed statement from the files and destroy it immediately if he has retained a microfilm or other photographic record, or in other cases after one year after the lapse. The filing officer shall so arrange matters by physical annexation of financing statements to continuation statements or other related filings, or by other means, that if he physically destroys the financing statements of a period more than five years past, those which have been continued by a continuation statement or which are still effective under subsection (6) shall be retained.

(4) Except as provided in subsection (7) a filing officer shall mark each statement with a file number and with the date and hour of filing and shall hold the statement or a microfilm or other photographic copy thereof for public inspection. In addition the filing officer shall index the statement according to the name of the debtor and shall note in the index the file number and the address of the debtor given in the statement.

(5) The uniform fee for filing and indexing and for stamping a copy furnished by the secured party to show the date and place of filing for an original financing statement or for a continuation statement shall be $.......... if the statement is in the standard form prescribed by the [Secretary of State] and otherwise shall be $.........., plus in each case, if the financing statement is subject to subsection (5) of Section 9–402, $....... The uniform fee for each name more than one required to be indexed shall be $......... The secured party may at his option show a trade name for any person and an extra uniform indexing fee of $......... shall be paid with respect thereto.

(6) If the debtor is a transmitting utility (subsection (5) of Section 9–401) and a filed financing statement so states, it is effective until a termination statement is filed. A real estate mortgage which is effective as a fixture filing under subsection (6) of Section 9–402 remains effective as a fixture filing until the mortgage is released or satisfied of record or its effectiveness otherwise terminates as to the real estate.

(7) When a financing statement covers timber to be cut or covers minerals or the like (including oil and gas) or accounts subject to subsection (5) of Section 9–103, or is filed as a fixture filing, [it shall be filed for record and] the filing officer shall index it under the names of the debtor and any owner of record shown on the financing statement in the same fashion as if they were the mortgagors in a mortgage of the real estate described, and, to the extent that the law of this state provides for indexing of mortgages under the name of the mortgagee, under the name of the secured party as if he were the mortgagee thereunder, or where indexing is by description in the same fashion as if the financing statement were a mortgage of the real estate described.

Note: *In states in which writings will not appear in the real estate records and indices unless actually recorded the bracketed language in subsection (7) should be used.*

Section 9–404. Termination Statement

(1) If a financing statement covering consumer goods is filed on or after ...., then within one month or within ten days following written demand by the debtor after there is no outstanding secured obligation and no commitment to make advances, incur obligations or otherwise give value, the secured party must file with each filing officer with whom the financing statement was filed, a termination statement to the effect that he no longer claims a security interest under the financing statement, which shall be identified by file number. In other cases whenever there is no outstanding secured obligation and no commitment to make advances, incur obligations or otherwise give value, the secured party must on written demand by the debtor send the debtor, for each filing officer with whom the financing statement was filed, a termination statement to the effect that he no longer claims a security interest under the financing statement, which shall be identified by file number. A termination statement signed by a person other than the secured party of record must be accompanied by a separate written statement of assignment signed by

the secured party of record complying with subsection (2) of Section 9–405, including payment of the required fee. If the affected secured party fails to file such a termination statement as required by this subsection, or to send such a termination statement within ten days after proper demand therefor, he shall be liable to the debtor for one hundred dollars, and in addition for any loss caused to the debtor by such failure.

(2) On presentation to the filing officer of such a termination statement he must note it in the index. If he has received the termination statement in duplicate, he shall return one copy of the termination statement to the secured party stamped to show the time of receipt thereof. If the filing officer has a microfilm or other photographic record of the financing statement, and of any related continuation statement, statement of assignment and statement of release, he may remove the originals from the files at any time after receipt of the termination statement, or if he has no such record, he may remove them from the files at any time after one year after receipt of the termination statement.

(3) If the termination statement is in the standard form prescribed by the [Secretary of State], the uniform fee for filing and indexing the termination statement shall be $......, and otherwise shall be $......, plus in each case an additional fee of $...... for each name more than one against which the termination statement is required to be indexed.

Note: *The date to be inserted should be the effective date of the revised Article 9.*

Section 9–405. Assignment of Security Interest; Duties of Filing Officer; Fees

(1) A financing statement may disclose an assignment of a security interest in the collateral described in the financing statement by indication in the financing statement of the name and address of the assignee or by an assignment itself or a copy thereof on the face or back of the statement. On presentation to the filing officer of such a financing statement the filing officer shall mark the same as provided in Section 9–403(4). The uniform fee for filing, indexing and furnishing filing data for a financing statement so indicating an assignment shall be $...... if the statement is in the standard form prescribed by the [Secretary of State] and otherwise shall be $......, plus in each case an additional fee of $...... for each name more than one against which the financing statement is required to be indexed.

(2) A secured party may assign of record all or part of his rights under a financing statement by the filing in the place where the original financing statement was filed of a separate written statement of assignment signed by the secured party of record and setting forth the name of the secured party of record and the debtor, the file number and the date of filing of the financing statement and the name and address of the assignee and containing a description of the collateral assigned. A copy of the assignment is sufficient as a separate statement if it complies with the preceding sentence. On presentation to the filing officer of such a separate statement, the filing officer shall mark such separate statement with the date and hour of the filing. He shall note the assignment on the index of the financing statement, or in the case of a fixture filing, or a filing covering timber to be cut, or covering minerals or the like (including oil and gas) or accounts subject to subsection (5) of Section 9–103, he shall index the assignment under the name of the assignor as grantor and, to the extent that the law of this state provides for indexing the assignment of a mortgage under the name of the assignee, he shall index the assignment of the financing statement under the name of the assignee. The uniform fee for filing, indexing and furnishing filing data about such a separate statement of assignment shall be $...... if the statement is in the standard form prescribed by the [Secretary of State] and otherwise shall be $......, plus in each case an additional fee of $...... for each name more than one against which the statement of assignment is required to be indexed. Notwithstanding the provisions of this subsection, an assignment of record of a security interest in a fixture contained in a mortgage effective as a fixture filing (subsection (6) of Section 9–402) may be made only by an assignment of the mortgage in the manner provided by the law of this state other than this Act.

(3) After the disclosure or filing of an assignment under this section, the assignee is the secured party of record.

Section 9–406. Release of Collateral; Duties of Filing Officer; Fees

A secured party of record may by his signed statement release all or a part of any collateral described in a filed financing statement. The statement of release is sufficient if it contains a description of the collateral being released, the name and address of the debtor, the name and address of the secured party, and the file number of the financing statement. A statement of release signed by a person other than the secured party of record must be accompanied by a separate written statement of assignment signed by the secured party of record and complying with subsection (2) of Section 9–405, including payment of the required fee. Upon presentation of such a statement of release to the filing officer he shall mark the statement with the hour and date of filing and shall note the same upon the margin of the index of the filing of the financing statement. The uniform fee for filing and noting such a statement of release shall be $...... if the statement is in the standard form prescribed by the [Secretary of State] and otherwise shall be $......, plus in each case an additional fee of $...... for each name more than one against which the statement of release is required to be indexed.

[Section 9–407. Information From Filing Officer]

[(1) If the person filing any financing statement, termination statement, statement of assignment, or statement of release, furnishes the filing officer a copy thereof, the filing officer shall upon request note upon the copy the file number and date and hour of the filing of the original and deliver or send the copy to such person.]

[(2) Upon request of any person, the filing officer shall issue his certificate showing whether there is on file on the date and hour stated therein, any presently effective financing statement naming a particular debtor and any statement of assignment thereof and if there is, giving the date and hour of filing of each such statement and the names and addresses of each secured party therein. The uniform fee for such a certificate shall be $...... if the request for the certificate is in the standard form prescribed by the [Secretary of State] and otherwise shall be $...... Upon request the filing officer shall furnish a copy of any filed financing statement or statement of assignment for a uniform fee of $...... per page.]

Note: *This section is proposed as an optional provision to require filing officers to furnish certificates. Local law and practices should be consulted with regard to the advisability of adoption.*

Section 9–408. Financing Statements Covering Consigned or Leased Goods

A consignor or lessor of goods may file a financing statement using the terms "consignor," "consignee," "lessor," "lessee" or the like instead of the terms specified in Section 9–402. The provisions of this Part shall apply as appropriate to such a financing statement but its filing shall not of itself be a factor in determining whether or not the consignment or lease is intended as security (Section 1–201(37)). However, if it is determined for other reasons that the consignment or lease is so intended, a security interest of the consignor or lessor which attaches to the consigned or leased goods is perfected by such filing.

Part 5 Default

Section 9–501. Default; Procedure When Security Agreement Covers Both Real and Personal Property

(1) When a debtor is in default under a security agreement, a secured party has the rights and remedies provided in this Part and except as limited by subsection (3) those provided in the security agreement. He may reduce his claim to judgment, foreclose or otherwise enforce the security interest by any available judicial procedure. If the collateral is documents the secured party may proceed either as to the documents or as to the goods covered thereby. A secured party in possession has the rights, remedies and duties provided in Section 9–207. The rights and remedies referred to in this subsection are cumulative.

(2) After default, the debtor has the rights and remedies provided in this Part, those provided in the security agreement and those provided in Section 9–207.

(3) To the extent that they give rights to the debtor and impose duties on the secured party, the rules stated in the subsections referred to below may not be waived or varied except as provided with respect to compulsory disposition of collateral (subsection (3) of Section 9–504 and Section 9–505) and with respect to redemption of collateral (Section 9–506) but the parties may by agreement determine the standards by which the fulfillment of these rights and duties is to be measured if such standards are not manifestly unreasonable:

(a) subsection (2) of Section 9–502 and subsection (2) of Section 9–504 insofar as they require accounting for surplus proceeds of collateral;

(b) subsection (3) of Section 9–504 and subsection (1) of Section 9–505 which deal with disposition of collateral;

(c) subsection (2) of Section 9–505 which deals with acceptance of collateral as discharge of obligation;

(d) Section 9–506 which deals with redemption of collateral; and

(e) subsection (1) of Section 9–507 which deals with the secured party's liability for failure to comply with this Part.

(4) If the security agreement covers both real and personal property, the secured party may proceed under this Part as to the personal property or he may proceed as to both the real and the personal property in accordance with his rights and remedies in respect of the real property in which case the provisions of this Part do not apply.

(5) When a secured party has reduced his claim to judgment the lien of any levy which may be made upon his collateral by virtue of any execution based upon the judgment shall relate back to the date of the perfection of the security interest in such collateral. A judicial sale, pursuant to such execution, is a foreclosure of the security interest by judicial procedure within the meaning of this section, and the secured party may purchase at the sale and thereafter hold the collateral free of any other requirements of this Article.

Section 9–502. Collection Rights of Secured Party

(1) When so agreed and in any event on default the secured party is entitled to notify an account debtor or the obligor on an instrument to make payment to him whether or not the assignor was theretofore making collections on the collateral, and also to take control of any proceeds to which he is entitled under Section 9–306.

(2) A secured party who by agreement is entitled to charge back uncollected collateral or otherwise to full or limited recourse against the debtor and who undertakes to collect from the account debtors or obligors must proceed in a commercially reasonable manner and may deduct his reasonable expense of realization from the collections. If the security agreement secures an indebtedness, the secured party must account to the debtor for any surplus, and unless otherwise agreed, the debtor is liable for any deficiency. But, if the underlying transaction was a sale of accounts or chattel paper, the debtor is entitled to any surplus or is liable for any deficiency only if the security agreement so provides.

Section 9–503. Secured Party's Right to Take Possession After Default

Unless otherwise agreed a secured party has on default the right to take possession of the collateral. In taking possession a secured party may proceed without judicial process if this can be done without breach of the peace or may proceed by action. If the security agreement so provides the secured party may require the debtor to assemble the collateral and make it available to the secured party at a place to be designated by the secured party which is reasonably convenient to both parties. Without removal a secured party may render equipment unusable, and may dispose of collateral on the debtor's premises under Section 9–504.

Section 9–504. Secured Party's Right to Dispose of Collateral After Default; Effect of Disposition

(1) A secured party after default may sell, lease or otherwise dispose of any or all of the collateral in its then condition or following any commercially reasonable preparation or processing. Any sale of goods is subject to the Article on Sales (Article 2). The proceeds of disposition shall be applied in the order following to

(a) the reasonable expenses of retaking, holding, preparing for sale or lease, selling, leasing and the like and, to the extent provided for in the agreement and not prohibited by law, the reasonable attorneys' fees and legal expenses incurred by the secured party;

(b) the satisfaction of indebtedness secured by the security interest under which the disposition is made;

(c) the satisfaction of indebtedness secured by any subordinate security interest in the collateral if written notification of demand therefor is received before distribution of the proceeds is completed. If requested by the secured party, the holder of a subordinate security interest must seasonably furnish reasonable proof of his interest, and unless he does so, the secured party need not comply with his demand.

(2) If the security interest secures an indebtedness, the secured party must account to the debtor for any surplus, and, unless otherwise agreed, the debtor is liable for any deficiency. But if the underlying transaction was a sale of accounts or chattel paper, the debtor is entitled to any surplus or is liable for any deficiency only if the security agreement so provides.

(3) Disposition of the collateral may be by public or private proceedings and may be made by way of one or more contracts. Sale or other disposition may be as a unit or in parcels and at any time and place and on any terms but every aspect of the disposition including the method, manner, time, place and terms must be commercially reasonable. Unless collateral is perishable or threatens to decline speedily in value or is of a type customarily sold on a recognized market, reasonable notification of the time and place of any public sale or reasonable notification of the time after which any private sale or other intended disposition is to be made shall be sent by the secured party to the debtor, if he has not signed after default a statement renouncing or modifying his right to notification of sale. In the case of consumer goods no other notification need be sent. In other cases notification shall be sent to any other secured party from whom the secured party has received (before sending his notification to the debtor or before the debtor's renunciation of his rights) written notice of a claim of an interest in the collateral. The secured party may buy at any public sale and if the collateral is of a type customarily sold in a recognized market or is of a type which is the subject of widely distributed standard price quotations he may buy at private sale.

(4) When collateral is disposed of by a secured party after default, the disposition transfers to a purchaser for value all of the debtor's rights therein, discharges the security interest under which it is made and any security interest or lien subordinate thereto. The purchaser takes free of all such rights and interests even though the secured party fails to comply with the requirements of this Part or of any judicial proceedings

(a) in the case of a public sale, if the purchaser has no knowledge of any defects in the sale and if he does not buy in collusion with the secured party, other bidders or the person conducting the sale; or

(b) in any other case, if the purchaser acts in good faith.

(5) A person who is liable to a secured party under a guaranty, indorsement, repurchase agreement or the like and who receives a transfer of collateral from the secured party or is subrogated to his rights has thereafter the rights and duties of the secured party. Such a transfer of collateral is not a sale or disposition of the collateral under this Article.

Section 9–505. Compulsory Disposition of Collateral; Acceptance of the Collateral as Discharge of Obligation

(1) If the debtor has paid sixty per cent of the cash price in the case of a purchase money security interest in consumer goods or sixty per cent of the loan in the case of another security interest in consumer goods, and has not signed after default a statement renouncing or modifying his rights under this Part a secured party who has taken possession of collateral must dispose of it under Section 9–504 and if he fails to do so within ninety days after he takes possession the debtor at his option may recover in conversion or under Section 9–507(1) on secured party's liability.

(2) In any other case involving consumer goods or any other collateral a secured party in possession may, after default, propose to retain the collateral in satisfaction of the obligation. Written notice of such proposal shall be sent to the debtor if he has not signed after default a statement renouncing or modifying his rights under this subsection. In the case of consumer goods no other notice need be given. In other cases notice shall be sent to any other secured party from whom the secured party has received (before sending his notice to the debtor or before the debtor's renunciation of his rights) written notice of a claim of an interest in the collateral. If the secured party receives objection in writing from a person entitled to receive notification within twenty-one days after the notice was sent, the secured party must dispose of the collateral under Section 9–504. In the absence of such written objection the secured party may retain the collateral in satisfaction of the debtor's obligation.

Section 9–506. Debtor's Right to Redeem Collateral

At any time before the secured party has disposed of collateral or entered into a contract for its disposition under Section 9–504 or before the obligation has been discharged under Section 9–505(2) the debtor or any other secured party may unless otherwise agreed in writing after default redeem the collateral by tendering fulfillment of all obligations secured by the collateral as well as the expenses reasonably incurred by the secured party in retaking, holding and preparing the collateral for disposition, in arranging for the sale, and to the extent provided in the agreement and not prohibited by law, his reasonable attorneys' fees and legal expenses.

Section 9–507. Secured Party's Liability for Failure to Comply with This Part

(1) If it is established that the secured party is not proceeding in accordance with the provisions of this Part disposition may be ordered or restrained on appropriate terms and conditions. If the disposition has occurred the debtor or any person entitled to notification or whose security interest has been made known to the secured party prior to the disposition has a right to recover from the secured party any loss caused by a failure to comply with the provisions of this Part. If the collateral is consumer goods, the debtor has a right to recover in any event an amount not less than the credit service charge plus ten per cent of the principal amount of the debt or the time price differential plus 10 per cent of the cash price.

(2) The fact that a better price could have been obtained by a sale at a different time or in a different method from that selected by the secured party is not of itself sufficient to establish that the sale was not made in a commercially reasonable manner. If the secured party either sells the collateral in the usual manner in any recognized market therefor or if he sells at the price current in such market at the time of his sale or if he has otherwise sold in conformity with reasonable commercial practices among dealers in the type of property sold he has sold in a commercially reasonable manner. The principles stated in the two preceding sentences with respect to sales also apply as may be appropriate to other types of disposition. A disposition which has been approved in any judicial proceeding or by any bona fide creditors' committee or representative of creditors shall conclusively be deemed to be commercially reasonable, but this sentence does not indicate that any such approval must be obtained in any case nor does it indicate that any disposition not so approved is not commercially reasonable.

[Articles 10 and 11 are omitted as unnecessary.]

GLOSSARY OF LEGAL TERMS AND DEFINITIONS

A

ab initio from the beginning

abandoned property discarded goods in which the owner has voluntarily relinquished all interest **417**

abstract of title a record of the history of the title to land as found in official records **1014**

abuse of civil legal process to make excessive and improper use of the right to sue in an attempt to exhaust someone into submission

acceptance the offeree's expressed assent to the offer in reliance on and in compliance with the offer **149**

acceptor the drawee on a draft who has assented in writing on the draft to pay it **602**

accession the increase in property by what it produces or by the addition of other property to it **399**

accommodation party a person who signs commercial paper as an accommodation to another person whose signature is on the instrument for the purpose of assisting the latter to obtain credit **609**

accord a new contract providing that, on its performance, a previous contract as well as the new contract are discharged **245**

accord and satisfaction a new contract (accord) that discharges a party from a previous contractual obligation; the old contract is discharged (satisfied) **180, 245, 710**

account a right to payment under a contract; "any right to payment for goods sold or leased or for services rendered which is not evidenced by an instrument or chattel paper, whether or not it has been earned by performance" UCC 9–106 **245, 1056**

account stated an account that has been settled and the matured items and balance expressly or impliedly agreed to by the parties **245**

accretion a method of obtaining title to another's land caused by gradual changes in the natural boundaries of such land **1017**

acknowledgement the formal written declaration, admission, or confirmation made by a person to a proper public official (usually a notary public) that he executed a particular legal instrument

act of God an unexpected force of nature **425**

action a judicial proceeding concerning legal interests

action to quiet title a legal proceeding initiated by a claimant to title in land affording any adverse parties opportunity to prove a claim to interest in the land or thereafter be barred from doing so **1019**

actual authority express and implied authority **292, 826**

ad litem during the action

additional living expense a homeowner's insurance policy provision that covers living expenses incurred by a homeowner forced to leave the home while repairs are being made **1117**

adhesion contract a standard form contract in which the weaker party has no realistic choice or opportunity to bargain **172, 1202**

adjudged the result of a formal legal process **190**

adjudicate to determine by judicial authority **669**

administrative law rules and regulations created by an administrative agency, thereby becoming law **33**

administrator (administratrix) a court-appointed man (woman) who acts as the intestate's personal representative **219, 1148**

administrator (administratrix) with the will annexed a court-appointed man (woman), who was not designated in a decedent's will, who acts as the decedent's personal representative **1148**

adverse possession a method of acquiring title to land by actual, exclusive, and continuous possession of land under color of title adverse or hostile to the true owner in an open and notorious manner for a statutory period of time **1015**

affiant the person who makes and signs an affidavit **1163**

affidavit the formal written statement of a person voluntarily confirmed by oath or affirmation before a public official with authority to administer oaths or affirmations (usually a notary public)

after-acquired property in security, property acquired after the security agreement is made **1057**

agency a legal relationship between two persons who agree that one is to act on behalf of the other, subject to the other's control **290, 826**

agent a person authorized to act on behalf of another and subject to the other's control; *see* **general agent, professional agent, special agent, universal agent 145, 290, 354, 826**

agreement a manifestation of mutual assent between parties by offer and acceptance **120**

air space, right to ownership of the air space above the surface of land

amicus curaie friend of the court

annuity an insurance policy that pays the insured a designated amount periodically, beginning at a date set in the policy **1100**

anticipatory breach a party's material breach of contract made by the party's repudiation before performance is due **239**

anticipatory repudiation a party's manifestation of an intent not to perform a contractual obligation, made before his or her performance is due; *see* **repudiation 270, 514**

antitrust laws laws that limit monopolies, combinations, and unfair restraints to help prevent the undue concentration of economic power **728**

apparent authority the power of a person (*A*) to act as though *A* were an agent, created by another's (*P*'s) manifestation to a third person (*T*) that *A* is *P*'s agent **292, 311, 811**

appellant a party who appeals a case decision against him or her **5, 1248**

appellee (respondent) a party against whom an appeal is taken **5, 1248**

applicant an individual or a firm seeking governmental permission to engage in some activity **774**

apprentice a student learning a particular craft **754**

arbitration a method for deciding disputes outside of court by persons called arbitrators, appointed by the disputing parties **20, 246, 1203**

arson the willful and malicious burning of the dwelling house of another (at common law); today, by statute, arson incudes one's own house and the buildings of another **67**

articles of incorporation the written application to the state for permission to incorporate **895**

artisan's lien a person's possessory lien on goods owned by another and improved at the owner's request

assault an unprivileged act by a person intentionally causing another to apprehend an immediate harmful or offensive bodily contact to the other **78**

assent a person's manifestation of approval of something; *see* **mutual assent** **81**

assignee the person to whom a contract right is transferred; in realty, the person to whom *all* the remaining term of a lease is transferred **257, 1031, 1056**

assignment the transfer of a contract right; in realty, a transfer by the lessee of *all* the remaining term of the lease **257, 1031, 1056**

assignor the transferor of a contract right; in realty, one who transfers *all* the remaining term of the lease **257, 1031**

assumption of a lease an agreement by an assignee with the assignor to become bound by all the terms and conditions in the original lease **1032**

assumption of risk voluntarily assuming a known risk of harm **87, 569**

attachment the seizure of tangible property by a proper public officer (usually a sheriff) pursuant to a writ of attachment pending an action

attempt in criminal law, a preparatory crime **70**

attest to witness **1140**

attractive nuisance a dangerous and attractive condition of realty that may lure children into trespassing **995**

auction a public sale of property by public outcry to the highest bidder **142**

auctioneer a person licensed by law to sell property of another at a public sale **295**

authority an agent's power to act for the principal in accordance with the principal's manifestation of consent to the agent; *see* **actual authority, apparent authority, customary authority, express authority, implied authority, incidental authority** **292, 310**

automobile liability insurance insurance that covers a driver who injures someone, or damages someone's property, in an automobile accident **1119**

avoid to void, annul

B

bad faith dishonesty in fact in the conduct or transaction concerned **1171**

bailee the person to whom goods are bailed **143, 410, 480, 1073**

bailee's lien the bailee's legal right to retain possession of the bailed goods as security for the obligation owing to the bailee, usually payment for the bailee's services and for materials supplied to the bailed goods **1073**

bailment a delivery of goods by a bailor to a bailee, which are to be returned to the bailor or as the bailor directs, in accordance with the bailment agreement **143, 295, 410, 928, 1073, 1160**

bailor the person who bails goods **143, 410**

bank *see* **collecting bank, depositary bank, intermediary bank, payor bank, presenting bank**

bankruptcy a federal procedure whereby a debtor's nonexempt assets are gathered together and used to discharge the debtor from most of his or her debts **1086**

bargain/negotiate terms used to indicate that both parties to a sales contract are aware of all the terms of the contract and that both parties exchanged value to establish the terms **466**

bargaining unit a group of employees appropriately joined together for the purpose of collective bargaining **758**

battery an act by a person intentionally causing harmful or offensive bodily contact with another **77**

bearer the person in possession of an instrument, document of title, or certificated security payable or deliverable to bearer or indorsed in blank (a signature without additional words) **430, 608**

beneficiary a person who is to receive a benefit; in insurance, the person designated in a life insurance policy to receive the death benefit **264, 406, 1116, 1160**

bid an offer; unless otherwise specifically indicated an auction is "with reserve," the auctioneer reserving the right to accept or reject any bid and a bid is an *offer;* while in an auction "without reserve" the auctioneer does not reserve such right and a bid is an *acceptance* of the auctioneer's offer to sell—in both auctions a bid may be withdrawn until the auctioneer announces completion of the sale

bilateral contract a contract in which the consideration is mutual promises **124**

bill of lading a document issued to the shipper by a carrier of goods **428, 493, 1195**

bill of sale a formal document used to transfer title to personal property **398**

binder an insurance company's memorandum of an oral contract of insurance pending the issuance of a formal policy

blank indorsement an indorsement that does not specify any particular indorsee; *see* **indorsement** **635**

blue-sky laws state laws regulating the sale and transfer of securities **940**

bona fide in good faith **358**

bona fide purchaser a purchaser for value in good faith and without notice of any adverse claim or defense with respect to what is being purchased; in corporations, a purchaser for value in good faith and without notice of any adverse claim, and who is either a holder of a certificated security or registered on the corporate books as the owner **936**

boycott the act of a combination of persons to cause business harm to another by refraining from doing business with that other and inducing others to do likewise; *see* **group boycott**

breach of contract wrongful nonperformance of a contractual promise **237, 269, 334**

breach of the peace a disturbance of public order by an act of violence, or by an act likely to produce violence, or which, by causing consternation and alarm, disturbs the peace and quiet of the community **1074**

breach of trust a trustee's violation of a trust duty **1170**

bribery the offering, giving, receiving, or soliciting of anything of value to influence action as an official or in discharge of legal or public duty **70**

broker a person authorized to represent another and negotiate for him or her with others **295**

bulk transfer "any transfer in bulk and not in the ordinary course of the transferor's business of a major part of the materials, supplies, merchandise or other inventory of an enterprise subject to Article 6" UCC 6–102(1) **503**

burglary the breaking and entering in the night of the structure (e.g., building) of another with the intent to commit a felony therein **70**

business interruption insurance insurance that covers lost revenues when a business is closed as the result of property damage **1102**

buyer in ordinary course of business "a person who, in good faith and without knowledge that the sale to him is in violation of the ownership rights or security interest of a third party in the goods, buys in ordinary course from a person in the business of selling goods of that kind but does not include a pawnbroker;" buying does not include a transfer for a past debt UCC 1–201(9) **484, 1073**

bylaws in corporations, rules and regulations of a corporation for its internal management and operation **898**

C

C.&F. cost plus freight **493**

C.I.F. cost, insurance, freight **493**

C.O.D. collect on delivery **483**

cancellation the nullification of a contractual obligation **249, 664**

capacity the legal ability to make a contract **119, 190**

capital corporate net assets

capital stock *see* **stated capital**

cartel a combination of private enterprises or states to control production, price, or distribution of like commodities or services **1208**

case law the law that comes from decided cases **34, 1193**

cashier's check a check drawn by a bank on itself and payable to the order of a payee **604**

caveat emptor let the buyer beware **131, 562**

caveat venditor let the seller beware **131**

certainty of terms test the promise must have certainty of terms in what it promises and what it asks for **141**

certificate of deposit a written "acknowledgement by a bank of receipt of money with an engagement to repay it," and which is in compliance with the UCC as being a negotiable instrument UCC 3–104(2)(c)

certiorari, writ of an appellate court's certification to an inferior court that a case will be reviewed by the appellate court

cestui que trust the beneficiary of a trust **1165**

challenge in a jury trial, objection by a party to an action to persons chosen for service on a jury to try a case who have not been selected properly, or who are not qualified or impartial **32**

Chapter 11 plan a plan for the reorganization of a business **1094**

Chapter 13 plan a plan for the payment of debts proposed by an individual as an alternative to a straight bankruptcy **1093**

charitable trust a trust created for a charitable purpose **1172**

charter articles of incorporation approved by the state **898**

chattel a tangible, movable thing **80, 396, 654, 1164**

chattel paper a writing or writings that evidence both a monetary obligation and a security interest in or lease of specific goods UCC 9–105(1)(b) **1056**

check a negotiable "draft drawn on a bank and payable on demand" UCC 3–104(2)(b) **69, 122, 598**

chose in action intangible personal property, such as an account receivable **1164**

close corporation a corporation in which managerial control is in the hands of the owners or shareholders **881**

closed container rule a bailee is not responsible for the contents of a closed container unless the bailee knows or should know the contents **412**

closed shop an employer who, by agreement with a union, will employ only union members **754**

code a comprehensive, systematic collection of statutes in a particular legal area **448**

codicil a writing executed with the same formality as a will, expressly referring to a prior will, by its terms either partially revoking or adding to the prior will by making changes or additions to the will and thereby becoming a supplemental part of the will to the extent of such changes or additions, or entirely revoking the prior will **1145**

collateral property subject to a security interest UCC 9–105(1)(c) **712, 1054**

collecting bank "any bank handling the item for collection except the payor bank" UCC 4–105(d) **612**

collision insurance insurance covering damage to the insured automobile resulting from a collision **1119**

Comments to the UCC comments that appear at the end of the Code sections; they are not part of the official Code, but they are provided by the drafters to help explain and interpret the Code **448**

commercial frustration an excuse offered by a party to a contract justifying nonperformance of an obligation, usually because performance has been made impossible in fact **241**

commercial unit "such a unit of goods as by commercial usage is a single whole for purposes of sale and division of which materially impairs its character or value on the market or in use" UCC 2–105(6) **496, 515**

common carrier a carrier that offers its services to the general public for a fee **424**

common law principles of nonstatutory law reflecting the customs and usages of society and found in judicial decisions **33, 121, 365, 454, 803, 1193**

common stock corporate stock with the ordinary rights of participation in a corporation; *see* **share of stock** **926**

community property a form of ownership by husband and wife of property acquired by their efforts during their marriage **405, 985**

comparative negligence a statute or doctrine in which negligence is measured in terms of percentage **87**

compensatory damages the money judicially awarded to an injured party to compensate for damage caused by another's wrongful conduct; *see* **damages** **270**

complaint the first pleading in a civil action **29, 1243**

composition (outside of bankruptcy) an agreement among some or all of the creditors with their insolvent or financially embarrassed debtor, each to take something less than what is owed to him or her and, on the debtor's performance, the debtor is discharged fully as to those creditors who are parties to the agreement **180**

comprehensive insurance insurance covering damage to the insured automobile resulting from causes other than collision **1119**

compromise an agreement resolving a dispute outside of court reached through concessions offered by the aggrieved parties **19**

concealment in insurance, the insured's intentional failure to disclose a material fact to the insurer **1107**

condemnation forcing a property owner to transfer property to a government in exchange for just compensation **991, 1015**

condition an uncertain event on the occurrence of which a contractual obligation is made contingent or dependent; *see* **condition concurrent, condition precedent,** and **condition subsequent 242, 492, 1027**

condition concurrent a condition that must occur at the same time as another condition; *see* **condition 243, 492**

condition precedent a condition that must occur or not occur before a dependent promise becomes performable; *see* **condition 243**

condition subsequent a condition, on the occurrence or nonoccurrence of which, after a promise becomes performable, excuses the duty of performance; *see* **condition 243**

conditional estate an estate where ownership is dependent upon some act or event **986**

conditional receipt a receipt that provides an applicant for life insurance with temporary coverage until the application is approved by the company **1115**

conditional sale a sale in which the seller reserves title until the buyer completes payments; now called a secured transaction under Article 9 of the Uniform Commercial Code **1057**

confession of judgment a party's consent to jurisdiction and judgment of a court without a trial in a civil case **252, 619, 828**

confirmation an assuring expression of understanding **456**

confirmation hearing the hearing at which a Chapter 13 plan is considered by the court **1093**

conforming goods those goods that are produced and tendered in accordance with the obligations under the contract **492**

confusion the mixing of chattels of like kind of different persons so that the chattels of one person cannot be distinguished from the chattels of the other persons **400**

consent a person's approval of something, made with full capacity, freely, and without fraud or mistake; in torts, such approval permitting what would otherwise be an intentional tort **81**

consequential (special) damages the money judicially awarded to an injured party for loss that the breaching party reasonably could foresee would be a result of his or her breach; *see* **damages 132, 270, 521**

consideration the legal price bargained for a promise and inducing a party to enter into a contract **119, 174**

consignee one to whom goods are shipped **427**

consignment the shipment of goods from one person to another **425, 463**

consignor one who ships goods to another **425**

consolidation in corporations, the combination of two or more corporations forming a new corporation **904**

conspiracy (criminal) a combination of persons for the purpose of committing an unlawful act **755**

constructive eviction a tenant's moving out of leased premises because the landlord caused the premises to become unfit for their intended use by the tenant **1028, 1036**

constructive notice knowledge of a fact presumed or imputed by law **1035, 1060**

consumer a person who buys goods for use primarily for personal, family, or household purposes **540**

consumer goods goods that "are used or bought for use primarily for personal, family, or household purposes" UCC 9–109(1) **1055**

contingent claim a claim not certain of occurring, depending on a possible future event **1089**

contract a promise that the law recognizes as creating a legal obligation of performance; *see* **"contract" of chance, contract under seal, executed contract, executory contract, express contract, formal contract, implied contract,** and **simple contract 121**

"contract" of chance an agreement creating a risk of loss **208**

contract to sell a contract to transfer title to goods in the future

contract under seal a contract that has a symbol attached to it attesting that it is a binding obligation **174**

contractual capacity *see* **capacity**

contribution in suretyship, the right of sureties who have paid the creditor to collect part of the payment from other sureties **1080**

contributory negligence plaintiff's conduct that falls below the standard to which he or she should conform for his or her own protection and that is a legally contributing cause with the defendant's negligence causing the plaintiff's harm; *see* **negligence 7, 86, 569**

conversion the tort of intentional interference with another's right to possession, control, and dominion of a chattel **339, 402, 484, 654**

conveyance the transfer of an interest in land

copyright a governmental grant of protection of original works in a tangible medium of expression **91, 542, 1205**

corporate express powers those powers specifically stated in the corporation's articles of incorporation and in the corporation statutes **912**

corporate implied powers those powers reasonably necessary to carry out the express powers **912**

corporation a legal entity created by statute authorizing an association of persons to carry on an enterprise; *see* **close corporation, *de jure* corporation, *de facto* corporation, professional corporation, subsidiary corporation 291, 752, 876**

cost-plus contract a contract in which the price is the cost of production or performance (whatever it turns out to be) plus an agreed-upon profit **142**

costs in litigation, allowable recoverable expense by a party in a legal proceeding

counterclaim a claim asserted by the defendant against the plaintiff's claim in a civil action **29, 225, 518, 1245**

counteroffer an offer that rejects a previous offer **145**

course of dealing "a sequence of previous conduct between the parties to a particular transaction which is fairly to be regarded as establishing a common basis of understanding for interpreting their expressions and other conduct" UCC 1–205(1) **150, 228, 475**

course of performance "where the contract for sale involves repeated occasions for performance by either party with knowledge of the nature of the performance and opportunity for objection to it by the other, any course of performance accepted or acquiesed in without objection shall be relevant to determine the meaning of the agreement" UCC 2–208(1) **475**

court a judicial tribunal **25**

covenant a promise as a part of a contract **994, 1027**

covenant running with the land the promise of an owner of land that binds future owners of the same land **994**

cover to seek a substitute performance of a contract **239, 519**

creditor one to whom money is owed **264**

creditors' committee in bankruptcy, a committee elected by the creditors to advise the trustee in bankruptcy **1088**

crime an act, committed or omitted, in violation of a public law governing it; *see* **felony** and **misdemeanor** **63, 205, 1164**

crime insurance insurance that protects the insured from losses due to criminal acts, such as burglary, against the insured **1102**

criminal conspiracy a combination of persons for the purpose of committing an unlawful act **755**

cross-examination a party's initial examination of a witness other than the party's own in a trial **32**

cumulative voting a method of voting whereby a shareholder has as many votes as he or she has shares of voting stock multiplied by the number of directors to be elected **929**

cure a seller's correction of his or her failure to deliver conforming goods under a contract for sale before the due date has expired **481, 497**

custom *see* **usage of trade**

customary authority implied authority to do those acts that conform to the general custom or usage; *see* **authority** **310, 811**

cy pres an equitable trust doctrine applicable particularly in charitable trusts whereby, by court order, the general trust purpose will be carried out as nearly as possible in accordance with the settlor's intent when the particular trust purpose cannot be carried out **1173**

D

d/b/a/ doing business as

damage loss or harm **270, 520**

damages the money judicially awarded to an injured party for another's wrongful conduct; *see* **compensatory damages, consequential (special) damages, incidental damages, liquidated damages, nominal damages,** and **punitive (exemplary) damages** **77, 239, 270, 327, 402, 1247**

***de facto* corporation** a corporation that has not complied substantially with the mandatory requirements of a valid state incorporation statute but has made a colorable attempt to do so, in good faith, and has begun to operate as a corporation **899**

***de jure* corporation** a corporation that has completely or substantially complied with the mandatory requirements of a valid state incorporation statute **899**

de novo anew; a trial de novo is a new trial

debtor one who owes money to another

decedent one who is dead **219, 1134**

deceit the tort of knowingly misrepresenting a material fact, intending to mislead another person by inducing the other person to rely on the misrepresentation and to act in a particular business transaction, causing financial damage to the other person **271, 333**

deed a formal document used to transfer title to real estate **397, 1000**

defamation a person's unprivileged, wrongful publication to a second person of a false and defamatory statement concerning a third person, harmful to the third person's reputation **50**

default a failure to perform a legal duty **222, 668**

defendant the party against whom a civil suit (or criminal action) is brought **5, 29, 1244**

deficiency judgment a judgment after foreclosure, against the borrower, for the remaining unpaid balance of the mortgage loan **1007**

defined benefit plan a plan under which the employee contributes an annual payment to the plan based upon a benefit expected to be received upon retirement **883**

defined contribution plan a plan under which the employer is required to contribute a specific amount annually to the plan for the employee's retirement **883**

delegation the transfer of one's duty to another, the transferor still being responsible for the duty **259, 314**

delivery a voluntary transfer of possession; in realty, the voluntary transfer of a deed with the intent thereby to transfer ownership of the realty **1002**

demise in realty, to lease or rent; in wills, trusts, and estates, death **1022, 1181**

demurrer a pleading that states that a preceding pleading does not state a cause of action

dependent promise a promise the performance of which is dependent upon the occurrence of a condition **242**

deposit rule an acceptance is effective when sent, though never received, if an authorized medium is timely used by the offeree **151**

depositary bank "the first bank to which an item is transferred for collection even though it is also the payor bank" UCC 4–105(a) **611**

deposition a written statement made by a person under oath or affirmation in a judicial proceeding where there is opportunity for cross-examination before trial **1245**

detriment the doing, or forbearing from doing, something by a party who had no previous legal obligation so to do or refrain from doing **175**

devise a testamentary gift of real property **1143**

devisee the beneficiary of a testamentary gift of real property **1143**

dictum that portion of a judge's opinion in a case that is not necessary to the decision of the case **1216**

directed verdict a jury verdict as directed by the judge **1247**

disaffirm to nullify one's previous consent **192**

discharge in contracts, termination of a contractual duty to perform a promise; under the UCC, cancellation and termination; in bankruptcy, a court order releasing the individual debtor from his or her debts after the estate has been liquidated and distributed **149, 236, 260, 708, 1091**

disclaimer denial of an obligation or a claim **415, 1165**

disclosed principal a person known, or who reasonably should be known, by a third party to be a principal for an agent **328**

dishonor the refusal of the drawee to accept the draft, or of the drawee, acceptor, or maker to pay the draft or note **607, 703**

distributor an independent contractor who sells on his or her own account, independent of the seller of goods to him or her **1196**

dividend a portion of corporate net profits or surplus set aside for distribution to the shareholders **926, 931**

divisible contract a contract that provides that performance of less than all the obligations on one side will become due by performance of less than all the obligations on the other side **212**

document of title a document evidencing that the person possessing it "is entitled to receive, hold, and dispose of the document and the goods it covers" UCC 1–201(15) **428, 1057, 1195**

documentary draft "any negotiable or nonnegotiable draft with accompanying documents, securities or other papers to be delivered against honor of the draft" UCC 4–104(f) **495**

domicile the state in which a person has his or her permanent home, not merely a residence **1135**

dominant tenement property that is benefited by an easement appurtenant in nearby land **989**

donee the recipient of a gift **264, 400**

donor the person who makes a gift **264, 400**

dower a widow's life estate in a portion of the land of her deceased husband; at common law but generally abolished by statute today **1003**

dowry traditionally, property that the wife brings to the marriage

draft a negotiable instrument containing an unconditional order (e.g., "pay") **598**

drawee the person on whom a draft is drawn and ordered to pay **69, 599**

drawer the person who initially draws or creates and signs a draft **69, 599**

due negotiation delivery of a negotiable document of title to a holder who purchases it for value, in good faith, and without notice of any claim or defense to the document **430**

durable power of attorney a statutory written power of attorney that will not terminate upon the principal's incapacity **297**

duress wrongful inducement to do that which a reasonable person would have been unable to resist **66, 166, 669**

duty a legal obligation not to interfere with another person's interest **257**

E

easement an irrevocable right to the limited use of another's land **220, 462, 988**

eleemosynary charitable, benevolent

emancipated minor a minor whose parents have given up their rights to take care of the minor and to have custody of and to claim the minor's earnings **156, 198**

embezzlement depriving someone of his or her property through breach of a trust relationship **69**

emblements what is sown and produced on the land **1029**

eminent domain government power to appropriate private land for public use on payment of just compensation without the owner's consent **1015**

employee as generally used, a servant agent, although some statutes are interpreted to give it a wider meaning **354**

employer a principal, or more specifically a master **354**

encumbrance a person's right in another person's property **546, 1003**

endowment insurance insurance that pays the policyholder a lump sum at a specified date **1114**

enforce to compel performance **205**

enforceable contract a contract that can be proved and enforced by the courts **218**

enjoining an order from a court to desist from doing

equipment goods that "are used or bought for use primarily in business (including farming or a profession) . . ." UCC 9–109(2) **1056**

equitable estoppel a doctrine that operates to prevent a person from denying anything to the contrary of that which, by the person's own deeds, acts, or representations, has been set forward as the truth **458**

equity principles of justice and fairness that developed when the relief at common law was inadequate **181**

escheat the transfer of property to the state when a person dies without heirs **399, 1015**

escrow the conditional delivery of property to a person who is to deal with it on the occurrence of specified conditions **277, 1031**

estate in realty, a bundle of ownership rights in, or powers over, realty; in bankruptcy, the debtor's legal or equitable interest in property on the date the case commences **986, 1087**

estoppel a principle of law stating that when one person "holds out" (represents) a material fact to another person, who changes his or her position materially to his or her prejudice in reasonable reliance on the holding out, the first person is "estopped" (prohibited) to deny what he or she asserted previously **403, 685, 809, 900**

et al. abbreviation of a Latin phrase meaning "and another" or "and others"

eviction the dispossession of a tenant from the leased premises **1027, 1037**

evidence a fact from which an inference can be drawn of another fact **32, 1247**

exclusive–dealing contract an agreement between a seller or lessor and a purchaser or lessee that the latter shall not use or deal in products of a competing seller or lessor **730**

exculpate to relieve from liability **1202**

exculpatory clause a clause that relieves a party from liability **169, 209, 512, 1030, 1171**

executed contract a contract that has been performed by all the parties to it; *see* **contract** **130, 236**

executor (executrix) a court-appointed man (woman) designated in a decedent's will as the decedent's personal representative **219, 406, 1148**

executory contract a contract that has not been performed by all the parties to it; *see* **contract** **130, 229, 237**

exemplary damages *see* **punitive damages**

exemption in bankruptcy, a debtor's property that is not liquidated and not distributed to creditors in bankruptcy **1090**

exoneration in suretyship, the surety's right to have a court compel the debtor to perform his or her promise to the surety to perform the debtor's obligation to his or her creditor to the extent of the debtor's available assets **1079**

express authority an agent's authority specifically expressed in the principal's manifestation to the agent; *see* **authority** **310, 826**

express contract an actual agreement of parties, the terms of which are stated in distinct and explicit language, either oral or in writing; *see* **contract** **124**

express trust a fiduciary relationship between persons in connection with property whereby one person called the "settlor" by his or her manifestation of intention causes property to be held by a person called the "trustee" for the benefit of a person called a "beneficiary" or *"cestui que trust,"* the trustee being under a duty so to deal with the property **1161**

express warranty a warranty expressed by a party; *see* **warranty** **542**

expropriation the taking of an owner's property by the government **1204**

F

F.A.S. free alongside **493**

F.O.B. free on board **483, 493**

factor a person in business for him- or herself with authority to buy goods, or to sell goods in his or her possession, in his or her own name for another **295**

factual impossibility the facts prevent performance of the promise **128**

false imprisonment (false arrest) an unprivileged act intentionally restraining the movement of another who is aware of such restraint **79**

farm products "crops or livestock or supplies used or produced in farming operations . . . in the possession of a debtor engaged in . . . farming operations" UCC 9–109(3) **1056**

featherbedding make-work arrangements for employees when there is no work for them to perform or their services are not required **760**

federal district court the trial level court of the federal legal system **27**

Federal Trade Commission a government body that monitors unfair competition and commercial practices **733**

fee simple absolute the greatest bundle of ownership rights in, and powers over, realty **986**

felony a serious crime for which, usually, the punishment can be more than one year in prison; *see* **crime** **63**

fiduciary a person with a duty to act primarily for the benefit of another **23, 167, 211, 292, 316, 667, 841, 895, 930, 1160**

financing statement a document filed by the secured party to give public notice of the security interest in personal property **1060**

firm offer under the UCC, a merchant's signed irrevocable offer to buy or sell goods, giving assurance that it will be kept open; consideration is not required, and its maximum time is three months **147, 470**

fixture a chattel that, under real estate law, has become permanently attached to realty and thus ceases to be a chattel and becomes part of the realty; it still can be used as collateral for a security interest **396, 982, 1071**

fixture filing filing a financing statement in the office where mortgages are recorded **1071**

floating lien a security device that covers after-acquired property and future advances **1057**

foreclosure the cutting off of an owner's interest in realty by sale pursuant to court decree **1006**

forfeiture to lose a legal right as a penalty **238**

forgery the unauthorized act of imitating or altering a writing with the intent to defraud and impose liability **69, 644**

formal contract a contract that must be in a certain form; *see* **contract** **122, 327, 596**

franchise a business relationship between a franchisor, who markets goods or services through a franchisee, who has the right to use the franchisor's trade name, trademark, and methods of operation **858**

fraud in contracts, a misrepresentation of fact, known to be false, intentionally made to induce another person to make or refrain from making a contract, and reasonably relied on by the other person **164, 219, 335**

freehold "an interest in land for a period of time the termination of which cannot be measured or computed exactly in terms of years, months, and days, and which is not terminable at the will of the transferor" Restatement of Property, sec. 8

freehold estates fee simple absolute, conditional, and life estates **1022**

fungible goods every unit of goods is the equivalent of any other like unit, either actually or by contract **412, 479, 570**

future goods "goods which are not both existing and identified" to the contract UCC 2–105(2) **452**

G

garnishee the person against whom a writ of garnishment is issued

garnishment a statutory proceeding begun by a judgment creditor to reach the intangible assets of the judgment debtor—e.g., the debtor's right to his or her salary—by writ of garnishment **1087**

general agent universal agent; an agent authorized to conduct a series of transactions involving a continuity of service **300**

general intangibles a catchall category covering a variety of personal property **1056**

general lien a lien on property other than the property on which services were rendered; *see* **lien**

general partnership a partnership as defined by the UPA; *see* **partnership** **802**

genuineness of assent reality of consent to an offer or acceptance **160**

gift a voluntary transfer of personal or real property by someone who is not to receive anything in return **400, 450**

gift causa mortis a conditional, revocable gift by someone facing imminent death from a present illness or impending peril **401**

good faith "honesty in fact in the conduct or transaction concerned" UCC 1–201(19) **484, 666**

goods tangible, movable things **120, 450, 1055, 1194**

grand jury a group of people selected to decide whether to recommend criminal prosecution of specified persons for the commission of crimes

grant in realty, a conveyance by deed **986**

grantee the person to whom a grant has been made **986**

grantor the person who has made a grant **986**

group boycott a concerted effort by a number of firms to avoid doing business with a particular individual or firm; *see* **boycott** **729**

guarantee (noun) the person to whom a guaranty is made; (verb) to make a guaranty

guarantor a type of surety **1076**

guaranty a type of suretyship **1076**

guardian a person legally entrusted with the custody and/or the property of another **196, 406, 1135**

guardian ad litem guardian for the legal action, appointed by a court

H

habendum that portion of a deed indicating the encumbrances burdening the estate **1005**

harm *see* **damage**

hearsay a matter not personally known but heard from others **744**

heirs persons who, by statute, are entitled to property not disposed of by a decedent's will **984, 1147**

historical school of jurisprudence a school of thought suggesting that law evolves from a nation's history **7**

holder "a person who is in possession of a document of title or an instrument or a certificated investment security drawn, issued, or indorsed to him or his order or to bearer or in blank" UCC 1–201(20); in corporations, the person in possession of a certificated security that flows to him or her either initially or by endorsement **608, 662, 937**

holder in due course (HIDC) the holder of a negotiable instrument who takes it for value, in good faith, and without notice that the instrument is overdue or has been dishonored or of any defense against, or claim to, the instrument by any person **597, 609, 635, 662**

holographic will a will that is entirely in the testator's handwriting **1138**

horizontal merger a merger of competing firms **731**

hot cargo agreement an agreement between an employer and a union that the employer is not to handle or otherwise deal with goods of another employer **761**

I

illegal contrary to law **205, 1164**

immunity exemption from liability **88**

implied authority an agent's authority that the agent reasonably can understand he or she has from the principal's manifestation to the agent, but not expressed therein; *see* **authority 310, 826**

implied contract an explicit agreement found from acts or conduct making it reasonable to conclude that a contract exists; *see* **contract 124**

implied warranty a warranty imposed by law; *see* **warranty 543**

impossibility performance cannot factually be done **241**

impostor (impersonator) a person who misrepresents himself or herself as another person **648**

in personam against the person **27**

in re in the matter of

in rem against the thing **27**

incidental authority implied authority to do what is incidental in carrying out the express authority; *see* **authority 310**

incidental damages the money judicially awarded to a nonbreaching party for expenses reasonably incurred by the nonbreaching party on the other party's breach; *see* **damages 270, 521**

incontestability clause a clause in a life insurance policy providing that the company may not contest coverage after the policy has been in effect for a stated time period **1115**

incorporator a persons who signs the articles of incorporation **895**

indemnity an absolute obligation to pay for another's loss **320, 710, 838, 1171**

independent contractor a person who contracts independently for him- or herself to render a result, and who is not acting on behalf of another nor subject to another's control **294, 334, 1196**

independent promise a promise the performance of which is not dependent upon the occurrence of a condition **242**

indorsee the person named by an indorser on an instrument to whom it is to be paid **608**

indorsement the indorser's signature on an instrument (or on a paper attached to it); *see* **blank indorsement, qualified indorsement, restrictive indorsement, special indorsement 608**

indorser the person who signs on an instrument (or on a paper attached to it) other than as a maker, drawer, or acceptor **607**

injunction a court order requiring a person to do or not to do something **269, 756**

injury the wrongful invasion of another person's interest **270, 541**

inland marine insurance insurance that covers goods that are being shipped **1102**

innkeeper operator of an establishment engaged in making lodging accommodations available to travelers **433**

insolvency in bankruptcy, when a debtor's assets are less than his or her liabilities; when the debtor "either has ceased to pay his debts in the ordinary course of business or cannot pay his debts as they become due or is insolvent within the meaning of the federal bankruptcy law" UCC 1–201(23) and Restatement (Second) of Contracts, sec. 252(2) **502, 607, 1089**

insolvent *see* **insolvency**

installment contract "one which requires or authorizes the delivery of goods in separate lots to be separately accepted" UCC 2–612(1) **497**

instrument a writing that evidences a right to payment of money, including negotiable instruments, and also certificated securities **1057**

insurable interest in insurance, an interest the insured has in the risk covered by the insurance contract; in sales, a person's interest in goods that can be insured against loss **478, 1105**

insurance a contract in which the insurer agrees to pay the insured for losses affecting the insured's interests **1102**

insured the person whose risk has been assumed by another (in the insurance contract) **1102**

insurer the person who assumes another's risk (in the insurance contract) **1102**

intention test the promise must cause the offeree reasonably to believe that the promise was intended to be an offer **142**

inter alia among other things or matters

inter vivos among living persons **401, 1162**

interest a person's desire that has been legally recognized as dominant over a similar desire of another person **256**

interlocutory order an intermediate court order pending a final decision

intermediary bank "any bank to which an item is transferred in course of collection except the depositary or payor bank" UCC 4–105(c) **613**

interpleader an equitable remedy of a person who has some thing but does not claim any interest in it, requesting the court to decide who, as between two or more claimants, is entitled to the thing **413**

interrogatory a written question **1245**

intestate (noun) a person who died without a will; (adjective) property not disposed of by a will **398**

inventory goods that are held for sale or lease **1056**

involuntary case a bankruptcy case in which the petition is filed by the creditors **1087**

ipso facto by the fact itself

J

joint liability in contracts, occurs when parties together obligate themselves to perform the same promise **126**

joint tenancy a form of ownership of property by more than one person with the right of survivorship **403, 812, 984, 1144**

joint venture an association of two or more persons as co-owners to engage in a limited business transaction for a profit **854, 1197**

journeyman a skilled craftsman **754**

judge the government officer who presides over a court **23**

judgment the final decision of a case by a court **32, 246**

jurisdiction the power of a court to hear and decide a case involving a person or subject matter properly brought before the court **25, 1200**

juristic by law **1165**

juristic person an artificial person created by law **1206**

jury trial jury, a group of people selected to decide the facts in a trial; grand jury, a group of people selected to decide whether to recommend criminal prosecution of specified persons for the commission of crimes **32, 1246**

jus tertii the right of a third party **710**

K

Keogh plan a pension plan for self-employed individuals **883**

L

laissez-faire a government policy of not interfering with business **727**

land a tangible, immovable thing

larceny the taking and carrying away of the personal property of another without the right to do so **69**

lateral support the physical support for the land surface

law norms established by the official leaders of society; also those interests recognized and secured by society **11**

law-government continuum a method of showing the numerous ways of constructing legal systems **11**

law merchant a body of law that developed by the customs and usages of merchants and that later became part of the common law **803**

lawyer a person who is licensed to practice law by advising and representing clients in legal matters **22**

lease of goods, a form of contract giving the lessee the exclusive right to use or possess the goods of the lessor for a stated period; of realty, a form of contract giving one person, the tenant (or lessee), the exclusive right to occupy for a period the realty of another, the landlord (or lessor) **410, 450, 1022**

leasehold estate the estate in realty owned by tenants **1022**

legacy a testamentary gift of personal property **1143**

legal in compliance with the law

legal rate of interest the maximum rate of interest fixed by statute where no rate of interest is fixed by the contract **207**

legal system a set of laws adopted by a society or group of people **4**

legality something that does not violate a statute or public policy as declared by the courts **119**

legatee the beneficiary of a testamentary gift of personal property **1143**

lessee a person who contracts with the owner of property to pay rent for the right to use, possess, or occupy the property

lessor an owner of property who contracts with another giving the other the right to use, possess, or occupy the property in exchange for rent

letter of credit "an engagement by a bank or other person made at the request of a customer and of a kind within the scope of UCC 5–102 that the issuer will honor drafts or other demands for payment upon compliance with the conditions specified in the" letter of credit UCC 5–103(1)(a); *see also* UCC 2–325(3) **1195**

libel a defamatory publication in written or other permanent form **93**

license permission to do something; in real property, a temporary, revocable right (privilege) to some limited use of another's land **988, 1198**

lien a legal right in another's property as security for the performance of an obligation; *see* **general lien, possessory lien,** and **specific lien** **186, 334, 432, 885, 988**

lien creditor a creditor with a judicial lien or a writ of execution **1090**

life estate an estate that lasts only for the length of a particular person's life **986**

limited partnership a partnership of one or more general partners and one or more limited partners formed in compliance with the Revised Uniform Limited Partnership Act (1976) with the 1985 amendments; *see* **partnership** **848**

liquidated claim a claim for an amount that is either certain, or ascertainable by mathematical calculation, or by operation of law

liquidated damages the money judicially awarded in the amount as agreed to by the parties in their contract at the time it was made as reasonable compensation for damage that may be caused by the wrongful conduct of one of the parties in the future; *see* **damages** **271, 532, 1030**

liquidated debt a debt whose amount has been agreed to by the parties or is ascertainable by a standard **180**

lis pendens a pending suit

listing an agency contract between a broker and a seller of realty **1011**

livery of seisin an ancient ceremony used to transfer ownership of land **1000**

locus in quo the place in which **417**

lost property goods in a place where they were not put by the owner, who does not know where they are **417**

M

mail box rule the rule in *Adams v. Lindsell:* an acceptance is effective when it is sent if the means of sending it were impliedly authorized by, for example, the offeror's use of the mails to send the offer **470**

majority in contracts, the legal age at which a minor becomes an adult; also, in voting, one more than half **193**

maker the person who initially makes and signs a promissory note **601**

malpractice insurance liability insurance that protects professional people (doctors, lawyers, accountants) against claims brought against them **1102**

manifestation of mutual assent offer and acceptance **161**

marshaling of assets an equitable doctrine that, when there are two classes of creditors, one class having recourse to more than one asset while the other class has recourse to only some but not all of those assets, creditors of the first class are to resort first to those assets not available to other creditors and then to the other assets available to the other creditors **819**

master a principal who has the right to control, or controls, the physical conduct of his or her servant agent **330**

material alteration "any alteration of an instrument is material which changes the contract of any party thereto in any respect" UCC 3–407(1) **473, 674**

mechanic's lien a statutory lien on real property given to a person who, pursuant to contract, has rendered labor or services, or supplied materials for the improvement of the property and who has not been paid

mediation the process of using a third party to bring disputants closer to resolution of their differences **21**

medium an agency, instrument, means, or channel **150**

mens rea the mental element required for a crime **64**

merchant "a person who deals in goods of the kind or otherwise by his occupation holds himself out as having knowledge or skill peculiar to the practices or goods involved in the transaction or to whom such knowledge or skill may be attributed by his employment of an agent or broker or other intermediary who by his occupation holds himself out as having such knowledge or skill" UCC 2–104(1) **147, 452**

merger in corporations, the absorption of one corporation by another corporation; *see* **horizontal merger, vertical merger 731, 903**

mineral right right to dig or mine the earth

minor a person who is under the age of full legal capacity

misdemeanor a crime for which the punishment is less than one year in prison and the possibility of a fine; *see* **crime 63**

misfeasance misdoing **330**

mislaid property goods that the owner has voluntarily laid down and forgotten where they were laid **417**

misrepresentation an assertion of what is not true **164**

mistake believing a fact to exist when it does not exist, or believing a fact not to exist when it does exist **162**

mitigation of damages a doctrine that imposes on the injured party the duty to minimize his or her damages after injury has been inflicted on him or her **1026**

monopoly *see* **pure monopoly**

mortgage a security interest in realty; also the instrument giving lenders the power to sell the mortgaged realty and to repay the debt when the borrower defaults on the payments **1006**

mortgagee the person to whom a mortgage has been given **1006**

mortgagor the person who has given a mortgage **1006**

motion a procedural device asking the court to take some action **1245**

mutual assent the meeting of the minds of both or all the parties to a contract **119, 139**

mutual company a company owned by the insureds **1103**

N

natural law an ideal or cosmic law **6**

navigable water a body of water that can support commerce between states **981**

necessaries those things needed for survival and to maintain social position in life **194**

negligence in conduct, failure to use the degree of care demanded by the circumstances; in tort, negligent conduct proximately causing injury to another person's interest; *see* **contributory negligence 7, 84, 335, 369, 564**

negotiable document a document of title stating that the goods covered by the document are to be delivered to bearer or to the order of someone **430**

negotiable instrument a writing signed by the maker or drawer containing an unconditional promise or order to pay a sum certain in money payable on demand or at a definite time to order or to bearer **596**

negotiable promissory note a written unconditional promise to pay a sum certain in money, payable on demand or at a definite time, payable to order or to bearer, and signed by the maker

negotiate to deliver a negotiable instrument, or document, or a certificated security to a holder **603**

negotiate/bargain terms used to indicate that both parties to a sales contract are aware of all the terms of the contract and that both parties exchanged value to establish the terms **466**

negotiation the delivery of negotiable paper to a person who thereby becomes a holder **632**

no arrival, no sale a term used by a seller when it is shipping goods and does not want to be liable if the goods do not arrive at their destination

nolo contendere no contest **962**

nominal damages the money judicially awarded to an injured party when no damage has occurred from another's wrongful conduct; *see* **damages 270, 520**

nonfeasance not doing **330**

nonperformance no performance

nonsuit termination of a lawsuit without a finding on the merits of the case

nontrading partnership a partnership in the business of selling only services; *see* **partnership 805**

no-par stock corporate stock that is issued without any stated nominal price; *see* **share of stock**

norm a group's standard of behavior **8**

notarize verification by a proper public official of the authenticity of a signature **1002**

notary public a public officer with the authority to administer oaths and affirmations and to attest and certify documents

novation a new contract in which one of the parties was not a party to the old contract and which immediately discharges the old contract **243, 266, 895**

NOW a negotiable order of withdrawal, as in a NOW account **694**

nuisance a tort concerned with a person's conduct that is a wrongful interference with the interest of other persons in their private and public use and enjoyment of land

null/nullity of no legal effect **206, 670**

nuncupative will an oral will as permitted by statute **1138**

O

objective evidence the words and conduct of the party, not the secret thoughts of the party **127**

obligee the person to whom a legal obligation is owed **124, 259**

obligor the person who owes a legal obligation **124, 259**

offer a promise proposed in exchange for another's act, forbearance, or return promise **140**

offeree the promisee to whom an offer is made **140**

offeror the promisor making an offer **140**

oligopoly a market in which there is a small number of sellers **728**

option the irrevocable offer in an option contract **145**

ordinance municipal legislation **991**

P

par value stock corporate stock that is issued for a stated certain minimum nominal price; *see* **share of stock**

paralegal an individual trained to assist lawyers in their practice **24**

pari delicto equal in legal fault or guilt

parol oral **227**

parol evidence oral testimony **458**

parol evidence rule a rule of law providing that, when there is a written contract, it cannot be contradicted (added to or varied) by any prior or contemporaneous oral agreement, or by a prior written agreement **227, 458**

parol lease a lease not reduced to writing **1023**

partial performance incomplete performance that is insufficient to accomplish, or that defeats, the main purpose of a contract **238**

partially disclosed principal a person whose identity is not disclosed to a third person who knows, or reasonably should know, that an agent is, or may be acting as, an agent for that principal whoever it may be **328**

partition a division of property between joint owners **323, 404**

partnership (general partnership) "an association of two or more persons to carry on as co-owners of a business for profit" UPA, sec. 6; *see* **limited partnership, nontrading partnership,** and **trading partnership 291, 752, 802**

patent a governmental grant of protection of an invention **91, 542, 1205**

payee the person to whose order the instrument is originally written **599**

payor bank "a bank by which an item is payable as drawn or accepted" UCC 4–105(b) **612**

per capita "by heads"; all persons who stand in the same degree of relationship to the intestate share equally in the estate without consideration of any right of representation **1148**

per curiam by the court, all the judges

per se in and of itself **1207**

per stirpes "by stocks, or by roots"; the survivors of their parent represent their parent and take the parent's share in an intestate's estate by such representation for division among themselves **1148**

peremptory challenge a challenge to an individual juror for which no cause need be stated. Only a limited number of peremptory challenges are allowed in each case **32**

perfection of a security interest when the creditor complies with Article 9 of the Uniform Commercial Code's requirements for perfection, giving priority over other claims **1060**

performance the fulfillment of a contractual obligation **236**

perjury knowingly falsely swearing under oath, or affirming, in a judicial or quasi-judicial proceeding **898**

perpetuities, rule against *see* **rule against perpetuities**

personal covenant a promise in a lease that does not touch and concern the realty **1032**

personal liability coverage a homeowner's insurance policy provision covering liability for accidents on or away from the insured property **1117**

personal or **limited defense** in negotiable instruments, a defense that is not to *contractual* liability on an instrument but, rather, is to *avoid* liability on an instrument; any defense that is not a real defense **676**

personal property (personalty) a movable thing, along with interests and rights in the thing **396, 448, 811, 982, 1138**

personal representative a court-appointed person to represent a decedent and administer his or her estate **1148**

personalty personal property *see* **personal property 982**

plaintiff the party who initiates a civil suit by filing a complaint in the proper court **5, 29, 1243**

pleadings the formal documents filed with a court that usually include the complaint, answer, and motions regarding them **29, 1245**

pledge the possessory security interest in bailed goods acquired by the bailee when there is a bailment for the purpose of security **712, 928, 1059, 1063**

police power the power of a state or federal government to legislate reasonably for the general public welfare **991**

possessory lien a lien that includes the right to possession of the property that is subject to the lien **334**

power of attorney written authority by a principal to an agent **297, 1176**

pre-emption to retain exclusively, supersede; the doctrine adopted by the U.S. Supreme Court that certain matters are of such a national character that federal laws pre-empt or take precedence over state laws **42**

pre-emptive right a shareholder's right to subscribe to a newly authorized issue of stock proportionate to his or her holdings in the corporation **935**

preference in bankruptcy, a debtor's transfer of his or her property, made when insolvent and within 90 days before a petition in bankruptcy was filed, which gives a creditor preferential treatment **1089**

preferred stock corporate stock with a preference over the common stock; *see* **share of stock 926**

prescription in real property, a method of obtaining the right to use of another's land as an easement by open and continuous possession and use of the land under a claim of right to such use for a statutory period of time **1017**

present sale a contract causing the immediate transfer of the title to goods for a price at the time the contract is made

presenting bank "any bank presenting an item except a payor bank" UCC 4–105(e) **613**

presentment "a demand for acceptance or payment made upon the maker, acceptor, drawee or other payor by or on behalf of the holder" UCC 3–504(1) **607, 703**

price discrimination the practice of offering the same product to different competing customers at different prices **734**

prima facie at first sight **132, 358, 1203**

primary parties parties (maker and acceptor) on a negotiable instrument who are absolutely liable for its payment according to the terms at the time they sign **606**

principal in agency, a person who has authorized an agent to act on his or her behalf and subject to his or her control; in money, the capital sum of a money debt; in suretyship, the debtor in a suretyship arrangement **290, 668, 1076**

priority/priorities in bankruptcy, claims that are paid first after the estate has been liquidated; in realty, the order in which claims against realty are satisfied **1010, 1091**

private carrier a carrier that does not offer its services to the general public **424**

privilege that which exempts a person from liability for his or her conduct which, but for the exemption, would subject the person to liability for such conduct **81**

privileged communication a communication between certain persons which, because of their relationship, is inadmissible in evidence without a waiver of the privilege **334, 1246**

privity a mutuality of relationship between persons or between persons and a particular transaction **90, 335, 554, 562**

privity of contract a legal relationship between two or more parties created by their contract **257, 1031**

privity of estate a legal relationship between two or more parties flowing from their ownership or possession of the same realty **1031**

pro rata distribution distribution in proportion to one's contribution, loan, or advance **504**

probate the procedure of proving to a proper court that an instrument is the will of a decedent **1146**

probate court a court that has jurisdiction over the estate of a deceased person **406, 1147**

procedural unconscionability circumstances, other than the contract terms, that cause the enforcement of the contract to be unreasonably excessive **132**

proceeds what the debtor receives when he or she disposes of collateral **1057**

professional agent a professional, independent contractor employed as a special agent **1011**

professional corporation a corporation formed by professionals (those who render personal services to the public of a type that requires a license or other legal authorization) **882**

promise an assurance or undertaking that something shall or shall not happen **123**

promisee the person to whom a promise is made **124**

promisor the person who makes a promise **124**

promissory estoppel an equitable principle of preventing injustice by enforcing a gratuitous promise as a contract, without consideration and agreement, the promisor reasonably expecting that his or her promise would be justifiably relied upon substantially by the promisee **181**

promissory note a written promise to pay money; *see* **negotiable promissory note** **122**

promoter a person who organizes and brings a corporation into existence **894**

promulgate proclaim **368**

proof of claim the claim filed by a creditor in a bankruptcy case **1089**

property a thing; also an interest or right in a thing; in trusts, an interest or right in a thing; not the thing itself **256, 396, 477, 804, 1134, 1160, 1194**

property interest a legally recognized and protected right in property **477**

proscribe to prohibit

protest in negotiable instruments, a formal certificate, issued by a properly authorized person, certifying that a foreign or international draft was duly presented for acceptance or payment and that it was dishonored **707**

proximate cause the cause of an injury without which the injury would not have occurred **86, 569**

proxy a shareholder's written authorization to another person to vote his or her shares at a corporate meeting; also the person with such authority **929**

public policy the concept of law under which the freedom to act is limited for the good of the community **205**

punitive (exemplary) damages the money judicially awarded to an injured party in excess of compensatory damages to punish for malicious, wanton, or intentional wrongful conduct; *see* **damages** **43, 77, 271, 331, 1088**

purchase money security interest "a security interest is a 'purchase money security interest' to the extent that it is (a) taken or retained by the seller of the collateral to secure all or part of its price; or (b) taken by a person who by making advances or incurring an obligation gives value to enable the debtor to acquire rights in or the use of collateral if such value is in fact so used." UCC 9–107 **1054**

purchaser one who makes a contract to buy goods **540**

pure competition a market in which many firms compete and no one firm has very much power **728**

pure monopoly a market in which there is a single firm with no competitors **728**

Q

qualified indorsement an indorsement that disclaims or qualifies the liability of the indorser on the instrument; *see* **indorsement** **639**

quantum meruit an action for services rendered based on an implied promise to pay plaintiff as much as plaintiff reasonably deserved to have for the plaintiff's services **270**

quasi as if

quasi contract a legal fiction invented by the common law to provide for a contract remedy where, in fact, there is no contract but where justice requires recovery as though there had been a promise **125**

question of fact a dispute over what happened **26**

question of law a dispute over the legal effect of what happened **26**

quiet title, action to a legal proceeding initiated by a claimant to title in land affording any adverse parties opportunity to prove a claim to interest in the land or thereafter be barred from doing so

quitclaim deed a document used in transferring the grantor's interest in realty, if any, without any warranties **1003**

quorum in corporations, the number of persons necessary to be present, or shares necessary to be represented, at a meeting in order to transact business **956**

R

R & D limited partnership a special kind of limited partnership allowing a limited partner to invest and claim a deduction on the investment as an expense in his or her business, although the limited partnership engages only in research and development and not sales **853**

ratification in contracts, a person's waiver of his or her power of avoidance; in agency, a person's manifested consent to be bound by another's previously unauthorized act made in the person's name and not binding on him or her **195, 301**

real or **universal defense** in negotiable instruments, a defense to *contractual* liability on an instrument **669**

real property (realty) land and immovable things attached to land, along with interests and rights in the land; also a freehold interest in land **396, 811, 982**

realty real property *see* **real property** **980**

receiver a person appointed by a court to receive, preserve, and manage property that is involved in litigation **811**

recognizance an obligation acknowledged by a person in a court to do something, such as to appear in court at a later time; for example, a personal bond **122**

recourse a right to resort to a person or to a thing **712**

redemption the reclaiming of a foreclosed ownership interest in realty **1007**

reformation an action to correct a writing so as to reflect correctly the intentions of the parties that mistakenly were not properly expressed in the writing **162, 273**

reimbursement one person's right against another to be repaid money paid on the other's behalf for which the latter was responsible; in suretyship, the surety's right to recover from the principal **320, 838, 1080**

rejection in contracts, the offeree's expression refusing the offer; in sales, the buyer's refusal to accept goods provided by the seller under a contract for sale **145, 515**

remainder that remaining part of an estate in land which, on the termination of a preceding estate, passes to someone other than the grantor **987**

remainderman a person who was not a grantor of an estate in land but who will acquire the remainder of an estate after a preceding estate has terminated

remedy the means by which a right is enforced or protected **269**

renunciation the abandonment of a right by a person **709**

replevin a common law form of action to regain possession of specific chattels

representation in insurance, a statement of fact made by the insured that is not a part of the insurance contract but, during negotiation, is made to induce formation of the contract **1107**

repudiation a party's manifestation of an intent not to perform an obligation; *see* **anticipatory repudiation**

res ipsa loquitur the thing speaks for itself **85, 564**

res judicata the thing has been adjudicated; the principle of law that, once a matter has been litigated and finally adjudicated, it should not be the subject of litigation again between the same parties

rescind to cancel, annul **161**

rescission cancellation **245**

respondeat superior let the master (superior) be responsible for the torts of his or her servant committed while acting within the scope of the servant's employment **331**

respondent (appellee) a party against whom an appeal is taken **5**

restitution a legal remedy restoring a party to his or her original position prior to the particular transaction **197, 273, 519**

restrictive indorsement an indorsement that determines the type of interest in the instrument being transferred; *see* **indorsement** **637**

reversion a future interest that will, or may, be returned to the grantor. In contrast, a remainder goes to one other than the grantor **987**

revocation in contracts, the offeror's recalling of the offeree's power to accept as contained in the offer **145**

right a legal claim by the owner of an interest that others shall not interfere with the owner's interest **256**

right of survivorship a relationship among co-owners where death of one owner causes the decedent's interest to be transferred to the remaining owners **984**

riparian relating to land abutting a body of water **981**

robbery the taking of money or goods of value from the person of another or in his or her presence, against that person's will, by force or fear **70**

rule against perpetuities the beneficiary of a trust, or of a contingent future interest in realty, must be identifiable at the time the trust or contingent future interest is created, or, in most states, within a period for the life of a person or persons in existence at the time the trust or contingent future interest is created and 21 years after the death of such person or persons **987, 1166**

S

sale the transfer "of title from seller to purchaser for a price" UCC 2–106(1) **410, 450, 1160**

sanction a group's technique for controlling its members **9**

satisfaction the discharge of an obligation by paying what is due **709**

seal a symbol attached to a writing attesting that it is a legal document

seasonably "an action is taken seasonably when it is taken at or within the time agreed or if no time is agreed at or within a reasonable time" UCC 1–204(3) **149**

secondary boycott the bringing of pressure by a union on a neutral party who will then pressure the employer with whom the union has a dispute **759**

secondary parties in negotiable instruments, parties on a negotiable instrument who are liable on the instrument only if certain conditions occur **606**

secured party a creditor with a security interest **1054**

secured transaction a transaction used to create a security interest **1054**

security in secured transactions, a creditor's interest in specific property, or in the obligation of a third person, as assurance for the performance of the debtor's obligation

security agreement "an agreement which creates or provides for a security interest" UCC 9–105(1)(l) **531, 1058**

security interest "an interest in personal property or fixtures which secures payment or performance of an obligation" UCC 1–201(37) **396, 450, 516, 531, 664, 982, 1054**

servant an agent whose physical conduct his or her master (principal) has the right to control or controls **330, 354**

service usually labor rendered by one person for another **451**

servient tenement property in which someone has an easement appurtenant **989**

settlor the person who has created an express trust **296, 1162**

several liability in contracts, occurs when the same performance is separately promised by each party **126**

shareholder (stockholder) the owner of a unit of interest in a corporation **876, 925**

share of stock a unit of interest in a corporation; *see* **common stock, no-par stock, par value stock, preferred stock,** and **treasury stock** **876, 924**

shelter provision obtaining rights by claiming "through" or "under" **642**

shipper-carrier a legal relationship between the shipper and the common carrier when goods have been delivered to the carrier for immediate shipment **427**

shop right an employer's free, nonexclusive, irrevocable, nonassignable license to use the invention or discovery of an employee who has used his or her employment time or the employer's facilities in connection with such invention or discovery

signed "includes any symbol executed or adopted by a party with the present intention to authenticate a writing" UCC 1–201(39) **147**

simple contract a contract that need not be in any particular form; *see* **contract 123, 326**

slander a defamatory publication by spoken words, gestures, or other nonpermanent form **93**

social engineering using the law to bring about societal change **12**

sole proprietorship a business owned and operated by one person **752**

special agent "an agent authorized to conduct a single transaction or a series of transactions not involving continuity of service" Restatement (Second) of Agency, sec. 3 **301, 1011**

special damages *see* **consequential damages**

special indorsement an indorsement that specifies a particular indorsee; *see* **indorsement 636**

specific lien a lien on the specific property on which services were rendered; *see* **lien**

specific performance the exact performance of a contract by a party as ordered by a court **272, 524**

standard an established measure **685**

stare decisis a principle of law stating that earlier cases that are similar should, if possible, be followed to decide current issues before the court **34**

state court of general jurisdiction the highest order state trial court **26**

stated capital (capital stock) generally, the money received by a corporation from the issuance of its shares exclusive of what has been allocated to capital surplus

state inferior court the lowest order of state trial court **25**

status quo the state of things at any given time

statute law created by a legislative body and approved by the executive **206, 1134**

statute of frauds a statute requiring that certain kinds of contracts be proved only by a proper writing **218, 455, 1023**

statute of limitations a statute limiting the time in which a claim may be asserted in court; expiration bars enforcement of the claim **183, 246, 533**

statutory law bills passed by a legislature and signed into law by the president or governor **33**

stay a halt **1088**

stock *see* **share of stock**

straight bill a non-negotiable bill of lading

strict liability absolute liability irrespective of the absence of negligence or fault **89, 566**

strict surety a co-debtor with the principal for the same obligation owing to the creditor

subagent the person appointed by an agent and as to whom the appointing agent is a principal **314**

subjectively existing only in one's mind **127**

sublet a transfer by the lessee of a *part* of the remaining term of the lease **1031**

subpoena an order to appear before a judicial or proper administrative body for the purpose of giving testimony **743**

subrogation the substitution of one person for another with reference to a claim or a right; in suretyship, the surety succeeds to the creditor's rights against the principal **689, 1080, 1108**

subsidiary corporation a corporation owned by another corporation **886, 1197**

substantial performance incomplete performance that is sufficient to accomplish, and does not defeat, the main purpose of a contract **238**

substantive law that part of the law that creates, defines, and regulates rights **212**

substantive unconscionability contract terms that cause one of the parties to be in too unequal or one-sided a bargaining position **132**

summary judgment a judgment rendered on a motion by a party in a civil action that, solely on the basis of the pleadings and affidavits, there is no genuine issue as to any material fact and that the moving party is entitled to judgment as a matter of law without the necessity of a trial on the facts **1246**

summons a writ or process served on the defendant in a civil action notifying him or her of the action and summoning him or her to appear and plead **29, 1244**

surety a person who promises the creditor to pay the principal's debt or to perform his or her obligation on the principal's nonperformance **190, 1076**

surety bond a promise by a professional surety to pay if the principal defaults or commits a wrongful act **1076**

suretyship a legal relationship in which one person (surety) and another person (principal, the debtor) are obligated to perform the same obligation to a third person (creditor) who is entitled to only one performance, and as between the surety and the principal the latter is to perform the obligation and is ultimately liable therefor **1075**

surface right the right to occupy the surface of a piece of land

survivorship, right of a relationship among co-owners where death of one owner causes his or her interest to be transferred to the remaining owners

T

technology a particular kind of property concerned with material things **1194**

tenancy a form of nonfreehold ownership in realty **987**

tenancy by entirety a form of co-ownership between husband and wife with the right of survivorship **404, 985**

tenancy in common a form of ownership of property by more than one person without survivorship **405, 812, 984**

tenant *see* **lease**

tender in contracts, an unconditional offer by one contracting party to perform, with present ability to do so; as a verb, to proffer, make available **237, 492, 711**

tenor what is stated as meant **687**

term insurance insurance sold for a specified time period, with no cash value **1114**

testamentary trust a trust created by the will of a decedent **1144, 1163**

testator (testatrix) a man (woman) who executes a will **1134**

title insurance insurance that covers the title to real estate **1101**

tort a civil (private) noncontractual wrong for which a court will give a remedy **63, 76, 205, 326, 541, 563, 840, 1164**

tortfeasor a person who has committed a tort

trade fixture a chattel attached to leased realty by a business tenant; it is usually treated as personal property **983**

trademark an identifying designation differentiating one's goods from those of another; "any word, name, symbol, or device, or any combination thereof, adopted and used by manufacturer or merchant to identify his goods and distinguish them from those manufactured by others" Lanham Act, sec. 5 **91, 861**

trading partnership a partnership in the business of buying and selling property; *see* **partnership** **805**

transfer (noun) a delivery of some thing

transferee one to whom another has transferred some thing **503**

transferor one who has transferred some thing to another **503**

treason a felony specifically defined by the U.S. Constitution **64**

treasure trove found buried treasure **418**

treasury stock corporate stock reacquired by the issuing corporation; *see* **share of stock** **935**

trespass (verb) to wrongfully interfere with another's possession of land or chattels **995**

trust a legal device whereby legal title to property is held by one person (a trustee) for the benefit of a beneficiary **190, 296, 406, 1135, 1160**

trust deed a deed given to a trustee, in trust, with the power to sell the land on default of the secured obligation **1007**

trust property the property held in trust, sometimes called the "trust res" **1160**

trustee a person who holds title to property in trust for the benefit of someone; in bankruptcy, the officer responsible for administering the debtor's estate; in realty, the one who holds the trust deed for the benefit of the lender **295, 1007, 1087, 1160**

tying arrangement an agreement between a seller or lessor and a purchaser or lessee that a sale or lease of a product to the latter is contingent upon the latter's purchase or lease of another product of the seller or lessor **730, 862, 1199**

U

ultra vires beyond the powers **883, 915**

unconscionable offensive to the conscience; immoderate, too one-sided **121, 168, 209, 449**

unconscionable contract a contract in which one of the parties is in too unequal or one-sided a bargaining position at the time the contract is made **130, 551**

undisclosed principal a person not known, or who is not reasonably known, to be a principal for an agent by a third party **328**

undue influence unfair persuasion by one who, because of his or her relationship with another, dominates the other **167, 1137**

unenforceable contract a contract that the courts will not enforce **130**

unfair labor practices tactics by an employer or a union that are legally prohibited as unfair **758**

Uniform Commercial Code a body of statutory law governing commercial transactions concerning personal property (movable things) **120**

unilateral contract a contract in which the consideration for a promise is an act or a forbearance **123**

uninsured motorist coverage insurance that pays all sums that the insured is entitled to recover when he or she is injured by an uninsured or a "hit and run" driver **1120**

union shop a shop or place of employment where the employer may hire non-union employees but after a short period of time, usually thirty days, the new employees must become members of the union or be discharged

universal agent an agent authorized by the principal to transact all business of every kind *see* **general agent** **301**

universal defense *see* **real** or **universal defense**

unjust enrichment a legal doctrine that prevents persons from profiting or enriching themselves inequitably at the expense of others **125**

unliquidated debt a debt whose amount has not been ascertained **180**

usage of trade "any practice or method of dealing having such regularity of observance in a place, vocation or trade as to justify an expectation that it will be observed with respect to the transaction in question" UCC 1–205(2); used synonymously with "custom" **228, 475, 704**

usury charging a rate of interest on a loan higher than that permitted by statute **207, 578, 670**

V

value any consideration sufficient to support a contract, a commitment to extend credit, or a past debt UCC 1–201(44) **664, 1059**

verdict a jury's finding of fact **32, 1247**

vertical merger a merger between a firm and one of its major suppliers or customers **731**

void of no legal effect **190**

void agreement an agreement that the law will not enforce as a legal obligation **128**

voidable contract a contract that can be avoided by one or more of the parties **129, 190**

voir dire the examination before trial of a prospective juror or witness in which he or she is to answer the questions truthfully **1246**

voluntary case a bankruptcy case in which the petition is filed by the debtor **1087**

voting trust a trust created by an agreement between the shareholders to transfer legal title to their voting stock to a party (trustee) who is authorized to vote the stock as a unit **930**

W

warehouse receipt a document issued to the bailor by a warehouseman **428**

warehouseman a person in the business of storing goods for a fee **426, 1063**

warranty an express or implied assurance that certain facts exist; in insurance, a statement of fact or a promise made by the insured that is part of the insurance contract and that must be true if the insurer is to be liable on the contract; in sales of goods, generally, an affirmation of fact or an express promise made by a seller or manufacturer of goods, or a promise implied in a sales transaction by law, that the goods sold are of a certain quality or will perform in a certain manner; *see* **express warranty** and **implied warranty** **261, 327, 541, 649, 1107**

warranty deed a deed conveying title and giving warranties to the grantee **1003**

water right a right to control of the water on the surface or under the ground

watered stock corporate stock reduced in value by the issuance of par value shares for less than their par value **939**

whole life insurance insurance for the entire life of the insured, with cash values that increase through the years **1114**

will a formal document that governs the transfer of property at death **398, 1134**

writ a court order

writ of execution a court order authorizing a sheriff or other proper legal officer to seize tangible property to satisfy a court judgment **413, 426**

writ of garnishment *see* **garnishment**

wrong the illegal invasion of another person's interest **77**

Y

yellow dog contract an agreement between an employer and employee that the employee will not be, nor continue to be, a member of a union **756**

Z

zoning the division of a geographical area by legislative regulation into districts, and the prescription and application of regulations concerning use and design of structures within those districts **783**

TABLE OF CASES

Note: Titles for cases featured at the end of chapters are printed in **boldface** type.

INDEX